CASES AND MATERIALS

EVIDENCE

TWELFTH EDITION

by

ROGER C. PARK
James Edgar Hervey Distinguished Professor of Law
University of California, Hastings College of Law

RICHARD D. FRIEDMAN
Alene and Allan F. Smith Professor of Law
University of Michigan Law School

FOUNDATION PRESS
2013

THOMSON REUTERS

University Casebook Series is a trademark registered in the U.S. Patent and Trademark Office.

© 1968, 1972, 1976, 1981, 1984, 1987, 1992, 1995, 1999, 2004 FOUNDATION PRESS
© 2005, 2009 THOMSON REUTERS/FOUNDATION PRESS
© 2013 by THOMSON REUTERS / FOUNDATION PRESS
> 1 New York Plaza, 34th Floor
> New York, NY 10004
> Phone Toll Free (877) 888-1330
> Fax (646) 424-5201
> foundation-press.com

Printed in the United States of America
ISBN: 978–1–60930–138–5

Mat #41265418

For Suzanne,
always my best friend,

R.C.P.

For Joanna,
with love and gratitude,

R.D.F.

PREFACE TO TWELFTH EDITION

We are pleased to present the Twelfth Edition of this coursebook, which was first published in 1968. This is the first edition that does not bear the names of any of the original authors, David Louisell, John Kaplan, and Jon Waltz. But it bears their mark throughout. We have preserved much of the substance of the early editions and have tried to preserve the style and flair that have made the book a successful teaching tool for so many years. At the same time, we have made many changes, both large and small, to ensure that the book remains fresh and up to date.

Throughout the book, we have replaced some old materials that we thought had become tired and dated. But we have not hesitated to retain older materials that still work well. We have, of course, introduced recent cases and other materials as well. At some points, we have replaced old writings of other authors with Notes of our own. In general, we have tried to tighten the book up, editing down cases that we thought were lengthier than necessary.

In addition, we have made these particular changes that seem worth noting:

In Chapter I, Jon Waltz's essay, *Making the Record*, retains its value, but it was showing its age in numerous small ways, some of them significant. So we have tried to update it, without altering its style or most of its substance.

We have substantially reorganized Chapter III and given it a new title. In prior editions, this chapter was titled *The Hearsay Rule* and it held off any discussion of the confrontation right to a subsection at the end, titled *The Future of Hearsay*. Especially in light of the transformation ushered in confrontation law ushered in by *Crawford v. Washington*, we believe this approach is no longer tenable. Accordingly, we now title the chapter *The Hearsay Rule and the Confrontation Right*. We introduce *Crawford* itself early and other Confrontation Clause cases as we address the hearsay subjects with which they are most closely connected. (There are now enough post-*Crawford* cases that we have had to compress our treatment of them; for example, we now include a description of the *Melendez-Diaz* case rather than an extended excerpt from it.) Throughout the chapter, we ask students (and teachers) to consider the relationship of hearsay and Confrontation Clause doctrines. We have also reorganized the presentation of the exceptions and exemptions to the hearsay rule. In response to comments from teachers, we have incorporated some traditional cases (though not ones used in prior editions) on the dying declaration exception. And we have folded into the hearsay chapter most of what was a separate chapter on forfeiture.

In what is now Chapter V, on non-governmental privileges, we have added a new subsection on inadvertent waiver.

What is now Chapter VII, covering writings, was particularly out of date, especially in its failure to cover electronically stored information, and so we have thoroughly revamped it.

In the preface to the Eleventh Edition, we noted that with some misgivings we were continuing the "one-book" approach of including appendices that contain the Federal Rules of Evidence, relevant legislative history of the Rules, and the California Evidence Code. The same note is appropriate here. (The Federal Rules reproduced here are the new version, revised throughout in 2011 as the result of a years-long restyling project.) Readers who appreciate this feature, or who dislike it, are invited to make their views known to the authors.

As in prior editions, we have sometimes deleted footnotes or citations (including citations with parentheticals) without any indication. Other deletions are indicated by the use of asterisks as ellipses.

We owe thanks to numerous people, including the staff of Foundation Press, for their patience and forbearance, and to Margaret Klocinski, for providing swift, capable, and cheerful secretarial assistance. As in the past, we have profited from the comments of many users of the book. Those who have contributed this way in the last couple of editions include David Leonard, whose untimely death leaves us deeply saddened, Jim Atkins, Norman Garland, Roger Kirst, John Leubsdorf, Christian Mammen, Paul McCaskle, Richard Marcus, Ruth Philips, and Peter Tillers. We owe special thanks to Fred Moss, who has made many helpful suggestions over several editions; we are glad that he continues to keep us on our toes. If we have omitted others by mistake, we offer apologies as well as thanks.

ROGER C. PARK
RICHARD D. FRIEDMAN

November 2012

SUMMARY OF CONTENTS

TABLE OF CONTENTS

TABLE OF CASES

The principal cases are in bold type.

TABLE OF CALIFORNIA EVIDENCE CODE SECTIONS

TABLE OF FEDERAL EVIDENCE RULES

UNIVERSITY CASEBOOK SERIES ®

EVIDENCE

TWELFTH EDITION

CHAPTER 1

MAKING THE RECORD;* TRIAL OBJECTIONS**

I.

"THE RECORD": WHAT IT MEANS AND HOW IT IS "MADE"

A.

The Meaning and Purpose of the Trial Record

Every experienced trial lawyer realizes that his or her cause may not prevail at the trial level and that the client may wish to appeal to a higher court if, in counsel's opinion, errors occurring at trial contributed significantly to the unhappy outcome. An experienced trial lawyer knows, therefore, that she must be in a position to show a reviewing court precisely what happened during the trial (and perhaps also at any important pretrial and out-of-court hearings or conferences). It follows that a lawyer must do two things at once—she must operate at two quite different levels—as she goes about the trial of her case. First, she must bend every proper effort to the winning of her client's case at the trial level, which means, essentially, that she must persuade the factfinder—judge or jury—of the rightness of her cause. Second, because counsel can never be absolutely certain of victory at the trial level, she must do everything she can to generate a record of the trial that will serve to convince a reviewing court that justice did not prevail in the court below.

An appellate court can neither speculate about what occurred at trial nor take on faith counsel's uncorroborated description of events in the lower court. A reviewing court can act only on the formal record of the trial that has been officially transmitted to it by the clerk of the trial court.

That record, assembled and bound into one or more volumes after the trial is over, includes all the pleadings in the case (Complaint, Answer, possibly a Reply and perhaps Cross-Complaints, Counterclaims, and Third-Party Complaints and the Answers or Replies to them). It will also include every other piece of paper that was filed during the course of the litigation: motions, supporting briefs, orders of the trial court, written stipulations of the parties, proposed jury instructions, journal entries, everything. The record also contains what in some jurisdictions is called the "Report of Proceedings." This is the verbatim transcript of any on-the-record proceedings in the case. There will be the actual trial transcript—the recordation of all

---

* Prepared by Professor Jon R. Waltz, and lightly edited by the current authors.
** Prepared by Professor Roger C. Park.

the words that were spoken by the trial's participants (judge, jurors, lawyers, witnesses, and perhaps others)—and there will be transcript from any on-the-record pre-trial or out-of-court hearings and conferences. Attached to the back of the trial transcript, or in the final volumes of a bulky record, will be the exhibits, received and unreceived, that were identified and offered at trial. The record, then, in all but the most minor of litigations, has three basic parts: (1) the litigation's paperwork, (2) the verbatim transcript of hearings, conferences, and trial testimony, and (3) the tangible exhibits that the parties offered into evidence. It will ordinarily contain less only if counsel have agreed to a "short" record, as when only designated portions of the record are needed for the effective presentation of an appeal.

B.

How the Record is Made

The active participants in a trial, which means the judge and the lawyers, literally "make" the trial record. They go about it almost as though they were dictating a non-fiction book, or the scenario for a documentary film, to an especially capable secretary. They create the record, in other words, with the assistance of that most important of courtroom functionaries, the court reporter. The reporter has a number of responsibilities during a trial but the most crucial one is the accurate recording of everything that is said by the participants. The reporter will record not only the testimony of the witnesses but the evidentiary objections and arguments of counsel and the comments, rulings, and instructions of the judge. The reporter will ordinarily also be assigned the job of placing identifying markings on tangible exhibits at offering counsel's request and will have the practical responsibility for taking care of the exhibits when they are not in use during the trial.

Traditionally, court reporters have recorded proceedings by means of high-speed shorthand or by mechanical means. The proficiency displayed by court reporters under even the most difficult heat-of-trial circumstances is almost invariably impressive. The confidence of courts and lawyers in the trial records produced by court reporters is reflected in statutes providing that these records are to be deemed *prima facie* correct (28 U.S.C. § 753(b)), and in such rules as Federal Rule of Civil Procedure 80 that provide that whenever the stenographically recorded testimony of a witness at a trial or hearing is admissible at a later trial, it may be proved by the court reporter's certified transcript of it. Perhaps the ultimate affirmation of the importance of the court reporter's product, the transcript, lies in those rulings—dating from the days when reporting by shorthand rather than mechanical means was the usual practice—that the plaintiff who lost in the trial court is entitled to a new trial if he is unable, because of the inability for any reason of the court reporter, or of a substitute for him, to make a transcript from the reporter's notes.

Difficulties of this sort are mitigated in those jurisdictions that have replaced traditional means by electronic audio recording. Electronic recording does not require the skill of traditional reporting, and is usually cheaper. It does not provide the participants with as good access to proceedings just held, and it entails the risk of machine failure. Also, a live reporter will know if she cannot understand what is being said, and the problem can be corrected immediately; with an automatic system, the problem may be discovered when it is too late to do anything about it.

However it is produced, the court reporter's transcript is an almost sacred thing. Although it is true in a general way that the reporter is subject to the trial court's direction, the court cannot curtail the performance of the reporter's essential duties. In other words, the parties' right to have a word-for-word record of everything said cannot be negated by a trial judge, no matter how much the judge might wish to interfere—possibly to excise his own errors or inappropriate language. Appellate courts have repeatedly held that a trial judge has no authority to order the court reporter to disregard his sworn obligation to make a complete transcript and some statutes specifically provide that a judge's overreaching in this regard is, in and of itself, prejudicial error. (Trial judges will, however, sometimes hold proceedings at sidebar or in chambers "off the record.")

It thus is no exaggeration to say that during a trial the judge and the lawyers are working with the court reporter in a joint effort that culminates in a complete record of the trial. Competent judges and attorneys are therefore continuously aware of the court reporter and his (or her) importance as the trial process unfolds. It may even be that verbatim court reporting sometimes promotes an attitude of stiffness, of undue formality, on counsel's part. On the whole, however, the influence of verbatim reporting, on all but those lawyers who are already gripped by a form of stage fright, is benign. Verbatim reporting tends to induce lawyers to be precise in their language, thorough and careful in their examinations. It tends to restrain the impetuous and the flamboyant. In short, it casts over all the trial participants a sense of the high responsibility engendered by the psychology of "making the record."

Recording the proceedings does not in itself generate a reliable transcript that can be read by persons without professional training. However the proceedings are recorded, the record must be transcribed if it is to be read. The trial record is so important that, in big cases that will bear the considerable expense involved, the parties often order daily transcript. Whether from notes or electronic recording, and perhaps with the aid of voice recognition software that is still far from perfect, a team of court reporters will provide counsel with a transcript of the day's proceedings shortly after the court recesses. Counsel will burn the midnight oil reading the transcript and indexing it in preparation for the days ahead. Otherwise, typed transcript is provided only as specifically ordered by court or counsel. If neither court nor counsel have any need for designated blocks of transcript during the trial, or if there is no appeal from verdict and judgment, the court reporter's notes or the audio recording may never be transcribed at all and a potentially taxable cost item of sizeable magnitude will be avoided.

Consciousness of the record and of the court reporter's part in the making of it has a discernible effect on the way the judge and counsel go about their work. In the first place, it is vital that, assuming traditional means are used, the court reporter be able to hear and understand everything that is said by the participants in a trial or hearing. It has been said, correctly, that it may even be more important that the reporter hear than the judge, the jurors, and the lawyers, since the reporter can then repeat from his notes any remarks unheard by them.

C.

Conduct of Lawyers that Hampers Court Reporters

Some years ago the National Shorthand Reporters Association catalogued some common practices of trial lawyers that create problems for court reporters. The most frustrating of them are paraphrased below.

1. *"Echoing."* A nervous trial lawyer, or one who is seeking an extra moment of time in which to frame his next question, sometimes engages in the practice known to court reporters as "echoing." That is, he constantly repeats the witness' response to a question.

Q. What is your name, sir?

A. Clyde Bushmat.

Q. Clyde Bushmat. Where do your reside?

A. At 3730 North Lake Shore Drive in Chicago, Illinois.

Q. 3730 North Lake Shore Drive, Chicago. And how old are you, sir?

A. I'll be forty-two next October 11.

Q. Forty-two in October. What is your present occupation?

Since he must take down everything that is said by the participants in a trial, this unnecessary repetition is distracting to the reporter, wasteful of trial time, and costly to the litigants.

2. *"Overlapping."* It is difficult for a court reporter, no matter how competent, to make an accurate and readable record when more than one person talks at the same time. The reporter may be unable to hear everything that is said or he may be unable to remember all of the overlapping statements long enough to sort out and record them while trying to keep up with the continuing testimony or argument. Counsel, although occasionally forced to prevent a witness from forging ahead with objectionable testimony, generally should avoid interruptions that result in broken sentences and garbled transcripts.

3. *Numbers.* What does a court reporter do when a trial lawyer says "twenty-one-O-two"? Does the lawyer mean 21.02, 2,102.00, or 20,102? Does

he mean dollars or something else? He should say, "Twenty-one dollars and two cents" if that is what he means. If he is dealing with a long number, such as the number of an insurance policy, counsel should avoid trying to give the millions, thousands, hundreds, and digits; he is likely to mix up not only himself, the judge, and the jury, but also the court reporter. It is simple enough to say, "Policy Number one-nine-four-seven-nine-six-three." References to dates can also be confusing. Counsel's reference to "October 11" can mean either October the 31st or October, 2011.

4. *Proper Names.* Many proper names have a similar sound. "White, Weit, Whyte, Wight, Wite, Wyatt." Counsel should be particularly careful to enunciate proper names slowly and clearly, in some instances spelling out the name or requesting the witness to do so. Indeed, counsel who is not known to the court reporter would do well to provide the correct spelling of her *own* name at the outset of the trial.

5. *Exhibits.* The Shorthand Reporters Association has observed that trial lawyers are often careless in the way they refer to exhibits. We shall be discussing the correct ways of marking and referring to exhibits. It is enough to mention here that court reporters do not appreciate the lawyer who gets his exhibit properly marked and then fails to make the intended use of the exhibit's number or letter. References to "this photograph" or "that letter" result in an incomprehensible record. Exhibits are marked *for identification.* Counsel's reference should be complete: "I hand you what has been marked Defendant's Exhibit Number 2 for Identification."

6. *Indications and Gestures.* Unclarified statements such as "About this long," "Approximately that far away," and "He had a jagged scar right here" may be comprehensible enough to those who were present in the trial court to see the witness' physical gestures but they become meaningless on the typed record. Either the witness will have to be asked to give an explicit oral response or, as we shall discuss later, counsel or the court will have to make a clarifying statement for the record.

7. *"Off the Record."* The practice of lawyers during depositions, pre-trial hearings and even occasionally in the midst of trial of directing the court reporter to go "off the record" is often confusing to the reporter. In some instances she may be unclear as to her authority to halt her note-taking, as when neither the trial judge nor opposing counsel has indicated his agreement that recordation can be interrupted; in others she may be uncertain as to precisely when recordation should recommence. If she is unclear of her authority, an experienced court reporter will simply continue to record. And whenever she halts recordation she will protect herself by making a notation in the transcript: "Whereupon discussion off the record was had."

Any confusion about when to resume note-taking can be far more embarrassing to counsel than it is to the reporter if counsel discovers later that an important concession or stipulation did not get on the record or got on it in such a truncated form that it is impossible to determine what it related to. Counsel should give a clear indication when they want to "go back on the record." It is easy to do. A hand signal may be all that is needed, or a statement by counsel such as "Let's go back on now. I want to put our stipulation on the record."

8. *Sidebar Conferences.* A variation on the off-the-record problem arises when counsel engage in whispered "sidebar" conferences—conferences occurring at the bench. These conferences, usually held in connection with an evidentiary objection, are calculated to be outside the jury's hearing but they may prove to be beyond the court reporter's hearing as well. If anything significant occurs during such a conference, such as a ruling by the judge or a stipulation between the parties, counsel should make certain that the reporter has been able to get it on the record.

9. *Abstruse Terminology.* In lawsuits that will involve substantial amounts of esoteric terminology, such as patent cases, counsel can contribute to the record's accuracy by supplying the reporter with a glossary of the specialized terms that are likely to come up.

10. *Reading Testimony into the Record.* In reading deposition testimony or previous trial testimony into the record, counsel should read slowly enough, and enunciate sharply enough, that the court reporter can follow. It helps the reporter if counsel always reads the words "Question" and "Answer" at the appropriate points. Better yet, if the court permits, counsel may read the questions and another person – perhaps a paralegal or a junior lawyer – may play the role of the witness, perhaps in the witness box, reading the answers that the witness actually gave on the prior occasion. Later, counsel should supply to the reporter the deposition or transcript from which she read. This will permit the reporter to check the accuracy of his notes against the written exhibit.

D.

Requesting the Making of a Record

It has already at least been implied that now and then a lawyer's making of the trial record involves little more than remembering to see to it that particular proceedings are "on the record"; that is, that they are being recorded by a court reporter. Many aspects of a litigated matter will not become part of the record unless counsel see to it, first, that there is a court reporter present and, second, that he is recording the proceedings. For example, there often will not be a reporter present at a pre-trial conference of the sort described in Rule 16 of the Federal Rules of Civil Procedure, or at conferences with the trial judge in his or her chambers, unless counsel requests that one be brought in when needed. Important matters, of both a procedural and an evidentiary nature, are frequently resolved at such sessions and a court reporter should be summoned in order that these stipulations can be put in the record.

In a few jurisdictions the court reporter will not record the examination of prospective jurors—the *voir dire*—or counsel's opening statements or closing arguments to the jury unless specifically instructed by the court or counsel to do so. Since error can occur during any of these trial phases (although it rarely does), counsel will request recordation in cases that can support the added expense. (He may also want the opening statements transcribed so that he can refer to them—his own or his adversary's—during his closing argument to the jury.)

Some courts, usually those of less than general jurisdiction (municipal courts, "small claims" courts, traffic courts, and the like), have no official court reporters regularly attached to them. Here the litigants have the obligation to provide and pay for the services of a qualified reporter. Often the parties agree to share the cost. Court reporters can be obtained from the same organizations that supply them for the taking of depositions.

E.

Requiring Audible Responses from Witnesses

The principal task of a court reporter, and it is a formidable one, is to take down testimony completely and accurately. The reporter ordinarily cannot take down an answer unless there has been an audible one; it is not the reporter's job to invent words that the witness did not speak. An alert court reporter may have time to insert in the record a bracketed statement of what the witness did—for example, "A: [Witness nodded in the affirmative.]"—but often the pace of the trial leaves no time for this. It is counsel's duty to obtain audible oral answers from witnesses or else, as will be described, he must himself insert an oral statement in the record. When a witness nods or gestures instead of answering audibly, counsel ordinarily should advise him that "The court reporter cannot get your answer unless you say it in words, sir."

F.

Statements for the Record

There are all manner of situations in which counsel or the court find it necessary to make a statement for the record. This means, in effect, that counsel or the trial judge is dictating a statement into the trial record; they, not a witness on the stand, speak and the court reporter takes down what they say as an integral part of the trial record.

Statements for the record are commonly employed to fill in testimonial gaps created by the witness, mentioned above, who provides inaudible or nonverbal responses. Instead of reminding the witness to give audible oral answers, assuming that such an answer was the appropriate mode of response to the question, examining counsel may turn to the court reporter and say, "Let the record show that the witness, in response to the question, nodded his head in the affirmative."

Sometimes witnesses, whether directed to do so or not, will respond to questions with their hands rather than vocally. Counsel inquires, "How long was the blade of the knife?" and the witness, instead of saying "About four inches," indicates the length with the thumb and index finger of one hand. In this situation counsel may make a statement for the record rather than insist on an oral response. "Let the record reflect that in answer to the question the witness, using the thumb and index finger of his right hand, indicated a length of approximately four inches." If opposing counsel objects to the statement, saying it looked more like three inches to her, counsel may have to call for an oral response. If opposing counsel remains silent, the statement for the record stands. If examining counsel inquires of opposing counsel, as out of courtesy he might, whether his statement for the record is satisfactory and gets an affirmative reply, the statement for the record rises to the level of a stipulation between counsel.

Whenever counsel expressly requests a witness to communicate information by means other than oral testimony, a statement for the record will be essential in order to avoid later confusion. Here a typical example involves the drama-conscious prosecutor who asks the witness,

Q. Do you see the man you have described anywhere in the courtroom?

A. I do.

Q. Please come down off the witness stand and place your hand on the shoulder of the man whom you have described as the one who assaulted the little girl. [Witness complies.]

BY THE PROSECUTOR: Let the record show that the witness crossed directly to the accused, Clyde Bushmat, and placed her hand on his right shoulder. [Or he may simply say, "Let the record show that the witness identified the accused."]

Sometimes a witness will give a response which, although oral and audible, nonetheless calls for a clarifying statement for the record.

Q. How far from the automobile were you when this happened?

A. Oh, about from here to the back wall of the courtroom.

BY EXAMINING COUNSEL: Let the record show that the witness has indicated a distance of approximately fifty feet. Does that meet with your approval, counsel?

BY OPPOSING COUNSEL: Yes, that seems about right.

A statement for the record can be used to place in the trial record pertinent matter that is not in dispute and would not be expected to come from a witness on the stand —matterthat, in a sense, is non-evidentiary. For example, it may from time to time be prudent to make a statement for the record to the effect that described proceedings or events took place while the jury was out, lest it later be suggested that comments, legal arguments, or events such as disruptions by defendants or spectators occurring during the period in question may have prejudiced the jury.

G.

Stipulations

Stipulations by counsel are a near relative of the sort of statements for the record that were discussed in the preceding section. As was suggested there, a statement for the record which opposing counsel affirmatively accepts as accurate rises to the level of a stipulation. An unchallenged statement for the record—one that is not objected to by the opposite side—probably qualifies as an implied stipulation. Stipulations can be extremely important in litigation. They are in the nature of contracts entered into by lawyers acting as special agents of their clients. These agreements between counsel can simplify and expedite trial and fill evidentiary gaps. But they are worse than useless unless they have been clearly made a part of the trial record.

A stipulation is simply a voluntary agreement entered into between counsel for the parties to a litigation respecting some matter that is before the trial court. In the absence of special circumstances that might induce a court to vacate it, a stipulation by counsel binds their principals, the clients. (Courts will usually vacate stipulations that were entered into by mistake, and they will always vacate those that were obtained by fraud or deceit.)

Stipulations can relate either to procedure or to evidence. Typical examples of procedural stipulations can be found in Rule 29 of the Federal Rules of Civil Procedure, which treats of "Stipulations About Discovery Procedure." (See also FRCP 15, which provides that a party, after the filing of a responsive pleading by the opposing side, can amend his or her pleading either with the trial court's permission "or with the opposing party's written consent.")

An evidentiary stipulation acts to admit or concede specified facts, relieving a party of the burden of making full-scale proof. Such an evidentiary stipulation constitutes a formal judicial admission—an abandonment of any contention to the contrary—and, unless vacated by the trial court, prevents those who enter into it from offering evidence to dispute it. It is identical in force to an admission contained in a pleading.

Complicated stipulations, like complex hypothetical questions to be posed to an expert witness, are usually written out by counsel and then edited. The final written product can then be filed in the case or read into the record. Simple, single-subject stipulations are stated for the record extemporaneously. Here the only problems involve (1) remembering to state the stipulation, (2) making certain that the court reporter is recording it, (3) making certain that the terms of the stipulation are clear and unambiguous, and (4) getting on the record opposing counsel's unqualified acquiescence in the stipulation.

Stipulations, whether entered into during a deposition, a pre-trial conference, or in the midst of trial, may evolve in a most informal way.

PLAINTIFF'S COUNSEL [speaking to defense counsel at a pre-trial conference]: Susan, will you agree to our photographs?

DEFENSE COUNSEL: What have you got, Charlie? I'll be glad to look at them. They're all in living color, I suppose?

PLAINTIFF'S COUNSEL: We're not using photos of the injuries, just some pictures of the accident site, the intersection. And they're black-and-white. We've got a group of four shots, taken about a month after the accident. There haven't been any changes out there and there's nothing staged. Just four shots of the intersection, East, West, North, South. Take a look.

DEFENSE COUNSEL: Well, these are all O.K., I think. Let's put it this way. I'll agree to yours if you'll agree to ours.

PLAINTIFF'S COUNSEL: I've seen yours and they're all right. Now these photos were all used in the depositions we took in this case and each one has an identifying mark put on it by the reporter at those depositions. We can use those numbers for now, and then change them at trial. Can we go on the record for this, Ms. Nixon?

THE COURT REPORTER: Yes, I'm ready.

PLAINTIFF'S COUNSEL: Let the record show that it is hereby stipulated by and between the parties to this action, through their counsel, that Plaintiff's Bushmat Deposition Exhibits Numbers 4, 5, 6, and 7 for Identification will be admissible in evidence at the trial of this case, without further foundation or proof, as being true and fair representations of what they purport to show. The same stipulation pertains to Defendant's Bushmat Deposition Exhibits C, D, E, F, and G for Identification. Is that satisfactory, Susan?

DEFENSE COUNSEL: Yes, that'll do it.

At trial, counsel will have the court reporter mark the deposition exhibits with new identifying numbers and letters with which the exhibits will be identified from then on. Each lawyer, when offering the exhibits, will inform the court that their admissibility has been stipulated by counsel. Each lawyer will repeat the full stipulation for the record and within the jury's hearing, thus making the record in an orderly and sequential manner. The exhibits will be received by the trial court without further foundation proof, although witnesses may make use of them as adjuncts to their testimony.

Stipulations are often entered into for the first time in the midst of trial. As one lawyer sets about laying the proper foundation for the introduction of a writing opposing counsel, seeing no reason not to spare his adversary from these laborious preliminaries, may interrupt to say, "We will stipulate that Plaintiff's Exhibit 10 for Identification is what it purports to be." The proposed stipulation, if accepted by offering counsel, serves to authenticate the document. Alert offering counsel will realize, however, that the proposed stipulation goes no further than that; by agreeing only that the writing "is what it purports to be," opposing counsel has reserved the right to assert objections based on evidentiary rules other than those governing authentication. It may go this way:

Q. Handing you what has been marked Plaintiff's Exhibit Number 10 for Identification, Mrs. Stitz, I'll ask you what it is, if you know?

A. This appears to be a letter dictated by my former employer, Mr. Morton P. Lishniss.

BY OPPOSING COUNSEL: Pardon me, counsel. We will stipulate that your Exhibit 10 is what it purports to be.

BY OFFERING COUNSEL: In that case, your Honor, we now offer in evidence what has been marked Plaintiff's Exhibit 10 for Identification.

BY OPPOSING COUNSEL: Well, now, just a moment. We object to it, your Honor. We agree that it is what it appears to be on its face, a letter from Lishniss to Bushmat dated April 1, 2011, but we don't think it has any relevance to this case. Furthermore, its receipt would violate the hearsay rule.

THE COURT: We'll take a brief recess while I hear argument from both sides on this.

Counsel will often be required by the trial court to accept any stipulation offered by the opposing side that unequivocally concedes everything that counsel would be entitled to show by making full proof. In such a situation the making of complete proof, the laying of every brick in the evidentiary foundation, would be a needless waste of time. On the other hand, offered stipulations do not always supply everything to which counsel is entitled. *See generally Old Chief v. United States*, 519 U.S. 172, 117 S.Ct. 644, 136 L.Ed.2d 574 (1997). In that situation she will be free to make a complete record on the matter in question. A common example has to do with the qualifications of an expert witness. Opposing counsel, desiring to keep the jury from hearing all of the witness' impressive credentials, may interrupt the preliminary examination to say, "We'll stipulate that Doctor Faust is a qualified orthopedist, your Honor." But such a stipulation does not give examining counsel everything to which she is entitled in a case that may involve a so-called battle of experts. In order to assign comparative weight to the opinions of opposing experts appearing in the case, the jurors are entitled to hear and assess the qualifications of each of them. And examining counsel is therefore entitled to make full proof of those qualifications, thus:

Q. Doctor, will you please give the court and jury your full name?

A. Myron L. Faust.

Q. Where do you reside?

A. 1000 Astor Place, Chicago, Illinois.

Q. What is your profession?

A. Physician and surgeon.

Q. Are you duly licensed to practice as a physician and surgeon in Illinois?

A. I am.

Q. What specialty, if any, have you made in your medical practice?

A. I specialize in orthopedic surgery.

Q. We will come back to that, Doctor. How long have you practiced medicine?

A. Twenty-six years this coming June.

Q. Of what medical school are you a graduate, Doctor Faust?

A. The Northwestern University Medical School in Chicago.

BY OPPOSING COUNSEL: Excuse me a moment. We're willing to stipulate that Doctor Faust is a qualified orthopedic surgeon and can testify here.

BY EXAMINING COUNSEL: We would prefer to make our proof on this, your Honor. The jury is entitled to hear his training and experience. The jurors have got to decide what weight to give his testimony and they can't very well do that without hearing his qualifications.

THE COURT: It would speed things up if you accepted the stipulation, counsel, but you can't be required to do so. You may proceed to establish the witness' qualifications.

Q. Very well, your Honor. Doctor Faust, what other training or study have you had?

BY OPPOSING COUNSEL: In view of our offer to stipulate, we object to this, your Honor.

THE COURT: Overruled.

II.

OFFERING EVIDENCE

Obviously, the making of a trial record consists in large part of offering evidence for the factfinder's consideration. The evidence will be in the form of oral testimony and tangible exhibits. The usual method for offering oral testimony into evidence is by engaging in the direct examination or cross-examination of a witness who has been called to the stand to testify under oath. (Sometimes oral testimony can also be offered by way of a deposition or a transcript of previously recorded testimony.) A tangible exhibit is ordinarily presented through a "sponsoring" witness who can identify or authenticate the item and reveal its relevance to some material issue in the case. After laying the necessary foundation, counsel will say something like "Your Honor, we now offer into evidence what has previously been marked Plaintiff's Exhibit Number 6 for Identification," at which point the trial court will rule on the offer, either receiving or rejecting it.

A.

Direct Examination of Witnesses

Unlike the practice in most European countries, where the witness merely stands up and delivers a long and sometimes rambling narrative concerning what he or she knows about the case, in Anglo-American law the witnesses relate their stories through the question-and-answer method. We require the witness to give his answers in response to relatively pointed questions so that the opposing counsel, forewarned by the question that the jury may be about to hear inadmissible material, can object in time to prevent receipt of the damaging answer.

In Anglo-American law not only must the parties proceed by question and answer, but they must adhere to certain forms of questions. And the restrictions are far more severe on the side calling the witness to the stand. The examination of one's own witness—direct examination as distinguished from cross-examination—is hedged about by a number of rules, the most familiar one being the rule against "leading" questions.

1. *Leading Questions.* A leading question is one that suggests its own answer. A typical leading question is, "You were driving your automobile well under the posted speed limit, isn't that so?" The witness may answer "Yes" but it is the attorney's version of the story that the jury hears. This type of question, at least when it goes to matters at the very heart of the case, is, with some exceptions that we will discuss, objectionable on direct examination. For example, Rule 611(c) of the Federal Rules of Evidence provides, "Leading questions should not be used on direct examination of except as necessary to develop the witness's testimony."

The notion has caught on that any question that can be answered "Yes" or "No" is automatically a leading one. This has led some lawyers to believe that they have only to preface their direct questions with "Did you or did you not * * * ? " or "What is the fact as to whether or not * * * ? " in order to avoid a successful objection. In fact, a question that is susceptible of a "Yes" or "No" response may be essentially non-leading, while the question with the seemingly neutral preface may strongly suggest the desired answer. The point is simply that although questions on direct examination can properly point the witness to a particular subject of inquiry, they should be reasonably balanced and neutral.

"Did you or did you not hear the man say, 'I just killed my wife'?" is a leading question, despite the seemingly neutral alternatives offered in the prefatory "Did you or did you not * * * ? " "And then did you hear the man say anything? " is technically leading but probably is permissible to suggest the desired topic of inquiry: what was *said* rather than what was *done* next. The wholly non-leading approach would be,

Q. What, if anything, happened next?

A. The man blurted out, "I just killed my wife!"

And everyone knows the all-time favorite non-leading question, "Directing your attention to April 1, 2011, I'll ask you whether anything unusual occurred?"—which may occasionally leave the witness totally baffled.

There are a number of situations in which leading questions are permitted even on direct examination.

(a.) Leading questions are allowed on preliminary matters that do not go to the heart of the case, and they are permitted to provide a transition from one subject of inquiry to another.

Q. And you are employed by the Acme Tool Company, I believe?

A. Yes.

Q. And have been for about ten years?

A. That's true.

* * *

Q. Now, Mr. Bushmat, turning to the day in question, were you and your family out driving in the country?

A. Yes, we were.

(b.) Leading questions are permitted with respect to undisputed matters where the question is used as a connective.

Q. You testified earlier, I believe, that you were driving at about thirty miles an hour, is that right?

A. Yes.

Q. Very well, then let me ask you this, * * *

(c.) An adverse or hostile witness can be asked leading questions. There is very little danger that such a witness would accept a false suggestion contained in a leading question. In the federal practice, leading questions can be put to "a witness identified with an adverse party." (Fed.R.Evid. 611(c)(2).)

(d.) Leading questions are allowed during direct examination when a witness gives "surprise" answers. Surprise is most commonly demonstrated where the witness' direct testimony is sharply at odds with his or her deposition testimony or with a previous statement. Of course, some courts suggest that examining counsel is not free to call a potentially adverse witness in the blind hope that his testimony will be helpful and then when it proves not to be, commence to lead and impeach him.

(e.) Leading questions may be allowed in connection with a witness of limited understanding, such as a child, an adult of diminished intelligence, or a person who is experiencing some language difficulty.

(f.) Leading questions can be put to a witness whose recollection has been exhausted but who apparently possesses additional information of a relevant sort. In other words, it is sometimes proper to refresh a witness' recollection by means of a leading question, thus—

Q. Can you remember the names of any other people who attended this meeting?

A. No, I can't. I know there were others but I just can't seem to come up with their names now.

Q. You have exhausted your recollection of those persons who were present?

A. I'm afraid so.

Q. Would it ring any bells if I suggested to you that Mr. Clyde Bushmat also attended that meeting?

A. You're right! Now I remember. Bushmat was there, too.

Some courts would require that counsel request permission before posing a leading question of this type. Immediately after receiving the response "I'm afraid so," counsel would inquire of the trial court, "Your Honor, may I ask the witness a leading question? His recollection is exhausted and yet he has indicated that he has additional knowledge." Under the circumstances indicated above, this request would undoubtedly be granted.

(g.) Hypothetical questions of the sort once commonly put to expert witnesses are intensely leading, up to a point, but they are permissible as a means of providing a factual basis for the expert's opinion.

Q. Doctor, I am going to ask you to assume that all of the following facts are true and then I will ask you for your opinion with respect to them. First, please assume that the plaintiff is a woman who on April 1, 2011, was thirty-five years of age. Assume that on that day she * * * [Counsel provides additional data, the truth of which is to be assumed by the witness.]

Now, assuming all of these facts to be true, do you have an opinion, based on a reasonable degree of medical certainty, as to whether the plaintiff's current condition was caused by the accident that she had on April 1, 2011?

A. I do.

Q. What is that opinion?

2. *Compound and Otherwise Confusing Questions.* In making the testimonial record, counsel should avoid the use of questions that will confuse or mislead the witness. The principal offender is the double or compound question, which may leave everyone in the courtroom baffled. Such questions result in ambiguous or incomplete responses.

Q. State where you were and whether at that time you had a conversation with Clyde Bushmat—was that his first name?—and, if so, what it was.

A. That's right, he said his first name was Clyde, and * * * What was the rest of your question?

BY EXAMINING COUNSEL: Would the court reporter please read the question back?

THE COURT: Maybe it would be better to ask him one question at a time, counsel. Put another question.

Questions should be brief, clear, and cast in reasonably simple terms. The use of negatives in questions is worth avoiding because they generate confusion.

Q. Actually, you don't know whether Bushmat was there, do you?

A. Yes.

THE COURT: Just one moment. Does the witness mean "Yes, I know," "Yes, it is true that I don't know," or "Yes, Bushmat was there"?

3. *Questions Assuming Unproved Facts.* The record cannot effectively be made by means of questions that assume the existence of facts that have neither been proved nor conceded. The classic example under this heading is "when did you stop beating your wife?" Nonexistent evidence cannot be supplied by means of "loaded" questions, since counsel is not testifying, and such questions only confuse the witness and the jury.

Expert Witnesses. The direct examination of an expert witness will differ somewhat from that of ordinary witnesses. This is true because of the operation of the so-called opinion rule. Generally speaking, witnesses are required to testify only about facts of which they have direct knowledge and they are not free to unburden themselves of opinions and beliefs about subjects on which any reasonably knowledgeable lay juror could form a conclusion. On the other hand, experts of one sort and another are allowed to express their opinions on relevant matters so long as a proper foundation has been laid.

An expert witness can state an opinion or conclusion if certain conditions are satisfied:

1. The validity of the opinion or conclusion must depend on special knowledge, experience, skill, or training not ordinarily found in lay jurors;

2. The witness must be qualified as an expert in the pertinent field;

3. She must possess a reasonable degree of certainty (probability) about her opinion or conclusion; and

4. Traditionally, in common law jurisdictions an expert witness could not testify as to an opinion without first making clear the case-specific facts on which it was based, and valid proof of those facts must have been offered in evidence. The expert might have observed some of those facts first-hand, or she may have been asked to accept hypothetically the truth of facts as to which other proof was given. As discussed below, the Federal Rules of Evidence promoted a loosening of these restrictions, and most states have followed suit. Experts in American courts may generally base an opinion on facts of a type on which experts in the field reasonably rely, even if no admissible evidence of those facts is presented; moreover, the expert need not state the facts on which she bases her opinion before giving the opinion itself. Whether, or the extent to which, constitutional constraints may limit the impact of this rule in criminal cases is a question not yet resolved at this writing.

Making the necessary record in connection with an expert witness involves two basic steps. First, he must be "qualified," that is, he must be asked a series of questions that will bring out his qualifications as an expert. Second, in some jurisdictions, and perhaps in some contexts in criminal cases, the record must show the data on which the witness' opinion is to be based.

"Qualifying" an Expert Witness. Needless to say, the qualifying questions will vary depending on the field of expertise that is involved.

There follows a typical sequence of direct questions aimed at qualifying a witness as a medical expert:

Q: Doctor, would you please state your full name and address for the court and jury?

A: Lenore T. Walsh, and I reside at 1213 North Lake Shore Drive, Chicago.

Q: What is your occupation or profession?

A: Physician.

Q: Are you licensed to practice as a physician in Illinois?

A: I am.

Q: Of what medical school are you a graduate?

A: Northwestern University Medical School, here in the city. I graduated in 1989.

Q: Are you in general practice or do you specialize?

A: I specialize.

Q: What is your specialty, Doctor?

A: Basically I'm a neurologist but my specialty is a narrow one, epilepsy and electroencephalography.

Q: Did you undergo special training for your specialty?

A: Yes, I did.

Q: Would tell us about it, please?

A: After graduating from medical school I went to Boston, to the Harvard Medical School, where I was an assistant in neuropathology. That's the study of manifestation of disease in nervous systems. I remained there one year and then I went to Johnson's Foundation for Medical Physics at the University of Pennsylvania, where I did research designed to provide us with improved diagnostic techniques for discovery and treatment of nervous diseases.

Q: What did you develop at Pennsylvania?

A: I developed a blood flow recording in the form of a needle that could be inserted in the large vein that drains blood from the brain, and I learned the technique for recording electroencephalograms from the body. I later applied this to recording the electric activity of the brain.

Q: That's what is called the electroencephalograph, right?

A: That's right.

Q: Can you describe to us, just in ordinary layman's language that we can all understand, how an electroencephalograph works?

A: [Witness complies.]

Q: And how long have you been taking electroencephalograms?

A: Since 1991.

Q: And have you read tracings since 1991?

A: Yes.

Q: Would you tell us approximately how many EEG's you have taken and interpreted?

A: I now have over 300 in my cross-index file, filed for diagnosis and for types of electroencephalogram abnormalities.

Q: Have you ever held a medical teaching position, Doctor Walsh?

A: Yes, I am professor of neurology at Northwestern.

Q: Are you a member of any learned medical societies?

A: Yes, quite a few. Besides the Illinois Medical Association, Chicago Medical Association, and American Medical Association, I am a member of the American Neurological Association, the American Academy of Neurologists, the American Epilepsy Society, the American Cerebral Society, and the American Electroencephalographic Association.

Q: Now, you indicated that you hold a teaching position at Northwestern's Medical School. Have you done teaching there concerning neurology and electroencephalograms?

A: Yes, those are my subject areas.

Q: You lecture to students on these subjects?

A: Yes, and to doctors.

Q: Have you ever written articles for medical journals on your specialty?

A: Yes, quite often.

Q: Would you give us some of the titles of your publications in learned journals?

A: [Witness complies.]

(At this point the witness would be tendered as an expert and opposing counsel would be permitted to engage in a *voir dire* examination, described hereafter, further to test the witness' level of expertise.)

Of course, the list of trained experts includes a broad range of persons who function in fields other than medicine but the mode of questioning to get their qualifications on the record is pretty much the same. Here is an example involving a trained expert from a field other than medicine:

Q: What is your name, please?

A: Milton F. Pine.

Q: And where do you live?

A: 630 North Beechwood Avenue, in Urbana, Illinois.

Q: What is your occupation?

A: I am on the faculty of the University of Illinois, Department of Forestry.

Q: Could you give us some notion of your background, sir?

A: Well, I had my undergraduate work at Purdue University in forestry. My Masters is from the New York State College of Forestry, and my Doctorate is from Yale University. At Yale I specialized in the field of wood properties, wood technology, and wood science.

Q: These are your specialties?

A: That's correct.

Q: Do you teach?

A: Yes, at Illinois, as I say. I teach those courses that have to do with the chemical, physical, and mechanical properties of wood.

Q: And when you speak of the properties of wood, what do you mean, just in everyday language?

A: [Witness explains his field in layman's terms.]

Q: Do you belong to any learned societies in your field of specialization?

A: Yes, I'm a member of the American Society for Testing and Materials. I am on two committees of the Society. I belong to the Forest Product Research Society and the American Wood Preservers Association.

Q: Have you had any experience with ladders, including the testing of them?

A: Yes, for the past twenty years or so. I have looked at a good many ladders, I can tell you, trying to find out why some of them failed. I have tested ladders, and I have tested components of ladders. I'm the author of an article, a technical report, on how one might use the weight of a ladder as a predictor of its bending strength and its service design.

Q: Could you tell us, Mr. Pine, if there are any standards that are used in the ladder industry?

A: Two main ones. The United States of America Standards Institute puts one out, Number A14.1. And the Underwriter's Laboratory has a standard on ladders.

Q: What is the purpose of publishing these standards for ladders?

A: [Witness explains that the standards are aimed at promoting the manufacture of safe, serviceable ladders.]

Q: And are you thoroughly familiar with these two standards?

A: Yes, indeed.

Q: Now, Mr. Pine, have you had occasion to examine Plaintiff's Exhibit 1 in this case, which is the ladder involved in the plaintiff's lawsuit?

A: Yes, at your request.

Q: Tell us what your examination consisted of.

A: [Witness complies.]

Q: Was your visual examination of Plaintiff's 1 sufficient for you to determine the cause of the collapse or breaking of this ladder?

A: Yes, it was.

Q: And you have an opinion about the cause?

A: Yes.

Q: What is that opinion?

A: The failure was a result of the cross-grain. The ladder's rails had less than 100 percent of their bending strength. It was a defect in the wood and it failed because of the defective wood.

There are those who have the mistaken belief that the title of "expert" can only be bestowed on a few members of professional groups who have a string of advanced degrees after their name. Some people think that only a scientist of one sort or another and perhaps a few engineers can rightly be called experts. But the term "expert" is far broader in meaning than this. Anyone who has ever tried to repair his own television set or automobile knows that some people are experts at these kinds of work and some are not. The proficient television repairer is an expert in his field even though a Ph.D. may be the last thing he ever hoped to acquire; the trained and experienced garage mechanic or plumber or brick mason is just as surely an expert as the most renowned neurosurgeon. The label "expert" applies to the sheet metal worker, the carpenter, the electrician, the candlestick maker. It applies to the firearms identification technician and those who are adept at fingerprint comparison. It applies to the police officer who knows how to use, interpret, and explain special equipment, such as radar vehicular speed measuring devices and equipment for measuring blood-alcohol ratios. As Rule 702 of the Federal Rules of Evidence points out, a witness may be qualified as an expert "by knowledge, skill, experience, training, or education."

And so counsel's qualifying questions sometimes focus on skill, knowledge, and experience rather than on educational background and memberships in learned societies. One short, somewhat unusual example will suffice. It combines expertise and personal knowledge.

Q: What is your name, young man?

A: Billy Walsh.

Q: Where do you live?

A: Here in Toledo.

Q: How old are you, Billy?

A: Eleven, pretty soon.

Q: How soon?

A: In two months, July.

Q: Do you have any hobbies, Billy; things you do for fun?

A: Yes.

Q: Name some of them, will you?

A: Baseball, swimming. I've got a little stamp collection. And I collect bugs.

Q: By that you mean insects?

A: That's the fancy name for them. I call 'em bugs.

Q: Good enough. How long have you been collecting bugs or insects?

A: For about four years.

Q: You collect them around here, around Toledo?

A: Yes, all around here, and out in the country, too.

Q: In the country around Toledo?

A: Yes, sir.

Q: Now, Billy, we have a question here as to whether a certain type of bug or insect is ever found around or in Toledo. In other words, in this part of the country. I want you to take a look at this bottle, which is marked Plaintiff's Exhibit Number 2. You'll see that there's a bug in the bottle. Turn the bottle all around and look at the bug and then tell us whether you have ever seen that kind of bug in or around Toledo, Ohio.

A: Sure, I have. I've got a whole box full of them in my room.

Q: Your witness, counsel.

At the conclusion of the direct questions aimed at qualifying a witness as an expert, and before examining counsel gets into substantive questions, opposing counsel is entitled to interrupt and engage in cross-examination as to the witness' expertise. This, somewhat confusingly, is often referred to as a *voir dire* of the witness. At this time the cross-examiner, believing the witness to be unqualified to express an "expert" opinion, makes his record. His cross-questions will be limited strictly to the matter of the witness' qualifications.

Hypothetical Questions to Experts. The medium of the hypothetical question has traditionally been employed where the expert witness does not have direct knowledge of the facts, or the evidence, on which an opinion is desired. Careful trial counsel will usually draft the hypothetical question well in advance of its use at trial. In doing this she will usually be assisted by the expert, thus making sure that all the essential facts are included in the question in a sensible sequence. At the beginning of a hypothetical question the witness is called upon to assume as true all of the facts that will be asserted by counsel in the body of the question. The body of the question then sets forth, in hypothetical form, the material facts as to which the expert's opinion is sought. (In the federal practice, as will be further explained later, it is not necessary to lay out *all* of the underlying facts, however. See Fed.R.Evid. 705: "Unless the court orders otherwise, an expert may state an opinion—and give the reasons for it—without first testifying to the underlying facts or data.") A hypothetical question's conclusion inquires whether the witness has an opinion, based upon a reasonable degree of certainty, regarding the assumed facts. Thus a hypothetical question may end this way:

Q: Doctor Faust, assuming all of these facts to be true, have you an opinion, based on a reasonable degree of certainty from a surgical point of view, whether the facts assumed in the question and the injury assumed, namely, the dislocation of the vertebrae, and the fracture of the lamina of the fifth cervical vertebra, are sufficient to cause the symptoms and the conditions assumed in my hypothetical question?

A: I do have an opinion.

Q: What is that opinion, doctor? [At this point any objection to the question will be made and ruled upon.]

Hypothetical Questions Under the Federal Rules of Evidence. The approach to expert testimony taken by the Federal Rules of Evidence is less limiting than the typical common law approach outlined above.

In the first place, Rule 703 provides that an expert witness can base his opinion testimony "on facts or data in the case that the expert has been made aware of or personally observed." This means that underlying facts or data can be gleaned not only from firsthand observation or from listening to testimony or a fullblown hypothetical question but also from a presentation made to the witness outside the courtroom. For example, this presentation might consist of showing an expert medical witness the pertinent medical records of the person about whose mental or physical condition the witness is to testify.

Q: Doctor Faust, prior to this trial did you, at my request, review all of the medical records of the plaintiff Clyde Bushmat, including his medical history?

A: I did, very thoroughly.

Q: And did you have occasion to examine Mr. Bushmat in your office?

A: Yes, I conducted a complete neurological examination.

Q: I will ask you whether, on the basis of your review of all his records and your clinical examination, you have formed an opinion, to a reasonable degree of medical certainty, regarding the cause of his reported back pain?

A: I have, yes.

Q: Would you please tell the court and jury what your opinion is, and your reasons for arriving at that opinion?

A: [Witness states his opinion and describes his reasons for reaching it, but does not describe—at least not in complete detail—the specific facts of the plaintiff's case.]

The expert's omission of all the facts underlying his or her opinion is explicitly authorized by the Federal Rules of Evidence. Rule 705 provides that an expert can testify to her conclusions and explain the reasons for them without prior in-court disclosure of the underlying facts or data, unless the trial judge requires disclosure.

This provision eliminates the necessity for lengthy and often tedious hypothetical questions, used as a vehicle for revealing the data on which an expert's opinion builds. However, Rule 705 does not do away with the hypothetical question absolutely; it simply does away with any absolute requirement that a hypothetical question, or a complete one, be used. The putting of a hypothetical question sometimes has its advantages as an educational device (or, to put it on a tactical plane, it permits counsel to summarize some of the evidence long before the time for her closing argument or summation) and trial lawyers do not invariably accept the rule's invitation to forgo their use altogether. What Rule 705 does do is permit some streamlining of expert testimony, either by omission of the hypothetical question or its abbreviation. The rule forecloses successful assignments of error based on a claim that opposing counsel's hypothetical was incomplete, that is, did not include every scrap of underlying data. Thus the rule should make counsel less nervous about the use of hypotheticals. In effect, Rule

705 places on the cross-examiner the burden of eliciting any weak, unreliable, or missing data. This strongly suggests that opposing counsel will be at a distinct disadvantage unless she has engaged in adequate pre-trial discovery. (Consult Federal Rule of Civil Procedure 26(b)(4).)

Laying the Foundation for Admission of Evidence. Before plunging into testimony on the merits the direct examiner of a witness usually finds it necessary to lay a preliminary foundation for the witness' testimony or for the admission of an exhibit that the witness is "sponsoring". For example, some foundation questions will be required to demonstrate that the witness is a percipient one; that is, that she was in a spatial and temporal position to obtain personal knowledge of the matters about which she is to testify. (Fed.R.Evid. 602 reads: "A witness may testify to a matter only if evidence is introduced sufficient to support a finding that the witness has personal knowledge of the matter. Evidence to prove personal knowledge may consist of the witness's own testimony.") This involves putting questions aimed at showing that the witness was in a position to see, hear, etc., the matters about which she is going to testify. It may not be much more complicated than inquiring, "About how far away were you from the two vehicles when you saw them collide?"

A foundation attesting relevance is also essential, although this is often self-evident from the natural flow of the witness' descriptive testimony. Still, careless trial counsel sometimes neglect it. It is not enough, in connection with a railroad grade crossing accident that occurred on April 1, 2007, to ask a witness who has been handed a photograph, "Is Plaintiff's Exhibit 9 for Identification a true and fair representation of the Madison Street grade crossing of the Illinois Central Railroad?" Time is frequently an indispensable ingredient of relevance; perhaps the characteristics of the grade crossing have changed significantly since April 1, 2007. A vital component of the relevance foundation for plaintiff's photograph is the time factor, since the factfinder requires assurance that the photograph accurately depicts the crossing's appearance at the *pertinent* time. Thus the proper sequence of examination would run something like this:

Q: As a result of your daily route to work, about which you have previously testified, were you familiar with the appearance of the Madison Street grade crossing of the Illinois Central Railroad as of April 1, 2007?

A: Yes, I had been over it, both ways, almost every day during both March and April of that year.

Q: Then I want you to cast your mind back to that time, April 1, 2007. I hand you what has been marked Plaintiff's Exhibit 9 for Identification and I'll ask you whether or not it is a true and fair representation of the Illinois Central's Madison Street grade crossing as it existed on April 1, 2007?

A: Yep, that's the way it looked back then.

Obviously, counsel often must lay a foundation—make a record—that demonstrates the existence of the essential elements of some evidentiary principle on which she intends to rely. Here a list of examples could be extended to cover every rule of admissibility. We can content ourselves with two examples that illustrate the meticulous making of the record preliminary to the offering of an item of evidence through an exception to the rule against hearsay. First, an example involving an item of past recollection recorded; then one involving a business record.

The past recollection recorded example (see Fed.R.Evid. 803(5)) comes from an insurance case. Counsel is trying to establish that a stolen Chinese painting had, at the pertinent time, been in the possession of her client, plaintiff Edman. The witness on the stand is an art dealer.

Q: As I understand it, then, you were in Mr. Edman's hotel room in London. He unwrapped the package, which was a sort of cylinder about a foot and a half long and as big around as your wrist, is that right?

A: That's correct, took the paper off of it.

Q: Can you describe what was in the package or tube?

A: Yes, I can. It was a Chinese scroll painting.

Q: A scroll, rolled up?

A: Yes, but Mr. Edman unrolled it on the table so I could examine it.

Q: What was it of, a landscape or figure or what?

A: Typical Chinese landscape.

Q: Did it bear any identifying markings of any kind?

A: It did.

Q: Please describe any identifying markings you saw on the Edman painting.

A: Well, I don't read old Chinese but there was a single Chinese character at the top of the painting, in the margin.

Q: You observed this marking on the painting?

A: Yes, but I couldn't read it, if that's what you're asking.

Q: I understand. But can you describe the mark to us? Do you recall what it looked like?

A: Vaguely. It had dots in it. Little circles. I can't give you a much better description. I don't remember it that well. It was just a Chinese character. Most Chinese pictures have a number of characters on them. The big one may be the artist's signature. The little ones along the side, made with a seal, are often collectors' marks.

Q: This painting had just one big character on it?

A: Yes.

Q: And you knew what that character looked like while you were there in Mr. Edman's hotel room?

A: Of course, I was looking right at it.

Q: Thank you. After you looked at the picture, what did you do?

* * *

Q: When you got back to your hotel room, what time was it, if you know?

A: It was 9:30.

Q: And you think you left Mr. Edman's room at about 9:15?

A: Yes. It was on the sixteenth floor and I was on the twenty-second. I'm being conservative but it took me a few minutes to get an elevator.

Q: When you got back to your own room, what did you do?

A: I sat down at the desk and made a memorandum of our meeting.

Q: The meeting with Mr. Edman?

A: Yes.

Q: What, in general, did you include in this memo?

A: There wasn't anything general about it. I put down everything that happened, what was said, the whole thing. I wanted some future protection.

Q: How would you characterize your memory of that meeting at the time you prepared your memo?

A: Perfect, excellent. I could remember everything that went on.

Q: Did you describe the Chinese character in your memo?

A: Not in words.

Q: Did you describe it at all?

A: Yes, I drew a sketch of it.

Q: You still remembered what it looked like?

A: Then, I did.

Q: But you don't now?

A: Not well enough to draw it again accurately, no. I see a lot of characters in my business.

Q: Don't we all? When you drew the sketch of the character that night, did you draw it accurately?

A: Yes.

Q: On what sort of paper did you draw it?

A: On the hotel stationery. Claridge's.

[To the court reporter]: I will ask the court reporter to mark this for identification as Plaintiff's Exhibit 6. [Reporter does so; counsel shows the exhibit to the judge and opposing counsel.]

Q: Handing you what has been marked Plaintiff's Exhibit 6 for Identification, I'll ask you if you know what it is?

A: Yes, this is my memo.

Q: In your longhand?

A: Yes.

Q: Made about 9:30 on the night of January 14, 2008?

A: That's right.

Q: Does Exhibit 6 contain the drawing or sketch about which you have just testified; the drawing or sketch you made of the Chinese character that was on the painting that Mr. Edman showed you that night?

A: Yes. Do you want me to point it out to you?

Q: Better yet, take this pencil and draw a circle around the sketch as it appears on Plaintiff's Exhibit 6 for Identification.

The foundation for a business record offered, for example, under Federal Rule of Evidence 803(6), will involve this sort of questioning:

Q: What is your name, sir?

A: Arthur L. Jackson, of 1300 Terrace Road, East Cleveland.

Q: What is your business or occupation, Mr. Jackson?

A: I'm a bookkeeper.

Q: Employed by whom?

A: Flashner Furniture Company, here in Cleveland.

Q: Were you employed by Flashner Furniture on March 17, 2006?

A: Yes.

Q: Who was in charge of the bookkeeping department there at that time?

A: I was, and I still am.

Q: Very good, sir. Were all the entries in the books and records of the Flashner Furniture Company kept and maintained by you?

A: Yes, and they were made under my supervision.

Q: What books or records of account did you use in 2006?

A: Same as now. A ledger, cash book, journal, and the invoice or sales book.

Q: Will you describe the method you followed in 2006 in keeping your books?

A: Sales tickets are made in paper for all sales and from there, posted to the general ledger, which we maintain digitally. The sales tickets are bound together in what we call a sales book. All receipts are also posted digitally to the ledger. The journal is used for general entries.

Q: I show you what has been marked Plaintiff's Exhibit 1 for Identification and ask you what it is, if you know?

A: It is a printout of the ledger account of Mr. Robert H. Watkins.

Q: How do you know that?

A: I printed it out myself this morning in response to a subpoena you issued to me. I brought it from my office.

Q: Was Plaintiff's Exhibit 1 made in the usual and ordinary course of your business, if you know?

A: Well, as I say, I just made the printout to comply with the subpoena. But the account that the printout reflects was kept in the ordinary course of our business.

Q: I show you Plaintiff's Exhibit 2 for Identification. Do you know what it is?

A: Yes, it is the sales book that I referred to earlier.

Q: Was Exhibit 2 prepared and kept under your supervision?

A: Yes, sir.

Q: In the usual course of business?

A: Certainly.

Q: In whose handwriting is Exhibit 2?

A: My assistant's.

Q: Who provided the information contained in Exhibit 2? Who transmitted that information to your assistant?

A: Our sales personnel.

Q: They are required to do that?

A: Yes, that's one of their duties.

Q: Did you bring Exhibit 2 here in response to my subpoena?

A: Yes. I would have brought them anyway, with or without.

Q: Thank you very much. It's just a formality. Did you bring them from your office at Flashner's?

A: I did. From the files.

Q: Who would have posted the items shown on Plaintiff's Exhibit 2, the sales book, to the ledger that yielded Exhibit 1?

A: My assistant.

Q: Would his doing this have been in accordance with regular practice in your business?

A: Yes, sir.

BY OFFERING COUNSEL: Your Honor, we now offer into evidence what have been marked Plaintiff's Exhibits 1 and 2.

THE COURT: They will be received.

Using an Interpreter. When a witness has a serious language barrier—when he or she speaks no English or very little—the testimonial record will have to be made with the assistance of a qualified interpreter. The interpreter must be shown to be disinterested and will be required to swear or affirm that he "will truly and correctly translate the questions of counsel from English to [German, Spanish, whatever the witness' language may be] and the answers of the witness from [German, Spanish] to English, so help me God." Counsel will frame her questions just as though she were questioning the witness directly in English. That is, counsel, looking at the witness on the stand and not at the interpreter, will inquire, "What happened next?"; she will not address her question to the interpreter, saying, "Now ask him what happened next." A useful precaution involves the making of an audio recording of any translated examination.

B.

Cross-Examination of Witnesses

As was suggested earlier, cross-examination is a much more flexible instrument than direct examination. It is hedged about by far fewer restrictive rules. Relevance is the principal test of a cross-question's propriety; relevance, and whether the cross-questions are ranging too far beyond the contours of opposing counsel's direct examination of the witness.

The proper purposes of cross-examination are numerous. At its most innocuous, cross-examination may do no more than clarify, supplement, or qualify the direct testimony of a not very damaging witness. However, cross-examination is usually used in a much more aggressive fashion. In an effort to weaken the witness' direct evidence, the cross-examiner's questions may challenge the sources of the witness' knowledge, together with his perception and his memory. The examiner may also try to demonstrate the witness' inability to describe events consistently and accurately. Cross-examination can be employed to extract admissions of fact that undermine the witness' direct testimony. And cross-examination can be used to impeach the witness' veracity, to cast a cloud on his truthfulness.

On one level a witness' veracity can be put in doubt by inquiries revealing an interest or partisanship, the existence of a bias or prejudice, which might lead him to misrepresent the facts or to twist them. That he is related to or friendly with the opposite party, or hostile to the examining side, can be developed, and any direct or indirect pecuniary interest in the outcome of the lawsuit can be gone into.

A witness can be impeached, on a somewhat different level, by cross-questions revealing that he has made prior out-of-court statements that are inconsistent with the answers he gave on his in-court direct examination. Occasionally a witness can also be impeached, on yet another level, by evidence of serious criminal convictions or prior "bad acts" tending to cast doubt on his current reliability.

It follows from what has just been said that counsel is free to use leading questions to make his or her record on cross-examination. (See, e.g., Fed.R.Evid. 611(c)(1), providing that "[o]rdinarily, the court should allow leading questions . . . on cross-examination") It is virtually impossible to conduct an impeaching cross-examination without asking leading questions. This does not mean, however, that excessively argumentative cross-questions will be countenanced by a trial court. It is one thing to inquire, in altogether leading fashion, "Isn't it a fact that on the night in question you could see only about ten or twelve feet ahead of you?" It is quite another thing, upon being given an unsatisfying response, heatedly to inquire, "Do you really expect the jury to believe that?" The first question is proper on cross-examination, there being scant risk that the opposing party's witness will accept the suggestion built into a leading question and supply the cross-examining party with a favorable but false answer. The second question is improper on either direct or cross-examination; it is unduly argumentative and contributes nothing of value to the trial record.

Questions assuming unproved facts ("loaded" questions), compound and otherwise confusing questions are no more allowable on cross-examination than they are on direct.

C.

Tangible Evidence

Standing in contrast to testimonial evidence is tangible evidence. Tangible evidence may be a writing, a murder weapon, the seized marijuana, a rusted metal container, the scar on a tort plaintiff's face. Putting writings to one side for a moment, because special rules have clustered around them, we can say that there are two basic types of tangible evidence: (1) real evidence, and (2) demonstrative evidence. And just as one must qualify oral testimony for admission into evidence by showing, for example, that the witness has personal knowledge of relevant facts, one must also qualify items of tangible evidence for receipt into evidence.

Tangible exhibits should be offered during the direct or re-direct examination of a party's witnesses and not during the cross-examination of the adverse party's witnesses. To put it a different way, *your* exhibits should be offered during *your* direct case, not opposing counsel's. It is not reversible error, however, to receive exhibits during cross-examination; the trial court can permit it and the parties can agree to it, expressly or by implication (as when no objection is interposed).

Real Evidence. This is "the real thing"—the actual murder weapon, not a mere example of a weapon of the type said to have been used in the alleged crime. Real evidence can be direct evidence, offered to establish facts about the tangible thing itself, such as the extent of plaintiff's disfigurement as a consequence of the observable facial scar. Real evidence can also be circumstantial, as when facts about an object are offered as the basis for an inference that some other fact is true; for example, rust inside a metal container implies the prior presence of moisture in the container.

The procedure for making the record in connection with real evidence is sometimes quite elaborate, depending on the nature of the particular exhibit. (It is usually easier to get a single letter into evidence than a patient's complete medical record, consisting of numerous separate records made by different authors at different times in different places for different reasons.) In general, there are six steps, all of them important:

1. *Marking for Identification.* In order to build a trial record that will be understandable and efficient to work with later on, counsel will cause real evidence to be marked or tagged for identification, usually by the court reporter. Thereafter, during her examination of witnesses, counsel will refer to the item by its identifying number or letter. Still later, when someone reads the typewritten trial record, she can readily associate the witness' testimony with the marked exhibits that are bound into the record either at the end of the transcribed testimony or, if the record is a lengthy one, in one or more separate volumes.

With experienced trial counsel the matter of marking exhibits for identification becomes almost automatic: when a trial lawyer picks something up with the intention of introducing it in evidence, she will first proceed to the court reporter and ask him to mark it in numerical or alphabetical sequence. Counsel will then subside into silence, since the reporter cannot record counsel's comments or continued questions to a witness while at the same time marking or tagging the exhibit. After the exhibit has been marked, counsel will as a matter of courtesy show the exhibit to the trial judge and opposing counsel unless they have already seen it or, in the case of a writing, diagram, chart, map, or the like, been provided by counsel with copies.

Step No. 1 goes this way, then:

OFFERING COUNSEL [having picked up a letter from the counsel table]: I will ask the court reporter to mark this for identification. If I recall correctly, this would be Plaintiff's 9.

COURT REPORTER [marking the exhibit]: Yes, this will be Plaintiff's 9.

OFFERING COUNSEL: Your Honor, I believe we gave you a Xerox copy of this letter. It is dated April 1, 2011, on the defendant's letterhead.

THE COURT: Yes, I have it.

OFFERING COUNSEL [addressing opposing counsel]: And we supplied you with a copy, too, did we not?

OPPOSING COUNSEL: Yes, we have our copy, although of course we reserve our right to object to it at the appropriate time.

OFFERING COUNSEL: Of course.

In complex litigations, counsel may have caused all or most of the tangible exhibits, especially writings, to be marked for identification prior to the onset of trial, often at a judicially supervised pre-trial conference at which objections to the exhibits were considered and ruled upon. (See III., Objections to Evidence, infra.)

2. *Laying the Necessary Foundation.* In the absence of a pretrial ruling or an agreement (stipulation) with opposing counsel that the exhibit is re-

ceivable, it will next be necessary to lay the foundation for admission of the item of real evidence. (See, e.g., Fed.R.Evid. 901.) This is usually accomplished through one or more witnesses who "sponsor" the exhibit, identifying (authenticating) it and illuminating its relevance to the issues in the case. Basically, this involves testifying that the exhibit is "the genuine article," "the real thing." Sometimes it involves testimony that the exhibit is a legitimate form of demonstrative evidence. Examination under Step No. 2 may proceed in this way:

BY OFFERING COUNSEL: Officer, I hand you what has been marked Prosecution Exhibit Number 1 for Identification and ask you if you know what it is?

A. Yes, I recognize it.

Q. What is it?

A. This is the knife that I found next to the victim's body that night.

Q. And by "this" you mean Prosecution Exhibit Number 1?

A. Yes, sir.

Q. How do you know that Prosecution Exhibit Number 1 is the same knife that you saw that night?

A. At that time I scratched the date and my initials on the handle of the knife, right here. [Indicating.]

If the witness, unlike the one in the preceding example, is unable to identify the exhibit to the exclusion of all similar objects, the chain of custody, without any hearsay links, must be traced in order to establish that the exhibit is "the real thing." This means that there will be a whole series of witnesses called to the stand, each one accounting for the period during which the exhibit was in his or her custody. In this manner each link in the chain of custody is forged and it is demonstrated that the exhibit is in fact "the genuine article."

If the condition of the object is significant, the sponsoring witness must be prepared to testify that its condition has not changed in any important way since the pertinent time, thus—

BY OFFERING COUNSEL: Mrs. Stitz, I show you Plaintiff's Exhibit Number 3 for Identification. Do you know what that is?

A. Yes, that's the tin can that I cut my hand on.

Q. How do you happen to know that?

A. It's been on a shelf in my kitchen ever since that day, except for the time I brought it to your office to show to you, and I brought it to court today myself.

Q. Can you tell us whether the condition of Exhibit Number 3 has changed since the day of your accident?

A. Just that there aren't any green beans in it any more. I cleaned it out.

Q. Otherwise it looks the same?

A. Yes, sir. You can still see the jagged metal protrusion that cut my hand. [Indicating.]

Finally, it should be mentioned that the record has not been satisfactorily made where the instrumentality of an alleged crime has not been linked to the crime and to the accused.

3. *Offering the Exhibit into Evidence.* The third step involves offering the exhibit into evidence once the proper foundation has been laid. Step No. 3, although sometimes forgotten by inexperienced trial counsel, is a mechanical one:

BY OFFERING COUNSEL: Your Honor, we now offer into evidence, as Plaintiff's Exhibit Number 1, what has previously been marked as Plaintiff's Exhibit Number 1 for Identification.

THE COURT: There being no objection, it will be received.

4. *Securing an Express Ruling on the Record.* In the preceding example the trial court made a prompt and explicit ruling on counsel's offer. Occasionally, however, counsel may find it necessary to request the court to make an unequivocal ruling. The trial court's silence in the face of an offer will not necessarily be taken, on review, as an acceptance of the offered evidence.

5. *A Precautionary Measure.* Cautious counsel, having obtained a ruling admitting his exhibit into evidence, may foreclose any possible future confusion by requesting the court reporter to scratch out the words "for Identification" in the exhibit-mark, thereby making it doubly clear that the exhibit was received in evidence.

6. *Showing or Reading the Exhibit to the Jury.* Now, for the first time, offering counsel is free to show the exhibit to the jurors or, in the case of written material, read it to them or direct the witness to read it to them. As a matter of courtesy, however, express permission to do so is usually requested of the trial judge.

BY OFFERING COUNSEL: Your Honor, may we now pass the exhibit, Plaintiff's Number 1, to the members of the jury for their examination?

THE COURT: You may.

Counsel will put no new questions to the witness on the stand until the jurors have had an opportunity to inspect the exhibit that has been handed to them. Alternatively, in the case of a writing, counsel might ask for permission to provide the jurors with duplicates or display the writing with a document camera.

So-called "testimonial exhibits," such as a deposition that has been placed in evidence or a learned treatise offered under Fed.R.Evid. 803(18), usually must be read into the record (in the fact-finders' hearing, of course) since most jurisdictions will not as a matter of course permit this sort of exhibit to be taken by the jurors to their deliberation room for examination along with the other exhibits in the case. (It is thought that giving the testimonial exhibit to the jurors might unduly highlight an isolated block of testimony.) Counsel can read the exhibit into the record herself or, in the case of a deposition or prior recorded testimony, she can put someone in the witness chair—another lawyer with whom she is associated, even a moonlighting actor hired as a deposition reader—to read the deponent's or witness' answers in response to counsel's reading of the questions contained in the deposition or transcript.

Demonstrative Evidence. This is *not* "the real thing." It is tangible material used for explanatory or illustrative purposes only: it is a visual aid, such as an anatomical model, a chart, a diagram, a map, a video recording, and the like. Evidence that is demonstrative only—that does not qualify as substantive evidence—is not ordinarily offered into evidence in the way real evidence is and it thus does not go to the jury's deliberation room. However, this does not mean that there is no foundational procedure, no record to be made, in connection with demonstrative material.

There are two basic types of demonstrative evidence. First there is "selected" demonstrative evidence, such as handwriting exemplars (specimens) used as standards of comparison by a handwriting expert. Then there is "prepared" or "reproduced" demonstrative evidence, such as the model or the diagram.

It is in connection with prepared or reproduced demonstrative material that there is the greatest risk of fabrication or distortion. The law seeks to minimize these risks by requiring certain testimonial assurances. These assurances are a part of the foundation, part of the record that must be made, as a precondition to the use of demonstrative materials in the courtroom.

In the first place, it is again true, as it usually is with real evidence, that conditions shown by the exhibit must not be significantly different from those that existed at the time of the events in question. If conceded changes are irrelevant, they must at least be accounted for, as, for example, in connection with a photograph of the accident site that reveals buildings constructed since the incident in question.

Secondly, there must be testimony that a particular demonstrative exhibit is a "true and fair representation" of what it purports to show. Thus a person familiar with the scene depicted in a photograph (it need not necessarily be the photographer) can lay the foundation for the photograph's use as an item of demonstrative material. In connection with motion picture film and tapes, there must be testimony from a knowledgeable witness that they have not been improperly edited by means of splicing, erasing and the like.

Writings. The evidentiary significance of writings frequently depends on their authorship. If the asserted letter of acceptance was dictated and signed by the defendant corporation's president, it will be a crucial item of evidence in a contract case; if it was signed by someone lacking any authority, real or apparent, to do so, it will be of no legal consequence. Accordingly, it often is necessary to make a record on the question of authorship. Is the writing truly what it purports to be on its face, a letter composed and signed by the defendant's president? A writing, in other words, is not receivable in evidence until it has been authenticated. (See e.g., Fed.R.Evid., Arts. IX–X.) Its genuineness must be demonstrated to the trial judge, as a preliminary matter, before the jury can consider it. It cannot be read or shown to the jury until the record has been made and the writing has been formally admitted into evidence by the judge.

A writing can be authenticated in a variety of ways:

1. By a notice or request to admit genuineness, as under Rule 36 of the Federal Rules of Civil Procedure.

2. By *direct* evidence that proves the handwriting in question. This can be either the identifying testimony of the writing's author, or the testimony of anyone who observed the writing being made.

3. By proving the handwriting *circumstantially,* which can be accomplished—

a. By the identifying testimony of someone who is familiar with the handwriting of the person in question;

b. By the testimony of a handwriting expert who compares the questioned handwriting with one or more genuine specimens; or

c. By letting the jurors themselves compare the questioned handwriting with genuine specimens (an approach which appeals to very few trial lawyers).

4. By reliance on common law, statutory or rules provisions that render some writings self-authenticating or that set up presumptions of authenticity. (A good example is the so-called ancient documents rule (see generally, Fed.R.Evid., Art. IX).)

The following is a simple example of direct authenticating testimony:

Q. Give your full name to the jury, please.

A. Clyde Bushmat.

Q. Your address?

A. 1313 Euclid Avenue, Cleveland, Ohio.

Q. What is your occupation?

A. I'm a deliveryman for C.D. Pigeon, a jewelry company here in the city.

Q. Do you know Morton P. Lishniss, the defendant in this case?

A. I do.

Q. How do you happen to know him?

A. I have delivered merchandise to him from time to time.

BY EXAMINING COUNSEL [to court reporter]: Please mark this Plaintiff's Exhibit Number 1 for Identification.

Q. Showing you what has just been marked Plaintiff's Exhibit Number 1 for Identification, Mr. Bushmat, I will ask you whether you have ever seen it before?

A. I've seen it before, yes.

Q. When, sir?

A. When I delivered the merchandise that's listed on it.

Q. On the occasion of that delivery did you see Morton P. Lishniss?

A. Sure I did.

Q. Tell us what happened.

A. I delivered the diamond necklace to Mr. Lishniss myself and I requested that he sign the receipt for it.

Q. Did he do so?

A. Yes, sir.

Q. How do you know he did?

A. I saw him do it.

Q. You saw him?

A. Yes I did. He signed it right there while I was watching him.

Q. Whose signature is this on Plaintiff's Exhibit Number 1 for Identification, Mr. Bushmat?

A. That's the signature that Mr. Lishniss made in my presence.

BY EXAMINING COUNSEL: We offer Plaintiff's Exhibit Number 1 for Identification as Plaintiff's Exhibit Number 1, your Honor.

THE COURT: It will be received.

If counsel is offering something other than the original of a writing his making of the record will include an indication of compliance with the "best evidence" rule. (See Fed.R.Evid., Art. X.) The following example begins in midstream:

Q. How many copies of the contract were signed, Ms. McLaren?

A. Just one.

Q. Who retained that? Who kept it?

A. I did.

Q. Do you have that original agreement that was executed by you and Mr. Bushmat?

A. No, I don't.

Q. Do you know where it is?

A. No, I do not. I can't find it.

Q. When did you last see it, Ms. McLaren?

A. The day we signed it.

Q. What did you do with it?

A. I put it in one of my desk drawers right after we executed it.

Q. Have you seen it since then?

A. No.

Q. When did you first look for it again?

A. About ten days ago, but I couldn't find it anywhere.

Q. Where did you search?

A. In my desk drawers, on top of the desk, all around my office, at home. Everywhere that I ordinarily keep papers. I looked everywhere.

Q. Have you tried to find it since then?

A. Yes. No luck.

Q. What do you think has happened to the original of the agreement?

A. Well, it's lost, that's all.

Q. Did you intentionally lose it or destroy it?

A. Of course not.

BY EXAMINING COUNSEL: Mark this Plaintiff's Exhibit Number 1 for Identification, if you please.

Q. Handing you what has been marked Plaintiff's Exhibit Number 1 for Identification, Ms. McLaren, I will inquire whether you have ever seen it before?

A. Oh, yes.

Q. Where and when?

A. In my office. I saw it there at the same time that the original agreement was executed. This is a Xerox copy of the original.

Q. Can you tell by looking at it whether or not it's a true and correct copy of the original?

A. Yes.

Q. Is it, or not?

A. Yes, it is. It was made that day, off the original. The Xerox shows the signatures, everything.

BY EXAMINING COUNSEL: We offer in evidence Plaintiff's Exhibit Number 1 for Identification.

THE COURT: It will be admitted as Plaintiff's Exhibit Number 1.

D.

Judicial Notice

Counsel who wish to take advantage of the time- and effort-saving judicial notice procedure should take care to make a proper record. Judicial notice satisfies in place of proof by admitted evidence if the fact to be noticed is (1) subject to common knowledge among reasonably informed persons in the jurisdiction or (2) capable of accurate and ready determination by resort to sources whose accuracy cannot reasonably be disputed.

If one or the other of these two bases for judicial notice is present, the taking of notice by a trial judge is mandatory if a proper record is made. This involves (1) an on-the-record request for the taking of judicial notice and for the giving of an appropriate jury instruction—"We ask the court to take judicial notice, and so instruct the jury, that the Chicago River runs backwards, away from and not into Lake Michigan"—and (2) presentation to the court, on the record, of any necessary back-up information such as an authoritative source of the sort mentioned in Federal Rule of Evidence 201(b)(2). The procedure might sound like this:

BY REQUESTING COUNSEL: Your Honor, we request the court to take judicial notice, and so instruct the jury, that December 29, 2011, fell on a Thursday.

THE COURT: Well, counsel, I don't know that as a fact and I doubt if it's common knowledge.

BY REQUESTING COUNSEL: Your Honor, I was just going to hand up to you a 2011 calendar published and distributed to lawyers by the Chicago Title & Trust Company.

THE COURT: All right, I see that Decembr 29 was a Thursday. I don't suppose opposing counsel wants a hearing on the accuracy of this calendar?

BY OPPOSING COUNSEL: That won't be necessary, your Honor.

THE COURT: Ladies and gentlemen of the jury, you are instructed to take it as established in this case, without further proof, that December 29, 2011, was a Thursday.

III.

OBJECTIONS TO EVIDENCE

A.

Party Responsibility for Making Objections

The rules of evidence can be made to work only if a party who contends that opposing counsel's question is improper or that certain evidence should be excluded promptly advises the trial judge, who is the umpire of the litigation, of the contention and the reasons for it. The initiative with respect to evidentiary objections lies with the parties, acting through their counsel, and not with the trial judge. This is simply another example of party responsibility in the adversary trial process. (See, e.g., Fed.R.Evid. 103.)

It is a responsibility gladly assumed by competent trial counsel, who dislike few things more than a trial judge's usurpation of the litigator's obligation to decide which objections, perhaps for purely tactical or strategic reasons, he will forgo. Thus it is unusual, although it would not be without precedent, to hear a judge exclude evidence to which counsel has not objected; a competent judge will do this only where the offered evidence is not only incompetent but also irrelevant or potentially unfairly prejudicial or where she is preserving the rights of an absent holder of some testimonial privilege. Occasionally, however, one encounters the sort of judge who, possibly because he is himself a frustrated trial lawyer, will interrupt testimony to inquire of one silent side, "Do I hear an objection?" With almost equal frequency one will hear the lawyer for that side respond, "You do not, your Honor." Counsel, for reasons of her own, has made a deliberate decision to dispense with any objection.

B.

Reasons for Forgoing Available Objections

No trial lawyer makes every evidentiary objection that may be open to him. There are a variety of reasons for this. (1) Trial counsel has no need or wish to complain about every innocuous leading question put by opposing counsel since the use of leading questions as to preliminary matters expedites the examination of witnesses, which is usually advantageous to all concerned and poses no real risk of prejudice. (2) Counsel may let a questionable objection go by the board because he does not want to run the risk that he will only underscore hurtful testimony. (3) He may abandon an available objection because he does not want to give the jurors the impression that he is excessively obstructive or that he distrusts them. (4) Often counsel forgoes objection because the evidence, although arguably inadmissible, actually in some way favors her client's cause. (5) And sometimes counsel remains silent because the opposing lawyer's offer of objectionable evidence "opens the door" for more important evidence that the silent lawyer hopes to offer later.

C.

Objections Made for Effect

The truth is that objections that go to nothing more important than the form of the question (e.g., leading) are as often made for jury-effect as they are for any weightier purpose. ("We've been very patient, your Honor, but the jurors might like to have a little more testimony from the witness and a little less from opposing counsel. This is all leading, your Honor, and we have to object to it.") Of course, the use of objections as an excuse to make speeches for the jurors' benefit is ethically questionable, as is their use solely to interrupt a damaging examination or to coach a witness who is undergoing effective cross-examination. The making of objections for improper purposes can bring an embarrassing admonition from the bench. Accordingly, many judges require that any argument in support of an objection be made at the bench, out of the jurors' hearing. Objecting counsel inquires, "May we approach the bench?" If the trial judge is receptive to argument on the objection, he or she will permit counsel to engage in a whispered sidebar presentation and may even adjourn to chambers if the arguments are likely to be extensive. Since jurors probably resent these mystifying huddles between the judge and the lawyers, there is all the more reason to forgo needless objections.

D.

Time for Objecting to Testimony: Waiver

Because the burden of interposing legitimate objections, to "protect the record," is lodged with counsel and not the trial court, the failure to make a timely objection, in proper form, to an offer of evidence will usually operate to waive any possible basis of complaint about its receipt. "Let him speak now or forever hold his peace" is as applicable at trials as it is at weddings.

An objection must be made as soon as the basis for it becomes apparent. Counsel is not free to sit back, gambling that the witness will give a harmless or even a favorable answer, and then object when the answer proves to be damaging. The trial court is likely to respond to the belated objection with a terse, "Asked and answered, counsel." Ordinarily examining counsel's question will by its own terms reveal that it calls for inadmissible testimony. Opposing counsel must make an effort to interpose his objection before the witness answers.

Q. What did your sister tell you about the incident that she had observed?

BY OPPOSING COUNSEL: Just one moment, please. We object, your Honor. It calls for hearsay and we ask that the witness not be permitted to answer.

THE COURT: The objection is sustained.

If the objection to a question is sustained before any answer is given but the terms of the question disclosed the expected answer, counsel can obtain an instruction to the jury that the question itself is not evidence in the case and should be wholly disregarded.

Q. Officer, did you issue a traffic ticket to the plaintiff?

PLAINTIFF'S COUNSEL: Now, we object to that question. Irrelevant.

THE COURT: Sustained.

PLAINTIFF'S COUNSEL: We ask that your Honor instruct the jury to disregard the implication contained in defense counsel's question.

THE COURT: Yes, the jurors are instructed to disregard the question completely. It is not evidence in this case and an objection to it has been sustained.

Of course, it is not always feasible neatly to insert one's objection between the question and the answer. For one thing, the witness may respond too quickly. All that opposing counsel can do in this situation is state her objection as soon as she can, adding a two-part request that the witness' answer be stricken and that the trial court instruct the jurors to disregard it. Sometimes an apparently unobjectionable question brings out an inadmissible answer. Here, obviously, counsel, be it examining counsel or opposing counsel, cannot phrase her objection until the infirmity in the witness' response emerges. Perhaps the answer is unresponsive, with the result that examining counsel is entitled to object. She will make what is sometimes referred to as an "after-objection":

Q. Did you observe the plaintiff enter the crosswalk?

A. Yes, and he appeared to be looking down at his feet instead of watching where he was going.

BY EXAMINING COUNSEL: Object to everything after the word "Yes" and ask that it go out, your Honor. We also ask that you instruct the jury to disregard everything except the answer "Yes" as being unresponsive to the question.

THE COURT: Your objection is sustained, and the jury is so instructed.

It is sometimes said that only examining counsel is entitled to object to an answer whose only infirmity is its lack of responsiveness. In other words, examining counsel is free to "adopt" an unresponsive but favorable answer, which he does either by expressly saying so or by the simple expedient of forgoing any objection to it. Opposing counsel, not being the author of the question, lacks standing to object to any unresponsive answer unless it is excludable on some evidentiary ground over and beyond unresponsiveness; for example, the witness' answer is not only unresponsive but also violative of the hearsay rule. Here are two examples of correct rulings:

BY PLAINTIFF'S COUNSEL: Did you observe the plaintiff enter the crosswalk?

A. Yes, and he looked in both directions first.

BY DEFENSE COUNSEL: Object, unresponsive.

BY PLAINTIFF'S COUNSEL: We adopt the entire answer, your Honor.

THE COURT: The objection will be overruled.

The result will be different if the witness' answer is varied somewhat.

BY PLAINTIFF'S COUNSEL: Did you observe the plaintiff enter the crosswalk?

A. No, I didn't, but my sister did and she said that the man looked both ways first.

BY DEFENSE COUNSEL: Object, unresponsive and hearsay, your Honor.

BY PLAINTIFF'S COUNSEL: We adopt the entire answer, your Honor.

THE COURT: The objection is sustained on the ground of hearsay.

Occasionally the inadmissibility of testimony does not emerge clearly until long after it has been received in evidence. This happens where it is revealed only after searching cross-examination that a witness' responses to direct examination were based on hearsay rather than personal knowledge, in which case opposing counsel will move to strike all of the witness' testimony and ask that the jurors be instructed to disregard it. It can also be said to happen in instances of so-called conditional relevance. When one side fails to "tie up" or "connect up" conditionally relevant evidence with other evidence that renders the earlier evidence relevant, a renewed objection to the earlier evidence will be sustained, it will be stricken, and the jury, upon request, will be ordered to disregard it in their deliberations.

Sometimes evidence is admissible only for a limited purpose. It may be admissible as to one party or for one purpose but not admissible as to another party or for some other purpose. For example, a witness' unsworn prior inconsistent statement may be admissible to impeach his credibility but not as substantive evidence of the truth of its contents. A prior criminal conviction may be receivable to impeach but not to prove that the accused is guilty of the current charge against him. Here counsel may wish to obtain an instruction that limits the evidence to its permissible scope. (This process is described in Fed.R.Evid. 105.)

E.

Objecting to Exhibits

Objections to an exhibit that constitutes real evidence will normally be made at the time the exhibit is formally offered in evidence. Offering counsel is entitled to accomplish the laying of the necessary evidentiary foundation for receipt of the exhibit. This he will do, as we have seen, through one or more "sponsoring" witnesses who are capable of identifying and otherwise authenticating the exhibit. Objections interjected before offering counsel has had a chance to lay the foundation for the exhibit would ordinarily be premature. Certainly an objection made at the juncture at which an exhibit is marked by the court reporter for identification would be premature in all but the most exceptional circumstances.

Q. Would you give the court and jury your full name, please?

A. Mrs. Irene Stitz.

Q. And where do you reside, Mrs. Stitz?

A. At 3730 North Lake Shore Drive, in Chicago, Illinois.

Q. What is your present occupation, Mrs. Stitz?

A. I am the Records Librarian at Jefferson Memorial Hospital here in the city.

Q. Would you describe your duties as a records librarian?

A. [Witness details her duties.]

Q. In response to a subpoena which I caused to be issued to you, Mrs. Stitz, have you brought anything with you to court today?

A. I have.

Q. What have you brought?

A. The records of Jefferson Memorial Hospital pertaining to a patient named Clyde Bushmat.

BY OPPOSING COUNSEL: Object, your Honor.

THE COURT: Overruled. Proceed.

Q. Would you hand that folder to me, please? [Witness hands folder to examining counsel.]

BY OFFERING COUNSEL: There appear to be nineteen pages or pieces of paper in the folder that the witness has handed to me. I will ask the court reporter to mark each separate page, front and back. What number have we reached with our exhibits at this point?

BY THE COURT REPORTER: This would be number 8.

BY OFFERING COUNSEL: Then we can begin with 8–A.

[Court reporter marks the group exhibit.]

Q. Mrs. Stitz, handing you what has been marked Plaintiff's Group Exhibit 8–A on the front and 8–B on the back, I'll ask you what it is.

BY OPPOSING COUNSEL: Objection, your Honor.

BY OFFERING COUNSEL: Your Honor, I haven't offered the exhibit yet. I've just barely gotten it marked for identification. May I have an opportunity to lay the proper foundation for its admission? I believe I can do that through this witness. Then I'll offer it and opposing counsel can then interpose any objection he may have.

THE COURT: The objection is overruled. You're jumping the gun, counsel. Wait until the exhibit is offered.

Q. Read the last question back, please.

Of course, an early objection, in advance of the offer, is appropriate if improper use of an exhibit is being made. If, for example, examining counsel displays the exhibit, such as a photograph or diagram, to the jury in ad-vance of its receipt in evidence, or if he asks the sponsoring witness to read a written exhibit to the jury prior to its receipt in evidence, an objection will be sustained.

BY THE COURT REPORTER [reading the last question to the wit-ness]: "Mrs. Stitz, handing you what has been marked Plaintiff's Group Exhibit 8–A on the front and 8–B on the back, I'll ask you what it is."

A. It is the admission sheet pertaining to Mr. Clyde Bushmat's admis-sion to Jefferson Memorial Hospital.

Q. Would you just read the first seven lines of that to the jury, please?

BY OPPOSING COUNSEL: Now, I object to any reading of this exhi-bit, your Honor. He's not doing what he said he would. He hasn't laid an adequate foundation for its admission and he hasn't offered it. It can't be read to the jury yet.

THE COURT: Sustained. Lay your foundation, counsel. Then we'll see whether this exhibit can be read to the jury.

Pre-Trial Objections to Exhibits in Complex Cases. In complex litiga-tions, or where particularly sensitive evidentiary questions are involved, counsel will seek pre-trial rulings on proposed items of evidence. For ex-ample, in federal practice the trial judge, by pre-trial order, may fix a time for listing and marking the documents to be offered by the parties and for inspection of the documents by the opposing parties for the purposes of (1) waiving formal authentication, (2) waiving objections on other grounds, and (3) filing written objections. At the final pre-trial conference the judge will often make unconditional rulings on counsel's objections. Documents ad-mitted in evidence unconditionally by pre-trial orders or rulings can then be used at trial without further order or ruling.

Occasionally the trial judge will make conditional pre-trial evidentiary rulings for the guidance of counsel. Documents admitted conditionally are reoffered during trial, at which time a further ruling, now unconditional, will be obtained.

Documents that have been unconditionally excluded at a pre-trial con-ference need not be reoffered during trial; indeed, to do so would ordinarily be improper.

In some jurisdictions lawyers who love the Latin speak of filing a mo-tion *in limine* (literally, "at the threshold") to obtain an advance-of-trial ruling on a controversial item of evidence. A pre-trial exclusionary ruling will prevent the embarrassing in-court offering of improper evidence. The process might go this way:

BY OBJECTING COUNSEL: Your Honor, there's a police accident re-port floating around in this case and it's full of typical bystander statements picked up by the investigating officer. I'll show it to you. You can see that it is the sort of report that is inadmissible under *Johnson v. Lutz* and under the Federal Rules, specifically, 803(8). We don't want this report to be offered at trial, in the presence of the jury, and we're making a motion *in limine* at this time that it be kept out.

THE COURT: This police report is plainly inadmissible. I am ruling that it will be excluded.

BY OPPOSING COUNSEL: Well, your Honor, can we at least make our offer of it at trial, so we can make a record on it?

THE COURT: No, you can't. You're making your record right now. Any reference during trial to this report and you'll have a mistrial. And I know I don't need to discuss contempt of court, counsel.

F.

Specificity of Objections

The question naturally comes up, how specific must an objection be? Is it enough simply to stand up and say, "Object, your Honor"? Is something more accomplished where counsel, after the fashion of Perry Mason and other lawyers whose practice is limited to television serials, intones, "Object, your Honor. Irrelevant, incompetent, and immaterial"? Or should a trial lawyer be quite specific: "Object, your Honor. Hearsay"? Or: "Object, the best evidence rule hasn't been satisfied"?

A reading of the countless cases dealing with specificity *versus* generality in the phrasing of objections would lead one to believe that the bare announcement that "I object" is insufficient and that even the somewhat more elaborate "Three I's," "Irrelevant, incompetent, and immaterial," which McCormick called a "meaningless ritual," are unavailing except perhaps to preserve the question of relevance. The codes and cases recommend that any objection be accompanied by a reasonably specific statement of the ground(s) for it. (See, e.g., Fed.R.Evid. 103(a)(1)(B)). For example, the objection "irrelevant and prejudicial" may not be enough to preserve for appeal the complaint that the opponent has violated the rule against character evidence. Similarly, a lawyer who objects by saying "no foundation" may well have forfeited the right to argue on appeal that the evidence should have been excluded as hearsay because there was inadequate foundation for a hearsay exception. In these two examples, the first lawyer should have objected on grounds of "improper character attack" or "Rule 404," while the second should have objected on grounds of hearsay.[1]

The idea is that a trial judge cannot be expected to recognize instantly the particular evidentiary rules applicable to the testimony and exhibits being offered in a given case. It may be asked, why should a judge be any

---

[1] See Roger C. Park, TRIAL OBJECTIONS HANDBOOK § 1.5 (2d ed. 2001) (discussing examples and collecting cases). For examples of common courtroom objections, see Part II of this chapter.

less equipped to detect the applicable rules than the lawyers appearing before her? The answer is that the lawyers have had the case for many months, even years, analyzing it and preparing it for trial; they have had plenty of time to get a firm grip on the evidentiary questions. Of course, the concept of adversariness is at work here. It is up to the contending lawyers, and not the judge, not only to make objections but to support them with reasons.

In making objections the trial lawyer will have three aims in mind, two of which are directly concerned with the "making" of the record. First, counsel is seeking to educate the trial judge on the rule or rules of evidence that authorize the objection and the exclusion of the challenged evidence. Counsel is being an advocate. Second, by being reasonably explicit, counsel is preserving a record for possible appeal in case the judge overrules his objection. Thirdly, and this is nothing more than the reverse of the same coin, he is making a record that will support the trial judge on appeal in the event that she sustains counsel's objection.

The rules regarding the required form of objections are heavily weighted in favor of the trial judge. If a generalized objection is made and overruled, appellate courts will not reverse unless a valid basis for the objection is perfectly clear. Obviously, in many situations of a recurring sort it would be a waste of time to require a recitation of reasons for a self-evident objection and the trial court is likely to rule before counsel can do more than say "I object." A common example would be the question that by its terms plainly seeks to elicit hearsay testimony. A simple "I object" should suffice to make the record here.

Occasionally it is also said that a general objection is enough where receipt of the offered evidence cannot be justified on any legal basis at all. However, it would be dangerous to gamble on the availability of this argument, which is often grounded on a lawyer's 20–20 hindsight. The rationale behind appellate courts' unwillingness to reverse on the basis of a trial judge's overruling of a general objection is that counsel should not be free to shift to the judge the burden of searching for an applicable exclusionary rule.

The rules also aid the trial judge when he or she has sustained a general objection—and here they redound to objecting counsel's benefit, too. On appeal the trial court will be upheld if there was any ground on which the evidence could properly have been excluded. It is assumed that the trial judge had the right reason in mind when he or she rejected the evidence. To sum up, then, a trial court will ordinarily be upheld on appeal whether it has sustained or overruled a general objection.

Where a specific objection ("Object, hearsay") is erroneously overruled, the record thus made will support a reversal if the evidence is unfairly prejudicial. If a specific objection is properly sustained, there obviously has been no reversible error. But what if the ground specified by court and counsel is invalid but there existed another and valid but unstated basis for the objection? Again, for common-sense reasons, the rule favors the trial judge and, indirectly, the objecting counsel. It is sometimes said that rejection of the evidence was not prejudicial since there was a good, albeit unmentioned, ground for its exclusion. A more sensible approach is to recognize how futile it would be to reverse the trial court, and remand the case for a new trial, for having rejected the evidence on the wrong ground, only to have the trial court exclude it for the right reason the second time around.

We have seen that an objector should be explicit about his or her legal grounds. The precise target at which the objection is aimed should also be made clear. An offer of evidence frequently consists of several statements or parts which make up a whole; for example, an entire deposition, a set of hospital records, or a transcript of previously recorded testimony may be tendered. If only portions of the offer are objectionable, counsel must point them out for the trial judge, who will not himself be required to sift the admissible from the inadmissible. Of course, the real fault may lie with the side offering the evidence as a unit. Where admissibility as a unit is questionable, counsel for the offering party probably should break down the evidence into its component parts, marking and offering those parts separately so that objections can be made and rulings secured in an efficient way. If this is inordinately time-consuming (it probably should have been done at a pre-trial conference), another approach is for offering counsel to see to it that each page of a voluminous exhibit bears a separate, sequential identifying number so that opposing counsel and the court can make convenient references to any portions objected to, thus:

BY OFFERING COUNSEL: Your Honor, we will ask the court reporter to mark the pages of this group exhibit [a group of medical records, for example] separately. There are twenty-four pages in the group, so they can be marked Plaintiff's Group Exhibit 3–A through 3–X for identification.

THE COURT: We'll just relax for a minute while the reporter marks the exhibits.

BY OPPOSING COUNSEL: Your Honor, we have an objection to 3–B and the reverse side of it, 3–C. That is the history sheet and it contains some inadmissible hearsay.

[Whereupon discussion out of the hearing of the jury is had.]

THE COURT: Certain deletions from exhibits 3–B and 3–C having been made, the objection will be overruled and Plaintiff's Group Exhibit 3–A through 3–X for Identification will be received in evidence as Plaintiff's Group Exhibit 3–A through 3–X.

A general objection is also unavailing where offered evidence is admissible against some parties, although not against all of them, or on a particular issue, although it is not admissible as to some other issue in the case. As was indicated earlier, it is objecting counsel's duty to couple with his or her objection a request that the evidence be restricted to the particular issue or party. This will be accomplished by means of a brief jury instruction.

BY OPPOSING COUNSEL: On behalf of the defendant Freightco, we object to the witness' testimony concerning what the defendant truck driver, Mr. Bushmat, may have said to plaintiff after the accident. It may be receivable against Bushmat because it was his own statement, but it certainly isn't binding on us, your Honor. He was not speaking about a matter within the scope of his employment.

THE COURT: The objection is well taken. The jury is instructed that the testimony they have just heard is received in evidence as against the defendant Bushmat only and is not to be considered by the jury in determining the liability, if any, of the defendant Freightco.

G.

Necessity for Repeating Objections

Where one side, through one or more witnesses, repeatedly offers similar evidence that opposing counsel considers inadmissible, an objection must be interposed each time the evidence is offered unless the trial court permits a single statement of the objection to stand as a "continuing" objection to the entire line of questioning or class of evidence. If opposing counsel's objection to the first of a string of offers of similar evidence is sustained, she will ordinarily find it necessary to object to each subsequent offer. If her initial objection is overruled, however, the trial court may allow a continuing objection in order to conserve time and save opposing counsel from seeming unduly obstructive in the eyes of the jurors.

BY EXAMINING COUNSEL: Had you received any previous complaints about bottles of Dispepsia Cola exploding?

BY OPPOSING COUNSEL: We object, your Honor. Irrelevant and immaterial, since notice is not an issue in this case.

THE COURT: Overruled, counsel. I'm inclined to let it in on the issue of punitive damages.

BY OPPOSING COUNSEL: Can the record show that our objection goes to all similar evidence that plaintiff's counsel may offer? May we have a standing objection, in other words?

THE COURT: You may. The record will show it.

To avoid any possibility of confusion, when additional evidence of the same type is later offered, opposing counsel should point out at least once that her earlier objection is applicable.

The failure to object to an inadmissible item of evidence may not preclude counsel from objecting successfully to subsequent efforts to offer more of the same. Some lawyers, not wishing to object excessively, will wait until it becomes unavoidably apparent that a type of evidence is potentially damaging before objecting to it. The deliberate waiver of objection as to the earlier evidence probably does not work a waiver as to later offers of similar evidence. For example, the fact that counsel permitted some hearsay to come in on a particular subject matter does not foreclose him from objecting to subsequent offers of additional hearsay on the same subject.

H.

Necessity for Obtaining a Ruling

The record in connection with an evidentiary objection has not been effectively made where no ruling from the trial judge has been obtained. It is the objector's burden to secure an express ruling on his objection. This is essential to appellate review since a trial judge's silence is not considered tantamount to an overruling of the objection. In the heat of trial the judge may neglect to make an explicit, audible ruling. If the matter is of any importance, objecting counsel can interrupt to forestall the witness from responding to the challenged question and can respectfully request an on-the-record ruling from the trial judge.

Q. What did your friend tell you about the incident?

BY OPPOSING COUNSEL: Object, your Honor, calls for hearsay.

BY EXAMINING COUNSEL: Well, it's perfectly relevant.

BY OPPOSING COUNSEL: It's still hearsay.

BY THE WITNESS: He told me * * *

BY OPPOSING COUNSEL: Just one moment, sir. Your Honor, we would appreciate your instructing the witness not to answer the question until your Honor has ruled. And we would like very much to have a ruling from your Honor on our hearsay objection.

THE COURT: Let me ponder this for a minute. The witness will not answer. Yes, the objection will be sustained. The question clearly calls for a hearsay response.

I.

Exceptions

At one time it was necessary, in many jurisdictions, for counsel to record an express exception to those evidentiary rulings of the trial court that counsel considered erroneous. Today this is rarely required. No longer does one hear the following exchange: "Object, your Honor, irrelevant." "Overruled, counsel." "Please note our exception." Instead, one encounters rules such as Federal Rule of Civil Procedure 46: "A formal exception to a ruling or order is unnecessary. When the ruling or order is requested or made, a party need only state the action that it wants the court to take or objects to, along with the grounds for the request or objection. * * * " Of course, it will subsequently be necessary to set up in a specific and detailed motion for new trial any assignments of error that are based on objections made during trial.

IV.

OFFER OF PROOF

A.

Offer of Evidence as Distinguished from Offer of Proof

In the trial practice the phrase "offer of proof" is something of a term of art. It is a somewhat confusing one because in litigation the word "offer", taken alone, has a common meaning all its own. The two terms need to be distinguished.

The "offer" is the last step, other than possible supportive argument, in the introduction of evidence. (We discussed the offering of evidence in section II, above.) The meaning of the word "offer" and of the synonymous phrase "offer of evidence" is perhaps most readily grasped when one thinks in terms of tangible evidence: writings, photographs, murder weapons, and the like. The proponent of a writing, for example, will cause it to be marked for identification and then will do the trial judge and opposing counsel the courtesy of letting them examine the exhibit preliminarily, if they are not already familiar with it as a consequence of pre-trial discovery. Counsel will then hand the exhibit to its "sponsoring" witness on the stand and pose questions aimed at authenticating the writing. When this process has been accomplished to the proponent's satisfaction, he will hand the exhibit to the judge and say, "Your Honor, we now offer in evidence what has been marked Plaintiff's Exhibit Number 1 for Identification."

As we have seen, one "offers" testimonial evidence, too, although there will be no need to say the word "offer" out loud. Counsel offers oral testimony simply by engaging in the direct examination or cross-examination of a witness on the stand.

The so-called offer of proof is something quite apart from the typical offer of evidence described above and in section II. The offer of proof can come into play before or during an offer of evidence. It can come into play when an objection is made, during the examination of a witness, to the offer either of tangible or testimonial evidence. The offer of proof also comes into play when counsel, with no objection pending and perhaps with no witness as yet on the stand, makes an offer to prove specified matters in order to induce a ruling by the trial court as to the relevance and competence of those matters. We consider first the offer of proof as it is made during the course of examination of a witness on the stand.

B.

Offer of Proof Made During the Examination of a Witness

The necessity for an offer of proof is most commonly encountered during the examination of a witness on the stand. Counsel poses a question to the witness in an effort to elicit testimony; she may value the anticipated testimony for its own sake or because it lays the authenticating or identifying foundation for the introduction of tangible evidence, such as a writing. Opposing counsel, for some stated reason rooted in the rules of evidence, makes a timely objection to counsel's question. Counsel for the introducing party (the "offering" party), either before or after the trial court's ruling on the objection, must make an offer of proof unless she is prepared to concede the merit of her opponent's objection.

The offer of proof has two legitimate purposes: (1) if properly made, it will permit the trial court to make a fully informed and, hopefully, correct ruling on the objection; (2) if the ruling is adverse to the introducing party and arguably erroneous, an adequate offer of proof is ordinarily essential to preserve the point for post-trial review.

Harold W. Huff, a Chicago trial lawyer of extensive experience, focused on appellate review when he described the purpose of an offer of proof:

* * * [S]ooner or later you can anticipate that you will be placed in a position in which you see your case disintegrating because the man [or woman] in the black robe will not receive your evidence.

What do you do in that situation? You make a record of what it was that you were not permitted to prove. The record is made, essentially, for the benefit of an appellate court.*

The offer of proof, as Huff indicates, is another aspect of "making the record" or "perfecting the record" for appeal. In the absence of an explicit offer of proof an appellate court often will have no sure way of knowing whether the trial court's evidentiary ruling was correct. Equally important, the reviewing court will have no sure way of knowing whether the loss of the excluded evidence was unfairly prejudicial to the introducing party's case; it can hardly weigh the importance of rejected evidence without knowing what that evidence would have been.

It has occasionally been suggested that the failure to make an offer of proof is excusable where the trial court has indicated to counsel in no uncertain terms that an offer would be useless. And a full offer of proof is unnecessary where described evidence has been rejected as a class by the trial court. Here in a very real sense the trial judge has made (and rejected) the

---

* H. Huff, Offers of Proof in Proceedings, Fifth Annual Trial Evidence Seminar (Ill.Inst. for Cont.Legal Ed.) 4 (1971).

offer of proof, as when he or she announces, "I'm not going to allow any evidence of previous reported explosions involving this type of glass container because I don't think any such reports could possibly be relevant to the present case."

It is ordinarily reversible error to refuse counsel an opportunity to make a proper offer of proof. A trial court's refusal to entertain an offer of proof is unjustifiable even where it is based on the court's knowledge of the witness' earlier testimony in the case since the current offer may embrace new matter. So important is counsel's freedom to make his or her record that it has been stated that any judicial discouraging of offers of proof is improper. However, a trial court need not hear lengthy offers where it is evident that the proposed evidence would not be admissible on any ground.

The necessity of an offer of proof after a sustained objection is generally limited to direct examination, the thought being that while counsel should experience no difficulty describing what his own witness would say in response to a question, he may not be equipped to predict precisely the response of an adverse witness. Certainly it would ordinarily be unfair for a trial court to require an offer of proof during cross-examination. However, enough must be done to show that the sustaining of an objection to a cross-question was error. The cross-question must on its face be proper. Counsel may have to elaborate somewhat to reveal what benefit he expects from his cross-question or line of cross-examination; in other words, it is as incumbent upon counsel during cross-examination as it is during direct examination to make clear the purpose, the materiality, of the anticipated response.

While it may be reasonably accurate to say that no offer of proof—certainly no very explicit or detailed one—is essential during cross-examination, it is also true that counsel is entirely free to make an offer during cross-examination if she can, and, in the absence of effective contradiction, the trial court can rely on it. If counsel has any reason to suspect that the point of her cross-examination is escaping the trial judge (and the sustaining of objections to it is an observable straw in the wind), she will be at pains to give at least some intimation of its purpose.

The required elements of an offer of proof made during the interrogation of a witness can rarely be found in procedural or evidentiary codes. At one time Rule 43(c) of the Federal Rules of Civil Procedure made at least a minimal effort to describe the mechanics of an offer of proof. It read in its entirety as follows:

Rule 43.

EVIDENCE

* * *

(c) Record of Excluded Evidence. In an action tried by a jury, if an objection to a question propounded to a witness is sustained by the court, the examining attorney may make a specific offer of what he expects to prove by the answer of the witness. The court may require the offer to be made out of the hearing of the jury. The court may add such other or further statement as clearly shows the character of the evidence, the form in which it was offered, the objection made, and the ruling thereon. In actions tried without a jury the same procedure may be followed, except that the court upon request shall take and report the evidence in full, unless it clearly appears that the evidence is not admissible on any ground or that the witness is privileged.

Rules such as FRCP 43(c) are never especially helpful to the practitioner because they are couched in general terms and leave so much to unwritten local practice. In one respect Rule 43(c) may even have been potentially misleading. The rule suggested that a lawyer whose evidence has been excluded "may" make an offer of proof. The word "may" could be read in the sense of "might." As we have said, the lawyer *can* make an offer of proof—it would ordinarily be reversible error to refuse him the opportunity to make a proper one—and usually he *must* make one if he is to preserve for review the propriety of the trial court's exclusionary ruling.

FRCP 43(c) has now been superseded by Federal Rule of Evidence 103, which reads in relevant part as follows:

Rule 103.

RULINGS ON EVIDENCE

(a) Preserving a Claim of Error. A party may claim error in a ruling to admit or exclude evidence only if the error affects a substantial right of the party and * * *

(2) if the ruling excludes evidence, a party informs the court of its substance by an offer of proof, unless the substance was apparent from the context. * * *

(c) Court's Statement About the Ruling; Directing an Offer of Proof. The court may make any statement about the character or form of the evidence, the objection made, and the ruling. The court may direct that an offer of proof be made in question-and-answer form.

(d) Preventing the Jury from Hearing Inadmissible Evidence. To the extent practicable, the court must conduct a jury trial so that inadmissible evidence is not suggested to the jury by any means.

Note that subdivision (c) of the Rule provides that the trial judge "may" direct that the offer of proof be made in question-and-answer form. This means that questions will be put to the witness by examining counsel and his or her responses will then constitute the offer; otherwise, examining counsel himself simply makes a narrative offer in his own words.

In the Advisory Committee's Preliminary Draft of the Federal Rules of Evidence the question-and-answer method was *required* in non-jury cases, presumably so that a reviewing court would have before it the precise evidentiary basis for possible final disposition of the case in the event of reversal for erroneous exclusion of evidence. This absolute requirement was thought to be an unnecessary intrusion upon judicial discretion and, on revision, it was dropped. It was realized that this requirement would foreclose the sort of offer of proof that is occasionally made with no witness on the stand.

There are three basic ways of making an offer of proof during the course of a witness' oral examination. These three methods can be labelled (1) the tangible offer, (2) the witness offer, and (3) the lawyer offer.

1. *Tangible Offer.* The tangible offer is easy enough. Any lawyer who knows how to mark, authenticate or identify, and offer into evidence an item of tangible evidence knows, almost *ipso facto*, how to make an offer of proof of the exhibit's contents if her offer of it is successfully objected to by opposing counsel. The proponent of the rejected exhibit need only hand it to the court reporter for inclusion in the trial record. (Or, if the exhibit happens to be a writing, such as a deposition, she might also, out of the jury's hearing, read it into the record at the time of its rejection, thereby ensuring its consideration in context.) Unlike received exhibits, the rejected item will not be handed to the jurors and will not go with them to their deliberation room. It will, however, find its way into the record on appeal, along with all other offered exhibits whether received or rejected. Counsel's only additional task may be to state for the record the evidential purpose of the evidence, if there exists any possibility that its function is unclear. She may also wish to be certain that the record reflects the trial judge's reasons for rejecting the exhibit since the judge may be focusing on a ground for rejection while erroneously disregarding a legitimate alternative basis for admission.

An offer of tangible proof that commingles admissible matter with inadmissible is not a good offer and its rejection *in toto* will not be reversible error. This is not to say that admissible portions of an offer are properly excludable merely because other portions are inadmissible. For example, the competency of a writing in its entirety is not essential to the receipt of unobjectionable parts. It simply means that the inadmissible portions must be omitted from the offer. More than this, it means that the obligation to screen out inadmissible matters belongs to counsel for the offering party; neither the trial court nor the objecting party is obliged to separate the admissible from the inadmissible.

The risk of rejection *in toto* is at its greatest in connection with "omnibus" offers or offers "in bulk." An unsegregated offer of all the hospital records pertaining to the plaintiff in a personal injury action would be a typical example of an omnibus or in bulk offer. Counsel cannot hope to produce error—to provide himself with an ace in the hole, so to speak—by offering, in bulk, a tall stack of pages comprising a patient's entire medical record, which may begin with an admission history, include laboratory and radiology reports, a report of operation, anesthesia record, progress notes, nurses' notes, and end with a discharge summary. The trial court's rejection of this offer is not improper where counsel has been accorded an opportunity to designate the admissible parts, even though buried in the pile are records which by themselves would be perfectly admissible. Counsel must offer only the admissible portions of his client's medical record or of any other writing or group of writings. Before making his offer he can pull out inadmissible items or mask or cut out inadmissible passages. (In one case it was suggested that a piece of paper might be pasted over the inadmissible part of a writing. However, experience teaches that jurors are inclined to peek. It is usually better to redact exhibits by more careful approaches, often presenting the jury with a copy from which the objectionable portions have been excised by electronic means)

Counsel must be specific as to what parts of a writing or group of writings are included in his offer of proof. It is not ordinarily enough to make a general representation that all objectionable parts will be deleted. Where an offer of a writing has been rejected, counsel cannot later insist that he offered only its receivable portions unless he in fact designated them explicitly at the trial level. When a writing is offered without such designations it is presumed that the entire exhibit is offered.

When a writing is offered as being impeaching, it is incumbent upon the proponent to isolate those portions thought to be receivable on this ground.

2. *Witness Offer.* The witness offer is an even more simple procedure than the tangible offer. When an objection has been made to a question put to a witness on the stand and an exclusionary ruling is made by the trial judge, examining counsel can make his or her offer of proof through the witness. Counsel simply proceeds with the examination of the witness, employing the usual question-and-answer method, and the witness' recorded responses, usually taken outside the jurors' hearing, constitute the offer of proof. This is the method adverted to in Rule 103(c) of the Federal Rules of Evidence, discussed above.

As in the case of tangible offers, counsel's only remaining task may be to explain the relevance of the offered testimony more fully than he or she did at the point of opposing counsel's successful objection to it. Again, offering counsel may want to be sure that the record accurately reflects the judge's reasons for excluding the testimony.

Normally, counsel should state for the record not only the purport (synopsized meaning) but the purpose (relevance, intended function) of the anticipated response. It is sometimes said that a formal offer of proof is unnecessary where counsel's question to a witness clearly calls for admissible evidence. For example, the Illinois Supreme Court has made a broad generalization on this point:

It is not necessary that offer of proof be made where the question shows the purpose and materiality of the evidence. It is not necessary that counsel state what the answer would be. If a question is in proper form and clearly admits of an answer relative [*sic*; relevant?] to the issues, the party by whom the question is propounded is not bound to state facts proposed to be proved by the answer unless the court requires him to do so.*

This sweeping language seems to disregard the circumstance that a question that quite plainly calls for an admissible answer may be little more than an exercise in optimism in the absence of some discernible assurance that the witness is not only able to answer counsel's question but to answer it favorably to his client's position. In most of the cases suggesting that a formal statement of the expected answer can safely be omitted, the record, in one way or another, showed unmistakably what counsel was after and what he or she was likely to have gotten had the witness been permitted to answer. Since appellate courts will not invariably presume that an unstated answer would be forthcoming and that it would be both relevant and favorable to the side represented by examining counsel, prudence will ordinarily dictate the making of a reasonably detailed offer of proof following an exclusionary ruling.

If rejection of the offered testimony was based on an exclusionary rule of evidence, such as the hearsay rule or some testimonial privilege, the offer of proof should include any information suggesting the inapplicability of the rule. (A collateral but obviously important possible advantage of a comprehensive and comprehensible offer of proof is that it may cause the trial judge to change his or her ruling.)

3. *Lawyer Offer.* Where it appears that a question in proper form was posed during the direct examination of a witness on the stand and that, upon objection by opposing counsel, the trial court ruled out the answer, examining counsel's offer of proof may consist of a statement to the court at the time of its ruling, and on the record, showing what the witness' answer would have been. Counsel's statement will include any additional matters essential to demonstrate that the described response would be relevant and otherwise admissible in evidence. Counsel's statement will also show that the response would benefit his client; that is, that it would be of such a character as could reasonably be expected to affect the finding of the jury in his client's favor.

This so-called lawyer offer will begin this way: the examining counsel poses a question to a witness on the stand, opposing counsel's objection to the question is sustained by the trial judge, and the examining counsel, to make the record for possible appeal, states to the judge, "Your Honor, through this witness we offer to prove [such-and-such]." Of course, there is no magic in the form of words employed in an offer of proof; examining counsel may say, "The witness, were he permitted to answer the last question, would have testified [to such-and-such]."

---

* Creighton v. Elgin, 387 Ill. 592, 606, 56 N.E.2d 825, 831 (1944), *quoted in*, *e.g.*, Schmitz v. Binette, 368 Ill.App.3d. 447, 453-54, 857 N.E.2d 846, 852 (1ˢᵗ Dist. 2006).

Ordinarily, the offer of proof should be made immediately after the adverse ruling that cut off the witness' response. Usually it is made out of the jury's presence, as is specifically suggested in Rule 103(d) of the Federal Rules of Evidence, quoted previously. Certainly the time for an offer has arrived when the trial court indicates unequivocally that it will permit no further inquiry along a particular line.

It has repeatedly been held that a lawyer offer is ineffective where the lawyer's statement of the anticipated answer goes beyond or is unresponsive to the question put to the witness. This rule seems as much an artificial device to avoid reversal as anything else, since counsel presumably could readily have put any number of additional questions to his witness. Furthermore, as will be discussed later, there is no pending question at all in the case of lawyer offers made prior to the calling of a witness to the stand. It is true, of course, that a methodical question and answer approach makes it easier for the opposing counsel to frame specific objections and this may be one reason for the rule. Perhaps this rule simply reflects persistent distrust of the lawyer offer. Although an unethical lawyer could as easily fabricate "anticipated" responsive answers as he could unresponsive ones, the better practice is to proceed by means of questions of limited scope, followed by the statement of an expected answer corresponding to the question.

A possible safeguard against a fabricated lawyer offer lies in the witness' ability—especially upon inquiry by a skeptical trial judge or opposing counsel—to contradict the offer, pointing out that in fact the stated answer would not be his response to the question asked. This, of course, assumes a witness who is sufficiently alert, sufficiently honest, and sufficiently brave to take exception to counsel's narrative.

C.

Offer of Proof Made With No Witness on the Stand

Few commentators on the making of the trial record have considered a special and sometimes difficult type of offer of proof, the type of offer that is made prior to any in-court testimony by a witness and thus obviously prior to any explicit objection and ruling. This is the second principal type of offer. It may be made because offering counsel has a number of witnesses, who are readily available but not presently in court, to establish a line of facts but the trial judge's rulings have strongly suggested that he would exclude their testimony. Such an offer can also be made to induce a ruling with respect to a line of facts. Counsel will make an offer when he is doubtful of the reception that his proposed evidence will receive from the trial judge and wishes to obtain a ruling, and make his record, without first going to the expense and inconvenience of calling and examining the witnesses involved. This approach permits a trial court, out of the jurors' hearings, to pre-test proposed evidence and avoid possible prejudicing of the jurors.

An offer of this second type will sound something like this in a simple case:

BY PLAINTIFF'S COUNSEL: Your Honor, we offer to prove in this case that the defendant had notice, repeated notice, that metal cans containing its product had exploded without warning, causing serious bodily injury. We can call to the stand six eye-witnesses to six separate incidents of this sort, all antedating the incident involving this plaintiff. Those witnesses are readily available on short notice.

COUNSEL FOR DEFENDANT: Well, we would object to that, your Honor. We don't think notice is an element in a strict liability case of this kind. Counsel is just trying to put in some inflammatory evidence.

COUNSEL FOR PLAINTIFF: If nothing else, your Honor, the proposed evidence would be relevant to our prayer for punitive damages.

THE COURT: The offer of proof will be denied. [Or, "The offer is sustained. You can have until tomorrow morning to get your witnesses here."]

When a trial court rejects an offer of proof of this second type it is taken to have conceded that counsel could have made the described proof if he had been permitted to proceed. The only open question is whether the facts embodied in the offer are properly admissible.

It is the burden of the offering party to include in his or her offer everything necessary to support the admissibility of the proposed evidence. This must be shown to the trial judge at the time of the making of the offer; if for some reason admissibility cannot be shown until a subsequent time during the trial, the offer, as will be more fully discussed later, should then be renewed. Where the facts supporting admissibility are unclear, no amount of hindsight at the appellate level will put the trial court in error for having rejected the offer.

For instance, an offer must be definite as to the time of events in order that the admissibility of the offer will be apparent. Thus the relevance of prior complaints concerning the condition of a stairway will depend in part on their nearness in point of time to the accident of which the plaintiff complains. Similarly, testimony regarding a post-accident inspection will be rejected where the offer fails to reveal its date.

Often it may also be essential to indicate other facets of relevance, such as similarity of conditions in connection with evidence of prior accidents and the like.

Furthermore, offering counsel may find it necessary to show that the offered evidence would not merely be cumulative to evidence already received in the case.

It will frequently be vital to include foundational elements in an offer of proof. These foundational elements are themselves to be found in the law of evidence. It may, for example, be necessary to state that offered out-of-court declarations would be admissible because they constituted excited utterances. To cite a much more common example, it may be crucial to include in the offer a clear indication that the witness whose testimony is being offered is qualified as an expert of some sort. Obviously, there is a serious flaw in an offer "to prove through Clyde Bushmat that cancer can be induced by trauma"; it will be necessary to include in the offer the fact that this is *Doctor* Clyde Bushmat, whose training, licensure, and experience equip him, in terms of the conventional wisdom respecting opinion evidence, to express a complex medical conclusion.

Much of this is simply one way or another of saying that an offer of proof must descend into specifics; it is not permissible to couch an offer in vague generalities. For instance, it is insufficient to announce that evidence will be adduced "to show bad faith," to show "insolvency," to show that goods for which a note was given "were not as represented," to show "bias and prejudice," or to show "surrounding circumstances and conditions." It is, in other words, not sufficient in an offer of proof to state ultimate facts that might be more appropriate to a pleading; thus reading the allegations of a pleading into the record will not result in an effective offer of proof. And if "ultimate" facts are not good enough it is doubly clear that broad-gauge conclusions are unavailing in an offer. An offer can be a summarization of proposed evidence but it must be cast in terms of evidentiary facts—what the proposed witnesses said, saw, heard, touched, or smelled; what the proposed items of tangible evidence reveal.

Needless to say, an offer that is based on nothing more than counsel's sense of hope and optimism is doomed. Thus the denial of an omnibus or "in bulk" offer is proper where the offering party, having neglected to employ pre-trial discovery devices to secure and examine the opposing party's records, bases his offer on nothing more than his unsubstantiated hope that those records might contain something helpful to his client. An offer of proof, in other words, must be made in good faith on the basis of evidence that is known to be available and beneficial.

As an offshoot of the basic premise that the offer must be in good faith, it is frequently asserted that the offering party must identify the witnesses who are in a position to testify to the matters described in the offer. From time to time this requirement has been pushed one long step farther, to demand a showing that the witness is presently in court and ready to testify. It is even occasionally suggested that a witness must be placed on the stand and the offer made through him. Any such requirement would effectively eliminate the second type of offer of proof and restrict counsel to the traditional post-objection witness offer.

It is clear enough, nonetheless, that an offer upon which counsel cannot possibly make good, because the necessary witnesses are unavailable to him, is properly rejected. This situation arises most commonly where witnesses, not previously subpoenaed by offering counsel, are shown to be beyond the trial court's subpoena power at the time of the offer of proof involving them. It is also plain that a trial judge, entertaining doubts about counsel's ability to make good on his offer, can insist on an offer made through one or more witnesses called to the stand (or to a pre-trial conference) in an out-of-court session. However, the weight of authority, which includes a decision of the United States Supreme Court, is to the effect that a lawyer offer, with no witness on the stand, is sufficient if an adequate demonstration of good faith is made. In Scotland County v. Hill* the Court said, "[I]f the trial court has doubts about the good faith of an offer of testimony, it can insist on the production of the witness, and upon some attempt to make the proof before it rejects the offer; but if it does reject it * * * and there is nothing else in the record to indicate bad faith, an appellate court must assume that the proof could have been made, and govern itself accordingly."

Offers of proof in more complex cases, and objections to such offers, are usually required to be in writing. As has been pointed out in the *Manual for Complex Litigation* followed by federal trial judges, this process is especially helpful in cases in which the parties expect to offer opinion evidence on complicated scientific, technical, or economic issues.

A typical written offer of proof in a complex case involving expertise will include (1) an identification of the expert, (2) a summary of his or her qualifications, (3) a detailed disclosure of the factual data and scientific, technical, or economic authorities and other material relied on by the expert in arriving at his or her opinion, (4) a clear statement of the expert's opinion, and (5) a summary of the reasons for the opinion.

In "big" cases it is also essential that there be pre-trial offers of deposition evidence, an opportunity to require the offeror to introduce additional portions of the deposition as provided in Federal Rules of Civil Procedure 32(a)(6), an opportunity to object to the offered deposition evidence, and rulings on any such objections.

Federal judges are accustomed to scheduling pre-trial offers of deposition evidence and the filing of objections, counter-offers, and suggested requirements under Rule 32(a)(6), supra. A useful, though old-fashioned, technique is for the deposition material offered by each party to be enclosed in brackets in a distinctive color on the outer margin of the deposition pages. Opposite these colored brackets the opposing counsel can mark his or her objections in abbreviated language such as "D Acme obj. hearsay." The trial court's ruling on designated deposition offers can be indicated in similar fashion so that the admitted portion of the deposition can easily be read into evidence from the original deposition. Of course, a modern court might instead deal with the deposition material in electronic form.

---

* 112 U.S. 183, 186, 5 S.Ct. 93, 28 L.Ed. 692 (1884).

D.

Renewing Offers of Proof

Occasionally a particular offer of proof must be made more than once or, more precisely, it must be renewed. This happens when an offer, defective when first made, is thereafter perfected. Sometimes an offer will be ruled premature because, for example, some element of its foundation is missing or because it has been made during the wrong stage of the trial. It is vital that counsel renew his or her offer after having adduced additional evidence by way of essential predicate; otherwise, the trial court is free to treat the earlier offer as having been abandoned.

A renewed offer may be necessary after counsel has put on proof rendering inapplicable some exclusionary rule of evidence, such as the best evidence rule. Where an offer of proof has been rebuffed because it was made during cross-examination of an adverse party's witness rather than in the offering party's own case, counsel usually must renew the offer at the appropriate juncture. Of course, express withdrawal of a question waives any error with respect to the treatment accorded an objection to it. There is, however, no need to make repeated offers of proof where the court has indicated that it will under no circumstances receive the indicated evidence or where the court has sustained an objection to an entire line of questioning. Federal Rule of Evidence 103(b) now codifies this rule in the federal courts, though in somewhat narrow terms:

(b) Not Needing to Renew an Objection or Offer of Proof. Once the court rules definitively on the record—either before or at trial—a party need not renew an objection or offer of proof to preserve a claim of error for appeal.

The need to renew an offer of proof after the taking of additional evidence can be avoided if in the original offer counsel expresses a willingness to connect up the offered evidence with other testimony that will render the offered evidence material. This is simply another way of saying that an offer of proof must be reasonably complete.

E.

Making Offers of Proof Outside the Jurors' Hearing

The trial court, for a fairly self-evident reason that we will come to shortly, will usually require that counsel present his or her offer of proof in such a way that although the court, opposing counsel, the witness (if any), and the court reporter can hear it, the jury cannot. A court has the right to insist that it be made out of the jury's hearing, and in some circumstances Fed.R.Evid. 103(d), quoted above, insists on that procedure. Some judicial hints to the contrary notwithstanding, a court is not invariably required to exercise this power, however. Whether an offer of proof shall be presented outside the jury's hearing is a question addressed to the trial judge's discretion.

It would be both disruptive and wasteful of time were a trial court to send the jury out for every offer of proof made during a trial, having in mind that many lawyer offers following objection are one brief sentence in length. Moreover, the content of many offers of proof is quite harmless. If the trial judge believes that an offer is of innocuous material she can properly permit it to be made in the jury's hearing, especially if there is no objection and if she instructs the jurors to disregard the procedure. If opposing counsel disputes the propriety of an offer made in the jury's hearing, he should indicate for the record the jury's presence since this circumstance may not otherwise be apparent unless the trial judge or the court reporter notes it.

Despite what has been said of the trial court's discretion, the potential for prejudice requires that all but the most neutral and routine offers of proof be presented outside the juror's hearing. The trial judge can send the jury out of the courtroom or she can retire to chambers if the offer is likely to be a lengthy one or if the risk of prejudice would be great were any juror to overhear it; otherwise, the judge can direct that the offer be made at a whispered sidebar conference. Of course, all of this suggests the wisdom of making important offers of proof at a pre-trial conference.

V.

THE INSTRUCTIONS TO THE JURY

A.

Making the Record on Instructions Given and Refused

In almost all jurisdictions, including those using court-approved "pattern" instructions, the trial judge will either require or at least permit participation by counsel in the preparation of the court's charge to the jury. In some jurisdictions counsel for each side prepares a complete proposed charge; in others counsel prepares only those instructions that apply, at least arguably, to his client's claims or affirmative defenses. Often counsel will have researched and briefed the underlying law and drafted the proposed instructions prior to the commencement of the trial. (Some jurisdictions require that proposed instructions be submitted to the trial judge at the beginning of the trial, although obviously they remain subject to modification as the trial unfolds.)

A conference on the charge is usually conducted in the trial judge's chambers after the parties have rested their cases and before their closing arguments commence. (Counsel prefer to have this conference before rather than after their closing arguments so that they can, with accuracy, make some reference in their arguments to the court's impending instructions.) At this conference the judge, after discussion with counsel, announces what instructions he or she will give to the jury. It is prudent to have a court reporter present to record the conference although some trial lawyers are content to have the words "Given ___" and "Refused ___" typed at the bottom of each of their requested instructions, the blank lines being for checkmarks. Counsel, having submitted his requested instructions separately ("Plaintiff's Requested Instruction No. 1," "Plaintiff's Requested Instruction No. 2," etc.), will place a check-mark after the appropriate term and deliver his set of requested instructions to the court reporter for inclusion in the record.

B.

Objecting to the Court's Instructions

If counsel has any objections to the jury instructions as given in open court, over and beyond those recorded during the aforementioned conference, she must make them out of the jury's hearing immediately after the trial judge has concluded the giving of the charge; otherwise, they are waived. (Grounds for objection may arise for the first time during the giving of the charge either because the judge was not explicit in describing some portion of the instructions during the pre-charge conference or because he or she has undertaken extemporaneous amendments to the charge that appeared to be decided upon in that conference.) A general exception to the instructions is insufficient to preserve error for appellate review. Counsel's objections must be specific, thus affording the judge an opportunity to correct any errors that he can be convinced he made. In other words, it is futile to approach the bench after the charge and say, "We object [or 'except'] to the charge in its entirety." Counsel must say something like "Your Honor, we object to your use of the word 'possible,' instead of the word 'probable,' in that portion of your instructions that dealt with the question of proximate cause."

VI.

VERDICTS

A.

General and Special Verdicts in Civil Cases

A jury's verdict in typical civil cases is usually a "general" verdict; that is, the jurors simply find for the plaintiff, stating the amount of damages they have decided to award to the plaintiff, or they find the defendant not liable. The jury's foreperson may enter its findings on printed verdict forms that are supplied to the jury by the trial court. These forms become a part of the trial record.

Many jurisdictions, including the federal, also provide for "special" verdicts. With this type of verdict, usually called for only in quite complicated lawsuits, the trial court directs the jury to make a specific written finding on each fact-issue in the case. The court either submits to the jurors written questions that are susceptible of categorical (Yes or No) or other brief answers, or it supplies them with written forms that embody the special findings that they could make under the pleadings and the evidence. These questions or special findings are submitted to the court by counsel for the side requesting them and the record regarding the court's giving or rejection of them is made in much the same way as it is with requested instructions, discussed in section V., above.

B.

Demand for Submission of Fact Issues

It is incumbent upon counsel to make a specific demand, on the record, that the trial court submit particular fact-issues to the jury under the special verdict procedure just described. The practice under Federal Rule of Civil Procedure 49 is typical and underscores this point. If in providing the jury with questions or special finding forms the federal court omits any issue of fact, each party is taken to waive its right to jury trial on that issue unless a specific, on-the-record demand is made before the jurors retire to deliberate. The trial judge can make his or her own finding as to any fact issue that was omitted without objection, just as though the court were sitting without a jury.

VII.

POLLING THE JURY

In litigation the moment of truth arrives with the reading of the jury's verdict. A buzzer has sounded; the word is that the jury is coming back. Court is reconvened. The jurors file into their places.

THE COURT: Have you reached a verdict?

THE FOREPERSON: We have, your Honor.

THE COURT: How do you find the defendant, guilty or not guilty?

THE FOREPERSON: Guilty, your Honor.

But perhaps this is not the moment of truth, after all. In many jurisdictions the losing side in either a criminal or a civil case is permitted to have the jurors polled with respect to the announced verdict. Upon request the judge will have the clerk or bailiff inquire of each juror, "Is this your true verdict?" Occasionally this polling process turns up improprieties that occurred during the jury's deliberations and that will require either further deliberations or perhaps even the declaring of a mistrial. (But see Fed.R.Evid. 606(b)(2), restricting jurors to a description of "extraneous prejudicial information," "outside influence," and a "mistake . . . made in entering the verdict on the verdict form.") The polling of the jury, and any comments made by the jurors during their interrogation, should be on the record.

VIII.

CONCLUSION

We have discussed the most important situations in which trial counsel must "make the record." Consciousness of the record and its significance can have a beneficial influence on a lawyer's effectiveness at the trial level. Awareness of the record induces counsel to make an orderly, logical presentation of evidence and argument. It also tends to inspire clarity of thought and speech. But sometimes counsel's ultimate reward, the real moment of truth, is found in the appellate courts, where the difference between affirmance and reversal may depend on his or her ability at perfecting the record.

EXAMPLES OF TRIAL OBJECTIONS*

Note: Some major objections, such as hearsay and lawyer-client privilege, are only briefly mentioned here because they are covered extensively elsewhere in this book.

Accrediting witness before impeachment

This objection is based on the rule that a witness's character may not be supported before it is attacked. Similarly, a witness's out-of-court statements cannot be admitted to bolster the witness's trial testimony unless the witness has been attacked for fabrication, undue influence, or improper motive.

Fed. R. Evid. 608, 801(d)(1)(B).

Argumentative

The essential feature of the "argumentative" objection is that counsel is making an argument that should be saved for the summation. In the summation, counsel is free to draw inferences from the testimony, to characterize it as believable or ridiculous, or to point out inconsistencies and improbabilities. Ordinarily, the questioning process should be limited to drawing information from the witnesses about what they observed. It should not be used to argue the believability of the testimony or the nature of the inferences that should be drawn from it. Thus, some judges would sustain an objection to a question such as "Doesn't it seem unlikely that you'd have had time to do all the things you've said you did in only three seconds?"

The "argumentative" objection is sometimes made as a substitute for the objection that counsel is harassing a witness. However, the element of attack or harassment is not the gist of the objection. The gist is the assertion that what counsel is doing should be saved for final argument.

---

* Prepared by Roger C. Park. Most of these examples are from entries in Park, QUICK REFERENCE GUIDE TO TRIAL OBJECTIONS (2002) a supplement to TRIAL OBJECTIONS HANDBOOK (2d ed. 2001).

Fed. R. Evid. 611(a)

Asked and answered

The statement "asked and answered" can mean either of two things: (1) the question is objectionable because it is repetitious, (2) The opponent's objection has been forfeited because the opponent did not object until after the witness had answered. Fed. R. Evid. 611.

Assumes a fact not in evidence

A question assumes a fact not in evidence when the questioner embeds an assertion about a fact not in evidence in a question that asks about another fact. For example, suppose that counsel is examining a witness who has testified that she fell to the floor. The witness has not explained how she fell. The question "When you slipped on the banana, did you land on your back?" would assume a fact not in evidence.

The question is objectionable because it is confusing and tricky. In the example, the accurate answer might be "Yes, I fell on my back, but I did not slip on a banana." The witness should not be burdened with spotting and denying the imbedded assertion. Instead, the questioner should be required to ask separately about the embedded fact.

A question that assumes a fact not in evidence is objectionable whether asked on direct or cross-examination. In this respect it differs from its close cousin the leading question. Leading questions are permissible on cross-examination.

Fed. R. Evid. 611(c).

Authentication lacking

"Authentication" simply refers to making a showing that a thing is what the offering party contends it is. For example: Is the computer that is offered into evidence the very computer that was stolen from the victim? Is the letter the actual letter that the plaintiff sent? Is the white powder the same powder that was found on the defendant's person when he was searched by the police? These are all questions of authentication.

In order to authenticate a document or tangible exhibit for purposes of admissibility, the party offering the exhibit need only offer evidence that is sufficient to justify a finding that the thing is what the party contends it is. The judge only determines whether a reasonable jury could find the thing to be authentic, not whether it is in fact authentic.

Fed. R. Evid. 901–02.

Best evidence rule (objection—not the best evidence)

If a proponent seeks to have a witness describe the contents of a document without producing the original document, then the objection "not the best evidence" applies. In many jurisdictions, including the federal courts, the requirement of an original also applies to recordings and photographs. The rule excludes oral testimony or other secondary evidence offered in lieu of the original writing, recording, or photograph. However, under the Federal Rules of Evidence a "duplicate" (e.g., photocopy) is admissible on the same basis as the original, unless there is a genuine issue of authenticity or it would otherwise be unfair to receive the duplicate in lieu of the original.

When the original (or a qualifying duplicate) is not available, then the attorney proposing to offer secondary evidence about contents must lay a foundation by establishing that the writing, recording, or photograph was lost or stolen; or was destroyed in good faith; or is in someone else's hands, and not obtainable by judicial process; or is in the possession of the opponent, and the opponent had notice, by the pleadings or otherwise.

Fed. R. Evid. 1001–08.

Broad (objection to question as "too broad")

The words "too broad" and "too general" are sometimes used to object to a question that calls for a narrative answer, and sometimes to object to a question that is confusing because it is not clear what the question refers to. The judge has discretion under Rule 611(a) to require that the question be made more specific.

Chain of custody defective

When a party contends that an exhibit is real evidence that actually played a role in the events giving rise to the case, a showing of the exhibit's chain of custody is required if the characteristics of the exhibit are not distinctive, and if substitution of an item of similar appearance would affect the probative value of the exhibit. For example, an exhibit consisting of a urine sample taken at the workplace, or drugs taken from a suspect, would need evidence of chain of custody in order to be admissible. The proponent would be required to show that the exhibit was handled and stored in a fashion that prevented substitution or tampering. If the exhibit was stored in an area accessible to persons who might have tampered with it, or if for a period the exhibit might have been in the hands of an unknown person, then the opponent should object on grounds that the chain of custody is defective.

Character, improper attack on

This objection, which can be expressed in various ways, invokes the basic rule against using evidence of character to show action in conformity therewith. It may also be used when character evidence is admissible but has been offered in improper form, as when reputation and opinion testimony is admissible but the proponent seeks to prove character by the forbidden route of using specific acts evidence. Fed. R. Evid. 404–05, 412–15, 608–09.

Characterization, improper

An assertion embedded in an attorney's question is an improper characterization if the attorney glosses the witness's prior testimony in a way that adds to it or changes it. For example, if a witness testifies that defendant's truck "turned" the corner, and the attorney then asks how fast the truck was going as it "careened" around the corner, the attorney has engaged in improper characterization. The characterization is objectionable because it may cause confusion about the actual content of the witness's testimony, and because it is a disguised form of testimony by the attorney.

Fed. R. Evid. 611(a).

Compound question

A compound question is one that asks about multiple things. Even if asked on cross, where leading questions are permissible, questions that throw three or four facts at the witness at once can be confusing. The trial judge has discretion under Rule 611 to require that the question be simplified.

Concealed during discovery

The trial judge has authority to exclude evidence that should have been revealed during discovery but that was not.

Conclusion, calls for

This objection asserts that the question calls for inadmissible lay opinion. Fed. R. Evid. 701.

Confrontation Clause violation

If a statement made by a witness who does not appear in court is characterized as testimonial in nature, then a prosecutor ordinarily may not introduce evidence of it against an accused, unless the accused has had an adequate opportunity to be confronted with the witness who made the testimonial statement and the witness is unavailable to testify at trial.

Confusing question

The trial judge has discretion to require that a confusing question be re-phrased.

Fed. R. Evid. 611(a).

Counsel is testifying

Often "counsel is testifying" is just another way of phrasing the leading question objection, but it seems to be a distinct objection when counsel makes an assertion without asking a question about it. For example, suppose that an attorney asks a "question" as follows: "The first car turned left.

What did the second car do?" If the witness in the above example has not testified about what the first car did, then the attorney cannot interject that fact. Assertions of fact that are not supported by the evidence, and that therefore rest upon the attorney's personal credit, are not permitted on either direct or cross examination.

Cross-examination beyond the scope of direct

Federal Rule 611(b) requires that cross-examination be limited to the subject matter of direct examination. Thus, if plaintiff calls defendant's former employee to testify on the issue whether the former employee was acting on behalf of the employer at the time of the accident, and defendant attempts to cross-examine on the issue of whether the former employee was exercising due care at the time, the plaintiff may properly object by saying "It's beyond the scope, your Honor."

Cumulative

The trial judge has discretion to exclude cumulative evidence that is a waste of time because too much other evidence of the same nature has already been received.

Fed. R. Evid. 403, 611(a).

Expert testimony objections

The following are examples of objections that might be made to expert testimony, depending on the jurisdiction:

Misleading hypothetical question

Opinion on ultimate issue

Opinion on law

No factual basis for opinion

Opinion rests on hearsay

Daubert not satisfied

Frye not satisfied

Opinion based on facts not in evidence

Expert not qualified

Witness not disclosed during discovery

Extrinsic evidence of inconsistent statement, no foundation for

Extrinsic evidence that a witness made a prior inconsistent statement is not admissible unless the witness is afforded an opportunity to explain or deny the prior inconsistent statement. Fed. R. Evid. 613(b).

Foundation lacking ("Objection—no foundation")

The "no foundation" objection is merely a way of stating that the opposing attorney has failed to do something that must be done as a prerequisite for introducing the evidence. The objection could refer to failure to lay the foundation for a hearsay exception, failure to authenticate an exhibit, failure to show that the witness has personal knowledge, or a variety of other grounds. Unless the ground for the objection is apparent from the context or unless the objection is explained in greater detail, this language will not preserve the objection on appeal.

Harassing the witness

There is no rule against asking insulting questions if they are pertinent and not repetitious, but an objection should be sustained if the attorney badgers the witness by asking the same question over and over, interjects pointless insults, or argues with the witness about the inferences to be drawn from the witness's answer. This objection usually overlaps with others, e.g. that the question is argumentative or that it has already been answered.

Fed. R. Evid. 611(a)(3).

Hearsay

This objection asserts that the opponent is offering an out-of-court statement to prove the truth of what it asserts, and that no hearsay exception or exemption applies. Fed. R. Evid. 801–807.

Impeachment, improper

This objection could be a claim that the witness is being impeached with extrinsic evidence on a collateral matter, that no foundation has been laid for extrinsic evidence of an inconsistent statement, that the witness is being improperly impeached with inadmissible convictions or bad acts, or a variety of other complaints. More specificity may be needed to preserve rights on appeal. See Fed. R. Evid. 608, 609, 613.

Insurance, reference to

This objection invokes the rule that evidence of insurance coverage is not admissible on the issue of liability. Fed. R. Evid. 411.

Irrelevant

Rule 401 provides that an item of evidence is relevant if it has "any tendency to make the existence of any fact that is of consequence to the determination of the action more probable or less probable than it would be without the evidence." Rule 402 provides that relevant evidence is admissible unless otherwise provided by rule or statute. Rule 403 provides that even if relevant, evidence may be excluded if its probative value is substantially outweighed by considerations of prejudice, waste of time, or confusion. Thus, under the federal rules, almost all evidence that will be offered by a rational lawyer is minimally relevant. The real question is usually not relevance, but whether the evidence passes muster under Rule 403. However, an objection that evidence is "irrelevant" is sometimes made as a loose way of expressing the idea that the probative value of the evidence is outweighed by the danger of prejudice, waste of time, or confusion.

Leading question

A question is leading when it suggests an answer, whatever the exact form of the question. Leading questions are generally prohibited on direct examination, but permitted on cross.

Leading questions are, however, permissible on direct when needed to develop testimony. For example:

1. Leading is permitted when the witness is a hostile witness, an adverse party, or a witness identified with an adverse party.

2. Leading is permitted when the question is a preliminary question about a fact not in dispute (here, leading does no harm and is useful in speeding up the trial).

3. Leading is permitted when the witness has knowledge but cannot testify without being led (as might be the case with a child witness or forgetful witness).

Fed. R. Evid. 611(c).

Misstates the testimony

In asking a question, an attorney will sometimes incorporate a misstatement of the witness's prior testimony. Misstatements of testimony confuse the jury and are objectionable under Rules 403 and 611.

Narrative answer, calls for

A question calls for a narrative answer if it invites the witness to give a lengthy freestyle answer. Because the question does not limit the witness's answer, the witness may stray into a description of inadmissible matters before opposing counsel has an opportunity to object. The trial judge has discretion under Rule 611(a) to require that questions be asked in a more specific fashion.

Nonresponsive answer

The examining attorney has the right to have the witness answer a proper question, and can ask the judge to instruct the witness to answer the question, not some other question. The attorney can also ask to strike the witness's answer.

Some judges maintain that the "nonresponsive answer" objection belongs only to the attorney who asked the question, not to the opposing counsel. It seems, however, that the witness who continually gives nonresponsive answers is in danger of straying into inadmissible matters, and that the trial judge should keep the witness in bounds by responding to a complaint from either side. If the trial judge will not sustain "nonresponsive" objections to testimony by an opponent's witness, a "narrative answer" objection can be made. Fed. R. Evid. 611(a).

Notes being used without foundation

Unless a foundation is laid for past recollection recorded or for some other hearsay exception, a witness may not read from notes while on the witness stand. However, the witness's notes may be used to refresh memory. When notes are used in this fashion, the judge should, upon request, rule that the notes must be taken away after having been shown to the witness.

Offer in compromise

Evidence of an offer to settle a case, or the settlement itself, is inadmissible to show liability or lack of liability. Under the federal rules, statements made as part of settlement negotiations are also inadmissible to show liability or lack of liability. However, settlement offers and statements are admissible if offered for some other purpose, such as showing the bias of a witness who received a payment in settlement from one of the parties.

Fed. R. Evid. 408.

Opinion rule violated

This objection asserts that the witness is being asked for an opinion that will be unhelpful or that the witness is not qualified to give. Fed. R. Evid. 701. Examples: "What was he thinking?" "Was he driving carelessly?" or (to a lay witness) "What caused the cancer?"

Personal knowledge, lack of

Rule 602 provides that "a witness may not testify to a matter unless evidence is introduced sufficient to support a finding that the witness has personal knowledge of the matter." Except when the witness is an expert, see Rule 703, the proponent must produce evidence that the witness perceived the matters described with his or her senses—i.e., saw, heard, tasted, smelled or felt the matter described.

The personal knowledge objection is sometimes confused with the hearsay objection. The two objections are distinct. If a witness testifies to a fact that can be perceived by the senses and does not purport to base his or her knowledge on another's statement, then the correct objection is lack of personal knowledge. If the witness's testimony is a description of an out-of-court statement, then the correct objection is hearsay.

Prejudicial

Evidence or argument is prejudicial when it creates a danger of misdecision that outweighs its potential contribution to accurate fact-finding. For example, one may object to gruesome photographs or inflammatory final argument as prejudicial. Under Rule 403, the trial judge has discretion to exclude evidence upon making a finding that its probative value is "substantially outweighed" by the danger of unfair prejudice.

Fed. R. Evid. 403.

Pretrial conference order, issue eliminated by

Under the Federal Rules of Civil Procedure, issues eliminated in the pretrial conference order may not be revived at trial unless necessary to prevent manifest injustice. Fed. R. Civ. P. 16(e). Hence, evidence of those issues is not admissible.

Prior crimes and other bad acts

See entry for improper attack on character.

Privilege

This family of objects asserts that the testimony is inadmissible because of an evidentiary privilege, such as the attorney-client privilege, the marital privileges, the doctor-patient privilege, the privilege for state secrets, etc. The specific privilege should be named in making the objection.

Propensity evidence

See entry for improper attack on character.

Rape shield statute

This is the objection that evidence of a sexual assault complainant's sexual reputation or sexual history is inadmissible because of rape shield legislation such as Fed. R. Evid. 412.

Re-direct examination beyond the scope of cross

Rule 611(a) gives the judge discretion to promote the orderly presentation of the evidence by restricting the redirect examination to matters covered on cross-examination.

Remedial measures evidence inadmissible

This is the objection that the evidence is inadmissible under the rule forbidding the use of evidence of subsequent remedial measures to show fault or defect. Fed. R. Evid. 407.

Repetitious question

The trial judge has authority to exclude repetitious questions under Rule 611(a), though there is some leeway, especially on cross, to ask them because the answers may shed light on credibility.

Rule 403

Rule 403 has become such a familiar rule that the rule number itself is sometimes used in making objections. The rule provides for exclusion of evidence on grounds of prejudice, waste of time, or confusion.

Settlement evidence inadmissible.

See entry for offers in compromise.

Specific acts not admissible to show character

This is an objection based on rules that require character to be shown by reputation or opinion testimony rather than by specific acts. See Fed. R. Evid. 405(a), 608(b).

Speculative

Objecting to a question as calling for "speculation" is another way of objecting to either (a) expressing an opinion, or (b) lack of personal knowledge. The "speculative" objection is often used when the witness is being asked to state what was in another person's mind, or to draw conclusions from other evidence.

Vague

The trial judge has discretion, under Rule 611(a), to sustain an objection to a question on grounds that its vagueness creates confusion or invites a narrative answer. Example: An attorney asks "When did he go to bed?" and it is not clear whether the attorney is asking about a particular night or a general habit.

Variance between pleading and proof

"Variance between pleading and proof" refers to an objection based upon the assertion that evidence is being offered on an issue that is not raised by the pleadings. Cf. Fed. R. Civ. P 15(b).

CHAPTER 2

RELEVANCE AND ITS COUNTERWEIGHTS

PART **A** Relevance to What?

PART **B** Relevance and Inference

PART **C** Probative Value Versus Prejudicial Effect

PART **D** Character and Habit

PART **E** Similar Happenings

PART **F** Subsequent Precautions

PART **G** Offers in Compromise

A. RELEVANCE TO WHAT?

The Judgment of Solomon
1 Kings 3:16–28 (c. 960 B.C.).*

Then there came two women that were harlots, to the king, and stood before him: And one of them said: "I beseech thee, my lord, I and this woman dwelt in one house, and I was delivered of a child with her in the chamber. And the third day, after that I was delivered, she also was delivered, and we were together, and no other person with us in the house, only we two. And this woman's child died in the night: for in her sleep she overlaid him. And rising in the dead time of the night, she took my child from my side, while I thy handmaid was asleep, and laid it in her bosom: and laid her dead child in my bosom. And when I rose in the morning to give my child suck, behold it was dead: but considering him more diligently when it was clear day, I found that it was not mine which I bore." And the other woman answered: "It is not so as thou sayest, but thy child is dead, and mine is alive." On the contrary she said: "Thou liest: for my child liveth, and thy child is dead." And in this manner they strove before the king. Then said the king: "The one saith, My child is alive, and thy child is dead. And the other answereth: Nay, but thy child is dead, and mine liveth." The king therefore said: "Bring me a sword." And when they had brought a sword before the king, "Divide," said he, "the living child in two, and give half to the one, and half to the other." But the woman whose child was alive, said to the king, (for her bowels were moved upon her child,) "I beseech thee, my lord, give her the child alive, and do not kill it." But the

---

* 1 Kings 3:16–28 (Douay–Rheims 1899 American Edition).

79

other said: "Let it be neither mine nor thine, but divide it." The king answered, and said: "Give the living child to this woman, and let it not be killed, for she is the mother thereof." And all Israel heard the judgment which the king had judged, and they feared the king, seeing that the wisdom of God was in him to do judgment.

Hart and McNaughton, Evidence and Inference in the Law
51–56 (1958).*

The kinds of evidence used by the law in making determinations of adjudicative fact are unlike those used by other disciplines in pursuance of their objectives.

The adjudicative facts of interest to the law, being historical facts, will rarely be triable by the experimental methods of the natural sciences. To be sure, ballistics tests in the murder case may prove beyond rational dispute that the bullet which killed the victim came from the defendant's gun. Laboratory tests in the breach-of-warranty case may settle beyond question the quality of the goods. And blood tests in the inheritance controversy may show that it is virtually impossible that the claimant was the child of the deceased. But these instances will be exceptional. For the most part the law must settle disputed questions of adjudicative fact by reliance upon the ambiguous implications of non-fungible "traces"—traces on human brains and on pieces of paper and traces in the form of unique arrangements of physical objects.

Furthermore, the law uses different evidence and uses it in a different way than other disciplines do even when those disciplines are similarly interested in the determination of historical facts. These differences result from the fact that what is involved, when the most distinctive practices of the law in the handling of evidence come into play, is the formal and official settlement of a controversy.

To understand the law's peculiar ways of treating evidence it is necessary to have some appreciation of the role which formal adjudication plays in the total functioning of the legal system.

A contested lawsuit is society's last line of defense in the indispensable effort to secure the peaceful settlement of social conflicts. In the overwhelming majority of instances, the general directions of the law function smoothly with no controversy whatever. When controversies do arise, the overwhelming majority of them are settled informally or, if formally, without a contest, as by plea of guilty in a criminal case. In almost all these situations lawyers are likely to handle evidence in the same common-sense fashion that anybody else would, unless special calculations are called for by a real possibility of formal litigation.

---

* The Hayden Colloquium on Scientific Concept and Method edited by Daniel Lerner. Copyright, 1958 by American Academy of Arts & Sciences, copyright, 1959 by The Free Press, Excerpts from material by Henry M. Hart, Jr., and John McNaughton.

When a question has reached the point of a contested trial, however, its whole context is changed. Victory, and not accommodation, is the objective of the parties. The adversary atmosphere and the delays of litigation naturally repel evidence, especially testimony and things under the control of disinterested persons, so that the litigants have available for use only the partisan and coerced residue after people with ingenuity have made themselves anonymous. That residue is culled by the parties with a view not so much to establishing the whole truth as to winning the case. And the evidence which survives this attrition (and the exclusionary rules of evidence described below) is communicated to the trier of fact in an emotion-charged setting.

In judging the law's handling of its task of fact-finding in this setting, it is necessary always to bear in mind that this is a last-ditch process in which something more is at stake than the truth only of the specific matter in contest. There is at stake also that confidence of the public generally in the impartiality and fairness of public settlement of disputes which is essential if the ditch is to be held and the settlements accepted peaceably.

The law does not require absolute assurance of the perfect correctness of particular decisions. While it is of course important that the court be right in its determinations of fact, it is also important that the court decide the case when the parties ask for the decision and on the basis of the evidence presented by the parties. A decision must be made now, one way or the other. To require certainty or even near-certainty in such a context would be impracticable and undesirable. The law thus compromises.

The compromise is expressed in the formulas used to guide decision of questions of adjudicative fact. In a criminal case, guilt need not be found beyond all doubt; the trier of the fact must be satisfied of the defendant's guilt only "beyond a reasonable doubt." In a civil case, the facts are ordinarily to be found on the basis of "a preponderance of the evidence"; this phrase is generally defined as meaning simply "more likely than not." The formula for determining whether a case should even be submitted to a jury assumes a wide leeway for differing judgments. The question for the trial judge is whether a "reasonable jury" on the evidence submitted could find that the facts have been proved by a preponderance of the evidence. The judge uses a similar formula in determining whether a verdict already rendered by the jury may stand, and so does the reviewing court in deciding whether to upset either the jury's verdict or the trial judge's own finding if the trial judge sat without a jury. * * *

The most conspicuous difference between the law's problems in determining historical facts and those of other disciplines lies in the procedure of decision. Other disciplines rely primarily on the method of inquiry, reflection, and report by trained investigators. In other disciplines the final conclusions as to key facts are drawn by experts, and the conclusions may be changed if they are found later—after further inquiry and reflection—to be wrong. The law, in contrast, depends in most formal proceedings upon presentation by the disputants in public hearing before an impartial tribunal, a tribunal previously uninformed about the matters in dispute. And findings of fact by the tribunal are usually final so far as the law is concerned.

Typical of such formal proceedings is the trial in court. A trial suffers from immobility. It suffers from shortage and inflexibility of time. It is dependent largely upon non-expert sources of information and upon non-expert evaluators of information (the jury). In addition, proof at a trial is rather strictly governed by procedural rules called rules of evidence.

James, Relevancy, Probability and the Law
29 Calif.L.Rev. 689 (1941).

Since scholars first attempted to treat the common law of evidence as a rational system, relevancy has been recognized as a basic concept underlying all further discussion. Thayer gave this recognition its classic form:

> "There is a principle—not so much a rule of evidence as a presupposition involved in the very conception of a rational system of evidence, as contrasted with the old formal and mechanical systems—which forbids receiving anything irrelevant, not logically probative."

> "The two leading principles should be brought into conspicuous relief, (1) that nothing is to be received which is not logically probative of some matter requiring to be proved; and (2) that everything which is thus probative should come in, unless a clear ground of policy or law excludes it."

* * * Relevancy, as the word itself indicates, is not an inherent characteristic of any item of evidence but exists as a relation between an item of evidence and a proposition sought to be proved. If an item of evidence tends to prove or to disprove any proposition, it is relevant to that proposition. If the proposition itself is one provable in the case at bar, or if it in turn forms a further link in a chain of proof the final proposition of which is provable in the case at bar, then the offered item of evidence has probative value in the case. Whether the immediate or ultimate proposition sought to be proved is provable in the case at bar is determined by the pleadings, by the procedural rules applicable thereto, and by the substantive law governing the case. Whether the offered item of evidence tends to prove the proposition at which it is ultimately aimed depends upon other factors, shortly to be considered. But because relevancy, as used by Thayer and in the Code, means tendency to prove a proposition properly provable in the case, an offered item of evidence may be excluded as "irrelevant" for either of these two quite distinct reasons: because it is not probative of the proposition at which it is directed, or because that proposition is not provable in the case.

* * * Let us analyze a single interesting case, Union Paint & Varnish Co. v. Dean,* an action of assumpsit to recover the purchase price of water-proof roof paint. The defendant relied upon the plaintiff's warranty that the

---

* 48 R.I. 288, 137 A. 469 (1927) [Eds.].

paint would wear for ten years, breach of which he sought to show by proof that another drum of paint of the same brand, which he had purchased six months earlier, not only had failed to prevent leaks but had ruined the shingles to which it had been applied. The drum of paint in issue, purchased just before leaks developed in the first roof painted, had never been opened. Reversing the trial court, the Supreme Court of Rhode Island held that the defendant's offer of proof (apparently almost the only evidence offered in defense) should have been received, saying:

> "If paint of the same brand, sold by the same concern under the same warranty within six months, had proved within that time to be not in conformity with the warranty, in that it was not only not suitable for stopping and preventing leaks but was actually injurious to a roof, a person might well hesitate before using more paint of the same brand when he had no reason to expect the second lot to be any better than the first."

Considered as evidence of the condition of the second drum of paint, proof of the results of use of the first is not very impressive. Waiving any doubts whether the leaks in the first roof were traceable to defects in paint in the first drum, there is no showing whether the defects in the first drum of paint were due to poor ingredients, to a poor formula, or to some error in preparation. If poor ingredients had been used, there is no showing that use of poor ingredients was a policy of, rather than an error of, the plaintiff company. It is easier to believe that one lot of defective paint went out than it is to believe that plaintiff customarily sold, under a ten-year guaranty, waterproof roof paint which would rot out shingles and cause leaks in six months. And the two drums of paint were probably not out of one lot; certainly there was no showing that they were. Proof of the condition of the paint in the first drum was of negligible value in judging the probable character of the paint in the second, unopened drum. It merely showed that plaintiff company sometimes sold bad paint. If the issue was whether the paint in the second drum *was* bad, an issue on which the defendant had the burden, the trial judge's ruling seems sound. At worst, the issue is close enough so that an appellate court should not reverse. Yet there is still a ring of reason to the supreme court's statement that "a person might well hesitate before using more paint of the same brand". He would hesitate to risk ruining a second roof even if he only feared that the second drum of paint might be no better than the first. And if he was reasonable in his hesitation, should the plaintiff be allowed to recover even if it could show at trial that the paint in the second drum was perfectly good? The defendant, reasonably hesitant to use the doubtful paint, by now has probably painted all of his roofs with some other paint and has no further use for the drum which he is tendering back to the vendor. If the customer is to be protected, even against proof that the second drum of paint was in fact satisfactory (as the writer should like to do in such a case), a novel rule of substantive law stands revealed behind a somewhat doubtful ruling on evidence.

But after excluding all cases which turn upon the materiality or immateriality under the pleadings and substantive law of ultimate propositions sought to be proved, there remain many cases in which there is no question of the materiality of the proposition sought to be proved and the probative value of the offered evidence is the real issue. These cases, and these alone, raise the problem of relevancy as a problem in the law of evidence. How should they be handled?

Thayer, after stating the principle which forbids receiving anything not "logically probative", excluded legal criteria from further operation, saying:

"How are we to know what these forbidden things are? Not by any rule of law. The law furnishes no test of relevancy. For this, it tacitly refers to logical and general experience,—assuming that the principles of reasoning are known to its judges and ministers, just as a vast multitude of other things are assumed as already sufficiently known to them." * * *

B. RELEVANCE AND INFERENCE

McCormick's Handbook on the Law of Evidence
316–17 (1954).*

Under our system, molded by the tradition of jury-trial and of predominantly oral proof, a party offers his evidence not in mass, but item by item. The problem of relevancy may arise as to each fact proposed to be elicited by successive questions of counsel, or by successive offers of writings or other objects. Such items are normally offered and admitted or rejected as units, though of course the judge will consider any proof already made by the proponent as indicating the bearing of the item offered, and may in his discretion ask the proponent what additional circumstances he expects to prove. But when it is offered and judged singly and in isolation, as it frequently is, it cannot be expected by itself to furnish conclusive proof of the ultimate fact to be inferred. Thus the common argument of the objector that the inference for which the fact is offered "does not necessarily follow" is untenable, as it supposes a standard of conclusiveness which probably no aggregation of circumstantial evidence, and certainly no single item thereof, could ever meet. This same practice of determining the admissibility of items of evidence singly as they are offered leads to another distinction, often stressed in judicial opinions. This is the distinction between relevancy and sufficiency. The test of relevancy, which is to be applied by the trial judge in determining whether a particular item or group of items of evidence is to be admitted, is a different and less stringent one than the standard used at a later stage in deciding whether all the evidence of the party on an issue is sufficient to permit the issue to go to the jury. A brick is not a wall.

NOTE: ASSESSING THE ENTIRE BODY OF EVIDENCE

As the McCormick excerpt emphasizes, the admissibility of evidence is largely determined item by item (though in some cases the admissibility of one item may depend on whether the proponent of that evidence is expected to introduce some other evidence). Ultimately, assessments must be made of the entire body of evidence that has been presented in the case.

We will consider these assessments on the assumption that the case is tried before a jury, and we'll begin by assuming further that the judge decides to submit the case to the jury. The judge will then instruct the jury on many matters, including the *standard of persuasion*. This is a measure a measure set by the law of how probable the trier of fact must assess a proposition to be if the trier is to determine that proposition in favor of a given party. Thus, in a criminal case, as indicated in the Hart and McNaughton piece, the jury may not find a criminal defendant guilty unless it concludes that facts supporting guilt are true *beyond a reasonable doubt*. This principle is based on the value judgment that it is far worse to find against the defendant if in fact he is innocent than to err in his favor if in fact he is guilty. In a civil case, we usually say that it is about as bad to make an error in favor of a civil defendant as it is to make an error in favor of the plaintiff. Accordingly, a verdict for the plaintiff is justified if it appears *more likely than not* that the facts support him. We may wonder whether the conduct of courts and juries actually matches judicial rhetoric in this respect; it may be that inertia, a tendency to preserve the status quo, tends to prevent plaintiffs from prevailing unless the facts appear *substantially* more likely than not in their favor. But in any event, the standard of persuasion is significantly more lenient in a civil case than in a criminal case.

So how does the jury determine whether the standard of persuasion has been met? For simplicity, let's focus on a civil case. The jurors must consider all the evidence in the case, plus all the knowledge of the world not particular to the case that they bring to court with them. Under one view, they must determine which better squares with all this, the set of stories favoring the plaintiff or the set of stories favoring the defendant.

Suppose Victor has been shot to death and his heirs bring a wrongful death action against Donald. Among the items of evidence presented by the plaintiffs are what purports to be a love letter that Donald wrote to Victor's wife Wanda, a few days before the shooting, and proof that a smoking pistol bearing Donald's fingerprints was found near Victor's body. Among the items of evidence that Victor presents is proof that he is a gentle soul who hated guns and that he told friends the day before the shooting that he was about to leave town.

Now, it would not be sensible for the jurors to consider each item of evidence in isolation. Nor would the jury have to make a series of intermediate findings of the type once suggested in analyzing a similar hypothetical by the great evidence scholar Edmund Morgan: "A man who writes a love letter to a woman is probably in love with her," "A man who loves a woman probably desires her for himself alone," "A man who loves a married woman and desired her for himself alone probably desired to get rid of her husband," and so forth.[1]

---

[1] EDMUND M. MORGAN, BASIC PROBLEMS OF EVIDENCE 185-88 (1961).

The case for the plaintiffs does not depend on a determination that such links are probable. The plaintiffs might even acknowledge that such links, taken by themselves, are improbable. But somehow Victor wound up dead with a smoking pistol bearing Donald's fingerprints lying beside him, and the jury must account for that and all the other evidence. The most plausible account, they might argue, is that Donald expressed his love for Wanda in the letter, overcame whatever resistance he had to violence, lied to his friends about his plans or perhaps changed them at the last minute, shot Donald and then panicked, leaving the gun behind. Donald, on the other hand, might argue that the best account is that he was framed; he wouldn't have been so stupid to leave a gun with his fingerprints behind after shooting someone, and besides he is not the type to have shot someone and he was out of town.

Note that each of these accounts may include a range of possibilities. Thus, the plaintiffs might not claim to know whether Donald lied about his plans or changed them, and Donald might not claim to know who framed him. That is why we say the jury's job may be conceived of as comparing rival *sets* of stories.[2] In any event, in most jurisdictions the jurors' job is not highly structured once the case is presented to them; they take into account the evidence as a whole and report their overall determination.

Now let's consider whether the case should be presented to the jury at all. In a civil case, this only makes sense if a reasonable jury could find either for the plaintiffs or for the defense. If a reasonable jury could only find for the plaintiffs, then they should win judgment as a matter of law, and if a reasonable jury could find only for the defense, then *it* should receive judgment as a matter of law. And so the judge as well as the jury has to make an overall assessment of the evidence, but only to determine whether the case should be submitted to the jury. In a criminal case, the prosecution cannot receive judgment as a matter of law – the accused cannot be found guilty without a verdict by the jury, assuming there is one. But if the judge determines that a reasonable jury could not conclude beyond a reasonable doubt that the accused is guilty, then the accused should win judgment as a matter of law.

Knapp v. State

Supreme Court of Indiana, 1907.
168 Ind. 153, 79 N.E. 1076.

■ GILLETT, J. Appellant appeals from a judgment in the above-entitled cause, under, which he stands convicted of murder in the first degree. Error is assigned on the overruling of a motion for new trial.

Appellant, as a witness in his own behalf, offered testimony tending to show a killing in self-defense. He afterwards testified, presumably for the purpose of showing that he had reason to fear the deceased, that before the killing he had heard that the deceased, who was the marshal of Hagerstown, had clubbed and seriously injured an old man in arresting him, and

---

[2] See generally Richard D. Friedman, *Infinite Strands, Infinitesimally Thin: Storytelling, Bayesianism, Hearsay and Other Evidence*, 14 CARDOZO L. REV. 79 (1992); Nancy Pennington & Reid Hastie, *A Cognitive Theory of Juror Decision Making: The Story Model*, 13 CARDOZO L. REV. 519 (1991).

that he died a short time afterwards. On appellant being asked, on cross-examination, who told him this, he answered: "Some people around Hagerstown there. I can't say as to who it was now." The state was permitted, on rebuttal, to prove by a physician, over the objection and exception of the defense, that the old man died of senility and alcoholism, and that there were no bruises or marks on his person. [Counsel for appellant contend that it was error to admit this testimony; that the question was as to whether he had, in fact, heard the story, and not as to its truth or falsity.] While it is laid down in the books that there must be an open and visible connection between the fact under inquiry and the evidence by which it is sought to be established, yet the connection thus required is in the logical processes only, for to require an actual connection between the two facts would be to exclude all presumptive evidence. Best on Evidence (Morgan's Ed.) § 90. Within settled rules, the competency of testimony depends largely upon its tendency to persuade the judgment. As said by Wharton: "Relevancy is that which conduces to the proof of a pertinent hypothesis." 1 Wharton, Ev. § 20. In Stevenson v. Stewart, 11 Pa. 307, it was said: "The competency of a collateral fact to be used as the basis of legitimate argument is not to be determined by the conclusiveness of the inferences it may afford in reference to the litigated fact. It is enough if these may tend in a slight degree to elucidate the inquiry, or to assist, though remotely, to a determination probably founded in truth."

We are of opinion that the testimony referred to was competent. While appellant's counsel are correct in their assertion that the question was whether appellant had heard a story to the effect that the deceased had offered serious violence to the old man, yet it does not follow that the testimony complained of did not tend to negative the claim of appellant as to what he had heard. One of the first principles of human nature is the impulse to speak the truth. "This principle," says Dr. Reid, whom Professor Greenleaf quotes at length in his work on Evidence (volume 1, § 7n), "has a powerful operation, even in the greatest liars, for where they lie once they speak truth 100 times." Truth speaking preponderating, it follows that to show that there was no basis in fact for the statement appellant claims to have heard had a tendency to make it less probable that his testimony on this point was true. Indeed, since this court has not, in cases where self-defense is asserted as a justification for homicide, confined the evidence concerning the deceased to character evidence, we do not perceive how, without the possibility of a gross perversion of right, the state could be denied the opportunity to meet in the manner indicated the evidence of the defendant as to what he had heard, where he, cunningly perhaps, denies that he can remember who gave him the information. The fact proved by the state tended to discredit appellant, since it showed that somewhere between the fact and the testimony there was a person who was not a truth speaker, and, appellant being unable to point to his informant, it must at least be said that the testimony complained of had a tendency to render his claim as to what he had heard less probable.

Judgment affirmed.

SHERROD v. BERRY, 856 F.2d 802 (7th Cir.1988) (en banc). This was a civil rights action by the father of Ronald Sherrod, a robbery suspect who had been killed by police. The police officers stopped a car occupied by two suspects and ordered them out of the car at gunpoint. The suspects at first refused to follow police commands to raise their hands. One of the officers testified that Sherrod made a "quick movement with his hand into his coat * * * [as if] he was going to reach for a weapon." At that point, the officer fired his revolver at Sherrod, killing him instantly. The trial judge admitted evidence that a search of the deceased failed to disclose that he was armed with a weapon. The jury found for the plaintiffs and returned a verdict of over a million dollars. The Seventh Circuit, sitting en banc, found reversible error in the admission of the evidence that Sherrod had been unarmed. The majority stated that "the reception of evidence or any information beyond that which Officer Berry had and reasonably believed at the time he fired his revolver is improper, irrelevant and prejudicial to the determination of whether Officer Berry acted reasonably 'under the circumstances.'"

C. PROBATIVE VALUE VERSUS PREJUDICIAL EFFECT

Old Chief v. United States

Supreme Court of the United States, 1997.
519 U.S. 172, 117 S.Ct. 644, 136 L.Ed.2d 574.

■ JUSTICE SOUTER delivered the opinion of the Court.

Subject to certain limitations, 18 U.S.C. § 922(g)(1) prohibits possession of a firearm by anyone with a prior felony conviction, which the government can prove by introducing a record of judgment or similar evidence identifying the previous offense. Fearing prejudice if the jury learns the nature of the earlier crime, defendants sometimes seek to avoid such an informative disclosure by offering to concede the fact of the prior conviction. The issue here is whether a district court abuses its discretion if it spurns such an offer and admits the full record of a prior judgment, when the name or nature of the prior offense raises the risk of a verdict tainted by improper considerations, and when the purpose of the evidence is solely to prove the element of prior conviction. We hold that it does.

I

In 1993, petitioner, Old Chief, was arrested after a fracas involving at least one gunshot. The ensuing federal charges included not only assault with a dangerous weapon and using a firearm in relation to a crime of violence but violation of 18 U.S.C. § 922(g)(1). This statute makes it unlawful for anyone "who has been convicted in any court of, a crime punishable by imprisonment for a term exceeding one year" to "possess in or affecting commerce, any firearm..." "[A] crime punishable by imprisonment for a term exceeding one year" is defined to exclude "any Federal or State offenses pertaining to antitrust violations, unfair trade practices, restraints of trade, or other similar offenses relating to the regulation of business practices" and "any State offense classified by the laws of the State as a misdemeanor and punishable by a term of imprisonment of two years or less." 18 U.S.C. § 921(a)(20).

The earlier crime charged in the indictment against Old Chief was assault causing serious bodily injury. Before trial, he moved for an order requiring the government "to refrain from mentioning—by reading the Indictment, during jury selection, in opening statement, or closing argument—and to refrain from offering into evidence or soliciting any testimony from any witness regarding the prior criminal convictions of the Defendant, *except* to state that the Defendant has been convicted of a crime punishable by imprisonment exceeding one (1) year." He said that revealing the name and nature of his prior assault conviction would unfairly tax the jury's capacity to hold the Government to its burden of proof beyond a reasonable doubt on current charges of assault, possession, and violence with a firearm, and he offered to "solve the problem here by stipulating, agreeing and requesting the Court to instruct the jury that he has been convicted of a crime punishable by imprisonment exceeding one (1) year[ ]." He argued that the offer to stipulate to the fact of the prior conviction rendered evidence of the name and nature of the offense inadmissible under Rule 403 of the Federal Rules of Evidence, the danger being that unfair prejudice from that evidence would substantially outweigh its probative value. * * *

The Assistant United States Attorney refused to join in a stipulation, insisting on his right to prove his case his own way, and the District Court agreed, ruling orally that, "If he doesn't want to stipulate, he doesn't have to." At trial, over renewed objection, the Government introduced the order of judgment and commitment for Old Chief's prior conviction. This document disclosed that on December 18, 1988, he "did knowingly and unlawfully assault Rory Dean Fenner, said assault resulting in serious bodily injury," for which Old Chief was sentenced to five years' imprisonment. The jury found Old Chief guilty on all counts, and he appealed.

The Ninth Circuit addressed the point with brevity:

> "Regardless of the defendant's offer to stipulate, the government is entitled to prove a prior felony offense through introduction of probative evidence." See United States v. Breitkreutz, 8 F.3d 688, 690 (9th Cir.1993) (citing United States v. Gilman, 684 F.2d 616, 622 (9th Cir.1982)). Under Ninth Circuit law, a stipulation is not proof, and, thus, it has no place in the FRE 403 balancing process.

> . . .

> "Thus, we hold that the district court did not abuse its discretion by allowing the prosecution to introduce evidence of Old Chief's prior conviction to prove that element of the unlawful possession charge."

We granted Old Chief's petition for writ of certiorari because the Courts of Appeals have divided sharply in their treatment of defendants' efforts to exclude evidence of the names and natures of prior offenses in cases like this. * * * We now reverse the judgment of the Ninth Circuit.

II

A

As a threshold matter, there is Old Chief's erroneous argument that the name of his prior offense as contained in the record of conviction is irrelevant to the prior-conviction element, and for that reason inadmissible under Rule 402 of the Federal Rules of Evidence. Rule 401 defines relevant evidence as having "any tendency to make the existence of any fact that is of consequence to the determination of the action more probable or less probable than it would be without the evidence." To be sure, the fact that Old Chief's prior conviction was for assault resulting in serious bodily injury rather than, say, for theft was not itself an ultimate fact, as if the statute had specifically required proof of injurious assault. But its demonstration was a step on one evidentiary route to the ultimate fact, since it served to place Old Chief within a particular sub-class of offenders for whom firearms possession is outlawed by § 922(g)(1). A documentary record of the conviction for that named offense was thus relevant evidence in making Old Chief's § 922(g)(1) status more probable than it would have been without the evidence.

Nor was its evidentiary relevance under Rule 401 affected by the availability of alternative proofs of the element to which it went, such as an admission by Old Chief that he had been convicted of a crime "punishable by imprisonment for a term exceeding one year" within the meaning of the statute. The 1972 Advisory Committee Notes to Rule 401 make this point directly:

> "The fact to which the evidence is directed need not be in dispute. While situations will arise which call for the exclusion of evidence offered to prove a point conceded by the opponent, the ruling should be made on the basis of such considerations as waste of time and undue prejudice (see Rule 403), rather than under any general requirement that evidence is admissible only if directed to matters in dispute." Advisory Committee's Notes on Fed. Rule Evid. 401, 28 U.S.C.App., p. 859.

If, then, relevant evidence is inadmissible in the presence of other evidence related to it, its exclusion must rest not on the ground that the other evidence has rendered it "irrelevant," but on its character as unfairly prejudicial, cumulative or the like, its relevance notwithstanding.

B

The principal issue is the scope of a trial judge's discretion under Rule 403, which authorizes exclusion of relevant evidence when its "probative value is substantially outweighed by the danger of unfair prejudice, confusion of the issues, or misleading the jury, or by considerations of undue delay, waste of time, or needless presentation of cumulative evidence." Old Chief relies on the danger of unfair prejudice.

1

The term "unfair prejudice," as to a criminal defendant, speaks to the capacity of some concededly relevant evidence to lure the factfinder into declaring guilt on a ground different from proof specific to the offense charged. So, the Committee Notes to Rule 403 explain, " 'Unfair prejudice' within its context means an undue tendency to suggest decision on an improper basis, commonly, though not necessarily, an emotional one."

Such improper grounds certainly include the one that Old Chief points to here: generalizing a defendant's earlier bad act into bad character and taking that as raising the odds that he did the later bad act now charged (or, worse, as calling for preventive conviction even if he should happen to be innocent momentarily). As then-Judge Breyer put it, "Although . . . 'propensity evidence' is relevant, the risk that a jury will convict for crimes other than those charged—or that, uncertain of guilt, it will convict anyway because a bad person deserves punishment—creates a prejudicial effect that outweighs ordinary relevance." United States v. Moccia, 681 F.2d 61, 63 (C.A.1 1982). * * *

Rule of Evidence 404(b) reflects this common law tradition by addressing propensity reasoning directly: "Evidence of other crimes, wrongs, or acts is not admissible to prove the character of a person in order to show action in conformity therewith." Fed. Rule Evid. 404(b). There is, accordingly, no question that propensity would be an "improper basis" for conviction and that evidence of a prior conviction is subject to analysis under Rule 403 for relative probative value and for prejudicial risk of misuse as propensity evidence. Cf. 1 J. Strong, McCormick on Evidence 780 (4th ed.1992) (hereinafter McCormick) (Rule 403 prejudice may occur, for example, when "evidence of convictions for prior, unrelated crimes may lead a juror to think that since the defendant already has a criminal record, an erroneous conviction would not be quite as serious as would otherwise be the case").

As for the analytical method to be used in Rule 403 balancing, two basic possibilities present themselves. An item of evidence might be viewed as an island, with estimates of its own probative value and unfairly prejudicial risk the sole reference points in deciding whether the danger substantially outweighs the value and whether the evidence ought to be excluded. Or the question of admissibility might be seen as inviting further comparisons to take account of the full evidentiary context of the case as the court understands it when the ruling must be made. This second approach would start out like the first but be ready to go further. On objection, the court would decide whether a particular item of evidence raised a danger of unfair prejudice. If it did, the judge would go on to evaluate the degrees of probative value and unfair prejudice not only for the item in question but for any actually available substitutes as well. If an alternative were found to have substantially the same or greater probative value but a lower danger of unfair prejudice, sound judicial discretion would discount the value of the item first offered and exclude it if its discounted probative value were substantially outweighed by unfairly prejudicial risk. As we will explain later on, the judge would have to make these calculations with an appreciation of the offering party's need for evidentiary richness and narrative integrity in presenting a case, and the mere fact that two pieces of evidence might go to the same point would not, of course, necessarily mean that only one of them might come in. It would only mean that a judge applying Rule 403 could reasonably apply some discount to the probative value of an item of evidence when faced with less risky alternative proof going to the same point. Even under this second approach, as we explain below, a defendant's Rule 403 objection offering to concede a point generally cannot prevail over the Government's choice to offer evidence showing guilt and all the circumstances surrounding the offense.[7]

The first understanding of the rule is open to a very telling objection. That reading would leave the party offering evidence with the option to structure a trial in whatever way would produce the maximum unfair prejudice consistent with relevance. He could choose the available alternative carrying the greatest threat of improper influence, despite the availability of less prejudicial but equally probative evidence. The worst he would have to fear would be a ruling sustaining a Rule 403 objection, and if that occurred, he could simply fall back to offering substitute evidence. This would be a strange rule. It would be very odd for the law of evidence to recognize the danger of unfair prejudice only to confer such a degree of autonomy on the party subject to temptation, and the Rules of Evidence are not so odd.

Rather, a reading of the companions to Rule 403, and of the commentaries that went with them to Congress, makes it clear that what counts as the Rule 403 "probative value" of an item of evidence, as distinct from its Rule 401 "relevance," may be calculated by comparing evidentiary alternatives. The Committee Notes to Rule 401 explicitly say that a party's concession is pertinent to the court's discretion to exclude evidence on the point conceded. Such a concession, according to the Notes, will sometimes "call for the exclusion of evidence offered to prove [the] point conceded by the opponent. . ." As already mentioned, the Notes make it clear that such rulings should be made not on the basis of Rule 401 relevance but on "such considerations as waste of time and undue prejudice (see Rule 403). . ." The Notes to Rule 403 then take up the point by stating that when a court considers "whether to exclude on grounds of unfair prejudice," the "availability of other means of proof may . . . be an appropriate factor." The point gets a reprise in the Notes to Rule 404(b), dealing with admissibility when a given evidentiary item has the dual nature of legitimate evidence of an element and illegitimate evidence of character: "No mechanical solution is offered.

---

[7] While our discussion has been general because of the general wording of Rule 403, our holding is limited to cases involving proof of felon status. On appellate review of a Rule 403 decision, a defendant must establish abuse of discretion, a standard that is not satisfied by a mere showing of some alternative means of proof that the prosecution in its broad discretion chose not to rely upon.

The determination must be made whether the danger of undue prejudice outweighs the probative value of the evidence in view of the availability of other means of proof and other facts appropriate for making decision of this kind under 403." Thus the notes leave no question that when Rule 403 confers discretion by providing that evidence "may" be excluded, the discretionary judgment may be informed not only by assessing an evidentiary item's twin tendencies, but by placing the result of that assessment alongside similar assessments of evidentiary alternatives. See 1 McCormick 782, and n. 41 (suggesting that Rule 403's "probative value" signifies the "marginal probative value" of the evidence relative to the other evidence in the case); 22 C. Wright & K. Graham, Federal Practice and Procedure § 5250, pp. 546–547 (1978) ("The probative worth of any particular bit of evidence is obviously affected by the scarcity or abundance of other evidence on the same point").

2

In dealing with the specific problem raised by § 922(g)(1) and its prior-conviction element, there can be no question that evidence of the name or nature of the prior offense generally carries a risk of unfair prejudice to the defendant. That risk will vary from case to case, for the reasons already given, but will be substantial whenever the official record offered by the government would be arresting enough to lure a juror into a sequence of bad character reasoning. Where a prior conviction was for a gun crime or one similar to other charges in a pending case the risk of unfair prejudice would be especially obvious, and Old Chief sensibly worried that the prejudicial effect of his prior assault conviction, significant enough with respect to the current gun charges alone, would take on added weight from the related assault charge against him.

The District Court was also presented with alternative, relevant, admissible evidence of the prior conviction by Old Chief's offer to stipulate, evidence necessarily subject to the District Court's consideration on the motion to exclude the record offered by the Government. Although Old Chief's formal offer to stipulate was, strictly, to enter a formal agreement with the Government to be given to the jury, even without the Government's acceptance his proposal amounted to an offer to admit that the prior-conviction element was satisfied, and a defendant's admission is, of course, good evidence. See Fed. Rule Evid. 801(d)(2)(A).

Old Chief's proffered admission would, in fact, have been not merely relevant but seemingly conclusive evidence of the element. The statutory language in which the prior-conviction requirement is couched shows no congressional concern with the specific name or nature of the prior offense beyond what is necessary to place it within the broad category of qualifying felonies, and Old Chief clearly meant to admit that his felony did qualify, by stipulating "that the Government has proven one of the essential elements of the offense." As a consequence, although the name of the prior offense may have been technically relevant, it addressed no detail in the definition of the prior-conviction element that would not have been covered by the stipulation or admission. Logic, then, seems to side with Old Chief.

3

There is, however, one more question to be considered before deciding whether Old Chief's offer was to supply evidentiary value at least equivalent to what the Government's own evidence carried. In arguing that the stipulation or admission would not have carried equivalent value, the Government invokes the familiar, standard rule that the prosecution is entitled to prove its case by evidence of its own choice, or, more exactly, that a criminal defendant may not stipulate or admit his way out of the full evidentiary force of the case as the government chooses to present it. The authority usually cited for this rule is Parr v. United States, 255 F.2d 86 (CA5), cert. denied, 358 U.S. 824 (1958), in which the Fifth Circuit explained that the "reason for the rule is to permit a party 'to present to the jury a picture of the events relied upon. To substitute for such a picture a naked admission might have the effect to rob the evidence of much of its fair and legitimate weight.'" 255 F.2d, at 88 (quoting *Dunning v. Maine Central R. Co.*, 91 Me. 87, 39 A. 352, 356 (1897)).

This is unquestionably true as a general matter. The "fair and legitimate weight" of conventional evidence showing individual thoughts and acts amounting to a crime reflects the fact that making a case with testimony and tangible things not only satisfies the formal definition of an offense, but tells a colorful story with descriptive richness. Unlike an abstract premise, whose force depends on going precisely to a particular step in a course of reasoning, a piece of evidence may address any number of separate elements, striking hard just because it shows so much at once; the account of a shooting that establishes capacity and causation may tell just as much about the triggerman's motive and intent. Evidence thus has force beyond any linear scheme of reasoning, and as its pieces come together a narrative gains momentum, with power not only to support conclusions but to sustain the willingness of jurors to draw the inferences, whatever they may be, necessary to reach an honest verdict. This persuasive power of the concrete and particular is often essential to the capacity of jurors to satisfy the obligations that the law places on them. Jury duty is usually unsought and sometimes resisted, and it may be as difficult for one juror suddenly to face the findings that can send another human being to prison, as it is for another to hold out conscientiously for acquittal. When a juror's duty does seem hard, the evidentiary account of what a defendant has thought and done can accomplish what no set of abstract statements ever could, not just to prove a fact but to establish its human significance, and so to implicate the law's moral underpinnings and a juror's obligation to sit in judgment. Thus, the prosecution may fairly seek to place its evidence before the jurors, as much to tell a story of guiltiness as to support an inference of guilt, to convince the jurors that a guilty verdict would be morally reasonable as much as to point to the discrete elements of a defendant's legal fault.

But there is something even more to the prosecution's interest in resisting efforts to replace the evidence of its choice with admissions and stipulations, for beyond the power of conventional evidence to support allegations and give life to the moral underpinnings of law's claims, there lies the need for evidence in all its particularity to satisfy the jurors' expectations about what proper proof should be. Some such demands they bring with them to the courthouse, assuming, for example, that a charge of using a firearm to commit an offense will be proven by introducing a gun in evidence. A prosecutor who fails to produce one, or some good reason for his failure, has something to be concerned about. "If [jurors'] expectations are not satisfied, triers of fact may penalize the party who disappoints them by drawing a negative inference against that party." Saltzburg, A Special Aspect of Relevance: Countering Negative Inferences Associated with the Absence of Evidence, 66 Calif. L.Rev. 1011, 1019 (1978) (footnotes omitted). Expectations may also arise in jurors' minds simply from the experience of a trial itself. The use of witnesses to describe a train of events naturally related can raise the prospect of learning about every ingredient of that natural sequence the same way. If suddenly the prosecution presents some occurrence in the series differently, as by announcing a stipulation or admission, the effect may be like saying, "never mind what's behind the door," and jurors may well wonder what they are being kept from knowing. A party seemingly responsible for cloaking something has reason for apprehension, and the prosecution with its burden of proof may prudently demur at a defense request to interrupt the flow of evidence telling the story in the usual way.

In sum, the accepted rule that the prosecution is entitled to prove its case free from any defendant's option to stipulate the evidence away rests on good sense. A syllogism is not a story, and a naked proposition in a courtroom may be no match for the robust evidence that would be used to prove it. People who hear a story interrupted by gaps of abstraction may be puzzled at the missing chapters, and jurors asked to rest a momentous decision on the story's truth can feel put upon at being asked to take responsibility knowing that more could be said than they have heard. A convincing tale can be told with economy, but when economy becomes a break in the natural sequence of narrative evidence, an assurance that the missing link is really there is never more than second best.

4

This recognition that the prosecution with its burden of persuasion needs evidentiary depth to tell a continuous story has, however, virtually no application when the point at issue is a defendant's legal status, dependent on some judgment rendered wholly independently of the concrete events of later criminal behavior charged against him. As in this case, the choice of evidence for such an element is usually not between eventful narrative and abstract proposition, but between propositions of slightly varying abstraction, either a record saying that conviction for some crime occurred at a certain time or a statement admitting the same thing without naming the particular offense. The issue of substituting one statement for the other normally arises only when the record of conviction would not be admissible for any purpose beyond proving status, so that excluding it would not deprive the prosecution of evidence with multiple utility; if, indeed, there were a justification for receiving evidence of the nature of prior acts on some issue other than status (*i.e.*, to prove "motive, opportunity, intent, preparation, plan, knowledge, identity, or absence of mistake or accident," Fed. Rule Evid. 404(b)), Rule 404(b) guarantees the opportunity to seek its admission. Nor can it be argued that the events behind the prior conviction are proper nourishment for the jurors' sense of obligation to vindicate the public interest. The issue is not whether concrete details of the prior crime should come to the jurors' attention but whether the name or general character of that crime is to be disclosed. Congress, however, has made it plain that distinctions among generic felonies do not count for this purpose; the fact of the qualifying conviction is alone what matters under the statute. "A defendant falls within the category simply by virtue of past conviction for any [qualifying] crime ranging from possession of short lobsters, see 16 U.S.C. § 3372, to the most aggravated murder." [United States v. Tavares, 21 F.3d 1, 4 (1st Cir.1994).]. The most the jury needs to know is that the conviction admitted by the defendant falls within the class of crimes that Congress thought should bar a convict from possessing a gun, and this point may be made readily in a defendant's admission and underscored in the court's jury instructions. Finally, the most obvious reason that the general presumption that the prosecution may choose its evidence is so remote from application here is that proof of the defendant's status goes to an element entirely outside the natural sequence of what the defendant is charged with thinking and doing to commit the current offense. Proving status without telling exactly why that status was imposed leaves no gap in the story of a defendant's subsequent criminality, and its demonstration by stipulation or admission neither displaces a chapter from a continuous sequence of conventional evidence nor comes across as an officious substitution, to confuse or offend or provoke reproach.

Given these peculiarities of the element of felony-convict status and of admissions and the like when used to prove it, there is no cognizable difference between the evidentiary significance of an admission and of the legitimately probative component of the official record the prosecution would prefer to place in evidence. For purposes of the Rule 403 weighing of the probative against the prejudicial, the functions of the competing evidence are distinguishable only by the risk inherent in the one and wholly absent from the other. In this case, as in any other in which the prior conviction is for an offense likely to support conviction on some improper ground, the only reasonable conclusion was that the risk of unfair prejudice did substantially outweigh the discounted probative value of the record of conviction, and it was an abuse of discretion to admit the record when an admission was available. What we have said shows why this will be the general rule when proof of convict status is at issue, just as the prosecutor's choice will generally survive a Rule 403 analysis when a defendant seeks to force the substitution of an admission for evidence creating a coherent narrative of his thoughts and actions in perpetrating the offense for which he is being tried.

The judgment is reversed, and the case is remanded to the Ninth Circuit for further proceedings consistent with this opinion.[11]

It is so ordered.

■ [Justice O'Connor, with whom The Chief Justice, Justice Scalia, and Justice Thomas joined, dissented. She did not believe "that it was *unfairly* prejudicial for the Government to establish an essential element of its case against petitioner with direct proof of his prior conviction."—Eds.]

Ballou v. Henri Studios, Inc.

United States Court of Appeals, Fifth Circuit, 1981.
656 F.2d 1147.

■ JERRE S. WILLIAMS, CIRCUIT JUDGE: The plaintiffs filed this diversity suit in Texas federal district court against Appellant Henri Studios, Inc., alleging that the death of Jesse Ballou [was] proximately caused by the negligence of Henri Studios' employee, John Woelfel, the driver of the truck.

Prior to trial, the plaintiffs filed a motion in limine seeking to prevent the introduction at trial of any evidence that Jesse Ballou was intoxicated at the time of the collision. Specifically, the motion in limine sought to exclude the results of a blood alcohol test . . . which reflected that his blood contained 0.24% alcohol by weight at the time of his death.

* * *

At the hearing, the plaintiffs sought to refute the results of the blood test through proof that Ballou was not intoxicated at the time of the collision.

To support their claim that Ballou was not intoxicated, the plaintiffs called to the stand Mrs. Eula Eisenhower, a registered nurse [who] testified that on the afternoon of June 14, 1977 [a few minutes before the collision], Jesse Ballou came to Dr. Washburn's office to have some stitches removed from his hand. She testified that in removing the stitches she was eighteen inches from Ballou's face, and that Ballou did not have alcohol on his breath and that she was positive that he was not intoxicated.

In response to the plaintiffs' arguments, Henri Studios outlined the chain of events leading from the removal of Ballou's body from his automobile through the chemists' analysis of one of the samples of his blood. [T]he defendant noted the chemists' deposition testimony that the test results indicated Ballou was grossly intoxicated at the time of the collision.

After hearing the foregoing arguments and testimony, the district judge sustained the motion in limine.

---

[11] In remanding, we imply no opinion on the possibility of harmless error, an issue not passed upon below.

* * *

In reviewing the district court's exclusion of the results of the blood alcohol test, it is important to note at the outset that even though this is a diversity case, the Federal Rules of Evidence govern the admissibility of evidence.

Under Rule 403 of the Federal Rules of Evidence, a district court may exclude evidence, even if relevant, "if its probative value is substantially outweighed by the danger of unfair prejudice." A trial court's ruling on admissibility under Rule 403's balancing test will not be overturned on appeal absent a clear abuse of discretion.

Although the district court neither stated with precision the grounds for its decision to exclude the results of the blood alcohol test nor specifically invoked Rule 403, the record clearly reveals that the court excluded the evidence because it believed that its prejudicial potential substantially outweighed its probative value. The court explicitly found that the evidence of Ballou's intoxication "would be too harmful" and "would be extremely prejudicial to the Plaintiff" because "it is never possible to judge the attitude of a Jury and how they are affected by the subject of alcohol." The court's comments also reveal that the court believed that the results of the blood alcohol test lacked "credibility." According to the court, its primary reason for determining that the test results lacked credibility was the testimony of Mrs. Eisenhower that Ballou was not intoxicated just a few minutes before the collision and Jim Middleton's testimony that it would probably take at least one hour of alcohol consumption to reach a blood alcohol level of 0.24%.

In challenging the district court's exclusion of the results of the blood alcohol test, Henri Studios argues, inter alia, (1) that the court's decision to believe Mrs. Eisenhower's testimony rather than the results of the blood alcohol test constituted a credibility choice which should properly have been reserved for the jury; and (2) that an adequate showing was made with respect to the chain of custody and lack of contamination of Ballou's body and blood samples, and that therefore any evidence concerning possible breaks in the chain of custody or contamination go to the weight and not the admissibility of the evidence. Because we agree with both of these contentions, and in addition conclude as a matter of law that the potential for unfair prejudice of the blood alcohol test did not substantially outweigh its probative value, we hold that the exclusion of the results of the test was an abuse of discretion requiring a reversal of the judgment and a new trial.

Henri Studios' argument that the district court made an impermissible credibility choice in deciding to believe Mrs. Eisenhower's testimony rather than the results of the blood alcohol test is well taken. It is clear that the district court credited Mrs. Eisenhower's testimony, and that her statement that Ballou was not intoxicated a few minutes before the collision was the primary basis for the court's decision that the results of the blood alcohol test were not worthy of belief. Of course, since the court found that the test results lacked credibility, they were assigned little or no probative value in the Rule 403 balancing test, which ultimately led to their exclusion from evidence.

Although we find the court's skepticism about the test results understandable in light of Mrs. Eisenhower's testimony, we cannot sanction the type of credibility choice made by the district court here. Under Fed.R.Evid. 104, a district court is authorized to conduct the balancing test required by Rule 403 outside the presence of the jury, in deciding the preliminary question of the admissibility of evidence. However, we have recently held that "Rule 403 does not permit exclusion of evidence because the judge does not find it credible." "Weighing probative value against unfair prejudice under [Rule] 403 means probative value with respect to a material fact *if the evidence is believed, not the degree the court finds it believable*." Rather than discounting the probative value of the test results on the basis of its perception of the degree to which the evidence was worthy of belief, the district court should have determined the probative value of the test results *if true*, and weighed that probative value against the danger of unfair prejudice, leaving to the jury the difficult choice of whether to credit the evidence.

* * *

The question remains whether the test results, when properly taken as true, have a potential for unfair prejudice that substantially outweighs their probative value. We hold as a matter of law that the potential for unfair prejudice of the test results does not substantially outweigh their probative value.

The results of the blood alcohol test indicate that Ballou was intoxicated at the time of the collision. Proof of Ballou's intoxication is, of course, highly relevant to and probative of one of the ultimate questions before the jury—Ballou's contributory negligence—and would doubtless have a major effect on the jury's apportionment of fault. On the other hand, in our view the potential prejudice of the test results is comparatively slight. As this court has consistently held, " 'unfair prejudice' as used in Rule 403 is not to be equated with testimony simply adverse to the opposing party. Virtually all evidence is prejudicial or it isn't material. The prejudice must be 'unfair.'" Unfair prejudice within the context of Rule 403 "means an undue tendency to suggest [a] decision on an improper basis, commonly, though not necessarily, an emotional one." Notes of the Advisory Committee on Proposed Federal Rules of Evidence, Rule 403. Although evidence of Ballou's intoxication would surely have an adverse effect on the plaintiffs' case, most of the potential prejudice flowing from the evidence cannot be considered to be unfair since Ballou's intoxication is unquestionably a legitimate ground for a finding of contributory negligence. While there is a slight possibility that evidence of Ballou's intoxication might adversely affect the jury's deliberation on issues other than Ballou's contributory negligence, this slight potential for unfair prejudice is virtually insignificant when compared with the high relevance and probative value of the evidence. We therefore conclude that the district court committed reversible error in excluding the results of the blood test under Rule 403 and that the judgment in favor of Yolanda and Terrence Ballou must be reversed and the cause remanded for a new trial.

See Federal Rules of Evidence 401, 402, 403; California Evidence Code §§ 210, 350, 351, 352. See also Waltz, *Judicial Discretion in the Admission of Evidence Under the Federal Rules of Evidence,* 79 Nw.U.L.Rev. 1097 (1984–1985).

HYPOTHETICALS

(1) P sues D for the wrongful death of H, her husband. H, a pedestrian, was struck and killed by D's car. D's answer admits liability. P offers evidence that D was driving while intoxicated, and that H was thrown 80 feet by the force of the impact. D objects to this evidence as irrelevant. Is D's objection proper?

(2) P sues D for damages for personal injuries to himself and for the wrongful death of P's wife arising out of D's rear-ending of P's car. P was in his car parked at a curb and his wife was at the car door, starting to get in. P also seeks damages for emotional trauma resulting from his presence at the scene of the accident. P testifies that he did not see his wife after the impact because he was rendered unconscious. D admits liability. P proffers photographs of his wife's body at the accident site to show the condition of her body as a result of the collision, the autopsy report, and testimony of the autopsy surgeon and a friend regarding the reconstruction of the wife's body required to permit an open coffin funeral. D makes an irrelevancy objection to P's proffered evidence. What result?

(3) D is charged with the sale of marijuana. The prosecutor introduces evidence that in the company of I, an informer, PO, a police officer, made a purchase of marijuana from D at D's residence. D's defense is a "frame-up"—that PO had the informer plant the marijuana in D's residence. D seeks to introduce evidence that before the alleged sale, D had filed a false arrest suit against the police department growing out of an arrest of D made nine months before the alleged sale. The prosecutor makes an irrelevancy objection to D's proffered evidence. What result?

(4) X is charged with the sale of heroin. A, an undercover police officer, testifies that she purchased heroin from X at approximately 8:00 p.m. on January 30, which was six months before X's arrest. X's defense is an alibi. He testifies that on January 30 he and his wife went to the Movie Theater and saw the movie "Airport," and that it was raining that night. X's wife corroborates his testimony. X calls the theater manager, who testifies that "Airport" was shown at the Movie Theater for seven days, from January 25 to January 31. X then calls B, a meteorologist, to testify that it rained on January 30 from 6:00 to 10:00 p.m., but not on any other day or night between January 25 and January 31. The prosecution makes an irrelevancy objection to B's testimony. What result?

(5) D is charged with forgery of a check and of using it to obtain cash from V, a grocer. D cashed a check drawn on an account of a foundation for which he

had worked. He allegedly endorsed the check with the forged signature of someone authorized to sign the check. The check was returned by the bank to V because the account on which it was drawn required two signatures, not one. D offers evidence that he made restitution to V a week after the incident. Should the prosecution's irrelevancy objection to D's proffered evidence be sustained?

Holmes v. South Carolina

United States Supreme Court, 2006.
547 U.S. 319, 126 S.Ct. 1727, 164 L.Ed.2d 503.

■ JUSTICE ALITO delivered the opinion of the Court.

This case presents the question whether a criminal defendant's federal constitutional rights are violated by an evidence rule under which the defendant may not introduce proof of third-party guilt if the prosecution has introduced forensic evidence that, if believed, strongly supports a guilty verdict.

On the morning of December 31, 1989, 86–year-old Mary Stewart was beaten, raped, and robbed in her home. She later died of complications stemming from her injuries. Petitioner was convicted by a South Carolina jury of murder, first-degree criminal sexual conduct, first-degree burglary, and robbery, and he was sentenced to death. The South Carolina Supreme Court affirmed his convictions and sentence, and this Court denied certiorari. Upon state post-conviction review, however, petitioner was granted a new trial.

At the second trial, the prosecution relied heavily on the following forensic evidence:

> "(1) [Petitioner's] palm print was found just above the door knob on the interior side of the front door of the victim's house; (2) fibers consistent with a black sweatshirt owned by [petitioner] were found on the victim's bed sheets; (3) matching blue fibers were found on the victim's pink nightgown and on [petitioner's] blue jeans; (4) microscopically consistent fibers were found on the pink nightgown and on [petitioner's] underwear; (5) [petitioner's] underwear contained a mixture of DNA from two individuals, and 99.99% of the population other than [petitioner] and the victim were excluded as contributors to that mixture; and (6) [petitioner's] tank top was found to contain a mixture of [petitioner's] blood and the victim's blood."

In addition, the prosecution introduced evidence that petitioner had been seen near Stewart's home within an hour of the time when, according to the prosecution's evidence, the attack took place.

As a major part of his defense, petitioner attempted to undermine the State's forensic evidence by suggesting that it had been contaminated and that certain law enforcement officers had engaged in a plot to frame him. Petitioner's expert witnesses criticized the procedures used by the police in handling the fiber and DNA evidence and in collecting the fingerprint evidence. Another defense expert provided testimony that petitioner cited as supporting his claim that the palm print had been planted by the police.

Petitioner also sought to introduce proof that another man, Jimmy McCaw White, had attacked Stewart. At a pretrial hearing, petitioner proffered several witnesses who placed White in the victim's neighborhood on the morning of the assault, as well as four other witnesses who testified that White had either acknowledged that petitioner was " 'innocent' " or had actually admitted to committing the crimes. One witness recounted that when he asked White about the "word . . . on the street" that White was responsible for Stewart's murder, White "put his head down and he raised his head back up and he said, well, you know I like older women." According to this witness, White added that "he did what they say he did" and that he had "no regrets about it at all." Another witness, who had been incarcerated with White, testified that White had admitted to assaulting Stewart, that a police officer had asked the witness to testify falsely against petitioner, and that employees of the prosecutor's office, while soliciting the witness' cooperation, had spoken of manufacturing evidence against petitioner. White testified at the pretrial hearing and denied making the incriminating statements. He also provided an alibi for the time of the crime, but another witness refuted his alibi.

The trial court excluded petitioner's third-party guilt evidence citing *State v. Gregory,* 198 S.C. 98, 16 S.E.2d 532 (1941), which held that such evidence is admissible if it " 'raise[s] a reasonable inference or presumption as to [the defendant's] own innocence' " but is not admissible if it merely " 'cast[s] a bare suspicion upon another' " or " 'raise[s] a conjectural inference as to the commission of the crime by another.' " On appeal, the South Carolina Supreme Court found no error in the exclusion of petitioner's third-party guilt evidence. Citing both *Gregory* and its later decision in *State v. Gay,* 343 S.C. 543, 541 S.E.2d 541 (2001), the State Supreme Court held that "where there is strong evidence of an appellant's guilt, especially where there is strong forensic evidence, the proffered evidence about a third party's alleged guilt does not raise a reasonable inference as to the appellant's own innocence." Applying this standard, the court held that petitioner could not "overcome the forensic evidence against him to raise a reasonable inference of his own innocence." We granted certiorari.

II

"[S]tate and federal rulemakers have broad latitude under the Constitution to establish rules excluding evidence from criminal trials." *United States v. Scheffer,* 523 U.S. 303, 308 (1998); see also *Crane v. Kentucky,* 476 U.S. 683, 689–690 (1986); *Marshall v. Lonberger,* 459 U.S. 422, 438, n. 6 (1983); *Chambers v. Mississippi,* 410 U.S. 284, 302–303 (1973); *Spencer v. Texas,* 385 U.S. 554, 564 (1967). This latitude, however, has limits. "Whether rooted directly in the Due Process Clause of the Fourteenth Amendment or in the Compulsory Process or Confrontation clauses of the Sixth Amendment, the Constitution guarantees criminal defendants 'a meaningful opportunity to present a complete defense.' " *Crane, supra,* at

690 (quoting *California v. Trombetta,* 467 U.S. 479, 485 (1984); citations omitted). This right is abridged by evidence rules that "infring[e] upon a weighty interest of the accused" and are " 'arbitrary' or 'disproportionate to the purposes they are designed to serve.' " *Scheffer, supra,* at 308 (quoting *Rock v. Arkansas,* 483 U.S. 44, 58, 56 (1987)).

This Court's cases contain several illustrations of "arbitrary" rules, *i.e.,* rules that excluded important defense evidence but that did not serve any legitimate interests. In *Washington v. Texas,* 388 U.S. 14 (1967), state statutes barred a person who had been charged as a participant in a crime from testifying in defense of another alleged participant unless the witness had been acquitted. As a result, when the defendant in *Washington* was tried for murder, he was precluded from calling as a witness a person who had been charged and previously convicted of committing the same murder. Holding that the defendant's right to put on a defense had been violated, we noted that the rule embodied in the statutes could not "even be defended on the ground that it rationally sets apart a group of persons who are particularly likely to commit perjury" since the rule allowed an alleged participant to testify if he or she had been acquitted or was called by the prosecution.

A similar constitutional violation occurred in *Chambers v. Mississippi, supra.* A murder defendant called as a witness a man named McDonald, who had previously confessed to the murder. When McDonald repudiated the confession on the stand, the defendant was denied permission to examine McDonald as an adverse witness based on the State's " 'voucher' rule," which barred parties from impeaching their own witnesses. *Id.,* at 294. In addition, because the state hearsay rule did not include an exception for statements against penal interest, the defendant was not permitted to introduce evidence that McDonald had made self-incriminating statements to three other persons. Noting that the State had not even attempted to "defend" or "explain [the] underlying rationale" of the "voucher rule," this Court held that "the exclusion of [the evidence of McDonald's out-of-court statements], coupled with the State's refusal to permit [the defendant] to cross-examine McDonald, denied him a trial in accord with traditional and fundamental standards of due process."

Another arbitrary rule was held unconstitutional in *Crane v. Kentucky, supra.* There, the defendant was prevented from attempting to show at trial that his confession was unreliable because of the circumstances under which it was obtained, and neither the State Supreme Court nor the prosecution "advanced any rational justification for the wholesale exclusion of this body of potentially exculpatory evidence."

In *Rock v. Arkansas, supra,* this Court held that a rule prohibiting hypnotically refreshed testimony was unconstitutional because "[w]holesale inadmissibility of a defendant's testimony is an arbitrary restriction on the right to testify in the absence of clear evidence by the State repudiating the validity of all post-hypnotic recollections." By contrast, in *United States v. Scheffer, supra,* we held that a rule excluding all polygraph evidence did not abridge the right to present a defense because the rule "serve[d] several legitimate interests in the criminal trial process," was "neither arbitrary nor disproportionate in promoting these ends," and did not "implicate a sufficiently weighty interest of the defendant."

While the Constitution thus prohibits the exclusion of defense evidence under rules that serve no legitimate purpose or that are disproportionate to the ends that they are asserted to promote, well-established rules of evidence permit trial judges to exclude evidence if its probative value is outweighed by certain other factors such as unfair prejudice, confusion of the issues, or potential to mislead the jury. See, *e.g.,* Fed. Rule Evid. 403; Uniform Rule of Evid. 45 (1953); ALI, Model Code of Evidence Rule 303 (1942); 3 J. Wigmore, Evidence §§ 1863, 1904 (1904). Plainly referring to rules of this type, we have stated that the Constitution permits judges "to exclude evidence that is 'repetitive . . ., only marginally relevant' or poses an undue risk of 'harassment, prejudice,[or] confusion of the issues.' " *Crane, supra,* at 689–690.

A specific application of this principle is found in rules regulating the admission of evidence proffered by criminal defendants to show that someone else committed the crime with which they are charged. See, *e.g.,* 41 C.J.S., Homicide § 216, pp. 56–58 (1991) ("Evidence tending to show the commission by another person of the crime charged may be introduced by accused when it is inconsistent with, and raises a reasonable doubt of, his own guilt; but frequently matters offered in evidence for this purpose are so remote and lack such connection with the crime that they are excluded"); 40A Am.Jur.2d, Homicide § 286, pp. 136–138 (1999) ("[T]he accused may introduce any legal evidence tending to prove that another person may have committed the crime with which the defendant is charged. . . [Such evidence] may be excluded where it does not sufficiently connect the other person to the crime, as, for example, where the evidence is speculative or remote, or does not tend to prove or disprove a material fact in issue at the defendant's trial" (footnotes omitted)). Such rules are widely accepted, and neither petitioner nor his *amici* challenge them here.

In *Gregory,* the South Carolina Supreme Court adopted and applied a rule apparently intended to be of this type, given the court's references to the "applicable rule" from Corpus Juris and American Jurisprudence:

> " '[E]vidence offered by accused as to the commission of the crime by another person must be limited to such facts as are inconsistent with his own guilt, and to such facts as raise a reasonable inference or presumption as to his own innocence; evidence which can have (no) other effect than to cast a bare suspicion upon another, or to raise a conjectural inference as to the commission of the crime by another, is not admissible. . . [B]efore such testimony can be received, there must be such proof of connection with it, such a train of facts or circumstances, as tends clearly to point out such other person as the guilty party.' " 198 S.C., at 104–105, 16 S.E.2d, at 534–535 (quoting 16 C.J., Criminal

Law § 1085, p. 560 (1918) and 20 Am.Jur., Evidence § 265, p. 254 (1939); footnotes omitted).

In *Gay* and this case, however, the South Carolina Supreme Court radically changed and extended the rule. In *Gay,* after recognizing the standard applied in *Gregory,* the court stated that "[i]n view of the strong evidence of appellant's guilt—especially the forensic evidence—... the proffered evidence ... did not raise 'a reasonable inference' as to appellant's own innocence." *Gay,* 343 S.C. at 550, 541 S.E.2d, at 545 (quoting *Gregory, supra,* at 104, 16 S.E.2d, at 534, in turn quoting 16 C.J., § 1085, at 560). Similarly, in the present case, as noted, the State Supreme Court applied the rule that "where there is strong evidence of [a defendant's] guilt, especially where there is strong forensic evidence, the proffered evidence about a third party's alleged guilt" may (or perhaps must) be excluded.

SC: Reasonable inference

Under this rule, the trial judge does not focus on the probative value or the potential adverse effects of admitting the defense evidence of third-party guilt. Instead, the critical inquiry concerns the strength of the prosecution's case: If the prosecution's case is strong enough, the evidence of third-party guilt is excluded even if that evidence, if viewed independently, would have great probative value and even if it would not pose an undue risk of harassment, prejudice, or confusion of the issues.

Furthermore, as applied in this case, the South Carolina Supreme Court's rule seems to call for little, if any, examination of the credibility of the prosecution's witnesses or the reliability of its evidence. Here, for example, the defense strenuously claimed that the prosecution's forensic evidence was so unreliable (due to mishandling and a deliberate plot to frame petitioner) that the evidence should not have even been admitted. The South Carolina Supreme Court responded that these challenges did not entirely "eviscerate" the forensic evidence and that the defense challenges went to the weight and not to the admissibility of that evidence. Yet, in evaluating the prosecution's forensic evidence and deeming it to be "strong"—and thereby justifying exclusion of petitioner's third-party guilt evidence—the South Carolina Supreme Court made no mention of the defense challenges to the prosecution's evidence.

Interpreted in this way, the rule applied by the State Supreme Court does not rationally serve the end that the *Gregory* rule and its analogues in other jurisdictions were designed to promote, *i.e.,* to focus the trial on the central issues by excluding evidence that has only a very weak logical connection to the central issues. The rule applied in this case appears to be based on the following logic: Where (1) it is clear that only one person was involved in the commission of a particular crime and (2) there is strong evidence that the defendant was the perpetrator, it follows that evidence of third-party guilt must be weak. But this logic depends on an accurate evaluation of the prosecution's proof, and the true strength of the prosecution's proof cannot be assessed without considering challenges to the reliability of the prosecution's evidence. Just because the prosecution's evidence, *if credited,* would provide strong support for a guilty verdict, it does not follow that evidence of third-party guilt has only a weak logical connection to the central issues in the case. And where the credibility of the prosecution's witnesses or the reliability of its evidence is not conceded, the strength of the prosecution's case cannot be assessed without making the sort of factual findings that have traditionally been reserved for the trier of fact and that the South Carolina courts did not purport to make in this case.

The rule applied in this case is no more logical than its converse would be, *i.e.,* a rule barring the prosecution from introducing evidence of a defendant's guilt if the defendant is able to proffer, at a pretrial hearing, evidence that, if believed, strongly supports a verdict of not guilty. In the present case, for example, the petitioner proffered evidence that, if believed, squarely proved that White, not petitioner, was the perpetrator. It would make no sense, however, to hold that this proffer precluded the prosecution from introducing its evidence, including the forensic evidence that, if credited, provided strong proof of the petitioner's guilt.

The point is that, by evaluating the strength of only one party's evidence, no logical conclusion can be reached regarding the strength of contrary evidence offered by the other side to rebut or cast doubt. Because the rule applied by the State Supreme Court in this case did not heed this point, the rule is "arbitrary" in the sense that it does not rationally serve the end that the *Gregory* rule and other similar third-party guilt rules were designed to further. Nor has the State identified any other legitimate end that the rule serves. It follows that the rule applied in this case by the State Supreme Court violates a criminal defendant's right to have " 'a meaningful opportunity to present a complete defense.' " *Crane,* 476 U.S., at 690 (quoting *Trombetta,* 467 U.S., at 485).

III

For these reasons, we vacate the judgment of the South Carolina Supreme Court and remand the case for further proceedings not inconsistent with this opinion.

Fighting Fire With Fire: Inadmissible Evidence as Opening the Door*

One party offers evidence which is inadmissible. Because the adversary fails to object, he has no opportunity to do so, or the judge erroneously overrules an objection, the inadmissible evidence comes in. Is the adversary entitled to answer this evidence, by testimony in denial or explanation of the facts so proved? The question has prompted a sharp split of authority. It has been asserted that in some jurisdictions the adversary is not entitled to meet the evidence, in others he may do so, and finally in still others he may do so if he would be prejudiced by denying him an opportunity to meet the evidence. However, in reaching these results, many decisions seem merely to affirm the trial judge's action. Most courts seem to subscribe to

---

* John W. Strong et al., 1 McCormick on Evidence § 57 (Practitioner's 5th ed. 1999).

the general proposition that "one who induces a trial court to let down the bars to a field of inquiry that is not competent or relevant to the issues cannot complain if his adversary is also allowed to avail himself of the opening." * * *

Appellate pronouncements afford little guidance on the question as to how the trial judge should deal with the problem. Because of the many variable factors affecting the solution in a particular case, the diverse situations do not lend themselves easily to neat generalizations. However, the published decisions do identify two key factors, the prejudicial nature of the evidence and whether the opponent made a timely objection to block the admission of the evidence. The following generalizations, having some support in the decisions, are submitted as reasonable:

(1) If the inadmissible evidence sought to be answered is irrelevant and not prejudice-arousing, the judge, to save time and to avoid distraction from the issues, should refuse to hear answering evidence; but if he does hear it, under the prevailing view the party opening the door has no standing to complain. Consider, for example, a case in which one party improperly injects evidence of the good character of one of his distant relatives who played a minor role in the litigated event. That type of evidence is unlikely to change the outcome of the trial; and it would hardly be an abuse of discretion for the judge to exclude the opponent's evidence attacking the relative's character.

(2) Suppose alternatively that the evidence, though inadmissible, is relevant to the issues and hence presumably damaging to the adversary's case, or though irrelevant is materially prejudicial and the adversary seasonably objected or moved to strike. Here the adversary should be entitled to give answering evidence as of right. By objecting he did his best to save the court from mistake. His remedy of assigning appellate error to the ruling is inadequate. He needs a fair opportunity to win his case at the trial level by refuting the damaging evidence. In many cases, the adversary simply cannot afford the expense of a second trial after an appeal. Assume that a litigant succeeds in introducing inadmissible evidence of his own good character. That evidence is much more likely to impact the verdict than testimony about a distant relative's character. * * *

(3) If the first inadmissible evidence is relevant, or though irrelevant is prejudicial, but the adversary has failed to object or to move to strike out where an objection might have avoided the harm, the allowance of answering evidence should rest in the judge's discretion. The judge ought to weigh the probable impact of the first evidence, the time and distraction incident to answering it, and the likely effectiveness of a curative instruction to the jury to disregard it. However, here several courts have indicated that introduction of the answering evidence is a matter of right and not allowed merely in the judge's discretion.

(4) In any event, if the inadmissible evidence or even the inquiry eliciting it is so prejudice-arousing that an objection or motion to strike would

not have erased the harm, the adversary should be entitled to answer it as of right.

The question discussed in this section as to rebutting inadmissible evidence differs from the issue of whether a party's introduction of evidence inadmissible under some exclusionary rule (such as hearsay) gives the adversary license to introduce other evidence which (1) is inadmissible under the same exclusionary rule but (2) bears on a different issue or is irrelevant to the original inadmissible evidence. The doctrine has not been extended that far; the door does not swing open that widely.

NOTE

CLARK v. STATE, 629 A.2d 1239 (Md. 1993). The defendant was convicted of rape, resisting arrest, and assault. To show the chain of custody of blood drawn from the defendant for a DNA test, the prosecution called a police officer who had witnessed the blood being drawn and had submitted the blood sample for testing. The blood had been drawn because the defendant was a suspect in another rape. On cross-examination, defense counsel asked the officer "and officer, what was your function in being there while this blood was drawn?" The officer started to answer "Recently I took a report on—" and the state's attorney interjected, "Your Honor, may we approach before the officer answers that"? The trial judge responded, "Overruled. Go ahead, officer, tell her and answer the question loud and clear" and the officer answered "Okay. Originally I answered to a call for a rape in the North Avenue, Curtin Avenue—area where a female reported that she was raped. And subsequently the suspect, Hammel Clark, was implicated as the suspect in this rape." This testimony revealed that the defendant had been suspected of a rape other than the one charged. The defense counsel wanted to question the witness further in order to reveal that the DNA test had exonerated the defendant in the other case. The trial judge refused to allow this further questioning. On appeal, the Court of Appeals of Maryland reversed, holding that the evidence should have been admitted under what it described as the doctrine of "curative admissibility." Once the officer blurted out the statement that the defendant was a suspect in another case, the defense was entitled to cure the damage by putting in otherwise inadmissible evidence. Striking the officer's testimony or giving a curative instruction would not have adequately repaired the damage.

D. CHARACTER AND HABIT

1. CHARACTER IN ISSUE

Cleghorn v. New York Central & H. River Ry. Co.

Court of Appeals of New York, 1874.
56 N.Y. 44.

■ CHURCH, CH. J. The accident was caused by the carelessness of the switchman, in neglecting to close the switch after the stock train had passed on to the side track, and in giving a false signal to the approaching passenger train, that the track was all right. It was a clear case of negligence; and for the injury to the plaintiff produced thereby the defendant is liable in this action. It is insisted that the court erred in admitting evidence of the intemperate habits of the switchman, and that the case of Warner v. N.Y.C.R.R. Co. is a direct authority against it. That was a case of injury at a road crossing. It was proved that the flagman neglected to give the customary signal, and was intoxicated at the time. The Commission of Appeals held it error to show previous habits of intemperance known to the officers of the company, upon the ground that such evidence had no bearing upon the question of negligence at the time. In that view the decision was right. Previous intoxication would not tend to establish an omission to give the signal on the occasion of the accident. In this case it was sought to be proved, not only that Hartman was intoxicated at the time of the accident, but that he was a man of intemperate habits, which were known by the agent of the company, having the power to employ and discharge him and other subordinates, with a view of claiming exemplary damages. For this purpose the evidence was competent. * * * [The court reversed the judgment on other grounds.]

Wellman, The Art of Cross–Examination
170–71 (rev. ed. 1923)

[Suit for libel. The defendant newspaper had published a front page attack upon the plaintiff opera manager which included the sentence:]

"My opinion of you is that you are the sort of man who would steal his mother's bones from the grave and sell them to buy flowers for a harlot."

The plaintiff testified in his own behalf. On cross-examination by Mr. Nicoll it developed that the plaintiff had written the editor who had composed the article an offensive note almost as violent as the one sued upon; that while manager of a trade journal he, himself, had been sued for libel, where the verdict was four thousand five hundred dollars against him; and that he was put upon the jail limits for failure to pay the judgment. It also appeared that he had been convicted of assault upon the opposing lawyer, a most respectable member of the bar; that he had been twice bankrupt; that his sister had recovered a judgment against him for money borrowed; and that his wife had been persuaded to help him in his business affairs and had been driven into bankruptcy on his account. During seven of the twenty years of his married life he kept a mistress, and even occupied, with her, on many occasions, a box in his own opera house directly over his wife's box. He also wrote her impassioned letters, and allowed her to use his wife's horses and carriages. The object of the cross-examiner was, of course, to show that the reputation of such a man could not be injured by anything a newspaper might say about him. The jury agreed with counsel that one thousand dollars out of the two hundred and fifty sued for was balm enough for his injured feelings.

In actions for defamation such as the one just described, it is always legitimate to attack the character of the plaintiff, whether or not he becomes a witness in his own behalf. The question in such cases is one of sound tactics rather than of professional ethics. The plaintiff's character is directly material on the issue as to how much he has been damaged by what the defendant has said or written of him.

Comment on Federal Rule of Evidence 405(b)

Rule 405(a) provides that when a person's character or a character trait may be offered, the proof may be testimony of the person's reputation or of another person's opinion as to the first person's character or trait. Rule 405(b) then provides: "When a person's character or character trait is an *essential element* of a charge, claim, or defense, the character or trait may also be proved by specific instances of the person's conduct" (emphasis added).

Character is an "essential element" only when it is an ultimate issue—that is, an issue that the law governing the "charge, claim or defense" makes determinative. When character is an ultimate issue, it is not being used as evidence of anything else. The proponent is not asking the trier to infer any other fact from the fact of character. Proof of character is an end in itself.

> *Example: Plaintiff sues defendant, claiming she was defamed when defendant called her a violent person. Defendant raises the defense of truth. In support of the defense, defendant offers evidence that plaintiff committed acts of violence.*

In the above example, evidence of specific acts is admissible. Character is an element or ultimate issue in the case. If defendant establishes that plaintiff has a violent character, defendant has established the defense of truth and defeated the plaintiff's claim. Character for violence is not being used to show anything other than character. The trier is not being asked to draw a conclusion about some further fact from the fact of violent character. Proving violent character is an end in itself.

When evidence of character is offered as circumstantial evidence to prove some other fact, then character is not an essential element.

> *Example: In a case in which the defendant is accused of assaulting Mr. X on January 10, 2012, evidence is offered about the defendant's character for violence.*

Here, character evidence is being offered as circumstantial evidence. Character is not an element or ultimate issue. It is merely an evidentiary fact. The evidence of violent character is offered for a further inference or conclusion of fact about *something other than character*—to wit, that the defendant in fact assaulted Mr. X on the day in question. In this example, proof of character is not an end in itself. The prosecution would not establish an element of its case merely by showing character. The defendant might have a violent character and still not have assaulted Mr. X—or he might have assaulted Mr. X even though he was very gentle. Even if the evidence fits an exception to the rule against character evidence—for example, because the defendant opened the door by offering defense character evidence—it may not be offered in the form of specific act testimony, because character is not an essential element.

HYPOTHETICAL

P, the widow of H, sues D in a wrongful death action arising out of H's death in 2011. P testifies on the issue of damages that she and H had a happy and affectionate marital relationship. D then proffers evidence that in 2002–05, H left P and lived with another woman in a meretricious relationship, and that H was convicted in 2008 of the offense of issuing checks without sufficient funds and received a year's jail sentence. P makes an inadmissible-character-evidence objection to D's proffered evidence. D contends that the proffered evidence establishes H's character traits for immorality and dishonesty and that these character traits are relevant to the issue of the pecuniary value of H's companionship to P, his widow. The trial judge overrules P's objection. Is this ruling correct?

2. CHARACTER AS CIRCUMSTANTIAL EVIDENCE

Michelson v. United States

Supreme Court of the United States, 1948.
335 U.S. 469, 69 S.Ct. 213, 93 L.Ed. 168.

■ MR. JUSTICE JACKSON delivered the opinion of the Court.

In 1947 petitioner Michelson was convicted of bribing a federal revenue agent. The Government proved a large payment by accused to the agent for the purpose of influencing his official action. The defendant, as a witness on his own behalf, admitted passing the money but claimed it was done in response to the agent's demands, threats, solicitations, and inducements that amounted to entrapment. It is enough for our purposes to say that determination of the issue turned on whether the jury should believe the agent or the accused.

On direct examination of defendant, his own counsel brought out that, in 1927, he had been convicted of a misdemeanor having to do with trading in counterfeit watch dials. On cross-examination it appeared that in 1930, in executing an application for a license to deal in second-hand jewelry, he answered "No" to the question whether he had theretofore been arrested or summoned for any offense.

Defendant called five witnesses to prove that he enjoyed a good reputation. Two of them testified that their acquaintance with him extended over a period of about thirty years and the others said they had known him at least half that long. A typical examination in chief was as follows:

"Q. Do you know the defendant Michelson? A. Yes.

"Q. How long do you know Mr. Michelson? A. About 30 years.

"Q. Do you know other people who know him? A. Yes.

"Q. Have you had occasion to discuss his reputation for honesty and truthfulness and for being a law-abiding citizen? A. It is very good.

"Q. You have talked to others? A. Yes.

"Q. And what is his reputation? A. Very good."

These are representative of answers by three witnesses; two others replied, in substance, that they never had heard anything against Michelson.

On cross-examination, four of the witnesses were asked, in substance, this question: "Did you ever hear that Mr. Michelson on March 4, 1927, was convicted of a violation of the trademark law in New York City in regard to watches?" This referred to the twenty-year-old conviction about which defendant himself had testified on direct examination. Two of them had heard of it and two had not.

To four of these witnesses the prosecution also addressed the question the allowance of which, over defendant's objection, is claimed to be reversible error:

"Did you ever hear that on October 11th, 1920, the defendant, Solomon Michelson, was arrested for receiving stolen goods?"

None of the witnesses appears to have heard of this.

The trial court asked counsel for the prosecution, out of presence of the jury, "Is it a fact according to the best information in your possession that Michelson was arrested for receiving stolen goods?" Counsel replied that it was, and to support his good faith exhibited a paper record which defendant's counsel did not challenge.

The judge also on three occasions warned the jury, in terms that are not criticized, of the limited purpose for which this evidence was received.[3]

Defendant-petitioner challenges the right of the prosecution so to cross-examine his character witnesses. The Court of Appeals held that it was permissible. The opinion, however, points out that the practice has been severely criticized and invites us, in one respect, to change the rule. Serious and responsible criticism has been aimed, however, not alone at the detail now questioned by the Court of Appeals but at common-law doctrine

---

[3] [The Court quoted from instructions given by the trial judge explaining that the evidence was to be used only to test the character witnesses' standard for assessing the reputation of the defendant, and not as evidence that the defendant had actually received stolen goods in 1920.]

on the whole subject of proof of reputation or character.[5] It would not be possible to appraise the usefulness and propriety of this cross-examination without consideration of the unique practice concerning character testimony, of which such cross-examination is a minor part.

Courts that follow the common-law tradition almost unanimously have come to disallow resort by the prosecution to any kind of evidence of a defendant's evil character to establish a probability of his guilt. Not that the law invests the defendant with a presumption of good character, but it simply closes the whole matter of character, disposition and reputation on the prosecution's case-in-chief. The State may not show defendant's prior trouble with the law, specific criminal acts, or ill name among his neighbors, even though such facts might logically be persuasive that he is by propensity a probable perpetrator of the crime.[8] The inquiry is not rejected because character is irrelevant; on the contrary, it is said to weigh too much with the jury and to so overpersuade them as to prejudge one with a bad general record and deny him a fair opportunity to defend against a particular charge. The overriding policy of excluding such evidence, despite its admitted probative value, is the practical experience that its disallowance tends to prevent confusion of issues, unfair surprise and undue prejudice.

But this line of inquiry firmly denied to the State is opened to the defendant because character is relevant in resolving probabilities of guilt. He may introduce affirmative testimony that the general estimate of his character is so favorable that the jury may infer that he would not be likely to commit the offense charged. This privilege is sometimes valuable to a defendant for this Court has held that such testimony alone, in some circumstances, may be enough to raise a reasonable doubt of guilt and that in the federal courts a jury in a proper case should be so instructed.

When the defendant elects to initiate a character inquiry, another anomalous rule comes into play. Not only is he permitted to call witnesses to testify from hearsay, but indeed such a witness is not allowed to base his testimony on anything but hearsay. What commonly is called "character evidence" is only such when "character" is employed as a synonym for "reputation." The witness may not testify about defendant's specific acts or courses of conduct or his possession of a particular disposition or of benign mental and moral traits; nor can he testify that his own acquaintance, observation, and knowledge of defendant leads to his own independent opinion that defendant possesses a good general or specific character, inconsis-

---

[5] A judge of long trial and appellate experience has uttered a warning which, in the opinion of the writer, we might well have heeded in determining whether to grant certiorari here: " * * * evidence of good character is to be used like any other, once it gets before the jury, and the less they are told about the grounds for its admission, or what they shall do with it, the more likely they are to use it sensibly. The subject seems to gather mist which discussion serves only to thicken, and which we can scarcely hope to dissipate by anything further we can add." * * *

[8] This would be subject to some qualification, as when a prior crime is an element of the later offense; for example, at a trial for being an habitual criminal. There are also well-established exceptions where evidence as to other transactions or a course of fraudulent conduct is admitted to establish fraudulent intent as an element of the crime charged. [Citations omitted.]

tent with commission of acts charged. The witness is, however, allowed to summarize what he has heard in the community, although much of it may have been said by persons less qualified to judge than himself. The evidence which the law permits is not as to the personality of defendant but only as to the shadow his daily life has cast in his neighborhood. This has been well described in a different connection as "the slow growth of months and years, the resultant picture of forgotten incidents, passing events, habitual and daily conduct, presumably honest because disinterested, and safer to be trusted because prone to suspect. * * * It is for that reason that such general repute is permitted to be proven. It sums up a multitude of trivial details. It compacts into the brief phrase of a verdict the teaching of many incidents and the conduct of years. It is the average intelligence drawing its conclusion."

While courts have recognized logical grounds for criticism of this type of opinion-based-on-hearsay testimony, it is said to be justified by "overwhelming considerations of practical convenience" in avoiding innumerable collateral issues which, if it were attempted to prove character by direct testimony, would complicate and confuse the trial, distract the minds of jurymen and befog the chief issues in the litigation.

Another paradox in this branch of the law of evidence is that the delicate and responsible task of compacting reputation hearsay into the "brief phrase of a verdict" is one of the few instances in which conclusions are accepted from a witness on a subject in which he is not an expert. However, the witness must qualify to give an opinion by showing such acquaintance with the defendant, the community in which he has lived and the circles in which he has moved, as to speak with authority of the terms in which generally he is regarded. To require affirmative knowledge of the reputation may seem inconsistent with the latitude given to the witness to testify when all he can say of the reputation is that he has "heard nothing against defendant." This is permitted upon assumption that, if no ill is reported of one, his reputation must be good.[13] But this answer is accepted only from a witness whose knowledge of defendant's habitat and surroundings is intimate enough so that his failure to hear of any relevant ill repute is an assurance that no ugly rumors were about.

Thus the law extends helpful but illogical options to a defendant. Experience taught a necessity that they be counterweighted with equally illogical conditions to keep the advantage from becoming an unfair and unreasonable one. The price a defendant must pay for attempting to prove his good name is to throw open the entire subject which the law has kept closed for his benefit and to make himself vulnerable where the law otherwise shields him. The prosecution may pursue the inquiry with contradictory witnesses to show that damaging rumors, whether or not well-grounded, were afloat—for it is not the man that he is, but the name that he has which is put in issue. Another hazard is that his own witness is subject to

---

[13] The law apparently ignores the existence of such human ciphers as Kipling's Tomlinson, of whom no ill is reported but no good can be recalled. They win seats with the righteous for character evidence purposes, however hard their lot in literature.

cross-examination as to the contents and extent of the hearsay on which he
bases his conclusions, and he may be required to disclose rumors and reports that are current even if they do not affect his own conclusion.[16] It may
test the sufficiency of his knowledge by asking what stories were circulat-
ing concerning events, such as one's arrest, about which people normally
comment and speculate. Thus, while the law gives defendant the option to
show as a fact that his reputation reflects a life and habit incompatible
with commission of the offense charged, it subjects his proof to tests of credibility designed to prevent him from profiting by a mere parade of parti-
sans.

To thus digress from evidence as to the offense to hear a contest as to
the standing of the accused, at its best opens a tricky line of inquiry as to a
shapeless and elusive subject matter. At its worst it opens a veritable Pan-
dora's box of irresponsible gossip, innuendo and smear. * * *

Wide discretion is accompanied by heavy responsibility on trial courts
to protect the practice from any misuse. The trial judge was scrupulous to
so guard it in the case before us. He took pains to ascertain, out of presence
of the jury, that the target of the question was an actual event, which
would probably result in some comment among acquaintances if not injury
to defendant's reputation. He satisfied himself that counsel was not merely
taking a random shot at a reputation imprudently exposed or asking a
groundless question to waft an unwarranted innuendo into the jury box.[18]

The question permitted by the trial court, however, involves several
features that may be worthy of comment. Its form invited hearsay; it asked
about an arrest, not a conviction, and for an offense not closely similar to
the one on trial; and it concerned an occurrence many years past.

---

[16] A classic example in the books is a character witness in a trial for murder. She testified
she grew up with defendant, knew his reputation for peace and quiet, and that it was good. On
cross-examination she was asked if she had heard that the defendant had shot anybody, and,
if so, how many. She answered, "Three or four," and gave the names of two but could not recall
the names of the others. She still insisted, however, that he was of "good character." The jury
seems to have valued her information more highly than her judgment, and on appeal from
conviction the cross-examination was held proper.

[18] This procedure was recommended by Wigmore. But analysis of his innovation emphasizes the way in which law on this subject has evolved from pragmatic considerations rather
than from theoretical consistency. The relevant information that it is permissible to lay before
the jury is talk or conversation about the defendant's being arrested. That is admissible
whether or not an actual arrest had taken place; it might even be more significant of repute if
his neighbors were ready to arrest him in rumor when the authorities were not in fact. But
before this relevant and proper inquiry can be made, counsel must demonstrate privately to
the court an irrelevant and possibly unprovable fact—the reality of arrest. From this permissible inquiry about reports of arrest, the jury is pretty certain to infer that defendant had in
fact been arrested and to draw its own conclusions as to character from that fact. The Wigmore suggestion thus limits legally relevant inquiries to those based on legally irrelevant facts
in order that the legally irrelevant conclusion which the jury probably will draw from the relevant questions will not be based on unsupported or untrue innuendo. It illustrates Judge
Hand's suggestion that the system may work best when explained least. Yet, despite its theoretical paradoxes and deficiencies, we approve the procedure as calculated in practice to hold
the inquiry within decent bounds.

Since the whole inquiry, as we have pointed out, is calculated to ascertain the general talk of people about defendant, rather that the witness' own knowledge of him, the form of inquiry, "Have you heard?" has general approval, and "Do you know?" is not allowed.

A character witness may be cross-examined as to an arrest whether or not it culminated in a conviction, according to the overwhelming weight of authority. This rule is sometimes confused with that which prohibits cross-examination to credibility by asking a witness whether he himself has been arrested.

Arrest without more does not, in law any more than in reason, impeach the integrity or impair the credibility of a witness. It happens to the innocent as well as the guilty. Only a conviction, therefore, may be inquired about to undermine the trustworthiness of a witness.

Arrest without more may nevertheless impair or cloud one's reputation. False arrest may do that. Even to be acquitted may damage one's good name if the community receives the verdict with a wink and chooses to remember defendant as one who ought to have been convicted. * * *

The inquiry as to an arrest is permissible also because the prosecution has a right to test the qualifications of the witness to bespeak the community opinion. If one never heard the speculations and rumors in which even one's friends indulge upon his arrest, the jury may doubt whether he is capable of giving any very reliable conclusions as to his reputation.

In this case the crime inquired about was receiving stolen goods; the trial was for bribery. The Court of Appeals thought this dissimilarity of offenses too great to sustain the inquiry in logic, though conceding that it is authorized by preponderance of authority. It asks us to substitute the Illinois rule which allows inquiry about arrest, but only for very closely similar if not identical charges, in place of the rule more generally adhered to in this country and in England. We think the facts of this case show the proposal to be inexpedient.

The good character which the defendant had sought to establish was broader than the crime charged and included the traits of "honesty and truthfulness" and "being a law-abiding citizen." Possession of these characteristics would seem as incompatible with offering a bribe to a revenue agent as with receiving stolen goods. The crimes may be unlike, but both alike proceed from the same defects of character which the witnesses said this defendant was reputed not to exhibit. It is not only by comparison with the crime on trial but by comparison with the reputation asserted that a court may judge whether the prior arrest should be made subject of inquiry. By this test the inquiry was permissible. It was proper cross-examination because reports of his arrest for receiving stolen goods, if admitted, would tend to weaken the assertion that he was known as an honest and law-abiding citizen. The cross-examination may take in as much ground as the testimony it is designed to verify. To hold otherwise would give defendant the benefit of testimony that he was honest and law-abiding in reputation when such might not be the fact; the refutation was founded on convictions equally persuasive though not for crimes exactly repeated in the present charge.

The inquiry here concerned an arrest twenty-seven years before the trial. Events a generation old are likely to be lived down and dropped from the present thought and talk of the community and to be absent from the knowledge of younger or more recent acquaintances. The court in its discretion may well exclude inquiry about rumors of an event so remote, unless recent misconduct revived them. But two of these witnesses dated their acquaintance with defendant as commencing thirty years before the trial. Defendant, on direct examination, voluntarily called attention to his conviction twenty years before. While the jury might conclude that a matter so old and indecisive as a 1920 arrest would shed little light on the present reputation and hence propensities of the defendant, we cannot say that, in the context of this evidence and in the absence of objection on this specific ground, its admission was an abuse of discretion.

We do not overlook or minimize the consideration that "the jury almost surely cannot comprehend the Judge's limiting instructions," which disturbed the Court of Appeals. The refinements of the evidentiary rules on this subject are such that even lawyers and judges, after study and reflection, often are confused, and surely jurors in the hurried and unfamiliar movement of a trial must find them almost unintelligible. However, limiting instructions on this subject are no more difficult to comprehend or apply than those upon various other subjects; for example, instructions that admissions of a co-defendant are to be limited to the question of his guilt and are not to be considered as evidence against other defendants, and instructions as to other problems in the trial of conspiracy charges. A defendant in such a case is powerless to prevent his cause from being irretrievably obscured and confused; but, in cases such as the one before us, the law foreclosed this whole confounding line of inquiry, unless defendant thought the net advantage from opening it up would be with him. Given this option, we think defendants in general and this defendant in particular have no valid complaint at the latitude which existing law allows to the prosecution to meet by cross-examination an issue voluntarily tendered by the defense.

We end, as we began, with the observation that the law regulating the offering and testing of character testimony may merit many criticisms. England, and some states have overhauled the practice by statute.[22] But the task of modernizing the longstanding rules on the subject is one of magnitude and difficulty which even those dedicated to law reform do not lightly undertake.

The law of evidence relating to proof of reputation in criminal cases has developed almost entirely at the hands of state courts of last resort, which have such questions frequently before them. This Court, on the other hand, has contributed little to this or to any phase of the law of evidence, for the reason, among others, that it has had extremely rare occasion to

---

[22] Criminal Evidence Act, 61 & 62, Vict. c. 36. * * *

decide such issues, as the paucity of citations in this opinion to our own writings attests. It is obvious that a court which can make only infrequent sallies into the field cannot recast the body of case law on this subject in many, many years, even if it were clear what the rules should be.

We concur in the general opinion of courts, textwriters and the profession that much of this law is archaic, paradoxical and full of compromises and compensations by which an irrational advantage to one side is offset by a poorly reasoned, counterprivilege to the other. But somehow it has proved a workable even if clumsy system when moderated by discretionary controls in the hands of a wise and strong trial court. To pull one misshapen stone out of the grotesque structure is more likely simply to upset its present balance between adverse interests than to establish a rational edifice.

The present suggestion is that we adopt for all federal courts a new rule as to cross-examination about prior arrest, adhered to by the courts of only one state and rejected elsewhere. The confusion and error it would engender would seem too heavy a price to pay for an almost imperceptible logical improvement, if any, in a system which is justified, if at all, by accumulated judicial experience rather than abstract logic.[25]

The judgment is

Affirmed.

[Justice Rutledge wrote a reflective dissent, joined by Justice Murphy. He defended the principle that the prosecution cannot introduce the subject of the defendant's character, so far as it bears on the probability that he committed the crime charged, but the defendant can. And he acknowledged that if the defendant chooses to present character evidence, the prosecution must be allowed to rebut. But he would have limited rebuttal "to inquiry concerning the witness' opportunity for knowing the accused and his reputation and to producing contrary evidence by other witnesses of the same general sort as that which is refuted"; he deemed it unacceptable, though, that "in the guise of 'testing the standards of the witness' when he speaks to reputation, the door has been thrown wide open to trying the defendant's whole life, both in general reputation and in specific incident." Justice Frankfurter wrote a concurring opinion, expressing sympathy with Justice Rutledge's general outlook but concluding that it was unwise to confine the discretion of trial judges in this matter.]

NOTE

Despite the fact that the *Michelson* case was decided in 1948, most of its propositions about character evidence are still good law. For example, it is still true, at least as a general matter, that (1) the prosecution cannot prove that the

---

[25] It must not be overlooked that abuse of cross-examination to test credibility carries its own corrective. Authorities on practice caution the bar of the imprudence as well as the unprofessional nature of attacks on witnesses or defendants which are likely to be resented by the jury. Wellman, Art of Cross Examination (1927) p. 167 et seq.

accused is more likely to have committed the crime charged because he has an evil character, Fed. R. Evid. 404(a), or because he has committed other bad acts in the past, Fed. R. Evid. 404(b); (2) the accused may, however, present evidence indicating that his character makes it less likely that he committed the crime (and note that if the accused does so, the prosecution may present character evidence in rebuttal), Fed. R. Evid. 404(b); (3) character witnesses can testify only as to general assessments as to the accused's character, and not as to specific acts, Fed. R. Evid. 405(a); and (4) on cross-examination of a character witness, inquiry as to specific incidents is permissible, in the discretion of the trial judge, *id.* The Federal Rules did, however, bring about one significant change in the form of character evidence: Opinion testimony as well as reputation testimony is now permitted. *Id.* That is, on direct examination a character witness for the accused may, contrary to *Michelson*, testify that based on her own "acquaintance, observation, and knowledge" of the accused she believes his character is inconsistent with commission of the crimes charged. And it is now permissible to cross-examine an opinion character witness by asking "Do you know" questions, as well as "Have you heard" questions, about specific acts of the defendant. See Advisory Committee Note, p. 1052.

Camus, The Stranger

79–81*

[The protagonist is awaiting trial before an Algerian Colonial Court on a charge of murder. The defense is self-defense. His lawyer visits him in jail] * * * [H]e said that they'd been making investigations into my private life. They had learned that my mother died recently in a home. Inquiries had been conducted at Marengo and the police informed that I'd shown "great callousness" at my mother's funeral.

"You must understand," the lawyer said, "that I don't relish having to question you about such a matter. But it has much importance, and, unless I find some way of answering the charge of 'callousness,' I shall be handicapped in conducting your defense. And that is where you, and only you, can help me."

He went on to ask if I had felt grief on that "sad occasion." The question struck me as an odd one; I'd have been much embarrassed if I'd had to ask anyone a thing like that.

I answered that, of recent years, I'd rather lost the habit of noting my feelings, and hardly knew what to answer. I could truthfully say I'd been quite fond of Mother—but really that didn't mean much. All normal people, I added as on afterthought, had more or less desired the death of those they loved, at some time or another.

Here the lawyer interrupted me, looking greatly perturbed.

"You must promise me not to say anything of that sort at the trial, or to the examining magistrate."

---

* Copyright, 1946 by Alfred A. Knopf, Inc. Vintage Books (A division of Random House)

I promised, to satisfy him, but I explained that my physical condition at any given moment often influenced my feelings. For instance, on the day I attended Mother's funeral, I was fagged out and only half awake. So, really, I hardly took stock of what was happening. Anyhow, I could assure him of one thing: that I'd rather Mother hadn't died.

The lawyer, however, looked displeased. "That's not enough," he said curtly.

After considering for a bit he asked me if he could say that on that day I had kept my feelings under control.

"No," I said. "That wouldn't be true."

He gave me a queer look, as if I slightly revolted him; then informed me, in an almost hostile tone, that in any case the head of the Home and some of the staff would be cited as witnesses.

"And that might do you a very nasty turn," he concluded.

When I suggested that Mother's death had no connection with the charge against me, he merely replied that this remark showed I'd never had any dealings with the law.

A.L.I., Model Penal Code
§ 251.2*

(6) Evidence. On the issue whether a place is a house of prostitution the following shall be admissible evidence: its general repute; the repute of the persons who reside in or frequent the place; the frequency, timing and duration of visits by non-residents * * *.

Maryland—District of Columbia—Virginia Criminal Practice Institute Trial Manual
2–7 (1964).**

2.03 Eliciting Testimony Regarding the Character Trait of Truth and Veracity.

1. What is your name, please?

2. Where do you reside, Mr. [name]?

3. Where are you employed?

4. How long have you worked there?

5. In what capacity?

---

* See Calif. Penal Code § 315.
** Copyright, 1964, by Lerner Law Book Co.

6. Do you know the defendant, [name]?

7. How long have you known him?

8. During that period, how often did you see him?

9. What was the nature of your association with him?

10. Did you know other people who knew him?

11. Did you discuss with these people, or hear discussed, the defendant's reputation for truth and veracity?

12. What generally is his reputation for truth and veracity among those people?

QUESTION

If Federal Rule of Evidence 405 applies, how might this series of questions be changed?

Theodore Roosevelt as Character Witness

10 Journal of the Cleveland Bar Assoc. 36 (Dec. 1938).

[Note—In this installment of the address which was delivered by President Frank J. Hogan, of the American Bar Association, before our members at the October meeting, we start with the entrance of the late President Theodore Roosevelt into the courtroom at Washington to testify as a character witness for Charles G. Glover, president of the largest national bank in the capital city.]

As Teddy Roosevelt stepped up into the room it appeared as though he had stepped on a button that would set off the applause, and first the applause started with hand clapping, and then everybody in the courtroom stood up. * * *

When quiet was restored and a few minutes passed and Roosevelt had waved to everybody whether he knew them or not, the Judge ascended the bench and we put Teddy on as the first witness.

Now, all of you, I don't know whether your rule is as strict with respect to reputation witnesses here, but in most states, of course, the witness is allowed to identify himself and then say he knows the defendant, and then he is asked whether the defendant's character or reputation for the trait involved is good or bad, and in some states they tie it down to good, bad or excellent, or very good, or something of that kind. In our jurisdiction we are allowed a little greater latitude, our Court of Appeals having held that one might have a good reputation or a superlatively good reputation, and that also we have a right to show who the character witness is so that the jury can give greater or less weight to the man who thus testifies.

But whether we had those rules of "good" or "bad" or monosyllabic responses would have made no difference to Roosevelt. Rules of evidence might be worshipped by a Wigmore, but if Roosevelt ever heard of them he heard of them only to laugh at them. (Laughter).

He was asked his name, and then many in the audience noticed what the older of this audience must know, that Theodore Roosevelt had a perpetually boy's changing voice [and] it gave a sort of an added, not practiced, unintentional emphasis to what he had to say.

And when we asked him his name, he said, "Theodore Roosevelt." (Voice breaking from bass to high-pitched). We asked what his profession was, and he said, "Write." (High-pitched voice). We asked where he lived; he said, "Used to be New York." (High-pitched voice). And then without imitating him any more I will tell you he went on that way, getting that up and down. It was fascinating when you realized that the man was intensely interested in what he was saying.

He was asked whether or not he had ever lived in Washington, and he twisted around to the jury, and he said, "May I state what happened without any further question?"

And I said, "Yes, go ahead."

He said, "I came to Washington as Civil Service Commissioner when conditions were very bad. Politics, politics, alone, governed whether—are any of you in the government service? Oh, no. I forgot jurymen can't be in the government service. Well, those of your neighbors would be shoved in and out of office all the time, and we were trying to make something permanent in the tenure of government officials, and we did it. But it was very routine: it wasn't exciting at all; and I was called back to New York—Judge, you will remember this; you are old enough to remember it—called back to New York, and when I got there I became Police Commissioner. Oh, gentlemen of the jury, I know I can't tell you stories about it today, but it was bully fun—it was bully fun. And I was interested in that. It's fine work where the policemen are generally honest policemen, and we made them honest in New York. We did, gentlemen of the jury, and the citizens of New York would be proud of our work. Oh, but I am getting off. I am coming back, Judge. I am coming back.

"Then I came to Washington as Assistant Secretary of the Navy. That got my interest. When this country gets a great big strong navy it won't have any reason to fear anybody, and people won't be going around saying, 'I didn't raise my son to be a soldier.' You won't hear that any more because the navy will take care of it. We need a strong navy.

"I know, Judge, you are just about to tell me, but I am coming now to it. That's when I was in Washington, though." (Laughter). "And at that time I opened—I know you want me, Mr. Hogan, to say this—I opened an account at the Riggs National Bank. You know, I had a deposit at the Riggs

National Bank ever since, and I had it because my faith in Mr. Glover was so great, I wouldn't take it out no matter where I lived."

There was still no stopping him. The district attorney had sense enough to know that if you stopped him you would be bowled over in some way.

He said, "Then came the Spanish–American War. That was terrible, but it was interesting, it was fine, and I had a real life for a while. Then I became governor of New York, so I was back there again for quite a while. Then, gentlemen of the jury, they made me Vice–President. It was the most terrible experience, a perfectly terrible experience. I don't think I would have lived through it if I had to take four years, but I had my account here at the Riggs National Bank as Vice-President just as I had it when I was President; and as you know, I was President for about seven and a half years, living here all the time, keeping my account at the Riggs National Bank.

"And by the way, Judge, I knew I had met you somewhere. I appointed you because of your civic righteousness, because of your interest in the poor of this city, on my committee to clean out the slums. That's what I did, and you were one of the best men on the committee I ever had. I know, gentlemen of the jury, you are glad to hear that about your Judge. I knew I recognized him. And you did splendid work." And the Judge, who was just on the soft and kindly side, was agreeing with my man, particularly when he said, "You did that splendid work." He went on for some time. Then he said, "Now, have I covered it?"

And I said, "Well, you have covered the fact that you had an account at the Riggs National Bank."

"And didn't I tell you why I put it there? Because of my confidence in Mr. Glover, because of his integrity, because of the splendid man he was and the fine bank he ran and what a fine credit it had all over the United States."

I said, "Yes, Colonel, you have told us that." Well; we were getting away with it. Now, we weren't doing anything wrong; we were simply presenting a man as nature had made him, and we could no more control him, parenthesis, if we wanted to, end parenthesis, (laughter) than could the judge or the jury, or the district attorney, had he attempted it.

Well, we went a little further—I won't go into all the details—and finally he was asked, "Do you know the reputation of Mr. Glover for honesty, probity, and integrity and veracity?" Getting them all in, you know.

He said, "Do I know it? Why, everybody in the city of Washington knows it. Of course. Nobody could live here, nobody could at any time have had any dealings that amounted to anything, and not know what his reputation is. It was"—

I said, "Just a moment, Colonel. You know that reputation, do you not? I am speaking now of his reputation in the community among people who knew him as you knew him."

"Well," he said "even everybody knew him, so everybody must have known the reputation as I knew it."

"All right. Now, Colonel, will you tell us what that reputation was?"

He pulled his chair forward almost to the edge of the jury platform, leaned over to the jury—he had very heavy hands, put them down on his knees, and he said "I knew Mr. Glover as a civic minded citizen who did more to make the national capital the perfectly beautiful, outstanding capital of the world that it is today than any other man that ever lived in America. I knew Mr. Glover as one who in all philanthropic and charitable enterprises—like the Judge; like you, Judge—would always come forward and respond, whether a neighbor or the President of the United States called him.

"I knew Mr. Glover in his home. We visited. My daughter was out there staying with his daughter. We visited out there. We visited as good old chums, because we have been very friendly, and I knew him as a family man loved by all of his own relatives and reverenced by all of his neighbors, and I knew Mr. Glover as a banker whose credit was so high, whose reputation was so fine, whose word was so good, that nobody ever questioned for a moment the safety of his deposit, whether it be large or small. That is the way I knew Mr. Glover."

And then the district attorney couldn't stand it any longer. He arose with a solemnity that I recall vividly to this day. He said, "If your Honor please, I move to strike out the entire answer of the witness. Colonel Roosevelt has said that he knew Mr. Glover in these various capacities, these various ways. He has not said a word about what his reputation was, and I move"—

The Court said, "I am with you, Mr. District Attorney; I will grant your motion," turned apologetically to Colonel Roosevelt and said, "Colonel, you have testified to your own knowledge of Mr. Glover. The rule is that you can testify only to general reputation, general repute. That's what you can do, and nothing more. So I'll have to strike out your answer. Now, please keep that in mind."

I said, "Go ahead, Colonel. Please give us your answer again, keeping the Judge's admonition in mind."

Again he turned to the Judge, again the thick finger went out. He said, "You are right. I should have known that. Thanks ever so much.

"Gentlemen of the jury, I knew Mr. Glover by general reputation and general repute—I'm right now, Judge, am I not? I am right now." (Laughter). And he went all over the whole thing again, with elaborations.

The district attorney whispered to me, "Oh, hell."

And I said, "I should have known better."

But there was no cross-examination. And then, as though that were not enough, Colonel Roosevelt, whom we had promised to let get the 11:00 o'clock train back to New York if he got through with his testimony as we thought he would, came over, and he was wearing his great big sombrero that all of you who ever saw him or pictures of him would recognize, that he always wore in campaign years, and he grabbed it and swished it in to the ladies. One of my associates was to take him to the train, and he had to pass right in front of the jury on his way out. Getting right in the middle in front of the jury, clenching his hand, using that terrific thick finger, he squatted himself as though for a football rush, and he said, "Judge or no Judge,"—* * * "Goodbye, gentlemen of the jury. I always like to appear before a jury of my fellow citizens, for you are rendering a public service. You are rendering a really great public service, just as much as the Judge there. You are here to do justice. That's why you are here—and I know you are going to do it, I know you are going to do it." (Laughter and applause).

With that he went out leaving the courtroom in a perfect storm of disorder. * * * Of course, may I add, again in parenthesis, that justice was done. (Laughter). * * *

QUESTION

If Federal Rule of Evidence 405 had applied, would the judge's initial ruling striking Roosevelt's testimony have been correct?

On methods of proving character, see Federal Rules of Evidence 405, and Advisory Committee's Note to Rule 405.

McCormick's Handbook on the Law of Evidence[*]
752–68 (6 ed. 2006).

§ 190. Bad character as evidence of criminal conduct: other crimes

---

This broad prohibition ["against using character evidence to prove conduct on a particular occasion," as under Federal Rule of Evidence 404,] includes the specific and frequently invoked rule that the prosecution may not introduce evidence of other criminal acts of the accused unless the evidence is introduced for some purpose other than to suggest that because the defendant is a person of criminal character,[6] it is more probable that he committed the crime for which he is on trial. * * * As [Rule 404(b)] indi-

---

[*] West Publishing Co. Reprinted with permission.

[6] Evidence of other crimes brought forth as circumstantial proof of guilt for the offense charged is sometimes called "extrinsic offense evidence." * * *

cates, there are numerous uses to which evidence of criminal acts may be put, and those enumerated are neither mutually exclusive nor collectively exhaustive.[9] * * * The permissible purposes include the following:

(1) To complete the story of the crime on trial by placing it in the context of nearby and nearly contemporaneous happenings.[11] * * * The phrases "same transaction" or, less happily, "res gestae" often are used to denote such evidence. This rational should be applied only when reference to the other crimes is essential to a coherent and intelligible description of the offense at bar.

(2) To prove the existence of a larger plan,[16] scheme, or conspiracy, of which the crime on trial is a part. For example, when a criminal steals a car to use it in a robbery, the automobile theft can be proved in a prosecution for the robbery. Although some courts construe "common plan" more broadly,[20] each crime should be an integral part of an over-arching plan explicitly conceived and executed by the defendant or his confederates.[21]

---

[9] * * * United States v. Tafoya, 757 F.2d 1522, 1525–28 (5th Cir.1985) (attempted assassinations to show unreported income on theory that "[i]t is unlikely that one would attempt three killings in exchange largely for expenses or continue killings for over a year if not paid for the first one"); State v. Jeffers, 661 P.2d 1105 (Ariz.1983) (murder defendant's prior assaults on witness and accomplice to explain why defendant did not report the murder promptly and to counter defendant's insinuation that the accomplice lied to gain immunity).

[11] United States v. Masters, 622 F.2d 83 (4th Cir.1980) (upholding admission of taped conversations of the defendant with undercover agents despite reference to other sales and acts on grounds that the evidence was necessary to complete the story of the crime on trial as well as to prove that the defendant was "dealing"; on the latter point, see supra § 187); * * * State v. Villavicencio, 388 P.2d 245 (Ariz.1964) (upholding introduction of evidence of sale of narcotics to one person in prosecution for sale to another, where evidence showed that both sales took place at same time and place); State v. Brown, 505 A.2d 1225, 1229–30 (Conn.1986) (evidence that robbery defendant was living with and receiving earnings of young prostitute admissible to complete the story, where prostitute suggested that defendant rob her customer); State v. Klotter, 142 N.W.2d 568 (Minn.1966) (where guns taken in burglary of sporting goods store and burglary that same night of home of friend of defendant's family located five miles away were found in defendant's possession, the events were "connected closely enough in time, place and manner").

[16] Lewis v. United States, 771 F.2d 454, 456 (10th Cir.1985) (testimony that defendant accused of burglary of a post office, first burglarized a garage to obtain a cutting torch that he then used in the post office burglary); * * * State v. Toshishige Yoshino, 364 P.2d 638 (Hawaii 1961) (evidence of first robbery admissible in prosecution for second where defendant and others robbed first victim and obtained from him the name and address of their next victim) * * *.

[20] See People v. Catlin, 26 P.3d 357 (Cal. 2001) (evidence that defendant poisoned his elderly mother with the herbicide paraquat was admissible, as part of a common plan, in prosecution for killing his fourth wife in the same manner); People v. Ewoldt, 867 P.2d 757 (Cal.1994) (overruling People v. Tassell, 679 P.2d 1 (Cal.1984), which held that evidence of uncharged misconduct is admissible to establish a common design or plan only if such evidence demonstrates a "single, continuing conception or plot" in favor of the view that such evidence is admissible if the uncharged misconduct "shares sufficient common features with the charged offenses to support the inference that both the uncharged misconduct and the charged offenses are manifestations of a common design or plan") * * *.

[21] United States v. Varoudakis, 233 F.3d 113, 119 (1st Cir.2000) (error to admit evidence of defendant's burning his car in on the theory that it, along with defendant's hiring someone to burn his failing restaurant two years later, were part of a common plan to collect insurance proceeds); United States v. O'Connor, 580 F.2d 38 (2d Cir.1978) (bribes six months earlier "not sufficiently probative of a definite project directed toward completion of the crime in question"); United States v. Anderson, 933 F.2d 1261 (5th Cir.1991) ("it is not enough to show that each crime was planned in the same way; rather, there must be some overall scheme of which each of the crimes is but a part"); United States v. Dothard, 666 F.2d 498, 502 (11th Cir.1982)

This will be relevant as showing motive, and hence the doing of the criminal act, the identity of the actor, or his intention.

(3) To prove other crimes by the accused so nearly identical in method as to earmark them as the handiwork of the accused.[22] Much more is demanded than the mere repeated commission of crimes of the same class, such as repeated murders,[23] robberies[24] or rapes.[25] The pattern and characteristics of the crimes must be so unusual and distinctive as to be like a signature. For example, in *Rex v. Smith*,[27] the "brides of the bath" case, George Joseph Smith was accused of murdering Bessie Mundy by drowning her in the small bathtub of their quarters in a boarding house. Mundy had left all her property to Smith in a will executed after a bigamous marriage ceremony. The trial court allowed the prosecution to show that Smith "married" several other women whom he drowned in their baths after they too left him their property. In all the drownings, Smith took elaborate steps to make it appear that he was not present during the drownings. The Court of Criminal Appeal affirmed the resulting conviction on the ground that the evidence in connection with Mundy's death alone made out a prima facie case, and the other incidents were properly admitted "for the purpose of shewing the design of the appellant."

(4) To show, by similar acts or incidents, that the act in question was not performed inadvertently, accidentally,[28] involuntarily,[29] or without

---

("Courts have admitted extrinsic act evidence to show a defendant's design or plan to commit the *specific* crime charged, but never to show a design or plan to commit '*crimes of the sort* with which he is charged' ") * * *.

[22] * * * The phrase of which authors of detective fiction are fond, *modus operandi*, may be employed in this context. * * *

[23] United States v. Woods, 484 F.2d 127, 134 (4th Cir.1973) (evidence that defendant accused of suffocating her eight-month-old pre-adoptive foster son had custody of or access to nine children who suffered at least 20 cyanotic episodes resulting in the death of seven of them "admissible generally under the accident and signature exceptions") * * *.

[24] United States v. Myers, 550 F.2d 1036, 1046 (5th Cir.1977), ("An early afternoon robbery of an outlying bank situated on a highway, by revolver-armed robbers wearing gloves and stocking masks, and carrying a bag for the loot, is not such an unusual crime that it tends to prove that one of the two individuals involved must have been the single bandit in a similar prior robbery.") * * *.

[25] Compare State v. Sauter, 232 P.2d 731, 732 (Mont.1951) (in charge of forcible rape in automobile after picking up victim in barroom, other rapes following similar pickups were "too common ... to have much evidentiary value in showing a systematic scheme or plan") with McGahee v. Massey, 667 F.2d 1357, 1360 (11th Cir.1982) (where man wearing a white, see-through bikini bathing suit approached a woman sunbathing at beach and raped her, it was within trial court's discretion to permit testimony that twice during the previous month the defendant, wearing a red see-through bathing suit, had exposed himself to other women at the same beach to demonstrate "the manner of operation, identity and type of clothing worn by the defendant"); Williams v. State, 110 So.2d 654, 663 (Fla.1959) (that defendant hid in back seat of woman's car at shopping center and fled when woman screamed admissible to prove that six weeks later the defendant raped another woman outside the same shopping center after hiding in the back seat of her car) * * *.

[27] 11 Cr. App. R. 229, 84 L.J.K.B. 2153 (1915), described in Marjoribanks, For the Defence: The Life of Edward Marshall Hall 321 (1929).

[28] * * * State v. Craig, 361 N.W.2d 206, 213 (Neb.1985) (15 prior incidents of mock wrestling with adopted daughter as prelude to fondling genitalia admissible to refute accused's claim that any disrobing in the course of wrestling with daughter on specific occasion charged was accidental) * * *

guilty knowledge.[30] *Rex v. Smith* falls in this category.[31] The death of one bride in the bath might be accident, but three drownings cannot be explained so innocently. Another classic example of the "improbability" logic is the "baby farming" case of *Makin v. Attorney General of New South Wales*.[32] The remains of thirteen infants were discovered in places where the couple, John and Sarah Makin were living or had lived, and the Crown charged the Makins with the murder of two of these children. One was identified by his clothing and hair. His mother testified that the Makins had agreed to adopt her son in exchange for only three pounds. The jury convicted the Makins of murdering the boy whose remains had been identified. On appeal, the couple argued that all the evidence concerning other missing children should not have been admitted. The Privy Council rejected this argument. Although its opinion did little to explain the basis for this conclusion, counsel for the Crown had stressed that "the recurrence of the unusual phenomenon of bodies of babies having been buried in an unexplained manner in a similar part of premises previously occupied" implied that the deaths were "wilful and not accidental." In these cases, the similarities between the act charged and the extrinsic acts need not be as extensive and striking as is required under purpose (3), and the various acts need not be manifestations of an explicit, unifying plan, as required for purpose (2).

(5) To establish motive.[35] The evidence of motive may be probative of the identity of the criminal[36] or of malice or specific intent.[37] This reasoning commonly is applied in cases in which a husband charged with murdering his wife had previously assaulted or threatened her, evincing not merely a general disposition toward violence, but a virulent hostility toward a specific individual. It should not apply when the "motive" is so common that the

---

[29] * * * United States v. Holman, 680 F.2d 1340, 1349 (11th Cir.1982) (other smuggling incidents to rebut defense of coercion); * * * United States v. Hearst, 563 F.2d 1331 (9th Cir.1977) (evidence of other crimes to negate anticipated defense of duress by publisher's daughter held for ransom by terrorist group and charged in bank robbery committed by group).

[30] Huddleston v. United States, 485 U.S. 681 (1988) (defendant's other sales of stolen property obtained from same suspicious source admissible to prove his knowledge that goods in question were stolen) * * *.

[31] Later incarnations of *Smith* include People v. Lisenba, 94 P.2d 569 (Cal. 1939), aff's, 313 U.S. 537 (1941) (drowning wives to collect insurance benefits), and State v. Langley, 354 N.W.2d 389 (Minn. 1984).

[32] [1894] App. C. 57 (P.C. 1893).

[35] United States v. Haldeman, 559 F.2d 31, 88 (D.C.Cir.1976) (evidence of conspiracy of government officials to break into psychiatrist's office to obtain records of an opponent of government's war policy admissible to show motive for Watergate cover-up conspiracy); * * * State v. Long, 244 P.2d 1033 (Or.1952) (testimony that defendant accused of murder used victim's truck to commit a robbery shortly afterward admissible) * * *.

[36] State v. Green, 652 P.2d 697, 701 (Kan.1982) (where the "defendant claimed in essence that someone had broken into his wife's house to rob her and inflicted the fatal wounds prior to his arrival ... evidence of the defendant's prior assaults on his wife was of great probative value on the issue of identity") * * *.

[37] United States v. Benton, 637 F.2d 1052, 1056 (5th Cir.1981), ("While motive is not an element of any offense charged ... appellant's knowledge that Zambito might implicate him in the Florida homicides constituted a motive for appellant wanting to kill Zambito.... This evidence of motivation was relevant as tending to show the participation of appellant in the crime and to show malice or intent which are elements of the crimes charged." * * *).

reasoning that establishes relevance verges on ordinary propensity reasoning.

An application of this principle to cases in which the defendant is charged with conduct that interferes with the enforcement of the law enables the prosecution to prove that the defendant committed a crime that motivated the interference. Finally, a variation of the reasoning permits proof of a consciousness of guilt as evidenced by criminal acts of the accused that are designed to obstruct justice[41] or to avoid punishment for a crime.[42]

(6) To establish opportunity, in the sense of access to or presence at the scene of the crime[44] or in the sense of possessing distinctive or unusual skills or abilities employed in the commission of the crime charged. For example, a defendant charged with a burglary in which a sophisticated alarm system was deactivated might be shown to have neutralized similar systems in the course of other burglaries.[46]

(7) To show, without considering motive, that defendant acted with malice, deliberation, or the requisite specific intent.[47] Thus, weapons seized in an arrest have been held admissible to show an "intent to promote and protect" a conspiracy to import illicit drugs.

(8) To prove identity. Although this is indisputably one of the ultimate purposes for which evidence of other criminal conduct will be received and frequently is included in the list of permissible purposes for other-crimes evidence, it is rarely a distinct ground for admission. Almost always, identity is the inference that flows from one or more of the theories just listed. The second (larger plan), third (distinctive device), and [fifth] (motive) seem to be most often relied upon to show identity. Certainly, the need to prove identity should not be, in itself, a ticket to admission. In addition, the courts tend to apply stricter standards when the desired inference pertains to identity as opposed to state of mind.

---

[41] People v. Spaulding, 141 N.E. 196 (Ill.1923) (killing sole eyewitness to crime) * * *.

[42] People v. Gambino, 145 N.E.2d 42 (Ill.1957) (escape and attempted escape while awaiting trial); State v. Brown, 372 P.2d 779 (Or.1962) (stealing cars to escape).

[44] United States v. DeJohn, 638 F.2d 1048, 1053 (7th Cir.1981) (testimony of YMCA security guard and city police officer revealing that on other occasions defendant had obtained checks from a mailbox at YMCA was "highly probative of defendant's opportunity to gain access to the mailboxes and obtain the checks that he cashed" with forged endorsements); State v. Lemon, 497 A.2d 713 (R.I.1985) (testimony that defendant robbed a restaurant in Providence admissible to refute alibi that he was in Boston at the time).

[46] See United States v. Barrett, 539 F.2d 244 (1st Cir.1976); cf. State v. Priebe, 22 N.W.2d 1 (Minn.1946) (shoplifting skills).

[47] * * * United States v. Beechum, 582 F.2d 898 (5th Cir.1978) (en banc) (evidence that defendant had possessed two stolen credit cards for ten months admissible to prove that he intended to keep a planted silver dollar taken from the mails rather than to return it to postal authorities, as he claimed, on the theory that "because the defendant had unlawful intent in the extrinsic offense, it is less likely that he had lawful intent in the present offense"); * * * But see * * * Ordover, Balancing the Presumptions of Guilt and Innocence, 38 Emory L.Rev. 135, 157 (1989) ("evidence of an unconnected prior crime is always evidence of propensity and never evidence of a specific intent to commit the crime charged").

(9) **To show a passion or propensity for unusual and abnormal sexual relations.** Initially, proof of other sex crimes was confined to offenses involving the same parties, but many jurisdictions now admit proof of other sex offenses with other persons, at least as to offenses involving sexual aberrations. Federal Rules of Evidence 413 and 414, added by Congress in 1994, allow the broadest conceivable use of "similar crimes" in sexual assault and child molestation cases, making "evidence of defendant's commission" of other such offenses "admissible . . . for its bearing on any matter to which it is relevant."

Unlike the other purposes for other-crimes evidence, the sex-crime exception [flouts] the general prohibition of evidence whose only purpose is to invite the inference that a defendant who committed a previous crime is disposed toward committing crimes, and therefore is more likely to have committed the one at bar. Although one can argue for such an exception in sex offense cases in which there is some question as to whether the alleged victim consented (or whether the accused might have thought there was consent),[57] a more sweeping exception is particularly difficult to justify. It rests either on an unsubstantiated empirical claim that one rather broad category of criminals are more likely to be repeat offenders than all others or on a policy of giving the prosecution some extra ammunition in its battle against alleged sex criminals.

(10) **To impeach an accused who takes the witness stand by introducing past convictions.**

A number of procedural and other substantive considerations also affect the admissibility of other crimes evidence pursuant to these ten exceptions. To begin with, the fact that the defendant is guilty of another relevant crime need not be proved beyond a reasonable doubt.* * * If the applicable standard is satisfied, then the other crimes evidence should be potentially admissible even if the defendant was acquitted of the other charge.

Second, the connection between the evidence and the permissible purpose should be clear, and the issue on which the other crimes evidence is said to bear should be the subject of a genuine controversy. For example, if the prosecution maintains that the other crime reveals defendant's guilty state of mind, then his intent should be disputed. Thus, if the defendant does not deny that the acts were deliberate, the prosecution may not introduce the evidence merely to show that the acts were not accidental. Likewise, if the accused does not deny performing the acts charged, the exceptions pertaining to identification are unavailing.

---

[57] See Bryden & Park, "Other Crimes" Evidence in Sex Offense Cases, 78 Minn. L. Rev. 529 (1994) (arguing that other-rape evidence should be admissible in acquaintance rape cases and child sexual abuse cases); Park, The Crime Bill of 1994 and the Law of Character Evidence: Congress Was Right About Consent Defense Cases, 22 Fordham Urb. L.J. 271 (1995); cf. Colb, "Whodunit" Versus "What Was Done": When to Admit Character Evidence in Criminal Cases, 79 N.C. L. Rev. 939 (2001) (advocating abolition of the ban against character evidence in cases in which "there is no dispute about identity").

Finally, even if one or more of the valid purposes for admitting other-crimes evidence is appropriately invoked, there is still the need to balance its probative value against the usual counterweights * * * When the sole purpose of the other-crimes evidence is to show some propensity to commit the crime at trial, there is no room for ad hoc balancing. The evidence is then unequivocally inadmissible—this is the meaning of the rule against other crimes evidence. But the fact that there is an accepted logical basis for the evidence other than the forbidden one of showing a proclivity for criminality does not ensure that the jury will not also rely on a defendant's apparent propensity toward criminal behavior. Accordingly, most authority recognizes that the problem is not merely one of pigeonholing, but of classifying and then balancing. In deciding whether the danger of unfair prejudice and the like substantially outweighs the incremental probative value, a variety of matters must be considered, including the strength of the evidence as to the commission of the other crime, the similarities between the crimes, the interval of time that has elapsed between the crimes, the need for the evidence, the efficacy of alternative proof, and the degree to which the evidence probably will rouse the jury to overmastering hostility.

HYPOTHETICALS

1. Defendant is charged with possession of marijuana with intent to sell. The prosecution produces evidence that 35 marijuana plants were found in defendant's back yard. The defendant testifies that he thought they were weeds. The prosecution offers evidence that fifteen years before the charged crime, defendant sold marijuana to an agent. Is it admissible?

2. Defendant is accused of bank robbery. The prosecution wishes to put in evidence that defendant is a drug addict. Could it be admissible?

3. Defendant is accused of murdering V. The prosecution offers evidence that a week before the alleged murder, defendant killed V's cat. Is it admissible?

4. Defendant is charged with assassinating the President. The prosecution offers evidence that not long after the assassination, the defendant shot a police officer when the officer stopped the defendant for a traffic violation. Could the evidence be admissible?

5. As a condition of parole, defendant was required to reside in the Eddy Corner Halfway House. The residents of Eddy Corner are allowed to go to work during the day, but in the evening they must return, sign in and stay overnight. On October 10, during the daytime, an armored truck was robbed in a location several miles from Eddy Corner. Defendant is charged with that crime. The prosecution wishes to offer evidence that defendant, because he was a convicted sex offender, was required to return to the Eddy Corner Halfway House every evening and that he did not return on October 10. Is the evidence admissible?

6. The defendant is accused of armed robbery. The victim picked defendant out of a line-up, but at trial she concedes she's not sure he's the robber. To show identity, the prosecution offers evidence that the defendant committed three

previous armed robberies in the past six months. It points to the word "identity" in Rule 404(b) and argues that it is not required to show any special similarity in the robberies. Defendant objects. What ruling?

United States v. Carrillo

United States Court of Appeals, Fifth Circuit, 1993.
981 F.2d 772.

■ DeMoss, Circuit Judge:

A jury found the defendant guilty of distribution of heroin and cocaine based on an undercover officer's testimony that he purchased a narcotics-filled balloon from the defendant. At trial, the defendant's alibi was mistaken identity: he claimed that the police officer misidentified him as the seller. The district court allowed the government to present evidence of two other sales of controlled substances by the defendant as modus operandi to help establish his identity as the drug seller in the present case. Carrillo challenges the admission of those extrinsic acts under the identity exception* of Federal Rule of Evidence 404(b). Because we hold that those acts do not bear a sufficient degree of similarity to the charged offense to mark it as the handiwork of the defendant, we vacate the conviction and remand for a new trial.

I. FACTS AND PROCEDURAL HISTORY

[The charged crime allegedly occurred on January 9, 1991. Alonzo, a San Antonio undercover officer, testified that on that date he made a narcotics purchase from Carrillo on a street near the Three Kings Lounge. According to Alonzo, he paid $20, and Carrillo took from his mouth and handed to Alonzo a balloon containing heroin and cocaine. Carrillo claimed alibi and mistaken identity, contending that he was several blocks away from the scene at the time of the transaction. The prosecution introduced, over Carrillo's objection, the testimony of two other officers as to other drug sales by Carrillo. One, Garcia, testified to making an undercover purchase of two bags of heroin on April 9, 1990, from a house about four blocks from the Three Kings Lounge. Garcia testified that he was third or fourth in line, and that Carrillo sold drugs to everybody present. The other officer, Peters, testified to arresting Carrillo after observing him conduct a drug transaction with a pregnant woman near the Three Kings Lounge on March 28, 1991; according to Peters, Carrillo possessed several balloons filled with heroin when arrested. Carrillo was convicted and appealed.]

---

* [The Court persists, as many do, in speaking of an identity "exception" to Fed. R. Evid. 404(b). But notice the actual structure of the Rule: It prescribes only a limited rule of exclusion—evidence of other crimes and bad acts "is not admissible to prove the character of a person in order to show action in conformity therewith." But such evidence may be admissible for other purposes—and identity is one of a non-exhaustive list of such other purposes. This, then, is not a broad rule of exclusion with multiple exceptions. Rather, it is a confined rule of exclusion, and there are many ways around it; Rule 404(b) does not purport to catalog all those ways. Eds.]

II. DISCUSSION

A. "The Test"

A district court's decision to admit evidence under Rule 404(b) is reviewed under an abuse of discretion standard. United States v. Anderson, 933 F.2d 1261, 1268 (5th Cir.1991). "Nevertheless, * * * [this court's] review of evidentiary rulings in criminal trials is necessarily heightened." Id. Federal Rule of Evidence 404(b), in issue here, states:

> [e]vidence of other crimes, wrongs, or acts is not admissible to prove the character of a person in order to show action in conformity therewith. It may, however, be admissible for other purposes, such as proof of motive, opportunity, intent, preparation, plan, knowledge, identity, or absence of mistake or accident * * *.*

The admissibility of extrinsic act evidence under Rule 404(b) is determined by application of the two-part test enunciated by this court in United States v. Beechum, 582 F.2d 898 (5th Cir.1978), cert. denied, 440 U.S. 920 (1979). "First, it must be determined that the extrinsic offense evidence is relevant to an issue other than the defendant's character." "Second, the evidence must possess probative value that is not substantially outweighed by its undue prejudice and must meet the other requirements of [Fed.R.Evid.] 403." Character evidence is not excluded because it has no probative value, but because it sometimes may lead a jury to convict the accused on the ground of bad character deserving punishment regardless of guilt.

B. "Application of the Test"

To support his contention that the district court erred in admitting evidence of the extrinsic acts, Carrillo relies on the case of United States v. Silva, 580 F.2d 144 (5th Cir.1978). In *Silva*, the defendant was convicted for distributing heroin and cocaine; he argued that testimony admitted by the trial court concerning a subsequent negotiation for the sale of heroin was inadmissible under the identity exception without a showing that it bore such a high degree of similarity as to mark it as the defendant's handiwork. The court agreed with the defendant: "[t]he identity exception has a much more limited scope; it is used either in conjunction with some other basis for admissibility or synonymously with modus operandi." The court stated an extrinsic offense is not admissible under 404(b) to show identity "merely because it is similar, but only if it bears such a high degree of similarity as to mark it as the handiwork of the accused." In the *Silva* case, the court held that "no such handiwork was * * * shown." Carrillo contends in the present case that the district court erred in admitting evidence of the extrinsic offenses because they were not so similar to the charged offense as to mark it as his handiwork.

---

* [Here, and throughout the book, quotations from Federal Rules in opinions are presented as they are in the opinions, and so do not reflect subsequent amendments.]

To refute Carrillo's contention, the government relies on the case of United States v. Torres–Flores, 827 F.2d 1031 (5th Cir.1987), where the court allowed evidence to be admitted showing that the defendant, accused of assaulting a border patrol officer, had previously been arrested at the same river checkpoint so as to place the defendant at the scene of the crime. We believe that the government's reliance on *Torres–Flores,* however, is misplaced because that case did not involve the modus operandi method of proving identity. In *Torres–Flores,* the defendant did not testify and thus the only evidence to corroborate the border patrol officer's testimony and place the defendant at the checkpoint during the commission of the offense was the testimony that he had been apprehended there twice before. The court did not hold that the evidence was admissible based on the uniqueness or similarity between the prior border crossings and the charged offense, but on the fact that the defendant had crossed there before and therefore was more likely to have been there on the day the charged offense occurred. Conversely, in the present case showing that Carrillo was in the area where the charged offense occurred adds little weight to the evidence against him since he doesn't deny being in the area—he claims that he was a few blocks away at the intersection of San Marcos and Buena Vista.

In that regard, the Fifth Circuit has recognized that evidence not constituting a signature or otherwise demonstrating a particular, identical modus operandi may nonetheless be admissible under the identity exception. In United States v. Evans, 848 F.2d 1352, 1360 (5th Cir.1988) (quoting 22 C. Wright & K. Graham, Federal Practice and Procedure § 5246, at 512 (1978)), modified on rehearing, 854 F.2d 56 (5th Cir.1988), this court stated:

> [t]he exception in Rule 404(b) for use of other crimes evidence will probably be used most often * * * '[t]o prove other like crimes by the accused so nearly identical in method as to earmark them as the handiwork of the accused.' This exception, often referred to as the 'handiwork or signature exception' or the exception for 'modus operandi' is, however, only one method by which other crimes can prove identity. It is important that courts recognize these different modes so as not to impose requirements, such as distinctive similarity, that apply only to the modus operandi method of identification, on different methods of using other crimes evidence to show identity.

While recognizing the different methods by which other crimes can prove identity and that only the modus operandi method needs to meet the handiwork or signature exception, here, it is abundantly clear that the government sought to introduce the extrinsic acts to prove identity by showing Carrillo's methods of selling heroin were so similar to the method used in the charged offense and so distinctive from the normal method as to mark it as his handiwork. The government sought to avail itself of the modus operandi method; and, as such, the government was required to show that evidence of the extrinsic acts was sufficiently similar to the charged offense and sufficiently unique from the common practice for it to do so. Carrillo's extrinsic offenses of selling heroin fail to satisfy those requirements.

Detective Alonzo himself testified that drug dealers and users frequent the area in which he made the drug purchase. He further stated that it is "very common" for a street dealer to distribute narcotics in a balloon; he explained that packaging the drug in this way allows the dealer to swallow it if a police officer approaches. Alonzo also testified that he had previously purchased narcotics in undercover operations when a dealer distributed the narcotics in a balloon. Alonzo did not testify to any characteristics of the purchase that was unique or would tend to mark the drug sale as the handiwork of the accused. In sum, the January 8 sale was a typical drug sale in a drug-ridden urban neighborhood where such transactions are commonplace. Thus, the testimony of Garcia and Peters did not corroborate the identity of the seller through unique or uncommon elements of the transaction. The evidence, in our opinion, did no more than to illustrate Carrillo's bad character and to show that he acted in conformity with that character on January 8. Such is not permissible; and, indeed, is the purpose behind the prohibition of propensity evidence in Rule 404(b). Therefore we hold that the trial court erred in admitting evidence of Carrillo's extrinsic offenses of selling heroin. * * *

California Constitution Art. 1, § 28 (Proposition 8)

(d) **Right to Truth-in-Evidence.** Except as provided by statute hereafter enacted by a two-thirds vote of the membership in each house of the Legislature, relevant evidence shall not be excluded in any criminal proceeding, including pretrial and post conviction motions and hearings, or in any trial or hearing of a juvenile for a criminal offense, whether heard in juvenile or adult court. Nothing in this section shall affect any existing statutory rule of evidence relating to privilege or hearsay, or Evidence Code, Sections 352, 782 or 1103. Nothing in this section shall affect any existing statutory or constitutional right of the press.

(Added by Initiative Measure, approved by the people, June 8, 1982, known as "The Victims' Bill of Rights").

NOTE

Proposition 8's statement that "relevant evidence shall not be excluded in any criminal proceeding" had potentially broad-ranging consequences. For example, it appeared to vitiate the rule against character evidence. Eventually, the California Supreme Court held that the ban on character evidence in CEC § 1101 survived Proposition 8, noting that the Legislature reenacted Section 1101 by more than a two-thirds vote when it amended the statute in 1986. See People v. Ewoldt, 867 P.2d 757 (1994).

United States v. Beasley

United States Court of Appeals, Seventh Circuit, 1987.
809 F.2d 1273.

■ EASTERBROOK, CIRCUIT JUDGE. [Beasley, an accomplished and respected chemist, was charged with seven counts of obtaining Dilaudid, a controlled substance, with intent to distribute, and two counts of attempting to obtain Dilaudid by misrepresenting the name of the person to appear on the prescription. Beasley allegedly obtained the prescriptions for large amounts of Dilaudid by telling an Indiana physician, Rucker, that he needed the drug to test his theory that large doses of tranquilizers and analgesics would help vegetables deal with stress better and therefore speed their absorption of nutrients and increase their rate of growth. Through several alleged confederates of Beasley, the prosecution offered evidence that Beasley continued to deal in drugs, not limited to Dilaudid, after the period covered by the indictment, which ended in March 1981. Beasley and some of the confederates allegedly went to several states "shopping for doctors" who would supply prescriptions. Margaret Walraven, a Dilaudid addict, testified that Marilyn Pierce, the daughter of one of Beasley's confederates, had also become addicted to Dilaudid and was committed to a mental hospital.]

The decision to admit the evidence [of other drug dealing by Beasley and his confederates] rested on a belief that the bad acts showed a "pattern" of crimes "especially close in time". Come the trial, however, the judge repeatedly told the jury that the sole purpose of admitting the evidence was to show Beasley's "intent". The judge tried to limit the jury's consideration in cautionary instructions as the evidence was admitted, and one of the instructions in the charge repeated this limitation.

The prosecutor tries to defend the decision on appeal by resurrecting the argument about "pattern". "Pattern" is missing not only in the instructions to the jury but also in Rule 404(b)'s list of permissible uses of bad act evidence. "Pattern" usually is a shorthand for a series of acts that collectively identify the offender—the ten bank robberies by a gang disguised by red polka dot bandannas, the series of counterfeit bills made by an engraver who never gets the Great Seal quite right, and so on. The pattern serves as the signature that enables the jury to determine that this offense, too, was committed by the defendant. This use of pattern to show identity, or sometimes the extent and membership of a conspiracy, is the usual one in this circuit, as in others.

When the similarity of the acts is used to identify the culprit, the proximity of the acts in time is important. Given enough time, similar crimes will be committed by other people, and the value of the other acts as an earmark is diminished. Thus many cases use language emphasizing proximity. But the many bad acts of which Beasley was accused during trial were not similar in the sense of demonstrating a modus operandi. None of the other bad acts involved duping a physician into making drugs available for "experiments." The episodes of "shopping for doctors" were similar to each other, but not to the crimes of which Beasley stood accused; Beasley's provision of Valium and codeine to his associates is not like the fraudulent acquisition of Dilaudid. * * * We therefore bypass the dispute that has occupied the parties about whether two or three years is "too remote" for the latter acts to be proximate in time. Questions about "how long is too long" do not have uniform answers; the answers depend on the theory that makes the evidence admissible. Here the acts are so dissimilar that their timing becomes unimportant.

Some language in the government's brief suggests that any commission of similar crimes is the sort of "pattern" that permits the evidence to come in. On this reasoning, one drug offense may be used to prove another, although a bank robbery could not be admitted in a drug prosecution. The prosecutor admits as limits the factors enumerated in cases such as United States v. Draiman, 784 F.2d 248, 254 (7th Cir.1986): the bad act evidence must be clear and convincing, must show a similar act close enough in time, must have value that outweighs the risk of unfair prejudice (the Rule 403 standard), and must be used to show something other than the defendant's propensity to commit similar crimes (the Rule 404(b) requirement). Yet in the prosecutor's view, to show similarity is to negate prejudice and the tendency of the evidence to condemn by besmirching character. Not so. The requirements are distinct. A rule that a judge may admit all evidence that the defendant committed crimes of similar varieties produces the gravest risk of offending the central prohibition of Rule 404(b): "Evidence of other crimes, wrongs, or acts is not admissible to prove the character of a person in order to show that he acted in conformity therewith." The inference from "pattern" by itself is *exactly* the forbidden inference that one who violated the drug laws on one occasion must have violated them on the occasion charged in the indictment. Unless something more than a pattern and temporal proximity is required, the fundamental rule is gone. This is why "pattern" is not listed in Rule 404(b) as an exception. Patterns of acts may *show* identity, intent, plan, absence of mistake, or one of the other listed grounds, but a pattern is not itself a reason to admit the evidence.

This brings into focus the instructions limiting the use of the evidence to proof of "intent". Patterns of similar acts may show intent, just as they may show identity. That the other bad acts came after the crimes charged in the indictment does not preclude their use to show intent.

Intent was an issue here. Beasley testified that he bought the drugs to conduct experiments, fed the drugs to his plants, and never distributed drugs to anyone. If this is true, he did not purchase with intent to distribute. The prosecutor claims that Beasley sold the Dilaudid to Brooks and perhaps others and did not conduct or intend to conduct experiments on the effects of narcotics on rutabagas or cauliflowers. A demonstration that in 1982 and 1983 Beasley, Rocky Terrell, and Carol Parks bilked other physicians into prescribing Dilaudid, which they resold, tends to show that Beasley acquired the Dilaudid in Indiana with the same intent. At the same time, the evidence inescapably creates a risk of the forbidden inference, that a person who violates the law at one time has a bad character and therefore violated the law at a different time. So although the episodes of "shopping for doctors" were relevant to show intent, they also had a potential for "unfair prejudice"—which the advisory committee's note to Rule 403 describes as "an undue tendency to suggest decision on an improper basis, commonly, though not necessarily, an emotional one." The sale of drugs brings emotions into play, especially when the evidence reveals that the drugs may have ruined Marilyn Pierce's life.

When the same evidence has legitimate and forbidden uses, when the introduction is valuable yet dangerous, the district judge has great discretion. There are no bright line rules; it is easy to identify polar cases but impossible to draw a line of demarcation. Appellate courts can contribute only modestly to the making of the best decision case by case. The decision must be made on the scene, and once the imponderables have been weighed there is little to be gained from weighing them again on appellate scales. The balance would not be systematically better the second time around, and the costs of second-guessing include new trials that may be less accurate as events become more remote. Trial judges have a comparative advantage because they alone see all the evidence in context, and the judicial system as a whole takes advantage of the division of labor.

Yet although appellate courts cannot often tell whether it was best, all things considered, to let in a given piece of evidence, it may be possible to tell whether the district court and the parties took the right things into account. A flaw in the process is easier to detect than is a flaw in the result—and over the run of cases the consistent operation of process is more important, too. The principled and just functioning of the judicial system depends on careful observation of the rules that focus attention on the proper grounds of decision. The rules deal in probabilities. We cannot know whether admission of the bad act evidence against Beasley changed the outcome or produced an improper conviction; we can be confident that repeated, careless use of bad act evidence will increase the probability of such unhappy outcomes.

The objective is not to enforce "rules"; Rules 403 and 404(b) establish standards rather than rules. It is to ensure that standards not be applied as if they were rules, as if they established mechanical indicia (such as "One drug offense may be used as evidence to prove any other"). The list of exceptions in Rule 404(b), if mechanically applied, would overwhelm the central principle. Almost *any* bad act evidence simultaneously condemns by besmirching character and by showing one or more of "motive, opportunity, intent, preparation, plan, knowledge, identity, or absence of mistake or accident", not to mention the "other purposes" of which this list is meant to be illustrative. We therefore repeat the theme that there must be a principled exercise of discretion. The district judge must both identify the exception that applies to the evidence in question and evaluate whether the evidence, although relevant and within the exception, is sufficiently probative to make tolerable the risk that jurors will act on the basis of emotion or an inference via the blackening of the defendant's character. Discretion, when exercised, will rarely be disturbed.

The record in this case does not show that the district judge took into account the power of this bad act evidence to impugn Beasley's character. The pretrial hearing was perfunctory. The district judge did not ask the prosecutor to explain what she expected to show. The only two comments by the court are "that seems to be admissible pattern evidence" and "[the acts] are especially close in time to be admissible". We have already explained why "pattern" evidence as such is excludable unless it shows one of the listed exceptions; the district court appeared to act on the opposite view. We have also explained why temporal proximity—if two or three years could be called "especially close in time"—does not support use of the evidence. And the court did not demonstrate an effort to determine the likely effect of the evidence in poisoning Beasley's character. The effect on Beasley's character may well have been the dominant one, indeed the principal reason why the prosecutor wanted to use the evidence. If Beasley's Ph.D. and scientific achievements might suggest to the jury that Beasley had a good character, the prosecutor wanted something that cut the other way.

If the power of the bad act evidence to show intent were obvious, and the danger of improper inferences low, we would not be concerned by the lack of balancing on the record. Judges need not explain the obvious, even briefly. We are not dealing, however, with transparently admissible evidence. Some seems almost transparently inadmissible. Evidence that Beasley gave Valium and codeine to two people in 1981 is not proof of the intent with which Beasley acquired Dilaudid—not unless any drug offense proves any other. Proof that Marilyn Pierce was addicted to Dilaudid and had to be committed to a mental hospital was gratuitous, much more likely to provoke an emotional reaction from the jurors than to help them understand Beasley's intent. Doubtless it was important to tell the jurors that Pierce, named on one prescription and whose apartment was a locus of sales, could not be present. It would have sufficed, however, for the judge to tell the jury that "for reasons beyond the prosecutor's control Marilyn Pierce cannot attend the trial" and to warn the jurors not to draw inferences for or against either party because of her absence. Or the court might have told the jury that Pierce was in a hospital and for medical reasons could not attend. The full reason for her absence—and the proof of the reason through Margaret Walraven, another Dilaudid addict—invited all the wrong kinds of inferences. Only the evidence that Beasley, Parks, and Rocky Terrell went "shopping for doctors" to acquire Dilaudid between 1982 and 1983 (or 1984) substantially implies intent to distribute in 1980, and even here the potential for an improper inference is strong enough to make its admission as part of the prosecutor's affirmative case not a foregone conclusion. The thoughtful exercise of discretion would have mattered. (Beasley took the stand and denied selling drugs to anyone * * *.)

It was certainly a mistake to admit the evidence about Pierce's mental condition; it was probably a mistake to admit the evidence about Valium and codeine; the use of the "shopping for doctors" incidents was sufficiently problematic that a more discriminating treatment by the district court was called for. * * *

Reversed in part and remanded.

United States v. Cunningham

United States Court of Appeals, Seventh Circuit, 1996.
103 F.3d 553.

■ POSNER, CHIEF JUDGE.

Constance Cunningham was sentenced to 84 months in prison after being convicted by a jury of tampering with a consumer product "with reckless disregard for the risk that another person will be placed in danger of death or bodily injury and under circumstances manifesting extreme indifference to such risk." 18 U.S.C. § 1365(a). Cunningham was a registered nurse at an Indiana hospital. The hospital staff discovered that syringes containing the powerful painkiller Demerol had been tampered with; in some instances the Demerol had been replaced with a saline solution. Cunningham was one of five nurses who, during a period when some of the syringes were known to have been tampered with, had access to the locked cabinet in which they were kept. All five nurses were interviewed by the police and denied having tampered with the syringes. But Cunningham acknowledged having once been a Demerol addict. She said the problem was in the past and to prove this she offered to have her blood and urine tested for Demerol. The blood test was negative but the urine test positive, which was consistent with recent use, since Demerol remains in the urinary tract longer than in the bloodstream. The government believes that Cunningham was stealing Demerol from the syringes in order to feed a Demerol addiction.

Cunningham argues that merely withholding pain medication does not "place" anyone "in danger of . . . bodily injury." The statute defines "bodily injury" to include "physical pain," but she argues that failing to relieve pain is not the same as causing pain. * * * [The Court rejected this argument in a paragraph—Eds.]

We must next consider whether the district judge abused his discretion in admitting evidence of prior "bad acts" of the defendant. Fed.R.Evid. 404(b). Four years before the tampering, Cunningham had pleaded guilty to stealing Demerol from the hospital at which she was then employed as a nurse under another name. Her nurse's license had been suspended, but it had later been reinstated subject to several conditions including that she submit to periodic drug testing. She falsified the results of some of these tests. The judge sustained an objection to placing the conviction in evidence but allowed in the suspension of her license because of her earlier theft of Demerol, the falsification of the test results, and the addiction that had led to the earlier theft and resulting suspension.

Rule 404(b) forbids the introduction of evidence of a person's prior conduct (wrongful or otherwise, but normally wrongful) for the purpose of showing a propensity to act in accordance with the character indicated by that conduct. So the fact that Cunningham had stolen Demerol in the past could not be introduced to show that she is likely to have stolen Demerol in the present. But evidence of prior conduct may be introduced (subject to the judge's power to exclude it under Rule 403 as unduly prejudicial, confusing, or merely cumulative) for other purposes, for example to show the defendant's motive for committing the crime with which he is charged.

motive

"Propensity" evidence and "motive" evidence need not overlap. They do not, for example, when past drug convictions are used to show that the defendant in a robbery case is an addict and his addiction is offered as the motive for the robbery. They do overlap when the crime is motivated by a taste for engaging in that crime or a compulsion to engage in it (an "addiction"), rather than by a desire for pecuniary gain or for some other advantage to which the crime is instrumental in the sense that it would not be committed if the advantage could be obtained as easily by a lawful route. Sex crimes provide a particularly clear example. Most people do not have a taste for sexually molesting children. As between two suspected molesters, then, only one of whom has a history of such molestation, the history establishes a motive that enables the two suspects to be distinguished. In 1994, Rule 414 was added to the Federal Rules of Evidence to make evidence of prior acts of child molestation expressly admissible, without regard to Rule 404(b). See also Rules 413 and 415. But the principle that we are discussing is not limited to sex crimes. A "firebug"—one who commits arson not for insurance proceeds or revenge or to eliminate a competitor, but for the sheer joy of watching a fire—is, like the sex criminal, a person whose motive to commit the crime with which he is charged is revealed by his past commission of the same crime. No special rule analogous to Rules 413 through 415 is necessary to make the evidence of the earlier crime admissible, because 404(b) expressly allows evidence of prior wrongful acts to establish motive. The greater the overlap between propensity and motive, the more careful the district judge must be about admitting under the rubric of motive evidence that the jury is likely to use instead as a basis for inferring the defendant's propensity, his habitual criminality, even if instructed not to. But the tool for preventing this abuse is Rule 403, not Rule 404(b).

We do not have a complete overlap between evidence of propensity and evidence of motive in this case. Most people don't *want* Demerol; being a Demerol addict gave Cunningham a motive to tamper with the Demerol-filled syringes that, so far as appears, none of the other nurses who had access to the cabinet in which the syringes were locked had. No one suggests that any of the five nurses might have wanted to steal Demerol in order to resell it rather than to consume it personally. Because Cunningham's addiction was not to *stealing* Demerol but to consuming it, this case is like *Moreno*, [People v. Moreno, 61 Cal.App.3d 688, 693–94 (1976)] where the defendant's sexual fetish supplied the motive for his stealing women's underwear, and *McConnell* [People v. McConnell, 335 N.W.2d 226, 230 (Mich.App.1983)], where the defendant's drug addiction supplied the motive to rob—he needed money to buy drugs. Cunningham was in a position to steal her drug directly.

The evidence of her addiction was thus admissible, unless the judge decided that its prejudicial effect—the effect that is inherent in any evidence that a jury, however instructed, might use to draw the forbidden inference that once a thief always a thief—clearly outweighed its probative value. He thought not, and we cannot say that this was an abuse of discretion. Remember that the judge excluded the evidence of Cunningham's conviction. That evidence would have been *de trop*, given the evidence of her addiction, which supplied the motive. What is more, the evidence of the conviction would not have distinguished between the addiction that furnished a motive to steal, and a propensity to steal—a nonaddict might steal drugs to resell them.

The evidence of Cunningham's suspension might seem to have been similarly superfluous and equivocal, as being merely the civil equivalent of the criminal conviction that the judge properly excluded. But the suspension, unlike the conviction, did not merely duplicate the evidence of Cunningham's addiction or insinuate a propensity to steal; it also provided essential background to the evidence of her having falsified the results of tests required as a condition of regaining her *license.* That evidence furnished the basis for an inference that she had falsified the test results in order to enable her to continue to feed her addiction without detection and without losing access to a "free" supply of the addictive substance, and so, like the addiction itself, established motive to tamper with the Demerol syringes. Granted, an alternative inference was that she had falsified the test results in order to be able to work as a nurse. But the jury was entitled to choose between these inferences, rather than having the evidence from which the inference was to be drawn withheld from them. Without knowing that she had been suspended, the jury would have wondered why she had been tested and had falsified the test results. The admission of bad-acts evidence to contextualize, and by contextualizing enable the jury to understand, other evidence is a recognized exception to the prohibition of bad-acts evidence.

With the challenged evidence in, Cunningham's last argument—that the evidence of her guilt was insufficient to convict her of product tampering beyond a reasonable doubt—collapses. One of the nurses was the thief, and only one—Cunningham—was shown to have a motive. Her lawyer could have tried to show that another one had a motive too (not necessarily the same motive), but he did not. As a consequence, there was little doubt of her guilt. And she did flunk the urine test.

Affirmed.

Tucker v. State

Supreme Court of Nevada, 1966.
82 Nev. 127, 412 P.2d 970.

■ THOMPSON, JUSTICE.

On May 7, 1957, Horace Tucker telephoned the police station and asked a detective to come to the Tucker home in North Las Vegas. Upon arrival the detective observed that Tucker had been drinking, was unshaven, and looked tired. Tucker led the detective to the dining room where one, Earl Kaylor, was dead on the floor. Kaylor had been shot several times. When asked what had happened, Tucker said that he (Tucker) had been sleeping in the bedroom, awakened, and walked to the dining room where he noticed Kaylor lying on the floor. Upon ascertaining that Kaylor was dead, Tucker telephoned the police station. He denied having killed Kaylor. A grand jury conducted an extensive investigation. However, an indictment was not returned as the grand jury deemed the evidence inconclusive. No one, including Tucker, has ever been charged with that killing.

On October 8, 1963, Horace Tucker telephoned the police and asked a sergeant to come to the Tucker home in North Las Vegas; that there was an old man dead there. Upon arrival the sergeant noticed that Tucker had been drinking. The body of Omar Evans was dead on the couch in the living room. Evans had been shot. Tucker stated that he (Tucker) had been asleep, awakened, and found Evans dead on the couch. Subsequently Tucker was charged with the murder of Evans. A jury convicted him of second degree murder.

At trial, over vehement objection, the court allowed the state to intro- duce evidence of the Kaylor homicide. The court reasoned that the circumstances of the deaths of Kaylor and Evans were sufficiently parallel to render admissible evidence of the Kaylor homicide to prove that Tucker intended to kill Evans, that the killing of Evans was part of a common scheme or plan in Tucker's mind, and also to negate any defense of accidental death. These limited purposes, for which the evidence was received and could be considered by the jury, were specified by court instruction as required by case law. We rule that evidence of the Kaylor homicide was not admissible for any purpose and that prejudicial error occurred when the court permitted the jury to hear and consider it.

Nevada exclude[s] any evidence which shows that the defendant committed other offenses unless relevant to prove the commission of the crime charged. The "unless" portion of the rule is stated in the form of exceptions. Thus we have held that evidence of an offense, other than that for which the accused is on trial, may be allowed as an exception if relevant to prove motive, identity, the absence of mistake or accident, or a common scheme or plan.

Whenever the problem of evidence of other offenses confronts a trial court, grave considerations attend. The danger of prejudice to the defendant is ever present, for the jury may convict now because he has escaped punishment in the past. Nor has the defendant been advised that he must be prepared to meet extraneous charges. Indeed, as our system of justice is accusatorial rather than inquisitorial, there is much to be said for the notion that the prosecution must prove the defendant guilty of the specific crime charged without resort to past conduct. Thus when the other offense sought to be introduced falls within an exception to the rule of exclusion, the trial court should be convinced that the probative value of such evidence outweighs its prejudicial effect. The reception of such evidence is justified by necessity and, if other evidence has substantially established the element of the crime involved (motive, intent, identity, absence of mistake, etc.), the probative value of showing another offense is diminished, and the trial court should rule it inadmissible even though relevant and within an exception to the rule of exclusion.

In the case at hand we need not consider whether evidence of the Kaylor homicide comes within one of the exceptions to the rule of exclusion, because the first requisite for admissibility is wholly absent—namely, that the defendant on trial committed the independent offense sought to be introduced. There is nothing in this record to establish that Tucker killed Kaylor. Anonymous crimes can have no relevance in deciding whether the defendant committed the crime with which he is charged. Kaylor's assailant remains unknown. A fortiori, evidence of that crime cannot be received in the trial for the murder of Evans.

We have not before had occasion to discuss the quantum of proof needed to establish that the defendant on trial committed the separate offense sought to be introduced. Here there was only conjecture and suspicion, aroused by the fact that Kaylor was found dead in Tucker's home. We now adopt the rule that, before evidence of a collateral offense is admissible for any purpose, the prosecution must first establish by plain, clear and convincing evidence, that the defendant committed that offense. Fundamental fairness demands this standard in order to preclude verdicts which might otherwise rest on false assumptions.

Reversed and remanded for new trial.

Huddleston v. United States

Supreme Court of the United States, 1988.
485 U.S. 681, 108 S.Ct. 1496, 99 L.Ed.2d 771.

■ [REHNQUIST, C.J., delivered the opinion for a unanimous Court.]

Federal Rule of Evidence 404(b) provides:

> "Other crimes, wrongs, or acts.—Evidence of other crimes, wrongs, or acts is not admissible to prove the character of a person in order to show that he acted in conformity therewith. It may, however, be admissible for other purposes, such as proof of motive, opportunity, intent, preparation, plan, knowledge, identity, or absence of mistake or accident."

This case presents the question whether the district court must itself make a preliminary finding that the Government has proved the "other act" by a preponderance of the evidence before it submits the evidence to the jury. We hold that it need not do so.

Petitioner, Guy Rufus Huddleston, was charged with one count of selling stolen goods in interstate commerce, 18 U.S.C. § 2315, and one count of possessing stolen property in interstate commerce, 18 U.S.C. § 659. The two counts related to two portions of a shipment of stolen Memorex video cassette tapes that petitioner was alleged to have possessed and sold, knowing that they were stolen.

The evidence at trial showed that a trailer containing over 32,000 blank Memorex video cassette tapes with a manufacturing cost of $4.53 per tape was stolen from the Overnight Express yard in South Holland, Illinois, sometime between April 11 and 15, 1985. On April 17, 1985, petitioner contacted Karen Curry, the manager of the Magic Rent-to-Own in Ypsilanti, Michigan, seeking her assistance in selling a large number of blank Memorex video cassette tapes. After assuring Curry that the tapes were not stolen, he told her he wished to sell them in lots of at least 500 at $2.75 to $3.00 per tape. Curry subsequently arranged for the sale of a total of 5,000 tapes, which petitioner delivered to the various purchasers—who apparently believed the sales were legitimate.

There was no dispute that the tapes which petitioner sold were stolen; the only material issue at trial was whether petitioner knew they were stolen. The district court allowed the Government to introduce evidence of "similar acts" under Rule 404(b), concluding that such evidence had "clear relevance as to [petitioner's knowledge],". The first piece of similar act evidence offered by the Government was the testimony of Paul Toney, a record store owner. He testified that in February 1985, petitioner offered to sell new 12□ black and white televisions for $28 a piece. According to Toney, petitioner indicated that he could obtain several thousand of these televisions. Petitioner and Toney eventually traveled to the Magic Rent-to-Own, where Toney purchased 20 of the televisions. Several days later, Toney purchased 18 more televisions.

The second piece of similar act evidence was the testimony of Robert Nelson, an undercover FBI agent posing as a buyer for an appliance store. Nelson testified that in May 1985, petitioner offered to sell him a large quantity of Amana appliances—28 refrigerators, 2 ranges, and 40 icemakers. Nelson agreed to pay $8,000 for the appliances. Petitioner was arrested shortly after he arrived at the parking lot where he and Nelson had agreed to transfer the appliances. A truck containing the appliances was stopped a short distance from the parking lot, and Leroy Wesby, who was driving the truck, was also arrested. It was determined that the appliances had a value of approximately $20,000 and were part of a shipment that had been stolen.

Petitioner testified that the Memorex tapes, the televisions, and the appliances had all been provided by Leroy Wesby, who had represented that all of the merchandise was obtained legitimately. Petitioner stated that he had sold 6,500 Memorex tapes for Wesby on a commission basis. Petitioner maintained that all of the sales for Wesby had been on a commission basis and that he had no knowledge that any of the goods were stolen.

In closing, the prosecution explained that petitioner was not on trial for his dealings with the appliances or the televisions. The district court instructed the jury that the similar acts evidence was to be used only to establish petitioner's knowledge, and not to prove his character. The jury convicted petitioner on the possession count only.

We granted certiorari, to resolve a conflict among the Courts of Appeals as to whether the trial court must make a preliminary finding before "similar acts" and other Rule 404(b) evidence is submitted to the jury. We conclude that such evidence should be admitted if there is sufficient evidence to support a finding by the jury that the defendant committed the similar act.

Federal Rule of Evidence 404(b)—which applies in both civil and criminal cases—generally prohibits the introduction of evidence of extrinsic acts that might adversely reflect on the actor's character, unless that evidence bears upon a relevant issue in the case such as motive, opportunity, or knowledge. Extrinsic acts evidence may be critical to the establishment of the truth as to a disputed issue, especially when that issue involves the actor's state of mind and the only means of ascertaining that mental state is by drawing inferences from conduct. The actor in the instant case was a criminal defendant, and the act in question was "similar" to the one with which he was charged. Our use of these terms is not meant to suggest that our analysis is limited to such circumstances.

Before this Court, petitioner argues that the district court erred in admitting Toney's testimony as to petitioner's sale of the televisions. The threshold inquiry a court must make before admitting similar acts evidence under Rule 404(b) is whether that evidence is probative of a material issue other than character. The Government's theory of relevance was that the televisions were stolen, and proof that petitioner had engaged in a series of sales of stolen merchandise from the same suspicious source would be strong evidence that he was aware that each of these items, including the Memorex tapes, was stolen. As such, the sale of the televisions was a "similar act" only if the televisions were stolen. Petitioner acknowledges that this evidence was admitted for the proper purpose of showing his knowledge that the Memorex tapes were stolen. He asserts, however, that the evidence should not have been admitted because the Government failed to prove to the district court that the televisions were in fact stolen.

Petitioner argues from the premise that evidence of similar acts has a grave potential for causing improper prejudice. For instance, the jury may choose to punish the defendant for the similar rather than the charged act, or the jury may infer that the defendant is an evil person inclined to violate the law. Because of this danger, petitioner maintains, the jury ought not to be exposed to similar act evidence until the trial court has heard the evidence and made a determination under Federal Rule of Evidence 104(a) that the defendant committed the similar act. Rule 104(a) provides that "[p]reliminary questions concerning the qualification of a person to be a witness, the existence of a privilege, or the admissibility of evidence shall be determined by the court, subject to the provisions of subdivision (b)." According to petitioner, the trial court must make this preliminary finding by at least a preponderance of the evidence.

We reject petitioner's position, for it is inconsistent with the structure of the Rules of Evidence and with the plain language of Rule 404(b). Article IV of the Rules of Evidence deals with the relevancy of evidence. Rules 401 and 402 establish the broad principle that relevant evidence—evidence that makes the existence of any fact at issue more or less probable—is admissible unless the Rules provide otherwise. Rule 403 allows the trial judge to exclude relevant evidence if, among other things, "its probative value is substantially outweighed by the danger of unfair prejudice." Rules 404 through 412 address specific types of evidence that have generated problems. Generally, these latter Rules do not flatly prohibit the introduction of such evidence but instead limit the purpose for which it may be introduced. Rule 404(b), for example, protects against the introduction of extrinsic act evidence when that evidence is offered solely to prove character. The text contains no intimation, however, that any preliminary showing is necessary before such evidence may be introduced for a proper purpose. If offered for such a proper purpose, the evidence is subject only to general strictures limiting admissibility such as Rules 402 and 403.

Petitioner's reading of Rule 404(b) as mandating a preliminary finding by the trial court that the act in question occurred not only superimposes a level of judicial oversight that is nowhere apparent from the language of that provision, but it is simply inconsistent with the legislative history behind Rule 404(b). The Advisory Committee specifically declined to offer any "mechanical solution" to the admission of evidence under 404(b). Advisory Committee's Notes on Fed.Rule Evid. 404(b), 18 U.S.C.App., p. 691. Rather, the Committee indicated that the trial court should assess such evidence under the usual rules for admissibility: "The determination must be made whether the danger of undue prejudice outweighs the probative value of the evidence in view of the availability of other means of proof and other factors appropriate for making decisions of this kind under Rule 403." Ibid.; see also S.Rep. No. 93–1277, p. 25 (1974) ("[I]t is anticipated that with respect to permissible uses for such evidence, the trial judge may exclude it only on the basis of those considerations set forth in Rule 403, i.e., prejudice, confusion or waste of time").

* * *

We conclude that a preliminary finding by the court that the Government has proved the act by a preponderance of the evidence is not called for under Rule 104(a).[6] This is not to say, however, that the Government may

---

[6] Petitioner also suggests that in performing the balancing prescribed by Federal Rule of Evidence 403, the trial court must find that the prejudicial potential of similar acts evidence

parade past the jury a litany of potentially prejudicial similar acts that have been established or connected to the defendant only by unsubstantiated innuendo. Evidence is admissible under Rule 404(b) only if it is relevant. "Relevancy is not an inherent characteristic of any item of evidence but exists only as a relation between an item of evidence and a matter properly provable in the case." Advisory Committee's Notes on Fed.Rule Evid. 401, 28 U.S.C.App., p. 688. In the Rule 404(b) context, similar act evidence is relevant only if the jury can reasonably conclude that the act occurred and that the defendant was the actor. See United States v. Beechum, 582 F.2d 898, 912–913 (C.A.5 1978) (en banc). In the instant case, the evidence that petitioner was selling the televisions was relevant under the Government's theory only if the jury could reasonably find that the televisions were stolen.

Such questions of relevance conditioned on a fact are dealt with under Federal Rule of Evidence 104(b). Beechum, supra, at 912–913; see also E. Imwinkelried, Uncharged Misconduct Evidence § 2.06 (1984). Rule 104(b) provides:

"When the relevancy of evidence depends upon the fulfillment of a condition of fact, the court shall admit it upon, or subject to, the introduction of evidence sufficient to support a finding of the fulfillment of the condition."

In determining whether the Government has introduced sufficient evidence to meet Rule 104(b), the trial court neither weighs credibility nor makes a finding that the Government has proved the conditional fact by a preponderance of the evidence. The court simply examines all the evidence in the case and decides whether the jury could reasonably find the conditional fact—here, that the televisions were stolen—by a preponderance of the evidence. The trial court has traditionally exercised the broadest sort of discretion in controlling the order of proof at trial, and we see nothing in the Rules of Evidence that would change this practice. Often the trial court may decide to allow the proponent to introduce evidence concerning a similar act, and at a later point in the trial assess whether sufficient evidence has been offered to permit the jury to make the requisite finding. If the proponent has failed to meet this minimal standard of proof, the trial court must instruct the jury to disregard the evidence.

We emphasize that in assessing the sufficiency of the evidence under Rule 104(b), the trial court must consider all evidence presented to the jury. "[I]ndividual pieces of evidence, insufficient in themselves to prove a point, may in cumulation prove it. The sum of an evidentiary presentation may

---

substantially outweighs its probative value unless the court concludes by a preponderance of the evidence that the defendant committed the similar act. We reject this suggestion because Rule 403 admits of no such gloss and because such a holding would be erroneous for the same reason that a preliminary finding under Rule 104(a) is inappropriate. We do, however, agree with the Government's concession at oral argument that the strength of the evidence establishing the similar act is one of the factors the court may consider when conducting the Rule 403 balancing.

well be greater than its constituent parts." Bourjaily v. United States, 483 U.S. 171 (1987). In assessing whether the evidence was sufficient to support a finding that the televisions were stolen, the court here was required to consider not only the direct evidence on that point—the low price of the televisions, the large quantity offered for sale, and petitioner's inability to produce a bill of sale—but also the evidence concerning petitioner's involvement in the sales of other stolen merchandise obtained from Wesby, such as the Memorex tapes and the Amana appliances. Given this evidence, the jury reasonably could have concluded that the televisions were stolen, and the trial court therefore properly allowed the evidence to go to the jury.

We share petitioner's concern that unduly prejudicial evidence might be introduced under Rule 404(b). See Michelson v. United States, 335 U.S. 469, 475–476 (1948). We think, however, that the protection against such unfair prejudice emanates not from a requirement of a preliminary finding by the trial court, but rather from four other sources: first, from the requirement of Rule 404(b) that the evidence be offered for a proper purpose; second, from the relevancy requirement of Rule 402—as enforced through Rule 104(b); third, from the assessment the trial court must make under Rule 403 to determine whether the probative value of the similar acts evidence is substantially outweighed by its potential for unfair prejudice, and fourth, from Federal Rule of Evidence 105, which provides that the trial court shall, upon request, instruct the jury that the similar acts evidence is to be considered only for the proper purpose for which it was admitted.

Affirmed.

NOTE: OTHER CRIME EVIDENCE OFFERED AGAINST A DEFENDANT WHO WAS ACQUITTED OF THE OTHER OFFENSE

In Dowling v. United States, 493 U.S. 342 (1990), the defendant was accused of robbing a bank while wearing a ski mask and carrying a small pistol. Relying on Fed. R. Evid. 404(b), the prosecution put in testimony that Dowling had committed another robbery while masked and armed in the same way. Dowling had been tried for the other robbery and acquitted. Dowling argued that the admission of this evidence violated the Double Jeopardy Clause.

The Supreme Court rejected his argument in a 6–3 decision. The Court acknowledged that the Double Jeopardy Clause did incorporate a doctrine of collateral estoppel. A man who robbed six poker players at the same time could not be tried for robbing one, acquitted, and then tried for robbing a second player. Ashe v. Swenson, 397 U.S. 436 (1970). In such a case, the prosecution would be attempting to relitigate the ultimate issue of the first case in violation of collateral estoppel doctrine. Here, however, the government was not attempting to relitigate the ultimate issue in the prior case. Instead, it was merely using the testimony about the other robbery as circumstantial evidence of the robbery charged in the present case. Even if the acquittal of the first robbery were taken as establishing that there was a reasonable doubt about whether Dowling committed the first robbery, that was not the issue in this case. Citing *Huddleston*, the Court noted that the prosecution did not have to prove that Dowling committed the first crime beyond a reasonable doubt. A jury might reasonably conclude that Dowling was the masked man who participated in the first robbery, even if it did not believe that he was guilty beyond a reasonable doubt. Therefore, collateral estoppel doctrine did not apply. The Court also rejected defendant's argument that the admission of the testimony about the other robbery was so unfair that it violated the Due Process Clause.

Perrin v. Anderson

United States Court of Appeals, Tenth Circuit, 1986.
784 F.2d 1040.

■ LOGAN, CIRCUIT JUDGE.

* * *

This is a 42 U.S.C. § 1983 civil rights action for compensatory and punitive damages arising from the death of Terry Kim Perrin. Plaintiff, administratrix of Perrin's estate and guardian of his son, alleged that defendants, Donnie Anderson and Roland Von Schriltz, members of the Oklahoma Highway Patrol, deprived Perrin of his civil rights when they shot and killed him while attempting to obtain information concerning a traffic accident in which he had been involved. The jury found in favor of defendants.

In this appeal plaintiff contends that the district court erred in admitting testimony by four police officers recounting previous violent encounters they had had with Perrin. * * *

A simple highway accident set off the bizarre chain of events that culminated in Perrin's death. The incident began when Perrin drove his car into the back of another car on an Oklahoma highway. After determining that the occupants of the car he had hit were uninjured, Perrin walked to his home, which was close to the highway.

Trooper Von Schriltz went to Perrin's home to obtain information concerning the accident. He was joined there by Trooper Anderson. They knocked on and off for ten to twenty minutes before persuading Perrin to open the door. Once Perrin opened the door, the defendant officers noticed Perrin's erratic behavior. The troopers testified that his moods would change quickly and that he was yelling that the accident was not his fault. Von Schriltz testified that he sensed a possibly dangerous situation and slowly moved his hand to his gun in order to secure its hammer with a leather thong. This action apparently provoked Perrin who then slammed the door. The door bounced open and Perrin then attacked Anderson. A fierce battle ensued between Perrin and the two officers, who unsuccessfully applied several chokeholds to Perrin in an attempt to subdue him. Eventually Anderson, who testified that he feared he was about to lose consciousness as a result of having been kicked repeatedly in the face and chest by Perrin, took out his gun, and, without issuing a warning, shot and killed Perrin. Anderson stated that he was convinced Perrin would have killed both officers had he not fired.

I

At trial the court permitted four police officers to testify that they had been involved previously in violent encounters with Perrin. These officers testified to Perrin's apparent hatred or fear of uniformed officers and his consistently violent response to any contact with them. For example, defendants presented evidence that on earlier occasions Perrin was completely uncontrollable and violent in the presence of uniformed officers. On one occasion he rammed his head into the bars and walls of his cell, requiring administration of a tranquilizer. Another time while barefoot, Perrin kicked loose a porcelain toilet bowl that was bolted to the floor. One officer testified that he encountered Perrin while responding to a public drunk call. Perrin attacked him, and during the following struggle Perrin tried to reach for the officer's weapon. The officer and his back-up had to carry Perrin handcuffed, kicking and screaming, to the squad car, where Perrin then kicked the windshield out of the car. Another officer testified that Perrin attacked him after Perrin was stopped at a vehicle checkpoint. During the ensuing struggle three policemen were needed to subdue Perrin, including one 6′2″ officer weighing 250 pounds and one 6′6″ officer weighing 350 pounds.

Defendants introduced this evidence to prove that Perrin was the first aggressor in the fight—a key element in defendants' self-defense claim. The court admitted the evidence over objection, under Federal Rules of Evidence provisions treating both character and habit evidence. Plaintiff contends this was error.

A

Section 404(a) of the Federal Rules of Evidence carefully limits the circumstances under which character evidence may be admitted to prove that an individual, at the time in question, acted in conformity with his character. This rule is necessary because of the high degree of prejudice that inheres in character evidence. *See* Fed.R.Evid. 404 advisory committee note.[*] In most instances we are unwilling to permit a jury to infer that an individual performed the alleged acts based on a particular character trait. The exceptions to Rule 404(a)'s general ban on the use of character evidence permit criminal defendants to offer evidence of their own character or of their victim's character. Fed.R.Evid. 404(a)(1)–(2). Not until such a defendant takes this initial step may the prosecution rebut by offering contrary character evidence. Although the Advisory Committee on the Rules of Evidence has observed that this rule "lies more in history and experience than in logic," it does seem desirable to afford a criminal defendant every opportunity to exonerate himself.[1] In offering such potentially prejudicial testi-

---

[*] See pp. 1045–1046.

[1] We agree with Professor Uviller's explanation of why a criminal defendant is entitled to use character evidence to a greater extent than a civil defendant:

"About the best one can do with this puzzle is to guess that somewhere, somehow the rule was relaxed to allow the criminal defendant with so much at stake and so little available

mony, the defendant of course proceeds at his own risk. Once he offers evidence of his or his victim's character, the prosecution may offer contrary evidence. Fed.R.Evid. 404(a)(1)–(2).

Although the literal language of the exceptions to Rule 404(a) applies only to criminal cases, we agree with the district court here that, when the central issue involved in a civil case is in nature criminal, the defendant may invoke the exceptions to Rule 404(a).

In a case of this kind, the civil defendant, like the criminal defendant, stands in a position of great peril. A verdict against the defendants in this case would be tantamount to finding that they killed Perrin without cause. The resulting stigma warrants giving them the same opportunity to present a defense that a criminal defendant could present. Accordingly we hold that defendants were entitled to present evidence of Perrin's character from which the jury could infer that Perrin was the aggressor. The self-defense claim raised in this case is not functionally different from a self-defense claim raised in a criminal case.[2]

Although we agree with the district court that character evidence was admissible in this case, we hold that the district court should not have permitted testimony about prior specific incidents.

Federal Rule of Evidence 405 establishes the permissible methods of proving character:

> "(a) **Reputation or opinion.** In all cases in which evidence of character or a trait of character of a person is admissible, proof may be made by testimony as to reputation or by testimony in the form of an opinion. On cross-examination, inquiry is allowable into relevant specific instances of conduct.

> (b) **Specific instances of conduct.** In cases in which character or a trait of character of a person is an essential element of a charge, claim, or defense, proof may also be made of specific instances of his conduct."

Testimony concerning specific instances of conduct is the most convincing, of course, but it also "possesses the greatest capacity to arouse prejudice, to confuse, to surprise and to consume time." Rule 405 therefore concludes that such evidence may be used only when character is in issue "in the strict sense."

---

in the way of conventional proof to have special dispensation to tell the factfinder just what sort of person he really is."

Uviller, Evidence of Character to Prove Conduct: Illusion, Illogic, and Injustice in the Courtroom, 130 U.Pa.L.Rev. 845, 855 (1982).

[2] Plaintiff also argues that, because defendants had no personal knowledge of Perrin's character, evidence of his character was irrelevant. Although plaintiff is correct that this evidence has no bearing on whether defendants had a reasonable fear of Perrin, it is directly relevant to the issue of who was the aggressor in the fight.

Character is directly in issue in the strict sense when it is "a material fact that under the substantive law determines rights and liabilities of the parties." In such a case the evidence is not being offered to prove that the defendant acted in conformity with the character trait; instead, the existence or nonexistence of the character trait itself "determines the rights and liabilities of the parties." In a defamation action, for example, the plaintiff's reputation for honesty is directly at issue when the defendant has called the plaintiff dishonest.

Defendants here offered character evidence for the purpose of proving that Perrin was the aggressor. "[E]vidence of a violent disposition to prove that the person was the aggressor in an affray" is given as an example of the circumstantial use of character evidence in the advisory committee notes for Fed.R.Evid. 404(a). When character is used circumstantially, only reputation and opinion are acceptable forms of proof. We therefore find that the district court erroneously relied upon the character evidence rules in permitting testimony about specific violent incidents involving Perrin.

B

Character and habit are closely akin. The district court found, alternatively, that the testimony recounting Perrin's previous violent encounters with police officers was admissible as evidence of a habit under Fed.R.Evid. 406. Here, we concur.

Rule 406 provides:

> "Evidence of the habit of a person * * *, whether corroborated or not and regardless of the presence of eyewitnesses, is relevant to prove that the conduct of the person * * * on a particular occasion was in conformity with the habit * * *."

The limitations on the methods of proving character set out in Rule 405 do not apply to proof of habit. Testimony concerning prior specific incidents is allowed.

This court has defined "habit" as "a regular practice of meeting a particular kind of situation with a certain type of conduct, or a reflex behavior in a specific set of circumstances." The advisory committee notes to Rule 406 state that, "[w]hile adequacy of sampling and uniformity of response are key factors, precise standards for measuring their sufficiency for evidence purposes cannot be formulated." That Perrin might be proved to have a "habit" of reacting violently to uniformed police officers seems rather extraordinary. We believe, however, that defendants did in fact demonstrate that Perrin repeatedly reacted with extreme aggression when dealing with uniformed police officers.

Four police officers testified to at least five separate violent incidents, and plaintiff offered no evidence of any peaceful encounter between Perrin and the police. Five incidents ordinarily would be insufficient to establish the existence of a habit. See Reyes v. Missouri Pacific Railway Co., 589 F.2d

791, 794–95 (5th Cir.1979) (four convictions for public intoxication in three and one-half years insufficient to prove habit). But defendants here had made an offer of proof of testimony from eight police officers concerning numerous different incidents. To prevent undue prejudice to plaintiff, the district court permitted only four of these witnesses to testify, and it explicitly stated that it thought the testimony of the four officers had been sufficient to establish a habit. We hold that the district court properly admitted this evidence pursuant to Rule 406. There was adequate testimony to establish that Perrin invariably reacted with extreme violence to any contact with a uniformed police officer.

Affirmed.

NOTE

Fed. R. Evid. 404(a)(1) and (a)(2) were amended in 2006 to make it clearer that they apply only in criminal cases.

QUESTIONS

Defendant (D) is charged with murder arising from a barroom brawl. In its opening statement, the defense states that the evidence will show that the alleged victim (V) was the first attacker and that the defendant acted in self-defense. In each of these cases, is the indicated evidence admissible?

1. D offers evidence that V had a bad reputation for violence.

2. D offers evidence that V previously shot someone in a fit of road rage.

3. D offers evidence that weeks before the incident that caused V's death, V attacked D in a fit of road rage.

4. D offers evidence that weeks before the fatal incident, he heard that V shot someone in a fit of road rage.

5. After the judge has admitted evidence about the bad reputation of V for violence, the prosecution offers evidence of the bad reputation of D for violence; D has not offered any evidence of D's own good character.

NOTE

See Federal Rules of Evidence 404, 405, and 803(21); California Evidence Code §§ 1100–1104 and § 1324.

Until several decades ago, the character of the victim was admissible on behalf of the defendant in one type of case other than that of self-defense—forcible rape. The cases were virtually unanimous that where the defendant had alleged consent as a defense, the "consenting character of the victim" could be shown to make consent more likely. After 1970, statutes in virtually every jurisdiction prohibited this, and did a good deal more as well. See Note, on

Rape Shield Legislation, p. 162, and *State v. Cassidy,* p. 163; see also Fed. Rules of Evidence 412, Cal. Evidence Code Sec. 1103.

Park, Leonard, Orenstein & Goldberg, Evidence Law
189-91 (3d ed. 2011).*

In most jurisdictions, character evidence is not admissible in civil cases as circumstantial evidence of conduct, and it is admissible in criminal cases only under prescribed exceptions. However, evidence of *habit* is freely admissible. The distinction between character and habit is largely a matter of degree. In describing the distinction, the advisory committee to the Federal Rules of Evidence quoted McCormick's classic definition:

> Character and habit are close akin. Character is a generalized description of one's disposition, or of one's disposition in respect to a general trait, such as honesty, temperance, or peacefulness. "Habit," in modern usage, both lay and psychological, is more specific. It describes one's regular response to a repeated specific situation. If we speak of character for care, we think of the person's tendency to act prudently in all the varying situations of life, in business, family life, in handling automobiles and in walking across the street. A habit, on the other hand, is the person's regular practice of meeting a particular kind of situation with a specific type of conduct, such as the habit of going down a particular stairway two stairs at a time, or of giving the hand-signal for a left turn, or of alighting from railway cars while they are moving. The doing of the habitual acts may become semi-automatic.[290]

The rules provide not only for the admission of habit evidence about human beings, but also for admission of evidence of the *routine practice* of a corporation or other organization. In contrast to the earlier practice of some jurisdictions, the Federal Rules contain no requirement that habit or routine practice be corroborated by other evidence; it can itself be sufficient to prove the doing of an act. Nor is there any rule that habit evidence is admissible only if eyewitness testimony is not available. One's habit—say, a habit of using seat belts—is admissible under the Federal Rules whether or

---

[290] Fed. R. Evid. 406 advisory committee's note (quoting Charles T. McCormick, McCormick on Evidence § 162, at 340 (1954)). *See also* Jones v. Southern Pac. R.R., 962 F.2d 447, 449 (5th Cir.1992) (habit evidence is superior to character evidence "because the uniformity of one's response to habit is far greater than the consistency with which one's conduct conforms to character"); Estate of Keys v. City of Harvey, 1996 WL 34422, at *2 (N.D.Ill.1996) (in wrongful death action stemming from killing by police sergeant, records of the sergeant's disciplinary and personnel files inadmissible under Fed. R. Evid. 406; records could only show a tendency to react violently to challenges to his authority, not conduct semi-automatic in nature; the degree of "specificity and frequency" of the action distinguishes habit evidence from impermissible character evidence); *cf.* Mobil Exploration & Producing U.S., Inc. v. Cajun Const. Servs., Inc., 45 F.3d 96, 100 (5th Cir.1995) (in suit claiming supplier had short-loaded its deliveries of limestone, trial court erroneously excluded evidence of supplier's method of loading its trucks; supplier's method of loading amounted to habit under Fed. R. Evid. 406 since the same procedure was used with such regularity as to amount to a routine business practice).

not eyewitnesses are also available who could testify that the person wore the seat belt on the occasion in question.

Examples of habit or routine practice include a doctor's regular practice of advising patients of risks of joint replacement surgery, to show that the advice was given on a particular occasion involving ankle replacement surgery;[291] a bar's regular practice of serving intoxicated persons, to support the inference that it did so on a particular occasion;[292] a drinker's habit of getting drunk at a particular social club nearly every weekend, to show intoxication at the time of a hit-and-run accident;[293] a railroad crew's practice of not blowing a whistle at a particular crossing,[294] or of operating a switch engine without a flagman in the street;[295] an undercover agent's routine practice of marking and sealing illicit drugs seized during an investigation, to show that the practice was followed on a particular occasion;[296] a nurse's routine practice of taking blood samples;[297] a business's routine practice of stamping mail with sufficient postage;[298] and a hospital's routine practices concerning the presentation and signing of medical malpractice arbitration forms.[299]

In general, habit evidence has tended to be evidence of responses, often semi-automatic, to relatively narrow specific situations. The evidence is sometimes rejected on grounds that the conduct is not sufficiently regular or that the trait in question is actually a trait of character.[300] On the other

---

[291] Bloskas v. Murray, 646 P.2d 907, 911 (Colo.1982). *See also* Meyer v. United States, 464 F.Supp. 317, 321 (D.Colo.1979) (dentist's practice of informing patients of the risks involved in extraction of third molars).

[292] Tommy's Elbow Room, Inc. v. Kavorkian, 727 P.2d 1038 (Alaska 1986).

[293] State v. Radziwil, 563 A.2d 856, 861 (N.J.Super.1989), *affirmed*, 582 A.2d 1003 (1990). *See also* Loughan v. Firestone Tire & Rubber Co., 749 F.2d 1519, 1522–24 (11th Cir.1985) (worker's habit of bringing cooler of beer to work on back of truck and drinking from it while working admissible as evidence of drunkenness on a particular occasion).

[294] Bradfield v. Illinois Central Gulf R.R., 505 N.E.2d 331 (Ill.1987).

[295] Williams v. Union Pac. R.R., 465 P.2d 975 (Kan.1970).

[296] State v. Van Sickle, 434 A.2d 31 (Me.1981).

[297] State v. Shelton, 176 N.W.2d 159, 161–62 (Iowa 1970).

[298] Swink & Co. v. Carroll McEntee & McGinley, Inc., 584 S.W.2d 393 (Ark.1979).

[299] McKinstry v. Valley Obstetrics–Gynecology Clinic, PC, 405 N.W.2d 88 (Mich.1987).

[300] See Neuren v. Adduci, Mastriani, Meeks & Schill, 43 F.3d 1507 (D.C.Cir.1995) (in an employment discrimination case, defendant's evidence that the plaintiff had experienced similar work-related problems, such as tardiness, on another job was inadmissible character evidence; court made no allusion to the "habit" theory of admissibility); Jones v. Southern Pac. R.R., 962 F.2d 447, 450 (5th Cir.1992) (evidence of nine violations in 29–year career as railroad engineer not admissible to prove habit of driving negligently); Smith v. State, 601 So.2d 201 (Ala.Crim.App.1992) (picking up prostitutes in certain area is not habit); Henry v. Cline, 626 S.W.2d 958 (Ark.1982) (testimony that witness had seen party drive on a road a dozen times and that party was speeding half the time not sufficient to establish habit; behavior not "nearly or completely involuntary"); Ritchey v. Murray, 625 S.W.2d 476 (Ark.1981) (tendency of driver to weave across centerline when reaching for chewing tobacco or delivering newspapers not sufficiently regular to constitute habit; no evidence that driver was delivering newspapers on occasion in question); Stapleton v. Great Lakes Chem. Corp., 616 So.2d 1311, 1317–18 (La.App.1993), vacated in part on other grounds 627 So.2d 1358 (1993) (harmless error for trial court to admit testimony of defendant's good driving record and awards for safe driving as habit evidence); State v. Lagasse, 410 A.2d 537, 542 (Me.1980) ("The tendency of a person to engage in violent acts while under the influence of intoxicating liquor does not establish 'the regular response to a repeated specific situation' necessary to constitute habit under M. R.

hand, where the need is great enough and the testimony convincing, some courts have treated rather broad traits as being "habit" traits.[301] There is much room for disagreement about just how much specificity is enough to establish habit.[302]

Habit evidence is often offered in civil cases to show a careful or careless habit. (In such instances, the evidence must actually demonstrate a habit, and not just a general tendency toward care or its opposite.) It should be noted, however, that although use of the habit concept is one way of justifying the receipt of other acts evidence in civil cases, it is not the only way. As already discussed, in both civil and criminal cases, evidence of uncharged misconduct (or of good conduct) may be admitted for one of the other purposes listed in Rule 404(b), as long as it is not offered for an inference about character. Thus, in a civil case in which a fire insurance company offers a defense of arson, the company may wish to offer evidence that other property belonging to the defendant had been destroyed by the defendant's arson. The commission of arson can hardly be regular enough to be considered a "habit," but if a distinctive modus operandi was involved, or if the arson was part of a common scheme or plan, it would be admissible under the principles of Rule 404(b).

See Federal Rules of Evidence 406; California Evidence Code § 1105.

Halloran v. Virginia Chemicals Inc.

Court of Appeals of New York, 1977.
41 N.Y.2d 386, 393 N.Y.S.2d 341, 361 N.E.2d 991.

■ BREITEL, CHIEF JUDGE.

Defendant Virginia Chemicals appeals in a personal injury products liability action. Plaintiff Frank Halloran, an automobile mechanic, obtained a verdict in his favor, after a jury trial on the issue of liability only, for injuries he sustained while using a can of refrigerant packaged and sold by the

---

Evid. 406"); De Matteo v. Simon, 812 P.2d 361, 362–63 (N.M.App.1991) (defendant's post-accident driving record not admissible to show a habit of negligence).

[301] See, e.g., Derring v. State, 619 S.W.2d 644 (Ark.1981) (regularity, reliability, and promptness of supposed victim admissible as habit evidence to show he would not have disappeared without foul play; query whether some of the traits described as habit should really be considered character).

[302] Compare Loughan v. Firestone Tire & Rubber Co., 749 F.2d 1519, 1522–24 (11th Cir.1985) (evidence that employee regularly drank on the job from cooler of beer he carried on his truck was admitted at trial for purposes of showing that employee was impaired at time of accident; held, showing of regularity was sufficient to establish habit under Rule 406, and evidence was admissible despite absence of direct evidence that employee drank on day of accident) with Reyes v. Missouri Pac. R.R., 589 F.2d 791 (5th Cir.1979) (four prior convictions for intoxication held inadmissible to show action in conformity; evidence was evidence of character, not habit, and hence forbidden). See 1 McCormick on Evidence § 195, at 826 n.8 (4th ed. John W. Strong ed. 1992) (probative force of habitual intoxication to prove intoxication on particular occasion depends on regularity of details of characteristic behavior).

chemical company. A divided Appellate Division affirmed, and certified a question of law for review in this court.

———————

There is one * * * issue meriting extended discussion: whether evidence that the injured mechanic had previously used an immersion heating coil to heat the can of the refrigerant should be admissible to show that on the particular occasion he was negligent and ignored the labeled warnings on the can [which cautioned against using an immersion coil]. Evidently relying on the rubric excluding prior instances of carelessness to create an inference of carelessness on a particular occasion, both the Trial Judge and the Appellate Division, save for two dissenting Justices, agreed that such evidence was not admissible.

There should be a reversal and a new trial. If plaintiff, when necessary to stimulate the flow of the refrigerant, a highly compressed liquefied gas, habitually or regularly used an immersion coil to heat the water in which the container was placed, evidence of that habit or regular usage should be admissible to prove he followed such a procedure on the day of the explosion. Evidence of habit or regular usage, if properly defined and therefore circumscribed, involves more than unpatterned occasional conduct, that is, conduct however frequent yet likely to vary from time to time depending upon the surrounding circumstances; it involves a repetitive pattern of conduct and therefore predictable and predictive conduct. On this view, the excluded evidence was offered to show a particular method of executing a task followed by the mechanic, who, on his own testimony, had serviced "hundreds" of air-conditioning units and used "thousands" of cans of the refrigerant. If on remittal the evidence tends to show that the mechanic used an immersion coil a sufficient number of times to warrant a finding of habit, or regular usage, it would be admissible to aid the jury on its inquiry whether he did so on the occasion in question.

On June 1, 1970, the day of the accident, Frank Halloran, a mechanic for 15 years, had been employed by the Hillcrest Service station for over three years. Among his duties was the servicing and charging of automobile air-conditioning units, a job for which he had been specially trained, and for which he used "all [his] own tools." The particular task involved that day was the changing of the air-conditioning compressor on a 1967 Chrysler automobile. Plaintiff testified that he had emptied the system, removed the old compressor, and installed a new one. He then began to charge the unit.

The first two cans of the refrigerant, Freon, flowed into the system without difficulty. By the time he was emptying the third can, however, plaintiff found it necessary to accelerate the flow of the refrigerant. The mechanic described how he filled an empty two-pound coffee tin with warm tap water, used a thermometer to determine that the water temperature was about 90 to 100 degrees, and inserted into the coffee tin the third can of Freon. Having a similar problem with the flow of the fourth can, Halloran again dropped the Freon into the warm water. Noticing that his low pressure gauge showed a rapid increase in the pressure, and aware that "something was wrong", Halloran reached down to remove the can from the water, but was too late. The can exploded before he could touch it.

Neither the thermometer Halloran claimed to have used nor the bottom of the exploded can of Freon was produced at trial. Halloran knew that excessive heating of the can would cause damage, and that the warnings on the can specified 130 degrees as the maximum permissible safe temperature. As discussed earlier, he proved no particular defect in the can, its contents, or in so much of the exploded can which was produced at the trial. Having worked alone that day, Halloran was the only eyewitness to the explosion.

Defendant Virginia Chemicals * * * sought to establish that it was Halloran's "usage and practice" to use an immersion coil to heat the water in which the Freon was placed. * * *

Of course, had an immersion heating coil been used at the time of the accident the unexplained and thus far unexplainable explosion would have been fully explained.

* * *

To be sure, Halloran's practice prior to June 1, 1970 is not conclusive proof of the method he employed in working on the 1967 Chrysler. * * * While courts of this State have in negligence cases traditionally excluded evidence of carefulness or carelessness as not probative of how one acted on a particular occasion, in other cases evidence of a consistent practice or method followed by a person has routinely been allowed * * *. That a kind of habit, practice, or method was proffered in this case to establish negligence should not, without more, affect its admissibility.

Because one who has demonstrated a consistent response under given circumstances is more likely to repeat that response when the circumstances arise again, evidence of habit has, since the days of the common-law reports, generally been admissible to prove conformity on specified occasions * * *. Hence, a lawyer, to prove due execution of a will, may testify that he always has wills executed according to statutory requirements. So, too, to prove that notice is mailed on a specified day of the month, one is allowed to testify that he is in the habit of being home on that day of the month to transact such business.

When negligence is at issue, however, New York courts have long resisted allowing evidence of specific acts of carelessness or carefulness to create an inference that such conduct was repeated when like circumstances were again presented. Hence, evidence of a plaintiff's habit of jumping on streetcars may not be offered to prove he was negligent on the day of the accident. Nor could testimony that the deceased had usually looked both ways before crossing railroad tracks be introduced to establish his care on the particular occasion. Whether a carryover from the prohibition against using so-called "character" evidence in civil cases, or grounded on the assumption that even repeated instances of negligence or care do not sufficiently increase the probability of like conduct on a particular occasion, the statement that evidence of habit or regular usage is never admissible to establish negligence is too broad (see 1 Wigmore, Evidence [3d ed.], § 97, esp. p. 532).

At least, as in this kind of case, where the issue involves proof of a deliberate and repetitive practice, a party should be able, by introducing evidence of such habit or regular usage, to allow the inference of its persistence, and hence negligence on a particular occasion (see McCormick, Evidence [2d ed.], § 195, advocating an even more expansive approach; see, also, 1 Wigmore, Evidence [3d ed.], § 97). Far less likely to vary with the attendant circumstances, such repetitive conduct is more predictive than the frequency (or rarity) of jumping on streetcars or exercising stop-look-and-listen caution in crossing railroad tracks. On no view, under traditional analysis, can conduct involving not only oneself but particularly other persons or independently controlled instrumentalities produce a regular usage because of the likely variation of the circumstances in which such conduct will be indulged. Proof of a deliberate repetitive practice by one in complete control of the circumstances is quite another matter and it should therefore be admissible because it is so highly probative.

As previously noted, Halloran, in the course of his work as a mechanic, had serviced "hundreds" of automobile air conditioners and had used "thousands" of cans of Freon. From his testimony at trial it seems clear that in servicing these units he followed, as of course he would, a routine. If, indeed, the use of an immersion coil tended to be part of this routine whenever it was necessary to accelerate the flow of the refrigerant, as he indicated was often the case, the jury should not be precluded from considering such evidence as an aid to its determination.

Of course, to justify introduction of habit or regular usage, a party must be able to show on *voir dire,* to the satisfaction of the Trial Judge, that he expects to prove a sufficient number of instances of the conduct in question * * *. If defendant's witness was prepared to testify to seeing Halloran using an immersion coil on only one occasion, exclusion was proper. If, on the other hand, plaintiff was seen a sufficient number of times, and it is preferable that defendant be able to fix, at least generally, the times and places of such occurrences, a finding of habit or regular usage would be warranted and the evidence admissible for the jury's consideration.

* * *

HYPOTHETICALS

(1) X, a prison inmate is charged with aggravated assault upon A, a fellow prisoner. The prosecution's case is that X and B, another inmate, assaulted A and stabbed him numerous times. X's defense is that his only part in the fray was to break up a fight between A and B. X calls Y, an inmate who did not witness the fight, to testify that he has known X for one month and that, in his opinion, X is a nonviolent man. The prosecutor makes an inadmissible-character-evidence objection to Y's proposed testimony. What result?

(2) X is charged with first degree murder of A, a police officer. B, a police officer, testifies that he was with A in a police car and that they stopped X, who was driving an automobile in an erratic fashion; that A asked X to step out and X complied; that A then asked X to raise his hands so he could be checked for weapons; that instead, X sprang back, drew a gun from a concealed holster under his shirt and began firing; that A was hit and died the next day; and that B succeeded in disarming X and placed him under arrest. The prosecution offers evidence that (a) X was on parole from a felony sentence in Illinois and his presence in California was in violation of his parole; (b) seven days before the charged offense X committed armed robbery of a market in Denver, Colorado; and (c) the automobile in which X was riding had been stolen from a San Francisco car dealer three days before the charged offense. The prosecutor announces that he is offering the above items of evidence on the issues of motive, intent, and premeditation. X makes an irrelevancy and inadmissible character evidence objection. How should the court rule?

(3) X is charged with grand theft from the person of A. X's defense is an alibi. A testifies that he is 85 years of age; that X approached him on the street, said he was celebrating the birth of a boy, put his arm around A, offered him a cigar and then left; and that immediately thereafter A noticed his wallet from his hip pocket was missing with its contents of $75. The prosecutor calls B and makes an offer of proof that he will testify that he is 84 years of age; that two months after the A incident, he was approached on the street by X who told him he was celebrating the birth of his first boy, offered him a cigar, put his arm around his waist, and asked for some street directions; that X pushed him slightly and then left; that B immediately felt for his wallet in his hip pocket and it was missing; and that he ran after X, saw him get into a car but could not catch him. The prosecutor states that B's testimony is offered on the issue of identity to prove modus operandi and common scheme or plan. X makes an irrelevancy and an inadmissible character-evidence objection. What result?

(4) X is charged with murder of A. X's version of events is that A, who lived in the same apartment building, was visiting X; that an argument developed and A took a karate stance and sprang at X; and that X wrestled A to the floor and stomped his foot in A's stomach. A died from injuries to the abdomen about two weeks later. In rebuttal, the prosecutor offers the following testimony: (1) the testimony of B that about two months before X's fight with A, he and X had a drunken quarrel; that X kicked him in the ribs, causing him to be hospitalized; and that X pleaded guilty to assault and battery; and (2) the testimony of C that he was a longtime acquaintance of X; that a year before X's fight with A, X and several others knocked him, C, down without reason; and that X then kicked him in the stomach. The prosecutor states that he is offering the testimony of B and C to establish X's modus operandi to use his feet in a fight. X makes an irrelevancy and an inadmissible character-evidence objection to the proposed testimony of B and C. What result?

(5) A sues X and the Y Bus Company for damages for personal injuries suffered in a collision between a bus driven by X, an employee of the Y Bus Company, and a car driven by A. A claims that X failed to stop at a stop sign. A calls B, who testifies that he has been a regular and daily rider on the bus driven by X during the six-month period preceding the accident, but that he was not on the bus the day of A's accident. A asks B whether, in this six-month period, X

habitually failed to come to a stop at the intersection where the accident took place. X and the Y Bus Company make an inadmissible-character and a habit-evidence objection to A's question. Should the objections be sustained?

NOTE ON RAPE SHIELD LEGISLATION*

Some common-law courts allowed rape defendants to introduce evidence about the victim's character for chastity. The evidence might take the form of testimony about the victim's reputation, or it might include testimony about specific sexual activity. The practice of receiving this evidence deterred victims from pursuing well-founded complaints because of fear of abuse and degradation in the courtroom. Its premise that consent with one partner is worthy evidence of consent with another is untenable in an age in which "one can presume that a woman will freely choose her partners, picking some and rejecting others, in line with highly personal standards not susceptible of generalization."[1] As part of a reform effort supported by the women's movement and by law enforcement officials, almost all state legislatures and Congress adopted "rape shield" legislation in the 1970's that limited the use of evidence of prior sexual conduct in sexual assault cases.

Rape shield legislation differs from state to state, but all statutes have at least one common feature: Evidence of reputation and sexual behavior is not admissible purely for purposes of showing unchaste character, as the basis for a further inference that the complainant consented to sex on the occasion in question. The statutes generally do allow prior sexual behavior to be admitted for certain limited purposes. Two widely recognized examples of admissible behavior are (a) the complainant's prior sexual behavior with the defendant, as opposed to behavior with other persons, and (b) evidence of the complainant's sexual behavior with other persons, when offered for purposes of explaining the physical consequences of the alleged rape—e.g., injury, the presence of semen, pregnancy, or venereal disease. Other examples of admissible behavior, though not universally recognized, involve evidence that is offered to show a possible motive for fabrication of the complaint, or to show other behavior closely similar to the behavior on the occasion in question. The statutes generally also have a procedural element, providing for hearings in limine on the issue of admissibility, and in some cases providing for in camera hearings to protect the victim's privacy. Indeed, some statutes do little more than set up a procedural mechanism for pretrial decision and call attention to the problem, providing only some general standard of admissibility, such as weighing prejudice against probative value.

---

* Based on R. Park, Trial Objections Handbook 37–38 (Shephard's McGraw–Hill, 1991).

[1] Berger, Man's Trial, Woman's Tribulation: Rape Cases in the Courtroom, 77 Colum.L.Rev. 1, 56 (1977).

State v. Cassidy

Appellate Court of Connecticut, 1985.
3 Conn.App. 374, 489 A.2d 386, cert. denied 196 Conn. 803, 492 A.2d 1239 (1985).

■ BORDEN, JUDGE.

* * *

The information arose out of an incident occurring on February 20, 1983. The jury could reasonably have found the following facts: The victim had previously been acquainted with the defendant, with whom she had engaged in sexual relations one or two times prior to the evening in question. Early in the morning hours of February 20, 1983, the victim went to a bar with a friend, where she saw the defendant. She accompanied him and some of his friends to an after-hours bar. They stayed there briefly and then went to the defendant's house. The victim went upstairs to the defendant's bedroom, undressed and got into the bed. She was, at that point, willing to have sexual relations with him.

At this stage in the events, the victim's and the defendant's recollections diverge. The victim recounted as follows: After she was in the bed, the defendant [started yelling threats and abuse. He then physically forced her to have oral, anal and vaginal intercourse with him.] Throughout the incident, the defendant called her obscene names and, in her estimation, acted "[l]ike a crazy person." The defendant then told her that she had two seconds to put her clothes on and leave or he would kill her. She quickly put on some of her clothes; the defendant got her coat and, pushing her out the door, said he never wanted to see her again and threatened to kill her if she called the police. She left the house and, after unsuccessfully attempting to get neighbors' help, flagged down a car which happened to be driven by a police officer. He took her to the police station. She was later taken to a hospital and treated for injuries.

The defendant's account was as follows: After the victim got into the bed, the defendant, * * * got into the bed with her [and engaged in intercourse]. She then asked if she could tie him up. He said no but asked if she would like to be tied up. She consented, and he tied her hands loosely in front of her with her stockings. * * * Then, * * * the complainant's "whole attitude changed * * * like she didn't consent to what we were doing." She started getting hysterical, screaming about her husband who was killed in Vietnam. She said she "shouldn't be doing this," and that she wanted to die and wanted to be with her husband. She untied her hands and started swinging at the defendant. He tried to get her off of him and slapped her. She fell onto the bed. The defendant got up, told the victim to put her clothes on and get out of his house, and went into the bathroom. When he returned to the bedroom, she was gone.

The defendant's principal claim on appeal arises from the exclusion of certain evidence by the trial court. Prior to trial, the defendant moved, pur-

appeal – exclusion of evidence

suant to General Statutes § 54–86f,[1] to offer evidence of the complainant's prior sexual conduct. The court permitted evidence of the prior sexual conduct between the defendant and the complainant but refused to admit evidence of a sexual encounter between the victim and another man, who testified in the absence of the jury as part of the defendant's offer of proof. This testimony was to the effect that she and he had gone to her home together about a year before the night in question. They had sexual relations, during which she began "going crazy" and screaming about her husband who was killed in Vietnam. The witness told her to forget about it and went to sleep. Nothing eventful happened for the rest of the night. The next morning she showed him pictures of her husband.

[handwritten margin note: Did not permit other man to testify]

The trial court excluded this testimony in the absence of an offer of proof by the defendant that the victim made a prior false complaint of sexual assault. The defendant argues that the evidence should have been admitted to show a pattern of conduct by the victim, and because it was highly relevant, probative and essential to the defense. He claims that applying the statute in this case violated his constitutional rights of confrontation and to present witnesses in his own behalf. We disagree.

[handwritten margin note: Trial Ct. – no false complaint.]

Statutes such as General Statutes § 54–86f, commonly known as rape shield statutes, have been enacted specifically to bar or limit the use of prior sexual conduct of an alleged victim of a sexual assault because it is such highly prejudicial material. Our legislature has determined that, except in specific instances, and taking the defendant's constitutional rights into account, evidence of prior sexual conduct is to be excluded for policy purposes. Some of these policies include protecting the victim's sexual privacy and shielding her from undue harassment, encouraging reports of sexual assault, and enabling the victim to testify in court with less fear of embarrassment. Other policies promoted by the law include avoiding prejudice to the victim, jury confusion and waste of time on collateral matters. The state's interests are substantial, but cannot by themselves outweigh the defendant's competing constitutional interests. The United States Supreme Court has looked to the facts and circumstances of the particular cases before it when determining if the state's interests in excluding evidence must yield to those interests of the defendant. See, e.g., Chambers v. Mississippi, 410 U.S. 284, 93 S.Ct. 1038, 35 L.Ed.2d 297 (1973). Likewise, we must analyze the defendant's constitutional claims in light of the facts of this particular case.

Under General Statutes § 54–86f, which has not been previously interpreted, evidence of the victim's prior sexual conduct is inadmissible un-

---

[1] [This statute, Connecticut's rape shield law, excludes evidence of the "sexual conduct of the victim" when introduced in a prosecution for criminal sexual conduct. The statute includes exceptions applicable if the "evidence is (1) offered by the defendant on the issue of whether the defendant was, with respect to the victim, the source of semen, disease, pregnancy or injury, or (2) offered by the defendant on the issue of credibility of the victim, provided the victim has testified on direct examination as to his or her sexual conduct, or (3) any evidence of sexual conduct with the defendant offered by the defendant on the issue of consent by the victim, when consent is raised as a defense by the defendant, or (4) otherwise so relevant and material to a critical issue in the case that excluding it would violate the defendant's constitutional rights."—Eds.]

less the trial court determines from an offer of proof at a hearing that it fits into one of the statute's exceptions. The defendant's argument focuses on exception (4) of § 54–86f, which permits evidence of prior sexual conduct if it is "so relevant and material to a critical issue in the case that excluding it would violate the defendant's constitutional rights."

must be "so relevant" that excluding violates D's const rights

This statute directs the court to examine the defendant's constitutional rights, implicating both his sixth amendment right to confront witnesses and his fourteenth amendment due process right to call witnesses on his own behalf. See Chambers v. Mississippi, supra, 410 U.S. 294, 93 S.Ct. 1045. * * *

6th – confrontation
14th – call witnesses

The court, in this case, was correct in noting that, unless the proffered testimony was to show that the victim previously made a false claim of sexual assault following the claimed similar, consensual sexual conduct, the evidence should be excluded. The relevant conduct was that between the defendant and the victim. Unless she had raised a false claim before, her conduct with another man had no bearing on her conduct with this defendant or on the credibility of her testimony in this case. * * *

* * * The defendant claims he had a right to present this evidence because it established a pattern of conduct by the victim, and it supported his defense of consent by showing another instance where the victim became irascible during a consensual sexual encounter.

* * *

The fact that about one year before the alleged assault occurred, the victim began a sexual episode with another man, became upset and changed her mind because of her feelings about her dead husband, does not tend to establish that, on this night, the victim became hysterical about her husband, screamed that she wanted to die and be with her dead husband, and struck the defendant. Particularly since there was also evidence of more recent nights which the defendant and the victim had spent together with no similar behavior by her, the defendant's version would not have been made more probable by this evidence.

One cannot logically infer that the victim acted in the manner described by the defendant simply because of a somewhat similar incident one year beforehand. The evidence, therefore, was legally irrelevant and was properly excluded without denying the defendant his constitutional rights.

Moreover, one similar instance is not sufficient to prove a pattern of conduct. Even in states which expressly permit evidence of prior sexual conduct to establish a pattern of conduct, evidence of one sexual encounter is not enough to do so. * * * No other instances of similar conduct were offered; the instances of prior sexual conduct between the defendant and the victim showed no pattern of the same type of behavior. The evidence was properly excluded, therefore, as insufficient to provide a basis for the inference that the victim acted as claimed by the defendant.

In holding that this single past instance of the victim's sexual conduct was properly excluded, we do not suggest that such evidence is never relevant or admissible. To be admissible, however, such evidence must fulfill the requirements of the statute within the context of the facts and circumstances of the case in which it arises. The evidence sought to be introduced in this case did not meet those requirements.[2]

There is no error.

Olden v. Kentucky

Supreme Court of the United States, 1988.
488 U.S. 227, 109 S.Ct. 480, 102 L.Ed.2d 513.

■ PER CURIAM. Petitioner James Olden and his friend Charlie Ray Harris, both of whom are black, were indicted for kidnapping, rape and forcible sodomy. The victim of the alleged crimes, Starla Matthews, a young white woman, gave the following account at trial: She and a friend, Regina Patton, had driven to Princeton, Kentucky, to exchange Christmas gifts with Bill Russell, petitioner's half-brother. After meeting Russell at a local car wash and exchanging presents with him, Matthews and Patton stopped in J.R.'s, a "bootlegging joint" serving a predominantly black clientele, to use the restroom. Matthews consumed several glasses of beer. As the bar became more crowded, she became increasingly nervous because she and Patton were the only white people there. When Patton refused to leave, Matthews sat at a separate table, hoping to demonstrate to her friend that she was upset. As time passed, however, Matthews lost track of Patton and became somewhat intoxicated. When petitioner told her that Patton had departed and had been in a car accident, she left the bar with petitioner and Harris to find out what had happened. She was driven in Harris's car to another location, where, threatening her with a knife, petitioner raped and sodomized her. Harris assisted by holding her arms. Later she was driven to a dump, where two other men joined the group. There, petitioner raped her once again. At her request, the men then dropped her off in the vicinity of Bill Russell's house.

On cross-examination, petitioner's counsel focused on a number of inconsistencies in Matthews' various accounts of the alleged crime. Matthews originally told the police that she had been raped by four men. Later, she claimed that she had been raped by only petitioner and Harris. At trial, she contended that petitioner was the sole rapist. Further, while Matthews testified at trial that petitioner had threatened her with a knife, she had not previously alleged that petitioner had been armed.

Russell, who also appeared as a State's witness, testified that on the evening in question he heard a noise outside his home and, when he went

---

[2] Before admitting evidence of prior sexual conduct, which otherwise meets the requirements of one of the statutory exceptions, General Statutes § 54–86f also requires balancing the probative value of the evidence with its prejudicial potential. We find this balancing test inapplicable to evidence fulfilling the requirements of subsection (4) because, if the defendant's constitutional rights would be violated by the exclusion of the evidence, no amount of prejudice to the victim could require its exclusion.

out to investigate, saw Matthews get out of Harris's car. Matthews immediately told Russell that she had just been raped by petitioner and Harris.

Petitioner and Harris asserted a defense of consent. According to their testimony, Matthews propositioned petitioner as he was about to leave the bar, and the two engaged in sexual acts behind the tavern. Afterwards, on Matthews' suggestion, Matthews, petitioner, and Harris left in Harris's car in search of cocaine. When they discovered that the seller was not at home, Matthews asked Harris to drive to a local dump so that she and petitioner could have sex once again. Harris complied. Later that evening, they picked up two other men, Richard Hickey and Chris Taylor, and drove to an establishment called "The Alley." Harris, Taylor, and Hickey went in, leaving petitioner and Matthews in the car. When Hickey and Harris returned, the men gave Hickey a ride to a store and then dropped Matthews off, at her request, in the vicinity of Bill Russell's home.

Taylor and Hickey testified for the defense and corroborated the defendants' account of the evening. While both acknowledged that they joined the group later than the time when the alleged rape occurred, both testified that Matthews did not appear upset. Hickey further testified that Matthews had approached him earlier in the evening at J.R.'s and told him that she was looking for a black man with whom to have sex. An independent witness also appeared for the defense and testified that he had seen Matthews, Harris and petitioner at a store called Big O's on the evening in question, that a policeman was in the store at the time, and that Matthews, who appeared alert, made no attempt to signal for assistance.

Although Matthews and Russell were both married to and living with other people at the time of the incident, they were apparently involved in an extramarital relationship. By the time of trial the two were living together, having separated from their respective spouses. Petitioner's theory of the case was that Matthews concocted the rape story to protect her relationship with Russell, who would have grown suspicious upon seeing her disembark from Harris's car. In order to demonstrate Matthews' motive to lie, it was crucial, petitioner contended, that he be allowed to introduce evidence of Matthews' and Russell's current cohabitation. Over petitioner's vehement objections, the trial court nonetheless granted the prosecutor's motion in limine to keep all evidence of Matthews' and Russell's living arrangement from the jury. Moreover, when the defense attempted to cross-examine Matthews about her living arrangements, after she had claimed during direct examination that she was living with her mother, the trial court sustained the prosecutor's objection.

Based on the evidence admitted at trial, the jury acquitted Harris of being either a principal or an accomplice to any of the charged offenses. Petitioner was likewise acquitted of kidnapping and rape. However, in a somewhat puzzling turn of events, the jury convicted petitioner alone of forcible sodomy. He was sentenced to ten years' imprisonment.

Petitioner appealed, asserting, inter alia, that the trial court's refusal to allow him to impeach Matthews' testimony by introducing evidence supporting a motive to lie deprived him of his Sixth Amendment right to confront witnesses against him. The Kentucky Court of Appeals upheld the conviction. The court specifically held that evidence that Matthews and Russell were living together at the time of trial was not barred by the State's rape shield law. Moreover, it acknowledged that the evidence in question was relevant to petitioner's theory of the case. But it held, nonetheless, that the evidence was properly excluded as "its probative value [was] outweighed by its possibility for prejudice." By way of explanation, the court stated: "[T]here were the undisputed facts of race; Matthews was white and Russell was black. For the trial court to have admitted into evidence testimony that Matthews and Russell were living together at the time of the trial may have created extreme prejudice against Matthews." Judge Clayton, who dissented but did not address the evidentiary issue, would have reversed petitioner's conviction both because he believed the jury's verdicts were "manifestly inconsistent," and because he found Matthews' testimony too incredible to provide evidence sufficient to uphold the verdict.

The Kentucky Court of Appeals failed to accord proper weight to petitioner's Sixth Amendment right "to be confronted with the witnesses against him." That right, incorporated in the Fourteenth Amendment and therefore available in state proceedings, Pointer v. Texas, 380 U.S. 400 (1965), includes the right to conduct reasonable cross-examination. Davis v. Alaska, 415 U.S. 308, 315–316 (1974).

In Davis v. Alaska, we observed that, subject to "the broad discretion of a trial judge to preclude repetitive and unduly harassing interrogation * * *, the cross-examiner has traditionally been allowed to impeach, i.e., discredit, the witness." Id., at 316. We emphasized that "the exposure of a witness' motivation in testifying is a proper and important function of the constitutionally protected right of cross-examination." Recently, in Delaware v. Van Arsdall, 475 U.S. 673 (1986), we reaffirmed Davis, and held that "a criminal defendant states a violation of the Confrontation Clause by showing that he was prohibited from engaging in otherwise appropriate cross-examination designed to show a prototypical form of bias on the part of the witness, and thereby 'to expose to the jury the facts from which jurors * * * could appropriately draw inferences relating to the reliability of the witness.'"

In the instant case, petitioner has consistently asserted that he and Matthews engaged in consensual sexual acts and that Matthews—out of her fear of jeopardizing her relationship with Russell—lied when she told Russell she had been raped and has continued to lie since. It is plain to us that "[a] reasonable jury might have received a significantly different impression of [the witness'] credibility had [defense counsel] been permitted to pursue his proposed line of cross-examination." Delaware v. Van Arsdall, supra, at 680.

The Kentucky Court of Appeals did not dispute, and indeed acknowledged, the relevance of the impeachment evidence. Nonetheless, without acknowledging the significance of, or even adverting to, petitioner's constitutional right to confrontation, the court held that petitioner's rights to effective cross-examination was outweighed by the danger that revealing Matthews' interracial relationship would prejudice the jury against her. While a trial court may, of course, impose reasonable limits on defense counsel's inquiry into the potential bias of a prosecution witness, to take account of such factors as "harassment, prejudice, confusion of the issues, the witness' safety, or interrogation that [would be] repetitive or only marginally relevant," Delaware v. Van Arsdall, supra, at 679, the limitation here was beyond reason. Speculation as to the effect of jurors' racial biases cannot justify exclusion of cross-examination with such strong potential to demonstrate the falsity of Matthews' testimony.

In Delaware v. Van Arsdall, supra, we held that "the constitutionally improper denial of a defendant's opportunity to impeach a witness for bias, like other Confrontation Clause errors, is subject to Chapman [v. California, 386 U.S. 18 (1967)] harmless-error analysis." Id., at 684. Thus we stated:

> "The correct inquiry is whether, assuming that the damaging potential of the cross-examination were fully realized, a reviewing court might nonetheless say that the error was harmless beyond a reasonable doubt. Whether such an error is harmless in a particular case depends upon a host of factors, all readily accessible to reviewing courts. These factors include the importance of the witness' testimony in the prosecution's case, whether the testimony was cumulative, the presence or absence of evidence corroborating or contradicting the testimony of the witness on material points, the extent of cross-examination otherwise permitted, and, of course, the overall strength of the prosecution's case." Ibid.

Here, Matthews' testimony was central, indeed crucial, to the prosecution's case. Her story, which was directly contradicted by that of petitioner and Harris, was corroborated only by the largely derivative testimony of Russell, whose impartiality would also have been somewhat impugned by revelation of his relationship with Matthews. Finally, as demonstrated graphically by the jury's verdicts, which cannot be squared with the State's theory of the alleged crime, and by Judge Clayton's dissenting opinion below, the State's case against petitioner was far from overwhelming. In sum, considering the relevant Van Arsdall factors within the context of this case, we find it impossible to conclude "beyond a reasonable doubt" that the restriction on petitioner's right to confrontation was harmless.

The motion for leave to proceed in forma pauperis and the petition for certiorari are granted, the judgment of the Kentucky Court of Appeals is reversed, and the case is remanded for further proceedings not inconsistent with this opinion.

It is so ordered.

[Justice Brennan took no part in the consideration or decision of this case.]

■ JUSTICE MARSHALL, dissenting.

I continue to believe that summary dispositions deprive litigants of a fair opportunity to be heard on the merits and create a significant risk that the Court is rendering an erroneous or ill-advised decision that may confuse the lower courts. I therefore dissent from the Court's decision today to reverse summarily the decision below.

NOTE

See Fed.R.Evid. 412, Cal.Evidence Code § 1103. See also Berger, "Man's Trial, Woman's Tribulation: Rape Cases in the Courtroom," 77 Colum.L.Rev. 1 (1977); S. Brownmiller, Against Our Will: Men, Women and Rape, (1975); and S. Estrich, Real Rape (1987).

UNITED STATES v. PLATERO, 72 F.3d 806 (10 Cir. 1995). Platero, a private security guard, was accused of raping Susan Francis. Francis had spent much of the evening with Vernon Laughlin (though she was married to another man). According to the couple, they had dinner at a restaurant, then went to a bar, and were headed out of town in Francis's car when Platero, impersonating a police officer, pulled them over. After questioning the couple, Platero said he would give Laughlin a break, and told him to walk away. After further questioning Francis and threatening her with charges, Platero handcuffed her and drove her away to a secluded place where, according to Francis, he raped her and forced her to have oral sex. Platero then drove her back to her car where Laughlin was waiting. Laughlin saw Francis buttoning up her blouse and fixing her clothes. Laughlin and Francis then drove away. She told him that she had been raped, and he drove her to a hospital.

At trial (in federal court, because the incident occurred on a Navajo reservation), Platero contended that the car had been stopped when he came up to it. He admitted having sex with Francis but contended that it was consensual. By the time of trial, Francis and Laughlin were living together. Platero sought to prove that the relationship had become an intimate one before the alleged rape; Anna Mike, Laughlin's former girlfriend, was willing to testify that she believed Francis and Laughlin had begun an affair two years before that time. The trial judge excluded the evidence and Platero was convicted. The appellate court reversed and remanded, holding that the admissibility of the evidence depended on whether there was an existing relationship between Francis and Laughlin at the time of the alleged crime; if there was, then *Olden* gave Platero a right to cross-examine Francis as to that relationship. On remand, the trial judge, making his own credibility determinations, concluded that no sexual relationship between Laughlin and Francis existed at the time of the alleged crime, and he let the conviction stand.

Platero appealed again, contending that the determination of whether the relationship existed should have been made by the jury, not by the judge. Though the prior decision had, according to the appellate court, left the matter to the judge, and under the doctrine of law of the case that might appear to be binding, there had been an intervening change of law. After the first appeal, Fed. R. Evid. 412(c) had been amended by removing a sentence that read: "Notwithstanding subdivision (b) of rule 104, if the relevancy of the evidence which the accused seeks to offer in the trial depends upon the fulfillment of a condition of fact, the court, at the hearing in chambers or at a subsequent hearing in chambers scheduled for such purpose, shall accept evidence on the issue of whether such condition of fact is fulfilled and shall determine such issue." The court noted that this provision had been constitutionally suspect. The court went on to hold that the determination of whether there had been a sexual relationship at the critical time was a matter of conditional relevance that should be determined by the jury. The court said, "If instead the trial judge proceeds to decide the preliminary relevancy-conditioned-on-fact issue against the proponent where the jury *could* reasonably find the fact to exist, the judge has violated the proponent's right to a jury trial * * *." The court concluded that Platero did present enough evidence to allow a jury to find reasonably that the relationship existed, that exclusion of the evidence was a violation of Platero's confrontation right under *Olden*, and that the error was not harmless.

Johnson v. Elk Lake School District

United States Court of Appeals, Third Circuit, 2002.
283 F.3d 138.

■ BECKER, CHIEF JUDGE.

This case arises out of plaintiff Betsy Sue Johnson's claim that her guidance counselor Wayne Stevens sexually harassed and abused her while she was a high school student in the Elk Lake School District.

* * *

I. Facts and Procedural History

Johnson entered the Elk Lake School District high school as a freshman in September 1991. Sometime in November or December of that year Johnson began making regular visits to Stevens's office to discuss family difficulties. Johnson contends that shortly thereafter, in December 1991, Stevens began sexually harassing and abusing her. She alleges that for the next two years Stevens repeatedly sent her letters, roses, cards, and other suggestive correspondence, attempted on numerous occasions to hug and kiss her without her consent, and at one point fondled her breasts and vagina.[The trial court granted summary judgment on plaintiff's claims against the school district but allowed her claims against Stevens to go to trial. The jury returned a verdict in favor of Stevens, from which Johnson appealed. Among the errors claimed on appeal was the exclusion of the other acts testimony described below.]

III. Exclusion of Radwanski's Testimony Under Rule 415

A. The Incident

During the course of the trial, Johnson attempted to introduce the testimony of Karen Radwanski, a teacher's associate in the high school's restaurant training program and a friend of Stevens, regarding an incident in which Stevens allegedly sexually assaulted her in the office of another teacher, Tony Blaisure. Radwanski had just walked into the office carrying lunch when Stevens allegedly picked her up and threw her over his shoulder. According to Radwanski, who was wearing a skirt at the time, Stevens's hand went up her skirt and touched her in the crotch area while he raised her off the floor. Stevens soon let her down to the floor and the two of them, along with Blaisure, proceeded to sit down and eat lunch together.

Whether Stevens's alleged touching of Radwanski's crotch was intentional or accidental is unclear from the record, as Radwanski offered somewhat inconsistent accounts of the incident. In her deposition Radwanski was asked whether Stevens's finger "lingered . . . on [her] crotch for any period of time." She responded, "I have to say no." In an earlier interview conducted by Johnson's attorney outside the presence of opposing counsel, Radwanski, under oath, was asked if Stevens had "left his hand [on her crotch] for a while, a moment, two moments or so," to which she responded, "Yeah." When asked during her deposition whether she thought the touching was intentional, Radwanski seemed unsure: "I guess maybe at the time I didn't feel right, but I guess the greater part of me not wanting to think anything was just like, you know, shrugged it off, no big deal."

* * *

C. History and Background of Rules 413–15

Federal Rules of Evidence 413–15 are relatively recent additions to the Rules, adopted by Congress as part of the Violent Crime Control and Law Enforcement Act of 1994. Evidence law has historically prohibited the admission into evidence of "other crimes, wrongs, or acts. . . to prove the character of a person in order to show action in conformity therewith." Fed. R. Evid. 404(b). Rules 413–15 establish exceptions to the general prohibition on character evidence in cases involving sexual assault and child molestation. Rules 413 and 414 apply to criminal proceedings, while Rule 415 applies to civil trials.

Ever since their initial proposal, Rules 413–15 have been met with hostility by the legal establishment. * * * Although Congress bypassed the ordinary rulemaking procedures when adopting Rules 413–15, the enacting legislation provided the Judicial Conference 150 days within which to make and submit alternative recommendations on the rules to Congress. The Judicial Conference's Advisory Committee on Evidence Rules, with what it noted was "highly unusual unanimity," ardently opposed the new rules, fearing that they "could diminish significantly the protections that have safeguarded persons accused in criminal cases and parties in civil cases against undue prejudice." Embracing the views of the Advisory Committee, the Conference recommended that Congress "reconsider its policy determinations underlying Evidence Rules 413–415" or, in the alternative, adopt amendments to Rules 404 and 405 proposed by the Advisory Committee. Congress rejected both alternatives, and the rules stand today as originally enacted.

D. Standards for Admission of Evidence under Rule 415

In order for evidence of a past act to be admitted under Rule 415, the District Court must determine whether the act satisfies the applicable definition of an "offense of sexual assault" provided by Rule 413(d). * * *

Although the language of Rule 413(d) is ambiguous as to whether the past "offense of sexual assault" must be a conviction, the legislative history of Rules 413–15 indicates that Congress intended to allow admission not only of prior convictions for sexual offenses, but also of uncharged conduct. * * *

[After citing references to legislative history that supported the point that the prior offense need not have resulted in conviction, the court went on to decide that there was sufficient evidence of the commission of a prior offense to satisfy the requirements of Fed. R. Evid. 104(b).]

Even if a trial court is satisfied that the proffered past act evidence satisfies Rule 104(b), however, it may still exclude it under Federal Rule of Evidence 403 * * * *

Having concluded that Rule 403 is applicable to Rules 413–15, we now turn to the manner in which the balancing inquiry ought to be performed. Relying on the legislative history, a number of courts and commentators have concluded that Rule 403 should be applied to Rules 413–15 with a thumb on the scale in favor of admissibility. * * * Indeed, in his speech that is referenced as part of the "authoritative" legislative history of Rules 413–15, [Justice Department lawyer] David Karp observed that there is "an underlying legislative judgment . . . that the sort of evidence that is admissible pursuant to proposed Rules 413–15 is typically relevant and probative, and that its probative value is normally not outweighed by any risk of prejudice or other adverse considerations."

In our view, this characterization of the role of Rule 403 is overly simplified. It makes sense when the past act sought to be introduced under Rules 413–15 is demonstrated with specificity, and is sufficiently similar to

---

* [As they were originally enacted, and as they stood at the time of the *Johnson* decision, Fed. R. Evid. 413 and 414 provided that evidence within each of the designated categories "is admissible, and may be considered for its bearing on any matter to which it is relevant." Similarly, Fed. R. Evid. 415 provided that evidence falling within its scope "is admissible and may be considered as provided in Rule 413 and Rule 414 of these rules. The court decided that the "is admissible" language did not deprive the trial court of discretion to exclude the evidence under Rule 403. In 2011, as part of the general restyling of the Federal Rules, these Rules were amended to provide that in each case "the court may admit" the prescribed evidence. Eds.]

When similar - congress
intended probative to
outweigh prejudicial effect.

the type of sexual assault allegedly committed by the defendant. *See United States v. Guardia*, 135 F.3d 1326, 1331 (10th Cir. 1998) (noting that "the similarity of the prior acts" to the acts at issue in the case is a factor to be considered in determining their probative value). In these archetypal cases, where the propensity inference that can be drawn from the past act evidence is greatest, Congress surely intended for the probative value of the evidence to outweigh its prejudicial effect, and, conversely, did not want Rule 403 factors such as undue delay, waste of time, confusion of the issues, etc., to justify exclusion.

not similar:

less probative value.

In other cases, however, where the past act is not substantially similar to the act for which the defendant is being tried, and/or where the past act cannot be demonstrated with sufficient specificity, the propensity inference provided by the past act is weaker, and no presumption in favor of admissibility is warranted. Where a past act cannot be shown with reasonable certainty, its probative value is reduced and it may prejudice the defendant unfairly, confuse the issues, mislead the jury, and result in undue delay and wasted time—all reasons for excluding evidence under Rule 403. The same can be said of evidence of past acts that are dissimilar to the act for which the defendant is being tried; in particular, the introduction of dissimilar past acts runs the risk of confusing the issues in the trial and wasting valuable time. Also relevant to the Rule 403 balancing analysis are the additional factors recognized by the Tenth Circuit in *Guardia*: "the closeness in time of the prior acts to the charged acts, the frequency of the prior acts, the presence or lack of intervening events, and the need for evidence beyond the testimony of the defendant and alleged victim." 135 F.3d at 1330 (internal citations omitted).

Finally, it bears repeating that despite these general guidelines, the Rule 403 balancing inquiry is, at its core, an essentially discretionary one that gives the trial court significant latitude to exclude evidence.

E. Discussion

Johnson contends that Radwanski's testimony as to the touching incident with Stevens qualified as an "offense of sexual assault" under Rules 413 and 415, and that the District Court therefore erred in excluding it. Moreover, at trial she objected to the fact that the Court did not hold an *in limine* hearing on the matter. We apply the legal standards described above, and review the District Court's evidentiary rulings for abuse of discretion, although our review of the Court's interpretation of the Federal Rules of Evidence is plenary.

Penn Law
must be intentionally

The District Court correctly noted that in order for the touching incident to qualify as an "offense of sexual assault" under Rule 413(d)'s definition, Pennsylvania law . . . requires that the touching have been done intentionally. * * *

In deciding to exclude Radwanski's testimony, the District Court did not indicate what standard for admission it was applying to the evidence. In keeping with *Huddleston*, the Court was not obliged to hold an *in limine* hearing, as requested by Johnson, or make a formal finding under Rule 104(a) when excluding the evidence. Under *Huddleston*, the Court needed only to ask itself whether a jury could reasonably find by a preponderance of the evidence that Stevens committed the act intentionally, provided that the Court was satisfied that the evidence need not be excluded under Rule 403. Although the Court did not say so explicitly, it appears to us that the Court concluded that Radwanski's testimony did not satisfy Rule 403, and it accordingly—and appropriately—bypassed the *Huddleston* reasonable jury determination.

The basis for the Court's Rule 403 determination seems to have been that Radwanski's equivocal testimony was insufficiently specific as to the intentionality of Stevens's conduct. The District Court stated, "I think there's insufficient evidence that the touching was in any way intentional. . .". Lacking more specific evidence of intentionality, the Court apparently concluded that the probative value of the evidence was slight and was outweighed by Rule 403's concerns of prejudice, undue delay, waste of time, etc. This judgment appears to us to be sound given the equivocal nature of Radwanski's testimony as regarding the intentionality of Stevens's conduct.

Additionally, we find the exclusion of the evidence justifiable for a reason not stressed by the District Court: the differences between Stevens's alleged assaults of Radwanski and Johnson. The former occurred in another teacher's office with that teacher present, involved an adult co-worker of Stevens, and consisted of a bizarre incident in which Stevens lifted Radwanski off the ground and placed her on his shoulders. The latter is said to have taken place with no one else present in Stevens's office, involved a minor to whom Stevens served as guidance counselor, and allegedly involved Stevens making more direct sexual advances upon a much younger female. In our view, these dissimilarities reduced significantly the probative value of Radwanski's testimony. The case law is in accord.

[margin note: differences b/t incident]

We also consider it relevant that the alleged touching of Radwanski appears to have been an isolated incident. Although Johnson presented evidence of rumors of Stevens acting inappropriately around female students in her attempt to attach § 1983 liability to the Administration, during her trial against Stevens she did not attempt to present any other evidence of offenses of sexual assault allegedly perpetrated by Stevens besides the lone incident with Radwanski. While the isolated nature of the incident alone would probably not be enough to warrant excluding it, we nevertheless consider it a relevant factor supporting the District Court's decision.

In sum, the uncertainty of the testimony regarding intentionality, the dissimilarities between the similar and alleged acts, and the isolated nature of the Radwanski incident reduced significantly the probative value of Radwanski's testimony. Given this reduced probative value, any presumption in favor of admissibility was unwarranted, and the District Court's exclusion of the evidence can be justified on grounds that its introduction might have prejudiced Stevens unfairly, misled the jury, confused the issues, and wasted valuable trial time. Accordingly, we cannot say that the Court abused its discretion in excluding Radwanski's testimony.

[Affirmed.]

NOTE

In People v. Watkins, 2012 WL 2076841 (Mich., June 8, 2012), the court decided that MCL 768.27a, a statutorily enacted state counterpart to Fed. R. Evid. 414, conflicts with and was intended to displace Mich. R. Evid. 404(b) in this context, but is subject to balancing under Mich. R. Evid. 403 (those two rules being state counterparts to the Federal Rules of the same numbers; Rule 404(b) excludes evidence of other wrongs offered "to prove the character of a person in order to show action in conformity therewith"). The court further held that, in conducting the balance under Rule 403, a trial judge should count other-acts evidence falling within the statute on the "probative value" side of the scale rather than on the "prejudicial effect" side, because to do otherwise would be to "resurrect" the applicability in this context of Rule 404(b), which the Legislature rejected in passing the statute.

Roger C. Park, Character at the Crossroads
49 Hastings L.J. 717, 758–64 (1998).

Recidivism and Comparative Propensity

Recidivism studies measure the rate of reversion to criminal behavior after a convicted perpetrator has been released from custody. Commentators have used information about recidivism rates as one yardstick for measuring the probative value of different types of character evidence. They have made the understandable assumption that the higher the rate of recidivism for a crime, the better the case for admission of propensity evidence when a defendant has been charged with that crime. For example, Professor Edward Imwinkelried asks us to think of the 1994 "crime bill" [the Violent Crime Control and Law Enforcement Act, which added Federal Rules of Evidence 413-415] as an experiment in selective abolition of the rule against character evidence.[121] He criticizes Congress for selecting the wrong crimes for the experiment. He argues that sex crimes have "minimal probative value as predictors of the accused's conduct," and suggests that "[i]t would make far more sense to initiate the experiment by selecting crimes with higher recidivism rates." Noting that in a leading study the reported recidivism rate for burglary was 31.9%, while for rape it was 7.7%, he suggests that burglary would have been a better candidate than rape. Similarly, Professor Katharine K. Baker states that:

> Advocates of Rule 413 also unabashedly and without proof suggest that rapists are more likely than other criminals to repeat their acts. The evidence that we have is to the contrary. A 1989 Bureau of Justice Statistics recidivism study found that only 7.7% of released rapists

---

[121] Edward J. Imwinkelried, *Undertaking the Task of Reforming the American Character Evidence Prohibition: The Importance of Getting the Experiment Off On the Right Foot*, 22 FORDHAM URB.L.J., 285, 287 (1995).

were re-arrested for rape. In contrast, 33.5% of released larcenists were re-arrested for larceny; 31.9% of released burglars were re-arrested for burglary; and 24.8% of drug offenders were re-arrested for drug offenses. Only homicide had a lower recidivism rate than rape. It is true that released rapists are more likely than other released prisoners to be re-arrested for rape, but that rapists are more likely than others to rape again does not distinguish rapists from other criminals. Larcenists are twenty-five percent more likely to be re-arrested for larceny than rapists are to be re-arrested for rape. Arguing from the statistics, a crime-based prior act exception is better suited to larcenists and drug offenders than to rapists.[125]

Recidivism data can indeed be helpful in assessing the probative value of other-crimes evidence. However, an assessment of the probative value of other-crime character evidence requires a comparison of the criminal propensity of prior offenders with the criminal propensity of other persons. To estimate comparative propensity, one needs to consider more than naked recidivism data. When a given crime has a low incidence in the general population, the probative value of evidence of another instance of the same crime will be greater than would have been the case had the crime been more common, even if the recidivism rate for the crime is low.

As an illustration, suppose burglary by parachute to be a crime separately defined by the criminal code. Were that the case, a prior instance of burglary by parachute, one that had no role in focusing suspicion on the defendant charged again with the same crime, would be more probative in a burglary by parachute case than a prior instance of common burglary in a common burglary case. That would be so even if burglars by parachute had the same absolute propensity to repeat the crime of burglary by parachute that common burglars had to repeat the crime of common burglary. That is, if 30% of all burglars by parachute repeated the crime of burglary by parachute, and 30% of all common burglars repeated the crime of common burglary, the other crime evidence would still be more probative in the burglary by parachute case. The absolute propensity of the parachute burglar would be the same as that of the common burglar, but the parachute burglar's comparative propensity would be much higher. A person with a burglary by parachute record would be many times more likely to commit that crime than a person chosen at random from the general population (or from the population of all burglars). This common-sense induction is reflected in the accepted rule that crimes that have a distinctive *modus operandi* are admissible to show propensity.[126]

---

[125] Katharine K. Baker, *Once a Rapist? Motivational and Relevancy in Rape Law*, 110 HARV.L.REV. 563, 578–79 (1997) (footnotes omitted) * * *.

[126] I am here using "propensity" simply to refer to a proclivity or tendency of the defendant. In modus operandi cases, like habit cases, evidence is offered to show a propensity that is considered to be more narrow than a trait of character. For example, evidence of a propensity to drown spouses in the bathtub, *see* Rex v. Smith, 11 Cr.App.R. 229, 84 L.J.K.B. 2153 (1915), or to warm freon by heating it with a coil, *see* Halloran v. Virginia Chemicals Inc., 361 N.E.2d 991, 996 (N.Y.1977), is considered not to be character evidence. American courts would, however, avoid the use of the word "propensity" in describing evidence considered to be

* * * [N]ote the following reported same-crime recidivism rates [from Allen J. Beck, Recidivism of Prisoners in 1983 (1989)]:

Rape..7.7%
Burglary...31.9%
Larceny 33.5%
Drugs..24.8%

From these figures, both Professors Imwinkelried and Baker separately conclude that rape is a relatively unpromising candidate for a same-crime exception because of rape's relatively low same-crime recidivism rate.

* * *

[I]t would make more sense to focus on what the data suggest about comparative propensity than on the naked recidivism rate. * * * Examining Table 2, one can see that prisoners released from a sentence of rape were 10.1 times more likely than the other prisoners to be re-arrested for rape, while prisoners released from burglary sentences were 2.3 times more likely than the other prisoners to be re-arrested for burglary. The figures for larceny and for drug offenses are even lower. Thus, the same-crime comparative propensity of the prisoners released from rape sentences appears to be higher than that of those released from sentences for burglary, larceny, or drug offenses. These comparative propensity statistics suggest that rape is a better candidate for an exception to a rule against other crimes evidence than those other offenses.[129]

Table 2. Same-Crime Comparative Propensity

		Ratio- Other Offenders	Ratio- General Population[129]
Rape arrests			
Previously held for—			
Rape 7.70%	Other 0.76%	10.1	163
Burglary arrests			
Previously held for—			
Burglary 31.90%	Other 13.70%	2.3	56
Larceny arrests			
Previously held for—			
Larceny 33.50%	Other 19.65%	1.7	19
Drug offense arrests			
Previously held for—			
Drug 24.80%	Other 17.06%	1.5	24

admissible under the modus or habit concepts, because "propensity" is considered a synonym for "character," and if deemed evidence of "character" the evidence would be inadmissible.

[129] The ratio was obtained by dividing the three-year arrest rate reported in the Beck study by three, then comparing that number with the arrest rate in the general population in 1986, as reported in Federal Bureau of Investigation, Crime in the United States 165 (1986).

QUESTIONS

Does the information set forth above justify Rule 413's sexual assault exception to the rule against character evidence?

Suppose that it could be established that a person who has once committed homicide is 200 times more likely to commit another homicide than a person who has no history of homicide. Would that fact justify allowing evidence of another homicide to be admitted as character evidence against a defendant accused of homicide?*

E. SIMILAR HAPPENINGS

Simon v. Kennebunkport

Supreme Judicial Court of Maine, 1980.
417 A.2d 982.

■ GLASSMAN, JUSTICE.

On the morning of July 22, 1977, the appellant, Irene Simon, sustained a broken hip when she stumbled and fell while walking on a sidewalk along Ocean Avenue in Kennebunkport. The elderly woman filed a complaint against the appellee, Town of Kennebunkport (Town), alleging that her injury was proximately caused by a defect in the design or construction of the sidewalk. Following a trial in the Superior Court, York County, the jury determined by special verdict that no defect in the sidewalk had proximately caused the appellant to fall, and judgment was entered for the appellee. The appellant contends that the presiding Justice erred in excluding evidence, offered to establish the defective condition of the sidewalk, that during the two years prior to the accident many other persons stumbled or fell at the location. We vacate the judgment.

Greg Quevillon and Anthony Cooper both operated businesses in the building in front of which the appellant fell. At trial Quevillon testified that the condition of the uneven, inclined sidewalk had not changed from the time it was constructed in 1974 or 1975 until the time of the accident in 1977. The appellant then attempted to elicit from this witness whether he had observed other persons fall at the location. The presiding Justice sustained the Town's objection, ruling that although the appellant could establish that the condition of the sidewalk had remained unchanged since its construction she could not offer evidence that other persons had fallen during this period. The appellant then represented that "if permitted to testify both Mr. Quevillon and Mr. Cooper would state that they saw nearly one person a day fall on that particular sidewalk, and * * * evidence of prior fall[s] is admissible where it goes to show a defect." Later, referring to the proposed testimony of Cooper, the appellant stated:

---

* On the comparative propensity of homicide offenders, see Roger C. Park, Character at the Crossroads, 49 Hastings L.J. 717, 727 n. 27 (1998). Park concludes that as with rapists, the comparative propensity of homicide offenders is very high; although they are unlikely to commit another homicide, they are many times (perhaps on the order of 200 times) more likely to do so than is a member of the general population.

My offer of proof is that if permitted to testify this witness would indicate that on similar conditions of weather, and under conditions where the road was identical to that, the condition of July 22, 1979 [sic], he saw approximately 100 people stumble or fall on that particular portion of the roadway.

* * *

In a negligence action, evidence of other similar accidents or occurrences may be relevant circumstantially to show a defective or dangerous condition, notice thereof or causation on the occasion in question. The absence of other accidents or occurrences may also be probative on these issues. Nevertheless, Maine courts, with only rare exceptions, traditionally excluded such evidence on the ground that it "tends to draw away the minds of the jury from the point in issue (negligence of the defendant at the time and place of the accident), and to excite prejudice, and mislead them; and, moreover, the adverse party, having no notice of such a course of evidence, is not prepared to rebut it."

The genesis of an inflexible rule excluding other-accident evidence is commonly believed to be the early Massachusetts case of Collins v. Inhabitants of Dorchester, 60 Mass. (6 Cush.) 396 (1850), which reasoned that such evidence was largely irrelevant, involved proof of collateral facts and engendered unfair surprise. The overwhelming majority of jurisdictions, including Massachusetts, have since either rejected or abandoned a positive rule of exclusion in favor of a standard of discretion. These courts hold that where the proponent can show that other accidents occurred under circumstances substantially similar to those prevailing at the time of the injury in question such evidence is admissible subject to exclusion by the trial court when the probative value of the evidence on the issues of defect, notice or causation is substantially outweighed by the danger of unfair prejudice or confusion of the issues or by consideration of undue delay.

A blanket rule of irrelevance is manifestly incompatible with modern principles of evidence. Although the introduction of other-accident evidence may carry with it the problems associated with inquiry into collateral matters, such evidence may also be highly probative on material issues of a negligence action, as illustrated by the instant case. Early cases failed to discern that admitting this evidence for its circumstantial force is not inconsistent with the fundamental principle that negligence liability is to be predicated on absence of due care under the circumstances at the time and place of injury. Although not rejecting prior case law, several later decisions of this Court appeared to eschew a *per se* rule as unnecessarily broad and to recognize that the similarity requirement, together with the trial court's discretion, adequately safeguards the proper use of this evidence.

Whatever the continued vitality following these cases of an absolute prohibition against other-accident evidence, it is clear that such a rule did not survive the adoption of our new Rules of Evidence in 1976. [The court reviews Maine Rules of Evidence 401–03, which are based on, and similar in substance to, Fed. R. Evid. 401–03.] As with other determinations of admissibility involving the balancing of probative value against prejudicial effect, the admission of other-accident evidence is committed to the sound discretion of the presiding Justice.[2]

In the case at bar, it is readily apparent that the ruling of the presiding Justice constituted an abuse of discretion which rose to the level of prejudicial error. Evidence that in the two years prior to the accident as many as one hundred persons stumbled or fell under similar circumstances at the same location, unchanged in condition, clearly satisfies the substantial-similarity foundational requirement and is highly probative on the material issue whether the sidewalk was in a defective condition at the time of the appellant's fall. As demonstrated by its prepared objection to the introduction of this evidence, the Town was well aware of the evidence before trial and therefore would not have been unfairly surprised by its admission. Because the evidence was to be offered through the personal observations of two witnesses, its introduction would not have consumed an inordinate amount of time or tended to confuse or excite the jury. The excluded evidence was crucial to the case of the appellant. The judgment of the Superior Court cannot stand.

* * *

All concurring.

Morris, Studies in the Law of Torts
87–89 (1952).[*]

* * * In the simple cases, safety-history evidence favorable to the defendant may be of greater weight than safety-history evidence favorable to the plaintiff. In Field v. Davis, the plaintiff was hurt when his mules backed his wagon out of the defendant's grain elevator and over the side of a railing-protected inclined roadway. The defendant was allowed to prove that thousands of wagons had been driven into his elevator and no other accident had ever happened on the incline. The jury might have been able to visualize the incline and appreciate its safety without such evidence; nevertheless, the fact that the plaintiff was injured is itself some slight evidence of danger, and the defendant deserves the protection of safety-history evidence—which tends to check the jury from formulating unsound general theories as to the danger of inclined roadways.

---

[2] At a later stage of the trial, the Town offered evidence that the appellant's husband, who was walking directly in front of the appellant at the time of the accident, did not fall as tending to show the absence of a defect in the sidewalk. Over the appellant's objection, the presiding Justice admitted this evidence, ruling that, unlike the excluded evidence of prior falls, the "non-fall" evidence related to the immediate time frame of the accident. In view of our disposition of this appeal, we need not decide whether this ruling, assigned as an additional ground of error by the appellant, constituted an abuse of discretion and, if so, whether the error was harmless. See M.R.Evid. 103(a).

The difference between evidence of safety history offered by a plaintiff and that offered by a defendant is illustrated perhaps more sharply in Charlton v. St. L. & S.F.R.R. The plaintiff's deceased, a brakeman, was knocked off a ladder on the side of a moving boxcar by a standpipe maintained near the tracks. Another brakeman was allowed to testify that he brushed his arm on the same standpipe under similar circumstances. The problem of danger seems so simple that, after proof of the distance between cars and the standpipe, jurors could probably decide this case without the second brakeman's testimony as well as they could with it. While this testimony probably did no harm, a trial judge who excluded it would not have abused his discretion. But if the railroad had offered to prove that no brakeman other than the deceased had ever been brushed by the standpipe, in spite of constant exposure, the evidence should be received. The deceased's injury was proof that such an accident could happen. Unless the distance was so large that a trainman could be hit only by assuming an unlikely posture, jurors with the actual dimensions of the clearance before them are not likely to judge the clearance safe. But the situation may be safer than it seems to those without actual experience in railroading. Therefore, a defendant's proof of favorable safety history has greater probative value in this kind of case than a plaintiff's proof of unfavorable safety history. * * *

HYPOTHETICAL

A sues the X Golf Course for damages for personal injuries arising out of a slip-and-fall accident. A, a business invitee of X, was proceeding from the parking lot to the starting area and was walking across a new, level, cement veranda that has a smooth surface. A was wearing golf shoes with half-worn spikes and her feet slipped from under her, causing her serious injury. X calls B, the manager of the golf course, to testify that, during the year the cement veranda has been in existence, she had never been informed of any accidents on this area other than A's, and that between 3500 and 4000 persons per month had traversed the area wearing golf shoes. A objects to B's proposed testimony on the grounds of irrelevancy and that such negative evidence is precluded by law. What result?

F. SUBSEQUENT PRECAUTIONS

Tuer v. McDonald

Court of Appeals of Maryland, 1997
701 A.2d 1101.

■ WILNER, JUDGE.

This is a medical malpractice action filed by Mary Tuer, the surviving spouse and personal representative of her late husband, Eugene, arising from Eugene's death at St. Joseph's Hospital on November 3, 1992. Although the hospital and several doctors were initially joined as defendants, we are concerned here only with the action against Mr. Tuer's two cardiac surgeons, Drs. McDonald and Brawley, and their professional association.

A jury in the Circuit Court for Baltimore County returned a verdict for those defendants, the judgment on which was affirmed by the Court of Special Appeals. *Tuer v. McDonald,* 112 Md.App. 121, 684 A.2d 478 (1996). We granted *certiorari* to consider whether the trial court erred in excluding evidence that, after Mr. Tuer's death, the defendants changed the protocol regarding the administration of the drug Heparin to patients awaiting coronary artery bypass surgery. The court's ruling was based on Maryland Rule 5–407, which renders evidence of subsequent remedial measures inadmissible to prove negligence or culpable conduct. We shall hold that the court did not err and therefore shall affirm the judgment of the Court of Special Appeals.

FACTUAL BACKGROUND

The relevant underlying facts are not in substantial dispute. Mr. Tuer, 63, had suffered from angina pectoris for about 16 years. In September, 1992, his cardiologist, Dr. Louis Grenzer, recommended that he undergo coronary artery bypass graft (CABG) surgery and referred him to the defendants for that purpose. The surgery was initially scheduled for November 9, 1992. On October 30, however, Mr. Tuer was admitted to St. Joseph's Hospital after suffering chest pains the night before, and the operation was rescheduled for the morning of November 2.

After a second episode of chest pain following Mr. Tuer's admission, Dr. Grenzer prescribed Atenolol, a beta blocker that reduces pressure on the heart, and Heparin, an anti-coagulant, to help stabilize the angina. The Heparin was administered intravenously throughout the weekend, and, with the other medication Mr. Tuer was receiving, it achieved its purpose; there were no further incidents of chest pains or shortness of breath. The defendants assumed responsibility for Mr. Tuer on November 1. Dr. McDonald was to perform the operation, with Dr. Brawley assisting.

The operation was scheduled to begin between 8:00 and 9:00 a.m. on November 2. In accordance with the protocol then followed by the defendants and by St. Joseph's Hospital, an anesthesiologist caused the administration of Heparin to be discontinued at 5:30 that morning. That was done to allow the drug to metabolize so that Mr. Tuer would not have an anti-coagulant in his blood when the surgery commenced.

Both Mr. Tuer and Dr. McDonald prepared for the 9:00 a.m. surgery. Shortly before the surgery was due to begin, however, Dr. McDonald was called to deal with an emergency involving another patient, whose condition was more critical than that of Mr. Tuer, and that required a three-to four-hour postponement of Mr. Tuer's operation. Mr. Tuer was taken to the coronary surgery unit (CSU) in the meanwhile, where he could be closely monitored. Dr. McDonald considered restarting the Heparin but decided not to do so.

Dr. McDonald next saw Mr. Tuer just after 1:00 p.m., when he was summoned to the CSU and found his patient short of breath and with arrhythmia and low blood pressure. Quickly thereafter, Mr. Tuer went into cardiac arrest. Appropriate resuscitation efforts, including some seven hours of surgery, were undertaken, and, although Mr. Tuer survived the operation, he died the next day. Following Mr. Tuer's death—apparently because of it—the defendants and St. Joseph's Hospital changed the protocol with respect to discontinuing Heparin for patients with unstable angina.[2] Under the new protocol, Heparin is continued until the patient is taken into the operating room; had that protocol been in effect on November 2, 1992, the Heparin would not have been discontinued at 5:30 a.m., and no issue would have arisen as to restarting it.

The admissibility of the change in protocol first came before the court through the defendants' motion *in limine* to exclude any reference to the change in practice. At a hearing on that motion, the plaintiff took alternative positions with respect to the admissibility of the evidence. First, she contended that, because the defendants were claiming that the protocol in place on November 2 was a correct one, consistent with the applicable standard of care, the new protocol was not really a remedial measure and, for that reason, did not fall under the Rule. The court rejected that approach, concluding that a defendant did not have to admit wrongdoing in order for a subsequent change to be regarded as remedial. The plaintiff has not pressed that argument in this appeal. She also asserted that the evidence would be admissible to show that restarting the Heparin was "feasible," to which the court responded that it would allow the evidence for that purpose if the feasibility of restarting the Heparin was denied by the defendants.[3] The defendants made clear that they did not intend to assert that the new protocol was not feasible and that they had no problem with the plaintiff asking Dr. McDonald whether Heparin could have been restarted. The court granted the motion subject to revisiting it "because of the way the trial goes."

The Heparin issue first arose at trial when the plaintiff called Dr. McDonald as an adverse witness. In direct examination, Dr. McDonald stated that he approved discontinuation of the Heparin at 5:30 so that it would metabolize before the scheduled surgery. That decision, he said, was taken to minimize the risk attendant to an inadvertent puncture of the carotid artery by the anesthesiologist.

Dr. McDonald explained that, in the initial stage of CABG surgery, the anesthesiologist inserts a catheter into the internal jugular vein in the neck and that the procedure for doing so involves, first, puncturing the vein with a needle and then, after inserting a guide wire, making an incision and in-

---

[2] Two of the testifying doctors described stable angina as a pattern of chest pain that is predictable—it will occur following a certain level of exercise or emotional distress, for example, and will be relieved when the exercise or distress stops or medication is taken. Unstable angina includes a sudden development of chest pain or a change in a pattern.

[3] As noted, under the new protocol the issue of restarting the Heparin would not have arisen, as the drug would not have been discontinued. The feasibility question related to the defendants' position that it was inadvisable for a patient to have Heparin in the bloodstream at the commencement of CABG surgery. That was the reason the Heparin was both discontinued and not restarted. The plaintiff's position was that Mr. Tuer could safely have undergone the CABG surgery with Heparin in his blood, and she wanted to use the new protocol to establish that fact.

serting the catheter. He pointed out that the jugular vein lies in close proximity to the carotid artery, which is a high pressure vessel that brings blood from the heart to the brain, and that, in his experience, there was a 5% to 10% incidence of the anesthesiologist inadvertently puncturing the carotid artery when attempting to insert the needle into the jugular vein. A puncture of the carotid artery, he said, could produce a serious bleeding problem, and it was for that reason that the protocol called for patients not to have an anticoagulant in their blood when the surgery commenced. He first said that he was unaware of whether any fatalities had resulted at St. Joseph's Hospital or in his particular practice from such an inadvertent puncture, but he did recall that they had had "some serious consequences from inadvertent carotid artery puncture in our hospital." In later testimony, he recounted that he was "very familiar with fatalities in the literature from inadvertent carotid puncture in patients who are having cardiac surgery." In response to a specific question, he confirmed that "the procedure in place on November the 2nd, 1992, at St. Joseph Hospital, for coronary artery bypass patients on Heparin therapy was to discontinue the Heparin three to four hours prior to the time of the surgery . . ." and that that practice and procedure "was required by the standard of care applicable at that time." He explained: "[t]hat is what we did at our hospital."

Following that answer, the plaintiff attempted to set up a basis for inquiring as to the subsequent change. He elicited from Dr. McDonald that there were no circumstances prior to November 2, 1992 in Dr. McDonald's practice at St. Joseph's Hospital in which a patient with Mr. Tuer's clinical profile—unstable angina stabilized in the hospital with Heparin therapy pending coronary bypass surgery—would not have had their Heparin discontinued three to four hours prior to their surgery. Dr. McDonald confirmed that "that was our policy at the time. It would have been a departure, and sitting here this morning I just can't think of a reason off hand why that could be." He added that he had considered restarting the Heparin once the surgery was postponed and elected not to do so because he did not want the drug in Mr. Tuer's blood when the surgery commenced. Counsel asked whether it was "feasible to restart Heparin for Mr. Tuer after your decision to postpone the surgery," but the court sustained an objection to that question. Counsel then inquired whether it was Dr. McDonald's contention "that it would have been *unsafe* to restart Mr. Tuer's Heparin after your decision to postpone his surgery," (emphasis added) to which the witness responded in the affirmative, for the reason already given.

With that answer, plaintiff urged that she was entitled to ask about the change in protocol for impeachment purposes—presumably to show that it is *not* unsafe to bring a patient into surgery with Heparin in his or her system. The court again rejected that argument, distinguishing between the situation presented, of the doctor changing his mind about the relative safety of the protocol, apparently as a result of the unfortunate death of Mr. Tuer, and the case of the doctor not really believing at the time that it would have been unsafe to restart the Heparin. The latter, the court concluded, would constitute grounds for impeachment, but not the former: "In order to impeach his opinion that it was unsafe on November the 1st, 1992, there need be evidence that he didn't think it was unsafe on November the 1st, 1992, not what he thought in January or February of 1993."

* * *

DISCUSSION

[After describing Maryland's common law approach to the admissibility of subsequent remedial measures, the Court noted that in 1994 the Court adopted Maryland Rule 5–407, whose language relevant to the issues of this case is the same as Fed.R.Evid. 407 as originally enacted.]

407 – reasons to exclude subsequent remedial measures –

The Federal Advisory Committee on Rules of Evidence, which drafted Fed.R.Evid. 407, offered two justifications for excluding evidence of subsequent remedial measures to prove culpability: first, that the subsequent conduct "is not in fact an admission, since the conduct is equally consistent with injury by mere accident or through contributory negligence," and second, the "social policy of encouraging people to take, or at least not discouraging them from taking, steps in furtherance of added safety." Although some commentators have since questioned the efficacy of the "social policy" argument (*see* 1 Saltzburg, Martin, and Capra, Federal Rules of Evidence Manual 481 (6th ed. 1994); 2 Mueller and Kirkpatrick, Federal Evidence § 127 (2d ed. 1994); 2 *Weinstein's Federal Evidence* § 407.03[3] (Matthew Bender 2d ed. 1997)), it was significant to the Advisory Committee and, together with the relevance argument, was sufficiently persuasive to cause the Federal rule to be proposed by the Supreme Court and adopted by Congress.[8]

* * *

The plaintiff offers two grounds for the admissibility of the change in procedure adopted after her husband's death, both hinging on Dr. McDonald's testimony and that of his expert witnesses regarding the risk associated with taking patients into CABG surgery with Heparin in their blood.

---

[8] Criticism of the "social policy" argument centers on the notion that an exclusionary rule is not necessary to impel corrective action—that a defendant who is able to do so would likely take corrective action even in the absence of such a rule. Professor Saltzburg offers a modified social policy argument in favor of the rule—that people who take post-accident safety measures are doing exactly what good citizens should do and that, so long as the relevance of those measures is not great, which he does not believe it is, courts should not sanction procedures which appear to punish praiseworthy behavior. LEMPERT & SALTZBURG, A MODERN APPROACH TO EVIDENCE 194 (2d ed. 1982). He and his co-authors Martin and Capra see far more force in the relevance basis of the rule, urging that "subsequent remedial measures are of marginal relevance in assessing the defendant's culpability or fault, and that this marginal relevance is almost always substantially outweighed by the risk of jury confusion created by the introduction of a subsequent remedial measure." SALTZBURG, MARTIN, AND CAPRA, *supra,* at 482. Professor McLain, who served as Special Reporter to the Rules Committee in the development of the Maryland Rules of Evidence, seems to concur in that last view, noting that subsequent remedial measure evidence "has *low probative value* with regard to negligence or fault" and that, to the extent it is not probative of fault but nonetheless suggests an awareness by the defendant that it had not met the standard of due care, "there is also the likelihood of *confusion of the jury and unfair prejudice.*" (Emphasis in original). LYNN MCLAIN, MARYLAND RULES OF EVIDENCE § 2,407.5 (1994 ed.).

That testimony, she urges, effectively controverted the feasibility of protecting patients with Heparin until taken into the operating room, which she was then entitled to establish through evidence of the revised protocol. That evidence was also admissible, she claims, to impeach Dr. McDonald's statement that restarting the drug would have been "unsafe." Although these arguments overlap, we shall deal with them separately.

Feasibility

Rule 5–407(b) exempts subsequent remedial measure evidence from the exclusionary provision of § (a) when it is offered to prove feasibility, if feasibility has been controverted. That raises two questions: what is meant by "feasibility" and was feasibility, in fact, controverted? These two questions also tend to overlap and are often dealt with together; whether a defendant has controverted feasibility may well depend on how one defines the term.

The exception allowing subsequent conduct evidence to show feasibility has been a troublesome one, especially in negligence cases, for, as Judge Weinstein points out, "negligence and feasibility [are] often indistinct issues. The feasibility of a precaution may bear on whether the defendant was negligent not to have taken the precaution sooner." 2 *Weinstein's Federal Evidence, supra,* § 407.04[3]. The Court of Special Appeals noted that two seemingly divergent approaches have been taken in construing the feasibility exception. Some courts have construed the word narrowly, disallowing evidence of subsequent remedial measures under the feasibility exception unless the defendant has essentially contended that the measures were not physically, technologically, or economically possible under the circumstances then pertaining. Other courts have swept into the concept of feasibility a somewhat broader spectrum of motives and explanations for not having adopted the remedial measure earlier, the effect of which is to circumscribe the exclusionary provision.

Feasibility exception (handwritten marginal note)

Courts in the first camp have concluded that feasibility is not controverted—and thus subsequent remedial evidence is not admissible under the Rule—when a defendant contends that the design or practice complained of was chosen because of its perceived comparative advantage over the alternative design or practice, or when the defendant merely asserts that the instructions or warnings given with a product were acceptable or adequate and does not suggest that additional or different instructions or warnings could not have been given, or when the defendant urges that the alternative would not have been effective to prevent the kind of accident that occurred.

Courts announcing a more expansive view have concluded that "feasible" means more than that which is merely possible, but includes that which is capable of being utilized successfully. In *Anderson v. Malloy,* 700 F.2d 1208 (8th Cir.1983), for example, a motel guest who was raped in her room and who sued the motel for failure to provide safe lodging, offered evidence that, after the event, the motel installed peepholes in the doors to the rooms. The appellate court held that the evidence was admissible in light of the defendant's testimony that it had considered installing peep-holes earlier but decided not to do so because (1) there were already windows next to the solid door allowing a guest to look out, and (2) based on the advice of the local police chief, peepholes would give a false sense of security. Although the motel, for obvious reasons, never suggested that the installation of peepholes was not possible, the court, over a strident dissent, concluded that, by inferring that the installation of peepholes would create a lesser level of security, the defendant had "controverted the feasibility of the installation of these devices."

* * *

The apparent divergence indicated by these cases may, at least to some extent, be less of a doctrinal division than a recognition that the concept of practicability is implicit in the notion of feasibility and allows some leeway in the application of the rule. Part of the problem is that dictionaries, which are often resorted to by the courts, contain several definitions of the word "feasible." Webster's New Universal Unabridged Dictionary (2d ed. 1983), for example, contains three definitions: (1) "that may be done, performed, executed, or effected; practicable; possible"; (2) "likely; reasonable; probable; as, a *feasible* story"; (3) "that may be used or dealt with successfully; as, land *feasible* for cultivation." Each of those definitions embody, to some extent, the concept of practicability. Some courts have tended to follow the first definition and have thus articulated the notion of feasibility in terms of that which physically, technologically, or economically is capable of being done; others, like the Eighth Circuit in *Anderson v. Malloy,* have latched on to the third definition, which brings more into play the concepts of value, effectiveness, and overall utility.

To some extent, the problem may be driven by special considerations arising from application of the rule to product liability cases, especially those grounded on strict liability. When the plaintiff is obliged to establish that there were feasible alternatives to the design, manufacturing method, or warnings used by the defendant, he or she necessarily injects the question of feasibility into the case, to which the defendant ordinarily responds by showing why those alternatives were not used. As Saltzburg, Martin, and Capra point out, if a remedial measure has, in fact, been taken that could have been taken earlier, the defendant is not likely to claim that the measure was not possible or practicable, and, indeed, defendants often are willing to stipulate to feasibility in order to avoid having the subsequent remedial evidence admitted. 1 Saltzburg, Martin and Capra, *supra,* 486. The issue arises when the defendant offers some other explanation for not putting the measure into effect sooner—often a judgment call as to comparative value or a trade-off between cost and benefit or between competing benefits—and the plaintiff characterizes that explanation as putting feasibility into issue. *See Rahmig v. Mosley Machinery Co.,* 226 Neb. 423, 412 N.W.2d 56 (1987).[9] To the extent there can be said to be a doctrinal split

---

[9] Wright and Graham note that many of the cases in which the feasibility exception has been invoked are product liability cases, and that "it may be that courts had intuitive appreciation of the inappropriateness of the traditional rule in that context and were using the 'excep-

among the courts, it seems to center on whether that kind of judgment call, which is modified later, suffices to allow the challenged evidence to be admitted.

That is essentially what occurred in this case. At no time did Dr. McDonald or any of his expert witnesses suggest that the Heparin could not have been restarted following the postponement of Mr. Tuer's surgery. Indeed, they indicated quite the opposite; Dr. McDonald, in fact, made clear that, had Mr. Tuer exhibited signs of renewed unstable angina, he would have restarted the Heparin. The only fair reading of his testimony and that of his supporting experts is that the protocol then in effect was the product of a professional judgment call that the risk to Mr. Tuer of having CABG surgery commence while there was a significant amount of Heparin in his blood outweighed the prospect of harm accruing from allowing him to remain Heparin-free for several hours.

Dr. McDonald's brief response to one question that, *at the time,* he regarded it as "unsafe" to restart the Heparin cannot be viewed in isolation but has to be read in the context of his whole testimony. Under any reasonable view of the meaning of feasibility, a flat assertion by a physician that the remedial measure was inappropriate because it was medically "unsafe" would ordinarily be tantamount to asserting that the measure was not feasible and would thus suffice to controvert the feasibility of the measure. In a medical context at least, feasibility has to include more than mere physical possibility; as we have so sadly learned from history, virtually anything can physically be done to the human body. The practice of medicine is quintessentially therapeutic in nature. Its purpose is to comfort and to heal, and a determination of whether a practice or procedure is feasible has to be viewed in that light. The assertion that a given course would be unsafe, in the sense that it would likely cause paramount harm to the patient, necessarily constitutes an assertion that the course would not be feasible. Dr. McDonald was not asserting, however, in any absolute sense, that restarting the Heparin would have been unsafe but only that, given the complications that could have arisen, and that, in other cases had arisen, from an inadvertent puncture of the carotid artery, weighed against Mr. Tuer's apparently stable condition at the time and the intensive monitoring he would receive during the waiting period, there was a relative safety risk that, at the time, he and the hospital believed was not worth taking. That does not, in our view, constitute an assertion that a restarting of the Heparin was not feasible. It was feasible but, in their view, not advisable.

Many factors

Impeachment

The exception in the Rule for impeachment has created some of the same practical and interpretive problems presented by the exception for establishing feasibility. As Saltzburg, Martin, and Capra point out, "almost any testimony given by defense witnesses could be contradicted at least in

---

tion' as an alternative to holding the rule inapplicable in strict liability." 23 WRIGHT AND GRAHAM, FEDERAL PRACTICE AND PROCEDURE § 5288 (footnote omitted) (1980 and 1997 Supp.).

some minimal way by a subsequent remedial measure. If the defendant's expert testifies that the product was safe, a subsequent remedial measure could be seen as contradicting that testimony. If the defendant is asked on cross-examination whether he thinks that he had taken all reasonable safety precautions, and answers in the affirmative, then a subsequent remedial measure can be seen as contradicting that testimony." 1 Saltzburg, Martin and Capra, *supra*, 487. *See also* 2 *Weinstein's Federal Evidence*, *supra*, § 407.07[1] at 407–32.

The prevailing, and pragmatically necessary, view is that the impeachment exception cannot be read in so expansive a manner. As Wright and Graham note, even at common law it would likely have been impermissible for the plaintiff to "have called the defendant to the stand, asked him if he thought he had been negligent, and impeached him with evidence of subsequent repairs if he answered 'no.' " 23 Wright and Graham, *supra*, § 5289, at 145 (1980).[10] Thus, as Saltzburg, Martin, and Capra point out, most courts have held that subsequent remedial measure evidence is not ordinarily admissible for impeachment "if it is offered for simple contradiction of a defense witness' testimony." 1 Saltzburg, Martin and Capra, *supra*, at 487.

To some extent, that begs the question; whether the evidence is allowed for impeachment seems to depend more on the nature of the contradiction than on the fact of it. In *Muzyka v. Remington Arms Co.*, 774 F.2d 1309, 1313 (5th Cir.1985), for example, where a defense witness asserted that the challenged product constituted "perhaps the best combination of safety and operation yet devised," a design change made after the accident but before the giving of that testimony was allowed as impeachment evidence, presumably to show either that the witness did not really believe that to be the case or that his opinion should not be accepted as credible. In *Dollar v. Long Mfg., N.C., Inc.*, 561 F.2d 613 (5th Cir.1977), the court allowed evidence of a post-accident letter by the manufacturer to its dealers warning of "death dealing propensities" of the product when used in a particular fashion to impeach testimony by the defendant's design engineer, who wrote the letter, that the product was safe to operate in that manner. *See also Patrick v. South Central Bell Tel. Co.*, 641 F.2d 1192 (6th Cir.1980) (evidence that defendant subsequently raised height of telephone lines admissible to impeach testimony that lines met minimum statutory height at time of accident). In these circumstances, the subsequent remedial measure

---

[10] The plaintiff has not made a separate issue of the court's disallowance of her question to Dr. McDonald and Dr. Fortuin of whether restarting the Heparin would have been feasible, although she has asked rhetorically what harm would have ensued from allowing the answer if feasibility was not being controverted. Although we need not answer that question, we do note, in the context of the impeachment issue, the view of the Alabama Supreme Court, expressed in *Blythe v. Sears, Roebuck & Co.*, 586 So.2d 861 (Ala.1991), *Phar-Mor, Inc. v. Goff*, 594 So.2d 1213 (Ala.1992), and *Baptist Med. Centers v. Trippe*, 643 So.2d 955 (Ala.1994), that "to impeach the credibility of a witness through the introduction of a subsequent remedial measure, the testimony providing grounds for impeachment must have been initiated by the witness." *Phar-Mor, Inc.*, supra, 594 So.2d at 1219. Because, the court said, the exception was created "to protect a plaintiff from an aggressive defendant attempting to manipulate the exclusionary nature of the rule for his own advantage, it follows that a plaintiff who is on the offensive should not be allowed to manipulate the impeachment exception in order to introduce evidence for purposes otherwise inadmissible." *Id.*

falls neatly within the scope of classic impeachment evidence and directly serves the purpose of such evidence—to cast doubt on the credibility of the witness's testimony; it is not a mere pretext for using the evidence to establish culpability. *Compare,* however, *Davenport v. Ephraim McDowell Mem. Hosp.,* 769 S.W.2d 56 (Ky.App.1988) (evidence that, after the decedent's death, the defendant reactivated alarms on heart monitoring machines held admissible to impeach defense testimony that the alarms had been made inoperative at the time of the event because they went off unnecessarily on false readings and were distracting to the nursing staff).

Consistent with the approach taken on the issue of feasibility, however, subsequent remedial measure evidence had been held inadmissible to impeach testimony that, at the time of the event, the measure was not believed to be as practical as the one employed (*Hardy v. Chemetron Corp.,* 870 F.2d 1007 (5th Cir.1989)), or that the defendant was using due care at the time of the accident (*Flaminio v. Honda Motor Co., Ltd., supra,* 733 F.2d 463).

[handwritten: at the time did not believe practical]

Largely for the reasons cited with respect to the feasibility issue, we do not believe that the change in protocol was admissible to impeach Dr. McDonald's brief statement that restarting the Heparin would have been unsafe. As we observed, that statement must be read in context, and, when so read, would not be impeached by the subsequent change in protocol. It is clear that Dr. McDonald made a judgment call based on his knowledge and collective experience at the time. He had read about and, in 5% to 10% of the cases had experienced, problems arising from an inadvertent puncture of the carotid artery; he had not experienced a patient in Mr. Tuer's circumstances dying from the lack of Heparin during a four-hour wait for surgery. He was aware that the same protocol, of allowing the Heparin to metabolize, was used at Johns Hopkins Hospital. The fact that the protocol was changed following Mr. Tuer's death in no way suggests that Dr. McDonald did not honestly believe that his judgment call was appropriate at the time. The only reasonable inference from his testimony, coupled with counsel's proffer as to why the protocol was changed, was that Dr. McDonald and his colleagues reevaluated the relative risks in light of what happened to Mr. Tuer and decided that the safer course was to continue the Heparin. That kind of reevaluation is precisely what the exclusionary provision of the Rule was designed to encourage.

[handwritten: had not experienced death from ≠ heparin]

JUDGMENT OF COURT OF SPECIAL APPEALS AFFIRMED, WITH COSTS.

NOT THE FEDERAL RULE

Rhode Island Rules of Evidence, 2003

Rule 407. Subsequent remedial measures.

When, after an event, measures are taken which, if taken previously, would have made the event less likely to occur, evidence of the subsequent measures is admissible.

Compare Federal Rule of Evidence 407; California Evidence Code § 1151.

HYPOTHETICALS

(1) A sues X for damages for personal injuries arising out of A's slipping and falling on steps in a store owned and operated by X. A testifies that a strip of abrasive tape on the step on which she slipped was worn, and that the step was slippery. X calls B, the store manager, who testifies that the tape strips on the steps were not worn and that the steps were not slippery. In rebuttal, A offers to prove that a week after A's accident, X replaced the old strips of tape with new ones, and A offers in evidence photographs of the steps with the new strips of tape. X objects to A's offer of proof on the ground of the policy exclusion of evidence of subsequent remedial conduct. What result? *Not Admissible*

(2) Assume the same facts as in Illustration (1), except that A adds to her offer of proof the fact that B, the store manager who testified for X, was the person who authorized installation of the new abrasive tape strips after A's accident. X makes the same objection that he makes in Illustration (1). How should the court rule? *Not Admissible Maybe*

(3) P, a savings company, sues D, a bank, for damages arising out of a long-period embezzlement of $500,000 by M, a manager of P's branch office. From time to time, M placed the embezzled funds in a personal account with D and subsequently made withdrawals by checks to herself until all funds were withdrawn. P claims D was negligent in permitting M to make deposits and withdrawals from this account. D's defense is that P was negligent in its accounting and auditing procedures, which allowed M to embezzle such a large amount without detection. After the embezzlement, P retained X, an accounting firm, to audit P and recommend accounting and auditing changes. P placed such recommended changes into effect after getting X's report. D makes a discovery motion to inspect and copy X's report. What result? *Not admissible*

G. OFFERS IN COMPROMISE

Davidson v. Prince

Court of Appeals of Utah, 1991.
813 P.2d 1225.

■ BILLINGS, ASSOCIATE PRESIDING JUDGE:

Appellant Grant Davidson was injured by a cow or a steer that had escaped from a wrecked truck driven by Erwin M. Prince, an employee of appellee Folkens Brothers Trucking. Subsequently, Davidson filed a negligence action against Prince and Folkens. A jury found appellees sixty percent negligent and appellant forty percent contributorily negligent. Based on this verdict, the judge entered a judgment in favor of appellant in the amount of $27,323.88 plus interest. Appellant moved for a new trial. The court denied this motion. Appellant appeals from the denial of his motion for a new trial. We affirm.

FACTS

On May 28, 1986, appellee was driving a truck containing animals. Appellee negligently overturned the truck, releasing animals onto the highway and into the surrounding area. Appellant was injured when he was attacked by a steer that had escaped from appellee's vehicle.

At trial, conflicting evidence was introduced regarding the proximity of appellant to the steer before the steer charged, ranging from forty feet to ten feet. Over appellant's objections, appellee's counsel introduced into evidence a statement from a letter written to the appellee wherein appellant estimated the distance as ten feet. Based on this evidence, appellee argued that appellant had cornered the steer and was therefore partly responsible for his injuries.

At trial, the jury awarded appellant total damages in the amount of $45,539.80. The jury, however, found appellant forty percent at fault and accordingly, appellant was ultimately awarded a judgment of only $27,323.88.

* * *

III. ADMISSION OF STATEMENT IN "SETTLEMENT" LETTER

Finally, appellant contends the trial court erred in allowing into evidence statements he made in a letter to appellee. Appellee's theory at trial was that appellant was negligent in cornering the steer which had escaped from appellee's truck. In support of this theory, appellee emphasized the distance between appellant and the animal at the time the animal charged. As noted earlier, appellant in deposition testimony estimated the distance to be approximately forty feet. Additional evidence was presented at trial that the distance may have been approximately twenty-two feet. At trial, appellee's counsel introduced a statement from a letter written to appellee wherein appellant estimated the distance at ten feet, a distance which tended to support appellee's theory. Appellant claims the trial court erred in admitting this statement because it was made as part of settlement negotiations.

The admissibility of settlement negotiations is governed by Utah Rule of Evidence 408 which states:

> Evidence of (1) furnishing or offering or promising to furnish, or (2) accepting or offering or promising to accept, a valuable consideration in compromising or attempting to compromise a claim which was disputed as to either validity or amount, is not admissible to prove liability for or invalidity of the claim or its amount. Evidence of conduct or statements made in compromise negotiations is likewise not admissi-

ble. This rule does not require the exclusion of any evidence otherwise discoverable merely because it is presented in the course of compromise negotiations. This rule also does not require exclusion when evidence is offered for another purpose, such as proving bias or prejudice of a witness, negativing a contention of undue delay, or proving an effort to obstruct a criminal investigation or prosecution.

Utah R.Evid. 408. This rule follows verbatim Federal Rule of Evidence 408 which was used as a model in drafting the Utah Rules. Accordingly, this court looks to federal law interpreting Federal Rule of Evidence 408 to define the contours of Utah Rule of Evidence 408.

"In order for the exclusionary rule to attach, the party seeking to have evidence of offers to compromise or statements made in the course thereof excluded must show that the discussions in question were made in 'compromise negotiations.'" 10 J. Moore & H. Bendix, Moore's Federal Practice § 408.04 (1988 & Supp.1990).

The letter in question, from appellant and his wife to appellee, begins by reviewing the factual circumstances of the accident[8] and it is in this factual recitation that appellant admits "he stopped and got out some 10 feet from the animal." Following this recitation of facts, the letter continues by stating, "[w]e don't intend to let you or that trucking company off, with a letter telling us that your [sic] not responsible." In conclusion, appellant's letter states, "[y]ou may speak with us directly or we can send it to lawyers and to court, you decide."

We believe the trial judge was correct in admitting the statement from the letter sent by appellant to appellee because the letter was not an offer to compromise appellant's claim, nor was it written as part of settlement negotiations. To the contrary, this letter is merely an attempt to inform appellee as to the facts of the incident. Furthermore, appellant in the letter

---

[8] This portion of the letter reads:

It appears you have been poorly informed as to Mr. Grant Davidson's injury claim.

Please allow us to clarify: Mr. Davidson while performing his job for the D & RGW Railroad, saw the injured cow sitting on the railroad. He stopped and got out some 10 feet from the animal. He made no move towards the injured cow but while standing still was charged. He fled the cow, but it caught him, goring him in the back and sending him air born for approximately 20 feet where he landed on the rail on his knee.

The attack continued with the cow attempting to trample Mr. Davidson to death, as he lay stunned with a concussion on the ground he pushed the animal off and escaped to the safety of a rail car.

The cow continued to charge repeatedly and finally moved off. It then charged many others before it was killed.

Mr. Davidson did not pursue, chase or attempt to move the cow. As it (the cow) was injured in the accident, it became abnormally dangerous.

We have been advised by legal counsel that the contents of a truck, when they spill and are dangerous (as this case) are the responsibility of the insurer when those dangerous contents injure innocent people.

Mr. Davidson has a permanent knee problem, and must wear a brace while doing any work. He's had 16 years with this job, which is now jeopardized by this injury. He has lost wages, has great suffering and now is going to be disabled the rest of his life.

demands payment in full of appellant's claim and its whole tenor is that appellant will not compromise one bit.[9] * * *

NOTE

In United States v. Mezzanatto, 513 U.S. 196 (1995), the Court faced a case in which, as a condition of starting a plea discussion, the prosecutor had required defendant to agree that any statements he made could be used to impeach his testimony at trial. When defendant's statements were in fact used for that purpose at trial, defendant objected. The Supreme Court upheld the trial judge's decision to admit the testimony. It held that rights under Fed. R. Evid. 410, like evidentiary rights generally, could be waived before trial. Such waivers are valid unless the defense makes an affirmative showing that the waiver was involuntary or unknowing. There was no such showing in the case at bar, where the defendant consulted with his lawyer after the prosecutor proposed the waiver.

HYPOTHETICALS

(1) A sues X and the Y Bus Company for damages for personal injuries suffered in a collision between an automobile driven by A and a bus owned by the Y Bus Company and driven by X, its employee. A makes an offer of proof that at the scene of the accident X made the statement, "I know I blew the stop sign, but will you take $100 in settlement? I know the company will pay that much." Both X and the Y Bus Company make objections that X's statement is hearsay and also barred by the rule against admissions made during settlement negotiations. Should the objection be sustained? *also admissible*

(2) A sues the X Insurance Company for damages for intentional infliction of mental distress. A carried a disability-insurance policy with X, which provided for monthly payments of $150 to A as long as a disability continued. A is hurt and has a permanent disability. X pays A $150 per month until she has been paid $2,500. X then stops the payments, and seeks cancellation of the policy on the ground that A had made misrepresentations at the time of the policy application. A offers evidence that X was acting in bad faith in asserting that A had made any misrepresentations to secure the policy. A offers in evidence a letter from X to A, in which X offered to compromise A's claim that the policy was valid by permitting A to retain the $2,500 in payments, in return for X's cancellation of the policy and A's execution of a release of X. X makes an objection that its letter is inadmissible as an offer to compromise a claim. What result? *Admissible*

---

[9] Even if appellant's letter was construed to be a statement made in settlement negotiations, courts construing Federal Rule of Evidence 408 and similar state rules have held that evidence of statements made in settlement negotiations can and should be admitted for purposes of impeachment. For example, in United States Aviation Underwriters, Inc. v. Olympia Wings, Inc., 896 F.2d 949 (5th Cir.1990), the court held that the trial court had properly acted within its discretion under Rule 408 when it admitted evidence of a settlement that was offered to impeach the plaintiff's earlier deposition testimony. In so holding, the court stated that Federal Rule of Evidence 408 "permits settlement evidence for any purpose except to prove or disprove liability or the amount of the claim."

* * *

Thus, even if appellant's letter to appellee were to be construed to have been made as part of settlement discussions, it could be admitted to impeach appellant's prior testimony regarding the distance between himself snd the steer prior to the accident.

CHAPTER 3

THE HEARSAY RULE AND THE CONFRONTATION RIGHT

PART **A** Rationales and Meanings: Definitions

PART **B** Exceptions and Exemptions

PART **C** A Recap

A. RATIONALES AND MEANINGS: DEFINITIONS

John George Phillimore, History and Principles of the Law of Evidence
157–64 (1850).

[Sir Walter Raleigh was tried in 1603 for participating in a conspiracy to dethrone King James I of England and to put Lady Arabella Stuart in his place, with the aid of Spanish money and intrigue. Sir Edward Coke, attorney-general, conducted the prosecution. The case against Raleigh depended heavily upon a confession made by an alleged conspirator, Lord Cobham, accusing Raleigh of participation in the plot. Cobham, who later retracted the accusation and then changed his story back again, was imprisoned in the Tower of London during Raleigh's trial and was not produced as a witness.]

Raleigh. "But it is strange to see how you press me still with my Lord Cobham, and yet will not produce him; it is not for gaining of time or prolonging my life that I urge this; HE IS IN THE HOUSE HARD BY, and may soon be brought hither; let him be produced, and if he will yet accuse me or avow this confession of his, it shall convict me and ease you of further proof."

Lord Cecil. "Sir Walter Raleigh presseth often that my Lord Cobham should be brought face to face; if he ask a thing of grace and favour, they must come from him only who can give them; but if he ask a matter of law, then, in order that we, who sit here as commissioners, may be satisfied, I desire to hear the opinions of my Lords, the judges, whether it may be done by law." The judges all answered, "that in respect it might be a mean to cover many with treasons, and might be prejudicial to the King, therefore, by the law, it was not sufferable."

Popham, C.J. "There must not such a gap be opened for the destruction of the King as would be if we should grant this; you plead hard for yourself, but the laws plead as hard for the King. Where no circumstances do concur to make a matter probable, then an accuser may be heard; but so many circumstances agreeing and confirming the accusation in this case, the accuser is not to be produced; for, having first confessed against himself voluntarily, and so charged another person, if we shall now hear him again in person, he may, for favour or fear, retract what formerly he hath said, and the jury may, by that means, be inveigled." * * *

Raleigh.—"I never had intelligence with Cobham since I came to the Tower." * * *

Lord Cecil.—"Sir Walter Raleigh, if my Lord Cobham will now affirm, that you were acquainted with his dealings with Count Aremberg, that you knew of the letter he received, that you were the chief instigator of him, will you then be concluded by it?"

Raleigh.—"Let my Lord Cobham speak before God and the King, and deny God and the King if he speak not truly, and will then say that ever I knew of Arabella's matter, or the money out of Spain, or the Surprising Treason, I will put myself upon it * * *." * * *

Lord Henry Howard.—"But what if my Lord Cobham affirm anything equivalent to this; what then?"

Raleigh.—"My Lord, I put myself upon it."

Attorney-General.—"I shall now produce a witness *vivâ voce:*"

He then produced one Dyer, a pilot, who, being sworn, said, "Being at Lisbon, there came to me a Portug[uese] gentleman, who asked me how the King of England did, and whether he was crowned? I answered him, that I hoped our noble king was well, and crowned by this; but the time was not come when I came from the coast [of] Spain. 'Nay,' said he, 'your king shall never be crowned, for Don Cobham and Don Raleigh will cut his throat before he come to be crowned.' And this, in time, was found to be spoken in mid July."

Raleigh.—"This is the saying of some wild Jesuit or beggarly priest; but what proof is it against me?"

Attorney-General.—"It must per force arise out of some preceding intelligence, and shews that your treason had wings." * * *

Thus on the single evidence of Cobham, never confronted with Raleigh, who retracted his confession, and then, according to the advocates of the Crown, recalled his retraction, did an English jury, to the amazement and horror of the bystanders, and the perpetual disgrace of the English name, find the most illustrious of their fellow subjects guilty of high treason.

Tribe, Triangulating Hearsay

87 Harvard Law Review 957, 958–61 (1974).*

I. THE TESTIMONIAL TRIANGLE

The basic hearsay problem is that of forging a reliable chain of infe-rences, from an act or utterance of a person not subject to contemporaneous in-court cross-examination about that act or utterance, to an event that the act or utterance is supposed to reflect. Typically, the first link in the re-quired chain of inferences is the link from the act or utterance to the belief it is thought to express or indicate. It is helpful to think of this link as in-volving a "trip" into the head of the person responsible for the act or utter-ance (the declarant) to see what he or she was really thinking when the act occurred. The second link is the one from the declarant's assumed belief to a conclusion about some external event that is supposed to have triggered the belief, or that is linked to the belief in some other way. This link in-volves a trip out of the head of the declarant, in order to match the decla-rant's assumed belief with the external reality sought to be demonstrated.

The trier must obviously employ such a chain of inferences whenever a witness testifies in court. But the process has long been regarded as partic-ularly suspect when the act or utterance is not one made in court, under oath, by a person whose demeanor at the time is witnessed by the trier, and under circumstances permitting immediate cross-examination by counsel in order to probe possible inaccuracies in the inferential chain. These inaccu-racies are usually attributed to the four testimonial infirmities of ambigui-ty, insincerity, faulty perception, and erroneous memory. In the absence of special reasons, the perceived untrustworthiness of such an out-of-court act or utterance has lead the Anglo-Saxon legal system to exclude it as hearsay despite its potentially probative value.

There exists a rather simple way of schematizing all of this in terms of an elementary geometric construct that serves to structure its several re-lated elements. The construct might be called the Testimonial Triangle. By making graphic the path of inferences, and by functionally grouping the problems encountered along the path, the triangle makes it easier both to identify when a hearsay problem exists and to structure consideration of the appropriateness of exceptions to the rule that bars hearsay inferences.

The diagram is as follows:

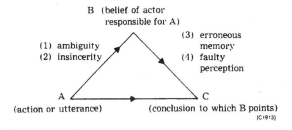

If we use the diagram to trace the inferential path the trier must follow, we begin at the lower left vertex of the triangle (A), which represents the declarant's (X's) act or assertion. The path first takes us to the upper vertex (B), representing X's belief in what his or her act or assertion suggests, and then takes us to the lower right vertex (C), representing the external reality suggested by X's belief. When "A" is used to prove "C" along the path through "B," a traditional hearsay problem exists and the use of the act or assertion as evidence is disallowed upon proper objection in the absence of some special reason to permit it.

It is of course a simple matter to locate the four testimonial infirmities on the triangle to show where and how they might impede the process of inference. To go from "A" to "B," the declarant's belief, one must remove the obstacles of (1) ambiguity and (2) insincerity. To go from "B" to "C," the external fact, one must further remove the obstacles of (3) erroneous memory and (4) faulty perception.

When it is possible to go directly from "A" to "C" with no detour through "B," there is no hearsay problem unless the validity of the trier's conclusion depends upon an implicit path through "B."[1] Suppose, for example, that the issue in a lawsuit is whether the Government took adequate safety precautions in connection with the nuclear test at Amchitka in 1971. James Schlesinger, then Chairman of the Atomic Energy Commission, "told reporters at Elmendorf Air Force Base outside Anchorage that he was taking his wife * * * and daughters * * * with him [to the site of the Amchitka blast] in response to Alaska Gov. William E. Egan's invitation. Egan strongly disapprove[d] of the test."[2] In these circumstances, the trip from "A," the Chairman's proposed travel with his family to the site of the blast, to "C," the conclusion that the blast was reasonably safe, may appear at first to be purely "circumstantial," but in fact that trip requires a journey into the Chairman's head and out again—a journey through the belief "B" suggested by his willingness to be near the blast with his family. The journey from "A" to "B" involves problems of possible ambiguity and of insincerity in that the Chairman was apparently seeking to dispel fears of danger, so that his act may not bespeak an actual belief in the test's safety. And the journey from "B" to "C" involves problems of memory and perception in that he may not have recalled all the relevant data and may have misperceived

---

[1] An uncompromising behaviorist might insist that no detour through mental states is ever necessary because every trip from an act or utterance "A" to a conclusion "C" is reducible to a circumstantial inference about the statistical frequency with which "C" is present when "A" is present. There are difficulties with accepting the behaviorist perspective as a coherent one. See Chomsky, A Review of B.F. Skinner's Verbal Behavior, 35 Language 26 (1959); Chomsky, The Case Against B.F. Skinner, New York Review of Books, Dec. 30, 1971, at 18. But even if one does adopt such a perspective, it does not follow that the trier's way of using the evidence "A" will in fact mirror that perspective, for the trier is likely to reason about states of mind even if it is in some sense incorrect or unnecessary to do so. Moreover, the connection between "A" and "C" may well be such that the frequency with which the latter accompanies the former depends upon the actor's testimonial capacities so that, even from a behaviorist perspective, information about a declarant's use of language, tendency to lie, eyesight, and so forth, may increase or decrease the statistical correlation between the utterance and the fact reported.

[2] Boston Globe, Nov. 5, 1971, at 16. The fact pattern of the Amchitka example is remarkably similar to a hypothetical presented by Baron Parke in his opinion in Wright v. Doe dem. Tatham (experienced ship captain inspecting and setting sail on a ship).

such data in the first instance, so that his belief in the test's safety, even if we assume the journey from "A" to "B" safely completed, may not correspond to the facts sought to be demonstrated. On both legs of the triangle, therefore, there are testimonial infirmities that cross-examination contemporaneous with the act "A" could help to expose.

By contrast, when the trier's inference can proceed from "A" directly to "C," the infirmities of hearsay do not arise. For example, the out-of-court statement "I can speak" would be admissible as nonhearsay to prove that the declarant was capable of speech, for it is the fact of his speaking rather than the content of the statement which permits the inference, and that involves no problems of the statement's ambiguity, or of sincerity, memory, or perception.

Park, Two Definitions of Hearsay*

Definitions of hearsay are usually either assertion-centered or declarant-centered. Under an assertion-centered definition, an out-of-court statement is hearsay when it is offered in evidence to prove the truth of the matter asserted. Under a declarant-centered definition, an out-of-court statement is hearsay when it depends for value upon the credibility of the declarant. The term "credibility" refers to the testimonial qualities of sincerity, narrative ability, memory, and perception.

Over much hearsay territory, the difference between the two definitions has no effect. Most utterances that are not hearsay under an assertion-centered definition would not be hearsay under a declarant-centered definition. However, the two definitions can produce different results in some cases. For example, suppose that a criminal defendant is charged with committing a crime in Miami. After the crime, the police questioned the defendant's wife, who told them that the defendant was with her in Honolulu on the evening of the crime. The wife's statement is demonstrably false, and the prosecution seeks to use her statement against the defendant for the inference that the wife lied because she knew the defendant to be guilty. Under an assertion-centered definition, the wife's statement is not hearsay because it is not offered to prove the truth of the matter asserted. Under a declarant-centered definition, her statement would be hearsay because the trier's use of it would require reliance on her powers of memory, perception, and narration. She might have been mistaken about the date on which her husband was in Honolulu or she might have misspoken the date. Even if she was trying to cover up for her husband because she believed him to be guilty, her belief might have been based upon misperception or misinterpretation.

Consider the hearsay triangle on p. 199. It is an illustration of the hearsay dangers. Under the declarant-centered definition, if the trier's use of an out-of-court statement involves hearsay dangers, then it is hearsay.

---

* Adapted from Park, "I Didn't Tell Them Anything About You": Implied Assertions as Hearsay Under the Federal Rules of Evidence, 74 Minn.L.Rev. 783, 783 (1990).

When the prosecution offers the wife's false alibi as evidence that her husband is guilty, the trier's inferential path requires a trip through the mind of the wife on the way to the conclusion that the husband is guilty. The first step requires the inference that her statement actually shows her belief that her husband is guilty of the crime charged. If language difficulties or mental lapses caused her to say "Honolulu" when she meant "Miami," or to say her husband's name when she meant to name someone else, the inference fails. If she lied to the police for some reason other than believing that her husband committed the crime charged, then the inference also fails.

The second step, from her belief that he committed the crime charged to the conclusion that he did in fact commit it, also involves hearsay dangers. Her belief might be mistaken. One reason is the danger of faulty perception illustrated in Professor Tribe's triangle. If she was speculating that her husband committed the crime charged, basing her belief on her imagination instead of her perception, then the inference fails. If she perceived something but misunderstood it (she thought her husband was plotting the crime when he was really plotting a surprise party), the inference also fails. Bad memory is another danger. If she was confused about when her husband went to Honolulu, then her bad memory about his trips might cause her to believe he was home at a time when he could have committed the crime charged when he was not. Cross-examination might help reveal some of these pitfalls.

McCormick's Handbook on the Law of Evidence
461 (1954).*

The requirement in the definition of hearsay is that the statement be offered to prove the truth of the matter asserted. What if the immediate purpose is to prove the fact asserted but the ultimate purpose is to draw a circumstantial inference of another fact, not asserted in the statement? Suppose the witness reports that D told him, a week before D's body was found in the bay, that he was planning to go fishing the next day with X in the latter's boat. If offered to show D's intent it is plainly hearsay, and it seems at least equally subject to the hearsay weaknesses if a further inference is to be built upon the inference that D's intent was what he said it was. Accordingly we find the courts treating the statement as hearsay wherever the *first* purpose is to prove the fact asserted in it, even though other secondary inferences are sought to be built upon the first.

See Federal Rules of Evidence 801(b), (c), 802; California Evidence Code § 1200.

---

* Copyright West Publishing Co., 1954.

Estate of Murdock

32 Muc. 352 (1983).*

■ KAPLAN, J. AND WALTZ, J. delivered the opinion of the court.

This is a dispute that could easily have been avoided by competent estate planning. But, unfortunately, what a lawyer could have done in two minutes in his office has required two years of expensive litigation. The case involves a contest between the children of Sarah Hayes Murdock by her first marriage (called hereinafter the Hayes children) and the children of Arthur G. Murdock by his first marriage (called hereinafter the Murdock children.)

Arthur G. Murdock had executed a will, leaving his entire estate to Sarah, his second wife, if she should survive him, but if she did not, then to his children by his first marriage (the Murdock children) in equal shares. Sarah Hayes Murdock, on the other hand, had made a substantially similar will, leaving her entire estate to Arthur G. Murdock, if he should survive her, and to her children by her first marriage (the Hayes children) if she survived him.

The problem, of course, comes from the fact that Sarah and Arthur were in their private airplane when it crashed, resulting in their deaths. Since this state has not adopted the Uniform Simultaneous Death Act, that becomes extremely important which would otherwise not have been a very significant issue—who died first?

Expert medical testimony was presented on both sides as to how long both Sarah and Arthur Murdock had lived after the crash. The crucial testimony at issue in this appeal was that of Deputy Sheriff Alfred Linden, who arrived at the scene of the crash some ten minutes after the crash. Linden testified that he saw immediately upon his arrival that Sarah was dead (in the interest of good taste, we will leave out his extremely graphic description of how he was able to determine that this was the case) and thereafter passed close to the other passenger, Arthur G. Murdock. The precise evidentiary ruling at issue here arose when Deputy Linden wished to testify that he heard Mr. Murdock whisper, "I'm still alive."

On objection, this evidence was excluded by the trial judge on the grounds that it was hearsay. Nor would the judge listen to any argument on this, saying:

> "The hearsay rule says you are not permitted to introduce an out-of-court statement, which this indubitably is, to show the truth of that statement which is exactly what you are trying to do here, counsel."

Unfortunately, the learned trial judge was wrong. Although the definition of hearsay, as given by the statutes and the common law, seems, by its words, to require the exclusion of the evidence at issue here, hearsay is re-

---

* M.U.C., the citation here, stands for made-up cases.

ally a type of reasoning not easily capturable in a few simple words. In essence, the hearsay rule precludes reliance on the credibility of an out-of-court declarant. By excluding hearsay, the law seeks to guarantee to the party against whom such evidence is sought to be introduced the right meaningfully to cross-examine the out-of-court declarant who is in substance, though not in form, the real witness against him. The opponent of the out-of-court hearsay statement sought to be related by the witness is denied the right to cross-examine the declarant on his perception, memory, sincerity and ability to communicate what he remembers.

In the case at bar, the forbidden hearsay reasoning would be as follows:

> "Arthur Murdock said he was alive; he was a man of principle, alert, and of sound faculties. He would never get something like that wrong, or lie about it."

The reasoning properly used here is not hearsay reasoning at all; it does not rely for its probative value on Arthur Murdock's perception, memory, sincerity and ability to communicate at the time he said the words. Rather we reason here from the converse. People who are dead do not say, "I am still alive"—or anything else. (Obviously for this purpose it would have made no difference whether Murdock had said, "I am dead.") If Arthur Murdock had said this—and the jury could so believe by weighing the testimony of Deputy Linden, who was subject to cross examination—then he was alive at the time.

Nor can we affirm the exclusion of the evidence on the principle that where a piece of evidence is admissible for one purpose (its non-hearsay purpose) and inadmissible for another (its hearsay purpose), the judge would have a discretion to exclude it on the ground that its prejudicial effect outweighed its probative value. Assuming this evidence could conceivably be used for a hearsay purpose, the non-hearsay purpose was so much more obvious and so clearly drowned out any hearsay reasoning (if indeed there were such) that any action of the trial judge in excluding it would be clear abuse of discretion.

Judgment reversed.

■ PARK, J., concurring.

I agree with the majority's conclusion and admire its lucid explanation.

It did not matter what Mr. Murdock said. The fact that he could say anything showed that he was still alive. The trier of fact was not being asked to use his whispering as an assertion at all. The fact that his statement was made, not anything it said, is what matters in this case.

I write to point out that the majority opinion stands only for the proposition that an utterance is not hearsay when its value at trial does not depend to any degree on the credibility of an out-of-court declarant. In such instances the utterance is not being used assertively.

The majority does not say that when use of a statement *does* require some dependence on the credibility of the declarant, then the statement is always hearsay.

Our code defines hearsay as an out-of-court assertion "offered in evidence to prove the truth of the matter asserted." Under that definition, a statement is sometimes not hearsay even though its value varies with the credibility of an out-of-court declarant. For an example, see the essay entitled "Two Definitions of Hearsay" on p. 201 of this casebook.

■ Friedman, J., concurring.

I am glad, nearly three decades later, to join the majority opinion of my late senior colleagues. They accurately state the law as of the time they wrote and as of now. And any other result would be silly. I also agree with the concurrence of my senior colleague Justice Park.

I do, however, want to add a few words about broader questions of policy. It will help to consider this hypothetical: Suppose that, following the example of John Adams,[1] Arthur Murdock's last words, uttered to Deputy Linden just seconds before he died, had been "Sarah is still alive." Under these altered facts, it is the Hayes children who seek to admit the evidence, and Arthur's statement is clearly hearsay: The statement is offered to prove that Sarah was indeed alive at the time that Arthur spoke, and its probative value with respect to that proposition depends on Arthur's having perceived that Sarah was still alive, remembered that fact by the time he spoke, and sincerely intended to convey that proposition to his listener. Accordingly, under the prevailing law, the statement is presumptively inadmissible. Therefore, unless the Hayes children can persuade the court that the statement fits within one of the many exceptions or exemptions to the rule against hearsay, the evidence will not be admitted. There are, however, many such exemptions. (I shall use this term as including exceptions as well.) Most of them carve out categories of statements that are supposedly particularly reliable. The basis for that conclusion is usually some form of cracker-barrel psychology, and the question of whether a particular exemption applies may raise numerous complex issues; it is not at all clear that any exemption would apply here.[2]

---

[1] Adams' last words are said to be, "Thomas Jefferson survives." But Adams, separated by more than 500 miles from Monticello, had no personal knowledge of the matter, and in fact Jefferson had died several hours earlier; both died on the 50th anniversary of the signing of the Declaration of Independence.

[2] In the hypothetical case, for example, the Hayes children might argue that the statement should be admitted as a statement of present sense impression, see Fed. R. Evid. 803(1) or as an excited utterance, see Fed. R. Evid., 803(2). These exceptions are based largely on the belief that "substantial contemporaneity of event and statement" or "a condition of excitement," respectively, makes "conscious misrepresentation" unlikely. Adv. Comm. Note. One familiar with the ease and speed with which some people lie to protect their interest, even while under considerable stress, might challenge that view. The Murdock children would no doubt argue that the statement was not sufficiently contemporaneous with his observation to

But what sense does this make? I assume that if Arthur were able to visit from the far side and testify, "Sarah was still alive when Deputy Linden came up to me," that evidence would be considered more probative than prejudicial and it would be admitted. If this is not so, the Deputy's testimony of what Arthur said can be excluded without considering the hearsay rule. So, assuming that it is so, why should the Deputy's testimony of what Arthur said be excluded?

True, the Deputy's testimony of what Arthur said is not as good as Arthur's own testimony. If Arthur were able to come to court, then perhaps that would be some ground for excluding the Deputy's testimony, to induce the Hayes children to present the better evidence, Arthur's own testimony. (Even that is doubtful, however, because unless the Hayes children were much better able than the Murdock children to produce Arthur, which seems unlikely, it might be enough to tell the Murdock children that if they want to examine Arthur they should bring him to court.) But Arthur is dead and in fact can't be brought back to life.

So the choice is between the Deputy's testimony of what Arthur said and not hearing from Arthur at all. Remember that by hypothesis Arthur's live testimony would be considered more probative than prejudicial. Given that, I think it is almost certain that the Deputy's testimony is also more probative than prejudicial. True, it is not as good as the live testimony, but the question now is whether it is better than nothing. It seems to me that a trier of fact, whether juror or judge, can take into account the facts that Arthur did not speak under oath and is not around to be cross-examined. (And of course, the trier can take into account any flaws in the Deputy's testimony; he *is* subject to cross.) Even if the trier would somewhat over-value the evidence by failing to take these defects into account – and some research suggests that jurors are more likely to *under*-value the evidence – I think it is highly unlikely that the trier would over-value it so greatly that the letting the trier know what Arthur said is worse for truth determination than shutting the trier's ears to it.

The situation would look very different if Arthur made his statement in contemplation of its use in litigation. Then admitting the statement would effectively allow Arthur to testify against the Hayes children without taking an oath or facing cross-examination. (If such a statement were offered against a criminal defendant, then its use should ordinarily be considered to violate the accused's right under the Sixth Amendment to the Constitution "to be confronted with the witnesses against him.") But it does not appear that Arthur's statement was made with litigation in mind.

This opinion, then, suggests that these are the questions that should determine the admissibility of statements like Arthur's hypothetical one: Would admitting the statement be effectively to allow a witness to testify outside a formal, adversative setting? Is the statement more probative

---

satisfy the first of these exceptions and that the second fails because there is no proof that he was in "a condition of excitement."

than prejudicial? Is the proponent much better able than the opponent to produce the person who made the statement? Some day, I hope the law of evidence will be revamped to reflect this view. But for now, we have to ask: Is it hearsay? Does it fit within an exemption to the hearsay rule?

Subramaniam v. Public Prosecutor

Judicial Committee of the Privy Council, 1956.
100 Solicitor's Journal 566.

This was an appeal, by special leave, by Subramaniam, a rubber tapper, from an order of the Supreme Court of the Federation of Malaya (Court of Appeal at Kuala Lumpur), dated 12th September, 1955, dismissing his appeal against a judgment and order of the High Court of Johore Bahru, whereby he was found guilty on a charge of being in possession of twenty rounds of ammunition without lawful authority, contrary to reg. 4(1)(*b*) of the Emergency Regulations, 1951, and sentenced to death. It was common ground that on 29th April, 1955, at a place in the Rengam District in the State of Johore, the appellant was found in a wounded condition by certain members of the security forces; that when he was searched there was found around his waist a leather belt with three pouches containing twenty live rounds of ammunition. The defense put forward was that he had been captured by terrorists, that at all material times he was acting under duress, and that at the time of his capture by the security forces he had formed the intention to surrender, with which intention he had come to the place where he was found. He gave evidence describing his capture and sought to give evidence of what the terrorists said to him, but the trial judge ruled that evidence of the conversation with the terrorists was not admissible unless they were called. The judge said that he could find no evidence of duress, and in the result the appellant, as stated, was convicted.

Mr. L. M. D. De Silva, giving the judgment said that the trial judge was in error in ruling out peremptorily the evidence of conversation between the terrorists and the appellant. Evidence of a statement made to a witness by a person who was not himself called as a witness might or might not be hearsay. It was hearsay and inadmissible when the object of the evidence was to establish the truth of what was contained in the statement. It was not hearsay and was admissible when it was proposed to establish by the evidence, not the truth of the statement, but the fact that it was made. Statements could have been made to the appellant by the terrorists which, whether true or not, if they had been believed by the appellant, might, within the meaning of s. 94 of the Penal Code of the Federated Malay States, reasonably have induced in him an apprehension of instant death if he failed to conform to their wishes. Thus a complete, or substantially complete, version according to the appellant of what was said to him by the terrorists and by him to them had been shut out, and their lordships had to consider whether, in the circumstances of this case, that exclusion of admissible evidence afforded sufficient reason for allowing the appeal. In Muhammad Nawaz v. King-Emperor, it was said: "Broadly speaking, the Judicial Committee will only interfere where there has been an infringement of the essential principles of justice. An obvious example would be * * * where [the accused] was not allowed to call relevant witnesses." In the present case the appellant had not been allowed to give relevant and admissible evidence, which was a circumstance very similar in its consequence to not being allowed "to call relevant witnesses." The appellant's version, if believed, could and might have afforded cogent evidence of duress brought to bear on him. He had not been allowed to give relevant and admissible evidence, and it could not be held with any confidence that had the excluded evidence, which went to the very root of the defense of duress, been admitted, the result of the trial would probably have been the same. Their lordships, for those reasons, had humbly advised Her Majesty that the appeal should be allowed.

Vinyard v. Vinyard Funeral Home, Inc.

St. Louis Court of Appeals, Missouri, 1968.
435 S.W.2d 392.

■ CLEMENS, COMMISSIONER.

Plaintiff got a verdict and $13,000 judgment for injuries from a fall on defendant's parking lot. (Plaintiff was the daughter-in-law of the corporate defendant's president.) Defendant appeals. * * *

[O]ne rainy night plaintiff slipped and fell when she stepped from a roughly paved surface onto a smoothly paved surface of a ramp in defendant's dimly lighted parking lot. * * *

* * *

Defendant's Point III concerns the admission of evidence that people complained to its officers and employees that the sealed surface was slippery when wet. Plaintiff offered this evidence to show that defendant knew its parking lot was slippery when wet. Witness Keith Vinyard was defendant's vice-president and plaintiff's husband. Testifying for plaintiff he was asked: "Now, Keith, after this sealer was put on did you receive any complaints from anyone visiting the funeral home?" Over defense objection that the question was hearsay unless limited to the same conditions as plaintiff's fall, the witness answered: "Yes, several people said it was slick." Later, witness Leroy Lucas, one of defendant's regular employees, was asked: "Did you yourself hear complaints of people that would come in and complain about it being slick when it was wet?" Over the defendant's hearsay objection Mr. Lucas answered: "I had heard different people comment on it that it was slick when it was wet."

These questions and answers were improper as hearsay if offered only to prove the fact that the sealed area was slick. But aside from the *fact* of slickness there was the issue of defendant's *knowledge* of slickness. Evidence of *complaints* of slickness made to defendant was relevant to the material issue of defendant's knowledge. As said in Miller v. Brunson Const. Co., Mo., 250 S.W.2d 958[9]: "Where, regardless of the truth or the falsity of a statement, the fact that it has been made is relevant, the hearsay rule does not apply, but the statement may be shown. Evidence as to the making of such statement is not secondary but primary, for the statement itself may constitute a fact in issue, or be circumstantially relevant as to the existence of such a fact."

The defendant's own witnesses later testified that the parking lot was slick when wet, and that the sealed upper area was slicker than the unsealed lower area. But to make her case the plaintiff was obliged to show that defendant's officers knew about the slickness. Under the circumstances of this case the trial court properly admitted evidence that this knowledge had come to them through complaints of patrons that the parking lot's sealed area was slick when wet.

Affirmed.

Johnson v. Misericordia Community Hospital

Court of Appeals of Wisconsin, 1980.
97 Wis.2d 521, 294 N.W.2d 501.

[Plaintiff sued the hospital for negligence in hiring one Dr. Salinsky and in allowing him to perform surgery on plaintiff's hip].

* * *

* * * [F]or Misericordia to be liable here, it must have failed to exercise that degree of care and skill usually exercised or maintained by other reputable hospitals in similar situations.

There was abundant expert testimony in this case regarding the procedures utilized by hospital committees to check a physician's references upon application for staff privileges, and the ease with which Misericordia could have had access to Dr. Salinsky's records. Once having obtained such records, Dr. Salinsky's incompetence would have been apparent to the executive committee of Misericordia Hospital.

* * *

Misericordia objects to the introduction of testimony regarding the restrictions imposed on Dr. Salinsky's practice at Doctors Hospital and to the introduction of Doctors Hospital medical executive committee reports dealing with the investigation and suspension of Dr. Salinsky's privileges. Misericordia similarly objects to the admission of testimony by the attorney for St. Anthony Hospital regarding the hospital's refusal to allow Dr. Salinsky on the staff. Finally, defendant objects to the introduction of documents concerning the action of the credentials committee of St. Anthony Hospital in regard to Dr. Salinsky's application.

The objections to the introduction of the minutes and records are based on hearsay. The trial court received the documents into evidence under the hearsay exception for records of regularly conducted activities. The trial court also noted that even if such records constituted medical opinions, they were not admitted to establish the truth of the opinions, but to show that such opinions did exist and should have been considered by those investigating Dr. Salinsky's application. We affirm the trial court.

Hearsay evidence is generally excluded as untrustworthy; lacking the traditional guarantees of oath, confrontation and cross-examination for the credibility of the out-of-court declarant. Thus hearsay rests its value upon the credibility of the out-of-court declarant. Misericordia claims that for these reasons, the individuals who comprised the committees and conducted the investigation leading to restriction and denial of staff privileges should have been present to testify. Nevertheless, Misericordia made no effort to prove the untruthfulness of the reports or to challenge the trustworthiness of physicians involved.

* * *

Based upon the facts as incorporated in this record, we affirm the trial court's receipt into evidence of the committee reports regarding Dr. Salinsky's professional competence. The reports were properly considered by the jury as evidence of the type of information available to Misericordia at the time of Dr. Salinsky's application for staff privileges.

The evidence concerning the "credentials process" was admissible to show the existence of information regarding Dr. Salinsky's professional qualifications and the availability of such knowledge to Misericordia's medical executive committee. Thus Misericordia should have known of the restrictions placed on Dr. Salinsky's practice by other Milwaukee hospitals and that one hospital had denied him staff privileges. Once admissible for the purpose of showing the existence and availability of information, Misericordia's remedy at trial was to ask for a limiting instruction if it believed that the evidence was to be used to establish Dr. Salinsky's incompetence. * * *

Misericordia also objects to the introduction into evidence of the testimony of Dr. Nesemann that between the years of 1967 and 1975, he had heard other physicians state that "Dr. Salinsky was incompetent as an orthopedic surgeon."

Again, as above, this evidence was admissible for the purpose of showing the availability of knowledge concerning Dr. Salinsky's competence. If counsel for Misericordia thought this evidence might be used for an improper purpose, a limiting instruction should have been requested.

Judgment affirmed.

Ries Biologicals, Inc. v. Bank of Santa Fe

United States Court of Appeals, Tenth Circuit, 1986.
780 F.2d 888.

■ CROW, DISTRICT JUDGE.

This is an appeal by the defendant, the Bank of Santa Fe, from a judgment for the plaintiff, Ries Biologicals, Inc., based upon the bank's alleged oral guarantee of payment for supplies delivered by Ries to Dialysis Management Systems, Inc. The trial court awarded the plaintiff $20,276.69 plus interest in the amount of $6,632.96, and costs including attorneys fees.

Ries Biologicals is a distributor of medical supplies. In 1979, Ries began selling supplies to Dialysis Management Systems, Inc. (DMS) a health care provider specializing in kidney dialysis, operating in New Mexico and adjacent states. DMS was experiencing financial problems quickly accumulating a debt to Ries Biologicals in the approximate amount of $42,000. Because of the size of this debt, in January of 1980 Ries refused to make further shipments to DMS except for cash on delivery. Sometime in the first quarter of 1980, Ries resumed shipments to DMS on credit. The trial court found that resumption of credit shipments resulted from Ries' reliance on the Bank's oral agreement to guarantee payment for orders which were approved in advance. From the time of the agreement until July 30, 1980, Ries made regular shipments to DMS based upon prior approval of the senior vice-president of the bank, Philip Levitt. * * *

Despite obtaining advance approval from the bank, Ries was not paid the full amount due for materials shipped under this arrangement. The trial court entered judgment in favor of Ries for the balance due.

* * *

The defendants contend that the trial court erroneously admitted testimony concerning Philip Levitt's oral, out-of-court statements guaranteeing payment for approved shipments. * * *

The oral statements of Philip Levitt were expressly offered for a nonhearsay purpose. The relevance of Levitt's statements is not their truth or falsity, rather it is the fact the statements were made. The relevance of the statements depends, therefore, not on the credibility of the out-of-court declarant, Philip Levitt, but on that of the testifying witness. See J. Weinstein & M. Berger, Weinstein's Evidence ¶ 801(c)[01]. There was no manifest error in the admission of testimony concerning the oral statements of Philip Levitt.

[Affirmed].

Strahorn, A Reconsideration of the Hearsay Rule and Admissions

85 U.Pa.L.Rev. 484, 490 (1937).*

Utterances as operative conduct

If the making of the utterance is the ultimate thing sought to be proven in the case, rather than a device for proving that thing, the suspicion of hearsay attaches the least. So it is that the topic of utterances as operative conduct is the one of simplest application under the hearsay rule. No question of possible testimonial or narrative use can arise when the speaking of the words determines the rights being litigated. Thus it is that such typical examples as the making of a promise, the speaking of a slander, the printing of a libel, the speaking of marriage vows are all species of extra-judicial utterances provable despite the hearsay rule because they are the operative conduct of the speaker. For them there is no possible question of the trustworthiness of the utterance. * * *

Fun–Damental Too, Ltd. v. Gemmy Industries Corp.

United States Court of Appeals, Second Circuit, 1997.
111 F.3d 993.

■ CARDAMONE, CIRCUIT JUDGE:

* * *

Plaintiff Fun–Damental Too, Ltd. (plaintiff or Fun–Damental) brought suit in the United States District Court for the Southern District of New York (Mukasey, J.) against defendants Gemmy Industries Corp. and Kay–Bee Toy & Hobby Shops, Inc. (defendants, appellants, or Gemmy and Kay–Bee) for trade dress infringement under the Lanham Act, as well as for claims alleging injury to its business under New York law. According to Fun–Damental's complaint, Gemmy copied the packaging of plaintiff's "Toilet Bank," a retail novelty item, for use with defendant's similar product, the "Currency Can" * * * *

Fun–Damental is a Pennsylvania limited partnership that develops and sells novelty toys and gifts, most of which feature some mechanism for producing sound. These products are known in the toy industry as "impulse items," because they are purchased based on a consumer's quick decision made while in the store, without comparison shopping or investigation. Fun–Damental sells its line of products through large chains such as Walgreen's, Service Merchandise and Toys 'R' Us, and through gift shops, hardware stores, college bookstores and other small retail outlets.

In 1992 plaintiff began developing the Toilet Bank, a toy coin bank closely resembling the familiar white tank toilet. An important feature of this product is its ability to simulate the flushing sound of a toilet when its handle is depressed. "Flushing" the Toilet Bank also enables coins placed in

---

* Copyright, 1936–1937 by The University of Pennsylvania.

the toilet bowl to drop into the bank's base. When development was completed in 1994, Fun–Damental began promoting its novelty coin bank through its catalogs and at trade shows. Consumers have since purchased more than 860,000 of these items at a retail price of $15 to $20 each.

In May 1995 defendant Kay–Bee, a major toy and novelty retailer, expressed interest in buying the Toilet Bank. But after examining a sample, Kay–Bee decided against carrying the product because of its high cost relative to other impulse items. In September 1995 Fun–Damental's sales manager visited Kay–Bee and noticed a toilet-shaped bank resembling the Toilet Bank on a shelf in the office of Kay–Bee's purchasing agent in charge of impulse items. The sales manager's request to examine the item more closely was turned down. In October Fun–Damental sent Kay–Bee a product notice requesting to examine a sample of the observed product for possible infringement. No sample was sent.

It turned out that defendant Gemmy, a novelty manufacturer, had approached Kay–Bee and supplied it with toilet-shaped coin banks similar to Fun–Damental's. Kay–Bee was able to purchase Gemmy's Currency Cans at a lower wholesale price than the Toilet Bank, and was therefore able to retail Gemmy's product at $9.99 each. The record reveals that when Gemmy's vice-president learned of Fun–Damental's Toilet Bank, he contacted his company's Chinese factory in May 1995 and asked it to design a similar product. In the design phase of the Currency Can, a sample of Fun–Damental's Toilet Bank was sent to Gemmy's Chinese manufacturer. The Gemmy official testified that the Currency Can was designed with dimensions virtually identical to those of the Toilet Bank in order to compete effectively with it.

* * *

Fun–Damental offered the direct testimony of its national sales manager to demonstrate actual confusion. He testified that some retail customers complained because they thought Fun–Damental was selling its Toilet Bank at a lower price to other retailers. Defendants argue that this evidence is inadmissible hearsay upon which the district court should not have relied and, even if admissible, it does not support a finding of actual confusion.

There is no hearsay problem. Hearsay is an out-of-court statement admitted for the truth of the matter asserted. *See* Fed. R. Evid. 801. The testimony in question was not offered to prove that Fun–Damental was actually selling to some retailers at lower prices, but was probative of the declarant's confusion. Further, Federal Rule of Evidence 803(3) allows statements, otherwise excluded as hearsay, to be received to show the declarant's then-existing state of mind. The district court properly considered the statements.

[After discussion of other issues, the district court's decision granting a preliminary injunction was affirmed.]

United States v. Hernandez

United States Court of Appeals, Fifth Circuit, 1985.
750 F.2d 1256.

■ ALVIN B. RUBIN, CIRCUIT JUDGE:

We reverse the conviction of Herminio Hernandez on two counts relating to possession and distribution of cocaine because the prosecuting attorney elicited inadmissible testimony from a government witness, a Drug Enforcement Administration (DEA) special agent, that U.S. Customs had identified Hernandez as a drug smuggler. The district judge overruled an objection to the testimony, and the prosecutor, in her closing argument to the jury, later emphasized this evidence, embellishing it to go even beyond the actual testimony.

Viewing the facts in the light most favorable to the government, the evidence showed that an informant, Gholson, accompanied by special agent Ana Saulnier, who posed as Gholson's wife, met Hernandez by prearrangement in a coffee shop. Hernandez offered to sell them a kilo of cocaine for $52,000. Hernandez, who took the stand, denies that the conversation at the coffee shop involved controlled substances. Later Gholson and agent Saulnier, the ostensible Mrs. Gholson, driving in an automobile, met Hernandez at a service station and followed Hernandez's car to his tire shop. There, in a back room, two packages of cocaine wrapped in newspaper lay atop a television tray table. Hernandez said he did not want to transact business in the presence of [Saulnier], so Saulnier left the room. Gholson then accepted the cocaine. As Gholson and Hernandez were proceeding to the place where payment was to be made, Hernandez was arrested.

Hernandez testified that he had been "set up" by Gholson. The conversation in the coffee shop, he said, concerned leasing a room at his tire shop to Gholson to be used to make pornographic films. He had led Gholson and Saulnier to his shop and had merely shown the room to Gholson, but he had not entered it. Hernandez, by cross-examination and other evidence, attacked Gholson's credibility. Gholson had been charged on numerous occasions with felony charges stemming from his involvement in the pornography business. He also had made his living as an informant for thirteen years, and was paid by the arrest, not the conviction. An officer of the Houston Police Department testified that his department had stopped using Gholson as an informant because they suspected him of making cases against innocent people. Thus, the case boiled down to the jury's acceptance of the version of the facts testified to by Gholson and Saulnier or Hernandez's version. Both sides, in oral argument, correctly referred to the testimony as a "swearing match."

Near the beginning of Saulnier's testimony, the following occurred:

Q. (Prosecutor) Now, Special Agent Saulnier, what first brought the attention of the Drug Enforcement Administration to Herminio Hernandez?

A. We received a referral by the U.S. Customs as Hernandez being a drug smuggler.

Mr. Suarez: Judge, may I object to this testimony * * *.

The Court: I'm going to overrule the objection.

The government's argument that this testimony was not hearsay and was relevant to show Saulnier's state of mind lacks merit. Saulnier's state of mind was not at issue. The testimony was, therefore, clearly hearsay. The referral was a "statement" other than one made by Saulnier * * * while testifying at trial, offered to prove the truth of the matter asserted (that Hernandez was a drug smuggler). The government's protestation that the evidence was not elicited to prove Hernandez was a drug smuggler, but merely to explain the motivation behind DEA's investigation is unconvincing from both a common sense perspective, and from the government's subsequent use of that testimony. * * *

The prosecuting attorney (who was not the Assistant U.S. Attorney who presented the case on appeal) was not content to leave bad enough alone. In her closing argument, she told the jury:

What kind of case has the government brought to you today? You heard testimony that this case, this defendant, was brought to the attention of the Drug Enforcement Administration through a referral from another law enforcement agency, United States Customs. And what was the nature of that referral? The nature of that referral was that this individual was a *known cocaine trafficer* [sic] * * *. (Emphasis added.)

* * * The government thus relied on the evidence not as proof of Saulnier's state of mind at the inception of the investigation, but as evidence of Hernandez's guilt. This type of evidence is inadmissible under Fed.R.Evid. 802.

The state of mind of the DEA agent for beginning an investigation of the defendant, was not relevant. * * *

Reversed.

HYPOTHETICALS

(1) X is prosecuted for assault with a deadly weapon on A by use of a billiard cue. X's defense is self-defense. In rebuttal the prosecution calls B, who proposes to testify that a week before the fight A told him that X had struck him several times with a baseball bat a month before in a sudden fit of temper. X makes a hearsay objection to B's testimony.

(2) X is prosecuted for murder of A. A died from a bullet wound received while in X's apartment. X's defense is that X was showing a pistol to A at A's request and that it accidentally went off as A was handling it. The prosecution calls B who proposes to testify that a week before A's death, A

[handwritten margin note: Non- Hearsay stmt stat of mind of victim.]

told him that X had threatened to kill A. X objects to B's testimony as hearsay.

(3) X is prosecuted for the murder of A, his wife. It is undisputed that while A was seated in a chair watching television, X pulled a pistol from his pocket and fired three shots into A, killing her instantly. *[handwritten: purpose]* In order to negate the intent requisite for first degree murder, X testifies to a history of marital difficulties, which he claims impaired his mental condition. In rebuttal, to prove A's state of mind shortly before her death, the prosecution calls B, who proposes to testify that in a telephone conversation with A on the day before her death, A said, *[handwritten: start]* "I know X is going to kill me. I wish he would hurry up and get it over with, because he will never let me leave him." X objects to B's proposed testimony on the grounds of hearsay.

[handwritten: Non Hearsay - goes to state of mind of victim. victim's fear is NOT relevant to the purpose for X]

United States v. Zenni

United States District Court, Eastern District of Kentucky, 1980.
492 F.Supp. 464.

■ BERTELSMAN, DISTRICT JUDGE.

This prosecution for illegal bookmaking activities presents a classic problem in the law of evidence, namely, whether implied assertions are hearsay. The problem was a controversial one at common law, the discussion of which has filled many pages in the treatises and learned journals. Although the answer to the problem is clear under the Federal Rules of Evidence, there has been little judicial treatment of the matter, and many members of the bar are unfamiliar with the marked departure from the common law the Federal Rules have effected on this issue.

FACTS

The relevant facts are simply stated. While conducting a search of the premises of the defendant, Ruby Humphrey, pursuant to a lawful search warrant which authorized a search for evidence of bookmaking activity, government agents answered the telephone several times. The unknown callers stated directions for the placing of bets on various sporting events. The government proposes to introduce this evidence to show that the callers believed that the premises were used in betting operations. The existence of such belief tends to prove that they were so used. The defendants object on the ground of hearsay.

COMMON LAW BACKGROUND

At common law, the hearsay rule applied "only to evidence of out-of-court statements offered for the purpose of proving that the facts are as asserted in the statement."

On the other hand, not all out-of-court expression is common law hearsay. For instance, an utterance offered to show the publication of a slander, or that a person was given notice of a fact, or orally entered into a contract, is not hearsay.

In the instant case, the utterances of the absent declarants are not offered for the truth of the words,[7] and the mere fact that the words were uttered has no relevance of itself. Rather they are offered to show the declarants' belief in a fact sought to be proved. At common law this situation occupied a controversial no-man's land. It was argued on the one hand that the out-of-court utterance was not hearsay, because the evidence was not offered for any truth stated in it, but for the truth of some other proposition inferred from it. On the other hand, it was also argued that the reasons for excluding hearsay applied, in that the evidence was being offered to show declarant's belief in the implied proposition, and he was not available to be cross-examined. Thus, the latter argument was that there existed strong policy reasons for ruling that such utterances were hearsay.

The classic case, which is discussed in virtually every textbook on evidence, is Wright v. Tatham, 7 Adolph. & E. 313, 386, 112 Eng.Rep. 488 (Exch. Ch. 1837), and 5 Cl. & F. 670, 739, 47 Rev.Rep. 136 (H.L.1838). Described as a "celebrated and hard-fought cause," Wright v. Tatham was a will contest, in which the will was sought to be set aside on the grounds of the incompetency of the testator at the time of its execution. The proponents of the will offered to introduce into evidence letters to the testator from certain absent individuals on various business and social matters. The purpose of the offer was to show that the writers of the letters believed the testator was able to make intelligent decisions concerning such matters, and thus was competent.

One of the illustrations advanced in the judicial opinions in Wright v. Tatham is perhaps even more famous than the case itself. This is Baron Parke's famous sea captain example. Is it hearsay to offer as proof of the seaworthiness of a vessel that its captain, after thoroughly inspecting it, embarked on an ocean voyage upon it with his family?

The court in Wright v. Tatham held that implied assertions of this kind were hearsay. The rationale, as stated by Baron Parke, was as follows:

> "The conclusion at which I have arrived is, that proof of a particular fact which is not of itself a matter in issue, but which is relevant only as implying a statement or opinion of a third person on the matter in issue, is inadmissible in all cases where such a statement or opinion not on oath would be of itself inadmissible; and, therefore, in this case the letters which are offered only to prove the competence of the testator, that is the truth of the implied statements therein contained, were properly rejected, as the mere statement or opinion of the writer would certainly have been inadmissible."

This was the prevailing common law view, where the hearsay issue was recognized. But frequently, it was not recognized. Thus, two federal appellate cases involving facts virtually identical to those in the case at bar

---

[7] That is, the utterance, "Put $2 to win on Paul Revere in the third at Pimlico," is a direction and not an assertion of any kind, and therefore can be neither true nor false.

did not even discuss the hearsay issue, although the evidence admitted in them would have been objectionable hearsay under the common law view.

THE FEDERAL RULES OF EVIDENCE

The common law rule that implied assertions were subject to hearsay treatment was criticized by respected commentators for several reasons. A leading work on the Federal Rules of Evidence [Weinstein's Evidence, ¶ 801(a)(01)], referring to the hotly debated question whether an implied assertion stands on better ground with respect to the hearsay rule than an express assertion, states:

> "By the time the federal rules were drafted, a number of eminent scholars and revisers had concluded that it does. Two principal arguments were usually expressed for removing implied assertions from the scope of the hearsay rule. First, when a person acts in a way consistent with a belief but without intending by his act to communicate that belief, one of the principal reasons for the hearsay rule—to exclude declarations whose veracity cannot be tested by cross-examination—does not apply, because the declarant's sincerity is not then involved. In the second place, the underlying belief is in some cases self-verifying:
>
> > 'There is frequently a guarantee of the trustworthiness of the inference to be drawn * * * because the actor has based his actions on the correctness of his belief, i.e., his actions speak louder than words.' "

In a frequently cited article [Judson F. Falknor, *The "Hear-Say" Rule as a "See-Do" Rule: Evidence of Conduct*, 33 Rocky Mt.L. Rev. 133 (1961)] the following analysis appears:

> "But ought the hearsay rule be deemed applicable to evidence of conduct? As McCormick has observed, the problem 'has only once received any adequate discussion in any decided case,' i.e., in Wright v. Tatham, already referred to. And even in that case the court did not pursue its inquiry beyond the point of concluding that evidence of an 'implied' assertion must necessarily be excluded wherever evidence of an 'express' assertion would be inadmissible. But as has been pointed out more than once (although I find no *judicial* recognition of the difference), the 'implied' assertion is, from the hearsay standpoint, not nearly as vulnerable as an express assertion of the fact which the evidence is offered to establish.
>
> "This is on the assumption that the conduct was 'nonassertive;' that the passers-by had their umbrellas up for the sake of keeping dry, not for the purpose of telling anyone it was raining; that the truck driver started up for the sake of resuming his journey, not for the purpose of telling anyone that the light had changed; that the vicar wrote the letter to the testator for the purpose of settling the dispute with the latter, rather than with any idea of expressing his opinion of the

testator's sanity. And in the typical 'conduct as hearsay' case this assumption will be quite justifiable.

"On this assumption, it is clear that evidence of conduct must be taken as freed from at least one of the hearsay dangers, i.e., mendacity. A man does not lie to himself. Put otherwise, if in doing what he does a man has no intention of asserting the existence or non-existence of a fact, it would appear that the trustworthiness of evidence of this conduct is the same whether he is an egregious liar or a paragon of veracity. Accordingly, the lack of opportunity for cross-examination in relation to his veracity or lack of it, would seem to be of no substantial importance. Accordingly, the usual judicial disposition to equate the 'implied' to the 'express' assertion is very questionable."

The drafters of the Federal Rules agreed with the criticisms of the common law rule that implied assertions should be treated as hearsay and expressly abolished it. They did this by providing that no oral or written expression was to be considered as hearsay, unless it was an "assertion" concerning the matter sought to be proved and that no nonverbal conduct should be considered as hearsay, unless it was intended to be an "assertion" concerning said matter.[18] The relevant provisions are:

Rule 801. "(a) Statement.—A *'statement'* is (1) an oral or written *assertion* or (2) nonverbal conduct of a person, if it is *intended by him as an assertion.*

* * *

(c) Hearsay. 'Hearsay' is a statement, other than one made by the declarant while testifying at the trial or hearing, offered in evidence to prove the truth of the matter asserted."

"Assertion" is not defined in the rules, but has the connotation of a forceful or positive declaration.

The Advisory Committee note concerning this problem states:

"The definition of 'statement' assumes importance because the term is used in the definition of hearsay in subdivision (c). The effect of the definition of 'statement' is to exclude from the operation of the hearsay rule all evidence of conduct, verbal or nonverbal, not intended as an assertion. The key to the definition is that nothing is an assertion unless intended to be one.

---

[18] See the sea captain illustration discussed, supra. In an unpublished ruling this court recently held admissible as non-hearsay the fact that a U.S. mining inspector ate his lunch in an area in a coal mine now alleged to have been unsafe, and that other inspectors who observed operations prior to a disastrous explosion issued no citations, when it would have been their duty to do so, if there had been safety violations. These non-assertive acts would have been hearsay under the rule of Wright v. Tatham but are not hearsay under Rule 801 of the Federal Rules of Evidence, because the inspectors did not intend to make assertions under the circumstances. Boggs v. Blue Diamond Coal Company (E.D.Ky. No. 77–69, Pikeville Division).

"It can scarcely be doubted that an assertion made in words is intended by the declarant to be an assertion. Hence verbal assertions readily fall into the category of 'statement.' Whether nonverbal conduct should be regarded as a statement for purposes of defining hearsay requires further consideration. Some nonverbal conduct, such as the act of pointing to identify a suspect in a lineup, is clearly the equivalent of words, assertive in nature, and to be regarded as a statement. Other nonverbal conduct, however, may be offered as evidence that the person acted as he did because of his belief in the existence of the condition sought to be proved, from which belief the existence of the condition may be inferred. This sequence is, arguably, in effect an assertion of the existence of the condition and hence properly includable within the hearsay concept. Admittedly evidence of this character is untested with respect to the perception, memory, and narration (or their equivalents) of the actor, but the Advisory Committee is of the view that these dangers are minimal in the absence of an intent to assert and do not justify the loss of the evidence on hearsay grounds. No class of evidence is free of the possibility of fabrication, but the likelihood is less with nonverbal than with assertive verbal conduct. The situations giving rise to the nonverbal conduct are such as virtually to eliminate questions of sincerity. Motivation, the nature of the conduct, and the presence or absence of reliance will bear heavily upon the weight to be given the evidence. Similar considerations govern nonassertive verbal conduct and verbal conduct which is assertive but offered as a basis for inferring something other than the matter asserted, also excluded from the definition of hearsay by the language of subdivision (c)." (Emphasis added).

This court, therefore, holds that, "Subdivision (a)(2) of Rule 801 removes implied assertions from the definition of statement and consequently from the operation of the hearsay rule."

Applying the principles discussed above to the case at bar, this court holds that the utterances of the betters telephoning in their bets were nonassertive verbal conduct, offered as relevant for an implied assertion to be inferred from them, namely that bets could be placed at the premises being telephoned. The language is not an assertion on its face, and it is obvious these persons did not intend to make an assertion about the fact sought to be proved or anything else.[21]

---

[21] A somewhat different type of analysis would be required by words non-assertive in form, but which under the circumstances might be intended as an assertion. For example, an inspector at an airport security station might run a metal detector over a passenger and say "go on through." In the absence of the inspector, would testimony of this event be objectionable hearsay, if offered for the proposition that the passenger did not have a gun on him at that time? Although Rule 801(a) does not seem to require a preliminary determination by the trial court whether verbal conduct is intended as an assertion, it is submitted that such a determination would be required in the example given. If an assertion were intended the evidence would be excluded. If not, it would be admissible. This result is implicit in the policy of the drafters of the Federal Rules of Evidence that the touchstone for hearsay is the intention to make an assertion.

As an implied assertion, the proffered evidence is expressly excluded from the operation of the hearsay rule by Rule 801 of the Federal Rules of Evidence, and the objection thereto must be overruled. An order to that effect has previously been entered.

NOTE

In Regina v. Kearley, 2 App. Cas. 228 (H.L. Eng. 1992), defendant was charged with possession of drugs with intent to supply. The police had raided defendant's flat, finding a modest quantity of drugs that could have been for personal use. Investigators remained on the premises for several hours. At trial, they testified that they intercepted ten telephone calls from persons seeking drugs and talked to seven people who visited the flat with requests for drugs. Citing *Wright v. Tatham*, discussed by *Zenni, supra* at 216, the House of Lords held that the statements of the callers and visitors were inadmissible hearsay. It indicated that evidence of a request to buy drugs, when offered as an "implied assertion" that defendant was a drug dealer, stood on the same footing as a statement expressly asserting that defendant was a drug dealer. But *Kearley* was reversed by Section 115 of the Criminal Justice Act of 2003, which makes the hearsay rule applicable in criminal proceedings only if

the purpose, or one of the purposes, of the person making the statement appears to the court to have been—

(a) to cause another person to believe the matter, or

(b) to cause another person to act or a machine to operate on the basis that the matter is as stated.

Thus, now an English court would say that the calls in *Kearley* were not hearsay; they were made not to persuade a person that the intended recipient was a drug dealer but simply to buy drugs. *See* Crown Prosecution Service, *Hearsay: Definition of a Statement,* http://www.cps.gov.uk/legal/h_to_k/ hearsay/#statement (last visited October 26, 2012); *see also, e.g.,* R v. Chrysostomou [2010] EWCA Crim 1403.

Commonwealth v. Knapp

Supreme Judicial Court of Massachusetts, 1830.
VII American State Trials 395, 515–516.

[John Francis Knapp was tried in 1830 for the murder of one Joseph White. The prosecution, headed by Daniel Webster, claimed that Knapp aided and abetted one Crowninshield, who actually struck the fatal blows. It was therefore crucial to the prosecution to show Crowninshield's guilt—even though Crowninshield himself had committed suicide before the trial. In his closing argument, Daniel Webster discussed the probative value of the suicide on the issue of Crowninshield's guilt—Eds.]

The fatal blow is given! and the victim passes, without a struggle or a motion, from the repose of sleep to the repose of death! It is the assassin's purpose to make sure work, and he yet plies the dagger, though it was obvious that life had been destroyed by the blow of the bludgeon. He even raises the aged arm, that he may not fail in his aim at the heart, and replaces it again over the wounds of the poignard! To finish the picture, he explores the wrist for the pulse! he feels it, and ascertains that it beats no longer! It is accomplished. The deed is done. He retreats, retraces his steps to the window, passes out through it, as he came in, and escapes. He has done the murder—no eye has seen him, no ear has heard him. The secret is his own, and it is safe!

Ah! gentlemen, that was a dreadful mistake. Such a secret can be safe nowhere. The whole creation of God has neither nook nor corner, where the guilty can bestow it, and say it is safe. Not to speak of that eye which glances through all disguises, and beholds everything, as in the splendor of noon, such secrets of guilt are never safe from detection, even by men. True it is, generally speaking, that "murder will out." True it is, that Providence hath so ordained, and doth so govern things, that those who break the great law of heaven, by shedding man's blood, seldom succeed in avoiding discovery. Especially, in a case exciting so much attention as this, discovery must come, and will come, sooner or later. A thousand eyes turn at once to explore every man, every thing, every circumstance, connected with the time and place; a thousand ears catch every whisper; a thousand excited minds intensely dwell on the scene, shedding all their light, and ready to kindle the slightest circumstance into a blaze of discovery. Meantime the guilty soul cannot keep its own secret. It is false to itself; or rather it feels an irresistible impulse of conscience to be true to itself. It labors under its guilty possession, and knows not what to do with it. The human heart was not made for the residence of such an inhabitant. It finds itself preyed on by a torment which it does not acknowledge to God nor man. A vulture is devouring it, and it can ask no sympathy or assistance, either from heaven or earth. The secret which the murderer possesses soon comes to possess him; and, like the evil spirits of which we read, it overcomes him, and leads him whithersoever it will. He feels it beating at his heart, rising to his throat, and demanding disclosure. He thinks the whole world sees it in his face, reads it in his eyes, and almost hears its workings in the very silence of his thoughts. It has become his master. It betrays his discretion, it breaks down his courage, it conquers his prudence. When suspicions, from without, begin to embarrass him, and the net of circumstance to entangle him, the fatal secret struggles with still greater violence to burst forth. It must be confessed, it will be confessed; there is no refuge from confession but suicide, and suicide is confession.

Morton, The Rothschilds[*]

49–50 (1962).

And there was no news more precious than the outcome of Waterloo. For days the London 'Change[1] had strained its ears. If Napoleon won, Eng-

---

[*] Copyright 1961 by The Curtis Publishing Co.
[1] The international currency exchange—Eds.

lish consols[2] were bound to drop. If he lost, the enemy empire would shatter and consols rise.

For thirty hours the fate of Europe hung veiled in cannon smoke. On June 19, 1815, late in the afternoon a Rothschild agent named Rothworth jumped into a boat at Ostend. In his hand he held a Dutch gazette still damp from the printer. By the dawn light of June 20 Nathan Rothschild stood at Folkstone harbor and let his eye fly over the lead paragraphs. A moment later he was on his way to London (beating Wellington's envoy by many hours) to tell the government that Napoleon had been crushed. Then he proceeded to the stock exchange.

Another man in his position would have sunk his worth into consols. But this was Nathan Rothschild. He leaned against "his" pillar. He did not invest. He sold. He dumped consols.

His name was already such that a single substantial move on his part sufficed to bear or bull an issue. Consols fell. Nathan leaned and leaned, and sold and sold. Consols dropped still more. "Rothschild knows," the whisper rippled through the 'Change. "Waterloo is lost."

Nathan kept on selling, his round face motionless and stern, his pudgy fingers depressing the market by tens of thousands of pounds with each sell signal. Consols dived, consols plummeted—until, a split second before it was too late, Nathan suddenly bought a giant parcel for a song. Moments afterwards the great news broke, to send consols soaring.

We cannot guess the number of hopes and savings wiped out by this engineered panic. We cannot estimate how many liveried servants, how many Watteaus and Rembrandts, how many thoroughbreds in his descendants' stables, the man by the pillar won that single day.

Sending a Message about Canadian Beef

In May, 2003, Canada's Prime Minister Jean Chrétien "ate a very public lunch of Alberta beef in a bid to combat a mad-cow scare."—Wall Street Journal, May 22, 2003, p. 1, col. 3.

See Federal Rules of Evidence § 801(a); Cal. Evidence Code § 225.

McCormick, The Borderland of Hearsay

39 Yale L.J. 489, 502–4 (1930).[*]

[The author, after discussing a number of cases including Wright v. Tatham, see p. 217, *supra*, concludes:]

---

[2] British government securities—Eds.

[*] Copyright 1929–1930 by The Yale Law Journal Company.

Probably the foregoing presents a fair sampling of the cases and comments pro and con on the question. From the data given it seems apparent, first, that Wright v. Tatham expresses the more generally accepted view in holding that conduct, even when not intended as assertive, is hearsay when offered to show the actor's belief and hence the truth of the belief, and second, that this view has, since the leading case, received such slight consideration in subsequent decisions which follow it, and has evoked such contrariety of opinion among the commentators (as well as a sprinkling of contrary decisions) that it is open for re-examination in the light of general policy.

It is only the technique of that general reconsideration that is of any real importance, and the assembling of the foregoing chance driftwood from the decisions is of value only so far as it clears the way for such a reconsideration. These decisions, though casual and inharmonious, serve chiefly to show the situations in real life which call for the application of such theory as we may adopt. And it is just here that the reader may ask, "Why assume that any one solution is likely to work for all the types of cases which seem to occur?" It will have been observed, certainly, that the cases fall into three groups. The first and simplest, for present purposes, are the cases of stark action with no element of communication at all. Such is the ship-captain example, see p. 217 and most of Parke's other illustrations. But in real life, as the cases show, the element of words enters in. Thus we may distinguish a second group where acts and words explaining them are offered together. Of this type is the evidence of the guest who refuses the hotel-room, objecting that it is too dark, offered to show the undesirability of the room, and the evidence of the rejection of similar goods as defective by other customers, to show breach of warranty. Finally, the third group comprises those cases where the conduct consists of words solely, but words not of *assertion,* but of *action,* such as an offer of a position (to show the *offeree's* skill) or the letters in Wright v. Tatham itself. It seems, however, that to base any difference in results on the mere circumstance that the conduct is verbal or non-verbal would be an undesirable rule of thumb not corresponding to any difference in probable trustworthiness.

If all three types, then, are to be treated alike, what shall that treatment be? The problem is one that will eventually be solved according as the profession adopts one or another general attitude toward the rules of proof. Possible attitudes might favor the admission of any and all offered items of proof, as seems to be the method in French criminal trials, or might lean toward vesting a large discretion in the trial judge to admit or exclude, guided only by certain general canons and standards, as seems to be the present English tendency, or, on the other hand, the attitude may remain one of adherence to the present system in vogue in the United States, of sharply defined rules prohibiting the admission of many rigidly classified types of evidence.

The advocates of entire exclusion of evidence of conduct to show belief, to show the truth of the fact believed, as being hearsay, hark back to the traditional technique of jury trial administration as it hardened in the eighteenth century. Judges then, to paraphrase a well-worn epigram, were surer about everything than judges today are about anything. That technique consisted of creating large, simple, but definite categories under which offered items of proof could be classified accurately and, above all, quickly. All the contents of each of these classes were either black or white, admissible or inadmissible. The largest of these categories of inadmissible evidence (though its recognition as such was later than we usually supposed) is that of hearsay. The advantages of these clear-cut rules of exclusion are obvious. They enable the lawyer preparing his case to know in advance with fair certainty what he can get in, and what he cannot. If a question as to admissibility does arise, the judge who has no time for subtle discrimination in the heat of trial can make a decision in his stride, as it were. This is splendid, and the only difficulty is that it does not work. The rule excluding all hearsay, clear and simple in its original form, when it was tested by the offer of particular hearsay evidence of a peculiarly indispensable or reliable kind cracked under the strain. To relieve the pressure, exception after exception was recognized until today the rule is riddled with thirteen or more exceptions. The exceptions are in some instances quite as rigidly defined as the rule itself.

To be contrasted with this sort of progress through the mitigation of a rigid rule by numerous rigid exceptions, is the different technique of development of such rules as, for example, those which provide for the order of presenting proof. These have from the outset been merely guides and not limits to the judge's discretion and consequently have never had to be complicated by exceptions. Would it not have been wiser to set up the hearsay rule also in some similar form, as for example: "Hearsay is inadmissible except where the judge in his discretion finds it needed and trustworthy"? The astonishing conservatism of most lawyers and of most judges drawn from their ranks, and their almost religious reverence for these mere procedural rules, will make progress towards such a result slow, but doubtless such a change is on the cards. At all events, newly evolved evidence rules are likely to be of that discretionary type.

Focusing these considerations upon our present problem, we find the orthodox, but not wholly settled or established, view to be that conduct to show belief, to show the fact believed, is invariably to be put in the "hearsay" category and banned as such. The result is that evidence which has the strongest circumstantial guaranties of reliability may be banned. Evidence that a doctor, since deceased, has operated upon a man for appendicitis, would be inadmissible as evidence that the patient actually had that disease. It is true, on the other hand, that very much of such conduct-evidence if admitted would be of trivial value and probably a general inclusionary rule, that all such evidence is admissible wherever the actor's testimony on the stand would be, would be only one degree better than wholesale exclusion. It would seem sensible to conclude that conduct (other than assertions) when offered to show the actor's beliefs and hence the truth of the facts so believed, being merely analogous to and not identical with typical hearsay, ought to be admissible whenever the trial judge in his discretion finds that the action so vouched the belief as to give reasonable assurance of trustworthiness.

Wilson v. Clancy

United States District Court for the District of Maryland, 1990.
747 F.Supp. 1154.

MEMORANDUM OPINION

■ SMALKIN, DISTRICT JUDGE.

This is a diversity case, in which the plaintiff, a disappointed testamentary beneficiary, brings a third-party malpractice suit against the attorney who drafted the 1987 Last Will and Testament of Dr. Thomas A. Hurney. The matter is before the Court on a summary judgment motion * * *.

[Most of the property held by Dr. and Mrs. Hurney was held in joint tenancy, with right of survivorship. Mrs. Hurney survived her husband. As a result, even though Dr. Hurney's 1987 will left the plaintiff half his residual estate, she received very little from the Hurneys. The plaintiff contended that Dr. Hurney intended for her to receive half the value of the couple's property, and that the malpractice of attorney Clancy, the defendant, defeated this intention. Clancy testified in a deposition that he had instructed Dr. Hurney that to make his intention effective he had to transfer assets from joint tenancy into his own name. If true, this fact would defeat plaintiff's claim.]

In an attempt to stave off summary judgment, plaintiff, in her opposition to summary judgment, has found a previously undiscovered witness, a Ms. Bouman, who had done Dr. Hurney's bookkeeping and tax work in the several years before his death. Her affidavit, submitted as Ex. 18 to plaintiff's summary judgment opposition, proffers testimony to the effect that neither Mr. Clancy nor Dr. Hurney ever mentioned to her that Dr. Hurney would need to change the titling of his assets in order to make the 1987 will effective. Plaintiff argues that, from this evidence, she is entitled to the inference that such advice was never given Dr. Hurney by Mr. Clancy, and that such inference is sufficient to carry the case to a jury.

The difficulty with this argument is that, in order to be sufficient to generate a triable dispute under Rule 56(c), affidavits must contain evidence that would be admissible at trial. Fed.R.Civ.P. 56(e).

At common law, there was substantial authority that the silence of an individual or group of individuals is hearsay, as an "implied assertion." *See* cases collected and discussed in Professor Morgan's famous article, "Hearsay Dangers and the Application of the Hearsay Concept," 62 Harv.L.Rev. 177, 213 (1948). It appears to be the intent of the limitation of the hearsay definition under Fed.R.Evid. 801(a)(2) to non-verbal conduct "intended by the [declarant] as an assertion" to do away with the notion that "implied assertions" are within the hearsay prohibition. *See McCor-*

mick on Evidence § 250 at 743 (1984). *See also* 4 J. Weinstein and M. Berger, *Weinstein's Evidence* ¶ 801(a)[01] at p. 801–61 (1990). Although there appears not to be any significant case law on this topic since the adoption of the Federal Rules of Evidence, and although a case might still be made for treating silence as hearsay, the Court is of the opinion that, as the cited authorities agree, silence, at least where there is no showing of intentional silence on a particular occasion intended as an assertion when the silence was kept, is no longer within the hearsay realm.

Nevertheless, even though the evidence is not hearsay, this Court would exclude it at trial under Fed.R.Evid. 403, because the probative value of silence, unless under circumstances that compel speech, is so weak and so fraught with speculation as to its reason that it is far outweighed by the prejudicial effect of introducing such evidence. * * *

Because of its very nature as the absence of any discernible action, silence on a topic in a situation such as this (where there is no specific stimulus identified calling for speech on that topic on a particular occasion) obviously starts out with a low degree of probative value, which then must be weighed against the danger of prejudice arising from allowing the trier of fact to speculate as to the reasons for that silence. Here, although Ms. Bouman gives her opinion (itself of questionable admissibility) that Dr. Hurney would have mentioned to her the need for retitling had Mr. Clancy advised him to do it, there might well have been a myriad of reasons, now unknowable, why Dr. Hurney never mentioned to her the need for retitling the property. Perhaps he just never got around to mentioning it, just as he never got around to doing it. Perhaps it just slipped his mind. Perhaps he didn't want Ms. Bouman to know what he was planning to do until he got around to doing it, or perhaps he didn't want her to know all the details of his estate planning (consistent with the fact, stated in her affidavit, that she never was shown the 1987 will). Or, perhaps, as plaintiff claims, Mr. Clancy never did tell Dr. Hurney to retitle the property.

The fact of the matter is that, because he is now dead, Dr. Hurney cannot be questioned as to the reasons for his silence, for which a number of speculative explanations could be laid before the jury, and, in the end, the jury would be left to guess the reason for it. In short, the Bouman affidavit is entirely too chimerical a basis for sending this case, full of sympathy for the disappointed plaintiff, to a jury.

* * *

For the reasons stated, an order will be entered separately, granting summary judgment to the defendant, with costs of these proceedings.

QUESTION

Plaintiff sued a railroad, claiming that while the Pullman car in which she had a berth was stopped for four hours in Cleveland, the car became extremely cold, aggravating her circulatory disease. The Pullman porter assigned to the car testified for the railroad that the temperature was normal and comfortable.

The trial judge permitted that evidence, but excluded testimony from the same witness that eleven other passengers in the same car made no complaint to him as to the temperature while in Cleveland. Was that ruling correct? Is Wilson v. Clancy distinguishable? See Silver v. New York Central Railroad, 105 N.E.2d 923 (Mass. 1952).

Morgan, Basic Problems of Evidence
248–50 (1961)*

C. Where the evidence of declarant's conduct is offered to prove that it truly reflected his then existing state of mind, his sincerity is necessarily involved. Thus where evidence of his abnormal objective conduct is offered as tending to prove his insanity, it has no value if it was feigned. His sincerity is a peculiarly important element where his conduct is a positive assertion and the issue is whether he was suffering an insane delusion that the assertion was true. Thus if a woman asserted "I am the Pope," and the issue is whether she had an insane delusion that she held that high office, her belief in the truth of the statement is determinative. And yet, the courts rarely, if ever, treat such evidence as hearsay, and Wigmore agrees, though Hinton dissented. Speaking generally, where evidence of the declarant's conduct, other than a direct assertion that he has a specified state of mind, is offered as tending to prove his state of mind at the time, and the state of mind at that time or at a later time only is in issue, the evidence is not classed as hearsay. This is difficult to harmonize with the theory of courts and commentators that one of the chief functions of cross-examination is to expose defects in sincerity, and with the accepted justification for most of the recognized exceptions to the hearsay rule on the ground that the circumstances of the utterance furnish a guaranty of sincerity.

United States v. Jaramillo–Suarez
United States Court of Appeals, Ninth Circuit, 1991.
950 F.2d 1378.

■ CANBY, CIRCUIT JUDGE:

[Defendant Suarez was accused of cocaine and conspiracy offenses. Part of the evidence against him was a "pay/owe sheet" that evidently recorded drug transactions. It had been found in an apartment frequented by Suarez.]

Analysis

I. *Pay/Owe Sheet*

Suarez contends that the district court erred by admitting into evidence a "pay/owe" sheet found at the San Juan Capistrano apartment. He claims the pay/owe sheet constitutes inadmissible hearsay not falling with-

---

* Joint Committee on Continuing Legal Education of The American Law Institute and The American Bar Association, Philadelphia, 1961.

in any of the exceptions allowed by the Federal Rules of Evidence.[3] Suarez further contends that, even if the pay/owe sheet falls within one of the hearsay exceptions, the government failed to lay the foundation required by United States v. Ordonez, 737 F.2d 793 (9th Cir.1983). Specifically, Suarez contends that the government failed to establish that he had authored or was in any way connected to the pay/owe sheet.

* * *

A. Hearsay

Initially, Suarez asks too much of *Ordonez* when he cites it for the proposition that drug-related documents are inadmissible for all purposes because they constitute hearsay. *Ordonez* simply holds that the rule against hearsay prohibits the admission of drug ledgers and pay/owe sheets to prove the truth of the matters asserted in them unless a proper foundation has been laid; *Ordonez* does not prohibit the use of the documents for all purposes. Most relevant for present purposes is our statement in *Ordonez* that the rule against hearsay does not stand as a bar to the admission of ledgers as "circumstantial evidence 'to show the character and use of the place where the [ledgers] were found * * *.'" The pay/owe sheet in the present case was admitted for the specific and limited purpose of showing the character and use of the San Juan Capistrano apartment. Its role is no different from that played by the very large amounts of cash found in the same apartment. Because the pay/owe sheet's probative value for the limited purpose for which it was admitted was independent of the truth of its contents, the rule against hearsay was not implicated and the requirement of "a proper foundational showing for admitting the records to prove the truth of the matters asserted" was not triggered.

Our conclusion is in accord with that of the Eighth Circuit in United States v. Wilson, 532 F.2d 641 (8th Cir.) cert. denied, 429 U.S. 846, 97 S.Ct. 128, 50 L.Ed.2d 117 (1976), a case we cited with approval in *Ordonez*. In *Wilson,* the court held that, although drug ledgers found at an apartment frequented by the defendants could not be used to prove the truth of the statements made in the ledgers, they were properly admitted as circumstantial evidence "that the apartment was being used for drug trafficking." The government was not required to prove the identity of the writer or writers. It was enough for the court that the government had established that the ledgers were found in one of the three houses the defendants frequented, even though that house was controlled by someone other than the defendants, and none of the defendants was present at the time the detective confiscated the ledger. In the present case, the government agent offered evidence that the pay/owe sheet was found in an apartment frequented by Suarez and rented to "Rick Suarez," and that other evidence such as vehicle registration slips belonging to Suarez were present in the apartment. The government's expert testified as to the nature of the document. This was enough of a showing to permit the pay/owe sheet to be ad-

---

[3] Specifically, Suarez argues that the document does not constitute an adoption or admission under Fed.R.Evid. 801(d)(2)(B) or a business record under 803(6).

mitted; the jury could consider the facts that the pay/owe sheet was evidence of drug-related activity, that it was linked to the San Juan Capistrano apartment, and that Suarez was also linked to the apartment.

In holding that drug-related documents may properly be admitted to prove the character and use of the place where found, we recognize the risk that the government or jury may erroneously rely on the document for the truth of the matters asserted therein. The trial court here was equally aware of the risk, and clearly instructed the jury that the sheet was "being admitted for the limited purpose of showing the character and use of the place where it was found and not for the truth of any matters asserted or whatever is on there says." The judge gave a similar instruction at the close of evidence. We conclude that the trial court adequately guarded against the risk of unfair prejudice.

United States v. Rhodes

Trial by General Court Martial,
Fort McNair, District of Columbia, 1958

[During February, 1958, Master Sergeant Roy A. Rhodes, United States Army, was tried by General Court Martial for having conspired with certain named and unnamed persons to violate the espionage laws of the United States by, among things, communicating information concerning the national defense to agents of the Union of Soviet Socialist Republics. Two of the accused's co-conspirators were alleged to be Col. Rudolph Ivanovich Abel and Lt. Col. Reino Hayhanen of the Soviet Secret Police. The evidence showed that in July, 1956, Abel had transmitted to Hayhanen some written information regarding the accused—whose code name was "Quebec"—which Abel had received from Moscow. The information was on "hard" film; Hayhanen had made "soft" film of it and hidden it in a hollowed-out bolt at his home in Peekskill, New York. The bolt and its contents were retrieved by agents of the Federal Bureau of Investigation and a copy of the piece of "soft" film was offered, over objection, and received at Rhodes' trial. The message on the piece of film is reproduced below. Counsel for the accused objected to receipt of this message on grounds of hearsay. On what basis was the exhibit received? Do you agree that it was properly admissible?—Eds.]

PROSECUTION EXHIBIT NO. 7.

QUEBEC, Roy A. Rhodes, born 1917 in Oilton, Oklahoma, U.S., senior sergeant of the War Ministry, former employee of the U.S. Military Attache Staff in our country. He was a chief of the garage of the Embassy.

He was recruited to our service in January 1952 in our country which he left in June 1953; recruited on the basis of compromising materials, but he is tied up to us with his receipts and information he had given in his own handwriting.

He had been trained in code work at the Ministry before he went to work at the Embassy, but as a code worker he was not used by the Embassy.

After he left our country he was to be sent to the school of communications of the Army C-I Service which is at the city of San Luis, California. He was to be trained there as a mechanic of the coding machines.

He fully agreed to continue to cooperate with us in the States or any other country. It was agreed that he was to have written to our Embassy here special letters, but we had received none during the last year.

It has been recently learned that Quebec is living in Red Bank, N.J. where he owns three garages. The garage job is being done by his wife. His own occupation at present is not known.

His father—Mr. W.A. Rhodes resides in the U.S. His brother is also in the States where he works as an engineer at an atomic plant in Camp, Georgia with a brother-in-law of his father.

Lilly, An Introduction to the Law of Evidence
245–46 (3d ed. 1996)*

Suppose that a child is taken to the defendant's house and molested. The victim subsequently describes to her mother what the house looked like and includes additional details about the appearance of the interior. At trial, the prosecutor introduces evidence describing the exterior and interior of the defendant's home. May the mother now testify as to her daughter's prior statements in which the child accurately recited what her captor's house looked like? If the prosecutor also supplied evidence that it was highly unlikely that the victim could have gained knowledge of these surroundings except by having been transported there on the occasion in question, the little girl's prior statements ought to be admissible to show her knowledge. Her statements would not be offered to prove the appearance of the defendant's house—this having been established by other evidence. Nor are they offered to prove the appearance of the house in which she was molested, although of course she could repeat her description of the surroundings from the witness stand. Her out-of-court description, congruent with the *actual physical* appearance of the defendant's home, constitutes convincing circumstantial evidence that she once saw it, at least if there is sufficient detail in her account to distinguish the house in question from other houses. See Bridges v. State, 247 Wis. 350, 19 N.W.2d 529 (1945), rehearing denied, 247 Wis. 350, 19 N.W.2d 862 (1945).

For a modern application of the *Bridges* principle, see United States v. Muscato, 534 F.Supp. 969 (E.D.N.Y.1982). There W gave an accurate extrajudicial description of a gun having unique features. The opportunities for gaining this knowledge, other than by actually seeing the weapon in the

---

* Copyright 1996 West Publishing Co.

circumstances claimed by W, were limited. The fact that W also identified the gun in the courtroom and was subject to cross-examination concerning other ways in which he might have gained knowledge of its appearance buttressed the prosecution's case for admissibility.

The trial judge in *Muscato* (Judge Jack Weinstein), after discussing *Bridges* and similar cases, allowed the previous description into evidence. He characterized the evidence, used not to prove the fact asserted but to prove the declarant's knowledge of the fact, as nonhearsay. Judge Weinstein acknowledged, however, that this kind of evidence might be highly influential to the jury, an influence that would be unwarranted if the witness might have gained his knowledge by more than one means. Nonetheless, in the case before him, not only was it unlikely that the witness gained the knowledge other than by seeing the gun (as claimed), but the witness also testified, identified the weapon again, and was subject to a full cross-examination about the source of his knowledge. Thus, applying Rule 403, the court ruled that the probative value of the nonhearsay, out-of-court declaration was not outweighed by the risk of jury misuse.

United States v. Brown

United States Court of Appeals, Fifth Circuit, 1977.
548 F.2d 1194.

■ JOHN R. BROWN, CHIEF JUDGE:

* * *

Defendant-Appellant Amos P. Brown, Sr., a part-time income tax preparer, was convicted by a jury on 12 counts of counseling, procuring and advising the preparation and presentation of fraudulent and false United States Individual Income Tax Returns for others in violation of 26 U.S.C.A. § 7206(2), Internal Revenue Code. * * * We find that the Trial Judge committed plain error by improperly admitting certain evidence which was highly prejudicial to the defendant. Accordingly, we reverse and remand for a new trial.

* * *

The Peacock's Tale

Among other evidence the Government also introduced the testimony of IRS agent Adrienne Peacock, who testified that between 90% and 95% of about 160 returns prepared by defendant contained overstated itemized deductions.

* * *

Hearsay

* * *

In this case, Peacock's testimony that between 90% and 95% of the returns she audited contained substantially overstated itemized deductions was introduced for the sole purpose of proving, circumstantially, the "willfulness" requirement of § 7206(2). In order to arrive at the conclusion that the deductions in these returns were overstated, Peacock's perusal of the 160 tax returns was not sufficient, since the returns obviously do not show on their face which deductions are overstated. [The record shows that Peacock must have gotten her "proof" of the overstatements through conversations with each of the taxpayers audited.] Presumably, the proof consisted either of statements by these taxpayers to Peacock that they all gave different information to the defendant tax preparer than defendant put down on their returns, or that they were unable to substantiate their deductions, because they did not have any (or had inadequate) supporting records. The proof might also have consisted of the fact that the IRS had legitimate disagreements with all or some of the deductions claimed. However, a prerequisite to this form of proof would be the initial conversation between Peacock and each taxpayer, so that Peacock could determine the bases for the deductions claimed.

The point to be emphasized, therefore, is that the information obtained by Peacock from the out-of-court statements made by the 160 taxpayers whose returns she audited, was absolutely vital to her ultimate in-court conclusion that between 90% and 95% of the 160 returns she audited contained substantially overstated itemized deductions. Because her testimony had to have been based directly on the out-of-court statements of these taxpayers, defendant had no opportunity to test their ultimate assumptions through cross-examination. He obviously could not cross-examine the taxpayers concerned, because they were not in court. He could not even cross-examine Peacock adequately, because she did not have with her any of the records of conversations she had had with these taxpayers, but was testifying solely from memory, in the most general, amorphous terms. Thus, the jury had no way to examine the trustworthiness of Peacock's testimony, because it could not examine the statements of the declarant taxpayers or others on which Peacock's testimony was directly and substantially founded. Given the rationale of the hearsay rule, a clearer case of hearsay testimony would be difficult to imagine.[1]

* * *

---

[1] Peacock's testimony also inescapably presented by implication the facts leading to her conclusion which she got from other nontestifying declarants, such as the taxpayers concerned. The implication was strong that she satisfied herself from talking to others that what the preparer entered was not what the taxpayer told him. It was an implied assertion that the defendant was responsible for the repetitious acts or practices from which the jury could infer the requisite willfulness. It was an assertion, in other words, of the ultimate fact that these faulty returns were due to defendant's acts.

The judgement of conviction against defendant is reversed, and the case remanded for new trial on all counts.

Reversed and remanded.

■ GEE, CIRCUIT JUDGE, dissenting:

The majority's characterization of Agent Peacock's testimony as "hearsay" represents an unprecedented departure from usual hearsay concepts * * * Agent Peacock's statements at trial were (1) that she personally audited all but two or three of the 163 tax returns prepared by appellant and audited by IRS, and (2) that her audit had determined that 90 to 95 percent of those returns contained overstated itemized deductions disallowed under IRS standards. Agent Peacock obviously testified from her own personal knowledge about the results of tax audits she conducted. In her testimony she neither related nor relied upon out-of-court statements by other persons.

It is too plain for argument that Peacock's testimony as to what she knew herself from the returns she individually audited does not fall within Rule 801's hearsay definition. An examination of the record reveals that *all* of Peacock's testimony was based on knowledge she personally acquired while auditing the tax returns prepared by Brown. In fact, the majority points to no *statement* whatever by Agent Peacock which it claims contains hearsay; she mentioned no statements others had made to her during the course of her audit. The majority objects, however, that Agent Peacock's audit necessarily rested on " 'proof' of the overstatements through conversations with each of the taxpayers audited." Since her testimony had to have been based directly on the out-of-court statements of these taxpayers who could not be cross-examined, it is said that "a clearer case of hearsay testimony would be difficult to imagine." I find little difficulty in doing so.

See Federal Rules of Evidence 602; California Evidence Code § 702.

City of Webster Groves v. Quick

St. Louis Court of Appeals, Missouri, 1959.
323 S.W.2d 386.

■ ANDERSON, JUDGE. This case arose upon the filing of a complaint against defendant in the City Court of Webster Groves, Missouri, for the violation of a speed ordinance of said city. * * *

Appellant's first point is that the court erred in permitting Police Officer Paillou to testify as to the readings of the electric timer showing defendant's speed at 40 miles per hour, for the reason that it constituted hearsay evidence.

There is no merit to the point made. The officer himself testified to the reading of the mechanism in question and not to what someone else had

told him; thus, the hearsay rule does not apply. The witness when testifying was under oath, and was thoroughly cross-examined, thus satisfying the principal requirements of the hearsay rule. Evidence is called hearsay when its probative force depends, in whole or in part, on the competency and credibility of some person other than the witness by whom it is sought to be produced. It is an extrajudicial utterance, including both oral statements and writings. The hearsay rule cannot be applied to what the witness, on the stand and subject to cross-examination, observed, either through his own senses or through the use of scientific instruments. If appellant's contention were sound then results of the use of a measuring device on some object to ascertain its length would be inadmissible; a doctor could not testify to what a fluoroscope revealed concerning the condition of his patient, and, likewise, he would not be permitted to testify as to the results heard through a stethoscope. Many other examples of the absurdity of such a rule could be cited. In such cases, as in the case at bar, the evidence as to the results obtained by the witness is not dependent on the perception, memory, and sincerity of an absent declarant. The circumstantial guarantee of trustworthiness is satisfied by the exercise of the right of cross-examination of the witness on the stand, both as to the results obtained and his testimony as to the reliability and accuracy of the device used. As to the latter, there was sufficient evidence in the case at bar. A police vehicle was operated through the device the morning defendant was arrested, and the device was found to be operating properly. In addition, the stop watch was tested during that week and the first week of the preceding and subsequent months. The witnesses to those facts were produced and were subjected to rigorous cross-examination. We rule there was no error in the court's ruling on the admission of the evidence in question.
* * *

[Affirmed]

Morgan, Hearsay and Non-Hearsay

48 Harv.L.Rev. 1138, 1145–6 (1935).*

[N]othing is more common than to allow a witness to rely upon a timepiece in stating the time of day when an event happened. If he should testify that he looked at a Western Union clock and noted the time, he would be considered as giving particularly accurate testimony, but would it not be anonymous hearsay upon anonymous hearsay? Certainly the person in charge of the master mechanism which regulated the clock consulted by the witness did not make the astronomical observations in accordance with which that clock was made to indicate the hour and minute of the day. Yet just as certainly an objection upon the ground of hearsay would receive scant attention. Only a little less easy is a demonstration of the hearsay element in the indication of time upon a sundial unless preceded by the testimony of a witness who checked it against his own astronomical observations. Much the same may be said of the automatic weighing machines which in return for a coin furnish a printed assertion of a person's weight,

---

and of non-automatic scales where the position of the marker which produces a balance of the beam announces the weight of the object upon the platform. In each of these cases, the anonymous maker or regulator of the machine intended that the reaction of the machine should operate as an assertion. In each of them he may have fixed the instrument so as to produce a false declaration, as where the faker who gambles upon his pretended ability to guess his victim's weight controls the balance by a hidden mechanism, or a practical joker sets a series of timepieces so as to cause another to miss an appointment. Generally speaking, however, the court regards these mechanisms as sufficiently accurate to justify a trier of fact in relying upon their reactions for most purposes, at least after a preliminary showing of reasonable accuracy. In other words, it takes judicial notice of the reliability of these sources of information under ordinary circumstances notwithstanding their hearsay character.

PROBLEMS

(1) Gary Rasp is charged with smothering Jane Gill to death in her bedroom. When her body was discovered, two days after her death, her African gray parrot Max was in his cage, dehydrated and hungry. Should Rasp be allowed to present the owner of the pet shop where Max was taken, that after Max regained his health he repeatedly cried out, "Richard, no, no, no!"? See *Parrot May Have the Answer to a Killing*, N.Y. Times, Nov. 12, 1993, p. B20 (noting private investigator's comment that Max was in a witness protection program and was now a macaw).

(2) Dewar is on trial for raping a woman in her bedroom. The victim testifies that she was able to call 911 surreptitiously during the rape, and that the perpetrator jumped out a window, leaving his T-shirt behind. Traynor, a police detective, is prepared to testify that he presented the shirt to Valiant, a bloodhound, and that when Valiant was later brought in the presence of Dewar Valiant barked insistently; according to Traynor, Valiant would do this only if he recognized Dewar as the source of the smell he had detected on the shirt. Dewar objects to the evidence as hearsay. What result?

Morgan, Evidence Exam, Summer Term, 1946, Harvard Law School

Which of the following items is hearsay?

_____ 1. On the issue whether X and D* were engaged to be married, D's statement to X, "I promise to marry you on June 1, 1931."

_____ 2. On the issue of the sanity of D, a woman, D's public statement, "I am the Pope."

_____ 3. On the issue of D's adverse possession of Blackacre, D's assertion, "I am the owner of this farm."

_____ 4. On the issue of X's provocation for assaulting Y, D's statement to X, her husband, "Y ravished me."

_____ 5. On the issue of D's consciousness after the attack, D's state-

---

* In each of the following questions concerning a statement made by D, that statement is of course, made out of court.

ment, "X shot me, as he often threatened to do."

____ 6. On the issue of identity of the shooter, D's statement in 5.

____ 7. On the issue whether X made threats to shoot D, D's statement in 5.

____ 8. On the issue of X's knowledge of speedily impending death, D's statement to X, "You have only a few minutes to live."

____ 9. In 8, X's out of court statement, "I realize that I am dying."

____ 10. On the issue whether a transfer of a chattel from D to X was a sale or gift, D's statement accompanying the transfer, "I am giving you this chattel as a birthday present."

____ 11. On the issue in 10, D's statement the day following the transfer, "I gave you the chattel as a birthday present."

* * *

____ 14. On the issue of damages to the family reputation in an action for the seduction of P's daughter, her reputation for chastity.

____ 15. On the issue of D's ill-feeling toward X, D's statement, "X is a liar and a hypocrite."

____ 16. On the issue of reasonableness of X's conduct, in the shooting of Y by X, D's statement to X, "Y has threatened to kill you on sight."

____ 17. On the issue in 16, Y's reputation, known to X, as a violent, quarrelsome man.

____ 18. Action for malicious prosecution of P by X on the charge of murdering Y. On the issue of probable cause, P's reputation as a gangster, known to X.

____ 19. In 18, Y's reputation, known to X, as a quiet, peace-loving citizen.

____ 20. On the issue of the terms of a contract with T negotiated by D, D's statement, "I am making this offer to you, as the agent of P."

____ 21. On the issue whether D was the agent of P, the statement in 20.

* * *

____ 23. As tending to prove X's honesty, the mere fact that D, X's employer, promoted him from the position of order clerk to cashier.

____ 24. As tending to prove D's guilt of the crime of killing X, the fact that D fled under suspicious circumstances immediately after X's murder, in order to draw suspicion upon himself.

____ 25. As tending to prove X's insanity, the fact that he was confined in an insane asylum.

____ 26. As tending to prove forgery of a will by X, D's angry statement to X, "Well, I never forged a will, anyway!"

____ 27. As tending to prove D's guilt of a particular criminal act, the fact that D fled under suspicious circumstances immediately after the criminal act was committed, solely in order to escape.

____ 28. On the issue whether a transfer of a chattel from D to X was a sale or a gift, D's statement accompanying the transfer, "Here is your birthday gift."

___ 29. As tending to prove that X was suffering from disease T, the mere fact that D, a physician, treated him for disease T.

___ 30. On the issue of D's adverse possession of Blackacre, D's statement, "I paid X $5000 for this farm."

___ 31. To show that X was ill, W offers to testify that X complained of pain in his chest.

___ 32. In a contest of a will on ground of forgery, to show testator's feelings toward X, the sole legatee, W offers to testify that testator had X arrested for forgery.

___ 33. In 32, for the same purpose, W offers to testify that testator ordered his superintendent to discharge X from testator's employ.

___ 34. In 32, for the same purpose, W offers to testify that testator falsely charged X with the crime of bigamy under such circumstances that testator must have known the charge to be false.

___ 35. Action for $500, the price of an automobile. Plea, payment. On the issue of payment, W offers to testify that he saw defendant hand plaintiff a $500 bill, and say: "This is the payment for that car."

___ 36. In 35, on the issue of payment, W offers to testify that on the following day [defendant] said to [plaintiff]: "I was glad to be able to pay you cash for that car."

___ 37. Action for conversion of an automobile. To prove value, plaintiff offers a receipt for the purchase price, $5000, signed by the dealer from whom he bought it.

___ 38. Action for personal injuries by a guest in an automobile against the owner. Defense, contributory negligence and assumption of risk. W offers to testify that an hour before the accident, in the presence of plaintiff, defendant, a mechanic said: "The spindle on that front wheel may break at any moment." If offered to show the spindle defective.

___ 39. The testimony in 38 offered as tending to show assumption of risk.

___ 40. As tending to show that D had never repaid a loan, W offers to testify that P hired W to collect the sum from D.

* * *

___ 44. As tending to show that D had a revolver at an affray, W offers to testify that as D passed W's house, W called his wife's attention to a revolver sticking out of D's pocket.

* * *

___ 48. W testified that he saw D do act X, and offers to testify: "I told M within one hour after the event that I had seen D do act X." Offered to show D's conduct.

* * *

___ 50. W testified that he saw D do act X, could not remember the date, but within an hour thereafter reported to M. M offers to testify that at 3:30 p.m. of June 1, 1944, W told M that he had just seen D do act X. M's testimony is offered to fix the time.

____ 51. To prove that the defendant committed the crime, the prosecution offers a confession made to police officers.

____ 52. To prove that the defendant committed the crime, the prosecution offers evidence that the defendant remained silent after being arrested for the crime.

____ 53. To prove that the defendant committed the crime, the prosecution offers into evidence a certified copy of a prior judgment of conviction for the same offense.

____ 54. To prove that the defendant committed the crime, the prosecution offers a witness to testify that he was present and observed the jury return a verdict of guilty in a prosecution of the defendant for a similar prior offense.

____ 55. To prove that her husband was insane, a wife offers evidence that he lived in a nest in the top of a tree for the last five years.

____ 56. In an action for breach of contract, the plaintiff offers into evidence an advertisement conceded to be that of the defendant offering a reward for certain information which the plaintiff claims to have provided.

____ 57. To prove that the defendant committed a crime, the prosecution offers evidence that the F.B.I. offered a reward for his capture.

____ 58. To prove that the defendant committed a crime, the prosecution offers evidence that the F.B.I. offered a reward for his capture.

____ 59. To prove paternity, the plaintiff offers evidence that the defendant referred to the child as "my son."

____ 60. To fix the time of a murder, the prosecution offers a witness who testifies that minutes after he heard the shot, he heard a clock chime three times.

____ 61. To prove adultery, the husband offers proof that a house guest after a visit had described to one of his cronies a birthmark that the accused wife has on an intimate part of her anatomy. The existence of the mark has previously been testified to by the husband while the wife has testified that only her parents and her husband knew of the mark.

____ 62. To prove that a couple is married, a witness is offered to testify that he heard the exchange of nuptial vows.

____ 63. To prove notice of a defect in the defendant's car in a personal injury suit, the plaintiff introduces evidence of the defendant's past attempts to repair his car.

____ 64. In a common disaster case, in order to establish survivorship, evidence is offered that after the accident one of the victims was heard to cry: "I'm alive."

____ 65. In a prosecution for the theft of valuable homing pigeons, evidence is offered that when the defendant's pigeon coop was opened, all of the birds flew to the home of the victim.

____ 66. In a prosecution for sale of pornography, the prosecution offers one hundred letters sent to the defendant's post office box, each of which says, in substance: "Send me some of those dirty books."

____ 67. Personal injury case. To show pain and suffering, plaintiff calls a nurse who testifies that the plaintiff was screaming when he was brought to the hospital.

____ 68. In a divorce case, after the husband has testified that his wife was always nagging him at the top of her voice, the wife calls a neighbor to testify that she never heard any nagging.

____ 69. In a paternity suit, the mother takes the stand and when asked to identify the father of her child, she points to the defendant.

____ 70. To prove that defendant is the father of her child, the mother offers a letter in evidence from defendant's attorney in which the attorney states that his client has admitted he is the father of the child.

____ 71. Personal injury litigation. Plaintiff testifies that there was a sign facing the intersection toward the direction that the defendant had come from without stopping and that sign said: "STOP".

____ 72. To prove that the insured under a life policy is dead, his wife offers a death certificate.

____ 73. In a plagiarism suit, the plaintiff testifies that he caught the defendant in his apartment copying portions of the plaintiff's typed manuscript in longhand on a sheet of paper.

____ 74. Murder prosecution. To support a self-defense claim, defendant introduces witnesses who testify that before the killing defendant told them he was afraid of the victim.

____ 75. To show that defendant was home and thus could have killed his wife the prosecution calls her paramour who testifies that when hubby was gone and the coast was clear, the wife always pulled down a shade on a particular window but when he was home the shade was always open. The prosecution calls a neighbor who testifies that on the night of the murder the shade was open.

Crawford v. Washington

Supreme Court of the United States, 2004.
541 U.S. 36, 124 S.Ct. 1354, 158 L.Ed.2d 177.

■ JUSTICE SCALIA delivered the opinion of the Court.

Petitioner Michael Crawford stabbed a man who allegedly tried to rape his wife, Sylvia. At his trial, the State played for the jury Sylvia's tape-recorded statement to the police describing the stabbing, even though he had no opportunity for cross-examination. The Washington Supreme Court upheld petitioner's conviction after determining that Sylvia's statement was reliable. The question presented is whether this procedure complied with the Sixth Amendment's guarantee that, "[i]n all criminal prosecutions, the accused shall enjoy the right . . . to be confronted with the witnesses against him."

I

[Michael Crawford was tried on charges of assault and attempted murder, growing out of a knife fight with Kenny Lee. Crawford acknowledged stabbing Lee but claimed self-defense; he had told police interrogators that he thought Lee was "goin' for something." Crawford's wife Sylvia, after having been read the *Miranda* warnings – she was suspected of having abetted her husband – gave police an audio-recorded account that was similar in many respects to Crawford's, but she appeared not to contend that Crawford was reaching for a weapon. Sylvia did not testify at trial because Michael did not waive Washington's marital privilege, which generally prevents the spouse of an accused from testifying against him absent consent. But that privilege did not extend to Sylvia's out-of-court statements, so the prosecution, over an objection based on the Confrontation Clause, played for the jury the recording of Sylvia's interrogation. In closing, the prosecution relied on Sylvia's account as refuting Crawford's claim of self-defense. Crawford was convicted and appealed. The then-prevailing doctrine governing the Confrontation Clause was developed by *Ohio v. Roberts*, 448 U.S. 56 (1980), and its progeny. Under that doctrine, the principal question in determining whether an out-of-court statement could be admitted for the truth of what it asserted notwithstanding the Clause was whether the statement was marked by sufficient "indicia of reliability." A statement could be deemed to satisfy this standard without more if it fit within a "firmly rooted hearsay exception"; otherwise, it could still satisfy the Confrontation Clause if it bore sufficient "individualized guarantees of trustworthiness." The Washington supreme court unanimously held that Sylvia's statement met this second standard: " '[W]hen a codefendant's confession is virtually identical [to, *i.e.*, interlocks with,] that of a defendant, it may be deemed reliable.' " The U.S. Supreme Court granted certiorari.]

II

* * * Petitioner argues that [the *Roberts*] test strays from the original meaning of the Confrontation Clause and urges us to reconsider it.

A

The Constitution's text does not alone resolve this case. One could plausibly read "witnesses against" a defendant to mean those who actually testify at trial, those whose statements are offered at trial, or something in-between. We must therefore turn to the historical background of the Clause to understand its meaning.

The right to confront one's accusers is a concept that dates back to Roman times. The founding generation's immediate source of the concept, however, was the common law. English common law has long differed from continental civil law in regard to the manner in which witnesses give testimony in criminal trials. The common-law tradition is one of live testimony in court subject to adversarial testing, while the civil law condones examination in private by judicial officers. See 3 W. Blackstone, Commentaries on the Laws of England 373–374 (1768).

Nonetheless, England at times adopted elements of the civil-law practice. Justices of the peace or other officials examined suspects and witnesses before trial. These examinations were sometimes read in court in lieu of live testimony, a practice that "occasioned frequent demands by the prisoner to have his 'accusers,' *i.e.* the witnesses against him, brought before him face to face." 1 J. Stephen, History of the Criminal Law of England 326 (1883). In some cases, these demands were refused.

* * *

The most notorious instances of civil-law examination occurred in the great political trials of the 16th and 17th centuries. One such was the 1603 trial of Sir Walter Raleigh for treason. Lord Cobham, Raleigh's alleged accomplice, had implicated him in an examination before the Privy Council and in a letter. At Raleigh's trial, these were read to the jury. Raleigh argued that Cobham had lied to save himself: "Cobham is absolutely in the King's mercy; to excuse me cannot avail him; by accusing me he may hope for favour." 1 D. Jardine, Criminal Trials 435 (1832). Suspecting that Cobham would recant, Raleigh demanded that the judges call him to appear, arguing that "[t]he Proof of the Common Law is by witness and jury: let Cobham be here, let him speak it. Call my accuser before my face. . ." 2 How. St. Tr., at 15–16. The judges refused, and, despite Raleigh's protestations that he was being tried "by the Spanish Inquisition," the jury convicted, and Raleigh was sentenced to death.

One of Raleigh's trial judges later lamented that " 'the justice of England has never been so degraded and injured as by the condemnation of Sir Walter Raleigh.' " 1 Jardine, *supra*, at 520. Through a series of statutory and judicial reforms, English law developed a right of confrontation that limited these abuses. For example, treason statutes required witnesses to confront the accused "face to face" at his arraignment. *E.g.*, 13 Car. 2, c. 1, § 5 (1661); see 1 Hale, *supra*, at 306. Courts, meanwhile, developed relatively strict rules of unavailability, admitting examinations only if the witness was demonstrably unable to testify in person. See *Lord Morley's Case*, 6 How. St. Tr. 769, 770–771 (H. L. 1666); 2 Hale, *supra*, at 284; 1 Stephen, *supra*, at 358. Several authorities also stated that a suspect's confession could be admitted only against himself, and not against others he implicated. * * *

One recurring question was whether the admissibility of an unavailable witness's pretrial examination depended on whether the defendant had had an opportunity to cross-examine him. In 1696, the Court of King's Bench answered this question in the affirmative, in the widely reported misdemeanor libel case of *King v. Paine*, 5 Mod. 163, 87 Eng. Rep. 584. The court ruled that, even though a witness was dead, his examination was not admissible where "the defendant not being present when [it was] taken before the mayor . . . had lost the benefit of a cross-examination." * * *

B

Controversial examination practices were also used in the Colonies. * * * A decade before the Revolution, England gave jurisdiction over Stamp Act offenses to the admiralty courts, which followed civil-law rather than common-law procedures and thus routinely took testimony by deposition or private judicial examination. Colonial representatives protested that the Act subverted their rights "by extending the jurisdiction of the courts of admiralty beyond its ancient limits." Resolutions of the Stamp Act Congress § 8th (Oct. 19, 1765). John Adams, defending a merchant in a high-profile admiralty case, argued: "Examinations of witnesses upon Interrogatories, are only by the Civil Law. Interrogatories are unknown at common Law, and Englishmen and common Lawyers have an aversion to them if not an Abhorrence of them."

Many declarations of rights adopted around the time of the Revolution guaranteed a right of confrontation. * * *

Early state decisions shed light upon the original understanding of the common-law right. *State v. Webb*, 2 N. C. 103 (1794) (*per curiam*), decided a mere three years after the adoption of the Sixth Amendment, held that depositions could be read against an accused only if they were taken in his presence. Rejecting a broader reading of the English authorities, the court held: "[I]t is a rule of the common law, founded on natural justice, that no man shall be prejudiced by evidence which he had not the liberty to cross examine." *Id.*, at 104.

* * * [The Court's description of other early state court cases has been omitted.—Eds.]

III

This history supports two inferences about the meaning of the Sixth Amendment.

A

First, the principal evil at which the Confrontation Clause was directed was the civil-law mode of criminal procedure, and particularly its use of *ex parte* examinations as evidence against the accused. It was these practices that the Crown deployed in notorious treason cases like Raleigh's; that the Marian statutes* invited; that English law's assertion of a right to confrontation was meant to prohibit; and that the founding-era rhetoric decried. The Sixth Amendment must be interpreted with this focus in mind.

---

* [The reference is to two statutes passed during the reign of Queen Mary in the 16th century that provided for examination of felony witnesses by justices of the peace; for many years, English courts allowed these examinations to be used at trial if the witness was unavailable. Eds.]

Accordingly, we once again reject the view that the Confrontation Clause applies of its own force only to in-court testimony, and that its application to out-of-court statements introduced at trial depends upon "the law of Evidence for the time being." 3 Wigmore § 1397, at 101; accord, *Dutton v. Evans*, 400 U.S. 74, 94 (1970) (Harlan, J., concurring in result). Leaving the regulation of out-of-court statements to the law of evidence would render the Confrontation Clause powerless to prevent even the most flagrant inquisitorial practices. Raleigh was, after all, perfectly free to confront those who read Cobham's confession in court.

This focus also suggests that not all hearsay implicates the Sixth Amendment's core concerns. An off-hand, overheard remark might be unreliable evidence and thus a good candidate for exclusion under hearsay rules, but it bears little resemblance to the civil-law abuses the Confrontation Clause targeted. On the other hand, *ex parte* examinations might sometimes be admissible under modern hearsay rules, but the Framers certainly would not have condoned them.

The text of the Confrontation Clause reflects this focus. It applies to "witnesses" against the accused—in other words, those who "bear testimony." 2 N. Webster, An American Dictionary of the English Language (1828). "Testimony," in turn, is typically "[a] solemn declaration or affirmation made for the purpose of establishing or proving some fact." *Ibid.* An accuser who makes a formal statement to government officers bears testimony in a sense that a person who makes a casual remark to an acquaintance does not. The constitutional text, like the history underlying the common-law right of confrontation, thus reflects an especially acute concern with a specific type of out-of-court statement.

Various formulations of this core class of "testimonial" statements exist: "*ex parte* in-court testimony or its functional equivalent—that is, material such as affidavits, custodial examinations, prior testimony that the defendant was unable to cross-examine, or similar pretrial statements that declarants would reasonably expect to be used prosecutorially," Brief for Petitioner 23; "extrajudicial statements . . . contained in formalized testimonial materials, such as affidavits, depositions, prior testimony, or confessions," *White v. Illinois*, 502 U.S. 346, 365 (1992) (Thomas, J., joined by Scalia, J., concurring in part and concurring in judgment); "statements that were made under circumstances which would lead an objective witness reasonably to believe that the statement would be available for use at a later trial," Brief for National Association of Criminal Defense Lawyers et al. as *Amici Curiae* 3. These formulations all share a common nucleus and then define the Clause's coverage at various levels of abstraction around it. Regardless of the precise articulation, some statements qualify under any definition—for example, *ex parte* testimony at a preliminary hearing.

Statements taken by police officers in the course of interrogations are also testimonial under even a narrow standard. Police interrogations bear a striking resemblance to examinations by justices of the peace in England. The statements are not *sworn* testimony, but the absence of oath was not dispositive. Cobham's examination was unsworn, see 1 Jardine, Criminal Trials, at 430, yet Raleigh's trial has long been thought a paradigmatic confrontation violation, see, *e.g.*, *Campbell*, 30 S.C.L., at 130. Under the Marian statutes, witnesses were typically put on oath, but suspects were not. Yet Hawkins and others went out of their way to caution that such unsworn confessions were not admissible against anyone but the confessor.

That interrogators are police officers rather than magistrates does not change the picture either. Justices of the peace conducting examinations under the Marian statutes were not magistrates as we understand that office today, but had an essentially investigative and prosecutorial function. England did not have a professional police force until the 19th century, so it is not surprising that other government officers performed the investigative functions now associated primarily with the police. The involvement of government officers in the production of testimonial evidence presents the same risk, whether the officers are police or justices of the peace.

In sum, even if the Sixth Amendment is not solely concerned with testimonial hearsay, that is its primary object, and interrogations by law enforcement officers fall squarely within that class.[4]

B

The historical record also supports a second proposition: that the Framers would not have allowed admission of testimonial statements of a witness who did not appear at trial unless he was unavailable to testify, and the defendant had had a prior opportunity for cross-examination. The text of the Sixth Amendment does not suggest any open-ended exceptions from the confrontation requirement to be developed by the courts. Rather, the "right . . . to be confronted with the witnesses against him," Amdt. 6, is most naturally read as a reference to the right of confrontation at common law, admitting only those exceptions established at the time of the founding. As the English authorities above reveal, the common law in 1791 conditioned admissibility of an absent witness's examination on unavailability and a prior opportunity to cross-examine. The Sixth Amendment therefore incorporates those limitations. The numerous early state decisions applying the same test confirm that these principles were received as part of the common law in this country.

We do not read the historical sources to say that a prior opportunity to cross-examine was merely a sufficient, rather than a necessary, condition for admissibility of testimonial statements. They suggest that this requirement was dispositive, and not merely one of several ways to establish reliability. This is not to deny, as THE CHIEF JUSTICE notes, that "[t]here were always exceptions to the general rule of exclusion" of hearsay evidence. Several had become well established by 1791. But there is scant

---

[4] We use the term "interrogation" in its colloquial, rather than any technical legal, sense. Cf. *Rhode Island v. Innis*, 446 U.S. 291, 300–301 (1980). Just as various definitions of "testimonial" exist, one can imagine various definitions of "interrogation," and we need not select among them in this case. Sylvia's recorded statement, knowingly given in response to structured police questioning, qualifies under any conceivable definition.

evidence that exceptions were invoked to admit *testimonial* statements against the accused in a *criminal* case.[6] Most of the hearsay exceptions covered statements that by their nature were not testimonial—for example, business records or statements in furtherance of a conspiracy. [We do not infer from these that the Framers thought exceptions would apply even to prior testimony.] * * *

do not apply to prior?

IV

Our case law has been largely consistent with these two principles. * * *[8]

Our cases have * * * remained faithful to the Framers' understanding: Testimonial statements of witnesses absent from trial have been admitted only where the declarant is unavailable, and only where the defendant has had a prior opportunity to cross-examine.[9]

V

Although the results of our decisions have generally been faithful to the original meaning of the Confrontation Clause, the same cannot be said of our rationales. *Roberts* conditions the admissibility of all hearsay evidence on whether it falls under a "firmly rooted hearsay exception" or bears "particularized guarantees of trustworthiness." This test departs from the historical principles identified above in two respects. First, it is too broad: It applies the same mode of analysis whether or not the hearsay consists of *ex parte* testimony. This often results in close constitutional scrutiny in cases that are far removed from the core concerns of the Clause. At the same time, however, the test is too narrow: It admits statements that *do* consist of *ex parte* testimony upon a mere finding of reliability. This malle-

---

[6] The one deviation we have found involves dying declarations. The existence of that exception as a general rule of criminal hearsay law cannot be disputed. Although many dying declarations may not be testimonial, there is authority for admitting even those that clearly are. We need not decide in this case whether the Sixth Amendment incorporates an exception for testimonial dying declarations. If this exception must be accepted on historical grounds, it is *sui generis.*

[8] One case arguably in tension with the rule requiring a prior opportunity for cross-examination when the proffered statement is testimonial is *White v. Illinois,* 502 U.S. 346 (1992), which involved, *inter alia,* statements of a child victim to an investigating police officer admitted as spontaneous declarations. It is questionable whether testimonial statements would ever have been admissible on that ground in 1791; to the extent the hearsay exception for spontaneous declarations existed at all, it required that the statements be made "immediat[ely] upon the hurt received, and before [the declarant] had time to devise or contrive any thing for her own advantage." *Thompson v. Trevanion,* Skin. 402, 90 Eng. Rep. 179 (K. B. 1694). In any case, the only question presented in *White* was whether the Confrontation Clause imposed an unavailability requirement on the types of hearsay at issue. The holding did not address the question whether certain of the statements, because they were testimonial, had to be excluded *even if* the witness was unavailable. We "[took] as a given * * * that the testimony properly falls within the relevant hearsay exceptions." *Id.,* at 351, n. 4.

[9] * * * If nothing else, the test we announce is an empirically accurate explanation of the results our cases have reached. * * * [W]e reiterate that, when the declarant appears for cross-examination at trial, the Confrontation Clause places no constraints at all on the use of his prior testimonial statements. * * * The Clause does not bar admission of a statement so long as the declarant is present at trial to defend or explain it. (The Clause also does not bar the use of testimonial statements for purposes other than establishing the truth of the matter asserted. See Tennessee v. Street, 471 U.S. 409, 414 (1985).)

able standard often fails to protect against paradigmatic confrontation violations.

Members of this Court and academics have suggested that we revise our doctrine to reflect more accurately the original understanding of the Clause. See, *e.g.*, *Lilly*, 527 U.S., at 140–143 (Breyer, J., concurring); *White*, 502 U.S., at 366 (Thomas, J., joined by Scalia, J., concurring in part and concurring in judgment); A. Amar, The Constitution and Criminal Procedure 125–131 (1997); Friedman, Confrontation: The Search for Basic Principles, 86 Geo. L.J. 1011 (1998). They offer two proposals: First, that we apply the Confrontation Clause only to testimonial statements, leaving the remainder to regulation by hearsay law—thus eliminating the overbreadth referred to above. Second, that we impose an absolute bar to statements that are testimonial, absent a prior opportunity to cross-examine—thus eliminating the excessive narrowness referred to above.

In *White*, we considered the first proposal and rejected it. Although our analysis in this case casts doubt on that holding, we need not definitively resolve whether it survives our decision today, because Sylvia Crawford's statement is testimonial under any definition. This case does, however, squarely implicate the second proposal.

A

Where testimonial statements are involved, we do not think the Framers meant to leave the Sixth Amendment's protection to the vagaries of the rules of evidence, much less to amorphous notions of "reliability." Certainly none of the authorities discussed above acknowledges any general reliability exception to the common-law rule. Admitting statements deemed reliable by a judge is fundamentally at odds with the right of confrontation. To be sure, the Clause's <u>ultimate goal</u> is to <u>ensure reliability of evidence,</u> but it is a procedural rather than a substantive guarantee. It commands, not that evidence be reliable, but that reliability be assessed in a particular manner: by testing in the crucible of cross-examination. The Clause thus reflects a judgment, not only about the desirability of reliable evidence (a point on which there could be little dissent), but about how reliability can best be determined. Cf. 3 Blackstone, Commentaries, at 373 ("This open examination of witnesses . . . is much more conducive to the clearing up of truth"); M. Hale, History and Analysis of the Common Law of England 258 (1713) (adversarial testing "beats and bolts out the Truth much better").

procedural reliability ↳ *cross*

The *Roberts* test allows a jury to hear evidence, untested by the adversary process, based on a mere judicial determination of reliability. It thus replaces the constitutionally prescribed method of assessing reliability with a wholly foreign one. In this respect, it is very different from exceptions to the Confrontation Clause that make no claim to be a surrogate means of assessing reliability. For example, the rule of forfeiture by wrongdoing (which we accept) extinguishes confrontation claims on essentially equitable grounds; it does not purport to be an alternative means of determining reliability. See *Reynolds v. United States*, 98 U.S. 145, 158–159 (1879). * * *

Dispensing with confrontation because testimony is obviously reliable is akin to dispensing with jury trial because a defendant is obviously guilty. This is not what the Sixth Amendment prescribes.

B

The legacy of *Roberts* in other courts vindicates the Framers' wisdom in rejecting a general reliability exception. The framework is so unpredictable that it fails to provide meaningful protection from even core confrontation violations.

Reliability is an amorphous, if not entirely subjective, concept. There are countless factors bearing on whether a statement is reliable; the nine-factor balancing test applied by the Court of Appeals below is representative. * * *

The unpardonable vice of the *Roberts* test, however, is not its unpredictability, but its demonstrated capacity to admit core testimonial statements that the Confrontation Clause plainly meant to exclude. Despite the plurality's speculation in *Lilly* [*v. Virginia*], 527 U.S., at 137, that it was "highly unlikely" that accomplice confessions implicating the accused could survive *Roberts*, courts continue routinely to admit them. * * * One recent study found that, after *Lilly*, appellate courts admitted accomplice statements to the authorities in 25 out of 70 cases—more than one-third of the time. Kirst, Appellate Court Answers to the Confrontation Questions in *Lilly v. Virginia*, 53 Syracuse L. Rev. 87, 105 (2003). Courts have invoked *Roberts* to admit other sorts of plainly testimonial statements despite the absence of any opportunity to cross-examine. See *United States v. Aguilar*, 295 F.3d 1018, 1021–1023 (CA9 2002) (plea allocution showing existence of a conspiracy); * * * *United States v. Papajohn*, 212 F.3d 1112, 1118–1120 (CA8 2000) (grand jury testimony). * * *

To add insult to injury, some of the courts that admit untested testimonial statements find reliability in the very factors that *make* the statements testimonial. As noted earlier, one court relied on the fact that the witness's statement was made to police while in custody on pending charges—the theory being that this made the statement more clearly against penal interest and thus more reliable. Other courts routinely rely on the fact that a prior statement is given under oath in judicial proceedings. That inculpating statements are given in a testimonial setting is not an antidote to the confrontation problem, but rather the trigger that makes the Clause's demands most urgent. It is not enough to point out that most of the usual safeguards of the adversary process attend the statement, when the single safeguard missing is the one the Confrontation Clause demands.

C

Roberts' failings were on full display in the proceedings below. Sylvia Crawford made her statement while in police custody, herself a potential suspect in the case. Indeed, she had been told that whether she would be released "depended on how the investigation continues." In response to often leading questions from police detectives, she implicated her husband in Lee's stabbing and at least arguably undermined his self-defense claim. Despite all this, the trial court admitted her statement, listing several reasons why it was reliable.⌈In its opinion reversing, the Court of Appeals listed several other reasons why the statement was *not* reliable. Finally, the State Supreme Court relied exclusively on the interlocking character of the statement and disregarded every other factor the lower courts had considered. The case is thus a self-contained demonstration of *Roberts*' unpredictable and inconsistent application. * * *⌉

We readily concede that we could resolve this case by simply reweighing the "reliability factors" under *Roberts* and finding that Sylvia Crawford's statement falls short. But we view this as one of those rare cases in which the result below is so improbable that it reveals a fundamental failure on our part to interpret the Constitution in a way that secures its intended constraint on judicial discretion. Moreover, to reverse the Washington Supreme Court's decision after conducting our own reliability analysis would perpetuate, not avoid, what the Sixth Amendment condemns. The Constitution prescribes a procedure for determining the reliability of testimony in criminal trials, and we, no less than the state courts, lack authority to replace it with one of our own devising.

We have no doubt that the courts below were acting in utmost good faith when they found reliability. The Framers, however, would not have been content to indulge this assumption. They knew that judges, like other government officers, could not always be trusted to safeguard the rights of the people; the likes of the dread Lord Jeffreys were not yet too distant a memory. They were loath to leave too much discretion in judicial hands. Cf. U.S. Const., Amdt. 6 (criminal jury trial); Amdt. 7 (civil jury trial); *Ring v. Arizona*, 536 U.S. 584, 611–612 (2002) (Scalia, J., concurring). By replacing categorical constitutional guarantees with open-ended balancing tests, we do violence to their design. Vague standards are manipulable, and, while that might be a small concern in run-of-the-mill assault prosecutions like this one, the Framers had an eye toward politically charged cases like Raleigh's—great state trials where the impartiality of even those at the highest levels of the judiciary might not be so clear. It is difficult to imagine *Roberts*' providing any meaningful protection in those circumstances.

* * *

Where nontestimonial hearsay is at issue, it is wholly consistent with the Framers' design to afford the States flexibility in their development of hearsay law—as does *Roberts*, and as would an approach that exempted such statements from Confrontation Clause scrutiny altogether. Where testimonial evidence is at issue, however, the Sixth Amendment demands what the common law required: unavailability and a prior opportunity for cross-examination. We leave for another day any effort to spell out a comprehensive definition of "testimonial."[10] Whatever else the term covers, it applies at a minimum to prior testimony at a preliminary hearing, before a grand jury, or at a former trial; and to police interrogations. These are the modern practices with closest kinship to the abuses at which the Confrontation Clause was directed.

In this case, the State admitted Sylvia's testimonial statement against petitioner, despite the fact that he had no opportunity to cross-examine her. That alone is sufficient to make out a violation of the Sixth Amendment. *Roberts* notwithstanding, we decline to mine the record in search of indicia of reliability. Where testimonial statements are at issue, the only indicium of reliability sufficient to satisfy constitutional demands is the one the Constitution actually prescribes: confrontation.

The judgment of the Washington Supreme Court is reversed, and the case is remanded for further proceedings not inconsistent with this opinion.

It is so ordered.

[Chief Justice Rehnquist, joined by Justice O'Connor, wrote a separate opinion concurring in the judgment. They did not believe that it was wise or necessary to overrule *Roberts*; the "interlocking nature" of the two confessions was simply a form of corroboration, and Idaho v. Wright, 497 U.S. 805 (1990), had held that reliability for purposes of *Roberts* could not be demonstrated by corroborating evidence.]

B. EXCEPTIONS AND EXEMPTIONS

1. ADMISSIONS

Reed v. McCord

Court of Appeals of New York, 1899.
160 N.Y. 330, 54 N.E. 737.

■ MARTIN, J. This action was to recover damages for personal injuries to the plaintiff's intestate which occasioned his death, and was based upon the alleged negligence of the defendant. * * *

The only remaining question is whether the statements of the defendant of the circumstances and cause of the accident to the plaintiff's intestate, made while a witness before the coroner, were competent and properly received. The defendant was called and sworn as a witness, and gave evidence as to the accident. Upon the trial of this action the official stenographer for the board of coroners was called and permitted, under the defendant's objection and exception, to testify that upon the hearing before the coroner the defendant gave evidence to the effect that all machines of

---

[10] We acknowledge THE CHIEF JUSTICE'S objection that our refusal to articulate a comprehensive definition in this case will cause interim uncertainty. But it can hardly be any worse than the status quo. The difference is that the *Roberts* test is *inherently*, and therefore *permanently*, unpredictable.

the make of the one in use when the decedent was killed were alike; that at the time of the injury the dog* of the machine was not in position, which caused the accident; and that "the man who had charge of it supposed the dog was in position, and he released his hold on the thing, and it commenced to revolve, and then he got down so as to put his foot on it, and it was going so rapidly that it slipped past." It was admitted that the defendant was not present when the accident occurred, and hence, it is obvious that his statement before the coroner was not based upon his personal knowledge, but upon what he had learned as to the situation and how the accident occurred. [The contention of the appellant is that, as his admissions were not based upon his personal knowledge, proof of them should have been excluded, and that his exception to their admission was well taken.] The defendant being a party to this action, his admissions against his own interest were evidence in favor of his adversary, if of a fact material to the issue. If he had merely admitted that he heard that the accident occurred in the manner stated, it would have been inadmissible, as then it would only have amounted to an admission that he had heard the statement which he repeated, and not to an admission of the facts included in it. That would have been in no sense an admission of any fact pertinent to the issue, but a mere admission of what he had heard, without adoption or indorsement. Such evidence is clearly inadmissible. Stephens v. Vroman, 16 N.Y. 381. But the admissions proved in this case were not of that character. They were plain admissions of facts and circumstances which attended the intestate's injury. In a civil action the admissions by a party of any fact material to the issue are always competent evidence against him, wherever, whenever, or to whomsoever made. * * * The theory upon which this class of evidence is held to be competent is that [it is highly improbable that a party will admit or state anything against himself or against his own interest unless it is true.] As the admissions testified to by the stenographer were of facts and circumstances which were material to the issue in this action, they were clearly competent, although not conclusive, evidence of the facts admitted. We find no error in the admission of this evidence, and, as no other questions are raised that we have jurisdiction to review, our conclusion is that the judgment should be affirmed. The judgment should be affirmed, with costs. All concur, except Parker, C. J., not voting, and O'Brien, J., dissenting. Judgment affirmed.

[handwritten margin note: logic for exception]

NOTES

Like many courts (and students) *Reed* refers to "admissions against * * * interest." That is a misleading phrase that it is best to avoid. Admissions do not have to be against the interest of the party at the time they are made. (Presumably, an admission is against the party's interest in the litigation at the time it is offered against the party.) Another doctrine, addressed below in subsection 6, provides an exception to the hearsay rule for a statement that was against the interests of the declarant at the time the statement was made.

---

* A clamp or catch.

The following quotation is from William Shakespeare's Othello, Act III, Sc. iii. The speaker is Iago.

* * * I lay with Cassio lately,

And being troubled with a raging tooth,

I could not sleep.

There are a kind of men so loose of soul,

That in their sleeps will mutter their affairs:

One of this kind is Cassio:

In sleep I heard him say "Sweet Desdemona,

Let us be wary, let us hide our loves;"

An then, sir, would he gripe and wring my hand,

Cry "O sweet creature!" and then kiss me hard,

As if he pluk'd up kisses by the roots,

That grew upon my lips: then laid his leg

Over my thigh, and sigh'd and kiss'd, and then

Cried "Cursed fate that gave thee to the Moor!"

Suppose Iago offers to testify to this effect at a trial of Cassio and Desdemona for adultery. Is this testimony hearsay? Would it on any ground be admissible against Cassio? Or Desdemona? Is it relevant?

United States v. Hoosier

United States Court of Appeals, Sixth Circuit, 1976.
542 F.2d 687.

■ Per Curiam.

Appellant seeks to overturn his jury conviction on one count of armed robbery of a federally insured bank. Four witnesses identified him, three of them positively, as the person who robbed the bank in Clarksville, Tennessee.

Another witness, Robert E. Rogers, testified that he had been with the robbery defendant before and after the bank robbery, that before the bank robbery defendant told him that he was going to rob a bank, and that three weeks after the bank robbery, he saw defendant with money and wearing what he thought were diamond rings, and that in the presence of defendant, the defendant's girl friend said concerning defendant's affluence at that point, "That ain't nothing, you should have seen the money we had in the hotel room," and that she spoke of "sacks of money." Although both defendant and his girl friend disputed these facts in their testimony, obviously the resolution of that fact dispute was for the jury, and we must assume the jury resolved it in favor of the government by its verdict of "guilty."

Appellant's sole appellate argument to this court, however, is that the testimony elicited from the fifth witness concerning appellant's girl friend's statement was inadmissible hearsay, and that it was reversible error for the District Judge to fail to grant the objection to its admission.

Relevant to this issue is Rule 801(d)(2)(B) of the Federal Rules of Evidence, which reads in applicable part:

> (2) Admission by party-opponent. The statement is offered against a party and is * * * (B) a statement of which he has manifested his adoption or belief in its truth, or * * *

The Advisory Committee's note concerning this rule is as follows:

> (B) Under established principles an admission may be made by adopting or acquiescing in the statement of another. While knowledge of contents would ordinarily be essential, this is not inevitably so: "X is a reliable person and knows what he is talking about." See McCormick § 246, p. 527, n. 15. Adoption or acquiescence may be manifested in any appropriate manner. When silence is relied upon, the theory is that the person would, under the circumstances, protest the statement made in his presence, if untrue. The decision in each case calls for an evaluation in terms of probable human behavior. In civil cases, the results have generally been satisfactory. In criminal cases, however, troublesome questions have been raised by decisions holding that failure to deny is an admission: the inference is a fairly weak one, to begin with; silence may be motivated by advice of counsel or realization that "anything you say may be used against you"; unusual opportunity is afforded to manufacture evidence; and encroachment upon the privilege against self-incrimination seems inescapably to be involved. However, recent decisions of the Supreme Court relating to custodial interrogation and the right to counsel appear to resolve these difficulties. Hence the rule contains no special provisions concerning failure to deny in criminal cases.

Fed.R.Evid. 801(d)(2)(B), Advisory Committee's Notes (1975).

Our analysis of our present problem is made in the context of the Advisory Committee note which is an appropriately guarded one. First, we note that the statement was made in appellant's presence, with only his girl friend and Rogers present. Since appellant had previously trusted Rogers sufficiently to tell him his plan to rob a bank, we see little likelihood that his silence in the face of these statements was due to "advice of counsel" or fear that anything he said might "be used against him." Under the total circumstances, we believe that probable human behavior would have been for appellant promptly to deny his girl friend's statement if it had not been true—particularly when it was said to a person to whom he had previously related a plan to rob a bank. While we agree with appellant's counsel that more is needed to justify admission of this statement than the mere presence and silence of the appellant, we observe that there was more in this record.

Finding no reversible error, the judgment of conviction is affirmed.

La Buy, Jury Instructions in Federal Criminal Cases
65 (1963).*

Section 6.15 Accusatory Statements

Evidence has been presented that statements accusing the defendant of the crime charged in the indictment were made in his presence, and that such statements were neither denied, nor objected to by him. If the jury finds that defendant actually heard and understood the accusatory statements, and that they were made under such circumstances that defendant would have denied them if they were not true, then the jury should consider whether defendant's silence was an admission of the truth of the statements. However, where defendant is under arrest, his silence in the face of accusatory statements does not in any way constitute an admission of the truth of the statements, nor create any inference of guilt.

The Gospel According to Luke*

" 'You are the Son of God, then?' they all said, and he replied, 'It is you who say I am.' They said, 'Need we call further witnesses? We have heard it ourselves from his own lips.'

"With that the whole assembly rose, and they brought him before Pilate. They opened the case against him by saying, 'We found this man subverting our nation, opposing the payment of taxes to Caesar, and claiming to be the Messiah, a king.' Pilate asked him, 'Are you the king of the Jews?' He replied, 'The words are yours.' "

Stephen Birmingham, "Our Crowd"
306–07 (1967).

One of [Otto Kahn's] first moves in 1903 was to hire a new impresario from Germany, Heinrich Conried, who, according to critics who instantly materialized, possessed no qualifications whatever. At the time, a writer for the New York *Herald* commented: "The only explanation of Kahn's motive in the Conried selection was that latter's very ignorance of music might have given his sponsor a chance to superintend, direct, and manage." The

---

* 7th Cir. Judicial Conference, West Pub. Co., 1963.
* Luke, 22:70–23:3; The New English Bible, 106–107 (1970).

same writer warned Mr. Kahn that Conried was "out for big game himself," and was "out to be the head of the opera not only in name but in fact also," and that Otto Kahn had used "Wall Street tactics" to get Conried appointed—rushing the new director in by getting busy board members to sign over their proxies to Kahn. (Kahn, who had already begun his lifetime practice of demanding that newspapers print retractions of stories he considered inexact, made no comment on this one, so we may assume it contains the truth.) *so outrageous that it doesn't require response?*

Admission by Silence—Another View

"In his funeral oration on Roscoe Conkling, Robert G. Ingersoll said: 'He was maligned, misrepresented and misunderstood, but he would not answer. He was as silent then as he is now—and his silence, better than any form of speech, refuted every charge.' George Bernard Shaw said: 'Silence is the most perfect expression of scorn.' "**

State v. Carlson

Supreme Court of Oregon, En Banc, 1991.
311 Or. 201, 808 P.2d 1002.

■ UNIS, JUSTICE.

Defendant appeals from his convictions for unlawful possession of a controlled substance, methamphetamine, ORS 475.992(4), and endangering the welfare of a minor, ORS 163.575. * * *

FACTS

On August 3, 1988, Officer Lewis was dispatched to an apartment in response to a report of a domestic dispute between defendant and his wife, Lisa. On his arrival, Lewis was met by Lisa, whom he later described as having a "very white" complexion, looking tired, "fairly depressed," "distraught," and "at her wit's end," being occasionally tearful, and "coming down off of methamphetamine." Also present were the minor daughter of Lisa and defendant, and Lisa's sister and her minor daughter. Defendant was not in the apartment at that time.

Lewis asked Lisa if there were any methamphetamine in the apartment. She responded by saying that "he probably took it all, but go ahead and look around; I don't care anymore." During his search of the apartment, Lewis found traces of methamphetamine on a mirror in the master bedroom that defendant and Lisa shared.

About 15 to 20 minutes later, Lewis, accompanied by a second police officer, met defendant in the parking lot of the apartment complex. Lewis noticed what appeared to be needle marks on defendant's arms. Without first advising defendant of his constitutional rights, Lewis asked defendant

** Commonwealth v. Dravecz, 424 Pa. 582, 585 n. 1, 227 A.2d 904, 906 n. 1 (1967).

about the needle marks. Defendant initially responded, "Yeah, I got a few tracks," and then said that the marks were injuries that he had received from working on a car. Lisa, who was present during the exchange and close enough to hear what was being said, broke in by yelling: "You liar, you got them from shooting up in the bedroom with all your stupid friends." Defendant "hung his head and shook his head back and forth."

[Over defendant's objection, the trial judge had admitted testimony about Lisa Carlson's accusation and the defendant's reaction to it.

[The court first considered defendant's argument that the evidence of defendant's statements to the police officer should have been excluded because defendant was not advised of his *Miranda* rights. It rejected this argument on grounds that the defendant was not in custody at the time of the incident. The court then turned to the issue whether Lisa Carlson's statement was inadmissible.]

The state first contends that Lewis' testimony about Lisa's accusatory statement ("[y]ou liar, you got [the marks on your arms] from shooting up in the bedroom [where the methamphetamine was found] with all your stupid friends") and defendant's nonverbal reaction thereto ("hung his head and shook his head back and forth") was properly admitted in evidence as an "adoptive admission" under OEC 801(4)(b)(B). Defendant responds that Lewis' testimony is inadmissible hearsay. See OEC 802 (rule against admission of hearsay). He argues, in essence, that his head shaking manifested his rejection, rather than his adoption, of his wife's accusation.

A threshold question in this case is whether the intent to adopt, agree or approve is a preliminary question of fact for the trial judge to decide under OEC 104(1) or a question of conditional relevancy under OEC 104(2).[a]
* * *

Few courts have addressed the issue whether manifestation of an adoption or a belief is a preliminary question of fact for the trial judge under a provision comparable to OEC 104(1) or a question of conditional relevancy under a provision comparable to OEC 104(2). Louisell & Mueller, supra, at 294, § 424. Courts, scholars and commentators who have spoken on the issue disagree on the answer. Some suggest that the question is one of conditional relevancy. See, e.g., United States v. Sears, 663 F.2d 896, 905 (9th Cir.1981), cert. den., 455 U.S. 1027, 102 S.Ct. 1731, 72 L.Ed.2d 148 (1982); United States v. Barletta, 652 F.2d 218, 219–20 (1st Cir.1981); Graham, Handbook of Federal Evidence 784, § 801.20 (3d ed 1991); McCormick, supra, at 799 n 14, § 269; but see id. at 135–36, § 53 (author's language suggests adoption is a question for the trial judge).

Others take the view that the issue is a preliminary question of fact for the trial judge under the federal counterpart to OEC 104(1). See, e.g., Wright & Graham, 21 Federal Practice and Procedure 260, § 5053 (judge

---

[a] OEC 104(1) and 104(2) are substantially similar to Fed.R.Evid. 104(a) and 104(b), respectively.—Eds.

determines issues including the admissibility of hearsay);   McCormick, Evidence 527, § 246 (1954) (implicit in principles stated);   Garland & Schmitz, Of Judges and Juries: A Proposed Revision of Federal Rule of Evidence 104, 23 UC Davis L Rev 77, 84 (1989).

For reasons that follow, we hold that whether the party intended to adopt, agree with or approve of the contents of the statement of another, a precondition to the admissibility of evidence offered under OEC 801(4)(b)(B), is a preliminary question of fact for the trial judge under OEC 104(1).

First, the wording of OEC 104(1) and the Legislative Commentary to that rule suggest that result. OEC 104(1) assigns to the trial judge the responsibility for making preliminary determinations regarding, inter alia, the "admissibility of evidence." Intent to adopt, agree or approve is a preliminary fact within the scope of OEC 104(1), because its proof concerns "the admissibility of evidence." * * *

Second, "[b]asically, Rule 104 divides the determination of preliminary facts between judge and jury along the rough line between 'competence' and 'relevance,' though it does not use this terminology." Wright and Graham, supra, at 259, § 5053. " 'Competency,' [in this context,] refers to whether evidence is admissible under one of the policy-based exclusionary rules [such as the rule against hearsay.]" Garland & Schmitz, supra, at 93. The intent to adopt, agree or approve involves a preliminary question of fact on which the competency, and thus the admissibility, of the evidence depends.

There exists an even more persuasive reason for holding that the predicate for admissibility of evidence under OEC 801(4)(b)(B) is an OEC 104(1) preliminary question of fact. The objection to admissibility, based on the rule against hearsay, furthers an important legal policy of preventing the trier of fact from considering the possible truthfulness of out-of-court statements, unless the statements have sufficient guarantees of trustworthiness. The purpose of the hearsay rule is to guard against the risks of misperception, misrecollection, misstatement, and insincerity, which are associated with statements of persons made out of court. Safeguards in the trial procedure, such as the immediate cross-examination of the witness and the opportunity of the trier of fact to observe the demeanor of the witness who swears or affirms under the penalty of perjury to tell the truth, are designed to reduce those risks.

There are several difficulties with leaving the question of intent to adopt, agree or approve to the jury as a question of conditional relevancy under OEC 104(2). If the OEC 104(2) conditional relevancy standard is employed, the legal policy underlying the hearsay rule would be furthered incompletely, if at all. The jury passing on the admission by conduct will have to hear not only evidence about the conduct and the surrounding circumstances, but also the out-of-court statement, as necessary predicates for understanding what the party allegedly adopted. For example, in the present case, the wife's accusatory statement to which defendant's nonverbal conduct is a response, would have to be admitted to give meaning to defendant's conduct, and the accusation is relevant to prove the truth of the accusation even though it may not be admissible for that purpose. A juror could (a) overlook the question of intent to adopt, agree or approve, and consider the truth of the matter asserted in the out-of-court statement, (b) use the out-of-court statement before considering and resolving the preliminary question of intent to adopt, agree or approve, or (c) consider the hearsay statement regardless of what conclusion is reached on the preliminary question of adoption or belief. See Garland & Schmitz, supra (pointing out these potential risks). If the evidence is inadmissible, i.e., the jury does not find the preliminary fact (intent to adopt, agree or approve) to exist, preventing jury contamination may prove impossible. Garland & Schmitz, supra, at 94. Additionally, a general verdict would not indicate the jury's resolution of whether intent to adopt existed. A record for appellate review would require a special set of preliminary jury findings.

In short, we believe that judicial intervention is required to prevent improper use of evidence. The preliminary question of intent to adopt, agree or approve, therefore, should be left to the trial judge under OEC 104(1).

Court's determination

In the present case, the preliminary question of fact for resolution by the trial judge under OEC 104(1) was whether the proponent of the evidence, the state, had established by a preponderance of the evidence (more likely than not) that defendant's nonverbal reaction to his wife's accusatory statement manifested defendant's intention to adopt, agree with or approve of the statement.

In the face of his wife's accusatory statement, defendant "hung his head and shook his head back and forth." Although the record discloses that Lewis twice demonstrated defendant's nonverbal reaction, it does not disclose whether defendant's shaking his head back and forth was positive or negative in character. Defendant essentially testified that he had not intended to adopt, agree with or approve of his wife's remarks and that he did not see any benefit in arguing with an irrational, mentally ill and angry woman.

Various factual hypotheses are suggested by defendant's ambiguous, nonverbal reaction. Head shaking back and forth generally means a negative reply. Village of New Hope v. Duplessie, 304 Minn. 417, 231 N.W.2d 548, 552 (1975) (quoting Bill v. Farm Bureau Ins. Co., 254 Iowa 1215, 119 N.W.2d 768, 773 (1963)). "[T]he lateral motion might * * * mean merely bewilderment or confusion, an 'I don't know' answer," id., a reluctance to engage in, or to continue, a dispute with his wife, a decision to stand mute in a situation that was intimidating by the presence of a police officer, or, as the state asserts in this case on appeal, an expression of dismay or resignation that his wife told the police the truth about how defendant obtained the needle marks on his arms.

We view the record consistent with the trial court's ruling on a preliminary question of fact under OEC 104(1), accepting reasonable inferences and reasonable credibility choices that the trial judge could have made.

* * * In the circumstances of this case, defendant's nonverbal reaction is so ambiguous that it cannot reasonably be deemed sufficient to establish that any particular interpretation, consistent with the trial judge's ruling, is more probably correct. [We hold, therefore, that there was insufficient evidence to support a finding by a preponderance of the evidence that defendant intended to adopt, agree with or approve the contents of his wife's accusatory statement. Accordingly, we hold that evidence of his wife's hearsay statement and defendant's nonverbal reaction thereto was not admissible under OEC 801(4)(b)(B). * * *]

[In the final part of its opinion, the court held Lisa Carlson's statement admissible as an excited utterance.]

QUESTION

Was Lisa's statement testimonial within the meaning of *Crawford*?

HYPOTHETICALS

(1) P sues D for damages for personal injuries arising out of an accident in which D was driving and P was a passenger. D testifies that as she was driving on an offramp of the freeway the throttle of her car stuck and she bent over to jiggle it loose; that as she bent over P reached through the steering wheel and blew the horn; that this so surprised her that she took her eyes off the road to look at P and the car then smashed into a telephone pole. P testifies that he never blew the horn or reached through the steering wheel. In an evidence-admissibility hearing before trial P makes an offer of proof as to an alleged admission made by D; that P and D had a conversation after P saw the police report for the first time; that the report contained D's statement about her leaning over and P's blowing the horn; that P made a telephone call to D and told her this was an untrue statement, and that D responded "Well, I did it because I was fearful over my insurance." D objects to P's offer of proof on grounds of hearsay. Should D's objection be sustained?

(2) A sues B for the price of goods sold to X Enterprises. A claims that B is a partner in X Enterprises. A testifies that, before he sold the goods to X Enterprises, he was at the X Enterprises office and X, the president, introduced him to B with the statement: "Meet my partner in X Enterprises, Ms. B," and that B then shook hands with A and said nothing. B moves to strike A's testimony as hearsay. What result?

La Buy, Jury Instructions in Federal Criminal Cases
63–64 (1963).*

Section 6.14 Exculpatory Statements

Evidence has been introduced that defendant made certain exculpatory statements outside of the courtroom explaining his actions to show that he was innocent of the crime charged in the indictment. Evidence contra-

---

* 7th Cir. Judicial Conference, West Pub. Co., 1963.

dicting such statements has also been introduced. If the jury finds that the exculpatory statements were untrue, and that the defendant made them voluntarily with knowledge of their falsity, the jury may consider the statements as circumstantial evidence of defendant's consciousness of guilt.

Mahlandt v. Wild Canid Survival & Research Center, Inc.

United States Court of Appeals, Eighth Circuit, 1978.
588 F.2d 626.

■ VAN SICKLE, DISTRICT JUDGE.

This is a civil action for damages arising out of an alleged attack by a wolf on a child. The sole issues on appeal are as to the correctness of three rulings which excluded conclusionary statements * * *. Two of them were made by a defendant, who was also an employee of the corporate defendant; and the third was in the form of a statement appearing in the records of a board meeting of the corporate defendant.

On March 23, 1973, Daniel Mahlandt, then 3 years, 10 months, and 8 days old, was sent by his mother to a neighbor's home on an adjoining street to get his older brother, Donald. Daniel's mother watched him cross the street, and then turned into the house to get her car keys. Daniel's path took him along a walkway adjacent to the Poos' residence. Next to the walkway was a five foot chain link fence to which Sophie had been chained with a six foot chain. In other words, Sophie was free to move in a half circle having a six foot radius on the side of the fence opposite from Daniel.

Sophie was a bitch wolf, 11 months and 28 days old, who had been born at the St. Louis Zoo, and kept there until she reached 6 months of age, at which time she was given to the Wild Canid Survival and Research Center, Inc. It was the policy of the Zoo to remove wolves from the Children's Zoo after they reached the age of 5 or 6 months. Sophie was supposed to be kept at the Tyson Research Center, but Kenneth Poos, as Director of Education for the Wild Canid Survival and Research Center, Inc., had been keeping her at his home because he was taking Sophie to schools and institutions where he showed films and gave programs with respect to the nature of wolves. Sophie was known as a very gentle wolf who had proved herself to be good natured and stable during her contacts with thousands of children, while she was in the St. Louis Children's Zoo.

* * *

A neighbor who was ill in bed in the second floor of his home heard a child's screams and went to his window, where he saw a boy lying on his back within the enclosure, with a wolf straddling him. The wolf's face was near Daniel's face, but the distance was so great that he could not see what the wolf was doing, and did not see any biting. Within about 15 seconds the neighbor saw Clarke Poos, about seventeen, run around the house, get the

wolf off of the boy, and disappear with the child in his arms to the back of
the house. Clarke took the boy in and laid him on the kitchen floor.

* * * An expert in the behavior of wolves stated that when a wolf licks
a child's face that it is a sign of care, and not a sign of attack; that a wolf's
wail is a sign of compassion, and an effort to get attention, not a sign of attack. * * * The defendant, Mr. Poos, arrived home while Daniel and his
mother were in the kitchen. After Daniel was taken in an ambulance, Mr.
Poos talked to everyone present, including a neighbor who came in. Within
an hour after he arrived home, Mr. Poos went to Washington University to
inform Owen Sexton, President of Wild Canid Survival and Research Center, Inc., of the incident. Mr. Sexton was not in his office so Mr. Poos left
the following note on his door:

> Owen, would you call me at home, 727–5080? Sophie bit a child that
> came in our back yard. All has been taken care of. I need to convey
> what happened to you. (Exhibit 11)

Denial of admission of this note is one of the issues on appeal.   *admissable?*

Later that day, Mr. Poos found Mr. Sexton at the Tyson Research Center and told him what had happened. Denial of plaintiff's offer to prove that
Mr. Poos told Mr. Sexton, that, "Sophie had bit a child that day," is the
second issue on appeal.

A meeting of the Directors of the Wild Canid Survival and Research
Center, Inc., was held on April 4, 1973. Mr. Poos was not present at that
meeting. The minutes of that meeting reflect that there was a "great deal
of discussion * * * about the legal aspects of the incident of Sophie biting
the child." Plaintiff offered an abstract of the minutes containing that reference. Denial of the offer of that abstract is the third issue on appeal.

Daniel had lacerations of the face, left thigh, left calf, and right thigh,
and abrasions and bruises of the abdomen and chest. Mr. Mahlandt was
permitted to state that Daniel had indicated that he had gone under the
fence. Mr. Mahlandt and Mr. Poos, about a month after the incident, examined the fence to determine what caused Daniel's lacerations. Mr. Mahlandt felt that they did not look like animal bites. The parallel scars on Daniel's thigh appeared to match the configuration of the barbs or tines on the
fence. The expert as to the behavior of wolves opined that the lacerations
were not wolf bites or wounds caused by wolf claws. * * *

The jury brought in a verdict for the defense.

The trial judge's rationale for excluding the note, the statement, and
the corporate minutes, was the same in each case. He reasoned that Mr.
Poos did not have any personal knowledge of the facts, and accordingly, the
first two admissions were based on hearsay; and the third admission contained in the minutes of the board meeting was subject to the same objection of hearsay, and unreliability because of lack of personal knowledge.

The Federal Rules of Evidence became effective in July 1975 (180 days after passage of the Act). Thus, at this time, there is very little case law to rely upon for resolution of the problems of interpretation.

The relevant rule here is: Rule 801(d)(2).

* * * [T]he statement in the note pinned on the door is not hearsay, and is admissible against Mr. Poos. It was his own statement, and as such was clearly different from the reported statement of another. Example, "I was told that * * *." It was also a statement of which he had manifested his adoption or belief in its truth. And the same observations may be made of the statement made later in the day to Mr. Sexton that, "Sophie had bit a child * * *."

Are these statements admissible against Wild Canid Survival and Research Center, Inc.? They were made by Mr. Poos when he was an agent or servant of the Wild Canid Survival and Research Center, Inc., and they concerned a matter within the scope of his agency, or employment, i.e., his custody of Sophie, and were made during the existence of that relationship.

* * * This is not an 801(d)(2)(C) situation because Mr. Poos was not authorized or directed to make a statement on the matter by anyone. * * * Weinstein's discussion of Rule 801(d)(2)(D) (Weinstein's Evidence § 801(d)(2)(D)(01), p. 801–137), states that:

> Rule 801(d)(2)(D) adopts the approach * * * which, as a general proposition, makes statement made by agents within the scope of their employment admissible * * *. Once agency, and the making of the statement while the relationship continues, are established, the statement is exempt from the hearsay rule so long as it relates to a matter within the scope of the agency.

After reciting a lengthy quotation which justifies the rule as necessary, and suggests that such admissions are trustworthy and reliable, Weinstein, states categorically that although an express requirement of personal knowledge on the part of the declarant of the facts underlying his statement is not written into the rule, it should be. He feels that is mandated by Rules 805 and 403.

Rule 805 recites, in effect, that a statement containing hearsay within hearsay is admissible, if each part of the statement falls within an exception to the hearsay rule. Rule 805, however, deals only with hearsay exceptions. A statement based [sic] on the personal knowledge of the declarant of facts underlying his statement is not the repetition of the statement of another, thus not hearsay. It is merely opinion testimony. Rule 805 cannot mandate the implied condition desired by Judge Weinstein.

Rule 403 provides for the exclusion of relevant evidence if its probative value is substantially outweighed by the danger of unfair prejudice, confusion of the issues, or misleading the jury, or by consideration of undue delay, waste of time, or needless presentation of cumulative evidence. Nor does Rule 403 mandate the implied condition desired by Judge Weinstein.

Thus, while both Rule 805 and Rule 403 provide additional bases for excluding otherwise acceptable evidence, neither rule mandates the introduction into Rule 801(d)(2)(D) of an implied requirement that the declarant have personal knowledge of the facts underlying his statement. So we conclude that the two statements made by Mr. Poos were admissible against Wild Canid Survival and Research Center, Inc.

Admissible !!

As to the entry in the records of a corporate meeting, the directors as primary officers of the corporation had the authority to include their conclusions in the record of the meeting. So the evidence would fall within 801(d)(2)(C) as to Wild Canid Survival and Research Center, Inc., and be admissible. * * *

But there was no servant, or agency, relationship which justified admitting the evidence of the board minutes as against Mr. Poos.

None of the conditions of 801(d)(2) cover the claim that minutes of a corporate board meeting can be used against a non-attending, nonparticipating employee of that corporation. The evidence was not admissible as against Mr. Poos.

There is left only the question of whether the trial court's rulings which excluded all three items of evidence are justified under Rule 403. He clearly found that the evidence was not reliable, pointing out that none of the statements were based on the personal knowledge of the declarant.

403 – was ov. reliable?

Again, that problem was faced by the Advisory Committee on Proposed Rules. In its discussion of 801(d)(2) exceptions to the hearsay rule, the Committee said:

> The freedom which admissions have enjoyed from technical demands of searching for an assurance of trustworthiness in some against-interest circumstances, and from the restrictive influences of the opinion rule and the rule requiring first hand knowledge, when taken with the apparently prevalent satisfaction with the results, calls for generous treatment of this avenue to admissibility. 28 U.S.C.A., Volume of Federal Rules of Evidence, Rule 801, p. 527, at p. 530.

So, here, remembering that relevant evidence is usually prejudicial to the cause of the side against which it is presented, and that the prejudice which concerns us is unreasonable prejudice; and applying the spirit of Rule 801(d)(2), we hold that Rule 403 does not warrant the exclusion of the evidence of Mr. Poos' statements as against himself or Wild Canid Survival and Research Center, Inc.

* * *

The judgment of the District Court is reversed and the matter remanded to the District Court for a new trial consistent with this opinion.

HYPOTHETICALS

(1) A, a painting subcontractor, sues X, a general contractor, for the balance due on a subcontract with X. A had been paid four progress payments, but X refused to pay the fifth and last progress payment on the ground that A's work was unsatisfactory. B was general superintendent for X and was authorized by X to approve and reject subcontractors' work and to approve progress payments to subcontractors accordingly. When A's painting job for X was 98 percent complete, B wrote a letter of recommendation for A, stating that A had completed the painting job for X to everyone's satisfaction. A offers B's letter in evidence. X objects that the letter is hearsay. What result under federal law? Under California law?

[handwritten margin note: B is an agent of X acting within scope?]

(2) A sues the X market for damages for personal injuries arising out of a slip-and-fall incident. A few minutes after A fell, B, the store manager, arrived and A pointed out a banana peel on the floor. C, a witness to the incident, proposes to testify for A that B then said to A, "Don't worry about this. We will pay your bills. It's the store's fault." X objects that C's testimony is hearsay. What result under federal law? Under California Law?

Big Mack Trucking Co., Inc. v. Dickerson

Supreme Court of Texas, 1973.
497 S.W.2d 283.

■ SAM D. JOHNSON, JUSTICE.

The wife and children of Willie Lee Dickerson have recovered damages for his wrongful death in an action against his employer, Big Mack Trucking Company, Inc. The court of civil appeals affirmed. We reverse.

Willie Dickerson and Ormand Leday were employees of Big Mack. Each was driving a truck-tractor pulling a flatbed trailer loaded with sheet steel across Texas from Eagle Pass to Arp. Both trucks stopped in Waco. Leday parked his truck fifteen to eighteen feet behind Dickerson's. Leday left his vehicle unattended. Dickerson got out of his truck and was standing behind his trailer with his back toward Leday's vehicle. Leday's unattended truck rolled forward striking Dickerson's trailer and crushing Dickerson between the two trucks. Dickerson was killed in the accident.

The present suit was * * * commenced against Big Mack and Leday. * * * After the verdict was returned, Leday was dismissed on plaintiffs' motion and judgment was rendered against Big Mack for $220,000.

The jury found that Leday was acting as an employee of Big Mack at the time of the accident, that Leday was guilty of two acts of negligence which also amounted to heedless and reckless disregard of the rights of others, and that those acts were proximate causes of the occurrence. The jury found actual damages in the aggregate amount of $220,000.

Big Mack applied for writ of error.

Big Mack asserts that there is "no evidence" to support the judgment against it because all the evidence of Leday's negligence and proximate cause was hearsay as to Big Mack. *Leday did not testify. No attempt was made to explain or justify the failure to call Leday, his absence, or his failure to give testimony.* The plaintiffs' theory of liability was predicated upon the fact that Leday's brakes were defective at the time he parked his truck. The only evidence tending to prove the circumstances of the accident or the elements necessary for plaintiffs' recovery came from two witnesses who could only testify what Leday had previously related to them. These two witnesses were Mr. David Stiles, the vice president of Big Mack, and Officer Henry Harwell, the investigating officer of the Waco Police Department.

Vice President Stiles testified that following the accident, Leday told him he had been having "air pressure troubles" and that he had not been maintaining the proper air pressure in his braking system. He further told Stiles that he had parked his truck behind Dickerson's truck, had gone off and left it and that when he returned he found the deceased crushed between the two trucks. In addition, Stiles, who was familiar with the proper operation of trucks, testified that if a truck was being operated under circumstances where the driver was having trouble with the brakes such as those related that it would be improper to park the truck on any kind of incline without scotching the wheels or putting it in gear.

The testimony of Officer Harwell was introduced by way of deposition. He testified that when he arrived that Dickerson was no longer there; that he had been removed by an ambulance. The two vehicles were still at the scene of the accident. Officer Harwell then related what Leday had told him: that he had been experiencing brake trouble with his truck in that the air pressure was running law [*sic*], that he was the operator of the back truck, that he parked his truck approximately fifteen to eighteen feet behind the decedent's truck and that when he left his truck Dickerson was standing at the back of Dickerson's truck eating off of the trailer.

Respondents assert that in an action against a servant and master, the master having been joined under respondeat superior, it is not necessary that the evidence proving the servant's negligence and proximate cause be competent evidence against the master in order to support a judgment against the master. The notion is that the master's derivative liability is imposed by law once the liability facts are proven by evidence competent against the servant.

We cannot accept such a view. The suggestion is that with respect to proof of the servant's liability, which we deem an essential element of plaintiffs' *case against the master,* the master loses the protection of the hearsay rule. Any reason which suggests that the master should lose the protection of that rule would also militate against the master's right to offer contrary evidence, to cross-examine plaintiffs' witnesses, to object to evidence on grounds other than hearsay, or, indeed, even to plead the general denial which requires the plaintiffs to prove the servant's liability in the first place. * * *

Since the evidence of Leday's negligence and proximate cause must be admissible against Big Mack in order to support the judgment against it, and since all evidence offered to prove those facts was hearsay, the question becomes whether the hearsay is admissible against Big Mack under any hearsay-rule exception known to Texas law.

The court of civil appeals held that Leday's statements to Stiles qualify against Big Mack as admissions of a party.[1] The theory is that Big Mack authorized Leday to speak to Stiles about the accident in Waco, and when Leday spoke he voiced, in contemplation of law, the position of Big Mack. We cannot agree. An agent's hearsay statements should be received against the principal as vicarious admissions only when the trial judge finds, as a preliminary fact, that the statements were authorized. The Restatement of Agency [§ 287] cautions that, in considering the breadth of an agent's authority when reporting details of an event to the principal, the court should notice the very likely limitation that the principal *intends* the agent's report to be made *only* to the principal or other person investigating the accident for the principal. If there be any special facts to show that Big Mack authorized Leday to speak to the world as well as to Stiles, those facts have not been introduced and so we follow the Restatement and hold that the Stiles testimony is not admissible under the admissions exception. In so holding we do not adopt § 287 of the Restatement as a hard and fast rule, but only observe it to the extent that it creates a rebuttable presumption of lack of authority.

The second theory of admissibility is that Leday's statements to Officer Harwell qualify as vicarious admissions. The Restatement rule noted above has no application since Officer Harwell was not investigating for the principal, Big Mack. Nevertheless, we must find that such statements were authorized by Big Mack, and in this inquiry we are mindful of the Wigmore-McCormick caveat against confusing the admissions exception with the res gestae, or spontaneous utterance, exception.

Of course, the authority to make admissions may be implied from express authority to do some other act. The question evolves, then, whether Leday's express authority to operate the truck may be a basis for implied authority to explain how the accident came to pass. Most authorities take the position that a driver's statements after an accident are not authorized by his employer. In terms of strictly consensual authority, we believe the well-advised employer would generally not authorize the driver to speak in these circumstances. There is, moreover, no basis for a claim of apparent authority since all events operating to establish liability for the injury have

---

[1] No doubt such statements are admissions of the party Leday, and so would be admissible over his hearsay objection. The pertinent question under our holding above is whether they are also admissions of Big Mack.

occurred at the time the statements are made, and there can be no pertinent detrimental reliance upon the driver's statements. There is no reason
peculiar to the case at bar why the general rule should not be followed.

Respondent assigns, as contrary authority, the cases of West Texas
Produce Co. v. Wilson; Dixie Motor Coach Corporation v. Meredith; Firestone Tire & Rubber Co. v. Rhodes; J. Weingarten, Inc. v. Reagan. We do
not think those cases require a different result. In *Wilson,* the president of
defendant corporation directed the investigating officers to question the
foreman on the day of the accident, and so the foreman's responses were
expressly authorized. The statements the driver made the following day
were not authorized and so were excluded. In *Meredith,* the bus driver's
post rem hearsay declarations were admitted, but the court of civil appeals
was of the opinion that there was no real dispute on the issue to which the
hearsay was relevant (i.e., defective brakes); the court's holding is only a
holding that, if error, it was harmless. The opinion in *Rhodes* indicates that
the witness never answered the question which sought to elicit the driver's
hearsay declarations; the court there held that "[a]n unanswered question,
although improper and duly excepted to, is not sufficient grounds for reversal of the case." In *Reagan,* the hearsay declarations of an employee of the
grocery store was admitted to show that the employee had knowledge of the
dangerous condition; its admission does not appear to have been challenged upon the basis that it also proved the fact of the dangerous condition. That is a viable distinction, and could properly have controlled the
decision of that case.[2]

The final theory of admissibility advanced by respondents is that Leday's statements to Officer Harwell were spontaneous exclamations. In order to so qualify, there must be some evidence of facts from which a trial
judge might infer that the declarant (Leday) was in such an emotional state
that he was incapable of that deliberation which might permit fabrication.
Spontaneity is the essence of the exception. The only evidence which tends
to show the time elapsed between the exciting event (Leday's discovery of
the accident) and Leday's statements to Officer Harwell is that when Harwell arrived, the ambulance had already taken Dickerson away. That alone
is clearly insufficient, and it is unaided by any mention by Officer Harwell
that the declarant appeared to be distraught. At all events, from the following colloquy it appears that the trial judge did not find the preliminary
facts constituting a spontaneous-exclamation predicate, but rather allowed
the Harwell deposition into evidence only as an admission. * * * After [the]
ruling by the trial judge, the only basis upon which we could hold the Harwell deposition admissible is to hold that Leday's hearsay declarations were
"spontaneous" as a matter of law. That we cannot do.

---

[2] We are aware that issue #2 inquired if Leday knew his brakes were defective, but an essential subsidiary question is whether the brakes were, in fact, defective. Evidence admitted
under a special rule-of-necessity, which liberalizes the admissions exception in a proponent's
effort to prove knowledge of a fact, cannot be used by indirection to prove existence of the fact
itself.

A great measure of trustworthiness stems from the fact that Leday's hearsay declarations were against his pecuniary interests. Our evidence law acknowledges this in the declarations against interest exception to the hearsay rule. However, it has long been the position of Texas jurisprudence that there should be a special *need* to rely on such hearsay, and consequently we require proof that the declarant was not available to testify at the trial. The instant record is wholly without proof of any attempt to establish that the hearsay declarant (Leday) was unavailable to testify. The exception therefore does not apply.

The judgments of the courts below are reversed, and the cause is remanded to the district court for a new trial.

Sabel v. Mead Johnson & Co.

United States District Court for the District of Massachusetts, 1990.
737 F.Supp. 135.

■ WOLF, DISTRICT JUDGE.

[A user of an antidepressant medication brought an action against a pharmaceutical manufacturer, claiming that the medication caused him to develop priapism. One of the issues was whether the tape of a meeting, convened by the manufacturer and attended by outside medical experts, was admissible when offered by the plaintiff against the defendant manufacturer.]

I. The Tucson Tape

The Tucson meeting was convened by Mead Johnson on March 21, 1983 to explore several aspects of the unexpected, but increasingly apparent association of Desyrel with priapism. The meeting was attended by five outside medical experts invited by Mead Johnson, as well as two employees of its Pharmaceutical Medical Services department. The meeting was chaired by Dr. Rubin Bressler, one of the outside experts, who had performed research sponsored by defendant in the past. One of the ten questions suggested for discussion at the meeting was "What should we tell the prescribing physician?" In general, topics discussed at the meeting included the potential pharmacological mechanisms by which Desyrel could cause priapism, possible avenues of research into the association of Desyrel with priapism, and what warnings to physicians should appropriately accompany Desyrel. * * *

Plaintiffs seek to introduce the tape and transcript as an admission of Mead Johnson under F.R.Ev. 801(d)(2), which provides, in pertinent part, that an out-of-court statement is not hearsay if "[t]he statement is offered against a party and is . . . (C) a statement by a person authorized by the party to make a statement concerning the subject, or (D) a statement by the party's agent or servant concerning a matter within the scope of the agency or employment, made during the existence of the relationship." Admissibility under these two provisions is governed not by the trustworthiness of the statement, but by the existence and scope of the principal-agent relationship as determined under the common law of agency. Plaintiffs have not carried their burden of demonstrating the existence of an agency relationship between defendant and the outside invitees. Thus, invitees' statements at the Tucson meeting are hearsay.

agency must be shown

An agency relationship has three essential characteristics: 1) the power of the agent to alter the legal relationships between the principal and third parties and the principal and himself; 2) the existence of a fiduciary relationship toward the principal with respect to matters within the scope of the agency; and 3) the right of the principal to control the agent's conduct with respect to matters within the scope of the agency. Restatement (Second) of Agency §§ 12–14 (1958). The courts have looked primarily at the issue of control in determining whether an agency relationship exists. *See United States v. Paxson*, 861 F.2d 730, 734 (D.C.Cir.1988) (admitting statement of corporate employee against corporate superior under Rule 801(d)(2)(D) where employee reported directly to superior); *United States v. Young*, 736 F.2d 565, 568 (10th Cir.1983) (same); *United States v. Mandel*, 591 F.2d 1347, 1368 (4th Cir.1979) (in criminal prosecution of governor, Rule 801(d)(2)(D) covered statements of governor's legislative aides, but not of state senators) * * *. Similarly, consent to control and to act in a fiduciary manner is important to a finding of an agency relationship. See *Abatti v. C.I.R.*, 644 F.2d 1385, 1390 (9th Cir.1981) (admitting binders prepared by defendant's accountant where accounting arrangements delegated to him); *United States v. Summers*, 598 F.2d 450, 459 (5th Cir.1979) (excluding taped statements of defendant's former agent on grounds that he could not be agent of defendant and informant for FBI at same time)* * *.

In the present case, it does not appear that Mead Johnson controlled the manner or means of discussion and analysis employed by the participants at the Tucson meeting. To the contrary, the tape and transcript of the meeting indicate it was a free-wheeling exchange of ideas, loosely moderated by one of the outside consultants.[1] It is not apparent who developed the agenda for the meeting. Although Mead Johnson financed the meeting and provided the factual information underlying the bulk of the discussion, there is no evidence in the transcript or otherwise that its employees sought to foreclose avenues of inquiry or to prevent the expression of potentially damaging ideas.

Proof against agency

In addition to Mead Johnson's apparent lack of control, there is no evidence that the consultants were empowered to speak or act on Mead Johnson's behalf. See *Ellis v. Kneifl*, 834 F.2d 128, 131 (8th Cir.1987) (statements of clerk of state court not admissible in suit against state court judge because clerk not authorized to act on judge's behalf). Mead Johnson never expressed an intent to be bound by the recommendations of the outside experts, nor did it even authorize or request them to prepare a written report on their findings and recommendations. The diversity of opinions expressed

---

[1] Although Dr. Bressler had apparently conducted research sponsored by Mead Johnson previous to the meeting, no evidence has been presented that he was an employee of Mead Johnson or that Mead Johnson controlled or influenced his research beyond the mere fact of sponsorship.

at the meeting, and the lack of resolution of differences among the experts, supports defendant's characterization of the meeting as a "brainstorming session," intended to generate ideas for defendant's further consideration, but not meant to establish its official position in any way.

F.R.Ev. 801(d)(2)(D) expanded the traditional admissions exception to the hearsay rule to include statements made by agents on matters within the scope of their agency, on the theory that an agent authorized to act on a principal's behalf is impliedly authorized to speak on the same matters. Here, however, plaintiffs have not shown that the consultants possessed the power to act on defendant's behalf in any respect, much less that they enjoyed the specific "speaking authority" contemplated by F.R.Ev. 801(d)(2)(C). Where defendant did not control the participants in the discussion, where the participants lacked the power to legally bind defendant through their statements and actions, and where the participants did not enter into a fiduciary relationship with defendant, the factors which support attribution of an agent's statements to her principal are completely missing. Mead Johnson could not control the actions or statements of the participants in the Tucson meeting; nor would it have had reason to do so, given the unforeseeability that the statements of those individuals would be attributed to it in a court of law.

The cases cited by plaintiffs in support of admission are distinguishable. In *Reid Brothers Logging Co. v. Ketchikan Pulp Co.*, 699 F.2d 1292, 1306 (9th Cir.)[1983], the court held that a report prepared by an employee of defendant's corporate parent on defendant's business operations was admissible under F.R.Ev. 801(d)(2)(C) as an admission of defendant. The author of the report was given full access to defendant's records and was aided by defendant's employees, and defendant circulated the report to its directors, officers and managers. Under such circumstances, the court concluded, the employee was authorized by defendant to make statements regarding its business operations and the defendant adopted these statements by adopting his report. Here, by contrast, Mead Johnson controlled the information given to the outside consultants, did not request or receive a final report from them, and did not adopt as its own the ideas expressed during the meeting. Moreover, the statements made by the experts were off-the-cuff, rather than opinions carefully formulated after thorough investigation and analysis. *Collins v. Wayne Corp.*, 621 F.2d 777 (5th Cir.1980), is distinguishable from the present case on essentially the same grounds. *Id.* at 780–82 (report of expert hired by defendant to investigate and analyze bus accident admissible under F.R.Ev. 801(d)(2)(C) because expert was a "speaking agent" of defendant).

[Judge Wolf ruled that the statements on the Tucson tape were inadmissible hearsay, with the exception of statements made by full-time Mead Johnson employees.]

United States v. DiDomenico

United States Court of Appeals for the Seventh Circuit, 1996.
78 F.3d 294.

[In the course of upholding a trial judge's decision to admit out-of-court statements under the exemption for statements of co-conspirators, Judge Posner made the following observations:]

[T]he principle that allows the admission of conspirator X to be treated as the admission of defendant conspirator Y, usable against Y as the admission of a party provided that the statement is made in furtherance of the conspiracy, disquiets those who believe that the concept of conspiracy gives prosecutors too much power. The rationalization for the principle is that conspirators are each others' agents (and therefore principals), and the principal is bound by the agent's words and deeds, provided they are within the scope of the agency, so that an admission by one is an admission by all and can be used against all as "their" admission.

This translation of commercial principles of agency into the law of evidence is one of the less impressive examples of what Coke called the "artificial reason" of the law. [The concern behind the hearsay principle is with the reliability of evidence rather than with the facilitation of enterprise]—and anyway the law of conspiracy is designed to discourage rather than to facilitate enterprise. Because a statement to be admissible as the statement of a party need not have been against interest when made (or at any time for that matter), the admissibility of such a statement cannot convincingly be grounded in the presumed trustworthiness of a statement that is against the utterer's self interest to give. The standard justification of its admissibility is a kind of estoppel or waiver theory, that a party should be entitled to rely on his opponent's statements. It has, it seems to us, rather little force as applied to the admissibility of coconspirator's statement. About all that can be said in favor of the rule is that since the statements of agents of legitimate enterprises are imputed to the enterprise through the operation of the law of agency on the party-admission rule, illegitimate enterprises, such as criminal conspiracies, should not receive more favorable treatment.

Whatever the justification for the rule—and there may be none—its dependence on agency principles makes the scope of the conspiracy critical. And a conspiracy, and a conspiracy to conceal an earlier, completed conspiracy, are two different conspiracies, like two different firms, and statements made in furtherance of the second, the cover-up conspiracy, are therefore not admissible in evidence to demonstrate participation in or the acts of the first conspiracy. But this is not such a case. * * * Statements designed to prevent a conspiracy from collapsing are not to be equated to statements designed to cover up a finished conspiracy. In the first case unlike the second there is only one conspiracy; the statements are made in an effort to shore it up and keep it going; they are therefore admissible against the conspirators.

United States v. Goldberg

United States Court of Appeals for the First Circuit, 1997.
105 F.3d 770.

■ BOUDIN, CIRCUIT JUDGE.

[Goldberg was convicted of federal fraud and tax offenses. On appeal, he challenged the admission against him of out-of-court statements by co-conspirators Lango and Clark.]

Goldberg does not dispute that Lango and Clark made the challenged statements during and in furtherance of the conspiracy, but he argues that the statements were not admissible against him because they were made before he joined. He relies heavily on our opinion in *United States v. Petrozziello*, 548 F.2d 20 (1st Cir.1977), where we said that "if it is more likely than not that the declarant and the defendant were members of a conspiracy when the hearsay statement was made, and that the statement was in furtherance of the conspiracy, the hearsay is admissible." *Id.* at 23.

Although this language has been cited with approval in a few later cases, it conflicts with *United States v. Baines*, 812 F.2d 41 (1st Cir.1987). *Baines* expressed the traditional notion that—insofar as hearsay is concerned—a late-joining conspirator takes the conspiracy as he finds it: "a conspiracy is like a train," and "when a party steps aboard, he is part of the crew, and assumes conspirator's responsibility for the existing freight. . ." *Id.* at 42; *accord, United States v. Saccoccia*, 58 F.3d 754, 778 (1st Cir.1995).

Frankly, the underlying co-conspirator exception to the hearsay rule makes little sense as a matter of evidence policy. No special guarantee of reliability attends such statements, save to the extent that they resemble declarations against interest. The exception derives from agency law, an analogy that is useful in some contexts but (as the Advisory Committee noted) is "at best a fiction" here. The most that can be said is that the co-conspirator exception to hearsay is of long standing and makes a difficult-to-detect crime easier to prove.

If starting afresh, one might argue that the narrow *Petrozziello* version of the exception should be preferred, if only because it accords better with the companion rule imposing substantive liability for other crimes committed during the conspiracy; a co-conspirator is held liable for foreseeable acts of others done in furtherance of the conspiracy but only if committed during the defendant's period of membership. Symmetry is at least convenient.

But we are not starting afresh. The broader *Baines* test describes the traditional approach, presumptively adopted by the Federal Rules of Evidence. It is followed in most circuits. Most important, it is the test in most of our own recent cases, including *Saccoccia,* decided only 19 months ago. This panel is arguably not free, but is in any event not inclined, to depart from *Saccoccia.* * * *

Affirmed.

United States v. Doerr

United States Court of Appeals, Seventh Circuit, 1989.
886 F.2d 944.

■ RIPPLE, CIRCUIT JUDGE.

[Defendants, Dale Doerr, John Paul Doerr, Archie Pixley and others, were charged with an unlawful prostitution conspiracy using the facilities of interstate commerce, and with tax crimes related to the enterprise.]

The prostitution activities underlying the offense alleged in Count One of the indictment were concentrated in three businesses that were part of an entity known as Worldwide Enterprises, Incorporated: the WW I Club, located in Kenosha County, Wisconsin; the Relaxation Health Systems massage parlor located next to the WW I Club in Kenosha County; and the WW II Club, located in Lake County, Illinois. The clubs were nude dancing establishments that served no food or alcoholic beverages. The testimony at trial revealed that the prostitution activities at the clubs were conducted pursuant to the following general procedure. A customer entering the club would be required to pay a cover charge. He would then be directed to a table and joined by a "dancer." After being seated, a waitress would approach the customer and ask him if he would like to purchase a drink (water or a soft drink) for himself and the dancer. Once the customer had purchased a drink, the waitress would return and ask the customer if he would like to go to a private area with the dancer. If the customer agreed and purchased a bottle of soda or water, at a cost of forty to fifty dollars, he would be taken to a "terrace," consisting of a number of booths, in the rear of the club. The customer would then be asked to buy additional bottles, and, once sufficient bottles had been purchased, the dancer would engage in sexual acts with the customer.

At the massage parlor, the customer would pay a flat fee for thirty minutes in a private room with a masseuse. The masseuse would then negotiate a "tip" with the customer. The amount of the tip would determine the degree of sexual contact that the masseuse had with the customer. At both the clubs and the massage parlor, customers could pay in cash or by credit card.

[Defendant-appellant asserted error in the admission of statements offered as co-conspirators' statements.]

The coconspirator exception to the hearsay rule, Fed.R.Evid. 801(d)(2)(E), provides that a statement is not hearsay if it is "offered against a party and is . . . a statement by a coconspirator of a party [made] during the course and in furtherance of the conspiracy." The appellants maintain that two out-of-court statements admitted at trial failed to satisfy the "in furtherance" requirement of the coconspirator exception. In the first challenged statement, Robert Meyer, a frequent customer at the Kenosha club, testified about a conversation between himself and Mr. Pixley in which the two discussed a red curtain at one of the clubs. Meyer testified that Mr. Pixley "mentioned that when he was hired back there that Josephine had a curtain put up in the terrace or the patio area, how ridiculous it was, it was asking for problems with the police." In the second challenged statement, John Patrick Doerr, Dale Doerr's half brother, testified that, in a conversation with his brother, Dale had laughed at him and said "I can't believe—I don't believe—I can't believe you don't know what's going on, or you didn't know what's going on." While conceding that these two statements may have been admissible against their declarants, Mr. Pixley and Dale Doerr, the appellants maintain that they should not have been admitted against the nondeclarant appellants because the statements were not made "in furtherance" of the conspiracy. Thus, they contend, Rule 801(d)(2)(E) was not satisfied.

We recently emphasized that the "in furtherance" requirement of Rule 801(d)(2)(E) is a limitation on the admissibility of coconspirators' statements that is meant to be taken seriously. See Garlington v. O'Leary, 879 F.2d 277, 283 (7th Cir.1989). As we explained in *Garlington,* a coconspirator's statement satisfies the "in furtherance" requirement "when the statement is 'part of the information flow between conspirators intended to help each perform his role.'" We further explained that statements "in furtherance" of a conspiracy can take many forms, including statements made to recruit potential coconspirators, statements seeking to control damage to an ongoing conspiracy, statements made to keep coconspirators advised as to the progress of the conspiracy, and statements made in an attempt to conceal the criminal objectives of the conspiracy. Narrative declarations, mere "idle chatter," and superfluous casual conversations, however, are not statements "in furtherance" of a conspiracy.

A district court's finding that a particular statement was made "in furtherance" is reviewed under a clearly erroneous standard. In addition, a court may conclude that the challenged statement was "in furtherance" even though "'the statement [was] susceptible of alternative interpretations.'" Id. at 628 (quoting United States v. Mackey, 571 F.2d 376, 383 (7th Cir.1978)). Moreover, the "in furtherance" requirement is satisfied so long "as some reasonable basis exists for concluding that the statement furthered the conspiracy.'" Id., quoted in Garlington, supra, at 283.

The government contends that the district court had a reasonable basis for concluding that Mr. Pixley's statements, described at trial by Meyer, were made "in furtherance" of the conspiracy. The government explains that, in addition to being a frequent customer, Robert Meyer had an interest in investing in the Kenosha club. Given this interest, the government asserts that "the trial court had a 'reasonable basis' for concluding that Pixley's comments were made in furtherance of the conspiracy since Pixley and Meyer had an interest in discussing ways that the club could improve and remain in operation." The government also contends that Dale Doerr's statement was "in furtherance" of the conspiracy, because it was a description of the clubs' illegal activities to John Patrick Doerr, a coconspirator who worked at the clubs as a manager and doorman.

We cannot accept the government's contentions. Therefore, we conclude that the district court erred in admitting the challenged testimony. Neither Mr. Pixley's statement nor Dale Doerr's statement was made "in furtherance" of the conspiracy. After reviewing Robert Meyer's testimony, we conclude that Mr. Pixley's discussion of the red curtain with Meyer cannot reasonably be characterized as part of an attempt to induce Meyer to join or assist the conspiracy. Instead, the statements are more accurately characterized as a narrative discussion of a past event. As such, they do not satisfy the "in furtherance" requirement of Rule 801(d)(2)(E).[7]

neither in furtherance

Similarly, Dale Doerr's statement to John Patrick Doerr fails to satisfy the "in furtherance" requirement. In making the statement recounted by John Patrick Doerr at trial, Dale was mocking his half-brother's ignorance of the clubs' unlawful activities; such a statement cannot be characterized as part of the normal information flow between coconspirators and in no way furthered the ends of the conspiracy. Thus, neither Mr. Pixley's statement nor Dale Doerr's statement should have been admitted under Rule 801(d)(2)(E). [The court went on to conclude, however, that admission of the statements was harmless error.]

QUESTIONS

Were the statements at issue in this case offered for a hearsay purpose? Were they testimonial within the meaning of *Crawford*?

Bourjaily v. United States

Supreme Court of the United States, 1987.
483 U.S. 171, 107 S.Ct. 2775, 97 L.Ed.2d 144.

■ CHIEF JUSTICE REHNQUIST delivered the opinion of the Court.

Federal Rule of Evidence 801(d)(2)(E) provides, "A statement is not hearsay if * * * [t]he statement is offered against a party and is * * * a statement by a coconspirator of a party during the course and in furtherance of the conspiracy." We granted certiorari to answer [among other questions] whether the court must determine by independent evidence that the conspiracy existed and that the defendant and the declarant were members of this conspiracy * * *

In May 1984, Clarence Greathouse, an informant working for the Federal Bureau of Investigation, arranged to sell a kilogram of cocaine to Angelo Lonardo. Lonardo agreed that he would find individuals to distribute the drug. When the sale became imminent, Lonardo stated in a tape-recorded telephone conversation that he had a "gentleman friend" who had some

---

[7] The district court itself had concluded that discussions between Mr. Pixley and Meyer regarding investment by Meyer in the club were not in furtherance of the conspiracy. The court had, however, concluded that Mr. Pixley's statements about the red curtain were "in furtherance," because they illustrate a "desire to increase the efficiency in the remunerative nature of the conspiracy." While the statements may in fact illustrate such a desire on the part of Mr. Pixley, the district court's finding does not explain how making this statement to Meyer in any way furthered the conspiracy.

questions to ask about the cocaine. In a subsequent telephone call, Greathouse spoke to the "friend" about the quality of the drug and the price. Greathouse then spoke again with Lonardo, and the two arranged the details of the purchase. They agreed that the sale would take place in a designated hotel parking lot, and Lonardo would transfer the drug from Greathouse's car to the "friend," who would be waiting in the parking lot in his own car. Greathouse proceeded with the transaction as planned, and FBI agents arrested Lonardo and petitioner immediately after Lonardo placed a kilogram of cocaine into petitioner's car in the hotel parking lot. In petitioner's car, the agents found over $20,000 in cash.

Petitioner was charged with conspiring to distribute cocaine, in violation of 21 U.S.C. § 846, and possession of cocaine with intent to distribute, a violation of 21 U.S.C. § 841(a)(1). The Government introduced, over petitioner's objection, Angelo Lonardo's telephone statements regarding the participation of the "friend" in the transaction. The District Court found that, considering the events in the parking lot and Lonardo's statements over the telephone, the Government had established by a preponderance of the evidence that a conspiracy involving Lonardo and petitioner existed, and that Lonardo's statements over the telephone had been made in the course of and in furtherance of the conspiracy. Accordingly, the trial court held that Lonardo's out-of-court statements satisfied Rule 801(d)(2)(E) and were not hearsay. Petitioner was convicted on both counts and sentenced to 15 years. The United States Court of Appeals for the Sixth Circuit affirmed. The Court of Appeals agreed with the District Court's analysis and conclusion that Lonardo's out-of-court statements were admissible under the Federal Rules of Evidence. The court also rejected petitioner's contention that because he could not cross-examine Lonardo, the admission of these statements violated his constitutional right to confront the witnesses against him. We affirm.

Before admitting a co-conspirator's statement over an objection that it does not qualify under Rule 801(d)(2)(E), a court must be satisfied that the statement actually falls within the definition of the Rule. There must be evidence that there was a conspiracy involving the declarant and the nonoffering party, and that the statement was made "in the course and in furtherance of the conspiracy." Federal Rule of Evidence 104(a) provides: "Preliminary questions concerning * * * the admissibility of evidence shall be determined by the court." Petitioner and respondent agree that the existence of a conspiracy and petitioner's involvement in it are preliminary questions of fact that, under Rule 104, must be resolved by the court. The Federal Rules, however, nowhere define the standard of proof the court must observe in resolving these questions.

We are therefore guided by our prior decisions regarding admissibility determinations that hinge on preliminary factual questions. We have traditionally required that these matters be established by a preponderance of proof. Evidence is placed before the jury when it satisfies the technical requirements of the evidentiary Rules, which embody certain legal and policy determinations. The inquiry made by a court concerned with these matters is not whether the proponent of the evidence wins or loses his case on the merits, but whether the evidentiary Rules have been satisfied. Thus, the evidentiary standard is unrelated to the burden of proof on the substantive issues, be it a criminal case or a civil case. The preponderance standard ensures that before admitting evidence, the court will have found it more likely than not that the technical issues and policy concerns addressed by the Federal Rules of Evidence have been afforded due consideration. * * * Therefore, we hold that when the preliminary facts relevant to Rule 801(d)(2)(E) are disputed, the offering party must prove them by a preponderance of the evidence.

Even though petitioner agrees that the courts below applied the proper standard of proof with regard to the preliminary facts relevant to Rule 801(d)(2)(E), he nevertheless challenges the admission of Lonardo's statements. Petitioner argues that in determining whether a conspiracy exists and whether the defendant was a member of it, the court must look only to independent evidence—that is, evidence other than the statements sought to be admitted. Petitioner relies on Glasser v. United States, 315 U.S. 60 (1942), in which this Court first mentioned the so-called "bootstrapping rule." The relevant issue in Glasser was whether Glasser's counsel, who also represented another defendant, faced such a conflict of interest that Glasser received ineffective assistance. Glasser contended that conflicting loyalties led his lawyer not to object to statements made by one of Glasser's co-conspirators. The Government argued that any objection would have been fruitless because the statements were admissible. The Court rejected this proposition:

> "[S]uch declarations are admissible over the objection of an alleged co-conspirator, who was not present when they were made, only if there is proof aliunde that he is connected with the conspiracy. . . Otherwise, hearsay would lift itself by its own bootstraps to the level of competent evidence." Id., at 74–75.

The Court revisited the bootstrapping rule in United States v. Nixon, 418 U.S. 683 (1974), where again, in passing, the Court stated, "Declarations by one defendant may also be admissible against other defendants upon a sufficient showing, _by independent evidence,_ of a conspiracy among one or more other defendants and the declarant and if the declarations at issue were in furtherance of that conspiracy." Id., at 701, and n. 14 (emphasis added) (footnote omitted). Read in the light most favorable to petitioner, Glasser could mean that a court should not consider hearsay statements at all in determining preliminary facts under Rule 801(d)(2)(E). Petitioner, of course, adopts this view of the bootstrapping rule. Glasser, however, could also mean that a court must have *some* proof aliunde, but may look at the hearsay statements themselves in light of this independent evidence to determine whether a conspiracy has been shown by a preponderance of the evidence. The Courts of Appeals have widely adopted the former view and held that in determining the preliminary facts relevant to co-conspirators' out-of-court statements, a court may not look at the hearsay statements themselves for their evidentiary value.

Both *Glasser* and *Nixon*, however, were decided before Congress enacted the Federal Rules of Evidence in 1975. These Rules now govern the treatment of evidentiary questions in federal courts. Rule 104(a) provides: "Preliminary questions concerning * * * the admissibility of evidence shall be determined by the court. * * * In making its determination it is not bound by the rules of evidence except those with respect to privileges." Similarly, Rule 1101(d)(1) states that the Rules of Evidence (other than with respect to privileges) shall not apply to "[t]he determination of questions of fact preliminary to admissibility of evidence when the issue is to be determined by the court under rule 104." The question thus presented is whether any aspect of *Glasser*'s bootstrapping rule remains viable after the enactment of the Federal Rules of Evidence.

Petitioner concedes that Rule 104, on its face, appears to allow the court to make the preliminary factual determinations relevant to Rule 801(d)(2)(E) by considering any evidence it wishes, unhindered by considerations of admissibility. That would seem to many to be the end of the matter. Congress has decided that courts may consider hearsay in making these factual determinations. Out-of-court statements made by anyone, including putative co-conspirators, are often hearsay. Even if they are, they may be considered, *Glasser* and the bootstrapping rule notwithstanding. But petitioner nevertheless argues that the bootstrapping rule, as most Courts of Appeals have construed it, survived this apparently unequivocal change in the law unscathed and that Rule 104, as applied to the admission of co-conspirator's statements, does not mean what it says. We disagree.

Petitioner claims that Congress evidenced no intent to disturb the bootstrapping rule, which was embedded in the previous approach, and we should not find that Congress altered the rule without affirmative evidence so indicating. It would be extraordinary to require legislative history to *confirm* the plain meaning of Rule 104. The Rule on its face allows the trial judge to consider any evidence whatsoever, bound only by the rules of privilege. We think that the Rule is sufficiently clear that to the extent that it is inconsistent with petitioner's interpretation of *Glasser* and *Nixon*, the Rule prevails.[2]

---

[2] The Advisory Committee Notes show that the Rule was not adopted in a fit of absent-mindedness. The Note to Rule 104 specifically addresses the process by which a federal court should make the factual determinations requisite to a finding of admissibility:

"If the question is factual in nature, the judge will of necessity receive evidence pro and con on the issue. The rule provides that the rules of evidence in general do not apply to this process. McCormick § 53, p. 123, n. 8, points out that the authorities are 'scattered and inconclusive,' and observes:

" 'Should the exclusionary law of evidence, "the child of the jury system" in Thayer's phrase, be applied to this hearing before the judge? Sound sense backs the view that it should not, and that the judge should be empowered to hear any relevant evidence, such as affidavits or other reliable hearsay.' " 28 U.S.C.App., p. 681 (emphasis added).

The Advisory Committee further noted, "An item, offered and objected to, may itself be considered in ruling on admissibility, though not yet admitted in evidence." Ibid. (emphasis added). We think this language makes plain the drafters' intent to abolish any kind of bootstrapping rule. Silence is at best ambiguous, and we decline the invitation to rely on speculation to import ambiguity into what is otherwise a clear rule.

* * *

We think that there is little doubt that a co-conspirator's statements could themselves be probative of the existence of a conspiracy and the participation of both the defendant and the declarant in the conspiracy. Petitioner's case presents a paradigm. The out-of-court statements of Lonardo indicated that Lonardo was involved in a conspiracy with a "friend." The statements indicated that the friend had agreed with Lonardo to buy a kilogram of cocaine and to distribute it. The statements also revealed that the friend would be at the hotel parking lot, in his car, and would accept the cocaine from Greathouse's car after Greathouse gave Lonardo the keys. Each one of Lonardo's statements may itself be unreliable, but taken as a whole, the entire conversation between Lonardo and Greathouse was corroborated by independent evidence. The friend, who turned out to be petitioner, showed up at the prearranged spot at the prearranged time. He picked up the cocaine, and a significant sum of money was found in his car. On these facts, the trial court concluded, in our view correctly, that the Government had established the existence of a conspiracy and petitioner's participation in it.

We need not decide in this case whether the courts below could have relied solely upon Lonardo's hearsay statements to determine that a conspiracy had been established by a preponderance of the evidence. To the extent that *Glasser* meant that courts could not look to the hearsay statements themselves for any purpose, it has clearly been superseded by Rule 104(a). It is sufficient for today to hold that a court, in making a preliminary factual determination under Rule 801(d)(2)(E), may examine the hearsay statements sought to be admitted. As we have held in other cases concerning admissibility determinations, "the judge should receive the evidence and give it such weight as his judgment and experience counsel." United States v. Matlock, 415 U.S. 164, 175 (1974). The courts below properly considered the statements of Lonardo and the subsequent events in finding that the Government had established by a preponderance of the evidence that Lonardo was involved in a conspiracy with petitioner. We have no reason to believe that the District Court's factfinding of this point was clearly erroneous. We hold that Lonardo's out-of-court statements were properly admitted against petitioner.

[Justice Stevens concurred, noting his view that the *Glasser* rule was that "[a]n otherwise inadmissible hearsay statement cannot provide the sole evidentiary support for its own admissibility," and that this rule was not affected by Rule 104.]

JUSTICE BLACKMUN, with whom JUSTICE BRENNAN and JUSTICE MARSHALL join, dissenting.

* * * [T]he independent-evidence requirement directly corresponds to the agency concept that an agent's statement cannot be used alone to prove the existence of the agency relationship.

"Evidence of a statement by an agent concerning the existence or extent of his authority is not admissible against the principal to prove its existence or extent, unless it appears *by other evidence* that the making of such statement was within the authority of the agent or, as to persons dealing with the agent, within the apparent authority or other power of the agent" (emphasis added). Restatement (Second) of Agency § 285 (1957).

See Levie, 52 Mich.L.Rev., at 1161. The reason behind this concept is that the agent's authority must be traced back to some act or statement by the alleged principal. See 1 F. Mechem, Law of Agency § 285, p. 205 (1914).

* * * [B]y explicitly retaining the agency rationale for the exemption, the Advisory Committee expressed its intention that the exemption would remain identical to the common-law rule and that it would not be expanded in any way. The Advisory Committee recognized that this agency rationale had been subject to criticism. The drafters of the American Law Institute's Model Code of Evidence had gone so far as to abandon the agency justification and had eliminated the "in furtherance of" requirement, observing that "[t]hese statements are likely to be true, and are usually made with a realization that they are against the declarant's interest." Model Code of Evidence, Rule 508(b) commentary, p. 251 (1942). The Advisory Committee, however, declined to accept without reservation a reliability foundation for Rule 801(d)(2)(E).

* * * [W]hen Rule 801(d)(2)(E) and Rule 104(a) are considered together—an examination that the Court neglects to undertake—there appears to be a conflict between the fact that no change in the co-conspirator hearsay exemption was intended by Rule 801(d)(2)(E) and the freedom that Rule 104(a) gives a trial court to rely on hearsay in resolving preliminary factual questions. Although one must be somewhat of an interpretative funambulist to walk between the conflicting demands of these Rules in order to arrive at a resolution that will satisfy their respective concerns, this effort is far to be preferred over accepting the easily available safety "net" of Rule 104(a)'s "plain meaning." The purposes of *both* Rules can be achieved by considering the relevant preliminary factual question for Rule 104(a) analysis to be the following: "whether a conspiracy that included the declarant and the defendant against whom a statement is offered has been demonstrated to exist on the basis of evidence *independent of the declarant's hearsay statements* " (emphasis added). Saltzburg & Redden, Federal Rules of Evidence Manual 735 (4th ed. 1986). This resolution sufficiently answers Rule 104(a)'s concern with allowing a trial court to consider hearsay in determining preliminary factual questions, because the only hearsay not available for its consideration is the statement at issue. The exclusion of the statement from the preliminary analysis maintains the common-law exemption unchanged.

QUESTIONS

Were Lonardo's statements offered for a hearsay purpose? Were they testimonial within the meaning of *Crawford*?

2. SPONTANEOUS AND CONTEMPORANEOUS EXCLAMATIONS

Hutchins & Slesinger, Some Observations on the Law of Evidence

28 Colum.L.Rev. 432 (1928).*

I. SPONTANEOUS EXCLAMATIONS

Spontaneous utterances, exclamations or declarations are, under certain conditions, admissible in evidence though the party who made them does not take the stand. According to most courts the occasion must be startling enough to cause shock, which in turn creates an emotional state. The utterance must be made under stress of that emotion; it must be "spontaneous and natural; impulsive and instinctive"; it should be immediate, or "so clearly connected (with the occasion) that the declaration may be said to be the spontaneous explanation of the real cause." Although in some jurisdictions there is insistence that the declaration be "contemporaneous" with the act, or "while the act is going on," the progressive view seems to be that the time interval, beyond which a declaration would no longer be spontaneous, is in the sound discretion of the trial court * * *.

The general theory under which these declarations are admissible has been well stated by Mr. Wigmore. "Under certain external circumstances of physical shock a state of nervous excitement may be produced which stills the reflective faculties and removes their control, so that the utterance which occurs is a spontaneous and sincere response to the actual sensations and perceptions already produced by the external shock." And "since this utterance is made under the immediate and controlled domination of the senses, and during the brief period when considerations of self-interest could not have been fully brought to bear by reasoned reflection, the utterances may be taken to be particularly trustworthy."

This reflective self-interest is a curious doctrine, dating back to a mentalist psychology, and the utilitarian philosophy that made use of it. Man's conduct, according to this theory of behavior, was always personally motivated, his acts being planned by an elaborate calculus of interests, immediate and remote. Since that calculus involved reflection, it clearly followed that by eliminating reflection, self-interested conduct became impossible. The entrance of instinct into psychology shifted the emphasis, without changing the fundamental idea, by putting self-interest on an instinctive basis. The modern tendency is to substitute groups of habits or habit patterns for such general concepts as self-interest. These, if they serve the self, may afterward be called self-interested. That they are not, in fact, due to a force or instinct of self-interest, is shown by their persistence beyond the point of general efficiency. The habit of saving money, for example, is, in certain circumstances, self-interested. But a person having the habit will tend to continue to save even when it is directly against his interest. Reflection plays a part, both in the formation of habits, and in resolving conflicts

---

* Copyright, 1928 By the Trustees of The Columbia Law Review.

between them. But once formed, they continue, on their own inertia, creating the illusion of a definite force.

To still, or circumvent this "force," the law relies in part on immediacy. The veracity of a response, according to the courts, varies directly with its speed. The desire to lie requires time and reflection to develop. And the intervention of reflection may be avoided by giving it no time to occur, thus rendering lying difficult, if not impossible.

In order to estimate the time required for reflection, it is necessary to know something of the difficulty of the task reflection is to perform. Ordinarily the choices are very simple ones, involving few alternatives. "John did it!" or "John did not do it!" The gentleman of after-dinner fame who, on being informed that his train had fallen over an embankment while he slept, cried, "Oh, my shoulder" in all probability did not take many moments to respond to the situation. If his general character is pointed to by way of explanation, the answer is simply that it is precisely that sort of character that the courts are guarding against.

A number of laboratory psychological experiments have been performed which throw some light on the problem under consideration. A subject is asked to disobey one of several orders, concealing from the examiner which order he has disobeyed. Or two subjects are sent out of the room, one to perform a series of acts, the other to do nothing, the actor trying to conceal his "crime." To each subject, then, is read a series of words, some of which are directly associated with the crimes in question, with the request that he respond as quickly as possible with the first word that comes to his mind, taking care, however, to avoid giving away his crime. All observers report a delay in reaction time to key words where deception is attempted, although Marston discovered a small group, which he called good liars, whose reaction time to significant words was actually faster than to the rest of the list. It seems, then, that the courts are on the right track in demanding speed as a guarantee of truth, or, at least of the absence of attempted falsehood. The difficulty comes when the speed is considered, not as a general idea, but quantitatively. Here we find that the difference in time between the ordinary reaction and the deception reaction to significant words is so slight, from .83 seconds to 3½ minutes, that it cannot be measured without the aid of instruments. The sound discretion of the trial judge, with the best of intention in these cases, is likely to be fallible.

But it will be remembered that speed is not the only guarantee of truthful response. In order more fully to guard against deceit, a good deal of reliance is placed on shock, and the emotion generated thereby, provided it is severe enough to still the reflective faculties. There is every reason to suppose that such an emotion would render difficult a consciously planned lie. As Mr. Watson inelegantly puts it, emotion is an affair of the guts, beyond control of the intellect, and pretty well running it during its active phase. It halts digestion, speeds up heart rate, increases blood pressure, creates general muscular tension throughout the body, pours sugar and adrenalin into the blood stream. These bodily changes are certainly discomforting to intellectual activity. They paralyze and distort it all along the line; unfortunately, while they make thinking difficult, they render observation and judgment all but impossible.

One need not be a psychologist to distrust an observation made under emotional stress; everybody accepts such statements with mental reservation. M. Gorphe cites the case of an excited witness to a horrible accident who erroneously declared that the coachman deliberately and vindictively ran down a helpless woman. Fiore tells of an emotionally upset man who testified that hundreds were killed in an accident; that he had seen their heads rolling from their bodies. In reality only one man was killed, and five others injured. Another excited gentleman took a pipe for a pistol. Besides these stories from real life, there are psychological experiments which point to the same conclusion. After a battle in a classroom, prearranged by the experimenter but a surprise to the students, each one was asked to write an account of the incident. The testimony of the most upset students was practically worthless, while those who were only slightly stimulated emotionally scored better than those left cold by the incident. Miss Hyde of Nebraska tells of an unpublished experiment, the results of which differed only in the general inaccuracy of all accounts, regardless of the amount of emotion generated. The conclusion drawn from these, and other similar experiments, is that "emotion may virtually hold connected perception in abeyance so that the subject has only isolated sensations to remember instead of a logically connected unit perception."

That participants, as well as bystanders, have their perceptions clouded by strong emotions will not be doubted. When a carriage containing the inevitable psychologist upset, that worthy gentleman amused himself and his companions by taking depositions while they awaited assistance. He had no known reality to check their stories against, but it was obvious that if any one was right, all the rest were wrong. That even trained observers are fallible is well brought out in an editorial in the *New York World* in which several accounts of newspaper reports of the striking of Kerensky on his recent visit to America are printed. Though the reporters were all experts, and sitting close to the platform, each one told a different story of what must have been a fairly simple event.

The result of these observations is a dilemma. From the point of view of subjective veracity, the speed the courts demand does not necessarily guarantee truth. And from the standpoint of objective accuracy, emotion is little better. If a speedy reaction means nothing without the aid of a stopwatch, an emotional reaction means nothing without eliminating the emotion. What the emotion gains by way of overcoming the desire to lie, it loses by impairing the declarant's power of observation. On the one hand, if reflective self-interest has not had a chance to operate because of emotional stress, then the statement should be excluded because of the probable inaccuracy of observation. On the other, if little emotion is involved, clearly a very short time is sufficient to allow reflected self-interest to assume full sway. On that basis there would seem to be no reason for this hearsay exception. In fact, the emphasis should be all the other way. On psychological grounds, the rule might very well read: Hearsay is inadmissible, especially (not except) if it is by a spontaneous exclamation.

Of course, such a result would be preposterous. The evidence is relevant and should be admitted unless it is so worthless as to mislead the tribunal or waste its time. It would do neither to a tribunal trained to decide the weight to be given to evidence in the light thrown by a knowledge of the background of the declarant, and the circumstances in which an exclamation was made. To this tribunal statements now viewed with suspicion because they are not made under emotional stress, would seem to represent more accurate observation for that very reason. Since an injured person is the one most affected by his injury, his observations would be considered less reliable than those of an uninjured motorman, brakeman, or engineer, and *a fortiori* less than those of a casual, unexcited bystander. And, according to this view, the best evidence of all is a statement made in immediate response to an external stimulus which produces no shock or nervous excitement whatever.

Professor Morgan's insistence on the admissibility of declarations closely connected in time with such a stimulus seems entirely justified. With emotion absent, speed present, and the person who heard the declaration on hand to be cross-examined, we appear to have an ideal exception to the hearsay rule. Statements by passengers before any damage has been done about the roughness of the train ride; observations as to the speed of a train as it is going by; remarks made on hearing a fight in progress some distance away; "why don't the train whistle?", spoken as the declarant saw it approaching the crossing;—all these are exclamations the value of which is indicated by the opportunity to cross-examine the hearer as to the surrounding circumstances, by the speed of the reaction, and the unemotional condition of the speaker.

Thus it appears that the spontaneous declarations regarded with least favor by the courts are more trustworthy than those which most of them admit without question: those where the trial judge rules that the statement was made under the influence of severe physical shock. It is by no means suggested, however, that these last should be excluded simply because other types of evidence assumed to be less reliable turn out, on investigation, to be more reliable. It is suggested, on the contrary, that all these varieties of declarations be admitted. If relevant they should go to the jury; for some are demonstrably more accurate than we have hitherto supposed, and those now admitted are not so inaccurate as to be arbitrarily excluded. To exclude any because they are not the immediate outpourings of an injured person is to insist on requirements shown to be artificial, if not mistaken.

Truck Insurance Exchange v. Michling

Supreme Court of Texas, 1963.
364 S.W.2d 172.

■ CULVER, JUSTICE.

This suit was brought by Mrs. Martha Michling and other statutory beneficiaries to recover death benefits provided by the Texas Workmen's Compensation Act. Judgment was rendered in favor of these beneficiaries by the trial court and the Court of Civil Appeals has affirmed.

The only evidence offered to prove that the deceased, Hugo Michling, sustained an accidental injury in the scope of his employment was that given by his wife, Mrs. Michling. She related that her husband left home to go to his place of work about 30 miles away on the morning of April 12, 1958, and at that time was apparently in good health; that she saw him when he got out of his car on his return home about 3:30 that afternoon and that "he sort of stumbled and caught himself and walked on up to the house and he said his head was hurting him terribly; he was batting his eyes and was very pale." She quoted him as saying that "he had hit his head on the bulldozer, the iron bar across the seat. It slipped off the hill and he hit his head." She also testified that he said "his head hurt so bad that he couldn't do anything else but had to put up the bulldozer and come home." Michling died at the hospital on May 11, 1958.

This case turns on the question of whether or not the foregoing testimony given by Mrs. Michling is admissible under the rule which admits res gestae* utterances as an exception to the hearsay rule.

This then brings us to the question of what are the general rules governing the admission of hearsay statements as res gestae. Wigmore in his work on Evidence, 3rd Edition, § 1747, has the following to say:

> "This general principle is based on the experience that, under certain external circumstances of physical shock, a stress of nervous excitement may be produced which stills the reflective faculties and removes their control, so that the utterance which then occurs is a spontaneous and sincere response to the actual sensations and perceptions already produced by the external shock. Since this utterance is made under the immediate and uncontrolled domination of the senses, and during the brief period when considerations of self-interest could not have been brought fully to bear by reasoned reflection, the utterance may be taken as particularly trustworthy (or, at least, as lacking the usual grounds of untrustworthiness), and thus as expressing the real tenor of the speaker's belief as to the facts just observed by him; and may therefore be received as testimony to those facts. * * *"

In § 1750 he sets out the requirements as follows:

---

* ["Res gestae" in many jurisdictions was the old fashioned name for what we now call "excited utterances" or "spontaneous exclamations."—Eds.]

"(a) Nature of the Occasion. There must be some *occurrence, startling enough* to produce this nervous excitement and render the utterance spontaneous and unreflecting. * * *."

"(b) Time of the Utterance. The utterance must have been *before there has been time to contrive and misrepresent, i.e.,* while the nervous excitement may be supposed still to dominate and the reflective powers to be yet in abeyance. This limitation is in practice the subject of most of the rulings.

"It is to be observed that the statements *need not be strictly contemporaneous* with the exciting cause; they may be subsequent to it, provided there has not been time for the exciting influence to lose its sway and to be dissipated. * * *

"Furthermore, there can be *no definite and fixed limit* of time. Each case must depend upon its own circumstances.

"(c) Subject of the Utterance. The utterance must *relate to the circumstances of the occurrence preceding it.* * * *."

The very unusual circumstance in this case is that the hearsay statement of Mrs. Michling is the only evidence of the event which gives rise to the statement. A hearsay statement, as res gestae, is admitted as an exception to the hearsay rule because it is made under circumstances which raise a reasonable presumption that it is the spontaneous utterance of thought created by or springing out of the occurrence itself and, so to speak, becomes a part of the occurrence. But in this case the only evidence of the occurrence is the hearsay statement. Thus the Court of Civil Appeals is conceding credit to a narrative to prove the very circumstances from which it is said to derive its credit. Its trustworthiness, as to the happening of an accident, is presumed from the influence of the accident which its trustworthiness is taken to prove. Thus this proof, to use a trite expression, is attempting to lift itself by its own bootstraps. There is not any independent proof that Hugo Michling suffered any injury at approximately the time and place alleged.

* * *

The medical testimony is that Michling died of a cerebral hemorrhage resulting from a congenital weakness in one of the blood vessels in the brain and that such a hemorrhage may be precipitated by a cough, a strain, a blow to the head or may occur spontaneously. The fact that Michling died from a cerebral hemorrhage does not necessarily indicate any accidental injury. There was no visible mark of any injury upon his head.

* * *

For declarations to be admissible in evidence as part of the res gestae they must be made in connection with an act proven. In other words there must be evidence of an act itself admissible in the case independently of the declaration that accompanies it.

As aptly said in 32 C.J.S. Evidence § 405:

> " * * * It is proceeding in a circle to use the declarations as proof of facts necessary to constitute declarations part of the res gestae."

* * *

Our holding in Wade v. Texas Employers' Ins. Ass'n, 150 Tex. 557, 244 S.W.2d 197 (1951) cited by the Court of Civil Appeals, is not an authority for the proposition that the statement made by Michling to his wife is admissible as evidence. In that case the deceased employee was at work when he made the statement that "this gas is about to get me," which was admitted as a res gestae utterance. But two of his fellow employees testified that there was an unusual amount of chlorine gas present when they were at work which was produced from nearby operations in a chemical plant. The proof of the occurrence, namely, the presence of chlorine gas, which gave rise to the statement, did not depend upon the statement of the deceased.

For the foregoing reasons the judgments of the trial court and of the Court of Civil Appeals are reversed and judgment here rendered in favor of petitioner, Truck Insurance Exchange.

Lira v. Albert Einstein Medical Center

Superior Court of Pennsylvania, 1989.
384 Pa.Super. 503, 559 A.2d 550.

■ WIEAND, JUDGE:

In this medical malpractice action, the trial court awarded a new trial on motion of the defendant-health care providers because of an erroneous evidentiary ruling which permitted a witness to testify that when the plaintiff-patient was examined by a non-testifying physician, the physician asked, "Who's the butcher who do this?" On appeal, the plaintiffs argue that the physician's declaration was properly received and did not warrant a new trial. * * * We affirm the order awarding a new trial.

[Plaintiffs Jose and Bonnie Lira alleged that plaintiff Bonnie Lira was injured while one of the defendants was inserting a nasogastric tube into her throat. The jury returned a verdict for the plaintiffs. Dr. Silberman, whose out-of-court statement is described in the following excerpt, was not a party to the lawsuit.]

When Jose Lira was called as a witness, he testified as follows:

[MR. LIRA]: I remember the day I take my wife to see [Dr. Silberman], and we wait like everybody else; and as our turn to sit there and see what's wrong, he put my wife in the chair—

[PLAINTIFF'S COUNSEL]: Were you in the room with your wife with the doctor?

[MR. LIRA]: I was with my wife in the room, yes, I was.

[PLAINTIFF'S COUNSEL]: And tell us what you observed.

[MR. LIRA]: My wife was following the instructions from the doctor, open your mouth, and the doctor is looking inside with some kind of instruments and lights, and he said: Who's the butcher who do this!

[DEFENSE COUNSEL]: Objection, Your Honor. In fact, I move for a mistrial with that statement, Your Honor.

THE COURT: Overruled.

Dr. Silberman was not present in court and did not testify. During closing argument to the jury, plaintiff's counsel referred to Lira's testimony, saying: "You will remember that Dr. Silberman examined her throat and asked Bonnie Lira, 'Who butchered you?' " A defense objection to the argument by plaintiff's counsel was sustained, and the jury was told that the testimony "was not proper testimony for you to consider." A motion for mistrial, however, was denied. In response to a defense motion for new trial, the trial court, with commendable candor, determined that its evidentiary ruling had been erroneous and, despite the subsequent sustaining of a defense objection to a reference to the testimony by plaintiff's counsel, may have contributed to the verdict. Therefore, a new trial was awarded. Plaintiffs argue on appeal that the physician's declaration was admissible as an excited utterance or present sense impression exception to the hearsay rule. We disagree.

Dr. Silberman's statement was clearly hearsay. It was an extrajudicial statement offered to prove the truth of the matter asserted, i.e., that Mrs. Lira had been "butchered." Hearsay evidence is inadmissible unless it falls within a recognized exception to the exclusionary rule. Even if it falls within an exception to the rule, however, hearsay evidence may not be received unless it is relevant and not excluded under another rule of evidence.

Appellants contend that Dr. Silberman's declaration was admissible under the "res gestae" exception. More specifically, they argue that it was admissible as an excited utterance or a present sense impression. An excited utterance is a spontaneous declaration by a person whose mind has been suddenly made subject to an overpowering emotion caused by some unexpected and shocking occurrence. When Dr. Silberman, an ear, nose and throat specialist, examined a patient who was complaining of a sore throat and difficulty in breathing, it cannot be said that his discovery of a throat abnormality was a shocking occurrence causing the specialist to be overcome with emotion. Dr. Silberman's declaration in this case simply was not an excited utterance.

Similarly, Dr. Silberman's extrajudicial declaration was not admissible as a present sense impression.

> Under this exception the necessity for the presence of a startling occurrence or accident to serve as a source of reliability is not required. The truthfulness of the utterance is dependent upon its spontaneity. It must be certain from the circumstances that the utterance is a reflex product of immediate sensual impressions, unaided by retrospective mental processes. Restated, the utterance must be "instinctive, rather than deliberate."

Commonwealth v. Farquharson, 467 Pa. 50, 68, 354 A.2d 545, 554 (1976), citing Commonwealth v. Coleman, 458 Pa. 112, 117, 326 A.2d 387, 389 (1974). Here, the evidence failed to establish that the declaration of Dr. Silberman, a throat specialist, was "instinctive, rather than deliberative—in short, the reflex product of immediate sensual impressions, unaided by retrospective mental action." Commonwealth v. Coleman, supra. It was, rather, an expression of opinion based on medical training and experience.

To permit a physician's extrajudicial statement of medical opinion, made upon examination of a patient, to be received in evidence as an excited utterance or under the present sense impression exception to the hearsay rule would run afoul not only of the hearsay exclusion but also of the rule which holds that expressions of medical opinion are generally inadmissible unless the physician expressing the opinion is available for cross-examination. In Ganster v. Western Pennsylvania Water Co., 349 Pa.Super. 561, 504 A.2d 186 (1985), the Superior Court said, in holding that the business records exception to the hearsay rule did not encompass opinion testimony:

> "Cross-examination," it has been said, "is a vital and fundamental part of a fair trial." Commonwealth v. Shirey, 333 Pa.Super. 85, 151, 481 A.2d 1314, 1350 (1984). Although the right of cross-examination is not absolute and although hearsay evidence may be received upon proof of exceptional circumstances, including factual evidence received under the business records in evidence exception, cross-examination is particularly important where it is the only means for testing the reliability of an opinion regarding disputed facts.

Id. 349 Pa.Super. at 573, 504 A.2d at 192.

Affirmed.

State v. Jones

Court of Appeals of Maryland, 1987.
311 Md. 23, 532 A.2d 169.

■ McAULIFFE, JUDGE.

A motorist testified that she had been sexually assaulted by a state trooper who stopped her for operating a vehicle without a tail light. The state trooper adamantly denied the charge. The deciding factor in the resolution of this dispute may well have been the hearsay statements of two unknown individuals heard over channel 19 of a citizens band radio. Our task is to decide whether the trial judge erred in admitting evidence of the statements.

At about 11 p.m. on October 15, 1983, Trooper First Class Jeffrey Jones of the Maryland State Police stopped a southbound 1972 Ford Pinto on Interstate Route 95, north of the Maryland House rest stop in Harford County. The stop was made because Trooper Jones could not determine whether the vehicle was displaying a rear license plate—a condition, it later turned out, that was caused by a short circuit in the tail light.

It is undisputed that Trooper Jones spoke with the female operator of the Pinto, and with her male friend, Willie Hooks, who was the owner of the vehicle and seated in the front passenger seat, and that at some point in time the female was seated in the trooper's cruiser. Why she entered the police cruiser, and what happened while she was there and shortly thereafter are facts sharply in dispute.

The complainant testified that Jones directed her to enter the cruiser to discuss his contention that she was operating in violation of the conditions of her New Jersey learner's permit. She said Jones told her she could drive only if accompanied by a New Jersey licensed driver, and because Hooks was licensed only in New York she was violating the law. She further related that Jones then said he would have to search her, and after handcuffing her put his hands in her pockets, unbuckled her belt, unzipped her jeans and pulled them down, and accomplished digital penetration after placing his hands under her panties. When she protested, he released her and she returned to the Pinto. She instructed Hooks, who was now behind the wheel, to obtain the trooper's tag number. At that point, however, the police cruiser left at a high rate of speed and without lights. Hooks gave chase, having observed that the complainant's belt buckle was loose and her jeans unzipped, and having learned from her that the officer "messed with her." According to the complainant and Hooks, their Pinto was no match for the police cruiser, and although they achieved speeds up to 70–80 miles per hour as they passed the Maryland House, they were never able to catch up to the cruiser. They then stopped at the first roadside emergency phone and reported the incident to the police. According to the complainant, she did not receive a summons or a warning ticket from Jones.

Jones testified that the complainant approached and entered his cruiser on her own initiative, while he was writing a warning ticket. He said she became upset when he explained that Hooks would have to drive the Pinto. He denied any physical contact with her, except to return her permit and to hand her a warning ticket.[1] Concerning his departure from the scene, Jones

---

[1] During the course of a subsequent investigation, Jones produced a copy of the warning ticket he said he issued to the complainant. The ticket was not signed by Jones or the complainant, an omission that Jones said represented an oversight on his part.

said he followed the Pinto into traffic and eventually passed it. He denied operating his vehicle without headlights.

Officer Kenneth Kinesman of the Maryland Toll Facility Police testified that at 11:30 p.m. on the night in question, he was dispatched to an emergency call box on the Harbor Tunnel Thruway, where he met the complainant and Hooks. He described the complainant as agitated, distraught, excited, and upset, and related her complaint that she had been "assaulted by a cop" on Interstate 95, north of the Maryland House. Officer Kinesman confirmed that the emergency call box used by the complainant was the first one available to southbound traffic after passing the Maryland House.

The evidence in controversy is that given by Trooper First Class William Byrd. It involves CB radio transmissions that Trooper Byrd said he heard while in his police cruiser at the Maryland House on the night in question, at some time between 11:00 and 11:30 p.m. To determine admissibility of the proffered evidence, Judge Brodnax Cameron, Jr. conducted a hearing out of the presence of the jury. At the hearing, Trooper Byrd testified he was monitoring channel 19 when he heard consecutive radio transmissions by persons he assumed were truckers. The two transmissions were:

1st Speaker: Look at Smokey Bear southbound with no lights on at a high rate of speed.

2nd Speaker: Look at that little car trying to catch up with him.

Trooper Byrd explained that among truckers and other citizens band radio aficionados "Smokey Bear" means a state trooper. Judge Cameron admitted the testimony, acknowledging that it was hearsay, but holding it was admissible under the present sense impression exception to the hearsay rule.[3] Jones was convicted of a third degree sexual offense, battery, and misconduct in office. He was given a sentence of two years imprisonment, of which 90 days was to be served and the balance suspended. He appealed, and the Court of Special Appeals reversed, Jones v. State, 65 Md.App. 121, 499 A.2d 511 (1985). Shortly thereafter, we decided Booth v. State, 306 Md. 313, 508 A.2d 976 (1986), discussing and approving the present sense impression exception to the hearsay rule. We granted certiorari in this case to consider the admissibility of the evidence in the light of *Booth*.

The principal reasons assigned by the Court of Special Appeals for the rejection of the evidence were the absence of an equally percipient witness to furnish corroboration and the absence of evidence sufficient to show the relevance of the statements. We address separately these and the other issues generated by this appeal.

---

[3] Judge Cameron noted in passing that the "man-bites-dog" character of a small civilian car chasing after a police car operating without headlights was the kind of startling event normally associated with the excited utterance exception to the hearsay rule. His holding, however, was grounded on the present sense impression exception, there being no evidence that the declarants spoke under the influence of excitement.

Variance in Testimony

At a bench conference requested by Respondent's counsel as Trooper Byrd was being called to the stand, the trial judge was informed that the State would attempt to elicit testimony concerning the statements heard on the CB radio. Respondent's counsel objected to any reference being made to the statements in the presence of the jury, and Judge Cameron agreed to excuse the jury when the testimony of Trooper Byrd reached that point. Consistent with this understanding, Trooper Byrd's initial testimony concerning the statements was given out of the presence of the jury. Following that testimony, and following argument by both counsel, Judge Cameron ruled the statements admissible, and the jury was recalled. As Jones points out, Trooper Byrd's testimony before the jury differed in some respects from that given before the judge. In first describing the statements he heard, Trooper Byrd cast them in the language of each declarant: "Look at Smokey Bear southbound with no lights on at a high rate of speed." "Look at that little car trying to catch up with him." Before the jury, Trooper Byrd cast his testimony in the narrative form:

> On the CB radio in the state police car, Channel 19, I overheard a trucker on the CB said [sic] that it was Smokey the Bear southbound in a police car with no lights on and right after that . . . another trucker on Channel 19 advised that there was a little car just took off behind Smokey the Bear trying to catch him at a high rate of speed.

Because the content of a statement may contain the requisite evidence of spontaneity, or of the fact that the statement is the product of personal perception by the declarant, *Booth,* supra, 306 Md. at 330, 508 A.2d 976, the wording of the statement may be important. Here, the statements in the form first related by Trooper Byrd are self-evidently spontaneous. However, the statements as related to the jury, at least when standing alone, give rise to questions concerning their spontaneity.[4]

The record discloses that Judge Cameron ruled on the admissibility of the statements based upon the initial testimony of Trooper Byrd. After the jury was recalled, and Trooper Byrd was asked to recount what he had heard, Respondent's counsel interposed a timely objection. However, counsel did not make any additional objection, or move to strike the answer, when Trooper Byrd gave what Respondent now suggests was a different version of the statements. Thus, Judge Cameron was given an opportunity to rule only on the basis of the testimony presented to him. He was never given an opportunity to determine whether the change in language would affect his ruling on admissibility. Nor was the prosecutor given an opportunity to inquire through further questioning whether the change in language

---

[4] The State suggests that the second declarant's reference to the fact that "a little car just took off" furnishes sufficient evidence that the speaker was describing something almost immediately after he observed it, and that because of the content and chronology of the two statements, a finding that the second statement was essentially contemporaneous with the occurrence necessarily implies a similar finding for the first statement. We need not address that contention.

reflected simply a different method of presenting the same information, or represented a change in Trooper Byrd's recollection of what had occurred. Although Respondent's counsel has fully preserved for review the question of admissibility based upon the testimony given at the hearing, he has not preserved any question concerning the possible legal effect of the change in words used to recount the statements.

Contemporaneousness

In Booth v. State, supra, 306 Md. at 324, 508 A.2d 976, we discussed the requirement that a statement of present sense impression be essentially contemporaneous with the event it describes:

> [B]ecause the presumed reliability of a statement of present sense impression flows from the fact of spontaneity, the time interval between observation and utterance must be very short. The appropriate inquiry is whether, considering the surrounding circumstances, sufficient time elapsed to have permitted reflective thought. See McCormick on Evidence § 298, at 862 (3d ed. E. Cleary 1984). In the words of Professor Jon Waltz, "absent some special corroborative circumstance, there should be no delay beyond an acceptable hiatus between perception and the cerebellum's construction of an uncalculated verbal description." Waltz, The Present Sense Impression Exception to the Rule Against Hearsay: Origins and Attributes, 66 Iowa L.Rev. 869, 880 (1981).

We also held that in some instances the content of the statement may furnish sufficient evidence of its spontaneity. Id. at 330–31, 508 A.2d 976. As conceded by Respondent's counsel at oral argument, the statements as related by Trooper Byrd to Judge Cameron are "self-evidently contemporaneous."

Personal Knowledge—Identity of Declarant

Jones contends, correctly, that the party offering the statement must show that the declarant spoke from personal knowledge. He also contends, incorrectly, that in every instance the identity of the declarant must be established. The contents of the two statements at issue in this case are sufficient to support the conclusion of the trial judge that the declarants spoke from first-hand knowledge. Additionally, we held in Booth that identification of the declarant is not an absolute prerequisite to introduction of the statement. What we said in Booth is dispositive of these issues:

> Although the declarant need not have been a participant in the perceived event, it is clear that the declarant must speak from personal knowledge, i.e., the declarant's own sensory perceptions. The more difficult question involves the quantity and quality of evidence required to demonstrate the existence of the requisite personal knowledge. We conclude that in some instances the content of the statement may itself be sufficient to demonstrate that it is more likely than not the product of personal perception, and in other instances extrinsic evidence may

be required to satisfy this threshold requirement of admissibility. Identification of the declarant, while often helpful in establishing that he or she was a percipient witness, is not a condition of admissibility. When the statement itself, or other circumstantial evidence demonstrates the percipiency of a declarant, whether identified or unidentified, this condition of competency is met. 306 Md. at 324–25, 508 A.2d 976 (footnote omitted).

Corroboration

The question of corroboration, considered in the context of the present sense impression exception, ordinarily relates to proof of first-hand knowledge or spontaneity. We have rejected the contention that corroboration by an equally percipient witness is invariably required as a condition to the admissibility of such a statement, while at the same time noting that in some instances extrinsic evidence in the nature of corroboration may be required. Booth, supra, 306 Md. at 327–30, 508 A.2d 976. Respondent puts a different spin on the argument in this case, contending that corroboration should be required to show that the witness is being truthful in recounting what he says he heard. In support of his contention, Respondent cites the following language of the Court of Special Appeals in this case:

> To permit evidence such as that of Byrd would throw open the door to imaginative, if not fabricated, present sense declarations between unknowns. Cross-examination of those witnesses is almost guaranteed to test absolutely nothing. *Jones v. State,* supra, 65 Md.App. at 126–27, 499 A.2d 511.

We cannot be certain whether the concern of the intermediate appellate court was directed to the possibility of fabrication by unknown declarants, or the danger that the witness on the stand could falsely testify that such a statement was made without serious fear of detection of his perjury. If it was the former, we are satisfied that the inherent trustworthiness of a statement of perception given contemporaneously with the event being described is sufficient to outweigh that concern. If it is the latter, we are willing to place our trust in the efficacy of the oath and of cross-examination, as we do in the case of any other witness who is present and testifying. There is no absolute safeguard against lying. An officer who would testify that he heard something when he did not could as well testify that he saw something when he did not. Trooper Byrd was sworn and subject to cross-examination. Respondent was at liberty to develop any bias the witness may have had, and to show whether Trooper Byrd knew the details of the alleged assault before he recounted the statements he allegedly heard. He was at liberty to argue the dangers of fabrication and the absence of corroboration. The jury was at liberty to reject, or accept and give appropriate weight to, the testimony that the statements were made.

We reverse and remand to permit consideration of additional issues raised by Respondent but not reached by the Court of Special Appeals.

See Federal Rules of Evidence 803(1) & (2); California Evidence Code § 1240.

HYPOTHETICALS

(1) Plaintiff, a pedestrian, sues Defendant for damages arising out of being struck by an automobile. Defendant's defense is that he was in the curb lane in his red car and that a blue car passed him in the next lane, striking Plaintiff, knocking her into the air and onto his red car. Plaintiff calls Paramedic, and represents that Paramedic will testify that she arrived on the scene ten minutes after the accident, and saw Plaintiff lying on the ground; that Plaintiff appeared to be in great pain but not in shock; that Paramedic said to Plaintiff, "Relax now, and take it easy;" and that Plaintiff then said, "Oh, my God! Help me! That red car hit me while I was in the crosswalk." Defendant makes a hearsay objection.

(2) Assume the same facts as in hypothetical (1). Defendant calls a police officer, and represents that the officer will testify that she arrived at the scene five minutes after the accident occurred; that a number of people were gathered around Plaintiff; and that she heard someone say, "That lady was hit by a blue car which didn't stop and she was thrown up in the air and landed on the red car," but doesn't know who made the statement. Plaintiff makes a hearsay objection.

(3) Prosecution of Accused for the kidnapping of and assault upon Victim. Victim suffered brain damage, and was hospitalized for seven weeks. S, Victim's sister, testified that one week after Victim came home from the hospital, S showed her a newspaper article containing a photograph of Accused. S testified that Victim's "immediate reaction was one of great distress," and that Victim "pointed to the picture and said very clearly, 'He killed me, he killed me.'" Accused objects that the statement is hearsay, and that it is not a spontaneous declaration because the startling event was the assault, which occurred eight weeks prior to the statement. What is the proper ruling on Accused's motion? See United States v. Napier, 518 F.2d 316 (9th Cir.1975).

(4) Prosecution for the theft of a truck. A state trooper testifies that after receiving a radio report of an abandoned stolen truck, he appealed for information over his citizen's band ("CB") radio. A "CB'er" reported that he saw two men walking away from the point where the truck had been abandoned.

A second "CB'er" informed him that the two men were seen walking five to six miles east of the truck's location. The two men were arrested five miles away from the truck, a few minutes after the first CB statement. Should the first statement have been admitted? See United States v. Cain, 587 F.2d 678 (5th Cir.1979).

Davis v. Washington

United States Supreme Court, 2006.
547 U.S. 813, 126 S.Ct. 2266, 165 L.Ed.2d 224.

■ JUSTICE SCALIA delivered the opinion of the Court.

These cases require us to determine when statements made to law enforcement personnel during a 911 call or at a crime scene are "testimonial" and thus subject to the requirements of the Sixth Amendment's Confrontation Clause.

I

A

The relevant statements in *Davis v. Washington,* No. 05–5224, were made to a 911 emergency operator on February 1, 2001. When the operator answered the initial call, the connection terminated before anyone spoke. She reversed the call, and Michelle McCottry answered. In the ensuing conversation, the operator ascertained that McCottry was involved in a domestic disturbance with her former boyfriend Adrian Davis, the petitioner in this case:

"911 Operator: Hello.

"Complainant: Hello.

"911 Operator: What's going on?

"Complainant: He's here jumpin' on me again.

"911 Operator: Okay. Listen to me carefully. Are you in a house or an apartment?

"Complainant: I'm in a house.

"911 Operator: Are there any weapons?

"Complainant: No. He's usin' his fists.

"911 Operator: Okay. Has he been drinking?

"Complainant: No.

"911 Operator: Okay, sweetie. I've got help started. Stay on the line with me, okay?

"Complainant: I'm on the line.

"911 Operator: Listen to me carefully. Do you know his last name?

"Complainant: It's Davis.

"911 Operator: Davis? Okay, what's his first name?

"Complainant: Adrian

"911 Operator: What is it?

"Complainant: Adrian.

"911 Operator: Adrian?

"Complainant: Yeah.

"911 Operator: Okay. What's his middle initial?

"Complainant: Martell. He's runnin' now."

As the conversation continued, the operator learned that Davis had "just r[un] out the door" after hitting McCottry, and that he was leaving in a car with someone else. McCottry started talking, but the operator cut her off, saying, "Stop talking and answer my questions." She then gathered more information about Davis (including his birthday), and learned that Davis had told McCottry that his purpose in coming to the house was "to get his stuff," since McCottry was moving. McCottry described the context of the assault, *id.*, at 12, after which the operator told her that the police were on their way. "They're gonna check the area for him first," the operator said, "and then they're gonna come talk to you."

The police arrived within four minutes of the 911 call and observed McCottry's shaken state, the "fresh injuries on her forearm and her face," and her "frantic efforts to gather her belongings and her children so that they could leave the residence." 154 Wash.2d 291, 296, 111 P.3d 844, 847 (2005) (en banc). * * *

McCottry presumably could have testified [at Davis's felony trial for violation of a non-contact order] as to whether Davis was her assailant, but she did not appear. Over Davis's objection, based on the Confrontation Clause of the Sixth Amendment, the trial court admitted the recording of her exchange with the 911 operator, and the jury convicted him. * * *

B

In *Hammon v. Indiana,* No. 05–5705, police responded late on the night of February 26, 2003, to a "reported domestic disturbance" at the home of Hershel and Amy Hammon. They found Amy alone on the front porch, appearing " 'somewhat frightened,' " but she told them that " 'nothing was the matter.' " She gave them permission to enter the house, where an officer saw "a gas heating unit in the corner of the living room" that had "flames coming out of the . . . partial glass front. There were pieces of glass on the ground in front of it and there was flame emitting from the front of the heating unit."

Hershel, meanwhile, was in the kitchen. He told the police "that he and his wife had 'been in an argument' but 'everything was fine now' and the argument 'never became physical.'" 829 N.E.2d, at 447. By this point Amy had come back inside. One of the officers remained with Hershel; the other went to the living room to talk with Amy, and "again asked [her] what had occurred." *Ibid.* . ... Hershel made several attempts to participate in Amy's conversation with the police, but was rebuffed. The officer later testified that Hershel "became angry when I insisted that [he] stay separated from Mrs. Hammon so that we can investigate what had happened." After hearing Amy's account, the officer "had her fill out and sign a battery affidavit." Amy handwrote the following: "Broke our Furnace & shoved me down on the floor into the broken glass. Hit me in the chest and threw me down. Broke our lamps & phone. Tore up my van where I couldn't leave the house. Attacked my daughter."

The State charged Hershel with domestic battery and with violating his probation. Amy was subpoenaed, but she did not appear at his subsequent bench trial. The State called the officer who had questioned Amy, and asked him to recount what Amy told him and to authenticate the affidavit. Hershel's counsel repeatedly objected to the admission of this evidence. At one point, after hearing the prosecutor defend the affidavit because it was made "under oath," defense counsel said, "That doesn't give us the opportunity to cross examine [the] person who allegedly drafted it. Makes me mad." *Id.,* at 19. Nonetheless, the trial court admitted the affidavit as a "present sense impression," *id.,* at 20, and Amy's statements as "excited utterances" that "are expressly permitted in these kinds of cases even if the declarant is not available to testify." *Id.,* at 40. * * *

The trial judge found Hershel guilty on both charges . . . [The Indiana Supreme Court affirmed, concluding that Amy's oral statement satisfied the state's hearsay exception for excited utterances, that this statement was not testimonial within the meaning of *Crawford*, and that, though the affidavit was testimonial and should not have been admitted, the error was harmless given that the trial was to the bench.]

II

* * * The character of the statements in the present cases is not as clear [as in *Crawford*], and these cases require us to determine more precisely which police interrogations produce testimony.

Without attempting to produce an exhaustive classification of all conceivable statements—or even all conceivable statements in response to police interrogation—as either testimonial or nontestimonial, it suffices to decide the present cases to hold as follows: Statements are nontestimonial when made in the course of police interrogation under circumstances objectively indicating that the primary purpose of the interrogation is to enable police assistance to meet an ongoing emergency. They are testimonial when the circumstances objectively indicate that there is no such ongoing emergency, and that the primary purpose of the interrogation is to establish or prove past events potentially relevant to later criminal prosecution.[1]

III

A

In *Crawford,* it sufficed for resolution of the case before us to determine that "even if the Sixth Amendment is not solely concerned with testimonial hearsay, that is its primary object, and interrogations by law enforcement officers fall squarely within that class." Moreover, as we have just described, the facts of that case spared us the need to define what we meant by "interrogations." The *Davis* case today does not permit us this luxury of indecision. The inquiries of a police operator in the course of a 911 call are an interrogation in one sense, but not in a sense that "qualifies under any conceivable definition." We must decide, therefore, whether the Confrontation Clause applies only to testimonial hearsay; and, if so, whether the recording of a 911 call qualifies.

The answer to the first question was suggested in *Crawford,* even if not explicitly held:

> "The text of the Confrontation Clause reflects this focus [on testimonial hearsay]. It applies to 'witnesses' against the accused-in other words, those who 'bear testimony.' 1 N. Webster, An American Dictionary of the English Language (1828). 'Testimony,' in turn, is typically 'a solemn declaration or affirmation made for the purpose of establishing or proving some fact.' *Ibid.* An accuser who makes a formal statement to government officers bears testimony in a sense that a person who makes a casual remark to an acquaintance does not."

A limitation so clearly reflected in the text of the constitutional provision must fairly be said to mark out not merely its "core," but its perimeter.

* * *

Most of the American cases applying the Confrontation Clause or its state constitutional or common-law counterparts involved testimonial statements of the most formal sort—sworn testimony in prior judicial proceedings or formal depositions under oath—which invites the argument that the scope of the Clause is limited to that very formal category. But the English cases that were the progenitors of the Confrontation Clause did not limit the exclusionary rule to prior court testimony and formal depositions,

---

[1] Our holding refers to interrogations because, as explained below, the statements in the cases presently before us are the products of interrogations—which in some circumstances tend to generate testimonial responses. This is not to imply, however, that statements made in the absence of any interrogation are necessarily nontestimonial. The Framers were no more willing to exempt from cross-examination volunteered testimony or answers to open-ended questions than they were to exempt answers to detailed interrogation. (Part of the evidence against Sir Walter Raleigh was a letter from Lord Cobham that was plainly *not* the result of sustained questioning. *Raleigh's Case,* 2 How. St. Tr. 1, 27 (1603).) And of course even when interrogation exists, it is in the final analysis the declarant's statements, not the interrogator's questions, that the Confrontation Clause requires us to evaluate.

see *Crawford*. In any event, we do not think it conceivable that the protections of the Confrontation Clause can readily be evaded by having a note-taking policeman *recite* the unsworn hearsay testimony of the declarant, instead of having the declarant sign a deposition. Indeed, if there is one point for which no case—English or early American, state or federal—can be cited, that is it.

The question before us in *Davis,* then, is whether, objectively considered, the interrogation that took place in the course of the 911 call produced testimonial statements. When we said in *Crawford* that "interrogations by law enforcement officers fall squarely within [the] class" of testimonial hearsay, we had immediately in mind (for that was the case before us) interrogations solely directed at establishing the facts of a past crime, in order to identify (or provide evidence to convict) the perpetrator. The product of such interrogation, whether reduced to a writing signed by the declarant or embedded in the memory (and perhaps notes) of the interrogating officer, is testimonial. It is, in the terms of the 1828 American dictionary quoted in *Crawford,* " '[a] solemn declaration or affirmation made for the purpose of establishing or proving some fact.' " (The solemnity of even an oral declaration of relevant past fact to an investigating officer is well enough established by the severe consequences that can attend a deliberate falsehood. [citations omitted]) A 911 call, on the other hand, and at least the initial interrogation conducted in connection with a 911 call, is ordinarily not designed primarily to "establis[h] or prov[e]" some past fact, but to describe current circumstances requiring police assistance.

The difference between the interrogation in *Davis* and the one in *Crawford* is apparent on the face of things. In *Davis,* McCottry was speaking about events *as they were actually happening,* rather than [describing past events.] Sylvia Crawford's interrogation, on the other hand, took place hours after the events she described had occurred. Moreover, any reasonable listener would recognize that McCottry (unlike Sylvia Crawford) was facing an ongoing emergency. Although one *might* call 911 to provide a narrative report of a crime absent any imminent danger, McCottry's call was plainly a call for help against a bona fide physical threat. Third, the nature of what was asked and answered in *Davis,* again viewed objectively, was such that the elicited statements were necessary to be able to *resolve* the present emergency, rather than simply to learn (as in *Crawford*) what had happened in the past. That is true even of the operator's effort to establish the identity of the assailant, so that the dispatched officers might know whether they would be encountering a violent felon. See, *e.g., Hiibel v. Sixth Judicial Dist. Court of Nev., Humboldt Cty.,* 542 U.S. 177, 186 (2004). And finally, the difference in the level of formality between the two interviews is striking. Crawford was responding calmly, at the station house, to a series of questions, with the officer-interrogator taping and making notes of her answers; McCottry's frantic answers were provided over the phone, in an environment that was not tranquil, or even (as far as any reasonable 911 operator could make out) safe.

We conclude from all this that the circumstances of McCottry's interrogation objectively indicate its primary purpose was to enable police assistance to meet an ongoing emergency. She simply was not acting as a *witness;* she was not *testifying.* What she said was not "a weaker substitute for live testimony" at trial, *United States v. Inadi,* 475 U.S. 387, 394 (1986), like Lord Cobham's statements in *Raleigh's Case,* 2 How. St. Tr. 1 (1603), or Jane Dingler's *ex parte* statements against her husband in *King v. Dingler,* 2 Leach 561, 168 Eng. Rep. 383 (1791), or Sylvia Crawford's statement in *Crawford.* In each of those cases, the *ex parte* actors and the evidentiary products of the *ex parte* communication aligned perfectly with their courtroom analogues. McCottry's emergency statement does not. No "witness" goes into court to proclaim an emergency and seek help.

Davis seeks to cast McCottry in the unlikely role of a witness by pointing to English cases. None of them involves statements made during an ongoing emergency. In *King v. Brasier,* 1 Leach 199, 168 Eng. Rep. 202 (1779), for example, a young rape victim, "immediately on her coming home, told all the circumstances of the injury" to her mother. The case would be helpful to Davis if the relevant statement had been the girl's screams for aid as she was being chased by her assailant. But by the time the victim got home, her story was an account of past events.

This is not to say that a conversation which begins as an interrogation to determine the need for emergency assistance cannot, as the Indiana Supreme Court put it, "evolve into testimonial statements," once that purpose has been achieved. In this case, for example, after the operator gained the information needed to address the exigency of the moment, the emergency appears to have ended (when Davis drove away from the premises). The operator then told McCottry to be quiet, and proceeded to pose a battery of questions. It could readily be maintained that, from that point on, McCottry's statements were testimonial, not unlike the "structured police questioning" that occurred in *Crawford.* This presents no great problem.* * *

B

Determining the testimonial or nontestimonial character of the statements that were the product of the interrogation in *Hammon* is a much easier task, since they were not much different from the statements we found to be testimonial in *Crawford.* It is entirely clear from the circumstances that the interrogation was part of an investigation into possibly criminal past conduct—as, indeed, the testifying officer expressly acknowledged. There was no emergency in progress; the interrogating officer testified that he had heard no arguments or crashing and saw no one throw or break anything. When the officers first arrived, Amy told them that things were fine, and there was no immediate threat to her person. When the officer questioned Amy for the second time, and elicited the challenged statements, he was not seeking to determine (as in *Davis*) "what is happening," but rather "what happened." Objectively viewed, the primary, if not indeed the sole, purpose of the interrogation was to investigate a possible crime—which is, of course, precisely what the officer *should* have done.

It is true that the *Crawford* interrogation was more formal. It followed a *Miranda* warning, was tape-recorded, and took place at the station house. While these features certainly strengthened the statements' testimonial aspect—made it more objectively apparent, that is, that the purpose of the exercise was to nail down the truth about past criminal events—none was essential to the point. It was formal enough that Amy's interrogation was conducted in a separate room, away from her husband (who tried to intervene), with the officer receiving her replies for use in his "investigat[ion]." What we called the "striking resemblance" of the *Crawford* statement to civil-law *ex parte* examinations is shared by Amy's statement here. Both declarants were actively separated from the defendant—officers forcibly prevented Hershel from participating in the interrogation. Both statements deliberately recounted, in response to police questioning, how potentially criminal past events began and progressed. And both took place some time after the events described were over. Such statements under official interrogation are an obvious substitute for live testimony, because they do precisely *what a witness does* on direct examination; they are inherently testimonial.[5]

Both Indiana and the United States as *amicus curiae* argue that this case should be resolved much like *Davis*. For the reasons we find the comparison to *Crawford* compelling, we find the comparison to *Davis* unpersuasive. The statements in *Davis* were taken when McCottry was alone, not only unprotected by police (as Amy Hammon was protected), but apparently in immediate danger from Davis. She was seeking aid, not telling a story about the past. McCottry's present-tense statements showed immediacy; Amy's narrative of past events was delivered at some remove in time from the danger she described. And after Amy answered the officer's questions, he had her execute an affidavit, in order, he testified, "[t]o establish events that have occurred previously."

Although we necessarily reject the Indiana Supreme Court's implication that virtually any "initial inquiries" at the crime scene will not be testimonial, we do not hold the opposite—that *no* questions at the scene will yield nontestimonial answers. We have already observed of domestic disputes that "[o]fficers called to investigate . . . need to know whom they are dealing with in order to assess the situation, the threat to their own safety, and possible danger to the potential victim." *Hiibel,* 542 U.S., at 186. Such exigencies may *often* mean that "initial inquiries" produce nontestimonial statements. But in cases like this one, where Amy's statements were nei-

---

[5] [Responding to the contention by Justice Thomas that the Court's opinion was not focused on the abuses that were the target of the Confrontation Clause, in particular the formal examinations taken by magistrates under the Marian statutes, the Court said:] We do not dispute that formality is indeed essential to testimonial utterance. But we no longer have examining Marian magistrates; and we do have, as our 18th-century forebears did not, examining police officers, see L. Friedman, *Crime and Punishment in American History* 67–68 (1993)—who perform investigative and testimonial functions once performed by examining Marian magistrates, see J. Langbein, *The Origins of Adversary Criminal Trial* 41 (2003). It imports sufficient formality, in our view, that lies to such officers are criminal offenses. Restricting the Confrontation Clause to the precise forms against which it was originally directed is a recipe for its extinction. Cf. *Kyllo v. United States,* 533 U.S. 27, 121 S.Ct. 2038, 150 L.Ed.2d 94 (2001).

ther a cry for help nor the provision of information enabling officers immediately to end a threatening situation, the fact that they were given at an
alleged crime scene and were "initial inquiries" is immaterial. Cf. *Crawford*.[6]

IV

Respondents in both cases, joined by a number of their *amici,* contend
that the nature of the offenses charged in these two cases—domestic violence—requires greater flexibility in the use of testimonial evidence. This
particular type of crime is notoriously susceptible to intimidation or coercion of the victim to ensure that she does not testify at trial. When this occurs, the Confrontation Clause gives the criminal a windfall. We may not,
however, vitiate constitutional guarantees when they have the effect of allowing the guilty to go free. Cf. *Kyllo v. United States,* 533 U.S. 27 (2001)
(suppressing evidence from an illegal search). But when defendants seek to
undermine the judicial process by procuring or coercing silence from witnesses and victims, the Sixth Amendment does not require courts to acquiesce. While defendants have no duty to assist the State in proving their
guilt, they *do* have the duty to refrain from acting in ways that destroy the
integrity of the criminal-trial system. We reiterate what we said in *Crawford:* that "the rule of forfeiture by wrongdoing ... extinguishes confrontation claims on essentially equitable grounds." That is, one who obtains the
absence of a witness by wrongdoing forfeits the constitutional right to confrontation.

* * *

We have determined that, absent a finding of forfeiture by wrongdoing,
the Sixth Amendment operates to exclude Amy Hammon's affidavit. . .

[Justice Thomas wrote a separate opinion, concurring in the judgment
in *Davis* and dissenting in *Hammon*, adhering to a view he had previously
expressed, that the scope of the Confrontation Clause is limited to "extrajudicial statements ... contained in formalized testimonial materials, such
as affidavits, depositions, prior testimony, or confessions." He pointed out
that "[i]n many, if not most, cases where police respond to a report of a
crime, whether pursuant to a 911 call from the victim or otherwise, the
purposes of an interrogation, viewed from the perspective of the police, are
both to respond to the emergency situation *and* to gather evidence." And he
contended that "the fact that the officer in *Hammon* was investigating Mr.
Hammon's past conduct does not foreclose the possibility that the primary
purpose of his inquiry was to assess whether Mr. Hammon constituted a
continuing danger to his wife, requiring further police presence or action."]

---

[6] Police investigations themselves are, of course, in no way impugned by our characterization of their fruits as testimonial. Investigations of past crimes prevent future harms and lead
to necessary arrests. While prosecutors may hope that inculpatory "nontestimonial" evidence
is gathered, this is essentially beyond police control. Their saying that an emergency exists
cannot make it be so. The Confrontation Clause in no way governs police conduct, because it is
the trial *use* of, not the investigatory *collection* of, ex parte testimonial statements which of-
fends that provision. But neither can police conduct govern the Confrontation Clause; testimonial statements are what they are.

Michigan v. Bryant

Supreme Court of the United States, 2011
131 S.Ct. 1143

■ JUSTICE SOTOMAYOR delivered the opinion of the Court.

* * *

I

Around 3:25 a.m. on April 29, 2001, Detroit, Michigan police officers responded to a radio dispatch indicating that a man had been shot. At the scene, they found the victim, Anthony Covington, lying on the ground next to his car in a gas station parking lot. Covington had a gunshot wound to his abdomen, appeared to be in great pain, and spoke with difficulty.

The police asked him what had happened, who had shot him, and where the shooting had occurred. Covington stated that Rick shot him at around 3 a.m. He also indicated that he had a conversation with Bryant, whom he recognized based on his voice, through the back door of Bryant's house. Covington explained that when he turned to leave, he was shot through the door and then drove to the gas station, where police found him.

Covington's conversation with the police ended within 5 to 10 minutes when emergency medical services arrived. Covington was transported to a hospital and died within hours. The police left the gas station after speaking with Covington, called for backup, and traveled to Bryant's house. They did not find Bryant there but did find blood and a bullet on the back porch and an apparent bullet hole in the back door. Police also found Covington's wallet and identification outside the house.

At trial, which occurred prior to our decisions in *Crawford* and *Davis*, the police officers who spoke with Covington at the gas station testified about what Covington had told them. The jury returned a guilty verdict on charges of second-degree murder, being a felon in possession of a firearm, and possession of a firearm during the commission of a felony.

[Although the trial court held that Covington's statements satisfied the excited-utterance exception to the hearsay rule, the Supreme Court of Michigan ultimately held that they should not have been admitted because they were testimonial for purposes of the Confrontation Clause.] The court did not address whether, absent a Confrontation Clause bar, the statements' admission would have been otherwise consistent with Michigan's hearsay rules or due process.* * *

II

* * * We * * * made clear in *Davis* that not all those questioned by the police are witnesses and not all interrogations by law enforcement officers, *Crawford,* are subject to the Confrontation Clause. * * *

[handwritten margin note: Not all interrogations Subject to Confrontation Clause]

* * * Even where such an interrogation is conducted with all good faith, introduction of the resulting statements at trial can be unfair to the accused if they are untested by cross-examination. Whether formal or informal, out-of-court statements can evade the basic objective of the Confrontation Clause, which is to prevent the accused from being deprived of the opportunity to cross-examine the declarant about statements taken for use at trial. When, as in *Davis,* the primary purpose of an interrogation is to respond to an ongoing emergency, its purpose is not to create a record for trial and thus is not within the scope of the Clause. But there may be *other* circumstances, aside from ongoing emergencies, when a statement is not procured with a primary purpose of creating an out-of-court substitute for trial testimony. In making the primary purpose determination, standard rules of hearsay, designed to identify some statements as reliable, will be relevant. Where no such primary purpose exists, the admissibility of a statement is the concern of state and federal rules of evidence, not the Confrontation Clause.

* * * [W]e confront for the first time circumstances in which the ongoing emergency discussed in *Davis* extends beyond an initial victim to a potential threat to the responding police and the public at large. This new context requires us to provide additional clarification with regard to what *Davis* meant by [the primary purpose of the interrogation is to enable police assistance to meet an ongoing emergency.] ~ would be non-testimonial

III

To determine whether the primary purpose of an interrogation is to enable police assistance to meet an ongoing emergency, which would render the resulting statements nontestimonial, we objectively evaluate the circumstances in which the encounter occurs and the statements and actions of the parties.

A

* * * [T]he relevant inquiry is not the subjective or actual purpose of the individuals involved in a particular encounter, but rather the purpose that reasonable participants would have had, as ascertained from the individuals' statements and actions and the circumstances in which the encounter occurred.

B

As our recent Confrontation Clause cases have explained, the existence of an ongoing emergency at the time of an encounter between an individual and the police is among the most important circumstances informing the primary purpose of an interrogation. * * * [4] Implicit in *Davis* is the idea that because the prospect of fabrication in statements given for the primary purpose of resolving that emergency is presumably significant-

---

[4] The existence of an ongoing emergency must be objectively assessed from the perspective of the parties to the interrogation at the time, not with the benefit of hindsight. * * *

ly diminished, the Confrontation Clause does not require such statements to be subject to the crucible of cross-examination.

This logic is not unlike that justifying the excited utterance exception in hearsay law. Statements relating to a startling event or condition made while the declarant was under the stress of excitement caused by the event or condition, Fed. Rule Evid. 803(2), are considered reliable because the declarant, in the excitement, presumably cannot form a falsehood. An ongoing emergency has a similar effect of focusing an individual's attention on responding to the emergency.

*** [T]he court below *** construed *Davis* to have decided more than it did and thus employed an unduly narrow understanding of ongoing emergency that *Davis* does not require.

First, the Michigan Supreme Court *** erroneously read *Davis* as deciding that the statements made after the defendant stopped assaulting the victim and left the premises did *not* occur during an ongoing emergency. We explicitly explained in *Davis,* however, that we were asked to review only the testimonial nature of Michelle McCottry's initial statements during the 911 call; we therefore merely *assumed* the correctness of the Washington Supreme Court's holding that admission of her other statements was harmless, without deciding whether those subsequent statements were also made for the primary purpose of resolving an ongoing emergency.

Second, by assuming that *Davis* defined the outer bounds of ongoing emergency, the Michigan Supreme Court failed to appreciate that whether an emergency exists and is ongoing is a highly context-dependent inquiry.*** Because *Davis* and *Hammon* were domestic violence cases, we focused only on the threat to the victims and assessed the ongoing emergency from the perspective of whether there was a continuing threat *to them*.

Domestic violence cases like *Davis* and *Hammon* often have a narrower zone of potential victims than cases involving threats to public safety. An assessment of whether an emergency that threatens the police and public is ongoing cannot narrowly focus on whether the threat solely to the first victim has been neutralized because the threat to the first responders and public may continue. ***

The Michigan Supreme Court also did not appreciate that the duration and scope of an emergency may depend in part on the type of weapon employed. *** If Hershel [Hammon] had been reported to be armed with a gun, however, separation by a single household wall might not have been sufficient to end the emergency.

The Michigan Supreme Court's failure to focus on the context-dependent nature of our *Davis* decision also led it to conclude that the medical condition of a declarant is irrelevant. *** The medical condition of the victim is important to the primary purpose inquiry to the extent that it sheds light on the ability of the victim to have any purpose at all in responding to police questions and on the likelihood that any purpose formed would necessarily be a testimonial one. The victim's medical state also provides important context for first responders to judge the existence and magnitude of a continuing threat to the victim, themselves, and the public. * * *

Finally, * * * [a]s *Davis* made clear, whether an ongoing emergency exists is simply one factor albeit an important factor that informs the ultimate inquiry regarding the primary purpose of an interrogation. Another factor the Michigan Supreme Court did not sufficiently account for is the importance of *informality* in an encounter between a victim and police. Formality is not the sole touchstone of our primary purpose inquiry because, although formality suggests the absence of an emergency and therefore an increased likelihood that the purpose of the interrogation is to establish or prove past events potentially relevant to later criminal prosecution, *Davis,* informality does not necessarily indicate the presence of an emergency or the lack of testimonial intent. The court below, however, too readily dismissed the informality of the circumstances in this case in a single brief footnote and in fact seems to have suggested that the encounter in this case was formal. * * * [T]he questioning in this case occurred in an exposed, public area, prior to the arrival of emergency medical services, and in a disorganized fashion. All of those facts make this case distinguishable from the formal station-house interrogation in *Crawford.*

C

In addition to the circumstances in which an encounter occurs, the statements and actions of both the declarant and interrogators provide objective evidence of the primary purpose of the interrogation. * * *

As the Michigan Supreme Court correctly recognized, *Davis* requires a combined inquiry that accounts for both the declarant and the interrogator. In many instances, the primary purpose of the interrogation will be most accurately ascertained by looking to the contents of both the questions and the answers. To give an extreme example, if the police say to a victim, "Tell us who did this to you so that we can arrest and prosecute them", the victim's response that "Rick did it", appears purely accusatory because by virtue of the phrasing of the question, the victim necessarily has prosecution in mind when she answers.

The combined approach also ameliorates problems that could arise from looking solely to one participant. Predominant among these is the problem of mixed motives on the part of both interrogators and declarants. Police officers in our society function as both first responders and criminal investigators. Their dual responsibilities may mean that they act with different motives simultaneously or in quick succession.

Victims are also likely to have mixed motives when they make statements to the police. During an ongoing emergency, a victim is most likely to want the threat to her and to other potential victims to end, but that does not necessarily mean that the victim wants or envisions prosecution of the assailant. A victim may want the attacker to be incapacitated temporarily or rehabilitated. * * *

The dissent suggests that we intend to give controlling weight to the intentions of the police. That is a misreading of our opinion. At trial, the declarant's statements, not the interrogator's questions, will be introduced to establis[h] the truth of the matter asserted, *Crawford,* and must therefore pass the Sixth Amendment test. In determining whether a declarant's statements are testimonial, courts should look to all of the relevant circumstances. Even Justice SCALIA concedes that the interrogator is relevant to this evaluation, and we agree that [t]he identity of an interrogator, and the content and tenor of his questions, can illuminate the primary purpose of the interrogation. The dissent criticizes the complexity of our approach, but we, at least, are unwilling to sacrifice accuracy for simplicity. Simpler is not always better, and courts making a primary purpose assessment should not be unjustifiably restrained from consulting all relevant information, including the statements and actions of interrogators. * * *

IV

As we suggested in *Davis,* when a court must determine whether the Confrontation Clause bars the admission of a statement at trial, it should determine the primary purpose of the interrogation by objectively evaluating the statements and actions of the parties to the encounter, in light of the circumstances in which the interrogation occurs. The existence of an emergency or the parties' perception that an emergency is ongoing is among the most important circumstances that courts must take into account in determining whether an interrogation is testimonial because statements made to assist police in addressing an ongoing emergency presumably lack the testimonial purpose that would subject them to the requirement of confrontation. As the context of this case brings into sharp relief, the existence and duration of an emergency depend on the type and scope of danger posed to the victim, the police, and the public. * * *

We first examine the circumstances in which the interrogation occurred. The parties disagree over whether there was an emergency when the police arrived at the gas station. Bryant argues, and the Michigan Supreme Court accepted, that there was no ongoing emergency because there . . . was no criminal conduct occurring. No shots were being fired, no one was seen in possession of a firearm, nor were any witnesses seen cowering in fear or running from the scene. Bryant, while conceding that a serious or life-threatening injury creates a medical emergency for a victim, further argues that a declarant's medical emergency is not relevant to the ongoing emergency determination.

In contrast, Michigan and the Solicitor General explain that when the police responded to the call that a man had been shot and found Covington bleeding on the gas station parking lot, they did not know who Covington was, whether the shooting had occurred at the gas station or at a different location, who the assailant was, or whether the assailant posed a continuing threat to Covington or others. * * *

* * * The officers * * * all agree that the first question was what happened? The answer was either I was shot or Rick shot me."

* * * Nothing Covington said to the police indicated that the cause of the shooting was a purely private dispute or that the threat from the shooter had ended. The record reveals little about the motive for the shooting. The police officers who spoke with Covington at the gas station testified that Covington did not tell them what words Covington and Rick had exchanged prior to the shooting. What Covington did tell the officers was that he fled Bryant's back porch, indicating that he perceived an ongoing threat. The police did not know, and Covington did not tell them, whether the threat was limited to him. The potential scope of the dispute and therefore the emergency in this case thus stretches more broadly than those at issue in *Davis* and *Hammon* and encompasses a threat potentially to the police and the public.

This is also the first of our post-*Crawford* Confrontation Clause cases to involve a gun. The physical separation that was sufficient to end the emergency in *Hammon* was not necessarily sufficient to end the threat in this case; Covington was shot through the back door of Bryant's house. Bryant's argument that there was no ongoing emergency because [n]o shots were being fired surely construes ongoing emergency too narrowly. * * *

At no point during the questioning did either Covington or the police know the location of the shooter. In fact, Bryant was not at home by the time the police searched his house at approximately 5:30 a.m. At some point between 3 a.m. and 5:30 a.m., Bryant left his house. At bottom, [there was an ongoing emergency here where an armed shooter, whose motive for and location after the shooting were unknown, had mortally wounded Covington within a few blocks and a few minutes of the location where the police found Covington.]

[margin handwritten note: ongoing emergency — armed shooter with unknown location]

This is not to suggest that the emergency continued until Bryant was arrested in California a year after the shooting. We need not decide precisely when the emergency ended because Covington's encounter with the police and all of the statements he made during that interaction occurred within the first few minutes of the police officers' arrival and well before they secured the scene of the shooting the shooter's last known location.

We reiterate, moreover, that the existence vel non of an ongoing emergency is not the touchstone of the testimonial inquiry; rather, the ultimate inquiry is whether the primary purpose of the interrogation [was] to enable police assistance to meet [the] ongoing emergency. *Davis.* We turn now to that inquiry, as informed by the circumstances of the ongoing emergency just described. The circumstances of the encounter provide important context for understanding Covington's statements to the police. * * * When he made the statements, Covington was lying in a gas station parking lot bleeding from a mortal gunshot wound to his abdomen. His answers to the police officers' questions were punctuated with questions about when emergency medical services would arrive. He was obviously in considerable pain and had difficulty breathing and talking. From this description of his condition and report of his statements, we cannot say that a person in Covington's situation would have had a primary purpose to establish or prove past events potentially relevant to later criminal prosecution.

For their part, the police responded to a call that a man had been shot. As discussed above, they did not know why, where, or when the shooting had occurred. Nor did they know the location of the shooter or anything else about the circumstances in which the crime occurred. The questions they asked what had happened, who had shot him, and where the shooting occurred were the exact type of questions necessary to allow the police to assess the situation, the threat to their own safety, and possible danger to the potential victim and to the public, including to allow them to ascertain whether they would be encountering a violent felon, *Davis*. In other words, they solicited the information necessary to enable them to meet an ongoing emergency.

Nothing in Covington's responses indicated to the police that, contrary to their expectation upon responding to a call reporting a shooting, there was no emergency or that a prior emergency had ended. Covington did indicate that he had been shot at another location about 25 minutes earlier, but he did not know the location of the shooter at the time the police arrived and, as far as we can tell from the record, he gave no indication that the shooter, having shot at him twice, would be satisfied that Covington was only wounded. In fact, Covington did not indicate any possible motive for the shooting, and thereby gave no reason to think that the shooter would not shoot again if he arrived on the scene. As we noted in *Davis,* initial inquiries may *often* . . . produce nontestimonial statements. The initial inquiries in this case resulted in the type of nontestimonial statements we contemplated in *Davis.*

Finally, we consider the informality of the situation and the interrogation. This situation is more similar, though not identical, to the informal, harried 911 call in *Davis* than to the structured, station-house interview in *Crawford.* As the officers' trial testimony reflects, the situation was fluid and somewhat confused . * * *

Because the circumstances of the encounter as well as the statements and actions of Covington and the police objectively indicate that the primary purpose of the interrogation was to enable police assistance to meet an ongoing emergency, *Davis,* Covington's identification and description of the shooter and the location of the shooting were not testimonial hearsay. The Confrontation Clause did not bar their admission at Bryant's trial.* * *

Justice KAGAN took no part in the consideration or decision of this case.

[Justice THOMAS concurred in the judgment. He repeated his criticisms of the "primary purpose" test but continued to adhere to the view that the historical practices falling within the Confrontation Clause were ones involving formality and solemnity, which he found lacking in the police interrogation of Covington.]

Justice SCALIA, dissenting.

Today's tale a story of five officers conducting successive examinations of a dying man with the primary purpose, not of obtaining and preserving his testimony regarding his killer, but of protecting him, them, and others from a murderer somewhere on the loose is so transparently false that professing to believe it demeans this institution. But reaching a patently incorrect conclusion on the facts is a relatively benign judicial mischief; it affects, after all, only the case at hand. In its vain attempt to make the incredible plausible, however or perhaps as an intended second goal today's opinion distorts our Confrontation Clause jurisprudence and leaves it in a shambles. Instead of clarifying the law, the Court makes itself the obfuscator of last resort. Because I continue to adhere to the Confrontation Clause that the People adopted, as described in *Crawford*, I dissent.

I

A

Crawford and *Davis* did not address whose perspective matters the declarant's, the interrogator's, or both when assessing the primary purpose of [an] interrogation. In those cases the statements were testimonial from any perspective. I think the same is true here, but because the Court picks a perspective so will I: The declarant's intent is what counts. In-court testimony is more than a narrative of past events; it is a solemn declaration made in the course of a criminal trial. For an out-of-court statement to qualify as testimonial, the declarant must intend the statement to be a solemn declaration rather than an unconsidered or offhand remark; and he must make the statement with the understanding that it may be used to invoke the coercive machinery of the State against the accused. See Friedman, *Grappling with the Meaning of Testimonial*, 71 Brooklyn L.Rev. 241, 259 (2005). That is what distinguishes a narrative told to a friend over dinner from a statement to the police. The hidden purpose of an interrogator cannot substitute for the declarant's intentional solemnity or his understanding of how his words may be used.

A declarant-focused inquiry is also the only inquiry that would work in every fact pattern implicating the Confrontation Clause. The Clause applies to volunteered testimony as well as statements solicited through police interrogation. An inquiry into an officer's purposes would make no sense when a declarant blurts out Rick shot me as soon as the officer arrives on the scene. I see no reason to adopt a different test one that accounts for an officer's intent when the officer asks what happened before the declarant makes his accusation. (This does not mean the interrogator is irrelevant. The identity of an interrogator, and the content and tenor of his questions, can bear upon whether a declarant intends to make a solemn statement, and envisions its use at a criminal trial. But none of this means that the interrogator's purpose matters.)

In an unsuccessful attempt to make its finding of emergency plausible, the Court instead adopts a test that looks to the purposes of both the police and the declarant. It claims that this is demanded by necessity, fretting that a domestic-violence victim may want her abuser briefly arrested presumably to teach him a lesson but not desire prosecution. I do not need to probe the purposes of the police to solve that problem. Even if a victim speaks to the police to establish or prove past events solely for the purpose of getting her abuser arrested, she surely knows her account is potentially relevant to later criminal prosecution should one ensue. * * *

The Court claims one affirmative virtue for its focus on the purposes of both the declarant and the police: It ameliorates problems that . . . arise when declarants have mixed motives. I am at a loss to know how. Sorting out the primary purpose of a declarant with mixed motives is sometimes difficult. But adding in the mixed motives of the police only compounds the problem. Now courts will have to sort through two sets of mixed motives to determine the primary purpose of an interrogation. And the Court's solution creates a mixed-motive problem where (under the proper theory) it does not exist viz., where the police and the declarant each have one motive, but those motives conflict. The Court does not provide an answer to this glaringly obvious problem, probably because it does not have one.

The only virtue of the Court's approach (if it can be misnamed a virtue) is that it leaves judges free to reach the fairest result under the totality of the circumstances. If the dastardly police trick a declarant into giving an incriminating statement against a sympathetic defendant, a court can focus on the police's intent and declare the statement testimonial. If the defendant deserves to go to jail, then a court can focus on whatever perspective is necessary to declare damning hearsay nontestimonial. And when all else fails, a court can mix-and-match perspectives to reach its desired outcome. * * *

B

Looking to the declarant's purpose (as we should), this is an absurdly easy case. Roughly 25 minutes after Anthony Covington had been shot, Detroit police responded to a 911 call reporting that a gunshot victim had appeared at a neighborhood gas station. They quickly arrived at the scene, and in less than 10 minutes five different Detroit police officers questioned Covington about the shooting. Each asked him a similar battery of questions: what happened and when, who shot the victim, and where did the shooting take place. After Covington would answer, they would ask follow-up questions, such as how tall is the shooter, [h]ow much does he weigh, what is the exact address or physical description of the house where the shooting took place, and what chain of events led to the shooting. The battery relented when the paramedics arrived and began tending to Covington's wounds.

From Covington's perspective, his statements had little value except to ensure the arrest and eventual prosecution of Richard Bryant. He knew the threatening situation had ended six blocks away and 25 minutes earlier when he fled from Bryant's back porch. * * * [I]t was entirely beyond imagination that Bryant would again open fire while Covington was surrounded by five armed police officers. And Covington knew the shooting was the work of a drug dealer, not a spree killer who might randomly threaten others.

Covington's knowledge that he had nothing to fear differs significantly from Michelle McCottry's state of mind during her frantic statements to a 911 operator at issue in *Davis.* * * * She did not have the luxuries of police protection and of time and space separating her from immediate danger that Covington enjoyed when he made his statements.

Covington's pressing medical needs do not suggest that he was responding to an emergency, but to the contrary reinforce the testimonial character of his statements. He understood the police were focused on investigating a past crime, not his medical needs. * * *

Neither Covington's statements nor the colloquy between him and the officers would have been out of place at a trial; it would have been a routine direct examination. Like a witness, Covington recounted in detail how a past criminal event began and progressed, and like a prosecutor, the police elicited that account through structured questioning. * * *

C

Worse still for the repute of today's opinion, this is an absurdly easy case even if one (erroneously) takes the interrogating officers' purpose into account. The five officers interrogated Covington primarily to investigate past criminal events. None absolutely none of their actions indicated that they perceived an imminent threat. They did not draw their weapons, and indeed did not immediately search the gas station for potential shooters. To the contrary, all five testified that they questioned Covington *before conducting any investigation at the scene.* Would this have made any sense if they feared the presence of a shooter? Most tellingly, none of the officers started his interrogation by asking what would have been the obvious first question if any hint of such a fear existed: Where is the shooter? * * *

D

A final word about the Court's active imagination. The Court invents a world where an ongoing emergency exists whenever an armed shooter, whose motive for and location after the shooting [are] unknown, . . . mortally wound [s] one individual within a few blocks and [25] minutes of the location where the police ultimately find that victim. Breathlessly, it worries that a shooter could leave the scene armed and ready to pull the trigger again. Nothing suggests the five officers in this case shared the Court's dystopian view of Detroit, where drug dealers hunt their shooting victim down and fire into a crowd of police officers to finish him off, or where spree killers shoot through a door and then roam the streets leaving a trail of bodies behind. Because almost 90 percent of murders involve a single victim, it is much more likely indeed, I think it certain that the officers viewed their encounter with Covington for what it was: an investigation into a past crime with no ongoing or immediate consequences.

The Court's distorted view creates an expansive exception to the Confrontation Clause for violent crimes. Because Bryant posed a continuing threat to public safety in the Court's imagination, the emergency persisted for confrontation purposes at least until the police learned his motive for and location after the shooting. It may have persisted in this case until the police secured the scene of the shooting two-and-a-half hours later.(The relevance of securing the scene is unclear so long as the killer is still at large especially if, as the Court speculates, he may be a spree-killer.) This is a dangerous definition of emergency. Many individuals who testify against a defendant at trial first offer their accounts to police in the hours after a violent act. If the police can plausibly claim that a potential threat to . . . the public persisted through those first few hours (and if the claim is plausible here it is always plausible) a defendant will have no constitutionally protected right to exclude the uncross-examined testimony of such witnesses. His conviction could rest (as perhaps it did here) solely on the officers' recollection at trial of the witnesses' accusations.

The Framers could not have envisioned such a hollow constitutional guarantee. No framing-era confrontation case that I know of, neither here nor in England, took such an enfeebled view of the right to confrontation. For example, *King v. Brasier,* 1 Leach 199, 200, 168 Eng. Rep. 202, 202 203 (K.B.1779), held inadmissible a mother's account of her young daughter's statements immediately on her coming home after being sexually assaulted. The daughter needed to testify herself. But today's majority presumably would hold the daughter's account to her mother a nontestimonial statement made during an ongoing emergency. She could not have known whether her attacker might reappear to attack again or attempt to silence the lone witness against him. Her mother likely listened to the account to assess the threat to her own safety and to decide whether the rapist posed a threat to the community that required the immediate intervention of the local authorities. Utter nonsense.

The 16th- and 17th-century English treason trials that helped inspire the Confrontation Clause show that today's decision is a mistake. The Court's expansive definition of an ongoing emergency and its willingness to consider the perspective of the interrogator and the declarant cast a more favorable light on those trials than history or our past decisions suggest they deserve. Royal officials conducted many of the *ex parte* examinations introduced against Sir Walter Raleigh and Sir John Fenwick while investigating alleged treasonous conspiracies of unknown scope, aimed at killing or overthrowing the King. Social stability in 16th- and 17th-century England depended mainly on the continuity of the ruling monarch, so such a conspiracy posed the most pressing emergency imaginable. Presumably, the royal officials investigating it would have understood the gravity of the situation and would have focused their interrogations primarily on ending the threat, not on generating testimony for trial. I therefore doubt that under the Court's test English officials acted improperly by denying Raleigh and Fenwick the opportunity to confront their accusers face to face."

Under my approach, in contrast, those English trials remain unquestionably infamous. Lord Cobham did not speak with royal officials to end an ongoing emergency. He was a traitor! He spoke, as Raleigh correctly observed, to establish Raleigh's guilt and to save his own life. Cobham's statements, when assessed from his perspective, had only a testimonial purpose. The same is true of Covington's statements here.

II

A

But today's decision is not only a gross distortion of the facts. It is a gross distortion of the law a revisionist narrative in which reliability continues to guide our Confrontation Clause jurisprudence, at least where emergencies and faux emergencies are concerned.

* * * The Court announces that in future cases it will look to standard rules of hearsay, designed to identify some statements as reliable, when deciding whether a statement is testimonial. *Ohio v. Roberts* said something remarkably similar: An out-of-court statement is admissible if it falls within a firmly rooted hearsay exception or otherwise bears adequate indicia of reliability. We tried that approach to the Confrontation Clause for nearly 25 years before *Crawford rejected* it as an unworkable standard unmoored from the text and the historical roots of the Confrontation Clause. * * *

Is it possible that the Court does not recognize the contradiction between its focus on reliable statements and *Crawford*'s focus on testimonial ones? Does it not realize that the two cannot coexist? Or does it intend, by following today's illogical roadmap, to resurrect *Roberts* by a thousand unprincipled distinctions without ever explicitly overruling *Crawford?* .* * *

[Justice Ginsburg also dissented. She agreed with Justice Scalia "that Covington's statements were testimonial and that '[t]he declarant's intent is what counts.'" She added: "Were the issue properly tendered here, I would take up the question whether the exception for dying declarations survives our recent Confrontation Clause decisions."]

3. STATE OF MIND

Adkins v. Brett

Supreme Court of California, 1920.
184 Cal. 252, 193 P. 251.

■ OLNEY, J. The action involved in the present appeal is one for damages for the alienation by the defendant of the plaintiff's wife. The cause was tried before a jury, a verdict was returned for the plaintiff, and from the judgment entered upon the verdict the defendant appeals.

The first point made on behalf of the defendant is that the verdict is not supported by the evidence. No question is made but that the evidence supports the conclusion that the husband had lost the affection of his wife, as a result of which she insisted upon a separation, or, if the testimony on behalf of the plaintiff be believed, as it must be taken it was by the jury, that acts of criminal conversation had taken place between the plaintiff's wife and the defendant. The particular in which it is claimed the evidence is insufficient is that, according to counsel's contention, it does not show that the defendant lured and enticed the plaintiff's wife from her husband, was her seducer, so to speak. Passing by the question as to whether or not evidence of adultery by a wife not shown to have theretofore lost her affection for her husband is not sufficient of itself to justify an inference of active seduction on the part of the man involved, it is sufficient for the purposes of this case to say that there was evidence of statements by the defendant to a male companion by the name of Tucker made by the day after a call by the two upon the wife as to what had taken place the night before, which, if true, justified the conclusion that the defendant was the active aggressor against the wife's resistance on the occasion when first they had criminal intercourse. It is only fair to say that the making of the statements was denied by the defendant, as was any guilty relation whatever on his part with the wife, and that the witness Tucker appears in anything but a creditable light. But evidence of the statements by the defendant was competent against him as admissions by him, and we cannot say that the jury was not justified in believing the evidence. It should also be said that there was considerable corroboration. The case is not one of a want of evidence in any particular, but of a flat conflict of evidence in nearly every particular, with gross perjury on one side or the other. Where the truth lay it was for the jury to determine.

The serious questions in the case arise in connection with the admission of evidence of conversations between the plaintiff and his wife, wherein the latter admitted or stated that she had gone automobile riding with the defendant, had dined with him, had received flowers from him, that he was able to give her a good time, and the plaintiff was not, that she intended to continue to accept the defendant's attentions and the plaintiff could do what he pleased about it, and that he was distasteful to her.

One objection to the evidence of these conversations, which may as well be disposed of at the outset as involving the most elementary principles of evidence, is that they were had without the presence of the defendant. The answer to this objection is that it is wholly immaterial whether the defendant was present or not. The competency of evidence of declarations or statements by a person other than the party to the action against whom they are introduced is not affected merely by the latter's presence or absence. If the evidence be not competent if the party against whom it is sought to introduce it was not present when the statements or declarations were made, no more is it competent if he were present. There are apparent

exceptions to this, but they are only apparent, and not real, exceptions. One
instance is that, when the party to the litigation was present and his conduct in response to the declarations or statements of others or his replies to
them are of such character as to amount to admissions by him, his conduct,
including his silence or want of action where an inference can fairly be
drawn from them, or his replies, may be shown in evidence against him,
and as a part of such conduct or replies the statements or declarations of
others to which they are a response. But the primary thing which is admitted in evidence in such a case is the party's own conduct or statements,
and, unless these are of such a character as to be relevant evidence against
him, the declarations or statements of others are not admissible simply because made in his presence. Another instance is where it is sought to
charge a party with notice or knowledge, and for that purpose evidence is
introduced of a statement made to him notifying or informing him.

The real objection to such evidence as that under consideration is that
it is hearsay. The evidence was plainly relevant; that is, it tended to prove
matters in issue, and was therefore admissible unless there is some rule of
exclusion applicable to it. The only rule of exclusion to which it can be subject is the rule against hearsay. The evidence was, in fact, hearsay, both as
to the past matters stated in the conversations and as to the wife's statements of her then feelings toward the plaintiff and the defendant. But the
rule is thoroughly well settled that, when the intention, feelings, or other
mental state of a certain person at a particular time, including his bodily
feelings, is material to the issues under trial, evidence of such person's declarations at the time indicative of his then mental state, even though hearsay, is competent as within an exception to the hearsay rule. In the present
case the state of the wife's feelings at the time of these conversations, both
toward her husband and toward the defendant, was material, and the conversations were indicative of her feelings, and, this being so, evidence of
them, was admissible to show her then state of feelings. This much can
hardly be questioned, in view of the settled character of the general rule
just stated, its plain applicability to just such cases as the present, and the
fact that it has very generally been so applied.

The difficulty in regard to such declarations as those involved here lies
in the fact that, while they may be competent upon the point of the wife's
feelings, they go very much further. They contain statements as to matters,
such as automobile rides, dinners, flowers, and attentions generally by the
defendant to the wife, as proof of which the statements are not within any
exception to the hearsay rule and are wholly incompetent. The situation is
intensified by the fact that those matters are themselves material to the
issues, and, if true, very detrimental to the defendant, so that the admission of the evidence involves the placing before the jury of evidence tending
to prove matters in issue, for proving which such evidence is not competent,
and the proof of which is very prejudicial to the party against whom it is
introduced.

Nevertheless, it is clear enough that the evidence, competent for the
purpose of showing the state of the wife's feelings, is not rendered incompe-

tent by the fact that it also tends to prove other material matters, to prove which it is not competent. The rule upon this point, which is one of well-nigh everyday application in actual trial, is thus stated by Wigmore (volume 1, p. 42):

> "In other words, when an evidentiary fact is offered for one purpose, and becomes admissible by satisfying all the rules applicable to it in that capacity, it is not inadmissible because it does not satisfy the rules applicable to it in some other capacity, and because the jury might improperly consider it in the latter capacity. This doctrine, although involving certain risks, is indispensable as a practical rule."

Cripe v. Cripe, supra, is an illustration of this. A father was sued by the wife of his son for the alienation from her of the son, and at the trial the following question was asked of the father as a witness:

> "After the marriage of your son and daughter, and before Dolly [the son's wife] left the ranch at Huasua in August, 1911, did your son ever tell you that Dolly drank to such an extent that he could not control her, or did he ever tell you during that time that she abused him so bad that he could not live with her?"

It is plain that as to the facts that the wife drank to excess and abused her husband, so that he could not live with her, the evidence was hearsay, was not within any exception to the hearsay rule, and was wholly incompetent, and at the same time those facts were material to the case, and, if true, very detrimental to the cause of the wife, so that the introduction of the evidence would be very prejudicial to her as to facts which the evidence was wholly incompetent to prove. Nevertheless the question was held to be proper, and the refusal of the trial court to permit it to be answered reversible error, on the ground that the testimony which it called for was competent to show the state of the son's feelings.

* * * In this situation there is little question but that Cripe v. Cripe should be followed. It is in accord with the great weight of authority and is but the application in this particular class of cases of a general rule of evidence, thoroughly well settled and applied in every kind of case, civil and criminal. One of the most frequent applications of it in civil cases is the admission of declarations by a testator when his mental capacity or his feelings are material. A notable instance of its application in a criminal case is Commonwealth v. Trefethen, where upon a trial for murder a statement of the decedent, a young unmarried woman, made shortly before her death, that she was five months pregnant, was held admissible for the purpose of showing that she believed this to be her condition, and therefore had a motive for committing suicide. Upon the point that such evidence, admissible to prove one fact, is not rendered inadmissible because tending to prove some other fact, to prove which it is not competent, the court said:

> "The most obvious distinction between speech and conduct is that speech is often not only an indication of the existing state of mind of the speaker, but a statement of a fact external to the mind, and as evi-

dence of that it is clearly hearsay. There is, of course, danger that a jury may not always observe this distinction, but that has not availed to exclude testimony which is admissible for one purpose, and not admissible for another to which there is danger the jury may apply it."

The rule, then, is that the admissibility of such evidence as that under discussion, admissible because competent as to one point, is not destroyed by its incompetency as to other points which it yet logically tends to prove. The danger, however, of the jury misusing such evidence and giving it weight in determining the points as to which it is incompetent is manifest. In such a situation, as Prof. Wigmore puts it immediately following the quotation already made, "the only question can be what the proper means are for avoiding the risk of misusing the evidence." Answering this question, Prof. Wigmore says:

"It is uniformly conceded that the instruction [to the jury] of the court [that the evidence is competent only as proof of one point and must not be considered as proof of others] suffices for that purpose; and the better opinion is that the opponent of the evidence must ask for that instruction; otherwise he may be supposed to have waived it as unnecessary for his protection."

The general correctness of this statement cannot be doubted. But we doubt if the learned author intended to say more than that the opponent of such evidence is always entitled to such an instruction for his protection, if he asks for it, and that generally it will suffice. But it is not difficult to imagine cases where it would not suffice, and the opponent could justly ask for more. The matter is largely one of discretion on the part of the trial judge. If the point to prove which the evidence is competent can just as well be proven by other evidence, or if it is of but slight weight or importance upon that point, the trial judge might well be justified in excluding it entirely, because of its prejudicial and dangerous character as to other points. A number of the authorities cited by defendant's counsel are distinguishable from the present case upon this ground. This would emphatically be true where there is good reason for believing that the real object for which the evidence is offered is not to prove the point for which it is ostensibly offered and is competent, but is to get before the jury declarations as to other points, to prove which the evidence is incompetent. The same thing would be true as to the introduction of repeated declarations, when once the point for which they are competent has been amply shown. It may also be that the portions of the declaration which there is danger may be misused by the jury are not so interwoven with the balance of the declaration but that they can be disassociated from it without impairing the meaning or effect of the declaration for the purpose for which it is admissible. In such a case evidence of such portions of the declaration may be excluded on proper objection, when offered, if there is opportunity for such objection, or, if there is not, may be stricken out on motion subsequently. The point of the matter is that the opponent of such evidence, so likely to be misused against him, is entitled to such protection against its misuse as can reasonably be given him without impairing the ability of the other party to prove his case, or depriving him of the use of competent evidence reasonably necessary for that purpose.

The question, then, in the present case in connection with the evidence of declarations of the wife reduces itself to a question as to whether the defendant was properly protected from the danger of this evidence being misused by the jury, and considered by them as proof of matters other than that for proving which it was admitted. We think that there can be no doubt but that the defendant was not properly protected in this respect. * * *

[The court holds that the instruction of the trial court was inadequate, and the judgment is reversed.]

HYPOTHETICALS

(1) On seeing Buzzy sitting in the ball park, Declarant said "I believe that's the man I saw running out of the bank." Declarant's statement is offered at trial to prove that Buzzy robbed the bank. Objection, hearsay. What result?

(2) To show Declarant's insanity, proponent offers testimony that Declarant said "I believe I am Napoleon." Objection, hearsay. What result?

(3) Declarant said of his older cousin, "I believe he's as sharp as he ever was." The statement is offered at trial to show that the older cousin was mentally competent at the time of the statement. Objection, hearsay. What result?

(4) Declarant wrote to his older cousin, "Please talk to my daughter Fuzzy, she's fallen in love with day trading and is going to lose all her money." The statement is offered at trial to show that the older cousin was mentally competent at the time. What result?

(5) Declarant has three children and one niece. On Day 5, Declarant allegedly gave the Eustace Diamonds to her niece. On Day 20, she died. Declarant's children claim the diamonds, saying that it would be unnatural for a mother to give a $100,000 diamond necklace to her niece instead of her children. They claim that the transfer was a loan, not a gift.

(a) Evidence is offered that on Day 1, Declarant said, "I love my niece more than my children." Objection, hearsay. What result?

(b) Evidence is offered that on Day 10, Declarant said, "I love my niece more than my children." Objection, hearsay. What result?

(c) Evidence is offered that on Day 10, Declarant said to the children at a family gathering, "I gave the Eustace Diamonds to Niece; too bad, kids!"

On the question of limited admissibility, see Federal Rules of Evidence 105; California Evidence Code § 355.

Mutual Life Insurance Co. of New York v. Hillmon

Supreme Court of the United States, 1892.
145 U.S. 285, 12 S.Ct. 909, 36 L.Ed. 706.

[Actions by Sallie E. Hillmon against two insurance companies to recover on policies on the life of her husband, John W. Hillmon. The chief issue was whether a body found at Crooked Creek was that of the insured Hillmon or, as contended by defendants, that of one Walters. To show that the body was that of Walters, defendants offered in evidence letters from Walters to his sister and fiance which expressed his intention to leave Wichita and go with Hillmon to Colorado, where Crooked Creek is located. The trial court rejected these letters. (For an interesting account of the history of this protracted litigation, involving the ouster during the Populist movement of three insurance companies from Kansas, see Wigmore, Problems of Judicial Proof, pp. 856–896 (1913))—Ed.]

MR. JUSTICE GRAY, after holding for the court that there had been a procedural error, continued:

There is, however, one question of evidence so important, so fully argued at the bar, and so likely to arise upon another trial, that it is proper to express an opinion upon it.

This question is of the admissibility of the letters written by Walters on the first days of March, 1879, which were offered in evidence by the defendants, and excluded by the court. In order to determine the competency of these letters, it is important to consider the state of the case when they were offered to be read.

The matter chiefly contested at the trial was the death of John W. Hillmon, the insured; and that depended upon the question whether the body found at Crooked Creek on the night of March 18, 1879, was his body, or the body of one Walters.

Much conflicting evidence had been introduced as to the identity of the body. The plaintiff had also introduced evidence that Hillmon and one Brown left Wichita in Kansas on or about March 5, 1879, and travelled together through Southern Kansas in search of a site for a cattle ranch, and that on the night of March 18, while they were in camp at Crooked Creek, Hillmon was accidentally killed, and that his body was taken thence and buried. The defendants had introduced evidence, without objection, that Walters left his home and his betrothed in Iowa in March, 1878, and was afterwards in Kansas until March, 1879; that during that time he corresponded regularly with his family and his betrothed; that the last letters received from him were one received by his betrothed on March 3 and postmarked at Wichita March 2, and one received by his sister about March 4 or 5, and dated at Wichita a day or two before; and that he had not been heard from since.

The evidence that Walters was at Wichita on or before March 5, and had not been heard from since, together with the evidence to identify as his the body found at Crooked Creek on March 18, tended to show that he went from Wichita to Crooked Creek between those dates. Evidence that just before March 5 he had the intention of leaving Wichita with Hillmon would tend to corroborate the evidence already admitted, and to show that he went from Wichita to Crooked Creek with Hillmon. Letters from him to his family and his betrothed were the natural, if not the only attainable, evidence of his intention.

not a memo exception

The position, taken at the bar, that the letters were competent evidence, within the rule stated in Nicholls v. Webb, as memoranda made in the ordinary course of business, cannot be maintained, for they were clearly not such.

But upon another ground suggested they should have been admitted. A man's state of mind or feeling can only be manifested to others by countenance, attitude or gesture, or by sounds or words, spoken or written. The nature of the fact to be proved is the same, and evidence of its proper tokens is equally competent to prove it, whether expressed by aspect or conduct, by voice or pen. When the intention to be proved is important only as qualifying an act, its connection with that act must be shown, in order to warrant the admission of declarations of the intention. But whenever the intention is of itself a distinct and material fact in a chain of circumstances, it may be proved by contemporaneous oral or written declarations of the party.

The existence of a particular intention in a certain person at a certain time being a material fact to be proved, evidence that he expressed that intention at that time is as direct evidence of the fact, as his own testimony that he then had that intention would be. After his death there can hardly be any other way of proving it; and while he is still alive, his own memory of his state of mind at a former time is no more likely to be clear and true than a bystander's recollection of what he then said, and is less trustworthy than letters written by him at the very time and under circumstances precluding a suspicion of misrepresentation.

The letters in question were competent, not as narratives of facts communicated to the writer by others, nor yet as proof that he actually went away from Wichita, but as evidence that, shortly before the time when other evidence tended to show that he went away, he had the intention of going, and of going with Hillmon, which made it more probable both that he did go and that he went with Hillmon, than if there had been no proof of such intention. In view of the mass of conflicting testimony introduced upon the question whether it was the body of Walters that was found in Hillmon's camp, this evidence might properly influence the jury in determining that question.

The rule applicable to this case has been thus stated by this court: "Wherever the bodily or mental feelings of an individual are material to be proved, the usual expressions of such feelings are original and competent evidence. Those expressions are the natural reflexes of what it might be impossible to show by other testimony. If there be such other testimony, this may be necessary to set the facts thus developed in their true light, and to give them their proper effect. As independent explanatory or corroborative evidence, it is often indispensable to the due administration of justice. Such declarations are regarded as verbal acts, and are as competent as any other testimony, when relevant to the issue. Their truth or falsity is an inquiry for the jury."

* * *

Upon principle and authority, therefore, we are of opinion that the two letters were competent evidence of the intention of Walters at the time of writing them, which was a material fact bearing upon the question in controversy; and that for the exclusion of these letters, as well as for the undue restriction of the defendants' challenges, the verdicts must be set aside, and a new trial had.

As the verdicts and judgments were several, the writ of error sued out by the defendants jointly was superfluous, and may be dismissed without costs; and upon each of the writs of error sued out by the defendants severally the order will be:

Judgment reversed, and case remanded to the Circuit Court, with directions to set aside the verdict and to order a new trial.

Shepard v. United States

Supreme Court of the United States, 1933.
290 U.S. 96, 54 S.Ct. 22, 78 L.Ed. 196.

■ MR. JUSTICE CARDOZO delivered the opinion of the Court.

The petitioner, Charles A. Shepard, a major in the medical corps of the United States army, has been convicted of the murder of his wife, Zenana Shepard, at Fort Riley, Kansas, a United States military reservation. The jury having qualified their verdict by adding thereto the words "without capital punishment" (18 U.S.C. § 567), the defendant was sentenced to imprisonment for life. The judgment of the United States District Court has been affirmed by the Circuit Court of Appeals for the Tenth Circuit, one of the judges of that court dissenting. A writ of certiorari brings the case here.

The crime is charged to have been committed by poisoning the victim with bichloride of mercury. The defendant was in love with another woman, and wished to make her his wife. There is circumstantial evidence to sustain a finding by the jury that to win himself his freedom he turned to poison and murder. Even so, guilt was contested and conflicting inferences are possible. The defendant asks us to hold that by the acceptance of incompetent evidence the scales were weighted to his prejudice and in the end to his undoing.

The evidence complained of was offered by the Government in rebuttal when the trial was nearly over. On May 22, 1929, there was a conversation in the absence of the defendant between Mrs. Shepard, then ill in bed, and

Clara Brown, her nurse. The patient asked the nurse to go to the closet in the defendant's room and bring a bottle of whisky that would be found upon a shelf. When the bottle was produced, she said that this was the liquor she had taken just before collapsing. She asked whether enough was left to make a test for the presence of poison, insisting that the smell and taste were strange. And then she added the words "Dr. Shepard has poisoned me."

The conversation was proved twice. After the first proof of it, the Government asked to strike it out, being doubtful of its competence, and this request was granted. A little later, however, the offer was renewed, the nurse having then testified to statements by Mrs. Shepard as to the prospect of recovery. "She said she was not going to get well; she was going to die." With the aid of this new evidence, the conversation already summarized was proved a second time. There was a timely challenge of the ruling.

She said, "Dr. Shepard has poisoned me." The admission of this declaration, if erroneous, was more than unsubstantial error * * * [The court held that the statement was not admissible under the dying declaration exception to the hearsay rule. The declarant had seemed to be on the road to recovery at the time she made the statement.]

We pass to the question whether the statements to the nurse, though incompetent as dying declarations, were admissible on other grounds.

The Circuit Court of Appeals determined that they were. Witnesses for the defendant had testified to declarations by Mrs. Shepard which suggested a mind bent upon suicide, or at any rate were thought by the defendant to carry that suggestion. More than once before her illness she had stated in the hearing of these witnesses that she had no wish to live; and had nothing to live for, and on one occasion she added that she expected some day to make an end to her life. This testimony opened the door, so it is argued, to declarations in rebuttal that she had been poisoned by her husband. They were admissible, in that view, not as evidence of the truth of what was said, but as betokening a state of mind inconsistent with the presence of suicidal intent.

(a) The testimony was neither offered nor received for the strained and narrow purpose now suggested as legitimate. It was offered and received as proof of a dying declaration. What was said by Mrs. Shepard lying ill upon her deathbed was to be weighed as if a like statement had been made upon the stand. The course of the trial makes this an inescapable conclusion. The Government withdrew the testimony when it was unaccompanied by proof that the declarant expected to die. Only when proof of her expectation had been supplied was the offer renewed and the testimony received again. For the reasons already considered, the proof was inadequate to show a consciousness of impending death and the abandonment of hope; but inadequate though it was, there can be no doubt of the purpose that it was understood to serve. There is no disguise of that purpose by counsel for the Government. They concede in all candor that Mrs. Shepard's accusation of her husband, when it was finally let in, was received upon the footing of a dying declaration, and not merely as indicative of the persistence of a will to live. Beyond question the jury considered it for the broader purpose, as the court intended that they should. A different situation would be here if we could fairly say in the light of the whole record that the purpose had been left at large, without identifying token. There would then be room for argument, that demand should have been made for an explanatory ruling. Here the course of the trial put the defendant off his guard. The testimony was received by the trial judge and offered by the Government with the plain understanding that it was to be used for an illegitimate purpose, gravely prejudicial. A trial becomes unfair if testimony thus accepted may be used in an appellate court as though admitted for a different purpose, unavowed and unsuspected. Such at all events is the result when the purpose in reserve is so obscure and artificial that it would be unlikely to occur to the minds of uninstructed jurors, and even if it did, would be swallowed up and lost in the one that was disclosed.

(b) Aside, however, from this objection, the accusatory declaration must have been rejected as evidence of a state of mind, though the purpose thus to limit it had been brought to light upon the trial. The defendant had tried to show by Mrs. Shepard's declarations to her friends that she had exhibited a weariness of life and a readiness to end it, the testimony giving plausibility to the hypothesis of suicide. By the proof of these declarations evincing an unhappy state of mind the defendant opened the door to the offer by the Government of declarations evincing a different state of mind, declarations consistent with the persistence of a will to live. The defendant would have no grievance if the testimony in rebuttal had been narrowed to that point. What the Government put in evidence, however, was something very different. It did not use the declarations by Mrs. Shepard to prove her present thoughts and feelings, or even her thoughts and feelings in times past. It used the declarations as proof of an act committed by some one else, as evidence that she was dying of poison given by her husband. This fact, if fact it was, the Government was free to prove, but not by hearsay declarations. It will not do to say that the jury might accept the declarations for any light that they cast upon the existence of a vital urge, and reject them to the extent that they charged the death to some one else. (Discrimination so subtle is a feat beyond the compass of ordinary minds.) The reverberating clang of those accusatory words would drown all weaker sounds. It is for ordinary minds, and not for psychoanalysts, that our rules of evidence are framed. They have their source very often in considerations of administrative convenience, of practical expediency, and not in rules of logic. When the risk of confusion is so great as to upset the balance of advantage, the evidence goes out. Thayer, Preliminary Treatise on the Law of Evidence, 266, 516; Wigmore, Evidence, §§ 1421, 1422, 1714.

These precepts of caution are a guide to judgment here. There are times when a state of mind, if relevant, may be proved by contemporaneous declarations of feeling or intent. Mutual Life Ins. Co. v. Hillmon. Thus, in proceedings for the probate of a will, where the issue is undue influence, the declarations of a testator are competent to prove his feelings for his relatives, but are incompetent as evidence of his conduct or of theirs. In suits for the alienation of affections, letters passing between the spouses are admissible in aid of a like purpose. * * * In damage suits for personal injuries, declarations by the patient to bystanders or physicians are evidence of sufferings or symptoms (Wigmore, §§ 1718, 1719), but are not received to prove the acts, the external circumstances, through which the injuries came about. * * * Even statements of past sufferings or symptoms are generally excluded, (Wigmore, § 1722[b]); though an exception is at times allowed when they are made to a physician. * * * So also in suits upon insurance policies, declarations by an insured that he intends to go upon a journey with another, may be evidence of a state of mind lending probability to the conclusion that the purpose was fulfilled. Mutual Life Ins. Co. v. Hillmon, supra. The ruling in that case marks the high water line beyond which courts have been unwilling to go. It has developed a substantial body of criticism and commentary.[*] Declarations of intention, casting light upon the future, have been sharply distinguished from declarations of memory, pointing backwards to the past. There would be an end, or nearly that, to the rule against hearsay if the distinction were ignored.

The testimony now questioned faced backward and not forward. This at least it did in its most obvious implications. What is even more important, it spoke to a past act, and more than that, to an act by some one not the speaker. Other tendency, if it had any, was a filament too fine to be disentangled by a jury.

The judgment should be reversed and the case remanded to the District Court for further proceedings in accordance with this opinion.

Reversed.

QUESTION

Was Mrs. Shepard's statement testimonial within the meaning of *Crawford*?

HYPOTHETICALS ON STATEMENTS BY HOMICIDE VICTIMS

A. Buzzy is being prosecuted for murder. The state offers testimony about a statement that the victim made before the victim's death.

1. The defense is accident. Buzzy claims he and the victim were cleaning Buzzy's hunting rifles when a rifle accidentally discharged, killing the victim. What arguments could the prosecutor make in favor of admitting the following statements?

     a. the victim told a friend, "I hate Buzzy."

     b. the victim told a friend, "Buzzy has been stalking me. He threatened to kill me."

---

[*] Maguire, The Hillmon Case, 38 Harv.L.Rev., 709, 721, 727; Seligman, An Exception to the Hearsay Rule, 26 Harv.L.Rev. 146; Chafee, Review of Wigmore's Treatise, 37 Harv.L.Rev., 513, 519.

2. The defense is self-defense. Buzzy claims that the victim attacked first. What arguments could the prosecutor make in favor of admitting the following statements?

    a. the victim told a friend, "I'm afraid of Buzzy."

    b. the victim told a friend, "Buzzy has been stalking me. He threatened to kill me."

B. Suppose Buzzy is charged with murder and the defense is identity. Buzzy claims that he was not involved in the crime at all and in fact did not even know the victim. The state offers testimony by a friend of the victim that on the day the victim was murdered, the victim said to the friend, "Buzzy is after me because I ripped him off. If I don't come back this afternoon call the police and tell them that Buzzy has me. I don't know his last name but here's his phone number." The victim then gave the friend a note that said, "Buzzy, 658–2789."

C. In one of the most famous trials of the late 20th century, O.J. Simpson was charged with the murder of Nicole Brown, who was his estranged wife, and a friend of hers who apparently happened on the scene. In an *in limine* ruling, the trial judge excluded evidence of certain statements by Brown, including one in which she allegedly told a friend that Simpson was following her and that she believed he was going to kill her (Ruling of Jan. 18, 1995, 1995 WL 21768, *4 (Cal.Super.Doc.)). Should the evidence have been admitted? Would it have made any difference if prosecution witnesses testified that Brown enraged the defendant on the night of the murder by rebuffing him at their daughter's dance recital, and the defendant testified that the couple's interaction at the dance recital was amicable and uneventful? Would it have made any difference if the defense had said, in its opening statement, that Brown and Simpson had a warm relationship even after their separation? See Rufo v. Simpson, 103 Cal.Rptr.2d 492 (2d Dist. Cal. 2001) (affirming permissive evidence rulings on appeal of civil wrongful death verdict against Simpson).

United States v. Pheaster

United States Court of Appeals, Ninth Circuit, 1976.
544 F.2d 353.

■ RENFREW, DISTRICT JUDGE:

I. FACTS

This case arises from the disappearance of Larry Adell, the 16-year-old son of Palm Springs multi-millionaire Robert Adell. At approximately 9:30 P.M. on June 1, 1974, Larry Adell left a group of his high school friends in a Palm Springs restaurant known as Sambo's North. He walked into the parking lot of the restaurant with the expressed intention of meeting a man named Angelo who was supposed to deliver a pound of free marijuana. Larry never returned to his friends in the restaurant that evening, and his family never saw him thereafter.

The long, agonizing, and ultimately unsuccessful effort to find Larry began shortly after his disappearance. At about 2:30 A.M. on June 2, 1974,

Larry's father was telephoned by a male caller who told him that his son was being held and that further instructions would be left in Larry's car in the parking lot of Sambo's North. Those instructions included a demand for a ransom of $400,000 for the release of Larry. [For a variety of reasons, and despite numerous attempts, the ransom was never delivered.]

When it appeared that further efforts to communicate with the kidnappers would be futile, the F.B.I. arrested appellants, who had been under surveillance for some time, in a coordinated operation on July 14, 1974.

* * *

Admissibility of Hearsay Testimony Concerning Statements of Larry Adell

Appellant Inciso argues that the district court erred in admitting hearsay testimony by two teenaged friends of Larry Adell concerning statements made by Larry on June 1, 1974, the day that he disappeared. Timely objections were made to the questions which elicited the testimony on the ground that the questions called for hearsay. In response, the Government attorney stated that the testimony was offered for the limited purpose of showing the "state of mind of Larry". After instructing the jury that it could only consider the testimony for that limited purpose and not for "the truth or falsity of what [Larry] said", the district court allowed the witnesses to answer the questions. Francine Gomes, Larry's date on the evening that he disappeared, testified that when Larry picked her up that evening, he told her that he was going to meet Angelo at Sambo's North at 9:30 P.M. to "pick up a pound of marijuana which Angelo had promised him for free". * * * She also testified that she had been with Larry on another occasion when he met a man named Angelo, and she identified the defendant as that man. Miss Gomes stated that it was approximately 9:15 P.M. when Larry went into the parking lot. Doug Sendejas, one of Larry's friends who was with him at Sambo's North just prior to his disappearance, testified that Larry had made similar statements to him in the afternoon and early evening of June 1st regarding a meeting that evening with Angelo. Mr. Sendejas also testified that when Larry left the table at Sambo's North to go into the parking lot, Larry stated that "he was going to meet Angelo and he'd be right back." * * *

Inciso's contention that the district court erred in admitting the hearsay testimony of Larry's friends is premised on the view that the statements could not properly be used by the jury to conclude that Larry did in fact meet Inciso in the parking lot of Sambo's North at approximately 9:30 P.M. on June 1, 1974. The correctness of that assumption is, in our view, the key to the analysis of this contention of error. The Government argues that Larry's statements were relevant to two issues in the case. First the statements are said to be relevant to an issue created by the defense when Inciso's attorney attempted to show that Larry had not been kidnapped but had disappeared voluntarily as part of a simulated kidnapping designed to extort money from his wealthy father from whom he was allegedly estranged. In his brief on appeal, Inciso concedes the relevance and, presumably, the admissibility of the statements to "show that Larry did not voluntarily disappear." However, Inciso argues that for this limited purpose, there was no need to name the person with whom Larry intended to meet, and that the district court's limiting instruction was insufficient to overcome the prejudice to which he was exposed by the testimony. Second, the Government argues that the statements are relevant and admissible to show that, as intended, Larry did meet Inciso in the parking lot at Sambo's North on the evening of June 1, 1974. If the Government's second theory of admissibility is successful, Inciso's arguments regarding the excision of his name from the statements admitted under the first theory is obviously mooted.

In determining the admissibility of the disputed evidence, we apply the standard of Rule 26 of the Federal Rules of Criminal Procedure which governed at the time of the trial below.* Under that standard, the District Court was required to decide issues concerning the "admissibility of evidence" according to the "principles of the common law as they may be interpreted by the courts of the United States in the light of reason and experience."

The Government's position that Larry Adell's statements can be used to prove that the meeting with Inciso did occur raises a difficult and important question concerning the scope of the so-called "*Hillmon* doctrine", a particular species of the "state of mind" exception to the general rule that hearsay evidence is inadmissible. The doctrine takes its name from the famous Supreme Court decision in Mutual Life Ins. Co. v. Hillmon, 145 U.S. 285 (1892). That the *Hillmon* doctrine should create controversy and confusion is not surprising, for it is an extraordinary doctrine. Under the state of mind exception, hearsay evidence is admissible if it bears on the state of mind of the declarant and if that state of mind is an issue in the case. For example, statements by a testator which demonstrate that he had the necessary testamentary intent are admissible to show that intent when it is in issue. The exception embodied in the *Hillmon* doctrine is fundamentally different, because it does not require that the state of mind of the declarant be an actual issue in the case. Instead, under the *Hillmon* doctrine the state of mind of the declarant is used inferentially to prove other matters which are in issue. Stated simply, the doctrine provides that when the performance of a particular act by an individual is an issue in a case, his intention (state of mind) to perform that act may be shown. From that intention, the trier of fact may draw the inference that the person carried out his intention and performed the act. Within this conceptual framework, hearsay evidence of statements by the person which tend to show his intention is deemed admissible under the state of mind exception. Inciso's objection to the doctrine concerns its application in situations in which the declarant has stated his intention to do something *with another person*, and the issue is whether he did so. There can be no doubt, that the theory of the *Hillmon* doctrine is different when the declarant's statement of intention necessarily requires the action of one or more others if it is to be fulfilled.

---

* The trial was held before the effective date of the Federal Rules of Evidence (Eds.).

* * *

The *Hillmon* doctrine has been applied by the California Supreme Court in People v. Alcalde, 24 Cal.2d 177, 148 P.2d 627 (1944). * * * In *Alcalde* the defendant was tried and convicted of first degree murder for the brutal slaying of a woman whom he had been seeing socially. One of the issues before the California Supreme Court was the asserted error by the trial court in allowing the introduction of certain hearsay testimony concerning statements made by the victim on the day of her murder. As in the instant case, the testimony was highly incriminating, because the victim reportedly said that she was going out with Frank, the defendant, on the evening she was murdered. On appeal, a majority of the California Supreme Court affirmed the defendant's conviction, holding that *Hillmon* was "the leading case on the admissibility of declarations of intent to do an act as proof that the act thereafter was accomplished."

* * *

* * * The court found no error in the trial court's admission of the disputed hearsay testimony. "Unquestionably the deceased's statement of her intent and the logical inference to be drawn therefrom, namely, that she was with the defendant that night, were relevant to the issue of the guilt of the defendant."

* * *

In addition to the decisions in *Hillmon* and *Alcalde*, support for the Government's position can be found in the California Evidence Code and the new Federal Rules of Evidence, although in each instance resort must be made to the comments to the relevant provisions.

Section 1250 of the California Evidence Code carves out an exception to the general hearsay rule for statements of a declarant's "then existing mental or physical state". The *Hillmon* doctrine is codified in Section 1250(2) which allows the use of such hearsay evidence when it "is offered to prove or explain acts or conduct of the declarant." The comment to Section 1250(2) states that, "Thus, a statement of the declarant's intent to do certain acts is admissible to prove that he did those acts." Although neither the language of the statute nor that of the comment specifically addresses the particular issue now before us, the comment does cite the *Alcalde* decision and, therefore, indirectly rejects the limitation urged by Inciso.

* * * Rule 803(3) provides an exemption from the hearsay rule for the following evidence:

"*Then existing mental, emotional, or physical condition.* A statement of the declarant's then existing state of mind, emotion, sensation, or physical condition (such as intent, plan, motive, design, mental feeling, pain, and bodily health), but not including a statement of memory or belief to prove the fact remembered or believed unless it relates to the execution, revocation, identification, or terms of declarant's will."

Although Rule 803(3) is silent regarding the *Hillmon* doctrine, both the Advisory Committee on the Proposed Rules and the House Committee on the Judiciary specifically addressed the doctrine. After noting that Rule 803(3) would not allow the admission of statements of memory, the Advisory Committee stated broadly that

> "The rule of Mutual Life Ins. Co. v. Hillmon [citation omitted] allowing evidence of intention as tending to prove the doing of the act intended, is, of course, left undisturbed." Note to Paragraph (3), 28 U.S.C.A. at 585.

Significantly, the Notes of the House Committee on the Judiciary regarding Rule 803(3) are far more specific and revealing:

> "However, the Committee intends that the Rule be construed to limit the doctrine of Mutual Life Insurance Co. v. Hillmon [citation omitted] so as to render statements of intent by a declarant admissible *only to prove his future conduct, not the future conduct of another person.*" House Report No. 93–650, Note to Paragraph (3), 28 U.S.C.A. at 579 (emphasis added).

Although the matter is certainly not free from doubt, we read the note of the Advisory Committee as presuming that the *Hillmon* doctrine would be incorporated in full force, including necessarily the application in *Hillmon* itself. The language suggests that the Advisory Committee presumed that such a broad interpretation was the prevailing common law position. The notes of the House Committee on the Judiciary are significantly different. The language used there suggests a legislative intention to cut back on what that body also perceived to be the prevailing common law view, namely, that the *Hillmon* doctrine could be applied to facts such as those now before us.

Although we recognize the force of the objection to the application of the *Hillmon* doctrine in the instant case,[18] we cannot conclude that the dis-

---

[18] Criticism of the *Hillmon* doctrine has come from very distinguished quarters, both judicial and academic. However, the position of the judicial critics is definitely the minority position, stated primarily in dicta and dissent.

In his opinion for the Court in *Shepard v. United States*, Justice Cardozo indicated in dicta an apparent hostility to the *Hillmon* doctrine. *Shepard* involved hearsay testimony of a dramatically different character from that in the instant case. The Court reviewed the conviction of an army medical officer for the murder of his wife by poison. The asserted error by the trial court was its admission, over defense objection, of certain hearsay testimony by Mrs. Shepard's nurse concerning statements that Mrs. Shepard had made during her final illness. The nurse's testimony was that, after asking whether there was enough whiskey left in the bottle from which she had drunk just prior to her collapse to make a test for poison, Mrs. Shepard stated, "Dr. Shepard has poisoned me." One theory advanced by the Government on appeal was that the testimony was admissible to show that Mrs. Shepard did not have suicidal tendencies and, thus, to refute the defense argument that she took her own life. The Court rejected that theory, holding that the testimony had not been admitted for the limited purpose suggested by the Government and that, even if it had been admitted for that purpose, its relevance was far outweighed by the extreme prejudice it would create for the defendant. In rejecting the Government's theory, the Court refused to "extend the state of mind exception to statements of memory." In his survey of the state of mind exception, Justice Cardozo appeared to suggest the *Hillmon* doctrine is limited to "suits upon insurance policies", although the cases cited by the Court in *Hillmon* refute that suggestion.

trict court erred in allowing the testimony concerning Larry Adell's statements to be introduced.

* * *

[Judgment affirmed.]

[Concurring and dissenting opinion omitted.]

QUESTION

Was Larry's statement testimonial within the meaning of *Crawford*?

HYPOTHETICALS

Let us assume that the issue is, "Was the declarant with Angelo that night?" Examine the following hypothetical statements made by the declarant the previous evening:

a. "I am going to the parking lot at Sambo's North tonight." (Other evidence shows that Angelo went there that night).

b. "Angelo is going to the parking lot at Sambo's North tonight." (Other evidence shows that the declarant went there that night).

c. "I am going to Angelo's apartment tonight."

d. "I will not go out with anyone other than Angelo tonight." (Other evidence showing that he went out with someone.)

The decision in *Shepard* was relied upon by Justice Traynor of the California Supreme Court in his vigorous dissent from the decision reached by the majority in *People v. Alcalde*. Justice Traynor argued that the victim's declarations regarding her meeting with Frank could not be used to "induce the belief that the defendant went out with the deceased, took her to the scene of the crime and there murdered her * * * without setting aside the rule against hearsay." Any other legitimate use of the declaration, in his opinion, was so insignificant that it was outweighed by the enormous prejudice to the defendant in allowing the jury to hear it.

Finally, the exhaustive analysis of a different, but related, hearsay issue by the Court of Appeals for the District of Columbia in *United States v. Brown*, provides inferential support for the position urged by Inciso. The issue in that case was the admissibility of hearsay testimony concerning a victim's extrajudicial declarations that he was "[f]rightened that he may be killed" by the defendant. After surveying the relevant cases, the court stated a "synthesis" of the governing principles. One of the cases which was criticized by the court was the decision of the California Supreme Court in *People v. Merkouris*, a case relied upon by the Government in the instant case. The court in Merkouris held that hearsay testimony showing the victim's fear of the defendant could properly be admitted to show the probable identity of the killer. The court in Brown expressed the following criticism of that holding, a criticism which might also apply to the application of the *Hillmon* doctrine in the instant case:

"Such an approach violates the fundamental safeguards necessary to the use of such testimony [citation omitted]. Through a circuitous series of inferences, the court reverses the effect of the statement so as to reflect on *defendant's* intent and actions rather than the state of mind of the declarant (victim). This is the very result that it is hoped the limiting instruction will prevent." 490 P.2d at 771 (emphasis in original).

For a frequently cited academic critique of the Hillmon doctrine, see Maguire, *The Hillmon Case—Thirty-Three Years After*, 38 Harv.L.Rev. 709 (1925).

e. "I am going to wait at home for Angelo until he picks me up and we will go out." (Other evidence shows that the declarant left his apartment that night).

f. "I am going out to meet Angelo in the parking lot at Sambo's tonight."

See Federal Rules of Evidence 803(3); California Evidence Code § 1250.

Zippo Manufacturing Co. v. Rogers Imports, Inc.

United States District Court, Southern District of New York, 1963.
216 F.Supp. 670.

■ FEINBERG, DISTRICT JUDGE. This case involves the attempt of a manufacturer of a popular cigarette lighter to keep others from imitating the lighter's shape and appearance. Plaintiff Zippo Manufacturing Company ("Zippo"), a Pennsylvania corporation, alleges both trademark infringement and unfair competition on the part of defendant Rogers, Inc.[1] ("Rogers"), a New York corporation by reason of Rogers' sale of pocket lighters closely resembling Zippo's. Plaintiff seeks injunctive relief, an accounting, and damages. * * *

Plaintiff Zippo has been primarily engaged in the manufacture of pocket lighters since 1932, and it has grown spectacularly over the years. Its annual national sales of these lighters grew from about 27,000 units in 1934 to over 3,180,00 in 1958, the year just prior to suit, and well over 4,000,000 in 1961. Today, Zippo produces more units than any other domestic lighter manufacturer. Its pocket lighters are made in two models, the "standard" and the "slim-lighter." The latter accounts for slightly less than twenty-five per cent of the number of pocket lighters sold by Zippo. * * *

After Rogers commenced marketing its allegedly offending lighters in 1957, Zippo began receiving Rogers lighters from consumers who wished to have them repaired through Zippo's free repair policy. At the time of trial, a total of 191 Rogers lighters had been received by Zippo in this manner. Zippo's policy was to return the lighter to the person from whom it was received, together with a form letter stating that the lighter was not a Zippo product, and, therefore, the company would not repair it. * * *

Plaintiff's unfair competition action will be considered first * * *

* * * [P]laintiff can obtain relief only if it meets its burden of proving that:

(1) Defendant's lighter copies plaintiff's lighter;

(2) A copied feature has acquired a special significance in the market identifying plaintiff as the source of the lighter, and that pur-

---

[1] Defendant was formerly known as Rogers Imports, Inc.

chasers are moved in any degree to buy the lighter because of its source ("secondary meaning");

(3) Such copied feature in defendant's lighter is likely to cause prospective purchasers to regard the lighter as coming from plaintiff;

(4) Such copied feature is nonfunctional. It should be noted, however, that even if the copied feature is functional, plaintiff may still be entitled to relief if defendant has not taken reasonable steps to set its lighter apart from plaintiff's in the public mind. * * *

Plaintiff has relied heavily on a consumer study to prove the elements of its case. This study was prepared and conducted by the sampling and market research firm of W.R. Simmons & Associates Research, Inc. Mr. Simmons, the head of this firm, and Donald F. Bowdren, the project supervisor, appeared as witnesses; both are qualified experts in the field of consumer surveys. Mr. Bowdren testified that the purpose of the study was to determine whether the physical attributes of the Zippo standard and slim-lighters serve as indicators of the source of the lighters to potential customers and whether the similar physical attributes of the Rogers lighters cause public confusion. The study or project consisted of three separate surveys. In Survey A, the respondents, or interviewees, were shown a Zippo standard lighter which had all the Zippo identification markings removed and were asked, among other things, what brand of lighter they thought it was and why. In Survey B, the same procedure was followed for the Zippo slim-lighter. In Survey C, respondents were shown a Rogers standard lighter that was being sold at the time of the survey, with all of its identifying markings, and they were asked, among other things, what brand of lighter they thought it was and why.

Mr. Simmons' testimony and the project report made clear the principles and procedures by which the surveys were conceived and conducted. Testimony to this effect is important, because it is well settled that the weight to be given a survey, assuming it is admissible, depends on the procedures by which the survey was created and conducted. * * *

There was no overlapping of respondents in the three surveys so that no one respondent would be influenced in one survey by his answers to another survey. The developmental phase of the project involved preparation of questions that could be handled properly by an interviewer, correctly understood by respondents and easily answered by them. This required several drafts of questionnaires and some pretesting. The "universe" to be studied consisted of all smokers aged eighteen years and older residing in the continental United States, which the research project indicated was approximately 115,000,000 ("the smoking population"). All percentage results in the surveys represent projected percentages of the smoking population.

The three separate surveys were conducted across a national probability sample of smokers, with a sample size of approximately 500 for each survey. The samples were chosen on the basis of data obtained from the

Bureau of Census by a procedure which started with the selection of fifty-three localities (metropolitan areas and non-metropolitan counties), and proceeded to a selection of 100 clusters within each of these localities—each cluster consisting of about 150–250 dwelling units—and then to approximately 500 respondents within the clusters. The manner of arriving at these clusters and respondents within each cluster was described in detail. The entire procedure was designed to obtain a representative sample of all smoking adults in the country. The procedures used to avoid sampling error and errors arising from other sources, the methods of processing, the instructions for the interviewers, and the approximate tolerance limits for a sample base of 500 were also described. Two of the interviewers testified that they were experienced in interviewing, explained the manner in which the interviews were conducted, and stated that they did not know the purpose of the surveys. All of the original responses to the questions as reported by these interviewers were made available in court.

Plaintiff also called Dr. Robert C. Sorensen as an expert in the field of survey research.[2] Dr. Sorensen stated that the project was conducted objectively and scientifically. Defendant does not deny this generally, but points to specific procedures and questions as being improper and buttresses its arguments with the testimony of its own expert, Professor Charles Winick.

Defendant objects to the admission of the surveys into evidence. It first contends that the surveys are hearsay. The weight of case authority, the consensus of legal writers, and reasoned policy considerations all indicate that the hearsay rule should not bar the admission of properly conducted public surveys. Although courts were at first reluctant to accept survey evidence or to give it weight, the more recent trend is clearly contrary. Surveys are now admitted over the hearsay objection on two technically distinct bases. Some cases hold that surveys are not hearsay at all; other cases hold that surveys are hearsay but are admissible because they are within the recognized exception to the hearsay rule for statements of present state of mind, attitude, or belief. Still other cases admit surveys without stating the ground on which they are admitted.

public survey

The cases holding that surveys are not hearsay do so on the basis that the surveys are not offered to prove the truth of what respondents said and, therefore, do not fall within the classic definition of hearsay. This approach has been criticized because, it is said, the answers to questions in a survey designed to prove the existence of a specific idea in the public mind are offered to prove the truth of the matter contained in these answers. Under this argument, when a respondent is asked to identify the brand of an unmarked lighter, the answer of each respondent who thinks the lighter is a Zippo is regarded as if he said, "I believe that this unmarked lighter is a Zippo." Since the matter to be proved in a secondary meaning case is respondent's belief that the lighter shown him is a Zippo lighter, a respondent's answer is hearsay in the classic sense. Others have criticized the non-hearsay characterization, regardless of whether surveys are offered to

---

[2] Dr. Sorensen is the co-author, *inter alia*, of R.C. Sorensen & T.C. Sorensen, The Admissibility and Use of Opinion Research Evidence, 28 N.Y.U.L.Rev. 1213 (1953).

prove the truth of what respondents said because the answers in a survey depend for their probative value on the sincerity of respondents. One of the purposes of the hearsay rule is to subject to cross-examination statements which depend on the declarant's narrative sincerity. * * * The answer of a respondent that he thinks an unmarked lighter is a Zippo is relevant to the issue of secondary meaning only if, in fact, the respondent really does believe that the unmarked lighter is a Zippo. Under this view, therefore, answers in a survey should be regarded as hearsay.

Regardless of whether the surveys in this case could be admitted under the non-hearsay approach, they are admissible because the answers of respondents are expressions of presently existing state of mind, attitude, or belief. There is a recognized exception to the hearsay rule for such statements, and under it the statements are admissible to prove the truth of the matter contained therein.

Even if the surveys did not fit within this exception, well reasoned authority justifies their admission under the following approach: the determination that a statement is hearsay does not end the inquiry into admissibility; there must still be a further examination of the need for the statement at trial and the circumstantial guaranty of trustworthiness surrounding the making of the statement. This approach has been used to justify the admissibility of a survey. Necessity in this context requires a comparison of the probative value of the survey with the evidence, if any, which as a practical matter could be used if the survey were excluded. If the survey is more valuable, then necessity exists for the survey, i.e., it is the inability to get "evidence of the same value" which makes the hearsay statement necessary. When, as here, the state of mind of the smoking population (115,000,000 people) is the issue, a scientifically conducted survey is necessary because the practical alternatives do not produce equally probative evidence. With such a survey, the results are probably approximately the same as would be obtained if each of the 115,000,000 people were interviewed. The alternative of having 115,000,000 people testify in court is obviously impractical. The alternatives of having a much smaller section of the public testify (such as eighty witnesses) or using expert witnesses to testify to the state of the public mind are clearly not as valuable because the inferences which can be drawn from such testimony to the public state of mind are not as strong or as direct as the justifiable inferences from a scientific survey.

The second element involved in this approach is the guaranty of trustworthiness supplied by the circumstances under which the out-of-court statements were made. A logical step in this inquiry is to see which of the hearsay dangers are present. With regard to these surveys: there is no danger of faulty memory; the danger of faulty perception is negligible because respondents need only examine two or three cigarette lighters at most; the danger of faulty narration is equally negligible since the answers called for are simple. The only appreciable danger is that the respondent is insincere. But this danger is minimized by the circumstances of this or any public opinion poll in which scientific sampling is employed, because members of the public who are asked questions about things in which they have no interest have no reason to falsify their feelings. While the sampling procedure substantially guarantees trustworthiness insofar as the respondent's sincerity is concerned, other survey techniques substantially insure trustworthiness in other respects. If questions are unfairly worded to suggest answers favorable to the party sponsoring the survey, the element of trustworthiness in the poll would be lacking. The same result would follow if the interviewers asked fair questions in a leading manner. Thus, the methodology of the survey bears directly on trustworthiness, as it does on necessity. Since the two elements of necessity and trustworthiness are satisfied, I would admit these surveys under this approach to the hearsay rule, even apart from the state of mind exception.[3]

Defendant's next objection to the surveys is that they should not have been conducted in respondents' homes but in stores, the actual places of purchase. While it may be that in general the store is the best place to measure the state of mind at the time of purchase, it would be virtually impossible to obtain a representative national sample if stores were used. [An interview at a respondent's home is probative of his state of mind at the time of purchase, although the deviation from the actual purchase situation should be considered in weighing the force of this evidence] Therefore, the surveys are not inadmissible merely because they were conducted in homes.

Location of survey

Defendant also objects to the surveys on the ground that they measured only the popularity of Zippo, as compared with the popularity of Rogers, and that this is not relevant to secondary meaning. However, I find that, by and large, the surveys did, as Dr. Sorenson testified, test brand identification and not brand popularity. They are, therefore, not incompetent because of the small elements of popularity which may have crept in, although that possibility should be considered in the weight to be given their results.

Defendant's next objection is to Survey C. In that survey, 34.7 per cent of respondents thought a Rogers lighter was a Zippo lighter, and plaintiff argues that this is probative of likelihood of confusion between the two lighters. However, respondents were not shown a Rogers display card when they made their mistaken identification. Therefore, defendant contends that the percentage of people who would mistakenly identify a Rogers ligh-

---

[3] Irvin v. State raises a possible objection not stressed by defendant—"multiple hearsay." The multiple hearsay argument is as follows: when answers made by respondents to interviewers are admissible under a hearsay exception, the interviewers can testify to these answers; but when the interviewers themselves do not testify but instead "tell" these answers to another person in the market research organization who then testifies as to the answers, this testimony is inadmissible hearsay because the witness is relating what the interviewers told him rather than what respondents in the survey told him. I conclude that this argument should not preclude the admission of a properly conducted survey, possibly because the business entries exception to the hearsay rule covers the transmission of the answers from the interviewers to other people in the organization, at least where the organization involved is in the business of conducting and reporting on surveys, or because considerations of necessity and trustworthiness justify an exception for the "second stage" of hearsay as well as for the original answers.

ter as a Zippo lighter would be smaller if the Rogers lighter were shown to them on a Rogers display card. This argument is probably correct. This does not mean, however, that the results of Survey C are inadmissible to prove that the appearance of the Rogers lighter is likely to confuse people into thinking that it is a Zippo lighter.

Defendant's argument is implicitly based on two assumptions: (1) that use of the Rogers display card in the interviews would have caused a great number of the respondents who thought the Rogers lighter was a Zippo lighter to give different answers; and (2) that the number left who, even after a display card was shown to them, would still confuse the Rogers lighter with a Zippo lighter would be statistically insignificant. However, these assumptions at best are too speculative to require exclusion of Survey C. Moreover, they are contradicted by other answers in Survey C, which show that about one-half of respondents who mistakenly thought that the Rogers lighter was a Zippo lighter actually saw something stamped on the bottom of the lighter (where the Rogers name was imprinted) and that over one-third of those who thought the Rogers lighter was a Zippo lighter actually saw the Rogers name stamped on the lighter. These results certainly give rise to the inference that if the Rogers display card had been shown to respondents, a significant number of people would have thought the Rogers lighter was a Zippo lighter anyway: although exposed to the display card, some would not have actually perceived the Rogers name, and others would have seen the Rogers name but would nonetheless think that the lighter was made by Zippo. Therefore, Survey C is not excluded. However, its weight on the issue of likelihood of confusion is less than it would be had a display card been used, and had the same number of respondents nonetheless identified the Rogers lighter as a Zippo lighter.

Defendant has other objections to admissibility of the surveys, e.g., that a survey is not the best way to prove secondary meaning, but none of these merit further discussion. Surveys A, B, and C were scientifically conducted by a competent and professional research firm, substantially in accordance with the recommendations of Recommended Procedures for the Trial of Protracted Cases. I conclude, therefore, that the surveys are admissible to show secondary meaning for the shape and appearance of the Zippo standard and slim-lighters and likelihood of confusion between these lighters and their Rogers counterparts.

[Judgment was rendered in accordance with the opinion]

HYPOTHETICALS

(1) P sues D for damages for wrongful death arising out of an automobile accident in which P's husband, H, was killed. P testifies that they had a warm and affectionate relationship during their five-year marriage, which ended with H's death. D calls X, a business associate of H, to testify that about six months before H's death, H said several times that he hated P and that he was very unhappy in his marriage. P makes a hearsay objection to X's testimony. What result?

(2) Assume the same facts as in Illustration (1). D proposes to have X also testify that on one occasion three months before H's death, H said: "I just can't forget that three months ago I caught P out with another man and that this has changed my love for her into hate." P makes a hearsay objection. What is the appropriate ruling?

(3) D is prosecuted for murder of B, his brother. D admits that he shot B but his defense is that the shooting was accidental. D calls PO, a police officer, to testify that several hours after the shooting he had a conversation with D in which D stated that he was just sick and grief-stricken over B's death. The prosecution makes a hearsay objection. Should the objection be sustained?

(4) X is prosecuted for the murder of A, his girl friend. A was shot to death in X's apartment. X's defense is that A was at his apartment and requested to see his gun collection, that he handed A a pistol, and that while A was examining it she dropped it and it went off, killing her. The prosecution calls B, A's girl friend, to testify that a week before the shooting A told her that she was afraid of X and was deathly afraid of guns. X makes a hearsay objection to B's proposed testimony. How should the court rule?

(5) Assume the same facts as in Illustration (4). X calls C, a friend of A, to testify that two weeks before the shooting, A told her that she was planning to go to Utah the following week and go deer hunting; that upon asking A how were things between her and X, A replied that she was very fond of X and liked to be around him. The prosecution makes a hearsay objection to C's proposed testimony. What result?

(6) Sarah is prosecuted for the murder of Sam. Sarah's defense is self-defense—that Sam was advancing on her with a knife, and that she shot him to protect herself. The prosecution calls W, a friend of Sam, to testify that on the day before the killing, Sam said to W "I am going to tell Sarah that I won't pay her the money I lost to her in that poker game. I might get killed over it but I'm going to do it." Sarah makes a hearsay objection to W's proposed testimony. How should the court rule?

4. Medical Diagnosis or Treatment

United States v. Tome

United States Court of Appeals for the Tenth Circuit, 1995
61 F.3d 1446

■ Tacha, Circuit Judge.

I. BACKGROUND

A jury convicted defendant Matthew Wayne Tome of aggravated sexual abuse * * * In his appeal to this court, defendant challenged the admissibility of the hearsay statements relayed by six witnesses. Each witness related out-of-court statements made by the child victim (A.T.). [The court previously held that the statements were admissible under Fed. R. Evid. 801(d)(1)(B) as prior consistent statements of A.T., Tome's daughter, offered to rebut the contention that she had fabricated her allegations under the influence of her mother, who was estranged from Tome, so that she would not have to live with him. The Supreme Court reversed, see p. 547, because the statements were made after the alleged motive to fabricate arose. On remand, the court had to determine whether the statements could come in under another rule of evidence.] * * *

III. DISCUSSION

A. Testimony of Karen Kuper, Laura Reich, and Jean Spiegel

We first address the testimony of three pediatricians who examined A.T. In their testimony, the three doctors relayed statements made by A.T. either before or during the doctors' physical examinations of the child. At trial, the district court admitted the doctors' hearsay testimony under both Rules 801(d)(1)(B) and 803(4).

* * * Rule 803(4) * * * makes admissible "[s]tatements made for purposes of medical diagnosis or treatment and describing medical history, or past or present symptoms, pain, or sensations, or the inception or general character of the cause or external source thereof insofar as reasonably pertinent to diagnosis or treatment." This exception is premised on the theory that a patient's statements to her physician are likely to be particularly reliable because the patient has a self-interested motive to be truthful: She knows that the efficacy of her medical treatment depends upon the accuracy of the information she provides to the doctor. *United States v. Joe,* 8 F.3d 1488, 1493 (10th Cir.1993), *cert. denied,* 510 U.S. 1184, 114 S.Ct. 1236, 127 L.Ed.2d 579 (1994). Stated differently, "a statement made in the course of procuring medical services, where the declarant knows that a false statement may cause misdiagnosis or mistreatment, carries special guarantees of credibility." *White v. Illinois,* 502 U.S. 346, 356, 112 S.Ct. 736, 743, 116 L.Ed.2d 848 (1992).

A declarant's statement to a physician that identifies the person responsible for the declarant's injuries is ordinarily inadmissible under Rule 803(4) because the assailant's identity is usually unnecessary either for accurate diagnosis or effective treatment. *Joe,* 8 F.3d at 1494. This court held in *Joe,* however, that a hearsay statement revealing the identity of a sexual abuser who is a member of the victim's family or household "is admissible under Rule 803(4) where the abuser has such an intimate relationship with the victim that the abuser's identity becomes 'reasonably pertinent' to the victim's proper treatment." In so holding, we reasoned that

> [a]ll victims of domestic sexual abuse suffer emotional and psychological injuries, the exact nature and extent of which depend on the identity of the abuser. The physician generally must know who the abuser was in order to render proper treatment because the physician's treatment will necessarily differ when the abuser is a member of the victim's family or household. In the domestic sexual abuse case, for example, the treating physician may recommend special therapy or counseling and instruct the victim to remove herself from the dangerous environment by leaving the home and seeking shelter elsewhere.

Although the victim in *Joe* was an adult, we stated that "the identity of the abuser is reasonably pertinent in virtually every domestic sexual assault case," including those in which the victim is a child. Thus, when a victim of domestic sexual abuse identifies her assailant to her physician, the physician's recounting of the identification is admissible under Rule 803(4) when it is "reasonably pertinent" to the victim's treatment or diagnosis. After reviewing the testimony of each pediatrician, we conclude that A.T.'s statements to those doctors were reasonably pertinent to her diagnosis or treatment.

1. Testimony of Karen Kuper

Kae Ecklebarger of Child Protection Services referred A.T. to Dr. Karen Kuper, a board certified pediatrician, for a physical examination. Kuper testified that she examined A.T. on two occasions, in September and October 1990. Prior to the first examination, Kuper interviewed A.T. Kuper testified that the purpose of the interview was "to ascertain exactly what injuries had occurred." In response to Kuper's questions, A.T. told Kuper about the sexual abuse, at times pointing to the appropriate areas of dolls to answer Kuper's questions. A.T. also identified defendant as her abuser. After the interview, Kuper performed a complete physical examination of A.T.

We find it clear that A.T.'s statement to Kuper was reasonably pertinent to Kuper's proper diagnosis and treatment of A.T. The information contained in the statement was important to Kuper's determination of A.T.'s condition. This statement was therefore admissible under Rule 803(4).

2. Testimony of Laura Reich

A.T. saw Dr. Laura Reich on September 21, 1990, for treatment of a skin rash in the vaginal area that was unrelated to any sexual abuse. At the time of Reich's examination of A.T., Reich was aware of the allegations of sexual abuse. Reich testified that, prior to conducting the physical examination, she asked A.T. several personal questions. One of these questions was whether "anybody had ever touched her in her private area." According to Reich's testimony, A.T. replied "that her father had put his thing in her." The remainder of Reich's testimony concerned her findings and conclusions from the physical examination.

Reich testified that the reason she had conducted a preexamination interview with A.T. was "that the child needs to be comfortable with me before I examine her." Because the adequacy of Reich's examination in part depended on the child's comfort with her, we find that A.T.'s statement was reasonably pertinent to Reich's diagnosis or treatment. It consequently was admissible under Rule 803(4).

3. Testimony of Jean Spiegel

Dr. Jean Spiegel, an assistant professor of pediatrics at the University of New Mexico, testified that she examined A.T. for the purpose of offering a second opinion as to whether the child had been sexually abused. Spiegel had extensive training in the area of child sexual abuse, and teaches other doctors how to examine children to detect molestation. Most of Spiegel's testimony focused on the technical aspects of her examination of A.T. and her conclusion that A.T. had experienced chronic vaginal penetration.

On redirect examination, Spiegel testified that A.T. told her where on her body she had been touched during the abuse. Spiegel did not ask, nor did A.T. volunteer, who had touched her. Clearly, A.T.'s statement regarding where she had been touched was pertinent to Spiegel's diagnosis of A.T. The district court therefore properly admitted the statement under Rule 803(4).

B. Testimony of Kae Ecklebarger

Kae Ecklebarger, a caseworker for Colorado Springs Child Protection Services, interviewed A.T. on August 29, 1990. Ecklebarger testified that during the interview, A.T. gave Ecklebarger a detailed account of the alleged abuse, at times using anatomically correct dolls to demonstrate what had occurred. Ecklebarger also testified that A.T. claimed she had told her grandmother and aunt of the abuse. * * *

For a hearsay statement to be admissible under Rule 803(4), the declarant need not have necessarily made the statement to a physician. As the advisory committee's note to the rule explains, "[s]tatements to hospital attendants, ambulance drivers, or even members of the family might be included." Accordingly, the government argues that A.T.'s statement to Ecklebarger is admissible because the job of a Child Protection Services caseworker "was equivalent to that of a doctor under Fed.R.Evid. 803(4)," and because A.T. understood that Ecklebarger's role was to "help kids."

As stated previously, however, the test for admissibility under Rule 803(4) is "whether the subject matter of the statements is reasonably pertinent to diagnosis or treatment." Ecklebarger neither diagnosed nor treated A.T. She described her role as "the initial short-term investigat[or]." Ecklebarger spoke to A.T. two times, after which "[t]he case was sent on to an ongoing protection worker." Clearly, Ecklebarger did not treat A.T. in any way.

Nor did Ecklebarger diagnose A.T. Indeed, Ecklebarger referred the child to Dr. Kuper for a medical opinion regarding the allegations of abuse. Moreover, Ecklebarger testified that she interviewed A.T. only to the extent necessary to make a decision whether a protective order was appropriate. Because Ecklebarger did not diagnose or treat A.T., the child's statement to Ecklebarger could not have been for the "purpose[ ] of medical diagnosis or treatment," and thus was not properly admitted under Rule 803(4). * * *

[The court also held that the statement could not be admitted under the residual exception to the hearsay rule.] The statement was therefore inadmissible hearsay, and the district court erred in admitting this testimony.

C. Testimony of Lisa Rocha

A.T. first mentioned the abuse to Lisa Rocha, who was A.T.'s babysitter during the summer of 1990. During her testimony, Rocha related two separate out-of-court statements by A.T.

The first occurred on August 22, 1990. Rocha testified that, while babysitting A.T. at Rocha's home on that day, A.T. spontaneously asked Rocha not to let her mother send her back to her father. When Rocha asked A.T. why she did not want to return to her father, A.T. replied, "Because my father gets drunk and he thinks I'm his wife." [The court rules that this statement could not be admitted under either Rule 803(3) or the residual exception; the Government apparently did not argue that Rule 803(4) applied.] * * *

A.T.'s second statement to Rocha occurred on August 27, 1990, at the home of A.T.'s mother, Beverly Padilla. Rocha had related A.T.'s August 22 statement to Padilla, and, after Padilla had unsuccessfully attempted to discuss the matter further with A.T., Padilla asked Rocha to broach the subject again with A.T. According to Rocha's testimony, when Rocha asked A.T. to explain her earlier remarks, A.T. described several details regarding one specific instance of abuse by her father. [The court held that the district court did not abuse its discretion in holding this statement inadmissible under the residual exception; again, the Government did not contend that it was admissible under Rule 803(4).]

D. Testimony of Beverly Padilla

Beverly Padilla, A.T.'s mother, testified that she was in another room of her apartment on August 27, 1990, when A.T. described her father's abuse to Rocha (A.T.'s second statement to Rocha). Padilla related to the jury a portion of A.T.'s statement to Rocha about the instance of abuse by her father. The district court admitted this testimony under Rule 801(d)(1)(B), and the government does not now argue that it was admissible under any other evidentiary rule. We likewise find no other basis on which this statement was admissible. Padilla's testimony regarding A.T.'s second statement to Rocha was therefore inadmissible hearsay.

[The court held that the error in admitting the statements of A.T. included in the testimony of Ecklebarger, Rocha, and Padilla was not harmless. Their testimony was "extremely compelling" and A.T.'s trial testimony "was not nearly as articulate or comprehensive in its description of the abuse."

[Judge Holloway dissented from the portion of the opinion dealing with the statements to to Drs. Kuper, Reich, and Spiegel. He wrote: "It is the patient's self-interest in furnishing accurate information which provides the guarantee of trustworthiness which justifies excepting these types of out-of-court statements from the general bar on the admission of hearsay. Thus, unless the declarant appreciates the fact that giving truthful information is necessary to ensure proper treatment or diagnosis, there is no guarantee of trustworthiness justifying the admission of the statement under Rule 803(4)." And in this case, he said, "there is no showing which demonstrates that A.T., who was four years old at the time of the alleged abuse, five at the time she saw Drs. Kuper and Reich, and six when she saw Dr. Spiegel, had the necessary understanding that 'the efficacy of her medical treatment depend[ed] upon the accuracy of the information she provide[d] to the doctor.'"]

QUESTIONS

(1) It does not appear that Dr. Spiegel was consulted for the purpose of treating A.T. or assisting those who did; rather, her opinion was sought in conjunction with the prosecution of Tome. Should this make a difference with respect to the hearsay exception? *See* Advisory Committee Note to FRE 803(4).

(2) Should A.T.'s statements to Dr. Spiegel be considered testimonial for purposes of the Confrontation Clause? *See, e.g.,* Commonwealth v. Allshouse, 36 A.3d 163 (2012), petition for certiorari pending.

(3) Suppose that Beverly Padilla, A.T.'s mother, made a statement to Dr. Kuper to assist in the doctor's treatment of A.T. Should that be considered testimonial?

(4) A personal injury action is brought by a plaintiff who slipped and fell in a supermarket. Should the plaintiff be allowed to introduce the following evidence?

> a. P complained "my neck hurts" to friends for weeks after the fall.
>
> *(A: Present state of mind/physical condition   Fed: Med diagnosis)*
>
> b. P told his doctor, "My neck has been hurting for six months."
>
> *Admit only under Fed. Not CA*
>
> c. P told the same thing to a non-treating doctor hired by his lawyer to give expert testimony at the trial.
>
> *Admit under Fed. Stmt for purposes of med diagnosis*
>
> d. P told the paramedic who came to the fall scene, "I slipped and fell on a banana that had been dropped by a stocker."

(5) In an action for termination of parental rights, the state offers evidence that a pediatrician asked a 5-year-old "What happened to your arm?" and the 5-year-old said "Buzzy burned me." Buzzy is the child's stepfather. Is the evidence admissible?

5. FORMER TESTIMONY

Travelers Fire Insurance Co. v. Wright

Supreme Court of Oklahoma, 1958.
322 P.2d 417, 70 A.L.R.2d 1170.

[Action by J.B. Wright and J.C. Wright to recover under the terms of two fire insurance policies. The defendant insurers defended on the ground that the fire that destroyed plaintiffs' property had been deliberately caused by plaintiff J.B. Wright with the intent to defraud the defendants.

Defendants alleged and proved that the plaintiffs were, at all pertinent times, business partners. There was a verdict and a judgment for plaintiffs, from which defendants appealed—Eds.]

■ JACKSON, JUSTICE. * * * Defendants called Wm. Holland Eppler and Albert Brown as witnesses. Each witness claimed his constitutional privilege against self-incrimination and refused to testify. The claim of each was granted by the trial court. Defendant then offered certified transcripts of testimony given by each witness in the trial of a criminal case wherein one of the plaintiffs herein, J.B. Wright, was charged with the crime of arson in connection with the fire involved in the instant case. Such testimony was to the effect that J.B. Wright, with the aid and assistance of the two named witnesses, actively procured the burning of the property. Each offer was rejected by the trial court. The court reporter who took the evidence in the criminal case testified as to the correctness of his transcript, the nature of the case in which the testimony was taken and the parties involved. In addition to offering the transcript, defendants offered to have the reporter read same in evidence.

* * *

It is quite often stated that before testimony can be taken from a former trial or proceeding and introduced in a subsequent trial there must be (1) an inability to obtain the testimony of the witness; (2) there must have been an opportunity to cross-examine the witness in the former trial; (3) there must be an identity, or substantial identity of issues, and (4) parties. These requirements are recognized in the Concordia case. The primary difficulty arises when we attempt to determine if there is an identity of issues. * * *

In the case before us, it appears that Eppler and Brown testified in the criminal case to establish the issue of whether J.B. Wright procured the burning of the building. Affirmative proof of this issue was necessary to establish his guilt. In the civil case before us the issue is whether J.B. Wright procured the burning of the building. Affirmative proof of this issue is necessary if defendants herein are to prevail. It may be that there were other issues sought to be proved by other witnesses in the instant case, but the issue sought to be established by Eppler and Brown in both the criminal and civil cases was whether J.B. Wright procured the burning of the building.

* * *

As a general proposition we think testimony from a criminal case can be introduced in a subsequent civil case where it appears that it is impossible to obtain the testimony of the witness who testified in the criminal case; that there was an opportunity to cross-examine the witness by the party against whom the testimony is sought to be used in the civil case, or by one whose motive and interest in cross-examining was the same; and that there is an identity of issues. * * *

[handwritten margin note:] prior opp for Cross

Is it material that one of the plaintiffs herein, J.C. Wright, was not a party defendant in the criminal case, and apparently did not participate in the alleged burning of the insured property? We think not.

The insurance policies herein, on which recovery is sought, provide that the defendant companies will not be liable for loss by fire caused by neglect of the insured to use all reasonable means to save and preserve the property at and after a loss. In 29 Am.Jur.Insurance § 1028, pp. 777 and 778, it is said:

> "On the other hand, an innocent partner cannot recover on an insurance policy upon partnership property wilfully burned by his co-partner, especially where the policy provides that the insured shall use all reasonable means at and after a fire to preserve the property."

This rule of law is supported by cases cited in American Jurisprudence and in an Annotation in 27 A.L.R. beginning at page 948.

Is it important that J.C. Wright did not have an opportunity to cross-examine in the criminal case? J.B. Wright had the same motive and interest in cross-examining the witnesses in the criminal case as would J.C. Wright in the instant case. The issues were the same in both cases. J.B. Wright had, and has, the same property interest as that of J.C. Wright. In 142 A.L.R. at page 696, the author quotes from 5 Wigmore on Evidence, 3rd ed. § 1368, as follows:

> "* * * The principle, then, is that where the interest of the person was calculated to induce equally as thorough a testing by cross-examination, then the present opponent has had adequate protection for the same end. Thus the requirement of identity of parties is after all only an incident or corollary of the requirement as to identity of issue. * * * It ought then, to be sufficient to inquire whether the former testimony was given upon such an issue that the party-opponent in that case had the same interest and motive in his cross-examination that the present opponent has."

The author of the Annotation concludes that the argument and position taken by Wigmore is supported by a considerable number of cases from various jurisdictions and cites the cases in support of that rule. We conclude that J.B. Wright's opportunity to cross-examine the witness in the criminal case on the same issue, and with the same interest and motives that J.C. Wright would have in the instant case, satisfies the rule of substantial identity of issues and parties and opportunity for satisfactory cross-examination.

From the foregoing it is seen that the question of substantial identity of parties is important only with regard to the parties as against whom such testimony is offered; therefore the fact that the state was J.B. Wright's adversary in the first case rather than the insurance companies is immaterial. Such fact has no bearing upon the question of whether there has been an adequate opportunity to thoroughly sift and test such testimony by cross-examination.

* * *

We have herein held that the court reporter should be permitted to relate and testify as to what both witnesses testified to in the criminal trial. This conclusion is upon the assumption that both witnesses, at the subsequent trial of this case, will be subpoenaed and will claim their privilege against self-incrimination, and that their claims will be granted. If so, their testimony is as unavailable as if they were dead.

The judgment is reversed and the cause remanded for a new trial in accordance with the views herein expressed.

DAVISON, HALLEY, JOHNSON, WILLIAMS and CARLILE, JJ., concur.

CORN, V.C.J., and BLACKBIRD, J., dissent.

See Federal Rules of Evidence 804(b)(1); California Rules of Evidence §§ 1290–1292.

NOTE—ISSUE PRECLUSION

When an issue that has been examined in a prior action arises in a second action:

1. Under the former testimony exception, testimony given in the first action may be admissible as evidence in the second. See Fed.R.Evid. 804(b)(1).

2. Under the exception for judgments of conviction, the judgment in the first action may be admissible as evidence in the second. See Fed.R.Evid. 803(22).

3. Under the doctrine of issue preclusion (also known as collateral estoppel) the judgment in the first action may, depending on the circumstances, preclude relitigation. If so, the issue has already been decided for purposes of the second action, and evidence on the precluded issue is not admissible. In contrast, when the judgment is used merely as evidence, it can be contradicted with other evidence and the second trier can reach a result different from the first trier.

Obviously, if issue preclusion applied in every case in which an issue had been examined in a prior lawsuit, there would be no occasion to create hearsay exceptions for prior testimony or for judgments. Often, however, issue preclusion does not apply despite the existence of overlapping lawsuits. For example, issue preclusion does not apply when the issue sought to be precluded was not actually litigated in the first action. For this reason, a conviction upon a plea of guilty does not have preclusive effect in later litigation, since nothing was litigated in the first action. (This continues to be the prevailing view, despite some distinguished opposition. See Shapiro, Should a Guilty Plea have Preclusive

Effect? 70 Iowa L. Rev. 27 (1984).) Preclusive effect may also be denied when determination of the issue was not essential to the judgment in the first action, or when the first action did not come to final judgment. See Restatement, Judgments, Second, § 27 (1982). Even when these conditions are satisfied, there are a variety of exceptions to the rule of preclusion. See Restatement, Judgments, Second, § 28 (1982) (exceptions for cases in which, for example, the procedures in the two courts are substantially different, the burden of proof has shifted, the public interest would be detrimentally affected, the second action was not foreseeable, or in which there was not an adequate opportunity or incentive to litigate in the first action).

Another obstacle to preclusion is the doctrine of mutuality of estoppel. Under traditional mutuality doctrine, a person who was not a party or privy to a prior lawsuit was neither bound by the prior suit nor permitted to take advantage of any determination made in the suit. The doctrine of mutuality was based on the notion that since the prior judgment could not have been used against a stranger to the prior suit had the decision been unfavorable to the stranger, fair play required that the stranger not be allowed to benefit from a favorable judgment. The doctrine treated persons equally when in fact they were in quite different situations. It treated a party who had an opportunity to litigate in the first action in the same way that it treated a non-party who had no opportunity.

The mutuality doctrine has been wholly or partly abandoned in many jurisdictions. A stranger to prior litigation is now often permitted to use issue preclusion against a party who had a full and fair opportunity to litigate in the prior action. Again, however, there are a number of exceptions for situations in which preclusion would have a detrimental effect on the public interest, or in which preclusion would be unfair to the precluded party. For example, if the first action was held in a court that did not allow discovery or did not follow rules of evidence, then many jurisdictions would not allow the issue to be precluded. See Restatement, Judgments, Second, § 29 (1982).

The once-prevalent refusal to treat criminal convictions as preclusive in subsequent civil cases was a specific application of the mutuality doctrine. (Perhaps other considerations, such as the absence of discovery in criminal actions and the danger that the criminal process would be abused by those with civil claims, have also had an impact.) The modern tendency, by no means universal, is toward expanding the situations in which prior convictions can be used to preclude relitigation of issues in civil cases. Where the convicted person seeks to profit from the crime, as when an arsonist sues the insurance company for the proceeds of fire insurance, courts are generally receptive toward preclusion. Many allow it in other situations, so long as there was a full and fair opportunity to defend the criminal prosecution and the convicted person cannot point to any defect in the proceeding. See Restatement of Judgments, Second, § 85(2)(a), Comment e thereto, and authorities cited in Comment e.

NOTE ON THE CONCEPT OF PREDECESSOR IN INTEREST

Federal Rule 804(b)(1) refers, in the civil context, to cross-examination by a "predecessor in interest." Professors Lilly, Capra, and Saltzburg describe the conventional understanding of this term in the following passage:[1]

> The phrase "predecessor in interest," which some courts use interchangeably with the phrase "parties in privity," has an exasperating imprecision about it. At common law, the expression generally refers to a predecessor from whom the present party received the right, interest or obligation that is at issue in the current litigation. For example, a decedent is a predecessor in interest to (or "in privity with") both her personal representative and those, such as heirs and legatees, who take from her. So, too, is the grantor of property a predecessor to the grantee.

A well-known case takes greater liberty with the term. In Lloyd v. American Export Lines, Inc., 580 F.2d 1179 (3d Cir.1978), a transcript of a Coast Guard hearing was offered in evidence in a civil action for injuries sustained during a shipboard fight. The transcript contained testimony about a life-endangering fight between an assistant engineer and an electrician on a merchant vessel. The Coast Guard had conducted the hearing for purposes of deciding whether to take disciplinary action against the electrician by suspending or revoking his merchant mariner's documents. American Export Lines offered the transcript for purposes of showing that the engineer, its opponent in the civil action, had started the fight. The court held that the Coast Guard was a "predecessor in interest" of the engineer for purposes of Rule 804(b)(1), so the transcript of the hearing was admissible as former testimony. The same alleged misconduct was involved in both the Coast Guard hearing and in the civil action. The court deemed the predecessor in interest requirement to be satisfied because the Coast Guard and the party against whom the testimony was offered in the civil action had similar interests in the two cases and a similar motive to cross-examine.

United States v. Salerno

Supreme Court of the United States, 1992.
505 U.S. 317.

■ JUSTICE THOMAS delivered the opinion of the Court.

Federal Rule of Evidence 804(b)(1) states an exception to the hearsay rule that allows a court, in certain instances, to admit the former testimony of an unavailable witness. We must decide in this case whether the Rule permits a criminal defendant to introduce the grand jury testimony of a witness who asserts the Fifth Amendment privilege at trial.

I

[Seven defendants, respondents in the Supreme Court, were indicted by a federal grand jury for various offenses related to their alleged participation in the Genovese Family of La Cosa Nostra. Among other offenses,

---

[1] Graham C. Lilly, Daniel J. Capra, & Stephen A. Saltzburg, PRINCIPLES OF EVIDENCE 328 (6th ed. 2012).

the Family allegedly used its influence to rig bidding for concrete contracts for large construction projects in Manhattan.] The Family purportedly allocated contracts for these projects among a so-called "Club" of six concrete companies in exchange for a share of the proceeds.

Much of the case concerned the affairs of the Cedar Park Concrete Construction Corporation (Cedar Park). Two of the owners of this firm, Frederick DeMatteis and Pasquale Bruno, testified before the grand jury under a grant of immunity. In response to questions by the United States, they repeatedly stated that neither they nor Cedar Park had participated in the Club. At trial, however, the United States attempted to show that Cedar Park, in fact, had belonged to the Club by calling two contractors who had taken part in the scheme and by presenting intercepted conversations among the respondents. The United States also introduced documents indicating that the Family had an ownership interest in Cedar Park.

[The defendants subpoenaed DeMatteis and Bruno as trial witnesses, but they invoked their Fifth Amendment privilege and refused to testify. The defendants offered the transcripts of the grand jury testimony of the two witnesses, arguing that they fell within the hearsay exception in Fed. R. Evid. 804(b)(1) for former testimony of an unavailable witness. The District Court refused to admit the transcripts, because there was no showing that before the grand jury the prosecution had a "similar motive" to develop the testimony to the one it would have at trial. The defendants were convicted. The United States Court of Appeals for the Second Circuit reversed, holding that, to maintain "adversarial fairness," the "similar motive" element of Rule 804(b)(1) should "evaporat[e]" when an accused offers against the Government grand jury testimony, procured by the Government under a grant immunity, given by a witness who refuses to testify at trial.]

II

The hearsay rule prohibits admission of certain statements made by a declarant other than while testifying at trial. See Rule 801(c) (hearsay definition), 802 (hearsay rule). The parties acknowledge that the hearsay rule, standing by itself, would have blocked introduction at trial of DeMatteis and Bruno's grand jury testimony. Rule 804(b)(1), however, establishes an exception to the hearsay rule for former testimony. This exception provides:

> "The following are not excluded by the hearsay rule if the declarant is unavailable as a witness:

> "(1) Former Testimony.—Testimony given as a witness at another hearing * * * if the party against whom the testimony is now offered * * * had an opportunity and similar motive to develop the testimony by direct, cross, or redirect examination."

We must decide whether the Court of Appeals properly interpreted Rule 804(b)(1) in this case.

The parties agree that DeMatteis and Bruno were "unavailable" to the defense as witnesses, provided that they properly invoked the Fifth Amendment privilege and refused to testify. See Rule 804(a)(1). They also agree that DeMatteis and Bruno's grand jury testimony constituted "testimony given as * * * witness[es] at another hearing." They disagree, however, about whether the "similar motive" requirement in the final clause of Rule 804(b)(1) should have prevented admission of the testimony in this case.

A

Nothing in the language of Rule 804(b)(1) suggests that a court may admit former testimony absent satisfaction of each of the Rule's elements. The United States thus asserts that, unless it had a "similar motive," we must conclude that the District Court properly excluded DeMatteis and Bruno's testimony as hearsay. The respondents, in contrast, urge us not to read Rule 804(b)(1) in a "slavishly literal fashion." Brief for Respondents at 31. They contend that "adversarial fairness" prevents the United States from relying on the similar motive requirement in this case. We agree with the United States.

When Congress enacted the prohibition against admission of hearsay in Rule 802, it placed 24 exceptions in Rule 803 and 5 additional exceptions in Rule 804. Congress thus presumably made a careful judgment as to what hearsay may come into evidence and what may not. To respect its determination, we must enforce the words that it enacted. * * *

The respondents' argument for a different result takes several forms. They first assert that adversarial fairness requires us to infer that Rule 804(b)(1) contains implicit limitations. They observe, for example, that the Advisory Committee Note to Rule 804 makes clear that the former testimony exception applies only to statements made under oath or affirmation, even though the Rule does not state this restriction explicitly. [That, however, is] not because adversarial fairness implies a limitation, but simply because the word "testimony" refers only to statements made under oath or affirmation. See Black's Law Dictionary 1476 (6th ed. 1990). We see no way to interpret the text of Rule 804(b)(1) to mean that defendants sometimes do not have to show "similar motive."

The respondents also assert that courts often depart from the Rules of Evidence to prevent litigants from presenting only part of the truth. For example, * * *the respondents maintain that, although parties may enjoy various testimonial privileges, they can forfeit these privileges by "opening the door" to certain subjects. In the respondents' view, the United States is attempting to use the hearsay rule like a privilege to keep DeMatteis and Bruno's grand jury testimony away from the jury. They contend, however, that adversarial fairness requires us to conclude that United States forfeited its right to object to admission of the testimony when it introduced contradictory evidence about Cedar Park.

This argument also fails. Even assuming that we should treat the hearsay rule like the rules governing testimonial privileges, we would not conclude that a forfeiture occurred here. Parties may forfeit a privilege by exposing privileged evidence, but do not forfeit one merely by taking a position that the evidence might contradict. In this case, . . the United States never presented to the jury any version of what DeMatteis and Bruno had said in the grand jury proceedings. Instead, it attempted to show Cedar Park's participation in the Club solely through other evidence available to the respondents. The United States never exposed the jury to anything analogous to a "privileged communication." The respondents' argument, accordingly, fails on its own terms.

The respondents finally argue that adversarial fairness may prohibit suppression of exculpatory evidence produced in grand jury proceedings. They note that, when this Court required disclosure of a grand jury transcript in Dennis v. United States, 384 U.S. 855, 86 S.Ct. 1840, 16 L.Ed.2d 973 (1966), it stated that "it is rarely justifiable for the prosecution to have exclusive access" to relevant facts. They allege that the United States nevertheless uses the following tactics to develop evidence in a one-sided manner: If a witness inculpates a defendant during the grand jury proceedings, the United States immunizes him and calls him at trial; however, if the witness exculpates the defendant, as Bruno and DeMatteis each did here, the United States refuses to immunize him and attempts to exclude the testimony as hearsay.[1] The respondents assert that dispensing with the "similar motive" requirement would limit these tactics.

We again fail to see how we may create an exception to Rule 804(b)(1). The Dennis case, unlike this one, did not involve a question about the admissibility of evidence. Rather, it concerned only the need to disclose a transcript to the defendants. Moreover, in Dennis, we did not hold that adversarial fairness required the United States to make the grand jury transcript available. Instead, we ordered disclosure under the specific language of Federal Rule of Criminal Procedure 6(e). In this case, the language of Rule 804(b)(1) does not support the respondents. Indeed, the respondents specifically ask us to ignore it. Neither Dennis nor anything else that the respondents have cited provides us with this authority.

B

The question remains whether the United States had a "similar motive" in this case. The United States asserts that the District Court specifically found that it did not and that we should not review its factual determinations. It also argues that a prosecutor generally will not have the same motive to develop testimony in grand jury proceedings as he does at trial. A prosecutor, it explains, must maintain secrecy during the investigatory stages of the criminal process and therefore may not desire to confront grand jury witnesses with contradictory evidence. It further states that a

---

[1] The respondents also suggest that, in the event that a witness chooses to testify at trial without immunity, the United States can impeach him with his grand jury testimony. See Fed.Rules Evid. 607, 801(d)(1)(A).

prosecutor may not know, prior to indictment, which issues will have importance at trial and accordingly may fail to develop grand jury testimony effectively.

The respondents disagree with both of the United States' arguments. They characterize the District Court's ruling as one of law, rather than fact, because the District Court essentially ruled that a prosecutor's motives at trial always differ from his motives in grand jury proceedings. The respondents contend further that the grand jury transcripts in this case actually show that the United States thoroughly attempted to impeach DeMatteis and Bruno. They add that, despite the United States' stated concern about maintaining secrecy, the United States revealed to DeMatteis and Bruno the identity of the major witnesses who testified against them at trial.

The Court of Appeals, as noted, erroneously concluded that the respondents did not have to demonstrate a similar motive in this case to make use of Rule 804(b)(1). It therefore declined to consider fully the arguments now presented by the parties about whether the United States had such a motive. Rather than to address this issue here in the first instance, we think it prudent to remand the case for further consideration.

It is so ordered.

[Justice Stevens dissented. He believed that, given that the testimony of the two witnesses was directly contrary to the prosecution's theory of the case and potentially devastating to that theory if believed, the prosecution had the same motive to cross-examine before the grand jury that it would have at trial; accordingly, he believed that the evidence satisfied Rule 804(b)(1). He recognized that the prosecution might decline to cross-examine before the grand jury for tactical reasons – perhaps fear that the witness would talk to the targets of the investigation, or a preference for using other means of impeachment – but he did not believe that this meant the prosecution lacked a similar motive to cross-examine. Justice Blackmun concurred in the Court's opinion, "with the understanding that it does not pass upon the weighty concerns, expressed by JUSTICE STEVENS, underlying the interpretation of [the] similar-motive requirement."]

HYPOTHETICALS

(1) X is prosecuted for robbery of A, a bartender. At X's preliminary hearing A testified as to the commission of the crime. In addition A stated the address of B Bar where he was then working, and his residence address, but indicated he planned to change his residence address very soon. At X's trial, the prosecutor offers in evidence the preliminary hearing transcript of A's testimony after calling C, a district attorney's investigator, who testifies that he had been unable to locate A; that A no longer worked at B Bar; and that the local phone book and voters' registration list did not contain A's name. On cross-examination by X, C testifies that he did not make inquiry at the Bartenders' Union nor the residence address A gave at the preliminary hearing, because A had said he was planning to move very soon. X makes a hearsay objection to the preliminary hearing transcript testimony of A. What result?

(2) X is prosecuted for robbery of A. The prosecutor offers in evidence the transcript of A's testimony given at the preliminary hearing after calling B, a district attorney's investigator, who testifies that a subpoena had been sent to A's place of employment but was not served because A was in New York; that an hour before testifying, he, B, had made a telephone call to A in New York and A told him that she planned to remain in New York for six months. Should X's hearsay objection to A's transcript testimony be sustained?

(3) A sues X for $1500 property damage to his automobile arising out of a rear-end collision. X takes A's deposition. A moves to New York after his deposition is taken and is living there at the time of trial. A's counsel offers A's deposition testimony in evidence after testifying that a few days before trial, A telephoned and said it was too expensive for him to come back to California and testify. X makes a hearsay objection to A's deposition testimony. What result?

(4) X, a police officer, pursued a suspect felon into a bar. X became involved in a dispute with A, the bar owner, regarding the whereabouts of the suspected felon. X claims that A struck him with a chair. X arrested A on the charge of battery upon a police officer. In the criminal trial of A, A testifies that he didn't touch X and that X struck him with his billy club. B, a bar patron who was present, testifies for A and corroborates A's version of what happened. A was acquitted and then sues X and Y City, X's employer, for damages for battery, false arrest, and imprisonment. At the trial of A's action against X and Y City, A establishes that B's whereabouts are unknown and that he used reasonable diligence to find B to serve him with a subpoena, but to no avail. A then offers in evidence a transcript of B's testimony given in A's criminal trial. X and Y City make hearsay objections. How should the court rule?

(5) D is charged with possession of narcotics. D is first arrested at his residence for an unrelated offense. At the time of his arrest, X resided with D. While D is in jail on the unrelated charge, P, a police officer, secures a search warrant for D's residence and discovers a home-constructed bedframe with hollowed out compartments in which P finds the narcotics. D testifies that he had no knowledge of the items in the bedframe compartments, that shortly before his arrest he had observed a pill vial in X's possession similar to the one found in the bedframe compartment, and that he had previously observed X injecting "speed". D offers in evidence in his defense under the former-testimony hearsay exception evidence given by X in another criminal case in a different county. In this prior case X testified for the prosecution as a witness to the murder of her husband, which took place one week after D's arrest. On cross-examination of X at the former trial, testimony was elicited from her that on the evening of the killing she was under the influence of narcotics, having earlier injected "speed"; that she was a narcotics addict and had possession of narcotics and the necessary paraphernalia for their use. At D's trial it is conceded that X is unavailable as a witness. D contends that X's former testimony is relevant on the question of D's lack of knowledge, possession, and control of the items discovered in the bedframe. The prosecutor makes a hearsay objection to the proffered former testimony of X. Should the prosecutor's motion be sustained?

6. DECLARATIONS AGAINST INTEREST

State v. English

Supreme Court of North Carolina, 1931.
201 N.C. 295, 159 S.E. 318.

Stephen English was convicted of murder in the second degree, and he appeals. * * *

[At trial, English had offered evidence that, the day after the murder, one David Locke was arrested, and that Locke admitted to three police officers that he (Locke) committed the murder. Defendant also offered testimony that Locke had described the contents of the house in which the victim was murdered and the condition of her body, apparently with substantial accuracy. Nonetheless, the authorities released Locke and prosecuted English, who was the husband of the murder victim. Locke did not testify at the trial of English, and his whereabouts were unknown. The trial judge excluded the testimony about Locke's confession.]

■ BROGDEN, J.

Is the voluntary confession of a third party, made to officers of the law, that he killed the deceased, detailing the circumstances, competent evidence in behalf of the defendant charged with the murder?

The admissibility of confessions of a third party in criminal actions has been bitterly assailed and warmly defended by courts and text-writers. The numerical weight of authority excludes such testimony. About one hundred years ago it appears in State v. May, 15 N.C. 328, that a defendant was charged with stealing a slave. At that time this was a capital felony in North Carolina, and the defendant having been convicted, the judgment of death was pronounced against him. In that case the defendant offered testimony that another man had confessed to stealing the slave and had made compensations therefor. The testimony was rejected. The court said: "Except the facts of the respective residences of the parties, which of themselves, do not tend to establish guilt in either of the parties, it is obvious, that all the evidence, as well that received as that rejected, consists of the acts and declarations of other persons, to which neither the State nor the prisoner is privy. I think the whole of it was inadmissible. The confession is plainly so. It is mere hearsay. It may seem absurd to one not accustomed to compare proofs, and estimate the weight of testimony according to the tests of veracity within our power, that an unbiased confession of one man that he is guilty of an offense with which another is charged, should not establish the guilt of him who confesses it, and by consequence, the innocence of the other, but the law must proceed on general principles; and it excludes such a confession upon the ground, that it is hearsay evidence—the words of a stranger to the parties, and not spoken on oath. Indeed, all hearsay might have more or less effect, and from some persons of good character, well known to the jury, it might avail much. Yet it is all rejected, with very few exceptions; which do not in terms or principle extend to this case. Even a judgment upon the plea of guilty could not be offered in evidence for or against another; much less a bare confession. As a declaration of another establishing his own guilt, the confession of a slave might be used upon the same principle."

The May Case is the original legal patriarch of an increasing line of legal descendants in this state. The states holding the same interpretation of the law are assembled in a note in the decision of Donnelly v. U.S., 228 U.S. 243, 33 S.Ct. 449, 461, 57 L.Ed. 820, Ann.Cas. 1913E, 710. The minority view is clearly and concisely stated by Mr. Justice Holmes who wrote a dissenting opinion in the Donnelly Case, supra, in which Justices Lurton and Hughes concurred. Justice Holmes said: "The confession of Joe Dick, since deceased, that he committed the murder for which the plaintiff in error was tried, coupled with circumstances pointing to its truth, would have a very strong tendency to make anyone outside of a court of justice believe that Donnelly did not commit the crime. I say this, of course, on the supposition that it should be proved that the confession really was made, and that there was no ground for connecting Donnelly with Dick. The rules of evidence in the main are based on experience, logic, and common sense, less hampered by history than some parts of the substantive law. There is no decision by this court against the admissibility of such a confession; the English cases since the separation of the two countries do not bind us; the exception to the hearsay rule in the case of declarations against interest is well known; no other statement is so much against interest as a confession of murder; it is far more calculated to convince than dying declarations, which would be let in to hang a man; * * * and when we surround the accused with so many safeguards, some of which seem to me excessive I think we ought to give him the benefit of a fact that, if proved, commonly would have such weight. The history of the law and the arguments against the English doctrine are so well and fully stated by Mr. Wigmore that there is no need to set them forth at greater length. 2 Wigmore, Ev. §§ 1476, 1477."

* * *

The great jurist who wrote the May Case * * * confesses that the holding might seem absurd to a layman, "but the law must proceed on general principles," and hence if proffered testimony is technically and legalistically hearsay, then the technical interpretation must prevail. Furthermore, the suggested possibility that some man accused of crime would procure a confession of guilt by a slave and thus escape punishment, might have been a consequence which law-writers of a hundred years ago were seeking to avoid.

The writer of this opinion, speaking for himself, strings with the minority, but it was the duty of the trial judge to apply the law as written, and the exceptions of the defendant are not sustained.

No error.

G.M. McKelvey Co. v. General Casualty Co. of America

Supreme Court of Ohio, 1957.
166 Ohio St. 401, 2 O.O.2d 345, 142 N.E.2d 854.

■ MATTHIAS, JUDGE. The issue raised by this appeal is whether, in a civil action against an insurer by an insured employer upon a policy of fidelity insurance protecting such employer from defalcations by his employees, written and signed confessions by certain employees admitting misappropriations of their employer's funds and stating the amounts of such misappropriations are admissible in evidence to prove both the fact and the amount of the loss.

* * *

One of the exceptions to the hearsay rule, which has been found to be based on trustworthiness or a probability of truthfulness and veracity, and which has arisen due to necessity, is a declaration against interest by a third party.

The courts, where confronted with a situation where death, absence from the jurisdiction or insanity makes a witness unavailable, and where such witness is the only source from which his evidence can be obtained, have held that as a matter of necessity a declaration by such witness against his interest should be admitted in evidence. The courts have reasoned that a person does not make statements against his own pecuniary interest unless they are true and have thus considered such statements trustworthy, even though there is no opportunity to confront the witness or to cross-examine him. 5 Wigmore on Evidence, 204, Section 1421.

Thus, the rule has arisen that a declaration against interest by one not a party or in privity with a party to an action is admissible in evidence, where (1) the person making such declaration is either dead or unavailable as a witness due to sickness, insanity or absence from the jurisdiction, (2) the declarant had peculiar means of knowing the facts which he stated, (3) the declaration was against his pecuniary or proprietary interest and (4) he had no probable motive to falsify the facts stated.

* * *

At least as applied to written and signed confessions, we are in accord with the rule as stated above, and we will consider the confessions of the employees in the instant case in relation to this rule. First, it is apparent from the record that the employees making them were unavailable as witnesses, having been summoned and not found in the jurisdiction by the sheriff. Second, certainly a person who commits an embezzlement has a peculiar means of knowing whether he embezzled and how much he took, and, from the record in the instant case, plaintiff's employees are the only persons who can accurately indicate both the fact and the amount of the embezzlements. Third, it was clearly not in their interest to state such facts, since such declarations render them civilly liable for the amounts of their defalcations. Fourth, there would certainly be no probable motive for plaintiff's employees to falsify the facts stated unless it would be to minimize the amount of their defalcations, and that question is not raised herein.

* * *

It is our conclusion that, in a civil action by an insured against his fidelity insurer to recover for defalcations by employees of the former, where such employees are unavailable as witnesses, they having been summoned and not found in the jurisdiction by the sheriff, written and signed confessions of such employees are admissible in evidence as declarations against interest as to both the fact and the amount of the loss.

For the reasons herein set out, the judgment of the Court of Appeals is affirmed.

Judgment affirmed.

■ WEYGANDT, C.J., and ZIMMERMAN, STEWART, BELL, TAFT and HERBERT, JJ., concur.

United States v. Barrett

United States Court of Appeals, First Circuit, 1976.
539 F.2d 244.

■ Before Coffin, Chief Judge, McEntee and Campbell, Circuit Judges.

■ LEVIN H. CAMPBELL, Circuit Judge.

Arthur Barrett appeals from his conviction after a jury trial for crimes arising from the theft and sale of a collection of postage stamps from the Cardinal Spellman Philatelic Museum in Weston, Massachusetts. [Barrett's nickname was "Bucky." Ben Tilley was allegedly a co-conspirator of Barrett's, but died prior to trial. "Buzzy" Adams testified at Barrett's trial as a government witness, in exchange for immunity from prosecution.]

* * *

Barrett * * * argues that the court below erred by refusing to admit the testimony of three defense witnesses. The first was James Melvin. Melvin testified that in February, 1974, he was at a card game on Bowdoin Street, in Dorchester, Massachusetts, with Ben Tilley. When Melvin was asked to recount a conversation which he had there with Tilley, the Government objected. Barrett made an offer of proof that Melvin would testify that Tilley had told Melvin "that he, Tilley, and Buzzy [Adams] were going to have some trouble from the people from California" with respect to the "stamp theft or matter" and that "[Melvin] asked him did he mean Bucky or Buzzy, and then he said, 'No, Bucky [Barrett] wasn't involved. It was Buzzy.'" Barrett argued at the bench that this testimony was admissible under Fed.R.Evid. 804(b)(3) as a declaration against self-interest, apparently on the theory that Tilley's display of inside knowledge of "the people from California," the stamp theft, and the identity of persons "involved", all tended against Tilley's penal interest at the time by advertising his likely complicity. The court excluded the proffered testimony as hearsay on the ground that the relevant part, that Buzzy, not Bucky, was involved, was not against Tilley's interest. The court said, "You are offering it not to prove anything prejudicial to the alleged maker of the statement but to prove that [Buzzy] rather than [Bucky] did it * * *." Barrett argues on appeal that the entire statement, including the portion exculpating Barrett, should have been admitted.

Rule 804(b)(3) of the new Federal Rules of Evidence provides, with an important qualification, for the admission of a statement by an unavailable declarant that at the time of making tended to subject him to criminal liability. The rule provides in pertinent part,

> "(b) *Hearsay exceptions.* The following are not excluded by the hearsay rule if the declarant is unavailable as a witness:

> * * *

> (3) *Statement against interest.* A statement which was at the time of its making so far contrary to the declarant's pecuniary or proprietary interest, or so far tended to subject him to civil or criminal liability * * * that a reasonable man in his position would not have made the statement unless he believed it to be true. A statement tending to expose the declarant to criminal liability and offered to exculpate the accused is not admissable [sic] unless corroborating circumstances clearly indicate the trustworthiness of the statement."

Rule 804(b)(3) is a departure from the principle laid down in Donnelly v. United States [1913], in which the Supreme Court endorsed the exclusion from evidence of a third party's extra-judicial confession to the murder for which the defendant was on trial. In conformity with English precedent, the *Donnelly* court limited the hearsay exception for declarations against interest to declarations against interest of a pecuniary character. Statements subjecting the declarant to criminal liability were held to be outside the exception.

Half a century later, when the present Federal Rules of Evidence were being formulated, *Donnelly* was in disfavor, and provision was made in the various drafts of the new code for the admission of declarations against penal interest. The text underwent several revisions prior to enactment. A provision forbidding prosecutorial use of third party statements or confessions which implicated an accused as well as the declarant was deleted, with the result that subject to sixth amendment and other constraints, a third party's out of court statements against penal interest may now be used against, as well as in favor of, an accused. And, more relevant here, the second sentence of clause (3) was rewritten to require that statements offered to exculpate the accused be corroborated so as to "clearly indicate the trustworthiness of the statement".

As submitted to Congress by the Supreme Court, the Rule required simply that a statement offered to exculpate the accused be corroborated. The Advisory Committee explained this requirement as a way of accommodating the common law's distrust of confessions offered to exculpate an accused:

"The refusal of the common law to concede the adequacy of a penal interest was no doubt indefensible in logic [citing Holmes' *Donnelly* dissent], but one senses in the decisions a distrust of evidence of confessions by third persons offered to exculpate the accused arising from suspicions of fabrication either of the fact of the making of the confession or in its contents, enhanced in either instance by the required unavailability of the declarant. Nevertheless, an increasing amount of decisional law recognizes exposure to punishment for crime as a sufficient stake. The requirement of corroboration is included in the rule in order to effect an accommodation between these competing considerations. When the statement is offered by the accused by way of exculpation, the resulting situation is not adapted to control by rulings as to the weight of the evidence, and hence the provision is cast in terms of a requirement preliminary to admissibility. The requirement of corroboration should be construed in such a manner as to effectuate its purpose of circumventing fabrication." [Citations omitted.]

Notes of Advisory Committee on Proposed Rules, at 28 U.S.C.A. Fed.R.Evid. 804.

The House Judiciary Committee strengthened this corroboration requirement by adding the present language. The Committee noted,

"[The Committee] believed * * * as did the [Supreme] Court [in its earlier version] that statements of this type tending to exculpate the accused are more suspect and so should have their admissibility conditioned upon some further provision insuring trustworthiness. The proposal in the Court Rule to add a requirement of simple corroboration was, however, deemed ineffective to accomplish this purpose since the accused's own testimony might suffice while not necessarily increasing the reliability of the hearsay statement. The Committee settled upon the language 'unless corroborating circumstances clearly indicate the trustworthiness of the statement' as affording a proper standard and degree of discretion. It was contemplated that the result in such cases as Donnelly v. United States where the circumstances plainly indicated reliability, would be changed."

Notes of Committee on the Judiciary, H.R.Rep. No. 93–650, Note to Subdivision (b)(3), at 28 U.S.C.A. Fed.R.Evid. 804, U.S.Code Cong. & Admin.News 1974, pp. 7051, 7089.

As finally enacted, Rule 804(b)(3) requires a two-stage analysis: first, do the offered remarks come within the hearsay exception as a "statement against interest"? and second, if they do, is there sufficient corroboration to clearly indicate trustworthiness? Here we believe that the remarks offered were statements against interest within the Rule, and that the district court should have gone on to determine whether there was sufficient corroboration so as to warrant their admission.

Turning to the first stage of analysis, we think that Tilley's alleged remarks sufficiently tended to subject him to criminal liability "that a reasonable man in his position would not have made the statement unless he believed it to be true." * * * A reasonable person would have realized that remarks of the sort attributed to Tilley strongly implied his personal participation in the stamp crimes and hence would tend to subject him to criminal liability. Though by no means conclusive, the statement would be important evidence against Tilley were he himself on trial for the stamp crimes. We cannot say, therefore, that it did not pose the sort of threat to Tilley's interest that the hearsay exception contemplates.

We do not overlook the fact that the proffered remarks came in the course of conversation with acquaintances over cards. In such circumstances, Tilley might not so readily have perceived the disserving character of what was said nor have expected his words to be repeated to the police. But we are unable to say that the contextual circumstances so far impugn the reliability presumed from the remarks' disserving character as to take them outside the first part of the Rule. * * * The factors in question seem better considered under the second part of the Rule in determining whether, overall, there is enough corroboration to "clearly indicate * * * trustworthiness."

Nor do we overlook the fact that exculpating Barrett was not in itself against Tilley's interest, since both could have participated in the crime. Tilley's remarks differ in this respect from the third-party confession in * * * *Donnelly*. In Barrett's trial, the relevance of Tilley's participation is limited to the credence it gives to his views on who else took part. The district court seemed to suggest that in order for exculpatory remarks such as Tilley's to be admissible as against interest, the innocence of the accused must itself be prejudicial to the declarant. On the present facts, we read the first part of Rule 804(b)(3) more broadly, and conclude that so much of Tilley's remarks as exculpated "Bucky" and inculpated "Buzzy" should here be considered as part of the statement against Tilley's interest.

Under the common law exception for declarations against interest, the treatment to be given portions of a declaration collateral to the declarant's interest has been the subject of much debate. A leading commentator, after acknowledging the traditional liberality with which courts have admitted collateral statements, has expressed the opinion that,

> "As long as the courts adhere to the exceptions to the hearsay rule it would be more reasonable to confine the use of statements against interest in all cases to the proof of the fact which is against interest, since the reliability of other parts of the statement is conjectural."

B. Jefferson, Declarations Against Interest: An Exception to the Hearsay Rule, 58 Harv.L.Rev. 1, 62–63 (1944). And more pointedly, in an article criticizing certain conventional exceptions to the hearsay rule, another author has said,

> "Nonetheless, the naming of another as a compatriot will almost never be against the declarant's own interest and thus will contain little assurance of reliability on this ground. * * * The invocation of a name may be gratuitous, may be deliberately false in order to gain advantages for the declarant greater than those that would flow from naming a real participant or no one at all, may be a cover for concealment purposes (another kind of 'advantage'), or may represent an effort to gain some kind of personal revenge." [Footnote omitted.]

D. Davenport, The Confrontation Clause and the Coconspirator Exception in Criminal Prosecutions: A Functional Analysis, 85 Harv.L.Rev. 1378, 1396 (1972).

There are two reasons, however, which make it difficult for us to agree with the district court's view of the statement in issue. First, the Buzzy-Bucky statement, especially in context, is itself arguably disserving to Tilley, since it strengthened the impression that he had an insider's knowledge of the crimes. And second, the case law, while far from settled, has tended to grant at least "[a] certain latitude as to contextual statements, neutral as to interest giving meaning to the declaration against interest * * *", McCormick on Evidence § 279(a), at 676 (2d ed. 1972). While we do not read the federal rule as incorporating the rather broad formulation put forward by Wigmore, who saw the against-interest exception as permitting reception not only of the "specific fact against interest, but also * * * *every fact contained in the same statement*", Wigmore, supra, § 1465, at 339 (emphasis in original), neither does it appear that Congress intended to constrict the scope of a declaration against interest to the point of excluding "collateral" material that, as here, actually tended to fortify the statement's disserving aspects. See Notes of Advisory Committee, supra; Notes of Committee on the Judiciary, supra. We hold that the Buzzy-Bucky remark was sufficiently integral to the entire statement, and the latter sufficiently against interest, as to come within the first part of Rule 804(b)(3).

It follows that the district court was under an obligation to determine, under the second sentence of the Rule, whether "corroborating circumstances clearly indicate[d] the trustworthiness of the statement", including, we would add, the trustworthiness of that part exculpating Barrett. We emphasize that admissibility is conditional upon separate compliance with that standard, which, it is clear from both the statutory language and the legislative history, is not an insignificant hurdle. * * * We would * * * make two observations to guide the district court's judgment, should the question arise upon retrial. [Elsewhere in its opinion, the court had decided that the conviction should be reversed because the trial court had erroneously excluded evidence about prior inconsistent statements of a government witness.—Eds.]

First we would not read the standard of trustworthiness as imposing a standard so strict as to be utterly unrealistic. Even in *Donnelly* * * * the evidence, while strongly corroborated, could have been disbelieved by the jury. On the other hand, there is no question but that Congress meant to preclude reception of exculpatory hearsay statements against penal interest unless accompanied by circumstances solidly indicating trustworthiness. This requirement goes beyond minimal corroboration. * * *

Second, in ruling on trustworthiness courts should be mindful of the possible relationship between constitutional cases * * * and the new federal rule. * * * Rule 804(b)(3) reflects Congress' attempt to strike a fair balance between exclusion of trustworthy evidence, as in * * * *Donnelly*, and indiscriminate admission of less trustworthy evidence which, because of the lack of opportunity for cross-examination and the absence of the declarant, is open to easy fabrication. Clearly the federal rule is no more restrictive than the Constitution permits, and may in some situations be more inclusive. * * *

QUESTIONS

In *Barrett*, as in *Salerno* and *English*, the hearsay evidence was offered by a criminal defendant. Should that fact affect the hearsay analysis? Note that, as explained in the *Barrett* opinion, at common law the hearsay exception for declarations against interest extended to statements against the declarant's pecuniary, but not penal, interest. That is, if making the statement would cost the declarant money, it could come within the exception, but not if making the statement would cost the declarant prison time or his life. Why, do you suppose? What is the most common circumstance in which one party will want to introduce a statement made by a declarant, not the party against whom the statement is offered, that was against the penal interest of the declarant when it was made?

GREEN v. GEORGIA, 442 U.S. 95, 99 S.Ct. 2150, 60 L.Ed.2d 738 (1979). Accused of murder, Green sought to introduce the testimony of Pasby that Moore, Green's confederate, had confessed to killing the victim after sending Green on an errand; Pasby had testified to that effect at the trial of Moore. Georgia adhered to the rule limiting the hearsay exception to statements against pecuniary interest, the evidence was excluded, and Green was convicted. The U.S. Supreme Court held that in the "unique circumstances" of this case, exclusion violated Green's rights under the Due Process Clause of the Fourteenth Amendment:

> The excluded testimony was highly relevant to a critical issue in the punishment phase of the trial, and substantial reasons existed to assume its reliability. Moore made his statement spontaneously to a close friend. The evidence corroborating the confession was ample, and indeed sufficient to procure a conviction of Moore and a capital sentence. The statement was against interest, and there was no reason to believe that Moore had any ulterior motive in making it. Perhaps most important, the State considered the testimony sufficiently reliable to use it against Moore, and to base a sentence of death upon it.

Williamson v. United States

Supreme Court of the United States, 1994.
512 U.S. 594, 114 S.Ct. 2431, 129 L.Ed.2d 476.

[Justice O'Connor, writing for six Justices, began as follows:]

In this case we clarify the scope of the hearsay exception for statements against penal interest. Fed. Rule Evid. 804(b)(3).

I

A deputy sheriff stopped the rental car driven by Reginald Harris for weaving on the highway. Harris consented to a search of the car, which revealed 19 kilograms of cocaine in two suitcases in the trunk. Harris was promptly arrested.

Shortly after Harris' arrest, Special Agent Donald Walton of the Drug Enforcement Administration (DEA) interviewed him by telephone. During that conversation, Harris said that he got the cocaine from an unidentified Cuban in Fort Lauderdale; that the cocaine belonged to petitioner Williamson; and that it was to be delivered that night to a particular dumpster. Williamson was also connected to Harris by physical evidence: The luggage bore the initials of Williamson's sister, Williamson was listed as an additional driver on the car rental agreement, and an envelope addressed to Williamson and a receipt with Williamson's girlfriend's address were found in the glove compartment.

Several hours later, Agent Walton spoke to Harris in person. During that interview, Harris said he had rented the car a few days earlier and had driven it to Fort Lauderdale to meet Williamson. According to Harris, he had gotten the cocaine from a Cuban who was Williamson's acquaintance, and the Cuban had put the cocaine in the car with a note telling Harris how to deliver the drugs. Harris repeated that he had been instructed to leave the drugs in a certain dumpster, to return to his car, and to leave without waiting for anyone to pick up the drugs.

Agent Walton then took steps to arrange a controlled delivery of the cocaine. But as Walton was preparing to leave the interview room, Harris "got out of [his] chair . . . and . . . took a half step toward [Walton] . . . and . . . said, . . . 'I can't let you do that,' threw his hands up and said 'that's not true, I can't let you go up there for no reason.'" Harris told Walton he had lied about the Cuban, the note, and the dumpster. The real story, Harris said, was that he was transporting the cocaine to Atlanta for Williamson, and that Williamson was traveling in front of him in another rental car. Harris added that after his car was stopped, Williamson turned around and drove past the location of the stop, where he could see Harris' car with its trunk open. Because Williamson had apparently seen the police searching the car, Harris explained that it would be impossible to make a controlled delivery.

Harris told Walton that he had lied about the source of the drugs because he was afraid of Williamson. Though Harris freely implicated himself, he did not want his story to be recorded, and he refused to sign a written version of the statement. Walton testified that he had promised to report any cooperation by Harris to the Assistant United States Attorney. Walton said Harris was not promised any reward or other benefit for cooperating.

[When called to testify at Williamson's trial, Harris refused, even though the prosecution gave him use immunity and the trial judge ordered him to testify and eventually held him in contempt. The judge then admitted Harris's statements incriminating Williamson, citing Fed.R.Evid. 804(b)(3). Williamson was convicted of cocaine-related offenses and eventually obtained review by the United States Supreme Court.]

* * * In our view, the most faithful reading of Rule 804(b)(3) is that it does not allow admission of non-self-inculpatory statements, even if they are made within a broader narrative that is generally self-inculpatory. The district court may not just assume for purposes of Rule 804(b)(3) that a statement is self-inculpatory because it is part of a fuller confession, and this is especially true when the statement implicates someone else. "[T]he arrest statements of a codefendant have traditionally been viewed with special suspicion. Due to his strong motivation to implicate the defendant and to exonerate himself, a codefendant's statements about what the defendant said or did are less credible than ordinary hearsay evidence." Lee v. Illinois, 476 U.S. 530, 541 (1986).

* * *

There are many circumstances in which Rule 804(b)(3) does allow the admission of statements that inculpate a criminal defendant. Even the confessions of arrested accomplices may be admissible if they are truly self-inculpatory, rather than merely attempts to shift blame or curry favor.

For instance, a declarant's squarely self-inculpatory confession—"yes, I killed X"—will likely be admissible under Rule 804(b)(3) against accomplices of his who are being tried under a co-conspirator liability theory. Likewise, by showing that the declarant knew something, a self-inculpatory statement can in some situations help the jury infer that his confederates knew it as well. And when seen with other evidence, an accomplice's self-inculpatory statement can inculpate the defendant directly: "I was robbing the bank on Friday morning," coupled with someone's testimony that the declarant and the defendant drove off together Friday morning, is evidence that the defendant also participated in the robbery.

Moreover, whether a statement is self-inculpatory or not can only be determined by viewing it in context. Even statements that are on their face neutral may actually be against the declarant's interest. "I hid the gun in Joe's apartment" may not be a confession of a crime; but if it is likely to help the police find the murder weapon, then it is certainly self-inculpatory. "Sam and I went to Joe's house" might be against the declarant's interest if a reasonable person in the declarant's shoes would realize that being linked to Joe and Sam would implicate the declarant in Joe and Sam's conspiracy. And other statements that give the police significant details about the crime may also, depending on the situation, be against the declarant's interest. The question under Rule 804(b)(3) is always whether the statement was sufficiently against the declarant's penal interest "that a reasonable person in the declarant's position would not have made the statement unless believing it to be true," and this question can only be answered in light of all the surrounding circumstances.

[After setting forth this approach, the Court ceased to speak with a majority voice. For herself and Justice Scalia, Justice O'Connor continued by saying that while some of Harris's confession would clearly have been admissible under Rule 804(b)(3), other parts, particularly the parts that implicated Williamson, did little to subject Harris to criminal liability. Since nothing in the record indicated that either of the courts below inquired whether each of the statements in Harris's confession was truly self-inculpatory, she favored remanding for a "fact-intensive inquiry" into this matter.]

[Justice Ginsburg, writing for four Justices, concurred in the judgment and agreed with the general analysis advanced by Justice O'Connor in the passage above. Unlike Justice O'Connor, however, she concluded that Harris's statements "do not fit, even in part, within the exception described in Rule 804(b)(3), for Harris' arguably inculpatory statements are too closely intertwined with his self-serving declarations to be ranked as trustworthy." She noted that Harris's statements "provided only marginal or cumulative evidence of his guilt. They project an image of a person acting not against his penal interest, but striving mightily to shift principal responsibility to someone else." For that reason, she would have held that none of Harris's statements were admissible under the declarations against interest exception. However, she concurred in the judgment remanding the case to the Court of Appeals for further consideration because she believed that the government should be given the opportunity to argue that the admission of the statements was harmless error.]

[Justice Kennedy, writing for a minority of three, concurred in the judgment remanding the case because he believed that the District Court should reconsider the admissibility of the evidence in light of the analysis set forth in his opinion. His analysis differed significantly, however, from that of the majority. Analyzing the text of the rule in light of the Advisory Committee Note and his interpretation of the common law, he would have construed the exception to apply to collateral statements that were connected with statements against interest. He would admit "neutral" collateral statements, but not "self-serving" collateral statements. He summarized his approach as follows:]

A court first should determine whether the declarant made a statement that contained a fact against penal interest. * * * If so, the court should admit all statements related to the precise statement against penal interest, subject to two limits. Consistent with the Advisory Committee Note, the court should exclude a collateral statement that is so self-serving as to render it unreliable (if, for example, it shifts blame to someone else for a crime the defendant could have committed). In addition, in cases where the statement was made under circumstances where it is likely that the declarant had a significant motivation to obtain favorable treatment, as when the government made an explicit offer of leniency in exchange for the declarant's admission of guilt, the entire statement should be inadmissible.

[The more restrictive approach of the majority, Justice Kennedy felt, would practically vitiate the exception for declarations against penal interest. Justice Scalia responded to Justice Kennedy in a brief separate opinion in which he argued that the exception would have plenty of life under the majority approach. As an example, he suggested that "if a lieutenant in an organized crime operation described the inner workings of an extortion and protection racket, naming some of the other actors and thereby inculpating himself on racketeering and/or conspiracy charges, I have no doubt that some of those remarks could be admitted as statements against penal interest."]

QUESTIONS

(1) On what basis would you expect *Williamson* to be decided if it had arisen after *Crawford*? Were Harris's statements testimonial within the meaning of *Crawford*? *Williamson* says that "a defendant's squarely self-inculpatory confession * * * will likely be admissible under Rule 804(b)(3) against accomplices of his who are being tried under a co-conspirator liability theory." Assuming that Rule 804(b)(3) removes the hearsay objection, how about the Confrontation Clause?

(2) Harris expressed fear of Williamson. If that fear was based on threats by Williamson after Harris's arrest that reasonably caused Harris to feel intimidated, should that affect the outcome of the case? What if Williamson's intimidating conduct occurred before the arrest and was not directed against Harris in particular – Williamson just did what he could to make clear that he was a tough person without scruples that would constrain him from doing what he felt he needed to for self-protection?

(3) In prison awaiting trial for a murder, Alfred tells Bob that Carol helped him commit the crime. Unbeknownst to Alfred, Bob has recorded the conversation surreptitiously. Is this statement testimonial within the meaning of *Crawford*? If the recording is properly authenticated, may it be offered against Alfred? Against Carol? *See* United States v. Pelletier, 666 F.3d 1 (1st Cir. 2011); United States v. Dale, 614 F.3d 942 (8th Cir. 2010).

HYPOTHETICALS

(1) X is prosecuted for possession of a marijuana cigarette that was found in a jacket in X's car. X's defense is that the jacket belonged to A. X calls A as a witness and A refuses to answer questions about the jacket on the ground of

the self-incrimination privilege. X then calls B, who will testify that A told him on the day before X's arrest that he had been riding with X and left his jacket in X's car. The prosecution makes a hearsay objection to B's proposed testimony. How should the court rule?

(2) X is charged with possession of heroin. The heroin was found in X's house while A was present. X establishes that A is in another state at the time of trial. X calls B, the wife of A, and offers to have her testify that A told her that the heroin found in X's house belonged to A. The prosecution makes a hearsay objection to B's testimony. What result? Should it matter whether under the laws of the jurisdiction A's statement to his wife was privileged and inadmissible against A?

(3) A is a guest in a car driven by B, which collides in an intersection with a car driven by X. A, B, and X all receive personal injuries. A sues X for damages, claiming that X ran the red light. X claims that B ran the red light. X offers testimony that B is in Europe. X then calls C and proposes that C will testify that a week after the accident B told him that his accident with X was all B's fault because he "blew the red light". Should A's hearsay objection to C's proposed testimony be sustained?

(4) A sues X in a paternity action, claiming that X is the father of a child born to A. X calls B who testifies that he (B) was a friend of C, a married man who now lives in Europe. X proposes to have B testify that C was formerly A's boss and that C told him (B) he (C) was having an affair with A during the time that A's child was conceived. A makes a hearsay objection to B's proposed testimony. What result?

(5) D is charged with murder of V, who was shot to death. The prosecution introduced testimony that D, along with another, was seen beating V prior to the shooting. There was no eyewitness testimony as to whether D did the shooting. Upon D's request, the trial judge conducts an evidence-admissibility hearing out of the presence of the jury. D calls X to testify about whether X did the shooting. X refuses to answer any questions on the ground of self-incrimination. D then calls A, who testifies that he was in the county jail with X and heard X state (1) that he had shot V in the chest and (2) that D was present trying to break up the fight. On cross-examination, A testifies that he also heard X say that X would "take the beef" because he was going to the Youth Authority and couldn't get hurt; that later, at the Youth Authority, he heard X state to a counselor that D had asked him to testify falsely on his behalf and had threatened to get him if he refused. D then offers to have A testify before the jury as to X's statements (1) that X had shot V and (2) that D was trying to break up the fight. The prosecutor makes a hearsay objection and D urges that X's statements would be admissible under the hearsay exception for a declaration against penal interest. The trial judge sustains the prosecutor's hearsay objection. Is this ruling appropriate?

See Federal Rules of Evidence 804(b)(3); California Evidence Code § 1230.

7. DYING DECLARATIONS AND FORFEITURE

Cairns, Law and the Social Sciences
173–74 (1935).*

* * * A large part of the business of psychology is to ascertain how people generally conduct themselves in certain situations; this is also, but to a much lesser extent, the concern of the law. If, for example, the courts decide that a dying declaration made by an individual, the manner of whose death is being investigated in a criminal proceeding, is admissible because the solemnity of the occasion is likely to impel truthfulness, they are making an assumption more properly describable as psychological than legal. In the establishing of the rule, which is perhaps rooted in a custom which goes back at least to the twelfth century, theological beliefs were perhaps a dominant factor. Psychology may or may not confirm the law's assumption but at least it would be wise for the courts to inquire what it has to offer. * * *

King John**
Act V, iv, 10–61.

SALISBURY

May this be possible? may this be true?

MELUN

Have I not hideous death within my view,

Retaining but a quantity of life,

Which bleeds away, even as a form of wax

Resolveth from his figure 'gainst the fire?

What in the world should make me now deceive,

Since I must lose the use of all deceit?

Why should I then be false, since it is true

That I must die here and live hence by truth?

I say again, * * *

---

* New York, Harcourt, Brace and Company, 1935.
** The Complete Works of Shakespeare, The Cambridge Edition Text, as edited by W. A. Wright (Rockwell Kent).

The Bedside of Lope De Vega[*]

* * * In 1635, Lope de Vega, the Spanish dramatist, earnestly asked those gathered at his bedside, "Am I really dying?" When they assured him that he was going fast, he explained, "All right then, I'll say it—Dante makes me sick."

The Last Words of Louis XVI[**]

The steps were steep, the king's hands were tied behind his back, and he was heavy and feeble from lack of exercise. It was unclear if he would even make it. There was a pause. Suddenly Edgeworth exhorted the king: *"Fils de Saint Louis, ascendez au ciel"* ("Son of Saint Louis, ascend to heaven")—or something to that effect; but whatever he said, it filled Louis with a blast of courage. The king hurried forward to the front of the platform, stood erect, and proudly sought to address the multitude. The head of the Paris National Guard signaled a drum roll; Louis commanded quiet. He now embraced the French not as accused and accusers, or counterrevolutionary and revolutionary, but as countryman and countrymen. "Frenchmen, I die innocent; it is from the scaffold and near to appearing before God that I tell you so. I pardon my enemies. I hope that the shedding of my blood will contribute to the happiness of France and you, unfortunate people"—but at that instant, the guard ordered, *"Tambours!"* and the din of fifteen drummers extinguished the rest.

Suddenly there was a grave silence. Louis was strapped to a plank, there was a hiss and then the thud of the heavy blade, and then for the barest of moments, a perfect stillness.

Stephen's Account[†]

The rule [admitting dying declarations] is in many ways remarkable. It has worked, I am informed, ill in India, into which country it has been introduced together with many other parts of the English law of evidence. * * * A remark made on the policy of the rule by a native of Madras shows how differently such matters are viewed in different parts of the world. "Such evidence," he said, "ought never to be admitted in any case. What motive for telling the truth can any man possibly have when he is at the point of death?"

---

[*] Ralph Slovenko, *The Impact of Profanity on Hearsay Evidence,* 1 Medicine and Law 397, 397 (1982).

[**] Jay Winik, The Great Upheaval 316–37 (2007).

[†] 1 Sir James Fitzjames Stephen, A History of the Criminal Law of England (1883).

* * *

R. v. Perry

Court of Criminal Appeal (England), 1909
[1909] 2 K.B. 697

The judgment of the COURT (Lord Alverstone C.J. Darling and A. T. Lawrence JJ.) was delivered by LORD ALVERSTONE C.J.

This appeal raises a very important question. The trial was one for murder arising out of the death of the girl Agnes Margaret Summersby through an illegal operation performed upon her. The evidence was not in all probability sufficient to secure the conviction of the prisoner apart from a dying declaration made by the deceased girl. [On the morning of April 16, 1909, several hours after a doctor said in her presence, in a subdued voice but loud enough that she could have heard him, that she might die at any moment, Agnes said to her sister Gertrude, "Oh, Gert, I shall go, but keep this a secret." She then described how the defendant performed an abortion on her. Agnes died that evening.] At the trial Lawrance J. admitted the declaration, but expressed the opinion that the case was one fit for appeal in order that a definite ruling might be given by this Court, if possible, as to the admissibility of the statement made by the deceased girl to her sister. Before dealing with the actual terms of the statement we desire to point out that the principle has been recognized for many years and can be expressed clearly and definitely. In our opinion that principle cannot be expressed in better terms than those used by Eyre C.B. in Rex v. Woodcock. He said:

> "Now the general principle on which this species of evidence is admitted is, that they are declarations made in extremity, when the party is at the point of death, and when every hope of this world is gone: when every motive to falsehood is silenced, and the mind is induced by the most powerful considerations to speak the truth; a situation so solemn and so awful is considered by the law as creating an obligation equal to that which is imposed by a positive oath administered in a Court of justice."

The expression "at the point of death" which is there used has given rise to some misapprehension, and in Reg. v. Osman 10 Lush L.J. said that there must be a settled hopeless expectation of "immediate death." We are of opinion that the presence or absence of expectation on the part of the declarant of immediate death is not the true test as to whether a statement as to the cause of death is admissible or not. Death must be imminent, but the material point is that the statement must be made when every hope of life has gone from the person making the statement. * * * It is also desirable to read a passage in the earlier part of the judgment in which Charles J. referred to the reasons why he differed from Lush L.J. He said: "In the latest case of all (Reg. v. Osman 16) Lush L.J. lays down the principle in these terms: 'A dying declaration is admitted in evidence because it is presumed that no person who is immediately going into the presence of his

Maker, will do so with a lie on his lips. But the person making the declaration must entertain a settled hopeless expectation of immediate death. If he thinks he will die to-morrow it will not do.' That is the judgment of Willes J. with this addition, that Lush L.J. inserts the word 'immediate' before death, and goes on to say: 'If he thinks he will die to-morrow it will not do.' With the greatest deference to the latter very learned judge I would rather prefer to adopt the language of Willes J. and say that the declarant must be under a 'settled hopeless expectation of death.' 'Immediate death' must be construed in the sense of death impending, not on the instant, but within a very very short distance indeed. These are the principles that have been laid down and are to guide me in the exercise of my judgment." In other words the test is whether all hope of life has been abandoned so that the person making the statement thinks that death must follow. In our opinion that is the true principle. * * *

We have communicated with Lawrance J., and he informs us that what he intended to express at the trial was that he thought it was a case in which this Court should have the opportunity of laying down the principle upon which the admissibility of evidence of such statements ought to be determined. He informs us that he has no doubt that the deceased girl had abandoned all hope of life at the time she made the statement. We are of opinion that the right view is that in determining whether a declaration is admissible in evidence the judge at the trial ought to consider whether the death of the deceased was imminent at the time the declaration was made and to determine from the language used by the deceased whether the statement was made at a time when the deceased had "a settled hopeless expectation of death." In the present case, if the expression "I shall go" is taken alone, it might mean I shall die some day; but, taking into consideration the whole sentence, we concur with the opinion of Lawrance J. that the statement was made by the deceased with the hopeless expectation of death. By the expression "hopeless expectation of death" I mean that the deceased had abandoned all hope of living. The statement is therefore admissible as a dying declaration made by her. On these grounds we are of opinion that the appeal must be dismissed.

QUESTION

Would Agnes' statement be considered testimonial within the meaning of *Crawford*?

State v. Williams

67 N.C. 12 (1872)

■ RODMAN, J.

* * * It is * * * clear that [dying] declarations are admissible only to those things to which the declarant would have been competent to testify if sworn in the case. Consequently, if they be not the statement of a fact, but merely the expression of the opinion of the deceased, they are inadmissible. And so, if merely hearsay, or irrelevant.

It is contended, for the prisoners, that the declarations in this case were nothing more than the expression of an opinion or belief.

The case states, that Lucinda Wainwright testified that the deceased said: He knew who shot him. To which she replied that she did not know. Then deceased said, it was Edward Williams, though I did not see him. Further, in reply to a question by witness as to who shot him, deceased said, I don't know what those poor creatures shot me for; it was Ed. Williams who shot me, though I did not see him.

The case further states that the deceased was shot after dark, while sitting in his house at the fire-place, with his right side near an aperture between the logs of the outer wall, about three inches wide. The shooting was done through the aperture by some person standing on the outside of the house. The wounds were in the right wrist and side.

It was said for the State that every allegation of the identity of a person is necessarily the expression of an opinion only, because it is a conclusion drawn from a comparison of the appearance of the person at one time, with the recollection of his appearance at some other time. This is true; but the admission of such evidence is an exception to the general rule excluding opinions, founded on the necessity of the case.

But there must be some limit to the exception: a witness cannot be allowed absolutely to substitute his judgment for that of the tribunal to whom the law has committed the decision of the fact. We think the limit may be drawn without any difficulty, and consistently with the habitual practice of Courts. Whenever the opinion of the witness upon such a question, or on one coming under the same rule, is the *direct* result of observation through his senses, the evidence is admitted. As, for example, when a witness has seen a person or object at several times, and expresses his opinion as to the identity of what he saw at one time with what he saw at another, as human language is inadequate to convey to the mind of another person fully and accurately the impression made upon the mind of the witness through his sense of sight, his opinion, as the result of that impression, is admitted, and is entitled to more or less weight, according to the circumstances. And although opinions, as derived, may sometimes be erroneous, yet they are not generally so, and when carefully weighed are sufficiently reliable for practical use in the ordinary affairs of life. The witness does not *unnecessarily* substitute his judgment for that of the tribunal.

But if the opinion of the witness is the result of a course of reasoning from collateral facts, it is inadmissible. As, for example, if at the time to which the question of identity applied he did not see or have the testimony of any sense as to the person in question, but believed it to have been him because he might have been there, and had a motive to have been there and to have done the act alleged. In such a case the tribunal is as competent to reason out the resultant opinion as the witness is; and by the theory of the law, it alone is competent to do so. To allow any influence to the opinion of the witness would be *unnecessarily* to substitute him to the function of the tribunal.

Now, to apply these views to the language of the deceased. * * * He appears to have had in his mind an idea of the distinction which I have been endeavoring to draw, and to have wished to exclude the conclusion that his opinion was anything more than one founded on an inference from facts and motives which he may have supposed to exist, but which even if they were in evidence on the trial, (as to which the case is silent,) do not affect the present question. The deceased excludes sight as a source of his opinion. A Court is not at liberty to conjecture, that he might have heard the prisoner and identified him in that way, especially as there is no suggestion of that sort in the evidence.

We think that, whether we take the words of the deceased alone, or in connection with the circumstances of the assault, they do not purport, and were not meant to state, the identity of Williams with the assailant, as a fact known through the senses, and that, consequently, they were inadmissible. * * *

Reade, J. *Dubitante.*

PER CURIAM. *Venire de novo.*

Garza v. Delta Tau Delta Fraternity National
Louisiana Court of Appeals, First Circuit, 2005
916 So. 2d 185

■ CARTER, C.J.

This matter comes before this court on a writ of certiorari granted to consider the res nova issue of whether a suicide note can qualify as a dying declaration, such that it may be admissible as an exception to the hearsay rule. * * *

On April 9, 2001, Courtney Garza, a twenty-one-year-old student at Southeastern University in Hammond, committed suicide by hanging herself in her parents' Baton Rouge home. Courtney left behind a handwritten, three-page suicide note, written on front and back, dated "04/08/01 Sunday 12:30." [Courtney Garza's parents brought a civil action against a national fraternity, the university, and other defendants, alleging that Courtney had been raped by a fraternity member as a result of defendants' negligence in failing to supervise activities at the fraternity, and that defendants also failed to provide adequate crisis intervention after the rape.]

The sole issue before this court is whether the trial court erred by admitting into evidence Courtney's suicide note pursuant to the dying declaration exception to the hearsay rule found in Louisiana Code of Evidence article 804 B(2). * * * "A statement made by a declarant while believing that [her] death was imminent, concerning the cause or circumstances of what [she] believed to be [her] impending death" is not excluded by the hearsay rule if the declarant is unavailable as a witness. LSA-C.E. art. 804 B(2). A court may look at the facts and circumstances surrounding the out-of-court statement to determine whether the declarant made the statements in the belief that death was imminent. If the circumstances do not satisfactorily disclose the declarant recognizes the solemn situation in which she is placed, the declaration should be rejected. The length of time elapsing between the making of the declaration and death is to be considered. The impression of an immediate death, not the rapid succession of death, is what makes the statement admissible. Relators contend death was not imminent as there is no evidence Courtney was injured at the time the note was written. As observed by relators, most of the jurisprudence involves dying declarations made after wounds have been inflicted on a declarant by a third person. However, there is no requirement in Article 804 B(2) that a wound or injury be inflicted prior to the making of a dying declaration. Nor does Article 804 B(2) require that death be by the hand of a third party. [There is nothing in Article 804 B(2) to prohibit a suicide note from being admitted as a dying declaration.] Courtney's written words expressly indicate an awareness of her impending death. She writes, "I thought I would've cut it short sometime before now. . . I'm still scared right now as I plan it out, but I'm really doing it this time." Her closing words are, "This is goodbye." The contents of Courtney's note reflect a settled expectation-a realization-that death was at hand. See Shepard v. United States.

Perhaps the greatest evidence that the statement was written with a belief that death was imminent, is the fact that Courtney took her own life soon after writing the dated note. The note is dated April 8, 2001, at 12:30; Courtney died April 9, 2001. Compare State v. Satterfield, 193 W.Va. 503, 457 S.E.2d 440, 450 (1995), wherein statements in a suicide note referenced events occurring less than twenty-four hours before the suicide. The suicide note was admissible as a dying declaration. In [United States v. Angleton, 269 F.Supp.2d 878 (S.D. Tex. 2003)], several suicide notes were offered and rejected as dying declarations. Two dated notes were written two weeks or more before the suicide, not "very shortly before the suicide." And, the evidence was insufficient to support a finding that the declarant committed suicide "soon after writing" the relevant parts of the undated notes. Unlike Angleton, in the instant case, Courtney died soon after writing her dated note.

To qualify as a dying declaration, the statement also must relate to the cause or circumstances of the declarant's death. The handwritten note offers insight into the circumstances leading to the suicide that shortly followed. Courtney wrote, "I guess I'll begin [and] explain what happened to me this semester. . . I hope you can read this. It explains it all for you." Courtney recounts past events, explaining the causes and circumstances she perceived to have brought her to suicide. See Angleton, 269 F.Supp.2d at 888.

* * * Finding no error in the trial court's judgment finding the note, as edited, admissible, we deny the writ.

McDONALD, J. dissenting.

Although I have the utmost respect for the excellent analysis of my colleagues, I am not convinced that the note in this case meets the criteria for a dying declaration. The "classic" dying declaration is made by a person near death from fatal wounds or illness, who makes a statement to a third party about who inflicted the wounds or caused the illness. The third party testifies as to the declarant's condition and the circumstances of the statement. Such a statement is made spontaneously by one who is unexpectedly facing imminent certain death. In contrast, a suicide note is a deliberate communication composed in advance of the act itself. The writer intends for the note to be found and read. Therefore, the writer may carefully and methodically select the words she wishes to use. The author has the opportunity tell some things and omit others, to accuse or exonerate, to clarify or confound, or even seek revenge against someone who is blameless. A person contemplating suicide, and leaving a note to be found after his death, would not be in fear of legal punishment. The writer of a suicide note might have a motive to implicate another other than the truth. He might be vindictive for reasons unrelated to the statements in the note. A declarant who has decided to commit suicide would have no fear, perhaps other than religious convictions which may or may not be present, of punishment for the criminal act asserted or for the falsity of the note.

Additionally, in reading Ms. Garza's note as a whole, it is not clear that she intended to immediately end her life. * * * [T]he note was written at least 12 hours and perhaps up to 36 hours or more prior to her death.

The dying declaration is a last gasp by someone who has been unexpectedly injured; a solemn yet spontaneous statement by someone who knows and believes that they cannot be saved from immediate death. The imminence of death is critical, and the declarant must believe that all hope of recovery is lost, that the damage has been done, and that death is certain to immediately follow. There is no hope, no ability to prevent or stop the looming and impending death. A spontaneous, unrehearsed statement by one who is a victim of violence and mortally wounded, is far different from a written, planned, and choreographed statement by one contemplating suicide. Not only are the motives, but the person contemplating suicide can change her mind and choose to live, while the mortally wounded victim of violence cannot. * * *

QUESTIONS

Suppose Courtney's suicide note had been introduced in a prosecution of the alleged rapist. Would it satisfy the dying declaration exception? Should it be considered testimonial within the meaning of *Crawford*? *Cf.* State v. Jensen, 331 Wis2d 440, 794 N.W.2d 482 (Wis. App. 2010) (husband accused of poisoning wife to death; wife made statements beforehand to effect that if anything happened to her husband should be first suspect).

See Federal Rules of Evidence 804(b)(2); California Evidence Code § 1242.

HYPOTHETICALS

(1) X is prosecuted for murder in shooting A to death in a barroom brawl. In defense, X calls B and makes an offer of proof that B will testify that she talked with A in the hospital the day before his death, that A had difficulty in breathing, and said: "I don't think I can make it. It was not X's fault, C was going after X with a knife before X drew his gun. C ducked when X fired and that's how I got shot." The prosecutor makes a hearsay objection to B's testimony and offers to prove by Y, a nurse, that five minutes before B talked with A, A told her that he was feeling fine and expected to be able to leave the hospital within a few days. The judge listens to the testimony of B and Y out of the presence of the jury and believes that both witnesses are telling the truth. Must she then admit A's statement in evidence?

(2) Assume the same facts as given in Illustration (1), except that the judge admits in evidence A's statement to B upon finding that the requirements of the dying declaration exception are satisfied. The prosecutor calls Y, the nurse, to testify before the jury to A's statement made to her. X objects that Y's testimony is inadmissible in view of the court's ruling admitting A's statement to B. What result?

Roger W. Kirst, Does Crawford Provide a Stable Foundation for Confrontation Doctrine?

71 Brook. L. Rev. 35 (2005)

* * *

1. Dying Declaration

[In *Crawford*, Justice Scalia conceded] that even a testimonial dying declaration might be admissible without confrontation. For that conclusion he cited English common law decisions and an English treatise. He suggested that this would be the only exception for a testimonial statement because it is sui generis in the English common law. * * * *Crawford* may suggest that any statement is admissible if it can be labeled a dying declaration, but there is still no case in which the Supreme Court has affirmed a conviction on that basis.

2. Forfeiture

Justice Scalia also endorsed a second exception to the bright-line rule for testimonial statements when he stated that "the rule of forfeiture by wrongdoing (which we accept) extinguishes confrontation claims on essentially equitable grounds." For this proposition, Justice Scalia used a "See" signal and cited *Reynolds v. United States* [98 U.S. 145 (1879)]. There are many questions about the forfeiture doctrine that were not discussed in this brief mention in *Crawford*. Justice Scalia did not discuss whether the original meaning of the Sixth Amendment had been followed in *Reynolds* in 1879. He did not suggest any limits on the rule of forfeiture that might be derived from *Reynolds*, even though elsewhere in *Crawford* he emphasized the need to read the facts of Supreme Court precedent precisely.

Reynolds did not involve an ordinary hearsay statement. The hearsay was prior testimony at an earlier trial of the same defendant under a different indictment. The defendant had been present and had a full opportunity to cross-examine. There was evidence that the defendant was actively involved in preventing the witness from testifying. * * * The Supreme Court * * * cited three American treatises as support for its statement that "if a witness is kept away by the adverse party, his testimony, taken on a former trial between the same parties upon the same issues, may be given in evidence."

Reynolds did not consider whether the forfeiture rule would apply if the defendant had killed the witness as part of the original crime without specifically intending to make the witness an unavailable hearsay declarant. That is a different kind of wrongdoing because its effect cannot be undone at the time of trial, while in *Reynolds* the defendant could have changed his mind and permitted the witness to attend and testify. *Reynolds* did not consider whether the defendant's wrongdoing would have mattered if the hearsay had been something other than prior testimony at a trial in which the defendant had already had one chance to confront the declarant.

In criticizing the reliability test, Justice Scalia wrote that "[d]ispensing with confrontation because testimony is obviously reliable is akin to dispensing with jury trial because a defendant is obviously guilty." That criticism could apply as well to some versions of a forfeiture rule. Should forfeiture depend on no more than a judicial finding that a defendant's alleged commission of the crime contributed to the unavailability of live testimony? That possibility would raise the question of whether dispensing with confrontation because the judge thinks the defendant is obviously guilty is akin to dispensing with the jury verdict because the defendant is obviously guilty. That question was not answered in *Reynolds* or *Crawford*.

Richard D. Friedman, Confrontation and the Definition of Chutzpa

31 Israel L. Rev. 507 (1997)

You may know the standard illustration of *chutzpa*—the man who kills both his parents and then begs the sentencing court to have mercy on an orphan. In this article, I discuss a case *of chutzpa* that is nearly as outlandish—the criminal defendant who, having rendered his victim unavailable to testify, contends that evidence of the victim's statement should not be admitted against him because to do so would violate his right to confront her. I contend that in a case like this the defendant should be deemed to have forfeited the confrontation right. On the same grounds, if the jurisdiction applies a rule against hearsay, he should be deemed to have forfeited the right to invoke it against evidence of the statement.

In one sense, this conclusion is very unstartling. Courts have held, in a variety of contexts, that if the accused has rendered a potential witness unavailable—whether by murder, concealment, intimidation, improper payment, or chicanery—the accused should be deemed to have forfeited the confrontation right or the hearsay objection. And this rule, which I shall call the forfeiture principle, has gained legislative recognition as well in some jurisdictions. * * *

I believe the forfeiture principle applies with full force, and without much controversy, when the declarant, the potential witness whose statement is at issue, is the victim of the crime alleged. My suggestion is that courts should be willing to apply the principle reflexively—that is, even when the act that rendered the declarant-victim unable to testify was the same criminal act for which the accused is now on trial.

QUESTION

Which is the best justification for the dying declaration-exception to the hearsay rule, and which best squares with the rationale of *Crawford* and justifies a qualification to the confrontation right – (a) the presumption that "no person who is immediately going into the presence of his Maker, will do so with a lie on his lips," (b) the probability that a person on the edge of death from a fatal blow will be motivated to blame the true perpetrator, not someone else, and will be unafraid to do so, or (c) the forfeiture principle?

Giles v. California

Supreme Court of the United States, 2008.
554 U.S. 353, 128 S.Ct. 2678, 171 L.Ed.2d 488

■ JUSTICE SCALIA delivered the opinion of the Court, except as to Part II–D–2.

We consider whether a defendant forfeits his Sixth Amendment right to confront a witness against him when a judge determines that a wrongful act by the defendant made the witness unavailable to testify at trial.

I

[Dwayne Giles shot to death his ex-girlfriend, Brenda Avie, outside the garage of his grandmother's house. At his murder trial, he testified that he acted in self-defense after Avie came to the house and threatened to kill him. The prosecution offered statements that Avie had made to a police officer responding to a domestic-violence report about three weeks before the shooting; Avie accused Giles of attempting to choke her, punching her, and threatening to kill her. Giles objected, but the trial court admitted the statements under a provision of California law that permits admission of out-of-court statements describing the infliction or threat of physical injury on a declarant when the declarant is unavailable to testify at trial and the prior statements are deemed trustworthy. Cal. Evid.Code Ann. § 1370 (West Supp.2008). Giles was convicted. *Crawford* and *Davis* were decided while the case was still on direct appellate review. Ultimately, the California Supreme Court, while noting that the parties did not dispute that Avie's statements were testimonial, held that Giles had forfeited the confrontation right because his intentional criminal act—killing Avie—had rendered her unavailable as a witness.]

II

* * * We held in *Crawford* that the Confrontation Clause is "most naturally read as a reference to the right of confrontation at common law, admitting only those exceptions established at the time of the founding." We therefore ask whether the theory of forfeiture by wrongdoing accepted by the California Supreme Court is a founding-era exception to the confrontation right.

A

We have previously acknowledged that two forms of testimonial statements were admitted at common law even though they were unconfronted. The first of these were declarations made by a speaker who was both on the brink of death and aware that he was dying. Avie did not make the unconfronted statements admitted at Giles' trial when she was dying, so her statements do not fall within this historic exception.

A second common-law doctrine, which we will refer to as forfeiture by wrongdoing, permitted the introduction of statements of a witness who was "detained" or "kept away" by the "means or procurement" of the defendant. * * *

The terms used to define the scope of the forfeiture rule suggest that the exception applied only when the defendant engaged in conduct *designed* to prevent the witness from testifying. * * *

Cases and treatises of the time indicate that a purpose-based definition of these terms governed. * * *

We are aware of no case in which the exception was invoked although the defendant had not engaged in conduct designed to prevent a witness from testifying, such as offering a bribe.

B

The manner in which the rule was applied makes plain that unconfronted testimony would *not* be admitted without a showing that the defendant intended to prevent a witness from testifying. In cases where the evidence suggested that the defendant had caused a person to be absent, but had not done so to prevent the person from testifying—as in the typical murder case involving accusatorial statements by the victim—the testimony was excluded unless it was confronted or fell within the dying-declaration exception. Prosecutors do not appear to have even *argued* that the judge could admit the unconfronted statements because the defendant committed the murder for which he was on trial. * * *

Many * * * cases excluded victims' statements when there was insufficient evidence that the witness was aware he was about to die. Courts in all these cases did not even consider admitting the statements on the ground that the defendant's crime was to blame for the witness's absence-even when the evidence establishing that was overwhelming. * * *

Judges and prosecutors also failed to invoke forfeiture as a sufficient basis to admit unconfronted statements in the cases that did apply the dying-declarations exception. * * *

The State and the dissent note that common-law authorities justified the wrongful-procurement rule by invoking the maxim that a defendant should not be permitted to benefit from his own wrong. But as the evidence amply shows, the "wrong" and the "evil Practices" to which these statements referred was conduct *designed* to prevent a witness from testifying. The absence of a forfeiture rule covering this sort of conduct would create an intolerable incentive for defendants to bribe, intimidate, or even kill witnesses against them. There is nothing mysterious about courts' refusal to carry the rationale further. The notion that judges may strip the defendant of a right that the Constitution deems essential to a fair trial, on the basis of a prior *judicial* assessment that the defendant is guilty as charged, does not sit well with the right to trial by jury. It is akin, one might say, to "dispensing with jury trial because a defendant is obviously guilty." *Crawford,* 541 U.S., at 62, 124 S.Ct. 1354.

C

Not only was the State's proposed exception to the right of confrontation plainly not an "exceptio[n] established at the time of the founding," *id.,* at 54, 124 S.Ct. 1354; it is not established in American jurisprudence *since* the founding. American courts never—prior to 1985—invoked forfeiture outside the context of deliberate witness tampering. * * *

In 1997, this Court approved a Federal Rule of Evidence, entitled "Forfeiture by wrongdoing," which applies only when the defendant "engaged or acquiesced in wrongdoing that was intended to, and did, procure the unavailability of the declarant as a witness." Fed. Rule of Evid. 804(b)(6). We have described this as a rule "which codifies the forfeiture doctrine." Davis v. Washington, 547 U.S. 813, 833 (2006). Every commentator we are aware of has concluded the requirement of intent "means that the exception applies only if the defendant has in mind the particular purpose of making the witness unavailable." The commentators come out this way because the dissent's claim that knowledge is sufficient to show intent is emphatically not the modern view.

In sum, our interpretation of the common-law forfeiture rule is supported by (1) the most natural reading of the language used at common law; (2) the absence of common-law cases *admitting* prior statements on a forfeiture theory when the defendant had not engaged in conduct designed to prevent a witness from testifying; (3) the common law's uniform exclusion of unconfronted inculpatory testimony by murder victims (except testimony given with awareness of impending death) in the innumerable cases in which the defendant was on trial for killing the victim, but was not shown to have done so for the purpose of preventing testimony; (4) a subsequent history in which the dissent's broad forfeiture theory has not been applied. The first two and the last are highly persuasive; the third is in our view conclusive.

D

* * *

2

* * * The "basic purposes and objectives" of forfeiture doctrine, [the dissent] says, require that a defendant who wrongfully caused the absence of a witness be deprived of his confrontation rights, whether or not there was any such rule applicable at common law.

If we were to reason from the "basic purposes and objectives" of the forfeiture doctrine, we are not at all sure we would come to the dissent's favored result. The common-law forfeiture rule was aimed at removing the otherwise powerful incentive for defendants to intimidate, bribe, and kill the witnesses against them—in other words, it is grounded in "the ability of courts to protect the integrity of their proceedings."*Davis*, 547 U.S., at 834, 126 S.Ct. 2266.The boundaries of the doctrine seem to us intelligently fixed so as to avoid a principle repugnant to our constitutional system of trial by jury: that those murder defendants whom the judge considers guilty (after less than a full trial, mind you, and of course before the jury has pronounced guilt) should be deprived of fair-trial rights, lest they benefit from their judge-determined wrong.† * * *

The larger problem with the dissent's argument, however, is that the guarantee of confrontation is no guarantee at all if it is subject to whatever exceptions courts from time to time consider "fair." It is not the role of courts to extrapolate from the words of the Sixth Amendment to the values behind it, and then to enforce its guarantees only to the extent they serve (in the courts' views) those underlying values. The Sixth Amendment seeks fairness indeed—but seeks it through very specific means (one of which is confrontation) that were the trial rights of Englishmen. It "does not suggest

---

† The dissent identifies one circumstance—and only one—in which a court may determine the outcome of a case before it goes to the jury: A judge may determine the existence of a conspiracy in order to make incriminating statements of co-conspirators admissible against the defendant under Federal Rule of Evidence 801(d)(2)(E). *Bourjaily v. United States*, 483 U.S. 171 (1987), held that admission of the evidence did not violate the Confrontation Clause because it "falls within a firmly rooted hearsay exception"—the test under *Ohio v. Roberts*, 448 U.S. 56, 66 (1980), the case that *Crawford* overruled. In fact it did not violate the Confrontation Clause for the quite different reason that it was not (as an incriminating statement in furtherance of the conspiracy would probably never be) testimonial. The co-conspirator hearsay rule does not pertain to a constitutional right and is in fact quite unusual.

We do not say, of course, that a judge can never be allowed to inquire into guilt of the charged offense in order to make a preliminary evidentiary ruling. That must sometimes be done under the forfeiture rule that we adopt—when, for example, the defendant is on trial for murdering a witness in order to prevent his testimony. But the exception to ordinary practice that we support is (1) needed to protect the integrity of court proceedings, (2) based upon longstanding precedent, and (3) much less expansive than the exception proposed by the dissent.

any open-ended exceptions from the confrontation requirement to be developed by the courts." *Crawford, supra,* at 54, 124 S.Ct. 1354.

E

The dissent closes by pointing out that a forfeiture rule which ignores *Crawford* would be particularly helpful to women in abusive relationships—or at least particularly helpful in punishing their abusers. Not as helpful as the dissent suggests, since only *testimonial* statements are excluded by the Confrontation Clause. Statements to friends and neighbors about abuse and intimidation, and statements to physicians in the course of receiving treatment would be excluded, if at all, only by hearsay rules, which are free to adopt the dissent's version of forfeiture by wrongdoing. In any event, we are puzzled by the dissent's decision to devote its peroration to domestic abuse cases. Is the suggestion that we should have one Confrontation Clause (the one the Framers adopted and *Crawford* described) for all other crimes, but a special, improvised, Confrontation Clause for those crimes that are frequently directed against women? Domestic violence is an intolerable offense that legislatures may choose to combat through many means—from increasing criminal penalties to adding resources for investigation and prosecution to funding awareness and prevention campaigns. But for that serious crime, as for others, abridging the constitutional rights of criminal defendants is not in the State's arsenal.

The domestic-violence context is, however, relevant for a separate reason. Acts of domestic violence often are intended to dissuade a victim from resorting to outside help, and include conduct designed to prevent testimony to police officers or cooperation in criminal prosecutions. Where such an abusive relationship culminates in murder, the evidence may support a finding that the crime expressed the intent to isolate the victim and to stop her from reporting abuse to the authorities or cooperating with a criminal prosecution—rendering her prior statements admissible under the forfeiture doctrine. Earlier abuse, or threats of abuse, intended to dissuade the victim from resorting to outside help would be highly relevant to this inquiry, as would evidence of ongoing criminal proceedings at which the victim would have been expected to testify. This is not, as the dissent charges, nothing more than "knowledge-based intent." (Emphasis deleted.)

The state courts in this case did not consider the intent of the defendant because they found that irrelevant to application of the forfeiture doctrine. This view of the law was error, but the court is free to consider evidence of the defendant's intent on remand.

* * *

We decline to approve an exception to the Confrontation Clause unheard of at the time of the founding or for 200 years thereafter. The judgment of the California Supreme Court is vacated, and the case is remanded for further proceedings not inconsistent with this opinion.

It is so ordered.

[Justice Thomas wrote a separate concurrence to note that he adhered to his view, expressed in *Davis*, that statements like the one made by Brenda Avie, which he regarded as indistinguishable from those involved in *Hammon* (decided together with *Davis*), are not testimonial; that question was not before the Court, however. Justice Alito also wrote a separate concurrence to make clear that he too was "not convinced" that the statement at issue fell within the Confrontation Clause; he made no attempt to distinguish *Hammon*, in which he had joined the majority.]

■ JUSTICE SOUTER, with whom JUSTICE GINSBURG joins, concurring in part.

I am convinced that the Court's historical analysis is sound and I join all but Part II–D–2 of the opinion. * * * It was, and is, reasonable to place the risk of untruth in an unconfronted, out-of-court statement on a defendant who meant to preclude the testing that confrontation provides. The importance of that intent in assessing the fairness of placing the risk on the defendant is most obvious when a defendant is prosecuted for the very act that causes the witness's absence, homicide being the extreme example. If the victim's prior statement were admissible solely because the defendant kept the witness out of court by committing homicide, admissibility of the victim's statement to prove guilt would turn on finding the defendant guilty of the homicidal act causing the absence; evidence that the defendant killed would come in because the defendant probably killed. The only thing saving admissibility and liability determinations from question begging would be (in a jury case) the distinct functions of judge and jury: judges would find by a preponderance of evidence that the defendant killed (and so would admit the testimonial statement), while the jury could so find only on proof beyond a reasonable doubt. Equity demands something more than this near circularity before the right to confrontation is forfeited, and more is supplied by showing intent to prevent the witness from testifying.

It is this rationale for the limit on the forfeiture exception rather than a dispositive example from the historical record that persuades me that the Court's conclusion is the right one in this case. The contrast between the Court's and Justice Breyer's careful examinations of the historical record tells me that the early cases on the exception were not calibrated finely enough to answer the narrow question here. The historical record as revealed by the exchange simply does not focus on what should be required for forfeiture when the crime charged occurred in an abusive relationship or was its culminating act; today's understanding of domestic abuse had no apparent significance at the time of the Framing, and there is no early example of the forfeiture rule operating in that circumstance.

Examining the early cases and commentary, however, reveals two things that count in favor of the Court's understanding of forfeiture when the evidence shows domestic abuse. The first is the substantial indication that the Sixth Amendment was meant to require some degree of intent to thwart the judicial process before thinking it reasonable to hold the confrontation right forfeited; otherwise the right would in practical terms boil down to a measure of reliable hearsay, a view rejected in *Crawford*. The second is the absence from the early material of any reason to doubt that the element of intention would normally be satisfied by the intent inferred on the part of the domestic abuser in the classic abusive relationship, which is meant to isolate the victim from outside help, including the aid of law enforcement and the judicial process. If the evidence for admissibility shows a continuing relationship of this sort, it would make no sense to suggest that the oppressing defendant miraculously abandoned the dynamics of abuse the instant before he killed his victim, say in a fit of anger. The Court's conclusion in Part II–E thus fits the rationale that equity requires and the historical record supports.

[Justice Breyer, joined by Justices Stevens and Kennedy, dissented. Part of his argument was historical. He contended that murder of the witness satisfied the standard of the old forfeiture cases, given the greatness of the wrong and the evidentiary advantage gained by the accused. He offered several arguments to explain the absence of any older cases in which forfeiture was applied even though the accused had not murdered the witness for the purpose of rendering her unavailable. One was that, in his view, under the older cases forfeiture doctrine did not have much force in the context of murder; a deposition of a crime victim taken pursuant to the Marian statutes could be admitted if and only if the accused had had an opportunity to cross-examine the deponent; this made forfeiture inapposite in cases like the present one. Recent cases had been willing to apply forfeiture even absent an opportunity for cross, and this was an "elephant of a change," acceptable to the majority as well as to the dissenters, in comparison to the "gnat"-like question of the required state of mind of the accused. Also, he noted, "The defendant's state of mind only arises as an issue in forfeiture cases where the witness has made prior statements against the defendant and where there is a possible motive for the killing other than to prevent the witness from testifying." This was likely to occur only in domestic violence cases, and 200 years ago a victim of non-fatal domestic violence was unlikely to make a testimonial statement about it. In response to the concern about a judge having to make a preliminary assessment of the defendant's wrongful act in order to determine whether the relevant statements should be admitted, he pointed out that "*any* forfeiture rule requires a judge to determine as a preliminary matter that the defendant's own wrongdoing caused the witness to be absent." Justice Breyer also argued that a "knowledge-based intent" approach to forfeiture was superior to a "purpose" approach. A "purpose" rule would find forfeiture only when the purpose of the defendant's action was to prevent testimony, whereas a "knowledge-based intent" rule would find forfeiture whenever the defendant would necessarily have known that his action would prevent the victim from testifying. Justice Breyer viewed the majority opinion as favoring a "purpose" approach, except perhaps in the context of domestic violence, where the majority "ends its opinion by creating a kind of presumption that will transform *purpose* into *knowledge-based intent*." He also analyzed Justice Souter's opinion, noting that it "seems to say that a showing of domestic abuse is sufficient to call into play the protection of the forfeiture rule in a trial for murder of the domestic abuse victim," and that this, in effect, eviscerated a purpose requirement in the domestic violence context. Thus, though he would have preferred a rule broadly rejecting a purpose requirement, he agreed with Justice Souter's formulation to the extent it "in effect presumes 'purpose' based on no more than evidence of a history of domestic violence."]

For a sharply critical view of *Giles*, contending that the dying declaration cases should be viewed as instances of forfeiture, see Richard D. Friedman, *Giles v. California: A Personal Reflection*, 13 Lewis & Clark L. Rev. 733 (2009).

---

8. PRIOR IDENTIFICATION

Weinstein's Evidence
Weinstein-Berger, 1975 (801–3).[*]

1975 AMENDMENT

Congress amended [Fed.Rule] 801(d)(1 by adding subparagraph (C) which excludes from the definition of hearsay a statement "of identification of a person made after perceiving him." * * *

The Report of the Senate Committee on the Judiciary considering the amendment explained this opposition as stemming from concern "that a conviction could be based upon such unsworn, out-of-court testimony." However, the Report noted that this was a misconception since all constitutional protections were retained and in addition, the requirements of Rule 801(d)(1) that the identifier be available for cross-examination at the trial is continued. The Report reads:

> The purpose of the provision was to make clear, in line with the recent law in the area, that nonsuggestive lineup, photographic and other identifications are not hearsay and therefore are admissible. In the lineup case of Gilbert v. California, the Supreme Court, noting the split of authority in admitting prior out-of-court identifications, stated, "The recent trend, however, is to admit the prior identification under the exception [to the hearsay rule] that admits as substantive evidence a prior communication by a witness who is available for cross-examination at the trial." And the Federal Courts of Appeals have generally admitted these identifications.

> * * *

In the course of processing the Rules of Evidence in the final weeks of the 93d Congress, the provision excluding such statements of identification from the hearsay category was deleted. Although there

---

[*] Copyright © 1975 By Matthew Bender & Company Incorporated.

was no suggestion in the committee report that prior identifications are not probative, concern was there expressed that a conviction could be based upon such unsworn, out-of-court testimony. Upon further reflection, that concern appears misdirected. First, this exception is addressed to the "admissibility" of evidence and not to the "sufficiency" of evidence to prove guilt. Secondly, except for the former testimony exception to the hearsay exclusion, all hearsay exceptions allow into evidence statements which may not have been made under oath. Moreover, under this rule, unlike a significant majority of the hearsay exceptions, the prior identification is admissible only when the person who made it testifies at trial and is subject to cross-examination. This assures that if any discrepancy occurs between the witness' in-court and out-of-court testimony, the opportunity is available to probe, with the witness under oath, the reasons for that discrepancy so that the trier of fact might determine which statement is to be believed.

Upon reflection, then, it appears the rule is desirable. Since these identifications take place reasonably soon after an offense has been committed, the witness' observations are still fresh in his mind. The identification occurs before his recollection has been dimmed by the passage of time. Equally as important, it also takes place before the defendant or some other party has had the opportunity, through bribe or threat, to influence the witness to change his mind.

* * *

HYPOTHETICALS

1. The victim in a robbery case, as the first prosecution witness, testifies that a masked stranger robbed him of his diamond ring at pistol-point. On direct examination, the witness also testifies that the next day, he told his roommate "I was mugged and the robber took my diamond ring." Objection, hearsay. Is the witness's statement to his roommate admissible on this foundation?

2. A witness testifies at trial that Becky robbed him. He points her out in the courtroom. Then he testifies that he also pointed her out in a pretrial lineup, when he said to the police officer who ran the lineup, "She's the one who robbed me." Is the out-of-court statement admissible?

3. After the robbery victim testified about the lineup, the police officer who ran the lineup gets on the stand and testifies that he saw the victim point to Becky and say "she's the one who robbed me." Admissible?

4. The robbery victim identifies Becky at the lineup, then dies. May the police officer then testify about the identification at the lineup?

United States v. Owens

Supreme Court of the United States, 1988.
484 U.S. 554, 108 S.Ct. 838, 98 L.Ed.2d 951.

■ JUSTICE SCALIA delivered the opinion of the Court.

This case requires us to determine whether either the Confrontation Clause of the Sixth Amendment or Rule 802 of the Federal Rules of Evidence bars testimony concerning a prior, out-of-court identification when the identifying witness is unable, because of memory loss, to explain the basis for the identification.

I

On April 12, 1982, John Foster, a correctional counselor at the federal prison in Lompoc, California, was attacked and brutally beaten with a metal pipe. His skull was fractured, and he remained hospitalized for almost a month. As a result of his injuries, Foster's memory was severely impaired. When Thomas Mansfield, an FBI agent investigating the assault, first attempted to interview Foster, on April 19, he found Foster lethargic and unable to remember his attacker's name. On May 5, Mansfield again spoke to Foster, who was much improved and able to describe the attack. Foster named respondent as his attacker and identified respondent from an array of photographs.

Respondent was tried in Federal District Court for assault with intent to commit murder under 18 U.S.C. § 113(a). At trial, Foster recounted his activities just before the attack, and described feeling the blows to his head and seeing blood on the floor. He testified that he clearly remembered identifying respondent as his assailant during his May 5th interview with Mansfield. On cross-examination, he admitted that he could not remember seeing his assailant. He also admitted that, although there was evidence that he had received numerous visitors in the hospital, he was unable to remember any of them except Mansfield, and could not remember whether any of these visitors had suggested that respondent was the assailant. Defense counsel unsuccessfully sought to refresh his recollection with hospital records, including one indicating that Foster had attributed the assault to someone other than respondent. Respondent was convicted and sentenced to 20 years' imprisonment to be served consecutively to a previous sentence.

On appeal, the United States Court of Appeals for the Ninth Circuit considered challenges based on the Confrontation Clause and Rule 802 of the Federal Rules of Evidence. By divided vote it upheld both challenges (though finding the Rule 802 violation harmless error), and reversed the judgment of the District Court. We granted certiorari to resolve the conflict with other Circuits on the significance of a hearsay declarant's memory loss both with respect to the Confrontation Clause and with respect to Rule 802.

II

The Confrontation Clause of the Sixth Amendment gives the accused the right "to be confronted with the witnesses against him." This has long been read as securing an adequate opportunity to cross-examine adverse witnesses. * * *

[The Court went on to hold that the Confrontation Clause was not violated by the admission of Foster's out-of-court statement. In the course of its opinion, it stated that:]

* * * "[T]he Confrontation Clause guarantees only 'an opportunity for effective cross-examination, not cross-examination that is effective in whatever way, and to whatever extent, the defense might wish.' " * * * It is sufficient that the defendant has the opportunity to bring out such matters as the witness's bias, his lack of care and attentiveness, his poor eyesight, and even (what is often a prime objective of cross-examination, see 3A J. Wigmore, Evidence § 995, pp. 931–932 (J. Chadbourn rev. 1970)) the very fact that he has a bad memory.

III

Respondent urges as an alternative basis for affirmance a violation of Federal Rule of Evidence 802, which generally excludes hearsay. Rule 801(d)(1)(C) defines as not hearsay a prior statement "of identification of a person made after perceiving the person," if the declarant "testifies at the trial or hearing and is subject to cross-examination concerning the statement." The Court of Appeals found that Foster's identification statement did not come within this exclusion because his memory loss prevented his being "subject to cross-examination concerning the statement." Although the Court of Appeals concluded that the violation of the Rules of Evidence was harmless (applying for purposes of that determination a "more-probable-than-not" standard, rather than the "beyond-a-reasonable-doubt" standard applicable to the Confrontation Clause violation), respondent argues to the contrary.

It seems to us that the more natural reading of "subject to cross-examination concerning the statement" includes what was available here. Ordinarily a witness is regarded as "subject to cross-examination" when he is placed on the stand, under oath, and responds willingly to questions. Just as with the constitutional prohibition, limitations on the scope of examination by the trial court or assertions of privilege by the witness may undermine the process to such a degree that meaningful cross-examination within the intent of the Rule no longer exists. But that effect is not produced by the witness' assertion of memory loss—which, as discussed earlier, is often the very result sought to be produced by cross-examination, and can be effective in destroying the force of the prior statement. Rule 801(d)(1)(C), which specifies that the cross-examination need only "concer[n] the statement," does not on its face require more.

This reading seems even more compelling when the Rule is compared with Rule 804(a)(3), which defines "[u]navailability as a witness" to include situations in which a declarant "testifies to a lack of memory of the subject matter of the declarant's statement." Congress plainly was aware of the recurrent evidentiary problem at issue here—witness forgetfulness of an underlying event—but chose not to make it an exception to Rule 801(d)(1)(C).

The reasons for that choice are apparent from the Advisory Committee's Notes on Rule 801 and its legislative history. The premise for Rule 801(d)(1)(C) was that, given adequate safeguards against suggestiveness, out-of-court identifications were generally preferable to courtroom identifications. Advisory Committee's Notes on Rule 801, 28 U.S.C.App., p. 717. Thus, despite the traditional view that such statements were hearsay, the Advisory Committee believed that their use was to be fostered rather than discouraged. Similarly, the House Report on the Rule noted that since, "[a]s time goes by, a witness' memory will fade and his identification will become less reliable," minimizing the barriers to admission of more contemporaneous identification is fairer to defendants and prevents "cases falling through because the witness can no longer recall the identity of the person he saw commit the crime." H.R.Rep. No. 94–355, p. 3 (1975). See also S.Rep. No. 94–199, p. 2 (1975). To judge from the House and Senate Reports, Rule 801(d)(1)(C) was in part directed to the very problem here at issue: a memory loss that makes it impossible for the witness to provide an in-court identification or testify about details of the events underlying an earlier identification.

Respondent argues that this reading is impermissible because it creates an internal inconsistency in the Rules, since the forgetful witness who is deemed "subject to cross-examination" under 801(d)(1)(C) is simultaneously deemed "unavailable" under 804(a)(3). This is the position espoused by a prominent commentary on the Rules, see 4 J. Weinstein & M. Berger, Weinstein's Evidence 801–120 to 801–121, 801–178 (1987). It seems to us, however, that this is not a substantive inconsistency, but only a semantic oddity resulting from the fact that Rule 804(a) has for convenience of reference in Rule 804(b) chosen to describe the circumstances necessary in order to admit certain categories of hearsay testimony under the rubric "Unavailability as a witness." These circumstances include not only absence from the hearing, but also claims of privilege, refusals to obey a court's order to testify, and inability to testify based on physical or mental illness or memory loss. Had the rubric instead been "unavailability as a witness, memory loss, and other special circumstances" there would be no apparent inconsistency with Rule 801, which is a definition section excluding certain statements entirely from the category of "hearsay." The semantic inconsistency exists not only with respect to Rule 801(d)(1)(C), but also with respect to the other subparagraphs of Rule 801(d)(1). It would seem strange, for example, to assert that a witness can avoid introduction of testimony from a prior proceeding that is inconsistent with his trial testimony, see Rule 801(d)(1)(A), by simply asserting lack of memory of the facts to which the prior testimony related. But that situation, like this one, presents the verbal curiosity that the witness is "subject to cross-examination" under Rule 801 while at the same time "unavailable" under Rule 804(a)(3). Quite obviously, the two characterizations are made for two entirely different purposes and there is no requirement or expectation that they should coincide.

For the reasons stated, we hold that neither the Confrontation Clause nor Federal Rule of Evidence 802 is violated by admission of an identification statement of a witness who is unable, because of a memory loss, to testify concerning the basis for the identification. The decision of the Court of Appeals is reversed, and the case is remanded for proceedings consistent with this opinion.

So ordered.

■ JUSTICE BRENNAN, with whom JUSTICE MARSHALL joins, dissenting.

* * * The principal witness against respondent was not the John Foster who took the stand in December 1983—that witness could recall virtually nothing of the events of April 12, 1982, and candidly admitted that he had no idea whether respondent had assaulted him. Instead, respondent's sole accuser was the John Foster who, on May 5, 1982, identified respondent as his attacker. This John Foster, however, did not testify at respondent's trial: the profound memory loss he suffered during the approximately 18 months following his identification prevented him from affirming, explaining, or elaborating upon his out-of-court statement just as surely and completely as his assertion of a testimonial privilege, or his death, would have. * * *

See Federal Rules of Evidence 801(d)(1); California Evidence Code § 1238.

HYPOTHETICALS

(1) X is prosecuted for robbery of A. A testifies that he was held up at gunpoint, that the next day he went to the police station and identified the man who robbed him, and that he is sure he picked the right man but can't remember now the person he identified. The prosecution then calls B, a police officer, and represents that B will testify that A came to the station the day after the crime and that, while X was being led through the hall, A yelled: "There goes the man who robbed me" and pointed at X. X makes a hearsay objection to B's proposed testimony. What result?

(2) Assume the same facts as in Illustration (1), except that A has no recollection of making a pretrial identification of X or any other person at the police station. The prosecution then offers B's testimony of A's pretrial identification of X at the police station. X makes a hearsay objection to B's testimony. How should the court rule?

9. PAST RECOLLECTION RECORDED

Baker v. State

Court of Special Appeals of Maryland, 1977.
35 Md.App. 593, 371 A.2d 699.

■ MOYLAN, JUDGE.

This appeal addresses the intriguing question of what latitude a judge should permit counsel when a witness takes the stand and says, "I don't remember." What are the available keys that may unlock the testimonial treasure vaults of the subconscious? What are the brush strokes that may be employed "to retouch the fading daguerreotype of memory?" The subject is that of Present Recollection Revived.[1]

The appellant, Teretha McNeil Baker, was convicted by a Baltimore City jury of both murder in the first degree and robbery. Although she raises two appellate contentions, the only one which we find it necessary to consider is her claim that the trial judge erroneously refused her the opportunity to refresh the present recollection of a police witness by showing him a report written by a fellow officer.

The ultimate source of most of the evidence implicating the appellant was the robbery and murder victim himself, Gaither Martin, a now-dead declarant who spoke to the jury through the hearsay conduit of Officer Bolton.[2] When Officer Bolton arrived at the crime scene, the victim told him that he had "picked these three ladies up * * * at the New Deal Bar"; that when he took them to their stated destination, a man walked up to the car and pulled him out; that "the other three got out and proceeded to kick him and beat him." It was the assertion made by the victim to the officer that established that his money, wallet and keys had been taken. The critical impasse, for present purposes, occurred when the officer was questioned, on cross-examination, about what happened en route to the hospital. The officer had received a call from Officer Hucke, of the Western District, apparently to the effect that a suspect had been picked up. Before proceeding to the hospital, Officer Bolton took the victim to the place where Officer Hucke was holding the appellant. The appellant, as part of this cross-examination, sought to elicit from the officer the fact that the crime victim confronted the appellant and stated that the appellant was not one of those persons who had attacked and robbed him. To stimulate the present memory of Officer Bolton, appellant's counsel attempted to show him the police report relating to that confrontation and prepared by Officer Hucke.

---

[1] Frequently and alternatively referred to as Present Recollection Refreshed.

[2] The exception to the Hearsay Rule urged by the State and utilized by the court to make the out-of-court assertion admissible was the "excited utterance" exception and not the "dying declaration" exception. We are not here considering the admissibility of this hearsay, but are rather assuming it to have been admissible.

The record establishes loudly and clearly that appellant's counsel sought to use the report primarily to refresh the recollection of Officer Bolton and that he was consistently and effectively thwarted in that attempt:

"BY MR. HARLAN:

Q. Do you have the report filed by Officer Hucke and Officer Saclolo or Saclolo?

A. Right, I have copies.

Q. Okay.

MR. DOORY: I would object to that, Your Honor.

THE COURT: I will sustain the objection. This is not his report.

BY MR. HARLAN:

Q. Can you look at this report and refresh your recollection as to whether or not you ever had the victim in a confrontation with Mrs. Baker?

MR. DOORY: Objection, Your Honor.

MR. HARLAN: He can refresh—

THE COURT: Well, he can refresh his recollection as to his personal knowledge. That's all right.

A. That is what I am saying, I don't know who it was that we confronted really.

BY MR. HARLAN:

Q. All right. Would you consult your report and maybe it will refresh your recollection.

THE COURT: I think the response is he doesn't know who—

MR. HARLAN: He can refresh his recollection if he looks at the report.

THE COURT: He can't refresh his recollection from someone else's report, Mr. Harlan.

MR. HARLAN: I would object, Your Honor. Absolutely he can.

THE COURT: You might object, but—

MR. HARLAN: You are not going to permit the officer to refresh his recollection from the police report?

THE COURT: No. It is not his report.

* * *

MR. HARLAN: Your Honor, I think I am absolutely within my rights to have a police officer read a report which mentions his name in it to see if it refreshes his recollection. If it doesn't refresh his recollection, then fine.

THE COURT: Well, he did that.

MR. HARLAN: You have not afforded him the opportunity to do that yet, Your Honor.

THE COURT: He says he does not know who it was before. So, he can't refresh his recollection if he does not know simply because someone else put some name in there.

MR. HARLAN: He has to read it to see if it refreshes his recollection, Your Honor.

THE COURT: We are reading from a report made by two other officers which is not the personal knowledge of this officer.

MR. HARLAN: I don't want him to read from that report. I want him to read it and see if it refreshes his recollection."

On so critical an issue as possible exculpation from the very lips of the crime victim, appellant was entitled to try to refresh the memory of the key police witness. She was erroneously and prejudicially denied that opportunity. The reason for the error is transparent. Because they both arise from the common seedbed of failed memory and because of their hauntingly parallel verbal rhythms and grammatical structures, there is a beguiling temptation to over analogize Present Recollection Revived and Past Recollection Recorded. It is a temptation, however, that must be resisted. The trial judge in this case erroneously measured the legitimacy of the effort to revive present recollection against the more rigorous standards for the admissibility of a recordation of past memory.

It is, of course, hornbook law that when a party seeks to introduce a record of past recollection, he must establish (1) that the record was made by or adopted by the witness at a time when the witness did have a recollection of the event and (2) that the witness can presently vouch for the fact that when the record was made or adopted by him, he knew that it was accurate. McCormick, Law of Evidence (1st Ed., 1954), describes the criteria, at 15:

"Appropriate safeguarding rules have been developed for this latter kind of memoranda, requiring that they must have been written by the witness or examined and found correct by him, and that they must have been prepared so promptly after the events recorded that these must have been fresh in the mind of the witness when the record was made or examined and verified by him. We have treated such memoranda separately, as an exception to the hearsay rule."

Had the appellant herein sought to offer the police report as a record of past recollection on the part of Officer Bolton, it is elementary that she would have had to show, *inter alia,* that the report had either been prepared by Officer Bolton himself or had been read by him and that he can now say that at that time he knew it was correct. Absent such a showing, the trial judge would have been correct in declining to receive it in evidence.

When dealing with an instance of Past Recollection Recorded, the reason for the rigorous standards of admissibility is quite clear. Those standards exist to test the competence of the report or document in question. Since the piece of paper itself, in effect, speaks to the jury, the piece of paper must pass muster in terms of its evidentiary competence.

The record speaks when there is evidence

Not so with Present Recollection Revived! By marked contrast to Past Recollection Recorded, no such testimonial competence is demanded of a mere stimulus to present recollection, for the stimulus itself is never evidence. Notwithstanding the surface similarity between the two phenomena, the difference between them could not be more basic. *It is the difference between evidence and non-evidence.* Of such mere stimuli or memory-prods, McCormick says "[T]he cardinal rule is that they are not evidence, but only aids in the giving of evidence." When we are dealing with an instance of Present Recollection Revived, the only source of evidence is the testimony of the witness himself. The stimulus may have jogged the witness's dormant memory, but the stimulus itself is not received in evidence. Dean McCormick makes it clear that even when the stimulus is a writing, when the witness "speaks from a memory thus revived, his testimony is what he says, not the writing." McCormick describes the psychological phenomenon in the following terms:

> "It is abundantly clear from every-day observation that the latent memory of an experience may be revived by an image seen, or a statement read or heard. It is a part of the group of phenomena which the classical psychologists have called the law of association. The recall of any part of a past experience tends to bring with it the other parts that were in the same field of awareness, and a new experience tends to stimulate the recall of other like experiences."

The psychological community is in full agreement with the legal community in assessing the mental phenomenon. See Cairn, Law and the Social Sciences 200 (1935):

> "In permitting a witness to refresh his recollection by consulting a memorandum, the courts are in accord with present psychological knowledge. A distinction is drawn, in the analysis of the memory process, between *recall,* which is the reproduction of what has been learned, and *recognition,* which is recall with a time-factor added, or an awareness that the recall relates to past experience. It is with rec-

ognition that the law is principally concerned in permitting a witness to revive his recollection. The psychological evidence is clear that in thus allowing to be brought to mind what has been forgotten, the law is following sound psychological procedure."

* * *

The catalytic agent or memory stimulator is put aside, once it has worked its psychological magic, and the witness then testifies on the basis of the now-refreshed memory. The opposing party, of course, has the right to inspect the memory aid, be it a writing or otherwise, and even to show it to the jury. This examination, however, is not for the purpose of testing the competence of the memory aid (for competence is immaterial where the thing in question is not evidence) but only to test whether the witness's memory has in truth been refreshed. As McCormick warns, "But the witness must swear that he is genuinely refreshed. * * * And he cannot be allowed to read the writing in the guise of refreshment, as a cloak for getting in evidence an inadmissible document." One of the most thorough reviews of this aspect of evidence law is found in the United States v. Riccardi, where the court said at 888:

> "In the case of present recollection revived, the witness, by hypothesis, relates his present recollection, and under oath and subject to cross-examination asserts that it is true; his capacities for memory and perception may be attacked and tested; his determination to tell the truth investigated and revealed; protestations of lack of memory, which escape criticism and indeed constitute a refuge in the situation of past recollection, recorded, merely undermine the probative worth of his testimony."

* * *

When the writing in question is to be utilized simply "to awaken a slumbering recollection of an event" in the mind of the witness, the writing may be a memorandum made by the witness himself, 1) even if it was not made immediately after the event, 2) even if it was not made of firsthand knowledge and 3) even if the witness cannot now vouch for the fact that it was accurate when made. It may be a memorandum made by one other than the witness, even if never before read by the witness or vouched for by him. It may be an Associated Press account. It may be a highly selective version of the incident at the hands of a Hemingway or an Eliot. All that is required is that it ignite the flash of accurate recall—that it accomplish the revival which is sought.

McCormick wrote to just such effect:

"[I]t is probable that most courts today when faced with the clear distinction between the two uses of the memoranda, will adhere to the 'classical' view that any memorandum or other object may be used as a stimulus to present memory, without restriction by rule as to authorship, guaranty of correctness, or time of making."

The Texas dean is in good company, for no less eminent an authority than Lord Ellenborough said in Henry v. Lee:

"If upon looking at *any* document he can so far refresh his memory as to recollect a circumstance, it is sufficient; and it makes no difference that the memorandum is not written by himself, for it is not the memorandum that is the evidence but the recollection of the witness."

Not only may the writing to be used as a memory aid fall short of the rigorous standards of competence required of a record of past recollection, the memory aid itself need not even be a writing. What may it be? It may be anything. It may be a line from Kipling or the dolorous refrain of "The Tennessee Waltz"; a whiff of hickory smoke; the running of the fingers across a swatch of corduroy; the sweet carbonation of a chocolate soda; the sight of a faded snapshot in a long-neglected album. All that is required is that it may trigger the Proustian moment.[3] It may be anything which produces the desired testimonial prelude, "It all comes back to me now."

* * *

Although the use of a memorandum of some sort will continue quantitatively to dominate the field of refreshing recollection, we are better able to grasp the process conceptually if we appreciate that the use of a memorandum as a memory aid is not a legal phenomenon unto itself but only an instance of a far broader phenomenon. In a more conventional mode, the process might proceed, "Your Honor, I am about to show the witness a written report, ask him to read it and then inquire if he can now testify from his own memory thus refreshed." In a far less conventional mode, the process could just as well proceed, "Your Honor, I am pleased to present to the court Miss Rosa Ponselle who will now sing 'Celeste Aida' for the witness, for that is what was playing on the night the burglar came through the window." Whether by conventional or unconventional means, precisely the same end is sought. One is looking for the effective elixir to revitalize dimming memory and make it live again in the service of the search for truth.

Even in the more conventional mode, it is quite clear that in this case the appropriate effort of the appellant to jog the arguably dormant memory of the key police witness on a vital issue was unduly and prejudicially restricted.

Judgments reversed; case remanded for a new trial; costs to be paid by mayor and city council of Baltimore.

---

[3] Marcel Proust, in his monumental epic In Remembrance of Things Past, sat, as a middle-aged man, sipping a cup of lime-flavored tea and eating a madeleine, a small French pastry. Through both media, two long-forgotten tastes from childhood were reawakened. By association, long forgotten memories from the same period of childhood came welling and surging back. Once those floodgates of recall were opened, seven volumes followed.

Adams v. The New York Central Railroad Co.

Court of Common Pleas, Cuyahoga County, Cleveland, Ohio, 1961.
Docket No. 724,072.

[This was an action for the recovery of damages for personal injuries. Defendant's theory was that the injury claimed by plaintiff had in fact never occurred and that plaintiff's quadraplegia stemmed from an injury antedating the claimed injury. One of the few ways in which defendant could hope to establish its theory was by introduction, as past recollection recorded, of a memorandum made by an insurance company employee of an interview with plaintiff. According to the memorandum, plaintiff had mentioned the antecedent injury but had made no reference to any injury of the sort claimed at trial. Following are key portions of the trial transcript showing the efforts of chief defense counsel, James C. Davis, Esq., of the Cleveland Bar, to secure admission of the memorandum—Eds.]

DIRECT EXAMINATION

BY MR. DAVIS:

Q. Will you state your name?

A. Eugene F. Raith.

Q. Where do you live?

A. I live at 20705 Harvard Road, Warrensville Heights, Ohio.

* * *

Q. What is your business?

A. Home Office Inspector, employed by the John Hancock Mutual Life Insurance Company.

Q. How long have you been employed with John Hancock?

A. 40 years.

Q. In your capacity with John Hancock, did you in 1957 call on a gentleman named Theodore H. Adams at a time when he was a patient in Highland View Hospital?

A. I did.

Q. What was your purpose in calling on Mr. Adams?

A. To seek any information to be used in evaluation of his disability claim that he had presented to our insurance company as an insured.

Q. At that time did you interview him?

A. I did.

Q. During the interview, or immediately thereafter, did you make a written record of what he told you—of the information you obtained?

A. Yes, sir.

* * *

Q. Do you have with you your file on this particular matter?

A. Yes.

Q. May I have it? First, the written record which you made, either during your interview or thereafter, was a record in longhand, was it not?

A. Yes.

Q. Have you ever testified as a witness before?

A. No.

Q. Well, it really is not as painful as it looks.

A. Thank you. I would change places with you.

* * *

Q. Now, Mr. Raith, do you at this time have any independent recollection of the subject-matter of the conversation between you and Mr. Adams—that is, what he told you and what you asked him—independent of the notes which you made at that time?

A. I do not.

Q. Do you recognize the gentleman at the end of the [counsel] table as the gentleman that you talked to?

A. I believe so.

Q. I hand you what has been marked Defendant's Exhibit OO. Now that piece of paper has writing on both sides, does it not?

A. Yes.

Q. Tell me, if you will, whether or not the notes that you made of your conversation with Mr. Adams appear on only one side or both sides of that page.

A. Only on one side.

* * *

Q. Now, was the information that is contained on the page that is marked Defendant's Exhibit OO * * * obtained entirely from the interview with Mr. Adams?

A. Yes, entirely from Mr. Adams.

Q. At the time you wrote that Exhibit OO * * * did it accurately record what he had told you?

A. Yes.

* * *

Q. Was [the interview] recorded in exactly the words which Mr. Adams gave you, or not?

A. I would be inclined to believe that when I talked to Mr. Adams I made notes rougher than these, and at the conclusion of the interview I made a recap. I say that because of the sequence; it would have been a recap of what I made previously. However, it came from Mr. Adams, no one else.

* * *

Q. Are there certain facts recorded on Exhibit OO?

A. Right.

Q. When did you record the facts on Exhibit OO with reference to the time of your interview with Mr. Adams?

A. At the time or shortly thereafter.

Q. Were the facts obtained from Mr. Adams accurately recorded by you on Exhibit OO?

A. Yes.

Q. At the time you made Defendant's Exhibit OO, did you or did you not know it was accurate so far as facts obtained by you from Mr. Adams were concerned?

A. I did.

Q. Without telling me what it is, Mr. Raith, is it not a fact that Defendant's Exhibit OO records the fact of an injury which Mr. Adams told you he had received?

A. Yes.

Q. Did you record whatever he told you about injuries?

A. I did.

MR. DAVIS: At this time defendant offers in evidence Defendant's Exhibit OO as evidence of past recollection recorded.

MR. DUDNIK: It is entirely improper.

THE COURT: We will recess until 1:30.

(Thereupon the jury left the Courtroom and the following further proceedings were had in the absence of the jury:)

THE COURT: Proceed, Mr. Davis.

MR. DAVIS: If the Court please, in these circumstances there are two ways in which a witness may properly proceed. First, he may look at a memorandum made at the time and, on the basis of his refreshed recollection, testify. Then he is testifying from his present recollection refreshed. On the other hand, the law is perfectly clear that a witness having no such present refreshed recollection may testify that he made a record of the event at a time in the past and that he knew at the time the record was made that the record was accurate. That record is admissible as past recollection recorded as distinguished from present recollection refreshed. Dean Wigmore says, in Volume 3, Section 734 of the third edition of his work on evidence. * * * [Quotation omitted.]

THE COURT: I will hear from Mr. Dudnik.

MR. DUDNIK: My associate, Mr. Nurenberg, will argue the point, your Honor.

MR. NURENBERG: These notes do not fill the bill. Office records might be permitted into evidence, providing certain qualifications are met. The witness stated that even by looking at the exhibit he can't refresh his recollection. * * * The witness said he saw Mr. Adams at Highland View Hospital and, apparently, he has some recollection. * * * The most important thing is that the document [Defendant's Exhibit OO], on its face is not a document at all. It is merely a piece of paper with some pencil jotting; this is not a document. * * * If I talk to you and I go home and jot down with pencil on a piece of paper what you told me, even though they are an accurate recollection * * * I can't come into Court and say they are what you told me, Judge White. I can't come into Court and introduce a pencil note. That is what they are trying to do. That is not past recollection recorded. Past recollection recorded is when a man, in the routine order of business, makes a certain document at or contemporaneous with the subject-matter, not a pencil jotting. * * * That is hearsay in its purest form. Every record is not *ipso facto* a business record.

* * *

MR. DAVIS: Your Honor, Mr. Dudnik has given you a case in 156 Northwestern at page 867. That is a case cited by Wigmore. If you will notice, Wigmore does not restrict past recollection recorded to papers that, in the technical sense, constitute business records. The very case cited to you by Mr. Dudnik involved a memorandum taken down by an insurance agent in connection with a policy.

* * *

THE COURT: The Court has examined, necessarily with some haste, the cases cited to it. * * * The fact that the witness has testified that his own recollection is not refreshed [by Defendant's Exhibit OO] persuades the Court that the exhibit is not admissible at this time.

* * *

Thereupon the defendant, further to maintain the issues on its part to be maintained, recalled as a witness, EUGENE F. RAITH, who, having been previously duly sworn, was examined and testified further as follows:

BY MR. DAVIS:

Q. Now, Mr. Raith, I hand you once more Defendant's Exhibit OO, and ask you if you will read it through again. To yourself, not out loud.

Q. Have you finished?

A. Yes, sir.

Q. Having read Exhibit OO, will you tell me whether or not your memory has been refreshed so that you now have a present recollection of your interview with Mr. Adams at Highland View Hospital, and of what he told you on that occasion?

A. No, it has not.

Q. It has not what?

A. It has not been refreshed by reading these notes.

Q. Then do you or do you not at this time have any present recollection of what Mr. Adams told you at the time you interviewed him at Highland View Hospital?

A. Other than these notes, I do not.

Q. Do the notes refresh your recollection so that you now have a recollection, or do they not?

A. No, they do not refresh my recollection.

* * *

Q. Now, at the time you made the writings on Exhibit OO, did you have a clear recollection of what Mr. Adams had told you?

A. Very clear.

MR. DAVIS: I reoffer Defendant's Exhibit OO, your Honor.

MR. DUDNIK: The same objection.

THE COURT: The objection is sustained.

MR. DAVIS: That is all, Mr. Raith.

NOTE

Do you agree with the rulings of the trial court? Did attorney Davis fail in some significant respect to lay the proper foundation for admission into evidence of the memorandum?

The trial of Adams v. The New York Central R.R. Co. resulted in a verdict for plaintiff in the sum of $300,000. In its motion for a new trial defendant argued that rejection of the proffered memorandum was prejudicial error. Before further proceedings were had, the case was settled for a sum substantially less than the verdict.

———————

See Federal Rules of Evidence 803(5), 612; California Evidence Code §§ 1237, 771.

———————

HYPOTHETICAL

(1) X is prosecuted for robbery. The prosecution calls A, who testifies that she saw the getaway car and noticed the license number, and that ten minutes later a police officer came to the scene and she told him exactly what license number she observed, but that she has no recollection now of that number. The prosecution then calls B, a police officer, who testifies that at the robbery scene A told him the license number of the getaway car she had seen and that he wrote correctly on a sheet in his book the number stated by A, and produces the sheet. The prosecutor asks B to read the license number written on the sheet. X makes a hearsay objection to the prosecutor's question. What result under California law? Under federal law?

10. BUSINESS AND PUBLIC RECORDS

Maryland—District of Columbia—Virginia Criminal Practice Institute Trial Manual
2-4, 2-5 (1964).*

2.02 Introducing Business Records**

1. Your Honor, I would like to have this instrument marked as defense exhibit # 1 for identification.

2. State your name.

3. Where do you reside, Mr. [witness]?

4. And what is your occupation?

5. Where are you employed?

6. What is the nature of your employer's business?

7. And what is the nature of your work there?

8. Were you so employed there on [date in question]?

9. Now, as the [position title], do you have responsibility of keeping the records concerning [subject matter]?

10. What is the method utilized for keeping these records?

11. Is this followed with respect to every [entry] [patient, etc.]?

12. I show you defendant's exhibit # 1 for identification, purporting to be [document title], and ask you whether these are the original records which you have kept in your position?

13. Were these records in your custody on [date]?

14. And were they in your custody prior to your bringing them to court this morning?

15. Where were they kept?

16. Were the entries made herein made shortly after the transaction they record?

17. Who provided the information contained therein?

18. Was it his duty to collect this data and pass it on to you?

---

* Copyright, 1964, by Lerner Law Book Company.

** On the authentication of writings, see Chapter I, Making the Record; Trial Objections, supra.

19. And were these entries made in the usual and ordinary course of business?

20. To the best of your knowledge, are they true and correct?

[Then move the admission of defense exhibit # 1 for identification into evidence.]

Johnson v. Lutz

Court of Appeals of New York, 1930.
253 N.Y. 124, 170 N.E. 517.

■ HUBBS, J. This action is to recover damages for the wrongful death of the plaintiff's intestate, who was killed when his motorcycle came into collision with the defendants' truck at a street intersection. There was a sharp conflict in the testimony in regard to the circumstances under which the collision took place. A policeman's report of the accident filed by him in the station house was offered in evidence by the defendants under section 374–a of the Civil Practice Act, and was excluded. The sole ground for reversal urged by the appellants is that said report was erroneously excluded. That section reads: "Any writing or record, whether in form of an entry in a book or otherwise, made as a memorandum or record of any act, transaction, occurrence or event, shall be admissible in evidence in proof of said act, transaction, occurrence or event, if the trial judge shall find that it was made in the regular course of any business, and that it was the regular course of such business to make such memorandum or record at the time of such act, transaction, occurrence or event, or within a reasonable time thereafter. All other circumstances of the making of such writing or record, including lack of personal knowledge by the entrant or maker, may be shown to affect its weight, but they shall not affect its admissibility. The term business shall include business, profession, occupation and calling of every kind."

Prior to the decision in the well-known case of Vosburgh v. Thayer, shopbooks could not be introduced in evidence to prove an account. The decision in that case established that they were admissible where preliminary proof could be made that there were regular dealings between the parties; that the plaintiff kept honest and fair books; that some of the articles charged had been delivered; and that the plaintiff kept no clerk. At that time it might not have been a hardship to require a shopkeeper who sued to recover an account to furnish the preliminary proof required by that decision. Business was transacted in a comparatively small way, with few, if any, clerks. Since the decision in that case, it has remained the substantial basis of all decisions upon the question in this jurisdiction prior to the enactment in 1928 of section 374–a, Civil Practice Act.

Under modern conditions, the limitations upon the right to use books of account, memoranda, or records, made in the regular course of business, often resulted in a denial of justice, and usually in annoyance, expense, and waste of time and energy. A rule of evidence that was practical a century ago had become obsolete. The situation was appreciated, and attention was called to it by the courts and textwriters.

The report of the Legal Research Committee of the Commonwealth Fund, published in 1927, by the Yale University Press, under the title, "The Law of Evidence—Some Proposals for Its Reform," dealt with the question in chapter 5, under the heading, "Proof of Business Transactions to Harmonize with Current Business Practice." That report, based upon extensive research, pointed out the confusion existing in decisions in different jurisdictions. It explained and illustrated the great need of a more practical, workable, and uniform rule, adapted to modern business conditions and practices. The chapter is devoted to a discussion of the pressing need of a rule of evidence which would "give evidential credit to the books upon which the mercantile and industrial world relies in the conduct of business." At the close of the chapter, the committee proposed a statute to be enacted in all jurisdictions. In compliance with such proposal the Legislature enacted section 374–a of the Civil Practice Act in the very words used by the committee.

It is apparent that the Legislature enacted section 374–a to carry out the purpose announced in the report of the committee. That purpose was to secure the enactment of a statute which would afford a more workable rule of evidence in the proof of business transactions under existing business conditions.

In view of the history of section 374–a and the purpose for which it was enacted, it is apparent that it was never intended to apply to a situation like that in the case at bar. The memorandum in question was not made in the regular course of any business, profession, occupation, or calling. The policeman who made it was not present at the time of the accident. The memorandum was made from hearsay statements of third persons who happened to be present at the scene of the accident when he arrived. It does not appear whether they saw the accident and stated to him what they knew, or stated what some other persons had told them.

The purpose of the Legislature in enacting section 374–a was to permit a writing or record, made in the regular course of business, to be received in evidence, without the necessity of calling as witnesses all of the persons who had any part in making it, provided the record was made as a part of the duty of the person making it, or on information imparted by persons who were under a duty to impart such information. The amendment permits the introduction of shopbooks without the necessity of calling all clerks who may have sold different items of account. It was not intended to permit the receipt in evidence of entries based upon voluntary hearsay statements made by third parties not engaged in the business or under any duty in relation thereto. It was said, in Mayor, etc., of New York City v. Second Ave. R. Co.: "It is a proper qualification of the rule admitting such evidence that the account must have been made in the ordinary course of business, and that it should not be extended so as to admit a mere private memorandum, not made in pursuance of any duty owing by the person making it, or when made upon information derived from another who made the communication casually and voluntarily, and not under the sanction of duty or other obligation."

An important consideration leading to the amendment was the fact that in the business world credit is given to records made in the course of business by persons who are engaged in the business upon information given by others engaged in the same business as part of their duty.

"Such entries are dealt with in that way in the most important undertakings of mercantile and industrial life. They are the ultimate basis of calculation, investment, and general confidence in every business enterprise. Nor does the practical impossibility of obtaining constantly and permanently the verification of every employee affect the trust that is given to such books. It would seem that expedients which the entire commercial world recognizes as safe could be sanctioned, and not discredited, by courts of justice. When it is a mere question of whether provisional confidence can be placed in a certain class of statements, there cannot profitably and sensibly be one rule for the business world and another for the court-room. The merchant and the manufacturer must not be turned away remediless because the methods in which the entire community places a just confidence are a little difficult to reconcile with technical judicial scruples on the part of the same persons who as attorneys have already employed and relied upon the same methods. In short, courts must here cease to be pedantic and endeavor to be practical." 3 Wigmore on Evidence (1923) § 1530, p. 278.

The Legislature has sought by the amendment to make the courts practical. It would be unfortunate not to give the amendment a construction which will enable it to cure the evil complained of and accomplish the purpose for which it was enacted. In construing it, we should not, however, permit it to be applied in a case for which it was never intended.

The judgment should be affirmed, with costs.

■ CARDOZO, C.J., and POUND, CRANE, LEHMAN, KELLOGG, and O'BRIEN, JJ., concur.

Judgment affirmed.

United States v. Vigneau
United States Court of Appeals for the First Circuit, 1999.
187 F.3d 70.

■ BOUDIN, CIRCUIT JUDGE.

Two brothers, Patrick and Mark Vigneau, were convicted after a lengthy trial on charges growing out of their participation in a drug distribution scheme. In this opinion, we consider Patrick Vigneau's claims of error. * * *

On this appeal, Patrick Vigneau's strongest claim is that the district court erred in allowing the government to introduce, without redaction and for all purposes, Western Union "To Send Money" forms, primarily in support of the money laundering charges. These forms, as a Western Union custodian testified, are handed by the sender of money to a Western Union agent after the sender completes the left side of the form by writing (1) the sender's name, address and telephone number; (2) the amount of the transfer; and (3) the intended recipient's name and location. The Western Union clerk then fills in the right side of the form with the clerk's signature, date, amount of the transfer and fee, and a computer-generated control number; but at least in 1995, Western Union clerks did not require independent proof of the sender's identity.

Western Union uses the control number affixed by the clerk to correlate the information on the "To Send Money" form with the corresponding "Received Money" form and with the canceled check issued by Western Union to pay the recipient. The original forms are usually discarded after six months, but the information provided by the sender, as well as the information from all records associated with the money transfer, are recorded in a computer database. In this case, for some transfers the government had the forms completed by the sender, but for most it had only the computer records.

The government introduced over 70 records of Western Union money transfers. Patrick Vigneau's name, address and phone number appeared as that of the sender on 21 of the "To Send Money" forms (11 other names, including fictional names and those of Mark Vigneau and of other defendants, appeared as those of the senders on the other forms), and those 21 forms corresponded to the 21 specific counts of money laundering on which Patrick Vigneau was ultimately convicted by the jury. Patrick Vigneau's most plausible objection, which was presented in the district court and is renewed on appeal, is that his name, address and telephone number on the "To Send Money" forms were inadmissible hearsay used to identify Patrick Vigneau as the sender.

Hearsay, loosely speaking, is an out-of-court statement offered in evidence to prove the truth of the matter asserted. Fed. R. Evid. 801(c). Whoever wrote the name "Patrick Vigneau" on the "To Send Money" forms was stating in substance: "I am Patrick Vigneau and this is my address and telephone number." Of course, if there were independent evidence that the writer was Patrick Vigneau, the statements would constitute party-opponent admissions and would fall within an exception to the rule against hearsay, Fed. R. Evid. 801(d)(2) (the rule says admissions are "not hearsay," but that is an academic refinement). However, the government cannot use the forms themselves as bootstrap-proof that Patrick Vigneau made the admission.[2]

---

[2] Hartzell v. United States, 72 F.2d 569, 578 (8th Cir.), cert. denied, 293 U.S. 621 (1934) * * * Partial bootstrapping is now explicitly permitted for certain hearsay exceptions, see Fed. R. Evid. 801(d)(2), on the premise that those hearsay exceptions turn upon facts resolved by the judge under Fed. R. Evid. 104(a), see Bourjaily v. United States, 483 U.S. 171 (1987); but the explicit exceptions do not include personal admissions, and whether the defendant signed the form may be governed instead by Fed. R. Evid. 104(b) as a matter of conditional relevance.

Instead, the government argues that the "To Send Money" forms and the computerized information reflecting those forms and the correlated material were admissible under the business records exception. Fed. R. Evid. 803(6). Rule 803(6) provides that business records are admissible where shown to be business records by a qualified witness, "unless the source of information or the method and circumstances of preparation indicate lack of trustworthiness." *Id.* The district judge accepted the view that the Western Union records were trustworthy and admitted the "To Send Money" forms (or equivalent computer records) without redaction and for all purposes, advising the jury that "what weight you give to them will be your choice."

The district judge was correct that the "To Send Money" forms literally comply with the business records exception because each form is a business record, and in this case, the computer records appeared to be a trustworthy account of what was recorded on the original "To Send Money" forms. The difficulty is that despite its language, the business records exception does not embrace statements contained within a business record that were made by one who is *not* a part of the business if the embraced statements are offered for their truth. The classic case is *Johnson v. Lutz*, 170 N.E. 517 (N. Y. 1930), which excluded an unredacted police report incorporating the statement of a bystander (even though the police officer recorded it in the regular course of business) because the informant was not part of that business. The Advisory Committee Notes to Rule 803(6) cite *Johnson v. Lutz* and make clear that the rule is intended to incorporate its holding.

Johnson v. Lutz is not a technical formality but follows directly from the very rationale for the business records exception. When a clerk records the receipt of an order over the telephone, the regularity of the procedure, coupled with business incentives to keep accurate records, provide reasonable assurance that the record thus made reflects the clerk's original entry. Thus the business record, although an out-of-court statement and therefore hearsay, is admitted without calling the clerk to prove that the clerk received an order.

But no such safeguards of regularity or business checks automatically assure the *truth* of a statement *to* the business by a stranger to it, such as that made by the bystander to the police officer or that made by the money sender who gave the form containing his name, address, and telephone number to Western Union. Accordingly, the *Johnson v. Lutz* gloss excludes this "outsider" information, where offered for its truth, unless some other hearsay exception applies to the outsider's own statement. This gloss on the business records exception, which the Federal Rules elsewhere call the "hearsay within hearsay" problem, Fed. R. Evid. 805, is well-settled in this circuit. Other circuits are in accord.

Of course, "hearsay within hearsay" is often trustworthy but hearsay is not automatically admissible merely because it is trustworthy. A residual hearsay exception exists *based* on case-specific findings of trustworthiness, but it is more stringent and requires, among other things, advance notice not here provided by the government. Fed. R. Evid. 807 (combining former Fed. R. Evid. 803(24) and Fed. R. Evid. 804(b)(5)). And precisely because hearsay law is now codified for the federal courts, the former freedom of federal judges to create new exceptions is now curtailed.

Nor does the reference to "trustworthiness" in the business records rule comprise an independent hearsay exception. Fed. R. Evid. 803(6). That reference was not designed to limit *Johnson v. Lutz* to untrustworthy statements—after all, the statement to the police officer was probably trustworthy—but rather to exclude records that would normally satisfy the business records exception (*e.g.*, the clerk's computerized record of calls received) where *inter alia* the opponent shows that the business record or system itself was not reliable (*e.g.*, the computer was defective).

Of course, in some situations, the statement by the "outsider" reflected in the business record may be admissible not for its truth but for some other purpose, but the disputed "To Send Money" forms here were admitted by the district court for all purposes, including as proof of the sender's identity. Possibly, the government could have argued as to Patrick Vigneau (it would be harder as to Mark) that other evidence of Patrick Vigneau's activities comprised circumstantial evidence that would permit a jury to conclude that he sent the specific forms bearing his name, Fed. R. Evid. 104(b); but apart from the need for a limiting instruction, Fed. R. Evid. 105, this presents a difficult issue that has not been argued and is not here resolved.

No doubt, the "To Send Money" forms were relevant to the government's case regardless of whether Patrick Vigneau (or any other named sender) was the person who made an individual transfer: they showed transfers of money from Rhode Island directed to Crandall and others that tended to support the general description of the drug and money laundering activities described by the government's witnesses. Thus, the forms could have been offered in redacted form, omitting the information identifying Patrick Vigneau as the sender of 21 of the forms. But that is not what happened.

Some cases have admitted under the business records exception "outsider" statements contained in business records, like the sender's name on the Western Union form, where there is evidence that the business itself used a procedure for *verifying* identity (*e.g.*, by requiring a credit card or driver's license). Probably the best analytical defense of this gloss is that in such a case, the verification procedure is circumstantial evidence of identity that goes beyond the mere bootstrap use of the name to establish identity. While this gloss may well represent a reasonable accommodation of conflicting values, verification was not Western Union's practice at the time.

The hearsay rule is an ancient and, even to most lawyers, a counter-intuitive restriction now riddled with many exceptions. However, the drafters chose to retain the hearsay rule, and any trial lawyer who has tried to cross-examine a witness whose story depends on the hearsay statements of others understands why. These are reasons enough to tread cautiously, quite apart from the Supreme Court's intermittent reliance on the Confrontation Clause to make the use of hearsay a potentially constitutional issue in criminal trials.

We thus conclude, in accord with the Tenth Circuit, that the sender name, address and telephone number on the forms should not have been admitted for their truth. There is no plausible claim of harmless error, as to 18 of the money laundering counts where, as here, the government might well have had difficulty in tying Patrick Vigneau to any of these 18 specific transactions except through the hearsay statements themselves.

[The convictions on 21 substantive counts of money laundering were vacated and remanded for new trial; convictions of other charges relating to the drug conspiracy were affirmed.]

HYPOTHETICALS

Examine the following hypotheticals involving a suit by A against B arising out of an automobile accident. What should be the result in each case?

The police report contains the following statement which the plaintiff seeks to introduce:

a. "I was standing at my beat and saw the red Chevrolet [which we now know to be the defendant's car] go through the red light and strike the green Ford [which other testimony shows to be the plaintiff's car]."

b. "I arrived at one thirty [which other evidence indicates was twenty minutes after the accident] and noticed a skid mark, which I measured at 93 feet leading directly to the rear wheels of the Chevrolet."

c. "I arrived within five seconds of the impact and heard a bystander scream, 'Did you see that crazy red car go through the red light?'"

d. "I arrived a few minutes after the accident and asked the driver in the red Chevrolet what happened. He stated that he had fallen asleep at the wheel and did not rightly know."

e. "I arrived a few minutes after the accident and Officer Jones approached me and said that he had seen the accident and that the red Chevrolet had gone through the red light and hit the green Ford."

f. "I arrived a few minutes after the accident and Officer Jones told me that she had gotten there just before I did and asked the Chevrolet driver what had happened and that he had said, 'I fell asleep at the wheel and I don't rightly know.'"

g. "I arrived twenty-five minutes after the accident and I asked a bystander what had happened. He said that he had seen it all and the red Chevrolet was going too fast and couldn't stop for the red light and went right through the red light and hit the green Ford."

Regarding multiple hearsay, see Federal Rules of Evidence 805; California Evidence Code § 1201.

United States v. Duncan

United States Court of Appeals, Fifth Circuit, 1990.
919 F.2d 981.

■ DUHÉ, CIRCUIT JUDGE.

The defendants raise a litany of issues to challenge their convictions for mail fraud and conspiracy. They contend that the district court improperly denied their motion for change of venue and erred in fourteen different evidentiary rulings. They also argue that the court erred by denying their motion for mistrial based on a comment by the judge and by refusing their proposed jury instructions. Finally, they assert that the evidence adduced at trial was insufficient to sustain their convictions and that the court imposed excessive sentences. We find no error and affirm the judgment of the district court.

FACTS

The defendants participated in a scheme to defraud insurance companies. Over a period of several years, each defendant purchased numerous hospitalization policies. Each policy provided that the insured would receive a predetermined sum of money for each day spent in the hospital, regardless of other coverage.

The indictment charged that on many occasions, the defendants sought admission to hospitals after reporting accidents that never occurred or after staging accidents. According to several witnesses, the defendants participated in planned collisions in which a driver, carrying a carload of conspirators, intentionally swerved out of his lane and careened into another car.

The evidence indicated that Samuel Duncan and Grace Duncan, husband and wife, were the ringleaders of the conspiracy. Each was hospitalized over twenty times and collected over $300,000 in insurance proceeds. Mr. Duncan's sister Gay Nell, another defendant, entered the hospital three times within a seven-month period and collected over $50,000. The insurance companies mailed the Duncans checks for these amounts.

The other four defendants were close friends and relatives of the Duncans. Each of the four was hospitalized between ten and nineteen times during a five-year period and each collected over $75,000. These defendants also received payments by mail.

The government indicted the seven defendants for mail fraud and conspiracy. After a two-week trial, the jury found all seven defendants guilty.

DISCUSSION

* * *

1. Admission of Records

The defendants first claim that the court erred in admitting into evidence the records of insurance companies. They challenge the admissibility of these records on a variety of grounds, arguing that (1) they were not sufficiently authenticated under rule 901; (2) they are not proper business records under rule 803(6); and (3) they were made by a person without personal knowledge in violation of rule 602.

Representatives of insurance companies came to court and authenticated the records. The prosecutor clearly established the prerequisites for admitting the records under the business records exception.[4] But the defendants argue that the insurance company records contained other unauthenticated medical records and statements by doctors. They contend that these medical records and statements are hearsay not falling within the business records exception of rule 803(6).

We reject this argument. The insurance companies compiled their records from the business records of hospitals. Because the medical records from which the insurance company records were made were themselves business records, there was no accumulation of inadmissible hearsay.

---

[4] For example, the following exchange occurred between the prosecutor and a witness:

Q. Your full name, Sir?

A. George Beverly Walker, Jr.

Q. And by whom are you employed?

A. J.C. Penney Life Insurance Company.

Q. And in what position?

A. Senior Vice President, Insurance Operations.

Q. Have you produced records of your corporation?

A. Yes I have.

Q. Pursuant to a subpoena?

A. Yes, Sir.

Q. Are these records kept in the regular course of your company's business?

A. Yes, they are.

Q. Are these records accurate?

A. Yes.

Q. Is it the regular practice of your company to keep such records?

A. Yes, it is.

    * * *

Q. [Let me] show you what's been marked for identification purposes as G–36–SDA, and ask you what is that?

A. This is a copy of the application by Samuel Duncan.* * * We have two applications as Mr. Duncan had two policies with our company. * * *

Q. Are you familiar with how your company generates and maintains and stores records?

A. Yes.

Q. How are these applications generated?

A. Through direct mail.

There is no requirement that the witness who lays the foundation be the author of the record or be able to personally attest to its accuracy. Furthermore, there is no requirement that the records be created by the business having custody of them.

Instead, the "primary emphasis of rule 803(6) is on the reliability or trustworthiness of the records sought to be introduced." The district court has great latitude on the issue of trustworthiness. Hospitals and insurance companies rely on these records in conducting business. We hold, therefore, that the district court did not err in admitting them under Federal Rule of Evidence 803(6) upon proper authentication by their custodian.

Even if the insurance company records contained some medical information not taken from actual hospital records, that information was admissible as nonhearsay evidence. The Federal Rules of Evidence exclude from the category of hearsay any "statement by a person authorized by the party to make a statement concerning the subject" and any "statement by the party's agent . . . concerning a matter within the scope of the agency." Fed.R.Evid. 801(d)(2)(C)–(D).

A patient routinely authorizes the release of medical records for use by insurance companies. A medical provider without express authority to release information would be acting as the patient's agent in obtaining payment of medical expenses from insurance companies. We therefore conclude that all information in the insurance company records was admissible either under the business records exception or as nonhearsay evidence. * * *

HYPOTHETICALS

Should a newspaper reporter's notes be admissible as a business record? A newspaper itself? A clipping from the newspaper's back-issue library?

Williams v. Alexander
Court of Appeals of New York, 1955.
309 N.Y. 283, 129 N.E.2d 417.

■ FULD, JUDGE. DESSI WILLIAMS was struck by defendant's automobile as he was crossing a street in Brooklyn, with the traffic light in his favor. His right leg fractured, he was taken to Kings County Hospital for treatment. At the trial, the testimony of the parties as to the manner in which the accident occurred was sharply discrepant. According to plaintiff, defendant's automobile approached the intersection, at which he was crossing, without diminishing speed and ran into him. Defendant, on the other hand, insisting that he had brought his car to a complete stop at the light, maintained that another vehicle had struck it from the rear and propelled it forward and upon plaintiff.

In the early stages of the trial, plaintiff introduced so much of the Kings County Hospital record as bore upon his injuries and their treatment. Counsel for defendant thereupon offered the balance of the record and it was received in evidence over plaintiff's objection. Specifically challenged by plaintiff as inadmissible hearsay was an entry to the effect that he had stated to a physician at the hospital that "he was crossing the street and an automobile ran into another automobile that was at a standstill, causing this car (standstill) to run into him". Plaintiff denied making any such statement, and the doctor who recorded it was not called as a witness.

Upon this appeal—following a verdict in defendant's favor and an affirmance by a divided Appellate Division—we are called upon to decide whether the statement attributed to plaintiff, relating the manner in which the accident occurred, was properly admitted in evidence as a memorandum or record made "in the regular course of * * * business". Civil Practice Act, § 374–a.

Section 374–a of the Civil Practice Act permits the introduction in evidence of "Any writing or record * * * made as a memorandum or record of any act, transaction, occurrence or event," despite its hearsay character, "if the trial judge shall find that it was made in the regular course of any business, and that it was the regular course of such business to make such memorandum or record at the time of such act, transaction, occurrence or event, or within a reasonable time thereafter." The term "business" is broadly defined as including "business, profession, occupation and calling of every kind", and among the records within the section's ambit are those that a hospital keeps in diagnosing and treating the ills of its patients.

The statute, similar to those in effect in most jurisdictions, is designed to harmonize the rules of evidence with modern business practice and give "evidential credit" to the memoranda or other writings upon which reliance is placed in the systematic conduct of business undertakings. It rests upon the probability of trustworthiness which inheres in such records, by virtue of the fact, first, that they are the "routine reflections of the day to day operations of a business", and, second, that it is the entrant's own obligation, and to his interest, to have them truthful and accurate, made and kept as they are with the knowledge, indeed, for the purpose, that they will be relied upon in the conduct of the enterprise. * * * [I]t is this element of trustworthiness, serving in place of the safeguards ordinarily afforded by confrontation and cross-examination, which justifies admission of the writing or record without the necessity of calling all the persons who may have had a hand in preparing it. And it was to assure such accuracy and reliability that the legislature made explicit the condition that the memorandum may be received in evidence—and this is the heart of the provision—only if it was "made in the regular course of [the] business, and * * * it was the regu- lar course of such business to make such memorandum".

As the statute makes plain, and we do not more than paraphrase it, entries in a hospital record may not qualify for admission in evidence unless made in the regular course of the "business" of the hospital, and for the purpose of assisting it in carrying on that "business." The business of a hospital, it is self-evident, is to diagnose and treat its patients' ailments. Consequently, the only memoranda that may be regarded as within the section's compass are those reflecting acts, occurrences or events that relate to diagnosis, prognosis or treatment or are otherwise "helpful to an understanding of the medical or surgical aspects of * * * [the particular patient's] hospitalization."

It follows from this that a memorandum made in a hospital record of acts or occurrences leading to the patient's hospitalization—such as a narration of the accident causing the injury—not germane to diagnosis or treatment, is not admissible under section 374–a, and so it has been almost universally held under the identical or similar statutes of other jurisdictions.

In the words of the Ohio court in Green v. City of Cleveland, typical of those found in the other cases, "it was the business of the hospital to diagnose plaintiff's condition and to treat her for her ailments, not to record a statement describing the cause of the accident in which plaintiff's injuries were sustained."

In some instances, perhaps, the patient's explanation as to how he was hurt may be helpful to an understanding of the medical aspects of his case; it might, for instance, assist the doctors if they were to know that the injured man had been struck by *an* automobile. However, whether the patient was hit by car A or car B, by car A under its own power or propelled forward by car B, or whether the injuries were caused by the negligence of the defendant or of another, cannot possibly bear on diagnosis or aid in determining treatment. That being so, entries of this sort, purporting to give particulars of the accident, which serve no medical purpose, may not be regarded as having been made in the regular course of the hospital's business. Indeed, in discussing the matter, Wigmore observed that the essential "Guarantee of Trustworthiness" rests upon the fact that "the physicians and nurses * * * themselves rely upon the record" and that the record is designed to be "relied upon in affairs of life and death." Such reasoning, however, will not support the use, or justify the receipt, of a statement detailing the circumstances of the accident where they are immaterial to, and were never intended to be relied upon in, the treatment of the patient. There is no need in that case for the physician to exercise care in obtaining and recording the information or to question the version, whatever it might be, that is given to him. The particulars may be a natural subject of the doctor's curiosity, but neither the inquiry nor the response properly belong in a record designed to reflect the regular course of the hospital's business.

In conclusion, then, that portion of the hospital record containing the statement assertedly made by plaintiff as to the manner in which the accident happened was erroneously admitted, and, since we cannot say that it did not influence the jury in arriving at its verdict for defendant, there must be a new trial.

The judgment of the Appellate Division and that of Trial Term should be reversed and a new trial granted, with costs to abide the event.

■ DESMOND, JUDGE (dissenting).

I see no error here, and no reason for retrying this simple question of fact.

Plaintiff, for his own convenience, chose to prove his injuries and the hospital treatment he received therefor, by putting a hospital record in evidence and without calling as a witness the physician who made the entries. In so doing, he of course vouched for the accuracy and regularity of that record. Defendant made no objection but in his turn offered in evidence so much of the same hospital record as showed a statement to the hospital physician by plaintiff that the accident had occurred in a manner quite different from that testified to at the trial by plaintiff. Plaintiff objected to any such "history" going into evidence. His alleged ground of objection was stated in the one word: "hearsay". That of course was meaningless in this context. An undoubted exception to the "hearsay" rule makes admissible extra-judicial declarations against interest. Plaintiff's declaration to the hospital physician as to the way the accident happened was directly probative evidence of a main fact in issue. It is, of course, conceivable (but unlikely) that by plaintiff's use of the word "hearsay" he referred to the failure of defendant to call as a witness the physician who had written up the notes. But plaintiff himself had put into evidence the (helpful to him) parts of that identical paper without calling the physician. Surely, plaintiff could not then demand that the other party prove the authenticity of the very record plaintiff had himself presented to the court. Since plaintiff had been allowed to prove by the record alone the diagnosis and treatment of his injuries, it would be absurd to forbid defendant using the same record, written in the same handwriting by the same physician at the same time, to prove an equally relevant, competent and material fact, that is, that plaintiff had stated to the physician that his injuries were caused in the manner asserted by defendant.

It follows from the above that section 374–a of the Civil Practice Act, our statutory rule as to admissibility of records made in the regular course of a business, has little or nothing to do with this case. What we have here is an admission against interest, proved not by the oral testimony of the person to whom it was made but by an authentic document already vouched for to the court by the opposing party himself.

But let us suppose that this is a section 374–a case. "Hospital records concededly are included within the records to which section 374–a of the Civil Practice Act is applicable." The physician who made the entries need not be called as a witness. True, as Judge Fuld points out, this court has not yet directly decided whether the section 374–a makes admissible that part of a hospital record which gives the history of the injury. But why should this court not adopt a practical and useful construction, rather than a narrow and unnecessarily restrictive one? And the statute itself seems to furnish the answer: "Any writing or record, whether in the form of an entry in a book or otherwise, made as a memorandum or record of any act, transaction, occurrence or event, shall be admissible in evidence in proof of said act, transaction, occurrence or event, if the trial judge shall find that it was made in the regular course of any business, and that it was the regular course of such business to make such memorandum or record at the time of such act, transaction, occurrence or event, or within a reasonable time thereafter." There is no reason why the "history" part of a hospital record, obtained not from unidentified persons but from the patient himself, should not be used in evidence against the patient. Of course, the writing must have been made in the regular course of the hospital's business and it must have been the regular course of the business of the hospital to make such entries. But in this case plaintiff did not object because of any failure to prove those requirements. Indeed, he could not, after himself bringing the record to court, reasonably urge that it was not the regularly made record of this hospital. And he knew, as we all do, that an examining physician, especially in a hospital receiving department, always inquires as to the cause of a trauma. Certainly, in the absence of any suspicious circumstance, it is not up to the courts to decide just how thoroughly a qualified physician may delve into the cause or occasion of the injuries he is diagnosing and treating. Anyhow, all this is by the statute's own words committed to the trial judge's discretion. It is he who is charged with passing on the question of whether the entry was regularly made. Here, no one suggested that it was not so made or called for proof that it was. The trial justice, therefore, had no reason for excluding it, particularly since there was no suggestion that the physician or the hospital had any interest in the case or any possible reason for falsifying these records.

This was a routine trial of a simple issue of fact. Plaintiff said the accident happened one way, defendant said that it happened another way. A hospital book brought to court by plaintiff showed that he himself had described the occurrence in the way that defendant described it. Plaintiff denied that he had made such a statement at the hospital. The jury settled that dispute. It is most unfortunate, especially in these days of congested calendars, that such a case must now be retried.

The judgment should be affirmed, with costs.

■ CONWAY, C.J., and FROESSEL and VAN VOORHIS, JJ., concur with FULD, J.

■ DESMOND, J., dissents in an opinion in which DYE and BURKE, JJ., concur.

Judgments reversed, etc.

See Federal Rules of Evidence 803(6)–(7); California Evidence Code §§ 1270–1272.

Hahnemann University Hospital v. Dudnick

Superior Court of New Jersey, Appellate Division, 1996.
678 A.2d 266.

■ VILLANUEVA, J.A.D. (Retired and temporarily assigned on recall).

* * *

This is a collection action for an outstanding balance due on a hospital bill incurred by defendant for treatment at the Hospital. * * * After a bench trial, the trial court found defendant liable for $1,111.11 plus interest and court costs.

On appeal defendant claims that the trial court erred by admitting into evidence computer printout records of the Hospital * * *.

I.

The records herein represent a classic example of the type of business records which have been historically accepted as an exception to the hearsay rule and were most recently recognized in *N.J.R.E.* 803(c)(6). Nonetheless, this case causes us to re-examine the law regarding admission into evidence of computer printouts.

During direct examination of plaintiff's witness Joseph Romano, plaintiff's counsel sought to introduce into evidence the computer printout of defendant's hospital bill. The witness provided testimony in order to establish a foundation to move the documents into evidence. Accordingly, the computer printout (1) was authenticated by a person who was in charge of the records and personally familiar with them, (2) was shown to reflect data recorded contemporaneously with the occurrence of the facts recorded in the usual course of the Hospital's regular practice. Plaintiff's foundation witness, as the custodian of records with knowledge of the billing procedures, certainly was qualified to testify as to the charges incurred by defendant as contained in the Hospital's bill.

Defendant cites *Monarch Federal Savings & Loan Ass'n v. Genser*, 156 *N.J.Super.* 107, 383 A.2d 475 (Ch.Div.1977), to argue that plaintiff failed to lay the requisite foundation under the business entry exception to the hearsay rule to admit a computer printout into evidence. That case sets forth an outdated six-prong test to be satisfied with respect to admission of computer printouts.* To the extent that *Monarch* suggests the application of special evidentiary requirements for computer-generated business records, we specifically disapprove it. * * *

Clearly, the climate of the use of computers in the mid–1990's is substantially different from that of the 1970's. In the 1970's, computers were

---

* The *Monarch* case required, among other things, that the foundation for computer records include testimony as to the competency of the computer operator; the type of computer used and its acceptance in the field; the procedure for the input and output of information, including controls, tests and checks for accuracy and reliability; and "the mechanical operations of the machine."—Eds.

relatively new, were not universally used and had no established standard of reliability. Now, computers are universally used and accepted, have become part of everyday life and work and are presumed reliable. * * *

Significantly, the *Monarch* case was decided before the adoption of the new *New Jersey Rules of Evidence* which became effective July 1, 1993. *Monarch* relied upon former *Evid.R.* 63(13):

> A writing offered as a memorandum or record of acts, conditions or events is admissible to prove the facts stated therein if the writing or the record upon which it is based was made in the regular course of a business, at or about the time of the act, condition or event recorded, and if the sources of information from which it was made and the method and circumstances of its preparation were such as to justify its admission.

Today's equivalent to this former rule, *N.J.R.E.* 803(c)(6), allows the following to be admitted in evidence:

> A statement contained in a writing or other record of acts, events, conditions, and, subject to Rule 808, opinions or diagnoses, made at or near the time of observation by a person with actual knowledge or from information supplied by such a person, if the writing or other record was made in the regular course of business and it was the regular practice of that business to make it, *unless the sources of information or the method, purpose or circumstances of preparation indicate that it is not trustworthy.*

> [Emphasis added.]

At the time *Monarch* was decided, the proponent of a business record had to show that the sources of information from which it was made and the method and circumstances of preparation justified its admission. The evidence rule in effect today is more relaxed than the rule which was in effect in 1977.

* * *

Expert testimony as to the reliability of the programs the computer uses or other technical aspects of its operation is unnecessary to find computer-generated records circumstantially reliable. A witness is competent to lay the foundation for systematically prepared computer records if the witness (1) can demonstrate that the computer record is what the proponent claims and (2) is sufficiently familiar with the record system used and (3) can establish that it was the regular practice of that business to make the record. * * *

There is no reason to believe that a computerized business record is not trustworthy unless the opposing party comes forward with some evidence to question its reliability. * * *

Plaintiff clearly established the reliability of the bill. The burden than shifted to defendant to offer some evidence that the bill was not reliable. Defendant failed to do so. Therefore, the bill was properly admitted.

[After disposing of other issues, the court affirmed the judgment.]

POTAMKIN CADILLAC CORP. v. B.R.I. COVERAGE CORP., 38 F.3d 627 (2d Cir.1994). Invoking the business records exception, the defendant proffered an accounting history that allegedly detailed all business transacted between the defendant and the plaintiff, including unreimbursed premium advances claimed by defendant in its counterclaim. It supported the proffer with an affidavit stating that its computer department had devised a program to scan its history tapes and extract pertinent information about transactions between the parties. Citing errors revealed by spot-checks against other records and noting the defendant's failure to make the source tapes available during discovery, the Court of Appeals held that the lower court acted within its discretion in excluding the evidence. Its opinion alluded both to trustworthiness concerns and to the requirement that the records be made in the regular course of business. On the latter point, it suggested that "the History required significant selection and interpretation of data, not simply a downloading of information previously computerized in the regular course of business." *Id.* at 633.

Palmer v. Hoffman

Supreme Court of the United States, 1943.
318 U.S. 109, 63 S.Ct. 477, 87 L.Ed. 645.

■ MR. JUSTICE DOUGLAS delivered the opinion of the Court.

This case arose out of a grade crossing accident which occurred in Massachusetts. Diversity of citizenship brought it to the federal District Court in New York. There were several causes of action. The first two were on behalf of respondent individually, one being brought under a Massachusetts statute (Mass.Gen.L. (1932) c. 160, §§ 138, 232), the other at common law. The third and fourth were brought by respondent as administrator of the estate of his wife and alleged the same common law and statutory negligence as the first two counts. On the question of negligence the trial court submitted three issues to the jury—failure to ring a bell, to blow a whistle, to have a light burning in the front of the train. The jury returned a verdict in favor of respondent individually for some $25,000 and in favor of respondent as administrator for $9,000. The District Court entered judgment on the verdict. The Circuit Court of Appeals affirmed, one judge dissenting. 129 F.2d 976. The case is here on a petition for a writ of certiorari which presents three points.

I. The accident occurred on the night of December 25, 1940. On December 27, 1940, the engineer of the train, who died before the trial, made a statement at a freight office of petitioners where he was interviewed by an assistant superintendent of the road and by a representative of the Massachusetts Public Utilities Commission. This statement was offered in evidence by petitioners under the Act of June 20, 1936, 49 Stat. 1561, 28 U.S.C. § 695.[1] They offered to prove (in the language of the Act) that the statement was signed in the regular course of business, it being the regular course of such business to make such a statement. Respondent's objection to its introduction was sustained.

We agree with the majority view below that it was properly excluded.

We may assume that if the statement was made "in the regular course" of business, it would satisfy the other provisions of the Act. But we do not think that it was made "in the regular course" of business within the meaning of the Act. The business of the petitioners is the railroad business. That business like other enterprises entails the keeping of numerous books and records essential to its conduct or useful in its efficient operation. Though such books and records were considered reliable and trustworthy for major decisions in the industrial and business world, their use in litigation was greatly circumscribed or hedged about by the hearsay rule— restrictions which greatly increased the time and cost of making the proof where those who made the records were numerous. It was that problem which started the movement towards adoption of legislation embodying the principles of the present Act. And the legislative history of the Act indicates the same purpose.

The engineer's statement which was held inadmissible in this case falls into quite a different category. It is not a record made for the systematic conduct of the business as a business. An accident report may affect that business in the sense that it affords information on which the management may act. It is not, however, typical of entries made systematically or as a matter of routine to record events or occurrences, to reflect transactions with others, or to provide internal controls. The conduct of a business commonly entails the payment of tort claims incurred by the negligence of its employees. But the fact that a company makes a business out of recording its employees' versions of their accidents does not put those statements in the class of records made "in the regular course" of the business within the meaning of the Act. If it did, then any law office in the land could follow the same course, since business as defined in the Act includes the professions. We would then have a real perversion of a rule designed to facilitate admission of records which experience has shown to be quite trustworthy. Any business by installing a regular system for recording and preserving its version of accidents for which it was potentially liable could qualify those reports under the Act. The result would be that the Act would cover any system of recording events or occurrences provided it was "regular" and

---

[1] "In any court of the United States and in any court established by Act of Congress, any writing or record, whether in the form of an entry in a book or otherwise, made as a memorandum or record of any act, transaction, occurrence, or event, shall be admissible as evidence of said act, transaction, occurrence, or event, if it shall appear that it was made in the regular course of any business, and that it was the regular course of such business to make such memorandum or record at the time of such act, transaction, occurrence, or event or within a reasonable time thereafter. All other circumstances of the making of such writing or record, including lack of personal knowledge by the entrant or maker, may be shown to affect its weight, but they shall not affect its admissibility. The term 'business' shall include business, profession, occupation, and calling of every kind."

though it had little or nothing to do with the management or operation of the business as such. Preparation of cases for trial by virtue of being a "business" or incidental thereto would obtain the benefits of this liberalized version of the early shop book rule. The probability of trustworthiness of records because they were routine reflections of the day to day operations of a business would be forgotten as the basis of the rule. Regularity of preparation would become the test rather than the character of the records and their earmarks of reliability acquired from their source and origin and the nature of their compilation. We cannot so completely empty the words of the Act of their historic meaning. If the Act is to be extended to apply not only to a "regular course" of a business but also to any "regular course" of conduct which may have some relationship to business, Congress not this Court must extend it. Such a major change which opens wide the door to avoidance of cross-examination should not be left to implication. Nor is it any answer to say that Congress has provided in the Act that the various circumstances of the making of the record should affect its weight, not its admissibility. That provision comes into play only in case the other requirements of the Act are met.

In short, it is manifest that in this case those reports are not for the systematic conduct of the enterprise as a railroad business. Unlike payrolls, accounts receivable, accounts payable, bills of lading and the like, these reports are calculated for use essentially in the court, not in the business. Their primary utility is in litigating, not in railroading.

Lewis v. Baker

United States Court of Appeals, Second Circuit, 1975.
526 F.2d 470.

■ WATERMAN, CIRCUIT JUDGE:

Plaintiff, Clifford J. Lewis Jr., brought this action in the United States District Court for the Southern District of New York alleging he suffered a disabling injury while employed by the Penn Central Railroad. Judgment was entered in favor of defendants after a jury trial. Plaintiff appeals and seeks a new trial on the * * * ground [that the] accident reports were improperly admitted into evidence. * * * Finding no merit to the above contention, we affirm.

On the date of his injury, October 26, 1969, plaintiff was employed as a freight brakeman or car dropper in the Penn Central railroad freight yard in Morrisville, Pennsylvania. His work called for him to move freight cars in a railroad yard by riding them down a slope while applying the brake manually. Plaintiff testified that immediately before the incident in question, he climbed onto the lead car of two box-cars, stationed himself on the rear brake platform of that car, applied the brake to test it, and found that the brake held. Upon his signal, another employee of the railroad released the two box-cars from the rest of the train at the top of a hill, at which time they started to roll down the slope. Plaintiff then started to turn the vertical brake wheel so that the car would slow down as it descended the slope and would ease into the train with which it was to couple on a track beyond the bottom of the slope. He claims that the brake did not hold, that the car continued to gather momentum, and that he then decided to leap off the car to avoid injury. As a result of the fall, he claims to have sustained substantial knee injury and the aggravation of a preexisting psychiatric condition which has precluded his returning to his job. There were no witnesses to the accident other than the plaintiff.

At the trial, defendants sought to rebut plaintiff's allegations of a faulty brake with evidence that the brake had functioned properly immediately prior to the accident when the plaintiff tested it, and immediately after the accident when it was checked in connection with the preparation of an accident report. It was the defendants' contention that plaintiff improperly set, or forgot to set, a necessary brake handle, panicked, and then leapt from the car.

In support of their interpretation of the events, defendants offered into evidence a "personal injury report" and an "inspection report." Frank Talbott, a trainmaster, testified that the personal injury report was signed by him and prepared under his supervision. The information had been provided to him by William F. Campbell, the night trainmaster. Talbott confirmed the authenticity of the record and testified that he was required to make out such reports of injuries as part of the regular course of business. At the trial David W. Halderman, an assistant general foreman for the defendants, identified the inspection report which had been prepared by Campbell and by Alfred Zuchero, a gang foreman. This report was based upon an inspection of the car Campbell and Zuchero had conducted less than four hours after the accident. Halderman testified that Zuchero was dead and that Campbell was employed by a railroad in Virginia. The latter was thus beyond the reach of subpoena. Halderman also confirmed that following every accident involving injury to an employee his office was required to complete inspection reports, and that such reports were regularly kept in the course of business. Over objection, the court admitted both reports into evidence.

* * *

As a preliminary matter, there is little doubt that these reports are each a "writing or record, whether in the form of an entry in a book or otherwise, made as a memorandum or record of any act, transaction, occurrence, or event * * * "28 U.S.C. § 1732 (1966). Furthermore, it is beyond dispute that these reports were made pursuant to a regular procedure at the railroad yard, and that Talbott, Campbell and Zuchero made the reports within a reasonable time after the accident. Appellant argues, however, that notwithstanding the presence of those factors which would indicate a full compliance with 28 U.S.C. § 1732, the Supreme Court's decision in Palmer v. Hoffman, 318 U.S. 109, 63 S.Ct. 477, 87 L.Ed. 645 (1943), precludes their admission into evidence. There the Court upheld the inadmissibility of an accident report offered by the defendant railroad that had been prepared by one of its locomotive engineers. The Court stated that since the report was not prepared "for the systematic conduct of the business as a business," it was not "made 'in the regular course' of the business" of the railroad. We find significant differences between the report and the circumstances of its making in that case and the facts here, and we uphold the district court's admission of the records below.

In *Palmer v. Hoffman,* the engineer preparing the report had been personally involved in the accident, and, as Circuit Judge Frank stated in his opinion for the Court of Appeals, the engineer knew "at the time of making it that he [was] very likely, in a probable law suit relating to that accident, to be charged with wrongdoing as a participant in the accident, so that he [was] almost certain, when making the memorandum or report, to be sharply affected by a desire to exculpate himself and to relieve himself or his employer of liability." Here there could have been no similar motivation on the part of Talbott, Campbell or Zuchero, for not one of them was involved in the accident, or could have possibly been the target of a lawsuit by Lewis. In United States v. New York Foreign Trade Zone Operators, 304 F.2d 792 (2d Cir.1962), we sustained the admissibility of a similar report by the co-employee of the injured party which had been prepared as part of the regular business of the defendant pier-owner and operator. As we explained there, the mere fact that a record might ultimately be of some value in the event of litigation does not *per se* mandate its exclusion. In *Palmer v. Hoffman,* "[o]bviously the Supreme Court was concerned about a likely untrustworthiness of materials prepared specifically by a prospective litigant for courtroom use." The fact that a report embodies an employee's version of the accident, or happens to work in favor of the entrant's employer, does not, without more, indicate untrustworthiness. In the absence of a motive to fabricate, a motive so clearly spelled out in *Palmer v. Hoffman,* the holding in that case is not controlling to emasculate the Business Records Act. Therefore the trial court must look to those earmarks of reliability which otherwise establish the trustworthiness of the record.

Here the ICC requires the employer to prepare and file monthly reports of all accidents involving railroad employees. Assistant general foreman Halderman testified that following every injury he was required to inspect the equipment involved and to report the results of the inspection on a regular printed form.[2] As we stated in Taylor v. Baltimore & Ohio R.R.

---

[2] 45 U.S.C. § 38 provides in relevant part:

It shall be the duty of the general manager, superintendent, or other proper officer of every common carrier engaged in interstate or foreign commerce by railroad to make to the Secretary of Transportation a monthly report, under oath, of all * * * accidents resulting in death or injury to any person.* * *

Although 45 U.S.C. § 41 provides that neither the report required by section 38 nor any part thereof "shall be admitted as evidence * * * in any suit or action for damages growing out of any matter mentioned in said report or investigation," we think it clear that the reports prepared by Talbott and by Campbell and Zuchero were not themselves monthly reports under section 41, and there is no indication that any part of the information contained in those reports will ever become part of the monthly report. Rather, it would appear that the forms completed by those employees were supplied by the employer, and that wholly different forms are utilized in complying with the federal reporting regulations, as prescribed by 49 C.F.R. § 225.1 et seq. Only the latter are barred by section 41 from admission in accident-related litigation.

Co., 344 F.2d 281 (2d Cir.1965), "[i]t would ill become a court to say that the regular making of reports required by law is not in the regular course of business." In addition to their use by the railroad in making reports to the ICC, the reports here were undoubtedly of utility to the employer in ascertaining whether the equipment involved was defective so that future accidents might be prevented. These factors, we think, are sufficient indicia of trustworthiness to establish the admissibility of the reports into evidence under the Federal Business Records Act.

Affirmed.

Sana v. Hawaiian Cruises, Ltd.

United States Court of Appeals, Ninth Circuit, 1999
181 F.3d 1041.

■ FARRIS, CIRCUIT JUDGE:

Peter Sana appeals from the judgment in favor of Hawaiian Cruises, Ltd. on his claim for maintenance and cure. We reverse.

[In 1995, Hawaiian Cruises hired Sana to work in the galley aboard the Navatek I, a vessel used for whale-watching cruises. After Sana left work on March 10, 1995, he ran into his father, who noticed that Sana was walking differently and that Sana's hands were "shivering or shaking." His father also observed swelling and a scratch right at Sana's hairline. Sana told him that he had bumped his head at work. He stayed home from work on March 12, 1995, and the next day he was taken to a hospital. Hospital workers noticed confused behavior, hysteria, and seizures, and they transferred Sana to the Straub Clinic. On March 16, he slipped into a coma, where he remained throughout the trial and appeal of this case. According to a medical expert at trial, Sana was suffering from viral encephalitis. Sana filed suit, claiming that his condition arose during his work with Hawaiian Cruises. He waived the right to jury trial.]

At trial, Sana attempted to call Don Beaudry, the president of Hawaiian Cruises' insurance company. A Beaudry Insurance agent named Michael Rutherford had investigated Sana's behavior on March 9 and 10. Rutherford's report contains transcripts of his interviews with two of Sana's co-workers, Christopher Kalani Kauhi and Saver Ruben, and with Sana's immediate supervisor John Michael Hudson. In the interviews, which took place a few days after Sana was admitted to the Straub Clinic, both Kauhi and Ruben state that Sana told them that he had bumped his head at work on March 10. Kauhi also claims that Sana was behaving abnormally that day. Hudson states that Sana told him that he felt sick on March 8. Since neither Rutherford nor Sana's co-workers were available to testify at trial, Sana hoped to establish through Beaudry that the Rutherford report was an admissible business record.

Rutherford and Coworkers unavailable

The court held that the Rutherford report contained inadmissible hearsay, and it refused to let Beaudry testify. * * * The court concluded that Sana did not prove that his illness manifested itself on or before

March 10, 1995, his last day of work. Therefore, he was not entitled to maintenance and cure. The court also denied Sana's Jones Act claims.

* * *

"[A] seaman who falls ill while in the service of his vessel is entitled to ... maintenance and cure." *Dragich v. Strika*, 309 F.2d 161, 163 (9th Cir.1962) (seaman who evidenced signs of Parkinson's disease aboard fishing vessel entitled to maintenance and cure). The obligation does not depend on the negligence or fault of the shipowner, nor is it limited to cases in which the seaman's employment caused his illness. *Id.* Traditionally, courts have construed this obligation liberally.

* * *

I. Did Sana fall ill while "in the service of his vessel"?

Sana argues that he experienced symptoms of encephalitis while he was still working on the Navatek I. Assuming that the court properly excluded the Rutherford report, Sana's only evidence to support this proposition is Dr. Pearce's opinion that he was infected by March 9. The court rejected this testimony, and it accepted the view of Drs. Pien and Nicholson that the origin and onset of the infection were impossible to determine. This resolution of the medical testimony was not clearly erroneous.

If the Rutherford report is admissible, Sana has a much better case. Hudson's statement establishes that Sana felt ill as early as March 8. Kauhi's statement shows that Sana was behaving abnormally on March 10. Taken together, these statements bolster Dr. Pearce's testimony that Sana was infected by March 9.

* * *

In *Stevens*, 82 F.3d at 1353, the Sixth Circuit affirmed a grant of maintenance and cure on similar facts. Stevens suffered a blow to the head when he fell on the deck of a towboat. According to a co-worker, Stevens suffered headaches for months, and his personality changed. The shipowner eventually fired him for threatening the same co-worker. Five months later, Stevens was diagnosed with a brain tumor. Both the district court and the Sixth Circuit concluded that he became sick while in the ship's service. Therefore, he was entitled to maintenance and cure.

Like Stevens, Sana exhibited the first signs of a severe illness while at work. Unlike Stevens, Sana deteriorated very shortly thereafter. This proximity makes Sana's case even stronger. In light of the inconclusive medical testimony presented by Hawaiian Cruises and the traditional liberality of the maintenance and cure remedy, the court's exclusion of the Rutherford report materially affected Sana's case.

II. Did the court abuse its discretion in excluding the Rutherford report?

The Rutherford report involves several layers of hearsay: (1) it is an unsworn, out-of-court statement by Rutherford; (2) it contains unsworn, out-of-court statements by Sana's co-workers; (3) which recall unsworn, out-of-court statements by Sana. For the document to be admissible, each layer of hearsay must satisfy an exception to the hearsay rule. *See* Fed.R.Evid. 805.

Sana argues that his statements to his co-workers are admissible under Fed.R.Evid. 803(3), which excepts from the hearsay rule statements "of the declarant's then existing . . . physical condition (such as . . . pain . . . and bodily health)." Hawaiian Cruises simply denies, without explanation, that this section applies. It is mistaken. The statements are admissible under Rule 803(3).

Sana argues that his co-workers' statements to Rutherford are admissions by a party-opponent under Fed.R.Evid. 801(d)(2)(D). Rule 801(d)(2)(D) provides that "[a] statement is not hearsay if [it] is offered against a party and is . . . a statement by the party's agent or servant concerning a matter within the scope of the agency or employment." The question is whether the statements of Kauhi, Ruben, and Hudson concerned a matter "within the scope of [their] employment."

Sana notes that his co-workers spoke to Rutherford while they were at work. He also points out that Hawaiian Cruises had a duty to investigate his injuries. * * * Sana contends that because Hawaiian Cruises had to investigate his claim, the cooperation of its employees was within the scope of their employment.

Hawaiian Cruises argues that Sana failed to prove that Kauhi, Ruben, and Hudson spoke to Rutherford in the scope of their employment. *See Oki Am., Inc. v. Microtech Intern., Inc.,* 872 F.2d 312, 314 (9th Cir.1989) (proponent of evidence has the burden of proof and must lay appropriate foundation). We conclude from the record that Sana's co-workers were acting within the scope of their employment. [Under controlling precedent, shipowners must] investigate a seaman's claims for maintenance and cure. Also, Hudson had an independent duty to monitor and report any injuries or illness among his staff. In all likelihood, Sana's co-workers would have been disciplined had they refused to share information with their employer's insurance investigator. The fact that the interviews were conducted on company time supports this view.

Sana argues that Rutherford's recorded version of the employee statements is an admissible business record under Fed.R.Evid. 803(6), which excepts from the hearsay rule

> [a] . . . report . . . of acts, events, [or] conditions . . . made at or near the time by . . . a person with knowledge, if kept in the ordinary course of a regularly conducted business activity, and if it was the regular practice of that business activity to make the . . . report . . . unless the source of

the information or the method or circumstances of preparation indicate lack of trustworthiness.

He claims that Rutherford's information gathering was a "regularly conducted business activity" on behalf of Beaudry Insurance. He also notes that the report was compiled on March 17, "at or near the time" of the recorded "events." Finally, Sana argues that the report is trustworthy, since Hawaiian Cruises had no incentive to generate evidence that he became ill at work.

Hawaiian Cruises argues that the Rutherford report is an accident report prepared in anticipation of litigation, and therefore it is not admissible as a business record. *See Palmer v. Hoffman,* 318 U.S. 109 (1943) (court properly barred defendant railroad from introducing engineer's internal accident report). It also claims that since Rutherford was investigating whether Sana had suffered a head injury aboard the Navatek I, his report is not trustworthy to show that he manifested signs of encephalitis there. Finally, Hawaiian Cruises points out that for a business record to be admissible, each contributor must act in the regular course of business. *See United States v. Pazsint,* 703 F.2d 420, 425 (9th Cir.1983) (court improperly admitted routinely recorded 911 tapes because callers had no duty to report information); *see also Clark v. City of Los Angeles,* 650 F.2d 1033, 1037 (9th Cir.1981) (purported business records "are admissible only if the observer or participant in furnishing the information to be recorded was acting routinely, under a duty of accuracy, with employer reliance on the result, or . . . in the regular course of business.") (citations omitted). Hawaiian Cruises argues that Kauhi, Ruben, and Hudson were not acting within the regular course of the vessel's business when they spoke to Rutherford.

* * * We conclude that the Rutherford report qualifies as a business record under Rule 803(6). Although Rutherford may have interviewed Sana's co-workers in anticipation of a potential claim, the rationale for excluding such reports is not present here. Courts are rightfully wary when parties create self-serving documents and seek to offer them as business records. Sana, however, sought to introduce a document created by Hawaiian Cruises' insurer, which had no incentive to gather evidence of Sana's illness.

Moreover, the report had other "circumstantial guarantees of trustworthiness." *See United States v. Scholl,* 166 F.3d 964, 978 (9th Cir.1999) (citation and internal quotation marks omitted). Rutherford had a duty to prepare an accurate report for Beaudry Insurance, which presumably relied on that report to adjust Sana's claim. Likewise, in light of Hawaiian Cruises' obligation to investigate claims for maintenance and cure, Kauhi, Ruben, and Hudson had a duty to report accurately any information relevant to such claims.

Although it is unlikely that Sana's co-workers dealt frequently with an insurance investigator, frequency need not be the only consideration when analyzing the meaning of "routinely" and "in the regular course of business." Webster's defines "routine" as "a regular course of procedure."

WEBSTER'S NEW COLLEGIATE DICTIONARY 1000 (1979). Although "regular" can mean "recurring . . . at fixed or uniform intervals," it can also mean "usual" or "ordinary." *Id.* at 966. Here, the shipowner's duty to investigate a seaman's injuries—and the employees' corresponding duty to cooperate in the investigation—drive the analysis of what is "regular." Fulfilling these obligations is a "usual" or "ordinary" fact of life for the maritime industry, which has the unique responsibility of providing maintenance and cure to injured workers. Thus, the contributions of Kauhi, Ruben, and Hudson to the Rutherford report were "routine" and "in the regular course of business." This conclusion is bolstered by the fact that the interviews were conducted on company time.

* * *

The court's refusal to allow Sana to introduce the Rutherford report through Beaudry was an abuse of discretion. The exclusion of this report materially affected Sana's case. Because the outcome may have been different if the report had been admitted, Sana is entitled to a new trial. * * *

Beech Aircraft Corp. v. Rainey

Supreme Court of the United States, 1988.
488 U.S. 153, 109 S.Ct. 439, 102 L.Ed.2d 445.

■ JUSTICE BRENNAN delivered the opinion of the Court [which was unanimous on the issue presented in this excerpt.]

I

This litigation stems from the crash of a Navy training aircraft at Middleton Field, Alabama, on July 13, 1982, which took the lives of both pilots on board, Lieutenant Commander Barbara Ann Rainey and Ensign Donald Bruce Knowlton. The accident took place while Rainey, a Navy flight instructor, and Knowlton, her student, were flying "touch-and-go" exercises in a T–34C Turbo–Mentor aircraft, number 3E955. Their aircraft and several others flew in an oval pattern, each plane making successive landing/takeoff maneuvers on the runway. Following its fourth pass at the runway, 3E955 appeared to make a left turn prematurely, cutting out the aircraft ahead of it in the pattern and threatening a collision. After radio warnings from two other pilots, the plane banked sharply to the right in order to avoid the other aircraft. At that point it lost altitude rapidly, crashed, and burned.

Because of the damage to the plane and the lack of any survivors, the cause of the accident could not be determined with certainty. The two pilots' surviving spouses brought a product liability suit against petitioners Beech Aircraft Corporation, the plane's manufacturer, and Beech Aerospace Services, which serviced the plane under contract with the Navy. The plaintiffs alleged that the crash had been caused by a loss of engine power, known as "rollback," due to some defect in the aircraft's fuel control system. The defendants, on the other hand, advanced the theory of pilot error, suggesting that the plane had stalled during the abrupt avoidance maneuver.

At trial, the only seriously disputed question was whether pilot error or equipment malfunction had caused the crash. Both sides relied primarily on expert testimony. One piece of evidence presented by the defense was an investigative report prepared by Lieutenant Commander William Morgan on order of the training squadron's commanding officer and pursuant to authority granted in the Manual of the Judge Advocate General. This "JAG Report," completed during the six weeks following the accident, was organized into sections labeled "finding of fact," "opinions," and "recommendations," and was supported by some 60 attachments. The "finding of fact" included statements like the following:

> "13. At approximately 1020, while turning crosswind without proper interval, 3E955 crashed, immediately caught fire and burned.

* * *

> "27. At the time of impact, the engine of 3E955 was operating but was operating at reduced power." App. 10–12.

[The "opinions" section of Morgan's report included a statement, which the trial judge admitted, that "The most probable cause of the accident was the pilots [sic] failure to maintain proper interval."]

II

Federal Rule of Evidence 803 provides that certain types of hearsay statements are not made excludable by the hearsay rule, whether or not the declarant is available to testify. Rule 803(8) defines the "public records and reports" which are not excludable, as follows:

> "Records, reports, statements, or data compilations, in any form, of public offices or agencies, setting forth (A) the activities of the office or agency, or (B) matters observed pursuant to duty imposed by law as to which matters there was a duty to report, * * * or (C) in civil actions and proceedings and against the Government in criminal cases, factual findings resulting from an investigation made pursuant to authority granted by law, unless the sources of information or other circumstances indicate lack of trustworthiness."

Controversy over what "public records and reports" are made not excludable by Rule 803(8)(C) has divided the federal courts from the beginning. In the present case, the Court of Appeals followed the "narrow" interpretation of Smith v. Ithaca Corp., 612 F.2d 215, 220–223 (C.A.5 1980), which held that the term "factual findings" did not encompass "opinions" or "conclusions." Courts of appeal other than those of the Fifth and Eleventh Circuits, however, have generally adopted a broader interpretation. For example, the Court of Appeals for the Sixth Circuit, in Baker v. Elcona Homes Corp., 588 F.2d 551, 557–558 (1978), cert. denied, 441 U.S. 933 (1979), held that "factual findings admissible under Rule 803(8)(C) may be those which are made by the preparer of the report from disputed evidence * * *." The other courts of appeal that have squarely confronted the issue

SC - fact based
opinions &conclusions
not excluded from

803 (8)(C)

have also adopted the broader interpretation. We agree and hold that factually based conclusions or opinions are not on that account excluded from the scope of Rule 803(8)(C).

Because the Federal Rules of Evidence are a legislative enactment, we turn to the "traditional tools of statutory construction," INS v. Cardoza–Fonseca, 480 U.S. 421, 446 (1987), in order to construe their provisions. We begin with the language of the Rule itself. Proponents of the narrow view have generally relied heavily on a perceived dichotomy between "fact" and "opinion" in arguing for the limited scope of the phrase "factual findings." Smith v. Ithaca Corp., supra, contrasted the term "factual findings" in Rule 803(8)(C) with the language of Rule 803(6) (records of regularly conducted activity), which expressly refers to "opinions" and "diagnoses." "Factual findings," the court opined, must be something other than opinions. Smith, supra, at 221–222.

For several reasons, we do not agree. In the first place, it is not apparent that the term "factual findings" should be read to mean simply "facts" (as opposed to "opinions" or "conclusions"). A common definition of "finding of fact" is, for example, "[a] conclusion by way of reasonable inference from the evidence." Black's Law Dictionary 569 (5th ed. 1979). To say the least, the language of the Rule does not compel us to reject the interpretation that "factual findings" includes conclusions or opinions that flow from a factual investigation. Second, we note that, contrary to what is often assumed, the language of the Rule does not state that "factual findings" are admissible, but that "*reports * * * setting forth * * * factual findings*" (emphasis added) are admissible. On this reading, the language of the Rule does not create a distinction between "fact" and "opinion" contained in such reports.

Turning next to the legislative history of Rule 803(8)(C), we find no clear answer to the question of how the Rule's language should be interpreted. Indeed, in this case the legislative history may well be at the origin of the dispute. Rather than the more usual situation where a court must attempt to glean meaning from ambiguous comments of legislators who did not focus directly on the problem at hand, here the Committees in both Houses of Congress clearly recognized and expressed their opinions on the precise question at issue. Unfortunately, however, they took diametrically opposite positions. Moreover, the two Houses made no effort to reconcile their views, either through changes in the Rule's language or through a statement in the Report of the Conference Committee.

The House Judiciary Committee, which dealt first with the proposed rules after they had been transmitted to Congress by this Court, included in its Report but one brief paragraph on Rule 803(8):

> "The Committee approved Rule 803(8) without substantive change from the form in which it was submitted by the Court. The Committee intends that the phrase 'factual findings' be strictly construed and that evaluations or opinions contained in public reports

house
↳
no

shall not be admissible under this Rule." H.R.Rep. No. 93–650, p. 14 (1973).

The Senate Committee responded at somewhat greater length, but equally emphatically:

> "The House Judiciary Committee report contained a statement of intent that 'the phrase "factual findings" in subdivision (c) be strictly construed and that evaluations or opinions contained in public reports shall not be admissible under this rule.' The committee takes strong exception to this limiting understanding of the application of the rule. We do not think it reflects an understanding of the intended operation of the rule as explained in the Advisory Committee notes to this subsection * * *. We think the restrictive interpretation of the House overlooks the fact that while the Advisory Committee assumes admissibility in the first instance of evaluative reports, they are not admissible if, as the rule states, 'the sources of information or other circumstances indicate lack of trustworthiness.'

* * *

> "The committee concludes that the language of the rule together with the explanation provided by the Advisory Committee furnish sufficient guidance on the admissibility of evaluative reports." S.Rep. No. 93–1277, p. 18 (1974).

Clearly this legislative history reveals a difference of view between the Senate and the House that affords no definitive guide to the congressional understanding. It seems clear however that the Senate understanding is more in accord with the wording of the Rule and with the comments of the Advisory Committee.

The Advisory Committee's comments are notable, first, in that they contain no mention of any dichotomy between statements of "fact" and "opinions" or "conclusions." What was on the Committee's mind was simply whether what it called "evaluative reports" should be admissible. Illustrating the previous division among the courts on this subject, the Committee cited numerous cases in which the admissibility of such reports had been both sustained and denied. It also took note of various federal statutes that made certain kinds of evaluative reports admissible in evidence. What is striking about all of these examples is that these were *reports that stated conclusions.* E.g., Moran v. Pittsburgh–Des Moines Steel Co., 183 F.2d 467, 472–473 (C.A.3 1950) (report of Bureau of Mines concerning the cause of a gas tank explosion admissible); Franklin v. Skelly Oil Co., 141 F.2d 568, 571–572 (CA10 1944) (report of state fire marshal on the cause of a gas explosion inadmissible); 42 U.S.C. § 269(b) (bill of health by appropriate official admissible as prima facie evidence of vessel's sanitary history and condition). The Committee's concern was clearly whether reports of this kind should be admissible. Nowhere in its comments is there the slightest indication that it even considered the solution of admitting only "factual" statements from such reports. Rather, the Committee referred throughout to "reports," without any such differentiation regarding the statements they contained. What the Committee referred to in the Rule's language as "reports * * * setting forth * * * factual findings" is surely nothing more or less than what in its commentary it called "evaluative reports." Its solution as to their admissibility is clearly stated in the final paragraph of its report on this Rule. That solution consists of two principles: First, "the rule * * * assumes admissibility in the first instance * * *." Second, it provides "ample provision for escape if sufficient negative factors are present."

Committee
– admissible
w/escape value

That "provision for escape" is contained in the final clause of the Rule: evaluative reports are admissible "unless the sources of information or other circumstances indicate lack of trustworthiness." This trustworthiness inquiry—and not an arbitrary distinction between "fact" and "opinion"—was the Committee's primary safeguard against the admission of unreliable evidence, and it is important to note that it applies to all elements of the report. Thus, a trial judge has the discretion, and indeed the obligation, to exclude an entire report or portions thereof—whether narrow "factual" statements or broader "conclusions"—that she determines to be untrustworthy. Moreover, safeguards built in to other portions of the Federal Rules, such as those dealing with relevance and prejudice, provide the court with additional means of scrutinizing and, where appropriate, excluding evaluative reports or portions of them. And of course it goes without saying that the admission of a report containing "conclusions" is subject to the ultimate safeguard—the opponent's right to present evidence tending to contradict or diminish the weight of those conclusions.

Our conclusion that neither the language of the Rule nor the intent of its framers calls for a distinction between "fact" and "opinion" is strengthened by the analytical difficulty of drawing such a line. It has frequently been remarked that the distinction between statements of fact and opinion is, at best, one of degree:

> "All statements in language are statements of opinion, i.e., statements of mental processes or perceptions. So-called 'statements of fact' are only more specific statements of opinion. What the judge means to say, when he asks the witness to state the facts, is: 'The nature of this case requires that you be more specific, if you can, in your description of what you saw.'" W. King & D. Pillinger, Opinion Evidence in Illinois 4 (1942) (footnote omitted), quoted in 3 J. Weinstein & M. Berger, Weinstein's Evidence ¶ 701[01], p. 701–6 (1988).

See also E. Cleary, McCormick on Evidence 27 (3d ed. 1984) ("There is no conceivable statement however specific, detailed and 'factual,' that is not in some measure the product of inference and reflection as well as observation and memory"); R. Lempert & S. Saltzburg, A Modern Approach to Evidence 449 (2d ed. 1982) ("A factual finding, unless it is a simple report of something observed, is an opinion as to what more basic facts imply"). Thus, the traditional requirement that lay witnesses give statements of fact rather than opinion may be considered, "[l]ike the hearsay and original documents rules * * * a 'best evidence' rule." McCormick, Opinion Evidence in Iowa, 19 Drake L.Rev. 245, 246 (1970).

In the present case, the trial court had no difficulty in admitting as a factual finding the statement in the JAG Report that "[a]t the time of impact, the engine of 3E955 was operating but was operating at reduced power." Surely this "factual finding" could also be characterized as an opinion, which the investigator presumably arrived at on the basis of clues contained in the airplane wreckage. Rather than requiring that we draw some inevitably arbitrary line between the various shades of fact/opinion that invariably will be present in investigatory reports, we believe the Rule instructs us—as its plain language states—to admit "reports * * * setting forth * * * factual findings." The Rule's limitations and safeguards lie elsewhere: First, the requirement that reports contain factual findings bars the admission of statements not based on factual investigation. Second, the trustworthiness provision requires the court to make a determination as to whether the report, or any portion thereof, is sufficiently trustworthy to be admitted.

A broad approach to admissibility under Rule 803(8)(C), as we have outlined it, is also consistent with the Federal Rules' general approach of relaxing the traditional barriers to "opinion" testimony. Rules 702–705 permit experts to testify in the form of an opinion, and without any exclusion of opinions on "ultimate issues." And Rule 701 permits even a lay witness to testify in the form of opinions or inferences drawn from her observations when testimony in that form will be helpful to the trier of fact. We see no reason to strain to reach an interpretation of Rule 803(8)(C) that is contrary to the liberal thrust of the Federal Rules.

We hold, therefore, that portions of investigatory reports otherwise admissible under Rule 803(8)(C) are not inadmissible merely because they state a conclusion or opinion. As long as the conclusion is based on a factual investigation and satisfies the Rule's trustworthiness requirement, it should be admissible along with other portions of the report. As the trial judge in this case determined that certain of the JAG Report's conclusions were trustworthy, he rightly allowed them to be admitted into evidence. * * *

[In a final portion of its opinion, the Court decided that the District Court erred in restricting the cross-examination of a witness concerning a document about which the witness had testified on direct.]

Richard D. Friedman, The Sky is Still Not Falling
20 J.L. & Pol'y 427 (2012)

Melendez-Diaz v. Massachusetts[, 557 U.S. 305 (2009),] * * * held that, at least as a general matter, forensic laboratory reports are testimonial for purposes of the Confrontation Clause. [The Court therefore held that the prosecution could not prove the substance of the report – that tested material contained cocaine – simply by introducing the report.] I regarded that basic holding as quite obvious—it was, as Justice Scalia's opinion for the majority said, a "rather straightforward application" of *Crawford*. But four justices, led by Justice Kennedy, dissented, and they, together with Massachusetts and its supporting amici (including the United States, thirty-five states, the District of Columbia, the National District Attorneys Association, and numerous local prosecutors), raised a flurry of arguments in opposition. This gave Justice Scalia a chance to clear away a good deal of underbrush, as one by one—quite correctly—he set these arguments aside.

- A lab report is ordinarily not accusatory. That does not matter—the Confrontation Clause is not limited to accusatory statements. Such a limitation would eviscerate the right, because in many cases there is no witness who can testify that she observed the accused committing a crime.

- An analyst who prepares a lab report is not an "ordinary" or "conventional" witness. The dissent raised several points in support of this rather odd assertion. The analyst writing the report was reporting near-contemporaneous observations. Not really true, responded Justice Scalia—the report was completed almost a week after performance of the tests—and immaterial in any event: A witness can testify about contemporaneous observances. The analyst who completed the report did not observe the crime itself or "any human action related to it." But again, so what? No one would deny, I suppose, that an observer who testifies to the state of the crime scene after the fact is a witness for Confrontation Clause purposes. She is reporting on information that may help the trier of fact determine whether a crime was committed and, if so, how. But the same is true of the lab analyst who testifies that a given substance contains cocaine. Finally, according to the dissent, the lab analyst is not testifying in response to police interrogation. That assertion is dubious at best: The lab analyst was responding to a police request. But the broader response is yet again, so what? The confrontation right is independent of, and much older than, the institutions of a police force or a public prosecutor. It is a right that the accused has with respect to the witness, and if the witness makes her statement on her own initiative that does not nullify the right.

- The lab report was, Massachusetts contended, a product of neutral, scientific testing, rather than an historical account subject to distortion. Once more, Justice Scalia challenged both the truth and the materiality of the premise. Lab testing, while usually accurate, is far from foolproof. Nor can agents of the government properly be called neutral in a criminal prosecution. But beyond that, *Crawford* forbids a court from trying to exempt species of evidence from the confrontation right on the ground that they are reliable and so cross-examination is unlikely to be productive.

- Massachusetts contended that the lab reports were akin to business records and so exempt from the Confrontation Clause. True, forensic lab reports are produced routinely—but to say that this is sufficient to guarantee admissibility would only mean that the confrontation rights of the accused are routinely violated. Forensic laboratory reports are routinely produced *for use in prosecution*, and that is what makes them testimonial. Statements genuinely falling within the hearsay exception for business records are not prepared for litigation purposes.[6] But beyond that, a statement cannot be exempted from the Confrontation Clause on the ground—part of the rejected *Roberts* doctrine—that it fits within a well-recognized hearsay exception. True, *Crawford* suggested that business records are typically not testimonial statements. But that was merely an empirical observation: If a statement satisfies the requirements for the hearsay exception, it will probably also be properly characterized as non-testimonial. That is not at all the same thing as saying that qualification as a business record *means* that the statement is not testimonial.

- Melendez-Diaz could have subpoenaed the lab analysts and made them his own witnesses. But, as the Court emphasized, that turns criminal procedure on its head. It is the prosecution's job, not the defense's, to produce the witnesses against the accused. The difference is not merely one of formality; it is far better for the defense if the prosecution produces its witness live and then the defense decides whether and how to cross-examine, than if the prosecution presents the testimony in written form and the defense can examine the witness only by calling her to the stand as part of his case.

- The practical burden on the courts of requiring lab analysts to testify, asserted those on the state side, would be intolerable. Once again, Justice Scalia challenged both the accuracy and the materiality of the premise. "[W]e may not disregard [the Confrontation Clause] at our convenience," he wrote. Besides, he doubted the "dire predictions" of disaster: "Perhaps the best indication that the sky will not fall [as a result of the decision] is that it has not done so already." That is, *Melendez-Diaz* had no impact on those states that already complied with the constitutional rule it required, and those states had not been led to ruin.

The majority opinion in *Melendez-Diaz* was quite wonderful. Point by point, it swept aside potential obstructions to the confrontation right that should never have been erected. But I confess that I found it disappointing in two respects. One was that the opinion secured only five votes—and the four dissenters seemed so ready to undercut *Crawford* severely, largely because of misguided concern that the practical consequences of the decision would be intolerable.

---

[6] E.g., *Palmer v. Hoffman*, 318 U.S. 109, 114 (1943), cited with approval by *Melendez-Diaz*, 129 S. Ct. at 2538.

The other respect was perhaps less to my credit. At the time, I had a petition for *certiorari* pending in *Briscoe v. Virginia*. The petition contended that Virginia did not satisfy the Confrontation Clause in providing that a lab certificate could be admissible but the accused could present the analyst as his own witness. The *Melendez-Diaz* decision, it appeared clear, had just resolved this issue in our favor—great news for my clients, but apparently precluding my hopes of arguing the issue in the Supreme Court. I, like most observers, expected that the Court would, as a matter of course, remand *Briscoe* to the Virginia Supreme Court for reconsideration in light of *Melendez-Diaz*. It was startling, therefore, when four days later the Court instead simply granted *certiorari*. There was widespread speculation that the four dissenters had decided to take *Briscoe* in hopes of undercutting *Melendez-Diaz*. The speculation gained credence from the fact that Justice David Souter, a member of the majority, had announced his retirement and his prospective successor, Sonia Sotomayor, was a former prosecutor.[7] Once again, state-side amici—including the United States, a majority of the states, and the District of Columbia—raised the catastrophic consequences that would occur if the defendant's position prevailed. But at the argument, it became quite clear that Justice Sotomayor was not about to undermine a seven-month-old precedent. Two weeks later, the Court did what observers had expected it to do in the first place, remanding the case for proceedings consistent with *Melendez-Diaz*.

But, of course, the matter did not rest there. Nine months later, the Court granted *certiorari* in *Bullcoming v. New Mexico*. The Court's makeup had shifted again—Justice Kagan had replaced Justice Stevens, a member of the *Melendez-Diaz* majority. In *Bullcoming*, unlike *Melendez-Diaz* and *Briscoe*, the prosecution had presented a live witness from the laboratory, rather than simply the report. [The report indicated that the accused's blood alcohol level, tested shortly after an auto accident, was very elevated.] But the witness was not the analyst who had performed the test and prepared the report, for he had been placed on unpaid administrative leave. I thought this case was extremely easy—after all, in his *Melendez-Diaz* dissent, Justice Kennedy noted that the Court had made clear that it "will not permit the testimonial statement of one witness to enter into evidence through the in-court testimony of a second . * * *" Perhaps for that reason, the United States did not appear as amicus in support of the state. But thirty-three states did, as well as organizations of prosecutors and medical examiners, and once again they focused on the practical consequences that would follow if the author of the report had to testify live. Nevertheless, I hoped that some or all of the *Melendez-Diaz* dissenters would acknowledge that the Court had decided that forensic lab reports are testimonial statements, and that it obviously followed that a surrogate witness could not testify ineas to the contents of a lab report stating events and results that the surrogates had not observed. In the end, Justice Kagan stayed with the majority, which once again—this time in an opinion by Justice Ginsburg—treated the case as virtually a foregone conclusion. But the

---

[7] During oral argument in *Briscoe*, Justice Scalia lent additional force to the speculation, suggesting that the Court had taken the case for no reason other than to consider overruling *Melendez-Diaz*.

bloc of four dissenters remained intact. Once again, Justice Kennedy took the lead, and this time some of his language seemed to indicate that he was ready to throw out the entire *Crawford* framework and return to something like that of *Roberts*.

Williams v. Illinois

Supreme Court of the United States, 2012
132 S.Ct. 2221

Justice ALITO announced the judgment of the Court and delivered an opinion, in which THE CHIEF JUSTICE, Justice KENNEDY, and Justice BREYER join.

In this case, we decide whether *Crawford v. Washington* precludes an expert witness from testifying in a manner that has long been allowed under the law of evidence. Specifically, does *Crawford* bar an expert from expressing an opinion based on facts about a case that have been made known to the expert but about which the expert is not competent to testify? We also decide whether *Crawford* substantially impedes the ability of prosecutors to introduce DNA evidence and thus may effectively relegate the prosecution in some cases to reliance on older, less reliable forms of proof.
* * *

I

A

[In February, 2000, a young woman, L.J., was abducted on a street in Chicago and raped and robbed. At a hospital, vaginal swabs were taken from her for a sexual assault kit. A police detective sent the kit to the Illinois State Police (ISP) lab. Brian Hapack, an ISP forensic scientist, confirmed the presence of semen on the swabs, and ISP later sent the kit, resealed, to Cellmark Diagnostics Laboratory in Germantown, Maryland. Some time later, Cellmark sent back a signed report with a male DNA profile that it said was produced from the semen on the swabs. [The report may be viewed at the blog post *The Cellmark report and what it shows*, available at <http://www.confrontationright.blogspot.com/2011/12/cellmark-report-and-what-it-shows.html> (last visited October 26, 2012). Eds.] After receiving the report, Sandra Lambatos, a forensic specialist at the ISP lab, conducted a computer search and determined that the Cellmark profile matched a profile produced by Karen Abbinanti, another ISP forensic analyst, from a sample of petitioner Williams' blood that had been taken after he was arrested on unrelated charges in August 2000; before that match was made, Williams had not previously been under suspicion for the assault on L.J. In April 2001, at a lineup conducted by the police, L.J. identified Williams as the assailant.

[Williams was tried on various charges before a state court judge. L.J. again identified him as the attacker. Hapack and Abbinanti each testified about the tests that they had performed. Lambatos also testified, among other things about the procedures used by ISP for maintaining a chain of custody of samples.]

The prosecutor asked Lambatos whether there was a computer match between the male DNA profile found in semen from the vaginal swabs of [L.J.] and [the] male DNA profile that had been identified from petitioner's blood sample. [Lambatos answered that there was. The prosecutor asked,] Did you compare the semen that had been identified by Brian Hapack from the vaginal swabs of [L.J.] to the male DNA profile that had been identified by Karen [Abbinanti] from the blood of [petitioner]?

Lambatos answered Yes. Defense counsel lodged an objection to the form of the question, but the trial judge overruled it. Lambatos then testified that, based on her own comparison of the two DNA profiles, she concluded that [petitioner] cannot be excluded as a possible source of the semen identified in the vaginal swabs, and that the probability of the profile's appearing in the general population was 1 in 8.7 quadrillion black, 1 in 390 quadrillion white, or 1 in 109 quadrillion Hispanic unrelated individuals. Asked whether she would call this a match to [petitioner], Lambatos answered yes, again over defense counsel's objection.

The Cellmark report itself was neither admitted into evidence nor shown to the factfinder. Lambatos did not quote or read from the report; nor did she identify it as the source of any of the opinions she expressed.

[The judge found Williams guilty, and the state intermediate appellate court and supreme court both affirmed the conviction. The state supreme court held that the report could not have been introduced to prove the truth of what it asserted, but that it was only introduced for the limited purpose of explaining the basis for [Lambatos's expert opinion].] * * *

II

* * * In concurrence [in *Bullcoming*], Justice SOTOMAYOR highlighted the importance of the fact that the forensic report had been admitted into evidence for the purpose of proving the truth of the matter it asserted. She emphasized that this [was] not a case in which an expert witness was asked for his independent opinion about underlying testimonial reports that were not themselves admitted into evidence. We would face a different question, she observed, if asked to determine the constitutionality of allowing an expert witness to discuss others' testimonial statements if the testimonial statements were not themselves admitted as evidence.

We now confront that question.

B

It has long been accepted that an expert witness may voice an opinion based on facts concerning the events at issue in a particular case even if the expert lacks first-hand knowledge of those facts.

At common law, courts developed two ways to deal with this situation. An expert could rely on facts that had already been established in the record. But because it was not always possible to proceed in this manner, and because record evidence was often disputed, courts developed the alternative practice of allowing an expert to testify in the form of a hypothetical question. Under this approach, the expert would be asked to assume the truth of certain factual predicates, and was then asked to offer an opinion based on those assumptions. * * *

There is a long tradition of the use of hypothetical questions in American courts. * * *

Modern rules of evidence continue to permit experts to express opinions based on facts about which they lack personal knowledge, but these rules dispense with the need for hypothetical questions. Under both the Illinois and the Federal Rules of Evidence, an expert may base an opinion on facts that are made known to the expert at or before the hearing, but such reliance does not constitute admissible evidence of this underlying information. Ill. Rule Evid. 703; Fed. Rule Evid. 703. Accordingly, *in jury trials,* both Illinois and federal law generally bar an expert from disclosing such inadmissible evidence.[2] In bench trials, however, both the Illinois and the Federal Rules place no restriction on the revelation of such information to the factfinder. When the judge sits as the trier of fact, it is presumed that the judge will understand the limited reason for the disclosure of the underlying inadmissible information and will not rely on that information for any improper purpose. As we have noted, [i]n bench trials, judges routinely hear inadmissible evidence that they are presumed to ignore when making decisions. *Harris v. Rivera,* 454 U.S. 339, 346, 102 S.Ct. 460, 70 L.Ed.2d 530 (1981) *(per curiam).* * * *

This feature of Illinois and federal law is important because *Crawford,* while departing from prior Confrontation Clause precedent in other respects, took pains to reaffirm the proposition that the Confrontation Clause does not bar the use of testimonial statements for purposes other than establishing the truth of the matter asserted, (citing *Tennessee v. Street,* 471 U.S. 409, 105 S.Ct. 2078, 85 L.Ed.2d 425).

III

A

In order to assess petitioner's Confrontation Clause argument, it is helpful to inventory exactly what Lambatos said on the stand about Cellmark. She testified to the truth of the following matters: Cellmark was an accredited lab; the ISP occasionally sent forensic samples to Cellmark for

---

[2] But disclosure of these facts or data to the jury is permitted if the value of disclosure substantially outweighs [any] prejudicial effect, Fed. Rule Evid. 703, or the probative value * * *outweighs the risk of unfair prejudice. *People v. Pasch,* 152 Ill.2d 133, 223, 178 Ill.Dec. 38, 604 N.E.2d 294, 333 (1992). When this disclosure occurs, the underlying facts are revealed to the jury for the limited purpose of explaining the basis for [the expert's] opinion and not for the truth of the matter asserted. *Id.,* at 176, 178 Ill.Dec. 38, 604 N.E.2d, at 311.

DNA testing; according to shipping manifests admitted into evidence, the ISP lab sent vaginal swabs taken from the victim to Cellmark and later received those swabs back from Cellmark; and, finally, the Cellmark DNA profile matched a profile produced by the ISP lab from a sample of petitioner's blood. Lambatos had personal knowledge of all of these matters, and therefore none of this testimony infringed petitioner's confrontation right.

Lambatos did not testify to the truth of any other matter concerning Cellmark. She made no other reference to the Cellmark report, which was not admitted into evidence and was not seen by the trier of fact. Nor did she testify to anything that was done at the Cellmark lab, and she did not vouch for the quality of Cellmark's work.

B

[Justice Alito characterizes the principal argument of the dissent as being based on the fact that Lambatos was able to testify that there was a computer match between Williams' DNA profile and the profile "found in semen from the vaginal swabs of [L.J.]"; if instead she had testified that the match was with the profile "produced by Cellmark," he thought, the dissent would not find her testimony problematic.]

The defect in this argument is that under Illinois law (like federal law) it is clear that the putatively offending phrase in Lambatos' testimony was not admissible for the purpose of proving the truth of the matter asserted *i.e.,* that the matching DNA profile was found in semen from the vaginal swabs. Rather, that fact was a mere premise of the prosecutor's question, and Lambatos simply assumed that premise to be true when she gave her answer indicating that there was a match between the two DNA profiles. There is no reason to think that the trier of fact took Lambatos' answer as substantive evidence to establish where the DNA profiles came from.

The dissent's argument would have force if petitioner had elected to have a jury trial. In that event, there would have been a danger of the jury's taking Lambatos' testimony as proof that the Cellmark profile was derived from the sample obtained from the victim's vaginal swabs. Absent an evaluation of the risk of juror confusion and careful jury instructions, the testimony could not have gone to the jury.

This case, however, involves *a bench trial* and we must assume that the trial judge understood that the portion of Lambatos' testimony to which the dissent objects was not admissible to prove the truth of the matter asserted. * * *

[T]he admissible evidence left little room for argument that the sample tested by Cellmark came from any source other than the victim's vaginal swabs.[7] This is so because there is simply no plausible explanation for how

---

[7] Our point is not that admissible evidence regarding the identity of the sample that Cellmark tested excuses the admission of testimonial hearsay on this matter. Rather, our point is that, because there was substantial (albeit circumstantial) evidence on this matter,

Cellmark could have produced a DNA profile that matched Williams' if Cellmark had tested any sample other than the one taken from the victim. If any other items that might have contained Williams' DNA had been sent to Cellmark or were otherwise in Cellmark's possession, there would have been a chance of a mix-up or of cross-contamination. But there is absolutely nothing to suggest that Cellmark had any such items. Thus, the fact that the Cellmark profile matched Williams the very man whom the victim identified in a lineup and at trial as her attacker was itself striking confirmation that the sample that Cellmark tested was the sample taken from the victim's vaginal swabs. For these reasons, it is fanciful to suggest that the trial judge took Lambatos' testimony as providing critical chain-of-custody evidence.

C

Other than the phrase that Lambatos used in referring to the Cellmark profile, no specific passage in the trial record has been identified as violating the Confrontation Clause, but it is nevertheless suggested that the State somehow introduced the substance of Cellmark's report into evidence. The main impetus for this argument appears to be the (erroneous) view that unless the substance of the report was sneaked in, there would be insufficient evidence in the record on two critical points: first, that the Cellmark profile was based on the semen in the victim's vaginal swabs and, second, that Cellmark's procedures were reliable. This argument is both legally irrelevant for present purposes and factually incorrect.

As to legal relevance, the question before us is whether petitioner's Sixth Amendment confrontation right was violated, not whether the State offered sufficient foundational evidence to support the admission of Lambatos' opinion about the DNA match. In order to prove these underlying facts, the prosecution relied on circumstantial evidence, and the Illinois courts found that this evidence was sufficient to satisfy state-law requirements regarding proof of foundational facts. * * *

It is not correct, however, that the trial record lacks admissible evidence with respect to the source of the sample that Cellmark tested or the reliability of the Cellmark profile. As to the source of the sample, the State offered conventional chain-of-custody evidence, namely, the testimony of the physician who obtained the vaginal swabs, the testimony of the police employees who handled and kept custody of that evidence until it was sent to Cellmark, and the shipping manifests, which provided evidence that the swabs were sent to Cellmark and then returned to the ISP lab. In addition, as already discussed, the match between the Cellmark profile and petitioner's profile was itself telling confirmation that the Cellmark profile was deduced from the semen on the vaginal swabs.

---

there is no reason to infer that the trier of fact must have taken Lambatos' statement as providing the missing link.

This match also provided strong circumstantial evidence regarding the reliability of Cellmark's work. Assuming (for the reasons discussed above) that the Cellmark profile was based on the semen on the vaginal swabs, how could shoddy or dishonest work in the Cellmark lab have resulted in the production of a DNA profile that just so happened to match petitioner's? If the semen found on the vaginal swabs was not petitioner's and thus had an entirely different DNA profile, how could sloppy work in the Cellmark lab have transformed that entirely different profile into one that matched petitioner's? And without access to any other sample of petitioner's DNA (and recall that petitioner was not even under suspicion at this time), how could a dishonest lab technician have substituted petitioner's DNA profile? Under the circumstances of this case, it was surely permissible for the trier of fact to infer that the odds of any of this were exceedingly low.

* * * [T]he truth of Lambatos' testimony, properly understood, was not dependent on the truth of any predicate facts. Lambatos testified that two DNA profiles matched. The correctness of this expert opinion, which the defense was able to test on cross-examination, was not in any way dependent on the origin of the samples from which the profiles were derived. Of course, Lambatos' opinion would have lacked probative value if the prosecution had not introduced other evidence to establish the provenance of the profiles, but that has nothing to do with the truth of her testimony.

The dissent is similarly mistaken in its contention that the Cellmark report was offered for its truth because that is all such basis evidence can be offered for. This view is directly contrary to the current version of Rule 703 of the Federal Rules of Evidence, which this Court approved and sent to Congress in 2000. Under that Rule, basis evidence that is not admissible for its truth may be disclosed even in a jury trial under appropriate circumstances. The purpose for allowing this disclosure is that it may assis[t] the jury to evaluate the expert's opinion. Advisory Committee's 2000 Notes on Fed. Rule Evid. 703. The Rule 703 approach, which was controversial when adopted, is based on the idea that the disclosure of basis evidence can help the factfinder understand the expert's thought process and determine what weight to give to the expert's opinion. For example, if the factfinder were to suspect that the expert relied on factual premises with no support in the record, or that the expert drew an unwarranted inference from the premises on which the expert relied, then the probativeness or credibility of the expert's opinion would be seriously undermined. The purpose of disclosing the facts on which the expert relied is to allay these fears to show that the expert's reasoning was not illogical, and that the weight of the expert's opinion does not depend on factual premises unsupported by other evidence in the record not to prove the truth of the underlying facts. * * *

IV

A

Even if the Cellmark report had been introduced for its truth, we would nevertheless conclude that there was no Confrontation Clause violation. The Confrontation Clause refers to testimony by witnesses against an accused. * * * The Court has * * * interpreted the Confrontation Clause as prohibiting modern-day practices that are tantamount to the abuses that gave rise to the recognition of the confrontation right. But any further expansion would strain the constitutional text.

The abuses that the Court has identified as prompting the adoption of the Confrontation Clause shared the following two characteristics: (a) they involved out-of-court statements having the primary purpose of accusing a targeted individual of engaging in criminal conduct and (b) they involved formalized statements such as affidavits, depositions, prior testimony, or confessions. In all but one of the post- *Crawford* cases[13] in which a Confrontation Clause violation has been found, both of these characteristics were present. The one exception occurred in *Hammon v. Indiana,* which was decided together with *Davis v. Washington,* but in *Hammon* and every other post-*Crawford* case in which the Court has found a violation of the confrontation right, the statement at issue had the primary purpose of accusing a targeted individual.

B

[The Court summarizes recent cases, characterizing *Hammon* as "the one case in which an informal statement was held to violate the Confrontation Clause."] In *Melendez Diaz* and *Bullcoming,* the Court held that the particular forensic reports at issue qualified as testimonial statements, but the Court did not hold that all forensic reports fall into the same category. Introduction of the reports in those cases ran afoul of the Confrontation Clause because they were the equivalent of affidavits made for the purpose of proving the guilt of a particular criminal defendant at trial. There was nothing resembling an ongoing emergency, as the suspects in both cases had already been captured, and the tests in question were relatively simple and can generally be performed by a single analyst. In addition, the technicians who prepared the reports must have realized that their contents (which reported an elevated blood-alcohol level and the presence of an illegal drug) would be incriminating.

C

The Cellmark report is very different. It plainly was not prepared for the primary purpose of accusing a targeted individual. In identifying the primary purpose of an out-of-court statement, we apply an objective test. We look for the primary purpose that a reasonable person would have ascribed to the statement, taking into account all of the surrounding circumstances.

Here, the primary purpose of the Cellmark report, viewed objectively, was not to accuse petitioner or to create evidence for use at trial. When the

---

[13] Experience might yet show that the holdings in those cases should be reconsidered for the reasons, among others, expressed in the dissents the decisions produced. Those decisions are not challenged in this case and are to be deemed binding precedents, but they can and should be distinguished on the facts here.

ISP lab sent the sample to Cellmark, its primary purpose was to catch a dangerous rapist who was still at large, not to obtain evidence for use against petitioner, who was neither in custody nor under suspicion at that time. Similarly, no one at Cellmark could have possibly known that the profile that it produced would turn out to inculpate petitioner or for that matter, anyone else whose DNA profile was in a law enforcement database. Under these circumstances, there was no prospect of fabrication and no incentive to produce anything other than a scientifically sound and reliable profile. * * *

It is also significant that in many labs, numerous technicians work on each DNA profile. When the work of a lab is divided up in such a way, it is likely that the sole purpose of each technician is simply to perform his or her task in accordance with accepted procedures.

Finally, the knowledge that defects in a DNA profile may often be detected from the profile itself provides a further safeguard. In this case, for example, Lambatos testified that she would have been able to tell from the profile if the sample used by Cellmark had been degraded prior to testing. As noted above, moreover, there is no real chance that sample contamination, sample switching, mislabeling, [or] fraud could have led Cellmark to produce a DNA profile that falsely matched petitioner. At the time of the testing, petitioner had not yet been identified as a suspect, and there is no suggestion that anyone at Cellmark had a sample of his DNA to swap in by malice or mistake. And given the complexity of the DNA molecule, it is inconceivable that shoddy lab work would somehow produce a DNA profile that just so happened to have the precise genetic makeup of petitioner, who just so happened to be picked out of a lineup by the victim. The prospect is beyond fanciful.

In short, the use at trial of a DNA report prepared by a modern, accredited laboratory bears little if any resemblance to the historical practices that the Confrontation Clause aimed to eliminate. *[Michigan v.] Bryant*, 131 S.Ct., at 1167 (THOMAS, J., concurring).

3

For the two independent reasons explained above, we conclude that there was no Confrontation Clause violation in this case. Accordingly, the judgment of the Supreme Court of Illinois is

Affirmed.

Justice BREYER, concurring.

This case raises a question that I believe neither the plurality nor the dissent answers adequately: How does the Confrontation Clause apply to the panoply of crime laboratory reports and underlying technical statements written by (or otherwise made by) laboratory technicians? In this context, what, if any, are the outer limits of the testimonial statements rule set forth in *Crawford v. Washington*?

* * * Lambatos' testimony did not introduce the Cellmark report (which other circumstantial evidence supported) for its truth. Rather, Lambatos used the Cellmark report only to indicate the underlying factual information upon which she based her independent expert opinion. Under well-established principles of evidence, experts may rely on otherwise inadmissible out-of-court statements as a basis for forming an expert opinion if they are of a kind that experts in the field normally rely upon. See Fed. Rule Evid. 703; Ill. Rule Evid. 703. Nor need the prosecution enter those out-of-court statements into evidence for their truth. That, the Illinois courts held, is just what took place here. * * *

Once one abandons the traditional rule, there would seem often to be no logical stopping place between requiring the prosecution to call as a witness one of the laboratory experts who worked on the matter and requiring the prosecution to call *all* of the laboratory experts who did so. Experts especially laboratory experts regularly rely on the technical statements and results of other experts to form their own opinions. The reality of the matter is that the introduction of a laboratory report involves layer upon layer of technical statements (express or implied) made by one expert and relied upon by another. Hence my general question: How does the Confrontation Clause apply to crime laboratory reports and underlying technical statements made by laboratory technicians? * * *

[Assuming] that the admissibility of [an] initial laboratory report into trial [is] directly at issue[, who] should the prosecution have * * * to call to testify? Only the analyst who signed the report noting the match? What if the analyst who made the match knew nothing about either the laboratory's underlying procedures or the specific tests run in the particular case? Should the prosecution then have had to call all potentially involved laboratory technicians to testify? Six to twelve or more technicians could have been involved. [In an Appendix, Justice Breyer presents what he calls "typically relevant laboratory procedures" involving multiple technicians.] * * *

The several different opinions filed today embody several serious, but different, approaches to the difficult general question. Yet none fully deals with the underlying question as to how, after *Crawford,* Confrontation Clause testimonial statement requirements apply to crime laboratory reports. * * *

Under these circumstances, I would have this case reargued. I would request the parties and *amici* to focus specifically upon the broader limits question. And I would permit them to discuss, not only the possible implications of our earlier post-*Crawford* opinions, but also any necessary modifications of statements made in the opinions of those earlier cases.

II

In the absence of reargument, I adhere to the dissenting view set forth in *Melendez Diaz* and *Bullcoming,* under which the Cellmark report would not be considered testimonial and barred by the Confrontation Clause. * * * That view * * * would leave the States with constitutional leeway to maintain traditional expert testimony rules as well as hearsay exceptions where there are strong reasons for doing so and *Crawford* 's basic rationale does not apply.

In particular, the States could create an exception that presumptively would allow introduction of DNA reports from accredited crime laboratories. The defendant would remain free to call laboratory technicians as witnesses. Were there significant reason to question a laboratory's technical competence or its neutrality, the presumptive exception would disappear, thereby requiring the prosecution to produce any relevant technical witnesses. Such an exception would lie outside *Crawford* 's constitutional limits. * * *

[T]he need for cross-examination is considerably diminished when the out-of-court statement was made by an accredited laboratory employee operating at a remove from the investigation in the ordinary course of professional work.

For one thing, as the hearsay exception itself reflects, alternative features of such situations help to guarantee its accuracy. * * * For another thing, the fact that the laboratory testing takes place behind a veil of ignorance makes it unlikely that a particular researcher has a defendant-related motive to behave dishonestly, say, to misrepresent a step in an analysis or otherwise to misreport testing results. The laboratory here, for example, did not know whether its test results might help to incriminate a particular defendant.

Further, the statements at issue, like those of many laboratory analysts, do not easily fit within the linguistic scope of the term testimonial statement as we have used that term in our earlier cases. * * * [H]ere the DNA report sought, not to accuse petitioner, but instead to generate objectively a profile of a then-unknown suspect's DNA from the semen he left in committing the crime.

Finally, to bar admission of the out-of-court records at issue here could undermine, not fortify, the accuracy of factfinding at a criminal trial. Such a precedent could bar the admission of other reliable case-specific technical information such as, say, autopsy reports. Autopsies, like the DNA report in this case, are often conducted when it is not yet clear whether there is a particular suspect or whether the facts found in the autopsy will ultimately prove relevant in a criminal trial. Autopsies are typically conducted soon after death. And when, say, a victim's body has decomposed, repetition of the autopsy may not be possible. What is to happen if the medical examiner dies before trial? * * *

In general, such a holding could also increase the risk of convicting the innocent. The New York County District Attorney's Office and the New York City Office of the Chief Medical Examiner tell us that the additional cost and complexity involved in requiring live testimony from perhaps dozens of ordinary laboratory technicians who participate in the preparation of a DNA profile may well force a laboratory to reduce the amount of DNA testing it conducts, and force prosecutors to forgo forensic DNA analysis in cases where it might be highly probative. In the absence of DNA testing, defendants might well be prosecuted solely on the basis of eyewitness testimony, the reliability of which is often questioned. * * *

Justice THOMAS, concurring in the judgment.

I agree with the plurality that the disclosure of Cellmark's out-of-court statements through the expert testimony of Sandra Lambatos did not violate the Confrontation Clause. I reach this conclusion, however, solely because Cellmark's statements lacked the requisite formality and solemnity to be considered   testimonial   for purposes of the Confrontation Clause. As I explain below, I share the dissent's view of the plurality's flawed analysis.

I

* * * Here, the State of Illinois contends that Cellmark's statements that it successfully derived a male DNA profile and that the profile came from L.J.'s swabs were introduced only to show the basis of Lambatos' opinion, and not for their truth. In my view, however, there was no plausible reason for the introduction of Cellmark's statements other than to establish their truth.

A

Illinois Rule of Evidence 703 (2011) and its federal counterpart permit an expert to base his opinion on facts about which he lacks personal knowledge and to disclose those facts to the trier of fact. Relying on these Rules, the State contends that the facts on which an expert's opinion relies are not to be considered for their truth, but only to explain the basis of his opinion. Accordingly, in the State's view, the disclosure of expert basis testimony does not implicate the Confrontation Clause.

I do not think that rules of evidence should so easily trump a defendant's confrontation right. To be sure, we should not lightly swee[p] away an accepted rule of federal or state evidence law when applying the Confrontation Clause. * * * And, we often presume that courts and juries follow limiting instructions. But we have recognized that concepts central to the application of the Confrontation Clause are ultimately matters of federal constitutional law that are not dictated by state or federal evidentiary rules. Likewise, we have held that limiting instructions may be insufficient in some circumstances to protect against violations of the Confrontation Clause. See *Bruton v. United States,* 391 U.S. 123 (1968).

Of particular importance here, we have made sure that an out-of-court statement was introduced for a *legitimate,* nonhearsay purpose before relying on the not-for-its-truth rationale to dismiss the application of the Confrontation Clause. See *Street* (emphasis added). In *Street,* the defendant testified that he gave a false confession because police coerced him into parroting his accomplice's confession. On rebuttal, the prosecution introduced the accomplice's confession to demonstrate to the jury the ways in which the two confessions differed. Finding no Confrontation Clause problem, this Court held that the accomplice's out-of-court confession was not introduced for its truth, but only to impeach the defendant's version of events. Although the Court noted that the confession was not hearsay under traditional rules of evidence, the Court did not accept that nonhearsay label at face value. Instead, the Court thoroughly examined the use of the out-of-court confession and the efficacy of a limiting instruction before concluding that the Confrontation Clause was satisfied [i]n this context.

Unlike the confession in *Street,* statements introduced to explain the basis of an expert's opinion are not introduced for a plausible nonhearsay purpose. There is no meaningful distinction between disclosing an out-of-court statement so that the factfinder may evaluate the expert's opinion and disclosing that statement for its truth. * * *[1]

Contrary to the plurality's suggestion, this commonsense conclusion is not undermined by any longstanding historical practice exempting expert basis testimony from the rigors of the Confrontation Clause. Prior to the adoption of the Federal Rules of Evidence in 1975, an expert could render an opinion based only on facts that the expert had personally perceived or facts that the expert learned at trial, either by listening to the testimony of other witnesses or through a hypothetical question based on facts in evidence. * * * In those situations, there was little danger that the expert would rely on testimonial hearsay that was not subject to confrontation because the expert and the witnesses on whom he relied were present at trial. It was not until 1975 that the universe of facts upon which an expert could rely was expanded to include facts of the case that the expert learned out of court by means other than his own perception. * * *

B

Those concerns are fully applicable in this case. Lambatos opined that petitioner's DNA profile matched the male profile derived from L.J.'s vaginal swabs. In reaching that conclusion, Lambatos relied on Cellmark's out-of-court statements that the profile it reported was in fact derived from L.J.'s swabs, rather than from some other source. Thus, the validity of Lambatos' opinion ultimately turned on the truth of Cellmark's statements. The plurality's assertion that Cellmark's statements were merely relayed to explain the assumptions on which [Lambatos'] opinion rest[ed], overlooks that the value of Lambatos' testimony depended on the truth of those very assumptions.

---

[1] The plurality relies heavily on the fact that this case involved a bench trial, emphasizing that a judge sitting as factfinder is presumed more so than a jury to understand the limited reason for the disclosure of basis testimony and to not rely on that information for any improper purpose. Even accepting that presumption, the point is not that the factfinder is unable to understand the restricted purpose for basis testimony. Instead, the point is that the purportedly limited reason for such testimony to aid the factfinder in evaluating the expert's opinion necessarily entails an evaluation of whether the basis testimony is true.

It is no answer to say that *other* nonhearsay evidence established the basis of the expert's opinion. Here, Lambatos disclosed Cellmark's statements that it generated a male DNA profile from L.J.'s swabs, but other evidence showed that L.J.'s swabs contained semen and that the swabs were shipped to and received from Cellmark. That evidence did not render Cellmark's statements superfluous. Of course, evidence that Cellmark received L.J.'s swabs and later produced a DNA profile is some indication that Cellmark in fact generated the profile from those swabs, rather than from some other source (or from no source at all). But the only direct evidence to that effect was Cellmark's statement, which Lambatos relayed to the factfinder. In any event, the factfinder's ability to rely on other evidence to evaluate an expert's opinion does not alter the conclusion that basis testimony is admitted for its truth. The existence of other evidence corroborating the basis testimony may render any Confrontation Clause violation harmless, but it does not change the purpose of such testimony and thereby place it outside of the reach of the Confrontation Clause. I would thus conclude that Cellmark's statements were introduced for their truth.

C

The plurality's contrary conclusion may seem of little consequence to those who view DNA testing and other forms of hard science as intrinsically reliable. But see *Melendez Diaz* (Forensic evidence is not uniquely immune from the risk of manipulation). Today's holding, however, will reach beyond scientific evidence to ordinary out-of-court statements. For example, it is not uncommon for experts to rely on interviews with third parties in forming their opinions. See, *e.g., People v. Goldstein,* 6 N.Y.3d 119, 123 124, 810 N.Y.S.2d 100, 843 N.E.2d 727, 729 730 (2005) (psychiatrist disclosed statements made by the defendant's acquaintances as part of the basis of her opinion that the defendant was motivated to kill by his feelings of sexual frustration).

It is no answer to say that safeguards in the rules of evidence will prevent the abuse of basis testimony. To begin with, courts may be willing to conclude that an expert is not acting as a mere condui[t] for hearsay, as long as he simply provides some opinion based on that hearsay. In addition, the hearsay may be the kind of fact on which experts in a field reasonably rely. Of course, some courts may determine that hearsay of this sort is not substantially more probative than prejudicial and therefore should not be disclosed under Rule 703. But that balancing test is no substitute for a constitutional provision that has already struck the balance in favor of the accused. See *Crawford* ([The Confrontation Clause] commands, not that evidence be reliable, but that reliability be assessed in a particular manner: by testing in the crucible of cross-examination).

II

A

Having concluded that the statements at issue here were introduced for their truth, I turn to whether they were testimonial for purposes of the

Confrontation Clause. * * * In light of its text, I continue to think that the Confrontation Clause regulates only the use of statements bearing indicia of solemnity. *Davis v. Washington* (THOMAS, J., concurring in judgment in part and dissenting in part).[5]

Applying these principles, I conclude that Cellmark's report is not a statement by a witnes[s] within the meaning of the Confrontation Clause. The Cellmark report lacks the solemnity of an affidavit or deposition, for it is neither a sworn nor a certified declaration of fact. Nowhere does the report attest that its statements accurately reflect the DNA testing processes used or the results obtained. The report is signed by two reviewers, but they neither purport to have performed the DNA testing nor certify the accuracy of those who did. And, although the report was produced at the request of law enforcement, it was not the product of any sort of formalized dialogue resembling custodial interrogation.

The Cellmark report is distinguishable from the laboratory reports that we determined were testimonial in *Melendez Diaz* and in *Bullcoming*. [In *Melendez-Diaz*, the analysts swore to the reports before a notary, and in *Bullcoming*,] the report, though unsworn, included a Certificate of Analyst signed by the forensic analyst who tested the defendant's blood sample. * * *

The dissent insists that the *Bullcoming* report and Cellmark's report are equally formal, separated only by such minutia as the fact that Cellmark's report is not labeled a certificate. To the contrary, what distinguishes the two is that Cellmark's report, in substance, certifies nothing. That distinction is constitutionally significant because the scope of the confrontation right is properly limited to extrajudicial statements similar in solemnity to the Marian examination practices that the Confrontation Clause was designed to prevent. * * *

Contrary to the dissent's suggestion, acknowledging that the Confrontation Clause is implicated only by formalized statements that are characterized by solemnity will not result in a prosecutorial conspiracy to elude confrontation by using only informal extrajudicial statements against an accused. As I have previously noted, the Confrontation Clause reaches bad-faith attempts to evade the formalized process. Moreover, the prosecution's use of informal statements comes at a price. As the dissent recognizes, such statements are less reliable than formalized statements, and therefore less persuasive to the factfinder. * * *

B

* * * The shortcomings of the original primary purpose test pale in comparison * * * to those plaguing the reformulated version that the plural-

---

[5] In addition, I have stated that, because the Confrontation Clause sought to regulate prosecutorial abuse occurring through use of *ex parte* statements, it also reaches the use of technically informal statements when used to evade the formalized process. *Davis.* But, in this case, there is no indication that Cellmark's statements were offered in order to evade confrontation.

ity suggests today. The new primary purpose test asks whether an out-of-court statement has the primary purpose of accusing a targeted individual of engaging in criminal conduct. That test lacks any grounding in constitutional text, in history, or in logic.

The new test first requires that an out-of-court statement be made for the purpose of proving the guilt of a *particular* criminal defendant. (emphasis added). Under this formulation, statements made before any suspect was identified are beyond the scope of the Confrontation Clause. There is no textual justification, however, for limiting the confrontation right to statements made after the accused's identity became known. To be sure, the Sixth Amendment right to confrontation attaches [i]n . . . criminal prosecutions, at which time the accused has been identified and apprehended. But the text of the Confrontation Clause does not constrain the time at which one becomes a witnes[s]. Indeed, we have previously held that a declarant may become a witnes[s] before the accused's prosecution. See *Crawford,*(rejecting the view that the Confrontation Clause applies only to in-court testimony).

Historical practice confirms that a declarant could become a witnes[s] before the accused's identity was known. As previously noted, the confrontation right was a response to *ex parte* examinations of witnesses in 16th-century England. Such examinations often occurred after an accused was arrested or bound over for trial, but some examinations occurred while the accused remained unknown or fugitive. J. Langbein, Prosecuting Crime in the Renaissance 90 (1974) (describing examples, including the deposition of a victim who was swindled out of 20 shillings by a cunning man). * * *

There is also little logical justification for the plurality's rule. The plurality characterizes Cellmark's report as a statement elicited by police and made by Cellmark not to accuse petitioner or to create evidence for use at trial, but rather to resolve the ongoing emergency posed by a dangerous rapist who was still at large. But, as I have explained, that distinction is unworkable in light of the mixed purposes that often underlie statements to the police. The difficulty is only compounded by the plurality's attempt to merge the purposes of both the police and the declarant.

But if one purpose must prevail, here it should surely be the evidentiary one, whether viewed from the perspective of the police, Cellmark, or both. The police confirmed the presence of semen on L.J.'s vaginal swabs on February 15, 2000, placed the swabs in a freezer, and waited until November 28, 2000, to ship them to Cellmark. Cellmark, in turn, did not send its report to the police until April 3, 2001, over a year after L.J.'s rape. Given this timeline, it strains credulity to assert that the police and Cellmark were primarily concerned with the exigencies of an ongoing emergency, rather than with producing evidence in the ordinary course.

In addition to requiring that an out-of-court statement targe[t] a particular accused, the plurality's new primary purpose test also considers whether the statement is so inherently inculpatory, that the declarant should have known that his statement would incriminate the accused. In this case, the plurality asserts that [t]he technicians who prepare a DNA profile generally have no way of knowing whether it will turn out to be incriminating or exonerating or both, and thus no one at Cellmark could have possibly known that the profile that it produced would turn out to inculpate petitioner.

Again, there is no textual justification for this limitation on the scope of the Confrontation Clause. In *Melendez Diaz,* we held that [t]he text of the [Sixth] Amendment contemplates two classes of witnesses those against the defendant and those in his favor. We emphasized that there is not a third category of witnesses, helpful to the prosecution, but somehow immune from confrontation. Thus, the distinction between those who make inherently inculpatory statements and those who make other statements that are merely helpful to the prosecution has no foundation in the text of the Amendment.

It is also contrary to history. * * * [n]either law nor practice limited *ex parte* examinations to those witnesses who made inherently inculpatory statements.

This requirement also makes little sense. A statement that is not facially inculpatory may turn out to be highly probative of a defendant's guilt when considered with other evidence. Recognizing this point, we previously rejected the view that a witness is not subject to confrontation if his testimony is inculpatory only when taken together with other evidence. *Melendez Diaz.* I see no justification for reviving that discredited approach, and the plurality offers none.[6]

3

Respondent and its *amici* have emphasized the economic and logistical burdens that would be visited upon States should every analyst who reports DNA results be required to testify at trial. These burdens are largely the product of a primary purpose test that reaches out-of-court statements well beyond the historical scope of the Confrontation Clause and thus sweeps in a broad range of sources on which modern experts regularly rely. The proper solution to this problem is not to carve out a Confrontation Clause exception for expert testimony that is rooted only in legal fiction. Nor is it to create a new primary purpose test that ensures that DNA evidence is treated differently. Rather, the solution is to adopt a reading of the Confrontation Clause that respects its historically limited application to a narrow class of statements bearing indicia of solemnity. In forgoing that approach, today's decision diminishes the Confrontation Clause's protection in cases where experts convey the contents of solemn, formalized statements to explain the bases for their opinions. These are the very cases

---

[6] The plurality states that its test will not prejudice any defendant who really wishes to probe the reliability of out-of-court statements introduced in his case because the person or persons who made the statements may always be subpoenaed by the defense and questioned at trial. *Melendez Diaz* rejected this reasoning as well, holding that the defendant's subpoena power is no substitute for the right of confrontation.

in which the accused *should* enjoy the right . . . to be confronted with the witnesses against him.

Justice KAGAN, with whom Justice SCALIA, Justice GINSBURG, and Justice SOTOMAYOR join, dissenting.

* * * Our Constitution contains a mechanism for catching [lab technicians'] errors the Sixth Amendment's Confrontation Clause. * * * In two decisions issued in the last three years, this Court held that if a prosecutor wants to introduce the results of forensic testing into evidence, he must afford the defendant an opportunity to cross-examine an analyst responsible for the test. Forensic evidence is reliable only when properly produced, and the Confrontation Clause prescribes a particular method for determining whether that has happened. * * * Hence the genius of an 18th-century device as applied to 21st-century evidence: Cross-examination of the analyst is especially likely to reveal whether vials have been switched, samples contaminated, tests incompetently run, or results inaccurately recorded.

Under our Confrontation Clause precedents, this is an open-and-shut case. The State of Illinois prosecuted Sandy Williams for rape based in part on a DNA profile created in Cellmark's laboratory. Yet the State did not give Williams a chance to question the analyst who produced that evidence. Instead, the prosecution introduced the results of Cellmark's testing through an expert witness who had no idea how they were generated. That approach no less (perhaps more) than the confrontation-free methods of presenting forensic evidence we have formerly banned deprived Williams of his Sixth Amendment right to confron[t] . . . the witnesses against him.

The Court today disagrees, though it cannot settle on a reason why. * * * In the pages that follow, I call Justice ALITO's opinion the plurality, because that is the conventional term for it. But in all except its disposition, his opinion is a dissent: Five Justices specifically reject every aspect of its reasoning and every paragraph of its explication. Justice THOMAS, for his part, contends that the Cellmark report is nontestimonial on a different rationale. But no other Justice joins his opinion or subscribes to the test he offers.

* * * I would choose another path to adhere to the simple rule established in our decisions, for the good reasons we have previously given. Because defendants like Williams have a constitutional right to confront the witnesses against them, I respectfully dissent from the Court's fractured decision. * * *

This case is of a piece [with *Melendez-Diaz* and *Bullcoming*]. * * * So under this Court's prior analysis, the substance of the report could come into evidence only if Williams had a chance to cross-examine the responsible analyst.

But that is not what happened. Instead, the prosecutor used Sandra Lambatos a state-employed scientist who had not participated in the testing as the conduit for this piece of evidence. * * * [I]t was Lambatos, rather than any Cellmark employee, who informed the trier of fact that the testing of L.J.'s vaginal swabs had produced a male DNA profile implicating Williams.

Have we not already decided this case? Lambatos's testimony is functionally identical to the surrogate testimony that New Mexico proffered in *Bullcoming,* which did nothing to cure the problem identified in *Melendez Diaz* (which, for its part, straightforwardly applied our decision in *Crawford*). Like the surrogate witness in *Bullcoming,* Lambatos could not convey what [the actual analyst] knew or observed about the events . . ., *i.e.,* the particular test and testing process he employed. *Bullcoming* * * * Indeed, Williams's lawyer was even more hamstrung than Bullcoming's. At least the surrogate witness in *Bullcoming* worked at the relevant laboratory and was familiar with its procedures. That is not true of Lambatos: She had no knowledge at all of Cellmark's operations. Indeed, for all the record discloses, she may never have set foot in Cellmark's laboratory.

Under our case law, that is sufficient to resolve this case. [W]hen the State elected to introduce the substance of Cellmark's report into evidence, the analyst who generated that report became a witness whom Williams had the right to confront. *Bullcoming.* As we stated just last year, Our precedent[s] cannot sensibly be read any other way. *Ibid.*

II

The plurality's primary argument to the contrary tries to exploit a limit to the Confrontation Clause recognized in *Crawford.* The Clause, we cautioned there, does not bar the use of testimonial statements for purposes other than establishing the truth of the matter asserted. [The plurality asserts] that Lambatos's recitation of Cellmark's findings, when viewed through the prism of state evidence law, was not introduced to establish the truth of any . . . matter concerning [the] Cellmark report. But five Justices agree, in two opinions reciting the same reasons, that this argument has no merit: Lambatos's statements about Cellmark's report went to its truth, and the State could not rely on her status as an expert to circumvent the Confrontation Clause's requirements.

[Justice Kagan describes Tennessee v. Street, cited by *Crawford.* Recall that in *Street,* the Court held that the trial court had not violated the accused's confrontation rights by allowing introduction of an accomplice's confession to rebut the accused's contention that his own confession was a forced repetition of the accomplice's.]

The situation could not be more different when a witness, expert or otherwise, repeats an out-of-court statement as the basis for a conclusion, because the statement's utility is then dependent on its truth. If the statement is true, then the conclusion based on it is probably true; if not, not. So to determine the validity of the witness's conclusion, the factfinder must assess the truth of the out-of-court statement on which it relies. * * * Unlike in *Street,* admission of the out-of-court statement in this context has no purpose separate from its truth; the factfinder can do nothing with it *except* assess its truth and so the credibility of the conclusion it serves to buttress.[1] * * *

The Cellmark report identified the rapist as having a particular DNA profile (think of it as the quintessential birthmark). The Confrontation Clause prevented the State from introducing that report into evidence except by calling to the stand the person who prepared it. So the State tried another route introducing the substance of the report as part and parcel of an expert witness's conclusion. In effect, Lambatos testified * * * : I concluded that Williams was the rapist because Cellmark, an accredited and trustworthy laboratory, says that the rapist has a particular DNA profile and, look, Williams has an identical one. * * * So if the plurality were right, the State would have a ready method to bypass the Constitution * * * ; a wink and a nod, and the Confrontation Clause would not pose a bar to forensic evidence. * * *

At bottom, the plurality's not-for-the-truth rationale is a simple abdication to state-law labels. Although the utility of the Cellmark statement that Lambatos repeated logically depended on its truth, the plurality thinks this case decided by an Illinois rule holding that the facts underlying an expert's opinion are not admitted for that purpose. * * * [But] in *Street*, we independently reviewed whether an out-of-court statement was introduced for its truth the very question at issue in this case. And in *Crawford*, we still more firmly disconnected the Confrontation Clause inquiry from state evidence law, by overruling an approach that looked in part to whether an out-of-court statement fell within a "firmly rooted hearsay exception". That decision made clear that the Confrontation Clause's protections are not coterminous with rules of evidence. So the plurality's state-law-first approach would be an about-face.

Still worse, that approach would allow prosecutors to do through subterfuge and indirection what we previously have held the Confrontation Clause prohibits. Imagine for a moment a poorly trained, incompetent, or dishonest laboratory analyst. (The analyst in *Bullcoming*, placed on unpaid leave for unknown reasons, might qualify.) Under our precedents, the prosecutor cannot avoid exposing that analyst to cross-examination simply by introducing his report. See *Melendez Diaz*. Nor can the prosecutor escape that fate by offering the results through the testimony of another analyst from the laboratory. See *Bullcoming*. But under the plurality's approach, the prosecutor could choose the analyst-witness of his dreams * * *, offer her as an expert (she knows nothing about the test, but boasts impressive degrees), and have her provide testimony identical to the best the actual tester might have given ("the DNA extracted from the vaginal swabs matched Sandy Williams's") all so long as a state evidence rule says that the purpose of the testimony is to enable the factfinder to assess the expert

---

[1] In responding to this reasoning, the plurality confirms it. According to the plurality, basis evidence supports the credibility of the expert's opinion by showing that he has relied on, and drawn logical inferences from, sound factual premises. Quite right. And that process involves assessing such premises' truth: If they are, as the majority puts it, unsupported by other evidence in the record or otherwise baseless, they will not allay [a factfinder's] fears about an expert's reasoning. I could not have said it any better.

opinion's basis. (And this tactic would not be confined to cases involving scientific evidence. As Justice THOMAS points out, the prosecutor could similarly substitute experts for all kinds of people making out-of-court statements.) The plurality thus would countenance the Constitution's circumvention. If the Confrontation Clause prevents the State from getting its evidence in through the front door, then the State could sneak it in through the back. What a neat trick but really, what a way to run a criminal justice system. No wonder five Justices reject it.

III

The plurality also argues, as a second, independent basis for its decision, that the Cellmark report falls outside the Confrontation Clause's ambit because it is nontestimonial. The plurality tries out a number of supporting theories, but all in vain: Each one either conflicts with this Court's precedents or misconstrues this case's facts. Justice THOMAS rejects the plurality's views for similar reasons as I do, thus bringing to five the number of Justices who repudiate the plurality's understanding of what statements count as testimonial. Justice THOMAS, however, offers a rationale of his own for deciding that the Cellmark report is nontestimonial. I think his essay works no better. When all is said and done, the Cellmark report is a testimonial statement.

A

According to the plurality, we should declare the Cellmark report nontestimonial because the use at trial of a DNA report prepared by a modern, accredited laboratory bears little if any resemblance to the historical practices that the Confrontation Clause aimed to eliminate. But we just last year treated as testimonial a forensic report prepared by a modern, accredited laboratory ; indeed, we declared that the report at issue fell within the core class of testimonial statements implicating the Confrontation Clause. *Bullcoming.* So the plurality must explain: What could support a distinction between the laboratory analysis there and the DNA test in this case?[4]

As its first stab, the plurality states that the Cellmark report was not prepared for the primary purpose of accusing a targeted individual. Where that test comes from is anyone's guess. Justice THOMAS rightly shows that it derives neither from the text nor from the history of the Confrontation Clause. And it has no basis in our precedents. We have previously

---

[4] Justice BREYER does not attempt to distinguish our precedents, opting simply to adhere to the dissenting view set forth in *Melendez Diaz* and *Bullcoming.* He principally worries that under those cases, a State will have to call to the witness stand [s]ix to twelve or more technicians who have worked on a report. But none of our cases including this one has presented the question of *how many* analysts must testify about a given report. (That may suggest that in most cases a lead analyst is readily identifiable.) The problem in the cases again, including this one is that *no* analyst came forward to testify. In the event that some future case presents the multiple-technician issue, the Court can focus on the broader limits' question that troubles Justice BREYER. But the mere existence of that question is no reason to wrongly decide the case before us which, it bears repeating, involved the testimony of not twelve or six or three or one, but zero Cellmark analysts.

asked whether a statement was made for the primary purpose of establishing past events potentially relevant to later criminal prosecution in other words, for the purpose of providing evidence. None of our cases has ever suggested that, in addition, the statement must be meant to accuse a previously identified individual; indeed, in *Melendez Diaz,* we rejected a related argument that laboratory analysts are not subject to confrontation because they are not accusatory witnesses.

Nor does the plurality give any good reason for adopting an accusation test. The plurality apparently agrees with Justice BREYER that prior to a suspect's identification, it will be unlikely that a particular researcher has a defendant-related motive to behave dishonestly. But surely the typical problem with laboratory analyses and the typical focus of cross-examination has to do with careless or incompetent work, rather than with personal vendettas. And as to that predominant concern, it makes not a whit of difference whether, at the time of the laboratory test, the police already have a suspect.

The plurality next attempts to invoke our precedents holding statements nontestimonial when made to respond to an ongoing emergency, rather than to create evidence for trial, here, the plurality insists, the Cellmark report's purpose was to catch a dangerous rapist who was still at large. But that is to stretch both our ongoing emergency test and the facts of this case beyond all recognition. We have previously invoked that test to allow statements by a woman who was being assaulted and a man who had just been shot. In doing so, we stressed the informal [and] harried nature of the statements, *Bryant* that they were made as, or minutes after, *id.,* the events they described actually happen [ed], *Davis* (emphasis deleted), by frantic victims of criminal attacks, *ibid.,* to officers trying to figure out what had . . . occurred and what threats remained, *Bryant.* On their face, the decisions have nothing to say about laboratory analysts conducting routine tests far away from a crime scene. And this case presents a peculiarly inapt set of facts for extending those precedents. Lambatos testified at trial that all reports in this case were prepared for this criminal investigation . . . [a]nd for the purpose of the eventual litigation in other words, for the purpose of producing evidence, not enabling emergency responders. And that testimony fits the relevant timeline. The police did not send the swabs to Cellmark until November 2008 nine months after L.J.'s rape and did not receive the results for another four months. That is hardly the typical emergency response.

Finally, the plurality offers a host of reasons for why reports like this one are reliable . * * * But once again: Been there, done that. In *Melendez Diaz,* this Court rejected identical arguments, noting extensive documentation of [s]erious deficiencies . . . in the forensic evidence used in criminal trials. Scientific testing is technical, to be sure; but it is only as reliable as the people who perform it. That is why a defendant may wish to ask the analyst a variety of questions: How much experience do you have? Have you ever made mistakes in the past? Did you test the right sample? Use the right procedures? Contaminate the sample in any way? Indeed, as scientific

evidence plays a larger and larger role in criminal prosecutions, those inquiries will often be the most important in the case.[6]

And *Melendez Diaz* made yet a more fundamental point in response to
claims of the *ber alles* reliability of scientific evidence: It is not up to us to
decide, *ex ante,* what evidence is trustworthy and what is not. That is because the Confrontation Clause prescribes its own procedure for determining the reliability of testimony in criminal trials. *Crawford.* That procedure is cross-examination. And [d]ispensing with [it] because testimony is
obviously reliable is akin to dispensing with jury trial because a defendant
is obviously guilty. *Id.*

So the plurality's second basis for denying Williams's right of confrontation also fails. The plurality can find no reason consistent with our precedents for treating the Cellmark report as nontestimonial. That is because
the report is, in every conceivable respect, a statement meant to serve as
evidence in a potential criminal trial. And that simple fact should be sufficient to resolve the question.

B

Justice THOMAS's unique method of defining testimonial statements
fares no better. [That] approach grants constitutional significance to minutia, in a way that can only undermine the Confrontation Clause's protections.

To see the point, start with precedent, because the Court rejected this
same kind of argument, as applied to this same kind of document, at
around this same time just last year. [In *Bullcoming,* the forensic report at
issue was not sworn before a notary public but the Court held it sufficient
that the certificate was "formalized in a signed document . . . headed a report."]

Now compare that checklist of material features to the report in this
case. The only differences are that Cellmark is a private laboratory under
contract with the State (which no one thinks relevant), and that the report
is not labeled a certificate. That amounts to (maybe) a nickel's worth of
difference: The similarities in form, function, and purpose dwarf the distinctions.* * * The difference in labeling a certificate in one case, a report
of laboratory examination in the other is not of constitutional dimension.

Indeed, Justice THOMAS's approach, if accepted, would turn the Confrontation Clause into a constitutional geegaw nice for show, but of little
value. The prosecution could avoid its demands by using the right kind of

---

[6] Both the plurality and Justice BREYER warn that if we require analysts to testify, we
will encourage prosecutors to forgo DNA evidence in favor of less reliable eyewitness testimony and so increase the risk of convicting the innocent. Neither opinion provides any evidence, even by way of anecdote, for that view, and I doubt any exists. DNA evidence is usually
the prosecutor's most powerful weapon, and a prosecutor is unlikely to relinquish it just because he must bring the right analyst to the stand.

forms with the right kind of language. * * * It is not surprising that no other Member of the Court has adopted this position.

IV

Before today's decision, a prosecutor wishing to admit the results of forensic testing had to produce the technician responsible for the analysis. That was the result of not one, but two decisions this Court issued in the last three years. But that clear rule is clear no longer. The five Justices who control the outcome of today's case agree on very little. Among them, though, they can boast of two accomplishments. First, they have approved the introduction of testimony at Williams's trial that the Confrontation Clause, rightly understood, clearly prohibits. Second, they have left significant confusion in their wake. What comes out of four Justices' desire to limit *Melendez Diaz* and *Bullcoming* in whatever way possible, combined with one Justice's one-justice view of those holdings, is to be frank who knows what. Those decisions apparently no longer mean all that they say. Yet no one can tell in what way or to what extent they are altered because no proposed limitation commands the support of a majority.

The better course in this case would have been simply to follow *Melendez Diaz* and *Bullcoming*. Precedent-based decisionmaking provides guidance to lower court judges and predictability to litigating parties. Today's plurality and concurring opinions, and the uncertainty they sow, bring into relief that judicial method's virtues. I would decide this case consistently with, and for the reasons stated by, *Melendez Diaz* and *Bullcoming*. And until a majority of this Court reverses or confines those decisions, I would understand them as continuing to govern, in every particular, the admission of forensic evidence.

I respectfully dissent.

HYPOTHETICAL

Defendant is accused of committing murder in a dwelling on Green Street. He will present an alibi defense, claiming that he was 600 miles away at the time of the crime. The prosecution has in its files the record of a traffic citation issued on the night of the murder to the defendant's sports utility vehicle for parking on the Green Street sidewalk near the crime scene. The citation contains the license number of the defendant's vehicle and the time and location of the parking infraction. It was issued by a police officer with general law enforcement duties who has no present memory of the vehicle or its license number. The murder had not been discovered at the time the citation was issued. The prosecution wishes to use the record of the citation at trial. Is the record testimonial within the meaning of *Crawford*? Assuming not, what hearsay exceptions might be applicable?

United States v. Grady

United States Court of Appeals, Second Circuit, 1976.
544 F.2d 598.

■ OAKES, CIRCUIT JUDGE:

The waves of tragedy from the internecine conflict in Northern Ireland have their ripple effects in this country. Appellants here are Frank Grady, a sympathizer with the Catholic minority in Ulster, and John Jankowski, a licensed firearms dealer in Yonkers, New York. Each was convicted of conspiracy to violate the federal firearms law, particularly 18 U.S.C. §§ 922(m) and 923, which together require a licensed firearms dealer to make true entries in a federal firearms record, and of ten substantive counts of making or causing to be made false entries as to ten .30-caliber semiautomatic rifles in Jankowski's record or "logbook"; Grady was also convicted of one count of unlawful exportation without a permit of these same rifles. * * *

* * *

IV. Admission of Irish Police Records.

Much is made in the briefs of the admission into evidence of records of the formidable-sounding Department of Industrial and Forensic Science of the Ministry of Commerce and of the Royal Ulster Constabulary. These were entitled "Material Forwarded for Examination" and "Order for Disposal of Firearms/Ammunition." The ground of objection was that the documents constituted inadmissible hearsay. * * *

For the limited purpose of showing that the specified weapons were found in Northern Ireland on dates subsequent to the May, 1970, purchases, however, we think the records were admissible under the public records exception to the hearsay rule, codified in Fed.R.Evid. 803(8)(B). Rule 803(8)(B) allows admission of records and reports of public offices or agencies setting forth "matters observed pursuant to duty imposed by law as to which matters there was a duty to report," but is subject to an exception for "matters observed by police officers and other law enforcement personnel." In adopting this exception, Congress was concerned about prosecutors attempting to prove their cases in chief simply by putting into evidence police officers' reports of their contemporaneous observations of crime. The reports admitted here were not of this nature; they did not concern observations by the Ulster Constabulary of the appellants' commission of crimes. Rather, they simply related to the routine function of recording serial numbers and receipt of certain weapons found in Northern Ireland. They did not begin to prove the Government's entire case; they were strictly routine records.

* * *

Judgments affirmed.

QUESTION

Does the result in *Grady* survive *Melendez-Diaz*? Is there further information you might want to know to be able to answer this question?

HYPOTHETICALS

(1) Plaintiff sues X Department Store for damages for injuries received in slipping on X's floor. Plaintiff claims she slipped and fell because the floor was highly waxed and polished and unduly slippery as a result. X offers in evidence a report prepared for X by B, the store manager. B is no longer in X's employ and could not be found to testify. X's evidence establishes that B's report was prepared the day after the accident, and that X's store manager customarily makes a report after an accident. B's report states that B arrived at the scene a few minutes after Plaintiff fell and while Plaintiff was still on the floor, and that B examined the floor and it was not highly waxed or polished but had a dull finish and was not slippery. Plaintiff objects to the report as hearsay. Should the objection be sustained?

(2) X is prosecuted for robbery. X's defense is an alibi. X testifies that he was in a distant city, having just registered at the Deluxe Motel at the time of the robbery. X calls a clerk at the Deluxe Motel, who identifies a registration card prepared by another clerk that shows that one X, with defendant's address, registered at the motel at the time of the robbery. The registration card does not bear any signature of the guest X on it. The clerk further testifies that motel clerks frequently fill out the registration card from information supplied by the guest and do not require a guest's signature. X offers the registration card in evidence. The prosecution makes a hearsay objection. What result?

(3) A sues X for fire damage to A's house. A had employed X, a general contractor, to remodel A's kitchen. Just before the work was completed, a fire started in the kitchen and caused the damage. A claims the fire resulted from X's negligence in leaving an open can of highly <u>inflammable</u> cabinet stain too close to the pilot of the water heater. X's defense is that the fire was the result of arson. After laying a proper foundation, X offers in evidence a report by a captain in the city fire department. The captain's report stated that his investigation of the fire included an inspection of the premises and conversations with A's neighbors, and that based upon this investigation, his conclusion was that the fire was of <u>incendiary origin</u>. A objects to the report as hearsay. Is A's objection proper?

Synonyms.

(4) P sues D for damages for injuries suffered in an automobile accident. P does not call a doctor to testify but offers into evidence the doctor's report. Foundation is established that the doctor's report is the only record kept by him in the ordinary course of business. The report recites that the doctor examined P on a certain date, had X-rays taken, and diagnosed a fracture of the femur. In a separate paragraph of the doctor's report, a prognosis is stated that, in the doctor's opinion, P will suffer permanent residuals of a limitation of motion. D makes a hearsay objection. How should the court rule?

(5) A sues X to recover the contract price of goods sold. A and X entered into a written contract for A to sell X 1,000 metric tons of lead fume. The contract price depended on the exact weight and metallic content of the lead fume deli-

vered by A. To prove the weight and metallic content, A testifies that she employed B, a highly respected assayer, to assay a sample of the lead fume; that she later went by B's office and received from a secretary a report on the letterhead of B, purporting to bear B's signature; that she is not, however, familiar with B's signature. A offers in evidence this report, which sets forth the weight and metallic content of a sample of the lead fume allegedly assayed by B. X makes a hearsay objection. What result?

(6) A sues X for damages for personal injuries and car property damage arising out of an automobile accident. A testifies that he went to Dr. B and C Hospital for treatment, and had his car repaired at D Garage. A offers in evidence bills or invoices, which he testifies as having been received from Dr. B, C Hospital, and D Garage. Each bill is stamped with the words "Payment Received." X makes a hearsay objection to the admissibility of the bills. How should the court rule?

(7) D is charged with robbery of V, a liquor store owner, at his store. V testifies that after the robbery he ran out of the store and obtained D's license number as D drove off. V testifies that the license number of the car was 468 ABC. D's car bore this license number. D calls a police records custodian, who identifies a police report of the event and establishes the foundation that it was made in the usual course of business and at or near the time of the robbery. A sentence in the report states that 30 minutes after the robbery, the police received a telephone call from A, a neighbor of V, who reported the license number of the robber's car as 416 ABC. D offers the police report in evidence. In response to the prosecutor's hearsay objection, D states that the report is being offered as nonhearsay to establish that a different license number had been reported, but that, if hearsay, the report is admissible under the official-record hearsay exception. Should the prosecutor's objection be sustained?

(8) Sam D is charged with perjury because he allegedly gave false testimony in the trial of a civil action. The prosecution's contention of the false testimony is that, in the civil action, Sam D identified himself by the name of John D, while his real name was Sam D, and that in qualifying to testify as an expert he said he was a standing consultant in engineering at the U.S. Bureau of Mines. The prosecution offers in evidence a writing stating that C, the signer, was the official custodian of records for the U.S. Bureau of Mines and that C had made a diligent search of the records of the U.S. Bureau of Mines and failed to find any record that any person by the name of Sam D or John D had been an engineering consultant. The writing bears a signature, C, as custodian of records of the U.S. Bureau of Mines, and has stamped thereon a seal purporting to be the seal of the U.S. Bureau of Mines. D makes a hearsay objection to the writing. What result?

11. MISCELLANEOUS EXCEPTIONS

A. PRIOR JUDGMENTS

Stroud v. Cook

District of Nevada, 1996.
931 F.Supp. 733.

■ EDWARD C. REED, JR., DISTRICT JUDGE.

Presently before the court for decision is defendant James Cook's Motion in Limine. Cook seeks to exclude from evidence the judgment of conviction entered against him on June 30, 1993 in the Eureka, Nevada Justice Court for violation of Nev. Rev. Stat. § 484.363.

This action arises out of the collision between the motor vehicles driven by Plaintiff Stroud and Defendant Cook, and the subsequent, and allegedly resultant, secondary collision between the plaintiff's automobile and the automobile driven by Defendant and Cross–Defendant Tinsley. The accident occurred on June 30, 1993, at the intersection of U.S. Highway 50 and State Route 278, near Eureka, Nevada. Defendant James Guy Cook was cited by an officer of the Nevada Highway Patrol for failing to use due care in the operation of his motor vehicle immediately prior to the accident, in violation of Nev. Rev. Stat. § 484.363. Cook was adjudged guilty of the violation, and fined $35.

Section 484.363 is a criminal statute punishing the failure to use due care in the operation of a motor vehicle. Plaintiff Stroud seeks to introduce the judgment of conviction as evidence of defendant Cook's negligence on the occasion of the motor vehicle accident from which this action arises. The court previously had occasion to rule on the effect of that judgment on this civil action. Plaintiff Stroud moved for summary judgment on the issue of defendant Cook's liability for Stroud's injuries resulting from the June 30, 1993 motor vehicle accident. Stroud argued that under Nev. Rev. Stat. § 41.133, Cook's conviction for violating Section 484.363 should operate to establish Cook's civil liability as a matter of law.

Judge Hagen ruled otherwise. Although the judgment of conviction would be admitted in evidence, that judgment would constitute only *prima facie* evidence of the facts necessary to sustain that conviction, i.e. the former judgment of the Eureka Justice Court would serve as establishing the fact of Cook's negligence, subject to rebuttal evidence.[1]

---

[1] In her summary judgment motion Stroud cited *Desert Cab Co. v. Marino*, 108 Nev. 32, 823 P.2d 898 (Nev. 1992) as authority for the proposition that Cook's traffic conviction should constitute "conclusive evidence" of his liability to her for her injuries. But in *Desert Cab*, the conviction being offered as "conclusive evidence" under Section 41.133 was for assault and battery, an intentional, violent person crime. Moreover, the Nevada Supreme Court in *Desert Cab* ruled only that the prior misdemeanor conviction "established the wrongfulness of [the person's] conduct." 823 P.2d at 900–901. The court stopped short of finding liability to be established as a matter of law. In the present action, Cook was convicted of a traffic violation and fined $35. The distinction between an assault and battery conviction and a relatively mi-

* * *

Plaintiff Stroud proposes to introduce in evidence a certified copy of the judgment of conviction entered by the Eureka Justice Court against Defendant Cook for failure to use due care in the operation of a motor vehicle. Defendant seeks to exclude the judgment from evidence. The court must decide whether such evidence is admissible under the federal rules.

Without question a judicial document such as a judgment is hearsay within the meaning of the federal evidence rules: It is a statement, made outside the proceedings in which it is offered in evidence, offered to prove the truth of the matter asserted therein, namely, that Defendant Cook did in fact fail to use due care while operating his motor vehicle on the occasion in question. The federal evidence rules exempt from the operation of the hearsay rule a judgment of a felony conviction. Fed. R. Evid. 803(22). Here, however, Plaintiff's Cook's conviction under Nev. Rev. Stat. § 484.363 was for a misdemeanor, not a felony. As hearsay, then, the judgment is excluded from evidence under the hearsay rule. Fed. R. Evid. 802. Unless some other hearsay exception applies, the judgment is inadmissible under the Federal Rules of Evidence.

The only other hearsay exception even arguably applicable to the judgment of conviction is the exception for "public records" under Fed. R. Evid. 803(8). Under Rule 803(8), documentary evidence otherwise excludable as hearsay is admissible when it takes the form of a record, report or statement by a public office or agency setting forth the activities of that office or agency. Fed. R. Evid. 803(8)(A). A judgment of conviction does "set forth the activities" of the court issuing the judgment to the extent that it memorializes the conviction, in the issuing court, of the defendant for the crime indicated on the judgment.

The drafters of the federal evidence rules plainly considered a felony conviction reliable enough to be admitted in evidence, and to that end crafted a specific hearsay exception for records of felony convictions. Fed. R. Evid. 803(22). On the other hand, the drafters appear to have deemed misdemeanor convictions too insubstantial to justify their admission in evidence in subsequent litigation: "Practical considerations require exclusion of convictions of minor offenses, not because the administration of justice in its lower echelons must be inferior, but because motivation to defend at this level is often minimal or nonexistent. . . Hence the rule includes only convictions of felony grade, measured by federal standards." Fed. R. Evid. 803 advisory committee's note.

At common law a judgment in a prior case was generally inadmissible. The drafters of the federal evidence rules saw fit to create an exception to the hearsay rule for *felony* convictions, but created no such exception for

---

nor traffic violation militates against the treatment of the latter as "conclusive" proof in a subsequent civil action. *See, e.g., Calusinski v. Kruger* 24 F.3d 931, 934 (7th Cir. 1994) (ruling prior conviction for resisting arrest of "sufficiently serious import" to merit treatment as prima facie evidence of facts upon which conviction rests).

misdemeanor convictions. The advisory committee notes to the "public records" exception, Fed. R. Evid. 803(8), contain no reference whatever to judicial records, but refer exclusively to the activities of executive agencies and offices.

On the other hand, the United States Court of Appeals for the Ninth Circuit, whose decisions bind this court, has several times flatly stated that misdemeanor convictions are admissible in evidence under the "public records" exception to the hearsay rule. *United States v. Loera*, 923 F.2d 725, 730 (9th Cir.1991); *United States v. Wilson*, 690 F.2d 1267, 1275 n. 2 (9th Cir.1982) * * *.

[While Judge Reed acknowledged that these cases appeared "to foreclose debate on this matter," establishing within the Ninth Circuit that "judgments of misdemeanor convictions are admissible under the 'public records' exception to the hearsay rule, he expressed misgivings. He noted that *Wilson*'s discussion of the subject was pure dictum relegated to a footnote and that *Loera* merely followed *Wilson*. By contrast, the treatment in *Nipper v. Snipes*, 7 F.3d 415, 417 (4th Cir. 1993), was

> grounded in its careful reading of the advisory committee notes to and the legislative history of the federal evidence rules. The logic of the *Nipper* court's *expressio unius, exclusio alterius* argument with respect to the special hearsay exception for felony convictions, and the corresponding absence of any such exception for past misdemeanor convictions, appears to this court unassailable. The drafters of the federal evidence rules plainly were capable of carving out exceptions to the hearsay rule for judicial documents. They did so for felonies, and declined to do so for misdemeanors. The Fourth Circuit in *Nipper* thereby advanced a powerful argument for the exclusion of past misdemeanor convictions under the Federal Rules of Evidence.

Nevertheless, Judge Reed indicated that another ground supported admissibility of Stroud's misdemeanor conviction. Although the Federal Rules of Evidence are "presumptively applicable in all federal trials," this was a diversity case, and a Nevada statute, Nev. Rev. Stat. § 41.133, provided:

> If an offender has been convicted of the crime which resulted in the injury to the victim, the judgment of conviction is conclusive evidence of all facts necessary to impose civil liability for the injury.

Under *Erie R.R. v. Tompkins*, 304 U.S. 64 (1938), therefore, § 41.133 governed if it was deemed substantive. Judge Reed concluded that this provision, which was part not of the evidence code but rather of "a chapter limiting liability of certain persons and preserving causes of actions for other persons," was indeed "a substantive expression of state policy." While recognizing that Judge Hagen's prior order might constitute "the law of the case" and so limit the impact of the statute so that it would constitute only prima facie evidence of Cook's negligence, Judge Reed nevertheless declared that it "substantially alters the burden of proof": "The state statute involved here essentially creates a presumption that a person convicted of a crime which resulted in injury is civilly liable to the injured person."]

See Federal Rules of Evidence 803(22); California Evidence Code §§ 1300–1302.

Comment to Calif.Evid.Code § 1301

If a person entitled to indemnity, or if the obligee under a warranty contract, complies with certain conditions relating to notice and defense, the indemnitor or warrantor is conclusively bound by any judgment recovered.

Where a judgment against an indemnitee or person protected by a warranty is not made conclusive on the indemnitor or warrantor, Section 1301 permits the judgment to be used as hearsay evidence in an action to recover on the indemnity or warranty. Section 1301 reflects the existing law relating to indemnity agreements. Civil Code § 2778(6). Section 1301 probably restates the law relating to warranties, too, but the law in that regard is not altogether clear.

B. TREATISES AND OTHER PROFESSIONAL LITERATURE

Wellman, The Art of Cross–Examination
73–78 (1903).

During the lifetime of Dr. J.W. Ranney there were few physicians in this country who were so frequently seen on the witness stand, especially in damage suits. So expert a witness had he become that Chief Justice Van Brunt many years ago is said to have remarked, "Any lawyer who attempts to cross-examine Dr. Ranney is a fool." A case occurred a few years before Dr. Ranney died, however, where a failure to cross-examine would have been tantamount to a confession of judgment, and the trial lawyer having the case in charge, though fully aware of the dangers, was left no alternative, and as so often happens where "fools rush in," made one of those lucky "bull's-eyes" that is perhaps worth recording. [Note: In later editions, Wellman acknowledged that he was the lucky fool, as well as the recipient of Justice Van Brunt's comment.] * * *

The cross-examiner first directed his questions toward developing before the jury the fact that the witness had been the medical expert for the New York, New Haven, and Hartford R.R. thirty-five years, for the New York Central R.R. forty years, for the New York and Harlem River R.R. twenty years, for the Erie R.R. fifteen years and so on until the doctor was forced to admit that he was so much in court as a witness in defence of these various railroads, and was so occupied with their affairs that he had but comparatively little time to devote to his reading and private practice.

Counsel (perfectly quietly). "Are you able to give us, doctor, the name of any medical authority that agrees with you when you say that the particular group of symptoms existing in this case points to one disease and one only?"

Doctor. "Oh, yes, Dr. Erskine* agrees with me."

Counsel. "Who is Dr. Erskine, if you please?"

Doctor (with a patronizing smile). "Well, Erskine was probably one of the most famous surgeons that England has ever produced." (There was a titter in the audience at the expense of counsel.)

Counsel. "What book has he written?"

Doctor (still smiling). "He has written a book called 'Erskine on the Spine,' which is altogether the best known work on the subject." (The titter among the audience grew louder.)

Counsel. "When was this book published?"

Doctor. "About ten years ago."

Counsel. "Well, how is it that a man, whose time is so much occupied as you have told us yours is, has leisure enough to look up medical authorities to see if they agree with him?"

Doctor (fairly beaming on counsel). "Well, Mr. _____, to tell you the truth, I have often heard of you, and I half suspected you would ask me some such foolish question; so this morning after my breakfast, and before starting for court, I took down from my library my copy of Erskine's book, and found that he agreed entirely with my diagnosis in this case." (Loud laughter at expense of counsel, in which the jury joined.)

Counsel (reaching under the counsel table and taking up his own copy of "Erskine on the Spine," and walking deliberately up to the witness). "Won't you be good enough to point out to me where Erskine adopts your view of this case?"

Doctor (embarrassed). "Oh, I can't do it now; it is a very thick book."

Counsel (still holding out the book to the witness). "But you forget, doctor, that thinking I might ask you some such foolish question, you examined your volume of Erskine this very morning after breakfast and before coming to court."

Doctor (becoming more embarrassed and still refusing to take the book). "I have not time to do it now."

---

* [In later editions, the name is spelled as Ericson. Neither is right. The reference is to Sir John Erichsen's famous work, ON CONCUSSION OF THE SPINE, NERVOUS SHOCK AND OTHER OBSCURE INJURIES OF THE NERVOUS SYSTEM: IN THEIR CLINICAL AND MEDICO-LEGAL ASPECTS, first published under that title in 1875.]

Counsel. "*Time!* —why, there is all the time in the world."

Doctor. (no answer).

Counsel and witness eye each other closely.

Counsel (sitting down, still eyeing witness). "I am sure the court will allow me to suspend my examination until you shall have had time to turn to the place you read this morning in that book, and can reread it now aloud to the jury."

Doctor. (no answer).

The court room was in deathly silence for fully three minutes. The witness *wouldn't* say anything, counsel for plaintiff *didn't dare* to say anything, and counsel for the city *didn't want* to say anything; he saw that he had caught the witness in a manifest falsehood, and that the doctor's whole testimony was discredited with the jury unless he could open to the paragraph referred to which counsel well knew did not exist in the whole work of Erskine.

At the expiration of a few minutes, Mr. Justice Barrett, who was presiding at the trial, turned quietly to the witness and asked him if he desired to answer the question, and upon his replying that he did not intend to answer it any further than he had already done, he was excused from the witness stand amid almost breathless silence in the court room.

———————

See Federal Rules of Evidence 803(18);   California Evidence Code §§ 721, 1341.

C. STATEMENTS DESCRIBING CHILD ABUSE OR SPOUSAL ABUSE

A number of states have adopted statutory exceptions to the hearsay rule for statements of children describing child abuse. The statutes commonly apply only if the child is either testifying or unavailable to testify, but unavailability is sometimes defined broadly to include situations in which the child is incompetent or would be traumatized by testimony. See Calif. Evid. Code § 1360 (child abuse hearsay exception) and § 240(c) (crime victim is "unavailable" as witness where testimony would cause trauma); Lucy S. McGough, Child Witnesses 144–48 (1994); Jean Montoya, *Child Hearsay Statutes*, 5 Psych. Pub. Pol. and L. 304 (1999). Most of these statutes were passed before the decision in *Crawford*. Whether, or when, they are constitutional as applied to statements that would be deemed testimonial if made by a competent adult remains a matter of doubt. Constitutional objections may also be raised to a California hearsay exception that is applicable to statements by adults subjected to physical abuse, for example to victims of spousal battery. See Calif. Evid. Code § 1370; *Note: the Problem of Using Hearsay in Domestic Violence Cases: Is a New Exception the Answer?* 49 Duke L.J. 1041 (2000).

12. THE RESIDUAL EXCEPTION AND POSSIBILITIES FOR FUTURE REFORM

McCormick, Law and the Future: Evidence
51 Nw.U.L.Rev. 218 (1956).**

* * * The group of rules about hearsay evidence may be liberalized and simplified. A distinctive and cherished ideal of our trial tradition is that evidence in the main should be limited to the statements in court of witnesses who have observed the facts and are produced for cross-examination. But the rational investigation of facts cannot always be so limited. In ordinary life we must base many of our important decisions upon letters, technical books and articles, word of mouth, account books—in short, upon hearsay. So ten to twenty (depending upon minuteness of classification) sharply defined exceptions have been hammered out. But a half-century ago the exceptions had become more or less crystallized and had ceased to grow. Already they were too numerous and too complex to be remembered reliably at the counsel table. They badly need to be consolidated and enlarged. One move in that direction is the Massachusetts hearsay statute which admits the declaration of a deceased person if the judge finds it was made in good faith upon personal knowledge. The English Evidence Act of 1938 admits a written hearsay statement, on personal knowledge, if the writer is unavailable for any reason. The Model Code would admit any hearsay statement, written or oral, based on personal knowledge, if the declarant is unavailable for any cause. Even bolder in conception are those decisions which seem to sanction the practice that when a statement does not fall within an existing exception it still may be admitted if the judge finds that there is a necessity for its use and that it was made under circumstances showing exceptional trustworthiness. These courageous judges have marked the way, and we may eventually see our hearsay canon restated in this fashion: a hearsay statement will be received if the judge finds that the need for and the probative value of the statement render it a fair means of proof under the circumstances. * * *

QUESTIONS

Does McCormick adequately provide for prosecution evidence? Assuming that there is no separate protection of the confrontation rights of an accused, does his approach make sense? What if there is a separate protection, such as the *Crawford* doctrine, of such rights? Putting aside confrontation concerns, and assuming that live testimony of the declarant would be admissible, should hearsay be presumptively inadmissible or presumptively admissible? That is, should it be excluded unless there is good reason to admit it, or admitted unless there is good reason to exclude it?

** Copyright, 1957 by Northwestern University of Law.

The British Solution for Civil Cases

Civil Evidence Act 1995 (c. 38)

Admissibility of hearsay evidence.

1.—(1) In civil proceedings evidence shall not be excluded on the ground that it is hearsay.

[Subsequent sections require that notice be given of intent to introduce previously inadmissible hearsay. They also state that provision may be made by rules of court for application of the hearsay ban to specified classes of proceedings or evidence, and that the parties may provide by agreement that the hearsay ban applies to a case in which they are involved.—Eds.]

Turbyfill v. International Harvester Co.

United States District Court, Eastern District of Michigan, 1980.
486 F.Supp. 232.

MEMORANDUM OPINION AND ORDER

■ JOINER, DISTRICT JUDGE.

The facts underlying plaintiff's claim for damages are as follows. Plaintiff visited defendant's used car lot with the purpose of purchasing a truck. [He] became interested in one particular truck, but because the truck wouldn't start, defendant's mechanic Oakley Anderson attempted, with the help of plaintiff, to get the truck started. Plaintiff was pouring gasoline from a small can into the carburetor when [a] companion attempted to start the engine. The engine backfired and ignited the can held by plaintiff, and plaintiff suffered severe burns on the upper part of his body.

* * * [P]laintiff * * * asserts that it was error for the court to admit into evidence the handwritten, unsworn account of the accident made by defendant's mechanic, Oakley Anderson. As noted above, Anderson was asked to get the truck started for plaintiff and was present when plaintiff was injured. Prior to trial, but after this suit was instituted, Anderson died. Defendant sought to have admitted Anderson's handwritten account of the accident. During the trial, Gordon Brown, Anderson's supervisor, testified that, upon learning of the accident on the afternoon that it happened, he instructed Anderson to "go into a room, fill out a statement and not talk to anyone else; write down anything that he knew about it, and everything." Anderson made a handwritten report of the incident as he was instructed to do. Brown testified that the document proffered by defendant was the account written by Anderson, stating that he was familiar with Anderson's handwriting and identifying the document as written by Anderson. Brown further stated that Anderson signed the account in his presence, although Anderson wrote it while he was alone in a room. The written statement was read to the jury, but the court did not allow the jury to see copies of the statement, declining to give Anderson's account of the accident any more weight than it would have had if Anderson had been alive to testify.

Anderson's written account of the accident was admitted into evidence to prove the truth of the matter asserted therein. It thus constituted hearsay evidence under Rule 801(c) of the Federal Rules of Evidence. Plaintiff objects to the admission of the Anderson statement on the ground that it does not fall within any of the hearsay exceptions embodied in F.R.E. 803 or 804, and is thus barred by F.R.E. 802, the general evidentiary rule barring the admission of hearsay.

The circumstances under which Anderson wrote his account of the accident were such as to persuade the court that the statement should be admitted under Rule 804(b)(5):*

A statement not specifically covered by any of the foregoing exceptions but having equivalent circumstantial guarantees of trustworthiness [is not excluded by the hearsay rule] if the court determines that (A) the statement is offered as evidence of a material fact; (B) the statement is more probative on the point for which it is offered than any other evidence which the proponent can procure through reasonable efforts; and (C) the general purposes of these rules and the interests of justice will best be served by admission of the statement into evidence.

Anderson's statement was written on the afternoon of the accident while the events were still fresh in his mind. Moreover, he wrote the account while he was alone in a room, without prompting or pressure by his superiors. These factors amply demonstrate that Anderson's statement had circumstantial guarantees of trustworthiness equivalent to those underlying the hearsay exceptions of both Rule 804 and Rule 803. Moreover, the statement was offered as proof of a material fact, and was more probative on the points for which it was offered than any other evidence which defendant could reasonably have obtained. Under these circumstances, it clearly served the interests of justice to admit the statement into evidence.

Moreover, it is worthy of note that admission of the Anderson statement was consistent with the policy underlying Rule 803(5) which provides:

A memorandum or record concerning a matter about which a witness once had knowledge but now has insufficient recollection to enable him to testify fully and accurately, shown to have been made or adopted by the witness when the matter was fresh in his memory and to reflect that knowledge correctly [is not excluded by the hearsay rule].

If Anderson had been alive and present to testify at the trial, and if he had suffered a loss of memory concerning the circumstances of the accident, his written account would have been admissible and could have been read to the jury. He wrote the statement on the afternoon of the accident, while the circumstances were still fresh in his mind. Moreover, the fact that he

---

* [As originally enacted, the Federal Rules of Evidence contained two identical residual exceptions, Rules 803(24) and 804(b)(5). Theoretically they could be different in effect because their substance was supposed to be determined by reference to different sets of exceptions. Ultimately, the two were combined into one separate residual exception, Rule 807. Eds.]

made his written account while alone in a room indicates that the account accurately reflects his knowledge of the events transcribed.

The above discussion demonstrates that Anderson's statement was properly admitted into evidence. Accordingly, plaintiff's motion for a new trial is denied.

Zenith Radio Corp. v. Matsushita Electrical Industrial Co., Ltd.

United States District Court, Eastern District of Pennsylvania, 1980.
505 F.Supp. 1190.

■ Edward R. Becker, Judge.

[Zenith contended that it had been victimized by a massive conspiracy of Japanese entities to destroy the American consumer electronics market by predatory pricing, financed by maintaining high, cartel-determined prices in Japan. This opinion was a monstrously long one, part of a series dealing with "myriad issues" raised during a pretrial evidentiary hearing, centering around the admissibility of diaries and other writings of officers of some of the Japanese companies and also of testimony given before the Japanese Federal Trade Commission ("JFTC") by employees of some of the companies. Zenith contended that these statements were admissible under various hearsay exceptions or exemptions—it invoked, with respect to one set or another of the statements, the exemptions for adoptive admissions, agency admissions, business records, former testimony, and statements against interest, as well as the residual exceptions. The judge wrote an encyclopedic analysis of these exemptions before deciding whether they were applicable to the case at hand. Among many topics, he offered an extensive discussion of the "near-miss" problem with respect to the residual exceptions.]

2. The "Near–Miss" Problem

The defendants contend that the residual hearsay exceptions cannot be invoked as the basis for the admissibility of evidence which is generically of a type covered by another specific hearsay exception, but which fails to meet the precise requirements of that specific exception.[90] For instance,

---

[90] In a related contention, the defendants have urged that if an item fails to meet the terms of one of the specific hearsay exceptions, it may not be offered under another of the specific exceptions. On this view, for instance, if a document is generically a business record, but fails to qualify for admission as such under Rule 803(6), it may not be offered under any other hearsay exception. We reject that view. There is nothing in the language or the structure of the hearsay rules to suggest that the specific exceptions are exclusive in their application, and the Judiciary Committees of both Houses of Congress expressly rejected the position advanced by the defendants in their comments on Rule 803(5). The House Committee stated:

> [I]t is the Committee's understanding that a memorandum or report, although barred under this Rule, would nonetheless be admissible if it came within another hearsay exception. This last stated principle is deemed applicable to all the hearsay rules.

House Report, U.S.Code Cong. & Admin.News 1974, p. 7087. The Senate Committee expressed its agreement with this principle, using virtually the same language as the House Committee. This clear statement of legislative intent precludes any assertion that the specific hearsay exceptions are exclusive of one another. In our view it does not, however, defeat de-

they contend that if a document is a "business record" it must qualify for admission under Rule 803(6), and not under the residual exceptions. The plaintiffs counter that there is no such rule of law, and cite a number of cases in which courts have considered the admissibility of evidence under the residual exceptions after finding that the evidence failed to meet the terms of one or more of the specific exceptions.

We agree in principle with the defendants. The Advisory Committee explained its proposed residual exception, which was broader than the one enacted by Congress, as designated for "new and presently unanticipated situations." The Senate Judiciary Committee, which drafted the present rule, commented that "an overly broad residual hearsay exception could emasculate the hearsay rule and the recognized exceptions or vitiate the rationale behind codification of the rules." The Senate Committee also stated its intent "that the residual hearsay exceptions will be used very rarely, and only in exceptional circumstances." U.S.Code Cong. & Admin.News 1974, p. 7066. We find it clear from the history of the rules that neither the Advisory Committee nor the Senate Judiciary Committee intended that the residual exceptions be used to qualify for admission evidence which is of a type covered by a specific exception, but which narrowly fails to meet the standards of the specific rule. Instead, they intended that the residual exceptions be used in exceptional and unanticipated situations which are not specifically covered by the specific exceptions.[91]

The defendants' position is also supported by a basic principle of statutory construction, which we find equally applicable to the Federal Rules of Evidence: that the specific controls the general. As the Supreme Court stated in Radzanower v. Touche Ross & Co., 426 U.S. 148, 153 (1976):

It is a basic principle of statutory construction that a statute dealing with a narrow, precise, and specific subject is not submerged by a later enacted statute covering a more generalized spectrum. "Where there is no clear intention otherwise, a specific statute will not be controlled or nullified by a general one, regardless of the priority of enactment." Morton v. Mancari, 417 U.S. 535, 550–551 (1974).

In conformity with this rule we conclude that the residual exceptions cannot be invoked when there is a specific exception which sets forth condi-

---

fendants' "near miss" contentions with respect to the residual exceptions. The quoted statement of the House Judiciary Committee cannot be applied to the residual exceptions, since the House Committee would have eliminated the residual exceptions entirely. The statement of the Senate Committee must be interpreted in light of that Committee's more specific comments on the residual exceptions, which we consider in the text.

[91] Mr. Justice Stewart, joined by Mr. Justice Marshall, has commented:

It seems to me open to serious doubt whether Rule 804(b)(5) was intended to provide case-by-case hearsay exceptions, or rather only to permit expansion of the hearsay exceptions by categories.

McKethan v. United States, 439 U.S. 936, 939 n. 3, denying cert. to United States v. Garner, 574 F.2d 1141 (4th Cir. 1978) (dissenting opinion). Although this statement is somewhat cryptic, we view it as a reference to the point at issue before us. * * *

tions governing the admissibility of a clearly defined category of hearsay evidence.

For example, the exception for former testimony, Rule 804(b)(1), applies to a clearly defined category of evidence and specifies conditions which must be met in order for evidence in that category to be admissible. We will thus not consider a proffer of former testimony under the residual exceptions if the testimony fails to meet the specific requirements of Rule 804(b)(1), such as unavailability of the declarant, and similarity of motive to develop the testimony at the former hearing. Some of the other specific hearsay exceptions similarly apply to a clearly defined category of evidence, and we would follow the "near miss" doctrine with respect to them as well, if the evidence before us were within those categories. E. g., Rule 803(18) (learned treatises); Rule 803(22) (judgment of previous conviction.)

However, most of the hearsay exceptions which plaintiffs invoke are not of this type. They do not apply to a clearly defined category of evidence, as the former testimony exception does. Instead, they apply to a relatively amorphous category of evidence which is delimited solely by the requirements set forth in the rule itself. For instance, the business records exception applies to any "memorandum, report, record, or data compilation, in any form" which satisfies certain additional requirements. Rule 804(b)(3) applies to any "statement" which is against the declarant's interest, as specified in that rule. We view rules 803(1) (present sense impression) and 803(5) (recorded recollection), under which the plaintiffs also offer the diaries and memoranda, as of the same character. We do not see how the "near miss" doctrine which defendants urge could practically be applied to those rules, without negating the residual exceptions altogether, a result which is plainly contrary to the intent of Congress.

Accordingly, although as we have stated we agree with the defendants' position in principle, we will not apply it to the evidence before us, except for former testimony, and we will consider plaintiffs' proffer under the residual exceptions. We note, however, that the considerations which we have reviewed in this section of our discussion are additional reasons to apply the express requirements of the residual exceptions most rigorously, so as not to vitiate the hearsay rule and the specific exceptions. * * *

[The court ruled that the testimony given before the JFTC was not admissible as former testimony against parties who were not parties to that proceeding, and that because of the "nearmiss" problem the residual exceptions could not apply. The court analyzed numerous other documents under the residual exceptions, but—without relying on the "near-miss" doctrine—held the exceptions inapplicable to all of them.]

Emerging Problems Under the Federal Rules of Evidence*

Rule 803(24): Other Exceptions

In 1983, the Litigation Section's first edition of this study pointed out that the residual exceptions "have been the focal point of considerable judicial activism * * *." This trend has continued unabated, with the exceptions generating some 50 reported decisions each year. For the most part, courts refer to 803(24) and 804(b)(5) interchangeably, without analyzing whether there are differences in application. [Rules 803(24) and 804(b)(5) are now Rule 807.—Eds.]

A few circuits claim to invoke the residual clause sparingly or only in exceptional circumstances. The Third Circuit has given the exceptions a "narrow focus." However, such language is often saved for the cases in which the court refuses to admit the hearsay pursuant to the residual clauses, and is conveniently absent from the numerous cases applying the exceptions. A court may even preface its remarks by indicating that 803(24) should be used "stintingly," and then hold that its requirements were met on this occasion. The current judicial view of the residual clause is reflected by *United States v. Cowley,*[155] which aptly referred to 803(24) as the "expanding exception."

Courts have encouraged the use of the residual clause by gratuitous comments about its applicability in situations where it is unclear whether the parties raised the issue. For example, the appeal in *U.S. v. Furst,*[157] focused on the residual clause although it had only been mentioned in passing below. In *United States v. Nivica,*[158] the appellate court even upheld the introduction of hearsay under the residual clause which the trial court had incorrectly admitted under 803(6). However, due to the residual clause notice requirements, *Nivica* should be limited to those cases in which the exception was properly raised in the trial court. The popularity of the residual clause is so great that it is not surprising to find it invoked in complex or controversial cases. For example, Oliver North's attorneys argued, *albeit* unsuccessfully, that excerpts of videotaped testimony should be admitted under 803(24).[159]

Near Misses

The expansive treatment of the residual clauses has been accelerated by the rejection of the "near miss" theory proposed by Judge Becker in *Zenith Radio Corp. v. Matsushita Elec. Indus. Co.*[160] Judge Becker had separated the specific hearsay exceptions into well defined categories and amorphous categories for purposes of determining whether a near miss

---

* Section of Litigation: American Bar Association © 1983 (notice), 1991 (near misses).

[155] 720 F.2d 1037, 1045 (9th Cir.1983), cert. denied, 465 U.S. 1029 (1984).

[157] 886 F.2d 558, 573–74 (3d Cir.1989), cert. denied, 110 S.Ct. 878 (1990).

[158] 887 F.2d 1110, 1127 (1st Cir.1989), cert. denied, 110 S.Ct. 1300 (1990).

[159] United States v. North, 713 F.Supp. 1450, 1451 (D.D.C.1989).

[160] 505 F.Supp. 1190, 1262–63 (E.D.Pa.1980).

could be admitted under the residual clause. He rejected the admission of near misses of specific categories such as former testimony, but permitted near misses of amorphous exceptions such as business records and present sense impressions. However, the Third Circuit in later reversing Judge Becker on evidentiary points, noted that this "theory puts the federal evidence rules back into the straightjacket from which the residual exceptions were intended to free them."[162] Recently, in *U.S. v. Furst*,[163] the Third Circuit explicitly held that 803(24) is available when the proponent fails to meet the standards set forth in the other exceptions.

Most cases which discuss the near miss exception reach the same result.[164] Most courts simply ignore the near miss issue when they admit hearsay ranging from grand jury testimony to not quite business or public records. On occasion, even the rare case which appears to approve the near miss theory can be otherwise explained. For example, in *United States v. York*,[165] the court stated that it would not admit a statement under 804(b)(5) if it did not meet 804(b)(3). Rather than approving a near miss theory, the court simply recognized that a statement which was not trustworthy enough be a declaration against penal interest, would also not meet the trustworthiness requirement of the residual clause.

Regardless of whether one believes that Judge Becker's theory of near misses fits more closely with the Rule's intention than present practice, it is clear that courts are almost uniformly applying the residual clause to near misses. Thus, it presently does not matter if a category of hearsay was specifically rejected as an exception when considering its admissibility under the catch-all provision. Indeed, it has been suggested that being a near miss may be a positive factor in evaluating trustworthiness. It is unlikely that this approach will change unless the Rule is modified or its use is limited by the Supreme Court.

* * *

[Notice]

The residual exceptions contain a notice requirement which was added by Congress to ensure fairness by allowing parties sufficient time before trial to prepare objections to the use of such hearsay statements.[226] A num-

---

[162] In re Japanese Elec. Products Antitrust Litig., 723 F.2d 238, 302 (3d Cir.1983), rev'd on other grounds, 475 U.S. 574 (1986).

[163] 886 F.2d 558, 573 (3d Cir.1989), cert. denied, 110 S.Ct. 878 (1990).

[164] For example, in United States v. Gotti, 641 F.Supp. 283, 289 (E.D.N.Y.1986), the judge found no reason in principle why a misdemeanor conviction not admissible under 803(22) should not be admitted under the residual clause. Similarly, United States v. Popenas, 780 F.2d 545, 547 (6th Cir.1985), specifically rejected the near miss reasoning concerning introduction of a prior inconsistent statement under the residual clause, because "we feel the district court's approach would render it (the exception) a nullity." United States v. Frazier, 678 F.Supp. 499, 503 (E.D.Pa.), aff'd, 806 F.2d 255 (3d Cir.1986), rejected the near miss approach in assessing the admissibility of a statement of a child who was the alleged victim of sexual abuse.

[165] 1989 WL 65167 n. 8 (N.D.Ill.1989).

[226] House Rep. No. 1597, 93rd Cong., 2d Sess. 11–12, 13 (1974). A proposal that notice *during* trial should suffice with respect to material submitted under the residual exceptions

ber of courts have read the notice requirement strictly, requiring formal pre-trial notice. In United States v. Oates, 560 F.2d 45 (2d Cir.1977), and United States v. Ruffin, 575 F.2d 346 (2d Cir.1978), detailed examinations of the legislative history led the Second Circuit to conclude that there was "absolutely no doubt that the requirement of advance notice [should] be rigidly enforced." However, both that court and others have read the notice requirement less strictly. In United States v. Muscato, 534 F.Supp. 969 (E.D.N.Y.1982), supra, Chief Judge Weinstein ruled that, where the objecting party had himself called the witness from whom the hearsay was adduced, had not taken the stand himself, and had not objected to the admission of the hearsay at trial on notice grounds, the objector had effectively waived any right to claim lack of notice. In United States v. Iaconetti, supra, the Second Circuit, while noting the legislative history and the general need to comply with the notice requirement, upheld Judge Weinstein's trial court ruling that hearsay material be admitted under the residual exception, despite the lack of notice, where the need for offering the material had not arisen until trial had commenced, the adverse party had received five days notice and the adverse party had not requested a continuance or otherwise indicated an inability to prepare for the testimony.

Similarly, in United States v. Leslie, 542 F.2d 285 (5th Cir.1976), supra, the Fifth Circuit deemed failure to comply with the notice requirements of Rule 803(24) harmless error, finding that the defendant had had "ample opportunity" to attack the trustworthiness of the material since he could not have failed to anticipate that the witnesses in question (his alleged accomplices) would be called. Although such anticipation may not necessarily include anticipation that specific hearsay may be offered under the residual exception, nevertheless several courts have interpreted the notice requirement flexibly where they found that the adverse party had not, or should not have been, surprised by the offer.[227]

It may be that all of the decisions rendered no injustice. Yet, there is a danger that these decisions will effectively write the notice requirement out of the rule. In future cases, it may be wise for trial judges to ascertain first why the rule-required notice was not given. If the party who failed to give notice sought the advantage of surprise, any claim of unfairness ought not be rejected out of hand. If, however, notice was not given because a party reasonably was unaware of the need to rely on a hearsay statement, the most timely notice under the circumstances is all that reasonably should be demanded. In close cases, however, the extent to which notice could not realistically have been given in advance may weigh heavily with a judge trying to decide whether tardy notice is sufficient to satisfy the rule and, in some criminal cases, the Confrontation Clause.

---

was rejected by the Joint Conference as inadequate to protect the rights of adverse parties. 120 Cong.Rec.H. 12256 (Dec. 18, 1974).

[227] See, e.g., Furtado v. Bishop, 604 F.2d 80 (1st Cir.1979), cert. denied 444 U.S. 1035, 100 S.Ct. 710, 62 L.Ed.2d 672 (1980); Piva v. Xerox Corp., 654 F.2d 591 (9th Cir.1981).

HYPOTHETICALS

1. Plaintiff offers in evidence a 19–year-old written inventory of personal effects. The judge concludes that the inventory was not prepared for the present litigation and that it is better evidence of the facts stated in it than the memory of witnesses with knowledge of matters so long past. May the judge admit the inventory in evidence under the residual exception to the hearsay rule? (In preparing an answer to this question, examine Fed.R.Evid. 803(16) and its Advisory Committee Note.)

2. Buzzy is accused of robbing a bank. The prosecution produces evidence that marked money from the bank was found in Buzzy's locker. Buzzy testifies that he won the money in a poker game. In rebuttal, the prosecution calls a witness who played in the poker game. The witness contradicts Buzzy, testifying that Buzzy *lost* money at the game.

Buzzy then calls another witness in an attempt to prove that he won money at the game. The witness was not present at the game, but after the game the witness heard Declarant tell Declarant's father, "Buzzy won everybody's money, including mine." The father responded angrily that he had warned Declarant not to gamble with Buzzy.

Is the testimony about what Declarant said admissible under a traditional exception? Under the residual exception?

3. A tractor-trailer driver hit a bridge abutment, sustaining injuries that a few days later caused his death. His family sued the manufacturer of the truck, claiming that defects in the truck caused the accident. The truck manufacturer claims that driver accidentally set his trousers on fire with a cigarette, then crashed while trying to put out the fire. It offers evidence that, while hospitalized after the accident, the driver told a family member that his trousers caught on fire and he was trying to put out the fire when he lost control and hit the bridge abutment. Is the statement admissible under a conventional exception? Under the residual exception?

C. A RECAP

McNaughton, Evidence Exam, Harvard Law School, First Semester, 1960–1961

B. 50 HEARSAY QUESTIONS

Each of the following questions has two parts. (a) Is the item hearsay? Answer "Yes" or "No." And (b), if hearsay, under what exception or exceptions might the item reasonably fall? In the blank following the question, write one of the following three things: (i) "Not applicable" (or "N/A") if the item is not hearsay; (ii) "None" if the hearsay link falls under no exception; (iii) the appropriate hearsay exception(s) under which the hearsay link might reasonably fall.

SPECIAL INFORMATION: (1) Even if the facts given are insufficient to supply all of the prerequisites of an exception, you should mention the exception if the facts given reasonably suggest and are not inconsistent with it. (2) Treat past recollection recorded, the business entry statute and present sense impression as separate exceptions to the hearsay rule.

If the item is multiple, or "totem pole," hearsay, indicate in some appropriate way which exceptions (if any) apply to which hearsay link.

Hearsay?

(Yes or No) ___

___ 76. Prosecution of D for killing V. On the issue of D's fear of V, W1 testifies that he heard W2 say to D, "V has knifed three people in the last year." (Exception(s) _____)

___ 77. Same as 76 except the issue is whether V or D was the aggressor. (Exception(s) _____ _____)

___ 78. On the issue whether P and D are bound by a contract, W testifies to D's statement to P, "I accept your offer." (Exception(s)_____ _____)

___ 79. Action P v. D for injuries sustained when P fell through termite-eaten boards on D's porch. (a) to prove that P was involved in such an accident, P offers the testimony of W: "D said that when he got home from work he heard that P had gone through the porch and that he thought it was too bad." (Exception(s) _____)

___ 80. — (b) to prove that P was involved in such an accident, P offers the testimony of W that N, a neighbor who had been on the porch with P, came rushing across the lawn shouting to D, "P has fallen through your porch." (Exception(s) _____ _____)

___ 81. — (c) to rebut evidence by D that he had no knowledge of P's alleged accident until 18 months after it was supposed to have occurred, P offers the testimony in 80. (Exception(s) _____ _____)

___ 82. — (d) to prove that P was involved in such an accident, P offers the transcript of D's testimony in prior litigation between him and his insurance company: "The boards on the porch were so weak that P went right through them." (Exception(s) _____ _____)

___ 83. Same as 79 except that W is dead and P is offering a transcript of W's testimony, to the indicated effect, given in a prior trial of the same cause. (Exception(s) _____ _____)

___ 84. As tending to show that D had a revolver in his possession, the state offers the testimony of W that, as D passed W's house, W called her husband's attention to a revolver sticking out of D's pocket. (Exception(s) _____ _____)

___   85. On the issue whether plaintiff's decedent (V) was still alive after his car was struck by the first of two cars, W (who was in V's car with V) testifies that, before the second car struck, V said, "My head hurts." (Exception(s) _____ _____)

___   86. On the issue of the existence of injuries to V's head caused by the first car, the testimony in 85. (Exception(s) _____ _____)

___   87. On the issue of the sanity of D, a woman, W testifies that D on numerous occasions said publicly, "I am the Pope." (Exception(s) _____ _____)

___   88. On the issue of D's guilt of the crime of killing V, W testifies that D told him that he (D) fled the scene immediately after V's murder. (Exception(s) _____ _____)

___   89. On the issue of X's sanity, W testifies that X was confined to an insane asylum. (Exception(s) _____ _____)

___   90. On the issue whether a transfer of a fountain pen from defendant (D) to plaintiff (P) was a sale or gift, P testifies that D made a statement accompanying the transfer, "I am giving you this pen as a birthday present." (Exception(s) _____ _____)

___   91. In 90, P testifies instead that D, the day following the transfer, said, "I gave you the pen as a birthday present." (Exception(s) _____ _____)

___   92. In 90, P testifies instead that D, the day before the transfer, said, "I plan to give you the pen as a birthday present." (Exception(s) _____ _____)

* * *

___   94. On the issue of plaintiff's (P's) having cancer, N (a nurse) testifies for D that E, a doctor, gave P X-Ray treatments. (Exception(s) _____ _____)

___   95. In 94, N testifies instead that she heard E tell P that P had cancer. (Exception(s) _____ _____)

___   96. In 94, instead of using N's testimony, D offers in evidence the hospital record containing a notation made by E to the effect that he had found a malignant tumor in P. (Exception(s) _____ _____)

___   97. Same as 96 except that the hospital record contains a notation by the hospital receptionist to the effect that P, on entering the hospital, said that he had "a cancerous tumor." (Exception(s) _____ _____)

___   98. On the issue of X's good eyesight, W testifies that Y, X's commanding officer, assigned X to the position of lookout on the ship. (Exception(s) _____ _____)

___   99. Action P v. D. On the issue of P's knowledge that D was in the city, D offers X's testimony that Z said to P, "D is in the city." (Exception(s) _____ _____)

___   100. The testimony in 99 offered to prove that D was in the city.

(Exception(s) _____ _____)

___ 101. Action P v. D. To prove that D was present in the city, D offers W's testimony that P said, "I know that D is in the city." (Exception(s) _____ _____)

___ 102. On the issue of witness W1's hostility toward defendant (D), W2 testifies for D that W1 said to D in an angry tone, while D remained silent, "Well, at least I've never stolen money from my employer like you have! " (Exception(s) _____ _____)

___ 103. On the issue of D's stealing money from his employer plaintiff (P) offers the evidence in 102. (Exception(s) _____ _____)

___ 104. To prove the license number of the car involved in a hit-run accident, P offers a crumpled slip of paper on which appears the number EE2468 and the testimony of a woman that, though she cannot now recall the number of the car, she did, while the number was fresh in her mind, write the number down on the piece of paper offered in evidence. (Exception(s) _____ _____)

___ 105. To prove the license number of the car involved in a hit-run accident, P offers a photograph of a retreating automobile bearing the license plate EE2468 and the testimony of a woman that, though she cannot now remember the number of the car, she did know it at the time and that she took the photograph offered in evidence of the accident car as it left the scene. (Exception(s) _____ _____)

* * *

___ 108. On the issue of the speed of a locomotive, P introduces the tape printed by an automatic speed-recording device in the train. (Exception(s) _____ _____)

___ 109. On the issue of D's guilt of a crime, P offers a moving picture of D re-enacting the crime. (Exception(s) _____ _____)

___ 110 On the issue of the voluntariness of D's confession, P offers the moving picture in 109. (Exception(s) _____ _____)

___ 111. On the issue of D's good faith in discharging X, an employee (W) testifies that the police chief told D that X had been caught burglarizing a store. (Exception(s) _____ _____)

___ 112. On the issue of D's good faith in discharging X, an employee, D testifies that W told him (D) that the police chief told W that X had been caught burglarizing a store. (Exception(s) _____ _____)

___ 113. On the issue of D's good faith in discharging X, an employee, W testifies that the police chief told W that he (the police chief) had told D that X had been caught burglarizing a store. (Exception(s) _____ _____)

* * *

____ 115. Action P v. D. W1 testifies for P that D's car was going "over 50 miles an hour." To impeach W1, D offers the testimony of W2 that W1 said a day after the accident that D was going "slow." (Exception(s) _____ _____)

____ 116. The evidence in 115 offered by D to prove that he (D) was going slowly. (Exception(s) _____ _____)

____ 117. In 115, W2 is a police officer with no present recollection of W1's statement, so D offers the officer's (W2's) accident report, made up the day after the accident, containing the alleged W1 statement. (Exception(s) _____ _____)

____ 118. To prove that X was ill, W testifies that X, at the time, complained of a pain in his chest. (Exception(s) _____ _____)

____ 119. Action P v. D for $800, the price of a used automobile. Plea, payment. On the issue of payment, W testifies that he saw D hand P $800 in cash and say, "This is the payment for that car." (Exception(s) _____ _____)

____ 120. Action P v. D for conversion of a new automobile. To prove value, P offers a receipt for the purchase price, $3000, signed by X, the dealer from whom P bought it. (Exception(s) _____ _____)

____ 121. Same as 120 except X is D. (Exception(s) _____ _____)

____ 122. Action for personal injuries by a guest in an automobile against the owner. On the issue of contributory negligence and assumption of risk, W testifies that an hour before the accident, a mechanic said to the owner in the presence of the guest, "The spindle on that front wheel may break at any moment." (Exception(s) _____ _____)

____ 123. The evidence in 122 offered to show that the spindle was defective. (Exception(s) _____ _____)

____ 124. As tending to prove title to Blackacre in defendant (D) by adverse possession under claim of title, D offers the testimony of W that plaintiff (P) said to his sister, "I've been down to the town meeting, and D is telling everyone that he owns Blackacre." (Exception(s) _____ _____)

____ 125. Action P v. D. To prove that A was an agent of D's, P offers the testimony of W that A said, "I am an agent of D's." (Exception(s) _____ _____)

QUESTION

Suppose that McNaughton's Question 117 is set in a criminal case: P died as a result of the accident and D is being charged with criminally negligent vehicular homicide. Assuming state hearsay law poses no obstacle, does the Confrontation Clause allow the prosecution to introduce W2's report?

CHAPTER 4

IMPEACHMENT AND REHABILITATION; CROSS-EXAMINATION

PART **A** Impeaching One's Own Witness and Other Forensic Problems

PART **B** Methods of Impeachment

A. IMPEACHING ONE'S OWN WITNESS AND OTHER FORENSIC PROBLEMS

Kaplan and Waltz, The Trial of Jack Ruby
120–121 (1965).*

* * * Unlike the practice in most European countries, where the witness merely stands up and delivers a long narrative concerning what he knows about the case, in Anglo-American law the witnesses relate their stories through the question-and-answer method. Although some lawyers argue that by focusing the witnesses' attention on specific details, our method actually is simpler and faster, most lawyers would agree that it is in fact slower and more cumbersome. The reason it is used is that the rules of evidence in our jurisprudence are vastly more detailed, complicated and strict than those of most other countries. Relying on a jury untrained in the law, we make every possible effort to keep from the jurors the sort of information which they might rely on but which experience teaches is either unfair to the defendant or for some reason dangerously misleading. We therefore require the witness to give his answers in response to relatively pointed questions so that the opposing attorney, forewarned by the question that the jury may be about to hear inadmissible material, can object in time to prevent receipt of the damaging answer.

In Anglo-American law not only must the parties proceed by question and answer, but they must adhere to certain forms of questions. And the restrictions are far more severe on the side calling the witness to the stand. The examination of one's own witness—direct examination as distinguished from cross-examination—must be made without the use of leading questions, that is, questions which suggest their own answer. A typical leading question is, "Was the defendant's black automobile going about fifty miles an hour when you first saw it on the right, bearing down on you?" The witness may answer "Yes," but it is the attorney's version of the story that the jury hears. Leading questions, although technically prohibited, are general-

---

ly used to save time on unimportant and background matters. "Is your name Joe Smith?" However, as soon as important matters are reached, most trial lawyers automatically switch from leading questions to avoid a barrage of objections which are properly sustained by the court.

* * *

[In contrast, the] cross-examiner can ask as many leading questions as he wishes and, if the answers prove unsatisfactory, he can go at the matter again and again in as many different ways as he can devise to press the witness into delivering the desired answers. * * *

Mathew, Forensic Fables by O
267–68 (1961).

THE BEGINNER WHO THOUGHT HE WOULD DO IT HIMSELF

A Beginner, in the Temporary Absence of his Leader, Found himself Opposed to a Big Pot in the Commercial Court. Though Greatly Alarmed, the Beginner Bore himself Bravely. To his Surprise and Delight the Beginner Managed to Cross-Examine the Big Pot's Principal Witness with Such Effect that he Needed a Good Deal of Rehabilitation. Rising to Re-Examine, the Big Pot Airily Observed to the Principal Witness: "I Suppose What You Meant by Your Last Answer was This," and Proceeded to Tell the Principal Witness Quite Clearly what he Meant. When the Beginner made a Dignified Protest the Judge Smilingly Suggested that the Big Pot might Shape his Question rather Differently. The Next Day the Beginner was in a County Court. The Plaintiff (for whom the Beginner Appeared) having Made an Awkward Admission to his Learned Friend on the Other Side, the Beginner Thought he would Employ the Excellent Formula of the Big Pot. He Did so. The Scene that Followed Beggars Description. The County Court Judge in a Voice of Thunder Ordered the Beginner to Sit Down. He then Rebuked the Beginner for his Gross Misconduct and Discussed the Question whether he would Commit him for Contempt, or Merely Report him to the General Council of the Bar. Finally he Expressed the Hope that the Incident would be a Lesson to the Beginner and Directed that the Case should be re-Heard on a Later Date before a Fresh Jury. Moral.—*Wait till You're a Big Pot.*

Susanna and the Elders*

[T]he two elders rising up in the midst of the people, laid their hands upon [Susanna's] head. And she weeping looked up to heaven, for her heart had confidence in the Lord.

---

* The story of Susanna is included in the Book of Daniel by the Catholic and Eastern Orthodox churches. The version presented here is taken, with some punctuation changes, from Daniel, 13:34-64, of the Douay-Rheims 1899 American Edition of the Bible. Most Protestant churches regard this portion of the Book as apocryphal, and it is not included in the Jewish Bible. Eds.]

And the elders said: "As we walked in the orchard alone, this woman came in with two maids, and shut the doors of the orchard, and sent away the maids from her. Then a young man that was there hid came to her, and lay with her. But we that were in a corner of the orchard, seeing this wickedness, ran up to them, and we saw them lie together. And him indeed we could not take, because he was stronger than us, and opening the doors he leaped out: But having taken this woman, we asked who the young man was, but she would not tell us: of this thing we are witnesses."

The multitude believed them as being the elders and the judges of the people, and they condemned her to death.

Then Susanna cried out with a loud voice, and said: "O eternal God, who knowest hidden things, who knowest all things before they come to pass, Thou knowest that they have borne false witness against me: and behold I must die, whereas I have done none of these things, which these men have maliciously forged against me."

And the Lord heard her voice. And when she was led to be put to death, the Lord raised up the holy spirit of a young boy, whose name was Daniel. And he cried out with a loud voice, "I am clear from the blood of this woman."

Then all the people turning themselves towards him, said: "What meaneth this word that thou hast spoken?"

But he standing in the midst of them, said: "Are ye so foolish, ye children of Israel, that without examination or knowledge of the truth, you have condemned a daughter of Israel? Return to judgment, for they have borne false witness against her."

So all the people turned again in haste, and the old men said to him: "Come, and sit thou down among us, and shew it as: seeing God hath given thee the honour of old age."

And Daniel said to the people: "Separate these two far from one another, and I will examine them."

So when they were put asunder one from the other, he called one of them, and said to him: "O thou that art grown old in evil days, now are thy sins come out, which thou hast committed before: In judging unjust judgments, oppressing the innocent, and letting the guilty to go free, whereas the Lord saith: 'The innocent and the just thou shalt not kill.' Now then, if thou sawest her, tell me under what tree thou sawest them conversing together."

He said: "Under a mastic tree."

And Daniel said: "Well hast thou lied against thy own head: for behold the angel of God having received the sentence of him, shall cut thee in two."

And having put him aside, he commanded that the other should come, and he said to him: "O thou seed of Chanaan, and not of Juda, beauty hath deceived thee, and lust hath perverted thy heart: Thus did you do to the daughters of Israel, and they for fear conversed with you: but a daughter of Juda would not abide your wickedness. Now therefore tell me, under what tree didst thou take them conversing together?"

And he answered: "Under a holm tree."

And Daniel said to him: "Well hast thou also lied against thy own head: for the angel of the Lord waiteth with a sword to cut thee in two, and to destroy you."

With that all the assembly cried out with a loud voice, and they blessed God, who saveth them that trust in him.

And they rose up against the two elders, (for Daniel had convicted them of false witness by their own mouth,) and they did to them as they had maliciously dealt against their neighbour, To fulfil the law of Moses: and they put them to death, and innocent blood was saved in that day.

But Helcias and his wife praised God, for their daughter Susanna, with Joakim her husband, and all her kindred, because there was no dishonesty found in her.

And Daniel became great in the sight of the people from that day, and thenceforward.

Gilbert Without Sullivan*

First briefs are always alarming, but few draw so much public attention as the following, which was delivered in 1863.

Mrs. Briggs had instructed her counsel that she was in the omnibus, a hymn book in her pocket, on her way to tea and prayers, when she was seized and monstrously accused of having just picked someone's pocket. The purse found on her must have been planted by some evil worldling. Counsel was holding his first brief and, determined to draw attention to the hymn-book, cross-examined the policeman with all the assurance he could muster.

GILBERT: You say you found the purse in her pocket, my man?

CONSTABLE: Yes, sir.

GILBERT: Did you find anything else?

CONSTABLE: Yes, sir.

GILBERT: What?

---

* Stephen Tumim, Great Legal Disasters 77–78, (Arthur Barker Limited, London, 1983).

CONSTABLE: Two other purses, a watch with the bow broken, three handkerchiefs, two silver pencil-cases, and a hymn-book.

Before Mrs. Briggs went below to start her eighteen-month sentence, she paused briefly to remove her boot and hurl it at her counsel, W.S. Gilbert (for it was he). "The language in which her ovation was couched was perfectly shocking," he noted soon afterwards. "The boot missed me, but hit a reporter on the head, and to this fact I am disposed to attribute the unfavourable light in which my search for the defence was placed in two or three leading daily papers next morning."

Gilbert practised at the bar for four years, with an average of five clients a year, and earned £ 75. Happily it was not long before he found more lucrative employment through meeting Arthur Sullivan in 1871.

Mathew, Forensic Fables by O
87–88 (1961).

MR. WHITEWIG AND THE RASH QUESTION

MR. WHITEWIG was Greatly Gratified when the Judge of Assize Invited him to Defend a Prisoner who was Charged with Having Stolen a Pair of Boots, a Mouse-Trap, and Fifteen Packets of Gold Flakes. It was his First Case and he Meant to Make a Good Show. Mr. Whitewig Studied the Depositions Carefully and Came to the Conclusion that a Skillful Cross-Examination of the Witnesses and a Tactful Speech would Secure the Acquittal of the Accused. When the Prisoner (an Ill-Looking Person) was Placed in the Dock, Mr. Whitewig Approached that Receptacle and Informed the Prisoner that he Might, if he Wished, Give Evidence on Oath. From the Prisoner's Reply (in which he Alluded to Grandmothers and Eggs) Mr. Whitewig Gathered that he did not Propose to Avail Himself of this Privilege. The Case Began. At First All Went Well. The Prosecutor* Admitted to Mr. Whitewig that he Could not be Sure that the Man he had Seen Lurking in the Neighbourhood of his Emporium was the Prisoner; and the Prosecutor's Assistant Completely Failed to Identify the Boots, the Mouse-Trap, or the Gold Flakes by Pointing to any Distinctive Peculiarities which they Exhibited. By the Time the Police Inspector Entered the Witness-Box Mr. Whitewig Felt that the Case was Won. Mr. Whitewig Cunningly Extracted from the Inspector the Fact that the Prisoner had Joined Up in 1914, and that the Prisoner's Wife was Expecting an Addition to her Family. He was about to Sit Down when a Final Question Occurred to him. "Having Regard to this Man's Record," he Stearnly Asked, "How Came You to Arrest him?" The Inspector Drew a Bundle of Blue Documents from the Recesses of his Uniform, and, Moistening his Thumb, Read therefrom. Mr. Whitewig Learned in Silent Horror that the Prisoner's Record Included Nine Previous Convictions. When the Prisoner was Asked whether he had

---

* [In this setting, the prosecutor is the victim of the crime, here a storekeeper, who is pressing charges. Eds].

Anything to say why Sentence should not be Passed Upon him, he Said some Very Disagreeable Things about the Mug who had Defended him.

Moral.—*Leave Well Alone.*

United States v. Hogan

United States Court of Appeals, Fifth Circuit, 1985.
763 F.2d 697.*

■ CLARK, CHIEF JUDGE:

I

Barry Kendall Hogan and Mark Bradford (Brad) Hogan appeal their conviction of importing marijuana and conspiracy to import and possess with the intent to distribute the drug. Because the government called a witness for the primary purpose of impeaching him with otherwise inadmissible hearsay evidence, we reverse.

II

At a jury trial, the government asserted that the Hogan brothers were implicated in an operation that smuggled marijuana from Mexico into Texas. The fulcrum of the government's proof was the testimony of Mark Carpenter, the pilot of Barry Hogan's airplane, allegedly used in the importing scheme. Carpenter was arrested on October 30, 1979 in Zacatecas, Mexico, shortly after landing at a deserted airstrip where the drug transfer was to occur. Found on the plane was a pouch containing $15,000. A truck parked near the landing strip contained approximately 6,000 pounds of marijuana. Carpenter and the two occupants of the truck were arrested and taken into custody by Mexican officials. A day or so later, Carpenter gave statements to Mexican and United States Drug Enforcement Agency (DEA) officials that implicated the Hogans and himself in the conspiracy. Carpenter remained incarcerated in Mexico for over twenty-eight months.

Following Carpenter's release and return to the United States, he was called to testify before the grand jury in a related case pending in the same court in which the Hogans were later to be tried, but before a different judge. Carpenter initially refused to testify. He was given immunity. He then denied that he or the Hogans had any involvement in a drug conspiracy and testified that his confessions while imprisoned in Mexico were wholly fabricated and resulted from torture. Carpenter was indicted for perjury, but that matter had not been concluded by the time of the Hogans' trial. The prosecutor in the Hogans' case was informed of Carpenter's reversal of position.

* * *

---

* [This decision was modified upon rehearing on grounds not relevant to the issue for which it is presented here. See United States v. Hogan, 771 F.2d 82 (5th Cir.1985). Eds.]

[The prosecutor told the jury that he anticipated that Carpenter would testify that the Hogans were not guilty and that his statements implicating them were the result of torture and other abuses. Assuming Carpenter testified that way, the prosecutor said, he would present the DEA agents to testify that Carpenter had inculpated the Hogans.]

The court permitted counsel for the Hogans to conduct a voir dire examination of Carpenter outside the presence of the jury. During that examination, Carpenter denied involvement in any drug smuggling operation and reaffirmed his grand jury testimony of torture and fabrication. Carpenter then testified before the jury as to these matters, and the witness again maintained that the confessions were coerced. Carpenter also stated that he complained of his abuse to United States Embassy officials during his incarceration.

Defense counsel conducted extensive cross-examination, exploring Carpenter's arrest and the extent of the alleged torture, and eliciting assertions that the Hogans were not involved. In the course of this examination, the defense introduced a 15-minute taped confession of Carpenter given to the DEA agents in Mexico. In the statement Carpenter directly linked the Hogans to the importation scheme.

Following Carpenter's testimony, the government called four DEA and embassy officials to impeach Carpenter's story of torture and fabrication. They testified that they observed no abuse of the prisoner, nor were they aware of any. In addition, two officials stated that at no time did Carpenter complain of mistreatment. Defendants twice objected to the use of such testimony as hearsay and improper impeachment, but these objections were overruled. The Hogans contend the use of such testimony constitutes reversible error. We agree, for the reasons stated in part III of this opinion.

* * *

III

The Hogans contend that the government called Carpenter solely to present otherwise inadmissible hearsay testimony to the jury under the guise of impeachment. Defendants claim this "straw-man" ploy violated the Federal Rules of Evidence (FRE), and deprived them of a fair trial.

The government first responds that the Hogans failed to object to the use of such testimony at trial and are therefore estopped from asserting the error on appeal. While the Hogans' objections discussed earlier are not paradigms, they clearly were sufficient to bring the issue to the attention of the trial court and thus preserve this ground for review. The government next contends that the Hogans waived this objection by failing to present authority to the court on the impeachment issue noted above. However, that request for briefing did not encompass the use of the hearsay evidence for impeachment. Thus we decline to hold that the failure to respond constituted a waiver of defendant's objection on this ground.

Next, the government contends that the extensive cross-examination of Carpenter concerning his torture and fabrication constituted a waiver of the objection to the use of such testimony. This contention is not well taken. When, in overruling an objection, the Court expressly sets the direction of trial proof, counsel does not waive the objection by thereafter conducting the defense in accord with the court's ruling.

The remainder of the contentions related to Carpenter's testimony and subsequent impeachment present more substantial issues. The prosecution contends that it has a right pursuant to FRE 607 to impeach its own witnesses. Rule 607 provides, "the credibility of a witness may be attacked by any party, including the party calling him." In addition, they assert that a prior inconsistent statement of the witness may be admitted to attack his credibility even if the statement tends to directly inculpate the defendant. These contentions are correct.

The rule in this Circuit, however, is that "the prosecutor may not use such a statement under the guise of impeachment for the *primary* purpose of placing before the jury substantive evidence which is not otherwise admissible." Every circuit to consider this question has ruled similarly.

Despite this consistent precedent, the government contends it has the right to place on the stand a witness whom it suspects will fabricate his story, despite indications by the witness that his story has changed. They assert that in the formal courtroom setting, where the witness must swear an oath before the judge and is subject to the penalties of perjury, the witness is under maximum compulsion to tell the truth. Under these conditions, the factfinder should be allowed to observe the witness's demeanor when confronted with the conflicting statements and decide which version is true. In addition, they point out that if the prosecution could not introduce the testimony of any witness who had once made incriminating statements but later announced that he would recant that story at trial, declarants could effectively negate all incriminating statements made during questioning.

The apparent conflict in theories is not real. The government may call a witness it knows may be hostile, and it may impeach that witness's credibility. Surprise is not a necessary prerequisite to impeaching one's own witness under FRE 607. The prosecution, however, may not call a witness it knows to be hostile for the *primary* purpose of eliciting otherwise inadmissible impeachment testimony, for such a scheme merely serves as a subterfuge to avoid the hearsay rule.

The danger in this procedure is obvious. The jury will hear the impeachment evidence, which is not otherwise admissible and is not substantive proof of guilt, but is likely to be received as such proof. The defendant thus risks being convicted on the basis of hearsay evidence that should bear only on a witness's credibility. Limiting instructions can ameliorate a jury's confusion. Because none were requested or given in this trial, we review whether the introduction of Carpenter's testimony and the subsequent impeachment evidence constituted plain error. We find that it did.

The prosecution announced to the jury that Carpenter would be hostile and that it would impeach him. This is not a case where the government needed to determine whether a witness would adhere to his story under oath and subject to perjury. In the cases recognizing the right to put the witness to a trial test, the witness had not testified under oath and subject to perjury. In contrast, Carpenter had already testified twice under oath, and both times he adhered to his account of fabrication. He testified at the grand jury proceedings in a related case and a perjury indictment *and conviction* resulted. He again testified on voir dire in this proceeding. The government was not entitled to another test of Carpenter's sworn testimony. It well knew what he would say under oath.

The government also contends that the primary purpose of calling Carpenter was to link the Hogans to the smuggling operation, and to help solidify in the jury's mind the drug operation, especially because Carpenter was the only conspirator apprehended at the scene of the crime. Again, while these are legitimate purposes for calling a witness, they can not be considered the primary purpose for calling Carpenter in this case. The testimony they knew he would give provided no link between the drug transaction in Mexico and the Hogans other than the undisputed fact that the plane belonged to Barry Hogan and that Carpenter was employed by Hogan. The primary if not sole purpose in calling him to testify again was focused on getting Carpenter's prior statements before the jury.

The government contends that even if its primary purpose in calling Carpenter to the stand was to elicit impeachment evidence, such evidence was independently admissible as substantive proof, and thus the introduction of Carpenter's testimony and the impeachment evidence constituted harmless error. The impeachment proof consisted exclusively of out of court statements offered to prove the truth thereof, and thus were hearsay. The prosecutor posits for the first time on appeal that this evidence could be admitted under the "catchall" exception to the hearsay rule, FRE 803(24), because it has equivalent guarantees of trustworthiness. We disagree. First, the prosecution failed to provide the Hogans with the required notice that it intended to rely on Rule 803(24). Second, at trial the prosecution failed to state this exception as a grounds for admission of the evidence. Instead, the government offered the evidence solely for impeachment. The trial court therefore never made the required findings under the exception concerning materiality, probity, trustworthiness, and conformity with the rules and the interests of justice. It is improper for this appellate forum to make these findings for the first time.

The admission of this evidence constituted plain, not harmless, error. Errors in the admission of evidence affecting the substantial rights of a party may be corrected on appeal, even if they were not brought to the attention of the trial court. FRE 103; Fed.R.Crim.P. 52(b). The danger that the uninstructed jury relied on the impeaching statements as substantive proof is great. In addition, in its closing arguments the government relied on Carpenter's hearsay statements to corroborate [another government witness's] testimony. This request for affirmative use of impeachment testimony as substantive evidence unfairly prejudiced the Hogans. The remaining evidence does not so overwhelmingly establish guilt that we could say the error is harmless under Fed.R.Crim.P. 52(a). The convictions of the Hogans must be reversed.

Ohio Rules of Evidence, 2003

Ohio R. Evid. 607. Impeachment

(A) Who May Impeach. The credibility of a witness may be attacked by any party except that the credibility of a witness may be attacked by the party calling the witness by means of a prior inconsistent statement only upon a showing of surprise and affirmative damage. This exception does not apply to statements admitted pursuant to Evid. R. 801(D)(1)(a), 801(D)(2), or 803.

(B) Impeachment: reasonable basis. A questioner must have a reasonable basis for asking any question pertaining to impeachment that implies the existence of an impeaching fact.

See Federal Rules of Evidence 607, 611; California Evidence Code §§ 764, 767, 776, 785.

B. METHODS OF IMPEACHMENT

1. IMPEACHMENT BY CONTRADICTION

State v. Oswalt

Supreme Court of Washington, 1963.
62 Wn.2d 118, 381 P.2d 617.

■ HAMILTON, JUDGE. Defendant appeals, upon a short record, from a conviction of robbery and first degree burglary. During trial, a defense of alibi was introduced. Error is assigned to the admission of certain rebuttal testimony, defendant contending such evidence constituted impeachment on a collateral matter.

The short record before us (testimony of two witnesses) indicates that on July 14, 1961, two armed men entered the King County residence of Frank L. Goodell. One man stood guard over a number of people at the home. The other man took Mr. Goodell to a Tradewell store and forced him to open the safe and turn over the money therein. Defendant was identified as one of the two men.

In presenting his defense of alibi, defendant called a Mr. August Ardiss of Portland, Oregon. On direct examination, Mr. Ardiss testified in substance that: his wife and he operated a restaurant in Portland; he was acquainted with the defendant, as a fairly regular patron of the restaurant; defendant was in the restaurant at such times on July 14, 1961, as to render it impossible, as a practical matter, for defendant to be in Seattle at the time of the offense charged; and he remembered this occasion because defendant had accompanied a restaurant employee to work, assisted in a part of her work, and escorted her home.

On cross-examination by the state, the following exchange took place:

"Q. To the best of your knowledge would you say Oswalt had been in every day for the last couple of months or did he miss occasional periods of three or four days, or what was it? A. No, I think he was in there every day. I really think he was in there every day. Q. For the last couple months? A. Yes."

In rebuttal, a police detective was permitted to testify, over defense objections, as follows:

"Q. Did you see and talk to the defendant Mr. Oswalt on June 12, 1961? A. I did. Q. And in what city did you talk to him? A. In the City of Seattle. Q. And did you during that conversation ask him how long he had been in this city of Seattle at that time? * * * A. I did. Q. And how long did he state he had been in the City of Seattle? A. He stated he had arrived in Seattle a couple days before I talked to him. Q. Did he state where he had come from? A. Portland, Oregon."

During colloquy between the trial court and counsel relative to the admissibility of the detective's testimony, the trial court commented: "There is no claim by Oswalt he wasn't in Seattle, Gilman [a codefendant] claims that, but Oswalt doesn't."

It is to the rebuttal testimony of the police detective that defendant assigns error. The state, in response, contends such testimony to be admissible not only because it challenges the credibility of witness Ardiss, but also establishes defendant's presence in Seattle preparatory to the offense.

It is a well recognized and firmly established rule in this jurisdiction, and elsewhere, that a witness cannot be impeached upon matters collateral to the principal issues being tried. [Citations omitted.]

The purpose of the rule is basically two-fold: (1) avoidance of undue confusion of issues, and (2) prevention of unfair advantage over a witness unprepared to answer concerning matters unrelated or remote to the issues at hand.

We, in common with other jurisdictions, have stated the test of collateralness to be: Could the fact, as to which error is predicated, have been shown in evidence for any purpose independently of the contradiction?

We are handicapped by the limited record before us in evaluating the relationship of the contradictory evidence in question to the general issues presented in the trial.

So far as appears by this record, the sole issue raised by defendant's defense of alibi, through the direct testimony of witness Ardiss, was whether or not the defendant was or could have been in Seattle at the time of the offense on July 14, 1961. The defendant did not contend or seek to prove by this witness that he had not been in Seattle prior to such date. Thus, for purposes of impeaching this witness, whether the defendant was in Seattle on a given occasion one month prior to July 14th, was irrelevant and collateral. While a cross-examiner is, within the sound discretion of the trial court, permitted to inquire into collateral matters testing the credibility of a witness, he does so at the risk of being concluded by the answers given.

The state, however, contends that the quoted testimony of Ardiss, as elicited by its cross-examination, carries with it an inference that defendant could not have been in Seattle sufficiently in advance of July 14, 1961, to have participated in necessary planning of and preparation for the offense. Upon the inference so erected, the state asserts the questioned testimony becomes material and admissible independently of its contradictory nature. The state further supports this argument by testimony elicited from the police detective to the effect that defendant admitted, in the interview of June 12, 1961, that he had purchased some adhesive tape.

Admittedly, relevant and probative evidence of preparations by an accused for the commission of a crime is admissible. Based upon the limited record before us, however, the state's argument requires us to speculate that the defendant could not readily commute between Portland and Seattle, and that his presence in Seattle and acquisition of adhesive tape, upon an isolated occasion approximately a month before the offense in question, constituted significant evidence of planning and preparation for the offense in question, the particular mechanics of which are unrevealed by the record. This we decline to do, absent effort upon the part of the state to obtain a more complete record.

Upon the record before us, we must conclude it was error to admit the questioned testimony. * * *

The judgment is reversed and the cause remanded for new trial.

■ OTT, C.J., AND DONWORTH, HUNTER, and FINLEY, JJ., concur.

QUESTIONS

1. Plaintiff's witness testifies as follows: "At 11:00 P.M. on June 13, I was driving home from the movie. Just as I got to Hyde and Lombard, the car behind me passed me going very fast and hit a man who was getting off a cable car." Can the opponent prove with extrinsic evidence that the witness was on the way home from a poker game rather than a movie?

Not closely connected
too separated from event

2. Suppose that the witness had been drinking in a bar instead of watching a movie. Could that fact be proven with extrinsic evidence?

vision of witness may be impaired — not collateral — impeachable

3. Suppose that the witness had been on a date with the plaintiff's brother on the evening of June 13. Could that fact be proven with extrinsic evidence?

4. Suppose a witness testifies, "I'm certain that the performance review meeting occurred on February 3, 2011. I'll never forget that day because right after I got out of the meeting, my daughter called and told me my house had burned down." Could the opponent prove with extrinsic evidence that the witness's house burned down on February 4, not February 3?

Closely connected enough to bring in extrinsic evidence

United States v. Copelin

United States Court of Appeals, District of Columbia Circuit, 1993.
996 F.2d 379.

■ MIKVA, CHIEF JUDGE:

Warren Ricardo Copelin appeals his conviction on one count of unlawful distribution of cocaine. He argues that the district court erred by permitting the government to cross-examine him concerning his three positive drug tests for cocaine while on pre-trial release. He further asserts that even if the district court did not err by admitting this evidence, it committed reversible error by doing so without issuing an immediate limiting instruction to the jury. Finally, Mr. Copelin contends that the district court's calculation of his sentence was improper because, in determining his base offense level, the judge considered a quantity of cocaine contained in a discarded bottle, even though Mr. Copelin was acquitted of the charge that he possessed the drugs in that bottle.

We find that the district court's decision to admit the evidence regarding the positive drug tests was proper, but that its failure to issue an immediate cautionary instruction informing the jury as to the permissible uses of that evidence constituted plain error. We therefore reverse the conviction and remand for a new trial. It thus is not necessary for us to reach the sentencing issue.

I. BACKGROUND

Vanessa Moore, an undercover District of Columbia police officer, pre-recorded the serial numbers of three bills and used them to purchase two rocks of crack cocaine, totalling .144 gram, from a man she maintains was Mr. Copelin. The man who sold her the crack produced the drugs from a brown medicine bottle. After making the purchase, Officer Moore broadcast a radio lookout and description of the suspect, and, within a few minutes, an arrest team stopped Mr. Copelin. Shortly thereafter, Officer Moore identified Mr. Copelin as the man who sold her drugs. When the arrest team officers searched Mr. Copelin, they found that he possessed the pre-recorded currency. At the scene of the arrest, one of the officers found a brown medicine bottle containing 5.634 grams of cocaine base lying on the ground.

Mr. Copelin was charged with the unlawful distribution of crack co-caine, in connection with the two rocks he allegedly sold the officer, and with possession with intent to distribute in excess of five grams of crack cocaine, in connection with the drugs contained in the bottle. At trial, Mr. Copelin contended that he had not made the sale. He argued that Officer Moore was mistaking him for a man named David Bailey, with whom he was playing dice around the time of the sale. Mr. Copelin and his corrobo-rating witnesses testified that they had seen Mr. Bailey repeatedly leave the dice game to engage in transactions. They further testified that money was rapidly changing hands during the game.

The jury found Mr. Copelin guilty of unlawful distribution, but not guilty of possession with intent to distribute the drugs in the brown medi-cine bottle. In calculating his sentence, however, the district court found by a preponderance of the evidence that he had possessed the 5.634 grams of cocaine in the bottle. The judge held that the "same course of conduct" pro-vision in the Sentencing Guidelines, U.S.S.G. § 1B1.3(a)(2), compelled him, in determining Mr. Copelin's sentence, to consider the quantity of crack in the bottle as well as in the two rocks purchased by Officer Moore. He sen-tenced Mr. Copelin to sixty-three months incarceration, to be followed by three years of supervised release.

II. ANALYSIS

Mr. Copelin's evidentiary claims concern a colloquy that occurred dur-ing the government's cross-examination of him at trial. The prosecutor asked him whether he knew that Mr. Bailey, the man Mr. Copelin contends actually made the sale, was in fact engaging in drug transactions during the dice game.

Q: All right. And did you ever see him engage in a transaction where you knew it for sure?

A: I would see money change hands, but other than seeing the actual drugs or anything, no, I haven't noticed.

Q: You didn't see any actual drugs?

A: No, sir.

Q: Would you know what they looked like if you saw them?

A: Yes. It's advertised on TV, too, sometimes in the commercials.

Q: You see drugs advertised on TV?

A: Yes, you know, on news or something like that.

Q: And that's the only time you've ever seen drugs?

A: Roughly, yes.

Q: Roughly?

A: Yes.

The prosecutor then requested a bench conference, during which he sought permission from the court to cross-examine Mr. Copelin as to his positive drug tests while he was on pretrial release.

> The defendant tested positive for cocaine on three separate occasions and I believe that provides a reasonable basis to assume that he has seen cocaine * * *. He's made a bald denial that he has ever seen cocaine aside from on TV right here on the stand. I believe that's false and as a result, I propose to cross-examine him on this, but I wanted to ask the Court about it in advance.

Over the objection of defense counsel, the trial judge, without explanation, permitted the prosecutor to proceed with this line of questioning.

Q: Now, Mr. Copelin, isn't it true that as a condition of your release pending trial in this case, you were required to report to the Pretrial Services Administration for drug testing?

A: Yes.

Q: And isn't it true that you tested positive for cocaine on June 13th, 1991?

A: Yes.

Q: And you tested positive for cocaine on June 14th, 1991.

A: Yes.

Q: And you tested positive for cocaine on June 21st, 1991?

A: I don't recall that one.

Q: You don't recall that one?

A: No, sir.

Q: But despite having tested positive for cocaine on at least two occasions, you're telling the ladies and gentlemen of the jury that you have never seen cocaine except on television?

A: It could be anywhere. I never seen it, never used it.

The government then went on to pursue other issues. Defense counsel did not request a limiting instruction, and the trial judge did not offer one *sua sponte,* either immediately after this dialogue or as part of his final charge to the jury.

Mr. Copelin argues that the district court should not have allowed the government to question him as to the positive drug tests. As an initial matter, however, he concedes, as he must, that although "prior bad acts" evidence is not admissible to show a defendant's propensity to commit the crime at issue, there are circumstances under which a court may admit such evidence. Rule 404(b) of the Federal Rules of Evidence states:

> Evidence of other crimes, wrongs, or acts is not admissible to prove the character of a person in order to show action in conformity therewith. It may, however, be admissible for other purposes, such as proof of motive, opportunity, intent, preparation, plan, knowledge, identity, or absence of mistake or accident * * *.

Although it is not one of the listed permissible purposes, an attempt to impeach through contradiction a defendant acting as a witness is indisputably a legitimate reason to introduce evidence of other crimes or wrongs. If "bad acts" evidence is offered for this reason, it is admissible unless "its probative value is substantially outweighed by the danger of unfair prejudice, confusion of the issues, or misleading the jury or by considerations of undue delay, waste of time, or needless presentation of cumulative evidence." Fed.R.Evid. 403.

Mr. Copelin levels several attacks against the district court's admission of the evidence concerning his positive drug tests. First, he contends that the government's line of inquiry violated the threshold requirement that impeachment evidence actually contradict the witness' testimony. This argument is unavailing, however, because Mr. Copelin's admission as to the positive drug tests clearly tended to contradict his earlier assertion that he had only seen drugs on television. Mr. Copelin responded to the government's initial queries by denying that he had ever had any direct acquaintance with narcotics. It was consequently proper for the district court to permit the government to impeach Mr. Copelin by attempting to demonstrate that this statement was false.

Mr. Copelin also claims that the government's method of impeachment violated the ban on the use of extrinsic evidence to impeach by contradiction on collateral matters. It is true that this Circuit generally follows the rule that "a witness may not be impeached by extrinsic evidence (contradiction by another witness or evidence) on a collateral issue." However, the rule disallowing the use of extrinsic evidence to impeach a witness as to a collateral matter is irrelevant to this case, because Mr. Copelin was impeached by his own statements on cross-examination, not by the testimony of another witness or by physical evidence. "[C]ases upholding a court's exclusion of *extrinsic* evidence offered to impeach a witness, on the ground of the issue's being 'collateral,' do not govern the scope of cross examination itself."

Mr. Copelin further argues that the government should not have been allowed to place inadmissible evidence before the jury by trapping him into opening the door by contradiction. He seems to suggest that the government's line of questioning was merely a ploy to smuggle in the evidence regarding the positive drug tests. But the courts have always recognized an important distinction between effective cross-examination and unfair tactics. When Mr. Copelin testified that he did not actually see David Bailey selling drugs, it was not entirely unnatural for the government to explore the basis for this response by inquiring whether Mr. Copelin had the ability to recognize drugs in the first place. As the Supreme Court has held in a related context, "If these questions would have been suggested to a reasonably competent cross-examiner * * * they were not 'smuggled in'; and forbidding the Government to impeach the answers to these questions by using contrary and reliable evidence in its possession fails to take account of our cases." United States v. Havens, 446 U.S. 620 (1980).

It may well be that the trial judge would have sustained timely objections by defense counsel to the prosecutor's questions concerning Mr. Copelin's ability to recognize drugs. Mr. Copelin's attorney did not issue any such objections, however, so in reviewing this aspect of the cross-examination, we are limited to correcting "plain errors." Fed.R.Crim.P. 52(b). The plain error exception to the contemporaneous objection requirement should be used sparingly, only for "particularly egregious errors," that "seriously affect the fairness, integrity or public reputation of judicial proceedings." The district court's failure to squelch the government's disputed line of questioning on its own initiative was certainly no plain error, if it was error at all.

[The Court next turned to Copelin's contention that, although he had not requested a limiting instruction at trial, the district court committed reversible error by failing to give one *sua sponte*. It agreed with that contention and reversed. This final aspect of the *Copelin* case was overruled in United States v. Rhodes, 62 F.3d 1449, 1453–54 (D.C. Cir. 1995). The *Rhodes* case held that Rule 105's requirement that an appropriate limiting instruction be given "upon request" placed upon counsel the burden of requesting the instruction, and it noted that counsel might decide not to make the request for tactical reasons.]

---

2. CHARACTER OF THE WITNESS

A. PRIOR BAD ACTS

United States v. Owens

United States Court of Military Appeals, 1985.
21 M.J. 117.

■ COX, JUDGE:

* * *

The circumstances surrounding appellant's conviction for unpremeditated murder were summarized by the court below as follows:

On 4 September 1981, Gari Owens was apprehended for the murder of his wife, Mary Owens. She died in the early morning hours of 4 September as a result of a single gunshot which entered her back causing a large laceration of the liver and perforation of the breathing muscle. Death was due to excessive bleeding. At the time Mary Owens had been driving the couple's Volkswagen Rabbit down the street from their quarters at Fort Campbell, Kentucky. Gari Owens held the 30.06 rifle mounted with a "Bushnell 4" telescopic sight which fired the fatal bullet.

At the trial the government introduced evidence to show that Gari Owens fired the weapon in anger following a domestic quarrel and that Owens intended his wife's death or grievous bodily harm. In defense Owens took the stand. An experienced hunter and marksman, Owens claimed that he had been standing in front of his house examining his rifle and that he had chambered a round and cleared the weapon by pulling the trigger. He maintained that his wife's death was a tragic accident.

* * *

* * * [A]ppellant was cross-examined as follows:

Questions by assistant trial counsel:

Q. Mr. Owens, isn't it a fact that as to your application for appointment as a Warrant Officer in the United States Army and the statement of personal history attached to it, that you knowingly omitted the fact from questions 19 and 18, that you had been convicted in Daleville, Alabama, for the possession of marihuana and marihuana paraphernalia in 1976?

A. No, sir.

Q. Is it not a fact that you intentionally omitted from both of these documents the fact that you had been arrested in 1976 in Daleville, Alabama, for assault and battery on your second wife, Mrs. Jennifer Conant Braun?

A. No, sir.

Q. Is it not a fact that you omitted from both of these documents, the fact that you had been convicted in Enterprise, Alabama, for carrying a .22 caliber pistol in your automobile without a permit in 1976?

A. It was admitted—it was omitted, rather. I did not knowingly omit it.

Q. You did not knowingly omit it?

A. I did not omit it.

Q. Mr. Owens, isn't it a fact that you knowingly omitted all three of these matters from those two documents because you realized that if you put them in there, you likely would not become the Warrant Officer that you wanted so badly to become?

A. No, Sir. That's not true.

After this cross-examination, defense counsel questioned appellant in detail about these omissions. He admitted to two prior convictions and provided explanations for the underlying conduct. He further explained the omission of this information from these forms. He testified that he informed the personnel specialists processing his application that he had a local marihuana offense and pistol offense. He asserted that he relied on these personnel specialists to properly process his application and signed the final papers without reading them. He made no admission concerning his prior arrest for assault or any claim that he disclosed this matter to them.

* * *

In the present case, trial counsel * * * was clearly authorized under Mil.R.Evid. 608(b) to impeach appellant by extracting on cross-examination his admission to a prior act of intentional falsehood under oath. In particular, he had a good-faith belief that appellant had previously failed to provide complete and truthful answers on his warrant-officer application. Since the prior convictions and arrests were the matters omitted in his answers, they were necessary and inseparable parts of this act of deceit. As such, they were clearly matters which were relevant within the meaning of Mil.R.Evid. 401 to establish appellant's prior act of falsehood. More importantly, the adverse nature of these omissions coupled with appellant's admitted interest in being selected reasonably tended to show these omissions were intentional.[2] The relevance of the suggested evidence was not obviated simply because the omissions pertained to additional acts of prior misconduct which might unfavorably reflect on appellant's character.

The relevance of the suggested evidence to show a prior act of deceit by appellant does not *per se* dictate its admissibility under the Military Rules of Evidence. Under Mil.R.Evid. 403, evidence relevant for a permissible purpose may still be found inadmissible "if its probative value is substantially outweighed by the danger of unfair prejudice." This additional requirement for admissibility precludes admission of relevant evidence which would tend to "*unduly* " prejudice an accused under the circumstances of a particular case.

---

[2] The suggested evidence of prior misconduct tended to show the omissions were substantial and material to the success of appellant's warrant-officer application. The Government argued that the more substantial and material the omission, the more likely that the omission was intentional on appellant's part. We note further that the more substantial and material the omissions, the less likely that personnel specialists would negligently omit responses given by appellant on the final form. In this light, the particular matters omitted were external circumstances which reflected on appellant's intent in submitting his application in an incomplete form. . . .

* * *

The record of trial in this case provides a firm basis for the conclusion that the suggested evidence had substantial probative value. First, the issue of appellant's prior falsehood was clearly a matter contested by the parties. Although after some evasion appellant admitted there were some omissions on his application, he steadfastly denied that he consciously and intentionally omitted the complete answers.[3] Second, other evidence to show appellant engaged in this act of deceit was not available to the Government. Under Mil.R.Evid. 608(b), the prosecution could not introduce extrinsic evidence of appellant's prior falsehood, by, for example, calling the personnel specialists who processed appellant's application. Finally, the strength of the suggested evidence to show appellant's prior falsehood was considerable. The number of omissions, their serious nature in terms of involvement with law enforcement authorities, and the potentially disqualifying character of the underlying offenses in terms of military promotion were substantial circumstances indicating deliberate deceit by appellant.

The military judge was also required to consider the tendency of the suggested evidence to unfairly prejudice appellant. He had to assess the suggested evidence in terms of its tendency to incite the members to irrational decision by its force on human emotion. The prior convictions and the prior arrest could naturally have led the members to find the appellant guilty because he was a "bad man." * * * In these circumstances and in view of the considerable probative value of the suggested evidence for a proper purpose, we hold that the military judge did not abuse his discretion under Mil.R.Evid. 403.

This holding does not extend to all the suggested evidence to which trial counsel was permitted to refer. The victim of appellant's purported assault and battery was identified as his second wife, Mrs. Jennifer Conant Braun. It is highly doubtful that the questions on the warrant-officer application intended to elicit this information as an essential part of a truthful and complete answer. In any event, its probative value, if any, on the issue of deceit was marginal if in fact the arrest and the basic underlying offense, assault and battery, had been omitted. Of course, the potential for prejudice was great in view of the fact that appellant was on trial for the murder of his third wife. This conclusion is buttressed by the fact that the military judge in his closing instructions referred to the suggested evidence of assault and battery as occurring "on an individual." Therefore, acknowledging the broad discretion of the military judge under Mil.R.Evid. 403, we nonetheless hold that the suggested evidence in this limited regard was inadmissible.

---

[3] Appellant admitted that complete and truthful answers to several questions on his warrant-officer application had been omitted. He asserted, however, that he did provide complete answers orally to the personnel specialists who processed his application; that they omitted the complete answers; and that he failed to read the completed forms before he signed them. In other words, he denied the impeaching fact sought to be proven by the Government, namely, that he knowingly and intentionally lied under oath or affirmation. See Mil.R.Evid. 608(b).

* * *

We have concluded that it was error for the military judge to allow trial counsel to suggest to the members in his cross-examination questions that appellant had previously been arrested for assault and battery on his second wife. However, appellant was entitled to a fair trial, not "an error-free, perfect trial." After considering the trial record as a whole, we are convinced beyond a reasonable doubt that this error did not prejudice appellant. Accordingly, he is not entitled to relief.

The decision of the United States Army Court of Military Review is affirmed.

* * *

An Illustration: Cross–Examination Well Prepared and Executed

Francis Wellman's classic *The Art of Cross-Examination* offers many instances of effective cross-examination. Recall the case of the expert who falsely claimed to have relied on a treatise that in fact provided no support for his testimony, pp. 468–470. Another good example, presented in the 1923 edition, pp. 37-41, featured Martin W. Littleton, who had first practiced law in Texas before moving to New York City, where he became a well-known political figure and member of the bar. Littleton's client, Henry E. Lazarus, was charged with bribing a senior Government inspector, Charles L. Fuller, to overlook the supposedly poor quality of hundreds of thousands of rubber coats that Lazarus supplied the Government during World War I. Fuller was the star witness for the prosecution, and Littleton did his homework.

In response to a question by Littleton, Fuller acknowledged signing an application for his job. Littleton then asked, "Did you swear to it?" and Fuller replied, "No, I did not swear to it." But Littleton had been able to get from Government files the original of the application. Upon being shown it, Fuller had to acknowledge that, though he had forgotten, he "must have sworn to it." Ultimately, under continued pressure from Littleton, he said flatly, "I swore to it."

This exchange followed:

Q. "Was your name Fuller?"

A. "Yes, sir."

Q. "Has your name always been Fuller?"

A. "No, sir."

Q. "What was your name?"

Over the witness's protest, Littleton was able to draw out that at times he had been known as Finkler. Littleton then move on to the substance of the application:

Q. "Now, Mr. Fuller, in your application you made to the Government, on which I showed you your signature and affidavit, you attached your picture, did you not?"

A. "Yes, sir."

Q. "And you stated in your application you were born in Atlanta, Georgia, did you not?"

A. "Yes, sir."

Q. "You were asked, when you sought this position, these questions: 'When employed, the years and the months,' and you wrote in, 'February, 1897 to August, 1917, number of years 20; Where employed—Brooklyn; Name of employer—Vulcan Proofing Company; Amount of salary,—$37.50 a week; also superintendent in the rubber and compound room.'"

Q. "You wrote that, didn't you?"

A. "Yes, sir."

Q. "And swore to that, didn't you?"

A. "Yes, sir."

Q. "Now, were you employed from February, 1897, to August, 1917, twenty years, with the Vulcan Proofing Company?"

A. "No sir."

Q. "That was not true, was it?"

A. "No, sir."

Q. "And had you been assistant superintendent of the rubber and compound room?"

A. "No, sir."

Q. "That was false, wasn't it?"

A. "Yes, sir."

Q. "'And through my experience as chief inspector of the rubber and slicker division,' that was false, wasn't it?"

A. "Yes, sir."

Q. "You knew it was false didn't you?"

A. "Yes, sir."

Q. "And you knew you were swearing to a falsehood when you swore to it?"

A. "Yes, sir."

Q. "And you swore to it intentionally?"

A. "Yes, sir."

Q. "And you knew you were committing perjury when you swore to it?"

A. "I did not look at it in that light."

Q. "Didn't you know you were committing perjury by swearing and pretending you had been twenty years in this business?"

A. "Yes, sir."

Q. "And you are swearing now, aren't you?"

A. "Yes, sir."

Q. "In a matter in which a man's liberty is involved?"

A. "Yes, sir."

Q. "And you know that the jury is to be called upon to consider whether you are worthy of belief or not, don't you?"

A. "Yes, sir."

Q. "When you swore to this falsehood deliberately, and wrote it in your handwriting, you knew it was false, you swore to it intentionally, and you knew that you were committing perjury, didn't you?"

A. "I did not look at it in that light."

Q. "Well, now, when you know you are possibly swearing away the liberty of a citizen of this community, do you look at it in the same light?"

A. "Yes, sir, I do."

Wellman recounts:

> Mr. Littleton then uncovered the fact that the witness, instead of having been twenty years superintendent of a rubber room with the Vulcan Proofing Company, as he had sworn in his own handwriting, was a stag entertainer in questionable houses, was a barker at a Coney

Island show, was an advance agent of a cheap road show and had been published in the paper as having drawn checks that were worthless, the witness fully admitting all of the details of his twenty years of questionable transactions. The result was his utter collapse so far as his credibility was concerned, and the Government's case collapsed with him.

Aron Steuer, Max D. Steuer: Trial Lawyer
48-52 (1950)

[Otto Foelker, a highly regarded member of Congress, accused Max Steuer's client of trying to bribe him while Foelker was a member of the state senate. After a chance meeting before trial, a Mr. Thain, who occupied law offices with Foelker, brought Steuer to the office to meet Foelker, but he was out. Certificates on the walls bore Foelker's signature in German script. Steuer expressed surprise.] His mental picture of Foelker's career was on the usual pattern of the crusader in politics. The first essential is that he be beholden to none. This most frequently results in a young man, from a secure background of position and affluence, both generally inherited. Mr. Thain gave an outline of Foelker's history. He was a German immigrant reaching this country in his early teens. After a short period in Troy, he settled in Brooklyn and attended public school. He left school early to go to work. He got a job in a law office, where he progressed from the minor tasks to a clerkship, eventually studying for the bar and being admitted. At the same time he interested himself in politics with the results already seen. So, in addition to being a knight errant he was also an Horatio Alger hero.

Now whatever Steuer may or may not have known about a Galahad career he was perfectly familiar with the life of the "Rags-to-Riches" type. He had lived it and when he got back to his office he compared his meager information with his intimate knowledge of the background. Two points loomed up. The first was that a man of that background gets rapid political preferment by being an asset first to a ward-heeler, then to a district leader. The most obvious service is the production of votes and the first vote to be produced is one's own. He decided to look into Foelker's voting record. It proved interesting. Foelker had followed the adage about voting early—by a year at least.

Secondly, in order to take the bar examination a candidate who is not a law-school graduate must pass a certain number of examinations set by the Board of Regents. The Regents examinations of those days were about the present equivalent of the graduation examinations for a junior high school. But they were all factual. An unprepared candidate could not pass them. There is obviously no way of knowing who won the battle of Lookout Mountain, the conjugations of the French irregular verbs or how to obtain the square root of X^2-Y^2 unless you have learned the answers. In the thumbnail sketch of Foelker, the necessary schooling was missing. He decided to find out how Foelker passed his Regents examinations.

Inquiry at the Board of Regents showed that the examination papers had been destroyed but the notation of the results, the correspondence and the like had been preserved. Foelker did remarkably well but the subject in which he must have been most proficient, German, did not appear in the list of his subjects. What writings there were from Foelker were not in a German script. And although Foelker had a residence and a business address at the time, the Regents Board were directed to correspond with him, care of Solinsky, at 54 Rutgers Street. Max Solinsky was traced and found. He proved to be a professional examination taker and was currently in Sing Sing prison for taking a civil-service examination under a false name.

That was all the ammunition there was, and it needed careful handling. In the first place there are the rules of evidence. When a witness takes the stand he puts his character in issue, and he can be cross-examined about anything in his life that will show he is not fit to be believed. But as to anything that he was not asked about on his direct examination, his answer is final and cannot be contradicted. For instance, if a lady takes the stand and testifies that the defendant stole her purse, you can call witnesses to show that she never had a purse, or that she was in Chicago at the time, or anything else to show that the purse was not stolen. But if you want to prove that she is no lady you must prove it out of her own mouth. You may have a dozen witnesses to show that she ran a gambling house, or tortured stray cats, or engaged in any number of activities that are not looked upon with approbation, but if she denies them (and you must ask her) that is the end of it.

Mr. Steuer had no illusions about Foelker's knowledge of this rule. If he was not already acquainted with it, he would be when he took the stand. Therefore he had to be so enmeshed by the time he was confronted with something important that a denial would be unavailing. But to get him in the toils would involve a series of questions about his schooling to which entirely credible answers would be that he did not remember. Who does remember at the age of 35 what he learned in school? Foelker had to have no excuse for not remembering. Mr. Steuer wrote Thain a letter telling him that he was going to question Foelker on these subjects, and asked him to refresh his recollection. If he ignored the request the jury would see that he had a good reason for doing it. On the other hand it would certainly warn Foelker that this incident was known and his care would make the questioning more difficult. It could not be helped. * * *

Note: Extrinsic Evidence Under Fed. R. Evid. 608(b)

Under Rule 608(b), the judge has discretion to permit a witness to be cross-examined about specific acts that reflect on character for truthfulness. If the witness denies the conduct, then, assuming the evidence is not admissible on some other ground, the cross-examiner must "take the answer." This does not mean that the cross-examiner is prohibited from further efforts to get the witness to admit the misconduct, but it does mean that "extrinsic evidence" of the misconduct is not admissible. The main purpose of this ban on extrinsic evidence is to prevent the waste of time and confusion that would occur if mini-trials were held about blemishes in each witness's past. Concerns about confusion of issues and unfair surprise also underlie the rule.

What constitutes extrinsic evidence? As the language of the rule itself makes clear, testimony about untruthful acts in a witness's past is not extrinsic evidence if it is extracted from the mouth of the witness being impeached by the evidence. Just as clearly, testimony by *another* witness who observed those acts *is* extrinsic evidence. Documentary proof of untruthful acts is also extrinsic evidence when it is necessary to call another witness to establish that the documents are genuine or to lay the foundation for their admission under an exception to the hearsay rule. Where, however, the foundation for an impeaching document can be laid through the testimony of the very witness whose character for truthfulness is being impeached, the danger that undue time will be consumed on side issues is lessened. Such documents are sometimes admitted despite the rule against extrinsic evidence, though generalizations are dangerous because caselaw pronouncements on the subject are divergent and often lacking in focus.[*]

QUESTIONS

The defense in a civil case has discovered that X, a witness for the plaintiff, lied on an employment application by claiming to have a Master's degree. In fact, X was expelled from graduate school for plagiarism before getting the degree. The evidence of X's lie on the application and his plagiarism has no relevance to the lawsuit other than its bearing on X's character for truthfulness.

1. Would it be permissible to ask X on cross-examination whether, in an application for employment, he falsely claimed to have a Master's degree?

2. If X denies that he claimed to have a Master's degree on the employment application, would it be permissible to refresh his memory by showing him the application?

3. If X denies committing plagiarism, should the cross-examiner be allowed to introduce into evidence a report by a school disciplinary committee finding that the witness committed plagiarism? Suppose that the witness, while denying plagiarism, admits that the report is an authentic report of the disciplinary committee?

4. Suppose that X denies committing plagiarism, and the cross-examiner produces a prior written statement by X confessing to plagiarism. Is the statement itself admissible if X admits making the statement but still denies committing plagiarism? If she denies making the statement?

------

[*] See authorities collected in Roger C. Park, David P. Leonard, Aviva A. Orenstein, and Steven H. Goldberg, EVIDENCE LAW 507-08 (3d. ed. 2011) and in 3 Christopher B. Mueller and Laird C. Kirkpatrick, FEDERAL EVIDENCE § 6.36 (3d. ed. 2007).

5. Would it be permissible to ask X on cross-examination, "Isn't it true that you were expelled from graduate school for plagiarism?"

United States v. Drake

United States Court of Appeals, Tenth Circuit, 1991.
932 F.2d 861.

■ ALDON J. ANDERSON, DISTRICT JUDGE.

[In a jury trial, Renee Roger Drake was convicted of fraud on the basis of allegations that he sought financing while concealing the existence of a third party's security interest in the collateral. He appealed.]

Cross–Examination of Appellant Drake.

At trial, a portion of Drake's defense centered on his claim that he was unaware of the Payne Company's security interest in after-acquired accounts receivable. Drake asserted that he believed ATIM [a corporation for which Drake, as Vice President for day-to-day operations, sought financing] had granted a security interest only in then existing accounts receivable. In support of this position, Drake testified that he had no formal training in business management. Drake noted that his background was as a business consultant with an emphasis on psychological applications and considerations in business management. Possibly in support of this argument, Mr. Drake was asked during direct examination, "Mr. Drake, basically, what is your background and education?" Drake answered, "Majored in psychology and the usual things that go along with a major." On cross-examination, Drake testified that he had a degree in psychology.

The assistant U.S. Attorney impeached Drake on this point through the use of prior inconsistent statements. Drake explained the inconsistencies by testifying, "No, I do not have a diploma that says I have 120 graduate hours. I have a completed major, and I did practice clinical psychology. It was at the University of Illinois and Roosevelt University... I would have completed it probably around [19]53 to '54."

The Assistant U.S. Attorney proceeded to cross-examine Drake on several other matters. Several hours later, after the noon break, the Assistant U.S. Attorney reopened her cross-examination of Drake with the following exchange:

Q. (By Ms. Robinson) I'm sorry. Mr. Drake, if we would clarify the record, is your testimony that you do or you do not have a degree in psychology?

A. I do not—

MR. SHARBUTT: I am going to object. I think we spent probably twenty minute [sic] on that this morning. I think he's answered that he does not have an official degree but he had the hours that were necessary in his major.

THE COURT: Overruled. Go ahead.

A. I do not have the official diploma document, no. I am not shown as a graduate per se of the institution of Roosevelt University in Chicago. I did complete my major which qualified me to practice.

Q. (By Ms. Robinson) All right. So when you testified under oath at the deposition and the trial that you had a B.A. degree, that was not a true statement?

A. I was in a hurry and that was wrong. I felt that way because I completed my major, and I was qualified for psychiatry—psychology. In reflection, yes, it was wrong.

Q. All right. Now, you also testified that you had done some work at the University of Illinois and then later you went to Roosevelt University, that is where you finished?

A. Yes.

Q. When you transferred from the University of Illinois to Roosevelt, did you transfer your credits from the University of Illinois?

A. Of course.

Q. All right. If the University of Illinois' records reflect that no credits were ever transferred, do you have any explanation for that?

A. I would have no explanation for that.

Q. Isn't it a fact that you didn't really have very many grades to transfer because most of your grades were flunking grades?

A. Not that I recall.

Q. And you left there in 1951 so it wouldn't be possible for you to stack up enough hours by 1954 or '55 to be close to a degree at Roosevelt University?

A. Not true.

Q. If the records reflect that you had Fs and Ds and a few Cs and only one B during your three semesters there, those records would be inaccurate?

A. At the University of Illinois?

Q. Yes.

A. I don't recall my records there. I just know they were transferred.

Q. Also, isn't it a fact that you were actually kicked out of the University of Illinois in 1951?

A. No.

Q. So if the records reflect that you were kicked out for falsifying facts in a disciplinary investigation, is your testimony that that would not be right?

MR. SHARBUTT: Your Honor, I'm going to object to this line of questions. This constant reference to records reflect, I think if there are some records, we should have them in evidence. They should be subject to proper ID, subject to foundation requirements rather than this line of questioning. I think if there are records that are going to be in evidence, let's get them in.

MS. ROBINSON: Your Honor, I have the custodian of the records upstairs in my office. I do have the record here. I imagine Mr. Drake has never seen this record or doesn't have it, but if Mr. Sharbutt wants to have it offered into evidence, I would have no objection.

MR. SHARBUTT: Your Honor, at this time Defendant Drake moves for mistrial on the grounds of this line of questioning. This line of questioning is only done, has no probative value with any of the facts that are to be presented to the jury, and it's merely to inflame the jury and on those grounds we move for mistrial.

THE COURT: Overruled. He may answer it. If you have your custodian here, why, we can get right into it.

Q. (By Ms. Robinson) All right. Mr. Drake, then, if the transcript and record from the University of Illinois indicates that you were dismissed from the university at the close of the second semester 1950 to 1951 for violation of terms of your probation and for falsification of facts in a disciplinary investigation, is it your testimony this document is not correct?

A. I would dispute that, yes.

The Assistant U.S. Attorney then moved to other subject areas.

Drake argues this line of questioning was improper on two grounds. First, the questions dealt with unfairly prejudicial and irrelevant material. Second, the questions themselves constituted the introduction of extrinsic evidence of specific instances of conduct offered in violation of Fed.R.Evid. 608(b). In general, the trial court has broad discretion in ruling on evidentiary matters. We may not reverse the trial court's evidentiary rulings "in the absence of an abuse of discretion."

We begin by examining whether the subject matter of the cross-examination was appropriate. As a preliminary matter during direct testimony, Drake testified that his educational background consisted of "a major in psychology." This testimony opened the area of Drake's educational background to cross-examination and provided a potential target for impeachment. Fed.R.Evid. 611(b).

In response to the prosecutor's exploration of Drake's educational background, Drake made certain factual assertions that created potential targets for impeachment. Drake initially stated that he had a degree in psychology. After being impeached through the use of prior inconsistent statements, Drake asserted that he had finished the requirements for a degree though he had not actually received one. The prosecutor later sought to impeach Drake on this and related points. The prosecutor did so by attempting to elicit admissions from Drake that his testimony was incorrect. Such a tactic is permissible to probe a witness' credibility through contradiction. The subject of the prosecutor's cross-examination was not, therefore, inappropriate.

Having determined that permitting the prosecutor to inquire into this subject matter on cross-examination was not inappropriate, the court must now determine whether the form of cross-examination permitted by the trial court was an abuse of discretion. Drake urges that the questions constituted the introduction of extrinsic evidence of specific instances of conduct in violation of Rule 608(b).

The questions posed by the prosecutor referred to the contents of school records not in evidence and specific instances of conduct approximately thirty years old. Cross-examination questions alone, however, cannot constitute extrinsic evidence. The court, therefore, rejects Drake's argument.

Though the questions asked did not constitute extrinsic evidence, they were arguably improper because they assumed facts not in evidence.[5] The questions implied that the records actually did support the facts asserted by the prosecutor. The contents of the records were not in evidence. The court, however, cannot find that any substantial right of Drake has been affected. Drake had already been effectively impeached on a closely related issue by the use of inconsistent statements. Furthermore, by the time Drake's counsel made the objection now being appealed, he had already permitted a number of almost identical questions to be posed. The damage had already been done by the time counsel raised the objection now on appeal. The court finds, therefore, that the trial court did not abuse its discretion nor thereby commit a harmful error.

* * *

AFFIRMED.

---

[5] The argument that the questions improperly assumed facts not in evidence better reflects the objection raised by Drake at trial than the extrinsic evidence argument now asserted on appeal. At trial, Drake did not contend that extrinsic evidence was inadmissible on these issues. In fact, Drake invited the introduction of extrinsic evidence. Drake merely objected to the reference to records not before the jury.

United States v. Saada

United States Court of Appeals for the Third Circuit, 2000.
212 F.3d 210.

■ HARRIS, DISTRICT JUDGE.

This appeal arises out of a factual setting of unusual corruption, involving a flooded portion of a warehouse resulting from a broken sprinkler head; a fraudulent insurance claim filed by a father and son; a cousin who took part in the scheme, but later testified against his relatives as a government witness, only to be caught on tape by the government encouraging an individual to falsely implicate someone in a different crime; and the use at trial of a statement by a deceased state court judge who had been removed from the bench and disbarred for unethical conduct. * * *

[Isaac Saada and his son Neil had been convicted of various fraud charges arising out of a scheme to cheat an insurance company. The government produced evidence that they staged a flooding in the warehouse of their business, Scrimshaw Handicrafts, by intentionally breaking a sprinkler head, causing a flood of dirty water to pour into a caged area containing valuable merchandise. One of those present was Tom Yaccarino, a vice-president of Scrimshaw and former New Jersey state court judge. They later submitted inflated claims for compensation for the damaged merchandise.]

Appellants contend that the District Court improperly admitted evidence of specific instances of misconduct by Yaccarino to impeach his credibility. The impetus for the admission of this evidence was the prior admission of a statement made by Yaccarino at the time of the water damage. Linda Chewning, a Scrimshaw employee, testified that she was working in the warehouse on the night in question. During cross-examination by defense counsel, she testified that Yaccarino had run into the office kitchen screaming words to the effect of "oh my God, Neil did something stupid, [threw] something, now he has got a mess. . . I can't believe it. He is so stupid. He threw it. He is stupid, he is dumb." Yaccarino was deceased at the time of trial. The District Court admitted his statement as hearsay under the excited utterance exception in Fed.R.Evid. 803(2).

Yaccarino's statement was important to appellants' defense because it purportedly provided contemporaneous evidence supporting their claim that Neil accidentally had broken the sprinkler head. Accordingly, the government sought to attack the statement by impeaching Yaccarino's credibility. The government asked the District Court to take judicial notice of two New Jersey Supreme Court decisions ordering Yaccarino's removal from the bench and disbarment for unethical conduct, as well as the factual details supporting those decisions, which reflected his unethical conduct.[9]

---

[9] The extent of Yaccarino's unethical conduct was substantial. Among other things, Yaccarino had attempted to buy real estate that was the subject of litigation before him and, after learning that the property owner had recorded incriminating statements he had made, Yaccarino attempted to persuade the property owner to submit a false affidavit or give false testi-

Appellants objected to that evidence on the grounds that the credibility of a hearsay declarant may not be impeached with extrinsic evidence of bad acts, and that the danger of unfair prejudice from this evidence substantially outweighed its probative value. Overruling these objections, the District Court took judicial notice of the two New Jersey Supreme Court decisions and their factual underpinnings. Appellants renew their objections to this evidence, and raise new challenges on the grounds that judicial notice of the facts in the two court opinions was not proper, and that the District Court conveyed an unfavorable assessment of Yaccarino's credibility to the jury in taking such judicial notice.

Appellants first argue that the judicially noticed evidence was admitted improperly because, although Federal Rule of Evidence 806 provides for the impeachment of a hearsay declarant, it limits that impeachment to "any evidence which would be admissible for [impeachment purposes] . . . if declarant had testified as a witness." Here, the judicially noticed evidence involved specific instances of Yaccarino's misconduct and, as the government acknowledged at trial, constituted extrinsic evidence. Federal Rule of Evidence 608(b) states:

> Specific instances of the conduct of a witness, for the purpose of attacking or supporting the witness' credibility, other than conviction of crime as provided in rule 609, may not be proved by extrinsic evidence. They may, however, in the discretion of the court, if probative of truthfulness or untruthfulness, be inquired into on cross-examination of the witness (1) concerning the witness' character for truthfulness or untruthfulness, or (2) concerning the character for truthfulness or untruthfulness of another witness as to which character the witness being cross-examined has testified.

Appellants argue that if Yaccarino had testified, Rule 608(b) would have prevented the government from introducing extrinsic evidence of his unethical conduct, and would have limited the government to questioning him about that conduct on cross-examination. Thus, appellants argue, judicial notice of the evidence constituted improper impeachment of a hearsay declarant. The government correctly avers that it would have been allowed to inquire into Yaccarino's misconduct on cross-examination if he had testified at trial because Rule 806 allows a party against whom a hearsay statement is admitted to call the declarant as a witness and "to examine the declarant on the statement as if under cross-examination." Because Yaccarino's death foreclosed eliciting the facts of his misconduct in this manner, the government argues that it was entitled to introduce extrinsic evidence of his misconduct. In effect, the government argues that, read in concert, Rules 806 and 608(b) permit the introduction of extrinsic evidence of misconduct when a hearsay declarant is unavailable to testify.

* * *

---

mony in court which would exonerate him. Yaccarino also failed to disclose his interest in two liquor licenses that he held in violation of New Jersey law.

We . . . conclude that Rule 806 does not modify Rule 608(b)'s ban on extrinsic evidence of prior bad acts in the context of hearsay declarants, even when those declarants are unavailable to testify. We perceive our holding to be dictated by the plain—albeit imperfectly meshed—language of Rules 806 and 608(b). As discussed, Rule 806 allows impeachment of a hearsay declarant only to the extent that impeachment would be permissible had the declarant testified as a witness, which, in the case of specific instances of misconduct, is limited to cross-examination under Rule 608(b). The asserted basis for declining to adhere to the clear thrust of these rules is that the only avenue for using information of prior bad acts to impeach the credibility of a witness—cross-examination—is closed if the hearsay declarant cannot be called to testify. We are unpersuaded by this rationale. First, the unavailability of the declarant will not always foreclose using prior misconduct as an impeachment tool because the witness testifying to the hearsay statement may be questioned about the declarant's misconduct—without reference to extrinsic evidence thereof—on cross-examination concerning knowledge of the declarant's character for truthfulness or untruthfulness. And, even if a hearsay declarant's credibility may not be impeached with evidence of prior misconduct, other avenues for impeaching the hearsay statement remain open. For example, the credibility of the hearsay declarant—and indeed that of the witness testifying to the hearsay statement—may be impeached with opinion and reputation evidence of character under Rule 608(a), evidence of criminal convictions under Rule 609, and evidence of prior inconsistent statements under Rule 613. The unavailability of one form of impeachment, under a specific set of circumstances, does not justify overriding the plain language of the Rules of Evidence.

We also read the language of Rule 806 implicitly to reject the asserted rationale for lifting the ban on extrinsic evidence. Rule 806 makes no allowance for the unavailability of a hearsay declarant in the context of impeachment by specific instances of misconduct, but makes such an allowance in the context of impeachment by prior inconsistent statements. Rule 613 requires that a witness be given the opportunity to admit or deny a prior inconsistent statement before extrinsic evidence of that statement may be introduced. If a hearsay declarant does not testify, however, this requirement will not usually be met. Rule 806 cures any problem over the admissibility of a non-testifying declarant's prior inconsistent statement by providing that evidence of the statement "is not subject to any requirement that the declarant may have been afforded an opportunity to deny or explain." *See generally* Fed.R.Evid. 806 advisory committee's notes. The fact that Rule 806 does not provide a comparable allowance for the unavailability of a hearsay declarant in the context of Rule 608(b)'s ban on extrinsic evidence indicates that the latter's ban on extrinsic evidence applies with equal force in the context of hearsay declarants.

In reaching this conclusion, we are mindful of its consequences. Upholding the ban on extrinsic evidence in the case of a hearsay declarant may require the party against whom the hearsay statement was admitted to call the declarant to testify, even though it was the party's adversary who adduced the statement requiring impeachment in the first place. And, as here, where the declarant is unavailable to testify, the ban prevents using evidence of prior misconduct as a form of impeachment, unless the witness testifying to the hearsay has knowledge of the declarant's misconduct. Nevertheless, these possible drawbacks may not override the language of Rules 806 and 608(b), and do not outweigh the reason for Rule 608(b)'s ban on extrinsic evidence in the first place, which is "to avoid minitrials on wholly collateral matters which tend to distract and confuse the jury . . . and to prevent unfair surprise arising from false allegations of improper conduct."

From our conclusion that the ban on extrinsic evidence of misconduct applies in the context of hearsay declarants, it follows that the District Court's ruling admitting evidence of Yaccarino's misconduct was based on an incorrect interpretation of Rules 806 and 608(b). We conclude, therefore, that the District Court erred in admitting such evidence. Nevertheless, we find the error to be harmless. * * *

See Federal Rules of Evidence 608(b); California Evidence Code § 787.

B. PRIOR CONVICTIONS

Reasoning About Defoe

At first I thought it was very unlikely, if Defoe committed robbery, he would be willing to lie about it. But now that I know he committed forgery a year before, that possibility seems substantially more likely[*]

United States v. Sanders

United States Court of Appeals, Fourth Circuit, 1992.
964 F.2d 295.

■ PHILLIPS, CIRCUIT JUDGE:

Carlos Sanders appeals his convictions for assault with a dangerous weapon with intent to do bodily harm in violation of 18 U.S.C. § 113(c), and for possession of contraband (a shank used in the assault) in violation of Virginia Code § 53.1–203(4), as assimilated by 18 U.S.C. § 13. Because we believe that the district court erred by admitting evidence of Sanders' prior convictions for assault and possession of a contraband shank and that the error was prejudicial as to his assault conviction, we reverse that conviction and remand for a new trial. But we find the error harmless as to his contraband possession conviction, and affirm it.

---

[*] Richard Friedman, Character Impeachment Evidence: Psycho–Bayesian[!?] Analysis and a Proposed Overhaul, 38 UCLA L.Rev. 637, 637 (1991) (prologue).

I

On March 6, 1990, Sanders and Ricky Alston, both inmates at Lorton Reformatory, were indicted for assault with intent to commit murder and possession of a knife or shank. The indictment charged Sanders and Alston with assaulting fellow inmate Bobby Jenkins with a shank on April 7, 1989.

Before trial, Sanders filed a motion *in limine* to exclude evidence of his prior convictions. Although the district court granted this motion in part by prohibiting the government from questioning Sanders about a stabbing for which he was acquitted and an armed robbery for which his conviction was reversed, the court declined to preclude the government from cross-examining Sanders about his prior assault and contraband possession convictions. The court ruled that the assault and contraband convictions were admissible under Federal Rules of Evidence 609(a) and 404(b).

After hearing the evidence, the jury acquitted Alston on the assault count and convicted Sanders of possession of a shank. The jury was unable to reach a verdict on the assault count against Sanders, however. The district court accordingly declared a mistrial as to that count and set it for retrial.

Before his second trial, Sanders renewed his motion *in limine* to exclude his previous convictions for assault and possession of contraband. The district court denied the renewed motion. At trial, Sanders testified that he had acted in self-defense, claiming that Jenkins had attacked him first. The government cross-examined Sanders about his prior convictions as follows:

Q: You testified on direct that you are a convicted felon.

A: Yes, sir.

Q: And in fact you were convicted in 1988 for committing an assault in Lorton, weren't you?

A: Yes, sir.

Q: And you were also convicted of prisoner in possession of contraband at that time?

A: Yes, sir.

Q: You were convicted because you stabbed an inmate named Silas Horn (phonetic)–

J.A. at 249. At this point, Sanders' counsel objected to any further questioning about the nature of the prior convictions and the district court sustained the objection. Trial was concluded in a half a day; the jury deliberated the rest of that day and into the next before returning a verdict of the lesser included offense of assault with a dangerous weapon with intent to do bodily harm. This appeal followed. Sanders challenges both his conviction of contraband possession on the first trial and of assault on the second.

II

Sanders argues that the district court abused its discretion by admitting evidence of his prior convictions under Federal Rules of Evidence 609(a) and 404(b), respectively. We address the admissibility of the prior convictions under each of these rules in turn.

A

At the time of trial,[3] Federal Rule of Evidence 609(a) provided that:

> For the purpose of attacking the credibility of a witness, evidence that the witness has been convicted of a crime shall be admitted if elicited from the witness or established by public record during cross-examination but only if the crime (1) was punishable by death or imprisonment in excess of one year under the law under which the witness was convicted, and the court determines that the probative value of admitting this evidence outweighs its prejudicial effect to the defendant, or (2) involved dishonesty or false statement, regardless of the punishment.

Sanders' convictions for assault and possession of contraband fall under 609(a)(1), and the district court therefore was required to balance the probative value of the evidence against its prejudicial effect in assessing its admissibility. Here, although evidence of the prior convictions may be thought somehow generally probative of Sanders' lack of credibility, they were extremely prejudicial since they involved the exact type of conduct for which Sanders was on trial.

We have recognized the prejudice that results from admitting evidence of a similar offense under Rule 609:

> Admission of evidence of a similar offense often does little to impeach the credibility of a testifying defendant while undoubtedly prejudicing him. The jury, despite limiting instructions, can hardly avoid drawing the inference that the past conviction suggests some probability that defendant committed the similar offense for which he is currently charged. The generally accepted view, therefore, is that evidence of similar offenses for impeachment purposes under Rule 609 should be admitted sparingly if at all.

United States v. Beahm, 664 F.2d 414, 418–19 (4th Cir.1981) (footnote omitted). In *Beahm,* the defendant was accused of taking indecent liberties with children, and the district court allowed admission of two prior convictions for similar offenses, one of which fell under Rule 609(b) because it was over ten years old. We found that the district court erred by admitting the

---

[3] The Rule has since been amended in a way irrelevant to this appeal. Fed.R.Evid. 609(a) (amendment effective Dec. 1, 1990).

prior convictions. In discussing the conviction that fell under Rule 609(a)(1), we explained:

> We think that it is doubtful if this conviction could ever serve as the basis for impeachment. It was remote in time, almost falling within the presumptive bar of Rule 609(b). It was for a similar offense, an odious one likely to inflame the jury and thus prejudice defendant. Moreover, it was an offense that had minimal if any bearing on the likelihood that defendant would testify truthfully. But in any event, defendant was denied the safeguards of Rule 609(a). The district court failed to determine as a prerequisite to use of the evidence that the probative value of the conviction for impeachment purposes outweighed its prejudicial effect to the defendant as required by Rule 609(a).

Although Sanders' prior convictions were not as remote in time as the prior conviction at issue in *Beahm,* all of the other reasons for holding the evidence inadmissible in *Beahm* apply equally well to Sanders. It is unclear whether and how the district court may have sought to balance the probative value of this evidence against its prejudicial effect, since at the hearing on Sanders' motion *in limine* the district judge simply stated, "[t]hey [the government] are entitled to go into that [Sanders' prior convictions] both on the question of intent and impeachment." Even if the district court had explicitly conducted a balancing inquiry before admitting this evidence, we would find the evidence inadmissible under Rule 609(a) because of the high likelihood of prejudice that accompanies the admission of such similar prior convictions. As we stated in *Beahm,*

> [w]here as here the offense sought to be admitted against defendant had little bearing on his propensity to tell the truth, the district court should have recognized that the substantial likelihood of prejudice outweighed the minimal impeachment value of the evidence, and refused to admit the evidence, . . . or at the very least limited disclosure to the fact of conviction without revealing its nature.

We therefore hold that Sanders' prior convictions were not admissible under Rule 609(a).

B

In the alternative, the district court held that Sanders' prior convictions were admissible under Rule 404(b) to show Sanders' intent to commit both crimes charged.

* * *

Since Sanders admitted the stabbing and claimed only that in doing so he acted in self-defense, the only factual issue in the case was whether that was the reason for the admitted act. The fact that Sanders had committed an assault on another prisoner and possessed contraband one year earlier had nothing to do with his reason for—his intent in—stabbing Jenkins. All that the evidence of the prior conviction of assault could possibly show was Sanders' propensity to commit assaults on other prisoners or his general propensity to commit violent crimes. The total lack of any probative value in the contraband possession conviction, except to show general criminal disposition, is even more <u>stark.</u> This is exactly the kind of propensity inference that Rule 404(b)'s built-in limitation was designed to prevent.

Unlike several of our cases relied upon by the government, this is not a case where prior convictions are relevant to the defendant's knowledge or absence of mistake. In contrast to the crimes involved in those cases, assault with a shank is not the kind of crime in which knowledge is even implicitly at issue. The government did not need to prove that Sanders knew how to stab Jenkins, that was not in issue. Sanders admitted the act, hence knowledge of how to do it, and that it was no mistake. Because Sanders' prior convictions could only "prove the character of [Sanders] in order to show action and conformity therewith," we hold that the district court erred in admitting this evidence under Rule 404(b).[4]

* * *

AFFIRMED IN PART, REVERSED IN PART, AND REMANDED.

■ NIEMEYER, CIRCUIT JUDGE, dissenting:

When Sanders claimed that he stabbed a fellow inmate in self defense, he placed at issue his intent which prompted or accompanied the stabbing. Because the government alleged that the stabbing was performed with assaultive intent, the issue was drawn. Although it is certainly true that Sanders' admission that he stabbed the inmate is relevant, the admission does not eliminate the need for determining whether self-defense provided the motive, as he claims, or the stabbing was accompanied by assaultive intent, as the government claims.

While I have had enormous difficulty in sorting out, in a principled manner, when evidence is not relevant to intent but "proves only criminal disposition," I have little difficulty in concluding that in this case intent was made an issue and that therefore evidence of a prior assault, which is probative of intent, is admissible under Rule 404(b). The admission of evidence is a matter of discretion committed to the trial court, and I cannot in the circumstances conclude that the district judge abused this discretion.

I would therefore affirm, and respectfully dissent.

---

[4] Admission of evidence under Rule 404(b) remains subject to the general limitation in Rule 403 that relevant evidence is admissible unless "its probative value is substantially outweighed by the danger of unfair prejudice * * *" Fed.R.Evidence 403. See Huddleston v. United States, 485 U.S. 681, 688, 108 S.Ct. 1496, 1500, 99 L.Ed.2d 771 (1988). Sanders argues that even if we did find that the prior crimes were relevant to proving intent, they should have been excluded under the Rule 403 balance. In view of our disposition, we need not address that alternative argument.

NOTE

A typical list of factors to be considered in deciding whether to exclude a prior conviction offered to impeach the accused is set forth in United States v. Sloman, 909 F.2d 176, 181 (6th Cir.1990). The factors listed there are:

1. The impeachment value of the prior crime.

2. The point in time of the conviction and the witness' subsequent history.

3. The similarity between the past crime and the charged crime.

4. The importance of the defendant's testimony.

5. The centrality of the credibility issue.

The third factor, similarity between the past crime and the charged crime, can have a double effect. When the issue is whether a prior conviction is admissible to impeach, similarity of the crimes cuts against admission of the evidence. The greater the similarity, the greater the danger that the jurors will use the prior crime as evidence of propensity to commit the charged crime, rather than using it properly as evidence of propensity to lie. In contrast, similarity weighs in favor of admission if the evidence is also offered under Rule 404(b) on the theory that it shows plan or modus operandi. If one takes this web of doctrine seriously, the accused must then argue that the prior crime falls within a middle area in which it is too similar to be received to impeach, but not similar enough to be received as substantive evidence.

Dont want too similar of crimes. if 609(a)

The first factor, impeachment value, reflects the belief that some felonies have a greater bearing on one's truth-telling than others. A classic example is the defendant who was previously convicted of killing a person in a duel, and who entered the duel because of an exaggerated sense of honor.

Defendants often argue that crimes of violence do not reflect on truth-telling as much as crimes of greed or dishonesty. Following this theory, one would think that sex crimes would rarely be admitted to impeach, especially when the past crime is similar to the one charged. Yet Bryden and Park[*] found that many modern courts are willing to admit prior sex crimes to impeach a defendant charged with rape. Although these authors support broadening the substantive admissibility of prior sex crimes in acquaintance rape cases, they argue that the impeachment theory is invalid:

> The impeachment theory of admission verges on being a transparent fiction. Few if any attorneys believe that juries actually follow the limiting instruction, or even understand it. In addition, it is doubtful that the evidence has significant value for its permitted purpose of determining credibility. It may be true that a convicted rapist is generally more likely to lie than a law-abiding person. When evidence is offered to impeach a defendant who testifies in his own defense at trial, however, the proposition that felons have a general propensity to lie is beside the point. If the accused is in fact innocent, he presumably will have no occasion to lie even if

---

[*] David P. Bryden and Roger C. Park, "Other Crimes" Evidence in Sex Offense Cases, 78 Minn.L.Rev. 529, 535–37 (1994).

he is a dishonest person, as shown by prior crimes. On the other hand, if he is guilty in fact, but has pleaded not guilty and testified on his own behalf, he presumably will lie about the rape, even if he is a generally truthful person and has no prior convictions. In either case, therefore, his prior conviction is unhelpful to the jury except for the forbidden purpose of determining whether he has a propensity to rape.

If the accused is innocent of the crime at bar, then prior-conviction impeachment defeats justice because it makes his denial appear false when it is not. If the accused is guilty, then prior-conviction impeachment still does not illuminate his truthfulness unless one assumes that a guilty person with a clean record would be less likely to lie to obtain an acquittal. In view of the guilty defendant's strong incentive to lie on the stand, it is doubtful that those with clean records are much more credible than those with prior convictions.

In short, the danger that the jury will use the evidence for the powerful and appealing, but forbidden, inference that the defendant has a tendency to rape outweighs its meager probative value for the permitted inference that the defendant has a greater-than-average propensity to lie. In any event, instructing a jury to follow only the permitted thought-path is like telling someone to ignore every flavor in an apple pie except the cinnamon.[20]

Can the same argument be made even when the prior crime is a crime of dishonesty, if the charged crime is a truly serious one? See generally Richard Friedman, Character Impeachment Evidence: Psycho–Bayesian [!?] Analysis and a Proposed Overhaul, 38 UCLA L.Rev. 637 (1991).

California Constitution Art. 1, § 28

(f)(4) **Use of Prior Convictions.** Any prior felony conviction of any person in any criminal proceeding, whether adult or juvenile, shall subsequently be used without limitation for purposes of impeachment or enhancement of sentence in any criminal proceeding. When a prior felony conviction is an element of any felony offense, it shall be proven to the trier of fact in open court.

(Added by Initiative Measure, approved by the people, June 8, 1982, known as "The Victims' Bill of Rights").

NOTES

On its face, Article I, § 28(f)(4) seems to mandate completely free impeachment with prior felony convictions. However, in People v. Castro, 696 P.2d 111 (1985), the California Supreme Court held that the amendment still left in place California Evidence Code § 352, and that under § 352, felony convictions were admissible to impeach only if they involved "moral turpitude."

---

[20] For an example of a social science study indicating that the limiting instruction does not function properly, see Roselle L. Wissler & Michael J. Saks, On the Inefficacy of Limiting Instructions: When Jurors Use Prior Conviction Evidence to Decide on Guilt, 9 Law & Hum. Behav. 37 (1985).

The related questions of which prior convictions *may* be used to impeach a witness and whether the trial judge should have discretion to *exclude* any such convictions have been a frequent source of contention throughout the history of the Federal Rules.

In keeping with traditional law, the Advisory Committee for the Rules proposed to make two categories of prior convictions admissible for impeachment: crimes punishable by death or imprisonment for at least one year (felonies) and crimes involving dishonesty or false statement (so-called *crimen falsi*). One of the Committee's early drafts of Rule 609(a), released for public comment, would have expressly given the trial judge discretion to exclude convictions falling within either category if it determined that their prejudicial effect substantially outweighed their probative value. Senator John McClellan of Arkansas vigorously objected to this provision, and when the Supreme Court submitted the Rules to Congress Rule 609 made no mention of the trial judge's discretion.

This Rule then became the subject of much debate in Congress. The House bill provided for impeachment *only* by crimes of dishonesty or false statement. The Senate Judiciary Committee proposed a modification of the House version; it would also have allowed use of felonies to impeach witnesses other than defendants. The full Senate, however, restored the Rule as it was submitted to Congress, allowing impeachment of any witness by either type of conviction. The Conference Committee adopted the Senate version, but with a modification: (1) A felony conviction could be admitted to impeach any witness, but only if the trial judge determined that the probative value of the conviction outweighed its prejudicial effect "to the defendant." Rule 609(a)(1). (2) Crimes of dishonesty or false statement "shall be admitted" to impeach any witness, without regard to the punishment imposed. Rule 609(a)(2).

The "to the defendant" language of Rule 609(a)(1) was a source of some confusion, as illustrated by Green v. Bock Laundry Machine Co., 490 U.S. 504, 109 S.Ct. 1981, 104 L.Ed.2d 557 (1989). Green, a prisoner, sued to recover for a workplace injury, the loss of an arm in a large drying machine, and he testified in his own behalf. The defendant sought to impeach him with his prior convictions for burglary and conspiracy to commit burglary. Green contended that those convictions should have been excluded because they were unduly prejudicial to him. The majority of a splintered Supreme Court held that Congress had meant what it said, sort of, when it said that prejudice "to the defendant" could be taken into account in determining whether a felony conviction could be admitted for impeachment. In the Court's view, the discretion to exclude on grounds of prejudice applied only when the witness was a criminal defendant. Green, a civil litigant, was out of luck; Rule 609(a)(1) mandated admission of his convictions.

The next year, the Court promulgated an amendment to the Rule providing a somewhat different resolution: If the witness being impeached is a criminal defendant testifying on his own behalf, a prior felony conviction (not involving dishonesty or false statement) may be admitted to impeach him only if the probative value outweighs the prejudicial impact, and if the witness is anyone else such a conviction may be admitted for impeachment if the usual stan-dard of Rule 403 – which puts thumb on the side of the scale favoring admissi-bility – is satisfied.

Rule 609(a)(2) also provided interpretive difficulties. Notwithstanding the seemingly unqualified "shall be admitted" language that governed it, some de-fendants contended that it was subject to the general balancing test of Rule 403. The courts roundly rejected this contention. For example, in United States v. Wong, 703 F.2d 65 (3d Cir. 1983), the accused, charged with seven-teen counts of mail fraud, among others, moved to preclude use of his two prior convictions, for mail fraud and Medicare fraud, on the ground that they would be more prejudicial than probative. But the court said:

> As the First Circuit has recently noted, Rule 403 was not designed to override more specific rules; rather it was "designed as a guide for the handling of situations for which no specific rules have been formulated."

> Rule 609(a) is such a specific rule. It was the product of extensive Congressional attention and considerable legislative compromise, clearly reflecting a decision that judges were to have no discretion to exclude *crimen falsi*.

In reviewing the history of the Rule, the court noted that the Chairman of the Subcommittee on Criminal Justice of the House Judiciary Committee said: "The conference rule provides that evidence of a conviction of a crime involving dishonesty or false statement may always be used to impeach." And the court also quoted the Conference Report: "Such convictions are particularly proba-tive of credibility and, under this rule, are always to be admitted."

A 2006 amendment to Rule 609(a)(2) was intended to resolve another un-certainty by making clear that, for example, a prior conviction for murder should not be considered one involving dishonesty or false statement even if the witness now being impeached acted deceitfully in the course of committing that particular crime. Rather, for a conviction to come within Rule 609(a)(2), the court must be able to determine readily that the witness could have been con-victed of the prior crime only if the trier of fact found, or the witness admitted, that he had acted deceitfully. Usually this determination can be made from the statutory elements of the prior crime, but it might be made from such materials as the indictment, jury instructions, or a statement of agreed facts. As an ex-ample, consider United States v. Jefferson, 623 F.3d 227, 233-34 (5th Cir. 2010). The court noted that if Jefferson testified and the prosecution offered his prior conviction for obstruction of justice, Rule 609(a)(2) would mandate admission. Although the statutory elements of obstruction of justice do not necessarily require dishonesty or false statement for conviction, the indictment in the earlier case charged that Jefferson knowingly and corruptly attempted to persuade a witness to lie to federal law enforcement authorities; therefore, it was apparent from the indictment that to convict him the factfinder had to find an act of dishonesty or false statement.

Rule 609(a) was further amended in 2011, without changing its substance, as part of the general restyling of the Federal Rules. As it now stands (and subject to limitations stated in the subsequent portions of Rule 609), Rule 609(a) provides the following:

• If the prior crime is a felony and the witness is *not* now the defendant in a criminal case, the trial court must admit the conviction, unless the court concludes that the evidence should be excluded under the usual standard of Rule 403. Subdiv. (a)(1)(A).

• If the prior crime is a felony and the witness *is* the defendant in a criminal case, the trial court must admit the conviction *if* its probative value outweighs its prejudicial effect on that defendant. Subdiv. (a)(1)(B).

• If the court can readily determine that establishing the elements of the prior crime required proof or admission of a dishonest act or false statement, then the evidence must be admitted, no matter what the punishment and whether or not the witness is now a criminal defendant. Subdiv. (a)(2).

United States v. Brackeen

United States Court of Appeals, Ninth Circuit, En Banc, 1992.
969 F.2d 827.

■ PER CURIAM:

This court has convened en banc to determine whether bank robbery necessarily involves "dishonesty," as that term is used in Federal Rule of Evidence 609(a)(2). The question arises in the context of whether a witness can be impeached by evidence of prior convictions. Faced with intra-circuit precedents which provide irreconcilably conflicting answers to the question, the original panel called *sua sponte* for en banc review. We now conclude that for purposes of Rule 609(a)(2) bank robbery is not per se a crime of "dishonesty."

FACTS AND PROCEEDINGS BELOW

Robert Nello Brackeen robbed three different banks, one bank a day on each of three separate days in July 1990. In the first robbery, Brackeen and an accomplice, Jermaine Moore, presented a threatening note to a teller. Bank surveillance photos showed Moore with a pistol, which he pointed at the teller. During the robbery, Brackeen and Moore acted in close proximity to each other. In the other two robberies, Brackeen was unarmed and apparently acted alone.

Brackeen was charged in a single indictment with one count of aiding and abetting an armed bank robbery, in violation of 18 U.S.C. §§ 2, 2113(a), 2113(d) (1988), and two counts of unarmed bank robbery, in violation of 18 U.S.C. § 2113(a). On September 24, 1990, Brackeen pleaded guilty to both unarmed bank robberies. On October 2, 1990, Brackeen went to trial on count one of the indictment, aiding and abetting Moore in the armed bank robbery. He claimed he did not know Moore had a gun.

On the second day of the two-day trial, Brackeen indicated he would testify, and objected before taking the stand to the use for impeachment of his guilty pleas to the two unarmed bank robberies. The court reserved its ruling on the objection until after Brackeen testified. Brackeen was the sole defense witness. On cross-examination, the court allowed impeachment with the guilty pleas.

The trial court's basis for admitting the prior guilty pleas as impeachment evidence was Federal Rule of Evidence 609(a)(2), which allows impeachment of a defendant by any crime involving "dishonesty or false statement." The court expressly refused to admit the pleas under Rule 609(a)(1), which allows impeachment using any felony "if the court determines that the probative value of admitting this evidence outweighs its prejudicial effect to the accused * * *." The court stated: "No. I don't think under Rule 609(a)(1) that I would let it in * * *. I don't think I could make that analysis under Rule 609(a)(1) so I'm going to base my ruling on Rule 609(a)(2) that this is a crime involving dishonesty and the government has an absolute right to use it to impeach him."

Brackeen appeals, claiming the impeachment was improper because (1) at the time of his trial, judgment had not yet been entered on his guilty pleas,[1] and (2) the guilty pleas were to bank robbery, a crime that does not involve "dishonesty or false statement" as required by Rule 609(a)(2). The original panel called for en banc proceedings to decide the second issue, and the full court granted en banc review.

ANALYSIS

* * * [T]he only issue in this case is whether bank robbery is per se a crime of "dishonesty" under Rule 609, regardless of the means by which it is perpetrated. * * *

Our first step in interpreting any statute or rule is to consider the plain meaning of the provision in question. Often, this will be the end of the analysis, because the words of the provision allow but one interpretation and preclude others.

Unfortunately, "dishonesty" has more than one meaning. In the dictionary, and in everyday use, "dishonesty" has two meanings, one of which includes, and one of which excludes, crimes such as bank robbery. In its broader meaning, "dishonesty" is defined as a breach of trust, a "lack of * * * probity or integrity in principle," "lack of fairness," or a "disposition to * * * betray." Webster's Third New International Dictionary 650 (1986 unabridged ed.). This dictionary states, under the heading "synonyms," that "dishonest may apply to any breach of honesty or trust, as lying, deceiving, cheating, stealing, or defrauding." Id. Bank robbery fits within this definition of "dishonesty" because it is a betrayal of principles of fairness and probity, a breach of community trust, like stealing.

In its narrower meaning, however, "dishonesty" is defined as deceitful behavior, a "disposition to defraud * * * [or] deceive," id., or a "[d]isposition to lie, cheat, or defraud," Black's Law Dictionary 421 (5th ed. 1979). Bank

---

[1] Brackeen did not raise this issue in the district court. Accordingly, we deem the issue waived, and do not consider it in this opinion.

robbery does not fit within this definition of "dishonesty" because it is a crime of violent, not deceitful, taking. Everyday usage mirrors the dictionary: we use "dishonesty" narrowly to refer to a liar, and broadly to refer to a thief.

Fortunately, we are not operating in a vacuum: while nothing in the *text* of Rule 609 indicates precisely what Congress meant when it used the term "dishonesty," we find guidance in the legislative history of the rule. As the Supreme Court has stated in another context, "[w]e begin by considering the extent to which the text of Rule 609 answers the question before us. Concluding that the text is ambiguous * * * we then seek guidance from legislative history * * *." Green v. Bock Laundry Machine Co., 490 U.S. 504, 508–09, 109 S.Ct. 1981, 1984, 104 L.Ed.2d 557 (1989). We look to the Advisory Committee's Note to the Rule, and to the relevant House and Senate Conference Committee Reports, which are legitimate sources of legislative history.

The legislative history of Rule 609 makes clear that Congress used the term "dishonesty" in the narrower sense, to mean only those crimes which involve deceit. The House Conference Committee Report on Rule 609 states:

> By the phrase "dishonesty and false statement" the Conference means crimes such as perjury or subornation of perjury, false statement, criminal fraud, embezzlement, or false pretense, or any other offense *in the nature of crimen falsi,* the commission of which involves some element of deceit, untruthfulness, or falsification bearing on the accused's propensity to testify truthfully. [Emphasis added by Court].

The Senate Judiciary Committee Report contains substantially the same language.

Bank robbery is not "in the nature of crimen falsi." Black's Law Dictionary defines "crimen falsi" as follows: "Term generally refers to crimes in the nature of perjury or subornation of perjury, false statement, criminal fraud, embezzlement, false pretense, or any other offense which involves some element of deceitfulness, untruthfulness, or falsification bearing on witness' propensity to testify truthfully." Black's Law Dictionary 335 (5th ed. 1979).

* * *

CONCLUSION

Congress intended Rule 609(a)(2) to apply only to those crimes that factually or by definition entail some element of misrepresentation or deceit, and not to " 'those crimes which, bad though they are, do not carry with them a tinge of falsification.' " We must follow Congress' intent. Brackeen's conviction is REVERSED, and the case is REMANDED for a new trial.

Abby's View

DEAR ABBY: My husband and I went on a two-week trip last year and hired a woman to stay in our home and look after our children.

After we came home, I couldn't find my favorite pair of earrings. They were only costume jewelry, but I liked them and wore them with many outfits.

Last evening my husband and I went to a movie, and as we came out, there was this friend who stayed at our home last year, wearing my earrings! Up until that time I wanted to believe that I had just misplaced them. Needless to say, I was shocked. Shall I ask her to return my earrings? Or should I just wait and hope she reads your column and brings them back?

MRS. A

DEAR MRS. A: Ask, but don't expect her to return them. Any one who would steal would probably lie.

HYPOTHETICALS

1. Betsy Borden is accused of murdering her father. In her defense, she calls her minister as a character witness. He testifies to her peaceable and nonviolent reputation. She also testifies in her own behalf to an alibi defense.

The prosecution has evidence that within the past five years Borden was convicted of the following offenses:

a. Petty larceny, a misdemeanor punishable by six months in jail. The conviction arose from a shoplifting episode in which Borden was caught leaving a department store with items concealed on her person. When questioned by store personnel, she said that she had bought the items in another store.

b. Disturbing the peace, a misdemeanor punishable by six months in jail. The conviction arose from an incident in which Borden disrupted a restaurant by throwing her meal at the server.

Should the prosecution be allowed to make use of the prior convictions in any way at trial?

2. Buzzy Bedford is the principal prosecution witness in the Borden case. He testifies that he was delivering newspapers on the morning of the murder and saw Borden leaving the house in which the crime was committed. To impeach Buzzy, the defense offers evidence that six weeks before his testimony in the present case, Buzzy was arrested for possession of marijuana with intent to sell. The case against Buzzy is still pending and has not resulted in his conviction. Should the evidence be admitted?

3. X is prosecuted for the offense of having sexual intercourse with A, his 13-year-old stepdaughter. A testifies, with minimal impeachment of her testimony. X testifies in denial of the charge. To impeach X, the prosecution propos-

es to establish, through cross-examination of X, that he has suffered prior felony convictions of rape, sale of heroin, and grand theft, all occurring within the 10-year-period prior to the offense charged, and all felonies punishable by more than one year. X requests the court to preclude such cross-examination. How should the court rule?

Luce v. United States

Supreme Court of the United States, 1984.
469 U.S. 38, 105 S.Ct. 460, 83 L.Ed.2d 443.

■ CHIEF JUSTICE BURGER delivered the opinion of the Court.

We granted certiorari to resolve a conflict among the Circuits as to whether the defendant, who did not testify at trial, is entitled to review of the District Court's ruling denying his motion to forbid the use of a prior conviction to impeach his credibility.

I

Petitioner was indicted on charges of conspiracy, and possession of cocaine with intent to distribute, in violation of 21 U.S.C. §§ 846 and 841(a)(1). During his trial in the United States District Court for the Western District of Tennessee, petitioner moved for a ruling to preclude the Government from using a 1974 state conviction to impeach him if he testified. There was no commitment by petitioner that he would testify if the motion were granted, nor did he make a proffer to the court as to what his testimony would be. In opposing the motion, the Government represented that the conviction was for a serious crime—possession of a controlled substance.

The District Court ruled that the prior conviction fell within the category of permissible impeachment evidence under Federal Rule of Evidence 609(a). The District Court noted, however, that the nature and scope of petitioner's trial testimony could affect the court's specific evidentiary rulings; for example, the court was prepared to hold that the prior conviction would be excluded if petitioner limited his testimony to explaining his attempt to flee from the arresting officers. However, if petitioner took the stand and denied any prior involvement with drugs, he could then be impeached by the 1974 conviction. Petitioner did not testify, and the jury returned guilty verdicts.

II

The United States Court of Appeals for the Sixth Circuit affirmed. 713 F.2d 1236 (1983). The Court of Appeals refused to consider petitioner's contention that the District Court abused its discretion in denying the motion *in limine*[2] without making an explicit finding that the probative value of

---

[2] "*In limine* " has been defined as "[o]n or at the threshold; at the very beginning; preliminarily." Black's Law Dictionary 708 (5th ed. 1979). We use the term in a broad sense to refer to any motion, whether made before or during trial, to exclude anticipated prejudicial evidence before the evidence is actually offered.

the prior conviction outweighed its prejudicial effect. The Court of Appeals held that when the defendant does not testify, the court will not review the District Court's *in limine* ruling.

Some other Circuits have permitted review in similar situations; we granted certiorari to resolve the conflict. We affirm.

III

It is clear, of course, that had petitioner testified and been impeached by evidence of a prior conviction, the District Court's decision to admit the impeachment evidence would have been reviewable on appeal along with any other claims of error. The Court of Appeals would then have had a complete record detailing the nature of petitioner's testimony, the scope of the cross-examination, and the possible impact of the impeachment on the jury's verdict.

A reviewing court is handicapped in any effort to rule on subtle evidentiary questions outside a factual context.[3] This is particularly true under Rule 609(a)(1), which directs the court to weigh the probative value of a prior conviction against the prejudicial effect to the defendant. To perform this balancing, the court must know the precise nature of the defendant's testimony, which is unknowable when, as here, the defendant does not testify.[4]

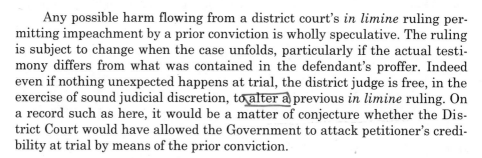

Any possible harm flowing from a district court's *in limine* ruling permitting impeachment by a prior conviction is wholly speculative. The ruling is subject to change when the case unfolds, particularly if the actual testimony differs from what was contained in the defendant's proffer. Indeed even if nothing unexpected happens at trial, the district judge is free, in the exercise of sound judicial discretion, to alter a previous *in limine* ruling. On a record such as here, it would be a matter of conjecture whether the District Court would have allowed the Government to attack petitioner's credibility at trial by means of the prior conviction.

When the defendant does not testify, the reviewing court also has no way of knowing whether the Government would have sought to impeach with the prior conviction. If, for example, the Government's case is strong, and the defendant is subject to impeachment by other means, a prosecutor might elect not to use an arguably inadmissible prior conviction.

Because an accused's decision whether to testify "seldom turns on the resolution of one factor," New Jersey v. Portash, 440 U.S. 450, 467, 99 S.Ct. 1292, 1301, 59 L.Ed.2d 501 (1979) (BLACKMUN, J., dissenting), a reviewing court cannot assume that the adverse ruling motivated a defendant's decision not to testify. In support of his motion a defendant might make a

---

[3] Although the Federal Rules of Evidence do not explicitly authorize *in limine* rulings, the practice has developed pursuant to the district court's inherent authority to manage the course of trials. See generally Fed.Rule Evid. 103(c); cf. Fed.Rule Crim.Proc. 12(e).

[4] Requiring a defendant to make a proffer of testimony is no answer; his trial testimony could, for any number of reasons, differ from the proffer.

commitment to testify if his motion is granted; but such a commitment is virtually risk free because of the difficulty of enforcing it.

Even if these difficulties could be surmounted, the reviewing court would still face the question of harmless error. Were *in limine* rulings under Rule 609(a) reviewable on appeal, almost any error would result in the windfall of automatic reversal; the appellate court could not logically term "harmless" an error that presumptively kept the defendant from testifying. Requiring that a defendant testify in order to preserve Rule 609(a) claims, will enable the reviewing court to determine the impact any erroneous impeachment may have had in light of the record as a whole; it will also tend to discourage making such motions solely to "plant" reversible error in the event of conviction.

* * *

We hold that to raise and preserve for review the claim of improper impeachment with a prior conviction, a defendant must testify. Accordingly, the judgment of the Court of Appeals is

Affirmed.

* * *

■ Justice Brennan, with whom Justice Marshall joins, concurring.

I join the opinion of the Court because I understand it to hold only that a defendant who does not testify at trial may not challenge on appeal an *in limine* ruling respecting admission of a prior conviction for purposes of impeachment under Rule 609(a) of the Federal Rules of Evidence. The Court correctly identifies two reasons for precluding appellate review unless the defendant testifies at trial. The careful weighing of probative value and prejudicial effect that Rule 609(a) requires of a district court can only be evaluated adequately on appeal in the specific factual context of a trial as it has unfolded. And if the defendant declines to testify, the reviewing court is handicapped in making the required harmless error determination should the district court's *in limine* ruling prove to have been incorrect.

I do not understand the Court to be deciding broader questions of appealability *vel non* of *in limine* rulings that do not involve Rule 609(a). * * *

NOTE

In Ohler v. United States, 529 U.S. 753 (2000), the defendant was charged with importation of marijuana and possession of marijuana with intent to sell. The government made a motion *in limine* asking the trial judge permit it to put into evidence the defendant's 1993 felony conviction for possession of methamphetamine. The defendant opposed the motion. On the first day of trial, the trial judge ruled that if defendant testified, evidence of her prior conviction would be admissible to impeach her under Rule 609. The defendant did testify. Defense counsel sought to "remove the sting" of her prior conviction by having her admit to it on direct examination, rather than remaining quiet about it and allowing the prosecution to reveal it to the jury for the first time on cross-examination. Citing *Luce*, a majority of the Supreme Court held that by revealing the conviction in her testimony on direct examination, the defendant forfeited the right to appeal the trial judge's prior decision that the conviction was admissible to impeach.

Forfeit right to appeal �'s

C. BAD REPUTATION FOR TRUTH AND VERACITY

O'Malley, Grenig & Lee, Federal Jury Practice and Instructions: Criminal

Vol. 1A, § 15.09 (6th ed. 2008)

§ 15.09 Credibility of witnesses—Bad reputation for truth and veracity.

The credibility of a *[witness] [defendant]* may be discredited or impeached by evidence showing that the general reputation of the *[witness] [defendant]* for truth and veracity is bad.

If you believe a *[witness] [defendant]* has been so impeached and thus discredited during this trial, it is your exclusive right to give the testimony of that impeached *[witness] [defendant]* such weight, if any, you think it deserves.

You may consider this evidence of bad reputation for truthfulness as one of the circumstances you assess in determining whether or not to believe the testimony of that *[witness] [defendant]*.

QUESTIONS

(1) Is this model instruction correct in giving the court the option of speaking of a defendant?

(2) Should this model instruction address opinion evidence as well as reputation evidence?

(3) Should it address evidence of good character as well as evidence of bad character?

(4) The first edition of the O'Malley, Grenig & Lee work said, "Evidence that the witness' reputation for truth and veracity has not been discussed or, if discussed, those traits of the witness' character have not been questioned, may be sufficient to warrant an inference of good reputation as to those traits of character." Mathes & Devitt, Federal Jury Practice § 9.10 (1965). Do you agree?

See Federal Rules of Evidence 608; California Evidence Code § 786.

HYPOTHETICAL

X is prosecuted for the sale of heroin to A, an informer for the police. A testifies that he made a purchase of heroin from X in a dimly lit bar, and that this was part of a "buy" program that covered a three-month period, with A's purchase from X coming in the second month. X's defense is an alibi. X calls B to testify that he has been a next-door neighbor to A for 10 years and has attended many social affairs which A also attended, and that A has a reputation in the community for having a bad memory. The prosecutor objects to the proposed testimony of B as improper impeachment evidence. What result?

3. PSYCHIATRIC CONDITION

United States v. Lindstrom

United States Court of Appeals, Eleventh Circuit, 1983.
698 F.2d 1154.

■ VANCE, CIRCUIT JUDGE:

[Dennis Slater and Joanne Lindstrom appealed convictions and sentences for mail fraud and conspiracy to commit mail fraud. The convictions centered around the activities of Bay Therapy, Inc., an entity that purported to provide physical therapy treatment to injured persons. The two defendants were among the owners of Bay Therapy. The indictment charged that the defendants, as part of a scheme to inflate medical costs and defraud insurance companies, caused patients to be sent to Bay Therapy for treatment they did not need and often did not receive. The government's key witness testified that during the period when she was overseeing operations at Bay Therapy, she had discussed alteration of the records with the defendants, that she and Lindstrom had in fact altered records, and that Slater and Lindstrom had ordered her to duplicate billing cards and that patients signed up for treatments they did not receive. The jury found both defendants guilty. One of their grounds for appeal was their contention that the trial judge improperly placed limitations on defense questioning of the government's chief witness relating to her prior psychiatric treatment and confinement.]

The sixth amendment to the United States Constitution mandates that a criminal defendant has the right "to be confronted with the witnesses against him." The Supreme Court has repeatedly emphasized that its "cases construing the [confrontation] clause hold that a primary interest secured by it is the right of cross-examination." * * *

One goal of effective cross-examination is to impeach the credibility of opposing witnesses. * * *

Certain forms of mental disorder have high probative value on the issue of credibility. Although the debate over the proper legal role of mental health professionals continues to rage, even those who would limit the availability of psychiatric evidence acknowledge that many types of "emotional or mental defect may materially affect the accuracy of testimony; a conservative list of such defects would have to include the psychoses, most or all of the neuroses, defects in the structure of the nervous system, mental deficiency, alcoholism, drug addiction and psychopathic personality." Juviler, Psychiatric Opinions as to Credibility of Witnesses: A Suggested Approach, 48 Cal.L.Rev. 648, 648 (1960). Mental illness may tend to produce bias in a witness' testimony. A psychotic's veracity may be impaired by lack of capacity to observe, correlate or recollect actual events. A paranoid person may interpret a reality skewed by suspicions, antipathies or fantasies. A schizophrenic may have difficulty distinguishing fact from fantasy and may have his memory distorted by delusions, hallucinations and paranoid thinking. A paranoid schizophrenic, though he may appear normal and his judgment on matters outside his delusional system may remain intact, may harbor delusions of grandeur or persecution that grossly distort his reactions to events. * * *

The government in this case contends that psychiatric evidence merely raises a collateral issue. But such labels cannot substitute for analysis. Whether called "collateral" or not, the issue of a witness' credibility is committed to the providence of the jury. Although the use of psychiatric evidence "does not fall within the traditional pattern of impeachment, the law should be flexible enough to make use of new resources." By this late date, use of this kind of evidence can hardly be termed "new."

At trial the defense sought to show that the key witness for the government was not credible, arguing that her motive for initiating and pursuing the investigation of Bay Therapy was based on hatred of the appellants. Lindstrom and Slater argued to the district court that this witness was carrying out a vendetta against them because she had not received a promised percentage of Bay Therapy when the business was sold. Appellants further sought to impeach the witness' credibility by demonstrating that her alleged vendetta resulted from a continuing mental illness, for which she had been periodically treated and confined. From public sources and from psychiatric records which the district court permitted defense counsel to review, the defense gathered material suggesting that in 1971 the witness was hospitalized following a serious suicide attempt; that in 1977 the witness, while she was running Bay Therapy, offered a patient of Bay Therapy $3,000 to murder the wife of the witness' alleged lover; that in 1978 she was involuntarily committed under Florida's Baker Act after taking an overdose of drugs; that in 1980 she was arrested and charged with aggravated assault for having allegedly fired a shotgun through the window of her purported lover's house; that following this incident she was briefly placed in a stockade until, at the urging of her psychiatrist, she was transferred to Hillsborough County Hospital where she was involuntarily committed under the Baker Act; that during this confinement she was diagnosed "schizophrenic reaction, chronic undifferentiated type" and described by the Chief of Psychology at Hillsborough as being "immature, egocentric, [and] manipulative," having superficial relationships causing "marital problems and sexual conflicts in general" and seeing authority as something to be manipulated for self gratification and as an obstacle; that an unsigned chart entry noted that the patient had a "history of hallucinations" and was "suicidal—homicidal and delusional." Through effective questioning in these areas, appellants contend that they could have shown the witness' past pattern of aggressive and manipulative conduct toward persons close to her and that they could have demonstrated the witness' motivation and determination in pursuing a vendetta.

The trial court, fearing that the defense would attempt to put the witness herself on trial, stated:

> I think we should discuss, too, the extent of the cross-examination of this witness in regard to these activities. I am trying to think this through. I am not fully convinced it's a 608–B question, although I think it's akin to that. But any questions along this line probably would go further than what seems to be envisioned by 608–B,[6] because you're testing the witness's credibility is what you're attempting to do, I would suppose. *So, within reason, there are two or three properly framed questions I'm going to allow you to at least let this jury know about the fact that this witness has had some mental and emotional problems in the past.*

I'm not going to allow the defense to try this witness, so to speak.

Three examples suffice to illustrate the extremely narrow limits within which the district judge permitted cross-examination of the witness.[7] First, the court refused to allow the defense to question the witness about the murder contract that she allegedly offered to a Bay Therapy patient. The defense proffered testimony by the patient to the effect that the witness had approached him and offered him $3,000 to shoot the wife of the witness' purported lover. The court sustained the government's objection to the questions, and also denied a defense request to ask the witness the questions out of the hearing of the jury. Secondly, the district court denied appellants the opportunity to cross-examine the witness about her own alleged attempt to shoot a shotgun through the window of her purported lover's house, after which she was committed under the Baker Act. Thirdly, the judge sustained the government's objection to defense questions focusing on whether, during her commitment, the witness had told hospital personnel that she had attempted suicide for the purpose of manipulating and punishing her boyfriend. Defense counsel proffered hospital records showing that the witness had in fact made such statements. During the ensuing side bar conference, defense counsel stated that the witness' history of ma-

---

[6] We agree with the trial court that Federal Rule of Evidence 608 is not controlling:

The credibility of a witness can always be attacked by showing that his capacity to observe, remember or narrate is impaired. Consequently, the witness' capacity at the time of the event, as well as at the time of trial, are significant. Defects of this nature reflect on mental capacity for truth-telling rather than on moral inducements for truth-telling, and consequently Rule 608 does not apply. J. Weinstein, Weinstein's Evidence § 607[4] (1981) (footnotes omitted) (emphasis in original).

[7] The district court did allow some cross-examination on the witness' psychiatric history. The defense was permitted to ask whether the witness had ever been committed under the Baker Act. Counsel elicited that she had been committed for three weeks in January, 1980, first at Hillsborough County and then at St. Joseph's Hospital. Further, the defense elicited that the witness had been involuntarily committed in 1978 * * *

nipulation was "the whole point of our defense. It's those people that cross her, Dennis Slater, Joanne Lindstrom, [or her alleged lover], she goes out to get them with a vendetta. She manipulated them. She did it to him on numerous occasions. She's doing the same thing to him. She's told two people that I have a witness for that she's out to get Dennis Slater."

These rulings by the district court constituted an abuse of discretion contradicting Supreme Court and former fifth circuit authority on the right of confrontation in general and the right to examine the psychiatric history of adverse witnesses in particular. In Greene v. Wainwright, 634 F.2d 272 (5th Cir.1981), the district court dismissed a petition for habeas corpus claiming a violation of the right to confrontation. The state trial judge had prohibited the defendant from questioning the state's chief witness about his "mental condition and about certain bizarre criminal actions." Id. at 274. "His credibility was crucial to the state's case." Id. at 275. The fifth circuit reversed, holding that the denial of an opportunity to present evidence regarding the "alleged recent history of mental instability * * * exceed[ed] any possible trial court discretion." Id. at 276.

We find Greene controls this issue. The restrictions on cross-examination in this case are even more egregious than those recently condemned in Greene, because the disputed medical records suggested a history of psychiatric disorders, manifesting themselves in violent threats and manipulative and destructive conduct having specific relevance to the facts at issue. As in Greene, the witness in question was the chief witness for the prosecution. She initiated and pursued the investigation of Bay Therapy. She was an insider to the fraud scheme, who testified in detail about the operation and about the activities of Slater and Lindstrom. We find the district court committed reversible error in unconstitutionally depriving appellants of their sixth amendment guarantee of the right to confrontation and cross-examination. * * *

HYPOTHETICALS

Plaintiff v. Acme Corporation in a product liability action. The plaintiff claims that Acme knowingly marketed an unsafe product. The plaintiff's key witness is a disgruntled former employee of Acme.

To impeach the former employee, Acme plans to offer the following evidence:

1. The witness lied on the resume that the witness submitted to Acme as part of his employment application.

2. The witness is a drug addict.

3. Just before quitting his job at Acme, the witness sabotaged his computer by erasing its hard disk.

4. The witness has secret plans to assassinate the Pope, the President, and the Dalai Lama.

May the witness be asked about these matters on cross-examination? Will extrinsic evidence be admissible if the witness denies the misconduct?

The Testimony of Dr. Binger

One of the most celebrated criminal cases of twentieth-century America was that of Alger Hiss, who among other distinctions had served as a law clerk to Justice Holmes, secretary-general of the United Nations Charter Conference, and president of the Carnegie Endowment for International Peace. Whittaker Chambers, a former Communist who had become a staunchly anti-Communist senior editor at Time Magazine, claimed that Hiss had passed State Department documents on to him in 1938. Before a Congressional committee – in which a freshman from California, Richard M. Nixon, played a leading role, and again before a federal grand jury, Hiss denied having done so, and denied having had any contact with Chambers after 1937. (He did acknowledge knowing Chambers, under a different name, at an earlier time.) The statute of limitations had passed on espionage, but Hiss was indicted for perjury.

At the first trial, in June 1949, the defense had a psychiatrist, Dr. Carl A.L. Binger, sit and take notes rather ostentatiously near Chambers as he testified. The trial judge, Samuel Kaufman, going against his initially stated inclination, allowed the defense to put Binger on the stand in an attempt to impeach Chambers. Hiss's counsel, the flamboyant Lloyd Paul Stryker, posed a hypothetical question that took 35 minutes to read. The prosecutor, Thomas Murphy, objected, calling the question an incomplete and misleading summation of Chambers' testimony "before the time of summations." The judge sustained the objection and excused Binger, explaining that " the record is sufficiently clear for the jury . . . to appraise the testimony of all the witnesses." Allen Weinstein, Perjury: The Hiss-Chambers Case 439-40 (1978). The trial ended with the jury hung, 8-4 for conviction.

Hiss was retried, beginning in November 1949, before a different judge, Henry W. Goddard. Goddard ruled formally ahead of time that Hiss could present expert impeachment testimony. *United States v. Hiss*, 88 F.Supp. 559 (S.D.N.Y. 1950) (noting that "the outcome of this trial is dependent to a great extent upon the testimony of one man—Whittaker Chambers" and that "Mr. Chambers' credibility is one of the major issues upon which the jury must pass"); *compare United States v. Barnard*, 490 F.2d 907, 912-13 (9th Cir. 1973) ("Credibility . . . is for the jury—the jury is the lie detector in the courtroom. * * * We think that the testimony of the type offered in this case should be received only in unusual cases, such as *United States v. Hiss*. And by referring to that case we are not saying that it would have been error to exclude the testimony there offered and received."), *cert. denied*, 416 U.S. 959, 94 S.Ct. 1976, 40 L.Ed.2d 310 (1974); *Bomas v. State*, 987 A.2d 98 (Md. 2010) (reviewing cases and concluding that the test for admissibility of expert testimony on the reliability of eyewitness identification is whether the testimony "will be of real appreciable help to the trier of fact in deciding the issue presented").

And so Dr. Binger took the stand as part of the defense case. After establishing Binger's credentials, Hiss's new lawyer, Claude B. Cross, established that Binger had personally observed Chambers testifying on five days at the first trial and on one day at the second trial. Cross then launched into an even longer hypothetical question that consumed forty pages of the trial transcript, Tr. 3611-3650, and was interrupted by the court's recess. Tr. 3632. The question emphasized unpleasant and unpalatable aspects of Chambers' personality and history, and presented a defense-oriented view of the facts of the case. At the conclusion, Cross asked Binger whether, assuming the facts as stated in the question to be true, and taking into account Binger's own personal observations and readings of Chambers' works, Binger had, "as a psychiatrist, an opinion within the bounds of reasonable medical certainty as to the mental condition of Whittaker Chambers." Binger said that he did – he thought that Chambers was a "psychopathic personality," which he defined as "a disorder of character, of which the outstanding features are behavior of what we call an amoral or an asocial and delinquent nature." Tr. 3650.

Binger reviewed what he regarded as symptoms of Chambers' mental illness – lies he had made, thefts of books, living with a woman "in an illicit relationship in his mother's house," Tr. 3677, "his untidiness, . . . his filthy mouth" (literally; a reference to his teeth and not to his choice of language), Tr. 3685, unstable attachments, and so forth. One of the "confirmatory" points cited by Binger was that during his testimony Chambers "frequently looked up at the ceiling as if trying to recall something that he had previously said." Tr. 3686.

The cross-examination by Murphy was long—filling over 250 transcript pages – and aggressive. Weinstein, *supra*, at 487-92. Murphy got Binger to acknowledge that the characterization of "psychopathic personality" was a rather vague catch-all. And, although Binger insisted repeatedly that no one factor was sufficient for his diagnosis—denying, for example, "that all people who neglect their teeth would be exhibiting some evidence of psychopathic personality," Tr. 3997—Murphy focused effectively on particulars. Binger had mentioned twenty lies (some of them to protect his Communist activities) by Chambers in his first 36 years. "What would par be?" Murphy asked. "How many lies is the normal person entitled to have in 36 years?" With considerable bravado, Murphy referred to Binger's testimony about Chambers having looked at the ceiling while testifying:

> Now, Doctor, we made a count this morning of the number of times that you looked at the ceiling, [and it came to] a total in 50 minutes of 59 times, and I was wondering, Doctor, whether that had any symptoms of a psychopathic personality."

"Not alone," was Binger's curt reply. Tr. 3830-31. With respect to thefts:

> Q. Did you ever take a hotel towel or a Pullman towel?
>
> A. I couldn't swear that I had or hadn't. I don't think so.
>
> Q. Well, if you did, Doctor, or if one of the jurors did, would you say that was evidence of a symptom of psychopathic personality?
>
> A. It would have no bearing.

Tr. 3893. As to untidiness, Albert Einstein, Will Rogers, Thomas Edison, and others were far from fastidious, weren't they? Tr. 3988-89. Chambers' 19-year marriage and ten-year tenure at Time suggested ability to form lasting relationships, didn't they? Tr. 3989-90. Binger responded that Chambers had been unstably attached to the Communist Party. Tr. 3991.

The defense presented the testimony of another expert, Dr. Henry A. Murray, a psychologist from Harvard Medical School, but he, too, seems not to have been persuasive in the end. Speaking of both experts, Judge Goddard instructed the jury:

> As is the case with all expert testimony, these opinions are purely advisory. You may reject their opinions entirely if you find the hypothetical situation presented to them in the question to be incomplete or incorrect or if you believe their reasons to be unsound or not convincing.
>
> An expert does not pass on the truth of the testimony included in a hypothetical question. * * *
>
> Now, you yourselves have seen and heard Mr. Chambers for several days while he was on the witness stand and you have heard all the evidence. It is for you to say how much weight, if any, you will give to the testimony of the experts—and of Mr. Chambers.

This time, the jury found Hiss guilty. He served three years and eight months in federal prison. He maintained his innocence until his death in 1996.

Witness' Claim That He Once Was Harlow Cast a Reasonable Doubt*

United Press International

* * * During two hours of testimony in a Miami fraud scam trial, [Perry Bond, the prosecution's star witness,] told how the scam worked.

Then it was defense lawyer James Jay Hogan's turn.

Hogan brought out a large square of cardboard covered with a sheet of paper. With a flourish, he uncovered his life-size exhibit—a picture of Jean Harlow in a bathing suit.

Hogan asked Bond if he recognized the picture of the platinum blond bombshell, a Hollywood sex symbol who died in 1937 at age 26.

Bond solemnly said he did.

Hogan asked if Bond had once occupied the body displayed in the picture.

Bond, born five years after Harlow's death, said he had.

[The prosecutor later said that Bond genuinely believed in the reincarnation and had not mentioned it, despite being asked if there was anything else about his life that the prosecutor should know. A mistrial was declared after the judge suffered an apparent heart attack.]

---

* Boston Globe—Oct 18, 1984 P 7.

HYPOTHETICAL

X is prosecuted for battery upon A, his girl friend. A testifies that she was trying to break off her relationship with X and that he got mad and beat her. On cross-examination, X asks A if it isn't true that she has been under the care of a psychiatrist for the last three years. The prosecutor makes an improper impeachment objection. X represents that he intends to prove that it was he who was trying to break off the relationship, because he found out that A had been under the care of a psychiatrist; that he never struck A at all; and that A's claim is a figment of her imagination. What ruling on the objection?

4. PRIOR STATEMENTS TO IMPEACH OR REHABILITATE

Coles v. Harsch

Supreme Court of Oregon, 1929.
129 Or. 11, 276 P. 248.

In this action the plaintiff sought to recover a judgment for $50,000 upon charges that the defendant had maliciously alienated the affections of plaintiff's wife by improper attentions shown to her in the years 1923, 1924, and 1925. * * * The verdict and judgment were in favor of the plaintiff in the sum of $17,500. The defendant appealed.

■ ROSSMAN, J. (after stating the facts as above). The defendant presents for our disposal several assignments of error. We shall first consider the one which is based upon the endeavor of the plaintiff to impeach the testimony of one James A. Thompson, who was one of the defendant's principal witnesses. In order to better understand the situation presented by this assignment of error, it seems desirable to state the following undisputed facts: While the parties were married to their former wives, the two couples belonged to the same social group; they frequently met at card parties, dances, and other social diversions, and frequently visited back and forth. The plaintiff contended that at some time in 1923 he noticed that the defendant was developing a propensity for wrestling with the plaintiff's wife, and engaging in other similar play with her. It was his contention that this propensity of the defendant did not abate with the passing of time, but that it grew more pronounced, and the plaintiff contended that it constituted one of the means which the defendant employed for winning the affections of the plaintiff's wife. This seems to be a rather unusual method of love making, yet if current reports are reliable, it is not the first instance where a cicisbeo has delved into the distant stone age and brought forth a somewhat rough and uncouth method of endearment, which well served his purpose, and brought about the desired result. Be this as it may, it will suffice to say that much time was consumed in the trial court in taking testimony concerning these wrestling and similar encounters and the extent to which other members of the parties participated in them; there was also testimony, not all in harmony, however, concerning the plaintiff's protests against the activities along these lines of his wife and the defendant and the latter's replies and rejoinders thereto.

As we have said, one of the defendant's principal witnesses was a Mr. James A. Thompson. The latter and his wife were members of this social group. His testimony, apparently important to the defendant, covered these wrestling encounters, the social diversions of the group, and the relationship between the defendant and Mrs. Coles, plaintiff's former wife. If his testimony was accepted as truthful by the jury, the defendant's conduct towards Mrs. Coles was the same as his conduct towards other women friends, and was proper and harmless. Apparently nothing developed upon cross-examination which obviously discredited this witness; but, upon rebuttal, the plaintiff was permitted over objection to testify that, "at the time I was in the garage where he works," Thompson told him that at a picnic held on the banks of the Pudding river the conduct of the defendant and Mrs. Coles towards each other was disgraceful. Before defendant's objection was ruled upon, plaintiff's counsel stated that the purpose of the contemplated answer was to "go to the credibility of Thompson." The objections of the defendant to the questions, which elicited the above answer, were specific and were reiterated; they were to the effect that, if the plaintiff sought this information to substantiate the charges of his complaint, the inquiry was in violation of the hearsay evidence rule: That if the plaintiff sought the answer for the purpose of impeaching Thompson, he had not laid the proper foundation by making a similar inquiry of Thompson accompanied with the details of time, place, and persons present. The merits of the first alternative of the objection are so self-evident, that we deem it necessary to set forth our consideration only of the second phase of the objection.

Section 864, Or.L., provides: "A witness may also be impeached by evidence that he has made, at other times, statements inconsistent with his present testimony; but before this can be done, the statements must be related to him, with the circumstances of times, places, and persons present; and he shall be asked whether he has made such statements, and if so, allowed to explain them. If the statements be in writing, they shall be shown to the witness before any question is put to him concerning them."

It is necessary, therefore, to examine the inquiries propounded to Thompson and determine whether a similar question was put to him which complied with this statutory rule. Pausing for a moment, it is worthwhile to observe that this requirement does not invoke an idle ceremony, but is intended to serve a useful purpose. Every witness, whose testimony is shown in conflict with a previous statement made by him, is not necessarily revealed thereby as a dishonest person; the impeachment, in many instances, may uncover only a faulty memory in the discredited witness. The requirement that the identifying circumstances of time, place, those present, and the statement that the witness then made shall be related to him, is founded upon the experience, which frequently presents itself in the courtroom, that a witness, who has stoutly denied having made an alleged statement, may finally blushingly and apologetically admit it, when the questioner throws into association with it identifying circumstances. It is a common observation that associated ideas, as they are related, one after another, not infrequently succeed in upturning a fact which previously had defied all efforts of recollection. And so this rule of evidence is intended to reveal not only the dishonest witness, but is also intended to afford all witnesses ample opportunity to recall a fact before they may be assailed as dishonest. The requirement also tends to reduce to the minimum a confusion of issues by eliminating unnecessary impeachments.

Approaching the statutory requirement thus broadly as one intended to serve a practical, useful end, let us see what the record presents. On direct examination Thompson was asked concerning a conversation he had had with the plaintiff at the Bybee Avenue Garage. The witness stated that the conversation occurred so long ago that his recollection had become somewhat vague, but he recalled that at that time the plaintiff said that his wife was going to get a divorce. No further questions were asked him on direct examination concerning that conversation. The time of this conversation was not fixed, nor were those present mentioned, and he was asked nothing concerning the Pudding river incident. On cross-examination he was asked whether he recalled "talking to Mr. Coles about that trip to the Pudding river." He replied in the negative. This was the only foundation laid for the impeaching question; we believe it was insufficient. It may be that Thompson was untruthful, but before the plaintiff could avail himself of such an argument he should have prepared the necessary premise by submitting to Thompson the alleged statement accompanied by the identifying circumstances. Since this was not done, error was committed when the impeaching witness was permitted to answer. * * *

[Reversed.]

Goldstein, Trial Technique
§ 601 (1935).*

§ 601. Former contradictory oral statements

In those instances where the lawyer is in possession of information as to verbal statements made by the witness which are directly contrary to his present testimony, the following procedure is suggested: First—get the witness to repeat upon cross-examination the statements that he has made on direct examination, then put a casual and general question as to whether or not he has ever made a statement to the contrary, at any time or place, then identify the person to whom the contradictory statement is purported to have been made, then direct his attention to the time, the place, and the exact language used or in substance, and again ask him whether or not he had made such contradictory statement. Upon his denial he might again be interrogated on the same question for psychological effect and upon a similar denial the witness should be excused.

After opponent's case is in and he rests, the lawyer should then produce the impeaching witness and prove the contradictory statement by him.

---

* Copyright 1935 by Callaghan & Co.

See Federal Rules of Evidence 613;   California Evidence Code §§ 769, 770.

Park, Leonard, Orenstein & Goldberg, Evidence Law

499–500 (3d ed. 2011)[*]

A prior inconsistent statement may not be proved with extrinsic evidence when the statement is being offered solely for collateral impeachment.[54] The impeachment is collateral when the statement is not independently relevant to some issue other than impeachment.[55]

Collateral impeachment out of the witness' own mouth is distinct from collateral impeachment with extrinsic evidence. An objection can still be made, but trial judges have wide discretion to allow collateral impeachment by cross-examination. When collateral questioning is allowed by the trial judge, the questioner is bound by the witness' answer. The questioner may not bring in another witness to prove that the out-of-court statement was made. To do so would violate the rule against using extrinsic evidence for collateral impeachment.[56]

For example, suppose that, in a sexual harassment case, the witness denies that anything improper happened at the office picnic. On cross-examination the witness is questioned about the witness' prior inconsistent statements about (a) what food was served at the picnic and (b) whether

---

[*] Copyright 2011, Thomson Reuters.

[54] 28 CHARLES A. WRIGHT & VICTOR J. GOLD, FEDERAL PRACTICE AND PROCEDURE (EVIDENCE) § 6206, at 537 (noting common-law rule, generally followed by federal courts, recognizing that when inconsistency relates to collateral matter, inconsistency cannot be proven by extrinsic evidence). . ..

[55] United States v. Roulette, 75 F.3d 418, 423 (8th Cir. 1996) (endorsing independent relevance test and finding it satisfied under facts of case); United States v. Laughlin, 772 F.2d 1382, 1393-94 (7th Cir.1985) (witness testified her defendant-husband only used drugs if his friends brought drugs to his house; extrinsic evidence she previously told FBI agent that her husband had "source" for drugs was independently relevant, in case where defendant was charged with possession of cocaine with intent to distribute); United States v. Nace, 561 F.2d 763, 771 (9th Cir. 1977) (where witness testified that he did not owe defendant any money but had listed loan as liability in his bankruptcy petition, defendant could not impeach witness with his bankruptcy petition statement because issue was whether defendant used extortion to get repayment of alleged loan, not whether witness had in fact borrowed money from the defendant); *cf.* United States v. Nazarenus, 983 F.2d 1480, 1485 (8th Cir. 1993) (improper to impeach defendant, who told police officer who stopped him on night of alleged sex crime that he had sped only to test car's alignment, with evidence that he frequently drove fast); see also 3A JOHN H. WIGMORE, EVIDENCE IN TRIALS AT COMMON LAW § 1020 (James H. Chadbourn rev. 1970).

[56] See, e.g., State v. Mangrum, 403 P.2d 925, 929 (Ariz. 1965) (opponent could inquire on cross-examination about witness' alleged statement that witness had testified falsely in unconnected case but could not bring in extrinsic evidence about alleged statement); 3A John H. Wigmore, EVIDENCE IN TRIALS AT COMMON LAW §§ 1020-23. See also United States v. Grooms, 978 F.2d 425, 428-29 (8th Cir. 1992) (in prosecution for child sex abuse, where victims' mother denied stating that victims' father coached their testimony, defendant may not call witness to testify that mother made statement because issue was collateral; in authors' opinion, court's conclusion is questionable because prior statement was relevant not only to mother's credibility but also to bias of child witness).

the defendant tried to kiss the plaintiff. The trial judge would have discretion to allow cross-examination about both issues. The question about what food was served deals with a collateral matter of no importance, but so long as the cross-examiner is content merely to ask questions of the witness being impeached, not much time is wasted. The answers may reveal a confused or forgetful witness. However, if the witness denies making an inconsistent statement about what food was served, then the cross-examiner cannot bring in another witness (extrinsic evidence) to prove the making of the statement, because an additional witness would be a waste of time. In contrast, if the prior inconsistent statement concerned something independently relevant—such as whether the defendant tried to kiss the plaintiff— then the extrinsic evidence would be admissible.

A prior inconsistent statement can be independently relevant because it goes to one of the substantive issues of the lawsuit, as in the example of the kiss at the picnic.[57] Alternatively, a prior inconsistent statement can be independently relevant because it goes to bias (e.g., the witness denies making a prior statement that he was paid for testimony) or perception (the witness denies having made a prior statement saying that he was drunk at the picnic).[58]

Morgan, Hearsay Dangers and the Application of the Hearsay Concept

62 Harv.L.Rev. 177, 192–93 (1948),[*] in Selected Writings on Evidence and Trial, 764, 774–75 (1957).[**]

Prior Declarations of Witness.—

* * * But there is one situation where the courts are prone to call hearsay what does not in fact involve in any substantial degree any of the hearsay risks. When the Declarant is also a witness, it is difficult to justify classifying as hearsay evidence of his own prior statements. This is especially true where Declarant as a witness is giving as part of his testimony his own prior statement. Although there are numerous dicta accepting Greenleaf's statement that hearsay is "that kind of evidence which does not derive its value solely from the credit to be given to the witness himself, but rests also, in part, on the veracity and competency of some other person," the dictum rarely becomes decision. The courts declare the prior statement to be hearsay because it was not made under oath, subject to the penalty for perjury or to the test of cross-examination. To which the answer might well be: "The declarant as a witness is now under oath and now purports to remember and narrate accurately. The adversary can now expose every element that may carry a danger of misleading the trier of fact both in the previous statement and in the present testimony, and the trier can judge whether

---

[57] 3A John H. Wigmore, Evidence in Trials at Common Law § 1021 (James H. Chadbourn rev., 1970).

[58] 3A JOHN H. WIGMORE, EVIDENCE IN TRIALS AT COMMON LAW § 1022 (James H. Chadbourn rev., 1970).

[*] Copyright, 1948, 1949 By The Harvard Law Review Association.

[**] West Publishing Co., St. Paul, 1957.

both the previous declaration and the present testimony are reliable in whole or in part." To this Mr. Justice Stone of the Minnesota Supreme Court, speaking of evidence of prior contradictory statements, has framed this reply:

> The chief merit of cross-examination is not that at some future time it gives the party opponent the right to dissect adverse testimony. Its principal virtue is in its immediate application of the testing process. Its strokes fall while the iron is hot. False testimony is apt to harden and become unyielding to the blows of truth in proportion as the witness has opportunity for reconsideration and influence by the suggestions of others, whose interest may be, and often is, to maintain falsehood rather than truth.

He adds "practical reasons" that receipt of such evidence would create temptation and opportunity to manufacture evidence and entrap witnesses, and would require admission of prior consistent statements. Why does falsehood harden any more quickly or unyieldingly than truth? What has become of the idea that truth is eternal and, though crushed to earth, will rise again? Isn't the opportunity for reconsideration and for baneful influence by others even more likely to color the later testimony than the prior statement? Furthermore, it must be remembered that the trier of fact is often permitted to hear these prior statements to impeach or rehabilitate the declarant-witness. In such event, of course, the trier will be told that he must not treat the statement as evidence of the truth of the matter stated. But to what practical effect? Wasn't Judge Swan right in saying, "Practically, men will often believe that if a witness has earlier sworn to the opposite of what he now swears to, he was speaking the truth when he first testified"? Do the judges deceive themselves or do they realize that they are indulging in a pious fraud? * * *

Tome v. United States

Supreme Court of the United States, 1995.
513 U.S. 150, 115 S.Ct. 696, 130 L.Ed.2d 574.

■ KENNEDY, J., announced the judgment of the Court and delivered the opinion of the Court with respect to Parts I, II–A, II–C, and III, in which Stevens, Scalia, Souter, and Ginsburg, JJ., joined, and an opinion with respect to Part II–B, in which Stevens, Souter, and Ginsburg, JJ., joined. Scalia, J., filed an opinion concurring in part and concurring in the judgment. Breyer, J., filed a dissenting opinion, in which Rehnquist, C.J., and O'Connor and Thomas, JJ., joined.

[Tome was charged with sexual abuse of his daughter, who was four at the time; the prosecution contended that the abuse occurred while the child, referred to as A.T., was in Tome's custody, on an Indian reservation. Tome, who was divorced from the child's mother, contended that the charges were concocted to prevent him from having custody of A.T. At trial in federal district court, A.T., then six and one half, testified for the Government, mainly by giving brief answers to leading questions. On cross-examination, A.T. was largely uncommunicative.]

After A.T. testified, the Government produced six witnesses who testified about a total of seven statements made by A.T. describing the alleged sexual assaults: A.T.'s babysitter recited A.T.'s statement to her on August 22, 1990, that she did not want to return to her father because he "gets drunk and he thinks I'm his wife"; the babysitter related further details given by A.T. on August 27, 1990, while A.T.'s mother stood outside the room and listened after the mother had been unsuccessful in questioning A.T. herself; the mother recounted what she had heard A.T. tell the babysitter; a social worker recounted details A.T. told her on August 29, 1990 about the assaults; and three pediatricians, Drs. Kuper, Reich and Spiegel, related A.T.'s statements to them describing how and where she had been touched by Tome. All but A.T.'s statement to Dr. Spiegel implicated Tome. (The physicians also testified that their clinical examinations of the child indicated that she had been subjected to vaginal penetrations. That part of the testimony is not at issue here.)

A.T.'s out-of-court statements, recounted by the six witnesses, were offered by the Government under Rule 801(d)(1)(B). The trial court admitted all of the statements over defense counsel's objection, accepting the Government's argument that they rebutted the implicit charge that A.T.'s testimony was motivated by a desire to live with her mother. The court also admitted A.T.'s August 22d statement to her babysitter under Rule 803(24), and the statements to Dr. Kuper (and apparently also to Dr. Reich) under Rule 803(4) (statements for purposes of medical diagnosis). The Government offered the testimony of the social worker under both Rules 801(d)(1)(B) and 803(24), but the record does not indicate whether the court ruled on the latter ground. No objection was made to Dr. Spiegel's testimony. Following trial, Tome was convicted and sentenced to 12 years imprisonment.

On appeal, the Court of Appeals for the Tenth Circuit affirmed, adopting the Government's argument that all of A.T.'s out-of-court statements were admissible under Rule 801(d)(1)(B) even though they had been made after A.T.'s alleged motive to fabricate arose. * * *

We granted certiorari and now reverse.

II

The prevailing common-law rule for more than a century before adoption of the Federal Rules of Evidence was that a prior consistent statement introduced to rebut a charge of recent fabrication or improper influence or motive was admissible if the statement had been made before the alleged fabrication, influence, or motive came into being, but it was inadmissible if made afterwards. As Justice Story explained: "[W]here the testimony is assailed as a fabrication of a recent date . . . in order to repel such imputation, proof of the *antecedent* declaration of the party may be admitted." Ellicott v. Pearl, 35 U.S. (10 Pet.) 412, 439, 9 L.Ed. 475 (1836) (emphasis supplied).

A

* * *

Rule 801 defines prior consistent statements as nonhearsay only if they are offered to rebut a charge of "recent fabrication or improper influence or motive." Fed.Rule Evid. 801(d)(1)(B). Noting the "troublesome" logic of treating a witness' prior consistent statements as hearsay at all (because the declarant is present in court and subject to cross-examination), the Advisory Committee decided to treat those consistent statements, once the preconditions of the Rule were satisfied, as nonhearsay and admissible as substantive evidence, not just to rebut an attack on the witness' credibility. See Advisory Committee Notes on Fed.Rule Evid. 801(d)(1), 28 U.S.C.App., p. 773. A consistent statement meeting the requirements of the Rule is thus placed in the same category as a declarant's inconsistent statement made under oath in another proceeding, or prior identification testimony, or admissions by a party opponent. See Fed.Rule Evid. 801.

The Rules do not accord this weighty, nonhearsay status to all prior consistent statements. To the contrary, admissibility under the Rules is confined to those statements offered to rebut a charge of "recent fabrication or improper influence or motive," the same phrase used by the Advisory Committee in its description of the "traditiona[l]" common law of evidence, which was the background against which the Rules were drafted. See Advisory Committee Notes, *supra*, at 773. Prior consistent statements may not be admitted to counter all forms of impeachment or to bolster the witness merely because she has been discredited. In the present context, the question is whether A.T.'s out-of-court statements rebutted the alleged link between her desire to be with her mother and her testimony, not whether they suggested that A.T.'s in-court testimony was true. The Rule speaks of a party rebutting an alleged motive, not bolstering the veracity of the story told.

This limitation is instructive, not only to establish the preconditions of admissibility but also to reinforce the significance of the requirement that the consistent statements must have been made before the alleged influence, or motive to fabricate arose. That is to say, the forms of impeachment within the Rule's coverage are the ones in which the temporal requirement makes the most sense. Impeachment by charging that the testimony is a recent fabrication or results from an improper influence or motive is, as a general matter, capable of direct and forceful refutation through introduction of out-of-court consistent statements that predate the alleged fabrication, influence or motive. A consistent statement that predates the motive is a square rebuttal of the charge that the testimony was contrived as a consequence of that motive. By contrast, prior consistent statements carry little rebuttal force when most other types of impeachment are involved. McCormick § 49, p. 105 ("When the attack takes the form of impeachment of character, by showing misconduct, convictions or bad reputation, it is generally agreed that there is no color for sustaining by consistent statements. The defense does not meet the assault." (footnote omitted)); see also 4 Wigmore § 1131, p. 293 ("The broad rule obtains in a few courts that consistent statements may be admitted *after* impeachment of any sort—in particular after any impeachment by *cross-examination*. But there is no reason for such a loose rule" (footnote omitted)).

There may arise instances when out-of-court statements that postdate the alleged fabrication have some probative force in rebutting a charge of fabrication or improper influence or motive, but those statements refute the charged fabrication in a less direct and forceful way. Evidence that a witness made consistent statements after the alleged motive to fabricate arose may suggest in some degree that the in-court testimony is truthful, and thus suggest in some degree that that testimony did not result from some improper influence; but if the drafters of Rule 801(d)(1)(B) intended to countenance rebuttal along that indirect inferential chain, the purpose of confining the types of impeachment that open the door to rebuttal by introducing consistent statements becomes unclear. If consistent statements are admissible without reference to the time frame we find imbedded in the Rule, there appears no sound reason not to admit consistent statements to rebut other forms of impeachment as well. Whatever objections can be leveled against limiting the Rule to this designated form of impeachment and confining the rebuttal to those statements made before the fabrication or improper influence or motive arose, it is clear to us that the drafters of Rule 801(d)(1)(B) were relying upon the common-law temporal requirement. * * *

* * *

C

The Government's final argument in favor of affirmance is that the common-law premotive rule advocated by petitioner is inconsistent with the Federal Rules' liberal approach to relevancy and with strong academic criticism, beginning in the 1940's, directed at the exclusion of out-of-court statements made by a declarant who is present in court and subject to cross-examination. This argument misconceives the design of the Rules' hearsay provisions.

Hearsay evidence is often relevant. * * * That does not resolve the matter, however. Relevance is not the sole criterion of admissibility. Otherwise, it would be difficult to account for the Rules' general proscription of hearsay testimony (absent a specific exception), see Fed.Rule Evid. 802, let alone the traditional analysis of hearsay that the Rules, for the most part, reflect. *Ibid.* ("The approach to hearsay in these rules is that of the common law... The traditional hearsay exceptions are drawn upon for the exceptions ..."). That certain out-of-court statements may be relevant does not dispose of the question whether they are admissible.

The Government's reliance on academic commentators critical of excluding out-of-court statements by a witness, is subject to like criticism. To be sure, certain commentators in the years preceding the adoption of the Rules had been critical of the common-law approach to hearsay, particularly its categorical exclusion of out-of-court statements offered for substantive purposes. See, *e.g.*, Weinstein, The Probative Force of Hearsay, 46 Iowa L.Rev. 331, 344–345 (1961) (gathering sources). General criticism was directed to the exclusion of a declarant's out-of-court statements where the declarant testified at trial. See, *e.g.*, Weinstein, *supra*, at 333 ("treating the out of court statement of the witness himself as hearsay" is a "practical absurdity in many instances"); Morgan, Hearsay Dangers and the Application of the Hearsay Concept, 62 Harv.L.Rev. 177, 192–196 (1948). As an alternative, they suggested moving away from the categorical exclusion of hearsay and toward a case-by-case balancing of the probative value of particular statements against their likely prejudicial effect. The Advisory Committee, however, was explicit in rejecting this balancing approach to hearsay:

> "The Advisory Committee has rejected this approach to hearsay as involving too great a measure of judicial discretion, minimizing the predictability of rulings, [and] enhancing the difficulties of preparation for trial." Advisory Committee's Introduction, *supra*, at 771.

Given the Advisory Committee's rejection of both the general balancing approach to hearsay, and of Uniform Rule 63(1), the Government's reliance on the views of those who advocated these positions is misplaced.

The statement-by-statement balancing approach advocated by the Government and adopted by the Tenth Circuit creates the precise dangers the Advisory Committee noted and sought to avoid: It involves considerable judicial discretion; it reduces predictability; and it enhances the difficulties of trial preparation because parties will have difficulty knowing in advance whether or not particular out-of-court statements will be admitted. See Advisory Committee's Introduction, *supra*, at 771.

D

The case before us illustrates some of the important considerations supporting the Rule as we interpret it, especially in criminal cases. If the Rule were to permit the introduction of prior statements as substantive evidence to rebut every implicit charge that a witness' in-court testimony results from recent fabrication or improper influence or motive, the whole emphasis of the trial could shift to the out-of-court statements, not the in-court ones. The present case illustrates the point. In response to a rather weak charge that A.T.'s testimony was a fabrication created so the child could remain with her mother, the Government was permitted to present a parade of sympathetic and credible witnesses who did no more than recount A.T.'s detailed out-of-court statements to them. Although those statements might have been probative on the question whether the alleged conduct had occurred, they shed but minimal light on whether A.T. had the charged motive to fabricate. At closing argument before the jury, the Government placed great reliance on the prior statements for substantive purposes but did not once seek to use them to rebut the impact of the alleged motive.

We are aware that in some cases it may be difficult to ascertain when a particular fabrication, influence, or motive arose. Yet, as the Government concedes, a majority of common-law courts were performing this task for well over a century, and the Government has presented us with no evidence that those courts, or the judicial circuits that adhere to the rule today, have been unable to make the determination. Even under the Government's hypothesis, moreover, the thing to be rebutted must be identified, so the date of its origin cannot be that much more difficult to ascertain. By contrast, as the Advisory Committee commented, the Government's approach, which would require the trial court to weigh all of the circumstances surrounding a statement that suggest its probativeness against the court's assessment of the strength of the alleged motive, would entail more of a burden, with no guidance to attorneys in preparing a case or to appellate courts in reviewing a judgment.

III

Courts must be sensitive to the difficulties attendant upon the prosecution of alleged child abusers. In almost all cases a youth is the prosecution's only eye witness. But "[t]his Court cannot alter evidentiary rules merely because litigants might prefer different rules in a particular class of cases." *United States v. Salerno*, 112 S.Ct. 2503, 2507 (1992). When a party seeks to introduce out-of-court statements that contain strong circumstantial indicia of reliability, that are highly probative on the material questions at trial, and that are better than other evidence otherwise available, there is no need to distort the requirements of Rule 801(d)(1)(B). If its requirements are met, Rule 803(24) exists for that eventuality. We intimate no view, however, concerning the admissibility of any of A.T.'s out-of-court statements under that section, or any other evidentiary principle. These matters, and others, are for the Court of Appeals to decide in the first instance.

Our holding is confined to the requirements for admission under Rule 801(d)(1)(B). The Rule permits the introduction of a declarant's consistent out-of-court statements to rebut a charge of recent fabrication or improper influence or motive only when those statements were made before the charged recent fabrication or improper influence or motive. These conditions of admissibility were not established here.

The judgment of the Court of Appeals for the Tenth Circuit is reversed, and the case is remanded for further proceedings consistent with this opinion.

It is so ordered.

[Justice Scalia concurred in the judgment and in all but Part II-B of Justice Kennedy's opinion (not presented here). In line with his general views on legislative history, he declined to join that portion of the opinion because it treated the Advisory Committee Notes as an indication of the purpose or intent of the drafters of the Rules. Justice Breyer, joined by Chief Justice Rehnquist and Justices O'Connor and Thomas, dissented. He believed that the question was whether the prior statements were relevant for impeachment purposes, and Rule 801(d)(1)(B), part of the codification of hearsay rules, did not address that issue.]

Minnesota Rules of Evidence (1998)

Rule 801(d). Statements which are not hearsay. A statement is not hearsay if—

(1) Prior statement by witness. The declarant testifies at the trial or hearing and is subject to cross-examination concerning the statement and the statement is * * *

(B) consistent with the declarant's testimony and helpful to the trier of fact in evaluating the declarant's credibility as a witness * * *

QUESTIONS

The Minnesota Rule is premised on the idea that if a prior consistent statement of a witness is helpful for evaluation of the witness's credibility, there is no harm in allowing it to be used also for the truth of what it assert, given that the witness is subject to cross-examination. Do you agree? Does it matter to your answer whether the prior statement contains information that the witness's courtroom testimony does not? Note that this was the situation in *Tome*: Testimony by adults related prior statements made by A.T. describing two acts of abuse that she did not discuss in her direct testimony. *See* Richard D. Friedman, *Prior Statements of a Witness: A Nettlesome Corner of the Hearsay Thicket*, 1995 Sup. Ct. Rev. 277.

See Federal Rules of Evidence 801(d)(1); California Evidence Code § 791, §§ 1235–36.

HYPOTHETICALS

(1) X is indicted for child molestation. The victim is A, his 12-year-old stepdaughter. At X's trial the prosecution calls A, who testifies that she has no recollection of any molestation by X, or of having testified before the grand jury. The prosecution seeks to read into the record a transcript of A's testimony before the grand jury, describing X's acts of molestation. X objects. Is X correct?

(2) X is charged with the murder of A by use of a beer bottle in a barroom fight. X claims that he struck in self-defense when A came at him with a knife. There were no witnesses to the killing. B testifies for X that shortly before the final encounter he saw A and X fighting in the bar with their fists, and that A was getting the best of it; that X was retreating as if he were trying to stop fighting; and that he, B, stepped in between A and X, stopped the fighting and then left the bar. On cross-examination, B has no recollection of making any

prior statement to C. The prosecution calls C to testify that a week after the killing B told him that X started the earlier fight with A and he (B) heard X say during that fight that he was going to get a gun and shoot A. X objects. What result?

(3) X is prosecuted for robbery of a gas station. Y, a codefendant, is tried first and convicted. At X's trial, the prosecutor calls Y who proves to be a recalcitrant witness and testifies that he and a friend had gone to the gas station together and that he, Y, had committed the robbery. Y gives an "I-don't-remember" answer to the prosecutor's question as to whether X was the friend with him at the gas station. In answer to the prosecutor's questions seeking a description of the friend, Y gives evasive and "I-don't-remember" answers. Y gives an "I-don't-remember" answer to the prosecutor's question as to whether Y had given a statement to B, a police officer, as to who was with him at the robbery. The prosecutor calls B and represents that B will testify that Y told him that X was his accomplice and told him the part each played in committing the robbery. X objects to B's proposed testimony, on the ground that Y's prior statements are not inconsistent with any of Y's testimony. How should the court rule?

(4) X is prosecuted for assault with a deadly weapon upon A. X calls B, who testifies that A was approaching X with a gun in his hand when struck by X with a billiard cue. On cross-examination, the prosecutor asks B, "Didn't you state after X's encounter with A that A had no weapon in his hand when he was struck by X with the billiard cue?" X makes a lack-of-foundation objection, in that no time, place, or persons present are given. Is X correct?

(5) On direct examination, a 90–year–old witness testifies to the details of a transaction that occurred 10 years before trial. The cross-examiner asks the witness to state his age, but asks no other questions. On re-direct, the proponent of the witness seeks to put in a memorandum that the witness wrote a few weeks after the transaction that described it in detail. Admissible?

5. BIAS

United States v. Abel

Supreme Court of the United States, 1984.
469 U.S. 45, 105 S.Ct. 465, 83 L.Ed.2d 450.

■ JUSTICE REHNQUIST delivered the opinion of the Court.

A divided panel of the Court of Appeals for the Ninth Circuit reversed respondent's conviction for bank robbery. The Court of Appeals held that the District Court improperly admitted testimony which impeached one of respondent's witnesses. We hold that the District Court did not err, and we reverse.

Respondent John Abel and two cohorts were indicted for robbing a savings and loan in Bellflower, Ca., in violation of 18 U.S.C. §§ 2113(a) and (d). The cohorts elected to plead guilty, but respondent went to trial. One of the cohorts, Kurt Ehle, agreed to testify against respondent and identify him as a participant in the robbery.

Respondent informed the District Court at a pretrial conference that he would seek to counter Ehle's testimony with that of Robert Mills. Mills was not a participant in the robbery but was friendly with respondent and with Ehle, and had spent time with both in prison. Mills planned to testify that after the robbery Ehle had admitted to Mills that Ehle intended to implicate respondent falsely, in order to receive favorable treatment from the government. The prosecutor in turn disclosed that he intended to discredit Mills' testimony by calling Ehle back to the stand and eliciting from Ehle the fact that respondent, Mills, and Ehle were all members of the "Aryan Brotherhood," a secret prison gang that required its members always to deny the existence of the organization and to commit perjury, theft, and murder on each member's behalf.

Defense counsel objected to Ehle's proffered rebuttal testimony as too prejudicial to respondent. After a lengthy discussion in chambers the District Court decided to permit the prosecutor to cross-examine Mills about the gang, and if Mills denied knowledge of the gang, to introduce Ehle's rebuttal testimony concerning the tenets of the gang and Mills' and respondent's membership in it. The District Court held that the probative value of Ehle's rebuttal testimony outweighed its prejudicial effect, but that respondent might be entitled to a limiting instruction if his counsel would submit one to the court.

At trial Ehle implicated respondent as a participant in the robbery. Mills, called by respondent, testified that Ehle told him in prison that Ehle planned to implicate respondent falsely. When the prosecutor sought to cross-examine Mills concerning membership in the prison gang, the District Court conferred again with counsel outside of the jury's presence, and ordered the prosecutor not to use the term "Aryan Brotherhood" because it was unduly prejudicial. Accordingly, the prosecutor asked Mills if he and respondent were members of a "secret type of prison organization" which had a creed requiring members to deny its existence and lie for each other. When Mills denied knowledge of such an organization the prosecutor recalled Ehle.

Ehle testified that respondent, Mills, and he were indeed members of a secret prison organization whose tenets required its members to deny its existence and "lie, cheat, steal [and] kill" to protect each other. The District Court sustained a defense objection to a question concerning the punishment for violating the organization's rules. Ehle then further described the organization and testified that "in view of the fact of how close Abel and Mills were" it would have been "suicide" for Ehle to have told Mills what Mills attributed to him. Respondent's counsel did not request a limiting instruction and none was given.

The jury convicted respondent. On his appeal a divided panel of the Court of Appeals reversed. The Court of Appeals held that Ehle's rebuttal testimony was admitted not just to show that respondent's and Mills' membership in the same group might cause Mills to color his testimony; the court held that the contested evidence was also admitted to show that because Mills belonged to a perjurious organization, he must be lying on the stand. This suggestion of perjury, based upon a group tenet, was impermissible. The court reasoned:

"It is settled law that the government may not convict an individual merely for belonging to an organization that advocates illegal activity. *** Rather, the government must show that the individual knows of and personally accepts the tenets of the organization. Neither should the government be allowed to impeach on the grounds of mere membership, since membership, without more, has no probative value. It establishes nothing about the individual's own actions, beliefs, or veracity."

The court concluded that Ehle's testimony implicated respondent as a member of the gang; but since respondent did not take the stand, the testimony could not have been offered to impeach him and it prejudiced him "by mere association."

We hold that the evidence showing Mills' and respondent's membership in the prison gang was sufficiently probative of Mills' possible bias towards respondent to warrant its admission into evidence. Thus it was within the District Court's discretion to admit Ehle's testimony, and the Court of Appeals was wrong in concluding otherwise.

Both parties correctly assume, as did the District Court and the Court of Appeals, that the question is governed by the Federal Rules of Evidence. But the Rules do not by their terms deal with impeachment for "bias," although they do expressly treat impeachment by character evidence and conduct, Rule 608, by evidence of conviction of a crime, Rule 609, and by showing of religious beliefs or opinion, Rule 610. Neither party has suggested what significance we should attribute to this fact. Although we are nominally the promulgators of the Rules, and should in theory need only to consult our collective memories to analyze the situation properly, we are in truth merely a conduit when we deal with an undertaking as substantial as the preparation of the Federal Rules of Evidence. In the case of these Rules, too, it must be remembered that Congress extensively reviewed our submission, and considerably revised it.

Before the present Rules were promulgated, the admissibility of evidence in the federal courts was governed in part by statutes or rules, and in part by case law. This Court had held in Alford v. United States, 282 U.S. 687 (1931) that a trial court must allow some cross-examination of a witness to show bias. This holding was in accord with the overwhelming weight of authority in the state courts as reflected in Wigmore's classic treatise on the law of evidence. Our decision in Davis v. Alaska, 415 U.S. 308 (1974) holds that the Confrontation Clause of the Sixth Amendment requires a defendant to have some opportunity to show bias on the part of a prosecution witness.

With this state of unanimity confronting the drafters of the Fed.Rules of Evid., we think it unlikely that they intended to scuttle entirely the evidentiary availability of cross-examination for bias. One commentator, recognizing the omission of any express treatment of impeachment for bias, prejudice, or corruption, observes that the Rules "clearly contemplate the use of the above-mentioned grounds of impeachment." E. Cleary, McCormick on Evidence, § 40 p. 85 (3d ed. 1984).

We think this conclusion is obviously correct. Rule 401 defines as "relevant evidence" evidence having any tendency to make the existence of any fact that is of consequence to the determination of the action more probable or less probable than it would be without the evidence. Rule 402 provides that all relevant evidence is admissible, except as otherwise provided by the United States Constitution, Act of Congress, or by applicable rule. A successful showing of bias on the part of a witness would have a tendency to make the facts to which he testified less probable in the eyes of the jury than it would be without such testimony.

* * *

Ehle's testimony about the prison gang certainly made the existence of Mills' bias towards respondent more probable. Thus it was relevant to support that inference. Bias is a term used in the "common law of evidence" to describe the relationship between a party and a witness which might lead the witness to slant, unconsciously or otherwise, his testimony in favor or against a party. Bias may be induced by a witness' like, dislike, or fear of a party, or by the witness' self-interest. Proof of bias is almost always relevant because the jury, as finder of fact and weigher of credibility, has historically been entitled to assess all evidence which might bear on the accuracy and truth of a witness' testimony. The "common law of evidence" allowed the showing of bias by extrinsic evidence, while requiring the cross-examiner to "take the answer of the witness" with respect to less favored forms of impeachment.

Mills' and respondent's membership in the Aryan Brotherhood supported the inference that Mills' testimony was slanted or perhaps fabricated in respondent's favor. A witness' and a party's common membership in an organization, even without proof that the witness or party has personally adopted its tenets, is certainly probative of bias. We do not read our holdings in Scales v. United States, 367 U.S. 203 (1961), and Brandenburg v. Ohio, 395 U.S. 444 (1969), to require a different conclusion. Those cases dealt with the constitutional requirements for convicting persons under the Smith Act and state syndicalism laws for belonging to organizations which espoused illegal aims and engaged in illegal conduct. Mills' and respondent's membership in the Aryan Brotherhood was not offered to convict either of a crime, but to impeach Mills' testimony. Mills was subject to no sanction other than that he might be disbelieved. Under these circumstances there is no requirement that the witness must be shown to have subscribed to all the tenets of the organization, either casually or in a manner sufficient to permit him to be convicted under laws such as those involved in *Scales* and *Brandenburg*. For purposes of the law of evidence the jury may be permitted to draw an inference of subscription to the tenets of the organization from membership alone, even though such an inference would not be sufficient to convict beyond a reasonable doubt in a criminal prosecution under the Smith Act.

Respondent argues that even if the evidence of membership in the prison gang were relevant to show bias, the District Court erred in permitting a full description of the gang and its odious tenets. Respondent contends that the District Court abused its discretion under Federal Rules of Evidence 403, because the prejudicial effect of the contested evidence outweighed its probative value. In other words, testimony about the gang inflamed the jury against respondent, and the chance that he would be convicted by his mere association with the organization outweighed any probative value the testimony may have had on Mills' bias.

Respondent specifically contends that the District Court should not have permitted Ehle's precise description of the gang as a lying and murderous group. Respondent suggests that the District Court should have cut off the testimony after the prosecutor had elicited that Mills knew respondent and both may have belonged to an organization together. This argument ignores the fact that the *type* of organization in which a witness and a party share membership may be relevant to show bias. If the organization is a loosely knit group having nothing to do with the subject matter of the litigation, the inference of bias arising from common membership may be small or nonexistent. If the prosecutor had elicited that both respondent and Mills belonged to the Book of the Month Club, the jury probably would not have inferred bias even if the District Court had admitted the testimony. The attributes of the Aryan Brotherhood—a secret prison sect sworn to perjury and self-protection—bore directly not only on the *fact* of bias but also on the *source* and *strength* of Mills' bias. The tenets of this group showed that Mills had a powerful motive to slant his testimony towards respondent, or even commit perjury outright.

A district court is accorded a wide discretion in determining the admissibility of evidence under the Federal Rules. Assessing the probative value of common membership in any particular group, and weighing any factors counseling against admissibility is a matter first for the district court's sound judgment under Rules 401 and 403 and ultimately, if the evidence is admitted, for the trier of fact.

Before admitting Ehle's rebuttal testimony, the District Court gave heed to the extensive arguments of counsel, both in chambers and at the bench. In an attempt to avoid undue prejudice to respondent the court ordered that the name "Aryan Brotherhood" not be used. The court also offered to give a limiting instruction concerning the testimony, and it sustained defense objections to the prosecutor's questions concerning the punishment meted out to unfaithful members. These precautions did not prevent *all* prejudice to respondent from Ehle's testimony, but they did in our opinion ensure that the admission of this highly probative evidence did not *unduly* prejudice respondent. We hold there was no abuse of discretion under Rule 403 in admitting Ehle's testimony as to membership and tenets.

* * *

The judgment of the Court of Appeals is

Reversed.

Waltz, Introduction to Criminal Evidence[*]
136–37 (3d ed.1991).

* * *

Proof of bias and the like is always relevant to credibility and can be inquired into thoroughly. This can run the gamut from showing that the accused's solitary alibi witness is his devoted wife to demonstrating that the witness on the stand has been bribed by the side whose cause his testimony favors.

Thus it can be brought out that an accomplice who has turned "State's evidence" was granted immunity from prosecution or promised a reduced sentence as a *quid pro quo* for testimony advantageous to the prosecution. Less dramatic circumstances can be revealed. Perhaps the defendant's witnesses can all be shown to be his relatives or close friends. Or perhaps—and this will be more difficult for the criminal investigator to develop—the defendant's witnesses, such as alibi witnesses, are persons over whom the defendant has some sort of hold. He has threatened them, or gotten others to threaten them, with bodily harm unless they testify in his favor. Threats to the witness's loved ones can be shown, as can threats to destroy the witness's business or reputation. Promises of a monetary or other type of reward for favorable testimony can be brought out.

Sometimes defense counsel, lacking anything more solid, will bear down on the fact that the prosecution's key witness has been housed in a good hotel, wined and dined, and supported financially pending and during the trial.

Example:

BY THE PROSECUTING ATTORNEY: Let's get this straight, Ms. Adams. You state, as I understand it, that the accused was with you during all of the night in question?

A. That's correct.

Q. It is a fact, is it not, that you have been living with the accused, although not married to him, for the past five years?

A. That's true. But we're going to get married sometime. He's promised me.

Q. That is your hope, is it?

A. Yes.

Q. You won't be able to get married if he goes to jail on this charge, will you?

A. No. Maybe I could wait for him.

Q. And the fact also is that the accused has been and is now your sole source of financial support, isn't that so?

A. Yes.

Q. And he could not continue to support you if he goes to prison, could he?

A. I guess not. They don't earn much in there.

Q. You have everything to gain if Charlie is acquitted and everything to lose if he is convicted, is that not correct?

A. Yes, but I'm not lying.

Q. Can you give the court and jury the name of any person who saw you and Charlie together on the night in question?

A. No.

It is proper to ask expert witnesses, such as a psychiatrist who has supported an insanity defense, whether he is being paid a fee for his testimony, although a carefully coached expert will usually sidestep this sort of cross-examination fairly artfully.

See Federal Rules of Evidence 806; California Evidence Code § 1202.

HYPOTHETICALS

(1) A sues X, a police officer, and Y City, X's employer, for damages for false imprisonment growing out of X's arrest of A in a barroom brawl. B, a witness for A, testifies that A was a mere bystander and not a party to the brawl. On cross-examination, X asks B if he had not, on two occasions, slashed tires on marked police cars and been convicted of malicious mischief for so doing. A objects that this is improper cross-examination and improper attempted impeachment of B. What result?

(2) A sues X, a police officer, and Y City, X's employer, for damages for false arrest and imprisonment growing out of X's arrest of A in a barroom brawl. B, a witness for A, testifies that A was a mere bystander and not a party to the brawl. On cross-examination, X seeks to question B to elicit that he had had three felony arrests by Y City police resulting in no convictions, and six arrests by Y City police resulting in misdemeanor convictions. A objects to this cross-examination as being irrelevant and improper

impeachment by specific instances of conduct. X asserts he is offering the evidence to prove bias by B against Y City police and against X as a police officer. Should A's objections be sustained?

CHAPTER 5

CONFIDENTIALITY AND CONFIDENTIAL COMMUNICATION

PART **A** The Attorney–Client Privilege

PART **B** Physician–Patient Privileges and Psychotherapist–Patient Privileges

PART **C** The Marital Privileges

PART **D** Miscellaneous Privileges

A. THE ATTORNEY–CLIENT PRIVILEGE

Jeremy Bentham, Rationale of Judicial Evidence
Vol. 5, pp. 302–304 (1827) (quoted in part in 8 Wigmore, Evidence, § 2291 pp. 549–550, McNaughton rev. 1961).

Lawyer and Client

English judges have taken care to exempt the professional members of the partnership from so unpleasant an obligation as that of rendering service to justice * * * When in consulting with a law advisor, attorney or advocate, a man has confessed his delinquency, or disclosed some fact which, if stated in court, might tend to operate in proof of it, such law adviser is not to be suffered to be examined as to any such point. The law adviser is neither to be compelled, nor so much as suffered, to betray the trust thus reposed in him. Not Suffered? Why not? Oh, because to betray a trust is treachery; and an act of treachery is an immoral act * * * But if such confidence, when reposed, is permitted to be violated, and if this be known, (which, if such be the law, it will be), the consequence will be, that no such confidence will be reposed. Not reposed?—Well: and if it be not, wherein will consist the mischief? The man by the supposition is guilty; if not, by the supposition there is nothing to betray: let the law adviser say every thing he has heard, every thing he can have heard from his client, the client cannot have any thing to fear from it * * * What then, will be the consequence? That a guilty person will not in general be able to derive quite so much assistance from his law adviser, in the way of concerting a false defence, as he may do at present. * * *

United States v. Woodruff

United States District Court, Eastern District of Pennsylvania, 1974.
383 F.Supp. 696.

MEMORANDUM AND ORDER

■ CLIFFORD SCOTT GREEN, DISTRICT JUDGE.

In this case, defendant Woodruff, who was free on bail pending trial of this matter, did not appear for trial. The government, which intends to seek an indictment against this defendant on charges of bail jumping, has requested this Court to order the public defender who represented this defendant to respond to the questions put to him by the government relating to whether or not he advised his client as to the time and place of the trial in this matter and further as to whether or not his client responded and acknowledged that he understood the time and place of the trial.

[T]he sole question before us is whether counsel is obligated to furnish this type of information when properly requested by the government. The essence of the question is whether the compelled disclosure which is sought will violate the attorney-client privilege. We grant the government's motion.

There is no doubt that the purpose of this rule is to promote the freedom of consultation of legal advisers by clients. We set out Judge Wyzanski's statement of the privilege.

"The privilege applies only if (1) the asserted holder of the privilege is or sought to become a client; (2) the person to whom the communication was made (a) is a member of the bar of a court, or his subordinate and (b) in connection with this communication is acting as a lawyer; (3) the communication relates to a fact of which his attorney was informed (a) by his client (b) without the presence of strangers (c) for the purpose of securing primarily either (i) an opinion on law or (ii) legal services or (iii) assistance in some legal proceeding, and not (d) for the purpose of committing a crime or tort; and (4) the privilege has been (a) claimed and (b) not waived by the client. United States v. United Shoe Machinery Corporation, (D.Mass.1950).

Two Circuit Courts have held that there is no breach of the attorney-client privilege in permitting a defendant's former counsel to testify that he had informed the defendant of the necessity of his appearance at a court proceeding and the time thereof. Both these cases involved prosecutions for violations of the statute under which the government intends to proceed against the present defendant. Both courts noted: that it is the duty of counsel to relay such instructions as an officer of the court; that, in this regard, defense counsel merely served as a conduit for the transmission of a message; and that, the transmission of such an instruction is not in the nature of a confidential communication.

Wigmore has helpfully analyzed the problem presented by this motion.

"The courts have not always used consistent language in answering the question whether the privilege is limited in some way to communications *necessary* or *material* or *relevant* to some purpose of the consultation.

"It should be clear, on the one hand, that the actual necessity of making a particular statement, or the materiality to the cause of a particular fact, cannot determine the answer, for the client cannot know what is necessary or material, and the object of the privilege is that he should be unhampered in his quest for advice. On the other hand, when he knowingly departs from that purpose and interjects other matters not relevant to it, he is in that respect not seeking legal advice, and the privilege does not design to protect him. The test is, therefore, not whether the fact or the statement is actually necessary or material or relevant to the subject of the consultation, but whether the statement is made as *a part of the purpose of the client* to obtain advice on that subject. Some such rule would seem to have been in the minds of all the judges in spite of the occasional apparent inconsistency of their utterances." 8 Wigmore, Evidence § 2310.

"A lawyer is sometimes employed without reference to his knowledge and discretion in the law—as where he is charged with finding a profitable investment for trust funds. * * * It is not easy to frame a definite test for distinguishing *legal from nonlegal advice*. Where the general purpose concerns legal rights and obligations, a particular incidental transaction would receive protection, though in itself it were merely commercial in nature—as where the financial condition of a shareholder is discussed in the course of a proceeding to enforce a claim against a corporation. But apart from such cases, the most that can be said by way of generalization is that a matter committed to a professional legal adviser *is prima facie so committed for the sake of the legal advice* which may be more or less desirable for some aspect of the matter, and is therefore within the privilege unless it clearly appears to be lacking in aspects requiring legal advice.

> Obviously, much depends upon the circumstances of the individual transactions." 8 Wigmore, Evidence § 2296.

There is no doubt that one could argue that holding these communications to be within the privilege would further the purpose of the privilege in that the disclosure by counsel will inhibit the development of trust on the part of clients and, as a consequence, inhibit full communication. However, the law has always recognized competing considerations, such as the necessity of the testimony of men [*sic*] in the enforcement of the criminal laws. Consequently, the scope and structure of the privilege is narrowed because of competing considerations.

Communications between counsel and defendant as to the trial date do not involve the subject matter of defendant's legal problem. Moreover, this is so clear that we need not be concerned in this regard with the factor of a client's uncertainty as to the relevancy of information which he imparts to

Notice of trial is not legal comms.
- not priv.

his attorney. Such communications are non-legal in nature. Counsel is simply performing a notice function. In fact, we take judicial notice that the courts generally rely upon counsel to perform such a function.

For this reason, and the fact that any communication from the attorney to the client in this regard was based on facts obtained by the attorney from a source other than his client, we hold that the transmission to defendant from the attorney of the fact of the time of trial is not privileged.

Defense counsel requests that we limit this disclosure to the situation when the attorney, himself, communicated this fact to the defendant. However, the rationale of our holding requires that the transmission of this information to defendant by defense counsel's office personnel is also outside the privilege. Also, defense counsel would have us exempt from disclosure other transmissions of this information to defendant by defense counsel which transmissions took place during strategy sessions concerning defendant's defense to this indictment. Both the rationale set out above and the fact that the questions proposed are specific and discrete, lead us to conclude that the transmission of the information in that context is also outside the privilege.

The communications involved here are not of the type that the client might arguably consider relevant to his legal problem. The information is not the type of non-legal information which is related to the client's legal problem and the advice he needs thereon and, for that reason, is not a protected incidental communication.

Finally, we also hold based on the reasoning above, that the communications of the defendant to defense counsel with respect to the trial date are outside the privilege.

Defense counsel has also indicated the peculiarly sensitive problem that a situation such as this presents for defense counsel of the Defender Association. We understand the singular problems that such counsel has in establishing a relationship of trust with their clients. Defense counsel suggests that this factor should be considered in shaping the attorney-client privilege in this context and/or that we should hold that disclosure under these circumstances would violate public policy. We decline to so hold. The impact of such a holding is difficult to foresee and, at least with respect to notice for court appearances, less drastic solutions to the problem should be created.

Upjohn Co. v. United States

Supreme Court of the United States, 1981.
449 U.S. 383, 101 S.Ct. 677, 66 L.Ed.2d 584.

■ JUSTICE REHNQUIST delivered the opinion of the Court.

We granted certiorari in this case to address important questions concerning the scope of the attorney-client privilege in the corporate context. We decline to lay down a broad rule or series of rules to govern all conceivable future questions in [the privilege] area. We can and do, however, conclude that the attorney-client privilege protects the communications involved in this case from compelled disclosure.

I

In January 1976 independent accountants conducting an audit of one of petitioner's foreign subsidiaries discovered that the subsidiary made payments to or for the benefit of foreign government officials in order to secure government business. The accountants so informed Mr. Gerard Thomas, petitioner's Vice President, Secretary, and General Counsel. He consulted with outside counsel and R.T. Parfet, Jr., petitioner's Chairman of the Board. It was decided that the company would conduct an internal investigation of what were termed "questionable payments." As part of this investigation the attorneys prepared a letter containing a questionnaire which was sent to "All Foreign General and Area Managers" over the Chairman's signature. The letter began by noting recent disclosures that several American companies made "possibly illegal" payments to foreign government officials and emphasized that the management needed full information concerning any such payments made by Upjohn. The letter indicated that the Chairman had asked Thomas, identified as "the company's General Counsel," "to conduct an investigation." The questionnaire sought detailed information concerning such payments. Managers were instructed to treat the investigation as "highly confidential" and not to discuss it with anyone other than Upjohn employees who might be helpful in providing the requested information. Responses were to be sent directly to Thomas. Thomas and outside counsel also interviewed the recipients of the questionnaire and some 33 other Upjohn officers or employees as part of the investigation.

On March 26, 1976, the company voluntarily submitted a preliminary report to the Securities and Exchange Commission on Form 8–K disclosing certain questionable payments. A copy of the report was simultaneously submitted to the Internal Revenue Service, which immediately began an investigation to determine the tax consequences of the payments. Special agents conducting the investigation were given lists by Upjohn of all those interviewed and all who had responded to the questionnaire. On November 23, 1976, the Service issued a summons demanding production of:

> "All files relative to the investigation conducted under the supervision of Gerard Thomas to identify payments to employees of foreign governments and any political contributions made by the Upjohn Company or any of its affiliates since January 1, 1971 and to determine whether any funds of the Upjohn Company had been improperly accounted for on the corporate books during the same period.

> "The records should include but not be limited to written questionnaires sent to managers of the Upjohn Company's foreign affiliates. * * *

The company declined to produce the documents specified in the second paragraph on the grounds that they were protected from disclosure by the attorney-client privilege. [T]he United States filed a petition seeking enforcement of the summons. [The District C]ourt adopted the recommendation of a Magistrate who concluded that the summons should be enforced. Petitioner appealed to the Court of Appeals for the Sixth Circuit which rejected the Magistrate's finding of a waiver of the attorney-client privilege, but agreed that the privilege did not apply "[t]o the extent that the communications were made by officers and agents not responsible for directing Upjohn's actions in response to legal advice * * * for the simple reason that the communications were not the 'client's.'" The court reasoned that accepting petitioner's claim for a broader application of the privilege would encourage upper-echelon management to ignore unpleasant facts and create too broad a "zone of silence." Noting that petitioner's counsel had interviewed officials such as the Chairman and President, the Court of Appeals remanded to the District Court so that a determination of who was within the "control group" could be made.

II

Federal Rule of Evidence 501 provides that "the privilege of a witness * * * shall be governed by the principles of the common law as they may be interpreted by the courts of the United States in light of reason and experience." The attorney-client privilege is the oldest of the privileges for confidential communications known to the common law. * * *

* * *

The Court of Appeals, however, considered the application of the privilege in the corporate context to present a "different problem," since the client was an inanimate entity and "only the senior management, guiding and integrating the several operations, * * * can be said to possess an identity analogous to the corporation as a whole." The first case to articulate the so-called "control group test" adopted by the court below, Philadelphia v. Westinghouse Electric Corp., reflected a similar conceptual approach:

> "Keeping in mind that the question is, Is it the corporation which is seeking the lawyer's advice when the asserted privileged communication is made?, the most satisfactory solution, I think, is that if the employee making the communication, of whatever rank he may be, is in a position to control or even to take a substantial part in a decision about any action which the corporation may take upon the advice of the attorney, * * * then, in effect, *he is (or personifies) the corporation* when he makes his disclosure to the lawyer and the privilege would apply." (Emphasis supplied.)

Such a view, we think, overlooks the fact that the privilege exists to protect not only the giving of professional advice to those who can act on it but also the giving of information to the lawyer to enable him to give sound and informed advice. The first step in the resolution of any legal problem is ascertaining the factual background and sifting through the facts.

In the case of the individual client the provider of information and the person who acts on the lawyer's advice are one and the same. In the corporate context, however, it will frequently be employees beyond the control group as defined by the court below—"officers and agents * * * responsible for directing [the company's] actions in response to legal advice"—who will possess the information needed by the corporation's lawyers. Middle-level—and indeed lower-level—employees can, by actions within the scope of their employment, embroil the corporation in serious legal difficulties, and it is only natural that these employees would have the relevant information needed by corporate counsel if he is adequately to advise the client with respect to such actual or potential difficulties. * * *

The control group test—adopted by the court below—frustrates the very purpose of the privilege by discouraging the communication of relevant information by employees of the client to attorneys seeking to render legal advice to the client corporation. The attorney's advice will also frequently be more significant to noncontrol group members than to those who officially sanction the advice, and the control group test makes it more difficult to convey full and frank legal advice to the employees who will put into effect the client corporation's policy.

[handwritten margin note: Control group test discourages comms by low level w/ info]

The narrow scope given the attorney-client privilege by the court below not only makes it difficult for corporate attorneys to formulate sound advice when their client is faced with a specific legal problem but also threatens to limit the valuable efforts of corporate counsel to ensure their client's compliance with the law. In light of the vast and complicated array of regulatory legislation confronting the modern corporation, corporations, unlike most individuals, "constantly go to lawyers to find out how to obey the law," particularly since compliance with the law in this area is hardly an instinctive matter. The test adopted by the court below is difficult to apply in practice, though no abstractly formulated and unvarying "test" will necessarily enable courts to decide questions such as this with mathematical precision. But if the purpose of the attorney-client privilege is to be served, the attorney and client must be able to predict with some degree of certainty whether particular discussions will be protected. An uncertain privilege, or one which purports to be certain but results in widely varying applications by the courts, is little better than no privilege at all. The very terms of the test adopted by the court below suggest the unpredictability of its application. The test restricts the availability of the privilege to those officers who play a "substantial role" in deciding and directing a corporation's legal response. Disparate decisions in cases applying this test illustrate its unpredictability.

The communications at issue were made by Upjohn employees[3] to counsel for Upjohn acting as such, at the direction of corporate superiors in

---

[3] Seven of the eighty-six employees interviewed by counsel had terminated their employment with Upjohn at the time of the interview. Petitioner argues that the privilege should nonetheless apply to communications by these former employees concerning activities during their period of employment. Neither the District Court nor the Court of Appeals had occasion to address this issue, and we decline to decide it without the benefit of treatment below.

order to secure legal advice from counsel. As the Magistrate found, "Mr. Thomas consulted with the Chairman of the Board and outside counsel and thereafter conducted a factual investigation to determine the nature and extent of the questionable payments *and to be in a position to give legal advice to the company with respect to the payments.*" (Emphasis supplied.) Information, not available from upper-echelon management, was needed to supply a basis for legal advice concerning compliance with securities and tax laws, foreign laws, currency regulations, duties to shareholders, and potential litigation in each of these areas. The communications concerned matters within the scope of the employees' corporate duties, and the employees themselves were sufficiently aware that they were being questioned in order that the corporation could obtain legal advice. The questionnaire identified Thomas as "the company's General Counsel" and referred in its opening sentence to the possible illegality of payments such as the ones on which information was sought. A statement of policy accompanying the questionnaire clearly indicated the legal implications of the investigation. The policy statement was issued "in order that there be no uncertainty in the future as to the policy with respect to the practices which are the subject of this investigation." It began "Upjohn will comply with all laws and regulations," and stated that commissions or payments "will not be used as a subterfuge for bribes or illegal payments" and that all payments must be "proper and legal." Any future agreements with foreign distributors or agents were to be approved "by a company attorney" and any questions concerning the policy were to be referred "to the company's General Counsel." This statement was issued to Upjohn employees worldwide, so that even those interviewees not receiving a questionnaire were aware of the legal implications of the interviews. Pursuant to explicit instructions from the Chairman of the Board, the communications were considered "highly confidential" when made, and have been kept confidential by the company. Consistent with the underlying purposes of the attorney-client privilege, these communications must be protected against compelled disclosure.

The Court of Appeals declined to extend the attorney-client privilege beyond the limits of the control group test for fear that doing so would entail severe burdens on discovery and create a broad "zone of silence" over corporate affairs. Application of the attorney-client privilege to communications such as those involved here, however, puts the adversary in no worse position than if the communications had never taken place. The privilege only protects disclosure of communications; it does not protect disclosure of the underlying facts by those who communicated with the attorney:

> "[T]he protection of the privilege extends only to *communications* and not to facts. A fact is one thing and a communication concerning that fact is an entirely different thing. The client cannot be compelled to answer the question, 'What did you say or write to the attorney?' but may not refuse to disclose any relevant fact within his knowledge merely because he incorporated a statement of such fact into his communication to his attorney." Philadelphia v. Westinghouse Electric Corp.

Here the Government was free to question the employees who communicated with Thomas and outside counsel. While it would probably be more convenient for the Government to secure the results of petitioner's internal investigation by simply subpoenaing the questionnaires and notes taken by petitioner's attorneys, such considerations of convenience do not overcome the policies served by the attorney-client privilege. As Justice Jackson noted in his concurring opinion in Hickman v. Taylor: "Discovery was hardly intended to enable a learned profession to perform its functions * * * on wits borrowed from the adversary."

* * * [W]e conclude that the narrow "control group test" sanctioned by the Court of Appeals in this case cannot, consistent with "the principles of the common law as * * * interpreted * * * in the light of reason and experience," govern the development of the law in this area. * * *

* * *

Accordingly, the judgment of the Court of Appeals is reversed, and the case remanded for further proceedings.

It is so ordered.

■ CHIEF JUSTICE BURGER, concurring in part and concurring in the judgment.

I join in [P]art I of the opinion of the Court and in the judgment. I agree fully with the Court's rejection of the so-called "control group" test, its reasons for doing so, and its ultimate holding that the communications at issue are privileged. As the Court states, however, "if the purpose of the attorney-client privilege is to be served, the attorney and client must be able to predict with some degree of certainty whether particular discussions will be protected." For this very reason, I believe that we should articulate a standard that will govern similar cases and afford guidance to corporations, counsel advising them, and federal courts.

The Court properly relies on a variety of factors in concluding that the communications now before us are privileged. Because of the great importance of the issue, in my view the Court should make clear now that, as a general rule, a communication is privileged at least when, as here, an employee or former employee speaks at the direction of the management with an attorney regarding conduct or proposed conduct within the scope of employment. The attorney must be one authorized by the management to inquire into the subject and must be seeking information to assist counsel in performing any of the following functions: (a) evaluating whether the employee's conduct has bound or would bind the corporation; (b) assessing the legal consequences, if any, of that conduct; or (c) formulating appropriate legal responses to actions that have been or may be taken by others with regard to that conduct. Other communications between employees and corporate counsel may indeed be privileged—as the petitioners and several amici have suggested in their proposed formulations—but the need for certainty does not compel us now to prescribe all the details of the privilege in this case. * * * Simply asserting that this failure "may to some slight extent undermine desirable certainty," neither minimizes the consequences of continuing uncertainty and confusion nor harmonizes the inherent dissonance of acknowledging that uncertainty while declining to clarify it within the frame of issues presented.

NOTE ON FEDERAL WORK PRODUCT DOCTRINE

During discovery, a claim of attorney-client privilege is likely to be accompanied by a claim that the material is protected under the Federal Rules of Civil Procedure as "work product" of the attorney or party. A limited "work product" protection is also recognized in criminal cases.

The civil "work product" protection has been codified in Fed.R.Civ.P. 26(b)(3). Under that rule, a party may obtain discovery of documents and tangible things prepared "in anticipation of litigation" by an attorney or agent of the opposing party only upon a showing of "substantial need" and a showing that the party seeking discovery cannot, without undue hardship, obtain the substantial equivalent from other sources.[1] Moreover, even if the requisite showing of need is made, the court must protect against disclosure of "the mental impressions, conclusions, opinions, or legal theories of an attorney or other representative of a party concerning the litigation."

There are several differences between the "work product" protection and the attorney-client privilege:

(1) Material that is covered by the attorney-client privilege cannot be discovered even if the opponent demonstrates that she has a special need for the material to prepare her case. Material that is covered only by work product protection can be discovered upon such a showing, at least if it does not reveal the mental impressions of the party's attorney or other representative.

(2) The attorney-client privilege applies only to confidential communications between the attorney (or attorney's representative) and the client (or client's representative). A much larger category of material is covered by the work product protection. For example, statements to an attorney by a witness who is not a client are covered. For that matter, an attorney need not be involved at all for the work product protection to take effect. For example, information gathered by the party or the party's agent (such as a claim adjuster) are covered by the work product doctrine so long as the information is gathered in anticipation of litigation, even if no attorney had been retained at the time of the information-gathering.

(3) The work product protection applies only to information gathered in "anticipation of litigation." The attorney-client privilege covers confidential communications to the lawyer seeking legal advice or services, whether or not litigation is expected.

---

[1] A person is, however, entitled to discover his or her own statement as a matter of course. For example, if the plaintiff gave a statement to the defendant's investigator, the plaintiff is entitled to have a copy of that statement without any showing of need.

See Federal Rules of Evidence 501; California Evidence Code §§ 911–913, 915–919.

City and County of San Francisco v. Superior Court

Supreme Court of California, 1951.
37 Cal.2d 227, 231 P.2d 26, 25 A.L.R.2d 1418.

■ TRAYNOR, JUSTICE. James Hession brought an action for personal injuries against the City and County of San Francisco and the Western Pacific Railroad Company. He alleged that he suffered brain concussion, nerve root damage, and nervous shock. At the request of Hession's attorneys, Dr. Joseph Catton, a physician specializing in nervous and mental diseases, twice gave Hession a neurological and psychiatric examination. In his deposition Dr. Catton testified that there was no physician-patient relationship between him and Hession; that he did not advise or treat Hession; that the sole purpose of the examination was to aid Hession's attorneys in the preparation of a lawsuit for Hession; and that he was the agent of the attorneys. He refused to answer questions regarding Hession's condition on the grounds that the information sought was privileged under subdivisions 2 and 4 of Section 1881 of the Code of Civil Procedure and that the questions called for "the use of faculties of a physician, neurologist, and psychiatrist and for an opinion based thereon, which opinion is a portion of my property which I do not wish to be deprived of without due compensation and arrangement having been made in relation thereto." Hession's counsel also claimed that the information was privileged.

Petitioner, the City and County of San Francisco, seeks a writ of mandamus to compel respondent court to order Dr. Catton to answer the questions.

[The court holds that the physician-patient privilege is inapplicable. Hession did not consult Dr. Catton for advice or treatment, and so there was no physician-patient relationship between the two. Moreover, even if there had been, under § 1881(4), bringing an action for personal injuries constituted a consent to testimony by any physician who treated the plaintiff for those injuries.]

The Attorney-Client Privilege

Although Dr. Catton can invoke no privilege of his own and there was no physician-patient privilege in this case, we have concluded that Dr. Catton was an intermediate agent for communication between Hession and his attorneys and that Hession may therefore invoke the attorney-client privilege under section 1881, subdivision (2) of the Code of Civil Procedure. That subdivision reads: "An attorney cannot, without the consent of his client, be examined as to any communication made by the client to him, or his advice given thereon in the course of professional employment; nor can an attorney's secretary, stenographer, or clerk be examined, without the consent of his employer, concerning any fact the knowledge of which has been acquired in such capacity." See also, Bus. & Prof.Code, § 6068(e). This privilege is strictly construed, since it suppresses relevant facts that may be necessary for a just decision. It cannot be invoked unless the client intended the communication to be confidential, and only communications made to an attorney in the course of professional employment are privileged.

* * *

The privilege embraces not only oral or written statements but actions, signs, or other means of communicating information by a client to his attorney. "[A]lmost any act, done by the client in the sight of the attorney and during the consultation, may conceivably be done by the client as the subject of a communication, and the only question will be whether, in the circumstances of the case, it was intended to be done as such. The client, supposedly, may make a specimen of his handwriting for the attorney's information, or may exhibit an identifying scar, or may show a secret token. If any of these acts are done as part of a communication to the attorney, and if further the communication is intended to be confidential * * *, the privilege comes into play." 8 Wigmore, supra, § 2306, p. 590.

Petitioner contends that under the express terms of section 1881(2) it is only the attorney and the attorney's secretary, stenographer, or clerk who cannot be examined, and that since Dr. Catton was not engaged in any of these capacities he cannot withhold the information requested.

The statute specifically extends the client's privilege to preclude examination of the attorney's secretary, stenographer, or clerk regarding information of communications between attorney and client acquired in such capacities, to rule out the possibility of their coming within the general rule that the privilege does not preclude the examination of a third person who overhears or otherwise has knowledge of communications between a client and his attorney. It does not follow, however, that intermediate agents of communication between attorney and client fall within that general rule. Had Hession himself described his condition to his attorneys there could be no doubt that the communication would be privileged and that neither the attorney nor Hession could be compelled to reveal it, even though a client is not listed in section 1881(2) among those who cannot be examined. It is no less the client's communication to the attorney when it is given by the client to an agent for transmission to the attorney, and it is immaterial whether the agent is the agent of the attorney, the client, or both.

"(T)he client's freedom of communication requires a liberty of employing other means than his own personal action. The privilege of confidence would be a vain one unless its exercise could be thus delegated. A communication, then by *any form of agency* employed or set in motion by the client is within the privilege.

"This of course includes communications through an *interpreter,* and also communications *through a messenger* or any other *agent of transmission,* as well as communications *originating with the client's agent* and made to the attorney. It follows, too, that the communications of the *attorney's agent* to the attorney are within the privilege, because the attorney's agent is also the client's sub-agent and is acting as such for the client."

8 Wigmore, supra, § 2317, pp. 616–617; * * * Thus, when communication by a client to his attorney regarding his physical or mental condition requires the assistance of a physician to interpret the client's condition to the attorney, the client may submit to an examination by the physician without fear that the latter will be compelled to reveal the information disclosed. In *Arnold v. City of Maryville,* and *McMillen v. Industrial Comm. of Ohio,* on which petitioner relies, it was held, as we hold in the present case, that there was no physician-patient privilege. In neither case, however, was the attorney-client privilege invoked or considered.

It is contended that the purpose of the patient-litigant exception in subdivision 4 of section 1881 would be defeated if the attorney-client privilege in subdivision 2 can be invoked to prevent a physician from divulging the results of his examination of a person for the purpose of aiding his attorneys in the preparation of an action for personal injuries. The two subdivisions relate to two separate and distinct privileges. Since there was no physician-patient relationship, there was no physician-patient privilege to waive; the whole of subdivision 4 including the exception was therefore inapplicable. It does not follow that if there is no physician-patient privilege there can be no attorney-client privilege. The patient-litigant exception applies only to the physician-patient privilege in subdivision 4 and there is no corresponding client-litigant exception in subdivision 2. Had Dr. Catton treated Hession before being asked to serve as an intermediate agent between Hession and his attorneys, the patient-litigant exception would apply and Dr. Catton would then have been like any other witness with knowledge of facts pertinent to an issue to be tried. The exception could not be defeated by asking the physician to reveal his knowledge of the facts to the attorneys, for a litigant cannot silence a witness by having him reveal his knowledge to the litigant's attorney. Similarly, if Dr. Catton should now treat Hession, any information acquired in the course of that treatment would not be privileged, although the results of his previous examinations and his reports to Hession's attorneys would be.

The alternative writ of mandamus is discharged, and the petition for the peremptory writ is denied.

■ Gibson, C.J., and Shenk, Edmonds, Carter, Schauer and Spence, JJ., concur.

Clark v. State

Court of Criminal Appeals, Texas, 1953.

159 Tex.Cr.R. 187, 261 S.W.2d 339. cert. denied 346 U.S. 855, 905, 74 S.Ct. 69(3),
217(2), 98 L.Ed. 369, 404.

■ MORRISON, JUDGE. The offense is murder; the punishment, death.

The deceased secured a divorce from appellant on March 25, 1952. That night she was killed, as she lay at home in her bed, as the result of a gunshot wound. From the mattress on her bed, as well as from the bed of her daughter, were recovered bullets which were shown by a firearms expert to have been fired by a .38 special revolver having Colt characteristics. Appellant was shown to have purchased a Colt .38 Detective Special some ten months prior to the homicide.

* * *

Marjorie Bartz, a telephone operator in the City of San Angelo, testified that at 2:49 in the morning of March 26, 1952, while on duty, she received a call from the Golden Spur Hotel; that at first she thought the person placing the call was a Mr. Cox and so made out the slip; but that she then recognized appellant's voice, scratched out the word "Cox" and wrote "Clark." She stated that appellant told her he wanted to speak to his lawyer, Jimmy Martin in Dallas, and that she placed the call to him at telephone number Victor 1942 in that city and made a record thereof, which record was admitted in evidence. Miss Bartz testified that, contrary to company rules, she listened to the entire conversation that ensued, and that it went as follows:

> The appellant: "Hello, Jimmy, I went to the extremes."
>
> The voice in Dallas: "What did you do?"
>
> The appellant: "I just went to the extremes."
>
> The voice in Dallas: "You got to tell me what you did before I can help."
>
> The appellant: "Well, I killed her."
>
> The voice in Dallas: "Who did you kill; the driver?"
>
> The appellant: "No, I killed her."
>
> The voice in Dallas: "Did you get rid of the weapon?"
>
> The appellant: "No, I still got the weapon."
>
> The voice in Dallas: "Get rid of the weapon and sit tight and don't talk to anyone, and I will fly down in the morning."

It was stipulated that the Dallas telephone number of appellant's attorney was Victor 1942.

* * *

[The court holds that evidence of the conversation is not rendered inadmissible by the fact that it was procured by eavesdropping.]

We now discuss the question of the privileged nature of the conversation. Wigmore on Evidence (Third Edition), Section 2326, reads as follows:

"The law provides subjective freedom for the client by assuring him of exemption from its processes of disclosure against himself or the attorney or their agents of communication. This much, but not a whit more, is necessary for the maintenance of the privilege. Since the means of preserving secrecy of communication are entirely in the client's hands, and since the privilege is a derogation from the general testimonial duty and should be strictly construed, it would be improper to extend its prohibition to third persons who obtain knowledge of the communications."

The precise question here presented does not appear to have been passed upon in this or other jurisdictions.

In Hoy v. Morris, Mass. (1859) a conversation between a client and his attorney was overheard by Aldrich, who was in the adjoining room. The Court therein said:

"Aldrich was not an attorney, not in any way connected with Mr. Todd; and certainly in no situation where he was either necessary or useful to the parties to enable them to understand each other. On the contrary, he was a mere bystander, and casually overheard conversation not addressed to him nor intended for his ear, but which the client and attorney meant to have respected as private and confidential. Mr. Todd could not lawfully have revealed it. But, in consequence of a want of proper precaution, the communications between him and his client were overheard by a mere stranger. As the latter stood in no relation of confidence to either of the parties, he was clearly not within the rule of exemption from giving testimony; and he might therefore, when summoned as a witness, be compelled to testify as to what he overheard, so far as it was pertinent to the subject matter of inquiry upon the trial * * *."

In Walker v. State, (Tex App. 1885) we find the following:

"Mrs. Bridges was not incompetent or disqualified because she was present and heard the confessions made by defendant, even assuming that the relation of attorney and client subsisted in fact between him and Culberson."

* * *

We hold that the trial court properly admitted the evidence of the telephone operator.

* * *

Finding no reversible error, the judgment of the trial court is affirmed.

On Appellant's Motion for Rehearing

■ Woodley, Judge., We are favored with masterful briefs and arguments in support of appellant's motion for rehearing including amicus curiae brief by an eminent and able Texas lawyer addressed to the question of privileged communications between attorney and client.

* * *

As to the testimony of the telephone operator regarding the conversation between appellant and Mr. Martin, the conversation is set forth in full in our original opinion. Our holding as to the admissibility of the testimony of the operator is not to be considered as authority except in comparable fact situations.

For the purpose of this opinion we assume that the Dallas voice was that of Mr. Martin, appellant's attorney. If it was not appellant's attorney the conversation was not privileged.

It is in the interest of public justice that the client be able to make a full disclosure to his attorney of all facts that are material to his defense or that go to substantiate his claim. The purpose of the privilege is to encourage such disclosure of the facts. But the interests of public justice further require that no shield such as the protection afforded to communications between attorney and client shall be interposed to protect a person who takes counsel on how he can safely commit a crime.

We think this latter rule must extend to one who, having committed a crime, seeks or takes counsel as to how he shall escape arrest and punishment, such as advice regarding the destruction or disposition of the murder weapon or of the body following a murder.

One who knowing that an offense has been committed conceals the offender or aids him to evade arrest or trial becomes an accessory. The fact that the aider may be a member of the bar and the attorney for the offender will not prevent his becoming an accessory.

Art. 77, P.C. defining an accessory contains the exception "One who aids an offender in making or preparing his defense at law" is not an accessory.

The conversation as testified to by the telephone operator is not within the exception found in Art. 77, P.C. When the Dallas voice advised appellant to "get rid of the weapon" (which advice the evidence shows was followed) such aid cannot be said to constitute aid "in making or preparing his defense at law". It was aid to the perpetrator of the crime "in order that he may evade arrest or trial."

Is such a conversation privileged as a communication between attorney and client?

If the adviser had been called to testify as to the conversation, would it not have been more appropriate for him to claim his privilege against self-incrimination rather than that the communication was privileged because it was between attorney and client?

Appellant, when he conversed with Mr. Martin, was not under arrest nor was he charged with a crime. He had just inflicted mortal wounds on his former wife and apparently had shot her daughter. Mr. Martin had acted as his attorney in the divorce suit which had been tried that day and had secured a satisfactory property settlement. Appellant called him and told him that he had gone to extremes and had killed "her", not "the driver". Mr. Martin appeared to understand these references and told appellant to get rid of "the weapon".

We are unwilling to subscribe to the theory that such counsel and advice should be privileged because of the attorney-client relationship which existed between the parties in the divorce suit. We think, on the other hand, that the conversation was admissible as not within the realm of legitimate professional counsel and employment.

The rule of public policy which calls for the privileged character of the communication between attorney and client, we think, demands that the rule be confined to the legitimate course of professional employment. It cannot consistent with the high purpose and policy supporting the rule be here applied.

The murder weapon was not found. The evidence indicates that appellant disposed of it as advised in the telephone conversation. Such advice or counsel was not such as merits protection because given by an attorney. It was not in the legitimate course of professional employment in making or preparing a defense at law.

Nothing is found in the record to indicate that appellant sought any advice from Mr. Martin other than that given in the conversation testified to by the telephone operator. We are not therefore dealing with a situation where the accused sought legitimate advice from his attorney in preparing his legal defense.

Some of the citations and quotations have been deleted from our original opinion.

We remain convinced that the appeal was properly disposed of on original submission.

Appellant's motion for rehearing is overruled.

Restatement of the Law Third—The Law Governing Lawyers*

§ 82. Client Crime Or Fraud

The attorney-client privilege does not apply to a communication occurring when a client:

(a) consults a lawyer for the purpose, later accomplished, of obtaining assistance to engage in a crime or fraud or aiding a third person to do so, or

(b) regardless of the client's purpose at the time of consultation, uses the lawyer's advice or other services to engage in or assist a crime or fraud.

Comment:

* * *

b. Rationale. When a client consults a lawyer intending to violate elemental legal obligations, there is less social interest in protecting the communication. Correlatively, there is a public interest in preventing clients from attempting to misuse the client-lawyer relationship for seriously harmful ends. Denying protection of the privilege can be founded on the additional moral ground that the client's wrongful intent forfeits the protection. The client can choose whether or not to commit or aid the act after consulting the lawyer and thus is able to avoid exposing secret communications. The exception does not apply to communications about client crimes or frauds that occurred prior to the consultation. Whether a communication relates to past or ongoing or future acts can be a close question. See Comment *e* hereto.

c. Intent of the client and lawyer. The client need not specifically understand that the contemplated act is a crime or fraud. The client's purpose in consulting the lawyer or using the lawyer's services may be inferred from the circumstances. It is irrelevant that the legal service sought by the client (such as drafting an instrument) was itself lawful.

Illustrations:

1. Client is a member of a group engaged in the ongoing enterprise of importing and distributing illegal drugs. Client has agreed with confederates, as part of the consideration for participating in the enterprise, that Client will provide legal representation for the confederates when necessary. Client and Lawyer agree that, for a substantial monthly retainer, Lawyer will stand ready to provide legal services in the event that Client or Client's associates encounter legal difficulties during the operation of the enterprise. In a communication that

---

otherwise qualifies as privileged under § 68,[1] Client informs Lawyer of the identities of confederates in the enterprise. Client continues to engage in the criminal enterprise following the communication. The crime-fraud exception renders nonprivileged the communications between Client and Lawyer, including identification of Client's confederates.

2. Client, who is in financial difficulty, consults Lawyer A concerning the sale of a parcel of real estate owned by Client. Lawyer A provides legal services in connection with the sale. Client then asks Lawyer A to represent Client in petitioning for bankruptcy. Lawyer A advises Client that the bankruptcy petition must list the sale of the real estate because it occurred within the year previous to the date of filing the petition. Client ends the representation. Client shortly thereafter hires Lawyer B. Omitting to tell Lawyer B about the land sale, Client directs Lawyer B to file a bankruptcy petition that does not disclose the proceeds of the sale. In a subsequent proceeding in which Client's fraud in filing the petition is in issue, a tribunal would be warranted in inferring that Client consulted Lawyer A with the purpose of obtaining assistance to defraud creditors in bankruptcy and thus that the communications between Client and Lawyer A concerning report of the land sale in the bankruptcy petition are not privileged. It would also suffice should the tribunal find that Client attempted to use Lawyer A's advice about the required contents of a bankruptcy petition to defraud creditors by withholding information about the land sale from Lawyer B.

A client could intend criminal or fraudulent conduct but not carry through the intended act. The exception should not apply in such circumstances, for it would penalize a client for doing what the privilege is designed to encourage—consulting a lawyer for the purpose of achieving law compliance. By the same token, lawyers might be discouraged from giving full and candid advice to clients about legally questionable courses of action. On the other hand, a client may consult a lawyer about a matter that constitutes a criminal conspiracy but that is later frustrated—and, in that sense, not later accomplished (cf. Subsection (a))—or, similarly, about a criminal attempt. Such a crime is within the exception stated in the Section if its elements are established.

The crime-fraud exception applies regardless of the fact that the client's lawyer is unaware of the client's intent. The exception also applies if the lawyer actively participates in the crime or fraud. However, if a client does not intend to commit a criminal or fraudulent act, the privilege protects the client's communication even if the client's lawyer acts with a criminal or fraudulent intent in giving advice.

---

[1] Restatement § 68 is the general definition of attorney-client privilege. It limits the privilege to communications made in confidence for the purpose of obtaining or providing legal assistance for the client, and notes that the privilege is subject to exceptions enumerated elsewhere in the Restatement.

Illustration:

> 3. Lawyer, in complicity with confederates who are not clients, is furthering a scheme to defraud purchasers in a public offering of shares of stock. Client, believing that the stock offering is legitimate and ignorant of facts indicating its wrongful nature, seeks to participate in the offering as an underwriter. In the course of obtaining legal advice from Lawyer, Client conveys communications to Lawyer that are privileged under § 68. The crime-fraud exception does not prevent Client from asserting the attorney-client privilege, despite Lawyer's complicity in the fraud.

Compare Illustration 1 to this Comment.

d. Kinds of illegal acts included within the exception. The authorities agree that the exception stated in this Section applies to client conduct defined as a crime or fraud. Fraud, for the purpose of the exception, requires a knowing or reckless misrepresentation (or nondisclosure when applicable law requires disclosure) likely to injure another (see Restatement Second, Torts § § 525–530 (defining elements of fraudulent misrepresentation)).

The evidence codes and judicial decisions are divided on the question of extending the exception to other wrongs such as intentional torts, which, although not criminal or fraudulent, have hallmarks of clear illegality and the threat of serious harm. Legislatures and courts classify illegal acts as crimes and frauds for purposes and policies different from those defining the scope of the privilege. Thus, limiting the exception to crimes and frauds produces an exception narrower than principle and policy would otherwise indicate. Nonetheless, the prevailing view limits the exception to crimes and frauds. The actual instances in which a broader exception might apply are probably few and isolated, and it would be difficult to formulate a broader exception that is not objectionably vague.

Consultation about some acts of civil disobedience is privileged under the Section, for example violations of a law based on a nonfrivolous claim that the law is unconstitutional. The same is true of a communication concerning a contempt sanction necessary to obtain immediate appellate review of an order whose validity is challenged in good faith. (See § 94, Comment *e*, & § 105, Comment *e*.) If, however, the client's position is that the law is valid but there is a superior moral justification for violating it, this Section applies if its conditions are otherwise satisfied.

e. Continuing crimes and frauds. The crime-fraud exception depends on a distinction between past client wrongs and acts that are continuing or will occur in the future. The exception does not apply to communications about client criminal or fraudulent acts that occurred in the past. Communications about past acts are necessary in defending against charges concerning such conduct and, for example, providing background for legal advice concerning a present transaction that is neither criminal nor fraudulent. The possible social costs of denying access to relevant evidence of past acts is accepted in order to realize the enhanced legality and fairness that confidentiality fosters (see § 68, Comment *c*).

The exception does apply to client crimes or frauds that are ongoing or continuing. With respect to past acts that have present consequences, such as the possession of stolen goods, consultation of lawyer and client is privileged if it addresses how the client can rectify the effects of the illegal act—such as by returning the goods to their rightful owner—or defending the client against criminal charges arising out of the offense.

Illustration:

4. Client consults Lawyer about Client's indictment for the crimes of theft and of unlawfully possessing stolen goods. Applicable law treats possession of stolen goods as a continuing offense. Client is hiding the goods in a secret place, knowing that they are stolen. Confidential communications between Client and Lawyer concerning the indictment for theft and possession and the facts underlying those offenses are privileged. Confidential communications concerning ways in which Client can continue to possess the stolen goods, including information supplied by Client about their present location, are not protected by the privilege because of the crime-fraud exception. Confidential communications about ways in which Client might lawfully return the stolen goods to their owner are privileged.

Strict limitation of the exception to ongoing or future crimes and frauds would prohibit a lawyer from testifying that a client confessed to a crime for which an innocent person is on trial. The law of the United Kingdom recognizes an exception in such cases. At least in capital cases, the argument for so extending the exception seems compelling. Compare also § 66 (disclosure to prevent loss of life or serious bodily injury, whether or not risk is created by wrongful client act).

f. Invoking the crime-fraud exception. The crime-fraud exception is relevant only after the attorney-client privilege is successfully invoked. The person seeking access to the communication then must present a prima facie case for the exception. A prima facie case need show only a reasonable basis for concluding that the elements of the exception (see Comment *d*) exist. The showing must be made by evidence other than the contested communication itself. Once a prima facie showing is made, the tribunal has discretion to examine the communication or hear testimony about it in camera, that is, without requiring that the communications be revealed to the party seeking to invoke the exception (see § 86, Comment *f*).

Unless the crime-fraud exception plainly applies to a client-lawyer communication, a lawyer has an obligation to assert the privilege (see § 63, Comment *b*).

g. Effects of the crime-fraud exception. A communication to which the crime-fraud exception applies is not privileged under § 68 for any purpose. Evidence of the communication is admissible in the proceeding in which that determination is made or in another proceeding. The privilege still applies, however, to communications that were not for a purpose included within this Section. For example, a client who consulted a lawyer about several different matters on several different occasions could invoke the privilege with respect to consultations concerning matters unrelated to the illegal acts (compare § 79, Comment *e*). With respect to a lawyer's duty not to use or disclose client information even if not privileged, see § 60; compare §§ 66–67.

United States v. Zolin

Supreme Court of the United States, 1989.
491 U.S. 554, 109 S.Ct. 2619, 105 L.Ed.2d 469.

[The Church of Scientology sought to prevent the IRS from obtaining access to tape recordings of meetings between Church representatives and legal counsel. The IRS argued that the tapes fell within the crime-fraud exception to the attorney-client privilege. It urged the District Court to listen to the tapes in camera to determine whether the exception applied. In support of its position, it submitted affidavits from an undercover agent who gave his reasons for believing that the tapes were relevant, and who provided a partial transcript of the contents of the tapes. The transcript had been obtained from a confidential source. For purposes of its decision, the Supreme Court assumed that the partial transcript had been obtained legally.]

■ JUSTICE BLACKMUN delivered the opinion of the Court [in which all the other Justices joined, except Justice Brennan, who took no part in the consideration or decision of the case].

[The Court first decided that neither Rule 104(a) nor the federal common law flatly prohibited in camera review of material claimed to be privileged. It continued:]

We turn to the question whether in camera review at the behest of the party asserting the crime-fraud exception is always permissible, or, in contrast, whether the party seeking in camera review must make some threshold showing that such review is appropriate. In addressing this question, we attend to the detrimental effect, if any, of in camera review on the policies underlying the privilege and on the orderly administration of justice in our courts. We conclude that some such showing must be made.

Our endorsement of the practice of testing proponents' privilege claims through in camera review of the allegedly privileged documents has not been without reservation. This Court noted in United States v. Reynolds, 345 U.S. 1 (1953), a case which presented a delicate question concerning the disclosure of military secrets, that "examination of the evidence, even by the judge alone, in chambers" might in some cases "jeopardize the security which the privilege is meant to protect." Analogizing to claims of Fifth Amendment privilege, it observed more generally: "Too much judicial inquiry into the claim of privilege would force disclosure of the thing the privilege was meant to protect, while a complete abandonment of judicial control would lead to intolerable abuses."

The Court in Reynolds recognized that some compromise must be reached. In Reynolds, it declined to "go so far as to say that the court *may automatically require* a complete disclosure to the judge before the claim of privilege will be accepted *in any case* " (emphasis added). 345 U.S., at 10. We think that much the same result is in order here.

A blanket rule allowing in camera review as a tool for determining the applicability of the crime-fraud exception, as Reynolds suggests, would place the policy of protecting open and legitimate disclosure between attorneys and clients at undue risk. There is also reason to be concerned about the possible due process implications of routine use of in camera proceedings. Finally, we cannot ignore the burdens in camera review places upon the district courts, which may well be required to evaluate large evidentiary records without open adversarial guidance by the parties.

There is no reason to permit opponents of the privilege to engage in groundless fishing expeditions, with the district courts as their unwitting (and perhaps unwilling) agents. Courts of Appeals have suggested that in camera review is available to evaluate claims of crime or fraud only "when justified," In re John Doe Corp., 675 F.2d, at 490, or "[i]n appropriate cases." In re Sealed Case, 219 U.S.App.D.C. 195,217, 676 F.2d 793, 815 (1982) (opinion of Wright, J.). Indeed, the Solicitor General conceded at oral argument (albeit reluctantly) that a district court would be mistaken if it reviewed documents in camera solely because "the government beg[ged it]" to do so, "with no reason to suspect crime or fraud." We agree.

In fashioning a standard for determining when in camera review is appropriate, we begin with the observation that "in camera inspection * * * is a smaller intrusion upon the confidentiality of the attorney-client relationship than is public disclosure." Fried, Too High a Price for Truth: The Exception to the Attorney–Client Privilege for Contemplated Crimes and Frauds, 64 N.C.L.Rev. 443, 467 (1986). We therefore conclude that a lesser evidentiary showing is needed to trigger in camera review than is required ultimately to overcome the privilege. Ibid. The threshold we set, in other words, need not be a stringent one.

We think that the following standard strikes the correct balance. Before engaging in in camera review to determine the applicability of the crime-fraud exception, "the judge should require a showing of a factual basis adequate to support a good faith belief by a reasonable person," Caldwell v. District Court, 644 P.2d 26, 33 (Colo.1982), that in camera review of the materials may reveal evidence to establish the claim that the crime-fraud exception applies.

Once that showing is made, the decision whether to engage in in camera review rests in the sound discretion of the district court. The court should make that decision in light of the facts and circumstances of the particular case, including, among other things, the volume of materials the district court has been asked to review, the relevant importance to the case of the alleged privileged information, and the likelihood that the evidence produced through in camera review, together with other available evidence then before the court, will establish that the crime-fraud exception does apply. The district court is also free to defer its in camera review if it concludes that additional evidence in support of the crime-fraud exception may be available that is not allegedly privileged, and that production of the additional evidence will not unduly disrupt or delay the proceedings.

C

The question remains as to what kind of evidence a district court may consider in determining whether it has the discretion to undertake an in camera review of an allegedly privileged communication at the behest of the party opposing the privilege. Here, the issue is whether the partial transcripts may be used by the IRS in support of its request for in camera review of the tapes.

The answer to that question, in the first instance, must be found in Rule 104(a), which establishes that materials that have been determined to be privileged may not be considered in making the preliminary determination of the existence of a privilege. Neither the District Court nor the Court of Appeals made factual findings as to the privileged nature of the partial transcripts, so we cannot determine on this record whether Rule 104(a) would bar their consideration.

Assuming for the moment, however, that no rule of privilege bars the IRS' use of the partial transcripts, we fail to see what purpose would be served by excluding the transcripts from the District Court's consideration. There can be little doubt that partial transcripts, or other evidence directly but incompletely reflecting the content of the contested communications, generally will be strong evidence of the subject matter of the communications themselves. Permitting district courts to consider this type of evidence would aid them substantially in rapidly and reliably determining whether in camera review is appropriate.

Respondents suggest only one serious countervailing consideration. In their view, a rule that would allow an opponent of the privilege to rely on such material would encourage litigants to elicit confidential information from disaffected employees or others who have access to the information. We think that deterring the aggressive pursuit of relevant information from third-party sources is not sufficiently central to the policies of the attorney-client privilege to require us to adopt the exclusionary rule urged by respondents. We conclude that the party opposing the privilege may use any nonprivileged evidence in support of its request for in camera review, even if its evidence is not "independent" of the contested communications as the Court of Appeals uses that term.[12]

---

[12] In addition, we conclude that evidence that is not "independent" of the contents of allegedly privileged communications—like the partial transcripts in this case—may be used not only in the pursuit of in camera review, but also may provide the evidentiary basis for the

D

In sum, we conclude that a rigid independent evidence requirement does not comport with "reason and experience," Fed.Rule Evid. 501, and we decline to adopt it as part of the developing federal common law of evidentiary privileges. We hold that in camera review may be used to determine whether allegedly privileged attorney-client communications fall within the crime-fraud exception. We further hold, however, that before a district court may engage in in camera review at the request of the party opposing the privilege, that party must present evidence sufficient to support a reasonable belief that in camera review may yield evidence that establishes the exception's applicability. Finally, we hold that the threshold showing to obtain in camera review may be met by using any relevant evidence, lawfully obtained, that has not been adjudicated to be privileged.

Because the Court of Appeals employed a rigid independent-evidence requirement which categorically excluded the partial transcripts and the tapes themselves from consideration, we vacate its judgment on this issue and remand the case for further proceedings consistent with this opinion. On remand, the Court of Appeals should consider whether the District Court's refusal to listen to the tapes in toto was justified by the manner in which the IRS presented and preserved its request for in camera review. In the event the Court of Appeals holds that the IRS' demand for review was properly preserved, the Court of Appeals should then determine, or remand the case to the District Court to determine in the first instance, whether the IRS has presented a sufficient evidentiary basis for in camera review, and whether, if so, it is appropriate for the District Court, in its discretion, to grant such review.

It is so ordered.

SWIDLER & BERLIN v. UNITED STATES, 524 U.S. 399 (1998). This case arose from the "Travelgate" investigation by Independent Counsel Kenneth Starr into whether obstruction of justice or other crimes occurred in connection with firing of employees in the White House Travel Office. Vincent Foster, Deputy White House Counsel, had consulted his personal attorney, James Hamilton, about possible investigations of the Travel Office firings. Foster committed suicide nine days after the consultation.

At the instance of the Independent Counsel, the grand jury subpoenaed Hamilton's handwritten notes of the consultation with Foster. Hamilton and his law firm filed a motion to quash, arguing that the notes were protected by the attorney-client privilege and by the work product privilege. The District Judge protected the documents from disclosure. The Independent Counsel appealed, and the Court of Appeals reversed the District

---

ultimate showing that the crime-fraud exception applies. We see little to distinguish these two uses: in both circumstances, if the evidence has not itself been determined to be privileged, its exclusion does not serve the policies which underlie the attorney-client privilege.

Court. The Supreme Court later summarized the decision of the Court of Appeals as follows:

> While recognizing that most courts assume the privilege survives death, the Court of Appeals noted that holdings actually manifesting the posthumous force of the privilege are rare. Instead, most judicial references to the privilege's posthumous application occur in the context of a well recognized exception allowing disclosure for disputes among the client's heirs. It further noted that most commentators support some measure of posthumous curtailment of the privilege. The Court of Appeals thought that the risk of posthumous revelation, when confined to the criminal context, would have little to no chilling effect on client communication, but that the costs of protecting communications after death were high. It therefore concluded that the privilege was not absolute in such circumstances, and that instead, a balancing test should apply. It thus held that there is a posthumous exception to the privilege for communications whose relative importance to particular criminal litigation is substantial. While acknowledging that uncertain privileges are disfavored, *Jaffee v. Redmond*, 518 U.S. 1, 17–18 (1996), the Court of Appeals determined that the uncertainty introduced by its balancing test was insignificant in light of existing exceptions to the privilege. The Court of Appeals also held that the notes were not protected by the work product privilege.

The Supreme Court granted certiorari and reversed the Court of Appeals, holding that the privilege survived death. It noted that the "great body" of caselaw precedent supported, either by holding or "considered dicta," the position that the privilege does survive in cases like the one before it; commentators had reached the same conclusion about the coverage of the privilege, though some had urged modification of the law. The Court also noted the danger that communications would be chilled if the privilege did not apply posthumously:

> Knowing that communications will remain confidential even after death encourages the client to communicate fully and frankly with counsel. While the fear of disclosure, and the consequent withholding of information from counsel, may be reduced if disclosure is limited to posthumous disclosure in a criminal context, it seems unreasonable to assume that it vanishes altogether. Clients may be concerned about reputation, civil liability, or possible harm to friends or family. Posthumous disclosure of such communications may be as feared as disclosure during the client's lifetime.

Six members of the Court joined in the majority opinion of Justice Rehnquist. Justice O'Connor wrote a dissenting opinion, in which Justice Scalia and Justice Thomas joined.

HYPOTHETICALS

(1) D is charged with furnishing a restricted dangerous drug to V, a minor. V testifies and identifies D as the person who gave her pills. After the first day

of trial, D disappears. A, D's attorney, testifies that D had expressed to him apprehension about whether V would show up to testify against him, and that upon seeing V enter the courtroom on the second day of trial, D departed. D is convicted by the jury. On appeal, D contends that it was error for the trial court to permit A to testify about D's communication to him as it violated D's lawyer-client privilege rights. Is D's contention correct?

(2) D is charged with exploding a destruction device, causing great bodily injury to V. V testifies about a bomb in a package exploding as he opened the package. While testifying, V draws on the blackboard a diagram of the bomb. The prosecutor calls B, the court bailiff, who testifies, without objection, that while V was drawing the diagram, B was seated near the far end of the jury box and heard D tell his lawyer: "It was not quite like that." D is convicted and makes a motion for a new trial on the ground that B's testimony was admitted in evidence in violation of D's lawyer-client privilege. How should the court rule?

(3) X is prosecuted for perjury. X previously had been convicted of assault with a deadly weapon and sentenced to prison. X filed a habeas corpus petition, alleging that he had entered a plea of guilty to the assault charge because A, his lawyer, had assured him that the judge, with the prosecutor's concurrence, had agreed to a county jail sentence. In the habeas corpus proceeding, A denied giving X any such assurance. The perjury prosecution is based on X's allegations in the habeas corpus petition. At the perjury trial, the prosecutor calls A to testify to the communications between him and X when he represented X on the assault charge. X claims the lawyer-client privilege to prevent A's testimony. What result?

(4) A was injured from a gas explosion occurring in a building under construction. A sues X, the contractor, and the Y Gas Co., which was installing gas equipment and machinery. Y Gas Co. files a cross-complaint against X. X takes the deposition of Z, an employee of Y Gas Co., who conducted an investigation of the explosion for Y. In answer to questions from X, Z testifies that he investigated the explosion upon the direction of his employer, Y Gas Co.; that he made a written report of the investigation; that one copy was sent to the accident-prevention department of the Y Gas Co. and the original was sent to the lawyer for Y Gas Co.; and that his job was to investigate all explosion-type accidents involving Y Gas Co.'s employees and equipment. Upon being asked what he discovered about the explosion and its cause, he answered that he had no present recollection and that he would have to look at his report. Y Gas Co.'s lawyer objects to Z's use of the report on the ground of the lawyer-client privilege. X seeks a court order to compel Z to answer the deposition questions through use of his report. How should the court rule?

(5) A sues the X Gas Service Station for damages for personal injuries arising out of a freeway accident. A's car was stopped on the freeway, with part of it in a travel lane. A was standing in back of his car when he was struck by an oncoming car driven by Y. A settled with Y. A testifies that before getting on the freeway he got oil and gas from X and that X's employee failed to fasten the hood, which suddenly flew open on the freeway, causing him to stop. X calls P, a police officer, to testify that several weeks after the accident he (P) telephoned Z, A's attorney, and advised him that if P couldn't get a statement from

A about how the accident happened, he would be forced to issue a traffic citation against A; that Z replied that A had been too ill to give a statement, but that Z knew the facts about the accident; that Z then said that A's engine had suddenly stopped and this was why A stopped; and that A first looked under the hood and then went to the back of his car to get some pliers when he was struck by Y's car. A objects to P's proposed testimony, on the ground that the lawyer-client privilege protects Z's disclosure to P of A's communication to Z. Is A's objection proper?

(6) A sues the X Hospital, a corporation, for damages for injuries suffered in falling out of a hospital bed while she was a patient. A makes a pretrial discovery motion for inspection and copying of a report of the incident prepared by B, an employee of the X Hospital, in possession of X's lawyer. X opposes the motion by asserting the lawyer-client privilege. X files a declaration by C, the X Hospital administrator, that states that a few days after the accident to A, he directed B, who is head of nursing services, to prepare a report of the accident on a form provided by the Y Insurance Co., the hospital's liability-insurance carrier. The form read at the top, "Confidential—to be prepared for use of hospital attorneys in case of litigation." The declaration also states that B prepared the report and that it was sent to Y Insurance Co. without any copy being held by the hospital. Other declarations filed by X indicate that B was not a witness to A's fall, and that Y Insurance Co. sent B's report to the X Hospital's lawyer. Should A's motion be granted?

(7) P sues D, a corporation, for damages arising out of a slip-and-fall accident at one of D's stores. At request of D's insurance carrier, D has M, the store manager, make a report of the accident. The report is transmitted to the carrier and then to defense counsel. P makes a discovery motion for inspection and copying of the report. D objects on the ground of the lawyer-client privilege. What result?

B. PHYSICIAN–PATIENT AND PSYCHOTHERAPIST–PATIENT PRIVILEGES

Prink v. Rockefeller Center, Inc.

Court of Appeals of New York, 1979.
48 N.Y.2d 309, 422 N.Y.S.2d 911, 398 N.E.2d 517.

■ MEYER, J.

The question presented by this appeal is whether evidentiary privileges prevent disclosure in a wrongful death action concerning the mental condition of the decedent whose unwitnessed death occurred under circumstances consistent with either negligence of the defendant or suicide.
* * *

Plaintiff is the administratrix of the estate of her husband, Robert Prink, who was an associate of a law firm whose offices were at 30 Rockefeller Plaza in New York City. On March 1, 1976, he was found dead on the sixth floor setback of the building. The window of the 36th floor office Mr. Prink had occupied was open. There were no eyewitnesses, but the deputy chief medical examiner noted on Mr. Prink's death certificate that Dr. Thomas Doyle, Mr. Prink's psychiatrist, had reported to him that Mr. Prink had been acutely tense and depressed.

Thereafter plaintiff commenced the present action against defendants, the owners and architects respectively of 30 Rockefeller Center, claiming that negligence in the design and installation of the window alcove desk at which decedent worked and in the maintenance of the window required that he kneel on the desk in order to open the window which was jammed, and that he lost his balance and fell when he attempted to do so. During the examination of plaintiff before trial she admitted that her husband had told her sometime before his death that he was seeing Dr. Doyle, a psychiatrist. * * * She also admitted that after her husband's death she had spoken with Dr. Doyle, but refused to disclose the content of the conversation, claiming privilege.[1] On defendants' motion for an order compelling plaintiff to testify concerning the content of her conversations with * * * Dr. Doyle, Special Term ordered the questions answered. The Appellate Division affirmed, but certified to us the question "Was the order of the Supreme Court, as affirmed by this Court, properly made?" We answer the certified question in the affirmative and, therefore, affirm the Appellate Division's order.

The initial inquiry is whether privilege ever attached. * * * Mrs. Prink did not consult Dr. Doyle as a patient. Mr. Prink did, however, and Dr. Doyle's information concerning him was therefore, "acquired in attending a patient in a professional capacity" within the meaning of * * * [the New York Statute] and for purposes of the present inquiry at least may be presumed to have been "necessary to enable him to act in that capacity" as required by that provision.

* * * [T]he physician-patient privilege is [not] terminated by death alone. * * * [The privilege applies] unless waived in some manner. To be borne in mind in deciding whether there has been a waiver is that * * * the physician-patient privilege belongs to the patient. * * * [I]t follows that Dr. Doyle's voluntary disclosures to the chief medical examiner and to Mrs. Prink after her husband's death, proper though they undoubtedly were as a matter of professional ethics cannot constitute a waiver making an otherwise privileged statement admissible. To hold that a recipient of confidential information by his sole fiat may destroy the privilege would be directly contrary to the salutary purpose for which the privilege was adopted.[2]

---

[1] While plaintiff's testimony concerning what Dr. Doyle told her is clearly hearsay, that would not protect her from the disclosure required by CPLR 3101 which requires revelation of inadmissible testimony that may lead to discovery of admissible evidence.

[2] To be distinguished, of course, is the common-law rule permitting an eavesdropper to testify concerning an otherwise privileged communication * * *. Thus, had Mrs. Prink overheard Dr. Doyle's conversation with her husband as an eavesdropper rather than having learned its content from the doctor she could be required to disclose its content. The distinction, perhaps filagree in nature, is between the unauthorized act of the recipient of the confidence and the act of the eavesdropper who unauthorizedly intrudes himself upon the confidential conference. It results, apparently, from the confidant's negligence in the eavesdropper situation in not assuring absolute secrecy at the time of disclosure, and the contradiction in

There is, however, another basis upon which we hold * * * the doctor-patient * * * privilege waived. The instant action is brought pursuant to EPTL 5–4.1, which authorizes an action for wrongful death only "for a wrongful act, neglect or default which *caused the decedent's death* against a person *who would have been liable to the decedent by reason of such wrongful conduct* if death had not ensued" (emphasis supplied). Thus to succeed in this action, which is wholly statutory in nature, plaintiff must establish that it could have been maintained by decedent had he survived * * * and that defendants' wrongful act caused his death. In final analysis, therefore, the issue is whether had Mr. Prink survived and brought the action he could successfully have resisted defendants' demand, in their effort to establish that his injuries resulted from attempted suicide rather than defendant's negligence, for disclosure of his conversations with Dr. Doyle * * * .

* * * [Because of] the unfairness of mulcting a defendant in damages without affording him an opportunity to prove his lack of culpability [cf. Chambers v. Mississippi], Mr. Prink as plaintiff could (not) assert * * * the physician-patient privilege (Koump v. Smith) to foreclose inquiry concerning whether his injury was the result of an attempt at suicide.

In *Koump* plaintiff demanded authorization * * * to obtain defendant's hospital record in an effort to show that defendant was intoxicated at the time his car crossed a center divider striking plaintiff's car and injuring plaintiff. We upheld defendant's claim of privilege in that case because defendant had done no more than deny plaintiff's allegation that defendant was intoxicated and plaintiff's only evidence of intoxication was an attorney's affidavit reciting that the police report of the accident contained a hearsay statement that defendant appeared intoxicated. Nevertheless, we recognized: "that by bringing or defending personal injury action in which mental or physical condition is affirmatively put in issue, a party *waives* the privilege" (emphasis in original).

Whatever the ultimate determination of the triers of fact may be in the present case and notwithstanding the presumption against suicide which they will have to consider in reaching their determination, we conclude that it is a matter of common knowledge which we can judicially notice * * * that many apparently accidental deaths are in fact suicides and that a wrongful death complaint predicated upon an alleged accidental fall from a 36th story window is sufficiently equivocal in that respect to put in issue, by plaintiff's affirmative act in bringing the action, decedent's mental condition * * * . To hold otherwise is to ignore the realities of the factual situation and to come perilously close to a taking of defendants' property without due process of law (cf. Chambers v. Mississippi). An additional reason, not however essential to our conclusion, for holding the (privilege) waived by the bringing of the action is that determination of the pecuniary injury sustained by Mr. Prink's death necessarily involved his mental condition.

---

terms that would be involved in taxing the confidant with negligence in relying upon the trust which is the very root of his relationship to the person in whom he has confided.

Bearing in mind the purpose for which the (privilege) in question (was) created, the affirmative stance of plaintiff who claims on behalf of decedent's distributees to have sustained pecuniary injury as a result of defendants' negligence, and the unfairness of permitting plaintiff to succeed by hiding behind the (privilege) asserted, we are satisfied on balance that the better policy is to hold the (privilege) waived. The basis for that conclusion * * * is set forth in Koump v. Smith, supra;   see, also, Wigmore, *op. cit.,* § 2380(a). * * *

Accordingly the certified question should be answered in the affirmative and the order of the Appellate Division should be affirmed.

* * *

Jaffee v. Redmond

Supreme Court of the United States, 1996.
518 U.S. 1, 116 S.Ct. 1923, 135 L.Ed.2d 337.

■ JUSTICE STEVENS delivered the opinion of the Court.

[While in the line of duty, Mary Lu Redmond, a police officer in Hoffman Estates, Illinois, shot and killed Ricky Allen. The Administrator of Allen's estate brought a federal action against Redmond and the village, claiming that the shooting was unjustified. In an account disputed by plaintiff's witnesses, Redmond testified that Allen disregarded her commands to drop a butcher's knife he was brandishing and appeared about to stab another man when she shot him.]

During pretrial discovery petitioner learned that after the shooting Redmond had participated in about 50 counseling sessions with Karen Beyer, a clinical social worker licensed by the State of Illinois and employed at that time by the Village of Hoffman Estates. Petitioner sought access to Beyer's notes concerning the sessions for use in cross-examining Redmond. Respondents vigorously resisted the discovery. They asserted that the contents of the conversations between Beyer and Redmond were protected against involuntary disclosure by a psychotherapist-patient privilege. The district judge rejected this argument. Neither Beyer nor Redmond, however, complied with his order to disclose the contents of Beyer's notes. At depositions and on the witness stand both either refused to answer certain questions or professed an inability to recall details of their conversations.

In his instructions at the end of the trial, the judge advised the jury that the refusal to turn over Beyer's notes had no "legal justification" and that the jury could therefore presume that the contents of the notes would have been unfavorable to respondents. The jury awarded petitioner $45,000 on the federal claim and $500,000 on her state-law claim.

The Court of Appeals for the Seventh Circuit reversed and remanded for a new trial. Addressing the issue for the first time, the court concluded that "reason and experience," the touchstones for acceptance of a privilege under Rule 501 of the Federal Rules of Evidence, compelled recognition of a psychotherapist-patient privilege. * * *

The Court of Appeals qualified its recognition of the privilege by stating that it would not apply if "in the interests of justice, the evidentiary need for the disclosure of the contents of a patient's counseling sessions outweighs that patient's privacy interests." Balancing those conflicting interests, the court observed, on the one hand, that the evidentiary need for the contents of the confidential conversations was diminished in this case because there were numerous eyewitnesses to the shooting, and, on the other hand, that Officer Redmond's privacy interests were substantial.[5] Based on this assessment, the court concluded that the trial court had erred by refusing to afford protection to the confidential communications between Redmond and Beyer.

The United States courts of appeals do not uniformly agree that the federal courts should recognize a psychotherapist privilege under Rule 501. Because of the conflict among the courts of appeals and the importance of the question, we granted certiorari. We affirm.

II

Rule 501 of the Federal Rules of Evidence authorizes federal courts to define new privileges by interpreting "common law principles . . . in the light of reason and experience." The authors of the Rule borrowed this phrase from our opinion in *Wolfle v. United States*, 291 U.S. 7, 12 (1934), which in turn referred to the oft-repeated observation that "the common law is not immutable but flexible, and by its own principles adapts itself to varying conditions." *Funk v. United States*, 290 U.S. 371, 383 (1933). See also *Hawkins v. United States*, 358 U.S. 74, 79 (1958) (changes in privileges may be "dictated by 'reason and experience' "). The Senate Report accompanying the 1975 adoption of the Rules indicates that Rule 501 "should be understood as reflecting the view that the recognition of a privilege based on a confidential relationship . . . should be determined on a case-by-case basis."[7] The Rule thus did not freeze the law governing the privileges of witnesses in federal trials at a particular point in our history, but rather directed federal courts to "continue the evolutionary development of testimonial privileges." *Trammel v. United States*, 445 U.S. 40, 47 (1980).

---

[5] "Her ability, through counseling, to work out the pain and anguish undoubtedly caused by Allen's death in all probability depended to a great deal upon her trust and confidence in her counselor, Karen Beyer. Officer Redmond, and all those placed in her most unfortunate circumstances, are entitled to be protected in their desire to seek counseling after mortally wounding another human being in the line of duty. An individual who is troubled as the result of her participation in a violent and tragic event, such as this, displays a most commendable respect for human life and is a person well-suited 'to protect and to serve.' " 51 F.3d, at 1358.

[7] In 1972 the Chief Justice transmitted to Congress proposed Rules of Evidence for United States Courts and Magistrates. 56 F.R.D. 183 (hereinafter Proposed Rules). The rules had been formulated by the Judicial Conference Advisory Committee on Rules of Evidence and approved by the Judicial Conference of the United States and by this Court. The proposed rules defined nine specific testimonial privileges, including a psychotherapist-patient privilege, and indicated that these were to be the exclusive privileges absent constitutional mandate. Congress rejected this recommendation in favor of Rule 501's general mandate.

The common-law principles underlying the recognition of testimonial privileges can be stated simply. " 'For more than three centuries it has now been recognized as a fundamental maxim that the public . . . has a right to every man's evidence. When we come to examine the various claims of exemption, we start with the primary assumption that there is a general duty to give what testimony one is capable of giving, and that any exemptions which may exist are distinctly exceptional, being so many derogations from a positive general rule.' " *United States v. Bryan*, 339 U.S. 323, 331 (1950) (quoting 8 J. Wigmore, Evidence § 2192, p. 64 (3d ed.1940)). Exceptions from the general rule disfavoring testimonial privileges may be justified, however, by a " 'public good transcending the normally predominant principle of utilizing all rational means for ascertaining the truth.' " *Trammel*, 445 U.S., at 50, quoting *Elkins v. United States*, 364 U.S. 206, 234 (1960) (Frankfurter, J., dissenting).

Guided by these principles, the question we address today is whether a privilege protecting confidential communications between a psychotherapist and her patient "promotes sufficiently important interests to outweigh the need for probative evidence. . ." 445 U.S., at 51. Both "reason and experience" persuade us that it does.

III

Like the spousal and attorney-client privileges, the psychotherapist-patient privilege is "rooted in the imperative need for confidence and trust." *Trammel*, 445 U.S., at 51. Treatment by a physician for physical ailments can often proceed successfully on the basis of a physical examination, objective information supplied by the patient, and the results of diagnostic tests. Effective psychotherapy, by contrast, depends upon an atmosphere of confidence and trust in which the patient is willing to make a frank and complete disclosure of facts, emotions, memories, and fears. Because of the sensitive nature of the problems for which individuals consult psychotherapists, disclosure of confidential communications made during counseling sessions may cause embarrassment or disgrace. For this reason, the mere possibility of disclosure may impede development of the confidential relationship necessary for successful treatment. As the Judicial Conference Advisory Committee observed in 1972 when it recommended that Congress recognize a psychotherapist privilege as part of the Proposed Federal Rules of Evidence, a psychiatrist's ability to help her patients

> "is completely dependent upon [the patients'] willingness and ability to talk freely. This makes it difficult if not impossible for [a psychiatrist] to function without being able to assure . . . patients of confidentiality and, indeed, privileged communication. Where there may be exceptions to this general rule . . ., there is wide agreement that confidentiality is a *sine qua non* for successful psychiatric treatment."

By protecting confidential communications between a psychotherapist and her patient from involuntary disclosure, the proposed privilege thus serves important private interests.

Our cases make clear that an asserted privilege must also "serv[e] public ends." *Upjohn Co. v. United States*, 449 U.S. 383, 389 (1981). Thus, the purpose of the attorney-client privilege is to "encourage full and frank communication between attorneys and their clients and thereby promote broader public interests in the observance of law and administration of justice." *Ibid.* And the spousal privilege, as modified in *Trammel*, is justified because it "furthers the important public interest in marital harmony," 445 U.S., at 53. The psychotherapist privilege serves the public interest by facilitating the provision of appropriate treatment for individuals suffering the effects of a mental or emotional problem. The mental health of our citizenry, no less than its physical health, is a public good of transcendent importance.[10]

In contrast to the significant public and private interests supporting recognition of the privilege, the likely evidentiary benefit that would result from the denial of the privilege is modest. If the privilege were rejected, confidential conversations between psychotherapists and their patients would surely be chilled, particularly when it is obvious that the circumstances that give rise to the need for treatment will probably result in litigation. Without a privilege, much of the desirable evidence to which litigants such as petitioner seek access—for example, admissions against interest by a party—is unlikely to come into being. This unspoken "evidence" will therefore serve no greater truth-seeking function than if it had been spoken and privileged.

That it is appropriate for the federal courts to recognize a psychotherapist privilege under Rule 501 is confirmed by the fact that all 50 States and the District of Columbia have enacted into law some form of psychotherapist privilege. We have previously observed that the policy decisions of the States bear on the question whether federal courts should recognize a new privilege or amend the coverage of an existing one. See *Trammel*, 445 U.S., at 48–50. Because state legislatures are fully aware of the need to protect the integrity of the factfinding functions of their courts, the existence of a consensus among the States indicates that "reason and experience" support recognition of the privilege. In addition, given the importance of the patient's understanding that her communications with her therapist will not be publicly disclosed, any State's promise of confidentiality would have little value if the patient were aware that the privilege would not be honored in a federal court. Denial of the federal privilege therefore would frustrate the purposes of the state legislation that was enacted to foster these confidential communications.

It is of no consequence that recognition of the privilege in the vast majority of States is the product of legislative action rather than judicial deci-

---

[10] This case amply demonstrates the importance of allowing individuals to receive confidential counseling. Police officers engaged in the dangerous and difficult tasks associated with protecting the safety of our communities not only confront the risk of physical harm but also face stressful circumstances that may give rise to anxiety, depression, fear, or anger. The entire community may suffer if police officers are not able to receive effective counseling and treatment after traumatic incidents, either because trained officers leave the profession prematurely or because those in need of treatment remain on the job.

sion. Although common-law rulings may once have been the primary source of new developments in federal privilege law, that is no longer the case. In *Funk v. United States*, 290 U.S. 371 (1933), we recognized that it is appropriate to treat a consistent body of policy determinations by state legislatures as reflecting both "reason" and "experience." *Id.*, at 376–381. That rule is properly respectful of the States and at the same time reflects the fact that once a state legislature has enacted a privilege there is no longer an opportunity for common-law creation of the protection. The history of the psychotherapist privilege illustrates the latter point. In 1972 the members of the Judicial Conference Advisory Committee noted that the common law "had indicated a disposition to recognize a psychotherapist-patient privilege when legislatures began moving into the field." Proposed Rules, 56 F.R.D., at 242 (citation omitted). The present unanimous acceptance of the privilege shows that the state lawmakers moved quickly. That the privilege may have developed faster legislatively than it would have in the courts demonstrates only that the States rapidly recognized the wisdom of the rule as the field of psychotherapy developed.[13]

The uniform judgment of the States is reinforced by the fact that a psychotherapist privilege was among the nine specific privileges recommended by the Advisory Committee in its proposed privilege rules. In *United States v. Gillock*, 445 U.S. 360, 367–368 (1980), our holding that Rule 501 did not include a state legislative privilege relied, in part, on the fact that no such privilege was included in the Advisory Committee's draft. The reasoning in *Gillock* thus supports the opposite conclusion in this case. In rejecting the proposed draft that had specifically identified each privilege rule and substituting the present more open-ended Rule 501, the Senate Judiciary Committee explicitly stated that its action "should not be understood as disapproving any recognition of a psychiatrist-patient ... privileg[e] contained in the [proposed] rules."

Because we agree with the judgment of the state legislatures and the Advisory Committee that a psychotherapist-patient privilege will serve a "public good transcending the normally predominant principle of utilizing all rational means for ascertaining truth," *Trammel*, 445 U.S., at 50, we hold that confidential communications between a licensed psychotherapist and her patients in the course of diagnosis or treatment are protected from compelled disclosure under Rule 501 of the Federal Rules of Evidence.[14]

IV

All agree that a psychotherapist privilege covers confidential communications made to licensed psychiatrists and psychologists. We have no he-

---

[13] Petitioner acknowledges that all 50 state legislatures favor a psychotherapist privilege. She nevertheless discounts the relevance of the state privilege statutes by pointing to divergence among the States concerning the types of therapy relationships protected and the exceptions recognized. A small number of state statutes, for example, grant the privilege only to psychiatrists and psychologists, while most apply the protection more broadly. . . . These variations in the scope of the protection are too limited to undermine the force of the States' unanimous judgment that some form of psychotherapist privilege is appropriate.

[14] Like other testimonial privileges, the patient may of course waive the protection.

sitation in concluding in this case that the federal privilege should also extend to confidential communications made to licensed social workers in the course of psychotherapy. The reasons for recognizing a privilege for treatment by psychiatrists and psychologists apply with equal force to treatment by a clinical social worker such as Karen Beyer. Today, social workers provide a significant amount of mental health treatment. Their clients often include the poor and those of modest means who could not afford the assistance of a psychiatrist or psychologist, but whose counseling sessions serve the same public goals. Perhaps in recognition of these circumstances, the vast majority of States explicitly extend a testimonial privilege to licensed social workers. We therefore agree with the Court of Appeals that "[d]rawing a distinction between the counseling provided by costly psychotherapists and the counseling provided by more readily accessible social workers serves no discernible public purpose."

We part company with the Court of Appeals on a separate point. We reject the balancing component of the privilege implemented by that court and a small number of States. Making the promise of confidentiality contingent upon a trial judge's later evaluation of the relative importance of the patient's interest in privacy and the evidentiary need for disclosure would eviscerate the effectiveness of the privilege. As we explained in *Upjohn*, if the purpose of the privilege is to be served, the participants in the confidential conversation "must be able to predict with some degree of certainty whether particular discussions will be protected. An uncertain privilege, or one which purports to be certain but results in widely varying applications by the courts, is little better than no privilege at all." 449 U.S., at 393.

These considerations are all that is necessary for decision of this case. A rule that authorizes the recognition of new privileges on a case-by-case basis makes it appropriate to define the details of new privileges in a like manner. Because this is the first case in which we have recognized a psychotherapist privilege, it is neither necessary nor feasible to delineate its full contours in a way that would "govern all conceivable future questions in this area." *Id.*, at 386.[19]

V

The conversations between Officer Redmond and Karen Beyer and the notes taken during their counseling sessions are protected from compelled disclosure under Rule 501 of the Federal Rules of Evidence. The judgment of the Court of Appeals is affirmed.

It is so ordered.

[Justice Scalia wrote a long and energetic dissent. Though he insisted that the question of whether there should be a psychotherapist-patient pri-

---

[19] Although it would be premature to speculate about most future developments in the federal psychotherapist privilege, we do not doubt that there are situations in which the privilege must give way, for example, if a serious threat of harm to the patient or to others can be averted only by means of a disclosure by the therapist.

vilege was too general for the case presented, he made his doubts as to its merits clear:

> When is it, one must wonder, that *the psychotherapist* came to play such an indispensable role in the maintenance of the citizenry's mental health? For most of history, men and women have worked out their difficulties by talking to, *inter alios*, parents, siblings, best friends, and bartenders-none of whom was awarded a privilege against testifying in court. Ask the average citizen: Would your mental health be more significantly impaired by preventing you from seeing a psychotherapist, or by preventing you from getting advice from your mom? I have little doubt what the answer would be. Yet there is no mother-child privilege.

> How likely is it that a person will be deterred from seeking psychological counseling, or from being completely truthful in the course of such counseling, because of fear of later disclosure in litigation? And even more pertinent to today's decision, to what extent will the evidentiary privilege reduce that deterrent? The Court does not try to answer the first of these questions; and it *cannot possibly have any notion* of what the answer is to the second, since that depends entirely upon the scope of the privilege, which the Court amazingly finds it "neither necessary nor feasible to delineate," ante, at 1932. If, for example, the psychotherapist can give the patient no more assurance than "A court will not be able to make me disclose what you tell me, unless you tell me about a harmful act," I doubt whether there would be much benefit from the privilege at all. * * *

> The Court confidently asserts that not much truth-finding capacity would be destroyed by the privilege anyway, since "[w]ithout a privilege, much of the desirable evidence to which litigants such as petitioner seek access . . . is unlikely to come into being." If that is so, how come psychotherapy got to be a thriving practice before the "psychotherapist privilege" was invented? Were the patients paying money to lie to their analysts all those years?

In Justice Scalia's view, the fact that some form of the privilege had been enacted into law by *legislatures* in all 50 states and the District of Columbia argued against, rather than in favor, of *judicial* adoption of such a privilege for the federal courts.

In a portion of the opinion joined by Chief Justice Rehnquist, Justice Scalia addressed what he considered to be the actual question presented by the case – whether there should be a privilege for psychotherapeutic counseling *with a social worker*.

> A licensed psychiatrist or psychologist is an expert in psychotherapy-and that may suffice (though I think it not so clear that this Court should make the judgment) to justify the use of extraordinary means to encourage counseling with him, as opposed to counseling with one's rabbi, minister, family, or friends. One must presume that a social

worker does *not* bring this greatly heightened degree of skill to bear, which is alone a reason for not encouraging that consultation as generously. Does a social worker bring to bear at least a significantly heightened degree of skill—more than a minister or rabbi, for example? I have no idea, and neither does the Court. The social worker in the present case, Karen Beyer, was a "licensed clinical social worker" in Illinois, a job title whose training requirements consist of a "master's degree in social work from an approved program," and "3,000 hours of satisfactory, supervised clinical professional experience." It is not clear that the degree in social work requires any training in psychotherapy. The "clinical professional experience" apparently will impart some such training, but only of the vaguest sort, judging from the Illinois Code's definition of "[c]linical social work practice," viz., "the providing of mental health services for the evaluation, treatment, and prevention of mental and emotional disorders in individuals, families and groups based on knowledge and theory of psychosocial development, behavior, psychopathology, unconscious motivation, interpersonal relationships, and environmental stress." Ch. 225, §20/3(5). But the rule the Court announces today—like the Illinois evidentiary privilege which that rule purports to respect, Ch. 225, §20/16—is not limited to "licensed clinical social workers," but includes all "licensed social workers." "Licensed social workers" may also provide "mental health services" as described in §20/3(5), so long as it is done under supervision of a licensed clinical social worker. And the training requirement for a "licensed social worker" consists of either (a) "a degree from a graduate program of social work" approved by the State, or (b) "a degree in social work from an undergraduate program" approved by the State, plus "3 years of supervised professional experience." Ch. 225, §20/9A. With due respect, it does not seem to me that any of this training is comparable in its rigor (or indeed in the precision of its subject) to the training of the other experts (lawyers) to whom this Court has accorded a privilege, or even of the experts (psychiatrists and psychologists) to whom the Advisory Committee and this Court proposed extension of a privilege in 1972. Of course these are only Illinois' requirements for "social workers." Those of other States, for all we know, may be even less demanding. Indeed, I am not even sure there is a nationally accepted definition of "social worker," as there is of psychiatrist and psychologist. It seems to me quite irresponsible to extend the so-called "psychotherapist privilege" to all licensed social workers, nationwide, without exploring these issues.

In closing, Justice Scalia emphasized, as he had at the outset, the loss to the truth-determining process of recognizing a privilege. He noted that numerous organizations had filed *amicus* briefs supporting a privilege, and that none were submitted in favor of the petitioner. "That is no surprise," he wrote.

There is no self-interested organization out there devoted to pursuit of the truth in the federal courts. The expectation is, however, that *this Court* will have that interest prominently—indeed, primarily—in mind. Today we have failed that expectation, and that responsibility. It is no small matter to say that, in some cases, our federal courts will be the tools of injustice rather than unearth the truth where it is available to be found. The common law has identified a few instances where that is tolerable. Perhaps Congress may conclude that it is also tolerable for the purpose of encouraging psychotherapy by social workers. But that conclusion assuredly does not burst upon the mind with such clarity that a judgment in favor of suppressing the truth ought to be pronounced by this honorable Court.]

People v. Sergio

Supreme Court, Kings County, New York, 2008.
21 Misc.3d 451, 864 N.Y.S.2d 264.

■ JOEL M. GOLDBERG, J.

[In response to a call, Diane Kasler, an emergency medical technician, came to the home of defendant Laura Sergio. On observing Sergio and traces of blood in the bathroom, she asked Sergio if she was or had been pregnant. Sergio answered , "No." Sergio was transported to Lutheran Medical Center. In part because of further statements she made there, the police were alerted that she had apparently just given birth but was not with the baby. After questioning Sergio's sister, the police found a newborn baby girl in a garbage bag outside the Sergios' home. The baby died soon after of exposure. Sergio was charged with murder.]

I. Applicability of the Physician–Patient Privilege

The People * * * contend that the privilege, as a matter of law, does not apply to the statement made to the EMS volunteer who was not a physician, or employed by a physician (i.e., the defendant responded "No" when asked by the EMS volunteer if she is or had been pregnant).

The People further argue, without any supporting detail, that the presence of the defendant's mother during her treatment at the Lutheran Medical Center constitutes a waiver of any confidentiality as to what transpired there. In response to this contention, the defense argues that the defendant's mother was not present during the privileged conversations at Lutheran Medical Center, and even if the defendant's mother was present at either the conversations at Lutheran Medical Center or the conversation with the EMS volunteer, those conversations were intended by the defendant to be confidential and, given the defendant's physical and mental condition at the time, the defendant was not capable of making a valid waiver of the privilege. * * *

The physician-patient privilege did not exist at common law. In 1829, New York became the first state to enact a physician-patient privilege statute. The physician-patient privilege is currently codified in CPLR 4504(a). The relevant text of the statute states, "[U]nless the patient waives the privilege, a person authorized to practice medicine, registered professional nursing, licensed practical nursing, dentistry, podiatry or chiropractic shall not be allowed to disclose any information which he acquired in attending a patient in a professional capacity, and which was necessary to enable him to act in that capacity."

Although in derogation of the common law, the physician-patient privilege is to be given a "broad and liberal construction to carry out its policy." Courts have "narrowly construed statutes limiting the privilege and rejected claims that there is a general public interest exception to CPLR 4504." The rationale supporting the privilege is that the protection of confidential information from involuntary disclosure will promote uninhibited communication between patient and physician for the purpose of obtaining appropriate medical treatment.

The privilege concerns not only the direct communication between the doctor and patient but other information acquired based on the relationship. The information that may qualify includes "not only communications received from the lips of the patient but such knowledge as may be acquired from the patient himself, the statements of others who may surround him at the time, or from observation of his appearance and symptoms." Alexander, Practice Commentaries, McKinney's Cons. Laws of N.Y., Book 7B, CPLR C4504: 2(b) quoting *Edington v. Mutual Life Insurance Co.,* 67 N.Y. 185, 194 (1876).

The information must also fall within "the realm" of medical diagnosis and treatment and prohibits physicians and other medical personnel, in the absence of a waiver by the patient, from revealing "any information which [they] acquired in attending a patient in a professional capacity, and which was necessary to enable [them] to act in that capacity."

The form in which the privileged information is stored, whether in the memory of the physician or medical records is irrelevant if the information qualifies for the privilege.

Except for the unique circumstances of this case, the People would not dispute a determination that the defendant's Lutheran Medical Center records would be covered by the privilege.

The People also do not argue that because the defendant's condition in Lutheran Medical Center would have been readily perceived by a lay person, the privilege does not apply. *See People v. Capra,* 17 N.Y.2d 670, 269 N.Y.S.2d 451, 216 N.E.2d 610 (1966) (privilege did not apply to emergency room doctor's observation of packet of heroine that fell from accident victim's boot); *Goldin v. Mejia,* 294 A.D.2d 231, 743 N.Y.S.2d 13 (1st Dept.2002) (privilege not applicable to hospital employee's observation of urine on bed and floor of patient's room). No witness from Lutheran Medical Center testified before the Grand Jury, and it cannot be determined from examination of the defendant's medical records alone if any of the observations or conclusions in those medical records would have been readily apparent to a lay person. Indeed, "medical records are not organized by the basis of what lay persons—as opposed to medical professionals—might discern". *Matter of Grand Jury Investigation in New York County*, 98 N.Y.2d at 531, 749 N.Y.S.2d 462, 779 N.E.2d 173.

A. Lutheran Medical Center

It is the People's principal contention that because the now deceased newborn baby girl was "a child," the information obtained from the defendant by Lutheran Medical Center was not protected by the privilege.

The People cite CPLR 4504(b), which in relevant part states, "a physician, dentist, podiatrist, chiropractor or nurse shall be required to disclose information indicating that *a patient* [emphasis supplied] who is under the age of sixteen years has been the victim of a crime," and argue that, therefore, invocation of the privilege in cases where a child has been murdered "is inappropriate."

However, CPLR 4504(b) applies only where the child is the patient, and in this case it was the defendant, not the child, who was the patient of Lutheran Medical Center. Similarly, pursuant to CPLR 4508(a)(3), certified social workers may testify about information acquired from a client under the age of sixteen indicating that the child has been the victim or subject of a crime where the child, not the parent, is the holder of the privilege.

Although society certainly has an interest in protecting children that may override its interest in fostering the confidentiality of the physician-patient relationship, because the deceased newborn was not the patient of Lutheran Medical Center the exception to the privilege contained in CPLR 4504(b) does not apply to the facts of this case.

Nevertheless, the above-noted specific CPLR exceptions where the child is the patient or client, express a clear legislative intent not to allow CPLR created privileges to obstruct judicial determinations regarding issues concerning the safety or welfare of children. *See also* Family Court Act 1046, which specifically states that in Family Court proceedings, neither the physician-patient nor several other listed CPLR privileges shall be grounds for excluding otherwise admissible evidence.

More persuasive is the People's reliance on Social Services Law 415 which requires immediate "reports of suspected child abuse or maltreatment" from persons or officials required to make such reports (i.e., "mandated reporters" such as physicians, registered nurses, emergency medical technicians, and hospital personnel engaged in the admission, examination, care or treatment of persons [Social Services Law 413(1)]). Social Service Law 415 also states that "notwithstanding the privileges set forth in article forty-five of the civil practice law and rules and any other provision of law to the contrary, mandated reporters . . . are required to comply with all requests for [relevant] records made by a child protective service . . . *of any patient or client* [emphasis supplied] that are essential to the investigation. . ." Section 415 further provides that written reports of child abuse or maltreatment by mandated reporters "shall be admissible in evidence *in any proceedings relating to child abuse or maltreatment* " [emphasis supplied].

Evidence of reports made pursuant to Social Service Law 415 is admissible in criminal prosecutions as well as child protective proceedings "where the defendant's statement triggers the requirement to report" even where the child was not the patient being treated. *People v. Gearhart,* 148 Misc.2d 249, 255, 560 N.Y.S.2d 247 (Nassau County Court 1990). *See also People v. Strawbridge,* 299 A.D.2d at 590–592, 751 N.Y.S.2d 606 (information provided pursuant to Social Services Law 415 by hospital personnel treating the mother of a deceased newborn can later be used in a criminal proceeding against the mother for murdering her child, although introduction of evidence at trial of the mother's entire health records concerning her pregnancy was error); *People v. Rodriguez,* 7 Misc.3d 1023(A), 2005 N.Y. Slip Op. 50715 (U), 2005 WL 1148695 (Suffolk County Court 2005) (Social Services Law exception to physician-patient privilege allows use in mother's criminal trial for murder of testimony concerning her condition and statements during her initial presentment in hospital emergency room, including her denial of being pregnant or having given birth up to the time the hospital staff called 911 to report a missing baby).

The defendant argues that the specific provisions of the Social Services Law requiring disclosure of abuse or maltreatment and allowing the use of the written reports in any related proceeding notwithstanding the physician-patient privilege are inapplicable to this case, because the child was deceased at the time of the Grand Jury presentation and there was obviously no danger of any future harm being caused to the child. However as noted above, the Third Department in *Strawbridge,* 299 A.D.2d at 592, 751 N.Y.S.2d 606, has expressly stated that the Social Service Law permits limited portions of hospital records of a mother's pregnancy to be admissible at her trial for murdering her child. The trial court in *Rodriguez,* 7 Misc.3d 1023(A), has also found the Social Services Law to allow for limited use of a mother's hospital records in her trial on similar charges.

Although the defendant's entire Lutheran Medical Center records were introduced in evidence before the Grand Jury, the only portion that was read to the Grand Jury stated, "25 year-old female, admitted on April 6, 2007, after a spontaneous vaginal delivery at home." There was also testimony from Police Office [Peter] Aponte (concerning which the ADA subsequently gave a limiting instruction) that, a "supervisor received a call from Lutheran Medical Center stating they had a female who apparently has given birth and the baby was not with the female."

The limited information about the defendant's having recently given birth and her missing baby was within the appropriate confines of the Social Service Law exception concerning information relating to reports of suspected child abuse or maltreatment. This limited information was required to be immediately disclosed pursuant to Social Service Law 415 and, pursuant to that statute and the above-cited cases, was also subject to being used in subsequent criminal proceedings relating to possible abuse or maltreatment of the child, regardless of whether the child was alive at the time of the proceedings.

Insofar as the hospital records may have contained additional medical information not within the exception to the physician-patient privilege of the Social Service Law, the defendant was not prejudiced by the failure to redact that information to the extent that the failure to redact impaired the integrity of the proceedings. Therefore, dismissal of the indictment for the failure to redact the Lutheran Medical Center records is not warranted. CPL 210.35(5).

B. *Defendant's Statements to EMT Kasler*

Neither CPLR 4504(a) nor any other statute specifically includes emergency medical technicians ("EMT's") among those to whom communications may be privileged. To the contrary, the Legislature has in Social Services Law 413 specifically included EMT's as well as physicians as mandated reporters of suspected child abuse or maltreatment. Thus, even if there is some legal rationale for judicially extending the privilege in this case to the defendant's statement to EMT Kasler, the same Social Service Law statutes that permitted disclosure to the Grand Jury of Lutheran Medical Center's determination that the defendant had recently given birth, would also permit the disclosure of the defendant's denial of that fact to EMT Kasler, who is also a mandated reporter of child abuse and maltreatment.

The People contend that regardless of whether the Social Services Law exception applies to EMT's, the defendant's statement to EMT Kasler was not covered by the privilege, *citing People v. Ackerson,* 149 Misc.2d 882, 566 N.Y.S.2d 833 (Monroe County Court, 1991) (EMT responding to scene of motor vehicle accident to stabilize injured allegedly intoxicated driver was not acting as an agent of a physician to obtain information for the physician's subsequent diagnosis and treatment and, therefore, the driver's statements to the EMT were not covered by the privilege).

The defendant contends that *Ackerson* should not be followed and, instead, argues that the privilege be applied, based upon a judicial determination that EMT Kasler, when asking the defendant if she had been pregnant, was acting as an agent of the doctors at Lutheran Medical Center. Indeed, other lower courts have not followed *Ackerson* and have applied the privilege to EMT's based upon the policy reasons underlying the privilege. *People v. Mirque,* 195 Misc.2d 375, 381, 758 N.Y.S.2d 471 (New York City Criminal Court, 2003) (information obtained by EMT from injured driver was required to be given to hospital emergency room personnel and, thus, the EMT was found to be acting as a "field agent" of the hospital medical staff despite the lack of any employment relationship); *People v. Hanf,* 159 Misc.2d 748, 611 N.Y.S.2d 85 (Monroe County Court, 1994) (found an EMT is specifically included in CPLR 4504[a] as a "person authorized to practice medicine").

As noted, it is not necessary to this decision to determine whether EMT Kasler was acting as a "field agent" for Lutheran Medical Center or whether she is "a person authorized to practice medicine" within the meaning of CPLR 4504(a). If the answer to these questions are in the negative, the privilege does not apply. If the answer to either question is affirmative, the exception to the privilege contained in the Social Service Law applies. In either situation, EMT Kasler's testimony before the Grand Jury did not disclose a confidential communication from the defendant in violation of the privilege.

C. *The Tarasoff Exception to the Privilege*

Although there is no general "public interest" exception to the privilege, New York has judicially recognized that the confidentiality obligations embodied in the privilege of CPLR 4504(a) must be overcome in those instances where silence would place an innocent person's life in jeopardy and that the disclosure of otherwise confidential information made under these circumstances may later be used against the patient in a criminal proceeding. *People v. Bierenbaum,* 301 A.D.2d 119, 141, 748 N.Y.S.2d 563 (1st Dept.2002), *lv. denied,* 99 N.Y.2d 626, 760 N.Y.S.2d 107, 790 N.E.2d 281 (2003), *cert. denied,* 540 U.S. 821, 124 S.Ct. 134, 157 L.Ed.2d 40 (2003). In *Bierenbaum,* the Appellate Division recognized the applicability to CPLR 4504(a) of the so-called " *Tarasoff* exception." *See Tarasoff v. Regents of University of Cal.,* 17 Cal.3d 425, 131 Cal.Rptr. 14, 551 P.2d 334 (1976) (when a psychotherapist determines that a patient presents a serious danger of violence to another, the psychotherapist incurs an obligation to use reasonable care to protect the intended victim against such danger and to take such steps as are necessary, including warning the victim and notifying the police of the specific details of the danger).

Bierenbaum, a circumstantial evidence case, involved a defendant convicted of murdering his wife whose body was never found, because allegedly the defendant, a licensed pilot, dropped the corpse into the Atlantic Ocean from a rented airplane. The trial evidence revealed that before the homicide, one of the defendant's treating psychiatrists had sent a " *Tarasoff* letter" to the defendant's wife warning her of the danger the psychiatrist believed the defendant posed to her.

The Appellate Division held that information about the defendant's expressed intentions to harm his wife made to his psychiatrist was properly introduced at the murder trial, *both* because the defendant had previously consented that his wife be informed and, "also because of the *Tarasoff* exception to CPLR 4504(a) privilege. That exception provides that for compelling policy reasons the privilege can be overcome when the patient demonstrates that he poses a clear and present danger to a third party—in this case his wife."

In this case, even in the absence of the specific provisions of the Social Services Law requiring limited disclosure by the hospital and the EMT of what they reasonably believed was evidence of child abuse or maltreatment, there was a common law obligation recognized by the *Tarasoff* exception for both the hospital and the EMT to make whatever disclosures would be necessary to determine if the life of the defendant's newborn baby was in danger.

The *Tarasoff* exception would be applicable to an emergency situation where either a child's or an adult's life was in danger, whereas the specific obligations of the Social Service Law protecting children would not apply to an endangered adult. If, for example, a patient in New York told his emergency room doctor that he was injured by the woman he was keeping locked up in chains in his basement, there would seem to be no question that, pursuant to the *Tarasoff* exception, the doctor would have an obligation to notify the police to rescue the woman. (Sending the woman a "warning letter" would not suffice, just as in this case nothing short of immediately notifying the police would have been a sufficient response to a mother denying having given birth and claiming no knowledge of the whereabouts of her newborn baby.)

Overcoming the privilege under these emergency circumstances would have a minimal, if any, negative affect on the goals underlying the privilege. A patient should have no expectation of confidentiality when the patient communicates information indicating that a third person's life may be in danger (regardless of whether that endangered person is a child or an adult). In this case, regardless of what may have been the defendant's own particular state of mind at the time of her statements to EMT Kasler and to the medical personnel at Lutheran Medical Center, no reasonable woman who had just given birth and whose baby was missing, would expect her denial of those facts to people treating her to be kept confidential from public officials responsible for locating and protecting the baby.

It is well-established constitutional doctrine that the police can enter premises without a search warrant to protect individuals in distress, to assist victims of crimes that have just occurred, or to investigate suspicious signs of impending danger. Considerations of "public safety" will also allow custodial interrogation without *Miranda* warnings. *New York v. Quarles,* 467 U.S. 649, 104 S.Ct. 2626, 81 L.Ed.2d 550 (1984). In both situations, the evidence acquired pursuant to these exceptions will be admissible in a criminal prosecution. Therefore, where a similar emergency exists and it is necessary to disclose an otherwise privileged communication to a physician in order to respond properly to that emergency, the patient should not expect that the disclosed communication will thereafter be confidential.

Accordingly, it was not a violation of the privilege for the People to put this limited information concerning the defendant's statement and medical condition before the Grand Jury. * * *

PROBLEM

In therapeutic sessions with his psychiatrist, Steven Chase makes statements threatening several specific people, including FBI agents. The psychiatrist, Kay Dieter, passes these threats along to the police, and eventually discusses them with the FBI; these discussions were proper under state law, which provides that, not withstanding a psychotherapist's ordinary duty of confidentiality, she may disclose confidentially received information that in her judgment "indicates a clear and immediate danger to others or to society." Chase is tried on charges of threatening violence to FBI agents. May Dr. Dieter testify about the statements he made to her? See United States v. Chase, 340 F.3d 978 (9th Cir. 2003) (noting spit in authority and holding that evidentiary privilege remains, notwithstanding lack of obligation of confidentiality). What if, after Chase first makes threatening comments, Dr. Dieter warns him that, because his statements suggest a clear and imminent danger to others, she will no longer treat such statements as confidential, and he continues to make threatening statements? See United States v. Auster, 517 F.3d 312 (5th Cir. 2008) (holding no privilege given lack of expectation of confidentiality).

See California Evidence Code §§ 1010–1017, 1024, 1027, 1028.

HYPOTHETICAL

A sues Dr. X for damages for injuries in a medical malpractice action. A's injuries were received when Dr. X performed angiogram tests on A. During the deposition of Dr. X, taken by A, Dr. X, claiming the physician-patient privilege, refuses to answer questions as to the names and addresses of other patients upon whom he performed angiogram tests, both before and after those performed on A, including two patients who developed complications from such tests. A moves for an order to compel Dr. X to answer these questions. Should A's motion be granted?

C. THE MARITAL PRIVILEGES

Trammel v. United States

Supreme Court of the United States, 1980.
445 U.S. 40, 100 S.Ct. 906, 63 L.Ed.2d 186.

■ MR. CHIEF JUSTICE BURGER delivered the opinion of the Court.

We granted certiorari to consider whether an accused may invoke the privilege against adverse spousal testimony so as to exclude the voluntary testimony of his wife. This calls for a re-examination of Hawkins v. United States.

I

On March 10, 1976, petitioner Otis Trammel was indicted with two others, Edwin Lee Roberts and Joseph Freeman, for importing heroin into the United States from Thailand and the Philippine Islands and for conspiracy to import heroin in violation of 21 U.S.C. §§ 952(a), 962(a), and 963. The indictment also named six unindicted co-conspirators, including petitioner's wife Elizabeth Ann Trammel.

According to the indictment, petitioner and his wife flew from the Philippines to California in August 1975, carrying with them a quantity of heroin. Freeman and Roberts assisted them in its distribution. Elizabeth Trammel then travelled to Thailand where she purchased another supply of the drug. On November 3, 1975, with four ounces of heroin on her person, she boarded a plane for the United States. During a routine customs search in Hawaii, she was searched, the heroin was discovered, and she was arrested. After discussions with Drug Enforcement Administration agents, she agreed to cooperate with the Government.

Prior to trial on this indictment, petitioner moved to sever his case from that of Roberts and Freeman. He advised the court that the Government intended to call his wife as an adverse witness and asserted his claim to a privilege to prevent her from testifying against him. At a hearing on the motion, Mrs. Trammel was called as a Government witness * * * . She testified that she and petitioner were married in May 1975 and that they remained married.[1] She explained that her cooperation with the Government was based on assurances that she would be given lenient treatment.[2] She then described, in considerable detail, her role and that of her husband in the heroin distribution conspiracy.

After hearing this testimony, the District Court ruled that Mrs. Trammel could testify in support of the Government's case to any act she observed during the marriage and to any communication "made in the presence of a third person"; however, confidential communications between petitioner and his wife were held to be privileged and inadmissible. The motion to sever was denied.

At trial, Elizabeth Trammel testified within the limits of the court's pretrial ruling; her testimony, as the Government concedes, constituted virtually its entire case against petitioner. He was found guilty on both the substantive and conspiracy charges * * *.

In the Court of Appeals petitioner's only claim of error was that the admission of the adverse testimony of his wife, over his objection, contravened this Court's teaching in Hawkins v. United States, and therefore constituted reversible error. The Court of Appeals rejected this contention. It concluded that *Hawkins* did not prohibit "the voluntary testimony of a spouse who appears as an unindicted co-conspirator under grant of immunity from the Government in return for her testimony."

II

The privilege claimed by petitioner has ancient roots. Writing in 1628, Lord Coke observed that "it hath been resolved by the Justices that a wife cannot be produced either against or for her husband." 1 Coke, A Commentarie upon Littleton 6b (1628). This spousal disqualification sprang from

---

[1] In response to the question whether divorce was contemplated, Mrs. Trammel testified that her husband had said that "I would go my way and he would go his." (App., at 27).

[2] The Government represents to the Court that Elizabeth Trammel has not been prosecuted for her role in the conspiracy.

two canons of medieval jurisprudence; first, the rule that an accused was not permitted to testify in his own behalf because of his interest in the proceeding; second, the concept that husband and wife were one, and that since the woman had no recognized separate legal existence, the husband was that one. From those two now long-abandoned doctrines, it followed that what was inadmissible from the lips of the defendant-husband was also inadmissible from his wife.

Despite its medieval origins, this rule of spousal disqualification remained intact in most common-law jurisdictions well into the 19th century. It was applied by this Court in Stein v. Bowman, in Graves v. United States, and again in Jin Fuey Moy v. United States, where it was deemed so well established a proposition as to "hardly requir[e] mention." Indeed, it was not until 1933, in Funk v. United States, that this Court abolished the testimonial disqualification in the federal courts, so as to permit the spouse of a defendant to testify in the defendant's behalf. *Funk,* however, left undisturbed the rule that either spouse could prevent the other from giving adverse testimony. The rule thus evolved into one of privilege rather than one of absolute disqualification. * * *

The modern justification for this privilege against adverse spousal testimony is its perceived role in fostering the harmony and sanctity of the marriage relationship. Notwithstanding this benign purpose, the rule was sharply criticized. Professor Wigmore termed it "the merest anachronism in legal theory and an indefensible obstruction to truth in practice." 8 Wigmore, § 2228 at 221. The Committee on the Improvement of the Law of Evidence of the American Bar Association called for its abolition. 63 American Bar Association Reports, at 594–595 (1938). In its place, Wigmore and others suggested a privilege protecting only private marital communications, modeled on the privilege between priest and penitent, attorney and client and physician and patient.[5]

These criticisms influenced the American Law Institute, which, in its 1942 Model Code of Evidence, advocated a privilege for marital confidences, but expressly rejected a rule vesting in the defendant the right to exclude all adverse testimony of his spouse. See American Law Institute, Model Code of Evidence, Rule 215 (1942). In 1953 the Uniform Rules of Evidence, drafted by the National Conference of Commissioners on Uniform State Laws, followed a similar course; it limited the privilege to confidential communications and "abolishe[d] the rule, still existing in some states, and largely a sentimental relic, of not requiring one spouse to testify against the other in a criminal action." See Rule 23(2) and comments. Several state legislatures enacted similarly patterned provisions into law.

---

[5] This Court recognized just such a confidential marital communications privilege in Wolfle v. United States and in Blau v. United States. In neither case, however, did the Court adopt the Wigmore view that the communications privilege be substituted *in place of* the privilege against adverse spousal testimony. The privilege as to confidential marital communications is not at issue in the instant case; accordingly, our holding today does not disturb *Wolfle* and *Blau.*

In Hawkins v. United States, this Court considered the continued vitality of the privilege against adverse spousal testimony in the federal courts. There the District Court had permitted petitioner's wife, over his objection, to testify against him. With one questioning concurring opinion, the Court held the wife's testimony inadmissible; it took note of the critical comments that the common-law rule had engendered but chose not to abandon it. Also rejected was the Government's suggestion that the Court modify the privilege by vesting it in the witness spouse, with freedom to testify or not independent of the defendant's control. The Court viewed this proposed modification as antithetical to the widespread belief, evidenced in the rules then in effect in a majority of the States and in England, "that the law should not force or encourage testimony which might alienate husband and wife, or further inflame existing domestic differences."

Hawkins, then, left the federal privilege for adverse spousal testimony where it found it, continuing "a rule which bars the testimony of one spouse against the other unless both consent." Accord, Wyatt v. United States.[7] However, in so doing, the Court made clear that its decision was not meant to "foreclose whatever changes in the rule may eventually be dictated by 'reason and experience.' "

III

A

The Federal Rules of Evidence acknowledge the authority of the federal courts to continue the evolutionary development of testimonial privileges in federal criminal trials "governed by the principles of the common law as they may be interpreted * * * in the light of reason and experience." Fed.Rule Evid. 501. The general mandate of Rule 501 was substituted by the Congress for a set of privilege rules drafted by the Judicial Conference Advisory Committee on Rules of Evidence and approved by the Judicial Conference of the United States and by this Court. That proposal defined nine specific privileges, including a husband-wife privilege which would have codified the *Hawkins* rule and eliminated the privilege for confidential marital communications. See Fed.Rule of Evid., Proposed Rule 505. In rejecting the proposed rules and enacting Rule 501, Congress manifested an affirmative intention not to freeze the law of privilege. Its purpose rather was to "provide the courts with the flexibility to develop rules of privilege on a case-by-case basis," 120 Cong.Rec. 40891 (1974) (statement of Rep. Hungate), and to leave the door open to change. * * *

Although Rule 501 confirms the authority of the federal courts to reconsider the continued validity of the *Hawkins* rule, the long history of the

---

[7] The decision in *Wyatt* recognized an exception to *Hawkins* for cases in which one spouse commits a crime against the other. This exception placed on the ground of necessity, was a longstanding one at common law. See Lord Audley's Case, 8 Wigmore § 2239. It has been expanded since then to include crimes against the spouse's property, see Herman v. United States, and in recent years crimes against children of either spouse, United States v. Allery. Similar exceptions have been found to the confidential marital communications privilege. See 8 Wigmore, § 2338.

privilege suggests that it ought not to be casually cast aside. That the privilege is one affecting marriage, home, and family relationships—already subject to much erosion in our day—also counsels caution. At the same time we cannot escape the reality that the law on occasion adheres to doctrinal concepts long after the reasons which gave them birth have disappeared and after experience suggests the need for change. This was recognized in *Funk* where the Court "decline[d] to enforce * * * ancient rule[s] of the common law under conditions as they now exist." For, as Mr. Justice Black admonished in another setting,"[w]hen precedent and precedent alone is all the argument that can be made to support a court-fashioned rule, it is time for the rule's creator to destroy it." Francis v. Southern Pacific Co. (Black, J., dissenting).

B

Since 1958, when *Hawkins* was decided, support for the privilege against adverse spousal testimony has been eroded further. Thirty-one jurisdictions, including Alaska and Hawaii, then allowed an accused a privilege to prevent adverse spousal testimony. The number has now declined to 24.[9] In 1974, the National Conference on Uniform States Laws revised its Uniform Rules of Evidence, but again rejected the *Hawkins* rule in favor of a limited privilege for confidential communications. See Uniform Rules of Evidence, Rule 504. That proposed rule has been enacted in Arkansas, North Dakota, and Oklahoma—each of which in 1958 permitted an accused to exclude adverse spousal testimony.[10] The trend in state law toward divesting the accused of the privilege to bar adverse spousal testimony has special relevance because of the law of marriage and domestic relations are concerns traditionally reserved to the states. Scholarly criticism of the *Hawkins* rule has also continued unabated.

---

[9] Eight states provide that one spouse is incompetent to testify against the other in a criminal proceeding: * * *.

Sixteen states provide a privilege against adverse spousal testimony and vest the privilege in both spouses or in the defendant-spouse alone; * * *.

Nine states entitle the witness-spouse alone to assert a privilege against adverse spousal testimony: * * *.

The remaining 17 states have abolished the privilege in criminal cases: * * *.

In 1901, Congress enacted a rule of evidence for the District of Columbia that made husband and wife "competent but not compellable to testify for or against each other," except as to confidential communications. This provision, which vests the privilege against adverse spousal testimony in the witness spouse, remains in effect. See 31 Stat. 1358, §§ 1068, 1069, recodified as D.C.Code § 14–306 (1973).

[10] In 1965, California took the privilege from the defendant-spouse and vested it in the witness-spouse, accepting a study commission recommendation that the "latter [was] more likely than the former to determine whether or not to claim the privilege on the basis of the probable effect on the marital relationship." See Cal.Evid.Code §§ 970–973 * * *.

Support for the common-law rule has also diminished in England. In 1972 a study group there proposed giving the privilege to the witness-spouse, on the ground that "if [the wife] is willing to give evidence * * * the law would be showing excessive concern for the preservation of marital harmony if it were to say she must not do so." Criminal Law Revision Committee, Eleventh Report Evidence (General), at 93.

C

Testimonial exclusionary rules and privileges contravene the fundamental principle that "the public * * * has a right to every man's evidence."
United States v. Bryan. As such, they must be strictly construed and accepted "only to the very limited extent that permitting a refusal to testify or
excluding relevant evidence has a public good transcending the normally
predominant principle of utilizing all rational means for ascertaining
truth." Elkins v. United States. Accord, United States v. Nixon. Here we
must decide whether the privilege against adverse spousal testimony promotes sufficiently important interests to outweigh the need for probative
evidence in the administration of criminal justice.

It is essential to remember that the *Hawkins* privilege is not needed to
protect information privately disclosed between husband and wife in the
confidence of the marital relationship—once described by this Court as "the
best solace of human existence." Those confidences are privileged under the
independent rule protecting confidential marital communications. The
Hawkins privilege is invoked, not to exclude private marital communications, but rather to exclude evidence of criminal acts and of communications made in the presence of third persons.

No other testimonial privilege sweeps so broadly. The privileges between priest and penitent, attorney and client, and physician and patient
limit protection to private communications. These privileges are rooted in
the imperative need for confidence and trust. The priest-penitent privilege
recognizes the human need to disclose to a spiritual counselor, in total and
absolute confidence, what are believed to be flawed acts or thoughts and to
receive priestly consolation and guidance in return. The lawyer-client privilege rests on the need for the advocate and counselor to know all that relates to the client's reasons for seeking representation if the professional
mission is to be carried out. Similarly, the physician must know all that a
patient can articulate in order to identify and to treat disease; barriers to
full disclosure would impair diagnosis and treatment.

The *Hawkins* rule stands in marked contrast to these three privileges.
Its protection is not limited to confidential communications; rather it permits an accused to exclude all adverse spousal testimony. As Jeremy Bentham observed more than a century and a half ago, such a privilege goes far
beyond making "every man's house his castle," and permits a person to
convert his house into "a den of thieves." 5 Rationale of Judicial Evidence
340 (1827). It "secures, to every man, one safe and unquestionable and ever
ready accomplice for every imaginable crime." Id., at 338.

The ancient foundations for so sweeping a privilege have long since
disappeared. Nowhere in the common-law world—indeed in any modern
society—is a woman regarded as chattel or demeaned by denial of a separate legal identity and the dignity associated with recognition as a whole
human being. Chip by chip, over the years those archaic notions have been
cast aside so that "[n]o longer is the female destined solely for the home

and the rearing of the family, and only the male for the marketplace and the world of ideas."

The contemporary justification for affording an accused such a privilege is also unpersuasive. When one spouse is willing to testify against the other in a criminal proceeding—whatever the motivation—their relationship is almost certainly in disrepair; there is probably little in the way of marital harmony for the privilege to preserve. In these circumstances, a rule of evidence that permits an accused to prevent adverse spousal testimony seems far more likely to frustrate justice than to foster family peace.[12] Indeed, there is reason to believe that vesting the privilege in the accused could actually undermine the marital relationship. For example, in a case such as this, the Government is unlikely to offer a wife immunity and lenient treatment if it knows that her husband can prevent her from giving adverse testimony. If the Government is dissuaded from making such an offer, the privilege can have the untoward effect of permitting one spouse to escape justice at the expense of the other. It hardly seems conducive to the preservation of the marital relation to place a wife in jeopardy solely by virtue of her husband's control over her testimony.

IV

Our consideration of the foundations for the privilege and its history satisfy us that "reason and experience" no longer justify so sweeping a rule as that found acceptable by the Court in *Hawkins*. Accordingly, we conclude that the existing rule should be modified so that the witness spouse alone has a privilege to refuse to testify adversely; the witness may be neither compelled to testify nor foreclosed from testifying. This modification—vesting the privilege in the witness spouse—furthers the important public interest in marital harmony without unduly burdening legitimate law enforcement needs.

Here, petitioner's spouse chose to testify against him. That she did so after a grant of immunity and assurances of lenient treatment does not render her testimony involuntary. Accordingly, the District Court and the Court of Appeals were correct in rejecting petitioner's claim of privilege, and the judgment of the Court of Appeals is affirmed.

Affirmed.

[Justice Stewart, who had concurred separately in *Hawkins*, did so again. In *Hawkins*, he expressed skepticism that the defendant ought to have a privilege to keep his spouse from testifying against him, but he also expressed doubt about a rule giving the spouse the choice whether to testify; he concluded that the issue was not properly presented in that case. In *Trammel*, he asserted that the decision was not justified by any change in

---

[12] It is argued that abolishing the privilege will permit the Government to come between husband and wife, pitting one against the other. That, too, misses the mark. Neither *Hawkins*, nor any other privilege, prevents the Government from enlisting one spouse to give information concerning the other or to aid in the other's apprehension. It is only the spouse's testimony in the courtroom that is prohibited.

perception brought on by "reason and experience." Rather, he said, "The fact of the matter is that the Court in this case simply accepts the very same arguments that the Court rejected when the Government first made them in the *Hawkins* case in 1958. I thought those arguments were valid then, and I think so now."]

See California Evidence Code §§ 970–973, 980–982, 984–987.

HYPOTHETICAL

X is prosecuted for murder of A, a liquor-store clerk, during a holdup. The murder remained unsolved for several years. X's participation became known after B, X's wife at the time, secured an annulment. The prosecutor calls B to testify that she had her marriage to X annulled about six months ago because she married X before her divorce from Y became final, and that on the night of A's murder, X came home and told her he had pulled a robbery at the liquor store and killed the clerk. X objects to B's proposed testimony on the ground of the privilege for marital communications. What result?

D. MISCELLANEOUS PRIVILEGES

1. CLERGY-COMMUNICANT PRIVILEGE

In re Grand Jury Investigation
United States Court of Appeals, Third Circuit, 1990
918 F.2d 374.

■BECKER, CIRCUIT JUDGE.

[In November 1985, in a formerly all-white neighborhood in Pittsburgh, Pennsylvania, a fire, determined likely to be the result of arson, broke out in a house recently bought by a black family. Next door to that house lived Mr. and Mrs. George Kampich, George Shaw, who was Mrs. Kampich's son from a prior marriage, and Patty DiLucente, Shaw's fiancée. Within several days of the fire, the four sought counseling from Rev. Ernest Knoche, pastor of a Lutheran church of which the Kampiches were members; Shaw and DiLucente were not members, though Shaw attended services occasionally. Shaw and DiLucente were married in June 1989. In November of that year, Knoche was subpoenaed to appear before a federal grand jury investigating possible crimes related to the fire; the government asserted that it had reason to believe the four next-door neighbors had participated in or planned the fire and discussed the matter with Knoche. Knoche asserted the clergy-communicant privilege.]

The government contends that * * * the presence at the counseling session of the fiancée (not yet a member of the family) was neither essential to nor in furtherance of any religiously motivated communications to the pastor on the part of the others present and therefore worked either to vitiate or to waive any privilege. In support of this argument, the government invokes the general principle that evidentiary privileges, which retard the search for truth, should be narrowly construed.

There is a relative dearth of federal precedent establishing the existence and contours of a clergy-communicant privilege.[2] * * * In accordance with [the standard established by Fed. R.Evid. 501], we must determine whether a clergy-communicant privilege in fact exists and, if it does, its relevant contours. * * *

I. FACTS AND PROCEDURAL HISTORY

In the course of [a hearing held to determine whether to compel Knoche's testimony], the district judge questioned the pastor about the extent of his family and group counseling, the parties involved in the discussion at issue, and the confidentiality of their communications. Pastor Knoche stated that family counseling, in contrast to individual counseling, constituted a typical and important part of his ministry. The Pastor also concurred with the district court's characterization of his ministry as founded upon the Judeo-Christian notion of redemption and forgiveness through counseling and prayer. The Pastor responded, further, that forthrightness and truthfulness on the part of participants, such as Mr. and Mrs. Kampich, Shaw, and DiLucente, are essential to proper counseling and, ultimately, to redemption. He concluded that those whom he spiritually counsels expect that he will keep any communications made to him in strict confidence.

The district court sustained Pastor Knoche's right to assert a clergy-communicant privilege and denied the government's motion to compel his testimony. * * * This appeal followed.

II. THE EXISTENCE AND CONTOURS OF A CLERGY–COMMUNICANT PRIVILEGE

* * *

A. The Clergy-Communicant Privilege and the History of Rule 501

[The court quotes at length deleted Federal Rule of Evidence 506 and the Advisory Committee Note to it; see Appendix C at pp. 1279–1281.

The reference in the Advisory Committee's Note to the group counseling practices common to the psychotherapist-patient relationship and the relationship of lawyers to multiple clients indicates that the Supreme Court did not view the privilege as limited solely to confidential relationships between two individuals. Given the requisite showing of confidentiality, proposed Rule 506 would have extended the clergy-communicant privilege to group discussions.

Although Congress chose not to adopt the proposed rules on privileges, it did not disapprove them.

* * *

---

[2] The privilege has variously been referred to as the priest-penitent, clergymen-penitent, communications to clergymen, and clergy-communicant privilege. We adopt the latter nomenclature.

We believe that the proposed rules provide a useful reference point and offer guidance in defining the existence and scope of evidentiary privileges in the federal courts. * * *

The history of the proposed Rules of Evidence reflects that the clergy-communicant rule was one of the least controversial of the enumerated privileges, merely defining a long-recognized principle of American law. Although most of the nine privileges set forth in the proposed rules were vigorously attacked in Congress, the privilege covering communications to members of the clergy was not. Indeed, virtually every state has recognized some form of clergy-communicant privilege.[10] * * *

B. Federal Judicial Precedents Recognizing a Clergy-Communicant Privilege

* * *

The Supreme Court, albeit in dicta, [has] acknowledged the existence of a "priest-penitent" privilege. See Trammel v. United States, 445 U.S. 40, 45, 100 S.Ct. 906, 909-10, 63 L.Ed.2d 186 (1980). * * * Critiquing an archaic and unduly expansive rule that permitted a defendant to exclude from evidence any adverse spousal testimony, the Court favorably referred to several privileges by analogy, among them, the "priest-penitent" privilege:

> The privileges between priest and penitent, attorney and client, and physician and patient limit protection to private communications. The privileges are rooted in the imperative need for confidence and trust. The priest-penitent privilege recognizes the human need to disclose to a spiritual counselor, in total and absolute confidence, what are believed to be flawed acts or thoughts and to receive priestly consolation and guidance in return.

Id. at 51, 100 S.Ct. at 913. * * *

C. The Scope and Contours of the Clergy–Communicant Privilege Adopted

* * * [W]e must attempt to balance the need for full disclosure of all probative evidence against the countervailing requirement of confidentiality that furthers the objectives underlying the privilege claimed. * * *

In determining whether a clergy-communicant privilege exists, we weigh Dean Wigmore's four fundamental prerequisites for a privilege against the disclosure of communications:

---

[10] [The court cites statutes of 39 states providing for a clergy-communicant evidentiary privilege.]

We note that, although the clergy-communicant privilege is part of the American tradition, it did not exist as part of the English common law. The climate of hostility in England toward the Roman Catholic Church during the Reformation largely accounts for the nonexistence of the privilege at common law. There is evidence to suggest, however, that as a matter of judicial discretion judges would often excuse members of the clergy from testifying about confidential communications.

(1) The communications must originate in a *confidence* that they will not be disclosed.

(2) This element of *confidentiality must be essential* to the full and satisfactory maintenance of the relation between the parties.

(3) The *relation* must be one which in the opinion of the community ought to be sedulously *fostered*.

(4) The *injury* that would inure to the relation by the disclosure of the communications must be *greater than the benefit* thereby gained for the correct disposal of litigation.

8 Wigmore at Sec. 2285 (footnote omitted) (emphasis in original).[12] The Advisory Committee Note to proposed Rule 506 adverts to these considerations and concludes that they "seem strongly to favor a privilege for confidential communications to clergymen."

* * * Both state and federal decisions have long recognized the privilege. The Supreme Court Rules Committee also recognized the privilege. That is doubtless because the clergy-communicant relationship is so important, indeed so fundamental to the western tradition, that it must be "sedulously fostered." Confidence is obviously essential to maintaining the clergy-communicant relationship. Although there are countervailing considerations, we have no doubt that the need for protecting the relationship outweighs them.

We believe that the privilege should apply to protect communications made (1) to a clergyperson[13] (2) in his or her spiritual and professional capacity (3) with a reasonable expectation of confidentiality. As is the case with the attorney-client privilege, the presence of third parties, if essential to and in furtherance of the communication, should not void the privilege. * * * In addition, we note our agreement with the tenor of the Advisory Committee's Note to proposed Rule 506, which extends the scope of the privilege to encompass not only communications between Roman Catholic

---

[12] In analyzing whether this privilege exists under federal common law, we have also considered the balancing process described by Judge Weinstein in United States v. King, 73 F.R.D. 103, 105 (E.D.N.Y.1976) * * *:

[T]he justifiable "principles of the common law" as they relate to matters of developing new privileges--those not firmly embedded in federal law--require the balancing of four factors: first, the federal government's need for the information being sought in enforcing its substantive and procedural policies; second, the importance of the relationship or policy sought to be furthered by the state rule of privilege and the probability that the privilege will advance that relationship or policy; third, in the particular case, the special need for the information sought to be protected; and fourth, in the particular case, the adverse impact on the local policy that would result from non-recognition of the privilege.

[13] We believe that Proposed Rule of Evidence 506(a)(1) provides a workable definition of a clergyperson: "A 'clergyman' is a minister, priest, rabbi, or other similar functionary of a religious organization, or an individual reasonably believed so to be by the person consulting him." By endorsing this definition of a clergyperson, we do not intimate that the privilege should be interpreted to comprehend communications to and among members of sects that denominate each and every member as clergy, proclaim that all communications have spiritual significance, or dictate that all communications among members, whether essential to and in furtherance of the purportedly privileged communication or not, shall be confidential

priests and their penitents, but also communications between clergy and communicants of other denominations.

* * * The precise scope of the privilege and its additional facets, such as whether a clergyperson should be required to disclose confidential communications when harm to innocent parties is threatened and imminent, are * * * most suitably left to case-by-case evolution.[15]

III. THE APPLICATION OF THE CLERGY-COMMUNICANT PRIVILEGE IN THIS CASE

* * *

The threshold criterion for deciding whether the privilege should attach—the criterion that the communication be made to a clergyperson—is clearly satisfied. Pastor Knoche is an ordained Lutheran minister. Whether the Kampiches, Shaw, and DiLucente communicated with Pastor Knoche in his spiritual or professional capacity, thus fulfilling the second prerequisite for attachment of the privilege, is less obvious. Whether the Kampiches', Shaw's, and DiLucente's communications to Knoche were made with a reasonable expectation of confidentiality, fulfilling the third prerequisite for the privilege's attachment, is also unclear.

The government, although not conceding the existence of the clergy-communicant privilege, maintains that DiLucente's presence during the Kampiches' and Shaw's conversation with Pastor Knoche undermines the confidentiality of this conversation for two reasons. The government contends, first, that any existing clergy-communicant privilege is inapplicable in this case because DiLucente was not related to the Kampiches and Shaw by either blood or marriage at the time the conversation took place. The government further contends that any privilege should be inapplicable because DiLucente's presence during the group discussion was neither essential to nor in furtherance of the purpose of the communication. * * *

The government is correct in observing that the traditional clergy-communicant privilege protected a penitential relationship in which a person privately confessed his or her sins to a priest, in order to receive some form of church sanctioned discipline or absolution. Neither family nor other types of group counseling fit neatly within this "one-to-one" model of the privilege. We have explained, however, that the modern view of the privilege is more expansive than the traditional one. We discern nothing in modern clergy-communicant privilege doctrine, as it finds expression in either proposed Rule 506 or the cases recognizing the privilege, that would limit the privilege's application solely to group discussions involving family members related by blood or marriage. Modern clergy-communicant privilege doctrine focuses, rather, on whether the presence of a third party is essential to or in furtherance of a communication to a member of the clergy. We think, consistent with the general constructional rule that evidentiary

---

[15] We also need not address at any length the question of who may assert the privilege. The authorities recognizing the privilege would allow it to be asserted, as it was here, by a clergyperson on behalf of a communicant. We need not reach the issue, therefore, of whether Pastor Knoche could assert the privilege on his own behalf. * * *

privileges should be narrowly construed, that recognition of the clergy-communicant privilege in this circumstance depends upon whether the third party's presence is essential to and in furtherance of a communication to a member of the clergy. As is the case with consultations between attorneys and clients, the presence of multiple parties, unrelated by blood or marriage, during discussions with a member of the clergy may, but will not necessarily, defeat the condition that communications be made with a reasonable expectation of confidentiality in order for the privilege to attach.

At the district court's hearing on the privilege, the testimony concerning whether the Kampiches, Shaw, and DiLucente reasonably expected that their communications to Pastor Knoche were confidential was sparse. [Knoche did testify that the session was held in confidence but the] district court neither inquired into whether the presence of each person at the discussion was essential to and in furtherance of the communications to the pastor nor made findings of fact on that issue.* * *

In order to determine [on remand] whether the Kampiches, Shaw, and DiLucente communicated with Pastor Knoche in his spiritual or professional capacity and with a reasonable expectation of confidentiality, * * * the district court may well have to inquire into the nature of the communicants' relationship as well as the pastoral counseling practices of the relevant synod of the Lutheran church. In order to decide, more particularly, whether members of this group reasonably expected that their communications to Pastor Knoche would be kept in confidence, the court may also find it necessary to inquire into whether the parties shared a commonality of interest at the time of the communication and, if so, in what respect. * * * In order to ascertain whether [DiLucente's] presence worked to vitiate or to waive the privilege, the court will have to inquire into whether the other group members, who apparently are subjects of the grand jury investigation, reasonably required her presence at the counselling session, either in furtherance of their communications to the pastor or to protect their interests. * * *

In its attempt to determine DiLucente's role in the group counseling session, * * * the district court may feel it necessary to seek some degree of disclosure of what was discussed with the pastor. We have, in other situations in which a privilege was implicated, recommended the use of in camera hearings, accompanied by a variety of options with respect to the presence or absence of counsel and the parties. We note, however, that the determination whether to conduct an in camera proceeding, as well as the anatomy of any such proceeding, in this situation will necessitate consideration of delicate first amendment issues, lest the hearing itself result in evisceration of the privilege. * * *

See California Evidence Code §§ 1030–1034; deleted Federal Rule of Evidence 506.

2. ACCOUNTANT–CLIENT PRIVILEGE

Note, Functional Overlap Between the Lawyer and Other Professionals: Its Implications for the Privileged Communications Doctrines

71 Yale L.J. 1226, 1247–49 (1962).*

THE ACCOUNTANT

At common law there was no testimonial privilege for communications between a man and his accountant, and courts continue to reject this claim of privilege unanimously. By enacting privileged communications statutes protecting confidences between accountants and their clients, fifteen American jurisdictions have changed the common law rule. Almost no case law exists which interprets these statutes. However, they may be narrowly construed if cases arise which invite their construction, since lawyers and jurists responding to our survey, leading commentators, legal organizations, and a number of federal courts disfavor this privilege. Almost certainly all the exceptions and limitations of the attorney-client privilege will be grafted onto these statutes. In a number of cases raising the question in States with such a privilege, federal courts have refused to apply the state accountant privilege statute, but have adhered to the common law rule. These cases involved either tax investigations or criminal prosecutions.

At first glance, it seems unfair that a conversation with a lawyer is protected while the same conversation if held with an accountant would not be. The possibility of an accountant-client privilege, however, is one which has not been enthusiastically embraced by all accountants. The American Institute of Certified Public Accountants officially opposes the privilege. The Executive Director of the National Society of Public Accountants explains this policy:

> Perhaps the reason for not pushing for privileged communication for our members practicing public accounting is the fact that much of their income is from tax work, and they maintain a good relationship with the Internal Revenue Service. There might be some question about cooperation and working relationships should there be privileged communication. Usually a client will tell the agent, "Go see my accountant." The agent would not be so amenable to this suggestion if the accountant were privileged.

Arguably, since the privilege is for the client's protection, not the professional's, the accountant's preference should defer to his client's. But no tension seems to exist between the views of the accountant and the client; a majority of the laymen surveyed who expressed an opinion disfavored the accountant privilege. Lawyers and judges, too, were heavily opposed, and accountants ambivalent at best. Thus, the practical political obstacles either to passage or successful administration of such a law are great.

Even discounting the public opinion against it, the accountant-client privilege is of dubious inherent desirability. It is likely that federal courts at least believe that an accountant-client privilege would greatly increase the government's difficulties in proving tax evasions. Tacit recognition of this privilege's obstructive effect is also found in the statutes of six of the fifteen States with this privilege. Those six suspend the privilege in criminal and bankruptcy cases. While personal counseling and advice about lawsuits may require guarantees of absolute confidentiality in order to be effectual, this is probably untrue of the tasks performed by the accountant—evidenced by the attitudes of their professional associations to the privilege. Although there is a functional overlap between accountants and attorneys, this is insufficient to justify a privilege for the former. The attorney-client privilege must cover all legitimate attorney tasks in order to shield those functions for which protection is essential. If the area of overlap could be separated, neither profession would be entitled to a privilege. In fact, courts have withdrawn the privilege from attorneys who were acting more like accountants than attorneys. Further, courts have curtailed accountant activity which resembled too closely the lawyer's work by declaring such tasks to have been unauthorized practice of law. In sum, therefore, the privilege should not be extended to the accountant.

See also California Evidence Code §§ 1050 (privilege to protect secrecy of vote), 1060 (privilege to protect trade secret), 1070 (newsman's refusal to disclose news source.)

3. PARENT–CHILD PRIVILEGE

In re Grand Jury
United States Court of Appeals, Third Circuit, 1997.
103 F.3d 1140.

■ GARTH, CIRCUIT JUDGE:

* * *

I.

[The Court considered together two appeals, one from the Virgin Islands and one from Delaware. In the Virgin Islands case, a grand jury subpoenaed a former FBI agent whose 18-year-old son was the target of its investigation as a result of "certain transactions" in which he was allegedly involved. Anticipating that he would be asked about conversations he had had with his son, the father moved to quash the subpoena.]

The father testified, at a hearing before the district court, that he and his son "ha[d] an excellent relationship, very close, very loving relationship." He further testified that if he were coerced into testifying against his son, "[their] relationship would dramatically change and the closeness that

[they] have would end. . ." The father further explained that the subpoena would impact negatively upon his relationship with his son:

> I will be living under a cloud in which if my son comes to me or talks to me, I've got to be very careful what he says, what I allow him to say. I would have to stop him and say, "you can't talk to me about that. You've got to talk to your attorney." It's no way for anybody to live in this country.

[On the basis of what it deemed to be governing law, the district court "regretfully decline[d]" to recognize a parent-child privilege."]

In the Delaware case, a sixteen year old minor daughter was subpoenaed to testify before the grand jury, as part of an investigation into her father's participation in an alleged interstate kidnapping of a woman who had disappeared. [A motion to quash made on behalf of the daughter and both her parents] sought to bar the testimony of the daughter claiming a parent-child privilege which would cover testimony and confidential communications. "[T]he privilege [was] claimed for confidential communications as well as for protection against being compelled to testify in a criminal proceeding".

[The district court concluded that there was "no recognized familial privilege," but that it should weigh the individuals' privacy interests against the government's interest in compelling the testimony; based on the government's *in camera ex parte* proffer, the district court concluded that the latter prevailed.]

* * *

III.

The central question in these appeals is one of first impression in this court: should we recognize a parent-child testimonial privilege? Appellants argue that recognition is necessary in order to advance important public policy interests such as the protection of strong and trusting parent-child relationships; the preservation of the family; safeguarding of privacy interests and protection from harmful government intrusion; and the promotion of healthy psychological development of children. These public policy arguments echo those advanced by academicians and other legal commentators in the myriad of law review articles discussing the parent-child testimonial privilege.

Although legal academicians appear to favor adoption of a parent-child testimonial privilege, no federal Court of Appeals and no state supreme court has recognized such a privilege. We too decline to recognize such a privilege * * * *

A. FEDERAL AND STATE COURTS HAVE DECLINED TO RECOGNIZE A PARENT–CHILD PRIVILEGE.

* * *

[The court's extensive review of the caselaw has been omitted.—Eds.]

B. THE STANDARDS PRESCRIBED BY FEDERAL RULE OF EVIDENCE 501 DO NOT SUPPORT THE CREATION OF A PRIVILEGE.

Federal Rule of Evidence 501 provides that "the privilege of a witness . . . shall be governed by the principles of the common law as they may be interpreted by the courts of the United States in the light of reason and experience." No such principle, interpretation, reason or experience has been drawn upon here.

It is true that Congress, in enacting Fed.R.Evid. 501, "manifested an affirmative intention not to freeze the law of privilege. Its purpose rather was to 'provide the courts with the flexibility to develop rules of privilege on a case-by-case basis,' and to leave the door open to change." *Trammel v. United States*, 445 U.S. 40, 47 (1980) (quoting 102 Cong. Rec. 40,891 (1974) (statement of Rep. William Hungate)). In doing so, however, we are admonished that privileges are generally disfavored; that " 'the public . . . has a right to every man's evidence' "; and that privileges are tolerable "only to the very limited extent that permitting a refusal to testify or excluding relevant evidence has a public good transcending the normally predominant principle of utilizing all rational means for ascertaining truth."

In keeping with these principles, the Supreme Court has rarely expanded common-law testimonial privileges. Following the Supreme Court's teachings, other federal courts, including this court, have likewise declined to exercise their power under Rule 501 expansively.

Neither the appellants nor the dissent has identified any principle of common law, and hence have proved no interpretation of such a principle. Nor has the dissent or the appellants discussed any common-law principle in light of reason and experience. Accordingly, no basis has been demonstrated for this court to adopt a parent-child privilege.

C. CREATING A PARENT–CHILD PRIVILEGE WOULD BE INCONSISTENT WITH THE TEACHINGS OF THE SUPREME COURT AND OF THIS COURT.

1. *Supreme Court*

* * * Notably, in recognizing a psychotherapist-patient privilege [in *Jaffe*], the Supreme Court relied on the fact that all fifty states had enacted some form of a psychotherapist privilege. The *Jaffee* Court explained that "it is appropriate to treat a consistent body of policy determinations by state legislatures as reflecting both 'reason' and 'experience.' " Here, by contrast, only four states have deemed it necessary to protect from disclosure, in any manner, confidential communications between children and their parents. * * * New York state courts have recognized a limited parent-child privilege, and Idaho and Minnesota have enacted limited statutory privileges protecting confidential communications by minors to their parents. In Massachusetts, * * * minor children are statutorily disqualified from testifying against their parents in criminal proceedings. No state within the Third Circuit has adopted a parent-child privilege.

* * *

The policy determinations of these four states do not constitute a "consistent body of policy determinations by state[s]" supporting recognition of a parent-child privilege. Indeed, if anything, the fact that the overwhelming majority of states have chosen *not* to create a parent-child privilege supports the opposite conclusion: "reason and experience" dictate that federal courts should refuse to recognize a privilege rejected by the vast majority of jurisdictions.

The *Jaffee* Court also relied on the fact that the psychotherapist-patient privilege was among the nine specific privileges recommended by the Advisory Committee on Rules of Evidence in 1972. Additionally, the *Jaffee* Court noted: "[O]ur holding [*United States v. Gillock*, 445 U.S. 360 (1980)] that Rule 501 did not include a state legislative privilege relied, in part, on the fact that no such privilege was included in the Advisory Committee's draft [of the proposed privilege rules]."

In the instant cases, in contrast to the psychotherapist-patient privilege recognized in *Jaffee*, the parent-child privilege, like the state legislative privilege rejected in *Gillock*, was not among the enumerated privileges submitted by the Advisory Committee. Although this fact, in and of itself, is not dispositive with respect to the question as to whether this court should create a privilege, it strongly suggests that the Advisory Committee, like the majority of state legislatures, did not regard confidential parent-child communications sufficiently important to warrant "privilege" protection.

A federal court should give due consideration, and accord proper weight, to the judgment of the Advisory Committee and of state legislatures on this issue when it evaluates whether it is appropriate to create a new privilege pursuant to Rule 501.

2. *Third Circuit*

* * * In contrast [to a clergy-communicant privilege, which the court recognized in *In re Grand Jury Investigation*, 918 F.2d 374 (3d Cir. 1990) (Becker, J.)], the parent-child privilege sought to be recognized here is of relatively recent vintage, and is virtually no more than the product of legal academicians. * * * *

Furthermore, an analysis of the four Wigmore factors, which Judge Becker used to buttress this court's disposition in *In re Grand Jury Investigation* [see above, p. 615 does not support the creation of a privilege. * * *

At least two of Wigmore's prerequisite conditions for creation of a federal common-law privilege are not met under the facts of these cases. We refer to the second and fourth elements of the Wigmore test.

First, confidentiality—in the form of a testimonial privilege—is not essential to a successful parent-child relationship, as required by the second factor. A privilege should be recognized only where such a privilege would be indispensable to the survival of the relationship that society deems should be fostered. For instance, because complete candor and full disclosure by the client is absolutely necessary in order for the attorney to function effectively, society recognizes an attorney-client privilege. Without a guarantee of secrecy, clients would be unwilling to reveal damaging information. As a corollary, clients would disclose negative information, which an attorney must know to prove effective representation, only if they were assured that such disclosures are privileged.

In contrast, it is not clear whether children would be more likely to discuss private matters with their parents if a parent-child privilege were recognized than if one were not. It is not likely that children, or even their parents, would typically be aware of the existence or non-existence of a testimonial privilege covering parent-child communications. On the other hand, professionals such as attorneys, doctors and members of the clergy would know of the privilege that attends their respective profession, and their clients, patients or parishioners would also be aware that their confidential conversations are protected from compelled disclosure.

Moreover, even assuming *arguendo* that children and their parents generally are aware of whether or not their communications are protected from disclosure, it is not certain that the existence of a privilege enters into whatever thought processes are performed by children in deciding whether or not to confide in their parents. Indeed, the existence or nonexistence of a parent-child privilege is probably one of the least important considerations in any child's decision as to whether to reveal some indiscretion, legal or illegal, to a parent. Moreover, it is unlikely that any parent would choose to deter a child from revealing a confidence to the parent solely because a federal court has refused to recognize a privilege protecting such communications from disclosure.

Finally, the proposed parent-child privilege fails to satisfy the fourth condition of the Wigmore test. As explained above, any injury to the parent-child relationship resulting from non-recognition of such a privilege would be relatively insignificant. In contrast, the cost of recognizing such a privilege is substantial: the impairment of the truth-seeking function of the judicial system and the increased likelihood of injustice resulting from the concealment of relevant information.

Moreover, because no clear benefit flows from the recognition of a parent-child privilege, any injury to the parent-child relationship caused by compelled testimony as to confidential communications is necessarily and substantially outweighed by the benefit to society of obtaining all relevant evidence in a criminal case. * * *

An even more compelling reason for rejecting a parent-child privilege stems from the fact that the parent-child relationship differs dramatically from other relationships. This is due to the unique duty owing to the child from the parent. A parent owes the duty to the child to nurture and guide the child. This duty is unusual because it inheres in the relationship and the relationship arises automatically at the child's birth.

If, for example, a fifteen year old unemancipated child informs her parent that she has committed a crime or has been using or distributing narcotics, and this disclosure has been made in confidence while the child is seeking guidance, it is evident to us that, regardless of whether the child consents or not, the parent must have the right to take such action as the parent deems appropriate *in the interest of the child*. That action could be commitment to a drug rehabilitation center or a report of the crime to the juvenile authorities. This is so because, in theory at least, juvenile proceedings are undertaken solely in the interest of the child. We would regard it intolerable in such a situation if the law intruded in the guise of a privilege, and silenced the parent because the child had a privilege to prevent disclosure.

This results in the analysis that any privilege, if recognized, must be dependent upon both the parent and child asserting it. However, in such a case, the privilege would disappear if the parent can waive it. It follows therefore that, if a child is able to communicate openly with a parent and seeks guidance from that parent, the entire basis for the privilege is destroyed if the child is required to recognize that confidence will be maintained only so long as the parent wants the conversation to be confidential. If, however, the parent can waive the privilege unilaterally, the goal of the privilege is destroyed. * * * It follows then that an effective parent-child privilege requires that the parent's lips be sealed but such a sealing would be inexcusable in the parent-child relationship. No government should have that power.

Indeed the obligation on the parent to act goes far beyond the parent's obligation to raise and nurture the child. Thus a parent-child privilege implicates considerations which are vastly different from the traditional privileges to which resort is had as analogues.

In sum, neither historical tradition, nor common-law principles, nor Wigmore formulations, nor the logic of privileges, nor the "reason and experience" of the various states supports creation of a parent-child privilege.

* * *

[Judge Mansmann wrote separately. He would have recognized a privilege for "compelled testimony concerning confidential communications made to a parent by his child in the course of seeking parental advice." Accordingly, while he concurred in the disposition of the Delaware case, he dissented from rejection of the claim of privilege in the Virgin Islands case.]

4. NEWS–PERSON'S PRIVILEGE

Matter of Farber

Supreme Court of New Jersey, 1978.
78 N.J. 259, 394 A.2d 330.

■ MOUNTAIN, J.

In these consolidated appeals The New York Times Company and Myron Farber, a reporter employed by the newspaper, challenge judgments entered against them in two related matters—one a proceeding in aid of a litigant (civil contempt), the other for criminal contempt of court. The proceedings were instituted in an ongoing murder trial now in its seventh month, as a result of the appellants' failure to comply with two *subpoena duces tecum,* directing them to produce certain documents and materials compiled by one or both of these appellants in the course of Farber's investigative reporting of certain allegedly criminal activities. Farber's investigations and reporting are said to have contributed largely to the indictment and prosecution of Dr. Mario E. Jascalevich for murder.[Farber wrote a series of articles in The Times contending that a surgeon to whom he referred as Dr. X – later identified as Jascalevich – had murdered numerous patients by using curare, a powerful muscle relaxant that can be lethal if not used in conjunction with artificial respiration.] Appellants moved unsuccessfully before Judge William J. Arnold, the trial judge in State v. Jascalevich, to quash the two subpoenas; an order was entered directing that the subpoenaed material be produced for *in camera* inspection by the court. The appellant's applications for a stay of Judge Arnold's order were denied successively by the Appellate Division of the Superior Court, by this Court, and by two separate Justices of the Supreme Court of the United States.

* * * A fine of $100,000 was imposed on The New York Times and Farber was ordered to serve six months in the Bergen County jail and to pay a fine of $1,000. Additionally, in order to compel production of the materials subpoenaed on behalf of Jascalevich, a fine of $5,000 per day for every day that elapsed until compliance with Judge Arnold's order was imposed upon The Times; Farber was fined $1,000 and sentenced to confinement in the county jail until he complied with the order.

* * *

I

The First Amendment

Appellants claim a privilege to refrain from revealing information sought by the *subpoenas duces tecum* essentially for the reason that were they to divulge this material, confidential sources of such information would be made public. Were this to occur, they argue, newsgathering and the dissemination of news would be seriously impaired, because much information would never be forthcoming to the news media unless the persons who were the sources of such information could be entirely certain that their identities would remain secret. The final result, appellants claim, would be a substantial lessening in the supply of available news on a variety of important and sensitive issues, all to the detriment of the public interest. They contend further that this privilege to remain silent with respect to confidential information and the sources of such information emanates from the "free speech" and "free press" clauses of the First Amendment.

In our view the Supreme Court of the United States has clearly rejected this claim [in Branzburg v. Hayes, 408 U.S. 665 (1972),] and has squarely held that no such First Amendment right exists.

* * *

Thus we do no weighing or balancing of societal interests in reaching our determination that the First Amendment does not afford appellants the privilege they claim. The weighing and balancing has been done by a higher court. * * *

II

The Shield Law*

In Branzburg v. Hayes, supra, the Court dealt with a newsman's claim of privilege based solely upon the First Amendment. As we have seen, this claim of privilege failed. In *Branzburg* no shield law was involved. Here we have a shield law, said to be as strongly worded as any in the country.

We read the legislative intent in adopting this statute in its present form as seeking to protect the confidential sources of the press as well as information so obtained by reporters and other news media representatives to the greatest extent permitted by the Constitution of the United States and that of the State of New Jersey. It is abundantly clear that appellants come fully within the literal language of the enactment. Extended discussion is quite unnecessary. Viewed solely as a matter of statutory construc-

---

* The term "shield law" is commonly and widely applied to statutes granting newsmen and other media representatives the privilege of declining to reveal confidential sources of information. The New Jersey shield law reads as follows:

Subject to Rule 37, a person engaged on, engaged in, connected with, or employed by news media for the purpose of gathering, procuring, transmitting, compiling, editing or disseminating news for the general public or on whose behalf news is so gathered, procured, transmitted, compiled, edited or disseminated has a privilege to refuse to disclose, in any legal or quasi-legal proceeding or before any investigative body, including, but not limited to, any court, grand jury, petit jury, administrative agency, the Legislature or legislative committee, or elsewhere:

a. The source, author, means, agency or person from or through whom any information was procured, obtained, supplied, furnished, gathered, transmitted, compiled, edited, disseminated, or delivered; and

b. Any news or information obtained in the course of pursuing his professional activities whether or not it is disseminated.

The provisions of this rule insofar as it relates to radio or television stations shall not apply unless the radio or television station maintains and keeps open for inspection, for a period of at least 1 year from the date of an actual broadcast or telecast, an exact recording, transcription, kinescopic film or certified written transcript of the actual broadcast or telecast.

tion, appellants are clearly entitled to the protections afforded by the act unless statutory exceptions including waiver are shown to apply. In view of the fundamental basis of our decision today, the question of waiver of privilege under the Shield Law need not be addressed by us.

III

The Sixth Amendment and its New Jersey Counterpart

Viewed on its face, considered solely as a reflection of legislative intent to bestow upon the press as broad a shield as possible to protect against forced revelation of confidential source materials, this legislation is entirely constitutional. Indeed, no one appears to have attacked its facial constitutionality.

It is, however, argued, and argued very strenuously, that if enforced under the facts of this case, the Shield Law violates the Sixth Amendment of the Federal Constitution as well as Article 1, ¶ 10 of the New Jersey Constitution. * * * Essentially the argument is this: The Federal and State Constitutions each provide that in all criminal prosecutions the accused shall have the right "to have compulsory process for obtaining witnesses in his favor." Dr. Jascalevich seeks to obtain evidence to use in preparing and presenting his defense in the ongoing criminal trial in which he has been accused of multiple murders. He claims to come within the favor of these constitutional provisions—which he surely does. Finally, when faced with the Shield Law, he invokes the rather elementary but entirely sound proposition that where Constitution and statute collide, the latter must yield. Subject to what is said below, we find this argument unassailable.

The compulsory process clause of the Sixth Amendment has never been elaborately explicated by the Supreme Court. Not until 1967, when it decided Washington v. Texas, had the clause been directly construed. Westen, Confrontation and Compulsory Process: A Unified Theory of Evidence for Criminal Cases, 91 Harv.L.Rev. 567, 586 (1978). In *Washington* the petitioner sought the reversal of his conviction for murder. A Texas statute at the time provided that persons charged or convicted as co-participants in the same crime could not testify for one another. One Fuller, who had already been convicted of the murder, was prevented from testifying by virtue of the statute. The record indicated that had he testified his testimony would have been favorable to petitioner. The Court reversed the conviction on the ground that petitioner's Sixth Amendment right to compulsory process had been denied. At the same time it determined that the compulsory process clause in the Sixth Amendment was binding on state courts by virtue of the due process clause of the Fourteenth Amendment. It will be seen that *Washington* is like the present case in a significant respect. The Texas statute and the Sixth Amendment could not both stand. The latter of course prevailed. So must it be here.

Quite recently, in United States v. Nixon, the Court dealt with another compulsory process issue. There the Special Prosecutor, Leon Jaworski, subpoenaed various tape recordings and documents in the possession of

President Nixon. The latter claimed an executive privilege and refused to deliver the tapes. The Supreme Court conceded that indeed there was an executive privilege and that although "[n]owhere in the Constitution * * * is there any explicit reference to a privilege of confidentiality, yet to the extent this interest relates to the effective discharge of a President's powers, it is constitutionally based." Despite this conclusion that at least to some extent a president's executive privilege derives from the Constitution, the Court nonetheless concluded that the demands of our criminal justice system required that the privilege must yield.

> We have elected to employ an adversary system of criminal justice in which the parties contest all issues before a court of law. The need to develop all relevant facts in the adversary system is both fundamental and comprehensive. The ends of criminal justice would be defeated if judgments were to be founded on a partial or speculative presentation of the facts. The very integrity of the judicial system and public confidence in the system depend on full disclosure of all the facts, within the framework of the rules of evidence. To ensure that justice is done, it is imperative to the function of courts that compulsory process be available for the production of evidence needed either by the prosecution or by the defense. [United States v. Nixon, supra.]

It is important to note that the Supreme Court in this case compelled the production of privileged material—the privilege acknowledged to rest in part upon the Constitution—even though there was no Sixth Amendment compulsion to do so. The Sixth Amendment affords rights to an accused but not to a prosecutor. The compulsion to require the production of the privileged material derived from the necessities of our system of administering criminal justice.

Article 1, ¶ 10 of the Constitution of the State of New Jersey contains, as we have seen, exactly the same language with respect to compulsory process as that found in the Sixth Amendment. * * * We hold that Article 1, ¶ 10 of our Constitution prevails over this statute, but in recognition of the strongly expressed legislative viewpoint favoring confidentiality, we prescribe the imposition of the safeguards set forth in Point IV below.

IV

Procedural Mechanism

Appellants insist that they are entitled to a full hearing on the issues of relevance, materiality and overbreadth of the subpoena. We agree. The trial court recognized its obligation to conduct such a hearing, but the appellants have aborted that hearing by refusing to submit the material subpoenaed for an *in camera* inspection by the court to assist it in determining the motion to quash. That inspection is no more than a procedural tool, a device to be used to ascertain the relevancy and materiality of that material. Such an *in camera* inspection is not in itself an invasion of the statutory privilege. Rather it is a preliminary step to determine whether, and if so to what extent, the statutory privilege must yield to the defendant's constitutional rights.

Appellants' position is that there must be a full showing and definitive judicial determination of relevance, materiality, absence of less intrusive access, and need, prior to any *in camera* inspection. The obvious objection to such a rule, however, is that it would, in many cases, effectively stultify the judicial criminal process. It might well do so here. The defendant properly recognizes Myron Farber as a unique repository of pertinent information. But he does not know the extent of this information nor is it possible for him to specify all of it with particularity, nor to tailor his subpoena to precise materials of which he is ignorant. Well aware of this, Judge Arnold refused to give ultimate rulings with respect to relevance and other preliminary matters until he had examined the material. We think he had no other course. It is not rational to ask a judge to ponder the relevance of the unknown.

* * *

While we agree, then, that appellants should be afforded the hearing they are seeking, one procedural aspect of which calls for their compliance with the order for *in camera* inspection, we are also of the view that they, and those who in the future may be similarly situated, are entitled to a preliminary determination before being compelled to submit the subpoenaed materials to a trial judge for such inspection. Our decision in this regard is not, contrary to the suggestion in some of the briefs filed with us, mandated by the First Amendment; for in addition to ruling generally against the representatives of the press in *Branzburg,* the Court particularly and rather vigorously, rejected the claims there asserted that before going before the grand jury, each of the reporters, at the very least, was entitled to a preliminary hearing to establish a number of threshold issues. Branzburg v. Hayes, supra. Rather, our insistence upon such a threshold determination springs from our obligation to give as much effect as possible, within ever-present constitutional limitations, to the very positively expressed legislative intent to protect the confidentiality and secrecy of sources from which the media derive information. To this end such a determination would seem a necessity.

The threshold determination would normally follow the service of a subpoena by a defendant upon a newspaper, a reporter or other representative of the media. The latter foreseeably would respond with a motion to quash. If the status of the movant—newspaper or media representative—were not conceded, then there would follow the taking of proofs leading to a determination that the movant did or did not qualify for the statutory privilege. Assuming qualification, it would then become the obligation of the defense to satisfy the trial judge, by a fair preponderance of the evidence including all reasonable inferences, that there was a reasonable probability or likelihood that the information sought by the subpoena was material and relevant to his defense, that it could not be secured from any less intrusive source, and that the defendant had a legitimate need to see and otherwise use it.

* * *

Although in this case the trial judge did not articulate the findings prescribed above, it is perfectly clear that on the record before him a conclusion of materiality, relevancy, unavailability of another source, as well as need was quite inescapable. * * *

* * * Two and a half months before his June 30th decision, Judge Arnold observed:

> The facts show that Farber has written articles for the *New York Times* about this matter, commencing in January 1976. According to an article printed in the *New York Times* (hereinafter the *Times*) on January 8, 1976, Farber showed Joseph Woodcock, the Bergen County Prosecutor at that time, a deposition not in the State's file and *provided additional information that convinced the prosecutor to reopen an investigation into some deaths that occurred at Riverdell Hospital.* [State v. Jascalevich; In the Matter of the Application of Myron Farber and the New York Times Company re: Sequestration (emphasis added).]

And

> The court has examined the news stories in evidence and they demonstrate exceptional quality, a grasp of intricate scientific knowledge, and a style of a fine journalist. *They, also, demonstrate considerable knowledge of the case before the court and deep involvement by Farber,* showing his attributes as a first-rate investigative reporter. However, if a newspaper reporter assumes the duties of an investigator, he must also assume the responsibilities of an investigator and be treated equally under the law, unless he comes under some exception.

In the same vein is a letter before the trial court dated January 14, 1977 from Assistant Prosecutor Moses to Judge Robert A. Matthews, sitting as a Presiding Judge in the Appellate Division, undertaking to explain "how the investigation, from which the [Jascalevich] indictment resulted, came to be reopened." In the course of that explanation it is revealed that sometime in the latter part of 1975 "a reporter for the *New York Times* began an investigation into the 1965–66 deaths and circumstances surrounding them. The results of the *New York Times* inquiry were made available to the Prosecutor. *It was thus determined that there were certain items which were not in the file of the Prosecutor.*" [Emphasis added.]

Further support for the determination that there is a reasonable probability that the subpoenaed materials meet the test formulated above appears in the following factual circumstances pointed to by this defendant and supported by documents and transcripts of testimony found in the appendix filed by the defendant:

1. A principal witness for the State is Dr. Michael Baden, a New York City Medical Examiner, who testified that Farber communicated with him prior to any official communication from the Prosecutor's office. The defendant would have one infer from this that Farber stimulated Baden's research into the causal connection among curare, the deaths, and Dr. Jascalevich, then turned the results of this joint effort over to the Prosecutor. (Trial testimony elicited from Dr. Baden after June 30th, the date of Judge Arnold's order, is said to furnish further support for this inference.) While no sinister implications need flow from this, it arguably serves to buttress the defense assertion that the driving power behind this prosecution is Farber, and hence such materials, if any, that he may be secreting are reasonably likely to bear on the guilt or innocence of Dr. Jascalevich.

2. Dr. Stanley Harris was a surgeon at the hospital where the criminal activities are said to have occurred. His suspicions are said to have been aroused by the unexplained deaths of some of his patients. Dr. Harris admits having spoken to Farber five times before the New York Times articles appeared and before his reinterview by the Prosecutor's office in 1976. He is characterized by the criminal defendant as his "principal accuser," and therefore whatever otherwise unavailable information Farber extracted from him would, with reasonable probability, bear upon Dr. Jascalevich's guilt or innocence.

3. Lee Henderson was an attendant at Seton Hall Medical School at a time when, according to one statement allegedly made by Dr. Jascalevich, the latter was performing certain tests on dogs in the School laboratory. The tests supposedly involved the effects of curare (a drug said to have been administered by the criminal defendant in producing the deaths of the victims). Henderson may very well have information touching upon Dr. Jascalevich's activities, if any, in the laboratory. After considerable effort Farber succeeded in tracking down Henderson in South Carolina. When a Prosecutor's investigator was later able to communicate with Henderson (having presumably been led to him by information furnished by Farber), the witness initially refused to give a statement (later supplied) for fear that it would conflict with a written statement previously furnished to Farber. The criminal defendant wishes to examine this earlier statement.

4. Herman Fuhr was an operating room attendant who opened Dr. Jascalevich's locker at Riverdell Hospital, where curare was allegedly stored. Farber interviewed him. He will not speak to defense representatives.

5. Dr. Charles Umberger was a toxicologist who worked on slides of one of the alleged victims. He gave notes to Farber who did not return them. Some of these notes are missing. Dr. Umberger died in 1977 before the defense could interview him.

6. Barbara Kenderes was a lab technician at the hospital. She gave a statement to a Prosecutor's detective in 1966, which the State

either has not furnished or cannot furnish to the defense. She testified before the grand jury in March, 1976. Several days later Mrs. Kenderes received a telephone call on her private, unlisted number from Myron Farber. During the course of the conversation he accused her of hiding something from him. She replied that, indeed, she was. Shortly thereafter, she received a call from Assistant Prosecutor Sybil Moses, who is handling the case. Mrs. Moses told Mrs. Kenderes that Myron Farber called her and said Mrs. Kenderes was hiding something. Mrs. Moses wanted to know what that was. Mrs. Kenderes replied that it was only the fact that she had appeared before the grand jury, which Mrs. Moses had cautioned her not to speak about. The only person to whom Mrs. Kenderes had given her private phone number in connection with this matter was Mrs. Moses. Again the inference defendant Jascalevich would have us draw is that early on there was complete cooperation and exchange of information between the Prosecutor's office and Farber, with the resultant likelihood that Farber is now, and for some time has been, in possession of material and relevant information not otherwise obtainable bearing on the guilt or innocence of Dr. Jascalevich.

We hasten to add that we need not, and do not, address (much less determine) the truth or falsity of these assertions. The point to be made is that these are the assertions of the criminal defendant supported by testimonial or documentary proof; and based thereon it is perfectly clear that there was more than enough before Judge Arnold to satisfy the tests formulated above. Of course all of this information detailed above has long been known to appellants. Accordingly we find that preliminary requirements for *in camera* inspection have been met.

* * *

[Chief Justice Hughes joined Justice Mountain's opinion but added a concurrence of his own. He thought that, although the trial judge should have made explicit references to the portion of the record justifying his decision, the record was clear enough; he also emphasized that *in camera* inspection was essential for a reasoned decision of the privilege claim. Justice Pashman dissented; he believed that the order of contempt violated due process because it was entered before Farber had an opportunity to marshall arguments against compelled *in camera* production of the subpoenaed documents. Justice Handler also dissented; he agreed that the newsman's privilege is not based on the First Amendment and that it must give way in appropriate circumstances to a criminal defendant's right to material evidence. But he thought that this case should be remanded for the trial judge to make a fuller statement as to why he believed in camera inspection was necessary. Farber spent a total of 40 days in jail, being finally released only after Jascalevich was acquitted. (Jascalevich's medical license was later revoked.) Governor Brendan Byrne later pardoned Farber and ordered that the criminal contempt fines of $101,000 be returned, though the civil contempt fines, totaling $185,000, remained.]

E. INADVERTENT WAIVER

Peterson v. Bernardi

United States District Court for the District of New Jersey, 2009.
262 F.R.D. 424.

■ JOEL SCHNEIDER, United States Magistrate Judge.

This matter is before the Court on plaintiff's Motion to Compel the Return of Inadvertently Produced Documents Pursuant to Fed.R.Civ.P. 26(b)(5)(B). The issue to be addressed is whether plaintiff waived any privilege or discovery protection applicable to documents that were inadvertently produced. * * * For the reasons to be discussed, plaintiff's motion is GRANTED in part and DENIED in part.

Background

By way of brief background, plaintiff alleges he was wrongfully imprisoned for over eighteen (18) years based on a false conviction for murder and rape. The essence of plaintiff's claim is that his conviction was based on the defendants' wrongful conduct. With the assistance of the Innocence Project the charges against plaintiff were dropped in May 2006, after DNA sample results indicated that the samples from the crime scene evidence did not match plaintiff's DNA profile.

Plaintiff filed his motion after he discovered that he inadvertently produced allegedly privileged and irrelevant documents. Plaintiff argues the documents are protected by the attorney client privilege and work product doctrine. Plaintiff also claims two documents are protected by the cleric penitent privilege. Plaintiff argues the documents should be returned because he took reasonable steps to prevent the inadvertent disclosure. Plaintiff alleges he was under time constraints to produce documents and his inadvertent production was only a small percentage of the total number of produced documents.[3]

Defendants argue that a weighing of the factors in *Ciba-Geigy Corp. v. Sandoz Ltd.,* 916 F.Supp. 404, 411 (D.N.J.1995), compels the conclusion that plaintiff's motion be denied. Defendants argue plaintiff cannot establish that he took reasonable steps to prevent the inadvertent disclosure. Defendants also argue the number and extent of plaintiff's disclosures support a finding of waiver. In addition, defendants argue plaintiff delayed seeking to rectify his disclosure and that the interests of justice are not

---

[3] Plaintiff's motion identified 156 allegedly privileged documents that should be returned. However, after the Court reviewed the documents *in camera* it was evident that some of the documents were not privileged. The Court then directed plaintiff's counsel to identify the documents genuinely at issue. On July 1, 2009, plaintiff identified approximately 135 documents that should be returned. It is again apparent that plaintiff's counsel did not carefully review the allegedly privileged documents. By way of example, plaintiff's list includes numerous letters from law students advising of their office schedule and other letters simply enclosing copies of public documents For the reasons discussed herein, these documents are clearly not privileged.

served by relieving plaintiff of his error. Defendants also argue that plaintiff has not established that the documents in question are privileged.

Discussion

* * * When deciding whether inadvertently produced documents should be returned a two-step analysis must be done. First, it must be determined if the documents in question are privileged. It is axiomatic that FRE 502 does not apply unless privileged or otherwise protected documents are produced. Second, if privileged documents were inadvertently produced then the three elements of FRE 502(b) must be satisfied (1) the disclosure must be inadvertent; (2) the holder of the privilege or protection took reasonable steps to prevent the disclosure, and; (3) the holder promptly took reasonable steps to rectify the error, including (if applicable) following Fed.R.Civ.P. 26(b)(5)(B). The disclosing party has the burden to prove that the elements of FRE 502(b) have been met.

FRE 502 does not change applicable case law which places the burden of proving that a privilege exists on the party asserting the privilege, in this case plaintiff. Except as to one category of documents discussed *infra,* the Court finds that plaintiff has not satisfied this threshold burden. Plaintiff's moving papers essentially make no attempt to establish that the documents in question are privileged or otherwise protected from discovery. Plaintiff simply attached a privilege log and assumed that all the listed documents are protected by the attorney client privilege and work product doctrine. Plaintiff's burden of proof is not satisfied by his broad unsupported allegations. *See NE Technologies, Inc. v. Evolving Systems, Inc.,* C.A. No. 06-6061(MLC), 2008 WL 4277668, at *5 (D.N.J. Sept.5, 2008) (citation omitted) (boiler plate objections, without an accompanying affidavit, lack specificity and constitute a waiver of such objections).

The Court recognizes that many of the documents at issue involve communications between plaintiff and the New Jersey Office of the Public Defender and the Innocence Project. However, not all communications between a client and lawyer are privileged. The attorney client privilege only insulates communications that assist the attorney to formulate and render legal advice. The privilege does not apply simply because a statement was made by or to an attorney. *HPD Laboratories, Inc. v. Clorox Company,* 202 F.R.D. 410, 414 (D.N.J.2001). Nor does the privilege attach simply because a statement conveys advice that is legal in nature. *Id.* The attorney client privilege only applies to disclosures necessary to obtain informed legal advice which might not have been made absent the privilege. *Id.* (citations omitted).

In addition to failing to establish the attorney client privilege, plaintiff also did not submit evidence that the produced documents were prepared in anticipation of litigation and primarily for the purpose of litigation. Plaintiff, therefore, has failed to establish that his documents are protected by the work product doctrine. *In re Gabapentin Patent Litigation,* 214 F.R.D. 178, 183 (D.N.J.2003); *Sealed Air,* 253 F.R.D. at 306-07. Given plaintiff's failure to establish the threshold requirement that his documents are protected from discovery, and except as otherwise discussed herein, plaintiff's motion is denied.

Even if plaintiff established that the documents in question were privileged, plaintiff's motion would still be denied except as to one category of documents. Plaintiff, not defendants, has the burden of proving that his documents were inadvertently produced. FRE 502(b) opts for a middle ground approach to determine if an inadvertent disclosure operates as a waiver. *See* Explanatory Note to FRE 502(b) (revised November 28, 2007).[3] [The court concludes that this approach is similar ot that previously sued by New Jersey courts.] Under [that] approach at least five factors are analyzed to determine if a waiver occurred (1) the reasonableness of the precautions taken to prevent inadvertent disclosure in view of the document production; (2) the number of inadvertent disclosures; (3) the extent of the disclosures; (4) any delay and measures taken to rectify the disclosure, and; (5) whether the overriding interests of justice would or would not be served by relieving the party of its error.

As to the first relevant factor for consideration, which is specifically referenced in FRE 502(b)(2), the Court finds that at best, plaintiff took minimal steps to protect against inadvertent disclosure. Plaintiff's moving papers only mention one step that was taken to prevent an inadvertent error [a]t each time [document production], plaintiff's counsel engaged in a privilege review. However, plaintiff does not state when his review occurred, how much time he took to review the documents, what documents were reviewed, and other basic details of the review process. The Court does not accept plaintiff's bare allegation that he conducted a privilege review as conclusive proof that he took reasonable steps to prevent an inadvertent production.

Plaintiff argues that in the course of his document review he identified a group of privileged documents, but the documents were mistakenly not separated, and inadvertently produced to defendants. However, plaintiff did not proffer any facts to establish that reasonable precautions were taken to prevent this from occurring. Nor does plaintiff explain how other allegedly privileged documents come to be inadvertently produced. For the purpose of deciding plaintiff's motion, the Court does not question the sincerity of plaintiff's argument that he did not intend to produce the documents in question. However, plaintiff's subjective intent is not controlling. All inadvertent disclosures are by definition unintentional.

As to the other factors relevant to whether an inadvertent production occurred, the Court finds that on the whole they weigh in favor of waiver. Although on a total percentage basis the number of disclosures is small (approximately 135 out of thousands produced), the nature of the disclo-

---

[3] The Note discusses a multi-factor test for determining whether inadvertent disclosure is a waiver. These factors include the reasonableness of precautions taken, the time taken to rectify the error, the scope of discovery, the extent of disclosure and the overriding issue of fairness. Other factors are the number of documents to be reviewed and the time constraints for production. *Id.* No one factor is dispositive. The rule * * * is really a set of non-determinative guidelines that vary from case to case and is designed to be flexible. *Id.*

sures is relevant. Most of the documents in question are exchanges between plaintiff and his counsel. These communications warranted a significant level of scrutiny. Further, 135 documents is not an insignificant number. As to plaintiff's efforts to rectify his error, the Court finds this factor neutral.[5] Although plaintiff did not alert defendants until months after his documents were produced when he was preparing for a deposition, plaintiff brought the error to defendants' attention within a week or two of his discovery. Plaintiff was not required to engage in a post-production review to determine whether any protected communication or information [was] * * * produced by mistake. *Explanatory Note, supra.*

The interests of fairness and justice would not be served by relieving plaintiff of the consequences of counsel's error. Parties must recognize that there are potentially harmful consequences if they do not take minimal precautions to prevent against the disclosure of privileged documents. Further, in contrast to the documents discussed *infra,* no unfairness or injustice would result from finding that a waiver occurred.[6]

The Court rejects plaintiff's argument that his inadvertent disclosure should be excused because his privilege review was conducted under extremely limited time constraints. Brief at 5. [The court points out that plaintiff completed document production late, nearly a year after the document request was first served.]

In sum, therefore, for all but a separate category of documents the Court denies plaintiff's motion. Since the documents are not privileged a FRE 502(b) analysis is not necessary. Even if the documents were privileged, plaintiff has not established that all the elements of FRE 502(b) were met. Plaintiff did not demonstrate that the documents were inadvertently produced within the meaning of FRE 502(b)(1). Plaintiff also did not establish that he took reasonable steps to prevent disclosure within the meaning of FRE 502(b)(2).

Documents P006988-6996

Despite the Court's ruling, however, the Court finds that documents P006988-6996 deserve special treatment. These nine (9) pages were prepared by student interns of the Innocence Project in 2003 and 2005 and describe in detail their litigation strategy and work product. The documents address in detail what plaintiff's attorneys and their representatives did to get plaintiff released from prison. In contrast to the other inadver-

---

[5] Plaintiff's counsel contends he did not discover he inadvertently produced documents until sometime after February 9, 2009 when he was preparing for plaintiff's scheduled March 3, 2009 deposition. On February 19, 2009, plaintiff identified the inadvertently produced documents in his log produced to defendant.

[6] The Court has reviewed all of the inadvertently produced documents. In the context of the primary issues to be litigated in the case, the documents will likely be inconsequential. (Nevertheless, as noted, they are discoverable). The Court reaches this conclusion because the documents generally discuss plaintiff's efforts from at least as early as 1990 to overturn his criminal conviction. This is not a disputed issue in the case. Further, on the whole the documents do not reveal any confidential information or attorney work product that in the Court's opinion will have a material impact on the outcome of the case.

tently produced documents, these documents are so obviously work product that no extrinsic evidence is necessary to establish this fact.

The Court's ruling is not made in a vacuum. The Court is mindful that the case involves plaintiff's claim that he was wrongfully imprisoned for eighteen years. It is undisputed that all charges against plaintiff were dropped in May 2006 even though he was convicted of rape and murder in 1989 and sentenced to life imprisonment. It is also undisputed that DNA tests in 2004 and 2005 on crime scene evidence did not match plaintiff. Given the nature of documents POO6988-6996, and the manner in which they were produced to defendants, the Court finds that the interests of fairness and justice are furthered by ruling that the work product protection attached to the documents was not waived.

The interests of fairness and justice are relevant factors to analyze to determine if inadvertently produced documents should be returned. Explanatory Note, supra * * * * See also Fed.R.Civ.P. 1 (the Federal Rules should be construed and administered to secure the just determination of every action and proceeding). The Court rules that the interests of fairness and justice so overwhelmingly favor plaintiff with regard to documents POO6988-6996, that they outweigh the fact that at best plaintiff's counsel exercised minimal precautions to protect the documents from inadvertent disclosure.

The application of FRE 502(b) was designed to be flexible. This flexibility authorizes the Court to find that a waiver did not occur in circumstances where an injustice to the client would result from a contrary ruling. It is rare that a Court will not find that a waiver occurred in an instance where a party presents only minimal evidence that it exercised reasonable precautions to prevent a waiver. This is one of those rare occurrences.

The Court does not believe that documents POO86988-6996 are determinative in the case. Although work product, the documents generally summarize events about which there is little dispute. In fact, an outside observer could reasonably opine that the documents help rather than hurt plaintiff's case. The Court would not be surprised if on reflection plaintiff decides to voluntarily produce the documents. Nevertheless, given the unusual circumstances of the case, the Court rules that plaintiff has the right to make an informed decision as to whether documents POO6988-6996 should be produced. The interests of fairness and justice demand no less. * * *

[The court's order required that defendants "must destroy or promptly return all copies of [documents POO86988-6996] and any copies they have, and take reasonable steps to retrieve all copies of the documents they distributed."]

CHAPTER 6

GOVERNMENTAL PRIVILEGES

United States v. Reynolds

Supreme Court of the United States, 1953.
345 U.S. 1, 73 S.Ct. 528, 97 L.Ed. 727.

■ MR. CHIEF JUSTICE VINSON delivered the opinion of the Court.

These suits under the Tort Claims Act[1] arise from the death of three civilians in the crash of a B–29 aircraft at Waycross, Georgia, on October 6, 1948. Because an important question of the Government's privilege to resist discovery[2] is involved, we granted certiorari.

The aircraft had taken flight for the purpose of testing secret electronic equipment, with four civilian observers aboard. While aloft, fire broke out in one of the bomber's engines. Six of the nine crew members, and three of the four civilian observers were killed in the crash.

The widows of the three deceased civilian observers brought consolidated suits against the United States. In the pretrial stages the plaintiffs moved, under Rule 34 of the Federal Rules of Civil Procedure,[3] for production of the Air Force's official accident investigation report and the statements of the three surviving crew members, taken in connection with the official investigation. The Government moved to quash the motion, claiming that these matters were privileged against disclosure pursuant to Air Force regulations promulgated under R.S. § 161.[4] The District Judge sus-

---

[1] 28 U.S.C. §§ 1346, 2674, 28 U.S.C.A. §§ 1346, 2674.

[2] Federal Rules of Civil Procedure, Rule 34, 28 U.S.C.A.

[3] "Rule 34. *Discovery and Production of Documents and Things for Inspection, Copying, or Photographing.* Upon motion of any party showing good cause therefore and upon notice to all other parties, and subject to the provisions of Rule 30(b), the court in which an action is pending may (1) order any party to produce and permit the inspection and copying or photographing, by or on behalf of the moving party, of any designated documents, papers, books, accounts, letters, photographs, objects, or tangible things, not privileged, which constitute or contain evidence relating to any of the matters within the scope of the examination permitted by Rule 26(b) and which are in his possession, custody, or control; or (2) order any party to permit entry upon designated land or other property in his possession or control for the purpose of inspecting, measuring, surveying, or photographing the property or any designated object or operation thereon within the scope of the examination permitted by Rule 26(b). The order shall specify the time, place, and manner of making the inspection and taking the copies and photographs and may prescribe such terms and conditions as are just."

[4] 5 U.S.C. § 22, 5 U.S.C.A. § 22:

"The head of each department is authorized to prescribe regulations, not inconsistent with law, for the government of his department, the conduct of its officers and clerks, the distribution and performance of its business, and the custody, use, and preservation of the records, papers, and property appertaining to it."

Air Force Regulation No. 62–7(5)(b) provides:

"Reports of boards of officers, special accident reports, or extracts therefrom will not be furnished or made available to persons outside the authorized chain of command without the specific approval of the Secretary of the Air Force."

tained plaintiffs' motion, holding that good cause for production had been shown.[5] The claim of privilege under R.S. § 161 was rejected on the premise that the Tort Claims Act, in making the Government liable "in the same manner" as a private individual[6] had waived any privilege based upon executive control over governmental documents.

Shortly after this decision, the District Court received a letter from the Secretary of the Air Force, stating that "it has been determined that it would not be in the public interest to furnish this report. * * *" The court allowed a rehearing on its earlier order, and at the rehearing the Secretary of the Air Force filed a formal "Claim of Privilege." This document repeated the prior claim based generally on R.S. § 161, and then stated that the Government further objected to production of the documents "for the reason that the aircraft in question, together with the personnel on board, were engaged in a highly secret mission of the Air Force." An affidavit of the Judge Advocate General, United States Air Force, was also filed with the court, which asserted that the demanded material could not be furnished "without seriously hampering national security, flying safety and the development of highly technical and secret military equipment." The same affidavit offered to produce the three surviving crew members, without cost, for examination by the plaintiffs. The witnesses would be allowed to refresh their memories from any statement made by them to the Air Force, and authorized to testify as to all matters except those of a "classified nature."

The District Court ordered the Government to produce the documents in order that the court might determine whether they contained privileged matter. The Government declined, so the court entered an order, under Rule 37(b)(2)(i),[7] that the facts on the issue of negligence would be taken as established in plaintiffs' favor. After a hearing to determine damages, final judgment was entered for the plaintiffs. The Court of Appeals affirmed, both as to the showing of good cause for production of the documents, and

---

[5] 10 F.R.D. 468.

[6] 28 U.S.C. § 2674, 28 U.S.C.A. § 2674:

"The United States shall be liable, respecting the provisions of this title relating to tort claims, in the same manner and to the same extent as a private individual under like circumstances, but shall not be liable for interest prior to judgment or for punitive damages."

[7] "Rule 37. Refusal to Make Discovery: Consequences

    * * *

"(b) Failure to Comply With Order.

    * * *

"(2) Other Consequences. If any party or an officer or managing agent of a party refuses to obey * * * an order made under Rule 34 to produce any document * * *, the court may make such orders in regard to the refusal as are just, and among others the following:

"(i) An order that the matters regarding which the questions were asked, or the character or description of the thing or land, or the contents of the paper, or the physical or mental condition of the party, or any other designated facts shall be taken to be established for the purposes of the action in accordance with the claim of the party obtaining the order; * * *"

as to the ultimate disposition of the case as a consequence of the Government's refusal to produce the documents.

We have had broad propositions pressed upon us for decision. On behalf of the Government it has been urged that the executive department heads have power to withhold any documents in their custody from judicial view if they deem it to be in the public interest.[9] Respondents have asserted that the executive's power to withhold documents was waived by the Tort Claims Act. Both positions have constitutional overtones which we find it unnecessary to pass upon, there being a narrower ground for decision.

The Tort Claims Act expressly makes the Federal Rules of Civil Procedure applicable to suits against the United States. The judgment in this case imposed liability upon the Government by operation of Rule 37, for refusal to produce documents under Rule 34. Since Rule 34 compels production only of matters "not privileged," the essential question is whether there was a valid claim of privilege under the Rule. We hold that there was, and that, therefore, the judgment below subjected the United States to liability on terms to which Congress did not consent by the Tort Claims Act.

We think it should be clear that the term "not privileged" as used in Rule 34, refers to "privileges" as that term is understood in the law of evidence. When the Secretary of the Air Force lodged his formal "Claim of Privilege," he attempted therein to invoke the privilege against revealing military secrets, a privilege which is well established in the law of evidence. The existence of the privilege is conceded by the court below, and, indeed, by the most outspoken critics of governmental claims to privilege.

Judicial experience with the privilege which protects military and state secrets has been limited in this country. English experience has been more extensive, but still relatively slight compared with other evidentiary privileges. Nevertheless, the principles which control the application of the privilege emerge quite clearly from the available precedents. The privilege belongs to the Government and must be asserted by it; it can neither be claimed nor waived by a private party. It is not to be lightly invoked. There must be a formal claim of privilege, lodged by the head of the department which has control over the matter, after actual personal consideration by that officer. The court itself must determine whether the circumstances are appropriate for the claim of privilege, and yet do so without forcing a disclosure of the very thing the privilege is designed to protect. The latter requirement is the only one which presents real difficulty. As to it, we find it helpful to draw upon judicial experience in dealing with an analogous privilege, the privilege against self-incrimination.

The privilege against self-incrimination presented the courts with a similar sort of problem. Too much judicial inquiry into the claim of privilege would force disclosure of the thing the privilege was meant to protect, while

---

[9] While claim of executive power to suppress documents is based more immediately upon R.S. § 161 (see supra, note 4), the roots go much deeper. It is said that R.S. § 161 is only a legislative recognition of an inherent executive power which is protected in the constitutional system of separation of power.

a complete abandonment of judicial control would lead to intolerable abuses. Indeed, in the earlier stages of judicial experience with the problem, both extremes were advocated, some saying that the bare assertion by the witness must be taken as conclusive, and others saying that the witness should be required to reveal the matter behind his claim of privilege to the judge for verification. Neither extreme prevailed, and a sound formula of compromise was developed. This formula received authoritative expression in this country as early as the Burr trial. There are differences in phraseology, but in substance it is agreed that the court must be satisfied from all the evidence and circumstances, and "from the implications of the question, in the setting in which it is asked, that a responsive answer to the question or an explanation of why it cannot be answered might be dangerous because injurious exposure could result." Hoffman v. United States. If the court is so satisfied, the claim of the privilege will be accepted without requiring further disclosure.

Regardless of how it is articulated, some like formula of compromise must be applied here. Judicial control over the evidence in a case cannot be abdicated to the caprice of executive officers. Yet we will not go so far as to say that the court may automatically require a complete disclosure to the judge before the claim of privilege will be accepted in any case. It may be possible to satisfy the court, from all the circumstances of the case, that there is a reasonable danger that compulsion of the evidence will expose military matters which, in the interest of national security, should not be divulged. When this is the case, the occasion for the privilege is appropriate, and the court should not jeopardize the security which the privilege is meant to protect by insisting upon an examination of the evidence, even by the judge alone, in chambers.

In the instant case we cannot escape judicial notice that this is a time of vigorous preparation for national defense. Experience in the past war has made it common knowledge that air power is one of the most potent weapons in our scheme of defense, and that newly developing electronic devices have greatly enhanced the effective use of air power. It is equally apparent that these electronic devices must be kept secret if their full military advantage is to be exploited in the national interest. On the record before the trial court it appeared that this accident occurred to a military plane which had gone aloft to test secret electronic equipment. Certainly there was a reasonable danger that the accident investigation report would contain references to the secret electronic equipment which was the primary concern of the mission.

Of course, even with this information before him, the trial judge was in no position to decide that the report was privileged until there had been a formal claim of privilege. Thus it was entirely proper to rule initially that petitioner had shown probable cause for discovery of the documents. Thereafter, when the formal claim of privilege was filed by the Secretary of the Air Force, under circumstances indicating a reasonable possibility that military secrets were involved, there was certainly a sufficient showing of privilege to cut off further demand for the document on the showing of necessity for its compulsion that had then been made.

In each case, the showing of necessity which is made will determine how far the court should probe in satisfying itself that the occasion for invoking the privilege is appropriate. Where there is a strong showing of necessity, the claim of privilege should not be lightly accepted, but even the most compelling necessity cannot overcome the claim of privilege if the court is ultimately satisfied that military secrets are at stake.[26] *A fortiori*, where necessity is dubious, a formal claim of privilege, made under the circumstances of this case, will have to prevail. Here, necessity was greatly minimized by an available alternative, which might have given respondents the evidence to make out their case without forcing a showdown on the claim of privilege. By their failure to pursue that alternative, respondents have posed the privilege question for decision with the formal claim of privilege set against a dubious showing of necessity.

There is nothing to suggest that the electronic equipment, in this case, had any causal connection with the accident. Therefore, it should be possible for respondents to adduce the essential facts as to causation without resort to material touching upon military secrets. Respondents were given a reasonable opportunity to do just that, when petitioner formally offered to make the surviving crew members available for examination. We think that offer should have been accepted.

Respondents have cited us to those cases in the criminal field, where it has been held that the Government can invoke its evidentiary privileges only at the price of letting the defendant go free. The rationale of the criminal cases is that, since the Government which prosecutes an accused also has the duty to see that justice is done, it is unconscionable to allow it to undertake prosecution and then invoke its governmental privileges to deprive the accused of anything which might be material to his defense. Such rationale has no application in a civil forum where the Government is not the moving party, but is a defendant only on terms to which it has consented.

The decision of the Court of Appeals is reversed and the case will be remanded to the District Court for further proceedings consistent with the views expressed in this opinion.

■ Reversed and remanded.

■ MR. JUSTICE BLACK, MR. JUSTICE FRANKFURTER, and MR. JUSTICE JACKSON dissented.

---

[26] See Totten v. United States, where the very subject matter of the action, a contract to perform espionage, was a matter of state secret. The action was dismissed on the pleadings without ever reaching the question of evidence, since it was so obvious that the action should never prevail over the privilege.

Evidentiary Privilege of "State Secrets" In Contract Action

55 Colum.L.Rev. 570–573 (1955).*

Defendant contracted to manufacture arming mechanisms for the United States Army. Plaintiff with whom he had subcontracted brought an action for breach of contract. Defendant moved to dismiss or, in the alternative, to stay all proceedings on the ground that prosecution and defense of the action would require disclosure of classified information in violation of the Espionage Act. *Held,* motions denied. Proceedings may continue along their ordinary course and the court if necessary will, at the appropriate time, take measures to ensure that national security is not endangered.

The courts have long recognized a privilege against disclosure of information affecting national security in essentially private litigation as well as when the government is a party. The basic policy underlying the decisions granting protection to state secrets is the paramount interest of the nation in safeguarding its military and diplomatic position, even to the subordination of individual interests.

Although the government has not raised the state secrets privilege while acting as plaintiff or prosecutor, it has asserted other privileges of nondisclosure resting upon different grounds. Ordinarily in these situations, however, the courts have not sustained the privilege where the defendant requested material documents in the government's possession. Apparently, the rationale of these decisions is that it is unconscionable to allow the government to initiate an action and then invoke a privilege that might deprive an accused of anything material to his defense. Although one case suggested that the government introduce secondary evidence in order to prevent disclosure, generally the courts have accommodated the conflicting interests of individuals and the government in favor of individuals. Thus, if the court finds that the information requested is material, the government is in the dilemma of either having to risk unsuccessful prosecution or being forced to disclose privileged information.

The government as defendant has not been estopped from raising the states secrets privilege by virtue of its consent to be sued. In United States v. Reynolds, the Supreme Court distinguished the role of government as prosecutor and reversed the trial court's finding of certain facts in favor of plaintiffs after the government had refused to produce documents in conformity with an order of the court. The Court noted the existence of international tension and emphasized that plaintiff had not demonstrated sufficient necessity to justify an order requiring initial disclosure to the judge of information involving ostensibly secret electronic data.

In private litigation the question of whether information comes within the states secrets privilege has been raised by motion or objection of a private party or by the court itself. The government's position in the matter, which may be stated by affidavit of the cognizant executive head—whether

---

the government intervenes as a party or not—is apparently the crucial factor in determining whether the privilege is to be sustained. Thus, if the court has evidence that the government does not object to the introduction of documents, a refusal to disclose may subject the objector to contempt proceedings.

Once a claim of privilege is properly made by the appropriate executive department head, the English view appears to be that whether there is a state secret involved is not justiciable. This view, granting the executive almost unlimited discretion, has been defended on the grounds that showing the information to the court may defeat the very secrecy required and that the court lacks the expertise that the executive possesses for a sound determination of the necessity for secrecy. *Reynolds,* while asserting the justiciable nature of the question, formulates a rule which considerably limits the court's discretion. If the government makes a showing that there is a reasonable danger that the evidence sought would expose military secrets, the privilege will be sustained without disclosure to the court. Although, theoretically, the showing required would be balanced against the opposing party's need, practically it appears that the government's burden of persuasion is relatively slight since the executive claim of secrecy is likely to be accepted on its face. Consequently, almost any assertion of privilege by the government will foreclose a private party's ability to litigate successfully.

The instant case in some measure reasserts judicial control over the privilege when a private party makes the claim, and the government apparently has not reviewed the question of secrecy in the light of the impending litigation. The decision does not require a disclosure of state secrets since production of classified documents or information was not requested by the opposing party or by the court. The court recognized that unauthorized disclosure by defendant would violate the espionage laws, but it apparently hoped to avoid the issue by taking a course of action which would stimulate the government to declassify the evidence, intervene in the action or arrange for a settlement between the parties. The court also reasoned that a dismissal might unjustly deprive plaintiff of his rights by precluding relief if declassification did not occur until after expiration of the statute of limitations and would encourage other litigants in the defendant's position to breach contracts and seek refuge under a privilege designed for the benefit of the state.

Although the prematureness of defendant's motions enabled the court to adjust the competing interests of nation and litigants, it is clear that the problem may be merely postponed. If plaintiff had utilized discovery mechanisms the court would have been faced with the issue of compulsion of the requested information. Assuming the court determines that state secrets are not involved and orders production, a refusal risks possible contempt of court or loss of the suit whereas compliance may entail violation of the espionage laws and exposure of the nation's secrets. A dismissal by the court after a decision that state secrets are involved may cause an injustice to a deserving plaintiff. Present procedures seem inadequate to equitably adjust the interests of nation and individual both in ascertaining the presence of state secrets and in disposing of the controversy once it is decided they are involved.

Perhaps, in the sub-contract situation, a solution might be reached along the following lines: A federal statute, based upon the power of the nation to protect itself, could require that sub-contracts let under a government prime contract and classified as affecting the national security contain a clause requiring the parties to arbitrate all disputes arising under the contract, the dispute would, however, only proceed to arbitration if the appropriate executive department head certified that there was a continued need for secrecy. If the executive declassified the contract or took no action within a reasonable time, the information would be deemed unprivileged and the clause inapplicable; the disputants would be free to litigate in the courts. Otherwise, an arbitrator would be chosen by the parties from a list provided by the executive department concerned, or if no choice could be agreed upon one would be designated by the department. The parties would be represented by counsel of their choice, or if necessary, because of security considerations, by appointed counsel. The arbitrator would be empowered to enter a default award after prescribed notice to a recalcitrant party. An award would be confirmable in any federal district court. Although the arbitrator's determination of the scope of the arbitration clause and the merits of the controversy would be final, an award would not be enforced if (1) the subject of the dispute had been declassified prior to arbitration proceedings, (2) reasonable notice was not given to a party against whom a default award was taken or, (3) the award was procured by means of fraud or corruption of the arbitrator.

At the minimum the proposal would ensure that individual interests receive a disposition on the merits while preserving the nation's interest in secrecy. Although parties would have to accept an arbitrator's disposition of the controversy with few of the safeguards of an independent judiciary, it is submitted that while the adjustment of individual and governmental interests requires something more than complete denial of relief to deserving litigants an effective security system precludes full judicial inquiry.

United States v. Nixon

Supreme Court of the United States, 1974.
418 U.S. 683, 94 S.Ct. 3090, 41 L.Ed.2d 1039.

■ MR. CHIEF JUSTICE BURGER delivered the opinion of the Court.

* * *

On March 1, 1974, a grand jury of the United States District Court for the District of Columbia returned an indictment charging seven named individuals[3] with various offenses, including conspiracy to defraud the United

---

[3] The seven defendants were John N. Mitchell, H.R. Haldeman, John D. Ehrlichman, Charles W. Colson, Robert C. Mardian, Kenneth W. Parkinson, and Gordon Strachan. Each had occupied either a position of responsibility on the White House staff or the Committee for the Re-election of the President. Colson entered a guilty plea on another charge and is no longer a defendant.

States and to obstruct justice. Although he was not designated as such in the indictment, the grand jury named the President, among others, as an unindicted coconspirator. On April 18, 1974, upon motion of the Special Prosecutor, see n. 8, infra, a subpoena *duces tecum* was issued pursuant to Rule 17(c) to the President by the United States District Court and made returnable on May 2, 1974. This subpoena required the production, in advance of the September 9 trial date, of certain tapes, memoranda, papers, transcripts or other writings relating to certain precisely identified meetings between the President and others. The Special Prosecutor was able to fix the time, place, and persons present at these discussions because the White House daily logs and appointment records had been delivered to him. On April 30, the President publicly released edited transcripts of 43 conversations; portions of 20 conversations subject to subpoena in the present case were included. On May 1, 1974, the President's counsel, filed a "special appearance" and a motion to quash the subpoena under Rule 17(c). This motion was accompanied by a formal claim of privilege. At a subsequent hearing, further motions to expunge the grand jury's action naming the President as an unindicted coconspirator and for protective orders against the disclosure of that information were filed or raised orally by counsel for the President.

On May 20, 1974, the District Court denied the motion to quash and the motions to expunge and for protective orders. It further ordered "the President or any subordinate officer, official, or employee with custody or control of the documents or objects subpoenaed," to deliver to the District Court, on or before May 31, 1974, the originals of all subpoenaed items, as well as an index and analysis of those items, together with tape copies of those portions of the subpoenaed recordings for which transcripts had been released to the public by the President on April 30. * * *

* * *

[The Court held that the order of the district judge was a final appealable order, despite the fact that no contempt adjudication had been made; that the matter was within the Supreme Court's jurisdiction, despite the fact that the two contending parties, the President and the Special Prosecutor, were both within the executive branch; and that the subpoena in question met the requirements of specificity of Rule 17 of the Federal Rules of Criminal Procedure. Then, it moved on to the privilege issue.]

IV

THE CLAIM OF PRIVILEGE

A

* * * [W]e turn to the claim that the subpoena should be quashed because it demands "confidential conversations between a President and his close advisors that it would be inconsistent with the public interest to produce." The first contention is a broad claim that the separation of powers doctrine precludes judicial review of a President's claim of privilege. The

second contention is that if he does not prevail on the claim of absolute privilege, the court should hold as a matter of constitutional law that the privilege prevails over the subpoena *duces tecum.*

In the performance of assigned constitutional duties each branch of the Government must initially interpret the Constitution, and the interpretation of its powers by any branch is due great respect from the others. The President's counsel, as we have noted, reads the Constitution as providing an absolute privilege of confidentiality for all Presidential communications. Many decisions of this Court, however, have unequivocally reaffirmed the holding of Marbury v. Madison, that "[i]t is emphatically the province and duty of the judicial department to say what the law is."

* * *

* * * Notwithstanding the deference each branch must accord the others, the "judicial Power of the United States" vested in the federal courts by Art. III, § 1, of the Constitution can no more be shared with the Executive Branch than the Chief Executive, for example, can share with the Judiciary the veto power, or the Congress share with the Judiciary the power to override a Presidential veto. Any other conclusion would be contrary to the basic concept of separation of powers and the checks and balances that flow from the scheme of a tripartite government. * * *

B

In support of his claim of absolute privilege, the President's counsel urges two grounds, one of which is common to all governments and one of which is peculiar to our system of separation of powers. The first ground is the valid need for protection of communications between high Government officials and those who advise and assist them in the performance of their manifold duties; the importance of this confidentiality is too plain to require further discussion. Human experience teaches that those who expect public dissemination of their remarks may well temper candor with a concern for appearances and for their own interests to the detriment of the decisionmaking process.[15] Whatever the nature of the privilege of confidentiality of Presidential communications in the exercise of Art. II powers, the privilege can be said to derive from the supremacy of each branch within its own assigned area of constitutional duties. Certain powers and privileges flow from the nature of enumerated powers;[16] the protection of the confi-

---

[15] There is nothing novel about governmental confidentiality. The meetings of the Constitutional Convention in 1787 were conducted in complete privacy. 1 M. Farrand, The Records of the Federal Convention of 1787, pp. xi–xxv (1911). Moreover, all records of those meetings were sealed for more than 30 years after the Convention. See 3 Stat. 475, 15th Cong., 1st Sess., Res. 8 (1818). Most of the Framers acknowledge that without secrecy no constitution of the kind that was developed could have been written. C. Warren, The Making of the Constitution 134–139 (1937).

[16] The Special Prosecutor argues that there is no provision in the Constitution for a Presidential privilege as to the President's communications corresponding to the privilege of Members of Congress under the Speech or Debate Clause. But the silence of the Constitution on this score is not dispositive. "The rule of constitutional interpretation announced in McCulloch v. Maryland, that that which was reasonably appropriate and relevant to the exercise of a

dentiality of Presidential communications has similar constitutional underpinnings.

The second ground asserted by the President's counsel in support of the claim of absolute privilege rests on the doctrine of separation of powers. Here it is argued that the independence of the Executive Branch within its own sphere, insulates a President from a judicial subpoena in an ongoing criminal prosecution, and thereby protects confidential Presidential communications.

However, neither the doctrine of separation of powers, nor the need for confidentiality of high-level communications, without more, can sustain an absolute, unqualified Presidential privilege of immunity from judicial process under all circumstances. The President's need for complete candor and objectivity from advisers calls for great deference from the courts. However, when the privilege depends solely on the broad, undifferentiated claim of public interest in the confidentiality of such conversations, a confrontation with other values arises. Absent a claim of need to protect military, diplomatic, or sensitive national security secrets, we find it difficult to accept the argument that even the very important interest in confidentiality of Presidential communications is significantly diminished by production of such material for *in camera* inspection with all the protection that a district court will be obliged to provide.

The impediment that an absolute, unqualified privilege would place in the way of the primary constitutional duty of the Judicial Branch to do justice in criminal prosecutions would plainly conflict with the function of the courts under Art. III. In designing the structure of our Government and dividing and allocating the sovereign power among three co-equal branches, the Framers of the Constitution sought to provide a comprehensive system, but the separate powers were not intended to operate with absolute independence.

"While the Constitution diffuses power the better to secure liberty, it also contemplates that practice will integrate the dispersed powers into a workable government. It enjoins upon its branches separateness but interdependence, autonomy but reciprocity." Youngstown Sheet & Tube Co. v. Sawyer (Jackson, J., concurring).

To read the Art. II powers of the President as providing an absolute privilege as against a subpoena essential to enforcement of criminal statutes on no more than a generalized claim of the public interest in confidentiality of nonmilitary and nondiplomatic discussions would upset the constitutional balance of "a workable government" and gravely impair the role of the courts under Art. III.

---

granted power was to be considered as accompanying the grant, has been so universally applied that it suffices merely to state it." Marshall v. Gordon.

C

Since we conclude that the legitimate needs of the judicial process may outweigh Presidential privilege, it is necessary to resolve those competing interests in a manner that preserves the essential functions of each branch. The right and indeed the duty to resolve that question does not free the Judiciary from according high respect to the representations made on behalf of the President.

The expectation of a President to the confidentiality of his conversations and correspondence, like the claim of confidentiality of judicial deliberations, for example, has all the values to which we accord deference for the privacy of all citizens and, added to those values, is the necessity for protection of the public interest in candid, objective, and even blunt or harsh opinions in Presidential decision-making. A President and those who assist him must be free to explore alternatives in the process of shaping policies and making decisions and to do so in a way many would be unwilling to express except privately. These are the considerations justifying a presumptive privilege for Presidential communications. The privilege is fundamental to the operation of Government and inextricably rooted in the separation of powers under the Constitution.[17] In Nixon v. Sirica, the Court of Appeals held that such Presidential communications are "presumptively privileged" and this position is accepted by both parties in the present litigation. We agree with Mr. Chief Justice Marshall's observation, therefore, that "[i]n no case of this kind would a court be required to proceed against the president as against an ordinary individual."

But this presumptive privilege must be considered in light of our historic commitment to the rule of law. This is nowhere more profoundly manifest than in our view that "the twofold aim [of criminal justice] is that guilt shall not escape or innocence suffer." We have elected to employ an adversary system of criminal justice in which the parties contest all issues before a court of law. The need to develop all relevant facts in the adversary system is both fundamental and comprehensive. The ends of criminal justice would be defeated if judgments were to be founded on a partial or speculative presentation of the facts. The very integrity of the judicial system and public confidence in the system depend on full disclosure of all the facts, within the framework of the rules of evidence. To ensure that justice is done, it is imperative to the function of courts that compulsory process be available for the production of evidence needed either by the prosecution or by the defense.

Only recently the Court restated the ancient proposition of law, albeit in the context of a grand jury inquiry rather than a trial,

"that 'the public * * * has a right to every man's evidence,' except for those persons protected by a constitutional, common-law, or statutory

---

[17] "Freedom of communication vital to fulfillment of the arms of wholesome relationships is obtained only by removing the specter of compelled disclosure. * * * [G]overnment * * * needs open but protected channels for the kind of plain talk that is essential to the quality of its functioning." Carl Zeiss Stiftung v. V.E.B. Carl Zeiss, Jena.

privilege, United States v. Bryan, 339 U.S. [323, 331, 70 S.Ct. 724, 730 (1950)]; Blackmer v. United States, 284 U.S. 421, 438 [52 S.Ct. 252, 76 L.Ed. 375] (1932) * * *" Branzburg v. Hayes. United States, 408 U.S. 665, 688 [92 S.Ct. 2646, 33 L.Ed.2d 626] (1972).

The privileges referred to by the Court are designed to protect weighty and legitimate competing interests. Thus, the Fifth Amendment to the Constitution provides that no man "shall be compelled in any criminal case to be a witness against himself." And, generally, an attorney or a priest may not be required to disclose what has been revealed in professional confidence. These and other interests are recognized in law by privileges against forced disclosure, established in the Constitution, by statute, or at common law. Whatever their origins, these exceptions to the demand for every man's evidence are not lightly created nor expansively construed, for they are in derogation of the search for truth.[18]

In this case the President challenges a subpoena served on him as a third party requiring the production of materials for use in a criminal prosecution; he does so on the claim that he has a privilege against disclosure of confidential communications. He does not place his claim of privilege on the ground they are military or diplomatic secrets. As to these areas of Art. II duties the courts have traditionally shown the utmost deference to Presidential responsibilities. In C. & S. Air Lines v. Waterman S.S. Corp., dealing with Presidential authority involving foreign policy considerations, the Court said:

"The President, both as Commander-in-Chief and as the Nation's organ for foreign affairs, has available intelligence services whose reports are not and ought not to be published to the world. It would be intolerable that courts, without the relevant information, should review and perhaps nullify actions of the Executive taken on information properly held secret."

In United States v. Reynolds, dealing with a claimant's demand for evidence in a Tort Claims Act case against the Government, the Court said:

"It may be possible to satisfy the court, from all the circumstances of the case, that there is a reasonable danger that compulsion of the evidence will expose military matters which, in the interest of national security, should not be divulged. When this is the case, the occasion for the privilege is appropriate, and the court should not jeopardize the security which the privilege is meant to protect by insisting upon an examination of the evidence, even by the judge alone, in chambers."

---

[18] Because of the key role of the testimony of witnesses in the judicial process, courts have historically been cautious about privileges. Mr. Justice Frankfurter, dissenting in Elkins v. United States, said of this: "Limitations are properly placed upon the operation of this general principle only to the very limited extent that permitting a refusal to testify or excluding relevant evidence has a public good transcending the normally predominant principle of utilizing all rational means for ascertaining truth."

No case of the Court, however, has extended this high degree of deference to a President's generalized interest in confidentiality. Nowhere in the Constitution, as we have noted earlier, is there any explicit reference to a privilege of confidentiality, yet to the extent this interest relates to the effective discharge of a President's powers, it is constitutionally based.

The right to the production of all evidence at a criminal trial similarly has constitutional dimensions. The Sixth Amendment explicitly confers upon every defendant in a criminal trial the right "to be confronted with the witnesses against him" and "to have compulsory process for obtaining witnesses in his favor." Moreover, the Fifth Amendment also guarantees that no person shall be deprived of liberty without due process of law. It is the manifest duty of the courts to vindicate those guarantees, and to accomplish that it is essential that all relevant and admissible evidence be produced.

In this case we must weigh the importance of the general privilege of confidentiality of Presidential communications in performance of the President's responsibilities against the inroads of such a privilege on the fair administration of criminal justice.[19] The interest in preserving confidentiality is weighty indeed and entitled to great respect. However, we cannot conclude that advisers will be moved to temper the candor of their remarks by the infrequent occasions of disclosure because of the possibility that such conversations will be called for in the context of a criminal prosecution.[20]

On the other hand, the allowance of the privilege to withhold evidence that is demonstrably relevant in a criminal trial would cut deeply into the guarantee of due process of law and gravely impair the basic function of the courts. A President's acknowledged need for confidentiality in the communications of his office is general in nature, whereas the constitutional need for production of relevant evidence in a criminal proceeding is specific and central to the fair adjudication of a particular criminal case in the administration of justice. Without access to specific facts a criminal prosecution may be totally frustrated. The President's broad interest in confidentiality

---

[19] We are not here concerned with the balance between the President's generalized interest in confidentiality and the need for relevant evidence in civil litigation, nor with that between the confidentiality interest and congressional demands for information, nor with the President's interest in preserving state secrets. We address only the conflict between the President's assertion of a generalized privilege of confidentiality and the constitutional need for relevant evidence in criminal trials.

[20] Mr. Justice Cardozo made this point in an analogous context, speaking for a unanimous Court in Clark v. United States, he emphasized the importance of maintaining the secrecy of the deliberations of a petit jury in a criminal case. "Freedom of debate might be stifled and independence of thought checked if jurors were made to feel that their arguments and ballots were to be freely published to the world." Nonetheless, the Court also recognized that isolated inroads on confidentiality designed to serve the paramount need of the criminal law would not vitiate the interests served by secrecy:

There is nothing novel about governmental confidentiality. The meetings of the Constitutional Convention in 1787 were conducted in complete privacy. 1 M. Farrand, The Records of the Federal Convention of 1787, pp. xi–xxv (1911). Moreover, all records of those meetings were sealed for more than 30 years after the Convention. See 3 Stat. 475, 15th Cong., 1st Sess., Res. 8 (1818). Most of the Framers acknowledge that without secrecy no constitution of the kind that was developed could have been written. C. Warren, The Making of the Constitution 134–139 (1937).

of communications will not be vitiated by disclosure of a limited number of conversations preliminarily shown to have some bearing on the pending criminal cases.

We conclude that when the ground for asserting privilege as to subpoenaed materials sought for use in a criminal trial is based only on the generalized interest in confidentiality, it cannot prevail over the fundamental demands of due process of law in the fair administration of criminal justice. The generalized assertion of privilege must yield to the demonstrated, specific, need for evidence in a pending criminal trial.

D

We have earlier determined that the District Court did not err in authorizing the issuance of the subpoena. If a President concludes that compliance with a subpoena would be injurious to the public interest he may properly, as was done here, invoke a claim of privilege on the return of the subpoena. Upon receiving a claim of privilege from the Chief Executive, it became the further duty of the District Court to treat the subpoenaed material as presumptively privileged and to require the Special Prosecutor to demonstrate that the Presidential material was "essential to the justice of the [pending criminal] case." United States v. Burr. Here the District Court treated the material as presumptively privileged, proceeded to find that the Special Prosecutor had made a sufficient showing to rebut the presumption, and ordered an *in camera* examination of the subpoenaed material. On the basis of our examination of the record we are unable to conclude that the District Court erred in ordering the inspection. Accordingly we affirm the order of the District Court that subpoenaed materials be transmitted to that court. We now turn to the important question of the District Court's responsibilities in conducting the *in camera* examination of Presidential materials or communications delivered under the compulsion of the subpoena *duces tecum*.

E

Enforcement of the subpoena *duces tecum* was stayed pending this Court's resolution of the issues raised by the petitions for certiorari. Those issues now having been disposed of, the matter of implementation will rest with the District Court. "[T]he guard, furnished to [the President] to protect him from being harassed by vexatious and unnecessary subpoenas, is to be looked for in the conduct of a [district] court after those subpoenas have issued; not in any circumstance, which is to precede their being issued." United States v. Burr, supra. Statements that meet the test of admissibility and relevance must be isolated; all other material must be excised. At this stage the District Court is not limited to representations of the Special Prosecutor as to the evidence sought by the subpoena; the material will be available to the District Court. It is elementary that *in camera* inspection of evidence is always a procedure calling for scrupulous protection against any release or publication of material not found by the court, at that stage, probably admissible in evidence and relevant to the issues of the trial for which it is sought. That being true of an ordinary situation, it is obvious that the District Court has a very heavy responsibility to see to it that Presidential conversations, which are either not relevant or not admissible, are accorded that high degree of respect due the President of the United States. Mr. Chief Justice Marshall, sitting as a trial judge in the *Burr* case, supra, was extraordinarily careful to point out that

> "[i]n no case of this kind would a court be required to proceed against the president as against an ordinary individual."

Marshall's statement cannot be read to mean in any sense that a President is above the law, but relates to the singularly unique role under Art. II of a President's communications and activities, related to the performance of duties under that Article. Moreover, a President's communications and activities encompass a vastly wider range of sensitive material than would be true of any "ordinary individual." It is therefore necessary[21] in the public interest to afford Presidential confidentiality the greatest protection consistent with the fair administration of justice. The need for confidentiality even as to idle conversations with associates in which casual reference might be made concerning political leaders within the country or foreign statesmen is too obvious to call for further treatment. We have no doubt that the District Judge will at all times accord to Presidential records that high degree of deference suggested in United States v. Burr, supra and will discharge his responsibility to see to it that until released to the Special Prosecutor no *in camera* material is revealed to anyone. This burden applies with even greater force to excised material; once the decision is made to excise, the material is restored to its privileged status and should be returned under seal to its lawful custodian.

* * *

Affirmed.

■ MR. JUSTICE REHNQUIST took no part in the consideration or decision of these cases.

NOTE

The investigation of President Bill Clinton by Independent Counsel Kenneth Starr and the investigation of Agriculture Secretary Mike Espy by Independent Counsel Donald Smaltz resulted in litigation about governmental privileges, but did not lead to new Supreme Court decisions on the subject. See *In re Sealed Case*, 121 F.3d 729 (D.C.Cir.1997) (held, executive privilege extends even to White House staff members not communicating directly with the President, but on facts of case privilege was pierced because Independent Counsel made sufficient showing of compelling need and inability to obtain information elsewhere); *In re Grand Jury Proceedings*, 5 F.Supp.2d 21 (D.D.C. 1998) (holding that OIC had made sufficient showing of need to overcome executive privi-

---

[21] When the subpoenaed material is delivered to the District Judge *in camera*, questions may arise as to the excising of parts, and it lies within the discretion of that court to seek the aid of the Special Prosecutor and the President's counsel for *in camera* consideration of the validity of particular excisions, whether the basis of excision is relevancy or admissibility or under such cases as United States v. Reynolds, or C. & S. Air Lines v. Waterman S.S. Corp.

lege), *aff'd sub nom. In re Lindsey,* 148 F.3d 1100 (D.C.Cir.), *cert. denied* 525 U.S. 996 (1998) (noting that President had not appealed from District Court decision that held that executive privilege had been pierced by adequate showing of need; appellate court ruled only on issue of governmental attorney-client privilege); *In re Sealed Case,* 148 F.3d 1073 (D.C.Cir.1998), *cert. denied* 525 U.S. 990 (1998) (held, no "protective function privilege" for Secret Service Officers guarding the President).

―――――――

See California Evidence Code § 1040.

United States v. Tzannos

United States Court of Appeals for the First Circuit, 2006.
460 F.3d 128.

■ Before LYNCH and HOWARD, CIRCUIT JUDGES, and STAFFORD,* K.

■ LYNCH, CIRCUIT JUDGE.

This is the government's appeal from a district court's suppression order.

The district court suppressed evidence, seized pursuant to a state court warrant, based on the defendant's allegations that the affidavit by a state trooper in support of the warrant application contained material misrepresentations. In essence, defendant argued, the affidavit referred to a confidential informant who did not exist.

* * *

I.

A. *The State Search Warrant Affidavit*

On August 28, 2003, Massachusetts State Trooper Pasquale Russolillo submitted an application for a search warrant to a magistrate in a state district court in East Boston, Massachusetts. Russolillo included a fourteen-page affidavit in support of the application. [The affidavit asserted that Tzannos was involved in bookmaking. Much of the basis for this assertion was information provided by a confidential informant, referred to as CI–1, who said that he had placed bets with Tzannos by calling (617) 567–6114 ("the 6114 line") and speaking with Tzannos directly.]

The affidavit recounted that on August 25, 2003, CI–1 and Russolillo placed a "controlled call" to Tzannos on the 6114 line. * * * The affidavit explained that in a controlled call, the police officer dials the number, waits until the target of the investigation answers, hands the phone to the informant, and then watches as the informant speaks to the target. CI–1 told

―――――――

* Of the Northern District of Florida, sitting by designation.

Russolillo that Tzannos was the person who answered the phone during the controlled call, and that Tzannos proceeded to give a rundown of the day's betting lines for baseball.

Russolillo's affidavit stated that CI–1 had provided information to Russolillo and other troopers in the past, and the information "has proven to be reliable and true." * * * The affidavit stated that CI–1 had also provided general intelligence information regarding other criminal matters, but that the affiant could not detail the particulars of these cases, because doing so would compromise the anonymity of the informant, making him "susceptible to physical harm and/or retribution."

* * *

B. *The State Search Warrant, the Search, and the Federal Indictment*

* * * The magistrate * * * issued the warrant. Massachusetts state police executed the warrant on August 28, 2003, and found a fully equipped gaming office. Officers seized gaming records, $10,200 in cash, and tape recorders and tapes that had been used to record conversations with customers. In addition, police found and seized a loaded pistol, two loaded revolvers, a sawed-off shotgun, various types of ammunition, three switchblade knives, a pair of brass knuckles, and a blowgun with needles.

On June 30, 2004, a federal grand jury indicted Tzannos on charges of violating 18 U.S.C. § 922(g)(1), which prohibits possession of firearms by convicted felons. The indictment stated that the offense "involved three to seven firearms" and that Tzannos possessed at least one of the firearms and at least one piece of ammunition "in connection with another felony offense, to wit: occupying a place for registering bets in violation of Mass. Gen. Laws [ ] ch. 271, § 17, a Massachusetts offense punishable by imprisonment for a term exceeding one year."

C. *The Franks Hearing and the Suppression Order*

* * * In his motion papers [seeking to challenge the accuracy of the affidavit], Tzannos argued that the affidavit had to be untruthful because (1) Russolillo swore that the informant placed calls to the 6114 line on four particular days, August 16, 17, 20, and 25, and spoke to Tzannos on each of those days, (2) the defense identified each and every caller to that number on those days and "ha[d] documentation to back it up," and (3) each and every one of those callers had signed a statement denying under oath that he or she was the informant. Tzannos argued that "[t]he only logical conclusion that one could possibly reach is that there was no informant, or at least that no informant did the things described in the [Russolillo] affidavit." Thus, Tzannos argued, if it were not true that the informant made gambling-related calls to Tzannos over the 6114 line on the four days, then it was necessarily true that no informant existed and that Russolillo had lied.

* * *

Tzannos focused his challenge on Russolillo's allegation that CI–1 had made a controlled call to Tzannos on August 25, 2003 on the 6114 line. Defense counsel represented that the ledger sheets [of gambling activity presented by him in connection with the motion] show that on August 25, only two individuals, "Jerry" and "Norton," called to place bets on the 6114 line. Counsel further represented that the tape is a recording of telephone calls made to the 6114 line on August 25, 2003, and that a transcript of that tape shows that only three people, "Paulie," "Jerry," and "Norton," made gaming-related calls that day to the 6114 line. Counsel then attached signed statements from "Paulie," "Jerry," and "Norton," swearing that "[a]t no time did I cooperate with the police, nor was I a confidential informant." * * *

[The government insisted] that there was no evidence that Russolillo had lied. It also explained that it could not divulge the identity of CI–1 publicly because doing so would endanger the informant's life. It represented that it was not authorized to disclose the informant's name without permission from the Department of Justice or the state Attorney General. The government offered instead to prove the veracity of Russolillo's affidavit and the existence of CI–1 in an ex parte, in camera proceeding, in which it would offer, inter alia, testimony of Russolillo revealing the identity of CI–1.

* * *

[At the start of the *"Franks"* hearing, held to determine the accuracy of the affidavit], the district court announced a procedure that neither party had proposed:

> [A]ccording to the defendant's proffer of evidence, there are three people [who] spoke [to Tzannos on August 25, 2003]: Paulie, Jerry[,] and Norton. So Paulie, Jerry[,] and Norton at the worst come in and testify that they are not the confidential informant. And I don't have to hear from anybody claiming to be the confidential informant.
>
> And if it turns out that I think that [the controlled] call was not made to [the 6114] line on August 25, 2003, I can determine that there is no basis for whatever exists and allow a motion to suppress, without violating the identity of the confidential informant.

Tzannos made no objections to the procedure; indeed, he indicated that the three individuals had already been summoned and that they were outside the courtroom at that moment and ready to testify. The government, however, was far less enthusiastic. It raised two main objections to the procedure. First, it argued that the procedure placed it in a double bind: if one of the three individuals were, in fact, CI–1, but testified on the stand to the contrary, the government would be placed in a position where it would be forced either to knowingly elicit and condone perjurious testimony or to "out" an informant and expose him or her to mortal danger. As a corollary of that argument, the government also noted that "if one of [the three] is the informant and tells the truth, then the Court is eliciting a statement that may get the person killed," which is "not [a] procedure that the government is prepared to participate in." Second, the government argued that there was a "fundamental flaw" in the procedure, which it could not explain in open court without providing information that would necessarily divulge CI–1's identity, but which it could explain "in one sentence ex parte [and] in camera." The government stressed that "the Court would not come out with the truthful and just result if the Court follow[ed] the procedure that the Court outlined."

The court refused to hear the government's explanation ex parte and in camera. It also refused the government's original proposal, which was to provide to the court evidence of the existence and identity of the informant ex parte and in camera. The court stated that "[t]here are two things I don't want": "one, I don't want to do an ex parte hearing," and "two, I don't want to know who the confidential informant is." It also explained:

> There is nothing absolute about the confidential informant and confidentiality. I mean, it has to be weighed under all the circumstances.

> I think my suggest[ed procedure] is a good one. I don't even want to know who the confidential informant is.

> I just want to know are these three people going to take the stand and say they are not. And if they take the stand and say they are not, then that is the end of it. I am not going to say who is it.

The court went further. It stated:

> [I]f it turns out that the defendant puts three people on the stand and the tapes verify that only these three people made phone calls and that's it, and none of the three is the confidential informant, that is it as far as I am concerned. I don't have to hear any more. I will allow the motion to suppress.

To the government's argument that "[t]he issue here is not whether the confidential informant gave somewhat incorrect or incomplete or any other degree of defective evidence" but "whether Trooper Russolillo lied under oath," the court stated: "I don't think I have to find that he lied. I can find that none of those three people is the confidential informant and that no other calls were made that day and that, therefore, there is no basis for whatever it was and then I am going to suppress it."

* * * [The government] agreed to stipulate that if the three individuals were called to testify, they would each testify that he had called Tzannos on August 25, 2003, and that he had never been a confidential informant or made a controlled call for Russolillo. The government emphasized, however, that it was making this stipulation "with the understanding that for the reasons previously explained the government cannot cross-examine these individuals to bring out the truth," and that "the government is not conceding the truth." The court then suppressed the evidence seized pursuant to the search warrant.

II.

* * *

A. *The Suppression Order*

"There is . . . a presumption of validity with respect to the affidavit supporting the search warrant." Franks, 438 U.S. at 171, 98 S.Ct. 2674. * * *

The alleged falsehood in the affidavit is that Trooper Russolillo fabricated the existence of a confidential informant. That Russolillo made the false statement knowingly and intelligently is shown, defendant says, by his having stated that he was present at the controlled call made by CI–1 to Tzannos on August 25, 2003 to the 6114 line. [The court reviewed the evidence bearing on whether Russolillo knowingly made a false statement.]

The district court did not make any explicit findings of fact at the *Franks* hearing. Nonetheless, it must implicitly have found that Tzannos's evidence was sufficient to show, by a preponderance of the evidence, that only "Paulie," "Jerry," and "Norton" made gambling-related calls to Tzannos on the 6114 line on August 25. Given the substantial gaps in the evidence, this finding was clear error and alone provides a basis for reversal.

* * *

There are further grounds, however, for reversing the suppression order. Even if Tzannos had proven his first assertion by a preponderance of the evidence, it does not follow that he proved by a preponderance of the evidence that no confidential informant exists.

Ultimately, Tzannos must demonstrate, by a preponderance of the evidence, that the affiant, Trooper Russolillo, rather than the informant, made a false statement knowingly and intentionally, or with reckless disregard for the truth. "Allegations of negligence or innocent mistake are insufficient,"*Franks*, 438 U.S. at 171, 98 S.Ct. 2674, as are allegations going to show that the informant relayed misinformation to the affiant * * *.

Tzannos has not contested the accuracy of any of the substantive information provided by CI–1 to Russolillo, and has not explained how Russolillo would have obtained such detailed and accurate information if CI–1 did not exist. Nor has Tzannos made any showing of why Russolillo would have reason to lie. He thus has not met his burden of showing that Russolillo made a false statement knowingly and intentionally, or with reckless disregard for the truth. To the extent that the district court held otherwise, it committed clear error. We hold that the court erred in suppressing the evidence.

B. *Problems with the District Court's Procedure at the Franks Hearing*

The government also appeals (1) the district court's refusal to hear the government's one-line explanation of why the procedure that the court devised for the Franks hearing was, in the government's view, flawed, and (2) the court's ultimate decision to go forward with the hearing without listening to that explanation.

At the *Franks* hearing, when the government asked to explain to the court, in one sentence, what the government argued was a "fundamental flaw" in the court's analysis, the court refused to hear the explanation ex parte and in camera, despite the government's entreaties that the way the court structured the proceeding would jeopardize the life of the informant and lead to a miscarriage of justice. The court in essence shifted the burden of proof to the government: short of proving CI–1's existence, there was no way the government could disprove the defendant's allegations.

The court's position effectively eliminated the privilege the government has under *Roviaro v. United States,* 353 U.S. 53, 77 S.Ct. 623, 1 L.Ed.2d 639 (1957),[8] to protect the identity of confidential informants. The court's refusal to hear the government's explanation and its insistence on going forward with the procedure of its own devising were thus an abuse of discretion.

In oft-quoted language, *Roviaro* stated:

> What is usually referred to as the informer's privilege is in reality the Government's privilege to withhold from disclosure the identity of persons who furnish information of violations of law to officers charged with enforcement of that law. The purpose of the privilege is the furtherance and protection of the public interest in effective law enforcement.

Id. at 59, 77 S.Ct. 623 (citations omitted). The privilege, while significant, is not absolute. Thus, "[w]here the disclosure of an informer's identity, or of the contents of his communication, is relevant and helpful to the defense of an accused, or is essential to a fair determination of a cause, the privilege must give way." *Id.* at 60–61, 77 S.Ct. 623; *see also id.* at 60, 77 S.Ct. 623 (holding that "where the disclosure of the contents of a communication will not tend to reveal the identity of an informer, the contents are not privileged," and that "[l]ikewise, once the identity of the informer has been disclosed to those who would have cause to resent the communication, the privilege is no longer applicable").

Ultimately, *Roviaro* requires a "balancing [of] the public interest in protecting the flow of information against the individual's right to prepare his defense." "Whether a proper balance . . . [requires] nondisclosure . . . must depend on the particular circumstances of each case, taking into con-

---

[8] Unlike *Roviaro,* the issue here is not the suppression of the informant's testimony, but rather the suppression of the fruits of the search pursuant to a warrant issued by a state court judge and presumed to be valid.

sideration the crime charged, the possible defenses, the possible significance of the informer's testimony, and other relevant factors." *Id.; see also McCray v. Illinois,* 386 U.S. 300, 311, 87 S.Ct. 1056, 18 L.Ed.2d 62 (1967). This court has stated that "when the government informant is not an actual participant or a witness to the offense, disclosure is required only in those exceptional cases where the defendant can point to some concrete circumstance that might justify overriding both the public interest in encouraging the flow of information, and the informant's private interest in his or her own safety." *United States v. Martinez,* 922 F.2d 914, 921 (1st Cir.1991).

Tzannos, as the party seeking disclosure, bore the burden of persuasion in this analysis. * * * This court has described this burden as a "heavy" one. *United States v. Robinson,* 144 F.3d 104, 106 (1st Cir.1998). The government argues that Tzannos has failed to meet this burden and that the court abused its discretion in implicitly holding otherwise.

For his part, Tzannos offers no arguments as to why disclosure of the confidential informant's identity was warranted in this case. Instead, Tzannos puts all of his stock in two arguments, of which we readily dispose. His first argument is that he never asked the court to order the disclosure of CI–1's identity and thus *Roviaro* does not even apply. The court's procedure, however, placed the government in a Catch–22: it could not participate in the *Franks* hearing without risking exposing its informant (or suborning perjury), and it could not explain to the court, beyond the other arguments it made, why the court's analysis was flawed without effectively disclosing the identity of its informant. That the court did not require the government to say the actual name of the informant is of little significance; it was requiring the government to provide information that would, for all practical purposes, divulge the informant's identity. "The privilege identified in *Roviaro* protects more than just the name of the informant and extends to information that would tend to reveal the identity of the informant." *United States v. Napier,* 436 F.3d 1133, 1136 (9th Cir.2006).

Tzannos's second argument as to why *Roviaro* does not apply is that "if one of the three would-be witnesses turned out to be CI–1, then that witness had voluntarily put himself in the position of having to admit being an informant." Tzannos's argument rests on mistaken premises: as we noted above, the *Roviaro* privilege does not belong to the informant, but rather to the government. Thus, even assuming that CI–1 was one of the three individuals identified by Tzannos, so long as that individual has not voluntarily disclosed his status as an informant to the defendant, the government may still invoke its "privilege to withhold from disclosure the identity of persons who furnish information of violations of law to officers charged with enforcement of that law." *Roviaro.*

The government emphatically argued that the particular circumstances of this case warranted protection of the informant's identity. It repeatedly stressed during the course of the *Franks* hearing and in its filings that CI–1 would likely be murdered if his identity were publicly disclosed.

It also pointed to Russolillo's affidavit, which stated that "traditional organized crime families (such as La Cosa Nostra or the Mafia) and other organized crime groups (such as the Winter Hill Gang) in the Boston area have been heavily involved in illegal gaming and bookmaking and have maintained a significant degree of control over organized bookmaking operations," and that "compromis[ing] the anonymity of the confidential reliable informant [would] mak[e] him/her susceptible to physical harm and/or retribution."

Against the government's interest in protecting the identity of the informant, we must balance "the fundamental requirements of fairness" and Tzannos's right to prepare his defense. *Roviaro*. Generally, the defendant's competing interests are of a lesser magnitude at the suppression stage than at trial. * * * [C]*f. McCray,* 386 U.S. at 312, 87 S.Ct. 1056 ("[T]he Court in the exercise of its power to formulate evidentiary rules for federal criminal cases has consistently declined to hold that an informer's identity need always be disclosed in a federal criminal trial, let alone in a preliminary hearing to determine probable cause for an arrest or search."). These interests are especially weak here, where the informant is not "the sole participant, other than the accused, in the transaction charged,"*Robinson,* 144 F.3d at 106; was not "the only witness in a position to amplify or contradict the testimony of government witnesses,"*Roviaro*; and in fact had no involvement whatsoever in the crime charged—to wit, possession of firearms and ammunition by a felon. Nor has Tzannos shown that the disclosure of the informant's identity would allow him to meet his burden under *Franks*.

Tzannos has failed to show why disclosure of the identity of CI–1 is warranted in the circumstances of this case. *See United States v. Brown,* 3 F.3d 673, 679 (3d Cir.1993) ("A defendant who merely hopes (without showing a likelihood) that disclosure will lead to evidence supporting suppression has not shown that disclosure will be 'relevant and helpful to the defense . . . or is essential to a fair determination[.]'" (omission in original) (quoting *Roviaro,* 353 U.S. at 60–61, 77 S.Ct. 623)). The district court's decision to go forward with its own procedure and to refuse to hear the government's ex parte, in camera explanation of why that procedure was problematic was an abuse of discretion.

III.

We *reverse* the district court's order suppressing the evidence and *remand* with instructions to deny the motion to suppress.

UNITED STATES v. MOUSSAOUI, 382 F.3d 453 (4th Cir. 2004). Moussaoui was charged with conspiracy in relation to the attacks of September 11, 2001; he was alleged to have been the so-called "20th hijacker," but the indictment charged crimes going beyond preparations for those attacks. He sought to take depositions of three alleged members of al Qaeda in custody of American armed forces. The district court found that their extensive knowledge of the September 11 plot might support Moussaoui's contention that he was not involved. The Government refused to make the witnesses available for depositions, but it did provide extracts from summaries of statements made by each of the three witnesses. The district court regarded these extracts as an inadequate substitute for deposition testimony. After extensive proceedings, the district court decided not to dismiss the indictment, but to preclude the possibility of the death penalty and to prohibit proof that Moussaoui was involved in, or knew about, the September 11 attacks.

On appeal, the Fourth Circuit (in an opinion that itself was heavily redacted for publication) indicated that the *Roviaro* standard would apply to this context; under that standard, a criminal defendant is entitled to the disclosure of classified information upon a showing that the information "is relevant and helpful to the defense . . . or is essential to a fair determination of a cause." The court accepted the Government's argument that producing the enemy combatant witnesses would impose substantial burdens on the Government; it might, for example, "have devastating effects" on continuing attempts to gather further information about them. But the court also concluded that the three witnesses could offer exculpatory testimony, supporting Moussaoui's contention that he was not involved in the September 11 attacks. Relying on *Roviaro* as well as other authorities, the court said:

> [I]t is clear that when an evidentiary privilege—even one that involves national security—is asserted by the Government in the context of its prosecution of a criminal offense, the "balancing" we must conduct is primarily, if not solely, an examination of whether the district court correctly determined that the information the Government seeks to withhold is material to the defense. We have determined that the enemy combatant witnesses can offer material testimony that is essential to Moussaoui's defense. . . Thus, the choice is the Government's whether to comply with those orders or suffer a sanction. * * *

> * * * We are thus left in the following situation: the district court has the power to order production of the enemy combatant witnesses and has properly determined that they could offer material testimony on Moussaoui's behalf, but the Government has refused to produce the witnesses. Under such circumstances, dismissal of the indictment is the usual course. *See, e.g.,* Jencks v. United States, 353 U.S. 657 (1957); *Roviaro*. Like the district court, however, we believe that a more measured approach is required. Additionally, we emphasize that no punitive sanction is warranted here because the Government has rightfully exercised its prerogative to protect national security interests by refusing to produce the witnesses.

For guidance, the court relied on the Classified Information Procedures Act (CIPA), 18 U.S.C.A.App. 3 §§ 1 *et seq.* For guidance. (In a previous stage of the litigation, the court had held that CIPA itself did not apply to the case; the provision most nearly applicable, § 4, concerns deletion of classified information from *documents* to be turned over to the defendant during discovery.) Under CIPA, dismissal would be appropriate "only if the government failed to provide an adequate substitute for the classified information, and the interests of justice would not be served by imposition of a lesser sanction." Further, "a substitution is an appropriate remedy when it will not materially disadvantage the defendant." The district court had concluded that the texts provided Moussaoui were an inadequate substitute. The court of appeals agreed that as they stood they were not adequate, but unlike the district court it concluded that the problems were remediable. The court of appeals asserted that those who had taken statements from the witnesses

> have a profound interest in obtaining accurate information from the witnesses and in reporting that information accurately to those who can use it to prevent acts of terrorism and to capture other al Qaeda operatives. These considerations provide sufficient indicia of reliability to alleviate the concerns of the district court.

The court of appeals concluded that the jury should be informed about the process by which the texts provided to it were created. Apparently (though it is difficult to be certain from the redacted opinion), it indicated that the witnesses' exact language should be used "to the greatest extent possible" in compiling those texts, and it called for "an interactive process among the parties and the district court," under which the defense would indicate the portions it wished to be admitted and the Government could then object or argue that additional portions should be included in the interests of completeness. Moussaoui asserted that allowing the government to include additional portions would result in inculpatory information being presented to the jury, in violation of his right to be confronted with adverse witnesses. The court, after discussing two (redacted) illustrations of how the completeness determination should be made, declared that the rule of completeness "is not to be used by the Government as a means of seeking the admission of inculpatory statements that neither explain nor clarify the statements designated by Moussaoui" but also advised that the defendant's ability to propose substitutions "is not a license to mislead the jury."

See California Evidence Code §§ 1041–1042.

HYPOTHETICALS

(1) D is charged with committing battery against PO, a police officer. D makes a pretrial discovery motion to have the prosecution obtain from the Police Department its personnel or disciplinary record file on PO for inspection and copying by D. D asserts in his motion that his defense will be self-defense in response to the use of excessive force by PO. D's motion is supported by affidavits setting forth (a) that two named persons who had filed complaints against PO for use of excessive force are unavailable for interview by D and that these persons' prior statements to police investigators are necessary for D's effective cross-examination of PO at trial; (b) that two other named persons had previously reported misconduct on the part of PO and are available as wit-

nesses but are unable to recall the details of the events and that the Police Department's files are necessary to refresh their recollection. The prosecutor claims the official information privilege as the person authorized by the Police Department to assert the privilege in opposition to D's motion. The trial judge makes an in camera inspection of the file in question and finds that the file does contain allegations by the four persons as set forth in D's affidavits. The trial judge then overrules the prosecutor's claim of privilege on the ground that the public-interest necessity for preserving the confidentiality of the information sought by D does not outweigh D's need for disclosure of the information to aid his defense in the interest of justice. Is this ruling of the trial judge correct?

(2) P sues D for damages for injuries received in an automobile accident on December 31, 2011. P alleges in her complaint that she lost a year's income of $100,000 for the year 2012, the year she was unable to work as a result of the accident. By a pretrial discovery motion, D seeks to inspect and copy P's copies of her federal and state income tax returns for the years 2010 and 2011, before the accident, and for 2012, the year after the accident. P resists D's motion on the ground of the official-information privilege. What result?

(3) A sues X for damages for injuries received in a collision between A's car and X's car. Shortly after the accident, A filed a claim for state disability-insurance benefits. The State Office for Disability Insurance Claims requests Dr. B to examine A for his ability or inability to work, and to make a confidential report to the state office. Dr. B examines A and sends his report to the state office. X takes Dr. B's deposition and has the state office served with a subpoena *duces tecum* to produce Dr. B's report at the deposition examination. A gives a written consent for the state office to disclose Dr. B's report to X. At the deposition examination, the state office claims an absolute privilege for nondisclosure. X seeks a court order to compel the state office to disclose Dr. B's report. How should the court rule?

(4) X is prosecuted for possession of heroin. At a pretrial hearing on X's motion to suppress, A, a police officer, testifies that he received a telephone call from a reliable informer who told him that X was selling heroin from her apartment and that she kept it in a telephone jack on the south wall of the bedroom; and that A then proceeded to X's apartment, without a warrant, found the heroin in the telephone jack and arrested X in the apartment. On cross-examination, A testifies that he did not learn from the informer whether he had ever been in X's apartment or in what way he obtained his information about the heroin location. X demands disclosure of the informer's identity, on the ground that there is the possibility that the informer could testify that another person put the heroin in the telephone jack, which would exonerate X of the heroin-possession charge. The prosecutor asserts the privilege for nondisclosure. Should the prosecutor's claim of privilege be sustained?

(5) "X" is prosecuted for the sale of heroin. At the preliminary hearing, A, a police officer, testifies that he gave an informer a ten-dollar bill dusted with fluorescent powder, that he watched the informer go into an apartment and later come out with a bindle of heroin, that A then knocked on the apartment door, that X opened the door and was placed under arrest, and that X had traces of fluorescent powder on his hands. In cross-examination of A, X asks the name of the informer. A claims the identity-of-informer privilege. What result?

CHAPTER 7

WRITINGS

PART **A** The Best Evidence Rule

PART **B** Authentication

A. THE BEST EVIDENCE RULE

McCormick, Evidence
409, 411–12 (1954).[*]

The specific tenor of [the best evidence rule] needs to be definitely stated and its limits clearly understood. The rule is this: in proving the terms of a writing, where such terms are material, the original writing must be produced, unless it is shown to be unavailable for some reason other than the serious fault of the proponent.

* * *

A rule which permitted the judge to insist that all evidence must pass his scrutiny as the "best" or most reliable means of proving the fact would be a sore incumbrance upon the parties, who in our system have the responsibility of proof. In fact, * * * no such general scrutiny is sanctioned, but only as to "writings" is a demand for the "best," the original, made. Accordingly, as to objects bearing no writing, the judge (unless in some exceptional cases when the exact features of the object have become as essential to the issue, as the precise words of a writing usually are) may not exclude oral testimony describing the object and demand that the object itself be produced. * * * If, however, the object, such as a policeman's badge, a revolver, an engagement ring, or a tombstone, bears a number or inscription the terms of which are relevant, we face the question, shall we treat it as a chattel or as a "writing"? Probably most modern cases would support the view advocated by Wigmore, that the judge shall have discretion, to follow the one analogy or the other in the light of such factors as the need for precise information as to the exact inscription, the ease or difficulty of production, and the simplicity or complexity of the inscription.

Meyers v. United States

United States Court of Appeals, District of Columbia, 1948.
84 U.S.App.D.C. 101, 171 F.2d 800,
cert. denied 336 U.S. 912, 69 S.Ct. 602, 93 L.Ed. 1076.

[This was a prosecution for subornation of perjury. At trial the prosecution sought to establish the content of one Lamarre's testimony before a United States Senate subcommittee. William P. Rogers, chief counsel to the committee (later Attorney General under President Eisenhower and Secretary of State under President Nixon), examined Lamarre before the subcommittee. The trial court allowed Rogers to testify as to the contents of Lamarre's testimony. Later, the Government introduced a stenographic transcript of that testimony.]

■ WILBUR K. MILLER, CIRCUIT JUDGE. * * * As applied generally in federal courts, the [best evidence] rule is limited to cases where the contents of a writing are to be proved. Here there was no attempt to prove the contents of a writing; the issue was what Lamarre had said, not what the transcript contained. The transcript made from shorthand notes of his testimony was, to be sure, evidence of what he had said, but it was not the only admissible evidence concerning it. Rogers' testimony was equally competent, and was admissible whether given before or after the transcript was received in evidence. Statements alleged to be perjurious may be proved by any person who heard them, as well as by a reporter who recorded them in shorthand. * * *

Rogers was not asked what the transcript contained but what Lamarre's testimony had been. * * *

Affirmed.

■ PRETTYMAN, CIRCUIT JUDGE (dissenting). * * * I am of opinion, and quite ready to hold, that the rules of evidence * * * are outmoded and at variance with known fact, and that the courts ought to establish a new and correct rule. The rationale of the so-called "best evidence rule" requires that a party having available evidence which is relatively certain may not submit evidence which is far less certain.

* * * As between two observers of an event, the law will not accept the evidence of one and exclude that of the other, because the law cannot say which is more accurate. But as between a document itself and a description of it, the law accepts the former and excludes the latter, because the former is certain and the latter is subject to many frailties. So as between the recollection of the parties to a contract evidenced by a writing and the writing itself, the law rejects the former and accepts the latter. To be sure, the writing may be attacked for forgery, alteration or some such circumstance. But absent such impeachment, the writing is immutable evidence from the date of the event, whereas human recollection is subject to many infirmities and human recitation is subject to the vices of prejudice and interest. Presented with that choice, the law accepts the certain and rejects the uncertain. * * *

It may be remarked at this point that the transcript in the case at bar is a document, not challenged for inaccuracy or alteration. It possesses every characteristic which the most literal devotee of established rules of evidence could ascribe to written evidence of a contract as justification for preference of such writing over the recollection of the parties.

In my view, the court iterates an error when it says that the best evidence rule is limited to cases where the contents of a writing are to be proved. The purpose of offering in evidence a "written contract" is not to prove the contents of the writing. The writing is not the contract; it is merely evidence of the contract. The contract itself is the agreement between the parties. Statutes such as the statute of frauds do not provide that a contract be in writing; they provide that the contract be evidenced by a writing, or that a written memorandum of it be made. The writing is offered as evidence of an agreement, not for the purpose of proving its own contents.

* * * From the theoretical point of view, the case poses this question: Given both (1) an accurate stenographic transcription of a witness' testimony during a two-day hearing and (2) the recollection of one of the complainants as to the substance of that testimony, is the latter admissible as evidence in a trial of the witness for perjury? I think not. To say that it is, is to apply a meaningless formula and ignore crystal-clear actualities. The transcript is, as a matter of simple, indisputable fact, the best evidence.
* * *

People v. Enskat

Appellate Department, Superior Court, Los Angeles County, California, 1971.
20 Cal.App.3d Supp. 1, 98 Cal.Rptr. 646.

■ ZACK, JUDGE. [Enskat was tried on charges of exhibiting an obscene motion picture. The prosecution presented photos of portions of the motion picture and oral testimony describing it, but it did not offer the motion picture itself into evidence. The trial court overruled Enskat's objection based on the best evidence rule; he was convicted and appealed. The appellate court first noted that under California's version of the rule, Evidence Code section 1500, a photographic transparency is a "writing," and so too is a motion picture, which is a series of such pictures on a celluloid strip.] Each picture in each frame is slightly different from the preceding one, so that when the film is moved through a projector, these individual pictures appear to merge into a continuous "moving" picture. This movement is only an optical illusion, for in actuality each separate picture is projected onto the screen for a split second, rapidly followed by the next one. That there *appears* to be a "motion picture" does not alter the fact that a series of single pictures on the filmstrip, each one a "writing," is casting an image on a screen.

Respondent argues, however, that it is not the film, but these light images on the screen, that constitute the offense of exhibiting an obscene motion picture. Respondent argues that as this moving image is unrecorded, it cannot be a writing, and therefore is not subject to the best evidence rule. This argument ignores the essential fact that the moving image is merely the consequence of passing a writing (the film) through a machine. Without the projector and the filmstrip, no moving image is cast at all. The content of the moving image, "evanescent" or not, is totally dependent upon the content of the filmstrip. Just as it is better for the trier of fact to read a document than have it described, it is better for the trier of fact to see a movie than have it described. The policy considerations upholding the rule for written documents apply with full force to movies as well. It is to be noted that the instant prosecution under Penal Code section 311.2 is for exhibiting *obscene matter*. The latter is defined in section 311, subdivisions (a)(2), (b) to include a "motion picture." It is the character of the contents of the motion picture exhibited which, strictly speaking is in issue, not the character of the images on the screen resulting from its exhibition.

[The court noted that if the accused were in possession or control when the prosecution was brought, and if he was given timely notice to produce it at trial but failed to do so, the prosecution could introduce secondary evidence – but the prosecution bore, and failed to carry, the burden of demonstrating that these conditions were met.]

The judgment is reversed, and the cause remanded for a new trial.

■ WHYTE, P.J., AND KATZ, J., concur.

United States v. Diaz-Lopez

United States Court of Appeals for the Ninth Circuit, 2010.
625 F.3d 1198.

Before: DIARMUID F. O'SCANNLAIN, RONALD M. GOULD and MILAN D. SMITH, JR., Circuit Judges.

OPINION

GOULD, Circuit Judge:

At a bench trial, Luis Diaz-Lopez (Diaz) was convicted of being a removed alien found in the United States in violation of 8 U.S.C. § 1326(a). Diaz contends that the district court erred in admitting testimony about the results of a database search introduced to show that Diaz had no permission to return, urging theories that the testimony lacked foundation and that it violated the best evidence rule. * * *

I

Diaz was born in and is a citizen of Mexico. On February 13, 2009, a Border Patrol agent found and arrested Diaz on a road in California, north of the United States-Mexico border. The government charged Diaz under 8 U.S.C. § 1326(a) with being a removed alien found in the United States without permission. At a bench trial, the government introduced testimony from a Border Patrol agent stating that he had performed a search of the Computer Linked Application Information Management System (CLAIMS) database using Diaz's name, alien number, and date of birth, and had found no record of Diaz having filed a Form I-212, which is the required application for permission to reapply for admission to the United States after having been previously removed.

The district court found Diaz guilty and sentenced him to twenty-one months in prison and three years of supervised release. This appeal followed.

II

Diaz appeals the district court judge's decision to admit the Border Patrol agent's testimony about the database search. He contends that the testimony lacked foundation and that it violated Federal Rule of Evidence 1002 (the best evidence rule). We review the district court's decision to admit this testimony for abuse of discretion. *United States v. Hernandez,* 109 F.3d 1450, 1452 (9th Cir.1997).

We reject Diaz's claim that the agent's testimony lacked foundation. * * *

III

Diaz next argues that the agent's testimony regarding the results of the CLAIMS database search violated Federal Rule of Evidence 1002, which codifies a principle long referred to at common law as the best evidence rule. *See* Fed.R.Evid. 1001-1008. Diaz's assertion challenging the testimony under the best evidence rule presents a question of first impression in our circuit. We must decide if testimony that a search of a computer database revealed no record of a matter violates the best evidence rule when it is offered without the production of an original printout showing the search results. We hold that it does not.

As we previously have observed, the best evidence rule requires not, as its common name implies, the best evidence in every case but rather the production of an original document instead of a copy. *Seiler v. Lucasfilm, Ltd.,* 808 F.2d 1316, 1318 (9th Cir.1986). Federal Rule of Evidence 1002, on its face, is simple and clear in its statement: To prove the content of a writing, recording, or photograph, the original writing, recording, or photograph is required, except as otherwise provided in these rules or by Act of Congress. Fed.R.Evid. 1002. For purposes of this rule, [w]ritings' and recordings' consist of letters, words, or numbers, or their equivalent, set down by handwriting, typewriting, printing, photostating, photographing, magnetic impulse, mechanical or electronic recording, or other form of data compilation. Fed.R.Evid. 1001. But despite its simple name and concise definition, experience has shown that application of this principle, as with other difficult questions of the law of evidence, may not safely be handled in slapdash fashion. John MacArthur Maguire, *Evidence: Common Sense and Common Law,* at v (1947).

The scope, application, and relevance of the best evidence doctrine have been debated by treatise-writers for centuries. Professor Thayer thought it would help to clear the subject, and keep our heads clear, if we drop the name and the notion of any specific rule of the Best Evidence. James Bradley Thayer, *A Preliminary Treatise on Evidence at the Common Law* 507 (1898). A century later, however, the name is still with us. Although the best evidence doctrine in the federal courts has since been refined to encompass only the requirement for originals set out in the Federal Rules of Evidence (and in no way involves comparing evidence to determine which is the best), it has also been enlarged to include not just writings, but also recordings and photographs. The modern doctrine appears to be a rule of evolving scope (applying to ever-increasing varieties of media) with less-frequent application (owing to the easy availability of exact duplicates, modern discovery procedures, and exceptions to the federal version of the best evidence rule).

The animating purpose of the best evidence rule has been persuasively summarized as follows:

> [P]resenting to a court the exact words of a writing is of more than average importance, particularly in the case of operative or dispositive instruments such as deeds, wills or contracts, where a slight variation of words may mean a great difference in rights. In addition, it is to be considered (1) that there has been substantial hazard of inaccuracy in some of the commonly utilized methods of making copies of writings, and (2) oral testimony purporting to give the terms of a writing from memory is probably subject to a greater risk of error than oral testimony concerning other situations generally. The danger of mistransmitting critical facts which accompanies the use of written copies or recollection, but which is largely avoided when an original writing is presented to prove its terms, justifies preference for original documents.

2 George E. Dix et al., *McCormick on Evidence* § 232 (Kenneth S. Broun, ed., 6th ed. 2009). Professor Wigmore offered a similar explanation of the fundamental notion of the best evidence rule:

> [I]n writings the smallest variation in words may be of importance... Thus the rule applies only to the *terms of the document,* and not to any *other facts about the document.* In other words, the rule ... does not apply to exclude testimony which concerns the document without aiming to establish its terms...

4 John Henry Wigmore, *Evidence in Trials at Common Law,* § 1242 at 574 (James H. Chadbourn rev. 1972).

We turn now to the issue presented by Diaz on this appeal. Diaz contends that, under Federal Rule of Evidence 1002, the government was required to produce an original to show that the CLAIMS database did not contain any record of Diaz having filed an I-212. When records or data are stored in a computer or similar device, any printout or other output readable by sight, shown to reflect the data accurately, is an original. Fed.R.Evid. 1001(3). Diaz argues that the government should have introduced a printout of the search results from the CLAIMS database rather than testimony from the agent performing the search.

Diaz is correct that the CLAIMS database falls within the scope of the best evidence rule, because the database is a "[w]riting[ ] or recording[ ] . . . set down by . . . magnetic impulse . . . or electronic recording, or other form of data compilation." Fed.R.Evid. 1001. The next question is whether the evidence was introduced [t]o prove the content of a writing, recording, or photograph. Fed.R.Evid. 1002. We conclude that it was not. The agent's testimony that he searched the database and found no record of Diaz having filed an I-212 is similar to testimony that an event did *not* occur because relevant records contain no mention of it. This negative type of testimony is usually held not to constitute proof of contents and thus not to require production of records. Dix et al., *supra,* at § 234 (emphasis in original). Indeed, the advisory committee's note to Rule 1002 states that the best evidence rule does not apply to testimony that books or records have been examined and found not to contain any reference to a designated matter. Fed.R.Evid. 1002, advisory committee's note.[2]

Diaz concedes that if no record were found pursuant to an agent's physical search of an A-file, testimony to that effect would be admissible under Federal Rule of Evidence 1002. However, Diaz asserts that, although the Rule applies to computer databases, the advisory committee note's limitation on the Rule applies only to searches of physical records. We decline to adopt such a position. First, we do not see any meaningful difference between a search of a physical file and a search of a database. Databases contain physical records, too, even if those records are not printed on paper. Second, the best evidence rule, like us, now survives in the twenty-first century. It is common sense, and not mere symmetry, to say that because the rule applies to computer databases, the rule's limitations must also apply to such databases. It is reasonable to apply the best evidence rule to new circumstances as technology evolves, but when the rule is extended, courts will necessarily be required to decide if the limits on the rule extend as well. When, by virtue of new technology, the best evidence rule can be applied to testimony about databases, the traditional limits on the rule should be properly extended as well.

Our decision here does not conflict with our holding in *United States v. Bennett,* 363 F.3d 947 (9th Cir.2004). There, we held that testimony about data retrieved from a boat's global positioning system (GPS) was barred by the best evidence rule because the testimony had been introduced to prove

---

[2] We have not passed explicitly on this issue, but other jurisdictions are in accord. *See* . . . *Allen v. Wells Fargo Bank Minn., N.A.,* 334 B.R. 746, 750 n. 7 (D.D.C.2005) (holding that the best evidence rule did not apply to testimony that voicemail logs did not contain a record of a message).

the content of the GPS, which, in turn, was evidence that the defendant had come from Mexico. But *Bennett* concerned testimony about the *contents* of the GPS data, not testimony about the *absence* of data. In that case, we concluded that "the GPS itself—or a printout or other representation of such data—. . . would have been the best evidence of the data showing [the defendant's] travels." *Id.* at 954 (citations omitted). We reached that decision because the testimony about the GPS data was introduced to prove its content (i.e., the location and travels of a boat). In Diaz's case, the government did not introduce testimony to prove the content of a writing; rather, the government introduced testimony to prove that a particular record was *not* part of the contents of a database. Moreover, the testimony about the search of the database was not testimony in which the smallest variation in words may be of importance. Wigmore, *supra; see also State v. Nano,* 273 Or. 366, 543 P.2d 660, 662 (1975) ("In the present case the witness testified to what the document did not contain; that is, the sales records did not show any sales of the calculators. . . [T]his is not testimony in which 'the smallest variation in words may be of importance.'" (quoting Wigmore, *supra*)).

It might be contended that, while "the smallest variation in words" is not of importance in the case of testimony regarding the negative results of a database search, such variations may well be significant if the testimony is offered to prove what particular search terms were used to search a database. However, even if Diaz had raised this argument, it would not aid his case. Any dispute about the particular search terms used by the agent for searching the CLAIMS database is not a dispute about the contents of the database, or about the contents of any records in the database, but rather a dispute about the specific actions performed by the agent. As a result, the best evidence rule would not apply because it applies only to writings, recordings, and photographs (as defined by Federal Rule of Evidence 1001), and not to actions. Moreover, even if the search terms used to search the database were genuinely in dispute, Diaz was free to cross-examine the agent who performed the search. Any doubts that might be raised by Diaz regarding the completeness of the search or the search terms used are a proper subject for a reasonable cross-examination, and go to the weight accorded to the testimony, not its admissibility under the best evidence rule. * * *

AFFIRMED.

Dale A. Nance, The Best Evidence Principle

73 Iowa L. Rev. 227 (1988)*

The first therefore, and most signal Rule, in relation to Evidence, is this, That a Man must have the utmost Evidence, the Nature of the Fact is capable of; For the Design of the Law is to come to rigid Demonstration in

---

Matters of Right, and there can be no Demonstration of a Fact without the best Evidence that the Nature of the Thing is capable of; less Evidence doth create but Opinion and Surmise, and does not leave a Man the entire Satisfaction, that arises from Demonstration.

—Chief Baron Geoffrey Gilbert (c.1726)[1]

* * * This Article runs against the tide, for my thesis is that there exists, even today, a principle of evidence law that a party should present to the tribunal the best evidence reasonably available on a litigated factual issue. This principle is not absolute, and in particular circumstances other considerations may override it or excuse its nonsatisfaction. Nevertheless, it is a general principle that manifests itself in a wide variety of concrete rules governing the trial process. In fact, it provides an organizing principle within the law of evidence. * * *

[T]his Article demonstrates that, putting aside the rules, such as those governing privileges, which are said to serve extrinsic social policies, the remaining evidentiary rules are more plausibly attributable to the epistemic concerns of a tribunal encountering the adversarial presentation of evidence than to judicial concerns about the irrational behavior of weak-minded lay jurors. This point coheres well with recent historical scholarship arguing that the modern rules of evidence were instituted primarily for the control of lawyers rather than for the control of juries.[12] Relatedly, our investigation undercuts at least one of the principal arguments for employing evidentiary rules in bench trials that are different from those applicable in jury trials. These arguments often proceed from the premise that the conventional rules are based upon a distrust of the trier of fact which, it is thought, is inappropriate when trial is to the judge. A theory of such rules that does not depend upon distrust of the jury would find confirmation in the long-prevailing principle that those rules apply in bench trials as well. * * *

The subtlety with which the best evidence principle often operates in the modern adversary process is exemplified by the case of *Linkhart v. Savely*[51] Defendant appealed a judgment in favor of the plaintiff on an assault and battery claim. The Supreme Court of Oregon reviewed, *inter alia*, the plaintiff's testimony that his eyesight was impaired by the attack, testimony that was not supported by any medical evidence. The court held that admission of the plaintiff's testimony on this point was error because the plaintiff failed to plead injury to his eyesight as an item of special damages. The decision thus appears to be based simply upon fairness to the defendant, a concern reflected in the state's pleading requirements and

---

[1] G. GILBERT, THE LAW OF EVIDENCE 3 4 (1st ed. 1754). [Note: Gilbert actually wrote the treatise, it appears, before 1710; he died in 1726, but it was not published until 1754. Eds.]

[12] See Langbein, The Criminal Trial Before the Lawyers, 45 U. CHI. L. REV. 263, 300 06 (1978); see also Langbein, Shaping the Eighteenth-Century Criminal Trial: A View from the Ryder Sources, 50 U. CHI. L. REV. 1, 123 34 (1983).

[51] 190 Or. 484, 227 P.2d 187 (1951).

their consequences in limiting materiality. The defendant was presumed unable to present adequate rebuttal evidence because of a lack of notice.

However, the court's application of the concept of special damages was questionable, for the defendant certainly had notice of plaintiff's claim of physical injuries adequate to allow defendant to identify during pretrial aspects of injury upon which evidence would be needed. The court hinted at the more important rationale by conspicuously taking judicial notice of the existence of 'accurate and scientific' tests for the impairment of eyesight. Such potential evidence, not presented by the plaintiff, is the kind of evidence to which the plaintiff would ordinarily be expected to have ready access as a consequence of medical diagnosis and treatment. This fact was apparently crucial, notwithstanding the argument that plaintiff's failure was harmless because the defendant had reasonable opportunity to acquire and introduce such evidence. The court's concern to be presented the best reasonably available evidence lies just beneath the surface of the decision.

A more recent case shows this concern penetrating the surface. In *People v. Park*,[55] the defendant appealed an unlawful possession conviction that was based principally upon a deputy sheriff's testimony, and the defendant's alleged oral confession, that the possessed substance was marijuana. The Supreme Court of Illinois held that the sheriff's testimony, based upon his supposed familiarity with 'marijuana's feel, smell, texture, and looks,' did not qualify as expert opinion. The court further held that without the sheriff's testimony there was insufficient evidence to support the conviction, a holding pointedly supported by judicially noticing the existence of highly reliable and readily available tests for the presence of cannabis. The court did not mention the possibility that the defendant could have acquired and presented such evidence.

As *Park* suggests, the best evidence obligation is an aspect of the due process of law that is constitutionally guaranteed to every person before being governmentally deprived of life, liberty, or property. While failure to present the best reasonably available package of evidence does not per se deprive the opponent of a fair trial, on occasion the circumstances may combine to give constitutional significance to a breach of the best evidence obligation. The most conspicuous example is the well-recognized obligation of the prosecution in criminal cases not knowingly to deceive the trier of fact or to allow its witnesses to attempt such deception by false testimony. In the various decisions that fill out this obligation, the prosecution was found to have been aware of the existence of highly probative evidence that it failed to present to the tribunal.

These examples of the best evidence principle at work, and the many others to be discussed, constitute a response to the weaknesses inherent in the adversary process and the incentives it creates for litigants. The argument presented here is that we should recognize them as such and appreciate the force of the principle they represent. Acceptance of this argument does not necessarily mean a dramatic change in the adversary process, let

---

[55] 72 Ill. 2d 203, 380 N.E.2d 795 (1978).

alone its wholesale rejection. To those who are inclined to see in the present thesis the specter of judicial control over fact gathering and the presentation of evidence, the simple response is that existing rules, whether or not based upon a best evidence principle, *do* interfere with litigant autonomy in the conduct of litigation, and many do so for best evidence reasons. The choice, therefore, is not accurately portrayed as one between complete litigant control and complete judicial control. There are many points along the spectrum between these extremes, and the law has settled, and moved and settled again many times, at some intermediate points. * * *

QUESTION

To what extent do you think the following rules reflect the best evidence principle as advocated by Nance?

(a) The rule prohibiting a lay witness from testifying about a matter absent proof that the witness has personal knowledge about the matter.

(b) The rule generally prohibiting the use of leading questions on direct examination. Fed. R. Evid. 611(c).

(c) The rule limiting lay witnesses' testimony in the form of opinions or inferences. Fed. R. Evid. 701.

(d) The rule against hearsay.

See Federal Rules of Evidence 1001–08; Chapter 1, pp. 70–71.

B. AUTHENTICATION

McCormick, Evidence
395–96 (1954).*

One who seeks to introduce evidence of a particular fact, or item of proof, must generally give evidence (or offer assurance that he will do so) of those circumstances which make this fact or item relevant to some issue in the case. In respect to writings one of the commonest and most obvious of these circumstances on which relevancy may depend is the *authorship* of the writing. By whom was it written, signed or adopted? Certainly any intelligible system of procedure must require that if the legal significance of the writing depends upon its authorship by a particular person, some showing must be made that he was the author, if the writing is to be accepted for consideration. The question is, what showing? In the everyday affairs of business and social life, the practice is to look first to the writing itself and if it bears the purported signature of X, or recites that it was made by him,

---

we assume if no question of authenticity is raised that the writing is what it purports to be, that is, the writing of X.

It is just here that the common law trial procedure departs sharply from men's customs in ordinary affairs, and adopts the opposite attitude, namely, that the purported signature or the recitation of authorship on the face of the writing will not be accepted as sufficient preliminary proof of authenticity to secure the admission of the writing in evidence. * * *

The term authentication is here used in the limited sense of proof of authorship. It is sometimes employed in a wider meaning, embracing all proof which may be required as a preliminary to the admission of a writing, chattel, photograph or the like. Thus in the case of business records not only is proof of authorship required for admission, but at common law various other facts such as that they were made in the course of the business must also be proved as part of the "foundation." Similarly the identity of a bullet offered in a murder case as the fatal bullet, or the correctness of a photograph would be part of the necessary foundation-proof for admission. * * *

United States v. Dockins

United States Court of Appeals, Fifth Circuit, 1993.
986 F.2d 888.

■ PATRICK E. HIGGINBOTHAM, CIRCUIT JUDGE:

* * *

III.

Dockins argues that the evidence was insufficient to support his convictions for illegal possession of a firearm by a convicted felon, 18 U.S.C. § 922(g)(1), and knowingly making false statements during the purchase of a firearm, 18 U.S.C. § 922(a)(6). Specifically, he argues the government failed to introduce any competent evidence of his status as a convicted felon, which was necessary to establish both offenses.

Without objection, the government introduced Exhibit 5, a judgment of conviction of Carl Tyron Smith on robbery charges in Colorado. The government attempted to link Dockins to this conviction through Exhibit 5a, a fingerprint card and police record sheet reflecting the arrest and conviction of Carl Smith. On its face, Exhibit 5a includes two official Denver Police Department documents. Agent Medley testified that he sent Exhibit 5a, along with handwriting exemplars, the original copy of the Form 4473, and a number of fingerprint cards, to the ATF Crime Laboratory. Medley said that Exhibit 5a included a fingerprint card from the Denver Police Department. Nancy Davis, a document examiner, testified that the signature of Carl Smith on the fingerprint card was written by Dockins. Next, the government called Rick Canty, a fingerprint expert, who testified that the fingerprints in Exhibit 5a matched the known fingerprints of Dockins. With Canty on the stand, the government offered Exhibit 5a into evidence. The court admitted the evidence over Dockins' objection on grounds of authentication.

After trial, Dockins moved for a Judgment of Acquittal Notwithstanding the Verdict or in the Alternative for a New Trial, claiming that Exhibits 5 and 5a had not been properly authenticated.[3] The court held a hearing on the authenticity of these two exhibits. Laurence Jantz, an officer of the Denver Police Department, testified that the documents in Exhibit 5a were exact copies of the records in his file. The court ruled that Exhibit 5 was properly admitted, because Dockins did not object. As to Exhibit 5a, the court ruled that it was not a self-authenticating document under Rule 902. Neither the fingerprint card nor the police record sheet is under seal and no public officer of the Denver Police Department certified under seal that the signature is genuine; the certification on the fingerprint card is only a rubber stamp. See Fed.R.Evid. 902(2), (4). The court, without relying on the testimony of Jantz, nevertheless found this exhibit to be admissible under Rule 901.

The parties agree that the documents comprising Exhibit 5a are not self-authenticating. Admissibility turns on Rule 901.[4] We do not require conclusive proof of authenticity, and Rule 901's list of illustrations is not exclusive.[5] The issue is whether the district court abused its discretion in finding that the government presented sufficient evidence *at trial* to support a finding that Exhibit 5a contained official Denver Police Department documents. We hold that it was an abuse of discretion to admit these documents.

Agent Medley testified that Exhibit 5a contained a fingerprint card from the Denver Police Department. However, he was simply testifying as to what appears on the face of the document. He had no knowledge, other than from reading the document, that the fingerprint card actually came from the Denver Police Department.[6] Furthermore, Davis and Canty simply compared the signature and fingerprints contained in Exhibit 5a with known samples from Dockins. Their testimony had nothing to do with whether these documents came from the Denver Police Department.

Our decision in [*United States v.*] *Jimenez Lopez* [873 F.2d 769, 772 (5th Cir.1989)] is instructive. That case also required proof of a prior conviction. The government offered a copy of the Record of Proceedings and Judgment asserted to be from the office of a United States Magistrate for

---

[3] Dockins also argued that these documents contained inadmissible hearsay; however, Dockins did not object on this ground at trial. Authentication is the only question before us.

[4] Rule 901. Requirement of Authentication or Identification

(a) General provision

The requirement of authentication or identification as a condition precedent to admissibility is satisfied by evidence sufficient to support a finding that the matter in question is what its proponent claims.

* * *

[5] None of the illustrations in 901(b) apply to this case.

[6] 901(b)(1) also does not apply for this reason.

the Southern District of California. Like this case, the document was not self-authenticating.[7] A border patrol agent, Johnston, testified that he personally requested the document and received it from a California border patrol agent who Johnston said procured it from the magistrate's court. In finding the document to have been properly admitted, we said,

> Without the testimony of Agent Johnston the admissibility of the document would have been doubtful. But Johnston's testimony as to the chain of custody of the photostatic copy combined with the internal indicia of reliability within the document itself justified the conclusion of the court that the document was admissible to prove its contents. Johnston was not testifying as custodian of the document. Rather, his testimony provided circumstantial evidence to support the conclusion that the document was an official record.

Medley was certainly not the custodian. Jantz was the custodian, but he did not testify at trial.[8] The government offered no circumstantial evidence at trial to support a finding that Exhibit 5a came from the Denver Police Department. Consequently, there was no basis for a reasonable jury to conclude that these documents were what they purported to be.

[In the final part of its opinion, the Court of Appeals deemed the admission of the evidence to be harmless error, on grounds that evidence other than exhibit 5(a) proved beyond a reasonable doubt that Dockins had a prior felony conviction]

■ Affirmed.

United States v. Hampton
United States Court of Appeals for the Seventh Circuit, 2006.
464 F.3d 687.

■ POSNER, CIRCUIT JUDGE.

[Hampton was a serial bank robber. An element of the crime was that the banks were federally insured at the time of the robberies. To prove this point, the Government relied in part on the testimony of bank employees and in part on photocopies purporting to be the certificates of insurance that the Federal Deposit Insurance Corporation had issued to the banks. The trial judge admitted this evidence, and defendant was convicted. On appeal, Judge Posner first decided that the photocopies were not self-authenticating as sealed documents under FRE 902(1): "[N]o seal was stamped on the copies. The copies were copies of sealed documents rather than sealed documents themselves. The rationale of Rule 902(1), according to the Committee Notes, is that a seal is difficult to forge. But that is not true of a copy of a seal—or at least the government has made no effort to show that the authenticity of the seal can be inferred with confidence from its copy." Judge Posner continued:]

---

[7] A signature on the document was illegible.

[8] If Jantz had testified at trial, Exhibit 5a would have been admissible under 901(b)(7).

Another federal rule of evidence, however, Rule 1005, provides that copies of public records are admissible if either a witness testifies that he compared the copy with the original and determined the copy to be accurate, or, in accordance with Rule 902(4), either the custodian of the original record, or someone else authorized to certify the accuracy of copies of it, certifies that it is an accurate copy. Some though not all of the bank employees testified that the photocopy the prosecutor showed them during their direct examination at trial was a copy of the certificate hanging on the wall of the bank, but there is no indication that that certificate was not itself a copy. One of these witnesses testified that the certificate was posted throughout his bank. Were those all originals? Does the FDIC issue multiple certificates for each branch office of an insured bank? There is no evidence bearing on the issue, and the government does not ask us to take judicial notice of the Corporation's practice.

Nevertheless we think the copies were admissible to establish the insured status of the banks as of the dates shown on the copies. The parties have managed to overlook provisions of the Federal Rules of Evidence which show that Rules 902(1), (4), and 1005 are not intended as straitjackets. Article IX of the rules deals with authentication and there we read that "the requirement of authentication or identification as a condition precedent to admissibility is satisfied by evidence sufficient to support a finding that the matter in question is what the proponent claims." Fed.R.Evid. 901(a). And in Article X, which deals with the admissibility of the contents of documents, we read that "a duplicate is admissible to the same extent as an original unless (1) a genuine question is raised as to the authenticity of the original or (2) in the circumstances it would be unfair to admit the duplicate in lieu of the original." Fed.R.Evid. 1003. And a photocopy (or equivalent chemical or electronic copy) is a "duplicate" within the meaning of the rule. Fed.R.Evid. 1001(4). These rules make clear that the principle enunciated in an 1807 case cited to us by the defendant that "authentication must not rest upon probability," *United States v. Burr,* 25 Fed. Cases 27, 28 (Cir.Ct.D.Va.1807), is no longer the law, even if it was said by Chief Justice Marshall in the treason trial of Aaron Burr.

The bank employees may conceivably have been mistaken about the insured status of their banks. But they all testified that they recognized the copies shown them by the prosecutor as copies of the certificates possessed by or posted in their banks, which is pretty compelling evidence that the copies were not forgeries prepared by or for, or somehow obtained by, the government. As between the parties' rival hypotheses—that the copies are genuine, as the government contends, and that they are forgeries, as the defendant contends—the defendant's hypothesis is so improbable that without some evidence to support the hypothesis no reasonable person would accept it. No such evidence was offered.

So we think the copies were admissible, and this kills the appeal. But the government would be wise in future cases to prove insured status more directly and conclusively than was done in this case, either by getting an affidavit from the FDIC confirming the insured status of the robbed bank, or by offering testimony by the bank employee who is the actual authorized custodian of the bank's FDIC certificate. The government was sloppy in this case, as in many others in which federally insured status is an element of the crime, probably because the matter is usually stipulated. But sloppiness is not a ground for reversal of a judgment.

Affirmed.

NOTE

In Keegan v. Green Giant Co., 150 Me. 283, 110 A.2d 599 (1954), plaintiff complained of injury produced by a piece of metal which had allegedly been included in a can of peas. To establish that the named defendant was the packer and distributor of the offending peas, plaintiff offered the metal can and the label surrounding it. The label read in part, "Green Giant Brand Great Big Tender Sweet Peas. Distributed by Green Giant Company." The Court held that exclusion of the exhibit was not error since the label had not been authenticated.

First State Bank of Denton v. Maryland Casualty Co.

United States Court of Appeals, Fifth Circuit, 1990.
918 F.2d 38.

■ JERRY E. SMITH, CIRCUIT JUDGE:

The plaintiff, First State Bank of Denton, acting as executor of the will of J.T. Mills, appeals from a jury verdict finding that a fire at the Millses' home was set intentionally. The plaintiff contends that the district court erred by allowing defendant Maryland Casualty Company (the "insurance company") to introduce a telephone conversation that occurred between a police dispatcher and an unknown male at the Mills' home. * * * Finding no reversible error, we affirm.

I.

The parties agree on the basic facts. The Millses' residence, which was insured by the Maryland Casualty Company, was completely destroyed by fire. Pursuant to Texas law, the policy provided that in case of total loss, Mills would receive $133,000, the entire face amount of the policy. After inspecting the site, however, the insurance company concluded that the fire was set intentionally and thus refused to make any payment on the policy.

The Millses brought suit to recover on their policy, but both of them died before the trial. The First State Bank of Denton continued the claim as executor. At trial, the insurance company introduced evidence showing that the Millses' house was unoccupied for several weeks prior to the fire but that a neighbor had seen a light in the home a few hours before the flames struck. The company also introduced the testimony of a witness who, right before the fire started, saw a pickup truck leaving the road which accesses the residence. Only Mills and his wife had a key to the house, and Mills owned a pickup truck.

The insurance company also showed that Mills was in financial trouble, as he had bought a second home before he had sold his first. For two years, Mills had attempted to sell his first home, but it had enkindled little interest; because of poor market conditions, the value of the home now was significantly less than the face value of the Millses' policy.

The company concluded by introducing evidence showing that Mills was not at his new home at the time of the fire. About fifteen minutes after the fire began, a police dispatcher attempted to contact Mills at his new residence to notify him of the fire. The dispatcher testified that when she called Mills there, at 1:00 a.m., an unidentified person replied that Mr. Mills was not home. Denton objected, believing this testimony to be unauthenticated and hearsay. The trial court allowed the insurance company to introduce the evidence. * * *

Fed.R.Evid. 901 provides that all evidence must be authenticated before being admitted and that this requirement is satisfied by evidence reliable enough to show that it is what its proponent claims it to be. The rule provides a laundry list of examples of proper authentication. Rule 901(b)(6) provides that authentication can occur for a

> [t]elephone conversation[ ], by evidence that a call was made to the number assigned at the time by the telephone company to a particular person or business, if (A) in the case of a person, circumstances, including self-identification, show the person answering to be the one called, or (B) in the case of a business, the call was made to a place of business and the conversation related to business reasonably transacted over the telephone.

The illustrations contained in rule 901(b) also provide that they only are examples and do not exhaust all possibilities.

Under the plain language of rule 901(b)(6), when a person places a call to a listed number, and the answering party identifies himself as the expected party, the call is properly authenticated. What is different about the present case is that the person who answered the phone did not identify himself as Mr. Mills; rather, he simply identified the residence as "the Millses' residence." The plaintiff contends that this does not fit within the illustration and that the phone call thus was unauthenticated.

What plaintiff ignores is that the illustrations are not exclusive, but are intended only to provide clear examples of properly authenticated evidence. All that is necessary in authenticating a phone call is that the proponent offer "sufficient authentication to make a *prima facie* case that would allow the issue of identity to be decided by the jury." *United States v. Register,* 496 F.2d 1072, 1077 (5th Cir.1974), *cert. denied,* 419 U.S. 1120, 95 S.Ct. 802, 42 L.Ed.2d 819 (1975).

The plaintiff's position, in demanding that the person answering the phone himself be the defendant, implicitly treats the authentication requirement as requiring an admission by a party opponent. This ignores the true reason for requiring the self-identification: The primary authentication occurs because the phone company usually is accurate. "The calling of a number assigned by the telephone company reasonably supports the assumption that the listing is correct and that the number is the one reached." Rule 901, advisory committee note example (6).

The self-identification supports this maxim by showing that the correct number was dialed. "In such a situation the accuracy of the telephone system, the probable absence of motive to falsify and the lack of opportunity for premeditated fraud all tend to support the conclusion that the self-identification of the speaker is reliable." E. Cleary, McCormick on Evidence § 226 at 698 (3d ed. 1984); accord Register, 496 F.2d at 1076–77.

The evidence in this case meets the *prima facie* standard established in *Register*. The dispatcher who called the Millses' residence on the night of the fire testified that she correctly dialed the Millses' number and that when she asked whether she had reached the Millses' residence, the person replied that "[t]his is the Millses' residence." Furthermore, when she asked whether Mr. Mills was home, the person answered, "J.T. Mills is not at home." * * *

There is little doubt that the dispatcher actually reached Mills's home. The trial court thus did not abuse its discretion by overruling the authentication objection. * * *

NOTE

See Federal Rules of Evidence 901–903; California Evidence Code §§ 1400–1402 and 1410–1421. For additional discussion of procedures for authentication of writings, see Chapter I, Making the Record, supra.

HYPOTHETICAL

A sues X for damages for personal injuries suffered in a two-car collision. A testifies that X ran a red light. A produces a letter addressed to him and bearing a signature, "X," which states that X ran the red light. A testifies that he received this letter through the mail about a week after the accident. A offers the letter in evidence. X makes a lack-of-authentication objection. What result?

Griffin v. State

Court of Appeals of Maryland, 2011.
419 Md. 343, 19 A.3d 415.

BATTAGLIA, J.

In this case, we are tasked with determining the appropriate way to authenticate, for evidential purposes, electronically stored information printed from a social networking website, in particular, MySpace.

Antoine Levar Griffin, Petitioner, seeks reversal of his convictions in the Circuit Court for Cecil County, contending that the trial judge abused his discretion in admitting, without proper authentication, what the State alleged were several pages printed from Griffin's girlfriend's MySpace profile.[9] The Court of Special Appeals determined that the trial judge did not abuse his discretion, and we granted Griffin's Petition for Writ of Certiorari * * * *

We shall hold that the pages allegedly printed from Griffin's girlfriend's MySpace profile were not properly authenticated pursuant to Maryland Rule 5–901 and shall, therefore, reverse the judgment of the Court of Special Appeals and remand the case for a new trial.

Griffin was charged in numerous counts with the shooting death, on April 24, 2005, of Darvell Guest at Ferrari's Bar in Perryville, in Cecil County. During his trial, the State sought to introduce Griffin's girlfriend's, Jessica Barber's, MySpace profile to demonstrate that, prior to trial, Ms. Barber had allegedly threatened another witness called by the State. The printed pages contained a MySpace profile in the name of "Sistasouljah," describing a 23 year-old female from Port Deposit, listing her birthday as "10/02/1983" and containing a photograph of an embracing couple. The printed pages also contained the following blurb:

FREE BOOZY!!!! JUST REMEMBER SNITCHES GET STITCHES!! U KNOW WHO YOU ARE!!

When Ms. Barber had taken the stand after being called by the State, she was not questioned about the pages allegedly printed from her MySpace profile.

Instead, the State attempted to authenticate the pages, as belonging to Ms. Barber, through the testimony of Sergeant John Cook, the lead investigator in the case. Defense counsel objected to the admission of the pages allegedly printed from Ms. Barber's MySpace profile, because the State could not sufficiently establish a "connection" between the profile and posting and Ms. Barber, and substantively, the State could not say with any certainty that the purported "threat" had any impact on the witness's testimony; the latter argument is not before us. * * *

The trial judge, thereafter, indicated that he would permit Sergeant Cook to testify in support of authentication of the redacted portion of the pages printed from MySpace, containing the photograph "of a person that looks like Jessica Barber" and the Petitioner, allegedly known as "Boozy," adjacent to a description of the woman as a 23 year-old from Port Deposit, and the blurb, stating "FREE BOOZY!!!! JUST REMEMBER SNITCHES GET STITCHES!! U KNOW WHO YOU ARE!!"

---

[9] To establish a "profile," a user needs only a valid email account [and to provide answers to a series of questions asking for personal data].

In lieu of Sergeant Cook's testimony, while maintaining his objection to the admissibility of the redacted MySpace page, defense counsel agreed to the following stipulation:

> If asked, Sergeant Cook would testify that he went onto the Internet to the website known as MySpace. . . [F]rom that site he downloaded some information of a posting that someone had put there.

> That posting contains a photograph which the witness would say he recognizes as a photograph of Jessica . . . Barber, who testified, . . . that she is the defendant's live-in fiance; and that it also contains a date of birth, to wit October 2nd, 1983, which the witness would testify is the date of birth that Jessica Barber gave as her date of birth.

> When the exhibit, the download, comes to you, you are going to see that it has a great—that most of its content has been redacted; that is, blacked out. That's because some of it, in my judgment, might tend to be inflammatory without proving anything one way or the other. There is one portion of it that will not be redacted when it comes to you, and this is the only portion of it which you should consider. And you certainly should not speculate as to what any of the redacted portions may be.

> The portion that will not be redacted says, just remember snitches get stitches. You will see that. The phrase is, just remember snitches get stitches. . . And . . . the witness would testify that the date it was retrieved was . . . December 5, 2006.

Whether the MySpace printout represents that which it purports to be, not only a MySpace profile created by Ms. Barber, but also upon which she had posted, "FREE BOOZY!!!! JUST REMEMBER SNITCHES GET STITCHES!! U KNOW WHO YOU ARE!!," is the issue before us.

* * * A number of social networking websites, such as MySpace, enable members "to create online 'profiles,' which are individual web pages on which members [can] post photographs, videos, and information about their lives and interests." *Doe v. MySpace, Inc.,* 474 F.Supp.2d 843, 845 (W.D.Tex.2007).

Anyone can create a MySpace profile at no cost, as long as that person has an email address and claims to be over the age of fourteen:

> MySpace users create profiles by filling out questionnaire-like web forms. Users are then able to connect their profiles to those of other users and thereby form communities. MySpace profiles contain several informational sections, known as "blurbs." These include two standard blurbs: "About Me" and "Who I'd Like to Meet." Users may supplement those blurbs with additional sections about their interests, general additional details, and other personal information. MySpace profiles also incorporate several multimedia features. For instance, users may post photos, music, videos, and web logs to their pages.

Richard M. Guo, *Stranger Danger and the Online Social Network,* 23 Berkeley Tech. L.J. 617, 621 (2008) (footnotes omitted). After a profile is established, the user may invite others to access her profile, as a "friend," who if the user accepts the befriending, can access her profile pages without further ado:

> Users establish virtual communities by linking their profiles in a process known as "friending" or "connecting." One user requests to add another as a friend, and the recipient may either accept or reject the invitation. If the recipient accepts, the profiles are linked and the connected members are generally able to view one another's online content without restriction. The network created by the linking process allows a user to chat with friends, display support for particular causes, "join interest groups dedicated to virtually any topic," and otherwise "hang out."

Nathan Petrashek, Comment, *The Fourth Amendment and the Brave New World of Online Social Networking,* 93 Marq. L.Rev. 1495, 1499–1500 (2009–2010) (footnotes omitted). Although a social networking site generally requires a unique username and password for the user to both establish a profile and access it, posting on the site by those that befriend the user does not.

The identity of who generated the profile may be confounding, because "a person observing the online profile of a user with whom the observer is unacquainted has no idea whether the profile is legitimate." Petrashek, 93 Marq. L.Rev. at 1499 n. 16. The concern arises because anyone can create a fictitious account and masquerade under another person's name or can gain access to another's account by obtaining the user's username and password:

> Although it may seem that, as creators of our own online social networking profiles, we are able to construct our own online persona, this is not always the case. There is no law that prevents someone from establishing a fake account under another person's name, so long as the purpose for doing so is not to deceive others and gain some advantage. Moreover, fragments of information, either crafted under our authority or fabricated by others, are available by performing a Google search . . . forever. Thus, online social networking poses two threats: that information may be (1) available because of one's own role as the creator of the content, or (2) generated by a third party, whether or not it is accurate.

> David Hector Montes, *Living Our Lives Online: The Privacy Implications of Online Social Networking,* Journal of Law and Policy for the Information Society, Spring 2009, at 507, 508. For instance, in one circumstance, Sophos, a Boston-based Internet security company, created a profile for a toy frog named "Freddi Staur," and nearly 200 Facebook users chose to add the frog as a "friend." Miller, 97 Ky. L.J. at 542.

> The possibility for user abuse also exists on MySpace, as illustrated by *United States v. Drew,* 259 F.R.D. 449 (D.C.D.Cal.2009), in which Lori Drew, a mother, was prosecuted under the Computer Fraud and Abuse Act,

18 U.S.C. § 1030, for creating a MySpace profile for a fictitious 16 year-old male named "Josh Evans." Drew had contacted a former friend of her daughter's, Megan Meier, through the MySpace network, using the Josh Evans screen name or pseudonym, and began to "flirt with her over a number of days." Drew then had "Josh" inform Megan that he no longer "liked her" and that "the world would be a better place without her in it," after which Megan killed herself. Thus, the relative ease with which anyone can create fictional personas or gain unauthorized access to another user's profile, with deleterious consequences, is the *Drew* lesson.

The potential for fabricating or tampering with electronically stored information on a social networking site, thus poses significant challenges from the standpoint of authentication of printouts of the site, as in the present case. * * *

Potential methods of authentication are illustrated in Rule 5–901(b) . . .[11] * * *

In the present case, Griffin argues that the State did not appropriately, for evidentiary purposes, authenticate the pages allegedly printed from Jessica Barber's MySpace profile, because the State failed to offer any extrinsic evidence describing MySpace, as well as indicating how Sergeant Cook obtained the pages in question and adequately linking both the profile and the "snitches get stitches" posting to Ms. Barber. The State counters that the photograph, personal information, and references to freeing "Boozy" were sufficient to enable the finder of fact to believe that the pages printed from MySpace were indeed Ms. Barber's.

We agree with Griffin and disagree with the State regarding whether the trial judge abused his discretion in admitting the MySpace profile as appropriately authenticated, with Jessica Barber as its creator and user, as well as the author of the "snitches get stitches" posting, based upon the inadequate foundation laid. We differ from our colleagues on the Court of Special Appeals, who gave short shrift to the concern that "someone other than the alleged author may have accessed the account and posted the message in question." While the intermediate appellate court determined that the pages allegedly printed from Ms. Barber's MySpace profile contained sufficient indicia of reliability, because the printout "featured a photograph of Ms. Barber and [Petitioner] in an embrace," and also contained the "user's birth date and identified her boyfriend as 'Boozy,'" the court failed to acknowledge the possibility or likelihood that another user could have created the profile in issue or authored the "snitches get stitches" posting.

We agree with Griffin that the trial judge abused his discretion in admitting the MySpace evidence pursuant to Rule 5–901(b)(4), because the picture of Ms. Barber, coupled with her birth date and location, were not

---

[11] We . . . highlight that a witness with knowledge, such as Ms. Barber, could be asked whether the MySpace profile was hers and whether its contents were authored by her; she, however, was not subject to such inquiry when she was called by the State.

sufficient "distinctive characteristics" on a MySpace profile to authenticate its printout, given the prospect that someone other than Ms. Barber could have not only created the site, but also posted the "snitches get stitches" comment. The potential for abuse and manipulation of a social networking site by someone other than its purported creator and/or user leads to our conclusion that a printout of an image from such a site requires a greater degree of authentication than merely identifying the date of birth of the creator and her visage in a photograph on the site in order to reflect that Ms. Barber was its creator and the author of the "snitches get stitches" language.[12]

In so holding, we recognize that other courts, called upon to consider authentication of electronically stored information on social networking sites, have suggested greater scrutiny because of the heightened possibility for manipulation by other than the true user or poster. In *Commonwealth v. Williams,* 456 Mass. 857, 926 N.E.2d 1162 (2010), the Supreme Judicial Court of Massachusetts considered the admission, over the defendant's objection, of instant messages a witness had received "at her account at MySpace." In the case, the defendant was convicted of the shooting death of Izaah Tucker, as well as other offenses. The witness, Ashlei Noyes, testified that she had spent the evening of the murder socializing with the defendant and that he had been carrying a handgun. She further testified that the defendant's brother had contacted her "four times on her MySpace account between February 9, 2007, and February 12, 2007," urging her "not to testify or to claim a lack of memory regarding the events of the night of the murder." At trial, Noyes testified that the defendant's brother, Jesse Williams, had a picture of himself on his MySpace account and that his MySpace screen name or pseudonym was "doit4it." She testified that she had received the messages from Williams, and the document printed from her MySpace account indicated that the messages were in fact sent by a user with the screen name "doit4it," depicting a picture of Williams.

The Supreme Judicial Court of Massachusetts determined that there was an inadequate foundation laid to authenticate the MySpace messages, because the State failed to offer any evidence regarding who had access to the MySpace page and whether another author, other than Williams, could have virtually-penned the messages:

> Although it appears that the sender of the messages was using Williams's MySpace Web "page," there is no testimony (from Noyes or another) regarding how secure such a Web page is, who can access a MySpace Web page, whether codes are needed for such access, etc. Analogizing a MySpace [message] to a telephone call, a witness's testimony that he or she has received an incoming call from a person

---

[12] The dissent minimizes as "the technological heebie jeebies" the challenges inherent in authenticating, for evidentiary purposes, social networking websites. *None* of the authorities cited by the dissent in support of its conclusion, however, even addresses the authentication of social networking sites. Only one case, *United States v. Gagliardi,* 506 F.3d 140, 151 (2d Cir.2007), involves digital communications, namely Internet chat room conversations, which the Second Circuit recognized were appropriately authenticated by witnesses who had participated in the "chats," clearly persons "with knowledge." *See* Federal Rule 901(b)(1). * * *

claiming to be "A," without more, is insufficient evidence to admit the call as a conversation with "A." Here, while the foundational testimony established that the messages were sent by someone with access to Williams's MySpace Web page, it did not identify the person who actually sent the communication. Nor was there expert testimony that no one other than Williams could communicate from that Web page. Testimony regarding the contents of the messages should not have been admitted.

Id. (citations omitted) The court emphasized that the State failed to demonstrate a sufficient connection between the messages printed from Williams's alleged MySpace account and Williams himself, with reference, for example, to Williams's use of an exclusive username and password to which only he had access. . .

Similarly, in *People v. Lenihan,* 30 Misc.3d 289, 911 N.Y.S.2d 588 (N.Y.Sup.Ct.2010), Lenihan challenged his second degree murder conviction because he was not permitted to cross-examine two witnesses called by the State on the basis of photographs his mother had printed from MySpace, allegedly depicting the witnesses and the victim making hand gestures and wearing clothing that suggested an affiliation with the "Crips" gang. The trial judge precluded Lenihan from confronting the witnesses with the MySpace photographs, reasoning that "[i]n light of the ability to 'photo shop,' edit photographs on the computer," Lenihan could not adequately authenticate the photographs.

In *United States v. Jackson,* 208 F.3d 633 (7th Cir.2000), Jackson was charged with mail and wire fraud and obstruction of justice after making false claims of racial harassment against the United Parcel Service in connection with an elaborate scheme in which she sent packages containing racial epithets to herself and to several prominent African–Americans purportedly from "racist elements" within UPS. At trial, Jackson sought to introduce website postings from "the Euro–American Student Union and Storm Front," in which the white supremacist groups gloated about Jackson's case and took credit for the UPS mailings. The court determined that the trial judge was justified in excluding the evidence because it lacked an appropriate foundation, namely that Jackson had failed to show that the web postings by the white supremacist groups who took responsibility for the racist mailings "actually were posted by the groups, as opposed to being slipped onto the groups' websites by Jackson herself, who was a skilled computer user."

The State refers us, however, to *In the Interest of F.P.,* 878 A.2d 91 (Pa.Super.Ct.2005), in which the Pennsylvania intermediate appellate court considered whether instant messages were properly authenticated pursuant to Pennsylvania Rule of Evidence 901(b)(4), providing that a document may be authenticated by distinctive characteristics or circumstantial evidence. In the case, involving an assault, the victim, Z.G., testified that the defendant had attacked him because he believed that Z.G. had stolen a DVD from him. The hearing judge, over defendant's objection, admitted instant messages from a user with the screen name "Icp4Life30" to and between "WHITEBOY Z 404." Z.G. testified that his screen name was "WHITEBOY Z 404" and that he had printed the instant messages from his computer. In the transcript of the instant messages, moreover, Z.G. asked "who is this," and the defendant replied, using his first name. Throughout the transcripts, the defendant threatened Z.G. with physical violence because Z.G. "stole off [him]." On appeal, the court determined that the instant messages were properly authenticated through the testimony of Z.G. and also because "Icp4Life30" had referred to himself by first name, repeatedly accused Z.G. of stealing from him, and referenced the fact that Z.G. had told high school administrators about the threats, such that the instant messages contained distinctive characteristics and content linking them to the defendant. *In the Interest of F.P.* is unpersuasive in the context of a social networking site, because the authentication of instant messages by the recipient who identifies his own "distinctive characteristics" and his having received the messages, is distinguishable from the authentication of a profile and posting printed from MySpace, by one who is neither a creator nor user of the specific profile.[13]

Similarly, the State relies upon an unreported opinion, *State v. Bell*, 2009 WL 1395857, 2009 Ohio App. LEXIS 2112 (Ohio Ct.App.2009), in which the defendant, convicted of multiple counts of child molestation, asserted that the trial judge improperly admitted "online conversations and email messages" on MySpace, purportedly involving Bell and one of his victims. The defendant argued that the messages were not properly authenticated, because his laptop "was turned on after it was seized," which he asserted altered hundreds of files on the hard drive. The appellate court rejected that argument because defense counsel had expressly approved the admission of the MySpace emails and messages. Griffin, in the present case, however, explicitly objected to the authenticity of the MySpace printout.

In the case sub judice, the MySpace printout was used to show that Ms. Barber had threatened a key witness, who the State had characterized as "probably the most important witness in this case;" the State highlighted

---

[13] We further note that authentication concerns attendant to e-mails, instant messaging correspondence, and text messages differ significantly from those involving a MySpace profile and posting printout, because such correspondences is sent directly from one party to an intended recipient or recipients, rather than published for all to see. *See Independent Newspapers, Inc. v. Brodie*, 407 Md. 415, 423, 966 A.2d 432, 437 (2009) (contrasting emails and instant messages with a "different category of Internet communications, in which users post statements to the world at large without specification," such as on social networking sites). *See also United States v. Safavian*, 435 F.Supp.2d 36, 41 (D.D.C.2006) (reasoning e-mails could be authenticated by comparison by the jury with those e-mails that had already been independently authenticated through the contents or in the email heading itself); *Commonwealth v. Amaral*, 78 Mass.App.Ct. 671, 674, 941 N.E.2d 1143, 1147 (2011) (reasoning that "[t]he actions of the defendant himself served to authenticate the e-mails," because one e-mail indicated that defendant would be at a certain place at a certain time and the defendant appeared at that place and time, and in another email, defendant provided his telephone number and immediately answered when the investigator called that number); *Dickens v. State*, 175 Md.App. 231, 238–40, 927 A.2d 32, 36–37 (2007) (reasoning text messages received on victim's cell phone were properly authenticated because the phone number on one message showed that it had come from defendant's phone and other messages referenced the defendant's right to see the couple's minor child and their wedding vows).

the importance of the "snitches get stitches" posting during closing argument, as follows:

> Sergeant Cook told you that he went online and went to a website called MySpace and found a posting that had been placed there by the defendant's girlfriend, Jessica Barber, recognized her picture, able to match up the date of birth on the posting with her date of birth, and the posting included these words, "Free Boozy. Just remember, snitches get stitches. You know who you are."

In addition, during rebuttal argument, the State again referenced the pages printed from MySpace, asserting that Ms. Barber had employed MySpace as a tool of intimidation against a witness for the State. It is clear, then, that the MySpace printout was a key component of the State's case; the error in the admission of its printout requires reversal.

In so doing, we should not be heard to suggest that printouts from social networking sites should never be admitted. Possible avenues to explore to properly authenticate a profile or posting printed from a social networking site, will, in all probability, continue to develop as the efforts to evidentially utilize information from the sites increases. A number of authentication opportunities come to mind, however.

The first, and perhaps most obvious method would be to ask the purported creator if she indeed created the profile and also if she added the posting in question, i.e. "[t]estimony of a witness with knowledge that the offered evidence is what it is claimed to be." Rule 5–901(b)(1). The second option may be to search the computer of the person who allegedly created the profile and posting and examine the computer's internet history and hard drive to determine whether that computer was used to originate the social networking profile and posting in question. One commentator, who serves as Managing Director and Deputy General Counsel of Stroz Friedberg, a computer forensics firm, notes that, "[s]ince a user unwittingly leaves an evidentiary trail on her computer simply by using it, her computer will provide evidence of her web usage." Seth P. Berman, et al., *Web 2. 0: What's Evidence Between "Friends"?*, Boston Bar J., Jan.-Feb.2009, at 5, 7.

A third method may be to obtain information directly from the social networking website that links the establishment of the profile to the person who allegedly created it and also links the posting sought to be introduced to the person who initiated it. This method was apparently successfully employed to authenticate a MySpace site in *People v. Clevenstine,* 68 A.D.3d 1448, 891 N.Y.S.2d 511 (2009). In the case, Richard Clevenstine was convicted of raping two teenage girls and challenged his convictions by asserting that the computer disk admitted into evidence, containing instant messages between him and the victims, sent via MySpace, was not properly authenticated. Specifically, Clevenstine argued that "someone else accessed his MySpace account and sent messages under his username." The Supreme Court of New York, Appellate Division, agreed with the trial judge that the MySpace messages were properly authenticated, because both victims testified that they had engaged in instant messaging conversations about sexual activities with Clevenstine through MySpace. In addition, an investigator from the computer crime unit of the State Police testified that "he had retrieved such conversations from the hard drive of the computer used by the victims." Finally, the prosecution was able to attribute the messages to Clevenstine, because a legal compliance officer for MySpace explained at trial that "the messages on the computer disk had been exchanged by users of accounts created by [Clevenstine] and the victims." The court concluded that such testimony provided ample authentication linking the MySpace messages in question to Clevenstine himself. * * *

HARRELL, J., dissenting in which MURPHY, J., joins.

I dissent from the Majority Opinion's holding that "the picture of Ms. Barber, coupled with her birth date and location, were not sufficient 'distinctive characteristics' on a MySpace profile to authenticate its [redacted] printout. . ."

Maryland Rule 5–901 ("Requirement of authentication or identification") derives from and is similar materially to Federal Rule of Evidence 901. * * * In construing and applying Federal Rule 901, federal courts have held almost unanimously that "a document is properly authenticated if a *reasonable juror could find in favor of authenticity." United States v. Gagliardi,* 506 F.3d 140, 151 (2d Cir.2007) (emphasis added) . . . Although, to date, we have not enunciated such a standard, because I think that the "reasonable juror" standard is consistent with Maryland Rule 5–901— requiring only " evidence *sufficient to support a finding* that the matter in question is what its proponent claims" (emphasis added)—I would adopt it. * * *

Applying that standard to the present case, a reasonable juror could conclude, based on the presence on the MySpace profile of (1) a picture of a person appearing to Sergeant Cook to be Ms. Barber posing with the defendant, her boyfriend; (2) a birth date matching Ms. Barber's; (3) a description of the purported creator of the MySpace profile as being a twenty-three year old from Port Deposit; and (4) references to freeing "Boozy" (a nickname for the defendant), that the redacted printed pages of the MySpace profile contained information posted by Ms. Barber.

I am not unmindful of the Majority Opinion's analysis relating to the concern that someone other than Ms. Barber could access or create the account and post the threatening message. The record, however, suggests no motive to do so. The technological heebie jeebies discussed in the Majority Opinion go, in my opinion, however, not to the admissibility of the printouts under Rule 5–901, but rather to the weight to be given the evidence by the trier of fact.

It has been said that the "purpose of authentication is to . . . filter untrustworthy evidence." *Phillip M. Adams & Assocs., L.L.C. v. Dell, Inc.,* 621 F.Supp.2d 1173, 1184 (D.Utah 2009). Like many filters that are unable to remove completely all impurities, Rule 5–901 does not act to disallow any and all evidence that may have "impurities" (i.e., in this case, evidence that could have come, conceivably, from a source other than the purported source). As long as a reasonable juror could conclude that the proffered evidence is what its proponent purports it to be, the evidence should be admitted. The potentialities that are of concern to the Majority Opinion are fit subjects for cross-examination or rebuttal testimony and go properly to the weight the fact-finder may give the print-outs. Accordingly, I dissent. * * *

CHAPTER 8

COMPETENCE OF WITNESSES

Hill v. Skinner

Court of Appeals of Ohio, 1947.
81 Ohio App. 375, 79 N.E.2d 787.

■ DOYLE, PRESIDING JUDGE. This is an action under the Ohio statute, Section 5838, General Code, seeking to hold the owners and harborers of a dog called "Chang" with liability for damages arising out of an episode in which the dog, Chang, is alleged to have seized with his teeth and injured a youngster aged approximately four, the petitioner herein.

A jury, upon trial, awarded damages in the amount of $500. The judgment rendered thereon, in the Court of Common Pleas of Summit county, is part of the final order from which this appeal is taken, and consideration will be first given to the legality of this money judgment.

1. The appellants say "There was no evidence of a 'bite' anywhere in the record from any of the witnesses save the plaintiff himself. Without this * * * minor's testimony there was evidence of injury only with barbed wire, glass, a gashed steel barrel and other dogs being present as explanation."

It is a fact that there is no *direct* testimony of this dog's attack except that given by the child. If this evidence has probative worth, and is competent, it, coupled with the circumstances and other facts shown to exist, is sufficient to furnish the degree of proof necessary to sustain the judgment.

Section 11493, General Code, reads:

"All persons are competent witnesses except those of unsound mind, and children under ten years of age who appear incapable of receiving just impressions of the facts and transactions respecting which they are examined, or of relating them truly."

The Supreme Court of this state has recently ruled on that part of this statute pertaining to witnesses claimed to be of "unsound mind."

"2. The competency of an insane person to testify as a witness lies in the discretion of the trial judge and a reviewing court will not disturb the ruling thereon where there is no abuse of discretion. State v. Wildman.

And in 2 Wigmore on Evidence (3 Ed.), Section 505, it is said:

"With reference to the general capacity to observe, recollect, and narrate, the same principles apply to Mental Immaturity that are applied to Mental Derangement."

The essential test of the competency of an infant witness is his comprehension of the obligation to tell the truth and his intellectual capacity of observation, recollection and communication. The nature of his conception of the obligation to tell the truth is of little importance if he shows that he will fulfill the obligation to speak truthfully as a duty which he owes a Diety or something held in reverence or regard, and if he has the intellectual capacity to communicate his observations and experiences.

The trial court, in chambers, examined the child at length, touching upon his qualifications to testify. Among other questions he was asked: "Do you know about telling the truth, what happens if you don't tell the truth?" and he answered, "They won't love me." Question: "Who won't love you?" Answer: "God won't love me." And in further answer to dozens of questions propounded by both the judge and counsel, the child demonstrated a capacity for memory of events, observation, recollection and communication.

Following this necessary and proper examination by the trial judge of the prospective witness, the court permitted him to testify. The child thereupon, direct examination, testified in part as follows:

"Q. Cary do you remember when you went over to Skinner's? A. Sure.

"Q. Tell the judge and jury what happened. A. The doggy bit me.

"Q. What doggy bit you? A. Skinner's doggy.

"Q. What were you doing with Skinner's dog? A. I was loving him.

"Q. How? A. Like that (indicating.)

"Q. You mean around his neck? A. Yes."

On cross-examination appears the following:

"Q. Where did Chang bite you, can you tell the ladies, take your fingers and show me where he bit you? A. He bit me when I was loving him.

"Q. Where did he bite you, did he bite you on the leg? A. No, he bite me on the head and on my mouth here (indicating.)"

As we view the testimony, the youthful narrator, except for a few non-responsive answers, clearly described and explained the circumstances giving rise to this action. The evidence considered as a whole describes the wandering of the child out onto his neighbor's yard and the subsequent attack of the dog, under circumstances clearly related by the child. There is nothing in the record to show, except through pure guess and speculation, that the head injuries resulted from any other cause.

Paraphrasing a syllabus in State v. Wildman, supra, to fit this case, the rule may be pronounced to be that the competency of a child of mental immaturity to testify as a witness lies in the discretion of the trial judge, and a reviewing court will not disturb the ruling thereon when there is no abuse of discretion. In the instant case we find no such abuse. We further find that the evidence in the record is such as to warrant the jury in finding in favor of the petitioner.

Judgment modified to provide for the destruction of the dog, as required by the Ohio statute, and as modified, affirmed.

PROBLEM

Brian Siler is accused of strangling his estranged wife Barbara to death. After Barbara was discovered hanging by a yellow cord tied to the track of the garage door of her home, police found the couple's three-year-old son, Nathan, asleep in his bedroom. Nathan told a detective, who was a trained police interviewer, that his mother was in the garage "sleep standing." In response to questioning, some of it leading, Nahan also said that the night before his father had scared him by knocking on the front door loudly, that his parents had argued loudly, and that his father had placed the "yellow thing" around his mother's neck.

May Nathan testify at trial to these propositions? If so, under what conditions? If not, is there any other way in which Nathan's account may be presented to the trier of fact? In particular, if the detective who interviewed him testified to what Nathan said, would that violate the Confrontation Clause? What if Nathan made the statements to a social worker, who met with him for therapeutic purposes; could she testify as to what he said? See State v. Siler, 876 N.E.2d 534 (Ohio 2007).

A NOTE ON COMPETENCE

The medieval jury was expected to be largely "self-informing"—that is, it was composed of knowledgeable men of the vicinity who were supposed to report the truth, at least largely on the basis of pre-existing knowledge. Indeed, while the jurors could go to a person's home to ask what he knew about a litigated matter, one who voluntarily came forward to share the same information was deemed to be a meddler and could be punished for *maintenance*. By the 16th century, the jury became more dependent on the testimony of witnesses, some of whom were *compelled* to testify by subpoena (and so not liable to be punished for maintenance); a key development was a statute of 1562-63 that imposed stiff penalties one anyone who declined to appear even after bring served ands offered reasonable compensation for attending.[14] It then became important to regulate who might testify and how.

Commentators have sometimes described four capacities—often identified by terms such as perception, memory, sincerity, and communication—that must be operating in order for a witness to give truthful testimony. That is, the witness must perceive the events or condition described accurately; retain an accurate memory of them through the time of the testimony and be able to summon the memory then; desire to communicate an accurate rendition of the

---

[14] *See, e.g.,* 8 John H. Wigmore, EVIDENCE 63-65 (McNaughton rev. 1961); Daniel Klerman, *Was the Jury Ever Self-Informing?*, 73 SO. CAL. L.

events or conditions she perceived; and make such a communication in a way that the trier of fact is likely to understand. A significant failure in any one of these capacities will lead the witness to testify inaccurately or not at all.

For several centuries, the common law's approach was to exclude various categories of witnesses whose testimony, for one reason or another, was thought not reliable. Interest in the case, infancy, limited mental capacity or mental derangement, infamy, and religious beliefs considered heretical were all grounds deemed sufficient to disqualify a person as a witness. Over time, the law recognized that it was self-defeating to prevent a person from testifying, and therefore deny the trier of fact the benefit of whatever information she might be able to offer, because of these characteristics. Most of them became instead potential grounds for impeachment.

Note that the first sentence of Federal Rule of Evidence 601 now provides, "Every person is competent to be a witness unless these rules provide otherwise." The rule is subject to three general qualifications, as well as narrower ones.

First, if state law provides the rule of decision on substantive law, then witness competency is also determined by state law. Some state laws are more restrictive than the Federal Rules. *See, e.g.,* Vt. Ev. R. 601(b).

Second, the proponent of the testimony of a non-expert witness must present evidence that the witness has personal knowledge of the matter to which she testifies. Fed. R. Evid. 602. If, for example, a prosecutor wishes to present the testimony of a witness describing a crime scene, ordinarily the witness would first testify that she personally witnessed the scene.

Third, the witness must take an oath or (for those who conscientiously decline to take oath) make an affirmation that indicates that the witness understands the solemn obligation to tell the truth. Fed. R. Evid. 603. The common law put great weight on the importance of the oath as a guarantor of truthful testimony. An oath was, in effect, a covenant with God; to lie under oath, therefore, was to risk eternal damnation. Accordingly, unwillingness or perceived inability to take a meaningful oath disqualified a person as a witness. Even today, unwillingness to take an oath or make an affirmation may prevent a witness from testifying. And it is arguable that the judge could decide that the witness simply lacks the mental capacity to satisfy Rule 603, *see* United States v. Ramirez, 871 F.2d 582, 584, *cert. denied,* 493 U.S. 841 (1989), but the proposition is debatable. *See* 27 Wright, Graham, Gold & Graham, Fed. Prac. & Proc. Evidence § 6005 (2d ed.).

Religious belief. The efficacy of the oath, in the view of the common law, was dependent on the witness's belief in a God who might punish such transgressions in an afterlife. Many potential witnesses were therefore disqualified because of their religious beliefs. Gradually, the states began removing this religious disability from testifying, though some still maintained that, while a non-believer was competent to testify, the lack of belief might still be shown for whatever bearing it had on the witness's credibility.[15] Ultimately, courts and

---

[15] See Case Comment, Witnesses – Religious Belief as Affecting Credibility, 17 HARV. L. REV. 286 (1904).

rulemakers came to regard as improper even this use of the witness's beliefs on matters of religion; note that Fed. R. Evid. 610 provides that such beliefs may not be used for the purpose of showing either that the witness's credibility is impaired or that it is enhanced.

Infancy and mental incompetence. Child witnesses have long posed a difficult problem for the courts. Although courts and commentators had sometimes taken a different view, a leading case in 1779, *R. v. Brasier*, 1 Leach, 168 E.R. 202 (K.B.), held that there is no minimum age for a witness, but that children as well as adults must testify under oath. That is still basically the law, except that modern courts will not usually insist that a child take a formal oath. The approach reflected in *Hill v. Skinner*, presented above, still prevails: It is generally enough if the court can satisfy itself that she has the testimonial capacities of perception, memory, and communication, and that she recognizes her obligation to tell the truth. Under one view, even if the child is deficient in one or more of these respects, and even if it is meaningless to think of her as presenting testimony in he usual sense, her rendition of events may still provide useful information for the trier of fact, and her deficiencies are unlikely to be overlooked.

Adults are generally presumed to have the mental competence to be able to testify, but it remains open to the opponent to contend that the witness lacks the capacity to be an acceptable witness.

Interest. For centuries, the common law disqualified from testifying in civil litigation, the parties, their spouses, and others who had a clear pecuniary interest in the matter. The thought was that their interest created too strong an incentive for perjury and would make their testimony too untrustworthy. But obviously the loss of potentially useful evidence was enormous. And if the interest was strong, presumably the jury would take that into account. England abolished the disqualification for civil non-parties in 1843 and for parties in 1851. Most American jurisdictions soon followed suit, legislating away these disqualifications. A witness's interest, or bias, remains as an important method of impeachment – indeed, sometimes it is constitutionally protected – but it will not keep a witness off the stand.

On the criminal side, the situation was different. Until the late 18th century and even later in some jurisdictions, most crimes were privately prosecuted. The victim, referred to as the prosecutor or prosecutrix, testified under oath (except in homicide prosecutions!). The accused, usually not represented by counsel, responded to the accusations, but he was not allowed to testify under oath. As defense lawyers became a greater part of the system, they usually kept their clients quiet. In 1864, Maine became the first jurisdiction in the common law world to allow the accused to testify under oath. The reform swept through most of the American states in the succeeding decades, and reached England in 1898. Georgia maintained the old rule into the 1960s. *See* Ferguson v. Georgia, 365 U.S. 570 (1961); Ga. Code §17-7-28 (enacted 1962; allowing accused to testify under oath).

The Dead Man's Statutes. When they abolished the disqualification for civil parties, many states retained it in one type of setting, defined by the so-called Dead Man's Statutes. These statutes operate on the premise that if two parties have dealings with each other and one then dies, it is unfair for the surviving party to testify against the estate of the other, whose lips have been sealed by death. By the late 20th century, most of the statutes had been repealed;[16] they often create a devastating loss of evidence, and it is not hard for the trier of fact to understand that because of death it is not hearing directly from one party to the controversy.

A handful of these statutes do survive, however, and where they do they tend to be quite complex. Here is New York's:

New York Civ. Prac. Law & Rules, § 4519

§ 4519. Personal transaction or communication between witness and decedent or mentally ill person.

Upon the trial of an action or the hearing upon the merits of a special proceeding, a party or a person interested in the event, or a person from, through or under whom such a party or interested person derives his interest or title by assignment or otherwise, shall not be examined as a witness in his own behalf or interest, or in behalf of the party succeeding to his title or interest against the executor, administrator or survivor of a deceased person or the committee of a mentally ill person, or a person deriving his title or interest from, through or under a deceased person or mentally ill person, by assignment, or otherwise, concerning a personal transaction or communication between the witness and the deceased person or mentally ill person, except where the executor, administrator, survivor, committee or person so deriving title or interest is examined in his own behalf, or the testimony of the mentally ill person or deceased person is given in evidence, concerning the same transaction or communication. A person shall not be deemed interested for the purposes of this section by reason of being a stockholder or officer of any banking corporation which is a party to the action or proceeding, or interested in the event thereof. No party or person interested in the event, who is otherwise competent to testify, shall be disqualified from testifying by the possible imposition of costs against him or the award of costs to him. A party or person interested in the event or a person from, through or under whom such a party or interested person derives his interest or title by assignment or otherwise, shall not be qualified for the purposes of this section, to testify in his own behalf or interest, or in behalf of the party succeeding to his title or interest, to personal transactions or communications with the donee of a power of appointment in an action or proceeding for the probate of a will, which exercises or attempts to exercise a power of appointment granted by the will of a donor of such power, or in an action or proceeding involving the construction of the will of the donee after its admission to probate.

Nothing contained in this section, however, shall render a person incompetent to testify as to the facts of an accident or the results therefrom where the proceeding, hearing, defense or cause of action involves a claim of negligence or contributory negligence in an action wherein one or more

---

[16] See generally Wesley P. Page, Dead Man Talking: a Historical Analysis of West Virginia's Dead Man's Statute and a Recommendation for Reform, 109 W.V. L. Rev. 897 (2007).

parties is the representative of a deceased or incompetent person based upon, or by reason of, the operation or ownership of a motor vehicle being operated upon the highways of the state, or the operation or ownership of aircraft being operated in the air space over the state, or the operation or ownership of a vessel on any of the lakes, rivers, streams, canals or other waters of this state, but this provision shall not be construed as permitting testimony as to conversations with the deceased.

And here is the California Law Revision Commission's explanation of that state's repeal of its dead man statute.

Comment to Section 1261—Law Revision Commission

The dead man statute (subdivision 3 of Section 1880 of the Code of Civil Procedure) prohibits a party who sues on a claim against a decedent's estate from testifying to any fact occurring prior to the decedent's death. The theory apparently underlying the statute is that it would be unfair to permit the surviving claimant to testify to such facts when the decedent is precluded by his death from doing so. To balance the positions of the parties, the living may not speak because the dead cannot.

The dead man statute operates unsatisfactorily. It prohibits testimony concerning matters of which the decedent had no knowledge and, hence, to which he could not have testified even if he had survived. It operates unevenly since it does not prohibit testimony relating to claims under, as distinguished from claims against, the decedent's estate even though the effect of such a claim may be to frustrate the decedent's plan for the disposition of his property. See the Law Revision Commission's Comment to Code of Civil Procedure Section 1880 and 1 Cal.Law Revision Comm'n, Rep., Rec. & Studies, Recommendation and Study Relating to the Dead Man Statute at D–1 (1957). The dead man statute excludes otherwise relevant and competent evidence—even if it is the only available evidence—and frequently this forces the courts to decide cases with a minimum of information concerning the actual facts. See the Supreme Court's complaint in Light v. Stevens, 159 Cal. 288, 292, 113 P. 659, 660 (1911) ("Owing to the fact that the lips of one of the parties to the transaction are closed by death and those of the other party by the law, the evidence on this question is somewhat unsatisfactory."). Hence, the dead man statute is not continued in the Evidence Code.

Under the Evidence Code, the positions of the parties are balanced by throwing more light, not less, on the actual facts. Repeal of the dead man statute permits the claimant to testify without restriction. To balance this advantage, Section 1261 permits hearsay evidence of the decedent's statements to be admitted. Certain safeguards—i.e., personal knowledge, recent perception, and circumstantial evidence of trustworthiness—are included in the section to provide some protection for the party against whom the statements are offered, for he has no opportunity to test the hearsay by cross-examination.

A NOTE ON COMPETENCE, CONTINUED

Infamy. At early common law a person who committed serious crimes was deemed infamous and stripped of various rights, among them the right to testify in a court of law. The rule of incompetence was justified largely on the basis that a person who had committed an infamous crime could not be trusted to tell the truth.

Ultimately, courts and rule-makers realized that this was a silly rule, rendering inadmissible too much evidence that might be persuasive to a trier of fact. In criminal cases particularly, it is often essential to rely on the testimony of witnesses who themselves have criminal records.

But was the evidence thus excluded helpful or harmful to the truth-determining process? The old attitude was the evidence could not have been good, because the source was so tainted. Some commentators resisted this idea, arguing that "there is no reason for believing that a person who has murdered will also lie."[17] But surely that is an overstatement. Antisocial personality disorder is defined as "a pervasive pattern of disregard for and violation of the rights of others since age 15 years," including at least three of a list of improper behaviors, including deception, such as repeated lying, repeated acts that are grounds for arrest, and aggressiveness, as indicated by physical fights or assaults.[18] In other words, though there certainly are gentle liars and honest murderers, the fact that a person violates one type of social norm makes it more likely that he will violate another.

Nevertheless, that does not mean that the testimony of a person who has committed serious crimes is worthless. He may, of course, have information that no one else has to offer. Indeed, prosecution of many crimes would be impossible if testimony of a former confederate of the accused were inadmissible. Even if the witness's credibility is not strong, he may be able to tell a story that is very compelling and that accounts for the evidence better than any alternative account. And there is no reason to suppose the trier of fact will be unable to take into account the witness's personal weaknesses. Indeed, in recent times the fear has been more that the jury might hold prior convictions excessively against a witness, especially a criminal defendant.

The modern approach, therefore, is not to preclude a witness from testifying because she has acted badly in the past. Rather, such bad behavior may, in tightly controlled circumstances, be used as a basis for impeaching the witness. Thus, proof of certain criminal convictions may be used for impeachment; the circumstances in which such impeachment is allowed are narrower when the witness is a criminal defendant than in other settings. And in the discretion of the trial court, an impeaching party may ask a witness about other bad acts the witness has committed that may suggest the witness has a bad character for

---

[17] Tracy, Handbook of the Law of Evidence (1952).

[18] Diagnostic and Statistical Manual of Mental Disorders (DSM IV-TR).

truthfulness—but the impeaching party may not prove such bad acts through the testimony of other witnesses. This topic is addressed in depth in Chapter IV.

Connection with the Tribunal. Though some states had provided that a judge could testify as a witness at a trial over which she was presiding, Fed. R. Evid. 605 does not allow this: It provides flatly that the judge presiding at the trial may not testify as a witness. Similarly, under Rule 606(a), a member of the jury may not testify at the trial of the case in which the juror is sitting. (Note how far we have come from the self-informing jury!) Rule 606(b) deals with a matter that frequently arises and is addressed by the *Tanner* decision, presented later in this chapter: In what circumstances may a juror testify after the verdict as part of an inquiry into the validity of the verdict?

Note that the disqualification of judges and juries does not extend to other court officers, such as the court clerk, the bailiff, or a stenographer. If, for example, the bailiff observes a party attempting to bribe a witness, he may testify to that. But if before trial it appears that a court officer will be a witness, presumably that person should not be assigned to the case.

Attorneys. The Federal Rules of Evidence, like most evidentiary codes, do not address the question of whether an attorney may testify in a trial in which she is representing a party. This matter is, however, addressed by the rules of professional responsibility, and the general rule is that she cannot. But there are qualifications and exceptions. Rule 3.7 of the American Bar Association's Model Rules of Professional Conduct provides as follows:

Rule 3.7 Lawyer As Witness

(a) A lawyer shall not act as advocate at a trial in which the lawyer is likely to be a necessary witness unless:

(1) the testimony relates to an uncontested issue;

(2) the testimony relates to the nature and value of legal services rendered in the case; or

(3) disqualification of the lawyer would work substantial hardship on the client.

(b) A lawyer may act as advocate in a trial in which another lawyer in the lawyer's firm is likely to be called as a witness unless precluded from doing so by Rule 1.7 or Rule 1.9. [These two Rules relate to conflicts of interest.]

In two significant respects, Rule 3.7 is more lenient than its predecessor, Disciplinary Rule 5-101(b) of the ABA's now superceded Model Code of Professional Responsibility. That Rule provided as a general matter that the lawyer should not even take employment in contemplated or pending litigation if it appeared obvious that the lawyer ought to be called as a witness; Rule 3.7, by contrast, allows the lawyer to take on the representation, but if the matter goes to trial and it still appears that she will be a witness she must turn the case over to someone else. Also, the older Rule operated with full force if the prospective witness was another lawyer in the same firm; subject to the ordinary rules on conflicts of interest, Rule 3.7 allows a lawyer to try a case at which another lawyer from her firm will testify.

Rock v. Arkansas

Supreme Court of the United States, 1987.
483 U.S. 44, 107 S.Ct. 2704, 97 L.Ed.2d 37.

■ JUSTICE BLACKMUN delivered the opinion of the Court [in which JUSTICES BRENNAN, MARSHALL, POWELL, and STEVENS joined].

The issue presented in this case is whether Arkansas' evidentiary rule prohibiting the admission of hypnotically refreshed testimony violated petitioner's constitutional right to testify on her own behalf as a defendant in a criminal case.

I

Petitioner Vickie Lorene Rock was charged with manslaughter in the death of her husband, Frank Rock, on July 2, 1983. A dispute had been simmering about Frank's wish to move from the couple's small apartment adjacent to Vickie's beauty parlor to a trailer she owned outside town. That night a fight erupted when Frank refused to let petitioner eat some pizza and prevented her from leaving the apartment to get something else to eat. When police arrived on the scene they found Frank on the floor with a bullet wound in his chest. Petitioner urged the officers to help her husband, and cried to a sergeant who took her in charge, "please save him" and "don't let him die." The police removed her from the building because she was upset and because she interfered with their investigation by her repeated attempts to use the telephone to call her husband's parents. According to the testimony of one of the investigating officers, petitioner told him that "she stood up to leave the room and [her husband] grabbed her by the throat and choked her and threw her against the wall and * * * at that time she walked over and picked up the weapon and pointed it toward the floor and he hit her again and she shot him."

Because petitioner could not remember the precise details of the shooting, her attorney suggested that she submit to hypnosis in order to refresh her memory. Petitioner was hypnotized twice by Doctor Betty Back, a licensed neuropsychologist with training in the field of hypnosis. Doctor Back interviewed petitioner for an hour prior to the first hypnosis session, taking notes on petitioner's general history and her recollections of the shooting. Both hypnosis sessions were recorded on tape. Petitioner did not relate any new information during either of the sessions, but, after the hypnosis, she was able to remember that at the time of the incident she had her thumb on the hammer of the gun, but had not held her finger on the trigger. She also recalled that the gun had discharged when her husband grabbed her arm during the scuffle. As a result of the details that petitioner was able to remember about the shooting, her counsel arranged for a gun expert to examine the handgun, a single action Hawes .22 Deputy Marshal.

That inspection revealed that the gun was defective and prone to fire, when hit or dropped, without the trigger's being pulled.

When the prosecutor learned of the hypnosis sessions, he filed a motion to exclude petitioner's testimony. The trial judge held a pre-trial hearing on the motion and concluded that no hypnotically refreshed testimony would be admitted. The court issued an order limiting petitioner's testimony to "matters remembered and stated to the examiner prior to being placed under hypnosis." At trial, petitioner introduced testimony by the gun expert, but the court limited petitioner's own description of the events on the day of the shooting to a reiteration of the sketchy information in Doctor Back's notes. The jury convicted petitioner on the manslaughter charge and she was sentenced to 10 years imprisonment and a $10,000 fine.

On appeal, the Supreme Court of Arkansas rejected petitioner's claim that the limitations on her testimony violated her right to present her defense. The court concluded that "the dangers of admitting this kind of testimony outweigh whatever probative value it may have," and decided to follow the approach of States that have held hypnotically refreshed testimony of witnesses inadmissible per se. Although the court acknowledged that "a defendant's right to testify is fundamental," it ruled that the exclusion of petitioner's testimony did not violate her constitutional rights. Any "prejudice or deprivation" she suffered "was minimal and resulted from her own actions and not by any erroneous ruling of the court." We granted certiorari, to consider the constitutionality of Arkansas' per se rule excluding a criminal defendant's hypnotically refreshed testimony.

II

Petitioner's claim that her testimony was impermissibly excluded is bottomed on her constitutional right to testify in her own defense. At this point in the development of our adversary system, it cannot be doubted that a defendant in a criminal case has the right to take the witness stand and to testify in his or her own defense. This, of course, is a change from the historic common-law view, which was that all parties to litigation, including criminal defendants, were disqualified from testifying because of their interest in the outcome of the trial. See generally 2 J. Wigmore, Evidence §§ 576, 579 (J. Chadbourn rev. 1979). The principal rationale for this rule was the possible untrustworthiness of a party's testimony. Under the common law, the practice did develop of permitting criminal defendants to tell their side of the story, but they were limited to making an unsworn statement that could not be elicited through direct examination by counsel and was not subject to cross-examination. Id., at § 579, p. 827.

This Court in Ferguson v. Georgia, 365 U.S. 570, 573–582 (1961), detailed the history of the transition from a rule of a defendant's incompetency to a rule of competency. As the Court there recounted, it came to be recognized that permitting a defendant to testify advances both the " 'detection of guilt' " and " 'the protection of innocence,' " and by the end of the second half of the 19th century, all States except Georgia had enacted statutes that declared criminal defendants competent to testify. * * *

The right to testify on one's own behalf at a criminal trial has sources in several provisions of the Constitution. It is one of the rights that "are essential to due process of law in a fair adversary process." Faretta v. California, 422 U.S. 806, 819, n. 15 (1975). The necessary ingredients of the Fourteenth Amendment's guarantee that no one shall be deprived of liberty without due process of law include a right to be heard and to offer testimony:

> "A person's right to reasonable notice of a charge against him, and *an opportunity to be heard in his defense*—a right to his day in court—are basic in our system of jurisprudence; and these rights include, as a minimum, a right to examine the witnesses against him, to offer testimony, and to be represented by counsel." (Emphasis added.) In re Oliver, 333 U.S. 257, 273 (1948).

* * *

The right to testify is also found in the Compulsory Process Clause of the Sixth Amendment, which grants a defendant the right to call "witnesses in his favor," a right that is guaranteed in the criminal courts of the States by the Fourteenth Amendment. Logically included in the accused's right to call witnesses whose testimony is "material and favorable to his defense," United States v. Valenzuela–Bernal, 458 U.S. 858, 867, is a right to testify himself, should he decide it is in his favor to do so. In fact, the most important witness for the defense in many criminal cases is the defendant himself. There is no justification today for a rule that denies an accused the opportunity to offer his own testimony. Like the truthfulness of other witnesses, the defendant's veracity, which was the concern behind the original common-law rule, can be tested adequately by cross-examination. * * *

The opportunity to testify is also a necessary corollary to the Fifth Amendment's guarantee against compelled testimony. In Harris v. New York, 401 U.S. 222, 230 (1971), the Court stated: "Every criminal defendant is privileged to testify in his own defense, or to refuse to do so." Id., at 225. Three of the dissenting Justices in that case agreed that the Fifth Amendment encompasses this right: "[The Fifth Amendment's privilege against self-incrimination] is fulfilled only when an accused is guaranteed the right 'to remain silent unless he chooses to speak in the unfettered exercise of his own will.' * * * The choice of whether to testify in one's own defense * * * is an exercise of the constitutional privilege." Id., at 230, quoting Malloy v. Hogan, 378 U.S. 1, 8 (1964). (Emphasis removed.)

III

The question now before the Court is whether a criminal defendant's right to testify may be restricted by a state rule that excludes her posthypnosis testimony. This is not the first time this Court has faced a constitutional challenge to a state rule, designed to ensure trustworthy evidence, that interfered with the ability of a defendant to offer testimony. In Washington v. Texas, 388 U.S. 14 (1967), the Court was confronted with a state statute that prevented persons charged as principals, accomplices, or accessories in the same crime from being introduced as witnesses for one another. The statute, like the original common-law prohibition on testimony by the accused, was grounded in a concern for the reliability of evidence presented by an interested party:

> "It was thought that if two persons charged with the same crime were allowed to testify on behalf of each other, 'each would try to swear the other out of the charge.' This rule, as well as the other disqualifications for interest, rested on the unstated premises that the right to present witnesses was subordinate to the court's interest in preventing perjury, and that erroneous decisions were best avoided by preventing the jury from hearing any testimony that might be perjured, even if it were the only testimony available on a crucial issue."

As the Court recognized, the incompetency of a codefendant to testify had been rejected on nonconstitutional grounds in 1918, when the Court, refusing to be bound by "the dead hand of the common-law rule of 1789," stated:

> " '[T]he conviction of our time [is] that the truth is more likely to be arrived at by hearing the testimony of all persons of competent understanding who may seem to have knowledge of the facts involved in a case, leaving the credit and weight of such testimony to be determined by the jury or by the court. . .' " 388 U.S., at 22, quoting Rosen v. United States, 245 U.S. 467, 471 (1918).

The Court concluded that this reasoning was compelled by the Sixth Amendment's protections for the accused. In particular, the Court reasoned that the Sixth Amendment was designed in part "to make the testimony of a defendant's witnesses admissible on his behalf in court."

With the rationale for the common-law incompetency rule thus rejected on constitutional grounds, the Court found that the mere presence of the witness in the courtroom was not enough to satisfy the Constitution's Compulsory Process Clause. By preventing the defendant from having the benefit of his accomplice's testimony, "the State *arbitrarily* denied him the right to put on the stand a witness who was physically and mentally capable of testifying to events that he had personally observed, and whose testimony would have been relevant and material to the defense."

Just as a State may not apply an arbitrary rule of competence to exclude a material defense witness from taking the stand, it also may not apply a rule of evidence that permits a witness to take the stand, but arbitrarily excludes material portions of his testimony. In Chambers v. Mississippi, 410 U.S. 284 (1973), the Court invalidated a State's hearsay rule on the ground that it abridged the defendant's right to "present witnesses in his own defense." Chambers was tried for a murder to which another person repeatedly had confessed in the presence of acquaintances. The State's hearsay rule, coupled with a "voucher" rule that did not allow the defendant to cross-examine the confessed murderer directly, prevented Chambers from introducing testimony concerning these confessions, which were critical to his defense. This Court reversed the judgment of conviction, holding that when a state rule of evidence conflicts with the right to present witnesses, the rule may "not be applied mechanistically to defeat the ends of justice," but must meet the fundamental standards of due process. In the Court's view, the State in Chambers did not demonstrate that the hearsay testimony in that case, which bore "assurances of trustworthiness" including corroboration by other evidence, would be unreliable, and thus the defendant should have been able to introduce the exculpatory testimony.

Of course, the right to present relevant testimony is not without limitation. The right "may, in appropriate cases, bow to accommodate other legitimate interests in the criminal trial process." But restrictions of a defendant's right to testify may not be arbitrary or disproportionate to the purposes they are designed to serve. In applying its evidentiary rules a State must evaluate whether the interests served by a rule justify the limitation imposed on the defendant's constitutional right to testify.

IV

The Arkansas rule enunciated by the state courts does not allow a trial court to consider whether posthypnosis testimony may be admissible in a particular case; it is a per se rule prohibiting the admission at trial of any defendant's hypnotically refreshed testimony on the ground that such testimony is always unreliable. Thus, in Arkansas, an accused's testimony is limited to matters that he or she can prove were remembered before hypnosis. This rule operates to the detriment of any defendant who undergoes hypnosis, without regard to the reasons for it, the circumstances under which it took place, or any independent verification of the information it produced.

In this case, the application of that rule had a significant adverse effect on petitioner's ability to testify. It virtually prevented her from describing any of the events that occurred on the day of the shooting, despite corroboration of many of those events by other witnesses. Even more importantly, under the court's rule petitioner was not permitted to describe the actual shooting except in the words contained in Doctor Back's notes. The expert's description of the gun's tendency to misfire would have taken on greater significance if the jury had heard petitioner testify that she did not have her finger on the trigger and that the gun went off when her husband hit her arm.

In establishing its per se rule, the Arkansas Supreme Court simply followed the approach taken by a number of States that have decided that hypnotically enhanced testimony should be excluded at trial on the ground that it tends to be unreliable. Other States that have adopted an exclusionary rule, however, have done so for the testimony of *witnesses,* not for the testimony of a *defendant.* The Arkansas Supreme Court failed to perform the constitutional analysis that is necessary when a defendant's right to testify is at stake.

Although the Arkansas court concluded that any testimony that cannot be proved to be the product of prehypnosis memory is unreliable, many courts have eschewed a per se rule and permit the admission of hypnotically refreshed testimony. Hypnosis by trained physicians or psychologists has been recognized as a valid therapeutic technique since 1958, although there is no generally accepted theory to explain the phenomenon, or even a consensus on a single definition of hypnosis. See Council on Scientific Affairs, Scientific Status of Refreshing Recollection by the Use of Hypnosis, 253 J.A.M.A. 1918, 1918–1919 (1985) (Council Report). The use of hypnosis in criminal investigations, however, is controversial, and the current medical and legal view of its appropriate role is unsettled.

Responses of individuals to hypnosis vary greatly. The popular belief that hypnosis guarantees the accuracy of recall is as yet without established foundation and, in fact, hypnosis often has no effect at all on memory. The most common response to hypnosis, however, appears to be an increase in both correct and incorrect recollections. Three general characteristics of hypnosis may lead to the introduction of inaccurate memories: the subject becomes "suggestible" and may try to please the hypnotist with answers the subject thinks will be met with approval; the subject is likely to "confabulate," that is, to fill in details from the imagination in order to make an answer more coherent and complete; and, the subject experiences "memory hardening," which gives him great confidence in both true and false memories, making effective cross-examination more difficult. See generally M. Orne, et al., Hypnotically Induced Testimony, in Eyewitness Testimony: Psychological Perspectives 171 (G. Wells and E. Loftus, eds., 1985); Diamond, Inherent Problems in the Use of Pretrial Hypnosis on a Prospective Witness, 68 Calif.L.Rev. 313, 333–342 (1980). Despite the unreliability that hypnosis concededly may introduce, however, the procedure has been credited as instrumental in obtaining investigative leads or identifications that were later confirmed by independent evidence. See, e.g., People v. Hughes, 59 N.Y.2d 523, 533, 453 N.E.2d 484, 488 (1983); see generally R. Udolf, Forensic Hypnosis 11–16 (1983).

The inaccuracies the process introduces can be reduced, although perhaps not eliminated, by the use of procedural safeguards. One set of suggested guidelines calls for hypnosis to be performed only by a psychologist or psychiatrist with special training in its use and who is independent of the investigation. See Orne, The Use and Misuse of Hypnosis in Court, 27 Int'l J. Clinical & Experimental Hypnosis 311, 335–336 (1979). These procedures reduce the possibility that biases will be communicated to the hypersuggestive subject by the hypnotist. Suggestion will be less likely also if the hypnosis is conducted in a neutral setting with no one present but the hypnotist and the subject. Tape or video recording of all interrogations, before, during, and after hypnosis, can help reveal if leading questions were asked. Id., at 336. Such guidelines do not guarantee the accuracy of the testimony, because they cannot control the subject's own motivations or any tendency to confabulate, but they do provide a means of controlling overt suggestions.

The more traditional means of assessing accuracy of testimony also remain applicable in the case of a previously hypnotized defendant. Certain information recalled as a result of hypnosis may be verified as highly accurate by corroborating evidence. Cross-examination, even in the face of a confident defendant, is an effective tool for revealing inconsistencies. Moreover, a jury can be educated to the risks of hypnosis through expert testimony and cautionary instructions. Indeed, it is probably to a defendant's advantage to establish carefully the extent of his memory prior to hypnosis, in order to minimize the decrease in credibility the procedure might introduce.

We are not now prepared to endorse without qualifications the use of hypnosis as an investigative tool; scientific understanding of the phenomenon and of the means to control the effects of hypnosis is still in its infancy. Arkansas, however, has not justified the exclusion of all of a defendant's testimony that the defendant is unable to prove to be the product of pre-hypnosis memory. A State's legitimate interest in barring unreliable evidence does not extend to per se exclusions that may be reliable in an individual case. Wholesale inadmissibility of a defendant's testimony is an arbitrary restriction on the right to testify in the absence of clear evidence by the State repudiating the validity of all posthypnosis recollections. The State would be well within its powers if it established guidelines to aid trial courts in the evaluation of posthypnosis testimony and it may be able to show that testimony in a particular case is so unreliable that exclusion is justified. But it has not shown that hypnotically enhanced testimony is always so untrustworthy and so immune to the traditional means of evaluating credibility that it should disable a defendant from presenting her version of the events for which she is on trial.

In this case, the defective condition of the gun corroborated the details petitioner remembered about the shooting. The tape recordings provided some means to evaluate the hypnosis and the trial judge concluded that Doctor Back did not suggest responses with leading questions. Those circumstances present an argument for admissibility of petitioner's testimony in this particular case, an argument that must be considered by the trial court. Arkansas' per se rule excluding all posthypnosis testimony infringes impermissibly on the right of a defendant to testify on his or her own behalf.

The judgment of the Supreme Court of Arkansas is vacated and the case is remanded to that court for further proceedings not inconsistent with this opinion.

It is so ordered.

[Chief Justice Rehnquist, with whom Justices White, O'Connor, and Scalia joined, dissented.They emphasized that the Court's decisions had established "that an individual's right to present evidence on his behalf is not absolute and must often times give way to countervailing considerations." Given especially that scientific understanding of hypnosis was "still in its infancy," they believed that the Court should accord greater respect to the state's choice of criminal trial rules and procedures.]

State v. Moore

Supreme Court of New Jersey, 2006.
902 A.2d 1212.

■ CHIEF JUSTICE PORITZ delivered the opinion of the Court.

This case returns to the Court after remand for a plenary hearing in respect of the continued viability of State v. Hurd, 86 N.J. 525, 432 A.2d 86 (1981), wherein the Court established guidelines for the admissibility of hypnotically refreshed testimony proffered by a witness in a criminal trial. Based on the record developed below, and the substantial body of case law that has considered the question since *Hurd* was decided, we have determined that a change in course is now warranted. We are no longer of the view that the *Hurd* guidelines can serve as an effective control for the harmful effects of hypnosis on the truth-seeking function that lies at the heart of our system of justice. Most important, we are not convinced that it is possible to know whether post-hypnotic testimony can ever be as reliable as testimony that is based on ordinary recall, even recognizing the myriad of problems associated with ordinary recall. We therefore conclude that the hypnotically refreshed testimony of a witness in a criminal trial is generally inadmissible and that *Hurd* should no longer be followed in New Jersey.

I.

[The victim, M.A., was awakened in her bed at 2:30 a.m. by a man who grabbed her neck and demanded money. He sexually assaulted and threatened her, telling her not to look at him. At one point, M.A. did open her eyes and looked up at him; he immediately told her to close her eyes, which she did. Several hours later, M.A. told police that her attacker might be an African–American man of medium build. Later that day, M.A. described her assailant as black in his late twenties to mid-thirties, with short hair and a short beard, wearing jeans. Because she saw him only once and was unable to provide sufficient information to develop a composite sketch, M.A. suggested hypnosis. Sixteen days later, M.A. visited the office of Dr. Samuel Babcock, a licensed clinical psychologist, to undergo hypnosis. Babcock first conducted a tape-recorded background interview with a police detective. He then conducted a private, tape-recorded, pre-hypnotic interview with M.A. M.A. described the lighting conditions in her bedroom at the time of the assault, explaining that the light was "enough to see . . . shadows and stuff . . . outlines of things, . . . but . . . nothing in detail." She also described how she saw the assailant's face only once, briefly, when he was standing over her bed. As a result, besides knowing that he was black, and that he had "what looked like a real light beard or more like shadows on his face[,] . . . nothing about his face caught [her] attention." She did not remember anything distinctive about either his eyes or his nose, but she thought he had a round face and that his legs looked as though they were muscular and stocky. When Babcock realized that M.A. was wearing contact lenses,] he asked how well she could see without them. M.A. responded that if an object is "a couple feet away . . . all I see is blur," and that her assailant had been "close enough to see but not in detail." While hypnotized, M.A. stated for the first time that she thought her assailant wore a tan suede jacket with a zipper and that he was a medium-skinned black male. As the session was ending but prior to bringing M.A. out of hypnosis, Dr. Babcock advised her that she would not be able to remember what they talked about, but that she "will remember the face [of her assailant], crystal clear, very clearly." Then, to ease her transition to a waking state, Dr. Babcock told her to sleep and switched off the tape during the last minutes of the session.

A few days later, M.A. chose defendant Clarence Moore from a photo array. Subsequently, she identified him from two more arrays, one of which was actually a photograph of a lineup. Moore was the only person common to all three. When she looked at the initial array, M.A. advised detectives that she recalled dirt near or on the pockets of her assailant's tan suede jacket.

[In pretrial proceedings, the court ruled that the hypnotic session had complied with the procedural guidelines established by *Hurd*.] The court therefore permitted M.A.'s testimony as refreshed recollection. The court also permitted the State to play a substantial portion of the recording of the hypnotic session for the jury. * * * [Apart from this evidence,] the State offered no corroborating evidence of M.A.'s identification of Moore.[2]

On the witness stand, M.A. made an in-court identification of Moore as the person who assaulted her. She admitted that during the attack she caught only a "glimpse" of his face in what could have been but a "split second" or "could have been more than that." M.A. maintained, however, that the glimpse was "enough to remember" and that Moore's face "was the same face." She further stated that there was "no question" but that the person she identified in the photo arrays was her assailant, recounting that when she picked Moore's photo she "recognize[d] that face, everything about it." Although she had described a person with a light beard during the police investigation (Moore actually had a mustache at the time of the assault), when she first identified Moore's photograph, M.A. testified, she "wasn't concerned with a beard or a mustache or any kind of facial hair[;] [she] was just looking at the whole face." In respect of the lighting conditions in her bedroom, M.A. testified that there was enough light to see facial features and to "remember someone." She also indicated that she was not wearing her contact lenses during the assault, but that she was able to see without them and, in fact, had driven without her lenses. When confronted with her prior statements regarding her inability to see objects

---

[2] M.A. testified that she recognized defendant's tan suede jacket and that it was the same as the jacket worn by her assailant; however, her recall of the jacket was derived from her hypnotically refreshed memory.

more than a few feet away without her contacts, M.A. responded that "before I was hypnotized that was accurate."

Finally, when questioned about the tan suede jacket she had identified, M.A. repeatedly stated she was sure it was the jacket worn by her assailant because she "could remember picturing him wearing it." A sergeant with the Atlantic County Prosecutor's Office testified at trial that M.A. knew the police had removed clothing from his house and that she may have been advised specifically that the clothes she was asked to identify were taken from his house. The sergeant also admitted that there was no other suede garment among the clothes M.A. viewed.

Most important, M.A. acknowledged that her recollection of her assailant had been altered by her hypnotic experience. She explained that hypnosis made her assailant's face "much clearer" with "the features . . . more detailed," that "[i]t was much easier to describe [his face] in more detail afterwards," and that her vision of his face and clothing appeared "brighter." Asked whether she would have recognized her assailant prior to being hypnotized, M.A. replied, "I think so, but I couldn't have been positive." She conveyed in her testimony a clear and strong conviction that Moore was the person who assaulted her. * * * [Moore was convicted on all counts, but the conviction was ultimately thrown out, primarily because of prosecutorial misconduct, by a federal appeals court. After considerable further proceedings before an anticipated retrial, the state supreme court directed the trial court to hold] a plenary hearing on the question "whether the assumptions and other factors reflected in *Hurd* regarding hypnotically-induced testimony remain valid and appropriate."

On remand, the trial court heard testimony from three experts. The court concluded that hypnotically refreshed testimony should be precluded; that "at the very least," the *Hurd* guidelines should be supplemented; and that, regardless of the decision on those two issues, M.A.'s testimony should be barred because Dr. Babcock did not comply with the *Hurd* guidelines. * * *

II.

Twenty-five years ago, in State v. Hurd, this Court was presented for the first time with the question "whether the testimony of a witness who has undergone hypnosis to refresh her recollection is admissible in a criminal trial and, if so, in what circumstances." After reviewing the expert testimony presented to the trial court, including the scientific literature available at the time, we held that a witness who has been hypnotized in an attempt to improve his or her recollection may testify at trial "subject to strict safeguards to ensure the reliability of the hypnotic procedure." * * *

In certain respects the facts undergirding the *Hurd* decision are similar to the facts here. In *Hurd*, Jane Sell had been attacked and stabbed while she was sleeping in her apartment. She was unable to identify her attacker, and consequently, the prosecutor's office recommended that she try hypnosis as a means of enhancing her recall. Sell agreed and, with two officers and a medical student present, underwent hypnosis by a psychiatrist. During the hypnotic session one of the officers asked her if the attacker was her ex-husband, Paul Hurd. Although she responded "[y]es," she was uncomfortable with her identification when she first came out of hypnosis. Days later, however, Sell came to the police station and identified Hurd as her attacker.

Hurd was charged with assault and other crimes. * * * [The question of admissibility of the victim's testimony was considered before trial by the state supreme court.]

Most important in respect of the question before us today, the *Hurd* Court reviewed the substantial extant authority discussing problems associated with post-hypnotic memory, noting that "while hypnosis often can produce remarkably accurate recall, it is also prone to yield sheer fantasy, willful lies, or a mixture of fact with gaps filled in by fantasy." Citing Dr. [Martin] Orne [a renowned expert on hypnosis, who had testified for the defense], the Court recognized three troubling concerns: that a person undergoing hypnosis is extremely vulnerable to suggestion, which even an expert observer may not be able to identify; that such a person loses critical judgment, and consequently will speculate and respond with greater confidence than other persons; and that memories evoked under hypnosis are often confounded with prior recall. Despite those concerns, the Court concluded that "a rule of per se inadmissibility is unnecessarily broad and will result in the exclusion of evidence that is as trustworthy as other eyewitness testimony."

Because the Court found that hypnotically refreshed testimony, in appropriate circumstances, could be as reliable as ordinary recall, it held that such testimony would be "admissible in a criminal trial if the trial court finds that the use of hypnosis in the particular case was reasonably likely to result in recall comparable in accuracy to normal human memory." To aid in that determination, the Court adopted the procedural safeguards suggested by Dr. Orne and directed trial courts to "evaluate both the kind of memory loss that hypnosis was used to restore and the specific technique employed." Under the safeguards, "a psychiatrist or psychologist experienced in the use of hypnosis must conduct the session"; that person "should be independent of and not regularly employed by the prosecutor, investigator or defense"; "any information given to the hypnotist by law enforcement personnel or the defense prior to the hypnotic session must be recorded, either in writing or another suitable form"; the hypnotist must elicit a detailed description of the facts from the subject before hypnosis; "all contacts between the hypnotist and the subject must be recorded"; and "only the hypnotist and the subject should be present during any phase of the hypnotic session." The burden of proof, by clear and convincing evidence, was assigned to the party offering the hypnotically refreshed testimony. * * * [The *Hurd* court concluded that these standards were not met. Two justices would have adopted a per se rule against the admissibility of "hypnotically induced testimony."]

III.

A.

[The court reviewed prior case law from various jurisdictions. Some, led by *State v. Mack*, 292 N.W.2d 764 (Minn. 1980), adopted a hard rule against "any evidence purportedly induced, refreshed or enhanced by hypnosis." Others concluded that the fact that a witness's testimony had been refreshed by hypnosis went only to the credibility of the witness and not to admissibility. Others adopted the intermediate position of *Hurd*, that hypnotically refreshed testimony could be introduced so long as prescribed procedural safeguards were followed.]

Finally, we note one other trend in respect of this issue. Nine states have adopted an alternative to the three approaches previously discussed (per se admissibility, procedural safeguards, and per se inadmissibility) known as the ad hoc approach. Those jurisdictions place "the burden on the state in each case to satisfy the trial court that the testimony of witnesses previously subjected to hypnotism is reliable." State v. Seager, 341 N.W.2d 420, 429 (Iowa 1983). Sometimes referred to as the "totality of the circumstances" test, this approach considers, among other things, whether the purpose of the hypnosis was therapeutic or investigative, whether corroborating evidence exists, and whether the post-hypnotic recollection was substantially similar to the pre-hypnotic recollection. The Supreme Court of Colorado, for example, has held that in determining admissibility, trial courts must consider the level of training and independence of the hypnotist, whether all contacts between the witness and the hypnotist were recorded, the circumstances under which the hypnosis occurred, and the appropriateness of hypnosis for the kind of memory loss involved. People v. Romero, 745 P.2d 1003, 1017 (Colo.1987), *cert. denied*, 485 U.S. 990, 108 S. Ct. 1296, 99 L. Ed. 2d 506 (1988).

* * * Today, as the debate continues, four states consider hypnotically refreshed testimony per se admissible, with the trier of fact determining its weight, six allow such testimony when certain procedural safeguards are met, twenty-six have adopted variations on the per se inadmissible rule, and nine have adopted some type of "totality of the circumstances" test.

B.

The four approaches described above had been adopted in at least some states by 1987, when the United States Supreme Court decided *Rock [v. Arkansas]*. * * *

VII.

Today we hold that in a criminal trial, the hypnotically refreshed testimony of a witness generally is inadmissible in New Jersey. Twenty-five years ago in *Hurd* this Court crafted a solution to the complex of problems raised when a witness testifies after undergoing hypnosis to improve his or her memory. Concerned about the reliability of hypnotically refreshed testimony, the Court established guidelines for conducting hypnotic sessions to ensure that the witness's refreshed memory would be as reliable as ordinary recall. On a defendant's claim that the prosecution violated the guidelines, *Hurd* required an inquiry to determine whether the challenged posthypnotic testimony could be put before the trier of fact. That approach, in the years since *Hurd*, has been challenged by the experts and rejected by the majority of courts considering the issue. Many of the jurisdictions that have declined to adopt *Hurd* have expressed concern about the inherent unreliability of hypnotically refreshed memory and the efficacy of the guidelines in controlling the adverse impacts of hypnosis. They have also rejected the New Jersey approach because it is time consuming and may lead to inconsistent results in cases that are similar on their facts.

Despite those concerns, we would not abandon the template established in *Hurd* unless we had become convinced that the scientific evidence presented below, and relied on by other courts, counsels another course. The difference between the testimony of the experts at the time *Hurd* was decided, and the experts who testified on remand in this case, is largely a difference in degree, not substance. Yet, that difference is telling. Although the scientific community has not reached a definitive consensus on the issue, more recent studies reaffirm and strengthen earlier understandings about how hypnosis affects both memory and attitude. We now conclude on the basis of this data that hypnotically refreshed testimony cannot meet the general acceptance standard of admissibility.

Moreover, there has been a shift in expert opinion suggesting that the problems associated with the use of hypnotically refreshed testimony are less amenable to correction through controls on the hypnotic process. Dr. Orne himself has concluded that the procedural safeguards he advocated in *Hurd* are inadequate to their purpose. We are unable to determine whether hypnotically refreshed testimony is as reliable as ordinary recall (a point important to the *Hurd* Court) or even to implement a process to ensure that such testimony can meet that criterion.

In sum, the experts that testified on remand agreed that hypnosis does not produce more accurate recall, but rather, instills a false confidence in the hypnotized individual thereby producing an aura of truthfulness that subverts effective cross-examination, a cornerstone of the adversarial system. Moreover, the cumulative import of the testimony below, the scientific literature, and the case law from other states is that there is at this point no way to gauge the reliability of hypnotically induced testimony. There is a consensus among scientists and clinical practitioners, including the experts below, that memory is reconstructive and that recall generally is a complicated process in which the individual draws material from many sources. In relation to hypnotically refreshed memory, specifically, because numerous factors "influence how events are perceived, [there are] psychologists and psychiatrists [who] believe hypnosis itself can affect recall." Webert, 40 *Am. Crim. L. Rev.* at 1304.

Most important here, the testifying experts and the scientific literature are consistent in their description of the effects of hypnosis—suggestibility, confabulation or "gap filling," pseudomemory or "false memory," memory hardening or "false confidence" in one's recollections, source amnesia, and loss of critical judgment. Antonia F. Giuliana, Note, *Between a Rock and a Hurd Place: Protecting the Criminal Defendant's Right to Testify After Her Testimony Has Been Hypnotically Refreshed*, 65 Fordham L. Rev. 2151, 2166–69 *(1997)*; Webert, 40 *Am. Crim. L. Rev.* at 1320–23; *see* Martin T. Orne, et al., *Hypnotically Refreshed Testimony: Enhanced Memory or Tampering with Evidence?, Issues and Practices in Criminal Justice*, Jan. 1985, at 5–27. In contrast, there is a lack of empirical evidence supporting the popular notion that hypnosis improves recall. Webert, 40 *Am. Crim. L. Rev.* at 1318–20; Nancy Mehrkens Steblay and Robert K. Bothwell, *Evidence for Hypnotically Refreshed Testimony: The View from the Laboratory*, 18 *Law & Hum. Behav.* 635, 648 (1994) ("[t]he hypothesized increase in recall accuracy for hypnotized subjects has not been substantiated by research to date."). In this vein, we add only that the general public believes that "hypnosis [is] a powerful tool to recover accurate memories." Webert, 40 *Am. Crim. L. Rev.* at 13–23. Eighty-eight percent of respondents in a 1999 survey agreed at some level that "hypnosis enables people to accurately remember things they could not otherwise remember." *Ibid.* (citing Myles E. Johnson & Coleen Hauk, *Beliefs and Opinions About Hypnosis Held by the General Public: A Systematic Evaluation*, 42 Am. J. Clinical Hypnosis 10, 17 (1999)). That confidence in the power of hypnosis to produce accurate recall affects individuals undergoing hypnosis who are convinced—wrongly—that they will remember precisely what happened to them after they are hypnotized, and affects jurors, who are likely to reach a favorable verdict when a witness has been hypnotized.

Finally, as was the trial court, we are most concerned that, after *Hurd* was decided, Dr. Orne repudiated the guidelines he had suggested because he concluded that information obtained through hypnosis is inherently unreliable and creates the risk of a "serious miscarriage of justice" if used in criminal trials. Giuliana, *supra*, 65 Fordham L. Rev. at 2154, n. 20 (citing Wayne G. Whitehouse et al., *Hypnotic Hypermnesia: Enhanced Memory Accessibility or Report Bias?*, 97 J. Abnormal Psychol. 289, 294 (1988)); *see also id.* at 2170 (quoting Dr. Orne's warning that " 'there is a considerable risk that the inherent unreliability of information confidently provided by a hypnotized witness may actually be detrimental to the truth-seeking process.' "). Other experts, also, have repeated Dr. Orne's conclusion that the probative value of hypnotically refreshed testimony is outweighed by the inherent risks of distorted recollection and false confidence. Steblay and Bothwell, 18 *Law & Hum. Behav.* at 636.

* * * Because we are no longer confident that procedural safeguards can guard effectively against the risks associated with hypnotically refreshed testimony, we reject the *Hurd* approach and hold that M.A.'s testimony is inadmissible.

Some further comments in respect of M.A.'s hypnosis are warranted. We observe first that in many respects the guidelines were not followed. For example, the psychologist conducting the hypnotic session testified at trial that he had a history of engagements by the prosecution, which raises questions about his independence, a guideline issue. Second, he told M.A. that he had hypnotized several rape victims and that she would remember the details of her assault "very clearly." That statement to M.A. to remember clearly the face of her assailant was sufficiently suggestive in and of itself to taint her post-hypnotic testimony and was, in any case another guideline violation. M.A. herself believed that after hypnosis her memory of the attack would be free from error and wanted to be hypnotized so that she accurately could identify her attacker. As a consequence of her belief and the hypnotist's suggestion, at trial M.A. testified with the utmost confidence in the truth of her identification of defendant, declaring then that hypnosis helped her to see "very clearly."

In some sense that fact pattern is a paradigm for what makes hypnosis unreliable and for why it should not be admissible. Most disturbing, M.A.'s pre-hypnotic memories were spare and unlikely to result in a confident identification of her attacker. There was virtually no other untainted corroborating evidence pointing to defendant.[12] Our concern for the victim, and for the horror of her assault, cannot override defendant's right to a fair trial in which evidence obtained through an unreliable procedure is excluded.

Under *Rock* a defendant may testify at his own trial after having been hypnotized. Regardless of our concerns about such testimony, we are constrained to accommodate defendants' rights in that setting. We are therefore, by this opinion, asking the Criminal Practice Committee to consider and recommend improvements to both the *Hurd* guidelines and the *Fertig* charge. There are suggestions in the record below and in the scientific literature that are available to the Committee as it undertakes its task.

VIII.

The conclusion of the trial court that hypnotically refreshed testimony should be inadmissible is affirmed. The matter is remanded to the Law Division for any further proceedings consonant with this opinion.

[Justice Rivera–Soto wrote separately, agreeing that M.A.'s post-hypnotic statements should be inadmissible but contending that "a defendant's constitutional right to testify on his own behalf and a victim's constitutional right to testify against the one who stands accused of harming that victim cannot be of unequal constitutional dignity." Therefore, he believed that "there is no principled basis on which to treat a victim's hypnotically refreshed testimony any differently than that of the defendant."]

---

[12] We note the State's concession in its brief that "without post-hypnotic testimony ..., there would not remain a viable prosecution."

Tanner v. United States

Supreme Court of the United States, 1987.
483 U.S. 107, 107 S.Ct. 2739, 97 L.Ed.2d 90.

■ JUSTICE O'CONNOR delivered the opinion of the Court.

Petitioners William Conover and Anthony Tanner were convicted of conspiring to defraud the United States in violation of 18 U.S.C. § 371, and of committing mail fraud in violation of 18 U.S.C. § 1341. * * *

The day before petitioners were scheduled to be sentenced, Tanner filed a motion, in which Conover subsequently joined, seeking continuance of the sentencing date, permission to interview jurors, an evidentiary hearing, and a new trial. According to an affidavit accompanying the motion, Tanner's attorney had received an unsolicited telephone call from one of the trial jurors, Vera Asbul. Juror Asbul informed Tanner's attorney that several of the jurors consumed alcohol during the lunch breaks at various times throughout the trial, causing them to sleep through the afternoons. The District Court continued the sentencing date, ordered the parties to file memoranda, and heard argument on the motion to interview jurors. The District Court concluded that juror testimony on intoxication was inadmissible under Federal Rule of Evidence 606(b) to impeach the jury's verdict. The District Court invited petitioners to call any nonjuror witnesses, such as courtroom personnel, in support of the motion for new trial. Tanner's counsel took the stand and testified that he had observed one of the jurors "in a sort of giggly mood" at one point during the trial but did not bring this to anyone's attention at the time. * * *

Following the hearing the District Court filed an order stating that "[o]n the basis of the admissible evidence offered I specifically find that the motions for leave to interview jurors or for an evidentiary hearing at which jurors would be witnesses is not required or appropriate." The District Court also denied the motion for new trial.

While the appeal of this case was pending before the Eleventh Circuit, petitioners filed another new trial motion based on additional evidence of jury misconduct. In another affidavit, Tanner's attorney stated that he received an unsolicited visit at his residence from a second juror, Daniel Hardy. Despite the fact that the District Court had denied petitioners' motion for leave to interview jurors, two days after Hardy's visit Tanner's attorney arranged for Hardy to be interviewed by two private investigators. The interview was transcribed, sworn to by the juror, and attached to the new trial motion. In the interview Hardy stated that he "felt like . . . the jury was on one big party." Hardy indicated that seven of the jurors drank alcohol during the noon recess. Four jurors, including Hardy, consumed between them "a pitcher to three pitchers" of beer during various recesses. Of the three other jurors who were alleged to have consumed alcohol, Hardy stated that on several occasions he observed two jurors having one or two mixed drinks during the lunch recess, and one other juror, who was also the foreperson, having a liter of wine on each of three occasions. Juror Hardy also stated that he and three other jurors smoked marijuana quite regularly during the trial. Moreover, Hardy stated that during the trial he observed one juror ingest cocaine five times and another juror ingest cocaine two or three times. One juror sold a quarter pound of marijuana to another juror during the trial, and took marijuana, cocaine, and drug paraphernalia into the courthouse. Hardy noted that some of the jurors were falling asleep during the trial, and that one of the jurors described himself to Hardy as "flying." Hardy stated that before he visited Tanner's attorney at his residence, no one had contacted him concerning the jury's conduct, and Hardy had not been offered anything in return for his statement. Hardy said that he came forward "to clear my conscience" and "[b]ecause I felt . . . that the people on the jury didn't have no business being on the jury. I felt . . . that Mr. Tanner should have a better opportunity to get somebody that would review the facts right." * * *

Petitioners argue that the District Court erred in not ordering an additional evidentiary hearing at which jurors would testify concerning drug and alcohol use during the trial. Petitioners assert that, contrary to the holdings of the District Court and the Court of Appeals, juror testimony on ingestion of drugs or alcohol during the trial is not barred by Federal Rule of Evidence 606(b). Moreover, petitioners argue that whether or not authorized by Rule 606(b), an evidentiary hearing including juror testimony on drug and alcohol use is compelled by their Sixth Amendment right to trial by a competent jury.

By the beginning of this century, if not earlier, the near-universal and firmly established common-law rule in the United States flatly prohibited the admission of juror testimony to impeach a jury verdict. See 8 J. Wigmore, Evidence § 2352, pp. 696–697 (J. McNaughton rev. ed. 1961) (common-law rule, originating from 1785 opinion of Lord Mansfield, "came to receive in the United States an adherence almost unquestioned").

Exceptions to the common-law rule were recognized only in situations in which an "extraneous influence," Mattox v. United States, 146 U.S. 140, 149 (1892), was alleged to have affected the jury. In *Mattox,* this Court held admissible the testimony of jurors describing how they heard and read prejudicial information not admitted into evidence. The Court allowed juror testimony on influence by outsiders in Parker v. Gladden, 385 U.S. 363, 365 (1966) (bailiff's comments on defendant), and Remmer v. United States, 347 U.S. 227, 228–230 (1954) (bribe offered to juror). See also Smith v. Phillips, 455 U.S. 209 (1982) (juror in criminal trial had submitted an application for employment at the District Attorney's office). In situations that did not fall into this exception for external influence, however, the Court adhered to the common-law rule against admitting juror testimony to impeach a verdict.

Lower courts used this external/internal distinction to identify those instances in which juror testimony impeaching a verdict would be admissible. The distinction was not based on whether the juror was literally inside or outside the jury room when the alleged irregularity took place; rather, the distinction was based on the nature of the allegation. Clearly a rigid distinction based only on whether the event took place inside or outside the jury room would have been quite unhelpful. For example, under a distinction based on location a juror could not testify concerning a newspaper read inside the jury room. Instead, of course, this has been considered an external influence about which juror testimony is admissible. Similarly, under a rigid locational distinction jurors could be regularly required to testify after the verdict as to whether they heard and comprehended the judge's instructions, since the charge to the jury takes place outside the jury room. Courts wisely have treated allegations of a juror's inability to hear or comprehend at trial as an internal matter.

Most significant for the present case, however, is the fact that lower federal courts treated allegations of the physical or mental incompetence of a juror as "internal" rather than "external" matters. In United States v. Dioguardi, 492 F.2d 70 (C.A.2 1974), the defendant Dioguardi received a letter from one of the jurors soon after the trial in which the juror explained that she had "eyes and ears that . . . see things before [they] happen," but that her eyes "are only partly open" because "a curse was put upon them some years ago." Armed with this letter and the opinions of seven psychiatrists that the letter suggested that the juror was suffering from a psychological disorder, Dioguardi sought a new trial or in the alternative an evidentiary hearing on the juror's competence. The District Court denied the motion and the Court of Appeals affirmed.

* * *

Substantial policy considerations support the common-law rule against the admission of jury testimony to impeach a verdict. As early as 1915 this Court explained the necessity of shielding jury deliberations from public scrutiny:

> "[L]et it once be established that verdicts solemnly made and publicly returned into court can be attacked and set aside on the testimony of those who took part in their publication and all verdicts could be, and many would be, followed by an inquiry in the hope of discovering something which might invalidate the finding. Jurors would be harassed and beset by the defeated party in an effort to secure from them evidence of facts which might establish misconduct sufficient to set aside a verdict. If evidence thus secured could be thus used, the result would be to make what was intended to be a private deliberation, the constant subject of public investigation—to the destruction of all frankness and freedom of discussion and conference." McDonald v. Pless, 238 U.S., at 267–268. * * *

There is little doubt that postverdict investigation into juror misconduct would in some instances lead to the invalidation of verdicts reached after irresponsible or improper juror behavior. It is not at all clear, however, that the jury system could survive such efforts to perfect it. Allegations of juror misconduct, incompetency, or inattentiveness, raised for the first time days, weeks, or months after the verdict, seriously disrupt the finality of the process. Moreover, full and frank discussion in the jury room, jurors' willingness to return an unpopular verdict, and the community's trust in a system that relies on the decisions of laypeople would all be undermined by a barrage of postverdict scrutiny of juror conduct.

Federal Rule of Evidence 606(b) is grounded in the common-law rule against admission of jury testimony to impeach a verdict and the exception for juror testimony relating to extraneous influences. * * *

[P]etitioners argue that substance abuse constitutes an improper "outside influence" about which jurors may testify under Rule 606(b). In our view the language of the Rule cannot easily be stretched to cover this circumstance. However severe their effect and improper their use, drugs or alcohol voluntarily ingested by a juror seems no more an "outside influence" than a virus, poorly prepared food, or a lack of sleep.

In any case, whatever ambiguity might linger in the language of Rule 606(b) as applied to juror intoxication is resolved by the legislative history of the Rule. * * *

[T]he legislative history demonstrates with uncommon clarity that Congress specifically understood, considered, and rejected a version of Rule 606(b) that would have allowed jurors to testify on juror conduct during deliberations, including juror intoxication. This legislative history provides strong support for the most reasonable reading of the language of Rule 606(b)—that juror intoxication is not an "outside influence" about which jurors may testify to impeach their verdict.

Finally, even if Rule 606(b) is interpreted to retain the common-law exception allowing postverdict inquiry of juror incompetence in cases of "substantial if not wholly conclusive evidence of incompetency," *Dioguardi,* 492 F.2d, at 80, the showing made by petitioners falls far short of this standard. The affidavits and testimony presented in support of the first new trial motion suggested, at worst, that several of the jurors fell asleep at times during the afternoons. The District Court Judge appropriately considered the fact that he had "an unobstructed view" of the jury, and did not see any juror sleeping. The juror affidavit submitted in support of the second new trial motion was obtained in clear violation of the District Court's order and the court's local rule against juror interviews, MD Fla. Rule 2.04(c); on this basis alone the District Court would have been acting within its discretion in disregarding the affidavit. In any case, although the affidavit of juror Hardy describes more dramatic instances of misconduct, Hardy's allegations of *incompetence* are meager. Hardy stated that the alcohol consumption he engaged in with three other jurors did not leave any of them intoxicated. App. to Pet. for Cert. 47 ("I told [the prosecutor] that we would just go out and get us a pitcher of beer and drink it, but as far as us being drunk, no we wasn't"). The only allegations concerning the jurors' ability to properly consider the evidence were Hardy's observations that some jurors were "falling asleep all the time during the trial," and that his own reasoning ability was affected on one day of the trial. These allegations would not suffice to bring this case under the common-law exception allowing postverdict inquiry when an extremely strong showing of incompetency has been made.

Petitioners also argue that the refusal to hold an additional evidentiary hearing at which jurors would testify as to their conduct "violates the sixth amendment's guarantee to a fair trial before an impartial and *competent* jury."

This Court has recognized that a defendant has a right to "a tribunal both impartial and mentally competent to afford a hearing." Jordan v. Massachusetts, 225 U.S. 167, 176 (1912). In this case the District Court held an evidentiary hearing in response to petitioners' first new trial motion at which the judge invited petitioners to introduce any admissible evidence in support of their allegations. At issue in this case is whether the Constitution compelled the District Court to hold an additional evidentiary hearing including one particular kind of evidence inadmissible under the Federal Rules.

As described above, long-recognized and very substantial concerns support the protection of jury deliberations from intrusive inquiry. Petitioners' Sixth Amendment interests in an unimpaired jury, on the other hand, are protected by several aspects of the trial process. The suitability of an individual for the responsibility of jury service, of course, is examined during *voir dire*. Moreover, during the trial the jury is observable by the court, by counsel, and by court personnel. Moreover, jurors are observable by each other, and may report inappropriate juror behavior to the court *before* they render a verdict. Finally, after the trial a party may seek to impeach the verdict by nonjuror evidence of misconduct. See United States v. Taliaferro, 558 F.2d 724, 725–726 (C.A.4 1977) (court considered records of club where jurors dined, and testimony of marshal who accompanied jurors, to determine whether jurors were intoxicated during deliberations). Indeed, in this case the District Court held an evidentiary hearing giving petitioners ample opportunity to produce nonjuror evidence supporting their allegations.

In light of these other sources of protection of petitioners' right to a competent jury, we conclude that the District Court did not err in deciding, based on the inadmissibility of juror testimony and the clear insufficiency of the nonjuror evidence offered by petitioners, that an additional postverdict evidentiary hearing was unnecessary. * * *

[Justice Marshall, with whom Justices Brennan, Blackmun, and Stevens joined, dissented from the portions of the majority opinion produced here. He emphasized that Rule 606(b) "is not applicable to juror testimony on matters *unrelated* to the jury's deliberations" and that the claim of juror misconduct and incompetency in this case involved "objectively verifiable conduct occurring prior to deliberations." He also believed that drugs and alcohol should count as "outside influences" on the jurors.]

See Federal Rules of Evidence 601–606; California Evidence Code §§ 700–704.

HYPOTHETICALS

(1) D is charged with the sale of heroin to X. The prosecution's evidence is that X, a known heroin addict, was given $300 by the police to purchase heroin from D at D's barbershop. The prosecution calls X, and D objects to any testimony from X on the ground that X is incompetent to be a witness by virtue of drug use. The trial court conducts an in-chambers hearing on the question. D calls P, a psychiatrist, who testifies that the use of LSD may confuse one's perception, thereby impairing the capacity to perceive or remember one's observations. In this case, however, P states that he did not personally interview X, and that his opinion testimony is based upon his experience with LSD users who had a history of suffering blackouts. The prosecutor calls X, who testifies to excessive use of drugs, including LSD, but denies ever passing out, freaking out, or having loss of memory from use of LSD. The trial judge then overrules D's incompetency objection. Is this ruling correct?

(2) A sues X for damages for personal injuries arising out of a two-car collision. A took X's deposition one month before trial. During her deposition, X testified that he had retrograde amnesia and could not remember the facts of the accident. At the trial, X takes the witness stand and her attorney asks her to relate how the accident happened. A objects that X is incompetent to testify in view of her deposition testimony. How should the court rule?

(3) Assume the same facts as in Hypothetical (2). A calls as a witness, C, who observed the accident after having escaped from a mental institution to which he had been committed as a manic-depressive psychotic. At the time of trial, C has been captured and is back in the institution. X objects to C as a witness, on the ground that C's commitment to a mental institution renders him incompetent to be a witness. How should the court rule?

(4) A sues X for damages for personal injuries arising out of a two-car, intersectional collision. A claims that X didn't stop at a stop sign. At a jury trial, A calls B to testify. X makes a lack-of-personal-knowledge objection. A represents that she will establish B's personal knowledge as B testifies. The trial judge permits B to testify conditionally, subject to X making a motion to strike. B then testifies that X "blew" the stop sign. On cross-examination, B finally admits that she reached the intersection just as the cars collided, and that she concluded that X blew the stop sign from observing the point of impact and from hearing other witnesses talk about what happened. X moves to strike B's testimony. What result?

CHAPTER 9

JUDICIAL NOTICE

PART **A** Adjudicative Facts

PART **B** Law and Legislative Facts

PART **C** Jury Notice

A. ADJUDICATIVE FACTS

De La Cruz v. City of Los Angeles

California Court of Appeal, Second District, Division 4, 2002.
2002 WL 358825.*

■ HASTINGS, J.

Appellant, on behalf of herself and as guardian ad litem for her minor daughter, appeals from a judgment entered in favor of the City of Los Angeles, after a jury deadlocked on the question of whether the City's negligent employee was acting within the scope of his employment when he injured appellant and her daughter. We find that the court did not have jurisdiction to enter the judgment as to appellant's second and third causes of action. We agree with the City's contention on cross-appeal that a damage award was unauthorized by law, and reverse that portion of the judgment as well.

BACKGROUND

Appellant Juana Mercado and her infant daughter, Leslie, were seriously injured when Bryce Wicks, a 28–year veteran of Los Angeles Police Department, struck them with his Bronco sport utility vehicle as they crossed Lankershim Boulevard at Arminta in the City of Los Angeles on October 16, 1997, at 7:50 p.m. Appellant was in the crosswalk with her father, pushing Leslie in a baby carriage, when she and Leslie were hit. The baby carriage, with Leslie still in it, was caught under Wicks's Bronco and dragged more that 600 feet until it became dislodged. Wicks left the scene of the accident without stopping. Witnesses reported that Wicks slowed down after the collision, appeared to look back, then sped away.

A witness gave investigating officers a partial license plate number, and the next day, a vehicle registration search turned up Wicks's Bronco as

---

* This opinion was not designated for publication, and therefore is subject to limitations on citation in litigation, pursuant to California Rule of Court 8.1115.

one of several possibly matching automobiles. On October 17, 1997, the investigating officers notified Captain Wahler, who was in charge of the North Hollywood Station where Wicks was employed in the Detective Division. Wicks, who was on duty at the time, was told to remain at the station, but when the investigating officers arrived, he had gone home. The investigating officers went there and found him dead. An inspection of the Bronco confirmed that it had been the vehicle that dragged the baby stroller.

Appellant brought an action on behalf of herself and her daughter against Wicks and the City of Los Angeles. Appellant charged Wicks and the City with negligence, and sought to recover from the City on the basis of respondeat superior, alleging that Wicks was acting in the course and scope of his employment at the time of the accident, under the "special errand" rule. * * * [The jury found that Wicks was negligent, and the plaintiff ultimately settled with Wick's estate. The jury divided six to six on the question of whether Wicks was acting within the scope of his employment at the time of the accident. The trial court subsequently entered a judgment of nonsuit against the plaintiff on her claim against the City.]

DISCUSSION

I

1. *The Procedural Issue*

[The court of appeal held that the judgment of nonsuit was procedurally defective.]

2. *The Merits of the Ruling*

Although we conclude that the judgment is void because of procedural error, the parties have fully briefed the merits of the ruling and the matter is being remanded for further proceedings. Because the legal issues will again be in play in the trial court, we address the merits for further guidance of the court. * * *

Appellant contends that the evidence that Wicks was acting within the scope of his employment was sufficient to withstand a motion for nonsuit. Under the doctrine of respondeat superior, the City would be liable for the damages caused by its employee Wicks, if Wicks was acting within the scope of his employment at the time of the accident. An employee acts within the course and scope of his employment when he engages in activities incident to his duties, or when his misconduct could have been reasonably foreseen by the employer.

Ordinarily, under the "going-and-coming rule," an employee is not considered to be acting within the scope of his or her employment while en route to work or home. Under the special-errand exception to the going-and-coming rule, however, "If the employee is not simply on his way from his home to his normal place of work or returning from said place to his home for his own purpose, but is coming from his home or returning to it on a special errand either as part of his regular duties or at a specific order or request of his employer, the employee is considered to be in the scope of his employment from the time that he starts on the errand until he has returned or until he deviates therefrom for personal reasons. [Citations.]" (*Boynton v. McKales* (1956) 139 Cal.App.2d 777, 789, 294 P.2d 733.)

"The attendance at a social function, although not forming part of the normal duties of the employee, may come under the 'special errand rule' if the function or the attendance was connected with the employment and for a material part intended to benefit the employer who requested or expected the employee to attend." *Id.* Even without direct evidence of benefit to the employer, the requisite connection may be shown by evidence that the function is a recognized, established, and encouraged custom, thus amounting to a "customary incident" of the employment relationship. (*Calrow v. Appliance Industries, Inc.* (1975) 49 Cal.App.3d 556, 570, 122 Cal.Rptr. 636.)

On October 16, 1997, Wicks attended a retirement party for two retiring employees of the North Hollywood Station, and appellant sought to prove that the party was a "special errand" from which Wicks was returning home at the time of the accident. The issue is a question of fact, and becomes a question of law only when the facts are undisputed and no conflicting inferences are possible. We agree with appellant that the evidence in the record is sufficient to support a finding of material benefit to the employer and a significant connection to Wicks's employment, as well as a recognized, established, and encouraged custom. * * *

A substantial deviation from the special errand is an exception to the special-errand doctrine. Thus, it became respondent's burden to establish the "exception to the exception" with evidence that Wicks had abandoned his employer's business for his own.

The evidence is silent on whether Wicks ever returned home that evening, or that he was on his way home when the accident occurred. Further, the accident did not occur on a route Wicks was known ever to have taken to return home. Thus, we cannot conclude one way or the other that Wicks had abandoned the special errand.

The scant evidence regarding Wicks's activity after leaving the retirement party was as follows: no one knew why Wicks was on Lankershim Boulevard at the time of the accident; Wicks lived in Acton, which is near Palmdale, and a "fair commute"; the retirement party was in Chatsworth, and Wicks's most direct route home from the party would have been to take the 118 Freeway north; whereas, the North Hollywood Station is near Burbank Boulevard and the Hollywood Freeway (I–170), and Wicks's most direct route home from the station was on the I–170 north; the party began at 4:00 p.m., and included a happy hour, then a meal, then the presentations, then "a lot more visiting"; and the accident occurred at approximately 7:50 p.m. No witness testified knowing what time Wicks left, but the party was still going on at 7:00 p.m., although most attendees had left by that time.[5]

Recognizing the problematic showing in the trial court, appellant has asked that we take judicial notice of several geographical facts, including the address of the North Hollywood Police Station, the proximity of Lankershim Boulevard to the Hollywood Freeway and the Golden State Freeway (I–5), which lead toward Palmdale. She has submitted map excerpts from the Thomas Guide for Los Angeles County (1999). She has also included counsel's declaration regarding his telephone call to the North Hollywood station to confirm the station's address.

Respondent contends that appellant's request for judicial notice is an improper attempt to place facts before the reviewing court that were not before the trial court. Respondent compares the request to that in *People v. Amador* (2000) 24 Cal.4th 387, 394, 100 Cal.Rptr.2d 617, 9 P.3d 993, where the Supreme Court refused to take judicial notice of maps and information from the United States Postal Service, because it was new evidence offered to support a contention which had not been before the trial court. We agree that the reviewing court will normally decline a request for judicial notice of matters that were not brought to the attention of the trial court or presented to the trier of fact. The reviewing court has the discretion, however, to grant judicial notice even when the information was not presented to the trial court, where the facts are not reasonably open to dispute, and the opposing party does not dispute them.

In any event, a geographical fact may deemed to have been brought to the attention of the trial court and trier of fact when it is probable that "every person in the courtroom at the trial, including judge, jury, counsel, witnesses, parties, and officers of the court, knew perfectly well what the character of the location was." (See *Varcoe v. Lee* (1919) 180 Cal. 338, 343, 181 P. 223.)* In this case, the trial took place in Burbank, North Hollywood's next-door neighbor, and the trial judge indicated that he was familiar with Lankershim Boulevard. Further, appellant, pointing to evidence that employees sometimes carpooled from the station, argued that the jury could reasonably infer that Wicks had returned to the station before going home. The comments of the court and counsel lead us to conclude that the general location of the station in relation to the accident scene was in issue and known to the parties, counsel, and the court.

The appellate court has the authority to take judicial notice of the distances between places. (* * * Evid.Code, §§ 452, 459.) A map is a proper

---

[5] Appellant's attorney argued to the trial court that he had done everything he could to produce evidence, but had been met with a "curtain of silence." That assertion, however, was supported by no evidence at all.

* [*Varcoe* held that a court could take judicial notice that Mission Street, between Twentieth and Twenty–Second Streets, in San Francisco is a business district, defined as "territory * * * contiguous to a public highway, which is at that point mainly built up with structures devoted to business," and therefore subject to a statutory speed limit of 15 mph.—Eds.]

subject of judicial notice (Evid.Code, §§ 452, subd. (h), 459, subd. (a) * * *), including the Thomas Brothers Guide.

We therefore exercise our discretion to take judicial notice that the accident occurred in the neighborhood of the North Hollywood Police Station, as well as other characteristics of the North Hollywood neighborhood: that Lankershim Boulevard is a north-south street that crosses Burbank Boulevard near the Hollywood Freeway (I–170); and that the I–170 and Lankershim both reach the Golden State Freeway (I–5), which leads northward out of the City of Los Angeles toward Palmdale. We decline to take judicial notice of the address of the station, however, since it was not discussed, and not, therefore in issue, and it is unlikely that the address was known to the court.

For the purposes of this review, it is not necessary to take judicial notice of more than we have. To amount to an abandonment of the special errand, any deviation would have to have been so "unusual or startling" as to be deemed a "complete departure" from the special errand. (See *Trejo v. Maciel* (1966) 239 Cal.App.2d 487, 497, 48 Cal.Rptr. 765.) Wicks's presence in the neighborhood of the station was not "unusual or startling," but a foreseeable deviation from the special errand. * * *

Wicks usually worked until 3:00 p.m., and the retirement party started around 4:00 p.m. Since he lived far away, it is reasonably foreseeable that Wicks would go to the party directly from work, and return to the station for some reason afterward. Indeed, people sometimes carpooled to retirement parties. The party lasted for several hours. It lasted until at least 7:00 p.m., and may have gone on some time more, since retirement parties usually included a happy hour, followed by a meal and presentations, and "a lot" of socializing afterward. The accident occurred at 7:50 p.m., a time consistent with attendance at a party lasting several hours and a trip back to the station.

Pointing out that no witness testified having known what time Wicks left the party, how he got to the party, or where he went when he left, respondent charges that it is mere conjecture that he returned to the station, or that if he did return, that it was close enough in time to the accident to permit an inference that any deviation was not substantial. "Although a judgment of nonsuit must not be reversed if plaintiff's proof raises nothing more than speculation, suspicion, or conjecture, reversal is warranted if there is 'some substance to plaintiff's evidence upon which reasonable minds could differ. . .' [Citations.]" (*Carson v. Facilities Development Co.* (1984) 36 Cal.3d 830, 839, 206 Cal.Rptr. 136, 686 P.2d 656.)

We agree that the evidence is thin, but the most important witness is dead, and appellant's case depended, to a very large extent, on inferences and circumstantial evidence. The proximity of the accident to the station, the time of the accident, the probable time the party lasted, the probability that Wicks went to the party directly from work due to his long commute, give rise to a reasonable inference that Wicks returned to the station after the party. Wicks's taking nearby Lankershim Boulevard was not so "unusual or startling" as to be deemed a "complete departure" from the special errand as a matter of law. We conclude that although the evidence was weak, it was sufficient to avoid nonsuit. * * *

■ We concur: EPSTEIN, ACTING P.J., and CURRY, J.

Fielding v. State

Court of Appeals of Alaska, 1992.
842 P.2d 614.

■ Before BRYNER, C.J., and COATS and MANNHEIMER, JJ.

OPINION

■ COATS, JUDGE.

Jim Fielding was convicted following a jury trial of driving while license suspended (DWLS). On appeal, he contends the trial court erred in instructing the jury that the Glenn Highway is a highway as that term is used in the DWLS statute. We reverse.

At trial, the primary fact in contention was whether Fielding drove on a highway or a vehicular way. *See* AS 28.15.291(a).[1] The defense claimed that Fielding drove within the parking lot of the Eagle River Department of Motor Vehicles, while the state alleged that Fielding drove from the parking lot onto the Glenn Highway.

At the close of the evidence, Fielding requested the court to instruct the jury that a shopping center parking lot is not a vehicular way or area. District Court Judge John D. Mason stated that he would comply with Fielding's request. However, the judge also ruled, over defense objection, that he would take judicial notice of the fact that the Glenn Highway is a highway. The court ultimately instructed the jury as follows:

> To find the defendant guilty of driving while his license was suspended, you must also find that the state has proved beyond a reasonable doubt that he drove on a "highway or vehicular way or area." The law defines a vehicular way or area as a way, path or area, other than a highway or private property.

---

[1] AS 28.15.291 reads in pertinent part as follows:

Driving while license canceled, suspended, revoked, or in violation of a limitation.

(a) a person is guilty of a class A misdemeanor if the person

(1) *drives a motor vehicle on a highway or vehicular way or area* at a time when that person's driver's license, privilege to drive, or privilege to obtain a license has been canceled, suspended, or revoked in this or another jurisdiction[.]

(Emphasis added.)

Alaska case law holds a shopping center parking lot is not a vehicular way or area.

It is clear, and the court so instructs you, that the Glenn Highway is a highway as used in the statute.

Jury Instruction No. 6 (emphasis added).

On appeal, Fielding claims, as he did below, that the trial court's instruction resulted in a directed verdict for the state on an essential element of the offense.

In order to convict Fielding, the jury was required to find that he drove on a highway or vehicular way or area. AS 28.15.291(a).[2] The manner in which the trial court took judicial notice of the Glenn Highway's status affected a substantial right of Fielding's: the right to have a jury decide every element of the crime. *See Smallwood v. State,* 781 P.2d 1000, 1003 (Alaska App.1989); *Sandstrom v. Montana,* 442 U.S. 510, 520, 99 S.Ct. 2450, 2457, 61 L.Ed.2d 39 (1979). We agree that the court's instruction amounted to a directed verdict for the prosecution on one of the essential elements of the charge; "the error in such a case is that the wrong entity judged the defendant guilty." *Smallwood,* 781 P.2d at 1003, citing *Rose v. Clark,* 478 U.S. 570, 578, 106 S.Ct. 3101, 3105, 92 L.Ed.2d 460 (1986).

Assuming that it was proper for the court to take judicial notice that the Glenn Highway was a highway for purposes of AS 28.15.291 and AS 28.40.100, the court's instruction to the jury was improper under Evidence Rule 203(c). Evidence Rule 203(c) provides in pertinent part that when a court takes judicial notice of a fact "[i]n a criminal case the court shall instruct the jury that it may, but is not required to, accept as conclusive any fact judicially noticed."

The state contends the court's error, while substantial, does not compel a reversal under the plain error rule because it was not prejudicial. However, in *Smallwood,* we determined that "harmless error principles should not be applied to a jury instruction which conclusively establishes an essential element of the crime charged." 781 P.2d at 1004. Thus, there is no need for further inquiry concerning the prejudice stemming from the court's order; the court's instruction, in depriving Fielding of his right to have the jury decide every element of the charge, was *per se* prejudicial.

Accordingly, the conviction is Reversed.

---

[2] AS 28.40.100(10) states:

(10) "highway" means the entire width between the boundary lines of every way that is publicly maintained when a part of it is open to the public for purposes of vehicular travel, including but not limited to every street and the Alaska state marine highway system but not vehicular ways or areas[.]

Comment, Judicial Notice by Appellate Courts of Facts and Foreign Laws Not Brought to the Attention of the Trial Court

42 Mich.L.Rev. 509 (1943).*

The doctrine of judicial notice represents one of the oldest and most valuable constituents of our jurisprudence. From the days of the Yearbooks, courts have noticed matters of many diverse kinds which they have considered (a) sufficiently notorious and (b) commonly recognized. Thus courts have recognized that games such as ping-pong are not "toys," that short delays often occur in mail deliveries, * * * that tobacco is a farm product, that the front fender of an automobile is about the height of a man's knee * * * that a mule is a dangerous instrumentality. * * * Today, as in earlier times, the doctrine remains a kind of common-sense "taking-for-granted" of certain facts which experience has shown need not be proved. To put the matter another way, it declares that there are certain propositions in a party's case as to which he will not be required to offer evidence. * * *

See Federal Rules of Evidence 201. California Evidence Code §§ 450–460. On judicial notice of foreign law see F.R.Civ.P. 44.1 and F.R.Cr.P. 26.1.

B. LAW AND LEGISLATIVE FACTS

Lilly, An Introduction to the Law of Evidence

19 (3d ed. 1996).*

The term "judicial notice" also applies to the process by which a judge, usually with the assistance of counsel, determines or discovers the procedural or substantive law in his or some other jurisdiction. Usually the judge can consult and apply statutes, regulations, and prior case law (precedents) whether or not such materials have been introduced into evidence. If counsel wishes the judge to consult a particular source, he simply calls the judge's attention to it and supplies a citation. However, in instances where there is no widely available source—in contrast with the general availability of American codes and case reports—it may be necessary for counsel formally to provide evidence of the pertinent rule of law. For example, foreign law, the content of which may pose difficulties of discovery and interpretation, is not routinely judicially noticed. Unless a statute provides for judicial notice, the content of the foreign law must be proved by official documents and, when necessary, expert witnesses. The treatment of municipal ordinances varies. Typically, these will not be noticed absent a statutory authorization; thus one relying upon such an ordinance may have to prove its content by an official or "true" copy.

McCormick on Evidence

vol. 2, 443–48 (Kenneth S. Broun, gen. ed. 6th ed. 2006).*

Social and Economic Data Used in Judicial Law–Making: "Legislative" Facts

It is conventional wisdom today to observe that judges not only are charged to find what the law is, but must regularly make new law when deciding upon the constitutional validity of a statute, interpreting a statute, or extending or restricting a common law rule. The very nature of the judicial process necessitates that judges be guided, as legislators are, by considerations of expediency and public policy.[5] They must, in the nature of things, act either upon knowledge already possessed or upon assumptions,[6] or upon investigation of the pertinent general facts, social,[7] economic,[8] political,[9] or scientific.[10] An older tradition once prescribed that judges should rationalize their result solely in terms of analogy to old doctrines, leaving the considerations of expediency unstated. Contemporary practice indicates that judges in their opinions should render explicit their policy judgments and the factual grounds therefor. These latter have been helpfully classed as "legislative facts," as contrasted with the "adjudicative facts" which are historical facts pertaining to the incidents which give rise to lawsuits.[11]

Constitutional cases argued in terms of due process typically involve reliance upon legislative facts for their proper resolution. Whether a statute enacted pursuant to the police power is valid, after all, involves a two-fold analysis. First, it must be determined that the enactment is designed to achieve an appropriate objective of the police power; that is, it must be designed to protect the public health, morals, safety, or general welfare. The second question is whether, in light of the data on hand, a legislature could reasonably have adopted the means they did to achieve the aim of their exercise of the police power. In Jay Burns Baking Co. v. Bryan,[14] for

---

* © 2006 Thomson/West.

[5] Benjamin N. Cardozo, The Nature of the Judicial Process, 113–125 (1921); Jerome Frank, Law and the Modern Mind, ch. 4 (1930).

[6] Village of Euclid v. Ambler Realty Co., 272 U.S. 365 (1926) (proper exercise of police power to exclude apartment houses from residential districts because they tend to be mere parasites and come near to being nuisances).

[7] Brown v. Board of Education, 347 U.S. 483 (1954) (racially segregated schools can never be equal notwithstanding their equality of teachers or equipment because the very act of segregation brands the segregated minority with a feeling of inferiority); Roe v. Wade, 410 U.S. 113 (1973) (canvass of historical, social and medical data in opinion articulating constitutional norms governing regulation of abortions).

[8] SEC v. Capital Gains Research Bureau, Inc., 300 F.2d 745 (2d Cir.1961). reversed 375 U.S. 180 (1963) (judicial notice taken that advice tendered by small advisory service could not influence stock market generally); same case, 375 U.S. 180 (1963) (judicial notice taken that the advice tendered could influence the market price).

[9] Baker v. Carr, 369 U.S. 186 (1962) (contemporary notions of justice require that equal apportionment of voting districts be made a legal and perforce largely mathematical question rather than a purely political one).

[10] Ballew v. Georgia, 435 U.S. 223 (1978) (critical evaluation of studies themselves to determine whether empirical data suggested that progressively smaller juries were less likely to engage in group deliberation).

[11] Davis, Administrative Law Treatise § 15.03 (1958).

[14] 264 U.S. 504 (1924).

example, the question was whether, concerned about consumers being misled by confusing sizes of bread, the Nebraska legislature could decree not only that the bakers bake bread according to distinctively different weights but that they wrap their product in wax paper lest any post-oven expansion of some loaves undo these distinctions. A majority of the court held the enactment unconstitutional because, in their opinion, the wrapping requirement was unreasonable. Mr. Justice Brandeis, correctly anticipating the decline of substantive due process, dissented, pointing out that the only question was whether the measure was a reasonable legislative response in light of the facts available to the legislators themselves. Then, in a marvelous illustration of the Brandeis brief technique, he recited page after page of data illustrating how widespread was the problem of short-weight and how, in light of nationwide experience, the statute appeared to be a reasonable response to the environmental situation.[16]

Given the bent to test due process according to the information available to the legislature, the truth-content of these data are not directly relevant. The question is whether sufficient data exist which could influence a reasonable legislature to act, not whether ultimately these data are true. This is not the same case as when a court proceeds to interpret a constitutional norm and, while they still rely upon data, the judges *qua* legislators themselves proceed to act as if the data were true. In Brown v. Board of Education,[18] for example, the Court faced the issue whether segregated schools, equal in facilities and faculty, could any longer be tolerated under the equal protection clause. The question was no longer whether a reasonable legislator could believe these schools could never be equal, but whether the *judges* believed that the very act of segregating branded certain children with a feeling of inferiority so deleterious that it would be impossible for them to obtain an equal education no matter how equal the facilities and teachers. Thus the intellectual legitimacy of this kind of decision turns upon the actual truth-content of the legislative facts taken into account by the judges who propound the decision. While not necessarily indisputably true, it would appear that these legislative facts must at least appear to be more likely than not true if the opinion is going to have the requisite intellectual legitimacy upon which the authority of judge-made rules is ultimately founded.[19]

---

[16] The opponents of a statute can resort to extra-record legislative facts to support their argument that it is invalid. In Jay Burns Baking Co. v. Bryan, 264 U.S. 504 (1924), the statute regulating bread sizes was struck down because it was "contrary to common experience and unreasonable to assume there could be any danger of * * * deception." See also Defiance Milk Products Co. v. Du Mond, 132 N.E.2d 829 (N.Y. 1956) (statute requiring inordinately large size cans for retail sale of evaporated skimmed milk held invalid because judicial notice was taken that it would be incredible to believe consumers needed protection against deception practiced with regard to the nature of this product).

[18] 347 U.S. 483 (1954), supplemented 349 U.S. 294 (1955).

[19] See, e.g., the reaction to Durham v. United States, 214 F.2d 862 (D.C.Cir.1954), wherein on the basis of psychiatric data the court formulated a new test for criminal insanity. Some psychiatrists accepted the result: Roche, Criminality and Mental Illness—Two Faces of the Same Coin, 22 U.Chi.L.Rev. 320 (1955). The American Law Institute rejected it. Model Penal Code, Tentative Draft No. 4, 159B60 (1955). See also Brown v. Board of Education, 347 U.S. 483 (1954), supplemented 349 U.S. 294 (1955), wherein for the psychological impact of segregation the court relied upon, inter alia, the work of Dr. Kenneth B. Clark. Dr. Clark felt com-

When it comes to the utilization of these lawmaking facts, three problems can beset constitutional law decisions. The first is that the forest can sometimes be lost sight of for the trees. That is to say, so much historical and sociological data are rehearsed that an opinion appears to be bottomed upon purely pragmatic considerations and not upon any compelling constitutional norm.[20] The second is that an outpouring of learning appears inordinate to the requirements of the problem at hand.[21] The third is that data can appear to be included as an exercise in fustian excess, often in a losing cause.[22] The first would appear to be a problem of draftsmanship, hard cases perhaps making bad law, but the latter two appear less defensible.

When making new common law, judges must, like legislators, do the best they can in assaying the data available to them and make the best decision they can concerning which course wisdom dictates they follow. Should they, for example, continue to invoke the common law rule of *caveat emptor* in the field of real property, or should they invoke a notion of implied warranty in the instance of the sale of new houses?[23] Should they require landlords of residential units to warrant their habitability and fitness for the use intended? While sociological, economic, political and moral doc-

---

pelled thereafter publicly to respond to critics of his work. Clark, The Desegregation Cases: Criticism of the Social Scientists Role, 5 Vill.L.Rev. 224, 236–40 (1960). But see Van den Haag, Social Science Testimony in the Desegregation Cases—A Reply to Professor Kenneth Clark, 6 Vill.L.Rev. 69 (1960).

[20] See particularly Chief Justice Burger's concurring opinion in Doe v. Bolton, 410 U.S. 179, 208 (1973) ("I am somewhat troubled that the Court has taken notice of various scientific and medical data in reaching its conclusion; however, I do not believe that the Court has exceeded the scope of judicial notice accepted in other contexts.").

[21] See, e.g., Justice Blackmun's opinion in Flood v. Kuhn, 407 U.S. 258. 260–264 (1972) (mythopoetic odyssey through nostalgia of baseball).

[22] See particularly Chief Justice Rehnquist's dissent in Texas v. Johnson, 491 U.S. 397 (1989) (patriotic effusions from Emerson, Francis Scott Key and Whittier massed in favor of respect for the flag) and Justice Brennan's dissent to the denial of certiorari in Glass v. Louisiana, 471 U.S. 1080 (1985) (vivid descriptions of bodily reactions to lethal doses of electricity injected by official executioners).

In Atkins v. Virginia, 536 U.S. 304 (2002), Justice Stevens wrote for the majority that contemporary standards of decency compelled the conclusion that the execution of a mentally retarded individual had become a cruel and unusual punishment not permitted by the 8th Amendment. The standard was derived from recent state legislation exempting these persons from execution. Although not a majority of states had yet so amended their laws, the amendments relied upon illustrated a consistency in the direction of change. Appended in a note were the results of opinion polls and the views of religious and professional organizations, together with a reference to world opinion. The Chief Justice took exception to the use of any standard other than a head count of state practice. Not only did he add an appendix designed to illustrate that polls were not dependable sources upon which to formulate any judgment, he signed off on his opinion with an abrupt "I dissent." Id. at 328–37 (dissenting opinion). Although respectfully dissenting, Justice Scalia made mock of the legislative facts and asserted that the case had not really been decided upon the "fabricated" national consensus but in cavalier fashion upon the personal feelings about the issue held by the majority. Id. at 347–49 (dissenting opinion).

[23] Schipper v. Levitt & Sons, Inc., 207 A.2d 314 (N.J.1965) (mass developer of homes who assembled final product out of component parts treated as a manufacturer and implied warranty imposed).

trine may abound about questions like this, none of these data are likely indisputable.[24]

Thus it is that, in practice, the legislative facts upon which judges rely when performing their lawmaking function are not indisputable. At the same time, cognizant of the fact that his decision as lawmaker can affect the public at large, in contradistinction to most rulings at trials which affect only the parties themselves, a judge is not likely to rely for his data only upon what opposing counsel tender him. Obviously enough, therefore, legislative facts tend to be the most elusive facts when it comes to propounding a codified system of judicial notice.[25] This seems to be confirmed by the fact that the Federal Rules of Evidence make no effort to regulate this type of judicial notice.[26]

There are, however, efforts being made to rationalize this subject-matter. If one were to examine social science materials looking for help in enunciating a rule of law, one would be searching for authority much in the same fashion as one would be if one were looking to unearth decisional precedential authority. This has suggested to Professors John Monahan and Laurens Walker that a foray into social science materials is more akin to an effort to answer a question of law than one of fact.[27]

Thus judges should not see themselves taking judicial notice of legislative facts but promulgating law. Social science materials would not be introduced into the system by expert testimony but by way of written briefs, and judges would have no hesitation at all carrying on their own independent researches. The very recognition that a question of law was involved would promote a more critical attitude toward these materials, because they would carry more *gravitas,* being law, than do the only arguably true episodic facts of the current approach. Soon enough a canon of precedential

---

[24] Lemle v. Breeden, 462 P.2d 470 (Haw. 1969) (application of implied warranty recognizes changes in history of leasing transactions and takes into account contemporary housing realities).

[25] In Hawkins v. United States, 358 U.S. 74 (1958) was based on the proposition that the testimony of one spouse against another would destroy their marriage. Justice Stewart suggested at the time that the proposition might well be nothing more than an unsound assumption in cases where the spouse's testimony was actually voluntary. Id. at 81–82 (concurring opinion). In 1980, the rule was modified to allow voluntary testimony. Trammel v. United States, 445 U.S. 40 (1980).

See particularly Davis, A System of Judicial Notice Based on Fairness and Convenience. in Perspectives of Law, 69, 82 (Pound ed. 1964) ("judge-made law would stop growing if judges, in thinking about questions of law and policy, were forbidden to take into account the facts they believe, as distinguished from facts which are 'clearly * * * within the domain of the indisputable.' ") If the data available on appeal are conflicting, however, a court can remand the case to trial so these data can be more effectively explored by introducing them there in the form of evidence subject to cross-examination. See, e.g., Borden's Farm Products Co. v. Baldwin, 293 U.S. 194 (1934).

[26] Fed.R.Evid. 201 does not purport to regulate the notice of legislative facts. The advisory committee note on Rule 201(a) nonetheless takes for granted the existence of legislative facts, observing simply that "no rule deals with judicial notice of legislative facts."

It has been suggested that the Rules ought to recognize explicitly that judicial notice can be taken of legislative facts, and such a fact be defined as one having "reasonable reliability." Revised Rule 202. 171 F.R.D. 330, 384–86.

[27] Monahan & Walker, Social Authority: Obtaining, Evaluating, and Establishing Social Science in Law, 134 U.Pa.L.Rev. 477 (1986).

authority would come into being based upon a calculus of the precise court which relied on particular data and the peer review each decision received in the law reviews and other opinions. Thus these materials could be quickly accessed by lower courts by simple reference and citation.

HYPOTHETICALS

(1) A sues X to recover on a promissory note in which X is the maker and B is the payee. A is B's assignee. X's defense is that the note was given in payment of B's services as a real estate broker and that B did not possess a broker's license. On direct examination, A is asked whether B, his assignor, was a licensed real estate broker. X makes an objection that A lacks personal knowledge. The judge announces that he knows B personally, and is taking judicial notice of the fact that B is a licensed real estate broker. Is the judge correct?

(2) In an action brought in state court in California, A sues X Construction Co. for damages for breach of a contract to build a brick chicken coop in Provo, Utah. X's defense is that it is illegal and impossible to build. At the trial, set for a two-day trial, X produces a volume labeled "Municipal Ordinances of Provo," and requests the court to take judicial notice of the fact that the building of brick chicken coops is prohibited by ordinance within the city of Provo. A objects on the ground that he has not been given advance notice of this judicial-notice request. What result?

C. JURY NOTICE

IV Wigmore, Evidence § 2570 (1904)*

Judicial Notice by the Jury's Own Knowledge. In general, the jury may in modern times act only upon evidence properly laid before them in the course of the trial. But so far as the matter in question is one upon which men in general have a common fund of experience and knowledge, through data notoriously accepted by all, the analogy of judicial notice obtains to some extent, and the jury are allowed to resort to this information in making up their minds. This doctrine, of course, has several aspects. From the point of view of the jury's duty, it appears as an exception to the rule that they must act only upon what is presented to them at the trial. From the point of view of the Hearsay rule, it may also be thought of as a partial exception to that. But additionally it must be considered from the present point of view, for it authorizes the party to ask the *jury to refer to their general knowledge* upon the matter in question, and thus in effect and to that extent makes it unnecessary for the party to offer evidence.

But the scope of this doctrine is narrow; it is strictly limited to a few matters of elemental experience in human nature, commercial affairs, and everyday life. Thus, the natural instincts of human conduct, with reference to care or negligence at the time of danger, may be considered, the dangerousness of smoking a pipe in a barn near the straw, the conditions affecting the various kinds of values, the intoxicating nature of a certain liquor,

---

* Copyright, 1904 by John H. Wigmore.

and even (though this illustrates how local conditions may affect the application) that a game played with bone-counters was played for money; but such a matter of private and variable belief as the character of a particular witness cannot be so taken into consideration by the jury.The range of such general knowledge is not precisely definable; but in these days when too much emphasis is placed, in the selection of jurors, on the blankness of their mental tablets, there can be no harm in the liberal application of the present principle.As a natural part of its doctrine, of course, these matters may be referred to by counsel in their arguments.

NOTE

In subsequent editions, Wigmore offered further examples. Thus, in one case a key witness who placed the accused on the ferry between Philadelphi and Camden on a crucial date referred to the ladies' cabin as being on the left side of the boat. Defense counsel in argument asserted that the ladies' cabin on that ferry was on the right side. The prosecutor interrupted to point out the absence of proof on the point. Defense counsel responded that "*the Court knows, the jury knows, the people know, and the prosecutor knows,* that the ladies' cabin on the boats of the Camden ferry is on the *right*-hand side." In another case, a juror explained an acquittal on the basis that the chief prosecution witness had said he was a carpenter, but had said that a pine door he was working on had cost $10 – but the juror was confident it cost no morethan $4.50. Wigmore also quote old cases drawing the distinction between general background knowledge and particular knowledge about the case. Thus, in *Rostad v. Portland R.L. & P. Co.*, 201 P. 184, 188 (Or. 1921), the court said:

> It is utterly impracticable in the administration of courts of justice to secure a juror whose mind is totally blank as to questions involved in the ordinary transactions of life. Triers of fact cannot, in the nature of things, be divested of general knowledge of practical affairs. The Court cannot do otherwise than to direct them to use such experiences as are common to all men in the decision of questions of fact.

Or, as the court said in Washburn v. Milwaukee & L.R. Co., 18 N.W. 328, 330-31 (Wis. 1884), "should a witness testify that at Boston on a certain day the sun arose at midnight, or that the Mississippi river empties into Lake Michigan, or that white is black, the testimony would be rejected at once." But:

> To allow jurors to make up their verdict on their individual knowledge of disputed facts material to the case, not testified to by them in court, or upon their private opinions, would be most dangerous and unjust. It would deprive the losing party of the right of cross-examination, and the benefit of all the tests of credibility which the law affords. Besides, the evidence of such knowledge, or of the grounds of such opinions, could not be preserved in a bill of exceptions or questioned on appeal.

Id. at 331.

United States v. Amado–Nunez

United States Court of Appeals for the First Circuit, 2004.
357 F.3d 119.

■ Before BOUDIN, CHIEF JUDGE, TORRUELLA and LYNCH, CIRCUIT JUDGES.

■ BOUDIN, CHIEF JUDGE.

This is an appeal by José Amado–Nú⬚ez following his conviction for transporting counterfeit tax stamps in interstate or foreign commerce. 18 U.S.C. § 2314 (2000). The appeal presents two issues, one evidentiary and the other of statutory construction. The background is as follows.

On November 25, 1999, Amado went through the primary customs screening point at the Luis Mu⬚oz Marin International Airport in San Juan, Puerto Rico. The later indictment described Amado as arriving on a flight from the Dominican Republic, but the prosecutor neglected to prove the origin point at trial. The inspector at the primary customs point randomly chose Amado for a more thorough examination and he was directed to a second inspector.

In the bottom of Amado's bag, the second inspector found packages of stamps that purported to be issued by the Puerto Rico Department of the Treasury. The inspector summoned a criminal investigator assigned to the customs service who, on examining what she believed to be tax stamps for coin-operated machines, noticed that many had duplicate serial numbers— which she did not think would occur if the stamps were genuine. * * * The agent took custody of 887 stamps, which were later determined to be counterfeit.

A federal grand jury indicted Amado for violating 18 U.S.C. § 2314 (2000). The third paragraph of this statute pertinently provides:

> Whoever, with unlawful or fraudulent intent, transports in interstate or foreign commerce any falsely made, forged, altered, or counterfeited securities or tax stamps, knowing the same to have been falsely made, forged, altered, or counterfeited . . . [s]hall be fined under this title or imprisoned not more than ten years, or both.

Exceptions appear in the final paragraph of section 2314 but none is claimed to be relevant in this case.

Amado was tried for this offense in a bench trial, consented to by both sides. Together with evidence of the initial seizure, the government presented (among other witnesses) several officials from the Puerto Rico Treasury Department who testified about the tax stamp regime in Puerto Rico and confirmed that the stamps in question were counterfeit. The defense presented no witnesses but preserved the objections raised on appeal by appropriate motions.

At the close of the case, the district judge determined that Amado was guilty of the offense charged; the oral decision from the bench was brief, but the district court had already addressed in writing a legal issue now raised on appeal. Thereafter Amado was sentenced to two years imprisonment. Amado now appeals, raising two arguments: that the evidence does not establish the interstate or foreign commerce element of the offense, and that the statute does not apply to the stamps in question.[1]

The evidentiary issue is easily framed. The prosecutor failed to offer direct evidence that Amado had arrived at the airport from the Dominican Republic or, indeed, from any foreign point. So, indulging inferences in favor of the verdict, the question is whether, from other fragments of evidence, a trier of facts could rationally conclude beyond a reasonable doubt that Amado had arrived from outside Puerto Rico.

The issue can be narrowed further. In describing the initial inspection of Amado's luggage, the inspector who found the stamps explained that her duties consisted of interviewing passengers and searching their luggage. She also made clear that she was talking about *arriving* passengers, saying: "We have to ask them where they come from, how long they stayed in whatever place they went, if they acquired any items in the place where they were visiting."

She also made it clear that Amado had gone through this process. After describing the primary and secondary inspection points, she said that Amado had presented himself at her secondary point and, when asked what she did when coming in contact with him, she described in generic terms the process of requesting the customs declaration card, asking the regular questions (such as "where are you coming from"), and searching the luggage. She then described the search of Amado's luggage and discovery of the stamps.

Based on this evidence, we think a trier could rationally conclude beyond a reasonable doubt that Amado had gone through this process as an arriving passenger from whom a customs declaration form is requested, who is asked about his origin point, and whose luggage is often or ordinarily searched upon arrival. The only remaining link in the chain is the proposition that passengers arriving from a foreign origin go through the customs process while domestic passengers do not; without this link Amado could have been arriving from a flight originating elsewhere in Puerto Rico, defeating the interstate or foreign commerce requirement.

That routine customs checks are done for foreign but not domestic flights is known to anyone who has done even a modicum of air travel; it is also known to many others who have merely met arriving friends and relatives or who have watched films or television programs or read books or newspapers that touch on air travel. Its truth can also be deduced, though this is quite a different matter, from a study of federal statutes, regulations governing customs inspections and reported decisions.

---

[1] Amado does not deny that the stamps were counterfeit and he does not contest two other elements of the statute, namely, that he acted "with unlawful or fraudulent intent" while "knowing" that the stamps were counterfeited.

A federal court can take judicial notice of "adjudicative facts"—facts about the parties or events involved in the case—if one of two tests is met and if the parties are given notice, Fed.R.Evid. 201. But that rule is irrelevant here because the practice of customs searches for foreign but not domestic arrivals is not an adjudicative fact, and Rule 201(b)'s limits do not apply to the vast array of "background" facts commonly considered by judges and juries in deciding cases. *See* Fed.R.Evid. 201(a) & advisory comm. note to 201(a).

These "background" or "evaluative" facts cover the whole range of human experience from the rough meaning of common terms ("city") to science (a full moon illuminates a scene) to human psychology (a witness who is related to one of the parties might be biased). *Id.* For example:

> When a witness says "car," everyone, judge and jury included, furnishes, from non-evidence sources within himself, the supplementing information that the "car" is an automobile, not a railroad car, that it is self-propelled, probably by an internal combustion engine, that it may be assumed to have four wheels with pneumatic rubber tires, and so on. The judicial process cannot construct every case from scratch, like Descartes creating a world based on the postulate Cogito, ergo sum. These items could not possibly be introduced into evidence, and no one suggests that they be.

Fed.R.Evid. advisory comm. note to 201(a); *see also* Mueller & Kirkpatrick, *1 Federal Evidence* § 57 (2d ed.1994); John H. Mansfield, *Jury Notice,* 74 Geo. L.J. 395 (1985).

Fact-finders rely upon such background references or propositions all the time in deciding whether something did or did not happen; and this is permissible, without resort to the machinery for noticing adjudicative facts. The background facts may be quite important, but by contrast to adjudicative facts, the parties do not have an advantage over the jury in access to evidence about them. This does not, of course, preclude the possibility of parties' seeking to offer evidence about them when they are important.

The level of reliability required is not often discussed in the cases; only rarely can an appeals court be sure (as we are here) that a specific background proposition was employed or, in the alternative, was logically necessary to the result. But refinement of the standard is unnecessary in this case, because we are certain enough that the proposition in this case— formal customs inspections are only for passengers arriving from foreign countries—is both familiar and true. So, there is no reason to worry here about whether and when a more vulnerable alleged background fact might be subject to attack.

Thus, the ultimate fact (that Amado arrived from a foreign country) did not need to be "judicially noticed" under Rule 201; rather, it could (quite easily) be inferred by the fact-finder from the background fact of general customs-service practice coupled with trial evidence that, on this occasion, Amado was interviewed at the secondary arrival customs inspection point and then was questioned and searched in the fashion described by the inspector and agent (both adjudicative facts but amply proved by evidence).

The same process of reasoning disposes of a variant theory offered by Amado to raise a reasonable doubt as to the commerce element, namely, that he might have been searched, regardless of whether he had traveled at all, by a customs-service representative patrolling the airport. There are other problems with this competing explanation but the evidence already described disposes of it without more: the testimony of the agent at the secondary arrival point makes clear that Amado was searched as an arriving passenger at a formal checkpoint and not through some random stop in the concourse.

[The court also rejected Amado's contention that the items seized from his suitcase were not tax stamps within the meaning of the statute.]

CHAPTER 10

THE BURDEN OF PROOF AND PRESUMPTIONS

PART **A** Civil Cases

PART **B** Criminal Cases

A. CIVIL CASES

James, Civil Procedure
248–266 (1965).*

§ 7.5. Burden of proof: The two meanings of the term. The term "burden of proof" is used in our law to refer to two separate and quite different concepts. The distinction was not clearly perceived until it was pointed out by James Bradley Thayer in 1898. The decisions before that time and many later ones are hopelessly confused in reasoning about the problem. The two distinct concepts may be referred to as (1) the risk of nonpersuasion, or the burden of persuasion or simply persuasion burden; (2) the duty of producing evidence, the burden of going forward with the evidence, or simply the production burden or the burden of evidence.

§ 7.9. Burden of proof: Presumptions. The word "presumption" is used to mean many different things, but this they all have in common: they involve a relationship between a proven or admitted fact or group of facts, *A,* and another fact or conclusion of fact, *B,* which is sought to be proven.

At one end of the scale is the presumption of law, or conclusive or irrebuttable presumption. If *A* is shown, then *B* is to be presumed without question and the court will not even receive evidence or entertain argument to show the nonexistence of *B.* And the court will direct a jury that if they find *A* to be proven they *must* also find *B.* The conclusive presumption is not really a procedural device at all. Rather it is a process of concealing by fiction a change in the substantive law. When the law conclusively presumes the presence of *B* from *A,* this means that the substantive law no longer requires the existence of *B* in cases where *A* is present, although it hesitates as yet to say so forthrightly. We shall not here deal further with conclusive presumptions. Our concern is with those often called "rebuttal presumptions of fact."

The word "presumption" is occasionally used to refer to the logical inference of one fact from the existence of another. The process of judicial proof is constantly calling on circumstantial evidence and the inferences which may be drawn from it. If Smith mails at a postbox a letter to Jones, with proper address and postage on the envelope, the trier may infer that Jones received the letter. From long skid marks on a pavement great speed on the part of the vehicle that made them may be inferred. From the blowing of a horn in certain circumstances it may be inferred that a driver then saw a pedestrian. From handwriting similarities identity of authorship of two documents may be inferred. And so on, ad infinitum. As we shall see, courts set limits to the drawing of inferences and will permit juries to draw only those which the courts consider rational. But if a court determines that B is a rational inference from A, then the trier of fact is free to draw that inference as a matter of general lay reasoning and persuasion without the aid of any special procedural rules pertaining to litigation. Since there are such special rules, since the word "presumption" is often used to refer to them, and since "inference" is the word generally used to refer to the process of drawing conclusions of fact on the basis of general lay reasoning and experience, it serves clarity and avoids confusion to observe this distinction between these two words.

Many careful courts and writers use the word "presumption" to refer only to a device for allocating the production burden. It operates thus: If B is presumed from A, then on a showing of A, B *must* be assumed by the trier in the absence of evidence of non-B. To put it another way, if A is shown, then the party who asserts non-B has the production burden on the issue of B vel non—that is, B's existence or nonexistence. The word "presumption" will be used here only in this way.

In some situations, to be sure, B may be the only rational inference from A (absent further evidence), and we have seen that in all such cases the production burden shifts under rules of general application. But courts and legislatures have created presumptions in cases where either (1) B would be a permissible inference from A, but not the *only* permissible one, or (2) B would not even be a permissible inference from A. In such situations a presumption has an artificial procedural force and effect (at the point where proponent rests his case) over and above the logical probative effect of the evidence. In the first situation just described a presumption would call for a directed verdict on the issue of B vel non, if the opponent also rests, while, as we have seen, without the presumption the proponent on that issue would be entitled only to have it go to the jury. In the second situation the presumption has a double effect. It protects the proponent from an adverse directed verdict on the issue (or nonsuit or dismissal), which he would otherwise suffer for want of sufficient evidence. It also entitles the proponent to a directed verdict in his own favor on the issue, absent any countervailing evidence. Later in this section we shall inquire whether a presumption may have any further, continuing effect after evidence to rebut it has been introduced.

From the above it appears that a presumption may have important consequences. What, then, are the bases upon which courts or legislatures will create presumptions? For the most part they are the same kinds of reasons that influence the allocation of the production burden generally, and these may be summed up as reasons of convenience, fairness, and policy. What is *likely*, for instance, is often presumed. Most men are sane, as the law reckons sanity, and most properly sent letters reach their destination. In the absence of any evidence pointing to an opposite conclusion in the case at hand, it is both convenient and fair to assume that *this* testator, or *this* man accused of crime was sane when he made the will or did the act charged as criminal; or that *this* properly mailed letter reached the addressee. If nothing else, these assumptions will save a lot of time and trouble in making ponderous proof in every case of matters which will be controverted in only a small minority of cases.

Access to evidence is often the basis for creating a presumption. When goods are damaged in a bailee's possession, for instance, the bailee can more easily find out what happened to them than the bailor, so it is fair to presume the bailee's negligence as an initial matter and put him to the production of exculpatory evidence if he has any. The owner of an automobile has better means of knowing whether the driver was in his service when it struck the plaintiff than has the plaintiff. In such a case also there is an increasingly strong policy to make an automobile owner pay for the damage it causes even where there is no agency in the legal sense. Fairness and policy therefore combine to justify a presumption of agency from the mere fact of ownership. Here, it may be noted, is a presumption (usually created by statute) in a situation where most courts would not permit an inference.

If there is a presumption operating in proponent's favor when he rests his case, two questions then arise: (1) what must the opponent do to lift the production burden then resting upon him, and (2) if the opponent does lift this burden, what (if any) further effect does the presumption have?

Let us take up the first of these questions. It can be rephrased in terms of the simple symbols we have been using. If from A there is a presumption of B, and A is shown,[1] what must the opponent do to escape a compulsory finding of B? The answer is that the opponent must introduce evidence which will justify a finding of non-B. This requirement has, to use Maguire's terms, both an extensive and an intensive aspect. To satisfy the extensive aspect, the evidence must cover the whole of B. Thus a presumption of negligence on the part of the charterers of a vessel turned over to them in good condition and sinking while in their control is not met by a showing of care during *part* of the time it was in their control. Such evidence is not enough to lift the production burden. To satisfy the intensive aspect of the requirement, the evidence must satisfy the qualitative tests of sufficiency of the evidence to show non-B.

---

[1] Of course the evidence tending to show A may itself fall short of compelling such a finding. If so it will be a question for the trier to decide whether A exists.

If, now, the opponent has lifted the production burden by rebutting evidence which satisfies the above standards, what happens to the presumption? The orthodox view, sired by Thayer, has it that the presumption is utterly destroyed and disappears, and this even though the trier disbelieves the countervailing evidence. If, for example, the addressee of a properly mailed letter testifies that he never received it, that testimony would, if believed, justify a finding of nonreceipt. It therefore satisfies the test of *sufficiency*—which is not concerned with *credibility*—whether it is believed or not. Under the orthodox view this testimony would, then, *end the presumption* even if everybody in the courtroom was convinced that the testimony was a lie. In the case put, the destruction of the presumption would not, however, compel a finding of nonreceipt because a properly addressed letter is so likely to reach its destination that a *rational inference* may be drawn that it did so. And while countervailing evidence banishes the artificial procedural effect given by a presumption to the facts proven, A (in this case the mailing of the letter, and so on), yet it does not destroy the rational probative effect of A. In our illustration, if the trier rejects the testimony of nonreceipt as false and believes the testimony as to proper mailing, it could and probably would find receipt as an inference from the mailing. On the suppositions here made, this result seems just and proper and the orthodox theory would not prevent it. But there are other situations wherein that view does present serious problems.

Suppose, first, that the mind of the trier in the case just described is in equipoise on all the evidence. If the proponent has the burden of persuading the trier of B's existence, he must lose. Does a presumption of B's existence from proof of A have any effect on the persuasion burden? The orthodox doctrine says emphatically not—it declares that the effect of a presumption is entirely spent in shifting the production burden, and it denies that the persuasion burden ever shifts. But why should this necessarily be so? We have seen that the considerations which determine the allocation of the persuasion burden are of the same kind as those which lead to the creation of presumptions. If the developments of a trial bring forth a situation which justifies a presumption in the proponent's favor, might not the same considerations (though not necessarily) be sufficient to call for placing the persuasion burden also on the opponent? Why should a presumption always have the minimum effect prescribed for it by orthodoxy? The reasons that bring it forth will vary from mere administrative convenience, the necessity for getting the ball rolling, so to speak, to very strong policy. Should not the force of a presumption "be tough or tender according to the nature and force of those reasons"? Some courts say frankly that it should, and that a presumption may sometimes shift the persuasion burden; but on this particular point the weight of authority is probably that it may not. This problem is of importance, but only in cases where the trier's mind is in equipoise at the end of its deliberations, a situation which probably does not occur very often.

There is another situation where the orthodox theory gives more trouble. As we have seen, the fact(s), A, which give rise to a presumption of B in many instances are not sufficient to warrant an *inference* of B. A familiar example is the fairly common presumption of agency from the fact of ownership of an automobile. Suppose the Plaintiff, injured by Owner's automobile driven by Driver, has no available evidence on the issue of agency except the adverse testimony of Owner and Driver, and therefore rests on a presumption of agency, ownership being proven or admitted. Suppose further that Owner, sole defendant, puts on his own testimony and that of Driver, both of whom deny agency. If this testimony banishes the presumption, you may have the anomaly that the trier must find nonagency, even though it thoroughly disbelieves the denial as self-serving perjury. Such a result does indeed offend common sense and justice, and most courts reject it, although it is hard to reconcile its rejection with the orthodox view. Once a presumption comes into play the tendency is to send the matter to the jury unless the evidence to rebut the presumption leaves no reasonable room for the jury's function.

If the issue is sent to the jury, the question arises in this situation, as in the illustration involving the mailing of the letter, whether the persuasion burden is to be placed on plaintiff or defendant. And here again most courts will probably put it on plaintiff.[2]

Another different problem has arisen in connection with presumptions. If a case goes to the jury, what if anything should be said to the jury about any presumptions which may have come into the case? The orthodox answer is unequivocal: nothing. If a presumption has been met with sufficient evidence, the presumption has vanished and the issue should go to the jury without mention of it. Of course, if the facts giving rise to the presumption also afford an inference, the jury may be told about the inference and if the word "presumption" is used so as to be clearly understood to mean only this permissible inference, choice of the wrong word may be harmless error.

Even where a court gives a presumption continuing effect after evidence has been introduced to rebut it, there is no need to mention the presumption to the jury and it is probably only confusing to do so. If the persuasion burden is shifted, that is the only burden the instructions need mention. If it is not, but the jury may find B if they disbelieve opponent's evidence of non-B, then a simple direction to that effect is all that is needed. The only justification for telling the jury about the presumption would be a desire to implement the policy behind the presumption by inviting the jury

---

2 * * *

The two alternative views set forth in the text are not the only possible ones, nor the only ones to attain some judicial support. Morgan, for example, lists the following: (1) The so-called orthodox view. (2) A presumption puts on the opponent the burden of persuading the jury "to believe so much of the evidence against the presumed fact as would justify a reasonable jury in finding against that fact." (3) It disappears when opponent puts in evidence upon which the trier's mind is in equipoise, if that evidence "is of the requisite quantity and quality to justify a reasonable jury in finding the non-existence of the presumed fact." (4) It puts on opponent "the burden of persuading the jury that the existence of the presumed fact is so doubtful that the jury cannot determine whether it exists." (5) It puts on opponent "the burden of persuading the jury that the presumed fact does not exist." (6) In addition to having one of the foregoing effects, the presumption is to be weighed by the jury together with the evidence in the case. (7) It may simply allow an inference of B from A when the ordinary rules of proof would not allow it. (8) It may compel the finding of B unconditionally, if A is found (the conclusive presumption).

to weigh it, in some vague manner not easy to understand or articulate, as they would a part of the evidence. But if policy demands additional force to the presumption, better ways than this can be devised for giving it.

Smith v. Rapid Transit, Inc.

Supreme Judicial Court of Massachusetts, 1945.
317 Mass. 469, 58 N.E.2d 754.

■ SPALDING, JUSTICE. The decisive question in this case is whether there was evidence for the jury that the plaintiff was injured by a bus of the defendant that was operated by one of its employees in the course of his employment. If there was, the defendant concedes that the evidence warranted the submission to the jury of the question of the operator's negligence in the management of the bus. The case is here on the plaintiff's exception to the direction of a verdict for the defendant.

These facts could have been found: While the plaintiff at about 1:00 A.M. on February 6, 1941, was driving an automobile on Main Street, Winthrop, in an easterly direction toward Winthrop Highlands, she observed a bus coming toward her which she described as a "great big, long, wide affair." The bus, which was proceeding at about forty miles an hour, "forced her to turn to the right," and her automobile collided with a "parked car." The plaintiff was coming from Dorchester. The department of public utilities had issued a certificate of public convenience or necessity to the defendant for three routes in Winthrop, one of which includes Main Street, and this was in effect in February, 1941. "There was another bus line in operation in Winthrop at that time but not on Main Street." According to the defendant's time-table, buses were scheduled to leave Winthrop Highlands for Maverick Square via Main Street at 12:10 A.M., 12:45 A.M., 1:15 A.M., and 2:15 A.M. The running time for this trip at that time of night was thirty minutes.

The direction of a verdict for the defendant was right. The ownership of the bus was a matter of conjecture. While the defendant had the sole franchise for operating a bus line on Main Street, Winthrop, this did not preclude private or chartered buses from using this street; the bus in question could very well have been one operated by someone other than the defendant. It was said in Sargent v. Massachusetts Accident Co. that it is "not enough that mathematically the chances somewhat favor a proposition to be proved; for example, the fact that colored automobiles made in the current year outnumber black ones would not warrant a finding that an undescribed automobile of the current year is colored and not black, nor would the fact that only a minority of men die of cancer warrant a finding that a particular man did not die of cancer." The most that can be said of the evidence in the instant case is that perhaps the mathematical chances somewhat favor the proposition that a bus of the defendant caused the accident. This was not enough. A "proposition is proved by a preponderance of the evidence if it is made to appear more likely or probable in the sense that actual belief in its truth, derived from the evidence, exists in the mind or minds of the tribunal notwithstanding any doubts that may still linger there."

Exceptions overruled.

Hart & McNaughton, Evidence and Inference in the Law
54–55 (1958).[*]

It may be suggested parenthetically at this point that, while it is clear that the law satisfies itself with less than certainty, it is not clear that the formulas mentioned above always describe correctly the degree of certainty which the law actually requires. Consider the formula that in a civil case the facts must be determined on a more-likely-than-not basis. In the first place, the probabilities are determined in a most subjective and unscientific way: the trier of fact simply asks itself which of the contesting contradictory propositions according to the trier's limited experience more nearly squares with the evidence. In the second place, the law refuses to honor its own formula when the evidence is coldly "statistical." A court would not, for example hold the government liable to a farmer for injuries inflicted on him by his mule frightened by a "buzzing" jet plane if the only evidence that the pilot was a member of the Air Force (rather than a civilian) was that most of the pilots flying jets that day were Air Force personnel. This would be true even though the farmer could show that as [many] as 70 or 80 per cent of the jet pilots in the vicinity that day were of the Air Force.

The court, on the other hand, would certainly allow recovery if the evidence was that 100 per cent of the pilots were Air Force personnel, and would probably allow it if all of them were except a negligible few. Similarly, the court might allow recovery if the farmer, instead of introducing the statistical evidence, testified that he got a fleeting glimpse of the pilot's cap and that it was distinctively Air Force headgear. The court somehow feels more comfortable permitting a finding to be based on such eye-witness testimony even though the probative value of such testimony is itself determined ultimately by home-spun "statistics" in the mind of the trier of fact and even though the eye-witness testimony is probably no more indicative of the truth than is the evidence as to the proportion of Air Force pilots in the air.

Even in the case as originally stated—with the farmer producing solely the statistical evidence—the court might allow recovery if the reason for the farmer's dearth of evidence is the irrelevant fact that the government refused without justification to cooperate in the farmer's search for the offending pilot. And, though according to the more-likely-than-not formula it is irrelevant, the court might be swayed in its demand for evidence by the size of the stakes—a more elaborate presentation would naturally be ex-

---

[*] The Hayden Colloquium on Scientific Concept and Method edited by Daniel Lerner, Copyright, 1958, by American Academy of Arts & Sciences, Copyright, 1959 by The Free Press: Excerpts from Material by Henry M. Hart, Jr., and John McNaughton.

pected if the farmer was claiming $100,000 in damages than if he was claiming $100.

Dyer v. MacDougall

United States Court of Appeals, Second Circuit, 1952.
201 F.2d 265.

■ L. HAND, CIRCUIT JUDGE. This case comes up on appeal by the plaintiff from a judgment summarily dismissing the third and fourth counts of a complaint for libel and slander. Two questions arise: (1) whether we have jurisdiction over the appeal; (2) whether the defendants showed that there was no "genuine issue" to try within the meaning of Rule 56(c) Fed.Rules Civ.Proc. 28 U.S.C. We may start with the amended complaint, which was filed on November 24, 1950. It was in four counts, of which the first alleged that the defendant, Albert E. MacDougall, had said of the plaintiff at a directors' meeting of the "Queensboro Corporation": "You are stabbing me in the back." The second count alleged that MacDougall had written a letter to one, Dorothy Russell Hope, the plaintiff's wife's sister, containing the words: "He"—the plaintiff—"has made false statements to my clients in Philadelphia," and "He has presented bills for work he has not done." The third count alleged that MacDougall had said to a lawyer, named Almirall, that a letter sent out by the plaintiff to the shareholders of the "Queensboro Corporation" was a "a blackmailing letter." The fourth count alleged that MacDougall's wife, as MacDougall's agent, had said to Mrs. Hope that the plaintiff had "written and sent out a blackmailing letter." On December 26, 1950, the defendants, before answer, moved for judgment summarily dismissing the second, third and fourth counts, supporting their motion by affidavits of MacDougall, MacDougall's wife, and Almirall, and by a deposition of Mrs. Hope, which the plaintiff himself had already taken. Each of the defendants unequivocally denied the utterance of the slanders attributed to him or her; and Almirall and Mrs. Hope denied that he or she had heard the slanders uttered. On his part the plaintiff replied with several affidavits of his own, the contents of all of which would, however, be inadmissible as evidence at a trial upon the issue of utterance. On January 24, 1951, the defendants filed an unverified answer denying the defamatory utterances, and on the same day they brought on their motion for hearing before Judge Kennedy. He offered the plaintiff an opportunity to take depositions of Mr. and Mrs. MacDougall and of Almirall, and a second deposition of Mrs. Hope; and by consent the case was then adjourned to allow the plaintiff to take the depositions. However, towards the end of October 1951, he told the court that he did not wish to do so, and on December 28, 1951 (the defendants having meanwhile withdrawn their motion as to the second count), the judge decided the defendants' motion by summarily dismissing the third and fourth counts on the ground that upon the trial the plaintiff would have no evidence to offer in support of the slanders except the testimony of witnesses, all of whom would deny their utterance. On this opinion he entered the judgment in suit on January 7, 1952, from which the plaintiff took no appeal within thirty days. However, on February 20, 1952, he wrote a letter to the judge, asking an extension under Rule 73(a) of thirty days within which to appeal; and this he followed on the 25th by a motion for a reargument, repeating his request for the extension. On March 4, 1952, the judge filed a second opinion, granting the reargument, but again deciding that counts three and four should be dismissed. However, he granted an extension of thirty days for the time to appeal, and, apparently, *sua sponte,* "certified" "that I did give an express direction for the entry of judgment, and that there is no reason for delay." On March 4, 1952, the plaintiff filed a notice of appeal from the judgment.

* * * The question is whether, in view of the defendants' affidavits and Mrs. Hope's deposition, there was any "genuine issue" under Rule 56(c) as to the utterance of the slanders. The defendants had the burden of proving that there was no such issue; on the other hand, at a trial the plaintiff would have the burden of proving the utterances; and therefore, if the defendants on the motion succeeded in proving that the plaintiff would not have enough evidence to go to the jury on the issue, the judgment was right. As the plaintiff has refused to avail himself of the privilege under Rule 56(f) of examining by deposition the witnesses whom the defendants proposed to call at the trial, we must assume that what they said in their affidavits they would have repeated in their depositions; and that what they would have said in their depositions, they would say at a trial, with one possible exception, the consideration of which we will postpone for the time being. With that reserve we will therefore first discuss the judgment on the assumption that the record before us contains all the testimony that would appear at a trial in support of the slanders. We have not forgotten that the plaintiff swears that his wife told him on March 8, 1950, that Mrs. Hope had said to her on March 7, 1950, that she, Mrs. Hope, could forgive the plaintiff "everything except that letter," meaning a letter, written by the plaintiff and addressed to the shareholders of the "Queensboro Corporation," which Mrs. MacDougall according to the complaint described as a "blackmailing letter." The plaintiff did not submit his wife's affidavit that Mrs. Hope had told her what he says his wife said to him she did; but we shall assume that such an affidavit is in the record. Mrs. Hope's putative declaration to Mrs. Dyer would of course be hearsay, but the plaintiff says that it would nevertheless be competent under the exception as to "spontaneous exclamations." We cannot agree. The time of Mrs. MacDougall's statement to Mrs. Hope is not fixed except that it is said to have been between December 13th and March 7th; and, strictly, we might dispose of the point because there is no reason to say that the interval was not two months. But let us suppose that Mrs. MacDougall had called up Mrs. Hope only the day before Mrs. Hope narrated the talk to her sister. The argument must be that the emotional stress set up in Mrs. Hope's mind by Mr. MacDougall's information endured for twenty-four hours and so far suspended her ordinary powers of deliberation as to make her declaration like the ejaculation of a person injured in an accident, or suddenly faced with a vital crisis. "The utterance must have been *before there has been time to contrive and fabricate,* i.e. while the nervous excitement may be supposed still to dominate and the reflective powers to be yet in abeyance." Wigmore § 1750(b). So we are to suppose that, when Mrs. Hope learned that her brother-in-law, whom incidentally she had recently "castigated," had sent out a letter that could be described as blackmailing MacDougall, it so far

obsessed her deliberative faculties that, although she did not call up her sister that day, she remained unable to "contrive or fabricate" for twenty-four hours. Unless we are altogether to abandon the hearsay rule, it is difficult to imagine a situation more appropriate for its application. Finally, any declaration of Mrs. Hope would be incompetent as contradictory of her testimony, if the plaintiff should call her as his witness. It is true that Rule 43(b) makes competent inconsistent statements of a witness called by a party, if the witness is the adverse party himself, but Mrs. Hope is not a party. If the plaintiff called her and she repeated her deposition, he could not use his wife's contradictory version of the interview between her and Mrs. MacDougall.

Hence, if the cause went to trial, the plaintiff would have no witnesses by whom he could prove the slanders alleged in the third and fourth counts, except the two defendants, Almirall and Mrs. Hope; and they would all deny that the slanders had been uttered. On such a showing how could he escape a directed verdict? It is true that the carriage, behavior, bearing, manner and appearance of a witness—in short, his "demeanor"—is a part of the evidence. The words used are by no means all that we rely on in making up our minds about the truth of a question that arises in our ordinary affairs, and it is abundantly settled that a jury is as little confined to them as we are. They may, and indeed they should, take into consideration the whole nexus of sense impressions which they get from a witness. This we have again and again declared, and have rested our affirmance of findings of fact of a judge, or of a jury, on the hypothesis that this part of the evidence may have turned the scale. Moreover, such evidence may satisfy the tribunal, not only that the witness' testimony is not true, but that the truth is the opposite of his story; for the denial of one, who has a motive to deny, may be uttered with such hesitation, discomfort, arrogance or defiance, as to give assurance that he is fabricating, and that, if he is, there is no alternative but to assume the truth of what he denies.

Nevertheless, although it is therefore true that in strict theory a party having the affirmative might succeed in convincing a jury of the truth of his allegations in spite of the fact that all the witnesses denied them, we think it plain that a verdict would nevertheless have to be directed against him. This is owing to the fact that otherwise in such cases there could not be an effective appeal from the judge's disposition of a motion for a directed verdict. He, who has seen and heard the "demeanor" evidence, may have been right or wrong in thinking that it gave rational support to a verdict; yet, since that evidence has disappeared, it will be impossible for an appellate court to say which he was. Thus, he would become the final arbiter in all cases where the evidence of witnesses present in court might be determinative. We need not say that in setting aside a verdict the judge has not a broader discretion than in directing one, for we have before us only the equivalent of a direction. It may be argued that such a ruling may deprive a party of a possibly rational verdict, and indeed that is theoretically true, although the occasions must be to the last degree rare in which the chance so denied is more than fanciful. Nevertheless we do not hesitate to set against the chance so lost, the protection of a review of the judge's decision.

There remains the second point which we reserved for separate discussion: i.e. whether by an examination in open court the plaintiff might extract from the four witnesses admissions which he would not have got on the depositions that he refused. Although this is also at best a tenuous possibility, we need not say that there could never be situations in which it might justify denying summary judgment. It might appear for example that upon a deposition a witness had been recalcitrant, or crafty, or defiant, or evasive, so that the immediate presence of a judge in a court-room was likely to make him tell more. That would be another matter; and it might be enough. But the plaintiff is in no position to invoke such a possibility for he has refused to try out these witnesses upon deposition, where he might discover whether there was any basis for supposing that awe of a judge was necessary to make them more amenable. A *priori* we will not assume that that is true. The course of procedural reform has all indeed been towards bringing witnesses before the tribunal when it is possible; but that is not so much because more testimony can be got out of them as because only so can the "demeanor" evidence be brought before the tribunal.

Judgment affirmed.

■ FRANK, CIRCUIT JUDGE (concurring).

1. The facts here are most peculiar, unlikely to recur often: The plaintiff in his complaint asserts that defendant slandered plaintiff in the plaintiff's absence but in the presence of only two other persons. If there were a trial, plaintiff could not himself testify, for he knows of his own knowledge none of the facts necessary to support his case. To prove his case, he would have to call the defendant who, in his oral testimony, would deny that he had uttered the alleged slanderous statement. For plaintiff is aware that the only two other possible witnesses he could summon would corroborate defendant; and, if he called them, he could not impeach them.

Judge Hand's opinion states that, if defendant and the other witnesses testified, the trial court, evaluating their credibility in the light of their demeanor as witnesses, could rationally find not only that defendant's denial was false but that the opposite was true, i.e., that defendant had made the slanderous statement. Yet Judge Hand holds that a trial judge in a jury trial of such a case would be obliged not to let the jury reach a verdict for plaintiff on that rational basis. As I understand Judge Hand, he says that the result of holding otherwise would be that the trial judge's disposition of a motion for a directed verdict (or a verdict n.o.v.) could not be effectively reviewed on appeal. On that ground alone—i.e., the supposed obstacle, in a jury trial of such a case, to review of a directed verdict— Judge Hand's opinion affirms the summary judgment for defendant here.

Since, then, the sole reason given in Judge Hand's opinion for affirmance is something peculiar to a jury trial, I take it that, were there a jury waiver here, so that if there were a trial, it would be a judge trial, Judge Hand would hold erroneous the summary judgment here. This is a curious distinction. It would make the propriety of a summary judgment in such a case turn exclusively on whether or not the parties, if entitled to any trial, are entitled to one by jury.[1] In such a case as this, it would prevent a jury from relying on demeanor but permit a judge in a judge trial to do so (although, if he did, his decision, in so far as he relied on demeanor, would not ordinarily be reviewable).

I agree with Judge Hand that (at least in some cases)[2] a trial judge should be allowed to find that a plaintiff has discharged his burden of proof when the judge disbelieves oral testimony all of which is adverse to plaintiff, solely because of the trial court's reaction to the witnesses' demeanor and there is no evidence for plaintiff except that "demeanor evidence."[3] But I think it most unfortunate to hold that this rule applies in judge trials and not in jury trials. Such a distinction should be avoided if possible.

But I read Judge Hand's opinion as saying it is unavoidable for the following reason: If, in a jury trial, the jury, solely on the basis of its evaluation of credibility as affected by the jury's reaction to a witness' demeanor, were allowed to bring in a plaintiff's verdict, then necessarily (says Judge Hand) the judge in that same trial could also properly take into account demeanor in passing on the defendant's motion for a directed verdict; but, were that true, the judge's action on the motion could never be reviewed, as demeanor cannot appear in the printed record on appeal.[4]

I cannot accept that distinction for the following reasons: Judge Hand argues from the alleged unreviewability of a directed verdict in a case like this, if demeanor were a factor. But this argument cuts too far. For, if Judge Hand is correct, the same difficulty will attend the review of any directed verdict in any case where any important evidence consists of oral testimony. In any such case, one could say, as Judge Hand says here: If the

---

[1] That is, whether or not they both have failed to demand a jury, or whether or not plaintiff seeks relief (e.g., specific performance) precluding a jury trial.

[2] This parenthetical qualification I shall explain later.

[3] We have already held that, solely on the basis of a trial judge's disbelief in the oral testimony of a plaintiff's witness—a disbelief resulting entirely from the witness' demeanor—the judge may decide for the defendant. [H]owever, the disbelief in this testimony—uncontradicted by anything other than the witnesses' demeanor—meant that plaintiff had not discharged his burden of proof. In the instant case, the question is whether plaintiff can discharge his burden of proof where the judge disbelieves the testimony of witnesses all of whom testified against him.

[4] This reasoning, spelled out more in detail, is as follows:

(a) If a jury, solely on the basis of its evaluation of credibility as affected by its reaction to a witness' demeanor in a case like this, could properly bring in a verdict for the plaintiff, then (says Judge Hand) necessarily a trial judge could also properly take into account credibility in the light of demeanor, and solely because of resulting evaluation of the witnesses' reliability, could grant or deny the defendant's motion for a directed verdict.

(b) But (says Judge Hand) if the trial judge could thus consider demeanor, then in no case where there was oral testimony could the grant or denial of a directed verdict motion ever be reviewed and reversed, because the printed record before the upper court necessarily omits demeanor.

(c) Since, however, such directed-verdict orders can and should be reviewable this follows according to Judge Hand:

(1) The jury in a case like this may not properly return a plaintiff's verdict on the sole basis of "demeanor evidence."

(2) Therefore in such a case, on defendant's motion for a directed verdict, the trial judge must disregard the possibility that, were the case allowed to go to the jury, it might decide for plaintiff on the sole basis of "demeanor evidence."

jury (should the case go to the jury) could rely on "demeanor evidence," then necessarily the trial judge could do likewise, on a motion for a directed verdict; and, if he could, no directed verdict would be reviewable when important testimony is oral. But this is exactly not the rule in the federal courts: The well-settled rule is that, in passing on a motion for a directed verdict, the trial judge always must utterly disregard his own views of witnesses' credibility, and therefore of their demeanor; that he believes or disbelieves some of the testimony is irrelevant. When asked to direct a verdict for the defendant, the judge must assume that if he lets the case go to the jury, the jurymen will believe all evidence—including "demeanor evidence"—favorable to the plaintiff. In other words, the judge must not deprive plaintiff of any advantage that plaintiff might derive from having the jury pass upon the oral testimony. Indeed, the important difference between a trial judge's power on a motion for a new trial and on a motion for a directed verdict is precisely that on a new-trial motion he may base his action on his belief or disbelief in some of the witnesses, while on a directed-verdict motion he may not.

Lurton, J., in a much quoted opinion,[5] expressed the difference thus: "We do not think * * * that it is a proper test of whether the court should direct a verdict, that the court, on weighing the evidence, would, upon motion, grant a new trial. * * * In passing upon such motions [for new trial] he is necessarily required to weigh the evidence * * *. But, in passing upon a motion to direct a verdict, his functions are altogether different. In the latter case we think he cannot properly undertake to weigh the evidence. His duty is to take that view of the evidence most favorable to the party against whom it is moved to direct a verdict, and from that evidence, and the inferences reasonably and justifiably to be drawn therefrom, determine whether or not, under the law, a verdict might be found for the party having the onus."

Taft, J., held similarly in Felton v. Spiro. The cases in accord are legion. They are excellently discussed by Judge Parker in Aetna Cas. & Sur. Co. v. Yeatts and by Judge Sibley in Marsh v. Illinois Central R. Co.

In Brady v. Southern Ry. Co., the Court said: "When the evidence is such that *without weighing the credibility of the witnesses* there can be but one reasonable conclusion as to the verdict, the court should determine the proceeding by non-suit, directed verdict or otherwise in accordance with the applicable practice without submission to the jury, or by judgment notwithstanding the verdict." (Emphasis added.) As Moore puts it, a motion for new trial may invoke "the exercise of the trial court's discretion, such as that the verdict is inadequate or excessive, or that the verdict is against the weight of the evidence. In reference to this latter matter this function of the motion for a new trial must be sharply distinguished from the motion for a

---

[5] Mt. Adams & E.P. Inclined Ry. Co. v. Lowery.

directed verdict."[6] A "verdict may be set aside as contrary to the preponderance of the evidence, although a directed verdict is not justified."[7]

On a motion for new trial, the judge acts "as the thirteenth juror", i.e., he evaluates the credibility of the orally-testifying witnesses and therefore their demeanor. But on a motion for a directed verdict he does not. The rule that a trial judge may legitimately consider demeanor in ordering new trials means that his new-trial orders are seldom reviewable; on the other hand, the rule that he may not legitimately consider demeanor in considering directed verdict motions means that his orders on such motions are readily reviewable.

Frequently this sort of case arises: The defendant urges his motion for a directed verdict on the ground that, although there is oral testimony, the record contains no testimony (or other evidence) from which any rational inference can be drawn for the existence of a fact indispensable to plaintiff's case. If the trial judge, then, directs a defendant's verdict,[8] the upper court, on appeal, in testing the propriety of his direction, adopts the postulate that the trial judge assumed that the jury, were it allowed to render a verdict, would regard the oral testimony—and therefore the witnesses' demeanor—in a manner most favorable to plaintiff. The upper court makes the same assumption; as a consequence, the trial judge's attitude towards that demeanor is not a factor on such an appeal, and so constitutes no obstacle to review.

If I am correct, there is no foundation for Judge Hand's distinction; and, as I gather that he would have held it error to enter summary judgment for defendant here, if there had been no jury demand, he should, I think, hold that the judgment here must be reversed, despite the request for trial by jury.

2. One can imagine a case in which a man would suffer a grave injustice, if it were the invariable rule that a plaintiff can never win a case when (1) he can offer only the oral testimony of the defendant, the one available witness, which is flatly and unswervingly against the plaintiff but (2) the jury (in a jury trial) or the judge (in a judge trial) is thoroughly convinced by that witness' demeanor that he is an unmitigated liar. On that account, I would oppose such a rule.

But this is not such a case. As already noted, the facts here are most unusual: The plaintiff asserts that in his absence he was slandered by defendant in the presence of but two other persons. As this fact is denied by all three, only plaintiff's own suit serves to publicize the alleged slander. In these peculiar circumstances, the plaintiff should not have the chance at a trial to discharge his burden of proof by nothing except the trial court's dis-

---

[6] Moore, Federal Practice (2d ed. 1951) § 50.02(1), p. 2317.

[7] Moore, loc. cit., § 50.03, p. 2318. See also § 50.11, pp. 2338–2339, and Wigmore, Evidence (3d ed.) § 2494, pp. 298–299.

[8] Or if he denies defendant's motion for such a verdict.

belief in the oral testimony of witnesses all of whom will deny that the alleged slanderous statement was made. Wherefore I concur.

Maguire, Evidence: Common Sense and Common Law
177–79, 182–84 (1947).[*]

* * * Now let us illustrate with a fascinating little case from which can be spun our whole discussion of these topics. Plaintiff sued defendant to quiet plaintiff's title to Blackacre. It seems to be assumed throughout that he had the burden of persuasion that he was the owner at the time he brought suit. Plaintiff alleged that he had acquired title on a specified date, and had ever since retained possession and title, but that defendant without right made some claim to Blackacre. Defendant admitted that plaintiff became owner of Blackacre on the date specified but denied that plaintiff was the present owner and also denied that defendant's claim was without right.

If on the issues shaped by these pleadings defendant had offered at trial evidence of acquisition of title to Blackacre by a sale for taxes, and plaintiff had given evidence tending to prove the sale invalid, apparently plaintiff would have had the burden of persuasion on the consequent issue. But that was not the way the parties tried the case. Plaintiff stood on the admission of the answer as to his acquisition of title and rested, urging that the status of ownership thus established was presumed to continue. Defendant, offering no evidence, moved for a non-suit. The motion was granted, and plaintiff appealed. Held error; reversed and remanded with a plain intimation that if defendant persisted in giving no evidence, judgment should be entered for plaintiff. Gatrell v. Salt Lake County; the court had trouble with the case; there are a brief main opinion, a slightly longer concurring opinion, and a still longer dissent.

The holding here is that although plaintiff had the ultimate burden of persuasion on the issue of continued ownership, the case had been left in a posture which cast upon defendant the burden of producing evidence on that issue. Evidently the cardinal point of the whole business is defendant's partial admission of plaintiff's allegations. The majority argue that this admission is in the nature of evidence conclusively establishing plaintiff's acquisition of title to Blackacre. Once getting title, plaintiff is presumed to retain title. Defendant has done nothing to displace or rebut this presumption. Therefore defendant could not win.

By reasoning thus the majority allow plaintiff to pick and choose among defendant's allegations, accepting the favorable and rejecting the unfavorable. The dissenter argues that plaintiff might not do this; he must take the bitter with the sweet; the whole matter is to be decided on the pleading level and, for purposes of pleading, defendant's denial of continued ownership nullifies the effect of his admission of plaintiff's acquisition of

---

[*] Copyright, 1947 by The Foundation Press, Inc.

title. The majority seems to deny that the problem is one of pleading, treating it rather as a problem of evidence. They assume in that aspect the propriety of plaintiff's taking what he likes, and only what he likes, from defendant's various utterances about the issue of ownership.

This controversy within the court is aside from our immediate interest. Let us grant the soundness of the majority's method of attack on the case and examine its elements. First, burden of persuasion—why was it upon plaintiff and what does the term signify when translated into mental operations of the trier of fact? As to placement of burden of persuasion, all sorts of explanatory formulae can be found in the books. It is with the party seeking to sustain an affirmative; it is determined by the form of the pleadings; it is to be borne by the party having peculiar knowledge of the facts; it is imposed on the party whose contentions depart further from normal likelihood. This plurality of so-called decisive factors proves forthwith that no single simple formula for allocating burden of persuasion will be found. All four factors mentioned might be found in the same case, some pointing to one litigant, some to the other. Here, as in many large legal problems, we must work out our answers issue by issue, taking into consideration all elements of fairness and expediency. Of course this does not mean that the answers have to be worked out case by case. As already remarked, precedents will build up for recurrent issues and these precedents will be serviceable analogies. It merely means that there is no wondrous touchstone to solve all problems without pain of thought.

Think back now to our *Gatrell* case about title to Blackacre. The decision rendered necessarily connoted that the finding *must* be for plaintiff unless defendant came forward with evidence to prove that plaintiff had somehow lost title between the date when he acquired it and the date when he began his suit. But, as a purely original proposition, there might be difference of opinion as to whether proof of getting title say in 1931 without more made it impossible reasonably to find that the grantee had lost title by say 1940. A lot could happen to shift ownership of Blackacre in nine years. Here, though, the courts step in with a judicial control. They say there is a presumption of continuance of the status of ownership, and that this presumption has an effect comparable to overwhelming proof in taking the issue out of debatability.

Here we had better slow down, make some comparisons, and take stock of difficulties. There is trouble with terminology. This word presumption has suffered badly from rough and careless handling. It has been used as a synonym for inference and sometimes as the operative part of weasel-worded formulae for saying that from the judicial or legislative point of view certain things are taken as so and attempts to contradict them will be futile. In the former usage the word has often been expanded into the term "presumption of fact" and in the latter into "presumption of law" or "conclusive presumption". As our text has shown, we are rejecting both these usages and employing presumption to denote the concept, illustrated specifically dozens of times in common and statute law, that when a designated basic fact or aggregate of facts exists, existence of another fact or aggregate of facts, called the presumed fact or facts, must be assumed in absence of adequate rebuttal. In the *Gatrell* case the basic fact was plaintiff's acquisition of title to Blackacre and the presumed fact the continuance of his ownership down to and through the date when he began his suit. This careful, particularized use of the word presumption, by the way, is getting more and more consistent acceptance in the courts; nobody has ever succeeded in making consistent the legislative use of this or any other important word.

Our text has steadily conceded that the state of decisive one-sidedness may not always be permanent. Temporarily overwhelming proof on an issue of fact may be met and controlled by counter-proof. Likewise the text has indicated that presumptions may be rebutted—that is, the presumed facts thrown open for deliberative findings instead of being coercively assumed. But a mighty battle has raged, and is still raging, over this matter of rebutting presumptions. Without being foolhardy enough to offer an infallible solution to terminate the battle for good and all, we should at least see what all the shooting is about.

It may be said that a presumption has both extensity and intensity. Rebuttal, we should expect, ought to be correspondingly wide and forceful. Suppose our presumption is that if a ship, hired under charter party, is turned over to the hirer in seaworthy condition and thereafter sinks, the sinking is due to the fault of the hirer. In case the rebuttal evidence offered by the hirer, when sued for damages because of the loss of the ship, tends to show due care on his part for *only a portion of the time* he controlled the ship, the evidence is not extensive enough to rebut the presumption. * * *

Legille v. Dann

United States Court of Appeals, District of Columbia Circuit, 1976.
544 F.2d 1.

■ SPOTTSWOOD W. ROBINSON, III, CIRCUIT JUDGE:

* * *

I

* * * On March 1, 1973, appellees' attorney mailed from East Hartford, Connecticut, to the Patent Office in Washington, D.C., a package containing four patent applications. Each of the applications had previously been filed in the Grand Duchy of Luxembourg, three on March 6, 1972, and the fourth on the following August 11. The package was marked "Airmail," bore sufficient airmail postage and was properly addressed. Delivery of air mail from East Hartford to Washington at that time was normally two days.

The applications were date-stamped "March 8, 1973," by the Patent Office. Each of the four applications was assigned that filing date on the ground that the stamped date was the date of receipt by the Patent Office. If the action of the Patent Office is to stand, three of appellees' applications, on which Luxembourg patents had been granted, fail in this country.

Appellees petitioned the Commissioner of Patents to reassign the filing date. The petition was denied. Appellees then sued in the District Court for a judgment directing the Commissioner to accord the applications a filing date not later than March 6, 1973. Both sides moved for summary judgment on the basis of the pleadings and affidavits respectively submitted. Not surprisingly, none of the affidavits reflected any direct evidence of the date on which the applications were actually delivered to the Patent Office.

The District Court correctly identified the central issue: "whether there exists a genuine issue of fact as to when these applications were received by the Patent Office." By the court's appraisal, appellees' suit was "predicated upon the legal presumption that postal employees discharge their duties in a proper manner and that properly addressed, stamped and deposited mail is presumed to reach the addressee in due course and without unusual delay, unless evidence to the contrary is proven." The court believed, however, that the Commissioner's position rested "primarily upon a presumption of procedural regularity based upon the normal manner, custom, practice and habit established for the handling of incoming mail at the Patent Office and upon the absence of evidence showing that the subject applications were not handled routinely in accordance with those established procedures." On this analysis, the court "concluded that the presumption relied upon by the [Commissioner] is insufficient to overcome the strong presumption that mails, properly addressed, having fully prepaid postage, and deposited in the proper receptacles, will be received by the addressee in the ordinary course of the mails." "This latter presumption," the court held, "can only be rebutted by proof of specific facts and not by invoking another presumption"; "the negative evidence in this case detailing the manner, custom, practice and habit of handling incoming mail by the Patent Office fails to overcome or rebut the strong presumption that the applications were timely delivered in the regular course of the mails to the Patent Office." In sum,

> [appellees] rely upon the strong presumption of the regularity of the mails to show that, in the normal course of postal business, these applications would be delivered within two days from March 1, 1973. [The Commissioner] does not show nor offer to show by way of any positive evidence that the presumption is inapplicable in this case. On the contrary, he relies on negative evidence as to custom, habit and usual procedure to create a conflicting presumption that the agency's business and procedure were followed in this case. Under the circumstances of this case, this Court holds, as a matter of law, that this presumption is insufficient to rebut or overcome the presumption of the regularity of the mails.

II

Proof that mail matter is properly addressed, stamped and deposited in an appropriate receptacle has long been accepted as evidence of delivery to the addressee. On proof of the foundation facts, innumerable cases recognize a presumption to that effect. Some presume more specifically that the delivery occurred in due course of the mails. The cases concede, however, that the presumption is rebuttable. We think the District Court erred in adhering to the presumption in the face of the evidentiary showing which the Commissioner was prepared to make.

Rebuttable presumptions[1] are rules of law attaching to proven evidentiary facts certain procedural consequences as to the opponent's duty to come forward with other evidence. In the instant case, the presumption would normally mean no more than that proof of proper airmailing of appellees' applications required a finding, in the absence of countervailing evidence, that they arrived at the Patent Office within the usual delivery time. There is abundant authority undergirding the proposition that, as a presumption, it did not remain viable in the face of antithetical evidence. As Dean Wigmore has explained, "the peculiar effect of a presumption 'of law' (that is, the real presumption) is merely to invoke a rule of law compelling the [trier of fact] to reach a conclusion in the absence of evidence to the contrary from the opponent. If the opponent does offer evidence to the contrary (sufficient to satisfy the judge's requirement of some evidence), the presumption disappears as a rule of law, and the case is in the [factfinder's] hands free from any rule." As more poetically the explanation has been put, "[p]resumptions * * * may be looked on as the bats of the law, flitting in the twilight, but disappearing in the sunshine of actual facts."

We are aware of the fact that this view of presumptions—the so-called "bursting bubble" theory—has not won universal acclaim. Nonetheless, it is the prevailing view, to which jurists preponderantly have subscribed; it is the view of the Supreme Court, and of this court as well. It is also the approach taken by the Model Code of Evidence and, very importantly, by the newly-adopted Federal Rules of Evidence.[2] These considerations hardly

---

[1] We distinguish the presumption "of law"—the procedural rule dictating a factual conclusion in the absence of contrary evidence—from the presumption "of fact," which in reality is not a presumption at all, see 9 J. Wigmore, Evidence § 2491 at 288–289 (3d ed. 1940), and from the "conclusive" presumption, which is actually a substantive rule of law. See 9 J. Wigmore, Evidence § 2492 (3d ed. 1940); C. McCormick, Evidence § 342 at 804 (2d ed. 1972). We also differentiate presumptions from inferences, a dissimilarity which "is subtle, but not unreal. A presumption, sometimes called a presumption of law, is an inference which the law directs the [trier of fact] to draw if it finds a given set of facts; an inference is a conclusion which the [trier of fact] is *permitted*, but not compelled, to draw from the facts."

[2] "In all civil actions and proceedings not otherwise provided for by Act of Congress or by these rules, a presumption imposes on the party against whom it is directed the burden of going forward with evidence to rebut or meet the presumption, but does not shift to such party the burden of proof in the sense of the risk of nonpersuasion, which remains throughout the trial upon the party on whom it was originally cast." Fed.R.Evid. 301. The history of this provision portrays a fluctuating evolution. As originally proposed by the Supreme Court, the presumptions governed were given the effect of placing on the opposing party the burden of establishing the nonexistence of the presumed fact, and "[t]he so-called 'bursting bubble' theory, under which a presumption vanishes upon the introduction of evidence which would support a finding of the nonexistence of the presumed fact, even though not believed, [was] rejected as according presumptions too 'slight and evanescent' an effect." Advisory Committee's Note to original Rule 301. The House Committee on the Judiciary agreed, but substituted a shift in the burden of going forward in place of a shift of the burden of proof, and conferred evidentiary value on the presumption. H.R.Rep. No. 93–650, 93d Cong., 1st Sess. 7 (1973), U.S. Code Cong. & Admin. News 1974, p. 7075. The Senate Committee on the Judiciary felt, however, that "the House amendment is ill-advised. * * * 'Presumptions are not evidence, but ways of dealing with evidence.' [footnote omitted]. This treatment requires juries to perform the task of considering 'as evidence' facts upon which they have no direct evidence and which may con-

leave us free to assume a contrary position. Beyond that, we perceive no legal or practical justification for preferring either of the two involved presumptions over the other. In light of the Commissioner's showing on the motions for summary judgment, then, we conclude that the District Court should have declined a summary disposition in favor of a trial.

III

Conservatively estimated, the Patent Office receives through the mails an average of at least 100,000 items per month. The procedures utilized for the handling of that volume of mail were meticulously described in an affidavit by an official of the Patent Office, whose principal duties included superintendence of incoming mail. Ordinary mail—other than special delivery, registered and certified—arrives at the Patent Office in bags, which are date-marked if the items contained were placed by the postal service in the Patent Office pouch earlier than the date of delivery of the bags. A number of readers open the wrappers, compare the contents against any included listing—such as a letter of transmittal or a return postcard—and note any discrepancy, and apply to at least the principal included paper a stamp recording thereon the receipt date and the reader's identification number. Another employee then applies to the separate papers the official mail-room stamp, which likewise records the date; the two stamps are used in order to minimize the chance of error. The date recorded in each instance is the date on which the Patent Office actually receives the particular bag of mail, or a previous date when the bag is so marked. From every indication, the affidavit avers, appellees' applications were not delivered to the Patent Office until March 8, 1973.

We cannot agree with the District Court that an evidentiary presentation of this caliber would do no more than raise "a presumption of procedural regularity" in the Patent Office. Certainly it would accomplish that much; it would cast upon appellees the burden of producing contradictory evidence, but its effect would not be exhausted at that point. The facts giving rise to the presumption would also have evidentiary force, and as evidence would command the respect normally accorded proof of any fact. In other words, the evidence reflected by the affidavit, beyond creation of a presumption of regularity in date-stamping incoming mail, would have probative value on the issue of date of receipt of appellees' applications; and even if the presumption were dispelled, that evidence would be entitled to consideration, along with appellees' own evidence, when a resolution of

---

fuse them in performance of their duties." S.Rep. No. 93–1277, 93d Cong., 2d Sess. 9–10 (1974), first quoting Hearings on H.R. 2463 Before the Senate Committee on Judiciary, 93d Cong., 2d Sess. 96 (1974) U.S. Code Cong. & Admin. News 1974, pp. 7051, 7056. The Senate Committee accordingly modified Rule 301 to its present form, and the Conference Committee adopted the Senate version. H.R.Rep. No. 93–1597, 93d Cong., 2d Sess. 5–6 (1974) U.S. Code Cong. & Admin. News 1974, p. 7098.

* * *

the issue is undertaken. And, clearly, a fact-finder convinced of the integrity of the Patent Office's mail-handling procedures would inexorably be led to the conclusion that appellees' applications simply did not arrive until the date which was stamped on them.

In the final analysis, the District Court's misstep was the treatment of the parties' opposing affidavits as a contest postulating a question of law as to the relative strength of the two presumptions rather than as a prelude to conflicting evidence necessitating a trial. Viewed as the mere procedural devices we hold that they are, presumptions are incapable of waging war among themselves. Even more importantly, the court's disposition of the case on a legal ruling disregarded the divergent inferences which the evidentiary tenders warranted, and consequently the inappropriateness of a resolution of the opposing claims by summary judgment. As only recently we said, "[t]he court's function is not to resolve any factual issue, but to ascertain whether any exists, and all doubts in that regard must be resolved against summary judgment." Here the District Court was presented with an issue of material fact as to the date on which appellees' applications were received by the Patent Office, and summary judgment was not in order.

The judgment appealed from is accordingly reversed, and the case is remanded to the District Court for further proceedings. The cross-motions for summary judgment will be denied, and the case will be set down for trial on the merits in regular course.

So ordered.

[The dissenting opinion of Judge Fahy is omitted.]

NOTE

See Federal Rules of Evidence 301–302, California Evidence Code §§ 110, 115, 500–502, 520–522, 550, 600–607, 620–624, 630–645, 660, 662–668.

Degnan, Syllabus on California Evidence Code

(11th Annual Summer Program for California Lawyers, U. of Calif. at Berkeley, 1965)
pp. 18–25.

B. Presumptions

The Code of Civil Procedure § 1957 divides all "indirect" (i.e., circumstantial) evidence into two forms or kinds, inferences and presumptions. In §§ 1958 and 1959 these two forms are defined. Without repeating the unnecessary division of § 1957, Evidence Code § 600 restates in more modern expression the substance of the existing definitions. An inference is a deduction which reasonable men could draw from another fact or facts which have been proved or established; a presumption is an assumption of fact that the law *requires* to be made when another fact or facts have been proved or established.

Evidence Code § 601 divides presumptions further into conclusive and rebuttable presumptions;   so does C.C.P. § 1961. Retention of the term "conclusive presumption" is unfortunate because the kinds of things described in §§ 621–624 are not presumptions at all but rules of law. None of the things which will subsequently be said about management of presumptions generally have any reference to conclusive presumptions.

There have been two perennially difficult problems about presumptions in civil cases in California. First to be treated is the difficult concept of the presumption as evidence. The second is what impact the presumption has on the burdens of producing evidence and of persuasion. These two will be discussed separately.

1. Presumptions as Evidence

All theories about presumption agree on one thing. If the basic facts which support the presumption are established, and there is no contradiction, the jury *must* find the presumed fact to be true. This is the result of C.C.P. § 1961, and it is much more explicitly stated in Evidence Code §§ 604 and 606. The difficulty under the C.C.P. was the meaning of the word "controverted" in § 1961. Did contradictory evidence so "controvert" the presumption that it disappeared entirely, never to be mentioned by judge or jury? Or was a controverted presumption merely no longer binding, but still retaining some probative force? In part because of some language (§§ 1957, 1963) which refers to presumptions as "evidence," the Supreme Court in Smellie v. Southern Pac. Co., 212 Cal. 540, 299 P. 529 (1931), held that presumptions are evidence, and that they continue in the case even after controverting evidence has been introduced. The jury should be so instructed. Although abundantly criticized, this holding has endured and is the prime basis for the instructions framed under BAJI series 135. The case also held that while a presumption could be totally dispelled by testimony, that could be accomplished only by the testimony the holder of the presumption offered on his own behalf, and not by that extracted from him under C.C.P. § 2055.

To meet this uniquely California view, Evidence Code § 600(a), after defining presumptions, expressly declares: "A presumption is not evidence." No longer should juries be instructed that it is evidence, and that it is to be weighed by them along with all other evidence on the particular issue. And there should no longer be a problem about whether the presumption is "dispelled" (i.e., totally eliminated) from the case in the sense of the *Smellie* opinion, for it was only as to the existence of the presumption as evidence that this question had any content.

2. The Two Kinds of Presumptions

Evidence Code § 601, after dividing presumptions into conclusive and rebuttable, further classifies the latter as those affecting only the burden of producing evidence and those also affecting the burden of proof. Each of these classes, and the consequences of the classification, is elaborated in §§ 603–606.

The basic theoretical dispute in other states and in the scholarly literature (somewhat concealed in California because of the doctrine that a presumption is evidence) has been about the effect of contrary or controverting evidence. One view, identified with Professors Thayer and Wigmore, has been that presumptions are created to resolve issues when no evidence has been produced on the point; when evidence is produced, the presumption is exhausted and plays no further role in the case. The burden of persuading the jury about the existence of the fact in question remains where it was at the outset. To the extent that the underlying facts of the presumption have some probative, circumstantial force (e.g., that a properly addressed and mailed letter was received) the jury may consider those facts, balancing them against the testimony of the other party that he did not receive it. But those basic facts, once contradicted, are not reinforced by the presumption.

The other major view, identified largely with Professors Morgan and McCormick and essentially adopted by the Uniform Rules of Evidence, is that a presumption that has a logical basis (again the letter doctrine) should not be robbed of its force merely by a denial or by the production of some evidence that, if believed, would support a finding. This view would continue the presumption in force, in the form of an instruction to the jury that if they believe that the basic facts exist they should find that the letter was received, unless the contrary evidence persuaded them (usually by a preponderance) that it was not achieved. Thus it may be that a party who started with the burden of proof on a given issue will have shifted that burden to the opponent by establishing the basic fact of a presumption.

No state has consistently followed either of these two theories. A court that solemnly declares that the burden of proof never shifts will, when encountering certain kinds of presumptions, declare that the presumption may be overcome only by persuasive evidence, and that the jury should find the presumed fact unless persuaded by the contrary evidence. Thus in California a child born of a married woman, or within ten months of the end of the marriage, is presumed to be the child of the husband, and that presumption can be overcome only by clear and convincing evidence.

The Law Revision Commission resolved the seeming contradiction between theories by determining that some presumptions are created merely to expedite the proof of law suits, or to shift to a person who has superior access to proof the obligation to come forward with an explanation of an event. § 603. These it classified as presumptions affecting only the burden of producing evidence. Under this section, the stages are:

(a) Evidence supporting the basic facts is produced by the party initially bearing the burden of proof. If no contrary evidence is produced the judge must direct the jury to find (or find himself) that the presumed fact exists if it or he believes the basic facts.

(b) If evidence sufficient to support a contrary finding is produced, the case goes to the jury without mention of the presumption; they resolve it as they would any case of conflicting inferences and testimony.

Some other presumptions founded more in policy considerations than in mere expedition are given greater force under §§ 605–606. The presumption of legitimacy found in § 661 is illustrative. The stages here are:

(a) Evidence supporting the basic facts is produced by the party initially bearing the burden of proof. If no contrary evidence is produced, the consequences are the same as above—a peremptory finding.

(b) If contrary evidence sufficient to support a finding is produced, the jury will be instructed that the husband bears the burden of persuading them that he is not the father.

Admittedly the classification of presumptions as one form or the other will not be a simple task. The code helps by classifying some of the standard and commonly encountered presumptions. As to others (either those found in other codes or in the case law), the judges must do as they have done before.

C. Prima Facie Evidence

Code of Civil Procedure § 1833 defines prima facie evidence as "that which suffices for the proof of a particular fact, until contradicted and overcome by other evidence." The phrase is troublesome because it has been and is used with several different meanings. To the original code commissioners, it meant evidence that "in the absence of all controlling evidence or discrediting circumstances, becomes conclusive of the fact; that is, it should operate upon the minds of the jury as decisive to found their verdict as to the fact." As such, it is hard to distinguish from a presumption. The term is often used also as the equivalent of a reasonable inference—evidence which, if believed, is sufficient to support but not to compel, a finding. And the code commissioners themselves often used it when the only probable purpose was to create a hearsay exception. E.g., C.C.P. §§ 1936, 1946. To avoid the confusion, the commission has eliminated from the Evidence Code both the definition and the usage of "prima facie." But the problem remains, for other codes contain many sections making one thing, usually a writing or recording prima facie evidence of some fact or facts. E.g., Health & S.C. § 10577 (death certificate). Sometimes the courts have treated these as presumptions affecting the burden of proof. At other times they appear to be regarded as merely shifting the burden of producing evidence.

Although the Commission eliminated the term from the Evidence Code, it could not eliminate the many instances in which the term is used in other codes. Section 602 therefore provides:

"A statute providing that a fact or group of facts is prima facie evidence of another fact establishes a rebuttable presumption."

Whether it is a presumption shifting the burden of producing evidence only, or one shifting the burden of proof as well, the courts must in each instance decide by ascertaining the legislative purpose. And in most instances, of course, the special statute will serve the additional purpose of creating a hearsay exception. Evidence Code § 1205 expressly disclaims any intention to repeal hearsay exceptions found in other codes.

In re Nicholas H.

Supreme Court of California, 2002.
46 P.3d 932.

■ BROWN, J.

A man who receives a child into his home and openly holds the child out as his natural child is presumed to be the natural father of the child. (Fam.Code, § 7611, subd. (d); hereafter section 7611(d).) The presumption that he is the natural father "is a rebuttable presumption affecting the burden of proof and may be rebutted in an appropriate action only by clear and convincing evidence." (§ 7612, subd. (a); hereafter section 7612(a).) The question presented by this case is whether a presumption arising under section 7611(d) is, under section 7612(a), necessarily rebutted when the presumed father seeks parental rights but admits that he is not the biological father of the child.

The answer to this question is of the gravest concern to the six-year-old boy involved in this case. While his presumed father is providing a loving home for him, his mother has not done so, and his biological father, whose identity has never been judicially determined, has shown no interest in doing so. Therefore, if, as the Court of Appeal concluded, the juvenile court had no discretion under section 7612(a) but to find that the presumption arising under section 7611(d) was rebutted by the presumed father's admission that he is not the biological father, this child will be rendered fatherless and homeless. * * *

[Nicholas was born to Kimberly on August 10, 1995. Thomas lived with Kimberly from May 1995 until December 1997 and from January 1999 until September 1999, was present at the birth and was named as the father on Nicholas's birth certificate. Thomas and Kimberly both agreed that Thomas was not Nicholas's natural father; apparently Kimberly and Thomas did not meet until after Kimberly was pregnant with Nicholas. Both Thomas and Kimberly had trouble with the law. In 1998, Thomas was arrested for battering Kimberly. In 1999, Kimberly was arrested for felony assault on Thomas. While Kimberly was in jail, Thomas took Nicholas to his home. When police later arrested Thomas for failure to complete an anger management class that was required as a result of his battery charge, they placed Nicholas in the custody of the Alameda County Social Services Agency. Thomas filed an action to obtain custody of Nicholas.]

Thomas has been the constant in Nicholas's life. As the Court of Appeal observed, in concluding the evidence "more than satisfied the requirements of section 7611(d)," Thomas has lived with Nicholas for long periods of time, he has provided Nicholas with significant financial support over the years, and he has consistently referred to and treated Nicholas as his son. "In addition, there is undisputed evidence that Nicholas has a strong emotional bond with Thomas and that Thomas is the only father Nicholas has ever know[n]."

Kimberly, on the other hand, has been a frail reed for Nicholas to lean upon. The investigation report prepared by a family services counselor stated that "information from friends and relatives of the family supported Thomas's allegations of Kimberly's drug use, transiency, lack of gainful employment and violence towards others." The juvenile court's finding that Nicholas had to be removed from her custody was based on the following grounds: "One, [Kimberly] continues to lead an unstable lifestyle, without housing or means of support of her own. . . Number two, Nicholas has continually stated he does not wish to reside with his mother because she is mean to him; she hits and slaps him; and she smokes weed. Three, and most importantly to me as I have observed [Kimberly's] demeanor throughout this case, particularly during her testimony, I have grown increasingly concerned about [her] mental and emotional health. . ."

Jason S., Kimberly claims, is Nicholas's biological father. However, Jason has not come forward to assert any parental rights he may have, and because the Agency has been unable to obtain enough information from Kimberly to locate Jason, his paternity could not be established.

On this record, the juvenile court found that the presumption under section 7611(d) that Thomas was Nicholas's natural father had not been rebutted. The court expressly rejected the contention that Thomas's admission that he is not Nicholas's biological father necessarily rebutted the presumption. "If I were to agree with County Counsel that [Thomas's] admission that he is not Nicholas's biological father rebuts the presumption, then what we would be doing is leaving Nicholas fatherless." * * *

Discussion

The Court of Appeal concluded that Thomas qualified as Nicholas's presumed father under section 7611(d), but that, under section 7612(a), his admission that he is not Nicholas's biological father necessarily rebutted that presumption.

The Court of Appeal reached the latter conclusion through the following analysis: "[T]he section 7611 presumption that a man is the 'natural father' of a child can be rebutted by 'clear and convincing evidence.' (§ 7612.) * * * " The Court of Appeal satisfied itself * * * that "courts construing sections 7611 and 7612 have assumed that natural means biological." Clear and convincing proof demands *a high probability*, the Court of Appeal observed. Accordingly, "when read in conjunction with section 7611," the Court of Appeal concluded, "section 7612 means that the presumption that a man is a child's natural father is rebutted by evidence establishing a high probability that the man is not the child's natural, biological father." Evidence establishing a high probability that Thomas is not Nicholas's biological father was adduced in this case, namely, the testimony of both Kimberly and Thomas under oath that Thomas is not Nicholas's biological father. Therefore, even though its decision would have the effect of rendering Nicholas fatherless, the Court of Appeal felt it was "not free to ignore the statute, which expressly states that the section 7611(d) presumption *is* rebutted by clear and convincing evidence that the presumed father is not the child's natural father." (Italics added.)

* * * [T]he Court of Appeal appears to have conflated two of the three subdivisions of section 7612. Subdivision (a) provides that "a presumption under Section 7611 is a rebuttable presumption affecting the burden of proof and *may* be rebutted *in an appropriate action* only by clear and convincing evidence." (Italics added.) Subdivision (c), on the other hand, provides that "[t]he presumption under Section 7611 *is* rebutted by a judgment establishing paternity of the child by another man." (Italics added.) No judgment establishing the paternity of another man has been entered here. Kimberly asserts Jason is Nicholas's biological father, but Jason has not come forward to affirm that claim and, indeed, has not even been located. (2) "A man who may be the father of a child, but whose biological paternity has not been established, or, in the alternative, has not achieved presumed father status, is an 'alleged' father. [Citation.]"

Our conclusion—that a man does not lose his status as a presumed father by admitting he is not the biological father—is also supported by subdivision (b) of section 7612. Subdivision (b) provides: "If two or more presumptions arise under section 7611 which conflict with each other, the presumption which on the facts is founded on the weightier considerations of policy and logic controls." As a matter of statutory construction, if the Legislature had intended that a man who is not a biological father cannot be a presumed father under section 7611, it would not have provided for such weighing, for among two competing claims for presumed father status under section 7611, there can be only one biological father. * * *

In a very recent case, [In re Kiana A., 93 Cal.App.4th 1109, 1118, 113 Cal.Rptr.2d 669 (2001)], two men qualified as presumed fathers of 13–year-old Kiana A. Mario A. qualified under subdivision (c)(1) of section 7611 because, after Kiana A.'s birth, he married her mother and his name appeared on her birth certificate. Kevin W. qualified under section 7611(d) because he received Kiana A. into his home and held her out as his child. The juvenile court weighed these conflicting presumptions against one another pursuant to section 7612, subdivision (b), which provides: "If two or more presumptions arise under Section 7611 which conflict with each other, the presumption which on the facts is founded on the weightier considerations of policy and logic controls." The evidence clearly supported the juvenile court's conclusion, the Court of Appeal held, that Kevin W.'s presumption was entitled to greater weight than Mario A.'s. "Mario A. was incarcerated at about the time of Kiana A.'s birth, has remained incarcerated continuously thereafter and was in prison for the entirety of his marriage to mother. Kiana A. is unaware of ever having seen Mario A. prior to his appearance in these proceedings and declared she does not acknowledge him as her father. [¶] Kevin W., on the other hand, has taken Kiana A. into his home, has cared for her needs, has held her out as his child and signed a declaration of paternity in juvenile court. . ." (*Kiana A.*, at pp. 1117–1118.)

Mario A. contended the juvenile court should have granted requests for genetic testing before it commenced the weighing process. The Court of Appeal rejected the contention on the ground Mario A. failed to seek genetic testing in the juvenile court. Moreover, the court went on to say, "Even if Mario A. could raise the issue at this juncture, it would fail because biological paternity by a competing presumptive father does not necessarily defeat a nonbiological father's presumption of paternity. Indeed, section 7612, subdivision (a), states a presumption of paternity 'may be rebutted in an appropriate action only by clear and convincing evidence.' . . . Thus, although the results of genetic testing constitute clear and convincing evidence, it does not follow that such evidence will rebut the presumption in every case. Rather, the statute seeks to protect presumptions of paternity, once they have arisen, from being set aside except upon clear and convincing evidence and only in an appropriate case." (*Kiana A.*, *supra*, 93 Cal.App.4th at pp. 1118–1119, italics omitted.) * * *

Conclusion

To review: Section 7612(a) provides that "a presumption under Section 7611 [that a man is the natural father of a child] is a rebuttable presumption affecting the burden of proof *and may be rebutted in an appropriate action* only by clear and convincing evidence." (Italics added.) When it used the limiting phrase *an appropriate action*, the Legislature was unlikely to have had in mind an action like this—an action in which no other man claims parental rights to the child, an action in which rebuttal of the section 7611(d) presumption will render the child fatherless. Rather, we believe the Legislature had in mind an action in which another candidate is vying for parental rights and seeks to rebut a section 7611(d) presumption in order to perfect his claim, or in which a court decides that the legal rights and obligations of parenthood should devolve upon an unwilling candidate. * * *

In this case it is not necessary to reach, and we do not reach, the question * * * whether, under section 7612, subdivision (b), biological paternity by a competing presumptive father necessarily defeats a nonbiological father's presumption of paternity. * * *

The judgment of the Court of Appeal is reversed and the matter remanded for further proceedings consistent with this opinion.

HYPOTHETICALS

(1) A sues X Insurance Company for $8000 damages for breach of a liability insurance policy. A had rear-ended B's car, injuring B. B sued A and got a judgment for $8000. X refused to defend A in B's lawsuit on the ground that the

policy had been canceled before the accident occurred. At A's trial against X, it is admitted that A paid a year's premium on the policy when it was issued six months before the accident. X's defense is that the policy had been canceled two months before the accident under a policy provision for ten days' notice to the insured and a return of the unused premium. X calls C, a clerk for X, who identifies a copy of a letter from X to A canceling the policy 15 days from the date of the letter, which was two months prior to the A–B accident. C also testifies that she personally mailed the original to A, properly addressed and stamped, and that she enclosed X's check to A for the unused premium. A calls Y who testifies that she and C lived together and that on the date C claims to have mailed the letter to A, C was home sick in bed and didn't go to work that day, the day before, or the day after. X requests the court to instruct the jury that if the jury finds that X's letter to A was correctly addressed and properly mailed, the jury must find that A received the letter in the ordinary course of mail. Should the court grant X's requested instruction?

(2) Assume the same facts as in Illustration (1). In addition to presenting Y's testimony, A testifies that she has lived continuously at the same address to which the canceling notice was allegedly mailed, but has never received any letter from X Insurance Company; that she had no other insurance on her car than the policy issued by X Insurance Company; and that she had driven continuously for five years preceding the accident and has always carried liability insurance coverage. X requests the court to instruct the jury that a letter correctly addressed and properly mailed is presumed to have been received in the ordinary course of mail. What result?

B. CRIMINAL CASES

Virginia v. Black

Supreme Court of the United States, 2003.
538 U.S. 343.

■ JUSTICE O'CONNOR announced the judgment of the Court and delivered the opinion of the Court with respect to Parts I, II, and III, and an opinion with respect to Parts IV and V, in which The Chief Justice, Justice Stevens, and Justice Breyer join.

In this case we consider whether the Commonwealth of Virginia's statute banning cross burning with "an intent to intimidate a person or group of persons" violates the First Amendment. Va.Code Ann. § 18.2–423 (1996). We conclude that while a State, consistent with the First Amendment, may ban cross burning carried out with the intent to intimidate, the provision in the Virginia statute treating any cross burning as prima facie evidence of intent to intimidate renders the statute unconstitutional in its current form.

I

Respondents Barry Black, Richard Elliott, and Jonathan O'Mara were convicted separately of violating Virginia's cross-burning statute, § 18.2–423. That statute provides:

"It shall be unlawful for any person or persons, with the intent of intimidating any person or group of persons, to burn, or cause to be burned, a cross on the property of another, a highway or other public place. Any person who shall violate any provision of this section shall be guilty of a Class 6 felony.

"Any such burning of a cross shall be prima facie evidence of an intent to intimidate a person or group of persons."

* * * At [Black's] trial, the jury was instructed that "intent to intimidate means the motivation to intentionally put a person or a group of persons in fear of bodily harm. Such fear must arise from the willful conduct of the accused rather than from some mere temperamental timidity of the victim." The trial court also instructed the jury that "the burning of a cross by itself is sufficient evidence from which you may infer the required intent." When Black objected to this last instruction on First Amendment grounds, the prosecutor responded that the instruction was "taken straight out of the [Virginia] Model Instructions."

* * * O'Mara pleaded guilty * * *, reserving the right to challenge the constitutionality of the cross-burning statute.

At Elliott's trial, * * * the court instructed the jury that the Commonwealth must prove that "the defendant intended to commit cross burning," that "the defendant did a direct act toward the commission of the cross burning," and that "the defendant had the intent of intimidating any person or group of persons." The court did not instruct the jury on the meaning of the word "intimidate," nor on the prima facie evidence provision of § 18.2–423. * * *

II

[The Court discussed at length the history of cross burning.]

In sum, while a burning cross does not inevitably convey a message of intimidation, often the cross burner intends that the recipients of the message fear for their lives. And when a cross burning is used to intimidate, few if any messages are more powerful.

III

* * *

The First Amendment permits Virginia to outlaw cross burnings done with the intent to intimidate because burning a cross is a particularly virulent form of intimidation. Instead of prohibiting all intimidating messages, Virginia may choose to regulate this subset of intimidating messages in light of cross burning's long and pernicious history as a signal of impending violence.

* * *

IV

* * *

The Supreme Court of Virginia has not ruled on the meaning of the prima facie evidence provision. It has, however, stated that "the act of burning a cross alone, with no evidence of intent to intimidate, will nonetheless suffice for arrest and prosecution and will insulate the Commonwealth from a motion to strike the evidence at the end of its case-in-chief." 262 Va., at 778, 553 S.E.2d, at 746. The jury in the case of Richard Elliott did not receive any instruction on the prima facie evidence provision, and the provision was not an issue in the case of Jonathan O'Mara because he pleaded guilty. The court in Barry Black's case, however, instructed the jury that the provision means: "The burning of a cross, by itself, is sufficient evidence from which you may infer the required intent." This jury instruction is the same as the Model Jury Instruction in the Commonwealth of Virginia. See Virginia Model Jury Instructions, Criminal, Instruction No. 10.250 (1998 and Supp.2001).

The prima facie evidence provision, as interpreted by the jury instruction, renders the statute unconstitutional. * * * As construed by the jury instruction, the prima facie provision strips away the very reason why a State may ban cross burning with the intent to intimidate. The prima facie evidence provision permits a jury to convict in every cross-burning case in which defendants exercise their constitutional right not to put on a defense. And even where a defendant like Black presents a defense, the prima facie evidence provision makes it more likely that the jury will find an intent to intimidate regardless of the particular facts of the case. The provision permits the Commonwealth to arrest, prosecute, and convict a person based solely on the fact of cross burning itself. * * *

V

With respect to Barry Black, we agree with the Supreme Court of Virginia that his conviction cannot stand, and we affirm the judgment of the Supreme Court of Virginia. With respect to Elliott and O'Mara, we vacate the judgment of the Supreme Court of Virginia, and remand the case for further proceedings.

It is so ordered.

[Justice Stevens wrote a one-paragraph concurrence emphasizing that cross burning with "an intent to intimidate" is a threat unprotected by the First Amendment.]

■ JUSTICE SCALIA, with whom JUSTICE THOMAS joins as to Parts I and II, concurring in part, concurring in the judgment in part, and dissenting in part.

* * *

I

Section 18.2–423 provides that the burning of a cross in public view "shall be prima facie evidence of an intent to intimidate." In order to determine whether this component of the statute violates the Constitution, it is necessary, first, to establish precisely what the presentation of prima facie evidence accomplishes.

Typically, "prima facie evidence" is defined as:

"Such evidence as, in the judgment of the law, is sufficient to establish a given fact . . . and which if not rebutted or contradicted, will remain sufficient. [Such evidence], if unexplained or uncontradicted, is sufficient to sustain a judgment in favor of the issue which it supports, but [it] may be contradicted by other evidence." Black's Law Dictionary 1190 (6th ed.1990).

The Virginia Supreme Court has, in prior cases, embraced this canonical understanding of the pivotal statutory language. * * *

The established meaning in Virginia, then, of the term "prima facie evidence" appears to be perfectly orthodox: It is evidence that suffices, on its own, to establish a particular fact. But it is hornbook law that this is true only to the extent that the evidence goes unrebutted. "Prima facie evidence of a fact is such evidence as, in judgment of law, is sufficient to establish the fact; and, *if not rebutted,* remains sufficient for the purpose." 7B Michie's Jurisprudence of Virginia and West Virginia § 32 (1998) (emphasis added).

To be sure, Virginia is entirely free, if it wishes, to discard the canonical understanding of the term "prima facie evidence." Its courts are also permitted to interpret the phrase in different ways for purposes of different statutes. In this case, however, the Virginia Supreme Court has done nothing of the sort. To the extent that tribunal has spoken to the question of what "prima facie evidence" means for purposes of § 18.2–423, it has not deviated a whit from its prior practice and from the ordinary legal meaning of these words. Rather, its opinion explained that under § 18.2–423, "the act of burning a cross alone, with no evidence of intent to intimidate, will . . . suffice for arrest and prosecution and will insulate the Commonwealth from a motion to strike the evidence at the end of its case-in-chief." Put otherwise, where the Commonwealth has demonstrated through its case in chief that the defendant burned a cross in public view, this is sufficient, at least until the defendant has come forward with rebuttal evidence, to create a jury issue with respect to the intent element of the offense.

It is important to note that the Virginia Supreme Court did not suggest (as did the trial court's jury instructions in respondent Black's case) that a jury may, in light of the prima-facie-evidence provision, ignore any rebuttal evidence that has been presented and, solely on the basis of a showing that the defendant burned a cross, find that he intended to intimidate. Nor, crucially, did that court say that the presentation of prima facie evidence is always sufficient to get a case to a jury, *i.e.,* that a court may never direct a verdict for a defendant who has been shown to have burned a cross in public view, even if, by the end of trial, the defendant has presented rebuttal evidence. Instead, according to the Virginia Supreme Court, the effect of the prima-facie-evidence provision is far more limited. It suffices to "insulate the Commonwealth from a motion to strike the evidence *at the end of its case-in-chief,*" but it does nothing more. 262 Va., at 778, 553 S.E.2d, at 746 (emphasis added). That is, presentation of evidence that a defendant burned a cross in public view is automatically sufficient, on its own, to support an inference that the defendant intended to intimidate *only until* the defendant comes forward with some evidence in rebuttal.

II

* * *

[Justice Scalia objected to what he called the plurality's "unprecedented decision facially to invalidate a statute in light of an errant jury instruction."]

III

As the analysis in Part I, *supra,* demonstrates, I believe the prima-facie-evidence provision in Virginia's cross-burning statute is constitutionally unproblematic. Nevertheless, because the Virginia Supreme Court has not yet offered an authoritative construction of § 18.2–423, I concur in the Court's decision to vacate and remand the judgment with respect to respondents Elliott and O'Mara. I also agree that respondent Black's conviction cannot stand. As noted above, the jury in Black's case was instructed that "[t]he burning of a cross, *by itself,* is sufficient evidence from which you may infer the required intent." (emphasis added). Where this instruction has been given, it is impossible to determine whether the jury has rendered its verdict (as it must) in light of the entire body of facts before it— *including* evidence that might rebut the presumption that the cross burning was done with an intent to intimidate—or, instead, has chosen to ignore such rebuttal evidence and focused exclusively on the fact that the defendant burned a cross.[6] * * * Because I believe the constitutional defect in Black's conviction is rooted in a jury instruction and not in the statute itself, I would not dismiss the indictment and would permit the Commonwealth to retry Black if it wishes to do so. * * *

■ JUSTICE SOUTER, with whom Justice Kennedy and Justice Ginsburg join, concurring in the judgment in part and dissenting in part.

* * *

---

[6] Though the jury may well have embraced the former (constitutionally permissible) understanding of its duties, that possibility is not enough to dissipate the cloud of constitutional doubt. See Sandstrom v. Montana, 442 U.S. 510, 517 (1979) (refusing to assume that the jury embraced a constitutionally sound understanding of an ambiguous instruction: "[W]e cannot discount the possibility that the jury may have interpreted the instruction [improperly]").

As I see the likely significance of the evidence provision, its primary effect is to skew jury deliberations toward conviction in cases where the evidence of intent to intimidate is relatively weak and arguably consistent with a solely ideological reason for burning. To understand how the provision may work, recall that the symbolic act of burning a cross, without more, is consistent with both intent to intimidate and intent to make an ideological statement free of any aim to threaten. One can tell the intimidating instance from the wholly ideological one only by reference to some further circumstance. In the real world, of course, and in real-world prosecutions, there will always be further circumstances, and the factfinder will always learn something more than the isolated fact of cross burning. Sometimes those circumstances will show an intent to intimidate, but sometimes they will be at least equivocal, as in cases where a white supremacist group burns a cross at an initiation ceremony or political rally visible to the public. In such a case, if the factfinder is aware of the prima facie evidence provision, as the jury was in respondent Black's case, the provision will have the practical effect of tilting the jury's thinking in favor of the prosecution. What is significant is not that the provision permits a factfinder's conclusion that the defendant acted with proscribable and punishable intent without any further indication, because some such indication will almost always be presented. What is significant is that the provision will encourage a factfinder to err on the side of a finding of intent to intimidate when the evidence of circumstances fails to point with any clarity either to the criminal intent or to the permissible one. The effect of such a distortion is difficult to remedy, since any guilty verdict will survive sufficiency review unless the defendant can show that, "viewing the evidence in the light most favorable to the prosecution, [no] rational trier of fact could have found the essential elements of the crime beyond a reasonable doubt." *Jackson v. Virginia*, 443 U.S. 307, 319 (1979). The provision will thus tend to draw nonthreatening ideological expression within the ambit of the prohibition of intimidating expression * * *.

* * * [T]he way to look at the prima facie evidence provision is to consider it for any indication of what is afoot. And if we look at the provision for this purpose, it has a very obvious significance as a mechanism for bringing within the statute's prohibition some expression that is doubtfully threatening though certainly distasteful. * * *

IV

I conclude that the statute under which all three of the respondents were prosecuted violates the First Amendment, since the statute's content-based distinction was invalid at the time of the charged activities, regardless of whether the prima facie evidence provision was given any effect in any respondent's individual case. * * * Accordingly, I concur in the Court's judgment as to respondent Black and dissent as to respondents Elliott and O'Mara.

■ JUSTICE THOMAS, dissenting.

In every culture, certain things acquire meaning well beyond what outsiders can comprehend. That goes for both the sacred, see *Texas v. Johnson,* 491 U.S. 397, 422–429 (1989) (REHNQUIST, C. J., dissenting) (describing the unique position of the American flag in our Nation's 200 years of history), and the profane. I believe that cross burning is the paradigmatic example of the latter.

I

* * * [T]his statute prohibits only conduct, not expression. And, just as one cannot burn down someone's house to make a political point and then seek refuge in the First Amendment, those who hate cannot terrorize and intimidate to make their point. * * *

II

Even assuming that the statute implicates the First Amendment, in my view, the fact that the statute permits a jury to draw an inference of intent to intimidate from the cross burning itself presents no constitutional problems. Therein lies my primary disagreement with the plurality.

A

"The threshold inquiry in ascertaining the constitutional analysis applicable to [a jury instruction involving a presumption] is to determine the nature of the presumption it describes." *Francis v. Franklin,* 471 U.S. 307, 313–314 (1985) (internal quotation marks omitted). We have categorized the presumptions as either permissive inferences or mandatory presumptions. *Id.,* at 314.

To the extent we do have a construction of this statute by the Virginia Supreme Court, we know that both the majority and the dissent agreed that the presumption was "a statutorily supplied *inference,*" 262 Va., at 778, 553 S.E.2d, at 746 (emphasis added); *id.,* at 795, 553 S.E.2d, at 755 (Hassell, J., dissenting) ("Code § 18.2–423 creates a statutory *inference*" (emphasis added)). Under Virginia law, the term "inference" has a well-defined meaning and is distinct from the term "presumption." *Martin v. Phillips*, 235 Va. 523, 526, 369 S.E.2d 397, 399 (1988).

"A presumption is a rule of law that compels the fact finder to draw a certain conclusion or a certain inference from a given set of facts.[1] The primary significance of a presumption is that it operates to shift to the opposing party the burden of producing evidence tending to rebut the presumption.[2] No presumption, however, can operate to shift the ultimate burden of persuasion from the party upon whom it was originally cast.

"[1] In contrast, an inference, sometimes loosely referred to as a presumption of fact, does not compel a specific conclusion. An inference merely applies to the rational potency or probative value of an evidentiary fact to which the fact finder may attach whatever force or weight it deems best. 9 J. Wigmore, Evidence in Trials at Common Law § 2491(1), at 304 (Chad.rev.1981).

"An inference, on the other hand, does not invoke this procedural consequence of shifting the burden of production. Id."

Ibid. (some citations omitted; emphasis added)

Both the majority and the dissent below classified the clause in question as an "inference," and I see no reason to disagree, particularly in light of the instructions given to the jury in Black's case, requiring it to find guilt beyond a reasonable doubt both as to the fact that "the defendant burned or caused to be burned a cross in a public place," and that "he did so with the intent to intimidate any person or group of persons," 262 Va., at 796, 553 S.E.2d, at 756 (Hassell, J., dissenting) (quoting jury instructions in Black's case).

Even though under Virginia law the statutory provision at issue here is characterized as an "inference," the Court must still inquire whether the label Virginia attaches corresponds to the categorization our cases have given such clauses. In this respect, it is crucial to observe that what Virginia law calls an "inference" is what our cases have termed a "permissive inference or presumption." *County Court of Ulster Cty. v. Allen*, 442 U.S. 140, 157 (1979).[3] Given that this Court's definitions of a "permissive inference" and a "mandatory presumption" track Virginia's definitions of "inference" and "presumption," the Court should judge the Virginia statute based on the constitutional analysis applicable to "inferences": they raise no constitutional flags unless there is "no rational way the trier could make the connection permitted by the inference." *Ibid.* As explained in Part I, *supra, not* making a connection between cross burning and intimidation would be irrational.

But even with respect to statutes containing a mandatory irrebuttable presumption as to intent, the Court has not shown much concern. For instance, there is no scienter requirement for statutory rape. That is, a person can be arrested, prosecuted, and convicted for having sex with a minor, without the government ever producing any evidence, let alone proving beyond a reasonable doubt, that a minor did not consent. In fact, "[f]or purposes of the child molesting statute . . . consent is irrelevant. The legisla-

---

[3] As the Court explained in *Allen,* a permissive inference or presumption "allows—but does not require—the trier of fact to infer the elemental fact from proof by the prosecutor of the basic one and which places no burden of any kind on the defendant. In that situation the basic fact may constitute prima facie evidence of the elemental fact.... Because this permissive presumption leaves the trier of fact free to credit or reject the inference and does not shift the burden of proof, it affects the application of the 'beyond a reasonable doubt' standard only if, under the facts of the case, there is no rational way the trier could make the connection permitted by the inference." 442 U.S., at 157 (citations omitted). By contrast, "[a] mandatory presumption ... may affect not only the strength of the 'no reasonable doubt' burden but also the placement of that burden; it tells the trier that he or they *must* find the elemental fact upon proof of the basic fact, at least unless the defendant has come forward with some evidence to rebut the presumed connection between the two facts." *Ibid.*

ture has determined in such cases that children under the age of sixteen (16) cannot, as a matter of law, consent to have sexual acts performed upon them, or consent to engage in a sexual act with someone over the age of sixteen (16)." *Warrick v. State*, 538 N.E.2d 952, 954 (Ind.App.1989) (citing Ind.Code § 35–42–4–3 (1988)). The legislature finds the behavior so reprehensible that the intent is satisfied by the mere act committed by a perpetrator. Considering the horrific effect cross burning has on its victims, it is also reasonable to presume intent to intimidate from the act itself.

Statutes prohibiting possession of drugs with intent to distribute operate much the same way as statutory rape laws. Under these statutes, the intent to distribute is effectively satisfied by possession of some threshold amount of drugs. As with statutory rape, the presumption of intent in such statutes is irrebuttable—not only can a person be arrested for the crime of possession with intent to distribute (or "trafficking") without any evidence of intent beyond quantity of drugs, but such person cannot even mount a defense to the element of intent. However, as with statutory rape statutes, our cases do not reveal any controversy with respect to the presumption of intent in these drug statutes.

Because the prima facie clause here is an inference, not an irrebuttable presumption, there is all the more basis under our due process precedents to sustain this statute. * * *

III

Because I would uphold the validity of this statute, I respectfully dissent.

See Federal Rules of Evidence 301–302; California Evidence Code § 646.

CHAPTER 11

OPINION, EXPERTISE AND EXPERTS; SCIENTIFIC AND DEMONSTRATIVE EVIDENCE

PART A Opinion, Expertise and Experts

PART B Scientific and Demonstrative Evidence

A. OPINION, EXPERTISE AND EXPERTS

Maguire, Evidence: Common Sense and Common Law
23–27 (1947).*

OPINION

Another kind of evidence toward which courts manifest hostility is described as opinion. Indications are not lacking that wiser members of bench and bar have come to consider this hostility rather overdone in the past. But, even when shrunk to diminished proportions by the best of common sense, the opinion rule is important enough to merit description as our second working tool.

In a way, all human assertions are opinions. It may have seemed pedantic to write, a few pages back, the phrase "manifestations of people's belief about * * * matters of fact" instead of merely saying "statements", but the wording was advisedly chosen. Our whole conscious life is a process of forming working beliefs or opinions from the evidence of our senses, few of them exactly accurate, most of them near enough correct for practical use, some of them seriously erroneous. Every assertion involves the expression of one or more of these opinions. A rule of evidence which called for the exclusion of opinion in this broad sense would therefore make trials quite impossible.

There certainly *is*, though, an exclusionary opinion rule. We can get a fair idea of its general scope by splitting opinions two different ways—first, into the categories of impulsive and deliberate opinions; second, into the categories of commonplace and expert opinions. When Professor Gray said in his teaching notes: "A witness may give his opinion when it is of a kind

---

which a normal man forms justly and correctly but on reasoning which is unconscious or difficult of analysis," he was using both these kinds of classification at once. The complement of his statement, phrased in broad terms without any attempt at meticulous exactitude, would be: "A non-expert witness may not give an opinion as to matters calling for expertness, nor may any witness give a deliberate opinion as to commonplace matters which can be analyzed or broken down into rudimental factors." While we shall have to say something more about expert testimony to round out the topic, this latter complementary statement contains the meat of the exclusionary opinion doctrine.

One great trouble with this doctrine is obviously difficulty in determining when its prohibition does, and when it does not, apply. But before taking up practical application and consequences, let us try to phrase the underlying concepts. It is, of course, plain good sense to refuse to let a non-expert purport to give evidence about matters he does not understand. He is more likely to mislead than to afford sound guidance. The trier of fact is equally capable of forming his own conclusions. By expanding this last statement we shall get a phrasing of the practice under which courts have tended to exclude testimony consciously cast in terms of opinion and referring to commonplace matters, whenever they believe this testimony can be broken down into its rudiments—that is, normally, into statements of perception from which the relevant opinion or conclusion is to be derived. It is fundamental to our method of litigating factual issues that the trier of fact, whether judge or juror, shall so far as his capacities and the nature of the issues permit draw for himself all the conclusions which build themselves into his determination. Witnesses are to state their perceptions of fact, the triers to appraise credibility, make findings of fundamental fact, and draw the inferences necessary to decision.

It scarcely needs illustration to show that restriction of layman's opinion testimony to the limits indicated by Gray can be the cause of endless difficulty. Indeed, this possibility has been painfully realized in practice. Great play has been made of distinction between "opinion" and "shorthand rendition of fact". Much dispute has arisen as to what matters are, and what are not, "difficult of analysis". In tort cases where plaintiffs have been hurt by falling down stairs, off platforms, into areas, along theatre aisles, and so forth, there is constant bickering as to whether witnesses may characterize the place or structure or condition as dangerous, or must confine themselves to attempted recital of its physical characteristics. So foreign to ordinary human communication has the latter method of expression proved in many of these trials as almost to tongue-tie the witnesses.

Some judges refuse to worry much about this difficulty of thought and statement. They have an easy practical solution based on the belief that a little superfluous opinion evidence in matters of this kind is not likely to do any great harm. What really counts is full presentation to the jury or judge of the evidence about rudimental facts, with free rein to draw the correct conclusions. If perchance some needless and maybe unserviceable expressions of opinion are mixed in by the fact witnesses, nothing worse than slight loss of time has been suffered; even in these terms, the lost minutes will probably be fewer than those resulting from frequent wrangles over admissibility. Rule 401 of the Model Code of Evidence is deliberately very liberal in this respect.

The emphasis just thrown upon the rudimental facts suggests an interesting parallel between opinion evidence and hearsay. Often a bare opinion, without exposition of its premises, and a bare hearsay assertion, without exposition of the declarant's power, opportunity, and inclination to perceive, remember, and narrate truly, are equally and for the same reason worthless as items of proof. The old Bible metaphor of the house built upon sand cannot safely be put out of mind until sound, solid rock foundation is shown. Indeed, the present author has asserted, and not altogether jocosely, that the hearsay rule is nothing more than a specialized manifestation of the opinion rule. Hearsay About Hearsay, 8 Univ.Chi.L.Rev. 621 (1941). The reasoning ventured is that hearsay is customarily offered without any adequate effort to demonstrate its value by evidence as to the reliability of the declarant; that an attempt to supply this defect by testimony of non-expert witnesses concerning his reliability would fail because on such an issue such witnesses are not deemed capable of giving effective evidence; but that an attempt to supply the defect by the testimony of a witness who could qualify as an expert on human credibility in general, and had adequate personal knowledge of the very declarant, might raise a meritorious contention.

Commonwealth v. Holden

Supreme Court of Pennsylvania, 1957.
390 Pa. 221, 134 A.2d 868.

[Prosecution for first degree murder. The court affirmed the judgment of conviction, holding the evidence sufficient. The court gave no attention to the point discussed in the following dissenting opinion—Eds.]

■ MUSMANNO, JUSTICE (dissenting). The Majority Opinion fails to discuss a very important matter raised by the defendant Charles Holden in his appeal to this Court for a new trial.

On December 31, 1955, between 5:15 and 6:40 a.m., Cora Smith was killed in her home as the result of being struck over the head. The defendant, Charles Holden, was accused, tried, and convicted of her murder. He maintained in his defense that he was innocent since he was not in the victim's home at the time of the brutal attack.

At the time of Holden's arrest, he was taken by the police to the home of a Ralph Jones who had been with Holden for several hours prior to the killing. In Holden's presence, Jones was questioned by the police. The matter of this questioning became a subject for inquiry at the later trial. The assistant district attorney representing the Commonwealth asked Jones if, at the time he was being quizzed by the police in Holden's presence, Holden did anything that was unusual. Jones replied:

> "Well, during the period of time that the detectives were questioning me in his presence, I believe one of them noticed him to sort of wink or something."

The assistant district attorney then asked Jones what Holden meant, and Jones replied:

> "I didn't rightfully know whether it was a wink or something that was in his eye."

The prosecuting attorney's question was a flagrant violation of the rules of evidence and should not have been permitted. What Jones may have thought that Holden meant by the wink, if it was a wink, was entirely speculative. The prosecuting attorney might just as well have asked: "What was Holden thinking of at the time?" In fact, the question imported that very type of query because obviously the eye, no matter how eloquent it is supposed to be in the minds of poets, novelists, and dreamers, is still not capable, by a blink, to telegraph complicated messages, unless, of course, the blinker and the blinkee have previously agreed upon a code.

When Jones replied that he did not know whether Holden had actually winked or had been troubled by a foreign substance in his eye, the Commonwealth's attorney asked him about a statement he had made to the police some time following the winking incident. On January 11th, a few days after the blinking affair, Captain Flynn of the City Detective Bureau asked Jones: "What did you take this wink to be?" and Jones replied:

> "I think he was trying to get me to make an alibi for him to cover up some of his actions and I don't know nothing about any of his actions."

Commonwealth's counsel sought to introduce this statement at the trial and defense counsel properly objected, explaining:

> "We object to that. Whatever it was, it wasn't made in the presence of the defendant, Charles Holden."

The objection was overruled and the jury was thus informed that the defendant endeavored to have Jones frame an alibi for him. On what evidence was this information based? On a wink.

And what did the wink say? I repeat:

"I think he was trying to get me to make an alibi for him to cover up some of his actions and I don't know nothing about any of his actions."

It will be noted that the stupendous and compendious wink not only solicited the fabrication of a spurious alibi but specified that it was "to cover up some of his actions." One movement of the eyelid conveyed a message of 21 words. Not even the most abbreviated Morse code could say so much with such little expenditure of muscular and mechanical power.

Although the statement of the interpretation of the wink is preposterous on its face, I can see how it could be made to seem very informative and convincing to the jury, since it was given to the jury with the Court's approval. If Holden had actually spoken to Jones the words which Jones related in his interpretation of the wink, no more effective admission of guilty knowledge could be imagined. Jones and Holden had been together prior to the killing. Holden tells Jones to make up an alibi so that Jones can extend their companionship of the evening to an hour including and beyond the time of the killing. And then Jones not only refuses to do what Holden asks him to do, but relates the criminal attempt on the part of Holden to suborn perjury.

But the fact of the matter is that Holden did not ask Jones to fabricate an alibi. He did not ask him to "cover up some of his actions." All that Holden did was to wink. No one knows whether he was trying to convey a message, whether he was attempting to shut out a strong ray of light, or whether a bit of dust troubled him at the moment. The Court, however, allowed the jury to believe that the wink was a semaphoric signal to Jones to commit perjury.

Was ever more ridiculous evidence presented in a murder trial? What is to happen to our rules of evidence in criminal trials if they can be breached so glaringly, without reproof or criticism by this Court? Holden was convicted and sentenced to life imprisonment. He might have been sentenced to death. On a wink.

And the Majority does not consider the matter of sufficient importance even to mention it.

If a witness is to be allowed to state what he believes a wink said, why should he not be allowed to interpret a cough? Or a sneeze? Or a grunt? Or a hiccough? Why should he indeed not be empowered to testify as to what is passing through an accused's brain? Why not permit mind readers to read a defendant's mind, and thus eliminate the jury system completely because who knows better than the defendant himself whether or not he committed the crime of which he stands accused?

The refusal of this Court to grant a new trial, with so momentous a violation of the defendant's rights, duly noted and excepted to on the record, would suggest that here the law has not only winked but closed both eyes.

Government of the Virgin Islands v. Knight

United States Court of Appeals, Third Circuit, 1993.
989 F.2d 619.

■ COWEN, CIRCUIT JUDGE.

[As defendant Henry Knight repeatedly struck Andreas Miller's head with a pistol, the gun discharged and killed Miller. As a result, Knight was indicted for second degree murder and two firearm violations. At trial, Knight admitted that he grabbed Miller and struck him with the gun several times, but claimed that the gun went off accidentally after Miller grabbed and squeezed Knight's pistol hand. Defense counsel also elicited eyewitness testimony that Knight never pointed the gun at Miller and never threatened to shoot him. The district court permitted this factual testimony, but precluded the eyewitness, as well as the investigating police officer, from offering their opinions that the firing of the gun was accidental. Defendant was found guilty of voluntary manslaughter and of the two weapons charges. One of his grounds of appeal was based on a claim that the trial judge erred in excluding the two opinions about whether the shooting was accidental.]

III. EXCLUSION OF LAY OPINION TESTIMONY

Knight argues that it was reversible error to exclude an eyewitness' and an investigating officer's testimony that the firing of the gun was an accident. We review the district court's exclusion of lay opinion testimony for abuse of discretion. Although we agree that the district court committed error by excluding the eyewitness' lay opinion, this error did not prejudice the defendant and therefore does not warrant a reversal of his conviction.

Federal Rule of Evidence 701 states:

If the witness is not testifying as an expert, the witness' testimony in the form of opinions or inferences is limited to those opinions or inferences which are (a) rationally based on the perception of the witness and (b) helpful to a clear understanding of the witness' testimony or the determination of a fact in issue.

The requirement that a lay opinion be rationally based on the witness' perception requires that the witness have firsthand knowledge of the factual predicates that form the basis for the opinion. Fed.R.Evid. 701(a) advisory committee's note. The district court properly excluded the investigating police officer's opinion because he did not observe the assault. In contrast, the eyewitness obviously had first-hand knowledge of the facts from which his opinion was formed.

Having met the firsthand knowledge requirement of Rule 701(a), the eyewitness' opinion was admissible if it would help the jury to resolve a disputed fact. The "modern trend favors admissibility of opinion testimony." The relaxation of the standards governing the admissibility of opinion testimony relies on cross-examination to reveal any weaknesses in the witness' conclusions. Fed.R.Evid. 701(b) advisory committee's note. If circumstances can be presented with greater clarity by stating an opinion, then that opinion is helpful to the trier of fact. Allowing witnesses to state their opinions instead of describing all of their observations has the further benefit of leaving witnesses free to speak in ordinary language.

In this case, an eyewitness' testimony that Knight fired the gun accidentally would be helpful to the jury. The eyewitness described the circumstances that led to his opinion. It is difficult, however, to articulate all of the factors that lead one to conclude a person did not intend to fire a gun. Therefore, the witness' opinion that the gunshot was accidental would have permitted him to relate the facts with greater clarity, and hence would have aided the jury. Based on an assessment of the witness' credibility, the jury then could attach an appropriate weight to this lay opinion.

Although the district court should not have excluded this opinion, the exclusion of the opinion was harmless error as it did not prejudice Knight. * * * During the government's closing argument, the prosecutor himself stated, "[The gunshot] may have been an accident. . . [The beating] resulted in an unintentional, perhaps—probably unintentional and perhaps accidental discharge of that gun." App. at 30. Under these circumstances, the trial court's ruling could not have significantly prejudiced Knight and a reversal of the conviction is not warranted.

Waltz, Introduction to Criminal Evidence
305–25 (3d ed.1991).*

OPINION, EXPERTISE, AND EXPERTS

A.

The Opinion Rule

Opinion Testimony by a Layman. The law of evidence includes a well-known general rule against testimony by laymen in the form of an *opinion* or *conclusion*. (In lawyer series on television one is forever hearing counsel say, "Object, Your Honor, calls for a conclusion!") Generally speaking, it is true that a layman, called to the stand to give testimony, must restrict himself to describing material facts about which he has firsthand know-

---

* Copyright, 1991, by Jon R. Waltz. Nelson-Hall Publishers, Chicago.

ledge. He cannot ordinarily unburden himself of opinions and conclusions which he has drawn from his firsthand observations. This is true for one of two reasons: either the lay witness is technically unqualified, for lack of some essential skill, training, or experience, to draw such a conclusion; or the jurors themselves are fully capable of drawing the right conclusion from the recited facts—and if they are, the witness's opinion testimony would invade the rightful province of the jury.

Not all jurisdictions enforce the opinion rule with equal force. Judges will be quick to exclude apparently baseless opinions on ultimate issues—for example, "In my opinion the defendant is guilty of this crime"—but may be slower to react to conclusory statements that do not go to the very heart of the case.

Furthermore, there are numerous realistic exceptions to the rule against opinion testimony. Most of them involve lay "shorthand" testimony where it is next to impossible to express the matter in any other way.

Examples:

a. *Matters of taste and smell*—"It smelled like gunpowder."

b. *Another's emotions*—"He seemed nervous."

c. *Vehicular speed*—"He was going very, very fast."

d. *Voice identification*—"I've known Clyde Bushmat for fifteen years and I'd recognize his voice anywhere. It was Bushmat's voice on the telephone."

e. *A witness's own intent, where relevant*—"I was planning on crossing the street."

f. *Genuineness of another's handwriting*—"That's my wife's signature."

g. *Another's irrational conduct*—"He was acting like a crazy man."

h. *Intoxication*—"The man was drunk."

Reasoning Behind the Rule Against Lay Opinion Testimony. A fundamental aspect of the reasoning underlying the opinion rule is that factual conclusions that are within the grasp or comprehension of the average layperson should be left to the jury, which supposedly is made up of just such average laypersons. If a juror can just as well arrive at his or her own conclusions by adding together the factual components provided by the witnesses, there is no need for the witnesses to inject their own conclusions.

Example a.:

In State v. Thorp, 72 N.C. 186 (1875), the defendant was charged with drowning her son Robert. The prosecution offered a witness who had known Robert. He testified that he was too far away from the defendant and the child she was holding to be certain that the child was Robert. He did testify, however, that it was "his best impression" that the child was Robert. The defendant's conviction was overturned on appeal because the witness had given prohibited opinion testimony.

Example b.:

In Commonwealth v. Holden, 134 A.2d 868 (1957), the accused was convicted of murder. While he was in custody he gave the police an alibi to the effect that he had been with one Ralph Jones at the crucial time. Jones, questioned by the police, denied this. During the questioning of Jones, the accused, who was present, had winked at him. At trial Jones testified about the wink and stated that he interpreted it as a signal to him to supply the defendant with an alibi. Although the accused's conviction was affirmed without consideration of the opinion rule problem in any detail, one justice of the Pennsylvania Supreme Court noted that Jones's testimony reflected an opinion.

Example c.:

In United States v. Schneiderman, 106 F.Supp. 892 (S.D.Cal.1952), the defendants were charged with Smith Act violations. The Government offered the testimony of former members of the Communist party that the defendants, by their actions, appeared to be members of the party. The trial court held that this was permissible since there was no other way the witnesses could convey to the jury what they had observed. (This was a questionable ruling, made during the era of Senator Joseph R. McCarthy.)

* * *

B.

Experts and Expertise

An Exception to the Opinion Rule. Opinion testimony by expert witnesses comes in through an important exception to the general rule against opinion testimony.

The Definition of "Expert." There are those who have the mistaken notion that the title of "expert" can properly be bestowed only on a few members of professional groups who have a cluster of postgraduate degrees after their names. Some people think that only a scientist of one sort or another and perhaps a few engineers can rightly be called experts. But the term "expert," at least in the law and in common sense, is far broader in meaning than this. Anyone who has ever tried to repair his own automobile or television set knows that some people are experts at these kinds of work and some are not. The proficient garage mechanic is an expert in his field even though a Ph.D. may be the last thing he ever hoped to acquire; the trained and experienced television repairman is just as surely an expert as the most renowned neurosurgeon. The same sort of thing can be said of the brick mason, the sheet metal worker, the plumber, the carpenter, and the electrician, just to name a few more genuine experts.

Getting closer to the immediate point, the label "expert" applies to the firearms identification technician and those who are proficient at fingerprint or handwriting comparison. And it applies to the policeman or policewoman who knows how to use, interpret, and explain special equipment, such as radar vehicular speed measuring devices and equipment for measuring blood-alcohol ratios. Thus a basic law dictionary, Black's, sweepingly defines experts as "men [and women] of science educated in the art, or persons possessing special or peculiar knowledge *acquired from practical experience*" (italics added).

The Four Basic Conditions of Expert Testimony. An expert witness, such as a pathologist or ballistics technician, can testify to an opinion, inference, or conclusion if four basic conditions are met:

(1) The opinions, inferences, or conclusions depend on special knowledge, skill, or training not within the ordinary experience of lay jurors;

(2) The witness must be shown to be qualified as a true expert in the particular field of expertise;

(3) The witness must testify to a reasonable degree of certainty (probability) regarding his or her opinion, inference, or conclusion; and

(4) Although this fourth condition is currently in the process of modification, at least in times past it has generally been true that an expert witness must first describe the data (facts) on which his or her opinion, inference, or conclusion is based or, in the alternative, he must testify in response to a hypothetical question that sets forth the underlying data.

Rationale Behind the Expert Witness Exception to the Rule Against Opinion Testimony. The reasoning behind letting expert witnesses give testimony in the form of opinions or conclusions is that experts have special training, knowledge, and skill in drawing conclusions from certain sorts of data that lay jurors do not have. Expert witnesses and their opinions are permissible only in areas in which lay jurors cannot draw conclusions unassisted or would find it difficult to do so.

* * *

Qualifying the Witness as an Expert. From what has been said thus far it follows that the exception for expert testimony is available only when the witness is shown to be a true expert in the field that is involved. Before a witness can testify to an expert opinion, examining counsel must lay the necessary foundation by bringing out the witness's training, experience, and special skills. Trial lawyers call this process "qualifying the witness."

At the conclusion of the direct questions aimed at qualifying the witness as an expert, and before examining counsel gets into the meat of the witness's testimony, opposing counsel is entitled to interrupt and engage in cross-examination as to the witness's expertise. This examination will be limited strictly to probing the witness's credentials as an expert.

Example a.:

BY THE PROSECUTING ATTORNEY: Give your full name if you would please.

A. Fred Stitz.

Q. Where do you live, Mr. Stitz?

A. In Chicago, Illinois. 373 West Pavon Street.

Q. What is your occupation or profession?

A. I'm an examiner of questioned documents.

Q. What does your work consist of?

A. I examine disputed documents and make reports as to their genuineness. I examine typewriting and matters of disputed interlineations, erasures, and deal with matters of papers, pens, and inks.

Q. How long have you had this profession?

A. I have been doing this work since 1965.

Q. Do you devote all of your time to this work?

A. Yes, I do.

Q. Have you ever testified before in a court regarding questioned documents?

A. I have testified in forty-two of the states and in Canada.

Q. Have you had any special study to prepare yourself to be an examiner of questioned documents?

A. Oh, yes. I have read all of the texts on the subject of questioned documents and on the related subjects that I mentioned. I have studied microscopy, inks and their manufacture, paper and paper manufacturing, and photography. I have all the necessary equipment. I have an office and a laboratory for my work and I exchange ideas constantly with other experts in this field.

Q. Where is your office and lab?

A. 662 North Pennell Street, Chicago.

Q. You are able, I take it, to compare handwriting of known origin with handwriting of unknown origin and form a conclusion or opinion as to whether they were written by the same person?

A. That's right.

Q. Then I will show you what has been marked Prosecution Exhibit Number 3 for Identification.

BY DEFENSE COUNSEL: Just a moment, if you please. May I ask this witness a few questions, Your Honor?

THE COURT: With respect to his qualifications?

BY DEFENSE COUNSEL: Yes.

THE COURT: You may proceed.

BY DEFENSE COUNSEL: Mr. Stitz, have you attended any special schools that teach one how to become a handwriting expert?

A. No, I don't think there are any.

Q. So you have no special degrees or certificates that reflect special study in a college or university?

A. No, I do not.

Q. Your supposed expertise is simply based on your own experience in examining documents, is that it?

A. That's right, and my reading and so on.

BY DEFENSE COUNSEL: Well, we have no strong objection to this witness testifying, Your Honor.

THE COURT: If that is supposed to be some kind of objection, counsel, it is overruled.

Example b.:

Q. What is your name, sir?

A. John V. DeMarco.

Q. Where do you live?

A. At the Belmont Hotel here in the city.

Q. What is your occupation or profession, sir?

A. I am a physician and toxicologist.

Q. Of what medical school are you a graduate, Doctor?

A. The Northwestern University Medical School in Chicago.

Q. When did you graduate?

A. In 1954.

Q. What was your undergraduate school?

A. The University of Michigan.

Q. What was your major field of study at Michigan?

A. Chemistry.

Q. After your graduation from medical school, what did you do?

A. I was with the Health Department in Chicago for three years and then in 1957 I became the toxicologist for the Coroner's Office in Chicago.

Q. Do you hold that position today?

A. Yes, I have held it continuously since 1957.

Q. What have your duties been as a toxicologist?

A. My duties involve the examination of organs for the presence of poisons and research concerning poisons. I have conducted many post mortems.

Q. About how many since 1957?

A. Probably around ten thousand. And I examined the organs of many people on whom I did not do a post mortem.

Q. Do you hold any teaching positions at the present time?

A. Yes, I am Professor of Toxicology at Rush Medical College in Chicago.

Q. How long have you had this professorship, Doctor DeMarco?

A. Since 1970.

Q. Have you ever written anything on the subject of toxicology?

A. Yes, I've written a number of articles on poisons and their detection. I have written chapters that were included in texts on toxicology, and I have delivered papers at professional seminars.

Q. Would you describe toxicology for us, Doctor?

A. It is the science that deals with toxic substances, poisons, their origin, and their detection by chemical or other means.

Q. When you speak of a poison, what precisely do you mean?

THE COURT: Just a moment, counsel. Are you now going to get into this witness's substantive testimony?

BY EXAMINING COUNSEL: That was my intention, Your Honor.

THE COURT: Let me inquire of opposing counsel whether she desires at this point to examine further into the witness's qualifications.

BY OPPOSING COUNSEL: We reserve the right to cross-examine Doctor DeMarco on the substance of his testimony, Your Honor, but we do not dispute his qualifications as an expert in the field of toxicology.

THE COURT: Very well. You may proceed, counsel.

BY EXAMINING COUNSEL: What is it that you mean when you talk of a poison, Doctor?

A. A poison is a substance which, when taken into the system, is capable of seriously affecting health adversely or of causing death, and that's its principal action.

Stipulating to the Witness's Expertise. Sometimes counsel, realizing that the opposing side's witness has impressive credentials that will probably awe the jurors, will try to prevent the jury from hearing them described. Counsel does this by offering to stipulate (agree) that the witness is qualified to testify as an expert, thereby magnanimously saving opposing counsel from having to elicit the witness's full catalogue of credentials through the questioning process. This gambit is not usually successful.

Opposing counsel is not obligated to accept an offered stipulation unless it gives everything that he or she would be entitled to prove with evidence. And counsel is entitled to prove his or her expert witness's qualifications in some detail; a mere stipulation that the witness is qualified to testify does not give the side offering the witness anything to which it is entitled. Experienced counsel will know that it is important to show the details of his or her expert's training and experience in any case in which there is to be a battle of experts. This is so because jurors must decide what weight to attach to the testimony of each side's experts. They can rationally apportion evidentiary weight only if they are in a position to compare the witnesses' relative qualifications.

Example:

Q. Doctor, will you give the jury your full name?

A. Jeffrey Eddy.

Q. Where do you reside?

A. 820 West Addison Street, Chicago, Illinois.

Q. What is your profession?

A. Physician and surgeon.

Q. What specialty, if any, have you made in your medical practice?

A. I specialize in neurosurgery.

Q. We'll come back to that, Doctor Eddy. How long have you practiced medicine?

A. Thirteen years this coming April.

Q. Of what medical school are you a graduate?

A. Northwestern University Medical School in Chicago.

Q. Have you done any postgraduate work?

BY OPPOSING COUNSEL: Pardon me just a moment. We would be willing to stipulate that Doctor Eddy is a qualified neurosurgeon and can testify here.

BY EXAMINING COUNSEL: We would rather make our proof on this, Your Honor. The jurors are entitled to hear his training and his experience in medicine and neurosurgery. They have to decide what weight to give his testimony, possibly in comparison with the testimony of an expert called by the other side, and they can't very well make that decision without hearing his qualifications in full.

THE COURT: It might speed things up a little if you accepted the stipulation, counsel, but I can't force you to do so. You may proceed to establish the witness's qualifications. Just don't get into the most minute details.

BY EXAMINING COUNSEL: Very well, Your Honor. We'll limit ourselves to the most important things. Doctor Eddy, have you had some postgraduate training?

BY OPPOSING COUNSEL: In view of our offer to stipulate, we object to counsel's going into this, Your Honor.

THE COURT: Overruled.

Sources of the Expert Witness's Data. Four sources of information are open to the expert witness in the formation of his or her opinions.

(1) The expert witness can express an opinion or conclusion based on facts personally observed by him, as occurs in the case of a medical examiner who renders a conclusion concerning cause of death on the basis of data clinically observed. (Such an expert can take into account facts communicated to him by another expert. For example, the medical examiner can base his opinion in part on the report of an X-ray technician. If the data upon which the expert bases his opinion or inference are of a type reasonably relied on by experts in the field when forming opinions or inferences on the subject in question, the data need not themselves be admissible in evidence through the expert.)

(2) An expert witness who has been present in the courtroom can base an opinion on the evidence adduced if that evidence is not in conflict. (An expert will not be permitted to weigh conflicting evidence since, unbeknownst to anyone, he or she might accord it a weight different from that given it by the jurors.)

(3) In some jurisdictions, notably the federal and those state jurisdictions that have adopted Rule 703 of the Federal Rules of Evidence, an expert witness can base his or her opinion on data made known to him/her in *advance* of the trial or hearing. Furthermore, the data thus conveyed to the expert need not itself be received in evidence and, even beyond that, need not necessarily be legally admissible. All that is required under rules such as Federal Rule of Evidence 703 is that the inadmissible evidence relied on by the expert have been of "a type reasonably relied upon by experts in the particular field in forming opinions or inferences upon the subject." * * *

(4) An expert witness can base an opinion on data conveyed to him or her by means of a hypothetical question that is drawn from the evidence introduced during the trial. * * *

Efforts to Eliminate the Hypothetical Question. Obviously, the hypothetical question is often awkward and hypertechnical. It is fraught with possibilities of reversible error. Hypothetical questions can be extremely time-consuming and they are frequently confusing to jurors. More often than not they are used by counsel to make an extra summation in the middle of the case. Although counsel may think there is some advantage in getting this opportunity to summarize the evidence far in advance of closing arguments, it is more likely that he is putting the jurors to sleep. Still, there are lawyers who believe that the hypothetical question represents the best method yet devised for extracting helpful opinions from an expert witness who is not directly familiar with the facts of the case.

Efforts are occasionally made to do away with the necessity for using hypothetical questions. For example, Rule 705 of the Federal Rules of Evidence would provide that an expert can testify in terms of opinion "without prior disclosure of the underlying facts or data." The major change intended to be accomplished by this language is the elimination of the necessity for the hypothetical question in eliciting expert testimony. Under Rule 705 examining counsel does not have to disclose underlying facts to his or her expert witness by means of a hypothetical question posed in open court as a preliminary to his or her opinion. The necessary data can be conveyed to the expert prior to his direct examination and it need not be disclosed during that examination. Of course, opposing counsel can cross-examine the expert about the data on which his opinion testimony is based.

* * *

Court-Appointed Experts. Ever since 1946 there has been a comprehensive federal procedure for court-appointed experts and many states have similar procedures. A federal trial judge can order the accused or the Government, or both, to show cause why expert witnesses should not be appointed and can request the parties to submit the names of possible witnesses. The judge can either appoint experts agreed upon by the parties or can appoint experts of his or her own selection. A court-appointed expert is informed of his or her duties by the judge, either in writing or at a conference at which the parties have an opportunity to take part. A court-appointed expert will inform the parties of his or her findings and can thereafter be called to the stand by the trial judge or any party to give testimony. Court-appointed experts are subject to full cross-examination by all parties.

Experts appointed by the trial court are most commonly encountered in cases in which it is suggested either that the accused was legally insane at the time of the offense charged or that the accused is presently incompetent to stand trial because of his inability to comprehend the proceedings and cooperate with his defense counsel. In such situations the trial court may appoint one or more psychiatrists to examine the accused and report.

The use of court-appointed experts occasionally avoids the frustrating phenomenon known as the battle of experts. Both sides in criminal and civil cases alike will shop for experts who are receptive to the position being taken by the side retaining them. Furthermore, some experts are in fact venal; one often hears remarks about "the best expert witness money can buy." And many reputable experts are unwilling to involve themselves in litigation. So, although the suggestion is occasionally made that court-appointed experts take on an aura of infallibility which they may not deserve, the trend is increasingly to provide for their use. The very availability of this appointment procedure reduces the need for resorting to it. This is because the mere possibility that the trial judge *might* appoint an objective, disinterested expert in a given case exerts a sobering influence on a party's expert and on the lawyer who is making use of his services.

Impeachment of Expert Witnesses. Aside from attacking his qualifications and disinterestedness or the thoroughness and competence of his investigation, there are two commonly encountered methods of attacking or impeaching an expert witness's opinion. They involve (1) contradictory material in authoritative publications in the field and (2) alteration of the facts of a hypothetical question put to the witness during his direct examination.

1. An expert witness can be confronted, on cross-examination, with contradictory material from authoritative published works in the pertinent field of expertise. In most jurisdictions it is not essential that the witness relied on the particular treatise or other items of literature in forming the conclusions given in his direct examination, although this was once a common requirement.

Example:

BY THE PROSECUTING ATTORNEY: Dr. Faust, you insisted in your direct testimony earlier this afternoon that a person who is a manic depressive may have a propensity for committing murder or assault to murder, didn't you?

A. Well, "insist" is a pretty strong word but that's what I said.

Q. And you believe your statement to be correct? You think it is medically and physically sound?

A. Certainly I do.

Q. Dr. Faust, at any given time a manic depressive can be in either the manic or exhilarated phase or the depressive, the subdued or depressed phase of the psychosis, can he not?

A. That's true.

Q. Would your statement about a propensity to commit violent acts be as true of a person in the depressive state as it would be of a person who was in a manic state?

A. I think so, yes.

Q. Do other psychiatrists agree with your position in this respect?

A. I don't know specifically but I would presume so. My position is the correct one.

Q. I see. Do you know Dr. Carl S. Milcher's work entitled *The Murderer's Mind?*

A. I know of it. Everyone does.

Q. Is Dr. Milcher a recognized authority on the psychotic condition of persons who have committed murder?

A. I would say so. He is a distinguished psychiatrist.

Q. And has done a great deal of work in this area?

A. Yes.

Q. Did you in any way rely on Dr. Milcher's work in forming your opinions regarding the accused in this case? [This question, although not required in a number of jurisdictions, is usually asked anyway.]

A. I may have unconsciously. His work is a part of the fund of knowledge that I carry around in my head.

Q. Dr. Faust, I hand you a copy of Dr. Milcher's book, *The Murderer's Mind*, published in 1988, which I have opened to page 492. On that page Dr. Milcher is discussing the manic depressive state, is he not? Take your time and look at it, Dr. Faust, and then you can answer.

A. Yes, he describes the state here.

Q. He mentions there that a person in the manic phase may have a propensity for murder or assault to murder, doesn't he?

A. Yes, he does.

Q. And Dr. Milcher is a widely recognized expert, is he not?

A. I said so.

Q. Yes, you did. Now look at the last full sentence on page 492 of Dr. Milcher's book. I want you to read that sentence to the court and jury. You can read it over to yourself first, if you want to, but then read it to the members of the jury, loud and clear.

A. [Reading.] "The depressive aspect of the illness manifests itself more commonly in suicide."

BY THE PROSECUTING ATTORNEY: Thank you, sir. That will be all.

2. Examining counsel will frequently omit certain facts from a hypothetical question put to his expert witness on direct examination. It is entirely permissible for opposing counsel to inquire whether consideration of the omitted facts would have an impact on the witness's opinion.

Example:

BY THE PROSECUTING ATTORNEY: Doctor Faust, if you were requested to assume these additional facts, which were not mentioned by defense counsel in his hypothetical question to you, namely [the omitted facts are recounted], would your opinion remain the same?

A. No, it wouldn't.

Q. What would your opinion be if we include those facts, Doctor?

A. [The witness gives his revised opinion.]

Sometimes facts included in a hypothetical question are later disproved by the evidence. In this situation the expert witness will be asked on cross-examination whether his conclusion would remain the same if those facts were eliminated from the hypothetical question.

Example:

BY THE PROSECUTING ATTORNEY: Doctor Faust, would your response to the hypothetical question have been different if in putting the question to you defense counsel had left out of consideration the statement that the blood found under the left shoulder was clotted?

A. My answer would have been different, yes.

* * *

Waltz & Inbau, Medical Jurisprudence
54–56 (1971).*

THE REQUIREMENT OF EXPERT TESTIMONY

The plaintiff in a medical malpractice action is ordinarily required to produce, in support of his claim, the testimony of qualified medical experts. This is true, as we have earlier said, because the technical aspects of his claim will ordinarily be far beyond the competence of the lay jurors whose duty it is to assess the defendant doctor's conduct. The plaintiff, himself a layman in most instances, is not free simply to enter the courtroom, announce under oath that the defendant surgeon amputated his leg instead of saving it, and then request the jury to find the surgeon negligent.

The jurors, possessing no special expertise in the relevant field, are incapable of judging whether the facts described by the plaintiff, even assuming an accurate narration by him, add up to negligent conduct. And the plaintiff himself is incompetent to supply guidance; he, too, lacks the training and experience that would qualify him to characterize the defendant's conduct. Unless the facts in our hypothetical amputation case spoke for themselves and unmistakably pointed to malpractice (the defendant, although operating in a fully equipped hospital, unaccountably removed plaintiff's leg with a dull ax), the judge would direct a verdict in defendant's favor immediately after the plaintiff's presentation of evidence. The judge would say that there had been a failure of proof on the issue of negligence, as to which the plaintiff had the burden of proof. Since the mere filing of a lawsuit, unsupported at trial by any probative evidence, does not entitle one to the payment of damages, the plaintiff here must lose. The plaintiff could hope to prevail only if he came to court backed by one or more qualified expert witnesses.

There is nothing unique about the requirement of expert testimony in medical malpractice cases. All sorts of lawsuits involve technical issues that exceed the competence of lay witnesses and lay jurors. A successful criminal prosecution may depend on the testimony of a firearms identification expert, a fingerprint expert, a handwriting expert, a pathologist, and a couple of psychiatrists. Many types of civil suits other than malpractice cases may call forth an array of essential experts: mechanical or aeronautical engineers and metallurgists in a case involving an airplane that allegedly crashed as a consequence of metal fatigue in the wing structure; pathologists in a product liability case against a food processor (was the corn borer that slipped into defendant's canned corn truly toxic?); handwriting experts in a will contest; accountants, entomologists, civil engineers—the catalog of potentially vital expert witnesses in civil cases goes on and on. It is so lengthy a list because lawsuits so often involve esoteric issues which a jury, unaided, could not possibly resolve on any basis other than guesswork. To the extent that it can, the Anglo-American system of justice pro-

---

* Copyright, 1971, by The Macmillan Company.

hibits verdicts having baseless speculation as their only support. The requirement of expert testimony on technical issues is one designed to avoid guesswork verdicts.

In short, lay jurors have a reasonable basis in their own life experience for deciding that it is negligent—that it poses an unreasonable risk of harm to others—to drive an automobile down the wrong side of the highway at ninety miles an hour; on the other hand, their life experience gives them no basis for assessing, for example, a delicate and difficult surgical procedure.

In our hypothetical malpractice case involving the defendant's amputation of plaintiff's leg, then, the plaintiff would be required to produce qualified medical experts who were prepared (1) to explain the accepted medical procedures and considerations applicable to plaintiff's condition and (2) to express an opinion, based on the proved facts, that the defendant surgeon had unjustifiably failed to follow those procedures or had followed them incompetently. In a less obvious case the plaintiff's experts would have to provide an answer to a third question—that is, whether the defendant's improper conduct probably was the cause of the plaintiff's injury. Indeed, in a less clear case than one involving an amputation it might even be essential that medical experts establish that the plaintiff had in fact suffered injury.

To recapitulate in sequence, in a typical medical malpractice lawsuit the plaintiff must put qualified medical experts on the witness stand to testify (1) that plaintiff suffered an injury that produced the disability and other ill effects claimed by him; (2) that the cause of this injury, or at least a significant contributing cause of it, was the professional services rendered by the defendant doctor; (3) that the standard methods, procedures, and treatments in cases such as plaintiff's were such-and-so; and (4) that defendant's professional conduct toward plaintiff fell below or otherwise unjustifiably departed from the described standard. In steps 1 and 2 the plaintiff's experts are used to establish damage and the causal connection with that damage of defendant's conduct. These two steps are common to every type of personal injury action, whether it be an automobile collision case or a medical malpractice case. Steps 3 and 4 are peculiar to professional negligence cases for they impart content and meaning to the generalized standard of care uniquely applicable to such cases.

NOTE: OBJECTIONS TO THE FORM OF EXPERT TESTIMONY

The federal rulemakers apparently intended to make major changes in the form of expert testimony, sweeping away most objections to form. The text below, based on a manual for practitioners,[3] describes the common-law objections to form and summarizes the changes that most commentators

---

[3] Roger C. Park, Trial Objections Handbook §§ 8:18–8:30 (2d ed. 2001).

thought the federal rules had brought. As you read the cases in this casebook involving testimony of police experts, consider whether the courts have followed the approach that is described below as the approach of the Federal Rules of Evidence.

Objection: No foundation showing factual basis for opinion

Suppose that an expert gives testimony in the form of an opinion without first revealing the factual basis for the opinion. To give an extreme example, the expert takes the stand and, after having been qualified, is asked the following questions, without any previous foundation:

Q. Do you have an opinion, to a reasonable medical certainty, about the cause of Billy Johnson's death?

A. Yes.

Q. What is your opinion?

A. The removal of his spleen during surgery caused him to lose his resistance to infection, and as a result he contracted an overwhelming infection that led to his death.

Q. In your opinion, was it sound medical practice to remove Billy's spleen?

A. No.

Q. In making his decision to remove Billy's spleen, did Dr. Smith exercise the professional care and skill ordinarily possessed by others in his profession in this community?

A. No, he did not.

Here, the doctor has not been shown to have personal knowledge. The doctor's opinion might be based on speculation or on unreliable hearsay. Therefore, common law courts took the position that, where the expert had no personal knowledge, his testimony had to be based on facts that had been admitted into evidence. Moreover, the nature of the facts relied upon had to be made specific, so that the trier of fact could reject the opinion if it rejected its factual basis. The examining attorney could specify the facts by asking hypothetical questions that incorporated testimony and exhibits that had been placed in evidence. A hypothetical question could ask the expert to assume the existence of certain facts specifically described by the attorney in the question, and to give an opinion based on those assumptions. An attorney's hypothetical question could also refer to testimony that the expert had heard or exhibits that the expert had examined, asking the expert to assume the accuracy of the testimony or exhibits in giving an opinion.

For example, suppose that hospital records and the treating doctor's testimony had been introduced into evidence in the splenectomy case described above. The nontreating expert might then be interrogated by a hypothetical question incorporating the facts in evidence ("Suppose that a twelve-year old boy suffered a fall that resulted in a two-centimeter laceration of the spleen, etc., etc., would it be sound medical practice to remove the spleen?") or by being asked to assume as true testimony that the expert had heard and exhibits that the expert had examined ("You heard the testimony of Dr. Roberts. Assume it to be true. Based on the facts stated by Dr. Roberts, do you have an opinion about whether it was sound medical practice to remove Billy's spleen?")

These forms of hypothetical questioning, while they were a logical outgrowth of the desire to show the trier the basis for the expert's opinion, were repeatedly criticized by scholars and reformers. Wigmore, in condemning the hypothetical question, said "Its abuses have become so obstructive and nauseous that no remedy short of extirpation will suffice." McCormick called the hypothetical question "a failure in practice and an obstruction to the administration of justice."

What was wrong with the hypothetical question? First, if the attorney asking the question were permitted to leave out certain material facts, then the question could become slanted. Suppose a case in which the patient's spleen was deeply lacerated. A question which asked whether it was sound practice to remove a spleen that had been bruised, but omitted to state that the spleen had also been deeply lacerated, would be misleading to the jury. In a welter of hypotheticals, cross-examination might not always be sufficient to cure the damage. Second, if the attorney were required to include all of the material facts in the hypothetical, the hypothetical could become so wordy that the jury might not be able to follow it. Third, the question of whether the hypothetical fairly included all of the material facts could lead to disputes and appeals. Fourth, many experts disliked the hypothetical question, feeling that their answers to a lawyer's hypothetical did not truly express their opinions. Finally, the hypothetical question could be misused to sum up the advocate's case repeatedly before final argument.

The drafters of the Federal Rules of Evidence did not prohibit the use of hypothetical questions. However, they accepted the view that hypothetical questions should not be required, and they framed the rules so that attorneys who preferred other forms of questioning would be able to avoid the use of hypotheticals. This result was accomplished through the joint operation of Rule 705 and Rule 703. Rule 705 permits an expert to give her opinion without prior disclosure of the underlying facts (unless the court directs otherwise). Rule 703 allows the expert to base an opinion on information provided before or during the hearing, and the information need not be admissible in evidence if it is of a type reasonably relied upon by experts in the field.

The same principle applies to questions that direct the expert's attention to prior testimony or to exhibits that have been admitted. Questions of this nature are permitted, but they are no longer necessary. Unless the judge in his discretion directs otherwise, the expert may testify to an opinion without first specifying the facts on which it is based. Moreover, the facts on which the opinion is based need not be facts that have been admitted into evidence, so long as they are facts on which experts in the field reasonably rely.

In the case of a medical expert, these rules mean that the expert can examine hospital records, talk to the patient and family members, and review reports by other doctors as a basis for testimony. When questioned at trial, the expert need not be asked a hypothetical question, but can simply be asked for an opinion based on the information reviewed. While it would ordinarily be wise, for purposes of persuasion, to have the expert first describe the facts upon which she bases the opinion, the rule does not erect an absolute requirement that this be done. Rule 705 provides that the expert may give an opinion without prior disclosure of the facts on which it is based, but also gives the trial judge discretion to require prior disclosure in appropriate cases.

Because Rule 705 allows the trial judge to require that the basis be set forth for an expert opinion, the objection that no factual foundation has been laid for the opinion is still plausible in a jurisdiction following the Federal Rules. However, the objection is addressed to the trial judge's discretion, not to an absolute rule. If the trial judge concludes that it is too burdensome to require the cross-examiner to elucidate the basis of the opposing expert's opinion, the trial judge may require the proponent of the expert to do so on direct examination.

In summary:

(1) In a jurisdiction following the common law approach, the objection that the expert is testifying to an opinion without first specifying the factual basis is still valid. The factual basis must be specified either (a) by showing that the expert has personal knowledge, or (b) by asking the expert a hypothetical question incorporating facts admitted into evidence, or (c) by having the expert listen to testimony and examine exhibits, and then asking a question that specifies the testimony and exhibits on which the expert is to rely.

(2) In a jurisdiction following the Federal Rules, the objection that the expert is testifying to an opinion without first specifying the factual basis is addressed to the discretion of the trial judge under Rule 705. The trial judge may either require that the basis be specified first, or may leave it to the cross-examiner to explore the factual basis for the opinion.

Objection: Improper Hypothetical Question

As noted above, both common law and Federal Rules jurisdictions permit hypothetical questions. Although lawyers in Federal Rules jurisdictions are not required to use hypothetical questions, many still do so. Hypothetical questions have some practical advantages: they are a way of controlling and focusing the expert witness, and they provide an opportunity to sum up damaging testimony in the middle of trial.

Hypothetical questions must be propounded in proper form. If a hypothetical question is phrased in a fashion that would mislead, confuse, or prejudice the trier of fact, then it is objectionable. In order to preserve rights on appeal, the objecting party should attempt to specify exactly why the hypothetical question is objectionable. For example, if the hypothetical question omits material undisputed facts, the objecting party should protect the record by designating what has been omitted.

Hypotheticals may be objectionable on any of the following grounds:

—*The Question Omits Material Facts That are Not in Dispute*

A hypothetical question may properly ask the witness to assume as true facts that are in dispute. For example, if one witness testifies that plaintiff was exposed to a toxic chemical and others testify that he was not, then the witness may properly be asked to assume that the plaintiff was exposed to the chemical, and to base an opinion on that assumption. In this sense, a hypothetical question may be slanted. It need not incorporate disputed testimony that is unfavorable to the party asking the question. It is up to the opposing party to ask the expert what his opinion would be on the assumption that the unfavorable testimony is true.

The hypothetical is improper, however, if it omits essential facts that are not in dispute. For example, in *Stumpf v. State Farm Mutual*,[2] the issue was whether the insured had made an intentionally false statement on an automobile insurance application when he stated that he did not have a mental or physical disability. The insured had been suffering from epilepsy for several years, but contended that it did not constitute a disability. His attorney asked the following question to a specialist in internal medicine who had been called as an expert witness:

"Doctor, assuming that you have a patient who is gainfully employed and has a history of infrequent epileptic seizures of the grand mal type over a period of years, takes regular oral medication for his epileptic condition three times daily; assume further that the patient, before suffering an epileptic seizure gets warning of the impending seizure sufficient to allow him to sit down and make adjustments, do you have

---

[2] 251 A.2d 362 (Md.1969).

an opinion, based on reasonable medical probability, whether that patient has a mental or physical disability?"

State Farm objected to this question on grounds that it omitted several material facts, and the trial court sustained the objection. The Court of Appeals affirmed, noting that the question omitted to note that the insured had also suffered petit mal seizures (which, unlike grand mal seizures, came upon him without warning) and that he had been discharged from the Marine Corps with a 30% disability because of epilepsy. These omissions rendered the question defective. The court stated that a hypothetical question " 'should contain a fair summary of the material facts in evidence essential to the formulation of a rational opinion concerning the matter to which it relates.' "

Courts have displayed various degrees of liberality in allowing the omission of undisputed facts from hypothetical questions. A certain amount of leeway is generally given, especially when the omission or misstatement of a fact is not materially misleading. After all, an alert cross-examiner has an opportunity to correct any misapprehension by asking the witness hypothetical questions that include the omitted facts. When, however, the omission of facts reduces the value of the resulting opinion to a point where its probative value is outweighed by dangers of prejudice or misleading the trier of fact, the question is objectionable.

—The Question Refers to Facts That are Not in Evidence

A hypothetical question can be objectionable because it adds facts that are not in evidence, either by interjecting totally new facts or by misstating the evidence to make it more favorable. For example, in *Stanley Co. of America v. Hercules Powder Co.*,[3] plaintiff claimed that an explosion in defendant's plant caused structural damage to plaintiff's theater. Plaintiff's expert on the cause of damage was asked to assume that there had been one explosion of 30,000 tons of nitroglycerin; the only evidence on the point indicated that there had been three separate smaller explosions adding up to 30,000 tons. The court reversed on grounds that the hypothetical question was improper.

Trial counsel are given some leeway in framing hypothetical questions; the addition of inconsequential facts, or the characterization of facts with a favorable slant, is often permitted. For example, in *Cortrim Mfg. Co. v. Smith*,[4] the expert was asked a question about whether an employee's exertion while "setting up" a large machine, a job characterized by the question as requiring a "tremendous amount" of stretching, bending and reaching down, could have contributed to the employee's fatal heart attack. In fact, the evidence showed that the employee had been engaged in adjusting the machine, not setting it up; and the words "tremendous amount" exagger-

---

[3] 108 A.2d 616 (N.J.1954).

[4] 570 S.W.2d 854 (Tenn.1978).

ated the amount of exertion involved. The trial court permitted the question and the appellate court affirmed, noting that the record indicated that the work did require somewhat strenuous effort and that the defendant had had the opportunity to restate the question on cross-examination.

—The Question Refers to Facts that are Irrelevant and Prejudicial

The previous objections dealt with hypothetical questions that omit facts in evidence or that add facts that are not in evidence. This objection deals with a question that incorporates facts properly in evidence, but uses facts that are irrelevant to the purported purpose of the question.

The proponent may not interject such facts in order to use the hypothetical question as a vehicle for making a final argument to the jury about matters that are not within the legitimate scope of the question. For example, in *Ingram v. McCuiston*[5] plaintiff's attorney asked the expert a 23–paragraph question, purportedly for purposes of asking for the expert's opinion about whether the plaintiff had been disabled by her injury. In the course of the question, he interjected statements that were relevant only to liability, not to damages. For example, he asserted that plaintiff had been hit from behind while stopped "in obedience to a traffic control device" and that plaintiff had slowed down because "she saw, and anyone who was properly observant could and should have seen" that the traffic ahead was slowing down. After enumerating a number of such statements, the court noted that "it was no part of the legitimate purpose of the hypothetical question under consideration to establish defendants' negligence" and condemned the question as "slanted and argumentative."

—The Question Requires the Expert's Opinion to Rest on the Opinion of Another

Sometimes an expert will be asked a hypothetical question that requires the expert to accept the opinion of another expert as the basis for an opinion. For example, one expert might express an opinion that the defendant had a certain type of organic brain damage. A second expert might be asked to assume, along with other matters, that the defendant had this type of brain damage, and then express an opinion about whether the defendant could distinguish right from wrong.

There is some authority, mainly in older cases, for the proposition that an expert cannot be asked to base an opinion upon opinions expressed by other experts. However, modern authority allows experts to base their opinions on those of others. As Wigmore stated, "There is no mysterious logical fatality in basing 'one expert opinion on another'; it is done every day in business and applied science."

---

[5] 134 S.E.2d 705 (N.C.1964).

The Federal Rules of Evidence allow an expert to use the opinions of others as an ingredient in forming the expert's own opinion. Rule 703 allows an expert's opinion to be based upon either facts or other "data," and the Advisory Committee Note to Rule 703 states that since a physician in medical practice may base a diagnosis upon "reports and opinions" from nurses, technicians, and other doctors, these sources ought to suffice for judicial purposes.

A different question arises when the expert, instead of using another's opinion as an ingredient in forming his or her own opinion, merely parrots the first expert's opinion. For example, suppose that a psychiatric expert merely reports that another psychiatrist had expressed the opinion that the defendant suffered from post-traumatic stress syndrome. In this case, where the expert is not expressing the expert's own opinion but merely relaying that of another, the testimony should be excluded.

Objection: The Expert's Opinion is Based Upon Facts Not in Evidence

The situations in which this objection may arise can be placed into two categories:

(1) Situations in which the expert is testifying in response to a hypothetical question in which the expert is asked to assume as true facts that are not in evidence. Asking the expert to assume the existence of these facts may make the question objectionable as misleading.

(2) Situations in which the expert is testifying from the expert's own knowledge, or from information supplied to the expert before trial, without the use of a hypothetical question.

In this second situation, the objection was a valid one in many common law jurisdictions. If the expert was testifying from the expert's own personal knowledge, then many jurisdictions required that the basis for the expert's opinion had to be described before the opinion was given. In other words, the expert had to describe the facts within the expert's personal knowledge before offering an opinion based upon those facts. Thus, a medical expert who examined the decedent would be required to describe the condition of the body before giving an opinion on the cause of death.

If the expert was not testifying from personal knowledge, it was necessary either to ask a hypothetical question incorporating facts that were in evidence, or to ask the expert to assume that certain testimony that had been given in the case was true. The expert who lacked personal knowledge could not testify on the basis of facts that were not in evidence.

The Federal Rules of Evidence have produced radical changes in this system of rules. It is no longer necessary that the expert testifying from personal knowledge describe the underlying facts before giving an opinion.

Rule 705 permits an expert to give an opinion without disclosing the facts on which it is based, unless the court directs otherwise.

Moreover, it is no longer necessary that the expert's testimony be based either on facts in evidence or on personal knowledge. The expert can, for example, use the report of another expert in forming an opinion, even if that report has not been introduced into evidence. Rule 703 allows the expert to base an opinion on information provided to the expert before or during the hearing, and the information need not be admissible in evidence if it is of a type reasonably relied upon by experts in the field.

Therefore, the objection that the expert's opinion is based upon facts not in evidence is no longer valid, in and of itself, in a jurisdiction that follows the Federal Rules of Evidence.

However, one may still object on grounds that the expert's opinion is based on evidence on which an expert may not reasonably rely.

Objection: The Expert's Testimony is Based on Inadmissible Hearsay

At common law, the expert's opinion had to be based on personal knowledge or on facts that were in evidence. Therefore, an expert's opinion could not be based on inadmissible hearsay. Under the Federal Rules, however, inadmissible hearsay is a permissible basis for an opinion, so long as the hearsay is the type of evidence reasonably relied upon by experts in the field. Rule 703 provides:

> The facts or data in the particular case upon which an expert bases an opinion or inference may be those perceived by or made known to him at or before the hearing. If of a type reasonably relied upon by experts in the particular field in forming opinions or inferences upon the subject, the facts or data need not be admissible in evidence.

The Advisory Committee's Note to Rule 703 indicates that the rule is intended to bring judicial practice "in line with the practice of the experts themselves when not in court." It notes that a physician in practice often relies upon hearsay, including statements by patients and relatives; reports from nurses, technicians, and other doctors; hospital records; and X-rays. Most of these are admissible in evidence, the Advisory Committee noted, but "only with the expenditure of substantial time in producing and examining various authenticating witnesses." Since the physician makes life-and-death decisions on the basis of such evidence, it ought to be good enough for judicial purposes.

The Committee recognized that some might fear that the rule was too liberal. It said that those who had that fear should take notice of the requirement that the facts or data "be of a type reasonably relied upon by experts in the particular field." It added that this requirement would require exclusion, for example, of "the opinion of an 'accidentologist' as to the point of impact in an automobile collision based on statements of bystanders."

An opinion by Judge Jack Weinstein provides a useful example of hearsay that was considered not to be the type of evidence on which an expert could reasonably rely under Rule 703. In *Lilley v. Dow Chemical Co.,*[6] the plaintiff's decedent had allegedly contracted cancer as a result of his contact with Agent Orange in Vietnam. On a motion for summary judgment, defendants claimed that there was insufficient evidence of cause to create a genuine issue of material fact. Plaintiff produced the affidavit of a qualified medical expert who concluded that the decedent's illness and death had been caused by contact with Agent Orange. The expert had based his opinion partly upon conversations with family members, whose information in turn came mainly from the decedent. They reported to the expert that decedent had been in contact with Agent Orange and not with other chemicals.

Judge Weinstein granted the motion for summary judgment, noting that the expert's opinion would not be admissible at trial. The expert's facts about the decedent's symptoms, habits, and background were based almost exclusively on hearsay that was not the type of hearsay on which physicians customarily rely in diagnosing illness. The wife's statements to the expert, for example, were not "the kind of reliable statements about direct observation of actions, contemporaneous statements and symptoms usually related by a spouse." Instead, she had "little or no contact with her husband for long periods of time and made no direct observations about his work or its effects upon him."

Judge Weinstein's opinion indicates that in some cases statements by a spouse might properly be considered by a medical expert in forming an opinion, as the Advisory Committee's Note to Rule 703 indicates. Here, however, the spouse's reports, themselves confused and based on hearsay, were simply not sufficiently reliable.

NOTE

Use of Rule 703 and state counterparts by prosecutors can pose problems under the Confrontation Clause, because of the possibility that the expert is being used effectively as a conduit for the presentation of testimonial statements without the accused having had an opportunity to be confronted with the makers of the statements. Note how the Supreme Court wrestled—perhaps inconclusively—with this problem in *Williams v. Illinois*, p. 439 *supra*.

---

[6] 611 F.Supp. 1267 (E.D.N.Y.1985).

State v. Odom

Supreme Court of New Jersey, 1989.
116 N.J. 65, 560 A.2d 1198.

■ HANDLER, J.

In this criminal appeal, the defendant was convicted of the possession of controlled dangerous substances with the intention to distribute. In the course of the trial, a police officer was qualified as an expert and permitted to testify that in his opinion the facts and circumstances surrounding the possession of the controlled dangerous substance indicated that they were possessed by the defendant not for personal use but with an intent to distribute them. A divided panel of the Appellate Division reversed the conviction. * * *

I.

At approximately 11:30 a.m. on January 31, 1986, Detective Timothy Jordan of the Paterson Police Department executed a search warrant at premises on North Main Street. Detective Jordan, along with Detectives Humphrey and Vaio, entered the attic apartment where they found defendant, Ernest Odom, and C.W., a juvenile. Defendant and C.W. were informed that the detectives were executing a search warrant. In the ensuing search, Detective Humphrey found a clear plastic bag containing eighteen vials of cocaine in crack form in the pillowcase on the bed. No other drugs or drug paraphernalia were found. The defendant was subsequently charged with possession of a controlled dangerous substance, cocaine, and possession of the same drug with intent to distribute.

At trial, the State offered Detective Sergeant Ronald Tierney as an expert in illegal narcotics. Defense counsel objected to the detective testifying, claiming the detective was unqualified because his experience was based on hearsay and his testimony would not assist the jury.

Detective Tierney had been a member of the Paterson Police force for sixteen and one-half years and had served with the narcotics squad for nine and one-half years. He had participated in over 8,000 investigations and had made approximately 4,000 narcotics arrests. The detective had also been involved in over 400 crack investigations and had spoken with crack dealers on over fifty occasions. He had arrested over 100 individuals distributing crack and had executed twenty search warrants where crack and crack paraphernalia were seized. In the past he had been qualified 1,000 times as an expert in trials involving narcotics distribution. The trial court found Detective Tierney qualified to testify as an expert.

The detective then testified about the packaging of crack, its street value, characteristics, and use. He was asked to assume the following facts, as adduced at trial, to be true: that a search warrant was executed, that eighteen vials of crack were found in a pillowcase in a bed in which defendant was found sleeping, that $24.00 was found in the apartment and that no other drug paraphernalia was found. He was asked based on his experiences and such facts if he had an opinion "whether Ernest Odom possessed 18 vials of crack for his own use or possessed them with the intent to distribute them." Defense counsel objected that the detective was incompetent to testify regarding state of mind. The court overruled the objection and the detective was again asked, "Do you have an opinion whether those 18 vials of crack were possessed for personal use or for the purpose of distributing them?" Detective Tierney stated that it was his opinion that the drugs were possessed with an intent to distribute them.

He then explained the basis for his opinion. He detailed the procedures for crack processing and packaging, the estimated value of a vial of crack, and the addictive impact of the drug. The detective also stated that the lack of paraphernalia relating to personal drug use was another factor considered in forming his opinion, noting that the distribution of crack required no paraphernalia.

Subsequently, defendant testified that he was a crack addict. He claimed he purchased all eighteen vials the night before for his personal use. According to defendant, he usually smoked the crack, using two pipes, which he kept in the closet but which were not found when the police searched the apartment. Thereafter, defendant was found guilty as charged.

As noted, the Appellate Division, in a reported decision, reversed defendant's conviction for possession of cocaine with intent to distribute and remanded the matter for a new trial. State v. Odom, 225 N.J.Super. 564, 543 A.2d 88 (1988). The majority found that the detective's opinion regarding defendant's purpose in possessing the drugs was not only unhelpful to the jury but that its probative value was outweighed by its potential for prejudice. The majority concluded that while expert testimony regarding the "use of and traffic in controlled dangerous substances" was permissible, an expert was precluded from expressing an opinion whether the circumstances of a particular case established an intent to distribute because that constituted a determination of the truth of the charge. The dissent, on the other hand, concluded that expert testimony in this area would be helpful to jurors and that a hypothetical question concerning intent was permissible.

II.

We have stated recently that the opinion of a duly-qualified expert may be presented to a jury if it will genuinely assist the jury in comprehending the evidence and determining issues of fact. The admissibility of expert testimony turns not on whether the subject matter is common or uncommon or whether many persons or few have knowledge of the matter, but [on] whether the witnesses offered as experts have peculiar knowledge or experience not common to the world which renders their opinions founded on such knowledge or experience any aid to the court or jury in determining the questions at issue.

Thus, the opinion of an expert can be admitted in evidence if it relates to a relevant subject that is beyond the understanding of the average person of ordinary experience, education, and knowledge. If the expert's testimony on such a subject would help the jury understand the evidence presented and determine the facts, it may be used as evidence. The witness offered as an expert must, of course, be suitably qualified and possessed of sufficient specialized knowledge to be able to express such an opinion and to explain the basis of that opinion. Once it is determined that this testimony will genuinely aid the jury, it can be admitted. Our Rules of Evidence codify these principles. Evid.R. 56(2). * * *

The defendant stresses that the expert's testimony in this case relating to certain underlying facts, such as the quality and quantity of the drugs, their packaging, their estimated value, and addictive characteristics, would have been sufficient to enable the jury to draw its own conclusions concerning the significance of defendant's possession. * * * It simply does not follow, however, that once the expert has revealed his knowledge and given such an explanation of underlying facts, average persons with ordinary backgrounds would then be able to appreciate whether possession of those drugs would be for personal use or for distribution. As stated in *State v. Perez,* "it is unreasonable to assume that the average lay person called to serve as a juror would necessarily know what a person who possessed [a certain quantity of drugs in certain circumstances] was going to do with it." 218 N.J.Super. at 485, 528 A.2d 56. The jury, though enlightened by the expert's explanation of the significance of surrounding facts, does not thereby become expert in the field. Thus, under these circumstances, the subject of intent or purpose in connection with the possession of unlawful drugs is a matter of specialized knowledge of experts. In this case, we are satisfied that the testimony of the expert covered a subject beyond the understanding of average persons and was genuinely helpful to the jury in understanding the evidence presented and determining important issues of fact.

The further criticism of the expert's testimony that was expressed by the majority below is that the opinion presented a view of the criminal guilt of the defendant, and, for that reason, should have been withheld from the jury.

We have repeatedly and consistently recognized that a jury's determination of criminal guilt or innocence is its exclusive responsibility. A jury's verdict of ultimate criminal liability can never be equated simply with its determination of underlying facts; the determination of guilt or innocence transcends the facts on which it is based, no matter how compelling or inexorable those facts may be. The determination of facts that serve to establish guilt or innocence is a function reserved exclusively to the jury. Hence, an expert's testimony that expresses a direct opinion that defendant is guilty of the crime charged is wholly improper. See, e.g., State v. Landeros, 20 N.J. 69, 74, 118 A.2d 521 (1955) (improper for expert, when asked if the defendant was guilty, to reply, "He is as guilty as Mrs. Murphy's pet pig."); see also Shutka v. Pennsylvania R.R. Co., 74 N.J.Super. 381, 401–02, 181 A.2d 400 (App.Div.1962) (court allowed expert opinion regarding the ultimate issue, noting, however, that expert testimony that expressed "his belief as to how the case should be decided" would be improper).

In this case, Detective Tierney did not express an opinion that defendant was guilty of the crime charged. Defendant contends, however, that the opinion went too far because it expressed the view that defendant possessed the drugs with the intent to distribute. The majority agreed that this opinion was improper because it embraced an ultimate issue bearing so directly on guilt that it must be reserved exclusively for the jury.

Perez suggests that an opinion does not go too far as long as it does not express the view that defendant is guilty of the crime charged. The court in *Perez* said that "nowhere do we find the record to indicate that [the expert] stated defendant was guilty of the charges against him." 218 N.J.Super. at 485, 528 A.2d 56. It pointed out that Evidence Rule 56(2) and (3) allows an expert to testify about areas of specialized knowledge if that testimony "will assist the trier of fact to understand the evidence or determine a fact in issue," even if that opinion embraces an ultimate issue to be determined by the jury. * * *

We are satisfied in this case that the detective's opinion was based exclusively on the surrounding facts relating to the quantity and packaging of the drugs and their addictive quality, as well as the absence of drug-use paraphernalia; his explanation of these facts was clearly founded on his experience and specialized knowledge as an expert. The conclusion he drew—that possession of these drugs was for the purpose of distribution— was similarly derived from his expertise. We therefore conclude that as long as the expert does not express his opinion of defendant's guilt but simply characterizes defendant's conduct based on the facts in evidence in light of his specialized knowledge, the opinion is not objectionable even though it embraces ultimate issues that the jury must decide.

Moreover, such an opinion is permissible although it is expressed in terms that parallel the language of the statutory offense when that language also constitutes the ordinary parlance or expression of persons in everyday life. See, e.g., State v. Morton, supra, 74 N.J.Super. at 531–32, 181 A.2d 785 (police officer in drunk-driving case allowed to testify that defendant was under the influence of alcohol); State v. Rucker, 46 N.J.Super 162, 166, 134 A.2d 409 (App.Div.) (police experts in gambling prosecution allowed to testify as experts that certain papers were for use in a lottery), certif. denied, 25 N.J. 102 (1957); State v. Smith, 21 N.J. 326, 334, 121 A.2d 729 (1956) (same); State v. Arthur, 70 N.J.L. 425, 57 A. 156 (Sup.Ct.1904) (same). * * *

It may be that an expert's opinion is expressed in such a way as to emphasize that the expert believes the defendant is guilty of the crime charged under the statute. This would be impermissible. Thus, in United States v. Scop, 846 F.2d 135, rev'd in part on rehearing, 856 F.2d 5 (2d Cir.1988), the court observed:

> None of our prior cases, however, has allowed testimony similar to [the expert's] repeated use of statutory and regulatory language indicating guilt. For example, telling the jury that a defendant acted as a "steerer" or participated in a narcotics transaction differs from opining that the defendant "possessed narcotics, to wit, heroin, with intent to sell," or "aided and abetted the possession of heroin with intent to sell," the functional equivalent of [the expert's] testimony in a drug case. [Id. at 142.]

Here, an expert in the use and distribution of unlawful drugs can assist the jury by offering his opinion based on special knowledge and experience about the characteristics that serve to identify drugs that are being held for sale or distribution. Further, an expert opinion that the drugs were held for distribution, even though expressed in words that are similar to the statutory definition of the offense, does not rise to the level of an assertion that the defendant committed the crime charged or is guilty of the statutory offense.

In sum, we are satisfied that the expert's opinion in this case was properly admitted. It covered a subject that was within the specialized knowledge of the expert, and thus beyond the understanding of persons of average knowledge, education, and experience; therefore, it was reasonably required to assist the jury in understanding the evidence and determining the facts. Further, although expressed in terms of ultimate issues of fact, namely, whether drugs were possessed with the intent to distribute, the expert's opinion did not impermissibly constitute the expression of a view that defendant was guilty of the crime charged.

III.

This does not mean that the question posed and answered by the expert in this case was proper. As demonstrated, the opinion was not objectionable on the grounds that it expressed a view on a subject that did not require expertise or a view that defendant was guilty of the crime charged. Nevertheless, there are aspects of the proposed testimony that are problematic. It is therefore important that trial courts and trial attorneys clearly understand the standards governing such expert testimony and that juries be carefully instructed on how to consider and use such testimony in their deliberations.

The majority below in part described such standards. It pointed out that in proffering the opinion of an expert in this kind of case, the hypothetical question should be carefully phrased to refer only to the testimony and evidence adduced

> about the manner of packaging and processing for use or distribution, the significance of various quantities and concentrations of narcotics, the roles of various drug paraphernalia, characteristics of the drugs themselves, the import of circumstances surrounding possession, the conduct of the possessor and the manner in which drugs may be secreted or otherwise possessed for personal use or distribution.

> [225 N.J.Super. at 573, 543 A.2d 88.]

Once this foundation has been laid, the expert should then be presented with a hypothetical question through which he or she can advise the jury of the significance of these facts on the issue of possession. Having set forth this information in the form of a hypothetical, the expert may be asked if, based on these assumed facts, he or she has an opinion whether the drugs were possessed for personal use or for the purpose of distribution.

It is also essential that the jury be advised, following the presentation of the expert's opinion, of the basis for that opinion. The hypothetical question should clearly indicate that it is the witness' opinion that is being sought and that that opinion was formed assuming the facts and circumstances adduced only at trial. It is important that the witness, and the jury, understand that the opinion cannot be based on facts that are not in evidence.

In addition, to the extent possible, the expert's answer should avoid the precise terminology of the statute defining the criminal offense and its necessary elements. While ordinary expression and plain language should not be distorted, statutory language should be paraphrased. Further, the defendant's name should not be used.

Finally, the trial court should carefully instruct the jury on the weight to be accorded to and the assessment of expert opinion testimony. It should be emphasized that the determination of ultimate guilt or innocence is to be made only by the jury.

In this case, the opinion of the expert was expressed in the ordinary language of average persons in everyday life. There was no undue repetition of the language of the statutory offense or references to the statutory offense. One aspect of the question, however, incorporated defendant's name in the hypothetical. Under the circumstances, however, the error is harmless. The jury was aware of defendant's admitted possession of the drugs.

The judgment below is reversed.

United States v. Scop

United States Court of Appeals, Second Circuit, 1988.
846 F.2d 135.

■ WINTER, CIRCUIT JUDGE:

In 1980 and 1981, appellants Alan Scop, Raphael Bloom, Herbert Stone and Jack Ringer were variously involved in the initial offering and subsequent trading of the stock of an automobile dealership. Each was indicted for mail fraud in violation of 18 U.S.C. § 1341 (1982), securities fraud in violation of Section 10(b) of the Securities Exchange Act of 1934, 15 U.S.C. § 78j(b) (1982), and conspiracy to commit those offenses in violation of 18 U.S.C. § 371 (1982).[4] Appellants Bloom and Stone were also charged with making false declarations before a grand jury in violation of 18 U.S.C. § 1623 (1982). After a jury trial before Judge Pollack, appellants were convicted on all counts.

Several investors in the dealership's stock testified at trial, but the government's case was based primarily upon the testimony of a co-conspirator who testified pursuant to a plea agreement and upon that of a government investigator who testified as an expert witness. On appeal, appellants argue inter alia that their mail fraud, securities fraud and conspiracy convictions are time-barred and that the government's expert witness was wrongly allowed to give opinions that embodied legal conclusions and were based upon his assessment of the credibility of the testimony of other witnesses.

Because we believe that the expert witness's opinions were inadmissible, we reverse all but the false-declaration convictions. * * *

[Defendants were investors and traders in the stock of European Auto Classics (EAC). The prosecution's evidence indicated that they became involved in a scheme with one Sarcinelli to inflate the price of the stock. Sarcinelli eventually turned against the defendants and became a government witness. Part of the scheme was described in his testimony as follows:]

Sarcinelli and his associates soon began bringing in customers for the stock and setting up "matched orders" or "matched trades" to be executed by Scop, Stone and Bloom. These "matched orders" involved Sarcinelli covering "both sides" of a transaction by providing the buyer, seller and price.

---

[4] The mail fraud statute, 18 U.S.C. § 1341, prohibits the use of the mails for the purpose of executing "any scheme or artifice to defraud."

Nevertheless, the stock price did not move as he had expected, reaching a price of no more than six cents per share. By late August or early September, Sarcinelli began to suspect that one of his partners was "back dooring" him by selling the stock on the open market, thereby undermining the scheme to control the stock's price. Sarcinelli severed all involvement in the scheme in November 1980.

After Sarcinelli withdrew, attempts to inflate the price of the stock appear to have ceased, and the stock generally declined, eventually becoming worthless. * * *

Whitten's Expert Testimony

The government called Stanley Whitten, the chief investigator for the SEC regional office in Chicago, as its final witness. Whitten had been a stockbroker for eight years prior to joining the SEC as an investigator in its Enforcement Division in 1974. He had spent over one thousand hours during four years of working on the present case and had interviewed approximately seventy witnesses. He had also assisted in the preparation of the indictment.

Whitten did not testify at trial as a witness with personal knowledge of relevant events. Claiming to be an expert in securities trading practices, he purported to base his testimony not on information obtained from his four-year investigation, but solely on the testimony and documentary evidence introduced at trial.

Whitten was allowed to answer over defense objections a question concerning his opinion as to whether there was a scheme to defraud investors in EAC stock from 1979 to 1982. He answered, "It is my opinion that the stock of European Auto Classics was manipulated and that certain individuals were active participants and material participants in the manipulation of that stock. And that these individuals engaged in a manipulative and fraudulent scheme in furtherance of that manipulation." Whitten consciously used the same formulation throughout his testimony. For example, when asked to name the "participants" in the scheme and the roles that they played, he corrected himself in mid-sentence to include the same elements in his answer: "I believe that the role at the inception, in terms of the participants and the manipulation—excuse me, the fraudulent manipulative practices that were engaged in. . ." He also repeatedly described the defendants as "active participants" and "material participants" in the manipulation of EAC stock. On cross-examination Whitten acknowledged that his positive assessment of the testimony of the government's witnesses, including Sarcinelli, was a basis for his opinions. * * *

We agree with defendants that Whitten's repeated statements embodying legal conclusions exceeded the permissible scope of opinion testimony under the Federal Rules of Evidence. It is true that Fed.R.Evid. 704 states that "testimony in the form of an opinion or inference otherwise admissible is not objectionable because it embraces an ultimate issue to be decided by the trier of fact." However, Rule 704 was not intended to allow experts to offer opinions embodying legal conclusions. [Here the court set forth the Advisory Committee's Note to Rule 704. See Appendix B.]

Had Whitten merely testified that controlled buying and selling of the kind alleged here can create artificial price levels to lure outside investors, no sustainable objection could have been made. Instead, however, Whitten made no attempt to couch the opinion testimony at issue in even conclusory factual statements but drew directly upon the language of the statute and accompanying regulations concerning "manipulation" and "fraud". See supra note 1. In essence, his opinions were legal conclusions that were highly prejudicial and went well beyond his province as an expert in securities trading. Moreover, because his opinions were calculated to "invade the province of the court to determine the applicable law and to instruct the jury as to that law," FAA v. Landy, 705 F.2d 624, 632 (2d Cir.), cert. denied, 464 U.S. 895, 104 S.Ct. 243, 78 L.Ed.2d 232 (1983), they could not have been helpful to the jury in carrying out its legitimate functions. "The admission of such testimony would give the appearance that the court was shifting to witnesses the responsibility to decide the case." Marx & Co. v. Diners' Club, Inc., 550 F.2d 505, 510 (2d Cir.) (citation omitted), cert. denied, 434 U.S. 861, 98 S.Ct. 188, 54 L.Ed.2d 134 (1977). "It is not for witnesses to instruct the jury as to applicable principles of law, but for the judge." Id. at 509–10; see also Torres v. County of Oakland, 758 F.2d 147, 150 (6th Cir.1985) ("The problem with testimony containing a legal conclusion is in conveying the witness' unexpressed, and perhaps erroneous, legal standards to the jury.").

"Manipulation," "scheme to defraud," and "fraud" are not self-defining terms but rather have been the subject of diverse judicial interpretations. * * *

The government argues, however, that Whitten's testimony was proper under three of our recent decisions upholding opinion testimony by government investigators. * * *

None of our prior cases, however, has allowed testimony similar to Whitten's repeated use of statutory and regulatory language indicating guilt. For example, telling the jury that a defendant acted as a "steerer" or participated in a narcotics transaction differs from opining that the defendant "possessed narcotics, to wit, heroin, with the intent to sell," or "aided and abetted the possession of heroin with intent to sell," the functional equivalent of Whitten's testimony in a drug case. It is precisely this distinction, between ultimate factual conclusions that are dispositive of particular issues if believed, e.g., medical causation, and "inadequately explored legal criteria," that is drawn by the Advisory Committee's Note.

We turn now to a second fatal objection to Whitten's opinion testimony. On cross-examination, defense counsel brought out that Whitten's opinions were based on his positive assessment of the trustworthiness and accuracy of the testimony of the government's witnesses, in particular that of Sarcinelli. We believe that expert witnesses may not offer opinions on relevant events based on their personal assessment of the credibility of another witness's testimony. The credibility of witnesses is exclusively for the determination by the jury, and witnesses may not opine as to the credibility of the testimony of other witnesses at the trial. Even apart from the gross invasion of the province of the jury that Whitten's testimony represented, his only claim to expertise was limited to securities trading and did not encompass the evaluation of testimony. Moreover, even expert witnesses possessed of medical knowledge and skills that relate directly to credibility may not state an opinion as to whether another witness is credible, United States v. Azure, 801 F.2d 336, 340–41 (8th Cir.1986), although such witnesses may be permitted to testify to relevant physical or mental conditions.

It is true that Rule 705 allows an expert to state an opinion without disclosing the basis for it, and that a cross-examiner thus may elect not to probe into whether an expert witness's personal assessment of other witnesses' credibility is a basis of the opinion. In a sense, therefore, defendants caused Whitten's credibility opinions to be exposed to the jury. Our objection to testimony on credibility is not limited, however, to the prejudicial effect such testimony may have on the jury. Rather, we believe that such testimony not only should be excluded as overly prejudicial but also renders inadmissible any secondary opinion based upon it. Our holding, therefore, is that witness A may not offer an opinion as to relevant facts based on A 's assessment of the trustworthiness or accuracy of witness B where B 's credibility is an issue to be determined by the trier of fact. Were we to rule otherwise, triers of fact would be called upon either to evaluate opinion testimony in ignorance of an important foundation for that opinion or to hear testimony that is otherwise inadmissible and highly prejudicial.

The present case exemplifies this dilemma. On the one hand, the jury could not accurately evaluate Whitten's testimony in ignorance of the fact that it was based in large part on his opinion that Sarcinelli was telling the truth. That judgment went well beyond the witness's purported expertise and vitiated whatever value his testimony had. On the other hand, testimony by one witness concerning the credibility of other testimony is objectionable in light of the presumption that the trier of fact is the best evaluator of credibility. Such testimony is thus not helpful to the trier of fact and is likely to be prejudicial.

Indeed, Whitten's offering of such an opinion was particularly objectionable. He had spent years investigating this case and had reached a conclusion well before trial as to the credibility of the various witnesses and parties. We believe it to be virtually impossible for an investigator so deeply involved in a case to put aside previous judgments regarding the credibility of witnesses and to render de novo judgments on their credibility after listening to the trial. Even if Whitten had such a sharply compartmentalized mind as to allow segregation of his various credibility analyses, such testimony by an investigator and opinions based thereon are clearly prejudicial when offered to a jury. * * * Certainly, the risk of a jury believing that an opinion offered as to credibility by an agent such as Whitten was based on his investigation as a whole rather than solely on evidence adduced at trial is particularly great.

We find nothing in Rule 703 inconsistent with our ruling. That Rule permits inadmissible evidence to be the basis of an expert's opinion where it is of "a type reasonably relied upon by experts in the particular field." As the Advisory Committee's Note makes plain in its illustration of decisions by physicians, the purpose of the rule is to align the law with the extrajudicial "practice of experts" who may base their opinions on technically inadmissible evidence, such as unauthenticated x-rays and oral reports by nurses. The Rule in no way purports to allow witnesses to assess the trustworthiness or accuracy of *testimony given in the same case* or to offer opinions based on such an assessment.

Our ruling thus does not preclude use of an expert such as Whitten to testify to methods by which share prices may be artificially inflated. Simple hypotheticals based on assumptions about testimony in the record can also be posed to the witness in a way that allows his or her opinions to be given but leaves the credibility issues to the jury. Our ruling thus also does not conflict with Rule 703's provision that the "facts or data in the particular case upon which an expert bases an opinion or inference may be thus . . . made known to the expert at . . . the hearing." Fed.R.Evid. 703; see also Fed.R.Evid. 703 Advisory Committee's Note ("expert [may] attend trial and hear the testimony establishing the facts"). Where such facts or data are based on the trial testimony of a witness whose credibility is not in dispute, the expert need not make a judgment about credibility. Where the credibility of the witness is an issue, the expert may assume the truth of his or her trial testimony and thereafter offer an opinion based on the substance of the testimony. There is thus no need for an expert to make, much less state to the jury, an assessment of credibility when offering an opinion based on trial testimony.

[The court concluded that the trial judge's treatment of Whitten's expert testimony was reversible error.]

■ PIERCE, CIRCUIT JUDGE, concurring:

I concur in all of Judge Winter's thorough opinion except for the portion discussing the "second fatal objection" to Whitten's expert testimony. A question remains in my mind as to whether Judge Winter's conclusion that "expert witnesses may not offer opinions on relevant events based on their personal assessment of the credibility of another witness's testimony" is consistent with Rules 703 and 705 of the Federal Rules of Evidence and the Advisory Committee Notes. As I understand it, the expert's reliance on the testimony of a witness whose credibility is in question may be brought out on cross-examination and may not affect the foundation for admission of the opinion itself. * * *

Ingram v. McCuiston

Supreme Court of North Carolina, 1964.
261 N.C. 392, 134 S.E.2d 705.

Plaintiff instituted this action to recover for personal injuries which she alleges she sustained on March 16, 1961 when the automobile of the defendant collided with the rear of her vehicle on South Tryon Street in the City of Charlotte. In broad outline the facts are these:

About 5:00 p.m. plaintiff, operating a Volkswagen, made a left turn from Woodlawn Road onto Tryon Street, a two-lane roadway at that point. At the same time, the defendant Linda Lee McCuiston was approaching this intersection from the north on Tryon Street in a Dodge automobile owned by her mother, the other defendant. The distance of the Dodge from the intersection at the time of plaintiff's entrance is a matter of dispute between the parties. After plaintiff had proceeded south on Tryon Street in front of the defendant for about two hundred and sixty feet, she stopped three to four feet behind the last car in a long line of traffic which was waiting on a red traffic signal at the Yorkmont Road intersection approximately five hundred and twenty feet ahead. The defendant's Dodge then collided with the rear of plaintiff's Volkswagen causing it to strike the car immediately in front. Again the evidence is conflicting. Plaintiff contends she came to a gradual stop; defendant contends she stopped suddenly. In the two impacts plaintiff sustained an injury to her neck and back which, in the opinion of Dr. Robert E. Miller, the orthopedic specialist who treated her, resulted in a five percent permanent disability to her neck and thoracic spine. Plaintiff was "a nervous type individual," and at the time of the collision she was three months pregnant. She contends that her nervous condition was so aggravated by the collision that in May 1962 she required psychiatric treatment. Plaintiff's psychiatrist, Dr. Thomas A. Wright, Jr., discharged her in August 1962 as much improved. In his opinion the emotional condition he observed in plaintiff at the time she was referred to him could have been produced by the automobile accident.

The pleadings and evidence raised issues of negligence, contributory negligence, and damages. The jury answered each in favor of the plaintiff and awarded her substantial damages. From judgment entered on the verdict the defendants appealed.

■ SHARP, JUSTICE. To establish the cause of plaintiff's injuries her counsel propounded to Dr. Miller a hypothetical question which covers six pages in

the record. The defendants' objections to this question, and to another
which incorporated it by reference, were overruled. The defendants assign
these rulings as error and contend that they were prejudicial because: (1)
The question was based on assumed facts of which there was no evidence;
(2) it was based in part on the opinion of another expert as to the plaintiff's
condition; (3) it included assumed facts totally unnecessary to enable the
doctor to form a satisfactory medical opinion; and (4) it was argumentative
and unduly colored the evidence in plaintiff's favor.

We have concluded that in order to discuss appellants' contentions in-
telligibly we are forced to reproduce the hypothetical question here. Therefore, it follows:

(1) Q. "Now, Dr. Miller, for the purpose of this hypothetical question,
assuming that the jury finds the facts to be, from the evidence, and by
its greater weight, that on March 16, 1961, and prior thereto, plaintiff
Betty Pat Ingram was in excellent physical, emotional and psychological health, and suffering from no disability whatsoever, being an extremely active person from birth, having been brought up on a farm
and actually worked in the fields, having held down a full-time job and
being gainfully employed as of March 16, 1961; and that on March 16,
1961, at approximately 4:50 P.M., plaintiff Betty Pat Ingram was operating her husband's car, a 1960 Volkswagen, two-door sedan automobile, proceeding in a westerly direction on Woodlawn Road just inside the city limits of Charlotte, Mecklenburg County, North Carolina,
and approaching the intersection of Woodlawn Road and South Tryon
Street.

(2) "That the plaintiff *safely* brought her car to a complete stop on
Woodlawn Road, in *lawful* obedience to a stop sign erected on said
Woodlawn Road, directing traffic to stop completely before entering
South Tryon Street, turning either left or right; and

(3) "That the plaintiff, after first having observed that no traffic was
approaching on South Tryon Street close enough or in such a manner
as to interfere with her safely entering South Tryon Street, and thus
after first observing that her actions would not affect the movement of
any other vehicle, and having given a *proper signal* of her intention to
turn to her left, did then *lawfully* make a left turn, entering South
Tryon Street and thereafter proceeding south along South Tryon St., in
the right-hand or westerly lane.

(4) "Assuming, further, that the jury should find from the evidence and
by its greater weight, that minor defendant Linda Lee McCuiston was
operating her mother's 1950 Dodge and traveling in a southerly direction on South Tryon Street, here in Charlotte, also, approaching the
intersection of South Tryon Street and Woodlawn Road, at approximately 4:57 P.M.; and

(5) "Further, that at the time mentioned herein, traffic was *extremely heavy* and practically bumper to bumper from the intersection of South Tryon Street and Woodlawn Road all the way down to the intersection of South Tryon Street or York Road and Yorkmont Road, and at which intersection there was located a red traffic light; and

(6) "That, as plaintiff Betty Pat Ingram started her left turn and started proceeding into South Tryon Street, *she saw, and anyone who was properly observant could and should have seen,* that the traffic south of Betty Pat Ingram's vehicle was just barely moving and obviously preparing to make a stop, in obedience to the traffic control device aforementioned; and

(7) "That, after the plaintiff had driven a very few feet south on South Tryon Street, she saw all of the cars, numbering between 15 and 20, south of her from a certain bridge on South Tryon Street all the way to the traffic signal aforementioned come to a complete stop, at which time the plaintiff also began slowing down and preparing to stop behind the long line of traffic;

(8) "Assuming, further, that the jury should find from the evidence and by its greater weight that when the plaintiff started slowing down and preparing to stop, as aforementioned, the minor defendant, Linda Lee McCuiston, was directly behind the plaintiff's vehicle, some two or three or more car-lengths north, traveling exactly the same direction in the same traffic lane; and

(9) "That the plaintiff had no difficulty in stopping her car and did stop her car three or four feet behind another vehicle operated by a Mr. Guy V. Soule, at a point near the center of the bridge on South Tryon Street, at which time the plaintiff was sitting with the brake pedal on her car completely and fully depressed; and

(10) "That a very short time after the plaintiff stopped her vehicle, *in obedience to the traffic control device and because of the traffic stopped ahead of her,* she observed the minor defendant approaching at a rapid rate of speed, but did not have time to brace herself properly before her car was struck, *and actually had no place to go in her car anyhow;* and that the minor defendant struck the rear of the 1960 Volkswagen with the front of her larger 1950 Dodge, with such force as to drive the plaintiff's automobile forward *and ram the same* into the rear of the vehicle in front of her, despite the locked brakes on the car; and

(11) "Assuming that the jury further finds from the evidence and by its greater weight that at the moment of the first impact, *when the defendant rammed the front of her car into the rear of the car the plaintiff was driving, the* car was suddenly thrown forward, with the result that the body of the plaintiff was thrown back, snapping and whipping her neck and upper portion of her body; and that at the time of the second

impact when the front of the plaintiff's car was driven by the force of the defendant's car into the rear of the vehicle operated by Mr. Guy V. Soule, that that impact caused the plaintiff's body to be *sharply* thrown forward, again snapping her neck in the manner of a whip and, likewise, throwing her suddenly and *with great force* forward, at which time her abdomen sustained, a *severe impact* with the steering wheel of the car the plaintiff was driving; and

(12) "Further, assuming the jury should find from the evidence and by its greater weight that the accident and the two impacts aforementioned subjected the plaintiff to a *severe jolt and strain,* the force of the two said impacts producing immediately excruciating pain *and agony,* in the plaintiff's neck, back, shoulder and arms; and

(13) "That at the time of the collision on March 16, 1961, the plaintiff had been pregnant for approximately three and a half months; and

(14) "Assuming, further, that the jury should find from the evidence and by its greater weight, that whereas plaintiff had not suffered any substantial emotional difficulty or disability prior to the accident, that the collision and the separate impact, coupled with the pregnant condition of the plaintiff, proximately caused the plaintiff from the date of the accident through the entire remainder of her pregnancy, up until the child was born on September 2, 1961, or for a period of more than five months, *constant mental anguish and shock,* caused by the *reasonable fear* that her serious personal injuries and the blow to her abdomen might cause her to sustain a miscarriage; and

(15) "Assuming, further, that the jury should find from the evidence and by its greater weight that the impact and the collision aforementioned subjected the plaintiff to *an extremely severe nervous and mental shock,* which permanently, to some extent, injured her nervous and mental systems, causing extensive and *permanent dislocation, psychoneurosis, nervous shock, nervousness, and traumatic neurosis or anxiety neurosis*, with the result that whereas plaintiff had never suffered such prior to the date of the accident, from the date of the accident and even for a considerable period of time after the birth of the plaintiff's baby, on September 2, 1961, the plaintiff suffered extremely from nightmares, worry and constant fear, and became in such a condition, as the result of the impact and the collision aforementioned, that she cried easily, became depressed and subject to suicidal tendencies; and

(16) "That her emotional condition became such that her orthopedic specialist, Dr. Robert E. Miller, referred her to a duly accredited psychiatrist, Dr. Thomas H. Wright, Jr., which psychiatrist diagnosed her condition as being an extremely depressive reaction, with nervous tension and depression greatly intensified since the date of the accident on March 16, 1961; and

(17) "That at the time the psychiatrist first examined the plaintiff in June of 1962, he found the plaintiff to have lost interest in life, being unable to concentrate and at times even not wishing to live; and

(18) "Assuming, further, that the jury finds from the evidence and by its greater weight that the plaintiff is still suffering emotional damage as the proximate result of the collision and the pain and suffering she endured, as above set out; and

(19) "Assuming, further, that from the time of the accident on March 16, 1961, despite extreme pain suffered in the neck, shoulder, back and other portions of the body, it was unsafe and impossible, safely, to take X-rays of the plaintiff, due to her pregnant condition, which in turn increased her anxiety and mental anguish; and

(20) "Assuming, further, that the jury should find from the evidence and by its greater weight that the plaintiff suffered from an extremely severe sprain of the cervical spine, thoracic spine, and the lumbar spine, and further, that the plaintiff presently is permanently partially disabled to the extent of 5% disability of said cervical spine, thoracic spine and lumbar spine; and

(21) "That the plaintiff, as a proximate result of the accident and the injuries sustained in the accident, has incurred medical expenses to date in the sum of approximately $600.00, including the cost of drugs and prescriptions, the charges to the Miller Clinic, the charges of the psychiatrist, the charges of the Presbyterian [Hospital] and the charges of the x-ray specialist, the charges for a special corrective girdle and for a cervical collar prescribed by the Miller Clinic; and

(22) "That the plaintiff would be likely to incur additional future medical expenses, directly attributable to her condition caused by the injuries; then

(23) "Assuming that the jury finds the above facts to be true, from the evidence and by its greater weight, then do you have an opinion satisfactory to yourself, as to whether or not the accident in which the plaintiff was involved on March 16, 1961, when the plaintiff was stopped in her husband's automobile on South Tryon Street, sitting with her foot on the brake, when the defendant *crashed* into the rear of the plaintiff's vehicle, *with tremendous force* and at a rapid rate of speed, driving the vehicle forward, and actually knocking the front of the plaintiff's vehicle into the rear of another vehicle, with the two separate impacts first knocking the plaintiff's body to the rear and then throwing the plaintiff's body to the front, *striking her abdomen, with a severe blow,* she being then and there three and a half months' pregnant, could or might have produced the severe nervous and mental shock, which injured her nervous and mental system, and further, could or might have produced the extensive and permanent psycho-

neurosis, nervous shock, nervous and traumatic neurosis, and further, could or might have caused the plaintiff to suffer from the nightmares, worry and constant fear, the depression and being subject to crying easily, and without reason and being subject to suicidal tendencies, and further, could or might have produced the 5% permanent partial disability to the cervical spine, the thoracic spine and the lumbar spine." (Italics ours).

The doctor answered that in his opinion the collision could or might have produced the conditions described.

The next question was:

"Q. Dr. Miller, assuming that the jury finds the facts to be from the evidence and by its greater weight, as set out in the hypothetical question that was just put to you, do you have an opinion satisfactory to yourself as to whether or not the plaintiff has sustained any permanent injury, mentally or emotionally, or whether she presently is still partially disabled from the standpoint of her mental health?

"A. Well, you have got an expert sitting back there in the Court. He can answer that question better than I can. * * * Yes, I have an opinion. The question is, of course, in two parts. One is whether she has permanent partial disability from the emotional status and I think she does. The other is as to the permanent anxiety, and there is some permanency."

Under our system the jury finds the facts and draws the inferences therefrom. The use of the hypothetical question is required if it is to have the benefit of expert opinions upon factual situations of which the experts have no personal knowledge. However, under the adversary method of trial, the hypothetical question has been so abused that criticism of it is now widespread and noted by every authority on evidence. E.g., Stansbury, N.C. Evidence, s. 137 (2d ed. 1963); McCormick on Evidence, s. 16; Ladd, Expert Testimony, 5 Vand.L.Rev. 414, 427. Wigmore has urged that the hypothetical question be abolished: "Its abuses have become so obstructive and nauseous that no remedy short of extirpation will suffice. It is a logical necessity, but a practical incubus; and logic must here be sacrificed. After all, Law (in Mr. Justice Holmes' phrase) is much more than Logic. It is a strange irony that the hypothetical question, which is one of the few truly scientific features of the rules of Evidence, should have become that feature which does most to disgust men of science with the law of Evidence." II Wigmore, Evidence, s. 686 (3d ed. 1940). The comment contained in 2 Jones, Evidence, s. 422 (5th ed. 1958) might well have been directed at the hypothetical question involved in this appeal.

"The most meritorious of the criticisms are that the questions are often slanted for partisan advantage and are often so long and involved as to confuse rather than assist the jury, and, like some appellate court opinions, contain detailed recitals of factual surplusage not essential to support the conclusion reached."

To be competent, a hypothetical question may include only facts which are already in evidence or those which the jury might logically infer therefrom. Jackson v. Stancil, 253 N.C. 291, 116 S.E.2d 817; Stansbury, N.C. Evidence, s. 137 (2d ed. 1963) and cases therein cited. After a careful examination of the record, we find no evidence to support the following facts which were assumed in the hypothetical question involved on this appeal: (Figures in parentheses refer to correspondingly numbered paragraphs of the question.)

1. That the plaintiff "was in excellent physical, emotional, and psychological health," (1). All the evidence indicates that plaintiff had "always had some nervousness." Indeed, she told Dr. Miller that she was "an extremely apprehensive type individual."

2. That as a result of the collision plaintiff "became depressed and subject to suicidal tendencies," (15). There was ample evidence that plaintiff was abnormally depressed after the accident and during her entire pregnancy. However, there is no evidence either that she developed suicidal tendencies or that she lost the desire to live, as paragraph (17) of the question assumes the psychiatrist "found." Depression and suicidal tendencies are not necessarily synonymous.

3. "That the plaintiff presently is permanently partially disabled to the extent of 5% disability of said cervical spine, thoracic spine and lumbar spine," (20), (23). The evidence of such disability related only to the neck and thoracic spine. The doctor testified to no such disability in the lumbar spine.

Defendants' objection that the hypothetical question asked Dr. Miller, an orthopedic surgeon, was based in part upon the opinion of Dr. Wright, a psychiatrist, must also be sustained. Paragraphs (16) and (17) of the question reveal its reference to Dr. Wright's diagnosis of the plaintiff's condition "as being an extremely depressive reaction, with nervous tension and depression greatly intensified since the date of the accident on March 16, 1961." The question does not assume that plaintiff was actually suffering from an extreme depressive reaction; it merely states that Dr. Wright made this diagnosis. The inclusion of such a statement violates the rule in this jurisdiction that the opinion of an expert witness may not be predicated in whole or in part upon the opinions, inferences, or conclusions of other witnesses, whether they be expert or lay, unless their testimony is put to him hypothetically as an assumed fact. State v. David, 222 N.C. 242, 22 S.E.2d 633. When the hypothetical question is properly asked the jury can determine whether the assumed facts have been proven and weigh the opinion of the expert accordingly. An excellent statement of this rule appears in Quimby v. Greenhawk, 166 Md. 335, 340, 171 A. 59, 61:

"Although a medical expert may base his opinion upon the facts testified to by another expert, the witness may not have submitted to him, as a part of the facts to be considered in the formation of his inference and conclusion, the opinion of such other expert on all or some of the facts to be considered by the witness from whom the answer is sought. To do so would destroy the premises of fact upon which an expert, by reason of his own peculiar technical skill and knowledge, is permitted to give in evidence his own inference and opinion."

The purpose of the first hypothetical question asked Dr. Miller was to elicit his opinion whether the collision on March 16, 1961 could have produced the five percent permanent disability which he found in plaintiff's neck and thoracic spine. The references therein to plaintiff's mental health had no bearing on the query whether the collision might have caused the injury to her neck and thoracic spine.

The purpose of the second question, which incorporated the first, was to find out whether, in his opinion, the plaintiff had sustained any permanent mental or emotional injury. As Dr. Miller himself told counsel, that question might have been more properly addressed to Dr. Wright, the psychiatrist. Furthermore, when paragraph (15) of the question stated that the collision on March 16, 1961 did proximately cause some "permanent dislocation, psychoneurosis, nervous shock, nervousness, and traumatic neurosis or anxiety neurosis," it assumed the very fact which plaintiff's counsel sought to establish by the doctor's opinion.

The references in the question to plaintiff's childhood on the farm, the route and manner of driving which brought her to Tryon Street immediately before the collision, her consultations with Dr. Wright and his diagnosis of her condition, the fact that her lumbar spine could not be X-rayed because of her pregnancy, and the cost of medical bills in the past and in the future were totally irrelevant to the question of causation. An examination of paragraphs (2), (3), (4), (5), (6), (16), (17), (18), (19), (21), and (22) discloses the validity of defendants' objection to the question on grounds that it contained an assumption of irrelevant facts. Each of the other paragraphs in question contain one or more references to facts which, more succinctly phrased, might be included in a properly stated question.

The italicized words in paragraphs (3), (6), (11), (12), (14), and (23) are examples of the repetitious, slanted, and argumentative words and phrases of which the defendants properly complain. It was no part of the legitimate purpose of the hypothetical question under consideration to establish defendants' negligence; nor are six pages required to state a proper hypothetical question based on the relevant evidence in this case. A shorter question should be no more difficult to frame and it will be easier for the court to rule upon and the jury to understand.

Defendants' assignments of error based on their objections to the hypothetical questions must be sustained. Since the case goes back for a new trial, it is not necessary to consider the other assignments involving questions which may not arise thereon.

New trial.

Waltz, The New Federal Rules of Evidence: An Analysis
112–113 (2d ed. 1975).*

Rule 705 is important and, rightly or wrongly, somewhat controversial. It provides that an expert can testify in terms of opinion "without prior disclosure of the underlying facts or data."

* * *

Rule 705 does not do away with the hypothetical question absolutely; it simply does away with any absolute requirement that a hypothetical be used by counsel. The use of the hypothetical question sometimes has its advantages and it remains to be seen whether trial lawyers will accept with any frequency this Rule's invitation to forego its use.

In any event, Rule 705 probably forecloses successful assignments of error based on a claim that opposing counsel's hypothetical question was incomplete, i.e., did not include all of the "underlying facts or data." In effect, the new rule places on the cross-examiner the burden of eliciting any missing data. Thus Rule 705 should serve to make examining counsel less nervous about the use of hypotheticals; no longer will it be essential to include each and every scrap of arguably pertinent data on pain of a successful objection or reversal.

* * *

People v. Gardeley
Supreme Court of California, 1996.
927 P.2d 713.

■ KENNARD, J.

At issue in this case are certain provisions of the Street Terrorism Enforcement and Prevention Act, also known as the STEP Act, enacted by the Legislature in 1988. Underlying the STEP Act was the Legislature's recognition that "California is in a state of crisis which has been caused by violent street gangs whose members threaten, terrorize, and commit a multitude of crimes against the peaceful citizens of their neighborhoods." The

---

* Copyright, 1975, by Multi-State Media, Inc.

act's express purpose was "to seek the eradication of criminal activity by street gangs."

As relevant here, the STEP Act imposes certain penal consequences when crimes are committed "for the benefit of, at the direction of, or in association with any *criminal street gang*." A "criminal street gang," as defined by the act, is any ongoing association of three or more persons that shares a common name or common identifying sign or symbol; has as one of its "primary activities" the commission of specified criminal offenses; and engages through its members in a "*pattern of criminal gang activity*." Under the act, "pattern of criminal gang activity" means that gang members have, within a certain time frame, committed or attempted to commit "two or more" of specified criminal offenses (so-called "predicate offenses").

Here, based on the jury's determination that the prosecution had satisfied the STEP Act requirements, the trial court imposed increased sentences as to both defendants. The Court of Appeal, however, struck the sentence enhancements on the ground that the prosecution had failed to prove the requisite "pattern of criminal gang activity." The Court of Appeal held that evidence of "two or more" predicate offenses by gang members can establish a "pattern of criminal gang activity" only if each such offense is shown to be "gang related." We disagree that the predicate offenses must be "gang related." We also disagree with the Court of Appeal's conclusion that the prosecution failed to prove the requisite pattern of criminal gang activity.

I

On August 4, 1992, about 2 a.m., Edward Bruno was riding in a car with some friends. Bruno, who had been drinking, needed to urinate. The car stopped near Farm Drive and Old Hillsdale Avenue in San Jose. While Bruno was relieving himself in the carport of an apartment complex, which happened to be in an area controlled by the Family Crip gang, he was approached by defendants Rochelle Lonel Gardeley and Tommie James Thompson, and one Tyrone Dermont Watkins. Gardeley shoved Bruno and asked, "What are you doing here, white boy?" Bruno pushed Gardeley back and punched him. Someone then hit Bruno in the head. When Bruno tried to get away, the three men pursued him. They knocked Bruno to the ground, repeatedly punched and kicked him, hit his thighs and rib cage with a bat or stick, and broke a large rock into pieces on his head. Taken from Bruno were a wristwatch, a gold neck chain, and $30. Bruno suffered an eye injury and multiple bruises, and required 20 stitches to his forehead. Apartment residents who witnessed the attack called the police. Minutes later, police officers stopped a car for speeding and making an illegal U-turn, and recovered from the ground outside the passenger door a plastic "baggie" containing .99 grams of cocaine. The driver of the car was defendant Thompson, and the passenger was defendant Gardeley, who had a bloody lip and blood on his T-shirt and arm.

Gardeley and Thompson were charged with attempted murder, assault with a deadly weapon, with a great bodily injury enhancement, and robbery. Each of these offenses was alleged to have been committed "for the benefit of, at the direction of, or in association with [a] criminal street gang." Both defendants were also charged with a fourth offense, committing an assault and/or battery "for the benefit of, at the direction of, or in association with, [a] criminal street gang;" additionally, defendant Gardeley was charged with possession of cocaine.[3]

At trial, the prosecution presented evidence regarding the attack on Edward Bruno. Thereafter, the prosecution called as a witness Detective Patrick Boyd of the San Jose Police Department, who had 23 years of experience in the investigation of criminal street gangs. Boyd had interviewed both defendants after their arrests in this case. Defendant Gardeley said that he had been a member of the Family Crip gang since 1983 and was known by the moniker or street name of "Trench." Defendant Thompson stated that he too was a Family Crip member and was known as "Capone." According to Thompson, the gang had approximately 70 active members. He admitted that he had been dealing cocaine at the apartment complex just before the confrontation with Bruno.

In the course of his testimony, Detective Boyd mentioned that he had also interviewed Tyrone Watkins, Bruno's third assailant. When the prosecutor then asked what Watkins had told Boyd, counsel for defendant Thompson objected on hearsay grounds. As an offer of proof, the prosecutor explained that he sought to elicit from Detective Boyd the statements made by Watkins, not "for the truth of the matter asserted," but to put before the jury facts on which Boyd could rely in rendering his expert opinion that the attack on Bruno "was gang activity in furtherance of . . . the Family Crip gang." The prosecutor added that he also intended to ask Detective Boyd "hearsay questions" about some prior criminal acts involving members of the Family Crip gang.

Out of the jury's presence, the trial court held a hearing to allow the prosecution to make an offer of proof regarding the statements by Watkins and the other "hearsay" evidence that it intended to present. At the hearing, Detective Boyd provided additional details of his familiarity with the criminal activities of the Family Crip gang. Thereafter, the trial court ruled that Boyd could testify as an expert on criminal gang activity.

In the jury's presence, the trial court overruled defendant Thompson's hearsay objection to the questions the prosecutor asked Detective Boyd about the Tyrone Watkins interview. The court then informed the jury that certain "hearsay" would be introduced pertaining to Tyrone Watkins and other matters, but that the jury "may not consider those [hearsay] state-

---

[3] For his part in the attack on Bruno, Tyrone Watkins was charged together with defendants Gardeley and Thompson. Before trial, however, Watkins entered guilty pleas to assault with a deadly weapon and committing a crime for the benefit of a criminal street gang.

ments for the truth of the matter, but only as they give rise ... to the expert opinion in which questions will be asked which will follow." Immediately thereafter Detective Boyd testified that Tyrone Watkins had said that his street name was "T–Bone," and that he had been a member of the Family Crip gang since 1988. Boyd added that several other individuals had also admitted to him their membership in the Family Crip gang.

The prosecutor asked Detective Boyd for his opinion as to the primary purpose or activity of the Family Crip gang. Detective Boyd responded that based on investigations of hundreds of gang-related offenses, conversations with defendants and other Family Crip members, as well as information from fellow officers and various law enforcement agencies, it was his opinion that the Family Crip gang's primary purpose was to sell narcotics, but that the gang also engaged in witness intimidation and other acts of violence to further its drug-dealing activities.

The prosecutor then gave Detective Boyd this scenario: "Assuming hypothetically that we have an incident that took place at about 2:00 a.m. on [Old] Hillsdale and Farm [in San Jose] in which Family Crip gang members were present and one of which is out attempting to sell cocaine and a second is found with cocaine near his possession when detained, and a white male is observed urinating in this area and a fight breaks out with the white male and then the white male is chased down by the three Family Crip gang members, severely beaten, threatened, they said they were gonna kill him, then he is robbed of money, necklace and a watch." The prosecutor asked whether in Detective Boyd's expert opinion the attack on the White male as just described was "gang related activity." Boyd replied that it was, calling it a "classic" example of how a gang uses violence to secure its drug-dealing stronghold.

Detective Boyd explained: It is common practice for several gang members acting in concert to assault a person in full view of residents of an area where the gang sells drugs. Such attacks serve to intimidate the residents and to dissuade them from reporting the gang's drug-dealing activities to police. Gang members typically view a dispute or argument with someone who is not a member of the gang as a "challenge" to the gang's authority, and they respond by trying to "dominate" the person physically, that is, they might "beat the person senseless, throw rocks over his head, kick him" and do this "where a lot of people can witness it." When gang members "terrorize people ... [who] have to live there," the "fear factor" allows the gang to "go right back to dope dealing" day after day in the same area.

Thereafter, the prosecutor questioned Detective Boyd regarding three separate criminal incidents. The most recent of the three was a May 2, 1992, shooting at an apartment complex involving defendant Thompson and one Mario Phipps, who Boyd confirmed was a Family Crip member. The second incident took place on July 17, 1989, in San Jose; it involved a threat against a drug dealer, Michael Halliburton, by defendant Gardeley and three other persons, who Detective Boyd knew to be members of the Family Crip gang. The third incident occurred on December 1, 1987, when two police officers observed defendant Gardeley and others in the vicinity of Nancy Lane and Florence in San Jose flagging down cars in a manner that the officers associated with the sale of narcotics; Gardeley fled, but when stopped by the officers was found to be in possession of crack cocaine. In the expert opinion of Detective Boyd, each of the three incidents just described was "gang related" criminal activity of the Family Crip gang.

The prosecutor then offered into evidence, without objection by the defense, certified copies of three informations together with abstracts of judgment and other official court records. The first information charged Mario Phipps (not a defendant in this case) with a May 2, 1992, shooting at an occupied dwelling with a shotgun; the second information charged defendant Gardeley with a July 17, 1989, incident of being an accessory to a felony; and the third information charged defendant Gardeley with a December 1, 1987, incident of cocaine possession. The three abstracts of judgment and other court records documented the convictions of Mario Phipps and of defendant Gardeley for the offenses charged in these informations.

The jury convicted defendants Gardeley and Thompson of attempted murder, and of assault with a deadly weapon with great bodily injury, and found true the allegations that the offenses had been committed "for the benefit of, at the direction of, or in association with [a] criminal street gang." The jury also convicted both defendants of committing assault and/or battery "for the benefit of, at the direction of, or in association with, [a] criminal street gang", and in addition convicted defendant Gardeley of possession of cocaine.[5] The trial court sentenced both defendants to state prison, Gardeley for 17 years, and Thompson for 9 years.[6] Both defendants appealed.

The Court of Appeal reversed the convictions under former subdivision (c) of section 186.22 (committing an assault and/or battery "for the benefit of, at the direction of, or in association with, [a] criminal street gang"), and struck the criminal street gang sentence enhancements that the trial court had imposed under subdivision (b)(1) of section 186.22, concluding that the prosecution had failed to prove the statutorily required "two or more" predicate offenses to establish that the Family Crip gang was a criminal street gang within the meaning of the statute; in all other respects, the court affirmed the judgments. The Court of Appeal reasoned that the prosecution had to prove not only the statutory requirements pertaining to predicate

---

[5] Bifurcated from the jury trial were allegations that defendant Gardeley had served a prior prison term (§ 667.5) and had suffered a previous conviction for a serious felony (§§ 667/1192.7). The trial court found both allegations to be true.

[6] Defendant Gardeley's seventeen-year prison term was comprised of nine years for attempted murder, two years concurrent for cocaine possession, a five-year serious felony enhancement, a one-year prior prison term enhancement, and a two-year "street gang" enhancement. * * *

offenses, but also that each such offense was "gang related." According to the Court of Appeal, Detective Boyd's expert opinion testimony that the three separate criminal incidents (involving defendants Gardeley and Thompson and other Family Crip members and committed before the charges in this case) were "gang related" was not competent evidence on the issue because Boyd's opinion was not based on facts in evidence and Boyd had no personal knowledge of the facts underlying the three incidents.

We granted the Attorney General's petition for review.

II

* * *

[T]o subject a defendant to the penal consequences of the STEP Act, the prosecution must prove that the crime for which the defendant was convicted had been "committed for the benefit of, at the direction of, or in association with any criminal street gang, with the specific intent to promote, further, or assist in any criminal conduct by gang members." In addition, the prosecution must prove that the gang (1) is an ongoing association of three or more persons with a common name or common identifying sign or symbol; (2) has as one of its primary activities the commission of one or more of the criminal acts enumerated in the statute; and (3) includes members who either individually or collectively have engaged in a "pattern of criminal gang activity" by committing, attempting to commit, or soliciting *two or more* of the enumerated offenses (the so-called "predicate offenses") during the statutorily defined period.

In the sections that follow, we explain how the prosecution here satisfied these statutory requirements.

III

We first consider the issue of gang expert testimony, which in this case was given by Detective Patrick Boyd of the San Jose Police Department.

California law permits a person with "special knowledge, skill, experience, training, or education" in a particular field to qualify as an expert witness (Evid. Code, § 720) and to give testimony in the form of an opinion (id., § 801). Under Evidence Code section 801, expert opinion testimony is admissible only if the subject matter of the testimony is "sufficiently beyond common experience that the opinion of an expert would assist the trier of fact." The subject matter of the culture and habits of criminal street gangs, of particular relevance here, meets this criterion.

Evidence Code section 801 limits expert opinion testimony to an opinion that is "[b]ased on matter . . . perceived by or personally known to the witness or made known to [the witness] at or before the hearing, whether or not admissible, that is of a type that reasonably may be relied upon by an expert in forming an opinion upon the subject to which [the expert] testimony relates. . ."

Generally, an expert may render opinion testimony on the basis of facts given "in a hypothetical question that asks the expert to assume their truth." (1 McCormick on Evidence (4th ed. 1992) § 14, p. 58.) Such a hypothetical question must be rooted in facts shown by the evidence, however.

Expert testimony may also be premised on material that is not admitted into evidence so long as it is material of a type that is reasonably relied upon by experts in the particular field in forming their opinions. Of course, any material that forms the basis of an expert's opinion testimony must be reliable. For "the law does not accord to the expert's opinion the same degree of credence or integrity as it does the data underlying the opinion. Like a house built on sand, the expert's opinion is no better than the facts on which it is based."

So long as this threshold requirement of reliability is satisfied, even matter that is ordinarily *inadmissible* can form the proper basis for an expert's opinion testimony. And because Evidence Code section 802 allows an expert witness to "state on direct examination the reasons for his opinion and the matter . . . upon which it is based," an expert witness whose opinion is based on such inadmissible matter can, when testifying, describe the material that forms the basis of the opinion. (*People v. Shattuck* (1895) 109 Cal. 673, 678 [42 P. 315] [medical expert could testify to patient's complaints in order "to give a clinical history of the case to understand the significance of her symptoms"]; *McElligott v. Freeland* (1934) 139 Cal.App. 143, 157–158 [33 P.2d 430] [certified public accountant could testify to information he relied on in property valuation]; see *People v. Wash* (1993) 6 Cal.4th 215, 251 [24 Cal.Rptr.2d 421, 861 P.2d 1107] [prosecution could elicit out-of-court statements relied on by the defense expert]; 2 McCormick on Evidence, *supra*, § 324.3, p. 372 [explaining that under rule 703, Fed. Rules Evid., which allows the expert to disclose to the trier of fact the basis for expert opinion, "[t]he result is that often the expert may testify to evidence even though it is inadmissible under the hearsay rule."].)

A trial court, however, "has considerable discretion to control the form in which the expert is questioned to prevent the jury from learning of incompetent hearsay." A trial court also has discretion "to weigh the probative value of inadmissible evidence relied upon by an expert witness . . . against the risk that the jury might improperly consider it as independent proof of the facts recited therein." This is because a witness's on-the-record recitation of sources relied on for an expert opinion does not transform inadmissible matter into "independent proof" of any fact.

Consistent with these well-settled principles, the trial court in this case ruled that Detective Boyd could testify as an expert witness and could reveal the information on which he had relied in forming his expert opinion, including hearsay.

After giving Detective Boyd a "hypothetical" based on the facts of the assault in this case on Edward Bruno by three Family Crip members, the prosecutor asked Boyd if in his expert opinion an attack as described would be "gang-related activity." Boyd responded that it was a "classic" example of gang-related activity, explaining that criminal street gangs rely on such violent assaults to frighten the residents of an area where the gang members sell drugs, thereby securing the gang's drug-dealing stronghold. From this expert testimony by Detective Boyd, the jury could reasonably conclude that the attack on Bruno by members of the Family Crip gang including defendants was committed "for the benefit of, at the direction of, or in association with" that gang, and "with the specific intent to promote, further, or assist in . . . criminal conduct by gang members" as specified in the STEP Act.

Detective Boyd's testimony also provided much of the evidence necessary to establish that the Family Crip gang met the STEP Act's definition of a "criminal street gang." (§ 186.22, subd. (f) [defining a criminal street gang as an "ongoing organization, association, or group of three or more persons, whether formal or informal, having as one of its primary activities the commission of one or more" criminal acts enumerated in subdivision (e) of the statute, and which has a "common name or common identifying sign or symbol, and whose members individually or collectively engage in or have engaged in a pattern of criminal gang activity."].)

Boyd testified that defendants Gardeley and Thompson admitted to membership in the Family Crips, and that Gardeley had been a member of the gang since 1983. Boyd also expressed his expert opinion that the primary activity of the Family Crip gang was the sale of narcotics, but that the gang also engaged in witness intimidation. (These are two of the offenses enumerated in subdivision (e) of section 186.22.) Boyd based this opinion on conversations with the defendants and with other Family Crip members, his personal investigations of hundreds of crimes committed by gang members, as well as information from his colleagues and various law enforcement agencies.

We conclude that this testimony by Detective Boyd provided a basis from which the jury could reasonably find that the Family Crip gang met the requirements of subdivision (f) of section 186.22 for a criminal street gang. * * * Thus, through Detective Boyd's expert testimony, the prosecution satisfied most of the requirements of the STEP Act to prove that the Family Crip gang was a "criminal street gang." But the prosecution still had to establish the additional statutory requirement that the gang's members "individually or collectively engage in or have engaged in a pattern of criminal gang activity" a point that we will discuss in the part that follows.

[In Parts IV and V of its opinion, the court held that the predicate of-fenses need not themselves be gang related, and that the prosecution had adequately proven a pattern of criminal gang activity.]

Conclusion

Through a combination of expert opinion testimony, documentary evidence of an uncharged crime, and testimony by percipient witnesses to the charged crimes in this case, the prosecution in this case met its burden of proving each of the several elements set forth by the Legislature in the Street Terrorism Enforcement and Prevention Act (also known as the STEP Act). Accordingly, for their roles in the brutal attack on Edward Bruno, Family Crip gang members Gardeley and Thompson are appropriately subject to the penal consequences of the STEP Act. We therefore reverse the judgment of the Court of Appeal insofar as it set aside defendants' convictions under former subdivision (c) and struck the increased prison terms imposed under subdivision (b)(1) of section 186.22.

United States v. Moore

United States Court of Appeals for the District of Columbia Circuit, 2011.
651 F.3d 30.

Before: SENTELLE, Chief Judge, and ROGERS and KAVANAUGH, Circuit Judges.

PER CURIAM:

[Numerous defendants were charged with various acts, including murder, in furtherance of an extensive drug conspiracy. The court rejected several grounds of appeal before turning to the government's use of an FBI agent as an overview witness.]

FBI Agent Daniel Sparks testified as the first witness in the government's case-in-chief. His testimony provided an overview of the government's case, setting forth for the jury the script of the testimony and evidence the jury could expect the government to present in its case-in-chief. Further, he expressed his opinion, based on his training and experience, about the nature of the investigation conducted in this case.

Appellants contend that the use of an overview witness as the government's first witness improperly permitted the government, over defense objections, to elicit FBI Agent Sparks's opinions about the charged crimes, the reasons for appellants' actions in various circumstances, the nature of the charged conspiracy and the relationships between co-conspirators, including the cooperating co-conspirators who testified as government witnesses, and the strength of the evidence—all before the government had presented any such evidence. Appellants suggest that FBI Agent Sparks's testimony left the impression for the jury that it should accept that the co-conspirator cooperating witnesses would fully and truthfully recount the events and impressions that he outlined in his testimony. Hence, the question is whether such overview testimony is permissible, and even if permissible with respect to the FBI agent's description of aspects of the pre-indictment investigation of which he had personal knowledge, whether the overview witness's testimony here caused substantial prejudice to appellants. . .

Until recently this court had not addressed the appropriateness of a government overview witness at the outset of its case, but had identified the "obvious dangers posed by summarization of evidence" by a non-expert witness called by the government during its case-in-chief in *United States v. Lemire*, 720 F.2d 1327, 1348 (D.C.Cir.1983). The analysis in *Lemire* is instructive. In that case, the government called toward the end of its case-in-chief an FBI agent, who was also a certified public accountant, "to summarize the evidence about the complex cash flow through offshore companies" in a prosecution for wire fraud, interstate transportation of proceeds of fraud, and conspiracy. The FBI agent "used four summary charts to re-examine th[e] evidence" already presented by the government "in a more organized fashion," and "prefaced each piece of his testimony by identifying the document in evidence from which he obtained the information." Upon defense objection that the FBI agent was an improper witness under Federal Rule of Evidence 602, the district court conducted a "full voir dire examination" before allowing the FBI agent to testify, "subject to limiting instructions that his testimony was explanatory and was not itself substantive evidence."

On appeal, this court held that the district court did not abuse its discretion in permitting the government to use a non-expert summary witness because neither Rule 602's literal language nor its overriding purpose was violated. [The FBI agent] did not testify about any of the events underlying the trial: he only summarized evidence about cash flows that several prior witnesses had already offered. As to that evidence, he testified from his personal knowledge of the transcripts and exhibits.

The court also noted that other courts had "permitted such summaries under Rule 1006, allowing for admission into evidence of summaries of documents too voluminous to be conveniently examined in court" even if the documents were already in evidence. That rule aside, the court observed that "[t]here is an established tradition that permits a summary of evidence to be put before the jury with proper limiting instructions." Nonetheless, this court concluded that the claim of unfair prejudice "raises more troubling concerns." Initially the court noted that the non-expert summary evidence was cumulative and subject to challenge under Rule 403 as more unfairly prejudicial than probative. It also acknowledged that a non-expert summary witness "can help the jury organize and evaluate evidence which is factually complex and fragmentally revealed in the testimony of a multitude of witnesses throughout the trial." But the court pointed to three "obvious dangers posed by summarization of evidence."

First, the jury might treat the summary evidence as additional or corroborative evidence that unfairly strengthens the government's case. The court was satisfied that for a summary witness there were adequate safeguards, including cross-examination and limiting instructions, that could be fashioned by the district court to prevent the jury from treating the summary evidence as substantive proof. The court emphasized that the defendant's challenge to the personal knowledge of the summary witness was not an issue because the witness "had carefully reviewed the charts and ensured that they reflected information contained in documents *already in evidence*." (emphasis added)

Second, summary witness testimony posed the risk that otherwise inadmissible evidence might be introduced. This concern was ameliorated, the court concluded, because "the judge, prosecutor and defense counsel all heard the evidence upon which [the witness] based his summary" and hence "he was unlikely to stray from that evidentiary base without quickly being stopped." Indeed, the court noted, "at one point the witness inadvertently started to discuss material not in evidence, and the prosecutor prevented him from doing so."

Third, a summary witness might permit the government to have an extra closing argument. The court noted, however, that the summary witness had made no "controversial inferences or pronounced judgment" and thus the district court had no need to interfere with the examination on this ground.

Other circuits to address the use of overview witnesses have reached uniformly negative conclusions in view of the serious dangers of prejudice to a fair trial. The Court of Appeals for the First, Second, and Fifth Circuits have held that the use of overview testimony by the government is a "troubling development" for this very reason. *United States v. Casas,* 356 F.3d 104, 120 (1st Cir.2004); *see also United States v. Garcia,* 413 F.3d 201 (2d Cir.2005); *United States v. Griffin,* 324 F.3d 330 (5th Cir.2003). As the First Circuit explained in describing the practice as "inherently problematic":

> [S]uch testimony raises the very real specter that the jury verdict could be influenced by statements of fact or credibility assessments in the overview but not in evidence. There is also the possibility that later testimony might be different than what the overview witness assumed; objections could be sustained or the witness could change his or her story. Overview testimony by government agents is especially problematic because juries may place greater weight on evidence perceived to have the imprimatur of the government.

Casas.

Approaching the question from a different perspective, the Second Circuit prohibited overview witnesses from giving lay opinions about anticipated evidence without satisfying the three requirements of Federal Rule of Evidence 701—that the witness's testimony (1) be based on his personal perception, (2) be helpful to the jury, and (3) not be based on scientific, technical, or other specialized knowledge. *See Garcia.* As regards the second factor, the Second Circuit dismissed the notion that an overview witness aided the jury by framing how the government's case-in-chief will unfold, observing that "[t]he law already provides an adequate vehicle for the government to 'help' the jury gain an overview of anticipated evidence as well as a preview of its theory of each defendant's culpability: the opening statement." To the extent the summary witness testified to the ultimate question of fact, the Second Circuit noted that "courts should be wary of opinion testimony whose 'sole function is to answer the same question that the trier of fact is to consider in its deliberations,'" *id.* at 210 (quoting 4 Weinstein's Federal Evidence § 701.05 (2d ed.2004), and citing Fed. R. Evid. 704 advisory committee's notes to 1972 proposed rules), observing that it had previously held in two other cases that it was "error to allow law enforcement witnesses to express opinions as to [the] defendants' culpability based on the totality of information gathered in the course of their investigations." The court held that "the foundation requirements of Rule 701 do not permit a law enforcement agent to testify to an opinion . . . based [on investigative work] and formed if the agent's reasoning process depended, in whole or in part, on his specialized training and experience."

This court recently observed that the First, Second, and Fifth Circuits "have viewed agents' hearsay-laden or hearsay-based overview testimony at the onset of trial as a rather blatant prosecutorial attempt to circumvent hearsay rules." *United States v. Smith,* 640 F.3d 358, 367 (D.C.Cir.2011) (citations omitted). In *Smith,* the defendant was charged with drug and firearm offenses. An FBI agent testified at the start of the trial that Smith and a co-conspirator "were working together putting their money together and going to New York to buy heroin." On appeal, Smith contended that the overview testimony—the single sentence—was based on inadmissible hearsay and thus violated Federal Rules of Evidence ("FRE") 701 and 802. Assuming the same prohibition against inadmissible hearsay testimony by an overview witness applied as in the other circuits, the court concluded that the FBI agent's objected-to single-sentence testimony was not based on otherwise inadmissible hearsay because the underlying statements were either admissions of a party-opponent or co-conspirator statements under FRE 801(d)(2), and if error, was harmless. The court reached the same ultimate conclusion with respect to the agent's lay opinion testimony about the meaning of slang used by Smith and his co-conspirators during recorded conversations; although the lay opinion testimony was inadmissible under FRE 701 because it was based on specialized knowledge gained from working on other drug investigations, the error was harmless because the agent would have qualified as an expert under FRE 702 and offered the same testimony.

The district court is ordinarily afforded broad discretion to determine the manner in which evidence will be received. But in *Lemire,* this court concluded that "the pervasiveness of the[ ] dangers [it had identified with summarization of evidence] requires that we review the use of a summary witness closely." Indeed, it was only "under appropriate circumstances with appropriate instructions" that this court "in the past approved the use of summary witnesses . . . in jury trials." *United States v. Microsoft Corp.,* 253 F.3d 34, 101 (D.C. Cir. 2001). We accordingly review FBI Agent Sparks's overview testimony closely, aware that there was no *voir dire* before his testimony and a limiting instruction was given to the jury only after he completed his testimony, and then only with regard to opinions, not otherwise described, that he may have offered while testifying.

All three dangers identified by this court in *Lemire* are evident from the record in this case: FBI Agent Sparks testified about evidence not yet presented while opining that the cooperating witnesses would present truthful evidence because they were insiders and were guilty themselves, strengthening the government's yet-to-be presented case and offering inadmissible evidence while providing the government with a second opening argument. For example, upon being shown a map of the District of Columbia, FBI Agent Sparks confirmed that the 31 circles located on the map accurately reflected the locations of the 31 charged murders, and that murders clustered in certain locations occurred toward the beginning of the charged conspiracy. But no such evidence was before the jury and FBI Agent Sparks did not purport to testify from personal knowledge of each murder. At other points, FBI Agent Sparks referred to witness testimony that was never presented to the jury during the course of the trial. In one exemplary circumstance, FBI Agent Sparks testified on redirect examination that co-conspirator Erskine Hartwell had described his role in the conspiracy as supplying drugs and introducing Moore and Gray to Oscar Veal. When asked by the district court whether this information was "based on what [Hartwell] told [him]," FBI Agent Sparks agreed, prompting the district court to state: "The jury is going to hear his testimony." Yet when asked only moments later by the prosecutor "if Erskine Hartwell will be a witness in this case or not," FBI Agent Sparks replied that he "d[idn't] know for sure if [Hartwell] will." From portions of the transcript submitted by the parties to this court, there is no indication that Hartwell testified at trial and hence "later testimony . . . differe[d] [from] what the overview witness assumed." *Casas.* The prosecutor thus impermissibly invited the jury to "rely upon the alleged facts in the [overview] as if [those] facts had already been proved." *Griffin,* 324 F.3d at 349.

Likewise, FBI Agent Sparks impermissibly commented on the strength of the government's yet-to-be introduced evidence, vouched for the credibility of witnesses the government intended to call at trial, and gave his per-

sonal opinion as to guilt or innocence. Weighing trial evidence and making
"[d]eterminations of credibility are for the jury," *United States v. Boyd,* 54
F.3d 868, 871 (D.C.Cir.1995), as is "draw[ing] the ultimate conclusion of
guilt or innocence," *United States v. Gaudin,* 515 U.S. 506, 514, 115 S.Ct.
2310, 132 L.Ed.2d 444 (1995). FBI Agent Sparks's testimony crossed the
line in a number of instances. For example, he testified that it was important, in his view, to use cooperating witnesses in this case because it was
"the only way" to gain "access to the inside information." Acknowledging
that cooperating witnesses were "themselves . . . criminals[,] unfortunately," he further testified that the cooperating co-conspirator witnesses nonetheless

> know what's going on, they have the information, they're the eyewit-
> nesses, ear-witnesses, they hear what these guys are talking about af-
> ter they commit a murder, they witness a murder, they know where
> the stash locations are for drugs. . . [T]hey are present when drug
> deals are done. They have been with these people day in and day out,
> and you need that kind of testimony. That's the only way to put these
> kind[s] of cases together.

He also testified that the goal in a debriefing session was to "[g]et [ ] complete and truthful information" and that it was important to "try and verify" the information "[j]ust to make sure the person is truthful, that they are
complete." On redirect examination, FBI Agent Sparks reinforced the notion that the cooperating witnesses were guilty of committing crimes in
their capacity as the defendants' co-conspirators:

> Q: You were asked a lot of questions on cross-examination about coo-
> perating witnesses, and you continually referred to them as criminals.
>
> A: Yes.
>
> Q: Any doubt in your mind about that?
>
> A: None whatsoever.

All of this was opinion testimony that went far beyond "constructing
the sequence of events in the investigation . . . to provide background information and to explain how and why the agents even came to be involved
with [a] particular defendant." *United States v. Flores–de–Jesús,* 569 F.3d
8, 19 (1st Cir.2009). Instead, these statements suggested both directly and
indirectly to the jury that an experienced and highly trained FBI agent had
determined that the cooperating co-conspirators who would testify at trial
were to be treated as credible witnesses and that appellants were guilty of
the charged crimes. The clear implication was that the government had
selected only truthful co-conspirator witnesses for the pre-indictment investigation, from whom the jury would hear during the trial.

In sum, FBI Agent Sparks's testimony was improper in offering his non-expert opinions about the charged conspiracy and appellants, vouching for the reliability of the investigation and of the cooperating co-conspirator witnesses the government planned to have testify at trial, and discussing evidence that had yet to be introduced. Given the dearth of taped conversations and videotaped evidence—none as to Moore—and almost exclusive reliance on co-conspirator cooperators' testimony, the government understandably might seek at the outset to enhance its case in the jury's mind with the imprimatur of an FBI agent. But the prosecutor went too far in questioning, allowing FBI Agent Sparks to act as an expert witness with respect to gang investigations and to refer to evidence that would never be introduced at trial. The district court, in turn, failed to sustain appropriate defense objections to FBI Agent Sparks's testimony that purported to offer opinion testimony and to confirm government evidence that had yet to be introduced.

. . . As the record here demonstrates, a trained law enforcement officer is likely to go as far as the questions allow, presenting a picture for the jury of a solid prosecution case based on his opinion of the strength and credibility of the witnesses the government plans to call to testify at trial for reasons made persuasive in view of the officer's training and experience. After-the-fact limiting instructions can, at best, mitigate prejudice, rather than invariably eliminate its effects completely. The view of the government's case has been implanted in the mind of the jury by an agent of the Federal Bureau of Investigation who worked on the case—he should know!

The government remains free to call as its first witness a law enforcement officer who is familiar with the pre-indictment investigation or was otherwise personally involved, where permissible under the Rules of Evidence and consistent with constitutional guarantees. Such a witness may, for example, be able to provide relevant background information as to the investigation's duration and scope or the methods of surveillance, based on personal knowledge. Put another way, a law enforcement officer may "describe a complicated government program in terms that do not address witness credibility," but he may not offer "tendentious testimony." *Griffin*, 324 F.3d at 349. Thus, FBI Agent Sparks could properly describe, based on his personal knowledge, how the gang investigation in this case was initiated, what law enforcement entities were involved, and what investigative techniques were used. What he could not do was present lay opinion testimony about investigative techniques in general and opine on what generally works and what does not, as illustrated by informants who pled guilty. Neither could he anticipate evidence that the government would hope to introduce at trial about the charged offenses or express an opinion, directly or indirectly, about the strength of that evidence or the credibility of any of the government's potential witnesses, including the cooperating co-conspirators.

Although the question is close, we conclude for the following reasons that the prejudice resulting from the admission of FBI Agent Sparks's overview testimony, to the extent it was inappropriate, was ameliorated: (1) Each instance of FBI Agent Sparks's improper testimony identified by appellants was later confirmed by admissible evidence at trial. (2) Appellants' defense was limited to cross-examining testifying cooperating coconspirators and other government witnesses. (3) The district court instructed at the conclusion of FBI Agent Sparks's testimony in the government's case-in-chief that the jury was to disregard any opinion testimony he offered. (4) There was overwhelming evidence of appellants' guilt. And as to some of his impermissible opinion testimony, FBI Agent Sparks might have qualified as an expert. Accordingly, the error did not "affect[ ] the outcome of the district court proceeding [ ]," *United States v. Sumlin,* 271 F.3d 274, 281 (D.C.Cir.2001), and hence appellants are not entitled to reversal of their convictions because of improper overview testimony by FBI Agent Sparks.

The inauspicious beginning of the government's case-in-chief is easily avoided in the future... [T]his court's long-held view of the purpose of the opening statement to the jury, namely to allow the prosecutor the opportunity to provide the jury with an objective overview of the evidence that the government intends to introduce at trial, has long afforded the prosecutor the opportunity to do that for which the prosecutor improperly used FBI Agent Sparks. This court now having made clear the exacerbated "obvious dangers" of the overview witness testifying about evidence yet to be admitted before the jury affords all parties clear direction to avoid unnecessary risks—for the prosecutor of an overturned conviction, for the defense of an unfair trial, and for the district court of having to retry a case. ***

United States v. Kristiansen

United States Court of Appeals, Eighth Circuit, 1990.
901 F.2d 1463.

■ HEANEY, SENIOR CIRCUIT JUDGE.

Kolby Kristiansen appeals from his conviction for escape from a halfway house facility. He raises two challenges to the conduct of the trial. First, the district court improperly excluded defense questions to an expert under Rule 704(b) while allowing prosecution questions that should have been excluded under the same rule. Second, the prosecution's closing argument was improper. We affirm.

I.

Kolby Kristiansen was transferred to a halfway house on April 18, 1988, prior to an anticipated release from confinement. On June 1, 1988, Kristiansen called the halfway house and informed them that he was sick and unable to return that night. He was told to keep them informed. He called again each of the next two days indicating that he was still ill. He was told to come back in and the authorities would help him get treatment. He failed to do so. On June 6, he was arrested by United States marshals outside his wife's residence. He was charged with escaping from custody. 18 U.S.C.A. § 751(a) (Supp.1990).

The defense's theory at trial was that Kristiansen was not guilty because he lacked, by reason of mental disease or defect, the willful intent to escape. The defense expert, Dr. Knowles, diagnosed Kristiansen as a cocaine addict and testified that Kristiansen had indicated that he was under the influence of cocaine at the time he failed to return. Dr. Knowles also testified that Kristiansen was suffering from psychosis, which can cause an individual to fail to appreciate the wrongfulness of their actions.

The prosecution called several witnesses to refute the defense theory. Kristiansen's counselor at the halfway house and a marshal who arrested him testified that they detected no evidence of alcohol or drug use in their encounters with Kristiansen. A second marshal testified that Kristiansen said that "he could have really stayed hidden out or on the run a lot longer if he didn't care for his family." Two expert witnesses for the government testified that Kristiansen had a history of drug abuse but both concluded that he was not delusional. The jury found Kristiansen guilty of escape.

II.

Federal Rule of Evidence 704(b) prohibits mental health experts from offering an opinion as to whether the defendant possessed the required mental state at the time of their crime. During direct examination, the defense attempted to ask Dr. Knowles: "Now, would an individual—would this severe mental disease or defect, which you've testified Mr. Kristiansen has, if an individual has that, affect the individual's ability to appreciate the nature and quality of the wrongfulness of his acts?" The court sustained the prosecution's objection because it felt that including the word "would" in the question asked for an answer that reached the ultimate issue. The defense also wanted to ask Dr. Knowles: "Dr. Knowles, do you have an opinion whether at the time of the commission of the alleged offense in this case, the defendant's judgment was so severely impaired as to render him incapable of appreciating the nature, quality and wrongfulness of his act?" [Trial transcript] at 94–95 (offer of proof). The court did not allow this question. The defense was allowed to ask, however, "Doctor, could the severe mental disease or defect that you have testified with regard to, could that affect the ability of an individual to appreciate the nature or the quality or the wrongfulness of his acts?"

Dr. Knowles also testified that Kristiansen exhibited antisocial behavior. The prosecution asked on cross-examination of Dr. Knowles what antisocial behavior involved. Dr. Knowles indicated that it consisted of a lack of conscience and added, without being prompted:

Because they are under no compunction to do right or to choose not to do wrong because they don't have that monitoring system that we all possess. So society treats them as being responsible for their behavior because they fail the test that the law has, they don't constitute the type of insanity or psychosis that constitutes a defense but they lack a very significant element of a normal functioning mind, so a sociopath will go through life leaving a path of waste and devastation behind him and yet he is [sic] wholly accountable because he lacks that single element of conscience that saves us from the same tragic consequences.

The prosecution followed up by asking: "So he is legally accountable for his acts as a sociopath?" A. "He is." Defense counsel did not object. During redirect, counsel asked the court if Knowles could be asked the previously disallowed defense questions in light of the cross-examination testimony. He argued that the door had been opened, but the court denied the request without explanation.

We review evidentiary rulings under the abuse of discretion standard. We have interpreted Rule 704(b) to exclude testimony that "specifically comments on the presence or absence of an element of the crime charged, . . . too conclusory to be helpful to the jury." United States v. Gipson, 862 F.2d 714, 716 (8th Cir.1988). We concluded that the trial court in Gipson properly excluded the question, " 'did [Gipson] have the requisite mental state to have willfully or intentionally attempted to escape,' " because it asked "for a mere legal conclusion." We approved asking the expert whether the defendant was suffering from a mental disease or defect at the time the crime was committed. Similarly, in United States v. Dubray, 854 F.2d 1099 (8th Cir.1988), we permitted a doctor to testify that the defendant was not suffering from psychosis at the time of the offense. We reasoned that this testimony related to the defendant's mental state which "has definite implications for the determination of Dubray's legal sanity," but that it did not state a legal conclusion "and did not state an opinion whether Dubray was able to appreciate the wrongfulness of his actions."

Under *Gipson* and *Dubray*, the defense clearly could ask whether Kristiansen was suffering from a mental disease or defect at the time of the offense. Just as clearly, the defense could not ask whether Kristiansen was unable to appreciate the nature and quality of his actions. The question the defense asked in its offer of proof was thus properly excluded. The more difficult question is whether the court erred in not permitting the defense to ask whether the mental disease or defect of the type that Kristiansen allegedly had would affect a person's ability to appreciate their actions.

We conclude that the defense should have been permitted to ask this question because it relates to the symptoms and qualities of the disease itself and does not call for an answer that describes Kristiansen's culpability at the time of the crime. Rule 704(b) was not meant to prohibit testimony that describes the qualities of a mental disease. "Under this proposal, expert psychiatric testimony would be limited to presenting and explaining their diagnoses, such as whether the defendant had a severe mental disease or defect and what the characteristics of such a disease or defect, if any, may have been." Comprehensive Crime Control Act of 1984, S.Rep. No. 225, 98th Cong., 2d Sess. 230 (1984). The fact that part of the wording of a question may track the legal test by asking if the disease prevents one suffering from the disease from understanding the nature and quality of an act does not violate the rule. The jury is left to ultimately decide whether the disease was so strongly present that the defendant himself suffered the effect of being unable to appreciate the quality of his act.

The court's error, however, was not prejudicial. The defense was permitted to ask if the mental condition Kristiansen allegedly suffered from "could" cause him to fail to appreciate the nature and quality of his actions. This question is sufficiently close in effect to a question substituting the word "would" that the court's error plainly did not affect the jury's decision. The defense was allowed to elicit testimony that Kristiansen suffered from a mental disease or defect and that the same type of disease or defect could affect his cognitive abilities.

The prosecution's questioning of Dr. Knowles presents a different problem. Asking the doctor if Kristiansen is legally accountable is clearly prohibited by Rule 704(b). Because the defense counsel did not object to this question or to his own witness' voluntary discourse on legal conclusions, we must decide only if it was error for the court not to overrule its previous decision preceding the defense's offer of proof and to allow the defense also to ask a question in violation of Rule 704(b). We hold that it was not error.

The defense counsel made a strategic choice to forego objecting to the prosecution's question and to his witness' testimony in the hopes that the court would allow him the same latitude. Counsel erred. The purpose of Rule 704(b) is to prevent a jury adjudicating an insanity claim from becoming thoroughly confused by medical experts' testimony about the ultimate legal issues. Senate Report at 223, 231. The proper course for the defense was to object to the prosecution's question rather than trying to use it as grounds for further violations of the rule. The district court has an obligation to minimize violations of the rules and was not required to even the playing field where no objection was made. The trial court could properly conclude that granting the request by the defense would be more prejudicial than helpful. Cf. Fed.R.Evid. 403. * * *

REPRISE: "FIGHTING FIRE WITH FIRE"

Recall an issue addressed in an excerpt from McCormick on Evidence presented at pages 106–108:* When a party puts in evidence that is inad-

---

* See also Roger C. Park, David. P. Leonard, Aviva Orenstein, and Steven H. Goldberg, EVIDENCE LAW 29–34 (3d ed. 2011).

missible, the opposing party may claim a right to fight back by putting in
counter-evidence that itself would normally be inadmissible. For example,
if a defendant blurts out an unsolicited assertion that he has never been
arrested, the door would be open for the opposing party to "fight fire with
fire" by putting in evidence of arrests.

In many situations, courts have held that the party who originally put
in the forbidden evidence has forfeited its objection to the opponent's counter-evidence and that the opponent may use otherwise inadmissible evidence to reduce the harm. However, if the opposing party had an opportunity to prevent the harm by making an objection and failed to object, the
trial judge may deny the opportunity to "fight fire with fire." Even if the
opposing party did object, the trial judge might exclude the opponent's
counter-evidence if the opponent was not very much harmed by the evidence and counter-evidence would be confusing and a waste of time. As
usual in evidence law, the trial court has broad discretion and will not
usually be reversed on appeal, whether it allows retaliation or not.

HYPOTHETICAL

P was injured by using a power rotary lawn mower manufactured by D
Mfg. Company. P sues D for damages, claiming that the lawn mower was defectively designed. P calls E, an expert on lawn mowers, to testify that the lawn
mower was defectively designed. E states that his opinion is based on (1) articles published in Reader's Digest, Today's Health and consumer-bulletin
magazines discussing the great number of injuries occurring from the use of
rotary power lawn mowers, and (2) statistical surveys on the same subject in a
book entitled, "Accidental Injuries Associated with Rotary Lawn Mowers," published by a department of the federal government. D moves to strike E's testimony on the ground that it is based on improper hearsay matter. The trial
judge denies D's motion. Is this a proper ruling?

B. SCIENTIFIC AND DEMONSTRATIVE EVIDENCE

The Case Against Expert Witnesses

by Walter Olson.
Fortune, September 25, 1989, 135–36, 138.*

Within the thriving business of suing people—what you might call the
disservice sector of the American economy—expert witnesses occupy a fast-
growing and controversial niche. Hardly a liability suit goes forward without an engineer or a doctor swearing that the product was misdesigned, or
the injury devastating, or the hospital negligent. The other side then calls
its expert to say the exact opposite. Both get paid handsomely.

Courts have always relied on expertise in one form or other. But sweeping changes in federal rules of evidence in the mid–1970s vastly widened the definition of an expert—and what that person can talk about. Says Jack Weinstein, a federal judge in Brooklyn: "An expert can be found to testify to the truth of almost any theory, no matter how frivolous." Unlike other witnesses, experts freely give opinions and can speak in the language of legal conclusions: "In my professional opinion, this was a clear case of malpractice." They are allowed to base their comments on evidence that for other witnesses would be inadmissible as hearsay. And they often make a big hit with juries.

No field is out of the experts' reach. Going through a nasty divorce? A forensic accountant will sketch a dazzlingly prosperous future for your spouse's business. Caught skimming the till? A hired psychologist will arouse sympathy with the jury by calling you a hapless victim of compulsive gambling syndrome. Your son was dropped from his college basketball team because of poor grades? A self-styled sportsologist can swear that if not for this unfairness Kevin could have earned $1 million a year with the pros.

A lively business has sprung up to bring lawyers and experts together. One of the biggest referral firms, Medical–Legal Consulting Service Inc. of Bethesda, Maryland, says it has 600 experts on call. If the first doctor it refers doesn't agree with your lawyer's theory on the case, the company promises to send over a second one free. Another firm, Medical Quality Foundation of Herndon, Virginia, has offered seminars on how lawyers can increase the size of jury awards. The referral services, and individual experts, put out colorful brochures listing the areas in which they can testify.

Exuberant ads in the back of *Trial* magazine, which is published by the Association of Trial Lawyers of America, tell the tale. One, headed "Heavyweight Malpractice Experts," features a photo of a man in a white clinical coat wearing boxing gloves. Other experts specialize in mishaps involving utility poles and so-called sport surfaces. Some ex-cops are eager to help in the growing area of "negligent security"—suits against the supermarket in whose parking lot you were assaulted, or the bank at whose automated cash machine you were robbed. "The more measured and impartial an expert is, the less likely he is to be used by either side," writes Professor John Langbein of the University of Chicago law school, who has himself testified. If the conscientious outsider resists the subtle pressure to get on the team by shading his opinions, he may not be called back. There seem to be plenty of willing replacements.

Experts in most demand are those with the surface polish that comes from previous trial combat. The more you appear in court, the more chances you get to appear again, picking up what you might call frequent-testifier bonus points. Counting in fees for strategy sessions, out-of-court appearances, and the like, just a few big cases may bring more to a professor than he normally makes in a year. If he or his consulting firm can swing a contingency deal—getting a share of the jury's award—the pay can be huge.

Hence the rise of the professional witness. "You see the same experts again and again around the country," says Arvin Maskin, a New York lawyer who helped defend the Agent Orange case for the U.S. government. Howard Balensweig, a semiretired Manhattan physician who spends much of his time as an expert in injury cases, says he averages $3,500 for a day in court and $2,500 for half a day.

Lawyers for Merrell Dow Pharmaceuticals have grown quite familiar with Dr. Alan K. Done, a Salt Lake City physician and toxicologist who travels around the country testifying that Bendectin, the company's anti-morning sickness drug, has caused or contributed to birth defects. Merrell Dow sends in mainstream experts of its own by the vanload, and usually wins. The Food and Drug Administration has approved Bendectin, stating specifically that it does not increase the risk of birth defects. The World Health Organization, which acts only in an advisory capacity to member countries, basically supports the FDA conclusion.

But when the occasional jury goes along with Dr. Done, the damages can be huge, $95 million in the case of one child. The judge rejected $75 million of that award. Other judgments against Merrell Dow keep getting thrown out by judges at trial or on appeal; federal judge Thomas Penfield Jackson cited the "now nearly universal scientific consensus" on the drug's safety. Still, because of the expense of litigation, Merrell Dow has stopped selling it.

The expert needn't convince; he does well to confuse. If even the pros can't seem to agree, the side with the weaker factual case at least manages to stay in the game. When a bewildered jury decides that the chemistry or geology or economics of the case must be just a matter of opinion, it will often follow its other instincts—especially the natural impulse to compensate a hardluck litigant at the expense of someone with money.

Among the claims that arouse the most sympathy in jurors are those of illness caused by pollution. In a typical pattern, neighbors of some chemical or nuclear facility come to court complaining that the plant has caused various ailments. Establishing a direct link between low-level toxins and specific illnesses has been difficult if not impossible. So the litigants, backed by their lawyers and a growing group of experts-for-hire, have developed a marvelously elastic theory: Pollution can suppress the immune system. Thus, it can be blamed for a wide range of common ailments from diabetes to learning problems, gallstones to hearing loss, depression to measles.

The experts—who call themselves clinical ecologists, practitioners of environmental medicine, or immunologists—aver that even minute exposures to man-made chemicals or radiation can alter the immune system.

The American Academy of Allergy and Immunology has repudiated the theory, as has the California Medical Association. Still, it plays well with juries. Yale law professor E. Donald Elliott says it has "dramatically changed the strategic balance in toxic tort cases."

A judge ordered Velsicol Chemical Co. to pay $22 million to a group of Toone, Tennessee, residents who claimed to have been harmed by leaks from a company landfill. Dr. Alan Levin, a San Francisco physician who treats AIDS patients, said of the plaintiffs: "In my opinion, their immune systems will never recover." (An appeals court later reversed part of the award and Velsicol settled the case, along with some other damage claims, for about $10 million.)

In a case brought by a group of Sedalia, Missouri, residents against Alcolac Inc., Arthur C. Zahalsky, who has a Ph.D. in microbiology and teaches immunology at Southern Illinois University, said several of the residents were suffering from "chemically induced AIDS," a dramatic malady unrecognized by mainstream science. The jury awarded $49 million in damages. The judge later set aside the ruling and ordered a new trial to recalculate damages. But the verdict of liability against Alcolac was allowed to stand by the Missouri Supreme Court. The company has asked the U.S. Supreme Court to review the case.

According to a court document, Zahalsky has no graduate credits in immunology, but he points out that such courses were not given when he went to school in the 1960s. He says he later audited courses in immunology at Washington University in St. Louis.

Questionable science used to be excluded on principle from the courtroom. Under the so-called Frye rule, named for a 1923 case, expert testimony could be admitted only if the scientific methods behind its conclusions would pass muster with most of those active in a particular field. The problem: What was a field, and who was active? Also, the courts in their caution tended to lag behind developments in forensic science.

Criticism intensified in the 1960s. Wasn't it elitist to insist on paper credentials before letting someone testify? What if the witness wanting to speak his piece, whose training had come in the school of hard knocks, turned out to be the next Galileo? Why waste time on what one court later dismissed as "scientific nose-counting"?

In 1975 Congress enacted new liberalized rules of evidence, and most states followed suit. Now all it takes to be an expert in many courts is a call from a lawyer. Trials filled with self-described accidentologists with coffee-pot-to-railroad-car expertise, human factor engineers, measurers and calibrators of workplace emotional trauma and post-one-thing-and-another-syndrome, and more. By no means are all these folks charlatans; many say perfectly commonsensical things in court. But in so doing they can add an aura of scientific authority to propositions ("It hurts to get fired") that juries could grasp on their own.

The let-it-all-in trend may have peaked in 1984 when the federal appeals court in Washington suggested that as long as a scientific proposition with very thin support had not been palpably disproved, it might be best to send it to a jury for a vote. But a reaction was already afoot. A federal judge in Kansas threw out a radiation claim based on testimony he felt the experts "would not dare report in a peer-reviewed format." Then Judge Weinstein in Brooklyn dismissed the remainder of the Agent Orange cases, saying the expert affidavits claiming to prove connections between various illnesses and use of the herbicide were just too flimsy. (Cold comfort for seven chemical companies that had already agreed to spring for $180 million to settle claims with a more or less identical basis.)

An even clearer call to action came in 1986 from federal appeals judge Patrick Higginbotham of Dallas, often mentioned as a future Supreme Court nominee. A Pan Am flight had crashed in New Orleans and lawyers were having the inevitable, ghoulish argument over what each passenger's death was worth. An economist hired by a bereaved family declared that a young man's struggling business had been headed for tremendous success: His after-inflation income would have climbed year after year in an unbroken line for the next 40 years, yet he would have found ways to keep his tax rate down to a thrifty 5%. And so members of his family lost $1,778,873 as their hypothetical inheritance (they were already on their way to an initial award from Pan Am of $3 million for other kinds of damages). Higginbotham called the economist's figures "completely airborne" and called for a new trial. "It is time," he said, "to take hold of expert testimony in federal trials."

More and more of his colleagues on the bench seem to agree. Two appeals decisions have recently backed the dismissal of Bendectin verdicts on scientific grounds; one was written by Judge Spottswood Robinson III, a Lyndon Johnson appointee from the D.C. circuit's liberal wing. In overturning the immune damage award against Velsicol based largely on Dr. Levin's testimony, another appeals court noted that leading professional societies "have rejected clinical ecology as an unproven methodology lacking any scientific base in either fact or theory." What Georgetown law professor Paul Rothstein calls the strict scrutiny faction among judges is fast gaining ground.

Plaintiffs' lawyers object to this know-it-when-I-see-it judicial approach to bad science. They also oppose tighter laws of evidence or some kind of modern Frye rule. They argue that thorough cross-examination is protection enough against the roving jack-of-all-testimony. New York lawyer Paul Rheingold ruefully recalls what happened when he brought in an all-purpose expert to opine on the supposedly defective design of a motorcycle. The defendant's attorney rose and asked: Didn't the witness also testify in auto cases? Yes. And ladder cases? On the attorney went, ticking off specialties from the expert's promotional brochure—glass, fires, TVs, explosions? Yes, yes, yes, yes—by which point the jury might not have believed the expert if he had told them the time of day.

The lawyers have a point: Cross-examination can be a good defense. The American Corporate Counsel Institute has begun keeping a database of hostile expert testimony so defendants can better expose weaknesses as cases accumulate.

Broader reform is clearly needed. Imperfect though it is, some sort of peer review is the ultimate answer. Juries deserve to know whether what they are being told would get a witness laughed out of an ordinary lab or hospital. To rely on judges' instincts about the validity of expert testimony is both not enough and too much. Courts may not be ready to return to the discipline symbolized by the Frye rule, but there are alternatives. Elliott of Yale suggests that dubious testimony could be countered by a court-appointed expert who would explain what mainstream practitioners of that particular branch of science might think of the witness's theories.

Since junk science has made companies so vulnerable to all kinds of claims, American business has everything to gain by ousting it from the courtroom. And the public at large could begin to regain some of its former confidence in the justice system. Cynical lawyers call their experts saxophones because they can be played with such virtuosity. Let's hope the brassier ones are muted before long.

Langbein, The German Advantage in Civil Procedure

52 U.Chi.L.Rev. 823, 835–36 (1985).[*]

The European jurist who visits the United States and becomes acquainted with our civil procedure typically expresses amazement at our witness practice. His amazement turns to something bordering on disbelief when he discovers that we extend the sphere of partisan control to the selection and preparation of experts. In the Continental tradition experts are selected and commissioned by the court, although with great attention to safeguarding party interests. In the German system, experts are not even called witnesses. They are thought of as "judges' aides."

Perverse incentives. At the American trial bar, those of us who serve as expert witnesses are known as "saxophones." This is a revealing term, as slang often is. The idea is that the lawyer plays the tune, manipulating the expert as though the expert were a musical instrument on which the lawyer sounds the desired notes. I sometimes serve as an expert in trust and pension cases, and I have experienced the subtle pressures to join the

---

[*] Copyright © 1985 by University of Chicago Law Review.

team—to shade one's views, to conceal doubt, to overstate nuance, to downplay weak aspects of the case that one has been hired to bolster. Nobody likes to disappoint a patron; and beyond this psychological pressure is the financial inducement. Money changes hands upon the rendering of expertise, but the expert can run his meter only so long as his patron litigator likes the tune. Opposing counsel undertakes a similar exercise, hiring and schooling another expert to parrot the contrary position. The result is our familiar battle of opposing experts. The more measured and impartial an expert is, the less likely he is to be used by either side.

At trial, the battle of experts tends to baffle the trier, especially in jury courts. If the experts do not cancel each other out, the advantage is likely to be with the expert whose forensic skills are the more enticing. The system invites abusive cross-examination. Since each expert is party-selected and party-paid, he is vulnerable to attack on credibility regardless of the merits of his testimony. A defense lawyer recently bragged about his technique of cross-examining plaintiffs' experts in tort cases. Notice that nothing in his strategy varies with the truthfulness of the expert testimony he tries to discredit:

> A mode of attack ripe with potential is to pursue a line of questions which, by their form and the jury's studied observation of the witness in response, will tend to cast the expert as a "professional witness." By proceeding in this way, the cross-examiner will reap the benefit of a community attitude, certain to be present among several of the jurors, that bias can be purchased, almost like a commodity.

Thus, the systematic incentive in our procedure to distort expertise leads to a systematic distrust and devaluation of expertise. Short of forbidding the use of experts altogether, we probably could not have designed a procedure better suited to minimize the influence of expertise.

Daubert v. Merrell Dow Pharmaceuticals, Inc.

Supreme Court of the United States, 1993.
509 U.S. 579.

■ JUSTICE BLACKMUN delivered the opinion of the Court.

In this case we are called upon to determine the standard for admitting expert scientific testimony in a federal trial.

I

Petitioners Jason Daubert and Eric Schuller are minor children born with serious birth defects. They and their parents sued respondent in California state court, alleging that the birth defects had been caused by the mothers' ingestion of Bendectin, a prescription anti-nausea drug marketed by respondent. Respondent removed the suits to federal court on diversity grounds.

After extensive discovery, respondent moved for summary judgment, contending that Bendectin does not cause birth defects in humans and that petitioners would be unable to come forward with any admissible evidence that it does. In support of its motion, respondent submitted an affidavit of Steven H. Lamm, physician and epidemiologist, who is a well-credentialed expert on the risks from exposure to various chemical substances. Doctor Lamm stated that he had reviewed all the literature on Bendectin and human birth defects—more than 30 published studies involving over 130,000 patients. No study had found Bendectin to be a human teratogen (i.e., a substance capable of causing malformations in fetuses). On the basis of this review, Doctor Lamm concluded that maternal use of Bendectin during the first trimester of pregnancy has not been shown to be a risk factor for human birth defects.

Petitioners did not (and do not) contest this characterization of the published record regarding Bendectin. Instead, they responded to respondent's motion with the testimony of eight experts of their own, each of whom also possessed impressive credentials. These experts had concluded that Bendectin can cause birth defects. Their conclusions were based upon "in vitro" (test tube) and "in vivo" (live) animal studies that found a link between Bendectin and malformations; pharmacological studies of the chemical structure of Bendectin that purported to show similarities between the structure of the drug and that of other substances known to cause birth defects; and the "reanalysis" of previously published epidemiological (human statistical) studies.

The District Court granted respondent's motion for summary judgment. The court stated that scientific evidence is admissible only if the principle upon which it is based is " 'sufficiently established to have general acceptance in the field to which it belongs.' " The court concluded that petitioners' evidence did not meet this standard. Given the vast body of epidemiological data concerning Bendectin, the court held, expert opinion which is not based on epidemiological evidence is not admissible to establish causation. Thus, the animal-cell studies, live-animal studies, and chemical-structure analyses on which petitioners had relied could not raise by themselves a reasonably disputable jury issue regarding causation. Petitioners' epidemiological analyses, based as they were on recalculations of data in previously published studies that had found no causal link between the drug and birth defects, were ruled to be inadmissible because they had not been published or subjected to peer review.

The United States Court of Appeals for the Ninth Circuit affirmed. Citing Frye v. United States, 54 App.D.C. 46, 47, 293 F. 1013, 1014 (1923), the court stated that expert opinion based on a scientific technique is inadmissible unless the technique is "generally accepted" as reliable in the relevant scientific community. The court declared that expert opinion based on a methodology that diverges "significantly from the procedures accepted by recognized authorities in the field . . . cannot be shown to be 'generally accepted as a reliable technique.' "

The court emphasized that other Courts of Appeals considering the risks of Bendectin had refused to admit reanalyses of epidemiological studies that had been neither published nor subjected to peer review. Those courts had found unpublished reanalyses "particularly problematic in light of the massive weight of the original published studies supporting [respondent's] position, all of which had undergone full scrutiny from the scientific community." Contending that reanalysis is generally accepted by the scientific community only when it is subjected to verification and scrutiny by others in the field, the Court of Appeals rejected petitioners' reanalyses as "unpublished, not subjected to the normal peer review process and generated solely for use in litigation." The court concluded that petitioners' evidence provided an insufficient foundation to allow admission of expert testimony that Bendectin caused their injuries and, accordingly, that petitioners could not satisfy their burden of proving causation at trial.We granted certiorari in light of sharp divisions among the courts regarding the proper standard for the admission of expert testimony. * * *

II

A

In the 70 years since its formulation in the *Frye* case, the "general acceptance" test has been the dominant standard for determining the admissibility of novel scientific evidence at trial. Although under increasing attack of late, the rule continues to be followed by a majority of courts, including the Ninth Circuit.

The *Frye* test has its origin in a short and citation-free 1923 decision concerning the admissibility of evidence derived from a systolic blood pressure deception test, a crude precursor to the polygraph machine. In what has become a famous (perhaps infamous) passage, the then Court of Appeals for the District of Columbia described the device and its operation and declared:

"Just when a scientific principle or discovery crosses the line between the experimental and demonstrable stages is difficult to define. Somewhere in this twilight zone the evidential force of the principle must be recognized, and while courts will go a long way in admitting expert testimony deduced from a well-recognized scientific principle or discovery, *the thing from which the deduction is made must be sufficiently established to have gained general acceptance in the particular field in which it belongs.*" (emphasis added).

Because the deception test had "not yet gained such standing and scientific recognition among physiological and psychological authorities as would justify the courts in admitting expert testimony deduced from the discovery, development, and experiments thus far made," evidence of its results was ruled inadmissible.

The merits of the *Frye* test have been much debated, and scholarship on its proper scope and application is legion. Petitioners' primary attack, however, is not on the content but on the continuing authority of the rule. They contend that the *Frye* test was superseded by the adoption of the Federal Rules of Evidence. We agree.

We interpret the legislatively-enacted Federal Rules of Evidence as we would any statute. Rule 402 provides the baseline:

> "All relevant evidence is admissible, except as otherwise provided by the Constitution of the United States, by Act of Congress, by these rules, or by other rules prescribed by the Supreme Court pursuant to statutory authority. Evidence which is not relevant is not admissible."

"Relevant evidence" is defined as that which has "any tendency to make the existence of any fact that is of consequence to the determination of the action more probable or less probable than it would be without the evidence." Rule 401. The Rule's basic standard of relevance thus is a liberal one.

Frye, of course, predated the Rules by half a century. In United States v. Abel, 469 U.S. 45 (1984), we considered the pertinence of background common law in interpreting the Rules of Evidence. We noted that the Rules occupy the field, but, quoting Professor Cleary, the Reporter, explained that the common law nevertheless could serve as an aid to their application:

> "In principle, under the Federal Rules no common law of evidence remains. 'All relevant evidence is admissible, except as otherwise provided * * *.' In reality, of course, the body of common law knowledge continues to exist, though in the somewhat altered form of a source of guidance in the exercise of delegated powers."

We found the common-law precept at issue in the Abel case entirely consistent with Rule 402's general requirement of admissibility, and considered it unlikely that the drafters had intended to change the rule. In Bourjaily v. United States, 483 U.S. 171 (1987), on the other hand, the Court was unable to find a particular common-law doctrine in the Rules, and so held it superseded.

Here there is a specific Rule that speaks to the contested issue. Rule 702, governing expert testimony, provides:

"If scientific, technical, or other specialized knowledge will assist the trier of fact to understand the evidence or to determine a fact in issue, a witness qualified as an expert by knowledge, skill, experience, training, or education, may testify thereto in the form of an opinion or otherwise."

Nothing in the text of this Rule establishes "general acceptance" as an absolute prerequisite to admissibility. Nor does respondent present any clear indication that Rule 702 or the Rules as a whole were intended to incorporate a "general acceptance" standard. The drafting history makes no mention of Frye, and a rigid "general acceptance" requirement would be at odds with the "liberal thrust" of the Federal Rules and their "general approach of relaxing the traditional barriers to 'opinion' testimony." Beech Aircraft Corp. v. Rainey, 488 U.S., at 169 (citing Rules 701 to 705). See also Weinstein, Rule 702 of the Federal Rules of Evidence is Sound; It Should Not Be Amended, 138 F.R.D. 631, 631 (1991) ("The Rules were designed to depend primarily upon lawyer-adversaries and sensible triers of fact to evaluate conflicts"). Given the Rules' permissive backdrop and their inclusion of a specific rule on expert testimony that does not mention "general acceptance," the assertion that the Rules somehow assimilated Frye is unconvincing. Frye made "general acceptance" the exclusive test for admitting expert scientific testimony. That austere standard, absent from and incompatible with the Federal Rules of Evidence, should not be applied in federal trials.

B

That the Frye test was displaced by the Rules of Evidence does not mean, however, that the Rules themselves place no limits on the admissibility of purportedly scientific evidence. Nor is the trial judge disabled from screening such evidence. To the contrary, under the Rules the trial judge must ensure that any and all scientific testimony or evidence admitted is not only relevant, but reliable.

The primary locus of this obligation is Rule 702, which clearly contemplates some degree of regulation of the subjects and theories about which an expert may testify. "If *scientific,* technical, or other specialized *knowledge will assist the trier of fact* to understand the evidence or to determine a fact in issue" an expert "may testify *thereto.*" The subject of an expert's testimony must be "scientific * * * knowledge."[8] The adjective "scientific" implies a grounding in the methods and procedures of science. Similarly, the word "knowledge" connotes more than subjective belief or unsupported speculation. The term "applies to any body of known facts or to any body of ideas inferred from such facts or accepted as truths on good grounds." Webster's Third New International Dictionary 1252 (1986). Of course, it would

---

[8] Rule 702 also applies to "technical, or other specialized knowledge." Our discussion is limited to the scientific context because that is the nature of the expertise offered here.

be unreasonable to conclude that the subject of scientific testimony must be "known" to a certainty; arguably, there are no certainties in science. See, e.g., Brief for Nicolaas Bloembergen et al. as Amici Curiae 9 ("Indeed, scientists do not assert that they know what is immutably 'true'—they are committed to searching for new, temporary theories to explain, as best they can, phenomena"); Brief for American Association for the Advancement of Science and the National Academy of Sciences as Amici Curiae 7–8 ("Science is not an encyclopedic body of knowledge about the universe. Instead, it represents a *process* for proposing and refining theoretical explanations about the world that are subject to further testing and refinement") (emphasis in original). But, in order to qualify as "scientific knowledge," an inference or assertion must be derived by the scientific method. Proposed testimony must be supported by appropriate validation—i.e., "good grounds," based on what is known. In short, the requirement that an expert's testimony pertain to "scientific knowledge" establishes a standard of evidentiary reliability.

Rule 702 further requires that the evidence or testimony "assist the trier of fact to understand the evidence or to determine a fact in issue." This condition goes primarily to relevance. "Expert testimony which does not relate to any issue in the case is not relevant and, ergo, non-helpful." 3 Weinstein & Berger ¶ 702[02], p. 702–18. See also United States v. Downing, 753 F.2d 1224, 1242 (C.A.3 1985) ("An additional consideration under Rule 702—and another aspect of relevancy—is whether expert testimony proffered in the case is sufficiently tied to the facts of the case that it will aid the jury in resolving a factual dispute"). The consideration has been aptly described by Judge Becker as one of "fit." "Fit" is not always obvious, and scientific validity for one purpose is not necessarily scientific validity for other, unrelated purposes. The study of the phases of the moon, for example, may provide valid scientific "knowledge" about whether a certain night was dark, and if darkness is a fact in issue, the knowledge will assist the trier of fact. However (absent creditable grounds supporting such a link), evidence that the moon was full on a certain night will not assist the trier of fact in determining whether an individual was unusually likely to have behaved irrationally on that night. Rule 702's "helpfulness" standard requires a valid scientific connection to the pertinent inquiry as a precondition to admissibility.

That these requirements are embodied in Rule 702 is not surprising. Unlike an ordinary witness, see Rule 701, an expert is permitted wide latitude to offer opinions, including those that are not based on first-hand knowledge or observation. See Rules 702 and 703. Presumably, this relaxation of the usual requirement of first-hand knowledge—a rule which represents "a 'most pervasive manifestation' of the common law insistence upon 'the most reliable sources of information,'" Advisory Committee's Notes on Fed.Rule Evid. 602 (citation omitted)—is premised on an assumption that the expert's opinion will have a reliable basis in the knowledge and experience of his discipline.

C

Faced with a proffer of expert scientific testimony, then, the trial judge must determine at the outset, pursuant to Rule 104(a), whether the expert is proposing to testify to (1) scientific knowledge that (2) will assist the trier of fact to understand or determine a fact in issue. This entails a preliminary assessment of whether the reasoning or methodology underlying the testimony is scientifically valid and of whether that reasoning or methodology properly can be applied to the facts in issue. We are confident that federal judges possess the capacity to undertake this review. Many factors will bear on the inquiry, and we do not presume to set out a definitive checklist or test. But some general observations are appropriate.

Ordinarily, a key question to be answered in determining whether a theory or technique is scientific knowledge that will assist the trier of fact will be whether it can be (and has been) tested. "Scientific methodology today is based on generating hypotheses and testing them to see if they can be falsified; indeed, this methodology is what distinguishes science from other fields of human inquiry." Green, at 645. See also C. Hempel, Philosophy of Natural Science 49 (1966) ("The statements constituting a scientific explanation must be capable of empirical test"); K. Popper, Conjectures and Refutations: The Growth of Scientific Knowledge 37 (5th ed. 1989) ("The criterion of the scientific status of a theory is its falsifiability, or refutability, or testability").

Another pertinent consideration is whether the theory or technique has been subjected to peer review and publication. Publication (which is but one element of peer review) is not a sine qua non of admissibility; it does not necessarily correlate with reliability, see S. Jasanoff, The Fifth Branch: Science Advisors as Policymakers 61–76 (1990), and in some instances well-grounded but innovative theories will not have been published, see Horrobin, The Philosophical Basis of Peer Review and the Suppression of Innovation, 263 J.Am.Med.Assn. 1438 (1990). Some propositions, moreover, are too particular, too new, or of too limited interest to be published. But submission to the scrutiny of the scientific community is a component of "good science," in part because it increases the likelihood that substantive flaws in methodology will be detected. See J. Ziman, Reliable Knowledge: An Exploration of the Grounds for Belief in Science 130–133 (1978); Relman and Angell, How Good Is Peer Review?, 321 New Eng.J.Med. 827 (1989). The fact of publication (or lack thereof) in a peer-reviewed journal thus will be a relevant, though not dispositive, consideration in assessing the scientific validity of a particular technique or methodology on which an opinion is premised.

Additionally, in the case of a particular scientific technique, the court ordinarily should consider the known or potential rate of error, see, e.g., United States v. Smith, 869 F.2d 348, 353–354 (C.A.7 1989) (surveying studies of the error rate of spectrographic voice identification technique), and the existence and maintenance of standards controlling the technique's operation. See United States v. Williams, 583 F.2d 1194, 1198 (C.A.2 1978) (noting professional organization's standard governing spectrographic analysis), cert. denied, 439 U.S. 1117 (1979).

Finally, "general acceptance" can yet have a bearing on the inquiry. A "reliability assessment does not require, although it does permit, explicit identification of a relevant scientific community and an express determination of a particular degree of acceptance within that community." United States v. Downing, 753 F.2d, at 1238. See also 3 Weinstein & Berger ¶ 702[03], pp. 702–41 to 702–42. Widespread acceptance can be an important factor in ruling particular evidence admissible, and "a known technique that has been able to attract only minimal support within the community," *Downing*, supra, at 1238, may properly be viewed with skepticism.

The inquiry envisioned by Rule 702 is, we emphasize, a flexible one. Its overarching subject is the scientific validity—and thus the evidentiary relevance and reliability—of the principles that underlie a proposed submission. The focus, of course, must be solely on principles and methodology, not on the conclusions that they generate.

Throughout, a judge assessing a proffer of expert scientific testimony under Rule 702 should also be mindful of other applicable rules. Rule 703 provides that expert opinions based on otherwise inadmissible hearsay are to be admitted only if the facts or data are "of a type reasonably relied upon by experts in the particular field in forming opinions or inferences upon the subject." Rule 706 allows the court at its discretion to procure the assistance of an expert of its own choosing. Finally, Rule 403 permits the exclusion of relevant evidence "if its probative value is substantially outweighed by the danger of unfair prejudice, confusion of the issues, or misleading the jury * * *." Judge Weinstein has explained: "Expert evidence can be both powerful and quite misleading because of the difficulty in evaluating it. Because of this risk, the judge in weighing possible prejudice against probative force under Rule 403 of the present rules exercises more control over experts than over lay witnesses." Weinstein, 138 F.R.D., at 632.

III

We conclude by briefly addressing what appear to be two underlying concerns of the parties and *amici* in this case. Respondent expresses apprehension that abandonment of "general acceptance" as the exclusive requirement for admission will result in a "free-for-all" in which befuddled juries are confounded by absurd and irrational pseudoscientific assertions. In this regard respondent seems to us to be overly pessimistic about the capabilities of the jury and of the adversary system generally. Vigorous cross-examination, presentation of contrary evidence, and careful instruction on the burden of proof are the traditional and appropriate means of attacking shaky but admissible evidence. See Rock v. Arkansas, 483 U.S. 44, 61 (1987). Additionally, in the event the trial court concludes that the scintilla of evidence presented supporting a position is insufficient to allow a reasonable juror to conclude that the position more likely than not is true, the court remains free to direct a judgment, and likewise to grant summary judgment * * * These conventional devices, rather than wholesale exclusion under an uncompromising "general acceptance" test, are the appropriate safeguards where the basis of scientific testimony meets the standards of Rule 702.

Petitioners and, to a greater extent, their *amici* exhibit a different concern. They suggest that recognition of a screening role for the judge that allows for the exclusion of "invalid" evidence will sanction a stifling and repressive scientific orthodoxy and will be inimical to the search for truth. It is true that open debate is an essential part of both legal and scientific analyses. Yet there are important differences between the quest for truth in the courtroom and the quest for truth in the laboratory. Scientific conclusions are subject to perpetual revision. Law, on the other hand, must resolve disputes finally and quickly. The scientific project is advanced by broad and wide-ranging consideration of a multitude of hypotheses, for those that are incorrect will eventually be shown to be so, and that in itself is an advance. Conjectures that are probably wrong are of little use, however, in the project of reaching a quick, final, and binding legal judgment—often of great consequence—about a particular set of events in the past. We recognize that, in practice, a gatekeeping role for the judge, no matter how flexible, inevitably on occasion will prevent the jury from learning of authentic insights and innovations. That, nevertheless, is the balance that is struck by Rules of Evidence designed not for the exhaustive search for cosmic understanding but for the particularized resolution of legal disputes.

IV

To summarize: "general acceptance" is not a necessary precondition to the admissibility of scientific evidence under the Federal Rules of Evidence, but the Rules of Evidence—especially Rule 702—do assign to the trial judge the task of ensuring that an expert's testimony both rests on a reliable foundation and is relevant to the task at hand. Pertinent evidence based on scientifically valid principles will satisfy those demands.

The inquiries of the District Court and the Court of Appeals focused almost exclusively on "general acceptance," as gauged by publication and the decisions of other courts. Accordingly, the judgment of the Court of Appeals is vacated and the case is remanded for further proceedings consistent with this opinion.

[The opinion of Chief Justice REHNQUIST, concurring in part and dissenting in part, has been omitted. Justice STEVENS joined in that opinion.]

GENERAL ELECTRIC CO. v. JOINER, 522 U.S. 136 (1997). Joiner, an electrician, worked with electrical transformers and came into contact with transformer fluid. The fluid in some of the transformers contained polychlorinated biphenyls (PCBs). After being diagnosed with small cell lung cancer, Joiner brought suit against General Electric, a manufacturer of transformers, and against two other defendants. Joiner offered expert testimony purporting to show a link between exposure to PCBs and small cell lung cancer. The District Court excluded Joiner's expert testimony on *Daubert* grounds and granted summary judgment against him. The Court of Appeals for the Eleventh Circuit reversed, stating that it would apply a "particularly stringent standard of review" to rulings on the admissibility of expert testimony and holding that the District Court had erred in excluding the testimony of Joiner's expert witnesses. The Supreme Court granted certiorari. The Court disagreed with the Eleventh Circuit about the standard of review for *Daubert* rulings, saying that the Eleventh Circuit's standard gave insufficient deference to the District Court. It reversed and remanded, holding that the abuse of discretion standard was the proper standard for review for all evidence rulings, including *Daubert* rulings. In the course of discussing whether the District Court had abused its discretion, the Supreme Court majority noted that

> Respondent points to *Daubert's* language that the "focus, of course, must be solely on principles and methodology, not on the conclusions that they generate." He claims that because the District Court's disagreement was with the conclusion that the experts drew from the studies, the District Court committed legal error and was properly reversed by the Court of Appeals. But conclusions and methodology are not entirely distinct from one another. Trained experts commonly extrapolate from existing data. But nothing in either *Daubert* or the Federal Rules of Evidence requires a district court to admit opinion evidence which is connected to existing data only by the *ipse dixit* of the expert. A court may conclude that there is simply too great an analytical gap between the data and the opinion proffered. That is what the District Court did here, and we hold that it did not abuse its discretion in so doing.

All of the Justices agreed that abuse of discretion was the appropriate standard. Justice Stevens dissented from the disposition, however, arguing that because the determination whether the District Court abused its discretion required further study of the record, the case should be remanded to the Court of Appeals.

Kumho Tire Company, Ltd. v. Carmichael

Supreme Court of the United States, 1999.
526 U.S. 137.

■ JUSTICE BREYER delivered the opinion of the Court.

In *Daubert v. Merrell Dow Pharmaceuticals, Inc.*, 509 U.S. 579 (1993), this Court focused upon the admissibility of scientific expert testimony. It pointed out that such testimony is admissible only if it is both relevant and reliable. And it held that the Federal Rules of Evidence "assign to the trial judge the task of ensuring that an expert's testimony both rests on a reliable foundation and is relevant to the task at hand." The Court also discussed certain more specific factors, such as testing, peer review, error rates, and "acceptability" in the relevant scientific community, some or all of which might prove helpful in determining the reliability of a particular scientific "theory or technique."

This case requires us to decide how *Daubert* applies to the testimony of engineers and other experts who are not scientists. We conclude that *Daubert*'s general holding—setting forth the trial judge's general "gatekeeping" obligation—applies not only to testimony based on "scientific" knowledge, but also to testimony based on "technical" and "other specialized" knowledge. See Fed. Rule Evid. 702. We also conclude that a trial court *may* consider one or more of the more specific factors that *Daubert* mentioned when doing so will help determine that testimony's reliability. But, as the Court stated in *Daubert*, the test of reliability is "flexible," and *Daubert*'s list of specific factors neither necessarily nor exclusively applies to all experts or in every case. Rather, the law grants a district court the same broad latitude when it decides *how* to determine reliability as it enjoys in respect to its ultimate reliability determination. See *General Electric Co. v. Joiner*, 522 U.S. 136, 143 (1997) (courts of appeals are to apply "abuse of discretion" standard when reviewing district court's reliability determination). Applying these standards, we determine that the District Court's decision in this case—not to admit certain expert testimony—was within its discretion and therefore lawful.

I

[A tire blew out on a minivan driven by Patrick Carmichael, causing the death of one passenger and severe injuries to others. Plaintiffs brought a diversity action against the tire's maker and distributor, claiming that the tire was defective. The issue before the Supreme Court was the admissibility of testimony of plaintiffs' expert on tire failure analysis, Dennis Carlson. Defendants had moved to exclude Carlson's testimony on *Daubert* grounds.

[Carlson claimed that he could distinguish between blow-outs caused by tire abuse and blow-outs caused by defects. He testified that if a blowout is not caused by tire separation resulting from "overdeflection" (underinflating the tire or putting too much weight on it), then ordinarily its cause is a defect in the tire. He claimed that damage due to overdeflection would result in certain physical symptoms, and identified four of them. He testified that at least two of these four symptoms had to be present before one could attribute tire separation to overdeflection. Carlson inspected Carmichael's tire. Although he conceded that "to a limited degree" the tire showed each of the four symptoms, he asserted that none of the symptoms were present to a significant degree. He concluded that the blowout was not caused by either overdeflection or a puncture, and hence that it must have been caused by a manufacturing or design defect.]

II

A

In *Daubert*, this Court held that Federal Rule of Evidence 702 imposes a special obligation upon a trial judge to "ensure that any and all scientific testimony . . . is not only relevant, but reliable." The initial question before us is whether this basic gatekeeping obligation applies only to "scientific" testimony or to all expert testimony. We, like the parties, believe that it applies to all expert testimony.

For one thing, Rule 702 itself says:

"If scientific, technical, or other specialized knowledge will assist the trier of fact to understand the evidence or to determine a fact in issue, a witness qualified as an expert by knowledge, skill, experience, training, or education, may testify thereto in the form of an opinion or otherwise."

This language makes no relevant distinction between "scientific" knowledge and "technical" or "other specialized" knowledge. It makes clear that any such knowledge might become the subject of expert testimony. In *Daubert*, the Court specified that it is the Rule's word "knowledge," not the words (like "scientific") that modify that word, that "establishes a standard of evidentiary reliability." Hence, as a matter of language, the Rule applies its reliability standard to all "scientific," "technical," or "other specialized" matters within its scope. We concede that the Court in *Daubert* referred only to "scientific" knowledge. But as the Court there said, it referred to "scientific" testimony "because that [wa]s the nature of the expertise" at issue.

Neither is the evidentiary rationale that underlay the Court's basic *Daubert* "gatekeeping" determination limited to "scientific" knowledge. *Daubert* pointed out that Federal Rules 702 and 703 grant expert witnesses testimonial latitude unavailable to other witnesses on the "assumption that the expert's opinion will have a reliable basis in the knowledge and experience of his discipline." 509 U.S., at 592 (pointing out that experts may testify to opinions, including those that are not based on firsthand knowledge or observation). The Rules grant that latitude to all experts, not just to "scientific" ones.

Finally, it would prove difficult, if not impossible, for judges to administer evidentiary rules under which a gatekeeping obligation depended upon a distinction between "scientific" knowledge and "technical" or "other specialized" knowledge. There is no clear line that divides the one from the others. Disciplines such as engineering rest upon scientific knowledge. Pure scientific theory itself may depend for its development upon observation and properly engineered machinery. And conceptual efforts to distinguish the two are unlikely to produce clear legal lines capable of application in particular cases. Cf. Brief for National Academy of Engineering as *Amicus Curiae* 9 (scientist seeks to understand nature while the engineer seeks nature's modification); Brief for Rubber Manufacturers Association as *Amicus Curiae* 14–16 (engineering, as an "applied science," relies on "scientific reasoning and methodology"); Brief for John Allen et al. as *Amici Curiae* 6 (engineering relies upon "scientific knowledge and methods"). * * *

We conclude that *Daubert*'s general principles apply to the expert matters described in Rule 702. The Rule, in respect to all such matters, "establishes a standard of evidentiary reliability." It "requires a valid . . . connection to the pertinent inquiry as a precondition to admissibility." And where such testimony's factual basis, data, principles, methods, or their application are called sufficiently into question, see Part III, *infra*, the trial judge must determine whether the testimony has "a reliable basis in the knowledge and experience of [the relevant] discipline."

B

The petitioners ask more specifically whether a trial judge determining the "admissibility of an engineering expert's testimony" *may* consider several more specific factors that *Daubert* said might "bear on" a judge's gate-keeping determination. These factors include:

—Whether a "theory or technique . . . can be (and has been) tested";

—Whether it "has been subjected to peer review and publication";

—Whether, in respect to a particular technique, there is a high "known or potential rate of error" and whether there are "standards controlling the technique's operation"; and

—Whether the theory or technique enjoys "general acceptance" within a "relevant scientific community."

Emphasizing the word "may" in the question, we answer that question yes.

Engineering testimony rests upon scientific foundations, the reliability of which will be at issue in some cases. In other cases, the relevant reliability concerns may focus upon personal knowledge or experience. As the Solicitor General points out, there are many different kinds of experts, and many different kinds of expertise. See Brief for United States as *Amicus Curiae* 18–19, and n. 5 (citing cases involving experts in drug terms, handwriting analysis, criminal *modus operandi*, land valuation, agricultural practices, railroad procedures, attorney's fee valuation, and others). Our emphasis on the word "may" thus reflects *Daubert*'s description of the Rule 702 inquiry as "a flexible one." *Daubert* makes clear that the factors it mentions do *not* constitute a "definitive checklist or test." And *Daubert* adds that the gatekeeping inquiry must be " 'tied to the facts' " of a particular "case." We agree with the Solicitor General that "[t]he factors identified in *Daubert* may or may not be pertinent in assessing reliability, depending on the nature of the issue, the expert's particular expertise, and the subject of his testimony." The conclusion, in our view, is that we can neither rule out, nor rule in, for all cases and for all time the applicability of the factors mentioned in *Daubert*, nor can we now do so for subsets of cases categorized by category of expert or by kind of evidence. Too much depends upon the particular circumstances of the particular case at issue.

Daubert itself is not to the contrary. It made clear that its list of factors was meant to be helpful, not definitive. Indeed, those factors do not all necessarily apply even in every instance in which the reliability of scientific testimony is challenged. It might not be surprising in a particular case, for example, that a claim made by a scientific witness has never been the subject of peer review, for the particular application at issue may never previously have interested any scientist. Nor, on the other hand, does the presence of *Daubert*'s general acceptance factor help show that an expert's testimony is reliable where the discipline itself lacks reliability, as, for example, do theories grounded in any so-called generally accepted principles of astrology or necromancy.

At the same time, and contrary to the Court of Appeals' view, some of *Daubert*'s questions can help to evaluate the reliability even of experience-based testimony. In certain cases, it will be appropriate for the trial judge to ask, for example, how often an engineering expert's experience-based methodology has produced erroneous results, or whether such a method is generally accepted in the relevant engineering community. Likewise, it will at times be useful to ask even of a witness whose expertise is based purely on experience, say, a perfume tester able to distinguish among 140 odors at a sniff, whether his preparation is of a kind that others in the field would recognize as acceptable.

We must therefore disagree with the Eleventh Circuit's holding that a trial judge may ask questions of the sort *Daubert* mentioned only where an expert "relies on the application of scientific principles," but not where an expert relies "on skill-or experience-based observation." We do not believe that Rule 702 creates a schematism that segregates expertise by type while mapping certain kinds of questions to certain kinds of experts. Life and the legal cases that it generates are too complex to warrant so definitive a match.

To say this is not to deny the importance of *Daubert*'s gatekeeping requirement. The objective of that requirement is to ensure the reliability and relevancy of expert testimony. It is to make certain that an expert, whether basing testimony upon professional studies or personal experience, employs in the courtroom the same level of intellectual rigor that characterizes the practice of an expert in the relevant field. Nor do we deny that, as stated in *Daubert*, the particular questions that it mentioned will often be appropriate for use in determining the reliability of challenged expert testimony. Rather, we conclude that the trial judge must have considerable leeway in deciding in a particular case how to go about determining whether particular expert testimony is reliable. That is to say, a trial court should consider the specific factors identified in *Daubert* where they are reasonable measures of the reliability of expert testimony.

C

The trial court must have the same kind of latitude in deciding *how* to test an expert's reliability, and to decide whether or when special briefing or other proceedings are needed to investigate reliability, as it enjoys when it decides *whether or not* that expert's relevant testimony is reliable. Our opinion in *Joiner* makes clear that a court of appeals is to apply an abuse-of-discretion standard when it "review[s] a trial court's decision to admit or exclude expert testimony." That standard applies as much to the trial court's decisions about how to determine reliability as to its ultimate conclusion. Otherwise, the trial judge would lack the discretionary authority needed both to avoid unnecessary "reliability" proceedings in ordinary cases where the reliability of an expert's methods is properly taken for granted, and to require appropriate proceedings in the less usual or more complex cases where cause for questioning the expert's reliability arises. Indeed, the Rules seek to avoid "unjustifiable expense and delay" as part of their search for "truth" and the "jus[t] determin[ation]" of proceedings. Fed. Rule Evid. 102. Thus, whether *Daubert*'s specific factors are, or are not, reasonable measures of reliability in a particular case is a matter that the law grants the trial judge broad latitude to determine. And the Eleventh Circuit erred insofar as it held to the contrary.

III

We further explain the way in which a trial judge "may" consider *Daubert*'s factors by applying these considerations to the case at hand, a matter that has been briefed exhaustively by the parties and their 19 *amici*. The District Court did not doubt Carlson's qualifications, which included a masters degree in mechanical engineering, 10 years' work at Michelin America,

Inc., and testimony as a tire failure consultant in other tort cases. Rather, it excluded the testimony because, despite those qualifications, it initially doubted, and then found unreliable, "the methodology employed by the expert in analyzing the data obtained in the visual inspection, and the scientific basis, if any, for such an analysis." After examining the transcript in "some detail," and after considering respondents' defense of Carlson's methodology, the District Court determined that Carlson's testimony was not reliable. It fell outside the range where experts might reasonably differ, and where the jury must decide among the conflicting views of different experts, even though the evidence is "shaky." In our view, the doubts that triggered the District Court's initial inquiry here were reasonable, as was the court's ultimate conclusion.

For one thing, and contrary to respondents' suggestion, the specific issue before the court was not the reasonableness *in general* of a tire expert's use of a visual and tactile inspection to determine whether overdeflection had caused the tire's tread to separate from its steel-belted carcass. Rather, it was the reasonableness of using such an approach, along with Carlson's particular method of analyzing the data thereby obtained, to draw a conclusion regarding *the particular matter to which the expert testimony was directly relevant*. That matter concerned the likelihood that a defect in the tire at issue caused its tread to separate from its carcass. The tire in question, the expert conceded, had traveled far enough so that some of the tread had been worn bald; it should have been taken out of service; it had been repaired (inadequately) for punctures; and it bore some of the very marks that the expert said indicated, not a defect, but abuse through overdeflection. The relevant issue was whether the expert could reliably determine the cause of *this* tire's separation.

Nor was the basis for Carlson's conclusion simply the general theory that, in the absence of evidence of abuse, a defect will normally have caused a tire's separation. Rather, the expert employed a more specific theory to establish the existence (or absence) of such abuse. Carlson testified precisely that in the absence of *at least two* of four signs of abuse (proportionately greater tread wear on the shoulder; signs of grooves caused by the beads; discolored sidewalls; marks on the rim flange) he concludes that a defect caused the separation. And his analysis depended upon acceptance of a further implicit proposition, namely, that his visual and tactile inspection could determine that the tire before him had not been abused despite some evidence of the presence of the very signs for which he looked (and two punctures).

For another thing, the transcripts of Carlson's depositions support both the trial court's initial uncertainty and its final conclusion. Those transcripts cast considerable doubt upon the reliability of both the explicit theory (about the need for two signs of abuse) and the implicit proposition (about the significance of visual inspection in this case). Among other things, the expert could not say whether the tire had traveled more than

10, or 20, or 30, or 40, or 50 thousand miles, adding that 6,000 miles was "about how far" he could "say with any certainty." The court could reasonably have wondered about the reliability of a method of visual and tactile inspection sufficiently precise to ascertain with some certainty the abuse-related significance of minute shoulder/center relative tread wear differences, but insufficiently precise to tell "with any certainty" from the tread wear whether a tire had traveled less than 10,000 or more than 50,000 miles. And these concerns might have been augmented by Carlson's repeated reliance on the "subjective[ness]" of his mode of analysis in response to questions seeking specific information regarding how he could differentiate between a tire that actually had been overdeflected and a tire that merely looked as though it had been. They would have been further augmented by the fact that Carlson said he had inspected the tire itself for the first time the morning of his first deposition, and then only for a few hours. (His initial conclusions were based on photographs.)

Moreover, prior to his first deposition, Carlson had issued a signed report in which he concluded that the tire had "not been . . . overloaded or underinflated," not because of the absence of "two of four" signs of abuse, but simply because "the rim flange impressions . . . were normal." That report also said that the "tread depth remaining was 3/32 inch," though the opposing expert's (apparently undisputed) measurements indicate that the tread depth taken at various positions around the tire actually ranged from .5/32 of an inch to 4/32 of an inch, with the tire apparently showing greater wear along *both* shoulders than along the center.

Further, in respect to one sign of abuse, bead grooving, the expert seemed to deny the sufficiency of his own simple visual-inspection methodology. He testified that most tires have some bead groove pattern, that where there is reason to suspect an abnormal bead groove he would ideally "look at a lot of [similar] tires" to know the grooving's significance, and that he had not looked at many tires similar to the one at issue.

Finally, the court, after looking for a defense of Carlson's methodology as applied in these circumstances, found no convincing defense. Rather, it found (1) that "none" of the *Daubert* factors, including that of "general acceptance" in the relevant expert community, indicated that Carlson's testimony was reliable, (2) that its own analysis "revealed no countervailing factors operating in favor of admissibility which could outweigh those identified in *Daubert*," and (3) that the "parties identified no such factors in their briefs." For these three reasons *taken together*, it concluded that Carlson's testimony was unreliable.

Respondents now argue to us, as they did to the District Court, that a method of tire failure analysis that employs a visual/tactile inspection is a reliable method, and they point both to its use by other experts and to Carlson's long experience working for Michelin as sufficient indication that that is so. But no one denies that an expert might draw a conclusion from a set of observations based on extensive and specialized experience. Nor does anyone deny that, as a general matter, tire abuse may often be identified by qualified experts through visual or tactile inspection of the tire. See Affidavit of H.R. Baumgardner 1–2, cited in Brief for National Academy of Forensic Engineers as *Amici Curiae* 16 (Tire engineers rely on visual examination and process of elimination to analyze experimental test tires). As we said before, the question before the trial court was specific, not general. The trial court had to decide whether this particular expert had sufficient specialized knowledge to assist the jurors "in deciding the particular issues in the case." 4 J. McLaughlin, Weinstein's Federal Evidence ¶ 702.05[1], p. 702–33 (2d ed.1998); see also Advisory Committee's Note on Proposed Fed. Rule Evid. 702, Preliminary Draft of Proposed Amendments to the Federal Rules of Civil Procedure and Evidence: Request for Comment 126 (1998) (stressing that district courts must "scrutinize" whether the "principles and methods" employed by an expert "have been properly applied to the facts of the case").

The particular issue in this case concerned the use of Carlson's two-factor test and his related use of visual/tactile inspection to draw conclusions on the basis of what seemed small observational differences. We have found no indication in the record that other experts in the industry use Carlson's two-factor test or that tire experts such as Carlson normally make the very fine distinctions about, say, the symmetry of comparatively greater shoulder tread wear that were necessary, on Carlson's own theory, to support his conclusions. Nor, despite the prevalence of tire testing, does anyone refer to any articles or papers that validate Carlson's approach. Compare Bobo, Tire Flaws and Separations, in Mechanics of Pneumatic Tires 636–637 (S. Clark ed.1981); C. Schnuth et al., Compression Grooving and Rim Flange Abrasion as Indicators of Over–Deflected Operating Conditions in Tires, presented to Rubber Division of the American Chemical Society, Oct. 21–24, 1997; J. Walter & R. Kiminecz, Bead Contact Pressure Measurements at the Tire–Rim Interface, presented to Society of Automotive Engineers, Feb. 24–28, 1975. Indeed, no one has argued that Carlson himself, were he still working for Michelin, would have concluded in a report to his employer that a similar tire was similarly defective on grounds identical to those upon which he rested his conclusion here. Of course, Carlson himself claimed that his method was accurate, but, as we pointed out in *Joiner*, "nothing in either *Daubert* or the Federal Rules of Evidence requires a district court to admit opinion evidence that is connected to existing data only by the *ipse dixit* of the expert."

Respondents additionally argue that the District Court too rigidly applied *Daubert*'s criteria. They read its opinion to hold that a failure to satisfy any one of those criteria automatically renders expert testimony inadmissible. The District Court's initial opinion might have been vulnerable to a form of this argument. There, the court, after rejecting respondents' claim that Carlson's testimony was "exempted from *Daubert*-style scrutiny" because it was "technical analysis" rather than "scientific evidence," simply added that "none of the four admissibility criteria outlined by the *Daubert* court are satisfied." Subsequently, however, the court granted respondents' motion for reconsideration. It then explicitly recognized that the relevant reliability inquiry "should be 'flexible,' "that its " 'overarching subject [should be] . . . validity' and reliability," and that "*Daubert* was intended neither to be exhaustive nor to apply in every case." And the court ultimately based its decision upon Carlson's failure to satisfy either *Daubert*'s factors or *any other* set of reasonable reliability criteria. In light of the record as developed by the parties, that conclusion was within the District Court's lawful discretion.

In sum, Rule 702 grants the district judge the discretionary authority, reviewable for its abuse, to determine reliability in light of the particular facts and circumstances of the particular case. The District Court did not abuse its discretionary authority in this case. Hence, the judgment of the Court of Appeals is

Reversed.

[Justice Scalia, with whom Justice O'Connor and Justice Thomas joined, concurred in the opinion of the Court but added that in some cases failure to apply one or another of the *Daubert* criteria might be unreasonable, and so an abuse of discretion. Justice Stevens, concurring in part and dissenting in part, joined in Parts I and II of the Court's opinion but would have stopped there, without deciding whether the trial judge abused his discretion in excluding Carlson's testimony.—Eds.]

Ellis v. State

Court of Criminal Appeals of Oklahoma, 1982.
643 P.2d 330.

On appeal from his conviction of Larceny of a Domestic Animal, in Kiowa County District Court, the appellant, in his single assignment of error, argues that the evidence was insufficient to sustain the verdict and that the trial court erred in failing to instruct the jury to acquit him.

On November 12, 1979, Richard Owens, the complaining witness, noticed that one of his newborn calves, a black baldy bull, was missing. Three (3) days later his son, Ray, observed a calf fitting the description of the missing calf, secreted in a shed with five (5) other calves on an adjoining neighbor's property. He notified the Sheriff's office, and the calves were transported to a storage barn pending further investigation. Jane Smith, the neighbor, testified that all the calves were the appellant's, who was residing with her, and that the shed was the property of a tenant who leased her land.

The following day, Kiowa County Undersheriff, Harlan Ross, took the calf in question to the Owens' pasture. The calf attempted to suckle several cows but was rebuffed. Then the mother cow came running across the open field bawling; she immediately licked the calf and without hesitation allowed it to nurse. According to the uncontroverted expert testimony of lifelong cattlemen who testified at trial, these actions of claiming a calf by a cow in an open field constitute the accepted test for determining maternal lineage.

Taking the stand in his own defense, the appellant testified that he purchased the calf from a friend. He further testified that at all times he had a sales slip to prove this purchase, but until trial never mentioned it to anyone. Leon Owens testified that on October 23, 1979, he sold a black, white-faced bull calf to the appellant.

Although the evidence in this case is wholly circumstantial it has established a prima facie case. * * * The trial court properly denied the appellant's motion for a directed verdict. This assignment of error is without merit.

For the above and foregoing reasons, the judgment and sentence appealed from is AFFIRMED.

United States v. Saelee

United States District Court for the District of Alaska, 2001.
162 F. Supp. 2d 1097.

■ H. RUSSEL HOLLAND, DISTRICT JUDGE.

Facts

Defendant Chan Ian Saelee was indicted on three counts of violating federal drug laws. Count III charges defendant with importing opium from Thailand in 1998 in violation of 21 U.S.C. §§ 952 and 960(b)(3). The opium in question was concealed in Butterfinger candy bars which appeared to have been express mailed from the United States but then returned to the sender after delivery was unsuccessful. The Government had John W. Cawley, III, a forensic document analyst with the United States Postal Inspection Service National Forensic Laboratory, compare hand printing exemplars provided by defendant with the hand printing on the address labels on the packages in question. Mr. Cawley concluded that defendant was the writer of one of the questioned writings and was probably the writer of another. The Government originally proposed to have Mr. Cawley testify as to his conclusions at trial, and defendant filed the instant motion to exclude all testimony by Mr. Cawley at trial.

In its first response to defendant's motion, the Government recognized that a *Daubert* hearing might be necessary to determine if Mr. Cawley's testimony was admissible but opposed excluding all of Mr. Cawley's testimony. The court tentatively scheduled a *Daubert* hearing for August 10,

2001. In the same order, the court directed the parties to file supplemental briefing on defendant's motion.

In its timely filed supplemental brief, the Government changed course and proposed to have Mr. Cawley testify only about the similarities and differences between the known writing and the questioned documents and not to have Mr. Cawley testify about his ultimate conclusions as to whether defendant authored the questioned documents. The Government argues that such comparison evidence is admissible pursuant to Rule 701, Federal Rules of Evidence, which governs the admissibility of lay opinion testimony. At first, defendant agreed that Mr. Cawley could testify under Rule 701. However, following a status conference, defendant filed an unopposed corrected response to the Government's Rule 701 proposal in which he disputed that Mr. Cawley's testimony would be admissible under Rule 701 and argued that Mr. Cawley's testimony, if admissible at all, could only be admissible under Rule 702, Federal Rules of Evidence, which governs the admissibility of expert testimony. Defendant continued to assert that a *Daubert* hearing was necessary to determine the admissibility of the comparison testimony.

The court agreed, and a *Daubert* hearing was held on August 10, 2001. At the *Daubert* hearing, the Government changed course once again and argued that Mr. Cawley's testimony was admissible under Federal Rule of Evidence 901, which deals with the authentication and identification of evidence. At the close of the *Daubert* hearing, the court granted defendant's motion *in limine* to exclude the hand printing comparison evidence at trial and advised the parties that a written order would follow.

Discussion

The question presented by defendant's motion *in limine* was whether the forensic document analyst's testimony as to whether defendant was the author of the questioned documents is admissible under the Federal Rules of Evidence. This question was narrowed when the Government decided not to have Mr. Cawley testify about his ultimate conclusions as to authorship of the questioned documents. The question facing the court at the *Daubert* hearing was whether the forensic document analyst's testimony about the similarities and differences between the known documents and the questioned documents was admissible under either Rule 701 or 702. On the basis of the record made at the *Daubert* hearing, the court answers both parts of this question in the negative.

Rule 701 governs the admissibility of opinion testimony by lay witnesses and provides:

> If the witness is not testifying as an expert, the witness' testimony in the form of opinions or inferences is limited to those opinions or inferences which are (a) rationally based on the perception of the witness,

(b) helpful to a clear understanding of the witness' testimony or the determination of a fact in issue, and (c) not based on scientific, technical, or other specialized knowledge within the scope of Rule 702.

In making its proposal to have Mr. Cawley testify under Rule 701, the Government relies on an unpublished case, *United States v. Santillan*, No. CR–96–40169 DLJ, (N.D. Ca. Dec. 3, 1999). In *Santillan*, the court allowed a forensic document examiner to offer comparison testimony under Rule 701, after finding that the testimony was inadmissible under Rule 702. The court noted that allowing a handwriting expert to testify under Rule 701 might raise a Rule 403 problem, but still found the testimony admissible.

Ignoring for the moment that *Santillan* is an unpublished case, *Santillan* was decided prior to the 2000 amendments to Rule 701; presumably the court would reach a much different conclusion if faced with the same issue today. In 2000, Rule 701 was amended to expressly limit lay opinion testimony to that which is *not* based on scientific, technical, or other specialized knowledge within the scope of Rule 702. The Advisory Committee Notes to the 2000 Amendments explain that the amendment was made "to eliminate the risk that the reliability requirements set forth in Rule 702 will be evaded through the simple expedient of proffering an expert in lay witness clothing," which is exactly what the Government is proposing to do here and what the Government was allowed to do in *Santillan*.

The court required that the parties pre-file in writing their witnesses' direct testimony for the *Daubert* hearing. The Government offered only the testimony of its forensic document analyst, Mr. Cawley. Mr. Cawley's pre-filed testimony is preceded by his *curriculum vitae*. There, Mr. Cawley sets out his employment as a "forensic document analyst" for the United States Postal Inspection Service. He sets forth his education, including training as a questioned documents examiner, the professional organizations of which he is a member (related to "forensic sciences" and document examination), and other "relevant" information including testifying as an expert in the field of questioned documents in various courts. In his report (which the Government treats as the written testimony), Mr. Cawley summarizes the examinations he has undertaken. He offers to provide for the Government testimony demonstrative of (1) his "scientific examination" of the defendant's known handwriting, (2) his "study of handwriting habits as the basis of handwriting identification principles," and (3) his "comparative evaluation" of the two writings (presumably the similarities and differences between known and questioned writings as now proposed by the Government).

While Mr. Cawley's written testimony discloses very little which is relevant to *Daubert* issues, it does disclose much about whether he is a lay witness or a purported expert. Plainly, Mr. Cawley is not a lay person who proposes to offer testimony based on sensory perception. Rather, he makes reference to handwriting identification *principles* and *scientific* examinations. Mr. Cawley would testify that he is a trained, forensic document analyst.

Mr. Cawley's testimony is plainly inadmissible under Rule 701 because of subsection (c) which precludes lay witness opinion testimony based on specialized knowledge. Any testimony Mr. Cawley would offer would be based on undisclosed handwriting principles, scientific examination of documents, and specialized knowledge gained through training and 24 years of experience as a document examiner. Such testimony must be analyzed under Rule 702 standards.

Rule 702 of the Federal Rules of Evidence governs the admission of expert testimony and provides:

> If scientific, technical, or other specialized knowledge will assist the trier of fact to understand the evidence or to determine a fact in issue, a witness qualified as an expert by knowledge, skill, experience, training, or education, may testify thereto in the form of an opinion or otherwise, if (1) the testimony is based upon sufficient facts or data, (2) the testimony is the product of reliable principles and methods, and (3) the witness has applied the principles and methods reliably to the facts of the case.

Rule 702 was amended in 2000 in response to *Daubert v. Merrell Dow Pharmaceuticals, Inc.*, 509 U.S. 579 (1993), and *Kumho Tire Co. v. Carmichael*, 526 U.S. 137 (1999). *Daubert* assigned a gatekeeping function to trial judges to exclude unreliable scientific expert testimony. *Kumho* extended this gatekeeping function not only to scientific testimony but also to all expert testimony.

As the Advisory Committee Notes to the 2000 Amendments indicate, "consistently with *Kumho*, the Rule as amended provides that all types of expert testimony present questions of admissibility for the trial court in deciding whether the evidence is reliable and helpful." The Court in *Daubert* set forth a non-exclusive list of factors for courts to consider in determining whether expert evidence is reliable. These factors are:

(1) whether the expert's theory or technique can be or has been tested;

(2) whether the expert's theory or technique has been subjected to peer review;

(3) the known or potential rate of error;

(4) the existence and maintenance of standards controlling the technique's operation; and

(5) general acceptance in the scientific community.

Kumho held that these factors may apply in a case dealing with non-scientific expert testimony as well. However, the Court in both cases emphasized that this is not an exclusive list and the factors that a court considers must "fit" the facts of the particular case.

Factors that "fit" the instant case are whether the theories and techniques of handwriting comparison have been tested, whether they have been subjected to peer review, the known or potential error rate of forensic document examiners, the existence of standards in making comparisons between known writings and questioned documents, and the general acceptance by the forensic evidence community.

The Government bears the burden of proving that its expert's proffered testimony is sufficiently reliable to be admissible under Rule 702. As already noted, the parties were ordered to file their direct testimony for the *Daubert* hearing prior to the hearing itself. Defendant filed an affidavit from Professor Michael J. Saks, a professor of both law and psychology who has done extensive work in the area of scientific evidence in general, and handwriting analysis in particular. The Government pre-filed a July 2, 2001, "Summary of Forensic Testimony". In fact, the Government's pre-filed testimony was Mr. Cawley's expert report. It contains Mr. Cawley's formal conclusions (which the Government has abandoned), the basis for the conclusions (which is itself conclusory), and a summary of examinations. The basis for Mr. Cawley's conclusions is stated to be "significant identifying characteristics." Mr. Cawley did not explain in his report nor at the *Daubert* hearing how one identifies such characteristics, what they mean, or how many are necessary for a positive opinion. Mr. Cawley testified at the *Daubert* hearing that his pre-filed testimony did not include any information about empirical testing of handwriting analysis, the known error rate in the field, peer review, or the standards that control in the field.

At the *Daubert* hearing, both Professor Saks and Mr. Cawley were cross-examined. Having heard the evidence, and applying the relevant *Daubert/Kumho* factors to that evidence, the only conclusion the court can reach is that the Government has failed to meet its burden of establishing that Mr. Cawley's testimony is sufficiently reliable to be admissible under Rule 702.

It is evident that the theories and techniques used in handwriting comparison could be empirically tested but, as Professor Saks' testimony illustrates, there has been an overall lack of such testing. At the *Daubert* hearing, Mr. Cawley testified that there has been at least one empirical study concerning the reliability of handwriting comparison, conducted for the FBI by Moshe Kam. According to Mr. Cawley, the Kam study determined that a document examiner could do what he said he could do, *i.e.*, compare a known document and a questioned document and offer an opinion about whether the writer of the known document was the writer of the questioned document. Mr. Cawley testified that the Kam study concluded that document examiners had an error rate of 6.5% and laypersons had an error rate of 38.6%. Cawley's testimony is in large part contradicted by Saks' testimony on the Kam studies. As detailed in Saks' affidavit, Kam actually conducted four studies, which Saks avers suffered from their own methodological problems. Ignoring that issue for now, the first study found that experts outperformed nonexperts but that the best nonexperts did about as well as the experts. The second study found the rate of true positives to be almost identical for experts and non-experts, while experts committed fewer false positives. The third study found an unexplained 41% improvement in laypersons' ability to avoid false positives. The fourth study tested the ability to determine whether a signature is genuine or not. Experts and laypersons had similar ability to detect forgeries; experts were slightly better at discerning genuine signatures than laypersons; experts incorrectly found forgeries to be genuine less often than laypersons, and experts incorrectly found genuine signatures to be forgeries less often than laypersons. From Saks' testimony it appears that, contrary to Mr. Cawley's testimony, the Kam studies did not conclusively establish that forensic document examiners can reliably do what they say they can do.

In addition to there being a lack of empirical evidence on the proficiency of document examiners, there has been little empirical testing done on the basic theories upon which the field is based. For instance, the basic premise on which document examiners work—namely, that no two persons write alike and that no one person writes the same all the time—has not even been adequately tested. In fact, Saks testified that one study suggested that this basic premise is not entirely true. A study done in 1958 found that the signatures of numerous people named "John Harris" were so similar that examiners could not distinguish one writer from another.

Also, there has never been any empirical research done on the theory of probability on which handwriting analysis is based. According to Professor Saks, the field of handwriting analysis is based on a theory of probability that "if we know the individual probabilities of a set of independent attributes, we can calculate the probability of their joint occurrence by multiplying them together." But, according to Saks, document examiners have never gone beyond stating this general theory. "They make no measurements, they make no calculations, and they report no probability of coincidental matches. In other words, they do not apply the theory to the practice at all." Mr. Cawley did not refute this testimony.

At the *Daubert* hearing, Mr. Cawley did attempt to refute the general notion that there has been little empirical research done in his field. He offered a four-page list of published and unpublished articles dealing with handwriting analysis. According to Mr. Cawley, these articles are written by forensic document examiners, and the published articles are presented at professional meetings for peer review. However, Mr. Cawley also testified that he did not know whether any of the articles discussed error rates, empirical testing, or coincidental matches, although he claimed to have read the articles. The list, without analysis of the substance of the articles, is of little use to the court. The court infers that most of the listed articles were written by proponents of the guild style (apprentice training) process of training handwriting examiners. This is Mr. Cawley's background. It is a training process little used today in professional and scientific callings. The list of articles gives the court no insight into whether there has been independent, empirical testing of the theories and techniques involved in handwriting comparison. The field of handwriting comparison also suffers from a lack of meaningful peer review. As Mr. Cawley testified, some articles are presented at professional meetings for review; nonetheless, there is no evidence that any of these articles are subjected to peer review by disinterested parties, such as academics.

There is little known about the error rates of forensic document examiners. The little testing that has been done raises serious questions about the reliability of methods currently in use. As to some tasks, there is a high rate of error and forensic document examiners may not be any better at analyzing handwriting than laypersons. This is illustrated not only in the Kam studies relied on by Mr. Cawley, but also in a series of proficiency tests carried out by Collaborative Testing Service under the supervision of the Forensic Sciences Foundation. In two such proficiency studies, the task for the examiners was to compare written letters in the natural hand of the writers with known exemplars of several suspects. In one study, the examiners were correct 89% of the time, but in the other only 52% of the time. In tests measuring their ability to determine if a signature was genuine, examiners were correct anywhere from 35% of the time to 100% of the time. A test involving hand printing produced only 13% correct answers. In a test asking examiners to identify the author of a forgery, the examiners were wrong 100% of the time. In a study conducted by Galbraith, laypersons were given the same material as experts were given in the 1987 proficiency study. The true positive accuracy rate of laypersons was the same as that of handwriting examiners; both groups were correct 52% of the time.

Mr. Cawley testified that he has experience in analyzing hand printing, which is what is involved here, and that hand printing has individual characteristics that can be compared. Mr. Cawley offered no evidence that this claim has been tested in any manner. It is not known whether printing is defendant's normal, natural manner of writing. Mr. Cawley may have been asked to compare an abnormal, unnatural writing style to the questioned address labels. The court has no insight into what requiring an abnormal, unnatural manner of writing would do to either the analysis or error rates. Professor Saks avers that any asserted special expertise in pointing out similarities or differences in hand printing has no empirical foundation of any kind. Nor did Mr. Cawley offer any specific evidence as to his proficiency in making hand printing comparisons, other than to state generally that he has examined thousands of documents. In fact, Mr. Cawley testified that his ability to make comparisons of hand printing was based on there being a sufficient quality and quantity of printing to compare. The quantity of printing in this case is printing on an address label, which the court presumes would be considered a very small quantity of printing.[22] The court infers that the very limited amount of questioned printing would diminish Mr. Cawley's ability to render an accurate opinion or make accurate comparisons irrespective of whether printing is defendant's normal, natural manner of writing.

The field of handwriting comparison also suffers from a lack of controlling standards. This was highlighted by Mr. Cawley's testimony at the *Daubert* hearing when he explained how he conducts a comparison of known handwriting with a questioned document. Generally using microscopic enlargements, he stated that he first determines whether the handwriting is normal, natural handwriting. Next, Mr. Cawley stated that he determines the characteristics of the writing, such as the flow, smoothness, pen impulse movements, etc. After having discerned the characteristics of the writing, Mr. Cawley said he makes side-by-side comparisons. Based on these comparisons, Mr. Cawley stated that he then can render an opinion about whether the author of the known writing was the author of the questioned document.

Missing from Mr. Cawley's description of how he makes comparisons and reaches ultimate conclusions is any testimony about the controlling standards used to make each of these determinations. The closest Mr. Cawley came to discussing any standards he employed was when he indicated that 25 samples of known writing were necessary for this process. Even then, he did not indicate what the effect would be on his ability to make comparisons or to reach an ultimate conclusion if he had a different number of samples or why 25 was the magic number. Above, the court infers that a limited quantity of questioned writing would detract from the reliability of the analysis; but in reality, we do not *know* whether there should be some minimal amount of questioned writing in order to arrive at a reliable opinion. The technique of comparing known writings with questioned documents appears to be entirely subjective and entirely lacking in controlling standards.

Finally, the evidence does indicate that there is general acceptance of the theories and techniques involved in the field of handwriting analysis among the closed universe of forensic document examiners. This proves nothing. Testimony from these experts has, until recently, been uncritically accepted as reliable in the courts. Having previously testified somewhere as an expert document examiner was usually sufficient qualification. "Courts have long received handwriting analysis testimony as admissible evidence." *United States v. Paul*, 175 F.3d 906, 910 n.2 (11th Cir. 1999). However, the fact that this type of evidence has been generally accepted in the past by

---

[22] Mr. Cawley had three questioned documents: address labels with "from" and "to" information. Mr. Cawley had 28 exemplars of defendant's known printing.

courts does not mean that it should be generally accepted now, after *Daubert* and *Kumho.*

Several other district courts that have recently considered whether testimony by a handwriting expert is admissible under Rule 702 have likewise found numerous problems with handwriting comparison testimony and severely limited it at trial. *See, United States v. Hines*, 55 F. Supp. 2d 62, 70–71 (D. Mass. 1999) (document examiner limited to testifying about the similarities between the known handwriting and the questioned document); *United States v. Van Wyk*, 83 F. Supp. 2d 515, 524 (D.N.J. 2000) (forensic stylistic expert limited to testifying about "the specific similarities and idiosyncracies between the known writings and the questioned writings, as well as testimony regarding, for example, how frequently or infrequently in his experience, he has seen a particular idiosyncrasy"); *United States v. Rutherford*, 104 F. Supp. 2d 1190, 1194 (D. Neb. 2000) (document examiner's testimony limited "to identifying and explaining the similarities and dissimilarities between the known exemplars and the questioned documents").

This court has gone one step further than other courts by excluding all of Mr. Cawley's testimony, including his comparison testimony. The Government has failed to prove that Mr. Cawley's proposed testimony as to similarity between known and questioned documents would be "the product of reliable principles and methods." Fed. R. Evid. 702(2). We do not know what principles of comparison Mr. Cawley would employ. We do not know what is required to have a valid similarity—one tending to prove that one person wrote both documents—nor do we know how many valid similarities are necessary to rule out the possibility that two people have essentially the same manner of writing the words in question. The Government would offer a witness as to similarities in handwriting who would speak with apparent authority on a subject in which he would appear to have special knowledge which the court is unable to evaluate on the present record. In the absence of tested principles for making comparisons, Mr. Cawley's testimony as to similarities would itself be nothing more than a set of subjective observations and little different from an unsupported opinion as to the fact of authorship of a document. Mr. Cawley's testimony is as likely to mislead a jury as to assist it in determining the facts of this case. It is therefore excluded entirely.

Contrary to the Government's argument at the *Daubert* hearing, nothing in Federal Rule of Evidence 901 demands a different result. At the *Daubert* hearing, the Government argued that Mr. Cawley's testimony must be admissible under Federal Rule of Evidence 901. Rule 901(a) provides that "[t]he requirement of authentication or identification as a condition precedent to admissibility is satisfied by evidence sufficient to support a finding that the matter in question is what its proponent claims." Rule 901(b) lists several examples of authentication or identification that conform with the rule, including one which allows for the "[c]omparison by the trier of fact or by expert witnesses with specimens which have been authenticated." Fed. R. Evid. 901(b)(3). In discussing Rule 901(b)(3), the Advisory Committee Notes specifically mention handwriting comparison testimony and state that "[e]xample (3) sets no higher standard for handwriting specimens and treats all comparison situations alike. . ."

The Government argues that Rule 901(b)(3) plainly contemplates the admission of comparison evidence by forensic document analysts and that to hold otherwise would render 901(b)(3) meaningless. The Government relies on *United States v. Jones*, 107 F.3d 1147 (6th Cir. 1997), in which the court considered the question of admissibility of a handwriting expert's testimony. The court concluded that handwriting analysis was not scientific evidence; but because this was pre-*Kumho*, the court did not apply the *Daubert* standards. Rather, the court considered whether handwriting analysis constituted "technical or other specialized knowledge" under the Federal Rules of Evidence and concluded that it did. In doing so, the court noted that:

> if we were to hold that handwriting analysis is not a field of expertise under the Federal Rules of Evidence, there would be no place for expert witnesses to compare writing on one document with that on another in order to authenticate a document. In other words, appellant's suggested approach would render Rule 901(b)(3) meaningless.

First of all, the court would point out that it is not holding that handwriting analysis can never be a field of expertise under the Federal Rules of Evidence. The court is merely holding that the Government has failed to meet its burden of establishing that the proffered expert testimony in this case is admissible under Rule 702. Second, even if the court were to hold that handwriting analysis is not a field of expertise under the rules, that would not render Rule 901(b)(3) meaningless. Rule 901(b)(3) does not deal exclusively with handwriting comparison, despite the fact that the Advisory Committee Notes for the rule discuss handwriting comparison testimony. Other types of comparison testimony are encompassed within the rule. Last, and most important, Rule 702 and Rule 901 must be read together. Rule 901(b)(3) contemplates testimony by an expert—but before an expert's testimony can be admitted, it must past through the gates of Rule 702. In this case, Mr. Cawley's testimony did not make it through the Rule 702 gate and, therefore, Rule 901 is irrelevant to the question of whether his testimony is admissible.

Conclusion

Defendant's motion *in limine* to exclude testimony of hand printing comparison evidence at trial is granted.

NOTE

The *Saelee* case is the high water mark for exclusion of expert testimony of forensic document examiners. As the citations in the *Saelee* case indicate, other courts have been more permissive about allowing these experts to testify. Some courts have permitted the examiner to describe similarities and differences between the questioned writing and the defendant's writing, but prohibit the examiner from offering an opinion as to whether or not the defendant is its author. Others have continued to allow the experts to testify without limit. For discussion, see David L. Faigman, David H. Kaye, Michael J. Saks, and Joseph Sanders, Science in the Law: Forensic Science Issues 113–193 (2002).

State v. Porter

Supreme Court of Connecticut, 1997.
698 A.2d 739.

■ BORDEN, JUSTICE.

The issues in this certified appeal are: (1) whether Connecticut should adopt as the standard for the admissibility of scientific evidence the standard set forth by the United States Supreme Court in *Daubert v. Merrell Dow Pharmaceuticals, Inc.,* 509 U.S. 579 (1993); and (2) whether Connecticut should abandon its traditional per se rule that polygraph evidence is inadmissible at trial. [The Court decided to adopt the *Daubert* standard. It then turned to a discussion of polygraph evidence:]

II

B

With this background in mind, we turn now to an assessment of the threshold validity, probative value, and prejudicial impact of polygraph evidence. In order to do so, it is necessary to understand some of the mechanics and theory behind the modern polygraph test.

1

Modern polygraph theory rests on two assumptions: (1) there is a regular relationship between deception and certain emotional states; and (2) there is a regular relationship between those emotional states and certain physiological changes in the body that can be measured and recorded. J. Tarantino, Strategic Use of Scientific Evidence (1988) § 6.01, p. 205. These physiological changes include fluctuations in heart rate and blood pressure, rate of breathing, and flow of electrical current through the body, and they are measured by a cardiosphygmograph, a pneumograph and a galvanometer, respectively. Id. These instruments, bundled together, form the basis of most modern polygraphs.

There is no question that a high quality polygraph is capable of accurately measuring the relevant physical characteristics. United States Congress, Office of Technology Assessment, "Scientific Validity of Polygraph Testing: A Review and Evaluation—A Technical Memorandum," OTA–TM–H–15 (1983) (OTA Memorandum), reprinted in 12 Polygraph 198, 201 (1983). Even polygraph advocates, however, acknowledge that "[n]o known physiological response or pattern of responses is unique to deception." D. Raskin, "The Polygraph in 1986: Scientific, Professional and Legal Issues Surrounding Application and Acceptance of Polygraph Evidence," 1986 Utah L.Rev. 29, 31 (1986). Indeed, "there is no reason to believe that lying produces distinctive physiological changes that characterize it and only it... [T]here is no set of responses—physiological or otherwise—that humans omit only when lying or that they produce only when telling the truth... No doubt when we tell a lie many of us experience an inner turmoil, but we experience similar turmoil when we are falsely accused of a crime, when we are anxious about having to defend ourselves against accusations, when we are questioned about sensitive topics—and, for that matter, when we are elated or otherwise emotionally stirred." (Citation omitted.) B. Kleinmuntz & J. Szucko, "On the Fallibility of Lie Detection," 17 Law & Society Rev. 85, 87 (1982). Thus, while a polygraph machine can accurately gauge a subject's *physiological* profile, it cannot, on its own, determine the nature of the underlying *psychological* profile. "The instrument cannot itself detect deception." OTA Memorandum, supra, reprinted in 12 Polygraph 196, statement of John Gibbons, Director of Office of Technology Assessment.

The polygraph examiner, therefore, is responsible for transforming the output of a polygraph machine from physiological data into an assessment of truth or deception. See, e.g., P. Giannelli, "Forensic Science: Polygraph Evidence: Part I," 30 Crim. L. Bull. 262, 264 (1994). This mission actually involves two separate tasks. First, the examiner must design and implement a polygraph test in such a way that the physiological data produced is properly linked to a subject's deceptiveness, and not just to his nervousness or other unrelated emotional responses. Id., 263. Second, even if the data produced *is* linked to a subject's deception, the examiner must interpret the data, that is, grade the test, correctly. Id., 264.

The "control question test" is the polygraph method most commonly used in criminal cases to link physiological responses to deception. See, e.g., C. Honts & M. Perry, "Polygraph Admissibility: Changes and Challenges," 16 Law & Hum. Behav. 357, 360 (1992). The control question test is based on the theory that fear of detection causes psychological stress. Under that test, therefore, the "polygraph instrument is measuring the fear of detection *rather than deception per se.*" (Emphasis added.) OTA Memorandum, supra, reprinted in 12 Polygraph 201.

In the control question test procedure, the polygrapher first conducts a pretest interview with the subject wherein the accuracy and reliability of the polygraph are emphasized.[41] This is done to aggravate the deceptive subject's fear of detection while calming the innocent subject, which is crucial given that the test's efficacy is based entirely on the subject's emotional state. All exam questions are then reviewed with the subject, in order to minimize the impact of surprise on the test results and to ensure that the subject understands the questions. The actual control question test consists of a sequence of ten to twelve questions, repeated several times. There are three categories of questions: neutral; relevant; and control. All questions are formulated by the polygrapher conducting the examination based on a review of the facts of the case.

A neutral question is entirely nonconfrontational and is designed to allow the polygrapher to get a baseline reading on the subject's physiological responses. A neutral question addresses a subject's name, age, address, or similar topic.

A relevant question is accusatory and directed specifically at the subject under investigation. "For example, in an assault investigation, a relevant question might be: 'On May 1, 1986, did you strike Mr. Jones (the alleged victim) with any part of your body?' "J. Tarantino, supra, § 6.09, p. 215.

A control question concerns "an act of wrongdoing of the same general nature as the main incident under investigation," and is designed to be "one to which the subject, in all probability, will lie or to which his answer will be of dubious validity in his own mind." J. Rat & F. Inbau, Truth and Deception (2d Ed.1977) p. 28. Control questions "cover many years in the prior life of the subject and are deliberately vague. Almost anyone would have difficulty answering them truthfully with a simple 'No.' "D. Raskin, supra, 1986 Utah L.Rev. 34. In an assault case, a control question might be: "Did you ever want to see anyone harmed?" J. Tarantino, supra, § 6.09, p. 215. Although few people honestly could deny these control questions categorically, they are "presented to the subject in a manner designed to lead him to believe that admissions would negatively influence the examiner's opinion and that strong reactions to those questions during the test would produce a deceptive result." D. Raskin, supra, 1986 Utah L.Rev. 34.[42]

---

[41] During the pretest interview, a "stimulation test" is often administered. "In this test, the examiner instructs the subject to choose a particular number or name from a preselected series. The polygraph examiner does not know which number or name the subject chooses. The polygraph examiner then instructs the subject to respond 'no' every time he is asked whether he chose a specific number or name. The qualified examiner should be able to determine which response is deceptive by evaluating the physical responses detected by the polygraph. The examiner then confronts the subject with his findings, causing the subject to be 'convinced' that the polygraph examination is effective." J. Tarantino, supra, § 6.11, p. 218. Occasionally, however, the correct response is determined by trickery, not polygraphy. J. Rat & F. Inbau, Truth and Deception (2d Ed.1977) pp. 42, 85 (stimulation test conducted using marked deck of cards).

[42] In other words, the control question test process requires that the examiner, during the pretest interview, manipulate the subject into both (1) lying on the control questions, out of

The theory behind the control question test is that "the truthful person will respond more to the control questions than to the relevant questions because they represent a greater threat to that person. For the same reason the deceptive person will respond more to the relevant questions than to the control questions." P. Giannelli, supra, 30 Crim. L. Bull. 266–67. Thus, in order for the test to work properly, both truthful and deceptive examinees must have particular mind sets during the exam. "The innocent examinee [must fear] that the polygraph examiner will pick up his deception [on the control question] and incorrectly conclude that he is also being deceptive about the relevant question." J. Tarantino, supra, § 6.09, p. 216. As a result, the innocent subject's physiological responses to the control question, stemming from this fear, will be greater than those to the relevant question, which the subject can answer honestly. A guilty subject, however, will be more worried about having his crime and deception exposed by the relevant question than he is about any control question issues. Accordingly, his physiological responses—prompted by his fear of detection—will be greater with regard to the relevant question than to the control question.

Under the control question test, the absolute measure of the subject's physiological responses to each question is unimportant. For example, the mere fact that a subject has a strong response to a relevant question can simply be indicative of nervousness and does not, by itself, indicate deception. Instead, the polygrapher looks to the *relative* strength of the responses to the control and relevant questions in order to determine truth or deception.[43] The art of the polygrapher lies in composing control and relevant questions that elicit the appropriate relative responses from truthful and deceitful parties. See generally *United States v. Kwong,* 69 F.3d 663, 668 (2d Cir.1995) (polygraph results excluded because examiner failed to formulate questions properly); J. McCall, supra, 1996 U. Ill. L.Rev. 378; D. Raskin, supra, 1986 Utah L.Rev. 47–49.

A control question exam ordinarily pairs relevant and control questions with some neutral questions interspersed. For example, a typical progression would be:

---

fear that the examiner will otherwise react negatively to the subject's prior antisocial conduct, and (2) fearing that this same deception will taint the entire exam.

[43] This process is what separates the control question test from the relevant-irrelevant polygraph test. In the latter test, there are no control questions, only relevant and irrelevant questions. A subject whose responses to the relevant questions are greater than those to the irrelevant questions is considered deceptive. Although still practiced by some polygraphers today; P. Giannelli, supra, 30 Crim.L.Bull. 266; the relevant-irrelevant test is almost universally rejected in the literature.

* * *

"1. (Neutral) Do you understand that I will ask only the questions we have discussed?

"2. (Pseudo–Relevant) Regarding whether you took that ring, do you intend to answer all of the questions truthfully?

"3. (Neutral) Do you live in the United States?

"4. (Control) During the first twenty-four years of your life, did you ever take something that did not belong to you?

"5. (Relevant) Did you take a ring from the Behavioral Sciences Building on July 1, 1985?

"6. (Neutral) Is your name Joanne?

"7. (Control) Between the ages of ten and twenty-four, did you ever do anything dishonest or illegal?

"8. (Relevant) Did you take that diamond ring from a desk in the Behavioral Sciences Building on July 1?

"9. (Neutral) Were you born in the month of February?

"10. (Control) Before 1984 did you ever lie to get out of trouble or to cause a problem for someone else?

"11. (Relevant) Were you in any way involved in the theft of that diamond ring from the Behavioral Sciences Building last July?" D. Raskin, supra, 1986 Utah L.Rev. 36. The entire sequence is normally gone through three times, after which the examiner scores the result to attempt to reach a determination of truthfulness or deception.

The most common technique for scoring polygraph charts is pure numerical grading. In the most prevalent numerical system, the polygrapher assigns a numerical value along the range of ▢3 to +3 to each pair of relevant and control questions. A score of +3 indicates a much stronger reaction to the control question than to the relevant question and, therefore, truthfulness; a score of -3 indicates a much stronger reaction to the relevant question and, therefore, deception; and a score of 0 indicates that there was no significant difference in response. The examiner considers only the polygraph chart in assigning these scores; no consideration is given to any subjective impressions regarding the subject's truthfulness that the examiner develops over the course of the exam. The scores for all question pairs in all three sequences are then totaled. If the sum is +6 or greater, the subject is classified as truthful; if the sum is -6 or lower, the subject is classified as deceptive; scores of -5 to +5 are deemed inconclusive. Computers are sometimes used to give more precise numerical scores to polygraph charts.

If an analysis of the first three charts produces inconclusive results, the examiner will often repeat the question sequence twice more. After that, however, further repetitions are generally considered meritless, as the subject will have become habituated to the test questions and, therefore, will no longer have sufficiently strong emotional responses for polygraph purposes. [45] Id., 37–40.

2

We now examine the validity of the results produced by the polygraph test.[46] The word "validity" has two meanings in the polygraph context: for the purposes of this discussion, they will be labeled "accuracy" and "predictive value." Courts generally do not specify to which concept they are referring when they address polygraph issues. Maintaining this distinction is

---

[45] The other main type of polygraph examination used in criminal matters is the guilty knowledge test. The guilty knowledge test "does not attempt to determine whether the [subject] is lying but, rather, whether he or she possesses guilty knowledge, that is, whether the [subject] recognizes the correct answers, from among several equally plausible but incorrect alternatives, to certain questions relating to a crime. For example, escaping through an alley a bank robber drops and leaves behind his hat. A likely suspect is later apprehended and, while attached to the polygraph, he is interrogated as follows:

"1. 'The robber in this case dropped something while escaping. If you are that robber, you will know what he dropped. Was it: a weapon? a face mask? a sack of money? his hat? his car keys?' ...

"Unlike the control question test, the accuracy of the guilty knowledge test does not depend upon the nature or degree of the subject's emotional concern. The physiological variables employed are not intended to measure emotional response but, rather, to signal the cognitive processes involved in the recognition of the correct alternative." D. Lykken, "The Case Against Polygraph Testing," in The Polygraph Test (A. Gale ed., 1988) pp. 111, 121–23.

"The guilty knowledge test assumes that the guilty subject will have a greater physical response to the 'significant alternative' than would a subject without any guilty knowledge." J. Tarantino, supra, § 6.13, p. 219. Advocates claim that the primary advantage of the guilty knowledge test is that recognition can be more directly measured by physiological data than can truth or deception. D. Lykken, "The Case Against Polygraph Testing," supra, pp. 121–23.

For the guilty knowledge test to work, however, there must be "concealed knowledge" that only the guilty party would know and recognize. This requirement greatly limits the number of cases in which the test can be utilized. P. Giannelli, supra, 30 Crim.L.Bull. 266. In any event, although the guilty knowledge test does have its advocates; D. Lykken, "The Case Against Polygraph Testing," supra, pp. 121–24; B. Kleinmuntz & J. Szucko, supra, 17 Law & Society Rev. 98; the guilty knowledge test's validity is as hotly debated as that of the control question test. C. Honts & M. Perry, supra, 16 Law & Hum. Behav. 359; D. Raskin, supra, 1986 Utah L.Rev. 31–32 n. 12 (many guilty people can pass guilty knowledge test). Because the validity of the guilty knowledge test is so uncertain, and because all of the prejudicial effects of allowing control question test evidence apply to guilty knowledge test evidence as well; see part II B 2 b of this opinion; we conclude that guilty knowledge test evidence must also be excluded from use in our courts.

[46] Although courts generally use the word "reliability" when discussing the polygraph test; see, e.g., *United States v. Crumby,* 895 F.Supp. 1354, 1358 (D.Ariz.1995) ("[t]he Court must consider whether polygraph evidence is *reliable* under *Daubert*"[emphasis added]); the concept to which the courts are referring is actually the test's "validity." In the polygraph context, reliability and validity have specialized meanings. Reliability refers only to reproducibility of results, or consistency, while validity relates to the test's actual ability to do what it claims to do, namely, detect deception. 1 C. McCormick, supra, § 206, p. 909 n. 28. Reliability is important, but the polygraph debate really centers around the test's validity. See generally S. Blinkhorn, "Lie Detection As a Psychometric Procedure," in The Polygraph Test (A. Gale ed., 1988) pp. 29, 31–35.

essential, however, if one is to evaluate fairly the validity of the polygraph test.

a

The "accuracy" of the polygraph test itself has two components: *sensitivity* and *specificity*. The polygraph's sensitivity is its ability to tell that a guilty person is, in fact, lying. If the polygraph test had a 90 percent sensitivity, then it would correctly label a deceptive subject as being deceptive 90 percent of the time. Thus, the test would incorrectly label a deceptive subject as being truthful 10 percent of the time; this mislabeling is called a "false negative" error. The polygraph's specificity is its ability to tell that an innocent person is, in fact, being truthful. If the polygraph test had an 80 percent specificity, then it would label a truthful subject as being truthful 80 percent of the time. The test would thus incorrectly label a truthful subject as being deceptive 20 percent of the time; this mislabeling is called a "false positive" error. It is generally agreed in the literature, by both advocates and critics, that polygraphs have greater sensitivity than specificity; that is, that false positives outnumber false negatives. See, e.g., C. Honts & M. Perry, supra, 16 Law & Hum. Behav. 362; see also *United States v. Galbreth,* 908 F.Supp. 877, 885 (D.N.M.1995).

There is wide disagreement, however, as to what the sensitivity and specificity values actually are for a well run polygraph exam. See generally 1 C. McCormick, supra, § 206, pp. 907–17. Dozens of studies of polygraph accuracy have been conducted. Id. They fall into two basic types, namely, laboratory simulations of crimes[47] and field studies based on data from polygraph examinations in actual criminal cases.[48] P. Giannelli, supra, 30 Crim. L. Bull. 270–73. The variance in expert opinion regarding polygraph accuracy arises from disagreements as to which methods and which studies within each method are methodologically valid. C. Honts & M. Perry, supra, 16 Law & Hum. Behav. 360.

Polygraph supporters base their accuracy estimates on both laboratory simulation and field studies. These advocates acknowledge that field studies are theoretically preferable for establishing the polygraph test's field accuracy, but they conclude that serious methodological difficulties inherent in such studies, such as establishing the actual guilt or innocence of

---

[47] "The most accepted type of laboratory study simulates a real crime in which subjects are randomly assigned to guilty and innocent treatment conditions.... Guilty subjects enact a realistic crime, and innocent subjects are merely told about the nature of the crime and do not enact it. All subjects are motivated to produce a truthful outcome, usually by a substantial cash bonus for passing the test." (Citations omitted.) D. Raskin, "Does Science Support Polygraph Testing?," in The Polygraph Test (A. Gale ed., 1988) pp. 96, 99.

[48] "The best available method for field research uses cases in which suspects were administered polygraph tests after which their guilt or innocence was established when the guilty person confessed. Other polygraph examiners are then asked to make diagnoses based solely on the polygraph charts from those tests without knowledge of the guilt or innocence of the subjects or the opinions of the original examiners. The decisions from these blind analyses are then compared to the confession criterion to estimate the accuracy of the polygraph tests." D. Raskin, supra, 1986 Utah L.Rev. 44.

the study subjects, make most of these studies unreliable. They think, however, that laboratory studies, when designed to approximate field conditions and when carefully conducted, *can* provide useful and valid data. See generally J. Kircher, S. Horowitz & D. Raskin, "Meta-analysis of Mock Crime Studies of the Control Question Polygraph Technique," 12 Law & Hum. Behav. 79, 80 (1988); see also C. Honts & M. Perry, supra, 16 Law & Hum. Behav. 361. David Raskin, perhaps the foremost polygraph advocate in the United States, recently reviewed the literature on polygraph studies and concluded that eight laboratory studies and four field studies of the control question test polygraph technique were methodologically valid. D. Raskin, "The Scientific Status of Research on Polygraph Techniques," in West Companion to Scientific Evidence 2 (Faigman et al. eds., forthcoming 1996), cited in C. Honts & B. Quick, "The Polygraph in 1995: Progress in Science and the Law," 71 N.D. L.Rev. 987, 995, 1018–19 (1995). The laboratory studies that Raskin cites, taken together, indicate that the polygraph test has an 89 percent sensitivity rate and a 91 percent specificity rate;[49] the field studies give an 87 percent sensitivity and a 59 percent specificity.[50] Id. Other studies indicate higher levels of accuracy. See generally P. Giannelli, supra, 30 Crim. L. Bull. 271–73; C. McCormick, supra, § 206, pp. 909–10. The United States Department of Defense, although acknowledging that more research needs to be done, concluded after a thorough review of the literature that there was no "data suggesting that the various polygraph techniques and applications . . . have high false positive or high false negative error rates." United States Department of Defense, The Accuracy and Utility of Polygraph Testing (1984) p. 63.

Critics, however, view the existing body of polygraph studies quite differently. First, although polygraph detractors agree with the advocates that most field studies are invalid due to methodological concerns, they disagree as to which tests *are* valid. David Lykken, a prominent polygraph critic, has concluded from the field tests he deems valid that the polygraph has a sensitivity of 84 percent and a specificity of only 53 percent. D. Lykken, "The Validity of Tests: Caveat Emptor," 27 Jurimetrics J. 263, 264 (1987).[51] Another critic has concluded that reliable field studies indicate that there is

---

[49] It is interesting that the recent laboratory studies cited here by Raskin as valid give *lower* aggregate rates for polygraph sensitivity and specificity than did those studies deemed reliable by him in an article he wrote ten years ago. D. Raskin, supra, 1986 Utah L.Rev. 43 (concluding that polygraph has 97 percent sensitivity and 92 percent specificity). It would appear that as testing has advanced, the validity of the polygraph has become more questionable.

[50] Pursuant to standard practice in calculating specificity and sensitivity, we exclude all of the inconclusive outcomes in the raw data from our calculations, because inconclusive results are not conclusions. See, e.g., C. Honts & B. Quick, supra, N.D.L.Rev. 996 n. 65.

[51] Lykken admittedly wrote this assessment before any of the recent field studies on which Raskin relies were published. Nonetheless, there is inarguably a fundamental schism in the type of field study that Raskin and Lykken will regard as valid. For example, the three studies that Lykken deems "scientifically credible"; D. Lykken, supra, 27 Jurimetrics J. 264; are specifically attacked by Raskin as not satisfying even "basic methodological requirements." D. Raskin & J. Kircher, "The Validity of Lykken's Criticisms: Fact or Fancy?," 27 Jurimetrics J. 271, 272 (1987).

"little or no case" for using the polygraph, and that "polygraph lie detection adds nothing positive to conventional approaches to interrogation and assessment." D. Carroll, "How Accurate Is Polygraph Lie Detection?," in The Polygraph Test (A. Gale ed., 1988) pp. 19, 28. After its own thorough review of the polygraph field studies, the United States Office of Technology Assessment concluded that "the cumulative research evidence suggest that . . . the polygraph test detects deception better than chance, but with significant error rates." OTA Memorandum, supra, reprinted in 12 Polygraph 200.

Moreover, polygraph critics argue that laboratory simulation studies are almost completely invalid. They point out that, although the accuracy of the control question test turns entirely on the subject having the "right" emotional responses, the emotional stimuli in the laboratory are completely different from those in the field. D. Carroll, "How Accurate Is Polygraph Lie Detection?," supra, p. 24. "In the mock crime paradigm . . . it is likely that volunteer subjects regard the experience as a kind of interesting game. Those persons instructed to commit the mock crime and to lie during the test no doubt feel a certain excitement, but not the guilt or fear of exposure that a real thief feels when tested for the police. Volunteers assigned to the innocent group have no reason at all to fear the relevant questions; they are not suspected of any wrongdoing and they will not be punished or defamed even if the test goes awry. On the other hand, the control questions used in laboratory studies . . . unlike the relevant questions, do refer to real-world events and, presumably, have the same embarrassing or disturbing effect on volunteer subjects that they have on criminal suspects. This is probably the reason why mock crime studies typically show a much lower rate of false positive errors than do studies of actual criminal interrogation in the field. Innocent suspects often fail police-administered tests . . . because they find the relevant questions more disturbing than the control questions, since they know they are in real jeopardy in respect to the accusations contained in the relevant questions while the controls involve no comparable risk. For the volunteer laboratory subject, this balance is reversed." D. Lykken, "The Case Against Polygraph Testing," in The Polygraph Test (A. Gale ed., 1988) pp. 111, 114–15.[52] Raskin has admitted that these concerns with laboratory simulations are significant. J. Kircher, S. Horowitz & D. Raskin, supra, 12 Law & Hum. Behav. 80, 88–89.

---

[52] Lykken describes a laboratory investigation that "succeeded in eliciting genuine concern in both the 'guilty' and 'innocent' examinees. [Two examiners] had forty-eight prison inmates tested in a mock crime situation. It was understood that each participant's bonus of $20 would be withheld if more than ten of the forty-eight subjects failed the polygraph test. Moreover, the names of inmates failing the test would be posted in the prison for all to see. The intent was to make both 'guilty' and 'innocent' subjects believe that, if they failed the test, they might be blamed by their fellow inmates for the loss of the $20, a considerable sum by prison standards. That this manipulation was successful is suggested by the fact that several inmates expressed their concern about the consequences of failing and a few actually declined to participate for that reason. Two skilled and experienced examiners administered control question tests and all charts were independently scored by both examiners.... [O]nly thirty of the forty-eight subjects were correctly classified. Excluding inconclusive tests, there were 13 percent false negative errors and 44 percent of the 'innocent' inmates were misclassified as deceptive." D. Lykken, "The Case Against Polygraph Testing," supra, p. 115.

Even if one accepts Raskin's field study estimates of accuracy over those of the polygraph critics, polygraph evidence is of questionable validity. Raskin's 87 percent sensitivity indicates a 13 percent false negative rate. In other words, 13 percent of those who are in fact deceptive will be labeled as truthful. Moreover, Raskin's 59 percent specificity indicates a 41 percent false positive rate. In other words, 41 percent of subjects who are, in fact, truthful will be labeled as deceptive.

b

In the previous section, we demonstrated that the basic *accuracy* of the polygraph test is still open to considerable debate. The actual *probative value* of polygraph evidence as a signifier of guilt or innocence, moreover, is even more questionable. This is because sensitivity, for example, only tells how likely a polygraph is to label accurately a person as deceptive *given that* the person really is lying. At trial, however, we would not yet know that a subject is deceptive—indeed, making that determination may be the entire point of the trial. Knowing how accurately the polygraph test labels deceptive people as deceptive is not, therefore, directly helpful. We are instead interested in a related, but distinct, question: how likely is it that a person really is lying given that the polygraph labels the subject as deceptive? This is called the "predictive value positive." Similarly, at trial we are not directly interested in the polygraph test's specificity, but rather in its "predictive value negative": how likely is it that a subject really is truthful given that the polygraph labels the subject as not deceptive?

Predictive value positive and predictive value negative depend on the sensitivity and specificity of the polygraph test, but also turn on the "base rate"[53] of deceptiveness among the people tested by the polygraph.[54] Unfor-

---

[53] The term "base rate" refers to the prevalence of a condition among the relevant tested population. In the context of the polygraph test, the base rate is the percentage of people who submit to a polygraph exam who are, in fact, deceptive on the exam. If, out of every 100 people who take a polygraph test, we could empirically demonstrate that fifty are, in fact, giving deceptive responses, then the base rate of deception would be 50 percent.

The base rate is important because it can greatly accentuate the impact of the false positive and false negative rates arising from any given specificity and sensitivity values. If one assumes base rates progressively higher than 50 percent, then, by definition, the number of deceptive examinees increases and the number of honest examinees decreases. A logical consequence is that, even holding specificity and sensitivity rates constant, as the base rate increases the number of false negatives (the labeling of deceptive subjects as truthful) also rises and the number of false positives (the labeling of truthful subjects as deceptive) falls, because only deceptive subjects produce false negatives and only truthful subjects produce false positives. Likewise, if one were to assume base rates progressively lower than 50 percent, then, even holding sensitivity and specificity constant, as the base rate falls the number of false positives will necessarily rise and the number of false negatives will fall.

For example, a very low base rate would dramatically emphasize the problem of false positives, even if sensitivity and specificity were both relatively high. Suppose that the polygraph has a sensitivity of 90 percent (and thus a false negative rate of 10 percent) and a specificity of 80 percent (and thus a false positive rate of 20 percent), and that the base rate of deception is 10 percent. If 100 subjects are tested, then the 10 percent base rate signifies that ten subjects

tunately, no reliable measure of this base rate currently exists if, indeed, one is possible at all. Raskin has claimed, on the basis of an analysis of a United States Secret Service study and on the basis of his own empirical experience, that only about 40 to 60 percent of criminal defendants who are willing to submit to polygraph tests are actually guilty. D. Raskin, supra, 1986 Utah L.Rev. 59–60. If a base rate of about 50 percent were correct, then, using Raskin's own field derived figures of 87 percent sensitivity and 59 percent specificity, the predictive value positive of the polygraph test would only be 68 percent and the predictive value negative would be 82 percent.[55] That is, even if we were to agree with all of Raskin's figures, we should only be 68 percent confident that a subject really is lying if the subject fails a polygraph exam, and only 82 percent confident that the subject is being truthful if the subject passes. Therefore, although the probative value of the polygraph test may be greater than that of a coin toss, it is not significantly greater, especially for failed tests.[56]

---

are deceptive and ninety are truthful. Given the specificity of 80 percent, seventy-two of the ninety truthful subjects will be labeled accurately as truthful (80 percent of ninety is seventy-two); the remaining eighteen truthful subjects will be mislabeled as deceptive due to the 20 percent false positive rate. Similarly, given the sensitivity of 90 percent, nine of the ten deceptive subjects will be labeled accurately as deceptive (90 percent of ten is nine); the remaining deceptive subject will be mislabeled as truthful due to the 10 percent false negative rate. These results can be summarized as follows:

	Innocent	Guilty
Pass	72	1
Fail	18	9

"A hundred people are tested: 81 percent are correctly classified; 90 percent of the guilty fail; 80 percent of the innocent pass. And yet of these who fail, only one in three is guilty." S. Blinkhorn, "Lie Detection As a Psychometric Procedure," in The Polygraph Test (A. Gale ed., 1988) pp. 29, 34.

[54] Predictive value positive (PVP) and predictive value negative (PVN) are determined by an equation involving the polygraph test's sensitivity and specificity, and the base rate of deception among the tested population. Mathematically, the relationship among these concepts is expressed as follows:

$$PVP= \frac{\Pi\eta}{\Pi(\eta + \Theta-1) + (1-\Theta)}$$

and:

$$PVN= \frac{\Theta(1-\Pi)}{\Theta(1-\Pi) + \Pi(1-\eta)}$$

where:
Π = the base rate of deception among people who choose to take the polygraph exam;
η = the polygraph test's sensitivity; and
Θ = the polygraph test's specificity.

See D. Kaye, "The Validity of Tests: Caveant Omnes," 27 Jurimetrics J. 349 (1987).

[55] The figures of 68 percent predictive value positive and 82 percent predictive value negative noted in the text of this opinion are the result of the application of the equation stated in footnote 54, using a base rate of 50 percent, a sensitivity rate of 87 percent, and a specificity rate of 59 percent.

[56] Even if we were to use only Raskin's laboratory derived values for sensitivity and specificity in calculating predictive value positive and predictive value negative, the polygraph test would still be of questionable worth. Assuming an 89 percent sensitivity, a 91 percent specificity and a base rate of 50 percent, the predictive value positive of the polygraph test is only 91

Furthermore, the 50 percent base rate that Raskin posits is far from universally accepted. "[T]he figures for [the base rate] that [Raskin] pull[s] out of the hat should not be taken as firm." D. Kaye, "The Validity of Tests: Caveant Omnes," 27 Jurimetrics J. 349, 357 (1987). Lykken posits, albeit with as equally sparse evidence as Raskin, that the base rate of guilt among people volunteering for a polygraph exam is 80 percent. D. Lykken, supra, 27 Jurimetrics J. 268. Using this base rate, the polygraph test's predictive value positive is 89 percent and its predictive value negative is 53 percent. Lykken's base rate, therefore, makes a failed test more probative than it is under Raskin's base rate, but makes a passed test much less probative.

The *specific* predictive value positive and predictive value negative figures generated by a particular set of assumptions, however, is not the significant point for the legal determination of whether to admit polygraph evidence. The point is that, given the complete absence of reliable data on base rates, we have no way of assessing the probative value of the polygraph test. Under one set of assumptions, a failed test has some significance, while a passed test does not; under another, the situation is reversed. The figures are further muddied when one recalls that the sensitivity and specificity of the polygraph are also hotly debated.

c

Countermeasures are also a concern with regard to polygraph validity. A countermeasure is any technique used by a deceptive subject to induce a false negative result and thereby pass the test. For a countermeasure to work on the control question test, all it must do is "change the direction of the differential reactivity between the relevant and control questions. . ." G. Gudjonsson, "How to Defeat the Polygraph Tests," in The Polygraph Test (A. Gale ed., 1988) pp. 126, 127.

It may be true that "subjects *without special training* in countermeasures are unable to beat the polygraph test, even if they have been provided with extensive information and suggestions on how they might succeed. . ."[57] (Citation omitted; emphasis added.) D. Raskin, "Hofmann, Hyp-

---

percent and the predictive value negative is only 89 percent. In other words, approximately one out of every ten polygraph examinations would still mislabel the subject.

We emphasize, moreover, that Raskin himself has never advocated assessing the validity of the polygraph examination solely by the use of laboratory data, without reference to field studies. Indeed, for the reasons set forth by the polygraph critics, we are persuaded that it would be reversible error for a trial court to follow such a procedure. Furthermore, to the extent that the previously mentioned figures may appear impressive to some, it is important to remember that, even if one does believe that use of laboratory derived values for sensitivity and specificity is appropriate, the assumed base rate of 50 percent underlying the calculations has essentially no empirical support.

[57] But see D. Lykken, supra, 27 Jurimetrics J. 267 ("As it happens, there is a simple, easily learned technique with which a guilty person can 'beat' the control question test. In one

nosis, and the Polygraph," 3 Utah B.J. 7, 8 (1990); G. Gudjonsson, "How to Defeat the Polygraph Tests," supra, p. 135. Yet as one polygraph supporter, Charles Honts, concedes, "studies have indicated that [expert-conducted] training in specific point countermeasures designed to increase [physiological responses to control questions] is effective in producing a substantial number of false negative outcomes. . ." C. Honts & B. Quick, supra, 71 N.D. L.Rev. 1001. Specifically, "[s]ubjects in these studies were informed about the nature of the control question test and were trained to recognize control and relevant questions. Countermeasure subjects were then instructed to employ a countermeasure (e.g., bite their tongue, press their toes to the floor, or count backward by seven) during the control question zones of a control question test. In one study, none of the guilty subjects who received this brief training was correctly detected. . . Across all of the studies more than 50% of the decisions on countermeasures subjects were incorrect." (Citation omitted.) C. Honts & M. Perry, supra, 16 Law & Hum. Behav. 374. Although we share Honts' hope that "the required [expert] training is . . . difficult to obtain"; C. Honts & B. Quick, supra, 71 N.D. L.Rev. 1001; we question whether such is the case and whether it would remain the case if polygraph examination of witnesses became common, especially given the apparent brevity and simplicity of the training in question.

3

With the foregoing information in mind, we will assume, without deciding, that polygraph evidence satisfies *Daubert*. Although the subjective nature and highly questionable predictive value of the polygraph test weigh heavily against admission, we assume that polygraph evidence may have enough demonstrated validity to pass the *Daubert* threshold for admissibility.

We conclude, however, that admission of the polygraph test would be highly detrimental to the operation of Connecticut courts, both procedurally and substantively. Moreover, as illustrated in part II B 2 b of this opinion, the probative value of polygraph evidence is very low, even if it satisfies *Daubert*. Accordingly, we also conclude that any limited evidentiary value that polygraph evidence does have is substantially outweighed by its prejudicial effects. We therefore reaffirm our per se rule against the use of polygraph evidence in Connecticut courts.

---

informal prison study, twenty-seven inmates accused of violating prison rules were given some fifteen minutes of instruction in this method [by a fellow inmate, based on information provided by Lykken] before reporting for a test concerned with the alleged infraction. Although all twenty-seven privately admitted their guilt, twenty-four of them managed to pass the polygraph.").

United States v. Piccinonna

United States Court of Appeals, Eleventh Circuit (En Banc), 1989.
885 F.2d 1529.

■ FAY, CIRCUIT JUDGE:

In this case, we revisit the issue of the admissibility at trial of polygraph expert testimony and examination evidence. Julio Piccinonna appeals his conviction on two counts of knowingly making false material
statements to a Grand Jury in violation of Title IV of the Organized Crime
Control Act of 1970. 18 U.S.C. 1623 (1982). Piccinonna argues that the trial
judge erred in refusing to admit the testimony of his polygraph expert and
the examination results. Because of the significant progress made in the
field of polygraph testing over the past forty years and its increasingly
widespread use, we reexamine our per se rule of exclusion and fashion new
principles to govern the admissibility of polygraph evidence. Accordingly,
we remand the case to the trial court to reconsider the admissibility of Piccinonna's polygraph test results in light of the principles we espouse today.

I. Background

Julio Piccinonna has been in the waste disposal business in South
Florida for over twenty-five years. In 1983, a Grand Jury conducted hearings to investigate antitrust violations in the garbage business. The government believed that South Florida firms in the waste disposal business
had agreed not to compete for each other's accounts, and to compensate one
another when one firm did not adhere to the agreement and took an account from another firm.

Piccinonna was compelled to testify before the Grand Jury pursuant to
a grant of immunity. The immunity, however, did not protect Piccinonna
from prosecution for perjury committed during his testimony. Piccinonna
testified that he had not heard of the agreement between garbage companies to refrain from soliciting each other's accounts and to compensate each
other for taking accounts. The Grand Jury, however, also heard testimony
from several witnesses involved in the disposal industry who implicated
Piccinonna in the garbage industry agreement. On August 1, 1985, Piccinonna was indicted on four counts of perjury.

Prior to trial, Piccinonna requested that the Government stipulate to
the admission into evidence of the results of a polygraph test which would
be administered subsequently. The Government refused to stipulate to the
admission of any testimony regarding the polygraph test or its results. Despite the Government's refusal, George B. Slattery, a licensed polygraph
examiner, tested Piccinonna on November 25, 1985. Piccinonna asserted
that the expert's report left no doubt that he did not lie when he testified
before the Grand Jury. On November 27, 1985, Piccinonna filed a motion
with the district court requesting a hearing on the admission of the poly-

graph testimony. On January 6, 1986, the district court held a hearing on the defendant's motions. Due to the per se rule, which holds polygraph evidence inadmissible in this circuit, the trial judge refused to admit the evidence. * * *

Piccinonna was convicted on two counts of making false material declarations concerning a matter the Grand Jury was investigating. * * * On appeal, Piccinonna urges us to modify our per se rule excluding polygraph evidence to permit its admission in certain circumstances.

II. The Per Se Rule

In federal courts, the admissibility of expert testimony concerning scientific tests or findings is governed by Rule 702 of the Federal Rules of Evidence. Rule 702 provides:

> If scientific, technical, or other specialized knowledge will assist the trier of fact to understand the evidence or to determine a fact in issue, a witness qualified as an expert by knowledge, skill, experience, training or education, may testify thereto in the form of an opinion or otherwise.

Fed.R.Evid. 702. Under this rule, to admit expert testimony the trial judge must determine that the expert testimony will be relevant and will be helpful to the trier of fact. In addition, courts require the proponent of the testimony to show that the principle or technique is generally accepted in the scientific community.

The general acceptance requirement originated in the 1923 case of Frye v. United States, 293 F. 1013 (D.C.Cir.1923). *Frye* involved a murder prosecution in which the trial court refused to admit results from a systolic blood pressure test, the precursor of the polygraph. The defendant appealed, arguing that the admissibility of the scientific test results should turn only on the traditional rules of relevancy and helpfulness to the trier of fact. The court of appeals disagreed and imposed the requirement that the area of specialty in which the court receives evidence must have achieved general acceptance in the scientific community. The court stated that "while courts will go a long way in admitting expert testimony deduced from a well-recognized scientific principle or discovery, the thing from which the deduction is made must be sufficiently established to have gained general acceptance in the particular field in which it belongs." The court concluded that the systolic blood pressure test lacked the requisite "standing and scientific recognition among physiological and psychological authorities."

Courts have applied the *Frye* standard to various types of scientific tests, including the polygraph. However, the *Frye* standard has historically been invoked only selectively to other types of expert testimony, and has been applied consistently only in cases where the admissibility of polygraph evidence was at issue. Most courts had little difficulty with the desirability of excluding polygraph evidence and thus, applied the *Frye* standard with little comment. This circuit also has consistently reaffirmed, with little discussion, the inadmissibility of polygraph evidence. . .

Recently, the application of the *Frye* standard to exclude polygraph evidence has been subject to growing criticism. Since the *Frye* decision, tremendous advances have been made in polygraph instrumentation and technique.[8] Better equipment is being used by more adequately trained polygraph administrators. Further, polygraph tests are used extensively by government agencies. Field investigative agencies such as the FBI, the Secret Service, military intelligence and law enforcement agencies use the polygraph. Thus, even under a strict adherence to the traditional *Frye* standard, we believe it is no longer accurate to state categorically that polygraph testing lacks general acceptance for use in all circumstances. For this reason, we find it appropriate to reexamine the per se exclusionary rule and institute a rule more in keeping with the progress made in the polygraph field.

III. Differing Approaches to Polygraph Admissibility

Courts excluding polygraph evidence typically rely on three grounds: 1) the unreliability of the polygraph test, 2) the lack of standardization of polygraph procedure, and 3) undue impact on the jury. Proponents of admitting polygraph evidence have attempted to rebut these concerns. With regard to unreliability, proponents stress the significant advances made in the field of polygraphy.[12] Professor McCormick argues that the fears of unreliability "are not sufficient to warrant a rigid exclusionary rule. A great deal of lay testimony routinely admitted is at least as unreliable and inaccurate, and other forms of scientific evidence involve risks of instrumental or judgmental error." McCormick, *supra*, § 206 at 629. Further, proponents argue that the lack of standardization is being addressed and will progressively be resolved as the polygraph establishes itself as a valid scientific test. Sevilla, *Polygraph 1984: Behind the Closed Door of Admissibility,* 16 U. West L.A.L.Rev. 5, 19 (1984).[13] Finally, proponents argue that there is no evidence that jurors are unduly influenced by polygraph evidence. *Id.* at

---

[8] Barland, Raskin, *"Detection of Deception,"* Electro-Dermal Activity in Psychological Research (1973); Barland, Raskin, *An Evaluation of Field Techniques in the Detection of Deception,* 12 Psychophysiology 321 (1975); Podlesny, Raskin, *Effectiveness of Techniques and Physiological Measurers in the Detection of Deception,* 15 Psychophysiology 344 (1978).

[12] Polygraph examiners contend that a properly administered polygraph test is a highly effective way to detect deception and cite figures between 92% and 100% for its accuracy. McCormick, *supra* § 206 at 626. Others suggest figures in the range of 63–72%. *Id.*

[13] For instance, Sevilla points out that experts in the polygraph field have developed detailed standards for administration of polygraph tests. The American Polygraph Association and state organizations have standards in their charters which members must follow as well. *See* Sevilla, *supra* at 19.

17. In fact, several studies refute the proposition that jurors are likely to give disproportionate weight to polygraph evidence.[14]

In the wake of new empirical evidence and scholarly opinion which have undercut many of the traditional arguments against admission of polygraph evidence, a substantial number of courts have revisited the admissibility question. Three roughly identifiable approaches to the problem have emerged. First, the traditional approach holds polygraph evidence inadmissible when offered by either party, either as substantive evidence or as relating to the credibility of a witness. Second, a significant number of jurisdictions permit the trial court, in its discretion, to receive polygraph evidence if the parties stipulate to the evidence's admissibility before the administration of the test and if certain other conditions are met. Finally, some courts permit the trial judge to admit polygraph evidence even in the absence of a stipulation, but only when special circumstances exist. In these jurisdictions, the issue is within the sound discretion of the trial judge. * * *

IV. Principles for Admissibility

* * *

[W]e believe the best approach in this area is one which balances the need to admit all relevant and reliable evidence against the danger that the admission of the evidence for a given purpose will be unfairly prejudicial. Accordingly we outline two instances where polygraph evidence may be admitted at trial, which we believe achieve the necessary balance.

A. *Stipulation*

The first rule governing admissibility of polygraph evidence is one easily applied. Polygraph expert testimony will be admissible in this circuit when both parties stipulate in advance as to the circumstances of the test and as to the scope of its admissibility. The stipulation as to circumstances must indicate that the parties agree on material matters such as the manner in which the test is conducted, the nature of the questions asked, and the identity of the examiner administering the test. The stipulation as to scope of admissibility must indicate the purpose or purposes for which the evidence will be introduced. Where the parties agree to both of these conditions in advance of the polygraph test, evidence of the test results is admissible.

---

[14] Carlson, Pasano & Jannunzzo, *The Effect of Lie Detector Evidence on Jury Deliberations: An Empirical Study,* 5 J. Pol. Sci. & Admin. 148; Markwart & Lynch, *The Effect of Polygraph Evidence on Mock Jury Decision-Making,* 7 J. Pol. Sci. & Admin. 324 (1979); Peters, *A Survey of Polygraph Evidence in Criminal Trials,* 68 A.B.A. J. 162, 165 (1982) (citing cases in which the jury verdict in criminal trials was at odds with the testimony of the polygraph examiner.)

B. *Impeachment or Corroboration*

The second situation in which polygraph evidence may be admitted is when used to impeach or corroborate the testimony of a witness at trial. Admission of polygraph evidence for these purposes is subject to three preliminary conditions. First, the party planning to use the evidence at trial must provide adequate notice to the opposing party that the expert testimony will be offered. Second, polygraph expert testimony by a party will be admissible only if the opposing party was given reasonable opportunity to have its own polygraph expert administer a test covering substantially the same questions. Failure to provide adequate notice or reasonable opportunity for the opposing side to administer its own test is proper grounds for exclusion of the evidence.

Finally, whether used to corroborate or impeach, the admissibility of the polygraph administrator's testimony will be governed by the Federal Rules of Evidence for the admissibility of corroboration or impeachment testimony. For example, Rule 608 limits the use of opinion or reputation evidence to establish the credibility of a witness in the following way: "[E]vidence of truthful character is admissible only after the character of the witness for truthfulness has been attacked by opinion or reputation evidence or otherwise." Thus, evidence that a witness passed a polygraph examination, used to corroborate that witness's in-court testimony, would not be admissible under Rule 608 unless or until the credibility of that witness were first attacked. Even where the above three conditions are met, admission of polygraph evidence for impeachment or corroboration purposes is left entirely to the discretion of the trial judge.

Neither of these two modifications to the per se exclusionary rule should be construed to preempt or limit in any way the trial court's discretion to exclude polygraph expert testimony on other grounds under the Federal Rules of Evidence. Our holding states merely that in the limited circumstances delineated above, the *Frye* general acceptance test does not act as a bar to admission of polygraph evidence as a matter of law. * * * Thus, we agree with the Ninth Circuit "that polygraph evidence should not be admitted, even for limited purposes, unless the trial court has determined that 'the probative value of the polygraph evidence outweighs the potential prejudice and time consumption involved in presenting such evidence.'"

Thus under the Federal Rules of Evidence governing the admissibility of expert testimony, the trial court may exclude polygraph expert testimony because 1) the polygraph examiner's qualifications are unacceptable; 2) the test procedure was unfairly prejudicial or the test was poorly administered; or 3) the questions were irrelevant or improper. The trial judge has wide discretion in this area, and rulings on admissibility will not be reversed unless a clear abuse of discretion is shown.

V. Conclusion

We neither expect nor hope that today's holding will be the final word within our circuit on this increasingly important issue. The advent of new and developing technologies calls for flexibility within the legal system so that the ultimate ends of justice may be served. It is unwise to hold fast to a familiar rule when the basis for that rule ceases to be persuasive. We believe that the science of polygraphy has progressed to a level of acceptance sufficient to allow the use of polygraph evidence in limited circumstances where the danger of unfair prejudice is minimized. We proceed with caution in this area because the reliability of polygraph testing remains a subject of intense scholarly debate. As the field of polygraph testing continues to progress, it may become necessary to reexamine the rules regarding the admissibility of polygraph evidence.

The judgment of conviction is VACATED and the case is REMANDED to the district court for further proceedings consistent with this opinion.

[Note: Part of the majority's discussion of judicial precedent has been redacted from the casebook excerpt. The majority's brief discussion of the scientific validity of polygraphy has, however, been reproduced in its entirety.

The opinion of Circuit Judge Johnson, in which Chief Judge Roney and Circuit Judges Hill and Clark joined, has also been omitted. Judge Johnson concurred in the portion of the majority opinion that allowed polygraph tests to be admitted on stipulation of both parties, but dissented from the portion finding the polygraph to be generally accepted in the scientific community and holding that results may be admitted even in the absence of stipulation.—Eds.]

United States v. Scheffer

Supreme Court of the United States, 1998.
523 U.S. 303.

■ JUSTICE THOMAS announced the judgment of the Court and delivered the opinion of the Court with respect to Parts I, II–A, and II–D, and an opinion with respect to Parts II–B and II–C, in which THE CHIEF JUSTICE, JUSTICE SCALIA, and JUSTICE SOUTER joined.

This case presents the question whether Military Rule of Evidence 707, which makes polygraph evidence inadmissible in court-martial proceedings, unconstitutionally abridges the right of accused members of the military to present a defense. We hold that it does not.

I

In March 1992, respondent Edward Scheffer, an airman stationed at March Air Force Base in California, volunteered to work as an informant on drug investigations for the Air Force Office of Special Investigations (OSI). His OSI supervisors advised him that, from time to time during the course of his undercover work, they would ask him to submit to drug testing and polygraph examinations. In early April, one of the OSI agents supervising respondent requested that he submit to a urine test. Shortly after providing the urine sample, but before the results of the test were known, respondent agreed to take a polygraph test administered by an OSI examiner. In the opinion of the examiner, the test "indicated no deception" when respondent denied using drugs since joining the Air Force.

On April 30, respondent unaccountably failed to appear for work and could not be found on the base. He was absent without leave until May 13, when an Iowa state patrolman arrested him following a routine traffic stop and held him for return to the base. OSI agents later learned that respondent's urinalysis revealed the presence of methamphetamine.

Respondent was tried by general court-martial on charges of using methamphetamine, failing to go to his appointed place of duty, wrongfully absenting himself from the base for 13 days, and, with respect to an unrelated matter, uttering 17 insufficient funds checks. He testified at trial on his own behalf, relying upon an "innocent ingestion" theory and denying that he had knowingly used drugs while working for OSI. On cross-examination, the prosecution attempted to impeach respondent with inconsistencies between his trial testimony and earlier statements he had made to OSI.

Respondent sought to introduce the polygraph evidence in support of his testimony that he did not knowingly use drugs. The military judge denied the motion, relying on Military Rule of Evidence 707, which provides, in relevant part:

"(a) Notwithstanding any other provision of law, the results of a polygraph examination, the opinion of a polygraph examiner, or any reference to an offer to take, failure to take, or taking of a polygraph examination, shall not be admitted into evidence."

The military judge determined that Rule 707 was constitutional because "the President may, through the Rules of Evidence, determine that credibility is not an area in which a fact finder needs help, and the polygraph is not a process that has sufficient scientific acceptability to be relevant." He further reasoned that the factfinder might give undue weight to the polygraph examiner's testimony, and that collateral arguments about such evidence could consume "an inordinate amount of time and expense."

Respondent was convicted on all counts and was sentenced to a bad-conduct discharge, confinement for 30 months, total forfeiture of all pay and allowances, and reduction to the lowest enlisted grade. The Air Force Court of Criminal Appeals affirmed in all material respects, explaining that

Rule 707 "does not arbitrarily limit the accused's ability to present reliable evidence."

By a 3–to–2 vote, the United States Court of Appeals for the Armed Forces reversed. Without pointing to any particular language in the Sixth Amendment, the Court of Appeals held that "[a] *per se* exclusion of polygraph evidence offered by an accused to rebut an attack on his credibility, . . . violates his Sixth Amendment right to present a defense."[3] Judge Crawford, dissenting, stressed that a defendant's right to present relevant evidence is not absolute, that relevant evidence can be excluded for valid reasons, and that Rule 707 was supported by a number of valid justifications. We granted certiorari, and we now reverse.

II

A defendant's right to present relevant evidence is not unlimited, but rather is subject to reasonable restrictions. See Taylor v. Illinois, 484 U.S. 400, 410 (1988); Rock v. Arkansas, 483 U.S. 44, 55 (1987); Chambers v. Mississippi, 410 U.S. 284, 295 (1973). A defendant's interest in presenting such evidence may thus " 'bow to accommodate other legitimate interests in the criminal trial process.' "*Rock, supra,* at 55 (quoting *Chambers, supra,* at 295). As a result, state and federal rulemakers have broad latitude under the Constitution to establish rules excluding evidence from criminal trials. Such rules do not abridge an accused's right to present a defense so long as they are not "arbitrary" or "disproportionate to the purposes they are designed to serve." Moreover, we have found the exclusion of evidence to be unconstitutionally arbitrary or disproportionate only where it has infringed upon a weighty interest of the accused.

Rule 707 serves several legitimate interests in the criminal trial process. These interests include ensuring that only reliable evidence is introduced at trial, preserving the jury's role in determining credibility, and avoiding litigation that is collateral to the primary purpose of the trial. The rule is neither arbitrary nor disproportionate in promoting these ends. Nor does it implicate a sufficiently weighty interest of the defendant to raise a constitutional concern under our precedents.

A

State and federal governments unquestionably have a legitimate interest in ensuring that reliable evidence is presented to the trier of fact in a criminal trial. Indeed, the exclusion of unreliable evidence is a principal objective of many evidentiary rules.

---

[3] In this Court, respondent cites the Sixth Amendment's Compulsory Process Clause as the specific constitutional provision supporting his claim. He also briefly contends that the "combined effect" of the Fifth and Sixth Amendments confers upon him the right to a "meaningful opportunity to present a complete defense," Crane v. Kentucky, 476 U.S. 683, 690 (1986) (citations omitted), and that this right in turn encompasses a constitutional right to present polygraph evidence to bolster his credibility.

The contentions of respondent and the dissent notwithstanding, there is simply no consensus that polygraph evidence is reliable. To this day, the scientific community remains extremely polarized about the reliability of polygraph techniques. 1 D. Faigman, D. Kaye, M. Saks, & J. Sanders, Modern Scientific Evidence 565, n. †; § 14–2.0, and § 14–3.0 (1997); see also 1 P. Giannelli & E. Imwinkelried, Scientific Evidence § 8–2(C), pp. 225–227 (2d ed. 1993) (hereinafter Giannelli & Imwinkelried); 1 J. Strong, McCormick on Evidence § 206, p. 909 (4th ed. 1992) (hereinafter McCormick). Some studies have concluded that polygraph tests overall are accurate and reliable. See, e.g., S. Abrams, The Complete Polygraph Handbook 190–191 (1968) (reporting the overall accuracy rate from laboratory studies involving the common "control question technique" polygraph to be "in the range of 87 percent"). Others have found that polygraph tests assess truthfulness significantly less accurately—that scientific field studies suggest the accuracy rate of the "control question technique" polygraph is "little better than could be obtained by the toss of a coin," that is, 50 percent. See Iacono & Lykken, The Scientific Status of Research on Polygraph Techniques: The Case Against Polygraph Tests, in 1 Modern Scientific Evidence, *supra*, § 14–5.3, p. 629 (hereinafter Iacono & Lykken).[6]

This lack of scientific consensus is reflected in the disagreement among state and federal courts concerning both the admissibility and the reliability of polygraph evidence. Although some Federal Courts of Appeal have abandoned the *per se* rule excluding polygraph evidence, leaving its admission or exclusion to the discretion of district courts under *Daubert*, see, *e.g.*, United States v. Posado, 57 F. 3d 428, 434 (C.A.5 1995); United States v. Cordoba, 104 F. 3d 225, 228 (C.A.9 1997), at least one Federal Circuit has recently reaffirmed its *per se* ban, see United States v. Sanchez, 118 F. 3d 192, 197 (C.A.4 1997), and another recently noted that it has "not decided whether polygraphy has reached a sufficient state of reliability to be admissible." United States v. Messina, 131 F. 3d 36, 42 (C.A.2 1997). Most States maintain *per se* rules excluding polygraph evidence. New Mexico is unique in making polygraph evidence generally admissible without the prior stipulation of the parties and without significant restriction. See

---

[6] The United States notes that in 1983 Congress' Office of Technology Assessment evaluated all available studies on the reliability of polygraphs and concluded that " '[o]verall, the cumulative research evidence suggests that when used in criminal investigations, the polygraph test detects deception better than chance, but with error rates that could be considered significant.' " Brief for United States 21 (quoting U.S. Congress, Office of Technology Assessment, Scientific Validity of Polygraph Testing: A Research Review and Evaluation—A Technical Memorandum 5 (OTA–TM–H–15, Nov. 1983)). Respondent, however, contends current research shows polygraph testing is reliable more than 90 percent of the time. Brief for Respondent 22 (citing J. Matte, Forensic Psychophysiology Using the Polygraph, 121–129 (1996)). Even if the basic debate about the reliability of polygraph technology itself were resolved, however, there would still be controversy over the efficacy of countermeasures, or deliberately adopted strategies that a polygraph examinee can employ to provoke physiological responses that will obscure accurate readings and thus "fool" the polygraph machine and the examiner. See, *e.g.*, Iacono & Lykken § 14–3.0.

N.M. Rule Evid. § 11–707.[8] Whatever their approach, state and federal courts continue to express doubt about whether such evidence is reliable.

The approach taken by the President in adopting Rule 707—excluding polygraph evidence in all military trials—is a rational and proportional means of advancing the legitimate interest in barring unreliable evidence. Although the degree of reliability of polygraph evidence may depend upon a variety of identifiable factors, there is simply no way to know in a particular case whether a polygraph examiner's conclusion is accurate, because certain doubts and uncertainties plague even the best polygraph exams. Individual jurisdictions therefore may reasonably reach differing conclusions as to whether polygraph evidence should be admitted. We cannot say, then, that presented with such widespread uncertainty, the President acted arbitrarily or disproportionately in promulgating a *per se* rule excluding all polygraph evidence.

[Part II–B of Justice Thomas's opinion argued that Rule 707 served a second legitimate governmental interest, that of "preserving the jury's core function of making credibility determinations in criminal trials." Part II–C argued that Rule 707 was a reasonable way of avoiding collateral litigation about matters such as whether the polygraph examiner was qualified or whether countermeasures had distorted the exam results. Only four members of the Court joined in Parts II–B and II–C—Eds.]

D

The three of our precedents upon which the Court of Appeals principally relied, Rock v. Arkansas, 483 U.S. 44 (1987), Washington v. Texas, 388 U.S. 14 (1967), and Chambers v. Mississippi, 410 U.S. 284 (1973), do not support a right to introduce polygraph evidence, even in very narrow circumstances. The exclusions of evidence that we declared unconstitutional in those cases significantly undermined fundamental elements of the accused's defense. Such is not the case here.

In *Rock*, the defendant, accused of a killing to which she was the only eyewitness, was allegedly able to remember the facts of the killing only after having her memory hypnotically refreshed. See Rock v. Arkansas, 483 U.S., at 46. Because Arkansas excluded all hypnotically refreshed testimony, the defendant was unable to testify about certain relevant facts, including whether the killing had been accidental. In holding that the exclusion

---

[8] Respondent argues that because the Government—and in particular the Department of Defense—routinely uses polygraph testing, the Government must consider polygraphs reliable. Governmental use of polygraph tests, however, is primarily in the field of personnel screening, and to a lesser extent as a tool in criminal and intelligence investigations, but not as evidence at trials. See Brief for United States 34, n. 17; Barland, The Polygraph Test in the USA and Elsewhere, in The Polygraph Test 76 (A. Gale ed. 1988). Such limited, out of court uses of polygraph techniques obviously differ in character from, and carry less severe consequences than, the use of polygraphs as evidence in a criminal trial. They do not establish the reliability of polygraphs as trial evidence, and they do not invalidate reliability as a valid concern supporting Rule 707's categorical ban.

of this evidence violated the defendant's "right to present a defense," we noted that the rule deprived the jury of the testimony of the only witness who was at the scene and had firsthand knowledge of the facts. Moreover, the rule infringed upon the accused's interest in testifying in her own defense—an interest that we deemed particularly significant, as it is the defendant who is the target of any criminal prosecution. For this reason, we stated that an accused ought to be allowed "to present his own version of events in his own words."

In *Washington*, the statutes involved prevented co-defendants or co-participants in a crime from testifying for one another and thus precluded the accused from introducing his accomplice's testimony that the accomplice had in fact committed the crime. In reversing Washington's conviction, we held that the Sixth Amendment was violated because "the State arbitrarily denied [the accused] the right to put on the stand a witness who was physically and mentally capable of testifying to events that he had personally observed."

In *Chambers*, we found a due process violation in the combined application of Mississippi's common law "voucher rule," which prevented a party from impeaching his own witness, and its hearsay rule that excluded the testimony of three persons to whom that witness had confessed. *Chambers* specifically confined its holding to the "facts and circumstances" presented in that case; we thus stressed that the ruling did not "signal any diminution in the respect traditionally accorded to the States in the establishment and implementation of their own criminal trial rules and procedures." *Chambers* therefore does not stand for the proposition that the accused is denied a fair opportunity to defend himself whenever a state or federal rule excludes favorable evidence.

Rock, Washington, and *Chambers* do not require that Rule 707 be invalidated, because, unlike the evidentiary rules at issue in those cases, Rule 707 does not implicate any significant interest of the accused. Here, the court members heard all the relevant details of the charged offense from the perspective of the accused, and the Rule did not preclude him from introducing any factual evidence. Rather, respondent was barred merely from introducing expert opinion testimony to bolster his own credibility. Moreover, in contrast to the rule at issue in *Rock*, Rule 707 did not prohibit respondent from testifying on his own behalf; he freely exercised his choice to convey his version of the facts to the court-martial members. We therefore cannot conclude that respondent's defense was significantly impaired by the exclusion of polygraph evidence. Rule 707 is thus constitutional under our precedents.

* * *

For the foregoing reasons, Military Rule of Evidence 707 does not unconstitutionally abridge the right to present a defense. The judgment of the Court of Appeals is reversed.

It is so ordered.

[The opinion of Justice Kennedy, with whom JUSTICE O'CONNOR, JUSTICE GINSBURG, and JUSTICE BREYER joined, concurring in part and concurring in the judgment, has been omitted.]

State v. Chapple

Supreme Court of Arizona, En Banc, 1983.
135 Ariz. 281, 660 P.2d 1208.

■ FELDMAN, JUSTICE.

Dolan Chapple was convicted on three counts of first degree murder * * *

FACTS

The instigator of this bizarre drama was Mel Coley, a drug dealer who resided in Washington, D.C., but who was also connected with dealers in Kansas City. Coley had a history of dealing with a supplier named Bill Varnes, who lived near Phoenix.

Coley had made a large number of drug deals through Malcolm Scott, a "middleman" who lived near Phoenix. Scott was also well acquainted with Varnes * * *.

Coley telephoned in early December 1977 and told Scott that he was interested in purchasing approximately 300 pounds of marijuana. He asked Scott to act as middleman in the transaction. Scott was to get $700 for his efforts. Scott testified that he called one or two of the Arizona suppliers with whom he was acquainted and found they could not supply the necessary quantity. He then called his sister, Pamela Buck, who was a "good friend" of Varnes and had worked with him in some drug deals. Scott asked Buck to contact her friend Varnes and see whether he could handle the sale. Buck talked to Varnes and reported to her brother that Varnes could supply the necessary amount of marijuana at an agreed upon price.

On the evening of December 10 or the early morning of December 11, 1977, Coley arrived at the Phoenix airport from Washington, D.C. Scott met him at the airport and found that Coley was accompanied by two strangers who were introduced as "Dee" and "Eric." Scott drove the three men to a trailer located at his parents' farm near Higley in Pinal County, Arizona. Scott had used this trailer in the past as a meeting place to consummate drug transactions. This meeting place was part of the service which Scott provided for his "finder's fee."

Coley, Dee and Eric spent the night at the trailer, while Scott returned to his residence in Mesa. The next morning Scott returned to the farm and took Coley to the airport where they picked up a brown leather bag. Back at the trailer, Scott observed Coley, Eric and Dee take four guns from the bag and clean them. Scott examined and handled one of the guns. Buck had also arrived at the trailer in Higley, and she and Dee were dispatched to Varnes' trailer in order to purchase a sample of the marijuana.

Later that morning the conversation between Coley, Eric and Dee indicated that it was likely there would be a "rip-off" of the marijuana and that Coley did not intend to pay for the goods. When Buck expressed to her brother the fear that Varnes would seek revenge if his goods were stolen, Scott told her not to worry because Varnes might never be seen again.

That evening, Scott and his sister met at the trailer with Coley, Eric and Dee. Varnes arrived with two companions, Eduardo Ortiz and Carlos Elsy. Ortiz and Elsy began to unload the marijuana and put it in the trailer.

After Ortiz and Elsy had finished unloading the marijuana and stacking it in the living room of the trailer, Dee suggested to Varnes that they go in the bedroom and "count the money." They started toward the bedroom and Buck went into the bathroom. A few moments later, Buck heard several shots, opened the bathroom door and ran out. Scott heard the shots while he was on the porch and saw a door of the trailer open. Elsy ran out, pursued by either Eric or Dee. After seeing Buck run out of the door at the other end of the trailer, Scott went back to the trailer and found Varnes dead in the bedroom of a gunshot wound to the head and Ortiz in the living room dead of a gunshot wound to the body. Subsequent ballistic tests showed they had been shot with different weapons. Elsy was outside, dead from a blow to the back of the head.

Dee and Eric then removed the marijuana from the trailer and loaded it into a car which Coley had directed Scott to buy the previous day.[1] Scott, Eric and Dee loaded the three bodies into the trunk of Varnes' car. That car was driven out to the desert, doused with gasoline and set afire. The trailer was cleaned to remove evidence of the crime and the carpet in the trailer was burned. The parties then left the scene of the crime and returned to Scott's house in Mesa. Eric and Dee asked for directions regarding the route to Kansas City and then left in the car containing the marijuana. Coley gave Scott and Buck $500 each. He then called the airport and reserved a seat to leave for Washington, D.C. under the name of "James Logan." Scott returned to the trailer and completed the cleanup. Fear or remorse, or

---

[1] Coley had given Scott $1,200 to buy a car. Scott got the car from "Harry the repo man" for $800, pocketing the difference.

both, drove Scott to seek the aid of a lawyer, who succeeded in negotiating an immunity deal for Scott and in getting him to surrender to the sheriff.

Defendant does not contest any of the foregoing facts. Defendant is accused of being "Dee." He denies this. At his extradition hearing in Illinois, seven witnesses placed him in Cairo, Illinois during the entire month of December 1977, three of them testifying specifically to his presence in that town on December 11, the day of the crime. The same witnesses testified for him in the trial at which he was convicted. No direct or circumstantial evidence of any kind connects defendant to the crime,[2] other than the testimony of Malcolm Scott and Pamela Buck, neither of whom had ever met the defendant before the crime and neither of whom saw him after the crime except at the trial. Defendant was apprehended and tried only because Malcolm Scott and Pamela Buck picked his photograph out of a lineup more than one year after the date of the crime; he was convicted because they later identified both the photographs and defendant himself at trial.

* * *

Defendant argued at trial, and urges here, that even if Scott and Buck are not lying, their identification was a case of mistaken identity. The argument is that Scott and Buck picked the wrong picture out of the photographic lineup and that their subsequent photographic and in-court identifications were part of the "feedback phenomenon" and are simply continuations or repetitions of the same mistake. To support this contention of mistaken identification, defendant offered expert testimony regarding the various factors that affect the reliability of identification evidence. For the most part, that testimony was rejected by the trial court as not being within the proper sphere of expert testimony.

* * *

EXPERT TESTIMONY REGARDING EYEWITNESS IDENTIFICATION

On learning of Mel Coley's participation in the crime, the sheriff's office quickly procured photographs of Coley, which were shown to Scott and Buck in a photographic lineup on December 16, 1977. Both of them identified Coley, thus providing law enforcement with the first step in its efforts to apprehend Dee and Eric. The detectives then showed Scott and Buck various photographs and lineups containing pictures of known acquaintances of Mel Coley. At this same session, Scott pointed to a picture of James Logan and stated that it resembled Dee, though he could not be sure. So far as the record shows, no follow-up was made of this tentative identification. One of the photographic lineups displayed to Scott, but not to

---

[2] Neither Coley, Eric nor Dee wore gloves during the events described. Latent fingerprints were found in the trailer and the vehicle containing the bodies, but did not match defendant's fingerprints.

Buck, contained a picture of the defendant, Dolan Chapple, but Scott did not identify him as Dee.

The police continued to show the witnesses photographic lineups in an attempt to obtain an identification of Dee. Police efforts were successful on January 27, 1979, when Scott was shown a nine-picture photo lineup. For the first time, this lineup included photos of both Eric Perry, who had already been tentatively identified by Scott and Buck, and of the defendant; however, James Logan's photo was not included. Upon seeing this lineup, Scott immediately recognized Eric's picture again. About ten minutes later, Scott identified defendant's picture as Dee. Scott was then shown the picture of defendant he had failed to identify at a previous session and asked to explain why he had not previously identified it. He stated that he had no recollection of having seen it before. After Scott had identified Dee and before he could talk to his sister, the police showed Buck the same lineup. Buck identified the defendant as Dee.

Defendant argues that the jury could have found the in-court identification unreliable for a variety of reasons. The defendant argues that the identification of Dee from photographic lineups in this case was unreliable because of the time interval which passed between the occurrence of the event and the lineup and because of the anxiety and tension inherent in the situation surrounding the entire identification process.[3] The defendant also argues that since Scott and Buck had smoked marijuana on the days of the crime, their perception would have been affected, making their identification through photographs less reliable. Further, defendant claims the January 27, 1979 identification of Dee by Scott and Buck from the photographic lineup was the product of an unconscious transfer. Defendant claims that Scott picked the picture of Dolan Chapple and identified it as Dee because he remembered that picture from the previous lineup (when he had not been able to identify defendant's picture). Defendant urges that the in-court identifications were merely reinforcements of the initial error. Further, defendant claims that the identification was made on the basis of subsequently acquired information which affected memory. Finally, defendant argues that the confidence and certainty which Scott and Buck displayed in making their in-court identification at trial had no relation whatsoever to the accuracy of that identification and was, instead, the product of other factors.

It is against this complicated background, with identification the one issue on which the guilt or innocence of defendant hinged, that defense counsel offered the testimony of an expert on eyewitness identification in order to rebut the testimony of Malcolm Scott and his sister, Pamela Buck.

---

[3] Buck and Scott both said they were frightened for their lives during the events. Since they are the only witnesses, one might assume they were also frightened and apprehensive during the time period when Eric and Dee were both at liberty.

The witness called by the defense was Dr. Elizabeth Loftus, a professor of psychology at the University of Washington. Dr. Loftus specializes in an area of experimental and clinical psychology dealing with perception, memory retention and recall. Her qualifications are unquestioned, and it may fairly be said that she "wrote the book" on the subject. The trial court granted the State's motion to suppress Dr. Loftus' testimony. Acknowledging that rulings on admissibility of expert testimony are within the discretion of the trial court, defendant contends that the court erred and abused its discretion in granting the motion to suppress Dr. Loftus' testimony.

The admissibility of expert testimony is governed by Rule 702, Ariz.R. of Evid. That rule states:

> If scientific, technical, or other specialized knowledge will assist the trier of fact to understand the evidence or to determine a fact in issue, a witness qualified as an expert by knowledge, skill, experience, training, or education, may testify thereto in the form of an opinion or otherwise.

> In what is probably the leading case on the subject, the Ninth Circuit affirmed the trial court's preclusion of expert evidence on eyewitness identification in United States v. Amaral. In its analysis, however, the court set out four criteria which should be applied in order to determine the admissibility of such testimony. These are: (1) qualified expert; (2) proper subject; (3) conformity to a generally accepted explanatory theory; and (4) probative value compared to prejudicial effect. Id. at 1153. We approve this test and find that the case at bar meets these criteria.

> We recognize that the cases that have considered the subject have uniformly affirmed trial court rulings denying admission of this type of testimony. However, a careful reading of these cases reveals that many of them contain fact situations which fail to meet the *Amaral* criteria or are decided on legal principles which differ from those we follow in Arizona. * * *

> Applying the *Amaral* test to the case at bench, we find from the record that the State has conceded that the expert was qualified and that the question of conformity to generally accepted explanatory theory is not raised and appears not to be a question in this case. The two criteria which must therefore be considered are (1) determination of whether the probative value of the testimony outweighs its possible prejudicial effect and (2) determination of whether the testimony was a proper subject.

(1) PROBATIVE VALUE *vs.* PREJUDICE

> The State argues that there would have been little probative value to the witness' testimony and great danger of unfair prejudice. The latter problem is claimed to arise from the fact that Loftus' qualifications were so impressive that the jury might have given improper weight to her testimo-

ny. We do not believe that this raises the issue of *unfair* prejudice. The contention of lack of probative value is based on the premise that the offer of proof showed that the witness would testify to general factors which were applicable to this case and affect the reliability of identification, but would not express any opinion with regard to the accuracy of the specific identification made by Scott and Buck and would not express an opinion regarding the accuracy percentage of eyewitness identification in general.

We believe that the "generality" of the testimony is a factor which favors admission. Witnesses are permitted to express opinions on ultimate issues but are not required to testify to an opinion on the precise questions before the trier of fact.

Most of the literature assumes that experts testify only in the form of opinions. The assumption is logically unfounded. [Rule 702] accordingly recognizes that an expert on the stand may give a dissertation or exposition of scientific or other principles relevant to the case, leaving the trier of fact to apply them to the facts. Since much of the criticism of expert testimony has centered upon the hypothetical question, it seems wise to recognize that opinions are not indispensable and to encourage the use of expert testimony in non-opinion form when counsel believes the trier can itself draw the requisite inference.

Fed.R. of Evid. 702 advisory committee note.

(2) PROPER SUBJECT

The remaining criterion at issue is whether the offered evidence was a proper subject for expert testimony. Ariz.R. of Evid. 702 allows expert testimony if it "will assist the trier of fact to understand the evidence or to determine a fact in issue." Put conversely, the test "is whether the subject of inquiry is one of such common knowledge that people of ordinary education could reach a conclusion as intelligently as the witness * * *." Furthermore, the test is not whether the jury could reach some conclusion in the absence of the expert evidence, but whether the jury is qualified without such testimony "to determine intelligently and to the best possible degree the particular issue without enlightenment from those having a specialized understanding of the subject. * * *" Fed.R.Evid. 702 advisory committee note (quoting Ladd, Expert Testimony, 5 Vand.L.Rev. 414, 418 (1952)).

In excluding the evidence in the case at bench, the trial judge stated:

I don't find anything that's been presented in the extensive discussions that I have read in your memorandum with regard to the fact that this expert is going to testify to anything that isn't within the common experience of the people on the jury, that couldn't really be covered in cross-examination of the witnesses who made the identification, and probably will be excessively argued in closing arguments to the jury.

This basis for the view that eyewitness identification is not a proper subject for expert testimony is the same as that adopted in United States v. Amaral, supra, and in the great majority of cases which have routinely followed *Amaral*.

However, after a careful review of these cases and the record before us, we have concluded that although the reasons cited by the trial judge would correctly permit preclusion of such testimony in the great majority of cases, it was error to refuse the testimony in the case at bench. In reaching this conclusion, we have carefully considered the offer of proof made by the defense in light of the basic concept of "proper subject" underlying Rule 702.

We note at the outset that the law has long recognized the inherent danger in eyewitness testimony.[4] Of course, it is difficult to tell whether the ordinary juror shares the law's inherent caution of eyewitness identification. Experimental data indicates that many jurors "may reach intuitive conclusions about the reliability of [such] testimony that psychological research would show are misguided." Note, Did Your Eyes Deceive You? Expert Psychological Testimony on the Unreliability of Eyewitness Identification, 29 Stan.L.Rev. 969, 1017 (1977).

Even assuming that jurors of ordinary education need no expert testimony to enlighten them to the danger of eyewitness identification, the offer of proof[5] indicated that Dr. Loftus' testimony would have informed the jury that there are many specific variables which affect the accuracy of identification and which apply to the facts of this case. For instance, while most jurors would no doubt realize that memory dims as time passes, Dr. Loftus presented data from experiments which showed that the "forgetting curve" is not uniform. Forgetting occurs very rapidly and then tends to level out; immediate identification is much more trustworthy than long-delayed identification. Thus, Scott's recognition of Logan's features as similar to those of Dee when Logan's picture was shown at the inception of the investigation is probably a more reliable identification than Scott's identification of Chapple's photograph in the photographic lineup thirteen months later. By the same token, Scott's failure to identify Chapple's photograph when it was first shown to him on March 26, 1978 (four months after the crime) and when Scott's ability to identify would have been far greater, is of key importance.

Another variable in the case is the effect of stress upon perception. Dr. Loftus indicated that research shows that most laymen believe that stress-

---

[4] "The vagaries of eye-witness identification are well know: the annals of criminal law are rife with instances of mistaken identification. * * * 'What is the worth of identification testimony even when uncontradicted? The identification of strangers is proverbially untrustworthy. The hazards of such testimony are established by a formidable number of instances in the records of English and American trials.'"

[5] The offer of proof was taken with Dr. Loftus on the stand and the jury excluded from the courtroom.

ful events cause people to remember "better" so that what is seen in periods of stress is more accurately related later. However, experimental evidence indicates that stress causes inaccuracy of perception with subsequent distortion of recall.

Dr. Loftus would also have testified about the problems of "unconscious transfer," a phenomenon which occurs when the witness confuses a person seen in one situation with the person seen in a different situation. Dr. Loftus would have pointed out that a witness who takes part in a photo identification session without identifying any of the photographs and who then later sees a photograph of one of those persons may relate his or her familiarity with the picture to the crime rather than to the previous identification session.

Another variable involves assimilation of post-event information. Experimental evidence, shown by Dr. Loftus, confirms that witnesses frequently incorporate into their identifications inaccurate information gained subsequent to the event and confused with the event. An additional problem is the "feedback factor." We deal here with two witnesses who were related and who, according to Loftus' interview, engaged in discussions with each other about the identification of Dee. Dr. Loftus, who interviewed them, emphasized that their independent descriptions of Dee at times utilized identical language. Dr. Loftus would have explained that through such discussions identification witnesses can reinforce their individual identifications. Such reinforcement will often tend to heighten the certainty of identification. The same may be said of the continual sessions that each witness had with the police in poring over large groups of photographs.[6]

The last variable in this case concerns the question of confidence and its relationship to accuracy. Dr. Loftus' testimony and some experimental data indicate that there is no relationship between the confidence which a witness has in his or her identification and the actual accuracy of that identification. Again, this factor was specifically tied to the evidence in the case before us since both Scott and Buck indicated in their testimony that they were absolutely sure of their identification. Evidently their demeanor on the witness stand showed absolute confidence.[7]

We cannot assume that the average juror would be aware of the variables concerning identification and memory about which Dr. Loftus was qualified to testify.

_____

[6] We do not suggest that the police attempted to prejudice the identification procedure. The facts show that the police were careful to avoid the possibility of prejudice. However, as Dr. Loftus pointed out, it is not possible to discuss identification of photographs with witnesses on seven different occasions, comprising a total of over 200 pictures, without giving the witness some "feedback" with respect to what the officers anticipate or expect the witness to find.

[7] We base this conclusion on statements the prosecutor made in closing argument and in defense counsel's attempts to argue that the jurors should not be misled by the confidence which the witnesses displayed in their identification testimony.

Depriving [the] jurors of the benefit of scientific research on eyewitness testimony force[d] them to search for the truth without full knowledge and opportunity to evaluate the strength of the evidence. In short, this deprivation prevent[ed] [the] jurors from having "the best possible degree" of "understanding the subject" toward which the law of evidence strives.

Note, supra, 29 Stan.L.Rev. at 1017–18. Thus, considering the standard of Rule 702, supra,—whether the expert testimony will assist the jury in determining an issue before them—and the unusual facts in this case, we believe that Dr. Loftus' offered evidence was a proper subject for expert testimony and should have been admitted.

Of course, the test is not whether we believe that under these facts the evidence was admissible, but whether the trial court abused its discretion in reaching the contrary conclusion. Our review of the record leads us to the following conclusions regarding the various factors which support admission or preclusion here. Among the factors considered are the following:

1. The facts were close and one of the key factual disputes to be resolved involved the accuracy of the eyewitness identification. The preclusion ruling undercut the entire evidentiary basis for defendant's arguments on this issue.

2. The testimony offered was carefully limited to an exposition of the factors affecting reliability, with experimental data supporting the witness' testimony and no attempt was made to have the witness render opinions on the actual credibility or accuracy of the identification witnesses. Issues of ultimate fact may be the subject of expert testimony, but witnesses are not "permitted as experts on how juries should decide cases." Ariz.R. of Evid. 704 comment.

3. On the other hand, we see no significant prejudice to the State in permitting the testimony; the problem of time is not present in this case, since time spent on the crucial issue of the case can not be considered as "undue" loss of time. No other significant factor weighing against admission of the evidence seems present.

4. No question exists with regard to three of the four criteria listed in United States v. Amaral, supra, being fulfilled by the factual situation present in this case.

5. The key issue here pertained to the fourth criterion—the question of whether Loftus' evidence was a "proper subject" for expert testimony.

As indicated above, the key to this issue is whether the testimony might assist the jury to resolve the issues raised by the facts. In making this determination, the trial court must first consider those contentions of ultimate fact raised by the party offering the evidence and supported by evidentiary facts in the record. It must then determine whether the expert testimony will assist in resolving the issues.

In our view, the record clearly shows that Dr. Loftus' testimony would have been of considerable assistance in resolving some of the factual contentions raised by the parties in this case. Examples follow:

First, the photographs in evidence show that there is a resemblance between Logan and Chapple. Scott told the police that Logan's photograph resembled Dee. Scott then failed to identify Chapple's photograph when it was first shown to him. Considering these facts, might Scott's comments regarding the Logan photographs be considered an identification? Should it be considered more accurate than his identification of Chapple from the photographic lineup almost one year later? Loftus' testimony regarding the forgetting curve would have assisted the jury in deciding this issue.

Second, assuming the jury disregarded, as was its right, Scott's and Buck's denial of having discussed Dee's description prior to the identification of January 27, 1979, did the feedback/after-acquired information phenomena play a part in Buck's identification of defendant on the cropped-hair lineup? We cannot assume that ordinary jurors would necessarily be aware of the impact of these factors.

Third. Logan and Chapple bear some resemblance. Logan's picture had been the object of some comment between Scott and the sheriff's deputies shortly after the killing. Although he professed to have no memory of it, Scott had seen a picture of the defendant within a few months of the shooting. Was Scott's identification of defendant on the January 27, 1979 lineup therefore influenced by an unconscious transfer of memory? Since Dee evidently looked like Logan and Chapple, was this transfer phenomenon with regard to their photographs more pronounced than it was with regard to other photographs which were shown to Scott on more than one occasion?

Fourth. Since a cropped-hair picture of Logan, who bore a resemblance to defendant and was tentatively identified by Scott soon after the killing, was not included in the lineup of January 1979, were Scott and Buck given a reasonable choice with respect to the photos which they examined on the occasion on which they identified Chapple?

Fifth. The opportunity for perception by the witnesses in this case was great. Most of us would assume that where the opportunity for perception has been significantly greater than the usual case, the recall of the witness and the subsequent identification must be correspondingly more accurate than in most cases. The expert testimony may well have led to the opposite conclusion, though Dr. Loftus admitted that none of her experiments had been based upon situations where the opportunity for perception had been similar to that of the case at bench. Nevertheless, it is implicit in Loftus' testimony that even in cases such as this, the other factors described by her can have a significant impact on the accuracy of later identification.

Sixth, did the witnesses' absolute confidence in the identification bear any relationship to the accuracy of that identification? Again, contrary to Dr. Loftus' opinion, most people might assume that it would.

Each of the factual issues described above is raised by evidentiary facts in the record or reasonable inferences from those facts. In effect, the trial judge ruled that all of the information necessary to resolve the conflicting factual contentions on these issues was within the common experience of the jurors and could be covered in cross-examination of the identification witnesses and argued to the jury.

It is difficult to support this conclusion. For instance, while jurors are aware that lapse of time may make identification less reliable, they are almost certainly unaware of the forgetting curve phenomenon and the resultant inference that a prompt tentative identification may be much more accurate than later positive identification. Similarly, cross-examination is unlikely to establish any evidentiary support for argument that eyewitnesses who have given similar nonfactual descriptions of the criminal may have been affected by the feedback phenomenon. Again, experimental data provides evidentiary support to arguments which might otherwise be unpersuasive because they seem contrary to common "wisdom."[8]

The phrase "within the discretion of the trial court" is often used but the reason for that phrase being applied to certain issues is seldom examined. One of the primary reasons an issue is considered discretionary is that its resolution is based on factors which vary from case to case and which involve the balance of conflicting facts and equitable considerations. Walsh v. Centeio, 692 F.2d 1239, 1242 (9th Cir.1982). Thus, the phrase "within the discretion of the trial court" does not mean that the court is free to reach any conclusion it wishes. It does mean that where there are opposing equitable or factual considerations, we will not substitute our judgment for that of the trial court.

Thus, while we have no problem with the usual discretionary ruling that the trier of facts needs no assistance from expert testimony on the question of reliability of identification, the unusual facts of this case compel the contrary conclusion. The preclusion ruling here was based upon a determination that the jury would not be assisted by expert testimony be-

---

[8] This problem is apparent on review of final argument. One example is that counsel for the State continually emphasized the degree of certainty of the witnesses and argued the consequent accuracy of the identification. Defense counsel asked the jury not to be misled by the certainty of the witnesses and argued that even people who are wrong are sometimes certain of their identification. No doubt the jury could understand that idea without having heard expert testimony, but we think it fair to say that experimental evidence showing the lack of correlation between certainty and reliability of even truthful witnesses might have given the argument some persuasive force.

cause the subjects embraced by that testimony could be elicited on cross-examination and argued without the evidentiary foundation. Preclusion here was not predicated upon a balancing of conflicting factual contentions or equitable considerations; it was based upon the court's own conclusion that scientific theory regarding the working of human memory could be developed on cross-examination and effectively argued without evidentiary foundation. The examples listed above demonstrate that under the facts here this conclusion was incorrect; there were a number of substantive issues of ultimate fact on which the expert's testimony would have been of significant assistance. Accordingly, we hold that the order precluding the testimony was legally incorrect and was unsupported by the record. It was, therefore, an abuse of discretion. Grant v. Public Service Company, 133 Ariz. 434, 652 P.2d 507 (1982).

In reaching this conclusion, we do not intend to "open the gates" to a flood of expert evidence on the subject. We reach the conclusion that Dr. Loftus should have been permitted to testify on the peculiar facts of this case and have no quarrel with the result reached in the vast majority of cases which we have cited above. The rule in Arizona will continue to be that in the usual case we will support the trial court's discretionary ruling on admissibility of expert testimony on eyewitness identification. Nor do we invite opinion testimony in even the most extraordinary case on the likelihood that a particular witness is correct or mistaken in identification or that eyewitness identification in general has a certain percentage of accuracy or inaccuracy.

* * *

■ HAYS, JUSTICE, dissenting:

I cannot agree with the majority's position that the trial court abused its discretion in excluding the testimony of an expert witness on eyewitness identification. With a view to preserving the integrity of the jury as finders of fact, I dissent in part. * * *

* * *

I also disagree with the majority's conclusion that the average juror does not know that immediate identification is much more trustworthy than long-delayed identification. The average juror may not know the technical terms for this phenomenon, but that is not relevant to his ability to assess a witness' credibility.

My concern here goes beyond the borders of this case. Once we have opened the door to this sort of impeaching testimony, what is to prevent experts from attacking any real or supposed deficiency in every other mental faculty? The peculiar risk of expert testimony with its scientific aura of trustworthiness and the possibility of undue prejudice should be respected.

I have great reluctance to permit academia to take over the fact-finding function of the jury. Although clothed in other guise, that will be the practical effect. With little to distinguish this case from the general rule against admitting expert testimony on eyewitness identification, we are left with no guidelines to decide the deluge of similar issues which are sure to result.

I dissent.

People v. Collins

Supreme Court of California, 1968.
68 Cal.2d 319, 66 Cal.Rptr. 497, 438 P.2d 33.

■ SULLIVAN, JUSTICE. We deal here with the novel question whether evidence of mathematical probability has been properly introduced and used by the prosecution in a criminal case. While we discern no inherent incompatibility between the disciplines of law and mathematics and intend no general disapproval or disparagement of the latter as an auxiliary in the fact-finding processes of the former, we cannot uphold the technique employed in the instant case. As we explain in detail infra, the testimony as to mathematical probability infected the case with fatal error and distorted the jury's traditional role of determining guilt or innocence according to long-settled rules. Mathematics, a veritable sorcerer in our computerized society, while assisting the trier of fact in the search for truth, must not cast a spell over him. We conclude that on the record before us defendant should not have had his guilt determined by the odds and that he is entitled to a new trial. We reverse the judgment.

A jury found defendant Malcolm Ricardo Collins and his wife defendant Janet Louise Collins guilty of second degree robbery (Pen.Code, §§ 211, 211a, 1157). Malcolm appeals from the judgment of conviction. Janet has not appealed.[1] * * *

At the seven-day trial the prosecution experienced some difficulty in establishing the identities of the perpetrators of the crime. The victim could not identify Janet and had never seen defendant. The identification by the witness Bass, who observed the girl run out of the alley and get into the automobile, was incomplete as to Janet and may have been weakened as to defendant. There was also evidence, introduced by the defense, that Janet had worn light-colored clothing on the day in question, but both the victim and Bass testified that the girl they observed had worn dark clothing.

In an apparent attempt to bolster the identifications, the prosecutor called an instructor of mathematics at a state college. Through this witness he sought to establish that, assuming the robbery was committed by a Cau-

---

[1] Hereafter, the term "defendant" is intended to apply only to Malcolm, but the term "defendants" to Malcolm and Janet.

casian woman with a blond ponytail who left the scene accompanied by a Negro with a beard and mustache, there was an overwhelming probability that the crime was committed by any couple answering such distinctive characteristics. The witness testified, in substance, to the "product rule," which states that the probability of the joint occurrence of a number of *mutually independent* events is equal to the product of the individual probabilities that each of the events will occur. *Without presenting any statistical evidence whatsoever in support of the probabilities for the factors selected,* the prosecutor then proceeded to have the witness *assume* probability factors for the various characteristics which he deemed to be shared by the guilty couple and all other couples answering to such distinctive characteristics.[2]

Applying the product rule to his own factors the prosecutor arrived at a probability that there was but one chance in 12 million that any couple possessed the distinctive characteristics of the defendants. Accordingly, under this theory, it was to be inferred that there could be but one chance in 12 million that defendants were innocent and that another equally distinctive couple actually committed the robbery. Expanding on what he had thus purported to suggest as a hypothesis, the prosecutor offered the completely unfounded and improper testimonial assertion that, in his opinion, the factors he had assigned were "conservative estimates" and that, in reality "the chances of anyone else besides these defendants being there, * * * having every similarity, * * * is somewhat like one in a billion."

---

[2] Although the prosecutor insisted that the factors he used were only for illustrative purposes—to demonstrate how the probability of the occurrence of mutually independent factors affected the probability that they would occur together—he nevertheless attempted to use factors which he personally related to the distinctive characteristics of defendants. In his argument to the jury he invited the jurors to apply their own factors, and asked defense counsel to suggest what the latter would deem as reasonable. The prosecutor himself proposed the individual probabilities set out in the table below. Although the transcript of the examination of the mathematics instructor and the information volunteered by the prosecutor at that time create some uncertainty as to precisely which of the characteristics the prosecutor assigned to the individual probabilities, he restated in his argument to the jury that they should be as follows:

	Characteristics	Individual Probability
A.	Partly yellow automobile	$\frac{1}{10}$
B.	Man with mustache	$\frac{1}{4}$
C.	Girl with ponytail	$\frac{1}{10}$
D.	Girl with blond hair	$\frac{1}{3}$
E.	Negro man with beard	$\frac{1}{10}$
F.	Interracial couple in car	$\frac{1}{1000}$

In his brief on appeal defendant agrees that the foregoing appeared on a table presented in the trial court.

Objections were timely made to the mathematician's testimony on the grounds that it was immaterial, that it invaded the province of the jury, and that it was based on unfounded assumptions. The objections were "temporarily overruled" and the evidence admitted subject to a motion to strike. When that motion was made at the conclusion of the direct examination, the court denied it, stating that the testimony had been received only for the "purpose of illustrating the mathematical probabilities of various matters, the possibilities for them occurring or re-occurring." * * *

As we shall explain, the prosecution's introduction and use of mathematical probability statistics injected two fundamental prejudicial errors into the case: (1) The testimony itself lacked an adequate foundation both in evidence and in statistical theory; and (2) the testimony and the manner in which the prosecution used it distracted the jury from its proper and requisite function of weighing the evidence on the issue of guilt, encouraged the jurors to rely upon an engaging but logically irrelevant expert demonstration, foreclosed the possibility of an effective defense by an attorney apparently unschooled in mathematical refinements, and placed the jurors and defense counsel at a disadvantage in sifting relevant fact from inapplicable theory.

We initially consider the defects in the testimony itself. As we have indicated, the specific technique presented through the mathematician's testimony and advanced by the prosecutor to measure the probabilities in question suffered from two basic and pervasive defects—an inadequate evidentiary foundation and an inadequate proof of statistical independence. First, as to the foundation requirement, we find the record devoid of any evidence relating to any of the six individual probability factors used by the prosecutor and ascribed by him to the six characteristics as we have set them out in footnote 10, ante. To put it another way, the prosecution produced no evidence whatsoever showing, or from which it could be in any way inferred, that only one out of every ten cars which might have been at the scene of the robbery was partly yellow, that only one out of every four men who might have been there wore a mustache, that only one out of every ten girls who might have been there wore a ponytail, or that any of the other individual probability factors listed were even roughly accurate.[3]

The bare, inescapable fact is that the prosecution made no attempt to offer any such evidence. Instead, through leading questions having perfunctorily elicited from the witness the response that the latter could not assign a probability factor for the characteristics involved,[4] the prosecutor

---

[3] We seriously doubt that such evidence could ever be compiled since no statistician could possibly determine after the fact which cars, or which individuals "might" have been present at the scene of the robbery; certainly there is no reason to suppose that the human and automotive populations of San Pedro, California, include all potential culprits—or, conversely, that all members of these populations are proper candidates for inclusion. Thus the sample from which the relevant probabilities would have to be derived is itself undeterminable.

[4] The prosecutor asked the mathematics instructor: "Now, let me see if you can be of some help to us with some independent factors, and you have some paper you may use. Your spe-

himself suggested what the various probabilities should be and these became the basis of the witness' testimony (see fn. 10, ante). It is a curious circumstance of this adventure in proof that the prosecutor not only made his own assertions of these factors in the hope that they were "conservative" but also in later argument to the jury invited the jurors to substitute their "estimates" should they wish to do so. We can hardly conceive of a more fatal gap in the prosecution's scheme of proof. A foundation for the admissibility of the witness' testimony was never even attempted to be laid, let alone established. His testimony was neither made to rest on his own testimonial knowledge nor presented by proper hypothetical questions based upon valid data in the record. In State v. Sneed, the court reversed a conviction based on probabilistic evidence, stating: "We hold that mathematical odds are not admissible as evidence to identify a defendant in a criminal proceeding *so long as the odds are based on estimates, the validity of which have [sic] not been demonstrated.*"

But, as we have indicated, there was another glaring defect in the prosecution's technique, namely an inadequate proof of the statistical independence of the six factors. No proof was presented that the characteristics selected were mutually independent, even though the witness himself acknowledged that such condition was essential to the proper application of the "product rule" or "multiplication rule."[5] To the extent that the traits or characteristics were not mutually independent (e.g. Negroes with beards and men with mustaches obviously represent overlapping categories[6]), the "product rule" would inevitably yield a wholly erroneous and exaggerated result even if all of the individual components had been determined with precision.

In the instant case, therefore, because of the aforementioned two defects—the inadequate evidentiary foundation and the inadequate proof of

---

cialty does not equip you, I suppose, to give us some probability of such things as a yellow car as contrasted with any other kind of car, does it? * * * I appreciate the fact that you can't assign a probability for a car being yellow as contrasted to some other car, can you? A. No, I couldn't."

[5] It is stated that: "A trait is said to be independent of a second trait when the occurrence or non-occurrence of one does not affect the probability of the occurrence of the other trait. The multiplication rule cannot be used without some degree of error where the traits are not independent."

[6] Assuming *arguendo* that factors B and E (see fn. 10, ante), were correctly estimated, nevertheless it is still arguable that most Negro men with beards *also* have mustaches (exhibit 3 herein, for instance, shows defendant with both a mustache and a beard, indeed in a hirsute continuum); if so, there is no basis for multiplying ¼ by $1/10$ to estimate the proportion of Negroes who wear beards *and* mustaches. Again, the prosecution's technique could *never* be meaningfully applied, since its accurate use would call for information as to the degree of interdependence among the six individual factors. (See Yamane, op. cit. supra.) Such information cannot be compiled, however, since the relevant sample necessarily remains unknown. (See fn. 10, ante.)

statistical independence—the technique employed by the prosecutor could only lead to wild conjecture without demonstrated relevancy to the issues presented. It acquired no redeeming quality from the prosecutor's statement that it was being used "for illustrative purposes" since, as we shall point out, the prosecutor's subsequent utilization of the mathematical testimony was not confined within such limits.

We now turn to the second fundamental error caused by the probability testimony. Quite apart from our foregoing objections to the specific technique employed by the prosecution to estimate the probability in question, we think that the entire enterprise upon which the prosecution embarked, and which was directed to the objective of measuring the likelihood of a random couple possessing the characteristics allegedly distinguishing the robbers, was gravely misguided. At best, it might yield an estimate as to how infrequently bearded Negroes drive yellow cars in the company of blond females with ponytails.

The prosecution's approach, however, could furnish the jury with absolutely no guidance on the crucial issue: *Of the admittedly few such couples, which one, if any, was guilty of committing this robbery?* Probability theory necessarily remains silent on that question, since no mathematical equation can prove beyond a reasonable doubt (1) that the guilty couple *in fact* possessed the characteristics described by the People's witnesses, or even (2) that only *one* couple possessing those distinctive characteristics could be found in the entire Los Angeles area.

As to the first inherent failing we observe that the prosecution's theory of probability rested on the assumption that the witnesses called by the People had conclusively established that the guilty couple possessed the precise characteristics relied upon by the prosecution. But no mathematical formula could ever establish beyond a reasonable doubt that the prosecution's witnesses correctly observed and accurately described the distinctive features which were employed to link defendants to the crime. Conceivably, for example, the guilty couple might have included a light-skinned Negress with bleached hair rather than a Caucasian blond; or the driver of the car might have been wearing a false beard as a disguise; or the prosecution's witnesses might simply have been unreliable.[7]

The foregoing risks of error permeate the prosecution's circumstantial case. Traditionally, the jury weighs such risks in evaluating the credibility and probative value of trial testimony, but the likelihood of human error or of falsification obviously cannot be quantified; that likelihood must therefore be excluded from any effort to assign a *number* to the probability of

---

[7] In the instant case, for instance, the victim could not state whether the girl had a ponytail, although the victim observed the girl as she ran away. The witness Bass, on the other hand, was sure that the girl whom he saw had a ponytail. The demonstration engaged in by the prosecutor also leaves no room for the possibility, although perhaps a small one, that the girl whom the victim and the witness observed was, in fact, the same girl.

guilt or innocence. Confronted with an equation which purports to yield a numerical index of probable guilt, few juries could resist the temptation to accord disproportionate weight to that index; only an exceptional juror, and indeed only a defense attorney schooled in mathematics, could successfully keep in mind the fact that the probability computed by the prosecution can represent, *at best,* the likelihood that a random couple would share the characteristics testified to by the People's witnesses—*not necessarily the characteristics of the actually guilty couple.*

As to the second inherent failing in the prosecution's approach, even assuming that the first failing could be discounted, the most a mathematical computation could *ever* yield would be a measure of the probability that a random couple would possess the distinctive features in question. In the present case, for example, the prosecution attempted to compute the probability that a random couple would include a bearded Negro, a blond girl with a ponytail, and a partly yellow car; the prosecution urged that this probability was no more than one in 12 million. Even accepting this conclusion as arithmetically accurate, however, one still could not conclude that the Collinses were probably *the* guilty couple. On the contrary, as we explain in the Appendix, the prosecution's figures actually implied a likelihood of over 40 percent that the Collinses could be "duplicated" by at least *one other couple who might equally have committed the San Pedro robbery.* Urging that the Collinses be convicted on the basis of evidence which logically establishes no more than this seems as indefensible as arguing for the conviction of X on the ground that a witness saw either X or X's twin commit the crime.

Again, few defense attorneys, and certainly few jurors, could be expected to comprehend this basic flaw in the prosecution's analysis. Conceivably even the prosecutor erroneously believed that his equation established a high probability that *no* other bearded Negro in the Los Angeles area drove a yellow car accompanied by a ponytailed blond. In any event, although his technique could demonstrate no such thing, he solemnly told the jury that he had supplied mathematical proof of guilt.

Sensing the novelty of that notion, the prosecutor told the jurors that the traditional idea of proof beyond a reasonable doubt represented "the most hackneyed, stereotyped, trite, misunderstood concept in criminal law." He sought to reconcile the jury to the risk that, under his "new math" approach to criminal jurisprudence, "on some rare occasion * * * an innocent person may be convicted." "Without taking that risk," the prosecution continued, "life would be intolerable * * * because * * * there would be immunity for the Collinses, for people who chose not to be employed to go down and push old ladies down and take their money and be immune because how could we ever be sure they are the ones who did it?"

In essence this argument of the prosecutor was calculated to persuade the jury to convict defendants whether or not they were convinced of their guilt to a moral certainty and beyond a reasonable doubt. (Pen.Code, § 1096.) Undoubtedly the jurors were unduly impressed by the mystique of the mathematical demonstration but were unable to assess its relevancy or value. Although we make no appraisal of the proper applications of mathematical techniques in the proof of facts, we have strong feelings that such applications, particularly in a criminal case, must be critically examined in view of the substantial unfairness to the defendant which may result from ill conceived techniques with which the trier of fact is not technically equipped to cope. We feel that the technique employed in the case before us falls into the latter category.

We conclude that the court erred in admitting over defendant's objection the evidence pertaining to the mathematical theory of probability and in denying defendant's motion to strike such evidence. * * *

The judgment is reversed.

■ TRAYNOR, C.J., and PETERS, TOBRINER, MOSK and BURKE, JJ., concur.

■ McCOMB, JUSTICE. I dissent. I would affirm the judgment in its entirety.

APPENDIX

If "Pr" represents the probability that a certain distinctive combination of characteristics, hereinafter designated "C," will occur jointly in a random couple, then the probability that C will *not* occur in a random couple is $(1-\text{Pr})$. Applying the product rule (see fn. 8, ante), the probability that C will occur in *none* of N couples chosen at random is $(1-\text{Pr})^N$, so that the probability of C occurring in *at least one* of N random couples is $[1-(1-\text{Pr})^N]$.

Given a particular couple selected from a random set of N, the probability of C occurring in that couple (i.e., Pr), multiplied by the probability of C occurring in none of the remaining N–1 couples (i.e., $(1-\text{Pr})^{N-1}$), yields the probability that C will occur in the selected couple and in no other. Thus the probability of C occurring in any particular couple, and in that couple alone, is $[(\text{Pr}) \times (1-\text{Pr})^{N-1}]$. Since this is true for each of the N couples, the probability that C will occur in precisely *one* of the N couples, without regard to which one, is $[(\text{Pr}) \times (1-\text{Pr})^{N-1}]$ added N times, because the probability of the occurrence of one of several *mutually exclusive* events is equal to the *sum* of the individual probabilities. Thus the probability of C occurring in *exactly one* of N random couples (*any* one, but *only* one) is $[(N) \times (\text{Pr}) \times (1-\text{Pr})^{N-1}]$.

By subtracting the probability that C will occur in *exactly one* couple from the probability that C will occur in *at least one* couple, one obtains the probability that C will occur in *more than one* couple: $[1-(1-\text{Pr})^N-(N) \times (\text{Pr}) \times (1-\text{Pr})^{N-1}]$. Dividing this difference by the probability that C will occur in at least one couple (i.e., dividing the difference by $[1-(1-\text{Pr})^N]$)

then yields *the probability that C will occur more than once in a group of N couples in which C occurs at least once.*

Turning to the case in which C represents the characteristics which distinguish a bearded Negro accompanied by a ponytailed blond in a yellow car, the prosecution sought to establish that the probability of C occurring in a random couple was 1/12,000,000—i.e., that $Pr = 1/12,000,000$. Treating this conclusion as accurate, it follows that, in a population of N random couples, the probability of C occurring *exactly once* is $[(N) \times (1/12,000,000) \times (1-1/12,000,000)^{N-1}]$. Subtracting this product from $[1-(1-1/12,000,000)^{N}]$, the probability of C occurring in *at least one* couple, and dividing the resulting difference by $[1-(1-1/12,000,000)^{N}]$, the probability that C will occur in at least one couple, yields the probability that C will occur more than once in a group of N random couples of which at least one couple (namely, the one seen by the witnesses) possesses characteristics C. In other words, the probability of *another* such couple in a population of N is the quotient A/B, where A designates the numerator $[1-(1-1/12,000,000)^{N}]-[(N) \times 1/12,000,000 \times (1-1/12,000,000)^{N-1}]$, and B designates the denominator $[1-(1-1/12,000,000)^{N}]$.

N which represents the total number of all couples who might conceivably have been at the scene of the San Pedro robbery, is not determinable, a fact which suggests yet another basic difficulty with the use of probability theory in establishing identity. One of the imponderables in determining N may well be the number of N-type couples in which a single person may participate. Such considerations make it evident that N, in the area adjoining the robbery, is in excess of several million; as N assumes values of such magnitude, the quotient A/B computed as above, representing the probability of a second couple as distinctive as the one described by the prosecution's witnesses, soon exceeds $4/10$. Indeed, as N approaches 12 million, this probability quotient rises to approximately 41 percent. We note parenthetically that if $1/N = Pr$, then as N increases indefinitely, the quotient in question approaches a limit of $(e-2)/(e-1)$, where "e" represents the transcendental number (approximately 2.71828) familiar in mathematics and physics.

Hence, even if we should accept the prosecution's figures without question, we would derive a probability of over 40 percent that the couple observed by the witnesses could be "duplicated" by at least one other equally distinctive interracial couple in the area, including a Negro with a beard and mustache, driving a partly yellow car in the company of a blond with a ponytail. Thus the prosecution's computations, far from establishing beyond a reasonable doubt that the Collinses were the couple described by the prosecution's witnesses, imply a very substantial likelihood that the area contained *more than one* such couple, and that a couple *other* than the Collinses was the one observed at the scene of the robbery.

NOTE

Even before People v. Collins, evidence scholars had taken an interest in the application of probability theory to courtroom situations. See, e.g., Kaplan, Decision Theory and the Factfinding Process, 20 Stan.L.Rev. 1065 (1968). The Collins case augmented this interest. It inspired an article, Finkelstein & Fairley, A Bayesian Approach to Identification Evidence, 83 Harv.L.Rev. 489 (1970), that argued that while *Collins* was correct on its facts, experts might in other cases properly use probability theory, in particular Bayes' theorem, to aid the jury in making identification decisions. The authors suggested a hypothetical case in which the defendant is accused of murdering his girlfriend. A partial palmprint was found on the knife that was used in the murder. It matches the defendant's palm. But it would also match the palm of one in a thousand people chosen at random, which means that in a metropolitan area hundreds of people would have the same palmprint characteristics. How is the jury to use that one in a thousand figure? Bayes' theorem, which provides a way of determining how an evaluation of probability based upon initial evidence should be modified in light of additional evidence, could be used to guide the jury. If the trier of fact believed that the prior probability of defendant's guilt was 25% (before taking the palmprint into account) then Bayes' theorem tells us that trier should believe that the posterior probability of guilt (after taking the palmprint into account) is 99.7%. The method often yields higher probabilities than intuition would yield. For example, if the prior probability is 25% and the palmprint is one in a hundred, then the posterior probability of guilt is 97%. (These calculations require that one assume (a) that the person who left the palmprint surely committed the murder, (b) that the expert's frequency figures are accurate, and (c) that there is no possibility of lab error, for example no possibility of a mixup in which someone else's palmprint was labeled as the defendant's.)

The proposition that the jury should be instructed about Bayes' theorem attracted the attention of a talented and resourceful debater, Laurence Tribe, then an assistant professor at the Harvard Law School. See Tribe, Trial by Mathematics: Precision and Ritual in the Legal Process, 84 Harv.L.Rev. 1329 (1971). Tribe pointed out a host of problems. It would be difficult to get jurors who are unused to formal probabilities to arrive at a consistent understanding of what they are supposed to do in formulating a prior probability. There is also a danger of "dwarfing soft variables"; that is, issues that cannot be quantified might be overlooked as the jury became mesmerized with those that could. Moreover, uncertainty about predicate facts can require the jury to make so many quantification decisions about so many issues that use of the theorem would be more confusing than helpful.

Although Tribe's view seems to have carried the day with regard to the use of Bayes' theorem in instructing the jury, the debate did stimulate interest in Bayes' theorem and probability theory. It has spawned a considerable body of "new evidence scholarship" that explores how probability theory might be used as a means of proof or as a way to help scholars model and evaluate trial processes—or even, as the following material indicates, to prove identity.

Dale A. Nance, Naturalized Epistemology and the Critique of Evidence Theory*

There is general recognition that a Bayesian analysis might, at least in theory, be useful in the context of scientific evidence with an explicitly statistical component. For example, it was suggested many years ago that Bayes' Theorem might be used to convey the significance of the "random match probability" for forensic identification evidence used in criminal trials. In a case in which a defendant matches a mark (for example, DNA profile or blood type) found at the scene of the crime, the random match probability is simply the chance that, though innocent, the defendant would—by mere coincidence—match that mark. This, in turn, is estimated by reference to the frequency of that mark in an appropriate suspect population.
* * *

The idea of Bayesian assistance is that jurors might be told the relative likelihood of getting a match under the hypothesis that the defendant is the source as compared to that of getting a match under the hypothesis that someone else (unknown and therefore statistically random as to the mark) is the source. For a random match probability of 0.04 (meaning that one out of twenty-five people on average share that mark), as an example, the expert would report to the jury that it is twenty-five times more likely that there would be a match if the defendant is the source than if some other unknown person is the source. (This presentation format will be called the "likelihood ratio format" in what follows.) Additionally, the same (or another) expert might illustrate for the jury the effect this likelihood ratio should have on various prior probabilities that the defendant is the source of the mark. That is, the jury might be shown a chart like the following, mapping prior probabilities (expressed as a percentage) to posterior probabilities for a likelihood ratio of twenty-five:

Prior Probability		Posterior Probability
0%	→	0%
5%	→	57%
10%	→	74%
15%	→	82%
20%	→	86%
25%	→	89%

---

* 87 Va. L. Rev. 1551, 1610–12 (2001). Reprinted with permission.93%

30%	$\rightarrow$	91%
35%	$\rightarrow$	93%
40%	$\rightarrow$	94%
45%	$\rightarrow$	95%
50%	$\rightarrow$	96%
55%	$\rightarrow$	96.8%
60%	$\rightarrow$	97.4%
65%	$\rightarrow$	97.9%
70%	$\rightarrow$	98.3%
75%	$\rightarrow$	98.7%
80%	$\rightarrow$	99.0%
85%	$\rightarrow$	99.3%
90%	$\rightarrow$	99.6%
95%	$\rightarrow$	99.8%
100%	$\rightarrow$	100%

(This presentation method will be called the "chart format" in what follows.) Neither the likelihood ratio format nor the chart format is commonly employed at this time in criminal cases in the United States, although they do appear in civil paternity cases and the occasional criminal case in which paternity is material. Most criminal courts, however, allow the presentation of the random match statistic, expressed either as a probability (for example, 0.04) or as a frequency (1 in 25, or 4%).

Lempert, The New Evidence Scholarship: Analyzing the Process of Proof*

The article which triggered widespread interest in the applicability of Bayesian reasoning to trial processes—and arguably still accounts for residual passion—was the comment of Finklestein and Fairley on *People v. Collins,* in which they argued that the real problem in that case lay not in the

---

* From P. Tillers & E. Green (eds.), Probability and Inference in the Law of Evidence, The Uses and Limits of Bayesianism 61, 62–63 (1988). Copyright 1988, Kluwer Academic Publishers.

prosecutor's attempt to use statistical reasoning but in his failure to offer
the jury statistical information in the form best suited to its decision-
making task—i.e., Bayes's Theorem. Professor Laurence Tribe, in his justly celebrated article *Trial by Mathematics,* took issue with Finklestein and
Fairley on both counts.

Among legal academics it is generally agreed that Tribe won this particular debate. As Professor Allen writes in his contribution to this volume,
"It is becoming increasingly obvious, for example, that Bayesian approaches can best be used heuristically as guides to rational thought and not as
specific blueprints for forensic decisionmaking." This conclusion, however,
is premature. Statistical evidence has figured in litigation for more than a
century, and in recent years has become increasingly common and complex.
For example, a recent LEXIS search of statistical terms done for the National Research Council reports:

> A search of published opinions in federal courts with a computer-based
> legal information retrieval system reveals the dramatic growth since
> 1960 in cases involving some form of statistical evidence. Between
> January 1960 and September 1979 the terms "statistic(s)" or "statis-
> tical" appeared in about 3,000 or 4% of 83,769 reported District Court
> opinions. In the Courts of Appeals, the same terms appeared in 1,671
> reported opinions.

These uses include not only statistical descriptions of samples and populations, but also uses of the kind Finklestein and Fairley proposed—as identification evidence.[9] With both sorts of uses problems arise because juries are
presented with frequentist statistics in situations where Bayesian approaches may be more appropriate to the task at hand.

I shall not dwell on this issue except to make one point. Many participants in [this] symposium paint with a broad brush in rejecting any place
for Bayesian models in trial processes. Often their arguments, or portions
of their arguments, read as if statistical evidence has no place at all in trials. Those who criticize Bayesian models of the legal process and the suggested application of Bayesian approaches at trial must confront the reality
that statistical evidence is offered in trials every day.

I do not mean to argue that this reality cannot be accommodated by
critics of Bayesian models or proposed applications. It is not difficult to imagine a place for statistical evidence in a theory that focuses, as do most
non-Bayesian theories of rational proof, on the relative weight of conflicting
evidence, the plausible generalizations that trial evidence allows, or the

---

[9] Examples include efforts to identify the accused as the criminal through blood traces or
hair samples. * * * Other kinds of identification evidence like fingerprints also depend on statistical inferences but the reliability of these tests is thought to be so high that their statistical
base may be neglected.

coherence of evidence with some larger plausible story. More difficult challenges for those who reject the Bayesian perspective are to explain why, if statistical evidence is presented at trials, frequentist approaches should be preferred to Bayesian ones, and to reevaluate arguments used to reject Bayesian approaches to proof where they do not accommodate the reality of the regular use of statistical evidence. Thus, arguments from the intuition that the law will not allow verdicts to rest on naked statistical evidence must accommodate or condemn a world in which the only admissible evidence of discrimination is embodied in a statistical model, or where the only admissible evidence linking the defendant to a crime is a hair match. If the answer is, as it appears implicitly to be in the case of fingerprint evidence, that the statistical probabilities are sufficiently high as to be unproblematic, an explanation is required of why one level of irreducible and undeniable uncertainty is tolerable and another is not.

The Red–Haired Soldier

S. found a red hair at the scene of the atrocity. From his forensic studies, he knew that one person in ten has red hair. On his way back to headquarters, he saw a red-haired soldier marching in a parade. "There is but one chance in ten," he thought, "that the hair I found at the scene came from someone other than that soldier."

People v. Mountain

Court of Appeals of New York, 1985.
486 N.E.2d 802.

* * *

On this appeal the defendant urges that the court erred in permitting the prosecutor to introduce evidence that the assailant's sperm contained type A blood, and allowing "references" to the defendant's blood type. He relies on People v. Robinson (27 NY2d 864).

In the *Robinson* case this court stated at page 865: "Proof that the defendant had type 'A' blood and that the semen found in and on the body of the decedent was derived from a man with type 'A' blood was of no probative value in the case against defendant in view of the large proportion of the general population having blood of this type and, therefore, should not have been admitted". * * *

The *Robinson* rule has been criticized by noted scholars, and in other jurisdictions has been universally rejected. For a time it appeared that Iowa would accept the rule but now it is clear that New York stands alone.

The basic problem with the rule is the premise on which it is founded. Although blood grouping may only serve to show that the defendant and the assailant are part of a large group having that particular characteristic, it does not follow that such proof completely lacks probative value. When identity is in issue, proof that the defendant and the perpetrator share similar physical characteristics is not rendered inadmissible simply because those characteristics are also shared by large segments of the population. For instance, evidence that the person who committed the crime was white would not be excluded although that may include 80% of the population. Similarly, evidence of a person's sex, which would include roughly 50% of the general population, is routinely accepted as having some probative value with respect to identification. Proof of such common characteristics, of little value individually, may acquire great probative value when considered cumulatively. Thus, the *Robinson* rule goes too far in holding that evidence showing that the defendant and the assailant have type A blood, is of no probative value merely because that includes 40% of the population.

It appears that the only justification for excluding such evidence is a fear that the jury may accord it undue weight, beyond its probative value, because of its scientific basis. That, however, can generally be avoided by instructions, where requested, emphasizing the fact that it is only circumstantial evidence and noting, perhaps, the percentage of the population involved. In cases where the defendant can show that the potential prejudice outweighs the probative value the court may in its discretion exclude the evidence.

In sum, there is no showing that the defendant was prejudiced by the blood test evidence in this case, and in future cases such evidence should be admissible unless prejudice is shown. * * *

1,000,000,000,000,000,000,000,000,000,000,000
to 1 Odds

According to a report in Newsday, a nurse from Brooklyn named Rose Grant went to the racetrack at Belmont Park on May 21, 1974. She wanted to place a $2 bet in each of the nine races on the "triple," which is called the trifecta at most tracks; to win, a bettor must pick in correct order the first-, second-, and third-place horses in the race. Grant had to leave early, though, so she wrote down her 27 picks and gave the sheet of paper along with a wrinkled $20 bill to Evelyn Jones, a lavatory matron, with the request that Jones place the bets. Grant later learned that her bet in the ninth race had won, with a payoff of $5,050. She returned to Belmont to get the ticket from Jones. But Jones told Grant that she had been unable to place the bets after all, and she handed back the paper that Grante had given her, together with a crisp $20 bill.

At a later time, Howard Graham, a retired restauranteur, turned in a winning ticket on the ninth-race triple; he said he had bought it himself. The ticket was the only one sold at Window 18 with the winning combination on that race.

Graham and Jones were eventually tried and convicted on criminal charges relating to the event. A key piece of evidence was a computer printout showing that a sequence of the bets that Grant had indicatged was in fact made at Window 18 on the day in question. According to the Newsday report, a Hofstra mathematics professor named Sylvia Pines testified that "the chances of two strangers deciding on their own to bet the same 27 choices in sequence at the same window the same day were 1,000,000,000,000,000,000,000,000,000,000 [one decillion] to 1."

QUESTIONS

Was the question that Prof. Pines attempted to answer the proper one? To calculate the odds that she did, what assumptions do you suppose she made?

NOTE: DNA AND OTHER EXONERATIONS

The National Registry of Exonerations, a joint project of the University of the Michigan Law School and the Center on Wrongful Convictions at Northwestern University School of Law, maintains a list of all known cases in the United States since 1989 in which a person was convicted of a crime an later exonerated (according to criteria prescribed by the Registry). See http://www.law.umich.edu/special/exoneration/Pages/about.aspx (last visited October 26, 2012). As of October 26, 2012, it included 1,000 exonerations. Not surprisingly, the number of exonerations based on DNA evidence has generally risen during that period, from a total of 16 in 1989-94 to a total of 111 in 2006-10. But the number of exonerations *not* based on DNA evidence has risen as well, and has remained higher, from a total of 76 in the earlier period to a total of 149 in the later period. The Registry's analysis of the first 873 cases indicates that the following were the principal factors contributing to mistaken convictions:

Factor	Percent of cases
Mistaken witness identification	43%
Perjury or false accusation	51%
False confession	15%
False or misleading forensic evidence	24%
Official misconduct	42%

(In some cases, more than one factor contributed to the conviction.) See also the website of The Innocence Project, <http://www.innocenceproject. org/understand/> (last visited October 26, 2012), which focuses on DNA exonerations. It reports that, of the first 225 such exonerations, eyewitness misidentification contributed in 173 (77%), unvalidated or improper forensics (such as hair microscopy and bite-mark and shoe comparisons) in 116 (52%), false confessions or admissions in 51 (23%), and informants or

snitches in 36 (21%). It also reports government misconduct and bad law-
yering as significant contributing factors.

Brown v. Farwell

United States Court of Appeals for the Ninth Circuit, 2008.
525 F.3d 787.

■ WARDLAW, CIRCUIT JUDGE:

At Petitioner Troy Brown's trial for sexual assault, the Warden and
State's ("Respondents") deoxyribonucleic acid ("DNA") expert provided critical testimony that was later proved to be inaccurate and misleading. Respondents have conceded at least twice that, absent this faulty DNA testimony, there was not sufficient evidence to sustain Troy's conviction. In
light of these extraordinary circumstances, we agree with District Judge
Philip M. Pro's conclusions that Troy was denied due process, and we affirm the district court's grant of Troy's petition for writ of habeas corpus.

[Troy Brown was tried and convicted in Nevada State Court of sexual
assault on a nine-year-old girl. The victim was uncertain and inconsistent
in her identification of the perpetrator of an assault that started while she
was sleeping in the bedroom of her trailer home. She was acquainted with
both Troy Brown and his brother Trent, and mentioned them as persons
whom the assailant resembled, but when the police showed her pictures
that included Troy's picture and pictures of people she did not know, she
was unable to identify Troy as her attacker. There was a difference between the victim's description of her attacker's clothing and what Troy was
wearing that night, and there was other circumstantial evidence that cast
doubt on Troy's guilt. The principal evidence presented against Troy at trial
came from prosecution DNA expert Renee Romero, who testified, among
other things, that there was a 99.99967 percent chance that Troy was the
assailant.]

On February 6, 2004, Troy filed his federal petition for writ of habeas
corpus pursuant to 28 U.S.C. § 2254, arguing, *inter alia,* violations of due
process and ineffective assistance of counsel. Judge Pro permitted Troy to
expand the record, admitting, among other things, an uncontested report
discrediting Romero's testimony by Dr. Laurence Mueller (the "Mueller Report"), a professor of Ecology and Evolutionary Biology at the University of
California, Irvine.

The district court granted Troy's petition. First, the district court concluded that, in light of the Mueller Report, Romero's testimony was unreliable. Absent that testimony, no rational trier of fact could conclude beyond
a reasonable doubt that Troy was guilty of each and every element of the
offenses with which he was charged. The district court also concluded that
Troy's attorney's failure to diligently defend against Respondents' DNA tes-

timony, as well as his failure to investigate the alibi of Henle, a potential suspect, amounted to ineffective assistance of counsel. Respondents timely appealed.

* * *

Troy asserts that there was insufficient evidence to convict him. His argument rests on the admission of Romero's later discredited testimony regarding the DNA evidence, which was introduced without rebuttal at trial. Respondents have conceded that absent introduction of Romero's DNA evidence, the remaining evidence is insufficient to sustain Troy's conviction. Having reviewed the record ourselves, we affirm the district court's conclusion that, had Romero's inaccurate and unreliable testimony on the DNA evidence been excluded, there would have been insufficient evidence to convict Troy on each essential element of the offenses beyond a reasonable doubt.

* * *

The Mueller Report indicates that Romero's testimony was unreliable for two main reasons. First, Romero testified that there was a 99.99967 percent chance that Troy's DNA was the same as the DNA discovered in Jane's underwear-or, in other words, that the science demonstrated a near 100 percent chance of Troy's guilt. This assertion was incorrect, as it falls directly into what has become known as the "prosecutor's fallacy." The prosecutor's fallacy occurs when the prosecutor elicits testimony that confuses source probability with random match probability. Put another way, a prosecutor errs when he "presents statistical evidence to suggest that the [DNA] evidence indicates the likelihood of the defendant's guilt rather than the odds of the evidence having been found in a randomly selected sample." *United States v. Shonubi,* 895 F.Supp. 460, 516 (E.D.N.Y.1995) (internal quotation marks and citation omitted), *vacated on other grounds,* 103 F.3d 1085 (2d Cir.1997); *see also United States v. Chischilly,* 30 F.3d 1144, 1157 (9th Cir.1994) ("To illustrate, suppose the . . . evidence establishes that there is a one in 10,000 chance of a random match. The jury might equate this likelihood with source probability by believing that there is a one in 10,000 chance that the evidentiary sample did not come from the defendant. This equation of random match probability with source probability is known as the prosecutor's fallacy."); Richard Lempert, *Some Caveats Concerning DNA as Criminal Identification Evidence,* 13 Cardozo L. Rev. 303, 305–06 (1991). Such a fallacy is dangerous, as the probability of finding a random match can be much higher than the probability of matching one individual, given the weight of the non-DNA evidence. *See* William C. Thompson and Edward L. Schumann, *Interpretation of Statistical Evidence in Criminal Trials,* 11 L. and Hum. Behav. 167, 170–71 (1987) (noting that the prosecutor's fallacy "could lead to serious error, particularly where the other evidence in the case is weak and therefore the prior probability of guilt is low").

Here, Romero initially testified that Troy's DNA matched the DNA found in Jane's underwear, and that 1 in 3,000,000 people randomly selected from the population would also match the DNA found in Jane's underwear (random match probability). After the prosecutor pressed her to put this another way, Romero testified that there was a 99.99967 percent chance that the DNA found in Jane's underwear was from Troy's blood (source probability). This testimony was misleading, as it improperly conflated random match probability with source probability. In fact, the former testimony (1 in 3,000,000) is the probability of a match between an innocent person selected randomly from the population; this is not the same as the probability that Troy's DNA was the same as the DNA found in Jane's underwear, which would prove his guilt. Statistically, the probability of guilt given a DNA match is based on a complicated formula known as Bayes's Theorem, *see id.* at 170–71 n. 2, and the 1 in 3,000,000 probability described by Romero is but one of the factors in this formula. Significantly, another factor is the strength of the non-DNA evidence. Here, Romero improperly conflated random match and source probability, an error that is especially profound given the weakness of the remaining evidence against Troy. In sum, Romero's testimony that Troy was 99.99967 percent likely to be guilty was based on her scientifically flawed DNA analysis, which means that Troy was most probably convicted based on the jury's consideration of false, but highly persuasive, evidence.

Second, Romero inaccurately minimized the likelihood that Troy's DNA would match one of his four brothers' DNA, thus underestimating the likelihood that one of Troy's brothers could have been the perpetrator. She testified that there was a 25 percent chance of two brothers sharing both alleles at one locus, and, using that figure, a 1/6500 chance that one of Troy's brothers would match Troy's DNA at all five loci. The Mueller Report indicated that Romero's calculation was incorrect, as the correct figure is 1/1024. More importantly, Romero's testimony is misleading because it presented the narrowest interpretation of the DNA evidence. Had Romero accounted for Troy's four brothers, two of whom lived in Carlin and two of whom lived in neighboring Utah, the chance that Troy's DNA would match at least one of his four brothers' DNA can increase to 1/66–almost one hundred times the probability asserted by Romero. This omission was especially egregious given that the victim, Jane, had twice identified Troy's brother, Trent, as the assailant. Again, Respondents introduced nothing to contradict the findings of the Mueller Report.

A federal court on habeas may exclude evidence admitted in the state court if the evidence "rendered[the] trial so fundamentally unfair as to violate federal due process." *Butcher v. Marquez,* 758 F.2d 373, 378 (9th Cir.1985). We agree with the district court that Romero's testimony was unreliable, as it was inaccurate and ignored logical implications about Troy's four brothers, each of whom lived in the general vicinity. Admission of this unreliable testimony most certainly rendered the trial fundamentally unfair, as even Respondents concede that "[t]here was insufficient evidence to convict the Defendant unless the DNA evidence established his guilt." Thus, the admission of Romero's unreliable and misleading testimony violated Troy's due process rights, and the district court did not err in excluding it. *See United States v. Scheffer,* 523 U.S. 303, 309, 118 S.Ct. 1261, 140 L.Ed.2d 413 (1998) ("State and Federal Governments unquestionably have a legitimate interest in ensuring that reliable evidence is presented to the trier of fact in a criminal trial. Indeed, the exclusion of unreliable evidence is a principal objective of many evidentiary rules.").

After excluding Romero's testimony, the district court weighed the sufficiency of the remaining evidence in the light most favorable to the prosecution, *Jackson,* 443 U.S. at 319, 99 S.Ct. 2781, and concluded that "there [is] sufficient conflicting testimony to raise a reasonable doubt in the mind of any rational trier of fact." On appeal, Respondents argue that there is much evidence to support the conviction. However, it is Respondents' burden to establish guilt beyond a reasonable doubt for each and every element of the offense, a burden that Respondents have not carried here.

* * *

Because we affirm the district court's grant of Troy Brown's habeas petition on due process grounds, we need not reach his arguments regarding ineffective assistance of counsel. The district court's grant of Troy's petition for writ of habeas corpus and reversal of his conviction is **AFFIRMED.** Respondents shall retry Troy within 180 days or shall release him from custody.

[The dissenting opinion of Circuit Judge O'Scannlain has been omitted.—Eds.]

Jonathan J. Koehler, DNA Matches and Statistics: Important Questions, Surprising Answers
76 Judicature 222 (1993).*

Since its introduction at trial in a Florida case in 1987, DNA profiling evidence has been used to find against defendants in more than a thousand criminal and civil cases. The technique initially was received by the courts and news media as a nearly foolproof means of identifying vicious criminals who left blood, hair, or semen at the scenes of their crimes, as well as biological fathers implicated in paternity lawsuits. There is now an increased awareness that DNA analyses are subject to error and more deserving of careful scrutiny.

This article asks and answers questions about the process involved in reporting DNA matches and their probative value. The validity of the underlying genetic theory is not questioned here. Instead, the focus is on the meaning and significance of reported matches, and the role the possibility of error should play in evaluating this evidence. These issues are not well understood by judges, attorneys, jurors, or, in many cases, DNA experts themselves.

Based on transcripts from criminal cases involving DNA evidence, it is clear that defense attorneys are greatly concerned with such issues as the procedural details of the DNA identification process, the acceptability of the technology in the scientific community, the size of the data bases used to make probability estimates, and the credentials of the prosecution's expert witnesses. Some useful points can indeed be made regarding each of these issues. Defense attorneys, however, are often so preoccupied with the scientific procedures that generated the DNA evidence that they fail to pursue important points related to the validity of the inferences that are drawn from the evidence. Defense attorneys also must understand the limited meaning of a reported match and the accompanying frequency statistics, and they must impress such an understanding on fact finders at trial.

The answers to some of the questions raised in this article may surprise readers. For example, it will be explained that a DNA expert cannot identify the probability that a defendant is the source of a hair, bloodstain, or semen stain recovered from the scene of the crime, or that a defendant is the father of a child. The expert can, with varying degrees of accuracy, estimate the frequency with which various characteristics might be expected to be found in a human biological sample. This information is probative, but an estimate of the probability that a defendant is the source of a particular trace requires an estimate about the strength of the relevant non-genetic evidence as well. The failure to understand this principle probably has been, and will continue to be, responsible for findings against defendants who would have been successful at trial if the evidence had been presented properly.

DNA typing

How does DNA typing work?

DNA is a long double-stranded molecule found in the chromosomes carried in the nuclei of all cells. It contains the genetic code that provides the blueprint for life. A typical DNA identification in criminal cases compares the DNA found in blood, semen, or hairs left at a crime scene with the DNA found in blood samples taken from the suspect. Unfortunately, it is not possible to observe a person's DNA directly through high-powered microscopes as we might observe other types of identification evidence, such as a piece of glass or a carpet fiber.

[At this point, Koehler describes the matching technology that was then extant, known as restriction fragment length polymorphism (or

RFLP), referred to in the Harlan Levy excerpt above. The DNA molecule was broken into long strands by an enzyme, and the lengths of the resulting fragments were analyzed through a process called electrophoresis, in which an electrical current caused shorter strands to move more than longer strands through a gel, eventually yielding an autoradiogram that bore a pattern of bands somewhat resembling a supermarket bar code. If the bands in two samples lined up, within a specified margin of error, a match was declared.

[RFLP testing is now virtually obsolete; it takes a long time and requires relatively large and fresh samples. The most commonly used method now is often referred to as PCR–STR testing—the acronyms standing for polymerase chain reaction and short tandem repeats. PCR is a technique by which the amount of available DNA can be rapidly and enormously amplified, meaning that even very tiny samples can be tested. STR testing analyzes the number of times a given sequence of proteins is repeated at a given location, or locus, on the DNA molecule. Thus, for example, at a given locus some people might have the sequence ATAT (two repeats), some might have three, others four, and so forth. The power of the STR technique comes from the facts that multiple loci are tested—13 is the standard in the United States—and that the number of repeats at any given locus is believed to be independent of the number of repeats at another locus. Thus, even though a substantial portion of the population might have the same number of repeats at a given locus, the probability is infinitesimally small that any two people, not identical twins, have the same number of repeats at 13 loci.]

DNA matches

Is DNA matching evidence probative?

Yes. After learning that a laboratory report indicates that trace evidence recovered from a crime scene matches the DNA profile of a defendant, fact finders in most cases generally should strengthen their beliefs that the defendant is the source of the trace and that the defendant is guilty of the crime.

Having said this, it is important to note that a reported DNA match does not require a belief in either proposition. First, the reported match may not be a "true" match; laboratories sometimes make mistakes. Second, even a rare DNA pattern may be shared by several others, particularly by relatives of the defendant. Third, even if the defendant is the source of the trace, there may be an innocent explanation. Perhaps the defendant innocently left the trace before or after the crime was committed. A Good Samaritan might, for example, run into the woods to save a woman screaming for help, cut himself on a tree branch, and bleed on the woman while trying to save her.

Finally, other evidence may suggest the defendant is neither the source of the trace nor guilty of the crime. An eyewitness may report that the defendant was not the one he or she saw at the crime scene. This testimony remains relevant no matter what results the DNA analyses yield. Indeed, a final judgment about whether a person is the source of an evidentiary trace or guilty of a crime must be based on the laboratory report and all other relevant evidence.

What does it mean when a DNA expert declares a match between a suspect and trace evidence recovered from the scene of a crime?

When scientists declare a DNA match between a person and an evidentiary trace, they are saying that the person might be the source of that trace. In other words, the person cannot be excluded as a possible source. But a match report does not necessarily mean the suspect is the source of the trace, or even that one can determine a probability that the matching person is the source.

Then what does the small probability that usually accompanies expert testimony of a DNA match mean?

The probability that accompanies a reported DNA match is the theoretical likelihood that a randomly selected person from the general population (or from the population of certain large ethnic or racial groups) would genetically match the trace evidence as well as the defendant. This probability, which may be referred to as the "random match probability," often (but not always) helps fact finders assess the probative significance of a match.

It is important to be clear about what the random match probability does not reflect. It does not tell us the "source probability," the likelihood that the defendant is the source of the trace, and it certainly does not tell us the "guilt probability," the likelihood that the defendant committed the crime in question. (See "Three probabilities" inset.) To assume otherwise is to commit the error of assuming that because it is known that (a) Jack the Ripper was left handed, (b) 10 percent of the population is left handed, and (c) I am left handed, there must therefore be a 10 percent chance that I am not Jack the Ripper. The fallacy here is in translating the handedness match evidence directly into a probability of innocence without considering the strength of other evidence for and against the proposition that I am Jack the Ripper. This same error is made when experts, attorneys, and judges identify the probability that a defendant is guilty based solely on DNA random match frequencies.[3]

---

[3] Consider the following exchange between an attorney and a DNA expert in one recent Texas case (Bethune v. State, 821 S.W.2d 222 (Tex.App.1991), transcript, p. 2327): Attorney: " * * * you're telling the members of this jury that there would [be] a one in 5 billion chance

Does the paternity index tell us the likelihood that an alleged father is the true father of a particular child?

No. Paternity indexes, like random match probabilities in criminal cases, identify the theoretical probability that a randomly selected person from a particular population would match as well. This information can be helpful to fact finders, but it should not be mistaken for an estimate of the probability that an alleged father is the true father of a particular child.

Does the probability of paternity supplied by the laboratories tell us how likely it is that an alleged father is the true father?

No. Despite the facts that many laboratories routinely provide a probability of paternity, and many courts support admission of this probability value into evidence, the laboratories are not in a position to supply such an estimate.

Can you provide an example to clarify this point?

Imagine two paternity cases, A and B. In case A, the alleged father denies having intercourse with the mother at or near the time of conception. The mother says otherwise. DNA blood analyses do not exclude the defendant as a potential father and yield a paternity index of 1,000. This means that the alleged father is 1,000 times more likely than a randomly selected man from the general population to produce children that have the genetic pattern of the child in question. Reflect for a moment on how likely it is that the alleged father is the true father of the child.

Now consider case B, which is identical in all respects, right down to the paternity index of 1,000. But here, an experienced physician testifies that the defendant had a vasectomy prior to the time of conception and that follow-up tests indicate he could not have fathered this or any other child. What is the likelihood that this alleged father is the true father?

If you believe that the alleged father in case B is less likely to be the true father than the alleged father in case A, you should be able to see why a laboratory analysis does not, by itself, determine the probability of paternity. A reasonable estimate of the probability of paternity can be made only after considering *all* relevant evidence. Proof of a successful vasectomy certainly provides at least some relevant evidence in case B. Failure to assign

---

that anybody else could have committed the crime; is that correct?" Witness: "One in 5 billion, correct."

different subjective probability of paternity estimates for cases A and B would suggest the vasectomy evidence has zero probative value.[4]

The prior probability assumption

If a probability of paternity computation requires knowledge of all relevant evidence—both genetic and nongenetic—how are paternity laboratories able to estimate this value?

As noted above, the laboratories compute probabilities of paternity by making a critical assumption about the strength of the nongenetic evidence. They assume the combined strength of all nongenetic evidence in every paternity case indicates that there is exactly a 50 percent chance the defendant is the father. This estimate, also known as a "prior probability" (i.e., probability of paternity prior to the introduction of laboratory evidence) is then combined with the paternity index to yield a probability of paternity. The combination is achieved by a mathematical technique called Bayes's Theorem.[5]

---

[4] There have been several cases in which large paternity indexes were obtained despite evidence of a successful vasectomy prior to conception. See e.g., Cole v. Cole, 328 S.E.2d 446 (N.C.App.1985); O'Bannon v. Azar, 435 So.2d 1144 (La.App. 4 Cir.1983).

[5] Bayes's theorem is a general method for updating probabilistic beliefs in the face of new evidence. It is based on the tenets of elementary probability theory. The odds form of Bayes's theorem is as follows:

$$\frac{P(H/E)}{P(-H/E)} = \frac{P(H)}{P(-H)} \times \frac{P(E/H)}{P(E/-H)}$$

P(H) and P(-H) refer to the unconditional probabilities that a hypothesis H is true and false respectively. These probabilities are commonly referred to as "prior probabilities" and their ratio is the "prior odds." P(E/H) and P(E/-H) refer to the information value of the evidence E if hypothesis H is true and false respectively. P(E/H) and P(E/-H) are called likelihoods and their ratio is the "likelihood ratio." P(H/E) and P(-H/E) are the probabilities that the hypothesis H is true and false in light of the evidence E. Their ratio is the "posterior odds," and it may be computed by multiplying the prior odds by the likelihood ratio.

In paternity cases, the 50 percent prior probability assumption is P(H), the paternity index is the likelihood ratio, and the odds in favor of paternity are the posterior odds ratio. Now, because the sum of two mutually exclusive and exhaustive outcomes equals 100 percent, if P(H)=50 percent, then P(-H)=50 percent. And when P(H)=50 percent, the prior odds ratio is 1, and the odds in favor of paternity are identical to the paternity index.

Returning to the example in the text, the odds in favor of paternity are:

$$\frac{P(Paternity\ /\ Paternity\ Index)}{P(Nonpaternity\ /\ Paternity\ Index)} = \frac{.50}{.50} \times \frac{1000}{1} = \frac{1000}{1}$$

The 1000/1 posterior odds of paternity correspond with a probability of paternity of 99.9 percent. Under the 50 percent prior probability assumption, the probability of paternity would be identical for Cases A and B in the text, despite their obvious evidentiary differences.

Is the 50 percent prior probability assumption reasonable?

No. The practice of assuming a 50 percent prior probability is misleading and potentially prejudicial to defendants.[6] The laboratories have no reason to assume that, prior to forensic analysis, there is a 50 percent chance that an alleged father is the true father of a particular child.[7]

Ideally, the scientists who conduct paternity tests should know nothing about the nongenetic evidence in the case so that their own analyses remain untainted.

How do the laboratories justify the use of a 50 percent prior probability?

The laboratories argue that the 50 percent prior probability of paternity is a neutral assumption because it does not indicate whether the proposition is more likely true or false. But why should an assumption be made when there is real evidence to be heard? Depending on the case, the nongenetic evidence may suggest probabilities that are much higher or lower than 50 percent. Use of the 50 percent prior says, in essence, that the nongenetic evidence in a case—including evidence of sterility or other possible fathers—is irrelevant.

There is also a legal objection to the 50 percent prior probability assumption. Even if forensic scientists were in a position to assess the strength of the nongenetic evidence in a case, it is not their function to do so. It is the fact finders' job alone to combine the strength of both the genetic and nongenetic evidence to arrive at a final judgment in each case.

Does the 50 percent prior probability assumption also arise in criminal contexts?

It does when forensic scientists testify about source probabilities or guilt probabilities (i.e., the probability that a defendant is the source of recovered trace evidence or the probability that a defendant is guilty of a particular crime). The major difference is that, in criminal cases, statements pertaining to source and guilt probabilities are made without explicit reference to the 50 percent prior probability assumption. The result is that judges and jurors are never told that the probability values they hear re-

---

[6] See Kaye, The Probability of an Ultimate Issue: The Strange Case of Paternity Testing, 75 Iowa L.Rev. 75–109 (1989); Kaye, Plemel as a primer on proving paternity. 24 Willamette L.Rev. 867–883 (1988). A majority of jurisdictions encourage, allow, or require the 50 percent prior probability estimate in paternity cases.

[7] An argument could be made that the true prior probability of paternity is substantially higher than 50 percent based on studies showing that approximately 70 percent of alleged fathers are, in fact, "guilty" of paternity. See Ellman & Kaye, Probabilities and proof: Can HLA and blood group testing prove paternity? 54 N.Y.U.L.Rev. 1131–1162, 1150 (1979). The authors argue that there are serious legal problems associated with using this general base rate as an estimate of an alleged father's prior probability of paternity (p. 1151–2).

quire an assumption about something the forensic scientist does not and
should not know anything about.

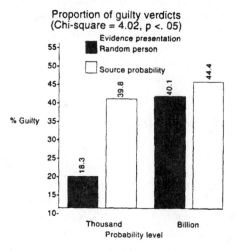

Why do laboratories continue to compute probabilities that require
use of the controversial 50 percent prior probability assumption?

It is hard to know for sure, but ignorance may be the best explanation.
Laboratory analysts are often unfamiliar with the subtle statistical issues
related to the interpretation of genetic matches. A less charitable explanation is that laboratory analysts provide probabilities of paternity and
source probabilities because they expect these to have a greater impact in
court than would other, more appropriate, characterizations of their findings. This increased impact lends power, prestige, and financial reward to
the forensic science profession.

Is there evidence that source probability characterizations of DNA
matching evidence increase the odds that jurors will return verdicts
against defendants?

Yes. Empirical research with mock jurors shows that when fact finders
are provided with source probability statements in a hypothetical murder
case, they are more likely to vote to convict the defendant.[8] As Figure 1 in-

---

[8] More than 300 jury-eligible students enrolled in graduate and undergraduate business
law classes at the University of Texas participated as mock jurors in experiments conducted
by the author. Subjects were provided with a one-page description of a hypothetical murder
case and asked to render a verdict and estimate the numerical probability that the defendant
killed the victim. Subjects were told that the evidence must satisfy them beyond a reasonable
doubt in order to render a guilty verdict.

Brief summaries of prosecution and defense arguments were included. Most subjects read
that forensic tests on a blood trace detected beneath the victim's fingernail could not rule out
the defendant as a possible source of the evidence. Next, the test results were presented in
terms of either a random match or source probability and included probability values at either
the one in one thousand or one in one billion levels. Subjects who did not receive forensic iden-

dicates, this is particularly true when relatively less extreme probabilities are involved.

In one study, subjects were provided with forensic matching evidence in one of two presentation modes (random match probability, source probability) at one of two probability levels (one in a thousand, one in a billion). For probability levels of one in a thousand, commission of the source probability error—reframing a source probability statement as a random match probability statement—dropped the conviction rate from 40 percent to 18 percent.[9]

Figure 1 also shows that reframing a source probability statement as a random match probability statement made little difference when the probability level was one in a billion. Because so many DNA cases include probability values in the billions, won't the impact of the source probability error be minimal in practice?

No. The National Academy of Sciences recently proposed a set of guidelines for computing DNA match probabilities that are more conservative than those previously used.[10] As these guidelines gain acceptance in the courts, we can expect to see fewer extremely small probabilities than we have seen thus far. Consequently, the empirical results associated with the source probability error will become increasingly relevant.

Relatives and subgroups

Are there grounds for disputing DNA frequency statistics in cases where a source probability error is not committed?

Yes. An important criticism of DNA frequency statistics is that they fail to take into account the population of interest. The frequency statistics computed by most laboratories compare the defendant to a randomly selected person in some general population (e.g., North American caucasians). Sometimes, these estimated frequencies are not as probative as the laboratories would have us believe. The main reason is that the general population may not be a fair genetic representation of the potential source

---

tification evidence were in the control group. The statistics provided in Figure 1 are the result of a loglinear analysis on the verdicts. The probability data, which were analyzed using analysis of variance, reflected a similar pattern. A complete experimental report is in preparation and may be obtained from the author.

[9] The hypothetical case used was designed to reflect a rough balance of incriminating and exculpatory evidence. Consequently, the conviction rates may be lower than might be expected in a typical murder case involving DNA evidence.

[10] The National Academy of Sciences initiated a study in January 1990 to examine the complex issues surrounding DNA evidence. The final report, issued in April 1992, recommended the use of more conservative techniques for estimating random match probabilities. Unless offset by an increase in the number of genetic characteristics examined, this will reduce the number of extremely small probability values produced by DNA laboratories. See DNA Technology in Forensic Science, supra n. 2, at chapter 3.

population, the group of people who might reasonably be the source of the recovered trace evidence.

What difference does this make?

It can make a big difference in cases where there is reason to believe that members of the potential source or suspect populations[11] are genetically similar to the defendant. Imagine a case in which the authorities strongly suspect that a rape was committed by one of three biological brothers. Imagine further that one of the brothers is charged with the crime, and that a three-probe[12] DNA analysis reveals that the frequency of the genetic pattern identified in both the defendant's blood and a sample of recovered semen is one in one million.

At first blush, the one in a million statistic appears to provide nearly conclusive proof that the defendant is the source of the recovered semen. But one must bear in mind that the probability that blood from one of the other brother-suspects would genetically match the recovered semen is far greater than the one in one million chance that a randomly selected person from the general population would match. According to genetic theory, the probability that at least one of the two brothers would also match on the three-probe analysis is more than 3 percent.[13] The fact that the pattern is rare in the general population makes little difference. Far more important is the fact that the population of potential donors of the trace evidence consists partly of people who are much more likely than a random person from the general population to have genetic traits that match those of the defendant.

The probabilities ordinarily generated by DNA laboratories make no allowance for possible genetic similarities among members of the potential source or suspect populations. This diminishes their usefulness in cases where the potential source population contains untested relatives of a defendant. Wherever possible, DNA analyses should be performed on the

---

[11] Although the potential source population is the population of interest, the suspect population will often be an acceptable substitute. The exception occurs when there are members of the potential source population who, for whatever reason, happen to be ruled out as suspects in the crime.

[12] Probes are fragments of radioactive DNA material that have been designed to attach to particular sections of DNA. After treatment, each probe produces one or two bands (resembling supermarket bar codes) that represent distinctive parts of a person's DNA pattern.

[13] The general formula for computing the probability of a match between brothers is $(.25 + .5p + 2p^2)^k$ where p = the average probability that two alleles will match, and k = the number of probes sites examined (DNA Technology in Forensic Science, supra n. 2, at 3–16). For DNA profiles consisting entirely of rare alleles, p approaches zero and there is a ¼ probability that two brothers will share a set of alleles at each probe site. In these cases, P (At least 1 of 2 brothers will also match on all 3 probes) = 1 – P (Neither brother matches on all 3 probes) = 1 – $[1 - (¼)^3]^2 = 1 - (63/64)^2 = 3.1$ percent. For alleles that are less rare, p is greater than zero and the probability that two brothers will share a set of alleles at each probe site is greater than ¼. In these cases, P (At least 1 of two brothers will also match on all 3 probes) may be considerably greater than 3.1 percent.

blood of close relatives who are members of the suspect population. In cases where this does not occur, the probative value of the probabilities may well be outweighed by its potential to mislead jurors.

What about cases in which the potential source population does not contain siblings or other close relatives?

Even in these cases, these are genetic subpopulations or substructures that may call into question the accuracy of general frequency statistics. Currently, there is substantial disagreement about how seriously these substructures undermine the general population frequency statistics.

Error

The role that error plays in the DNA typing process is a source of great controversy. Two major categories of error exist: false positives and false negatives. A false positive error occurs when a laboratory erroneously reports that a defendant is the likely source of a matching trace. A false negative error occurs when a laboratory erroneously reports that a defendant is not the source of a trace. Most of the discussion of laboratory error to date has focused on the possibility of false positive error. On the one side, DNA experts testifying for the prosecution argue that it is nearly impossible to obtain a false positive error. Such testimony appears to be motivated by definitions of false positive error that exclude consideration of human error or coincidental matches. On the other side, defense experts argue not only that errors can and do occur, but that the forensic science community has conspired to cover them up.

Why worry about the possibility of false positive errors when provided with probabilities that are as small as those typically encountered in DNA cases (e.g., one in a million, one in a billion)?

As discussed earlier, sometimes there is good reason to question the relevance of reported DNA probabilities that are based on general populations. But even when the reported probabilities are regarded as accurate indicators of a chance match in the relevant population, these values are not synonymous with the false positive error rate.

The frequency with which a genetic pattern occurs corresponds with one type of false positive error—namely, coincidental match. But what really is important is the error rate across all types of false positive errors. As noted earlier, it is necessary to know how often a laboratory declares a match between two samples when, in fact, the samples are from different sources. To answer this question, the possibility of a variety of human errors must be considered. These errors—many of which have been documented—can include transcription errors, sample mix-ups, measurement errors, tampering, and fraud.

How can we measure the aggregate false positive error rate, which takes into account both the probability of coincidental matches and all forms of human error in DNA testing?

Blind proficiency tests. Laboratories can be provided with known pairs of samples, ostensibly as part of their routine case work, and asked to make match judgments about them. The false positive error rate is the proportion of sample pairs that were not produced from a common source, yet are reported as matches. Few proficiency tests have been conducted to date, and those that have been conducted were generally nonblind.

What is wrong with nonblind proficiency tests?

Nonblind proficiency tests may not provide a good indicator of the error rate in actual case work because the technicians may be unusually diligent and cautious when they know they are being observed and tested. For example, the observed technicians may be reluctant to declare matches in ambiguous situations to avoid the stigma of having committed a false positive error.

Can the false positive error rate of a particular DNA laboratory or lab technician be determined in the absence of data from blind proficiency tests?

Not exactly, but there are ways to handle this problem. Here is one idea: The results of nonblind proficiency tests that have been performed may be combined and averaged to provide a lower-bound estimate of the false positive error rate (i.e., a minimum error rate) for a laboratory or lab technician whose error rate is unknown. Thus, if the average error rate in testing is 2 percent, then it should be concluded that laboratories make errors at least 2 percent of the time.

There are several reasons why the proficiency test error rate should be used as a lower-bound estimate rather than as a best estimate. First, the openness of nonblind tests makes them less sensitive to false positive error. The probability of false positive error also is diminished in many proficiency tests because the samples used are generally easier to work with and analyze than those in actual case work. Finally, as a matter of legal policy, defendants should be given the benefit of the doubt when it comes to estimating the error rate associated with the analyses that matched their own blood with an incriminating trace.

A related idea is to report the false positive error rate as the largest false positive error rate that is consistent with the combined false positive error rates obtained in proficiency tests. The advantage of this approach is that it contains an incentive for DNA laboratories to submit to and perform well in large-scale proficiency tests. The burden would then shift to the individual laboratories to present evidence that their own false positive error rates are lower than this value.

According to proficiency test data conducted to date, what is the false positive error rate of DNA analyses?

First, it must be noted that proficiency test results to date are extremely limited. Much more proficiency testing under reasonably realistic conditions is needed before confident estimates can be made. But based on the little evidence available to date, a reasonable estimate of the false positive error rate is 1–4 percent. In 1987 and 1988, the California Association of Crime Laboratory Directors conducted proficiency tests with three DNA laboratories. In an initial study, two out of 110 reported matches were false positives. In a follow-up study, one out of an estimated 120 reported matches were false positives. More recent proficiency tests involving many more labs reflect a similar or slightly higher false positive error rate.

It should be noted that many laboratories conduct internal proficiency tests and report that errors are rare. These tests, however, are generally shrouded in secrecy and are so obviously self-serving that it is hard to know how to assess their significance. After considering all available evidence, the bottom line is that the laboratories seem to make many more accurate match declarations than inaccurate ones. But before deciding that an error rate of, say, 1 percent is acceptable or even "good," consider the error rate that would be tolerated in a commercial airliner (where an "error" is defined as a potentially fatal mistake). Even seemingly low rates of error may be intolerable when the cost of the error is sufficiently high.

What is an appropriate legal policy for divulging DNA laboratory error rates at trial?

A good argument can be made for requiring DNA laboratories to provide fact finders with conservatively high estimates of their false positive error rates when they provide testimony about genetic matches. By the same token, laboratories should be required to divulge their estimated false negative error rate in cases where exclusions are reported.

A valuable but limited tool

DNA identification evidence has been, and probably will continue to be, extremely valuable in obtaining criminal convictions. Jurors frequently report that such evidence is convincing. In many cases, this is as it should be. DNA evidence can provide a powerful link between a defendant, a crime scene, and a victim. It is also useful in determining paternity.

It is imperative, however, that judges, attorneys, jurors, and experts understand the meaning of a reported match and the conditions in which it should have more and less impact on judgments. Experts must be discouraged from overstating the probative significance of a match (i.e., no source

or guilt probability statements) and encouraged to discuss the significance
of relatives and subpopulations in the potential source population. They
should also provide candid testimony about the potential for error in DNA
analyses. But when zealous experts are not forthcoming about the limitations and shortcomings of DNA evidence, defense attorneys must be prepared to identify and explain the relevant issues in cross-examination and
with experts of their own.

Three probabilities

Random Match Probability: The probability that a person selected at
random from a particular population would match the trace evidence as
well as the suspect. A random match probability of .001 indicates that the
trace evidence would match about 10 people in a population of 10,000 and
would not match the remaining 9,990 people. Based on the genetic test
alone, each of the 10 matchees is a possible source of the trace, while all of
the 9,990 nonmatchees may be excluded as possible sources.

Source Probability: The probability that the suspect is the source of
the recovered trace evidence. The source probability is not, simply, one mi-
nus the random match probability, as many people seem to believe. The
source probability is affected by the random match probability, but it is also
affected by an estimate of the number of other people who might be the
source, their relation to the suspect, and the particular circumstances surrounding the trace evidence.

Guilt Probability: The probability that the suspect is guilty of the
crime in question. This computation requires an estimate of both the
strength of the genetic matching evidence and the strength of the nongenetic evidence in the case. Genetic evidence that supports an inference of
guilt can be offset by nongenetic evidence that supports an inference of innocence. Likewise, genetic evidence that supports an inference of innocence
(e.g., hairs recovered from a crime scene that do not match those of the
suspect) may be offset by nongenetic evidence that supports an inference of
guilt (e.g., credible eyewitness testimony that places the suspect at the
crime scene).

Margaret A. Berger, Laboratory Error Seen Through the Lens of Science and Policy[*]

30 U.C. Davis L. Rev. 1081 (1997).

* * *

I. Is Laboratory Error a "Scientific" Fact?

A. Must the Error Rate Be Combined with the RMP?

Requiring the rate of profile matching due to laboratory error to be combined with the RMP [random match probability] would mean that an expert witness would not be allowed to testify to statistics that refer solely to the probability that a person randomly selected from the population has the same DNA profile as the evidence sample. This result is the goal of a number of commentators who have strenuously urged that a report on the frequency of matching DNA profiles is meaningless unless laboratory error is taken into account. Furthermore, they claim that scientific principles compel the conclusion that only a combined statistic is significant in a court of law. Their position is perhaps best approached with the help of a beguiling, but I will argue, ultimately misleading, baseball analogy offered by Professor Jonathan Koehler, a leading proponent of this view.

Professor Koehler's example is as follows: Suppose, he says that the fielder "makes throwing errors fewer than one time in a million, but makes fielding errors two percent of the time." If we are trying to estimate the error rate on the fielder's next attempt (due to either throwing or fielding) the chance of an error is at least two percent because he has to field the ball before he can throw it. Even if the fielder's throwing improves so that he now throws imperfectly only once in a hundred million times, his overall error rate will not improve. Professor Koehler concludes that "just as the infielder's two percent fielding error rate sets a lower bound threshold for error estimates, the forensic scientist's laboratory error rate sets a lower bound for false positive match reports." In other words, according to Professor Koehler, even if the probability of a random match of the DNA profile in question is one in a hundred million, if the laboratory makes errors two percent of the time, the RMP is irrelevant.

* * *

However calculated, the laboratory error rate differs radically from the error rates in baseball. The baseball analogy is misleading. In baseball, each time the infielder handles the ball we know from the official scorer whether or not an error occurred. The result is an error rate that is based on each chance the infielder has for a play.

There is no error rate based on the real tests a laboratory performs. Instead, a surrogate error rate is calculated on the basis of open or blind proficiency testing done on specially constructed samples. Statisticians know that a meaningful estimate of a particular laboratory's error rate on proficiency testing cannot be ascertained. Such a calculation would require more proficiency tests than any laboratory will ever perform. And even were it possible for a particular laboratory to conduct enough blind sufficiency testing to be statistically meaningful, arriving at a representative error rate would still entail considerable guesswork due to the nature of DNA testing and proficiency testing. Because an accurate estimate of a particular laboratory's rate is unattainable either by counting errors it made in real cases or by looking at its record on proficiency testing, it is, therefore, pointless to argue that *Daubert* demands that DNA evidence "should not be admitted unless a laboratory can offer a reliable estimate of *its* false positive error rate."

Of course, Professor Koehler understands that the probability of error in a particular laboratory cannot be computed. Instead, he suggests that proficiency test results should be pooled in order to estimate an "industry-wide" error rate, and that this pooled rate will be reported as the applicable laboratory error in a particular case. The pooled proficiency test approach pretends that all laboratories are the same, despite the reality that some laboratories are better than others, and despite the fact that case-specific information will be available about how the laboratory performed in the case at hand. It also assumes, without proof, that sufficient proficiency testing is done to arrive at a meaningful estimate of industry-wide laboratory error. The objective of proficiency testing is not to measure error, but to allow laboratories to evaluate their performance, a somewhat different question. Furthermore, the amount of testing that is required (by voluntary standards or legislative directive) is not determined solely by how much performance review is appropriate. Especially in an era of budgetary constraints, cost as well as benefit affects the volume of testing. Proficiency testing is expensive and time-consuming; personnel who could be working on pending cases are instead spending their time designing tests, taking tests, and grading tests. Therefore, the data available for calculating industry-wide error rates are the product of pragmatic and evaluative concerns rather than a scientific approach to quantifying error.

This leap from a real case error rate to a surrogate proficiency test-based error rate to a pooled error rate to the rate for a particular laboratory may be the best that a statistician can do. But does this mean that the result is "scientific"? Does this calculation provide a "satisfactory approximation" of the error that occurred in the laboratory in question?

I would argue that it does not, not only for the reasons stated above, but also because Professor Koehler's baseball analogy is misleading in another respect as well. It suggests that the fielder's lifetime error rate is a constant that will apply to each subsequent play. But this is a meaningless fiction to any fan knowledgeable about the infielder's current playing abilities. Similarly, the historical industry-wide error rate will not be sufficiently helpful in evaluating a laboratory's performance in a particular case at a particular moment in time. The historical pooled rate will include performance errors that no longer occur because of quality control and quality assurance programs, as well as interpretive errors experienced with now obsolete methodologies. The rate may not take into account the fact that error rates in homicides and assaults differ markedly from those experienced with rapes, where the presence of the rape victim's DNA in the crime sample ensures that certain kinds of error cannot occur. Furthermore, because proficiency test rates are derived from simulations, they are impervious to the possibility that in real cases other evidence, such as the existence of an iron-clad alibi, retesting, or laboratory review procedures may unearth a mistake, which the laboratory will correct.

Although Professor Koehler concedes that the error rate ought to be adjusted when "[c]ase-specific circumstances . . . suggest that error is more or less likely to arise," he relies on another analogy to argue that it would be unscientific to ignore pooled error rates just because specific facts may alter the probability of error in a given case. He claims that the invariable existence of "unique circumstances . . . does not itself provide reason to disregard industry-wide error rate estimates any more than the fact of human uniqueness provides physicians with reason to disregard medical studies about likely responses to various drugs and procedures," or the Federal Aviation Administration to ignore errors that lead to airplane crashes. These analogies miss the point. The question under discussion is not whether, and under what circumstances, laboratory error may have probative value. The question is whether the scientific validity of pooled error rates is such that, under *Daubert,* evidence of a DNA match is meaningless unless it is either combined with, or accompanied by, this pooled proficiency test-based error rate.

The RMP conveys accurate information to the fact-finder about the distinctiveness of the DNA profile in question. No scientific principle dictates that this significance is worthless without a pooled surrogate inexact approximation of an error rate.

* * *

[One] possible justification for a special error rule for DNA evidence rests on the evidence's arcane nature. Unlike fingerprint evidence, which rests on a theory that is readily understandable and visible—it is easy to see that the whorls on one's fingers do not match those of others in the room—DNA alleles are invisible, and theories of population genetics are complex. The argument here is that the mysterious nature of DNA profiling makes it appear infallible, and therefore not subject to error.

Some commentators would extend this rationale—that jurors need to know that error does occur even in connection with abstruse and seemingly irrefutable evidence—to all scientific evidence. They would require the prosecution to make an error rate part of its case-in-chief because they believe that scientific evidence is so compelling that jurors will ignore the possibility of laboratory error.

Singling out DNA or other scientific evidence for special treatment is inconsistent with the law's reaction to the possibility of error in other contexts. There are other kinds of evidence that jurors may consistently overvalue. A considerable body of empirical research suggests that jurors may accord eyewitness testimony far more probative value than it deserves. Until now, the data concerning error in eyewitness cases were derived from simulations that perhaps do not reflect what happens when there is a genuine crime. If, however, we are wary of extrapolating error from staged events, we now have another source for error rates. Data are accumulating, and could be collected more systematically, on how often an eyewitness identification in an actual case is contradicted by a DNA test that exonerates the accused. In addition, a growing number of rape convictions based on eyewitness testimony are being overturned after post-conviction DNA testing. Despite these real case data that confirm the research findings on mistaken identifications, the law rarely acknowledges that jurors ought to be informed that their confidence in the accuracy of eyewitness testimony may be misplaced. Even in a case that hinges exclusively on eyewitness identification, not only is the prosecution under no obligation to furnish error rates, but usually the defense is precluded from calling expert witnesses to educate jurors about the prevalence of eyewitness error. In light of this unwillingness, even for impeachment, to make use of eyewitness error about which we know quite a bit, it seems rather inconsistent to take the radical step of conditioning the admissibility of DNA evidence on pooled proficiency test-based error rates, even though there is virtually no data on how jurors process RMPs or error rates.

* * *

Interpretative errors, which are a significant component of laboratory error, are not invisible when defendants are provided with adequate documentation of the laboratory's operation. Mistakes in applying proper scientific principles can then be attacked with the assistance of existing evidentiary and procedural rules. Counsel can cross-examine the prosecution's experts about how they reached their conclusions, dispute their opinions with the help of the learned treatise rule, and call experts of their own. Prosecution experts can also be cross-examined about the possibility of performance errors or the procedures that the laboratory employs to minimize their occurrence. In addition, courts have the power to enlist the assistance of court-appointed experts. Procedures such as duplicate testing by the prosecution, retesting by the defense, and testing all crime scene samples eliminate the possibility of many laboratory performance errors, which may also be detectable through scrutiny of the laboratory's internal documentation.

* * *

Requiring an error rate as part of the prosecution's case for fear the jury will not properly assess the evidence against the defendant is reminiscent of a now generally outmoded common law approach to evidence. Burdens, such as the requirement of corroboration, were placed on the prosecution to protect the innocent instead of trusting jurors to weigh the evidence in the case. We have abandoned this distrust of jurors in recent years, and should not now readopt fixed evaluation of evidence requirements without some demonstration that defendants are at greater risk in DNA cases than in criminal cases in general. The demand for incorporating an error lower bound into presentations of DNA evidence obscures the fact that, in the great majority of cases, no laboratory error will have occurred.

* * *

Assuming that the problems in quantifying adjusted laboratory error could be overcome, a very questionable supposition, is it worthwhile to burden the prosecution with this issue? The consequence would be that, at least potentially, a laboratory error rate would have to be calculated for each case in which DNA evidence is offered. Such a case-specific estimate threshold to the admissibility of DNA evidence might engulf courts in costly and protracted in limine hearings if the defense disagreed with the prosecution's calculation. Furthermore, if the available research is correct in concluding that laboratory error rates by themselves are ineffectual, then the time and effort devoted to establishing an acceptable case-specific estimate would be non-productive unless, perhaps, it were combined with the RMP. A combined statistic, however, so underestimates the probative value of a DNA match in the great majority of cases that, as a matter of policy, we ought not deprive ourselves of this evidence—at least until we have a more sound basis for concluding that more mistaken convictions occur because of inaccurate DNA results than occur with all the other forensic techniques for which no error rate is required.

* * *

Two different fallacies need to be avoided in presenting statistical evidence. The "prosecutor's fallacy" occurs when a prosecutor suggests that the evidence indicates the likelihood of the defendant's guilt, rather than the odds of a match, given that defendant is not the source. Furthermore, even in the absence of prosecution insinuation, the danger persists that jurors will transpose the conditional probability, despite the court's or experts' instructions explaining the RMP.

If the RMP estimate were limited by the laboratory error rate, however, explanations by the court and experts of the meaning of the single adjusted statistic would reveal that this is a RMP estimate modified to account for the probability of laboratory error in this case. Is it not perhaps possible that a reference to error *in this case* would make jurors even more prone to assume that the adjusted figure must represent the odds of guilt *in this case*? Even if the probability were much higher than a pure random match probability, a juror who thinks that the statistic means that there is only a one in five thousand chance that defendant is not guilty may conclude that the reasonable doubt standard has been satisfied.

The "defendant's fallacy" occurs when defense counsel suggests, or jurors conclude, that anyone with the same profile as the defendant is as likely as the defendant to be the source of the crime scene sample. In other words, if the error-adjusted probability is one in five thousand and the crime occurred in a city of five million, jurors might erroneously conclude that one thousand other equally likely suspects exist. This fallacy, which current research indicates is more likely to sway jurors than the "prosecutor's fallacy," results from the jury's failure to evaluate the non-DNA evidence that tends to incriminate the defendant, but not a random member of the population. Larger probabilities such as would result with an error-adjusted statistic are likely to fuel this type of erroneous juror reasoning—a probability of one in one thousand might lead some to conclude that there are five thousand potential culprits in our hypothetical city.

* * *

CONCLUSION

DNA evidence is extremely powerful and we rightly fear that innocent persons might be convicted if DNA matches result from laboratory error. We also know that it is no more possible to eliminate all sources of error in connection with DNA testing than with any other kind of evidence, including fingerprints. Before we overreact by restricting the probative value of DNA evidence in every case, we need to take two steps.

First, we need to decrease the possibility of error in laboratories as much as possible. As discussed above, a principal argument for conditioning the admissibility of DNA evidence on a laboratory error rate is that such a rule will have a prophylactic effect in minimizing error. There are more direct ways of achieving the same result, however, without skewing evidentiary principles. Forensic laboratories could be made independent of police control. Courts could pressure laboratories into seeking accreditation by refusing to qualify experts from unaccredited laboratories. Courts could also insist, as a minority of courts do, that DNA evidence will not be admitted if the laboratory involved failed to follow proper protocols. Courts could instruct jurors about laboratory quality control and assurance programs to permit them to draw a negative inference about the quality of the DNA evidence if such procedures had not been followed.

Second, we need to make sure that our traditional mechanisms are functioning effectively. Defense counsel must be given adequate procedural tools, such as discovery and access to experts, in order to deal with DNA evidence. We also need more information about how to make DNA evidence—and other statistical data—more comprehensible to jurors.

We should take these steps before we engage in an expensive and time-consuming quest for an elusive statistic about error that is unlikely to improve our fact-finding system. The very limited available research suggests that error rates by themselves will not have any impact. A combined error and RMP statistic may confuse jurors further or perhaps make them more cynical about the operation of the judicial system. Given these choices, neither science nor policy requires a special burden-shifting rule for DNA cases to handle the possibility of laboratory error.

NOTE

In a news conference on November 12, 1997, FBI officials announced a policy under which FBI DNA analysts would testify that an individual was the "source" of a DNA sample "to a reasonable degree of scientific certainty" when the random match probability was smaller than one in 260 billion. FDCH Political Transcripts, November 12, 1997. FBI analysts will, however, continue to testify in a less positive fashion where random match probabilities are larger, for example when they are testifying about results of mitochondrial DNA analysis, a relatively new technique. See Mark Hansen, *A Comeback for Hair Evidence*, ABA Journal, May, 1998 (" 'We always say it's maternally inherited and it's not unique to the individual,' says Mark Wilson, the FBI's program manager for mitochondrial DNA analysis. 'And we always tell them it cannot be used as a means of positive identification.' ")

QUESTIONS ON PROBABILITY AND PROOF

A. Consider the following statements of probability. Do they reflect errors?

1. The red-haired soldier, *supra*, reprinted here for convenience:

    S. found a red hair at the scene of the atrocity. From his forensic studies, he knew that one person in ten has red hair. On his way back to headquarters, he saw a red-haired soldier marching in a parade. "There is but one chance in ten," he thought, "that the hair I found at the scene came from someone other than that soldier."

2. The following testimony about a DNA match:

Q: And in your profession and in the scientific field when you say match what do you mean?

A: They are identical.

Q: So the blood on the blanket can you say that it came from Sayeh Rivaz-far [the victim]?

A: With great certainty I can say that those two DNA samples match and they are identical. And with population statistics we can derive a probability of it being anyone other than that victim.

Q: What is that probability in this case?

A: In this case that probability is that it is one in 7 million chances that it could be anyone other than the victim.

[From Koehler, 34 Jurimetrics J. 21, 25 (1993)]

3. Victor's reasoning:

Victor was startled when the lab results came back. He tested positive for syphilis. His doctor told him that the lab's false positive error rate was one in 100. He thought, "This isn't fair. I've never had sexual contact with anyone. Yet the odds are almost a hundred to one that I have syphilis."4. Ernies's reasoning:

> Ernie was planning his trip to Pamplona. "There are two ways I could get hurt," he thought. "There is about a one in a hundred chance of getting gored by a bull, and about a one in a million chance of dying in an airline crash. Therefore my overall chances of getting hurt are about one in half a million."

B. Suppose that your opponent argued the "prosecutor's fallacy" (that the 1/200 population frequency of the incriminating trait means that there is a 1/200 chance that the defendant who possesses it is innocent) to the jury. What argument could you make in response?

C. Suppose that your opponent argued the "defense counsel's fallacy" (e.g., that the fact that there are 10,000 other men in the area with the same genetic markers means that the the odds are 10,000:1 that the defendant is innocent). What argument could you make in response?

Houts, Photographic Misrepresentation

Matthew Bender & Co.; San Francisco; 1964, pp. 5–46 to 5–49.

[8]—Lens Performance: Position of Automobiles

* * *

Figures 54 & 55 are taken from the same camera position behind the convertible automobile. A short focal length lens is used in *Figure 54*. This makes it appear that there is a substantial distance between the two vehicles and that perhaps the driver of the convertible would have had ample time to stop when the other car pulled out in front of him. *Figure 55* was taken with a long focal length lens which "pulls" the two vehicles together, making it appear that the driver of the convertible would not have had time to stop. * * *

Figure 54

Figure 55

Waltz, Introduction to Criminal Evidence

417–423 (3d ed.1991).[*]

DEMONSTRATIVE EVIDENCE

A.

Historical Background

It is pointed out in [an earlier chapter] that demonstrative evidence is to be distinguished from real evidence in that demonstrative evidence consists of tangible materials that are used for illustrative or explanatory purposes only and do not purport to be "the real thing"—the murder weapon, the burglary tools actually used by the accused, the heroin seized by the narcotics agents when they arrested the defendant. It was also mentioned in [an earlier chapter] that there are two basic types of demonstrative evidence: (1) *selected* demonstrative evidence, such as handwriting exemplars, and (2) *prepared* or *reproduced* demonstrative evidence, such as a sketch or diagram * * *. In this chapter we go into somewhat greater depth in describing types of demonstrative evidence and the range of possible objections to its use.

There has been a resurgence of interest in the imaginative use of demonstrative evidence, after a lengthy period during which trial lawyers were reluctant to rely on it for fear of causing an adverse reaction by jurors who might draw the implication that an essentially weak case was being overproved by means of unsubstantial gimmickry. Unquestionably, the use of demonstrative evidence has had its ups and downs, as the following commentary—made almost a hundred years ago—attests:

> In the early and rude ages there was a strong leaning toward the adoption of demonstrative and practical tests upon disputed questions. Doubting Thomases demanded the satisfaction of their senses. * * * As society grew civilized and refined, it seemed disposed to despise these demonstrative methods, and inclined more to the preference of a narration, at second-hand, by eye and ear witnesses. But in this busy century there seems to have been a relapse toward the earlier experimental spirit, and a disposition to make assurance doubly sure by any practical method addressed to the senses. (Browne, Practical Tests in Evidence, 4 Green Bag 510 (1892).)

Of course, there is nothing inherently wrong with evidence which is addressed to some sense other than that of hearing. One character in the musical <u>My Fair Lady</u> may have unwittingly summed up the attitude of many jury members when she said, "Words, words, words—I'm sick of words. Is that all you [lawyers] can do? *Show me!*" (Italics added.)

---

[*] Copyright, 1991, by Jon R. Waltz. Nelson–Hall Publishers, Chicago.

For a number of years now, trial lawyers have paid increasing attention to demonstrative evidence as a means of *showing* the elements of a case to the fact-finder.

Perhaps the earliest reported use of demonstrative evidence was in the Case of *James Watson, the elder, Surgeon, on an Indictment charging him with High Treason,* 32 Howard State Trials 1 (1817). There was offered into evidence in that case a sketch of a flag that allegedly had been used to whip up a "treasonous assemblage" in England. Defense counsel objected, arguing that the flag "was a matter of verbal description not of description by drawing." The trial judge sneered and overruled the objection: "Can there be any objection to the production of a drawing, or a model, as illustrative of evidence? Surely there is nothing in the objection."

Another leading case, this time arising in America but not many years after the Watson trial, is Commonwealth v. Webster, 5 Cush. 295 (Sup.Jud.Ct.Mass.1850). Professor Webster had been charged with murdering Doctor Parkman and burning his body in a furnace. A mold of Doctor Parkman's jaw, made several years previously when he had been fitted for dentures, taken together with some teeth that had survived the furnace fire, was credited with securing Webster's conviction.

Today the propriety, in fact the wisdom, of using demonstrative evidence to help jurors follow the trial evidence goes pretty much without question in many cases, both criminal and civil. Objections to demonstrative evidence are frequently voiced, however.

B.

Bases for Objection to Demonstrative Evidence

Misguided Objections. Some objections to demonstrative evidence are misguided and will be swiftly overruled. Occasionally a lawyer will become confused about the proper application of the best evidence rule, discussed [earlier], and contend that the "original," and not "a mere example," must be produced in court. Thus one hears about the Texas judge who prohibited the use of a skeletal model because it did not consist of the very bones of the complaining witness (who was not dead). This judge had forgotten, if he ever knew, that the best evidence rule applies only to written documents.

Then, too, one sometimes encounters a misguided hearsay objection to demonstrative evidence. Defense counsel leaps up to object to the prosecution's offer of a witness's freehand sketch of a crime scene, asking, "How can we cross-examine a sketch, Your Honor?" What this objection misses, of course, is the fact that the sketch is being offered as a part of the testimony of a witness on the stand who is fully subject to confrontation and cross-examination.

Objections Grounded on Lack of Verity or Accuracy. As was suggested in [an earlier chapter], dealing with the perfecting of the trial record, a proper foundation or predicate must be laid before an item of demonstrative evidence can successfully be offered. The witness who is in a position to "sponsor" (authenticate) the exhibit must identify it and verify, the accuracy of whatever it portrays. This does not mean that the sponsoring witness must be the person who took the photograph or prepared the drawing, chart, or map.

Example:

BY THE PROSECUTING ATTORNEY: Officer Ham, you have testified that you were present, in your investigative capacity, at the scene of the murders, isn't that correct?

A. That's right, I was in the room for maybe three hours.

Q. And you have testified to its general layout and appearance, have you not?

A. I have.

Q. To your knowledge, were photographs of the room taken while you were there?

A. Yes, our photographer took a number of shots of the place.

Q. Officer Ham, I now hand you what previously has been marked Prosecution Exhibit 12 for Identification, being a photographic print, and ask you whether or not it is a fair and accurate representation of the room at 421 Melrose Street on the day in question?

A. Yes, sir, it is. That's exactly the way it looked.

BY THE PROSECUTING ATTORNEY: Your Honor, we offer prosecution's 12 into evidence.

BY DEFENSE COUNSEL: We have no objection.

THE COURT: The exhibit will be received.

There can be no stronger an objection to demonstrative evidence than that it is not a fair representation of what it supposedly depicts. If, for example, a photograph or map significantly distorts relevant aspects of the scene depicted, it will be subject to successful objection, or at least to an instruction that the jury is to disregard the distorted parts.

Occasionally photographs can be obtained only after autopsy procedures have in a sense distorted the picture of a deceased: the head has been shaved; large incisions have been made; sutures may be visible. Still, the tendency is to admit such photographs if they add to the case anything of real probative value. Thus in Young v. State, the court, commenting on the receipt in evidence of post-autopsy photographs, said, "[T]he fact that the ghastly appearance of the wounds, even though such appearance was heightened by the shaving of the head and the use of mercurochrome * * * did not make [the photographs] inadmissible."

So long as the color has not been artificially and misleadingly heightened, there is a trend toward preferring natural color to black-and-white photographs. Some years ago Professor Conrad, an authority on photographic evidence, wrote, "[W]e have used black and white photographs for so long that we accept them as the real thing. Actually, black and white photography is considered an abstract medium and does not represent reality as such. * * * The inherent realism of color photography has been urged [as preferable to black and white]. * * * " (Conrad, Evidential Aspects of Color Photography, 4 Jour. of Forensic Science 176, 178 (1959).)

The fact that a photograph or other item of demonstrative evidence has been retouched or marked will not, in and of itself, result in inadmissibility. For example, in State v. Weston, plaster casts of a body containing gunshot wounds had been prepared prior to autopsy. Many small blue dots had been placed on the casts by a witness who compared the casts with the body in order to distinguish the bullet wounds from air bubbles in the plaster casts. When the casts were offered in evidence to exemplify the location of the bullet wounds, defense counsel objected that "after the blue dots which indicate the wounds had been placed upon the cast it was no longer * * * a true representation of deceased's forearm and hand." The Oregon Supreme Court laid down the applicable principles:

> The jury was amply informed that the sole purpose of the blue dots was to indicate the presence of the wounds. Since the jurors could rightfully look at the indications of the wounds, we cannot understand how the help which these small dots gave them in locating the wounds would have prejudiced any interest properly claimed by the defendant. * * *
>
> [W]e deduce the rule that maps, photographs et cetera, containing markings, are not inadmissible if they are otherwise relevant and if the individual who made the mark or wrote the legend was familiar with the facts and so testifies, or if some other witness, familiar with the facts, adopts the mark or legend as his own. (See also Busch, Photographic Evidence, 4 DePaul Law Rev. 195 (1955).)

Models are sometimes rejected by trial courts because they may be misleading or confusing due to difference in scale.

Example A:

San Mateo County v. Christian, ("While models may frequently be of great assistance to a court and jury, it is common knowledge that, even when constructed to scale, they may frequently, because of the great disparity in size between the model and the original, also be very misleading. * * * ").

Example B:

Martindale v. City of Mountain View, (in assault and battery case, testimony was that victim had been beaten with 2□ stick; offer in evidence of axe handle 3□ long rejected).

Courts are suspicious of filmed reenactments and posed photographs, lest they be misleading. A leading case, Richardson v. Missouri-K.T.R. Co. of Texas, arose on the civil side. To establish that the plaintiff himself had been negligent, the defendant introduced a color film showing plaintiff's shop foreman demonstrating how plaintiff's hand *"could* be caught and run through the blades" of a shaping machine (italics added). The foreman testified that "he did not know how the fingers of [plaintiff] were caught in the machine and therefore his experiments did not undertake to show how [plaintiff] was operating it at the time."

The Texas court brushed aside the plaintiff's objections to this filmed reenactment. "In the final analysis," the court said, "the increased danger of fraud peculiar to posed photographs must be weighed against their communicative value. Only the additional danger of fraud or suggestion separates this question from that of the admissibility of ordinary photographs."

In line with the Richardson decision, posed and photographed reenactments of a crime are sometimes admitted in evidence after a careful foundation, which manifests the accuracy of the reenactment, has been laid by the prosecuting attorney.

Gruesome Films and Photographs. As was intimated earlier, another prime basis of objections to demonstrative evidence is that the motion picture or still photograph is gruesome and inflammatory; in other words, that its potential for prejudice to the accused's right to a fair trial outweighs whatever probative worth it may have. An objection of this sort is directed to the trial judge's discretion.

A photograph or motion picture is not inadmissible simply because it is gruesome. That has been understood ever since the opinion in Franklin v. State involving some gruesome photographs:

The throat of the deceased was cut; the character of the wound was important * * *; the man was killed and buried * * *; we cannot conceive of a more impartial and truthful witness than the sun, as its light stamps and seals the similitude of the wound on the photograph put before the jury; it would be more accurate than the memory of witnesses, and as the object of all evidence is to show the truth, why should not this dumb [in the sense of mute] witness show it?

Ever since *Franklin* it has been the rule that photographs and films are not rendered inadmissible simply because they depict in a graphic way the details of a shocking or revolting crime. They will be deemed inadmissible only if they are irrelevant to the issues in the case or where their probative worth is outweighed by their potential for unfair prejudice.

Example A:

Johnson v. Commonwealth (hideous photographs showing mangled body in morgue, *held*, admissible to support autopsy surgeon's explanatory testimony).

Example B:

Henninger v. State (three gruesome photographs showing knife wounds in back, partially severed head, and pantyhose wrapped around neck, *held*, admissible to establish identity of accused, cause of death, and to rebut claim of self-defense).

Appellate courts will conclude that it was an abuse of judicial discretion to receive gruesome photographs only when they were unnecessary, cumulative to the narrative testimony of witnesses, or where, although of minimal evidentiary value, they have been overemphasized to the jury. Thus it may be error to admit gruesome photographs when the testimony of an available pathologist would do just as well. In an early California case, Thrall v. Smiley, the court rejected drawings of the defendant's damaged teeth, noting that the sketches were not "necessary to illustrate the fact asserted [since] the extent of the injury could be as well understood from the statement of the dentist who repaired them." And projecting color slides of the deceased's wounds for a full half day during a four and one-half day trial has led to reversal. Some additional examples are given below:

Example A:

Commonwealth v. Dankel (where only factual dispute was whether accused aided in burglary during which a homicide occurred, introduction by prosecution of four gruesome photographs of victim, showing face eroded by ammonia burns, was reversible error).

Example B:

Terry v. State (where bruises and other injuries sustained by infant homicide victim had already been shown with pre-autopsy photographs, it was prejudicial error to receive four post-autopsy photographs depicting massive mutilation to child caused by autopsy procedures).

Example C:

> Beagles v. State (where defense in first degree murder case admitted victim's death, the cause of death, and her identity, the admission of numerous gruesome color photographs of the victim was error: "Photographs should be received in evidence with great caution and photographs which show nothing more than a gory or gruesome portrayal should not be admitted.").

Trial judges will protect an accused against the use of demonstrative evidence the primary purpose of which is to whip jurors into a vindictive mood. But demonstrative evidence has a firmly settled place in criminal litigation. If it is used sparingly, with scrupulous accuracy, and only when it holds out genuine promise of making the case more readily understandable by judge and jurors, courts can be expected to be liberal in their rulings on the admissibility question.

APPENDIX A

FEDERAL RULES OF EVIDENCE

Including Amendments Effective December 1, 2011.

Table of Rules

ARTICLE I. General Provisions

ARTICLE X. CONTENTS OF WRITINGS, RECORDINGS, AND PHOTOGRAPHS

ARTICLE XI. MISCELLANEOUS RULES

ARTICLE I. GENERAL PROVISIONS

Rule 101
SCOPE; DEFINITIONS

(a) SCOPE. These rules apply to proceedings in United States courts. The specific courts and proceedings to which the rules apply, along with exceptions, are set out in Rule 1101.

(b) DEFINITIONS. In these rules:

(1) "civil case" means a civil action or proceeding;

(2) "criminal case" includes a criminal proceeding;

(3) "public office" includes a public agency;

(4) "record" includes a memorandum, report, or data compilation;

(5) a "rule prescribed by the Supreme Court" means a rule adopted by the Supreme Court under statutory authority; and

(6) a reference to any kind of written material or any other medium includes electronically stored information.

(Pub.L. 93–595, § 1, Jan. 2, 1975, 88 Stat. 1929; Mar. 2, 1987, eff. Oct. 1, 1987; Apr. 25, 1988, eff. Nov. 1, 1988; Apr. 22, 1993, eff. Dec. 1, 1993; Apr. 26, 2011, eff. Dec. 1, 2011.)

Rule 102
PURPOSE

These rules should be construed so as to administer every proceeding fairly, eliminate unjustifiable expense and delay, and promote the development of evidence law, to the end of ascertaining the truth and securing a just determination.

(Pub.L. 93–595, § 1, Jan. 2, 1975, 88 Stat.1929; Apr. 26, 2011, eff. Dec. 1, 2011.)

Rule 103
RULINGS ON EVIDENCE

(a) PRESERVING A CLAIM OF ERROR. A party may claim error in a ruling to admit or exclude evidence only if the error affects a substantial right of the party and:

(1) if the ruling admits evidence, a party, on the record:

(A) timely objects or moves to strike; and

(B) states the specific ground, unless it was apparent from the context; or

(2) if the ruling excludes evidence, a party informs the court of its substance by an offer of proof, unless the substance was apparent from the context.

(b) NOT NEEDING TO RENEW AN OBJECTION OR OFFER OF PROOF. Once the court rules definitively on the record—either before or at trial—a party need not renew an objection or offer of proof to preserve a claim of error for appeal.

(c) COURT'S STATEMENT ABOUT THE RULING; DIRECTING AN OFFER OF PROOF. The court may make any statement about the character or form of the evidence, the objection made, and the ruling. The court may direct that an offer of proof be made in question and answer form.

(d) PREVENTING THE JURY FROM HEARING INADMISSIBLE EVIDENCE. To the extent practicable, the court must conduct a jury trial so that inadmissible evidence is not suggested to the jury by any means.

(e) TAKING NOTICE OF PLAIN ERROR. A court may take notice of a plain error affecting a substantial right, even if the claim of error was not properly preserved.

(Pub.L. 93–595, § 1, Jan. 2, 1975, 88 Stat. 1929; Apr. 17, 2000, eff. Dec. 1, 2000; Apr. 26, 2011, eff. Dec. 1, 2011.)

Rule 104
PRELIMINARY QUESTIONS

(a) IN GENERAL. The court must decide any preliminary question about whether a witness is qualified, a privilege exists, or evidence is admissible. In so deciding, the court is not bound by evidence rules, except those on privilege.

—(b) RELEVANCE THAT DEPENDS ON A FACT. When the relevance of evidence depends on whether a fact exists, proof must be introduced sufficient to support a finding that the fact does exist. The court may admit the proposed evidence on the condition that the proof be introduced later.

(c) CONDUCTING A HEARING SO THAT THE JURY CANNOT HEAR IT. The court must conduct any hearing on a preliminary question so that the jury cannot hear it if:

(1) the hearing involves the admissibility of a confession;

(2) a defendant in a criminal case is a witness and so requests; or

(3) justice so requires.

(d) CROSS–EXAMINING A DEFENDANT IN A CRIMINAL CASE. By testifying on a preliminary question, a defendant in a criminal case does not become subject to cross examination on other issues in the case.

(e) EVIDENCE RELEVANT TO WEIGHT AND CREDIBILITY. This rule does not limit a party's right to introduce before the jury evidence that is relevant to the weight or credibility of other evidence.

(Pub.L. 93–595, § 1, Jan. 2, 1975, 88 Stat.1930; Mar. 2, 1987, eff. Oct. 1, 1987; Apr. 26, 2011, eff. Dec. 1, 2011.)

Rule 105
LIMITING EVIDENCE THAT IS NOT ADMISSIBLE AGAINST OTHER PARTIES OR FOR OTHER PURPOSES

If the court admits evidence that is admissible against a party or for a purpose—but not against another party or for another purpose—the court, on timely request, must restrict the evidence to its proper scope and instruct the jury accordingly.

(Pub.L. 93–595, § 1, Jan. 2, 1975, 88 Stat. 1930; Apr. 26, 2011, eff. Dec. 1, 2011.)

Rule 106
REMAINDER OF OR RELATED WRITINGS OR RECORDED STATEMENTS

If a party introduces all or part of a writing or recorded statement, an adverse party may require the introduction, at that time, of any other part—or any other writing or recorded statement—that in fairness ought to be considered at the same time.

(Pub.L. 93–595, § 1, Jan. 2, 1975, 88 Stat. 1930; Mar. 2, 1987, eff. Oct. 1, 1987; Apr. 26, 2011, eff. Dec. 1, 2011.)

ARTICLE II. JUDICIAL NOTICE

Rule 201
JUDICIAL NOTICE OF ADJUDICATIVE FACTS

(a) SCOPE. This rule governs judicial notice of an adjudicative fact only, not a legislative fact.

(b) KINDS OF FACTS THAT MAY BE JUDICIALLY NOTICED. The court may judicially notice a fact that is not subject to reasonable dispute because it:

(1) is generally known within the trial court's territorial jurisdiction; or

(2) can be accurately and readily determined from sources whose accuracy cannot reasonably be questioned.

(c) TAKING NOTICE. The court:

(1) may take judicial notice on its own; or

(2) must take judicial notice if a party requests it and the court is supplied with the necessary information.

(d) TIMING. The court may take judicial notice at any stage of the proceeding.

(e) OPPORTUNITY TO BE HEARD. On timely request, a party is entitled to be heard on the propriety of taking judicial notice and the nature of the fact to be noticed. If the court takes judicial notice before notifying a party, the party, on request, is still entitled to be heard.

(f) Instructing the Jury. In a civil case, the court must instruct the jury to accept the noticed fact as conclusive. In a criminal case, the court must instruct the jury that it may or may not accept the noticed fact as conclusive.

(Pub.L. 93–595, § 1, Jan. 2, 1975, 88 Stat. 1930; Apr. 26, 2011, eff. Dec. 1, 2011.)

ARTICLE III. PRESUMPTIONS IN CIVIL CASES

Rule 301
PRESUMPTIONS IN CIVIL CASES GENERALLY

In a civil case, unless a federal statute or these rules provide otherwise, the party against whom a presumption is directed has the burden of producing evidence to rebut the presumption. But this rule does not shift the burden of persuasion, which remains on the party who had it originally.

(Pub.L. 93–595, § 1, Jan. 2, 1975, 88 Stat. 1931; Apr. 26, 2011, eff. Dec. 1, 2011.)

Rule 302
APPLYING STATE LAW TO PRESUMPTIONS IN CIVIL CASES

In a civil case, state law governs the effect of a presumption regarding a claim or defense for which state law supplies the rule of decision.

(Pub.L. 93–595, § 1, Jan. 2, 1975, 88 Stat. 1931; Apr. 26, 2011, eff. Dec. 1, 2011.)

ARTICLE IV. RELEVANCE AND ITS LIMITS

Rule 401
TEST FOR RELEVANT EVIDENCE

Evidence is relevant if:

(a) it has any tendency to make a fact more or less probable than it would be without the evidence; and

(b) the fact is of consequence in determining the action.

(Pub.L. 93–595, § 1, Jan. 2, 1975, 88 Stat.1931; Apr. 26, 2011, eff. Dec. 1, 2011.)

Rule 402
GENERAL ADMISSIBILITY OF RELEVANT EVIDENCE

Relevant evidence is admissible unless any of the following provides otherwise:

- the United States Constitution;

- a federal statute;

- these rules; or

- other rules prescribed by the Supreme Court.

Irrelevant evidence is not admissible.

(Pub.L. 93–595, § 1, Jan. 2, 1975, 88 Stat. 1931; Apr. 26, 2011, eff. Dec. 1, 2011.)

Rule 403
EXCLUDING RELEVANT EVIDENCE FOR PREJUDICE, CONFUSION, WASTE OF TIME, OR OTHER REASONS

The court may exclude relevant evidence if its probative value is substantially outweighed by a danger of one or more of the following: unfair prejudice, confusing the issues, misleading the jury, undue delay, wasting time, or needlessly presenting cumulative evidence.

(Pub.L. 93–595, § 1, Jan. 2, 1975, 88 Stat. 1932; Apr. 26, 2011, eff. Dec. 1, 2011.)

Rule 404
CHARACTER EVIDENCE; CRIMES OR OTHER ACTS

(a) CHARACTER EVIDENCE.

(1) *Prohibited Uses.* Evidence of a person's character or character trait is not admissible to prove that on a particular occasion the person acted in accordance with the character or trait.

(2) *Exceptions for a Defendant or Victim in a Criminal Case.* The following exceptions apply in a criminal case:

(A) a defendant may offer evidence of the defendant's pertinent trait, and if the evidence is admitted, the prosecutor may offer evidence to rebut it;

(B) subject to the limitations in Rule 412, a defendant may offer evidence of an alleged victim's pertinent trait, and if the evidence is admitted, the prosecutor may:

(i) offer evidence to rebut it; and

(ii) offer evidence of the defendant's same trait; and

(C) in a homicide case, the prosecutor may offer evidence of the alleged victim's trait of peacefulness to rebut evidence that the victim was the first aggressor.

(3) *Exceptions for a Witness.* Evidence of a witness's character may be admitted under Rules 607, 608, and 609.

(b) CRIMES, WRONGS, OR OTHER ACTS.

(1) *Prohibited Uses.* Evidence of a crime, wrong, or other act is not admissible to prove a person's character in order to show that on a particular occasion the person acted in accordance with the character.

(2) *Permitted Uses;* Notice in a Criminal Case. This evidence may be admissible for another purpose, such as proving motive, opportunity, intent, preparation, plan, knowledge, identity, absence of mistake, or lack of accident. On request by a defendant in a criminal case, the prosecutor must:

(A) provide reasonable notice of the general nature of any such evidence that the prosecutor intends to offer at trial; and

(B) do so before trial—or during trial if the court, for good cause, excuses lack of pretrial notice.

(Pub.L. 93–595, § 1, Jan. 2, 1975, 88 Stat.1932; Mar. 2, 1987, eff. Oct. 1, 1987; Apr. 30, 1991, eff. Dec. 1, 1991; Apr. 17, 2000, eff. Dec. 1, 2000; Apr. 12, 2006, eff. Dec. 1, 2006; Apr. 26, 2011, eff. Dec. 1, 2011.)

Rule 405
METHODS OF PROVING CHARACTER

(a) BY REPUTATION OR OPINION. When evidence of a person's character or character trait is admissible, it may be proved by testimony about the person's reputation or by testimony in the form of an opinion. On cross examination of the character witness, the court may allow an inquiry into relevant specific instances of the person's conduct.

(b) BY SPECIFIC INSTANCES OF CONDUCT. When a person's character or character trait is an essential element of a charge, claim, or defense, the character or trait may also be proved by relevant specific instances of the person's conduct.

(Pub.L. 93–595, § 1, Jan. 2, 1975, 88 Stat. 1932; Mar. 2, 1987, eff. Oct. 1, 1987; Apr. 26, 2011, eff. Dec. 1, 2011.)

Rule 406
HABIT; ROUTINE PRACTICE

Evidence of a person's habit or an organization's routine practice may be admitted to prove that on a particular occasion the person or organization acted in accordance with the habit or routine practice. The court may admit this evidence regardless of whether it is corroborated or whether there was an eyewitness.

(Pub.L. 93–595, § 1, Jan. 2, 1975, 88 Stat. 1932; Apr. 26, 2011, eff. Dec. 1, 2011.)

Rule 407
SUBSEQUENT REMEDIAL MEASURES

When measures are taken that would have made an earlier injury or harm less likely to occur, evidence of the subsequent measures is not admissible to prove:

- negligence;

- culpable conduct;

- a defect in a product or its design; or

- a need for a warning or instruction.

But the court may admit this evidence for another purpose, such as impeachment or—if disputed—proving ownership, control, or the feasibility of precautionary measures.

(Pub.L. 93–595, § 1, Jan. 2, 1975, 88 Stat. 1932; Apr. 11, 1997, eff. Dec. 1, 1997; Apr. 26, 2011, eff. Dec. 1, 2011.)

Rule 408
COMPROMISE OFFERS AND NEGOTIATIONS

(a) PROHIBITED USES. Evidence of the following is not admissible—on behalf of any party—either to prove or disprove the validity or amount of a disputed claim or to impeach by a prior inconsistent statement or a contradiction:

(1) furnishing, promising, or offering—or accepting, promising to accept, or offering to accept—a valuable consideration in compromising or attempting to compromise the claim; and

(2) conduct or a statement made during compromise negotiations about the claim—except when offered in a criminal case and when the negotiations related to a claim by a public office in the exercise of its regulatory, investigative, or enforcement authority.

(b) EXCEPTIONS. The court may admit this evidence for another purpose, such as proving a witness's bias or prejudice, negating a contention of undue delay, or proving an effort to obstruct a criminal investigation or prosecution.

(Pub.L. 93–595, § 1, Jan. 2, 1975, 88 Stat. 1933; Apr. 12, 2006, eff. Dec. 1, 2006; Apr. 26, 2011, eff. Dec. 1, 2011.)

Rule 409
OFFERS TO PAY MEDICAL AND SIMILAR EXPENSES

Evidence of furnishing, promising to pay, or offering to pay medical, hospital, or similar expenses resulting from an injury is not admissible to prove liability for the injury.

(Pub.L. 93–595, § 1, Jan. 2, 1975, 88 Stat.1933; Apr. 26, 2011, eff. Dec. 1, 2011.)

Rule 410
PLEAS, PLEA DISCUSSIONS, AND RELATED STATEMENTS

(a) PROHIBITED USES. In a civil or criminal case, evidence of the following is not admissible against the defendant who made the plea or participated in the plea discussions:

(1) a guilty plea that was later withdrawn;

(2) a nolo contendere plea;

(3) a statement made during a proceeding on either of those pleas under Federal Rule of Criminal Procedure 11 or a comparable state procedure; or

(4) a statement made during plea discussions with an attorney for the prosecuting authority if the discussions did not result in a guilty plea or they resulted in a later withdrawn guilty plea.

(b) EXCEPTIONS. The court may admit a statement described in Rule 410(a)(3) or (4):

(1) in any proceeding in which another statement made during the same plea or plea discussions has been introduced, if in fairness the statements ought to be considered together; or

(2) in a criminal proceeding for perjury or false statement, if the defendant made the statement under oath, on the record, and with counsel present.

(Pub.L. 93–595, § 1, Jan. 2, 1975, 88 Stat. 1933; Pub.L. 94–149, § 1(9), Dec. 12, 1975, 89 Stat. 805; Apr. 30, 1979, eff. Dec. 1, 1980; Apr. 26, 2011, eff. Dec. 1, 2011.)

Rule 411
LIABILITY INSURANCE

Evidence that a person was or was not insured against liability is not admissible to prove whether the person acted negligently or otherwise wrongfully. But the court may admit this evidence for another purpose, such as proving a witness's bias or prejudice or proving agency, ownership, or control.

(Pub.L. 93–595, § 1, Jan. 2, 1975, 88 Stat.1933; Mar. 2, 1987, eff. Oct. 1, 1987; Apr. 26, 2011, eff. Dec. 1, 2011.)

Rule 412
SEX–OFFENSE CASES: THE VICTIM'S SEXUAL
BEHAVIOR OR PREDISPOSITION

(a) PROHIBITED USES. The following evidence is not admissible in a civil or criminal proceeding involving alleged sexual misconduct:

(1) evidence offered to prove that a victim engaged in other sexual behavior; or

(2) evidence offered to prove a victim's sexual predisposition.

(b) EXCEPTIONS.

(1) *Criminal Cases*. The court may admit the following evidence in a criminal case:

(A) evidence of specific instances of a victim's sexual behavior, if offered to prove that someone other than the defendant was the source of semen, injury, or other physical evidence;

(B) evidence of specific instances of a victim's sexual behavior with respect to the person accused of the sexual misconduct, if offered by the defendant to prove consent or if offered by the prosecutor; and

(C) evidence whose exclusion would violate the defendant's constitutional rights.

(2) *Civil Cases.* In a civil case, the court may admit evidence offered to prove a victim's sexual behavior or sexual predisposition if its probative value substantially outweighs the danger of harm to any victim and of unfair prejudice to any party. The court may admit evidence of a victim's reputation only if the victim has placed it in controversy.

(c) PROCEDURE TO DETERMINE ADMISSIBILITY.

(1) *Motion.* If a party intends to offer evidence under Rule 412(b), the party must:

(A) file a motion that specifically describes the evidence and states the purpose for which it is to be offered;

(B) do so at least 14 days before trial unless the court, for good cause, sets a different time;

(C) serve the motion on all parties; and

(D) notify the victim or, when appropriate, the victim's guardian or representative.

(2) *Hearing.* Before admitting evidence under this rule, the court must conduct an in camera hearing and give the victim and parties a right to attend and be heard. Unless the court orders otherwise, the motion, related materials, and the record of the hearing must be and remain sealed.

(d) DEFINITION OF "VICTIM." In this rule, "victim" includes an alleged victim.

(Added Pub.L. 95–540, § 2(a), Oct. 28, 1978, 92 Stat. 2046, and amended Pub.L. 100–690, Title VII, § 7046(a), Nov. 18, 1988, 102 Stat. 4400; Apr. 29, 1994, eff. Dec. 1, 1994; Pub.L. 103–322, Title IV, § 40141(b), Sept. 13, 1994, 108 Stat. 1919; Apr. 26, 2011, eff. Dec. 1, 2011.)

Rule 413
SIMILAR CRIMES IN SEXUAL–ASSAULT CASES

(a) PERMITTED USES. In a criminal case in which a defendant is accused of a sexual assault, the court may admit evidence that the defendant committed any other sexual assault. The evidence may be considered on any matter to which it is relevant.

(b) DISCLOSURE TO THE DEFENDANT. If the prosecutor intends to offer this evidence, the prosecutor must disclose it to the defendant, including witnesses' statements or a summary of the expected testimony. The prosecutor must do so at least 15 days before trial or at a later time that the court allows for good cause.

(c) EFFECT ON OTHER RULES. This rule does not limit the admission or consideration of evidence under any other rule.

(d) DEFINITION OF "SEXUAL ASSAULT." In this rule and Rule 415, "sexual assault" means a crime under federal law or under state law (as "state" is defined in 18 U.S.C. § 513) involving:

(1) any conduct prohibited by 18 U.S.C. chapter 109A;

(2) contact, without consent, between any part of the defendant's body—or an object—and another person's genitals or anus;

(3) contact, without consent, between the defendant's genitals or anus and any part of another person's body;

(4) deriving sexual pleasure or gratification from inflicting death, bodily injury, or physical pain on another person; or

(5) an attempt or conspiracy to engage in conduct described in subparagraphs (1)–(4).

(Added Pub.L. 103–322, Title XXXII, § 320935(a), Sept. 13, 1994, 108 Stat. 2136; Apr. 26, 2011, eff. Dec. 1, 2011.)

Rule 414
SIMILAR CRIMES IN CHILD–MOLESTATION CASES

(a) PERMITTED USES. In a criminal case in which a defendant is accused of child molestation, the court may admit evidence that the defendant committed any other child molestation. The evidence may be considered on any matter to which it is relevant.

(b) DISCLOSURE TO THE DEFENDANT. If the prosecutor intends to offer this evidence, the prosecutor must disclose it to the defendant, including witnesses' statements or a summary of the expected testimony. The prosecutor must do so at least 15 days before trial or at a later time that the court allows for good cause.

(c) EFFECT ON OTHER RULES. This rule does not limit the admission or consideration of evidence under any other rule.

(d) DEFINITION OF "CHILD" AND "CHILD MOLESTATION." In this rule and Rule 415:

(1) "child" means a person below the age of 14; and

(2) "child molestation" means a crime under federal law or under state law (as "state" is defined in 18 U.S.C. § 513) involving:

> (A) any conduct prohibited by 18 U.S.C. chapter 109A and committed with a child;

> (B) any conduct prohibited by 18 U.S.C. chapter 110;

> (C) contact between any part of the defendant's body—or an object—and a child's genitals or anus;

> (D) contact between the defendant's genitals or anus and any part of a child's body;

> (E) deriving sexual pleasure or gratification from inflicting death, bodily injury, or physical pain on a child; or

> (F) an attempt or conspiracy to engage in conduct described in subparagraphs (A)–(E).

(Added Pub.L. 103–322, Title XXXII, § 320935(a), Sept. 13, 1994, 108 Stat. 2135; Apr. 26, 2011, eff. Dec. 1, 2011.)

Rule 415
SIMILAR ACTS IN CIVIL CASES INVOLVING SEXUAL ASSAULT OR CHILD MOLESTATION

(a) PERMITTED USES. In a civil case involving a claim for relief based on a party's alleged sexual assault or child molestation, the court may admit evidence that the party committed any other sexual assault or child molestation. The evidence may be considered as provided in Rules 413 and 414.

(b) DISCLOSURE TO THE OPPONENT. If a party intends to offer this evidence, the party must disclose it to the party against whom it will be offered, including witnesses' statements or a summary of the expected testimony. The party must do so at least 15 days before trial or at a later time that the court allows for good cause.

(c) EFFECT ON OTHER RULES. This rule does not limit the admission or consideration of evidence under any other rule.

(Added Pub.L. 103–322, Title XXXII, § 320935(a), Sept. 13, 1994, 108 Stat. 2137; Apr. 26, 2011, eff. Dec. 1, 2011.)

ARTICLE V. PRIVILEGES

Rule 501
PRIVILEGE IN GENERAL

The common law—as interpreted by United States courts in the light of reason and experience—governs a claim of privilege unless any of the following provides otherwise:

- the United States Constitution;

- a federal statute; or

- rules prescribed by the Supreme Court.

But in a civil case, state law governs privilege regarding a claim or defense for which state law supplies the rule of decision.

(Pub.L. 93–595, § 1, Jan. 2, 1975, 88 Stat. 1933; Apr. 26, 2011, eff. Dec. 1, 2011.)

Rule 502
ATTORNEY–CLIENT PRIVILEGE AND WORK PRODUCT; LIMITATIONS ON WAIVER

The following provisions apply, in the circumstances set out, to disclosure of a communication or information covered by the attorney client privilege or work product protection.

(a) DISCLOSURE MADE IN A FEDERAL PROCEEDING OR TO A FEDERAL OFFICE OR AGENCY; SCOPE OF A WAIVER. When the disclosure is made in a federal proceeding or to a federal office or agency and waives the attorney client privilege or work product protection, the waiver extends to an undisclosed communication or information in a federal or state proceeding only if:

(1) the waiver is intentional;

(2) the disclosed and undisclosed communications or information concern the same subject matter; and

(3) they ought in fairness to be considered together.

(b) INADVERTENT DISCLOSURE. When made in a federal proceeding or to a federal office or agency, the disclosure does not operate as a waiver in a federal or state proceeding if:

(1) the disclosure is inadvertent;

(2) the holder of the privilege or protection took reasonable steps to prevent disclosure; and

(3) the holder promptly took reasonable steps to rectify the error, including (if applicable) following Federal Rule of Civil Procedure 26(b)(5)(B).

(c) DISCLOSURE MADE IN A STATE PROCEEDING. When the disclosure is made in a state proceeding and is not the subject of a state court order concerning waiver, the disclosure does not operate as a waiver in a federal proceeding if the disclosure:

(1) would not be a waiver under this rule if it had been made in a federal proceeding; or

(2) is not a waiver under the law of the state where the disclosure occurred.

(d) CONTROLLING EFFECT OF A COURT ORDER. A federal court may order that the privilege or protection is not waived by disclosure connected with the litigation pending before the court—in which event the disclosure is also not a waiver in any other federal or state proceeding.

(e) CONTROLLING EFFECT OF A PARTY AGREEMENT. An agreement on the effect of disclosure in a federal proceeding is binding only on the parties to the agreement, unless it is incorporated into a court order.

(f) CONTROLLING EFFECT OF THIS RULE. Notwithstanding Rules 101 and 1101, this rule applies to state proceedings and to federal court annexed and federal court mandated arbitration proceedings, in the circumstances set out in the rule. And notwithstanding Rule 501, this rule applies even if state law provides the rule of decision.

(g) DEFINITIONS. In this rule:

(1) "attorney client privilege" means the protection that applicable law provides for confidential attorney client communications; and

(2) "work product protection" means the protection that applicable law provides for tangible material (or its intangible equivalent) prepared in anticipation of litigation or for trial.

(Pub.L. 110–322, § 1(a), Sept. 19, 2008, 122 Stat. 3537; Apr. 26, 2011, eff. Dec. 1, 2011.)

ARTICLE VI. WITNESSES

Rule 601
COMPETENCY TO TESTIFY IN GENERAL

Every person is competent to be a witness unless these rules provide otherwise. But in a civil case, state law governs the witness's competency regarding a claim or defense for which state law supplies the rule of decision.

(Pub.L. 93–595, § 1, Jan. 2, 1975, 88 Stat.1934; Apr. 26, 2011, eff. Dec. 1, 2011.)

Rule 602
NEED FOR PERSONAL KNOWLEDGE

A witness may testify to a matter only if evidence is introduced sufficient to support a finding that the witness has personal knowledge of the matter. Evidence to prove personal knowledge may consist of the witness's own testimony. This rule does not apply to a witness's expert testimony under Rule 703.

(Pub.L. 93–595, § 1, Jan. 2, 1975, 88 Stat. 1934; Mar. 2, 1987, eff. Oct. 1, 1987; Apr. 25, 1988, eff. Nov. 1, 1988; Apr. 26, 2011, eff. Dec. 1, 2011.)

Rule 603
OATH OR AFFIRMATION TO TESTIFY TRUTHFULLY

Before testifying, a witness must give an oath or affirmation to testify truthfully. It must be in a form designed to impress that duty on the witness's conscience.

(Pub.L. 93–595, § 1, Jan. 2, 1975, 88 Stat. 1934; Mar. 2, 1987, eff. Oct. 1, 1987; Apr. 26, 2011, eff. Dec. 1, 2011.)

Rule 604
INTERPRETER

An interpreter must be qualified and must give an oath or affirmation to make a true translation.

(Pub.L. 93–595, § 1, Jan. 2, 1975, 88 Stat. 1934; Mar. 2, 1987, eff. Oct. 1, 1987; Apr. 26, 2011, eff. Dec. 1, 2011.)

Rule 605
JUDGE'S COMPETENCY AS A WITNESS

The presiding judge may not testify as a witness at the trial. A party need not object to preserve the issue.

(Pub.L. 93–595, § 1, Jan. 2, 1975, 88 Stat. 1934; Apr. 26, 2011, eff. Dec. 1, 2011.)

Rule 606
JUROR'S COMPETENCY AS A WITNESS

(a) AT THE TRIAL. A juror may not testify as a witness before the other jurors at the trial. If a juror is called to testify, the court must give a party an opportunity to object outside the jury's presence.

(b) DURING AN INQUIRY INTO THE VALIDITY OF A VERDICT OR INDICTMENT.

(1) *Prohibited Testimony or Other Evidence.* During an inquiry into the validity of a verdict or indictment, a juror may not testify

about any statement made or incident that occurred during the jury's deliberations; the effect of anything on that juror's or another juror's vote; or any juror's mental processes concerning the verdict or indictment. The court may not receive a juror's affidavit or evidence of a juror's statement on these matters.

(2) *Exceptions.* A juror may testify about whether:

(A) extraneous prejudicial information was improperly brought to the jury's attention;

(B) an outside influence was improperly brought to bear on any juror; or

(C) a mistake was made in entering the verdict on the verdict form.

(Pub.L. 93–595, § 1, Jan. 2, 1975, 88 Stat. 1934; Pub.L. 94–149, § 1(10), Dec. 12, 1975, 89 Stat. 805; Mar. 2, 1987, eff. Oct. 1, 1987; Apr. 12, 2006, eff. Dec. 1, 2006; Apr. 26, 2011, eff. Dec. 1, 2011.)

Rule 607
WHO MAY IMPEACH A WITNESS

Any party, including the party that called the witness, may attack the witness's credibility.

(Pub.L. 93–595, § 1, Jan. 2, 1975, 88 Stat.1934; Mar. 2, 1987, eff. Oct. 1, 1987; Apr. 26, 2011, eff. Dec. 1, 2011.)

Rule 608
A WITNESS'S CHARACTER FOR TRUTHFULNESS OR UNTRUTHFULNESS

(a) REPUTATION OR OPINION EVIDENCE. A witness's credibility may be attacked or supported by testimony about the witness's reputation for having a character for truthfulness or untruthfulness, or by testimony in the form of an opinion about that character. But evidence of truthful character is admissible only after the witness's character for truthfulness has been attacked.

(b) SPECIFIC INSTANCES OF CONDUCT. Except for a criminal conviction under Rule 609, extrinsic evidence is not admissible to prove specific instances of a witness's conduct in order to attack or support the witness's character for truthfulness. But the court may, on cross examination, allow them to be inquired into if they are probative of the character for truthfulness or untruthfulness of:

(1) the witness; or

(2) another witness whose character the witness being cross examined has testified about.

By testifying on another matter, a witness does not waive any privilege against self incrimination for testimony that relates only to the witness's character for truthfulness.

(Pub.L. 93–595, § 1, Jan. 2, 1975, 88 Stat.1935; Mar. 2, 1987, eff. Oct. 1, 1987; Apr. 25, 1988, eff. Nov. 1, 1988; Mar. 27, 2003, eff. Dec. 1, 2003; Apr. 26, 2011, eff. Dec. 1, 2011.)

Rule 609
IMPEACHMENT BY EVIDENCE OF A CRIMINAL CONVICTION

(a) IN GENERAL. The following rules apply to attacking a witness's character for truthfulness by evidence of a criminal conviction:

(1) for a crime that, in the convicting jurisdiction, was punishable by death or by imprisonment for more than one year, the evidence: (felony)

(A) must be admitted, subject to Rule 403, in a civil case or in a criminal case in which the witness is not a defendant; and

(B) must be admitted in a criminal case in which the witness is a defendant, if the probative value of the evidence outweighs its prejudicial effect to that defendant; and

(2) for any crime regardless of the punishment, the evidence must be admitted if the court can readily determine that establishing the elements of the crime required proving—or the witness's admitting—a dishonest act or false statement.

(b) LIMIT ON USING THE EVIDENCE AFTER 10 YEARS. This subdivision (b) applies if more than 10 years have passed since the witness's conviction or release from confinement for it, whichever is later. Evidence of the conviction is admissible only if:

(1) its probative value, supported by specific facts and circumstances, substantially outweighs its prejudicial effect; and

(2) the proponent gives an adverse party reasonable written notice of the intent to use it so that the party has a fair opportunity to contest its use.

(c) EFFECT OF A PARDON, ANNULMENT, OR CERTIFICATE OF REHABILITATION. Evidence of a conviction is not admissible if:

(1) the conviction has been the subject of a pardon, annulment, certificate of rehabilitation, or other equivalent procedure based on a finding that the person has been rehabilitated, and the person has not been convicted of a later crime punishable by death or by imprisonment for more than one year; or

(2) the conviction has been the subject of a pardon, annulment, or other equivalent procedure based on a finding of innocence.

(d) JUVENILE ADJUDICATIONS. Evidence of a juvenile adjudication is admissible under this rule only if:

(1) it is offered in a criminal case;

(2) the adjudication was of a witness other than the defendant;

(3) an adult's conviction for that offense would be admissible to attack the adult's credibility; and

(4) admitting the evidence is necessary to fairly determine guilt or innocence.

(e) PENDENCY OF AN APPEAL. A conviction that satisfies this rule is admissible even if an appeal is pending. Evidence of the pendency is also admissible.

(Pub.L. 93–595, § 1, Jan. 2, 1975, 88 Stat.1935; Mar. 2, 1987, eff. Oct. 1, 1987; Jan. 26, 1990, eff. Dec. 1, 1990; Apr. 12, 2006, eff. Dec. 1, 2006; Apr. 26, 2011, eff. Dec. 1, 2011.)

Rule 610
RELIGIOUS BELIEFS OR OPINIONS

Evidence of a witness's religious beliefs or opinions is not admissible to attack or support the witness's credibility.

(Pub.L. 93–595, § 1, Jan. 2, 1975, 88 Stat.1936; Mar. 2, 1987, eff. Oct. 1, 1987; Apr. 26, 2011, eff. Dec. 1, 2011.)

Rule 611
MODE AND ORDER OF EXAMINING WITNESSES AND PRESENTING EVIDENCE

(a) CONTROL BY THE COURT; PURPOSES. The court should exercise reasonable control over the mode and order of examining witnesses and presenting evidence so as to:

(1) make those procedures effective for determining the truth;

(2) avoid wasting time; and

(3) protect witnesses from harassment or undue embarrassment.

(b) SCOPE OF CROSS–EXAMINATION. Cross examination should not go beyond the subject matter of the direct examination and matters affecting the witness's credibility. The court may allow inquiry into additional matters as if on direct examination.

(c) LEADING QUESTIONS. Leading questions should not be used on direct examination except as necessary to develop the witness's testimony. Ordinarily, the court should allow leading questions:

(1) on cross examination; and

(2) when a party calls a hostile witness, an adverse party, or a witness identified with an adverse party.

(Pub.L. 93–595, § 1, Jan. 2, 1975, 88 Stat. 1936; Mar. 2, 1987, eff. Oct. 1, 1987; Apr. 26, 2011, eff. Dec. 1, 2011.)

Rule 612
WRITING USED TO REFRESH A WITNESS'S MEMORY

(a) SCOPE. This rule gives an adverse party certain options when a witness uses a writing to refresh memory:

(1) while testifying; or

(2) before testifying, if the court decides that justice requires the party to have those options.

(b) ADVERSE PARTY'S OPTIONS; DELETING UNRELATED MATTER. Unless 18 U.S.C. § 3500 provides otherwise in a criminal case, an adverse party is entitled to have the writing produced at the hearing, to inspect it, to cross examine the witness about it, and to introduce in evidence any portion that relates to the witness's testimony. If the producing party claims that the writing includes unrelated matter, the court must examine the writing in camera, delete any unrelated portion, and order that the rest be delivered to the adverse party. Any portion deleted over objection must be preserved for the record.

(c) FAILURE TO PRODUCE OR DELIVER THE WRITING. If a writing is not produced or is not delivered as ordered, the court may issue any appropriate order. But if the prosecution does not comply in a criminal case, the court must strike the witness's testimony or—if justice so requires—declare a mistrial.

(Pub.L. 93–595, § 1, Jan. 2, 1975, 88 Stat. 1936; Mar. 2, 1987, eff. Oct. 1, 1987; Apr. 26, 2011, eff. Dec. 1, 2011.)

Rule 613
WITNESS'S PRIOR STATEMENT

(a) SHOWING OR DISCLOSING THE STATEMENT DURING EXAMINATION. When examining a witness about the witness's prior statement, a party need not show it or disclose its contents to the witness. But the party must, on request, show it or disclose its contents to an adverse party's attorney.

(b) EXTRINSIC EVIDENCE OF A PRIOR INCONSISTENT STATEMENT. Extrinsic evidence of a witness's prior inconsistent statement is admissible only if the witness is given an opportunity to explain or deny the statement and an adverse party is given an opportunity to examine the witness about it, or if justice so requires. This subdivision (b) does not apply to an opposing party's statement under Rule 801(d)(2).

(Pub.L. 93–595, § 1, Jan. 2, 1975, 88 Stat.1936; Mar. 2, 1987, eff. Oct. 1, 1987; Apr. 25, 1988, eff. Nov. 1, 1988; Apr. 26, 2011, eff. Dec. 1, 2011.)

Rule 614
COURT'S CALLING OR EXAMINING A WITNESS

(a) CALLING. The court may call a witness on its own or at a party's request. Each party is entitled to cross examine the witness.

(b) EXAMINING. The court may examine a witness regardless of who calls the witness.

(c) OBJECTIONS. A party may object to the court's calling or examining a witness either at that time or at the next opportunity when the jury is not present.

(Pub.L. 93–595, § 1, Jan. 2, 1975, 88 Stat.1937; Apr. 26, 2011, eff. Dec. 1, 2011.)

Rule 615
EXCLUDING WITNESSES

At a party's request, the court must order witnesses excluded so that they cannot hear other witnesses' testimony. Or the court may do so on its own. But this rule does not authorize excluding:

(a) a party who is a natural person;

(b) an officer or employee of a party that is not a natural person, after being designated as the party's representative by its attorney;

(c) a person whose presence a party shows to be essential to presenting the party's claim or defense; or

(d) a person authorized by statute to be present.

(Pub.L. 93–595, § 1, Jan. 2, 1975, 88 Stat.1937; Mar. 2, 1987, eff. Oct. 1, 1987; Apr. 25, 1988, eff. Nov. 1, 1988; Pub.L. 100–690, Nov. 18, 1988, Title VII, § 7075(a), 102 Stat. 4405; Apr. 24, 1998, eff. Dec. 1, 1998; Apr. 26, 2011, eff. Dec. 1, 2011.)

ARTICLE VII. OPINIONS AND EXPERT TESTIMONY

Rule 701
OPINION TESTIMONY BY LAY WITNESSES

If a witness is not testifying as an expert, testimony in the form of an opinion is limited to one that is:

(a) rationally based on the witness's perception;

(b) helpful to clearly understanding the witness's testimony or to determining a fact in issue; and

(c) not based on scientific, technical, or other specialized knowledge within the scope of Rule 702.

(Pub.L. 93–595, § 1, Jan. 2, 1975, 88 Stat.1937; Mar. 2, 1987, eff. Oct. 1, 1987; Apr. 17, 2000, eff. Dec. 1, 2000; Apr. 26, 2011, eff. Dec. 1, 2011.)

Rule 702
TESTIMONY BY EXPERT WITNESSES

A witness who is qualified as an expert by knowledge, skill, experience, training, or education may testify in the form of an opinion or otherwise if:

(a) the expert's scientific, technical, or other specialized knowledge will help the trier of fact to understand the evidence or to determine a fact in issue;

(b) the testimony is based on sufficient facts or data;

(c) the testimony is the product of reliable principles and methods; and

(d) the expert has reliably applied the principles and methods to the facts of the case.

(Pub.L. 93–595, § 1, Jan. 2, 1975, 88 Stat. 1937; Apr. 17, 2000, eff. Dec. 1, 2000; Apr. 26, 2011, eff. Dec. 1, 2011.)

Rule 703
BASES OF AN EXPERT'S OPINION TESTIMONY

An expert may base an opinion on facts or data in the case that the expert has been made aware of or personally observed. If experts in the particular field would reasonably rely on those kinds of facts or data in forming an opinion on the subject, they need not be admissible for the opinion to be admitted. But if the facts or data would otherwise be inadmissible, the proponent of the opinion may disclose them to the jury only if their probative value in helping the jury evaluate the opinion substantially outweighs their prejudicial effect.

(Pub.L. 93–595, § 1, Jan. 2, 1975, 88 Stat.1937; Mar. 2, 1987, eff. Oct. 1, 1987; Apr. 17, 2000, eff. Dec. 1, 2000; Apr. 26, 2011, eff. Dec. 1, 2011.)

Rule 704
OPINION ON AN ULTIMATE ISSUE

(a) IN GENERAL—NOT AUTOMATICALLY OBJECTIONABLE. An opinion is not objectionable just because it embraces an ultimate issue.

(b) Exception. In a criminal case, an expert witness must not state an opinion about whether the defendant did or did not have a mental state or condition that constitutes an element of the crime charged or of a defense. Those matters are for the trier of fact alone.

(Pub.L. 93–595, § 1, Jan. 2, 1975, 88 Stat. 1937; Pub.L. 98–473, Title IV, § 406, Oct. 12, 1984, 98 Stat. 2067; Apr. 26, 2011, eff. Dec. 1, 2011.)

Rule 705
DISCLOSING THE FACTS OR DATA UNDERLYING AN EXPERT'S OPINION

Unless the court orders otherwise, an expert may state an opinion—and give the reasons for it—without first testifying to the underlying facts or data. But the expert may be required to disclose those facts or data on cross examination.

(Pub.L. 93–595, § 1, Jan. 2, 1975, 88 Stat. 1938; Mar. 2, 1987, eff. Oct. 1, 1987; Apr. 22, 1993, eff. Dec. 1, 1993; Apr. 26, 2011, eff. Dec. 1, 2011.)

Rule 706
COURT–APPOINTED EXPERT WITNESSES

(a) Appointment Process. On a party's motion or on its own, the court may order the parties to show cause why expert witnesses should not be appointed and may ask the parties to submit nominations. The court may appoint any expert that the parties agree on and any of its own choosing. But the court may only appoint someone who consents to act.

(b) Expert's Role. The court must inform the expert of the expert's duties. The court may do so in writing and have a copy filed with the clerk or may do so orally at a conference in which the parties have an opportunity to participate. The expert:

(1) must advise the parties of any findings the expert makes;

(2) may be deposed by any party;

(3) may be called to testify by the court or any party; and

(4) may be cross examined by any party, including the party that called the expert.

(c) Compensation. The expert is entitled to a reasonable compensation, as set by the court. The compensation is payable as follows:

(1) in a criminal case or in a civil case involving just compensation under the Fifth Amendment, from any funds that are provided by law; and

(2) in any other civil case, by the parties in the proportion and at the time that the court directs—and the compensation is then charged like other costs.

(d) DISCLOSING THE APPOINTMENT TO THE JURY. The court may authorize disclosure to the jury that the court appointed the expert.

(e) PARTIES' CHOICE OF THEIR OWN EXPERTS. This rule does not limit a party in calling its own experts.

(Pub.L. 93–595, § 1, Jan. 2, 1975, 88 Stat.1938; Mar. 2, 1987, eff. Oct. 1, 1987; Apr. 26, 2011, eff. Dec. 1, 2011.)

ARTICLE VIII. HEARSAY

Rule 801
DEFINITIONS THAT APPLY TO THIS ARTICLE; EXCLUSIONS FROM HEARSAY

(a) STATEMENT. "Statement" means a person's oral assertion, written assertion, or nonverbal conduct, if the person intended it as an assertion.

(b) DECLARANT. "Declarant" means the person who made the statement.

(c) HEARSAY. "Hearsay" means a statement that:

(1) the declarant does not make while testifying at the current trial or hearing; and

(2) a party offers in evidence to prove the truth of the matter asserted in the statement.

(d) STATEMENTS THAT ARE NOT HEARSAY. A statement that meets the following conditions is not hearsay:

(1) *A Declarant–Witness's Prior Statement.* The declarant testifies and is subject to cross examination about a prior statement, and the statement:

(A) is inconsistent with the declarant's testimony and was given under penalty of perjury at a trial, hearing, or other proceeding or in a deposition;

(B) is consistent with the declarant's testimony and is offered to rebut an express or implied charge that the declarant recently fabricated it or acted from a recent improper influence or motive in so testifying; or

(C) identifies a person as someone the declarant perceived earlier.

995

Not exception (803,804) but rather exclusion to hearsay.

(2) *An Opposing Party's Statement.* The statement is offered against an opposing party and:

(A) was made by the party in an individual or representative capacity;

(B) is one the party manifested that it adopted or believed to be true;

(C) was made by a person whom the party authorized to make a statement on the subject;

(D) was made by the party's agent or employee on a matter within the scope of that relationship and while it existed; or

(E) was made by the party's coconspirator during and in furtherance of the conspiracy.

The statement must be considered but does not by itself establish the declarant's authority under (C); the existence or scope of the relationship under (D); or the existence of the conspiracy or participation in it under (E).

(Pub.L. 93–595, § 1, Jan. 2, 1975, 88 Stat.1938; Pub.L. 94–113, § 1, Oct. 16, 1975, 89 Stat. 576; Mar. 2, 1987, eff. Oct. 1, 1987; Apr. 11, 1997, eff. Dec. 1, 1997; Apr. 26, 2011, eff. Dec. 1, 2011.)

Rule 802
THE RULE AGAINST HEARSAY

Hearsay is not admissible unless any of the following provides otherwise:

- a federal statute;

- these rules; or

- other rules prescribed by the Supreme Court.

(Pub.L. 93–595, § 1, Jan. 2, 1975, 88 Stat. 1939; Apr. 26, 2011, eff. Dec. 1, 2011.)

Rule 803
EXCEPTIONS TO THE RULE AGAINST HEARSAY— REGARDLESS OF WHETHER THE DECLARANT IS AVAILABLE AS A WITNESS

The following are not excluded by the rule against hearsay, regardless of whether the declarant is available as a witness:

(1) *Present Sense Impression.* A statement describing or explaining an event or condition, made while or immediately after the declarant perceived it.

(2) *Excited Utterance.* A statement relating to a startling event or condition, made while the declarant was under the stress of excitement that it caused.

(3) *Then–Existing Mental, Emotional, or Physical Condition.* A statement of the declarant's then existing state of mind (such as motive, intent, or plan) or emotional, sensory, or physical condition (such as mental feeling, pain, or bodily health), but not including a statement of memory or belief to prove the fact remembered or believed unless it relates to the validity or terms of the declarant's will.

(4) *Statement Made for Medical Diagnosis or Treatment.* A statement that:

    (A) is made for—and is reasonably pertinent to—medical diagnosis or treatment; and

    (B) describes medical history; past or present symptoms or sensations; their inception; or their general cause.

(5) *Recorded Recollection.* A record that:

    (A) is on a matter the witness once knew about but now cannot recall well enough to testify fully and accurately;

    (B) was made or adopted by the witness when the matter was fresh in the witness's memory; and

    (C) accurately reflects the witness's knowledge.

    If admitted, the record may be read into evidence but may be received as an exhibit only if offered by an adverse party.

(6) *Records of a Regularly Conducted Activity.* A record of an act, event, condition, opinion, or diagnosis if:

    (A) the record was made at or near the time by—or from information transmitted by—someone with knowledge;

    (B) the record was kept in the course of a regularly conducted activity of a business, organization, occupation, or calling, whether or not for profit;

    (C) making the record was a regular practice of that activity;

    (D) all these conditions are shown by the testimony of the custodian or another qualified witness, or by a certification that complies with Rule 902(11) or (12) or with a statute permitting certification; and

(E) neither the source of information nor the method or circumstances of preparation indicate a lack of trustworthiness.

(7) *Absence of a Record of a Regularly Conducted Activity.* Evidence that a matter is not included in a record described in paragraph (6) if:

(A) the evidence is admitted to prove that the matter did not occur or exist;

(B) a record was regularly kept for a matter of that kind; and

(C) neither the possible source of the information nor other circumstances indicate a lack of trustworthiness.

(8) *Public Records.* A record or statement of a public office if:

(A) it sets out:

(i) the office's activities;

(ii) a matter observed while under a legal duty to report, but not including, in a criminal case, a matter observed by law enforcement personnel; or

not against Δ in criminal case

(iii) in a civil case or against the government in a criminal case, factual findings from a legally authorized investigation; and

(B) neither the source of information nor other circumstances indicate a lack of trustworthiness.

(9) *Public Records of Vital Statistics.* A record of a birth, death, or marriage, if reported to a public office in accordance with a legal duty.

(10) *Absence of a Public Record.* Testimony—or a certification under Rule 902—that a diligent search failed to disclose a public record or statement if the testimony or certification is admitted to prove that:

(A) the record or statement does not exist; or

(B) a matter did not occur or exist, if a public office regularly kept a record or statement for a matter of that kind.

(11) *Records of Religious Organizations Concerning Personal or Family History.*

A statement of birth, legitimacy, ancestry, marriage, divorce, death, relationship by blood or marriage, or similar facts of personal or family history, contained in a regularly kept record of a religious organization.

(12) *Certificates of Marriage, Baptism, and Similar Ceremonies.* A statement of fact contained in a certificate:

(A) made by a person who is authorized by a religious organization or by law to perform the act certified;

(B) attesting that the person performed a marriage or similar ceremony or administered a sacrament; and

(C) purporting to have been issued at the time of the act or within a reasonable time after it.

(13) *Family Records.* A statement of fact about personal or family history contained in a family record, such as a Bible, genealogy, chart, engraving on a ring, inscription on a portrait, or engraving on an urn or burial marker.

(14) *Records of Documents That Affect an Interest in Property.* The record of a document that purports to establish or affect an interest in property if:

(A) the record is admitted to prove the content of the original recorded document, along with its signing and its delivery by each person who purports to have signed it;

(B) the record is kept in a public office; and

(C) a statute authorizes recording documents of that kind in that office.

(15) *Statements in Documents That Affect an Interest in Property.* A statement contained in a document that purports to establish or affect an interest in property if the matter stated was relevant to the document's purpose—unless later dealings with the property are inconsistent with the truth of the statement or the purport of the document.

(16) *Statements in Ancient Documents.* A statement in a document that is at least 20 years old and whose authenticity is established.

(17) *Market Reports and Similar Commercial Publications.* Market quotations, lists, directories, or other compilations that are generally relied on by the public or by persons in particular occupations.

(18) *Statements in Learned Treatises, Periodicals, or Pamphlets.* A statement contained in a treatise, periodical, or pamphlet if:

(A) the statement is called to the attention of an expert witness on cross examination or relied on by the expert on direct examination; and

(B) the publication is established as a reliable authority by the expert's admission or testimony, by another expert's testimony, or by judicial notice.

If admitted, the statement may be read into evidence but not received as an exhibit.

(19) *Reputation Concerning Personal or Family History.* A reputation among a person's family by blood, adoption, or marriage—or among a person's associates or in the community—concerning the person's birth, adoption, legitimacy, ancestry, marriage, divorce, death, relationship by blood, adoption, or marriage, or similar facts of personal or family history.

(20) *Reputation Concerning Boundaries or General History.* A reputation in a community—arising before the controversy—concerning boundaries of land in the community or customs that affect the land, or concerning general historical events important to that community, state, or nation.

(21) *Reputation Concerning Character.* A reputation among a person's associates or in the community concerning the person's character.

(22) *Judgment of a Previous Conviction.* Evidence of a final judgment of conviction if:

    (A) the judgment was entered after a trial or guilty plea, but not a nolo contendere plea;

    (B) the conviction was for a crime punishable by death or by imprisonment for more than a year;

    (C) the evidence is admitted to prove any fact essential to the judgment; and

    (D) when offered by the prosecutor in a criminal case for a purpose other than impeachment, the judgment was against the defendant.

The pendency of an appeal may be shown but does not affect admissibility.

(23) *Judgments Involving Personal, Family, or General History, or a Boundary.* A judgment that is admitted to prove a matter of personal, family, or general history, or boundaries, if the matter:

    (A) was essential to the judgment; and

    (B) could be proved by evidence of reputation.

(24) [*Other Exceptions.*] [Transferred to Rule 807.]

(Pub.L. 93–595, § 1, Jan. 2, 1975, 88 Stat. 1939; Pub.L. 94–149, § 1(11), Dec. 12, 1975, 89 Stat. 805; Mar. 2, 1987, eff. Oct. 1, 1987; Apr. 11, 1997, eff. Dec. 1, 1997; Apr. 17, 2000, eff. Dec. 1, 2000; Apr. 26, 2011, eff. Dec. 1, 2011.)

Rule 804
EXCEPTIONS TO THE RULE AGAINST HEARSAY—WHEN THE DECLARANT IS UNAVAILABLE AS A WITNESS

(a) CRITERIA FOR BEING UNAVAILABLE. A declarant is considered to be unavailable as a witness if the declarant:

(1) is exempted from testifying about the subject matter of the declarant's statement because the court rules that a privilege applies;

(2) refuses to testify about the subject matter despite a court order to do so;

(3) testifies to not remembering the subject matter;

(4) cannot be present or testify at the trial or hearing because of death or a then existing infirmity, physical illness, or mental illness; or

(5) is absent from the trial or hearing and the statement's proponent has not been able, by process or other reasonable means, to procure:

(A) the declarant's attendance, in the case of a hearsay exception under Rule 804(b)(1) or (6); or

(B) the declarant's attendance or testimony, in the case of a hearsay exception under Rule 804(b)(2), (3), or (4).

But this subdivision (a) does not apply if the statement's proponent procured or wrongfully caused the declarant's unavailability as a witness in order to prevent the declarant from attending or testifying.

(b) THE EXCEPTIONS. The following are not excluded by the rule against hearsay if the declarant is unavailable as a witness:

(1) *Former Testimony.* Testimony that:

(A) was given as a witness at a trial, hearing, or lawful deposition, whether given during the current proceeding or a different one; and

(B) is now offered against a party who had—or, in a civil case, whose predecessor in interest had—an opportunity and similar motive to develop it by direct, cross , or redirect examination.

(2) *Statement Under the Belief of Imminent Death.* In a prosecution for homicide or in a civil case, a statement that the declarant, while believing the declarant's death to be imminent, made about its cause or circumstances.

(3) *Statement Against Interest.* A statement that:

(A) a reasonable person in the declarant's position would have made only if the person believed it to be true because, when made, it was so contrary to the declarant's proprietary or pecuniary interest or had so great a tendency to invalidate the declarant's claim against someone else or to expose the declarant to civil or criminal liability; and

(B) is supported by corroborating circumstances that clearly indicate its trustworthiness, if it is offered in a criminal case as one that tends to expose the declarant to criminal liability.

(4) *Statement of Personal or Family History.* A statement about:

(A) the declarant's own birth, adoption, legitimacy, ancestry, marriage, divorce, relationship by blood, adoption, or marriage, or similar facts of personal or family history, even though the declarant had no way of acquiring personal knowledge about that fact; or

(B) another person concerning any of these facts, as well as death, if the declarant was related to the person by blood, adoption, or marriage or was so intimately associated with the person's family that the declarant's information is likely to be accurate.

(5) [*Other Exceptions.*] [Transferred to Rule 807.]

(6) *Statement Offered Against a Party That Wrongfully Caused the Declarant's Unavailability.* A statement offered against a party that wrongfully caused—or acquiesced in wrongfully causing—the declarant's unavailability as a witness, and did so intending that result.

(Pub.L. 93–595, § 1, Jan. 2, 1975, 88 Stat. 1942; Pub.L. 94–149, § 1(12), (13), Dec. 12, 1975, 89 Stat. 806; Mar. 2, 1987, eff. Oct. 1, 1987; Pub.L. 100–690, Title VII, § 7075(b), Nov. 18, 1988, 102 Stat. 4405; Apr. 11, 1997, eff. Dec. 1, 1997; Apr. 28, 2010, eff. Dec. 1, 2010; Apr. 26, 2011, eff. Dec. 1, 2011.)

Rule 805
HEARSAY WITHIN HEARSAY

Hearsay within hearsay is not excluded by the rule against hearsay if each part of the combined statements conforms with an exception to the rule.

(Pub.L. 93–595, § 1, Jan. 2, 1975, 88 Stat. 1943; Apr. 26, 2011, eff. Dec. 1, 2011.)

Rule 806
ATTACKING AND SUPPORTING THE DECLARANT'S CREDIBILITY

When a hearsay statement—or a statement described in Rule 801(d)(2)(C), (D), or (E)—has been admitted in evidence, the declarant's credibility may be attacked, and then supported, by any evidence that would be admissible for those purposes if the declarant had testified as a witness. The court may admit evidence of the declarant's inconsistent statement or conduct, regardless of when it occurred or whether the declarant had an opportunity to explain or deny it. If the party against whom the statement was admitted calls the declarant as a witness, the party may examine the declarant on the statement as if on cross examination.

(Pub.L. 93–595, § 1, Jan. 2, 1975, 88 Stat. 1943; Mar. 2, 1987, eff. Oct. 1, 1987; Apr. 11, 1997, eff. Dec. 1, 1997; Apr. 26, 2011, eff. Dec. 1, 2011.)

Rule 807
RESIDUAL EXCEPTION

(a) IN GENERAL. Under the following circumstances, a hearsay statement is not excluded by the rule against hearsay even if the statement is not specifically covered by a hearsay exception in Rule 803 or 804:

(1) the statement has equivalent circumstantial guarantees of trustworthiness;

(2) it is offered as evidence of a material fact;

(3) it is more probative on the point for which it is offered than any other evidence that the proponent can obtain through reasonable efforts; and

(4) admitting it will best serve the purposes of these rules and the interests of justice.

(b) NOTICE. The statement is admissible only if, before the trial or hearing, the proponent gives an adverse party reasonable notice of the intent to offer the statement and its particulars, including the declarant's name and address, so that the party has a fair opportunity to meet it. (Added Apr. 11, 1997, eff. Dec. 1, 1997; Apr. 26, 2011, eff. Dec. 1, 2011.)

ARTICLE IX. AUTHENTICATION AND IDENTIFICATION

Rule 901
AUTHENTICATING OR IDENTIFYING EVIDENCE

(a) IN GENERAL. To satisfy the requirement of authenticating or identifying an item of evidence, the proponent must produce evidence sufficient to support a finding that the item is what the proponent claims it is.

(b) EXAMPLES. The following are examples only—not a complete list—of evidence that satisfies the requirement:

(1) *Testimony of a Witness with Knowledge.* Testimony that an item is what it is claimed to be.

(2) *Nonexpert Opinion About Handwriting.* A nonexpert's opinion that handwriting is genuine, based on a familiarity with it that was not acquired for the current litigation.

(3) *Comparison by an Expert Witness or the Trier of Fact.* A comparison with an authenticated specimen by an expert witness or the trier of fact.

(4) *Distinctive Characteristics and the Like.* The appearance, contents, substance, internal patterns, or other distinctive characteristics of the item, taken together with all the circumstances.

(5) *Opinion About a Voice.* An opinion identifying a person's voice—whether heard firsthand or through mechanical or electronic transmission or recording—based on hearing the voice at any time under circumstances that connect it with the alleged speaker.

(6) *Evidence About a Telephone Conversation.* For a telephone conversation, evidence that a call was made to the number assigned at the time to:

    (A) a particular person, if circumstances, including self identification, show that the person answering was the one called; or

    (B) a particular business, if the call was made to a business and the call related to business reasonably transacted over the telephone.

(7) *Evidence About Public Records.* Evidence that:

    (A) a document was recorded or filed in a public office as authorized by law; or

    (B) a purported public record or statement is from the office where items of this kind are kept.

(8) *Evidence About Ancient Documents or Data Compilations.* For a document or data compilation, evidence that it:

    (A) is in a condition that creates no suspicion about its authenticity;

    (B) was in a place where, if authentic, it would likely be; and

    (C) is at least 20 years old when offered.

(9) *Evidence About a Process or System.* Evidence describing a process or system and showing that it produces an accurate result.

(10) *Methods Provided by a Statute or Rule.* Any method of authentication or identification allowed by a federal statute or a rule prescribed by the Supreme Court.

(Pub.L. 93–595, § 1, Jan. 2, 1975, 88 Stat.1943; Apr. 26, 2011, eff. Dec. 1, 2011.)

Rule 902
EVIDENCE THAT IS SELF–AUTHENTICATING

The following items of evidence are self authenticating; they require no extrinsic evidence of authenticity in order to be admitted:

(1) *Domestic Public Documents That Are Sealed and Signed.* A document that bears:

(A) a seal purporting to be that of the United States; any state, district, commonwealth, territory, or insular possession of the United States; the former Panama Canal Zone; the Trust Territory of the Pacific Islands; a political subdivision of any of these entities; or a department, agency, or officer of any entity named above; and

(B) a signature purporting to be an execution or attestation.

(2) *Domestic Public Documents That Are Not Sealed but Are Signed and Certified.* A document that bears no seal if:

(A) it bears the signature of an officer or employee of an entity named in Rule 902(1)(A); and

(B) another public officer who has a seal and official duties within that same entity certifies under seal—or its equivalent—that the signer has the official capacity and that the signature is genuine.

(3) *Foreign Public Documents.* A document that purports to be signed or attested by a person who is authorized by a foreign country's law to do so. The document must be accompanied by a final certification that certifies the genuineness of the signature and official position of the signer or attester—or of any foreign official whose certificate of genuineness relates to the signature or attestation or is in a chain of certificates of genuineness relating to the signature or attestation. The certification may be made by a secretary of a United States embassy or legation; by a consul general, vice consul, or consular agent of the United States; or by a diplomatic or consular official of the foreign country assigned or accredited to the United States. If all parties have been given a reasonable opportunity to investigate the document's authenticity and accuracy, the court may, for good cause, either:

(A) order that it be treated as presumptively authentic without final certification; or

(B) allow it to be evidenced by an attested summary with or without final certification.

(4) *Certified Copies of Public Records.* A copy of an official record—or a copy of a document that was recorded or filed in a public office as authorized by law—if the copy is certified as correct by:

(A) the custodian or another person authorized to make the certification; or

(B) a certificate that complies with Rule 902(1), (2), or (3), a federal statute, or a rule prescribed by the Supreme Court.

(5) *Official Publications.* A book, pamphlet, or other publication purporting to be issued by a public authority.

(6) *Newspapers and Periodicals.* Printed material purporting to be a newspaper or periodical.

(7) *Trade Inscriptions and the Like.* An inscription, sign, tag, or label purporting to have been affixed in the course of business and indicating origin, ownership, or control.

(8) *Acknowledged Documents.* A document accompanied by a certificate of acknowledgment that is lawfully executed by a notary public or another officer who is authorized to take acknowledgments.

(9) *Commercial Paper and Related Documents.* Commercial paper, a signature on it, and related documents, to the extent allowed by general commercial law.

(10) *Presumptions Under a Federal Statute.* A signature, document, or anything else that a federal statute declares to be presumptively or prima facie genuine or authentic.

(11) *Certified Domestic Records of a Regularly Conducted Activity.* The original or a copy of a domestic record that meets the requirements of Rule 803(6)(A)–(C), as shown by a certification of the custodian or another qualified person that complies with a federal statute or a rule prescribed by the Supreme Court. Before the trial or hearing, the proponent must give an adverse party reasonable written notice of the intent to offer the record—and must make the record and certification available for inspection—so that the party has a fair opportunity to challenge them.

(12) *Certified Foreign Records of a Regularly Conducted Activity.* In a civil case, the original or a copy of a foreign record that meets the requirements of Rule 902(11), modified as follows: the certification, rather than complying with a federal statute or Supreme Court rule, must be signed in a manner that, if falsely made, would subject the maker to a criminal penalty in the country where the certification is

signed. The proponent must also meet the notice requirements of Rule 902(11).

(Pub.L. 93–595, § 1, Jan. 2, 1975, 88 Stat. 1944; Mar. 2, 1987, eff. Oct. 1, 1987; Apr. 25, 1988, eff. Nov. 1, 1988; Apr. 17, 2000, eff. Dec. 1, 2000; Apr. 26, 2011, eff. Dec. 1, 2011.)

Rule 903
SUBSCRIBING WITNESS'S TESTIMONY

A subscribing witness's testimony is necessary to authenticate a writing only if required by the law of the jurisdiction that governs its validity.

(Pub.L. 93–595, § 1, Jan. 2, 1975, 88 Stat.1945; Apr. 26, 2011, eff. Dec. 1, 2011.)

ARTICLE X. CONTENTS OF WRITINGS, RECORDINGS AND PHOTOGRAPHS

Rule 1001
DEFINITIONS THAT APPLY TO THIS ARTICLE

In this article:

(a) A "writing" consists of letters, words, numbers, or their equivalent set down in any form.

(b) A "recording" consists of letters, words, numbers, or their equivalent recorded in any manner.

(c) A "photograph" means a photographic image or its equivalent stored in any form.

(d) An "original" of a writing or recording means the writing or recording itself or any counterpart intended to have the same effect by the person who executed or issued it. For electronically stored information, "original" means any printout—or other output readable by sight—if it accurately reflects the information. An "original" of a photograph includes the negative or a print from it.

(e) A "duplicate" means a counterpart produced by a mechanical, photographic, chemical, electronic, or other equivalent process or technique that accurately reproduces the original.

(Pub.L. 93–595, § 1, Jan. 2, 1975, 88 Stat. 1945; Apr. 26, 2011, eff. Dec. 1, 2011.)

Rule 1002
REQUIREMENT OF THE ORIGINAL

An original writing, recording, or photograph is required in order to prove its content unless these rules or a federal statute provides otherwise. (Pub.L. 93–595, § 1, Jan. 2, 1975, 88 Stat. 1946; Apr. 26, 2011, eff. Dec. 1, 2011.)

Rule 1003
ADMISSIBILITY OF DUPLICATES

A duplicate is admissible to the same extent as the original unless a genuine question is raised about the original's authenticity or the circumstances make it unfair to admit the duplicate.

(Pub.L. 93–595, § 1, Jan. 2, 1975, 88 Stat. 1946; Apr. 26, 2011, eff. Dec. 1, 2011.)

Rule 1004
ADMISSIBILITY OF OTHER EVIDENCE OF CONTENT

An original is not required and other evidence of the content of a writing, recording, or photograph is admissible if:

(a) all the originals are lost or destroyed, and not by the proponent acting in bad faith;

(b) an original cannot be obtained by any available judicial process;

(c) the party against whom the original would be offered had control of the original; was at that time put on notice, by pleadings or otherwise, that the original would be a subject of proof at the trial or hearing; and fails to produce it at the trial or hearing; or

(d) the writing, recording, or photograph is not closely related to a controlling issue.

(Pub.L. 93–595, § 1, Jan. 2, 1975, 88 Stat. 1946; Mar. 2, 1987, eff. Oct. 1, 1987; Apr. 26, 2011, eff. Dec. 1, 2011.)

Rule 1005
COPIES OF PUBLIC RECORDS TO PROVE CONTENT

The proponent may use a copy to prove the content of an official record—or of a document that was recorded or filed in a public office as authorized by law—if these conditions are met: the record or document is otherwise admissible; and the copy is certified as correct in accordance with Rule 902(4) or is testified to be correct by a witness who has compared it with the original. If no such copy can be obtained by reasonable diligence, then the proponent may use other evidence to prove the content.

(Pub.L. 93–595, § 1, Jan. 2, 1975, 88 Stat. 1946; Apr. 26, 2011, eff. Dec. 1, 2011.)

Rule 1006
SUMMARIES TO PROVE CONTENT

The proponent may use a summary, chart, or calculation to prove the content of voluminous writings, recordings, or photographs that cannot be conveniently examined in court. The proponent must make the originals or duplicates available for examination or copying, or both, by other parties at a reasonable time and place. And the court may order the proponent to produce them in court.

(Pub.L. 93–595, § 1, Jan. 2, 1975, 88 Stat. 1946; Apr. 26, 2011, eff. Dec. 1, 2011.)

Rule 1007
TESTIMONY OR STATEMENT OF A PARTY TO PROVE CONTENT

The proponent may prove the content of a writing, recording, or photograph by the testimony, deposition, or written statement of the party against whom the evidence is offered. The proponent need not account for the original.

(Pub.L. 93–595, § 1, Jan. 2, 1975, 88 Stat. 1947; Mar. 2, 1987, eff. Oct. 1, 1987; Apr. 26, 2011, eff. Dec. 1, 2011.)

Rule 1008
FUNCTIONS OF THE COURT AND JURY

Ordinarily, the court determines whether the proponent has fulfilled the factual conditions for admitting other evidence of the content of a writing, recording, or photograph under Rule 1004 or 1005. But in a jury trial, the jury determines—in accordance with Rule 104(b)—any issue about whether: *sufficiency standard*

(a) an asserted writing, recording, or photograph ever existed;

(b) another one produced at the trial or hearing is the original; or

(c) other evidence of content accurately reflects the content.

(Pub.L. 93–595, § 1, Jan. 2, 1975, 88 Stat. 1947; Apr. 26, 2011, eff. Dec. 1, 2011.)

ARTICLE XI. MISCELLANEOUS RULES

Rule 1101
APPLICABILITY OF THE RULES

(a) TO COURTS AND JUDGES. These rules apply to proceedings before:

- United States district courts;

- United States bankruptcy and magistrate judges;

- United States courts of appeals;

- the United States Court of Federal Claims; and

- the district courts of Guam, the Virgin Islands, and the Northern Mariana Islands.

(b) TO CASES AND PROCEEDINGS. These rules apply in:

- civil cases and proceedings, including bankruptcy, admiralty, and maritime cases;

- criminal cases and proceedings; and

- contempt proceedings, except those in which the court may act summarily.

(c) RULES ON PRIVILEGE. The rules on privilege apply to all stages of a case or proceeding.

(d) EXCEPTIONS. These rules—except for those on privilege—do not apply to the following:

    (1) the court's determination, under Rule 104(a), on a preliminary question of fact governing admissibility;

    (2) grand jury proceedings; and

    (3) miscellaneous proceedings such as:

- extradition or rendition;

- issuing an arrest warrant, criminal summons, or search warrant;

- a preliminary examination in a criminal case;

- sentencing;

- granting or revoking probation or supervised release; and

- considering whether to release on bail or otherwise.

(e) OTHER STATUTES AND RULES. A federal statute or a rule prescribed by the Supreme Court may provide for admitting or excluding evidence independently from these rules.

(Pub.L. 93–595, § 1, Jan. 2, 1975, 88 Stat. 1947; Pub.L. 94–149, § 1(14), Dec. 12, 1975, 89 Stat. 806; Pub.L. 95–598, Title II, § 251, Nov. 6, 1978, 92 Stat. 2673; Pub.L. 97–164, Title I, § 142, Apr. 2, 1982, 96 Stat. 45; Mar. 2, 1987, eff. Oct. 1, 1987; Apr. 25, 1988, eff. Nov. 1, 1988; Pub.L. 100–690, Title VII, § 7075(c), Nov. 18, 1988, 102 Stat. 4405; Apr. 22, 1993, eff. Dec. 1, 1993; Apr. 26, 2011, eff. Dec. 1, 2011.)

Rule 1102
AMENDMENTS

These rules may be amended as provided in 28 U.S.C. § 2072.

(Pub.L. 93–595, § 1, Jan. 2, 1975, 88 Stat.1948; Apr. 30, 1991, eff. Dec. 1, 1991; Apr. 26, 2011, eff. Dec. 1, 2011.)

Rule 1103
TITLE

These rules may be cited as the Federal Rules of Evidence.

(Pub.L. 93–595, § 1, Jan. 2, 1975, 88 Stat.1948; Apr. 26, 2011, eff. Dec. 1, 2011.)

SELECTED LEGISLATIVE HISTORY OF THE FEDERAL RULES OF EVIDENCE FOR UNITED STATES COURTS AND MAGISTRATES

Editors' Note: Appendix A presents the Federal Rules of Evidence as they stand at the time this volume goes to press. This version of the Rules, which went into effect on December 1, 2011, was drafted as part of the federal rulemakers' restyling project. The Advisory Committee's explanation of guidelines for restyling the Rules, taken from its Note to Rule 101, follows immediately below this prefatory note. There follow selections from the legislative history of each Rule, including the Advisory Committee Notes. We have not included some Notes that have little or no substance; for example, in 1987 many of the Rules were amended to render them gender-neutral, and we have not included the Notes on those changes. Similarly, for most of the Rules, the Advisory Committee Notes for the 2011 restyling followed this form:

Rule ___

Committee Note

The language of Rule ___ has been amended as part of the general restyling of the Evidence Rules to make them more easily understood and to make style and terminology consistent throughout the rules. These changes are intended to be stylistic only. There is no intent to change any result in any ruling on evidence admissibility.

Committee Notes consisting of nothing more than this paragraph are not presented here.

––––––

Committee Note Explaining 2011 Restyling

The Style Project

The Evidence Rules are the fourth set of national procedural rules to be restyled. The restyled Rules of Appellate Procedure took effect in 1998. The restyled Rules of Criminal Procedure took effect in 2002. The restyled

Rules of Civil Procedure took effect in 2007. The restyled Rules of Evidence apply the same general drafting guidelines and principles used in restyling the Appellate, Criminal, and Civil Rules.

1. General Guidelines

Guidance in drafting, usage, and style was provided by Bryan Garner, *Guidelines for Drafting and Editing Court Rules,* Administrative Office of the United States Courts (1969) and Bryan Garner, *Dictionary of Modern Legal Usage* (2d ed. 1995). *See also* Joseph Kimble, *Guiding Principles for Restyling the Civil Rules,* in *Preliminary Draft of Proposed Style Revision of the Federal Rules of Civil Procedure,* at page x (Feb. 2005) (available at http://www.uscourts.gov/uscourts/RulesAndPolicies/rules/Prelim_draft_pro posed_pt1.pdf); Joseph Kimble, *Lessons in Drafting from the New Federal Rules of Civil Procedure,* 12 Scribes J. Legal Writing 25 (2008–2009). For specific commentary on the Evidence restyling project, see Joseph Kimble, *Drafting Examples from the Proposed New Federal Rules of Evidence,* 88 Mich. B.J. 52 (Aug. 2009); 88 Mich. B.J. 46 (Sept. 2009); 88 Mich. B.J. 54 (Oct. 2009); 88 Mich. B.J. 50 (Nov. 2009).

2. Formatting Changes

Many of the changes in the restyled Evidence Rules result from using format to achieve clearer presentations. The rules are broken down into constituent parts, using progressively indented subparagraphs with headings and substituting vertical for horizontal lists. "Hanging indents" are used throughout. These formatting changes make the structure of the rules graphic and make the restyled rules easier to read and understand even when the words are not changed. Rules 103, 404(b), 606(b), and 612 illustrate the benefits of formatting changes.

3. Changes to Reduce Inconsistent, Ambiguous, Redundant, Repetitive, or Archaic Words

The restyled rules reduce the use of inconsistent terms that say the same thing in different ways. Because different words are presumed to have different meanings, such inconsistencies can result in confusion. The restyled rules reduce inconsistencies by using the same words to express the same meaning. For example, consistent expression is achieved by not switching between "accused" and "defendant" or between "party opponent" and "opposing party" or between the various formulations of civil and criminal action/case/proceeding.

The restyled rules minimize the use of inherently ambiguous words. For example, the word "shall" can mean "must," "may," or something else, depending on context. The potential for confusion is exacerbated by the fact the word "shall" is no longer generally used in spoken or clearly written English. The restyled rules replace "shall" with "must," "may," or "should," depending on which one the context and established interpretation make correct in each rule.

The restyled rules minimize the use of redundant "intensifiers." These are expressions that attempt to add emphasis, but instead state the obvious and create negative implications for other rules. The absence of intensifiers in the restyled rules does not change their substantive meaning. *See, e.g.,* Rule 104(c) (omitting "in all cases"); Rule 602 (omitting "but need not"); Rule 611(b) (omitting "in the exercise of discretion").

The restyled rules also remove words and concepts that are outdated or redundant.

4. Rule Numbers

The restyled rules keep the same numbers to minimize the effect on research. Subdivisions have been rearranged within some rules to achieve greater clarity and simplicity.

5. No Substantive Change

The Committee made special efforts to reject any purported style improvement that might result in a substantive change in the application of a rule. The Committee considered a change to be "substantive" if any of the following conditions were met:

    a. Under the existing practice in any circuit, the change could lead to a different result on a question of admissibility (e.g., a change that requires a court to provide either a less or more stringent standard in evaluating the admissibility of particular evidence);

    b. Under the existing practice in any circuit, it could lead to a change in the procedure by which an admissibility decision is made (e.g., a change in the time in which an objection must be made, or a change in whether a court must hold a hearing on an admissibility question);

    c. The change would restructure a rule in a way that would alter the approach that courts and litigants have used to think about, and argue about, questions of admissibility (e.g., merging Rules 104(a) and 104(b) into a single subdivision); or

    d. The amendment would change a "sacred phrase" – one that has become so familiar in practice that to alter it would be unduly disruptive to practice and expectations. Examples in the Evidence Rules include "unfair prejudice" and "truth of the matter asserted."

———

Selected Legislative History of Individual Rules

ARTICLE I. GENERAL PROVISIONS

Rule 101

Note by Federal Judicial Center

The rule enacted by the Congress is the rule prescribed by the Supreme Court without change.

Advisory Committee's Note

Rule 1101 specifies in detail the courts, proceedings, questions, and stages of proceedings to which the rules apply in whole or in part.

Advisory Committee's Note to 2011 Amendment

The language of Rule 101 has been amended, and definitions have been added, as part of the general restyling of the Evidence Rules to make them more easily understood and to make style and terminology consistent throughout the rules. These changes are intended to be stylistic only. There is no intent to change any result in any ruling on evidence admissibility.

The reference to electronically stored information is intended to track the language of Fed. R. Civ. P. 34. * * *

Rule 102

Note by Federal Judicial Center

The rule enacted by the Congress is the rule prescribed by the Supreme Court without change.

Advisory Committee's Note

For similar provisions see Rule 2 of the Federal Rules of Criminal Procedure, Rule 1 of the Federal Rules of Civil Procedure, California Evidence Code § 2, and New Jersey Evidence Rule 5.

Rule 103

Note by Federal Judicial Center

The rule enacted by the Congress is the rule prescribed by the Supreme Court, amended by substituting "court" in place of "judge," with appropriate pronominal change.

Advisory Committee's Note

Subdivision (a) states the law as generally accepted today. Rulings on evidence cannot be assigned as error unless (1) a substantial right is affected, and (2) the nature of the error was called to the attention of the judge, so as to alert him to the proper course of action and enable opposing counsel to take proper corrective measures. The objection and the offer of proof are the techniques for accomplishing these objectives. For similar provisions see Uniform Rules 4 and 5; California Evidence Code §§ 353 and 354; Kansas Code of Civil Procedure §§ 60–404 and 60–405. The rule does not purport to change the law with respect to harmless error. See 28 USC § 2111, F.R.Civ.P. 61, F.R.Crim.P. 52, and decisions construing them. The status of constitutional error as harmless or not is treated in Chapman v. California, 386 U.S. 18, 87 S.Ct. 824, 17 L.Ed.2d 705 (1967), reh. denied id. 987, 386 U.S. 987, 87 S.Ct. 1283, 18 L.Ed.2d 241.

Subdivision (b). The first sentence is the third sentence of Rule 43(c) of the Federal Rules of Civil Procedure[1] virtually verbatim. Its purpose is to reproduce for an appellate court, insofar as possible, a true reflection of what occurred in the trial court. The second sentence is in part derived from the final sentence of Rule 43(c).[1] It is designed to resolve doubts as to what testimony the witness would have in fact given, and, in nonjury cases, to provide the appellate court with material for a possible final disposition of the case in the event of reversal of a ruling which excluded evidence. See 5 Moore's Federal Practice § 43.11 (2d ed. 1968). Application is made discretionary in view of the practical impossibility of formulating a satisfactory rule in mandatory terms.

Subdivision (c). This subdivision proceeds on the supposition that a ruling which excludes evidence in a jury case is likely to be a pointless procedure if the excluded evidence nevertheless comes to the attention of the jury. Bruton v. United States, 391 U.S. 123 (1968). Rule 43(c) of the Federal Rules of Civil Procedure provides: "The court may require the offer to be made out of the hearing of the jury." In re McConnell, 370 U.S. 230, 82 S.Ct. 1288, 8 L.Ed.2d 434 (1962), left some doubt whether questions on which an offer is based must first be asked in the presence of the jury. The subdivision answers in the negative. The judge can foreclose a particular line of testimony and counsel can protect his record without a series of questions before the jury, designed at best to waste time and at worst "to waft into the jury box" the very matter sought to be excluded.

Subdivision (d). This wording of the plain error principle is from Rule 52(b) of the Federal Rules of Criminal Procedure. While judicial unwillingness to be constricted by mechanical breakdowns of the adversary system has been more pronounced in criminal cases, there is no scarcity of decisions to the same effect in civil cases. In general, see Campbell, Extent

---

[1] Rule 43(c) of the Federal Rules of Civil Procedure was deleted by order of the Supreme Court entered on November 20, 1972, 93 S.Ct. 3073, 3075, 3076, 3077, 34 L.Ed.2d lxv, ccv, ccviii, which action was affirmed by the Congress in P.L. 93–595 § 3 (January 2, 1975).

to Which Courts of Review Will Consider Questions Not Properly Raised and Preserved, 7 Wis.L.Rev. 91, 160 (1932); Vestal, Sua Sponte Consideration in Appellate Review, 27 Fordham L.Rev. 477 (1958–59); 64 Harv.L.Rev. 652 (1951). In the nature of things the application of the plain error rule will be more likely with respect to the admission of evidence than to exclusion, since failure to comply with normal requirements of offers of proof is likely to produce a record which simply does not disclose the error.

Advisory Committee's Note to 2000 Amendment

The amendment applies to all rulings on evidence whether they occur at or before trial, including so-called "*in limine*" rulings. One of the most difficult questions arising from *in limine* and other evidentiary rulings is whether a losing party must renew an objection or offer of proof when the evidence is or would be offered at trial, in order to preserve a claim of error on appeal. Courts have taken differing approaches to this question. Some courts have held that a renewal at the time the evidence is to be offered at trial is always required. *See, e.g., Collins v. Wayne Corp.*, 621 F.2d 777 (5th Cir. 1980). Some courts have taken a more flexible approach, holding that renewal is not required if the issue decided is one that (1) was fairly presented to the trial court for an initial ruling, (2) may be decided as a final matter before the evidence is actually offered, and (3) was ruled on definitively by the trial Judge. *See, e.g., Rosenfeld v. Basquiat*, 78 F.3d 84 (2d Cir. 1996) (admissibility of former testimony under the Dead Man's Statute; renewal not required). Other courts have distinguished between objections to evidence, which must be renewed when evidence is offered, and offers of proof, which need not be renewed after a definitive determination is made that the evidence is inadmissible. *See, e.g., Fusco v. General Motors Corp.*, 11 F.3d 259 (1st Cir. 1993). Another court, aware of this Committee's proposed amendment, has adopted its approach. *Wilson v. Williams*, 182 F.3d 562 (7th Cir. 1999) (en banc). Differing views on this question create uncertainty for litigants and unnecessary work for the appellate courts.

The amendment provides that a claim of error with respect to a definitive ruling is preserved for review when the party has otherwise satisfied the objection or offer of proof requirements of Rule 103(a). When the ruling is definitive, a renewed objection or offer of proof at the time the evidence is to be offered is more a formalism than a necessity. *See* Fed.R.Civ.P. 46 (formal exceptions unnecessary); Fed.R.Cr.P. 51 (same); *United States v. Mejia–Alarcon*, 995 F.2d 982, 986 (10th Cir. 1993) ("Requiring a party to renew an objection when the district court has issued a definitive ruling on a matter that can be fairly decided before trial would be in the nature of a formal exception and therefore unnecessary."). On the other hand, when the trial court appears to have reserved its ruling or to have indicated that the ruling is provisional, it makes sense to require the party to bring the issue to the court's attention subsequently. *See, e.g., United States v. Vest*, 116 F.3d 1179, 1188 (7th Cir. 1997) (where the trial court ruled *in limine* that testimony from defense witnesses could not be admitted, but allowed the defendant to seek leave at trial to call the witnesses should their testimony turn out to be relevant, the defendant's failure to seek such leave at trial meant that it was "too late to reopen the issue now on appeal"); *United States v. Valenti*, 60 F.3d 941 (2d Cir. 1995) (failure to proffer evidence at trial waives any claim of error where the trial judge had stated that he would reserve judgment on the *in limine* motion until he had heard the trial evidence).

The amendment imposes the obligation on counsel to clarify whether an *in limine* or other evidentiary ruling is definitive when there is doubt on that point. *See, e.g., Walden v. Georgia–Pacific Corp.*, 126 F.3d 506, 520 (3d Cir. 1997) (although "the district court told plaintiffs' counsel not to reargue every ruling, it did not countermand its clear opening statement that all of its rulings were tentative, and counsel never requested clarification, as he might have done.").

Even where the court's ruling is definitive, nothing in the amendment prohibits the court from revisiting its decision when the evidence is to be offered. If the court changes its initial ruling, or if the opposing party violates the terms of the initial ruling, objection must be made when the evidence is offered to preserve the claim of error for appeal. The error, if any, in such a situation occurs only when the evidence is offered and admitted. *United States Aviation Underwriters, Inc. v. Olympia Wings, Inc.*, 896 F.2d 949, 956 (5th Cir. 1990) ("objection is required to preserve error when an opponent, or the court itself, violates a motion *in limine* that was granted"); *United States v. Roenigk*, 810 F.2d 809 (8th Cir. 1987) (claim of error was not preserved where the defendant failed to object at trial to secure the benefit of a favorable advance ruling).

A definitive advance ruling is reviewed in light of the facts and circumstances before the trial court at the time of the ruling. If the relevant facts and circumstances change materially after the advance ruling has been made, those facts and circumstances cannot be relied upon on appeal unless they have been brought to the attention of the trial court by way of a renewed, and timely, objection, offer of proof, or motion to strike. *See Old Chief v. United States*, 519 U.S. 172, 182, n.6 (1997) ("it is important that a reviewing court evaluate the trial court's decision from its perspective when it had to rule and not indulge in review by hindsight."). Similarly, if the court decides in an advance ruling that proffered evidence is admissible subject to the eventual introduction by the proponent of a foundation for the evidence, and that foundation is never provided, the opponent cannot claim error based on the failure to establish the foundation unless the opponent calls that failure to the court's attention by a timely motion to strike or other suitable motion. *See Huddleston v. United States*, 485 U.S. 681, 690, n.7 (1988) ("It is, of course, not the responsibility of the judge *sua sponte* to ensure that the foundation evidence is offered; the objector must move to strike the evidence if at the close of the trial the offeror has failed to satisfy the condition.").

Nothing in the amendment is intended to affect the provisions of Fed.R.Civ.P. 72(a) or 28 U.S.C. § 636(b)(1) pertaining to nondispositive pretrial rulings by magistrate judges in proceedings that are not before a magistrate judge by consent of the parties. Fed. R. Civ. P. 72(a) provides that a party who fails to file a written objection to a magistrate judge's nondispositive order within ten days of receiving a copy "may not thereafter assign as error a defect" in the order. 28 U.S.C. § 636(b)(1) provides that any party "may serve and file written objections to such proposed findings and recommendations as provided by rules of court" within ten days of receiving a copy of the order. Several courts have held that a party must comply with this statutory provision in order to preserve a claim of error. *See, e.g., Wells v. Shriner's Hospital*, 109 F.3d 198, 200 (4th Cir. 1997) ("[i]n this circuit, as in others, a party 'may' file objections within ten days or he may not, as he chooses, but he 'shall' do so if he wishes further consideration."). When Fed.R.Civ.P. 72(a) or 28 U.S.C. § 636(b)(1) is operative, its requirement must be satisfied in order for a party to preserve a claim of error on appeal, even where Evidence Rule 103(a) would not require a subsequent objection or offer of proof.

Nothing in the amendment is intended to affect the rule set forth in *Luce v. United States*, 469 U.S. 38 (1984), and its progeny. The amendment provides that an objection or offer of proof need not be renewed to preserve a claim of error with respect to a definitive pretrial ruling. *Luce* answers affirmatively a separate question: whether a criminal defendant must testify at trial in order to preserve a claim of error predicated upon a trial court's decision to admit the defendant's prior convictions for impeachment. The *Luce* principle has been extended by many lower courts to other situations. *See United States v. DiMatteo*, 759 F.2d 831 (11th Cir. 1985) (applying *Luce* where the defendant's witness would be impeached with evidence offered under Rule 608). *See also United States v. Goldman*, 41 F.3d 785, 788 (1st Cir. 1994) ("Although *Luce* involved impeachment by conviction under Rule 609, the reasons given by the Supreme Court for requiring the defendant to testify apply with full force to the kind of Rule 403 and 404 objections that are advanced by *Goldman* in this case."); *Palmieri v. DeFaria*, 88 F.3d 136 (2d Cir. 1996) (where the plaintiff decided to take an adverse judgment rather than challenge an advance ruling by putting on evidence at trial, the *in limine* ruling would not be reviewed on appeal); *United States v. Ortiz*, 857 F.2d 900 (2d Cir. 1988) (where uncharged misconduct is ruled admissible if the defendant pursues a certain defense, the defendant must actually pursue that defense at trial in order to preserve a claim of error on appeal); *United States v. Bond*, 87 F.3d 695 (5th Cir. 1996) (where the trial court rules *in limine* that the defendant would waive his fifth amendment privilege were he to testify, the defendant must take the stand and testify in order to challenge that ruling on appeal).

The amendment does not purport to answer whether a party who objects to evidence that the court finds admissible in a definitive ruling, and who then offers the evidence to "remove the sting" of its anticipated prejudicial effect, thereby waives the right to appeal the trial court's ruling. *See, e.g., United States v. Fisher*, 106 F.3d 622 (5th Cir. 1997) (where the trial judge ruled *in limine* that the government could use a prior conviction to impeach the defendant if he testified, the defendant did not waive his right to appeal by introducing the conviction on direct examination); *Judd v. Rodman*, 105 F.3d 1339 (11th Cir. 1997) (an objection made *in limine* is sufficient to preserve a claim of error when the movant, as a matter of trial strategy, presents the objectionable evidence herself on direct examination to minimize its prejudicial effect); *Gill v. Thomas*, 83 F.3d 537, 540 (1st Cir. 1996) ("by offering the misdemeanor evidence himself, Gill waived his opportunity to object and thus did not preserve the issue for appeal"); *United States v. Williams*, 939 F.2d 721 (9th Cir. 1991) (objection to impeachment evidence was waived where the defendant was impeached on direct examination).

Rule 104

Note by Federal Judicial Center

The rule enacted by the Congress is the rule prescribed by the Supreme Court, amended by substituting "court" in place of "judge," with appropriate pronominal change, and by adding to subdivision (c) the concluding phrase, "or when an accused is a witness, if he so requests."[1]

Advisory Committee's Note

Subdivision (a). The applicability of a particular rule of evidence often depends upon the existence of a condition. Is the alleged expert a qualified physician? Is a witness whose former testimony is offered unavailable? Was a stranger present during a conversation between attorney and client? In each instance the admissibility of evidence will turn upon the answer to the question of the existence of the condition. Accepted practice, incorporated in the rule, places on the judge the responsibility for these determinations. McCormick § 53; Morgan, Basic Problems of Evidence 45–50 (1962).

To the extent that these inquiries are factual, the judge acts as a trier of fact. Often, however, rulings on evidence call for an evaluation in terms of a legally set standard. Thus when a hearsay statement is offered as a declaration against interest, a decision must be made whether it possesses the required against-interest characteristics. These decisions, too, are made by the judge.

In view of these considerations, this subdivision refers to preliminary requirements generally by the broad term "questions," without attempt at specification.

This subdivision is of general application. It must, however, be read as subject to the special provisions for "conditional relevancy" in subdivision (b) and those for confessions in subdivision (c).

---

[1] The effect of the amendment was to restore language included in the 1971 Revised Draft of the Proposed Rules but deleted before the rules were presented to and prescribed by the Supreme Court.

If the question is factual in nature, the judge will of necessity receive evidence pro and con on the issue. The rule provides that the rules of evidence in general do not apply to this process. McCormick § 53, p. 123, n. 8, points out that the authorities are "scattered and inconclusive," and observes:

"Should the exclusionary law of evidence, 'the child of the jury system' in Thayer's phrase, be applied to this hearing before the judge? Sound sense backs the view that it should not, and that the judge should be empowered to hear any relevant evidence, such as affidavits or other reliable hearsay."

This view is reinforced by practical necessity in certain situations. An item, offered and objected to, may itself be considered in ruling on admissibility, though not yet admitted in evidence. Thus the content of an asserted declaration against interest must be considered in ruling whether it is against interest. Again, common practice calls for considering the testimony of a witness, particularly a child, in determining competency. Another example is the requirement of Rule 602 dealing with personal knowledge. In the case of hearsay, it is enough, if the declarant "so far as appears [has] had an opportunity to observe the fact declared." McCormick, § 10, p. 19.

If concern is felt over the use of affidavits by the judge in preliminary hearings on admissibility, attention is directed to the many important judicial determinations made on the basis of affidavits. Rule 47 of the Federal Rules of Criminal Procedure provides:

"An application to the court for an order shall be by motion. *** It may be supported by affidavit."

The Rules of Civil Procedure are more detailed. Rule 43(e), dealing with motions generally, provides:

"When a motion is based on facts not appearing of record the court may hear the matter on affidavits presented by the respective parties, but the court may direct that the matter be heard wholly or partly on oral testimony or depositions."

Rule 4(g) provides for proof of service by affidavit. Rule 56 provides in detail for the entry of summary judgment based on affidavits. Affidavits may supply the foundation for temporary restraining orders under Rule 65(b).

The study made for the California Law Revision Commission recommended an amendment to Uniform Rule 2 as follows:

"In the determination of the issue aforesaid [preliminary determination], exclusionary rules shall not apply, subject, however, to Rule 45 and any valid claim of privilege." Tentative Recommendation and a Study Relating to the Uniform Rules of Evidence (Article VIII, Hearsay), Cal.Law Revision Comm'n, Rep., Rec. & Studies, 470 (1962).

The proposal was not adopted in the California Evidence Code. The Uniform Rules are likewise silent on the subject. However, New Jersey Evidence Rule 8(1), dealing with preliminary inquiry by the judge, provides:

> "In his determination the rules of evidence shall not apply except for Rule 4 [exclusion on grounds of confusion, etc.] or a valid claim of privilege."

Subdivision (b). In some situations, the relevancy of an item of evidence, in the large sense, depends upon the existence of a particular preliminary fact. Thus when a spoken statement is relied upon to prove notice to X, it is without probative value unless X heard it. Or if a letter purporting to be from Y is relied upon to establish an admission by him, it has no probative value unless Y wrote or authorized it. Relevance in this sense has been labelled "conditional relevancy." Morgan, Basic Problems of Evidence 45–46 (1962). Problems arising in connection with it are to be distinguished from problems of logical relevancy, e.g. evidence in a murder case that accused on the day before purchased a weapon of the kind used in the killing, treated in Rule 401.

If preliminary questions of conditional relevancy were determined solely by the judge, as provided in subdivision (a), the functioning of the jury as a trier of fact would be greatly restricted and in some cases virtually destroyed. These are appropriate questions for juries. Accepted treatment, as provided in the rule, is consistent with that given fact questions generally. The judge makes a preliminary determination whether the foundation evidence is sufficient to support a finding of fulfillment of the condition. If so, the item is admitted. If after all the evidence on the issue is in, pro and con, the jury could reasonably conclude that fulfillment of the condition is not established, the issue is for them. If the evidence is not such as to allow a finding, the judge withdraws the matter from their consideration. Morgan, *supra;* California Evidence Code § 403; New Jersey Rule 8(2). See also Uniform Rules 19 and 67.

The order of proof here, as generally, is subject to the control of the judge.

Subdivision (c). Preliminary hearings on the admissibility of confessions must be conducted outside the hearing of the jury. See Jackson v. Denno, 378 U.S. 368, 84 S.Ct. 1774, 12 L.Ed.2d 908 (1964).[2] Otherwise, detailed treatment of when preliminary matters should be heard outside the hearing of the jury is not feasible. The procedure is time consuming. Not infrequently the same evidence which is relevant to the issue of establishment of fulfillment of a condition precedent to admissibility is also relevant to weight or credibility, and time is saved by taking foundation proof in the

---

[2] At this point the Advisory Committee's Note to the 1971 Revised Draft contained the sentence, "Also, due regard for the right of an accused not to testify generally in the case requires that he be given an option to testify out of the presence of the jury upon preliminary matters." The statement was deleted in view of the deletion from the rule, mentioned in the preceding footnote.

presence of the jury. Much evidence on preliminary questions, though not relevant to jury issues, may be heard by the jury with no adverse effect. A great deal must be left to the discretion of the judge who will act as the interests of justice require.

Report of the House Committee on the Judiciary

Rule 104(c) as submitted to the Congress provided that hearings on the admissibility of confessions shall be conducted outside the presence of the jury and hearings on all other preliminary matters should be so conducted when the interests of justice require. The Committee amended the Rule to provide that where an accused is a witness as to a preliminary matter, he has the right, upon his request, to be heard outside the jury's presence. Although recognizing that in some cases duplication of evidence would occur and that the procedure could be subject to abuse, the Committee believed that a proper regard for the right of an accused not to testify generally in the case dictates that he be given an option to testify out of the presence of the jury on preliminary matters.

The Committee construes the second sentence of subdivision (c) as applying to civil actions and proceedings as well as to criminal cases, and on this assumption has left the sentence unamended.

Advisory Committee's Note

Subdivision (d). The limitation upon cross-examination is designed to encourage participation by the accused in the determination of preliminary matters. He may testify concerning them without exposing himself to cross-examination generally. The provision is necessary because of the breadth of cross-examination [possible] under Rule 611(b).

The rule does not address itself to questions of the subsequent use of testimony given by an accused at a hearing on a preliminary matter. See Walder v. United States, 347 U.S. 62 (1954); Simmons v. United States, 390 U.S. 377 (1968); Harris v. New York, 401 U.S. 222 (1971).

Report of Senate Committee on the Judiciary

Under rule 104(c) the hearing on a preliminary matter may at times be conducted in front of the jury. Should an accused testify in such a hearing, waiving his privilege against self-incrimination as to the preliminary issue, rule 104(d) provides that he will not generally be subject to cross-examination as to any other issue. This rule is not, however, intended to immunize the accused from cross-examination where, in testifying about a preliminary issue, he injects other issues into the hearing. If he could not be cross-examined about any issues gratuitously raised by him beyond the scope of the preliminary matters, injustice might result. Accordingly, in order to prevent any such unjust result, the committee intends the rule to be construed to provide that the accused may subject himself to cross-examination as to issues raised by his own testimony upon a preliminary matter before a jury.

Advisory Committee's Note

Subdivision (e). For similar provisions see Uniform Rule 8; California Evidence Code § 406; Kansas Code of Civil Procedure § 60–408; New Jersey Evidence Rule 8(1).

Rule 105

Note by Federal Judicial Center

The rule enacted by the Congress is the rule prescribed by the Supreme Court as Rule 106, amended by substituting "court" in place of "judge." Rule 105 as prescribed by the Court, which was deleted from the rules enacted by the Congress, is set forth in the Appendix hereto, together with a statement of the reasons for the deletion.

Advisory Committee's Note

A close relationship exists between this rule and Rule 403[,] which requires exclusion when "probative value is substantially outweighed by the danger of unfair prejudice, confusion of the issues, or misleading the jury." The present rule recognizes the practice of admitting evidence for a limited purpose and instructing the jury accordingly. The availability and effectiveness of this practice must be taken into consideration in reaching a decision whether to exclude for unfair prejudice under Rule 403. In Bruton v. United States, 391 U.S. 123 (1968), the Court ruled that a limiting instruction did not effectively protect the accused against the prejudicial effect of admitting in evidence the confession of a codefendant which implicated him. The decision does not, however, bar the use of limited admissibility with an instruction where the risk of prejudice is less serious.

Similar provisions are found in Uniform Rule 6; California Evidence Code § 355; Kansas Code of Civil Procedure § 60–406; New Jersey Evidence Rule 6. The wording of the present rule differs, however, in repelling any implication that limiting or curative instructions are sufficient in all situations.

Report of House Committee on the Judiciary

Rule 106 as submitted by the Supreme Court (now Rule 105 in the bill) dealt with the subject of evidence which is admissible as to one party or for one purpose but is not admissible against another party or for another purpose. The Committee adopted this Rule without change on the understanding that it does not affect the authority of a court to order a severance in a multi-defendant case.

Rule 106

Note by Federal Judicial Center

The rule enacted by the Congress is the rule prescribed by the Supreme Court as Rule 107 without change.

Advisory Committee's Note

The rule is an expression of the rule of completeness. McCormick § 56. It is manifested as to depositions in Rule 32(a)(4) of the Federal Rules of Civil Procedure, of which the proposed rule is substantially a restatement.

The rule is based on two considerations. The first is the misleading impression created by taking matters out of context. The second is the inadequacy of repair work when delayed to a point later in the trial. See McCormick § 56; California Evidence Code § 356. The rule does not in any way circumscribe the right of the adversary to develop the matter on cross-examination or as part of his own case.

For practical reasons, the rule is limited to writings and recorded statements and does not apply to conversations.

ARTICLE II. JUDICIAL NOTICE

Rule 201

[**Editorial Note:** The 2011 restyling resulted in renumbering some of the subdivisions of Rule 201. The substance of the original subdivisions (c) and (d) is now contained in subdivision (c), the substance of the original subdivision (f) is now contained in subdivision (d), and the substance of the orginal dubdivsion (g) is now contained in subdivision (f).]

Note by Federal Judicial Center

The rule enacted by the Congress is the rule prescribed by the Supreme Court with the following changes:

In subdivisions (c) and (d) the words "judge or" before "court" were deleted.

Subdivision (g) as it is shown was substituted in place of, "The judge shall instruct the jury to accept as established any facts judicially noticed." The substituted language is from the 1969 Preliminary Draft. 46 F.R.D. 161, 195.

Advisory Committee's Note

Subdivision (a). This is the only evidence rule on the subject of judicial notice. It deals only with judicial notice of "adjudicative" facts. No rule deals with judicial notice of "legislative" facts. Judicial notice of matters of foreign law is treated in Rule 44.1 of the Federal Rules of Civil Procedure and Rule 26.1 of the Federal Rules of Criminal Procedure.

The omission of any treatment of legislative facts results from fundamental differences between adjudicative facts and legislative facts. Adjudicative facts are simply the facts of the particular case. Legislative facts, on the other hand, are those which have relevance to legal reasoning and the lawmaking process, whether in the formulation of a legal principle or ruling by a judge or court or in the enactment of a legislative body. The terminology was coined by Professor Kenneth Davis in his article An Approach to Problems of Evidence in the Administrative Process, 55 Harv.L.Rev. 364, 404–407 (1942). The following discussion draws extensively upon his writings. In addition, see the same author's Judicial Notice, 55 Colum.L.Rev. 945 (1955); Administrative Law Treatise, ch. 15 (1958); A System of Judicial Notice Based on Fairness and Convenience, in Perspectives of Law 69 (1964).

The usual method of establishing adjudicative facts is through the introduction of evidence, ordinarily consisting of the testimony of witnesses. If particular facts are outside the area of reasonable controversy, this process is dispensed with as unnecessary. A high degree of indisputability is the essential prerequisite.

Legislative facts are quite different. As Professor Davis says:

> "My opinion is that judge-made law would stop growing if judges, in thinking about questions of law and policy, were forbidden to take into account the facts they believe, as distinguished from facts which are 'clearly * * * within the domain of the indisputable.' Facts most needed in thinking about difficult problems of law and policy have a way of being outside the domain of the clearly indisputable." A System of Judicial Notice Based on Fairness and Convenience, supra, at 82.

An illustration is Hawkins v. United States, 358 U.S. 74, 79 S.Ct. 136, 3 L.Ed.2d 125 (1958), in which the Court refused to discard the common law rule that one spouse could not testify against the other, saying, "Adverse testimony given in criminal proceedings would, we think, be likely to destroy almost any marriage." This conclusion has a large intermixture of fact, but the factual aspect is scarcely "indisputable." See Hutchins and Slesinger, Some Observations on the Law of Evidence—Family Relations, 13 Minn.L.Rev. 675 (1929). If the destructive effect of the giving of adverse testimony by a spouse is not indisputable, should the Court have refrained from considering it in the absence of supporting evidence?

> "If the Model Code or the Uniform Rules had been applicable, the Court would have been barred from thinking about the essential factual ingredient of the problems before it, and such a result would be obviously intolerable. What the law needs at its growing points is more, not less, judicial thinking about the factual ingredients of prob-

lems of what the law ought to be, and the needed facts are seldom 'clearly' indisputable." Davis, supra, at 83.

Professor Morgan gave the following description of the methodology of determining domestic law:

"In determining the content or applicability of a rule of domestic law, the judge is unrestricted in his investigation and conclusion. He may reject the propositions of either party or of both parties. He may consult the sources of pertinent data to which they refer, or he may refuse to do so. He may make an independent search for persuasive data or rest content with what he has or what the parties present. * * * [T]he parties do no more than to assist; they control no part of the process." Morgan, Judicial Notice, 57 Harv.L.Rev. 269, 270–271 (1944).

This is the view which should govern judicial access to legislative facts. It renders inappropriate any limitation in the form of indisputability, any formal requirements of notice other than those already inherent in affording opportunity to hear and be heard and exchanging briefs, and any requirement of formal findings at any level. It should, however, leave open the possibility of introducing evidence through regular channels in appropriate situations. See Borden's Farm Products Co. v. Baldwin, 293 U.S. 194, 55 S.Ct. 187, 79 L.Ed. 281 (1934), where the cause was remanded for the taking of evidence as to the economic conditions and trade practices underlying the New York Milk Control Law.

Similar considerations govern the judicial use of non-adjudicative facts in ways other than formulating laws and rules. Thayer described them as a part of the judicial reasoning process.

"In conducting a process of judicial reasoning, as of other reasoning, not a step can be taken without assuming something which has not been proved; and the capacity to do this with competent judgment and efficiency, is imputed to judges and juries as part of their necessary mental outfit." Thayer, Preliminary Treatise on Evidence 279–280 (1898).

As Professor Davis points out, A System of Judicial Notice Based on Fairness and Convenience, in Perspectives of Law 69, 73 (1964), every case involves the use of hundreds or thousands of non-evidence facts. When a witness in an automobile accident case says "car," everyone, judge and jury included, furnishes, from non-evidence sources within himself, the supplementing information that the "car" is an automobile, not a railroad car, that it is self-propelled, probably by an internal combustion engine, that it may be assumed to have four wheels with pneumatic rubber tires, and so on. The judicial process cannot construct every case from scratch, like Descartes creating a world based on the postulate Cogito, ergo sum. These items could not possibly be introduced into evidence, and no one suggests that they be. Nor are they appropriate subjects for any formalized treatment of judicial notice of facts. See Levin and Levy, Persuading the Jury with Facts Not in Evidence: The Fiction-Science Spectrum, 105 U.Pa.L.Rev. 139 (1956).

Another aspect of what Thayer had in mind is the use of non-evidence facts to appraise or assess the adjudicative facts of the case. Pairs of cases from two jurisdictions illustrate this use and also the difference between non-evidence facts thus used and adjudicative facts. In People v. Strook, 347 Ill. 460, 179 N.E. 821 (1932), venue in Cook County had been held not established by testimony that the crime was committed at 7956 South Chicago Avenue, since judicial notice would not be taken that the address was in Chicago. However, the same court subsequently ruled that venue in Cook County was established by testimony that a crime occurred at 8900 South Anthony Avenue, since notice would be taken of the common practice of omitting the name of the city when speaking of local addresses, and the witness was testifying in Chicago. People v. Pride, 16 Ill.2d 82, 156 N.E.2d 551 (1959). And in Hughes v. Vestal, 264 N.C. 500, 142 S.E.2d 361 (1965), the Supreme Court of North Carolina disapproved the trial judge's admission in evidence of a state-published table of automobile stopping distances on the basis of judicial notice, though the court itself had referred to the same table in an earlier case in a "rhetorical and illustrative" way in determining that the defendant could not have stopped her car in time to avoid striking a child who suddenly appeared in the highway and that a nonsuit was properly granted. Ennis v. Dupree, 262 N.C. 224, 136 S.E.2d 702 (1964). See also Brown v. Hale, 263 N.C. 176, 139 S.E.2d 210 (1964); Clayton v. Rimmer, 262 N.C. 302, 136 S.E.2d 562 (1964). It is apparent that this use of non-evidence facts in evaluating the adjudicative facts of the case is not an appropriate subject for a formalized judicial notice treatment.

In view of these considerations, the regulation of judicial notice of facts by the present rule extends only to adjudicative facts.

What, then, are "adjudicative" facts? Davis refers to them as those "which relate to the parties," or more fully:

"When a court or an agency finds facts concerning the immediate parties—who did what, where, when, how, and with what motive or intent—the court or agency is performing an adjudicative function, and the facts are conveniently called adjudicative facts. * * *

"Stated in other terms, the adjudicative facts are those to which the law is applied in the process of adjudication. They are the facts that normally go to the jury in a jury case. They relate to the parties, their activities, their properties, their businesses." 2 Administrative Law Treatise 353.

Subdivision (b). With respect to judicial notice of adjudicative facts the tradition has been one of caution in requiring that the matter be beyond reasonable controversy. This tradition of circumspection appears to be soundly based, and no reason to depart from it is apparent. As Professor Davis says:

> "The reason we use trial-type procedure, I think, is that we make the practical judgment, on the basis of experience, that taking evidence, subject to cross-examination and rebuttal, is the best way to resolve controversies involving disputes of adjudicative facts, that is, facts pertaining to the parties. The reason we require a determination on the record is that we think fair procedure in resolving disputes of adjudicative facts calls for giving each party a chance to meet in the appropriate fashion the facts that come to the tribunal's attention, and the appropriate fashion for meeting disputed adjudicative facts includes rebuttal evidence, cross-examination, usually confrontation, and argument (either written or oral or both). The key to a fair trial is opportunity to use the appropriate weapons (rebuttal evidence, cross-examination, and argument) to meet adverse materials that come to the tribunal's attention." A System of Judicial Notice Based on Fairness and Convenience, in Perspectives of Law 69, 93 (1964).

The rule proceeds upon the theory that these considerations call for dispensing with traditional methods of proof only in clear cases. Compare Professor Davis' conclusion that judicial notice should be a matter of convenience, subject to requirements of procedural fairness. Id., 94.

This rule is consistent with Uniform Rule 9(1) and (2) which limit judicial notice of facts to those "so universally known that they cannot reasonably be the subject of dispute," those "so generally known or of such common notoriety within the territorial jurisdiction of the court that they cannot reasonably be the subject of dispute," and those "capable of immediate and accurate determination by resort to easily accessible sources of indisputable accuracy." The traditional textbook treatment has included these general categories (matters of common knowledge, facts capable of verification), McCormick §§ 324, 325, and then has passed on into detailed treatment of such specific topics as facts relating to the personnel and records of the court, id. § 327, and other governmental facts, id. § 328. The California draftsmen, with a background of detailed statutory regulation of judicial notice, followed a somewhat similar pattern. California Evidence Code §§ 451, 452. The Uniform Rules, however, were drafted on the theory that these particular matters are included within the general categories and need no specific mention. This approach is followed in the present rule.

The phrase "propositions of generalized knowledge," found in Uniform Rule 9(1) and (2) is not included in the present rule. It was, it is believed, originally included in Model Code Rules 801 and 802 primarily in order to afford some minimum recognition to the right of the judge in his "legislative" capacity (not acting as the trier of fact) to take judicial notice of very limited categories of generalized knowledge. The limitations thus imposed have been discarded herein as undesirable, unworkable, and contrary to existing practice. What is left, then, to be considered, is the status of a "proposition of generalized knowledge" as an "adjudicative" fact to be noticed judicially and communicated by the judge to the jury. Thus viewed, it is considered to be lacking practical significance. While judges use judicial notice of "propositions of generalized knowledge" in a variety of situations: determining the validity and meaning of statutes, formulating common law rules, deciding whether evidence should be admitted, assessing the sufficiency and effect of evidence, all are essentially nonadjudicative in nature. When judicial notice is seen as a significant vehicle for progress in the law, these are the areas involved, particularly in developing fields of scientific knowledge. See McCormick 712. It is not believed that judges now instruct juries as to "propositions of generalized knowledge" derived from encyclopedias or other sources, or that they are likely to do so, or, indeed, that it is desirable that they do so. There is a vast difference between ruling on the basis of judicial notice that radar evidence of speed is admissible and explaining to the jury its principles and degree of accuracy, or between using a table of stopping distances of automobiles at various speeds in a judicial evaluation of testimony and telling the jury its precise application in the case. For cases raising doubt as to the propriety of the use of medical texts by lay triers of fact in passing on disability claims in administrative proceedings, see Sayers v. Gardner, 380 F.2d 940 (6th Cir.1967); Ross v. Gardner, 365 F.2d 554 (6th Cir.1966); Sosna v. Celebrezze, 234 F.Supp. 289 (E.D.Pa.1964); Glendenning v. Ribicoff, 213 F.Supp. 301 (W.D.Mo.1962).

Subdivisions (c) and (d). Under subdivision (c) the judge has a discretionary authority to take judicial notice, regardless of whether he is so requested by a party. The taking of judicial notice is mandatory, under subdivision (d), only when a party requests it and the necessary information is supplied. This scheme is believed to reflect existing practice. It is simple and workable. It avoids troublesome distinctions in the many situations in which the process of taking judicial notice is not recognized as such.

Compare Uniform Rule 9 making judicial notice of facts universally known mandatory without request, and making judicial notice of facts generally known in the jurisdiction or capable of determination by resort to accurate sources discretionary in the absence of request but mandatory if request is made and the information furnished. But see Uniform Rule 10(3), which directs the judge to decline to take judicial notice if available information fails to convince him that the matter falls clearly within Uniform Rule 9 or is insufficient to enable him to notice it judicially. Substantially the same approach is found in California Evidence Code §§ 451–453 and in New Jersey Evidence Rule 9. In contrast, the present rule treats alike all adjudicative facts which are subject to judicial notice.

Subdivision (e). Basic considerations of procedural fairness demand an opportunity to be heard on the propriety of taking judicial notice and the tenor of the matter noticed. The rule requires the granting of that opportunity upon request. No formal scheme of giving notice is provided. An adversely affected party may learn in advance that judicial notice is in contemplation, either by virtue of being served with a copy of a request by another party under subdivision (d) that judicial notice be taken, or through an advance indication by the judge. Or he may have no advance notice at all. The likelihood of the latter is enhanced by the frequent failure to recognize judicial notice as such. And in the absence of advance notice, a request made after the fact could not in fairness be considered untimely. See the provision for hearing on timely request in the Administrative Procedure Act, 5 U.S.C. § 556(e). See also Revised Model State Administrative Procedure Act (1961), 9C U.L.A. § 10(4) (Supp.1967).

Subdivision (f). In accord with the usual view, judicial notice may be taken at any stage of the proceedings, whether in the trial court or on appeal. Uniform Rule 12;　California Evidence Code § 459;　Kansas Rules of Evidence § 60–412;　New Jersey Evidence Rule 12;　McCormick § 330, p. 712.

Subdivision (g). Much of the controversy about judicial notice has centered upon the question whether evidence should be admitted in disproof of facts of which judicial notice is taken.

The writers have been divided. Favoring admissibility are Thayer, Preliminary Treatise on Evidence 308 (1898);　9 Wigmore § 2567;　Davis, A System of Judicial Notice Based on Fairness and Convenience, in Perspectives of Law, 69, 76–77 (1964). Opposing admissibility are Keeffe, Landis and Shaad, Sense and Nonsense about Judicial Notice, 2 Stan.L.Rev. 664, 668 (1950); McNaughton, Judicial Notice—Excerpts Relating to the Morgan-Whitmore Controversy, 14 Vand.L.Rev. 779 (1961); Morgan, Judicial Notice, 57 Harv.L.Rev. 269, 279 (1944); McCormick 710–711. The Model Code and the Uniform Rules are predicated upon indisputability of judicially noticed facts.

The proponents of admitting evidence in disproof have concentrated largely upon legislative facts. Since the present rule deals only with judicial notice of adjudicative facts, arguments directed to legislative facts lose their relevancy.

Report of House Committee on the Judiciary

Rule 201(g) as received from the Supreme Court provided that when judicial notice of a fact is taken, the court shall instruct the jury to accept that fact as established. Being of the view that mandatory instruction to a jury in a criminal case to accept as conclusive any fact judicially noticed is inappropriate because contrary to the spirit of the Sixth Amendment right to a jury trial, the Committee adopted the 1969 Advisory Committee draft of this subsection, allowing a mandatory instruction in civil actions and proceedings and a discretionary instruction in criminal cases.

Advisory Committee's Note (Continued)

[The following portion of the Advisory Committee's Note is from the 1969 Preliminary Draft, 46 F.R.D. 161, 204.]

Within its relatively narrow area of adjudicative facts, the rule contemplates there is to be no evidence before the jury in disproof in civil cases. The judge instructs the jury to take judicially noticed facts as conclusive. This position is justified by the undesirable effects of the opposite rule in limiting the rebutting party, though not his opponent, to admissible evidence, in defeating the reasons for judicial notice, and in affecting the substantive law to an extent and in ways largely unforeseeable. Ample protection and flexibility are afforded by the broad provision for opportunity to be heard on request set forth in subdivision (e).

Criminal cases are treated somewhat differently in the rule. While matters falling within the common fund of information supposed to be possessed by jurors need not be proved, State v. Dunn, 221 Mo. 530, 120 S.W. 1179 (1909), these are not, properly speaking, adjudicative facts but an aspect of legal reasoning. The considerations which underlie the general rule that a verdict cannot be directed against the accused in a criminal case seem to foreclose the judge's directing the jury on the basis of judicial notice to accept as conclusive any adjudicative facts in the case. State v. Main, 94 R.I. 338, 180 A.2d 814 (1962); State v. Lawrence, 120 Utah 323, 234 P.2d 600 (1951). Cf. People v. Mayes, 113 Cal. 618, 45 P. 860 (1896); Ross v. United States, 374 F.2d 97 (8th Cir.1967). However, this view presents no obstacle to the judge's advising the jury as to a matter judicially noticed, if he instructs them that it need not be taken as conclusive.

Note on Judicial Notice of Law (by the Advisory Committee)

By rules effective July 1, 1966, the method of invoking the law of a foreign country is covered elsewhere. Rule 44.1 of the Federal Rules of Civil Procedure; Rule 26.1 of the Federal Rules of Criminal Procedure. These two new admirably designed rules are founded upon the assumption that the manner in which law is fed into the judicial process is never a proper concern of the rules of evidence but rather of the rules of procedure. The Advisory Committee on Evidence, believing that this assumption is entirely correct, proposes no evidence rule with respect to judicial notice of law, and suggests that those matters of law which, in addition to foreign-country law, have traditionally been treated as requiring pleading and proof and more recently as the subject of judicial notice be left to the Rules of Civil and Criminal Procedure.

ARTICLE III. PRESUMPTIONS IN CIVIL ACTIONS AND PROCEEDINGS

Rule 301

Note by Federal Judicial Center

The bill passed by the House substituted a substantially different rule in place of that prescribed by the Supreme Court. The Senate bill substituted yet a further version, which was accepted by the House, was enacted by the Congress, and is the rule shown above. The earlier versions are set forth in the Appendix hereto.

Report of Senate Committee on the Judiciary

This rule governs presumptions in civil cases generally. Rule 302 provides for presumptions in cases controlled by State law.

As submitted by the Supreme Court, presumptions governed by this rule were given the effect of placing upon the opposing party the burden of establishing the nonexistence of the presumed fact, once the party invoking the presumption established the basic facts giving rise to it.

Instead of imposing a burden of persuasion on the party against whom the presumption is directed, the House adopted a provision which shifted the burden of going forward with the evidence. They further provided that "even though met with contradicting evidence, a presumption is sufficient evidence of the fact presumed, to be considered by the trier of fact." The effect of the amendment is that presumptions are to be treated as evidence.

The committee feels the House amendment is ill-advised. As the joint committees (the Standing Committee on Practice and Procedure of the Judicial Conference and the Advisory Committee on the Rules of Evidence) stated: "Presumptions are not evidence, but ways of dealing with evidence."[1] This treatment requires juries to perform the task of considering "as evidence" facts upon which they have no direct evidence and which may confuse them in performance of their duties. California had a rule much like that contained in the House amendment. It was sharply criticized by Justice Traynor in Speck v. Sarver[2] and was repealed after 93 troublesome years.[3]

Professor McCormick gives a concise and compelling critique of the presumption as evidence rule:

Another solution, formerly more popular than now, is to instruct the jury that the presumption is 'evidence', to be weighed and considered

---

[1] Hearings Before the Committee on the Judiciary, United States Senate, H.R. 5463, p. 56.

[2] 20 Cal.2d 585, 594, 128 P.2d 16, 21 (1942).

[3] Cal.Ev.Code 1965 § 600.

with the testimony in the case. This avoids the danger that the jury may infer that the presumption is conclusive, but it probably means little to the jury, and certainly runs counter to accepted theories of the nature of evidence.[4]

For these reasons the committee has deleted that provision of the House-passed rule that treats presumptions as evidence. The effect of the rule as adopted by the committee is to make clear that while evidence of facts giving rise to a presumption shifts the burden of coming forward with evidence to rebut or meet the presumption, it does not shift the burden of persuasion on the existence of the presumed facts. The burden of persuasion remains on the party to whom it is allocated under the rules governing the allocation in the first instance.

The court may instruct the jury that they may infer the existence of the presumed fact from proof of the basic facts giving rise to the presumption. However, it would be inappropriate under this rule to instruct the jury that the inference they are to draw is conclusive.

Conference Report

The House bill provides that a presumption in civil actions and proceedings shifts to the party against whom it is directed the burden of going forward with evidence to meet or rebut it. Even though evidence contradicting the presumption is offered, a presumption is considered sufficient evidence of the presumed fact to be considered by the jury. The Senate amendment provides that a presumption shifts to the party against whom it is directed the burden of going forward with evidence to meet or rebut the presumption, but it does not shift to that party the burden of persuasion on the existence of the presumed fact.

Under the Senate amendment, a presumption is sufficient to get a party past an adverse party's motion to dismiss made at the end of his case-in-chief. If the adverse party offers no evidence contradicting the presumed fact, the court will instruct the jury that if it finds the basic facts, it may presume the existence of the presumed fact. If the adverse party does offer evidence contradicting the presumed fact, the court cannot instruct the jury that it may *presume* the existence of the presumed fact from proof of the basic facts. The court may however, instruct the jury that it may infer the existence of the presumed fact from proof of the basic facts.

The Conference adopts the Senate amendment.

Rule 302

Note by Federal Judicial Center

The rule enacted by the Congress is the rule prescribed by the Supreme Court, amended by adding "and proceedings" after "actions."

---

[4] McCormick, Evidence, 669 (1954); id 825 (2d ed. 1972).

Advisory Committee's Note

A series of Supreme Court decisions in diversity cases leaves no doubt of the relevance of Erie Railroad Co. v. Tompkins, 304 U.S. 64, 58 S.Ct. 817, 82 L.Ed. 1188 (1938), to questions of burden of proof. These decisions are Cities Service Oil Co. v. Dunlap, 308 U.S. 208, 60 S.Ct. 201, 84 L.Ed. 196 (1939), Palmer v. Hoffman, 318 U.S. 109, 63 S.Ct. 477, 87 L.Ed. 645 (1943), and Dick v. New York Life Ins. Co., 359 U.S. 437, 79 S.Ct. 921, 3 L.Ed.2d 935 (1959). They involved burden of proof, respectively, as to status as bona fide purchaser, contributory negligence, and nonaccidental death (suicide) of an insured. In each instance the state rule was held to be applicable. It does not follow, however, that all presumptions in diversity cases are governed by state law. In each case cited, the burden of proof question had to do with a substantive element of the claim or defense. Application of the state law is called for only when the presumption operates upon such an element. Accordingly the rule does not apply state law when the presumption operates upon a lesser aspect of the case, i.e. "tactical" presumptions.

The situations in which the state law is applied have been tagged for convenience in the preceding discussion as "diversity cases." The designation is not a completely accurate one since *Erie* applies to any claim or issue having its source in state law, regardless of the basis of federal jurisdiction, and does not apply to a federal claim or issue, even though jurisdiction is based on diversity. Vestal, Erie R. R. v. Tompkins: A Projection, 48 Iowa L.Rev. 248, 257 (1963); Hart and Wechsler, The Federal Courts and the Federal System, 697 (1953); 1A Moore, Federal Practice ¶ 0.305[3] (2d ed. 1965); Wright, Federal Courts, 217–218 (1963). Hence the rule employs, as appropriately descriptive, the phrase "as to which state law supplies the rule of decision." See A.L.I. Study of the Division of Jurisdiction Between State and Federal Courts, § 2344(c), p. 40, P.F.D. No. 1 (1965).

ARTICLE IV. RELEVANCY AND ITS LIMITS

Rule 401

Note by Federal Judicial Center

The rule enacted by the Congress is the rule prescribed by the Supreme Court without change.

Advisory Committee's Note

Problems of relevancy call for an answer to the question whether an item of evidence, when tested by the processes of legal reasoning, possesses sufficient probative value to justify receiving it in evidence. Thus, assessment of the probative value of evidence that a person purchased a revolver shortly prior to a fatal shooting with which he is charged is a matter of analysis and reasoning.

The variety of relevancy problems is coextensive with the ingenuity of counsel in using circumstantial evidence as a means of proof. An enormous number of cases fall in no set pattern, and this rule is designed as a guide for handling them. On the other hand, some situations recur with sufficient frequency to create patterns susceptible of treatment by specific rules. Rule 404 and those following it are of that variety; they also serve as illustrations of the application of the present rule as limited by the exclusionary principles of Rule 403.

Passing mention should be made of so-called "conditional" relevancy. Morgan, Basic Problems of Evidence 45–46 (1962). In this situation, probative value depends not only upon satisfying the basic requirement of relevancy as described above but also upon the existence of some matter of fact. For example, if evidence of a spoken statement is relied upon to prove notice, probative value is lacking unless the person sought to be charged heard the statement. The problem is one of fact, and the only rules needed are for the purpose of determining the respective functions of judge and jury. See Rules 104(b) and 901. The discussion which follows in the present note is concerned with relevancy generally, not with any particular problem of conditional relevancy.

Relevancy is not an inherent characteristic of any item of evidence but exists only as a relation between an item of evidence and a matter properly provable in the case. Does the item of evidence tend to prove the matter sought to be proved? Whether the relationship exists depends upon principles evolved by experience or science, applied logically to the situation at hand. James, Relevancy, Probability and the Law, 29 Calif.L.Rev. 689, 696, n. 15 (1941), in Selected Writings on Evidence and Trial 610, 615, n. 15 (Fryer ed. 1957). The rule summarizes this relationship as a "tendency to make the existence" of the fact to be proved "more probable or less probable." Compare Uniform Rule 1(2) which states the crux of relevancy as "a tendency in reason," thus perhaps emphasizing unduly the logical process and ignoring the need to draw upon experience or science to validate the general principle upon which relevancy in a particular situation depends.

The standard of probability under the rule is "more * * * probable than it would be without the evidence." Any more stringent requirement is unworkable and unrealistic. As McCormick § 152, p. 317, says, "A brick is not a wall," or, as Falknor, Extrinsic Policies Affecting Admissibility, 10 Rutgers L.Rev. 574, 576 (1956), quotes Professor McBaine, "* * * [I]t is not to be supposed that every witness can make a home run." Dealing with probability in the language of the rule has the added virtue of avoiding confusion between questions of admissibility and questions of the sufficiency of the evidence.

The rule uses the phrase "fact that is of consequence to the determination of the action" to describe the kind of fact to which proof may properly be directed. The language is that of California Evidence Code § 210; it has the advantage of avoiding the loosely used and ambiguous word "material." Tentative Recommendation and a Study Relating to the Uniform Rules of Evidence (Art. I. General Provisions), Cal. Law Revision Comm'n, Rep., Rec. & Studies, 10–11 (1964). The fact to be proved may be ultimate, intermediate, or evidentiary; it matters not, so long as it is of consequence in the determination of the action. Cf. Uniform Rule 1(2) which requires that the evidence relate to a "material" fact.

The fact to which the evidence is directed need not be in dispute. While situations will arise which call for the exclusion of evidence offered to prove a point conceded by the opponent, the ruling should be made on the basis of such considerations as waste of time and undue prejudice (see Rule 403), rather than under any general requirement that evidence is admissible only if directed to matters in dispute. Evidence which is essentially background in nature can scarcely be said to involve disputed matter, yet it is universally offered and admitted as an aid to understanding. Charts, photographs, views of real estate, murder weapons, and many other items of evidence fall in this category. A rule limiting admissibility to evidence directed to a controversial point would invite the exclusion of this helpful evidence, or at least the raising of endless questions over its admission. Cf. California Evidence Code § 210, defining relevant evidence in terms of tendency to prove a disputed fact.

Rule 402

Note by Federal Judicial Center

The rule enacted by the Congress is the rule prescribed by the Supreme Court, with the first sentence amended by substituting "prescribed" in place of "adopted", and by adding at the end thereof the phrase "pursuant to statutory authority."

Advisory Committee's Note

The provisions that all relevant evidence is admissible, with certain exceptions, and that evidence which is not relevant is not admissible are "a presupposition involved in the very conception of a rational system of evidence." Thayer, Preliminary Treatise on Evidence 264 (1898). They constitute the foundation upon which the structure of admission and exclusion rests. For similar provisions see California Evidence Code §§ 350, 351. Provisions that all relevant evidence is admissible are found in Uniform Rule 7(f); Kansas Code of Civil Procedure § 60–407(f); and New Jersey Evidence Rule 7(f); but the exclusion of evidence which is not relevant is left to implication.

Not all relevant evidence is admissible. The exclusion of relevant evidence occurs in a variety of situations and may be called for by these rules, by the Rules of Civil and Criminal Procedure, by Bankruptcy Rules, by Act of Congress, or by constitutional considerations.

Succeeding rules in the present article, in response to the demands of particular policies, require the exclusion of evidence despite its relevancy. In addition, Article V recognizes a number of privileges; Article VI imposes limitations upon witnesses and the manner of dealing with them; Article

VII specifies requirements with respect to opinions and expert testimony; Article VIII excludes hearsay not falling within an exception; Article IX spells out the handling of authentication and identification; and Article X restricts the manner of proving the contents of writings and recordings.

The Rules of Civil and Criminal Procedure in some instances require the exclusion of relevant evidence. For example, Rules 30(b) and 32(a)(3) of the Rules of Civil Procedure, by imposing requirements of notice and unavailability of the deponent, place limits on the use of relevant depositions. Similarly, Rule 15 of the Rules of Criminal Procedure restricts the use of depositions in criminal cases, even though relevant. And the effective enforcement of the command, originally statutory and now found in Rule 5(a) of the Rules of Criminal Procedure, that an arrested person be taken without unnecessary delay before a commissioner or other similar officer is held to require the exclusion of statements elicited during detention in violation thereof. Mallory v. United States, 354 U.S. 449, 77 S.Ct. 1356, 1 L.Ed.2d 1479 (1957); 18 U.S.C. § 3501(c).

While congressional enactments in the field of evidence have generally tended to expand admissibility beyond the scope of the common law rules, in some particular situations they have restricted the admissibility of relevant evidence. Most of this legislation has consisted of the formulation of a privilege or of a prohibition against disclosure. 8 U.S.C. § 1202(f), records of refusal of visas or permits to enter United States confidential, subject to discretion of Secretary of State to make available to court upon certification of need;   10 U.S.C. § 3693, replacement certificate of honorable discharge from Army not admissible in evidence; 10 U.S.C. § 8693, same as to Air Force;   11 U.S.C. § 25(a)(10), testimony given by bankrupt on his examination not admissible in criminal proceedings against him, except that given in hearing upon objection to discharge;   11 U.S.C. § 205(a), railroad reorganization petition, if dismissed, not admissible in evidence;   11 U.S.C. § 403(a), list of creditors filed with municipal composition plan not an admission;   13 U.S.C. § 9(a), census information confidential, retained copies of reports privileged;   47 U.S.C. § 605, interception and divulgence of wire or radio communications prohibited unless authorized by sender. These statutory provisions would remain undisturbed by the rules.

The rule recognizes but makes no attempt to spell out the constitutional considerations which impose basic limitations upon the admissibility of relevant evidence. Examples are evidence obtained by unlawful search and seizure, Weeks v. United States, 232 U.S. 383, 34 S.Ct. 341, 58 L.Ed. 652 (1914); Katz v. United States, 389 U.S. 347, 88 S.Ct. 507, 19 L.Ed.2d 576 (1967); incriminating statement elicited from an accused in violation of right to counsel, Massiah v. United States, 377 U.S. 201, 84 S.Ct. 1199, 12 L.Ed.2d 246 (1964).

Report of House Committee on the Judiciary

Rule 402 as submitted to the Congress contained the phrase "or by other rules adopted by the Supreme Court". To accommodate the view that the Congress should not appear to acquiesce in the Court's judgment that it has authority under the existing Rules Enabling Acts to promulgate Rules of Evidence, the Committee amended the above phrase to read "or by other rules prescribed by the Supreme Court pursuant to statutory authority" in this and other Rules where the reference appears.

Rule 403

Note by Federal Judicial Center

The rule enacted by the Congress is the rule prescribed by the Supreme Court without change.

Advisory Committee's Note

The case law recognizes that certain circumstances call for the exclusion of evidence which is of unquestioned relevance. These circumstances entail risks which range all the way from inducing decision on a purely emotional basis, at one extreme, to nothing more harmful than merely wasting time, at the other extreme. Situations in this area call for balancing the probative value of and need for the evidence against the harm likely to result from its admission. Slough, Relevancy Unraveled, 5 Kan.L.Rev. 1, 12–15 (1956); Trautman, Logical or Legal Relevancy—A Conflict in Theory, 5 Van.L.Rev. 385, 392 (1952); McCormick § 152, pp. 319–321. The rules which follow in this Article are concrete applications evolved for particular situations. However, they reflect the policies underlying the present rule, which is designed as a guide for the handling of situations for which no specific rules have been formulated.

Exclusion for risk of unfair prejudice, confusion of issues, misleading the jury, or waste of time, all find ample support in the authorities. "Unfair prejudice" within its context means an undue tendency to suggest decision on an improper basis, commonly, though not necessarily, an emotional one.

The rule does not enumerate surprise as a ground for exclusion, in this respect following Wigmore's view of the common law. 6 Wigmore § 1849. Cf. McCormick § 152, p. 320, n. 29, listing unfair surprise as a ground for exclusion but stating that it is usually "coupled with the danger of prejudice and confusion of issues." While Uniform Rule 45 incorporates surprise as a ground and is followed in Kansas Code of Civil Procedure § 60–445, surprise is not included in California Evidence Code § 352 or New Jersey Rule 4, though both the latter otherwise substantially embody Uniform Rule 45. While it can scarcely be doubted that claims of unfair surprise may still be justified despite procedural requirements of notice and instrumentalities of discovery, the granting of a continuance is a more appropriate remedy than exclusion of the evidence. Tentative Recommendation and a Study Relating to the Uniform Rules of Evidence (Art. VI. Extrinsic Policies Affecting Admissibility), Cal. Law Revision Comm'n, Rep., Rec. & Studies, 612 (1964). Moreover, the impact of a rule excluding evidence on the ground of surprise would be difficult to estimate.

In reaching a decision whether to exclude on grounds of unfair prejudice, consideration should be given to the probable effectiveness or lack of effectiveness of a limiting instruction. See Rule 106[105] and Advisory Committee's Note thereunder. The availability of other means of proof may also be an appropriate factor.

Rule 404

[**Editorial Note:** As a result of the 2011 restyling, the designation of subdivsions of Rule 404(a) has changed. The substance of the introductory portion of the original Rule 404(a) is now contained in subdivision (a)(1); the substance of the first portion of subdivision (a)(1) as it stood before the restyling is now contained in subdivision (a)(2)(A); the substance of the latter portion of subdivision (a)(1) and of the first portion of subdivision (a)(2) as they stood before the restyling are now contained in subdivision (a)(2)(B); and the substance of the latter portion of subdivision (a)(2) as it stood before the restyling is now contained in subdivision (a)(2)(C).]

Note by Federal Judicial Center

The rule enacted by the Congress is the rule prescribed by the Supreme Court, with the second sentence of subdivision (b) amended by substituting "It may, however, be admissible" in place of "This subdivision does not exclude the evidence when offered."

Advisory Committee's Note

Subdivision (a). This subdivision deals with the basic question whether character evidence should be admitted. Once the admissibility of character evidence in some form is established under this rule, reference must then be made to Rule 405, which follows, in order to determine the appropriate method of proof. If the character is that of a witness, see Rules 608 and 609 for methods of proof.

Character questions arise in two fundamentally different ways. (1) Character may itself be an element of a crime, claim, or defense. A situation of this kind is commonly referred to as "character in issue." Illustrations are: the chastity of the victim under a statute specifying her chastity as an element of the crime of seduction, or the competency of the driver in an action for negligently entrusting a motor vehicle to an incompetent driver. No problem of the general relevancy of character evidence is involved, and the present rule therefore has no provision on the subject. The only question relates to allowable methods of proof, as to which see Rule 405, immediately following. (2) Character evidence is susceptible of being used for the purpose of suggesting an inference that the person acted on the occasion in question consistently with his character. This use of character is often described as "circumstantial." Illustrations are: evidence of a violent disposition to prove that the person was the aggressor in an affray, or evidence of honesty in disproof of a charge of theft. This circumstantial use of character evidence raises questions of relevancy as well as questions of allowable methods of proof.

In most jurisdictions today, the circumstantial use of character is rejected but with important exceptions: (1) an accused may introduce pertinent evidence of good character (often misleadingly described as "putting his character in issue"), in which event the prosecution may rebut with evidence of bad character; (2) an accused may introduce pertinent evidence of the character of the victim, as in support of a claim of self-defense to a charge of homicide or consent in a case of rape, and the prosecution may introduce similar evidence in rebuttal of the character evidence, or, in a homicide case, to rebut a claim that deceased was the first aggressor, however proved; and (3) the character of a witness may be gone into as bearing on his credibility. McCormick §§ 155–161. This pattern is incorporated in the rule. While its basis lies more in history and experience than in logic an underlying justification can fairly be found in terms of the relative presence and absence of prejudice in the various situations. Falknor, Extrinsic Policies Affecting Admissibility, 10 Rutgers L.Rev. 574, 584 (1956); McCormick § 157. In any event, the criminal rule is so deeply imbedded in our jurisprudence as to assume almost constitutional proportions and to override doubts of the basic relevancy of the evidence.

The limitation to pertinent traits of character, rather than character generally, in paragraphs (1) and (2) is in accordance with the prevailing view. McCormick § 158, p. 334. A similar provision in Rule 608, to which reference is made in paragraph (3), limits character evidence respecting witnesses to the trait of truthfulness or untruthfulness.

The argument is made that circumstantial use of character ought to be allowed in civil cases to the same extent as in criminal cases, i.e. evidence of good (nonprejudicial) character would be admissible in the first instance, subject to rebuttal by evidence of bad character. Falknor, Extrinsic Policies Affecting Admissibility, 10 Rutgers L.Rev. 574, 581–583 (1956); Tentative Recommendation and a Study Relating to the Uniform Rules of Evidence (Art. VI. Extrinsic Policies Affecting Admissibility), Cal. Law Revision Comm'n, Rep., Rec. & Studies, 657–658 (1964). Uniform Rule 47 goes farther, in that it assumes that character evidence in general satisfies the conditions of relevancy, except as provided in Uniform Rule 48. The difficulty with expanding the use of character evidence in civil cases is set forth by the California Law Revision Commission in its ultimate rejection of Uniform Rule 47, id., 615:

> "Character evidence is of slight probative value and may be very prejudicial. It tends to distract the trier of fact from the main question of what actually happened on the particular occasion. It subtly permits the trier of fact to reward the good man and to punish the bad man because of their respective characters despite what the evidence in the case shows actually happened."

Much of the force of the position of those favoring greater use of character evidence in civil cases is dissipated by their support of Uniform Rule 48 which excludes the evidence in negligence cases, where it could be expected to achieve its maximum usefulness. Moreover, expanding concepts of "character," which seem of necessity to extend into such areas as psychiatric evaluation and psychological testing, coupled with expanded admissibility, would open up such vistas of mental examinations as caused the Court concern in Schlagenhauf v. Holder, 379 U.S. 104, 85 S.Ct. 234, 13 L.Ed.2d 152 (1964). It is believed that those espousing change have not met the burden of persuasion.

Subdivision (b) deals with a specialized but important application of the general rule excluding circumstantial use of character evidence. Consistently with that rule, evidence of other crimes, wrongs, or acts is not admissible to prove character as a basis for suggesting the inference that conduct on a particular occasion was in conformity with it. However, the evidence may be offered for another purpose, such as proof of motive, opportunity, and so on, which does not fall within the prohibition. In this situation the rule does not require that the evidence be excluded. No mechanical solution is offered. The determination must be made whether the danger of undue prejudice outweighs the probative value of the evidence in view of the availability of other means of proof and other factors appropriate for making decisions of this kind under Rule 403. Slough and Knightly, Other Vices, Other Crimes, 41 Iowa L.Rev. 325 (1956).

Report of House Committee on the Judiciary

The second sentence of Rule 404(b) as submitted to the Congress began with the words "This subdivision does not exclude the evidence when offered". The Committee amended this language to read "It may, however, be admissible", the words used in the 1971 Advisory Committee draft, on the ground that this formulation properly placed greater emphasis on admissibility than did the final Court version.

Report of Senate Committee on the Judiciary

This rule provides that evidence of other crimes, wrongs, or acts is not admissible to prove character but may be admissible for other specified purposes such as proof of motive.

Although your committee sees no necessity in amending the rule itself, it anticipates that the use of the discretionary word "may" with respect to the admissibility of evidence of crimes, wrongs, or acts is not intended to confer any arbitrary discretion on the trial judge. Rather, it is anticipated that with respect to permissible uses for such evidence, the trial judge may exclude it only on the basis of those considerations set forth in Rule 403, i.e. prejudice, confusion or waste of time.

Advisory Committee's Note to 1991 Amendment

Rule 404(b) has emerged as one of the most cited Rules in the Rules of Evidence. And in many criminal cases evidence of an accused's extrinsic acts is viewed as an important asset in the prosecution's case against an accused. Although there are a few reported decisions on use of such evidence by the defense, see, e.g., United States v. McClure, 546 F.2d 670 (5th Cir.1977) (acts of informant offered in entrapment defense), the overwhelming number of cases involve introduction of that evidence by the prosecution.

The amendment to Rule 404(b) adds a pretrial notice requirement in criminal cases and is intended to reduce surprise and promote early resolution on the issue of admissibility. The notice requirement thus places Rule 404(b) in the mainstream with notice and disclosure provisions in other rules of evidence. See, e.g., Rule 412 (written motion of intent to offer evidence under rule), Rule 609 (written notice of intent to offer conviction older than 10 years), Rule 803(24) and 804(b)(5) (notice of intent to use residual hearsay exceptions).

The Rule expects that counsel for both the defense and the prosecution will submit the necessary request and information in a reasonable and timely fashion. Other than requiring pretrial notice, no specific time limits are stated in recognition that what constitutes a reasonable request or disclosure will depend largely on the circumstances of each case. Compare Fla.Stat.Ann. § 90.404(2)(b) (notice must be given at least 10 days before trial) *with* Tex.R.Evid. 404(b) (no time limit).

Likewise, no specific form of notice is required. The Committee considered and rejected a requirement that the notice satisfy the particularity requirements normally required of language used in a charging instrument. Cf. Fla.Stat.Ann. § 90.404(2)(b) (written disclosure must describe uncharged misconduct with particularity required of an indictment or information). Instead, the Committee opted for a generalized notice provision which requires the prosecution to apprise the defense of the general nature of the evidence of extrinsic acts. The Committee does not intend that the amendment will supercede other rules of admissibility or disclosure, such as the Jencks Act, 18 U.S.C. § 3500, et. seq. nor require the prosecution to disclose directly or indirectly the names and addresses of its witnesses, something it is currently not required to do under Federal Rule of Criminal Procedure 16.

The amendment requires the prosecution to provide notice, regardless of how it intends to use the extrinsic act evidence at trial, i.e., during its case-in-chief, for impeachment, or for possible rebuttal. The court in its discretion may, under the facts, decide that the particular request or notice was not reasonable, either because of the lack of timeliness or completeness. Because the notice requirement serves as condition precedent to admissibility of 404(b) evidence, the offered evidence is inadmissible if the court decides that the notice requirement has not been met.

Nothing in the amendment precludes the court from requiring the government to provide it with an opportunity to rule *in limine* on 404(b) evidence before it is offered or even mentioned during trial. When ruling *in limine,* the court may require the government to disclose to it the specifics of such evidence which the court must consider in determining admissibility.

The amendment does not extend to evidence of acts which are "intrinsic" to the charged offense, see United States v. Williams, 900 F.2d 823 (5th Cir.1990) (noting distinction between 404(b) evidence and intrinsic offense evidence). Nor is the amendment intended to redefine what evidence would otherwise be admissible under Rule 404(b). Finally, the Committee does not intend through the amendment to affect the role of the court and the jury in considering such evidence. See Huddleston v. United States, 485 U.S. 681, (1988).

Advisory Committee's Note to 2000 Amendment to Rule 404(a)

Rule 404(a)(1) has been amended to provide that when the accused attacks the character of an alleged victim under subdivision (a)(2) of this Rule, the door is opened to an attack on the same character trait of the accused. Current law does not allow the government to introduce negative character evidence as to the accused unless the accused introduces evidence of good character. *See, e.g., United States v. Fountain,* 768 F.2d 790 (7th Cir. 1985) (when the accused offers proof of self-defense, this permits proof of the alleged victim's character trait for peacefulness, but it does not permit proof of the accused's character trait for violence).

The amendment makes clear that the accused cannot attack the alleged victim's character and yet remain shielded from the disclosure of equally relevant evidence concerning the same character trait of the accused. For example, in a murder case with a claim of self-defense, the accused, to bolster this defense, might offer evidence of the alleged victim's violent disposition. If the government has evidence that the accused has a violent character, but is not allowed to offer this evidence as part of its rebuttal, the jury has only part of the information it needs for an informed assessment of the probabilities as to who was the initial aggressor. This may be the case even if evidence of the accused's prior violent acts is admitted under Rule 404(b), because such evidence can be admitted only for limited purposes and not to show action in conformity with the accused's character on a specific occasion. Thus, the amendment is designed to permit a more balanced presentation of character evidence when an accused chooses to attack the character of the alleged victim.

The amendment does not affect the admissibility of evidence of specific acts of uncharged misconduct offered for a purpose other than proving character under Rule 404(b). Nor does it affect the standards for proof of character by evidence of other sexual behavior or sexual offenses under Rules

412–415. By its placement in Rule 404(a)(1), the amendment covers only proof of character by way of reputation or opinion.

The amendment does not permit proof of the accused's character if the accused merely uses character evidence for a purpose other than to prove the alleged victim's propensity to act in a certain way. *See United States v. Burks*, 470 F.2d 432, 434–5 (D.C. Cir. 1972) (evidence of the alleged victim's violent character, when known by the accused, was admissible "on the issue of whether or not the defendant reasonably feared he was in danger of imminent great bodily harm"). Finally, the amendment does not permit proof of the accused's character when the accused attacks the alleged victim's character as a witness under Rule 608 or 609.

The term "alleged" is inserted before each reference to "victim" in the Rule, in order to provide consistency with Evidence Rule 412.

Advisory Committee's Note to 2006 Amendment to Rule 404(a)

The Rule has been amended to clarify that in a civil case evidence of a person's character is never admissible to prove that the person acted in conformity with the character trait. The amendment resolves the dispute in the case law over whether the exceptions in subdivisions (a)(1) and (2) permit the circumstantial use of character evidence in civil cases. *Compare Carson v. Polley*, 689 F.2d 562, 576 (5th Cir. 1982) ("when a central issue in a case is close to one of a criminal nature, the exceptions to the Rule 404(a) ban on character evidence may be invoked"), *with SEC v. Towers Financial Corp.*, 966 F.Supp. 203 (S.D.N.Y. 1997) (relying on the terms "accused" and "prosecution" in Rule 404(a) to conclude that the exceptions in subdivisions (a)(1) and (2) are inapplicable in civil cases). The amendment is consistent with the original intent of the Rule, which was to prohibit the circumstantial use of character evidence in civil cases, even where closely related to criminal charges. *See Ginter v. Northwestern Mut. Life Ins. Co.*, 576 F.Supp. 627, 629–30 (D. Ky. 1984) ("It seems beyond peradventure of doubt that the drafters of F.R.Evi. 404(a) explicitly intended that all character evidence, except where 'character is at issue' was to be excluded" in civil cases).

The circumstantial use of character evidence is generally discouraged because it carries serious risk of prejudice, confusion and delay. *See Michelson v. United States*, 335 U.S. 469, 476 (1948) ("The overriding policy of excluding such evidence, despite its admitted probative value, is the practical experience that its disallowance tends to prevent confusion of issues, unfair surprise and undue prejudice."). In criminal cases, the so-called "mercy rule" permits a criminal defendant to introduce evidence of pertinent character traits of the defendant and the victim. But that is because the accused, whose liberty is at stake, may need "a counterweight against the strong investigative and prosecutorial resources of the government." C. Mueller & L. Kirkpatrick, *Evidence: Practice Under the Rules*, pp. 264–5 (2d ed. 1999). See also Richard Uviller, *Evidence of Character to Prove*

Conduct: Illusion, Illogic, and Injustice in the Courtroom, 130 U.Pa.L.Rev. 845, 855 (1982) (the rule prohibiting circumstantial use of character evidence "was relaxed to allow the criminal defendant with so much at stake and so little available in the way of conventional proof to have special dispensation to tell the factfinder just what sort of person he really is"). Those concerns do not apply to parties in civil cases.

The amendment also clarifies that evidence otherwise admissible under Rule 404(a)(2) may nonetheless be excluded in a criminal case involving sexual misconduct. In such a case, the admissibility of evidence of the victim's sexual behavior and predisposition is governed by the more stringent provisions of Rule 412.

Nothing in the amendment is intended to affect the scope of Rule 404(b). While Rule 404(b) refers to the "accused," the "prosecution," and a "criminal case," it does so only in the context of a notice requirement. The admissibility standards of Rule 404(b) remain fully applicable to both civil and criminal cases.

Rule 405

Note by Federal Judicial Center

The rule enacted by the Congress is the rule prescribed by the Supreme Court without change. The bill reported by the House Committee on the Judiciary deleted the provision in subdivision (a) for making proof by testimony in the form of an opinion, but the provision was reinstated on the floor of the House. See Congressional Record, February 6, 1974 (daily ed. pp. H546–H549).

Advisory Committee's Note

The rule deals only with allowable methods of proving character, not with the admissibility of character evidence, which is covered in Rule 404.

Of the three methods of proving character provided by the rule, evidence of specific instances of conduct is the most convincing. At the same time it possesses the greatest capacity to arouse prejudice, to confuse, to surprise, and to consume time. Consequently the rule confines the use of evidence of this kind to cases in which character is, in the strict sense, in issue and hence deserving of a searching inquiry. When character is used circumstantially and hence occupies a lesser status in the case, proof may be only by reputation and opinion. These latter methods are also available when character is in issue. This treatment is, with respect to specific instances of conduct and reputation, conventional contemporary common law doctrine. McCormick § 153.

In recognizing opinion as a means of proving character, the rule departs from usual contemporary practice in favor of that of an earlier day. See 7 Wigmore § 1986, pointing out that the earlier practice permitted opinion and arguing strongly for evidence based on personal knowledge and belief as contrasted with "the secondhand, irresponsible product of multiplied guesses and gossip which we term 'reputation'." It seems likely that the persistence of reputation evidence is due to its largely being opinion in disguise. Traditionally character has been regarded primarily in moral overtones of good and bad: chaste, peaceable, truthful, honest. Nevertheless, on occasion nonmoral considerations crop up, as in the case of the incompetent driver, and this seems bound to happen increasingly. If character is defined as the kind of person one is, then account must be taken of varying ways of arriving at the estimate. These may range from the opinion of the employer who has found the man honest to the opinion of the psychiatrist based upon examination and testing. No effective dividing line exists between character and mental capacity, and the latter traditionally has been provable by opinion.

According to the great majority of cases, on cross-examination inquiry is allowable as to whether the reputation witness has heard of particular instances of conduct pertinent to the trait in question. Michelson v. United States, 335 U.S. 469, 69 S.Ct. 213, 93 L.Ed. 168 (1948); Annot., 47 A.L.R.2d 1258. The theory is that, since the reputation witness relates what he has heard, the inquiry tends to shed light on the accuracy of his hearing and reporting. Accordingly, the opinion witness would be asked whether he knew, as well as whether he had heard. The fact, is, of course, that these distinctions are of slight if any practical significance, and the second sentence of subdivision (a) eliminates them as a factor in formulating questions. This recognition of the propriety of inquiring into specific instances of conduct does not circumscribe inquiry otherwise into the bases of opinion and reputation testimony.

The express allowance of inquiry into specific instances of conduct on cross-examination in subdivision (a) and the express allowance of it as part of a case in chief when character is actually in issue in subdivision (b) contemplate that testimony of specific instances is not generally permissible on the direct examination of an ordinary opinion witness to character. Similarly as to witnesses to the character of witnesses under Rule 608(b). Opinion testimony on direct in these situations ought in general to correspond to reputation testimony as now given, i.e., be confined to the nature and extent of observation and acquaintance upon which the opinion is based. See Rule 701.

Rule 406

Note by Federal Judicial Center

The rule enacted by the Congress is subdivision (a) of the rule prescribed by the Supreme Court. Subdivision (b) of the Court's rule was deleted for reasons stated in the Report of the House Committee on the Judiciary set forth below. The subdivision is included in the Appendix.

Advisory Committee's Note

Subdivision (a). An oft-quoted paragraph, McCormick, § 162, p. 340, describes habit in terms effectively contrasting it with character:

> "Character and habit are close akin. Character is a generalized description of one's disposition, or of one's disposition in respect to a general trait, such as honesty, temperance, or peacefulness. 'Habit,' in modern usage, both lay and psychological, is more specific. It describes one's regular response to a repeated specific situation. If we speak of character for care, we think of the person's tendency to act prudently in all the varying situations of life, in business, family life, in handling automobiles and in walking across the street. A habit, on the other hand, is the person's regular practice of meeting a particular kind of situation with a specific type of conduct, such as the habit of going down a particular stairway two stairs at a time, or of giving the hand-signal for a left turn, or of alighting from railway cars while they are moving. The doing of the habitual acts may become semi-automatic."

Equivalent behavior on the part of a group is designated "routine practice of an organization" in the rule.

Agreement is general that habit evidence is highly persuasive as proof of conduct on a particular occasion. Again quoting McCormick § 162, p. 341:

> "Character may be thought of as the sum of one's habits though doubtless it is more than this. But unquestionably the uniformity of one's response to habit is far greater than the consistency with which one's conduct conforms to character or disposition. Even though character comes in only exceptionally as evidence of an act, surely any sensible man in investigating whether X did a particular act would be greatly helped in his inquiry by evidence as to whether he was in the habit of doing it."

When disagreement has appeared, its focus has been upon the question what constitutes habit, and the reason for this is readily apparent. The extent to which instances must be multiplied and consistency of behavior maintained in order to rise to the status of habit inevitably gives rise to differences of opinion. Lewan, Rationale of Habit Evidence, 16 Syracuse L.Rev. 39, 49 (1964). While adequacy of sampling and uniformity of response are key factors, precise standards for measuring their sufficiency for evidence purposes cannot be formulated.

The rule is consistent with prevailing views. Much evidence is excluded simply because of failure to achieve the status of habit. Thus, evidence of intemperate "habits" is generally excluded when offered as proof of drunkenness in accident cases, Annot., 46 A.L.R.2d 103, and evidence of other assaults is inadmissible to prove the instant one in a civil assault action, Annot., 66 A.L.R.2d 806. In Levin v. United States, 119 U.S.App.D.C. 156, 338 F.2d 265 (1964), testimony as to the religious "habits" of the accused, offered as tending to prove that he was at home observing the Sabbath rather than out obtaining money through larceny by trick, was held properly excluded:

> "It seems apparent to us that an individual's religious practices would not be the type of activities which would lend themselves to the characterization of 'invariable regularity.' [1 Wigmore 520.] Certainly the very volitional basis of the activity raises serious questions as to its invariable nature, and hence its probative value." Id. at 272.

These rulings are not inconsistent with the trend towards admitting evidence of business transactions between one of the parties and a third person as tending to prove that he made the same bargain or proposal in the litigated situation. Slough, Relevancy Unraveled, 6 Kan.L.Rev. 38–41 (1957). Nor are they inconsistent with such cases a Whittemore v. Lockheed Aircraft Corp., 65 Cal.App.2d 737, 151 P.2d 670 (1944), upholding the admission of evidence that plaintiff's intestate had on four other occasions flown planes from defendant's factory for delivery to his employer airline, offered to prove that he was piloting rather than a guest on a plane which crashed and killed all on board while en route for delivery.

A considerable body of authority has required that evidence of the routine practice of an organization be corroborated as a condition precedent to its admission in evidence. Slough, Relevancy Unraveled, 5 Kan.L.Rev. 404, 449 (1957). This requirement is specifically rejected by the rule on the ground that it relates to the sufficiency of the evidence rather than admissibility. A similar position is taken in New Jersey Rule 49. The rule also rejects the requirement of the absence of eyewitnesses, sometimes encountered with respect to admitting habit evidence to prove freedom from contributory negligence in wrongful death cases. For comment critical of the requirements see Frank J., in Cereste v. New York, N. H. & H. R. Co., 231 F.2d 50 (2d Cir.1956), cert. denied 351 U.S. 951, 76 S.Ct. 848, 100 L.Ed. 1475, 10 Vand.L.Rev. 447 (1957); McCormick § 162, p. 342. The omission of the requirement from the California Evidence Code is said to have effected its elimination. Comment, Cal.Ev.Code § 1105.

Report of House Committee on the Judiciary

Rule 406 as submitted to Congress contained a subdivision (b) providing that the method of proof of habit or routine practice could be "in the form of an opinion or by specific instances of conduct sufficient in number to warrant a finding that the habit existed or that the practice was routine." The Committee deleted this subdivision believing that the method of proof of habit and routine practice should be left to the courts to deal with on a case-by-case basis. At the same time, the Committee does not intend that its action be construed as sanctioning a general authorization of opinion evidence in this area.

Rule 407

Note by Federal Judicial Center

The rule enacted by the Congress is the rule prescribed by the Supreme Court without change.

Original Advisory Committee's Note

The rule incorporates conventional doctrine which excludes evidence of subsequent remedial measures as proof of an admission of fault. The rule rests on two grounds. (1) The conduct is not in fact an admission, since the conduct is equally consistent with injury by mere accident or through contributory negligence. Or, as Baron Bramwell put it, the rule rejects the notion that "because the world gets wiser as it gets older, therefore it was foolish before." Hart v. Lancashire & Yorkshire Ry. Co., 21 L.T.R. N.S. 261, 263 (1869). Under a liberal theory of relevancy this ground alone would not support exclusion as the inference is still a possible one. (2) The other, and more impressive, ground for exclusion rests on a social policy of encouraging people to take, or at least not discouraging them from taking, steps in furtherance of added safety. The courts have applied this principle to exclude evidence of subsequent repairs, installation of safety devices, changes in company rules, and discharge of employees, and the language of the present rule is broad enough to encompass all of them. See Falknor, Extrinsic Policies Affecting Admissibility, 10 Rutgers L.Rev. 574, 590 (1956).

The second sentence of the rule directs attention to the limitations of the rule. Exclusion is called for only when the evidence of subsequent remedial measures is offered as proof of negligence or culpable conduct. In effect it rejects the suggested inference that fault is admitted. Other purposes are, however, allowable, including ownership or control, existence of duty, and feasibility of precautionary measures, if controverted, and impeachment. 2 Wigmore § 283; Annot., 64 A.L.R.2d 1296. Two recent federal cases are illustrative. Boeing Airplane Co. v. Brown, 291 F.2d 310 (9th Cir.1961), an action against an airplane manufacturer for using an allegedly defectively designed alternator shaft which caused a plane crash, upheld the admission of evidence of subsequent design modification for the purpose of showing that design changes and safeguards were feasible. And Powers v. J. B. Michael & Co., 329 F.2d 674 (6th Cir.1964), an action against a road contractor for negligent failure to put out warning signs, sustained the admission of evidence that defendant subsequently put out signs to show that the portion of the road in question was under defendant's control. The requirement that the other purpose be controverted calls for a automatic exclusion unless a genuine issue be present and allows the opposing party to lay the groundwork for exclusion by making an admission. Otherwise the factors of undue prejudice, confusion of issues, misleading the jury, and waste of time remain for consideration under Rule 403.

For comparable rules, see Uniform Rule 51; California Evidence Code § 1151; Kansas Code of Civil Procedure § 60–451; New Jersey Evidence Rule 51.

Advisory Committee's Note to 1997 Amendment

The amendment to Rule 407 makes two changes in the rule. First, the words "an injury or harm allegedly caused by" were added to clarify that the rule applies only to changes made after the occurrence that produced the damages giving rise to the action. Evidence of measures taken by the defendant prior to the "event" causing "injury or harm" do not fall within the exclusionary scope of Rule 407 even if they occurred after the manufacture or design of the product. See *Chase v. General Motors Corp.*, 856 F.2d 17, 21–22 (4th Cir.1988).

Second, Rule 407 has been amended to provide that evidence of subsequent remedial measures may not be used to prove "a defect in a product, a defect in a product's design, or a need for a warning or instruction." This amendment adopts the view of a majority of the circuits that have interpreted Rule 407 to apply to products liability actions. See *Raymond v. Raymond Corp.*, 938 F.2d 1518, 1522 (1st Cir. 1991); *In re Joint Eastern District and Southern District Asbestos Litigation v. Armstrong World Industries. Inc.*, 995 F.2d 343, 345 (2d Cir.1993); *Cann v. Ford Motor Co.*, 658 F.2d 54, 60 (2d Cir.1981), cert. denied, 456 U.S. 960 (1982); *Kelly v. Crown Equipment Co.*, 970 F.2d 1273, 1275 (3d Cir.1992); *Werner v. Upjohn Co., Inc.*, 628 F.2d 848, 856 (4th Cir. 1980), *cert. denied*, 449 U.S. 1080 (1981); *Grenada Steel Industries, Inc. v. Alabama Oxygen Co., Inc.*, 695 F.2d 883, 887 (5th Cir.1983); *Bauman v. Volkswagenwerk Aktiengesellschaft*, 621 F.2d 230, 232 (6th Cir.1980); *Flaminio v. Honda Motor Company. Ltd.*, 733 F.2d 463, 469 (7th Cir.1984); *Gauthier v. AMF, Inc.*, 788 F.2d 634, 636–37 (9th Cir.1986).

Although this amendment adopts a uniform federal rule, it should be noted that evidence of subsequent remedial measures may be admissible pursuant to the second sentence of Rule 407. Evidence of subsequent measures that is not barred by Rule 407 may still be subject to exclusion on Rule 403 grounds when the dangers of prejudice or confusion substantially outweigh the probative value of the evidence.

Advisory Committee's Note to 2011 Amendment

* * * Rule 407 previously provided that evidence was not excluded if offered for a purpose not explicitly prohibited by the Rule. To improve the language of the Rule, it now provides that the court may admit evidence if offered for a permissible purpose. There is no intent to change the process for admitting evidence covered by the Rule. It remains the case that if offered for an impermissible purpose, it must be excluded, and if offered for a purpose not barred by the Rule, its admissibility remains governed by the general principles of Rules 402, 403, 801, etc.

Rule 408

Note by Federal Judicial Center

The rule enacted by the Congress is the rule prescribed by the Supreme Court, amended by the insertion of the third sentence. Other amendments, proposed by the House bill, were not enacted, for reasons stated in the Report of the Senate Committee on the Judiciary and in the Conference Report, set forth below.

Advisory Committee's Note

As a matter of general agreement, evidence of an offer to compromise a claim is not receivable in evidence as an admission of, as the case may be, the validity or invalidity of the claim. As with evidence of subsequent remedial measures, dealt with in Rule 407, exclusion may be based on two grounds. (1) The evidence is irrelevant, since the offer may be motivated by a desire for peace rather than from any concession of weakness of position. The validity of this position will vary as the amount of the offer varies in relation to the size of the claim and may also be influenced by other circumstances. (2) A more consistently impressive ground is promotion of the public policy favoring the compromise and settlement of disputes. McCormick §§ 76, 251. While the rule is ordinarily phrased in terms of offers of compromise, it is apparent that a similar attitude must be taken with respect to completed compromises when offered against a party thereto. This latter situation will not, of course, ordinarily occur except when a party to the present litigation has compromised with a third person.

The same policy underlies the provision of Rule 68 of the Federal Rules of Civil Procedure that evidence of an unaccepted offer of judgment is not admissible except in a proceeding to determine costs.

The practical value of the common law rule has been greatly diminished by its inapplicability to admissions of fact, even though made in the course of compromise negotiations, unless hypothetical, stated to be "without prejudice," or so connected with the offer as to be inseparable from it. McCormick § 251, pp. 540–541. An inevitable effect is to inhibit freedom of communication with respect to compromise, even among lawyers. Another effect is the generation of controversy over whether a given statement falls within or without the protected area. These considerations account for the expansion of the rule herewith to include evidence of conduct or statements made in compromise negotiations, as well as the offer or completed compromise itself. For similar provisions see California Evidence Code §§ 1152, 1154.

The policy considerations which underlie the rule do not come into play when the effort is to induce a creditor to settle an admittedly due amount for a lesser sum. McCormick § 251, p. 540. Hence the rule requires that the claim be disputed as to either validity or amount.

The final sentence of the rule serves to point out some limitations upon its applicability. Since the rule excludes only when the purpose is proving the validity or invalidity of the claim or its amount, an offer for another purpose is not within the rule. The illustrative situations mentioned in the rule are supported by the authorities. As to proving bias or prejudice of a witness, see Annot., 161 A.L.R. 395, contra, Fenberg v. Rosenthal, 348 Ill.App. 510, 109 N.E.2d 402 (1952), and negativing a contention of lack of due diligence in presenting a claim, 4 Wigmore § 1061. An effort to "buy off" the prosecution or a prosecuting witness in a criminal case is not within the policy of the rule of exclusion. McCormick § 251, p. 542.

For other rules of similar import, see Uniform Rules 52 and 53; California Evidence Code §§ 1152, 1154; Kansas Code of Civil Procedure §§ 60–452, 60–453; New Jersey Evidence Rules 52 and 53.

Report of House Committee on the Judiciary

Under existing federal law evidence of conduct and statements made in compromise negotiations is admissible in subsequent litigation between the parties. The second sentence of Rule 408 as submitted by the Supreme Court proposed to reverse that doctrine in the interest of further promoting non-judicial settlement of disputes. Some agencies of government expressed the view that the Court formulation was likely to impede rather than assist efforts to achieve settlement of disputes. For one thing, it is not always easy to tell when compromise negotiations begin, and informal dealings end. Also, parties dealing with government agencies would be reluctant to furnish factual information at preliminary meetings; they would wait until "compromise negotiations" began and thus hopefully effect an immunity for themselves with respect to the evidence supplied. In light of these considerations the Committee recast the Rule so that admissions of liability or opinions given during compromise negotiations continue inadmissible, but evidence of unqualified factual assertions is admissible. The latter aspect of the Rule is drafted, however, so as to preserve other possible objections to the introduction of such evidence. The Committee intends no modification of current law whereby a party may protect himself from future use of his statements by couching them in hypothetical conditional form.

Report of Senate Committee on the Judiciary

This rule as reported makes evidence of settlement or attempted settlement of a disputed claim inadmissible when offered as an admission of liability or the amount of liability. The purpose of this rule is to encourage settlements which would be discouraged if such evidence were admissible.

Under present law, in most jurisdictions, statements of fact made during settlement negotiations, however, are excepted from this ban and are admissible. The only escape from admissibility of statements of fact made in a settlement negotiation is if the declarant or his representative expressly states that the statement is hypothetical in nature or is made without prejudice. Rule 408, as submitted by the Court reversed the traditional rule. It would have brought statements of fact within the ban and made them, as well as an offer of settlement, inadmissible.

The House amended the rule and would continue to make evidence of facts disclosed during compromise negotiations admissible. It thus reverted to the traditional rule. The House committee report states that the committee intends to preserve current law under which a party may protect himself by couching his statements in hypothetical form.[1] The real impact of this amendment, however, is to deprive the rule of much of its salutary effect. The exception for factual admissions was believed by the Advisory Committee to hamper free communication between parties and thus to constitute an unjustifiable restraint upon efforts to negotiate settlements—the encouragement of which is the purpose of the rule. Further, by protecting hypothetically phrased statements, it constituted a preference for the sophisticated, and a trap for the unwary.

Three States which had adopted rules of evidence patterned after the proposed rules prescribed by the Supreme Court opted for versions of rule 408 identical with the Supreme Court draft with respect to the inadmissibility of conduct or statements made in compromise negotiations.[2]

For those reasons, the committee has deleted the House amendment and restored the rule to the version submitted by the Supreme Court with one additional amendment. This amendment adds a sentence to insure that evidence, such as documents, is not rendered inadmissible merely because it is presented in the course of compromise negotiations if the evidence is otherwise discoverable. A party should not be able to immunize from admissibility documents otherwise discoverable merely by offering them in a compromise negotiation.

Conference Report

The House bill provides that evidence of admissions of liability or opinions given during compromise negotiations is not admissible, but that evidence of facts disclosed during compromise negotiations is not inadmissible by virtue of having been first disclosed in the compromise negotiations. The Senate amendment provides that evidence of conduct or statements made in compromise negotiations is not admissible. The Senate amendment also provides that the rule does not require the exclusion of any evidence otherwise discoverable merely because it is presented in the course of compromise negotiations.

The House bill was drafted to meet the objection of executive agencies that under the rule as proposed by the Supreme Court, a party could present a fact during compromise negotiations and thereby prevent an opposing party from offering evidence of that fact at trial even though such

---

[1] See Report No. 93–650, dated November 15, 1973.

[2] Nev.Rev.Stats. § 48.105; N.Mex.Stats.Anno. (1973 Supp.) § 20–4–408; West's Wis.Stats.Anno. (1973 Supp.) § 904.08.

evidence was obtained from independent sources. The Senate amendment expressly precludes this result.

The Conference adopts the Senate amendment.

Advisory Committee's Note to 2006 Amendment to Rule 408

Rule 408 has been amended to settle some questions in the courts about the scope of the Rule, and to make it easier to read. First, the amendment provides that Rule 408 does not prohibit the introduction in a criminal case of statements or conduct during compromise negotiations regarding a civil dispute by a government regulatory, investigative, or enforcement agency. *See e.g., United States v. Prewitt*, 34 F.3d 436, 439 (7th Cir. 1994) (admissions of fault made in compromise of a civil securities enforcement action were admissible against the accused in a subsequent criminal action for mail fraud). Where an individual makes a statement in the presence of government agents, its subsequent admission in a criminal, case should not be unexpected. The individual can seek to protect against subsequent disclosure through negotiation and agreement with the civil regulator or an attorney for the government.

Statements made in compromise negotiations of a claim by a government agency may be excluded in criminal cases where the circumstances so warrant under Rule 403. For example, if an individual was unrepresented at the time the statement was made in a civil enforcement proceeding, its probative value in a subsequent criminal case may be minimal. But there is no absolute exclusion imposed by Rule 408.

In contrast, statements made during compromise negotiations of other disputed claims are not admissible in subsequent criminal litigation, when offered to prove liability for, invalidity of, or amount of those claims. When private parties enter into compromise negotiations they cannot protect against the subsequent use of statements in criminal cases by way of private ordering. The inability to guarantee protection against subsequent use could lead to parties refusing to admit fault, even if by doing so they could favorably settle the private matter. Such a chill on settlement negotiations would be contrary to the policy of Rule 408.

The amendment distinguishes statements and conduct (such as a direct admission of fault) made in compromise negotiations of a civil claim by a government agency from an offer or acceptance of a compromise of such a claim. An offer or acceptance of a compromise of any civil claim is excluded under the Rule if offered against the defendant as an admission of fault. In that case, the predicate for the evidence would be that the defendant, by compromising with the government agency, has admitted the validity and amount of the civil claim, and that this admission has sufficient probative value to be considered as evidence of guilt. But unlike a direct statement of fault, an offer or acceptance of a compromise is not very probative of the defendant's guilt. Moreover, admitting such an offer or acceptance could deter a defendant from settling a civil regulatory action, for fear of evidentiary use in a subsequent criminal action. *See, e.g.,* Fishman, *Jones on Evidence, Civil and Criminal*, § 22:16 at 199, n.83 (7th ed., 2000) ("A target of a potential criminal investigation may be unwilling to settle civil claims against him if by doing so he increases the risk of prosecution and conviction.").

The amendment retains the language of the original rule that bars compromise evidence only when offered as evidence of the "validity," "invalidity," or "amount" of the disputed claim. The intent is to retain the extensive case law finding Rule 408 inapplicable when compromise evidence is offered for a purpose other than to prove the validity, invalidity, or amount of a disputed claim. *See, e.g., Athey v. Farmers Ins. Exchange*, 234 F.3d 357 (8th Cir. 2000) (evidence of settlement offer by insurer was properly admitted to prove insurer's bad faith); *Coakley & Williams v. Structural Concrete Equip.*, 973 F.2d 349 (4th Cir. 1992) (evidence of settlement is not precluded by Rule 408 where offered to prove a party's intent with respect to the scope of release); *Cates v. Morgan Portable Bldg. Corp.*, 708 F.2d 683 (7th Cir. 1985) (Rule 408 does not bar evidence of a settlement when offered to prove a breach of the settlement agreement, as the purpose of the evidence is to prove the fact of settlement as opposed to the validity or amount of the underlying claim); *Uforma/Shelby Bus. Forms. Inc. v. NLRB*, 111 F.3d 1284 (6th Cir. 1997) (threats made in settlement negotiations were admissible; Rule 408 is inapplicable when the claim is based upon a wrong that is committed during the course of settlement negotiations). So for example Rule 408 is inapplicable if offered to show that a party made fraudulent statements in order to settle a litigation.

The amendment does not affect the case law providing that Rule 408 is inapplicable when evidence of the compromise is offered to prove notice, *See e.g., United States v. Austin*, 54 F.3d 394 (7th Cir. 1995) (no error to admit evidence of the defendant's settlement with the FTC, because it was offered to prove that the defendant was on notice that subsequent similar conduct was wrongful); *Spell v. McDaniel*, 824 F.2d 1380 (4th Cir. 1987) (in a civil rights action alleging that an officer used excessive force, a prior settlement by the City of another brutality claim was properly admitted to prove that the City was on notice of aggressive behavior by police officers).

The amendment prohibits the use of statements made in settlement negotiations when offered to impeach by prior inconsistent statement or through contradiction. Such broad impeachment would tend to swallow the exclusionary rule and would impair the public policy of promoting settlements. *See McCormick on Evidence* at 186 (5th ed. 1999) ("Use of statements made in compromise negotiations to impeach the testimony of a party, which is not specifically treated in Rule 408, is fraught with danger of misuse of the statements to prove liability, threatens frank interchange of information during negotiations, and generally should not be permitted."). *See also EEOC v. Gear Petroleum, Inc.*, 948 F.2d 1542 (10th Cir. 1991) (letter sent as part of settlement negotiation cannot be used to impeach defense witnesses by way of contradiction or prior inconsistent statement;

such broad impeachment would undermine the policy of encouraging uninhibited settlement negotiations).

The amendment makes clear that Rule 408 excludes compromise evidence even when a party seeks to admit its own settlement offer or statements made in settlement negotiations. If a party were to reveal its own statement or offer, this could itself reveal the fact that the adversary entered into settlement negotiations. The protections of Rule 408 cannot be waived unilaterally because the Rule, by definition, protects both parties from having the fact of negotiation disclosed to the jury. Moreover, proof of statements and offers made in settlement would often have to be made through the testimony of attorneys, leading to the risks and costs of disqualification. *See generally Pierce v. F.R. Tripler & Co.*, 955 F.2d 820, 828 (2d Cir. 1992) (settlement offers are excluded under Rule 408 even if it is the offeror who seeks to admit them; noting that the "widespread admissibility of the substance of settlement offers could bring with it a rash of motions for disqualification of a party's chosen counsel who would likely become a witness at trial").

The sentence of the Rule referring to evidence "otherwise discoverable" has been deleted as superfluous. *See, e.g.*, Advisory Committee Note to Maine Rule of Evidence 408 (refusing to include the sentence in the Maine version of Rule 408 and noting that the sentence "seems to state what the law would be if it were omitted"); Advisory Committee Note to Wyoming Rule of Evidence 408 (refusing to include the sentence in Wyoming Rule 408 on the ground that it was "superfluous"). The intent of the sentence was to prevent a party from trying to immunize admissible information, such as a pre-existing document, through the pretense of disclosing it during compromise negotiations. *See Ramada Development Co. v. Rauch*, 644 F.2d 1097 (5th Cir. 1981). But even without the sentence, the Rule cannot be read to protect pre-existing information simply because it was presented to the adversary in compromise negotiations.

Advisory Committee's Note to 2011 Amendment

* * * Rule 408 previously provided that evidence was not excluded if offered for a purpose not explicitly prohibited by the Rule. To improve the language of the Rule, it now provides that the court may admit evidence if offered for a permissible purpose. There is no intent to change the process for admitting evidence covered by the Rule. It remains the case that if offered for an impermissible purpose, it must be excluded, and if offered for a purpose not barred by the Rule, its admissibility remains governed by the general principles of Rules 402, 403, 801, etc.

The Committee deleted the reference to "liability" on the ground that the deletion makes the Rule flow better and easier to read, and because "liability" is covered by the broader term "validity." Courts have not made substantive decisions on the basis of any distinction between validity and liability. No change in current practice or in the coverage of the Rule is intended.

Rule 409

Note by Federal Judicial Center

The rule enacted by the Congress is the rule prescribed by the Supreme Court without change.

Advisory Committee's Note

The considerations underlying this rule parallel those underlying Rules 407 and 408, which deal respectively with subsequent remedial measures and offers of compromise. As stated in Annot., 20 A.L.R.2d 291, 293:

"[G]enerally, evidence of payment of medical, hospital, or similar expenses of an injured party by the opposing party, is not admissible, the reason often given being that such payment or offer is usually made from humane impulses and not from an admission of liability, and that to hold otherwise would tend to discourage assistance to the injured person."

Contrary to Rule 408, dealing with offers of compromise, the present rule does not extend to conduct or statements not a part of the act of furnishing or offering or promising to pay. This difference in treatment arises from fundamental differences in nature. Communication is essential if compromises are to be effected, and consequently broad protection of statements is needed. This is not so in cases of payments or offers or promises to pay medical expenses, where factual statements may be expected to be incidental in nature.

For rules on the same subject, but phrased in terms of "humanitarian motives," see Uniform Rule 52; California Evidence Code § 1152; Kansas Code of Civil Procedure § 60–452; New Jersey Evidence Rule 52.

Rule 410

Note by Federal Judicial Center

The rule prescribed by the Supreme Court consisted only of the first sentence of the rule enacted by the Congress, exclusive of the introductory phrase, "Except as otherwise provided by Act of Congress". Reasons for the amendments are stated in the Report of the House Committee on the Judiciary, Senate Committee on the Judiciary, and Conference, set forth below. See also the explanation by Chairman Hungate in the Congressional Record, December 18, 1974, H12253.

Advisory Committee's Note

Withdrawn pleas of guilty were held inadmissible in federal prosecutions in Kercheval v. United States, 274 U.S. 220, 47 S.Ct. 582, 71 L.Ed. 1009 (1927). The Court pointed out that to admit the withdrawn plea would effectively set at naught the allowance of withdrawal and place the accused in a dilemma utterly inconsistent with the decision to award him a trial. The New York Court of Appeals, in People v. Spitaleri, 9 N.Y.2d 168, 212 N.Y.S.2d 53, 173 N.E.2d 35 (1961), reexamined and overturned its earlier decisions which had allowed admission. In addition to the reasons set forth in Kercheval, which was quoted at length, the court pointed out that the effect of admitting the plea was to compel defendant to take the stand by way of explanation and to open the way for the prosecution to call the lawyer who had represented him at the time of entering the plea. State court decisions for and against admissibility are collected in Annot., 86 A.L.R.2d 326.

Pleas of *nolo contendere* are recognized by Rule 11 of the Rules of Criminal Procedure, although the law of numerous States is to the contrary. The present rule gives effect to the principal traditional characteristic of the *nolo* plea, i.e. avoiding the admission of guilt which is inherent in pleas of guilty. This position is consistent with the construction of Section 5 of the Clayton Act, 15 U.S.C. § 16(a), recognizing the inconclusive and compromise nature of judgments based on *nolo* pleas. General Electric Co. v. City of San Antonio, 334 F.2d 480 (5th Cir.1964); Commonwealth Edison Co. v. Allis-Chalmers Mfg. Co., 323 F.2d 412 (7th Cir.1963), cert. denied 376 U.S. 939, 84 S.Ct. 794, 11 L.Ed.2d 659; Armco Steel Corp. v. North Dakota, 376 F.2d 206 (8th Cir.1967); City of Burbank v. General Electric Co., 329 F.2d 825 (9th Cir.1964). See also state court decisions in Annot., 18 A.L.R.2d 1287, 1314.

Exclusion of offers to plead guilty or *nolo* has as its purpose the promotion of disposition of criminal cases by compromise. As pointed out in McCormick § 251, p. 543.

> "Effective criminal law administration in many localities would hardly be possible if a large proportion of the charges were not disposed of by such compromises."

See also People v. Hamilton, 60 Cal.2d 105, 32 Cal.Rptr. 4, 383 P.2d 412 (1963), discussing legislation designed to achieve this result. As with compromise offers generally, Rule 408, free communication is needed, and security against having an offer of compromise or related statement admitted in evidence effectively encourages it.[1]

Limiting the exclusionary rule to use against the accused is consistent with the purpose of the rule, since the possibility of use for or against other persons will not impair the effectiveness of withdrawing pleas or the freedom of discussion which the rule is designed to foster. See A.B.A. Standards Relating to Pleas of Guilty § 2.2 (1968). See also the narrower provisions of New Jersey Evidence Rule 52(2) and the unlimited exclusion provided in California Evidence Code § 1153.

---

[1] The rule as enacted, it should be noted, allows use of the statements for impeachment or in a subsequent prosecution for perjury or false statement.

Report of House Committee on the Judiciary

The Committee added the phrase "Except as otherwise provided by Act of Congress" to Rule 410 as submitted by the Court in order to preserve particular congressional policy judgments as to the effect of a plea of guilty or of nolo contendere. See 15 U.S.C. 16(a). The Committee intends that its amendment refers to both present statutes and statutes subsequently enacted.

Report of Senate Committee on the Judiciary

As adopted by the House, rule 410 would make inadmissible pleas of guilty or nolo contendere subsequently withdrawn as well as offers to make such pleas. Such a rule is clearly justified as a means of encouraging pleading. However, the House rule would then go on to render inadmissible for any purpose statements made in connection with these pleas or offers as well.

The committee finds this aspect of the House rule unjustified. Of course, in certain circumstances such statements should be excluded. If, for example, a plea is vitiated because of coercion, statements made in connection with the plea may also have been coerced and should be inadmissible on that basis. In other cases, however, voluntary statements of an accused made in court on the record, in connection with a plea, and determined by a court to be reliable should be admissible even though the plea is subsequently withdrawn. This is particularly true in those cases where, if the House rule were in effect, a defendant would be able to contradict his previous statements and thereby lie with impunity.[2] To prevent such an injustice, the rule has been modified to permit the use of such statements for the limited purposes of impeachment and in subsequent perjury or false statement prosecutions.

Conference Report

The House bill provides that evidence of a guilty or nolo contendere plea, of an offer of either plea, or of statements made in connection with such pleas or offers of such pleas, is inadmissible in any civil or criminal action, case or proceeding against the person making such plea or offer. The Senate amendment makes the rule inapplicable to a voluntary and reliable statement made in court on the record where the statement is offered in a subsequent prosecution of the declarant for perjury or false statement.

The issues raised by Rule 410 are also raised by proposed Rule 11(e)(6) of the Federal Rules of Criminal Procedure presently pending before Congress. This proposed rule, which deals with the admissibility of pleas of guilty or nolo contendere, offers to make such pleas, and statements made in connection with such pleas, was promulgated by the Supreme Court on April 22, 1974, and in the absence of congressional action will become effec-

---

[2] See Harris v. New York, 401 U.S. 222 (1971).

tive on August 1, 1975. The conferees intend to make no change in the presently-existing case law until that date, leaving the courts free to develop rules in this area on a case-by-case basis.

The Conferees further determined that the issues presented by the use of guilty and nolo contendere pleas, offers of such pleas, and statements made in connection with such pleas or offers, can be explored in greater detail during Congressional consideration of Rule 11(e)(6) of the Federal Rules of Criminal Procedure. The Conferees believe, therefore, that it is best to defer its effective date until August 1, 1975. The Conferees intend that Rule 410 would be superseded by any subsequent Federal Rule of Criminal Procedure or Act of Congress with which it is inconsistent, if the Federal Rule of Criminal Procedure or Act of Congress takes effect or becomes law after the date of the enactment of the act establishing the rules of evidence.

The conference adopts the Senate amendment with an amendment that expresses the above intentions.

1975 and 1980 Amendments

[We have omitted the legislative history of the 1975 and 1980 amendments to Rule 410. For documents from that history, see 1976 U.S.Code Cong. & Ad. News 713, 714 (Conference Report on 1975 amendment) and 77 F.R.D. 507, 533 (Advisory Committee Note to 1980 amendment).—Eds.]

Rule 411

Note by Federal Judicial Center

The rule enacted by the Congress is the rule prescribed by the Supreme Court without change.

Advisory Committee's Note

The courts have with substantial unanimity rejected evidence of liability insurance for the purpose of proving fault, and absence of liability insurance as proof of lack of fault. At best the inference of fault from the fact of insurance coverage is a tenuous one, as is its converse. More important, no doubt, has been the feeling that knowledge of the presence or absence of liability insurance would induce juries to decide cases on improper grounds. McCormick § 168; Annot., 4 A.L.R.2d 761. The rule is drafted in broad terms so as to include contributory negligence or other fault of a plaintiff as well as fault of a defendant.

The second sentence points out the limits of the rule, using well established illustrations. Id.

For similar rules see Uniform Rule 54; California Evidence Code § 1155; Kansas Code of Civil Procedure § 60–454; New Jersey Evidence Rule 54.

Advisory Committee's Note to 2011 Amendment

* * * Rule 411 previously provided that evidence was not excluded if offered for a purpose not explicitly prohibited by the Rule. To improve the language of the Rule, it now provides that the court may admit evidence if offered for a permissible purpose. There is no intent to change the process for admitting evidence covered by the Rule. It remains the case that if offered for an impermissible purpose, it must be excluded, and if offered for a purpose not barred by the Rule, its admissibility remains governed by the general principles of Rules 402, 403, 801, etc.

Rule 412

Advisory Committee's Note

Editors' Note: Congress originally enacted Rule 412 in 1978. The original version applied exclusively to criminal cases. Similar "rape shield statutes" had already been enacted by many states. The discussion in the House of Representatives which preceded enactment of original Rule 412 follows this introduction.

In 1994 the Judicial Conference proposed to the Supreme Court a revision of Rule 412 which, among other things, extended shield protection to civil cases. The Supreme Court, in its April 29, 1994 order, withheld approval of that part of the rule, though it approved the other revisions in Rule 412. In a letter to the Chair of the Executive Committee of the Judicial Conference, Chief Justice Rehnquist explained:

> Some members of the Court expressed the view that the amendment might exceed the scope of the Court's authority under the Rules Enabling Act, which forbids the enactment of rules that "abridge, enlarge, or modify any substantive right." 28 U.S.C. § 2072(b). This Court recognized in *Meritor Saving Bank v. Vinson*, 477 U.S. 57, 69 (1986), that evidence of an alleged victim's "sexually provocative speech or dress" may be relevant in workplace harassment cases, and some Justices expressed concern that the proposed amendment might encroach on the rights of defendants.

(Letter of Chief Justice Rehnquist to Judge John F. Gerry, April 29, 1994.)

Ultimately, any issue under the Rules Enabling Act was rendered moot: Congress enacted the Advisory Committee's version and extended shield protection to civil cases as part of the Violent Crime Control and Law Enforcement Act of 1994 (Pub. L. No. 103–322, 108 Stat. 1796).

1978 HOUSE OF REPRESENTATIVES DEBATE

The following debate in the House of Representatives of October 10, 1978, preceded passage of H.R. 4727, which enacted Rule 412. The debate appears in 124 Cong.Record, at page H. 34912.

Mr. MANN. Mr. Speaker, I yield myself such time as I may consume.

Mr. Speaker, for many years in this country, evidentiary rules have permitted the introduction of evidence about a rape victim's prior sexual conduct. Defense lawyers were permitted great latitude in bringing out intimate details about a rape victim's life. Such evidence quite often serves no real purpose and only results in embarrassment to the rape victim and unwarranted public intrusion into her private life.

The evidentiary rules that permit such inquiry have in recent years come under question; and the States have taken the lead to change and modernize their evidentiary rules about evidence of a rape victim's prior sexual behavior. The bill before us similarly seeks to modernize the Federal evidentiary rules.

The present Federal Rules of Evidence reflect the traditional approach. If a defendant in a rape case raises the defense of consent, that defendant may then offer evidence about the victim's prior sexual behavior. Such evidence may be in the form of opinion evidence, evidence of reputation, or evidence of specific instances of behavior. Rule 404(a)(2) of the Federal Rules of Evidence permits the introduction of evidence of a "pertinent character trait." The advisory committee note to that rule cites, as an example of what the rule covers, the character of a rape victim when the issue is consent. Rule 405 of the Federal Rules of Evidence permits the use of opinion or reputation evidence or the use of evidence of specific behavior to show a character trait.

Thus, Federal evidentiary rules permit a wide ranging inquiry into the private conduct of a rape victim, even though that conduct may have at best a tenuous connection to the offense for which the defendant is being tried.

H.R. 4727 amends the Federal Rules of Evidence to add a new rule, applicable only in criminal cases, to spell out when, and under what conditions, evidence of a rape victim's prior sexual behavior can be admitted. The new rule provides that reputation or opinion evidence about a rape victim's prior sexual behavior is not admissible. The new rule also provides that a court cannot admit evidence of specific instances of a rape victim's prior sexual conduct except in three circumstances.

The first circumstance is where the Constitution requires that the evidence be admitted. This exception is intended to cover those infrequent instances where, because of an unusual chain of circumstances, the general rule of inadmissibility, if followed, would result in denying the defendant a constitutional right.

The second circumstance in which the defendant can offer evidence of specific instances of a rape victim's prior sexual behavior is where the defendant raises the issue of consent and the evidence is of sexual behavior with the defendant. To admit such evidence, however, the court must find that the evidence is relevant and that its probative value outweighs the danger of unfair prejudice.

The third circumstance in which a court can admit evidence of specific instances of a rape victim's prior sexual behavior is where the evidence is of behavior with someone other than the defendant and is offered by the defendant on the issue of whether or not he was the source of semen or injury. Again, such evidence will be admitted only if the court finds that the evidence is relevant and that its probative value outweighs the danger of unfair prejudice.

The new rule further provides that before evidence is admitted under any of these exceptions, there must be an in camera hearing—that is, a proceeding that takes place in the judge's chambers out of the presence of the jury and the general public. At this hearing, the defendant will present the evidence he intends to offer and be able to argue why it should be admitted. The prosecution, of course, will be able to argue against that evidence being admitted.

The purpose of the in camera hearing is twofold. It gives the defendant an opportunity to demonstrate to the court why certain evidence is admissible and ought to be presented to the jury. At the same time, it protects the privacy of the rape victim in those instances when the court finds that evidence is inadmissible. Of course, if the court finds the evidence to be admissible, the evidence will be presented to the jury in open court.

The effect of this legislation, therefore, is to preclude the routine use of evidence of specific instances of a rape victim's prior sexual behavior. Such evidence will be admitted only in clearly and narrowly defined circumstances and only after an in camera hearing. In determining the admissibility of such evidence, the court will consider all of the facts and circumstances surrounding the evidence, such as the amount of time that lapsed between the alleged prior act and the rape charged in the prosecution. The greater the lapse of time, of course, the less likely it is that such evidence will be admitted.

Mr. Speaker, the principal purpose of this legislation is to protect rape victims from the degrading and embarrassing disclosure of intimate details about their private lives. It does so by narrowly circumscribing when such evidence may be admitted. It does not do so, however, by sacrificing any constitutional right possessed by the defendant. The bill before us fairly balances the interests involved—the rape victim's interest in protecting her private life from unwarranted public exposure; the defendant's interest in being able adequately to present a defense by offering relevant and probative evidence; and society's interest in a fair trial, one where unduly prejudicial evidence is not permitted to becloud the issues before the jury.

I urge support of the bill.

Mr. WIGGINS. Mr. Speaker, I yield myself such time as I may consume.

(Mr. WIGGINS asked and was given permission to revise and extend his remarks.)

Mr. WIGGINS. Mr. Speaker, this legislation addresses itself to a subject that is certainly a proper one for our consideration. Many of us have been troubled for years about the indiscriminate and prejudicial use of testimony with respect to a victim's prior sexual behavior in rape and similar cases. This bill deals with that problem. It is not, in my opinion, Mr. Speaker, a perfect bill in the manner in which it deals with the problem, but my objections are not so fundamental as would lead me to oppose the bill.

I think, Mr. Speaker, that it is unwise to adopt a per se rule absolutely excluding evidence of reputation and opinion with respect to the victim—and this bill does that—but it is difficult for me to foresee the specific case in which such evidence might be admissible. The trouble is this, Mr. Speaker: None of us can foresee perfectly all of the various circumstances under which the propriety of evidence might be before the court. If this bill has a defect, in my view it is because it adopts a per se rule with respect to opinion and reputation evidence.

Alternatively we might have permitted that evidence to be considered in camera as we do other evidence under the bill.

I should note, however, in fairness, having expressed minor reservations, that the bill before the House at this time does improve significantly upon the bill which was presented to our committee.

I will not detail all of those improvements but simply observe that the bill upon which we shall soon vote is a superior product to that which was initially considered by our subcommittee.

Mr. Speaker, I ask my colleagues to vote for this legislation as being, on balance, worthy of their support, and urge its adoption.

I reserve the balance of my time.

Mr. MANN. Mr. Speaker, this legislation has more than 100 cosponsors, but its principal sponsor, as well as its architect is the gentlewoman from New York (Ms. Holtzman). As the drafter of the legislation she will be able to provide additional information about the probable scope and effect of the legislation.

I yield such time as she may consume to the gentlewoman from New York (Ms. Holtzman).

(Ms. HOLTZMAN asked and was given permission to revise and extend her remarks.)

Ms. HOLTZMAN. Mr. Speaker, I would like to begin first by complimenting the distinguished gentleman from South Carolina (Mr. Mann), the chairman of the subcommittee, for his understanding of the need for corrective legislation in this area and for the fairness with which he has conducted the subcommittee hearings. I would like also to compliment the other members of the subcommittee, including the gentleman from California (Mr. Wiggins).

Too often in this country victims of rape are humiliated and harassed when they report and prosecute the rape. Bullied and cross-examined about their prior sexual experiences, many find the trial almost as degrading as the rape itself. Since rape trials become inquisitions into the victim's morality, not trials of the defendant's innocence or guilt, it is not surprising that it is the least reported crime. It is estimated that as few as one in ten rapes is ever reported.

Mr. Speaker, over 30 States have taken some action to limit the vulnerability of rape victims to such humiliating cross-examination of their past sexual experiences and intimate personal histories. In federal courts, however, it is permissible still to subject rape victims to brutal cross-examination about their past sexual histories. H.R. 4727 would rectify this problem in Federal courts and I hope, also serve as a model to suggest to the remaining states that reform of existing rape laws is important to the equity of our criminal justice system.

H.R. 4727 applies only to criminal rape cases in Federal courts. The bill provides that neither the prosecution nor the defense can introduce any reputation or opinion evidence about the victim's past sexual conduct. It does permit, however, the introduction of specific evidence about the victim's past sexual conduct in three very limited circumstances.

First, this evidence can be introduced if it deals with the victim's past sexual relations with the defendant and is relevant to the issue of whether she consented. Second, when the defendant claims he had no relations with the victim, he can use evidence of the victim's past sexual relations with others if the evidence rebuts the victim's claim that the rape caused certain physical consequences, such as semen or injury. Finally, the evidence can be introduced if it is constitutionally required. This last exception, added in subcommittee, will insure that the defendant's constitutional rights are protected.

Before any such evidence can be introduced, however, the court must determine at a hearing in chambers that the evidence falls within one of the exceptions.

Furthermore, unless constitutionally required, the evidence of specific instances of prior sexual conduct cannot be introduced at all it if would be more prejudicial and inflammatory than probative.

Mr. Speaker, I urge adoption of this bill. It will protect women from both injustice and indignity.

Mr. MANN. Mr. Speaker, I have no further requests for time, and I yield back the balance of my time.

Mr. WIGGINS. Mr. Speaker, I have no further requests for time, and yield back the balance of my time.

The SPEAKER pro tempore. The question is on the motion offered by the gentleman from South Carolina (Mr. Mann) that the House suspend the rules and pass the bill H.R. 4727, as amended.

The question was taken; and (two-thirds having voted in favor thereof) the rules were suspended and the bill, as amended, was passed.

ADVISORY COMMITTEE NOTES

1994 Amendments

Rule 412 has been revised to diminish some of the confusion engendered by the original rule and to expand the protection afforded alleged victims of sexual misconduct. Rule 412 applies to both civil and criminal proceedings. The rule aims to safeguard the alleged victim against the invasion of privacy, potential embarrassment and sexual stereotyping that is associated with public disclosure of intimate sexual details and the infusion of sexual innuendo into the factfinding process. By affording victims protection in most instances, the rule also encourages victims of sexual misconduct to institute and to participate in legal proceedings against alleged offenders.

Rule 412 seeks to achieve these objectives by barring evidence relating to the alleged victim's sexual behavior or alleged sexual predisposition, whether offered as substantive evidence or for impeachment, except in designated circumstances in which the probative value of the evidence significantly outweighs possible harm to the victim.

The revised rule applies in all cases involving sexual misconduct without regard to whether the alleged victim or person accused is a party to the litigation. Rule 412 extends to "pattern" witnesses in both criminal and civil cases whose testimony about other instances of sexual misconduct by the person accused is otherwise admissible. When the case does not involve alleged sexual misconduct, evidence relating to a third-party witness' alleged sexual activities is not within the ambit of Rule 412. The witness will, however, be protected by other rules such as Rules 404 and 608, as well as Rule 403.

The terminology "alleged victim" is used because there will frequently be a factual dispute as to whether sexual misconduct occurred. It does not connote any requirement that the misconduct be alleged in the pleadings. Rule 412 does not, however, apply unless the person against whom the evidence is offered can reasonably be characterized as a "victim of alleged sexual misconduct." When this is not the case, as for instance in a defamation action involving statements concerning sexual misconduct in which the evidence is offered to show that the alleged defamatory statements were true or did not damage the plaintiff's reputation, neither Rule 404 nor this rule will operate to bar the evidence; Rules 401 and 403 will continue to control. Rule 412 will, however, apply in a Title VII action in which the plaintiff has alleged sexual harassment.

The reference to a person "accused" is also used in a non-technical sense. There is no requirement that there be a criminal charge pending against the person or even that the misconduct would constitute a criminal offense. Evidence offered to prove allegedly false prior claims by the victim is not barred by Rule 412. However, this evidence is subject to the requirements of Rule 404.

Subdivision (a). As amended, Rule 412 bars evidence offered to prove the victim's sexual behavior and alleged sexual predisposition. Evidence, which might otherwise be admissible under Rules 402, 404(b), 405, 607, 608, 609 or some other evidence rule, must be excluded if Rule 412 so requires. The word "other" is used to suggest some flexibility in admitting evidence "intrinsic" to the alleged sexual misconduct. *Cf.* Committee Note to 1991 amendment to Rule 404(b).

Past sexual behavior connotes all activities that involve actual physical conduct, i.e. sexual intercourse and sexual contact, or that imply sexual intercourse or sexual contact. See, e.g., United States v. Galloway, 937 F.2d 542 (10th Cir.1991), cert. denied, 506 U.S. 957 (1992) (use of contraceptives inadmissible since use implies sexual activity); United States v. One Feather, 702 F.2d 736 (8th Cir.1983) (birth of an illegitimate child inadmissible); State v. Carmichael, 727 P.2d 918, 925 (Kan.1986) (evidence of venereal disease inadmissible). In addition, the word "behavior" should be construed to include activities of the mind, such as fantasies or dreams. See 23 C. Wright & K. Graham, Jr., Federal Practice and Procedure, § 5384 at p. 548 (1980) ("While there may be some doubt under statutes that require 'conduct,' it would seem that the language of Rule 412 is broad enough to encompass the behavior of the mind.").

The rule has been amended to also exclude all other evidence relating to an alleged victim of sexual misconduct that is offered to prove a sexual predisposition. This amendment is designed to exclude evidence that does not directly refer to sexual activities or thoughts but that the proponent believes may have a sexual connotation for the factfinder. Admission of such evidence would contravene Rule 412's objectives of shielding the alleged victim from potential embarrassment and safeguarding the victim against stereotypical thinking. Consequently, unless the (b)(2) exception is satisfied, evidence such as that relating to the alleged victim's mode of dress, speech, or life-style will not be admissible.

The introductory phrase in subdivision (a) was deleted because it lacked clarity and contained no explicit reference to the other provisions of the law that were intended to be overridden. The conditional clause, "except as provided in subdivisions (b) and (c)" is intended to make clear that evidence of the types described in subdivision (a) is admissible only under the strictures of those sections.

The reason for extending the rule to all criminal cases is obvious. The strong social policy of protecting a victim's privacy and encouraging victims to come forward to report criminal acts is not confined to cases that involve a charge of sexual assault. The need to protect the victim is equally great when a defendant is charged with kidnapping, and evidence is offered, either to prove motive or as background, that the defendant sexually assaulted the victim.

The reason for extending Rule 412 to civil cases is equally obvious. The need to protect alleged victims against invasions of privacy, potential embarrassment, and unwarranted sexual stereotyping, and the wish to encourage victims to come forward when they have been sexually molested do not disappear because the context has shifted from a criminal prosecution to a claim for damages or injunctive relief. There is a strong social policy in not only punishing those who engage in sexual misconduct, but in also providing relief to the victim. Thus, Rule 412 applies in any civil case in which a person claims to be the victim of sexual misconduct, such as actions for sexual battery or sexual harassment.

Subdivision (b). Subdivision (b) spells out the specific circumstances in which some evidence may be admissible that would otherwise be barred by the general rule expressed in subdivision (a). As amended, Rule 412 will be virtually unchanged in criminal cases, but will provide protection to any person alleged to be a victim of sexual misconduct regardless of the charge actually brought against an accused. A new exception has been added for civil cases.

In a criminal case, evidence may be admitted under subdivision (b)(1) pursuant to three possible exceptions, provided the evidence also satisfies other requirements for admissibility specified in the Federal Rules of Evidence, including Rule 403. Subdivisions (b)(1)(A) and (b)(1)(B) require proof in the form of specific instances of sexual behavior in recognition of the limited probative value and dubious reliability of evidence of reputation or evidence in the form of an opinion.

Under subdivision (b)(1)(A), evidence of specific instances of sexual behavior with persons other than the person whose sexual misconduct is alleged may be admissible if it is offered to prove that another person was the source of semen, injury or other physical evidence. Where the prosecution has directly or indirectly asserted that the physical evidence originated with the accused, the defendant must be afforded an opportunity to prove that another person was responsible. See United States v. Begay, 937 F.2d 515, 523 n. 10 (10th Cir.1991). Evidence offered for the specific purpose identified in this subdivision may still be excluded if it does not satisfy Rules 401 or 403. See, e.g., United States v. Azure, 845 F.2d 1503, 1505–06 (8th Cir.1988) (10 year old victim's injuries indicated recent use of force; court excluded evidence of consensual sexual activities with witness who testified at in camera hearing that he had never hurt victim and failed to establish recent activities).

Under the exception in subdivision (b)(1)(B), evidence of specific instances of sexual behavior with respect to the person whose sexual misconduct is alleged is admissible if offered to prove consent, or offered by the prosecution. Admissible pursuant to this exception might be evidence of prior instances of sexual activities between the alleged victim and the accused, as well as statements in which the alleged victim expresses an intent to engage in sexual intercourse with the accused, or voiced sexual fantasies involving that specific accused. In a prosecution for child sexual abuse, for example, evidence of uncharged sexual activity between the accused and the alleged victim offered by the prosecution may be admissible pursuant to Rule 404(b) to show a pattern of behavior. Evidence relating to the victim's alleged sexual predisposition is not admissible pursuant to this exception.

Under subdivision (b)(1)(C), evidence of specific instances of conduct may not be excluded if the result would be to deny a criminal defendant the protections afforded by the Constitution. For example, statements in which the victim has expressed an intent to have sex with the first person encountered on a particular occasion might not be excluded without violating the due process right of a rape defendant seeking to prove consent. Recognition of this basic principle was expressed on subdivision (b)(1) of the original rule. The United States Supreme Court has recognized that in various circumstances a defendant may have a right to introduce evidence otherwise precluded by an evidence rule under the Confrontation Clause. See, e.g., Olden v. Kentucky, 488 U.S. 227 (1988) (defendant in rape cases had right to inquire into alleged victim's cohabitation with another man to show bias).

Subdivision (b)(2) governs the admissibility of otherwise proscribed evidence in civil cases. It employs a balancing test rather than the specific exceptions stated in subdivision (b)(1) in recognition of the difficulty of foreseeing future developments in the law. Greater flexibility is needed to accommodate evolving causes of action such as claims for sexual harassment.

The balancing test requires the proponent of the evidence, whether plaintiff or defendant, to convince the court that the probative value of the proffered evidence "substantially outweighs the danger of harm to any victim and of unfair prejudice of any party." This test for admitting evidence offered to prove sexual behavior or sexual propensity in civil cases differs in three respects from the general rule governing admissibility set forth in Rule 403. First, it reverses the usual procedure spelled out in Rule 403 by shifting the burden to the proponent to demonstrate admissibility rather than making the opponent justify exclusion of the evidence. Second, the standard expressed in subdivision (b)(2) is more stringent than in the original rule; it raises the threshold for admission by requiring that the probative value of the evidence *substantially* outweigh the specified dangers. Finally, the Rule 412 test puts "harm to the victim" on the scale in addition to prejudice to the parties.

Evidence of reputation may be received in a civil case only if the alleged victim has put his or her reputation into controversy. The victim may do so without making a specific allegation in a pleading. *Cf.* Fed.R.Civ.P. 35(a).

Subdivision (c). Amended subdivision (c) is more concise and understandable than the subdivision it replaces. The requirement of a motion before trial is continued in the amended rule, as is the provision that a late motion may be permitted for good cause shown. In deciding whether to permit late filing, the court may take into account the conditions previously included in the rule: namely whether the evidence is newly discovered and could not have been obtained earlier through the existence of due diligence, and whether the issue to which such evidence relates has newly arisen in the case. The rule recognizes that in some instances the circumstances that justify an application to introduce evidence otherwise barred by Rule 412 will not become apparent until trial.

The amended rule provides that before admitting evidence that falls within that prohibition of Rule 412(a), the court must hold a hearing in camera at which the alleged victim and any party must be afforded the right to be present and an opportunity to be heard. All papers connected with the motion of a hearing on the motion and any record must be kept and remain under seal during the course of trial and appellate proceedings unless otherwise ordered. This is to assure that the privacy of the alleged victim is preserved in all cases in which the court rules that proffered evidence is not admissible, and in which the hearing refers to matters that are not received, or are received in another form.

The procedures set forth in subdivision (c) do not apply to discovery of a victim's past sexual conduct or predisposition in civil cases, which will be continued to be governed by Fed. R. Civ. P. 26. In order not to undermine the rationale of Rule 412, however, courts should enter appropriate orders pursuant to Fed. R. Civ. P. 26 (c) to protect the victim against unwarranted inquiries and to ensure confidentiality. Courts should presumptively issue protective orders barring discovery unless the party seeking discovery makes a showing that the evidence sought to be discovered would be relevant under the facts and theories of the particular case, and cannot be obtained except through discovery. In an action for sexual harassment, for instance, while some evidence of the alleged victim's sexual behavior and/or predisposition in the workplace may perhaps be relevant, non-work place conduct will usually be irrelevant. *Cf.* Burns v. McGregor Electronic Industries, Inc., 989 F.2d 959, 962–63 (8th Cir.1993) (posing for a nude magazine outside work hours is irrelevant to issue of unwelcomeness of sexual advances at work). Confidentiality orders should be presumptively granted as well.

One substantive change made in subdivision (c) is the elimination of the following sentence: "Notwithstanding subdivision (b) of Rule 104, if the relevancy of the evidence which the accused seeks to offer in trial depends upon the fulfillment of a condition of fact, the court, at the hearing in chambers or at a subsequent hearing in chambers scheduled for such purpose, shall accept evidence on the issue of whether such condition of fact is fulfilled and shall determine such issue." On its face, this language would appear to authorize a trial judge to exclude evidence of past sexual conduct between an alleged victim and an accused or a defendant in a civil case based upon the judge's belief that such past acts did not occur. Such an authorization raises questions of invasion of the right to a jury trial under the Sixth and Seventh Amendments. See 1 S. Saltzburg & M. Martin, Federal Rules of Evidence Manual, 396–97 (5th ed. 1990).

The Advisory Committee concluded that the amended rule provided adequate protection for all persons claiming to be the victims of sexual misconduct, and that it was inadvisable to continue to include a provision in the rule that has been confusing and that raises substantial constitutional issues.

[The Advisory Committee Note was adopted by the Congressional Conference Report accompanying Pub.L. 103–322. See H.R. Conf. Rep. No. 103–711, 103rd Cong., 2nd Sess., 383 (1994).]

Rules 413–415

Editors' Note: Rules 413, 414, and 415 were passed by Congress as part of the Violent Crime Control and Law Enforcement Act of 1994, Pub.L. No. 103–322 (September 13, 1994). The statute gave the Judicial Conference of the United States 150 days to provide Congress a report containing recommendations for amending these Rules. The Judicial Conference responded by opposing Rules 413–415 and recommending no change in existing law. As a second choice, the Conference recommended a redrafting of the legislation to adopt a flexible approach that would give judges greater authority to exclude than that provided by Rules 413–415. Despite this opposition, Congress adopted Rules 413, 414, and 415 without change and they became effective on July 9, 1995.

Rules 413, 414, and 415 were not part of the Federal Rules of Evidence; thus, there is no Advisory Committee note. What follows is the floor statement of Representative Susan Molinari, the Principal House Sponsor of Rules 413, 414, and 415 [140 Cong.Rec. H8991–92 (daily ed. Aug. 21, 1994)]:

Mr. Speaker, the revised conference bill contains a critical reform that I have long sought to protect the public from crimes of sexual violence— general rules of admissibility in sexual assault and child molestation cases for evidence that the defendant has committed offenses of the same type on other occasions. The enactment of this reform is first and foremost a triumph for the public—for the women who will not be raped and the children who will not be molested because we have strengthened the legal system's tools for bringing the perpetrators of these atrocious crimes to justice.

Senator DOLE and I initially proposed this reform in February of 1991 in the Women's Equal Opportunity Act bill, and we later re-introduced it in the Sexual Assault Prevention Act bills of the 102d and 103d Congresses. The proposal also enjoyed the strong support of the Administration in the 102d Congress, and was included in President Bush's violent crime bill of that Congress, S. 635. The Senate passed the proposed rules on Nov. 5, 1993, by a vote of 75 to 19, in a crime bill amendment offered by Senator DOLE. This Chamber endorsed the same rules on June 29, 1994, by a vote of 348 to 62, through a motion to instruct conferees that I offered.

The rules in the revised conference bill are substantially identical to our earlier proposals. We have agreed to a temporary deferral of the effective date of the new rules, pending a report by the Judicial Conference, in order to accommodate procedural objections raised by opponents of the reform. However, regardless of what the Judicial Conference may recommend, the new rules will take effect within at most 300 days of the enactment of this legislation, unless repealed or modified by subsequent legislation.

The need for these rules, their precedential support, their interpretation, and the issues and policy questions they raise have been analyzed at length in the legislative history of this proposal. I would direct the Members' attention particularly to two earlier statements:

The first is the portion of the section-by-section analysis accompanying these rules in section 801 of S. 635, which President Bush transmitted to Congress in 1991. That statement appears on pages S3238 [to] S3242 of the daily edition of the CONGRESSIONAL RECORD for March 13, 1991.

The second is the prepared text of an address—entitled "Evidence of Propensity and Probability in Sex Offense Cases and Other Cases"—by Senior Counsel David J. Karp of the Office of Policy Development of the U.S. Department of Justice. Mr. Karp, who is the author of the new evidence rules, presented this statement on behalf of the Justice Department to the Evidence Section of the Association of American Law Schools on January 9, 1993. The statement provided a detailed account of the views of the legislative sponsors and the Administration concerning the proposed reform, and should also be considered an authoritative part of its legislative history.

These earlier statements address the issues raised by this reform in considerable detail. In my present remarks, I will simply emphasize the following essential points:

The new rules will supersede in sex offense cases the restrictive aspects of Federal Rule of Evidence 404(b). In contrast to Rule 404(b)'s general prohibition of evidence of character or propensity, the new rules for sex offense cases authorize admission and consideration of evidence of an uncharged offense for its bearing "on any matter to which it is relevant." This includes the defendant's propensity to commit sexual assault or child molestation offenses, and assessment of the probability or improbability that the defendant has been falsely or mistakenly accused of such an offense.

In other respects, the general standards of the rules of evidence will continue to apply, including the restrictions on hearsay evidence and the court's authority under Evidence Rule 403 to exclude evidence whose probative value is substantially outweighed by its prejudicial effect. Also, the government—or the plaintiff in a civil case—will generally have to disclose to the defendant any evidence that is to be offered under the new rules at least 15 days before trial.

The proposed reform is critical to the protection of the public from rapists and child molesters, and is justified by the distinctive characteristics of the cases it will affect. In child molestation cases, for example, a history of similar acts tends to be exceptionally probative because it shows an unusual disposition of the defendant—a sexual or sado-sexual interest in children—that simply does not exist in ordinary people. Moreover, such cases require reliance on child victims whose credibility can readily be attacked in the absence of substantial corroboration. In such cases, there is a compelling public interest in admitting all significant evidence that will illumine the credibility of the charge and any denial by the defense.

Similarly, adult-victim sexual assault cases are distinctive, and often turn on difficult credibility determinations. Alleged consent by the victim is rarely an issue in prosecutions for other violent crimes—the accused mugger does not claim that the victim freely handed over [his] wallet as a gift—but the defendant in a rape case often contends that the victim engaged in consensual sex and then falsely accused him. Knowledge that the defendant has committed rapes on other occasions is frequently critical in assessing the relative plausibility of these claims and accurately deciding cases that would otherwise become unresolvable swearing matches.

The practical effect of the new rules is to put evidence of uncharged offenses in sexual assault and child molestation cases on the same footing as other types of relevant evidence that are not subject to a special exclusionary rule. The presumption is in favor of admission. The underlying legislative judgment is that the evidence admissible pursuant to the proposed rules is typically relevant and probative, and that its probative value is normally not outweighed by any risk of prejudice or other adverse effects.

In line with this judgment, the rules do not impose arbitrary or artificial restrictions on the admissibility of evidence. Evidence of offenses for which the defendant has not previously been prosecuted or convicted will be admissible, as well as evidence of prior convictions. No time limit is imposed on the uncharged offenses for which evidence may be admitted; as a practical matter, evidence of other sex offenses by the defendant is often probative and properly admitted, notwithstanding very substantial lapses of time in relation to the charged offense or offenses. See, e.g., United States v. Hadley, 918 F.2d 848, 850–51 (9th Cir.1990), cert. dismissed, 506 U.S. 19 (1992) (evidence of offenses occurring up to 15 years earlier admitted); State v. Plymate, 345 N.W.2d 327 (Neb.1984) (evidence of defendant's commission of other child molestations more than 20 years earlier admitted).

Finally, the practical efficacy of these rules will depend on faithful execution by judges of the will of Congress in adopting this critical reform. To implement the legislative intent, the courts must liberally construe these rules to provide the basis for a fully informed decision of sexual assault and child molestation cases, including assessment of the defendant's propensities and questions of probability in light of the defendant's past conduct.

* * *

Editors' Note: The following is a section-by-section analysis (referred to by Representative Molinari in her statement above) accompanying section 801 of S.635, which President Bush proposed to Congress in 1991. [137 Cong. Rec. S3238–420 (daily ed. March 13, 1991)].

VIII. SEXUAL VIOLENCE AND CHILD ABUSE

Sec. 801. Admissibility of Evidence of Similar Crimes in Sexual Assault and Child Molestation Cases

In cases where the defendant is accused of committing an offense of sexual assault or child molestation, courts in the United States have traditionally favored the broad admission at trial of evidence of the defendant's prior commission of similar crimes. The contemporary edition of Wigmore's treatise describes this tendency as follows (IA Wigmore's Evidence § 62.2 (Tillers rev. 1983)):

> "[T]here is a strong tendency in prosecutions for sex offenses to admit evidence of the accused's sexual proclivities. Do such decisions show that the general rule against the use of propensity evidence against an accused is not honored in sex offense prosecutions? We think so.

> "[S]ome states and courts have forthrightly and expressly recogniz[ed] a 'lustful disposition' or sexual proclivity exception to the general rule barring the use of character evidence against an accused. . . [J]urisdictions that do not expressly recognize a lustful disposition exception may effectively recognize such an exception by expansively interpreting in prosecutions for sex offenses various well-established exceptions to the character evidence rule. The exception for common

scheme or design is frequently used, but other exceptions are also used."

More succinctly, the Supreme Court of Wyoming observed in Elliot v. State, 600 P.2d 1044, 1047–48 (1979):

> "[I]n recent years a preponderance of the courts have sustained the admissibility of the testimony of third persons as to prior or subsequent similar crimes, wrongs or acts in cases involving sexual offenses. . . [I]n cases involving sexual assaults, such as incest, and statutory rape with family members as the victims, the courts in recent years have almost uniformly admitted such testimony."

The willingness of the courts to admit similar crimes evidence in prosecutions for serious sex crimes is of great importance to effective prosecution in this area, and hence to the public's security against dangerous sex offenders. In a rape prosecution, for example, disclosure of the fact that the defendant has previously committed other rapes is frequently critical to the jury's informed assessment of the credibility of a claim by the defense that the victim consented and that the defendant is being falsely accused.

The importance of admitting this type of evidence is still greater in child molestation cases. Such cases regularly present the need to rely on the testimony of child victim-witnesses whose credibility can readily be attacked in the absence of substantial corroboration. In such cases, the public interest in admitting all significant evidence that will illumine the credibility of the charge and any denial by the defense is truly compelling.

Notwithstanding the salutary tendency of the courts to admit evidence of other offenses by the defendant in such cases, the current state of the law in this area is not satisfactory. The approach of the courts has been characterized by considerable uncertainty and inconsistency. Not all courts have recognized the area of sex offense prosecutions as one requiring special standards or treatment, and those which have adopted admission rules on varying scope and rationale.

Moreover, even where the courts have traditionally favored admission of "similar crimes evidence" in sex offense prosecutions, the continuation of this approach has been jeopardized by recent developments. These developments include the widespread adoption by the states of codified rules of evidence modeled on the Federal Rules of Evidence, which make no special allowance for admitting similar crimes evidence in sex offense cases. They also include the limitation of evidence of other sexual activity by the *victim* under "rape victim shield laws," which has given rise to an argument that it would be unfair or inappropriate to be more permissive in admitting evidence of the commission of other sex crimes by the defendant.

Section 801 of title VIII would amend the Federal Rules of Evidence to ensure an appropriate scope of admission for evidence of similar crimes by defendants accused of serious sex crimes. The section adds three new Rules (proposed Rules 413, 414, and 415), which state general rules of admissibility for such evidence. The proposed new rules would apply directly in federal cases, and would have broader significance as a potential model for state reforms.

The remainder of this explanation of section 801 is set out in several parts. Part A briefly discusses the meaning and operation of the proposed new rules of evidence. Part B sets out the background of these rules in terms of the historical development and contemporary formulation of the rules of evidence, and explains why legislation addressing this issue is particularly critical at this point in time. Part C discusses the adequacy of the formulation of the proposed rules to meet concerns about the possibility of undue prejudice or other unfairness to defendants, and sets out affirmative considerations supporting the rules. Part D responds to the argument that "rape victim shield laws," which limit admission of evidence of other acts by the victim, entail a like restriction on admission of similar crimes evidence in relation to the defendant. Part E responds to other objections that might be raised to the proposal.

A. The Proposed Rules

Proposed Rule 413 relates to criminal prosecutions for sexual assault. Paragraph (a) provides that evidence of the defendant's commission of other sexual assaults is admissible in such cases. If such evidence were admitted under the Rule, it could be considered for its bearing on any matter to which it is relevant. For example, it could be considered as evidence that the defendant has the motivation or disposition to commit sexual assaults, and a lack of effective inhibitions against acting on such impulses, and as evidence bearing on the probability or improbability that the defendant was falsely implicated in the offense of which he is presently accused. These grounds of relevance are more fully discussed in part C infra.

Paragraph (b) of proposed Rule 413 generally requires pre-trial disclosure of evidence to be offered under the Rule. This is designed to provide the defendant with notice of the evidence that will be offered, and a fair opportunity to develop a response. The Rule sets a normal minimum period of 15 days notice, but the court could allow notice at a later time for good cause, such as later discovery of evidence admissible under the rule. In such a case, it would, of course, be within the court's authority to grant a continuance if the defense needed additional time for preparation.

Paragraph (c) makes clear that proposed Rule 413 is not meant to be the exclusive avenue for introducing evidence of other crimes by the defendant in sexual assault prosecutions, and that the admission and consideration of such evidence under other rules will not be limited or impaired. For example, evidence that could be offered under proposed Rule 413 will often be independently admissible for certain purposes under Rule 609 (impeachment) or Rule 404(b) (evidence of matters other than "character").

Paragraph (d) defines the term "offense of sexual assault." The definition would apply both in determining whether a currently charged federal offense is an offense of sexual assault for purposes of the Rule, and in determining whether an uncharged offense qualifies as an offense of sexual assault for purposes of admitting evidence of its commission under the Rule. The definition covers federal and state offenses involving the types of conduct prohibited by the chapter of the criminal code relating to sexual abuse (chapter 109A of title 18, U.S. Code) in light of subparagraph (1), and other federal and state offenses that satisfy the general criteria set out in subparagraphs (2)–(5).

Rule 414 concerns criminal prosecutions for child molestation. Its provisions are parallel to those of the sexual assault rule (Rule 413), and should be understood in the same sense, except that the relevant class of offenses is child molestations rather than sexual assaults. The definition of child molestation offenses set out in paragraph (d) of this Rule differs from the corresponding definition of sexual assault offenses in Rule 413 in that (1) it provides that the offense must be committed in relation to a child, defined as a person below the age of fourteen, (2) it includes the child exploitation offenses of chapter 110 of the criminal code within the relevant category, and (3) it does not condition coverage of offenses on a lack of consent by the child-victim.

Rule 415 applies the same rules to civil actions in which a claim for damages or other relief is predicated on the defendant's alleged commission of an offense of sexual assault or child molestation. Evidence of the defendant's commission of other offenses of the same type would be admissible, and could be considered for its bearing on any matter to which it is relevant.

B. Background in the Law of Evidence

The common law has traditionally limited the admission of evidence of a defendant's commission of offenses other than the particular crime for which he is on trial. This limitation, however, has never been absolute. The Supreme Court has summarized the general position of the common law on this issue as follows:

> "Alongside the general principle that prior offenses are inadmissible, despite their relevance to guilt . . . the common law developed broad, vaguely defined exceptions—such as proof of intent, identify, malice, motive, and plan—whose application is left largely to the discretion of the trial judge. . . In short, the common law, like our decision in [Spencer v. Texas], implicitly recognized that any unfairness resulting from admitting prior convictions was more often than not balanced by its probative value and permitted the prosecution to introduce such evidence without demanding any particularly strong justification. (Marshall v. Lonberger, 459 U.S. 422, 438–39 n. 6 (1983))."

The Federal Rules of Evidence—which went into effect in 1975—follow the general pattern of traditional evidence rules, in that they reflect a general presumption against admitting evidence of uncharged offenses, but recognize various exceptions to this principle. One exception is set out in Rule 609. Rule 609 incorporates a restricted version of the traditional rule admitting, for purposes of impeachment, evidence of a witness's prior conviction for felonies or crimes involving dishonesty or false statement. The other major provision under which evidence of uncharged offenses may be admitted is Rule 404(b). That rule provides that such evidence is not admissible for the purpose of proving the "character" of the accused, but that it may be admitted as proof concerning any non-character issue:

(b) Other crimes, wrongs, or acts. Evidence of other crimes, wrongs, or acts is not admissible to prove the character of a person in order to show action in conformity therewith. It may, however, be admissible for other purposes, such as proof of motive, opportunity, intent, preparation, plan, knowledge, identity, or absence of mistake or accident.

Rule 404(b), however, makes no special allowance for admission of evidence of other "crimes, wrongs, or acts" in sex offense prosecutions. There was perhaps little reason for the framers of the Federal Rules of Evidence to focus on this issue, since sex offense prosecutions were not, at the time, a significant category of federal criminal jurisdiction.

This omission has been widely reproduced in codified state rules of evidence, whose formulation has been strongly influenced by the Federal Rules. The practical effect of this development is that the authority of the courts to admit evidence of uncharged offenses in prosecutions for sexual assaults and child molestations has been clouded, even in states that have traditionally favored a broad approach to admission in this area.

The actual responses of the courts to this development have varied. For example, in State v. McKay, 787 P.2d 479 (Or.1990), in which the defendant was accused of molesting his stepdaughter, the court admitted evidence of prior acts of molestation by the defendant against the girl. The court reached this result by stipulating that evidence of a predisposition to commit sex crimes against the victim of the charged offense was not evidence of "character" for purposes of the state's version of Rule 404(b), although it apparently would have regarded evidence of a general disposition to commit sex crimes as impermissible "character" evidence.

In Elliot v. State, 600 P.2d 1044 (1979), the Supreme Court of Wyoming reached a broader result supporting admission, despite a state rule that was essentially the same as Federal Rule 404(b). This was also a prosecution for child molestation. Evidence was admitted that the defendant had attempted to molest the older sister of the victim of the charged offense on a number of previous occasions. The court reconciled this result with Rule 404(b) by indicating that proof of prior acts of molestation would generally be admissible as evidence of "motive"—one of the traditional "exception" categories that is explicitly mentioned in Rule 404(b). Id. at 1048–49.

In contrast, in Getz v. State, 538 A.2d 726 (1988), the Supreme Court of Delaware overturned the defendant's conviction for raping his 11 year old daughter because evidence that he had also molested her on other occasions was admitted. The court stated that "a lustful disposition or sexual propensity exception to [Rule] 404(b)'s general prohibitions ... is almost universally recognized in cases involving proof of prior incestuous relations between the defendant and the complaining victim," but that "courts which have rejected this blanket exception have noted that in the absence of a materiality nexus such propensity evidence is difficult to reconcile with the restrictive language of [Rule] 404(b)." The court went on to hold that the disputed evidence in the case was impermissible evidence of character and could not be admitted under the state's Rule 404(b).

The foregoing decisions illustrate the increased jeopardy that the current formulation of the Federal Rules of Evidence has created for effective prosecution in sex offense cases. While the law in this area has never been a model of clarity and consistency, the widespread adoption of codified state rules based on the Federal Rules has aggravated its shortcomings. In jurisdictions that have such codified rules, the courts are no longer free to recognize straightforwardly the need for rules of admission tailored to the distinctive characteristics of sex offense cases or other distinctive categories of crimes. Important evidence of guilt may consequently be excluded in such cases.

Where the courts do admit such evidence, it may require a forced effort to work around the language and standard interpretation of codified rules that restrict admission, or may depend on unpredictable decisions by individual trial judges to allow admission under other "exception" categories. The establishment of clear, general rules of admission, as set out in proposed Rules 413–415, would resolve these problems under current law in federal proceedings, and would provide a model for comparable reforms in state rules of evidence.

C. Evidence of Motivation and Probability

Rules restricting the admission of evidence of uncharged misconduct by the defendant have traditionally been justified on two main grounds:

First, there is the concern over lack of fair notice to the defendant, if evidence of "bad acts" with which he has not formally been charged could freely be offered at trial. In the absence of limitations on such evidence, it has been argued, "a defendant could be confronted at trial with evidence implicating him in an unpredictable range of prior acts of misconduct extending over the whole course of his life, and would be denied a fair opportunity to prepare a defense to the accusations he would face at trial." The Admission of Criminal Histories at Trial, 22 U. Mich. J.L. Ref. 707, 728 (1989).

Second, there is the concern that evidence of other offenses or misconduct by the defendant is likely to be prejudicial or distracting, and that the potential for prejudice and distraction outweighs its probative value. Statements of this concern are sometimes accompanied by assertions that such evidence is of little probative value, merely being an indication of the defendant's "character." In light of the potential such evidence holds for prejudicing the defendant, it is argued, the general authority of the trial judge to exclude evidence that is unduly prejudicial or distracting (F.R.E. 403) is inadequate, and categorical rules of exclusion must be adopted for such evidence.

The first concern—relating to fair notice—can readily be answered in connection with proposed Rules 413–15. The Rules do not authorize an open-ended enquiry into all the "bad acts" the defendant may have committed in the course of his life, but only admit evidence of other serious criminal acts which are of the same type as the offense with which the defendant is formally charged. More importantly, the Rules specifically require prior disclosure to the defendant of the evidence that will be offered against him.

The second general concern about evidence of uncharged acts—a risk of prejudice or distraction that generally outweighs its probative value—is also adequately addressed by the limitations on the admission of evidence under the proposed rules. The rules do not admit evidence that merely indicates that the defendant is generally of "bad character," or even that he has a general disposition to engage in crime. Rather, to be admissible, the evidence must relate to other crimes by the defendant that are of the same type—sexual assault or child molestation—as the crime with which he is formally charged.

In general, the probative value of such evidence is strong, and is not outweighed by any overriding risk of prejudice. The relevance of such evidence will normally be apparent on at least two grounds—as evidence that the defendant has the motivation or disposition to commit such offenses, and as evidence of the improbability that the defendant has been falsely or mistakenly accused of the crime.

Evidence of Motivation. One of the traditional "exception" categories that has been explicitly carried forward in F.R.E. 404(b) is admission of evidence of "other crimes, wrongs, or acts" to establish "motive." For example, in a prosecution for embezzlement, evidence may be admitted of other acts by the defendant which indicate that he was in financial straits, to show that he would have had a motive or committing a crime that offered monetary gain. Or in a prosecution for a hate crime—such as a lynching or assault with apparent racial motivation—evidence may be admitted of other acts by the defendant that manifest a general animosity towards the victim's racial group for the purpose of establishing motive.

The admissibility of evidence of similar crimes under the proposed new rules is analogous to the current "motive" exception, and is justifiable on similar grounds. The proposed sexual assault rule (Rule 413), as noted above, does not indiscriminately admit evidence of other bad things the defendant may have done, but only evidence of his commission of other criminal sexual assaults. In other words, the evidence must be of such a character as to indicate that the defendant has the unusual combination of aggressive and sexual impulses that motivates the commission of such crimes, and a lack of effective inhibitions against acting on such impulses.

Where there is evidence that the defendant has such impulses—and has acted on them in the past—a charge of sexual assault has far greater plausibility than if there were no evidence of such a disposition on the part of the defendant. See generally The Admission of Criminal Histories at Trial, 22 U. Mich. J.L. Ref. 707, 725–26 (1989). This seems to be the main point underlying the judicial decisions that have straightforwardly admitted evidence of similar crimes in sex offense cases as evidence of the defendant's "lustful disposition."

The case for admission on these grounds is equally strong, if not stronger, in child molestation cases. Evidence of other acts of molestation indicates that the defendant has a type of desire or impulse—a sexual or sado-sexual interest in children—that simply does not exist in ordinary people. In such cases, the evidence is generally relevant as proof of "motive" in common sense terms, and admission could normally be sustained even under the current Rules on a sufficiently broad reading of the "motive" exception category. See Elliott v. State, 600 P.2d 1044, 1048–49 (Wyo.1979).

Evidence of Improbability. Existing exceptions to the general presumption against admitting evidence of uncharged offenses are sometimes justified on grounds of probability (in Wigmore's terminology, the "doctrine of chances"). For example, one of the "exception" categories mentioned in F.R.E. 404(b) is for proof of "intent." Under this exception, evidence of similar crimes may be admitted to rebut a defense that the defendant engaged in allegedly criminal conduct accidentally, or otherwise lacked the state of mind required for its commission. The rationale commonly given for this exception is the probative value such evidence has on account of the inherent improbability that a person will innocently or inadvertently engage in similar, potentially criminal conduct on a number of different occasions. See Imwinkelried, Uncharged Misconduct Evidence § 5.05 (1984).

Probabilistic reasoning of this type is not limited to proof of the mental element of the offense, but may also be used to support the admission of evidence establishing the defendant's commission of the charged criminal conduct:

"[For example, suppose] that the defendant is charged with arson. The defendant claims that the fire was accidental. The cases routinely permit the prosecutor to show other acts of arson by the defendant and even non-arson fires at premises owned by the defendant. In these cases, the courts invoke the doctrine of chances. The courts reason that as the number of incidents increases, the objective probability of accident decreases. Simply stated, it is highly unlikely that a single person would be victimized by so many similar accidental fires in a short period of time. The coincidence defies common sense and is too peculiar. (Imwinkelried, *Uncharged Misconduct Evidence* § 4.01 (1984))."

Turning to the case of sex offense prosecutions, similar considerations of probability provide support for a general rule of admission for similar crimes evidence. It is inherently improbable that a person whose prior acts show that he is in fact a rapist or child molester would have the bad luck to be later hit with a false accusation of committing the same type of crime, or that a person would fortuitously be subject to multiple false accusations by a number of different victims. These points may be seen more clearly by considering the major elements of a sex offense prosecution.

In general, to obtain a conviction for a sexual assault, the government must prove that (1) the alleged sexual conduct actually took place, (2) the victim did not consent, (3) the defendant was the person who engaged in the conduct, and (4) the defendant acted with the culpable state of mind required for the commission of the offense. The elements in a child molestation case are similar, except that proof of non-consent by the victim is normally not required.

With respect to the third and fourth elements—the defendant's identity as the perpetrator and satisfaction of the mental element—similar crimes evidence will often be admissible even under a codified rule modeled on F.R.E. 404(b). Proof of "identity", and proof of "intent" or "knowledge," are explicitly mentioned as examples of permissible "non-character" uses of such evidence in the Rule.

In comparison, admission of such evidence on the first and second issues—the occurrence of the alleged act and the victim's lack of consent—is more problematic under a codified rule of this type. However, on these issues as well, similar crimes evidence is likely to have a high degree of probative value on grounds of probability.

For example, consider a case in which the defense attacks the victim's assertion that she did not consent, or represents that the whole incident was made up by the victim. Suppose further that there is practically conclusive evidence that the defendant has in fact committed one or more sexual assaults on other occasions, such as a prior conviction of the defendant on a charge of rape. In the presence of such evidence, the defense's claim of consent, or claim that the whole incident did not occur, would usually amount to a contention that the victim fabricated a false charge of rape against a person who just happened to be a rapist. The improbability of such a coincidence gives similar crimes evidence a high degree of probative value, and supports its admission, in such a case.

As a second example, consider a case like that described above, but with similar crimes evidence of a less conclusive character. For example, suppose the evidence is the testimony of another woman that the defendant raped her on a different occasion, though the defendant has not been prosecuted for that offense. In such a case, the defendant's alleged commission of rape on the earlier occasion, as well as his guilt of the presently charged offense, would be open to question.

Nevertheless, the "doctrine of chances" legitimately applies to such a case as well. If the defense concedes that the earlier rape occurred, then the case is essentially the same as the preceding one. If the defense disputes both the charged offense and the uncharged offense, this amounts to a claim that not just one but two women have made false charges of rape against the defendant. Here as well, the improbability of multiple false charges gives similar crimes evidence of [sic] high degree of probative value.

The force of the argument from improbability may be reduced if there is reason to believe that the formal charge and the accusation of an uncharged offense were not generated independently of each other. For example, where the identity of the offender is an issue, it may appear that a witness' identification of the defendant as the man who raped her could have been influenced by knowledge that the victim of the charged offense had previously identified the same man as her assailant.

In such a case, however, the defense would be free to bring out the possible connection of the charges, and the jury would consider that factor in assessing the significance of the evidence. Similar crimes evidence under the proposed rules is no different in this respect from other forms of regularly admissible evidence, whose normal probative force may also be reduced by special factors in some cases. In relation to evidence admissible under the proposed rules, as with other forms of evidence, the general standards of the Rules of Evidence and the processes of adversarial presentation and testing of evidence can properly be relied on to provide a fair picture of the relevant facts as the basis for the jury's decision.

D. The Import of Rape Victim Shield Laws

Within the past twenty years, virtually all American jurisdictions have adopted "rape victim shield laws," which limit enquiry in rape trials into the past sexual history of the victim. The shield laws have overturned earlier evidentiary rules and doctrines which tended to be highly permissive in allowing exploration of the victim's prior sexual activity in rape cases.

The pertinent provision in federal law is F.R.E. 412, which generally bars the admission in federal sexual abuse prosecutions of evidence of the victim's past sexual behavior. The Rule recognizes exceptions to this general presumption of non-admissibility for cases where admission of such evidence is constitutionally required or other specified circumstances give it an unusually high degree of relevance.

The argument has been made that the elimination of broad rules of admission for other acts of the victim in rape cases makes it improper to continue or adopt broad rules of admission for uncharged acts of the accused. If the victim is not to be taxed with evidence of unrelated conduct on her part, the argument goes, why should the defendant be taxed with evidence of other things he has done, which also have no direct relationship to the charged offense?

This argument, however, is not well-founded. The rules of evidence do not generally aim at a superficial neutrality between rules of admission affecting the victim and the defendant. Rather, the formulation of such rules must depend on a rational consideration of the relevant policies. The sound policies that underlie the rape victim shield laws provide no support for comparable restrictions in relation to the conduct of the defendant. The differences between the two contexts include the following:

First, there is a basic difference in the probative value of the evidence that is subject to exclusion under such rules. In the ordinary case, enquiry by the defense into the past sexual behavior of the victim in a rape case will show at most that she has engaged in some sexual activity prior to or outside of marriage—a circumstance that does not distinguish her from most of the rest of the population, and that normally has little probative value on the question whether she consented to the sexual acts involved in the charged offense. In contrast, evidence showing that the defendant has committed rapes on other occasions places him in a small class of depraved criminals, and is likely to be highly probative in relation to the pending charge. The difference in typical probative [sic] alone is sufficient to refute facile equations between evidence of other sexual behavior by the victim and evidence of other violent sex crimes by the defendant.

Second, the rape victim shield laws serve the important purpose of encouraging victims to report rapes and cooperate in prosecution by not requiring them to undergo public exposure of their personal sexual histories as a consequence of doing so. Rules limiting disclosure at trial of the defendant's commission of other rapes do not further any comparable public purpose, because the defendant's cooperation is not required to carry out the prosecution.

Third, the victim shield laws serve the important purpose of safeguarding the privacy of rape victims. The unrelated sexual activity of the victim is generally no one's business but her own, and should not be exposed in the absence of compelling justification. In contrast, violent sex crimes are not private acts, and the defendant can claim no legitimate interest in suppressing evidence that he has engaged in such acts when it is relevant to the determination of a later criminal charge.

E. Other Issues

This final part of this explanation of section 801 addresses two further objections to the proposed rules—the objection that the prosecutor should be barred from introducing evidence of uncharged offenses in order to require him to formally charge all the offenses he wishes to prove at trial, and the objection that fairness to the defendant or other policies require that some time limit be imposed on the uncharged offenses that could be admitted under the proposed rules.

The decision whether to charge an offense. With respect to the first objection, it should be noted that the prosecutor has practical incentives to charge fully, regardless of any compulsion arising from the rules restricting evidence of uncharged misconduct. Charging a larger number of counts tends to reduce the risk that the defendant will be entirely acquitted if the jury is not persuaded concerning a particular charge or charges. Moreover, charging more counts creates the possibility of conviction on a larger number of counts, and conviction on a larger number of counts tends to result in a higher penalty. Under the federal sentencing guidelines, for example, uncharged offenses may be given some weight in sentencing, but the largest determinants of the sentence are normally the offenses for which the defendant is convicted and his record of prior convictions.

Moreover, even if it were thought that additional incentives or requirements were needed to ensure fuller charging of available offenses, a general presumption against admitting evidence of uncharged offenses would be an unsound means of promoting this objective. In many cases it is impossible, or undesirable for entirely legitimate reasons, to charge certain offenses, but admitting evidence of such offenses is valid and important for their bearing on a charged offense.

For example, the uncharged offenses may have taken place in a different jurisdiction. This would occur in a state prosecution of a rapist or child molester whose earlier known crimes were committed in a different state. It would also occur in a federal prosecution of a rapist or molester whose earlier offenses were committed within the jurisdiction of a state or states, but outside of federal jurisdiction. In such a case, it is legally impossible for the prosecutor to charge the earlier offenses; if they are to be disclosed in the prosecution, it must be through uncharged misconduct evidence.

A second example is situations in which there is insufficient evidence or other practical difficulties in prosecuting all of the defendant's prior offenses as separate counts, but the evidence regarding the earlier offenses is legitimately relevant to proof of the charged offense.

A common fact-pattern of this type involves fathers or stepfathers who are accused of molesting their daughters. The formally charged offenses in such a case may be limited to a particular act of molestation or a limited number of acts that happened to come to the attention of an adult witness (such as the defendant's wife). However, the victim will often testify in such a case that the molestation had been going on for a long time. A sister or sisters of the victim of the charged offense may also testify that the father had molested them as well over an extended period of time.

Charging all the prior offenses in such a case may be neither feasible nor desirable. The acts of molestation may number in the hundreds; the victim may be unable to recall most of them with any specificity; and the evidence supporting them individually would only be the uncorroborated testimony of a child victim-witness. Nevertheless, evidence that the charged offense was part of a broader pattern of molestation may be important to put the charge in perspective, and most courts have admitted such testimony by the victim. See, e.g., State v. Graham, 641 S.W.2d 102, 104–05 (Mo.1982). As Getz v. State, 538 A.2d 726 (Del.1988), illustrates, however, a court may regard such admission as problematic or simply prohibited under the restrictive standards of Rule 404(b).

Time limitation. Proposed Rules 413–15 do not place any particular time limit on the unchanged offenses that may be offered in evidence. The view underlying this formulation is that a lapse of time from the uncharged offense may properly be considered by the jury for any bearing it may have on the evidence's probative value, but that there is no justification for categorically excluding offenses that occurred before some arbitrarily specified temporal limit.

There is no magic line in time beyond which similar crimes evidence generally ceases to be relevant to the determination of a pending charge. This point is reflected in the current formulation of Rule 404(b), which does not specify any particular limit for admitting "non-character" evidence under the various categories it enumerates.

While there does not appear to be any precedent supporting a definite time limit on similar crimes evidence, some judicial decisions have given weight to the question of temporal proximity in a more flexible manner in deciding on the admission of such evidence in sex offense prosecutions. However, the rationales for this approach in such cases do not necessarily apply in connection with the proposed new rules. The admission of such evidence in past decisions has usually depended on ad hoc applications of other "exception" categories, such as proof of "a common scheme or plan," which comes with their own built-in limitations. If admission is thought to depend on a showing that the charged offense and uncharged offenses were part of a single on-going plan to engage in a series of sexual assaults, then too large a temporal spread among the offenses may weigh against such a finding. The theories of relevance underlying the proposed rules, however, do not depend on such a determination.

Concerns over fair notice to the defendant might also be thought to support a restrictive approach to admitting evidence of older offenses, on the view that there is a greater risk of unfair surprise if the defendant is initially confronted at trial with evidence of events that are far removed in time from the charged offense. Under the proposed rules, however, this concern is adequately met by the requirement of prior disclosure to the defendant of the evidence that will be offered.

Under the current rule admitting prior convictions for purposes of impeachment, as formulated in F.R.E. 609, prior convictions are presumptively inadmissible if they fall beyond a ten-year time period. However, the traditional version of the impeachment rule automatically admitted evidence of prior felony and *crimen falsi* convictions without limitation of time, on the view that temporal proximity (or the lack of it) should go to probative value rather than admissibility. The validity of the codified federal rule's contrary approach is open to question. See generally The Admission of Criminal Histories at Trial, 22 U. Mich. J.L. Ref. 707, 769 (1989).

Moreover, the impeachment rule has sometimes been criticized on the ground that it theoretically admits prior convictions only for the limited purpose of impeachment, but that the jury may realistically consider this information as affirmative evidence of guilt once it is admitted. The suspicion that evidence admitted pursuant to the rule may be misused for purposes that are not legally authorized may partially explain the view that additional restrictions on the range of admissible convictions should be imposed, including the presumptive time limit that now appears in Rule 609.

No similar considerations support a time limit on admission under proposed Rules 413–15. The basic scope of the proposed rules is narrower than the impeachment rule in that their application is confined to sexual assault and child molestation cases, and only evidence of crimes of the same type as the charged offense may be shown. Within this clearly defined range, the normal probative value of similar crimes evidence is sufficiently great to support a general rule of admission, and consideration of such evidence for its bearing on any matter to which it is relevant. In contrast to the impeachment rule, there is no risk that evidence admitted under the proposed new rules will be considered for a prohibited purpose, since the rules do not limit the purposes for which such evidence may be considered.

Statement by David J. Karp

[The following excerpt is from the prepared text of an address presented by Mr. Karp, Senior Counsel, Office of Policy Development, United States Department of Justice, to the Evidence Section of the Association of American Law Schools on January 9, 1993, and referenced in Representative Molinari's remarks, supra, at p. 1074. The full address is reprinted at 70 Chi.–Kent L. Rev. 15 (1994)—Eds]

My subject today is the admission of evidence of uncharged crimes against the defendant, with particular reference to the use of such evidence in sex offense cases.

Public attention has been focused on this issue by the William Kennedy Smith case in Florida. As everyone knows, the case involved a sexual assault prosecution, in which the court excluded evidence that the defendant had engaged in sexual assaults against a number of other women.

However, the proposal for reform in this area pre-dates that particular case. It initially appeared in February of 1991 in bills introduced by Representative Susan Molinari and Senator Robert Dole. The bills proposed a general rule of admissibility in sexual assault and child molestation cases for evidence that the defendant has committed offenses of the same type on other occasions. The same proposal has subsequently been introduced in a number of other bills. These include the two violent crime bills that President Bush transmitted to the 102d Congress, and the proposed "Sexual Assault Prevention Act of 1992."

My discussion of this proposal will be in three parts. First, I will briefly describe the proposed new rules for sex offense cases and their intended operation. Second, I will discuss the arguments that have been made in support of these rules by the legislative sponsors and the Administration. Third, I will try to relate the proposed reform to broader issues in the law of evidence.

* * *

I. The Proposed Rules

The legislative proposal would add three new rules to the Federal Rules of Evidence. The first of these, proposed Rule 413, would apply to sexual assault cases. The basic rule of admissibility, set out in subdivision (a) of the rule, reads as follows: "In a criminal case in which the defendant is accused of an offense of sexual assault, evidence of the defendant's commission of another offense or offenses of sexual assault is admissible, and may be considered for its bearing on any matter to which it is relevant."

Proposed Rule 414 states a parallel principle for criminal cases involving child molestation: Evidence that the defendant committed offenses of the same type on other occasions would be admissible. Proposed Rule 415 makes the same rules applicable in civil cases. Hence, for example, in a civil suit for damages by a rape victim, evidence of the defendant's commission of rapes on other occasions would be admissible.

All of the proposed rules include certain safeguards for the defendant. The prosecutor—or the plaintiff in a civil case—would be required to disclose the evidence of the uncharged offenses to the defendant, including statements of witnesses or a summary of the substance of any testimony that is expected to be offered. This prevents unfair surprise and ensures that the defendant will have an opportunity to prepare any response or rebuttal.

The following points should be noted concerning the interpretation and application of these rules:

First, the proposed rules of admissibility mean what they say. Evidence admitted under the rules could be considered for its bearing on any matter to which it is relevant. This includes questions of the defendant's propensity or disposition to commit sex crimes. Evidence Rule 404(b)'s prohibition of "character" evidence would be superseded in this context.

Second, these rules are rules of admissibility, and not mandatory rules of admission. The general standards of the rules of evidence would apply to evidence offered under these rules, including the limitations of hearsay evidence, and the authority of the court to exclude relevant evidence under Rule 403. However, the rules would eliminate in sex offense cases the special restrictions on evidence of uncharged acts, where the acts are crimes of the same type as the charged offense. The analysis statement for the proposed Sexual Assault Prevention Act explained the effect of this change as follows:

> [E]vidence admissible pursuant to these rules would remain subject to the normal authority of the court to exclude evidence pursuant to F.R.E. 403 if the evidence's probative value is "substantially outweighed by the danger of unfair prejudice" or other adverse effects noted in that rule.

> It is not expected, however, that evidence admissible pursuant to proposed Rules 413–15 would often be excluded on the basis of Rule 403. Rather, the effect of the new rules is to put evidence of uncharged offenses in sexual assault and child molestation cases on the same footing as other types of evidence that are not subject to a special exclusionary rule. The presumption is in favor of admission. The underlying legislative judgment is that the sort of evidence that is admissible pursuant to proposed Rules 413–15 is typically relevant and probative, and that its probative value is normally not outweighed by any risk of prejudice or other adverse considerations.

Finally, the standard of proof with respect to uncharged offenses under the new rules would be governed by the Supreme Court's decision in Huddleston v. United States. In Huddleston, the Supreme Court held that information about uncharged offenses may be admitted conditionally, and that such offenses may properly be considered so long as a jury could reasonably conclude by a preponderance that the offenses occurred. While the case was directly concerned with admission under Rule 404(b), its reasoning on these points is also applicable to the proposed new rules for sex offense cases.

II. Arguments for the Proposed Rules

The proposal of these rules presupposes that they will be more effective than the current rules in promoting accurate fact-finding and achieving just results. What are the policy considerations supporting this view? Let's start with common sense.

One obvious ground is considerations of probability. The defense in a rape case will claim that the police or victim fingered the wrong man, or that the victim consented and then made up a false charge, or that the claim that a rape occurred is a complete fabrication. If the direct evidence of guilt is not conclusive, there may be no adequate basis for excluding these possibilities.

Evidence that the defendant has committed sexual assaults on other occasions, however, often puts an entirely different light on the matter. It would be quite a coincidence if a person who just happened to be a chronic rapist was falsely or mistakenly implicated in a later crime of the same type. In conjunction with the direct evidence of guilt, knowledge of the defendant's past behavior may foreclose reasonable doubt as to guilt in a case that would otherwise be inconclusive.

The second common sense ground for admitting and considering this type of evidence is the ground that the existing rules most strongly condemn—the inference concerning propensity or disposition. If we put aside preconceptions for the moment, however, the inference is certainly not an unreasonable one.

Ordinary people do not commit outrages against others because they have relatively little inclination to do so, and because any inclination in that direction is suppressed by moral inhibitions and fear of the practical risks associated with the commission of crimes. A person with a history of rape or child molestation stands on a different footing. His past conduct provides evidence that he has the combination of aggressive and sexual impulses that motivates the commission of such crimes, that he lacks effective inhibitions against acting on these impulses, and that the risks involved do not deter him. A charge of rape or child molestation has greater plausibility against a person with such a background.

In addition to these general grounds, the statements supporting the legislative proposal have pointed to the strength of the public interest in admitting all significant evidence of guilt in sex offense cases. This reflects in part the typically secretive nature of such crimes, and resulting lack of neutral witnesses in most cases; the difficulty of stopping rapists and child molesters because of the reluctance of many victims to report the crime or testify; and the gravity of the danger to the public if a rapist or child molester remains at large.

In cases involving adult victims, the issue of consent is a further reason. In violent crimes other than sexual assaults, there is rarely any colorable defense that the defendant's conduct was not criminal because of consent by the victim. The accused mugger does not claim that the victim freely handed over his wallet as a gift. In contrast, claims are regularly heard in rape cases that the victim engaged in consensual sex with the defendant and then falsely accused him. In such instances, knowledge that the defendant has committed rapes on other occasions is frequently critical in assessing the relative plausibility of these conflicting claims and accurately deciding cases that would otherwise become unresolvable swearing matches.

In child molestation cases, the importance of admitting similar crimes evidence is equally great, if not greater. Such cases regularly present the need to rely on the testimony of child victim-witnesses whose credibility can readily be attacked in the absence of substantial corroboration. In this context, the public interest in admitting all significant evidence that will illumine the credibility of the charge and any denial by the defense is truly compelling.

What can be said on the other side of the issue? Let me start by addressing the three standard justifications for restricting evidence of uncharged acts.

One ground is the need to provide fair notice to the defendant concerning the matters he will have to respond to at trial. The proposed rules meet this concern by requiring full disclosure to the defendant of the evidence that will be offered in support of the uncharged offenses. This is more than the defendant would be entitled to in connection with a formally charged offense.

The second standard rationale for limiting evidence of uncharged acts is the need to establish reasonable limits on the scope of the proceedings. The concern here is diffusing the focus of the proceedings and distracting the trier through prolonged explorations of the defendant's personal history.

The proposed rules also incorporate features which are responsive to this concern. They do not indiscriminately admit evidence of all the bad things the defendant may have done in the course of his life, but only admit evidence of criminal offenses of the same type as those with which he is formally charged. This limits the number of incidents for which evidence may be offered. In addition, the requirement of similarity in kind to the charged offense tends to ensure that the uncharged acts will have a high degree of probative value, and will not be mere distractions from the main issues.

In some instances, the operation of the proposed rules will complicate the proceedings. However, even if a large number of incidents are brought in, the complexity will not exceed that of a trial in which several counts are charged, or a large number of uncharged incidents are brought in under existing rules. For example, in the Atlanta child-murders case in 1982, the defendant Wayne Williams was formally charged with two murders, but evidence linking him to ten other killings was also presented. Similarly, if the defendant in a rape case has passed through life leaving a trail of women who say that he raped them, that fact is singular enough to justify the time required for presenting it to the jury.

The third standard rationale for the existing restriction is the concern over prejudice. The claim here, of course, is not just that admission of evidence of uncharged offenses increases the probability of conviction. That point is true, but admission of any other persuasive evidence of guilt has the same effect.

Rather, the "prejudice" rationale maintains that this type of evidence carries an unacceptable risk of convicting the innocent. This is premised on the view that jurors are likely to accord prior offenses more weight than they rationally merit as evidence of guilt, and are likely to return unwarranted convictions based on antagonism against the defendant that results from knowledge of his other offenses.

There is, however, no means of determining a priori whether particular categories of evidence are likely to be more prejudicial than probative. The lesson must be learned from experience, and in the context of sex offense prosecutions, the lesson of experience seems to point in the other direction. Courts in the United States have traditionally been inclined to admit evidence of other sex crimes by the defendant in sex offense prosecutions. In some states, this has involved the formal recognition of special case law rules of admissibility in sex offense cases.

Special rules of this sort have become less common in the past few decades, in part because of the widespread adoption of codified evidence rules that appear to leave no room for them. However, the same practical result is often achieved by stretching the existing rules. The contemporary edition of Wigmore's Evidence has described this tendency as follows:

> [T]here is a strong tendency in prosecutions for sex offenses to admit evidence of the accused's sexual proclivities. Do such decisions show that the general rule against the use of propensity evidence against an accused is not honored in sex offense prosecutions? We think so. . . [S]ome states and courts have . . . forthrightly and expressly recogniz[ed] a "lustful disposition" or sexual proclivity exception to the general rule barring the use of character evidence against an accused. . . [J]urisdictions that do not expressly recognize a lustful disposition exception may effectively recognize such an exception by expansively interpreting in prosecutions for sex offenses various well-established exceptions to the character evidence rule.

Finally, the statements supporting the legislative proposal have addressed two more specific objections.

The first of these is an alleged inconsistency with the rape victim shield laws. American jurisdictions have generally adopted rules that narrowly limit inquiry into unrelated sexual behavior of the alleged victim in rape cases. If the victim has immunity from disclosure of what she has done in the past, the argument runs, then why should the defendant be taxed with his past misconduct?

However, this objection is superficial. The shield laws further two important policies: First, they promote cooperation in the prosecution of sex offenses by not requiring the victim to suffer exposure of her sexual history as the price for doing so. Second, they safeguard the privacy of rape victims. There are no comparable policies supporting non-disclosure of the defendant's acts. The defendant's cooperation is not required for prosecution. Violent sex crimes are not private acts, and the defendant can claim no privacy interest in suppressing them when they are relevant to the determination of a later criminal charge.

In addition, there is a distinction in terms of probative value. The complainant in a rape prosecution is usually just a woman who had the bad luck to be raped. Inquiry into her sexual history will normally disclose nothing that particularly distinguishes her from the general population, and typically has little probative value on the question whether she consented to sex in the charged incident and fabricated a false accusation.

In contrast, evidence showing that the defendant has committed sexual assaults on other occasions places him in a small class of depraved criminals, and is likely to be highly probative in relation to the pending charge. The difference in typical probative value alone is sufficient to refute facile equations between evidence of other sexual behavior by the victim and evidence of other violent sex crimes by the defendant.

The second specific objection to the proposal is that it is too broad because it allows evidence of uncharged offenses for which the defendant has never been prosecuted, as well as evidence of prior convictions for sex crimes. One response is that the approach of the proposed new rules is no different in this respect than current Rule 404(b). The admission of evidence under the current rule is not conditioned on a prior conviction or other prior determination that the defendant committed the uncharged offenses. The following additional points may be noted in response to this criticism:

First, there is no disadvantage to the defendant if he is only formally charged with a particular offense, and other (uncharged) offenses are offered as supporting evidence. The defendant has the same rights and opportunities to respond to evidence of uncharged offenses that he has in relation to a formally charged offense, including the assistance of counsel, cross-examination of witnesses, and presentation of rebuttal evidence. In addition, under the proposed new rules, the prosecutor would be required to make a full disclosure to the defendant of the evidence to be offered to establish an uncharged offense. Hence, the defendant's procedural rights under the proposed rules exceed those which he would have if he were formally charged with all offenses.

Second, rapists and child molesters frequently commit numerous crimes before being apprehended and prosecuted, and it is often impossible to join all offenses for trial in a single forum. This occurs, for example, in the case of a rapist or child molester who commits crimes in a number of different states, or who commits some crimes in state jurisdiction and others in federal jurisdiction. If the jury is to be made aware of all relevant criminal conduct of the defendant, this can only be accomplished in such a case through the admission of evidence of uncharged crimes.

Third, it also commonly happens in rape and child molestation cases that the victim is too traumatized, intimidated, or humiliated to file a complaint and go through the full course of proceedings in a criminal prosecution. Nevertheless, the victims in such cases are often willing to bear the more limited burden of testifying at the offender's trial for raping or molesting another person, when they find out that the person who marred their lives has also victimized others. Barring such testimony whenever the victims cannot take the stress of going through a full prosecution would enable rapists and child molesters to benefit from their success in traumatizing the victims of their crimes.

Fourth, evidence which links the defendant to several other rapes or child molestations may be highly probative when taken in the aggregate, even if it does not warrant charging separate counts based on all the individual incidents. As the Supreme Court observed in the Huddleston case, "individual pieces of evidence, insufficient in themselves to prove a point, may in cumulation prove it. The sum of an evidentiary presentation may well be greater than its constituent parts."

Fifth, the fact that the evidence supporting uncharged offenses may fall short of establishing their occurrence beyond a reasonable doubt is not a valid basis for barring the admission and consideration of such evidence. A defendant's commission of an offense with which he is formally charged must be proved beyond a reasonable doubt because we are unwilling to pronounce a person guilty of a crime—and to subject him to criminal punishment—unless guilt is established with a high degree of certainty. This does not mean, however, that the truth or validity of any particular piece of supporting evidence must be shown beyond a reasonable doubt.

In this respect, evidence admitted under the proposed new rules for sex offense cases would be assessed in essentially the same way as evidence of uncharged offenses that is admitted under current Rule 404(b). The defendant cannot be convicted for these offenses; they are admitted only for their bearing on the defendant's commission of the formally charged offense. If there are weaknesses in the government's evidence supporting the uncharged offenses, then the jury will be less persuaded of their occurrence, and their probative value as evidence of the charged offense is reduced accordingly. However, the strength of the supporting evidence generally goes to probative value rather than to admissibility. Evidence of this type is properly considered so long as the jury could reasonably conclude that the defendant committed the uncharged offense. No preliminary finding that the defendant committed the uncharged offense is required before evidence of the offense can be admitted, much less a finding that it occurred beyond a reasonable doubt.

* * *

In closing, I would suggest that the current rules are subject to criticism on two grounds. First, they are inadequate in providing the trier with information that is reasonably necessary to achieve just results in sex offense prosecutions, and hence inadequate to protect people from a particularly dangerous class of criminals. Now as in the past, many courts attempt to get around the restrictions, but there is no reliability in the results of this effort. The evidence that is needed to establish the guilt of rapists and child molesters is often subject to exclusion.

The result is cases in which everyone who is fully informed about the case—the police, the prosecutor, the victim, the judge, the defendant's lawyer, even spectators in the courtroom—is persuaded that the defendant did it, because the combination of the direct evidence and knowledge of the defendant's past conduct forecloses any genuine doubt on that point. Only the people who are actually responsible for deciding the case are denied the critical information.

The second criticism is the resulting distortions in the law. The vagueness of the standards of Rule 404(b) ensures considerable variation in their application by the courts, and this tendency is magnified in sex offense cases by the special pressures courts have felt to find some way of getting the evidence in. People's security against sexual violence should not have to depend on the willingness of courts to stretch evidentiary rules in particular cases.

The legislative proposal I have discussed provides a reasonable and honest alternative. It permits the use of evidence of other sex crimes in sex offense cases, while providing appropriate safeguards of fairness for the defendant. No fictions of limited admissibility are relied on; evidence admitted under the new rules would be subject to rational assessment. The result would be a major step forward in achieving justice and protecting people from one of the most atrocious forms of criminal violence.

ARTICLE V. PRIVILEGES

Rule 501

Note by Federal Judicial Center

The rules enacted by the Congress substituted the single Rule 501 in place of the 13 rules dealing with privilege prescribed by the Supreme Court as Article V. The 13 superseded rules, with Advisory Committee's Notes, are included in the Appendix. The reasons given in support of the congressional action are stated in the Report of the House Committee on the Judiciary, the Report of the Senate Committee on the Judiciary, and Conference Report, set forth below.

Report of House Committee on the Judiciary

Article V as submitted to Congress contained thirteen Rules. Nine of those Rules defined specific non-constitutional privileges which the federal courts must recognize (i.e. required reports, lawyer-client, psychotherapist-patient, husband-wife, communications to clergymen, political vote, trade secrets, secrets of state and other official information, and identity of informer). Another Rule provided that only those privileges set forth in Article V or in some other Act of Congress could be recognized by the federal courts. The three remaining Rules addressed collateral problems as to waiver of privilege by voluntary disclosure, privileged matter disclosed under compulsion or without opportunity to claim privilege, comment upon or inference from a claim of privilege, and jury instruction with regard thereto.

The Committee amended Article V to eliminate all of the Court's specific Rules on privileges. Instead, the Committee, through a single Rule, 501, left the law of privileges in its present state and further provided that privileges shall continue to be developed by the courts of the United States under a uniform standard applicable both in civil and criminal cases. That standard, derived from Rule 26 of the Federal Rules of Criminal Procedure, mandates the application of the principles of the common law as interpreted by the courts of the United States in the light of reason and experience. The words "person, government, State, or political subdivision thereof" were added by the Committee to the lone term "witnesses" used in Rule 26 to make clear that, as under present law, not only witnesses may have privileges. The Committee also included in its amendment a proviso modeled after Rule 302 and similar to language added by the Committee to Rule 601 relating to the competency of witnesses. The proviso is designed to require the application of State privilege law in civil actions and proceedings governed by Erie R. Co. v. Tompkins, 304 U.S. 64 (1938), a result in accord with current federal court decisions. See Republic Gear Co. v. Borg-Warner Corp., 381 F.2d 551, 555–556 n. 2 (2d Cir.1967). The Committee deemed the proviso to be necessary in the light of the Advisory Committee's view (see its note to Court Rule 501) that this result is not mandated under *Erie*.

The rationale underlying the proviso is that federal law should not supersede that of the States in substantive areas such as privilege absent a compelling reason. The Committee believes that in civil cases in the federal courts where an element of a claim or defense is not grounded upon a federal question, there is no federal interest strong enough to justify departure from State policy. In addition, the Committee considered that the Court's proposed Article V would have promoted forum shopping in some civil actions, depending upon differences in the privilege law applied as among the State and federal courts. The Committee's proviso, on the other hand, under which the federal courts are bound to apply the State's privilege law in actions founded upon a State-created right or defense, removes the incentive to "shop".

Report of Senate Committee on the Judiciary

Article V as submitted to Congress contained 13 rules. Nine of those rules defined specific nonconstitutional privileges which the Federal courts must recognize (i.e., required reports, lawyer-client, psychotherapist-patient, husband-wife, communications to clergymen, political vote, trade secrets, secrets of state and other official information, and identity of informer). Many of these rules contained controversial modifications or restrictions upon common law privileges. As noted supra, the House amended article V to eliminate all of the Court's specific rules on privileges. Through a single rule, 501, the House provided that privileges shall be governed by the principles of the common law as interpreted by the courts of the United

States in the light of reason and experience (a standard derived from rule 26 of the Federal Rules of Criminal Procedure) except in the case of an element of a civil claim or defense as to which State law supplies the rule of decision, in which event state privilege law was to govern.

The committee agrees with the main thrust of the House amendment: that a federally developed common law based on modern reason and experience shall apply except where the State nature of the issues renders deference to State privilege law the wiser course, as in the usual diversity case. The committee understands that thrust of the House amendment to require that State privilege law be applied in "diversity" cases (actions on questions of State law between citizens of different States arising under 28 U.S.C. § 1332). The language of the House amendment, however, goes beyond this in some respects, and falls short of it in others: State privilege law applies even in nondiversity, Federal question civil cases, where an issue governed by State substantive law is the object of the evidence (such issues do sometimes arise in such cases); and, in all instances where State privilege law is to be applied, e.g., on proof of a State issue in a diversity case, a close reading reveals that State privilege law is not to be applied unless the matter to be proved is an element of that state claim or defense, as distinguished from a step along the way in the proof of it.

The committee is concerned that the language used in the House amendment could be difficult to apply. It provides that "in civil actions * * * with respect to an element of a claim or defense as to which State law supplies the rule of decision," State law on privilege applies. The question of what is an element of a claim or defense is likely to engender considerable litigation. If the matter in question constitutes an element of a claim, State law supplies the privilege rule; whereas if it is a mere item of proof with respect to a claim, then, even though State law might supply the rule of decision, Federal law on the privilege would apply. Further, disputes will arise as to how the rule should be applied in an antitrust action or in a tax case where the Federal statute is silent as to a particular aspect of the substantive law in question, but Federal cases had incorporated State law by reference to State law.[1] Is a claim (or defense) based on such a reference a claim or defense as to which federal or State law supplies the rule of decision?

Another problem not entirely avoidable is the complexity or difficulty the rule introduces into the trial of a Federal case containing a combination of Federal and State claims and defenses, e.g. an action involving Federal antitrust and State unfair competition claims. Two different bodies of privilege law would need to be consulted. It may even develop that the same

---

[1] For a discussion of reference to State substantive law, see note on Federal Incorporation by Reference of State Law, Hart & Wechsler, The Federal Courts and the Federal System, pp. 491–94 (2d ed. 1973).

witness-testimony might be relevant on both counts and privileged as to one but not the other.[2]

The formulation adopted by the House is pregnant with litigious mischief. The committee has, therefore, adopted what we believe will be a clearer and more practical guideline for determining when courts should respect State rules of privilege. Basically, it provides that in criminal and Federal question civil cases, federally evolved rules on privilege should apply since it is Federal policy which is being enforced.[3] Conversely, in diversity cases where the litigation in question turns on a substantive question of State law, and is brought in the Federal courts because the parties reside in different States, the committee believes it is clear that State rules of privilege should apply unless the proof is directed at a claim or defense for which Federal law supplies the rule of decision (a situation which would not commonly arise.)[4] It is intended that the State rules of privilege should apply equally in original diversity actions and diversity actions removed under 28 U.S.C. § 1441(b).

Two other comments on the privilege rule should be made. The committee has received a considerable volume of correspondence from psychiatric organizations and psychiatrists concerning the deletion of rule 504 of the rule submitted by the Supreme Court. It should be clearly understood that, in approving this general rule as to privileges, the action of Congress should not be understood as disapproving any recognition of a psychiatrist-patient, or husband-wife, or any other of the enumerated privileges contained in the Supreme Court rules. Rather, our action should be understood as reflecting the view that the recognition of a privilege based on a confidential relationship and other privileges should be determined on a case-by-case basis.

Further, we would understand that the prohibition against spouses testifying against each other is considered a rule of privilege and covered by this rule and not by rule 601 of the competency of witnesses.

---

[2] The problems with the House formulation are discussed in Rothstein. The Proposed Amendments to the Federal Rules of Evidence, 62 Georgetown University Law Journal 125 (1973) at notes 25, 26 and 70–74 and accompanying text.

[3] It is also intended that the Federal law of privileges should be applied with respect to pendant State law claims when they arise in a Federal question case.

[4] While such a situation might require use of two bodies of privilege law, federal and state, in the same case, nevertheless the occasions on which this would be required are considerably reduced as compared with the House version, and confined to situations where the Federal and State interests are such as to justify application of neither privilege law to the case as a whole. If the rule proposed here results in two conflicting bodies of privilege law applying to the same piece of evidence in the same case, it is contemplated that the rule favoring reception of the evidence should be applied. This policy is based on the present rule 43(a) of the Federal Rules of Civil Procedure which provides: In any case, the statute or rule which favors the reception of the evidence governs and the evidence shall be presented according to the most convenient method prescribed in any of the statutes or rules to which reference is herein made.

Conference Report

Rule 501 deals with the privilege of a witness not to testify. Both the House and Senate bills provide that federal privilege law applies in criminal cases. In civil actions and proceedings, the House bill provides that state privilege law applies "to an element of a claim or defense as to which State law supplies the rule of decision." The Senate bill provides that "in civil actions and proceedings arising under 28 U.S.C. § 1332 or 28 U.S.C. § 1335, or between citizens of different States and removed under 28 U.S.C. § 1441(b) the privilege of a witness, person, government, State or political subdivision thereof is determined in accordance with State law, unless with respect to the particular claim or defense, Federal law supplies the rule of decision."

The wording of the House and Senate bills differs in the treatment of civil actions and proceedings. The rule in the House bill applies to evidence that relates to "an element of a claim or defense." If an item of proof tends to support or defeat a claim or defense, or an element of a claim or defense, and if state law supplies the rule of decision for that claim or defense, then state privilege law applies to that item of proof.

Under the provision in the House bill, therefore, state privilege law will usually apply in diversity cases. There may be diversity cases, however, where a claim or defense is based upon federal law. In such instances, federal privilege law will apply to evidence relevant to the federal claim or defense. See Sola Electric Co. v. Jefferson Electric Co., 317 U.S. 173 (1942).

In nondiversity jurisdiction civil cases, federal privilege law will generally apply. In those situations where a federal court adopts or incorporates state law to fill interstices or gaps in federal statutory phrases, the court generally will apply federal privilege law. As Justice Jackson has said:

> A federal court sitting in a non-diversity case such as this does not sit as a local tribunal. In some cases it may see fit for special reasons to give the law of a particular state highly persuasive or even controlling effect, but in the last analysis its decision turns upon the law of the United States, not that of any state.

D'Oench, Duhme & Co. v. Federal Deposit Insurance Corp., 315 U.S. 447, 471 (1942) (Jackson, J., concurring). When a federal court chooses to absorb state law, it is applying the state law as a matter of federal common law. Thus, state law does not supply the rule of decision (even though the federal court may apply a rule derived from state decisions), and state privilege law would not apply. See C.A. Wright, Federal Courts 251–252 (2d ed. 1970); Holmberg v. Armbrecht, 327 U.S. 392 (1946); DeSylva v. Ballentine, 351 U.S. 570, 581 (1956); 9 Wright & Miller, Federal Rules and Procedure § 2408.

In civil actions and proceedings, where the rule of decision as to a claim or defense or as to an element of a claim or defense is supplied by state law, the House provision requires that state privilege law apply.

The Conference adopts the House provision.

Rule 502

Rule 502 was adopted by Pub. L. 110–322, 122 Stat. 3538, signed into law on Sept. 19, 2008. By the terms of the statute, the Rule applies "in all proceedings commenced after the date of enactment of this Act and, insofar as is just and practicable, in all proceedings pending on such date of enactment."

Explanatory Note on Evidence Rule 502 Prepared by the Judicial Conference Advisory Committee on Evidence Rules (Revised 11/28/2007)

This new rule has two major purposes:

1) It resolves some longstanding disputes in the courts about the effect of certain disclosures of communications or information protected by the attorney-client privilege or as work product–specifically those disputes involving inadvertent disclosure and subject matter waiver.

2) It responds to the widespread complaint that litigation costs necessary to protect against waiver of attorney-client privilege or work product have become prohibitive due to the concern that any disclosure (however innocent or minimal) will operate as a subject matter waiver of all protected communications or information. This concern is especially troubling in cases involving electronic discovery. *See, e.g., Hopson v. City of Baltimore*, 232 F.R.D. 228, 244 (D.Md. 2005) (electronic discovery may encompass "millions of documents" and to insist upon "record-by-record pre-production privilege review, on pain of subject matter waiver, would impose upon parties costs of production that bear no proportionality to what is at stake in the litigation").

The rule seeks to provide a predictable, uniform set of standards under which parties can determine the consequences of a disclosure of a communication or information covered by the attorney-client privilege or work-product protection. Parties to litigation need to know, for example, that if they exchange privileged information pursuant to a confidentiality order, the court's order will be enforceable. Moreover, if a federal court's confidentiality order is not enforceable in a state court then the burdensome costs of privilege review and retention are unlikely to be reduced.

The rule makes no attempt to alter federal or state law on whether a communication or information is protected under the attorney-client privilege or work-product immunity as an initial matter. Moreover, while establishing some exceptions to waiver, the rule does not purport to supplant applicable waiver doctrine generally.

The rule governs only certain waivers by disclosure. Other common-law waiver doctrines may result in a finding of waiver even where there is no disclosure of privileged information or work product. *See, e.g., Nguyen v. Excel Corp.*, 197 F.3d 200 (5th Cir. 1999) (reliance on an advice of counsel defense waives the privilege with respect to attorney-client communications pertinent to that defense); *Ryers v. Burleson*, 100 F.R.D. 436 (D.D.C. 1983) (allegation of lawyer malpractice constituted a waiver of confidential communications under the circumstances). The rule is not intended to displace or modify federal common law concerning waiver of privilege or work product where no disclosure has been made.

Subdivision (a). The rule provides that a voluntary disclosure in a federal proceeding or to a federal office or agency, if a waiver, generally results in a waiver only of the communication or information disclosed; a subject matter waiver (of either privilege or work product) is reserved for those unusual situations in which fairness requires a further disclosure of related, protected information, in order to prevent a selective and misleading presentation of evidence to the disadvantage of the adversary. *See, e.g., In re United Mine Workers of America Employee Benefit Plans Litig.*, 159 F.R.D. 307, 312 (D.D.C. 1994) (waiver of work product limited to materials actually disclosed, because the party did not deliberately disclose documents in an attempt to gain a tactical advantage). Thus, subject matter waiver is limited to situations in which a party intentionally puts protected information into the litigation in a selective, misleading and unfair manner. It follows that an inadvertent disclosure of protected information can never result in a subject matter waiver. *See* Rule 502(b). The rule rejects the result in *In re Sealed Case*, 877 F.2d 976 (D.C.Cir. 1989), which held that inadvertent disclosure of documents during discovery automatically constituted a subject matter waiver.

The language concerning subject matter waiver "ought in fairness"–is taken from Rule 106, because the animating principle is the same. Under both Rules, a party that makes a selective, misleading presentation that is unfair to the adversary opens itself to a more complete and accurate presentation.

To assure protection and predictability, the rule provides that if a disclosure is made at the federal level, the federal rule on subject matter waiver governs subsequent state court determinations on the scope of the waiver by that disclosure.

Subdivision (b). Courts are in conflict over whether an inadvertent disclosure of a communication or information protected as privileged or work product constitutes a waiver. A few courts find that a disclosure must be intentional to be a waiver. Most courts find a waiver only if the disclosing party acted carelessly in disclosing the communication or information and failed to request its return in a timely manner. And a few courts hold that any inadvertent disclosure of a communication or information protected under the attorney-client privilege or as work product constitutes a waiver without regard to the protections taken to avoid such a disclosure.

See generally Hopson v. City of Baltimore, 232 F.R.D. 228 (D.Md. 2005), for a discussion of this case law.

The rule opts for the middle ground: inadvertent disclosure of protected communications or information in connection with a federal proceeding or to a federal office or agency does not constitute a waiver if the holder took reasonable steps to prevent disclosure and also promptly took reasonable steps to rectify the error. This position is in accord with the majority view on whether inadvertent disclosure is a waiver.

Cases such as *Lois Sportswear, U.S.A., Inc. v. Levi Strauss & Co.,* 104 F.R.D. 103, 105 (S.D.N.Y. 1985) and *Hartford Fire Ins. Co. v. Garvey,* 109 F.R.D. 323, 332 (N.D.Cal. 1985), set out a multifactor test for determining whether inadvertent disclosure is a waiver. The stated factors (none of which is dispositive) are the reasonableness of precautions taken, the time taken to rectify the error, the scope of discovery, the extent of disclosure and the overriding issue of fairness. The rule does not explicitly codify that test, because it is really a set of non-determinative guidelines that vary from case to case. The rule is flexible enough to accommodate any of those listed factors. Other considerations bearing on the reasonableness of a producing party's efforts include the number of documents to be reviewed and the time constraints for production. Depending on the circumstances, a party that uses advanced analytical software applications and linguistic tools in screening for privilege and work product may be found to have taken "reasonable steps" to prevent inadvertent disclosure. The implementation of an efficient system of records management before litigation may also be relevant.

The rule does not require the producing party to engage in a post-production review to determine whether any protected communication or information has been produced by mistake. But the rule does require the producing party to follow up on any obvious indications that a protected communication or information has been produced inadvertently.

The rule applies to inadvertent disclosures made to a federal office or agency, including but not limited to an office or agency that is acting in the course of its regulatory, investigative or enforcement authority. The consequences of waiver, and the concomitant costs of pre-production privilege review, can be as great with respect to disclosures to offices and agencies as they are in litigation.

Subdivision (c). Difficult questions can arise when 1) a disclosure of a communication or information protected by the attorney-client privilege or as work product is made in a state proceeding, 2) the communication or information is offered in a subsequent federal proceeding on the ground that the disclosure waived the privilege or protection, and 3) the state and federal laws are in conflict on the question of waiver. The Committee determined that the proper solution for the federal court is to apply the law that is most protective of privilege and work product. If the state law is more protective (such as where the state law is that an inadvertent disclosure can never be a waiver), the holder of the privilege or protection may well have relied on that law when making the disclosure in the state proceeding. Moreover, applying a more restrictive federal law of waiver could impair the state objective of preserving the privilege or work-product protection for disclosures made in state proceedings. On the other hand, if the federal law is more protective, applying the state law of waiver to determine admissibility in federal court is likely to undermine the federal objective of limiting the costs of production.

The rule does not address the enforceability of a state court confidentiality order in a federal proceeding, as that question is covered both by statutory law and principles of federalism and comity. *See* 28 U.S.C. § 1738 (providing that state judicial proceedings "shall have the same full faith and credit in every court within the United States . . . as they have by law or usage in the courts of such State . . . from which they are taken"). *See also Tucker v. Ohtsu Tire & Rubber Co.*, 191 F.R.D. 495, 499 (D.Md. 2000) (noting that a federal court considering the enforceability of a state confidentiality order is "constrained by principles of comity, courtesy, and . . . federalism"). Thus, a state court order finding no waiver in connection with a disclosure made in a state court proceeding is enforceable under existing law in subsequent federal proceedings.

Subdivision (d). Confidentiality orders are becoming increasingly important in limiting the costs of privilege review and retention, especially in cases involving electronic discovery. But the utility of a confidentiality order in reducing discovery costs is substantially diminished if it provides no protection outside the particular litigation in which the order is entered. Parties are unlikely to be able to reduce the costs of pre-production review for privilege and work product if the consequence of disclosure is that the communications or information could be used by non-parties to the litigation.

There is some dispute on whether a confidentiality order entered in one case is enforceable in other proceedings. *See generally Hopson v. City of Baltimore*, 232 F.R.D. 228 (D.Md. 2005), for a discussion of this case law. The rule provides that when a confidentiality order governing the consequences of disclosure in that case is entered in a federal proceeding, its terms are enforceable against non-parties in any federal or state proceeding. For example, the court order may provide for return of documents without waiver irrespective of the care taken by the disclosing party; the rule contemplates enforcement of "claw-back" and "quick peek" arrangements as a way to avoid the excessive costs of pre-production review for privilege and work product. *See Zubulake v. UBS Warburg LLC*, 216 F.R.D. 280, 290 (S.D.N.Y. 2003) (noting that parties may enter into "so-called 'claw-back' agreements that allow the parties to forego privilege review altogether in favor of an agreement to return inadvertently produced privilege documents"). The rule provides a party with a predictable protection from a court order–predictability that is needed to allow the party to plan in advance to limit the prohibitive costs of privilege and work product review and retention.

Under the rule, a confidentiality order is enforceable whether or not it memorializes an agreement among the parties to the litigation. Party agreement should not be a condition of enforceability of a federal court's order.

Under subdivision (d), a federal court may order that disclosure of privileged or protected information "in connection with" a federal proceeding does not result in waiver. But subdivision (d) does not allow the federal court to enter an order determining the waiver effects of a separate disclosure of the same information in other proceedings, state or federal. If a disclosure has been made in a state proceeding (and is not the subject of a state-court order on waiver), then subdivision (d) is inapplicable. Subdivision (c) would govern the federal court's determination whether the state-court disclosure waived the privilege or protection in the federal proceeding.

Subdivision (e). Subdivision (e) codifies the well-established proposition that parties can enter an agreement to limit the effect of waiver by disclosure between or among them. Of course such an agreement can bind only the parties to the agreement. The rule makes clear that if parties want protection against non-parties from a finding of waiver by disclosure, the agreement must be made part of a court order.

Subdivision (f). The protections against waiver provided by Rule 502 must be applicable when protected communications or information disclosed in federal proceedings are subsequently offered in state proceedings. Otherwise the holders of protected communications and information, and their lawyers, could not rely on the protections provided by the Rule, and the goal of limiting costs in discovery would be substantially undermined. Rule 502(f) is intended to resolve any potential tension between the provisions of Rule 502 that apply to state proceedings and the possible limitations on the applicability of the Federal Rules of Evidence otherwise provided by Rules 101 and 1101.

The rule is intended to apply in all federal court proceedings, including court-annexed and court-ordered arbitrations, without regard to any possible limitations of Rules 101 and 1101. This provision is not intended to raise an inference about the applicability of any other rule of evidence in arbitration proceedings more generally.

The costs of discovery can be equally high for state and federal causes of action, and the rule seeks to limit those costs in all federal proceedings, regardless of whether the claim arises under state or federal law. Accordingly, the rule applies to state law causes of action brought in federal court.

Subdivision (g). The rule's coverage is limited to attorney-client privilege and work product. The operation of waiver by disclosure, as applied to other evidentiary privileges, remains a question of federal common law. Nor does the rule purport to apply to the Fifth Amendment privilege against compelled self-incrimination.

The definition of work product "materials" is intended to include both tangible and intangible information. *See In re Cendant Corp. Sec. Litig.,* 343 F.3d 658, 662 (3d Cir. 2003) ("work product protection extends to both tangible and intangible work product").

Report of Senate Committee on the Judiciary

* * *

I. BACKGROUND AND PURPOSE OF THE BILL

A. BACKGROUND

An efficient and cost-effective discovery process is important to preserving the integrity of our legal system. The costs of discovery have increased dramatically in recent years as the proliferation of email and other forms of electronic record-keeping have multiplied the number of documents litigants must review to protect privileged material. Outdated law affecting inadvertent disclosure coupled with the stark increase in discovery materials has led to dramatic litigation cost increases.

Currently, the inadvertent production of even a single privileged document puts the producing party at significant risk. If a privileged document is disclosed, a court may find that the waiver applies not only to that specific document and case but to all other documents and cases concerning the same subject matter. Furthermore, the privilege can be waived even if the party took reasonable steps to avoid disclosing it.

The increased use of email and other electronic media in today's business environment have exacerbated the problems with the current doctrine on waiver. Electronic information is even more voluminous and dispersed than traditional record-keeping methods, greatly increasing the time needed to review and separate privileged from non-privileged material. As the time spent reviewing documents has increased, so too has the amount of money litigants on all sides must spend to protect against the potential waiver of privilege.

In his floor statement introducing legislation to correct this problem, Senator Leahy observed:

Billions of dollars are spent each year in litigation to protect against the inadvertent disclosure of privileged materials. With the routine use of email and other electronic media in today's business environment, discovery can encompass millions of documents in a given case, vastly expanding the risks of inadvertent disclosure. The rule proposed by the Standing Committee is aimed at adapting to the new realities that accompany today's modes of communication, and reducing the burdens associated with the conduct of diligent electronic discovery.

In his statement supporting the proposed legislation, co-sponsor Senator Specter remarked:

Current law on attorney-client privilege and work product is responsible in large part for the rising costs of discovery–especially electronic discovery. Right now, it is far too easy to inadvertently lose–or "waive" the privilege. A single inadvertently disclosed document can result in waiving the privilege not only as to what was produced, but as to all documents on the same subject matter. In some courts, a waiver may be found even if the producing party took reasonable steps to avoid disclosure. Such waivers will not just affect the case in which the accidental disclosure is made, but will also impact other cases filed subsequently in State or Federal courts.

In sum, though most documents produced during discovery have little value, lawyers must nevertheless conduct exhaustive reviews to prevent the inadvertent disclosure of privileged material. In addition to the amount of resources litigants must dedicate to preserving privileged material, the fear of waiver also leads to extravagant claims of privilege, further undermining the purpose of the discovery process. Consequently, the costs of privilege review are often wholly disproportionate to the overall cost of the case.

B. PURPOSE OF THE BILL

The bill addresses these problems by providing a predictable and consistent standard to govern the waiver of privileged information. It improves the efficiency of the discovery process while preserving accountability. Furthermore, it does not alter federal or state law on whether information is protected by the attorney-client privilege or work product doctrine in the first instance, but merely modifies the consequences of inadvertent disclosure once a privilege is found to exist.

The bill provides a new Federal Rule of Evidence 502 to limit the consequences of inadvertent disclosure, thereby relieving litigants of the burden that a single mistake during the discovery process can cost them the protection of a privilege. It provides that if there is a waiver of privilege, it applies only to the specific information disclosed and not the broader subject matter unless the holder has intentionally used the privileged information in a misleading fashion. An inadvertent disclosure of privileged information does not constitute a waiver as long as the holder took reasonable steps to prevent disclosure and acted promptly to retrieve the mistakenly disclosed information.

The bill provides a new rule to ensure that parties will take advantage of its protections by remaining enforceable in subsequent proceedings. If a federal court enters an order finding that an inadvertent disclosure of privileged information does not constitute a waiver, that order will be enforceable against persons in federal or state proceedings. This protects the rule's ability to limit discovery costs by ensuring that parties in any given case will know they can rely on the new waiver rules in subsequent proceedings.

Importantly, the bill respects federal-state comity. The bill will ensure that if there is a disclosure of privileged information at the federal level then courts must honor Rule 502 in any subsequent state proceedings. If there is a disclosure in a state proceeding, then admissibility in any subsequent federal proceeding will be determined by the law that is most protective against waiver. However, it does not apply to any disclosure made in a state proceeding that is later introduced in a subsequent state proceeding.

Litigants recognize the need to adopt a new waiver doctrine to adapt to the effects of changing technology in the business environment. The bill has attracted widespread support from major legal organizations representing stakeholders on all sides of modern litigation. Among those groups voicing support for the measure are the American Bar Association, American College of Trial Lawyers, U.S. Chamber of Commerce, former Chairs of the Section of Litigation of the American Bar Association, Lawyers for Civil Justice, and several private law firms. * * *

CONGRESSIONAL RECORD—HOUSE

Sept. 8, 2008, pp. H7817–19

Ms. JACKSON–LEE of Texas. * * * Doing the research on this legislation and spending time with a number of lawyers, and the American Bar Association, Mr. Speaker, I can assure you that this has no negative impact on those lawyers representing defendants or those lawyers representing plaintiffs. In fact, unlike the courthouse and the courtroom, plaintiff lawyers and defendant lawyers, the plaintiff bar and the defendant bar, have come together in a unanimous voice, indicating that this will in fact enhance their ability to represent their clients and to ensure that they may have the broadest based discovery possible. * * *

Fast-moving litigation or expensive and vast litigation has both plaintiff and defendant shooting back and forth various documents, particularly in extensive discovery. In the course of the kind of voluminous discovery that often takes place, this can happen, where a privileged document is seen by the other party.

When vast amounts of documents are transmitted and stored electronically and can be searched and collected in the same manner, it is all too easy for a document containing privileged information to be overlooked, despite careful efforts to prevent it. * * *

Unfortunately, the case law has not kept up with these developments of expedited discovery and the electronic use of passing documents. Outdated legal precedents from an earlier era continue to create uncertainty. There are precedents, for example, holding that an inadvertent disclosure of a single document or communication not only can waive the privilege as to that one item, but can result in a blanket waiver as to all information concerning the same subject. That can collapse a case.

Concern about the potential adverse consequences has in recent years forced clients and their lawyers to undertake exhaustive, time-consuming, and expensive examination of documents item by item, often page by page, before they can be comfortable turning them over in discovery. That impacts, of course, negatively plaintiffs and defendants.

The document reviews can be grossly disproportionate in cost to the stakes of the underlying litigation and significantly impede the efficient processing of cases through the courts. * * *

The rule we are submitting today, submitted to Congress last year by the Judicial Conference, is a product of careful deliberations in its Advisory Committee on Evidence Rules, informed by years of examination of the issue in its Committee on Rules of Practice and Procedure. * * *

The proposed rule has now also undergone careful review in the House, as well as the Senate. During its consideration in the House Judiciary Committee, a number of questions arose regarding the scope and contours of the effect of the proposed rule on current law regarding attorney-client privilege and work product protection. * * *

The Judicial Conference was able to answer all these questions satisfactorily, without need to revise the text of the rule as submitted to Congress. In order to further reduce any potential uncertainty regarding how the rule is to be interpreted and applied, the committee has asked and the Judicial Conference has agreed to augment the explanatory note. I would like to insert the agreed addendum to the explanatory note in the Record at this point.

STATEMENT of CONGRESSIONAL INTENT REGARDING RULE 502 of THE FEDERAL RULES of EVIDENCE

During consideration of this rule in Congress, a number of questions were raised about the scope and contours of the effect of the proposed rule on current law regarding attorney-client privilege and work-product protection. These questions were ultimately answered satisfactorily, without need to revise the text of the rule as submitted to Congress by the Judicial Conference.

In general, these questions are answered by keeping in mind the limited though important purpose and focus of the rule. The rule addresses only the effect of disclosure, under specified circumstances, of a communication that is otherwise protected by attorney-client privilege, or of information that is protected by work-product protection, on whether the disclosure itself operates as a waiver of the privilege or protection for purposes of admissibility of evidence in a federal or state judicial or administrative proceeding. The rule does not alter the substantive law regarding attorney-client privilege or work-product protection in any other respect, including the burden on the party invoking the privilege (or protection) to prove that the particular information (or communication) qualifies for it. And it is not intended to alter the rules and practices governing use of information outside this evidentiary context.

Some of these questions are addressed more specifically below, in order to help further avoid uncertainty in the interpretation and application of the rule.

Subdivision (a)—Disclosure vs. Use

This subdivision does not alter the substantive law regarding when a party's strategic use in litigation of otherwise privileged information obliges that party to waive the privilege regarding other information concerning the same subject matter, so that the information being used can be fairly considered in context. One situation in which this issue arises, the assertion as a defense in patent-infringement litigation that a party was relying on advice of counsel, is discussed elsewhere in this.

Note. In this and similar situations, under subdivision (a)(1) the party using an attorney-client communication to its advantage in the litigation has, in so doing, intentionally waived the privilege as to other communications concerning the same subject matter, regardless of the circumstances in which the communication being so used was initially disclosed.

Subdivision (b)—Fairness Considerations

The standard set forth in this subdivision for determining whether a disclosure operates as a waiver of the privilege or protection is, as explained elsewhere in this Note, the majority rule in the federal courts. The majority rule has simply been distilled here into a standard designed to be predictable in its application. This distillation is not intended to foreclose notions of fairness from continuing to inform application of the standard in all aspects as appropriate in particular cases–for example, as to whether steps taken to rectify an erroneous inadvertent disclosure were sufficiently prompt under subdivision (b)(3) where the receiving party has relied on the information disclosed.

Subdivisions (a) and (b)—Disclosures to Federal Office or Agency

This rule, as a Federal Rule of Evidence, applies to admissibility of evidence. While subdivisions (a) and (b) are written broadly to apply as appropriate to disclosures of information to a federal office or agency, they do not apply to uses of information–such as routine use in government publications–that fall outside the evidentiary context. Nor do these subdivisions relieve the party seeking to protect the information as privileged from the burden of proving that the privilege applies in the first place.

Subdivision (d)—Court Orders

This subdivision authorizes a court to enter orders only in the context of litigation pending before the court. And it does not alter the law regarding waiver of privilege resulting from having acquiesced in the use of otherwise privileged information. Therefore, this subdivision does not provide a basis for a court to enable parties to agree to a selective waiver of the privilege, such as to a federal agency conducting an investigation, while preserving the privilege as against other parties seeking the information. This subdivision is designed to enable a court to enter an order, whether on motion of one or more parties or on its own motion, that will allow the parties to conduct and respond to discovery expeditiously, without the need for exhaustive pre-production privilege reviews, while still preserving each party's right to assert the privilege to preclude use in litigation of information disclosed in such discovery. While the benefits of a court order under this subdivision would be equally available in government enforcement actions as in private actions, acquiescence by the disclosing party in use by the federal agency of information disclosed pursuant to such an order would still be treated as under current law for purposes of determining whether the acquiescence in use of the information, as opposed to its mere disclosure, effects a waiver of the privilege. The same applies to acquiescence in use by another private party.

Moreover, whether the order is entered on motion of one or more parties, or on the court's own motion, the court retains its authority to include the conditions it deems appropriate in the circumstances.

Subdivision (e)—Party Agreements

This subdivision simply makes clear that while parties to a case may agree among themselves regarding the effect of disclosures between each other in a federal proceeding, it is not binding on others unless it is incorporated into a court order. This subdivision does not confer any authority on a court to enter any order regarding the effect of disclosures. That authority must be found in subdivision (d), or elsewhere.
* * *

ARTICLE VI. WITNESSES

Rule 601

Note by Federal Judicial Center

The first sentence of the rule enacted by the Congress is the entire rule prescribed by the Supreme Court, without change. The second sentence was added by congressional action.

Advisory Committee's Note

This general ground-clearing eliminates all grounds of incompetency not specifically recognized in the succeeding rules of this Article. Included among the grounds thus abolished are religious belief, conviction of crime, and connection with the litigation as a party or interested person or spouse of a party or interested person. With the exception of the so-called Dead Man's Acts, American jurisdictions generally have ceased to recognize these grounds.

The Dead Man's Acts are surviving traces of the common law disqualification of parties and interested persons. They exist in variety too great to convey conviction of their wisdom and effectiveness. These rules contain no provision of this kind. * * *

No mental or moral qualifications for testifying as a witness are specified. Standards of mental capacity have proved elusive in actual application. A leading commentator observes that few witnesses are disqualified on that ground. Weihofen, Testimonial Competence and Credibility, 34 Geo.Wash.L.Rev. 53 (1965). Discretion is regularly exercised in favor of allowing the testimony. A witness wholly without capacity is difficult to imagine. The question is one particularly suited to the jury as one of weight and credibility, subject to judicial authority to review the sufficiency of the evidence. 2 Wigmore §§ 501, 509. Standards of moral qualification in practice consist essentially of evaluating a person's truthfulness in terms of his own answers about it. Their principal utility is in affording an opportunity on voir dire examination to impress upon the witness his moral duty. This result may, however, be accomplished more directly, and without haggling in terms of legal standards, by the manner of administering the oath or affirmation under Rule 603.

Admissibility of religious belief as a ground of impeachment is treated in Rule 610. Conviction of crime as a ground of impeachment is the subject of Rule 609. Marital relationship is the basis for privilege under Rule 505. Interest in the outcome of litigation and mental capacity are, of course, highly relevant to credibility and require no special treatment to render them admissible along with other matters bearing upon the perception, memory, and narration of witnesses.

Report of House Committee on the Judiciary

Rule 601 as submitted to the Congress provided that "Every person is competent to be a witness except as otherwise provided in these rules." One effect of the Rule as proposed would have been to abolish age, mental capacity, and other grounds recognized in some State jurisdictions as making a person incompetent as a witness. The greatest controversy centered around the Rule's rendering inapplicable in the federal courts the so-called Dead Man's Statutes which exist in some States. Acknowledging that there is substantial disagreement as to the merit of Dead Man's Statutes, the Committee nevertheless believed that where such statutes have been enacted they represent State policy which should not be overturned in the absence of a compelling federal interest. The Committee therefore amended the Rule to make competency in civil actions determinable in accordance with State law with respect to elements of claims or defenses as to which State law supplies the rule of decision. Cf. Courtland v. Walston & Co., Inc., 340 F.Supp. 1076, 1087–1092 (S.D.N.Y.1972).

Report of Senate Committee on the Judiciary

The amendment to rule 601 parallels the treatment accorded rule 501 discussed immediately above.

Conference Report

Rule 601 deals with competency of witnesses. Both the House and Senate bills provide that federal competency law applies in criminal cases. In civil actions and proceedings, the House bill provides that state competency law applies "to an element of a claim or defense as to which State law supplies the rule of decision." The Senate bill provides that "in civil actions and proceedings arising under 28 U.S.C. § 1332 or 28 U.S.C. § 1335, or between citizens of different States and removed under 28 U.S.C. § 1441(b) the competency of a witness, person, government, State or political subdivision thereof is determined in accordance with State law, unless with respect to the particular claim or defense, Federal law supplies the rule of decision."

The wording of the House and Senate bills differs in the treatment of civil actions and proceedings. The rule in the House bill applies to evidence that relates to "an element of a claim or defense." If an item of proof tends to support or defeat a claim or defense, or an element of a claim or defense, and if state law supplies the rule of decision for that claim or defense, then state competency law applies to that item of proof.

For reasons similar to those underlying its action on Rule 501, the Conference adopts the House provision.

Rule 602

Note by Federal Judicial Center

The rule enacted by the Congress is the rule prescribed by the Supreme Court without change.

Advisory Committee's Note

" * * * [T]he rule requiring that a witness who testifies to a fact which can be perceived by the senses must have had an opportunity to observe, and must have actually observed the fact" is a "most pervasive manifestation" of the common law insistence upon "the most reliable sources of information." McCormick § 10, p. 19. These foundation requirements may, of course, be furnished by the testimony of the witness himself; hence personal knowledge is not an absolute but may consist of what the witness thinks he knows from personal perception. 2 Wigmore § 650. It will be observed that the rule is in fact a specialized application of the provisions of Rule 104(b) on conditional relevancy.

This rule does not govern the situation of a witness who testifies to a hearsay statement as such, if he has personal knowledge of the making of the statement. Rules 801 and 805 would be applicable. This rule would, however, prevent him from testifying to the subject matter of the hearsay statement, as he has no personal knowledge of it.

The reference to Rule 703 is designed to avoid any question of conflict between the present rule and the provisions of that rule allowing an expert to express opinions based on facts of which he does not have personal knowledge.

Rule 603

Note by Federal Judicial Center

The rule enacted by the Congress is the rule prescribed by the Supreme Court without change.

Advisory Committee's Note

The rule is designed to afford the flexibility required in dealing with religious adults, atheists, conscientious objectors, mental defectives, and children. Affirmation is simply a solemn undertaking to tell the truth; no special verbal formula is required. As is true generally, affirmation is recognized by federal law. "Oath" includes affirmation, 1 U.S.C. § 1; judges and clerks may administer oaths and affirmations, 28 U.S.C. §§ 459, 953; and affirmations are acceptable in lieu of oaths under Rule 43(d) of the Federal Rules of Civil Procedure. Perjury by a witness is a crime, 18 U.S.C. § 1621.

Rule 604

Note by Federal Judicial Center

The rule enacted by the Congress is the rule prescribed by the Supreme Court without change.

Advisory Committee's Note

The rule implements Rule 43(f) of the Federal Rules of Civil Procedure and Rule 28(b) of the Federal Rules of Criminal Procedure, both of which contain provisions for the appointment and compensation of interpreters.

Rule 605

Note by Federal Judicial Center

The rule enacted by the Congress is the rule prescribed by the Supreme Court without change.

Advisory Committee's Note

In view of the mandate of 28 U.S.C. § 455 that a judge disqualify himself in "any case in which he * * * is or has been a material witness," the likelihood that the presiding judge in a federal court might be called to testify in the trial over which he is presiding is slight. Nevertheless the possibility is not totally eliminated.

The solution here presented is a broad rule of incompetency, rather than such alternatives as incompetency only as to material matters, leaving the matter to the discretion of the judge, or recognizing no incompetency. The choice is the result of inability to evolve satisfactory answers to questions which arise when the judge abandons the bench for the witness stand. Who rules on objections? Who compels him to answer? Can he rule impartially on the weight and admissibility of his own testimony? Can he be impeached or cross-examined effectively? Can he, in a jury trial, avoid conferring his seal of approval on one side in the eyes of the jury? Can he, in a bench trial, avoid an involvement destructive of impartiality? The rule of general incompetency has substantial support. See Report of the Special Committee on the Propriety of Judges Appearing as Witnesses, 36 A.B.A.J. 630 (1950); cases collected in Annot. 157 A.L.R. 311; McCormick § 68, p. 147; Uniform Rule 42; California Evidence Code § 703; Kansas Code of Civil Procedure § 60–442; New Jersey Evidence Rule 42. Cf. 6 Wigmore § 1909, which advocates leaving the matter to the discretion of the judge, and statutes to that effect collected in Annot. 157 A.L.R. 311.

The rule provides an "automatic" objection. To require an actual objection would confront the opponent with a choice between not objecting, with the result of allowing the testimony, and objecting, with the probable result of excluding the testimony but at the price of continuing the trial before a judge likely to feel that his integrity had been attacked by the objector.

Rule 606

Note by Federal Judicial Center

The rule enacted by the Congress is the rule prescribed by the Supreme Court, amended only by the addition of the concluding phrase "for these purposes." The bill originally passed by the House did not contain in the first sentence the prohibition as to matters or statements during the deliberations or the clause beginning "except."

Advisory Committee's Note

Subdivision (a). The considerations which bear upon the permissibility of testimony by a juror in the trial in which he is sitting as juror bear an obvious similarity to those evoked when the judge is called as a witness. See Advisory Committee's Note to Rule 605. The judge is not, however in this instance so involved as to call for departure from usual principles requiring objection to be made; hence the only provision on objection is that opportunity be afforded for its making out of the presence of the jury. Compare Rule 605.

Subdivision (b). Whether testimony, affidavits, or statements of jurors should be received for the purpose of invalidating or supporting a verdict or indictment, and if so, under what circumstances, has given rise to substantial differences of opinion. The familiar rubric that a juror may not impeach his own verdict, dating from Lord Mansfield's time, is a gross oversimplification. The values sought to be promoted by excluding the evidence include freedom of deliberation, stability and finality of verdicts, and protection of jurors against annoyance and embarrassment. McDonald v. Pless, 238 U.S. 264, 35 S.Ct. 783, 59 L.Ed. 1300 (1915). On the other hand, simply putting verdicts beyond effective reach can only promote irregularity and injustice. The rule offers an accommodation between these competing considerations.

The mental operations and emotional reactions of jurors in arriving at a given result would, if allowed as a subject of inquiry, place every verdict at the mercy of jurors and invite tampering and harassment. See Grenz v. Werre, 129 N.W.2d 681 (N.D.1964). The authorities are in virtually complete accord in excluding the evidence. Fryer, Note on Disqualification of Witnesses, Selected Writings on Evidence and Trial 345, 347 (Fryer ed. 1957); Maguire, Weinstein, et al., Cases on Evidence 887 (5th ed. 1965); 8 Wigmore § 2349 (McNaughton Rev.1961). As to matters other than mental operations and emotional reactions of jurors, substantial authority refuses to allow a juror to disclose irregularities which occur in the jury room, but allows his testimony as to irregularities occurring outside and allows outsiders to testify as to occurrences both inside and out. 8 Wigmore § 2354 (McNaughton Rev.1961). However, the door of the jury room is not necessarily a satisfactory dividing point, and the Supreme Court has refused to accept it for every situation. Mattox v. United States, 146 U.S. 140, 13 S.Ct. 50, 36 L.Ed. 917 (1892).

Under the federal decisions the central focus has been upon insulation of the manner in which the jury reached its verdict, and this protection extends to each of the components of deliberation, including arguments, statements, discussions, mental and emotional reactions, votes, and any other feature of the process. Thus testimony or affidavits of jurors have been held incompetent to show a compromise verdict, Hyde v. United States, 225 U.S. 347, 382 (1912); a quotient verdict, McDonald v. Pless, 238 U.S. 264 (1915); speculation as to insurance coverage, Holden v. Porter, 405 F.2d 878 (10th Cir.1969), Farmers Coop. Elev. Ass'n v. Strand, 382 F.2d 224, 230 (8th Cir.1967), cert. denied 389 U.S. 1014; misinterpretation of instructions, Farmers Coop. Elev. Ass'n v. Strand, supra; mistake in returning verdict, United States v. Chereton, 309 F.2d 197 (6th Cir.1962); interpretation of guilty plea by one defendant as implicating others, United States v. Crosby, 294 F.2d 928, 949 (2d Cir.1961). The policy does not, however, foreclose testimony by jurors as to prejudicial extraneous information or influences injected into or brought to bear upon the deliberative process. Thus a juror is recognized as competent to testify to statements by the bailiff or the introduction of a prejudicial newspaper account into the jury room, Mattox v. United States, 146 U.S. 140 (1892). See also Parker v. Gladden, 385 U.S. 363 (1966).

This rule does not purport to specify the substantive grounds for setting aside verdicts for irregularity; it deals only with the competency of jurors to testify concerning those grounds.

See also Rule 6(e) of the Federal Rules of Criminal Procedure and 18 U.S.C. § 3500, governing the secrecy of grand jury proceedings. The present rule does not relate to secrecy and disclosure but to the competency of certain witnesses and evidence.

Report of House Judiciary Committee

As proposed by the Court, Rule 606(b) limited testimony by a juror in the course of an inquiry into the validity of a verdict or indictment. He could testify as to the influence of extraneous prejudicial information brought to the jury's attention (e.g. a radio newscast or a newspaper account) or an outside influence which improperly had been brought to bear upon a juror (e.g. a threat to the safety of a member of his family), but he could not testify as to other irregularities which occurred in the jury room. Under this formulation a quotient verdict could not be attacked through the testimony of a juror, nor could a juror testify to the drunken condition of a fellow juror which so disabled him that he could not participate in the jury's deliberations.

The 1969 and 1971 Advisory Committee drafts would have permitted a member of the jury to testify concerning these kinds of irregularities in the jury room. The Advisory Committee note in the 1971 draft stated that " * * * the door of the jury room is not a satisfactory dividing point, and the Supreme Court has refused to accept it." The Advisory Committee further commented that—

The trend has been to draw the dividing line between testimony as to mental processes, on the one hand, and as to the existence of conditions or occurrences of events calculated improperly to influence the verdict, on the other hand, without regard to whether the happening is within or without the jury room. * * * The jurors are the persons who know what really happened. Allowing them to testify as to matters other than their own reactions involves no particular hazard to the values sought to be protected. The rule is based upon this conclusion. It makes no attempt to specify the substantive grounds for setting aside verdicts for irregularity.

Objective jury misconduct may be testified to in California, Florida, Iowa, Kansas, Nebraska, New Jersey, North Dakota, Ohio, Oregon, Tennessee, Texas, and Washington.

Persuaded that the better practice is that provided for in the earlier drafts, the Committee amended subdivision (b) to read in the text of those drafts.

Report of Senate Judiciary Committee

As adopted by the House, this rule would permit the impeachment of verdicts by inquiry into, not the mental processes of the jurors, but what happened in terms of conduct in the jury room. This extension of the ability to impeach a verdict is felt to be unwarranted and ill-advised.

The rule passed by the House embodies a suggestion by the Advisory Committee of the Judicial Conference that is considerably broader than the final version adopted by the Supreme Court, which embodied long-accepted Federal law. Although forbidding the impeachment of verdicts by inquiry into the jurors' mental processes, it deletes from the Supreme Court version the proscription against testimony "as to any matter or statement occurring during the course of the jury's deliberations." This deletion would have the effect of opening verdicts up to challenge on the basis of what happened during the jury's internal deliberations, for example, where a juror alleged that the jury refused to follow the trial judge's instructions or that some of the jurors did not take part in deliberations.

Permitting an individual to attack a jury verdict based upon the jury's internal deliberations has long been recognized as unwise by the Supreme Court. In McDonald v. Pless, the Court stated:

* * *

[L]et it once be established that verdicts solemnly made and publicly returned into court can be attacked and set aside on the testimony of those who took part in their publication and all verdicts could be, and many would be, followed by an inquiry in the hope of discovering something which might invalidate the finding. Jurors would be harassed and beset by the defeated party in an effort to secure from them evidence of facts which might establish misconduct sufficient to set aside a verdict. If evidence thus secured could be thus used, the result would be to make what was intended to be a private deliberation, the constant subject of public investigation—to the destruction of all frankness and freedom of discussion and conference.[2]

* * *

As it stands then, the rule would permit the harassment of former jurors by losing parties as well as the possible exploitation of disgruntled or otherwise badly-motivated ex-jurors.

Public policy requires a finality to litigation. And common fairness requires that absolute privacy be preserved for jurors to engage in the full and free debate necessary to the attainment of just verdicts. Jurors will not be able to function effectively if their deliberations are to be scrutinized in post-trial litigation. In the interest of protecting the jury system and the citizens who make it work, rule 606 should not permit any inquiry into the internal deliberations of the jurors.

Conference Report

Rule 606(b) deals with juror testimony in an inquiry into the validity of a verdict or indictment. The House bill provides that a juror cannot testify about his mental processes or about the effect of anything upon his or another juror's mind as influencing him to assent to or dissent from a verdict or indictment. Thus, the House bill allows a juror to testify about objective matters occurring during the jury's deliberation, such as the misconduct of another juror or the reaching of a quotient verdict. The Senate bill does not permit juror testimony about any matter or statement occurring during the course of the jury's deliberations. The Senate bill does provide, however, that a juror may testify on the question whether extraneous prejudicial information was improperly brought to the jury's attention and on the question whether any outside influence was improperly brought to bear on any juror.

The Conference adopts the Senate amendment. The Conferees believe that jurors should be encouraged to be conscientious in promptly reporting to the court misconduct that occurs during jury deliberations.

Advisory Committee's Note to 2006 Amendment to Rule 606(b)

Rule 606(b) has been amended to provide that juror testimony may be used to prove that the verdict reported was the result of a mistake entering the verdict on the verdict form. The amendment responds to a divergence between the text of the Rule and the case law that has established an exception for proof of clerical errors. *See, e.g., Plummer v. Springfield Term.*

---

[2] 238 U.S. 264, at 267 (1915).

Ry., 5 F.3d 1, 3 (1st Cir. 1993) ("A number of circuits hold, and we agree, that juror testimony regarding an alleged clerical error, such as announcing a verdict different than that agreed upon, does not challenge the validity of the verdict or the deliberation of mental processes, and therefore is not subject to rule 606(b)."); *Teevee Toons, Inc., v. MP3 Com, Inc.,* 148 F.Supp.2d 276, 278 (S.D.N.Y. 2001) (noting that Rule 606(b) has been silent regarding inquiries designed to confirm the accuracy of a verdict).

In adopting the exception for proof of mistakes in entering the verdict on the verdict form, the amendment specifically rejects the broader exception, adopted by some courts, permitting the use of juror testimony to prove that the jurors were operating under a misunderstanding about the consequences of the result that they agreed upon. *See, e.g., Attridge v. Cencorp Div. of Dover Techs. Int'l. Inc.,* 836 F.2d 113, 116 (2d Cir. 1987*); Eastridge Development Co. v. Halpert Associates, Inc.,* 853 F.2d 772 (10th Cir. 1988). The broader exception is rejected because an inquiry into whether the jury misunderstood or misapplied an instruction goes to the jurors' mental processes underlying the verdict, rather than the verdict's accuracy in capturing what the jurors had agreed upon. *See, e.g., Karl v. Burlington Northern R.R.,* 880 F.2d 68, 74 (8th Cir. 1989) (error to receive juror testimony on whether verdict was the result of jurors' misunderstanding of instructions: "The jurors did not state that the figure written by the foreman was different from that which they agreed upon, but indicated that the figure the foreman wrote down was intended to be a net figure, not a gross figure. Receiving such statements violates Rule 606(b) because the testimony relates to how the jury interpreted the court's instructions, and concerns the jurors' 'mental processes,' which is forbidden by the rule."); *Robles v. Exxon Corp.,* 862 F.2d 1201, 1208 (5th Cir. 1989) ("the alleged error here goes to the substance of what the jury was asked to decide, necessarily implicating the jury's mental processes insofar as it questions the jury's understanding of the court's instructions and application of those instructions to the facts of the case"). Thus, the exception established by the amendment is limited to cases such as "where the jury foreperson wrote down, in response to an interrogatory, a number different from that agreed upon by the jury, or mistakenly stated that the defendant was 'guilty' when the jury had actually agreed that the defendant was not guilty." *Id.*

It should be noted that the possibility of errors in the verdict form will be reduced substantially by polling the jury. Rule 606(b) does not, of course, prevent this precaution. *See* 8 C. Wigmore, *Evidence*, § 2350 at 691 (McNaughton ed. 1961) (noting that the reasons for the rule barring juror testimony, "namely, the dangers of uncertainty and of tampering with the jurors to procure testimony, disappear in large part if such investigation as may be desired is *made by the judge* and takes place *before the jurors' discharge* and separation") (emphasis in original). Errors that come to light after polling the jury "may be corrected on the spot, or the jury may be sent out to continue deliberations, or, if necessary, a new trial may be ordered." C. Mueller & L. Kirkpatrick, *Evidence Under the Rules* at 671 (2d ed. 1999) (citing *Sincox v. United States,* 571 F.2d 876, 878–79 (5th Cir. 1978)).

Rule 607

Note by Federal Judicial Center

The rule enacted by the Congress is the rule prescribed by the Supreme Court without change.

Advisory Committee's Note

The traditional rule against impeaching one's own witness is abandoned as based on false premises. A party does not hold out his witnesses as worthy of belief, since he rarely has a free choice in selecting them. Denial of the right leaves the party at the mercy of the witness and the adversary. If the impeachment is by a prior statement, it is free from hearsay dangers and is excluded from the category of hearsay under Rule 801(d)(1). Ladd, Impeachment of One's Own Witness—New Developments, 4 U.Chi.L.Rev. 69 (1936); McCormick § 38; 3 Wigmore §§ 896–918. The substantial inroads into the old rule made over the years by decisions, rules, and statutes are evidence of doubts as to its basic soundness and workability. Cases are collected in 3 Wigmore § 905. Revised Rule 32(a)(1) of the Federal Rules of Civil Procedure allows any party to impeach a witness by means of his deposition, and Rule 43(b) has allowed the calling and impeachment of an adverse party or person identified with him. Illustrative statutes allowing a party to impeach his own witness under varying circumstances are Ill.Rev.Stats.1967, c. 110, § 60; Mass.Laws Annot.1959, c. 233 § 23; 20 N.M.Stats.Annot.1953, § 20–2–4; N.Y. CPLR § 4514 (McKinney 1963); 12 Vt.Stats.Annot.1959, §§ 1641a, 1642. Complete judicial rejection of the old rule is found in United States v. Freeman, 302 F.2d 347 (2d Cir.1962). The same result is reached in Uniform Rule 20; California Evidence Code § 785; Kansas Code of Civil Procedure § 60–420. See also New Jersey Evidence Rule 20.

Rule 608

Note by Federal Judicial Center

The rule enacted by the Congress is the rule prescribed by the Supreme Court, changed only by amending the second sentence of subdivision (b). The sentence as prescribed by the Court read: "They may, however, if probative of truthfulness or untruthfulness and not remote in time, be inquired into on cross-examination of the witness himself or on cross-examination of a witness who testifies to his character for truthfulness or untruthfulness." The effect of the amendments was to delete the phrase "and not remote in time," to add the phrase "in the discretion of the court," and otherwise only to clarify the meaning of the sentence. The reasons for the amendments are stated in the Report of the House Committee on the Judiciary, set forth below. See also Note to Rule 405(a) by Federal Judicial Center, supra.

Advisory Committee's Note

Subdivision (a). In Rule 404(a) the general position is taken that character evidence is not admissible for the purpose of proving that the person acted in conformity therewith, subject, however, to several exceptions, one of which is character evidence of a witness as bearing upon his credibility. The present rule develops that exception.

In accordance with the bulk of judicial authority, the inquiry is strictly limited to character for veracity, rather than allowing evidence as to character generally. The result is to sharpen relevancy, to reduce surprise, waste of time, and confusion, and to make the lot of the witness somewhat less unattractive. McCormick § 44.

The use of opinion and reputation evidence as means of proving the character of witnesses is consistent with Rule 405(a). While the modern practice has purported to exclude opinion, witnesses who testify to reputation seem in fact often to be giving their opinions, disguised somewhat misleadingly as reputation. See McCormick § 44. And even under the modern practice, a common relaxation has allowed inquiry as to whether the witnesses would believe the principal witness under oath. United States v. Walker, 313 F.2d 236 (6th Cir.1963), and cases cited therein; McCormick § 44, pp. 94–95, n. 3.

Character evidence in support of credibility is admissible under the rule only after the witness' character has first been attacked, as has been the case at common law. Maguire, Weinstein, et al., Cases on Evidence 295 (5th ed. 1965); McCormick § 49, p. 105; 4 Wigmore § 1104. The enormous needless consumption of time which a contrary practice would entail justifies the limitation. Opinion or reputation that the witness is untruthful specifically qualifies as an attack under the rule, and evidence of misconduct, including conviction of crime, and of corruption also fall within this category. Evidence of bias or interest does not. McCormick § 49; 4 Wigmore §§ 1106, 1107. Whether evidence in the form of contradiction is an attack upon the character of the witness must depend upon the circumstances. McCormick § 49. Cf. 4 Wigmore §§ 1108, 1109.

As to the use of specific instances on direct by an opinion witness, see the Advisory Committee's Note to Rule 405, supra.

Subdivision (b). In conformity with Rule 405, which forecloses use of evidence of specific incidents as proof in chief of character unless character is an issue in the case, the present rule generally bars evidence of specific instances of conduct of a witness for the purpose of attacking or supporting his credibility. There are, however, two exceptions: (1) specific instances are provable when they have been the subject of criminal conviction, and (2) specific instances may be inquired into on cross-examination of the principal witness or of a witness giving an opinion of his character for truthfulness.

(1) Conviction of crime as a technique of impeachment is treated in detail in Rule 609, and here is merely recognized as an exception to the general rule excluding evidence of specific incidents for impeachment purposes.

(2) Particular instances of conduct, though not the subject of criminal conviction, may be inquired into on cross-examination of the principal witness himself or of a witness who testifies concerning his character for truthfulness. Effective cross-examination demands that some allowance be made for going into matters of this kind, but the possibilities of abuse are substantial. Consequently safeguards are erected in the form of specific requirements that the instances inquired into be probative of truthfulness or its opposite * * *. Also, the overriding protection of Rule 403 requires that probative value not be outweighed by danger of unfair prejudice, confusion of issues, or misleading the jury, and that of Rule 611 bars harassment and undue embarrassment.

The final sentence constitutes a rejection of the doctrine of such cases as People v. Sorge, 301 N.Y. 198, 93 N.E.2d 637 (1950), that any past criminal act relevant to credibility may be inquired into on cross-examination, in apparent disregard of the privilege against self-incrimination. While it is clear that an ordinary witness cannot make a partial disclosure of incriminating matter and then invoke the privilege on cross-examination, no tenable contention can be made that merely by testifying he waives his right to foreclose inquiry on cross-examination into criminal activities for the purpose of attacking his credibility. So to hold would reduce the privilege to a nullity. While it is true that an accused, unlike an ordinary witness, has an option whether to testify, if the option can be exercised only at the price of opening up inquiry as to any and all criminal acts committed during his lifetime, the right to testify could scarcely be said to possess much vitality. In Griffin v. California, 380 U.S. 609, 85 S.Ct. 1229, 14 L.Ed.2d 106 (1965), the Court held that allowing comment on the election of an accused not to testify exacted a constitutionally impermissible price, and so here. While no specific provision in terms confers constitutional status on the right of an accused to take the stand in his own defense, the existence of the right is so completely recognized that a denial of it or substantial infringement upon it would surely be of due process dimensions. See Ferguson v. Georgia, 365 U.S. 570, 81 S.Ct. 756, 5 L.Ed.2d 783 (1961); McCormick § 131; 8 Wigmore § 2276 (McNaughton Rev.1961). In any event, wholly aside from constitutional considerations, the provision represents a sound policy.

Report of House Committee on the Judiciary

The second sentence of Rule 608(b) as submitted by the Court permitted specific instances of misconduct of a witness to be inquired into on cross-examination for the purpose of attacking his credibility, if probative of truthfulness or untruthfulness, "and not remote in time." Such cross-examination could be of the witness himself or of another witness who testifies as to "his" character for truthfulness or untruthfulness.

The Committee amended the Rule to emphasize the discretionary power of the court in permitting such testimony and deleted the reference to remoteness in time as being unnecessary and confusing (remoteness from time of trial or remoteness from the incident involved?). As recast, the Committee amendment also makes clear the antecedent of "his" in the original Court proposal.

Advisory Committee Note to 2003 Amendment to Rule 608(b)

The Rule has been amended to clarify that the absolute prohibition on extrinsic evidence applies only when the sole reason for proffering that evidence is to attack or support the witness' character for truthfulness. *See* United States v. Abel, 469 U.S. 45 (1984); United States v. Fusco, 748 F.2d 996 (5th Cir. 1984) (Rule 608(b) limits the use of evidence "designed to show that the witness has done things, unrelated to the suit being tried, that make him more or less believable per se"); Ohio R. Evid. 608(b). On occasion the Rule's use of the overbroad term "credibility" has been read "to bar extrinsic evidence for bias, competency and contradiction impeachment since they too deal with credibility." American Bar Association Section of Litigation, *Emerging Problems Under the Federal Rules of Evidence* at 161 (3d ed. 1998). The amendment conforms the language of the Rule to its original intent, which was to impose an absolute bar on extrinsic evidence only if the sole purpose for offering the evidence was to prove the witness' character for veracity. *See* Advisory Committee Note to Rule 608(b) (stating that the Rule is "[i]n conformity with Rule 405, which forecloses use of evidence of specific incidents as proof in chief of character unless character is in issue in the case. . .").

By limiting the application of the Rule to proof of a witness' character for truthfulness, the amendment leaves the admissibility of extrinsic evidence offered for other grounds of impeachment (such as contradiction, prior inconsistent statement, bias and mental capacity) to Rules 402 and 403. *See, e.g.,* United States v. Winchenbach, 197 F.3d 548 (1st Cir. 1999) (admissibility of a prior inconsistent statement offered for impeachment is governed by Rules 402 and 403, not Rule 608(b)); *United States v. Tarantino*, 846 F.2d 1384 (D.C. Cir. 1988) (admissibility of extrinsic evidence offered to contradict a witness is governed by Rules 402 and 403); *United States v. Lindemann*, 85 F.3d 1232 (7th Cir. 1996) (admissibility of extrinsic evidence of bias is governed by Rules 402 and 403).

It should be noted that the extrinsic evidence prohibition of Rule 608(b) bars any reference to the consequences that a witness might have suffered as a result of an alleged bad act. For example, Rule 608(b) prohibits counsel from mentioning that a witness was suspended or disciplined for the conduct that is the subject of impeachment, when that conduct is offered only to prove the character of the witness. *See* United States v. Davis, 183 F.3d 231, 257, n.12 (3d Cir. 1999) (emphasizing that in attacking the defendant's character for truthfulness "the government cannot make reference to Davis's forty-four day suspension or that Internal Affairs found that he lied about" an incident because "[s]uch evidence would not only be hearsay to the extent it contains assertion of fact, it would be inadmissible extrinsic evidence under Rule 608(b)"). *See also* Stephen A. Saltzburg, *Impeaching the Witness: Prior Bad Acts and Extrinsic Evidence*, 7 Crim. Just. 28, 31 (Winter 1993) ("counsel should not be permitted to circumvent the no-extrinsic-evidence provision by tucking a third person's opinion about prior acts into a question asked of the witness who has denied the act.").

For purposes of consistency the term "credibility" has been replaced by the term "character for truthfulness" in the last sentence of subdivision (b). The term "credibility" is also used in subdivision (a). But the Committee found it unnecessary to substitute "character for truthfulness" for "credibility" in Rule 608(a), because subdivision (a)(1) already serves to limit impeachment to proof of such character.

Rules 609(a) and 610 also use the term "credibility" when the intent of those Rules is to regulate impeachment of a witness' character for truthfulness. No inference should be derived from the fact that the Committee proposed an amendment to Rule 608(b) but not to Rules 609 and 610.

Advisory Committee's Note to 2011 Amendment

* * * The Committee is aware that the Rule's limitation of bad-act impeachment to "cross-examination" is trumped by Rule 607, which allows a party to impeach witnesses on direct examination. Courts have not relied on the term "on cross-examination" to limit impeachment that would otherwise be permissible under Rules 607 and 608. The Committee therefore concluded that no change to the language of the Rule was necessary in the context of a restyling project.

Rule 609

Note by Federal Judicial Center on the original Rule

Subdivision (a) of the rule prescribed by the Supreme Court was revised successively in the House, in the Senate, and in the Conference. The nature of the rule prescribed by the Court, the various amendments, and the reasons therefor are stated in the Report of the House Committee on the Judiciary, the Report of the Senate Committee on the Judiciary, and the Conference Report, set forth below.

Subdivision (b) of the rule prescribed by the Supreme Court was also revised successively in the House, in the Senate, and in the Conference. The nature of the rule prescribed by the Court, those amendments, and the reasons therefor are likewise stated in the Report of the House Committee on the Judiciary, the Report of the Senate Committee on the Judiciary, and the Conference Report, set forth below.

Subdivision (c) enacted by the Congress is the subdivision prescribed by the Supreme Court, with amendments and reasons therefor stated in the Report of the House Committee on the Judiciary, set forth below.

Subdivision (d) enacted by the Congress is the subdivision prescribed by the Supreme Court, amended in the second sentence by substituting "court" in place of "judge" and by adding the phrase "in a criminal case."

Subdivision (e) enacted by the Congress is the subdivision prescribed by the Supreme Court without change.

Materials related to Rule 609(a) as originally enacted

Advisory Committee's Note

As a means of impeachment, evidence of conviction of crime is significant only because it stands as proof of the commission of the underlying criminal act. There is little dissent from the general proposition that at least some crimes are relevant to credibility but much disagreement among the cases and commentators about which crimes are usable for this purpose. See McCormick § 43; 2 Wright, Federal Practice and Procedure: Criminal § 416 (1969). The weight of traditional authority has been to allow use of felonies generally, without regard to the nature of the particular offense, and of *crimen falsi* without regard to the grade of the offense. This is the view accepted by Congress in the 1970 amendment of § 14–305 of the District of Columbia Code, P.L. 91–358, 84 Stat. 473. Uniform Rule 21 and Model Code Rule 106 permit only crimes involving "dishonesty or false statement." Others have thought that the trial judge should have discretion to exclude convictions if the probative value of the evidence of the crime is substantially outweighed by the danger of unfair prejudice. Luck v. United States, 121 U.S.App.D.C. 151, 348 F.2d 763 (1965); McGowan, Impeachment of Criminal Defendants by Prior Convictions, 1970 Law & Soc. Order 1. * * *

The proposed rule incorporates certain basic safeguards, in terms applicable to all witnesses but of particular significance to an accused who elects to testify. These protections include the imposition of definite time limitations, giving effect to demonstrated rehabilitation, and generally excluding juvenile adjudications.

Subdivision (a). For purposes of impeachment, crimes are divided into two categories by the rule: (1) those of what is generally regarded as felony grade, without particular regard to the nature of the offense, and (2) those involving dishonesty or false statement, without regard to the grade of the offense. Provable convictions are not limited to violations of federal law. By reason of our constitutional structure, the federal catalog of crimes is far from being a complete one, and resort must be had to the laws of the states for the specification of many crimes. For example, simple theft as compared with theft from interstate commerce. Other instances of borrowing are the Assimilative Crimes Act, making the state law of crimes applicable to the special territorial and maritime jurisdiction of the United States, 18 U.S.C. § 13, and the provision of the Judicial Code disqualifying persons as jurors on the grounds of state as well as federal convictions, 28 U.S.C. § 1865. For evaluation of the crime in terms of seriousness, reference is made to the congressional measurement of felony (subject to imprisonment in excess of one year) rather than adopting state definitions which vary considerably. See 28 U.S.C. § 1865, supra, disqualifying jurors for conviction in state or federal court of crime punishable by imprisonment for more than one year.

Report of the House Committee on the Judiciary

Rule 609(a) as submitted by the Court was modeled after Section 133(a) of Public Law 91–358, 14 D.C.Code 305(b)(1), enacted in 1970. The Rule provided that:

> For the purpose of attacking the credibility of a witness, evidence that he has been convicted of a crime is admissible but only if the crime (1) was punishable by death or imprisonment in excess of one year under the law under which he was convicted or (2) involved dishonesty or false statement regardless of the punishment.

As reported to the Committee by the Subcommittee, Rule 609(a) was amended to read as follows:

> For the purpose of attacking the credibility of a witness, evidence that he has been convicted of a crime is admissible only if the crime (1) was punishable by death or imprisonment in excess of one year, unless the court determines that the danger of unfair prejudice outweighs the probative value of the evidence of the conviction, or (2) involved dishonesty or false statement.

In full committee, the provision was amended to permit attack upon the credibility of a witness by prior conviction only if the prior crime involved dishonesty or false statement. While recognizing that the prevailing doctrine in the federal courts and in most States allows a witness to be impeached by evidence of prior felony convictions without restriction as to type, the Committee was of the view that, because of the danger of unfair prejudice in such practice and the deterrent effect upon an accused who might wish to testify, and even upon a witness who was not the accused, cross-examination by evidence of prior conviction should be limited to those kinds of convictions bearing directly on credibility, i.e., crimes involving dishonesty or false statement.

Report of the Senate Committee on the Judiciary

As proposed by the Supreme Court, the rule would allow the use of prior convictions to impeach if the crime was a felony or a misdemeanor if the misdemeanor involved dishonesty or false statement. As modified by the House, the rule would admit prior convictions for impeachment purposes only if the offense, whether felony or misdemeanor, involved dishonesty or false statement.

The committee has adopted a modified version of the House-passed rule. In your committee's view, the danger of unfair prejudice is far greater when the accused, as opposed to other witnesses, testifies, because the jury may be prejudiced not merely on the question of credibility but also on the ultimate question of guilt or innocence. Therefore, with respect to defendants, the committee agreed with the House limitation that only offenses involving false statement or dishonesty may be used. By that phrase, the committee means crimes such as perjury or subornation of perjury, false statement, criminal fraud, embezzlement or false pretense, or any other offense, in the nature of crimen falsi the commission of which involves some element of untruthfulness, deceit or falsification bearing on the accused's propensity to testify truthfully.

With respect to other witnesses, in addition to any prior conviction involving false statement or dishonesty, any other felony may be used to impeach if, and only if, the court finds that the probative value of such evidence outweighs its prejudicial effect against the party offering that witness.

Notwithstanding this provision, proof of any prior offense otherwise admissible under rule 404 could still be offered for the purposes sanctioned by that rule. Furthermore, the committee intends that notwithstanding this rule, a defendant's misrepresentation regarding the existence or nature of prior convictions may be met by rebuttal evidence, including the record of such prior convictions. Similarly, such records may be offered to rebut representations made by the defendant regarding his attitude toward or willingness to commit a general category of offense, although denials or other representations by the defendant regarding the specific conduct which forms the basis of the charge against him shall not make prior convictions admissible to rebut such statement.

In regard to either type of representation, of course, prior convictions may be offered in rebuttal only if the defendant's statement is made in response to defense counsel's questions or is made gratuitously in the course of cross-examination. Prior convictions may not be offered as rebuttal evidence if the prosecution has sought to circumvent the purpose of this rule by asking questions which elicit such representations from the defendant.

One other clarifying amendment has been added to this subsection, that is, to provide that the admissibility of evidence of a prior conviction is permitted only upon cross-examination of a witness. It is not admissible if a person does not testify. It is to be understood, however, that a court record of a prior conviction is admissible to prove that conviction if the witness has forgotten or denies its existence.

Conference Report

The House bill provides that the credibility of a witness can be attacked by proof of prior conviction of a crime only if the crime involves dishonesty or false statement. The Senate amendment provides that a witness' credibility may be attacked if the crime (1) was punishable by death or imprisonment in excess of one year under the law under which he was convicted or (2) involves dishonesty or false statement, regardless of the punishment.

The Conference adopts the Senate amendment with an amendment. The Conference amendment provides that the credibility of a witness, whether a defendant or someone else, may be attacked by proof of a prior conviction but only if the crime: (1) was punishable by death or imprisonment in excess of one year under the law under which he was convicted and the court determines that the probative value of the conviction outweighs its prejudicial effect to the defendant; or (2) involved dishonesty or false statement regardless of the punishment.

By the phrase "dishonesty and false statement" the Conference means crimes such as perjury or subornation of perjury, false statement, criminal fraud, embezzlement, or false pretense, or any other offense in the nature of crimen falsi, the commission of which involves some element of deceit, untruthfulness, or falsification bearing on the accused's propensity to testify truthfully.

The admission of prior convictions involving dishonesty and false statement is not within the discretion of the Court. Such convictions are peculiarly probative of credibility and, under this rule, are always to be admitted. Thus, judicial discretion granted with respect to the admissibility of other prior convictions is not applicable to those involving dishonesty or false statement.

With regard to the discretionary standard established by paragraph (1) of rule 609(a), the Conference determined that the prejudicial effect to be weighed against the probative value of the conviction is specifically the prejudicial effect *to the defendant*. The danger of prejudice to a witness other than the defendant (such as injury to the witness' reputation in his community) was considered and rejected by the Conference as an element to be weighed in determining admissibility. It was the judgment of the Conference that the danger of prejudice to a nondefendant witness is outweighed by the need for the trier of fact to have as much relevant evidence on the issue of credibility as possible. Such evidence should only be excluded where it presents a danger of improperly influencing the outcome of the trial by persuading the trier of fact to convict the defendant on the basis of his prior criminal record.

Materials related to Rule 609(b) as originally enacted

Advisory Committee's Note

Subdivision (b). Few statutes recognize a time limit on impeachment by evidence of conviction. However, practical considerations of fairness and relevancy demand that some boundary be recognized. See Ladd, Credibility Tests—Current Trends, 89 U.Pa.L.Rev. 166, 176–177 (1940). This portion of the rule is derived from the proposal advanced in Recommendation Proposing in Evidence Code, § 788(5), p. 142, Cal.Law Rev.Comm'n (1965), though not adopted. See California Evidence Code § 788.

Report of the House Committee on the Judiciary

Rule 609(b) as submitted by the Court was modeled after Section 133(a) of Public Law 91–358, 14 D.C.Code 305(b)(2)(B), enacted in 1970. The Rule provided:

> Evidence of a conviction under this rule is not admissible if a period of more than ten years has elapsed since the date of the release of the witness from confinement imposed for his most recent conviction, or the expiration of the period of his parole, probation, or sentence granted or imposed with respect to his most recent conviction, whichever is the later date.

Under this formulation, a witness' entire past record of criminal convictions could be used for impeachment (provided the conviction met the standard of subdivision (a)), if the witness had been most recently released from confinement, or the period of his parole or probation had expired, within ten years of the conviction.

The Committee amended the Rule to read in the text of the 1971 Advisory Committee version to provide that upon the expiration of ten years from the date of a conviction of a witness, or of his release from confinement for that offense, that conviction may no longer be used for impeachment. The Committee was of the view that after ten years following a person's release from confinement (or from the date of his conviction) the probative value of the conviction with respect to that person's credibility diminished to a point where it should no longer be admissible.

Report of the Senate Committee on the Judiciary

Although convictions over ten years old generally do not have much probative value, there may be exceptional circumstances under which the conviction substantially bears on the credibility of the witness. Rather than exclude all convictions over 10 years old, the committee adopted an amendment in the form of a final clause to the section granting the court discretion to admit convictions over 10 years old, but only upon a determination by the court that the probative value of the conviction supported by specific facts and circumstances, substantially outweighs its prejudicial effect.

It is intended that convictions over 10 years old will be admitted very rarely and only in exceptional circumstances. The rules provide that the decision be supported by specific facts and circumstances thus requiring the court to make specific findings on the record as to the particular facts and circumstances it has considered in determining that the probative value of the conviction substantially outweighs its prejudicial impact. It is expected that, in fairness, the court will give the party against whom the conviction is introduced a full and adequate opportunity to contest its admission.

Conference Report

The House bill provides in subsection (b) that evidence of conviction of a crime may not be used for impeachment purposes under subsection (a) if more than ten years have elapsed since the date of the conviction or the date the witness was released from confinement imposed for the conviction, whichever is later. The Senate amendment permits the use of convictions older than ten years, if the court determines, in the interests of justice, that the probative value of the conviction, supported by specific facts and circumstances, substantially outweighs its prejudicial effect.

The Conference adopts the Senate amendment with an amendment requiring notice by a party that he intends to request that the court allow him to use a conviction older than ten years. The Conferees anticipate that a written notice, in order to give the adversary a fair opportunity to contest the use of the evidence, will ordinarily include such information as the date of the conviction, the jurisdiction, and the offense or statute involved. In order to eliminate the possibility that the flexibility of this provision may impair the ability of a party-opponent to prepare for trial, the Conferees intend that the notice provision operate to avoid surprise.

Maerials related to Rule 609(c) as originally enacted

Advisory Committee's Note

Subdivision (c). A pardon or its equivalent granted solely for the purpose of restoring civil rights lost by virtue of a conviction has no relevance to an inquiry into character. If, however, the pardon or other proceeding is hinged upon a showing of rehabilitation the situation is otherwise. The result under the rule is to render the conviction inadmissible. The alternative of allowing in evidence both the conviction and the rehabilitation has not been adopted for reasons of policy, economy of time, and difficulties of evaluation.

A similar provision is contained in California Evidence Code § 788. Cf. A.L.I. Model Penal Code, Proposed Official Draft § 306.6(3)(e) (1962), and discussion in A.L.I. Proceedings 310 (1961).

Pardons based on innocence have the effect, of course, of nullifying the conviction *ab initio*.

Report of House Committee on the Judiciary

Rule 609(c) as submitted by the Court provided in part that evidence of a witness' prior conviction is not admissible to attack his credibility if the conviction was the subject of a pardon, annulment, or other equivalent procedure, based on a showing of rehabilitation, and the witness has not been convicted of a subsequent crime. The Committee amended the Rule to provide that the "subsequent crime" must have been "punishable by death or imprisonment in excess of one year", on the ground that a subsequent conviction of an offense not a felony is insufficient to rebut the finding that the witness has been rehabilitated. The Committee also intends that the words "based on a finding of the rehabilitation of the person convicted" apply not only to "certificate of rehabilitation, or other equivalent procedure", but also to "pardon" and "annulment."

Materials related to Rule 609(d) as originally enacted

Advisory Committee's Note

Subdivision (d). The prevailing view has been that a juvenile adjudication is not usable for impeachment. Thomas v. United States, 74 App.D.C. 167, 121 F.2d 905 (1941); Cotton v. United States, 355 F.2d 480 (10th Cir.1966). This conclusion was based upon a variety of circumstances. By virtue of its informality, frequently diminished quantum of required proof, and other departures from accepted standards for criminal trials under the theory of *parens patriae,* the juvenile adjudication was considered to lack the precision and general probative value of the criminal conviction. While In re Gault, 387 U.S. 1, 87 S.Ct. 1428, 18 L.Ed.2d 527 (1967), no doubt eliminates these characteristics insofar as objectionable, other obstacles remain. Practical problems of administration are raised by the common provisions in juvenile legislation that records be kept confidential and that they be destroyed after a short time. While *Gault* was skeptical as to the realities of confidentiality of juvenile records, it also saw no constitutional obstacles to improvement. 387 U.S. at 25, 387 U.S. 1. See also Note, Rights and Rehabilitation in the Juvenile Courts, 67 Colum.L.Rev. 281, 289 (1967). In addition, policy considerations much akin to those which dictate exclusion of adult convictions after rehabilitation has been established strongly suggest a rule of excluding juvenile adjudications. Admittedly, however, the rehabilitative process may in a given case be a demonstrated failure, or the strategic importance of a given witness may be so great as to require the overriding of general policy in the interests of particular justice. See Giles v. Maryland, 386 U.S. 66, 87 S.Ct. 793, 17 L.Ed.2d 737 (1967). Wigmore was outspoken in his condemnation of the disallowance of juvenile adjudications to impeach, especially when the witness is the complainant in a case of molesting a minor. 1 Wigmore § 196; 3 id. §§ 924a, 980. The rule recognizes discretion in the judge to effect an accommodation among these various factors by departing from the general principle of exclusion. In deference to the general pattern and policy of juvenile statutes, however, no discretion is accorded when the witness is the accused in a criminal case.

Subdivision (e). The presumption of correctness which ought to attend judicial proceedings supports the position that pendency of an appeal does not preclude use of a conviction for impeachment. United States v. Empire Packing Co., 174 F.2d 16 (7th Cir.1949), cert. denied 337 U.S. 959, 69 S.Ct. 1534, 93 L.Ed. 1758; Bloch v. United States, 226 F.2d 185 (9th

Cir.1955), cert. denied 350 U.S. 948, 76 S.Ct. 323, 100 L.Ed. 826 and 353 U.S. 959, 77 S.Ct. 868, 1 L.Ed.2d 910; and see Newman v. United States, 331 F.2d 968 (8th Cir.1964). Contra, Campbell v. United States, 85 U.S.App.D.C. 133, 176 F.2d 45 (1949). The pendency of an appeal is, however, a qualifying circumstance properly considerable.

Advisory Committee's Note to 1990 Amendment to Rule 609

The amendment to Rule 609(a) makes two changes in the rule. The first change removes from the rule the limitation that the conviction may only be elicited during cross-examination, a limitation that virtually every circuit has found to be inapplicable. It is common for witnesses to reveal on direct examination their convictions to "remove the sting" of the impeachment. See e.g., United States v. Bad Cob, 560 F.2d 877 (8th Cir.1977). The amendment does not contemplate that a court will necessarily permit proof of prior convictions through testimony, which might be time-consuming and more prejudicial than proof through a written record. Rules 403 and 611(a) provide sufficient authority for the court to protect against unfair or disruptive methods of proof.

The second change effected by the amendment resolves an ambiguity as to the relationship of Rules 609 and 403 with respect to impeachment of witnesses other than the criminal defendant. See, Green v. Bock Laundry Machine Co., 490 U.S. 504, 109 S.Ct. 1981 (1989). The amendment does not disturb the special balancing test for the criminal defendant who chooses to testify. Thus, the rule recognizes that, in virtually every case in which prior convictions are used to impeach the testifying defendant, the defendant faces a unique risk of prejudice—i.e., the danger that convictions that would be excluded under Fed.R.Evid. 404 will be misused by a jury as propensity evidence despite their introduction solely for impeachment purposes. Although the rule does not forbid all use of convictions to impeach a defendant, it requires that the government show that the probative value of convictions as impeachment evidence outweighs their prejudicial effect.

Prior to the amendment, the rule appeared to give the defendant the benefit of the special balancing test when defense witnesses other than the defendant were called to testify. In practice, however, the concern about unfairness to the defendant is most acute when the defendant's own convictions are offered as evidence. Almost all of the decided cases concern this type of impeachment, and the amendment does not deprive the defendant of any meaningful protection, since Rule 403 now clearly protects against unfair impeachment of any defense witness other than the defendant. There are cases in which a defendant might be prejudiced when a defense witness is impeached. Such cases may arise, for example, when the witness bears a special relationship to the defendant such that the defendant is likely to suffer some spill-over effect from impeachment of the witness.

The amendment also protects other litigants from unfair impeachment of their witnesses. The danger of prejudice from the use of prior convictions is not confined to criminal defendants. Although the danger that prior convictions will be misused as character evidence is particularly acute when the defendant is impeached, the danger exists in other situations as well. The amendment reflects the view that it is desirable to protect all litigants from the unfair use of prior convictions, and that the ordinary balancing test of Rule 403, which provides that evidence shall not be excluded unless its prejudicial effect substantially outweighs its probative value, is appropriate for assessing the admissibility of prior convictions for impeachment of any witness other than a criminal defendant.

The amendment reflects a judgment that decisions interpreting Rule 609(a) as requiring a trial court to admit convictions in civil cases that have little, if anything, to do with credibility reach undesirable results. See, e.g., Diggs v. Lyons, 741 F.2d 577 (3d Cir.1984), cert. denied, 471 U.S. 1078 (1985). The amendment provides the same protection against unfair prejudice arising from prior convictions used for impeachment purposes as the rules provide for other evidence. The amendment finds support in decided cases. See, e.g., Petty v. Ideco, 761 F.2d 1146 (5th Cir.1985); Czajka v. Hickman, 703 F.2d 317 (8th Cir.1983).

Fewer decided cases address the question whether Rule 609(a) provides any protection against unduly prejudicial prior convictions used to impeach government witnesses. Some courts have read Rule 609(a) as giving the government no protection for its witnesses. See, e.g., United States v. Thorne, 547 F.2d 56 (8th Cir.1976); United States v. Nevitt, 563 F.2d 406 (9th Cir.1977), cert. denied, 444 U.S. 847 (1979). This approach also is rejected by the amendment. There are cases in which impeachment of government witnesses with prior convictions that have little, if anything, to do with credibility may result in unfair prejudice to the government's interest in a fair trial and unnecessary embarrassment to a witness. Fed.R.Evid. 412 already recognizes this and excluded certain evidence of past sexual behavior in the context of prosecutions for sexual assaults.

The amendment applies the general balancing test of Rule 403 to protect all litigants against unfair impeachment of witnesses. The balancing test protects civil litigants, the government in criminal cases, and the defendant in a criminal case who calls other witnesses. The amendment addresses prior convictions offered under Rule 609, not for other purposes, and does not run afoul, therefore, of Davis v. Alaska, 415 U.S. 308 (1974). Davis involved the use of a prior juvenile adjudication not to prove a past law violation, but to prove bias. The defendant in a criminal case has the right to demonstrate the bias of a witness and to be assured a fair trial, but not to unduly prejudice a trier of fact. See generally Rule 412. In any case in which the trial court believes that confrontation rights require admission of impeachment evidence, obviously the Constitution would take precedence over the rule.

The probability that prior convictions of an ordinary government witness will be unduly prejudicial is low in most criminal cases. Since the behavior of the witness is not the issue in dispute in most cases, there is little chance that the trier of fact will misuse the convictions offered as impeachment evidence as propensity evidence. Thus, trial courts will be skeptical when the government objects to impeachment of its witnesses with prior convictions. Only when the government is able to point to a real danger of prejudice that is sufficient to outweigh substantially the probative value of the conviction for impeachment purposes will the conviction be excluded.

The amendment continues to divide subdivision (a) into subsections (1) and (2) thus facilitating retrieval under current computerized research programs which distinguish the two provisions. The Committee recommended no substantive change in subdivision (a)(2), even though some cases raise a concern about the proper interpretation of the words "dishonesty or false statement." These words were used but not explained in the original Advisory Committee Note accompanying Rule 609. Congress extensively debated the rule, and the Report of the House and Senate Conference Committee states that "[b]y the phrase 'dishonesty and false statement,' the Conference means crimes such as perjury, subornation of perjury, false statement, criminal fraud, embezzlement, or false pretense, or any other offense in the nature of crimen falsi, commission of which involves some element of deceit, untruthfulness, or falsification bearing on the accused's propensity to testify truthfully." The Advisory Committee concluded that the Conference Report provides sufficient guidance to trial courts and that no amendment is necessary, notwithstanding some decisions that take an unduly broad view of "dishonesty," admitting convictions such as for bank robbery or bank larceny. Subsection (a)(2) continues to apply to any witness, including a criminal defendant.

Finally, the Committee determined that it was unnecessary to add to the rule language stating that, when a prior conviction is offered under Rule 609, the trial court is to consider the probative value of the prior conviction for impeachment not for other purposes. The Committee concluded that the title of the rule, its first sentence, and its placement among the impeachment rules clearly establish that evidence offered under Rule 609 is offered only for purposes of impeachment.

Advisory Committee's Note to 2006 Amendment to Rule 609

The amendment provides that Rule 609(a)(2) mandates the admission of evidence of a conviction only when the conviction required the proof of (or in the case of a guilty plea, the admission of) an act of dishonesty or false statement. Evidence of all other convictions is inadmissible under this subsection, irrespective of whether the witness exhibited dishonesty or made a false statement in the process of the commission of the crime of conviction. Thus, evidence that the witness was convicted for a crime of violence, such as murder, is not admissible under Rule 609(a)(2), even if the witness acted deceitfully in the course of committing the crime.

The amendment is meant to give effect to the legislative intent to limit the convictions that are to be automatically admitted under subdivision (a)(2). The Conference Committee provided that by "dishonesty and false statement" it meant "crimes such as perjury, subornation of perjury, false statement, criminal fraud, embezzlement, or false pretense, or any other offense in the nature of *crimen falsi*, the commission of which involves some element of deceit, untruthfulness, or falsification bearing on the [witness's] propensity to testify truthfully." Historically, offenses classified as *crimina falsi* have included only those crimes in which the ultimate criminal act was itself an act of deceit. *See* Green, *Deceit and the Classification of Crimes: Federal of Rule of Evidence 609(a)(2) and the Origins of* Crimen Falsi, 90 J. Crim. L. & Criminology 1087 (2000).

Evidence of crimes in the nature of *crimen falsi* must be admitted under Rule 609(a)(2), regardless of how such crimes are specifically charged. For example, evidence that a witness was convicted of making a false claim to a federal agent is admissible under this subdivision regardless of whether the crime was charged under a section that expressly references deceit (*e.g.*, 18 U.S.C. § 1001, Material Misrepresentation to the Federal Government) or a section that does not (*e.g.* 18 U.S.C. § 1503, Obstruction of Justice).

The amendment requires that the proponent have ready proof that the conviction required the factfinder to find, or the defendant to admit, an act of dishonesty or false statement. Ordinarily, the statutory elements of the crime will indicate whether it is one of dishonesty or false statement. Where the deceitful nature of the crime is not apparent from the statute and the face of the judgment—as, for example, where the conviction simply records a finding of guilt for a statutory offense that does not reference deceit expressly—a proponent may offer information such as an indictment, a statement of admitted facts, or jury instructions to show that the factfinder had to find, or the defendant had to admit, an act of dishonesty or false statement in order for the witness to have been convicted. *Cf.* Taylor v. United States, 495 U.S. 575, 602 (1990) (providing that a trial court may look to a charging instrument or jury instructions to ascertain the nature of a prior offense where the statute is insufficiently clear on its face); *Shepard v. United States*, 125 S.Ct. 1254 (2005) (the inquiry to determine whether a guilty plea to a crime defined by a nongeneric statute necessarily admitted elements of the generic offense was limited to the charging document's terms, the terms of a plea agreement or transcript of colloquy between judge and defendant in which the factual basis for the plea was confirmed by the defendant, or a comparable judicial record). But the amendment does not contemplate a "minitrial" in which the court plumbs the record of the previous proceeding to determine whether the crime was in the nature of *crimen falsi*.

The amendment also substitutes the term "character for truthfulness" for the term "credibility" in the first sentence of the Rule. The limitations of Rule 609 are not applicable if a conviction is admitted for a purpose other than to prove the witness's character for untruthfulness. *See, e.g.*, United States v. Lopez, 979 F.2d 1024 (5th Cir. 1992) (Rule 609 was not applicable where the conviction was offered for purposes of contradiction). The use of the term "credibility" in subdivision (d) is retained, however, as that subdivision is intended to govern the use of a juvenile adjudication for any type of impeachment.

Rule 610

Note by Federal Judicial Center

The rule enacted by the Congress is the rule prescribed by the Supreme Court without change.

Advisory Committee's Note

While the rule forecloses inquiry into the religious beliefs or opinions of a witness for the purpose of showing that his character for truthfulness is affected by their nature, an inquiry for the purpose of showing interest or bias because of them is not within the prohibition. Thus disclosure of affiliation with a church which is a party to the litigation would be allowable under the rule. Cf. Tucker v. Reil, 51 Ariz. 357, 77 P.2d 203 (1938). To the same effect, though less specifically worded, is California Evidence Code § 789. See 3 Wigmore § 936.

Rule 611

Note by Federal Judicial Center

Subdivision (a) of the rule enacted by the Congress is the subdivision prescribed by the Supreme Court, amended only by substituting "court" in place of "judge."

Subdivision (b) of the rule enacted by the Congress is substantially different from the subdivision prescribed by the Supreme Court. The nature of the changes and the reasons therefor are stated in the Report of the House Committee on the Judiciary, set forth below.

The first two sentences of subdivision (c) of the rule enacted by the Congress are the same as prescribed by the Supreme Court. The third sentence has been amended in the manner and for the reasons stated in the Report of the House Committee on the Judiciary, set forth below.

Advisory Committee's Note

Subdivision (a). Spelling out detailed rules to govern the mode and order of interrogating witnesses and presenting evidence is neither desirable nor feasible. The ultimate responsibility for the effective working of the adversary system rests with the judge. The rule sets forth the objectives which he should seek to attain.

Item (1) restates in broad terms the power and obligation of the judge as developed under common law principles. It covers such concerns as whether testimony shall be in the form of a free narrative or responses to specific questions, McCormick § 5, the order of calling witnesses and presenting evidence, 6 Wigmore § 1867, the use of demonstrative evidence, McCormick § 179, and the many other questions arising during the course of a trial which can be solved only by the judge's common sense and fairness in view of the particular circumstances.

Item (2) is addressed to avoidance of needless consumption of time, a matter of daily concern in the disposition of cases. A companion piece is found in the discretion vested in the judge to exclude evidence as a waste of time in Rule 403(b).

Item (3) calls for a judgment under the particular circumstances whether interrogation tactics entail harassment or undue embarrassment. Pertinent circumstances include the importance of the testimony, the nature of the inquiry, its relevance to credibility, waste of time, and confusion. McCormick § 42. In Alford v. United States, 282 U.S. 687, 694, 51 S.Ct. 218, 75 L.Ed. 624 (1931), the Court pointed out that, while the trial judge should protect the witness from questions which "go beyond the bounds of proper cross-examination merely to harass, annoy or humiliate," this protection by no means forecloses efforts to discredit the witness. Reference to the transcript of the prosecutor's cross-examination in Berger v. United States, 295 U.S. 78, 55 S.Ct. 629, 79 L.Ed. 1314 (1935), serves to lay at rest any doubts as to the need for judicial control in this area.

The inquiry into specific instances of conduct of a witness allowed under Rule 608(b) is, of course, subject to this rule.

Subdivision (b)[*]. The tradition in the federal courts and in numerous state courts has been to limit the scope of cross-examination to matters testified to on direct, plus matters bearing upon the credibility of the witness. Various reasons have been advanced to justify the rule of limited cross-examination. (1) A party vouches for his own witness but only to the extent of matters elicited on direct. Resurrection Gold Mining Co. v. Fortune Gold Mining Co., 129 Fed. 668, 675 (8th Cir.1904), quoted in Maguire, Weinstein, et al., Cases on Evidence 277 n. 38 (5th ed. 1965). But the concept of vouching is discredited, and Rule 6–07[607] rejects it. (2) A party cannot ask his own witness leading questions. This is a problem properly solved in terms of what is necessary for a proper development of the testimony rather than by a mechanistic formula similar to the vouching concept. See discussion under subdivision (c). (3) A practice of limited cross-examination promotes orderly presentation of the case. Finch v. Weiner, 109 Conn. 616, 145 Atl. 31 (1929). In the opinion of the Advisory Committee this latter reason has merit. It is apparent, however, that the rule of limited cross-examination thus viewed becomes an aspect of the judge's general control over the mode and order of interrogating witnesses and presenting evidence, to be administered as such. The matter is not one in which involvement at the appellate level is likely to prove fruitful. See, for example,

---

[*] The Advisory Committee's Note to subdivision (b) is from the 1969 Preliminary Draft. 46 F.R.D. 161, 304.

Moyer v. Aetna Life Ins. Co., 126 F.2d 141 (3d Cir.1942); Butler v. New York Central R. Co., 253 F.2d 281 (7th Cir.1958); United States v. Johnson, 285 F.2d 35 (9th Cir.1960); Union Automobile Indemnity Ass'n v. Capitol Indemnity Ins. Co., 310 F.2d 318 (7th Cir.1962). In view of these considerations, the rule is phrased in terms of a suggestion rather than a mandate to the trial judge.

The qualification "as if on direct examination," applicable when inquiry into additional matters is allowed is designed to terminate at that point the asking of leading questions as a matter of right and to bring into operation subdivision (c) of the rule.

The rule does not purport to determine the extent to which an accused who elects to testify thereby waives his privilege against self-incrimination. The question is a constitutional one, rather than a mere matter of administering the trial. Under Simmons v. United States, 390 U.S. 377 (1968), no general waiver occurs when the accused testifies on such preliminary matters as the validity of a search and seizure or the admissibility of a confession. Rule 1–04(d) [104(d)], supra. When he testifies on the merits, however, can he foreclose inquiry into an aspect or element of the crime by avoiding it on direct? The affirmative answer given in Tucker v. United States, 5 F.2d 818 (8th Cir.1925), is inconsistent with the description of the waiver as extending to "all other relevant facts" in Johnson v. United States, 318 U.S. 189, 195 (1943). See also Brown v. United States, 356 U.S. 148 (1958). The situation of an accused who desires to testify on some but not all counts of a multiple-count indictment is one to be approached, in the first instance at least, as a problem of severance under Rule 14 of the Federal Rules of Criminal Procedure. Cross v. United States, 335 F.2d 987 (D.C.Cir.1964). Cf. United States v. Baker, 262 F.Supp. 657, 686 (D.D.C.1966). In all events, the extent of the waiver of the privilege against self-incrimination ought not to be determined as a by-product of a rule on scope of cross-examination.

Report of House Committee on the Judiciary

As submitted by the Court, Rule 611(b) provided:

A witness may be cross-examined on any matter relevant to any issue in the case, including credibility. In the interests of justice, the judge may limit cross-examination with respect to matters not testified to on direct examination.

The Committee amended this provision to return to the rule which prevails in the federal courts and thirty-nine State jurisdictions. As amended, the Rule is in the text of the 1969 Advisory Committee draft. It limits cross-examination to credibility and to matters testified to on direct examination, unless the judge permits more, in which event the cross-examiner must proceed as if on direct examination. This traditional rule facilitates orderly presentation by each party at trial. Further, in light of existing discovery procedures, there appears to be no need to abandon the traditional rule.

Report of Senate Committee on the Judiciary

Rule 611(b) as submitted by the Supreme Court permitted a broad scope of cross-examination: "cross-examination on any matter relevant to any issue in the case" unless the judge, in the interests of justice, limited the scope of cross-examination.

The House narrowed the Rule to the more traditional practice of limiting cross-examination to the subject matter of direct examination (and credibility), but with discretion in the judge to permit inquiry into additional matters in situations where that would aid in the development of the evidence or otherwise facilitate the conduct of the trial.

The committee agrees with the House amendment. Although there are good arguments in support of broad cross-examination from prospectives of developing all relevant evidence, we believe the factors of insuring an orderly and predictable development of the evidence weigh in favor of the narrower rule, especially when discretion is given to the trial judge to permit inquiry into additional matters. The committee expressly approves this discretion and believes it will permit sufficient flexibility allowing a broader scope of cross-examination whenever appropriate.

The House amendment providing broader discretionary cross-examination permitted inquiry into additional matters only as if on direct examination. As a general rule, we concur with this limitation, however, we would understand that this limitation would not preclude the utilization of leading questions if the conditions of subsection (c) of this rule were met, bearing in mind the judge's discretion in any case to limit the scope of cross-examination.[1]

Further, the committee has received correspondence from Federal judges commenting on the applicability of this rule to section 1407 of title 28. It is the committee's judgment that this rule as reported by the House is flexible enough to provide sufficiently broad cross-examination in appropriate situations in multidistrict litigation.

Advisory Committee's Note

Subdivision (c). The rule continues the traditional view that the suggestive powers of the leading question are as a general proposition undesirable. Within this tradition, however, numerous exceptions have achieved recognition: The witness who is hostile, unwilling, or biased; the child witness or the adult with communication problems; the witness whose recollection is exhausted; and undisputed preliminary matters. 3 Wigmore §§ 774–778. An almost total unwillingness to reverse for infractions has been manifested by appellate courts. See cases cited in 3 Wigmore § 770.

---

[1] See McCormick on Evidence, §§ 24–26 (especially 24) (2d ed. 1972).

The matter clearly falls within the area of control by the judge over the mode and order of interrogation and presentation and accordingly is phrased in words of suggestion rather than command.

The rule also conforms to tradition in making the use of leading questions on cross-examination a matter of right. The purpose of the qualification "ordinarily" is to furnish a basis for denying the use of leading questions when the cross-examination is cross-examination in form only and not in fact, as for example the "cross-examination" of a party by his own counsel after being called by the opponent (savoring more of re-direct) or of an insured defendant who proves to be friendly to the plaintiff.

The final sentence deals with categories of witnesses automatically regarded and treated as hostile. Rule 43(b) of the Federal Rules of Civil Procedure has included only "an adverse party or an officer, director, or managing agent of a public or private corporation or of a partnership or association which is an adverse party." This limitation virtually to persons whose statements would stand as admissions is believed to be an unduly narrow concept of those who may safely be regarded as hostile without further demonstration. See, for example, Maryland Casualty Co. v. Kador, 225 F.2d 120 (5th Cir.1955), and Degelos v. Fidelity and Casualty Co., 313 F.2d 809 (5th Cir.1963), holding despite the language of Rule 43(b) that an insured fell within it, though not a party in an action under the Louisiana direct action statute. The phrase of the rule, "witness identified with" an adverse party, is designed to enlarge the category of persons thus callable.

Report of House Committee on the Judiciary

The third sentence of Rule 611(c) as submitted by the Court provided that:

> In civil cases, a party is entitled to call an adverse party or witness identified with him and interrogate by leading questions.

The Committee amended this Rule to permit leading questions to be used with respect to any hostile witness, not only an adverse party or person identified with such adverse party. The Committee also substituted the word "When" for the phrase "In civil cases" to reflect the possibility that in criminal cases a defendant may be entitled to call witnesses identified with the government, in which event the Committee believed the defendant should be permitted to inquire with leading questions.

Report of Senate Committee on the Judiciary

As submitted by the Supreme Court, the rule provided: "In civil cases, a party is entitled to call an adverse party or witness identified with him and interrogate by leading questions."

The final sentence of subsection (c) was amended by the House for the purpose of clarifying the fact that a "hostile witness"—that is a witness who is hostile in fact—could be subject to interrogation by leading questions. The rule as submitted by the Supreme Court declared certain witnesses hostile as a matter of law and thus subject to interrogation by leading questions without any showing of hostility in fact. These were adverse parties or witnesses identified with adverse parties. However, the wording of the first sentence of subsection (c) while generally prohibiting the use of leading questions on direct examination, also provides "except as may be necessary to develop his testimony." Further, the first paragraph of the Advisory Committee note explaining the subsection makes clear that they intended that leading questions could be asked of a hostile witness or a witness who was unwilling or biased and even though that witness was not associated with an adverse party. Thus, we question whether the House amendment was necessary.

However, concluding that it was not intended to affect the meaning of the first sentence of the subsection and was intended solely to clarify the fact that leading questions are permissible in the interrogation of a witness, who is hostile in fact, the committee accepts that House amendment.

The final sentence of this subsection was also amended by the House to cover criminal as well as civil cases. The committee accepts this amendment, but notes that it may be difficult in criminal cases to determine when a witness is "identified with an adverse party," and thus the rule should be applied with caution.

Rule 612

Note by Federal Judicial Center

The rule enacted by the Congress is the rule prescribed by the Supreme Court, amended by substituting "court" in place of "judge," with appropriate pronominal change, and in the first sentence, by substituting "the writing" in place of "it" before "produced," and by substituting the phrase "(1) while testifying, or (2) before testifying if the court in its discretion determines it is necessary in the interests of justice" in place of "before or while testifying." The reasons for the latter amendment are stated in the Report of the House Committee on the Judiciary, set forth below.

Advisory Committee's Note

The treatment of writings used to refresh recollection while on the stand is in accord with settled doctrine. McCormick § 9, p. 15. The bulk of the case law has, however, denied the existence of any right to access by the opponent when the writing is used prior to taking the stand, though the judge may have discretion in the matter. Goldman v. United States, 316 U.S. 129, 62 S.Ct. 993, 86 L.Ed. 1322 (1942); Needelman v. United States, 261 F.2d 802 (5th Cir.1958), cert. dismissed 362 U.S. 600, 80 S.Ct. 960, 4 L.Ed.2d 980, rehearing denied 363 U.S. 858, 80 S.Ct. 1606, 4 L.Ed.2d 1739, Annot., 82 A.L.R.2d 473, 562 and 7 A.L.R.3d 181, 247. An increasing group of cases has repudiated the distinction, People v. Scott, 29 Ill.2d 97, 193

N.E.2d 814 (1963); State v. Mucci, 25 N.J. 423, 136 A.2d 761 (1957); State v. Hunt, 25 N.J. 514, 138 A.2d 1 (1958); State v. Deslovers, 40 R.I. 89, 100 A. 64 (1917), and this position is believed to be correct. As Wigmore put it, "the risk of imposition and the need of safeguard is just as great" in both situations. 3 Wigmore § 762, p. 111. To the same effect is McCormick § 9, p. 17.

The purpose of the phrase "for the purpose of testifying" is to safeguard against using the rule as a pretext for wholesale exploration of an opposing party's files and to insure that access is limited only to those writings which may fairly be said in fact to have an impact upon the testimony of the witness.

The purpose of the rule is the same as that of the *Jencks* statute, 18 U.S.C. § 3500: to promote the search of credibility and memory. The same sensitivity to disclosure of government files may be involved; hence the rule is expressly made subject to the statute, subdivision (a) of which provides: "In any criminal prosecution brought by the United States, no statement or report in the possession of the United States which was made by a Government witness or prospective Government witness (other than the defendant) shall be the subject of subpena, discovery, or inspection until said witness has testified on direct examination in the trial of the case." Items falling within the purview of the statute are producible only as provided by its terms, Palermo v. United States, 360 U.S. 343, 351 (1959), and disclosure under the rule is limited similarly by the statutory conditions. With this limitation in mind, some differences of application may be noted. The *Jencks* statute applies only to statements of witnesses; the rule is not so limited. The statute applies only to criminal cases; the rule applies to all cases. The statute applies only to government witnesses; the rule applies to all witnesses. The statute contains no requirement that the statement be consulted for purposes of refreshment before or while testifying; the rule so requires. Since many writings would qualify under either statute or rule, a substantial overlap exists, but the identity of procedures makes this of no importance.

The consequences of nonproduction by the government in a criminal case are those of the *Jencks* statute, striking the testimony or in exceptional cases a mistrial. 18 U.S.C. § 3500(d). In other cases these alternatives are unduly limited, and such possibilities as contempt, dismissal, finding issues against the offender, and the like are available. See Rule 16(g) of the Federal Rules of Criminal Procedure and Rule 37(b) of the Federal Rules of Civil Procedure for appropriate sanctions.

Report of House Committee on the Judiciary

As submitted to Congress, Rule 612 provided that except as set forth in 18 U.S.C. 3500, if a witness uses a writing to refresh his memory for the purpose of testifying, "either before or while testifying," an adverse party is entitled to have the writing produced at the hearing, to inspect it, to cross-examine the witness on it, and to introduce in evidence those portions relating to the witness' testimony. The Committee amended the Rule so as still to require the production of writings used by a witness while testifying, but to render the production of writings used by a witness to refresh his memory before testifying discretionary with the court in the interests of justice, as is the case under existing federal law. See Goldman v. United States, 316 U.S. 129 (1942). The Committee considered that permitting an adverse party to require the production of writings used before testifying could result in fishing expeditions among a multitude of papers which a witness may have used in preparing for trial.

The Committee intends that nothing in the Rule be construed as barring the assertion of a privilege with respect to writings used by a witness to refresh his memory.

Rule 613

Note by Federal Judicial Center

The rule enacted by the Congress is the rule prescribed by the Supreme Court, amended only by substituting "nor" in place of "or" in subdivision (a).

Advisory Committee's Note

Subdivision (a). The Queen's Case, 2 Br. & B. 284, 129 Eng.Rep. 976 (1820), laid down the requirement that a cross-examiner, prior to questioning the witness about his own prior statement in writing, must first show it to the witness. Abolished by statute in the country of its origin, the requirement nevertheless gained currency in the United States. The rule abolishes this useless impediment, to cross-examination. Ladd, Some Observations on Credibility: Impeachment of Witnesses, 52 Cornell L.Q. 239, 246–247 (1967); McCormick § 28; 4 Wigmore §§ 1259–1260. Both oral and written statements are included.

The provision for disclosure to counsel is designed to protect against unwarranted insinuations that a statement has been made when the fact is to the contrary.

The rule does not defeat the application of Rule 1002 relating to production of the original when the contents of a writing are sought to be proved. Nor does it defeat the application of Rule 26(b)(3) of the Rules of Civil Procedure, as revised, entitling a person on request to a copy of his own statement, though the operation of the latter may be suspended temporarily.

Subdivision (b). The familiar foundation requirement that an impeaching statement first be shown to the witness before it can be proved by extrinsic evidence is preserved but with some modifications. See Ladd, Some Observations on Credibility: Impeachment of Witnesses, 52 Cornell L.Q. 239, 247 (1967). The traditional insistence that the attention of the witness be directed to the statement on cross-examination is relaxed in favor of simply providing the witness an opportunity to explain and the opposite party an opportunity to examine on the statement, with no specification of any particular time or sequence. Under this procedure, several collusive witnesses can be examined before disclosure of a joint prior inconsistent statement. See Comment to California Evidence Code § 770. Also, dangers of oversight are reduced. See McCormick § 37, p. 68.

In order to allow for such eventualities as the witness becoming unavailable by the time the statement is discovered, a measure of discretion is conferred upon the judge. Similar provisions are found in California Evidence Code § 770 and New Jersey Evidence Rule 22(b).

Under principles of *expression unius* the rule does not apply to impeachment by evidence of prior inconsistent conduct. The use of inconsistent statements to impeach a hearsay declaration is treated in Rule 806.

Rule 614

Note by Federal Judicial Center

The rule enacted by the Congress is the rule prescribed by the Supreme Court, amended only by substituting "court" in place of "judge," with conforming pronominal changes.

Advisory Committee's Note

Subdivision (a). While exercised more frequently in criminal than in civil cases, the authority of the judge to call witnesses is well established. McCormick § 8, p. 14; Maguire, Weinstein, et al., Cases on Evidence 303–304 (5th ed. 1965); 9 Wigmore § 2484. One reason for the practice, the old rule against impeaching one's own witness, no longer exists by virtue of Rule 607, supra. Other reasons remain, however, to justify the continuation of the practice of calling court's witnesses. The right to cross-examine, with all it implies, is assured. The tendency of juries to associate a witness with the party calling him, regardless of technical aspects of vouching, is avoided. And the judge is not imprisoned within the case as made by the parties.

Subdivision (b). The authority of the judge to question witnesses is also well established. McCormick § 8, pp. 12–13; Maguire, Weinstein, et al., Cases on Evidence 737–739 (5th ed. 1965); 3 Wigmore § 784. The authority is, of course, abused when the judge abandons his proper role and assumes that of advocate, but the manner in which interrogation should be conducted and the proper extent of its exercise are not susceptible of formulation in a rule. The omission in no sense precludes courts of review from continuing to reverse for abuse.

Subdivision (c). The provision relating to objections is designed to relieve counsel of the embarrassment attendant upon objecting to questions by the judge in the presence of the jury, while at the same time assuring that objections are made in apt time to afford the opportunity to take possible corrective measures. Compare the "automatic" objection feature of Rule 605 when the judge is called as a witness.

Rule 615

Note by Federal Judicial Center

The rule enacted by the Congress is the rule prescribed by the Supreme Court, amended only by substituting "court," in place of "judge," with conforming pronominal changes.

Advisory Committee's Note

The efficacy of excluding or sequestering witnesses has long been recognized as a means of discouraging and exposing fabrication, inaccuracy, and collusion. 6 Wigmore §§ 1837–1838. The authority of the judge is admitted, the only question being whether the matter is committed to his discretion or one of right. The rule takes the latter position. No time is specified for making the request.

Several categories of persons are excepted. (1) Exclusion of persons who are parties would raise serious problems of confrontation and due process. Under accepted practice they are not subject to exclusion. 6 Wigmore § 1841. (2) As the equivalent of the right of a natural-person party to be present, a party which is not a natural person is entitled to have a representative present. Most of the cases have involved allowing a police officer who has been in charge of an investigation to remain in court despite the fact that he will be a witness. United States v. Infanzon, 235 F.2d 318 (2d Cir.1956); Portomene v. United States, 221 F.2d 582 (5th Cir.1955); Powell v. United States, 208 F.2d 618 (6th Cir.1953); Jones v. United States, 252 F.Supp. 781 (W.D.Okl.1966). Designation of the representative by the attorney rather than by the client may at first glance appear to be an inversion of the attorney-client relationship, but it may be assumed that the attorney will follow the wishes of the client, and the solution is simple and workable. See California Evidence Code § 777. (3) The category contemplates such persons as an agent who handled the transaction being litigated or an expert needed to advise counsel in the management of the litigation. See 6 Wigmore § 1841, n. 4.

Report of Senate Committee on the Judiciary

Many district courts permit government counsel to have an investigative agent at counsel table throughout the trial although the agent is or may be a witness. The practice is permitted as an exception to the rule of exclusion and compares with the situation defense counsel finds himself in—he always has the client with him to consult during the trial. The investigative agent's presence may be extremely important to government counsel, especially when the case is complex or involves some specialized subject matter. The agent, too, having lived with the case for a long time, may be able to assist in meeting trial surprises where the best-prepared counsel would otherwise have difficulty. Yet, it would not seem the Government could often meet the burden under rule 615 of showing that the agent's presence is essential. Furthermore, it could be dangerous to use the agent as a witness as early in the case as possible, so that he might then help counsel as a nonwitness, since the agent's testimony could be needed in rebuttal. Using another, nonwitness agent from the same investigative agency would not generally meet government counsel's needs.

This problem is solved if it is clear that investigative agents are within the group specified under the second exception made in the rule, for "an officer or employee of a party which is not a natural person designated as its representative by its attorney." It is our understanding that this was the intention of the House committee. It is certainly this committee's construction of the rule.

ARTICLE VII. OPINIONS AND EXPERT TESTIMONY

Rule 701

Note by Federal Judicial Center

The rule enacted by the Congress is the rule prescribed by the Supreme Court without change.

Advisory Committee's Note

The rule retains the traditional objective of putting the trier of fact in possession of an accurate reproduction of the event.

Limitation (a) is the familiar requirement of first-hand knowledge or observation.

Limitation (b) is phrased in terms of requiring testimony to be helpful in resolving issues. Witnesses often find difficulty in expressing themselves in language which is not that of an opinion or conclusion. While the courts have made concessions in certain recurring situations, necessity as a standard for permitting opinions and conclusions has proved too elusive and too unadaptable to particular situations for purposes of satisfactory judicial administration. McCormick § 11. Moreover, the practical impossibility of determining by rule what is a "fact," demonstrated by a century of litigation of the question of what is a fact for purposes of pleading under the Field Code, extends into evidence also. 7 Wigmore § 1919. The rule assumes that the natural characteristics of the adversary system will generally lead to an acceptable result, since the detailed account carries more conviction than the broad assertion, and a lawyer can be expected to display his witness to the best advantage. If he fails to do so, cross-examination and argument will point up the weakness. See Ladd, Expert Testimony, 5 Vand.L.Rev. 414, 415–417 (1952). If, despite these considerations, attempts are made to introduce meaningless assertions which amount to little more than choosing up sides, exclusion for lack of helpfulness is called for by the rule.

The language of the rule is substantially that of Uniform Rule 56(1). Similar provisions are California Evidence Code § 800; Kansas Code of Civil Procedure § 60–456(a); New Jersey Evidence Rule 56(1).

Advisory Committee's Note to 2000 Amendment

Rule 701 has been amended to eliminate the risk that the reliability requirements set forth in Rule 702 will be evaded through the simple expedient of proffering an expert in lay witness clothing. Under the amendment, a witness' testimony must be scrutinized under the rules regulating expert opinion to the extent that the witness is providing testimony based on scientific, technical, or other specialized knowledge within the scope of Rule 702. *See generally Asplundh Mfg. Div. v. Benton Harbor Eng'g*, 57 F.3d 1190 (3d Cir. 1995). By channeling testimony that is actually expert testimony to Rule 702, the amendment also ensures that a party will not evade the expert witness disclosure requirements set forth in Fed.R.Civ.P. 26 and Fed.R.Crim.P. 16 by simply calling an expert witness in the guise of a layperson. *See* Joseph, *Emerging Expert Issues Under the 1993 Disclosure Amendments to the Federal Rules of Civil Procedure*, 164 F.R.D. 97, 108 (1996) (noting that "there is no good reason to allow what is essentially surprise expert testimony," and that "the Court should be vigilant to preclude manipulative conduct designed to thwart the expert disclosure and discovery process"). *See also United States v. Figueroa–Lopez*, 125 F.3d 1241,1246 (9th Cir. 1997) (law enforcement agents testifying that the defendant's conduct was consistent with that of a drug trafficker could not testify as lay witnesses; to permit such testimony under Rule 701 "subverts the requirements of Federal Rule of Criminal Procedure 16(a)(1)(E)").

The amendment does not distinguish between expert and lay *witnesses*, but rather between expert and lay *testimony*. Certainly it is possible for the same witness to provide both lay and expert testimony in a single case. *See, e.g.,* United States v. Figueroa–Lopez, 125 F.3d 1241, 1246 (9th Cir.1997) (law enforcement agents could testify that the defendant was acting suspiciously, without being qualified as experts; however, the rules on experts were applicable where the agents testified on the basis of extensive experience that the defendant was using code words to refer to drug quantities and prices). The amendment makes clear that any part of a witness' testimony that is based upon scientific, technical, or other specialized knowledge within the scope of Rule 702 is governed by the standards of Rule 702 and the corresponding disclosure requirements of the Civil and Criminal Rules.

The amendment is not intended to affect the "prototypical example[s] of the type of evidence contemplated by the adoption of Rule 701 relat[ting] to the appearance of persons or things, identity, the manner of conduct, competency of a person, degrees of light or darkness, sound, size, weight, distance, and an endless number of items that cannot be described factually in words apart from inferences." *Asplundh Mfg. Div. v. Benton Harbor Eng'g*, 57 F.3d 1190, 1196 (3d Cir. 1995).

For example, most courts have permitted the owner or officer of a business to testify to the value or projected profits of the business, without the necessity of qualifying the witness as an accountant, appraiser, or similar expert. *See, e.g.,* Lightning Lube, Inc. v. Witco Corp. 4 F.3d 1153 (3d Cir.1993) (no abuse of discretion in permitting the plaintiff's owner to give lay opinion testimony as to damages, as it was based on his knowledge and participation in the day-to-day affairs of the business). Such opinion testimony is admitted not because of experience, training or specialized knowledge within the realm of an expert, but because of the particularized knowledge that the witness has by virtue of his or her position in the business. The amendment does not purport to change this analysis. Similarly, courts have permitted lay witnesses to testify that a substance appeared to be a narcotic, so long as a foundation of familiarity with the substance is established. *See, e.g., United States v. Westbrook,* 896 F.2d 330 (8th Cir. 1990) (two lay witnesses who were heavy amphetamine users were properly permitted to testify that a substance was amphetamine; but it was error to permit another witness to make such an identification where she had no experience with amphetamines). Such testimony is not based on specialized knowledge within the scope of Rule 702, but rather is based upon a layperson's personal knowledge. If, however, that witness were to describe how a narcotic was manufactured, or to describe the intricate workings of a narcotic distribution network, then the witness would have to qualify as an expert under Rule 702. *United States v. Figueroa–Lopez, supra.*

The amendment incorporates the distinctions set forth in State v. Brown, 836 S.W.2d 530, 529 (1992), a case involving former Tennessee Rule of Evidence 701, a rule that precluded lay witness testimony based on "special knowledge." In *Brown,* the court declared that the distinction between lay and expert witness testimony is that lay testimony "results from a process of reasoning familiar in everyday life," while expert testimony "results from a process of reasoning which can be mastered only by specialists in the field." The court in *Brown* noted that a lay witness with experience could testify that a substance appeared to be blood, but that a witness would have to qualify as an expert before he could testify that bruising around the eyes is indicative of skull trauma. That is the kind of distinction made by the amendment to this Rule.

Advisory Committee's Note to 2011 Amendment

* * * The Committee deleted all reference to an "inference" on the grounds that the deletion made the Rule flow better and easier to read, and because any "inference" is covered by the broader term "opinion." Courts have not made substantive decisions on the basis of any distinction between an opinion and an inference. No change in current practice is intended.

Rule 702

Note by Federal Judicial Center

The rule enacted by the Congress is the rule prescribed by the Supreme Court without change.

Advisory Committee's Note

An intelligent evaluation of facts is often difficult or impossible without the application of some scientific, technical, or other specialized knowledge. The most common source of this knowledge is the expert witness, although there are other techniques for supplying it.

Most of the literature assumes that experts testify only in the form of opinions. The assumption is logically unfounded. The rule accordingly recognizes that an expert on the stand may give a dissertation or exposition of scientific or other principles relevant to the case, leaving the trier of fact to apply them to the facts. Since much of the criticism of expert testimony has centered upon the hypothetical question, it seems wise to recognize that opinions are not indispensable and to encourage the use of expert testimony in non-opinion form when counsel believes the trier can itself draw the requisite inference. The use of opinions is not abolished by the rule, however. It will continue to be permissible for the expert to take the further step of suggesting the inference which should be drawn from applying the specialized knowledge to the facts. See Rules 703 to 705.

Whether the situation is a proper one for the use of expert testimony is to be determined on the basis of assisting the trier. "There is no more certain test for determining when experts may be used than the common sense inquiry whether the untrained layman would be qualified to determine intelligently and to the best possible degree the particular issue without enlightenment from those having a specialized understanding of the subject involved in the dispute." Ladd, Expert Testimony, 5 Vand.L.Rev. 414, 418 (1952). When opinions are excluded, it is because they are unhelpful and therefore superfluous and a waste of time. 7 Wigmore § 1918.

The rule is broadly phrased. The fields of knowledge which may be drawn upon are not limited merely to the "scientific" and "technical" but extend to all "specialized" knowledge. Similarly, the expert is viewed, not in a narrow sense, but as a person qualified by "knowledge, skill, experience, training or education." Thus within the scope of the rule are not only experts in the strictest sense of the word, e.g. physicians, physicists, and architects, but also the large group sometimes called "skilled" witnesses, such as bankers or landowners testifying to land values.

Advisory Committee's Note to 2000 Amendment

Rule 702 has been amended in response to *Daubert v. Merrell Dow Pharmaceuticals, Inc.*, 509 U.S. 579 (1993), and to the many cases applying *Daubert*, including *Kumho Tire Co. v. Carmichael*, 119 S.Ct. 1167 (1999). In

Daubert the Court charged trial judges with the responsibility of acting as gatekeepers to exclude unreliable expert testimony, and the Court in *Kumho* clarified that this gatekeeper function applies to all expert testimony, not just testimony based in science. See also *Kumho*, 119 S.Ct. at 1178 (citing the Committee Note to the proposed amendment to Rule 702, which had been released for public comment before the date of the *Kumho* decision). The amendment affirms the trial court's role as gatekeeper and provides some general standards that the trial court must use to assess the reliability and helpfulness of proffered expert testimony. Consistently with *Kumho*, the Rule as amended provides that all types of expert testimony present questions of admissibility for the trial court in deciding whether the evidence is reliable and helpful. Consequently, the admissibility of all expert testimony is governed by the principles of Rule 104(a). Under that Rule, the proponent has the burden of establishing that the pertinent admissibility requirements are met by a preponderance of the evidence. *See Bourjaily v. United States*, 483 U.S. 171 (1987).

Daubert set forth a non-exclusive checklist for trial courts to use in assessing the reliability of scientific expert testimony. The specific factors explicated by the *Daubert* Court are (1) whether the expert's technique or theory can be or has been tested that is, whether the expert's theory can be challenged in some objective sense, or whether it is instead simply a subjective, conclusory approach that cannot reasonably be assessed for reliability; (2) whether the technique or theory has been subject to peer review and publication; (3) the known or potential rate of error of the technique or theory when applied; (4) the existence and maintenance of standards and controls; and (5) whether the technique or theory has been generally accepted in the scientific community. The Court in *Kumho* held that these factors might also be applicable in assessing the reliability of non-scientific expert testimony, depending upon "the particular circumstances of the particular case at issue." 119 S.Ct. at 1175.

No attempt has been made to "codify" these specific factors. *Daubert* itself emphasized that the factors were neither exclusive nor dispositive. Other cases have recognized that not all of the specific *Daubert* factors can apply to every type of expert testimony. In addition to *Kumho*, 119 S.Ct. at 1175, *see Tyus v. Urban Search Management*, 102 F.3d 256 (7th Cir. 1996) (noting that the factors mentioned by the Court in *Daubert* do not neatly apply to expert testimony from a sociologist). *See also Kannankeril v. Terminix Int'l, Inc.*, 128 F.3d 802, 809 (3d Cir. 1997) (holding that lack of peer review or publication was not dispositive where the expert's opinion was supported by "widely accepted scientific knowledge"). The standards set forth in the amendment are broad enough to require consideration of any or all of the specific *Daubert* factors where appropriate.

Courts both before and after *Daubert* have found other factors relevant in determining whether expert testimony is sufficiently reliable to be considered by the trier of fact. These factors include:

(1) Whether experts are "proposing to testify about matters growing naturally and directly out of research they have conducted independent of the litigation, or whether they have developed their opinions expressly for purposes of testifying." *Daubert v. Merrell Dow Pharmaceuticals, Inc.*, 43 F.3d 1311, 1317 (9th Cir. 1995).

(2) Whether the expert has unjustifiably extrapolated from an accepted premise to an unfounded conclusion. *See* General Elec. Co. v. Joiner, 522 U.S. 136, 146 (1997) (noting that in some cases a trial court "may conclude that there is simply too great an analytical gap between the data and the opinion proffered").

(3) Whether the expert has adequately accounted for obvious alternative explanations. *See* Claar v. Burlington N.R.R., 29 F.3d 499 (9th Cir. 1994) (testimony excluded where the expert failed to consider other obvious causes for the plaintiff's condition). *Compare Ambrosini v. Labarraque*, 101 F.3d 129 (D.C. Cir. 1996) (the possibility of some uneliminated causes presents a question of weight, so long as the most obvious causes have been considered and reasonably ruled out by the expert).

(4) Whether the expert "is being as careful as he would be in his regular professional work outside his paid litigation consulting." *Sheehan v. Daily Racing Form, Inc.*, 104 F.3d 940, 942 (7th Cir. 1997). *See Kumho Tire Co. v. Carmichael*, 119 S.Ct. 1167, 1176 (1999) (*Daubert* requires the trial court to assure itself that the expert "employs in the courtroom the same level of intellectual rigor that characterizes the practice of an expert in the relevant field.").

(5) Whether the field of expertise claimed by the expert is known to reach reliable results for the type of opinion the expert would give. *See* Kumho Tire Co. v. Carmichael, 119 S.Ct. 1167, 1175 (1999) (*Daubert's* general acceptance factor does not "help show that an expert's testimony is reliable where the discipline itself lacks reliability, as, for example, do theories grounded in any so-called generally accepted principles of astrology or necromancy."); *Moore v. Ashland Chemical, Inc.*, 151 F.3d 269 (5th Cir. 1998) (en banc) (clinical doctor was properly precluded from testifying to the toxicological cause of the plaintiff's respiratory problem, where the opinion was not sufficiently grounded in scientific methodology); *Sterling v. Velsicol Chem. Corp.*, 855 F.2d 1188 (6th Cir. 1988) (rejecting testimony based on "clinical ecology" as unfounded and unreliable).

All of these factors remain relevant to the determination of the reliability of expert testimony under the Rule as amended. Other factors may also be relevant. See Kumho, 119 S.Ct. 1167, 1176 ("[W]e conclude that the trial judge must have considerable leeway in deciding in a particular case how to go about determining whether particular expert testimony is reliable."). Yet no single factor is necessarily dispositive of the reliability of a particular expert's testimony. *See, e.g., Heller v. Shaw Industries, Inc.*, 167

F.3d 146, 155 (3d Cir. 1999) ("not only must each stage of the expert's testimony be reliable, but each stage must be evaluated practically and flexibly without bright-line exclusionary (or inclusionary) rules."); *Daubert v. Merrell Dow Pharmaceuticals, Inc.*, 43 F.3d 1311, 1317, n.5 (9th Cir. 1995) (noting that some expert disciplines "have the courtroom as a principal theatre of operations" and as to these disciplines "the fact that the expert has developed an expertise principally for purposes of litigation will obviously not be a substantial consideration.").

A review of the caselaw after *Daubert* shows that the rejection of expert testimony is the exception rather than the rule. *Daubert* did not work a "seachange over federal evidence law," and "the trial court's role as gatekeeper is not intended to serve as a replacement for the adversary system." *United States v. 14.38 Acres of Land Situated in* Leflore County, Mississippi, 80 F.3d 1074, 1078 (5th Cir. 1996). As the Court in *Daubert* stated: "Vigorous cross-examination, presentation of contrary evidence, and careful instruction on the burden of proof are the traditional and appropriate means of attacking shaky but admissible evidence." 509 U.S. at 595. Likewise, this amendment is not intended to provide an excuse for an automatic challenge to the testimony of every expert. *See Kumho Tire Co. v. Carmichael*, 119 S.Ct. 1167, 1176 (1999) (noting that the trial judge has the discretion "both to avoid unnecessary 'reliability' proceedings in ordinary cases where the reliability of an expert's methods is properly taken for granted, and to require appropriate proceedings in the less usual or more complex cases where cause for questioning the expert's reliability arises.").

When a trial court, applying this amendment, rules that an expert's testimony is reliable, this does not necessarily mean that contradictory expert testimony is unreliable. The amendment is broad enough to permit testimony that is the product of competing principles or methods in the same field of expertise. *See, e.g.*, Heller v. Shaw Industries, Inc., 167 F.3d 146, 160 (3d Cir. 1999) (expert testimony cannot be excluded simply because the expert uses one test rather than another, when both tests are accepted in the field and both reach reliable results). As the court stated in *In re Paoli R. R. Yard PCB Litigation*, 35 F.3d 717, 744 (3d Cir. 1994), proponents "do not have to demonstrate to the judge by a preponderance of the evidence that the assessments of their experts are correct, they only have to demonstrate by a preponderance of evidence that their opinions are reliable. . . The evidentiary requirement of reliability is lower than the merits standard of correctness." *See also Daubert v. Merrell Dow Pharmaceuticals, Inc.*, 43 F.3d 1311, 1318 (9th Cir. 1995) (scientific experts might be permitted to testify if they could show that the methods they used were also employed by "a recognized minority of scientists in their field."); *Ruiz-Troche v. Pepsi Cola*, 161 F.3d 77, 85 (1st Cir. 1998) ("*Daubert* neither requires nor empowers trial courts to determine which of several competing scientific theories has the best provenance.").

The Court in *Daubert* declared that the "focus, of course, must be solely on principles and methodology, not on the conclusions they generate."

509 U.S. at 595. Yet as the Court later recognized, "conclusions and methodology are not entirely distinct from one another." *General Elec. Co. v. Joiner*, 522 U.S. 136, 146 (1997). Under the amendment, as under *Daubert*, when an expert purports to apply principles and methods in accordance with professional standards, and yet reaches a conclusion that other experts in the field would not reach, the trial court may fairly suspect that the principles and methods have not been faithfully applied. *See Lust v. Merrell Dow Pharmaceuticals, Inc.*, 89 F.3d 594, 598 (9th Cir. 1996). The amendment specifically provides that the trial court must scrutinize not only the principles and methods used by the expert, but also whether those principles and methods have been properly applied to the facts of the case. As the court noted in *In re Paoli R.R. Yard PCB Litig.*, 35 F.3d 717, 745 (3d Cir. 1994), "*any* step that renders the analysis unreliable . . . renders the expert's testimony inadmissible. *This is true whether the step completely changes a reliable methodology or merely misapplies that methodology.*"

If the expert purports to apply principles and methods to the facts of the case, it is important that this application be conducted reliably. Yet it might also be important in some cases for an expert to educate the factfinder about general principles, without ever attempting to apply these principles to the specific facts of the case. For example, experts might instruct the factfinder on the principles of thermodynamics, or bloodclotting, or on how financial markets respond to corporate reports, without ever knowing about or trying to tie their testimony into the facts of the case. The amendment does not alter the venerable practice of using expert testimony to educate the factfinder on general principles. For this kind of generalized testimony, Rule 702 simply requires that: (1) the expert be qualified; (2) the testimony address a subject matter on which the factfinder can be assisted by an expert; (3) the testimony be reliable; and (4) the testimony "fit" the facts of the case.

As stated earlier, the amendment does not distinguish between scientific and other forms of expert testimony. The trial court's gatekeeping function applies to testimony by any expert. *See Kumho Tire Co. v. Carmichael*, 119 S.Ct. 1167, 1171 (1999) ("We conclude that *Daubert's* general holding—setting forth the trial judge's general 'gatekeeping' obligation—applies not only to testimony based on 'scientific' knowledge, but also to testimony based on 'technical' and 'other specialized' knowledge."). While the relevant factors for determining reliability will vary from expertise to expertise, the amendment rejects the premise that an expert's testimony should be treated more permissively simply because it is outside the realm of science. An opinion from an expert who is not a scientist should receive the same degree of scrutiny for reliability as an opinion from an expert who purports to be a scientist. *See Watkins v. Telsmith, Inc.*, 121 F.3d 984, 991 (5th Cir. 1997) ("[I]t seems exactly backwards that experts who purport to rely on general engineering principles and practical experience might escape screening by the district court simply by stating that their conclusions were not reached by any particular method or technique."). Some types of expert testimony will be more objectively verifiable, and subject to the expectations of falsifiability, peer review, and publication, than others. Some types of expert testimony will not rely on anything like a scientific method, and so will have to be evaluated by reference to other standard principles attendant to the particular area of expertise. The trial judge in all cases of proffered expert testimony must find that it is properly grounded, well-reasoned, and not speculative before it can be admitted. The expert's testimony must be grounded in an accepted body of learning or experience in the expert's field, and the expert must explain how the conclusion is so grounded. *See, e.g.,* American College of Trial Lawyers, *Standards and Procedures for Determining the Admissibility of Expert Testimony after Daubert,* 157 F.R.D. 571, 579 (1994) ("[W]hether the testimony concerns economic principles, accounting standards, property valuation or other non-scientific subjects, it should be evaluated by reference to the 'knowledge and experience' of that particular field.").

The amendment requires that the testimony must be the product of reliable principles and methods that are reliably applied to the facts of the case. While the terms "principles" and "methods" may convey a certain impression when applied to scientific knowledge, they remain relevant when applied to testimony based on technical or other specialized knowledge. For example, when a law enforcement agent testifies regarding the use of code words in a drug transaction, the principle used by the agent is that participants in such transactions regularly use code words to conceal the nature of their activities. The method used by the agent is the application of extensive experience to analyze the meaning of the conversations. So long as the principles and methods are reliable and applied reliably to the facts of the case, this type of testimony should be admitted.

Nothing in this amendment is intended to suggest that experience alone—or experience in conjunction with other knowledge, skill, training or education—may not provide a sufficient foundation for expert testimony. To the contrary, the text of Rule 702 expressly contemplates that an expert may be qualified on the basis of experience. In certain fields, experience is the predominant, if not sole, basis for a great deal of reliable expert testimony. *See, e.g., United States v. Jones,* 107 F.3d 1147 (6th Cir. 1997) (no abuse of discretion in admitting the testimony of a handwriting examiner who had years of practical experience and extensive training, and who explained his methodology in detail); *Tassin v. Sears Roebuck,* 946 F.Supp. 1241, 1248 (M.D. La. 1996) (design engineer's testimony can be admissible when the expert's opinions "are based on facts, a reasonable investigation, and traditional technical/mechanical expertise, and he provides a reasonable link between the information and procedures he uses and the conclusions he reaches"). *See also Kumho Tire Co. v. Carmichael,* 119 S.Ct. 1167, 1178 (1999) (stating that "no one denies that an expert might draw a conclusion from a set of observations based on extensive and specialized experience.").

If the witness is relying solely or primarily on experience, then the witness must explain how that experience leads to the conclusion reached, why that experience is a sufficient basis for the opinion, and how that experience is reliably applied to the facts. The trial court's gatekeeping function requires more than simply "taking the expert's word for it." *See* Daubert v. Merrell Dow Pharmaceuticals, Inc., 43 F.3d 1311, 1319 (9th Cir. 1995) ("We've been presented with only the experts' qualifications, their conclusions and their assurances of reliability. Under *Daubert*, that's not enough."). The more subjective and controversial the expert's inquiry, the more likely the testimony should be excluded as unreliable. *See O'Conner v. Commonwealth Edison Co.*, 13 F.3d 1090 (7th Cir. 1994) (expert testimony based on a completely subjective methodology held properly excluded). *See also Kumho Tire Co. v. Carmichael*, 119 S.Ct. 1167, 1176 (1999) ("[I]t will at times be useful to ask even of a witness whose expertise is based purely on experience, say, a perfume tester able to distinguish among 140 odors at a sniff, whether his preparation is of a kind that others in the field would recognize as acceptable.").

Subpart (1) of Rule 702 calls for a quantitative rather than qualitative analysis. The amendment requires that expert testimony be based on sufficient underlying "facts or data." The term "data" is intended to encompass the reliable opinions of other experts. See the original Advisory Committee Note to Rule 703. The language "facts or data" is broad enough to allow an expert to rely on hypothetical facts that are supported by the evidence. *Id.*

When facts are in dispute, experts sometimes reach different conclusions based on competing versions of the facts. The emphasis in the amendment on "sufficient facts or data" is not intended to authorize a trial court to exclude an expert's testimony on the ground that the court believes one version of the facts and not the other.

There has been some confusion over the relationship between Rules 702 and 703. The amendment makes clear that the sufficiency of the basis of an expert's testimony is to be decided under Rule 702. Rule 702 sets forth the overarching requirement of reliability, and an analysis of the sufficiency of the expert's basis cannot be divorced from the ultimate reliability of the expert's opinion. In contrast, the "reasonable reliance" requirement of Rule 703 is a relatively narrow inquiry. When an expert relies on inadmissible information, Rule 703 requires the trial court to determine whether that information is of a type reasonably relied on by other experts in the field. If so, the expert can rely on the information in reaching an opinion. However, the question whether the expert is relying on a *sufficient* basis of information—whether admissible information or not—is governed by the requirements of Rule 702.

The amendment makes no attempt to set forth procedural requirements for exercising the trial court's gatekeeping function over expert testimony. *See* Daniel J. Capra, *The Daubert Puzzle*, 38 Ga. L. Rev. 699, 766 (1998) ("Trial courts should be allowed substantial discretion in dealing with *Daubert* questions; any attempt to codify procedures will likely give rise to unnecessary changes in practice and create difficult questions for appellate review."). Courts have shown considerable ingenuity and flexibility in considering challenges to expert testimony under *Daubert*, and it is contemplated that this will continue under the amended Rule. *See, e.g., Cortes–Irizarry v. Corporacion Insular*, 111 F.3d 184 (1st Cir. 1997) (discussing the application of *Daubert* in ruling on a motion for summary judgment); *In re Paoli R.R. Yard PCB Litig.*, 35 F.3d 717, 736, 739 (3d Cir. 1994) (discussing the use of *in limine* hearings); *Claar v. Burlington N.R.R.*, 29 F.3d 499, 502–05 (9th Cir. 1994) (discussing the trial court's technique of ordering experts to submit serial affidavits explaining the reasoning and methods underlying their conclusions).

The amendment continues the practice of the original Rule in referring to a qualified witness as an "expert." This was done to provide continuity and to minimize change. The use of the term "expert" in the Rule does not, however, mean that a jury should actually be informed that a qualified witness is testifying as an "expert." Indeed, there is much to be said for a practice that prohibits the use of the term "expert" by both the parties and the court at trial. Such a practice "ensures that trial courts do not inadvertently put their stamp of authority" on a witness's opinion, and protects against the jury's being "overwhelmed by the so-called 'experts'." Hon. Charles Richey, *Proposals To Eliminate the Prejudicial Effect of the Use of the Word "Expert" Under the Federal Rules of Evidence in* Criminal and Civil Jury Trials, 154 F.R.D. 537, 559 (1994) (setting forth limiting instructions and a standing order employed to prohibit the use of the term "expert" in jury trials).

Rule 703

Note by Federal Judicial Center

The rule enacted by the Congress is the rule prescribed by the Supreme Court without change.

Advisory Committee's Note

Facts or data upon which expert opinions are based may, under the rule, be derived from three possible sources. The first is the firsthand observation of the witness, with opinions based thereon traditionally allowed. A treating physician affords an example. Rheingold, The Basis of Medical Testimony, 15 Vand.L.Rev. 473, 489 (1962). Whether he must first relate his observations is treated in Rule 705. The second source, presentation at the trial, also reflects existing practice. The technique may be the familiar hypothetical question or having the expert attend the trial and hear the testimony establishing the facts. Problems of determining what testimony the expert relied upon, when the latter technique is employed and the testimony is in conflict, may be resolved by resort to Rule 705. The third source contemplated by the rule consists of presentation of data to the expert outside of court and other than by his own perception. In this respect the rule is designed to broaden the basis for expert opinions beyond that current in many jurisdictions and to bring the judicial practice into line with the practice of the experts themselves when not in court. Thus a physician in his own practice bases his diagnosis on information from numerous sources and of considerable variety, including statements by patients and relatives, reports and opinions from nurses, technicians and other doctors, hospital records, and X rays. Most of them are admissible in evidence, but only with the expenditure of substantial time in producing and examining various authenticating witnesses. The physician makes life-and-death decisions in reliance upon them. His validation, expertly performed and subject to cross-examination, ought to suffice for judicial purposes. Rheingold, supra, at 531; McCormick § 15. A similar provision is California Evidence Code § 801(b).

The rule also offers a more satisfactory basis for ruling upon the admissibility of public opinion poll evidence. Attention is directed to the validity of the techniques employed rather than to relatively fruitless inquiries whether hearsay is involved. See Judge Feinberg's careful analysis in Zippo Mfg. Co. v. Rogers Imports, Inc., 216 F.Supp. 670 (S.D.N.Y.1963). See also Blum et al., The Art of Opinion Research: A Lawyer's Appraisal of an Emerging Service, 24 U.Chi.L.Rev. 1 (1956); Bonynge, Trademark Surveys and Techniques and Their Use in Litigation, 48 A.B.A.J. 329 (1962); Zeisel, The Uniqueness of Survey Evidence, 45 Cornell L.Q. 322 (1960); Annot., 76 A.L.R.2d 919.

If it be feared that enlargement of permissible data may tend to break down the rules of exclusion unduly, notice should be taken that the rule requires that the facts or data "be of a type reasonably relied upon by experts in the particular field." The language would not warrant admitting in evidence the opinion of an "accidentologist" as to the point of impact in an automobile collision based on statements of bystanders, since this requirement is not satisfied. See Comment, Cal.Law Rev.Comm'n, Recommendation Proposing an Evidence Code 148–150 (1965).

Advisory Committee's Note to 2000 Amendment

Rule 703 has been amended to emphasize that when an expert reasonably relies on inadmissible information to form an opinion or inference, the underlying information is not admissible simply because the opinion or inference is admitted. Courts have reached different results on how to treat inadmissible information when it is reasonably relied upon by an expert in forming an opinion or drawing an inference. *Compare United States v. Rollins*, 862 F.2d 1282 (7th Cir. 1988) (admitting, as part of the basis of an FBI agent's expert opinion on the meaning of code language, the hearsay statements of an informant), with *United States v. 0.59 Acres of Land*, 109 F.3d 1493 (9th Cir. 1997) (error to admit hearsay offered as the basis of an expert opinion, without a limiting instruction). Commentators have also taken differing views. *See, e.g.*, Ronald Carlson, *Policing the Bases of Modern Expert Testimony*, 39 Vand. L. Rev. 577 (1986) (advocating limits on the jury's consideration of otherwise inadmissible evidence used as the basis for an expert opinion); Paul Rice, *Inadmissible Evidence as a Basis for Expert Testimony: A Response to Professor Carlson;* 40 Vand. L. Rev. 583 (1987) (advocating unrestricted use of information reasonably relied upon by an expert).

When information is reasonably relied upon by an expert and yet is admissible only for the purpose of assisting the jury in evaluating an expert's opinion, a trial court applying this Rule must consider the information's probative value in assisting the jury to weigh the expert's opinion on the one hand, and the risk of prejudice resulting from the jury's potential misuse of the information for substantive purposes on the other. The information may be disclosed to the jury, upon objection, only if the trial court finds that the probative value of the information in assisting the jury to evaluate the expert's opinion substantially outweighs its prejudicial effect. If the otherwise inadmissible information is admitted under this balancing test, the trial judge must give a limiting instruction upon request, informing the jury that the underlying information must not be used for substantive purposes. *See* Rule 105. In determining the appropriate course, the trial court should consider the probable effectiveness or lack of effectiveness of a limiting instruction under the particular circumstances.

The amendment governs only the disclosure to the jury of information that is reasonably relied on by an expert, when that information is not admissible for substantive purposes. It is not intended to affect the admissibility of an expert's testimony. Nor does the amendment prevent an expert from relying on information that is inadmissible for substantive purposes.

Nothing in this Rule restricts the presentation of underlying expert facts or data when offered by an adverse party. *See* Rule 705. Of course, an adversary's attack on an expert's basis will often open the door to a proponent's rebuttal with information that was reasonably relied upon by the expert even if that information would not have been discloseable initially under the balancing test provided by this amendment. Moreover, in some circumstances the proponent might wish to disclose information that is relied upon by the expert in order to "remove the sting" from the opponent's anticipated attack, and thereby prevent the jury from drawing an unfair negative inference. The trial court should take this consideration into account in applying the balancing test provided by this amendment.

This amendment covers facts or data that cannot be admitted for any purpose other than to assist the jury to evaluate the expert's opinion. The balancing test provided in this amendment is not applicable to facts or data that are admissible for any other purpose but have not yet been offered for such a purpose at the time the expert testifies.

The amendment provides a presumption against disclosure to the jury of information used as the basis of an expert's opinion and not admissible for any substantive purpose, when that information is offered by the proponent of the expert. In a multi-party case, where one party proffers an expert whose testimony is also beneficial to other parties, each such party should be deemed a "proponent" within the meaning of the amendment.

Advisory Committee's Note to 2011 Amendment

* * * The Committee deleted all reference to an "inference" on the grounds that the deletion made the Rule flow better and easier to read, and because any "inference" is covered by the broader term "opinion." Courts have not made substantive decisions on the basis of any distinction between an opinion and an inference. No change in current practice is intended.

Rule 704

Note by Federal Judicial Center

The rule [initially] enacted by the Congress is the rule prescribed by the Supreme Court without change. [Rule 704(b) was added by Congress in 1984. Eds.]

Advisory Committee's Note

Subdivision (a). The basic approach to opinions, lay and expert, in these rules is to admit them when helpful to the trier of fact. In order to render this approach fully effective and to allay any doubt on the subject, the so-called "ultimate issue" rule is specifically abolished by the instant rule.

The older cases often contained strictures against allowing witnesses to express opinions upon ultimate issues, as a particular aspect of the rule against opinions. The rule was unduly restrictive, difficult of application, and generally served only to deprive the trier of fact of useful information. 7 Wigmore §§ 1920, 1921; McCormick § 12. The basis usually assigned for the rule, to prevent the witness from "usurping the province of the jury," is aptly characterized as "empty rhetoric." 7 Wigmore § 1920, p. 17. Efforts to meet the felt needs of particular situations led to odd verbal circumlocutions which were said not to violate the rule. Thus a witness could express his estimate of the criminal responsibility of an accused in terms of sanity or insanity, but not in terms of ability to tell right from wrong or other more modern standard. And in cases of medical causation, witnesses were sometimes required to couch their opinions in cautious phrases of "might or could," rather than "did," though the result was to deprive many opinions of the positiveness to which they were entitled, accompanied by the hazard of a ruling of insufficiency to support a verdict. In other instances the rule was simply disregarded, and, as concessions to need, opinions were allowed upon such matters as intoxication, speed, handwriting, and value, although more precise coincidence with an ultimate issue would scarcely be possible.

Many modern decisions illustrate the trend to abandon the rule completely. People v. Wilson, 25 Cal.2d 341, 153 P.2d 720 (1944), whether abortion necessary to save life of patient; Clifford-Jacobs Forging Co. v. Industrial Comm., 19 Ill.2d 236, 166 N.E.2d 582 (1960), medical causation; Dowling v. L.H. Shattuck, Inc., 91 N.H. 234, 17 A.2d 529 (1941), proper method of shoring ditch; Schweiger v. Solbeck, 191 Or. 454, 230 P.2d 195 (1951), cause of landslide. In each instance the opinion was allowed.

The abolition of the ultimate issue rule does not lower the bars so as to admit all opinions. Under Rules 701 and 702, opinions must be helpful to the trier of fact, and Rule 403 provides for exclusion of evidence which wastes time. These provisions afford ample assurances against the admission of opinions which would merely tell the jury what result to reach, somewhat in the manner of the oath-helpers of an earlier day. They also stand ready to exclude opinions phrased in terms of inadequately explored legal criteria. Thus the question, "Did T have capacity to make a will?" would be excluded, while the question, "Did T have sufficient mental capacity to know the nature and extent of his property and the natural objects of his bounty and to formulate a rational scheme of distribution?" would be allowed. McCormick § 12.

For similar provisions see Uniform Rule 56(4); California Evidence Code § 805; Kansas Code of Civil Procedure § 60–456(d); New Jersey Evidence Rule 56(3).

Rule 704(b)

Report of the Senate Committee on the Judiciary (1984)

The purpose of this amendment is to eliminate the confusing spectacle of competing expert witnesses testifying to directly contradictory conclusions as to the ultimate legal issue to be found by the trier of fact. Under this proposal, expert psychiatric testimony would be limited to presenting and explaining their diagnoses, such as whether the defendant had a severe mental disease or defect and what the characteristics of such a disease or defect, if any, may have been. The basis for this limitation on expert testimony in insanity cases is ably stated by the American Psychiatric Association:

> [I]t is clear that psychiatrists are experts in medicine, not the law. As such, it is clear that the psychiatrist's first obligation and expertise in the courtroom is to "do psychiatry," i.e., to present medical information and opinion about the defendant's mental state and motivation and to explain in detail the reason for his medical-psychiatric conclusions. When, however, "ultimate issue" questions are formulated by the law and put to the expert witness who must then say "yea" or "nay," then the expert witness is required to make a leap in logic. He no longer addresses himself to medical concepts but instead must infer or intuit what is in fact unspeakable, namely, the probable relationship between medical concepts and legal or moral constructs such as free will. These impermissible leaps in logic made by expert witnesses confuse the jury. [Footnote omitted.] Juries thus find themselves listening to conclusory and seemingly contradictory psychiatric testimony that defendants are either "sane" or "insane" or that they do or do not meet the relevant legal test for insanity. This state of affairs does

considerable injustice to psychiatry and, we believe, possibly to criminal defendants. In fact, in many criminal insanity trials both prosecution and defense psychiatrists do agree about the nature and even the extent of mental disorder exhibited by the defendant at the time of the act.

Psychiatrists, of course, must be permitted to testify fully about the defendant's diagnosis, mental state and motivation (in clinical and common sense terms) at the time of the alleged act so as to permit the jury or judge to reach the ultimate conclusion about which they and only they are expert. Determining whether a criminal defendant was legally insane is a matter for legal fact-finders, not for experts.

Moreover, the rationale for precluding ultimate opinion psychiatric testimony extends beyond the insanity defense to any ultimate mental state of the defendant that is relevant to the legal conclusion sought to be proven. The Committee has fashioned its Rule 704 provision to reach all such "ultimate" issues, e.g., premeditation in a homicide case, or lack of predisposition in entrapment.

Advisory Committee's Note to 2011 Amendment

* * * The Committee deleted all reference to an "inference" on the grounds that the deletion made the Rule flow better and easier to read, and because any "inference" is covered by the broader term "opinion." Courts have not made substantive decisions on the basis of any distinction between an opinion and an inference. No change in current practice is intended.

Rule 705

Note by Federal Judicial Center

The rule enacted by the Congress is the rule prescribed by the Supreme Court, amended only by substituting "court" in place of "judge."

Advisory Committee's Note

The hypothetical question has been the target of a great deal of criticism as encouraging partisan bias, affording an opportunity for summing up in the middle of the case, and as complex and time consuming. Ladd, Expert Testimony, 5 Vand.L.Rev. 414, 426–427 (1952). While the rule allows counsel to make disclosure of the underlying facts or data as a preliminary to the giving of an expert opinion, if he chooses, the instances in which he is required to do so are reduced. This is true whether the expert bases his opinion on data furnished him at secondhand or observed by him at firsthand.

The elimination of the requirement of preliminary disclosure at the trial of underlying facts or data has a long background of support. In 1937 the Commissioners on Uniform State Laws incorporated a provision to this effect in their Model Expert Testimony Act, which furnished the basis for Uniform Rules 57 and 58. Rule 4515, N.Y. CPLR (McKinney 1963), provides:

> "Unless the court orders otherwise, questions calling for the opinion of an expert witness need not be hypothetical in form, and the witness may state his opinion and reasons without first specifying the data upon which it is based. Upon cross-examination, he may be required to specify the data * * *."

See also California Evidence Code § 802; Kansas Code of Civil Procedure §§ 60–456, 60–457; New Jersey Evidence Rules 57, 58.

If the objection is made that leaving it to the cross-examiner to bring out the supporting data is essentially unfair, the answer is that he is under no compulsion to bring out any facts or data except those unfavorable to the opinion. The answer assumes that the cross-examiner has the advance knowledge which is essential for effective cross-examination. This advance knowledge has been afforded, though imperfectly, by the traditional foundation requirement. Rule 26(b)(4) of the Rules of Civil Procedure, as revised, provides for substantial discovery in this area, obviating in large measure the obstacles which have been raised in some instances to discovery of findings, underlying data, and even the identity of the experts. Friedenthal, Discovery and Use of an Adverse Party's Expert Information, 14 Stan.L.Rev. 455 (1962).

These safeguards are reinforced by the discretionary power of the judge to require preliminary disclosure in any event.

Advisory Committee's Note to 1993 Amendment

This rule, which relates to the manner of presenting testimony at trial, is revised to avoid an arguable conflict with revised Rules 26(a)(2)(B) and 26(e)(1) of the Federal Rules of Civil Procedure or with revised Rule 16 of the Federal Rules of Criminal Procedure, which require disclosure in advance of trial of the basis and reasons for an expert's opinions.

If a serious question is raised under Rule 702 or 703 as to the admissibility of expert testimony, disclosure of the underlying facts or data on which opinions are based may, of course, be needed by the court before deciding whether, and to what extent, the person should be allowed to testify. This rule does not preclude such an inquiry.

Advisory Committee's Note to 2011 Amendment

* * * The Committee deleted all reference to an "inference" on the grounds that the deletion made the Rule flow better and easier to read, and because any "inference" is covered by the broader term "opinion." Courts have not made substantive decisions on the basis of any distinction be-

tween an opinion and an inference. No change in current practice is intended.

Rule 706

[Editorial Note: As a result of the 2011 restyling, the substance of subdivision (a) of Rule 706 was divided into two subdivisions, (a) and (b). The substance of former subdivsions (b), (c), and (d) is now in subdivsions (c), (d), and (e), respectively.]

Note by Federal Judicial Center

The rule enacted by the Congress is the rule prescribed by the Supreme Court, amended by substituting "court" in place of "judge," with conforming pronominal changes, and, in subdivision (b), by substituting the phrase "and civil actions and proceedings" in place of "and cases" before "involving" in the second sentence.

Advisory Committee's Note

The practice of shopping for experts, the venality of some experts, and the reluctance of many reputable experts to involve themselves in litigation, have been matters of deep concern. Though the contention is made that court appointed experts acquire an aura of infallibility to which they are not entitled, Levy, Impartial Medical Testimony—Revisited, 34 Temple L.Q. 416 (1961), the trend is increasingly to provide for their use. While experience indicates that actual appointment is a relatively infrequent occurrence, the assumption may be made that the availability of the procedure in itself decreases the need for resorting to it. The ever-present possibility that the judge *may* appoint an expert in a given case must inevitably exert a sobering effect on the expert witness of a party and upon the person utilizing his services.

The inherent power of a trial judge to appoint an expert of his own choosing is virtually unquestioned. Scott v. Spanjer Bros., Inc., 298 F.2d 928 (2d Cir.1962); Danville Tobacco Assn. v. Bryant-Buckner Associates, Inc., 333 F.2d 202 (4th Cir.1964); Sink, The Unused Power of a Federal Judge to Call His Own Expert Witnesses, 29 S.Cal.L.Rev. 195 (1956); 2 Wigmore § 563, 9 id. § 2484; Annot., 95 A.L.R.2d 383. Hence the problem becomes largely one of detail.

The New York plan is well known and is described in Report by Special Committee of the Association of the Bar of the City of New York: Impartial Medical Testimony (1956). On recommendation of the Section of Judicial Administration, local adoption of an impartial medical plan was endorsed by the American Bar Association. 82 A.B.A.Rep. 184–185 (1957). Descriptions and analyses of plans in effect in various parts of the country are found in Van Dusen, A United States District Judge's View of the Impartial Medical Expert System, 32 F.R.D. 498 (1963); Wick and Kightlinger, Impartial Medical Testimony Under the Federal Civil Rules: A Tale of

Three Doctors, 34 Ins. Counsel J. 115 (1967); and numerous articles collected in Klein, Judicial Administration and the Legal Profession 393 (1963). Statutes and rules include California Evidence Code §§ 730–733; Illinois Supreme Court Rule 215(d), Ill.Rev.Stat.1969, c. 110A, § 215(d); Burns Indiana Stats.1956, § 9–1702; Wisconsin Stats.Annot.1958, § 957.27.

In the federal practice, a comprehensive scheme for court appointed experts was initiated with the adoption of Rule 28 of the Federal Rules of Criminal Procedure in 1946. The Judicial Conference of the United States in 1953 considered court appointed experts in civil cases, but only with respect to whether they should be compensated from public funds, a proposal which was rejected. Report of the Judicial Conference of the United States 23 (1953). The present rule expands the practice to include civil cases.

Subdivision (a) is based on Rule 28 of the Federal Rules of Criminal Procedure, with a few changes, mainly in the interest of clarity. Language has been added to provide specifically for the appointment either on motion of a party or on the judge's own motion. A provision subjecting the court appointed expert to deposition procedures has been incorporated. The rule has been revised to make definite the right of any party, including the party calling him, to cross-examine.

Subdivision (b) combines the present provision for compensation in criminal cases with what seems to be a fair and feasible handling of civil cases, originally found in the Model Act and carried from there into Uniform Rule 60. See also California Evidence Code §§ 730–731. The special provision for Fifth Amendment compensation cases is designed to guard against reducing constitutionally guaranteed just compensation by requiring the recipient to pay costs. See Rule 71A(l) of the Rules of Civil Procedure.

Subdivision (c) seems to be essential if the use of court appointed experts is to be fully effective. Uniform Rule 61 so provides.

Subdivision (d) is in essence the last sentence of Rule 28(a) of the Federal Rules of Criminal Procedure.

ARTICLE VIII. HEARSAY

Advisory Committee's Note

Introductory Note: The Hearsay Problem

The factors to be considered in evaluating the testimony of a witness are perception, memory, and narration. Morgan, Hearsay Dangers and the Application of the Hearsay Concept, 62 Harv.L.Rev. 177 (1948), Selected Writings on Evidence and Trial 764, 765 (Fryer ed. 1957); Shientag, Cross-Examination—A Judge's Viewpoint, 3 Record 12 (1948); Strahorn, A Reconsideration of the Hearsay Rule and Admissions, 85 U.Pa.L.Rev. 484, 485 (1937), Selected Writings, supra, 756, 757; Weinstein, Probative Force of

Hearsay, 46 Iowa L.Rev. 331 (1961). Sometimes a fourth is added, sincerity, but in fact it seems merely to be an aspect of the three already mentioned.

In order to encourage the witness to do his best with respect to each of these factors, and to expose any inaccuracies which may enter in, the Anglo-American tradition has evolved three conditions under which witnesses will ideally be required to testify: (1) under oath, (2) in the personal presence of the trier of fact, (3) subject to cross-examination.

(1) Standard procedure calls for the swearing of witnesses. While the practice is perhaps less effective than in an earlier time, no disposition to relax the requirement is apparent, other than to allow affirmation by persons with scruples against taking oaths.

(2) The demeanor of the witness traditionally has been believed to furnish trier and opponent with valuable clues. Universal Camera Corp. v. N.L.R.B., 340 U.S. 474, 495–496, 71 S.Ct. 456, 95 L.Ed. 456 (1951); Sahm, Demeanor Evidence: Elusive and Intangible Imponderables, 47 A.B.A.J. 580 (1961), quoting numerous authorities. The witness himself will probably be impressed with the solemnity of the occasion and the possibility of public disgrace. Willingness to falsify may reasonably become more difficult in the presence of the person against whom directed. Rules 26 and 43(a) of the Federal Rules of Criminal and Civil Procedure, respectively, include the general requirement that testimony be taken orally in open court. The Sixth Amendment right of confrontation is a manifestation of these beliefs and attitudes.

(3) Emphasis on the basis of the hearsay rule today tends to center upon the condition of cross-examination. All may not agree with Wigmore that cross-examination is "beyond doubt the greatest legal engine ever invented for the discovery of truth," but all will agree with his statement that it has become a "vital feature" of the Anglo-American system. 5 Wigmore § 1367, p. 29. The belief, or perhaps hope, that cross-examination is effective in exposing imperfections of perception, memory, and narration is fundamental. Morgan, Foreword to Model Code of Evidence 37 (1942).

The logic of the preceding discussion might suggest that no testimony be received unless in full compliance with the three ideal conditions. No one advocates this position. Common sense tells that much evidence which is not given under the three conditions may be inherently superior to much that is. Moreover, when the choice is between evidence which is less than best and no evidence at all, only clear folly would dictate an across-the-board policy of doing without. The problem thus resolves itself into effecting a sensible accommodation between these considerations and the desirability of giving testimony under the ideal conditions.

The solution evolved by the common law has been a general rule excluding hearsay but subject to numerous exceptions under circumstances supposed to furnish guarantees of trustworthiness. Criticisms of this scheme are that it is bulky and complex, fails to screen good from bad hearsay realistically, and inhibits the growth of the law of evidence.

Since no one advocates excluding all hearsay, three possible solutions may be considered: (1) abolish the rule against hearsay and admit all hearsay; (2) admit hearsay possessing sufficient probative force, but with procedural safeguards; (3) revise the present system of class exceptions.

(1) Abolition of the hearsay rule would be the simplest solution. The effect would not be automatically to abolish the giving of testimony under ideal conditions. If the declarant were available, compliance with the ideal conditions would be optional with either party. Thus the proponent could call the declarant as a witness as a form of presentation more impressive than his hearsay statement. Or the opponent could call the declarant to be cross-examined upon his statement. This is the tenor of Uniform Rule 63(1), admitting the hearsay declaration of a person "who is present at the hearing and available for cross-examination." Compare the treatment of declarations of available declarants in Rule 801(d)(1) of the instant rules. If the declarant were unavailable, a rule of free admissibility would make no distinctions in terms of degrees of noncompliance with the ideal conditions and would exact no quid pro quo in the form of assurances of trustworthiness. Rule 503 of the Model Code did exactly that, providing for the admissibility of any hearsay declaration by an unavailable declarant, finding support in the Massachusetts act of 1898, enacted at the instance of Thayer, Mass.Gen.L.1932, c. 233 § 65, and in the English act of 1938, St.1938, c. 28, Evidence. Both are limited to civil cases. The draftsmen of the Uniform Rules chose a less advanced and more conventional position. Comment, Uniform Rule 63. The present Advisory Committee has been unconvinced of the wisdom of abandoning the traditional requirement of some particular assurance of credibility as a condition precedent to admitting the hearsay declaration of an unavailable declarant.

In criminal cases, the Sixth Amendment requirement of confrontation would no doubt move into a large part of the area presently occupied by the hearsay rule in the event of the abolition of the latter. The resultant split between civil and criminal evidence is regarded as an undesirable development.

(2) Abandonment of the system of class exceptions in favor of individual treatment in the setting of the particular case, accompanied by procedural safeguards, has been impressively advocated. Weinstein, The Probative Force of Hearsay, 46 Iowa L.Rev. 331 (1961). Admissibility would be determined by weighing the probative force of the evidence against the possibility of prejudice, waste of time, and the availability of more satisfactory evidence. The bases of the traditional hearsay exceptions would be helpful in assessing probative force. Ladd, The Relationship of the Principles of Exclusionary Rules of Evidence to the Problem of Proof, 18 Minn.L.Rev. 506 (1934). Procedural safeguards would consist of notice of intention to use hearsay, free comment by the judge on the weight of the evidence, and a greater measure of authority in both trial and appellate judges to deal

with evidence on the basis of weight. The Advisory Committee has rejected this approach to hearsay as involving too great a measure of judicial discretion, minimizing the predictability of rulings, enhancing the difficulties of preparation for trial, adding a further element to the already over-complicated congeries of pretrial procedures, and requiring substantially different rules for civil and criminal cases. The only way in which the probative force of hearsay differs from the probative force of other testimony is in the absence of oath, demeanor, and cross-examination as aids in determining credibility. For a judge to exclude evidence because he does not believe it has been described as "altogether atypical, extraordinary. * * *" Chadbourn, *Bentham and the Hearsay Rule—A Benthamic View of Rule 63(4)(c) of the Uniform Rules of Evidence*, 75 Harv.L.Rev. 932, 947 (1962).

(3) The approach to hearsay in these rules is that of the common law, i.e., a general rule excluding hearsay, with exceptions under which evidence is not required to be excluded even though hearsay. The traditional hearsay exceptions are drawn upon for the exceptions, collected under two rules, one dealing with situations where availability of the declarant is regarded as immaterial and the other with those where unavailability is made a condition to the admission of the hearsay statement. Each of the two rules concludes with a provision for hearsay statements not within one of the specified exceptions "but having comparable [equivalent] circumstantial guarantees of trustworthiness." Rules 803(24) and 804(b)(6)[5]. This plan is submitted as calculated to encourage growth and development in this area of the law, while conserving the values and experience of the past as a guide to the future.

Confrontation and Due Process

Until very recently, decisions invoking the confrontation clause of the Sixth Amendment were surprisingly few, a fact probably explainable by the former inapplicability of the clause to the states and by the hearsay rule's occupancy of much the same ground. The pattern which emerges from the earlier cases invoking the clause is substantially that of the hearsay rule, applied to criminal cases: an accused is entitled to have the witnesses against him testify under oath, in the presence of himself and trier, subject to cross-examination; yet considerations of public policy and necessity require the recognition of such exceptions as dying declarations and former testimony of unavailable witnesses. Mattox v. United States, 156 U.S. 237, 15 S.Ct. 337, 39 L.Ed. 409 (1895); Motes v. United States, 178 U.S. 458, 20 S.Ct. 993, 44 L.Ed. 1150 (1900); Delaney v. United States, 263 U.S. 586, 44 S.Ct. 206, 68 L.Ed. 462 (1924). Beginning with Snyder v. Massachusetts, 291 U.S. 97, 54 S.Ct. 330, 78 L.Ed. 674 (1934), the Court began to speak of confrontation as an aspect of procedural due process, thus extending its applicability to state cases and to federal cases other than criminal. The language of *Snyder* was that of an elastic concept of hearsay. The deportation case of Bridges v. Wixon, 326 U.S. 135, 65 S.Ct. 1443, 89 L.Ed. 2103 (1945), may be read broadly as imposing a strictly construed right of confrontation in all kinds of cases or narrowly as the product of a failure of the

Immigration and Naturalization Service to follow its own rules. In re Oliver, 333 U.S. 257, 68 S.Ct. 499, 92 L.Ed. 682 (1948), ruled that cross-examination was essential to due process in a state contempt proceeding, but in United States v. Nugent, 346 U.S. 1, 73 S.Ct. 991, 97 L.Ed. 1417 (1953), the court held that it was not an essential aspect of a "hearing" for a conscientious objector under the Selective Service Act. Stein v. New York, 346 U.S. 156, 196, 73 S.Ct. 1077, 97 L.Ed. 1522 (1953), disclaimed any purpose to read the hearsay rule into the Fourteenth Amendment, but in Greene v. McElroy, 360 U.S. 474, 79 S.Ct. 1400, 3 L.Ed.2d 1377 (1959), revocation of security clearance without confrontation and cross-examination was held unauthorized, and a similar result was reached in Willner v. Committee on Character, 373 U.S. 96, 83 S.Ct. 1175, 10 L.Ed.2d 224 (1963). Ascertaining the constitutional dimensions of the confrontation-hearsay aggregate against the background of these cases is a matter of some difficulty, yet the general pattern is at least not inconsistent with that of the hearsay rule.

In 1965 the confrontation clause was held applicable to the states. Pointer v. Texas, 380 U.S. 400, 85 S.Ct. 1065, 13 L.Ed.2d 923 (1965). Prosecution use of former testimony given at a preliminary hearing where petitioner was not represented by counsel was a violation of the clause. The same result would have followed under conventional hearsay doctrine read in the light of a constitutional right to counsel, and nothing in the opinion suggests any difference in essential outline between the hearsay rule and the right of confrontation. In the companion case of Douglas v. Alabama, 380 U.S. 415, 85 S.Ct. 1074, 13 L.Ed.2d 934 (1965), however, the result reached by applying the confrontation clause is one reached less readily via the hearsay rule. A confession implicating petitioner was put before the jury by reading it to the witness in portions and asking if he made that statement. The witness refused to answer on grounds of self-incrimination. The result, said the Court, was to deny cross-examination, and hence confrontation. True, it could broadly be said that the confession was a hearsay statement which for all practical purposes was put in evidence. Yet a more easily accepted explanation of the opinion is that its real thrust was in the direction of curbing undesirable prosecutorial behavior, rather than merely applying rules of exclusion, and that the confrontation clause was the means selected to achieve this end. Comparable facts and a like result appeared in Brookhart v. Janis, 384 U.S. 1, 86 S.Ct. 1245, 16 L.Ed.2d 314 (1966).

The pattern suggested in *Douglas* was developed further and more distinctly in a pair of cases at the end of the 1966 term. United States v. Wade, 388 U.S. 218, 87 S.Ct. 1926, 18 L.Ed.2d 1149 (1967), and Gilbert v. California, 388 U.S. 263, 87 S.Ct. 1951, 18 L.Ed.2d 1178 (1967), hinged upon practices followed in identifying accused persons before trial. This pretrial identification was said to be so decisive an aspect of the case that accused was entitled to have counsel present; a pretrial identification made in the absence of counsel was not itself receivable in evidence and, in addition, might fatally infect a courtroom identification. The presence of counsel at the earlier identification was described as a necessary prerequisite for "a meaningful confrontation at trial." United States v. Wade, supra, 388 U.S. at p. 236, 87 S.Ct. at p. 1937. *Wade* involved no evidence of the fact of a prior identification and hence was not susceptible of being decided on hearsay grounds. In *Gilbert,* witnesses did testify to an earlier identification, readily classifiable as hearsay under a fairly strict view of what constitutes hearsay. The Court, however, carefully avoided basing the decision on the hearsay ground, choosing confrontation instead. 388 U.S. 263, 272, n. 3, 87 S.Ct. 1951. See also Parker v. Gladden, 385 U.S. 363, 87 S.Ct. 468, 17 L.Ed.2d 420 (1966), holding that the right of confrontation was violated when the bailiff made prejudicial statements to jurors, and Note, 75 Yale L.J. 1434 (1966).

Under the earlier cases, the confrontation clause may have been little more than a constitutional embodiment of the hearsay rule, even including traditional exceptions but with some room for expanding them along similar lines. But under the recent cases the impact of the clause clearly extends beyond the confines of the hearsay rule. These considerations have led the Advisory Committee to conclude that a hearsay rule can function usefully as an adjunct to the confrontation right in constitutional areas and independently in nonconstitutional areas. In recognition of the separateness of the confrontation clause and the hearsay rule, and to avoid inviting collisions between them or between the hearsay rule and other exclusionary principles, the exceptions set forth in Rules 803 and 804 are stated in terms of exemption from the general exclusionary mandate of the hearsay rule, rather than in positive terms of admissibility. See Uniform Rule 63(1) to (31) and California Evidence Code §§ 1200–1340.

Rule 801

Note by Federal Judicial Center

The rule enacted by the Congress is the rule prescribed by the Supreme Court, with two amendments to subdivision (d)(1). The first of these amendments inserted in item (A), after "testimony," the phrase "and was given under oath subject to the penalty of perjury at a trial, hearing, or other proceeding, or in a deposition." The other amendment consisted of the deletion of item (C), which dealt with prior statements of identification. The reasons for these amendments are stated in the Report of the House Committee on the Judiciary, the Report of the Senate Committee on the Judiciary, and the Conference Report, set forth below.

Advisory Committee's Note

Subdivision (a). The definition of "statement" assumes importance because the term is used in the definition of hearsay in subdivision (c). The effect of the definition of "statement" is to exclude from the operation of the hearsay rule all evidence of conduct, verbal or nonverbal, not intended as an assertion. The key to the definition is that nothing is an assertion unless intended to be one.

It can scarcely be doubted that an assertion made in words is intended by the declarant to be an assertion. Hence verbal assertions readily fall into the category of "statement." Whether nonverbal conduct should be regarded as a statement for purposes of defining hearsay requires further consideration. Some nonverbal conduct, such as the act of pointing to identify a suspect in a lineup, is clearly the equivalent of words, assertive in nature, and to be regarded as a statement. Other nonverbal conduct, however, may be offered as evidence that the person acted as he did because of his belief in the existence of the condition sought to be proved, from which belief the existence of the condition may be inferred. This sequence is, arguably, in effect an assertion of the existence of the condition and hence properly includable within the hearsay concept. See Morgan, Hearsay Dangers and the Application of the Hearsay Concept, 62 Harv.L.Rev. 177, 214, 217 (1948), and the elaboration in Finman, Implied Assertions as Hearsay: Some Criticisms of the Uniform Rules of Evidence, 14 Stan.L.Rev. 682 (1962). Admittedly evidence of this character is untested with respect to the perception, memory, and narration (or their equivalents) of the actor, but the Advisory Committee is of the view that these dangers are minimal in the absence of an intent to assert and do not justify the loss of the evidence on hearsay grounds. No class of evidence is free of the possibility of fabrication, but the likelihood is less with nonverbal than with assertive verbal conduct. The situations giving rise to the nonverbal conduct are such as virtually to eliminate questions of sincerity. Motivation, the nature of the conduct, and the presence or absence of reliance will bear heavily upon the weight to be given the evidence. Falknor, The "Hear-Say" Rule as a "See-Do" Rule: Evidence of Conduct, 33 Rocky Mt.L.Rev. 133 (1961). Similar considerations govern nonassertive verbal conduct and verbal conduct which is assertive but offered as a basis for inferring something other than the matter asserted, also excluded from the definition of hearsay by the language of subdivision (c).

When evidence of conduct is offered on the theory that it is not a statement, and hence not hearsay, a preliminary determination will be required to determine whether an assertion is intended. The rule is so worded as to place the burden upon the party claiming that the intention existed; ambiguous and doubtful cases will be resolved against him and in favor of admissibility. The determination involves no greater difficulty than many other preliminary questions of fact. Maguire, The Hearsay System: Around and Through the Thicket, 14 Vand.L.Rev. 741, 765–767 (1961).

For similar approaches, see Uniform Rule 62(1); California Evidence Code §§ 225, 1200; Kansas Code of Civil Procedure § 60–459(a); New Jersey Evidence Rule 62(1).

Subdivision (c). The definition follows along familiar lines in including only statements offered to prove the truth of the matter asserted. McCormick § 225; 5 Wigmore § 1361, 6 id. § 1766. If the significance of an offered statement lies solely in the fact that it was made, no issue is raised as to the truth of anything asserted, and the statement is not hearsay.

Emich Motors Corp. v. General Motors Corp., 181 F.2d 70 (7th Cir.1950), rev'd on other grounds 340 U.S. 558, 71 S.Ct. 408, 95 L.Ed. 534, letters of complaint from customers offered as a reason for cancellation of dealer's franchise, to rebut contention that franchise was revoked for refusal to finance sales through affiliated finance company. The effect is to exclude from hearsay the entire category of "verbal acts" and "verbal parts of an act," in which the statement itself affects the legal rights of the parties or is a circumstance bearing on conduct affecting their rights.

The definition of hearsay must, of course, be read with reference to the definition of statement set forth in subdivision (a).

Testimony given by a witness in the course of court proceedings is excluded since there is compliance with all the ideal conditions for testifying.

Subdivision (d). Several types of statements which would otherwise literally fall within the definition are expressly excluded from it:

(1) *Prior statement by witness.* Considerable controversy has attended the question whether a prior out-of-court statement by a person now available for cross-examination concerning it, under oath and in the presence of the trier of fact, should be classed as hearsay. If the witness admits on the stand that he made the statement and that it was true, he adopts the statement and there is no hearsay problem. The hearsay problem arises when the witness on the stand denies having made the statement or admits having made it but denies its truth. The argument in favor of treating these latter statements as hearsay is based upon the ground that the conditions of oath, cross-examination, and demeanor observation did not prevail at the time the statement was made and cannot adequately be supplied by the later examination. The logic of the situation is troublesome. So far as concerns the oath, its mere presence has never been regarded as sufficient to remove a statement from the hearsay category, and it receives much less emphasis than cross-examination as a truth-compelling device. While strong expressions are found to the effect that no conviction can be had or important right taken away on the basis of statements not made under fear of prosecution for perjury, Bridges v. Wixon, 326 U.S. 135, 65 S.Ct. 1443, 89 L.Ed. 2103 (1945), the fact is that, of the many common law exceptions to the hearsay rule, only that for reported testimony has required the statement to have been made under oath. [Note, however, that rule 801(d)(1)(A), as enacted by Congress, requires that a prior inconsistent statement have been made under oath.]

Nor is it satisfactorily explained why cross-examination cannot be conducted subsequently with success. The decisions contending most vigorously for its inadequacy in fact demonstrate quite thorough exploration of the weaknesses and doubts attending the earlier statement. State v. Saporen, 205 Minn. 358, 285 N.W. 898 (1939); Ruhala v. Roby, 379 Mich. 102, 150 N.W.2d 146 (1967); People v. Johnson, 68 Cal.2d 646, 68 Cal.Rptr. 599, 441 P.2d 111 (1968). In respect to demeanor, as Judge Learned Hand observed in Di Carlo v. United States, 6 F.2d 364 (2d Cir.1925), when the jury decides that the truth is not what the witness says now, but what he said before, they are still deciding from what they see and hear in court. The bulk of the case law nevertheless has been against allowing prior statements of witnesses to be used generally as substantive evidence. Most of the writers and Uniform Rule 63(1) have taken the opposite position.

The position taken by the Advisory Committee in formulating this part of the rule is founded upon an unwillingness to countenance the general use of prior prepared statements as substantive evidence, but with a recognition that particular circumstances call for a contrary result. The judgment is one more of experience than of logic. The rule requires in each instance, as a general safeguard, that the declarant actually testify as a witness, and it then enumerates three situations in which the statement is excepted from the category of hearsay. Compare Uniform Rule 63(1) which allows any out-of-court statement of a declarant who is present at the trial and available for cross-examination.

(A) Prior inconsistent statements traditionally have been admissible to impeach but not as substantive evidence. Under the rule they are substantive evidence. As has been said by the California Law Revision Commission with respect to a similar provision:

"Section 1235 admits inconsistent statements of witnesses because the dangers against which the hearsay rule is designed to protect are largely nonexistent. The declarant is in court and may be examined and cross-examined in regard to his statements and their subject matter. In many cases the inconsistent statement is more likely to be true than the testimony of the witness at the trial because it was made nearer in time to the matter to which it relates and is less likely to be influenced by the controversy that gave rise to the litigation. The trier of fact has the declarant before it and can observe his demeanor and the nature of his testimony as he denies or tries to explain away the inconsistency. Hence, it is in as good a position to determine the truth or falsity of the prior statement as it is to determine the truth or falsity of the inconsistent testimony given in court. Moreover, Section 1235 will provide a party with desirable protection against the 'turncoat' witness who changes his story on the stand and deprives the party calling him of evidence essential to his case." Comment, California Evidence Code § 1235. See also McCormick § 39. The Advisory Committee finds these views more convincing than those expressed in People v. Johnson, 68 Cal.2d 646, 68 Cal.Rptr. 599, 441 P.2d 111 (1968). The constitutionality of the Advisory Committee's view was upheld in California v. Green, 399 U.S. 149, 90 S.Ct. 1930, 26 L.Ed.2d 489 (1970). Moreover, the requirement that the statement be inconsistent with the testimony given assures a thorough exploration of both versions while the witness is on the stand and bars any general and indiscriminate use of previously prepared statements.

[Note that the Rule as enacted by the Congress also requires that the prior inconsistent statements have been made under oath. Eds.]

Report of House Committee on the Judiciary

Present federal law, except in the Second Circuit, permits the use of prior inconsistent statements of a witness for impeachment only. Rule 801(d)(1) as proposed by the Court would have permitted all such statements to be admissible as substantive evidence, an approach followed by a small but growing number of State jurisdictions and recently held constitutional in California v. Green, 399 U.S. 149 (1970). Although there was some support expressed for the Court Rule, based largely on the need to counteract the effect of witness intimidation in criminal cases, the Committee decided to adopt a compromise version of the Rule similar to the position of the Second Circuit. The Rule as amended draws a distinction between types of prior inconsistent statements (other than statements of identification of a person made after perceiving him which are currently admissible, see United States v. Anderson, 406 F.2d 719, 720 (4th Cir.), cert. denied, 395 U.S. 967 (1969)) and allows only those made while the declarant was subject to cross-examination at a trail [trial] or hearing or in a deposition, to be admissible for their truth. Compare United States v. De-Sisto, 329 F.2d 929 (2d Cir.), cert. denied, 377 U.S. 979 (1964); United States v. Cunningham, 446 F.2d 194 (2d Cir.1971) (restricting the admissibility of prior inconsistent statements as substantive evidence to those made under oath in a formal proceeding, but not requiring that there have been an opportunity for cross-examination). The rationale for the Committee's decision is that (1) unlike in most other situations involving unsworn or oral statements, there can be no dispute as to whether the prior statement was made; and (2) the context of a formal proceeding, an oath, and the opportunity for cross-examination provide firm additional assurances of the reliability of the prior statement.

Report of Senate Committee on the Judiciary

Rule 801 defines what is and what is not hearsay for the purpose of admitting a prior statement as substantive evidence. A prior statement of a witness at a trial or hearing which is inconsistent with his testimony is, of course, always admissible for the purpose of impeaching the witness' credibility.

As submitted by the Supreme Court, subdivision (d)(1)(A) made admissible as substantive evidence the prior statement of a witness inconsistent with his present testimony.

The House severely limited the admissibility of prior inconsistent statements by adding a requirement that the prior statement must have been subject to cross-examination, thus precluding even the use of grand jury statements. The requirement that the prior statement must have been subject to cross-examination appears unnecessary since this rule comes into play only when the witness testifies in the present trial. At that time, he is on the stand and can explain an earlier position and be cross-examined as to both.

The requirement that the statement be under oath also appears unnecessary. Notwithstanding the absence of an oath contemporaneous with the statement, the witness, when on the stand, qualifying or denying the prior statement, is under oath. In any event, of all the many recognized exceptions to the hearsay rule, only one (former testimony) requires that the out-of-court statement have been made under oath. With respect to the lack of evidence of the demeanor of the witness at the time of the prior statement, it would be difficult to improve upon Judge Learned Hand's observation that when the jury decides that the truth is not what the witness says now but what he said before, they are still deciding from what they see and hear in court.[1]

The rule as submitted by the Court has positive advantages. The prior statement was made nearer in time to the events, when memory was fresher and intervening influences had not been brought into play. A realistic method is provided for dealing with the turncoat witness who changes his story on the stand.[2]

New Jersey, California, and Utah have adopted a rule similar to this one; and Nevada, New Mexico, and Wisconsin have adopted the identical Federal rule.

For all of these reasons, we think the House amendment should be rejected and the rule as submitted by the Supreme Court reinstated.[3]

Conference Report

The House bill provides that a statement is not hearsay if the declarant testifies and is subject to cross-examination concerning the statement and if the statement is inconsistent with his testimony and was given under oath subject to cross-examination and subject to the penalty of perjury at a trial or hearing or in a deposition. The Senate amendment drops the requirement that the prior statement be given under oath subject to cross-examination and subject to the penalty of perjury at a trial or hearing or in a deposition.

The Conference adopts the Senate amendment with an amendment, so that the rule now requires that the prior inconsistent statement be given under oath subject to the penalty of perjury at a trial, hearing, or other proceeding, or in a deposition. The rule as adopted covers statements before a grand jury. Prior inconsistent statements may, of course, be used for impeaching the credibility of a witness. When the prior inconsistent state-

---

[1] Di Carlo v. United States, 6 F.2d 364 (2d Cir.1925).

[2] See Comment, California Evidence Code § 1235; McCormick, Evidence, § 38 (2nd ed. 1972).

[3] It would appear that some of the opposition to this Rule is based on a concern that a person could be convicted solely upon evidence admissible under this Rule. The Rule, however, is not addressed to the question of the sufficiency of evidence to send a case to the jury, but merely as to its admissibility. Factual circumstances could well arise where, if this were the sole evidence, dismissal would be appropriate.

ment is one made by a defendant in a criminal case, it is covered by Rule 801(d)(2).

Advisory Committee's Note

(B) Prior consistent statements traditionally have been admissible to rebut charges of recent fabrication or improper influence or motive but not as substantive evidence. Under the rule they are substantive evidence. The prior statement is consistent with the testimony given on the stand, and, if the opposite party wishes to open the door for its admission in evidence, no sound reason is apparent why it should not be received generally.

Report of Senate Committee on the Judiciary

As submitted by the Supreme Court and as passed by the House, subdivision (d)(1)(c)[C] of rule 801 made admissible the prior statement identifying a person made after perceiving him. The committee decided to delete this provision because of the concern that a person could be convicted solely upon evidence admissible under this subdivision.

Conference Report

The House bill provides that a statement is not hearsay if the declarant testifies and is subject to cross-examination concerning the statement and the statement is one of identification of a person made after perceiving him. The Senate amendment eliminated this provision.

The Conference adopts the Senate amendment.

Editorial Note

Subdivision (d)(1)(C) was included in the rule as prescribed by the Supreme Court but was deleted by the Congress in enacting the rules, as indicated in the Conference Report above. However, the subdivision was restored by Act effective Oct. 31, 1975. Therefore the Advisory Committee's Note to the subdivision is now reprinted below, followed by the Note to subdivision (d)(2).

Advisory Committee's Note

(C) The admission of evidence of identification finds substantial support, although it falls beyond a doubt in the category of prior out-of-court statements. Illustrative are People v. Gould, 54 Cal.2d 621, 7 Cal.Rptr. 273, 354 P.2d 865 (1960); Judy v. State, 218 Md. 168, 146 A.2d 29 (1958); State v. Simmons, 63 Wash.2d 17, 385 P.2d 389 (1963); California Evidence Code § 1238; New Jersey Evidence Rule 63(1)(c); N.Y.Code of Criminal Procedure § 393–b. Further cases are found in 4 Wigmore § 1130. The basis is the generally unsatisfactory and inconclusive nature of courtroom identifications as compared with those made at an earlier time under less suggestive conditions. The Supreme Court considered the admissibility of evidence of prior identification in Gilbert v. California, 388 U.S. 263, 87 S.Ct.

1951, 18 L.Ed.2d 1178 (1967). Exclusion of lineup identification was held to be required because the accused did not then have the assistance of counsel. Significantly, the Court carefully refrained from placing its decision on the ground that testimony as to the making of a prior out-of-court identification ("That's the man") violated either the hearsay rule or the right of confrontation because not made under oath, subject to immediate cross-examination, in the presence of the trier. Instead the Court observed:

> "There is a split among the States concerning the admissibility of prior extra-judicial identifications, as independent evidence of identity, both by the witness and third parties present at the prior identification. See 71 A.L.R.2d 449. It has been held that the prior identification is hearsay, and, when admitted through the testimony of the identifier, is merely a prior consistent statement. The recent trend, however, is to admit the prior identification under the exception that admits as substantive evidence a prior communication by a witness who is available for cross-examination at the trial. See 5 A.L.R.2d Later Case Service 1225–1228. * * * " 388 U.S. at 272, n. 3, 87 S.Ct. at 1956.

(2) *Admissions.* Admissions by a party-opponent are excluded from the category of hearsay on the theory that their admissibility in evidence is the result of the adversary system rather than satisfaction of the conditions of the hearsay rule. Strahorn, A Reconsideration of the Hearsay Rule and Admissions, 85 U.Pa.L.Rev. 484, 564 (1937); Morgan, Basic Problems of Evidence 265 (1962); 4 Wigmore § 1048. No guarantee of trustworthiness is required in the case of an admission. The freedom which admissions have enjoyed from technical demands of searching for an assurance of trustworthiness in some against-interest circumstance, and from the restrictive influences of the opinion rule and the rule requiring firsthand knowledge, when taken with the apparently prevalent satisfaction with the results, calls for generous treatment of this avenue to admissibility.

The rule specifies five categories of statements for which the responsibility of a party is considered sufficient to justify reception in evidence against him:

(A) A party's own statement is the classic example of an admission. If he has a representative capacity and the statement is offered against him in that capacity, no inquiry whether he was acting in the representative capacity in making the statement is required; the statement need only be relevant to representative affairs. To the same effect is California Evidence Code § 1220. Compare Uniform Rule 63(7), requiring a statement to be made in a representative capacity to be admissible against a party in a representative capacity.

(B) Under established principles an admission may be made by adopting or acquiescing in the statement of another. While knowledge of contents would ordinarily be essential, this it not inevitably so: "X is a reliable person and knows what he is talking about." See McCormick § 246, p. 527, n. 15. Adoption or acquiescence may be manifested in any appropriate manner. When silence is relied upon, the theory is that the person would, under the circumstances, protest the statement made in his presence, if untrue. The decision in each case calls for an evaluation in terms of probable human behavior. In civil cases, the results have generally been satisfactory. In criminal cases, however, troublesome questions have been raised by decisions holding that failure to deny is an admission: the inference is a fairly weak one, to begin with; silence may be motivated by advice of counsel or realization that "anything you say may be used against you"; unusual opportunity is afforded to manufacture evidence; and encroachment upon the privilege against self-incrimination seems inescapably to be involved. However, recent decisions of the Supreme Court relating to custodial interrogation and the right to counsel appear to resolve these difficulties. Hence the rule contains no special provisions concerning failure to deny in criminal cases.

(C) No authority is required for the general proposition that a statement authorized by a party to be made should have the status of an admission by the party. However, the question arises whether only statements to third persons should be so regarded, to the exclusion of statements by the agent to the principal. The rule is phrased broadly so as to encompass both. While it may be argued that the agent authorized to make statements to his principal does not speak for him, Morgan, Basic Problems of Evidence 273 (1962), communication to an outsider has not generally been thought to be an essential characteristic of an admission. Thus a party's books or records are usable against him, without regard to any intent to disclose to third persons. 5 Wigmore § 1557. See also McCormick § 78, pp. 159–161. In accord is New Jersey Evidence Rule 63(8)(a). Cf. Uniform Rule 63(8)(a) and California Evidence Code § 1222 which limit status as an admission in this regard to statements authorized by the party to be made "for" him, which is perhaps an ambiguous limitation to statements to third persons. Falknor, Vicarious Admissions and the Uniform Rules, 14 Vand.L.Rev. 855, 860–861 (1961).

(D) The tradition has been to test the admissibility of statements by agents, as admissions, by applying the usual test of agency. Was the admission made by the agent acting in the scope of his employment? Since few principals employ agents for the purpose of making damaging statements, the usual result was exclusion of the statement. Dissatisfaction with this loss of valuable and helpful evidence has been increasing. A substantial trend favors admitting statements related to a matter within the scope of the agency or employment. Grayson v. Williams, 256 F.2d 61 (10th Cir.1958); Koninklijke Luchtvaart Maatschappij N.V. KLM Royal Dutch Airlines v. Tuller, 110 U.S.App.D.C. 282, 292 F.2d 775, 784 (1961); Martin v. Savage Truck Lines, Inc., 121 F.Supp. 417 (D.D.C.1954), and numerous state court decisions collected in 4 Wigmore, 1964 Supp., pp. 66–73, with comments by the editor that the statements should have been excluded as not within scope of agency. For the traditional view see Northern Oil Co. v. Socony Mobil Oil Co., 347 F.2d 81, 85 (2d Cir.1965) and cases cited therein.

Similar provisions are found in Uniform Rule 63(9)(a), Kansas Code of Civil Procedure § 60–460(i)(1), and New Jersey Evidence Rule 63(9)(a).

(E) The limitation upon the admissibility of statements of co-conspirators to those made "during the course and in furtherance of the conspiracy" is in the accepted pattern. While the broadened view of agency taken in item (iv) might suggest wider admissibility of statements of co-conspirators, the agency theory of conspiracy is at best a fiction and ought not to serve as a basis for admissibility beyond that already established. See Levie, Hearsay and Conspiracy, 52 Mich.L.Rev. 1159 (1954); Comment, 25 U.Chi.L.Rev. 530 (1958). The rule is consistent with the position of the Supreme Court in denying admissibility to statements made after the objectives of the conspiracy have either failed or been achieved. Krulewitch v. United States, 336 U.S. 440, 69 S.Ct. 716, 93 L.Ed. 790 (1949); Wong Sun v. United States, 371 U.S. 471, 490, 83 S.Ct. 407, 9 L.Ed.2d 441 (1963). For similarly limited provisions see California Evidence Code § 1223 and New Jersey Rule 63(9)(b). Cf. Uniform Rule 63(9)(b).

Report of Senate Committee on the Judiciary

The House approved the long-accepted rule that "a statement by a co-conspirator of a party during the course and in furtherance of the conspiracy" is not hearsay as it was submitted by the Supreme Court. While the rule refers to a coconspirator, it is this committee's understanding that the rule is meant to carry forward the universally accepted doctrine that a joint venturer is considered as a coconspirator for the purposes of this rule even though no conspiracy has been charged. United States v. Rinaldi, 393 F.2d 97, 99 (2d Cir.), cert. denied 393 U.S. 913 (1968); United States v. Spencer, 415 F.2d 1301, 1304 (7th Cir.1969).

Advisory Committee's Note to 1997 Amendment

Rule 801(d)(2) has been amended in order to respond to three issues raised by *Bourjaily v. United States*, 483 U.S. 171 (1987). First, the amendment codifies the holding in Bourjaily by stating expressly that a court shall consider the contents of a coconspirator's statement in determining "the existence of the conspiracy and the participation therein of the declarant and the party against whom the statement is offered." According to *Bourjaily*, Rule 104(a) requires these preliminary questions to be established by a preponderance of the evidence.

Second, the amendment resolves an issue on which the Court had reserved decision. It provides that the contents of the declarant's statement do not alone suffice to establish a conspiracy in which the declarant and the defendant participated. The court must consider in addition the circumstances surrounding the statement, such as the identity of the speaker, the context in which the statement was made, or evidence corroborating the contents of the statement in making its determination as to each preliminary question. This amendment is in accordance with existing practice. Every court of appeals that has resolved this issue requires some evidence in addition to the contents of the statement. *See e.g., United States v. Beckham*, 968 F.2d 47, 51 (D.C.Cir.1992); *United States v. Sepulveda*, 15 F.3d 1161, 1181–82 (lst Cir. 1993), *cert. denied*, 512 U.S. 1223 (1994); United States v. Daly, 842 F.2d 1380, 1386 (2d Cir.), *cert. denied*, 488 U.S. 821 (1988); United States v. Clark, 18 F.3d 1337, 1341–42 (6th Cir.), *cert. denied*, 513 U.S. 852 (1994); *United States v. Zambrana*, 841 F.2d 1320, 1344–45 (7th Cir.1988); *United States v. Silverman*, 861 F.2d 571, 577 (9th Cir. 1988); *United States v. Gordon*, 844 F.2d 1397, 1402 (9th Cir.1988); *United States v. Hernandez*, 829 F.2d 988, 993 (10th Cir. 1987), *cert. denied*, 485 U.S. 1013 (1988); *United States v. Byrom*, 910 F.2d 725, 736 (11th Cir.1990).

Third, the amendment extends the reasoning of *Bourjaily* to statements offered under subdivisions (C) and (D) of Rule 801(d)(2). In *Bourjaily*, the Court rejected treating foundational facts pursuant to the law of agency in favor of an evidentiary approach governed by Rule 104(a). The Advisory Committee believes it appropriate to treat analogously preliminary questions relating to the declarant's authority under subdivision (C), and the agency or employment relationship and scope thereof under subdivision (D).

Advisory Committee's Note to 2011 Amendment

* * * Statements falling under the hearsay exclusion provided by Rule 801(d)(2) are no longer referred to as "admissions" in the title to the subdivision. The term "admissions" is confusing because not all statements covered by the exclusion are admissions in the colloquial sense—a statement can be within the exclusion even if it "admitted" nothing and was not against the party's interest when made. The term "admissions" also raises confusion in comparison with the Rule 804(b)(3) exception for declarations against interest. No change in application of the exclusion is intended.

Rule 802

Note by Federal Judicial Center

The rule enacted by the Congress is the rule prescribed by the Supreme Court, amended by substituting "prescribed" in place of "adopted" and by inserting the phrase "pursuant to statutory authority."

Advisory Committee's Note

The provision excepting from the operation of the rule hearsay which is made admissible by other rules adopted by the Supreme Court or by Act of Congress continues the admissibility thereunder of hearsay which would not qualify under these Evidence Rules. The following examples illustrate the working of the exception:

Federal Rules of Civil Procedure

Rule 4(g): proof of service by affidavit.

Rule 32: admissibility of depositions.

Rule 43(e): affidavits when motion based on facts not appearing of record.

Rule 56: affidavits in summary judgment proceedings.

Rule 65(b): showing by affidavit for temporary restraining order.

Federal Rules of Criminal Procedure

Rule 4(a): affidavits to show grounds for issuing warrants.

Rule 12(b)(4): affidavits to determine issues of fact in connection with motions.

Acts of Congress

10 U.S.C. § 7730: affidavits of unavailable witnesses in actions for damages caused by vessel in naval service, or towage or salvage of same, when taking of testimony or bringing of action delayed or stayed on security grounds.

29 U.S.C. § 161(4): affidavit as proof of service in NLRB proceedings.

38 U.S.C. § 5206: affidavit as proof of posting notice of sale of unclaimed property by Veterans Administration.

Rule 803

Note by Federal Judicial Center

The rule enacted by the Congress retains the 24 exceptions set forth in the rule prescribed by the Supreme Court. Three of the exceptions, numbered (6), (8), and (24) have been amended in respects that may fairly be described as substantial. Others, numbered (5), (7), (14), and (16), have been amended in lesser ways. The remaining 17 are unchanged. The amendments are, in numerical order, as follows.

Exception (5) as prescribed by the Supreme Court was amended by inserting after "made" the phrase "or adopted by the witness."

Exception (6) as prescribed by the Supreme Court was amended by substituting the phrase, "if kept in the course of a regularly conducted business activity, and if it was the regular practice of that business activity to make the memorandum, report, record, or data compilation, all," in place of "all in the course of a regularly conducted activity"; by substituting "source" in place of "sources"; by substituting the phrase, "the method or circumstances of preparation," in place of "other circumstances"; and by adding the second sentence.

Exception (7) as prescribed by the Supreme Court was amended by substituting the phrase, "kept in accordance with the provisions of paragraph (6)," in place of "of a regularly conducted activity." The exception prescribed by the Supreme Court included a comma after "memoranda," while the congressional enactment does not.

Exception (8) as prescribed by the Supreme Court was amended by inserting in item (B) after "law" the phrase, "as to which matters there was a duty to report, excluding, however, in criminal cases matters observed by police officers and other law enforcement personnel," and by substituting in item (C) the phrase "civil actions and proceedings," in place of "civil cases."

Exception (14) as prescribed by the Supreme Court was amended by substituting "authorizes" in place of "authorized."

Exception (16) as prescribed by the Supreme Court was amended by substituting the phrase, "the authenticity of which," in place of "whose authenticity."

Exception (24) as prescribed by the Supreme Court was amended by substituting "equivalent" in place of "comparable," and adding all that appears after "trustworthiness" in the exception as enacted by the Congress.

Advisory Committee's Note

The exceptions are phrased in terms of nonapplication of the hearsay rule, rather than in positive terms of admissibility, in order to repel any implication that other possible grounds for exclusion are eliminated from consideration.

The present rule proceeds upon the theory that under appropriate circumstances a hearsay statement may possess circumstantial guarantees of trustworthiness sufficient to justify nonproduction of the declarant in person at the trial even though he may be available. The theory finds vast support in the many exceptions to the hearsay rule developed by the common law in which unavailability of the declarant is not a relevant factor. The present rule is a synthesis of them, with revision where modern developments and conditions are believed to make that course appropriate.

In a hearsay situation, the declarant is, of course, a witness, and neither this rule nor Rule 804 dispenses with the requirement of firsthand knowledge. It may appear from his statement or be inferable from circumstances. See Rule 602.

Exceptions (1) and (2). In considerable measure these two examples overlap, though based on somewhat different theories. The most significant practical difference will lie in the time lapse allowable between event and statement.

The underlying theory of Exception (1) is that substantial contemporaneity of event and statement negative the likelihood of deliberate or conscious misrepresentation. Moreover, if the witness is the declarant, he may be examined on the statement. If the witness is not the declarant, he may be examined as to the circumstances as an aid in evaluating the statement. Morgan, Basic Problems of Evidence 340–341 (1962).

The theory of Exception (2) is simply that circumstances may produce a condition of excitement which temporarily stills the capacity of reflection and produces utterances free of conscious fabrication. 6 Wigmore § 1747, p. 135. Spontaneity is the key factor in each instance, though arrived at by somewhat different routes. Both are needed in order to avoid needless niggling.

While the theory of Exception (2) has been criticized on the ground that excitement impairs accuracy of observation as well as eliminating conscious fabrication, Hutchins and Slesinger, Some Observations on the Law of Evidence: Spontaneous Exclamations, 28 Colum.L.Rev. 432 (1928), it finds support in cases without number. See cases in 6 Wigmore § 1750; Annot. 53 A.L.R.2d 1245 (statements as to cause of or responsibility for motor vehicle accident); Annot., 4 A.L.R.3d 149 (accusatory statements by homicide victims). Since unexciting events are less likely to evoke comment, decisions involving Exception (1) are far less numerous. Illustrative are Tampa Elec. Co. v. Getrost, 151 Fla. 558, 10 So.2d 83 (1942); Houston Oxygen Co. v. Davis, 139 Tex. 1, 161 S.W.2d 474 (1942); and cases cited in McCormick § 273, p. 585, n. 4.

With respect to the *time element,* Exception (1) recognizes that in many, if not most, instances precise contemporaneity is not possible, and hence a slight lapse is allowable. Under Exception (2) the standard of measurement is the duration of the state of excitement. "How long can excitement prevail? Obviously there are no pat answers and the character of the transaction or event will largely determine the significance of the time factor." Slough, Spontaneous Statements and State of Mind, 46 Iowa L.Rev. 224, 243 (1961); McCormick § 272, p. 580.

Participation by the declarant is not required: a non-participant may be moved to describe what he perceives, and one may be startled by an event in which he is not an actor. Slough, supra; McCormick, supra; 6 Wigmore § 1755; Annot., 78 A.L.R.2d 300.

Whether *proof of the startling event* may be made by the statement itself is largely an academic question, since in most cases there is present at least circumstantial evidence that something of a startling nature must have occurred. For cases in which the evidence consists of the condition of the declarant (injuries, state of shock), see Insurance Co. v. Mosely, 75 U.S. (8 Wall.) 397, 19 L.Ed. 437 (1869); Wheeler v. United States, 93 U.S.App.D.C. 159, 211 F.2d 19 (1953), cert. denied 347 U.S. 1019, 74 S.Ct. 876, 98 L.Ed. 1140; Wetherbee v. Safety Casualty Co., 219 F.2d 274 (5th Cir.1955); Lampe v. United States, 97 U.S.App.D.C. 160, 229 F.2d 43 (1956). Nevertheless, on occasion the only evidence may be the content of the statement itself, and rulings that it may be sufficient are described as "increasing," Slough, supra at 246, and as the "prevailing practice," McCormick § 272, p. 579. Illustrative are Armour & Co. v. Industrial Commission, 78 Colo. 569, 243 P. 546 (1926); Young v. Stewart, 191 N.C. 297, 131 S.E. 735 (1926). Moreover, under Rule 104(a) the judge is not limited by the hearsay rule in passing upon preliminary questions of fact.

Proof of declarant's perception by his statement presents similar considerations when declarant is identified. People v. Poland, 22 Ill.2d 175, 174 N.E.2d 804 (1961). However, when declarant is an unidentified bystander, the cases indicate hesitancy in upholding the statement alone as sufficient, Garrett v. Howden, 73 N.M. 307, 387 P.2d 874 (1963); Beck v. Dye, 200 Wash. 1, 92 P.2d 1113 (1939), a result which would under appropriate circumstances be consistent with the rule.

Permissible *subject matter* of the statement is limited under Exception (1) to description or explanation of the event or condition, the assumption being that spontaneity, in the absence of a startling event, may extend no farther. In Exception (2), however, the statement need only "relate" to the startling event or condition, thus affording a broader scope of subject matter coverage. 6 Wigmore §§ 1750, 1754. See Sanitary Grocery Co. v. Snead, 67 App.D.C. 129, 90 F.2d 374 (1937), slip-and-fall case sustaining admissibility of clerk's statement, "That has been on the floor for a couple of hours," and Murphy Auto Parts Co., Inc. v. Ball, 101 U.S.App.D.C. 416, 249 F.2d 508 (1957), upholding admission, on issue of driver's agency, of his statement that he had to call on a customer and was in a hurry to get home. Quick, Hearsay, Excitement, Necessity and the Uniform Rules: A Reappraisal of Rule 63(4), 6 Wayne L.Rev. 204, 206–209 (1960).

Similar provisions are found in Uniform Rule 63(4)(a) and (b); California Evidence Code § 1240 (as to Exception (2) only); Kansas Code of Civil Procedure § 60–460(d)(1) and (2); New Jersey Evidence Rule 63(4).

Exception (3) is essentially a specialized application of Exception (1), presented separately to enhance its usefulness and accessibility. See McCormick §§ 265, 268.

The exclusion of "statements of memory or belief to prove the fact remembered or believed" is necessary to avoid the virtual destruction of the hearsay rule which would otherwise result from allowing state of mind, provable by a hearsay statement, to serve as the basis for an inference of the happening of the event which produced the state of mind. Shepard v. United States, 290 U.S. 96, 54 S.Ct. 22, 78 L.Ed. 196 (1933); Maguire, The Hillmon Case—Thirty-three Years After, 38 Harv.L.Rev. 709, 719–731 (1925); Hinton, States of Mind and the Hearsay Rule, 1 U.Chi.L.Rev. 394, 421–423 (1934). The rule of Mutual Life Ins. Co. v. Hillmon, 145 U.S. 285, 12 S.Ct. 909, 36 L.Ed. 706 (1892), allowing evidence of intention as tending to prove the doing of the act intended, is, of course, left undisturbed.

The carving out, from the exclusion mentioned in the preceding paragraph, of declarations relating to the execution, revocation, identification, or terms of declarant's will represents an *ad hoc* judgment which finds ample reinforcement in the decisions, resting on practical grounds of necessity and expediency rather than logic. McCormick § 271, pp. 577–578; Annot., 34 A.L.R.2d 588, 62 A.L.R.2d 855. A similar recognition of the need for and practical value of this kind of evidence is found in California Evidence Code § 1260.

Report of House Committee on the Judiciary

Rule 803(3) was approved in the form submitted by the Court to Congress. However, the Committee intends that the Rule be construed to limit the doctrine of Mutual Life Insurance Co. v. Hillmon, 145 U.S. 285, 295–300 (1892), so as to render statements of intent by a declarant admissible only to prove his future conduct, not the future conduct of another person.

Advisory Committee's Note

Exception (4). Even those few jurisdictions which have shied away from generally admitting statements of present condition have allowed them if made to a physician for purposes of diagnosis and treatment in view of the patient's strong motivation to be truthful. McCormick § 266, p. 563. The same guarantee of trustworthiness extends to statements of past conditions and medical history, made for purposes of diagnosis or treatment. It also extends to statements as to causation, reasonably pertinent to the same purposes, in accord with the current trend, Shell Oil Co. v. Industrial Commission, 2 Ill.2d 590, 119 N.E.2d 224 (1954); McCormick § 266, p. 564; New Jersey Evidence Rule 63(12)(c). Statements as to fault would not ordinarily qualify under this latter language. Thus a patient's statement that he was struck by an automobile would qualify but not his statement that the car was driven through a red light. Under the exception the statement need not have been made to a physician. Statements to hospital attendants, ambulance drivers, or even members of the family might be included.

Conventional doctrine has excluded from the hearsay exception, as not within its guarantee of truthfulness, statements to a physician consulted only for the purpose of enabling him to testify. While these statements were not admissible as substantive evidence, the expert was allowed to state the basis of his opinion, including statements of this kind. The distinction thus called for was one most unlikely to be made by juries. The rule accordingly rejects the limitation. This position is consistent with the provision of Rule 703 that the facts on which expert testimony is based need not be admissible in evidence if of a kind ordinarily relied upon by experts in the field.

Report of House Committee on the Judiciary

After giving particular attention to the question of physical examination made solely to enable a physician to testify, the Committee approved Rule 803(4) as submitted to Congress, with the understanding that it is not intended in any way to adversely affect present privilege rules or those subsequently adopted.

Report of Senate Committee on the Judiciary

The House approved this rule as it was submitted by the Supreme Court "with the understanding that it is not intended in any way to adversely affect present privilege rules." We also approve this rule, and we would point out with respect to the question of its relation to privileges, it must be read in conjunction with rule 35 of the Federal Rules of Civil Procedure which provides that whenever the physical or mental condition of a party (plaintiff or defendant) is in controversy, the court may require him to submit to an examination by a physician. It is these examinations which will normally be admitted under this exception.

Advisory Committee's Note

Exception (5). A hearsay exception for recorded recollection is generally recognized and has been described as having "long been favored by the federal and practically all the state courts that have had occasion to decide the question." United States v. Kelly, 349 F.2d 720, 770 (2d Cir.1965), citing numerous cases and sustaining the exception against a claimed denial of the right of confrontation. Many additional cases are cited in Annot., 82 A.L.R.2d 473, 520. The guarantee of trustworthiness is found in the reliability inherent in a record made while events were still fresh in mind and accurately reflecting them. Owens v. State, 67 Md. 307, 316, 10 A. 210, 212 (1887).

The principal controversy attending the exception has centered, not upon the propriety of the exception itself, but upon the question whether a preliminary requirement of impaired memory on the part of the witness should be imposed. The authorities are divided. If regard be had only to the accuracy of the evidence, admittedly impairment of the memory of the witness adds nothing to it and should not be required. McCormick § 277, p. 593; 3 Wigmore § 738, p. 76; Jordan v. People, 151 Colo. 133, 376 P.2d 699 (1962), cert. denied 373 U.S. 944, 83 S.Ct. 1553, 10 L.Ed.2d 699; Hall v. State, 223 Md. 158, 162 A.2d 751 (1960); State v. Bindhammer, 44 N.J. 372, 209 A.2d 124 (1965). Nevertheless, the absence of the requirement, it is believed, would encourage the use of statements carefully prepared for purposes of litigation under the supervision of attorneys, investigators, or claim adjusters. Hence the example includes a requirement that the witness not have "sufficient recollection to enable him to testify fully and accurately." To the same effect are California Evidence Code § 1237 and New Jersey Rule 63(1)(b), and this has been the position of the federal courts. Vicksburg & Meridian R.R. v. O'Brien, 119 U.S. 99, 7 S.Ct. 118, 30 L.Ed. 299 (1886); Ahern v. Webb, 268 F.2d 45 (10th Cir.1959); and see N.L.R.B. v. Hudson Pulp and Paper Corp., 273 F.2d 660, 665 (5th Cir.1960); N.L.R.B. v. Federal Dairy Co., 297 F.2d 487 (1st Cir.1962). But cf. United States v. Adams, 385 F.2d 548 (2d Cir.1967).

No attempt is made in the exception to spell out the method of establishing the initial knowledge or the contemporaneity and accuracy of the record, leaving them to be dealt with as the circumstances of the particular case might indicate. Multiple person involvement in the process of observing and recording, as in Rathbun v. Brancatella, 93 N.J.L. 222, 107 A. 279 (1919), is entirely consistent with the exception.

Locating the exception at this place in the scheme of the rules is a matter of choice. There were two other possibilities. The first was to regard the statement as one of the group of prior statements of a testifying witness which are excluded entirely from the category of hearsay by Rule 801(d)(1). That category, however, requires that declarant be "subject to cross-examination," as to which the impaired memory aspect of the exception raises doubts. The other possibility was to include the exception among those covered by Rule 804. Since unavailability is required by that rule and lack of memory is listed as a species of unavailability by the definition of the term in Rule 804(a)(3), that treatment at first impression would seem appropriate. The fact is, however, that the unavailability requirement of the exception is of a limited and peculiar nature. Accordingly, the exception is located at this point rather than in the context of a rule where unavailability is conceived of more broadly.

Report of House Committee on the Judiciary

Rule 803(5) as submitted by the Court permitted the reading into evidence of a memorandum or record concerning a matter about which a witness once had knowledge but now has insufficient recollection to enable him to testify accurately and fully, "shown to have been made when the matter was fresh in his memory and to reflect that knowledge correctly." The Committee amended this Rule to add the words "or adopted by the witness" after the phrase "shown to have been made", a treatment consistent with the definition of "statement" in the Jencks Act, 18 U.S.C. 3500. Moreover, it is the Committee's understanding that a memorandum or report, although barred under this Rule, would nonetheless be admissible if it came within another hearsay exception. This last stated principle is deemed applicable to all the hearsay rules.

Report of Senate Committee on the Judiciary

Rule 803(5) as submitted by the Court permitted the reading into evidence of a memorandum or record concerning a matter about which a witness once had knowledge but now has insufficient recollection to enable him to testify accurately and fully, "shown to have been made when the matter was fresh in his memory and to reflect that knowledge correctly." The House amended the rule to add the words "or adopted by the witness" after the phrase "shown to have been made," language parallel to the Jencks Act.[1]

---

[1] 18 U.S.C. § 3500.

The committee accepts the House amendment with the understanding and belief that it was not intended to narrow the scope of applicability of the rule. In fact, we understand it to clarify the rule's applicability to a memorandum adopted by the witness as well as one made by him. While the rule as submitted by the Court was silent on the question of who made the memorandum, we view the House amendment as a helpful clarification, noting, however, that the Advisory Committee's note to this rule suggests that the important thing is the accuracy of the memorandum rather than who made it.

The committee does not view the House amendment as precluding admissibility in situations in which multiple participants were involved.

When the verifying witness has not prepared the report, but merely examined it and found it accurate, he has adopted the report, and it is therefore admissible. The rule should also be interpreted to cover other situations involving multiple participants, e.g., employer dictating to secretary, secretary making memorandum at direction of employer, or information being passed along a chain of persons, as in Curtis v. Bradley.[2]

The committee also accepts the understanding of the House that a memorandum or report, although barred under this rule, would nonetheless be admissible if it came within another hearsay exception. We consider this principle to be applicable to all the hearsay rules.

Advisory Committee's Note

Exception (6) represents an area which has received much attention from those seeking to improve the law of evidence. The Commonwealth Fund Act was the result of a study completed in 1927 by a distinguished committee under the chairmanship of Professor Morgan. Morgan et al., The Law of Evidence: Some Proposals for its Reform 63 (1927). With changes too minor to mention, it was adopted by Congress in 1936 as the rule for federal courts. 28 U.S.C. § 1732. A number of states took similar action. The Commissioners on Uniform State Laws in 1936 promulgated the Uniform Business Records as Evidence Act, 9A U.L.A. 506, which has acquired a substantial following in the states. Model Code Rule 514 and Uniform Rule 63(13) also deal with the subject. Difference of varying degrees of importance exist among these various treatments.

These reform efforts were largely within the context of business and commercial records, as the kind usually encountered, and concentrated considerable attention upon relaxing the requirement of producing as witnesses, or accounting for the nonproduction of, all participants in the process of gathering, transmitting, and recording information which the common law had evolved as a burdensome and crippling aspect of using records of this type. In their areas of primary emphasis on witnesses to be

---

[2] 65 Conn. 99, 31 Atl. 591 (1894). See also, Rathbun v. Brancatella, 93 N.J.L. 222, 107 Atl. 279 (1919); see also McCormick on Evidence, § 303 (2d ed. 1972).

called and the general admissibility of ordinary business and commercial records, the Commonwealth Fund Act and the Uniform Act appear to have worked well. The exception seeks to preserve their advantages.

On the subject of what witnesses must be called, the Commonwealth Fund Act eliminated the common law requirement of calling or accounting for all participants by failing to mention it. United States v. Mortimer, 118 F.2d 266 (2d Cir.1941); La Porte v. United States, 300 F.2d 878 (9th Cir.1962); McCormick § 290, p. 608. Model Code Rule 514 and Uniform Rule 63(13) did likewise. The Uniform Act, however, abolished the common law requirement in express terms, providing that the requisite foundation testimony might be furnished by "the custodian or other qualified witness." Uniform Business Records as Evidence Act, § 2; 9A U.L.A. 506. The exception follows the Uniform Act in this respect.

The element of unusual reliability of business records is said variously to be supplied by systematic checking, by regularity and continuity which produce habits of precision, by actual experience of business in relying upon them, or by a duty to make an accurate record as part of a continuing job or occupation. McCormick §§ 281, 286, 287; Laughlin, Business Entries and the Like, 46 Iowa L.Rev. 276 (1961). The model statutes and rules have sought to capture these factors and to extend their impact by employing the phrase "regular course of business," in conjunction with a definition of "business" far broader than its ordinarily accepted meaning. The result is a tendency unduly to emphasize a requirement of routineness and repetitiveness and an insistence that other types of records be squeezed into the fact patterns which give rise to traditional business records. * * *

Amplification of the kinds of activities producing admissible records has given rise to problems which conventional business records by their nature avoid. They are problems of the source of the recorded information, of entries in opinion form, of motivation, and of involvement as participant in the matters recorded.

Sources of information presented no substantial problem with ordinary business records. All participants, including the observer or participant furnishing the information to be recorded, were acting routinely, under a duty of accuracy, with employer reliance on the result, or in short "in the regular course of business." If, however, the supplier of the information does not act in the regular course, an essential link is broken; the assurance of accuracy does not extend to the information itself, and the fact that it may be recorded with scrupulous accuracy is of no avail. An illustration is the police report incorporating information obtained from a bystander: the officer qualifies as acting in the regular course but the informant does not. The leading case, Johnson v. Lutz, 253 N.Y. 124, 170 N.E. 517 (1930), held that a report thus prepared was inadmissible. Most of the authorities have agreed with the decision. Gencarella v. Fyfe, 171 F.2d 419 (1st Cir.1948); Gordon v. Robinson, 210 F.2d 192 (3d Cir.1954); Standard Oil Co. of California v. Moore, 251 F.2d 188, 214 (9th Cir.1957), cert. denied 356 U.S. 975, 78 S.Ct. 1139, 2 L.Ed.2d 1148; Yates v. Bair Transport, Inc.,

249 F.Supp. 681 (S.D.N.Y.1965); Annot., 69 A.L.R.2d 1148. Cf. Hawkins v. Gorea Motor Express, Inc., 360 F.2d 933 (2d Cir.1966). Contra, 5 Wigmore § 1530a, n. 1, pp. 391–392. The point is not dealt with specifically in the Commonwealth Fund Act, the Uniform Act, or Uniform Rule 63(13). However, Model Code Rule 514 contains the requirement "that it was the regular course of that business for one with personal knowledge * * * to make such a memorandum or record or to transmit information thereof to be included in such a memorandum or record * * *." The rule follows this lead in requiring an informant with knowledge acting in the course of the regularly conducted activity.

Entries in the form of opinions were not encountered in traditional business records in view of the purely factual nature of the items recorded, but they are now commonly encountered with respect to medical diagnoses, prognoses, and test results, as well as occasionally in other areas. The Commonwealth Fund Act provided only for records of an "act, transaction, occurrence, or event," while the Uniform Act, Model Code Rule 514, and Uniform Rule 63(13) merely added the ambiguous term "condition." The limited phrasing of the Commonwealth Fund Act, 28 U.S.C. § 1732, may account for the reluctance of some federal decisions to admit diagnostic entries. New York Life Ins. Co. v. Taylor, 79 U.S.App.D.C. 66, 147 F.2d 297 (1944); Lyles v. United States, 103 U.S.App.D.C. 22, 254 F.2d 725 (1957), cert. denied 356 U.S. 961, 78 S.Ct. 997, 2 L.Ed.2d 1067; England v. United States, 174 F.2d 466 (5th Cir.1949); Skogen v. Dow Chemical Co., 375 F.2d 692 (8th Cir.1967). Other federal decisions, however, experienced no difficulty in freely admitting diagnostic entries. Reed v. Order of United Commercial Travelers, 123 F.2d 252 (2d Cir.1941); Buckminster's Estate v. Commissioner of Internal Revenue, 147 F.2d 331 (2d Cir.1944); Medina v. Erickson, 226 F.2d 475 (9th Cir.1955); Thomas v. Hogan, 308 F.2d 355 (4th Cir.1962); Glawe v. Rulon, 284 F.2d 495 (8th Cir.1960). In the state courts, the trend favors admissibility. Borucki v. MacKenzie Bros. Co., 125 Conn. 92, 3 A.2d 224 (1938); Allen v. St. Louis Public Service Co., 365 Mo. 677, 285 S.W.2d 663, 55 A.L.R.2d 1022 (1956); People v. Kohlmeyer, 284 N.Y. 366, 31 N.E.2d 490 (1940); Weis v. Weis, 147 Ohio St. 416, 72 N.E.2d 245 (1947). In order to make clear its adherence to the latter position the rule specifically includes both diagnoses and opinions, in addition to acts, events, and conditions, as proper subjects of admissible entries.

Problems of the motivation of the informant have been a source of difficulty and disagreement. In Palmer v. Hoffman, 318 U.S. 109, 63 S.Ct. 477, 87 L.Ed. 645 (1943), exclusion of an accident report made by the since deceased engineer, offered by defendant railroad trustees in a grade crossing collision case, was upheld. The report was not "in the regular course of business," not a record of the systematic conduct of the business as a business, said the Court. The report was prepared for use in litigating, not railroading. While the opinion mentions the motivation of the engineer only obliquely, the emphasis on records of routine operations is significant only by virtue of impact on motivation to be accurate. Absence of routineness raises lack of motivation to be accurate. The opinion of the Court of Appeals had gone beyond mere lack of motive to be accurate: the engineer's statement was "dripping with motivations to misrepresent." Hoffman v. Palmer, 129 F.2d 976, 991 (2d Cir.1942). The direct introduction of motivation is a disturbing factor, since absence of motive to misrepresent has not traditionally been a requirement of the rule; that records might be self-serving has not been a ground for exclusion. Laughlin, Business Records and the Like, 46 Iowa L.Rev. 276, 285 (1961). As Judge Clark said in his dissent, "I submit that there is hardly a grocer's account book which could not be excluded on that basis." 129 F.2d at 1002. A physician's evaluation report of a personal injury litigant would appear to be in the routine of his business. If the report is offered by the party at whose instance it was made, however, it has been held inadmissible, Yates v. Bair Transport, Inc., 249 F.Supp. 681 (S.D.N.Y.1965), otherwise if offered by the opposite party, Korte v. New York, N.H. & H.R. Co., 191 F.2d 86 (2d Cir.1951), cert. denied 342 U.S. 868, 72 S.Ct. 108, 96 L.Ed. 652.

The decisions hinge on motivation and which party is entitled to be concerned about it. Professor McCormick believed that the doctor's report or the accident report were sufficiently routine to justify admissibility. McCormick § 287, p. 604. Yet hesitation must be experienced in admitting everything which is observed and recorded in the course of a regularly conducted activity. Efforts to set a limit are illustrated by Hartzog v. United States, 217 F.2d 706 (4th Cir.1954), error to admit worksheets made by since deceased deputy collector in preparation for the instant income tax evasion prosecution, and United States v. Ware, 247 F.2d 698 (7th Cir.1957), error to admit narcotics agents' records of purchases. See also Exception (8), infra, as to the public record aspects of records of this nature. Some decisions have been satisfied as to motivation of an accident report if made pursuant to statutory duty, United States v. New York Foreign Trade Zone Operators, 304 F.2d 792 (2d Cir.1962); Taylor v. Baltimore & O.R. Co., 344 F.2d 281 (2d Cir.1965), since the report was oriented in a direction other than the litigation which ensued. Cf. Matthews v. United States, 217 F.2d 409 (5th Cir.1954). The formulation of specific terms which would assure satisfactory results in all cases is not possible. Consequently the rule proceeds from the base that records made in the course of a regularly conducted activity will be taken as admissible but subject to authority to exclude if "the sources of information or other circumstances indicate lack of trustworthiness."

Occasional decisions have reached for enhanced accuracy by requiring involvement as a participant in matters reported. Clainos v. United States, 82 U.S.App.D.C. 278, 163 F.2d 593 (1947), error to admit police records of convictions; Standard Oil Co. of California v. Moore, 251 F.2d 188 (9th Cir.1957), cert. denied 356 U.S. 975, 78 S.Ct. 1139, 2 L.Ed.2d 1148, error to admit employees' records of observed business practices of others. The rule includes no requirement of this nature. Wholly acceptable records may involve matters merely observed, e.g. the weather.

The form which the "record" may assume under the rule is described broadly as a "memorandum, report, record, or data compilation, in any form." The expression "data compilation" is used as broadly descriptive of any means of storing information other than the conventional words and figures in written or documentary form. It includes, but is by no means limited to, electronic computer storage. The term is borrowed from revised Rule 34(a) of the Rules of Civil Procedure.

Report of House Committee on the Judiciary

Rule 803(6) as submitted by the Court permitted a record made "in the course of a regularly conducted activity" to be admissible in certain circumstances. The Committee believed there were insufficient guarantees of reliability in records made in the course of activities falling outside the scope of "business" activities as that term is broadly defined in 28 U.S.C. 1732. Moreover, the Committee concluded that the additional requirement of Section 1732 that it must have been the regular practice of a business to make the record is a necessary further assurance of its trustworthiness. The Committee accordingly amended the Rule to incorporate these limitations.

Report of Senate Committee on the Judiciary

Rule 803(6) as submitted by the Supreme Court permitted a record made in the course of a regularly conducted activity to be admissible in certain circumstances. This rule constituted a broadening of the traditional business records hearsay exception which has been long advocated by scholars and judges active in the law of evidence.

The House felt there were insufficient guarantees of reliability of records not within a broadly defined business records exception. We disagree. Even under the House definition of "business" including profession, occupation, and "calling of every kind," the records of many regularly conducted activities will, or may be, excluded from evidence. Under the principle of ejusdem generis, the intent of "calling of every kind" would seem to be related to work-related endeavors—e.g., butcher, baker, artist, etc.

Thus, it appears that the records of many institutions or groups might not be admissible under the House amendments. For example, schools, churches, and hospitals will not normally be considered businesses within the definition. Yet, these are groups which keep financial and other records on a regular basis in a manner similar to business enterprises. We believe these records are of equivalent trustworthiness and should be admitted into evidence.

Three states, which have recently codified their evidence rules, have adopted the Supreme Court version of rule 803(6), providing for admission of memoranda of a "regularly conducted activity." None adopted the words "business activity" used in the House amendment.[3]

Therefore, the committee deleted the word "business" as it appears before the word "activity". The last sentence then is unnecessary and was also deleted.

It is the understanding of the committee that the use of the phrase "person with knowledge" is not intended to imply that the party seeking to introduce the memorandum, report, record, or data compilation must be able to produce, or even identify, the specific individual upon whose first-hand knowledge the memorandum, report, record or data compilation was based. A sufficient foundation for the introduction of such evidence will be laid if the party seeking to introduce the evidence is able to show that it was the regular practice of the activity to base such memorandums, reports, records, or data compilations upon a transmission from a person with knowledge, e.g., in the case of a content of a shipment of goods, upon a report from the company's receiving agent or in the case of a computer printout, upon a report from the company's computer programmer or one who has knowledge of the particular record system. In short, the scope of the phrase "person with knowledge" is meant to be coterminous with the custodian of the evidence or other qualified witness. The committee believes this represents the desired rule in light of the complex nature of modern business organizations.

Conference Report

The House bill provides in subsection (6) that records of a regularly conducted "business" activity qualify for admission into evidence as an exception to the hearsay rule. "Business" is defined as including "business, profession, occupation and calling of every kind." The Senate amendment drops the requirement that the records be those of a "business" activity and eliminates the definition of "business." The Senate amendment provides that records are admissible if they are records of a regularly conducted "activity."

The Conference adopts the House provision that the records must be those of a regularly conducted "business" activity. The Conferees changed the definition of "business" contained in the House provision in order to make it clear that the records of institutions and associations like schools, churches and hospitals are admissible under this provision. The records of public schools and hospitals are also covered by Rule 803(8), which deals with public records and reports.

---

[3] See Nev.Rev.Stats. § 15.135; N.Mex.Stats. (1973 Supp.) § 20–4–803(6); West's Wis.Stats.Anno. (1973 Supp.) § 908.03(6).

Advisory Committee's Note to 2000 Amendment to
Rule 803(6)

The amendment provides that the foundation requirements of Rule 803(6) can be satisfied under certain circumstances without the expense and inconvenience of producing time-consuming foundation witnesses. Under current law, courts have generally required foundation witnesses to testify. *See, e.g., Tongil Co., Ltd v. Hyundai Merchant Marine Corp.*, 968 F.2d 999 (9th Cir. 1992) (reversing a judgment based on business records where a qualified person filed an affidavit but did not testify). Protections are provided by the authentication requirements of Rule 902(11) for domestic records, Rule 902(12) for foreign records in civil cases, and 18 U.S.C. § 3505 for foreign records in criminal cases.

Advisory Committee's Note

Exception (7). Failure of a record to mention a matter which would ordinarily be mentioned is satisfactory evidence of its nonexistence. Uniform Rule 63(14), Comment. While probably not hearsay as defined in Rule 801, supra, decisions may be found which class the evidence not only as hearsay but also as not within any exception. In order to set the question at rest in favor of admissibility, it is specifically treated here. McCormick § 289, p. 609; Morgan, Basic Problems of Evidence 314 (1962); 5 Wigmore § 1531; Uniform Rule 63(14); California Evidence Code § 1272; Kansas Code of Civil Procedure § 60–460(n); New Jersey Evidence Rule 63(14).

Report of House Committee on the Judiciary

Rule 803(7) as submitted by the Court concerned the *absence* of entry in the records of a "regularly conducted activity." The Committee amended this Rule to conform with its action with respect to Rule 803(6).

Advisory Committee's Note

Exception (8). Public records are a recognized hearsay exception at common law and have been the subject of statutes without number. McCormick § 291. See, for example, 28 U.S.C. § 1733, the relative narrowness of which is illustrated by its nonapplicability to nonfederal public agencies, thus necessitating resort to the less appropriate business record exception to the hearsay rule. Kay v. United States, 255 F.2d 476 (4th Cir.1958). The rule makes no distinction between federal and nonfederal offices and agencies.

Justification for the exception is the assumption that a public official will perform his duty properly and the unlikelihood that he will remember details independently of the record. Wong Wing Foo v. McGrath, 196 F.2d 120 (9th Cir.1952), and see Chesapeake & Delaware Canal Co. v. United States, 250 U.S. 123, 39 S.Ct. 407, 63 L.Ed. 889 (1919). As to items (A) and (B), further support is found in the reliability factors underlying records of regularly conducted activities generally. See Exception (6), supra.

(A) Cases illustrating the admissibility of records of the office's or agency's own activities are numerous. Chesapeake & Delaware Canal Co. v. United States, 250 U.S. 123, 39 S.Ct. 407, 63 L.Ed. 889 (1919), Treasury records of miscellaneous receipts and disbursements; Howard v. Perrin, 200 U.S. 71, 26 S.Ct. 195, 50 L.Ed. 374 (1906), General Land Office records; Ballew v. United States, 160 U.S. 187, 16 S.Ct. 263, 40 L.Ed. 388 (1895), Pension Office records.

(B) Cases sustaining admissibility of records of matters observed are also numerous. United States v. Van Hook, 284 F.2d 489 (7th Cir.1960), remanded for resentencing 365 U.S. 609, 81 S.Ct. 823, 5 L.Ed.2d 821, letter from induction officer to District Attorney, pursuant to army regulations, stating fact and circumstances of refusal to be inducted; T'Kach v. United States, 242 F.2d 937 (5th Cir.1957), affidavit of White House personnel officer that search of records showed no employment of accused, charged with fraudulently representing himself as an envoy of the President; Minnehaha County v. Kelley, 150 F.2d 356 (8th Cir.1945); Weather Bureau records of rainfall; United States v. Meyer, 113 F.2d 387 (7th Cir.1940), cert. denied 311 U.S. 706, 61 S.Ct. 174, 85 L.Ed. 459, map prepared by government engineer from information furnished by men working under his supervision.

(C) The more controversial area of public records is that of the so-called "evaluative" report. The disagreement among the decisions has been due in part, no doubt, to the variety of situations encountered, as well as to differences in principle. Sustaining admissibility are such cases as United States v. Dumas, 149 U.S. 278, 13 S.Ct. 872, 37 L.Ed. 734 (1893), statement of account certified by Postmaster General in action against postmaster; McCarty v. United States, 185 F.2d 520 (5th Cir.1950), reh. denied 187 F.2d 234, Certificate of Settlement of General Accounting Office showing indebtedness and letter from Army official stating Government had performed, in action on contract to purchase and remove waste food from Army camp; Moran v. Pittsburgh-Des Moines Steel Co., 183 F.2d 467 (3d Cir.1950), report of Bureau of Mines as to cause of gas tank explosion; Petition of W——, 164 F.Supp. 659 (E.D.Pa.1958), report by Immigration and Naturalization Service investigator that petitioner was known in community as wife of man to whom she was not married. To the opposite effect and denying admissibility are Franklin v. Skelly Oil Co., 141 F.2d 568 (10th Cir.1944), State Fire Marshal's report of cause of gas explosion; Lomax Transp. Co. v. United States, 183 F.2d 331 (9th Cir.1950), Certificate of Settlement from General Accounting Office in action for naval supplies lost in warehouse fire; Yung Jin Teung v. Dulles, 229 F.2d 244 (2d Cir.1956), "Status Reports" offered to justify delay in processing passport applications. * * * Various kinds of evaluative reports are admissible under federal statutes: 7 U.S.C. § 78, findings of Secretary of Agriculture prima facie evidence of true grade of grain; 7 U.S.C. § 210(f), findings of Secretary of Agriculture prima facie evidence in action for damages against stockyard owner; 7 U.S.C. § 292, order by Secretary of Agriculture prima facie evidence in judicial enforcement proceedings against producers association monopoly; 7 U.S.C. § 1622(h), Department of Agriculture inspection certificates of products shipped in interstate commerce prima facie evidence; 8 U.S.C. § 1440(c), separation of alien from military service on conditions other than honorable provable by certificate from department in proceedings to revoke citizenship; 18 U.S.C. § 4245, certificate of Director of Prisons that convicted person has been examined and found probably incompetent at time of trial prima facie evidence in court hearing on competency; 42 U.S.C. § 269(b), bill of health by appropriate official prima facie evidence of vessel's sanitary history and condition and compliance with regulations; 46 U.S.C. § 679, certificate of consul presumptive evidence of refusal of master to transport destitute seamen to United States. While these statutory exceptions to the hearsay rule are left undisturbed, Rule 802, the willingness of Congress to recognize a substantial measure of admissibility for evaluative reports is a helpful guide.

Factors which may be of assistance in passing upon the admissibility of evaluative reports include: (1) the timeliness of the investigation, McCormick, Can the Courts Make Wider Use of Reports of Official Investigations? 42 Iowa L.Rev. 363 (1957); (2) the special skill or experience of the official, id., (3) whether a hearing was held and the level at which conducted, Franklin v. Skelly Oil Co., 141 F.2d 568 (10th Cir.1944); (4) possible motivation problems suggested by Palmer v. Hoffman, 318 U.S. 109, 63 S.Ct. 477, 87 L.Ed. 645 (1943). Others no doubt could be added.

The formulation of an approach which would give appropriate weight to all possible factors in every situation is an obvious impossibility. Hence the rule, as in Exception (6), assumes admissibility in the first instance but with ample provision for escape if sufficient negative factors are present. In one respect, however, the rule with respect to evaluative reports under item (C) is very specific: they are admissible only in civil cases and against the government in criminal cases in view of the almost certain collision with confrontation rights which would result from their use against the accused in a criminal case.

Report of House Committee on the Judiciary

The Committee approved Rule 803(8) without substantive change from the form in which it was submitted by the Court. The Committee intends that the phrase "factual findings" be strictly construed and that evaluations or opinions contained in public reports shall not be admissible under this Rule.

CONGRESSIONAL RECORD—HOUSE

Feb. 6, 1974, pp. H563–565

Amendment offered by Ms. Holtzman

Ms. HOLTZMAN. Mr. Chairman, I offer an amendment.

The Clerk read as follows:

Amendment offered by Ms. Holtzman: On page 94, line 11, after the word "law" and before the comma, insert the following: "as to which matters there was a duty to report".

Ms. HOLTZMAN. Mr. Chairman, I will try to be very brief, because it is late in the day.

My amendment is offered to clarify and narrow a provision on the hearsay rule (Rule 803(8)(B)). This rule now provides that if any Government employee in the course of his duty observes something—in fact, anything—and makes a report of that observation, that report can be entered into evidence at a trial whether criminal or civil, without the opportunity to cross-examine the author of the report.

While I respect Government employees, I think we would all concede that they are fallible, exactly like every other human. We do not provide such broad exceptions to the hearsay rule for ordinary mortals.

My amendment makes it crystal clear that random observations by a Government employee cannot be introduced as an exception to the hearsay rule and be insulated from cross-examination. My amendment would allow reports of "matters observed" by a public official only if he had a duty to report about such matters. One operating under such a duty is far more likely to observe and report accurately.

I urge adoption of this amendment in order to narrow and restrict the broad exception to the hearsay rule in the bill.

Mr. HUNGATE. Mr. Chairman, I rise in opposition to the amendment.

This is a matter that was considered in the subcommittee, and we decided to stay with the language as presented to the House here, which states as follows:

Records, reports, statements, or data compilations, in any form, of public offices or agencies, setting forth (A) the activities of the office or agency, or (B) matters observed pursuant to duty imposed by law. * * *

Mr. Chairman, this is where the point of disagreement occurred. We stayed with that version of the bill, and I would recommend that version to the Committee of the Whole House.

Mr. DANIELSON. Mr. Chairman, I rise in support of the amendment offered by the gentlewoman from New York (Ms. Holtzman).

I think if we leave this language in the proposed bill, we are opening the door to a host of problems, the like of which we have probably never seen in a trial court.

I think the proper approach, in order to eliminate this, is simply to adopt the gentlewoman's amendment, and eliminate this provision, simply because there is absolutely no restriction on the sort of material which could come in under the language as proposed.

I urge the adoption of the gentlewoman's amendment.

Mr. DENNIS. Mr. Chairman, I rise in support of the gentlewoman's amendment.

So that the committee will know what we are talking about here, this permits the introduction in evidence as an exception to the hearsay rule of public records and reports, statements, or data compilations in any form of matters observed pursuant to duty imposed by law. The gentlewoman would add "as to which matters there was a duty to report."

Again it is a matter of judgment, but the difference would be this: Supposing you had a divorce case and you tried to put in a report of a social worker, rather than putting the social worker on the stand; under the committee's language anything she said in the report which would be observed by her pursuant to her general duties would be admissible. Under the amendment, only those things as to which she had some duty to make a report would be admissible.

If the law required her to observe and report certain things about a condition in the home, that could come in, but if she put in a lot of other stuff there, she could not put that in without calling her as a witness and giving the opposition a chance to cross examine her.

On the whole I think the amendment improves the bill, and I support it.

The CHAIRMAN. The question is on the amendment offered by the gentlewoman from New York (Ms. Holtzman).

The amendment was agreed to.

Amendment offered by Mr. Dennis

Mr. DENNIS. Mr. Chairman, I offer an amendment.

The Clerk read as follows:

Amendment offered by Mr. Dennis: On page 94, line 11 of the bill, after the word "law", insert the words "excluding, however, in criminal cases matters observed by police officers and other law enforcement personnel".

Mr. DENNIS. Mr. Chairman, this goes to the same subject matter as the last amendment. It deals with official statements and reports.

What I am saying here is that in a criminal case, only, we should not be able to put in the police report to prove your case without calling the policeman. I think in a criminal case you ought to have to call the policeman on the beat and give the defendant the chance to cross examine him, rather than just reading the report into evidence. That is the purpose of this amendment.

Ms. HOLTZMAN. Mr. Chairman, I rise in support of the amendment.

I will be very brief again.

I commend my colleague for raising this point. Again his purpose is to restrict the possible abuse of hearsay evidence.

I think the gentleman's amendment is very valuable and reaffirms the right of cross examination to the accused. It also permits those engaged in civil trials the right of cross examination. Cross-examination guarantees of due process of law and a fair trial.

(Ms. HOLTZMAN asked and was given permission to revise and extend her remarks.)

Mr. SMITH of New York. Mr. Chairman, I rise in opposition to the amendment.

Mr. Chairman, in reading this amendment it seems to me that the effect of the gentleman's amendment is to treat police officers and other law enforcement officers as second-class citizens, because we have already agreed that we are going to allow in as exceptions to the hearsay rule matters observed pursuant to duty imposed by law. The gentleman from Indiana would exclude from that as follows: "Excluding however, in criminal cases, matters observed by police officers and other law enforcement personnel." This would be so even though they were matters observed pursuant to a duty imposed by law.

I just think we are treading in an area the impact of which will be very unfortunate and the effect of which is to make police officers and law enforcement officers second-class citizens and persons less trustworthy than social workers or garbage collectors.

Mr. DENNIS. Mr. Chairman, will the gentleman yield?

Mr. SMITH of New York. I will be glad to yield to the gentleman from Indiana.

Mr. DENNIS. Mr. Chairman, I would like to say on that point that of course that is not my idea. I think the point is that we are dealing here with criminal cases, and in a criminal case the defendant should be confronted with the accuser to give him the chance to cross examine. This is not any reflection on the police officer, but in a criminal case that is the type of report with which, in fact, one is going to be concerned.

Mr. JOHNSON of Colorado. Mr. Chairman, will the gentleman yield?

Mr. SMITH of New York. I yield to the gentleman from Colorado.

Mr. JOHNSON of Colorado. Mr. Chairman, as an ex-prosecutor I cannot imagine that the gentleman would be advocating that a policeman's report could come in to help convict a man, and not have the policeman himself subject to cross-examination.

Is that what the gentleman is advocating?

Mr. SMITH of New York. That is what I am advocating in that the policeman's report, if he is not available, should be admissible when it is made pursuant to a duty imposed on that law enforcement officer by law. This is the amendment we have just adopted, and for other public officers these police reports ought to be admissible, whatever their probative value might be.

Mr. JOHNSON of Colorado. Mr. Chairman, if the gentleman will yield further, as I said, I was a prosecutor in a State court, and there were so many cases where good cross-examination indicated a lack of investigative ability on the part of the man who made the report that I became more and more convinced that good cross-examination was one of the principal elements in any criminal trial. If the officer who made the investigation is not available for cross-examination, then you cannot have a fair trial.

I cannot believe the gentleman would be saying that we should be able to convict people where the police officer's statement is not subject to cross-examination.

Mr. SMITH of New York. All I am saying to the gentleman from Colorado is that—and I will concede that the gentleman has probably had greater experience in this field than I have had—all I am saying is that it seems to me that it should be allowed for the jury to consider such a report, together with all of the other aspects of the case, if this report was made by a police officer pursuant to a duty imposed upon that police officer by law.

I will have to admit to the gentleman from Colorado that it is not the best evidence.

Mr. JOHNSON of Colorado. If the gentleman will yield still further, I will have to say that in my opinion the Supreme Court would have to ultimately declare that kind of a rule unconstitutional if we did pass it, and that the present amendment is one that would have to be passed if we are going to preserve the rights and traditions of individuals that have been in existence since 1066—I think that is when it started.

Mr. BRASCO. Mr. Chairman, I move to strike the requisite number of words.

(Mr. BRASCO asked and was given permission to revise and extend his remarks.)

Mr. BRASCO. Mr. Chairman, I would like to ask the author of the amendment, the gentleman from Indiana (Mr. Dennis) a question. I am deeply disturbed and troubled about these rules that have been brought out today.

It seems to me that many critical areas have been overlooked.

One of the basic tenets of our law is that one should be confronted by one's accuser and be able to cross-examine the accuser.

There are many, many exceptions to the hearsay rule here.

As I understand it the gentleman from New York (Mr. Smith) is advocating, in opposition to the amendment offered by the gentleman from Indiana (Mr. Dennis) that if a police officer made a report that he saw Mr. X with a gun on such and such an occasion, and then thereafter that police officer is unavailable that that statement could be used in a criminal trial against Mr. X without the defense attorney having the opportunity to cross examine the officer with respect to his position with relation to Mr. X, the time of the day, whether he was under a light, or whether there was no light, how much time did he have in which to see the gun, and all other observations relevant to the case.

Mr. DENNIS. Mr. Chairman, I would say in answer to the question raised by the gentleman from New York (Mr. Brasco) that if the statements of the police officer in his report would, in the language of this bill, be "matters observed pursuant to a duty imposed by law, and as to which he was under a duty to make a report," and I rather think they might be, that then what the gentleman says is true, and would be true.

I am trying to remove that possibility, by saying that the rule will not apply in the case the gentleman is talking about.

Mr. BRASCO. I support the gentleman. I am just standing up talking, because I cannot believe that we would for one moment entertain any other rule. I would hope we would do it with all cases of hearsay.

Mr. HUNT. Mr. Chairman, will the gentleman yield?

Mr. BRASCO. I will be glad to yield to the gentleman from New Jersey if the gentleman wishes me to yield to him.

Mr. HUNT. I had no intention of getting into this argument, but when the gentleman brings in the word "investigator," then I have to get in.

Mr. BRASCO. I did not say it.

Mr. HUNT. I know the gentleman from New York did not, but it was discussed. The only time I can recall in my 34 years of law enforcement that a report of an investigator was admissible in court was to test the credibility of an officer. We would never permit a report to come in unchallenged. We would never even think about bringing in a report in lieu of the officer being there to have that officer cross-examined; but reports were admitted as evidentiary fact for the purpose of testing the officer's credibility and perhaps to refresh his memory. That has always been the rule of law in the State of New Jersey, and I hope it will always remain that way—and even the Federal canons.

Mr. BRASCO. I do not think that the gentleman's amendment interferes with that at all. I think what he is talking about is that the prosecution could use this to prove its case in chief with the possibility of no other evidence being presented.

Mr. HUNT. He is talking about bringing the report in in lieu of an officer, and that certainly is not the case.

Mr. DENNIS. Mr. Chairman, will the gentleman yield?

Mr. BRASCO. I yield to the gentleman from Indiana.

Mr. DENNIS. I thank the gentleman for yielding. I certainly agree this amendment has nothing to do with what my friend, the gentleman from New Jersey, is talking about. This applies only to a hearsay exception, where it would be attempted to bring this report in instead of the officer to prove one's case in chief, which one could do if we do not pass this amendment; but we could still use the report to contradict him and cross-examine him.

Mr. HUNT. Certainly, but the gentleman is speaking of the best evidence available then in lieu of the direct evidence.

Mr. DENNIS. I say we should bring in the man who saw it and put him on the stand.

Mr. HUNT. Certainly, the gentleman is right.

The CHAIRMAN. The question is on the amendment offered by the gentleman from Indiana (Mr. Dennis).

The amendment was agreed to.

Report of Senate Committee on the Judiciary

The House approved rule 803(8), as submitted by the Supreme Court, with one substantive change. It excluded from the hearsay exception reports containing matters observed by police officers and other law enforcement personnel in criminal cases. Ostensibly, the reason for this exclusion is that observations by police officers at the scene of the crime or the apprehension of the defendant are not as reliable as observations by public officials in other cases because of the adversarial nature of the confrontation between the police and the defendant in criminal cases.

The committee accepts the House's decision to exclude such recorded observations where the police officer is available to testify in court about his observation. However, where he is unavailable as unavailability is defined in rule 804(a)(4) and (a)(5), the report should be admitted as the best available evidence. Accordingly, the committee has amended rule 803(8) to refer to the provision of rule 804(b)(5), which allows the admission of such reports, records or other statements where the police officer or other law enforcement officer is unavailable because of death, then existing physical or mental illness or infirmity, or not being successfully subject to legal process. [This version of rule 804(b)(5) was not included in the rules as enacted.]

The House Judiciary Committee report contained a statement of intent that "the phrase 'factual findings' in subdivision (c) be strictly construed and that evaluations or opinions contained in public reports shall not be admissible under this rule." The committee takes strong exception to this limiting understanding of the application of the rule. We do not think it reflects an understanding of the intended operation of the rule as explained in the Advisory Committee notes to this subsection. The Advisory Committee notes on subsection (c) of this subdivision point out that various kinds of evaluative reports are now admissible under Federal statutes. 7 U.S.C. § 78, findings of Secretary of Agriculture prima facie evidence of true grade of grain; 42 U.S.C. § 269(b), bill of health by appropriate official prima facie evidence of vessel's sanitary history and condition and compliance with regulations. These statutory exceptions to the hearsay rule are preserved. Rule 802. The willingness of Congress to recognize these and other such evaluative reports provides a helpful guide in determining the kind of reports which are intended to be admissible under this rule. We think the restrictive interpretation of the House overlooks the fact that while the Advisory Committee assumes admissibility in the first instance of evaluative reports, they are not admissible if, as the rule states, "the sources of information or other circumstances indicate lack of trustworthiness."

The Advisory Committee explains the factors to be considered:

* * *

Factors which may be of assistance in passing upon the admissibility of evaluative reports include: (1) the timeliness of the investigation, McCormick, Can the Courts Make Wider Use of Reports of Official Investigations? 42 Iowa L.Rev. 363 (1957); (2) the special skill or experience of the official, id.; (3) whether a hearing was held and the level at which conducted, Franklin v. Skelly Oil Co., 141 F.2d 568 (10th Cir.1944): (4) possible motivation problems suggested by Palmer v.

Hoffman, 318 U.S. 109, 63 S.Ct. 477, 87 L.Ed. 645 (1943). Others no doubt could be added.[4]

* * *

The committee concludes that the language of the rule together with the explanation provided by the Advisory Committee furnish sufficient guidance on the admissibility of evaluative reports.

Conference Report

The Senate amendment adds language, not contained in the House bill, that refers to another rule that was added by the Senate in another amendment (Rule 804(b)(5)—Criminal law enforcement records and reports).

In view of its action on Rule 804(b)(5) (Criminal law enforcement records and reports), the Conference does not adopt the Senate amendment and restores the bill to the House version.

Advisory Committee's Note

Exception (9). Records of vital statistics are commonly the subject of particular statutes making them admissible in evidence, Uniform Vital Statistics Act, 9C U.L.A. 350 (1957). The rule is in principle narrower than Uniform Rule 63(16) which includes reports required of persons performing functions authorized by statute, yet in practical effect the two are substantially the same. Comment Uniform Rule 63(16). The exception as drafted is in the pattern of California Evidence Code § 1281.

Exception (10). The principle of proving nonoccurrence of an event by evidence of the absence of a record which would regularly be made of its occurrence, developed in Exception (7) with respect to regularly conducted [business] activities, is here extended to public records of the kind mentioned in Exceptions (8) and (9). 5 Wigmore § 1633(6), p. 519. Some harmless duplication no doubt exists with Exception (7). For instances of federal statutes recognizing this method of proof, see 8 U.S.C. § 1284(b), proof of absence of alien crewman's name from outgoing manifest prima facie evidence of failure to detain or deport, and 42 U.S.C. § 405(c)(3), (4)(B), (4)(C), absence of HEW record prima facie evidence of no wages or self-employment income.

The rule includes situations in which absence of a record may itself be the ultimate focal point of inquiry, e.g. People v. Love, 310 Ill. 558, 142 N.E. 204 (1923), certificate of Secretary of State admitted to show failure to file documents required by Securities Law, as well as cases where the absence of a record is offered as proof of the nonoccurrence of an event ordinarily recorded.

---

[4] Advisory Committee's notes, to rule 803(8)(c).

The refusal of the common law to allow proof by certificate of the lack of a record or entry, has no apparent justification, 5 Wigmore § 1678(7), p. 752. The rule takes the opposite position, as do Uniform Rule 63(17); California Evidence Code § 1284; Kansas Code of Civil Procedure § 60–460(c); New Jersey Evidence Rule 63(17). Congress has recognized certification as evidence of the lack of a record. 8 U.S.C. § 1360(d), certificate of Attorney General or other designated officer that no record of Immigration and Naturalization Service of specified nature or entry therein is found, admissible in alien cases.

Exception (11). Records of activities of religious organizations are currently recognized as admissible at least to the extent of the business records exception to the hearsay rule, 5 Wigmore § 1523, p. 371, and Exception (6) would be applicable. However, both the business record doctrine and Exception (6) require that the person furnishing the information be one in the business or activity. The result is such decisions as Daily v. Grand Lodge, 311 Ill. 184, 142 N.E. 478 (1924), holding a church record admissible to prove fact, date, and place of baptism, but not age of child except that he had at least been born at the time. In view of the unlikelihood that false information would be furnished on occasions of this kind, the rule contains no requirement that the informant be in the course of the activity. See California Evidence Code § 1315 and Comment.

Exception (12). The principle of proof by certification is recognized as to public officials in Exceptions (8) and (10), and with respect to authentication in Rule 902. The present exception is a duplication to the extent that it deals with a certificate by a public official, as in the case of a judge who performs a marriage ceremony. The area covered by the rule is, however, substantially larger and extends the certification procedure to clergymen and the like who perform marriages and other ceremonies or administer sacraments. Thus certificates of such matters as baptism or confirmation, as well as marriage, are included. In principle they are as acceptable evidence as certificates of public officers. See 5 Wigmore § 1645, as to marriage certificates. When the person executing the certificate is not a public official, the self-authenticating character of documents purporting to emanate from public officials, see Rule 902, is lacking and proof is required that the person was authorized and did make the certificate. The time element, however, may safely be taken as supplied by the certificate, once authority and authenticity are established, particularly in view of the presumption that a document was executed on the date it bears.

For similar rules, some limited to certificates of marriage, with variations in foundation requirements, see Uniform Rule 63(18); California Evidence Code § 1316; Kansas Code of Civil Procedure § 60–460(p); New Jersey Evidence Rule 63(18).

Exception (13). Records of family history kept in family Bibles have by long tradition been received in evidence. 5 Wigmore §§ 1495, 1496, citing numerous statutes and decisions. See also Regulations, Social Security Administration, 20 C.F.R. § 404.703(c), recognizing family Bible entries as proof of age in the absence of public or church records. Opinions in the area also include inscriptions on tombstones, publicly displayed pedigrees, and engravings on rings. Wigmore, supra. The rule is substantially identical in coverage with California Evidence Code § 1312.

Report of House Committee on the Judiciary

The Committee approved this Rule in the form submitted by the Court, intending that the phrase "Statements of fact concerning personal or family history" be read to include the specific types of such statements enumerated in Rule 803(11).

Advisory Committee's Note

Exception (14). The recording of title documents is a purely statutory development. Under any theory of the admissibility of public records, the records would be receivable as evidence of the contents of the recorded document, else the recording process would be reduced to a nullity. When, however, the record is offered for the further purpose of proving execution and delivery, a problem of lack of firsthand knowledge by the recorder, not present as to contents, is presented. This problem is solved, seemingly in all jurisdictions, by qualifying for recording only those documents shown by a specified procedure, either acknowledgement or a form of probate, to have been executed and delivered. 5 Wigmore §§ 1647–1651. Thus what may appear in the rule, at first glance, as endowing the record with an effect independently of local law and inviting difficulties of an *Erie* nature under Cities Service Oil Co. v. Dunlap, 308 U.S. 208, 60 S.Ct. 201, 84 L.Ed. 196 (1939), is not present, since the local law in fact governs under the example.

Exception (15). Dispositive documents often contain recitals of fact. Thus a deed purporting to have been executed by an attorney in fact may recite the existence of the power of attorney, or a deed may recite that the grantors are all the heirs of the last record owner. Under the rule, these recitals are exempted from the hearsay rule. The circumstances under which dispositive documents are executed and the requirement that the recital be germane to the purpose of the document are believed to be adequate guarantees of trustworthiness, particularly in view of the nonapplicability of the rule if dealings with the property have been inconsistent with the document. The age of the document is of no significance, though in practical application the document will most often be an ancient one. See Uniform Rule 63(29), Comment.

Similar provisions are contained in Uniform Rule 63(29); California Evidence Code § 1330; Kansas Code of Civil Procedure § 60–460(aa); New Jersey Evidence Rule 63(29).

Exception (16). Authenticating a document as ancient, essentially in the pattern of the common law, as provided in Rule 901(b)(8), leaves open as a separate question the admissibility of assertive statements contained therein as against a hearsay objection. 7 Wigmore § 2145a. Wigmore further states that the ancient document technique of authentication is universally conceded to apply to all sorts of documents, including letters, records, contracts, maps, and certificates, in addition to title documents, citing numerous decisions. Id. § 2145. Since most of these items are significant evidentially only insofar as they are assertive, their admission in evidence must be as a hearsay exception. But see 5 id. § 1573, p. 429, referring to recitals in ancient deeds as a "limited" hearsay exception. The former position is believed to be the correct one in reason and authority. As pointed out in McCormick § 298, danger of mistake is minimized by authentication requirements, and age affords assurance that the writing antedates the present controversy. See Dallas County v. Commercial Union Assurance Co., 286 F.2d 388 (5th Cir.1961), upholding admissibility of 58-year-old newspaper story. Cf. Morgan, Basic Problems of Evidence 364 (1962), but see id. 254.

For a similar provision, but with the added requirement that "the statement has since generally been acted upon as true by persons having an interest in the matter," see California Evidence Code § 1331.

Exception (17). Ample authority at common law supported the admission in evidence of items falling in this category. While Wigmore's text is narrowly oriented to lists, etc., prepared for the use of a trade or profession, 6 Wigmore § 1702, authorities are cited which include other kinds of publications, for example, newspaper market reports, telephone directories, and city directories. Id. §§ 1702–1706. The basis of trustworthiness is general reliance by the public or by a particular segment of it, and the motivation of the compiler to foster reliance by being accurate.

For similar provisions, see Uniform Rule 63(30); California Evidence Code § 1340; Kansas Code of Civil Procedure § 60–460(bb); New Jersey Evidence Rule 63(30). Uniform Commercial Code § 2–724 provides for admissibility in evidence of "reports in official publications or trade journals or in newspapers or periodicals of general circulation published as the reports of such [established commodity] market."

Exception (18). The writers have generally favored the admissibility of learned treatises, McCormick § 296, p. 621; Morgan, Basic Problems of Evidence 366 (1962); 6 Wigmore § 1692, with the support of occasional decisions and rules, City of Dothan v. Hardy, 237 Ala. 603, 188 So. 264 (1939); Lewandowski v. Preferred Risk Mut. Ins. Co., 33 Wis.2d 69, 146 N.W.2d 505 (1966), 66 Mich.L.Rev. 183 (1967); Uniform Rule 63(31); Kansas Code of Civil Procedure § 60–460(cc), but the great weight of authority has been that learned treatises are not admissible as substantive evidence though usable in the cross-examination of experts. The foundation of the minority view is that the hearsay objection must be regarded as unimpressive when directed against treatises since a high standard of accuracy is engendered by various factors: the treatise is written primarily and impartially for professionals, subject to scrutiny and exposure for inaccuracy, with the reputation of the writer at stake. 6 Wigmore § 1692. Sound as this position may be with respect to trustworthiness, there is, nevertheless, an additional difficulty in the likelihood that the treatise will be misunderstood and misapplied without expert assistance and supervision. This difficulty is recognized in the cases demonstrating unwillingness to sustain findings relative to disability on the basis of judicially noticed medical texts. Ross v. Gardner, 365 F.2d 554 (6th Cir.1966); Sayers v. Gardner, 380 F.2d 940 (6th Cir.1967); Colwell v. Gardner, 386 F.2d 56 (6th Cir.1967); Glendenning v. Ribicoff, 213 F.Supp. 301 (W.D.Mo.1962); Cook v. Celebrezze, 217 F.Supp. 366 (W.D.Mo.1963); Sosna v. Celebrezze, 234 F.Supp. 289 (E.D.Pa.1964); and see McDaniel v. Celebrezze, 331 F.2d 426 (4th Cir.1964). The rule avoids the danger of misunderstanding and misapplication by limiting the use of treatises as substantive evidence to situations in which an expert is on the stand and available to explain and assist in the application of the treatise if desired. The limitation upon receiving the publication itself physically in evidence, contained in the last sentence, is designed to further this policy.

The relevance of the use of treatises on cross-examination is evident. This use of treatises has been the subject of varied views. The most restrictive position is that the witness must have stated expressly on direct his reliance upon the treatise. A slightly more liberal approach still insists upon reliance but allows it to be developed on cross-examination. Further relaxation dispenses with reliance but requires recognition as an authority by the witness, developable on cross-examination. The greatest liberality is found in decisions allowing use of the treatise on cross-examination when its status as an authority is established by any means. Annot., 60 A.L.R.2d 77. The exception is hinged upon this last position, which is that of the Supreme Court, Reilly v. Pinkus, 338 U.S. 269, 70 S.Ct. 110, 94 L.Ed. 63 (1949), and of recent well considered state court decisions, City of St. Petersburg v. Ferguson, 193 So.2d 648 (Fla.App.1966), cert. denied Fla., 201 So.2d 556; Darling v. Charleston Memorial Community Hospital, 33 Ill.2d 326, 211 N.E.2d 253 (1965); Dabroe v. Rhodes Co., 64 Wash.2d 431, 392 P.2d 317 (1964).

In Reilly v. Pinkus, supra, the Court pointed out that testing of professional knowledge was incomplete without exploration of the witness' knowledge of and attitude toward established treatises in the field. The process works equally well in reverse and furnishes the basis of the rule.

The rule does not require that the witness rely upon or recognize the treatise as authoritative, thus avoiding the possibility that the expert may at the outset block cross-examination by refusing to concede reliance or authoritativeness. Dabroe v. Rhodes Co., supra. Moreover, the rule avoids the unreality of admitting evidence for the purpose of impeachment only, with an instruction to the jury not to consider it otherwise. The parallel to the treatment of prior inconsistent statements will be apparent. See Rules 613(b) and 801(d)(1).

Exceptions (19), (20), and (21). Trustworthiness in reputation evidence is found "when the topic is such that the facts are likely to have been inquired about and that persons having personal knowledge have disclosed facts which have thus been discussed in the community; and thus the community's conclusion, if any has been formed, is likely to be a trustworthy one." 5 Wigmore § 1580, p. 444, and see also § 1583. On this common foundation, reputation as to land boundaries, customs, general history, character, and marriage have come to be regarded as admissible. The breadth of the underlying principle suggests the formulation of an equally broad exception, but tradition has in fact been much narrower and more particularized, and this is the pattern of these exceptions in the rule.

Exception (19) is concerned with matters of personal and family history. Marriage is universally conceded to be a proper subject of proof by evidence of reputation in the community. 5 Wigmore § 1602. As to such items as legitimacy, relationship, adoption, birth, and death, the decisions are divided. Id. § 1605. All seem to be susceptible to being the subject of well founded repute. The "world" in which the reputation may exist may be family, associates, or community. This world has proved capable of expanding with changing times from the single uncomplicated neighborhood, in which all activities take place, to the multiple and unrelated worlds of work, religious affiliation, and social activity, in each of which a reputation may be generated. People v. Reeves, 360 Ill. 55, 195 N.E. 443 (1935); State v. Axilrod, 248 Minn. 204, 79 N.W.2d 677 (1956); Mass.Stat.1947, c. 410, M.G.L.A. c. 233 § 21A; 5 Wigmore § 1616. The family has often served as the point of beginning for allowing community reputation. 5 Wigmore § 1488. For comparable provisions see Uniform Rule 63(26), (27)(c); California Evidence Code §§ 1313, 1314; Kansas Code of Civil Procedure § 60–460(x), (y)(3); New Jersey Evidence Rule 63(26), (27)(c).

The first portion of Exception (20) is based upon the general admissibility of evidence of reputation as to land boundaries and land customs, expanded in this country to include private as well as public boundaries. McCormick § 299, p. 625. The reputation is required to antedate the controversy, though not to be ancient. The second portion is likewise supported by authority, id., and is designed to facilitate proof of events when judicial notice is not available. The historical character of the subject matter dispenses with any need that the reputation antedate the controversy with respect to which it is offered. For similar provisions see Uniform Rule 63(27)(a), (b); California Evidence Code §§ 1320–1322; Kansas Code of Civil Procedure § 60–460(y), (1), (2); New Jersey Evidence Rule 63(27)(a), (b).

Exception (21) recognizes the traditional acceptance of reputation evidence as a means of proving human character. McCormick §§ 44, 158. The exception deals only with the hearsay aspect of this kind of evidence. Limitations upon admissibility based on other grounds will be found in Rules 404, relevancy of character evidence generally, and 608, character of witness. The exception is in effect a reiteration, in the context of hearsay, of Rule 405(a). Similar provisions are contained in Uniform Rule 63(28); California Evidence Code § 1324; Kansas Code of Civil Procedure § 60–460(z); New Jersey Evidence Rule 63(28).

Exception (22). When the status of a former judgment is under consideration in subsequent litigation, three possibilities must be noted: (1) the former judgment is conclusive under the doctrine of res judicata, either as a bar or a collateral estoppel; or (2) it is admissible in evidence for what it is worth; or (3) it may be of no effect at all. The first situation does not involve any problem of evidence except in the way that principles of substantive law generally bear upon the relevancy and materiality of evidence. The rule does not deal with the substantive effect of the judgment as a bar or collateral estoppel. When, however, the doctrine of res judicata does not apply to make the judgment either a bar or a collateral estoppel, a choice is presented between the second and third alternatives. The rule adopts the second for judgments of criminal conviction of felony grade. This is the direction of the decisions, Annot., 18 A.L.R.2d 1287, 1299, which manifest an increasing reluctance to reject *in toto* the validity of the law's factfinding processes outside the confines of res judicata and collateral estoppel. While this may leave a jury with the evidence of conviction but without means to evaluate it, as suggested by Judge Hinton, Note 27 Ill.L.Rev. 195 (1932), it seems safe to assume that the jury will give it substantial effect unless defendant offers a satisfactory explanation, a possibility not foreclosed by the provision. But see North River Ins. Co. v. Militello, 104 Colo. 28, 88 P.2d 567 (1939), in which the jury found for plaintiff on a fire policy despite the introduction of his conviction for arson. For supporting federal decisions see Clark, J., in New York & Cuba Mail S.S. Co. v. Continental Cas. Co., 117 F.2d 404, 411 (2d Cir.1941); Connecticut Fire Ins. Co. v. Ferrara, 277 F.2d 388 (8th Cir.1960).

Practical considerations require exclusion of convictions of minor offenses, not because the administration of justice in its lower echelons must be inferior, but because motivation to defend at this level is often minimal or nonexistent. Cope v. Goble, 39 Cal.App.2d 448, 103 P.2d 598 (1940); Jones v. Talbot, 87 Idaho 498, 394 P.2d 316 (1964); Warren v. Marsh, 215 Minn. 615, 11 N.W.2d 528 (1943); Annot., 18 A.L.R.2d 1287, 1295–1297; 16 Brooklyn L.Rev. 286 (1950); 50 Colum.L.Rev. 529 (1950); 35 Cornell L.Q. 872 (1950). Hence the rule includes only convictions of felony grade, measured by federal standards.

Judgments of conviction based upon pleas of *nolo contendere* are not included. This position is consistent with the treatment of *nolo* pleas in Rule 410 and the authorities cited in the Advisory Committee's Note in support thereof.

While these rules do not in general purport to resolve constitutional issues, they have in general been drafted with a view to avoiding collision with constitutional principles. Consequently the exception does not include evidence of the conviction of a third person, offered against the accused in a criminal prosecution to prove any fact essential to sustain the judgment of conviction. A contrary position would seem clearly to violate the right of confrontation. Kirby v. United States, 174 U.S. 47, 19 S.Ct. 574, 43 L.Ed. 890 (1899), error to convict of possessing stolen postage stamps with the only evidence of theft being the record of conviction of the thieves. The situation is to be distinguished from cases in which conviction of another person is an element of the crime, e.g. 15 U.S.C. § 902(d), interstate shipment of firearms to a known convicted felon, and, as specifically provided, from impeachment.

For comparable provisions see Uniform Rule 63(20); California Evidence Code § 1300; Kansas Code of Civil Procedure § 60–460(r); New Jersey Evidence Rule 63(20).

Exception (23). A hearsay exception in this area was originally justified on the ground that verdicts were evidence of reputation. As trial by jury graduated from the category of neighborhood inquests, this theory lost its validity. It was never valid as to chancery decrees. Nevertheless the rule persisted, though the judges and writers shifted ground and began saying that the judgment or decree was as good evidence as reputation. See City of London v. Clerke, Carth. 181, 90 Eng.Rep. 710 (K.B. 1691); Neill v. Duke of Devonshire, 8 App.Cas. 135 (1882). The shift appears to be correct, since the process of inquiry, sifting, and scrutiny which is relied upon to render reputation reliable is present in perhaps greater measure in the process of litigation. While this might suggest a broader area of application, the affinity to reputation is strong, and paragraph (23) goes no further, not even including character.

The leading case in the United States, Patterson v. Gaines, 47 U.S. (6 How.) 550, 599, 12 L.Ed. 553 (1847), follows in the pattern of the English decisions, mentioning as illustrative matters thus provable: manorial rights, public rights of way, immemorial custom, disputed boundary, and pedigree. More recent recognition of the principle is found in Grant Bros. Construction Co. v. United States, 232 U.S. 647, 34 S.Ct. 452, 58 L.Ed. 776 (1914), in action for penalties under Alien Contract Labor Law, decision of board of inquiry of Immigration Service admissible to prove alienage of laborers, as a matter of pedigree; United States v. Mid-Continent Petroleum Corp., 67 F.2d 37 (10th Cir.1933), records of commission enrolling Indians admissible on pedigree; Jung Yen Loy v. Cahill, 81 F.2d 809 (9th Cir.1936), board decisions as to citizenship of plaintiff's father admissible in proceeding for declaration of citizenship. Contra, In re Estate of Cunha, 49 Haw. 273, 414 P.2d 925 (1966).

[**Editorial Note:** As originally passed, Rule 803 included a residual exception, Rule 803(24). In 1997, this exception and an identical counterpart, Rule 804(b)(5), were incorporated in a new Rule 807. Materials related to the former rules are therefore presented in conjunction with Rule 807.]

Rule 804

Note by Federal Judicial Center

The rule prescribed by the Supreme Court was amended by the Congress in a number of respects as follows:

Subdivision (a). Paragraphs (1) and (2) were amended by substituting "court" in place of "judge," and paragraph (5) was amended by inserting "(or in the case of a hearsay exception under subdivision (b)(2), (3), or (4), his attendance or testimony)".

Subdivision (b). Exception (1) was amended by inserting "the same or" after "course of," and by substituting the phrase "if the party against whom the testimony is now offered, or, in a civil action or proceeding, a predecessor in interest, had an opportunity and similar motive to develop the testimony by direct, cross, or redirect examination" in place of "at the instance of or against a party with an opportunity to develop the testimony by direct, cross, or redirect examination, with motive and interest similar to those of the party against whom now offered."

Exception (2) as prescribed by the Supreme Court, dealing with statements of recent perception, was deleted by the Congress. It is included in the Appendix hereto as an aid to interpretation. Exception (2) as enacted by the Congress is Exception (3) prescribed by the Supreme Court, amended by inserting at the beginning, "In a prosecution for homicide or in a civil action or proceeding".

Exception (3) as enacted by the Congress is Exception (4) prescribed by the Supreme Court, amended in the first sentence by deleting, after "another," the phrase "or to make him an object of hatred ridicule, or disgrace," and amended in the second sentence by substituting, after "unless," the phrase, "corroborating circumstances clearly indicate the trustworthiness of the statement," in place of "corroborated."

Exception (4) as enacted by the Congress is Exception (5) prescribed by the Supreme Court without change.

Exception (5) as enacted by the Congress is Exception (6) prescribed by the Supreme Court, amended by substituting "equivalent" in place of "comparable" and by adding all after "trustworthiness."

Advisory Committee's Note

As to firsthand knowledge on the part of hearsay declarants, see the introductory portion of the Advisory Committee's Note to Rule 803.

Subdivision (a). The definition of unavailability implements the division of hearsay exceptions into two categories by Rules 803 and 804(b).

At common law the unavailability requirement was evolved in connection with particular hearsay exceptions rather than along general lines. For example, see the separate explications of unavailability in relation to former testimony, declarations against interest, and statements of pedigree, separately developed in McCormick §§ 234, 257, and 297. However, no reason is apparent for making distinctions as to what satisfies unavailability for the different exceptions. The treatment in the rule is therefore uniform although differences in the range of process for witnesses between civil and criminal cases will lead to a less exacting requirement under item (5). See Rule 45(e) of the Federal Rules of Civil Procedure and Rule 17(e) of the Federal Rules of Criminal Procedure.

Five instances of unavailability are specified:

(1) Substantial authority supports the position that exercise of a claim of privilege by the declarant satisfies the requirement of unavailability (usually in connection with former testimony). Wyatt v. State, 35 Ala.App. 147, 46 So.2d 837 (1950); State v. Stewart, 85 Kan. 404, 116 P. 489 (1911); Annot., 45 A.L.R.2d 1354; Uniform Rule 62(7)(a); California Evidence Code § 240(a)(1); Kansas Code of Civil Procedure § 60–459(g)(1). A ruling by the judge is required, which clearly implies that an actual claim of privilege must be made.

(2) A witness is rendered unavailable if he simply refuses to testify concerning the subject matter of his statement despite judicial pressures to do so, a position supported by similar considerations of practicality. Johnson v. People, 152 Colo. 586, 384 P.2d 454 (1963); People v. Pickett, 339 Mich. 294, 63 N.W.2d 681, 45 A.L.R.2d 1341 (1954). Contra, Pleau v. State, 255 Wis. 362, 38 N.W.2d 496 (1949).

(3) The position that a claimed lack of memory by the witness of the subject matter of his statement constitutes unavailability likewise finds support in the cases, though not without dissent. McCormick § 234, p. 494. If the claim is successful, the practical effect is to put the testimony beyond reach, as in the other instances. In this instance, however, it will be noted that the lack of memory must be established by the testimony of the witness himself, which clearly contemplates his production and subjection to cross-examination.

Report of House Committee on the Judiciary

Rule 804(a)(3) was approved in the form submitted by the Court. However, the Committee intends no change in existing federal law under which the court may choose to disbelieve the declarant's testimony as to his lack of memory. See United States v. Insana, 423 F.2d 1165, 1169–1170 (2d Cir.), cert. denied, 400 U.S. 841 (1970).

Advisory Committee's Note

(4) Death and infirmity find general recognition as grounds. McCormick §§ 234, 257, 297; Uniform Rule 62(7)(c); California Evidence Code § 240(a)(3); Kansas Code of Civil Procedure § 60–459(g)(3); New Jersey Evidence Rule 62(6)(c). See also the provisions on use of depositions in Rule 32(a)(3) of the Federal Rules of Civil Procedure and Rule 15(e) of the Federal Rules of Criminal Procedure.

(5) Absence from the hearing coupled with inability to compel attendance by process or other reasonable means also satisfies the requirement. McCormick § 234; Uniform Rule 62(7)(d) and (e); California Evidence Code § 240(a)(4) and (5); Kansas Code of Civil Procedure § 60–459(g)(4) and (5); New Jersey Rule 62(6)(b) and (d). See the discussion of procuring attendance of witnesses who are nonresidents or in custody in Barber v. Page, 390 U.S. 719, 88 S.Ct. 1318, 20 L.Ed.2d 255 (1968).

If the conditions otherwise constituting unavailability result from the procurement or wrongdoing of the proponent of the statement, the requirement is not satisfied. * * *

Report of House Committee on the Judiciary

Rule 804(a)(5) as submitted to the Congress provided, as one type of situation in which a declarant would be deemed "unavailable", that he be "absent from the hearing and the proponent of his statement has been unable to procure his attendance by process or other reasonable means." The Committee amended the Rule to insert after the word "attendance" the parenthetical expression "(or, in the case of a hearsay exception under subdivision (b)(2), (3), or (4), his attendance or testimony)". The amendment is designed primarily to require that an attempt be made to depose a witness (as well as to seek his attendance) as a precondition to the witness being deemed unavailable. The Committee, however, recognized the propriety of an exception to this additional requirement when it is the declarant's former testimony that is sought to be admitted under subdivision (b)(1).

Report of Senate Committee on the Judiciary

Subdivision (a) of rule 804 as submitted by the Supreme Court defined the conditions under which a witness was considered to be unavailable. It was amended in the House.

The purpose of the amendment, according to the report of the House Committee on the Judiciary, is "primarily to require that an attempt be made to depose a witness (as well as to seek his attendance) as a precondition to the witness being unavailable."[1]

Under the House amendment, before a witness is declared unavailable, a party must try to depose a witness (declarant) with respect to dying

---

[1] H.Rept. 93–650, at p. 15.

declarations, declarations against interest, and declarations of pedigree. None of these situations would seem to warrant this needless, impractical and highly restrictive complication. A good case can be made for eliminating the unavailability requirement entirely for declarations against interest cases.[2]

In dying declaration cases, the declarant will usually, though not necessarily, be deceased at the time of trial. Pedigree statements which are admittedly and necessarily based largely on word of mouth are not greatly fortified by a deposition requirement.

Depositions are expensive and time-consuming. In any event, deposition procedures are available to those who wish to resort to them. Moreover, the deposition procedures of the Civil Rules and Criminal Rules are only imperfectly adapted to implementing the amendment. No purpose is served unless the deposition, if taken, may be used in evidence. Under Civil Rule (a)(3) and Criminal Rule 15(e), a deposition, though taken, may not be admissible, and under Criminal Rule 15(a) substantial obstacles exist in the way of even taking a deposition.

For these reasons, the committee deleted the House amendment.

The committee understands that the rule as to unavailability, as explained by the Advisory Committee "contains no requirement that an attempt be made to take the deposition of a declarant." In reflecting the committee's judgment, the statement is accurate insofar as it goes. Where, however, the proponent of the statement, with knowledge of the existence of the statement, fails to confront the declarant with the statement at the taking of the deposition, then the proponent should not, in fairness, be permitted to treat the declarant as "unavailable" simply because the declarant was not amenable to process compelling his attendance at trial. The committee does not consider it necessary to amend the rule to this effect because such a situation abuses, not conforms to, the rule. Fairness would preclude a person from introducing a hearsay statement on a particular issue if the person taking the deposition was aware of the issue at the time of the deposition but failed to depose the unavailable witness on that issue.

Conference Report

Subsection (a) defines the term "unavailability as a witness". The House bill provides in subsection (a)(5) that the party who desires to use the statement must be unable to procure the declarant's attendance by process or other reasonable means. In the case of dying declarations, statements against interest and statements of personal or family history, the House bill requires that the proponent must also be unable to procure the declarant's *testimony* (such as by deposition or interrogatories) by process or other reasonable means. The Senate amendment eliminates this latter provision.

---

[2] Uniform rule 63(10); Kan.Stat.Anno. 60–460(j); 2A N.J.Stats.Anno. 84–63(10).

The Conference adopts the provision contained in the House bill.

Advisory Committee's Note

Subdivision (b). Rule 803, supra, is based upon the assumption that a hearsay statement falling within one of its exceptions possesses qualities which justify the conclusion that whether the declarant is available or unavailable is not a relevant factor in determining admissibility. The instant rule proceeds upon a different theory: hearsay which admittedly is not equal in quality to testimony of the declarant on the stand may nevertheless be admitted if the declarant is unavailable and if his statement meets a specified standard. The rule expresses preferences: testimony given on the stand in person is preferred over hearsay, and hearsay, if of the specified quality, is preferred over complete loss of the evidence of the declarant. The exceptions evolved at common law with respect to declarations of unavailable declarants furnish the basis for the exceptions enumerated in the proposal. The term "unavailable" is defined in subdivision (a).

Exception (1). Former testimony does not rely upon some set of circumstances to substitute for oath and cross-examination, since both oath and opportunity to cross-examine were present in fact. The only missing one of the ideal conditions for the giving of testimony is the presence of trier and opponent ("demeanor evidence"). This is lacking with all hearsay exceptions. Hence it may be argued that former testimony is the strongest hearsay and should be included under Rule 803, supra. However, opportunity to observe demeanor is what in a large measure confers depth and meaning upon oath and cross-examination. Thus in cases under Rule 803 demeanor lacks the significance which it possesses with respect to testimony. In any event, the tradition, founded in experience, uniformly favors production of the witness if he is available. The exception indicates continuation of the policy. This preference for the presence of the witness is apparent also in rules and statutes on the use of depositions, which deal with substantially the same problem.

Under the exception, the testimony may be offered (1) against the party *against* whom it was previously offered or (2) against the party *by* whom it was previously offered. In each instance the question resolves itself into whether fairness allows imposing, upon the party against whom now offered, the handling of the witness on the earlier occasion. (1) If the party against whom now offered is the one against whom the testimony was offered previously, no unfairness is apparent in requiring him to accept his own prior conduct of cross-examination or decision not to cross-examine. Only demeanor has been lost, and that is inherent in the situation. (2) If the party against whom now offered is the one *by* whom the testimony was offered previously, a satisfactory answer becomes somewhat more difficult. One possibility is to proceed somewhat along the line of an adoptive admission, i.e. by offering the testimony proponent in effect adopts it. However, this theory savors of discarded concepts of witnesses' belonging to a party, of litigants' ability to pick and choose witnesses, and of vouching for one's own witnesses. Cf. McCormick § 246, pp. 526–527; 4 Wigmore § 1075. A more direct and acceptable approach is simply to recognize direct and redirect examination of one's own witness as the equivalent of cross-examining an opponent's witness. Falknor, Former Testimony and the Uniform Rules: A Comment, 38 N.Y.U.L.Rev. 651, n. 1 (1963); McCormick § 231, p. 483. See also 5 Wigmore § 1389. Allowable techniques for dealing with hostile, double-crossing, forgetful, and mentally deficient witnesses leave no substance to a claim that one could not adequately develop his own witness at the former hearing. An even less appealing argument is presented when failure to develop fully was the result of a deliberate choice.

The common law did not limit the admissibility of former testimony to that given in an earlier trial of the same case, although it did require identity of issues as a means of insuring that the former handling of the witness was the equivalent of what would now be done if the opportunity were presented. Modern decisions reduce the requirement to "substantial" identity. McCormick § 233. Since identity of issues is significant only in that it bears on motive and interest in developing fully the testimony of the witness, expressing the matter in the latter terms is preferable. Id. Testimony given at a preliminary hearing was held in California v. Green, 399 U.S. 149, 90 S.Ct. 1930, 26 L.Ed.2d 489 (1970), to satisfy confrontation requirements in this respect.

As a further assurance of fairness in thrusting upon a party the prior handling of the witness, the common law also insisted upon identity of parties, deviating only to the extent of allowing substitution of successors in a narrowly construed privity. Mutuality as an aspect of identity is now generally discredited, and the requirement of identity of the offering party disappears except as it might affect motive to develop the testimony. Falknor, supra, at 652; McCormick § 232, pp. 487–488. The question remains whether strict identity, or privity, should continue as a requirement with respect to the party against whom offered. * * *

Report of House Committee on the Judiciary

Rule 804(b)(1) as submitted by the Court allowed prior testimony of an unavailable witness to be admissible if the party against whom it is offered or a person "with motive and interest similar" to his had an opportunity to examine the witness. The Committee considered that it is generally unfair to impose upon the party against whom the hearsay evidence is being offered responsibility for the manner in which the witness was previously handled by another party. The sole exception to this, in the Committee's view, is when a party's predecessor in interest in a civil action or proceeding had an opportunity and similar motive to examine the witness. The Committee amended the Rule to reflect these policy determinations.

Advisory Committee's Note

Exception (3)[now exception 2]. The exception is the familiar dying declaration of the common law, expanded somewhat beyond its traditionally narrow limits. While the original religious justification for the exception may have lost its conviction for some persons over the years, it can scarcely be doubted that powerful psychological pressures are present. See 5 Wigmore § 1443 and the classic statement of Chief Baron Eyre in Rex v. Woodcock, 1 Leach 500, 502, 168 Eng.Rep. 352, 353 (K.B.1789).

The common law required that the statement be that of the victim, offered in a prosecution for criminal homicide. Thus declarations by victims in prosecutions for other crimes, e.g. a declaration by a rape victim who dies in childbirth, and all declarations in civil cases were outside the scope of the exception. An occasional statute has removed these restrictions, as in Colo.R.S. § 52–1–20, or has expanded the area of offenses to include abortions, 5 Wigmore § 1432, p. 224, n. 4. Kansas by decision extended the exception to civil cases. Thurston v. Fritz, 91 Kan. 468, 138 P. 625 (1914). While the common law exception no doubt originated as a result of the exceptional need for the evidence in homicide cases, the theory of admissibility applies equally in civil cases * * *. The same considerations suggest abandonment of the limitation to circumstances attending the event in question, yet when the statement deals with matters other than the supposed death, its influence is believed to be sufficiently attenuated to justify the limitation. Unavailability is not limited to death. See subdivision (a) of this rule. Any problem as to declarations phrased in terms of opinion is laid at rest by Rule 701, and continuation of a requirement of first-hand knowledge is assured by Rule 602.

Comparable provisions are found in Uniform Rule 63(5); California Evidence Code § 1242; Kansas Code of Civil Procedure § 60–460(e); New Jersey Evidence Rule 63(5).

Report of House Committee on the Judiciary

Rule 804(b)(3) as submitted by the Court (now Rule 804(b)(2) in the bill) proposed to expand the traditional scope of the dying declaration exception (i.e. a statement of the victim in a homicide case as to the cause or circumstances of his believed imminent death) to allow such statements in all criminal and civil cases. The Committee did not consider dying declarations as among the most reliable forms of hearsay. Consequently, it amended the provision to limit their admissibility in criminal cases to homicide prosecutions, where exceptional need for the evidence is present. This is existing law. At the same time, the Committee approved the expansion to civil actions and proceedings where the stakes do not involve possible imprisonment, although noting that this could lead to forum shopping in some instances.

Advisory Committee's Note

Exception (4)[now exception 3]. The circumstantial guaranty of reliability for declarations against interest is the assumption that persons do not make statements which are damaging to themselves unless satisfied for good reason that they are true. Hileman v. Northwest Engineering Co., 346 F.2d 668 (6th Cir.1965). If the statement is that of a party, offered by his opponent, it comes in as an admission, Rule 803(d)(2), and there is no occasion to inquire whether it is against interest, this not being a condition precedent to admissibility of admissions by opponents.

The common law required that the interest declared against be pecuniary or proprietary but within this limitation demonstrated striking ingenuity in discovering an against-interest aspect. Higham v. Ridgway, 10 East 109, 103 Eng.Rep. 717 (K.B.1808); Reg. v. Overseers of Birmingham, 1 B. & S. 763, 121 Eng.Rep. 897 (Q.B.1861); McCormick, § 256, p. 551 nn. 2 and 3.

The exception discards the common law limitation and expands to the full logical limit. One result is to remove doubt as to the admissibility of declarations tending to establish a tort liability against the declarant or to extinguish one which might be asserted by him, in accordance with the trend of the decisions in this country. McCormick, § 254, pp. 548–549. * * * And finally, exposure to criminal liability satisfies the against-interest requirement. The refusal of the common law to concede the adequacy of a penal interest was no doubt indefensible in logic, see the dissent of Mr. Justice Holmes in Donnelly v. United States, 228 U.S. 243, 33 S.Ct. 449, 57 L.Ed. 820 (1913), but one senses in the decisions a distrust of evidence of confessions by third persons offered to exculpate the accused arising from suspicions of fabrication either of the fact of the making of the confession or in its contents, enhanced in either instance by the required unavailability of the declarant. Nevertheless, an increasing amount of decisional law recognizes exposure to punishment for crime as a sufficient stake. People v. Spriggs, 60 Cal.2d 868, 36 Cal.Rptr. 841, 389 P.2d 377 (1964); Sutter v. Easterly, 354 Mo. 282, 189 S.W.2d 284 (1945); Band's Refuse Removal, Inc. v. Fairlawn Borough, 62 N.J.Super. 522, 163 A.2d 465 (1960); Newberry v. Commonwealth, 191 Va. 445, 61 S.E.2d 318 (1950); Annot., 162 A.L.R. 446. The requirement of corroboration is included in the rule in order to effect an accommodation between these competing considerations. When the statement is offered by the accused by way of exculpation, the resulting situation is not adapted to control by rulings as to the weight of the evidence, and hence the provision is cast in terms of a requirement preliminary to admissibility. Cf. Rule 406(a). The requirement of corroboration should be construed in such a manner as to effectuate its purpose of circumventing fabrication.

Ordinarily the third-party confession is thought of in terms of exculpating the accused, but this is by no means always or necessarily the case: it may include statements implicating him, and under the general theory of declarations against interest they would be admissible as related statements. Douglas v. Alabama, 380 U.S. 415, 85 S.Ct. 1074, 13 L.Ed.2d 934 (1965), and Bruton v. United States, 389 U.S. 818, 88 S.Ct. 126, 19 L.Ed.2d 70 (1967), both involved confessions by codefendants which implicated the accused. While the confession was not actually offered in evidence in *Douglas,* the procedure followed effectively put it before the jury, which the Court ruled to be error. Whether the confession might have been admissible as a declaration against penal interest was not considered or discussed. *Bruton* assumed the inadmissibility, as against the accused, of the implicating confession of his codefendant, and centered upon the question of the effectiveness of a limiting instruction. These decisions, however, by no means require that all statements implicating another person be excluded from the category of declarations against interest. Whether a statement is in fact against interest must be determined from the circumstances of each case. Thus a statement admitting guilt and implicating another person, made while in custody, may well be motivated by a desire to curry favor with the authorities and hence fail to qualify as against interest. See the dissenting opinion of Mr. Justice White in *Bruton*. On the other hand, the same words spoken under different circumstances, e.g., to an acquaintance, would have no difficulty in qualifying. The rule does not purport to deal with questions of the right of confrontation.

The balancing of self-serving against disserving aspects of a declaration is discussed in McCormick § 256.

For comparable provisions, see Uniform Rule 63(10); California Evidence Code § 1230; Kansas Code of Civil Procedure § 60–460(j); New Jersey Evidence Rule 63(10).

Report of House Committee on the Judiciary

Rule 804(b)(4) as submitted by the Court (now Rule 804(b)(3) in the bill) provided as follows:

Statement against interest.—A statement which was at the time of its making so far contrary to the declarant's pecuniary or proprietary interest or so far tended to subject him to civil or criminal liability or to render invalid a claim by him against another or to make him an object of hatred, ridicule, or disgrace, that a reasonable man in his position would not have made the statement unless he believed it to be true. A statement tending to exculpate the accused is not admissible unless corroborated.

The Committee determined to retain the traditional hearsay exception for statements against pecuniary or proprietary interest. However, it deemed the Court's additional references to statements tending to subject a declarant to civil liability or to render invalid a claim by him against another to be redundant as included within the scope of the reference to statements against pecuniary or proprietary interest. See Gichner v. Antonio Troiano Tile and Marble Co., 410 F.2d 238 (D.C.Cir.1969). Those additional references were accordingly deleted.

The Court's Rule also proposed to expand the hearsay limitation from its present federal limitation to include statements subjecting the declarant to criminal liability and statements tending to make him an object of hatred, ridicule, or disgrace. The Committee eliminated the latter category from the subdivision as lacking sufficient guarantees of reliability. See United States v. Dovico, 380 F.2d 325, 327 nn. 2, 4 (2d Cir.), cert. denied,

389 U.S. 944 (1967). As for statements against penal interest, the Committee shared the view of the Court that some such statements do possess adequate assurances of reliability and should be admissible. It believed, however, as did the Court, that statements of this type tending to exculpate the accused are more suspect and so should have their admissibility conditioned upon some further provision insuring trustworthiness. The proposal in the Court Rule to add a requirement of simple corroboration was, however, deemed ineffective to accomplish this purpose since the accused's own testimony might suffice while not necessarily increasing the reliability of the hearsay statement. The Committee settled upon the language "unless corroborating circumstances clearly indicate the trustworthiness of the statement" as affording a proper standard and degree of discretion. It was contemplated that the result in such cases as Donnelly v. United States, 228 U.S. 243 (1913), where the circumstances plainly indicated reliability, would be changed. The Committee also added to the Rule the final sentence from the 1971 Advisory Committee draft, designed to codify the doctrine of Bruton v. United States, 391 U.S. 123 (1968). The Committee does not intend to affect the existing exception to the *Bruton* principle where the co-defendant takes the stand and is subject to cross-examination, but believed there was no need to make specific provision for this situation in the Rule, since in that event the declarant would not be "unavailable".

Report of Senate Committee on the Judiciary

The rule defines those statements which are considered to be against interest and thus of sufficient trustworthiness to be admissible even though hearsay. With regard to the type of interest declared against, the version submitted by the Supreme Court included inter alia, statements tending to subject a declarant to civil liability or to invalidate a claim by him against another. The House struck these provisions as redundant. In view of the conflicting case law construing pecuniary or proprietary interests narrowly so as to exclude, e.g., tort cases, this deletion could be misconstrued.

Three States which have recently codified their rules of evidence have followed the Supreme Court's version of this rule, i.e., that a statement is against interest if it tends to subject a declarant to civil liability.[3]

The committee believes that the reference to statements tending to subject a person to civil liability constitutes a desirable clarification of the scope of the rule. Therefore, we have reinstated the Supreme Court language on this matter.

The Court rule also proposed to expand the hearsay limitation from its present federal limitation to include statements subjecting the declarant to statements tending to make him an object of hatred, ridicule, or disgrace. The House eliminated the latter category from the subdivision as lacking sufficient guarantees of reliability. Although there is considerable support

---

[3]   Nev.Rev.Stats.   § 51.345;   N.Mex.Stats.   (1973   Supp.)   § 20–4–804(4);   West's Wis.Stats.Anno. (1973 Supp.) § 908–045(4).

for the admissibility of such statements (all three of the State rules referred to supra, would admit such statements), we accept the deletion by the House.

The House amended this exception to add a sentence making inadmissible a statement or confession offered against the accused in a criminal case, made by a codefendant or other person implicating both himself and the accused. The sentence was added to codify the constitutional principle announced in Bruton v. United States, 391 U.S. 123 (1968). *Bruton* held that the admission of the extrajudicial hearsay statement of one codefendant inculpating a second codefendant violated the confrontation clause of the sixth amendment.

The committee decided to delete this provision because the basic approach of the rules is to avoid codifying, or attempting to codify, constitutional evidentiary principles, such as the fifth amendment's right against self-incrimination and, here, the sixth amendment's right of confrontation. Codification of a constitutional principle is unnecessary and, where the principle is under development, often unwise. Furthermore, the House provision does not appear to recognize the exceptions to the *Bruton* rule, e.g. where the codefendant takes the stand and is subject to cross examination; where the accused confessed, see United States v. Mancusi, 404 F.2d 296 (2d Cir.1968), cert. denied 397 U.S. 942 (1970); where the accused was placed at the scene of the crime, see United States v. Zelker, 452 F.2d 1009 (2d Cir.1971). For these reasons, the committee decided to delete this provision.

Conference Report

The Senate amendment to subsection (b)(3) provides that a statement is against interest and not excluded by the hearsay rule when the declarant is unavailable as a witness, if the statement tends to subject a person to civil or criminal liability or renders invalid a claim by him against another. The House bill did not refer specifically to civil liability and to rendering invalid a claim against another. The Senate amendment also deletes from the House bill the provision that subsection (b)(3) does not apply to a statement or confession, made by a codefendant or another, which implicates the accused and the person who made the statement, when that statement or confession is offered against the accused in a criminal case.

The Conference adopts the Senate amendment. The Conferees intend to include within the purview of this rule, statements subjecting a person to civil liability and statements rendering claims invalid. The Conferees agree to delete the provision regarding statements by a codefendant, thereby reflecting the general approach in the Rules of Evidence to avoid attempting to codify constitutional evidentiary principles.

Advisory Committee's Note to 2010 Amendment to
Rule 804(b)(3)

Rule 804(b)(3) has been amended to provide that the corroborating circumstances requirement applies to all declarations against penal interest offered in criminal cases. A number of courts have applied the corroborating circumstances requirement to declarations against penal interest offered by the prosecution, even though the text of the Rule did not so provide. *See, e.g., United States v. Alvarez*, 584 F.2d 694, 701 (5th Cir. 1978) ("by transplanting the language governing exculpatory statements onto the analysis for admitting inculpatory hearsay, a unitary standard is derived which offers the most workable basis for applying Rule 804(b)(3)"); *United States v. Shukri*, 207 F.3d 412 (7th Cir. 2000) (requiring corroborating circumstances for against-penal-interest statements offered by the government). A unitary approach to declarations against penal interest assures both the prosecution and the accused that the Rule will not be abused and that only reliable hearsay statements will be admitted under the exception.

All other changes to the structure and wording of the Rule are intended to be stylistic only. There is no intent to change any other result in any ruling on evidence admissibility.

The amendment does not address the use of the corroborating circumstances for declarations against penal interest offered in civil cases.

In assessing whether corroborating circumstances exist, some courts have focused on the credibility of the witness who relates the hearsay statement in court. But the credibility of the witness who relates the statement is not a proper factor for the court to consider in assessing corroborating circumstances. To base admission or exclusion of a hearsay statement on the witness's credibility would usurp the jury's role of determining the credibility of testifying witnesses.

Advisory Committee's Note to 2011 Amendment to Rule 804

No style changes were made to Rule 804(b)(3), because it was already restyled in conjunction with a substantive amendment, effective December 1, 2010.

Advisory Committee's Note

Exception (5)[now exception 4]. The general common law requirement that a declaration in this area must have been made *ante litem motam* has been dropped, as bearing more appropriately on weight than admissibility. See 5 Wigmore § 1483. Item (i) specifically disclaims any need of firsthand knowledge respecting declarant's own personal history. In some instances it is self-evident (marriage) and in others impossible and traditionally not required (date of birth). Item (ii) deals with declarations concerning the history of another person. As at common law, declarant is qualified if related by blood or marriage. 5 Wigmore § 1489. In addition, and contrary to the common law, declarant qualifies by virtue of intimate association with the family. Id., § 1487. The requirement sometimes encountered that when the subject of the statement is the relationship between two other persons the declarant must qualify as to both is omitted. Relationship is reciprocal. Id., § 1491.

For comparable provisions, see Uniform Rule 63(23), (24), (25); California Evidence Code §§ 1310, 1311; Kansas Code of Civil Procedure § 60–460(u), (v), (w); New Jersey Evidence Rules 63(23), 63(24), 63(25).

[**Editorial Note:** As originally passed, Rule 804(b) included a residual exception, Rule 804(b)(5). In 1997, this exception and an identical counterpart, Rule 803(24), were incorporated in a new Rule 807. Materials related to the former rules are therefore presented in conjunction with Rule 807.]

Conference Report

Senate Provision Deleted

The Senate amendment adds a new hearsay exception [804(b)(5)], not contained in the House bill, which provides that certain law enforcement records are admissible if the officer-declarant is unavailable to testify or be present because of (1) death or physical or mental illness or infirmity or (2) absence from the proceeding and the proponent of the statement has been unable to procure his attendance by process or other reasonable means.

The Conference does not adopt the Senate amendment, preferring instead to leave the bill in the House version, which contained no such provision.

Rule 804(b)(6)

1997 Advisory Committee's Note

Subdivision (b)(6). Rule 804(b)(6) has been added to provide that a party forfeits the right to object on hearsay grounds to the admission of a declarant's prior statement when the party's deliberate wrongdoing or acquiescence therein procured the unavailability of the declarant as a witness. This recognizes the need for a prophylactic rule to deal with abhorrent behavior "which strikes at the heart of the system of justice itself." *United States v. Mastrangelo*, 693 F.2d 269, 273 (2d Cir.1982), *on remand*, 561 F.Supp. 1114 (E.D.N.Y.) (1983), *aff'd.*, 722 F.2d 13 (2d Cir.1983), *cert. denied*, 467 U.S. 1204 (1984). The wrongdoing need not consist of a criminal act. The rule applies to all parties, including the government.

Every circuit that has resolved the question has recognized the principle of forfeiture by misconduct, although the tests for determining whether there is a forfeiture have varied. *See, e.g., United States v. Aguiar*, 975 F.2d 45, 47 (2d Cir.1992); *United States v. Potamitis*, 739 F.2d 784, 789 (2d Cir.), *cert. denied*, 469 U.S. 918 (1984); *Steele v. Taylor*, 684 F.2d 1193, 1199 (6th Cir.1982), *cert. denied*, 460 U.S. 1053 (1983); *United States v. Balano*,

618 F.2d 624, 629 (10th Cir.1979), *cert. denied*, 449 U.S. 840 (1980); *United States v. Carlson*, 547 F.2d 1346, 1358–59 (8th Cir.1976), *cert. denied*, 431 U.S. 914 (1977). The foregoing cases apply a preponderance of the evidence standard. *Contra United States v. Thevis*, 665 F.2d 616, 631 (5th Cir.) (clear and convincing standard), *cert. denied*, 459 U.S. 825 (1982). The usual Rule 104(a) preponderance of the evidence standard has been adopted in light of the behavior the new Rule 804(b)(6) seeks to discourage.

Rule 805

Note by Federal Judicial Center

The rule enacted by the Congress is the rule prescribed by the Supreme Court without change.

Advisory Committee's Note

On principle it scarcely seems open to doubt that the hearsay rule should not call for exclusion of a hearsay statement which includes a further hearsay statement when both conform to the requirements of a hearsay exception. Thus a hospital record might contain an entry of the patient's age based on information furnished by his wife. The hospital record would qualify as a regular entry except that the person who furnished the information was not acting in the routine of the business. However, her statement independently qualifies as a statement of pedigree (if she is unavailable) or as a statement made for purposes of diagnosis or treatment, and hence each link in the chain falls under sufficient assurances. Or, further to illustrate, a dying declaration may incorporate a declaration against interest by another declarant. See McCormick § 290, p. 611.

Rule 806

Note by Federal Judicial Center

The rule enacted by the Congress is the rule prescribed by the Supreme Court, amended by inserting the phrase "or a statement defined in Rule 801(d)(2), (C), (D), or (E)."

Advisory Committee's Note

The declarant of a hearsay statement which is admitted in evidence is in effect a witness. His credibility should in fairness be subject to impeachment and support as though he had in fact testified. See Rules 608 and 609. There are however, some special aspects of the impeaching of a hearsay declarant which require consideration. These special aspects center upon impeachment by inconsistent statement, arise from factual differences which exist between the use of hearsay and an actual witness and also between various kinds of hearsay, and involve the question of applying to declarants the general rule disallowing evidence of an inconsistent statement to impeach a witness unless he is afforded an opportunity to deny or explain. See Rule 613(b).

The principal difference between using hearsay and an actual witness is that the inconsistent statement will in the case of the witness almost inevitably of necessity in the nature of things be a *prior* statement, which it is entirely possible and feasible to call to his attention, while in the case of hearsay the inconsistent statement may well be a *subsequent* one, which practically precludes calling it to the attention of the declarant. The result of insisting upon observation of this impossible requirement in the hearsay situation is to deny the opponent, already barred from cross-examination, any benefit of this important technique of impeachment. The writers favor allowing the subsequent statement. McCormick § 37, p. 69; 3 Wigmore § 1033. The cases, however, are divided. Cases allowing the impeachment include People v. Collup, 27 Cal.2d 829, 167 P.2d 714 (1946); People v. Rosoto, 58 Cal.2d 304, 23 Cal.Rptr. 779, 373 P.2d 867 (1962); Carver v. United States, 164 U.S. 694, 17 S.Ct. 228, 41 L.Ed. 602 (1897). Contra, Mattox v. United States, 156 U.S. 237, 15 S.Ct. 337, 39 L.Ed. 409 (1895); People v. Hines, 284 N.Y. 93, 29 N.E.2d 483 (1940). The force of *Mattox,* where the hearsay was the former testimony of a deceased witness and the denial of use of a subsequent inconsistent statement was upheld, is much diminished by *Carver,* where the hearsay was a dying declaration and denial of use of a subsequent inconsistent statement resulted in reversal. The difference in the particular brand of hearsay seems unimportant when the inconsistent statement is a *subsequent* one. True, the opponent is not totally deprived of cross-examination when the hearsay is former testimony or a deposition but he is deprived of cross-examining on the statement or along lines suggested by it. Mr. Justice Shiras, with two justices joining him, dissented vigorously in *Mattox.*

When the impeaching statement was made *prior* to the hearsay statement, differences in the kinds of hearsay appear which arguably may justify differences in treatment. If the hearsay consisted of a simple statement by the witness, e.g. a dying declaration or a declaration against interest, the feasibility of affording him an opportunity to deny or explain encounters the same practical impossibility as where the statement is a subsequent one, just discussed, although here the impossibility arises from the total absence of anything resembling a hearing at which the matter could be put to him. The courts by a large majority have ruled in favor of allowing the statement to be used under these circumstances. McCormick § 37, p. 69; 3 Wigmore § 1033. If, however, the hearsay consists of former testimony or a deposition, the possibility of calling the prior statement to the attention of the witness or deponent is not ruled out, since the opportunity to cross-examine was available. It might thus be concluded that with former testimony or depositions the conventional foundation should be insisted upon. Most of the cases involve depositions, and Wigmore describes them as divided. 3 Wigmore § 1031. Deposition procedures at best are cumbersome and expensive, and to require the laying of the foundation may impose an undue burden. Under the federal practice, there is no way of knowing with certainty at the time of taking a deposition whether it is merely for discovery or will ultimately end up in evidence. With respect to both former testimony and depositions the possibility exists that knowledge of the statement might not be acquired until after the time of the cross-examination. Moreover, the expanded admissibility of former testimony and depositions under Rule 804(b)(1) calls for a correspondingly expanded approach to impeachment. The rule dispenses with the requirement in all hearsay situations, which is readily administered and best calculated to lead to fair results.

Notice should be taken that Rule 26(f) of the Federal Rules of Civil Procedure, as originally submitted by the Advisory Committee, ended with the following:

> " * * * and, without having first called them to the deponent's attention, may show statements contradictory thereto made at any time by the deponent."

This language did not appear in the rule as promulgated in December, 1937. See 4 Moore's Federal Practice ¶¶ 26.01[9], 26.35 (2d ed.1967). In 1951, Nebraska adopted a provision strongly resembling the one stricken from the federal rule:

> "Any party may impeach any adverse deponent by self-contradiction without having laid foundation for such impeachment at the time such deposition was taken." R.S.Neb. § 25–1267.07.

For similar provisions, see Uniform Rule 65; California Evidence Code § 1202; Kansas Code of Civil Procedure § 60–462; New Jersey Evidence Rule 65.

The provision for cross-examination of a declarant upon his hearsay statement is a corollary of general principles of cross-examination. A similar provision is found in California Evidence Code § 1203.

Report of Senate Committee on the Judiciary

Rule 906[806], as passed by the House and as proposed by the Supreme Court provides that whenever a hearsay statement is admitted, the credibility of the declarant of the statement may be attacked, and if attacked may be supported, by any evidence which would be admissible for those purposes if the declarant had testified as a witness. Rule 801 defines what is a hearsay statement. While statements by a person authorized by a party-opponent to make a statement concerning the subject, by the party-opponent's agent or by a coconspirator of a party—see rule 801(d)(2)(C), (D) and (E)—are traditionally defined as exceptions to the hearsay rule, rule 801 defines such admission by a party-opponent as statements which are not hearsay. Consequently, rule 806 by referring exclusively to the admission of hearsay statements, does not appear to allow the credibility of the declarant to be attacked when the declarant is a coconspirator, agent or authorized spokesman. The committee is of the view that such statements should open the declarant to attacks on his credibility. Indeed, the reason such statements are excluded from the operation of rule 806 is likely attributable to the drafting technique used to codify the hearsay rule, viz. some statements, instead of being referred to as exceptions to the hearsay rule, are defined as statements which are not hearsay. The phrase "or a statement defined in rule 801(d)(2)(C), (D) and (E)" is added to the rule in order to subject the declarant of such statements, like the declarant of hearsay statements, to attacks on his credibility.[1]

Conference Report

The Senate amendment permits an attack upon the credibility of the declarant of a statement if the statement is one by a person authorized by a party-opponent to make a statement concerning the subject, only by an agent of a party-opponent, or one by a coconspirator of the party-opponent, as these statements are defined in Rules 801(d)(2)(C), (D) and (E). The House bill has no such provision.

The Conference adopts the Senate amendment. The Senate amendment conforms the rule to present practice.

Rule 807

[Editorial Note: As presented by the Supreme Court, the Federal Rules included two identical residual hearsay exceptions, Rules 803(24) and 804(b)(6); these were enacted, with the latter renumbered as (b)(5). In 1997, these rules were combined into a new Rule 807. Materials pertaining to the original rules follow.]

Advisory Committee's Note to Original Rule 803(24)
(Now 807)

Exception (24). The preceding 23 exceptions of Rule 803 and the first five [four] exceptions of Rule 804(b), infra, are designed to take full advantage of the accumulated wisdom and experience of the past in dealing with hearsay. It would, however, be presumptuous to assume that all possible desirable exceptions to the hearsay rule have been catalogued and to pass the hearsay rule to oncoming generations as a closed system. Exception (24) and its companion provision in Rule 804(b)(6)[5] are accordingly included. They do not contemplate an unfettered exercise of judicial discretion, but they do provide for treating new and presently unanticipated situations which demonstrate a trustworthiness within the spirit of the specifically stated exceptions. Within this framework, room is left for growth and development of the law of evidence in the hearsay area, consistently with the broad purposes expressed in Rule 102. See Dallas County v. Commercial Union Assur. Co., 286 F.2d 388 (5th Cir.1961).

---

[1] The committee considered it unnecessary to include statements contained in rule 801(d)(2)(A) and (B)—the statement by the party-opponent himself or the statement of which he has manifested his adoption—because the credibility of the party-opponent is always subject to an attack on his credibility.

Advisory Committee's Note to Original Rule 804(b)(5)
(now 807)

Exception (6)[5]. In language and purpose, this exception is identical with Rule 803(24). See the Advisory Committee's Note to that provision.

Report of House Committee on the Judiciary

The proposed Rules of Evidence submitted to Congress contained identical provisions in Rules 803 and 804 (which set forth the various hearsay exceptions), to the effect that the federal courts could admit any hearsay statement not specifically covered by any of the stated exceptions, if the hearsay statement was found to have "comparable circumstantial guarantees of trustworthiness."

The Committee deleted these provisions (proposed rules 803(24) and 804(b)(6)) as injecting too much uncertainty into the law of evidence and impairing the ability of practitioners to prepare for trial. It was noted that Rule 102 directs the courts to construe the Rules of Evidence so as to promote "growth and development." The Committee believed that if additional hearsay exceptions are to be created, they should be by amendments to the Rules, not on a case-by-case basis.

Report of Senate Committee on the Judiciary

The proposed Rules of Evidence submitted to Congress contained identical provisions in rules 803 and 804 (which set forth the various hearsay exceptions), admitting any hearsay statement not specifically covered by any of the stated exceptions, if the hearsay statement was found to have "comparable circumstantial guarantees of trustworthiness." The House deleted these provisions (proposed rules 803(24) and 804(b)(6)) as injecting "too much uncertainty" into the law of evidence and impairing the ability of practitioners to prepare for trial. The House felt that rule 102, which directs the courts to construe the Rules of Evidence so as to promote growth and development, would permit sufficient flexibility to admit hearsay evidence in appropriate cases under various factual situations that might arise.

We disagree with the total rejection of a residual hearsay exception. While we view rule 102 as being intended to provide for a broader construction and interpretation of these rules, we feel that, without a separate residual provision, the specifically enumerated exceptions could become tortured beyond any reasonable circumstances which they were intended to include (even if broadly construed). Moreover, these exceptions, while they reflect the most typical and well recognized exceptions to the hearsay rule, may not encompass every situation in which the reliability and appropriateness of a particular piece of hearsay evidence make clear that it should be heard and considered by the trier of fact.

The committee believes that there are certain exceptional circumstances where evidence which is found by a court to have guarantees of trustworthiness equivalent to or exceeding the guarantees reflected by the presently listed exceptions, and to have a high degree of probativeness and necessity could properly be admissible.

The case of Dallas County v. Commercial Union Assoc. Co., Ltd., 286 F.2d 388 (5th Cir.1961) illustrates the point. The issue in that case was whether the tower of the county courthouse collapsed because it was struck by lightning (covered by insurance) or because of structural weakness and deterioration of the structure (not covered). Investigation of the structure revealed the presence of charcoal and charred timbers. In order to show that lightning may not have been the cause of the charring, the insurer offered a copy of a local newspaper published over 50 years earlier containing an unsigned article describing a fire in the courthouse while it was under construction. The Court found that the newspaper did not qualify for admission as a business record or an ancient document and did not fit within any other recognized hearsay exception. The court concluded, however, that the article was trustworthy because it was inconceivable that a newspaper reporter in a small town would report a fire in the courthouse if none had occurred. See also United States v. Barbati, 284 F.Supp. 409 (E.D.N.Y.1968).

Because exceptional cases like the *Dallas County* case may arise in the future, the committee has decided to reinstate a residual exception for rules 803 and 804(b).

The committee, however, also agrees with those supporters of the House version who felt that an overly broad residual hearsay exception could emasculate the hearsay rule and the recognized exceptions or vitiate the rationale behind codification of the rules.

Therefore, the committee has adopted a residual exception for rules 803 and 804(b) of much narrower scope and applicability than the Supreme Court version. In order to qualify for admission, a hearsay statement not falling within one of the recognized exceptions would have to satisfy at least four conditions. First, it must have "equivalent circumstantial guarantees of trustworthiness." Second, it must be offered as evidence of a material fact. Third, the court must determine that the statement "is more probative on the point for which it is offered than any other evidence which the proponent can procure through reasonable efforts." This requirement is intended to insure that only statements which have high probative value and necessity may qualify for admission under the residual exceptions. Fourth, the court must determine that "the general purposes of these rules and the interests of justice will best be served by admission of the statement into evidence."

It is intended that the residual hearsay exceptions will be used very rarely, and only in exceptional circumstances. The committee does not intend to establish a broad license for trial judges to admit hearsay statements that do not fall within one of the other exceptions contained in rules 803 and 804(b). The residual exceptions are not meant to authorize major judicial revisions of the hearsay rule, including its present exceptions. Such major revisions are best accomplished by legislative action. It is intended that in any case in which evidence is sought to be admitted under these subsections, the trial judge will exercise no less care, reflection and caution than the courts did under the common law in establishing the now-recognized exceptions to the hearsay rule.

In order to establish a well-defined jurisprudence, the special facts and circumstances which, in the court's judgment, indicates that the statement has a sufficiently high degree of trustworthiness and necessity to justify its admission should be stated on the record. It is expected that the court will give the opposing party a full and adequate opportunity to contest the admission of any statement sought to be introduced under these subsections.

Conference Report on Rule 803(24)

The Senate amendment adds a new subsection, (24), which makes admissible a hearsay statement not specifically covered by any of the previous twenty-three subsections, if the statement has equivalent circumstantial guarantees of trustworthiness and if the court determines that (A) the statement is offered as evidence of a material fact; (B) the statement is more probative on the point for which it is offered than any other evidence the proponent can procure through reasonable efforts; and (C) the general purposes of these rules and the interests of justice will best be served by admission of the statement into evidence.

The House bill eliminated a similar, but broader, provision because of the conviction that such a provision injected too much uncertainty into the law of evidence regarding hearsay and impaired the ability of a litigant to prepare adequately for trial.

The Conference adopts the Senate amendment with an amendment that provides that a party intending to request the court to use a statement under this provision must notify any adverse party of this intention as well as of the particulars of the statement, including the name and address of the declarant. This notice must be given sufficiently in advance of the trial or hearing to provide any adverse party with a fair opportunity to prepare to contest the use of the statement.

[**Editorial Note:** The Conference Report included a comment on what became Rule 804(b)(5), identical to the above comment on Rule 803(24) except that it began: "The Senate amendment adds a new subsection, (b)(6)[5], which makes admissible a hearsay statement not specifically covered by any of the five previous subsections . . ."]

1997 Advisory Committee Note to Rule 807

The contents of Rule 803(24) and Rule 804(b)(5) have been combined and transferred to a new Rule 807. This was done to facilitate additions to Rule 803 and 804. No change in meaning is intended.

ARTICLE IX. AUTHENTICATION AND IDENTIFICATION

Rule 901

Note by Federal Judicial Center

The rule enacted by the Congress is the rule prescribed by the Supreme Court, amended in subdivision (b)(10) by substituting "prescribed" in place of "adopted," and by adding "pursuant to statutory authority."

Advisory Committee's Note

Subdivision (a). Authentication and identification represent a special aspect of relevancy. Michael and Adler, Real Proof, 5 Vand.L.Rev. 344, 362 (1952); McCormick §§ 179, 185; Morgan, Basic Problems of Evidence 378 (1962). Thus a telephone conversation may be irrelevant because on an unrelated topic or because the speaker is not identified. The latter aspect is the one here involved. Wigmore describes the need for authentication as "an inherent logical necessity." 7 Wigmore § 2129, p. 564.

This requirement of showing authenticity or identity falls in the category of relevancy dependent upon fulfillment of a condition of fact and is governed by the procedure set forth in Rule 104(b).

The common law approach to authentication of documents has been criticized as an "attitude of agnosticism," McCormick, Cases on Evidence 388, n. 4 (3rd ed. 1956), as one which "departs sharply from men's customs in ordinary affairs," and as presenting only a slight obstacle to the introduction of forgeries in comparison to the time and expense devoted to proving genuine writings which correctly show their origin on their face, McCormick § 185, pp. 395, 396. Today, such available procedures as requests to admit and pretrial conference afford the means of eliminating much of the need for authentication or identification. Also, significant inroads upon the traditional insistence on authentication and identification have been made by accepting as at least prima facie genuine items of the kind treated in Rule 902, infra. However, the need for suitable methods of proof still remains, since criminal cases pose their own obstacles to the use of preliminary procedures, unforeseen contingencies may arise, and cases of genuine controversy will still occur.

Subdivision (b). The treatment of authentication and identification draws largely upon the experience embodied in the common law and in statutes to furnish illustrative applications of the general principle set forth in subdivision (a). The examples are not intended as an exclusive enumeration of allowable methods but are meant to guide and suggest, leaving room for growth and development in this area of the law.

The examples relate for the most part to documents, with some attention given to voice communications and computer print-outs. As Wigmore noted, no special rules have been developed for authenticating chattels. Wigmore, Code of Evidence § 2086 (3rd ed.1942).

It should be observed that compliance with requirements of authentication or identification by no means assures admission of an item into evidence, as other bars, hearsay for example, may remain.

Example (1) contemplates a broad spectrum ranging from testimony of a witness who was present at the signing of a document to testimony establishing narcotics as taken from an accused and accounting for custody through the period until trial, including laboratory analysis. See California Evidence Code § 1413, eyewitness to signing.

Example (2) states conventional doctrine as to lay identification of handwriting, which recognizes that a sufficient familiarity with the handwriting of another person may be acquired by seeing him write, by exchanging correspondence, or by other means, to afford a basis for identifying it on subsequent occasions. McCormick § 189. See also California Evidence Code § 1416. Testimony based upon familiarity acquired for purposes of the litigation is reserved to the expert under the example which follows.

Example (3). The history of common law restrictions upon the technique of proving or disproving the genuineness of a disputed specimen of handwriting through comparison with a genuine specimen, by either the testimony of expert witnesses or direct viewing by the triers themselves, is detailed in 7 Wigmore §§ 1991–1994. In breaking away, the English Common Law Procedure Act of 1854, 17 and 18 Vict., c. 125, § 27, cautiously allowed expert or trier to use exemplars "proved to the satisfaction of the judge to be genuine" for purposes of comparison. The language found its way into numerous statutes in this country, e.g., California Evidence Code §§ 1417, 1418. While explainable as a measure of prudence in the process of breaking with precedent in the handwriting situation, the reservation to the judge of the question of the genuineness of exemplars and the imposition of an unusually high standard of persuasion are at variance with the general treatment of relevancy which depends upon fulfillment of a condition of fact. Rule 104(b). No similar attitude is found in other comparison situations, e.g., ballistics comparison by jury, as in Evans v. Commonwealth, 230 Ky. 411, 19 S.W.2d 1091 (1929), or by experts, Annot., 26 A.L.R.2d 892, and no reason appears for its continued existence in handwriting cases. Consequently Example (3) sets no higher standard for handwriting specimens and treats all comparison situations alike, to be governed by Rule 104(b). This approach is consistent with 28 U.S.C. § 1731: "The admitted or proved handwriting of any person shall be admissible, for purposes of comparison, to determine genuineness of other handwriting attributed to such person."

Precedent supports the acceptance of visual comparison as sufficiently satisfying preliminary authentication requirements for admission in evidence. Brandon v. Collins, 267 F.2d 731 (2d Cir.1959); Wausau Sulphate Fibre Co. v. Commissioner of Internal Revenue, 61 F.2d 879 (7th Cir.1932); Desimone v. United States, 227 F.2d 864 (9th Cir.1955).

Example (4). The characteristics of the offered item itself, considered in the light of circumstances, afford authentication techniques in great variety. Thus a document or telephone conversation may be shown to have emanated from a particular person by virtue of its disclosing knowledge of facts known peculiarly to him; Globe Automatic Sprinkler Co. v. Braniff, 89 Okl. 105, 214 P. 127 (1923); California Evidence Code § 1421; similarly, a letter may be authenticated by content and circumstances indicating it was in reply to a duly authenticated one. McCormick § 192; California Evidence Code § 1420. Language patterns may indicate authenticity or its opposite. Magnuson v. State, 187 Wis. 122, 203 N.W. 749 (1925); Arens and Meadow, Psycholinguistics and the Confession Dilemma, 56 Colum.L.Rev. 19 (1956).

Example (5). Since aural voice identification is not a subject of expert testimony, the requisite familiarity may be acquired either before or after the particular speaking which is the subject of the identification, in this respect resembling visual identification of a person rather than identification of handwriting. Cf. Example (2), supra, People v. Nichols, 378 Ill. 487, 38 N.E.2d 766 (1941); McGuire v. State, 200 Md. 601, 92 A.2d 582 (1952); State v. McGee, 336 Mo. 1082, 83 S.W.2d 98 (1935).

Example (6). The cases are in agreement that a mere assertion of his identity by a person talking on the telephone is not sufficient evidence of the authenticity of the conversation and that additional evidence of his identity is required. The additional evidence need not fall in any set pattern. Thus the content of his statements or the reply technique, under Example (4), supra, or voice identification under Example (5), may furnish the necessary foundation. Outgoing calls made by the witness involve additional factors bearing upon authenticity. The calling of a number assigned by the telephone company reasonably supports the assumption that the listing is correct and that the number is the one reached. If the number is that of a place of business, the mass of authority allows an ensuing conversation if it relates to business reasonably transacted over the telephone, on the theory that the maintenance of the telephone connection is an invitation to do business without further identification. Mattan v. Hoover Co., 350 Mo. 506, 166 S.W.2d 557 (1942); City of Pawhuska v. Crutchfield, 147 Okl. 4, 293 P. 1095 (1930); Zurich General Acc. & Liability Ins. Co. v. Baum, 159 Va. 404, 165 S.E. 518 (1932). Otherwise, some additional circumstance of identification of the speaker is required. The authorities divide on the question whether the self-identifying statement of the person answering suffices. Example (6) answers in the affirmative on the assumption that usual conduct respecting telephone calls furnish adequate assurances of regularity, bearing in mind that the entire matter is open to exploration before the trier of fact. In general, see McCormick § 193; 7 Wigmore § 2155; Annot., 71 A.L.R. 5, 105 id. 326.

Example (7). Public records are regularly authenticated by proof of custody, without more. McCormick § 191; 7 Wigmore §§ 2158, 2159. The example extends the principle to include data stored in computers and similar methods, of which increasing use in the public records area may be expected. See California Evidence Code §§ 1532, 1600.

Example (8). The familiar ancient document rule of the common law is extended to include data stored electronically or by other similar means. Since the importance of appearance diminishes in this situation, the importance of custody or place where found increases correspondingly. This expansion is necessary in view of the widespread use of methods of storing data in forms other than conventional written records.

Any time period selected is bound to be arbitrary. The common law period of 30 years is here reduced to 20 years, with some shift of emphasis from the probable unavailability of witnesses to the unlikeliness of a still viable fraud after the lapse of time. The shorter period is specified in the English Evidence Act of 1938, 1 & 2 Geo. 6, c. 28, and in Oregon R.S.1963, § 41.360(34). See also the numerous statutes prescribing periods of less than 30 years in the case of recorded documents. 7 Wigmore § 2143.

The application of Example (8) is not subject to any limitation to title documents or to any requirement that possession, in the case of a title document, has been consistent with the document. See McCormick § 190.

Example (9) is designed for situations in which the accuracy of a result is dependent upon a process or system which produces it. X rays afford a familiar instance. Among more recent developments is the computer, as to which see Transport Indemnity Co. v. Seib, 178 Neb. 253, 132 N.W.2d 871 (1965); State v. Veres, 7 Ariz.App. 117, 436 P.2d 629 (1968); Merrick v. United States Rubber Co., 7 Ariz.App. 433, 440 P.2d 314 (1968); Freed, Computer Print-Outs as Evidence, 16 Am.Jur.Proof of Facts 273; Symposium, Law and Computers in the Mid-Sixties, ALI–ABA (1966); 37 Albany L.Rev. 61 (1967). Example (9) does not, of course, foreclose taking judicial notice of the accuracy of the process or system.

Example (10). The example makes clear that methods of authentication provided by Act of Congress and by the Rules of Civil and Criminal Procedure or by Bankruptcy Rules are not intended to be superseded. Illustrative are the provisions for authentication of official records in Civil Procedure Rule 44 and Criminal Procedure Rule 27, for authentication of records of proceedings by court reporters in 28 U.S.C. § 753(b) and Civil Procedure Rule 80(c), and for authentication of depositions in Civil Procedure Rule 30(f).

Rule 902

Note by Federal Judicial Center

The rule enacted by the Congress is the rule prescribed by the Supreme Court, amended as follows:

Paragraph (4) was amended by substituting "prescribed" in place of "adopted," and by adding "pursuant to statutory authority."

Paragraph (8) was amended by substituting "in the manner provided by law by" in place of "under the hand and seal of."

Advisory Committee's Note

Case law and statutes have, over the years, developed a substantial body of instances in which authenticity is taken as sufficiently established for purposes of admissibility without extrinsic evidence to that effect, sometimes for reasons of policy but perhaps more often because practical considerations reduce the possibility of unauthenticity to a very small dimension. The present rule collects and incorporates these situations, in some instances expanding them to occupy a larger area which their underlying considerations justify. In no instance is the opposite party foreclosed from disputing authenticity.

Paragraph (1). The acceptance of documents bearing a public seal and signature, most often encountered in practice in the form of acknowledgments or certificates authenticating copies of public records, is actually of broad application. Whether theoretically based in whole or in part upon judicial notice, the practical underlying considerations are that forgery is a crime and detection is fairly easy and certain. 7 Wigmore § 2161, p. 638; California Evidence Code § 1452. More than 50 provisions for judicial notice of official seals are contained in the United States Code.

Paragraph (2). While statutes are found which raise a presumption of genuineness of purported official signatures in the absence of an official seal, 7 Wigmore § 2167; California Evidence Code § 1453, the greater ease of effecting a forgery under these circumstances is apparent. Hence this paragraph of the rule calls for authentication by an officer who has a seal. Notarial acts by members of the armed forces and other special situations are covered in paragraph (10).

Paragraph (3). provides a method for extending the presumption of authenticity to foreign official documents by a procedure of certification. It is derived from Rule 44(a)(2) of the Rules of Civil Procedure but is broader in applying to public documents rather than being limited to public records.

Paragraph (4). The common law and innumerable statutes have recognized the procedure of authenticating copies of public records by certificate. The certificate qualifies as a public document, receivable as authentic when in conformity with paragraph (1), (2), or (3). Rule 44(a) of the Rules of Civil Procedure and Rule 27 of the Rules of Criminal Procedure have provided authentication procedures of this nature for both domestic and foreign public records. It will be observed that the certification procedure here provided extends only to public records, reports, and recorded documents, all including data compilations, and does not apply to public documents generally. Hence documents provable when presented in original form under paragraphs (1), (2), or (3) may not be provable by certified copy under paragraph (4).

Paragraph (5). Dispensing with preliminary proof of the genuineness of purportedly official publications, most commonly encountered in connection with statutes, court reports, rules, and regulations, has been greatly enlarged by statutes and decisions. 5 Wigmore § 1684. Paragraph (5), it will be noted, does not confer admissibility upon all official publications; it merely provides a means whereby their authenticity may be taken as established for purposes of admissibility. Rule 44(a) of the Rules of Civil Procedure has been to the same effect.

Paragraph (6). The likelihood of forgery of newspapers or periodicals is slight indeed. Hence no danger is apparent in receiving them. Establishing the authenticity of the publication may, of course, leave still open questions of authority and responsibility for items therein contained. See 7 Wigmore § 2150. Cf. 39 U.S.C. § 4005(b), public advertisement prima facie evidence of agency of person named, in postal fraud order proceeding; Canadian Uniform Evidence Act, Draft of 1936, printed copy of newspaper prima facie evidence that notices or advertisements were authorized.

Paragraph (7). Several factors justify dispensing with preliminary proof of genuineness of commercial and mercantile labels and the like. The risk of forgery is minimal. Trademark infringement involves serious penalties. Great efforts are devoted to inducing the public to buy in reliance on brand names, and substantial protection is given them. Hence the fairness of this treatment finds recognition in the cases. Curtiss Candy Co. v. Johnson, 163 Miss. 426, 141 So. 762 (1932), Baby Ruth candy bar; Doyle v. Continental Baking Co., 262 Mass. 516, 160 N.E. 325 (1928), loaf of bread; Weiner v. Mager & Throne, Inc., 167 Misc. 338, 3 N.Y.S.2d 918 (1938), same. And see W.Va.Code 1966, § 47–3–5, trade-mark on bottle prima facie evidence of ownership. Contra, Keegan v. Green Giant Co., 150 Me. 283, 110 A.2d 599 (1954); Murphy v. Campbell Soup Co., 62 F.2d 564 (1st Cir.1933). Cattle brands have received similar acceptance in the western states. Rev.Code Mont. 1947, § 46–606; State v. Wolfley, 75 Kan. 406, 89 P.

1046 (1907); Annot., 11 L.R.A.(N.S.) 87. Inscriptions on trains and vehicles are held to be prima facie evidence of ownership or control. Pittsburgh, Ft. W. & C. Ry. v. Callaghan, 157 Ill. 406, 41 N.E. 909 (1895); 9 Wigmore § 2510a. See also the provision of 19 U.S.C. § 1615(2) that marks, labels, brands, or stamps indicating foreign origin are prima facie evidence of foreign origin of merchandise.

Paragraph (8). In virtually every state, acknowledged title documents are receivable in evidence without further proof. Statutes are collected in 5 Wigmore § 1676. If this authentication suffices for documents of the importance of those affecting titles, logic scarcely permits denying this method when other kinds of documents are involved. Instances of broadly inclusive statutes are California Evidence Code § 1451 and N.Y.CPLR 4538, McKinney's Consol.Laws 1963.

Report of House Committee on the Judiciary

Rule 902(8) as submitted by the Court referred to certificates of acknowledgment "under the hand and seal of" a notary public or other officer authorized by law to take acknowledgments. The Committee amended the Rule to eliminate the requirement, believed to be inconsistent with the law in some States, that a notary public must affix a seal to a document acknowledged before him. As amended the Rule merely requires that the document be executed in the manner prescribed by State law.

Advisory Committee's Note

Paragraph (9). Issues of the authenticity of commercial paper in federal courts will usually arise in diversity cases, will involve an element of a cause of action or defense, and with respect to presumptions and burden of proof will be controlled by Erie Railroad Co. v. Tompkins, 304 U.S. 64, 58 S.Ct. 817, 82 L.Ed. 1188 (1938). Rule 302, supra. There may, however, be questions of authenticity involving lesser segments of a case or the case may be one governed by federal common law. Clearfield Trust Co. v. United States, 318 U.S. 363, 63 S.Ct. 573, 87 L.Ed. 838 (1943). Cf. United States v. Yazell, 382 U.S. 341, 86 S.Ct. 500, 15 L.Ed.2d 404 (1966). In these situations, resort to the useful authentication provisions of the Uniform Commercial Code is provided for. While the phrasing is in terms of "general commercial law," in order to avoid the potential complications inherent in borrowing local statutes, today one would have difficulty in determining the general commercial law without referring to the Code. See Williams v. Walker-Thomas Furniture Co., 121 U.S.App.D.C. 315, 350 F.2d 445 (1965). Pertinent Code provisions are sections 1–202, 3–307, and 3–510, dealing with third-party documents, signatures on negotiable instruments, protests, and statements of dishonor.

Report of House Committee on the Judiciary

The Committee approved Rule 902(9) as submitted by the Court. With respect to the meaning of the phrase "general commercial law", the Committee intends that the Uniform Commercial Code, which has been adopted in virtually every State, will be followed generally, but that federal commercial law will apply where federal commercial paper is involved. See Clearfield Trust Co. v. United States, 318 U.S. 363 (1943). Further, in those instances in which the issues are governed by Erie R. Co. v. Tompkins, 304 U.S. 64 (1938), State law will apply irrespective of whether it is the Uniform Commercial Code.

Advisory Committee's Note

Paragraph (10). The paragraph continues in effect dispensations with preliminary proof of genuineness provided in various Acts of Congress. See, for example, 10 U.S.C. § 936, signature, without seal, together with title, prima facie evidence of authenticity of acts of certain military personnel who are given notarial powers; 15 U.S.C. § 77f(a), signature on SEC registration presumed genuine; 26 U.S.C. § 6064, signature to tax return prima facie genuine.

Advisory Committee's Note to 2000 Amendment

The amendment adds two new paragraphs to the rule on self-authentication. It sets forth a procedure by which parties can authenticate certain records of regularly conducted activity, other than through the testimony of a foundation witness. See the amendment to Rule 803(6). 18 U.S.C. § 3505 currently provides a means for certifying foreign records of regularly conducted activity in criminal cases, and this amendment is intended to establish a similar procedure for domestic records, and for foreign records offered in civil cases.

A declaration that satisfies 28 U.S.C. § 1746 would satisfy the declaration requirement of Rule 902(11), as would any comparable certification under oath.

The notice requirement in Rules 902(11) and (12) is intended to give the opponent of the evidence a full opportunity to test the adequacy of the foundation set forth in the declaration.

Rule 903

Note by Federal Judicial Center

The rule enacted by the Congress is the rule prescribed by the Supreme Court without change.

Advisory Committee's Note

The common law required that attesting witnesses be produced or accounted for. Today the requirement has generally been abolished except with respect to documents which must be attested to be valid, e.g. wills in some states. McCormick § 188. Uniform Rule 71; California Evidence Code

§ 1411; Kansas Code of Civil Procedure § 60–468; New Jersey Evidence Rule 71; New York CPLR Rule 4537.

ARTICLE X. CONTENTS OF WRITINGS, RECORDINGS, AND PHOTOGRAPHS

Rule 1001

[**Editorial Note:** As a result of the 2011 restyling, the designation of the subdivisions of Rule 1001 has changed. The substance of former subdivision (1) is now contained in subdivisions (a) and (b). The substance of former subdivisions (2), (3), and (4) is now contained in subdivisions (c), (d), and (e), respectively.]

Note by Federal Judicial Center

The rule enacted by the Congress is the rule prescribed by the Supreme Court, amended in paragraph (2) by inserting "video tapes."

Advisory Committee's Note

In an earlier day, when discovery and other related procedures were strictly limited, the misleading named "best evidence rule" afforded substantial guarantees against inaccuracies and fraud by its insistence upon production of original documents. The great enlargement of the scope of discovery and related procedures in recent times has measurably reduced the need for the rule. Nevertheless important areas of usefulness persist: discovery of documents outside the jurisdiction may require substantial outlay of time and money; the unanticipated document may not practically be discoverable; criminal cases have built-in limitations on discovery. Cleary and Strong, The Best Evidence Rule: An Evaluation in Context, 51 Iowa L.Rev. 825 (1966).

Paragraph (1). Traditionally the rule requiring the original centered upon accumulations of data and expressions affecting legal relations set forth in words and figures. This meant that the rule was one essentially related to writings. Present day techniques have expanded methods of storing data, yet the essential form which the information ultimately assumes for usable purposes is words and figures. Hence the considerations underlying the rule dictate its expansion to include computers, photographic systems, and other modern developments.

Report of House Committee on the Judiciary

The Committee amended this Rule expressly to include "video tapes" in the definition of "photographs."

Advisory Committee's Note

Paragraph (3). In most instances, what is an original will be self-evident and further refinement will be unnecessary. However, in some instances particularized definition is required. A carbon copy of a contract executed in duplicate becomes an original, as does a sales ticket carbon copy given to a customer. While strictly speaking the original of a photograph might be thought to be only the negative, practicality and common usage require that any print from the negative be regarded as an original. Similarly, practicality and usage confer the status of original upon any computer printout. Transport Indemnity Co. v. Seib, 178 Neb. 253, 132 N.W.2d 871 (1965).

Paragraph (4). The definition describes "copies" produced by methods possessing an accuracy which virtually eliminates the possibility of error. Copies thus produced are given the status of originals in large measure by Rule 1003, infra. Copies subsequently produced manually, whether handwritten or typed, are not within the definition. It should be noted that what is an original for some purposes may be a duplicate for others. Thus a bank's microfilm record of checks cleared is the original as a record. However, a print offered as a copy of a check whose contents are in controversy is a duplicate. This result is substantially consistent with 28 U.S.C. § 1732(b). Compare 26 U.S.C. § 7513(c), giving full status as originals to photographic reproductions of tax returns and other documents, made by authority of the Secretary of the Treasury, and 44 U.S.C. § 399(a), giving original status to photographic copies in the National Archives.

Rule 1002

Note by Federal Judicial Center

The rule enacted by the Congress is the rule prescribed by the Supreme Court without change.

Advisory Committee's Note

The rule is the familiar one requiring production of the original of a document to prove its contents, expanded to include writings, recordings, and photographs, as defined in Rule 1001(1) and (2), supra.

Application of the rule requires a resolution of the question whether contents are sought to be proved. Thus an event may be proved by nondocumentary evidence, even though a written record of it was made. If, however, the event is sought to be proved by the written record, the rule applies. For example, payment may be proved without producing the written receipt which was given. Earnings may be proved without producing books of account in which they are entered. McCormick § 198; 4 Wigmore § 1245. Nor does the rule apply to testimony that books or records have been examined and found not to contain any reference to a designated matter.

The assumption should not be made that the rule will come into operation on every occasion when use is made of a photograph in evidence. On the contrary, the rule will seldom apply to ordinary photographs. In most instances a party *wishes* to introduce the item and the question raised is the propriety of receiving it in evidence. Cases in which an offer is made of the testimony of a witness as to what he saw in a photograph or motion picture, without producing the same, are most unusual. The usual course is for a witness on the stand to identify the photograph or motion picture as a correct representation of events which he saw or of a scene with which he is familiar. In fact he adopts the picture as his testimony, or, in common parlance, uses the picture to illustrate his testimony. Under these circumstances, no effort is made to prove the contents of the picture, and the rule is inapplicable. Paradis, The Celluloid Witness, 37 U.Colo.L.Rev. 235, 249–251 (1965).

On occasion, however, situations arise in which contents are sought to be proved. Copyright, defamation, and invasion of privacy by photograph or motion picture falls in this category. Similarly as to situations in which the picture is offered as having independent probative value, e.g. automatic photograph of bank robber. See People v. Doggett, 83 Cal.App.2d 405, 188 P.2d 792 (1948), photograph of defendants engaged in indecent act; Mouser and Philbin, Photographic Evidence—Is There a Recognized Basis for Admissibility? 8 Hastings L.J. 310 (1957). The most commonly encountered of this latter group is of course, the X ray, with substantial authority calling for production of the original. Daniels v. Iowa City, 191 Iowa 811, 183 N.W. 415 (1921); Cellamare v. Third Ave. Transit Corp., 273 App.Div. 260, 77 N.Y.S.2d 91 (1948); Patrick & Tillman v. Matkin, 154 Okl. 232, 7 P.2d 414 (1932); Mendoza v. Rivera, 78 P.R.R. 569 (1955).

It should be noted, however, that Rule 703, supra, allows an expert to give an opinion based on matters not in evidence, and the present rule must be read as being limited accordingly in its application. Hospital records which may be admitted as business records under Rule 803(6) commonly contain reports interpreting X rays by the staff radiologist, who qualifies as an expert, and these reports need not be excluded from the records by the instant rule.

The reference to Acts of Congress is made in view of such statutory provisions as 26 U.S.C. § 7513, photographic reproductions of tax returns and documents, made by authority of the Secretary of the Treasury, treated as originals, and 44 U.S.C. § 399(a), photographic copies in National Archives treated as originals.

Rule 1003

Note by Federal Judicial Center

The rule enacted by the Congress is the rule prescribed by the Supreme Court without change.

Advisory Committee's Note

When the only concern is with getting the words or other contents before the court with accuracy and precision, then a counterpart serves equally as well as the original, if the counterpart is the product of a method which insures accuracy and genuineness. By definition in Rule 1001(4), supra, a "duplicate" possesses this character.

Therefore, if no genuine issue exists as to authenticity and no other reason exists for requiring the original, a duplicate is admissible under the rule. This position finds support in the decisions, Myrick v. United States, 332 F.2d 279 (5th Cir.1963), no error in admitting photostatic copies of checks instead of original microfilm in absence of suggestion to trial judge that photostats were incorrect; Johns v. United States, 323 F.2d 421 (5th Cir.1963), not error to admit concededly accurate tape recording made from original wire recording; Sauget v. Johnston, 315 F.2d 816 (9th Cir.1963), not error to admit copy of agreement when opponent had original and did not on appeal claim any discrepancy. Other reasons for requiring the original may be present when only a part of the original is reproduced and the remainder is needed for cross-examination or may disclose matters qualifying the part offered or otherwise useful to the opposing party. United States v. Alexander, 326 F.2d 736 (4th Cir.1964). And see Toho Bussan Kaisha, Ltd. v. American President Lines, Ltd., 265 F.2d 418, 76 A.L.R.2d 1344 (2d Cir.1959).

Report of House Committee on the Judiciary

The Committee approved this Rule in the form submitted by the Court, with the expectation that the courts would be liberal in deciding that a "genuine question is raised as to the authenticity of the original."

Rule 1004

[**Editorial Note:** As a result of the 2011 restyling, the subdivsions of Rule 1004, formerly numbered from (1) to (4), are now lettered from (a) to (d), respectively.]

Note by Federal Judicial Center

The rule enacted by the Congress is the rule prescribed by the Supreme Court without change.

Advisory Committee's Note

Basically the rule requiring the production of the original as proof of contents has developed as a rule of preference: if failure to produce the original is satisfactorily explained, secondary evidence is admissible. The instant rule specifies the circumstances under which production of the original is excused.

The rule recognizes no "degrees" of secondary evidence. While strict logic might call for extending the principle of preference beyond simply preferring the original, the formulation of a hierarchy of preferences and a procedure for making it effective is believed to involve unwarranted complexities. Most, if not all, that would be accomplished by an extended scheme of preferences will, in any event, be achieved through the normal motivation of a party to present the most convincing evidence possible and the arguments and procedures available to his opponent if he does not. Compare McCormick § 207.

Paragraph (1). Loss or destruction of the original, unless due to bad faith of the proponent, is a satisfactory explanation of nonproduction. McCormick § 201.

Report of House Committee on the Judiciary

The Committee approved Rule 1004(1) in the form submitted to Congress. However, the Committee intends that loss or destruction of an original by another person at the instigation of the proponent should be considered as tantamount to loss or destruction in bad faith by the proponent himself.

Advisory Committee's Note

Paragraph (2). When the original is in the possession of a third person, inability to procure it from him by resort to process or other judicial procedure is a sufficient explanation of nonproduction. Judicial procedure includes subpoena duces tecum as an incident to the taking of a deposition in another jurisdiction. No further showing is required. See McCormick § 202.

Paragraph (3). A party who has an original in his control has no need for the protection of the rule if put on notice that proof of contents will be made. He can ward off secondary evidence by offering the original. The notice procedure here provided is not to be confused with orders to produce or other discovery procedures, as the purpose of the procedure under this rule is to afford the opposite party an opportunity to produce the original, not to compel him to do so. McCormick § 203.

Paragraph (4). While difficult to define with precision, situations arise in which no good purpose is served by production of the original. Examples are the newspaper in an action for the price of publishing defendant's advertisement, Foster-Holcomb Investment Co. v. Little Rock Publishing Co., 151 Ark. 449, 236 S.W. 597 (1922), and the streetcar transfer of plaintiff claiming status as a passenger, Chicago City Ry. Co. v. Carroll, 206 Ill. 318, 68 N.E. 1087 (1903). Numerous cases are collected in McCormick § 200, p. 412, n. 1.

Rule 1005

Note by Federal Judicial Center

The rule enacted by the Congress is the rule prescribed by the Supreme Court without change.

Advisory Committee's Note

Public records call for somewhat different treatment. Removing them from their usual place of keeping would be attended by serious inconvenience to the public and to the custodian. As a consequence judicial decisions and statutes commonly hold that no explanation need be given for failure to produce the original of a public record. McCormick § 204; 4 Wigmore §§ 1215–1228. This blanket dispensation from producing or accounting for the original would open the door to the introduction of every kind of secondary evidence of contents of public records were it not for the preference given certified or compared copies. Recognition of degrees of secondary evidence in this situation is an appropriate *quid pro quo* for not applying the requirement of producing the original.

The provisions of 28 U.S.C. § 1733(b) apply only to departments or agencies of the United States. The rule, however, applies to public records generally and is comparable in scope in this respect to Rule 44(a) of the Rules of Civil Procedure.

Rule 1006

Note by Federal Judicial Center

The rule enacted by the Congress is the rule prescribed by the Supreme Court without change.

Advisory Committee's Note

The admission of summaries of voluminous books, records, or documents offers the only practicable means of making their contents available to judge and jury. The rule recognizes this practice, with appropriate safeguards. 4 Wigmore § 1230.

Rule 1007

Note by Federal Judicial Center

The rule enacted by the Congress is the rule prescribed by the Supreme Court without change.

Advisory Committee's Note

While the parent case, Slatterie v. Pooley, 6 M. & W. 664, 151 Eng.Rep. 579 (Exch. 1840), allows proof of contents by evidence of an oral admission by the party against whom offered, without accounting for nonproduction of the original, the risk of inaccuracy is substantial and the decision is at odds with the purpose of the rule giving preference to the original. See 4 Wigmore § 1255. The instant rule follows Professor McCormick's suggestion of limiting this use of admissions to those made in the course of giving testimony or in writing. McCormick § 208, p. 424. The limitation of course, does not call for excluding evidence of an oral admission when nonproduction of the original has been accounted for and secondary evidence generally has become admissible. Rule 1004, supra.

A similar provision is contained in New Jersey Evidence Rule 70(1) (h).

Rule 1008

Note by Federal Judicial Center

The rule enacted by the Congress is the rule prescribed by the Supreme Court, amended by substituting "court" in place of "judge," and by adding at the end of the first sentence the phrase "in accordance with the provisions of rule 104."

Advisory Committee's Note

Most preliminary questions of fact in connection with applying the rule preferring the original as evidence of contents are for the judge, under the general principles announced in Rule 104, supra. Thus, the question whether the loss of the originals has been established, or of the fulfillment of other conditions specified in Rule 1004, supra, is for the judge. However, questions may arise which go beyond the mere administration of the rule preferring the original and into the merits of the controversy. For example, plaintiff offers secondary evidence of the contents of an alleged contract, after first introducing evidence of loss of the original, and defendant counters with evidence that no such contract was ever executed. If the judge decides that the contract was never executed and excludes the secondary evidence, the case is at an end without ever going to the jury on a central issue. Levin, Authentication and Content of Writings, 10 Rutgers L.Rev. 632, 644 (1956). The latter portion of the instant rule is designed to insure treatment of these situations as raising jury questions. The decision is not one for uncontrolled discretion of the jury but is subject to the control exercised generally by the judge over jury determinations. See Rule 104(b), supra.

For similar provisions, see Uniform Rule 70(2); Kansas Code of Civil Procedure § 60–467(b); New Jersey Evidence Rule 70(2), (3).

ARTICLE XI. MISCELLANEOUS RULES

Rule 1101

Note by Federal Judicial Center

The rule enacted by the Congress is the rule prescribed by the Supreme Court, amended as follows:

Subdivision (a) was amended in the first sentence by inserting "the Court of Claims" and by inserting "actions, cases, and." It was amended in the second sentence by substituting "terms" in place of "word," by inserting the phrase "and 'court'," and by adding "commissioners of the Court of Claims."

Subdivision (b) was amended by substituting "civil actions and proceedings" in place of "civil actions," and by substituting "criminal cases and proceedings" in place of "criminal proceedings."

Subdivision (c) was amended by substituting "rule" in place of "rules" and by changing the verb to the singular.

Subdivision (d) was amended by deleting "those" after "other than" and by substituting "Rule 104" in place of "Rule 104(a)."

Subdivision (e) was amended by substituting "prescribed" in place of "adopted" and by adding "pursuant to statutory authority." The form of the statutory citations was also changed.

Advisory Committee's Note

Subdivision (a). [This portion of the Advisory Committee's Note discussed the courts for which the various enabling acts granted the Supreme Court power to prescribe rules. These acts did not extend to the Court of Claims. Congressional enactment of the rules rendered the discussion moot.]

Report of House Committee on the Judiciary

Subdivision (a) as submitted to the Congress, in stating the courts and judges to which the Rules of Evidence apply, omitted the Court of Claims and commissioners of that Court. At the request of the Court of Claims, the Committee amended the Rule to include the Court and its commissioners within the purview of the Rules.

Advisory Committee's Note

Subdivision (b) is a combination of the language of the enabling acts, supra, with respect to the kinds of proceedings in which the making of rules is authorized. It is subject to the qualifications expressed in the subdivisions which follow.

Subdivision (c), singling out the rules of privilege for special treatment, is made necessary by the limited applicability of the remaining rules.

Subdivision (d). The rule is not intended as an expression as to when due process or other constitutional provisions may require an evidentiary hearing. Paragraph (1) restates, for convenience, the provisions of the second sentence of Rule 104(a), supra. See Advisory Committee's Note to that rule.

(2) While some states have statutory requirements that indictments be based on "legal evidence," and there is some case law to the effect that the

rules of evidence apply to grand jury proceedings, 1 Wigmore § 4(5), the Supreme Court has not accepted this view. In Costello v. United States, 350 U.S. 359, 76 S.Ct. 406, 100 L.Ed. 397 (1956), the Court refused to allow an indictment to be attacked, for either constitutional or policy reasons, on the ground that only hearsay evidence was presented.

> "It would run counter to the whole history of the grand jury institution, in which laymen conduct their inquiries unfettered by technical rules. Neither justice nor the concept of a fair trial requires such a change." Id. at 364.

The rule as drafted does not deal with the evidence required to support an indictment.

(3) The rule exempts preliminary examinations in criminal cases. Authority as to the applicability of the rules of evidence to preliminary examinations has been meagre and conflicting. Goldstein, The State and the Accused: Balance of Advantage in Criminal Procedure, 69 Yale L.J. 1149, 1168, n. 53 (1960); Comment, Preliminary Hearings on Indictable Offenses in Philadelphia, 106 U. of Pa.L.Rev. 589, 592–593 (1958). Hearsay testimony is, however, customarily received in such examinations. Thus in a Dyer Act case, for example, an affidavit may properly be used in a preliminary examination to prove ownership of the stolen vehicle, thus saving the victim of the crime the hardship of having to travel twice to a distant district for the sole purpose of testifying as to ownership. It is believed that the extent of the applicability of the Rules of Evidence to preliminary examinations should be appropriately dealt with by the Federal Rules of Criminal Procedure which regulate those proceedings.

Extradition and rendition proceedings are governed in detail by statute. 18 U.S.C. §§ 3181–3195. They are essentially administrative in character. Traditionally the rules of evidence have not applied. 1 Wigmore § 4(6). Extradition proceedings are accepted from the operation of the Rules of Criminal Procedure. Rule 54(b)(5) of Federal Rules of Criminal Procedure.

The rules of evidence have not been regarded as applicable to sentencing or probation proceedings, where great reliance is placed upon the presentence investigation and report. Rule 32(c) of the Federal Rules of Criminal Procedure requires a presentence investigation and report in every case unless the court otherwise directs. In Williams v. New York, 337 U.S. 241, 69 S.Ct. 1079, 93 L.Ed. 1337 (1949), in which the judge overruled a jury recommendation of life imprisonment and imposed a death sentence, the Court said that due process does not require confrontation or cross-examination in sentencing or passing on probation, and that the judge has broad discretion as to the sources and types of information relied upon. Compare the recommendation that the substance of all derogatory information be disclosed to the defendant, in A.B.A. Project on Minimum Standards for Criminal Justice, Sentencing Alternatives and Procedures § 4.4, Tentative Draft (1967, Sobeloff, Chm.). Williams was adhered to in Specht v. Patterson, 386 U.S. 605, 87 S.Ct. 1209, 18 L.Ed.2d 326 (1967), but not extended to a proceeding under the Colorado Sex Offenders Act, which was said to be a new charge leading in effect to punishment, more like the recidivist statutes where opportunity must be given to be heard on the habitual criminal issue.

Warrants for arrest, criminal summonses, and search warrants are issued upon complaint or affidavit showing probable cause. Rules 4(a) and 41(c) of the Federal Rules of Criminal Procedure. The nature of the proceedings makes application of the formal rules of evidence inappropriate and impracticable.

Criminal contempts are punishable summarily if the judge certifies that he saw or heard the contempt and that it was committed in the presence of the court. Rule 42(a) of the Federal Rules of Criminal Procedure. The circumstances which preclude application of the rules of evidence in this situation are not present, however, in other cases of criminal contempt.

Proceedings with respect to release on bail or otherwise do not call for application of the rules of evidence. The governing statute specifically provides:

> "Information stated in, or offered in connection with, any order entered pursuant to this section need not conform to the rules pertaining to the admissibility of evidence in a court of law." 18 U.S.C.A. § 3146(f).

This provision is consistent with the type of inquiry contemplated in A.B.A. Project on Minimum Standards for Criminal Justice, Standards Relating to Pretrial Release, § 4.5(b), (c), p. 16 (1968). The references to the weight of the evidence against the accused, in Rule 46(a) (1), (c) of the Federal Rules of Criminal Procedure and in 18 U.S.C.A. § 3146(b), as a factor to be considered, clearly do not have in view evidence introduced at a hearing under the rules of evidence.

The rule does not exempt habeas corpus proceedings. The Supreme Court held in Walker v. Johnston, 312 U.S. 275, 61 S.Ct. 574, 85 L.Ed. 830 (1941), that the practice of disposing of matters of fact on affidavit, which prevailed in some circuits, did not "satisfy the command of the statute that the judge shall proceed 'to determine the facts of the case, by hearing the testimony and arguments.' " This view accords with the emphasis in Townsend v. Sain, 372 U.S. 293, 83 S.Ct. 745, 9 L.Ed.2d 770 (1963), upon trial-type proceedings, id. 311, 372 U.S. 293 with demeanor evidence as a significant factor, id. 322, 372 U.S. 293 in applications by state prisoners aggrieved by unconstitutional detentions. Hence subdivision (e) applies the rules to habeas corpus proceedings to the extent not inconsistent with the statute.

Subdivision (e). In a substantial number of special proceedings, *ad hoc* evaluation has resulted in the promulgation of particularized evidentiary provisions, by Act of Congress or by rule adopted by the Supreme Court. Well adapted to the particular proceedings, though not apt candidates for inclusion in a set of general rules, they are left undisturbed. Otherwise, however, the rules of evidence are applicable to the proceedings enumerated in the subdivision.

Report of House Committee on the Judiciary

Subdivision (b) [e] was amended merely to substitute positive law citations for those which were not.

Rule 1102

Note by Federal Judicial Center

This rule was not included among those prescribed by the Supreme Court. The rule prescribed by the Court as 1102 now appears as 1103.

Rule 1103

Note by Federal Judicial Center

The rule enacted by the Congress is the rule prescribed by the Supreme Court as Rule 1102 without change.

APPENDIX C

APPENDIX OF DELETED AND SUPERSEDED MATERIALS WITH NOTES

[Rules originally prescribed by the Supreme Court but deleted from the rules enacted by Congress in 1975]

Table of Rules

Rule 105
SUMMING UP AND COMMENT BY JUDGE

[Not enacted.]

After the close of the evidence and arguments of counsel, the judge may fairly and impartially sum up the evidence and comment to the jury upon the weight of the evidence and the credibility of the witnesses, if he also instructs the jury that they are to determine for themselves the weight of the evidence and the credit to be given to the witnesses and that they are not bound by the judge's summation or comment.

Note by Federal Judicial Center

The foregoing rule prescribed by the Supreme Court was deleted from the rules enacted by the Congress.

Advisory Committee's Note

The rule states the present rule in the federal courts. Capital Traction Co. v. Hof, 174 U.S. 1, 13–14, 19 S.Ct. 580, 43 L.Ed. 873 (1899). The judge must, of course, confine his remarks to what is disclosed by the evidence. He cannot convey to the jury his purely personal reaction to credibility or to the merits of the case; he can be neither argumentative nor an advocate. Quercia v. United States, 289 U.S. 466, 469, 53 S.Ct. 698, 77 L.Ed. 1321 (1933); Billeci v. United States, 87 U.S.App.D.C. 274, 184 F.2d 394, 402, 24 A.L.R.2d 881 (1950). For further discussion see the series of articles by Wright, The Invasion of Jury: Temperature of the War, 27 Temp.L.Q. 137 (1953), Instructions to the Jury: Summary Without Comment, 1954 Wash.U.L.Q. 177, Adequacy of Instructions to the Jury, 53 Mich.L.Rev. 505, 813 (1955); A.L.I. Model Code of Evidence, Comment to Rule 8; Maguire, Weinstein, et al., Cases and Materials on Evidence 737–740 (5th ed. 1965); Vanderbilt, Minimum Standards of Judicial Administration 224–229 (1949).

Report of the House Committee on the Judiciary

Rule 105 as submitted by the Supreme Court concerned the issue of summing up and comment by the judge. It provided that after the close of the evidence and the arguments of counsel, the presiding judge could fairly and impartially sum up the evidence and comment to the jury upon its weight and the credibility of the witnesses, if he also instructed the jury that it was not bound thereby and must make its own determination of those matters. The Committee recognized that the Rule as submitted is consistent with long standing and current federal practice. However, the aspect of the Rule dealing with the authority of a judge to comment on the weight of the evidence and the credibility of witnesses—an authority not granted to judges in most State courts—was highly controversial. After much debate the Committee determined to delete the entire Rule, intending that its action be understood as reflecting no conclusion as to the merits of the proposed Rule and that the subject should be left for separate consideration at another time.

Report of Senate Committee on the Judiciary

This rule as submitted by the Supreme Court permitted the judge to sum up and comment on the evidence. The House struck the rule.

The committee accepts the House action with the understanding that the present Federal practice, taken from the common law, of the trial judge's discretionary authority to comment on and summarize the evidence is left undisturbed.

Rule 301
PRESUMPTIONS IN GENERAL IN CIVIL ACTIONS AND PROCEEDINGS

[As passed by House of Representatives]

In all civil actions and proceedings not otherwise provided for by Act of Congress or by these rules, a presumption imposes on the party against whom it is directed the burden of going forward with the evidence, and, even though met with contradicting evidence, a presumption is sufficient evidence of the fact presumed, to be considered by the trier of the facts.

Note by Federal Judicial Center

Neither of the above versions of Rule 301 was enacted.

Advisory Committee's Note

This rule governs presumptions generally. See Rule 302 for presumptions controlled by state law and Rule 303 for those against an accused in a criminal case.

Presumptions governed by this rule are given the effect of placing upon the opposing party the burden of establishing the nonexistence of the presumed fact, once the party invoking the presumption establishes the basic facts giving rise to it. The same considerations of fairness, policy, and probability which dictate the allocation of the burden of the various elements of a case as between the prima facie case of a plaintiff and affirmative defenses also underlie the creation of presumptions. These considerations are not satisfied by giving a lesser effect to presumptions. Morgan and Maguire, Looking Backward and Forward at Evidence, 50 Harv.L.Rev. 909, 913 (1937); Morgan, Instructing the Jury upon Presumptions and Burden of Proof, 47 Harv.L.Rev. 59, 82 (1933); Cleary, Presuming and Pleading: An Essay on Juristic Immaturity, 12 Stan.L.Rev. 5 (1959).

The so-called "bursting bubble" theory, under which a presumption vanishes upon the introduction of evidence which would support a finding of the nonexistence of the presumed fact, even though not believed, is rejected as according presumptions too "slight and evanescent" an effect. Morgan and Maguire, supra, at p. 913.

In the opinion of the Advisory Committee, no constitutional infirmity attends this view of presumptions. In Mobile, J. & K. C. R. Co. v. Turnipseed, 219 U.S. 35, 31 S.Ct. 136, 55 L.Ed. 78 (1910), the Court upheld a Mississippi statute which provided that in actions against railroads proof of injury inflicted by the running of trains should be prima facie evidence of negligence by the railroad. The injury in the case had resulted from a derailment. The opinion made the points (1) that the only effect of the statute was to impose on the railroad the duty of producing some evidence to the contrary, (2) that an inference may be supplied by law if there is a rational connection between the fact proved and the fact presumed, as long as the opposite party is not precluded from presenting his evidence to the contrary, and (3) that considerations of public policy arising from the character of the business justified the application in question. Nineteen years later, in Western & Atlantic R. Co. v. Henderson, 279 U.S. 639, 49 S.Ct. 445, 73 L.Ed. 884 (1929), the Court overturned a Georgia statute making railroads liable for damages done by trains, unless the railroad made it appear that reasonable care had been used, the presumption being against the railroad.

The declaration alleged the death of plaintiff's husband from a grade crossing collision, due to specified acts of negligence by defendant. The jury were instructed that proof of the injury raised a presumption of negligence; the burden shifted to the railroad to prove ordinary care; and unless it did so, they should find for plaintiff. The instruction was held erroneous in an opinion stating (1) that there was no rational connection between the mere fact of collision and negligence on the part of anyone, and (2) that the statute was different from that in *Turnipseed* in imposing a burden upon the railroad. The reader is left in a state of some confusion. Is the difference between a derailment and a grade crossing collision of no significance? Would the *Turnipseed* presumption have been bad if it had imposed a burden of persuasion on defendant, although that would in nowise have impaired its "rational connection"? If *Henderson* forbids imposing a burden of persuasion on defendants, what happens to affirmative defenses?

Two factors serve to explain *Henderson*. The first was that it was common ground that negligence was indispensable to liability. Plaintiff thought so, drafted her complaint accordingly, and relied upon the presumption. But how in logic could the same presumption establish her alternative grounds of negligence that the engineer was so blind he could not see decedent's truck and that he failed to stop after he saw it? Second, take away the basic assumption of no liability without fault, as *Turnipseed* intimated might be done ("considerations of public policy arising out of the character of the business"), and the structure of the decision in *Henderson* fails. No question of logic would have arisen if the statute had simply said: a prima facie case of liability is made by proof of injury by a train; lack of negligence is an affirmative defense, to be pleaded and proved as other affirmative defenses. The problem would be one of economic due process only. While it seems likely that the Supreme Court of 1929 would have voted that due process was denied, that result today would be unlikely. See, for example, the shift in the direction of absolute liability in the consumer cases. Prosser, The Assault upon the Citadel (Strict Liability to the Consumer), 69 Yale L.J. 1099 (1960).

Any doubt as to the constitutional permissibility of a presumption imposing a burden of persuasion of the nonexistence of the presumed fact in civil cases is laid at rest by Dick v. New York Life Ins. Co., 359 U.S. 437, 79 S.Ct. 921, 3 L.Ed.2d 935 (1959). The Court unhesitatingly applied the North Dakota rule that the presumption against suicide imposed on defendant the burden of proving that the death of insured, under an accidental death clause, was due to suicide.

"Proof of coverage and of death by gunshot wound shifts the burden to the insurer to establish that the death of the insured was due to his suicide." 359 U.S. at 443, 79 S.Ct. at 925.

"In a case like this one, North Dakota presumes that death was accidental and places on the insurer the burden of proving that death resulted from suicide." Id. at 446, 79 S.Ct. at 927.

The rational connection requirement survives in criminal cases, Tot v. United States, 319 U.S. 463, 63 S.Ct. 1241, 87 L.Ed. 1519 (1943), because the Court has been unwilling to extend into that area the greater-includes-the-lesser theory of Ferry v. Ramsey, 277 U.S. 88, 48 S.Ct. 443, 72 L.Ed. 796 (1928). In that case the Court sustained a Kansas statute under which bank directors were personally liable for deposits made with their assent and with knowledge of insolvency, and the fact of insolvency was prima facie evidence of assent and knowledge of insolvency. Mr. Justice Holmes pointed out that the state legislature could have made the directors personally liable to depositors in every case. Since the statute imposed a less stringent liability, "the thing to be considered is the result reached, not the possibly inartificial or clumsy way of reaching it." Id. at 94, 48 S.Ct. at 444. Mr. Justice Sutherland dissented: though the state could have created an absolute liability, it did not purport to do so; a rational connection was necessary, but lacking, between the liability created and the prima facie evidence of it; the result might be different if the basis of the presumption were being open for business.

The Sutherland view has prevailed in criminal cases by virtue of the higher standard of notice there required. The fiction that everyone is presumed to know the law is applied to the substantive law of crimes as an alternative to complete unenforceability. But the need does not extend to criminal evidence and procedure, and the fiction does not encompass them. "Rational connection" is not fictional or artificial, and so it is reasonable to suppose that Gainey should have known that his presence at the site of an illicit still could convict him of being connected with (carrying on) the business, United States v. Gainey, 380 U.S. 63, 85 S.Ct. 754, 13 L.Ed.2d 658 (1965), but not that Romano should have known that his presence at a still could convict him of possessing it, United States v. Romano, 382 U.S. 136, 86 S.Ct. 279, 15 L.Ed.2d 210 (1965).

In his dissent in Gainey, Mr. Justice Black put it more artistically:

"It might be argued, although the Court does not so argue or hold, that Congress if it wished could make presence at a still a crime in itself, and so Congress should be free to create crimes which are called 'possession' and 'carrying on an illegal distillery business' but which are defined in such a way that unexplained presence is sufficient and indisputable evidence in all cases to support conviction for those offenses. See Ferry v. Ramsey, 277 U.S. 88, 48 S.Ct. 443, 72 L.Ed. 796. Assuming for the sake of argument that Congress could make unexplained presence a criminal act, and ignoring also the refusal of this Court in other cases to uphold a statutory presumption on such a theory, see Heiner v. Donnan, 285 U.S. 312, 52 S.Ct. 358, 76 L.Ed. 772, there is no indication here that Congress intended to adopt such a misleading method of draftsmanship, nor in my judgment could the statutory provisions if so construed escape condemnation for vagueness, under the principles applied in Lanzetta v. New Jersey, 306 U.S. 451, 59 S.Ct. 618, 83 L.Ed. 888, and many other cases." 380 U.S. at 84, n. 12, 85 S.Ct. at 766.

And the majority opinion in *Romano* agreed with him:

"It may be, of course, that Congress has the power to make presence at an illegal still a punishable crime, but we find no clear indication that it intended to so exercise this power. The crime remains possession, not presence, and with all due deference to the judgment of Congress, the former may not constitutionally be inferred from the latter." 382 U.S. at 144, 86 S.Ct. at 284.

The rule does not spell out the procedural aspects of its application. Questions as to when the evidence warrants submission of a presumption and what instructions are proper under varying states of fact are believed to present no particular difficulties.

Report of House Committee on the Judiciary

Rule 301 as submitted by the Supreme Court provided that in all cases a presumption imposes on the party against whom it is directed the burden of proving that the nonexistence of the presumed fact is more probable than its existence. The Committee limited the scope of Rule 301 to "civil actions and proceedings" to effectuate its decision not to deal with the question of presumptions in criminal cases. (See note on Rule 303 in discussion of Rules deleted). With respect to the weight to be given a presumption in a civil case, the Committee agreed with the judgment implicit in the Court's version that the so-called "bursting bubble" theory of presumptions, whereby a presumption vanishes upon the appearance of any contradicting evidence by the other party, gives to presumptions too slight an effect. On the other hand, the Committee believed that the Rule proposed by the Court, whereby a presumption permanently alters the burden of persuasion, no matter how much contradicting evidence is introduced—a view shared by only a few courts—lends too great a force to presumptions. Accordingly, the Committee amended the Rule to adopt an intermediate position under which a presumption does not vanish upon the introduction of contradicting evidence, and does not change the burden of persuasion; instead it is merey deemed sufficient evidence of the fact presumed, to be considered by the jury or other finder of fact.

Rule 303
PRESUMPTIONS IN CRIMINAL CASES

[Not enacted.]

(a) Scope. Except as otherwise provided by Act of Congress, in criminal cases, presumptions against an accused, recognized at common law or created by statute, including statutory provisions that certain facts are prima facie evidence of other facts or of guilt, are governed by this rule.

(b) Submission to jury. The judge is not authorized to direct the jury to find a presumed fact against the accused. When the presumed fact establishes guilt or is an element of the offense or negatives a defense, the judge may submit the question of guilt or of the existence of the presumed fact to the jury, if, but only if, a reasonable juror on the evidence as a whole, including the evidence of the basic facts, could find guilt or the presumed fact beyond a reasonable doubt. When the presumed fact has a lesser effect, its existence may be submitted to the jury if the basic facts are supported by substantial evidence, or are otherwise established, unless the evidence as a whole negatives the existence of the presumed fact.

(c) Instructing the jury. Whenever the existence of a presumed fact against the accused is submitted to the jury, the judge shall give an instruction that the law declares that the jury may regard the basic facts as sufficient evidence of the presumed fact but does not require it to do so. In addition, if the presumed fact establishes guilt or is an element of the offense or negatives a defense, the judge shall instruct the jury that its existence must, on all the evidence, be proved beyond a reasonable doubt.

Note by Federal Judicial Center

The foregoing rule prescribed by the Supreme Court was deleted from the rules enacted by the Congress.

Advisory Committee's Note

Subdivision (a). This rule is based largely upon A.L.I. Model Penal Code § 1.12(5) P.O.D. (1962) and United States v. Gainey, 380 U.S. 63, 85 S.Ct. 754, 13 L.Ed.2d 658 (1965). While the rule, unlike the Model Penal Code provision, spells out the effect of common law presumptions as well as those created by statute, cases involving the later are no doubt of more frequent occurrence. Congress has enacted numerous provisions to lessen the burden of the prosecution, principally though not exclusively in the fields of narcotics control and taxation of liquor. Occasionally, in the pattern of the usual common law treatment of such matters as insanity, they take the form of assigning to the defense the responsibility of raising specified matters as affirmative defenses, which are not within the scope of these rules. See Comment, A.L.I. Model Penal Code § 1.13, T.D. No. 4 (1955). In other instances they assume a variety of forms which are the concern of this rule. The provision may be that proof of a specified fact (possession or presence) is sufficient to authorize conviction. 26 U.S.C. § 4704(a), unlawful to buy or sell opium except from original stamped package—absence of stamps from package prima facie evidence of violation by person in possession; 26 U.S.C. § 4724(c), unlawful for person who has not registered and paid special tax to possess narcotics—possession presumptive evidence of violation. Sometimes the qualification is added, "unless the defendant explains the possession [presence] to the satisfaction of the jury." 18 U.S.C. § 545, possession of unlawfully imported goods sufficient for conviction of smuggling, unless explained; 21 U.S.C. § 174, possession sufficient for conviction of buying or selling narcotics known to have been imported unlawfully, unless explained. See also 26 U.S.C. § 5601(a)(1), (a)(4), (a)(8), (b)(1), (b)(2), (b)(4), relating to distilling operations. Another somewhat different pattern makes possession evidence of a particular element of the crime. 21 U.S.C. § 176b, crime to furnish unlawfully imported heroin to juveniles—possession sufficient proof of unlawful importation, unless explained; 50 U.S.C.A.App. § 462(b), unlawful to possess draft card not lawfully issued to holder, with intent to use for purposes of false identification—possession sufficient evidence of intent, unless explained. See also 15 U.S.C. § 902(f), (i).

Differences between the permissible operation of presumptions against the accused in criminal cases and in other situations prevent the formulation of a comprehensive definition of the term "presumption," and none is attempted. Nor do these rules purport to deal with problems of the validity of presumptions except insofar as they may be found reflected in the formulation of permissible procedures.

The presumption of innocence is outside the scope of the rule and unaffected by it.

Subdivisions (b) and (c). It is axiomatic that a verdict cannot be directed against the accused in a criminal case, 9 Wigmore § 2495, p. 312, with the corollary that the judge is without authority to direct the jury to find against the accused as to any element of the crime, A.L.I. Model Penal Code § 1.12(1) P.O.D. (1962). Although arguably the judge could direct the jury to find against the accused as to a lesser fact, the tradition is against it, and this rule makes no use of presumptions to remove any matters from final determination by the jury.

The only distinction made among presumptions under this rule is with respect to the measure of proof required in order to justify submission to the jury. If the effect of the presumption is to establish guilt or an element of the crime or to negative a defense, the measure of proof is the one widely accepted by the Courts of Appeals as the standard for measuring the sufficiency of the evidence in passing on motions for directed verdict (now judgment of acquittal): an acquittal should be directed when reasonable jurymen must have a reasonable doubt. Curley v. United States, 81 U.S.App.D.C. 389, 160 F.2d 229 (1947), cert. denied 331 U.S. 837; United States v. Honeycutt, 311 F.2d 660 (4th Cir.1962); Stephens v. United States, 354 F.2d 999 (5th Cir.1965); Lambert v. United States, 261 F.2d 799 (5th Cir.1958); United States v. Leggett, 292 F.2d 423 (6th Cir.1961); Cape v. United States, 283 F.2d 430 (9th Cir.1960); Cartwright v. United States, 335 F.2d 919 (10th Cir.1964). Cf. United States v. Gonzales Castro, 228 F.2d 807 (2d Cir.1956); United States v. Masiello, 235 F.2d 279 (2d Cir.1956), cert. denied Stickel v. United States, 352 U.S. 882, 77 S.Ct. 100, 1 L.Ed.2d 79; United States v. Feinberg, 140 F.2d 592 (2d Cir.1944). But cf. United States v. Arcuri, 282 F.Supp. 347 (E.D.N.Y.1968), aff'd. 405 F.2d 691, cert. denied 395 U.S. 913; United States v. Melillo, 275 F.Supp. 314 (E.D.N.Y.1967). If the presumption operates upon a lesser aspect of the case than the issue of guilt itself or an element of the crime or negativing a defense, the required measure of proof is the less stringent one of substantial evidence, consistently with the attitude usually taken with respect to particular items of evidence. 9 Wigmore § 2497, p. 324.

The treatment of presumptions in the rule is consistent with United States v. Gainey, 380 U.S. 63, 85 S.Ct. 754, 13 L.Ed.2d 658 (1965), where the matter was considered in depth. After sustaining the validity of the provision of 26 U.S.C. § 5601(b)(2) that presence at the site is sufficient to convict of the offense of carrying on the business of distiller without giving bond, unless the presence is explained to the satisfaction of the jury, the Court turned to procedural considerations and reached several conclusions. The power of the judge to withdraw a case from the jury for insufficiency of evidence is left unimpaired; he may submit the case on the basis of presence alone, but he is not required to do so. Nor is he precluded from rendering judgment notwithstanding the verdict. It is proper to tell the jury about the "statutory inference," if they are told it is not conclusive. The jury may still acquit, even if it finds defendant present and his presence is unexplained. [Compare the mandatory character of the instruction condemned in Bollenbach v. United States, 326 U.S. 607, 66 S.Ct. 402, 90 L.Ed. 350 (1946).] To avoid any implication that the statutory language relative to explanation be taken as directing attention to failure of the accused to testify, the better practice, said the Court, would be to instruct the jury that they may draw the inference unless the evidence provides a satisfactory explanation of defendant's presence, omitting any explicit reference to the statute.

The Final Report of the National Commission on Reform of Federal Criminal Laws § 103(4) and (5) (1971) contains a careful formulation of the consequences of a statutory presumption with an alternative formulation set forth in the Comment thereto, and also of the effect of a prima facie case. In the criminal code there proposed, the terms "presumption" and "prima facie case" are used with precision and with reference to these meanings. In the federal criminal law as it stands today, these terms are not used with precision. Moreover, common law presumptions continue. Hence it is believed that the rule here proposed is better adapted to the present situation until such time as the Congress enacts legislation covering the subject, which the rule takes into account. If the subject of common law presumptions is not covered by legislation, the need for the rule in that regard will continue.

Report of House Committee on the Judiciary

Rule 303, as submitted by the Supreme Court was directed to the issues of when, in criminal cases, a court may submit a presumption to a jury and the type of instruction it should give. The Committee deleted this Rule since the subject of presumptions in criminal cases is addressed in detail in bills now pending before the Committee to revise the federal criminal code. The Committee determined to consider this question in the course of its study of these proposals.

Rule 406
HABIT; ROUTINE PRACTICE

[Subdivision (b) not enacted.]

(b) Method of proof. Habit or routine practice may be proved by testimony in the form of an opinion or by specific instances of conduct sufficient in number to warrant a finding that the habit existed or that the practice was routine.

Advisory Committee's Note

* * *

Subdivision (b). Permissible methods of proving habit or routine conduct include opinion and specific instances sufficient in number to warrant a finding that the habit or routine practice in fact existed. Opinion evidence must be "rationally based on the perception of the witness" and helpful, under the provisions of Rule 701. Proof by specific instances may be controlled by the overriding provisions of Rule 403 for exclusion on grounds of prejudice, confusion, misleading the jury, or waste of time. Thus the illustrations following A.L.I. Model Code of Evidence Rule 307 suggests the possibility of admitting testimony by W that on numerous occasions he had been with X when X crossed a railroad track and that on each occasion X had first stopped and looked in both directions, but discretion to exclude offers of 10 witnesses, each testifying to a different occasion.

Similar provisions for proof by opinion or specific instances are found in Uniform Rule 50 and Kansas Code of Civil Procedure § 60–450. New Jersey Rule 50 provides for proof by specific instances but is silent as to opinion. The California Evidence Code is silent as to methods of proving habit, presumably proceeding on the theory that any method is relevant and all relevant evidence is admissible unless otherwise provided. Tentative Recommendation and a Study Relating to the Uniform Rules of Evidence (Art. VI. Extrinsic Policies Affecting Admissibility), Rep., Rec. & Study, Cal. Law Rev. Comm'n 620 (1964).

Report of House Committee on the Judiciary

[Reasons for deleting subdivision (b) are stated in the report, which is set forth in the main text under rule 406, supra.]

ARTICLE V. PRIVILEGES

Note by Federal Judicial Center

The 13 rules numbered 501–513 prescribed by the Supreme Court as Article V were replaced by a single rule 501 in the rules enacted by the Congress. The rules are included here for informational purposes only.

Rule 501
PRIVILEGES RECOGNIZED ONLY AS PROVIDED

[Not enacted.]

Except as otherwise required by the Constitution of the United States or provided by Act of Congress, and except as provided in these rules or in other rules adopted by the Supreme Court, no person has a privilege to:

(1) Refuse to be a witness; or

(2) Refuse to disclose any matter; or

(3) Refuse to produce any object or writing; or

(4) Prevent another from being a witness or disclosing any matter or producing any object or writing.

Advisory Committee's Note

No attempt is made in these rules to incorporate the constitutional provisions which relate to the admission and exclusion of evidence, whether denominated as privileges or not. The grand design of these provisions does not readily lend itself to codification. The final reference must be the provisions themselves and the decisions construing them. Nor is formulating a rule an appropriate means of settling unresolved constitutional questions.

Similarly, privileges created by act of Congress are not within the scope of these rules. These privileges do not assume the form of broad principles; they are the product of resolving particular problems in particular terms. Among them are included such provisions as 13 U.S.C. § 9, generally prohibiting official disclosure of census information and conferring a privileged status on retained copies of census reports; 42 U.S.C. § 2000e–5(a), making inadmissible in evidence anything said or done during Equal Employment Opportunity conciliation proceeding; 42 U.S.C. § 2240, making required reports of incidents by nuclear facility licensees inadmissible in actions for damages; 45 U.S.C. §§ 33, 41, similarly as to reports of accidents by railroads; 49 U.S.C. § 1441(e), declaring C.A.B. accident investigation reports inadmissible in actions for damages. The rule leaves them undisturbed.

The reference to other rules adopted by the Supreme Court makes clear that provisions relating to privilege in those rules will continue in operation. See, for example, the "work product" immunity against discovery spelled out under the Rules of Civil Procedure in Hickman v. Taylor, 329 U.S. 495, 67 S.Ct. 385, 91 L.Ed. 451 (1947), now formalized in revised Rule 26(b) (3) of the Rules of Civil Procedure, and the secrecy of grand jury proceedings provided by Criminal Rule 6.

With respect to privileges created by state law, these rules in some instances grant them greater status than has heretofore been the case by according them recognition in federal criminal proceedings, bankruptcy, and federal question litigation. See Rules 502 and 510. There is, however, no provision generally adopting state-created privileges.

In federal criminal prosecutions the primacy of federal law as to both substance and procedure has been undoubted. See, for example, United States v. Krol, 374 F.2d 776 (7th Cir.1967), sustaining the admission in a federal prosecution of evidence obtained by electronic eavesdropping, despite a state statute declaring the use of these devices unlawful and evidence obtained therefrom inadmissible. This primacy includes matters of privilege. As stated in 4 Barron, Federal Practice and Procedure § 2151, p. 175 (1951):

"The determination of the question whether a matter is privileged is governed by federal decisions and the state statutes or rules of evidence have no application."

In Funk v. United States, 290 U.S. 371, 54 S.Ct. 212, 78 L.Ed. 369 (1933), the Court had considered the competency of a wife to testify for her husband and concluded that, absent congressional action or direction, the federal courts were to follow the common law as they saw it "in accordance with present day standards of wisdom and justice." And in Wolfle v. United States, 291 U.S. 7, 54 S.Ct. 279, 78 L.Ed. 617 (1934), the Court said with respect to the standard appropriate in determining a claim of privilege for an alleged confidential communication between spouses in a federal criminal prosecution:

"So our decision here, in the absence of Congressional legislation on the subject, is to be controlled by common law principles, not by local statute." Id., 13, 54 S.Ct. at 280.

On the basis of *Funk* and *Wolfle,* the Advisory Committee on Rules of Criminal Procedure formulated Rule 26, which was adopted by the Court. The pertinent part of the rule provided:

"The * * * privileges of witnesses shall be governed, except when an act of Congress or these rules otherwise provide, by the principles of the common law as they may be interpreted * * * in the light of reason and experience."

As regards bankruptcy, section 21(a) of the Bankruptcy Act provides for examination of the bankrupt and his spouse concerning the acts, conduct, or property of the bankrupt. The Act limits examination of the spouse to business transacted by her or to which she is a party but provides "That the spouse may be so examined, any law of the United States or of any State to the contrary notwithstanding." 11 U.S.C. § 44(a). The effect of the quoted language is clearly to override any conflicting state rule of incompetency or privilege against spousal testimony. A fair reading would also indicate an overriding of any contrary state rule of privileged confidential spousal communications. Its validity has never been questioned and seems most unlikely to be. As to other privileges, the suggestion has been made that state law applies, though with little citation of authority, 2 Moore's Collier on Bankruptcy ¶ 21.13, p. 297 (14th ed. 1961). This position seems to be contrary to the expression of the Court in McCarthy v. Arndstein, 266 U.S. 34, 39, 45 S.Ct. 16, 69 L.Ed. 158 (1924), which speaks in the pattern of Rule 26 of the Federal Rules of Criminal Procedure:

"There is no provision [in the Bankruptcy Act] prescribing the rules by which the examination is to be governed. These are, impliedly, the general rules governing the admissibility of evidence and the competency and compellability of witnesses."

With respect to federal question litigation, the supremacy of federal law may be less clear, yet indications that state privileges are inapplicable preponderate in the circuits. In re Albert Lindley Lee Memorial Hospital, 209 F.2d 122 (2d Cir.1953), cert. denied Cincotta v. United States, 347 U.S. 960, 74 S.Ct. 709, 98 L.Ed. 1104; Colton v. United States, 306 F.2d 633 (2d Cir.1962); Falsone v. United States, 205 F.2d 734 (5th Cir.1953); Fraser v. United States, 145 F.2d 139 (6th Cir.1944), cert. denied 324 U.S. 849, 65 S.Ct. 684, 89 L.Ed. 1409; United States v. Brunner, 200 F.2d 276 (6th Cir.1952). Contra, Baird v. Koerner, 279 F.2d 623 (9th Cir.1960). Additional decisions of district courts are collected in Annot., 95 A.L.R.2d 320, 336. While a number of the cases arise from administrative income tax investigations, they nevertheless support the broad proposition of the inapplicability of state privileges in federal proceedings.

In view of these considerations, it is apparent that, to the extent that they accord state privileges standing in federal criminal cases, bankruptcy, and federal question cases, the rules go beyond what previously has been thought necessary or proper.

On the other hand, in diversity cases, or perhaps more accurately cases in which state law furnishes the rule of decision, the rules avoid giving state privileges the affect which substantial authority has thought necessary and proper. Regardless of what might once have been thought to be the command of Erie R. Co. v. Tompkins, 304 U.S. 64, 58 S.Ct. 817, 82 L.Ed. 1188 (1938), as to observance of state created privileges in diversity cases, Hanna v. Plumer, 380 U.S. 460, 85 S.Ct. 1136, 14 L.Ed.2d 8 (1965), is believed to locate the problem in the area of choice rather than necessity. Wright, Procedural Reform: Its Limitations and Its Future, 1 Ga.L.Rev. 563, 572–573 (1967). Contra, Republic Gear Co. v. Borg-Warner Corp., 381 F.2d 551, 555, n. 2 (2d Cir.1967), and see authorities there cited. Hence all significant policy factors need to be considered in order that the choice may be a wise one.

The arguments advanced in favor of recognizing state privileges are: a state privilege is an essential characteristic of a relationship or status created by state law and thus is substantive in the *Erie* sense; state policy ought not to be frustrated by the accident of diversity; the allowance or denial of a privilege is so likely to affect the outcome of litigation as to encourage forum selection on that basis, not a proper function of diversity jurisdiction. There are persuasive answers to these arguments.

(1) As to the question of "substance," it is true that a privilege commonly represents an aspect of a relationship created and defined by a State. For example, a confidential communications privilege is often an incident of marriage. However, in litigation involving the relationship itself, the privilege is not ordinarily one of the issues. In fact, statutes frequently make the communication privilege inapplicable in cases of divorce. McCormick § 88, p. 177. The same is true with respect to the attorney-client privilege when the parties to the relationship have a falling out. The reality of the matter is that privilege is called into operation, not when the relation giving rise to the privilege is being litigated, but when the litigation involves something substantively devoid of relation to the privilege. The appearance of privilege in the case is quite by accident, and its effect is to block off the tribunal from a source of information. Thus its real impact is on the method of proof in the case, and in comparison any substantive aspect appears tenuous.

(2) By most standards, criminal prosecutions are attended by more serious consequences than civil litigation, and it must be evident that the criminal area has the greatest sensitivity where privilege is concerned. Nevertheless, as previously noted, state privileges traditionally have given way in federal criminal prosecutions. If a privilege is denied in the area of greatest sensitivity, it tends to become illusory as a significant aspect of the relationship out of which it arises. For example, in a state having by statute an accountant's privilege, only the most imperceptible added force would be given the privilege by putting the accountant in a position to assure his client that, while he could not block disclosure in a federal criminal prosecution, he could do so in diversity cases as well as in state court proceedings. Thus viewed, state interest in privilege appears less substantial than at first glance might seem to be the case.

Moreover, federal interest is not lacking. It can scarcely be contended that once diversity is invoked the federal government no longer has a legitimate concern in the quality of judicial administration conducted under its aegis. The demise of conformity and the adoption of the Federal Rules of Civil Procedure stand as witness to the contrary.

(3) A large measure of forum shopping is recognized as legitimate in the American judicial system. Subject to the limitations of jurisdiction and the relatively modest controls imposed by venue provisions and the doctrine of forum non conveniens, plaintiffs are allowed in general a free choice of forum. Diversity jurisdiction has as its basic purpose the giving of a choice, not only to plaintiffs but, in removal situations, also to defendants. In principle, the basis of the choice is the supposed need to escape from local prejudice. If the choice were tightly confined to that basis, then complete conformity to local procedure as well as substantive law would be required. This, of course, is not the case, and the choice may in fact be influenced by a wide range of factors. As Dean Ladd has pointed out, a litigant

may select the federal court "because of the federal procedural rules, the liberal discovery provisions, the quality of jurors expected in the federal court, the respect held for federal judges, the control of federal judges over a trial, the summation and comment upon the weight of evidence by the judge, or the authority to grant a new trial if the judge regards the verdict against the weight of the evidence." Ladd, Privileges, 1969 Ariz.St.L.J. 555, 564. Present Rule 43(a) of the Civil Rules specifies a broader range of admissibility in federal than in state courts and makes no exception for diversity cases. Note should also be taken that Rule 26(b) (2) of the Rules of Civil Procedure, as revised, allows discovery to be had of liability insurance, without regard to local state law upon the subject.

When attention is directed to the practical dimensions of the problem, they are found not to be great. The privileges affected are few in number. Most states provide a physician-patient privilege; the proposed rules limit the privilege to a psychotherapist-patient relationship. See Advisory Committee's Note to Rule 504. The area of marital privilege under the proposed rules is narrower than in most states. See Rule 505. Some states recognize privileges for journalists and accountants; the proposed rules do not.

Physician-patient is the most widely recognized privilege not found in the proposed rules. As a practical matter it was largely eliminated in diversity cases when Rule 35 of the Rules of Civil Procedure became effective in 1938. Under that rule, a party physically examined pursuant to court order, by requesting and obtaining a copy of the report or by taking the deposition of the examiner, waives any privilege regarding the testimony of every other person who has examined him in respect of the same condition. While waiver may be avoided by neither requesting the report nor taking the examiner's deposition, the price is one which most litigant-patients are probably not prepared to pay.

Rule 502
REQUIRED REPORTS PRIVILEGED BY STATUTE

[Not enacted.]

A person, corporation, association, or other organization or entity, either public or private, making a return or report required by law to be made has a privilege to refuse to disclose and to prevent any other person from disclosing the return or report, if the law requiring it to be made so provides. A public officer or agency to whom a return or report is required by law to be made has a privilege to refuse to disclose the return or report if the law requiring it to be made so provides. No privilege exists under this rule in actions involving perjury, false statements, fraud in the return or report, or other failure to comply with the law in question.

Advisory Committee's Note

Statutes which require the making of returns or reports sometimes confer on the reporting party a privilege against disclosure, commonly coupled with a prohibition against disclosure by the officer to whom the report is made. Some of the federal statutes of this kind are mentioned in the Advisory Committee's Note to Rule 501, supra. See also the Note to Rule 402, supra. A provision against disclosure may be included in a statute for a variety of reasons, the chief of which are probably assuring the validity of the statute against claims of self-incrimination, honoring the privilege against self-incrimination, and encouraging the furnishing of the required information by assuring privacy.

These statutes, both state and federal, may generally be assumed to embody policies of significant dimension. Rule 501 insulates the federal provisions against disturbance by these rules; the present rule reiterates a result commonly specified in federal statutes and extends its application to state statutes of similar character. Illustrations of the kinds of returns and reports contemplated by the rule appear in the cases, in which a reluctance to compel disclosure is manifested. In re Reid, 155 F. 933 (E.D.Mich.1906), assessor not compelled to produce bankrupt's property tax return in view of statute forbidding disclosure; In re Valecia Condensed Milk Co., 240 F. 310 (7th Cir.1917), secretary of state tax commission not compelled to produce bankrupt's income tax returns in violation of statute; Herman Bros. Pet Supply, Inc. v. N.L.R.B., 360 F.2d 176 (6th Cir.1966), subpoena denied for production of reports to state employment security commission prohibited by statute, in proceeding for back wages. And see the discussion of motor vehicle accident reports in Krizak v. W.C. Brooks & Sons, Inc., 320 F.2d 37, 42–43 (4th Cir.1963). Cf. In re Hines, 69 F.2d 52 (2d Cir.1934).

Rule 503
LAWYER–CLIENT PRIVILEGE

[Not enacted.]

(a) Definitions. As used in this rule:

(1) A "client" is a person, public officer, or corporation, association, or other organization or entity, either public or private, who is rendered professional legal services by a lawyer, or who consults a lawyer with a view to obtaining professional legal services from him.

(2) A "lawyer" is a person authorized, or reasonably believed by the client to be authorized, to practice law in any state or nation.

(3) A "representative of the lawyer" is one employed to assist the lawyer in the rendition of professional legal services.

(4) A communication is "confidential" if not intended to be disclosed to third persons other than those to whom disclosure is in furtherance of the rendition of professional legal services to the client or those reasonably necessary for the transmission of the communication.

(b) General rule of privilege. A client has a privilege to refuse to disclose and to prevent any other person from disclosing confidential communications made for the purpose of facilitating the rendition of professional legal services to the client, (1) between himself or his representative and his lawyer or his lawyer's representative, or (2) between his lawyer and the lawyer's representative, or (3) by him or his lawyer to a lawyer representing another in a matter of common interest, or (4) between representatives of the client or between the client and a representative of the client, or (5) between lawyers representing the client.

(c) Who may claim the privilege. The privilege may be claimed by the client, his guardian or conservator, the personal representative of a deceased client, or the successor, trustee, or similar representative of a corporation, association, or other organization, whether or not in existence. The person who was the lawyer at the time of the communication may claim the privilege but only on behalf of the client. His authority to do so is presumed in the absence of evidence to the contrary.

(d) Exceptions. There is no privilege under this rule:

(1) Furtherance of crime or fraud. If the services of the lawyer were sought or obtained to enable or aid anyone to commit or plan to commit what the client knew or reasonably should have known to be a crime or fraud; or

(2) Claimants through same deceased client. As to a communication relevant to an issue between parties who claim through the same deceased client, regardless of whether the claims are by testate or intestate succession or by *inter vivos* transaction; or

(3) Breach of duty by lawyer or client. As to a communication relevant to an issue of breach of duty by the lawyer to his client or by the client to his lawyer; or

(4) Document attested by lawyer. As to a communication relevant to an issue concerning an attested document to which the lawyer is an attesting witness; or

(5) Joint clients. As to a communication relevant to a matter of common interest between two or more clients if the communication was made by any of them to a lawyer retained or consulted in common, when offered in an action between any of the clients.

Advisory Committee's Note

Subdivision (a). (1) The definition of "client" includes governmental bodies, Connecticut Mutual Life Ins. Co. v. Shields, 18 F.R.D. 448 (S.D.N.Y.1955); People ex rel. Department of Public Works v. Glen Arms Estate, Inc., 230 Cal.App.2d 841, 41 Cal.Rptr. 303 (1964); Rowley v. Ferguson, 48 N.E.2d 243 (Ohio App. 1942); and corporations, Radiant Burners, Inc. v. American Gas Assn., 320 F.2d 314 (7th Cir.1963). Contra, Gardner, A Personal Privilege for Communications of Corporate Clients—Paradox or

Public Policy, 40 U.Det.L.J. 299, 323, 376 (1963). The definition also extends the status of client to one consulting a lawyer preliminarily with a view to retaining him, even though actual employment does not result. McCormick, § 92, p. 184. The client need not be involved in litigation; the rendition of legal service or advice under any circumstances suffices. 8 Wigmore § 2294 (McNaughton Rev. 1961). The services must be professional legal services; purely business or personal matters do not qualify. McCormick § 92, p. 184.

The rule contains no definition of "representative of the client." In the opinion of the Advisory Committee, the matter is better left to resolution by decision on a case-by-case basis. The most restricted position is the "control group" test, limiting the category to persons with authority to seek and act upon legal advice for the client. See *e.g.*, City of Philadelphia v. Westinghouse Electric Corp., 210 F.Supp. 483 (E.D.Pa.1962), mandamus and prohibition denied sub nom. General Electric Co. v. Kirkpatrick, 312 F.2d 742 (3d Cir.), cert. denied 372 U.S. 943; Garrison v. General Motors Corp., 213 F.Supp. 515 (S.D.Cal.1963); Hogan v. Zletz, 43 F.R.D. 308 (N.D.Okla.1967), aff'd sub nom. Natta v. Hogan, 392 F.2d 686 (10th Cir.1968); Day v. Illinois Power Co., 50 Ill.App.2d 52, 199 N.E.2d 802 (1964). Broader formulations are found in other decisions. See, e.g., United States v. United Shoe Machinery Corp., 89 F.Supp. 357 (D.Mass.1950); Zenith Radio Corp. v. Radio Corp. of America, 121 F.Supp. 792 (D.Del.1954); Harper & Row Publishers, Inc. v. Decker, 423 F.2d 487 (7th Cir.1970), aff'd without opinion by equally divided court 400 U.S. 955 (1971), reh. denied 401 U.S. 950; D.I. Chadbourne, Inc. v. Superior Court, 60 Cal.2d 723, 36 Cal.Rptr. 468, 388 P.2d 700 (1964). Cf. Rucker v. Wabash R. Co., 418 F.2d 146 (7th Cir.1969). See generally, Simon, The Attorney-Client Privilege as Applied to Corporations, 65 Yale L.J. 953, 956–966 (1956); Note, Attorney-Client Privilege for Corporate Clients: The Control Group Test, 84 Harv.L.Rev. 424 (1970).

The status of employees who are used in the process of communicating, as distinguished from those who are parties to the communication, is treated in paragraph (4) of subdivision (a) of the rule.

(2) A "lawyer" is a person licensed to practice law in any state or nation. There is no requirement that the licensing state or nation recognize the attorney-client privilege, thus avoiding excursions into conflict of laws questions. "Lawyer" also includes a person reasonably believed to be a lawyer. For similar provisions, see California Evidence Code § 950.

(3) The definition of "representative of the lawyer" recognizes that the lawyer may, in rendering legal services, utilize the services of assistants in addition to those employed in the process of communicating. Thus the definition includes an expert employed to assist in rendering legal advice. United States v. Kovel, 296 F.2d 918 (2d Cir.1961) (accountant). Cf. Himmelfarb v. United States, 175 F.2d 924 (9th Cir.1949). It also includes an expert employed to assist in the planning and conduct of litigation, though not one employed to testify as a witness. Lalance & Grosjean Mfg. Co. v. Haberman Mfg. Co., 87 F. 563 (S.D.N.Y.1898), and see revised Civil Rule

26(b) (4). The definition does not, however, limit "representative of the lawyer" to experts. Whether his compensation is derived immediately from the lawyer or the client is not material.

(4) The requisite confidentiality of communication is defined in terms of intent. A communication made in public or meant to be relayed to outsiders or which is divulged by the client to third persons can scarcely be considered confidential. McCormick § 95. The intent is inferable from the circumstances. Unless intent to disclose is apparent, the attorney-client communication is confidential. Taking or failing to take precautions may be considered as bearing on intent.

Practicality requires that some disclosure be allowed beyond the immediate circle of lawyer-client and their representatives without impairing confidentiality. Hence the definition allows disclosure to persons "to whom disclosure is in furtherance of the rendition of professional legal services to the client," contemplating those in such relation to the client as "spouse, parent, business associate, or joint client." Comment, California Evidence Code § 952.

Disclosure may also be made to persons "reasonably necessary for the transmission of the communication," without loss of confidentiality.

Subdivision (b) sets forth the privilege, using the previously defined terms: client, lawyer, representative of the lawyer, and confidential communication.

Substantial authority has in the past allowed the eavesdropper to testify to overheard privileged conversations and has admitted intercepted privileged letters. Today, the evolution of more sophisticated techniques of eavesdropping and interception calls for abandonment of this position. The rule accordingly adopts a policy of protection against these kinds of invasion of the privilege.

The privilege extends to communications (1) between client or his representative and lawyer or his representative, (2) between lawyer and lawyer's representative, (3) by client or his lawyer to a lawyer representing another in a matter of common interest, (4) between representatives of the client or the client and a representative of the client, and (5) between lawyers representing the client. All these communications must be specifically for the purpose of obtaining legal services for the client; otherwise the privilege does not attach.

The third type of communication occurs in the "joint defense" or "pooled information" situation, where different lawyers represent clients who have some interests in common. In Chahoon v. Commonwealth, 62 Va. 822 (1871), the court said that the various clients might have retained one attorney to represent all; hence everything said at a joint conference was privileged, and one of the clients could prevent another from disclosing what the other had himself said. The result seems to be incorrect in overlooking a frequent reason for retaining different attorneys by the various clients, namely actually or potentially conflicting interests in addition to the common interest which brings them together. The needs of these cases seem better to be met by allowing each client a privilege as to his own statements. Thus if all resist disclosure, none will occur. Continental Oil Co. v. United States, 330 F.2d 347 (9th Cir.1964). But, if for reasons of his own, a client wishes to disclose his own statements made at the joint conference, he should be permitted to do so, and the rule is to that effect. The rule does not apply to situations where there is no common interest to be promoted by a joint consultation, and the parties meet on a purely adversary basis. Vance v. State, 190 Tenn. 521, 230 S.W.2d 987 (1950), cert. denied 339 U.S. 988, 70 S.Ct. 1010, 94 L.Ed. 1389. Ct. Hunydee v. United States, 355 F.2d 183 (9th Cir.1965).

Subdivision (c). The privilege is, of course, that of the client, to be claimed by him or by his personal representative. The successor of a dissolved corporate client may claim the privilege. California Evidence Code § 953; New Jersey Evidence Rule 26(1). Contra, Uniform Rule 26(1).

The lawyer may not claim the privilege on his own behalf. However, he may claim it on behalf of the client. It is assumed that the ethics of the profession will require him to do so except under most unusual circumstances. American Bar Association, Canons of Professional Ethics, Canon 37. His authority to make the claim is presumed unless there is evidence to the contrary, as would be the case if the client were now a party to litigation in which the question arose and were represented by other counsel. Ex parte Ex parte Lipscomb, 111 Tex. 409, 239 S.W. 1101 (1922).

Subdivision (d) in general incorporates well established exceptions.

(1) The privilege does not extend to advice in aid of future wrongdoing. 8 Wigmore § 2298 (McNaughton Rev. 1961). The wrongdoing need not be that of the client. The provision that the client knew or reasonably should have known of the criminal or fraudulent nature of the act is designed to protect the client who is erroneously advised that the proposed action is within the law. No preliminary finding that sufficient evidence aside from the communication has been introduced to warrant a finding that the services were sought to enable the commission of a wrong is required. Cf. Clark v. United States, 289 U.S. 1, 15–16, 53 S.Ct. 465, 77 L.Ed. 993 (1933); Uniform Rule 26(2)(a). While any general exploration of what transpired between attorney and client would, of course, be inappropriate, it is wholly feasible, either at the discovery stage or during trial, so to focus the inquiry by specific questions as to avoid any broad inquiry into attorney-client communications. Numerous cases reflect this approach.

(2) Normally the privilege survives the death of the client and may be asserted by his representative. Subdivision (c), supra. When, however, the identity of the person who steps into the client's shoes is in issue, as in a will contest, the identity of the person entitled to claim the privilege remains undetermined until the conclusion of the litigation. The choice is

thus between allowing both sides or neither to assert the privilege, with authority and reason favoring the latter view. McCormick § 98; Uniform Rule 26(2)(b); California Evidence Code § 957; Kansas Code of Civil Procedure § 60–426(b)(2); New Jersey Evidence Rule 26(2)(b).

(3) The exception is required by considerations of fairness and policy when questions arise out of dealings between attorney and client, as in cases of controversy over attorney's fees, claims of inadequacy of representation, or charges of professional misconduct. McCormick § 95; Uniform Rule 26(2)(c); California Evidence Code § 958; Kansas Code of Civil Procedure § 60–426(b)(3); New Jersey Evidence Rule 26(2)(c).

(4) When the lawyer acts as attesting witness, the approval of the client to his so doing may safely be assumed, and waiver of the privilege as to any relevant lawyer-client communications is a proper result. McCormick § 92, p. 184; Uniform Rule 26(2)(d); California Evidence Code § 959; Kansas Code of Civil Procedure § 60–426(b)(d) [*sic*].

(5) The subdivision states existing law. McCormick § 95, pp. 192–193. For similar provisions, see Uniform Rule 26(2)(e); California Evidence Code § 962; Kansas Code of Civil Procedure § 60–426(b)(4); New Jersey Evidence Rule 26(2). The situation with which this provision deals is to be distinguished from the case of clients with a common interest who retain different lawyers. See subdivision (b)(3) of this rule, supra.

Rule 504
PSYCHOTHERAPIST-PATIENT PRIVILEGE

[Not enacted]

(a) Definitions.

(1) A "patient" is a person who consults or is examined or interviewed by a psychotherapist.

(2) A "psychotherapist" is (A) a person authorized to practice medicine in any state or nation, or reasonably believed by the patient so to be, while engaged in the diagnosis or treatment of a mental or emotional condition, including drug addiction, or (B) a person licensed or certified as a psychologist under the laws of any state or nation, while similarly engaged.

(3) A communication is "confidential" if not intended to be disclosed to third persons other than those present to further the interest of the patient in the consultation, examination, or interview, or persons reasonably necessary for the transmission of the communication, or persons who are participating in the diagnosis and treatment under the direction of the psychotherapist, including members of the patient's family.

(b) General rule of privilege. A patient has a privilege to refuse to disclose and to prevent any other person from disclosing confidential communications, made for the purposes of diagnosis or treatment of his mental or emotional condition, including drug addiction, among himself, his psychotherapist, or persons who are participating in the diagnosis or treatment under the direction of the psychotherapist, including members of the patient's family.

(c) Who may claim the privilege. The privilege may be claimed by the patient, by his guardian or conservator, or by the personal representative of a deceased patient. The person who was the psychotherapist may claim the privilege but only on behalf of the patient. His authority so to do is presumed in the absence of evidence to the contrary.

(d) Exceptions.

(1) Proceedings for hospitalization. There is no privilege under this rule for communications relevant to an issue in proceedings to hospitalize the patient for mental illness, if the psychotherapist in the course of diagnosis or treatment has determined that the patient is in need of hospitalization.

(2) Examination by order of judge. If the judge orders an examination of the mental or emotional condition of the patient, communications made in the course thereof are not privileged under this rule with respect to the particular purpose for which the examination is ordered unless the judge orders otherwise.

(3) Condition an element of claim or defense. There is no privilege under this rule as to communications relevant to an issue of the mental or emotional condition of the patient in any proceeding in which he relies upon the condition as an element of his claim or defense, or, after the patient's death, in any proceeding in which any party relies upon the condition as an element of his claim or defense.

Advisory Committee's Note

The rules contain no provision for a general physician-patient privilege. While many states have by statute created the privilege, the exceptions which have been found necessary in order to obtain information required by the public interest or to avoid fraud are so numerous as to leave little if any basis for the privilege. Among the exclusions from the statutory privilege, the following may be enumerated; communications not made for purposes of diagnosis and treatment; commitment and restoration proceedings; issues as to wills or otherwise between parties claiming by succession from the patient; actions on insurance policies; required reports (venereal diseases, gunshot wounds, child abuse); communications in furtherance of crime or fraud; mental or physical condition put in issue by patient (personal injury cases); malpractice actions; and some or all criminal prosecutions. California, for example, excepts cases in which the patient puts his condition in issue, all criminal proceedings, will and similar contests, malpractice cases, and disciplinary proceedings, as well as certain other situations, thus leaving virtually nothing covered by the privilege. California

Evidence Code §§ 990–1007. For other illustrative statutes see Ill.Rev.Stat.1967, c. 51, § 5.1; N.Y.C.P.L.R. § 4504; N.C.Gen.Stat.1953, § 8–53. Moreover, the possibility of compelling gratuitous disclosure by the physician is foreclosed by his standing to raise the question of relevancy. See Note on "Official Information" Privilege following Rule 509, infra.

The doubts attendant upon the general physician-patient privilege are not present when the relationship is that of psychotherapist and patient. While the common law recognized no general physician-patient privilege, it had indicated a disposition to recognize a psychotherapist-patient privilege, Note, Confidential Communications to a Psychotherapist: A New Testimonial Privilege, 47 Nw.U.L.Rev. 384 (1952), when legislatures began moving into the field.

The case for the privilege is convincingly stated in Report No. 45, Group for the Advancement of Psychiatry 92 (1960):

"Among physicians, the psychiatrist has a special need to maintain confidentiality. His capacity to help his patients is completely dependent upon their willingness and ability to talk freely. This makes it difficult if not impossible for him to function without being able to assure his patients of confidentiality and, indeed, privileged communication. Where there may be exceptions to this general rule * * *, there is wide agreement that confidentiality is a *sine qua non* for successful psychiatric treatment. The relationship may well be likened to that of the priest-penitent or the lawyer-client. Psychiatrists not only explore the very depths of their patients' conscious, but their unconscious feelings and attitudes as well. Therapeutic effectiveness necessitates going beyond a patient's awareness and, in order to do this, it must be possible to communicate freely. A threat to secrecy blocks successful treatment."

A much more extended exposition of the case for the privilege is made in Slovenko, Psychiatry and a Second Look at the Medical Privilege, 6 Wayne L.Rev. 175, 184 (1960), quoted extensively in the careful Tentative Recommendation and Study Relating to the Uniform Rules of Evidence (Article V. Privileges), Cal.Law Rev. Comm'n, 417 (1964). The conclusion is reached that Wigmore's four conditions needed to justify the existence of a privilege are amply satisfied.

Illustrative statutes are Cal.Evidence Code §§ 1010–1026; Ga.Code § 38–418 (1961 Supp.);Conn.Gen.Stat., § 52–146a (1966 Supp.); Ill.Rev.Stat.1967, c. 51, § 5.2.

While many of the statutes simply place the communications on the same basis as those between attorney and client, 8 Wigmore § 2286, n. 23 (McNaughton Rev.1961), basic differences between the two relationships forbid resorting to attorney-client save as a helpful point of departure. Goldstein and Katz, Psychiatrist-Patient Privilege: The GAP Proposal and the Connecticut Statute, 36 Conn.B.J. 175, 182 (1962).

Subdivision (a). (1) The definition of patient does not include a person submitting to examination for scientific purposes. Cf. Cal.Evidence Code § 1101. Attention is directed to 42 U.S.C. 242(a)(2), as amended by the Drug Abuse and Control Act of 1970, P.L. 91–513, authorizing the Secretary of Health, Education, and Welfare to withhold the identity of persons who are the subjects of research on the use and effect of drugs. The rule would leave this provision in full force. See Rule 501.

(2) The definition of psychotherapist embraces a medical doctor while engaged in the diagnosis or treatment of mental or emotional conditions, including drug addiction, in order not to exclude the general practitioner and to avoid the making of needless refined distinctions concerning what is and what is not the practice of psychiatry. The requirement that the psychologist be in fact licensed, and not merely be believed to be so, is believed to be justified by the number of persons, other than psychiatrists, purporting to render psychotherapeutic aid and the variety of their theories. Cal.Law Rev. Comm'n, supra, at pp. 434–437.

The clarification of mental or emotional condition as including drug addition is consistent with current approaches to drug abuse problems. See, e.g., the definition of "drug dependent person" in 42 U.S.C. 201(q), added by the Drug Abuse Prevention and Control Act of 1970, P.L. 91–513.

(3) Confidential communication is defined in terms conformable with those of the lawyer-client privilege, Rule 503(a)(4), supra, with changes appropriate to the difference in circumstance.

Subdivisions (b) and (c). The lawyer-client rule is drawn upon for the phrasing of the general rule of privilege and the determination of those who may claim it. See Rule 503(b) and (c).

The specific inclusion of communications made for the diagnosis and treatment of drug addiction recognizes the continuing contemporary concern with rehabilitation of drug dependent persons and is designed to implement that policy by encouraging persons in need thereof to seek assistance. The provision is in harmony with Congressional actions in this area. See 42 U.S.C. § 260, providing for voluntary hospitalization of addicts or persons with drug dependence problems and prohibiting use of evidence of admission or treatment in any proceeding against him, and 42 U.S.C. § 3419 providing that in voluntary or involuntary commitment of addicts the results of any hearing, examination, test, or procedure used to determine addiction shall not be used against the patient in any criminal proceeding.

Subdivision (d). The exceptions differ substantially from those of the attorney-client privilege, as a result of the basic differences in the relationships. While it has been argued convincingly that the nature of the psychotherapist-patient relationship demands complete security against legally coerced disclosure in all circumstances, Louisell, The Psychologist in Today's Legal World: Part II, 41 Minn.L.Rev. 731, 746 (1957), the committee of psychiatrists and lawyers who drafted the Connecticut statute concluded that in three instances the need for disclosure was sufficiently great to justify the risk of possible impairment of the relationship. Goldstein and Katz, Psychiatrist-Patient Privilege: The GAP Proposal and the Connecticut Statute, 36 Conn.B.J. 175 (1962). These three exceptions are incorporated in the present rule.

(1) The interests of both patient and public call for a departure from confidentiality in commitment proceedings. Since disclosure is authorized only when the psychotherapist determines that hospitalization is needed, control over disclosure is placed largely in the hands of a person in whom the patient has already manifested confidence. Hence damage to the relationship is unlikely.

(2) In a court ordered examination, the relationship is likely to be an arm's length one, though not necessarily so. In any event, an exception is necessary for the effective utilization of this important and growing procedure. The exception, it will be observed, deals with a court ordered examination rather than with a court appointed psychotherapist. Also, the exception is effective only with respect to the particular purpose for which the examination is ordered. The rule thus conforms with the provisions of 18 U.S.C. § 4244 that no statement made by the accused in the course of an examination into competency to stand trial is admissible on the issue of guilt and of 42 U.S.C. § 3420 that a physician conducting an examination in a drug addiction commitment proceeding is a competent and compellable witness.

(3) By injecting his condition into litigation, the patient must be said to waive the privilege, in fairness and to avoid abuses. Similar considerations prevail after the patient's death.

Rule 505
HUSBAND–WIFE PRIVILEGE

[Not enacted.]

(a) General rule of privilege. An accused in a criminal proceeding has a privilege to prevent his spouse from testifying against him.

(b) Who may claim the privilege. The privilege may be claimed by the accused or by the spouse on his behalf. The authority of the spouse to do so is presumed in the absence of evidence to the contrary.

(c) Exceptions. There is no privilege under this rule (1) in proceedings in which one spouse is charged with a crime against the person or property of the other or of a child of either, or with a crime against the person or property of a third person committed in the course of committing a crime against the other, or (2) as to matters occurring prior to the marriage, or (3) in proceedings in which a spouse is charged with importing an alien for prostitution or other immoral purpose in violation of 8 U.S.C. § 1328, with transporting a female in interstate commerce for immoral purposes or other offense in violation of 18 U.S.C. §§ 2421–2424, or with violation of other similar statutes.

Advisory Committee's Note

Subdivision (a). Rules of evidence have evolved around the marriage relationship in four respects: (1) incompetency of one spouse to testify for the other; (2) privilege of one spouse not to testify against the other; (3) privilege of one spouse not to have the other testify against him; and (4) privilege against disclosure of confidential communications between spouses, sometimes extended to information learned by virtue of the existence of the relationship. Today these matters are largely governed by statutes.

With the disappearance of the disqualification of parties and interested persons, the basis for spousal incompetency no longer existed, and it, too, virtually disappeared in both civil and criminal actions. Usually reached by statute, this result was reached for federal courts by the process of decision. Funk v. United States, 290 U.S. 371, 54 S.Ct. 212, 78 L.Ed. 369 (1933). These rules contain no recognition of incompetency of one spouse to testify for the other.

While some 10 jurisdictions recognize a privilege not to testify against one's spouse in a criminal case, and a much smaller number do so in civil cases, the great majority recognizes no privilege on the part of the testifying spouse, and this is the position taken by the rule. Compare Wyatt v. United States, 362 U.S. 525, 80 S.Ct. 901, 4 L.Ed.2d 931 (1960), a Mann Act prosecution in which the wife was the victim. The majority opinion held that she could not claim privilege and was compellable to testify. The holding was narrowly based: The Mann Act presupposed that the women with whom it dealt had no independent wills of their own, and this legislative judgment precluded allowing a victim-wife an option whether to testify, lest the policy of the statute be defeated. A vigorous dissent took the view that nothing in the Mann Act required departure from usual doctrine, which was conceived to be one of allowing the injured party to claim or waive privilege.

About 30 jurisdictions recognize a privilege of an accused in a criminal case to prevent his or her spouse from testifying. It is believed to represent the one aspect of marital privilege the continuation of which is warranted. In Hawkins v. United States, 358 U.S. 74, 79 S.Ct. 136, 3 L.Ed.2d 125 (1958) it was sustained. Cf. McCormick § 66; 8 Wigmore § 2228 (McNaughton Rev.1961): Comment, Uniform Rule 23(2).

The rule recognizes no privilege for confidential communications. The traditional justifications for privileges not to testify against a spouse and not to be testified against by one's spouse have been the prevention of marital dissension and the repugnancy of requiring a person to condemn or be condemned by his spouse. 8 Wigmore §§ 2228, 2241 (McNaughton Rev.1961). These considerations bear no relevancy to marital communications. Nor can it be assumed that marital conduct will be affected by a privilege for confidential communications of whose existence the parties in all likelihood are unaware. The other communication privileges, by way of contrast, have as one party a professional person who can be expected to inform the other of the existence of the privilege. Moreover, the relationships from which those privileges arise are essentially and almost exclusively verbal in nature, quite unlike marriage. See Hutchins and Slesinger, Some Observations on the Law of Evidence: Family Relations, 13 Minn.L.Rev. 675 (1929). Cf. McCormick § 90; 8 Wigmore § 2337 (McNaughton Rev.1961). The parties are not spouses if the marriage was a sham, Lutwak v. United States, 344 U.S. 604 (1953), or they have been divorced, Barsky v. United States, 339 F.2d 180 (9th Cir.1964), and therefore the privilege is not applicable.

Subdivision (b). This provision is a counterpart of Rules 503(c), 504(c), and 506(c). Its purpose is to provide a procedure for preventing the taking of the spouse's testimony notably in grand jury proceedings, when the accused is absent and does not know that a situation appropriate for a claim of privilege is presented. If the privilege is not claimed by the spouse, the protection of Rule 512 is available.

Subdivision (c) contains three exceptions to the privilege against spousal testimony in criminal cases.

(1) The need of limitation upon the privilege in order to avoid grave injustice in cases of offenses against the other spouse or a child of either can scarcely be denied. Wigmore § 2239 (McNaughton Rev.1961). The rule therefore disallows any privilege against spousal testimony in these cases and in this respect is in accord with the result reached in Wyatt v. United States, 362 U.S. 525, 80 S.Ct. 901, 4 L.Ed.2d 931 (1960), a Mann Act prosecution, denying the accused the privilege of excluding his wife's testimony, since she was the woman who was transported for immoral purposes.

(2) The second exception renders the privilege inapplicable as to matters occurring prior to the marriage. This provision eliminates the possibility of suppressing testimony by marrying the witness.

(3) The third exception continues and expands established Congressional policy. In prosecutions for importing aliens for immoral purposes, Congress has specifically denied the accused any privilege not to have his spouse testify against him. 8 U.S.C. § 1328. No provision of this nature is included in the Mann Act, and in Hawkins v. United States, 358 U.S. 74, 79 S.Ct. 136, 3 L.Ed.2d 125 (1958), the conclusion was reached that the common law privilege continued. Consistency requires similar results in the two situations. The rule adopts the Congressional approach, as based upon a more realistic appraisal of the marriage relationship in cases of this kind, in preference to the specific result in *Hawkins*. Note the common law treatment of pimping and sexual offenses with third persons as exceptions to marital privilege. 8 Wigmore § 2239 (McNaughton Rev.1961).

With respect to bankruptcy proceedings, the smallness of the area of spousal privilege under the rule and the general inapplicability of privileges created by state law render unnecessary any special provision for examination of the spouse of the bankrupt, such as that now contained in section 21(a) of the Bankruptcy Act. 11 U.S.C. § 44(a).

For recent statutes and rules dealing with husband-wife privileges, see California Evidence Code §§ 970–973, 980–987; Kansas Code of Civil Procedure §§ 60–423(b), 60–428; New Jersey Evidence Rules 23(2), 28.

Rule 506
COMMUNICATIONS TO CLERGYMEN

[Not enacted.]

(a) Definitions. As used in this rule:

(1) A "clergyman" is a minister, priest, rabbi, or other similar functionary of a religious organization, or an individual reasonably believed so to be by the person consulting him.

(2) A communication is "confidential" if made privately and not intended for further disclosure except to other persons present in furtherance of the purpose of the communication.

(b) General rule of privilege. A person has a privilege to refuse to disclose and to prevent another from disclosing a confidential communication by the person to a clergyman in his professional character as spiritual adviser.

(c) Who may claim the privilege. The privilege may be claimed by the person, by his guardian or conservator, or by his personal representative if he is deceased. The clergyman may claim the privilege on behalf of the person His authority so to do is presumed in the absence of evidence to the contrary.

Advisory Committee's Note

The considerations which dictate the recognition of privileges generally seem strongly to favor a privilege for confidential communications to clergymen. During the period when most of the common law privileges were taking shape, no clear-cut privilege for communications between priest and penitent emerged. 8 Wigmore § 2394 (McNaughton Rev.1961). The English political climate of the time may well furnish the explanation. In this country, however,the privilege has been recognized by statute in about two-thirds of the states and occasionally by the common law process of decision. Id., § 2395; Mullen v. United States, 105 U.S.App.D.C. 25, 263 F.2d 275 (1959).

Subdivision (a). Paragraph (1) defines a clergyman as a "minister, priest, rabbi, or other similar functionary of a religious organization." The concept is necessarily broader than that inherent in the ministerial exemption for purposes of Selective Service. See United States v. Jackson, 369 F.2d 936 (4th Cir.1966). However, it is not so broad as to include all self-denominated "ministers." A fair construction of the language requires that the person to whom the status is sought to be attached be regularly engaged in activities conforming at least in a general way with those of a Catholic priest, Jewish rabbi, or minister of an established Protestant denomination, though not necessarily on a full-time basis. No further specification seems possible in view of the lack of licensing and certification procedures for clergymen. However, this lack seems to have occasioned no particular difficulties in connection with the solemnization of marriages, which suggests that none may be anticipated here. For similar definitions of "clergyman" see California Evidence Code § 1030; New Jersey Evidence Rule 29.

The "reasonable belief" provision finds support in similar provisions for lawyer-client in Rule 503 and for psychotherapist-patient in Rule 504. A parallel is also found in the recognition of the validity of marriages performed by unauthorized persons if the parties reasonably believed them legally qualified. Harper and Skolnick, Problems of the Family 153 (Rev.Ed.1962).

(2) The definition of "confidential" communication is consistent with the use of the term in Rule 503(a)(5) for lawyer-client and in Rule 504(a)(3) for psychotherapist-patient, suitably adapted to communications to clergymen.

Subdivision (b). The choice between a privilege narrowly restricted to doctrinally required confessions and a privilege broadly applicable to all confidential communications with a clergyman in his professional character as spiritual adviser has been exercised in favor of the latter. Many clergymen now receive training in marriage counseling and the handling of personality problems. Matters of this kind fall readily into the realm of the spirit. The same considerations which underlie the psychotherapist-patient privilege of Rule 504 suggest a broad application of the privilege for communications to clergymen.

State statutes and rules fall in both the narrow and the broad categories. A typical narrow statute proscribes disclosure of "a confession * * * made * * * in the course of discipline enjoined by the church to which he belongs." Ariz.Rev.Stats.Ann.1956, § 12–2233. See also California Evidence Code § 1032; Uniform Rule 29. Illustrative of the broader privilege are statutes applying to "information communicated to him in a confidential manner, properly entrusted to him in his professional capacity, and necessary to enable him to discharge the functions of his office according to the usual course of his practice or discipline, wherein such person so communicating * * * is seeking spiritual counsel and advice," Fla.Stats.Ann.1960, § 90.241, or to any "confidential communication properly entrusted to him in his professional capacity, and necessary and proper to enable him to discharge the functions of his office according to the usual course of practice or discipline," Iowa Code Ann.1950, § 622.10. See also Ill.Rev.Stats.1967, c. 51, § 48.1; Minn.Stats.Ann.1945, § 595.02(3); New Jersey Evidence Rule 29.

Under the privilege as phrased, the communicating person is entitled to prevent disclosure not only by himself but also by the clergyman and by eavesdroppers. For discussion see Advisory Committee's Note under lawyer-client privilege, Rule 503(b).

The nature of what may reasonably be considered spiritual advice makes it unnecessary to include in the rule a specific exception for communications in furtherance of crime or fraud, as in Rule 503(d)(1).

Subdivision (c) makes clear that the privilege belongs to the communicating person. However, a prima facie authority on the part of the clergyman to claim the privilege on behalf of the person is recognized. The discipline of the particular church and the discreetness of the clergyman are believed to constitute sufficient safeguards for the absent communicating person. See Advisory Committee's Note to the similar provision with respect to attorney-client in Rule 503(c).

Rule 507
POLITICAL VOTE

[Not enacted.]

Every person has a privilege to refuse to disclose the tenor of his vote at a political election conducted by secret ballot unless the vote was cast illegally.

Advisory Committee's Note

Secrecy in voting is an essential aspect of effective democratic government, insuring free exercise of the franchise and fairness in elections. Secrecy after the ballot has been cast is as essential as secrecy in the act of voting. Nutting, Freedom of Silence: Constitutional Protection Against Governmental Intrusion in Political Affairs, 47 Mich.L.Rev. 181, 191 (1948). Consequently a privilege has long been recognized on the part of a voter to decline to disclose how he voted. Required disclosure would be the exercise of "a kind of inquisitorial power unknown to the principles of our government and constitution, and might be highly injurious to the suffrages of a free people, as well as tending to create cabals and disturbances between contending parties in popular elections." Johnston v. Charleston, 1 Bay 441, 442 (S.C.1795).

The exception for illegally cast votes is a common one under both statutes and case law, Nutting, supra, at p. 192; 8 Wigmore § 2214, p. 163 (McNaughton Rev.1961). The policy considerations which underlie the privilege are not applicable to the illegal voter. However, nothing in the exception purports to foreclose an illegal voter from invoking the privilege against self-incrimination under appropriate circumstances.

For similar provisions, see Uniform Rule 31; California Evidence Code § 1050; Kansas Code of Civil Procedure § 60–431; New Jersey Evidence Rule 31.

Rule 508
TRADE SECRETS

[Not enacted.]

A person has a privilege, which may be claimed by him or his agent or employee, to refuse to disclose and to prevent other persons from disclosing a trade secret owned by him, if the allowance of the privilege will not tend to conceal fraud or otherwise work injustice. When disclosure is directed, the judge shall take such protective measure as the interests of the holder of the privilege and of the parties and the furtherance of justice may require.

Advisory Committee's Note

While sometimes said not to be a true privilege, a qualified right to protection against disclosure of trade secrets has found ample recognition, and, indeed, a denial of it would be difficult to defend. 8 Wigmore § 2212(3) (McNaughton Rev.1961). And see 4 Moore's Federal Practice 30.12 and 34.15 (2nd ed. 1963 and Supp.1965) and 2A Barron and Holtzoff, Federal Practice and Procedure § 715.1 (Wright ed. 1961). Congressional policy is reflected in the Securities Exchange Act of 1934, 15 U.S.C. § 78x, and the Public Utility Holding Company Act of 1933, id. § 79v, which deny the Securities and Exchange Commission authority to require disclosure of trade secrets or processes in applications and reports. See also Rule 26(c)(7) of the Rules of Civil Procedure, as revised, mentioned further hereinafter.

Illustrative cases raising trade-secret problems are: E.I. Du Pont de Nemours Powder Co. v. Masland, 244 U.S. 100, 37 S.Ct. 575, 61 L.Ed. 1016 (1917), suit to enjoin former employee from using plaintiff's secret processes, countered by defense that many of the processes were well known to the trade; Segal Lock & Hardware Co. v. FTC, 143 F.2d 935 (2d Cir.1944), question whether expert locksmiths employed by FTC should be required to disclose methods used by them in picking petitioner's "pick-proof" locks; Dobson v. Graham, 49 F. 17 (E.D.Pa.1889), patent infringement suit in which plaintiff sought to elicit from former employees now in the hire of defendant the respects in which defendant's machinery differed from plaintiff's patented machinery; Putney v. Du Bois Co., 240 Mo.App. 1075, 226 S.W.2d 737 (1950), action for injuries allegedly sustained from using defendant's secret formula dishwashing compound. See 8 Wigmore § 2212(3) (McNaughton Rev.1961); Annot., 17 A.L.R.2d 383; 49 Mich.L.Rev. 133 (1950). The need for accommodation between protecting trade secrets, on the one hand, and eliciting facts required for full and fair presentation of a case, on the other hand, is apparent. Whether disclosure should be required depends upon a weighing of the competing interests involved against the background of the total situation, including consideration of such factors as the dangers of abuse, good faith, adequacy of protective measures, and the availability of other means of proof.

The cases furnish examples of the bringing of judicial ingenuity to bear upon the problem of evolving protective measures which achieve a degree of control over disclosure. Perhaps the most common is simply to take testimony *in camera*. Annot., 62 A.L.R.2d 509. Other possibilities include making disclosure to opposing counsel but not to his client, E.I. Du Pont de Nemours Powder Co. v. Masland, 244 U.S. 100, 37 S.Ct. 575, 61 L.Ed. 1016 (1917); making disclosure only to the judge (hearing examiner), Segal Lock & Hardware Co. v. FTC, 143 F.2d 935 (2d Cir.1944); and placing those present under oath not to make disclosure, Paul v. Sinnott, 217 F.Supp. 84 (W.D.Pa.1963).

Rule 26(c) of the Rules of Civil Procedure, as revised, provides that the judge may make "any order which justice requires to protect a party or person from annoyance, embarrassment, oppression, or undue burden or expense, including one or more of the following: * * * (7) that a trade secret or other confidential research, development, or commercial information not be disclosed or be disclosed only in a designated way * * *." While the instant evidence rule extends this underlying policy into the trial, the difference in circumstances between discovery stage and trial may well be such as to require a different ruling at the trial.

For other rules recognizing privilege for trade secrets, see Uniform Rule 32; California Evidence Code § 1060; Kansas Code of Civil Procedure § 60–432; New Jersey Evidence Rule 32.

Rule 509
SECRETS OF STATE AND OTHER   OFFICIAL INFORMATION

[Not enacted.]

(a) Definitions.

(1) Secret of state. A "secret of state" is a governmental secret relating to the national defense or the international relations of the United States.

(2) Official information. "Official information" is information within the custody or control of a department or agency of the government the disclosure of which is shown to be contrary to the public interest and which consists of: (A) intragovernmental opinions or recommendations submitted for consideration in the performance of decisional or policymaking functions, or (B) subject to the provisions of 18 U.S.C. § 3500, investigatory files compiled for law enforcement purposes and not otherwise available, or (C) information within the custody or control of a governmental department or

agency whether initiated within the department or agency or acquired by it in its exercise of its official responsibilities and not otherwise available to the public pursuant to 5 U.S.C. § 552.

(b) General rule of privilege. The government has a privilege to refuse to give evidence and to prevent any person from giving evidence upon a showing of reasonable likelihood of danger that the evidence will disclose a secret of state or official information, as defined in this rule.

(c) Procedures. The privilege for secrets of state may be claimed only by the chief officer of the government agency or department administering the subject matter which the secret information sought concerns, but the privilege for official information may be asserted by any attorney representing the government. The required showing may be made in whole or in part in the form of a written statement. The judge may hear the matter in chambers, but all counsel are entitled to inspect the claim and showing and to be heard thereon, except that, in the case of secrets of state, the judge upon motion of the government, may permit the government to make the required showing in the above form *in camera*. If the judge sustains the privilege upon a showing *in camera,* the entire text of the government's statements shall be sealed and preserved in the court's records in the event of appeal. In the case of privilege claimed for official information the court may require examination *in camera* of the information itself. The judge may take any protective measure which the interests of the government and the furtherance of justice may require.

(d) Notice to government. If the circumstances of the case indicate a substantial possibility that a claim of privilege would be appropriate but has not been made because of oversight or lack of knowledge, the judge shall give or cause notice to be given to the officer entitled to claim the privilege and shall stay further proceedings a reasonable time to afford opportunity to assert a claim of privilege.

(e) Effect of sustaining claim. If a claim of privilege is sustained in a proceeding to which the government is a party and it appears that another party is thereby deprived of material evidence, the judge shall make any further orders which the interests of justice require, including striking the testimony of a witness, declaring a mistrial, finding against the government upon an issue as to which the evidence is relevant, or dismissing the action.

Advisory Committee's Note

Subdivision (a). (1) The rule embodies the privilege protecting military and state secrets described as "well established in the law of evidence," United States v. Reynolds, 345 U.S. 1, 6, 73 S.Ct. 528, 97 L.Ed. 727 (1953), and as one "the existence of which has never been doubted," 8 Wigmore § 2378, p. 794 (McNaughton Rev.1961).

The use of the term "national defense," without attempt at further elucidation, finds support in the similar usage in statutory provisions relating to the crimes of gathering, transmitting, or losing defense information, and gathering or delivering defense information to aid a foreign government. 18 U.S.C. §§ 793, 794. See also 5 U.S.C. § 1002; 50 U.S.C.App. § 2152(d). In determining whether military or state secrets are involved, due regard will, of course, be given to classification pursuant to executive order.

(2) The rule also recognizes a privilege for specified types of official information and in this respect is designed primarily to resolve questions of the availability to litigants of data in the files of governmental departments and agencies. In view of the lesser danger to the public interest than in cases of military and state secrets, the official information privilege is subject to a generally overriding requirement that disclosure would be contrary to the public interest. It is applicable to three categories of information.

(A) Intergovernmental opinions or recommendations submitted for consideration in the performance of decisional or policy making functions. The policy basis of this aspect of the privilege is found in the desirability of encouraging candor in the exchange of views within the government. Kaiser Aluminum & Chemical Corp. v. United States, 141 Ct.Cl. 38, 157 F.Supp. 939 (1958); Davis v. Braswell Motor Freight Lines, Inc., 363 F.2d 600 (5th Cir.1966); Ackerly v. Ley, 420 F.2d 1336 (D.C.Cir.1969). A privilege of this character is consistent with the Freedom of Information Act, 5 U.S.C. § 552(b)(5), and with the standing of the agency to raise questions of relevancy, though not a party, recognized in such decisions as Boeing Airplane Co. v. Coggeshall, 108 U.S.App.D.C. 106, 280 F.2d 654, 659 (1960) (Renegotiation Board) and Freeman v. Seligson, 132 U.S.App.D.C. 56, 405 F.2d 1326, 1334 (1968) (Secretary of Agriculture).

(B) Investigatory files compiled for law enforcement purposes. This category is expressly made subject to the provisions of the Jencks Act, 18 U.S.C. § 3500, which insulates prior statements or reports of government witnesses in criminal cases against subpoena, discovery, or inspection until the witness has testified on direct examination at the trial but then entitles the defense to its production. Rarely will documents of this nature be relevant until the author has testified and thus placed his credibility in issue. Further protection against discovery of government files in criminal cases is found in Criminal Procedure Rule 16(a) and (b). The breadth of discovery in civil cases, however, goes beyond ordinary bounds of relevancy and raises problems calling for the exercise of judicial control, and in making provision for it the rule implements the Freedom of Information Act, 18 U.S.C. § 552(b)(7).

(C) Information exempted from disclosure under the Freedom of Information Act, 5 U.S.C. § 552. In 1958 In 1958 the old "housekeeping" statute which had been relied upon as a foundation for departmental regulations curtailing disclosure was amended by adding a provision that it did not authorize withholding information from the public. In 1966 the Congress enacted the Freedom of Information Act for the purpose of making information in the files of departments and agencies, subject to certain specified exceptions, available to the mass media and to the public generally. 5 U.S.C. § 552. These enactments are significant expressions of Congressional policy. The exceptions in the Act are not framed in terms of evidentiary privilege, thus recognizing by clear implication that the needs of litigants may stand on somewhat different footing from those of the public generally. Nevertheless, the exceptions are based on values obviously entitled to weighty consideration in formulating rules of evidentiary privilege. In some instances in these rules, exceptions in the Act have been made the subject of specific privileges, e.g., military and state secrets in the present rule and trade secrets in Rule 508. The purpose of the present provision is to incorporate the remaining exceptions of the Act into the qualified privilege here created, thus subjecting disclosure of the information to judicial determination with respect to the effect of disclosure on the public interest. This approach appears to afford a satisfactory resolution of the problems which may arise.

Subdivision (b). The rule vests the privileges in the government where they properly belong rather than a party or witness. See United States v. Reynolds, supra, p. 7, 345 U.S. 1. The showing required as a condition precedent to claiming the privilege represents a compromise between complete judicial control and accepting as final the decision of a departmental officer. See Machin v. Zuckert, 114 U.S.App.D.C. 335, 316 F.2d 336 (1963), rejecting in part a claim of privilege by the Secretary of the Air Force and ordering the furnishing of information for use in private litigation. This approach is consistent with *Reynolds*.

Subdivision (c). In requiring the claim of privilege for state secrets to be made by the chief departmental officer, the rule again follows *Reynolds,* insuring consideration by a high-level officer. This provision is justified by the lesser participation by the judge in cases of state secrets. The full participation by the judge in official information cases, on the contrary, warrants allowing the claim of privilege to be made by a government attorney.

Subdivision (d) spells out and emphasizes a power and responsibility on the part of the trial judge. An analogous provision is found in the requirement that the court certify to the Attorney General when the constitutionality of an act of Congress is in question in an action to which the government is not a party. 28 U.S.C. § 2403.

Subdivision (e). If privilege is successfully claimed by the government in litigation to which it is not a party, the effect is simply to make the evidence unavailable, as though a witness had died or claimed the privilege against self-incrimination, and no specification of the consequences is necessary. The rule therefore deals only with the effect of a successful claim of privilege by the government in proceedings to which it is a party. Reference to other types of cases serves to illustrate the variety of situations which may arise and the impossibility of evolving a single formula to be applied automatically to all of them. The privileged materials may be the statement of government witness, as under the *Jencks* statute, which provides that, if the government elects not to produce the statement, the judge is to strike the testimony of the witness, or that he may declare a mistrial if the interests of justice so require. 18 U.S.C. § 3500(d). Or the privileged materials may disclose a possible basis for applying pressure upon witnesses. United States v. Beekman, 155 F.2d 580 (2d Cir.1946). Or they may bear directly upon a substantive element of a criminal case, requiring dismissal in the event of a successful claim of privilege. United States v. Andolschek, 142 F.2d 503 (2d Cir.1944); and see United States v. Reynolds, 345 U.S. 1, 73 S.Ct. 528, 97 L.Ed. 727 (1953). Or they may relate to an element of a plaintiff's claim against the government, with the decisions indicating unwillingness to allow the government's claim of privilege for secrets of state to be used as an offensive weapon against it. United States v. Reynolds, supra; Republic of China v. National Union Fire Ins. Co., 142 F.Supp. 551 (D.Md.1956).

Rule 510
IDENTITY OF INFORMER

[Not enacted.]

(a) Rule of privilege. The government or a state or subdivision thereof has a privilege to refuse to disclose the identity of a person who has furnished information relating to or assisting in an investigation of a possible violation of law to a law enforcement officer or member of a legislative committee or its staff conducting an investigation.

(b) Who may claim. The privilege may be claimed by an appropriate representative of the government, regardless of whether the information was furnished to an officer of the government or of a state or subdivision thereof. The privilege may be claimed by an appropriate representative of a state or subdivision if the information was furnished to an officer thereof, except that in criminal cases the privilege shall not be allowed if the government objects.

(c) Exceptions.

(1) Voluntary disclosure; informer a witness. No privilege exists under this rule if the identity of the informer or his interest in the subject matter of his communication has been disclosed to those who would have cause to resent the communication by a holder of the privilege or by the informer's own action or if the informer appears as a witness for the government.

(2) Testimony on merits. If it appears from the evidence in the case or from other showing by a party that an informer may be able to give testimony necessary to a fair determination of the issue of guilt or innocence in a criminal case or a material issue on the merits in a civil case to which the government is a party, and the government invokes the privilege, the judge shall give the government an opportunity to show *in camera* facts relevant to determining whether the informer can, in fact, supply that testimony. The showing will ordinarily be in the form of affidavits, but the judge may

direct that testimony be taken if he finds that the matter cannot be resolved satisfactorily upon affidavit. If the judge finds that there is a reasonable probability that the informer can give the testimony, and the government elects not to disclose his identity, the judge on motion of the defendant in a criminal case shall dismiss the charges to which the testimony would relate, and the judge may do so on his own motion. In civil cases, he may make any order that justice requires. Evidence submitted to the judge shall be sealed and preserved to be made available to the appellate court in the event of an appeal, and the contents shall not otherwise be revealed without consent of the government. All counsel and parties shall be permitted to be present at every stage of proceedings under this subdivision except a showing *in camera,* at which no counsel or party shall be permitted to be present.

(3) Legality of obtaining evidence. If information from an informer is relied upon to establish the legality of the means by which evidence was obtained and the judge is not satisfied that the information was received from an informer reasonably believed to be reliable or credible, he may require the identity of the informer to be disclosed. The judge shall, on request of the government, direct that the disclosure be made *in camera.* All counsel and parties concerned with the issue of legality shall be permitted to be present at every stage of proceedings under this subdivision except a disclosure *in camera,* at which no counsel or party shall be permitted to be present. If disclosure of the identity of the informer is made *in camera,* the record thereof shall be sealed and preserved to be made available to the appellate court in the event of an appeal, and the contents shall not otherwise be revealed without consent of the government.

Advisory Committee's Note

The rule recognizes the use of informers as an important aspect of law enforcement, whether the informer is a citizen who steps forward with information or a paid undercover agent. In either event, the basic importance of anonymity in the effective use of informers is apparent, Bocchicchio v. Curtis Publishing Co., 203 F.Supp. 403 (E.D.Pa.1962), and the privilege of withholding their identity was well established at common law. Roviaro v. United States, 353 U.S. 53, 59, 77 S.Ct. 623, 1 L.Ed.2d 639 (1957); McCormick § 148; 8 Wigmore § 2374 (McNaughton Rev.1961).

Subdivision (a). The public interest in law enforcement requires that the privilege be that of the government, state, or political subdivision, rather than that of the witness. The rule blankets in as an informer anyone who tells a law enforcement officer about a violation of law without regard to whether the officer is one charged with enforcing the particular law. The rule also applies to disclosures to legislative investigating committees and their staffs, and is sufficiently broad to include continuing investigations.

Although the tradition of protecting the identity of informers has evolved in an essentially criminal setting, noncriminal law enforcement situations involving possibilities of reprisal against informers fall within the purview of the considerations out of which the privilege originated. In Mitchell v. Roma, 265 F.2d 633 (3d Cir.1959), the privilege was given effect with respect to persons informing as to violations of the Fair Labor Standards Act, and in Wirtz v. Continental Finance & Loan Co., 326 F.2d 561 (5th Cir.1964), a similar case, the privilege was recognized, although the basis of decision was lack of relevancy to the issues in the case.

Only identity is privileged; communications are not included except to the extent that disclosure would operate also to disclose the informer's identity. The common law was to the same effect. 8 Wigmore § 2374, at p. 765 (McNaughton Rev.1961). See also Roviaro v. United States, supra, 353 U.S. at p. 60, 353 U.S. 53; Bowman Dairy Co. v. United States, 341 U.S. 214, 221, 71 S.Ct. 675, 95 L.Ed. 879 (1951).

The rule does not deal with the question whether presentence reports made under Criminal Procedure Rule 32(c) should be made available to an accused.

Subdivision (b). Normally the "appropriate representative" to make the claim will be counsel. However, it is possible that disclosure of the informer's identity will be sought in proceedings to which the government, state, or subdivision, as the case may be, is not a party. Under these circumstances effective implementation of the privilege requires that other representatives be considered "appropriate." See, for example, Bocchicchio v. Curtis Publishing Co., 203 F.Supp. 403 (E.D.Pa.1962), a civil action for libel, in which a local police officer not represented by counsel successfully claimed the informer privilege.

The privilege may be claimed by a state or subdivision of a state if the information was given to its officer, except that in criminal cases it may not be allowed if the government objects.

Subdivision (c) deals with situations in which the informer privilege either does not apply or is curtailed.

(1) If the identity of the informer is disclosed, nothing further is to be gained from efforts to suppress it. Disclosure may be direct, or the same practical effect may result from action revealing the informer's interest in the subject matter. See, for example, Westinghouse Electric Corp. v. City of Burlington, 122 U.S.App.D.C. 65, 351 F.2d 762 (1965), on remand City of Burlington v. Westinghouse Electric Corp., 246 F.Supp. 839 (D.D.C.1965), which held that the filing of civil antitrust actions destroyed as to plaintiffs the informer privilege claimed by the Attorney General with respect to complaints of criminal antitrust violations. While allowing the privilege in effect to be waived by one not its holder, i.e. the informer himself, is something of a novelty in the law of privilege, if the informer chooses to reveal his identity, further efforts to suppress it are scarcely feasible.

The exception is limited to disclosure to "those who would have cause to resent the communication," in the language of Roviaro v. United States,

353 U.S. 53, 60, 77 S.Ct. 623, 1 L.Ed.2d 639 (1957), since disclosure otherwise, e.g., to another law enforcing agency, is not calculated to undercut the objects of the privilege.

If the informer becomes a witness for the government, the interests of justice in disclosing his status as a source of bias or possible support are believed to outweigh any remnant of interest in nondisclosure which then remains. See Harris v. United States, 371 F.2d 365 (9th Cir.1967), in which the trial judge permitted detailed inquiry into the relationship between the witness and the government. Cf. Attorney General v. Briant, 15 M. & W. 169, 153 Eng.Rep. 808 (Exch.1846). The purpose of the limitation to witnesses for the government is to avoid the possibility of calling persons as witnesses as a means of discovery whether they are informers.

(2) The informer privilege, it was held by the leading case, may not be used in a criminal prosecution to suppress the identity of a witness when the public interest in protecting the flow of information is outweighed by the individual's right to prepare his defense. Roviaro v. United States, supra. The rule extends this balancing to include civil as well as criminal cases and phrases it in terms of "a reasonable probability that the informer may be able to give testimony necessary to a fair determination of the issue of guilt or innocence in a criminal case or of a material issue on the merits in a civil case." Once the privilege is invoked a procedure is provided for determining whether the informer can in fact supply testimony of such nature as to require disclosure of his identity, thus avoiding a "judicial guessing game" on the question. United States v. Day, 384 F.2d 464, 470 (3d Cir.1967). An investigation *in camera* is calculated to accommodate the conflicting interests involved. The rule also spells out specifically the consequences of a successful claim of the privilege in a criminal case; the wider range of possibilities in civil cases demands more flexibility in treatment. See Advisory Committee's Note to Rule 509(e), supra.

(3) One of the acute conflicts between the interest of the public in nondisclosure and the avoidance of unfairness to the accused as a result of nondisclosure arises when information from an informer is relied upon to legitimate a search and seizure by furnishing probable cause for an arrest without a warrant or for the issuance of a warrant for arrest or search. McCray v. Illinois, 386 U.S. 300, 87 S.Ct. 1056, 18 L.Ed.2d 62 (1967), rehearing denied 386 U.S. 1042. A hearing *in camera* provides an accommodation of these conflicting interests. United States v. Jackson, 384 F.2d 825 (3d Cir.1967). The limited disclosure to the judge avoids any significant impairment of secrecy, while affording the accused a substantial measure of protection against arbitrary police action. The procedure is consistent with McCray and the decisions there discussed.

Rule 511
WAIVER OF PRIVILEGE BY VOLUNTARY DISCLOSURE

[Not enacted.]

A person upon whom these rules confer a privilege against disclosure of the confidential matter or communication waives the privilege if he or his predecessor while holder of the privilege voluntarily discloses or consents to disclosure of any significant part of the matter or communication. This rule does not apply if the disclosure is itself a privileged communication.

Advisory Committee's Note

The central purpose of most privileges is the promotion of some interest or relationship by endowing it with a supporting secrecy or confidentiality. It is evident that the privilege should terminate when the holder by his own act destroys this confidentiality. McCormick §§ 87, 97, 106; 8 Wigmore §§ 2242, 2327–2329, 2374, 2389–2390 (McNaughton Rev.1961).

The rule is designed to be read with a view to what it is that the particular privilege protects. For example, the lawyer-client privilege covers only communications, and the fact that a client has discussed a matter with his lawyer does not insulate the client against disclosure of the subject matter discussed, although he is privileged not to disclose the discussion itself. See McCormick § 93. The waiver here provided for is similarly restricted. Therefore a client, merely by disclosing a subject which he had discussed with his attorney, would not waive the applicable privilege; he would have to make disclosure of the communication itself in order to effect a waiver.

By traditional doctrine, waiver is the intentional relinquishment of a known right. Johnson v. Zerbst, 304 U.S. 458, 464, 58 S.Ct. 1019, 82 L.Ed. 1461 (1938). However, in the confidential privilege situations, once confidentiality is destroyed through voluntary disclosure, no subsequent claim of privilege can restore it, and knowledge or lack of knowledge of the existence of the privilege appears to be irrelevant. California Evidence Code § 912; 8 Wigmore § 2327 (McNaughton Rev.1961).

Rule 512
PRIVILEGED MATTER DISCLOSED UNDER
COMPULSION OR WITHOUT OPPORTUNITY TO CLAIM
PRIVILEGE

[Not enacted.]

Evidence of a statement or other disclosure of privileged matter is not admissible against the holder of the privilege if the disclosure was (a) compelled erroneously or (b) made without opportunity to claim the privilege.

Advisory Committee's Note

Ordinarily a privilege is invoked in order to forestall disclosure. However, under some circumstances consideration must be given to the status and effect of a disclosure already made. Rule 511, immediately preceding, gives voluntary disclosure the effect of a waiver, while the present rule covers the effect of disclosure made under compulsion or without opportunity to claim the privilege.

Confidentiality, once destroyed, is not susceptible of restoration, yet some measure of repair may be accomplished by preventing use of the evidence against the holder of the privilege. The remedy of exclusion is therefore made available when the earlier disclosure was compelled erroneously or without opportunity to claim the privilege.

With respect to erroneously compelled disclosure, the argument may be made that the holder should be required in the first instance to assert the privilege, stand his ground, refuse to answer, perhaps incur a judgment of contempt, and exhaust all legal recourse, in order to sustain his privilege. See Fraser v. United States, 145 F.2d 139 (6th Cir.1944), cert. denied 324 U.S. 849, 65 S.Ct. 684, 89 L.Ed. 1409; United States v. Johnson, 76 F.Supp. 538 (M.D.Pa.1947), aff'd 165 F.2d 42 (3d Cir.1947), cert. denied 332 U.S. 852, 68 S.Ct. 355, 92 L.Ed. 422, reh. denied 333 U.S. 834, 68 S.Ct. 457, 92 L.Ed. 1118. However, this exacts of the holder greater fortitude in the face of authority than ordinary individuals are likely to possess, and assumes unrealistically that a judicial remedy is always available. In self-incrimination cases, the writers agree that erroneously compelled disclosures are inadmissible in a subsequent criminal prosecution of the holder, Maguire, Evidence of Guilt 66 (1959); McCormick § 127; 8 Wigmore § 2270 (McNaughton Rev.1961), and the principle is equally sound when applied to other privileges. The modest departure from usual principles of res judicata which occurs when the compulsion is judicial is justified by the advantage of having one simple rule, assuring at least one opportunity for judicial supervision in every case.

The second circumstance stated as a basis for exclusion is disclosure made without opportunity to the holder to assert his privilege. Illustrative possibilities are disclosure by an eavesdropper, by a person used in the transmission of a privileged communication, by a family member participating in psychotherapy, or privileged data improperly made available from a computer bank.

Rule 513
COMMENT UPON OR INFERENCE FROM CLAIM OF PRIVILEGE; INSTRUCTION

[Not enacted.]

(a) **Comment or inference not permitted.** The claim of a privilege, whether in the present proceeding or upon a prior occasion, is not a proper subject of comment by judge or counsel. No inference may be drawn there-from.

(b) Claiming privilege without knowledge of jury. In jury cases, proceedings shall be conducted, to the extent practicable, so as to facilitate the making of claims of privilege without the knowledge of the jury.

(c) Jury instruction. Upon request, any party against whom the jury might drawn an adverse inference from a claim of privilege is entitled to an instruction that no inference may be drawn therefrom.

Advisory Committee's Note

Subdivision (a). In Griffin v. California, 380 U.S. 609, 614, 85 S.Ct. 1229, 14 L.Ed.2d 106 (1965), the Court pointed out that allowing comment upon the claim of a privilege "cuts down on the privilege by making its assertion costly." Consequently it was held that comment upon the election of the accused not to take the stand infringed upon his privilege against self-incrimination so substantially as to constitute a constitutional violation. While the privileges governed by these rules are not constitutionally based, they are nevertheless founded upon important policies and are entitled to maximum effect. Hence the present subdivision forbids comment upon the exercise of a privilege, in accord with the weight of authority. Courtney v. United States, 390 F.2d 521 (9th Cir.1968); 8 Wigmore §§ 2243, 2322, 2386; Barnhart, Privilege in the Uniform Rules of Evidence, 24 Ohio St.L.J. 131, 137–138 (1963). Cf. McCormick § 80.

Subdivision (b). The value of a privilege may be greatly depreciated by means other than expressly commenting to a jury upon the fact that it was exercised. Thus, the calling of a witness in the presence of the jury and subsequently excusing him after a sidebar conference may effectively convey to the jury the fact that a privilege has been claimed, even though the actual claim has not been made in their hearing. Whether a privilege will be claimed is usually ascertainable in advance and the handling of the entire matter outside the presence of the jury is feasible. Destruction of the privilege by innuendo can and should be avoided. Tallo v. United States, 344 F.2d 467 (1st Cir.1965); United States v. Tomaiolo, 249 F.2d 683 (2d Cir.1957); San Fratello v. United States, 343 F.2d 711 (5th Cir.1965); Courtney v. United States, 390 F.2d 521 (9th Cir.1968); 6 Wigmore § 1808, pp. 275–276; 6 U.C.L.A.L.Rev. 455 (1959). This position is in accord with the general agreement of the authorities that an accused cannot be forced to make his election not to testify in the presence of the jury. 8 Wigmore § 2268, p. 407 (McNaughton Rev.1961).

Unanticipated situations are, of course, bound to arise, and much must be left to the discretion of the judge and the professional responsibility of counsel.

Subdivision (c). Opinions will differ as to the effectiveness of a jury instruction not to draw an adverse inference from the making of a claim of privilege. See Bruton v. United States, 389 U.S. 818, 88 S.Ct. 126, 19 L.Ed.2d 70 (1967). Whether an instruction shall be given is left to the sound judgment of counsel for the party against whom the adverse inference may be drawn. The instruction is a matter of right, if requested. This is the result reached in Bruno v. United States, 308 U.S. 287, 60 S.Ct. 198, 84 L.Ed. 257 (1939), holding that an accused is entitled to an instruction under the statute (now 18 U.S.C. § 3481) providing that his failure to testify creates no presumption against him.

The right to the instruction is not impaired by the fact that the claim of privilege is by a witness, rather than by a party, provided an adverse inference against the party may result.

Rule 804
HEARSAY EXCEPTIONS: DECLARANT UNAVAILABLE

[Subdivision (b)(2) not enacted.]

* * *

(b) Hearsay exceptions. The following are not excluded by the hearsay rule if the declarant is unavailable as a witness:

* * *

(2) *Statement of recent perception.* A statement, not in response to the instigation of a person engaged in investigating, litigating, or settling a claim, which narrates, describes, or explains an event or condition recently perceived by the declarant, made in good faith, not in contemplation of pending or anticipated litigation in which he was interested, and while his recollection was clear.

Note by Federal Judicial Center

Hearsay exception (b)(2) is set forth above as prescribed by the Supreme Court. It was not included in the rules enacted by the Congress but is reproduced here for such value as it may have for purposes of interpretation.

Advisory Committee's Note

Exception (2). The rule finds support in several directions. The well known Massachusetts Act of 1898 allows in evidence the declaration of any deceased person made in good faith before the commencement of the action and upon personal knowledge. Mass.G.L., c. 233, § 65. To the same effect is R.I.G.L. § 9–19–11. Under other statutes, a decedent's statement is admissible on behalf of his estate in actions against it, to offset the presumed inequality resulting from allowing a surviving opponent to testify. California Evidence Code § 1261; Conn.G.S., § 52–172; and statutes collected in 5 Wigmore § 1576. See also Va.Code § 8–286, allowing statements made when capable by a party now incapable of testifying.

In 1938 the Committee on Improvements in the Law of Evidence of the American Bar Association recommended adoption of a statute similar to that of Massachusetts but with the concept of unavailability expanded to include, in addition to death, cases of insanity or inability to produce a witness or take his deposition. 63 A.B.A. Reports 570, 584, 600 (1938). The same year saw enactment of the English Evidence Act of 1938, allowing written statements made on personal knowledge, if declarant is deceased or otherwise unavailable or if the court is satisfied that undue delay or expense would otherwise be caused, unless declarant was an interested person in pending or anticipated relevant proceedings. Evidence Act of 1938, 1 & 2 Geo. 6, c. 28; Cross on Evidence 482 (3rd ed. 1967).

Model Code Rule 503(a) provided broadly for admission of any hearsay declaration of an unavailable declarant. No circumstantial guarantees of trustworthiness were required. Debate upon the floor of the American Law Institute did not seriously question the propriety of the rule but centered upon what should constitute unavailability. 18 A.L.I. Proceedings 90–134 (1941).

The Uniform Rules draftsman took a less advanced position, more in the pattern of the Massachusetts statute, and invoked several assurances of accuracy: recency of perception, clarity of recollection, good faith, and antecedence to the commencement of the action. Uniform Rule 63(4)(c).

Opposition developed to the Uniform Rule because of its countenancing of the use of statements carefully prepared under the tutelage of lawyers, claim adjusters, or investigators with a view to pending or prospective litigation. Tentative Recommendation and a Study Relating to the Uniform Rules of Evidence (Art. VIII. Hearsay Evidence), Cal.Law Rev.Comm'n, 318 (1962); Quick, Excitement, Necessity and the Uniform Rules: A Reappraisal of Rule 63(4), 6 Wayne L.Rev. 204, 219–224 (1960). To meet this objection, the rule excludes statements made at the instigation of a person engaged in investigating, litigating, or settling a claim. It also incorporates as safeguards the good faith and clarity of recollection required by the Uniform Rule and the exclusion of a statement by a person interested in the litigation provided by the English act.

With respect to the question whether the introduction of a statement under this exception against the accused in a criminal case would violate his right of confrontation, reference is made to the last paragraph of the Advisory Committee's Note under Exception (1), supra.

Report of House Committee on the Judiciary

Rule 804(b)(2), a hearsay exception submitted by the Court, titled "Statement of recent perception", read as follows:

A statement, not in response to the instigation of a person engaged in investigating, litigating, or settling a claim, which narrates, describes, or explains an event or condition recently perceived by the declarant, made in good faith, not in contemplation of pending or anticipated litigation in which he was interested, and while his recollection was clear.

The Committee eliminated this Rule as creating a new and unwarranted hearsay exception of great potential breadth. The Committee did not believe that statements of the type referred to bore sufficient guarantees of trustworthiness to justify admissibility.

APPENDIX D

EVIDENCE CODE

An act to establish an Evidence Code, thereby consolidating and revising the law relating to evidence; amending various sections of the Business and Professions Code, Civil Code, Code of Civil Procedure, Corporations Code, Government Code, Health and Safety Code, Penal Code, and Public Utilities Code to make them consistent therewith; adding Sections 164.5, 3544, 3545, 3546, 3547, and 3548 to the Civil Code; adding Sections 631.7 and 1908.5 to the Code of Civil Procedure; and repealing legislation inconsistent therewith.

Enacted by Stats.1965, c. 299
Operative January 1, 1967.

The people of the State of California do enact as follows:

Division 1

PRELIMINARY PROVISIONS AND CONSTRUCTION

8. Construction of tenses.

9. Construction of gender references.

10. Construction of singular and plural.

11. "Shall" and "may".

12. Operative date of code; effect on pending proceedings.

§ 1
Short title

This code shall be known as the Evidence Code. (*Stats.1965, c. 299, § 2, operative Jan. 1, 1967.*)

§ 2
Abrogation of common law rule of strict construction; liberal construction

The rule of the common law, that statutes in derogation thereof are to be strictly construed, has no application to this code. This code establishes the law of this state respecting the subject to which it relates, and its provisions are to be liberally construed with a view to effecting its objects and promoting justice. (*Stats.1965, c. 299, § 2, operative Jan. 1, 1967.*)

§ 3
Severability

If any provision or clause of this code or application thereof to any person or circumstances is held invalid, such invalidity shall not affect other provisions or applications of the code which can be given effect without the invalid provision or application, and to this end the provisions of this code are declared to be severable. (*Stats.1965, c. 299, § 2, operative Jan. 1, 1967.*)

§ 4
Construction of code

Unless the provision or context otherwise requires, these preliminary provisions and rules of construction shall govern the construction of this code. (*Stats.1965, c. 299, § 2, operative Jan. 1, 1967.*)

§ 5
Construction of headings

Division, chapter, article, and section headings do not in any manner affect the scope, meaning, or intent of the provisions of this code. (*Stats.1965, c. 299, § 2, operative Jan. 1, 1967.*)

§ 6
References to statutes; application

Whenever any reference is made to any portion of this code or of any other statute, such reference shall apply to all amendments and additions heretofore or hereafter made. (*Stats.1965, c. 299, § 2, operative Jan. 1, 1967.*)

§ 7
Definitions

Unless otherwise expressly stated:

(a) "Division" means a division of this code.

(b) "Chapter" means a chapter of the division in which that term occurs.

(c) "Article" means an article of the chapter in which that term occurs.

(d) "Section" means a section of this code.

(e) "Subdivision" means a subdivision of the section in which that term occurs.

(f) "Paragraph" means a paragraph of the subdivision in which that term occurs. (*Stats.1965, c. 299, § 2, operative Jan. 1, 1967.*)

§ 8
Construction of tenses

The present tense includes the past and future tenses; and the future, the present. (*Stats.1965, c. 299, § 2, operative Jan. 1, 1967.*)

§ 9
Construction of gender references

The masculine gender includes the feminine and neuter. (*Stats.1965, c. 299, § 2, operative Jan. 1, 1967.*)

§ 10
Construction of singular and plural

The singular number includes the plural; and the plural, the singular. (*Stats.1965, c. 299, § 2, operative Jan. 1, 1967.*)

§ 11
"Shall" and "may"

"Shall" is mandatory and "may" is permissive. (*Stats.1965, c. 299, § 2, operative Jan. 1, 1967.*)

§ 12
Operative date of code; effect on pending proceedings

(a) This code shall become operative on January 1, 1967, and shall govern proceedings in actions brought on or after that date and, except as provided in subdivision (b), further proceedings in actions pending on that date.

(b) Subject to subdivision (c), a trial commenced before January 1, 1967, shall not be governed by this code. For the purpose of this subdivision:

(1) A trial is commenced when the first witness is sworn or the first exhibit is admitted into evidence and is terminated when the issue upon which such evidence is received is submitted to the trier of fact. A new trial, or a separate trial of a different issue, commenced on or after January 1, 1967, shall be governed by this code.

(2) If an appeal is taken from a ruling made at a trial commenced before January 1, 1967, the appellate court shall apply the law applicable at the time of the commencement of the trial.

(c) The provisions of Division 8 (commencing with Section 900) relating to privileges shall govern any claim of privilege made after December 31, 1966. (*Stats.1965, c. 299, § 2, operative Jan. 1, 1967.*)

Division 2

WORDS AND PHRASES DEFINED

§ 100
Application of definitions

Unless the provision or context otherwise requires, these definitions govern the construction of this code. (*Stats.1965, c. 299, § 2, operative Jan. 1, 1967.*)

§ 105
Action

"Action" includes a civil action and a criminal action. (*Stats.1965, c. 299, § 2, operative Jan. 1, 1967.*)

§ 110
Burden of producing evidence

"Burden of producing evidence" means the obligation of a party to introduce evidence sufficient to avoid a ruling against him on the issue. (*Stats.1965, c. 299, § 2, operative Jan. 1, 1967.*)

§ 115
Burden of proof

"Burden of proof" means the obligation of a party to establish by evidence a requisite degree of belief concerning a fact in the mind of the trier of fact or the court. The burden of proof may require a party to raise a reasonable doubt concerning the existence or nonexistence of a fact or that he establish the existence or nonexistence of a fact by a preponderance of the evidence, by clear and convincing proof, or by proof beyond a reasonable doubt.

Except as otherwise provided by law, the burden of proof requires proof by a preponderance of the evidence. (*Stats.1965, c. 299, § 2, operative Jan. 1, 1967.*)

§ 120
Civil action

"Civil action" includes civil proceedings. (*Stats.1965, c. 299, § 2, operative Jan. 1, 1967.*)

§ 125
Conduct

"Conduct" includes all active and passive behavior, both verbal and nonverbal. (*Stats.1965, c. 299, § 2, operative Jan. 1, 1967.*)

§ 130
Criminal action

"Criminal action" includes criminal proceedings. (*Stats.1965, c. 299, § 2, operative Jan. 1, 1967.*)

§ 135
Declarant

"Declarant" is a person who makes a statement. (*Stats.1965, c. 299, § 2, operative Jan. 1, 1967.*)

§ 140
Evidence

"Evidence" means testimony, writings, material objects, or other things presented to the senses that are offered to prove the existence or nonexistence of a fact. (*Stats.1965, c. 299, § 2, operative Jan. 1, 1967.*)

§ 145
The hearing

"The hearing" means the hearing at which a question under this code arises, and not some earlier or later hearing. (*Stats.1965, c. 299, § 2, operative Jan. 1, 1967.*)

§ 150
Hearsay evidence

"Hearsay evidence" is defined in Section 1200. (*Stats.1965, c. 299, § 2, operative Jan. 1, 1967.*)

§ 160
Law

"Law" includes constitutional, statutory, and decisional law. (*Stats.1965, c. 299, § 2, operative Jan. 1, 1967.*)

§ 165
Oath

"Oath" includes affirmation or declaration under penalty of perjury. (*Stats.1965, c. 299, § 2, operative Jan. 1, 1967.*)

§ 170
Perceive

"Perceive" means to acquire knowledge through one's senses. (*Stats.1965, c. 299, § 2, operative Jan. 1, 1967.*)

§ 175
Person

"Person" includes a natural person, firm, association, organization, partnership, business trust, corporation, limited liability company, or public entity. (*Stats.1965, c. 299, § 2, operative Jan. 1, 1967. Amended by Stats.1994, c. 1010 (S.B.2053), § 103.*)

§ 177
Dependent person

"Dependent person" means any person who has a physical or mental impairment that substantially restricts his or her ability to carry out normal activities or to protect his or her rights, including, but not limited to, persons who have physical or developmental disabilities or whose physical or mental abilities have significantly diminished because of age. "Dependent person" includes any person who is admitted as an inpatient to a 24–hour health facility, as defined in Sections 1250, 1250.2, and 1250.3 of the Health and Safety Code. (*Added by Stats.2004, c. 823 (A.B.20), § 2.*)

§ 180
Personal property

"Personal property" includes money, goods, chattels, things in action, and evidences of debt. (*Stats.1965, c. 299, § 2, operative Jan. 1, 1967.*)

§ 185
Property

"Property" includes both real and personal property. (*Stats.1965, c. 299, § 2, operative Jan. 1, 1967.*)

§ 190
Proof

"Proof" is the establishment by evidence of a requisite degree of belief concerning a fact in the mind of the trier of fact or the court. (*Stats.1965, c. 299, § 2, operative Jan. 1, 1967.*)

§ 195
Public employee

"Public employee" means an officer, agent, or employee of a public entity. (*Stats.1965, c. 299, § 2, operative Jan. 1, 1967.*)

§ 200
Public entity

"Public entity" includes a nation, state, county, city and county, city, district, public authority, public agency, or any other political subdivision or public corporation, whether foreign or domestic. (*Stats.1965, c. 299, § 2, operative Jan. 1, 1967.*)

§ 205
Real property

"Real property" includes lands, tenements, and hereditaments. (*Stats.1965, c. 299, § 2, operative Jan. 1, 1967.*)

§ 210
Relevant evidence

"Relevant evidence" means evidence, including evidence relevant to the credibility of a witness or hearsay declarant, having any tendency in reason to prove or disprove any disputed fact that is of consequence to the determination of the action. (*Stats.1965, c. 299, § 2, operative Jan. 1, 1967.*)

§ 220
State

"State" means the State of California, unless applied to the different parts of the United States. In the latter case, it includes any state, district, commonwealth, territory, or insular possession of the United States. (*Stats.1965, c. 299, § 2, operative Jan. 1, 1967.*)

§ 225
Statement

"Statement" means (a) oral or written verbal expression or (b) nonverbal conduct of a person intended by him as a substitute for oral or written verbal expression. (*Stats.1965, c. 299, § 2, operative Jan. 1, 1967.*)

§ 230
Statute
"Statute" includes a treaty and a constitutional provision. (*Stats.1965, c. 299, § 2, operative Jan. 1, 1967.*)

§ 235
Trier of fact
"Trier of fact" includes (a) the jury and (b) the court when the court is trying an issue of fact other than one relating to the admissibility of evidence. (*Stats.1965, c. 299, § 2, operative Jan. 1, 1967.*)

§ 240
Unavailable as a witness

(a) Except as otherwise provided in subdivision (b), "unavailable as a witness" means that the declarant is any of the following:

(1) Exempted or precluded on the ground of privilege from testifying concerning the matter to which his or her statement is relevant.

(2) Disqualified from testifying to the matter.

(3) Dead or unable to attend or to testify at the hearing because of then-existing physical or mental illness or infirmity.

(4) Absent from the hearing and the court is unable to compel his or her attendance by its process.

(5) Absent from the hearing and the proponent of his or her statement has exercised reasonable diligence but has been unable to procure his or her attendance by the court's process.

(6) Persistent in refusing to testify concerning the subject matter of the declarant's statement despite having been found in contempt for refusal to testify.

(b) A declarant is not unavailable as a witness if the exemption, preclusion, disqualification, death, inability, or absence of the declarant was brought about by the procurement or wrongdoing of the proponent of his or her statement for the purpose of preventing the declarant from attending or testifying.

(c) Expert testimony that establishes that physical or mental trauma resulting from an alleged crime has caused harm to a witness of sufficient severity that the witness is physically unable to testify or is unable to testify without suffering substantial trauma may constitute a sufficient showing of unavailability pursuant to paragraph (3) of subdivision (a). As used in this section, the term "expert" means a physician and surgeon, including a psychiatrist, or any person described by subdivision (b), (c), or (e) of Section 1010.

The introduction of evidence to establish the unavailability of a witness under this subdivision shall not be deemed procurement of unavailability, in absence of proof to the contrary. (*Stats.1965, c. 299, § 2, operative Jan. 1, 1967. Amended by Stats.1984, c. 401, § 1; Stats.1988, c. 485, § 1; Stats.2010, c. 537 (A.B.1723), § 1.*)

§ 250
Writing

"Writing" means handwriting, typewriting, printing, photostating, photographing, photocopying, transmitting by electronic mail or facsimile, and every other means of recording upon any tangible thing, any form of communication or representation, including letters, words, pictures, sounds, or symbols, or combinations thereof, and any record thereby created, regardless of the manner in which the record has been stored. (*Stats.1965, c. 299, § 2, operative Jan. 1, 1967. Amended by Stats.2002, c. 945 (A.B.1962), § 1.*)

§ 255
Original

"Original" means the writing itself or any counterpart intended to have the same effect by a person executing or issuing it. An "original" of a photograph includes the negative or any print therefrom. If data are stored in a computer or similar device, any printout or other output readable by sight, shown to reflect the data accurately, is an "original." (*Added by Stats.1977, c. 708, p. 2268, § 1.*)

§ 260
Duplicate

A "duplicate" is a counterpart produced by the same impression as the original, or from the same matrix, or by means of photography, including enlargements and miniatures, or by mechanical or electronic rerecording, or by chemical reproduction, or by other equivalent technique which accurately reproduces the original. (*Added by Stats.1977, c. 708, p. 2268, § 2.*)

Division 3

GENERAL PROVISIONS

CHAPTER 1. APPLICABILITY OF CODE

Section
300. Applicability of code.

§ 300
Applicability of code

Except as otherwise provided by statute, this code applies in every action before the Supreme Court or a court of appeal or superior court, including proceedings in such actions conducted by a referee, court commissioner, or similar officer, but does not apply in grand jury proceedings. (*Stats.1965, c. 299, § 2, operative Jan. 1, 1967. Amended by Stats.1967, c. 17, p. 836, § 35; Stats.1998, c. 931 (S.B.2139), § 141, eff. Sept. 28, 1998; Stats.2002, c. 784 (S.B.1316), § 101.*)

CHAPTER 2. PROVINCE OF COURT AND JURY

Section
310. Questions of law for court.
311. Foreign law applicable; law undetermined; procedures.
312. Jury as trier of fact.

§ 310
Questions of law for court

(a) All questions of law (including but not limited to questions concerning the construction of statutes and other writings, the admissibility of evidence, and other rules of evidence) are to be decided by the court. Determination of issues of fact preliminary to the admission of evidence are to be decided by the court as provided in Article 2 (commencing with Section 400) of Chapter 4.

(b) Determination of the law of an organization of nations or of the law of a foreign nation or a public entity in a foreign nation is a question of law to be determined in the manner provided in Division 4 (commencing with Section 450). (*Stats.1965, c. 299, § 2, operative Jan. 1, 1967.*)

§ 311
Foreign law applicable; law undetermined; procedures

If the law of an organization of nations, a foreign nation or a state other than this state, or a public entity in a foreign nation or a state other than this state, is applicable and such law cannot be determined, the court may, as the ends of justice require, either:

(a) Apply the law of this state if the court can do so consistently with the Constitution of the United States and the Constitution of this state; or

(b) Dismiss the action without prejudice or, in the case of a reviewing court, remand the case to the trial court with directions to dismiss the action without prejudice. (*Stats.1965, c. 299, § 2, operative Jan. 1, 1967.*)

§ 312
Jury as trier of fact

Except as otherwise provided by law, where the trial is by jury:

(a) All questions of fact are to be decided by the jury.

(b) Subject to the control of the court, the jury is to determine the effect and value of the evidence addressed to it, including the credibility of witnesses and hearsay declarants. (*Stats.1965, c. 299, § 2, operative Jan. 1, 1967.*)

CHAPTER 3. ORDER OF PROOF

Section
320. Power of court to regulate order of proof.

§ 320
Power of court to regulate order of proof
Except as otherwise provided by law, the court in its discretion shall regulate the order of proof. (*Stats.1965, c. 299, § 2, operative Jan. 1, 1967.*)

CHAPTER 4. ADMITTING AND EXCLUDING EVIDENCE

ARTICLE 1. GENERAL PROVISIONS

§ 350
Only relevant evidence admissible
No evidence is admissible except relevant evidence. (*Stats.1965, c. 299, § 2, operative Jan. 1, 1967.*)

§ 351
Admissibility of relevant evidence
Except as otherwise provided by statute, all relevant evidence is admissible. (*Stats.1965, c. 299, § 2, operative Jan. 1, 1967.*)

§ 351.1
Polygraph examinations; results, opinion of examiner or reference; exclusion
(a) Notwithstanding any other provision of law, the results of a polygraph examination, the opinion of a polygraph examiner, or any reference to an offer to take, failure to take, or taking of a polygraph examination, shall not be admitted into evidence in any criminal proceeding, including pretrial and post conviction motions and hearings, or in any trial or hearing of a juvenile for a criminal offense, whether heard in juvenile or adult court, unless all parties stipulate to the admission of such results.

(b) Nothing in this section is intended to exclude from evidence statements made during a polygraph examination which are otherwise admissible. (*Added by Stats.1983, c. 202, § 1, eff. July 12, 1983.*)

§ 352
Discretion of court to exclude evidence

The court in its discretion may exclude evidence if its probative value is substantially outweighed by the probability that its admission will (a) necessitate undue consumption of time or (b) create substantial danger of undue prejudice, of confusing the issues, or of misleading the jury. (*Stats.1965, c. 299, § 2, operative Jan. 1, 1967.*)

§ 352.1
Criminal sex acts; victim's address and telephone number

In any criminal proceeding under Section 261, 262, or 264.1, subdivision (d) of Section 286, or subdivision (d) of Section 288a of the Penal Code, or in any criminal proceeding under subdivision (c) of Section 286 or subdivision (c) of Section 288a of the Penal Code in which the defendant is alleged to have compelled the participation of the victim by force, violence, duress, menace, or threat of great bodily harm, the district attorney may, upon written motion with notice to the defendant or the defendant's attorney, if he or she is represented by an attorney, within a reasonable time prior to any hearing, move to exclude from evidence the current address and telephone number of any victim at the hearing.

The court may order that evidence of the victim's current address and telephone number be excluded from any hearings conducted pursuant to the criminal proceeding if the court finds that the probative value of the evidence is outweighed by the creation of substantial danger to the victim.

Nothing in this section shall abridge or limit the defendant's right to discover or investigate the information. (*Added by Stats.1985, c. 335, § 3. Amended by Stats.1996, c. 1075 (S.B.1444), § 5.*)

§ 353
Erroneous admission of evidence; effect

A verdict or finding shall not be set aside, nor shall the judgment or decision based thereon be reversed, by reason of the erroneous admission of evidence unless:

(a) There appears of record an objection to or a motion to exclude or to strike the evidence that was timely made and so stated as to make clear the specific ground of the objection or motion; and

(b) The court which passes upon the effect of the error or errors is of the opinion that the admitted evidence should have been excluded on the ground stated and that the error or errors complained of resulted in a miscarriage of justice. (*Stats.1965, c. 299, § 2, operative Jan. 1, 1967.*)

§ 354
Erroneous exclusion of evidence; effect

A verdict or finding shall not be set aside, nor shall the judgment or decision based thereon be reversed, by reason of the erroneous exclusion of evidence unless the court which passes upon the effect of the error or errors is of the opinion that the error or errors complained of resulted in a miscarriage of justice and it appears of record that:

(a) The substance, purpose, and relevance of the excluded evidence was made known to the court by the questions asked, an offer of proof, or by any other means;

(b) The rulings of the court made compliance with subdivision (a) futile; or

(c) The evidence was sought by questions asked during cross-examination or recross-examination. (*Stats.1965, c. 299, § 2, operative Jan. 1, 1967.*)

§ 355
Limited admissibility

When evidence is admissible as to one party or for one purpose and is inadmissible as to another party or for another purpose, the court upon request shall restrict the evidence to its proper scope and instruct the jury accordingly. (*Stats.1965, c. 299, § 2, operative Jan. 1, 1967.*)

§ 356
Entire act, declaration, conversation, or writing to elucidate part offered

Where part of an act, declaration, conversation, or writing is given in evidence by one party, the whole on the same subject may be inquired into by an adverse party; when a letter is read, the answer may be given; and when a detached act, declaration, conversation, or writing is given in evidence, any other act, declaration, conversation, or writing which is necessary to make it understood may also be given in evidence. (*Stats.1965, c. 299, § 2, operative Jan. 1, 1967.*)

ARTICLE 2. PRELIMINARY DETERMINATIONS ON ADMISSIBILITY OF EVIDENCE

Section
400. Preliminary fact defined.
401. Proffered evidence defined.
402. Procedure for determining foundational and other preliminary facts.
403. Determination of foundational and other preliminary facts where relevancy, personal knowledge, or authenticity is disputed.
404. Determination of whether proffered evidence is incriminatory.
405. Determination of foundational and other preliminary facts in other cases.
406. Evidence affecting weight or credibility.

§ 400
Preliminary fact defined

As used in this article, "preliminary fact" means a fact upon the existence or nonexistence of which depends the admissibility or inadmissibility of evidence. The phrase "the admissibility or inadmissibility of evidence" includes the qualification or disqualification of a person to be a witness and the existence or nonexistence of a privilege. (*Stats.1965, c. 299, § 2, operative Jan. 1, 1967.*)

§ 401
Proffered evidence defined

As used in this article, "proffered evidence" means evidence, the admissibility or inadmissibility of which is dependent upon the existence or nonexistence of a preliminary fact. (*Stats.1965, c. 299, § 2, operative Jan. 1, 1967.*)

§ 402
Procedure for determining foundational and other preliminary facts

(a) When the existence of a preliminary fact is disputed, its existence or nonexistence shall be determined as provided in this article.

(b) The court may hear and determine the question of the admissibility of evidence out of the presence or hearing of the jury; but in a criminal action, the court shall hear and determine the question of the admissibility of a confession or admission of the defendant out of the presence and hearing of the jury if any party so requests.

(c) A ruling on the admissibility of evidence implies whatever finding of fact is prerequisite thereto; a separate or formal finding is unnecessary unless required by statute. (*Stats.1965, c. 299, § 2, operative Jan. 1, 1967.*)

§ 403
Determination of foundational and other preliminary facts where relevancy, personal knowledge, or authenticity is disputed

(a) The proponent of the proffered evidence has the burden of producing evidence as to the existence of the preliminary fact, and the proffered evidence is inadmissible unless the court finds that there is evidence sufficient to sustain a finding of the existence of the preliminary fact, when:

(1) The relevance of the proffered evidence depends on the existence of the preliminary fact;

(2) The preliminary fact is the personal knowledge of a witness concerning the subject matter of his testimony;

(3) The preliminary fact is the authenticity of a writing; or

(4) The proffered evidence is of a statement or other conduct of a particular person and the preliminary fact is whether that person made the statement or so conducted himself.

(b) Subject to Section 702, the court may admit conditionally the proffered evidence under this section, subject to evidence of the preliminary fact being supplied later in the course of the trial.

(c) If the court admits the proffered evidence under this section, the court:

(1) May, and on request shall, instruct the jury to determine whether the preliminary fact exists and to disregard the proffered evidence unless the jury finds that the preliminary fact does exist.

(2) Shall instruct the jury to disregard the proffered evidence if the court subsequently determines that a jury could not reasonably find that the preliminary fact exists. (*Stats.1965, c. 299, § 2, operative Jan. 1, 1967.*)

§ 404
Determination of whether proffered evidence is incriminatory

Whenever the proffered evidence is claimed to be privileged under Section 940, the person claiming the privilege has the burden of showing that the proffered evidence might tend to incriminate him; and the proffered evidence is inadmissible unless it clearly appears to the court that the proffered evidence cannot possibly have a tendency to incriminate the person claiming the privilege. (*Stats.1965, c. 299, § 2, operative Jan. 1, 1967.*)

§ 405
Determination of foundational and other preliminary facts in other cases

With respect to preliminary fact determinations not governed by Section 403 or 404:

(a) When the existence of a preliminary fact is disputed, the court shall indicate which party has the burden of producing evidence and the burden of proof on the issue as implied by the rule of law under which the question arises. The court shall determine the existence or nonexistence of the preliminary fact and shall admit or exclude the proffered evidence as required by the rule of law under which the question arises.

(b) If a preliminary fact is also a fact in issue in the action:

(1) The jury shall not be informed of the court's determination as to the existence or nonexistence of the preliminary fact.

(2) If the proffered evidence is admitted, the jury shall not be instructed to disregard the evidence if its determination of the fact differs from the court's determination of the preliminary fact. (*Stats.1965, c. 299, § 2, operative Jan. 1, 1967.*)

§ 406
Evidence affecting weight or credibility

This article does not limit the right of a party to introduce before the trier of fact evidence relevant to weight or credibility. (*Stats.1965, c. 299, § 2, operative Jan. 1, 1967.*)

CHAPTER 5. WEIGHT OF EVIDENCE GENERALLY

Section
410. Direct evidence defined.
411. Direct evidence of one witness sufficient.
412. Party having power to produce better evidence.
413. Party's failure to explain or deny evidence.

§ 410
Direct evidence defined

As used in this chapter, "direct evidence" means evidence that directly proves a fact, without an inference or presumption, and which in itself, if true, conclusively establishes that fact. (*Stats.1965, c. 299, § 2, operative Jan. 1, 1967.*)

§ 411
Direct evidence of one witness sufficient

Except where additional evidence is required by statute, the direct evidence of one witness who is entitled to full credit is sufficient for proof of any fact. (*Stats.1965, c. 299, § 2, operative Jan. 1, 1967.*)

§ 412
Party having power to produce better evidence

If weaker and less satisfactory evidence is offered when it was within the power of the party to produce stronger and more satisfactory evidence, the evidence offered should be viewed with distrust. (*Stats.1965, c. 299, § 2, operative Jan. 1, 1967.*)

§ 413
Party's failure to explain or deny evidence

In determining what inferences to draw from the evidence or facts in the case against a party, the trier of fact may consider, among other things, the party's failure to explain or to deny by his testimony such evidence or facts in the case against him, or his willful suppression of evidence relating thereto, if such be the case. (*Stats.1965, c. 299, § 2, operative Jan. 1, 1967.*)

Division 4

JUDICIAL NOTICE

Section
450. Judicial notice may be taken only as authorized by law.
451. Matters which must be judicially noticed.
452. Matters which may be judicially noticed.

§ 450
Judicial notice may be taken only as authorized by law

Judicial notice may not be taken of any matter unless authorized or required by law. (*Stats.1965, c. 299, § 2, operative Jan. 1, 1967.*)

§ 451
Matters which must be judicially noticed

Judicial notice shall be taken of the following:

(a) The decisional, constitutional, and public statutory law of this state and of the United States and the provisions of any charter described in Section 3, 4, or 5 of Article XI of the California Constitution.

(b) Any matter made a subject of judicial notice by Section 11343.6, 11344.6, or 18576 of the Government Code or by Section 1507 of Title 44 of the United States Code.

(c) Rules of professional conduct for members of the bar adopted pursuant to Section 6076 of the Business and Professions Code and rules of practice and procedure for the courts of this state adopted by the Judicial Council.

(d) Rules of pleading, practice, and procedure prescribed by the United States Supreme Court, such as the Rules of the United States Supreme Court, the Federal Rules of Civil Procedure, the Federal Rules of Criminal Procedure, the Admiralty Rules, the Rules of the Court of Claims, the Rules of the Customs Court, and the General Orders and Forms in Bankruptcy.

(e) The true signification of all English words and phrases and of all legal expressions.

(f) Facts and propositions of generalized knowledge that are so universally known that they cannot reasonably be the subject of dispute. (*Stats.1965, c. 299, § 2, operative Jan. 1, 1967. Amended by Stats.1971, c. 438, p. 881, § 88; Stats.1972, c. 764, p. 1373, § 1; Stats.1982, c. 454, p. 1835, § 20; Stats.1985, c. 106, § 32; Stats.1986, c. 248, § 43.*)

§ 452
Matters which may be judicially noticed

Judicial notice may be taken of the following matters to the extent that they are not embraced within Section 451:

(a) The decisional, constitutional, and statutory law of any state of the United States and the resolutions and private acts of the Congress of the United States and of the Legislature of this state.

(b) Regulations and legislative enactments issued by or under the authority of the United States or any public entity in the United States.

(c) Official acts of the legislative, executive, and judicial departments of the United States and of any state of the United States.

(d) Records of (1) any court of this state or (2) any court of record of the United States or of any state of the United States.

(e) Rules of court of (1) any court of this state or (2) any court of record of the United States or of any state of the United States.

(f) The law of an organization of nations and of foreign nations and public entities in foreign nations.

(g) Facts and propositions that are of such common knowledge within the territorial jurisdiction of the court that they cannot reasonably be the subject of dispute.

(h) Facts and propositions that are not reasonably subject to dispute and are capable of immediate and accurate determination by resort to sources of reasonably indisputable accuracy. (*Stats.1965, c. 299, § 2, operative Jan. 1, 1967.*)

§ 452.5
Criminal conviction records; computer-generated records; admissibility

(a) The official acts and records specified in subdivisions (c) and (d) of Section 452 include any computer-generated official court records, as specified by the Judicial Council which relate to criminal convictions, when the record is certified by a clerk of the superior court pursuant to Section 69844.5 of the Government Code at the time of computer entry.

(b) An official record of conviction certified in accordance with subdivision (a) of Section 1530 is admissible pursuant to Section 1280 to prove the commission, attempted commission, or solicitation of a criminal offense, prior conviction, service of a prison term, or other act, condition, or event recorded by the record. (*Added by Stats.1996, c. 642 (A.B.1387), § 3. Amended by Stats.2002, c. 784 (S.B.1316), § 102.*)

2002 Amendment

§ 453
Compulsory judicial notice upon request

The trial court shall take judicial notice of any matter specified in Section 452 if a party requests it and:

(a) Gives each adverse party sufficient notice of the request, through the pleadings or otherwise, to enable such adverse party to prepare to meet the request; and

(b) Furnishes the court with sufficient information to enable it to take judicial notice of the matter. (*Stats.1965, c. 299, § 2, operative Jan. 1, 1967.*)

§ 454
Information that may be used in taking judicial notice

(a) In determining the propriety of taking judicial notice of a matter, or the tenor thereof:

(1) Any source of pertinent information, including the advice of persons learned in the subject matter, may be consulted or used, whether or not furnished by a party.

(2) Exclusionary rules of evidence do not apply except for Section 352 and the rules of privilege.

(b) Where the subject of judicial notice is the law of an organization of nations, a foreign nation, or a public entity in a foreign nation and the court resorts to the advice of persons learned in the subject matter, such advice, if not received in open court, shall be in writing. (*Stats.1965, c. 299, § 2, operative Jan. 1, 1967.*)

§ 455
Opportunity to present information to court

With respect to any matter specified in Section 452 or in subdivision (f) of Section 451 that is of substantial consequence to the determination of the action:

(a) If the trial court has been requested to take or has taken or proposes to take judicial notice of such matter, the court shall afford each party reasonable opportunity, before the jury is instructed or before the cause is submitted for decision by the court, to present to the court information relevant to (1) the propriety of taking judicial notice of the matter and (2) the tenor of the matter to be noticed.

(b) If the trial court resorts to any source of information not received in open court, including the advice of persons learned in the subject matter, such information and its source shall be made a part of the record in the action and the court shall afford each party reasonable opportunity to meet such information before judicial notice of the matter may be taken. (*Stats.1965, c. 299, § 2, operative Jan. 1, 1967.*)

§ 456
Noting denial of request to take judicial notice

If the trial court denies a request to take judicial notice of any matter, the court shall at the earliest practicable time so advise the parties and indicate for the record that it has denied the request. (*Stats.1965, c. 299, § 2, operative Jan. 1, 1967.*)

§ 457
Instructing jury on matter judicially noticed

If a matter judicially noticed is a matter which would otherwise have been for determination by the jury, the trial court may, and upon request shall, instruct the jury to accept as a fact the matter so noticed. (*Stats.1965, c. 299, § 2, operative Jan. 1, 1967.*)

§ 458
Judicial notice by trial court in subsequent proceedings

The failure or refusal of the trial court to take judicial notice of a matter, or to instruct the jury with respect to the matter, does not preclude the trial court in subsequent proceedings in the action from taking judicial notice of the matter in accordance with the procedure specified in this division. (*Stats.1965, c. 299, § 2, operative Jan. 1, 1967.*)

§ 459
Judicial notice by reviewing court

(a) The reviewing court shall take judicial notice of (1) each matter properly noticed by the trial court and (2) each matter that the trial court was required to notice under Section 451 or 453. The reviewing court may take judicial notice of any matter specified in Section 452. The reviewing court may take judicial notice of a matter in a tenor different from that noticed by the trial court.

(b) In determining the propriety of taking judicial notice of a matter, or the tenor thereof, the reviewing court has the same power as the trial court under Section 454.

(c) When taking judicial notice under this section of a matter specified in Section 452 or in subdivision (f) of Section 451 that is of substantial consequence to the determination of the action, the reviewing court shall comply with the provisions of subdivision (a) of Section 455 if the matter was not theretofore judicially noticed in the action.

(d) In determining the propriety of taking judicial notice of a matter specified in Section 452 or in subdivision (f) of Section 451 that is of substantial consequence to the determination of the action, or the tenor thereof, if the reviewing court resorts to any source of information not received in open court or not included in the record of the action, including the advice of persons learned in the subject matter, the reviewing court shall afford each party reasonable opportunity to meet such information before judicial notice of the matter may be taken. (*Stats.1965, c. 299, § 2, operative Jan. 1, 1967.*)

§ 460
Appointment of expert by court

Where the advice of persons learned in the subject matter is required in order to enable the court to take judicial notice of a matter, the court on its own motion or on motion of any party may appoint one or more such persons to provide such advice. If the court determines to appoint such a person, he shall be appointed and compensated in the manner provided in Article 2 (commencing with Section 730) of Chapter 3 of Division 6. (*Stats.1965, c. 299, § 2, operative Jan. 1, 1967.*)

Division 5

BURDEN OF PROOF; BURDEN OF PRODUCING EVIDENCE; PRESUMPTIONS AND INFERENCES

Chapter 1

BURDEN OF PROOF

ARTICLE 1. GENERAL

§ 500
Party who has the burden of proof

Except as otherwise provided by law, a party has the burden of proof as to each fact the existence or nonexistence of which is essential to the claim for relief or defense that he is asserting. (*Stats.1965, c. 299, § 2, operative Jan. 1, 1967.*)

§ 501
Criminal actions; statutory assignment of burden of proof; controlling section

Insofar as any statute, except Section 522, assigns the burden of proof in a criminal action, such statute is subject to Penal Code Section 1096. (*Stats.1965, c. 299, § 2, operative Jan. 1, 1967.*)

§ 502
Instructions on burden of proof

The court on all proper occasions shall instruct the jury as to which party bears the burden of proof on each issue and as to whether that burden requires that a party raise a reasonable doubt concerning the existence or nonexistence of a fact or that he establish the existence or nonexistence of a fact by a preponderance of the evidence, by clear and convincing proof, or by proof beyond a reasonable doubt. (*Stats.1965, c. 299, § 2, operative Jan. 1, 1967.*)

ARTICLE 2. BURDEN OF PROOF ON SPECIFIC ISSUES

Section
520. Claim that person is guilty of crime or wrongdoing.
521. Claim that person did not exercise care.
522. Claim that person is or was insane.
523. Historic locations of water; claims involving state land patents or grants.
524. Burden of proof in cases involving State Board of Equalization; unreasonable search or access to records prohibited; taxpayer defined.

§ 520
Claim that person is guilty of crime or wrongdoing

The party claiming that a person is guilty of crime or wrongdoing has the burden of proof on that issue. (*Stats.1965, c. 299, § 2, operative Jan. 1, 1967.*)

§ 521
Claim that person did not exercise care

The party claiming that a person did not exercise a requisite degree of care has the burden of proof on that issue. (*Stats.1965, c. 299, § 2, operative Jan. 1, 1967.*)

§ 522
Claim that person is or was insane

The party claiming that any person, including himself, is or was insane has the burden of proof on that issue. (*Stats.1965, c. 299, § 2, operative Jan. 1, 1967.*)

§ 523
Historic locations of water; claims involving state land patents or grants

In any action where the state is a party, regardless of who is the moving party, where (a) the boundary of land patented or otherwise granted by the state is in dispute, or (b) the validity of any state patent or grant dated prior to 1950 is in dispute, the state shall have the burden of proof on all issues relating to the historic locations of rivers, streams, and other water bodies and the authority of the state in issuing the patent or grant.

This section is not intended to nor shall it be construed to supersede existing statutes governing disputes where the state is a party and regarding title to real property. (*Added by Stats.1994, c. 128 (S.B.1429), § 2.*)

§ 524
Burden of proof in cases involving State Board of Equalization; unreasonable search or access to records prohibited; taxpayer defined

(a) Notwithstanding any other provision of law, in a civil proceeding to which the State Board of Equalization is a party, that board shall have the burden of proof by clear and convincing evidence in sustaining its assertion of a penalty for intent to evade or fraud against a taxpayer, with respect to any factual issue relevant to ascertaining the liability of a taxpayer.

(b) Nothing in this section shall be construed to override any requirement for a taxpayer to substantiate any item on a return or claim filed with the State Board of Equalization.

(c) Nothing in this section shall subject a taxpayer to unreasonable search or access to records in violation of the United States Constitution, the California Constitution, or any other law.

(d) For purposes of this section, "taxpayer" includes a person on whom fees administered by the State Board of Equalization are imposed. (*Added by Stats.2010, c. 168 (A.B.2195), § 1.*)

CHAPTER 2. BURDEN OF PRODUCING EVIDENCE

Section
550. Party who has the burden of producing evidence.

§ 550
Party who has the burden of producing evidence

(a) The burden of producing evidence as to a particular fact is on the party against whom a finding on that fact would be required in the absence of further evidence.

(b) The burden of producing evidence as to a particular fact is initially on the party with the burden of proof as to that fact. (*Stats.1965, c. 299, § 2, operative Jan. 1, 1967.*)

CHAPTER 3. PRESUMPTIONS AND INFERENCES

ARTICLE 1. GENERAL

Section
600. Presumption and inference defined.
601. Classification of presumptions.
602. Statute making one fact prima facie evidence of another fact.
603. Presumption affecting the burden of producing evidence defined.
604. Effect of presumption affecting burden of producing evidence.
605. Presumption affecting the burden of proof defined.
606. Effect of presumption affecting burden of proof.
607. Effect of certain presumptions in a criminal action.

§ 600
Presumption and inference defined

(a) A presumption is an assumption of fact that the law requires to be made from another fact or group of facts found or otherwise established in the action. A presumption is not evidence.

(b) An inference is a deduction of fact that may logically and reasonably be drawn from another fact or group of facts found or otherwise established in the action. (*Stats.1965, c. 299, § 2, operative Jan. 1, 1967.*)

The definition of a presumption in Section 600 is substantially the same as that contained in Code of Civil Procedure Section 1959: "A presumption is a deduction which the law expressly directs to be made from particular facts." Section 600 was derived from Rule 13 of the Uniform Rules of Evidence and supersedes Code of Civil Procedure Section 1959.

The second sentence of subdivision (a) may be unnecessary in light of the definition of "evidence" in Section 140—"testimony, writings, material objects, or other things presented to the senses that are offered to prove the existence or nonexistence of a fact." Presumptions, then, are not "evidence" but are conclusions that the law requires to be drawn (in the absence of a sufficient contrary showing) when some other fact is proved or otherwise established in the action.

Nonetheless, the second sentence has been added here to repudiate specifically the rule of Smellie v. Southern Pac. Co., 212 Cal. 540, 299 Pac. 529 (1931). That case held that a presumption is evidence that must be weighed against conflicting evidence; and in Scott v. Burke, 39 Cal.2d 388, 247 P.2d 313 (1952), the Supreme Court held that conflicting presumptions must be weighed against each other. These decisions require the jury to perform an intellectually impossible task. The jury is required to weigh the testimony of witnesses and other evidence as to the circumstances of a particular event against the fact that the law requires an opposing conclusion in the absence of contrary evidence and to determine which "evidence" is of greater probative force. Or else, the jury is required to accept the fact that the law requires two opposing conclusions and to determine which required conclusion is of greater probative force.

Moreover, the doctrine that a presumption is evidence imposes upon the party with the burden of proof a much higher burden of proof than is warranted. For example, if a party with the burden of proof has a presumption invoked against him and if the presumption remains in the case as evidence even though the jury believes that he has produced a preponderance of the evidence, the effect is that he must produce some additional but unascertainable quantum of proof in order to dispel the effect of the presumption. See Scott v. Burke, 39 Cal.2d 388, 405–406, 247 P.2d 313, 323–324 (1952) (dissenting opinion). The doctrine that a presumption is evidence gives no guidance to the jury or to the parties as to the amount of this additional proof. The most that should be expected of a party in a civil case is that he prove his case by a preponderance of the evidence (unless some specific presumption or rule of law requires proof of a particular issue by clear and convincing evidence). The most that should be expected of the prosecution in a criminal case is that it establishes the defendant's guilt beyond a reasonable doubt. To require some additional quantum of proof, unspecified and uncertain in amount, to dispel a presumption which persists as evidence in the case unfairly weights the scales of justice against the party with the burden of proof.

To avoid the confusion engendered by the doctrine that a presumption is evidence, this code describes "evidence" as the matters presented in judicial proceedings and uses presumptions solely as devices to aid in determining the facts from the evidence presented.

The definition of "inference" in subdivision (b) restates in substance the definition contained in Code of Civil Procedure Sections 1958 and 1960. Under the Evidence Code, an inference is not itself evidence; it is the result of reasoning from evidence.

In the sections that follow, the Evidence Code classifies presumptions and lists a number of specific presumptions. Some presumptions that have been listed in the Code of Civil Procedure have not been listed as presumptions in the Evidence Code. But the fact that a statutory presumption has been repealed will not preclude the drawing of any appropriate inferences from the facts that would have given rise to the presumption. And, in appropriate cases, the court may instruct the jury on the propriety of drawing particular inferences.

§ 601
Classification of presumptions

A presumption is either conclusive or rebuttable. Every rebuttable presumption is either (a) a presumption affecting the burden of producing evidence or (b) a presumption affecting the burden of proof. (*Stats.1965, c. 299, § 2, operative Jan. 1, 1967.*)

§ 602
Statute making one fact prima facie evidence of another fact

A statute providing that a fact or group of facts is prima facie evidence of another fact establishes a rebuttable presumption. (*Stats.1965, c. 299, § 2, operative Jan. 1, 1967.*)

§ 603
Presumption affecting the burden of producing evidence defined

A presumption affecting the burden of producing evidence is a presumption established to implement no public policy other than to facilitate the determination of the particular action in which the presumption is applied. (*Stats.1965, c. 299, § 2, operative Jan. 1, 1967.*)

§ 604
Effect of presumption affecting burden of producing evidence

The effect of a presumption affecting the burden of producing evidence is to require the trier of fact to assume the existence of the presumed fact unless and until evidence is introduced which would support a finding of its nonexistence, in which case the trier of fact shall determine the existence or nonexistence of the presumed fact from the evidence and without regard to the presumption. Nothing in this section shall be construed to prevent the drawing of any inference that may be appropriate. (*Stats.1965, c. 299, § 2, operative Jan. 1, 1967.*)

Section 604 describes the manner in which a presumption affecting the burden of producing evidence operates. Such a presumption is merely a preliminary assumption in the absence of contrary evidence, *i.e.,* evidence sufficient to sustain a finding of the nonexistence of the presumed fact. If contrary evidence is introduced, the trier of fact must weigh the inferences arising from the facts that gave rise to the presumption against the contrary evidence and resolve the conflict. For example, if a party proves that a letter was mailed, the trier of fact is required to find that the letter was received in the absence of any believable contrary evidence. However, if the adverse party denies receipt, the presumption is gone from the case. The trier of fact must then weigh the denial of receipt against the inference of receipt arising from proof of mailing and decide whether or not the letter was received.

If a presumption affecting the burden of producing evidence is relied on, the judge must determine whether there is evidence sufficient to sustain a finding of the nonexistence of the presumed fact. If there is such evidence, the presumption disappears and the judge need say nothing about it in his instructions. If there is not evidence sufficient to sustain a finding of the nonexistence of the presumed fact, the judge should instruct the jury concerning the presumption. If the basic fact from which the presumption arises is established (by the pleadings, by stipulation, by judicial notice, etc.) so that the existence of the basic fact is not a question of fact for the jury, the jury should be instructed that the presumed fact is also established. If the basic fact is a question of fact for the jury, the judge should charge the jury that, if it finds the basic fact, the jury must also find the presumed fact. Morgan, Basic Problems of Evidence 36–38 (1957).

Of course, in a criminal case, the jury has the *power* to disregard the judge's instructions and find a defendant guilty of a lesser crime than that shown by the evidence or acquit a defendant despite the facts established by the undisputed evidence. *Cf.* People v. Powell, 34 Cal.2d 196, 208 P.2d 974 (1949); Pike, What is Second Degree Murder in California?, 9 So.Cal.L.Rev. 112, 128–132 (1936). Nonetheless, the jury should be instructed on the rules of law applicable, including those rules of law called presumptions. The fact that the jury may choose to disregard the applicable rules of law should not affect the nature of the instructions given. See People v. Lem You, 97 Cal. 224, 32 Pac. 11 (1893); People v. Macken, 32 Cal.App.2d 31, 89 P.2d 173 (1939) .

§ 605
Presumption affecting the burden of proof defined

A presumption affecting the burden of proof is a presumption established to implement some public policy other than to facilitate the determination of the particular action in which the presumption is applied, such as the policy in favor of establishment of a parent and child relationship, the validity of marriage, the stability of titles to property, or the security of those who entrust themselves or their property to the administration of others. (*Stats.1965, c. 299, § 2, operative Jan. 1, 1967. Amended by Stats.1975, c. 1244, p. 3201, § 12.*)

§ 606
Effect of presumption affecting burden of proof

The effect of a presumption affecting the burden of proof is to impose upon the party against whom it operates the burden of proof as to the non-existence of the presumed fact. (*Stats.1965, c. 299, § 2, operative Jan. 1, 1967.*)

Section 606 describes the manner in which a presumption affecting the burden of proof operates. In the ordinary case, the party against whom it is invoked will have the burden of proving the nonexistence of the presumed fact by a preponderance of the evidence. Certain presumptions affecting the burden of proof may be overcome only by clear and convincing proof. When such a presumption is relied on, the party against whom the presumption operates will have a heavier burden of proof and will be required to persuade the trier of fact of the nonexistence of the presumed fact by proof " 'sufficiently strong to command the unhesitating assent of every reasonable mind.§ " Sheehan v. Sullivan, 126 Cal. 189, 193, 58 Pac. 543 (1899).

If the party against whom the presumption operates already has the same burden of proof as to the nonexistence of the presumed fact that is assigned by the presumption, the presumption can have no effect on the case and no instruction in regard to the presumption should be given. See Speck v. Sarver, 20 Cal.2d 585, 590, 128 P.2d 16, 19 (1942) (dissenting opinion by Traynor, J.); Morgan, Instructing the Jury Upon Presumptions and Burden of Proof, 47 Harv.L.Rev. 59, 69 (1933). If the evidence is not sufficient to sustain a finding of the nonexistence of the presumed fact, the judge's instructions will be the same as if the presumption were merely a presumption affecting the burden of producing evidence. See the Comment to Section 604. If there is evidence of the nonexistence of the presumed fact, the judge should instruct the jury on the manner in which the presumption affects the factfinding process. If the basic fact from which the presumption arises is so established that the existence of the basic fact is not a question of fact for the jury (as, for example, by the pleadings, by judicial notice, or by stipulation of the parties), the judge should instruct the jury that the existence of the presumed fact is to be assumed until the jury is persuaded to the contrary by the requisite degree of proof (proof by a preponderance of the evidence, clear and convincing proof, etc.). See McCormick, Evidence § 317 at 672 (1954). If the basic fact is a question of fact for the jury, the judge should instruct the jury that, if it finds the basic fact, it must also find the presumed fact unless persuaded of the nonexistence of the presumed fact by the requisite degree of proof. Morgan, Basic Problems of Evidence 38 (1957).

In a criminal case, a presumption affecting the burden of proof may be relied upon by the prosecution *to establish an element of the crime* with which the defendant is charged. The effect of the presumption on the factfinding process and the nature of the instructions in such a case are described in Section 607 and the Comment thereto. On other issues, a presumption affecting the burden of proof will have the same effect in a criminal case as it does in a civil case, and the instructions will be the same.

§ 607
Effect of certain presumptions in a criminal action

When a presumption affecting the burden of proof operates in a criminal action to establish presumptively any fact that is essential to the defendant's guilt, the presumption operates only if the facts that give rise to the presumption have been found or otherwise established beyond a reasonable doubt and, in such case, the defendant need only raise a reasonable doubt as to the existence of the presumed fact. (*Stats.1965, c. 299, § 2, operative Jan. 1, 1967.*)

If a presumption affecting the burden of proof is relied upon by the prosecution in a criminal case to establish a fact essential to the defendant's guilt, the defendant will not be required to overcome the presumption by clear and convincing evidence or even by a preponderance of the evidence; the defendant will be required merely to raise a reasonable doubt as to the existence of the presumed fact. This is the effect of a presumption in a criminal case under existing law. People v. Hardy, 33 Cal.2d 52, 198 P.2d 865 (1948); People v. Scott, 24 Cal.2d 774, 151 P.2d 517 (1944); People v. Agnew, 16 Cal.2d 655, 107 P.2d 601 (1940).

Instructions in criminal cases on presumptions affecting the burden of proof will be similar to the instructions given on presumptions and on issues where the defendant has the burden of proof under existing law. Where no evidence has been introduced to show the nonexistence of the presumed fact, the court should instruct the jury that, if it finds beyond a reasonable doubt the facts giving rise to the presumption, it should also find the presumed fact. Where some evidence of the nonexistence of the presumed fact has been introduced, the court should instruct the jury that, if it finds beyond a reasonable doubt the facts giving rise to the presumption, it should also find the presumed fact unless the contrary evidence has raised a reasonable doubt as to the existence of the presumed fact. *Cf.* People v. Hardy, 33 Cal.2d 52, 63–64, 198 P.2d 865, 871–872 (1948); People v. Agnew, 16 Cal.2d 655, 661-667, 107 P.2d 601, 603-607 (1940); People v. Martina, 140 Cal.App.2d 17, 25, 294 P.2d 1015, 1019 (1956). The judge must be careful to specify that a presumption is rebutted by any evidence that raises a reasonable doubt as to the presumed fact. In the absence of this qualification, the jury may be led to believe that the defendant has the burden of disproof of the presumed fact by a preponderance of the evidence and the instruction will be erroneous. People v. Agnew, 16 Cal.2d 655, 107 P.2d 601 (1940). *Cf.* People v. Hardy, 33 Cal.2d 52, 198 P.2d 865 (1948).

Of course, in a criminal case, the jury may choose to disregard the instructions relating to presumptions. But this should not affect the duty of the court to instruct the jury on the rules of law, including presumptions, applicable to the case. See the Comment to Section 604.

Section 607 does not apply to the "presumption" of sanity. Under the Evidence Code, the burden of proof on the issue of sanity is allocated by Section 522, and there is no "presumption" of sanity. See Evidence Code § 522 and the Comment thereto. Hence, notwithstanding the provisions of Section 607, a defendant who pleads insanity has the burden of proving by a preponderance of the evidence that he was insane. See the Comment to Section 501.

ARTICLE 2. CONCLUSIVE PRESUMPTIONS

Section
620. Conclusive presumptions.
621. Repealed.
621.1. Repealed.
622. Facts recited in written instrument.
623. Estoppel by own statement or conduct.
624. Estoppel of tenant to deny title of landlord.

§ 620
Conclusive presumptions

The presumptions established by this article, and all other presumptions declared by law to be conclusive, are conclusive presumptions. (*Stats.1965, c. 299, § 2, operative Jan. 1, 1967.*)

§ 621
Repealed by Stats.1992, c. 162 (A.B.2650), § 8, operative
Jan. 1, 1994

§ 621.1
Repealed by Stats.1993, c. 219 (A.B.1500), § 76

§ 622
Facts recited in written instrument

The facts recited in a written instrument are conclusively presumed to be true as between the parties thereto, or their successors in interest; but this rule does not apply to the recital of a consideration. (*Stats.1965, c. 299, § 2, operative Jan. 1, 1967.*)

§ 623
Estoppel by own statement or conduct

Whenever a party has, by his own statement or conduct, intentionally and deliberately led another to believe a particular thing true and to act upon such belief, he is not, in any litigation arising out of such statement or conduct, permitted to contradict it. (*Stats.1965, c. 299, § 2, operative Jan. 1, 1967.*)

§ 624
Estoppel of tenant to deny title of landlord

A tenant is not permitted to deny the title of his landlord at the time of the commencement of the relation. (*Stats.1965, c. 299, § 2, operative Jan. 1, 1967.*)

ARTICLE 3. PRESUMPTIONS AFFECTING THE BURDEN OF PRODUCING EVIDENCE

Section

§ 630
Presumptions affecting the burden of producing evidence

The presumptions established by this article, and all other rebuttable presumptions established by law that fall within the criteria of Section 603, are presumptions affecting the burden of producing evidence. (*Stats.1965, c. 299, § 2, operative Jan. 1, 1967.*)

§ 631
Money delivered by one to another

Money delivered by one to another is presumed to have been due to the latter. (*Stats.1965, c. 299, § 2, operative Jan. 1, 1967.*)

§ 632
Thing delivered by one to another

A thing delivered by one to another is presumed to have belonged to the latter. (*Stats.1965, c. 299, § 2, operative Jan. 1, 1967.*)

§ 633
Obligation delivered up to the debtor

An obligation delivered up to the debtor is presumed to have been paid. (*Stats.1965, c. 299, § 2, operative Jan. 1, 1967.*)

§ 634
Person in possession of order on self

A person in possession of an order on himself for the payment of money, or delivery of a thing, is presumed to have paid the money or delivered the thing accordingly. (*Stats.1965, c. 299, § 2, operative Jan. 1, 1967.*)

§ 635
Obligation possessed by creditor

An obligation possessed by the creditor is presumed not to have been paid. (*Stats.1965, c. 299, § 2, operative Jan. 1, 1967.*)

§ 636
Payment of earlier rent or installments

The payment of earlier rent or installments is presumed from a receipt for later rent or installments. (*Stats.1965, c. 299, § 2, operative Jan. 1, 1967.*)

§ 637
Ownership of things possessed

The things which a person possesses are presumed to be owned by him. (*Stats.1965, c. 299, § 2, operative Jan. 1, 1967.*)

§ 638
Property ownership acts

A person who exercises acts of ownership over property is presumed to be the owner of it. (*Stats.1965, c. 299, § 2, operative Jan. 1, 1967.*)

§ 639
Judgment correctly determines rights of parties

A judgment, when not conclusive, is presumed to correctly determine or set forth the rights of the parties, but there is no presumption that the facts essential to the judgment have been correctly determined. (*Stats.1965, c. 299, § 2, operative Jan. 1, 1967.*)

§ 640
Writing truly dated

A writing is presumed to have been truly dated. (*Stats.1965, c. 299, § 2, operative Jan. 1, 1967.*)

§ 641
Letter received in ordinary course of mail

A letter correctly addressed and properly mailed is presumed to have been received in the ordinary course of mail. (*Stats.1965, c. 299, § 2, operative Jan. 1, 1967.*)

§ 642
Conveyance by person having duty to convey real property

A trustee or other person, whose duty it was to convey real property to a particular person, is presumed to have actually conveyed to him when such presumption is necessary to perfect title of such person or his successor in interest. (*Stats.1965, c. 299, § 2, operative Jan. 1, 1967.*)

§ 643
Authenticity of ancient document

A deed or will or other writing purporting to create, terminate, or affect an interest in real or personal property is presumed to be authentic if it:

(a) Is at least 30 years old;

(b) Is in such condition as to create no suspicion concerning its authenticity;

(c) Was kept, or if found was found, in a place where such writing, if authentic, would be likely to be kept or found; and

(d) Has been generally acted upon as authentic by persons having an interest in the matter. (*Stats.1965, c. 299, § 2, operative Jan. 1, 1967.*)

§ 644
Book purporting to be published by public authority

A book, purporting to be printed or published by public authority, is presumed to have been so printed or published. (*Stats.1965, c. 299, § 2, operative Jan. 1, 1967.*)

§ 645
Book purporting to contain reports of cases

A book, purporting to contain reports of cases adjudged in the tribunals of the state or nation where the book is published, is presumed to contain correct reports of such cases. (*Stats.1965, c. 299, § 2, operative Jan. 1, 1967.*)

§ 645.1
Printed materials purporting to be particular newspaper or periodical

Printed materials, purporting to be a particular newspaper or periodical, are presumed to be that newspaper or periodical if regularly issued at average intervals not exceeding three months. (*Added by Stats.1986, c. 330, § 1.*)

§ 646
Res ipsa loquitur; instruction

(a) As used in this section, "defendant" includes any party against whom the res ipsa loquitur presumption operates.

(b) The judicial doctrine of res ipsa loquitur is a presumption affecting the burden of producing evidence.

(c) If the evidence, or facts otherwise established, would support a res ipsa loquitur presumption and the defendant has introduced evidence which would support a finding that he was not negligent or that any negligence on his part was not a proximate cause of the occurrence, the court may, and upon request shall, instruct the jury to the effect that:

(1) If the facts which would give rise to a res ipsa loquitur presumption are found or otherwise established, the jury may draw the inference from such facts that a proximate cause of the occurrence was some negligent conduct on the part of the defendant; and

(2) The jury shall not find that a proximate cause of the occurrence was some negligent conduct on the part of the defendant unless the jury believes, after weighing all the evidence in the case and drawing such inferences therefrom as the jury believes are warranted, that it is more probable than not that the occurrence was caused by some negligent conduct on the part of the defendant. (*Added by Stats.1970, c. 69, p. 83, § 1.*)

§ 647
Return of process served by registered process server

The return of a process server registered pursuant to Chapter 16 (commencing with Section 22350) of Division 8 of the Business and Professions Code upon process or notice establishes a presumption, affecting the burden of producing evidence, of the facts stated in the return. (*Added by Stats.1978, c. 528, p. 1687, § 1.*)

ARTICLE 4. PRESUMPTIONS AFFECTING THE BURDEN OF PROOF

Section
660. Presumptions affecting the burden of proof.
661. Repealed.

§ 660
Presumptions affecting the burden of proof

The presumptions established by this article, and all other rebuttable presumptions established by law that fall within the criteria of Section 605, are presumptions affecting the burden of proof. (*Stats.1965, c. 299, § 2, operative Jan. 1, 1967.*)

§ 661
Repealed by Stats.1975, c. 1244, p. 3202, § 14

§ 662
Owner of legal title to property is owner of beneficial title

The owner of the legal title to property is presumed to be the owner of the full beneficial title. This presumption may be rebutted only by clear and convincing proof. (*Stats.1965, c. 299, § 2, operative Jan. 1, 1967.*)

§ 663
Ceremonial marriage

A ceremonial marriage is presumed to be valid. (*Stats.1965, c. 299, § 2, operative Jan. 1, 1967.*)

§ 664
Official duty regularly performed

It is presumed that official duty has been regularly performed. This presumption does not apply on an issue as to the lawfulness of an arrest if it is found or otherwise established that the arrest was made without a warrant. (*Stats.1965, c. 299, § 2, operative Jan. 1, 1967.*)

The first sentence of Section 664 restates and supersedes subdivision 15 of Code of Civil Procedure Section 1963.

Under existing law, there is a common law presumption that an arrest made without a warrant is unlawful. People v. Agnew, 16 Cal.2d 655, 107 P.2d 601 (1940). Under this common law presumption, if a person arrests another without the color of legality provided by a warrant, the person making the arrest must prove the circumstances that justified the arrest without a warrant. Badillo v. Superior Court, 46 Cal.2d 269, 294 P.2d 23 (1956); Dragna v. White, 45 Cal.2d 469, 471, 289 P.2d 428 (1955) ("Upon proof of [arrest without process] the burden is on the defendants to prove justification for the arrest."). The second sentence of Section 664 makes it clear that the presumption of regular performance of official duty is inapplicable whenever facts have been established that give rise to the common law presumption regarding the illegality of an arrest made without a warrant.

§ 665
Ordinary consequences of voluntary act

A person is presumed to intend the ordinary consequences of his voluntary act. This presumption is inapplicable in a criminal action to establish the specific intent of the defendant where specific intent is an element of the crime charged. (*Stats.1965, c. 299, § 2, operative Jan. 1, 1967.*)

Section 665 restates and supersedes the presumption in subdivision 3 of Code of Civil Procedure Section 1963. The second sentence in this section also appears in Section 668 (restating the presumption in subdivision 2 of Code of Civil Procedure Section 1963). These sentences reflect the fact that it is error to rely on these presumptions when specific intent is in issue in a criminal case. See People v. Snyder, 15 Cal.2d 706, 104 P.2d 639 (1940); People v. Maciel, 71 Cal.App. 213, 234 Pac. 877 (1925).

§ 666
Judicial action in lawful exercise of jurisdiction

Any court of this state or the United States, or any court of general jurisdiction in any other state or nation, or any judge of such a court, acting as such, is presumed to have acted in the lawful exercise of its jurisdiction. This presumption applies only when the act of the court or judge is under collateral attack. (*Stats.1965, c. 299, § 2, operative Jan. 1, 1967.*)

Section 666 restates and supersedes the presumption in subdivision 16 of Code of Civil Procedure Section 1963. Under existing law, the presumption applies only to courts of general jurisdiction; the presumption has been held inapplicable to a superior court in California when acting in a special or limited jurisdiction. Estate of Sharon, 179 Cal. 447, 177 Pac. 283 (1918). The presumption also has been held inapplicable to courts of inferior jurisdiction. Santos v. Dondero, 11 Cal.App.2d 720, 54 P.2d 764 (1936). There is no reason to perpetuate this distinction insofar as the courts of California and of the United States are concerned. California's municipal and justice courts are served by able and conscientious judges and are no more likely to act beyond their jurisdiction than are the superior courts. Moreover, there is no reason to suppose that a superior court or a federal court is less respectful of its jurisdiction when acting in a limited capacity (for example, as a juvenile court) than it is when acting in any other capacity. Section 666, therefore, applies to any court or judge of any court of California or of the United States. So far as other states are concerned, the distinction is still applicable, and the presumption applies only to courts of general jurisdiction.

Under Section 666, as under existing law, the presumption applies only when the act of the court or judge is under collateral attack. See City of Los Angeles v. Glassell, 203 Cal. 44, 262 Pa. 1084 (1928).

§ 667
Death of person not heard from in five years

A person not heard from in five years is presumed to be dead. (*Stats.1965, c. 299, § 2, operative Jan. 1, 1967. Amended by Stats.1983, c. 201, § 1.*)

§ 668
Unlawful intent

An unlawful intent is presumed from the doing of an unlawful act. This presumption is inapplicable in a criminal action to establish the specific intent of the defendant where specific intent is an element of the crime charged. (*Stats.1965, c. 299, § 2, operative Jan. 1, 1967.*)

Section 668 restates and supersedes the presumption in subdivision 2 of Code of Civil Procedure Section 1963. See the Comment to Section 665.

§ 669
Due care; failure to exercise

(a) The failure of a person to exercise due care is presumed if:

(1) He violated a statute, ordinance, or regulation of a public entity;

(2) The violation proximately caused death or injury to person or property;

(3) The death or injury resulted from an occurrence of the nature which the statute, ordinance, or regulation was designed to prevent; and

(4) The person suffering the death or the injury to his person or property was one of the class of persons for whose protection the statute, ordinance, or regulation was adopted.

(b) This presumption may be rebutted by proof that:

(1) The person violating the statute, ordinance, or regulation did what might reasonably be expected of a person of ordinary prudence, acting under similar circumstances, who desired to comply with the law; or

(2) The person violating the statute, ordinance, or regulation was a child and exercised the degree of care ordinarily exercised by persons of his maturity, intelligence, and capacity under similar circumstances, but the presumption may not be rebutted by such proof if the violation occurred in the course of an activity normally engaged in only by adults and requiring adult qualifications. (*Added by Stats.1967, c. 650, p. 2004, § 1.*)

§ 669.1
Standards of conduct for public employees; presumption of failure to exercise due care

A rule, policy, manual, or guideline of state or local government setting forth standards of conduct or guidelines for its employees in the conduct of their public employment shall not be considered a statute, ordinance, or regulation of that public entity within the meaning of Section 669, unless the rule, manual, policy, or guideline has been formally adopted as a statute, as an ordinance of a local governmental entity in this state empowered to adopt ordinances, or as a regulation by an agency of the state pursuant to the Administrative Procedure Act (Chapter 3.5 (commencing with Section 11340) of Division 3 of Title 2 of the Government Code), or by an agency of the United States government pursuant to the federal Administrative Procedure Act (Chapter 5 (commencing with Section 5001) of Title 5 of the United States Code). This section affects only the presumption set forth in Section 669, and is not otherwise intended to affect the admissibility or inadmissibility of the rule, policy, manual, or guideline under other provisions of law. (*Added by Stats.1987, c. 1201, § 13; Stats.1987, c. 1207, § 2.*)

§ 669.5
Ordinances limiting building permits or development of buildable lots for residential purposes; impact on supply of residential units; actions challenging validity

(a) Any ordinance enacted by the governing body of a city, county, or city and county which (1) directly limits, by number, the building permits that may be issued for residential construction or the buildable lots which may be developed for residential purposes, or (2) changes the standards of residential development on vacant land so that the governing body's zoning is rendered in violation of Section 65913.1 of the Government Code is presumed to have an impact on the supply of residential units available in an area which includes territory outside the jurisdiction of the city, county, or city and county.

(b) With respect to any action which challenges the validity of an ordinance specified in subdivision (a) the city, county, or city and county enacting the ordinance shall bear the burden of proof that the ordinance is necessary for the protection of the public health, safety, or welfare of the population of the city, county, or city and county.

(c) This section does not apply to state and federal building code requirements or local ordinances which (1) impose a moratorium, to protect the public health and safety, on residential construction for a specified period of time, if, under the terms of the ordinance, the moratorium will cease when the public health or safety is no longer jeopardized by the construction, (2) create agricultural preserves under Chapter 7 (commencing with Section 51200) of Part 1 of Division 1 of Title 5 of the Government Code, or (3) restrict the number of buildable parcels or designate lands within a zone for nonresidential uses in order to protect agricultural uses as defined in subdivision (b) of Section 51201 of the Government Code or open-space land as defined in subdivision (b) of Section 65560 of the Government Code.

(d) This section shall not apply to a voter approved ordinance adopted by referendum or initiative prior to the effective date of this section which (1) requires the city, county, or city and county to establish a population growth limit which represents its fair share of each year's statewide population growth, or (2) which sets a growth rate of no more than the average population growth rate experienced by the state as a whole. Paragraph (2) of subdivision (a) does not apply to a voter-approved ordinance adopted by referendum or initiative which exempts housing affordable to persons and families of low or moderate income, as defined in Section 50093 of the Health and Safety Code, or which otherwise provides low- and moderate-income housing sites equivalent to such an exemption. (*Added by Stats.1980, c. 1144, p. 3703, § 2. Amended by Stats.1988, c. 541, § 1.*)

§ 670
Payments by check

(a) In any dispute concerning payment by means of a check, a copy of the check produced in accordance with Section 1550 of the Evidence Code, together with the original bank statement that reflects payment of the check by the bank on which it was drawn or a copy thereof produced in the same manner, creates a presumption that the check has been paid.

(b) As used in this section:

(1) "Bank" means any person engaged in the business of banking and includes, in addition to a commercial bank, a savings and loan association, savings bank, or credit union.

(2) "Check" means a draft, other than a documentary draft, payable on demand and drawn on a bank, even though it is described by another term, such as "share draft" or "negotiable order of withdrawal."

(Added by Stats.1992, c. 914 (S.B.833), § 51. Amended by Stats.2001, c. 854 (S.B.205), § 3.)

Division 6

WITNESSES

CHAPTER 1. COMPETENCY

§ 700
General rule as to competency

Except as otherwise provided by statute, every person, irrespective of age, is qualified to be a witness and no person is disqualified to testify to any matter. (*Stats.1965, c. 299, § 2, operative Jan. 1, 1967. Amended by Stats.1985, c. 884, § 1.*)

§ 701
Disqualification of witness

(a) A person is disqualified to be a witness if he or she is:

(1) Incapable of expressing himself or herself concerning the matter so as to be understood, either directly or through interpretation by one who can understand him; or

(2) Incapable of understanding the duty of a witness to tell the truth.

(b) In any proceeding held outside the presence of a jury, the court may reserve challenges to the competency of a witness until the conclusion of the direct examination of that witness. (*Stats.1965, c. 299, § 2, operative Jan. 1, 1967. Amended by Stats.1985, c. 884, § 2.*)

§ 702
Personal knowledge of witness

(a) Subject to Section 801, the testimony of a witness concerning a particular matter is inadmissible unless he has personal knowledge of the matter. Against the objection of a party, such personal knowledge must be shown before the witness may testify concerning the matter.

(b) A witness§ personal knowledge of a matter may be shown by any otherwise admissible evidence, including his own testimony. (*Stats.1965, c. 299, § 2, operative Jan. 1, 1967.*)

§ 703
Judge as witness

(a) Before the judge presiding at the trial of an action may be called to testify in that trial as a witness, he shall, in proceedings held out of the presence and hearing of the jury, inform the parties of the information he has concerning any fact or matter about which he will be called to testify.

(b) Against the objection of a party, the judge presiding at the trial of an action may not testify in that trial as a witness. Upon such objection, the judge shall declare a mistrial and order the action assigned for trial before another judge.

(c) The calling of the judge presiding at a trial to testify in that trial as a witness shall be deemed a consent to the granting of a motion for mistrial, and an objection to such calling of a judge shall be deemed a motion for mistrial.

(d) In the absence of objection by a party, the judge presiding at the trial of an action may testify in that trial as a witness. (*Stats.1965, c. 299, § 2, operative Jan. 1, 1967.*)

Under existing law, a judge may be called as a witness even if a party objects, but the judge in his discretion may order the trial to be postponed or suspended and to take place before another judge. Code Civ.Proc. § 1883 (superseded by Evidence Code §§ 703 and 704). But see People v. Connors, 77 Cal.App. 438, 450–457, 246 Pac. 1072, 1076–1079 (1926) (dictum) (abuse of discretion for the presiding judge to testify to important and necessary facts).

Section 703, however, precludes the judge from testifying if a party objects. Before the judge may be called to testify in a civil or criminal action, he must disclose to the parties out of the presence and hearing of the jury the information he has concerning the case. After such disclosure, if no party objects, the judge is permitted—but not required—to testify.

Section 703 is based on the fact that examination and cross-examination of a judge-witness may be embarrassing and prejudicial to a party. By testifying as a witness for one party a judge appears in a partisan attitude before the jury. Objections to questions and to his testimony must be ruled on by the witness himself. The extent of cross-examination and the introduction of impeaching and rebuttal evidence may be limited by the fear of appearing to attack the judge personally. For these and other reasons, Section 703 is preferable to Code of Civil Procedure Section 1883.

Subdivision (c) is designed to prevent a plea of double jeopardy by a defendant who either calls or objects to the calling of the judge to testify. Under subdivision (c), the defendant will, in effect, have consented to the mistrial and thus waived any objection to a retrial. See Witkin, California Crimes § 193 (1963).

§ 703.5
Judges, arbitrators or mediators as witnesses; subsequent civil proceeding

No person presiding at any judicial or quasi-judicial proceeding, and no arbitrator or mediator, shall be competent to testify, in any subsequent civil proceeding, as to any statement, conduct, decision, or ruling, occurring at or in conjunction with the prior proceeding, except as to a statement or conduct that could (a) give rise to civil or criminal contempt, (b) constitute a crime, (c) be the subject of investigation by the State Bar or Commission on Judicial Performance, or (d) give rise to disqualification proceedings under paragraph (1) or (6) of subdivision (a) of Section 170.1 of the Code of Civil Procedure. However, this section does not apply to a mediator with regard to any mediation under Chapter 11 (commencing with Section 3160) of Part 2 of Division 8 of the Family Code. (*Added by Stats.1979, c. 205, p. 449, § 1. Amended by Stats.1980, c. 290, p. 617, § 1; Stats.1988, c. 281, § 1; Stats.1990, c. 1491 (A.B.3765), § 13; Stats.1993, c. 114 (A.B.1757), § 1; Stats.1993, c. 1261 (S.B.401), § 5; Stats.1994, c. 1269 (A.B.2208), § 7.)*

§ 704
Juror as witness

(a) Before a juror sworn and impaneled in the trial of an action may be called to testify before the jury in that trial as a witness, he shall, in proceedings conducted by the court out of the presence and hearing of the remaining jurors, inform the parties of the information he has concerning any fact or matter about which he will be called to testify.

(b) Against the objection of a party, a juror sworn and impaneled in the trial of an action may not testify before the jury in that trial as a witness. Upon such objection, the court shall declare a mistrial and order the action assigned for trial before another jury.

(c) The calling of a juror to testify before the jury as a witness shall be deemed a consent to the granting of a motion for mistrial, and an objection to such calling of a juror shall be deemed a motion for mistrial.

(d) In the absence of objection by a party, a juror sworn and impaneled in the trial of an action may be compelled to testify in that trial as a witness. (*Stats.1965, c. 299, § 2, operative Jan. 1, 1967.*)

Under existing law, a juror may be called as a witness even if a party objects, but the judge in his discretion may order the trial to be postponed or suspended and to take place before another jury. Code Civ.Proc. § 1883 (superseded by Evidence Code §§ 703 and 704). Section 704, on the other hand, prevents a juror from testifying before the jury if any party objects.

A juror-witness is in an anomalous position. He manifestly cannot weigh his own testimony impartially. A party affected adversely by the juror's testimony is placed in an embarrassing position. He cannot freely cross-examine or impeach the juror for fear of antagonizing the juror—and perhaps his fellow jurors as well. And, if he does not attack the juror's testimony, the other jurors may give his testimony undue weight. For these and other reasons, Section 704 forbids jurors to testify over the objection of any party.

Before a juror may be called to testify before the jury in a civil or criminal action, he is required to disclose to the parties out of the presence and hearing of the remaining jurors the information he has concerning the case. After such disclosure, if no party objects, the juror is required to testify. If a party objects, the objection is deemed a motion for mistrial and the judge is required to declare a mistrial and order the action assigned for trial before another jury.

Section 704 is concerned only with the problem of a juror who is called to testify before the jury. Section 704 does not deal with *voir dire* examinations of jurors, with testimony of jurors in post-verdict proceedings (such as on motions for new trial), or with the testimony of jurors on any other matter that is to be decided by the court. *Cf.* Evidence Code § 1150 and the Comment thereto.

Subdivision (c) is designed to prevent a plea of double jeopardy by a defendant who either calls or objects to the calling of the juror to testify. Under subdivision (c), the defendant will, in effect, have consented to the mistrial and thus waived any objection to a retrial. See Witkin, California Crimes § 193 (1963).

CHAPTER 2. OATH AND CONFRONTATION

Section

§ 710
Oath required

Every witness before testifying shall take an oath or make an affirmation or declaration in the form provided by law, except that a child under the age of 10 or a dependent person with a substantial cognitive impairment, in the court's discretion, may be required only to promise to tell the truth. (*Stats.1965, c. 299, § 2, operative Jan. 1, 1967. Amended by Stats.1988, c. 486, § 1; Stats.2004, c. 823 (A.B.20), § 3.*)

§ 711
Confrontation

At the trial of an action, a witness can be heard only in the presence and subject to the examination of all the parties to the action, if they choose to attend and examine. (*Stats.1965, c. 299, § 2, operative Jan. 1, 1967.*)

§ 712
Blood samples; technique in taking; affidavits in criminal actions; service; objections

Notwithstanding Sections 711 and 1200, at the trial of a criminal action, evidence of the technique used in taking blood samples may be given by a registered nurse, licensed vocational nurse, or licensed clinical laboratory technologist or clinical laboratory bioanalyst, by means of an affidavit. The affidavit shall be admissible, provided the party offering the affidavit as evidence has served all other parties to the action, or their counsel, with a copy of the affidavit no less than 10 days prior to trial. Nothing in this section shall preclude any party or his counsel from objecting to the introduction of the affidavit at any time, and requiring the attendance of the affiant, or compelling attendance by subpoena. (*Added by Stats.1978, c. 93, p. 256, § 1, eff. April 14, 1978.*)

CHAPTER 3. EXPERT WITNESSES

ARTICLE 1. EXPERT WITNESSES GENERALLY

§ 720
Qualification as an expert witness

(a) A person is qualified to testify as an expert if he has special knowledge, skill, experience, training, or education sufficient to qualify him as an expert on the subject to which his testimony relates. Against the objection of a party, such special knowledge, skill, experience, training, or education must be shown before the witness may testify as an expert.

(b) A witness§ special knowledge, skill, experience, training, or education may be shown by any otherwise admissible evidence, including his own testimony. (*Stats.1965, c. 299, § 2, operative Jan. 1, 1967.*)

§ 721
Cross-examination of expert witness

(a) Subject to subdivision (b), a witness testifying as an expert may be cross-examined to the same extent as any other witness and, in addition, may be fully cross-examined as to (1) his or her qualifications, (2) the subject to which his or her expert testimony relates, and (3) the matter upon which his or her opinion is based and the reasons for his or her opinion.

(b) If a witness testifying as an expert testifies in the form of an opinion, he or she may not be cross-examined in regard to the content or tenor of any scientific, technical, or professional text, treatise, journal, or similar publication unless any of the following occurs:

(1) The witness referred to, considered, or relied upon such publication in arriving at or forming his or her opinion.

(2) The publication has been admitted in evidence.

(3) The publication has been established as a reliable authority by the testimony or admission of the witness or by other expert testimony or by judicial notice.

If admitted, relevant portions of the publication may be read into evidence but may not be received as exhibits. (*Stats.1965, c. 299, § 2, operative Jan. 1, 1967. Amended by Stats.1997, c. 892 (S.B.73), § 11.*)

§ 722
Credibility of expert witness

(a) The fact of the appointment of an expert witness by the court may be revealed to the trier of fact.

(b) The compensation and expenses paid or to be paid to an expert witness by the party calling him is a proper subject of inquiry by any adverse party as relevant to the credibility of the witness and the weight of his testimony. (*Stats.1965, c. 299, § 2, operative Jan. 1, 1967.*)

§ 723
Limit on number of expert witnesses

The court may, at any time before or during the trial of an action, limit the number of expert witnesses to be called by any party. (*Stats.1965, c. 299, § 2, operative Jan. 1, 1967.*)

ARTICLE 2. APPOINTMENT OF EXPERT WITNESS BY COURT

Section
730. Appointment of expert by court.
731. Payment of court-appointed expert.
732. Calling and examining court-appointed expert.
733. Right to produce other expert evidence.

§ 730
Appointment of expert by court

When it appears to the court, at any time before or during the trial of an action, that expert evidence is or may be required by the court or by any party to the action, the court on its own motion or on motion of any party may appoint one or more experts to investigate, to render a report as may be ordered by the court, and to testify as an expert at the trial of the action relative to the fact or matter as to which the expert evidence is or may be required. The court may fix the compensation for these services, if any, rendered by any person appointed under this section, in addition to any service as a witness, at the amount as seems reasonable to the court.

Nothing in this section shall be construed to permit a person to perform any act for which a license is required unless the person holds the appropriate license to lawfully perform that act. (*Added by Stats.1979, c. 746, p. 2592, § 3, operative Jan. 1, 1983. Amended by Stats.1990, c. 295 (A.B.3371), § 1.*)

§ 731
Payment of court-appointed expert

(a)(1) In all criminal actions and juvenile court proceedings, the compensation fixed under Section 730 shall be a charge against the county in which the action or proceeding is pending and shall be paid out of the treasury of that county on order of the court.

(2) Notwithstanding paragraph (1), if the expert is appointed for the court's needs, the compensation shall be a charge against the court.

(b) In any county in which the superior court so provides, the compensation fixed under Section 730 for medical experts appointed for the court's needs in civil actions shall be a charge against the court. In any county in which the board of supervisors so provides, the compensation fixed under Section 730 for medical experts appointed in civil actions * * *, for purposes

<u>other than the court's needs,</u> shall be a charge against and paid out of the treasury of <u>that</u> county on order of the court.

(c) Except as otherwise provided in this section, in all civil actions, the compensation fixed under Section 730 shall, in the first instance, be apportioned and charged to the several parties in <u>a</u> proportion as the court may determine and may thereafter be taxed and allowed in like manner as other costs. (*Added by Stats.1979, c. 746, § 5, operative Jan. 1, 1983. Amended by Stats.2012, c. 470 (A.B.1529), § 8.*)

§ 732
Calling and examining court-appointed expert

Any expert appointed by the court under Section 730 may be called and examined by the court or by any party to the action. When such witness is called and examined by the court, the parties have the same right as is expressed in Section 775 to cross-examine the witness and to object to the questions asked and the evidence adduced. (*Stats.1965, c. 299, § 2, operative Jan. 1, 1967.*)

§ 733
Right to produce other expert evidence

Nothing contained in this article shall be deemed or construed to prevent any party to any action from producing other expert evidence on the same fact or matter mentioned in Section 730; but, where other expert witnesses are called by a party to the action, their fees shall be paid by the party calling them and only ordinary witness fees shall be taxed as costs in the action. (*Stats.1965, c. 299, § 2, operative Jan. 1, 1967.*)

CHAPTER 4. INTERPRETERS AND TRANSLATORS

Section

§ 750
Rules relating to witnesses apply to interpreters and translators

A person who serves as an interpreter or translator in any action is subject to all the rules of law relating to witnesses. (*Stats.1965, c. 299, § 2, operative Jan. 1, 1967.*)

§ 751
Oath required of interpreters and translators

(a) An interpreter shall take an oath that he or she will make a true interpretation to the witness in a language that the witness understands and that he or she will make a true interpretation of the witness§ answers to questions to counsel, court, or jury, in the English language, with his or her best skill and judgment.

(b) In any proceeding in which a deaf or hard-of-hearing person is testifying under oath, the interpreter certified pursuant to subdivision (f) of Section 754 shall advise the court whenever he or she is unable to comply with his or her oath taken pursuant to subdivision (a).

(c) A translator shall take an oath that he or she will make a true translation in the English language of any writing he or she is to decipher or translate.

(d) An interpreter regularly employed by the court and certified or registered in accordance with Article 4 (commencing with Section 68560) of Chapter 2 of Title 8 of the Government Code, or a translator regularly employed by the court, may file an oath as prescribed by this section with the clerk of the court. The filed oath shall serve for all subsequent court proceedings until the appointment is revoked by the court. (*Stats.1965, c. 299, § 2, operative Jan. 1, 1967. Amended by Stats.1984, c. 30, § 1, eff. March 7, 1984; Stats.1990, c. 1450 (S.B.2046), § 1; Stats.1997, c. 376 (A.B.1445), § 1.*)

§ 752
Interpreters for witnesses; compensation

(a) When a witness is incapable of understanding the English language or is incapable of expressing himself or herself in the English language so as to be understood directly by counsel, court, and jury, an interpreter whom * * * the witness can understand and who can understand * * * the witness shall be sworn to interpret for * * * the witness.

(b) The record shall identify the interpreter¢a,¢a who may be appointed and compensated as provided in Article 2 (commencing with Section 730) of Chapter 3¢d * * *, with that compensation charged as follows:

(1) In all criminal actions and juvenile court proceedings, the compensation for an interpreter under this section shall be a charge against the court.

(2) In all civil actions, the compensation for an interpreter under this section shall, in the first instance, be apportioned and charged to the several parties in a proportion as the court may determine and may thereafter be taxed and allowed in a like manner as other costs. (*Stats.1965, c. 299, § 2, operative Jan. 1, 1967. Amended by Stats.1984, c. 30, § 2, eff. March 7, 1984; Stats.1984, c. 768, § 1; Stats.2012, c. 470 (A.B.1529), § 9.*)

§ 753
Translators of writings; compensation

(a) When the written characters in a writing offered in evidence are incapable of being deciphered or understood directly, a translator who can decipher the characters or understand the language shall be sworn to decipher or translate the writing.

(b) The record shall identify the translator, who may be appointed and compensated as provided in Article 2 (commencing with Section 730) of Chapter 3 * * *, with that compensation charged as follows:

(1) In all criminal actions and juvenile court proceedings, the compensation for a translator under this section shall be a charge against the court.

(2) In all civil actions, the compensation for a translator under this section shall, in the first instance, be apportioned and charged to the several parties in a proportion as the court may determine and may thereafter be taxed and allowed in like manner as other costs. (*Stats.1965, c. 299, § 2, operative Jan. 1, 1967. Amended by Stats.1984, c. 30, § 3, eff. March 7, 1984; Stats.2012, c. 470 (A.B.1529), § 10.*)

§ 754
Deaf or hearing impaired persons; interpreters; qualifications; guidelines; compensation; questioning; use of statements

(a) As used in this section, "individual who is deaf or hearing impaired" means an individual with a hearing loss so great as to prevent his or her understanding language spoken in a normal tone, but does not include an individual who is hearing impaired provided with, and able to fully participate in the proceedings through the use of, an assistive listening system or computer-aided transcription equipment provided pursuant to Section 54.8 of the Civil Code.

(b) In any civil or criminal action, including, but not limited to, any action involving a traffic or other infraction, any small claims court proceeding, any juvenile court proceeding, any family court proceeding or service, or any proceeding to determine the mental competency of a person, in any court-ordered or court-provided alternative dispute resolution, including mediation and arbitration, or any administrative hearing, where a party or witness is an individual who is deaf or hearing impaired and the individual who is deaf or hearing impaired is present and participating, the proceedings shall be interpreted in a language that the individual who is deaf or hearing impaired understands by a qualified interpreter appointed by the court or other appointing authority, or as agreed upon.

(c) For purposes of this section, "appointing authority" means a court, department, board, commission, agency, licensing or legislative body, or other body for proceedings requiring a qualified interpreter.

(d) For the purposes of this section, "interpreter" includes, but is not limited to, an oral interpreter, a sign language interpreter, or a deaf-blind interpreter, depending upon the needs of the individual who is deaf or hearing impaired.

(e) For purposes of this section, "intermediary interpreter" means an individual who is deaf or hearing impaired, or a hearing individual who is able to assist in providing an accurate interpretation between spoken English and sign language or between variants of sign language or between American Sign Language and other foreign languages by acting as an intermediary between the individual who is deaf or hearing impaired and the qualified interpreter.

(f) For purposes of this section, "qualified interpreter" means an interpreter who has been certified as competent to interpret court proceedings by a testing organization, agency, or educational institution approved by the Judicial Council as qualified to administer tests to court interpreters for individuals who are deaf or hearing impaired.

(g) In the event that the appointed interpreter is not familiar with the use of particular signs by the individual who is deaf or hearing impaired or his or her particular variant of sign language, the court or other appointing authority shall, in consultation with the individual who is deaf or hearing impaired or his or her representative, appoint an intermediary interpreter.

(h) Prior to July 1, 1992, the Judicial Council shall conduct a study to establish the guidelines pursuant to which it shall determine which testing organizations, agencies, or educational institutions will be approved to administer tests for certification of court interpreters for individuals who are deaf or hearing impaired. It is the intent of the Legislature that the study obtain the widest possible input from the public, including, but not limited to, educational institutions, the judiciary, linguists, members of the State Bar, court interpreters, members of professional interpreting organizations, and members of the deaf and hearing-impaired communities. After obtaining public comment and completing its study, the Judicial Council shall publish these guidelines. By January 1, 1997, the Judicial Council shall approve one or more entities to administer testing for court interpreters for individuals who are deaf or hearing impaired. Testing entities may include educational institutions, testing organizations, joint powers agencies, or public agencies.

Commencing July 1, 1997, court interpreters for individuals who are deaf or hearing impaired shall meet the qualifications specified in subdivision (f).

(i) Persons appointed to serve as interpreters under this section shall be paid, in addition to actual travel costs, the prevailing rate paid to persons employed by the court to provide other interpreter services unless such service is considered to be a part of the person's regular duties as an employee of the state, county, or other political subdivision of the state. Except as provided in subdivision (j), payment of the interpreter's fee shall be a charge against the * * * court. Payment of the interpreter's fee in administrative proceedings shall be a charge against the appointing board or authority.

(j) Whenever a peace officer or any other person having a law enforcement or prosecutorial function in any criminal or quasi-criminal investigation or non-court proceeding questions or otherwise interviews an alleged victim or witness who demonstrates or alleges deafness or hearing impairment, a good faith effort to secure the services of an interpreter shall be made, without any unnecessary delay unless either the individual who is deaf or hearing impaired affirmatively indicates that he or she does not need or cannot use an interpreter, or an interpreter is not otherwise required by Title II of the Americans with Disabilities Act of 1990 (Public Law 101–336) [1] and federal regulations adopted thereunder. Payment of the interpreter's fee shall be a charge against the county, or other political subdivision of the state, in which the action is pending.

(k) No statement, written or oral, made by an individual who the court finds is deaf or hearing impaired in reply to a question of a peace officer, or any other person having a law enforcement or prosecutorial function in any criminal or quasi-criminal investigation or proceeding, may be used against that individual who is deaf or hearing impaired unless the question was accurately interpreted and the statement was made knowingly, voluntarily, and intelligently and was accurately interpreted, or the court makes special findings that either the individual could not have used an interpreter or an interpreter was not otherwise required by Title II of the Americans with Disabilities Act of 1990 (Public Law 101–336) and federal regulations adopted thereunder and that the statement was made knowingly, voluntarily, and intelligently.

(*l*) In obtaining services of an interpreter for purposes of subdivision (j) or (k), priority shall be given to first obtaining a qualified interpreter.

(m) Nothing in subdivision (j) or (k) shall be deemed to supersede the requirement of subdivision (b) for use of a qualified interpreter for individuals who are deaf or hearing impaired participating as parties or witnesses in a trial or hearing.

(n) In any action or proceeding in which an individual who is deaf or hearing impaired is a participant, the appointing authority shall not commence proceedings until the appointed interpreter is in full view of and spatially situated to assure proper communication with the participating individual who is deaf or hearing impaired.

(o) Each superior court shall maintain a current roster of qualified interpreters certified pursuant to subdivision (f). (*Stats.1965, c. 299, § 2, operative Jan. 1, 1967. Amended by Stats.1977, c. 1182, p. 3873, § 1; Stats.1984, c. 768, § 2; Stats.1989, c. 1002, § 2; Stats.1990, c. 1450 (S.B.2046), § 2; Stats.1991, c. 883 (S.B.585), § 1; Stats.1992, c. 118 (S.B.16), § 1, eff. July 7, 1992; Stats.1992, c. 913 (A.B.1077), § 14; Stats.1995, c. 143 (A.B.1833), § 1, eff. July 18, 1995; Stats.2012, c. 470 (A.B.1529), § 11.*)

[1] 42 U.S.C.A. §12101 et seq.

§ 754.5
Privileged statements; deaf or hearing impaired persons; use of interpreter

Whenever an otherwise valid privilege exists between an individual who is deaf or hearing impaired and another person, that privilege is not waived merely because an interpreter was used to facilitate their communication. (*Added by Stats.1990, c. 1450 (S.B.2046), § 3. Amended by Stats.1992, c. 913 (A.B.1077), § 15.*)

§ 755
Hearings or proceedings related to domestic violence; party not proficient in English; interpreters; fees

(a) In any action or proceeding under Division 10 (commencing with Section 6200) of the Family Code, and in any action or proceeding under the Uniform Parentage Act (Part 3 (commencing with Section 7600) of Division 12 of the Family Code) or for dissolution or nullity of marriage or legal separation of the parties in which a protective order has been granted or is being sought pursuant to Section 6221 of the Family Code, in which a party does not proficiently speak or understand the English language, and that party is present, an interpreter, as provided in this section, shall be present to interpret the proceedings in a language that the party understands, and to assist communication between the party and his or her attorney. Notwithstanding this requirement, a court may issue an ex parte order pursuant to Sections 2045 and 7710 of, and Article 1 (commencing with Section 6320) of Chapter 2 of Part 4 of Division 10 of the Family Code, without the presence of an interpreter. The interpreter selected shall be certified pursuant to Article 4 (commencing with Section 68560) of Chapter 2 of Title 8 of the Government Code, unless the court in its discretion appoints an interpreter who is not certified.

(b) The fees of interpreters utilized under this section shall be paid as provided in subdivision (b) of Section 68092 of the Government Code. However, the fees of an interpreter shall be waived for a party who needs an interpreter and appears in forma pauperis pursuant to Section 68511.3 of the Government Code. The Judicial Council shall amend subdivision (i) of California Rule of Court 985 and revise its forms accordingly by July 1, 1996.

(c) In any civil action in which an interpreter is required under this section, the court shall not commence proceedings until the appointed interpreter is present and situated near the party and his or her attorney. However, this section shall not prohibit the court from doing any of the following:

(1) Issuing an order when the necessity for the order outweighs the necessity for an interpreter.

(2) Extending the duration of a previously issued temporary order if an interpreter is not readily available.

(3) Issuing a permanent order where a party who requires an interpreter fails to make appropriate arrangements for an interpreter after receiving proper notice of the hearing with information about obtaining an interpreter.

(d) This section does not prohibit the presence of any other person to assist a party.

(e) A local public entity may, and the Judicial Council shall, apply to the appropriate state agency that receives federal funds authorized pursuant to the federal Violence Against Women Act (P.L. 103–322) for these federal funds or for funds from sources other than the state to implement this section. A local public entity and the Judicial Council shall comply with the requirements of this section only to the extent that any of these funds are made available.

(f) The Judicial Council shall draft rules and modify forms necessary to implement this section, including those for the petition for a temporary restraining order and related forms, to inform both parties of their right to an interpreter pursuant to this section. (*Added by Stats.1995, c. 888 (S.B.982), § 1.*)

§ 755.5
Medical examinations; parties not proficient in English language; interpreters; fees; admissibility of record

(a) During any medical examination, requested by an insurer or by the defendant, of a person who is a party to a civil action and who does not proficiently speak or understand the English language, conducted for the purpose of determining damages in a civil action, an interpreter shall be present to interpret the examination in a language that the person understands. The interpreter shall be certified pursuant to Article 8 (commencing with Section 11435.05) of Chapter 4.5 of Part 1 of Division 3 of Title 2 of the Government Code.

(b) The fees of interpreters used under subdivision (a) shall be paid by the insurer or defendant requesting the medical examination.

(c) The record of, or testimony concerning, any medical examination conducted in violation of subdivision (a) shall be inadmissible in the civil action for which it was conducted or any other civil action.

(d) This section does not prohibit the presence of any other person to assist a party.

(e) In the event that interpreters certified pursuant to Article 8 (commencing with Section 11435.05) of Chapter 4.5 of Part 1 of Division 3 of Title 2 of the Government Code cannot be present at the medical examination, upon stipulation of the parties the requester specified in subdivision (a) shall have the discretionary authority to provisionally qualify and use other interpreters. (*Added by Stats.1992, c. 1302 (A.B.3107), § 5, eff. Sept. 30, 1992. Amended by Stats.1995, c. 938 (S.B.523), § 8, operative July 1, 1997.*)

CHAPTER 5. METHOD AND SCOPE OF EXAMINATION

ARTICLE 1. DEFINITIONS

§ 760
Direct examination

"Direct examination" is the first examination of a witness upon a matter that is not within the scope of a previous examination of the witness. (*Stats.1965, c. 299, § 2, operative Jan. 1, 1967.*)

§ 761
Cross-examination

"Cross-examination" is the examination of a witness by a party other than the direct examiner upon a matter that is within the scope of the direct examination of the witness. (*Stats.1965, c. 299, § 2, operative Jan. 1, 1967.*)

§ 762
Redirect examination

"Redirect examination" is an examination of a witness by the direct examiner subsequent to the cross-examination of the witness. (*Stats.1965, c. 299, § 2, operative Jan. 1, 1967.*)

§ 763
Recross-examination

"Recross-examination" is an examination of a witness by a cross-examiner subsequent to a redirect examination of the witness. (*Stats.1965, c. 299, § 2, operative Jan. 1, 1967.*)

§ 764
Leading question

A "leading question" is a question that suggests to the witness the answer that the examining party desires. (*Stats.1965, c. 299, § 2, operative Jan. 1, 1967.*)

ARTICLE 2. EXAMINATION OF WITNESSES

Section
765. Court to control mode of interrogation.
766. Responsive answers.
767. Leading questions.
768. Writings.
769. Inconsistent statement or conduct.
770. Evidence of inconsistent statement of witness; exclusion; exceptions.
771. Production of writing used to refresh memory.
772. Order of examination.
773. Cross-examination.
774. Re-examination.
775. Court may call witnesses.
776. Examination of adverse party or person identified with adverse party.
777. Exclusion of witness.
778. Recall of witness.

§ 765
Court to control mode of interrogation

(a) The court shall exercise reasonable control over the mode of interrogation of a witness so as to make interrogation as rapid, as distinct, and as effective for the ascertainment of the truth, as may be, and to protect the witness from undue harassment or embarrassment.

(b) With a witness under the age of 14 or a dependent person with a substantial cognitive impairment, the court shall take special care to protect him or her from undue harassment or embarrassment, and to restrict the unnecessary repetition of questions. The court shall also take special care to ensure that questions are stated in a form which is appropriate to the age or cognitive level of the witness. The court may, in the interests of justice, on objection by a party, forbid the asking of a question which is in a form that is not reasonably likely to be understood by a person of the age or cognitive level of the witness. (*Stats.1965, c. 299, § 2, operative Jan. 1, 1967. Amended by Stats.1985, c. 884, § 3; Stats.1986, c. 1051, § 1; Stats.2004, c. 823 (A.B.20), § 4.*)

§ 766
Responsive answers

A witness must give responsive answers to questions, and answers that are not responsive shall be stricken on motion of any party. (*Stats.1965, c. 299, § 2, operative Jan. 1, 1967.*)

§ 767
Leading questions

(a) Except under special circumstances where the interests of justice otherwise require:

(1) A leading question may not be asked of a witness on direct or redirect examination.

(2) A leading question may be asked of a witness on cross-examination or recross-examination.

(b) The court may, in the interests of justice permit a leading question to be asked of a child under 10 years of age or a dependent person with a substantial cognitive impairment in a case involving a prosecution under Section 273a, 273d, 288.5, 368, or any of the acts described in Section 11165.1 or 11165.2 of the Penal Code. (*Stats.1965, c. 299, § 2, operative Jan. 1, 1967. Amended by Stats.1984, c. 1423, § 1, eff. Sept. 26, 1984; Stats.1995, c. 87 (A.B.355), § 1; Stats.2004, c. 823 (A.B.20), § 5.*)

Subdivision (a) restates the substance of and supersedes the last sentence of Section 2046 of the Code of Civil Procedure. Subdivision (b) is based on and supersedes a phrase that appears in Code of Civil Procedure Section 2048.

The exception stated at the beginning of the section continues the present law that permits leading questions on direct examination where there is little danger of improper suggestion or where such questions are necessary to obtain relevant evidence. This would permit leading questions on direct examination for preliminary matters, refreshing recollection, and examining handicapped witnesses, expert witnesses, and hostile witnesses. See Witkin, California Evidence §§ 591, 592 (1958); 3 Wigmore, Evidence § 769 *et seq.* (3d ed. 1940). The court may also forbid the asking of leading questions on cross-examination where the witness is biased in favor of the cross-examiner and would be unduly susceptible to the influence of questions that suggested the desired answer. See 3 Wigmore, Evidence § 773 (3d ed. 1940).

§ 768
Writings

(a) In examining a witness concerning a writing, it is not necessary to show, read, or disclose to him any part of the writing.

(b) If a writing is shown to a witness, all parties to the action must be given an opportunity to inspect it before any question concerning it may be asked of the witness. (*Stats.1965, c. 299, § 2, operative Jan. 1, 1967.*)

Existing law apparently does not require that a writing (other than one containing prior inconsistent statements used for impeachment purposes) be shown to a witness before he can be examined concerning it. Section 2054 of the Code of Civil Procedure, which seems to so require, actually requires only that the adverse party be given an opportunity to inspect any writing that is *actually shown* to a witness before the witness can be examined concerning the writing. See People v. Briggs, 58 Cal.2d 385, 413, 24 Cal.Rptr. 417, 435, 374 P.2d 257, 275 (1962); People v. Keyes, 103 Cal.App. 624, 284 Pac. 1096 (1930) (hearing denied); People v. De Angelli, 34 Cal.App. 716, 168 Pac. 699 (1917). Section 768 clarifies whatever doubt may exist in this regard by declaring that such a writing need not be shown to the witness before he can be examined concerning it. Of course, the best evidence rule may in some cases preclude eliciting testimony concerning the content of a writing. See Evidence Code § 1500 and the Comment thereto.

Insofar as Section 768 relates to prior inconsistent statements that are in writing, see the Comment to Section 769.

Subdivision (b) of Section 768 preserves the right of the adverse party to inspect a writing that is *actually shown* to a witness before the witness can be examined concerning it. As indicated above, this preserves the existing requirement declared in Code of Civil Procedure Section 2054. However, the right of inspection has been extended to all parties to the action.

§ 769
Inconsistent statement or conduct

In examining a witness concerning a statement or other conduct by him that is inconsistent with any part of his testimony at the hearing, it is not necessary to disclose to him any information concerning the statement or other conduct. (*Stats.1965, c. 299, § 2, operative Jan. 1, 1967.*)

Section 769 is consistent with the existing California law regarding the examination of a witness concerning prior inconsistent *oral* statements. Under existing law, a party need not disclose to a witness any information concerning a prior inconsistent *oral* statement of the witness before asking him questions about the statement. People v. Kidd, People v. Kidd, 56

Cal.2d 759, 765, 16 Cal.Rptr. 793, 796–797, 366 P.2d 49, 52–53 (1961); People v. Campos, 10 Cal.App.2d 310, 317, 52 P.2d 251, 254 (1935). However, if a witness§ prior inconsistent statements are in *writing* or, as in the case of former oral testimony, have been reduced to writing, "they must be shown to the witness before any question is put to him concerning them." Code Civ.Proc. § 2052 (superseded by Evidence Code § 768); Umemoto v. McDonald, 6 Cal.2d 587, 592, 58 P.2d 1274, 1276 (1936).

Section 769 eliminates the distinction made in existing law between oral and written statements and permits a witness to be asked questions concerning a prior inconsistent statement, whether written or oral, even though no disclosure is made to him concerning the prior statement. (Whether a foundational showing is required before other evidence of the prior statement may be admitted is not covered in Section 769; the prerequisites for the admission of such evidence are set forth in Section 770.) The disclosure of inconsistent written statements that is required under existing law limits the effectiveness of cross-examination by removing the element of surprise. The forewarning gives the dishonest witness the opportunity to reshape his testimony in conformity with the prior statement. The existing rule is based on an English common law rule that has been abandoned in England for 100 years. See McCormick, Evidence § 28 at 53 (1954).

§ 770
Evidence of inconsistent statement of witness; exclusion; exceptions

Unless the interests of justice otherwise require, extrinsic evidence of a statement made by a witness that is inconsistent with any part of his testimony at the hearing shall be excluded unless:

(a) The witness was so examined while testifying as to give him an opportunity to explain or to deny the statement; or

(b) The witness has not been excused from giving further testimony in the action. (*Stats.1965, c. 299, § 2, operative Jan. 1, 1967.*)

§ 771
Production of writing used to refresh memory

(a) Subject to subdivision (c), if a witness, either while testifying or prior thereto, uses a writing to refresh his memory with respect to any matter about which he testifies, such writing must be produced at the hearing at the request of an adverse party and, unless the writing is so produced, the testimony of the witness concerning such matter shall be stricken.

(b) If the writing is produced at the hearing, the adverse party may, if he chooses, inspect the writing, cross-examine the witness concerning it, and introduce in evidence such portion of it as may be pertinent to the testimony of the witness.

(c) Production of the writing is excused, and the testimony of the witness shall not be stricken, if the writing:

(1) Is not in the possession or control of the witness or the party who produced his testimony concerning the matter; and

(2) Was not reasonably procurable by such party through the use of the court's process or other available means. (*Stats.1965, c. 299, § 2, operative Jan. 1, 1967.*)

Section 771 grants to an adverse party the right to inspect any writing used to refresh a witness§ recollection, whether the writing is used by the witness while testifying or prior thereto. The right of inspection granted by Section 771 may be broader than the similar right of inspection granted by Section 2047 of the Code of Civil Procedure, for Section 2047 has been interpreted by the courts to grant a right of inspection of only those writings used by the witness while he is testifying. People v. Gallardo, 41 Cal.2d 57, 257 P.2d 29 (1953); People v. Grayson, 172 Cal.App.2d 372, 341 P.2d 820 (1959); Smith v. Smith, 135 Cal.App.2d 100, 286 P.2d 1009 (1955). In a criminal case, however, the defendant can compel the prosecution to produce any written statement of a prosecution witness relating to matters covered in the witness§ testimony. People v. Estrada, 54 Cal.2d 713, 7 Cal.Rptr. 897, 355 P.2d 641 (1960). The extent to which the public policy reflected in criminal discovery practice overrides the restrictive interpretation of Code of Civil Procedure Section 2047 is not clear. See Witkin, California Evidence § 602 (Supp. 1963). In any event, Section 771 follows the lead of the criminal cases, such as People v. Silberstein, 159 Cal.App.2d Supp. 848, 323 P.2d 591 (1958) (defendant entitled to inspect police report used by police officer to refresh his recollection *before* testifying), and grants a right of inspection without regard to when the writing is used to refresh recollection. If a witness§ testimony depends upon the use of a writing to refresh his recollection, the adverse party's right to inspect the writing should not be made to depend upon the happenstance of when the writing is used.

Subdivision (b) gives an adverse party the right to introduce the refreshing memorandum into evidence. An adverse party has a similar right under Code of Civil Procedure Section 2047, which is superseded by this section. This right is not unlimited, however. Only those parts of the refreshing memorandum that are pertinent to the testimony given by the witness are admissible under this rule. *Cf.* People v. Silberstein, 159 Cal.App.2d Supp. 848, 851–852, 323 P.2d 591, 593 (1958) ("the right to inspect [a refreshing writing] cannot be denied although its admission in evidence may be refused if ′ ′ ′ its contents are immaterial"); Dragash v. Western Pac. R.R., 161 Cal.App.2d 233, 326 P.2d 649 (1958). See also Evidence Code § 356 and the Comment thereto.

Subdivision (c) excuses the nonproduction of the memory-refreshing writing where the writing cannot be produced through no fault of the witness or the party eliciting his testimony concerning the matter. The rule is analogous to the rule announced in People v. Parham, 60 Cal.2d 378, 33 Cal.Rptr. 497, 384 P.2d 1001 (1963), which affirmed an order denying defendant's motion to strike certain witnesses§ testimony where the witnesses§ prior statements were withheld by the Federal Bureau of Investigation.

It should be noted that there is no restriction in the Evidence Code on the means that may be used to refresh recollection. Thus, the limitations on the types of writings that may be used as recorded memory under Section 1237 do not limit the types of writings that may be used to refresh recollection under Section 771.

§ 772
Order of examination

(a) The examination of a witness shall proceed in the following phases: direct examination, cross-examination, redirect examination, re-cross-examination, and continuing thereafter by redirect and re-cross-examination.

(b) Unless for good cause the court otherwise directs, each phase of the examination of a witness must be concluded before the succeeding phase begins.

(c) Subject to subdivision (d), a party may, in the discretion of the court, interrupt his cross-examination, redirect examination, or re-cross-examination of a witness, in order to examine the witness upon a matter not within the scope of a previous examination of the witness.

(d) If the witness is the defendant in a criminal action, the witness may not, without his consent, be examined under direct examination by another party. (*Stats.1965, c. 299, § 2, operative Jan. 1, 1967.*)

Subdivision (a) codifies existing but nonstatutory California law. See Witkin, California Evidence § 576 at 631 (1958).

Subdivision (b) is based on and supersedes the second sentence of Section 2045 of the Code of Civil Procedure. The language of the existing section has been expanded, however, to require completion of each phase of examination of the witness, not merely the direct examination.

Under subdivision (c), as under existing law, a party examining a witness under cross-examination, redirect examination, or re-cross-examination may go beyond the scope of the initial direct examination if the court permits. See Code Civ.Proc. §§ 2048 (last clause), 2050; Witkin, California Evidence §§ 627, 697 (1958). Under the definition in Section 760, such an extended examination is direct examination. *Cf.* Code Civ.Proc. § 2048 ("such examination is to be subject to the same rules as a direct examination"). Such direct examination may, however, be subject to the rules applicable to a cross-examination by virtue of the provisions of Section 776, 804, or 1203.

Subdivision (d) states an exception for the defendant-witness in a criminal action that reflects existing law. See Witkin, California Evidence § 629 at 676 (1958).

§ 773
Cross-examination

(a) A witness examined by one party may be cross-examined upon any matter within the scope of the direct examination by each other party to the action in such order as the court directs.

(b) The cross-examination of a witness by any party whose interest is not adverse to the party calling him is subject to the same rules that are applicable to the direct examination. (*Stats.1965, c. 299, § 2, operative Jan. 1, 1967.*)

§ 774
Re-examination

A witness once examined cannot be reexamined as to the same matter without leave of the court, but he may be reexamined as to any new matter upon which he has been examined by another party to the action. Leave may be granted or withheld in the court's discretion. (*Stats.1965, c. 299, § 2, operative Jan. 1, 1967.*)

§ 775
Court may call witnesses

The court, on its own motion or on the motion of any party, may call witnesses and interrogate them the same as if they had been produced by a party to the action, and the parties may object to the questions asked and the evidence adduced the same as if such witnesses were called and examined by an adverse party. Such witnesses may be cross-examined by all parties to the action in such order as the court directs. (*Stats.1965, c. 299, § 2, operative Jan. 1, 1967.*)

The power of the judge to call *expert* witnesses is well recognized by statutory and case law in California. Code Civ.Proc. § 1871 (recodified as Section 723 and Article 2 (commencing with Section 730) of Chapter 3); Penal Code § 1027; Citizens State Bank v. Castro, 105 Cal.App. 284, 287 Pac. 559 (1930). See also Code Civ.Proc. §§ 1884 and 1885 (interpreters), continued in substance by Chapter 4 (commencing with Section 750).

The power of the judge to call other witnesses is also recognized by case law. Travis v. Southern Pac. Co., 210 Cal.App.2d 410, 425, 26 Cal.Rptr. 700, 707–708 (1962) ("[W]e have been cited to no case, nor has our independent research disclosed any case, dealing with a civil action in which a witness has been called to the stand by the court, over objection of a party. However, we can see no difference in this respect between a civil and a criminal case. In both, the endeavor of the court and the parties should be to get at the truth of the matter in contest. Fundamentally, there is no reason why the court in the interests of justice should not call to the stand anyone who appears to have relevant, competent and material information.").

Of course, the judge would be guilty of misconduct were he to show partiality or bias in calling and interrogating witnesses. See 2 Witkin, California Procedure, Trial §§ 14–17 (1954).

§ 776
Examination of adverse party or person identified with adverse party

(a) A party to the record of any civil action, or a person identified with such a party, may be called and examined as if under cross-examination by any adverse party at any time during the presentation of evidence by the party calling the witness.

(b) A witness examined by a party under this section may be cross-examined by all other parties to the action in such order as the court directs; but, subject to subdivision (e), the witness may be examined only as if under redirect examination by:

(1) In the case of a witness who is a party, his own counsel and counsel for a party who is not adverse to the witness.

(2) In the case of a witness who is not a party, counsel for the party with whom the witness is identified and counsel for a party who is not adverse to the party with whom the witness is identified.

(c) For the purpose of this section, parties represented by the same counsel are deemed to be a single party.

(d) For the purpose of this section, a person is identified with a party if he is:

(1) A person for whose immediate benefit the action is prosecuted or defended by the party.

(2) A director, officer, superintendent, member, agent, employee, or managing agent of the party or of a person specified in paragraph (1), or any public employee of a public entity when such public entity is the party.

(3) A person who was in any of the relationships specified in paragraph (2) at the time of the act or omission giving rise to the cause of action.

(4) A person who was in any of the relationships specified in paragraph (2) at the time he obtained knowledge of the matter concerning which he is sought to be examined under this section.

(e) Paragraph (2) of subdivision (b) does not require counsel for the party with whom the witness is identified and counsel for a party who is not adverse to the party with whom the witness is identified to examine the witness as if under redirect examination if the party who called the witness for examination under this section:

(1) Is also a person identified with the same party with whom the witness is identified.

(2) Is the personal representative, heir, successor, or assignee of a person identified with the same party with whom the witness is identified. (*Stats.1965, c. 299, § 2, operative Jan. 1, 1967. Amended by Stats.1967, c. 650, p. 2005, § 2.*)

§ 777
Exclusion of witness

(a) Subject to subdivisions (b) and (c), the court may exclude from the courtroom any witness not at the time under examination so that such witness cannot hear the testimony of other witnesses.

(b) A party to the action cannot be excluded under this section.

(c) If a person other than a natural person is a party to the action, an officer or employee designated by its attorney is entitled to be present. (*Stats.1965, c. 299, § 2, operative Jan. 1, 1967.*)

§ 778
Recall of witness

After a witness has been excused from giving further testimony in the action, he cannot be recalled without leave of the court. Leave may be granted or withheld in the court's discretion. (*Stats.1965, c. 299, § 2, operative Jan. 1, 1967.*)

CHAPTER 6. CREDIBILITY OF WITNESSES

ARTICLE 1. CREDIBILITY GENERALLY

§ 780
Testimony; proof of truthfulness; considerations

Except as otherwise provided by statute, the court or jury may consider in determining the credibility of a witness any matter that has any tendency in reason to prove or disprove the truthfulness of his testimony at the hearing, including but not limited to any of the following:

(a) His demeanor while testifying and the manner in which he testifies.

(b) The character of his testimony.

(c) The extent of his capacity to perceive, to recollect, or to communicate any matter about which he testifies.

(d) The extent of his opportunity to perceive any matter about which he testifies.

(e) His character for honesty or veracity or their opposites.

(f) The existence or nonexistence of a bias, interest, or other motive.

(g) A statement previously made by him that is consistent with his testimony at the hearing.

(h) A statement made by him that is inconsistent with any part of his testimony at the hearing.

(i) The existence or nonexistence of any fact testified to by him.

(j) His attitude toward the action in which he testifies or toward the giving of testimony.

(k) His admission of untruthfulness. (*Stats.1965, c. 299, § 2, operative Jan. 1, 1967.*)

§ 782
Sexual offenses; evidence of sexual conduct of complaining witness; procedure for admissibility; treatment of resealed affidavits

(a) In any of the circumstances described in subdivision (c), if evidence of sexual conduct of the complaining witness is offered to attack the credibility of the complaining witness under Section 780, the following procedure shall be followed:

(1) A written motion shall be made by the defendant to the court and prosecutor stating that the defense has an offer of proof of the relevancy of evidence of the sexual conduct of the complaining witness proposed to be presented and its relevancy in attacking the credibility of the complaining witness.

(2) The written motion shall be accompanied by an affidavit in which the offer of proof shall be stated. The affidavit shall be filed under seal and only unsealed by the court to determine if the offer of proof is sufficient to order a hearing pursuant to paragraph (3). After that determination, the affidavit shall be resealed by the court.

(3) If the court finds that the offer of proof is sufficient, the court shall order a hearing out of the presence of the jury, if any, and at the hearing allow the questioning of the complaining witness regarding the offer of proof made by the defendant.

(4) At the conclusion of the hearing, if the court finds that evidence proposed to be offered by the defendant regarding the sexual conduct of the complaining witness is relevant pursuant to Section 780, and is not inadmissible pursuant to Section 352, the court may make an order stating what evidence may be introduced by the defendant, and the nature of the questions to be permitted. The defendant may then offer evidence pursuant to the order of the court.

(5) An affidavit resealed by the court pursuant to paragraph (2) shall remain sealed, unless the defendant raises an issue on appeal or collateral review relating to the offer of proof contained in the sealed document. If the defendant raises that issue on appeal, the court shall allow the Attorney General and appellate counsel for the defendant access to the sealed affidavit. If the issue is raised on collateral review, the court shall allow the district attorney and defendant's counsel access to the sealed affidavit. The use of the information contained in the affidavit shall be limited solely to the pending proceeding.

(b) As used in this section, "complaining witness" means:

(1) The alleged victim of the crime charged, the prosecution of which is subject to this section, pursuant to paragraph (1) of subdivision (c).

(2) An alleged victim offering testimony pursuant to paragraph (2) or (3) of subdivision (c).

(c) The procedure provided by subdivision (a) shall apply in any of the following circumstances:

(1) In a prosecution under Section 261, 262, 264.1, 286, 288, 288a, 288.5, or 289 of the Penal Code, or for assault with intent to commit, attempt to commit, or conspiracy to commit any crime defined in any of those sections, except if the crime is alleged to have occurred in a local detention facility, as defined in Section 6031.4 of the Penal Code, or in the state prison, as defined in Section 4504.

(2) When an alleged victim testifies pursuant to subdivision (b) of Section 1101 as a victim of a crime listed in Section 243.4, 261, 261.5, 269, 285, 286, 288, 288a, 288.5, 289, 314, or 647.6 of the Penal Code, except if the

crime is alleged to have occurred in a local detention facility, as defined in Section 6031.4 of the Penal Code, or in the state prison, as defined in Section 4504 of the Penal Code.

(3) When an alleged victim of a sexual offense testifies pursuant to Section 1108, except if the crime is alleged to have occurred in a local detention facility, as defined in Section 6031.4 of the Penal Code, or in the state prison, as defined in Section 4504 of the Penal Code. (*Added by Stats.1974, c. 569, p. 1388, § 1. Amended by Stats.1981, c. 726, p. 2876, § 1; Stats.1987, c. 177, § 1; Stats.1989, c. 1402, § 2; Stats.1996, c. 1075 (S.B.1444), § 6; Stats.2004, c. 61 (A.B.2829), § 1; Stats.2006, c. 225 (A.B.1996), § 1; Stats.2007, c. 130 (A.B.299), § 83.*)

§ 783
Sexual harassment, sexual assault, or sexual battery cases; admissibility of evidence of plaintiff's sexual conduct; procedure

In any civil action alleging conduct which constitutes sexual harassment, sexual assault, or sexual battery, if evidence of sexual conduct of the plaintiff is offered to attack credibility of the plaintiff under Section 780, the following procedures shall be followed:

(a) A written motion shall be made by the defendant to the court and the plaintiff's attorney stating that the defense has an offer of proof of the relevancy of evidence of the sexual conduct of the plaintiff proposed to be presented.

(b) The written motion shall be accompanied by an affidavit in which the offer of proof shall be stated.

(c) If the court finds that the offer of proof is sufficient, the court shall order a hearing out of the presence of the jury, if any, and at the hearing allow the questioning of the plaintiff regarding the offer of proof made by the defendant.

(d) At the conclusion of the hearing, if the court finds that evidence proposed to be offered by the defendant regarding the sexual conduct of the plaintiff is relevant pursuant to Section 780, and is not inadmissible pursuant to Section 352, the court may make an order stating what evidence may be introduced by the defendant, and the nature of the questions to be permitted. The defendant may then offer evidence pursuant to the order of the court. (*Added by Stats.1985, c. 1328, § 3.*)

ARTICLE 2. ATTACKING OR SUPPORTING CREDIBILITY

Section
785. Parties may attack or support credibility.
786. Character evidence generally.
787. Specific instances of conduct.
788. Prior felony conviction.

789. Religious belief.
790. Good character of witness.
791. Prior consistent statement of witness.

§ 785
Parties may attack or support credibility

The credibility of a witness may be attacked or supported by any party, including the party calling him. (*Stats.1965, c. 299, § 2, operative Jan. 1, 1967.*)

§ 786
Character evidence generally

Evidence of traits of his character other than honesty or veracity, or their opposites, is inadmissible to attack or support the credibility of a witness. (*Stats.1965, c. 299, § 2, operative Jan. 1, 1967.*)

§ 787
Specific instances of conduct

Subject to Section 788, evidence of specific instances of his conduct relevant only as tending to prove a trait of his character is inadmissible to attack or support the credibility of a witness. (*Stats.1965, c. 299, § 2, operative Jan. 1, 1967.*)

§ 788
Prior felony conviction

For the purpose of attacking the credibility of a witness, it may be shown by the examination of the witness or by the record of the judgment that he has been convicted of a felony unless:

(a) A pardon based on his innocence has been granted to the witness by the jurisdiction in which he was convicted.

(b) A certificate of rehabilitation and pardon has been granted to the witness under the provisions of Chapter 3.5 (commencing with Section 4852.01) of Title 6 of Part 3 of the Penal Code.

(c) The accusatory pleading against the witness has been dismissed under the provisions of Penal Code Section 1203.4, but this exception does not apply to any criminal trial where the witness is being prosecuted for a subsequent offense.

(d) The conviction was under the laws of another jurisdiction and the witness has been relieved of the penalties and disabilities arising from the conviction pursuant to a procedure substantially equivalent to that referred to in subdivision (b) or (c). (*Stats.1965, c. 299, § 2, operative Jan. 1, 1967.*)

Under Section 787, evidence of specific instances of a witness§ conduct is inadmissible for the purpose of attacking or supporting his credibility. Section 788 states an exception to this general rule where the evidence of the witness§ misconduct consists of his conviction of a felony. A judgment of conviction that is offered to prove that the person adjudged guilty committed the crime is hearsay. See Evidence Code §§ 1200 and 1300 and the Comments thereto. But the hearsay objection to the evidence specified in Section 788 is overcome by the declaration in the section that such evidence "may be shown" for the purpose of attacking a witness§ credibility.

Section 788 is based on Section 2051 of the Code of Civil Procedure. Under Section 788, as under Section 2051, only the testimony of the witness himself or the record of the judgment of conviction may be used to prove the fact of conviction. As Section 788 is, in substance, a recodification of the existing law, it will have no effect on the case-developed rules limiting the circumstances under which a witness may be asked whether he was convicted of a felony. See People v. Perez, 58 Cal.2d 229, 23 Cal.Rptr. 569, 373 P.2d 617 (1962); People v. Darnold, 219 Cal.App.2d 561, 33 Cal.Rptr. 369 (1963).

Subdivision (a) prohibits the use of a conviction to attack the credibility of a witness if a pardon has been granted to the witness on the ground that he was innocent and was erroneously convicted. Subdivision (a) changes the existing California law. Under the existing law, the conviction is admissible to attack credibility, and the pardon—even though based on innocence—is admissible merely to mitigate the effect of the conviction. People v. Hardwick, 204 Cal. 582, 269 Pac. 427 (1928).

Subdivision (b) recodifies the provision of Section 2051 that prohibits the use of a conviction to attack credibility if a pardon has been granted upon the basis of a certificate of rehabilitation. See also Code Civ.Proc. § 2065.

Subdivision (c) recodifies the existing law that prohibits the use of a conviction to attack the credibility of a witness if the conviction has been set aside under Penal Code Section 1203.4. See People v. Mackey, 58 Cal.App. 123, 208 Pac. 135 (1922). The exception that permits the use of such a conviction to attack the credibility of a criminal defendant who testifies as a witness also reflects existing law. See People v. James, 40 Cal.App.2d 740, 105 P.2d 947 (1940).

Subdivision (d) merely provides that a witness who has been relieved of the penalties and disabilities of a prior conviction under the laws of another jurisdiction will be subject to attacks on his credibility under the same conditions that would be applicable if such relief had been granted him under the laws of California.

§ 789
Religious belief

Evidence of his religious belief or lack thereof is inadmissible to attack or support the credibility of a witness. (*Stats.1965, c. 299, § 2, operative Jan. 1, 1967.*)

§ 790
Good character of witness

Evidence of the good character of a witness is inadmissible to support his credibility unless evidence of his bad character has been admitted for the purpose of attacking his credibility. (*Stats.1965, c. 299, § 2, operative Jan. 1, 1967.*)

§ 791
Prior consistent statement of witness

Evidence of a statement previously made by a witness that is consistent with his testimony at the hearing is inadmissible to support his credibility unless it is offered after:

(a) Evidence of a statement made by him that is inconsistent with any part of his testimony at the hearing has been admitted for the purpose of attacking his credibility, and the statement was made before the alleged inconsistent statement; or

(b) An express or implied charge has been made that his testimony at the hearing is recently fabricated or is influenced by bias or other improper motive, and the statement was made before the bias, motive for fabrication, or other improper motive is alleged to have arisen. (*Stats.1965, c. 299, § 2, operative Jan. 1, 1967.*)

CHAPTER 7. HYPNOSIS OF WITNESSES

Section
795. Testimony of hypnosis subject; admissibility; conditions.

§ 795
Testimony of hypnosis subject; admissibility; conditions

(a) The testimony of a witness is not inadmissible in a criminal proceeding by reason of the fact that the witness has previously undergone hypnosis for the purpose of recalling events that are the subject of the witness's testimony, if all of the following conditions are met:

(1) The testimony is limited to those matters that the witness recalled and related prior to the hypnosis.

(2) The substance of the prehypnotic memory was preserved in a writing, audio recording, or video recording prior to the hypnosis.

(3) The hypnosis was conducted in accordance with all of the following procedures:

(A) A written record was made prior to hypnosis documenting the subject's description of the event, and information that was provided to the hypnotist concerning the subject matter of the hypnosis.

(B) The subject gave informed consent to the hypnosis.

(C) The hypnosis session, including the pre- and post-hypnosis interviews, was video recorded for subsequent review.

(D) The hypnosis was performed by a licensed physician and surgeon, psychologist, licensed clinical social worker, licensed marriage and family therapist, or licensed professional clinical counselor experienced in the use of hypnosis and independent of and not in the presence of law enforcement, the prosecution, or the defense.

(4) Prior to admission of the testimony, the court holds a hearing pursuant to Section 402 at which the proponent of the evidence proves by clear and convincing evidence that the hypnosis did not so affect the witness as to render the witness's prehypnosis recollection unreliable or to substantially impair the ability to cross-examine the witness concerning the witness's prehypnosis recollection. At the hearing, each side shall have the right to present expert testimony and to cross-examine witnesses.

(b) Nothing in this section shall be construed to limit the ability of a party to attack the credibility of a witness who has undergone hypnosis, or to limit other legal grounds to admit or exclude the testimony of that witness. (*Added by Stats.1984, c. 479, § 1. Amended by Stats.1987, c. 285, § 1; Stats.1996, c. 67 (A.B.2296), § 1; Stats.2002, c. 1013 (S.B.2026), § 77; Stats.2009, c. 88 (A.B.176), § 34; Stats.2011, c. 381 (S.B.146), § 20.*)

Division 7

OPINION TESTIMONY AND SCIENTIFIC EVIDENCE

CHAPTER 1. EXPERT AND OTHER OPINION TESTIMONY

ARTICLE 1. EXPERT AND OTHER OPINION TESTIMONY GENERALLY

Section

800. Lay witnesses; opinion testimony.
801. Expert witnesses; opinion testimony.
802. Statement of basis of opinion.
803. Opinion based on improper matter.
804. Opinion based on opinion or statement of another.
805. Opinion on ultimate issue.

§ 800
Lay witnesses; opinion testimony

If a witness is not testifying as an expert, his testimony in the form of an opinion is limited to such an opinion as is permitted by law, including but not limited to an opinion that is:

(a) Rationally based on the perception of the witness; and

(b) Helpful to a clear understanding of his testimony. (*Stats.1965, c. 299, § 2, operative Jan. 1, 1967.*)

§ 801
Expert witnesses; opinion testimony

If a witness is testifying as an expert, his testimony in the form of an opinion is limited to such an opinion as is:

(a) Related to a subject that is sufficiently beyond common experience that the opinion of an expert would assist the trier of fact; and

(b) Based on matter (including his special knowledge, skill, experience, training, and education) perceived by or personally known to the witness or made known to him at or before the hearing, whether or not admissible, that is of a type that reasonably may be relied upon by an expert in forming an opinion upon the subject to which his testimony relates, unless an expert is precluded by law from using such matter as a basis for his opinion. (*Stats.1965, c. 299, § 2, operative Jan. 1, 1967.*)

§ 802
Statement of basis of opinion

A witness testifying in the form of an opinion may state on direct examination the reasons for his opinion and the matter (including, in the case of an expert, his special knowledge, skill, experience, training, and education) upon which it is based, unless he is precluded by law from using such reasons or matter as a basis for his opinion. The court in its discretion may require that a witness before testifying in the form of an opinion be first examined concerning the matter upon which his opinion is based. (*Stats.1965, c. 299, § 2, operative Jan. 1, 1967.*)

§ 803
Opinion based on improper matter

The court may, and upon objection shall, exclude testimony in the form of an opinion that is based in whole or in significant part on matter that is not a proper basis for such an opinion. In such case, the witness may, if there remains a proper basis for his opinion, then state his opinion after excluding from consideration the matter determined to be improper. (*Stats.1965, c. 299, § 2, operative Jan. 1, 1967.*)

§ 804
Opinion based on opinion or statement of another

(a) If a witness testifying as an expert testifies that his opinion is based in whole or in part upon the opinion or statement of another person, such other person may be called and examined by any adverse party as if under cross-examination concerning the opinion or statement.

(b) This section is not applicable if the person upon whose opinion or statement the expert witness has relied is (1) a party, (2) a person identified with a party within the meaning of subdivision (d) of Section 776, or (3) a witness who has testified in the action concerning the subject matter of the opinion or statement upon which the expert witness has relied.

(c) Nothing in this section makes admissible an expert opinion that is inadmissible because it is based in whole or in part on the opinion or statement of another person.

(d) An expert opinion otherwise admissible is not made inadmissible by this section because it is based on the opinion or statement of a person who is unavailable for examination pursuant to this section. (*Stats.1965, c. 299, § 2, operative Jan. 1, 1967.*)

§ 805
Opinion on ultimate issue

Testimony in the form of an opinion that is otherwise admissible is not objectionable because it embraces the ultimate issue to be decided by the trier of fact. (*Stats.1965, c. 299, § 2, operative Jan. 1, 1967.*)

ARTICLE 2. EVIDENCE OF MARKET VALUE OF PROPERTY

Section

§ 810
Application of article

(a) Except where another rule is provided by statute, this article provides special rules of evidence applicable to any action in which the value of property is to be ascertained.

(b) This article does not govern ad valorem property tax assessment or equalization proceedings. (*Added by Stats.1965, c. 1151, p. 2904, § 4, operative Jan. 1, 1967. Amended by Stats.1978, c. 294, p. 615, § 3; Stats.1980, c. 381, p. 757, § 1.*)

§ 811
Value of property

As used in this article, "value of property" means market value of any of the following:

(a) Real property or any interest therein.

(b) Real property or any interest therein and tangible personal property valued as a unit. (*Added by Stats.1965, c. 1151, p. 2904, § 4, operative Jan. 1, 1967. Amended by Stats.1975, c. 1240, p. 3202, § 15, operative July 1, 1976; Stats.1978, c. 294, p. 615, § 4; Stats.1980, c. 381, p. 757, § 2.*)

§ 812
Market value; interpretation of meaning

This article is not intended to alter or change the existing substantive law, whether statutory or decisional, interpreting the meaning of "market value," whether denominated "fair market value" or otherwise. (*Added by Stats.1965, c. 1151, p. 2904, § 4, operative Jan. 1, 1967. Amended by Stats.1975, c. 1240, p. 3202, § 16, operative July 1, 1976; Stats.1978, c. 294, p. 615, § 5.*)

§ 813
Value of property; authorized opinions; view of property; admissible evidence

(a) The value of property may be shown only by the opinions of any of the following:

(1) Witnesses qualified to express such opinions.

(2) The owner or the spouse of the owner of the property or property interest being valued.

(3) An officer, regular employee, or partner designated by a corporation, partnership, or unincorporated association that is the owner of the property or property interest being valued, if the designee is knowledgeable as to the value of the property or property interest.

(b) Nothing in this section prohibits a view of the property being valued or the admission of any other admissible evidence (including but not limited to evidence as to the nature and condition of the property and, in an eminent domain proceeding, the character of the improvement proposed to be constructed by the plaintiff) for the limited purpose of enabling the court, jury, or referee to understand and weigh the testimony given under subdivision (a); and such evidence, except evidence of the character of the improvement proposed to be constructed by the plaintiff in an eminent domain proceeding, is subject to impeachment and rebuttal.

(c) For the purposes of subdivision (a), "owner of the property or property interest being valued" includes, but is not limited to, the following persons:

(1) A person entitled to possession of the property.

(2) Either party in an action or proceeding to determine the ownership of the property between the parties if the court determines that it would not be in the interest of efficient administration of justice to determine the issue of ownership prior to the admission of the opinion of the party. (*Added by Stats.1965, c. 1151, p. 2904, § 4, operative Jan. 1, 1967. Amended by Stats.1978, c. 294, p. 615, § 6; Stats.1980, c. 381, p. 757, § 3.*)

§ 814
Matter upon which opinion must be based

The opinion of a witness as to the value of property is limited to such an opinion as is based on matter perceived by or personally known to the witness or made known to the witness at or before the hearing, whether or not admissible, that is of a type that reasonably may be relied upon by an expert in forming an opinion as to the value of property, including but not limited to the matters listed in Sections 815 to 821, inclusive, unless a witness is precluded by law from using such matter as a basis for an opinion. (*Added by Stats.1965, c. 1151, p. 2904, § 4, operative Jan. 1, 1967. Amended by Stats.1975, c. 1240, p. 3202, § 17, operative July 1, 1976; Stats.1980, c. 381, p. 757, § 4.*)

§ 814.5
Repealed by Stats.1971, c. 1574, p. 3154, § 1.4, operative July 1, 1972

§ 815
Sales of subject property

When relevant to the determination of the value of property, a witness may take into account as a basis for an opinion the price and other terms and circumstances of any sale or contract to sell and purchase which included the property or property interest being valued or any part thereof if the sale or contract was freely made in good faith within a reasonable time before or after the date of valuation, except that in an eminent domain proceeding where the sale or contract to sell and purchase includes only the property or property interest being taken or a part thereof, such sale or contract to sell and purchase may not be taken into account if it occurs after the filing of the lis pendens. (*Added by Stats.1965, c. 1151, p. 2904, § 4, operative Jan. 1, 1967. Amended by Stats.1978, c. 294, p. 615, § 7.*)

§ 816
Comparable sales

When relevant to the determination of the value of property, a witness may take into account as a basis for his opinion the price and other terms and circumstances of any sale or contract to sell and purchase comparable property if the sale or contract was freely made in good faith within a reasonable time before or after the date of valuation. In order to be considered comparable, the sale or contract must have been made sufficiently near in time to the date of valuation, and the property sold must be located sufficiently near the property being valued, and must be sufficiently alike in respect to character, size, situation, usability, and improvements, to make it clear that the property sold and the property being valued are comparable in value and that the price realized for the property sold may fairly be considered as shedding light on the value of the property being valued. (*Added by Stats.1965, c. 1151, p. 2904, § 4, operative Jan. 1, 1967.*)

§ 817
Leases of subject property

(a) Subject to subdivision (b), when relevant to the determination of the value of property, a witness may take into account as a basis for an opinion the rent reserved and other terms and circumstances of any lease which included the property or property interest being valued or any part thereof which was in effect within a reasonable time before or after the date of valuation, except that in an eminent domain proceeding where the lease includes only the property or property interest being taken or a part thereof, such lease may not be taken into account in the determination of the value of property if it is entered into after the filing of the lis pendens.

(b) A witness may take into account a lease providing for a rental fixed by a percentage or other measurable portion of gross sales or gross income from a business conducted on the leased property only for the purpose of arriving at an opinion as to the reasonable net rental value attributable to the property or property interest being valued as provided in Section 819 or determining the value of a leasehold interest. (*Added by Stats.1965, c. 1151, § 4, operative Jan. 1, 1967. Amended by Stats.1978, c. 294, p. 616, § 8.*)

§ 818
Comparable leases

For the purpose of determining the capitalized value of the reasonable net rental value attributable to the property or property interest being valued as provided in Section 819 or determining the value of a leasehold interest, a witness may take into account as a basis for his opinion the rent reserved and other terms and circumstances of any lease of comparable property if the lease was freely made in good faith within a reasonable time before or after the date of valuation. (*Added by Stats.1965, c. 1151, p. 2904, § 4, operative Jan. 1, 1967.*)

§ 819
Capitalization of income

When relevant to the determination of the value of property, a witness may take into account as a basis for his opinion the capitalized value of the reasonable net rental value attributable to the land and existing improvements thereon (as distinguished from the capitalized value of the income or profits attributable to the business conducted thereon). (*Added by Stats.1965, c. 1151, p. 2904, § 4, operative Jan. 1, 1967.*)

§ 820
Reproduction cost

When relevant to the determination of the value of property, a witness may take into account as a basis for his opinion the value of the property or property interest being valued as indicated by the value of the land together with the cost of replacing or reproducing the existing improvements thereon, if the improvements enhance the value of the property or property interest for its highest and best use, less whatever depreciation or obsolescence the improvements have suffered. (*Added by Stats.1965, c. 1151, p. 2904, § 4, operative Jan. 1, 1967.*)

§ 821
Conditions in general vicinity of subject property

When relevant to the determination of the value of property, a witness may take into account as a basis for his opinion the nature of the improvements on properties in the general vicinity of the property or property interest being valued and the character of the existing uses being made of such properties. (*Added by Stats.1965, c. 1151, p. 2904, § 4, operative Jan. 1, 1967.*)

§ 822
Matter upon which opinion may not be based

(a) In an eminent domain or inverse condemnation proceeding, notwithstanding the provisions of Sections 814 to 821, inclusive, the following matter is inadmissible as evidence and shall not be taken into account as a basis for an opinion as to the value of property:

(1) The price or other terms and circumstances of an acquisition of property or a property interest if the acquisition was for a public use for which the property could have been taken by eminent domain.

The price or other terms and circumstances shall not be excluded pursuant to this paragraph if the proceeding relates to the valuation of all or part of a water system as defined in Section 240 of the Public Utilities Code.

(2) The price at which an offer or option to purchase or lease the property or property interest being valued or any other property was made, or the price at which the property or interest was optioned, offered, or listed for sale or lease, except that an option, offer, or listing may be introduced by a party as an admission of another party to the proceeding; but nothing in this subdivision permits an admission to be used as direct evidence upon any matter that may be shown only by opinion evidence under Section 813.

(3) The value of any property or property interest as assessed for taxation purposes or the amount of taxes which may be due on the property, but nothing in this subdivision prohibits the consideration of actual or estimated taxes for the purpose of determining the reasonable net rental value attributable to the property or property interest being valued.

(4) An opinion as to the value of any property or property interest other than that being valued.

(5) The influence upon the value of the property or property interest being valued of any noncompensable items of value, damage, or injury.

(6) The capitalized value of the income or rental from any property or property interest other than that being valued.

(b) In an action other than an eminent domain or inverse condemnation proceeding, the matters listed in subdivision (a) are not admissible as evidence, and may not be taken into account as a basis for an opinion as to the value of property, except to the extent permitted under the rules of law otherwise applicable. (*Added by Stats.1965, c. 1151, p. 2904, § 4, operative Jan. 1, 1967. Amended by Stats.1978, c. 294, p. 616, § 9; Stats.1980, c. 381, p. 758, § 5; Stats.1986, c. 1238, § 2; Stats.1987, c. 1278, § 1; Stats.2000, c. 948 (A.B.321), § 1.*)

§ 823
Property with no relevant, comparable market

Notwithstanding any other provision of this article, the value of property for which there is no relevant, comparable market may be determined by any method of valuation that is just and equitable. (*Added by Stats.1980, c. 381, p. 758, § 6. Amended by Stats.1992, c. 7 (S.B.821), § 4.*)

§ 824
Nonprofit, special use property

(a) Notwithstanding any other provision of this article, a just and equitable method of determining the value of nonprofit, special use property, as defined by Section 1235.155 of the Code of Civil Procedure, for which there is no relevant, comparable market, is the cost of purchasing land and the reasonable cost of making it suitable for the conduct of the same nonprofit, special use, together with the cost of constructing similar improvements. The method for determining compensation for improvements shall be as set forth in subdivision (b).

(b) Notwithstanding any other provision of this article, a witness providing opinion testimony on the value of nonprofit, special use property, as defined by Section 1235.155 of the Code of Civil Procedure, for which there is no relevant, comparable market, shall base his or her opinion on the value of reproducing the improvements without taking into consideration any depreciation or obsolescence of the improvements.

(c) This section does not apply to actions or proceedings commenced by a public entity or public utility to acquire real property or any interest in real property for the use of water, sewer, electricity, telephone, natural gas, or flood control facilities or rights-of-way where those acquisitions neither require removal or destruction of existing improvements, nor render the property unfit for the owner's present or proposed use. (*Added by Stats.1992, c. 7 (S.B.821), § 5.*)

ARTICLE 3. OPINION TESTIMONY ON PARTICULAR
SUBJECTS

Section
870. Opinion as to sanity.

§ 870
Opinion as to sanity

A witness may state his opinion as to the sanity of a person when:

(a) The witness is an intimate acquaintance of the person whose sanity is in question;

(b) The witness was a subscribing witness to a writing, the validity of which is in dispute, signed by the person whose sanity is in question and the opinion relates to the sanity of such person at the time the writing was signed; or

(c) The witness is qualified under Section 800 or 801 to testify in the form of an opinion. (*Stats.1965, c. 299, § 2, operative Jan. 1, 1967.*)

CHAPTER 2. BLOOD TESTS TO DETERMINE PATERNITY [REPEALED]

§§ 890 to 895
Repealed by Stats.1992, c. 162 (A.B.2650), § 9, operative Jan. 1, 1994

§ 895.5
Repealed by Stats.1993, c. 219 (A.B.1500), § 77

§§ 896, 897
Repealed by Stats.1992, c. 162 (A.B.2650), § 9, operative Jan. 1, 1994

Division 8

PRIVILEGES

CHAPTER 1. DEFINITIONS

§ 900
Application of definitions

Unless the provision or context otherwise requires, the definitions in this chapter govern the construction of this division. They do not govern the construction of any other division. (*Stats.1965, c. 299, § 2, operative Jan. 1, 1967.*)

§ 901
Proceeding

"Proceeding" means any action, hearing, investigation, inquest, or inquiry (whether conducted by a court, administrative agency, hearing officer, arbitrator, legislative body, or any other person authorized by law) in which, pursuant to law, testimony can be compelled to be given. (*Stats.1965, c. 299, § 2, operative Jan. 1, 1967.*)

§ 902
Civil proceeding

"Civil proceeding" means any proceeding except a criminal proceeding. (*Stats.1965, c. 299, § 2, operative Jan. 1, 1967.*)

§ 903
Criminal proceeding

"Criminal proceeding" means:

(a) A criminal action; and

(b) A proceeding pursuant to Article 3 (commencing with Section 3060) of Chapter 7 of Division 4 of Title 1 of the Government Code to determine whether a public officer should be removed from office for willful or corrupt misconduct in office. (*Stats.1965, c. 299, § 2, operative Jan. 1, 1967.*)

§ 905
Presiding officer

"Presiding officer" means the person authorized to rule on a claim of privilege in the proceeding in which the claim is made. (*Stats.1965, c. 299, § 2, operative Jan. 1, 1967.*)

CHAPTER 2. APPLICABILITY OF DIVISION

Section
910. Applicability of division.

§ 910
Applicability of division

Except as otherwise provided by statute, the provisions of this division apply in all proceedings. The provisions of any statute making rules of evidence inapplicable in particular proceedings, or limiting the applicability of rules of evidence in particular proceedings, do not make this division inapplicable to such proceedings. (*Stats.1965, c. 299, § 2, operative Jan. 1, 1967.*)

CHAPTER 3. GENERAL PROVISIONS RELATING TO PRIVILEGES

Section

§ 911
Refusal to be or have another as witness, or disclose or produce any matter

Except as otherwise provided by statute:

(a) No person has a privilege to refuse to be a witness.

(b) No person has a privilege to refuse to disclose any matter or to refuse to produce any writing, object, or other thing.

(c) No person has a privilege that another shall not be a witness or shall not disclose any matter or shall not produce any writing, object, or other thing. (*Stats.1965, c. 299, § 2, operative Jan. 1, 1967.*)

§ 912
Waiver of privilege

(a) Except as otherwise provided in this section, the right of any person to claim a privilege provided by Section 954 (lawyer–client privilege), 980 (privilege for confidential marital communications), 994 (physician–patient privilege), 1014 (psychotherapist–patient privilege), 1033 (privilege of penitent), 1034 (privilege of clergyman), 1035.8 (sexual assault counselor-victim privilege), or 1037.5 (domestic violence counselor-victim privilege) is waived with respect to a communication protected by the privilege if any holder of the privilege, without coercion, has disclosed a significant part of the communication or has consented to disclosure made by anyone. Consent to disclosure is manifested by any statement or other conduct of the holder of the privilege indicating consent to the disclosure, including failure to claim the privilege in any proceeding in which the holder has the legal standing and opportunity to claim the privilege.

(b) Where two or more persons are joint holders of a privilege provided by Section 954 (lawyer–client privilege), 994 (physician–patient privilege), 1014 (psychotherapist–patient privilege), 1035.8 (sexual assault counselor-victim privilege), or 1037.5 (domestic violence counselor- victim privilege), a waiver of the right of a particular joint holder of the privilege to claim the privilege does not affect the right of another joint holder to claim the privilege. In the case of the privilege provided by Section 980 (privilege for confidential marital communications), a waiver of the right of one spouse to claim the privilege does not affect the right of the other spouse to claim the privilege.

(c) A disclosure that is itself privileged is not a waiver of any privilege.

(d) A disclosure in confidence of a communication that is protected by a privilege provided by Section 954 (lawyer–client privilege), 994 (physician–patient privilege), 1014 (psychotherapist–patient privilege), 1035.8 (sexual assault counselor-victim privilege), or 1037.5 (domestic violence counselor-victim privilege), when disclosure is reasonably necessary for the accomplishment of the purpose for which the lawyer, physician, psychotherapist, sexual assault counselor, or domestic violence counselor was consulted, is not a waiver of the privilege. (*Stats.1965, c. 299, § 2, operative Jan. 1, 1967. Amended by Stats.1980, c. 917, p. 2915, § 1; Stats.2002, c. 72 (S.B.2061), § 1; Stats.2004, c. 405 (S.B.1796), § 1.*)

§ 913
Comment on, and inferences from, exercise of privilege

(a) If in the instant proceeding or on a prior occasion a privilege is or was exercised not to testify with respect to any matter, or to refuse to disclose or to prevent another from disclosing any matter, neither the presiding officer nor counsel may comment thereon, no presumption shall arise because of the exercise of the privilege, and the trier of fact may not draw any inference therefrom as to the credibility of the witness or as to any matter at issue in the proceeding.

(b) The court, at the request of a party who may be adversely affected because an unfavorable inference may be drawn by the jury because a privilege has been exercised, shall instruct the jury that no presumption arises because of the exercise of the privilege and that the jury may not draw any inference therefrom as to the credibility of the witness or as to any matter at issue in the proceeding. (*Stats.1965, c. 299, § 2, operative Jan. 1, 1967.*)

§ 914
Determination of claim of privilege; limitation on punishment for contempt

(a) The presiding officer shall determine a claim of privilege in any proceeding in the same manner as a court determines such a claim under Article 2 (commencing with Section 400) of Chapter 4 of Division 3.

(b) No person may be held in contempt for failure to disclose information claimed to be privileged unless he has failed to comply with an order of a court that he disclose such information. This subdivision does not apply to any governmental agency that has constitutional contempt power, nor does it apply to hearings and investigations of the Industrial Accident Commission, nor does it impliedly repeal Chapter 4 (commencing with Section 9400) of Part 1 of Division 2 of Title 2 of the Government Code. If no other statutory procedure is applicable, the procedure prescribed by Section 1991 of the Code of Civil Procedure shall be followed in seeking an order of a court that the person disclose the information claimed to be privileged. (*Stats.1965, c. 299, § 2, operative Jan. 1, 1967.*)

§ 915
Disclosure of privileged information or attorney work product in ruling on claim of privilege

(a) Subject to subdivision (b), the presiding officer may not require disclosure of information claimed to be privileged under this division or attorney work product under subdivision (a) of Section 2018.030 of the Code of Civil Procedure in order to rule on the claim of privilege; provided, however, that in any hearing conducted pursuant to subdivision (c) of Section 1524 of the Penal Code in which a claim of privilege is made and the court determines that there is no other feasible means to rule on the validity of the claim other than to require disclosure, the court shall proceed in accordance with subdivision (b).

(b) When a court is ruling on a claim of privilege under Article 9 (commencing with Section 1040) of Chapter 4 (official information and identity of informer) or under Section 1060 (trade secret) or under subdivision (b) of Section 2018.030 of the Code of Civil Procedure (attorney work product) and is unable to do so without requiring disclosure of the information claimed to be privileged, the court may require the person from whom disclosure is sought or the person authorized to claim the privilege, or both, to disclose the information in chambers out of the presence and hearing of all persons except the person authorized to claim the privilege and any other persons as the person authorized to claim the privilege is willing to have present. If the judge determines that the information is privileged, neither the judge nor any other person may ever disclose, without the consent of a person authorized to permit disclosure, what was disclosed in the course of the proceedings in chambers. (*Stats.1965, c. 299, § 2, operative Jan. 1, 1967. Amended by Stats.1979, c. 1034, p. 3572, § 1; Stats.2001, c. 812 (A.B.223), § 13; Stats.2004, c. 182 (A.B.3081), § 29, operative July 1, 2005.*)

§ 916
Exclusion of privileged information where persons authorized to claim privilege are not present

(a) The presiding officer, on his own motion or on the motion of any party, shall exclude information that is subject to a claim of privilege under this division if:

(1) The person from whom the information is sought is not a person authorized to claim the privilege; and

(2) There is no party to the proceeding who is a person authorized to claim the privilege.

(b) The presiding officer may not exclude information under this section if:

(1) He is otherwise instructed by a person authorized to permit disclosure; or

(2) The proponent of the evidence establishes that there is no person authorized to claim the privilege in existence. (*Stats.1965, c. 299, § 2, operative Jan. 1, 1967.*)

§ 917. Presumption that certain communications are confidential; privileged character of electronic communications

(a) If a privilege is claimed on the ground that the matter sought to be disclosed is a communication made in confidence in the course of the lawyer-client, physician-patient, psychotherapist-patient, clergy-penitent, husband-wife, sexual assault counselor-victim, or domestic violence counselor-victim relationship, the communication is presumed to have been made in confidence and the opponent of the claim of privilege has the burden of proof to establish that the communication was not confidential.

(b) A communication between persons in a relationship listed in subdivision (a) does not lose its privileged character for the sole reason that it is communicated by electronic means or because persons involved in the delivery, facilitation, or storage of electronic communication may have access to the content of the communication.

(c) For purposes of this section, "electronic" has the same meaning provided in Section 1633.2 of the Civil Code. (*Stats.1965, c. 299, § 2, operative Jan. 1, 1967. Amended by Stats.2002, c. 72 (S.B.2061), § 2; Stats.2003, c. 468 (S.B.851), § 2; Stats.2004, c. 183 (A.B.3082), § 93; Stats.2006, c. 689 (S.B.1743), § 2.*)

§ 918
Error in overruling claim of privilege

A party may predicate error on a ruling disallowing a claim of privilege only if he is the holder of the privilege, except that a party may predicate error on a ruling disallowing a claim of privilege by his spouse under Section 970 or 971. (*Stats.1965, c. 299, § 2, operative Jan. 1, 1967.*)

§ 919
Admissibility where disclosure erroneously compelled; claim of privilege; coercion

(a) Evidence of a statement or other disclosure of privileged information is inadmissible against a holder of the privilege if:

(1) A person authorized to claim the privilege claimed it but nevertheless disclosure erroneously was required to be made; or

(2) The presiding officer did not exclude the privileged information as required by Section 916.

(b) If a person authorized to claim the privilege claimed it, whether in the same or a prior proceeding, but nevertheless disclosure erroneously was required by the presiding officer to be made, neither the failure to refuse to disclose nor the failure to seek review of the order of the presiding officer requiring disclosure indicates consent to the disclosure or constitutes a waiver and, under these circumstances, the disclosure is one made under coercion. (*Stats.1965, c. 299, § 2, operative Jan. 1, 1967. Amended by Stats.1974, c. 227, p. 426, § 1.*)

§ 920
Implied repeal of other statutes related to privileges

Nothing in this division shall be construed to repeal by implication any other statute relating to privileges. (*Stats.1965, c. 299, § 2, operative Jan. 1, 1967.*)

CHAPTER 4. PARTICULAR PRIVILEGES

ARTICLE 1. PRIVILEGE OF DEFENDANT IN CRIMINAL CASE

Section
930. Privilege not to be called as a witness and not to testify.

§ 930
Privilege not to be called as a witness and not to testify

To the extent that such privilege exists under the Constitution of the United States or the State of California, a defendant in a criminal case has a privilege not to be called as a witness and not to testify. (*Stats.1965, c. 299, § 2, operative Jan. 1, 1967.*)

ARTICLE 2. PRIVILEGE AGAINST SELF–INCRIMINATION

Section
940. Privilege against self-incrimination.

§ 940
Privilege against self-incrimination

To the extent that such privilege exists under the Constitution of the United States or the State of California, a person has a privilege to refuse to disclose any matter that may tend to incriminate him. (*Stats.1965, c. 299, § 2, operative Jan. 1, 1967.*)

ARTICLE 3. LAWYER–CLIENT PRIVILEGE

Section
950. Lawyer.
951. Client.
952. Confidential communication between client and lawyer.
953. Holder of the privilege.
954. Lawyer-client privilege.
955. When lawyer required to claim privilege.
956. Exception: Crime or fraud.
956.5. Exception: Prevention of criminal act likely to result in death or substantial bodily harm.
957. Exception: Parties claiming through deceased client.
958. Exception: Breach of duty arising out of lawyer-client relationship.
959. Exception: Lawyer as attesting witness.
960. Exception: Intention of deceased client concerning writing affecting property interest.
961. Exception: Validity of writing affecting property interest.
962. Exception: Joint clients.

§ 950
Lawyer

As used in this article, "lawyer" means a person authorized, or reasonably believed by the client to be authorized, to practice law in any state or nation. (*Stats.1965, c. 299, § 2, operative Jan. 1, 1967.*)

§ 951
Client

As used in this article, "client" means a person who, directly or through an authorized representative, consults a lawyer for the purpose of retaining the lawyer or securing legal service or advice from him in his professional capacity, and includes an incompetent (a) who himself so consults the lawyer or (b) whose guardian or conservator so consults the lawyer in behalf of the incompetent. (*Stats.1965, c. 299, § 2, operative Jan. 1, 1967.*)

§ 952
Confidential communication between client and lawyer

As used in this article, "confidential communication between client and lawyer" means information transmitted between a client and his or her lawyer in the course of that relationship and in confidence by a means which, so far as the client is aware, discloses the information to no third persons other than those who are present to further the interest of the client in the consultation or those to whom disclosure is reasonably necessary for the transmission of the information or the accomplishment of the purpose for which the lawyer is consulted, and includes a legal opinion formed and the advice given by the lawyer in the course of that relationship. (*Stats.1965, c. 299, § 2, operative Jan. 1, 1967. Amended by Stats.1967, c. 650, p. 2006, § 3; Stats.1994, c. 186 (A.B.2662), § 1; Stats.1994, c. 587 (A.B.3600), § 9; Stats.2002, c. 72 (S.B.2061), § 3.*)

§ 953
Holder of the privilege

As used in this article, "holder of the privilege" means:

(a) The client, if the client has no guardian or conservator.

(b) A guardian or conservator of the client, if the client has a guardian or conservator.

(c) The personal representative of the client if the client is dead, including a personal representative appointed pursuant to Section 12252 of the Probate Code.

(d) A successor, assign, trustee in dissolution, or any similar representative of a firm, association, organization, partnership, business trust, corporation, or public entity that is no longer in existence. (*Stats.1965, c.*

299, § 2, operative Jan. 1, 1967. Amended by Stats.2009, c. 8 (A.B.1163), § 1.)

§ 954
Lawyer-client privilege

Subject to Section 912 and except as otherwise provided in this article, the client, whether or not a party, has a privilege to refuse to disclose, and to prevent another from disclosing, a confidential communication between client and lawyer if the privilege is claimed by:

(a) The holder of the privilege;

(b) A person who is authorized to claim the privilege by the holder of the privilege; or

(c) The person who was the lawyer at the time of the confidential communication, but such person may not claim the privilege if there is no holder of the privilege in existence or if he is otherwise instructed by a person authorized to permit disclosure.

The relationship of attorney and client shall exist between a law corporation as defined in Article 10 (commencing with Section 6160) of Chapter 4 of Division 3 of the Business and Professions Code and the persons to whom it renders professional services, as well as between such persons and members of the State Bar employed by such corporation to render services to such persons. The word "persons" as used in this subdivision includes partnerships, corporations, limited liability companies, associations and other groups and entities. *(Stats.1965, c. 299, § 2, operative Jan. 1, 1967. Amended by Stats.1968, c. 1375, p. 2695, § 2; Stats.1994, c. 1010 (S.B.2053), § 104.)*

§ 955
When lawyer required to claim privilege

The lawyer who received or made a communication subject to the privilege under this article shall claim the privilege whenever he is present when the communication is sought to be disclosed and is authorized to claim the privilege under subdivision (c) of Section 954. *(Stats.1965, c. 299, § 2, operative Jan. 1, 1967.)*

§ 956
Exception: Crime or fraud

There is no privilege under this article if the services of the lawyer were sought or obtained to enable or aid anyone to commit or plan to commit a crime or a fraud. *(Stats.1965, c. 299, § 2, operative Jan. 1, 1967.)*

§ 956.5
Exception: Prevention of criminal act likely to result in death or substantial bodily harm

There is no privilege under this article if the lawyer reasonably believes that disclosure of any confidential communication relating to representation of a client is necessary to prevent a criminal act that the lawyer reasonably believes is likely to result in the death of, or substantial bodily harm to, an individual. (*Added by Stats.1993, c. 982 (S.B.645), § 8. Amended by Stats.2003, c. 765 (A.B.1101), § 2, operative July 1, 2004; Stats.2004, c. 183 (A.B.3082), § 94.*)

§ 957
Exception: Parties claiming through deceased client

There is no privilege under this article as to a communication relevant to an issue between parties all of whom claim through a deceased client, regardless of whether the claims are by testate or intestate succession, nonprobate transfer, or inter vivos transaction. (*Stats.1965, c. 299, § 2, operative Jan. 1, 1967. Amended by Stats.2009, c. 8 (A.B.1163), § 2.*)

§ 958
Exception: Breach of duty arising out of lawyer-client relationship

There is no privilege under this article as to a communication relevant to an issue of breach, by the lawyer or by the client, of a duty arising out of the lawyer-client relationship. (*Stats.1965, c. 299, § 2, operative Jan. 1, 1967.*)

§ 959
Exception: Lawyer as attesting witness

There is no privilege under this article as to a communication relevant to an issue concerning the intention or competence of a client executing an attested document of which the lawyer is an attesting witness, or concerning the execution or attestation of such a document. (*Stats.1965, c. 299, § 2, operative Jan. 1, 1967.*)

§ 960
Exception: Intention of deceased client concerning writing affecting property interest

There is no privilege under this article as to a communication relevant to an issue concerning the intention of a client, now deceased, with respect to a deed of conveyance, will, or other writing, executed by the client, purporting to affect an interest in property. (*Stats.1965, c. 299, § 2, operative Jan. 1, 1967.*)

§ 961
Exception: Validity of writing affecting property interest

There is no privilege under this article as to a communication relevant to an issue concerning the validity of a deed of conveyance, will, or other writing, executed by a client, now deceased, purporting to affect an interest in property. (*Stats.1965, c. 299, § 2, operative Jan. 1, 1967.*)

§ 962
Exception: Joint clients

Where two or more clients have retained or consulted a lawyer upon a matter of common interest, none of them, nor the successor in interest of any of them, may claim a privilege under this article as to a communication made in the course of that relationship when such communication is offered in a civil proceeding between one of such clients (or his successor in interest) and another of such clients (or his successor in interest). (*Stats.1965, c. 299, § 2, operative Jan. 1, 1967.*)

ARTICLE 4. PRIVILEGE NOT TO TESTIFY AGAINST SPOUSE

Section
970. Spouse's privilege not to testify against spouse; exceptions.
971. Privilege not to be called as a witness against spouse.
972. Exceptions to privilege.
973. Waiver of privilege.

§ 970
Spouse's privilege not to testify against spouse; exceptions

Except as otherwise provided by statute, a married person has a privilege not to testify against his spouse in any proceeding. (*Stats.1965, c. 299, § 2, operative Jan. 1, 1967.*)

§ 971
Privilege not to be called as a witness against spouse

Except as otherwise provided by statute, a married person whose spouse is a party to a proceeding has a privilege not to be called as a witness by an adverse party to that proceeding without the prior express consent of the spouse having the privilege under this section unless the party calling the spouse does so in good faith without knowledge of the marital relationship. (*Stats.1965, c. 299, § 2, operative Jan. 1, 1967.*)

§ 972
Exceptions to privilege

A married person does not have a privilege under this article in:

(a) A proceeding brought by or on behalf of one spouse against the other spouse.

(b) A proceeding to commit or otherwise place his or her spouse or his or her spouse's property, or both, under the control of another because of the spouse's alleged mental or physical condition.

(c) A proceeding brought by or on behalf of a spouse to establish his or her competence.

(d) A proceeding under the Juvenile Court Law, Chapter 2 (commencing with Section 200) of Part 1 of Division 2 of the Welfare and Institutions Code.

(e) A criminal proceeding in which one spouse is charged with:

(1) A crime against the person or property of the other spouse or of a child, parent, relative, or cohabitant of either, whether committed before or during marriage.

(2) A crime against the person or property of a third person committed in the course of committing a crime against the person or property of the other spouse, whether committed before or during marriage.

(3) Bigamy.

(4) A crime defined by Section 270 or 270a of the Penal Code.

(f) A proceeding resulting from a criminal act which occurred prior to legal marriage of the spouses to each other regarding knowledge acquired prior to that marriage if prior to the legal marriage the witness spouse was aware that his or her spouse had been arrested for or had been formally charged with the crime or crimes about which the spouse is called to testify.

(g) A proceeding brought against the spouse by a former spouse so long as the property and debts of the marriage have not been adjudicated, or in order to establish, modify, or enforce a child, family or spousal support obligation arising from the marriage to the former spouse; in a proceeding brought against a spouse by the other parent in order to establish, modify, or enforce a child support obligation for a child of a nonmarital relationship of the spouse; or in a proceeding brought against a spouse by the guardian of a child of that spouse in order to establish, modify, or enforce a child support obligation of the spouse. The married person does not have a privilege under this subdivision to refuse to provide information relating to the issues of income, expenses, assets, debts, and employment of either spouse, but may assert the privilege as otherwise provided in this article if other information is requested by the former spouse, guardian, or other parent of the child.

Any person demanding the otherwise privileged information made available by this subdivision, who also has an obligation to support the child for whom an order to estabish[1], modify, or enforce child support is sought, waives his or her marital privilege to the same extent as the spouse as provided in this subdivision. (*Stats.1965, c. 299, § 2, operative Jan. 1,*

1967. Amended by Stats.1975, c. 71, p. 132, § 2; Stats.1982, c. 256, p. 833, § 1; Stats.1983, c. 244, § 1; Stats.1986, c. 769, § 1, eff. Sept. 15, 1986; Stats.1989, c. 1359, § 9.7.)

[1] So in enrolled bill.

§ 973. Waiver of privilege

(a) Unless erroneously compelled to do so, a married person who testifies in a proceeding to which his spouse is a party, or who testifies against his spouse in any proceeding, does not have a privilege under this article in the proceeding in which such testimony is given.

(b) There is no privilege under this article in a civil proceeding brought or defended by a married person for the immediate benefit of his spouse or of himself and his spouse. (*Stats.1965, c. 299, § 2, operative Jan. 1, 1967.*)

ARTICLE 5. PRIVILEGE FOR CONFIDENTIAL MARITAL COMMUNICATIONS

Section
980. Confidential marital communication privilege.
981. Exception: Crime or fraud.
982. Commitment or similar proceedings.
983. Competency proceedings.
984. Proceeding between spouses.
985. Criminal proceedings.
986. Juvenile court proceedings.
987. Communication offered by spouse who is criminal defendant.

§ 980
Confidential marital communication privilege

Subject to Section 912 and except as otherwise provided in this article, a spouse (or his guardian or conservator when he has a guardian or conservator), whether or not a party, has a privilege during the marital relationship and afterwards to refuse to disclose, and to prevent another from disclosing, a communication if he claims the privilege and the communication was made in confidence between him and the other spouse while they were husband and wife. (*Stats.1965, c. 299, § 2, operative Jan. 1, 1967.*)

§ 981
Exception: Crime or fraud

There is no privilege under this article if the communication was made, in whole or in part, to enable or aid anyone to commit or plan to commit a crime or a fraud. (*Stats.1965, c. 299, § 2, operative Jan. 1, 1967.*)

§ 982
Commitment or similar proceedings

There is no privilege under this article in a proceeding to commit either spouse or otherwise place him or his property, or both, under the control of another because of his alleged mental or physical condition. (*Stats.1965, c. 299, § 2, operative Jan. 1, 1967.*)

§ 983
Competency proceedings

There is no privilege under this article in a proceeding brought by or on behalf of either spouse to establish his competence. (*Stats.1965, c. 299, § 2, operative Jan. 1, 1967.*)

§ 984
Proceeding between spouses

There is no privilege under this article in:

(a) A proceeding brought by or on behalf of one spouse against the other spouse.

(b) A proceeding between a surviving spouse and a person who claims through the deceased spouse, regardless of whether such claim is by testate or intestate succession or by inter vivos transaction. (*Stats.1965, c. 299, § 2, operative Jan. 1, 1967.*)

§ 985
Criminal proceedings

There is no privilege under this article in a criminal proceeding in which one spouse is charged with:

(a) A crime committed at any time against the person or property of the other spouse or of a child of either.

(b) A crime committed at any time against the person or property of a third person committed in the course of committing a crime against the person or property of the other spouse.

(c) Bigamy.

(d) A crime defined by Section 270 or 270a of the Penal Code. (*Stats.1965, c. 299, § 2, operative Jan. 1, 1967. Amended by Stats.1975, c. 71, p. 133, § 3.*)

§ 986
Juvenile court proceedings

There is no privilege under this article in a proceeding under the Juvenile Court Law, Chapter 2 (commencing with Section 200) of Part 1 of

Division 2 of the Welfare and Institutions Code. (*Stats.1965, c. 299, § 2, operative Jan. 1, 1967. Amended by Stats.1982, c. 256, p. 833, § 2.*)

§ 987
Communication offered by spouse who is criminal defendant

There is no privilege under this article in a criminal proceeding in which the communication is offered in evidence by a defendant who is one of the spouses between whom the communication was made. (*Stats.1965, c. 299, § 2, operative Jan. 1, 1967.*)

ARTICLE 6. PHYSICIAN–PATIENT PRIVILEGE

§ 990
Physician

As used in this article, "physician" means a person authorized, or reasonably believed by the patient to be authorized, to practice medicine in any state or nation. (*Stats.1965, c. 299, § 2, operative Jan. 1, 1967.*)

§ 991
Patient

As used in this article, "patient" means a person who consults a physician or submits to an examination by a physician for the purpose of securing a diagnosis or preventive, palliative, or curative treatment of his physical or mental or emotional condition. (*Stats.1965, c. 299, § 2, operative Jan. 1, 1967.*)

§ 992
Confidential communication between patient and physician

As used in this article, "confidential communication between patient and physician" means information, including information obtained by an examination of the patient, transmitted between a patient and his physician in the course of that relationship and in confidence by a means which, so far as the patient is aware, discloses the information to no third persons other than those who are present to further the interest of the patient in the consultation or those to whom disclosure is reasonably necessary for the transmission of the information or the accomplishment of the purpose for which the physician is consulted, and includes a diagnosis made and the advice given by the physician in the course of that relationship. (*Stats.1965, c. 299, § 2, operative Jan. 1, 1967. Amended by Stats.1967, c. 650, p. 2006, § 4.*)

§ 993
Holder of the privilege

As used in this article, "holder of the privilege" means:

(a) The patient when he has no guardian or conservator.

(b) A guardian or conservator of the patient when the patient has a guardian or conservator.

(c) The personal representative of the patient if the patient is dead. (*Stats.1965, c. 299, § 2, operative Jan. 1, 1967.*)

§ 994
Physician-patient privilege

Subject to Section 912 and except as otherwise provided in this article, the patient, whether or not a party, has a privilege to refuse to disclose, and to prevent another from disclosing, a confidential communication between patient and physician if the privilege is claimed by:

(a) The holder of the privilege;

(b) A person who is authorized to claim the privilege by the holder of the privilege; or

(c) The person who was the physician at the time of the confidential communication, but such person may not claim the privilege if there is no holder of the privilege in existence or if he or she is otherwise instructed by a person authorized to permit disclosure.

The relationship of a physician and patient shall exist between a medical or podiatry corporation as defined in the Medical Practice Act and the patient to whom it renders professional services, as well as between such patients and licensed physicians and surgeons employed by such corporation to render services to such patients. The word "persons" as used in this subdivision includes partnerships, corporations, limited liability companies, associations, and other groups and entities. (*Stats.1965, c. 299, § 2, operative Jan. 1, 1967. Amended by Stats.1968, c. 1375, p. 2696, § 3; Stats.1980, c. 1313, p. 4532, § 12; Stats.1994, c. 1010 (S.B.2053), § 105.*)

§ 995
When physician required to claim privilege

The physician who received or made a communication subject to the privilege under this article shall claim the privilege whenever he is present when the communication is sought to be disclosed and is authorized to claim the privilege under subdivision (c) of Section 994. (*Stats.1965, c. 299, § 2, operative Jan. 1, 1967.*)

§ 996
Patient-litigant exception

There is no privilege under this article as to a communication relevant to an issue concerning the condition of the patient if such issue has been tendered by:

(a) The patient;

(b) Any party claiming through or under the patient;

(c) Any party claiming as a beneficiary of the patient through a contract to which the patient is or was a party; or

(d) The plaintiff in an action brought under Section 376 or 377 of the Code of Civil Procedure for damages for the injury or death of the patient. (*Stats.1965, c. 299, § 2, operative Jan. 1, 1967.*)

§ 997
Exception: crime or tort

There is no privilege under this article if the services of the physician were sought or obtained to enable or aid anyone to commit or plan to commit a crime or a tort or to escape detection or apprehension after the commission of a crime or a tort. (*Stats.1965, c. 299, § 2, operative Jan. 1, 1967.*)

§ 998
Criminal proceeding

There is no privilege under this article in a criminal proceeding. (*Stats.1965, c. 299, § 2, operative Jan. 1, 1967.*)

§ 999
Communication relating to patient condition in proceeding to recover damages; good cause

There is no privilege under this article as to a communication relevant to an issue concerning the condition of the patient in a proceeding to recover damages on account of the conduct of the patient if good cause for disclosure of the communication is shown. (*Stats.1965, c. 299, § 2, operative Jan. 1, 1967. Amended by Stats.1975, c. 318, p. 764, § 1.*)

§ 1000
Parties claiming through deceased patient

There is no privilege under this article as to a communication relevant to an issue between parties all of whom claim through a deceased patient, regardless of whether the claims are by testate or intestate succession or by inter vivos transaction. (*Stats.1965, c. 299, § 2, operative Jan. 1, 1967.*)

§ 1001
Breach of duty arising out of physician-patient relationship

There is no privilege under this article as to a communication relevant to an issue of breach, by the physician or by the patient, of a duty arising out of the physician-patient relationship. (*Stats.1965, c. 299, § 2, operative Jan. 1, 1967.*)

§ 1002
Intention of deceased patient concerning writing affecting property interest

There is no privilege under this article as to a communication relevant to an issue concerning the intention of a patient, now deceased, with respect to a deed of conveyance, will, or other writing, executed by the patient, purporting to affect an interest in property. (*Stats.1965, c. 299, § 2, operative Jan. 1, 1967.*)

§ 1003
Validity of writing affecting property interest

There is no privilege under this article as to a communication relevant to an issue concerning the validity of a deed of conveyance, will, or other writing, executed by a patient, now deceased, purporting to affect an interest in property. (*Stats.1965, c. 299, § 2, operative Jan. 1, 1967.*)

§ 1004
Commitment or similar proceeding

There is no privilege under this article in a proceeding to commit the patient or otherwise place him or his property, or both, under the control of another because of his alleged mental or physical condition. (*Stats.1965, c. 299, § 2, operative Jan. 1, 1967.*)

§ 1005
Proceeding to establish competence

There is no privilege under this article in a proceeding brought by or on behalf of the patient to establish his competence. (*Stats.1965, c. 299, § 2, operative Jan. 1, 1967.*)

§ 1006
Required report

There is no privilege under this article as to information that the physician or the patient is required to report to a public employee, or as to information required to be recorded in a public office, if such report or record is open to public inspection. (*Stats.1965, c. 299, § 2, operative Jan. 1, 1967.*)

§ 1007
Proceeding to terminate right, license or privilege

There is no privilege under this article in a proceeding brought by a public entity to determine whether a right, authority, license, or privilege (including the right or privilege to be employed by the public entity or to hold a public office) should be revoked, suspended, terminated, limited, or conditioned. (*Stats.1965, c. 299, § 2, operative Jan. 1, 1967.*)

ARTICLE 7. PSYCHOTHERAPIST–PATIENT PRIVILEGE

1023. Exception: Proceeding to determine sanity of criminal defendant.
1024. Exception: Patient dangerous to himself or others.
1025. Exception: Proceeding to establish competence.
1026. Exception: Required report.
1027. Exception: Child under 16 victim of crime.
1028. Repealed.

§ 1010
Psychotherapist

As used in this article, "psychotherapist" means a person who is, or is reasonably believed by the patient to be:

(a) A person authorized to practice medicine in any state or nation who devotes, or is reasonably believed by the patient to devote, a substantial portion of his or her time to the practice of psychiatry.

(b) A person licensed as a psychologist under Chapter 6.6 (commencing with Section 2900) of Division 2 of the Business and Professions Code.

(c) A person licensed as a clinical social worker under Article 4 (commencing with Section 4996) of Chapter 14 of Division 2 of the Business and Professions Code, when he or she is engaged in applied psychotherapy of a nonmedical nature.

(d) A person who is serving as a school psychologist and holds a credential authorizing that service issued by the state.

(e) A person licensed as a marriage and family therapist under Chapter 13 (commencing with Section 4980) of Division 2 of the Business and Professions Code.

(f) A person registered as a psychological assistant who is under the supervision of a licensed psychologist or board certified psychiatrist as required by Section 2913 of the Business and Professions Code, or a person registered as a marriage and family therapist intern who is under the supervision of a licensed marriage and family therapist, a licensed clinical social worker, a licensed psychologist, or a licensed physician and surgeon certified in psychiatry, as specified in Section 4980.44 of the Business and Professions Code.

(g) A person registered as an associate clinical social worker who is under supervision as specified in Section 4996.23 of the Business and Professions Code.

(h) A person exempt from the Psychology Licensing Law pursuant to subdivision (d) of Section 2909 of the Business and Professions Code who is under the supervision of a licensed psychologist or board certified psychiatrist.

(i) A psychological intern as defined in Section 2911 of the Business and Professions Code who is under the supervision of a licensed psychologist or board certified psychiatrist.

(j) A trainee, as defined in subdivision (c) of Section 4980.03 of the Business and Professions Code, who is fulfilling his or her supervised practicum required by subparagraph (B) of paragraph (1) of subdivision (d) of Section 4980.36 of, or subdivision (c) of Section 4980.37 of, the Business and Professions Code and is supervised by a licensed psychologist, a board certified psychiatrist, a licensed clinical social worker, a licensed marriage and family therapist, or a licensed professional clinical counselor.

(k) A person licensed as a registered nurse pursuant to Chapter 6 (commencing with Section 2700) of Division 2 of the Business and Professions Code, who possesses a master's degree in psychiatric-mental health nursing and is listed as a psychiatric-mental health nurse by the Board of Registered Nursing.

(l) An advanced practice registered nurse who is certified as a clinical nurse specialist pursuant to Article 9 (commencing with Section 2838) of Chapter 6 of Division 2 of the Business and Professions Code and who participates in expert clinical practice in the specialty of psychiatric-mental health nursing.

(m) A person rendering mental health treatment or counseling services as authorized pursuant to Section 6924 of the Family Code.

(n) A person licensed as a professional clinical counselor under Chapter 16 (commencing with Section 4999.10) of Division 2 of the Business and Professions Code.

(o) A person registered as a clinical counselor intern who is under the supervision of a licensed professional clinical counselor, a licensed marriage and family therapist, a licensed clinical social worker, a licensed psychologist, or a licensed physician and surgeon certified in psychiatry, as specified in Sections 4999.42 to 4999.46, inclusive, of the Business and Professions Code.

(p) A clinical counselor trainee, as defined in subdivision (g) of Section 4999.12 of the Business and Professions Code, who is fulfilling his or her supervised practicum required by paragraph (3) of subdivision (c) of Section 4999.32 of, or paragraph (3) of subdivision (c) of Section 4999.33 of, the Business and Professions Code, and is supervised by a licensed psychologist, a board-certified psychiatrist, a licensed clinical social worker, a licensed marriage and family therapist, or a licensed professional clinical counselor. (*Stats.1965, c. 299, § 2, operative Jan. 1, 1967. Amended by Stats.1967, c. 1677, p. 4211, § 3; Stats.1970, c. 1396, p. 2624, § 1.5; Stats.1970, c. 1397, p. 2626, § 1.5; Stats.1972, c. 888, p. 1584, § 1; Stats.1974, c. 546, p. 1359, § 16; Stats.1983, c. 928, § 8; Stats.1987, c. 724, § 1; Stats.1988, c. 488, § 1; Stats.1989, c. 1104, § 37; Stats.1990, c. 662*

(A.B.3613), § 1; Stats.1992, c. 308 (A.B.3035), § 2; Stats.1994, c. 1270 (A.B.2659), § 1; Stats.2001, c. 142 (S.B.716), § 1; Stats.2001, c. 420 (A.B.1253), § 1, eff. Oct. 2, 2001; Stats.2001, c. 420 (A.B.1253), § 1.5, eff. Oct. 2, 2001, operative Jan. 1, 2002; Stats.2009, c. 26 (S.B.33), § 21; Stats.2011, c. 381 (S.B.146), § 21.)

§ 1010.5
Privileged communication between patient and educational psychologist

A communication between a patient and an educational psychologist, licensed under Article 5 (commencing with Section 4986) of Chapter 13 of Division 2 of the Business and Professions Code, shall be privileged to the same extent, and subject to the same limitations, as a communication between a patient and a psychotherapist described in subdivisions (c), (d), and (e) of Section 1010. *(Added by Stats.1985, c. 545, § 1.)*

§ 1011
Patient

As used in this article, "patient" means a person who consults a psychotherapist or submits to an examination by a psychotherapist for the purpose of securing a diagnosis or preventive, palliative, or curative treatment of his mental or emotional condition or who submits to an examination of his mental or emotional condition for the purpose of scientific research on mental or emotional problems. *(Stats.1965, c. 299, § 2, operative Jan. 1, 1967.)*

§ 1012
Confidential communication between patient and psychotherapist

As used in this article, "confidential communication between patient and psychotherapist" means information, including information obtained by an examination of the patient, transmitted between a patient and his psychotherapist in the course of that relationship and in confidence by a means which, so far as the patient is aware, discloses the information to no third persons other than those who are present to further the interest of the patient in the consultation, or those to whom disclosure is reasonably necessary for the transmission of the information or the accomplishment of the purpose for which the psychotherapist is consulted, and includes a diagnosis made and the advice given by the psychotherapist in the course of that relationship. *(Stats.1965, c. 299, § 2, operative Jan. 1, 1967. Amended by Stats.1967, c. 650, p. 2006, § 5; Stats.1970, c. 1396, p. 2625, § 2; Stats.1970, c. 1397, p. 2627, § 2.)*

§ 1013
Holder of the privilege

As used in this article, "holder of the privilege" means:

(a) The patient when he has no guardian or conservator.

(b) A guardian or conservator of the patient when the patient has a guardian or conservator.

(c) The personal representative of the patient if the patient is dead. (*Stats.1965, c. 299, § 2, operative Jan. 1, 1967.*)

§ 1014
Psychotherapist-patient privilege; application to individuals and entities

Subject to Section 912 and except as otherwise provided in this article, the patient, whether or not a party, has a privilege to refuse to disclose, and to prevent another from disclosing, a confidential communication between patient and psychotherapist if the privilege is claimed by:

(a) The holder of the privilege.

(b) A person who is authorized to claim the privilege by the holder of the privilege.

(c) The person who was the psychotherapist at the time of the confidential communication, but the person may not claim the privilege if there is no holder of the privilege in existence or if he or she is otherwise instructed by a person authorized to permit disclosure.

The relationship of a psychotherapist and patient shall exist between a psychological corporation as defined in Article 9 (commencing with Section 2995) of Chapter 6.6 of Division 2 of the Business and Professions Code, a marriage and family therapist corporation as defined in Article 6 (commencing with Section 4987.5) of Chapter 13 of Division 2 of the Business and Professions Code, a licensed clinical social workers corporation as defined in Article 5 (commencing with Section 4998) of Chapter 14 of Division 2 of the Business and Professions Code, or a professional clinical counselor corporation as defined in Article 7 (commencing with Section 4999.123) of Chapter 16 of Division 2 of the Business and Professions Code, and the patient to whom it renders professional services, as well as between those patients and psychotherapists employed by those corporations to render services to those patients. The word "persons" as used in this subdivision includes partnerships, corporations, limited liability companies, associations, and other groups and entities. (*Stats.1965, c. 299, § 2, operative Jan. 1, 1967. Amended by Stats.1969, c. 1436, p. 2943, § 1; Stats.1972, c. 1286, p. 2569, § 6; Stats.1989, c. 1104, § 38; Stats.1990, c. 605 (S.B.2245), § 1; Stats.1994, c. 1010 (S.B.2053), § 106; Stats.2002, c. 1013 (S.B.2026), § 78; Stats.2011, c. 381 (S.B.146), § 22.*)

§ 1014.5
Repealed by Stats.1994, c. 1270 (A.B.2659), § 2

§ 1015
When psychotherapist required to claim privilege

The psychotherapist who received or made a communication subject to the privilege under this article shall claim the privilege whenever he is present when the communication is sought to be disclosed and is authorized to claim the privilege under subdivision (c) of Section 1014. (*Stats.1965, c. 299, § 2, operative Jan. 1, 1967.*)

§ 1016
Exception: Patient-litigant exception

There is no privilege under this article as to a communication relevant to an issue concerning the mental or emotional condition of the patient if such issue has been tendered by:

(a) The patient;

(b) Any party claiming through or under the patient;

(c) Any party claiming as a beneficiary of the patient through a contract to which the patient is or was a party; or

(d) The plaintiff in an action brought under Section 376 or 377 of the Code of Civil Procedure for damages for the injury or death of the patient. (*Stats.1965, c. 299, § 2, operative Jan. 1, 1967.*)

§ 1017
Exception: Psychotherapist appointed by court or board of prison terms

(a) There is no privilege under this article if the psychotherapist is appointed by order of a court to examine the patient, but this exception does not apply where the psychotherapist is appointed by order of the court upon the request of the lawyer for the defendant in a criminal proceeding in order to provide the lawyer with information needed so that he or she may advise the defendant whether to enter or withdraw a plea based on insanity or to present a defense based on his or her mental or emotional condition.

(b) There is no privilege under this article if the psychotherapist is appointed by the Board of Prison Terms to examine a patient pursuant to the provisions of Article 4 (commencing with Section 2960) of Chapter 7 of Title 1 of Part 3 of the Penal Code. (*Stats.1965, c. 299, § 2, operative Jan. 1, 1967. Amended by Stats.1967, c. 650, p. 2007, § 6; Stats.1987, c. 687, § 1.*)

§ 1018
Exception: Crime or tort

There is no privilege under this article if the services of the psychotherapist were sought or obtained to enable or aid anyone to commit or plan to commit a crime or a tort or to escape detection or apprehension after the commission of a crime or a tort. (*Stats.1965, c. 299, § 2, operative Jan. 1, 1967.*)

§ 1019
Exception: Parties claiming through deceased patient

There is no privilege under this article as to a communication relevant to an issue between parties all of whom claim through a deceased patient, regardless of whether the claims are by testate or intestate succession or by inter vivos transaction. (*Stats.1965, c. 299, § 2, operative Jan. 1, 1967.*)

§ 1020
Exception: Breach of duty arising out of psychotherapist-patient relationship

There is no privilege under this article as to a communication relevant to an issue of breach, by the psychotherapist or by the patient, of a duty arising out of the psychotherapist-patient relationship. (*Stats.1965, c. 299, § 2, operative Jan. 1, 1967.*)

§ 1021
Exception: Intention of deceased patient concerning writing affecting property interest

There is no privilege under this article as to a communication relevant to an issue concerning the intention of a patient, now deceased, with respect to a deed of conveyance, will, or other writing, executed by the patient, purporting to affect an interest in property. (*Stats.1965, c. 299, § 2, operative Jan. 1, 1967.*)

§ 1022
Exception: Validity of writing affecting property interest

There is no privilege under this article as to a communication relevant to an issue concerning the validity of a deed of conveyance, will, or other writing, executed by a patient, now deceased, purporting to affect an interest in property. (*Stats.1965, c. 299, § 2, operative Jan. 1, 1967.*)

§ 1023
Exception: Proceeding to determine sanity of criminal defendant

There is no privilege under this article in a proceeding under Chapter 6 (commencing with Section 1367) of Title 10 of Part 2 of the Penal Code initiated at the request of the defendant in a criminal action to determine his sanity. (*Stats.1965, c. 299, § 2, operative Jan. 1, 1967.*)

§ 1024
Exception: Patient dangerous to himself or others

There is no privilege under this article if the psychotherapist has reasonable cause to believe that the patient is in such mental or emotional condition as to be dangerous to himself or to the person or property of another and that disclosure of the communication is necessary to prevent the threatened danger. (*Stats.1965, c. 299, § 2, operative Jan. 1, 1967.*)

§ 1025
Exception: Proceeding to establish competence

There is no privilege under this article in a proceeding brought by or on behalf of the patient to establish his competence. (*Stats.1965, c. 299, § 2, operative Jan. 1, 1967.*)

§ 1026
Exception: Required report

There is no privilege under this article as to information that the psychotherapist or the patient is required to report to a public employee or as to information required to be recorded in a public office, if such report or record is open to public inspection. (*Stats.1965, c. 299, § 2, operative Jan. 1, 1967.*)

§ 1027
Exception: Child under 16 victim of crime

There is no privilege under this article if all of the following circumstances exist:

(a) The patient is a child under the age of 16.

(b) The psychotherapist has reasonable cause to believe that the patient has been the victim of a crime and that disclosure of the communication is in the best interest of the child. (*Added by Stats.1970, c. 1397, p. 2627, § 3.*)

§ 1028
Repealed by Stats.1985, c. 1077, §§ 1, 2

ARTICLE 8. CLERGY PENITENT PRIVILEGES

Section
1030. Member of the clergy.
1031. Penitent.
1032. Penitential communication.
1033. Privilege of penitent.

1034. Privilege of clergy.

§ 1030
Member of the clergy

As used in this article, a "member of the clergy" means a priest, minister, religious practitioner, or similar functionary of a church or of a religious denomination or religious organization. (*Stats.1965, c. 299, § 2, operative Jan. 1, 1967. Amended by Stats.2002, c. 806 (A.B.3027), § 19.*)

§ 1031
Penitent

As used in this article, "penitent" means a person who has made a penitential communication to a member of the clergy. (*Stats.1965, c. 299, § 2, operative Jan. 1, 1967. Amended by Stats.2002, c. 806 (A.B.3027), § 20.*)

§ 1032
Penitential communication

As used in this article, "penitential communication" means a communication made in confidence, in the presence of no third person so far as the penitent is aware, to a member of the clergy who, in the course of the discipline or practice of the clergy member's church, denomination, or organization, is authorized or accustomed to hear those communications and, under the discipline or tenets of his or her church, denomination, or organization, has a duty to keep those communications secret. (*Stats.1965, c. 299, § 2, operative Jan. 1, 1967. Amended by Stats.2002, c. 806 (A.B.3027), § 21.*)

§ 1033
Privilege of penitent

Subject to Section 912, a penitent, whether or not a party, has a privilege to refuse to disclose, and to prevent another from disclosing, a penitential communication if he or she claims the privilege. (*Stats.1965, c. 299, § 2, operative Jan. 1, 1967. Amended by Stats.2002, c. 806 (A.B.3027), § 22.*)

§ 1034
Privilege of clergy

Subject to Section 912, a member of the clergy, whether or not a party, has a privilege to refuse to disclose a penitential communication if he or she claims the privilege. (*Stats.1965, c. 299, § 2, operative Jan. 1, 1967. Amended by Stats.2002, c. 806 (A.B.3027), § 23.*)

ARTICLE 8.5. SEXUAL ASSAULT COUNSELOR–VICTIM PRIVILEGE

Section
1035. Victim.
1035.2. Sexual assault counselor.

§ 1035
Victim

As used in this article, "victim" means a person who consults a sexual assault counselor for the purpose of securing advice or assistance concerning a mental, physical, or emotional condition caused by a sexual assault. (*Added by Stats.1980, c. 917, p. 2916, § 2. Amended by Stats.2006, c. 689 (S.B.1743), § 4.*)

§ 1035.2
Sexual assault counselor

As used in this article, "sexual assault counselor" means any of the following:

(a) A person who is engaged in any office, hospital, institution, or center commonly known as a rape crisis center, whose primary purpose is the rendering of advice or assistance to victims of sexual assault and who has received a certificate evidencing completion of a training program in the counseling of sexual assault victims issued by a counseling center that meets the criteria for the award of a grant established pursuant to Section 13837 of the Penal Code and who meets one of the following requirements:

(1) Is a psychotherapist as defined in Section 1010; has a master's degree in counseling or a related field; or has one year of counseling experience, at least six months of which is in rape crisis counseling.

(2) Has 40 hours of training as described below and is supervised by an individual who qualifies as a counselor under paragraph (1). The training, supervised by a person qualified under paragraph (1), shall include, but not be limited to, the following areas:

(A) Law.

(B) Medicine.

(C) Societal attitudes.

(D) Crisis intervention and counseling techniques.

(E) Role playing.

(F) Referral services.

(G) Sexuality.

(b) A person who is employed by any organization providing the programs specified in Section 13835.2 of the Penal Code, whether financially compensated or not, for the purpose of counseling and assisting sexual assault victims, and who meets one of the following requirements:

(1) Is a psychotherapist as defined in Section 1010; has a master's degree in counseling or a related field; or has one year of counseling experience, at least six months of which is in rape assault counseling.

(2) Has the minimum training for sexual assault counseling required by guidelines established by the employing agency pursuant to subdivision (c) of Section 13835.10 of the Penal Code, and is supervised by an individual who qualifies as a counselor under paragraph (1). The training, supervised by a person qualified under paragraph (1), shall include, but not be limited to, the following areas:

(A) Law.

(B) Victimology.

(C) Counseling.

(D) Client and system advocacy.

(E) Referral services. (*Added by Stats.1980, c. 917, p. 2916, § 2. Amended by Stats.1983, c. 580, § 1; Stats.1983, c. 1072, § 1; Stats.1990, c. 1342 (S.B.2501), § 1; Stats.2006, c. 689 (S.B.1743), § 5.*)

§ 1035.4
Confidential communication between the sexual assault counselor and the victim; disclosure

As used in this article, "confidential communication between the sexual assault counselor and the victim" means information transmitted between the victim and the sexual assault counselor in the course of their relationship and in confidence by a means which, so far as the victim is aware, discloses the information to no third persons other than those who are present to further the interests of the victim in the consultation or those to whom disclosures are reasonably necessary for the transmission of the information or an accomplishment of the purposes for which the sexual assault counselor is consulted. The term includes all information regarding the facts and circumstances involving the alleged sexual assault and also includes all information regarding the victim's prior or subsequent sexual conduct, and opinions regarding the victim's sexual conduct or reputation in sexual matters.

The court may compel disclosure of information received by the sexual assault counselor which constitutes relevant evidence of the facts and circumstances involving an alleged sexual assault about which the victim is complaining and which is the subject of a criminal proceeding if the court determines that the probative value outweighs the effect on the victim, the treatment relationship, and the treatment services if disclosure is compelled. The court may also compel disclosure in proceedings related to child abuse if the court determines the probative value outweighs the effect on the victim, the treatment relationship, and the treatment services if disclosure is compelled.

When a court is ruling on a claim of privilege under this article, the court may require the person from whom disclosure is sought or the person authorized to claim the privilege, or both, to disclose the information in chambers out of the presence and hearing of all persons except the person authorized to claim the privilege and such other persons as the person authorized to claim the privilege is willing to have present. If the judge determines that the information is privileged and must not be disclosed, neither he or she nor any other person may ever disclose, without the consent of a person authorized to permit disclosure, what was disclosed in the course of the proceedings in chambers.

If the court determines certain information shall be disclosed, the court shall so order and inform the defendant. If the court finds there is a reasonable likelihood that particular information is subject to disclosure pursuant to the balancing test provided in this section, the following procedure shall be followed:

(1) The court shall inform the defendant of the nature of the information which may be subject to disclosure.

(2) The court shall order a hearing out of the presence of the jury, if any, and at the hearing allow the questioning of the sexual assault counselor regarding the information which the court has determined may be subject to disclosure.

(3) At the conclusion of the hearing, the court shall rule which items of information, if any, shall be disclosed. The court may make an order stating what evidence may be introduced by the defendant and the nature of questions to be permitted. The defendant may then offer evidence pursuant to the order of the court. Admission of evidence concerning the sexual conduct of the complaining witness is subject to Sections 352, 782, and 1103. (*Added by Stats.1980, c. 917, p. 2916, § 2. Amended by Stats.1983, c. 1072, § 2.*)

§ 1035.6
Holder of the privilege

As used in this article, "holder of the privilege" means:

(a) The victim when such person has no guardian or conservator.

(b) A guardian or conservator of the victim when the victim has a guardian or conservator.

(c) The personal representative of the victim if the victim is dead. (*Added by Stats.1980, c. 917, p. 2916, § 2.*)

§ 1035.8
Sexual assault counselor privilege

A victim of a sexual assault, whether or not a party, has a privilege to refuse to disclose, and to prevent another from disclosing, a confidential communication between the victim and a sexual assault counselor if the privilege is claimed by any of the following:

(a) The holder of the privilege;

(b) A person who is authorized to claim the privilege by the holder of the privilege; or

(c) The person who was the sexual assault counselor at the time of the confidential communication, but that person may not claim the privilege if there is no holder of the privilege in existence or if he or she is otherwise instructed by a person authorized to permit disclosure. (*Added by Stats.1980, c. 917, p. 2916, § 2. Amended by Stats.2006, c. 689 (S.B.1743), § 6.*)

§ 1036
Claim of privilege by sexual assault counselor

The sexual assault counselor who received or made a communication subject to the privilege under this article shall claim the privilege if he or she is present when the communication is sought to be disclosed and is authorized to claim the privilege under subdivision (c) of Section 1035.8. (*Added by Stats.1980, c. 917, p. 2916, § 2. Amended by Stats.2006, c. 689 (S.B.1743), § 7.*)

§ 1036.2
Sexual assault

As used in this article, "sexual assault" includes all of the following:

(a) Rape, as defined in Section 261 of the Penal Code.

(b) Unlawful sexual intercourse, as defined in Section 261.5 of the Penal Code.

(c) Rape in concert with force and violence, as defined in Section 264.1 of the Penal Code.

(d) Rape of a spouse, as defined in Section 262 of the Penal Code.

(e) Sodomy, as defined in Section 286 of the Penal Code, except a violation of subdivision (e) of that section.

(f) A violation of Section 288 of the Penal Code.

(g) Oral copulation, as defined in Section 288a of the Penal Code, except a violation of subdivision (e) of that section.

(h) Sexual penetration, as defined in Section 289 of the Penal Code.

(i) Annoying or molesting a child under 18, as defined in Section 647a of the Penal Code.

(j) Any attempt to commit any of the above acts. (*Added by Stats.1980, c. 917, p. 2916, § 2. Amended by Stats.1988, c. 102, § 1; Stats.2001, c. 854 (S.B.205), § 4.*)

ARTICLE 8.7. DOMESTIC VIOLENCE COUNSELOR–VICTIM PRIVILEGE

Section
1037. Victim.
1037.1. Domestic violence counselor; qualifications; domestic violence victim service organization.
1037.2. Confidential communication; compulsion of disclosure by court; claim of privilege.
1037.3. Child abuse; reporting.
1037.4. Holder of the privilege.
1037.5. Privilege of refusal to disclose communication; claimants.
1037.6. Claim of privilege by counselor.
1037.7. Domestic violence.
1037.8. Notice; limitations on confidential communications.

§ 1037
Victim

As used in this article, "victim" means any person who suffers domestic violence, as defined in Section 1037.7. (*Added by Stats.1986, c. 854, § 1.*)

§ 1037.1
Domestic violence counselor; qualifications; domestic violence victim service organization

(a)(1) As used in this article, "domestic violence counselor" means a person who is employed by a domestic violence victim service organization, as defined in this article, whether financially compensated or not, for the purpose of rendering advice or assistance to victims of domestic violence and who has at least 40 hours of training as specified in paragraph (2).

(2) The 40 hours of training shall be supervised by an individual who qualifies as a counselor under paragraph (1), and who has at least one year of experience counseling domestic violence victims for the domestic violence victim service organization. The training shall include, but need not be limited to, the following areas: history of domestic violence, civil and criminal law as it relates to domestic violence, the domestic violence victim-counselor privilege and other laws that protect the confidentiality of

victim records and information, societal attitudes towards domestic violence, peer counseling techniques, housing, public assistance and other financial resources available to meet the financial needs of domestic violence victims, and referral services available to domestic violence victims.

(3) A domestic violence counselor who has been employed by the domestic violence victim service organization for a period of less than six months shall be supervised by a domestic violence counselor who has at least one year of experience counseling domestic violence victims for the domestic violence victim service organization.

(b) As used in this article, "domestic violence victim service organization" means a nongovernmental organization or entity that provides shelter, programs, or services to victims of domestic violence and their children, including, but not limited to, either of the following:

(1) Domestic violence shelter-based programs, as described in Section 18294 of the Welfare and Institutions Code.

(2) Other programs with the primary mission to provide services to victims of domestic violence whether or not that program exists in an agency that provides additional services. (*Added by Stats.1986, c. 854, § 1. Amended by Stats.1990, c. 1342 (S.B.2501), § 2; Stats.2007, c. 206 (S.B.407), § 2.*)

§ 1037.2
Confidential communication; compulsion of disclosure by court; claim of privilege

(a) As used in this article, "confidential communication" means any information, including, but not limited to, written or oral communication, transmitted between the victim and the counselor in the course of their relationship and in confidence by a means which, so far as the victim is aware, discloses the information to no third persons other than those who are present to further the interests of the victim in the consultation or those to whom disclosures are reasonably necessary for the transmission of the information or an accomplishment of the purposes for which the domestic violence counselor is consulted. The term includes all information regarding the facts and circumstances involving all incidences of domestic violence, as well as all information about the children of the victim or abuser and the relationship of the victim with the abuser.

(b) The court may compel disclosure of information received by a domestic violence counselor which constitutes relevant evidence of the facts and circumstances involving a crime allegedly perpetrated against the victim or another household member and which is the subject of a criminal proceeding, if the court determines that the probative value of the information outweighs the effect of disclosure of the information on the victim, the counseling relationship, and the counseling services. The court may compel disclosure if the victim is either dead or not the complaining witness in a criminal action against the perpetrator. The court may also compel disclosure in proceedings related to child abuse if the court determines that the probative value of the evidence outweighs the effect of the disclosure on the victim, the counseling relationship, and the counseling services.

(c) When a court rules on a claim of privilege under this article, it may require the person from whom disclosure is sought or the person authorized to claim the privilege, or both, to disclose the information in chambers out of the presence and hearing of all persons except the person authorized to claim the privilege and such other persons as the person authorized to claim the privilege consents to have present. If the judge determines that the information is privileged and shall not be disclosed, neither he nor she nor any other person may disclose, without the consent of a person authorized to permit disclosure, any information disclosed in the course of the proceedings in chambers.

(d) If the court determines that information shall be disclosed, the court shall so order and inform the defendant in the criminal action. If the court finds there is a reasonable likelihood that any information is subject to disclosure pursuant to the balancing test provided in this section, the procedure specified in subdivisions (1), (2), and (3) of Section 1035.4 shall be followed. (*Added by Stats.1986, c. 854, § 1. Amended by Stats.2007, c. 206 (S.B.407), § 3.*)

§ 1037.3
Child abuse; reporting

Nothing in this article shall be construed to limit any obligation to report instances of child abuse as required by Section 11166 of the Penal Code. (*Added by Stats.1986, c. 854, § 1.*)

§ 1037.4
Holder of the privilege

As used in this article, "holder of the privilege" means:

(a) The victim when he or she has no guardian or conservator.

(b) A guardian or conservator of the victim when the victim has a guardian or conservator, unless the guardian or conservator is accused of perpetrating domestic violence against the victim. (*Added by Stats.1986, c. 854, § 1. Amended by Stats.2007, c. 206 (S.B.407), § 4.*)

§ 1037.5
Privilege of refusal to disclose communication; claimants

A victim of domestic violence, whether or not a party to the action, has a privilege to refuse to disclose, and to prevent another from disclosing, a confidential communication between the victim and a domestic violence counselor in any proceeding specified in Section 901 if the privilege is claimed by any of the following persons:

(a) The holder of the privilege.

(b) A person who is authorized to claim the privilege by the holder of the privilege.

(c) The person who was the domestic violence counselor at the time of the confidential communication. However, that person may not claim the privilege if there is no holder of the privilege in existence or if he or she is otherwise instructed by a person authorized to permit disclosure. (*Added by Stats.1986, c. 854, § 1. Amended by Stats.2007, c. 206 (S.B.407), § 5.*)

§ 1037.6
Claim of privilege by counselor

The domestic violence counselor who received or made a communication subject to the privilege granted by this article shall claim the privilege whenever he or she is present when the communication is sought to be disclosed and he or she is authorized to claim the privilege under subdivision (c) of Section 1037.5. (*Added by Stats.1986, c. 854, § 1.*)

§ 1037.7
Domestic violence

As used in this article, "domestic violence" means "domestic violence" as defined in Section 6211 of the Family Code. (*Added by Stats.1993, c. 219 (A.B.1500), § 77.4.*)

§ 1037.8

Notice; limitations on confidential communications

A domestic violence counselor shall inform a domestic violence victim of any applicable limitations on confidentiality of communications between the victim and the domestic violence counselor. This information may be given orally. (*Added by Stats.2002, c. 629 (S.B.1735), § 1.*)

ARTICLE 8.8. HUMAN TRAFFICKING CASEWORKER– VICTIM PRIVILEGE

Section
1038. Privilege.
1038.1. Compulsion of disclosure by court.
1038.2. Definitions.

§ 1038
Privilege

(a) A trafficking victim, whether or not a party to the action, has a privilege to refuse to disclose, and to prevent another from disclosing, a confidential communication between the victim and a human trafficking caseworker if the privilege is claimed by any of the following persons:

(1) The holder of the privilege.

(2) A person who is authorized to claim the privilege by the holder of the privilege.

(3) The person who was the human trafficking caseworker at the time of the confidential communication. However, that person may not claim the privilege if there is no holder of the privilege in existence or if he or she is otherwise instructed by a person authorized to permit disclosure. The human trafficking caseworker who received or made a communication subject to the privilege granted by this article shall claim the privilege whenever he or she is present when the communication is sought to be disclosed and he or she is authorized to claim the privilege under this section.

(b) A human trafficking caseworker shall inform a trafficking victim of any applicable limitations on confidentiality of communications between the victim and the caseworker. This information may be given orally. (*Added by Stats.2005, c. 240 (A.B.22), § 4.*)

§ 1038.1
Compulsion of disclosure by court

(a) The court may compel disclosure of information received by a human trafficking caseworker that constitutes relevant evidence of the facts and circumstances involving a crime allegedly perpetrated against the victim and that is the subject of a criminal proceeding, if the court determines that the probative value of the information outweighs the effect of disclosure of the information on the victim, the counseling relationship, and the counseling services. The court may compel disclosure if the victim is either dead or not the complaining witness in a criminal action against the perpetrator.

(b) When a court rules on a claim of privilege under this article, it may require the person from whom disclosure is sought or the person authorized to claim the privilege, or both, to disclose the information in chambers out of the presence and hearing of all persons except the person authorized to claim the privilege and those other persons that the person authorized to claim the privilege consents to have present.

(c) If the judge determines that the information is privileged and shall not be disclosed, neither he nor she nor any other person may disclose, without the consent of a person authorized to permit disclosure, any information disclosed in the course of the proceedings in chambers. If the court determines that information shall be disclosed, the court shall so order and inform the defendant in the criminal action. If the court finds there is a reasonable likelihood that any information is subject to disclosure pursuant to the balancing test provided in this section, the procedure specified in paragraphs (1), (2), and (3) of Section 1035.4 shall be followed. (*Added by Stats.2005, c. 240 (A.B.22), § 4.*)

§ 1038.2
Definitions

(a) As used in this article, "victim" means any person who is a "trafficking victim" as defined in Section 236.1.[1]

(b) As used in this article, "human trafficking caseworker" means any of the following:

(1) A person who is employed by any organization providing the programs specified in Section 18294 of the Welfare and Institutions Code, whether financially compensated or not, for the purpose of rendering advice or assistance to victims of human trafficking, who has received specialized training in the counseling of human trafficking victims, and who meets one of the following requirements:

(A) Has a master's degree in counseling or a related field; or has one year of counseling experience, at least six months of which is in the counseling of human trafficking victims.

(B) Has at least 40 hours of training as specified in this paragraph and is supervised by an individual who qualifies as a counselor under subparagraph (A), or is a psychotherapist, as defined in Section 1010. The training, supervised by a person qualified under subparagraph (A), shall include, but need not be limited to, the following areas: history of human trafficking, civil and criminal law as it relates to human trafficking, societal attitudes towards human trafficking, peer counseling techniques, housing, public assistance and other financial resources available to meet the financial needs of human trafficking victims, and referral services available to human trafficking victims. A portion of this training must include an explanation of privileged communication.

(2) A person who is employed by any organization providing the programs specified in Section 13835.2 of the Penal Code, whether financially compensated or not, for the purpose of counseling and assisting human trafficking victims, and who meets one of the following requirements:

(A) Is a psychotherapist as defined in Section 1010, has a master's degree in counseling or a related field, or has one year of counseling experience, at least six months of which is in rape assault counseling.

(B) Has the minimum training for human trafficking counseling required by guidelines established by the employing agency pursuant to subdivision (c) of Section 13835.10 of the Penal Code, and is supervised by an individual who qualifies as a counselor under subparagraph (A). The training, supervised by a person qualified under subparagraph (A), shall include, but not be limited to, law, victimology, counseling techniques, client and system advocacy, and referral services. A portion of this training must include an explanation of privileged communication.

(c) As used in this article, "confidential communication" means information transmitted between the victim and the caseworker in the course of their relationship and in confidence by a means which, so far as the victim is aware, discloses the information to no third persons other than those who are present to further the interests of the victim in the consultation or those to whom disclosures are reasonably necessary for the transmission of the information or an accomplishment of the purposes for which the human trafficking counselor is consulted. It includes all information regarding the facts and circumstances involving all incidences of human trafficking.

(d) As used in this article, "holder of the privilege" means the victim when he or she has no guardian or conservator, or a guardian or conservator of the victim when the victim has a guardian or conservator. (*Added by Stats.2005, c. 240 (A.B.22), § 4.*)

[1] See Penal Code § 236.1.

ARTICLE 9. OFFICIAL INFORMATION AND IDENTITY OF INFORMER

Section

§ 1040
Privilege for official information

(a) As used in this section, "official information" means information acquired in confidence by a public employee in the course of his or her duty and not open, or officially disclosed, to the public prior to the time the claim of privilege is made.

(b) A public entity has a privilege to refuse to disclose official information, and to prevent another from disclosing official information, if the privilege is claimed by a person authorized by the public entity to do so and:

(1) Disclosure is forbidden by an act of the Congress of the United States or a statute of this state; or

(2) Disclosure of the information is against the public interest because there is a necessity for preserving the confidentiality of the information that outweighs the necessity for disclosure in the interest of justice; but no

privilege may be claimed under this paragraph if any person authorized to do so has consented that the information be disclosed in the proceeding. In determining whether disclosure of the information is against the public interest, the interest of the public entity as a party in the outcome of the proceeding may not be considered.

(c) Notwithstanding any other provision of law, the Employment Development Department shall disclose to law enforcement agencies, in accordance with the provisions of subdivision (k) of Section 1095 and subdivision (b) of Section 2714 of the Unemployment Insurance Code, information in its possession relating to any person if an arrest warrant has been issued for the person for commission of a felony. (*Stats.1965, c. 299, § 2, operative Jan. 1, 1967. Amended by Stats.1984, c. 1127, § 2.*)

§ 1041
Privilege for identity of informer

(a) Except as provided in this section, a public entity has a privilege to refuse to disclose the identity of a person who has furnished information as provided in subdivision (b) purporting to disclose a violation of a law of the United States or of this state or of a public entity in this state, and to prevent another from disclosing such identity, if the privilege is claimed by a person authorized by the public entity to do so and:

(1) Disclosure is forbidden by an act of the Congress of the United States or a statute of this state; or

(2) Disclosure of the identity of the informer is against the public interest because there is a necessity for preserving the confidentiality of his identity that outweighs the necessity for disclosure in the interest of justice; but no privilege may be claimed under this paragraph if any person authorized to do so has consented that the identity of the informer be disclosed in the proceeding. In determining whether disclosure of the identity of the informer is against the public interest, the interest of the public entity as a party in the outcome of the proceeding may not be considered.

(b) This section applies only if the information is furnished in confidence by the informer to:

(1) A law enforcement officer;

(2) A representative of an administrative agency charged with the administration or enforcement of the law alleged to be violated; or

(3) Any person for the purpose of transmittal to a person listed in paragraph (1) or (2).

(c) There is no privilege under this section to prevent the informer from disclosing his identity. (*Stats.1965, c. 299, § 2, operative Jan. 1, 1967.*)

§ 1042
Adverse order or finding in certain cases

(a) Except where disclosure is forbidden by an act of the Congress of the United States, if a claim of privilege under this article by the state or a public entity in this state is sustained in a criminal proceeding, the presiding officer shall make such order or finding of fact adverse to the public entity bringing the proceeding as is required by law upon any issue in the proceeding to which the privileged information is material.

(b) Notwithstanding subdivision (a), where a search is made pursuant to a warrant valid on its face, the public entity bringing a criminal proceeding is not required to reveal to the defendant official information or the identity of an informer in order to establish the legality of the search or the admissibility of any evidence obtained as a result of it.

(c) Notwithstanding subdivision (a), in any preliminary hearing, criminal trial, or other criminal proceeding, any otherwise admissible evidence of information communicated to a peace officer by a confidential informant, who is not a material witness to the guilt or innocence of the accused of the offense charged, is admissible on the issue of reasonable cause to make an arrest or search without requiring that the name or identity of the informant be disclosed if the judge or magistrate is satisfied, based upon evidence produced in open court, out of the presence of the jury, that such information was received from a reliable informant and in his discretion does not require such disclosure.

(d) When, in any such criminal proceeding, a party demands disclosure of the identity of the informant on the ground the informant is a material witness on the issue of guilt, the court shall conduct a hearing at which all parties may present evidence on the issue of disclosure. Such hearing shall be conducted outside the presence of the jury, if any. During the hearing, if the privilege provided for in Section 1041 is claimed by a person authorized to do so or if a person who is authorized to claim such privilege refuses to answer any question on the ground that the answer would tend to disclose the identity of the informant, the prosecuting attorney may request that the court hold an in camera hearing. If such a request is made, the court shall hold such a hearing outside the presence of the defendant and his counsel. At the in camera hearing, the prosecution may offer evidence which would tend to disclose or which discloses the identity of the informant to aid the court in its determination whether there is a reasonable possibility that nondisclosure might deprive the defendant of a fair trial. A reporter shall be present at the in camera hearing. Any transcription of the proceedings at the in camera hearing, as well as any physical evidence presented at the hearing, shall be ordered sealed by the court, and only a court may have access to its contents. The court shall not order disclosure, nor strike the testimony of the witness who invokes the privilege, nor dismiss the criminal proceeding, if the party offering the witness refuses to disclose the identity of the informant, unless, based upon the evidence presented at the hearing held in the presence of the defendant and his counsel and the evidence presented at the in camera hearing, the court concludes that there is a reasonable possibility that nondisclosure might deprive the defendant of a fair trial. (*Stats.1965, c. 299, § 2, operative Jan. 1, 1967. Amended Stats.1965, c. 937, p. 2549, § 2, operative Jan. 1, 1967; Stats.1969, c. 1412, p. 2891, § 1.*)

§ 1043
Peace or custodial officer personnel records; discovery or disclosure; procedure

(a) In any case in which discovery or disclosure is sought of peace or custodial officer personnel records or records maintained pursuant to Section 832.5 of the Penal Code or information from those records, the party seeking the discovery or disclosure shall file a written motion with the appropriate court or administrative body upon written notice to the governmental agency which has custody and control of the records. The written notice shall be given at the times prescribed by subdivision (b) of Section 1005 of the Code of Civil Procedure. Upon receipt of the notice the governmental agency served shall immediately notify the individual whose records are sought.

(b) The motion shall include all of the following:

(1) Identification of the proceeding in which discovery or disclosure is sought, the party seeking discovery or disclosure, the peace or custodial officer whose records are sought, the governmental agency which has custody and control of the records, and the time and place at which the motion for discovery or disclosure shall be heard.

(2) A description of the type of records or information sought.

(3) Affidavits showing good cause for the discovery or disclosure sought, setting forth the materiality thereof to the subject matter involved in the pending litigation and stating upon reasonable belief that the governmental agency identified has the records or information from the records.

(c) No hearing upon a motion for discovery or disclosure shall be held without full compliance with the notice provisions of this section except upon a showing by the moving party of good cause for noncompliance, or upon a waiver of the hearing by the governmental agency identified as having the records. (*Added by Stats.1978, c. 630, p. 2082, § 1. Amended by Stats.1989, c. 693, § 7; Stats.2002, c. 391 (A.B.2040), § 1.*)

§ 1044
Medical or psychological history records; right of access

Nothing in this article shall be construed to affect the right of access to records of medical or psychological history where such access would otherwise be available under Section 996 or 1016. (*Added by Stats.1978, c. 630, p. 2082, § 2.*)

§ 1045
Peace or custodial officers; access to records of complaints, investigations of complaints, or discipline imposed; relevancy; protective orders

(a) Nothing in this article shall be construed to affect the right of access to records of complaints, or investigations of complaints, or discipline imposed as a result of those investigations, concerning an event or transaction in which the peace officer or custodial officer, as defined in Section 831.5 of the Penal Code, participated, or which he or she perceived, and pertaining to the manner in which he or she performed his or her duties, provided that information is relevant to the subject matter involved in the pending litigation.

(b) In determining relevance, the court shall examine the information in chambers in conformity with Section 915, and shall exclude from disclosure:

(1) Information consisting of complaints concerning conduct occurring more than five years before the event or transaction that is the subject of the litigation in aid of which discovery or disclosure is sought.

(2) In any criminal proceeding the conclusions of any officer investigating a complaint filed pursuant to Section 832.5 of the Penal Code.

(3) Facts sought to be disclosed that are so remote as to make disclosure of little or no practical benefit.

(c) In determining relevance where the issue in litigation concerns the policies or pattern of conduct of the employing agency, the court shall consider whether the information sought may be obtained from other records maintained by the employing agency in the regular course of agency business which would not necessitate the disclosure of individual personnel records.

(d) Upon motion seasonably made by the governmental agency which has custody or control of the records to be examined or by the officer whose records are sought, and upon good cause showing the necessity thereof, the court may make any order which justice requires to protect the officer or agency from unnecessary annoyance, embarrassment or oppression.

(e) The court shall, in any case or proceeding permitting the disclosure or discovery of any peace or custodial officer records requested pursuant to Section 1043, order that the records disclosed or discovered may not be used for any purpose other than a court proceeding pursuant to applicable law. (*Added by Stats.1978, c. 630, p. 2082, § 3. Amended by Stats.1982, c. 946, p. 3432, § 1; Stats.2002, c. 391 (A.B.2040), § 2.*)

§ 1046
Allegation of excessive force by peace or custodial officer; copy of police or crime report

In any case, otherwise authorized by law, in which the party seeking disclosure is alleging excessive force by a peace officer or custodial officer, as defined in Section 831.5 of the Penal Code, in connection with the arrest of that party, or for conduct alleged to have occurred within a jail facility, the motion shall include a copy of the police report setting forth the circumstances under which the party was stopped and arrested, or a copy of the crime report setting forth the circumstances under which the conduct is alleged to have occurred within a jail facility. (*Added by Stats.1985, c. 539, § 1. Amended by Stats.2002, c. 391 (A.B.2040), § 3.*)

§ 1047
Records of peace or custodial officers; exemption from disclosure

Records of peace officers or custodial officers, as defined in Section 831.5 of the Penal Code, including supervisorial officers, who either were not present during the arrest or had no contact with the party seeking disclosure from the time of the arrest until the time of booking, or who were not present at the time the conduct is alleged to have occurred within a jail facility, shall not be subject to disclosure. (*Added by Stats.1985, c. 539, § 2. Amended by Stats.2002, c. 391 (A.B.2040), § 4.*)

ARTICLE 10. POLITICAL VOTE

Section
1050. Privilege to protect secrecy of vote.

§ 1050
Privilege to protect secrecy of vote

If he claims the privilege, a person has a privilege to refuse to disclose the tenor of his vote at a public election where the voting is by secret ballot unless he voted illegally or he previously made an unprivileged disclosure of the tenor of his vote. (*Stats.1965, c. 299, § 2, operative Jan. 1, 1967.*)

ARTICLE 11. TRADE SECRET

Section
1060. Privilege to protect trade secret.
1061. Procedure for assertion of trade secret privilege.
1062. Exclusion of public from criminal proceeding; motion; contents; hearing; determination.
1063. Sealing of articles protected by protective order; procedures.

§ 1060
Privilege to protect trade secret

If he or his agent or employee claims the privilege, the owner of a trade secret has a privilege to refuse to disclose the secret, and to prevent another from disclosing it, if the allowance of the privilege will not tend to conceal fraud or otherwise work injustice. (*Stats.1965, c. 299, § 2, operative Jan. 1, 1967.*)

§ 1061. Procedure for assertion of trade secret privilege

(a) For purposes of this section, and Sections 1062 and 1063:

(1) "Trade secret" means "trade secret," as defined in subdivision (d) of Section 3426.1 of the Civil Code, or paragraph (9) of subdivision (a) of Section 499c of the Penal Code.

(2) "Article" means "article," as defined in paragraph (2) of subdivision (a) of Section 499c of the Penal Code.

(b) In addition to Section 1062, the following procedure shall apply whenever the owner of a trade secret wishes to assert his or her trade secret privilege, as provided in Section 1060, during a criminal proceeding:

(1) The owner of the trade secret shall file a motion for a protective order, or the people may file the motion on the owner's behalf and with the owner's permission. The motion shall include an affidavit based upon personal knowledge listing the affiant's qualifications to give an opinion concerning the trade secret at issue, identifying, without revealing, the alleged trade secret and articles which disclose the secret, and presenting evidence that the secret qualifies as a trade secret under either subdivision (d) of Section 3426.1 of the Civil Code or paragraph (9) of subdivision (a) of Section 499c of the Penal Code. The motion and affidavit shall be served on all parties in the proceeding.

(2) Any party in the proceeding may oppose the request for the protective order by submitting affidavits based upon the affiant's personal knowledge. The affidavits shall be filed under seal, but shall be provided to the owner of the trade secret and to all parties in the proceeding. Neither the owner of the trade secret nor any party in the proceeding may disclose the affidavit to persons other than to counsel of record without prior court approval.

(3) The movant shall, by a preponderance of the evidence, show that the issuance of a protective order is proper. The court may rule on the request without holding an evidentiary hearing. However, in its discretion, the court may choose to hold an in camera evidentiary hearing concerning disputed articles with only the owner of the trade secret, the people's representative, the defendant, and defendant's counsel present. If the court holds such a hearing, the parties§ right to examine witnesses shall not be

used to obtain discovery, but shall be directed solely toward the question of whether the alleged trade secret qualifies for protection.

(4) If the court finds that a trade secret may be disclosed during any criminal proceeding unless a protective order is issued and that the issuance of a protective order would not conceal a fraud or work an injustice, the court shall issue a protective order limiting the use and dissemination of the trade secret, including, but not limited to, articles disclosing that secret. The protective order may, in the court's discretion, include the following provisions:

(A) That the trade secret may be disseminated only to counsel for the parties, including their associate attorneys, paralegals, and investigators, and to law enforcement officials or clerical officials.

(B) That the defendant may view the secret only in the presence of his or her counsel, or if not in the presence of his or her counsel, at counsel's offices.

(C) That any party seeking to show the trade secret, or articles containing the trade secret, to any person not designated by the protective order shall first obtain court approval to do so:

(i) The court may require that the person receiving the trade secret do so only in the presence of counsel for the party requesting approval.

(ii) The court may require the person receiving the trade secret to sign a copy of the protective order and to agree to be bound by its terms. The order may include a provision recognizing the owner of the trade secret to be a third-party beneficiary of that agreement.

(iii) The court may require a party seeking disclosure to an expert to provide that expert's name, employment history, and any other relevant information to the court for examination. The court shall accept that information under seal, and the information shall not be disclosed by any court except upon termination of the action and upon a showing of good cause to believe the secret has been disseminated by a court-approved expert. The court shall evaluate the expert and determine whether the expert poses a discernible risk of disclosure. The court shall withhold approval if the expert's economic interests place the expert in a competitive position with the victim, unless no other experts are available. The court may interview the expert in camera in aid of its ruling. If the court rejects the expert, it shall state its reasons for doing so on the record and a transcript of those reasons shall be prepared and sealed.

(D) That no articles disclosing the trade secret shall be filed or otherwise made a part of the court record available to the public without approval of the court and prior notice to the owner of the secret. The owner of the secret may give either party permission to accept the notice on the owner's behalf.

(E) Other orders as the court deems necessary to protect the integrity of the trade secret.

(c) A ruling granting or denying a motion for a protective order filed pursuant to subdivision (b) shall not be construed as a determination that the alleged trade secret is or is not a trade secret as defined by subdivision (d) of Section 3426.1 of the Civil Code or paragraph (9) of subdivision (a) of Section 499c of the Penal Code. Such a ruling shall not have any effect on any civil litigation.

(d) This section shall have prospective effect only and shall not operate to invalidate previously entered protective orders. (*Added by Stats.1990, c. 149 (A.B.2986), § 1. Amended by Stats.1990, c. 714 (A.B.2553), § 1; Stats.2002, c. 784 (S.B.1316), § 103.*)

§ 1062
Exclusion of public from criminal proceeding; motion; contents; hearing; determination

(a) Notwithstanding any other provision of law, in a criminal case, the court, upon motion of the owner of a trade secret, or upon motion by the People with the consent of the owner, may exclude the public from any portion of a criminal proceeding where the proponent of closure has demonstrated a substantial probability that the trade secret would otherwise be disclosed to the public during that proceeding and a substantial probability that the disclosure would cause serious harm to the owner of the secret, and where the court finds that there is no overriding public interest in an open proceeding. No evidence, however, shall be excluded during a criminal proceeding pursuant to this section if it would conceal a fraud, work an injustice, or deprive the People or the defendant of a fair trial.

(b) The motion made pursuant to subdivision (a) shall identify, without revealing, the trade secrets which would otherwise be disclosed to the public. A showing made pursuant to subdivision (a) shall be made during an in camera hearing with only the owner of the trade secret, the People's representative, the defendant, and defendant's counsel present. A court reporter shall be present during the hearing. Any transcription of the proceedings at the in camera hearing, as well as any articles presented at that hearing, shall be ordered sealed by the court and only a court may allow access to its contents upon a showing of good cause. The court, in ruling upon the motion made pursuant to subdivision (a), may consider testimony presented or affidavits filed in any proceeding held in that action.

(c) If, after the in camera hearing described in subdivision (b), the court determines that exclusion of trade secret information from the public is appropriate, the court shall close only that portion of the criminal proceeding necessary to prevent disclosure of the trade secret. Before granting the motion, however, the court shall find and state for the record that the moving party has met its burden pursuant to subdivision (b), and that the closure of that portion of the proceeding will not deprive the People or the defendant of a fair trial.

(d) The owner of the trade secret, the People, or the defendant may seek relief from a ruling denying or granting closure by petitioning a higher court for extraordinary relief.

(e) Whenever the court closes a portion of a criminal proceeding pursuant to this section, a transcript of that closed proceeding shall be made available to the public as soon as practicable. The court shall redact any information qualifying as a trade secret before making that transcript available.

(f) The court, subject to Section 867 of the Penal Code, may allow witnesses who are bound by a protective order entered in the criminal proceeding protecting trade secrets, pursuant[1] to Section 1061, to remain within the courtroom during the closed portion of the proceeding. (*Added by Stats.1990, c. 149 (A.B.2986), § 2. Amended by Stats.1990, c. 714 (A.B.2553), § 2.*)

[1]So in enrolled bill.

§ 1063
Sealing of articles protected by protective order; procedures

The following provisions shall govern requests to seal articles which are protected by a protective order entered pursuant to Evidence Code Section 1060 or 1061:

(a) The People shall request sealing of articles reasonably expected to be filed or admitted into evidence as follows:

(1) No less than 10 court days before trial, and no less than five court days before any other criminal proceeding, the People shall file with the court a list of all articles which the People reasonably expect to file with the court, or admit into evidence, under seal at that proceeding. That list shall be available to the public. The People may be relieved from providing timely notice upon showing that exigent circumstances prevent that notice.

(2) The court shall not allow the listed articles to be filed, admitted into evidence, or in any way made a part of the court record otherwise open to the public before holding a hearing to consider any objections to the People's request to seal the articles. The court at that hearing shall allow those objecting to the sealing to state their objections.

(3) After hearing any objections to sealing, the court shall conduct an in camera hearing with only the owner of the trade secret contained within those articles, the People's representative, defendant, and defendant's counsel present. The court shall review the articles sought to be sealed, evaluate objections to sealing, and determine whether the People have sa-

tisfied the constitutional standards governing public access to articles which are part of the judicial record. The court may consider testimony presented or affidavits filed in any proceeding held in that action. The People, defendant, and the owner of the trade secret may file affidavits based on the affiant's personal knowledge to be considered at that hearing. Those affidavits are to be sealed and not released to the public, but shall be made available to the parties. The court may rule on the request to seal without taking testimony. If the court takes testimony, examination of witnesses shall not be used to obtain discovery, but shall be directed solely toward whether sealing is appropriate.

(4) If the court finds that the movant has satisfied appropriate constitutional standards with respect to sealing particular articles, the court shall seal those articles if and when they are filed, admitted into evidence, or in any way made a part of the court record otherwise open to the public. The articles shall not be unsealed absent an order of a court upon a showing of good cause. Failure to examine the court file for notice of a request to seal shall not constitute good cause to consider objections to sealing.

(b) The following procedure shall apply to other articles made a part of the court record:

(1) Where any articles protected by a protective order entered pursuant to Section 1060 or 1061 are filed, admitted into evidence, or in any way made a part of the court record in such a way as to be otherwise open to the public, the People, a defendant, or the owner of a trade secret contained within those articles may request the court to seal those articles.

(2) The request to seal shall be made by noticed motion filed with the court. It may also be made orally in court at the time the articles are made a part of the court record. Where the request is made orally, the movant must file within 24 hours a written description of that request, including a list of the articles which are the subject of that request. These motions and lists shall be available to the public.

(3) The court shall promptly conduct hearings as provided in paragraphs (2), (3), and (4) of subdivision (a). The court shall, pending the hearings, seal those articles which are the subject of the request. Where a request to seal is made orally, the court may conduct hearings at the time the articles are made a part of the court record, but shall reconsider its ruling in light of additional objections made by objectors within two court days after the written record of the request to seal is made available to the public.

(4) Any articles sealed pursuant to these hearings shall not be unsealed absent an order of a court upon a showing of good cause. Failure to examine the court file for notice of a request to seal shall not constitute good cause to consider objections to sealing. (*Added by Stats.1990, c. 714 (A.B.2553), § 3.*)

CHAPTER 5. IMMUNITY OF NEWSMAN FROM CITATION FOR CONTEMPT

Section

1070. Refusal to disclose news source.

§ 1070
Refusal to disclose news source

(a) A publisher, editor, reporter, or other person connected with or employed upon a newspaper, magazine, or other periodical publication, or by a press association or wire service, or any person who has been so connected or employed, cannot be adjudged in contempt by a judicial, legislative, administrative body, or any other body having the power to issue subpoenas, for refusing to disclose, in any proceeding as defined in Section 901, the source of any information procured while so connected or employed for publication in a newspaper, magazine or other periodical publication, or for refusing to disclose any unpublished information obtained or prepared in gathering, receiving or processing of information for communication to the public.

(b) Nor can a radio or television news reporter or other person connected with or employed by a radio or television station, or any person who has been so connected or employed, be so adjudged in contempt for refusing to disclose the source of any information procured while so connected or employed for news or news commentary purposes on radio or television, or for refusing to disclose any unpublished information obtained or prepared in gathering, receiving or processing of information for communication to the public.

(c) As used in this section, "unpublished information" includes information not disseminated to the public by the person from whom disclosure is sought, whether or not related information has been disseminated and includes, but is not limited to, all notes, outtakes, photographs, tapes or other data of whatever sort not itself disseminated to the public through a medium of communication, whether or not published information based upon or related to such material has been disseminated. (*Stats.1965, c. 299, § 2, operative Jan. 1, 1967. Amended by Stats.1971, c. 1717, p. 3658, § 1; Stats.1972, c. 1431, p. 3126, § 1; Stats.1974, c. 1323, p. 2877, § 1; Stats.1974, c. 1456, p. 3184, § 2.*)

Division 9

EVIDENCE AFFECTED OR EXCLUDED BY EXTRINSIC POLICIES

CHAPTER 1. EVIDENCE OF CHARACTER, HABIT, OR CUSTOM

§ 1100
Manner of proof of character

Except as otherwise provided by statute, any otherwise admissible evidence (including evidence in the form of an opinion, evidence of reputation, and evidence of specific instances of such person's conduct) is admissible to prove a person's character or a trait of his character. (*Stats.1965, c. 299, § 2, operative Jan. 1, 1967.*)

§ 1101
Evidence of character to prove conduct

(a) Except as provided in this section and in Sections 1102, 1103, 1108, and 1109, evidence of a person's character or a trait of his or her character (whether in the form of an opinion, evidence of reputation, or evidence of specific instances of his or her conduct) is inadmissible when offered to prove his or her conduct on a specified occasion.

(b) Nothing in this section prohibits the admission of evidence that a person committed a crime, civil wrong, or other act when relevant to prove some fact (such as motive, opportunity, intent, preparation, plan, knowledge, identity, absence of mistake or accident, or whether a defendant in a prosecution for an unlawful sexual act or attempted unlawful sexual act did not reasonably and in good faith believe that the victim consented) other than his or her disposition to commit such an act.

(c) Nothing in this section affects the admissibility of evidence offered to support or attack the credibility of a witness. (*Stats.1965, c. 299, § 2, operative Jan. 1, 1967. Amended by Stats.1986, c. 1432, § 1; Stats.1995, c. 439 (A.B.882), § 1; Stats.1996, c. 261 (S.B.1876), § 1.*)

§ 1102
Opinion and reputation evidence of character of criminal defendant to prove conduct

In a criminal action, evidence of the defendant's character or a trait of his character in the form of an opinion or evidence of his reputation is not made inadmissible by Section 1101 if such evidence is:

(a) Offered by the defendant to prove his conduct in conformity with such character or trait of character.

(b) Offered by the prosecution to rebut evidence adduced by the defendant under subdivision (a). (*Stats.1965, c. 299, § 2, operative Jan. 1, 1967.*)

§ 1103. Character evidence of crime victim to prove conduct; evidence of defendant's character or trait for violence; evidence of manner of dress of victim; evidence of complaining witness§ sexual conduct

(a) In a criminal action, evidence of the character or a trait of character (in the form of an opinion, evidence of reputation, or evidence of specific instances of conduct) of the victim of the crime for which the defendant is being prosecuted is not made inadmissible by Section 1101 if the evidence is:

(1) Offered by the defendant to prove conduct of the victim in conformity with the character or trait of character.

(2) Offered by the prosecution to rebut evidence adduced by the defendant under paragraph (1).

(b) In a criminal action, evidence of the defendant's character for violence or trait of character for violence (in the form of an opinion, evidence of reputation, or evidence of specific instances of conduct) is not made inadmissible by Section 1101 if the evidence is offered by the prosecution to prove conduct of the defendant in conformity with the character or trait of character and is offered after evidence that the victim had a character for violence or a trait of character tending to show violence has been adduced by the defendant under paragraph (1) of subdivision (a).

(c)(1) Notwithstanding any other provision of this code to the contrary, and except as provided in this subdivision, in any prosecution under Section 261, 262, or 264.1 of the Penal Code, or under Section 286, 288a, or 289 of the Penal Code, or for assault with intent to commit, attempt to commit, or conspiracy to commit a crime defined in any of those sections, except where the crime is alleged to have occurred in a local detention facility, as defined in Section 6031.4, or in a state prison, as defined in Section 4504, opinion evidence, reputation evidence, and evidence of specific instances of the complaining witness§ sexual conduct, or any of that evidence, is not admissible by the defendant in order to prove consent by the complaining witness.

(2) Notwithstanding paragraph (3), evidence of the manner in which the victim was dressed at the time of the commission of the offense shall not be admissible when offered by either party on the issue of consent in any prosecution for an offense specified in paragraph (1), unless the evidence is determined by the court to be relevant and admissible in the interests of justice. The proponent of the evidence shall make an offer of proof outside the hearing of the jury. The court shall then make its determination and at that time, state the reasons for its ruling on the record. For the purposes of this paragraph, "manner of dress" does not include the condition of the victim's clothing before, during, or after the commission of the offense.

(3) Paragraph (1) shall not be applicable to evidence of the complaining witness§ sexual conduct with the defendant.

(4) If the prosecutor introduces evidence, including testimony of a witness, or the complaining witness as a witness gives testimony, and that evidence or testimony relates to the complaining witness§ sexual conduct, the defendant may cross-examine the witness who gives the testimony and offer relevant evidence limited specifically to the rebuttal of the evidence introduced by the prosecutor or given by the complaining witness.

(5) Nothing in this subdivision shall be construed to make inadmissible any evidence offered to attack the credibility of the complaining witness as provided in Section 782.

(6) As used in this section, "complaining witness" means the alleged victim of the crime charged, the prosecution of which is subject to this subdivision. (*Stats.1965, c. 299, § 2, operative Jan. 1, 1967. Amended by Stats.1974, c. 569, p. 1388, § 2; Stats.1981, c. 726, p. 2876, § 2; Stats.1990, c. 268 (A.B.2615), § 1; Stats.1991, c. 16 (A.B.263), § 1, eff. March 18, 1991; Stats.1996, c. 1075 (S.B.1444), § 7; Stats.1998, c. 127 (A.B.1926), § 1.*)

§ 1104
Character trait for care or skill

Except as provided in Sections 1102 and 1103, evidence of a trait of a person's character with respect to care or skill is inadmissible to prove the quality of his conduct on a specified occasion. (*Stats.1965, c. 299, § 2, operative Jan. 1, 1967.*)

§ 1105
Habit or custom to prove specific behavior

Any otherwise admissible evidence of habit or custom is admissible to prove conduct on a specified occasion in conformity with the habit or custom. (*Stats.1965, c. 299, § 2, operative Jan. 1, 1967.*)

§ 1106
Sexual harassment, sexual assault, or sexual battery cases; opinion or reputation evidence of plaintiff's sexual conduct; inadmissibility; exception; cross-examination

(a) In any civil action alleging conduct which constitutes sexual harassment, sexual assault, or sexual battery, opinion evidence, reputation evidence, and evidence of specific instances of plaintiff's sexual conduct, or any of such evidence, is not admissible by the defendant in order to prove consent by the plaintiff or the absence of injury to the plaintiff, unless the injury alleged by the plaintiff is in the nature of loss of consortium.

(b) Subdivision (a) shall not be applicable to evidence of the plaintiff's sexual conduct with the alleged perpetrator.

(c) If the plaintiff introduces evidence, including testimony of a witness, or the plaintiff as a witness gives testimony, and the evidence or testimony relates to the plaintiff's sexual conduct, the defendant may cross-examine the witness who gives the testimony and offer relevant evidence limited specifically to the rebuttal of the evidence introduced by the plaintiff or given by the plaintiff.

(d) Nothing in this section shall be construed to make inadmissible any evidence offered to attack the credibility of the plaintiff as provided in Section 783. (*Added by Stats.1985, c. 1328, § 4.*)

§ 1107
Intimate partner battering and its effects; expert testimony in criminal actions; sufficiency of foundation; abuse and domestic violence; applicability to Penal Code; impact on decisional law

(a) In a criminal action, expert testimony is admissible by either the prosecution or the defense regarding intimate partner battering and its effects, including the nature and effect of physical, emotional, or mental abuse on the beliefs, perceptions, or behavior of victims of domestic violence, except when offered against a criminal defendant to prove the occurrence of the act or acts of abuse which form the basis of the criminal charge.

(b) The foundation shall be sufficient for admission of this expert testimony if the proponent of the evidence establishes its relevancy and the proper qualifications of the expert witness. Expert opinion testimony on intimate partner battering and its effects shall not be considered a new scientific technique whose reliability is unproven.

(c) For purposes of this section, "abuse" is defined in Section 6203 of the Family Code, and "domestic violence" is defined in Section 6211 of the Family Code and may include acts defined in Section 242, subdivision (e) of Section 243, Section 262, 273.5, 273.6, 422, or 653m of the Penal Code.

(d) This section is intended as a rule of evidence only and no substantive change affecting the Penal Code is intended.

(e) This section shall be known, and may be cited, as the Expert Witness Testimony on Intimate Partner Battering and Its Effects Section of the Evidence Code.

(f) The changes in this section that become effective on January 1, 2005, are not intended to impact any existing decisional law regarding this section, and that decisional law should apply equally to this section as it refers to "intimate partner battering and its effects" in place of "battered women's syndrome." (*Added by Stats.1991, c. 812 (A.B.785), § 1. Amended by Stats.1992, c. 163 (A.B.2641), § 72, operative Jan. 1, 1994; Stats.1993, c. 589 (A.B.2211), § 60; Stats.1993, c. 219 (A.B.1500), § 77.5; Stats.2000, c. 1001 (S.B.1944), § 1; Stats.2004, c. 609 (S.B.1385), § 1.*)

§ 1108
Evidence of another sexual offense by defendant; disclosure; construction of section

(a) In a criminal action in which the defendant is accused of a sexual offense, evidence of the defendant's commission of another sexual offense or offenses is not made inadmissible by Section 1101, if the evidence is not inadmissible pursuant to Section 352.

(b) In an action in which evidence is to be offered under this section, the people shall disclose the evidence to the defendant, including statements of witnesses or a summary of the substance of any testimony that is expected to be offered in compliance with the provisions of Section 1054.7 of the Penal Code.

(c) This section shall not be construed to limit the admission or consideration of evidence under any other section of this code.

(d) As used in this section, the following definitions shall apply:

(1) "Sexual offense" means a crime under the law of a state or of the United States that involved any of the following:

(A) Any conduct proscribed by Section 243.4, 261, 261.5, 262, 264.1, 266c, 269, 286, 288, 288a, 288.2, 288.5, or 289, or subdivision (b), (c), or (d) of Section 311.2 or Section 311.3, 311.4, 311.10, 311.11, 314, or 647.6, of the Penal Code.

(B) Any conduct proscribed by Section 220 of the Penal Code, except assault with intent to commit mayhem.

(C) Contact, without consent, between any part of the defendant's body or an object and the genitals or anus of another person.

(D) Contact, without consent, between the genitals or anus of the defendant and any part of another person's body.

(E) Deriving sexual pleasure or gratification from the infliction of death, bodily injury, or physical pain on another person.

(F) An attempt or conspiracy to engage in conduct described in this paragraph.

(2) "Consent" shall have the same meaning as provided in Section 261.6 of the Penal Code, except that it does not include consent which is legally ineffective because of the age, mental disorder, or developmental or physical disability of the victim. (*Added by Stats.1995, c. 439 (A.B.882), § 2. Amended by Stats.2001, c. 517 (A.B.380), § 1; Stats.2002, c. 194 (A.B.2252), § 1; Stats.2002, c. 828 (A.B.2499), § 1.*)

§ 1109
Evidence of defendant's other acts of domestic violence

(a)(1) Except as provided in subdivision (e) or (f), in a criminal action in which the defendant is accused of an offense involving domestic violence, evidence of the defendant's commission of other domestic violence is not made inadmissible by Section 1101 if the evidence is not inadmissible pursuant to Section 352.

(2) Except as provided in subdivision (e) or (f), in a criminal action in which the defendant is accused of an offense involving abuse of an elder or dependent person, evidence of the defendant's commission of other abuse of an elder or dependent person is not made inadmissible by Section 1101 if the evidence is not inadmissible pursuant to Section 352.

(3) Except as provided in subdivision (e) or (f) and subject to a hearing conducted pursuant to Section 352, which shall include consideration of any corroboration and remoteness in time, in a criminal action in which the defendant is accused of an offense involving child abuse, evidence of the defendant's commission of child abuse is not made inadmissible by Section 1101 if the evidence is not inadmissible pursuant to Section 352. Nothing in this paragraph prohibits or limits the admission of evidence pursuant to subdivision (b) of Section 1101.

(b) In an action in which evidence is to be offered under this section, the people shall disclose the evidence to the defendant, including statements of witnesses or a summary of the substance of any testimony that is expected to be offered, in compliance with the provisions of Section 1054. 7 of the Penal Code.

(c) This section shall not be construed to limit or preclude the admission or consideration of evidence under any other statute or case law.

(d) As used in this section:

(1) "Abuse of an elder or dependent person" means physical or sexual abuse, neglect, financial abuse, abandonment, isolation, abduction, or other treatment that results in physical harm, pain, or mental suffering, the deprivation of care by a caregiver, or other deprivation by a custodian or provider of goods or services that are necessary to avoid physical harm or mental suffering.

(2) "Child abuse" means an act proscribed by Section 273d of the Penal Code.

(3) "Domestic violence" has the meaning set forth in Section 13700 of the Penal Code. Subject to a hearing conducted pursuant to Section 352, which shall include consideration of any corroboration and remoteness in time, "domestic violence" has the further meaning as set forth in Section 6211 of the Family Code, if the act occurred no more than five years before the charged offense.

(e) Evidence of acts occurring more than 10 years before the charged offense is inadmissible under this section, unless the court determines that the admission of this evidence is in the interest of justice.

(f) Evidence of the findings and determinations of administrative agencies regulating the conduct of health facilities licensed under Section 1250 of the Health and Safety Code is inadmissible under this section. *(Added by Stats.1996, c. 261 (S.B.1876), § 2. Amended by Stats.1998, c. 707 (S.B.1682), § 1; Stats.2000, c. 97 (A.B.2063), § 1; Stats.2004, c. 116 (A.B.141), § 1; Stats.2004, c. 823 (A.B.20), § 6.5; Stats.2005, c. 464 (A.B.114), § 1.)*

CHAPTER 2. MEDIATION

1127. Attorney's fees and costs.
1128. Subsequent trials; references to mediation.

§ 1115
Definitions

For purposes of this chapter:

(a) "Mediation" means a process in which a neutral person or persons facilitate communication between the disputants to assist them in reaching a mutually acceptable agreement.

(b) "Mediator" means a neutral person who conducts a mediation. "Mediator" includes any person designated by a mediator either to assist in the mediation or to communicate with the participants in preparation for a mediation.

(c) "Mediation consultation" means a communication between a person and a mediator for the purpose of initiating, considering, or reconvening a mediation or retaining the mediator. (*Added by Stats.1997, c. 772 (A.B.939), § 3.*)

§ 1116
Effect of chapter

(a) Nothing in this chapter expands or limits a court's authority to order participation in a dispute resolution proceeding. Nothing in this chapter authorizes or affects the enforceability of a contract clause in which parties agree to the use of mediation.

(b) Nothing in this chapter makes admissible evidence that is inadmissible under Section 1152 or any other statute. (*Added by Stats.1997, c. 772 (A.B.939), § 3.*)

§ 1117
Application of chapter

(a) Except as provided in subdivision (b), this chapter applies to a mediation as defined in Section 1115.

(b) This chapter does not apply to either of the following:

(1) A proceeding under Part 1 (commencing with Section 1800) of Division 5 of the Family Code or Chapter 11 (commencing with Section 3160) of Part 2 of Division 8 of the Family Code.

(2) A settlement conference pursuant to Rule 3.1380 of the California Rules of Court. (*Added by Stats.1997, c. 772 (A.B.939), § 3. Amended by Stats.2007, c. 130 (A.B.299), § 84.*)

§ 1118
Oral agreements

An oral agreement "in accordance with Section 1118" means an oral agreement that satisfies all of the following conditions:

(a) The oral agreement is recorded by a court reporter or reliable means of audio recording.

(b) The terms of the oral agreement are recited on the record in the presence of the parties and the mediator, and the parties express on the record that they agree to the terms recited.

(c) The parties to the oral agreement expressly state on the record that the agreement is enforceable or binding, or words to that effect.

(d) The recording is reduced to writing and the writing is signed by the parties within 72 hours after it is recorded. (*Added by Stats.1997, c. 772 (A.B.939), § 3. Amended by Stats.2009, c. 88 (A.B.176), § 35; Stats.2010, c. 328 (S.B.1330), § 64.*)

§ 1119
Written or oral communications during mediation process; admissibility

Except as otherwise provided in this chapter:

(a) No evidence of anything said or any admission made for the purpose of, in the course of, or pursuant to, a mediation or a mediation consultation is admissible or subject to discovery, and disclosure of the evidence shall not be compelled, in any arbitration, administrative adjudication, civil action, or other noncriminal proceeding in which, pursuant to law, testimony can be compelled to be given.

(b) No writing, as defined in Section 250, that is prepared for the purpose of, in the course of, or pursuant to, a mediation or a mediation consultation, is admissible or subject to discovery, and disclosure of the writing shall not be compelled, in any arbitration, administrative adjudication, civil action, or other noncriminal proceeding in which, pursuant to law, testimony can be compelled to be given.

(c) All communications, negotiations, or settlement discussions by and between participants in the course of a mediation or a mediation consultation shall remain confidential. (*Added by Stats.1997, c. 772 (A.B.939), § 3.*)

§ 1120
Evidence otherwise admissible

(a) Evidence otherwise admissible or subject to discovery outside of a mediation or a mediation consultation shall not be or become inadmissible or protected from disclosure solely by reason of its introduction or use in a mediation or a mediation consultation.

(b) This chapter does not limit any of the following:

(1) The admissibility of an agreement to mediate a dispute.

(2) The effect of an agreement not to take a default or an agreement to extend the time within which to act or refrain from acting in a pending civil action.

(3) Disclosure of the mere fact that a mediator has served, is serving, will serve, or was contacted about serving as a mediator in a dispute. (*Added by Stats.1997, c. 772 (A.B.939), § 3.*)

§ 1121
Mediator's reports and findings

Neither a mediator nor anyone else may submit to a court or other adjudicative body, and a court or other adjudicative body may not consider, any report, assessment, evaluation, recommendation, or finding of any kind by the mediator concerning a mediation conducted by the mediator, other than a report that is mandated by court rule or other law and that states only whether an agreement was reached, unless all parties to the mediation expressly agree otherwise in writing, or orally in accordance with Section 1118. (*Added by Stats.1997, c. 772 (A.B.939), § 3.*)

§ 1122
Communications or writings; conditions to admissibility

(a) A communication or a writing, as defined in Section 250, that is made or prepared for the purpose of, or in the course of, or pursuant to, a mediation or a mediation consultation, is not made inadmissible, or protected from disclosure, by provisions of this chapter if either of the following conditions is satisfied:

(1) All persons who conduct or otherwise participate in the mediation expressly agree in writing, or orally in accordance with Section 1118, to disclosure of the communication, document, or writing.

(2) The communication, document, or writing was prepared by or on behalf of fewer than all the mediation participants, those participants expressly agree in writing, or orally in accordance with Section 1118, to its disclosure, and the communication, document, or writing does not disclose anything said or done or any admission made in the course of the mediation.

(b) For purposes of subdivision (a), if the neutral person who conducts a mediation expressly agrees to disclosure, that agreement also binds any other person described in subdivision (b) of Section 1115. (*Added by Stats.1997, c. 772 (A.B.939), § 3.*)

§ 1123
Written settlement agreements; conditions to admissibility

A written settlement agreement prepared in the course of, or pursuant to, a mediation, is not made inadmissible, or protected from disclosure, by provisions of this chapter if the agreement is signed by the settling parties and any of the following conditions are satisfied:

(a) The agreement provides that it is admissible or subject to disclosure, or words to that effect.

(b) The agreement provides that it is enforceable or binding or words to that effect.

(c) All parties to the agreement expressly agree in writing, or orally in accordance with Section 1118, to its disclosure.

(d) The agreement is used to show fraud, duress, or illegality that is relevant to an issue in dispute. (*Added by Stats.1997, c. 772 (A.B.939), § 3.*)

§ 1124
Oral agreements; conditions to admissibility

An oral agreement made in the course of, or pursuant to, a mediation is not made inadmissible, or protected from disclosure, by the provisions of this chapter if any of the following conditions are satisfied:

(a) The agreement is in accordance with Section 1118.

(b) The agreement is in accordance with subdivisions (a), (b), and (d) of Section 1118, and all parties to the agreement expressly agree, in writing or orally in accordance with Section 1118, to disclosure of the agreement.

(c) The agreement is in accordance with subdivisions (a), (b), and (d) of Section 1118, and the agreement is used to show fraud, duress, or illegality that is relevant to an issue in dispute. (*Added by Stats.1997, c. 772 (A.B.939), § 3.*)

§ 1125
End of mediation; satisfaction of conditions

(a) For purposes of confidentiality under this chapter, a mediation ends when any one of the following conditions is satisfied:

(1) The parties execute a written settlement agreement that fully resolves the dispute.

(2) An oral agreement that fully resolves the dispute is reached in accordance with Section 1118.

(3) The mediator provides the mediation participants with a writing signed by the mediator that states that the mediation is terminated, or words to that effect, which shall be consistent with Section 1121.

(4) A party provides the mediator and the other mediation participants with a writing stating that the mediation is terminated, or words to that effect, which shall be consistent with Section 1121. In a mediation involving more than two parties, the mediation may continue as to the remaining parties or be terminated in accordance with this section.

(5) For 10 calendar days, there is no communication between the mediator and any of the parties to the mediation relating to the dispute. The mediator and the parties may shorten or extend this time by agreement.

(b) For purposes of confidentiality under this chapter, if a mediation partially resolves a dispute, mediation ends when either of the following conditions is satisfied:

(1) The parties execute a written settlement agreement that partially resolves the dispute.

(2) An oral agreement that partially resolves the dispute is reached in accordance with Section 1118.

(c) This section does not preclude a party from ending a mediation without reaching an agreement. This section does not otherwise affect the extent to which a party may terminate a mediation. (*Added by Stats.1997, c. 772 (A.B.939), § 3.*)

§ 1126
Protections before and after mediation ends

Anything said, any admission made, or any writing that is inadmissible, protected from disclosure, and confidential under this chapter before a mediation ends, shall remain inadmissible, protected from disclosure, and confidential to the same extent after the mediation ends. (*Added by Stats.1997, c. 772 (A.B.939), § 3.*)

§ 1127
Attorney's fees and costs

If a person subpoenas or otherwise seeks to compel a mediator to testify or produce a writing, as defined in Section 250, and the court or other adjudicative body determines that the testimony or writing is inadmissible under this chapter, or protected from disclosure under this chapter, the court or adjudicative body making the determination shall award reasonable attorney's fees and costs to the mediator against the person seeking the testimony or writing. (*Added by Stats.1997, c. 772 (A.B.939), § 3.*)

§ 1128
Subsequent trials; references to mediation

Any reference to a mediation during any subsequent trial is an irregularity in the proceedings of the trial for the purposes of Section 657 of the Code of Civil Procedure. Any reference to a mediation during any other subsequent noncriminal proceeding is grounds for vacating or modifying the decision in that proceeding, in whole or in part, and granting a new or further hearing on all or part of the issues, if the reference materially affected the substantial rights of the party requesting relief. (*Added by Stats.1997, c. 772 (A.B.939), § 3.*)

CHAPTER 3. OTHER EVIDENCE AFFECTED OR EXCLUDED
BY EXTRINSIC POLICIES

Section

§ 1150
Evidence to test a verdict

(a) Upon an inquiry as to the validity of a verdict, any otherwise admissible evidence may be received as to statements made, or conduct, conditions, or events occurring, either within or without the jury room, of such a character as is likely to have influenced the verdict improperly. No evidence is admissible to show the effect of such statement, conduct, condition, or event upon a juror either in influencing him to assent to or dissent from the verdict or concerning the mental processes by which it was determined.

(b) Nothing in this code affects the law relating to the competence of a juror to give evidence to impeach or support a verdict. (*Stats.1965, c. 299, § 2, operative Jan. 1, 1967.*)

§ 1151
Subsequent remedial conduct

When, after the occurrence of an event, remedial or precautionary measures are taken, which, if taken previously, would have tended to make the event less likely to occur, evidence of such subsequent measures is inadmissible to prove negligence or culpable conduct in connection with the event. (*Stats.1965, c. 299, § 2, operative Jan. 1, 1967.*)

§ 1152
Offers to compromise

(a) Evidence that a person has, in compromise or from humanitarian motives, furnished or offered or promised to furnish money or any other thing, act, or service to another who has sustained or will sustain or claims that he or she has sustained or will sustain loss or damage, as well as any conduct or statements made in negotiation thereof, is inadmissible to prove his or her liability for the loss or damage or any part of it.

(b) In the event that evidence of an offer to compromise is admitted in an action for breach of the covenant of good faith and fair dealing or violation of subdivision (h) of Section 790.03 of the Insurance Code, then at the request of the party against whom the evidence is admitted, or at the request of the party who made the offer to compromise that was admitted, evidence relating to any other offer or counteroffer to compromise the same or substantially the same claimed loss or damage shall also be admissible for the same purpose as the initial evidence regarding settlement. Other than as may be admitted in an action for breach of the covenant of good faith and fair dealing or violation of subdivision (h) of Section 790.03 of the Insurance Code, evidence of settlement offers shall not be admitted in a motion for a new trial, in any proceeding involving an additur or remittitur, or on appeal.

(c) This section does not affect the admissibility of evidence of any of the following:

(1) Partial satisfaction of an asserted claim or demand without questioning its validity when such evidence is offered to prove the validity of the claim.

(2) A debtor's payment or promise to pay all or a part of his or her preexisting debt when such evidence is offered to prove the creation of a

new duty on his or her part or a revival of his or her preexisting duty. (*Stats.1965, c. 299, § 2, operative Jan. 1, 1967. Amended by Stats.1967, c. 650, p. 2007, § 7; Stats.1987, c. 496, § 1.*)

§ 1152.5
Repealed by Stats.1997, c. 772 (A.B.939), § 5

§ 1152.6
Repealed by Stats.1997, c. 772 (A.B.939), § 6

§ 1153
Offer to plead guilty or withdrawn plea of guilty by criminal defendant

Evidence of a plea of guilty, later withdrawn, or of an offer to plead guilty to the crime charged or to any other crime, made by the defendant in a criminal action is inadmissible in any action or in any proceeding of any nature, including proceedings before agencies, commissions, boards, and tribunals. (*Stats.1965, c. 299, § 2, operative Jan. 1, 1967.*)

§ 1153.5
Offer for civil resolution of crimes against property

Evidence of an offer for civil resolution of a criminal matter pursuant to the provisions of Section 33 of the Code of Civil Procedure, or admissions made in the course of or negotiations for the offer shall not be admissible in any action. (*Added by Stats.1982, c. 1518, p. 5890, § 2.*)

§ 1154
Offer to discount a claim

Evidence that a person has accepted or offered or promised to accept a sum of money or any other thing, act, or service in satisfaction of a claim, as well as any conduct or statements made in negotiation thereof, is inadmissible to prove the invalidity of the claim or any part of it. (*Stats.1965, c. 299, § 2, operative Jan. 1, 1967.*)

§ 1155
Liability insurance

Evidence that a person was, at the time a harm was suffered by another, insured wholly or partially against loss arising from liability for that harm is inadmissible to prove negligence or other wrongdoing. (*Stats.1965, c. 299, § 2, operative Jan. 1, 1967.*)

§ 1156
Records of medical or dental study of in–hospital staff committee

(a) In-hospital medical or medical-dental staff committees of a licensed hospital may engage in research and medical or dental study for the purpose of reducing morbidity or mortality, and may make findings and recommendations relating to such purpose. Except as provided in subdivision (b), the written records of interviews, reports, statements, or memoranda of such in-hospital medical or medical-dental staff committees relating to such medical or dental studies are subject to Title 4 (commencing with Section 2016.010) of Part 4 of the Code of Civil Procedure (relating to discovery proceedings) but, subject to subdivisions (c) and (d), shall not be admitted as evidence in any action or before any administrative body, agency, or person.

(b) The disclosure, with or without the consent of the patient, of information concerning him to such in-hospital medical or medical-dental staff committee does not make unprivileged any information that would otherwise be privileged under Section 994 or 1014; but, notwithstanding Sections 994 and 1014, such information is subject to discovery under subdivision (a) except that the identity of any patient may not be discovered under subdivision (a) unless the patient consents to such disclosure.

(c) This section does not affect the admissibility in evidence of the original medical or dental records of any patient.

(d) This section does not exclude evidence which is relevant evidence in a criminal action. (*Stats.1965, c. 299, § 2, operative Jan. 1, 1967. Amended by Stats.1975, c. 674, p. 1468, § 1; Stats.2004, c. 182 (A.B.3081), § 30, operative July 1, 2005.*)

§ 1156.1
Records of medical or psychiatric studies of quality assurance committees

(a) A committee established in compliance with Sections 4070 and 5624 of the Welfare and Institutions Code may engage in research and medical or psychiatric study for the purpose of reducing morbidity or mortality, and may make findings and recommendations to the county and state relating to such purpose. Except as provided in subdivision (b), the written records of interviews, reports, statements, or memoranda of such committees relating to such medical or psychiatric studies are subject to Title 4 (commencing with Section 2016.010) of Part 4 of the Code of Civil Procedure but, subject to subdivisions (c) and (d), shall not be admitted as evidence in any action or before any administrative body, agency, or person.

(b) The disclosure, with or without the consent of the patient, of information concerning him or her to such committee does not make unprivileged any information that would otherwise be privileged under Section 994 or 1014. However, notwithstanding Sections 994 and 1014, such information is subject to discovery under subdivision (a) except that the identity of any patient may not be discovered under subdivision (a) unless the patient consents to such disclosure.

(c) This section does not affect the admissibility in evidence of the original medical or psychiatric records of any patient.

(d) This section does not exclude evidence which is relevant evidence in a criminal action. (*Added by Stats.1982, c. 234, p. 767, § 4, eff. June 2, 1982. Amended by Stats.2004, c. 182 (A.B.3081), § 31, operative July 1, 2005.*)

§ 1157
Proceedings and records of organized committees having responsibility of evaluation and improvement of quality of care; exceptions

(a) Neither the proceedings nor the records of organized committees of medical, medical-dental, podiatric, registered dietitian, psychological, marriage and family therapist, licensed clinical social worker, professional clinical counselor, or veterinary staffs in hospitals, or of a peer review body, as defined in Section 805 of the Business and Professions Code, having the responsibility of evaluation and improvement of the quality of care rendered in the hospital, or for that peer review body, or medical or dental review or dental hygienist review or chiropractic review or podiatric review or registered dietitian review or veterinary review or acupuncturist review committees of local medical, dental, dental hygienist, podiatric, dietetic, veterinary, acupuncture, or chiropractic societies, marriage and family therapist, licensed clinical social worker, professional clinical counselor, or psychological review committees of state or local marriage and family therapist, state or local licensed clinical social worker, state or local licensed professional clinical counselor, or state or local psychological associations or societies having the responsibility of evaluation and improvement of the quality of care, shall be subject to discovery.

(b) Except as hereinafter provided, no person in attendance at a meeting of any of those committees shall be required to testify as to what transpired at that meeting.

(c) The prohibition relating to discovery or testimony does not apply to the statements made by any person in attendance at a meeting of any of those committees who is a party to an action or proceeding the subject matter of which was reviewed at that meeting, or to any person requesting hospital staff privileges, or in any action against an insurance carrier alleging bad faith by the carrier in refusing to accept a settlement offer within the policy limits.

(d) The prohibitions in this section do not apply to medical, dental, dental hygienist, podiatric, dietetic, psychological, marriage and family therapist, licensed clinical social worker, professional clinical counselor, veterinary, acupuncture, or chiropractic society committees that exceed 10 percent of the membership of the society, nor to any of those committees if any person serves upon the committee when his or her own conduct or practice is being reviewed.

(e) The amendments made to this section by Chapter 1081 of the Statutes of 1983, or at the 1985 portion of the 1985–86 Regular Session of the Legislature, at the 1990 portion of the 1989–90 Regular Session of the Legislature, at the 2000 portion of the 1999–2000 Regular Session of the Legislature, or at the 2011 portion of the 2011–12 Regular Session of the Legislature, do not exclude the discovery or use of relevant evidence in a criminal action. (*Added by Stats.1968, c. 1122, p. 2138, § 1. Amended by Stats.1975, c. 674, p. 1468, § 2; Stats.1978, c. 7, p. 62, § 1, eff. Feb. 10, 1978; Stats.1978, c. 503, p. 1648, § 2; Stats.1982, c. 705, p. 2864, § 3; Stats.1983, c. 289, § 3; Stats.1983, c. 422, § 1; Stats.1983, c. 1081, § 2.5; Stats.1985, c. 725, § 1; Stats.1990, c. 196 (A.B.1565), § 2; Stats.1994, c. 815 (S.B.1279), § 3; Stats.2000, c. 136 (A.B.2374), § 1; Stats.2011, c. 381 (S.B.146), § 23.*)

§ 1157.5
Organized committee of nonprofit medical care foundation or professional standards review organization; proceedings and records

Except in actions involving a claim of a provider of health care services for payment for such services, the prohibition relating to discovery or testimony provided by Section 1157 shall be applicable to the proceedings or records of an organized committee of any nonprofit medical care foundation or professional standards review organization which is organized in a manner which makes available professional competence to review health care services with respect to medical necessity, quality of care, or economic justification of charges or level of care. (*Added by Stats.1973, c. 848, p. 1515, § 1. Amended by Stats.1980, c. 524, p. 1461, § 1.*)

§ 1157.6
Proceedings and records of quality assurance committees for county health facilities

Neither the proceedings nor the records of a committee established in compliance with Sections 4070 and 5624 of the Welfare and Institutions Code having the responsibility of evaluation and improvement of the quality of mental health care rendered in county operated and contracted mental health facilities shall be subject to discovery. Except as provided in this section, no person in attendance at a meeting of any such committee shall be required to testify as to what transpired thereat. The prohibition relating to discovery or testimony shall not apply to the statements made by any person in attendance at such a meeting who is a party to an action or proceeding the subject matter of which was reviewed at such meeting, or to any person requesting facility staff privileges. (*Added by Stats.1982, c. 234, p. 767, § 5, eff. June 2, 1982.*)

§ 1157.7
Application of Section 1157 discovery or testimony prohibitions; application of public records and meetings provisions

The prohibition relating to discovery or testimony provided in Section 1157 shall be applicable to proceedings and records of any committee established by a local governmental agency to monitor, evaluate, and report on the necessity, quality, and level of specialty health services, including, but not limited to, trauma care services, provided by a general acute care hospital which has been designated or recognized by that governmental agency as qualified to render specialty health care services. The provisions of Chapter 3.5 (commencing with Section 6250) of Division 7 of Title 1 of the Government Code and Chapter 9 (commencing with Section 54950) of Division 2 of Title 5 of the Government Code shall not be applicable to the committee records and proceedings. (*Added by Stats.1983, c. 1237, § 1.*)

§ 1158
Inspection and copying of patient's records; authorization; failure to comply; costs

Whenever, prior to the filing of any action or the appearance of a defendant in an action, an attorney at law or his or her representative presents a written authorization therefor signed by an adult patient, by the guardian or conservator of his or her person or estate, or, in the case of a minor, by a parent or guardian of the minor, or by the personal representative or an heir of a deceased patient, or a copy thereof, a physician and surgeon, dentist, registered nurse, dispensing optician, registered physical therapist, podiatrist, licensed psychologist, osteopathic physician and surgeon, chiropractor, clinical laboratory bioanalyst, clinical laboratory technologist, or pharmacist or pharmacy, duly licensed as such under the laws of the state, or a licensed hospital, shall make all of the patient's records under his, hers or its custody or control available for inspection and copying by the attorney at law or his, or her, representative, promptly upon the presentation of the written authorization.

No copying may be performed by any medical provider or employer enumerated above, or by an agent thereof, when the requesting attorney has employed a professional photocopier or anyone identified in Section 22451 of the Business and Professions Code as his or her representative to obtain or review the records on his or her behalf. The presentation of the authorization by the agent on behalf of the attorney shall be sufficient proof that the agent is the attorney's representative.

Failure to make the records available, during business hours, within five days after the presentation of the written authorization, may subject the person or entity having custody or control of the records to liability for all reasonable expenses, including attorney's fees, incurred in any proceeding to enforce this section.

All reasonable costs incurred by any person or entity enumerated above in making patient records available pursuant to this section may be charged against the person whose written authorization required the availability of the records.

"Reasonable cost," as used in this section, shall include, but not be limited to, the following specific costs: ten cents ($0.10) per page for standard reproduction of documents of a size 8½ by 14 inches or less; twenty cents ($0.20) per page for copying of documents from microfilm; actual costs for the reproduction of oversize documents or the reproduction of documents requiring special processing which are made in response to an authorization; reasonable clerical costs incurred in locating and making the records available to be billed at the maximum rate of sixteen dollars ($16) per hour per person, computed on the basis of four dollars ($4) per quarter hour or fraction thereof; actual postage charges; and actual costs, if any, charged to the witness by a third person for the retrieval and return of records held by that third person.

Where the records are delivered to the attorney or the attorney's representative for inspection or photocopying at the record custodian's place of business, the only fee for complying with the authorization shall not exceed fifteen dollars ($15), plus actual costs, if any, charged to the record custodian by a third person for retrieval and return of records held offsite by the third person. *(Added by Stats.1968, c. 1122, p. 2138, § 2. Amended by Stats.1970, c. 556, p. 1077, § 1; Stats.1974, c. 250, p. 461, § 1; Stats.1974, c. 667, p. 1530, § 1; Stats.1975, c. 563, p. 1144, § 1; Stats.1978, c. 493, p. 1625, § 1; Stats.1980, c. 697, p. 2099, § 1; Stats.1986, c. 603, § 5; Stats.1987, c. 19, § 1, eff. May 12, 1987; Stats.1993, c. 226 (A.B.1987), § 9; Stats.1997, c. 442 (A.B.758), § 15.)*

§ 1159
Animal experimentation in product liability actions

(a) No evidence pertaining to live animal experimentation, including, but not limited to, injury, impact, or crash experimentation, shall be admissible in any product liability action involving a motor vehicle or vehicles.

(b) This section shall apply to cases for which a trial has not actually commenced, as described in paragraph (6) of subdivision (a) of Section 581 of the Code of Civil Procedure, on January 1, 1993. *(Added by Stats.1992, c. 188 (A.B.3691), § 1.)*

§ 1160
Admissibility of expressions of sympathy or benevolence; definitions

(a) The portion of statements, writings, or benevolent gestures expressing sympathy or a general sense of benevolence relating to the pain, suffering, or death of a person involved in an accident and made to that person or to the family of that person shall be inadmissible as evidence of an admission of liability in a civil action. A statement of fault, however, which is part of, or in addition to, any of the above shall not be inadmissible pursuant to this section.

(b) For purposes of this section:

(1) "Accident" means an occurrence resulting in injury or death to one or more persons which is not the result of willful action by a party.

(2) "Benevolent gestures" means actions which convey a sense of compassion or commiseration emanating from humane impulses.

(3) "Family" means the spouse, parent, grandparent, stepmother, stepfather, child, grandchild, brother, sister, half brother, half sister, adopted children of parent, or spouse's parents of an injured party.

(Added by Stats.2000, c. 195 (A.B.2804), § 1.)

§ 1161
Human trafficking; admissibility of evidence of engagement in commercial sexual act by victim or sexual history of victim

Section operative if Initiative Measure (Prop. 35) is approved at the Nov. 6, 2012 election; see Preface for election results (for electronic publications, see Evidence Code Refs & Annos).

(a) Evidence that a victim of human trafficking, as defined in Section 236.1 of the Penal Code, has engaged in any commercial sexual act as a result of being a victim of human trafficking is inadmissible to prove the victim's criminal liability for any conduct related to that activity.

(b) Evidence of sexual history or history of any commercial sexual act of a victim of human trafficking, as defined in Section 236.1 of the Penal Code, is inadmissible to attack the credibility or impeach the character of the victim in any civil or criminal proceeding. (*Added by Initiative Measure (Prop. 35, § 4, operative if approved at the Nov. 6, 2012 election).*)

Division 10

HEARSAY EVIDENCE

Chapter 1. GENERAL PROVISIONS

In some situations, hearsay evidence is admitted because there is either some exceptional need for the evidence or some circumstantial probability of its truthworthiness, or both. People v. Brust, 47 Cal.2d 776, 785, 306 P.2d 480, 484 (1957); Turney v. Sousa, 146 Cal.App.2d 787, 791, 304 P.2d 1025, 1027–1028 (1956). Even though it may be necessary or desirable to permit certain hearsay evidence to be admitted despite the fact that the adverse party had no opportunity to cross-examine the declarant when the hearsay statement was made, there seems to be no reason to prohibit the adverse party from cross-examining the declarant concerning the statement. The policy in favor of cross-examination that underlies the hearsay rule, therefore, indicates that the adverse party should be accorded the right to call the declarant of a statement received in evidence and to cross-examine him concerning his statement.

Section 1203, therefore, reverses (insofar as a hearsay declarant is concerned) the traditional rule that a witness called by a party is a witness for that party and may not be cross-examined by him. Because a hearsay declarant is in practical effect a witness against the party against whom his hearsay statement is admitted, Section 1203 gives that party the right to call and cross-examine the hearsay declarant concerning the subject matter of the hearsay statement just as he has the right to cross-examine the witnesses who appear personally and testify against him at the trial.

Subdivisions (b) and (c) make Section 1203 inapplicable in certain situations where it would be inappropriate to permit a party to examine a hearsay declarant as if under cross-examination. Thus, for example, subdivision (b) does not permit counsel for a party to examine his own client as if under cross-examination merely because a hearsay statement of his client has been admitted; and, because a party should not have the right to cross-examine his own witness merely because the adverse party has introduced a hearsay statement of the witness, witnesses who have testified in the action concerning the subject matter of the statement are not subject to examination under Section 1203.

Subdivision (d) makes it clear that the unavailability of a hearsay declarant for examination under Section 1203 has no effect on the admissibility of his hearsay statements. The subdivision forestalls any argument that availability of the declarant for examination under Section 1203 is an additional condition of admissibility for hearsay evidence.

§ 1203.1
Hearsay offered at preliminary examination; application of § 1203

Section 1203 is not applicable if the hearsay statement is offered at a preliminary examination, as provided in Section 872 of the Penal Code. (*Added by Initiative Measure (Prop. 115), approved June 5, 1990, eff. June 6, 1990.*)

§ 1200
The hearsay rule

(a) "Hearsay evidence" is evidence of a statement that was made other than by a witness while testifying at the hearing and that is offered to prove the truth of the matter stated.

(b) Except as provided by law, hearsay evidence is inadmissible.

(c) This section shall be known and may be cited as the hearsay rule. (*Stats.1965, c. 299, § 2, operative Jan. 1, 1967.*)

Section 1200 states the hearsay rule. It defines hearsay evidence and provides that such evidence is inadmissible unless it meets the conditions of an exception established by law. Chapter 2 (commencing with Section 1220) of this division contains a series of exceptions to the hearsay rule. Other exceptions may be found in other statutes or in decisional law. But the fact that certain evidence meets the requirements of an exception to the hearsay rule does not necessarily make such evidence admissible. The exception merely provides that such evidence is not inadmissible under the hearsay rule. If there is some other rule of law—such as privilege or the best evidence rule—that makes the evidence inadmissible, the court is not authorized to admit the evidence merely because it falls within an exception to the hearsay rule. See also Evidence Code § 352.

Although the California courts have excluded hearsay evidence since the earliest days of the State (see, *e.g.,* People v. Bob, 29 Cal.2d 321, 175 P.2d 12 (1946) (1946); Kilburn v. Ritchie, 2 Cal. 145 (1852)), the hearsay rule has never been clearly stated in statutory form. Code of Civil Procedure Section 1845 (superseded by Evidence Code Section 702) has at times been considered to be the statutory basis for the hearsay rule. People v. Spriggs, 60 Cal.2d 868, 872, 36 Cal.Rptr. 841, 844, 389 P.2d 377, 380 (1964). Analytically, however, Section 1845 does not deal with hearsay at all; it deals only with the requirement of personal knowledge. It is true that the section provides that there is an exception to the personal knowledge requirement "in those few express cases in which ' ' ' the declarations of others, are admissible"; but "this section is inaccurate, so far as it refers to [this] exception. In such case the witness testifies merely to the making of the declaration, which he must have heard in order to be a competent witness to testify to it, and hence, the fact to which he testifies is a fact within his own knowledge, derived from his own perceptions." Sneed v. Marysville Gas etc. Co., 149 Cal. 704, 708, 87 Pac. 376, 378 (1906).

"Hearsay evidence" is defined in Section 1200 as "evidence of a statement that was made other than by a witness while testifying at the hearing and that is offered to prove the truth of the matter stated." Under this definition, as under existing case law, a statement that is offered for some purpose other than to prove the fact stated therein is not hearsay. Smith v. Whittier, 95 Cal. 279, 30 Pac. 529 (1892). See Witkin, California Evidence §§ 215–218 (1958).

The word "statement" used in the definition of "hearsay evidence" is defined in Section 225 as "oral or written verbal expression" or "nonverbal conduct . . . intended . . . as a substitute for oral or written verbal expression." Hence, evidence of a person's conduct out of court is not inadmissible under the hearsay rule expressed in Section 1200 unless that conduct is clearly assertive in character. Nonassertive conduct is not hearsay.

Some California cases have regarded evidence of nonassertive conduct as hearsay evidence if it is offered to prove the actor's belief in a particular fact as a basis for an inference that the fact believed is true. See, *e.g.,* Estate of De Laveaga, 165 Cal. 607, 624, 133 Pac. 307, 314 (1913) ("the manner in which a person whose sanity is in question was treated by his family is not, taken alone, competent substantive evidence tending to prove insanity, for it is a mere extra-judicial expression of opinion on the part of the family"); People v. Mendez, 193 Cal. 39, 52, 223 Pac. 65, 70 (1924) ("circumstances of flight [of other persons from the scene of a crime] are in the nature of confessions ′ ′ ′ and are, therefore, in the nature of hearsay evidence") (overruled on other grounds in People v. McCaughan, 49 Cal.2d 409, 420, 317 P.2d 974, 981 (1957)).

Other California cases, however, have held that evidence of nonassertive conduct is not hearsay even though offered to prove that the belief giving rise to the conduct was based on fact. See, *e.g.,* People v. Reifenstuhl, 37 Cal.App.2d 402, 99 P.2d 564 (1940) (hearing denied) (incoming telephone calls made for the purpose of placing bets admissible over hearsay objection to prove that place of reception was bookmaking establishment).

Under the Evidence Code, nonassertive conduct is not regarded as hearsay for two reasons. *First,* one of the principal reasons for the hearsay rule—to exclude declarations where the veracity of the declarant cannot be tested by cross-examination—does not apply because such conduct, being nonassertive, does not involve the veracity of the declarant. *Second,* there is frequently a guarantee of the trustworthiness of the inference to be drawn from such nonassertive conduct because the actor has based his actions on the correctness of his belief, *i.e.,* his actions speak louder than words.

Of course, if the probative value of evidence of nonassertive conduct is outweighed by the probability that such evidence will be unduly prejudicial, confuse the issues, mislead the jury, or consume too much time, the judge may exclude the evidence under Section 352.

Under Section 1200, exceptions to the hearsay rule may be found either in statutes or in decisional law. Under existing law, too, the courts have recognized exceptions to the exclusionary rule in addition to those exceptions expressed in the statutes. See People v. Spriggs, 60 Cal.2d 868, 874, 36 Cal.Rptr. 841, 844, 389 P.2d 377, 380 (1964).

§ 1201
Multiple hearsay

A statement within the scope of an exception to the hearsay rule is not inadmissible on the ground that the evidence of such statement is hearsay evidence if such hearsay evidence consists of one or more statements each of which meets the requirements of an exception to the hearsay rule. (*Stats.1965, c. 299, § 2, operative Jan. 1, 1967. Amended by Stats.1967, c. 650, p. 2007, § 8.*)

§ 1202
Credibility of hearsay declarant

Evidence of a statement or other conduct by a declarant that is inconsistent with a statement by such declarant received in evidence as hearsay evidence is not inadmissible for the purpose of attacking the credibility of the declarant though he is not given and has not had an opportunity to explain or to deny such inconsistent statement or other conduct. Any other evidence offered to attack or support the credibility of the declarant is admissible if it would have been admissible had the declarant been a witness at the hearing. For the purposes of this section, the deponent of a deposition taken in the action in which it is offered shall be deemed to be a hearsay declarant. (*Stats.1965, c. 299, § 2, operative Jan. 1, 1967.*)

§ 1203
Cross-examination of hearsay declarant

(a) The declarant of a statement that is admitted as hearsay evidence may be called and examined by any adverse party as if under cross-examination concerning the statement.

(b) This section is not applicable if the declarant is (1) a party, (2) a person identified with a party within the meaning of subdivision (d) of Section 776, or (3) a witness who has testified in the action concerning the subject matter of the statement.

(c) This section is not applicable if the statement is one described in Article 1 (commencing with Section 1220), Article 3 (commencing with Section 1235), or Article 10 (commencing with Section 1300) of Chapter 2 of this division.

(d) A statement that is otherwise admissible as hearsay evidence is not made inadmissible by this section because the declarant who made the statement is unavailable for examination pursuant to this section. (*Stats.1965, c. 299, § 2, operative Jan. 1, 1967.*)

Hearsay evidence is generally excluded because the declarant was not in court and not subject to cross-examination before the trier of fact when he made the statement. People v. Bob, 29 Cal.2d 321, 325, 175 P.2d 12, 15 (1946).

§ 1204
Hearsay statement offered against criminal defendant

A statement that is otherwise admissible as hearsay evidence is inadmissible against the defendant in a criminal action if the statement was made, either by the defendant or by another, under such circumstances that it is inadmissible against the defendant under the Constitution of the United States or the State of California. (*Stats.1965, c. 299, § 2, operative Jan. 1, 1967.*)

Section 1204 is a statutory recognition that hearsay evidence that fits within an exception to the hearsay rule may nonetheless be inadmissible under the Constitution of the United States or the Constitution of California. Thus, Section 1220, which creates an exception for the statements of a party, is subject to the constitutional rule excluding evidence of involuntary confessions against a criminal defendant.

In People v. Underwood, 61 Cal.2d 113, 37 Cal.Rptr. 313, 389 P.2d 937 (1964), the California Supreme Court held that a prior inconsistent statement of a witness could not be introduced to impeach him in a criminal action when the statement would have been inadmissible as an involuntary confession if the witness had been the defendant. To the extent that the Underwood decision is based on constitutional principles, its effect is continued by Section 1204 and its principle is made applicable to all hearsay statements.

Insofar as the Constitution of the United States is concerned, Section 1204 refers only to those rules required to be observed in state proceedings. It is not intended to make applicable in proceedings in California courts those rules the United States Constitution requires to be observed only in federal proceedings.

§ 1205

No implied repeal

Nothing in this division shall be construed to repeal by implication any other statute relating to hearsay evidence. (*Stats.1965, c. 299, § 2, operative Jan. 1, 1967.*)

Chapter 2. EXCEPTIONS TO THE HEARSAY RULE

ARTICLE 1. CONFESSIONS AND ADMISSIONS

Section

1220. Admission of party.
1221. Adoptive admission.
1222. Authorized admission.
1223. Admission of co-conspirator.
1224. Statement of declarant whose liability or breach of duty is in issue.
1225. Statement of declarant whose right or title is in issue.
1226. Statement of minor child in parent's action for child's injury.
1227. Statement of declarant in action for his wrongful death.
1228. Admissibility of certain out-of-court statements of minors under the age of 12; establishing elements of certain sexually oriented crimes; notice to defendant.
1228.1. Signature of parent or guardian on child welfare services case plan; acceptance of services; use in court of law; failure to cooperate.

§ 1220
Admission of party

Evidence of a statement is not made inadmissible by the hearsay rule when offered against the declarant in an action to which he is a party in either his individual or representative capacity, regardless of whether the statement was made in his individual or representative capacity. (*Stats.1965, c. 299, § 2, operative Jan. 1, 1967.*)

§ 1221
Adoptive admission

Evidence of a statement offered against a party is not made inadmissible by the hearsay rule if the statement is one of which the party, with knowledge of the content thereof, has by words or other conduct manifested his adoption or his belief in its truth. (*Stats.1965, c. 299, § 2, operative Jan. 1, 1967.*)

§ 1222
Authorized admission

Evidence of a statement offered against a party is not made inadmissible by the hearsay rule if:

(a) The statement was made by a person authorized by the party to make a statement or statements for him concerning the subject matter of the statement; and

(b) The evidence is offered either after admission of evidence sufficient to sustain a finding of such authority or, in the court's discretion as to the order of proof, subject to the admission of such evidence. (*Stats.1965, c. 299, § 2, operative Jan. 1, 1967.*)

§ 1223
Admission of co-conspirator

Evidence of a statement offered against a party is not made inadmissible by the hearsay rule if:

(a) The statement was made by the declarant while participating in a conspiracy to commit a crime or civil wrong and in furtherance of the objective of that conspiracy;

(b) The statement was made prior to or during the time that the party was participating in that conspiracy; and

(c) The evidence is offered either after admission of evidence sufficient to sustain a finding of the facts specified in subdivisions (a) and (b) or, in the court's discretion as to the order of proof, subject to the admission of such evidence. (*Stats.1965, c. 299, § 2, operative Jan. 1, 1967.*)

§ 1224
Statement of declarant whose liability or breach of duty is in issue

When the liability, obligation, or duty of a party to a civil action is based in whole or in part upon the liability, obligation, or duty of the declarant, or when the claim or right asserted by a party to a civil action is barred or diminished by a breach of duty by the declarant, evidence of a statement made by the declarant is as admissible against the party as it would be if offered against the declarant in an action involving that liability, obligation, duty, or breach of duty. (*Stats.1965, c. 299, § 2, operative Jan. 1, 1967.*)

§ 1225
Statement of declarant whose right or title is in issue

When a right, title, or interest in any property or claim asserted by a party to a civil action requires a determination that a right, title, or interest exists or existed in the declarant, evidence of a statement made by the declarant during the time the party now claims the declarant was the holder of the right, title, or interest is as admissible against the party as it would be if offered against the declarant in an action involving that right, title, or interest. (*Stats.1965, c. 299, § 2, operative Jan. 1, 1967.*)

§ 1226
Statement of minor child in parent's action for child's injury

Evidence of a statement by a minor child is not made inadmissible by the hearsay rule if offered against the plaintiff in an action brought under Section 376 of the Code of Civil Procedure for injury to such minor child. (*Stats.1965, c. 299, § 2, operative Jan. 1, 1967.*)

§ 1227
Statement of declarant in action for his wrongful death

Evidence of a statement by the deceased is not made inadmissible by the hearsay rule if offered against the plaintiff in an action for wrongful death brought under Section 377 of the Code of Civil Procedure. (*Stats.1965, c. 299, § 2, operative Jan. 1, 1967.*)

§ 1228
Admissibility of certain out-of-court statements of minors under the age of 12; establishing elements of certain sexually oriented crimes; notice to defendant

Notwithstanding any other provision of law, for the purpose of establishing the elements of the crime in order to admit as evidence the confession of a person accused of violating Section 261, 264.1, 285, 286, 288, 288a, 289, or 647a of the Penal Code, a court, in its discretion, may determine that a statement of the complaining witness is not made inadmissible by the hearsay rule if it finds all of the following:

(a) The statement was made by a minor child under the age of 12, and the contents of the statement were included in a written report of a law enforcement official or an employee of a county welfare department.

(b) The statement describes the minor child as a victim of sexual abuse.

(c) The statement was made prior to the defendant's confession. The court shall view with caution the testimony of a person recounting hearsay where there is evidence of personal bias or prejudice.

(d) There are no circumstances, such as significant inconsistencies between the confession and the statement concerning material facts establishing any element of the crime or the identification of the defendant, that would render the statement unreliable.

(e) The minor child is found to be unavailable pursuant to paragraph (2) or (3) of subdivision (a) of Section 240 or refuses to testify.

(f) The confession was memorialized in a trustworthy fashion by a law enforcement official.

If the prosecution intends to offer a statement of the complaining witness pursuant to this section, the prosecution shall serve a written notice upon the defendant at least 10 days prior to the hearing or trial at which the prosecution intends to offer the statement.

If the statement is offered during trial, the court's determination shall be made out of the presence of the jury. If the statement is found to be admissible pursuant to this section, it shall be admitted out of the presence of the jury and solely for the purpose of determining the admissibility of the confession of the defendant. (*Added by Stats.1984, c. 1421, § 1. Amended by Stats.1985, c. 1572, § 1, eff. Oct. 2, 1985.*)

§ 1228.1
Signature of parent or guardian on child welfare services case plan; acceptance of services; use in court of law; failure to cooperate

(a) Except as provided in subdivision (b), neither the signature of any parent or legal guardian on a child welfare services case plan nor the acceptance of any services prescribed in the child welfare services case plan by any parent or legal guardian shall constitute an admission of guilt or be used as evidence against the parent or legal guardian in a court of law.

(b) A parent's or guardian's failure to cooperate, except for good cause, in the provision of services specified in the child welfare services case plan may be used as evidence, if relevant, in any hearing held pursuant to Section 366.21, 366.22, or 388 of the Welfare and Institutions Code and at any jurisdictional or dispositional hearing held on a petition filed pursuant to Section 300, 342, or 387 of the Welfare and Institutions Code. (*Added by Stats.1995, c. 540 (A.B.1523), § 1. Amended by Stats.1997, c. 793 (A.B.1544), § 1.*)

ARTICLE 2. DECLARATIONS AGAINST INTEREST

Section
1230. Declarations against interest.

§ 1230
Declarations against interest

Evidence of a statement by a declarant having sufficient knowledge of the subject is not made inadmissible by the hearsay rule if the declarant is unavailable as a witness and the statement, when made, was so far contrary to the declarant's pecuniary or proprietary interest, or so far subjected him to the risk of civil or criminal liability, or so far tended to render invalid a claim by him against another, or created such a risk of making him an object of hatred, ridicule, or social disgrace in the community, that a reasonable man in his position would not have made the statement unless he believed it to be true. (*Stats.1965, c. 299, § 2, operative Jan. 1, 1967.*)

Except for the requirement that the declarant be shown to be unavailable as a witness, Section 1230 codifies the hearsay exception for declarations against interest as that exception has been developed by the California courts (People v. Spriggs, 60 Cal.2d 868, 36 Cal.Rptr. 841, 389 P.2d 377 (1964)) and possibly expends the exception. It is not clear whether the existing exception for declarations against interest applies to statements that make the declarant an object of hatred, ridicule, or social disgrace in the community.

Under existing law, a declaration against interest is admissible regardless of the availability of the declarant to testify as a witness. People v. Spriggs, 60 Cal.2d 868, 36 Cal.Rptr. 841, 389 P.2d 377 (1964). Section 1230, however, conditions admissibility upon the unavailability of the declarant in order to require the proponent of the evidence to use the in-court testimony of the declarant if it is possible to do so. If the declarant disappoints the proponent and testifies inconsistently, the proponent may then show the prior inconsistent statement as substantive evidence of the facts stated. See Evidence Code § 1235 and the Comment thereto.

Section 1230 supersedes the partial and inaccurate statements of the exception for declarations against interest found in Code of Civil Procedure Sections 1853, 1870(4), and 1946(1). See People v. Spriggs, 60 Cal.2d 868, 871–872, 36 Cal.Rptr. 841, 844–845, 389 P.2d 377, 380–381 (1964). The requirement that the declarant have "sufficient knowledge of the subject" continues the similar common law requirement stated in Code of Civil Procedure Section 1853 that the declarant must have had some peculiar means—such as personal observation—for obtaining accurate knowledge of the matter stated. See 5 Wigmore, Evidence § 1471 (3d ed. 1940).

ARTICLE 2.5. SWORN STATEMENTS REGARDING GANG– RELATED CRIMES

Section

1231. Prior statements of deceased declarant; hearsay exception.
1231.1. Statements made by deceased declarant; admissibility; notice of statement to adverse party.
1231.2. Administer and certify oaths.
1231.3. Testimony of law enforcement officer; hearsay.
1231.4. Cause of death; deceased declarant.

§ 1231
Prior statements of deceased declarant; hearsay exception

Evidence of a prior statement made by a declarant is not made inadmissible by the hearsay rule if the declarant is deceased and the proponent of introducing the statement establishes each of the following:

(a) The statement relates to acts or events relevant to a criminal prosecution under provisions of the California Street Terrorism Enforcement and Prevention Act (Chapter 11 (commencing with Section 186.20) of Title 7 of Part 1 of the Penal Code).

(b) A verbatim transcript, copy, or record of the statement exists. A record may include a statement preserved by means of an audio or video recording or equivalent technology.

(c) The statement relates to acts or events within the personal knowledge of the declarant.

(d) The statement was made under oath or affirmation in an affidavit; or was made at a deposition, preliminary hearing, grand jury hearing, or other proceeding in compliance with law, and was made under penalty of perjury.

(e) The declarant died from other than natural causes.

(f) The statement was made under circumstances that would indicate its trustworthiness and render the declarant's statement particularly worthy of belief. For purposes of this subdivision, circumstances relevant to the issue of trustworthiness include, but are not limited to, all of the following:

(1) Whether the statement was made in contemplation of a pending or anticipated criminal or civil matter, in which the declarant had an interest, other than as a witness.

(2) Whether the declarant had a bias or motive for fabricating the statement, and the extent of any bias or motive.

(3) Whether the statement is corroborated by evidence other than statements that are admissible only pursuant to this section.

(4) Whether the statement was a statement against the declarant's interest. (*Added by Stats.1997, c. 499 (S.B.941), § 1.*)

§ 1231.1
Statements made by deceased declarant; admissibility; notice of statement to adverse party

A statement is admissible pursuant to Section 1231 only if the proponent of the statement makes known to the adverse party the intention to offer the statement and the particulars of the statement sufficiently in advance of the proceedings to provide the adverse party with a fair opportunity to prepare to meet the statement. (*Added by Stats.1997, c. 499 (S.B.941), § 1.*)

§ 1231.2
Administer and certify oaths

A peace officer may administer and certify oaths for purposes of this article. (Added by Stats.1997, c. 499 (S.B.941), § 1. Amended by Stats.1998, c. 606 (S.B.1880), § 2.)

§ 1231.3
Testimony of law enforcement officer; hearsay

Any law enforcement officer testifying as to any hearsay statement pursuant to this article shall either have five years of law enforcement experience or have completed a training course certified by the Commission on Peace Officer Standards and Training which includes training in the investigation and reporting of cases and testifying at preliminary hearings and trials. (*Added by Stats.1997, c. 499 (S.B.941), § 1.*)

§ 1231.4
Cause of death; deceased declarant

If evidence of a prior statement is introduced pursuant to this article, the jury may not be told that the declarant died from other than natural causes, but shall merely be told that the declarant is unavailable. (*Added by Stats.1997, c. 499 (S.B.941), § 1.*)

ARTICLE 3. PRIOR STATEMENTS OF WITNESSES

Section
1235. Inconsistent statements.
1236. Prior consistent statements.
1237. Past recollection recorded.
1238. Prior identification.

§ 1235
Inconsistent statements

Evidence of a statement made by a witness is not made inadmissible by the hearsay rule if the statement is inconsistent with his testimony at the hearing and is offered in compliance with Section 770. (*Stats.1965, c. 299, § 2, operative Jan. 1, 1967.*)

§ 1236
Prior consistent statements

Evidence of a statement previously made by a witness is not made inadmissible by the hearsay rule if the statement is consistent with his testimony at the hearing and is offered in compliance with Section 791. (*Stats.1965, c. 299, § 2, operative Jan. 1, 1967.*)

§ 1237
Past recollection recorded

(a) Evidence of a statement previously made by a witness is not made inadmissible by the hearsay rule if the statement would have been admissible if made by him while testifying, the statement concerns a matter as to which the witness has insufficient present recollection to enable him to testify fully and accurately, and the statement is contained in a writing which:

(1) Was made at a time when the fact recorded in the writing actually occurred or was fresh in the witness§ memory;

(2) Was made (i) by the witness himself or under his direction or (ii) by some other person for the purpose of recording the witness§ statement at the time it was made;

(3) Is offered after the witness testifies that the statement he made was a true statement of such fact; and

(4) Is offered after the writing is authenticated as an accurate record of the statement.

(b) The writing may be read into evidence, but the writing itself may not be received in evidence unless offered by an adverse party. (*Stats.1965, c. 299, § 2, operative Jan. 1, 1967.*)

Section 1237 provides a hearsay exception for what is usually referred to as "past recollection recorded." Although the provisions of Section 1237 are taken largely from the provisions of Section 2047 of the Code of Civil Procedure, there are some substantive differences between Section 1237 and existing law.

The existing law requires that a foundation be laid for the admission of such evidence by showing (1) that the writing recording the statement was made by the witness or under his direction, (2) that the writing was made at the time when the fact recorded in the writing actually occurred or at another time when the fact was fresh in the witness§ memory, and (3) that the witness "knew that the same was correctly stated in the writing." Under Section 1237, however, the writing may be made not only by the witness himself or under his direction but also by some other person for the purpose of recording the witness§ statement at the time it was made. In addition, Section 1237 permits testimony of the person who recorded the statement to be used to establish that the writing is a correct record of the statement. Sufficient assurance of the trustworthiness of the statement is provided if the declarant is available to testify that he made a true statement and if the person who recorded the statement is available to testify that he accurately recorded the statement.

Under subdivision (b), as under existing law, the statement is read into evidence but may not itself be introduced in evidence by its proponent. See Anderson v. Souza, 38 Cal.2d 825, 243 P.2d 497 (1952). The adverse party, however, may introduce the writing as evidence. *Cf.* Horowitz v. Fitch, 216 Cal.App.2d 303, 30 Cal.Rptr. 882 (1963) (dictum).

§ 1238
Prior identification

Evidence of a statement previously made by a witness is not made inadmissible by the hearsay rule if the statement would have been admissible if made by him while testifying and:

(a) The statement is an identification of a party or another as a person who participated in a crime or other occurrence;

(b) The statement was made at a time when the crime or other occurrence was fresh in the witness§ memory; and

(c) The evidence of the statement is offered after the witness testifies that he made the identification and that it was a true reflection of his opinion at that time. (*Stats.1965, c. 299, § 2, operative Jan. 1, 1967.*)

ARTICLE 4. SPONTANEOUS, CONTEMPORANEOUS, AND DYING DECLARATIONS

Section
1240. Spontaneous statement.
1241. Contemporaneous statement.
1242. Dying declaration.

§ 1240
Spontaneous statement

Evidence of a statement is not made inadmissible by the hearsay rule if the statement:

(a) Purports to narrate, describe, or explain an act, condition, or event perceived by the declarant; and

(b) Was made spontaneously while the declarant was under the stress of excitement caused by such perception. (*Stats.1965, c. 299, § 2, operative Jan. 1, 1967.*)

§ 1241
Contemporaneous statement

Evidence of a statement is not made inadmissible by the hearsay rule if the statement:

(a) Is offered to explain, qualify, or make understandable conduct of the declarant; and

(b) Was made while the declarant was engaged in such conduct. (*Stats.1965, c. 299, § 2, operative Jan. 1, 1967.*)

Under existing law, where a person's conduct or act is relevant but is equivocal or ambiguous, the statements accompanying it may be admitted to explain and make the conduct or act understandable. Code Civ.Proc. § 1850 (superseded by Evidence Code § 1241); Witkin, California Evidence § 216 (1958). Some writers do not regard evidence of this sort as hearsay evidence, but the definition in Section 1200 seems applicable to many of the statements received under this exception. *Cf.* 6 Wigmore, Evidence § 1772 et seq. (1940). Section 1241 removes any doubt that might otherwise exist concerning the admissibility of such evidence under the hearsay rule.

§ 1242
Dying declaration

Evidence of a statement made by a dying person respecting the cause and circumstances of his death is not made inadmissible by the hearsay rule if the statement was made upon his personal knowledge and under a sense of immediately impending death. (*Stats.1965, c. 299, § 2, operative Jan. 1, 1967.*)

ARTICLE 5. STATEMENTS OF MENTAL OR PHYSICAL STATE

Section
1250. Statement of declarant's then existing mental or physical state.
1251. Statement of declarant's previously existing mental or physical state.
1252. Restriction on admissibility of statement of mental or physical state.
1253. Statements for purposes of medical diagnosis or treatment; contents of statement; child abuse or neglect; age limitations.

§ 1250
Statement of declarant's then existing mental or physical state

(a) Subject to Section 1252, evidence of a statement of the declarant's then existing state of mind, emotion, or physical sensation (including a statement of intent, plan, motive, design, mental feeling, pain, or bodily health) is not made inadmissible by the hearsay rule when:

(1) The evidence is offered to prove the declarant's state of mind, emotion, or physical sensation at that time or at any other time when it is itself an issue in the action; or

(2) The evidence is offered to prove or explain acts or conduct of the declarant.

(b) This section does not make admissible evidence of a statement of memory or belief to prove the fact remembered or believed. (*Stats.1965, c. 299, § 2, operative Jan. 1, 1967.*)

Section 1250 provides an exception to the hearsay rule for statements of the declarant's *then* existing mental or physical state. Under Section 1250, as under existing law, a statement of the declarant's state of mind at the time of the statement is admissible when the then existing state of mind is itself an issue in the case. Adkins v. Brett, 184 Cal. 252, 193 Pac. 251 (1920). A statement of the declarant's then existing state of mind is also admissible when relevant to show the declarant's state of mind at a time prior or subsequent to the statement. Watenpaugh v. State Teachers§ Retirement System, 51 Cal.2d 675, 336 P.2d 165 (1959); Whitlow v. Durst, 20 Cal.2d 523, 127 P.2d 530 (1942); Estate of Anderson, 185 Cal. 700, 198 Pac. 407 (1921); Williams v. Kidd, 170 Cal. 631, 151 Pac. 1 (1915). Section 1250 also makes a statement of then existing state of mind admissible to "prove or explain acts or conduct of the declarant." Thus, a statement of the declarant's intent to do certain acts is admissible to prove that he did those acts. People v. Alcalde, 24 Cal.2d 177, 148 P.2d 627 (1944); Benjamin v. District Grand Lodge No. 4, 171 Cal. 260, 152 Pac. 731 (1915). Statements of then existing pain or other bodily condition also are admissible to prove the existence of such condition. Bloomberg v. Laventhal, 179 Cal. 616, 178 Pac. 496 (1919); People v. Wright, 167 Cal. 1, 138 Pac. 349 (1914).

A statement is not admissible under Section 1250 if the statement was made under circumstances indicating that the statement is not trustworthy. See Evidence Code § 1252 and the Comment thereto.

In light of the definition of "hearsay evidence" in Section 1200, a distinction should be noted between the use of a declarant's statements of his then existing mental state to prove such mental state and the use of a declarant's statements of other facts as circumstantial evidence of his mental state. Under the Evidence Code, no hearsay problem is involved if the declarant's statements are not being used to prove the truth of their contents but are being used as circumstantial evidence of the declarant's mental state. See the Comment to Section 1200.

Section 1250(b) does not permit a statement of memory or belief to be used to prove the fact remembered or believed. This limitation is necessary to preserve the hearsay rule. Any statement of a past event is, of course, a statement of the declarant's then existing state of mind—his memory or belief—concerning the past event. If the evidence of that state of mind—the statement of memory—were admissible to show that the fact remembered or believed actually occurred, any statement narrating a past event would be, by a process of circuitous reasoning, admissible to prove that the event occurred.

The limitation in Section 1250(b) is generally in accord with the law developed in the California cases. Thus, in Estate of Anderson, 185 Cal. 700, 198 Pac. 407 (1921), a testatrix, after the execution of a will, declared, in effect, that the will had been made at an aunt's request; this statement was held to be inadmissible hearsay "because it was merely a declaration as to a past event and was not indicative of the condition of mind of the testatrix at the time she made it." 185 Cal. at 720, 198 Pac. at 415 (1921).

A major exception to the principle expressed in Section 1250(b) was created in People v. Merkouris, 52 Cal.2d 672, 344 P.2d 1 (1959). That case held that certain murder victims§ statements relating threats by the defendant were admissible to show the victims§ mental state—their fear of the defendant. Their fear was not itself an issue in the case, but the court held that the fear was relevant to show that the defendant had engaged in conduct engendering the fear, *i.e.,* that the defendant had in fact threatened them. That the defendant had threatened them was, of course, relevant to show that the threats were carried out in the homicide. Thus, in effect, the court permitted the statements to be used to prove the truth of the matters stated in them. In People v. Purvis, 56 Cal.2d 93, 13 Cal.Rptr. 801, 362 P.2d 713 (1961), the doctrine of the Merkouris case was limited to cases where identity is an issue; however, at least one subsequent decision has applied the doctrine where identity was not in issue. See People v. Cooley, 211 Cal.App.2d 173, 27 Cal.Rptr. 543 (1962).

The doctrine of the Merkouris case is repudiated in Section 1250(b) because that doctrine undermines the hearsay rule itself. Other exceptions to the hearsay rule are based on some indicia of reliability peculiar to the evidence involved. People v. Brust, 47 Cal.2d 776, 785, 306 P.2d 480, 484 (1957). The exception created by Merkouris is not based on any probability of reliability; it is based on a rationale that destroys the very foundation of the hearsay rule.

To be distinguished from the Merkouris decision, however, are certain other cases in which the statements of a murder victim were used to prove or explain subsequent acts of the *decedent,* and not as a basis for inferring that the defendant did the acts charged in the statements. See, *e.g.,* People v. Atchley, 53 Cal.2d 160, 172, 346 P.2d 764, 770 (1959); People v. Finch, 213 Cal.App.2d 752, 765, 29 Cal.Rptr. 420, 427 (1963). Statements of a decedent's then existing fear—*i.e.,* his state of mind—may be offered under Section 1250, as under existing law, either to prove that fear when it is itself in issue or to prove or explain the decedent's subsequent conduct. Statements of a decedent narrating threats or brutal conduct by some other person may also be used as circumstantial evidence of the decedent's fear—his state of mind—when that fear is itself in issue or when it is relevant to prove or explain the decedent's subsequent conduct; and, for that purpose, the evidence is not subject to a hearsay objection because it is not offered to prove the truth of the matter stated. See the Comment to Section 1200. See also the Comment to Section 1252. But when such evidence is used as a basis for inferring that the alleged threatener must have made threats, the evidence falls within the language of Section 1250(b) and is inadmissible hearsay evidence.

§ 1251
Statement of declarant's previously existing mental or physical state

Subject to Section 1252, evidence of a statement of the declarant's state of mind, emotion, or physical sensation (including a statement of intent, plan, motive, design, mental feeling, pain, or bodily health) at a time prior to the statement is not made inadmissible by the hearsay rule if:

(a) The declarant is unavailable as a witness; and

(b) The evidence is offered to prove such prior state of mind, emotion, or physical sensation when it is itself an issue in the action and the evidence is not offered to prove any fact other than such state of mind, emotion, or physical sensation. (*Stats.1965, c. 299, § 2, operative Jan. 1, 1967.*)

§ 1252
Restriction on admissibility of statement of mental or physical state

Evidence of a statement is inadmissible under this article if the statement was made under circumstances such as to indicate its lack of trustworthiness. (*Stats.1965, c. 299, § 2, operative Jan. 1, 1967.*)

§ 1253
Statements for purposes of medical diagnosis or treatment; contents of statement; child abuse or neglect; age limitations

Subject to Section 1252, evidence of a statement is not made inadmissible by the hearsay rule if the statement was made for purposes of medical diagnosis or treatment and describes medical history, or past or present symptoms, pain, or sensations, or the inception or general character of the cause or external source thereof insofar as reasonably pertinent to diagnosis or treatment. This section applies only to a statement made by a victim who is a minor at the time of the proceedings, provided the statement was made when the victim was under the age of 12 describing any act, or attempted act, of child abuse or neglect. "Child abuse" and "child neglect," for purposes of this section, have the meanings provided in subdivision (c) of Section 1360. In addition, "child abuse" means any act proscribed by Chapter 5 (commencing with Section 281) of Title 9 of Part 1 of the Penal Code committed against a minor. (*Added by Stats.1995, c. 87 (A.B.355), § 2.*)

ARTICLE 6. STATEMENTS RELATING TO WILLS AND TO CLAIMS AGAINST ESTATES

Section
1260. Statements concerning declarant's will or revocable trust.
1261. Statement of decedent offered in action against his estate.

§ 1260
Statements concerning declarant's will or revocable trust

(a) Except as provided in subdivision (b), evidence of any of the following statements made by a declarant who is unavailable as a witness is not made inadmissible by the hearsay rule:

(1) That the declarant has or has not made a will or established or amended a revocable trust.

(2) That the declarant has or has not revoked his or her will, revocable trust, or an amendment to a revocable trust.

(3) That identifies the declarant's will, revocable trust, or an amendment to a revocable trust.

(b) Evidence of a statement is inadmissible under this section if the statement was made under circumstances that indicate its lack of trustworthiness. (*Stats.1965, c. 299, § 2, operative Jan. 1, 1967. Amended by Stats.2010, c. 106 (S.B.1041), § 1.*)

§ 1261
Statement of decedent offered in action against his estate

(a) Evidence of a statement is not made inadmissible by the hearsay rule when offered in an action upon a claim or demand against the estate of the declarant if the statement was made upon the personal knowledge of the declarant at a time when the matter had been recently perceived by him and while his recollection was clear.

(b) Evidence of a statement is inadmissible under this section if the statement was made under circumstances such as to indicate its lack of trustworthiness. (*Stats.1965, c. 299, § 2, operative Jan. 1, 1967.*)

ARTICLE 7. BUSINESS RECORDS

Section
1270. A business.
1271. Admissible writings.
1272. Absence of entry in business records.

§ 1270
A business

As used in this article, "a business" includes every kind of business, governmental activity, profession, occupation, calling, or operation of institutions, whether carried on for profit or not. (*Stats.1965, c. 299, § 2, operative Jan. 1, 1967.*)

§ 1271
Admissible writings

Evidence of a writing made as a record of an act, condition, or event is not made inadmissible by the hearsay rule when offered to prove the act, condition, or event if:

(a) The writing was made in the regular course of a business;

(b) The writing was made at or near the time of the act, condition, or event;

(c) The custodian or other qualified witness testifies to its identity and the mode of its preparation; and

(d) The sources of information and method and time of preparation were such as to indicate its trustworthiness. (*Stats.1965, c. 299, § 2, operative Jan. 1, 1967.*)

§ 1272
Absence of entry in business records

Evidence of the absence from the records of a business of a record of an asserted act, condition, or event is not made inadmissible by the hearsay rule when offered to prove the nonoccurrence of the act or event, or the nonexistence of the condition, if:

(a) It was the regular course of that business to make records of all such acts, conditions, or events at or near the time of the act, condition, or event and to preserve them; and

(b) The sources of information and method and time of preparation of the records of that business were such that the absence of a record of an act, condition, or event is a trustworthy indication that the act or event did not occur or the condition did not exist. (*Stats.1965, c. 299, § 2, operative Jan. 1, 1967.*)

ARTICLE 8. OFFICIAL RECORDS AND OTHER OFFICIAL WRITINGS

Section
1280. Record by public employee.
1281. Vital statistics records.
1282. Finding of presumed death by authorized federal employee.
1283. Record by federal employee that person is missing, captured, beleaguered, besieged, detained, or dead.
1284. Statement of absence of public record.

§ 1280
Record by public employee

Evidence of a writing made as a record of an act, condition, or event is not made inadmissible by the hearsay rule when offered in any civil or criminal proceeding to prove the act, condition, or event if all of the following applies:

(a) The writing was made by and within the scope of duty of a public employee.

(b) The writing was made at or near the time of the act, condition, or event.

(c) The sources of information and method and time of preparation were such as to indicate its trustworthiness. (*Stats.1965, c. 299, § 2, operative Jan. 1, 1967. Amended by Stats.1996, c. 642 (A.B.1387), § 4.*)

§ 1281
Vital statistics records

Evidence of a writing made as a record of a birth, fetal death, death, or marriage is not made inadmissible by the hearsay rule if the maker was required by law to file the writing in a designated public office and the writing was made and filed as required by law. (*Stats.1965, c. 299, § 2, operative Jan. 1, 1967.*)

§ 1282
Finding of presumed death by authorized federal employee

A written finding of presumed death made by an employee of the United States authorized to make such finding pursuant to the Federal Missing Persons Act (56 Stats. 143, 1092, and P.L. 408, Ch. 371, 2d Sess. 78th Cong.; 50 U.S.C. App. 1001–1016), as enacted or as heretofore or hereafter amended, shall be received in any court, office, or other place in this state as evidence of the death of the person therein found to be dead and of the date, circumstances, and place of his disappearance. (*Stats.1965, c. 299, § 2, operative Jan. 1, 1967.*)

§ 1283
Record by federal employee that person is missing, captured, beleaguered, besieged, detained, or dead

An official written report or record that a person is missing, missing in action, interned in a foreign country, captured by a hostile force, beleaguered by a hostile force, besieged by a hostile force, or detained in a foreign country against his will, or is dead or is alive, made by an employee of the United States authorized by any law of the United States to make such report or record shall be received in any court, office, or other place in this state as evidence that such person is missing, missing in action, interned in a foreign country, captured by a hostile force, beleaguered by a hostile force, besieged by a hostile force, or detained in a foreign country against his will, or is dead or is alive. (*Stats.1965, c. 299, § 2, operative Jan. 1, 1967.*)

§ 1284
Statement of absence of public record

Evidence of a writing made by the public employee who is the official custodian of the records in a public office, reciting diligent search and failure to find a record, is not made inadmissible by the hearsay rule when offered to prove the absence of a record in that office. (*Stats.1965, c. 299, § 2, operative Jan. 1, 1967.*)

Just as the existence and content of a public record may be proved under Section 1530 by a copy accompanied by the attestation or certificate of the custodian reciting that it is a copy, the absence of such a record from a particular public office may be proved under Section 1284 by a writing made by the custodian of the records in that office stating that no such record was found after a diligent search. The writing must, of course, be properly authenticated. See Evidence Code §§ 1401, 1453. See also Code Civ.Proc. § 1893 (public official, on demand, must, furnish certificate or its equivalent that he did not find a designated writing after a diligent search). The exception is justified by the likelihood that such a statement made by the custodian of the records is accurate and by the necessity for providing a simple and inexpensive method of proving the absence of a public record.

ARTICLE 9. FORMER TESTIMONY

Section

§ 1290
Former testimony

As used in this article, "former testimony" means testimony given under oath in:

(a) Another action or in a former hearing or trial of the same action;

(b) A proceeding to determine a controversy conducted by or under the supervision of an agency that has the power to determine such a controversy and is an agency of the United States or a public entity in the United States;

(c) A deposition taken in compliance with law in another action; or

(d) An arbitration proceeding if the evidence of such former testimony is a verbatim transcript thereof. (*Stats.1965, c. 299, § 2, operative Jan. 1, 1967.*)

§ 1291
Former testimony offered against party to former proceeding

(a) Evidence of former testimony is not made inadmissible by the hearsay rule if the declarant is unavailable as a witness and:

(1) The former testimony is offered against a person who offered it in evidence in his own behalf on the former occasion or against the successor in interest of such person; or

(2) The party against whom the former testimony is offered was a party to the action or proceeding in which the testimony was given and had the right and opportunity to cross-examine the declarant with an interest and motive similar to that which he has at the hearing.

(b) The admissibility of former testimony under this section is subject to the same limitations and objections as though the declarant were testifying at the hearing, except that former testimony offered under this section is not subject to:

(1) Objections to the form of the question which were not made at the time the former testimony was given.

(2) Objections based on competency or privilege which did not exist at the time the former testimony was given. (*Stats.1965, c. 299, § 2, operative Jan. 1, 1967.*)

Section 1291 provides a hearsay exception for former testimony offered against a person who was a party to the proceeding in which the former testimony was given. For example, if a series of cases arises involving several plaintiffs and but one defendant, Section 1291 permits testimony given in the first trial to be used against the defendant in a later trial if the conditions of admissibility stated in the section are met.

Former testimony is admissible under Section 1291 only if the declarant is unavailable as a witness.

Paragraph (1) of subdivision (a) of Section 1291 provides for the admission of former testimony if it is offered against the party who offered it in the previous proceeding. Since the witness is no longer available to testify, the party's previous direct and redirect examination should be considered an adequate substitute for his present right to cross-examine the declarant.

Paragraph (2) of subdivision (a) of Section 1291 provides for the admissibility of former testimony where the party against whom it is now offered had the right and opportunity in the former proceeding to cross-examine the declarant with an interest and motive similar to that which he now has. Since the party has had his opportunity to cross-examine, the primary objection to hearsay evidence—lack of opportunity to cross-examine the declarant—is not applicable. On the other hand, paragraph (2) does not make the former testimony admissible where the party against whom it is offered did not have a similar interest and motive to cross-examine the declarant. The determination of similarity of interest and motive in cross-examination should be based on practical considerations and not merely on the similarity of the party's position in the two cases. For example, testimony contained in a deposition that was taken, but not offered in evidence at the trial, in a different action should be excluded if the judge determines that the deposition was taken for discovery purposes and that the party did not subject the witness to a thorough cross-examination because he sought to avoid a premature revelation of the weakness in the testimony of the witness or in the adverse party's case. In such a situation, the party's interest and motive for cross-examination on the previous occasion would have been substantially different from his present interest and motive.

Section 1291 supersedes Code of Civil Procedure Section 1870(8) which permits former testimony to be admitted in a civil case only if the former proceeding was an action between the same parties or their predecessors in interest, relating to the same matter, or was a former trial of the action in which the testimony is offered. Section 1291 will also permit a broader range of hearsay to be introduced against the defendant in a criminal action than has been permitted under Penal Code Section 686. Under that section, former testimony has been admissible against the defendant in a criminal action only if the former testimony was given in the same action—at the preliminary examination, in a deposition, or in a prior trial of the action. Likewise, Section 1291 will permit a broader range of hearsay to be introduced against the prosecution in a criminal action since the people of the State of California are a party to all criminal actions. See Penal Code § 684.

Subdivision (b) of Section 1291 makes it clear that objections based on the competence of the declarant or on privilege are to be determined by reference to the time the former testimony was given. Existing California law is not clear on this point; some California decisions indicate that competency and privilege are to be determined as of the time the former testimony was given, but others indicate that these matters are to be determined as of the time the former testimony is offered in evidence. See Tentative Recommendation and a Study Relating to the Uniform Rules of Evidence (Article VIII. Hearsay Evidence), 6 Cal.Law Revision Comm'n, Rep., Rec. & Studies Appendix at 581–585 (1964).

Subdivision (b) also provides that objections to the form of the question may not be used to exclude the former testimony. Where the former testimony is offered under paragraph (1) of subdivision (a), the party against whom the former testimony is now offered phrased the question himself; and where the former testimony is admitted under paragraph (2) of subdivision (a), the party against whom the testimony is now offered had the opportunity to object to the form of the question when it was asked on the former occasion. Hence, the party is not permitted to raise this technical objection when the former testimony is offered against him.

§ 1292
Former testimony offered against person not a party to former proceeding

(a) Evidence of former testimony is not made inadmissible by the hearsay rule if:

(1) The declarant is unavailable as a witness;

(2) The former testimony is offered in a civil action; and

(3) The issue is such that the party to the action or proceeding in which the former testimony was given had the right and opportunity to cross-examine the declarant with an interest and motive similar to that which the party against whom the testimony is offered has at the hearing.

(b) The admissibility of former testimony under this section is subject to the same limitations and objections as though the declarant were testifying at the hearing, except that former testimony offered under this section is not subject to objections based on competency or privilege which did not exist at the time the former testimony was given. (*Stats.1965, c. 299, § 2, operative Jan. 1, 1967.*)

Section 1292 provides a hearsay exception for former testimony given at the former proceeding by a person who is now unavailable as a witness when such former testimony is offered against a person who was not a party to the former proceeding but whose motive for cross-examination is similar to that of a person who had the right and opportunity to cross-examine the declarant when the former testimony was given. For example, if one occurrence gives rise to a series of cases involving one defendant and several plaintiffs, Section 1292 permits testimony given against the plaintiff in the first action to be used against a different plaintiff in a subsequent action if the conditions of admissibility stated in the section are met.

Code of Civil Procedure Section 1870(8) (which is superseded by this article) authorizes the admission of former testimony only if it was given in another action between the same parties and involving the same matter. Section 1292 substitutes for these restrictive requirements what is, in effect, a more flexible "trustworthiness" approach characteristic of other hearsay exceptions. The trustworthiness of the former testimony is sufficiently guaranteed because the former adverse party had the right and opportunity to cross-examine the declarant with an interest and motive similar to that of the present adverse party. Although the party against whom the former testimony is offered did not himself have an opportunity to cross-examine the witness on the former occasion, it can be generally assumed that most prior cross-examination is adequate if the same stakes are involved. If the same stakes are not involved, the difference in interest or motivation would justify exclusion. Even where the prior cross-examination was inadequate, there is better reason here for providing a hearsay exception than there is for many of the presently recognized exceptions to the hearsay rule. As Professor McCormick states:

> I suggest that if the witness *is* unavailable, then the need for the sworn, transcribed former testimony in the ascertainment of truth is so great, and its reliability so far superior to most, if not all the other types of oral hearsay coming in under the other exceptions, that the requirements of identity of parties and issues be dispensed with. This dispenses with the opportunity for cross-examination, that great characteristic weapon of our adversary system. But the other types of admissible oral hearsay, admissions, declarations against interest, statements about bodily symptoms, likewise dispense with cross-examination, for declarations having far less trustworthiness than the sworn testimony in open court, and with a far greater hazard of fabrication or mistake in the reporting of the declaration by the witness. [McCormick, Evidence § 238 at 501 (1954).]

Section 1292 does not make former testimony admissible in a criminal case. This limitation preserves the right of a person accused of crime to confront and cross-examine the witnesses against him. When a person's life or liberty is at stake—as it is in a criminal action—the defendant should not be compelled to rely on the fact that another person has had an opportunity to cross-examine the witness.

Subdivision (b) of Section 1292 makes it clear that objections based on competency or privilege are to be determined by reference to the time when the former testimony was given. Existing California law is not clear on this point; some California decisions indicate that competency and privilege are to be determined as of the time the former testimony was given, but others indicate that these matters are to be determined as of the time the former testimony is offered in evidence. See Tentative Recommendation and a Study Relating to the Uniform Rules of Evidence (Article VIII. Hearsay Evidence), 6 Cal.Law Revision Comm'n, Rep., Rec. & Studies Appendix, at 581–585 (1964).

§ 1293
Former testimony by minor child complaining witness at preliminary examination

(a) Evidence of former testimony made at a preliminary examination by a minor child who was the complaining witness is not made inadmissible by the hearsay rule if:

(1) The former testimony is offered in a proceeding to declare the minor a dependent child of the court pursuant to Section 300 of the Welfare and Institutions Code.

(2) The issues are such that a defendant in the preliminary examination in which the former testimony was given had the right and opportunity to cross-examine the minor child with an interest and motive similar to that which the parent or guardian against whom the testimony is offered has at the proceeding to declare the minor a dependent child of the court.

(b) The admissibility of former testimony under this section is subject to the same limitations and objections as though the minor child were testifying at the proceeding to declare him or her a dependent child of the court.

(c) The attorney for the parent or guardian against whom the former testimony is offered or, if none, the parent or guardian may make a motion to challenge the admissibility of the former testimony upon a showing that new substantially different issues are present in the proceeding to declare the minor a dependent child than were present in the preliminary examination.

(d) As used in this section, "complaining witness" means the alleged victim of the crime for which a preliminary examination was held.

(e) This section shall apply only to testimony made at a preliminary examination on and after January 1, 1990. (*Added by Stats.1989, c. 322, § 1.*)

§ 1294
Unavailable witnesses; prior inconsistent statements; preliminary hearing or prior proceeding

(a) The following evidence of prior inconsistent statements of a witness properly admitted in a preliminary hearing or trial of the same criminal matter pursuant to Section 1235 is not made inadmissible by the hearsay rule if the witness is unavailable and former testimony of the witness is admitted pursuant to Section 1291:

(1) A video recorded statement introduced at a preliminary hearing or prior proceeding concerning the same criminal matter.

(2) A transcript, containing the statements, of the preliminary hearing or prior proceeding concerning the same criminal matter.

(b) The party against whom the prior inconsistent statements are offered, at his or her option, may examine or cross-examine any person who testified at the preliminary hearing or prior proceeding as to the prior inconsistent statements of the witness. (*Added by Stats.1996, c. 560 (A.B.2483), § 1. Amended by Stats.2009, c. 88 (A.B.176), § 36.*)

ARTICLE 10. JUDGMENTS

Section

1302. Judgment determining liability of third person.

§ 1300
Judgment of conviction of crime punishable as felony

Evidence of a final judgment adjudging a person guilty of a crime punishable as a felony is not made inadmissible by the hearsay rule when offered in a civil action to prove any fact essential to the judgment whether or not the judgment was based on a plea of nolo contendere. (*Stats.1965, c. 299, § 2, operative Jan. 1, 1967. Amended by Stats.1982, c. 390, p. 1724, § 2.*)

§ 1301
Judgment against person entitled to indemnity

Evidence of a final judgment is not made inadmissible by the hearsay rule when offered by the judgment debtor to prove any fact which was essential to the judgment in an action in which he seeks to:

(a) Recover partial or total indemnity or exoneration for money paid or liability incurred because of the judgment;

(b) Enforce a warranty to protect the judgment debtor against the liability determined by the judgment; or

(c) Recover damages for breach of warranty substantially the same as the warranty determined by the judgment to have been breached. (*Stats.1965, c. 299, § 2, operative Jan. 1, 1967.*)

§ 1302
Judgment determining liability of third person

When the liability, obligation, or duty of a third person is in issue in a civil action, evidence of a final judgment against that person is not made inadmissible by the hearsay rule when offered to prove such liability, obligation, or duty. (*Stats.1965, c. 299, § 2, operative Jan. 1, 1967.*)

ARTICLE 11. FAMILY HISTORY

Section
1310. Statement concerning declarant's own family history.
1311. Statement concerning family history of another.
1312. Entries in family records and the like.
1313. Reputation in family concerning family history.
1314. Reputation in community concerning family history.
1315. Church records concerning family history.
1316. Marriage, baptismal and similar certificates.

§ 1310
Statement concerning declarant's own family history

(a) Subject to subdivision (b), evidence of a statement by a declarant who is unavailable as a witness concerning his own birth, marriage, divorce, a parent and child relationship, relationship by blood or marriage, race, ancestry, or other similar fact of his family history is not made inadmissible by the hearsay rule, even though the declarant had no means of acquiring personal knowledge of the matter declared.

(b) Evidence of a statement is inadmissible under this section if the statement was made under circumstances such as to indicate its lack of trustworthiness. (*Stats.1965, c. 299, § 2, operative Jan. 1, 1967. Amended by Stats.1975, c. 1244, p. 3202, § 15.*)

§ 1311
Statement concerning family history of another

(a) Subject to subdivision (b), evidence of a statement concerning the birth, marriage, divorce, death, parent and child relationship, race, ancestry, relationship by blood or marriage, or other similar fact of the family history of a person other than the declarant is not made inadmissible by the hearsay rule if the declarant is unavailable as a witness and:

(1) The declarant was related to the other by blood or marriage; or

(2) The declarant was otherwise so intimately associated with the other's family as to be likely to have had accurate information concerning the matter declared and made the statement (i) upon information received from the other or from a person related by blood or marriage to the other or (ii) upon repute in the other's family.

(b) Evidence of a statement is inadmissible under this section if the statement was made under circumstances such as to indicate its lack of trustworthiness. (*Stats.1965, c. 299, § 2, operative Jan. 1, 1967. Amended by Stats.1975, c. 1244, p. 3202, § 16.*)

§ 1312
Entries in family records and the like

Evidence of entries in family Bibles or other family books or charts, engravings on rings, family portraits, engravings on urns, crypts, or tombstones, and the like, is not made inadmissible by the hearsay rule when offered to prove the birth, marriage, divorce, death, parent and child relationship, race, ancestry, relationship by blood or marriage, or other similar fact of the family history of a member of the family by blood or marriage. (*Stats.1965, c. 299, § 2, operative Jan. 1, 1967. Amended by Stats.1975, c. 1244, p. 3202, § 17.*)

§ 1313
Reputation in family concerning family history

Evidence of reputation among members of a family is not made inadmissible by the hearsay rule if the reputation concerns the birth, marriage, divorce, death, parent and child relationship, race, ancestry, relationship by blood or marriage, or other similar fact of the family history of a member of the family by blood or marriage. (*Stats.1965, c. 299, § 2, operative Jan. 1, 1967. Amended by Stats.1975, c. 1244, p. 3202, § 18.*)

§ 1314
Reputation in community concerning family history

Evidence of reputation in a community concerning the date or fact of birth, marriage, divorce, or death of a person resident in the community at the time of the reputation is not made inadmissible by the hearsay rule. (*Stats.1965, c. 299, § 2, operative Jan. 1, 1967.*)

§ 1315
Church records concerning family history

Evidence of a statement concerning a person's birth, marriage, divorce, death, parent and child relationship, race, ancestry, relationship by blood or marriage, or other similar fact of family history which is contained in a writing made as a record of a church, religious denomination, or religious society is not made inadmissible by the hearsay rule if:

(a) The statement is contained in a writing made as a record of an act, condition, or event that would be admissible as evidence of such act, condition, or event under Section 1271; and

(b) The statement is of a kind customarily recorded in connection with the act, condition, or event recorded in the writing. (*Stats.1965, c. 299, § 2, operative Jan. 1, 1967. Amended by Stats.1975, c. 1244, p. 3203, § 19.*)

§ 1316
Marriage, baptismal and similar certificates

Evidence of a statement concerning a person's birth, marriage, divorce, death, parent and child relationship, race, ancestry, relationship by blood or marriage, or other similar fact of family history is not made inadmissible by the hearsay rule if the statement is contained in a certificate that the maker thereof performed a marriage or other ceremony or administered a sacrament and:

(a) The maker was a clergyman, civil officer, or other person authorized to perform the acts reported in the certificate by law or by the rules, regulations, or requirements of a church, religious denomination, or religious society; and

(b) The certificate was issued by the maker at the time and place of the ceremony or sacrament or within a reasonable time thereafter. (*Stats.1965, c. 299, § 2, operative Jan. 1, 1967. Amended by Stats.1975, c. 1244, p. 3203, § 20.*)

ARTICLE 12. REPUTATION AND STATEMENTS CONCERNING COMMUNITY HISTORY, PROPERTY INTERESTS, AND CHARACTER

Section

§ 1320
Reputation concerning community history

Evidence of reputation in a community is not made inadmissible by the hearsay rule if the reputation concerns an event of general history of the community or of the state or nation of which the community is a part and the event was of importance to the community. (*Stats.1965, c. 299, § 2, operative Jan. 1, 1967.*)

§ 1321
Reputation concerning public interest in property

Evidence of reputation in a community is not made inadmissible by the hearsay rule if the reputation concerns the interest of the public in property in the community and the reputation arose before controversy. (*Stats.1965, c. 299, § 2, operative Jan. 1, 1967.*)

§ 1322
Reputation concerning boundary or custom affecting land

Evidence of reputation in a community is not made inadmissible by the hearsay rule if the reputation concerns boundaries of, or customs affecting, land in the community and the reputation arose before controversy. (*Stats.1965, c. 299, § 2, operative Jan. 1, 1967.*)

§ 1323
Statement concerning boundary

Evidence of a statement concerning the boundary of land is not made inadmissible by the hearsay rule if the declarant is unavailable as a witness and had sufficient knowledge of the subject, but evidence of a statement is not admissible under this section if the statement was made under circumstances such as to indicate its lack of trustworthiness. (*Stats.1965, c. 299, § 2, operative Jan. 1, 1967.*)

§ 1324
Reputation concerning character

Evidence of a person's general reputation with reference to his character or a trait of his character at a relevant time in the community in which he then resided or in a group with which he then habitually associated is not made inadmissible by the hearsay rule. (*Stats.1965, c. 299, § 2, operative Jan. 1, 1967.*)

ARTICLE 13. DISPOSITIVE INSTRUMENTS AND ANCIENT WRITINGS

Section
1330. Recitals in writings affecting property.
1331. Recitals in ancient writings.

§ 1330
Recitals in writings affecting property

Evidence of a statement contained in a deed of conveyance or a will or other writing purporting to affect an interest in real or personal property is not made inadmissible by the hearsay rule if:

(a) The matter stated was relevant to the purpose of the writing;

(b) The matter stated would be relevant to an issue as to an interest in the property; and

(c) The dealings with the property since the statement was made have not been inconsistent with the truth of the statement. (*Stats.1965, c. 299, § 2, operative Jan. 1, 1967.*)

§ 1331
Recitals in ancient writings

Evidence of a statement is not made inadmissible by the hearsay rule if the statement is contained in a writing more than 30 years old and the statement has been since generally acted upon as true by persons having an interest in the matter. (*Stats.1965, c. 299, § 2, operative Jan. 1, 1967.*)

ARTICLE 14. COMMERCIAL, SCIENTIFIC, AND SIMILAR PUBLICATIONS

Section
1340. Publications relied upon as accurate in the course of business.
1341. Publications concerning facts of general notoriety and interests.

§ 1340
Publications relied upon as accurate in the course of business

Evidence of a statement, other than an opinion, contained in a tabulation, list, directory, register, or other published compilation is not made inadmissible by the hearsay rule if the compilation is generally used and relied upon as accurate in the course of a business as defined in Section 1270. (*Stats.1965, c. 299, § 2, operative Jan. 1, 1967.*)

§ 1341
Publications concerning facts of general notoriety and interests

Historical works, books of science or art, and published maps or charts, made by persons indifferent between the parties, are not made inadmissible by the hearsay rule when offered to prove facts of general notoriety and interest. (Stats.1965, c. 299, § 2, operative Jan. 1, 1967.)

ARTICLE 15. DECLARANT UNAVAILABLE AS WITNESS

Section
1350. Unavailable declarant; hearsay rule.

§ 1350
Unavailable declarant; hearsay rule

(a) In a criminal proceeding charging a serious felony, evidence of a statement made by a declarant is not made inadmissible by the hearsay rule if the declarant is unavailable as a witness, and all of the following are true:

(1) There is clear and convincing evidence that the declarant's unavailability was knowingly caused by, aided by, or solicited by the party against whom the statement is offered for the purpose of preventing the arrest or prosecution of the party and is the result of the death by homicide or the kidnapping of the declarant.

(2) There is no evidence that the unavailability of the declarant was caused by, aided by, solicited by, or procured on behalf of, the party who is offering the statement.

(3) The statement has been memorialized in a tape recording made by a law enforcement official, or in a written statement prepared by a law enforcement official and signed by the declarant and notarized in the presence of the law enforcement official, prior to the death or kidnapping of the declarant.

(4) The statement was made under circumstances which indicate its trustworthiness and was not the result of promise, inducement, threat, or coercion.

(5) The statement is relevant to the issues to be tried.

(6) The statement is corroborated by other evidence which tends to connect the party against whom the statement is offered with the commission of the serious felony with which the party is charged. The corroboration is not sufficient if it merely shows the commission of the offense or the circumstances thereof.

(b) If the prosecution intends to offer a statement pursuant to this section, the prosecution shall serve a written notice upon the defendant at least 10 days prior to the hearing or trial at which the prosecution intends to offer the statement, unless the prosecution shows good cause for the failure to provide that notice. In the event that good cause is shown, the defendant shall be entitled to a reasonable continuance of the hearing or trial.

(c) If the statement is offered during trial, the court's determination shall be made out of the presence of the jury. If the defendant elects to testify at the hearing on a motion brought pursuant to this section, the court shall exclude from the examination every person except the clerk, the court reporter, the bailiff, the prosecutor, the investigating officer, the defendant and his or her counsel, an investigator for the defendant, and the officer having custody of the defendant. Notwithstanding any other provision of law, the defendant's testimony at the hearing shall not be admissible in any other proceeding except the hearing brought on the motion pursuant to this section. If a transcript is made of the defendant's testimony, it shall be sealed and transmitted to the clerk of the court in which the action is pending.

(d) As used in this section, "serious felony" means any of the felonies listed in subdivision (c) of Section 1192.7 of the Penal Code or any violation of Section 11351, 11352, 11378, or 11379 of the Health and Safety Code.

(e) If a statement to be admitted pursuant to this section includes hearsay statements made by anyone other than the declarant who is unavailable pursuant to subdivision (a), those hearsay statements are inadmissible unless they meet the requirements of an exception to the hearsay rule. (*Added by Stats.1985, c. 783, § 1. Amended by Stats.2001, c. 854 (S.B.205), § 5.*)

ARTICLE 16. STATEMENTS BY CHILDREN UNDER THE AGE OF 12 IN CHILD NEGLECT AND ABUSE PROCEEDINGS

Section
1360. Statements describing an act or attempted act of child abuse or neglect; criminal prosecutions; requirements.

§ 1360
Statements describing an act or attempted act of child abuse or neglect; criminal prosecutions; requirements

(a) In a criminal prosecution where the victim is a minor, a statement made by the victim when under the age of 12 describing any act of child abuse or neglect performed with or on the child by another, or describing any attempted act of child abuse or neglect with or on the child by another, is not made inadmissible by the hearsay rule if all of the following apply:

(1) The statement is not otherwise admissible by statute or court rule.

(2) The court finds, in a hearing conducted outside the presence of the jury, that the time, content, and circumstances of the statement provide sufficient indicia of reliability.

(3) The child either:

(A) Testifies at the proceedings.

(B) Is unavailable as a witness, in which case the statement may be admitted only if there is evidence of the child abuse or neglect that corroborates the statement made by the child.

(b) A statement may not be admitted under this section unless the proponent of the statement makes known to the adverse party the intention to offer the statement and the particulars of the statement sufficiently in advance of the proceedings in order to provide the adverse party with a fair opportunity to prepare to meet the statement.

(c) For purposes of this section, "child abuse" means an act proscribed by Section 273a, 273d, or 288.5 of the Penal Code, or any of the acts described in Section 11165.1 of the Penal Code, and "child neglect" means any of the acts described in Section 11165.2 of the Penal Code. (*Added by Stats.1995, c. 87 (A.B.355), § 3.*)

ARTICLE 17. PHYSICAL ABUSE

Section

§ 1370
Threat of infliction of injury

(a) Evidence of a statement by a declarant is not made inadmissible by the hearsay rule if all of the following conditions are met:

(1) The statement purports to narrate, describe, or explain the infliction or threat of physical injury upon the declarant.

(2) The declarant is unavailable as a witness pursuant to Section 240.

(3) The statement was made at or near the time of the infliction or threat of physical injury. Evidence of statements made more than five

years before the filing of the current action or proceeding shall be inadmissible under this section.

(4) The statement was made under circumstances that would indicate its trustworthiness.

(5) The statement was made in writing, was electronically recorded, or made to a physician, nurse, paramedic, or to a law enforcement official.

(b) For purposes of paragraph (4) of subdivision (a), circumstances relevant to the issue of trustworthiness include, but are not limited to, the following:

(1) Whether the statement was made in contemplation of pending or anticipated litigation in which the declarant was interested.

(2) Whether the declarant has a bias or motive for fabricating the statement, and the extent of any bias or motive.

(3) Whether the statement is corroborated by evidence other than statements that are admissible only pursuant to this section.

(c) A statement is admissible pursuant to this section only if the proponent of the statement makes known to the adverse party the intention to offer the statement and the particulars of the statement sufficiently in advance of the proceedings in order to provide the adverse party with a fair opportunity to prepare to meet the statement. (*Added by Stats.1996, c. 416 (A.B.2068), § 2, eff. Sept. 4, 1996. Amended by Stats.2000, c. 1001 (S.B.1944), § 2.*)

§ 1380
Elder and dependent adults; statements by victims of abuse

(a) In a criminal proceeding charging a violation, or attempted violation, of Section 368 of the Penal Code, evidence of a statement made by a declarant is not made inadmissible by the hearsay rule if the declarant is unavailable as a witness, as defined in subdivisions (a) and (b) of Section 240, and all of the following are true:

(1) The party offering the statement has made a showing of particularized guarantees of trustworthiness regarding the statement, the statement was made under circumstances which indicate its trustworthiness, and the statement was not the result of promise, inducement, threat, or coercion. In making its determination, the court may consider only the circumstances that surround the making of the statement and that render the declarant particularly worthy of belief.

(2) There is no evidence that the unavailability of the declarant was caused by, aided by, solicited by, or procured on behalf of, the party who is offering the statement.

(3) The entire statement has been memorialized in a videotape recording made by a law enforcement official, prior to the death or disabling of the declarant.

(4) The statement was made by the victim of the alleged violation.

(5) The statement is supported by corroborative evidence.

(6) The victim of the alleged violation is an individual who meets both of the following requirements:

(A) Was 65 years of age or older or was a dependent adult when the alleged violation or attempted violation occurred.

(B) At the time of any criminal proceeding, including, but not limited to, a preliminary hearing or trial, regarding the alleged violation or attempted violation, is either deceased or suffers from the infirmities of aging as manifested by advanced age or organic brain damage, or other physical, mental, or emotional dysfunction, to the extent that the ability of the person to provide adequately for the person's own care or protection is impaired.

(b) If the prosecution intends to offer a statement pursuant to this section, the prosecution shall serve a written notice upon the defendant at least 10 days prior to the hearing or trial at which the prosecution intends to offer the statement, unless the prosecution shows good cause for the failure to provide that notice. In the event that good cause is shown, the defendant shall be entitled to a reasonable continuance of the hearing or trial.

(c) If the statement is offered during trial, the court's determination as to the availability of the victim as a witness shall be made out of the presence of the jury. If the defendant elects to testify at the hearing on a motion brought pursuant to this section, the court shall exclude from the examination every person except the clerk, the court reporter, the bailiff, the prosecutor, the investigating officer, the defendant and his or her counsel, an investigator for the defendant, and the officer having custody of the defendant. Notwithstanding any other provision of law, the defendant's testimony at the hearing shall not be admissible in any other proceeding except the hearing brought on the motion pursuant to this section. If a transcript is made of the defendant's testimony, it shall be sealed and transmitted to the clerk of the court in which the action is pending. (*Added by Stats.1999, c. 383 (A.B.526), § 1.*)

§ 1390
Statements against parties involved in causing unavailability of declarant as witness

(a) Evidence of a statement is not made inadmissible by the hearsay rule if the statement is offered against a party that has engaged, or aided and abetted, in the wrongdoing that was intended to, and did, procure the unavailability of the declarant as a witness.

(b)(1) The party seeking to introduce a statement pursuant to subdivision (a) shall establish, by a preponderance of the evidence, that the elements of subdivision (a) have been met at a foundational hearing.

(2) The hearsay evidence that is the subject of the foundational hearing is admissible at the foundational hearing. However, a finding that the elements of subdivision (a) have been met shall not be based solely on the unconfronted hearsay statement of the unavailable declarant, and shall be supported by independent corroborative evidence.

(3) The foundational hearing shall be conducted outside the presence of the jury. However, if the hearing is conducted after a jury trial has begun, the judge presiding at the hearing may consider evidence already presented to the jury in deciding whether the elements of subdivision (a) have been met.

(4) In deciding whether or not to admit the statement, the judge may take into account whether it is trustworthy and reliable.

(c) This section shall apply to any civil, criminal, or juvenile case or proceeding initiated or pending as of January 1, 2011.

(d) This section shall remain in effect only until January 1, 2016, and as of that date is repealed, unless a later enacted statute, that is enacted before January 1, 2016, deletes or extends that date. If this section is repealed, the fact that it is repealed, should it occur, shall not be deemed to give rise to any ground for an appeal or a postverdict challenge based on its use in a criminal or juvenile case or proceeding before January 1, 2016. (*Added by Stats.2010, c. 537 (A.B.1723), § 2. Amended by Stats.2011, c. 296 (A.B.1023), § 90.*)

Repeal

For repeal of this section, see its terms.

Division 11

WRITINGS

CHAPTER 1. AUTHENTICATION AND PROOF OF WRITINGS

ARTICLE 1. REQUIREMENT OF AUTHENTICATION

Section
1400. Authentication.
1401. Authentication required.
1402. Authentication of altered writings.

§ 1400
Authentication

Authentication of a writing means (a) the introduction of evidence sufficient to sustain a finding that it is the writing that the proponent of the
evidence claims it is or (b) the establishment of such facts by any other
means provided by law. (*Stats.1965, c. 299, § 2, operative Jan. 1, 1967.*)

§ 1401
Authentication required

(a) Authentication of a writing is required before it may be received in
evidence.

(b) Authentication of a writing is required before secondary evidence of
its content may be received in evidence. (*Stats.1965, c. 299, § 2, operative
Jan. 1, 1967.*)

The requirement of authentication stated in subdivision (a) reflects existing law. Ten Winkel v. Anglo California Sec. Co., 11 Cal.2d 707, 81 P.2d
958 (1938). However, the requirement has never been stated in the California statutes.

Some cases have indicated that authentication is not necessary under
certain circumstances, as, for example, when the execution of the writing is
not in issue. See People v. Adamson, 118 Cal.App.2d 714, 258 P.2d 1020
(1953). This is true, however, only if "authentication" is construed narrowly
to refer only to proof of due execution. The Evidence Code defines the term
more broadly and requires all writings to be authenticated. The writing
involved in the Adamson case was a letter that a witness claimed he had
received and acted upon. Under the Evidence Code, the requirement of authentication would require a showing that the letter offered in evidence
was in fact the one received and acted upon; and this is the preliminary
showing that was found sufficient in the Adamson case.

The "writing" referred to in subdivision (a) is any writing offered in
evidence; although it may be either an original or a copy, it must be authenticated before it may be received in evidence.

Authentication of a writing does not in and of itself authorize the writing to be admitted in evidence. The writing, of course, must be relevant and

not be made inadmissible by any exclusionary rule—*e.g.,* the hearsay rule, the best evidence rule, or the rule excluding a coerced confession. Thus, Section 1401 merely requires that an otherwise admissible writing be authenticated before it may be received in evidence.

Subdivision (b) of Section 1401 requires that a writing be authenticated even when it is not offered in evidence but is sought to be proved by a copy or by testimony as to its content under the circumstances permitted by Sections 1500–1510 (the best evidence rule). This is declarative of existing California law. Spottiswood v. Weir, 80 Cal. 448, 22 Pac. 289 (1889); Smith v. Brannan, 13 Cal. 107, 115 (1859); Smith v. Brannan, 13 Cal. 107, 115 (1859); Forman v. Goldberg, 42 Cal.App.2d 308, 316–317, 108 P.2d 983, 988 (1941). Under Section 1401, therefore, if a person offers in evidence a copy of a writing, he must make a sufficient preliminary showing of the authenticity of both the copy and the original (*i.e.,* the writing sought to be proved by the copy).

In some instances, however, authentication of a copy will provide the necessary evidence to authenticate the original writing at the same time. For example: If a copy of a recorded deed is offered in evidence, Section 1401 requires that the copy be authenticated—proved to be a copy of the official record. It also requires that the official record be authenticated—proved to be the official record—because the official record is a writing of which secondary evidence of its content is being offered. Finally, Section 1401 requires the original deed itself to be authenticated—proved to have been executed by its purported maker—for it, too, is a writing of which secondary evidence of its content is being offered. The copy offered in evidence may be authenticated by the attestation or certification of the official custodian of the record as provided by Section 1530. Under Section 1530, the authenticated copy is prima facie evidence of the existence and content of the official record itself. Thus, the authenticated copy supplies the necessary authenticating evidence for the official record. Under Section 1600, the official record is prima facie evidence of the existence and content of the original deed and of its execution by its purported maker; hence, the official record is the requisite authenticating evidence for the original deed. Thus, the duly attested or certified copy of the record meets the requirement of authentication for the copy itself, for the official record, and for the original deed.

§ 1402
Authentication of altered writings

The party producing a writing as genuine which has been altered, or appears to have been altered, after its execution, in a part material to the question in dispute, must account for the alteration or appearance thereof. He may show that the alteration was made by another, without his concurrence, or was made with the consent of the parties affected by it, or otherwise properly or innocently made, or that the alteration did not change the meaning or language of the instrument. If he does that, he may give the writing in evidence, but not otherwise. (*Stats.1965, c. 299, § 2, operative Jan. 1, 1967.*)

ARTICLE 2. MEANS OF AUTHENTICATING AND PROVING WRITINGS

Section
1410. Article not exclusive.
1410.5. Graffiti constitutes a writing; admissibility.
1411. Subscribing witness§ testimony unnecessary.
1412. Use of other evidence when subscribing witness§ testimony required.
1413. Witness to the execution of a writing.
1414. Admission of authenticity; acting upon writing as authentic.
1415. Authentication by handwriting evidence.
1416. Proof of handwriting by person familiar therewith.
1417. Comparison of handwriting by trier of fact.
1418. Comparison of writing by expert witness.
1419. Exemplars when writing is more than 30 years old.
1420. Authentication by evidence of reply.
1421. Authentication by content.

§ 1410
Article not exclusive

Nothing in this article shall be construed to limit the means by which a writing may be authenticated or proved. (*Stats.1965, c. 299, § 2, operative Jan. 1, 1967.*)

§ 1410.5
Graffiti constitutes a writing; admissibility

(a) For purposes of this chapter, a writing shall include any graffiti consisting of written words, insignia, symbols, or any other markings which convey a particular meaning.

(b) Any writing described in subdivision (a), or any photograph thereof, may be admitted into evidence in an action for vandalism, for the purpose of proving that the writing was made by the defendant.

(c) The admissibility of any fact offered to prove that the writing was made by the defendant shall, upon motion of the defendant, be ruled upon outside the presence of the jury, and is subject to the requirements of Sections 1416, 1417, and 1418. (*Added by Stats.1989, c. 660, § 1.*)

§ 1411
Subscribing witness§ testimony unnecessary

Except as provided by statute, the testimony of a subscribing witness is not required to authenticate a writing. (*Stats.1965, c. 299, § 2, operative Jan. 1, 1967.*)

§ 1412
Use of other evidence when subscribing witness§ testimony required

If the testimony of a subscribing witness is required by statute to authenticate a writing and the subscribing witness denies or does not recollect the execution of the writing, the writing may be authenticated by other evidence. (*Stats.1965, c. 299, § 2, operative Jan. 1, 1967.*)

§ 1413
Witness to the execution of a writing

A writing may be authenticated by anyone who saw the writing made or executed, including a subscribing witness. (*Stats.1965, c. 299, § 2, operative Jan. 1, 1967.*)

Section 1413 restates and supersedes the provisions of subdivisions 1 and 3 of Code of Civil Procedure Section 1940.

Section 1413 refers to writings that were "made" as well as "executed" in order to include all kinds of writings, not merely those bearing a signature. See Evidence Code § 250, defining "writing."

§ 1414
Admission of authenticity; acting upon writing as authentic

A writing may be authenticated by evidence that:

(a) The party against whom it is offered has at any time admitted its authenticity; or

(b) The writing has been acted upon as authentic by the party against whom it is offered. (*Stats.1965, c. 299, § 2, operative Jan. 1, 1967.*)

§ 1415
Authentication by handwriting evidence

A writing may be authenticated by evidence of the genuineness of the handwriting of the maker. (*Stats.1965, c. 299, § 2, operative Jan. 1, 1967.*)

§ 1416
Proof of handwriting by person familiar therewith

A witness who is not otherwise qualified to testify as an expert may state his opinion whether a writing is in the handwriting of a supposed writer if the court finds that he has personal knowledge of the handwriting of the supposed writer. Such personal knowledge may be acquired from:

(a) Having seen the supposed writer write;

(b) Having seen a writing purporting to be in the handwriting of the supposed writer and upon which the supposed writer has acted or been charged;

(c) Having received letters in the due course of mail purporting to be from the supposed writer in response to letters duly addressed and mailed by him to the supposed writer; or

(d) Any other means of obtaining personal knowledge of the handwriting of the supposed writer. (*Stats.1965, c. 299, § 2, operative Jan. 1, 1967.*)

§ 1417
Comparison of handwriting by trier of fact

The genuineness of handwriting, or the lack thereof, may be proved by a comparison made by the trier of fact with handwriting (a) which the court finds was admitted or treated as genuine by the party against whom the evidence is offered or (b) otherwise proved to be genuine to the satisfaction of the court. (*Stats.1965, c. 299, § 2, operative Jan. 1, 1967.*)

§ 1418
Comparison of writing by expert witness

The genuineness of writing, or the lack thereof, may be proved by a comparison made by an expert witness with writing (a) which the court finds was admitted or treated as genuine by the party against whom the evidence is offered or (b) otherwise proved to be genuine to the satisfaction of the court. (*Stats.1965, c. 299, § 2, operative Jan. 1, 1967.*)

§ 1419
Exemplars when writing is more than 30 years old

Where a writing whose genuineness is sought to be proved is more than 30 years old, the comparison under Section 1417 or 1418 may be made with writing purporting to be genuine, and generally respected and acted upon as such, by persons having an interest in knowing whether it is genuine. (*Stats.1965, c. 299, § 2, operative Jan. 1, 1967.*)

§ 1420
Authentication by evidence of reply

A writing may be authenticated by evidence that the writing was received in response to a communication sent to the person who is claimed by the proponent of the evidence to be the author of the writing. (*Stats.1965, c. 299, § 2, operative Jan. 1, 1967.*)

§ 1421
Authentication by content

A writing may be authenticated by evidence that the writing refers to or states matters that are unlikely to be known to anyone other than the person who is claimed by the proponent of the evidence to be the author of the writing. (*Stats.1965, c. 299, § 2, operative Jan. 1, 1967.*)

ARTICLE 3. PRESUMPTIONS AFFECTING ACKNOWLEDGED WRITINGS AND OFFICIAL WRITINGS

Section
1450. Classification of presumptions in article.
1451. Acknowledged writings.
1452. Official seals.
1453. Domestic official signatures.
1454. Foreign official signatures.

§ 1450
Classification of presumptions in article

The presumptions established by this article are presumptions affecting the burden of producing evidence. (*Stats.1965, c. 299, § 2, operative Jan. 1, 1967.*)

§ 1451
Acknowledged writings

A certificate of the acknowledgment of a writing other than a will, or a certificate of the proof of such a writing, is prima facie evidence of the facts recited in the certificate and the genuineness of the signature of each person by whom the writing purports to have been signed if the certificate meets the requirements of Article 3 (commencing with Section 1180) of Chapter 4, Title 4, Part 4, Division 2 of the Civil Code. (*Stats.1965, c. 299, § 2, operative Jan. 1, 1967.*)

§ 1452
Official seals

A seal is presumed to be genuine and its use authorized if it purports to be the seal of:

(a) The United States or a department, agency, or public employee of the United States.

(b) A public entity in the United States or a department, agency, or public employee of such public entity.

(c) A nation recognized by the executive power of the United States or a department, agency, or officer of such nation.

(d) A public entity in a nation recognized by the executive power of the United States or a department, agency, or officer of such public entity.

(e) A court of admiralty or maritime jurisdiction.

(f) A notary public within any state of the United States. (*Stats.1965, c. 299, § 2, operative Jan. 1, 1967.*)

§ 1453
Domestic official signatures

A signature is presumed to be genuine and authorized if it purports to be the signature, affixed in his official capacity, of:

(a) A public employee of the United States.

(b) A public employee of any public entity in the United States.

(c) A notary public within any state of the United States. (*Stats.1965, c. 299, § 2, operative Jan. 1, 1967.*)

§ 1454
Foreign official signatures

A signature is presumed to be genuine and authorized if it purports to be the signature, affixed in his official capacity, of an officer, or deputy of an officer, of a nation or public entity in a nation recognized by the executive power of the United States and the writing to which the signature is affixed is accompanied by a final statement certifying the genuineness of the signature and the official position of (a) the person who executed the writing or (b) any foreign official who has certified either the genuineness of the signature and official position of the person executing the writing or the genuineness of the signature and official position of another foreign official who has executed a similar certificate in a chain of such certificates beginning with a certificate of the genuineness of the signature and official position of the person executing the writing. The final statement may be made only by a secretary of an embassy or legation, consul general, consul, vice consul, consular agent, or other officer in the foreign service of the United States stationed in the nation, authenticated by the seal of his office. (*Stats.1965, c. 299, § 2, operative Jan. 1, 1967.*)

CHAPTER 2. SECONDARY EVIDENCE OF WRITINGS

ARTICLE 1. PROOF OF THE CONTENT OF A WRITING

Section

1523. Oral testimony of the content of a writing; admissibility.

§§ 1500 to 1511
Repealed

§§ 1500 to 1511
Repealed by Stats.1998, c. 100 (S.B.177), § 1, operative Jan. 1, 1999

§ 1520
Content of writing; proof

The content of a writing may be proved by an otherwise admissible original. (*Added by Stats.1998, c. 100 (S.B.177), § 2, operative Jan. 1, 1999.*)

§ 1521
Secondary evidence rule

(a) The content of a writing may be proved by otherwise admissible secondary evidence. The court shall exclude secondary evidence of the content of writing if the court determines either of the following:

(1) A genuine dispute exists concerning material terms of the writing and justice requires the exclusion.

(2) Admission of the secondary evidence would be unfair.

(b) Nothing in this section makes admissible oral testimony to prove the content of a writing if the testimony is inadmissible under Section 1523 (oral testimony of the content of a writing).

(c) Nothing in this section excuses compliance with Section 1401 (authentication).

(d) This section shall be known as the "Secondary Evidence Rule." (*Added by Stats.1998, c. 100 (S.B.177), § 2, operative Jan. 1, 1999.*)

§ 1522
Additional grounds for exclusion of secondary evidence

(a) In addition to the grounds for exclusion authorized by Section 1521, in a criminal action the court shall exclude secondary evidence of the content of a writing if the court determines that the original is in the proponent's possession, custody, or control, and the proponent has not made the original reasonably available for inspection at or before trial. This section does not apply to any of the following:

(1) A duplicate as defined in Section 260.

(2) A writing that is not closely related to the controlling issues in the action.

(3) A copy of a writing in the custody of a public entity.

(4) A copy of a writing that is recorded in the public records, if the record or a certified copy of it is made evidence of the writing by statute.

(b) In a criminal action, a request to exclude secondary evidence of the content of a writing, under this section or any other law, shall not be made in the presence of the jury. (*Added by Stats.1998, c. 100 (S.B.177), § 2, operative Jan. 1, 1999.*)

§ 1523
Oral testimony of the content of a writing; admissibility

(a) Except as otherwise provided by statute, oral testimony is not admissible to prove the content of a writing.

(b) Oral testimony of the content of a writing is not made inadmissible by subdivision (a) if the proponent does not have possession or control of a copy of the writing and the original is lost or has been destroyed without fraudulent intent on the part of the proponent of the evidence.

(c) Oral testimony of the content of a writing is not made inadmissible by subdivision (a) if the proponent does not have possession or control of the original or a copy of the writing and either of the following conditions is satisfied:

(1) Neither the writing nor a copy of the writing was reasonably procurable by the proponent by use of the court's process or by other available means.

(2) The writing is not closely related to the controlling issues and it would be inexpedient to require its production.

(d) Oral testimony of the content of a writing is not made inadmissible by subdivision (a) if the writing consists of numerous accounts or other writings that cannot be examined in court without great loss of time, and the evidence sought from them is only the general result of the whole. (*Added by Stats.1998, c. 100 (S.B.177), § 2, operative Jan. 1, 1999.*)

ARTICLE 2. OFFICIAL WRITINGS AND RECORDED WRITINGS

Section
1530. Copy of writing in official custody.
1531. Certification of copy for evidence.
1532. Official record of recorded writing.

§ 1530
Copy of writing in official custody

(a) A purported copy of a writing in the custody of a public entity, or of an entry in such a writing, is prima facie evidence of the existence and content of such writing or entry if:

(1) The copy purports to be published by the authority of the nation or state, or public entity therein in which the writing is kept;

(2) The office in which the writing is kept is within the United States or within the Panama Canal Zone, the Trust Territory of the Pacific Islands, or the Ryukyu Islands, and the copy is attested or certified as a correct copy of the writing or entry by a public employee, or a deputy of a public employee, having the legal custody of the writing; or

(3) The office in which the writing is kept is not within the United States or any other place described in paragraph (2) and the copy is attested as a correct copy of the writing or entry by a person having authority to make attestation. The attestation must be accompanied by a final statement certifying the genuineness of the signature and the official position of (i) the person who attested the copy as a correct copy or (ii) any foreign official who has certified either the genuineness of the signature and official position of the person attesting the copy or the genuineness of the signature and official position of another foreign official who has executed a similar certificate in a chain of such certificates beginning with a certificate of the genuineness of the signature and official position of the person attesting the copy. Except as provided in the next sentence, the final statement may be made only by a secretary of an embassy or legation, consul general, consul, vice consul, or consular agent of the United States, or a diplomatic or consular official of the foreign country assigned or accredited to the United States. Prior to January 1, 1971, the final statement may also be made by a secretary of an embassy or legation, consul general, consul, vice consul, consular agent, or other officer in the foreign service of the United States stationed in the nation in which the writing is kept, authenticated by the seal of his office. If reasonable opportunity has been given to all parties to investigate the authenticity and accuracy of the documents, the court may, for good cause shown, (i) admit an attested copy without the final statement or (ii) permit the writing or entry in foreign custody to be evidenced by an attested summary with or without a final statement.

(b) The presumptions established by this section are presumptions affecting the burden of producing evidence. (*Stats.1965, c. 299, § 2, operative Jan. 1, 1967. Amended by Stats.1970, c. 41, p. 60, § 1, eff. April 3, 1970.*)

§ 1531
Certification of copy for evidence

For the purpose of evidence, whenever a copy of a writing is attested or certified, the attestation or certificate must state in substance that the copy is a correct copy of the original, or of a specified part thereof, as the case may be. (*Stats.1965, c. 299, § 2, operative Jan. 1, 1967.*)

§ 1532
Official record of recorded writing

(a) The official record of a writing is prima facie evidence of the existence and content of the original recorded writing if:

(1) The record is in fact a record of an office of a public entity; and

(2) A statute authorized such a writing to be recorded in that office.

(b) The presumption established by this section is a presumption affecting the burden of producing evidence. (*Stats.1965, c. 299, § 2, operative Jan. 1, 1967.*)

ARTICLE 3. PHOTOGRAPHIC COPIES AND PRINTED REPRESENTATIONS OF WRITINGS

Section
1550. Photographic copies made as business records.
1550. Types of evidence as writing admissible as the writing itself.
1550.1. Admissibility of reproductions of files, records, writings, photographs, and fingerprints.
1551. Photographic copies where original destroyed or lost.
1552. Printed representation of computer-generated information.
1553. Printed representation of video or digital images.

§ 1550
Photographic copies made as business records

Section prior to amendment by Stats.2002, c. 124 (A.B.2033), § 1. See, also, section as amended by Stats.2002, c. 124 (A.B.2033), § 1.

A nonerasable optical image reproduction provided that additions, deletions, or changes to the original document are not permitted by the technology, a photostatic, microfilm, microcard, miniature photographic, or other photographic copy or reproduction, or an enlargement thereof, of a writing is as admissible as the writing itself if the copy or reproduction was made and preserved as a part of the records of a business (as defined by Section 1270) in the regular course of that business. The introduction of the copy, reproduction, or enlargement does not preclude admission of the original writing if it is still in existence. A court may require the introduction of a hard copy printout of the document. (*Stats.1965, c. 299, § 2, operative Jan. 1, 1967. Amended by Stats.1992, c. 876 (A.B.3296), § 10.*)

§ 1550
Types of evidence as writing admissible as the writing itself

Section as amended by Stats.2002, c. 124 (A.B.2033), § 1. See, also, section prior to amendment by Stats.2002, c. 124 (A.B.2033), § 1.

(a) If made and preserved as a part of the records of a business, as defined in Section 1270, in the regular course of that business, the following types of evidence of a writing are as admissible as the writing itself:

(1) A nonerasable optical image reproduction or any other reproduction of a public record by a trusted system, as defined in Section 12168.7 of the Government Code, if additions, deletions, or changes to the original document are not permitted by the technology.

(2) A photostatic copy or reproduction.

(3) A microfilm, microcard, or miniature photographic copy, reprint, or enlargement.

(4) Any other photographic copy or reproduction, or an enlargement thereof.

(b) The introduction of evidence of a writing pursuant to subdivision (a) does not preclude admission of the original writing if it is still in existence. A court may require the introduction of a hard copy printout of the document. (*Stats.1965, c. 299, § 2, operative Jan. 1, 1967. Amended by Stats.1992, c. 876 (A.B.3296), § 10; Stats.2002, c. 124 (A.B.2033), § 1, operative contingent.*)

Operative Effect

Stats.2002, c. 124 (A.B.2033), § 2, provides that this act shall become operative on the date the Secretary of State adopts uniform standards for storing and recording permanent and nonpermanent documents in electronic media as required by Government Code § 12168.7.

§ 1550.1
Admissibility of reproductions of files, records, writings, photographs, and fingerprints

Reproductions of files, records, writings, photographs, fingerprints or other instruments in the official custody of a criminal justice agency that were microphotographed or otherwise reproduced in a manner that conforms with the provisions of Section 11106.1, 11106.2, or 11106.3 of the Penal Code shall be admissible to the same extent and under the same circumstances as the original file, record, writing or other instrument would be admissible. (*Added by Stats.2004, c. 65 (A.B.883), § 1.*)

§ 1551
Photographic copies where original destroyed or lost

A print, whether enlarged or not, from a photographic film (including a photographic plate, microphotographic film, photostatic negative, or similar reproduction) of an original writing destroyed or lost after such film was taken or a reproduction from an electronic recording of video images on magnetic surfaces is admissible as the original writing itself if, at the time of the taking of such film or electronic recording, the person under whose direction and control it was taken attached thereto, or to the sealed container in which it was placed and has been kept, or incorporated in the film or electronic recording, a certification complying with the provisions of Section 1531 and stating the date on which, and the fact that, it was so taken under his direction and control. (*Stats.1965, c. 299, § 2, operative Jan. 1, 1967. Amended by Stats.1969, c. 646, p. 1298, § 1.*)

§ 1552
Printed representation of computer-generated information

(a) A printed representation of computer information or a computer program is presumed to be an accurate representation of the computer information or computer program that it purports to represent. This presumption is a presumption affecting the burden of producing evidence. If a party to an action introduces evidence that a printed representation of computer information or computer program is inaccurate or unreliable, the party introducing the printed representation into evidence has the burden of proving, by a preponderance of evidence, that the printed representation is an accurate representation of the existence and content of the computer information or computer program that it purports to represent.

(b) Subdivision (a) applies to the printed representation of computer-generated information stored by an automated traffic enforcement system.

(c) Subdivision (a) shall not apply to computer-generated official records certified in accordance with Section 452.5 or 1530. (*Added by Stats.1998, c. 100 (S.B.177), § 4, operative Jan. 1, 1999. Amended by Stats.2012, c. 735 (S.B.1303), § 1.*)

§ 1553
Printed representation of video or digital images

(a) A printed representation of images stored on a video or digital medium is presumed to be an accurate representation of the images it purports to represent. This presumption is a presumption affecting the burden of producing evidence. If a party to an action introduces evidence that a printed representation of images stored on a video or digital medium is inaccurate or unreliable, the party introducing the printed representation into evidence has the burden of proving, by a preponderance of evidence, that the printed representation is an accurate representation of the existence and content of the images that it purports to represent.

(b) Subdivision (a) applies to the printed representation of video or photographic images stored by an automated traffic enforcement system. *(Added by Stats.1998, c. 100 (S.B.177), § 5, operative Jan. 1, 1999. Amended by Stats.2012, c. 735 (S.B.1303), § 2.)*

ARTICLE 4. PRODUCTION OF BUSINESS RECORDS

Section

1560. Compliance with subpoena duces tecum for business records.
1561. Affidavit accompanying records.
1562. Admissibility of affidavit and copy of records.
1563. One witness and mileage fee.
1564. Personal attendance of custodian and production of original records.
1565. Service of more than one subpoena duces tecum.
1566. Applicability of article.
1567. Employee income and benefit information; forms completed by employer; support modification or termination proceedings.

§ 1560
Compliance with subpoena duces tecum for business records

(a) As used in this article:

(1) "Business" includes every kind of business described in Section 1270.

(2) "Record" includes every kind of record maintained by a business.

(b) Except as provided in Section 1564, when a subpoena duces tecum is served upon the custodian of records or other qualified witness of a business in an action in which the business is neither a party nor the place where any cause of action is alleged to have arisen, and the subpoena requires the production of all or any part of the records of the business, it is sufficient compliance therewith if the custodian or other qualified witness delivers by mail or otherwise a true, legible, and durable copy of all of the records described in the subpoena to the clerk of the court or to another person described in subdivision (d) of Section 2026.010 of the Code of Civil Procedure, together with the affidavit described in Section 1561, within one of the following time periods:

(1) In any criminal action, five days after the receipt of the subpoena.

(2) In any civil action, within 15 days after the receipt of the subpoena.

(3) Within the time agreed upon by the party who served the subpoena and the custodian or other qualified witness.

(c) The copy of the records shall be separately enclosed in an inner envelope or wrapper, sealed, with the title and number of the action, name of witness, and date of subpoena clearly inscribed thereon; the sealed envelope or wrapper shall then be enclosed in an outer envelope or wrapper, sealed, and directed as follows:

(1) If the subpoena directs attendance in court, to the clerk of the court.

(2) If the subpoena directs attendance at a deposition, to the officer before whom the deposition is to be taken, at the place designated in the subpoena for the taking of the deposition or at the officer's place of business.

(3) In other cases, to the officer, body, or tribunal conducting the hearing, at a like address.

(d) Unless the parties to the proceeding otherwise agree, or unless the sealed envelope or wrapper is returned to a witness who is to appear personally, the copy of the records shall remain sealed and shall be opened only at the time of trial, deposition, or other hearing, upon the direction of the judge, officer, body, or tribunal conducting the proceeding, in the presence of all parties who have appeared in person or by counsel at the trial, deposition, or hearing. Records that are original documents and that are not introduced in evidence or required as part of the record shall be returned to the person or entity from whom received. Records that are copies may be destroyed.

(e) As an alternative to the procedures described in subdivisions (b), (c), and (d), the subpoenaing party in a civil action may direct the witness to make the records available for inspection or copying by the party's attorney, the attorney's representative, or deposition officer as described in Section 2020.420 of the Code of Civil Procedure, at the witness§ business address under reasonable conditions during normal business hours. Normal business hours, as used in this subdivision, means those hours that the business of the witness is normally open for business to the public. When provided with at least five business days§ advance notice by the party's attorney, attorney's representative, or deposition officer, the witness shall designate a time period of not less than six continuous hours on a date certain for copying of records subject to the subpoena by the party's attorney, attorney's representative, or deposition officer. It shall be the responsibility of the attorney's representative to deliver any copy of the records as directed in the subpoena. Disobedience to the deposition subpoena issued pursuant to this subdivision is punishable as provided in Section 2020.240 of the Code of Civil Procedure. (*Stats.1965, c. 299, § 2, operative Jan. 1, 1967. Amended by Stats.1969, c. 199, p. 484, § 2; Stats.1982, c. 452, p. 1824, § 2.5; Stats.1984, c. 481, § 2; Stats.1986, c. 603, § 6; Stats.1991, c. 1090 (A.B.1484), § 14; Stats.1997, c. 442 (A.B.758), § 16; Stats.1999, c. 444 (A.B.794), § 4; Stats.2000, c. 287 (S.B.1955), § 1; Stats.2004, c. 182 (A.B.3081), § 32, operative July 1, 2005; Stats.2004, c. 162 (A.B.1249), § 1; Stats.2005, c. 294 (A.B.333), § 18; Stats.2006, c. 538 (S.B.1852), § 155.)*

§ 1561
Affidavit accompanying records

(a) The records shall be accompanied by the affidavit of the custodian or other qualified witness, stating in substance each of the following:

(1) The affiant is the duly authorized custodian of the records or other qualified witness and has authority to certify the records.

(2) The copy is a true copy of all the records described in the subpoena duces tecum, or pursuant to subdivision (e) of Section 1560 the records were delivered to the attorney, the attorney's representative, or deposition officer for copying at the custodian's or witness§ place of business, as the case may be.

(3) The records were prepared by the personnel of the business in the ordinary course of business at or near the time of the act, condition, or event.

(4) The identity of the records.

(5) A description of the mode of preparation of the records.

(b) If the business has none of the records described, or only part thereof, the custodian or other qualified witness shall so state in the affidavit, and deliver the affidavit and those records that are available in one of the manners provided in Section 1560.

(c) Where the records described in the subpoena were delivered to the attorney or his or her representative or deposition officer for copying at the custodian's or witness§ place of business, in addition to the affidavit required by subdivision (a), the records shall be accompanied by an affidavit by the attorney or his or her representative or deposition officer stating that the copy is a true copy of all the records delivered to the attorney or his or her representative or deposition officer for copying. (*Stats.1965, c. 299, § 2, operative Jan. 1, 1967. Amended by Stats.1969, c. 199, p. 484, § 3; Stats.1986, c. 603, § 7; Stats.1987, c. 19, § 2, eff. May 12, 1987; Stats.1996, c. 146 (A.B.3001), § 1; Stats.1999, c. 444 (A.B.794), § 5.*)

§ 1562
Admissibility of affidavit and copy of records

If the original records would be admissible in evidence if the custodian or other qualified witness had been present and testified to the matters stated in the affidavit, and if the requirements of Section 1271 have been met, the copy of the records is admissible in evidence. The affidavit is admissible as evidence of the matters stated therein pursuant to Section 1561 and the matters so stated are presumed true. When more than one person has knowledge of the facts, more than one affidavit may be made. The presumption established by this section is a presumption affecting the burden of producing evidence. (*Stats.1965, c. 299, § 2, operative Jan. 1, 1967. Amended by Stats.1989, c. 1416, § 31; Stats.1996, c. 146 (A.B.3001), § 2.*)

Section 1562 supersedes the provisions of Code of Civil Procedure Section 1998.2. Under Section 1998.2, the presumption provided in this section could be overcome only by a preponderance of the evidence. Section 1562, however, classifies the presumption as one affecting the burden of producing evidence only. See Evidence Code §§ 603 and 604 and the Comments thereto. Section 1562 makes it clear, too, that the presumption relates only to the truthfulness of the matters required by Section 1561 to be stated in the affidavit.

§ 1563
One witness and mileage fee

(a) This article shall not be interpreted to require tender or payment of more than one witness fee and one mileage fee or other charge, to a witness or witness§ business, unless there is an agreement to the contrary between the witness and the requesting party.

(b) All reasonable costs incurred in a civil proceeding by any witness which is not a party with respect to the production of all or any part of business records the production of which is requested pursuant to a subpoena duces tecum may be charged against the party serving the subpoena duces tecum.

(1) "Reasonable cost," as used in this section, shall include, but not be limited to, the following specific costs: ten cents ($0.10) per page for standard reproduction of documents of a size 8 1/2 by 14 inches or less; twenty cents ($0.20) per page for copying of documents from microfilm; actual costs for the reproduction of oversize documents or the reproduction of documents requiring special processing which are made in response to a subpoena; reasonable clerical costs incurred in locating and making the records available to be billed at the maximum rate of twenty-four dollars ($24) per hour per person, computed on the basis of six dollars ($6) per quarter hour or fraction thereof; actual postage charges; and the actual cost, if any, charged to the witness by a third person for the retrieval and return of records held offsite by that third person.

(2) The requesting party, or the requesting party's deposition officer, shall not be required to pay those costs or any estimate thereof prior to the time the records are available for delivery pursuant to the subpoena, but the witness may demand payment of costs pursuant to this section simultaneous with actual delivery of the subpoenaed records, and until payment is made, is under no obligation to deliver the records.

(3) The witness shall submit an itemized statement for the costs to the requesting party, or the requesting party's deposition officer, setting forth the reproduction and clerical costs incurred by the witness. Should the costs exceed those authorized in paragraph (1), or the witness refuses to

produce an itemized statement of costs as required by paragraph (3), upon demand by the requesting party, or the requesting party's deposition officer, the witness shall furnish a statement setting forth the actions taken by the witness in justification of the costs.

(4) The requesting party may petition the court in which the action is pending to recover from the witness all or a part of the costs paid to the witness, or to reduce all or a part of the costs charged by the witness, pursuant to this subdivision, on the grounds that those costs were excessive. Upon the filing of the petition the court shall issue an order to show cause and from the time the order is served on the witness the court has jurisdiction over the witness. The court may hear testimony on the order to show cause and if it finds that the costs demanded and collected, or charged but not collected, exceed the amount authorized by this subdivision, it shall order the witness to remit to the requesting party, or reduce its charge to the requesting party by an amount equal to, the amount of the excess. In the event that the court finds the costs excessive and charged in bad faith by the witness, the court shall order the witness to remit the full amount of the costs demanded and collected, or excuse the requesting party from any payment of costs charged but not collected, and the court shall also order the witness to pay the requesting party the amount of the reasonable expenses incurred in obtaining the order including attorney's fees. If the court finds the costs were not excessive, the court shall order the requesting party to pay the witness the amount of the reasonable expenses incurred in defending the petition, including attorney's fees.

(5) If a subpoena is served to compel the production of business records and is subsequently withdrawn, or is quashed, modified or limited on a motion made other than by the witness, the witness shall be entitled to reimbursement pursuant to paragraph (1) for all costs incurred in compliance with the subpoena to the time that the requesting party has notified the witness that the subpoena has been withdrawn or quashed, modified or limited. In the event the subpoena is withdrawn or quashed, if those costs are not paid within 30 days after demand therefor, the witness may file a motion in the court in which the action is pending for an order requiring payment, and the court shall award the payment of expenses and attorney's fees in the manner set forth in paragraph (4).

(6) Where the records are delivered to the attorney, the attorney's representative, or the deposition officer for inspection or photocopying at the witness§ place of business, the only fee for complying with the subpoena shall not exceed fifteen dollars ($15), plus the actual cost, if any, charged to the witness by a third person for retrieval and return of records held offsite by that third person. If the records are retrieved from microfilm, the reasonable cost, as defined in paragraph (1), shall also apply.

(c) When the personal attendance of the custodian of a record or other qualified witness is required pursuant to Section 1564, in a civil proceeding, he or she shall be entitled to the same witness fees and mileage permitted in a case where the subpoena requires the witness to attend and testify before a court in which the action or proceeding is pending and to any additional costs incurred as provided by subdivision (b). (*Stats.1965, c. 299, § 2, operative Jan. 1, 1967. Amended by Stats.1972, c. 396, p. 719, § 1; Stats.1981, c. 1014, p. 3913, § 2; Stats.1982, c. 452, p. 1825, § 3; Stats.1986, c. 603, § 8; Stats.1987, c. 19, § 3, eff. May 12, 1987; Stats.1997, c. 442 (A.B.758), § 17; Stats.1999, c. 444 (A.B.794), § 6.*)

Fees and Charges

Commissioner's authority to increase or decrease fees, and schedule of fees and charges, see Insurance Code § 12978.

§ 1564
Personal attendance of custodian and production of original records

The personal attendance of the custodian or other qualified witness and the production of the original records is not required unless, at the discretion of the requesting party, the subpoena duces tecum contains a clause which reads:

"The personal attendance of the custodian or other qualified witness and the production of the original records are required by this subpoena. The procedure authorized pursuant to subdivision (b) of Section 1560, and Sections 1561 and 1562, of the Evidence Code will not be deemed sufficient compliance with this subpoena." (*Stats.1965, c. 299, § 2, operative Jan. 1, 1967. Amended by Stats.1984, c. 603, § 2; Stats.1986, c. 603, § 9; Stats.1987, c. 19, § 4, eff. May 12, 1987.*)

§ 1565
Service of more than one subpoena duces tecum

If more than one subpoena duces tecum is served upon the custodian of records or other qualified witness and the personal attendance of the custodian or other qualified witness is required pursuant to Section 1564, the witness shall be deemed to be the witness of the party serving the first such subpoena duces tecum. (*Stats.1965, c. 299, § 2, operative Jan. 1, 1967. Amended by Stats.1969, c. 199, p. 485, § 4.*)

§ 1566
Applicability of article

This article applies in any proceeding in which testimony can be compelled. (*Stats.1965, c. 299, § 2, operative Jan. 1, 1967.*)

§ 1567
Employee income and benefit information; forms completed by employer; support modification or termination proceedings

A completed form described in Section 3664 of the Family Code for income and benefit information provided by the employer may be admissible in a proceeding for modification or termination of an order for child, family, or spousal support if both of the following requirements are met:

(a) The completed form complies with Sections 1561 and 1562.

(b) A copy of the completed form and notice was served on the employee named therein pursuant to Section 3664 of the Family Code. (*Added by Stats.1995, c. 506 (A.B.413), § 1.*)

CHAPTER 3. OFFICIAL WRITINGS AFFECTING PROPERTY

Section
1600. Record of document affecting property interest.
1601. Proof of content of lost official record affecting property.
1602. Repealed.
1603. Deed by officer in pursuance of court process.
1604. Certificate of purchase or of location of lands.
1605. Authenticated Spanish title records.

§ 1600
Record of document affecting property interest

(a) The record of an instrument or other document purporting to establish or affect an interest in property is prima facie evidence of the existence and content of the original recorded document and its execution and delivery by each person by whom it purports to have been executed if:

(1) The record is in fact a record of an office of a public entity; and

(2) A statute authorized such a document to be recorded in that office.

(b) The presumption established by this section is a presumption affecting the burden of proof. (*Stats.1965, c. 299, § 2, operative Jan. 1, 1967. Amended by Stats.1967, c. 650, p. 2007, § 9.*)

§ 1601
Proof of content of lost official record affecting property

(a) Subject to subdivisions (b) and (c), when in any action it is desired to prove the contents of the official record of any writing lost or destroyed by conflagration or other public calamity, after proof of such loss or destruction, the following may, without further proof, be admitted in evidence to prove the contents of such record:

(1) Any abstract of title made and issued and certified as correct prior to such loss or destruction, and purporting to have been prepared and made in the ordinary course of business by any person engaged in the business of preparing and making abstracts of title prior to such loss or destruction; or

(2) Any abstract of title, or of any instrument affecting title, made, issued, and certified as correct by any person engaged in the business of insuring titles or issuing abstracts of title to real estate, whether the same was made, issued, or certified before or after such loss or destruction and whether the same was made from the original records or from abstract and notes, or either, taken from such records in the preparation and upkeeping of its plant in the ordinary course of its business.

(b) No proof of the loss of the original writing is required other than the fact that the original is not known to the party desiring to prove its contents to be in existence.

(c) Any party desiring to use evidence admissible under this section shall give reasonable notice in writing to all other parties to the action who have appeared therein, of his intention to use such evidence at the trial of the action, and shall give all such other parties a reasonable opportunity to inspect the evidence, and also the abstracts, memoranda, or notes from which it was compiled, and to take copies thereof. (*Stats.1965, c. 299, § 2, operative Jan. 1, 1967.*)

§ 1602
Repealed by Stats.1967, c. 650, p. 2008, § 10

§ 1603
Deed by officer in pursuance of court process

A deed of conveyance of real property, purporting to have been executed by a proper officer in pursuance of legal process of any of the courts of record of this state, acknowledged and recorded in the office of the recorder of the county wherein the real property therein described is situated, or the record of such deed, or a certified copy of such record, is prima facie evidence that the property or interest therein described was thereby conveyed to the grantee named in such deed. The presumption established by this section is a presumption affecting the burden of proof. (*Stats.1965, c. 299, § 2, operative Jan. 1, 1967. Amended by Stats.1967, c. 650, p. 2008, § 11.*)

§ 1604
Certificate of purchase or of location of lands

A certificate of purchase, or of location, of any lands in this state, issued or made in pursuance of any law of the United States or of this state, is prima facie evidence that the holder or assignee of such certificate is the owner of the land described therein; but this evidence may be overcome by proof that, at the time of the location, or time of filing a preemption claim on which the certificate may have been issued, the land was in the adverse possession of the adverse party, or those under whom he claims, or that the adverse party is holding the land for mining purposes. (*Stats.1965, c. 299, § 2, operative Jan. 1, 1967.*)

§ 1605
Authenticated Spanish title records

Duplicate copies and authenticated translations of original Spanish title papers relating to land claims in this state, derived from the Spanish or Mexican governments, prepared under the supervision of the Keeper of Archives, authenticated by the Surveyor–General or his successor and by the Keeper of Archives, and filed with a county recorder, in accordance with Chapter 281 of the Statutes of 1865–66, are admissible as evidence with like force and effect as the originals and without proving the execution of such originals. (*Stats.1965, c. 299, § 2, operative Jan. 1, 1967. Amended by Stats.1967, c. 650, p. 2008, § 12.*)

INDEX

References are to Pages